CHAMBERS

CROSSWORD COMPLETER

an alternate letter word list

New edition

With a foreword by
Don Manley

CHAMBERS

CHAMBERS
An imprint of Chambers Harrap Publishers Ltd
7 Hopetoun Crescent
Edinburgh EH7 4AY

www.chambers.co.uk

This edition first published Chambers 2001
First edition W & R Chambers 1987
Second edition Chambers 1995

We have made every effort to mark as such all words which we believe to be trademarks. We should also like to make it clear that the presence of a word in this book, whether marked or unmarked, in no way affects its legal status as a trademark.

A CIP catalogue record for this book is available from the British Library.

ISBN 0550 12013 0

Designed and typeset in Great Britain by Chambers Harrap Publishers Ltd
Printed and bound in Great Britain by Cox & Wyman Ltd, Reading, Berkshire

Contributors

Editor
Una McGovern

Consultant Editor
Catherine Schwarz

Computerization
Peter Schwarz

Prepress
Hannah Perry

The editors would also like to acknowledge the valuable contribution made to the planning of this book by Elaine Higgleton

Foreword

The standard crossword in daily newspapers is based on a grid of black and white squares, so most answers to the clues have alternate letters 'checked' by letters of crossing answers. The other letters are said to be 'unchecked'. This means that you may find yourself with a grid entry like this, with the odd letters checked:

A_A_E_(where the answer could be AZALEA)

or like this, with the even letters checked:

_A_A_E (where the answer could be PARADE)

Chambers Crossword Completer is a unique 'alternate letter dictionary' that helps the solver (or indeed the setter) to fill in the crossword grid — and this new edition is based on *Chambers Crossword Dictionary*. As well as single words and abbreviations, it introduces phrases, some plurals and verb endings, and a vast array of proper nouns beyond those in *The Chambers Dictionary*, which was used for previous editions. You will now find, for the first time, 'fair game', 'soldiers', 'pervaded', 'papering', and 'Bayreuth' — not to mention neighbours 'Babe Ruth' and 'Kate Bush'. Additional material from *The Chambers Dictionary* is also included — but some words that are more likely to appear only in more difficult puzzles on barred grids (without the traditional alternate letter-checking) have been omitted to make room for entries that will be more useful for everyday solvers.

A word that can be spelled with or without an initial capital letter, sometimes with different meanings, is given the symbol ▫. Accents have been retained since they often point to separate word meanings (eg 'pate' and 'pâté') or to the foreign origin of the word. Hyphenated and unhyphenated forms have often been shown, again as reflecting different meanings or usages. Registered trade names have also been noted. All these devices will help the solver to track down words and their meanings.

Entries, ranging from 4 letters to 15 letters, are arranged by length and then alphabetically according to the alternate letters. These letters are shown in capitals at the side for the first word in the group for which they are relevant (AA for A_A_ and so on). For ease of reference the book is divided into two sections. The first section gives entries according to the alphabetical order of the even letters (_A_A to _Y_T_M_T_Z_T_O_) and the second section gives them according to the order of the odd (A_A_ to Z_G_O_M_U_T_I_S).

You won't *always* manage to pop *Chambers Crossword Completer* into your briefcase, I am sure, but when you arrive home frustrated by the gaps in 17 across, you'll be able to look up CEOE and write in 'Cherokee', knowing that one of life's little loose ends has been tied up!

Don Manley
Oxford 2001

Words arranged according to EVEN LETTERS

4 letters – even

AA baba, Capa, Cara, Cava, Dada, Dana, data, Daya, Gaea, gaga, Gaia, gala, Gama, ha-ha, haka, IAEA, IATA, Java, Kaba, kaka, Kama, kana, kara❑, kata, kava, Lada®, la-la, Lara, lava, Maia, mama, Maya, Naha, nana❑, napa, Nara, paca, papa❑, para, RADA, raga, raja, Rama, Rana, saga, Saha, San'a, Sara, sa sa, sasa, taha, taka, tala, Tana, ta-ta, taxa, Vasa, Zama, Zara

AB barb❑, daub, garb, iamb, jamb, lamb❑, SATB

AC laic, marc❑, RADC, RAEC, RAMC, RAOC, talc, WAAC, Waac, bald, band, bard, baud, bawd, card, daud, dawd, Fahd, fard, gaud, gawd, hand, hard, haud, laid, land❑, lard, laud❑, maid, Maud, nard, paid, pard, raid, rand❑, said, sand❑, sard, wadd, wald, wand, ward❑, yard

AE Aare, babe❑, bake, bale, bane, bare, base, bate, Cade, cafe, café, cage❑, cake, came, cane, cape, care, case, cave, dace, dale, dame, Dane, dare, date, Dave, daze, ease, face, fade, fake, fame, fane, fare, fate, Faye, faze, gage, gale❑, game, gape, gate, gave, Gaye, gaze, hade, hake, hale❑, hame, hare❑, hate, have, haze, jade❑, Jake, Jane, jape, kale, kame, Kate, Kaye, lace, lade, lake, lame, lamé, lane, late, Laue, lave, laze, mace❑, made, mage, Mahe, make, male, Malé, mane, mare, mase, mate, maze, name, nape, nave, naze, pace, page❑, pale, pane, pare, pate, paté, pâté, pave, race, rage, rake, rale, râle, rape, rare, rase, rate, rave, raze, sade❑, safe, sage, sake, sale, same, sane, sate, save, SAYE, Tafe, take, tale, tame, tane, tape, Tate, vale, vane, vase, wade❑, wage, wake, wale, wane, ware, wave, Yale, yare

AF baff, barf, BASF, calf, daff, faff, half, IAAF, MAFF, naff, naif, naïf, RAAF, Taff, WAAF, waif, yaff

AG bang, dang, fang, gang, Haig, hang, Lang, marg, pang, ragg, rang, sang, tang, vang, Wang

AH Bach, bash, bath❑, cash❑, dash, each, fash, gash, hash, hath, kaph, Kath, lash, lath, Mach, mash, Nash, oath, pash, path, rash, sash, tanh, tash, tath, wash, Zach

AI Bali, bani, Bari, cadi, Cali, capi, Dali, Gabi, haji, Iasi, kadi, kaki, kali❑, kazi, lari, magi, Mali, Maui, maxi, Nazi, Pali, qadi, rabi❑, raki, ram i, rani, Ravi, Safi, saki❑, sari, sati, tali, Tati, taxi, vagi, wadi, zati

AJ hadj, hajj

AK back, balk, bank, bark, bask, calk, cask, dank, dark, faik, fank, gawk, hack, haik, hank❑, hark, hawk, jack❑, kark, lack, lank, lark, lawk, mack❑, mark❑, mask, nark, pack, paik, park❑, rack, raik, rank, sack, sank, Sark, tack, talk, tank, task, walk, wank, Wark, wauk, yack, yank❑, Zack

AL Baal, bail, ball❑, bawl, call, Carl, caul, dahl❑, Dáil, earl, fail, fall, Gael, Gail, gall❑, gaol

Words marked ❑ can also be spelled with an initial capital letter

Gaul
hail
hall❑
harl
haul
jail
kail
Karl
mail
mall
marl
maul
nail
pail
pall
Paul
pawl
rail
sail
Saul
Taal
tail
tall
Vaal
wail
wall
waul
wawl
yawl
AM balm
barm
calm
farm
gaum
haem
halm
harm
hawm
ma'am
maim
malm
marm
palm
warm
AN Bain
Bann
barn
Caen
Cahn
Cain
damn
darn
dawn❑
eaon
earn
fain
faun
fawn
gain
hain
Hawn
Iain
Jain
jann
kaon
lain
larn
lawn
main
Mann
maun
naan
pain
pawn
rain
sawn
tarn
vain
wain❑
warn
yarn
yawn
AO Cano
Caro
Cato
dado
faro❑
Gabo
halo
haro
Iago
jato
Kano
kayo
mako
Mayo
NATO
Nato
Pavo
sago
taco
taro
Waco
AP camp❑
carp
damp
gamp
gasp
gaup
gawp
harp❑
hasp
jaup
lamp
Lapp
palp
parp
ramp
rasp
tamp
vamp
warp
wasp
yapp
yawp
AR Baer
BAgr
BAOR
fair
haar
hair❑
lair
Mayr
pair
parr❑
Saar
AS Babs
bags
bars
bass
bats
bays
cars
Cass
Cats
DAFS
dais
days❑
Eads
eats
fans
gags
Hals
jaws❑
Laos
lass
lats
laws
Mars
mass❑
oafs
Oaks
OAPs
oats
pass
RAeS
Rais
Rams
rats
rays
sans
sass
Tass
tats
taws
wads
ways
yaws
AT baft
baht
bait
bant
Bart
bast❑
cant
can't
cart
cast
daft
dart
d'art
daut
dawt
east
fact
fast
gait
gant
GATT
haft
halt
hart
hast
Kant
kart
last
Maat
malt
mart
mast
matt❑
NAHT
oast
pact
pant
part
past
raft
rait
rant
rapt
SALT
salt
tact
Taft
Tait
tart
tatt
taut
vant
vast
waft
wait
Walt
want
wart
wast
watt❑
AU Baku
Danu
kagu
KANU
Oahu
raku
tabu
vatu
Yalu
ZANU
ZAPU
AV Maev
AW BASW
AX calx
faix
Manx
Marx
PABX
AY baby
cagy
Cary
cavy
Daly
Davy
easy
gamy
Gary
hazy
Katy
lacy
lady
lazy
many
Mary
maty
mazy
Nagy
nary
navy
pacy
racy
vary
wady
waly
wany
wary
wavy
waxy
zany
AZ Baez
jazz
Katz
razz
BA abba❑
ABTA
BC BBBC
BBFC
BD abed
ibid
IBRD
BE Abbe
abbé❑
able
oboe
BL Abel
obol
BN Oban
Obon
BO CBSO
Ebro
BP tbsp
BS à bas
Abos
ibis
Ibos
obos
BT abet
a bit
abut
BX ibex
BY Abby
ably
obey
CA UCCA
CB scab
CC AC/DC
ECSC
CD acid
ecad
iced
scad
SCID
scud❑
CE ache
acme
acne
acre❑
ecce
eche
GCSE
oche
CF RCAF
CG DCMG
GCMG
KCMG
RCOG
scag
CL Icel
kcal
NCCL
SCCL
CM BCom
ICBM
scam
scum
CN icon
scan
CO DCVO
echo❑
GCVO
ICAO
KCVO
CP RCMP
CQ GCHQ
NCVQ
CR acer
scar
scur
CS ACAS
acts
PCAS
RCVS
SCPS
UCAS
CT ACTT
echt
scat
Scot
scut
CU ecru
CV CCTV
CW scow
CX Ickx
CY achy
DA Edda
Edna
idea
MDMA
odea
PDSA
DE Adie
a due
adze
edge
Edie
idle❑
Odie
DL idol
idyl
DM Adam
Edam
idem
DN Aden
Eden
Odin
DP SDLP
DR Adar
Edur
Oder
DS ados
Gdns
Ides
odds
Odes
udos
VDQS
DT advt
edit
Udet
DV HDTV
DY Addy
D-Day
eddy❑
edgy
idly
EA beta
ceca
feta❑
geta
Hera
keta
Leda
Lena
leva
mega
mesa
Neva
sera
seta
Tema
UEFA
Veda
Vega

Vela
vena
Vera
Zena
ZETA
zeta❑
EB BEAB
CEGB
herb
kerb
Serb
verb
Webb
EC merc
Merc®
NEDC
NERC
OEEC
SERC
ED bead
bend
dead❑
deed
feed
fend
feud
geld
head
heed
held
herd
lead
lend
lewd
mead❑
meld
mend
need
nerd
OECD
read❑
redd
reed❑
rend
retd
Revd
seed
send
tend
veld
vend
weed
weld
wend
EE Bede
cede
cere
cete
dele
deme
fête
gene❑
Gere
hebe❑
he-he
hele
heme
here
jeté
leve
mene
mere
mete
névé
Peke
Pele
Pete
REME
Rene
René
rete
sere
were
we're
we've
EF beef
deaf
delf
Jeff
kerf
leaf
pelf
reef
self
serf
teff
EG BEng
berg❑
Leng
EH Beth
eech
hech
heth
kesh
Leah
lech
mesh
pech
pegh
resh
sech
Seth
tech
teth
yeah
yech
EI Bedi
cedi
Ceri
deli
Devi
feni
Kemi
kepi
Levi
peri
semi
semi-
Seti
yeti
EK beak
beck❑
berk
deck
deek
desk
geck
geek
heck
jerk
keck
keek
leak
leek
meek
neck
peak
peck❑
peek
perk
reck
reek
seek
teak
weak
week
welk
yerk
EL bell❑
ceil
cell
deal❑
dell
feel
fell❑
heal
heel
heil!
hell❑
he'll
herl
jeel
jell
keel
meal
mell
mewl
Neal
Neil
Nell
peal
peel❑
real
reel
seal
seel
seil
sell
teal
TEFL
tell
TESL
veal
veil
weal
weel
Weil
well❑
we'll
yell
zeal
EM beam
berm
deem
germ
geum
helm
leam
neum
perm❑
seam
seem
team
teem
term
yelm
EN aeon
bean❑
been
Behn
bein
Benn
Bern
dean❑
Dern
fern
gean
Hern
jean❑
Kean
keen
kern❑
lean❑
León
mean
mein
neon
peen
pein
Penn
peon
rein
Sean
seen
sewn
teen
tern
vein
Venn
wean
zein
EO Belo
demo
Devo
hero❑
Leto
memo
Nero
pepo
peso
redo
Reno
repo
sego
veto
zero
EP beep
deep
Depp
geep
heap
help
hemp
jeep❑
keep
kelp
Kemp
leap
leep
neap
neep
peep
reap
repp
seep
temp
weep
yelp
EQ SEAQ
seqq
ER bear
beer❑
dear
deer
fear
gear
hear
heir
jeer
Lear
leer
Meir
near
ne'er
pear
peer
rear
sear
seer
serr
tear
teer
veer
wear
weir
year
ES Bess
Debs
fees
fegs
fess
gems❑
geos
Gers
hers
Hess
jess❑
keks
lees
legs
lens
less
LETS
mess
mews
ness
news
peas
Pécs
Reds
seas
Tees
Tess
yes's
Zeus
ET beat
beet
belt
bent
Bert
best❑
Celt
cent
cert
debt
deft
dent
feat
feet
felt
fest
gelt
gent❑
Gert
heat
heft
jest
kelt❑
Kent
kept
Kett
leet
left
lent❑
lest
meat
meet
melt
neat
nest
nett
newt
next
peat
pelt
PERT
pert
pest
regt
rent❑
rept
rest
seat
sect
Sekt
sent
sept
sett
sext
teat
tent
test
text
vent
vest
weet
weft
welt
went
wept
west❑
zest
EU beau
Cebu
Jehu
menu
Pegu
Peru
zebu
EV derv
perv
EW meow
EX Leix
EY bevy
defy
demy
deny
dewy
levy
rely
sexy
very
EZ Benz
Getz
Jeez
Lenz
lezz
Metz
FA Afra
EFTA
Efta

4 _F_C

Offa
FC NFSC
FD IFAD
FE NFSE
FI NFWI
FO Afro
BFPO
FR afar
Ifor
NFER
FS EFTS
mfrs
UFOs
FU WFTU
FW a few
FX Sfax
FY iffy
GA Agra
Ogma
GD aged
GE agee
ague
ogee
ogle
ogre
GG agog
GI Agni
CGLI
GL egal
GM ogam
GN agin
Egon
GR agar
GS ages
eggs
GU TGWU
GY Aggy
eggy
ugly
HA rhea❑
shea
Shia
Shi'a
shwa
Thea
whoa
HB Ahab
chub
HC chic❑
choc
HD Chad
shad
shed
she'd
thud
whid
who'd
HE ghee
Rhee
shoe
thee
whee
HF chef
HG chug
shag
shog
thig
thug
Whig
HH shah❑
HI dhai
Shri
Thai
HL dhal
Phil
Phyl
Rhyl
shul
HM ahem
chum
sham
Shem
shim
them
wham❑
whim
whom
HN Chan
chin
chon
khan❑
phon
Rhun
shin
shun
than
then
thin
Thun
when
whin
HO Ohio
shoo
Theo
thro
thro'
HP chap
chip
chop
Shep
ship
shop
whap
whip
whop
HR char
Cher
Thar
Thor
whe'r
whir
HS DHSS
mhos
OHMS
ohos
rhos
Rhys
shes
she's
this
thus
who's
HT chat❑
chit
chut
ghat
khat
phut
shit
shot
shut
that
what
whet
whit❑
HU thou
HV chiv
HW chew
chow
dhow
phew
Shaw
show
thaw
thew
whew
whow
HY ahoy
Chay
they
whey
HZ chez
phiz
whiz
IA Aïda
Biwa
Ciba
CIPA
diva❑
FIFA
giga
gila
Gina
Gita
hila
hiya
Jima
kina
Lima
lira
Lisa
Liza
mica
mina
Mira
Nina
nipa
Nita
Oita
pica
pika
pila
pipa
Pisa
pita
RIBA
Riga
RIPA
Rita
riza
sika
sima
Sita
Siva
Tina
vina
visa
Vita
viva
IB CICB
CIOB
limb
IC C-in-C
disc
NIRC
RISC
zinc
ID bind
bird❑
died
find
gild
gird
hind
Kidd
kind
lied
Lind
mild
mind❑
pied
rind
sild
sind
tied
tind
wild
wind
yird
IE aide
aîné
bide
bike
bile
bise
bite
cide
cine
cite
dice
dike
dime
dine
dire
dite
dive
Eire
FIDE
fife❑
fike
file
fine
fire
five
gibe
Gide
gite
gîte
give
hide
hike
hire
Hite
hive
jibe
jive
kibe
kine
kite
lice
life
like
lime
line
lire
Lise
lite
live
mice
mike❑
mile
mime
mine
mire
mite
nice❑
Nike
Nile
nine
pice
pike
pile
pine❑
pipe
rice❑
ride❑
rife
rile
rime
ripe
rise
rite
rive
side
sile
sine
sipe
sire
site
size
tice
tide
tile
time❑
tine
tire
vice
vide
vile
vine
vire
vite
vive
wide
wife
wile
wine
wipe
wire
wise❑
wite
yike
zine
IF biff
fief
jiff
miff
niff
Piaf
riff
tiff
ziff
IG DIng
ding
Eigg
king❑
ling
Ming
ping
Rigg
ring
sing
Tigg
ting
wing
zing
IH dich
dish
fish❑
Gish
high
mish
nigh
pish
pith
rich❑
sigh
Sikh
sith
tich
wish
with
II Ci-xi
Didi
Dini
Fiji
Gigi
hi-fi
hili
Jixi
kiwi
MIDI
midi
mini
Mini®
miri
nidi
nisi
pili
titi
ziti
IK bilk
dick❑
dink
dirk❑
disk
fink
firk
gink
hick❑
jink
kick
kink
kirk❑
lick
link
lirk
Mick
milk
mink
mirk
nick❑
oink
pick
pink
rick❑
rink
risk
sick
silk
sink
tick
tink
wick❑
wink
IL bill❑
birl
dial
dill
dirl
fill

gill□
girl
hill□
jill□
Kiel
kill
lill
mill□
nirl
pill
rial
riel
rill
sial
sill
till
tirl
vial
viol
will□
IM film
firm
Liam
RIAM
IN bien
Dian
Dion
Finn
girn
hisn
his'n
jinn
kiln
Lian
lien
limn
linn
lion□
mien
pion
Sian
sien
sign
Sion
Wien
Xi'an
Zion
IO Biko
Biro
Biro®
ciao
cito
dido□
fico
FIFO
figo
filo
fino
GIGO
giro
jiao
kilo□
kino
lido
LIFO
lilo□
limo
lino
mico
Miró
miso
rivo
silo
tiro
Tito
Vigo
vino
wino
Zibo
IP gimp
limp
LISP
lisp
pimp
risp
WIMP
wimp
wisp
IR bier
birr
Dior
fiar
kier
liar
MICR
pier
tier
tirr
vier
IS AIDS
Aids
aims
airs
bias□
bits
dies
digs
diss
fibs
fils
gios
hips
hiss□
hits
kids
kiss□
Lias
lies
lips
MIPS
mips
mirs
miss
oils
pics
pigs□
Pils
pins
Pius
RICS
SIDS
Sims
ties
tips
tits
wits
IT ain't
airt
bint
Biot
Birt
bitt
cist
diet□
dint
dirt
fiat
Fiat®
fist
GIFT
gift
gilt
girt
gist
hilt
hint
hist
jilt
kilt
kist
lift
lilt
lint
list
milt
mint
mist
mitt
oint
Pict
pint
pint-
Pitt
rift
riot
ritt
sift
silt
sist
tift
tilt
tint
vint
wilt
wist
Witt
ZIFT
Zift
IU BIFU
Gifu
Kivu
lieu
rimu
IV Kiev
MIRV
IW view
IX jinx
minx
IY airy
city
lily□
limy
Livy
miry
oily
piny
pioy
pipy
pity
pixy
ricy
rimy
tidy
tiny
viny
wily
winy
wiry
IZ Diaz
Díaz
fizz
hizz
jizz
Linz
tizz
zizz
JE ajee
JR ajar
JX Ajax
KA okra
skua
KD skid
KE Skye
KG skag
skug
KL skol
KM skim
KN akin
ikon
skin
KP skep
skip
KR sker
KS skis
KT ikat
skat
skit
KW skew
KY okay
LA alga
Alma
Elba
Ella
Elma
flea
glia
ilea
ilia
Olga
olla
plea
ulna
LB blab
bleb
blob
blub
club
flab
glib
glob
pleb
slab
slob
slub
LC Alec
bloc
flic
LD Aled
bled□
blvd
clad
clod
glad
plod
sled
slid
LE alae
alee
aloe
blae
blue
clue
Elbe
Elle
else
flee
floe
flue
glee
glue
Klee
Mlle
plié
sloe
slue
LF alef
alif
clef
LG blag
clag
clog
flag□
fleg
flog
glug
plug
slag
slog
slug
LH blah
LI glei
LK Blok
flak
LL Elul
LM alum
Blum
clam
Clem
glam
glom
glum
plim
plum
slam
slim
slum
ylem
LN Alan
Alun
clan
élan
flan
glen□
Glyn
plan
LO Algo
also
alto
Cleo
Clio
oleo
olio
LP blip
clap
clip
clop
flap
flip
flop
glop
plap
plop
slap
slip
slop
LR blur□
flor
slur
LS alas
alms
Alps
plus
LT a lot
blat
blet
blot
clot
Elat
flat
flit
glut
plot
slat
slit
slot
slut
LV Olav
Slav
LW alow
blew
blow
claw
clew□
flaw
flew
flow
glow
slew
slow
LX Alex
flax
flex
flux
ilex
LY Algy
ally□
clay□
cloy
flay
fley
gley
play
ploy
slay
MA Emma
YMCA
MD amid
ME smee□
MG smog
smug
MH GmbH
MK amok
Omsk
MM imam
MN amen
Amin
G-man
Oman
omen
MO ambo
ammo
HMSO
IMRO
umbo
MR Amur
emir
Omar
smur
MS Ames
Amis
Amos

Words marked □ can also be spelled with an initial capital letter

BMus
DMus
Mmes
Xmas
MT emit
omit
SMMT
smut
MU GMWU
MW smew
MX Amex
MY Emmy
NA anna❑
CNAA
ENSA
Inca
Inga
inia
INLA
NB knob
knub
PNdB
RNIB
snab
snib
snob
snub
ND Enid
RNID
sned
snod
NE Anne
ante
Inge
in re
knee
once
unbe
NF SNCF
NG knag
snag
snig
snog
snug❑
NH ankh
inch
NI anti
RNLI
unci
NL anil❑
BNFL
NM RNCM
NN in on
NO info
inro
into
on to
onto
unco
undo
NP knap
snap
snip

NQ GNVQ
NR gnar
knar
knur
RNVR
NS anas
ana's
anis
anus
gnus
Ines
onus
RNAS
NT gnat
in it
inst
knit
knot
Knut
onst
snot
unit
NU unau
NW anew
enew
enow
gnaw
knew
know
snow❑
NX Knox
onyx
UNIX
Unix
UNIX®
NY Andy
Angy
envy
inby
Indy
inky
inly
only
NZ Inez
OA bora
coca
coda
cola
coma
Cora
coxa
Doha
Doña
dopa
Dora
EOKA
fora
Goya
Hova
Iona
iota
Iowa
kola

kora
Kota
Lola
mona❑
mora
moxa
noma
Nora
nova
roma
Rona
Rosa
rota
soca
soda
sofa
sola
soma❑
soya
toga
yoga
Zola
OB AOCB
bomb
boob
Cobb
comb
doab
sorb
tomb
womb
OC douc
torc
zoic
OD bold
bond❑
cold
cord
Dodd
fold
fond
food
ford❑
Ford®
goad
gold❑
good
Hoad
hold
hood❑
Joad
load
loid
lord❑
loud
Mold
Mond
mood
pond
road
roed
rood
sold

toad❑
Todd
told
void
woad
wold
wood❑
word
you'd
OE a one
bode
boke
bole
bone
bore
Bose
code
C of E
coke
Coke®
cole❑
come
cone
cope❑
core
cote
cove
coze
doge
dole❑
dome
done
dope
Doré
dose
dote
dove❑
doze
fore
gone
gore❑
hoke
hole
home❑
hone
hope❑
hose
Hove
Howe
jobe
joke
Jove
Kobe
lobe
lode
loge
Lomé
lone
lope
lore
lose
love
mode

moke
mole❑
mope
more❑
mose
moue
move
moze
node
nole
none
nope
nose
note
ooze
poke
pole❑
pome
pone
pope❑
pore
pose
pote
robe
rode
roke
role
rôle
Rome
rone
rope
rore
rose❑
rosé
rote
roué
rove
Rowe
sole❑
some
sore
to be
toke
tole
tome
tone
tope
tore
tose
tote
toze
vole
vote
woke
wore
yoke
zone
OF boff
coff
coif
doff
golf❑
goof

gowf
hoof
howf
loaf
poof
pouf
Rolf
roof
sowf
toff
wolf❑
woof
OG bong
Borg
DOCG
dong
Doug
gong
Hogg
long❑
Moog®
nong
pong
Roeg
song
tong
OH bosh
both
cosh
dosh
doth
Foch
gosh
Goth
josh❑
Koch
koph
loch
loth
moth❑
Noah
nosh
pooh❑
posh
qoph
Roth
tosh
yodh
yogh
OI foci
Gobi
Holi
Hopi
Jodi
Joni
lobi
loci
Logi
Loki
loti
modi
MORI
nodi

nori
roti
soli
sori
Toni
topi
tori
yogi
OK boak
book
cock
conk
cook❑
cork❑
dock
dork
folk
fork
hock
hoik
honk
hook❑
howk
Jock
jook
jouk
kook
lock❑
look
mock
monk❑
nock
nook
pock
Polk
pook
pork
pouk
rock
rook❑
soak
sock
sook
souk
tock
tonk
took
work
yolk
York
zonk
OL boil
boll
Böll
bowl
coal
coil
Coll
cool
cowl
doll
dowl

foal
foil
fool❑
foul
fowl
goal
gowl
howl❑
Jodl
Joel
jowl
kohl❑
loll
moll❑
noel❑
Noël
nowl
poll❑
pool
roil
roll
soil
soul❑
toil
toll
tool
wool
yowl
OM Böhm
boom
Colm
coom
corm
doom
dorm
foam
form
gorm
holm
loam
loom
Noam
norm
poem
roam
Röhm
room
soum
toom
WORM
worm
zoom
ON Bonn
boon
born❑
boun
Cohn
coin
conn
corn
do in
down
föhn
go in
go on
gown
horn
Joan
john❑
join
koan
Köln
loan
loin
loon
lown
moan
moon
morn
noon
noun
porn
roan
soon
sorn
sown
torn
town
worn
OO boko
Boro
boyo
coco
Como
Cono
dodo
do to
go to
Gozo
hobo
homo
koto
lobo
logo
Lomo
Mojo
mono
Moro
no go
no-no
poco
pogo
polo❑
Polo®
ro-ro
soho
so-ho
solo
so so
so-so
Soto
to-do
Togo
toho
Tojo
Toto
yo-ho
yo-yo
OP Bopp
comp
coop
co-op
coup
dorp
do up
goop
go up
hoop
loop
loup
moop
moup
pomp
poop
Popp
romp
roop
roup
soap
soop
soup
yomp
yoop
OR boar
Boer
Bohr
boor
coir
doer
door
dour
four
goer
hoar
hour
lour
moor❑
poor
pour
roar
soar
sour
torr
tour
your
OS Bors
boss
bows
cops
cows
dohs
Dons
Dors
doss
foes
foss
gods
goes
goys
hoas
hohs
hols
Homs
hors
Jobs
joes
Joss
Lois
Loos
loss
lots
Mons
moss❑
nobs
noes
nous
oops
pods
pons
pots
Ross
Rous
rows
so as
S. of S.
sols
soss
togs
tons
tops
toss
Voss
vows
OT boat
bolt❑
boot❑
bott
bout
coat
colt❑
Colt®
coot
Copt
cost
doat
dolt
don't
dort
dost
dout
font
foot❑
fort
go at
goat❑
go it
gout
Govt
holt
hoot
host
jolt
loft
loot❑
lost
lout
moat
moot
most
Mott
nowt
Oort
poet
port
post
pott
pout
root
rort
rout
soft
soot
sort
to a T
toot
tort
tout
volt
wont
won't
woot
woo't
wort
yont
OU motu
non-U
tofu
tolu
OX coax
hoax
roux❑
OY body
bogy
bony
cony
copy
cosy
do by
dopy
dory
dozy
fogy
foxy
go by
goby
go-by
goey
gory
holy
homy
Jody
joey❑
Jouy
lory
mopy
nosy
oozy
poky
poly
pony
posy
poxy
ropy
Rory
rosy
Soay
Toby
tody
Tony
Tory
towy❑
OZ Lódz
PA Apia
CPSA
NPFA
PB SPAB
PC epic
IPCC
OPEC
spec
SPUC
uPVC
PD spud
PE apse
CPRE
épée
spae
Spee
PF IPPF
PG CPAG
PH Ipoh
opah
PK SPCK
PL opal
Opel®
PM spam❑
PN open
span
spin
spun
up on
upon
PO oppo
up to
PR spar
spur
PS Apis
Apus
EPNS
EPOS
epos
IPCS
opus
PT spat
spit
spot
up at
PV spiv
PW spew
PX APEX
apex
PY spay
Spey
spry❑
upby
RA area
aria
Irma
mRNA
proa
tRNA
urea
RB Arab
crab❑
crib
drab
drub
frab
grab
grub
prob
RC Eric
uric
WRAC
RD arid
brad
crad
cred
crud
Fred
grid
prod❑
trad
trod
RE Arne
arse
brae
Brie
Cree
dree
Erie
erne
Erse
free
FRSE
gree
grue
orle
pree
Prue
tree
true
urge
RF Graf
Orff
prof
tref
WRAF
RG areg
brag
brig

brog
crag
drag
drug
frag
frig
frog❑
grig
grog
prig
prog
trig
trog
trug
RH arch
pruh
SRCh
RK arak
trek
Uruk
RL Aral
aryl
oral
RM Aram
arum
Bram
brim
cram❑
dram
drum
from
gram❑
grim
IRBM
LRAM
pram
prim
PROM
prom
tram
trim❑
VRAM
RN Aran
Arun
bran❑
bren
Bryn
Erin
gran
grin
Iran
iron
Oran
wren❑
RO arco
Argo
arvo
brio
Brno
ergo
or so
proo
trio

RP crap
crop
drap
drip
drop
drop-
frap
FRCP
grip
LRCP
MRCP
prep
prop
trap
trip
wrap
RQ Iraq
RR brrr
RS Ares
arms
arts
BRCS
Bros
crus
ergs
Eros
FRCS
GRAS
Gris
Grus
iris❑
kris
LRCS
pros
très
WRNS
WRVS
RT aret
brat
brit❑
brut
crit
drat
erst
fret
frit
grit
grot
prat
trot❑
writ
RU Frau
prau
Urdu
RW arow
a-row
braw
brew
brow
craw
crew
crow❑
draw

drew❑
grew
grow
prow
trow
RX crux❑
oryx
T Rex
Trix
RY army
arty
bray
Cray
dray
drey
fray
Frey
Gray
grey❑
Kray
orgy
pray
prey
tray
trey
troy❑
Urey
X-ray
RZ Druz
friz
Graz
SA Asia
asta
Isla
ossa
RSSA
USIA
SB RSPB
SC ESRC
RSNC
SD used
SE Ashe
esse
isle
OSCE
SF as if
as of
USAF
SI asci
Asti
SSSI
SN ISBN
ISDN
SO as to
Esso
Oslo
RSNO
SP ASAP
asap
RSVP
VSOP
SR åsar
Msgr

PSBR
tsar
user
USSR
SS as is
CSYS
ISIS
Isis
tsps
ST isn't
psst
SU CSEU
Esau
SY ashy
espy
I say!
I-spy
TA stoa
TB stab
stub
TC BTEC
otic
STUC
TD stud
TE PTFE
stye
TG stag
TH etch
itch
Ptah
Utah
TL CTOL
et al
HTML
it'll
STOL
VTOL
TM atom
fthm
item
stem
stum
TN Aten
Eton
stun
TO Otho
otto❑
St-Lô
TP atap
atop
http
step❑
stop
TR star
stir
TS Otis
Utes
utis
TT at it
stet
stot
TV HTLV
TW stew

stow
TY stay
UA aura
BUPA
Cuba
Duma
hula
juga
Jura
kuna
Lüda
pula❑
puma
pupa
rusa
sura
Susa
Suva
tuba
tufa
Tula
tuna
UB bulb
curb
dumb
MusB
numb
UD auld
Budd
bund
curd
fund
hued
Hurd
IUCD
Kurd
Lund
MusD
nurd
quad
quid
quod
rudd
surd
turd
UE cube
cure❑
curé
cute
duce
dude
duke
dune
dupe
Duse
Duve
euge
Euwe
fume
fuse
huge
Hume
iure

jube
Jude
juke
June
jure
jute❑
Luce
luge
Luke
lure
lute
mule
mure
muse❑
mute
nude
NUPE
Ouse
puce
puke
pule
pure
rude❑
rule
rume
rune
ruse❑
Suke
sure
tube
tune
yuke
Yule
Zuse
UF buff
bumf
cuff
duff
fuff
guff
gulf
huff
luff
muff
puff
ruff
surf
tuff
turf
UG bung
dung
hung
Jung
lung
quag
rung
sung
UH bush❑
cush
dush
gush
Hugh
hush

Lugh
lush
much
mush
ouch
ouph
push
rush❑
Ruth
such
sukh
tush
UI Audi®
fuci
Fuji®
kuri
muti
puri
Pu Yi
Sufi
Tupí
Wuxi
Zuni
Zuñi
UK buck❑
bulk
bunk
burk
busk
duck
dunk
dusk
funk
gunk
huck
hulk
hunk
husk
junk
luck
lurk
muck❑
murk
musk
puck❑
punk
ruck
rusk❑
suck
sulk
sunk
tuck❑
Turk
tusk
yuck
UL buhl
bull❑
burl
cull
curl
dual
duel
dull❑

fuel
full
furl
gull
gurl
hull❑
hurl
lull
mull❑
murl
null
nurl
pull
purl
Tull
wull
UM culm
Guam
UN burn
Dunn
guan
Gunn
Kuhn
muon
Nunn
quin
ruin
turn
vuln
yuan
UO auto
bubo
euro❑
Hugo
judo
Juno
ludo
muso
ouzo
Puzo
sumo
yuko
UP bump
burp
cusp
dump

gulp
gump
hump
jump
lump
mump
pulp❑
pump
quep
quip
rump
rurp
sump
tump
yump
UR burr
curr
Muir
puer
purr
Ruhr
suer
US bugs
cuss
duds
dues
duos
fuss
guns
guts
huis
Huss
lues
muss
nuts
puns
puss
runs
suds
suss
wuss
UT aunt
bunt
bust
butt❑
cult

curt
duct
duet
dunt
dust
fust
gust
hunt❑
hurt❑
just
Kurt
lunt
lust
must
mutt
oust
punt
putt
quat
quit
runt
rust❑
suet
suit
tuft
yurt
UU guru
juju
ju-ju
kudu
luau
Lulu
Oulu
sulu
tutu❑
Wuhu
Zulu
UW AUEW
UY buoy
bury❑
busy
Dufy
duly
Dury
duty
fumy

fury❑
Huey
Judy
July
jury
Lucy
ou ay
puly
puny
quay
ruby❑
ruly
Suky
Susy
Suzy
UZ buzz
fuzz
lutz
quiz
Suez
VA DVLA
NVLA
VD avid
Ovid
VE Evie
evoe
VI TVEI
VL evil
oval
vvll
VM ovum
VN Avon
Evan
even
Ivan
Ivon
oven
VR aver
ever
Ivor
over
VS aves
Ives
Yves
VV Lvov
VW avow

WA YWCA
WB swab
WC KWAC
KWIC
KWOC
WD awed
owed
swad
WE AWRE
owre
swee
twee
WG swag
swig
twig
WI lwei
SWRI
WL AWOL
WM dwam
swam
swim
swum
WN Ewan
Ewen
Gwen
Gwyn
Owen
swan❑
twin
WP swap
swop
WR ewer
ower
WS Owls
WT swat
swot
twit
WY away
awry
M-way
sway
WZ swiz
XA ixia
XD axed
XE axle
XL axel

axil
XM exam
XN axon
exon
oxen
XO expo
XR exor
XS axes
axis
exes
Oxus
XT exit
YA cyma
Lyra
myna
Myra
SYHA
YB BYOB
YC sync
YD Byrd
synd
tynd
tyn'd
wynd
YE byre
byte
cyme
dyke
dyne
Eyre
gybe
gyre
gyve
hype
kyle
Lyle
Lyme
lyre
lyse
pyre
Ryde
Ryle
syne
sype
tyke
Tyne

type
tyre❑
YG Byng
YH ayah
myth
YK Eyck
YM lyam
YN ayin
cyan
hyen
hymn
Lynn
Ryan
syen
wynn
YO hypo
typo
tyro
YP gymp
YR Ayer
Györ
Iyar
YS byes
eyas
eyes
oyes
YT cyst
eyot
kyat
ryot
YX lynx❑
YZ oyez
ZA Ezra
ZC NZBC
ZL Ozal
ZM azym
ZN azan
ZR czar
ZS Uzis
ZV Azov
ZY Ozzy
ZZ Aziz

5 letters – even

AA Bahai
Baha'i
Bajan
banal
Barak
basal
Bayan
cabal
cacao
camas

canal
carat
Cavan
Dakar
daman
Danae
Davao
Dayan
fanal
farad

Farah
fatal
galah
gazar
hakam
halal
Halas
Hamad
Hasan
Jamal

japan❑
Kamal
Kanak
Karaj
Karan
kayak
Kazak
Kazan
Laban
Lanai

La Paz
lavas
lazar
Macao
macaw
madam
malax
Malay
manat
Marat

Masai
Masan
naiad
nasal
natal❑
naval
nawab
paean
pagan
Palau

papal
papaw
pavan
pawaw
Qatar
Rabat
radar
rajah
ramal
Raman
ratan
Sabal
Sadat
Sagan
Sakai
salad
Salam
Sarah
Satan
satay
tapas
Tatar
vagal
vasal
zakat
AB Bambi
bar-b-q
cabby
Darby
daube
gabby❏
Galba
garbo❏
iambi
jambo
Ka'aba
lay by
mamba
mambo
maybe
rabbi
samba
sambo
tabby
Tambo
AC baccy
BArch
batch
caeca
catch
Dacca
dance
Darcy
fancy
farce
fasci
ganch
hatch
lance❏
larch
latch
-mancy
march❏
match
Nance
nancy❏
narco
narcs
natch
parch
Pasch
patch
rance
ranch
sauce
saucy
Vance
watch
AD Baade
baddy
Banda
b and b
Bände
bandy
bawdy
caddy
can do
C and W
candy❏
daddy
Dagda
D and C
dandy
faddy
Faldo
G and T
garda❏
Gaudí
gauds
gaudy
h and c
hands
handy
hardy❏
Haydn
I-and-I
Kandy
LAMDA
Lando
lands
lardy
Lauda
lauds
Magda
Mahdi
Mandy
mardy
Maude
paddy❏
panda
pandy
pardi
pardy
ragde
R and B
rands
randy❏
S and M
sands❏
sandy❏
tardy
V and A
waddy
Waldo
Wanda
-wards
AE babel❏
Baden
Bader
bagel
baked
baker❏
baler
based
bases
Bates
caber
cadet
caged
cagey
camel
cameo
caper
Capet
carer
caret
Carey
cases
cater
caver
daker
Dalek
Dales
dated
daven
dazed
eager
eared
easel
eaten
eater
eaves
faced
facer
facet
faded
faked
faker
famed
fated
fazed
Galen
games
gamey
gaper
gases
gated
Gates
gavel
Haber
Hades
Hagen
Haley
harem
hated
Havel
haven
haver
haves
Hayes
hazel❏
jaded
jäger
jakes
James
Janet
japer
Jared
Karen
label
laced
laden
lager
Laker
lapel
Lares
laser
lated
laten
later
latex
laver❏
Lawes
layer
Mabel
maker❏
Mamet
maned
Manes
Manet
Marey
maser
mated
mater
matey
maven
Mayer
Nader
naked
named
nares
nates
navel
oaken
oared
oases
oaten
Oates
oaves
pacer
pacey
pager
Paget
Paley
panel
paper
pareo
pareu
paten
pater❏
paved
payee
payer
racer
races
rager
rakee
raker
ramen
ranee
ratel
rates
ravel❏
raven
raver
razee
saker
Salem
samey
saree
sated
saved
saver
savey
sawed
sayer
tabes
tacet
taken
taker
tales
tamed
tamer
taper
tapes
tawer
taxed
taxes
valet
vaned
varec
wader
wafer
waged
wager
wages
waken
Waler
Wales
waney
wares
water
waved
waver
waves
waxed
waxen
Yates
AF Banff
calfs
daffy
gaffe
Haifa
halfs
Jaffa
NAAFI
nakfa
samfu
Taffy
AG badge
baggy
bangs
barge
cadge
cargo
dagga
daggy
darga
faugh
gauge
jaggy
kanga❏
laigh
Lange
large
largo
laugh
Madge
Manga
mange
mango
mangy
marge
Margo
NALGO
Paige
pangs
parge
ragga
raggy
range
rangy
saggy
saiga
sarge
Taegu
taiga
tanga❏
tango❏
tangy
targe
Waugh
AH basho❏
bathe
baths
cache
Cathy
dacha

Farhi
kasha
Kathy
lathe
lathi
laths
Macha
macho
maths
nache
Nashe
oaths
pasha
pashm
paths
Sacha
Sachs
sadhe
sadhu
Sasha
tache
washy
yacht
AI BASIC
basic□
Basie
basil□
basin
basis
batik
cabin
Cádiz
calif
Carib
cavil
Dalit
David
Davie
Davis
davit
eat in
facia
fakir
gamin
Gavin
habit
hakim
ham it
Hasid
Jamie
Jamil
Janis
kalif
kamik
Karin
Kasim
Katie
Kavir
lakin
lamia□
Laois
lapis
Latin
lay in
Mafia
magic
Malin
Mamie
mania
manic
Maria
Marie
mavin
mavis□
maxim□
Nadia
nadir
Namib
oasis□
Palin
panic
Paris
patio
Pavia
pay in
rabid
Rabin
radii
radio
radix
Rajiv
ramie
ramin
rapid
ratio
ravin
Sadie
Safin
sahib
Salic
Samit
sapid
Sapir
Satie
satin
savin
sayid
tacit
Tamil
Tania
tapir
Tariq
taxis
Vadim
valid
vapid
varix
vatic
Wasim
way in
wazir
x-axis
y-axis
zayin
AJ banjo
Baoji
ganja
hadji
hajji
kanji
zanja
AK Banks
gawky
hacks
haiku
Hanks
hanky
Hawke
Hawks
jacks
Kafka
Laika
lanky
larks
Laski
lawks
maiko
manky
marka
marks□
narky
parka
parky
pawky
Ranke
sarky
tacky
talks
tanka
Tarka
wacko
wacky
AL badly
Baily
balls
bally
Basle
baulk
Bayle
cable
calla
Carla
Carly
caulk
daily
dally
eagle□
early
fable
Falla
falls
fatly
fault
gable□
gaily
Galle
gally
Gavle
Gayle
Halle
Hallé
hallo
haply
haulm
Kahlo
Karla
ladle
Lalla
laxly
Layla
madly
Malle
manly
maple
marly
matlo
nabla
pally
paoli
patly
Paula
Pauli
rails
rally
rawly
sable
sadly
Sails
sally□
Sayle
tabla
table□
tally
vault
walla
wally□
wanly
waulk
AM balmy
barmy
damme
gamma
gammy
halma
hammy
jammy
kamme
karma
magma
Malmo
Malmö
mamma
Palma
palmy
Parma
Saame
salmi
Sammy
tammy□
AN banns
Caine
canny
Carné
carny
Danny
daunt
fains
faint
Fanny
fauna□
gains
garni
gaunt
hadn't
Hanno
hasn't
haunt
jaunt
Laing
Larne
laund
Maine
Mainz
manna
Manny
Marne
Nanna
nanny
Paine
pains
paint
panne
Patna
Raine
rainy
saint
sauna
say no
Taino
taint
taunt
tawny
Varna
vaunt
Warne
Wayne
AO Aaron
bacon□
Baloo
Balor
baron
baton
bayou
Caboc
Cabot
CAFOD
canoe
canon
Canon®
capon
capos
capot
carob
carol□
dados
dagos
Damon
Davos
fados
Fanon
Gabon
Gabor
gajos
galop
Gamow
gapós
halon
halos
Hanoi
haros
havoc
jabot
Jacob
Jason
jatos
kagos
kapok
Karoo
kayos
kazoo
Lagos
lay on
Mâcon
mad on
ma foi
magot
major□
makos
manor
manos
mason□
Mayon
mayor
Mayow
nabob
napoo
Naxos
pacos
paeon
Paros
Patos
racon
radon
Ramos
rat on
rayon
razoo
razor
sabot
sajou
salon
Samoa
Samos
sapor
sarod
saros
savoy
Saxon

5 _A_P_

taboo
tabor
tacos
talon
taros
tarot
taxon
wagon
wahoo
yahoo
Yalow
AP campy
carpi
gappy
happy
harpy
jaspe
kappa
Nampo
nappa
nappe
nappy
palpi
pappy
Ralph
raspy
sappy
Tampa
taupe
waspy
yappy
Zappa
zappy
AQ Zarqa
AR Baird
bairn
bajra
Barra
barre
Barry
Basra
cadre
cairn
Cairo
CAMRA
Capra
Capri
Carré
carry
dairy
eagre
Fabre
fairy
Fauré
Garry
Gauri
hairy
harry□
Hatra
karri
kauri
labra
laird

Larry
Laura
macro
Maori
marry
nacre
NACRO
Nacro
naira
Nauru
padre
paire
pairs
parry□
sabra
sabre
sacra
saury
tarry
zabra
zaire□
AS bags I
Bakst
balsa
bassi
canst
cause
daisy□
false□
farse
Farsi
fatso
Faust
gassy
gauss□
hadst
halse
harsh
Hausa
karst
karsy
lapse
lasso
manse
marsh□
massé
palsy
pansy□
parse
Parsi
passé
patsy□
pause
raise
salsa
sassy
says I
say-so
tansy
tarsi
Tasso
tawse
Vaasa

valse
waist
AT Aalto
BAFTA
Bafta
balti
Bantu
Barth
basta
baste
batts
battu
batty□
cacti
canto
caste
catty
Dante
darts
earth□
facts
faith□
fatty
haith
Haiti
Hants
Harte
hasta
haste
hasty
Hatty
laity
latte
Malta
malty
manta
Marty
NAFTA
Nafta
nasty
natty
panto
pants
parts
party
pasta
paste
pasty
Patti
patty□
pay TV
raita
ratty□
saith
Sakti
salto
salts
salty
Sarto
sauté
tanto
tarty
taste

tasty
tatty
Waite
Waits
waltz
warty
waste
AU Babur
Calum
Camus
caput
dam up
datum
eat up
Faruq
gamut
garum
Hague
ham up
Janus
Kabul
kaput
Laius
lap up
lay up
magus
manus
Nahum
Namur
oakum
Padua
pay up
ramus
tabus
Tagus
talus
Tatum
vacua
Vaduz
vague
value
varus
wax up
Yakut
zap up
AV calve
carve
halva
halve
larva
Maeve
mauve
naevi
naive
naïve
navvy
salve
salvo
savvy
valve
varve
waive
AW fatwa

AY calyx
Katya
many a
nary a
satyr
Tanya
AZ baize
Bazza
gauze
gauzy
Gazza
jazzy
karzy
Lanza
Lao Zi
lazzi
maize
Manzú
matzo
Taizé
tazze
BA abeam
Abram
I-beam
obeah
Q-boat
U-boat
BC abaca
abaci
aback
BD abide
abode
a'body
BE abbey
Ibsen
objet
BF abaft
BI aboil
abrim
abrin
BJ Abuja
BK Mbeki
BL obeli
oboli
BM H-bomb
BN ebony
U-bend
BO abbot
abhor
ablow
Ibrox
BP tbsps
BR abord
abort
BS abase
abash
abask
abuse
abyss
obese
BT abate
kbyte
Obote

BU Abdul
about
BV above
ab ovo
BY abaya
BZ abuzz
Ibiza
CA act as
éclat
OCCAM
occam
ocean
octad
octal
scrag
scram
scrap
CB scuba
CC acock
CD acidy
scads
scudi
CE acres
G-clef
ocker
ocrea
octet
scree
screw
CF sci-fi
scoff
scuff
CI acrid
actin
scail
scrim
scrip
CL acold
E. coli
icily
oculi
scald
scale
scalp
scaly
scold
scull
t-cell
CM BComm
scamp
CN acini
icing
scant
scena
scene
scent
scone
CO act on
actor
McCoy
scion
scoop□
scoot

CP scapa
scape
scapi
scope
CR acari
Accra
acorn
ochre
ochry
scare
scarf
scarp
scart
scary
score
scorn
scurf
CS scuse
CT acute
ICFTU
scats
Scots
Scott
scuta
scute
UCATT
CU act up
actus
ice up
ictus
occur
scaup
scaur
scoup
scour
scout
scrub
scrum
CW schwa
scowl
scowp
DA adman
Adnan
Edgar
ideal
ideas
DB adobe
DC edict
educe
DE added
adder
adeem
adieu
Adler
ad rem
edged
edger
edges
Edred
idler
udder
DF edify
DG adage
Adige
DH Idaho
DI Addie
add in
addio
ad lib
ad-lib
admin
admit
admix
Eddie
Edwin
Idris
Oddie
DL addle
Adela
Adèle
Adolf
adult
Idola
idyll
Ndola
oddly
DM Adams
DN Adana
Idunn
DO add-on
ad hoc
adios
adiós
CD-ROM
idiom
idiot
odeon
odsos
DP adapt
adept
adopt
DR adore
adorn
DT add to
Aditi
adyta
Edith
Odets
DU add up
à deux
odium
odour
EA bedad
begad
began
begar
Behan
Behar
belay
Bevan
cedar
debag
debar
decay
defat
degas❑
delay
deman
Desai
Dewar
feral
fetal
getas
get at
geyan
hejab
hemal
he-man
hexad
Ieuan
jehad
kebab
kenaf
legal
leman
medal
Medan
Megan
Merak
metal
ne has
Neman
Nepal
ne was
pecan
pedal
pekan
penal
Pesah
petal
petar
re-bar
recal
recap
regal
Regan
rehab
relax❑
relay
renal
Renan
repay
resay
SECAM
sedan❑
see as
sepad
sepal
setae
telae
teras
Texas
Vedas
VE day
vegan
velar
venae
venal
EB Beebe
debby❑
derby❑
gerbe
get by
herbs
lesbo
let be
Melba
Newby
o'erby
set by
yerba
EC beach
beech
belch❑
bench❑
cerci
de-ice
Dench
deuce
fence
fetch
hence
keech
ketch
leach
leech
Leica®
letch
mecca❑
mercy❑
peace
peach
pence
perch
Percy
reach
react
recce
reccy
Reich
retch
teach❑
tench
terce
vetch
Welch
wench
ED beads
beady
bendy
deeds
geode
Gerda
heady
Heidi
herds
Jedda
kendo
Leeds
Lendl
Meade
Meads
neddy❑
needs
needy
nerdy
Penda
perdy
ready
reddy
reedy
seedy
teddy❑
Vedda
veldt
Verdi
weedy
Wendy
Zelda
EE bedel
bedew
begem
beget
belee
Belém
benet
Benét
beret
beset
betel
bevel
bewet
bezel
Ceres
defer
Deneb
denet
Derek
desex
deter
fever❑
fewer
fezes
genet❑
Hefei
Hegel
Helen
Heyer
jewel
Kesey
keyed
Léger
lenes
leper
levee
level
lever
Lewes
Medea
Médée
melee
mêlée
Menem
meter
Meyer
nevel
never
newel
Peres
peter❑
rebec
rebel
refer
remex
Renée
renew
repel
reset
revel
revet
Reyes
Seder
Seles
semen
sesey
seven
sever
sewed
sewer
sexed
seyen
te-hee
telex
tenet
tepee
Tevet
Texel
veney
vexed
weber❑
Weser
xebec
Yemen
yeses
EF beefs
beefy
be off
deify
delfs
delft❑
feoff
Geoff
leafy
neafe
reify
selfs
serfs
EG beige
cerge
deign
feign
hedge
heigh
Helga
henge
hewgh
kedge
ledge

5 _E_H_

legge
leggy
Leigh
let go
merge
neigh
Peggy
reign
sedge
sedgy
serge
tenge
terga
venge
verge
wedge
wedgy
weigh
EH Bethe
Delhi
hecht
meths
EI aecia
Aegir
aegis
aesir
bedim
befit
begin□
belie
Benin
Bevin
bewig
Cecil
cedis
Celia
debit
Delia
demit
denim
Denis
derig
devil
eerie
Felix
fetid
gelid
genic
genie
genii
geoid
get in
get it
helix
hem in
kelim
Kevin
key in
Le Cid
leg it
legit
Lenin
lenis
lepid
let in
Levin
Levis®
lewis□
lexis
media
medic
merit
metif
Métis
nelis
pen in
penis
Pepin
peril
pewit
rebid
récit
refit
rejig
re-jig
relic
remit
renig
renin
resin
resit
Revie
Selim
sepia
serif
serin
set in
telia
tepid
Vedic
vegie
xenia
xeric
EK beaky
Becky
decko
dekko
fenks
gecko
geeky
jerky
kecks
leaky
nerka
Peake
peaky
pecke
perky
pesky
reaks
welkt
EL Bella
belle□
bells
belly
ceili
cello
dealt
Della
fella
felly
ferly
gelly
heald
Hekla
hello□
jelly
Kelly
Leila
meals
mealy
Neale
nelly□
newly
realm
redly
repla
reply
Sella
sells
teals
telly
tesla□
veily
weald
Weill
Wells
welly
wetly
EM beams
derma
femme
fermi□
gemma□
germs
herms
Jemma
jemmy
lemma
neume
Reims
seame
seamy
terms
Weems
Yerma
EN beano
being
benny□
Berne
cerne
Denny
feint
fenny
ferny
Heine
Heinz
henna
jeans□
Jenna
jenny□
Keane
Kenny
Lenny
Leona
leone
meane
means
meant
meany
Peano
penna
penne
penny□
peony
reins
seine□
senna□
teend
teens
teeny
teind
terne
veiny
Verne
weeny
EO Aesop
bebop
befog
below
besom
besot
bet on
celom
décor
decoy
Defoe
Delos
demob
demon
demos
depot
detox
Devon
felon
fetor
gemot
genoa□
get on
helot
Herod
heroe
heron
jeton
lemon
lenos
Leroy
let on
Médoc
melon
Melos
memos
meson
metol□
me-too
Nepos
Pecos
peeoy
pekoe
pepos
Perón
pesos
rejón
repos
repot
segos
Señor
sepoy
set on
tenon
tenor
venom
xenon
xerox
Xerox®
zeros
EP delph
heaps
kelpy
Kempe
kempt
peepe
peppy
recpt
seepy
SERPS
Serps
tempi
tempo
tempt
weepy
ER beard
beery
Beira
Berra
berry□
Debra
decry
ferry□
gears
genre
Gerry
heard
heart
heirs
Henri
henry□
jerry□
Jewry
Kerry
learn
leery
merry
metre
metro
Negro
Nehru
pearl□
Pears
Peary
Pedro
peers
peery
perry□
Petra
rearm
repro
retro
retry
Segrè
serre
serry
tears
teary
terry□
tetra
weary
weird
yearn
years
zebra
ES beast
Bessy
Betsy
cease
cense
cesse
deism
deist
dense
feast
feese
fesse
geese
gesso
heist
Hesse
Jesse
Jessy
Kelso
lease
leash
least
leese
Mensa
mense
messy
Meuse
neese
newsy
Pepsi®
perse
reast
reest
reist
reuse
re-use
sease

Words marked □ can also be spelled with an initial capital letter

seism
sensa
sense
sessa
tease
temse
tense
terse
TESSA
Tessa
verse
verso
welsh□
yeast
Zeiss
ET berth
Betty
death
debts
deity□
delta□
depth
feats
Feste
fetta
Geeta
gents
get to
Getty
heath□
hefty
hertz□
Hetty
jetty
Keats
Keith
Leith
lenti
lento
lepta
Letty
Meath
meaty
neath
Nesta
Netta
Netty
peaty
Perth
pesto
petty
recta
recti
recto
Reith
SEATO
seats
see to
set to
set-to
teeth
tenth
tents

testa
tests
testy
vertu
vesta□
Yeats
zesty
EU beaut
beaux
begum
begun
Cetus
debug
debus
debut
début
degum
demur
fed up
femur
fetus
gee up
gen up
genus
get up
get-up
het up
Jesus
jésus
leg-up
lemur
Lepus
let up
let-up
nexus
pep up
rebus
rebut
recur
Remus
rerun
revue
sebum
sedum
segue
Seoul
serum
set up
set-up
sew up
tee up
velum
venue
Venus
EV bevvy
deave
deeve
delve
heave
heavy
helve
keeve
leave

Nerva
nerve
Nervi
nervy
peavy
peeve
perve
reeve□
selva
serve
servo
verve
weave
EW be two
fetwa
EX Benxi
EY bedye
beryl□
Beuys
Debye
Denys
Kenya
Lenya
Meryl
Pepys
EZ feeze
heeze
Jeeze
Kenzo
lezzy
mezzo
neeze
Penza
seaze
seize
senza
FA aflaj
offal
OFGAS
Ofgas
OFWAT
Ofwat
FE after
offer
OFTEL
Oftel
often
FG of age
FI affix
afrit
Effie
of kin
FL of old
FO afoot
Ffion
if not
OFLOT
Oflot
FR afire
FS of use
FT off to
FU afoul
GA eggar

ogham
GE aglee
aglet
agley
Agnes
Agnew
agree
egger
egret
ngwee
GI again
Aggie
ngaio□
oggin
ogmic
GL agile
GM agami
GN Agana
agent
aging
agony
Nguni
GO agios
aglow
agood
egg on
igloo
Ogdon
GP agape
Egypt
GR aggro
agora
GS agist
egest
GT agate
aguti
GV agave
ogive
HA ahead
Ahmad
Ahvaz
cheap
cheat
chiao
phial
Rhian
sheaf
sheal
shear
Shiah
shoal
thraw
uhlan
wheat
HB Chiba
dhobi
Sheba
HC chack
check
chica
chick
chock
chuck□

shack
shock
shuck
theca
thick
whack
which
Which?
HD chide
khadi
Rhoda
rhody
shade
shady
Zhu De
HE Ahmed
cheek
cheep
cheer
chief
Khmer
Shaef
sheel
sheen□
sheep
sheer
sheet
shiel
shies
shlep
shoes
shred
shrew
thief
three
threw
wheel
HF chafe
chaff
chuff
shaft
shift
theft
whiff
HG phage
shogi
thigh
HI Chaim
chain□
chair
choir
Chris
Ohrid
sheik
their
thrip
HJ shoji
HK choke
choko
choky
Dhaka
khaki
shake

shako
shaky
HL ahold
ahull
chalk
chela
child
Chile
chill
chyle
ghyll
phyla
shale
shall
shaly
shelf
shell
she'll
shill
shily
Shula
shule
shuln
shuls
shyly
thilk
thole
tholi
Thule
whale□
whelk
whelp
while
whole
HM champ
chime
chimo
chomp
chump
chyme
rhomb
rhumb
rhyme
shame
theme
thumb
thump
thyme
thymi
HN ahind
ahint
bhang
chant
china□
chine
chink□
chino
chunk
Ghana
Ghent
ohone
phang
phone

Words marked □ can also be spelled with an initial capital letter

5 _H_O_

Rhine
rhino
Rhona
Rhône
Shane
shank
shan't
shine
shiny
Shona
shone
shunt
thane❑
thank
thing
think❑
thong
whang
whine
whiny
HO a hoot
chaos
Chios
Chloe
choof
oh boy!
phlox
shook
shool
shoot
shrow
throb
throe
throw
whoop
HP chaps
chops
I hope
shape❑
ships
HR Ahern
chard
chark
charm
charr
chart
chary
chert
chirk
chirl
chirm
chirp
chirr
chirt
chord
chore
churl
churn
churr
NHBRC
O'Hara
O'Hare
shard

share
shark❑
sharp❑
sherd
shire❑
shirk
shirr
shirt
shore
shorn
short❑
Tharp
Thera
there
therm
Thira
third
thirl
Thora
thorn
uhuru
wharf
where
whirl
whirr
whore
whorl
HS chase❑
chasm
chess❑
chest
chose
ghost❑
Lhasa
phase
phese
shush
these
those
whish
whisk
whisp
whiss
whist
whose
Xhosa
HT Chita
chute
dhoti
Ghats
photo
rhyta
Shute
theta
Thoth
white❑
HU choux
ghoul
rheum
Shaun
shout
shrub
shrug

shtum
shtup
thous
thrum
uh-huh
whaup
HV chevy
chive
chivy
shave
shiva❑
shove
HW chewy
shawl
shawm
Shawn
shown
showy
HY ghayn
shoyu
they'd
HZ chizz
whizz
IA Aidan
aim at
bigae
Bihar
binal
cigar❑
Dinah
dinar
Dirac
divan
Eilat
filar
final
hi-hat
hijab
hit at
jihad
Jinan
Kitaj
Lifar
lilac
liras
litas
Micah
micas
Midas
Milan
minar
minas
MIRAS
nicad
Nicam
nidal
nikau
Nisan
nizam
Pilao
pilau
pilaw
pipal

rimae
rival
riyal
Silas
sisal
sitar
sit at
Sivan
tidal
Tikal
titan❑
vicar
Vidal
Vidar
Vijay
viral
vital
vitas
vivat
Wigan
IB bimbo
kimbo
Libby
Limbi
limbo❑
nimbi
NIMBY
Nimby
Niobe
sit by
Tibby
IC aitch
birch
bitch
cinch
circa
Circe
disco
ditch
filch
finch
fitch
hilch
hitch
milch
mince
mitch
niece
piccy
piece
pinch
pitch
Ricci
since
tinct
titch
wilco
wince
winch
witch
zilch
zinco
ID biddy❑

birds
Cindy
diddy
diode
giddy
Hilda
Hindi
Hindu
kiddy
kinda
kindy
Linda
Lindy
Middx
middy
misdo
Sindy
Sindy®
tilde
widdy
Wilde
wilds
windy
IE Aiden
aides
aînée
airer
bidet
biker
Binet
biped
biter
Bizet
cider
cited
CITES
civet
dicey
dimer
diner
diver
Dives
DIYer
eider
Eiger
Fides
fifer
filed
filer
files
filet
finer
fines
fired
firer
fiver
fives
fixed
fixer
giber
Giles
gilet
gimel

given
giver
hiker
Hines
hired
hirer
hi-tec
hives
jiver
kiley
libel
lifer
liger
liked
liken
limey
lined
linen
liner
lines
liven
liver
lives
miler
miles❑
mimer
miner
miser
mixed
mixer
nicer
Nigel
Niger
Nîmes
NIREX
nisei
Niven
oiled
oiler
pilea
piled
pilei
piles
piper❑
pipes
pixel
ricey
rider
riled
Riley
ripen
riser
rivel
river
rivet
sided
Sikes
silex
sinew
siren❑
sixer
sized
sizer

Tiber
tiger
tiled
tiler
timer
times
tinea
tined
tired
Tiree
vibes
vibex
video
vinew
viper
vireo
vires
vixen□
w iden
widen
wiles
winey
wiper
wired□
wirer
wived
wives
wizen
yikes
zineb
IF CIPFA
jiffy
LIFFE
miffy
niffy
IG Biggs
biggy
bilge
binge
bingo
ciggy
dinge
dingo
dingy
dirge
fidge
fingi
Giggs
hinge
jingo□
Kings
liege
Liège
lingo
midge
mingy
piggy□
pingo
ridge
rings
siege
singe
tinge
virga
Virgo
wings□
zingy
IH Aisha
bight
dicht
dishy
eight
fiche
fight
fishy
hight
hithe
kithe
light
lithe
litho
miche
might
niche
night
pithy
right
RIPHH
sight
sithe
tight
tithe
Wight
withe
withy
II bid in
bifid
cilia
civic
civil
dig in
digit
Dilip
dinic
dip in
dixie
finis
fit in
hit it
Jilin
kilim
kinin
licit
limit
lipid
Livia
livid
mimic
Mimir
minim
mirin
mix in
mix it
nitid
nixie
oidia
Oisin
pipit
pixie
rigid
sit in
sit-in
tibia
tie in
tie-in
timid
vigil
virid
visie
visit
vivid
IJ ninja
rioja□
IK dicky□
dinky□
Hicks
kicks
Kinks
kinky
links
Micky
milky
Nicky
picky
Ricky
Rilke
risky
silky
tikka
IL aioli
aïoli
aisle
bible□
bield
bills
billy□
dials
dilly
dimly
field□
filly
fitly
Gigli
girly
hilly
Killy
Lille
lisle
Mills
Mitla
Niall
piel'd
qibla
rifle
sidle
sigla
silly
Tilly
title
villa□
villi
viola□
wield
Wills
willy□
yield
IM biome
disme
films
filmy
Fiume
gimme
gismo
gizmo
hiems
Jimmy
Miami
Niamh
pigmy
sigma
Timmy
Wilma
IN Diana
Diane
diene
eigne
fiend
finny
Fiona
giant□
Ginny
hinny
jinni
Jinny
kiang
liana□
liane
Milne
ninny
piano□
pinna
Siena
signs
tinny
zirna
IO bigot
bijou
Biros
bison
bitos
ciaos
Cimon
didos
die of
Dijon
divot
ficos
figos
finos
fit on
Fitou
fix on
gigot
giros
hit on
kilos
kinos
Kirov
lidos
linos
miaow
micos
mid-on
milos
minor
Minos
misos
Nikon®
Nilot
Nimoy
ninon
Nixon
picot
pilot
pilow
pin on
piton
pivot
Ripon
rivos
Sidon
silos
Simon
sit on
Ticos
tigon
Timon
Timor
Titov
vinos
visor
vizor
widow
win on
winos
IP cippi
dippy
hippo
hippy
Kipps
Lippi
lippy
nippy
Pippa
pippy
timps
Wimpy
wispy
zippy
IR cirri
diary
fibre
fibro
fiery
fiord
Kiera
Libra
litre
micra
micro
mikra
mitre
nitre
Piers
Sitra
tiara
IS Ailsa
cissy□
dipso
ditsy
first
Gipsy
Hirst
kiosk
midst
Minsk
missy
rinse
sissy
tipsy
IT biota
birth
bitte
bitty
dicta
dirty
ditto
ditty
fifth
fifty
filth
firth
gifts
girth
hints
kilty
kitty□
linty
mirth
misty
Mitty
nifty
ninth
nitty
pieta□
pietà□
piety
pinta□
pinto□
piste
pitta
sieth
sixte
sixth
sixty
tilth
virtu
vista

vitta
width
witty
IU bid up
dig up
fit up
fit-up
fix up
gigue
hilum
Linus
lit up
miaul
minus
mix up
mix-up
pin up
pin-up
pious
pipul
pique
piqué
rig up
rip up
sinus
Sioux
sit up
situs
tie up
tie-up
Timur
titup
Titus
virus
Vitus
zip up
IV bivvy
civvy
divvy
lieve
sieve
IW Kitwe
IY Dilys
Libya
sibyl❑
vinyl
IZ ditzy
dizzy
fizzy
Liszt
Pinza
pizza
ritzy
tizzy
winze
JC eject
JN djinn
JR fjord
Njord
KA Akbar
Akram
skean
Skeat

skoal
KE skeet
skier
skies
skyer
UKAEA
KF skiff
KI skail
skein
KL Akela
skald
skelp
skill
skulk
skull
KM Nkomo
skimp
KN skank
skink
skint
skunk
KO I know
skeos
skios
KP okapi
KR skirl
skirr
skirt
skyre
KS ukase
KT skate
skite
skyte
KU Aksum
ek dum
KV skive
KY okays
LA Alban
algae
alias
Allah
Allan
allay
altar❑
bleak
blear
bleat
bloat
clean
clear
cleat
cloak
Elgar
eliad
elvan
Elway
float
fly at
gleam
glean
glial
gloat
ileac

iliac
plead
pleat
ulnae
ulnar
Ulsan
LB alibi
clubs
fly-by
glebe
globe
plebs
slubb
LC Alice
black❑
Bloch
block
clack
cleck
click
clock❑
cluck
elect
Flack
fleck
flick
flock
glacé
Gluck
place
pluck
slack
slice
slick
LD blade
Clyde
elide
elude
glade
glide
slade❑
slide
LE Albee
alder
alien❑
Allen
alley
alter
bleed
bleep
blues❑
bluey
cleek
clues
elder
Ellen
elver
elves
fleer
fleet❑
flier
flies
flyer

gleek
gleet
glued
gluey
Milles
olden
older
Olsen
Olwen
plier
plies
sleek
sleep
sleet
ulcer
LF aleft
aloft
bluff
cleft
cliff
Clift
flaff
fluff
pluff
LG align
Bligh
elegy
ology
Sligo
slugs
LH aloha
alpha❑
LI Alcis
Alfie
algid
alkie
Allie
all in
all-in
blain
Blair
claim
El Cid
elfin
Ellie
Ellis
Elsie
Elvis
flail
flair
fluid
glair
Klein
oldie
oleic
olein
Ollie
Olwin
plaid
plain
plait
slain
LJ Flo-Jo

LK alike
Blake
bloke
flake
flaky
fluke
fluky
glike
slake
LL alula
slily
slyly
LM Alamo
blame
blimp❑
blimy
clamp
climb
clime
clomp
clump
elemi
flame
fleme
flimp
flume
flump
glume
Klimt
llama
plumb
plume
plump
plumy
slime
slimy
slump
ulema
LN Åland
aline
alone
along
Blanc
bland
blank
blend
blind❑
blini
blink
blond
blunk
blunt❑
clang
clank
cline
cling
clink
clint❑
clone
clonk
clunk
eland
flank

fling
flint
flong
flunk
Flynn
gland
Glenn
glent
glint
Ilona
klang
Kline
plane
plank
plans
plant
plink
plonk
plunk
slang
slant
sling
slink
LO ALGOL
Algol
all of
allot
allow
alloy
aloof
altos
blood❑
bloom❑
bloop
Cleon
cloot
elbow
Eliot
Elroy
Elton
flood
floor
fluor
gloom
gloop
gluon
kloof
oleos
olios
plook
sloom
sloop
LP aleph
clipe
clype
elope
flype
glyph
slept
slope❑
slops
slopy
slype

Words marked ❑ can also be spelled with an initial capital letter

LR alarm
alert
blare
blurb
blurt
Clara
Clare
Clark
clart
clary
clerk
flare
flirt
flora❑
glare
glory
Klerk
slurp
ultra
ultra-
Uluru
LS blasé
blast
bless
bliss❑
blush
clash❑
clasp
class
close❑
flash
flask
flesh
flisk
floss
flush
glass❑
gloss
plash
plasm
plush
slash
slish
slosh
slush
LT alate
all to
all-to
BLitt
blitz
Blyth
cloth
DLitt
elate
elite
élite
elute
flite
flute❑
fluty
flyte
glitz
Klute
plate
Plath
Plato
Pluto
slate
slaty
sloth❑
zloty
LU album
aloud
blaud
Claud
claut
cloud
clour
clout
Fleur
flour
flout
fly up
glaum
glaur
ileum
ilium
oleum
plouk
LV alive
Clive
glove
olive❑
slave
slive
LW alowe
blown
blows
blowy
claws
clown
flown
LY Al Ayn
aleye
cloye
Clwyd
Elwyn
Floyd
Lloyd
Olwyn
playa
LZ blaze
Eliza
glaze
plaza
MA Amman
embar
embay
smear
umiak
MC amici
amuck
smack
smock
MD amide
ME amber❑
embed
ember
emcee
Emden
emmer
emmew
imbed
immew
impel
umbel
umber
MG amigo
image
imago
Omagh
omega
MH imshi
imshy
Omaha
MI ambit
amnia
amnio
email
e-mail❑
Emmie
impis
MK Smike
smoke
smoky
ML amble
ample
amply
Emily
emule
Imola
imply
n mile
small
smalt
smell
smelt
smile
smolt
MN amend
amine
amino
among
emend
IMunE
MO ambos
ammon
embog
embox
smoor
smoot
umbos
MR D-mark
emery❑
emure
Imari
ombre
ombré
smarm
smart❑
smirk
smore
umbra
MS a mass
amass
Amish
amiss❑
amuse
omasa
smash
UMIST
MT amate
Amati
amity
emote
empty
RMetS
smite
smith❑
Smuts
MU amour
embus
imbue
ombus
ombús
MV amove
MW BMEWS
MY Emlyn
Emmys
Emrys
Omiya
MZ amaze
NA antae
antar
Anwar
Anzac
Incan
in-car
inlay
Inman
Invar®
knead
on tap
Snead
sneak
sneap
unbag
unbar
uncap
unhat
Uniat
unlay
unman
unpay
unsay
untax
NB knobs
NC enact
Enoch
knack
knock
on ice
snack
sneck
snick
UNHCR
ND anode
snide
UNIDO
NE Andes
angel❑
anger
annex
ended
Ender
enmew
enter
Enzed
index
infer
in few
inlet
inner
Innes
in rem
INSET
inset
inter
kneed
knee'd
kneel
oncer
onset
sneer
snoek
unbed
under
unget
unmet
unmew
unpen
Unser
unset
unsew
unsex
unwed
NF in-off
knife
on-off
snafu
sniff
snift
snuff
unify
NG Inigo
Onega
snags
NI Anaïs
Angie
Annie
antic
anvil
Anzio
enfix
entia
India
Indic
indie
infix
ink in
intil
Inuit
snail
undid
unfit
unfix
unhip
unlid
unlit
unpin
unrig
unrip
untie
until
untin
unwit
unzip
NK ensky
snake
snaky
snoke
NL anele
angle❑
ankle
in all
in alt
inkle
knell
knelt
knoll
uncle
NM anima
anomy
enema
enemy
gnome
Mneme
NN an-end
anent
inane
in one
Inön
on end
NO ancon
anion
annoy
end-on
endow
enjoy
enrol
Ensor
envoy
in for
ingot
in tow
onion
snood
snook

snool
snoop
snoot
unbox
uncos
ungod
union
NP inapt
inept
snipe
snips
unapt
NR Andre
angry
antra
Enard
entry
gnarl
gnarr
inarm
Indra
indri
inert
infra
inorb
intro
inure
inurn
knurl
knurr
snare
snarl
snore
snort
unarm
NS angst
anise
gnash
in use
knish
knosp
snash
NT Anita
Knott
uneth
UNITA
unite
units
unity❏
NU Angus
annul
endue
end up
ennui
ensue
in bud
incur
incus
indue
Indus
in fun
in pup
input
in sum
knout
on cue
one up
snout❏
uncut
undue
ungum
NV knave
NW in two
knowe
known
snowk
snowy❏
UNRWA
NY inbye
OA Bolan
bolas
borak
borax
Cohan
comae
Copán
coral❏
coram
coxae
domal
Donal
Donau
focal
foray
go bad
go far
go mad
gonad
gopak
Gopal
Hogan
Honan
Hovas
Jonah
Kodak®
Koran
lobar
local
Loman
loran❏
lovat
loyal
modal
molal
molar
molas
monad
Morag
moral
moray❏
nodal
nomad
Norah
novae
novas
no way
noway
polar
Qoran
Rohan
roman❏
romas
roral
rowan❏
royal
so far
SOGAT
solar
somas
sonar
today
toga'd
tolar
tonal
topaz
Torah
total
vocab
vocal
volae
volar
woman❏
Wotan
Zohar
zonae
zonal
OB bobby❏
bombe
bombs
boobs
booby
combe
combo
Cosby
doubt
forby
gobbi
Gobbo
Hobbs
hobby
kombu
lobby
Tomba
tombs
womby
yobbo
zombi
Zorba
OC bonce
Bosch
botch
coach
coact
cocci
conch
couch❏
dolce
force
Gooch
hoick
hooch
hotch
Joyce
loach
Lorca
Monck
mooch
Mosca
mouch
nonce
notch
poach
ponce
poncy
pooch
porch
pouch
roach❏
Royce
souce
souct
torch
Tosca
touch
voice
voici
vouch
yoick
OD Aoede
Bondi
bonds
boody
cords
dowdy
Fonda
Golda
good-o
goods
goody
Gouda
Honda
horde
Korda
loads
lords❏
mondo
moody❏
noddy
roads
Roddy
rondo
rowdy
Soddy
soldi
sonde
toady
toddy
tondi
tondo
woods❏
woody
words
wordy
zonda
OE bogey
boned
boner
bones❏
bored
borer
bowed
bowel
bower
boxer❏
codex
Cohen
coley
comer
comet❏
coney
cooee
copec
coper
Corea
cored
corer
coven
cover
covet
covey
cowed
cower
Cowes
cozen
domed
donee
doped
dopey
Dover
dowel
dower
doyen
dozen
fogey
fovea
foxed
Foxes
foyer
Gödel
gofer
golem
Gomel
goner
gooey
go red
Gower
holed
holey
Homer
homes
homey
honey
hooey
Hosea
hosen
hoses
hotel❏
hovel
hover
joker
jokes
jokey
Jones
kopek
lobed
loden
loner
Loren
loser
loved
lover
lower
model
modem
mohel
Monet
money❏
moped
moper
morel
mores
Mosel
Moses
mosey
motel
moten
motet
moved
mover
moves
mower
Nobel
nones
nonet
nosed
nosey
noted
notes
novel
poker
posed
poser
power
robes
Robey
rodeo❏
Roger
romeo❏
roneo
roped
ropey
Roses
roset
Rouen
rover
rowel
rower
sober

soles
Soper
Soter
sowed
Soyer
token
to let
topee
toper
totem
towel
tower
toyer
voces
Vogel
vomer
voter
vowel
Woden
woken
women
wooer
wowee
yodel
yoked
yokel
OF comfy
Corfu
go off
goofy❑
hoofs
loofa
loofs
roofs
sol-fa
sowff
toffs
Wolfe
OG bodge
Boggs
boggy
bongo
bouge
bough
conga
congé
Congo
CORGI
corgi
cough
dodge
dodgy
doggo
doggy
donga
dough
foggy
forge
forgo
Golgi
gorge
gouge
Gough

lodge❑
lough
moggy
podgy
pongo❑
pongy
porge
Porgy
rouge
rough
soggy
sough
Tonga
tongs
Torga
tough
Volga
wodge
wonga
wongi
Yonge
OH Boche
Botha
bothy
foehn
hoo-ha
Hoxha
Kochi
mocha
Moche
Moshe
moths
Sochi
Sophy
tophi
OI bogie
boric
Boris
Bowie
bow in
box in
colic
Colin
comic
conic
Corin
dolia
Dolin
Doria
Doric
Doris
eosin
folia
folic
folio
gonia
goyim
hog it
hop it
ionic❑
Jodie
Josie
logic

loris
Louie
louis❑
modii
Moria
motif
movie
noria
podia
polio
pop in
posit
potin
robin❑
Rodin
roric
rorid
Rosie
rosin
rotis
Sofia
solid
Sonia
sonic
Tobin
Tobit
tonic
topic
toric❑
torii
to wit
toxic
toxin
vomit
yogic
yogin
zoris
zowie
OJ kopje
OK books
bosky
cocky
Cooke
corky
folks
Gorky
hokku
hooka
Hooke
hooky
kooky
Korky
Locke
locks
looks
poake
polka
pooka
porky
pouke
rocks
rocky❑
rooky

socks
vodka
wonky
works
yonks
OL Boole
boult❑
bowls
Boyle
colly
COSLA
coyly
do-all
doily
dolly❑
dowle
Doyle
Foale
folly
fonly
fowls
goals
godly
golly
Gould
holla
hollo
holly❑
hooly
hotly
Hoyle
Joely
jolly
Jools
joule❑
jowly
koala
lolly
lowly
Molly
mooli
mould
moult
noble
nobly
Polly
Poole
poult
Roald
Rolli
Rolls
Rolls®
rotls
socle
Solly
toile
tools
voila
voilà
voile
woold
Woolf
world❑

would
yodle
you'll
OM comma
coomb
corms
Cosmo
dogma
dolma
dooms
dormy
foamy
forme
korma
loamy
momma
mommy
Norma
poems
rooms
roomy
Somme
tommy❑
Worms
wormy
ON Boann
boing
bonny❑
Boone
borne
bound
bowne
Boyne
coins
corni
corny
count
doing
Donna
Donne
doona
Doone
downs❑
downy
found
fount
go and
going
gonna
horny
hound
Johns
joint
koine❑
loony
Lorna
lowne
moony
Morna
mound
mount
no end
no one

no-one
nouny
poind
point
Poona
porno
pound❑
round
royne
Soane
sonny
sound
sownd
tonne
towny
wound
xoana
young❑
zoons
OO bokos
bolos
boron
bosom
boson
bozos
COBOL
cocoa
cocos
codon
cohos
colon
Colón
Conor
Corot
dodos
do for
dojos
donor
gobos
go for
Gogol
hobos
Hohot
Honor
hoo-oo
HOTOL
hot on
kolos
Koror
kotos
kotow
locos
logos
lotos
low on
mojos
mokos
Monod
monos
moron
Moros
motor
nomoi

Words marked ❑ can also be spelled with an initial capital letter

no-nos
no-no's
not on
polos
pot on
potoo
robot
ro-ros
rotor
Sodom
Solon
solos
Solow
son of
sopor
tocos
to-dos
tohos
tokos
topoi
zobos
OP coapt
coopt
co-opt
corps
coupe
coupé
coypu
go ape
Hoops
hoppy
loopy
loupe
morph
oomph
Poopó
poppy
poupe
poupt
RoSPA
soapy
soppy
soupy
OR board
Bosra
bourn
cobra
copra
court❑
cowry
dobra
Doors
Douro
dowry
go dry
gourd
hoard
hoary
houri
koori
Loire
Lorre
lorry
Lowry
Moira
moire
moiré
Monro
Moore
mourn
sopra
sorry
Tours
worry
you're
yours
OS boast
Boise
boost
bossy
bouse
coast
COHSE
copse
Doisy
dorsa
douse
dowse
foist
fossa
fosse
goose
gorse
gorsy
gosse
hoast
hoist
Holst
hoosh
horse
horst
horsy
house❑
joist
Jooss
joust
loess
loose
louse
lousy
lowse
moist
moose
Morse
mossy
mouse
mousy
noise
noisy
noose
Norse
poesy
poise
popsy
roast
roist
roose
roost
rouse
roust
royst
sonsy
Sousa
souse
sowse
toast
Tomsk
Topsy
torso❑
tossy
touse
towse
woosh
worse
worst
OT aorta
Aosta
bolts
booth❑
boots
booty
bow to
coate
coati
Comte
contd
costa
costs
cotta
dotty
foots
footy
forte❑
forth❑
forty
Fouts
gotta
gouty
hosta
hosts
kofta
loath
lofty
lotto
Louth
molto
monte
month
Mopti
motte
motto
mouth
nod to
north❑
potto
potty
pouty
roate
roots❑
rorty
route
softy
Solti
sooth
sooty
south❑
sowth
tooth
torte
Volta
volte
worth
youth
OU bob up
bogus
bolus
bonus
bosun
Colum
Comus
do out
focus
fog up
forum❑
go out
hocus
ho-hum
Horus
hot up
Iomud
locum
locus
lotus
mogul
mop up
mop-up
Mosul
Motus
not up
novum
pop up
pop-up
pot up
rogue
Rogun
sorus
tog up
ton-up
top up
toque
torus
tot up
vogue❑
yokul
OV loave
Soave
solve
Volvo®
you've
OW Conwy
Loewe
OY Konya
polyp
polys
Powys
Robyn
Sonya
Tokyo
Tonys
OZ booze
boozy
gonzo
Monza
Pozzo
toaze
touze
towze
woozy
PA apeak
apian
appal
Oprah
speak
spean
spear
splat
splay
sprag
sprat
spray
uplay
PC apace
epact
epoch
space
speck
specs
spica❑
spice
spick
spicy
PD epode
spade❑
spode❑
PE apeek
après
speed
speel
Speer
spiel
spies
spree
upjet
upper
upset
Ypres
PG apage
PH spahi
PI aphid
aphis
April
apsis
BPhil
MPhil
optic❑
Spain
speir
split❑
spoil
sprig
sprit
uptie
PK Speke
spike
spiky
spoke
PL apple
apply
aptly
spall
spalt
speld
spell
spelt
spile
spill
spilt
PM spume
spumy
PN aping
Epona
opine
spane
spang
spank
spend
spent
spine
spiny
spunk
upend
up-end
PO apoop
apron
ephod
EPROM
Epsom
oppos
spoof
spook
spool
spoom
spoon
spoor
sprog
spy on
up for
up top
PR apart
apery
Aphra
aport
appro
EPSRC
Op Art
opera
PPARC
spare

spark❑
sperm
spire
spirt
spore
sport
spurn
Spurs
spurt
PS apish
spasm
PT apt to
Opitz
spate
spite
spitz❑
spots
sputa
PU appui
appuy
opium
spout
sprue
PW spawn
PX epoxy
PY upbye
PZ spazz
QA equal
squab
squad
squat
squaw
QB Aqaba
QI equip
squib
squid
squit
QU Equus
RA argal
Arian
A-road
arrah
Arran
arras❑
array
artal
Aryan
bread
break
bream❑
Brian
briar
broad
Bryan
creak
cream
croak
Croat
dread
dream
drear
dryad
freak
friar
great❑
groan
groat
Kraak
kraal
oread
organ
prial
Priam
pro-am
tread
treat
triad
trial
troat
urban❑
ureal
urial
urman
wreak
RB bribe
grebe
Krebs
oribi
probe
tribe
RC areca
Arica
brace
bract
brick
Broca
broch
Bruce
crack
Crécy
crick❑
Croce
crock
Draco
erect
erica❑
eruct
fract
frock
GRACE
grace❑
Greco
grice
oracy
price❑
prick
pricy
trace
track
tract
Tracy
trice
trick
truce
truck
wrack
wreck
wrick
RD Brady
Breda
bride
credo
crude
crudy
erode
Freda
grade❑
irade
Prado
predy
pride❑
Prodi
prude
trade
Trudy
RE Arden
ariel❑
Aries
Arles
armed
breed
brief
brier
creed
creek❑
creel
creep
crier
cries
cruel
cruet
dried
drier
dryer
erven
freed
freer
fried
frier
fryer
greed❑
Greek
green❑
Greer
greet
grief
Grieg
gruel
irked
order
oriel
ormer
preen
proem
treen
trees
tried
trier❑
urger
RF craft
croft
draff
draft
drift
graff
graft
griff
gruff
kraft
trefa
RG Bragg
dregs
drugs
Frege
Frigg
tragi
RH Archy
Brahe
prahu
RI argil
arris
artic
braid❑
brail
brain
broil
bruit
Craig
drail
drain
droit
druid❑
Ernie
frail
fruit
grail❑
grain
Greig
groin
krait
Mr Big
orbit
orgia
orpin
orris
Praia
pry in
traik
trail
train
trait
ureic
vraic
RK brake
broke
crake
drake❑
grike
proke
RL Arkle
brill
brûlé
drill
drily
droll
dryly
frill
grill
krill
prill
prole
tra-la
trill
troll
truly
Urals
wryly
RM aroma
cramp
crème
crime
crimp
crome
crumb
crump
drama
DRAMs
frame
Frome
frump
grime
grimy
grume
grump
Prima
prime
primo
primp
primy
promo
tramp
tromp
trump
RN arena
aren't
brand
Brent
brine
bring
brink❑
briny
Bruno
brunt
crane❑
crank
crine
crone
crony
drank
drant
drink
drone
drunk
franc
frank❑
frena
Frink
frond
front
grand
grant❑
grind
grunt
Irena
Irene
irons❑
irony
krans
kranz
Krenz
krona
krone
prana
prang
prank
prink
print
prone
prong
pronk
prune
trant
trend
Trent
Trina
trine
trunk
urent
urine
wring
wrong
RO arbor
argol
argon
Argos
argot
ariot
Arnor
arrow❑
arson
arvos
brood
brook❑
broom
Creon
crook
croon
cruor
cry on
Drood
drook
drool
droop
ergot
Errol
error
groom
Kreon

kroon
Ordos
Orion
orlop
Orson
Orton
Oryol
prior
proof
Pryor
trios
Troon
troop
try on
try-on
vroom
RP crape
craps
crepe
crèpe
crêpe
crept
crêpy
crypt
drape
drupe
erupt
grape
graph
GRAPO
Grapo
gripe
grope
Krupp
trape
tripe
trope
RQ Iraqi
RR frore
prore
Truro
RS arise
brash
brass
Brest
brisk
brose
brush
crash□
crass
cress
crest
crisp
cross
crush
crust
dress
dross
Druse
erase
Ernst
erose
frass
fresh
frisk
frost□
frush
grasp
grass□
grise
grist
gross
Grosz
Irish
prese
press
prise
prism
prose
Prost
prosy
trash
tress
Trish
truss
trust
tryst
wrest
wrist
RT arête
arett
Arita
Brett
broth
brute
crate
Crete
Erato
frati
fritz
froth
grate
Greta
grits
irate
orate
prate
trite
troth
truth
urate
wrath
write
wrote
wroth
RU Arbus
argue
Argun
Argus
Århus
Arius
Braun
croup
cry up
drouk
dry up
dry-up
fraud
Freud
fry-up
group
grout
proud
Prout
trout
RV brave
bravo□
breve
crave
drive
drove
grave
gravy
grove□
privy
prove
Provo
RW brawl
brawn
brown□
crawl
Crewe
crowd
crown
drawl
drawn
drown
frown
growl
grown
prawn
prowl
trawl
trews
Urawa
RX proxy
Trixy
RY Freya
RZ braze
craze
crazy
Druze
frizz
froze
graze
prize
SA ASEAN
Asean
Asian
Aslan
Assad
assai
Assam
assay
Aswan
as was
asway
CS gas
essay
Isaac
Islam
Islay
oscar□
pshaw
psoas
USDAW
usual
SC NSPCC
psych
RSPCA
SD aside
A-side
SE ashen
Asher
ashes
ashet
askew
ASLEF
as new
aspen□
as per
asses
asset
aster
as yet
as-yet
esker
Essen
Essex
ester
islet
osier
usher
SG usage
V-sign
SI ASCII
asdic□
a snip
aspic
astir
Essie
g-suit□
NSAID
ossia
Ossis
Ostia
Q-ship
SK Osaka
SL Isold
istle
psalm
SN asana
as one
using
SO Ascot
as for
as how
as now
Astor
escot
estop
g-spot
MSDOS
MS-DOS
MS-DOS®
SR Astra®
users
usure
usurp
usury
SS RSFSR
SU ascus
issue
Issus
pseud
use up
TA atlas□
atman
at par
attar
at war
stead□
steak
steal
steam
stean
stoae
stoai
stoas
stoat
strad
strap
straw□
stray
TB Stubb
TC stack
Stacy
stich
stick
stock
stuck
Utica
TD étude
study
TE at sea
Ethel
ether
other
Otley
otter
Staël
steed
steek
steel□
steen
steep
steer
sties
stoep
strep
strew
styes
utter
TF staff
stiff
stuff
TG stage
stagy
TH itchy
TI atria
atrip
attic□
ethic
staid
stain
stair
stein□
stoic
stoit
stria
strig
strip
TK stake
stoke
TL at all
atilt
atoll
ettle
Italy
stale
stalk
stall
stele
stell
stilb
stile
still
stilt
stole
style
styli
utile
TM atomy
etyma
items
stamp
stoma
stomp
stumm
stump
styme
TN at one
atone
atony
stand
stend
Steno
stent
sting
stink
stint
stone□
stonk
stony
stung
stunt
TO Athos
ethos

Words marked □ can also be spelled with an initial capital letter

stood
stook
stool
stoop
strop
TP steps
stipe
stope
stupa
stupe
TR stare
stark
Starr
stars
START
start
stere
stern❑
store
stork
storm
story
Sturt
styre
uteri
U-turn
TS stash
TT state
styte
TU stoup
stout
strum
strut
TV stave
Steve
stive
stove
TW stewy
Stowe
TX ataxy
TY ethyl
stays
UA aurae
aural
auras
buran
Busan
Cuban
Dubai
ducal
ducat
Dukas
Dumas
fugal
gulag
human
Judah
Judas
jumar
jurat
kulak
Kumar
kunar
Lucan
Lucas
lunar
Murad
mural
Murat
NUAAW
pumas
pupae
pupal
pupas
Pusan
Quran
Qur'an
rural
sugar❑
sumac
surah
sural
Surat
Susan
tubae
tubal
tubas
tunas
Wuhan
UB busby❑
curbs
dumbo❑
gumbo
hubby
jumbo
outby
put by
rugby❑
rumba
tubby
turbo
UC Buick®
bunce
bunch
bunco
butch❑
Cuzco
dunce
dunch
Dutch
gulch
hunch
hutch
juice
juicy
lunch
lurch
mulch
mulct
munch❑
Musca
ounce
Pucci
punch❑
quack
quick
succi
sulci
yucca
UD buddy
fundi
funds
Fundy
guide
Lundy
muddy
Murdo
Nuada
Oujda
outdo
quids
ruddy
suede
UE Auden
auger
aurei
Buber
buses
buyer
cupel
cured
duped
Drer
duvet
Euler
fumes
fumet
Funen
fused
fusee
gules
Hubel
julep
luces
Luger
Luger®
lumen
Lurex®
luxes
muted
numen
Nupes
ousel
outer
ouzel
puler
purée
Pusey
queen❑
queer
quiet
ruled
ruler
rules
rumen
rupee
suber
super
tubed
tuber
tuned
tuner
tutee
UF buffa
buffe
buffi
buffo
cuffo
cuffs
Duffy
huffy
luffa
puffy
quaff
quiff
surfy
tuffe
turfs
turfy
UG budge❑
buggy
bulge❑
bulgy
burgh❑
Durga
fudge
fuggy
fungi
gunge
gungy
judge❑
lunge
lungi
lurgi
lurgy
muggy
Mungo
nudge
outgo
pudgy
purge
Rudge
surge
vulgo
UH aught
bushy
cushy
duchy
Fuchs
gushy
Mucha
musha
mushy
nucha
ought
ouphe
pushy
ruche
sushi
UI audio
audit
auric
auxin
Bunin
burin
buy in
cubic
cubit
cumin
cupid❑
curie❑
curio
cut in
cutis
cut it
Dupin
fusil
Fuxin
humic
humid
Julia
Julie
Kufic
Lucia
lucid
ludic
lug in
lupin
lurid
mucid
music
musit
nudie
pubis
Pugin
Punic
pupil
Purim
purin
put in
Putin
quail
quoin
quoit
rub in
runic
run in
run-in
Sufis
Sukie
Sunil
Susie
tulip
tumid
tunic
Tunis
tupik
Turin
UK Bubka
Buck's
bulky
bunko
Burke
dumky
dusky
funky
hucks
hunky
husks
husky
junky
lucky❑
mucky
murky
musky
pukka
punka
quake
quaky
sucks!
sulks
sulky
Turki
Turku
tusky
yucky
yukky
UL bugle
build
built
bulla
bulls
bully
burly
curly
Duala
dully
duple
duply
fugle
fully
guild
guile
guilt
gully
hullo
Lully
Nuala
qualm
quell
quill
Quilp
quilt
rumly
Sulla
sully❑
surly
tulle
UM Burma
dummy
duomi
duomo
guimp
gummy
lumme
lummy
mummy
NUGMW

Words marked ❑ can also be spelled with an initial capital letter

Nurmi
rummy
tummy
yummy
UN Bueno
bunny
Burns
burnt
Duane
funny
guana
guano
gunny
Husni
Jumna
Khne
Luing
quant□
quint
quonk
ruins
runny
Sunna
Sunni
sunny
tunny
zurna
UO auloi
autos
budos
Blow
buxom
Cukor
Dukou
Duroc
duros
euros
futon
Huron
husos
Junor
jupon
juror
kudos
ludos
Luton
Luxor
Luzon
musos
out of
ouzos
put on
put-on
run on
sudor
sumos
Suwon
Tudor
tutor
Yukon
UP bumph
bumpy
cuppa
dumps
dumpy
guppy
humph□
humpy
jumpy
lumpy
mumps
NUCPS
pulpy
puppy
yuppy
UR Buerk
Burra
burro
curry□
furry
guard
Huari
hurra
hurry
kukri
lucre
Munro
outré
quark
quart
quern
query
quire
quirk
quirt
sucre□
Sun Ra
supra
surra
sutra
US buist
bursa□
burst
bussu
curse
cursi
dulse
dunsh
fussy
guess
guest
guise
gutsy
hurst□
hussy
Kursk
mumsy
mussy
nurse□
pulse
purse
pursy
pussy
quash
quasi
quasi-
quest
sudsy
Tulsa
wurst
UT aunty
Bunty
busty
butte
butty
due to
duets
duett
dusty
furth
fusty
gusto
gusty
gutta
junta
junto
jutty
lusty
mufti
Muntz
musth
musty
nutty
out to
putti
put to
putto
putty
quite
Quito
quits
quota
quote
run to
rusty
rutty
Suita
suite
tufty
tutti
tutty
UU augur
butut
buy up
cut up
durum
fucus
fugue
gum up
humus
lupus□
mucus
mug up
put up
queue
rub up
Rufus
run up
run-up
sum up
sun-up
tuque
UV curve
curvy
guava
luvvy
suave
vulva
UY Surya
UZ furze
fuzzy
huzza
kudzu
muzzy
VA avian
VC evict
VD evade
VI avail
avoid
Avril
ovoid
VK evoke
VL Ávila
NVALA
ovoli
ovolo
ovule
uvula
VN avine
Evans
evens
event
Ivana
ovine
VR avert
Avery
evert□
every□
ivory□
ovary
overt
VS avast
kvass
VT Evita
ovate
Ovett
WA sweal
swear
sweat
tweak
WB swabs
WC AWACS
twice
WD swede□
WE a-week
aweel
awned
owlet
owner
sweel
sweep
sweet
tweed□
tweer
tweet
twyer
WF swift□
WG swage
WI await
swain
Twain
WK awake
Iwaki
WL dwale
dwell
Pwyll
swale
SWALK
swell
swill
twill
WM swami
swamp
WN a-wing
Dwane
dwine
Gwent
Owens
owing
swank
swine
swing
swung
twang
twine
twink
twins□
twiny
WO ewhow
swoon
swoop
WP SWAPO
Swapo
swept
swipe
WR award
aware
dwarf
sward
swarf
swarm
swerf
swirl
sword
sworn
twerp
twire
twirl
twirp
WS awash□
ewest
swash
swish
Swiss
twist□
UWIST
WT swath
swits
twite
WU awful
own up
two-up
WY swayl
WZ Swazi
XA axial
exeat
expat
ex-pat
OXFAM
Uxmal
XC exact
XD exude
oxide
XE excel
expel
oxter
XI oxlip
XL axile
exalt
exile
exult
ixtle
XO axiom
expos
extol
XR exert
extra
exurb
XS exist
XT exits
YA by far
by law
by-law
byway
cycad
Dylan
gyral
hyrax
my hat!
mynah
pygal
Syrah
YC lynch□
synch
YD Byrds
Hyads
Lynda
tynde
YE by sea
cyder
Dyfed
dykey
gyves
hymen
hyper
Hywel
Myles
Ryder

ryper
Tyler
tyned
Wyler
xylem
YF nyaff
YG Synge
YH Aysha
hypha
kythe
myths
YI by air
cynic
Cyril
eyrie
Eytie
hyoid
kylie❑
Lydia
lyric
lysis
pyxis❑
Sybil
Syria
YL ayelp
cycle
nyala
YM pygmy
YN ayont
dying
gynny
hyena
lying
Lynne
Lyons
Myrna
vying
Wynne
YO by now
Byron
Cynon
hypos
kyloe
Myron
nylon
pylon
synod
Tylor
typos
Tyson
xylol
YP lymph
nymph
sylph
YR aygre
hydra❑
hydro
Lycra®
myrrh
YS gypsy❑
Nyasa
Tysse
YT Byatt
Eyeti
Kyoto
synth
typto
xyst i
YU Cyrus
eye up
gyrus
syrup
ZC Czech
ZD azide
ZE Aztec
Uzbek
ZI azoic
Izmir
Ozzie
ZM azyme
ZN azine
ozone
ZO ZZ Top
ZR azure

6 letters – even

AAA banana
cabala
Canada
fa la la
Havana
jacana
jataka
kabala
kamala❑
Kanaka
katana
Malaga
Manama
mañana
maraca
masala
Nacala
nagana
panada
panama❑
papaya
Paraná
pataca
Sahara
Salala
samara❑
Tamara
Tarawa
Zapata
AAC QARANC
AAD canard
Harald
hazard
Layard
maraud
tabard
vaward
AAE canapé
carafe
damage
facade
façade❑
garage
hamate
Harare
karate
lanate
Madame
manage
palace
palate
parade❑
pavane
rafale
ramate
ravage
savage
savate
takahe
tamale❑
vacate
AAG Malang
Padang
Pahang
satang
AAH camash
Kazakh
Namath
paraph
Wabash
AAI calami
dalasi
Hawaii
Malawi
nagari
safari
salami
tamari
uakari
AAK damask
Lanark
padauk
AAL Bacall
Mayall
AAM napalm
salaam
AAN Danaan
Gawain
papain
AAO Bamako
da capo
galago
kakapo
Malabo
Nagano
Navaho
Navajo
AAR bazaar
AAS badass
Calais
camass
Casals
harass
madams
Manaus
Naiads
AAT basalt
caract
savant
vacant
AAU Makalu
Xanadu
AAY canary
galaxy
malady
panary
papacy
salary
vagary
AAZ pazazz
ABA balboa❑
cambia
lambda
Zambia
ABB baobab
ABC iambic
tambac
ABD barbed
day bed
daybed
pay bed
rabbed
tabbed
ABE babble
barbie❑
Barbie®
bauble
cabbie
dabble
gabble
gamble
garble
hamble
jabble
marble
rabble
ramble
wamble
warble
ABG gasbag
may bug
ragbag
ratbag
ABH casbah❑
kasbah❑
ABK jambok
ABL barbel
gambol
ABN carbon
Harbin
Vauban
ABO bamboo
gabbro
ABR barber❑
camber
dauber
gabber
gambir
jabber
nabber
sambar
sambur
yabber
ABS garbos
iambus
jambos
lay-bys
mambos
rabbis
sambos
zambos
ABT barbet
gambit
rabbet
rabbit❑
Talbot
ABV Tambov
ABX hatbox
haybox
ABY carboy
dawbry
day-boy
marbly
ACA fascia
Garcia
kaccha
Marcia
ACD rancid
ACE gauche
Parcae
ACI Ranchi
ACL caecal
cancel
faecal
Marcel
parcel
PASCAL
pascal❑
rascal
ACM caecum
talcum
ACN cancan
can-can
earcon
falcon
garçon
gascon
ACO gaucho
ACP madcap
ACR cancer❑
dancer❑
lancer
lascar
saucer
ACS Baucis
calces
cascos
caucus
darcys
faeces
falces
fasces
fauces
Jancis
lances
Marcos
Marcus
narcos
ACT fat cat
faucet
lancet❑
mascot
ACY catchy
far cry
patchy
War Cry
war cry
warcry
ADA Kandla
Sandra
ADC bardic
ADD banded
candid
handed
landed
padded
sanded
ADE caddie
candle
caudle
daddle
daidle
dandle
dawdle

faddle
handle
Hardie
laddie
paddle
pardie
raddle
saddle
waddle
Yardie
ADG bandog
wardog
ADI Gandhi
gardai
ADL caudal
Handel
Randal
sandal
vandal□
ADM randem
random□
tandem
ADN Camden
Cardin
garden□
Handan
hand in
hand on
harden
Hayden
Haydon
lardon
madden
maiden
pardon
pardon?
randon
sadden
Varden
Vardon
Walden
warden
ADO nardoo
vaudoo
wandoo
ADP hard up
hard-up
laid up
paid-up
ADR Baader
Balder
bandar
Calder
dander
Gaidar
gander
ladder
Länder
larder
Lauder
madder
pander
raider
sander
sawder
wander
warder
ADS caddis
Galdós
Sardis
ADT bandit
Bardot
ADU landau
saddhu
ADY baldly
hardly
man-day
May Day
mayday□
tawdry
AEA camera
favela
galena
Ganesa
macera
Pamela
tapeta
Valera
valeta
Walesa
zareba
AED fag end
fag-end
far end
hareld
lag-end
AEE gamete
manège
paleae
raceme
sapele
taleae
Varèse
AEF care of
make of
AEH daleth
Gareth
lamedh
samekh
varech
AEI Nägeli
AEL Cavell
AEM hareem
AEN baleen
cage in
casein
casern
cave in
cave-in
cavern
ease in
fade in
fade-in
Hadean
have on
lateen
make on
rake in
sateen
take in
take on
tavern
Vänern
wade in
AEO came to
gazebo
have to
Maceio
make do
make-do
make go
sapego
Sasebo
take to
wake to
wave to
AEP ease up
fade up
have up
lace-up
made up
made-up
make up
make-up
rake up
rave-up
save up
take up
take-up
wake up
AER career
pasear
AES cameos
capers
caress
papers
save us
Sayers
Waters
AET cadent
caveat
gape at
gaze at
have at
have it
haven't
lament
latent
latest
make at
make it
parent
patent
take it
talent
AEU bateau
gateau
gâteau
Maseru
Rameau
AEY bakery
barely
basely
calefy
eatery
gaiety
gamely
lamely
lately
namely
napery
Naseby
palely
papery
rakery
rarefy
rarely
safely
safety
sagely
sanely
Savery
tabefy
tamely
Valéry
wafery
watery
AEZ kameez
AFA Jaffna
raffia
AFE baffle
raffle
waffle
yaffle
zaffre
AFL bagful
earful
lawful
manful
panful
AFN Baffin
AFO samfoo
AFR gaffer
Kaffer
pay for
zaffer
AFY gadfly
mayfly
naffly
sawfly
AGA kangha
Pangea
AGD fagged
fanged
jagged
ragged
AGE bangle
bargee
cangle
daggle
dangle
gaggle
gangue
gargle
haggle
jangle
langue
Maggie
maigre
mal gré
malgré
mangle
raggle
taigle
tangle
waggle
wangle
AGI Bangui
Haggai
AGM targum□
AGN bang on
hang in
hang on
jargon
largen
margin
Saigon
Sargon
waggon
Yangon
AGO Baggio
dayglo
Fangio
AGP bang up
hang up
hang-up
AGR badger□
banger
Bangor
cadger
dagger
danger
ganger
hangar
hanger
laager
langur
larger
manger
ranger
saggar
sagger
Sanger
yagger
AGS fangos
Ganges
haggis
largos
laughs
tangos
Vargas
AGT catgut
caught
faggot
gadget
maggot
naught
parget
target
taught
waught
AGY gangly
jangly
mangey
Sangay
tangly
Tanguy
waggly
AHA raphia□
AHD dashed
lashed
washed
AHE daphne□
mashie
AHL Rachel
Warhol
AHM fathom
mayhem
sachem
AHN Aachen
bash on
cash in
fat hen
Nathan
Pathan
AHO Pashto
AHP cash up
wash up
AHR basher
bather
Cather
Dasher
father□
gather
Hathor
lather
Madhur
masher
Mather
rasher
rather
washer
AHS Aarhus
bathos
Jan Hus
laches
machos
nachos
Paphos
pathos
rachis
AHT cachet
sachet
AHW cashew
haw-haw
AHY eathly
gashly
rashly

sashay
AIA capita
Davina
farina
Fatima
Jamila
Janina
Kariba
Karina
la-di-da
lamina
Latina
manila❑
marina❑
maxima
patina
Sabina
salina
saliva
vagina
AIC maniac
manioc
AID varied
AIE barite
canine
dative
facile
famine
gamine
halide
halite
Janice
Janine
labile
malice
marine
Maxine
Nadine
narine
native
Racine
rapine
ravine
Sabine
saline
satire
savine
valine
valise
wahine
AIF tariff
AIG baking
bating
caking
caning
caring
casing
caving
Daqing
daring
dating
Ealing
easing

eating
facing
fading
faking
gaming
gaping
gating
gazing
having
japing
lacing
lading
lazing
making
mating
naming
paling
paring
paving
paying
racing
raging
raring
rating
raving
razing
saving
saying
taking
taxing
waking
waning
waving
AIH banish
caliph
Danish
famish
garish
Hadith
Hamish
latish
lavish
oafish
palish
pariah
parish
radish
rakish
ravish
vanish
AII Marini
tahini
Tahiti
wapiti
AIL Daniel
facial
garial
gavial
labial
narial
racial
radial
samiel

AIM barium
labium
Maoism
Nazism
racism
radium
sadism
Taoism
Valium®
AIN banian
cation
Dalian
Damian
Damien
Darién
Fabian
fanion
kalian
magian
Malian
malign
Marian
Marion
nation
Parian
radian
ration
Salian
Samian
talion
wanion
AIO calico
casino
katipo
Marino
Pacino
AIP magilp
AIR caviar
Napier
pavior
rapier
Xavier
AIS babies
basics
caries
danios
Darius
Davies
Fabius
facies
habits
ladies
Marius
matins
navies
patios
rabies
radios
radius
rapids
ratios
sanies
taxies

AIT galiot
lariat
Maoist
racist
rapist
sadist
Taoist
AIU jabiru
AIY cagily
cavity
easily
family
gasify
hazily
ladify
laxity
lazily
matily
mazily
Nazify
pacify
parity
racily
ramify
rarity
ratify
salify
sanify
sanity
satiny
vanity
warily
wavily
waxily
AJL Banjul
AJN gaijin
Taejon
AJR gas jar
AJS banjos
kanjis
AJT fan-jet
gas jet
ramjet
AJX banjax
AJY Sanjay
AKA markka
Saskia
AKD marked
masked
narked
packed
parked
racked
sacked
AKE cackle
darkle
fankle
hackle
hankie
mackle
parkie
rankle
tackle

talkie
Yankee
AKF back of
talk of
AKI naskhi
AKL Baikal
jackal
Wankel
AKN bank on
catkin
darken
harken
jack in
Larkin
napkin
pack in
parkin
Rankin
tack on
walk on
walk-on
AKO talk to
AKP back up
backup
back-up
hack up
jack up
mark up
mark-up
pack up
park up
talk up
tank up
AKR backer
banker
barker❑
canker
dacker
daiker
hacker
hanker
hawker
Lasker
marker
masker
packer❑
Parker
racker
ranker
talker
tanker
walker❑
AKS Backus
Barkis
Fawkes
maikos
sankos
tankas
AKT balk at
bark at
basket
casket
gasket

hack it
jacket
market
nark at
nark it!
packet
racket
Rajkat
talk at
walk it
AKY darkly
hackly
jacksy
lackey
lankly
Mackay
rankly
ALA dahlia
halloa
paella
pallia
ALC Gaelic
Gallic
garlic
ALD ballad
called
callid
fabled
failed
gabled
galled
jailed
mailed
pallid
sailed
tailed
walled
ALE Gaulle
Hadlee
pallae
ALH wallah
ALL Callil
fallal
hallal
ALM Baalim
Callum
Harlem
vallum
ALN ballon
call in
call on
fail in
fallen
fall in
fall on
Fallon
gallon
kaolin
Mallon
marlin
Marlon
pall on
raglan❑

wall in
ALO Callao
fall to
halloo
ALP ball up
call up
call-up
gallop
Gallup
haul up
nail up
wallop
wall up
ALR bailer
caller
fabler
gaoler
Haller
jailer
jailor
Mahler
Mailer
nailer
pallor
sailer□
sailor
tailor
tatler
Taylor
wailer
Waller
ALS Callas
callus
caules
Dallas
Eagles
fables
Faulks
gallus
hallos
Laclos
Majlis
matlos
Nablus
Naples
Wallis
ALT ballet
ballot
callet
carlot
eaglet
gallet
hamlet□
harlot
haslet
mallet
pallet
rail at
tablet
wallet
ALV maglev
Pavlov
ALW ballow
callow
Carlow
fallow
gallow
hallow
Harlow
lay low
mallow
matlow
sallow
tallow
wallow
ALX hallux
ALY bailey□
barley
call by
Cawley
faulty
galley
Halley
Hayley
Manley
Marley
parlay
parley
valley
waylay
Y-alloy
AMA kalmia
Saimaa
AMC haemic
karmic
tarmac
AMD farmed
harmed
jammed
Mahmud
maimed
Talmud
AME mammae
AMG malmag
AMH warmth
AML Carmel
haemal
mammal
AMM Dammam
AMN barman
batman
caiman
Carmen
cayman
daemon
daimon
gammon
hamman
Harman
Jarman
layman
madman
mammon
Paxman
Rahman
salmon
Tasman
Vatman
Wadman
Yasmin
AMO warm to
AMP warm up
warm-up
AMR farmer
hammer□
mammer
palmar
palmer□
rammer
Taimyr
Taymyr
yammer
AMS Cadmus
Lammas
magmas
Patmos
salmis
AMT dammit
mammet
marmot
AMW haymow
AMX Mad Max
AMY calmly
warmly
AMZ Tammuz
ANA Jamnia
Kaunda
Narnia
pa'anga
taenia
ANB Zainab
Zaynab
ANC tannic
AND banned
canned
damned□
darned
earned
maenad
manned
pained
tanned
ANE Cannae
faunae
jaunce
jaunse
launce
pawnee□
sarnie
ANF warn of
ANH gaunch
Hannah
haunch
launch
paunch
raunch
ANL carnal
darnel
faunal
tarnal
ANM magnum
ANN cannon□
dawn on
fawn on
gain on
Hainan
rain in
Tainan
tannin
ANO bagnio
ANP Carnap
catnap
catnip
ANR banner
darner
dauner
dawner
earner
Fafnir
fawner
garner□
Gaynor
manner
Marner
pawner
Ratner
tanner
Wagner
warner□
ANS Barnes
Cannes
faunas
Faunus
Kaunas
Magnus
pannus
QARNNS
Saints
Tainos
ANT Barnet
cannot
gainst
gannet
garnet
magnet
walnut
ANY barney□
Cagney
carney
dainty
fainly
gainly
Hannay
jaunty
mainly
maundy
painty
tannoy□
Tawney
vainly
AOA Canova
Carola
dagoba
Dakota
Ladoga
Lakota
Nagoya
pagoda
pakora
Paloma
payola
samosa
Tacoma
AOD day-old
gadoid
ganoid
haloid
Harold
kayoed
AOE cajole
Capone
Capote
Carole
day one
galore
hamose
Lahore
parole
radome
ramose
Salome
Tagore
vamose
AOF day off
eat off
far-off
lay off
lay-off
pay off
pay-off
AOG Datong
kalong
sarong
AOH galosh
AOI caroli
Jacobi
satori
AOK Farouk
paiock
pajock
AON baboon
Eamonn
Haroun
lagoon
maroon
racoon
ratoon
sagoin
saloon
AOO Barolo
palolo
AOR favour
Kapoor
labour
savour
valour
vapour
AOS dadoes
famous
Faroes
Galois
haloes
hamous
kaross
kayoes
patois
ramous
taboos
Yahoos
AOT cavort
dacoit
dakoit
day out
eat out
fag out
fan out
far out
far-out
galoot
Lamont
lavolt
lay out
layout
mahout
map out
pad out
pan out
pay out
ragout
way out
way-out
AOY barony
canopy
jalopy
paeony
parody
APA yarpha
APD napped
sapped
warped
APE dapple
magpie
Marple
salpae
sample
sapple
API Taipei
APK kalpak
APL carpal
carpel
palpal
rappel
APN camp on
dampen
happen
harp on
hatpin
jampan

parpen
sampan
sanpan
taipan
tampon
APO Sappho
APR camper
carper
Caspar
damper
dapper
gasper
gawper
hamper
harper
Jaipur
jasper❑
Kanpur
Kaspar
lapper
mapper
Nagpur
pamper
pauper
Raipur
ramper
rapper
sapper❑
tamper
wapper
warper
yapper
zapper
APS Campos
campus
carpus
palpus
pampas
pappus
salpas
APT carpet
lappet
Rajput
tappet
APV Karpov
APW pawpaw
APY camply
damply
AQE barque
basque❑
caique
calque
manqué
marque
masque
AQO Banquo
ARB Zagreb
ARC BAgric
fabric
ARD barred
Garrod
haired
hatred

Madrid
marred
paired
ramrod
sacred
wax-red
ARE Barrie
Carrie
Laurie
Lawrie
Nairne
ARL barrel
carrel❑
laurel❑
patrol
sacral
ARM Bairam
marram
sacrum
vagrom
Wagram
ARN barren
Dacron®
Darren
garran
garron
hadron
Lauren
macron
matron
natron
patron
warren❑
ARO hairdo
Karroo
ARP larrup
pair up
satrap
ARS Cairns
Harris
macros
madras❑
Maoris
Taurus
walrus
ART carrot
garret
garrot
parrot
ARW barrow❑
Darrow
farrow❑
harrow❑
Jarrow
marrow
narrow
yarrow
ARX matrix
ARY fairly
Man Ray
warrey
ARZ Tabriz
ASA fatsia

Marsha
nausea❑
ASC parsec
ASD Hassid
lapsed
massed
raised
ASE Bassae
Cassie
dassie
hassle
lassie❑
Maisie
Parsee
says he
ASF bags of
massif
ASL causal
damsel
eassel
eassil
Faisal
Faysal
Kassel
tarsal
tassel
vassal
ASM balsam
hansom
passim
ransom
ASN Carson
Casson
damson
Dawson
Hamsun
Hassan
Jansen
Lawson
Manson
Nansen
parson
pass on
raisin
Samson
Samsun
sarsen
Tamsin
Watson
ASO Cassio
ASP pass up
ASR caesar❑
hawser
kaiser❑
Mauser
Nasser
parser
pauser
raiser
ASS bassos
cassis
fatsos
gadsos

Kansas
lassos
masses
Massys
pass as
tarsus❑
AST basset
Cassat
wadset
ASU Nassau
ASW Warsaw
ASY Bassey
gansey
Gatsby
Jansky
karsey
marshy
pass by
Ramsay
ATA Eartha
mantra
mantua❑
Martha
tantra❑
ATC Baltic
haptic
lactic
mantic
mastic
tactic
ATD casted
halted
malted
masted
matted
parted
salted
want ad
wanted
wasted
ATE battle
cantle
castle❑
cattle
daftie
Hattie
mantle❑
Mattie
rattle❑
Sartre
tattie
tattle
wattle
Xanthe
ATF part of
ATG ragtag
ATI canthi
ATK Bartók
ATL battel
cartel
cautel
dactyl
hartal

mantel
martel
pastel
ATM bantam
partim
tam-tam
ATN batten
caftan
canton❑
carton
cast on
daft on
dalton❑
Danton
Dayton
fasten
fatten
Galton
hasten
kaftan
latten
marten
martin❑
Martyn
panton
patten❑
Patton
Paxton
Payton
rattan
ratten
tartan
tauten
wait on
Walton
want in
wanton
Warton
ATO Castro
LAUTRO
tattoo
ATP cast up
laptop
tart up
wait up
want up
ATR banter
barter
baster
batter
canter
cantor
captor
Carter
caster
castor❑
darter
Easter
factor
falter
gaiter
garter
halter

hatter
karter
latter
martyr
master
matter
natter
palter
pastor
patter
rafter
ranter
raptor
raster
ratter
sartor
tartar❑
taster
tatter
waiter
Walter
wanter
waster
yatter
ATS bastos
cactus
cantos
cantus
mantis
mantos
Nantes
pantos
pastis
QANTAS
Qantas
saltos
saltus
Santos
sautés
ATT Lartet
past it
ATU Baotou
Lao-tzu
ATY Bantry
daftly
earthy
gantry
lastly
paltry
pantry
partly
pastry
raptly
saltly
tartly
tautly
vastly
AUA Cayuga
datura
Kaluga
lacuna
Laputa
macula

manuka
papula
radula
valuta
Varuna
yakuza
AUD salued
valued
AUE Canute
Danube
Mabuse
manure
mature
nature□
papule
salute
AUF Ranulf
AUH Baruch
AUI Batumi
Faludi
hamuli
kabuki
ramuli
saluki
AUK Zanuck
AUL casual
manual
Raquel
Samuel
AUM vacuum
AUN saguin
Saturn
AUO Caruso
lanugo
Majuro
Maputo
AUP gazump
AUR jaguar
Jaguar®
valuer
AUS Jaques
maquis
values
AUT NAS/UWT
AVA Latvia
salvia
AVD halved
valved
AVE larvae
AVK Narvik
AVL carvel
larval
marvel
AVN Calvin
Marvin
mauvin
AVR calver
carver□
marver
salver
waiver
AVS calves
canvas
cauves
halves
Jarvis
naevus
parvis
salvos
Walvis
AVY Garvey
Harvey
savvey
AWG earwig
AWH fatwah
wah-wah
Yahweh
AWL qawwal
AWN Darwin
Taiwan
AWY Galway
say why
AXS calxes
AYD Dafydd
sayyid
AYE Kabyle
AYF wary of
AYI papyri
AYN banyan
baryon
canyon
AYR Baeyer
lawyer
Magyar
sawyer□
AYS Satyrs
AYX larynx
AYY ladyfy
AZC Balzac
AZE dazzle
razzle
AZG Danzig
AZI banzai
AZN Tarzan
AZP jazz up
AZR mahzor
panzer
AZS matzos
tazzas
BAD aboard
abraid
BAE ablate
ablaze
abrade
oblate
BAN obtain
BAO Abbado
BAS abdabs
BAT ablaut
oblast
BAY abbacy
BCA Abacha
BCE obeche
BCS abacus
ibices
BDC EBCDIC
BDM ibidem
BDN Abadan
Ibadan
BEE abrégé
BEL abseil
BES abbess
abbeys
objets
obsess
BET abject
absent
object
obtest
obvert
BEY ubiety
BIE oblige
BIG B B King
ebbing
BIH abeigh
BIN O'Brien
obsign
BIS ablins
BIT oboist
BLA abulia
BLS obelus
obolus
BMY Abomey
BNI Ubangi
BOB absorb
BOD abroad
BOG oblong
BOM abloom
BOT Abbott
BQE ubique
BRI sbirri
BRN Oberon
BRT aburst
BSD abased
abused
BSI Ubasti
BSR abuser
BTF a bit of
BTR obiter
BTS abatis
BUD abound
absurd
BUE abduce
abjure
objure
obtuse
BUH ablush
BUT abduct
abrupt
BXS ibexes
CAE ice age
ice axe
octane
octave
scrape
CAF sclaff
CAK ack-ack
CAL acrawl
scrawl
CAM scrawm
CAO octavo
CAR éclair
CAS oceans
Octans
scraps
CAT octant□
CAY occamy
CBG act big
CBY scabby
CCA acacia
CCE icicle
CCP icecap
CDA acedia
CDC acidic
CDM McAdam
CDY acidly
CEA eczema
schema
sclera
CED screed
CEE accede
Achebe
ocreae
scheme
CEK screak
CEM scream
CEN McBean
screen
CES access
screws
CET accent
accept
Eckert
CEY screwy
CFR act for
CIE accite
active
scribe
scrive
CIG aching
acting
I Ching
CIH scaith
CIK Schick
tchick
CIM Actium
schism
CIN action
CIO schizo
CIP scrimp
CIT schist
script
CIY acuity
CLA scilla
scolia
Scylla
CLE scalae
CLI ocelli
CLP schlep
CLR ocular
scalar
CLS oculus
scales□
CLT ocelot
sculpt
CMI scampi
CML scamel
CMN acumen
CMY scummy
CNC iconic
scenic
CNE sconce
scunge
CNH a cinch
CNL SCONUL
CNS acinus
scenes
CNT econut
CNY scanty
COC echoic
COD accord
COE eclose
ochone
COI octopi
COK o'clock
COL school
scroll
COP scroop
COS across
actors
echoes
scions
Y-cross
COT accost
act out
ice out
COY ectopy
CPE scopae
CPI scyphi
CPO Scipio
CPS Scopas
CRA Icaria
ochrea
scarpa
scoria
CRB scarab
CRD scared
scored
CRE accrue
écarté
J-curve
scarce
Scarfe
scorse
CRH scorch
CRI octroi
CRR scarer
scorer
CRS Icarus
scarfs
scores
CRY scurfy
scurry
scurvy
CSY O'Casey
CTC acetic
CTE scathe
scythe
CTH scotch□
scutch
CTL acetyl
scutal
CTM scutum
CTR scoter
CTY McStay
scatty
CUE accuse
acture
Scouse
CUF scruff
CUL actual
CUO scruto
CUP scrump
CUS schuss
CUT acquit
occult
CUY occupy
CWN McEwan
CZY scuzzy
DAD Edward
DAE ideate
DAI Adjani
DAS ideals
DBD odd bod
DBE edible
DEB adverb
DEE adhere
DEG Edberg
DES adieus
DET advent□
advert
DEX adieux
DEY Eddery
DGO adagio
DIA Edwina
DIE admire
advice
advise
DIG adding
edging
DIH Edrich
oddish
DIN Adrian
DIS add-ins
addios
DIT addict
adrift
DIY oddity
DLD addled
DLT odd lot
DNA Gdynia
DNC Edenic
DNE Odense
DNK Gdansk
DNS Adonis
DOB adsorb
DOH Ed Koch
DOK Adcock

DON adjoin
DOS add-ons
odious
DOT adroit
DOY idiocy
DRD adored
DRR adorer
DSA Odessa
DSN Edison
odds-on
DTE Odette
DTR editor
DUD Edmund
DUE adduce
adjure
DUS odeums
DUT adduct
adjust
EAA Gemara
Kerala
Megara
Nevada
Renata
terata
zenana
EAB bedaub
decarb
EAD belaud
Benaud
demand
Gerald
Gerard
herald
petard
regard
remand
repand
retard
reward
Weland
EAE aerate
became
bedaze
behave
belace
be made
bename
berate
betake
beware
cetane
debase
debate
decade
decane
deface
defame
delate
derate
female
Hecate
hexane
legate
let-a-be
menace
ménage
metage
negate
New Age
pedate
pelage
pesade
rebate
regale
relate
remake
re-make
rename
resale
retake
sedate
senate❑
serape
sesame
sewage
EAF behalf
decaff
EAG Hegang
Penang
EAH bedash
detach
Pesach
rehash
seraph
EAI gelati
Nepali
EAK debark
demark
Newark
reback
remark
EAL becall
befall
bewail
derail
detail
devall
recall
rerail
retail
EAM becalm
EAN Derain
detain
Pétain
regain
remain
retain
EAO legato
pedalo
rebato
EAP decamp
revamp
EAR repair
EAS Le Mans
lemans
repass
EAT Béjart
Besant
bezant
decant
depart
desalt
levant❑
pedant
recant
recast
redact
repast
secant
sejant
tenant
EAU déjà vu
EAY be easy
denary
legacy
EBA jerboa
EBD webbed
EBE Debbie
feeble
Herbie
Kemble
leg bye
pebble
remble
semble
EBG bedbug
tea bag
EBK reebok
EBL gerbil
herbal
verbal
EBN Reuben
EBR Berber
member
EBS Lesbos
EBT Nesbit
Tebbit
EBW Benbow
EBY feebly
pebbly
sea boy
ECD deuced
ECE fescue
rescue
Seb Coe
ECL cercal
mescal
pencil
tercel
ECN beacon
deacon❑
Deccan
leucin
nem con
ECO re-echo
Velcro®
ECP redcap
red-cap
sea cap
teacup
ECR de-icer
fencer
mercer❑
Redcar
ECS recces
reccos
seccos
ECT tercet
ECW sea cow
ECX Merckx
ECY descry
tetchy
EDD beaded
bended
headed
mended
needed
seeded
wedded
EDE beadle❑
Deidre
heddle
meddle
needle
peddle
perdie
reddle
vendee
EDG sea dog
EDH Jeddah
EDI Sendai
EDL feudal
Kendal
Mendel
EDM seldom
EDN deaden
dead on
dead-on
feed in
feed on
head-on
held in
leaden
lead in
lead-in
lead on
Leiden
Leyden
read in
redden
send on
tendon
Verdun
Weldon
EDO lead to
EDP feed up
head up
read up
send up
send-up
EDR bender
deodar
feeder
fender❑
gender
header
herder❑
leader
lender
mender
reader
render
sender
tedder
tender
vender
vendor
weeder
welder
weldor
EDS Deedes
EDT geddit
EDW meadow
EDY deadly
Hendry
heyday
lewdly
needly
EEA genera
Geneva
Helena
never a
oedema
pereia
peseta
pesewa
semeia
Seneca
Serena
Teresa
veleta
EEB reverb
EED behead
defend
depend
legend
nereid
reread
tele-ad
EEE delete
lexeme
Melete
recede
re-cede
red-eye
renege
revere❑
secede
Selene
Semele
sememe
serene
severe
venewe
EEF hereof
EEK bedeck
EEL cereal
repeal
retell
reveal
Sewell
EEM beseem
beteem
redeem
Te Deum
EEN Aegean
bemean
decern
demean
hele in
herein
hereon
secern
Severn
Webern
wedeln
EEO hereto
hetero
teredo
EEP beweep
EER meneer
meteor
rehear
veneer
EES Aeneas
jewels
levers
Peters
recess
revels
revers
tenets
EET behest
bereft
cement
deceit
decent
defeat
defect
deject
dement
desert
detect
detest
devest
fewest
newest
recent
refect
regent
reheat
reject
relent
repeat
repent
resect
resent
revert

6 _E_E_Y

revest
select
EEY celery
hereby
heresy
Hevesy
Jeremy
merely
remedy
tepefy
EFC deific
EFD leafed
EFE neaffe
EFL keffel
EFN deafen
EFP beef up
EFR heifer
hey for
reefer
yen for
EFS reffos
EFT see fit
EFY belfry
deafly
let fly
EGA zeugma
EGD legged
merged
wedged
EGE beagle❑
dengue
gee-gee
league
meagre
reggae
Reggie
teagle
EGH length
EGL beigel
Bengal
EGM tergum
EGN Bergen
Keegan
Reagan
EGO Reggio
EGR beggar
Berger
Geiger
hedger
ledger
merger
Seeger
verger
Wenger
Yeager
EGS Fergus
EGT height
weight
EGU Bengpu
EGW gewgaw
EHA peshwa
tephra
EHD meshed❑
method
EHE lechwe
lethee
rechie
tee-hee
EHL bethel
lethal
EHM Ken Hom
Newham
pelham❑
EHN peahen
EHO Jethro
techno
EHR aether
Ben-Hur
lecher
menhir
nether
tether
wether
zephyr
EHT Bechet
red hot
red-hot
EHW heehaw
nephew
reshow
EIA Celina
De Sica
hegira❑
Hejira
Jemima
Medina
Petipa
Regina
retina
Selina
vesica
EID begild
behind
Hesiod
period
rebind
remind
EIE aedile
Belize
beside
betide
betime
cerise
decide
defile
define
demise
Denise
deride
derive
desire
device
devise
feline
ferine
mediae
Medise
Medize
nerine
pelite
penile
petite
rebite
Recife
recipe
recite
rediae
refine
regime
régime
reline
relive
remise
repine
reside
resile
retire
revile
revise
revive
sedile
senile
serine
Venice
venite
EIF belief
relief
EIG Bering
ceding
Peking
seeing
sewing
vexing
EIH fetish
Hewish
Jewish
nebish
newish
perish
relish
zenith
EII Gemini
Medici
periti
EIK be sick
EIL aerial
Belial
denial
ferial
genial
medial
menial
Meriel
mesial
refill
retial
serial
venial
xenial
EIM cerium
helium
medium
sexism
tedium
verism
EIN benign
design
Fenian
legion
lesion
median
region
resign
re-sign
EIO De Niro
DeVito
medico
merino
Mexico
pepino
EIP megilp
EIR defier
denier
métier
relier
senior
EIS bekiss
Delius
demies
denims
genius❑
Helios
merits
nelies
relics
remiss
series
EIT begift
demist
depict
desist
dewitt
relict
resist
sexist
Vedist
verist
EIW review
EIY Cecily
dewily
eerily
ferity
geminy
lenify
lenity
levity
verify
verily
verity❑
EJY deejay
dee-jay
EKD beaked
decked
peaked
EKE deckle
heckle
keckle
EKL Terkel
EKN beckon
jerkin
meeken
perkin
reckon
weaken
welkin
EKO seek to
EKP perk up
EKR beaker
Becker
Dekker
Necker
pecker
seeker
Wesker
EKS deckos
dekkos
geckos
EKT Becket
EKY Leakey
meekly
weakly
weekly
ELC Belloc
ELD healed
heeled
keeled
sealed
veiled
wealk'd
ELE cellae
jeelie
keelie
Leslie
mealie
wellie
ELG jet-lag
reflag
ELH fellah
health
wealth
ELM bedlam
beflum
peplum
vellum
ELN Berlin
Ceylon
deal in
Declan
heel in
Mellon
merlin❑
merlon
Teflon®
tell on
ELO Serlio
ELP dewlap
sell up
well up
ELR cellar
dealer
de-blur
feeler
feller
healer
Heller
Kepler
medlar
Mellor
pedlar
peeler
sealer
seller
teller❑
Weller
ELS Aeolus
cellos
Hellas
hellos
jellos
realms
realos
Welles
ELT Merlot
pellet
reflet
reglet
yell at
zealot
ELW bellow❑
fellow
mellow
reflow
yellow❑
ELX deflex
reflex
reflux
ELY berley
Bexley
deploy
fealty
Healey
Henley
leally
Lesley
medley
really
replay
Wesley
EMA Hermia
EMC dermic
heamic
EMD desmid
permed
red mud
termed
EME gemmae
hermae
EML dermal

vermil
EMN Beamon
fenman
gemmen
german❑
Henman
Herman
hetman
Kelman
key man
leg-man
Lemmon
merman
met man
new man
Newman
penman
seaman❑
sermon
tegmen
vermin
yeoman
yeomen
yes-man
EMP team up
EMR beamer
Mesmer
seamer
Weimar
EMS dermis
Hermes
kermes
kermis
lemmas
Seamas
Seamus
Seumas
vermes
vermis
EMT besmut
cermet
Dermot
Fermat
Heimat
helmet
hermit
Mehmet
pelmet
permit
EMX Tex-Mex
EMY seemly
termly
ENA Deanna
hernia
ENC fennec
neanic
END penned
veined
ENE beanie
Bernie
Deanne
Jeanie
Leanne

Leonie
meanie
peenge
pennae
Rennie
séance
ENL fennel
kennel
kernel
regnal
vernal
ENN Heenan
keen on
lean on
Lennon
Memnon
pennon
rein in
rennin
Vernon
ENO keen to
lean-to
ENP sewn up
ENR Jenner
keener
Lerner
tenner
weaner
ENS beanos
Dennis
Keynes
Lemnos
Meknès
Rennes
segnos
tennis
ENT be in it
Bennet
jennet
Nernst
peanut
rennet
sennet
ENW begnaw
ENY dernly
Heaney
keenly
leanly
meanly
teensy
EOA fedora❑
femora
hebona
pelota
remora
Señora
Verona
EOB desorb
resorb
EOC heroic
EOD behold
beyond
devoid

keloid
record
reload
reword
second
vetoed
EOE aerobe
become
be done
before
begone
behove
decode
decoke
delope
démodé
demote
denote
depone
depose
devote
Eeyore
genome
hexose
Jerome
ketone
metope
peyote
rebore
remote
remove
repone
repose
revoke
rezone
setose
veloce
venose
EOF get off
let off
let-off
set off
set-off
EOG belong
Mekong
EOH zeroth
EOI neroli
EOK rework
EOL befool
befoul
behowl
bemoil
betoil
recoil
EOM deform
reform
re-form
EON bemoan
dehorn
heroin
reborn
recoin
rejoin

renown❑
zero in
EOO De Bono
de novo
zeloso
EOP recoup
EOR detour
devour
memoir
Renoir
retour
velour
EOS betoss
deboss
heroes
serous
venous
vetoes
EOT bed out
Benoît
besort
decoct
dehort
deport
devout
get out
get-out
let out
let-out
Mel Ott
peg out
reboot
red out
report
resort
retort
revolt
set out
wet out
EOY felony
lemony
melody❑
memory
EPD heaped
keypad
peapod
EPE kelpie
people
sempre
teepee
temple❑
weepie
EPL peepul
pen-pal
EPN bedpan
be up in
deepen
hempen
keep in
keep on
reopen
tenpin
weapon

EPO keep to
EPP heap up
keep up
leap up
EPR beeper
helper
keeper
kelper❑
kemper
pepper
reaper
Semper
temper
weeper
yelper
EPS delphs
herpes
Kempis
tempos
EPT bespot
despot
keep at
leap at
sexpot
teapot
EPY deeply
net pay
EQE jerque
ERA kerria
ERC Cedric
ferric
metric
tenrec
ERD feared
seared
see red
tetrad
ERE dear me
decree
degree
George
hearse
Legree
Pearce
Petrie
Searle
serrae
terrae
ERG defrag
Gehrig
red rag
ERH dearth
hearth
search
ERL neural
petrel
petrol
ERM betrim
EEPROM
megrim
Red Rum
ERN bear on
Hebron

Herren
neuron
perron
tear in
Tehran
wear on
ERO weirdo
ERP bear up
bedrop
beer-up
de trop
gear up
let rip
tear up
ERR bearer
hearer
jeerer
terror
wearer
ERS debris
débris
derris
des res
henrys
métros
pearls
repros
retros
serras
Sèvres
ERT Beirut
ferret
jeer at
Meerut
peer at
regret
sea rat
secret
Seurat
tear at
wet rot
ERU Debreu
ERV Henry V
ERW Hebrew
ERY betray
bewray
dearly
defray
Delroy
hearty
near by
nearby
near-by
nearly
pearly
rearly
yearly
ESA geisha
Red Sea
ESD jessed
new-sad
tensed
versed

Words marked ❑ can also be spelled with an initial capital letter

ESE Bessie
jessie❑
lessee
measle
ESL deasil
new sol
teasel
vessel
weasel
ESM jetsam
ESN Besson
kelson
lessen
lesson
Mersin
Neeson
nelson❑
peason
pepsin
person
reason
season
telson
Velsen
ESP mess up
ESR censer
censor
geyser
leaser
lesser
lessor
sensor
teaser
verser
ESS beasts
Celsus
census
lenses
menses
Messrs
mewses
senses
sepses
sepsis
versos
versus
Wessis
yesses
EST bedsit
bed-sit
jet set
pet-sit
ESW leasow
seesaw
ESY feisty
jersey❑
kersey
measly
Mersey
Tersky
yeasty
ETA bertha❑
centra
kentia
ETC Celtic
hectic
Keltic
lentic
peptic
septic
ETD belted
bestud
debted
dented
heated
heptad
melted
netted
pentad
petted
rested
seated
tested
vested
ETE beetle
Beetle®
Bertie
centre
debtee
fettle
gentle
Gertie
kettle
leftie
Lettie
mestee
mettle
nestle
nettle
pestle
pettle
seethe
settee
settle
teethe
testee
Westie
ETL dental
dentil
festal
lentil
mental
rectal
rental
ventil
vestal
ETM rectum
restem
septum
ETN beaten
Beaton
Beeton
bent on
Benton
dentin
Heston
jetton
Keaton
Kenton
lectin
Lenten
lepton
Merton
neaten
nekton
newton❑
pecten
pectin
rest on
Retton
sexton
Teuton
ETO gentoo
next to
ETP beat up
beat-up
belt up
heat up
meet up
pent-up
ETR beater
belter
bestir
better
bettor
debtor
dexter❑
fester
fetter
getter
heater
hector❑
Hester
jester
kelter
lector
Lester
letter
mentor
nectar
Nestor
neuter
pester
pewter
rector
renter
rester
Reuter
sector
setter
teeter
tenter
tester
tetter
vector
venter
welter
wester
zester
ETS centos
cestus
depths
gentes
lentos
meatus
mentos
rectos
rectus
set-tos
set-to's
vestas
ETT beat it
septet
sestet
sextet
ETW bestow
ETX Pentax®
Semtex®
vertex
ETY Beatty
beltry
deftly
featly
gently
gentry
heathy
meetly
neatly
nextly
peltry
pertly
sentry
vestry
EUA beluga
cesura
Hecuba
medusa❑
nebula
Neruda
Petula
Uemura
veduta
EUB benumb
EUD fecund
gerund
Pequod
refund
retund
secund
EUE Beaune
bemuse
be sure
deduce
defuse
de jure
delude
deluge
de luxe
deluxe
de-luxe
demure
denude
depute
detune
ferule
jejune
legume
peruke
peruse
rebuke
recure
recuse
reduce
refuge
refuse
refute
repure
repute
resume
résumé
retuse
secure
seduce
tenure
vedute
velure
venule
EUF rebuff
EUG bedung
EUI veduti
EUK beduck
begunk
debunk
EUL becurl
sequel
sexual
EUN beguin
repugn
return
re-turn
sequin
EUO tenuto
EUS femurs
lemurs
serums
tenues
EUT bedust
deduct
Jesuit
penult
requit
result
EUU Telugu
EUY beauty
deputy
penury
EUZ Perutz
EVA Dervla
EVC pelvic
EVD fervid
leaved
nerved
peeved
EVE oeuvre
EVL devvel
serval
weevil
Yeovil
EVN heaven❑
kelvin❑
leaven
Leuven
Melvin
Melvyn
Mervyn
EVR beaver
Denver
heaver
server
weaver❑
weever
EVS beeves
delves
Jeeves
Jervis
leaves
Leavis
nerves
pelves
pelvis
Reeves
selvas
selves
EVT velvet
vervet
EVX cervix
EVY peavey
EWE wee-wee
EWT peewit
EWY keyway
leeway
EXS Xerxes
EYL Jekyll
EYN rely on
EYU see you
EZE teazle
EZG Herzog
EZL Denzil
teazel
EZR geezer
EZS fezzes
mezzos
FAD afeard
afraid
FAE aflame
efface
of late
FAR affair
FAY Offaly
FCT offcut
FED afield
offend
FEE effete
FEH afresh
FES afters
FET affect
effect
eftest

FHN Afghan
FIA Africa
FIE office
FIG offing
FIH offish
FII Uffizi
FIM affirm
FIY effigy
FKY off-key
FLX efflux
FNF a fan of
FNY if only
FOD afford
FOE of note
of yore
FOT afloat
afront
effort
FPS EFTPOS
FPT off pat
FRY affray
FST offset
FTD OFSTED
Ofsted
FUE effuse
FVR Q-fever
GAA Aglaia
iguana
GAE agnate
O-grade
GAL agnail
GAT aghast
GCP eggcup
GDR Agadir
GED agreed
GEM agleam
GES egress
ogress
GET Egbert
GIE ignite
GIG ageing
GIH ogrish
GIM ageism
egoism
GIS ngaios
Ogmios
GIT ageist
egoist
GIY uglify
uglily
GMC ogamic
GMD agamid
GNA agenda
Uganda
GNG eggnog
GNS Ngunis
GNY agency
GOD age-old
GOE ignore
GOT Egmont
GOY ignomy
GPE agapae
GRC agaric
GRT agorot
Ugarit
GSA egesta
GSI Agassi
GTA Agatha
kgotla
GTO Agatho
GUI agouti
GVL ogival
GZD agazed
HAE ohmage
phrase
sheave
the axe
HAH sheath
thrash
HAK chiack
chyack
shrank
thwack
HAL thrall
HAN thrawn
HAO cheapo
HAS shears
shoals
HAT thwart
HBA phobia
HBC phobic
HBK rhebok
HBS Thebes
HBX the box
HBY chubby
shabby
HCA cha-cha
HCE phocae
thecae
HCI chichi
HCL thecal
HCO whacko
HCS checks
chicks
phocas
shucks
HCY chicly
HDC Chadic
HDD shaded
HDE Phèdre
rhodie
HDF shaduf
HDH whidah
whydah
HDR chadar
chador
chider
HDS Rhodes
HDW shadow
HDY shoddy
the day
the dry
HEA Sheela
Sheena
HED shield
shrewd
the end
thread
HEE cheese
pheese
pheeze
phoebe❑
Sheene
thieve
threne
wheeze
HEH thresh
wheech
HEM phlegm
HEP threap
threep
HER oh dear!
HES cheers
sheets
shreds
wheels
HET threat
HEY cheeky
cheery
cheesy
sheeny
wheezy
HFD chafed
HFI shufti
HFR chafer
HFW the few
HFY shifty
shufty
The Fly
whiffy
HGE bhagee
chigoe
HGN shogun
HGS thighs
HGY shaggy
HIA sheila❑
HIE chaise
choice
Shiite
shrike
shrine
shrive
theine
thrice
thrive
HIH sheikh
HIK shriek
shrink
HIL shrill
thrill
HIM chrism
Shiism
theism
HIP shrimp
HIS chains
chairs
Rheims
theirs
thrips
HIT Christ
shrift
theist
thrift
HJS shojis
HKA chakra
chukka
HKD choked
The Kid
HKI bhakti
Shakti
HKL shekel
HKN shaken
HKR choker
shaker
HKS chokos
shakes
shakos
HKT Phuket
HKV Zhukov
HLA Khalsa
Khulna
Shelta
Thalia
Thelma
HLD Khalid
HLE chelae
shelve
HLF khalif
HLG the leg
HLH Shiloh
HLI chilli
thalli
tholoi
HLM phylum
shalom
HLN chalan
Chilon
HLO phyllo
HLP Philip
HLR choler
thaler
whaler
HLS Phelps
shells
Thales
whiles
HLT chalet
shalot
the lot
whilst
HLW the Law
HLY chalky
chilly
Philby
shelty
whilly
wholly
HMA ahimsa
rhumba
HMB the mob
HMC chemic
HMD rhymed
shamed
HMI rhombi
HML thymol
HMN shaman
HMR rhymer
Shamir
HMS shamus❑
Thames
Thomas
thymus
HMT the Met
HMY chummy
shammy
whammy
whimsy
HNA khanga
Rhonda
HNC phonic
HNE chance
change
thence
whence
whinge
HNI bhindi
Changi
HNL Chanel
phenol
phenyl
rhinal
HNO Shinto
HNP chin up
shin up
HNR shiner
thenar
whiner
HNS chinks
chinos
rhinos
thanks
things
whenas
HNT the Net
the net
HNU Chonju
HNW the now
HNY chancy
Chaney
chunky
phoney
shandy❑
shanny
shanty
shindy
shinny
shinty
thingy
thinly
whinny
HNZ chintz
HOD shroud
shrowd
HOE choose
chrome
shoole
the one
throne
HOF shroff
HOG throng
HOH whoosh
HOI dhooti
HOK shtook
HOM phloem
shtoom
HON shoo-in
thrown
HOS shmoes
throes
whoops
HOT throat
HOY choosy
phooey
theory
HPD shaped
HPL Bhopal
chapel
HPN chip in
chop in
Chopin
whip in
HPP chop up
whip up
HPR shaper
HPT chop at
shop at
HPY chippy
choppy
whippy
HQE cheque
HRA charka
chorea
choria
dharma
sharia
Sherpa
HRB cherub
HRC Chirac
HRD shared
the red
HRE charge
Cherie
chirre
Sharpe
Thorpe
HRF Sharif
sherif
HRH church❑
HRI thyrsi
HRL bharal
choral
Sheryl
HRN Charon
Chiron
Sharon
shoran
HRO gherao
Thurso

Words marked ❑ can also be spelled with an initial capital letter

HRR sharer
HRS chorus
pharos
shares
shorts
wharfs
HRT thirst
HRX thorax
HRY cherry□
chirpy
sherry□
shirty
shorty
thirty
thorny
wherry
whirry
HRZ Shiraz
HSC physic
HSD Chasid
HSE chassé
chaste
Thisbe
HSL chesil
chisel
HSM the sum
HSN chosen
the Son
The Sun
Xhosan
HSO physio
HSR chaser
HSS phases
rhesus
theses
thesis
HST whisht
HSY chesty
whisky
HTC photic
HTE Lhotse
HTF what if
what of
HTH thatch
HTM rhythm
HTN Bhutan
chitin
photon
shut in
shut-in
whet on
whiten
HTO Bhutto
ghetto
the two
what ho
whatso
HTP chat up
shut up
HTS photos
that is
whites
White's

HTY chatty
chitty
Whitby
HUD should
HUE chouse
HUH chough
sheuch
though
thrush
wheugh
HUK shrunk
HUM shtumm
HUS shrubs
HUT thrust
HUY rheumy
HVD shaved
HVL shovel
HVN shaven
HVR shaver
shiver
shover
HVS chives
HVT Shevat
HVY chivvy
HWB the Web
HWD showed
thawed
HWO The Who
HWP chew up
show up
HWR shower
HWZ The Wiz
HYE they're
they've
HYL they'll
HZG phizog
IAA cicada
cicala
piraña
Tirana
vihara
vimana
IAD ligand
lizard□
ribald
riband
vizard
wizard
IAE binate
dilate
finale
fixate
ligase
ligate
micate
mid-age
mirage
Miyake
Pilate
pirate
silage
tirade
tisane

visage
vivace
Zidane
IAF pilaff
IAH Riyadh
Sirach
IAI Divali
Diwali
Kigali
IAK hijack
IAM disarm
misaim
IAO mikado□
Pisano
virago
IAS rivals
Titans
vitals
IAU Timaru
IAY bigamy
binary
Hilary
litany
milady
piracy
IAZ pizazz
IBD disbud
ribbed
IBE dibble
jirble
kibble
liable
nibble
nimble
Ribble
timbre
viable
wimble
IBG air bag
airbag
bin-bag
kitbag
Liebig
IBN gibbon□
Lisbon
ribbon□
IBO Bilbao
IBR bibber
Cibber
dibber
disbar
fibber
Finbar
gibber
libber
limber
timber
IBS Airbus®
bilbos
bimbos
himbos
limbos
nimbus

timbós
IBT gibbet
Lisbet
tidbit
titbit
IBY nimbly
ICD diacid
viscid
ICE circle
fiacre
miscue
ICI kimchi
litchi
ICL fiscal
ICM sitcom
ICN niacin
piecen
zircon
ICP hiccup
ICR mincer
pincer
wincer
ICS circus
ciscos
discos
discus
pieces
Pincus
Pisces
viscus
zincos
ICT big cat
ICY Binchy
Biscay
bitchy
pitchy
titchy
IDD gilded
lidded
minded
rinded
winded
IDE birdie
diddle
fiddle
girdle
kindle
middle
piddle
riddle
tiddle
widdle
IDF kind of
IDH Jiddah
IDK dik-dik
IDM diadem
wisdom□
IDN hidden
linden
midden
milden
ridden
Sinden

IDP bind up
giddap
giddup
tied up
wind up
wind-up
IDR bidder
binder
birder
cinder
didder
finder
gilder
girder
hinder
kidder
lieder
minder
Pindar
tinder
Wilder
winder
Zinder
IDW mildew
window
IDY air-dry
fiddly
kindly
midday
mildly
tiddly
vildly
wildly
IEA cinema
kinema
pineta
Ribena®
Rijeka
Rivera
IED Aideed
big end
Sinéad
IEE give me
misère
picene
IEF wide of
IEH hi-tech
wideth
IEI Himeji
Ligeti
Sileni
IEL lineal
IEM pileum
IEN Aileen
bite in
dine on
dive on
Eileen
fire on
Gideon
give in
give on
live in

live-in
live on
pigeon
ride on
side-on
Simeon
wigeon
wire in
wivern
IEO Cicero
libero
live to
Pinero
wise to
IEP fire up
give up
hike up
line up
line-up
pile up
pile-up
pipe up
ride up
rise up
size up
wipe up
wise up
IER linear
IES biceps
cizers
divers
Hibees
pileus
sinews
Sirens
videos
vireos
IET bisect
digest
direct
divert
divest
finest
fire at
give it
silent
virent
wisest
IEY cicely□
finely
finery
likely
live by
lively□
livery
misery
nicely
nicety
ninety
nitery
ripely
rivery
sinewy

timely
vilely
vinery
vively
widely
wifely
winery
wisely
IFD miffed
IFE piaffe
piffle
siffle
IFL Eiffel
fitful
sinful
tinful
wilful
IFN tiffin
IFR aim for
die for
differ
dig for
niffer
pilfer
titfer
IFT misfit
IFX kid-fox
IFY Liffey
IGD hinged
ridged
ringed
tin god
wigged
winged
IGE biggie
bingle
dingle
giggle
higgle
jiggle
jingle
mingle
niggle
piggie
pingle
single
tingle
wiggle
IGG fisgig
fizgig
IGI nilgai
IGL Fingal
Virgil
IGN airgun
big gun
pidgin
piggin
ring in
six-gun
virgin□
IGO gingko
Ningbo
IGP ring up
IGR bigger
digger
finger□
ginger□
jigger
ligger
linger
Pilger
pinger
rigger
ringer
singer□
Tigger
winger
zinger
IGS bingos
biogas
dinges
Hingis
Mingus
pingos
IGT fidget
giggit
king it
midget
Piaget
widget
wing it
IGU nilgau
IGY dinghy
giggly
jingly
kingly
singly
wiggly
IHA lithia
Mishna
IHC lithic
IHD dished
niched
IHE Fichte
lichee
Michie
Richie
IHH eighth
IHI pithoi
Tishri
IHL Nichol
IHM dirham
IHN lichen
nigh on
richen
siphon
Sirhan
sithen
wish on
within
Yichun
IHO righto
IHP bishop□
dish up
fish up
high up
high-up
hip-hop
mishap
IHR cipher
cither
dither
either
fisher□
higher□
hither
lither
mither
wisher
wither
zither
IHS dishes
Fishes
lights
lithos
nights
riches
rights
sithes
tights
IHT Bichat
big hit
mishit
tin hat
with it
IHU Vishnu
IHY eighty
highly
mighty
nighly
nighty
richly
IIA minima
silica
IIE divide
divine
finite
liaise
simile
tibiae
virile
IIG aiding
ailing
airing
biking
biting
diving
filing
firing
fixing
gibing
giving
hiding
hiring
kiting
liking
liming
lining
living
mixing
piling
pining
piping
riding□
rising
siding
siting
sizing
tiling
timing
tiring
viking□
wiring
Xining
IIH finish
Lilith
linish
widish
III bikini□
Figini
miriti
Rimini
IIK tisick
IIL filial
finial
tibial
IIM cilium
Miriam
sizism
IIN Lilian
minion
Ninian
pinion
simian
titian□
vision
Vivian
Vivien
IIO aikido
libido
IIR vizier
IIS cities
civics
limits
Sirius
tibias
IIU milieu
Titipu
IIY airily
citify
dimity
fixity
minify
nidify
oilily
Sicily
tidily
tinily
vilify
vivify
wilily
wirily
IIZ Nimitz
IJG jig-jog
IJS ninjas
IKD linked
nicked
picked
pinked
wicked
wiz kid
IKE dickie□
fickle
pickle□
Pinkie
sickie
sickle
tickle
tinkle
Wilkie
winkle
IKF sick of
IKK Kirkuk
Wim Kok
IKL nickel
IKM dinkum
Sikkim
IKN Dicken
Dickon
fink on
firkin
kick in
libken
misken
pick on
pipkin
sicken
silken
sink in
Sir Ken
siskin
IKO ginkgo
IKP link up
link-up
pick up
pick-up
IKR bicker
bilker
dicker
hicker
kicker
milker
nicker
picker
ricker
sinker
ticker
tinker
wicker
winker
yikker
IKS pinkos
sickos
Wilkes
IKT pick at
picket
ticket
wicket
wink at
IKY dickey
Kirkby
miskey
sickly
tinkly
ILD filled
killed
misled
titled
willed
ILE gillie
girlie
Killie
Lillie
Millie
Willie
ILG mid-leg
ILH kiblah
ILI nielli
ILL Hillel
ILN Dillon
fill in
fill-in
tiglon
Villon
violin
ILO billy-o
niello
will do
ILP fillip
fill up
Hislop
kill up
ILR filler
Hitler
killer
Midler
miller□
pillar
rifler
tiller
ILS fields□
villus
Willis
ILT billet
fillet
gillet
gimlet
millet□
piglet□
rillet
violet□
willet
ILV Kislev
ILW billow
lie low
pillow
willow
ILY Finlay

6 _I_M_C

Finley
Lilley
Millay
mislay
Ridley
Sibley
Sisley
wieldy
IMC filmic
IMD rimmed
IME Timmie
IML dismal
hiemal
IMN airman
binman
Birman
disman
firman
Gilman
hit man
hit-man
Kidman
oilman
pitman❑
Tilman
Timman
Wigman
Xiamen
IMP firm up
IMR dimmer
gimmor
simmer
IMS gismos
gizmos
litmus
Titmus
IMT kismet❑
IMY dismay
firmly
Niamey
INA Bianca
Lianna
sienna
Vienna
zinnia
INC bionic
picnic
IND finned
nid-nod
pioned
tinned
INE Dianne
dinnle
Dionne
fiancé
jinnee
Lianne
Minnie
pinnae
Winnie
INF sign of
INH Jinnah
INL dirndl

Lionel
signal
simnel
INM lignum
INN finnan
lignin
mignon
sign on
INP kidnap
sign up
INR dinner
girner
limner
pioner
signer
Signor
sinner
Wiener
winner
INS pianos
viands
Widnes
INT linnet❑
lionet
pignut
signet
SI unit
INW minnow
winnow
INY Disney
Finney
kidney
Pitney
Sidney
IOA aikona
eidola
Ginola
kia-ora
mimosa
Nicola
Winona
IOC fi donc!
IOD lipoid
milord
IOE dipole
Nicole
Nilote
pilose
pinole
ribose
Simone
IOF aim off
die off
hit off
mid-off
rip off
rip-off
tip off
tip-off
IOG qi gong
Viborg
IOH kibosh
IOI Biloxi

IOM simoom
ION disown
Minoan
simoon
IOO gigolo
kimono
vigoro
IOR rigour
vigour
IOS didoes
vinous
IOT die out
dig out
dim out
dim-out
fit out
hit out
kit out
pig out
rig out
rig-out
sit out
tip out
win out
IOX bijoux
IOY Kid Ory
simony
IOZ Milosz
IPC biopic
hippic
IPD hipped
hispid
limpid
lipped
ripped
tipped
IPE Dieppe
dimple
fipple
hippie
hirple
Niepce
nipple
pimple
ripple
simple
sipple
tipple
wimple
yippee
IPL dispel
IPN kirpan
lippen
Nippon
pippin
Rippon
tiepin
IPR diaper
dipper
kipper
lisper
nipper❑
Nippur

simper
sipper
zipper
IPS cippus
gippos
hippos
IPT big pot
limpet
pit-pat
sippet
tinpot
tippet
IPU piupiu
IPY biopsy
jimply
limply
pimply
ripply
simply
IQE bisque
cirque
risqué
IRA sierra❑
IRB midrib
mihrab
IRC citric
nitric
ric-rac
IRD fibred
IRE Bierce
fierce
pierce❑
Pierre
tierce
IRG oil rig
IRL fibril
IRM Vikram
IRN citrin
citron
fibrin
Kieran
Kieron
micron
Mirren
IRR mirror
IRS cirrus
citrus
fibros
micros
Tigris
IRT tirrit
ISA fiesta
Fiesta®
miasma
siesta
vizsla
ISD biased
missed
pissed
ISE birsle
Cissie
fissle
hirsle

missee
tissue
ISH kirsch
kitsch
ISI Giusti
ISL diesel❑
hirsel
missal
tinsel
Wiesel
ISM dim sum
jissom
lissom
ISN bisson
Gibson
Nilsen
Pilsen
Wilson
ISO fiasco
giusto
ISR kisser
rinser
ISS dieses
diesis
dipsos
lisses
miasms
misses
missis
missus
nisses
IST Bisset
misset
Tilsit
ISU Bissau
ISW jigsaw
jig-saw
ripsaw
ISY Kinsey
Kirsty
pigsty
Wimsey
ITA sistra
ITC biotic
ITD fitted
gifted
hinted
jilted
kilted
lifted
pitted
tilted
wilted
ITE bistre
kiltie
kirtle
kittle
little
pintle
Sittwe
tiptoe
tittle
virtue

vittae
wintle
ITL distal
distil
kittul
lintel
pistil
pistol❑
rictal
ITM diatom
dictum
victim
ITN biotin
bitten
Fintan
Hilton
kitten
listen
Liston
Milton
Minton
mitten
piston
Wilton
ITO bistro
Giotto
ITP big top
lift up
mist up
silt up
tiptop
tittup
ITR bister
bitter
dieter
filter
fitter
jitter
kilter
lictor
Lister
litter
mister
Pictor
Pinter
pitter
rioter
sifter
sinter
sister
sitter
titter
victor❑
winter
witter
ITS dittos
hiatus
pintos
rictus
Sixtus
ITT diktat
hint at
ITY filthy

Words marked ❑ can also be spelled with an initial capital letter

wintry
wistly
IUA fibula
vicuna
vicuña
IUD liquid
piqued
IUE dilute
disuse
figure
fixure
minute
misuse
pilule
titule
IUL ritual
visual
IUR liquor
IUT minuet
piquet❑
IVA Silvia
IVN silvan
IVR silver❑
IWG bigwig
wigwag
IWM wigwam
IWN Kirwan
IWR viewer
IWS Biswas
view as
IWT dimwit
nitwit
IWY airway
midway❑
rid way
IXD jinxed
IXN dioxin
IYN Binyon
Libyan
Pinyin
IYO Tim Yeo
IYP tidy up
tidyup
IYY cityfy
IZA piazza
IZE fizzle
Lizzie
mizzle
sizzle
IZG zigzag
IZN gizzen
mizzen
IZO Rizzio
IZR fizzer
rizzar
rizzer
rizzor
IZS diazos
JBA Ojibwa
JNI djinni
KBB skibob
KDO skidoo
KDY skiddy
KEE ekuele
O'Keefe
KIG skiing
KIH skaith
skyish
KIP skrimp
KLA skolia
KLB Skylab
KLY skelly
skilly
KMO akimbo
KMY skimpy
KNP skin up
KNY skinny
KOA Akmola
KOH skoosh
KOT eke out
KPE Skopje
KPS okapis
KPT skip it!
KRS Skiros
KRY skerry
KTH sketch
KTR skater
KUP skrump
KVR skiver
KVY skivvy
KWD skewed
KWR skewer
LAA alpaca
cloaca
LAC Altaic
LAD Eluard
LAE alkane
Alsace
cleave
Eliade
eluate
old age
oleate
please
sleave
sleaze
Sloane
ullage
LAH bleach
fly ash
pleach
LAI alkali
LAO El Paso
LAS always
floats
LAT eluant
olfact
pliant❑
LAY Albany
bleary
floaty
sleazy
LBL global
LBN globin
LBT all but
LBY flabby
glibly
old boy
plebby
slobby
slubby
LCA Alicia
LCD placid
LCE cliché
cloche
flèche
plicae
LCI flocci
LCL glycol
LCN flacon
LCR placer
slicer
LCS flicks
flocks
glacis
ilices
places
slacks
LCT elicit
placet
LCY plucky
LDD sleded
LDE bludge
fledge
gledge
kludge
pledge
sledge
sludge
LDF glad of
LDN plod on
LDR glider
slider
LDS Gladys
LDY clodly
gladly
sludgy
LEE alkene
allege
allele
Cleese
fleece
sleeve
LEH fleech
LEN Alleyn
alpeen
clue in
LEO Cluedo®
LEP clue up
LES alleys
Elaeis
Olbers
pliers
LET albeit
Albert
client
eldest
eluent
fluent
oldest
LEY bluely
bluesy
fleecy
sleepy
sleety
LFN olefin
LFR all for
LFY fluffy
LGE plague
LGL Glagol
plagal
LGN flagon
plug in
slogan
LGP a leg up
clog up
LGT alight
blight
flight
plight
slight
slog at
LGY cloggy
LHA Althea
LHM Oldham
LHT old hat
old-hat
LIA El Giza
Eloisa
Elvira
Ulrica
ultima
LID allied
illiad
pleiad
LIE al fine
alpine
Blaise
Claire
Elaine
Eloise
plaice
sluice
LIG flying
slairg
LIH bluish
elfish
elvish
oldish
sleigh
LIM allium
LIN Albion
ultion
LIO albino
El Niño
ultimo
LIS Aldiss
allies
oldies
LIT plaint
LIY ploidy
LJH Elijah
LKN sloken
LKY Blakey
blokey
flukey
LLG old lag
LLM slalom
LMA alumna
LMD plumed
LME flambé
LMI alumni
LMN Altman
old man
Ullman
LMP clam up
LMS flames
LMX climax
LMY blimey
clammy
clumpy
clumsy
flimsy
glumly
plummy
slimly
slummy
slumpy
LNA Blanda
Glenda
Glinka
LNC clinic
LND cloned
LNE blende
blonde
blunge
elance
flange
flense
glance
plunge
LNH blanch❑
blench
clench
clinch
flench
flinch
planch
plinth
LNK Planck
LNL clonal
LNM plenum
LNO Alonso
Blanco
LNR Elinor
planar
planer
LNS blinds
blinis
Glenys
Glynis
llanos
planks
plants
LNT planet
LNY blanky
blenny
Clancy
clingy
clunky
flinty
flunky
plenty❑
slangy
slinky
LOA glioma
LOD almond
LOE alcove
Al Gore
all one
LOF ill off
LOH sloosh
LOK Alcock
LOS allons
floods
LOT Alcott
all out
all-out
almost
fly out
Olcott
LOY bloody
floozy
gloomy
LPE elapse
LPN clap on
slip in
slip on
slip-on
LPO Aleppo
LPP slap-up
slip up
slip-up
LPR eloper
LPT Elspet
LPY flappy
floppy
slip by
slippy
sloppy
LQE claque
clique
plaque
LRA gloria❑
LRC Alaric
cleric
LRD Alfred
flared
florid
LRE Clarke
florae
LRL floral
plural
LRN aldrin❑
florin
LRS claros
flares
floras

Words marked ❑ can also be spelled with an initial capital letter

Flores
LRT claret
floret
LRY blurry
clergy
flirty
flurry
slurry
LSA Alaska
Elisha
plasma
LSD closed
LSE plissé
LSI Alessi
LSN Alison
LSR Glaser
LSS Blasis
pluses
LST all set
closet
LSY classy
flashy
fleshy
flossy
glassy
glossy
I'll say!
plushy
slushy
LTA elytra
LTD elated
fluted
plated
slated
LTE blithe
clothe
LTF a lot of
LTH blotch
clatch
clutch
fletch
flitch
glitch
LTI glutei
LTL flotel
LTN Blyton
Cloten
gluten
platan
platen
LTO blotto
LTP blot up
LTR plater
ulster
LTS cloths
flatus
plates
zlotys
LTY flatly
glitzy
LUA pleura
LUE allude
allure

blouse
Claude
clause
flouse
illude
illume
ill-use
LUH Clough
floush
plough
sleuth
slouch
slough❑
LUN Alcuin
LUS albums
clouts
LUT flaunt
LUY cloudy
floury
glaury
LVA Flavia
Olivia
LVC Old Vic
Slavic
LVK Slovak
LVN alevin
cloven
eleven
flavin
sloven
LVR claver
clever
clover
glover
Oliver
plover
slaver
sliver
LVS claves
cloves
Clovis
gloves
LWD flawed
flewed
LWN blow in
LWP blow up
Blow-Up
blow-up
clew up
slow up
LWR blower
flower
glower
LWT blow it
LWY blowsy
blowzy
flyway
slowly
LXA alexia❑
LXI Alexei
LXN Blixen
flaxen
klaxon

LXR elixir
flexor
plexor
LXS Alexis
ilexes
plexus
LYD gleyed
played
LYE alkyne
Olwyne
LYN play on
LYP play up
LYR E-layer
flayer
F-layer
player❑
slayer
LYT play at
play it
LYY clayey
LZD glazed
LZN blazon
LZR blazer
LZS blazes
MAA impala
MAE embale
embase
empale
imbase
impale
impave
MAH smeath
MAK embank
embark
imbark
immask
MAL Amdahl
emball
MAM embalm
MAR impair
MAT impact
impart
umlaut
MAY smeary
MBL Amabel
MDE smudge
MDS emydes
MDT amidst
MDY smudgy
MEA amoeba
MED impend
MEE ampere
Ampère
impede
MEH emmesh
immesh
smeeth
MES Amiens
embers
MGA smegma
MGE émigré
MGN Imogen
MGS amigos

imagos
MGY smoggy
smugly
MIA amrita
MIE empire❑
imbibe
umpire
MIH impish
MIM omnium❑
MIN amnion
MIS Emmies
impies
MKD smoked
MKR smoker
MKS smokos
MLA Amelia
Emilia
Imelda
MLI smalti
MLM emblem
MLR smiler
MLS smalls
umbles
MLT amulet
smilet
MLX smilax
MLY employ
smelly
smiley
MNA Amanda
amenta
omenta
MND omened
MNE Amun-Re
MNS amends
MOC Imbolc
MOE impone
impose
MOH smooch
smooth
MOS emboss
MOT import
impost
MOY embody
MRA omertà
Smyrna
MRE amerce
embrue
emerge
imbrue
umbrae
MRH smirch
MRL amoral
umbral
MRO embryo
MRS umbras
MRY smarmy
smarty
MSD amused
MSM omasum
MSN Empson
MSS emesis
tmeses

MTC emetic
MTH smutch
MTR emptor
smiter
MTS Smiths
MTY smithy
smutty
MUD imbued
MUE immune
immure
impure
impute
MUH ambush
smouch
MUN impugn
MUT amount
MVE B-movie
MZD amazed
MZN amazon❑
NAA Ankara
Annaba
indaba
NAB enjamb
NAC in banc
NAD enlard
in hand
inlaid
inland
inward
on hand
onward
unhand
unpaid
unsaid
NAE anlage
ansate
encage
encase
encave
enface
engage
engagé
enlace
enrage
entame
in care
incase
incave
infame
inhale
inmate
in name
innate
insane
intake
invade
on sale
unbare
uncage
uncape
uncase
uncate
undate

unease
Uniate
unlace
unlade
unmade
unmake
unrake
unsafe
untame
unware
NAF in calf
NAG An Wang
NAH aneath
encash
in cash
on oath
uneath
unlash
NAI incavi
NAK unbark
unmask
unpack
untack
NAL and all
engaol
entail
enwall
inwall
on call
onfall
unnail
NAN in pain
in vain
NAO enhalo
NAP encamp
unhasp
NAR unfair
unhair
NAS annals
in-laws
in mass
in rags
NAT endart
enrapt
indart
in fact
infant
in part
intact
in want
unlast
NAY infamy
sneaky
uneasy
unwary
NBE enable
unable
NBS anabas
Anubis
NBY knobby
snobby
snubby
NCF UNICEF

NCP ink cap
ink-cap
NCS snacks
NDC anodic
NDE cnidae
on edge
snudge
unedge
NDL anodal
NDY any day
one day
NEA Angela
Anneka
entera
injera
NED in deed
indeed
in need
intend
on-lend
unbend
undead
unhead
unlead
unread
NEE annexe
en fête
entêté
in fere
inhere
sneeze
unhele
NEF undeaf
unself
NEH enmesh
inmesh
NEK undeck
NEL anneal
unreal
unreel
unseal
unseel
unveil
unwell
NEM Anselm
enseam
inseem
unhelm
unseam
unteam
NEN intern
unrein
unseen
NEO Angelo
NER endear
ensear
unbear
ungear
NES Enders
Engels
unless
NET incept
in debt
indent
infect
infeft
infest
ingest
inject
in jest
insect
insert
intent
invent
invert
invest
unbelt
unbent
unnest
unrest
unseat
untent
unwept
NEY Annecy
sneezy
NFC unific
NFX in a fix
NFY sniffy
snuffy
NGA enigma
NGN Onegin
NGR onager
NGT anight
knight□
NGY knaggy
snaggy
snugly
NHA Anthea
NHD unshod
NHE unshoe
NHM anthem
NHN Anshan
Inchon
NHP inship
unship
NHR anchor
anther
NHT in that
unshut
NHW and how
anyhow
on show
unthaw
NIA angina
Annika
Indira
in rixa
NID engild
engird
enwind
in bird
in kind
invis'd
inwind
unbind
ungird
unkind
untied
unwind
NIE endive
engine
ensile
entice
entire
incise
incite
in line
inside
in time
invite
Ondine
on file
on fire
on hire
on-line
onside
on-site
on time
undine
unhive
unlike
unlime
unline
unlive
unripe
untile
unwire
unwise
unwive
NIG Anning
ending
enring
unking
NIH enrich
in with
inwith
on high
unwish
NII uncini
NIK enlink
inwick
on tick
unlink
unpick
NIL infill
O'Neill
uncial
unwill
NIM indium
infirm
NIN ensign
Indian
NIO indigo
in vivo
NIS antics
Ennius
gneiss
in bits
on-dits
unbias
undies
unkiss
NIT anoint
enlist
indict
insist
unbitt
NIU in situ
NIW in view
on view
NIY enmity
entity
untidy
NJM in a jam
NLA Antlia
NLC en bloc
NLD angled
unclad
NLE unglue
NLG unclog
unplug
NLN inulin
NLR angler
antler
NLS Anglos
NLT anklet
englut
NLW inflow
onflow
NLX influx
NLY anally
in play
snelly
NMC gnomic
NME anomie
gnomae
NML animal
enamel
NMN gnomon
one-man
NMS animus
enemas
gnomes
NNM anonym
NNT unknit
unknot
NOA Ancona
ancora
Angola
angora□
NOB entomb
enwomb
untomb
NOD any old
enfold
infold
inroad
in word
on hold
uncord
unfold
ungord
unload
unlord
untold
NOE Ankole
any one
anyone
encode
encore
engore
enrobe
enzone
income
Indore
in-joke
in love
insole
intone
invoke
snooze
uncope
undone
unlove
unpope
unrobe
unrope
unyoke
NOF one-off
unroof
NOG on song
NOK enlock
inlock
in work
inwork
uncock
uncork
undock
unhook
unlock
unwork
NOL ensoul
entoil
in foal
insoul
uncoil
uncool
uncowl
unfool
unroll
unsoul
NOM inform
unform
NON enjoin
inborn
unborn
ungown
unsown
NOO in toto
NOP inhoop
unhoop
NOR indoor
unmoor
NOS ingoes
Onions
NOT enroot
inmost
in sort
oncost
on foot
unbolt
uncolt
unroot
NOY Antony
incony
oniony
snoopy□
snooty
snoozy
unholy
NPC on spec
NPD uniped
unipod
NPN inspan
NPP snap up
NPR on a par
sniper
unspar
NPS snipes
NPY snappy
NQE unique
NRA Andrea
anuria
NRD inbred
Ingrid
inured
snared
NRE enfree
entrée
untrue
NRH enarch
NRK anorak
NRM antrum
in trim
untrim
NRN intron
NRP entrap
enwrap
inwrap
unwrap
NRR snarer
snorer
NRS Andros
in arms
indris
Ingres
intros
NRT in a rut
NRW Andrew
in a row
undraw
NRY energy
gnarly
in-tray
knurly
snarly
unpray
NSD UNCSTD

Words marked □ can also be spelled with an initial capital letter

unused
NSE enisle
in esse
inisle
NSN UNISON
unison
NSO UNESCO
NSR Dnestr
NSS enoses
enosis
gnoses
NSX unisex
NTC anetic
NTD UNCTAD
united□
NTH snatch
snitch
NTL instil
NTO anatto
one-two
NTP in step
instep
unstep
unstop
NTR instar
uniter
NTS Unitas
NTW unstow
NTY knotty
snotty
NUA pneuma
ungula
NUE endure
ennuyé
ensure
incuse
induce
infuse
inhume
injure
insure
in tune
unrule
unsure
untune
NUF engulf
ingulf
unturf
NUG unsung
NUH enough
inrush
onrush
NUI annuli
NUK in luck
unhusk
untuck
NUL annual
in full
uncurl
unfurl
ungual
NUN in turn
unturn

NUS ungues
unguis
NUT induct
Innuit
insult
intuit
unhurt
unjust
unsuit
NUY injury
on duty
snouty
unbury
unduly
unruly
NVL snivel
NVN uneven
NVS knives
NWR answer
NWS in twos
know as
NWT gnaw at
NWY anyway
in a way
one-way
NXA anoxia
NXC anoxic
NYC in sync
NYE enzyme
oneyre
NYR oneyer
NYT encyst
NZY snazzy
OAA Douala
Roxana
somata
sonata
Toyama
OAC mosaic□
OAD coward□
Donald
dotard
Godard
go hard
Howard
Poland
Roland
Ronald
togaed
to hand
woman'd
OAE borage
borate
donate
dosage
dotage
folate
forage
for aye
homage
Horace
lobate
locale

locate
lovage
morale
nonage
nonane
notate
pomace
pomade
potage
romage
rosace
rotate
Roxane
solace
to date
towage
voyage
OAG go bang
go hang
OAH potash
OAI romaji
Romani
Somali
OAK go back
Mohawk
OAL for all
go bail
morall
no ball
sod all
OAN domain
OAO dorado
Monaco
potato
Tobago
tomato
wo ha ho
OAR hot air
mohair
OAS morals
morass
noways
Romans
today's
OAT Bogart
cobalt
comart
dotant
go-cart
go fast
go-kart
go past
Hobart
Mozart
Pop Art
sonant
volant
OAU nogaku
OAX boyaux
OAY botany□
Bovary
covary
go easy

nonary
not any
notary
oogamy
Romany
rosary
rotary
so many
votary
OBC tombac
OBD bombed
forbid
hotbed
mobbed
morbid
not bad
robbed
too bad
OBE bobble
cobble
corbie
doable
double
double-
foible
forbye
gobble
hobble
nobble
Robbie
rouble
sombre
wobble
zombie
OBK tombak
OBL corbel
OBN bobbin
bonbon
dobbin
OBO booboo
boo-boo
OBR bomber
cobber
comber
dobber
jobber
robber
towbar
OBS bombos
combos
Forbes
Hobbes
yobbos
OBT combat
fox-bat
gobbet
hobbit
Korbut
nobbut
sorbet
wombat
you bet
OBY bobbly

Bombay
bow-boy
cowboy
Dombey
doubly
lowboy
tomboy
Tor Bay
Torbay
toy boy
toyboy
wobbly
OCA concha
OCD forced
roscid
voiced
OCE bouclé
conche
douche
potche
touché
OCM non-com
OCN mod con
toucan
OCO honcho
poncho
OCP mob-cap
toecap
OCR concur
forcer
soccer
OCS coccos
coccus
conchs
forces
hoicks
yoicks
zoccos
OCT bobcat
low-cut
tomcat
Top Cat
OCU roucou
OCW Moscow
OCX coccyx
OCY botchy
conchy
notchy
pouchy
touchy
ODC Nordic
ODD aoudad
corded
folded
goaded
hooded
loaded□
sordid
wooded
ODE boodle
coddle
doddle
doodle

fondle
fondue
foodie
Goldie
Hoddle
noddle
noodle
poodle
roadie
toddle
ODF fond of
hold of
ODG hot dog
hot-dog
top dog
ODH doodah
good-oh
houdah
howdah
ODK pondok
ODL Goidel
rondel
ODM condom
goddam
ODN Borden
Cobden
cordon
fold in
Godden
golden
Gooden
Gordon
hold in
hold on
houdan
hoyden
Jordan
London
louden
sodden
sold on
wooden
ODO hold to
hoodoo
koodoo
voodoo
word go
ODP fold up
hold up
hold-up
road up
ODR border□
condor
dodder
donder
fodder
folder
Gondor
holder
loader
moider
Mordor
polder

Words marked □ can also be spelled with an initial capital letter

ponder
powder
solder
wonder□
yonder
ODS hordes
rondos
tondos
ODT Bordet
hold it!
ODY boldly
coldly
Corday
fondly
goodly
hobday
hold by
lordly
loudly
Monday
wordly
OEA bodega
monera
novena
Rowena
Topeka
womera
OED dog end
dog-end
Howerd
token'd
OEE cohere
Eocene
foveae
Göreme
Jolene
Rovere
toneme
OEF come of
OEH Joseph
OEI boleti
Boveri
OEK copeck
kopeck
to seek
OEL boreal
do well
Dowell
foveal
go well
Howell
Jowell
Lovell
Lowell
Powell
to sell
OEN Boleyn
come in
come on
come-on
done in
Doreen
dote on
govern
home in
Joleen
modern
move in
move on
Noreen
poteen
rope in
solemn
vote in
OEO bolero□
Boléro
comedo
come to
forego
more so
non-ego
pomelo
Soweto
Toledo
torero
OEP bone up
come up
done up
hole up
move up
move-up
nose up
tone up
OER co-heir
no fear
poseur
to-tear
voyeur
OES bogeys
Boreas
bowels
coleus
covers
dozens
fogeys
lovers
moneys
no less
novels
pokeys
pose as
powers
rodeos
Rogers
Romeos
Sobers
soleus
voters
vowess
OET cogent
come at
covert
foment
forest
go west
honest
lowest
modest
molest
moment
potent
Robert
rodent
so be it
OEU Moreau
Roseau
OEY bowery
come by
comedy
comely
gone by
homely
lonely
lovely
moiety
solely
sorely
OEZ Lorenz
OFB confab
OFD hoofed
roofed
OFE coffee
pouffe
toffee
OFH loofah
OFL joyful
potful
woeful
OFN boffin
coffin
for fun
OFR coffer
confer
goffer
golfer
hoofer
loafer
not far
roofer
OFT comfit
confit
goof it
hoof it
non-fat
soffit
Wolfit
OFW too few
OFX confix
forfex
Koufax
OFY botfly
dor-fly
OGA Borgia
loggia
OGD dogged
forged
gorged
OGE boggle
bon gré
boogie
bougie
coggle
goggle
google
joggle
loggie
moggie
morgue
pongee
soigné
soogee
toggle
tongue
woggle
OGI Mowgli
OGL Dougal
googol
OGN Coggan
gorgon□
long on
Morgan
noggin
Top Gun
OGO gorgio
OGR codger
conger
cougar
dodger
dogger□
forger
gorger
Hoggar
jogger
lodger
longer
monger
Polgar
OGS bongos
Borges
borgos
pongos
sorgos
Vosges
OGT bought
forget
forgot
fought
gorget
hogget
nougat
nought
rotgut
OGY coggly
doughy
googly
longly
OHA Joshua
Sophia
OHC Gothic
OHE Sophie
OHH hoo-hah
OHI kowhai
OHL Köchel
OHM Bochum
Botham
OHN Cochin
lochan
so then
OHO boohoo
boo-hoo
Rothko
yoo-hoo
OHP nosh-up
OHR bother
cosher
fother
gopher
josher
kosher
mother
pother
rother
tocher
tother
t'other
OHT rochet
so that
so what?
top hat
top-hat
Tophet
OHV moshav
OHW forhow
no-show
OHY poshly
OIA Aouita
coaita
Konica®
Lolita
Louisa
Monica
nomina
OIC oomiac
zodiac□
OID copied
do bird
Gobind
Govind
honied
monied
OIE bodice
bolide
bovine
cosine
cotise
docile
dorise
dorize
do time
Fokine
go live
iodide
iodine
iodise
iodize
ionise
ionize
Kosice
Louise
mobile□
motile
motive
no-side
notice
no time
novice
nowise
oolite
police□
polite
votive
OIG Boeing
boring
boxing
coming
coping
coving
doning
doping
doting
dozing
foxing
holing
homing
hoping
joking
losing
loving
lowing
moping
moving
nosing
noting
oozing
posing
roving
rowing
towing
toying
voting
Woking
wooing
OIH boyish
dovish
do with
eolith
go with
goyish
modish
morish
polish□
Romish
OII solidi
yogini
OIK Kodiak
oomiak
Yorick
OIL jovial

Words marked □ can also be spelled with an initial capital letter

6 _O_I_M

oorial
social
OIM corium
eonism
holism
monism
podium
sodium
OIN Ionian
Lorien
lotion
motion❑
notion
potion
OIO Comino
domino❑
Lobito
solito
OIR copier
cosier
cozier
foliar
hosier
OIS bodies
bogies
fogies
folios
golias
Möbius
monies
movies
pokies
polios
sonics
Tobias
to bits
Tonies
OIT aorist
forint
holist
monist
soviet❑
OIY bodily
codify
comity
cosily
gorily
holily
homily
modify
nosily
notify
oozily
policy
polity
ropily
rosily
rosiny
Torify
OIZ Dönitz
OJB hobjob
OJE conjee
OJM log-jam
OJN donjon
OJY popjoy
OKD booked
cooked
corked
forked
hooked
locked
soaked
worked
zonked
OKE bookie
cockle
cookie
folkie
honkie
kookie
nookie
rookie
yorkie❑
OKH hookah
OKN bodkin
book in
lock in
lock on
look in
look-in
look on
work in
work-in
work on
OKO look to
OKP cock up
cock-up
cook up
fork up
hook up
hook-up
lock up
lock-up
look up
mock up
mock-up
soak up
soakup
work up
OKR cocker
conker
cooker
corker
corkir
Fokker
forker
hooker❑
korkir
locker
looker
mocker
porker
rocker
soaker
worker
yorker
OKS jockos
work as
OKT docket
hook it
locket
look at
pocket
rocket
socket
work at
OKY donkey
folksy
hockey
jockey
low-key
monkey
OLD boiled
bowled
coiled
foiled
jowled
mobled
pooled
rolled
soiled
OLE boulle
collie
goalie
goolie
Joelle
Noelle
OLG dog-leg
loglog
OLH moolah
OLM coelom
Moslem
Mowlam
OLN goblin
Joplin
pollan
pollen
poplin
roll in
roll on
roll-on
Toulon
OLP dollop
doll up
foul up
foul-up
gollop
lollop
roll up
roll-up
OLR boiler
bowler
coaler
collar
cooler
dollar
fowler❑
gollar
holler
howler
loller
poplar
roller❑
toiler
OLS boules
coulis
Fowles
hollos
nobles
oodles
poules
worlds
OLT cool it
goblet
job-lot
not let
toilet
OLW follow
go slow
go-slow
hollow
OLX pollex
Pollux
OLY Bowlby
coolly
foully
hooley
Mosley
motley
mouldy
Sorley
volley
woolly
OLZ Boulez
OMA Nouméa
OMC cosmic
formic
OMD doomed
formed
roomed
OME commie
coombe
dormie
OML formal
normal
Rommel
OMN bogman
common
con man
Corman
cowman
dolmen
Forman
Mormon
Norman
rodman
to a man
zoom in
OMP loom up
OMR dormer
former
roamer
roomer
wormer
OMS commis
commos
Cosmas
cosmos
dolmas
Holmes
houmus
OMT bon mot
commit
format
motmot
OMX commix
ONA cornea
cornua
Joanna
ONB hobnob
ONC cognac
OND corned
Gounod
horned
joined
ONE Bonnie
bounce
Connie
Donnie
Joanie
Joanne
jounce
lounge
pounce
townee
townie
ONL nounal
ONN born in
horn in
join in
Poznan
ONO Borneo
go in to
go into
soon to
ONP join up
ONR coiner
Connor
corner
Donner
downer
joiner
moaner
mooner
sooner
ONS bounds
doings
donnés
points
pounds
rounds
ONT bonnet
cobnut
coin it
cornet
go on at
hornet
sonnet
soon at
ONW for now
how now
ONY Bonney
bouncy
bounty❑
county
Hornby
mornay❑
mounty❑
Rodney
Rooney
OOA Bogotá
corona
Dodoma
Honora
jojoba
Pomona
Somoza
Toyota
Toyota®
Yo-Yo Ma
OOD go cold
kobold
no good
no-good
toroid
toxoid
OOE bog-ore
coyote
for one
go home
jocose
morose
nodose
no joke
no more
not one
to come
to-come
tofore
OOF fob off
lop off
nod off
pop off
top off
OOG oolong
so long
so long!
so-long
OOH golosh
OOI colobi
Moroni
Potosí
OON cocoon
cojoin
do down
go down
godown
so soon

OOO corozo
Komodo
Kosovo
rococo□
yo-ho-ho
OOR colour
dolour
go sour
honour□
OOS cohoes
colons
dodoes
goboes
hoboes
joyous
mojoes
nodous
no-noes
porous
OOT bow out
cohort
co-host
cop out
cop-out
not out
not-out
to boot
top out
OOY bosomy
colony
monody
nobody
oology
polony
OPA cowpea
hoop-la
OPD looped
pooped
torpid
OPE corpse
couple
hoopoe
hopple
koppie
popple
souple
topple
toupee
OPH oompah
OPL compel
gospel
OPM pompom
OPN coupon
Jospin
loipen
OPO go up to
poo-poo
OPP coop up
joy-pop
soup up
vox pop
OPR bopper
cooper□
copper
Cowper
hopper□
looper
lopper
mopper
popper□
romper
topper
torpor
OPS compos
corpus
OPT cowpat
hotpot
moppet
Pol Pot
poppet
OPX cowpox
OPY comply
Pompey
OQE mosque
torque
ORD Conrad
con-rod
forrad
horrid
hot rod
Modred
moored
soured
torrid
ORE bo tree
bourse
coarse
coerce
corrie
course
cowrie
gourde
hoarse
Moerae
Monroe
soirée
source
ORG toerag
ORH fourth
Howrah
ORI Moirai
ORK Tobruk
ORL corral
sorrel
ORM pogrom
ORN Conran
poprin
ORO hooroo
journo
ORR horror
pourer
roarer
Rohrer
tourer
ORS boards
courts
Morris
Morris®
morros
Norris
zorros
ORT Dorrit
forrit
Poirot
worrit
ORW borrow
sorrow
ORY dourly
hooray
hourly
poorly
Rob Roy
sourly
OSD bossed
doused
MOSSAD
poised
roused
soused
OSE fo'c'sle
fossae
mossie
mousle
mousse
not see
nousle
Sousse
sowsse
tousle
Wopsle
OSF lots of
tons of
toss of
OSH borsch
OSI bonsai
OSL consul
dorsal
dossal
dossel
fossil
housel
morsal
morsel
podsol
tonsil
woosel
OSM dorsum
possum
OSN Boyson
cousin
Dobson
godson
horson
Jolson
Jonson
loosen
poison
Robson
Roisin
tocsin
worsen
OSO so as to
OSP gossip
toss up
toss-up
OSR bowser
dosser
dowser
fossor
mouser
rouser
worser
wowser
OSS bosses
corsos
gooses
horses
houses
louses
noesis
souses
torsos
OST corset
cosset
Dorset
posset
OSU Honshu
OSY Dorsey
fousty
horsey
mousey
Wolsey
OTA contra
footra
foutra
Nootka
Portia
rostra
OTC aortic
Coptic
noetic
nostoc
poetic
zoetic
OTD coated
dotted
foetid
footed
lofted
moated
posted
potted
rooted
routed
sorted
wonted
OTE boatie
bootee
Bootle
bottle
bow-tie
costae
Dottie
footie
footle
goatee
Goethe
goitre
goutte
jostle
loathe
Lottie
Moltke
mottle
postie
softie
soothe
sortie
to a tee
tootle
OTF sort of
OTG Sontag
OTH hootch
OTL coital
costal
foetal
fontal
hostel
mortal
portal
postal
postil
OTM bottom□
tom-tom
OTN Bolton
bon ton
Boston
cotton
molten
Morton
rotten
soften
soft on
torten
OTO lost to
too-too
wont to
OTR boater
co-star
coster
cottar
cotter
doctor
footer
foster□
fouter
hooter
hotter
jotter
loiter
looter
low-tar
mortar
porter□
poster
potter
pouter
powter
rooter
rorter
roster
rotter
sorter
souter
tolter
totter
touter
zoster
OTS Boötes
Coates
coitus
contos
Cortes
Cortés
foetus
fortes
fortis
lottos
mouths
pontes
pottos
tortes
youths
OTT foot it
tomtit
tom-tit
OTW kowtow
OTX cortex
vortex
OTY costly
Holtby
Horthy
mostly
mouthy
poetry
portly
rootsy
softly
toothy
tootsy
worthy
OUA copula
koruna
Yoruba
OUD jocund
rotund
OUE cohune
lobule
module
nodule
solute
volume
volute
OUH go bush
so much
OUI gomuti
lobuli
loculi

moduli
toruli
OUN Coburn
column
OUO colugo
modulo
OUS forums
locums
Pogues
OUT coquet
go bust
locust
loquat
robust
roquet
yogurt
OUU Mobutu
OVE louvre❑
OVL coeval
OVR bovver
do over
go over
Hoover
soever
solver
OVS corves
Corvus
hooves
loaves
looves
wolves
OVT Jouvet
OVX convex
OVY convey
convoy
OWB cobweb❑
OWL go AWOL
OWN Colwyn
Godwin
OWP doo-wop
OWR hot war
OWT godwit
OWW powwaw
powwow
OWY go away
go awry
Norway
OXR coaxer
hoaxer
OYA Kolyma
OYB corymb
OYE oocyte
OYI polypi
OYN Jolyon
ronyon
OYP copy up
cosy up
OYS polyps
OYT nor yet
OYY Toryfy
OZE foozle
mozzie
nozzle
sozzle
touzle
OZI borzoi
OZL podzol
OZO zoozoo
OZR boozer
rozzer
OZT howzat
PAD uphaud
upland
upward
PAE L-plate
opiate
update
uprate
uptake
PAH splash
PAL sprawl
PAN sprain
PAT upcast
PAY apiary
PCD spaced
spiced
PCE apache❑
specie
spicae
PCL apical
PCR spacer
PCS apices
spicas
PCY specky
PDL apodal
PDR spader
spider
PDS spados
PDX spadix
PED append
spread
uplead
PEE a piece
apiece
sphere
PEH speech
PEI ephebi
PEL appeal
PEN spleen
PEO speedo
PEP upkeep
PER appear
upbear
uprear
uptear
PET upbeat
PEY speedy
PFR opt for
PGE apogee
PGT spight
spigot
PHT upshot
PIA optima
PID upbind
upwind
up-wind
PIE ophite
splice
spline
sprite
Updike
uprise
upside
PIF spliff
PIG opting
spring❑
spying
upping
PIH uppish
up with
PIL uphill
PIN option
PIS aphids
optics
speiss
splits
spoils
PIT splint
spoilt
sprint
uplift
uprist
PIX sphinx❑
PIY uppity
PIZ spritz
PKD spiked
PKN spoken
PLH spilth
PLO apollo❑
PLS apples
PLW upblow
upflow
PMN apeman
PND opened
PNE sponge
PNL spinal
spinel
PNM eponym
PNP open up
PNR opener
PNS Spinks
PNT spinet
upknit
PNW C P Snow
PNY openly
spongy
spunky
POA apnoea
POB aplomb
POD uphold
upload
POE appose
oppose
uprose
POH splosh
POK uplock
uplook
POL upcoil
uproll
PON up town
uptown
POR uproar
POT opt out
opt-out
sprout
spy out
upmost
uproot
up to it
POY spooky
PPE epopee
PQE opaque
PRA Sparta
spirea
PRD spared
PRE sparge
sparse
sperre
spurge
PRH eparch
PRL spiral
PRN Oparin
spur on
PRO Oporto
PRS sparks
sports
PRT spirit
PRW upgrow
PRY sparky
sparry
sporty
spurry
PSS eposes
opuses
PTA aphtha
PTE spathe
PTM sputum
PTN spot on
spot-on
PTY apathy
spotty
PUE spouse
spruce
PUG sprung
PUH sprush
PUK spruik
PUN oppugn
upturn
PUS Ophuls
PVN spavin
PVY spivvy
PWR spewer
PWY upsway
PXF a pox of
PXN a pox on
PXS apexes
PYY spryly
PZA epizoa
PZM apozem
QAA squama
QAE equate
square
QAH squash
QAK squawk
QAL squail
squall
QEK squeak
QEL squeal
QIA Aquila
QIE equine
équipe
squire
QIF squiff
QIH squish
QIL squill
QIM squirm
QIO Aquino
QIR squier
squirr
QIS squids
QIT squint
squirt
QIY equity
squiny
RAA arcana
armada
errata
organa
Oriana
RAD Artaud
briard
Erhard
errand
try and
RAE arcade
arcane
crease
create
grease❑
greave
ornate
urbane
RAH Armagh
breach
breath
broach
preach
wreath
wroath
RAI argali
Armani
RAK arrack
RAM orgasm
RAN ordain
RAO Arcaro
Armado
RAS briars
broads
Dryads
Frears
groats
Oreads
organs
trials
RAT arrant
breast
dreamt
errant
truant
RAY creaky
creamy
creasy
croaky
dreamy
dreary
freaky
friary
greasy
treaty
RAZ ersatz
RBC arabic❑
RBE arable
Crabbe
treble
RBL tribal
RBR briber
prober
RBT grab at
RBY crabby
drably
grabby
grubby
trebly
RCA Tricia
RCD graced
RCE crèche
Gracie
oracle❑
troche
RCL uracil
RCM drachm
RCR bracer
grocer
tracer
trocar
RCS braces
crocus
cruces
fracas
grices
précis
prices
traces
tracks
tricks
RCT Brecht
fricht
tricot
RCW Cracow
RCY cricky
pricey
Tracey
tricky
RDA uredia
RDD eroded
RDE bridge
Bridie
bridle

Words marked ❑ can also be spelled with an initial capital letter

Brodie
cradle
dredge
drudge
fridge
grudge
trudge
RDL bridal
credal
RDN Dryden
RDR grader
trader
RDS credos
irides
RDT credit
RDY aridly
cruddy
Freddy
Friday
REA fraena
Frieda
Ortega
RED friend
REE breeze
creese
freeze
frieze
Graeme
Greece
Greene
grieve
kreese
prieve
REH breech
creesh
REI Ormeli
REL ordeal
Orwell
REN orcein
REO true to
RER arrear
RES briefs
creeps
greens
orders
RET ardent
arrest
Ernest
orient
priest
urgent
REY artery
breezy
briery
creepy
freely
greedy
greeny
orrery
troely
RFB prefab
RFD trifid
RFE griffe
trifle
trofie
RFL armful
artful
ireful
RFR prefer
try for
RFT Arafat
profit
RFX orifex
prefix
RFY crafty
dry-fly
RGC tragic
RGD Brigid
frigid
RGE brigue
brogue
Brugge
dragée
drogue
Prague
RGL frugal
RGN Aragon
drag on
dragon□
Oregon
Origen
origin
orogen
trigon
trogon
RGP drag up
RGR Kruger
RGS Briggs
Bruges
gregos
tragus
troggs
RGT aright
bright□
Brigit
fright
wright□
RGU gru-gru
RGY craggy
drag by
druggy
froggy□
groggy
trigly
RHA Brahma
RHC Orphic
RHD arched
orchid
RHE Archie
RHL archil
orchel
orchil
RHM Arnhem
Graham
RHN orphan
urchin
RHR archer□
Arthur
RHS Brahms
orthos
RHY archly
RIA arnica
troika
urtica
RID braird
RIE araise
arrive
arsine
braide
Braine
braise
bruise
cruise□
dry ice
ermine
fraise
greige
Irvine
oroide
orpine
praise
pruine
ureide
ursine
RIG crying
drying
erring
irking
Irving
prying
trying
urging
RIH graith
wraith
RIM erbium
truism
RIN Arrian
RIO Orsino
RIS armies
brains
fruits
grains
traits
RIT aroint
artist
RIY brainy
fruity
grainy
RJL frijol
RJN Trajan
Trojan
RKN broken
kraken
RKR broker
RKS Drake's
irokos
RKW Kraków
RKY crikey
RLA aralia
brolga
RLC frolic
Uralic
RLE grille
grilse
or else
Tralee
RLG PROLOG
RLI arilli
RLM prelim
RLN Dralon®
RLS frills
proles
RLT armlet
RLV Krylov
RLX prolix
RLY brolly
drolly
frilly
orally
trilby□
trolly
RMC eremic
RMD premed
primed
RME gramme
trompe
RMH grumph
RMI dromoi
Urumqi
RML brumal
primal
RMN Bremen
cram in
Truman
RMO Dromio
RMP drum up
Mrs Mop
RMR framer
primer
tremor
trimer
RMS Aramis
crumbs
grumps
primos
Primus
promos
tramps
RMT Gromit
prompt
RMY Brumby
crumby
crummy
frumpy
Grammy
grimly
grumly
grumpy
primly
trimly
RNA Brenda
crania
Granta
Urania
RNC irenic
ironic
uranic
RNE brenne
Brontë
bronze
cringe
France
fringe
grange□
grunge
orange□
or snee
prance
prince□
trance
RNH branch
brunch
cranch
crunch
drench
French
Granth
trench
wrench
RNI Brunei
RNK Franck
RNL Brunel
crenel
crinal
trinal
urinal
RNM crinum
frenum
RNN Cronin
kronen
RNO Brando
bronco
Cranko
drongo
Franco
pronto
Trento
RNR kroner
kronor
krónur
pruner
RNS crants
Cronus
drinks
Erinys
Kronos
pranks
trunks
Uranus
RNT Brandt
RNW ere now
erenow
RNY brandy
branny
bronzy
cranky
cranny
frenzy
fringy
granny
grungy
Orkney
tranny
trendy
RNZ krantz
ROA areola
ROD Arnold
ROE arkose
Brooke
creole□
groove
oriole
triode
ROF cry off
ROH brooch
ROI ariosi
ROO arioso
ROR arbour
ardour
armour
ROS Brooks
proofs
Proops
troops
ROT cry out
dry out
pry out
try out
try-out
ROU ormolu
ROY Briony
broody
bryony□
droopy□
groovy
priory
RPA grappa
RPC tropic
RPD tripod
RPE frappé
triple
RPL propel
propyl
RPN drop in
drop-in
drop on
trepan
RPO troppo
RPP crop up
prop up
trip up
wrap up
RPR draper
groper
proper
RPS cripes
Cripps
trapes

Words marked □ can also be spelled with an initial capital letter

tripos
RPT armpit
RPY crappy
drop by
dropsy
prepay
preppy
triply
trippy
trophy
RQE Braque
RRL crural
RRN dry run
RSA arista
crissa
frusta
Orissa
Prisca
Trisha
RSD irised
Prasad
RSE crosse
Crusoe
wrasse
RSH Frisch
RSN Bryson
orison
prison
RSO fresco
Fresno
presto
RSR eraser
Fraser
RSS crases
crises
crisis
crusts
irises
krises
preses
uruses
RST preset
prosit
RSV Brasov
RSY brassy
brisky
crispy
Crosby
crusty
dressy
drossy
frisky
frosty
grassy
grisly
prissy
trashy
tressy
trusty
wristy
RTA Aretha
protea
RTC arctic❑
critic
erotic
RTE writhe
RTH crotch
crutch
wretch
RTK Bratsk
RTL brutal
RTM pro tem
RTN Breton
Briton
Bruton
craton
cretin
gratin
proton
triton❑
RTO grotto
RTR crater❑
frater
grater
orator
ureter
writer
RTS Brutus
gratis
Pratt's
RTX pre-tax
RTY Bratby
bratty
frothy
gritty
grotty
pretty
RUA trauma
Ursula
RUD around
Freund
ground
RUE arouse
crouse
grouse
ordure
triune
troupe
RUH crouch
drouth
grouch
trough
RUI arguli
RUL Breuil
RUR arguer
RUS trouts
RUT draunt
irrupt
Proust
RUX Proulx
RUY argufy
croupy
RVA hryvna
trivia
RVD gravid
proved
RVL drivel
frivol
gravel
grovel
travel
RVN craven
driven
graven
Previn
proven
RVR driver
drover
graver
Trevor
RVS bravos
droves
graves❑
Provos
Treves
RVT cravat
grivet
privet
trivet
RWD brewed
RWE Browne
browse
drowse
prawle
RWH growth
RWL crewel
trowel
RWN draw in
draw on
grow on
prewyn
RWO grow to
RWP brew up
draw up
grow up
RWR brewer❑
drawer
grower
RWS crowds
RWT frowst
RWY brawly
brawny
browny
drowsy
frowsy
frowzy
growly
RXE Trixie
wraxle
RXS braxas
cruxes
praxis
RYA Freyja
RYD frayed
RYE arayse
argyle
groyne
RYF Cruyff
RYH Irtysh
RYN crayon
prey on
RYO pray to
RYR prayer
RYT aroynt
RYY greyly
RZD crazed
grazed
prized
RZL Brazil
frazil
RZN brazen
frozen
RZO Arezzo
RZR Frazer
grazer
RZS prizes
RZY frizzy
Grozny
SAA Asmara
Tswana
SAD Asgard
island
Oswald
usward
SAE a shade
escape
estate
SAL assail
Ismail
Israel
SAM aswarm
SAP escarp
SAS Isaacs
SAT askant
aslant
assart
SBE usable
SBL Isabel
Ishbel
Isobel
SBR isobar
SBY usably
SCE psyche
SCO psycho
SDD Ashdod
SDO used to
SDP used up
SED ascend
Ostend
SEE Essene
SEL a steal
as well
osteal
SEM esteem
SEN astern
SEP asleep
SES assess
assets
SET ascent
aspect
assent
assert
Osbert
ostent
SFL useful
SFR ask for
SHA asthma
ischia
SHL isohel
SHN as then
SHR Escher
Esther
Ussher
SHW eschew
SIE aspire
assize
oscine
SIH Isaiah
SIK aspick
SIL aswirl
SIM osmium
SIN assign
Ossian
SIO Eskimo
SIT assist
T-shirt
SIY ossify
SLA Isolda
SLE Isolde
SLM asylum
SLO as also
SLR ashlar
ashler
ostler
SLS Psalms
SLY Ashley
SMR isomer
SMV Asimov
SNE usance
SOE ashore
aslope
osmose
SOL assoil
SOT assort
escort
Escort®
SPC RSSPCC
SRD Astrid
SRL astral
SRM as from
ashram
SRR usurer
SRS Esdras
Osiris
SRT astrut
esprit
SRW escrow
SRY astray
estray
osprey
SSO Osasco
STE tsetse
STN Ashton
SUA oscula
SUE assume
assure
astute
SUH as much
as such
SUO escudo
pseudo
SUT Iseult
Ust'-Urt
TAA Ottawa
strata
TAD at hand
strand
Utgard
TAE at ease
ethane
strafe
strake
TAF straff
TAH attach
strath
TAK attack
straik
TAL St Paul
TAN at dawn
attain
strain
TAO St-Malo
Strabo
Strato
TAP stramp
TAS it says
straps
TAT at last
strait
Stuart
TAY steady
steamy
strawy
TBE stable
TBS Stubbs
TBY stably
stubby
TCA atocia
TCO stucco
TCS stacks
sticks
stocks
TCY Stacey
sticky
stocky
TDA stadia
TDE stodge
TDO studio
TDS at odds
Études
TDY stodgy
TED attend
TEE Athene
ethene
Steele
steeve
TEF itself
TEK streak

streek
TEL atweel
streel
TEM stream
TEP Streep
TES Athens
Atreus
others
stress
TET at best
at rest
attent
attest
street
TEY steely
TFA Staffa
TFE stifle
TFS Staffs
TFY stiffy
stuffy
TGA stigma
TGD staged
TGR stager
TGY stagey
THR etcher
THT at that
TIA Attila
striga
TIE attire
striae
stride
strife
strike
stripe
strive
TIG a'thing
string
TIK at risk
TIL atrial
TIM atrium
TIS ethics
stairs
TIT atwixt
strict
TIU Itaipu
TIY stripy
TKR stoker□
TKS stakes
stokes□
TLA Stella
TLC italic
TLD stolid
styled
TLE Attlee
stelae
TLG stalag
TLN etalon
Stalin
stolen
stolon
TLO Otello
TLR stelar
TLS stalls

stylos
stylus
TMA stemma
TMC atomic
TME stemme
stymie
TMN ataman
etymon
stamen
TMO a tempo
TMS stumps
TMY stumpy
TNA stanza
TNC ethnic
TND stoned
TNE at once
stance
stanze
TNH stanch
stench
TNL atonal
TNO stanzo
TNR stoner
TNS stones
stunts
TNY stingy
TOA stroma
TOD Atwood
strond
Stroud
TOE at home
at-home
otiose
O'Toole
stooge
stoope
strobe
stroke
TOG strong□
TOK at work
TOL stroll
TOM stroam
TON attorn
St John
TOS stools
TOT at most
strout
utmost
TPA utopia□
TPD stupid
TPE staple
steppe
TPL stipel
TPN step in
step on
stop in
TPO stop-go
TPP step up
step-up
stop up
TPR stupor
TPS stapes
stipes

Stopes
TPT stop at
TPY stop by
TRA pteria
TRB athrob
TRC steric
TRD stored
TRE starve
Sterne
TRH starch
TRL sterol
TRM iterum
TRO stereo
TRP stir up
TRS stirps
stores
storms
storys
uterus
TRX storax
TRY starry
storey
stormy
sturdy
TSS ptoses
stasis
TTC static
TTD at stud
stated
TTE statue
TTH stitch
TTM statim
TTR stater
stator
TTS otitis
status
TUA struma
TUD stound
TUE attune
TUG strung
TUH a touch
stoush
TUK struck
TUS at outs
TUT strunt
TVN Steven
TVS staves
St Ives
TWD stewed
TWR stower
TXA ataxia
TYE ethyne
TYN stay in
stay on
TYR stayer
TYT stay at
UAA Guyana
kumara
Lusaka
UAC Judaic
UAD Cunard
UAE aubade
butane

curare
curate
humane
jubate
jugate
lunate
luxate
Mugabe
mutate
nutate
outage
pupate
rugate
sudate
tubate
UAH sumach
UAI jupati
rubati
UAK Eubank
out-ask
UAN Husain
UAO bumalo
fugato
Lugano
rubato
turaco
UAR au pair
UAS humans
Lukacs
Lukács
UAT au fait
Kuwait
mutant
nutant
subact
UAU Tuvalu
UAY curacy
lunacy
queasy
sugary
UBA Puebla
Rubbra
UBB hubbub
UBC Quebec
UBD curbed
dubbed
numbed
outbid
sunbed
turbid
UBE bubble
bumble□
burble
fumble
hubbie
Hubble
humble
jumble
mumble
nubble
outbye
rubble
rumble

suable
tumble
UBG bum bag
humbug
UBL bulbul
UBN dubbin
Durban
turban
UBO pueblo□
UBR cumber
Dunbar
Humber
lubber
lumbar
lumber
number
rubber
tubber
UBS bumbos
gumbos
jumbos
rumbos
turbos
UBT burbot
numbat
turbit
turbot
UBW sunbow
UBY bubbly
dumbly
humbly
numbly
suably
UCA fulcra
Murcia
puncta
UCE Dulcie
muscle
nuncle
quiche
Runcie
tusche
UCK Dubcek
UCL buccal
furcal
sulcal
UCN Duncan
Tuscan
Vulcan
UCO nuncio
UCP hub-cap
UCS buncos
cuscus
guacos
juncos
sulcus
Turcos
UCT dulcet
muscat□
UCY bunchy
muscly
outcry
punchy

UDA Buddha
tundra
UDD funded
UDE buddle
bundle
cuddle
Culdee
curdle
Dundee
fuddle
guddle
huddle
hurdle
muddle
nurdle
puddle
ruddle
subdue
sundae
UDG gun dog
UDH purdah
UDM dumdum
UDN burden
Eusden
gulden
Mukden
sudden
UDP huddup
UDR funder
judder
murder
rudder
sunder
UDS fundus
UDT pundit
UDW sundew
UDY cuddly
run dry
Sunday
sundry
UEA eureka
UEB superb
UEE Eugene
quaere
tuyère
UEF sure of
UEI Fuseli
humeri
UEK Lübeck
rule OK
UEM museum
UEN dudeen
lutein
muse on
tune in
tureen
UEO pukeko
tupelo
UEP dude up
tune up
UER auteur
fureur
UES aureus

buyers
duress
duvets
lumens
Queens
Rubens
UET Hubert
humect
lucent
Rupert
UEU bureau
Juneau
UEY cutely
hugely
mutely
nudely
purely
rubefy
rudely
rudery
surely
surety
tumefy
UFD puffed
ruffed
turfed
UFE duffle
muffle
purfle
ruffle
UFL cupful
duffel
fulfil
jugful
mugful
rueful
tubful
UFN Buffon
muffin
puffin
puff on
UFP buff up
puff up
UFR buffer
but for
buy for
duffer
furfur
gun for
out for
puffer
put for
sub for
suffer
surfer
UFT buffet
outfit
tuffet
UFU subfeu
UFW curfew
guffaw
UFX outfox
suffix

UGA quagga
UGD bugged
judged
rugged
sun-god
turgid
UGE budgie
bungle
burgee
burgle
Duggie
guggle
gurgle
juggle
jungle
puggle
UGL cudgel
fungal
UGN Kurgan
outgun
UGO gung-ho
UGP bung up
hung up
hung-up
UGR bugger
bulgur
burger
Fugger
hunger
lugger
mugger
rugger
tugger
turgor
vulgar
UGS Burgos
fungus
Judges
mungos
outgas
Tungus
UGT budget
nugget
UGU kung fu
UGY hungry
jungly
quaggy
UHD bushed
hushed
pushed
rushed
UHE euchre
Hughie
nuchae
UHG quahog
UHL burhel
bushel
nuchal
UHM Durham
UHN Buchan
Fushun
push in
UHO Pushto

tu-whoo
UHP hush up
push up
UHR author
gusher
Luther
Nuphar
pusher
wuther
UHS bushes
Hughes
much as
such as
UHT cushat
rush at
sunhat
UHU Fuzhou
Pushtu
Suzhou
Xuzhou
UHY lushly
UIA Auriga
lumina
numina
Rubina
rumina
UID buried
UIE audile
Eunice
futile
lumine
lupine
munite
murine
mutine
nubile
pumice
purine
rutile
supine
UIG buying
curing
duping
during
fuming
fusing
luring
musing
outing
puking
puling
ruling
tubing
tuning
Turing
UIH Judith
mulish
Munich
punish
quaich
rupiah
Zurich
UIL Auriel

Auriol
burial
Muriel
UIM autism
Cubism
curium
mutism
nudism
purism□
Sufism
UIN bunion
fusion
Julian
Lucian
Nubian
turion
UIO subito
UIR Cuvier
junior
UIS audios
curios
duties
Furies
Julius
kumiss
Lucius
pupils
quoits
UIT Cubist
Juliet
lutist
nudist
purist
quaint
UIY aurify
busily
humify
munify
mutiny
nudity
punily
purify
purity
UJB Punjab
UKA Gurkha
quokka
UKC Turkic
UKD rucked
tucked
UKE buckle
huckle
junkie
muckle
ruckle
runkle
suckle
UKH punkah
UKM bunkum
UKN Culkin
dusken
muck in
Ruskin
suck in

sunken
tuck in
UKO cuckoo
UKP buck up
fuck up
muck up
suck up
tuck up
UKR bunker
busker
duiker
mucker
pucker
Quaker
sucker
tusker
UKS bunkos
Butkus
ruckus
UKT bucket
junket
musket
Sukkot
tucket
UKX musk ox
UKY duskly
turkey□
ULA qualia
ULC public
ULD curled
dulled
Euclid
ULE bullae
ULF full of
ULH Guelph
mullah
quelch
ULI nuclei
ULK suslik
ULM Muslim
ULN Butlin
Dublin
dunlin
Lublin
muflon
muslin
pull in
pull on
purlin
sullen
ULP burlap
curl up
Dunlop
full up
pull up
ULR bugler
buller
butler□
curler
cutler
Fuller
Muller
Müller

purler
ULS Dulles
hullos
qualms
ULT bullet
cutlet
gullet
Gullit
mullet
outlet
pullet
sublet
sunlit
ULW curlew
Ludlow
outlaw
run low
ULX duplex
ULY burley
dually
Dudley
guilty
gulley
hurley
Huxley
Lumley
outlay
pulley
UMD gummed
UME bummle
summae
UMG nutmeg
UML hummel
kümmel
pummel
UMN cummin
gunman
outman
summon
Tubman
UMR bummer
fulmar
Gummer
mummer
murmur
rummer
summer□
UMS duomos
hummus
UMT submit
summit
UMU muu-muu
UMX lummox
UNA duenna
guinea□
Luanda
quanta
quinta
UNC muonic
UND burned
ruined
turned
UNE nuance

Words marked □ can also be spelled with an initial capital letter

quince□
quinte
UNH quench
Sunnah
UNL funnel
gunnel
quinol
runnel
tunnel
UNN burn in
guenon
turn in
turn on
turn-on
UNO quango
turn to
UNP burn up
turnip
turn up
turn-up
UNR gunner
Murner
ruiner
runner
turner□
UNS guanos
UNT burnet□
punnet
UNY Burney
Gurney
quinsy
UOA aurora□
cupola
Euboea
Europa
mucosa
UOD cuboid
fucoid
UOE Aurore
dumose
Europe
furore
rugose
UOF buy off
cut off
cut-off
fub off
put off
put-off
Rudolf
run off
run-off
UOG dugong
oulong
UOI judogi
Lugosi
zufoli
UOL nut oil
UON suborn
UOP Euro-MP
UOR humour
rumour
tumour
UOS aurous
buboes
Du Bois
dumous
fumous
humous
jurors
mucous
rufous
rugous
UOT buy out
buyout
buy-out
cut out
cut-out
dugout
Du Pont
jut out
put out
rub out
run out
sus out
UOY eulogy
UPA sulpha
UPD cupped
dumped
humped
UPE purple
rumple
supple
yuppie
UPN dump on
jump on
lumpen
Turpin
UPO Bumppo
UPP bump up
jump up
jump-up
pump up
UPR bumper
dumper
jumper
Kuiper
supper
UPS rumpus
UPT jump at
output
pulpit
puppet
put-put
UPW Quapaw
UPY Murphy
supply
UQE pulque
URA nutria
URC cupric
rubric
URD outred
putrid
URE quarte
URG Runrig
Tuareg
URH hurrah
URK tugrik
URL burrel
URM quorum
URN fun run
Gudrun
outrun
URO quarto
URQ Tubruq
URR Führer
URS burros
Durres
fueros
guiros
hubris
mucros
Munros
URT Gujrat
gutrot
turret
URW burrow
furrow
URY Aubrey
Audrey
hurray
Murray
quarry
quirky
surrey□
URZ Juárez
quartz
USA Russia
subsea
USD cursed
cussed
USE Aussie
bursae
Gussie
nursle
puisne
pursue
tussle
USH putsch
USI muesli
Russki
USL mussel
pussel
USM outsum
USN Bunsen
Hudson
Hun Sen
nuts on
Tucson
tutsan
USR bursar
cursor
fusser
guiser
hussar
pulsar
purser
quasar
tusser
USS busses
guests
tussis
UST gusset
outset
outsit
russet
subset
sunset
USY gun-shy
Russky
UTA lustra
quotha
UTC cultic
fustic
luetic
rustic
UTD gutted
quoted
rusted
rutted
suited
tufted
UTE auntie□
bustle
buttle
guttae
guttle
hurtle
hustle
justle
lustre
puttee
rustle
subtle□
suttee
suttle
turtle
UTI duetti
UTM custom
tum-tum
UTN Austen
Austin
burton□
butt in
button
Buxton
Dustin
hunt in
Huston
Hutton
Justin
Multan
muntin
mutton
sultan
suntan
Sutton
UTO just so
UTP bust up
bust-up
dust-up
hunt up
outtop
UTR Bunter
butter
cuiter
Custer
cutter
duster
guitar
gutter
hunter□
Hutter
muster
mutter
nutter
ouster
punter
putter
suitor
UTS Curtis
duetts
juntos
Muftis
puntos
quotas
UTT tut-tut
UTX surtax
UTY curtly
curtsy
justly
subtly
sultry
suttly
UUA lunula
UUB suburb
UUE future
jujube
suture
tubule
UUG fu yung
UUH Duluth
eunuch
UUI cumuli
tumuli
UUL Buñuel
mutual
UUN auburn
autumn
UUT august□
tumult
UUY augury
luxury
UVD curved
fulvid
UVE luvvie
UVL pulvil
UVR quaver
quiver
UVS turves
UVT curvet
UVY purvey
survey
UWR tulwar
UWT outwit
UWY runway
subway
UYE Quayle
UYH gunyah
UYM yum-yum
UYN Bunyan
UYP bunyip
buoy up
UZE fuzzle
guzzle
muzzle
nuzzle
puzzle
wuzzle
UZN Curzon
UZR buzzer
UZS putzes
VAE aviate
VAY aviary
VCT avocet
VDE Evadne
VDN avidin
VDR evader
VDY avidly
VEO Oviedo
VEX Evreux
VIA Aveira
VLE avulse
evolve
evulse
svelte
uvulae
VLN Avalon
Evelyn
VLR ovular
uvular
VLS Aviles
uvulas
VLY evilly
ovally
VNE avenge
avenue
evince
Evonne
Yvonne
VNF even if
VNI avanti
VNN even on
VNO even so
VNP even up
VNS even as
events
VNY evenly
VRA Avarua
VRE averse
VRK Dvorák
VRL Averil
VRM DVD-ROM
VRO ever so
overdo
VRY overby
overly
VSA Avesta

Words marked □ can also be spelled with an initial capital letter

VSS avisos
VTE Yvette
VTH kvetch
VTR avatar
VUH avouch
VUT avaunt
VWD avowed
VWL avowal
VWR avower
WAY sweaty
WBT two-bit
WCA kwacha
WDN Sweden
WDY swaddy
WEE a'where
tweeze
WEL awheel
WEN a wheen
WES owners
sweets
WEY sweety
tweedy
tweely
WGY twiggy
WIE a while
WIG awning
WIH aweigh
owlish
WKN awaken
WLE twelve
WLS swells
WLT twilit
WMY swampy
WNA Gwenda
kwanza
Rwanda
WND twined
WNE swinge
twinge
WNN swan in
WNP swan up
WNR twiner
WNY swanky
twenty
WOH swoosh
WPY two-ply
WRA Swarga
WRE swarve
swerve
WRS dwarfs
swarms
WRY owerby
QWERTY
qwerty
twirly
WSY twisty
WTE swathe
WTH swatch
switch□
twitch
WTP swot up
WTS awetos
WVL swivel
WWY two-way
WYD swayed
WYE Swayze
XAB excamb
XAD expand
XAE exhale
XAL oxtail
XAT extant
XCT Exocet®
XDS exodus□
XED exceed
expend
extend
XES excess
XET except
expect
expert
exsect
exsert
extent
XGN oxygen
XIE excise
excite
expire
XIY expiry
XLC oxalic
XLD exiled
XLP oxslip
XLS oxalis
XMN axeman
XMT exempt
XOD Oxford
XOE expose
exposé
XOR Exmoor
XOT exhort
export
extort
XRS extras
XSS axises
XTC exotic
XTR Exeter
XUE excuse
exhume
XUN expugn
XUT exeunt
XYD ox-eyed
YAA Aymara
YAD by hand
YAE aye-aye
byname
gyrate
lyrate
Mycale
mygale
zymase
YAF by half
YAH bypath
YAL by rail
YAO dynamo
YAS bypass
YAT dynast
Tybalt
tyrant
YAY my lady
YBE bye-bye
YBK dybbuk
YBL cymbal
symbol
YCS Lyncis
YDC syndic
YDG pye-dog
YDL Myrdal
YDS Hyades
YEA hyaena
YEE Cybele
Cyrene
pyrene
xylene
YEF myself
YEM lyceum
YEN wyvern
YFL eyeful
YFT fylfot
YHA Pythia
YHC mythic
YHE hyphae
lychee
YHL hyphal
YHN by then
hyphen
python
syphon
Typhon
YHR cypher
sypher
YHS sythes
typhus
YIC Syriac
YID myriad
YIE byline
lysine
pyrite
YIG typing
YIH tykish
YII cytisi
YIM Myriam
YIN Syrian
Tyrian
YIS lyrics
YIT typist
YIX syrinx□
YIY typify
YKN ryokan
YLC cyclic
YLN myelin
YLS Byblos
cyclos
nyalas
YLT eyelet
YLW bye-law
YLY by-play
YMA pyemia
YNA Nyanja
YNC hypnic
pyknic
YNL hymnal
YNN cyanin
YNR pyoner
YNS Cygnus
YNT cygnet
YNY gynney
Sydney
YOA myxoma
YOB Ty Cobb
YOD ayword
by road
byroad
byword
cytoid
hypoid
jymold
My Lord
my word
xyloid
YOE bygone
by Jove
by rote
cymose
Mysore
pyrope
Tyrone
zygote
YOG Nyborg
YOH kybosh
YOM byroom
YON tycoon
YOS pylons
syboes
sybows
YOT my foot!
YPA myopia
YPC myopic
YPN tympan
YPS Nymphs
YRA hydria
YRC Cymric
hydric
synroc
YRD hybrid
YRO Pyrrho
YRS Cyprus
hydros
Hydrus
YSA Ayesha
YSM gypsum
YSN myosin
YSP hyssop
YSS cyeses
YSU Kyushu
YSY Lynsey
YTC cystic
mystic
YTE Eyetie
Myrtle
YTL hyetal
YTM system
YTR oyster
YTS syrtes
YTX syntax
YUY syrupy
YVA Sylvia
YVE sylvae
YVN sylvan
YXS lynxes
ZEK Ozbeck
ZGD Szeged
ZLA azalea
ZLD Ozalid®
ZNL azonal
ZRS Azores
Ozarks

7 letters – even

AAA Bahamas
bananas
Calabar
caracal
Caracas
caravan
caraway
Catalan
Daya Bay
eat away
faraday□
faraway
far-away
gala day
Galahad
Halakah
jacamar
Java Man
Karajan
macadam
maracas
Maracay
palamae
palatal
pan-Arab
Ramadan
Sabahan
Saharan
Savalas
waratah
yatagan
AAB caramba
Garamba
AAC balance
Jamaica
Lamarck
Tabasco®
vacancy
valance
AAD calando
AAE Banares
cabaret□
cadaver
caramel
caravel
damaged
damages
falafel
Galatea
Janácek
Java Sea
Kara Sea
lazaret
manager
manatee
naiades
palaver
panacea
parapet
para-red

ravaged
ravager
ravages
Saracen
Sarazen
tabaret
tanager
Yanayev
AAG yaranga
AAH calathi
Halacha
Karachi
Malachi
Natasha
panache
paratha
AAI canakin
cap-a-pie
cap-à-pie
carabid
Catania
fanatic
faradic
Gagarin
Latakia
malaria
manakin
Mazarin
Natalia
Natalie
navarin
paladin
Paradip
patagia
ramakin
ratafia
Salamis
Samaria
satanic
tamarin
Vasarib
AAK karaoke
malarky
AAL banally
Caballé
capable
capably
datable
eatable
fatally
hatable
makable
manacle
namable
nasally
papally
parable
payable
ratable
ratably
salably
savable
sayable

tamable
taxable
taxably
AAM mahatma□
paracme
AAN ca' canny
lasagna
lasagne
savanna
AAO Badajoz
Balaton
cabanos
camaron
caracol
galagos
kakapos
lavabos
Layamon
macacos
marabou
matador
Navahos
Navajos
pakapoo
parados
paradox
paragon
paramos
parasol
Parazoa
sabayon
sapajou
Saratov
Tagálog
AAR catarrh
cavalry
macabre
AAS babassu
Bahaism
Baha'ism
Bahaist
Dadaism
Dadaist
Lamaism
Lamaist
malaise
AAT canasta
Jakarta
rabatte
Taranto
AAU calamus
caracul
Damasus
karakul
Kara Kum
labarum
Lazarus
macaque
Malamud
Managua
AAY paranym
AAZ palazzi
palazzo

ABA Cambrai
catboat
wax bean
Zambian
ABB war baby
ABC iambics
pay back
Tarbuck
ABD carbide
lambada
ABE babbler
baubles
dabbler
darbies
gabbler
gambier
gambler
gambrel
garbled
has-been
mad-bred
marbled
marbles
rambler
warbler
ABG Babbage
cabbage
gamboge
garbage
ABI cambric
far be it
parboil
ABL barbule
cabbala
falbala
fan belt
kabbala
ragbolt
waxbill
waybill
ABM car bomb
ABN bambini
carbine
hatband
jawbone
lambent
nabbing
rabbins
ABO daybook
day-book
gabbros
rag-book
ABR Aalborg
Banbury
Barbara
Cadbury
halberd
halbert
Hamburg
hauberk
lambert□
lay bare
Marburg

Max Born
Raeburn
Rambert
tambura
Warburg
ABS had best
lambast
ABT Babbitt
Lambeth
Macbeth
rabbity
Sabbath
ABU cambium
harbour
jambeux
tambour
ABY jambiya
ABZ Zambezi
ACA Barclay
catch at
fascial
Mancham
Marceau
Marcian
panchax
paschal□
ACC Babcock
dawcock
Hancock
haycock
ACD bar code
cascade
saccade
ACE catcher
catches
darcies
fancied
fancier
Haeckel
hatchel
hatchet
manchet
marcher
marches
matched
matches
Nancies
Natchez
parched
rancher
ratchet
satchel
Tancred
watched
watcher
ACF calcify
farcify
ACI bacchii
catch it
MacCaig
pay cain
watch in
watch it!

ACK oatcake
pancake
ACL bascule
bauchle
calculi
catcall
MacColl
Malcolm
Mauchly
parcels
Pascale
saccule
sacculi
saucily
vascula
ACM catch me
sarcoma
Satchmo
ACN balcony
calcine
dancing
fascine
larceny
Mancini
Marconi
nascent
vaccine
ACO catch on
eat crow
gauchos
halcyon
Laocoon
raccoon
ranchos
salchow
sanchos
ACR baccare
d'accord
day care
lancers□
mascara
ACS carcase
carcass
fascism
fascist
Marcuse
Pat Cash
sarcasm
ACT calcite
falcate
Fawcett
marcato
paucity
saccate
Walcott
ACU Bacchus
calcium
catch up
farceur
match up
patch up
patch-up
rancour

Words marked □ can also be spelled with an initial capital letter

raucous
sanctum
Sanctus
sarcous
watch up
ADA bandeau
band-saw
cardiac
handbag
handsaw
hard hat
Pandean
sandbag
sand bar
sandbar
ADB bad debt
habdabs
ADC Candace
Candice
candock
haddock
haiduck
paddock
ADD candida❑
Candide
ADE candied
candies
dawdler
Gardner
handled
handler
Handley
handsel
handset
Lardner
mandrel
raddled
saddler
sand eel
waddler
ADF Cardiff
dandify
Gaddafi
laid off
Macduff
ward off
ADG bandage
yardage
ADI baldric
Baldwin
Band-aid®
hard-hit
mandril
maudlin
sandpit
Vaudois
ADK hardoke
vandyke❑
zaddiks
ADL bawdily
candela
dandily
Gandalf

gaudily
handily
hardily
mandala
Mandela
rag-doll
Randall
Randolf
sandfly
tardily
ADN balding
bandana
Bandung
Cardano
carding
gardens
Haldane
Harding
Jardine
landing
padding
raiding
Sandino
sardine
wadding
yardang
ADO Caedmon
caldron
hands on
hands-on
laid low
lardoon
mandioc
sandbox
sandboy
ADR caldera❑
eat dirt
gaudery
Ian Dury
Pandora
yard-arm
ADS caddish
caddyss
faddish
hardest
Kaddish
laddish
Mahdist
Qaddish
tax disc
ADT bandits
caudate
mandate
ADU candour
carduus
eardrum
handful
handgun
hand out
handout
hand-out
hands up
hard put

sardius
vaudoux
ADW lay down
Sandown
ADX handaxe
ADY man-days
AEA camerae
cameras
cane rat
catenae
catenas
caveman
Danelaw
Fareham
gateway
have way
kamerad
Lake Van
lateral
make law
make war
make way
paterae
rare gas
rate-cap
Sazerac®
wage war
AEB Catesby
AEC cadence
faience
faïence
latency
valency
Van Eyck
AED calends
fazenda
kalends
AEE caterer
haverer
have sex
latexes
layered
make wet
paperer
racemed
safe bet
sakeret
tagetes
tapered
Tavener
wagerer
wakened
watered
waterer
wavelet
waverer
AEF ease off
face-off
make off
rake-off
take off
take-off
wave off

AEG have a go
have-a-go
Marengo
parerga
Raleigh
Raleigh®
AEH Ganesha
AEI caved-in
gametic
hare lip
javelin
Ladenis
paresis
paretic
racemic
ramekin
rarebit
ravelin
take aim
take air
taken in
Valerie
AEL cadelle
Capella
dazedly
eagerly
fadedly
gazelle
jadedly
labella
lamella
nacelle
nakedly
pale ale
patella
sacella
AEM Palermo
AEN cayenne❑
ha'penny
pageant
Ravenna
Salerno
taverna
AEO Bagehot
based on
Bateson
Camelot
Cameron
care for
gazebos
have got
have-not
Jameson
L'Age d'Or
later on
make for
matelot
name for
pageboy
saveloy
save you
take for
AEP Mazeppa

AER cave art
Madeira
AES Vanessa
AET Barents
Barentz
Canetti
cater to
cavetti
cavetto
eager to
galette
gazette
jadeite
Janetta
Janette
Lacerta
layette
magenta
majesty
Nanette
palette
Papeete
parents
ramenta
Valetta
waken to
AEU baleful
bale out
baneful
base out
bateaux
cadeaux
careful
caseous
dareful
easeful
face out
fade out
fade-out
fateful
gaseous
gateaus
gâteaux
hateful
have fun
make out
pace out
taken up
take out
tapetum
wakeful
AEW Max Euwe
AEZ cadenza
AFA half-cap
half-day
halfway
Kaufman
saffian
AFC maffick
AFE baffled
Cadfael
gauffer
Jaffrey

raffler
Raffles
tax-free
AFI halfwit
half-wit
Mayfair
parfait
AFL bagfuls
canfuls
fanfold
hatfuls
jarfuls
panfuls
vatfuls
AFN barfing
half one
naffing
AFO damfool
saffron❑
AFR bad form
Camford
fanfare
hay fork
hayfork
malform
Salford
warfare
Watford
AFS catfish
gabfest
garfish
hagfish
raffish
AFT taffeta
AFU Balfour
half-cut
Mahfouz
AFW half two
AGA gang saw
gangway
Gaughan
hangman
laugh at
Maugham
pangram
tangram
Vaughan
AGD raggedy
AGE cargoes
fangled
gangrel
haggler
Haughey
Langley
Maigret
mangled
mangler
mangoes
Pangaea
Tangier
tangled
wangler
AGF bang off
hang off
AGG baggage
Van Gogh
AGI bargain
barge in
ganglia
Gauguin
languid
sangria
AGL baggily
largely
nargile
oak-gall
tangelo
AGM Targums
war game
AGN Baggins
banging
cadging
far gone
gagging
gauging
hanging
lagging
margins
nagging
panging
ragging
ranging
sagging
Sargent
tangent
waygone
AGO Bangkok
Habgood
hangdog
jargoon
Langton
languor
Rangoon
AGR Calgary
daggers
day-girl
Gargery
haggard❑
Jaggers
laggard
Langtry
Margery
waggery
AGS haggish
largess
largest
largish
waggish
AGT gangsta
haughty
maggoty
Margate
naughty
Targets
AGU bang out
hang out
hangout
hang-out
langour
Margaux
AGZ Yangtze
AHA Baghdad
each way
fat head
fathead
fat-head
Lachlan
Mashhad
pathway
warhead
washday
yashmak
AHD cathode
rawhide
AHE cashier
dasheen
pay heed
Rachael
Raphael
AHF dash off
AHH naphtha
AHI daphnia
Daphnis
Samhain
AHK dasheki
dashiki
AHL manhole
AHM fathoms
pay home
sashimi
AHN bashing
dab hand
dashing
each one
Hamhung
lashing
machine
manhunt
saphena
washing
AHO cash box
fashion
manhood
AHR Cathari
Cathars
Earhart
hachure
lathery
saxhorn
Zachary
AHS hashish
pachisi
tachism
tachist
AHT Japheth
machete
AHU bashful
Bath bun
bathtub
dash out
kashrus❑
kashrut❑
lash out
man-hour
wash out
washout
wash-out
AHY Kathryn
AIA basilar
Caliban
capital❑
caritas
fajitas
habitat
Halifax
laminae
laminar
magical
marital
matinal
maximal
radical
talipat
taxicab
vanitas
Vatican
AIB marimba
paxiuba
Savimbi
AIC tapioca
AID Cabinda
Matilda
may I add
AIE cabinet
calices
calipee
caliver
carices
Galilee
Galilei
Galileo
latices
Latimer
mariner
matinee
matinée
natives
radices
salices
samisen
satinet
talipes
varices
AIF Dario Fo
satisfy
AIG ratings
savings
sayings
takings
AIH Lapiths
malicho
Tabitha
AII basidia
canikin
Habibie
Hamitic
Hasidic
Hasidim
Kalinin
Lavinia
manikin
maximin
Namibia
pacific❑
Palikir
salicin
satiric
AIK panicky
AIL bacilli
Camilla
Daniela
dariole
mamilla
manilla
maxilla
panicle
papilla
rabidly
radiale
radicle
rapidly
ravioli
tacitly
validly
vanilla
vapidly
variola
AIN A A Milne
Mariana
nations
patient
radiant
rations
salient
sapient
valiant
variant
AIO calicos
caribou
CARICOM
casinos
Davison
haricot
janitor
Ladinos
lay it on
Madison
malison
manihoc
maticos
parison
paritor
talipot
Vavilov
AIR calibre

Words marked ❑ can also be spelled with an initial capital letter

caviare
laniard
Salieri
AIS Mafiosi
mafioso❑
Matisse
may I ask
AIT Batista
eat into
Jacinta
jacinth❑
labiate
Lafitte
lay into
radiate
Sagitta
satiate
satiety
variate
variety
AIU Calicut
carious
fatigue
habitué
halibut
Latinus
Manipur
Marinus
maximum
sanious
saviour❑
Tacitus
various
zap it up
AIY Marilyn
AJA San Juan
AJB Panjabi
AJC carjack
man jack
manjack
AJE banjoes
AJN mah-jong
Nanjing
AJR Marjory
AJS San José
AKA hacksaw
jackdaw
Jack Tar
Jack tar
markkaa
markkas
packman
pack rat
pack-rat
Rackham
walkway
AKC pack ice
AKE Backley
hackler
hackney❑
nankeen
rankled
tackler

AKF back off
hack off
jack off
mark off
pack off
walk off
AKG package
AKI banksia
Jacklin
talk big
AKL Gaskell
lankily
Maskell
pawkily
tackily
AKN backing
balking
banking
basking
Dawkins
hacking
hawking❑
Hawkins
Hawkyns
lacking
mankind
marking
Nanking
napkins
packing
racking
Rankine
ranking
sacking
sarking
talking
walking
wanking
AKO backlog
I ask you!
jackpot
Jackson
tank top
AKR backare
backers
Falkirk
hackery
jankers
Sankara
tankard
AKS dankish
darkish
hawkish
jackass
mawkish
AKT packets
rackets
AKU back out
mark out
sackbut
sackful
talk out
tankful

walk out
walk-out
AKV Markova
AKY lackeys
ALA Caelian
hallway
MacLean
Maclean
mailman
payload
pay-load
railway
tableau
ALB wallaby
ALC bad luck
fallacy
Gallice
Laplace
Matlock
padlock
Wallace
warlock
ALD bag lady
ballade
ALE Baalbek
dallier
earlier
haulier
nail-bed
rallier
tailles
tallies
wallies
ALF bailiff
call off
fall off
fall-off
haul off
Karloff
tail off
wall off
ALG haulage
tallage
ALH tally-ho
ALI haploid
São Luis
tabloid
tail fin
ALK catlike
manlike
man-like
sawlike
warlike
ALL Carlyle
day-lily
may-lily
ALN calling
Carling
cauline
darling❑
daylong
failing
falling

gallant
galling
garland❑
kaoline
Lallans
Marlene
marline
mauling
Oakland
Paulina
Pauline
Pauling
railing
sailing
sapling
tabling
tail end
tail-end
tailing
tallent
Tallinn
wailing
Wayland
ALO ball-boy
balloon
call for
earldom
fall for
Gaeldom
galleon
Gallios
galliot
galloon
MacLeod
Macleod
tallboy
Walloon
ALR Ballard
callers
failure
gallery
Law Lord
mallard
Mallory
nailery
Paul Pry
warlord
ALS ballast
gallise
Gaulish
hapless
hatless
lawless
oarless
Sallust
ALT cable TV
Hazlitt
La Plata
tallith
ALU bail out
balls up
balls-up
bawl out

callous
call out
fall due
fall guy
fall out
fallout
gallium
gallnut
haul out
malleus
nail gun
pailful
pallium
parlour
parlous
ALV baclava
baklava
pavlova❑
ALW gallows
Harlowe
Marlowe
matlows
sallowy
ALY Hakluyt
valleys
ALZ gallize
AMA oatmeal
AMC gammock
hammock
AMD man-made
AME Daimler
Daimler®
Daumier
malmsey
AMF palm off
AMI barmaid
gas main
AML balmily
hammily
mammals
AMN calmant
calming
carmine
catmint
caymans
farming
garment
Gaumont
Hammond
harmony
jasmine❑
lamming
maiming
payment
raiment
Raymond
Salmond
salmons
AMO bad mood
daimios
Marmion
palmtop
AMR earmark

Hammers
mammary
Marmara
palmyra
saimiri
waymark
AMS farmost
gas mask
oak moss
palmist
warmish
AMT Hammett
magmata
mammoth
marmite❑
Nasmyth
palmate
tagmata
AMU cadmium
farm out
harmful
ANA balneal
gainsay
Rain Man
taeniae
taenias
ANB Barnaby
wannabe
ANC bannock
jannock
Larnaca
Rannoch
AND Maenads
ANE daunder
daunted
fainted
haunted
haunter
Laender
launder
maunder
nannies
painted
painter
pannier
Rainier
sainted
saunter
tainted
vaunter
ANF carnify
damnify
magnify
warn off
ANG carnage
ANH paunchy
raunchy
ANL cannily
cannula
damn all
faintly
gauntly
Parnell

saintly
ANM magnums
ANN bar none
Canning
cannons
damning
darning
dawning
earning
fawning
gaining
Manning
Nanning
raining
tanning
warning
yawning
ANO bagnios
daunton
rainbow
Taunton
ANR Barnard
laundry
manners
tannery
ANS badness
carnose
earnest
Farnese
farness
fatness
gabnash
garnish
gayness
harness
Jainism
laxness❑
madness
mannish
pannose
rawness
sadness
tarnish
varnish
wanness
ANT Hamnett
kainite
magnate
magneto
say no to
ANU Dawn Run
earn out
gainful
hafnium
hahnium
painful
ANW bad news
barn owl
ANY carneys
AOA man-o'-war
mayoral
samosas
samovar

AOB j'adoube
AOC Iacocca
Majorca
AOD Lagonda®
lay odds
AOE baloney
baronet
bayonet
cajoler
halogen
Hanover
jaconet
lay open
Mahomet
Samoyed
wagoner
AOH Laroche
panocha
AOI Aaronic
calorie
carotid
carotin
laconic
lanolin
major in
masonic❑
parodic
parotid
sagouin
saponin
valonia
AOK bazooka
bazouki
paiocke
pajocke
palooka
AOL cagoule
kagoule
panoply
AON Garonne
kayoing
Madonna
AOO gasohol
manoaos
Nabokov
palolos
AOP jaloppy
AOR masonry
savoury
vapoury
AOS carouse
jalouse
papoose
vamoose
AOT cahoots
dacoity
fagotti
garotte
gavotte
hap'orth
LaCoste
lavolta
AOU baroque❑

Canopus
AOY Carolyn
paronym
APA Caspian
Sampras
APC ratpack
Tampico
tappice
APE camp-bed
Dampier
dappled
Harpies
lamprey
Magpies
nappies
sampler
APG rampage
API nauplii
Sapphic
Tarpeia
APK garpike
APL happily
Kampala
maypole
tadpole
Walpole
wax palm
APN capping
carping
gasping
jampani
kampong
lapping
mapping
napping
rampant
ramping
rasping
salpinx
sapping
tapping
wappend
zampone
zamponi
APO camphor
campion❑
Hampton
harpoon
lampoon
Rajpoot
rampion
tampion
APP bagpipe
APR car port
carport
Jaspers
mappery
pampero
rampart
rapport
Sapporo
vampire
APS Bagpuss

Campese
dampish
harpist
pappose
vampish
wampish
waspish
waypost
APT palpate
warpath
APU camp out
carpyus
Naipaul
pappous
AQE banquet
Jacques
lacquer
marquee
Márquez
parquet
racquet
AQI marquis
Pasquil
Tarquin
ARA Fairfax
fairway
Hadrian
Marryat
Mauriac
patrial
saurian
Taurean
Zairean
ARB Nairobi
ARC barrack
caprice
Garrick
hayrick
Maurice
parrock
Patrick
rat race
ARD hag-ride
ARE barrier
carrier
farrier
Gabriel
hairnet
harried
harrier
Harriet
Laertes
married
Maureen
tarrier
ARF caprify
pair off
ARG barrage
farrago
ARI Bahrain
carry it
hairpin
Lacroix

ram-raid
ARJ naartje
ARK paprika
ARL carrell
Carroll
fairily
jam roll
laurels
payroll
ARM macramé
San Remo
ARN barring
caprine
earring
fairing
gas ring
jarring
Katrina
latrine
padrone
padroni
pairing
patrons
Sabrina
vagrant
warrant
warring
ARO barrios
bar-room
carrion
carry on
carry-on□
day room
day-room
fair do's
gadroon
hairdos
patriot
taproom
warrior
ARP satrapy
ARS fairish
Ian Rush
matrass
sacrist
ART Carrott
carroty
Jarrett
narrate
ARU Babrius
carry up
haircut
Malraux
ARW marrowy
narrows
ASA batsman
capstan
cat's paw
cat's-paw
darshan
daystar
Harstad
marshal
oarsman
pan-Slav
rakshas
ramstam
tar-seal
Waksman
ASB sassaby
ASC carsick
car-sick
cassock
hassock
ransack
ASD Matsudo
passade
Tayside
wayside
ASE banshee
Causley
Dansker
falsies
fatsoes
gagster
hamster
harshen
hassled
hayseed
lassoes
paisley□
palsied
parsley
passkey
tarsier
waisted
ASF falsify
pass off
salsify
ASG massage
passage
paysage
sausage
ASI catsuit
caustic
lawsuit
parsnip
warship
wassail
ASL capsule
falsely
harshly
Mansell
Marsala
Walsall
ASM Lakshmi
Ransome
satsuma□
ASN Cassini
causing
gassing
lapsang
Massine
paisano
Parsons
passant
passing
pausing
raising
war song
war-song
ASO bassoon
caisson
earshot
mansion
Marston
pass for
passion□
Sassoon
says you
ASR caesura
Hansard
Hans Arp
Kayseri
maestri
maestro
mansard
San Siro
ASS bassist
AST falsity
gap site
passata
varsity
ASU caesium
Cassius
danseur
masseur
pas seul
pass out
ASV cassava
massive
passive
ASY cat's eye
janskys
ASZ capsize
man-size
ATA Bartram
Dantean
Eastham
Eastman
factual
Haitian
Kantian
lacteal
last man
mantram
mantrap
martial□
Martian
Matthau
partial
part way
salt pan
Watteau
ATB mastaba
ATC last act
lattice
mattock
tactics
ATE Barthes
battler
battles
canteen
earthen
farther
fartlek
Fastnet
Gautier
Hartley
mantoes
martlet
Matthew
narthex
panther
panties
pantler
parties
partner
saltier
sautées
tartlet
tattler
waltzer
wastrel
wattled
wax tree
ATF caitiff
cart off
cast off
cast-off
mastiff
part-off
Santa Fe
wait off
ATG vantage
wastage
wattage
ATI bad trip
Caitlín
captain
day trip
factoid
fantail
gastric
gastrin
mastoid
nartjie
Tantric
wagtail
xanthic
ATK partake
ATL cattily
earthly
hastily
Mantell
nastily
nattily
nautili
pantile
pastels
saltily
tactile
tastily
tattily
ATM daytime
pastime
ragtime
Sao Tomé
São Tomé
wartime
ATN baiting
Banting
basting
batting
canting
Cantona
casting
Daytona
East End
easting
farting
fasting
fast one
gas tank
Gatting
Haitink
halting
karting
lasting
malting
Martina
Martine
martini
matting
panting
parting
pasting
ranting
saltant
salting
tartane
tasting
tatting
wafting
waiting
wanting
wasting
ATO bastion
caption
cartoon
caution
faction
hautboy
paction
pant for
wait for
warthog
ATR bad turn
bastard
battery
capture
cattery
dastard
eastern□
factors

Words marked □ can also be spelled with an initial capital letter

factory
jam tart
lantern
martyry
mastery
matters
pastern
pasture
pattern
rafters
rapture
saltire ❑
tantara
tatters
wafture
war-torn
ATS baptise
baptism
baptist
fantasy
fastish
fattish
Kantism
Kantist
lactose
maltase
Maltese
maltose
Nastase
saltish
ATT cantata
hastate
lactate
partita
partite
party to
saltate
saltato
ATU cast out
hauteur
last out
Malthus
paste-up
Pasteur
salt out
tactful
tantrum
want out
ATV captive
factive
ATX Martext
ATZ baptize
AUA faculae
hamular
hanuman ❑
lacunae
maculae
macular
Madurai
natural
paludal
papulae
papular
radulae
radular
samurai
tabulae
tabular
AUC Nabucco
AUD Yaoundé
AUE caducei
calumet
Capulet
manurer
papules
saluter
AUH capuche
AUI Bakunin
manumit
AUK mazurka
zakuski
AUL vacuole
vaguely
AUM vacuums
AUN calumny
valuing
AUO baguios
lanugos
AUP galumph
Ranulph
AUR January
saguaro
vaquero
AUS casuist
AUT faculty
fatuity
vacuity
valuate
Vanuatu
AUU fatuous
hamulus
pabulum
ramulus
vacuous
AUZ Jacuzzi®
AVA Latvian
AVE salvoes
AVG salvage
AVI mauvein
naevoid
AVL Marvell
marvels
naively
naïvely
AVN Calvino
carving
Galvani
mauvine
parvenu
waiving
AVR carvery
Danvers
halvers
Harvard
Malvern
AVS canvass
Fauvism
Fauvist
harvest
parvise
AVT naïveté
naivety
naïvety
Parvati
salvete
valvate
AVU carve up
carve-up
AWA narwhal
AWC Gatwick
Harwich
Warwick
AWE mayweed
oarweed
ragweed
Salween
say when
AWL catwalk
Falwell
gadwall
jaywalk
maxwell ❑
qawwali
AWN lapwing
waxwing
AWO barwood
camwood
Harwood
Larwood
sapwood
AWR haywire
nayward
nayword
ragwork
ragworm
ragwort
vanward
war-worn
waxwork
wayward
wayworn
AWS fanwise
Mae West
mapwise
AXA faux pas
Manx cat
Manxman
AXM faux ami
AXS Marxism
Marxist
AXT bauxite
AYA Lady Day
Taiyuan
AYE barytes
calyces
calyxes
AYI babysit
baby-sit
satyric
satyrid
AYL Dalyell
AYN varying
AYO Babylon
AYR halyard
lanyard
lawyers
AYS babyish
calypso ❑
zanyism
AYU papyrus
AZE dazzled
dazzler
AZH matzahs
AZL jazzily
AZN calzone
calzoni
canzoni
fanzine
Manzoni
war zone
AZO Lanzhou
AZR mamzers
AZT matzoth
AZZ pazzazz
BAA Abraham
abraxas
ebb away
BAE abraded
BAI Ibrahim
BAO abrazos
Absalom
BBN Mbabane
BCN abscind
abscond
obscene
BCR obscure
BCS abscess
abscise
BDA a bad hat
Abidjan
Obadiah
BDB abide by
BDG a bad egg
BDN abiding
BDO Abaddon
BEC abreact
absence
BES abreast
obverse
BET objects
W B Yeats
BEU obsequy
BEV observe
BGI abigail ❑
BIE obliged
BIG abridge
BIT absinth
obviate
BIU oblique
obvious
BLN abalone
BLR Abelard
obolary
BLS abolish
obelise
obelisk
Tbilisi
BLT ability
BLZ obelize
BMN Abu Mena
BMS abomasa
BNO abandon
BNS ebonise
BNT ebonite
BNZ ebonize
BOE abdomen
BOI obconic
BOK abrooke
BON abjoint
BOU obloquy
BOV absolve
BRA Aberfan
Iberian
BRD obtrude
BSA abysmal
BSE abashed
BSI NBC suit
BST obesity
BSV abusive
BTD ebb tide
ebbtide
BTE abetter
BTF a bit off
BTI abattis
abstain
BTN abating
BTO abettor
BTR abature
BUH ébauche
BUI Aboukir
aboulia
BVT obovate
CAC scraich
scranch
scratch
CAE ectases
McLaren
scraped
scraper
CAG scraggy
scraigh
scraugh
CAI oceanic
octadic
Octavia
sciatic
scrapie
CAL actable
scrawly
CAN scrawny
CAO Actaeon
Ecuador
ichabod
octagon
octavos

Words marked ❑ can also be spelled with an initial capital letter

CAP échappé
schappe
scrappy
CAU Oceanus
CBE scabies
CBI scabrid
CBL scabble
scybala
CBR iceberg
CCA acacias
CCB ice cube
CCD ecocide
CCL ice-cold
CDA Acadian
CDD act dido
CDE scudder
CDF acidify
CDL scuddle
CDM academe
academy
CDT acidity
CEA à cheval
CEC science❑
screech
CEE schemer
screwer
CEG acreage
CEI screw it
CEL McNeill
Scheele
Uccello
CEM ack-emma
CEO ache for
Acheron
Acheson
echelon
CET octette
CEU screw up
screw-up
CEV screeve
CEZ scherzi
scherzo
CFA scoff at
CFE scoffer
CFI scaffie
CFL Scafell
scuffle
CFO ice floe
CHR Eckhart
CIA scribal
CIC scritch
CIE scriber
CIG accinge
CII accidie
CIL Schiele
CIN actions
echidna
CIO Schipol
schizos
CIP scrimpy
CIS eclipse❑
CIU echinus
Ictinus
occiput
CIV achieve
scrieve
CLA ocellar
CLC schlich
schlock
CLD occlude
CLE scalder
scalpel
scolder
sculler
CLG ecology
CLI acclaim
scaldic
CLN Iceland
scalene
scaleni
scaling
CLO scallop
CLP schlepp
CLS oculist
schloss❑
CLT acolyte
oculate
CLU ocellus
scale up
CMA scumbag
CMC schmuck
CMD Schmidt
CME scamper
schmoes
scummer
CML scamble
scumble
CNA scandal
CNE scanner
scented
scunner
CNF iconify
CNH acantha
CNL scantle
scantly
schnell
CNM economy
CNO McEnroe
O'Connor
CNP schnaps
CNR e contra
scenery
schnorr
CNS iciness
iconise
CNT aconite
CNZ iconize
COA acrobat
scholar
COE ice over
October
scooped
scooper
scooter
COG McGough
Scrooge
scrouge
COI acromia
ectopia
ectopic
scholia
COL schoole
schools
CON account
echoing
COO ectozoa
COS accoast
echoise
McCoist
COT sciolto
COU eclogue
octopus
scoop up
scrotum
COY acronym
COZ echoize
CPC ice pick
CPE scupper
CPI sceptic
CPL scapple
scapula
CPR sceptre❑
CRA accrual
ochreae
Scarman
scoriae
CRD McBride
CRE scarlet❑
scarper
scarred
scarves
scorner
CRF scarify
scorify
CRI acerbic
Scorpio
CRN eccrine
ocarina
scaring
CRS actress
CRT accrete
CRU ochrous
scare up
CRY Ackroyd
CSO scissor
CTC Scotice
CTE scatter
SCOTVEC
Scotvec
scutter
CTF acetify
Scotify
CTI Scottie
CTL acutely
scuttle
CTM scotoma
CTN acetone
CTO schtook
schtoom
CTP ecotype
CTR Scutari
CTS ecstasy❑
CTT acetate
scutate
CTU acetous
CUC scrunch
CUE accused
accuser
ictuses
McQueen
scourer
Scouter
CUF scruffy
CUG scourge
CUL a couple
octuple
scruple
CUM scrummy
CUO act upon
scrutos
CUP scrumpy
CUR acquire
actuary
CUS accurse
CUT actuate
act up to
occur to
CUU scrub up
CWE scowder
CWN Schwann
CYI acrylic
ecdysis
CYL Ucayali
CZN scazons
DAC advance
DAD Edwards
DAE P D James
DAI Idi Amin
DAL ideally
DAN R D Laing
DBE edibles
DBL oddball
DCA edictal
DCT edacity
educate
DDL a doddle
DEA adrenal
DED addenda
DEE odd-even
DES adverse
DET added to
DEU edge out
DFC edifice
DFS odd fish
DGO adagios
DIA admiral
DIE admired
admirer
advised
adviser
L-driver
DII adhibit
DIN Adriana
DIO Addison
advisor
DLA Edelman
DLI idyllic
DLS idolise
idolism
idolist
odalisk
DLT adulate
DLZ idolize
DMN adamant
oddment
DMO Adamson
DNN adenine
DNS adonise
oddness
DNZ adonize
DOE Ed Moses
DOI idiotic
DOR adjourn
DPE adapted
adapter
adopted
DPI edaphic
DPL adeptly
DPO adaptor
DPS adipose
DRE adorned
DRN adoring
DRS address
adpress
DRU odorous
DSE odyssey
DSR odd sort
DTN editing
DTO edition
DTU edit out
DUC adjunct
DUG adjudge
DUT add up to
EAA decanal
get away
getaway
Medawar
Metaxas
peg away
EAC debauch
penance
rematch
tenancy
EAD regards
rewards
veranda
EAE aerated
belated
Benares
debased
debaser
debated
debater
decayed
defaced

Words marked ❑ can also be spelled with an initial capital letter

defacer
defamed
defamer
delayed
delayer
dewater
fedayee
felafel
Gemayel
H E Bates
legatee
menacer
menaces
Penates
related
relater
relaxed
retaker
velamen
EAG derange
melange
mélange
rebadge
EAH seraphs
EAI ceramic
denarii
fedarie
gelatin
heparin
hepatic
keratin
Melanie
melanin
Nepalis
pelagic
regalia
relax in
relaxin
sematic
senarii
Tel Aviv
vedalia
velaria
Xenakis
EAL debacle
débâcle
default
details
legally
mesally
penally
regally
Renault
retable
tenable
venally
EAM De Palma
EAN Cézanne
Dehaene
Geraint
remains
repaint
Sedaine

EAO celadon
decagon
decapod
hexagon
hexapod
Lebanon
legatos
levator
megaton
melanos
pedalos
senator
telamon
venator
EAR hetaera
hetaira
Le Carré
Le Havre
repairs
EAS because
degauss
relapse
EAT de facto
Lepanto
penalty
pesante
regatta
Vedanta
EAU Belarus
Dedalus
devalue
Pegasus
renague
revalue
tetanus
EBA lee beam
lesbian
membral
Serbian
EBC get back
nebbich
peg back
redback
set back
setback
EBE herblet
keg beer
pebbled
pebbles
Peebles
EBF verbify
EBG herbage
EBI Leibniz
EBL cembali
netball
EBM sex bomb
EBN henbane
verbena
webbing
EBO set book
EBR Berbera
Hepburn
Herbert

members
newborn
Newbury
Seaborg
EBS herbist
nebbish
sea bass
verbose
EBU be about
terbium
ECA Beecham
redcoat
ECC meacock
peacock❑
ECE beached
bencher
Meacher
Mencken
reaches
rescuer
teacher
ECF mercify
ECI fence in
helcoid
percoid
reechie
teach-in
ECK teacake
ECL descale
get cold
key-cold
rescale
re-scale
Seacole
ECM leucoma
welcome
ECN descant
descend
descent
fencing
leucine
peccant
per cent
red cent
rescind
ECO Lenclos
tercios
ECP percept
ECR key card
Leuctra
mercury❑
peccary
red card
rescore
ECS percuss
tea cosy
ECT react to
ECU fetch up
ketchup
Mencius
mesclun
new chum
Peachum

ECV peccavi
EDA deadpan
dead-pan
Feldman
headman
headway
EDC vendace
verdict
EDD Ken Dodd
EDE Beddoes
Dead Sea
dead set
headset
meddler
needled
peddler
readies
red deer
seedbed
EDF fend off
head off
lead off
read off
re-edify
send off
send-off
EDG Bendigo
EDI Hendrix
tendril
EDL deedily
headily
needily
readily
Rendell
seedily
Weddell
EDN beading
bedding
bending
dead end
feeding
feuding
heading
heeding
herding
leading
lending
mending
needing
pendant
pendent
pending
reading❑
Redding
rending
sending
tending
vending
verdant
wedding
weeding
welding
EDO dendron

head boy
head for
herdboy
let drop
send for
tendron
EDR leaders
perdure
verdure
Wenders
EDS geodesy
herdess
reddish
EDT Perdita
ready to
EDU heedful
lead out
needful
read out
send out
weed out
EDW bed down
get down
let down
let-down
meadows
meadowy
new dawn
peg down
set down
EDY dead-eye
EDZ Mendoza
EEA bemedal
federal
general
Genevan
level at
pesewas
Rebekah
renewal
Senegal
Sénégal
several
Teheran
telefax
vegetal
veteran
Yerevan
EEC beseech
decency
defence
Rebecca
recency
regency❑
tedesca
Terence
EED legends
Nereids
EEE bejewel
Celebes
Demeter
fevered
geneses

Words marked ❑ can also be spelled with an initial capital letter

get even
Jezebel
Le Fever
leveret
Nemeses
referee
reneger
renewed
renewer
revered
reverer
seceder
severed
venerer
EEG demerge
deterge
remerge
revenge
Selenga
EEI bedevil
benefit
generic
genesis□
genetic
heretic
nemesia
nemesis□
revel in
reverie
Seferis
selenic
Venetia
zetetic
EEL cereals
Fenella
vexedly
EEM beteeme
EEN Gehenna
EEO develop
Fénelon
hebenon
Hereros
heteros
reredos
teredos
EEP receipt
EER cerebra
pereira
relearn
revelry
EES decease
recense
release
reverse
EET beneath
celesta
celeste
defer to
deserts
détente
genette
here's to
memento

refer to
seventh
seventy
EEU Benelux
cereous
keyed up
keyed-up
level up
mete out
renegue
réseaus
réseaux
revenue
Severus
EEV bereave
deceive
Deneuve
deserve
receive
reserve
EFA red flag
EFC perfect
EFD perfidy
EFE feoffee
feoffer
Jeffrey
leaflet
set free
EFG leafage
EFI set fair
EFL beefalo
let fall
menfolk
penfold
tenfold
EFM perfume
perfumy
EFN beefing
EFO feoffor
seafood
self-sow
serfdom
webfoot
EFR Bedford
deiform
fee-farm
perform
Redford
Seifert
Seyfert
Telford
welfare
Wexford
EFS Belfast
perfuse
selfish
EFT Heifetz
EFW peafowl
EGA Belgian
Bergman
Sea Goat
verglas
EGE beagler

Bee Gees
feigned
feigner
leaguer
Lenglen
weigher
EGG lee-gage
EGH heigh-ho
lengths
lengthy
EGI hedge in
penguin
weigh in
weigh-in
EGL Bengali
pergola
seagull
weigela
EGM Bergama
Bergamo
net game
EGN begging
Ben Gunn
hedging
merging
o'ergang
reagent
V-engine
verging
EGO let go of
verge on
EGR beggary
ledgers
sea-girt
EGT Reigate
weighty
EGU Belgium
Bergius
Sergius
weigh up
EGW gewgaws
sea gown
EHA Heshvan
lethean
per head
recheat
redhead
red heat
EHD methods
EHE lethied
Sekhmet
EHH Jephtha
EHI Mechlin
technic
EHL Bexhill
keyhole
New Hall
techily
EHM bethumb
bethump
EHN Bethany
bethink
methane

Metheny
rethink
EHO nephron
EHP perhaps
reshape
EHR becharm
be there
bewhore
get here
lechery
leghorn□
Pechora
EHT pet hate
rechate
EHU Cepheus
EHV beehive
yeshiva
EIA decimal
Delilah
devisal
genital
helical
helipad
lexical
medical
metical
Mexican
oedipal□
pedicab
pelican□
pemican
recital
retinae
retinal
retinas
retiral
revisal
revival
seminal
seminar
vesicae
vesical
EIC bewitch
dehisce
menisci
EID Belinda
EIE bedizen
besides
betimes
decibel
decided
decider
defiled
defined
definer
Delibes
deliver
Demirel
demi-sec
denizen
derider
derived
desired

Désirée
devisee
deviser
Devizes
helices
helixes
merited
pedicel
perigee
recipes
reciter
refined
refiner
regimen
reliver
remiges
resider
retired
reviler
reviser
revived
reviver
Yenisei
EIF beliefs
EIG besiege
let it go
EIH bedight
Belisha
benight
delight
Jericho
EII aecidia
Cecilia
deficit
delimit
deliria
felicia□
Geminis
Letitia
lewisia
pelitic
periwig
revisit
Semitic
sericin
EIL betitle
cedilla
de Mille□
gelidly
legible
legibly
Neville
pedicle
petiole
reticle
Seville
tepidly
vehicle
vesicle
vexilla
EIM mediums
EIN defiant
deviant

legions
lenient
mediant
reliant
EIO be big on
benison
debitor
demigod
devisor
Femidom®
get in on
get it on
heritor
leg-iron
let in on
lexicon
medicos
merinos
peridot
retinol
venison
EIP periapt
EIR devilry
Kenitra
retiary
EIS Melissa
Métisse
pelisse
EIT deviate
genista
get in to
get into
let into
mediate
rebirth
seriate
EIU bezique
devious
Lepidus
Oedipus
perique
repique
residua
residue
retinue
serious
tedious
EIV believe
relieve
relievo
EIW reviews
EJD Hey Jude
EJN Beijing
EJR perjure
perjury
EKA Beckham
weekday
EKD Beskids
EKE geckoes
heckler
necklet
EKF jerk off
EKG leakage
EKI necktie
EKL deskill
jerkily
perkily
peskily
reskill
EKN decking
Jenkins
leaking
necking
Perkins
reeking
seeking
weekend
EKO desktop
let know
seek for
EKR Selkirk
EKS peckish
EKT Beckett
EKU deck out
leak out
seek out
ELA aeolian
feel-bad
feel sad
hell-cat
new leaf
Perlman
realgar
red lead
tea leaf
ELB Jellyby
ELC deflect
fetlock
hemlock
neglect
re-elect
reflect
replace
replica
sea lace
sea-loch
wedlock
yelloch
ELD ceilidh
seclude
ELE Belleek
jellied
replier
ELF jellify
New Left
peel off
reel off
seal off
see life
sell off
tell off
well off
well-off
ELG geology
realign
sea legs
ELH fellahs
healthy
wealthy
ELI declaim
new-laid
reclaim
well-lit
ELK sea-like
ELL cellule
real ale
tell all
ELM Bellamy
deplume
ELN beeline
Bellini
Bellona
ceiling
Cellini
dealing
decline
deplane
feeling
Fellini
Geelong
healing
Hellene
peeling
recline
red-line
reeling
replant
sealant
selling
setline
telling
veiling
Weiland
welling
wetland
yelling
Zealand
ELO begloom
bell-boy
bell-hop
Berlioz
feel for
hellion
keelson
new look
realtor
sea lion
sell for
ELR declare
De Klerk
deplore
Mellors
Sellers
ELS cellist
declass
get less
get lost
get lost!
hellish
keyless
legless
realise
realism□
realist
recluse
sexless
ELT deflate
deplete
fellate
neolith
pellets
perlite
reality
reflate
replete
reply to
zeolite
ELU becloud
deal out
jealous
sell out
sell-out
well-run
zealous
ELV beslave
hellova
replevy
ELW bellows
fellows
yellowy
ELZ realize
EMA besmear
Permian
red meat
vermian
EMC Wemmick
EMD Bermuda
Kermode
EME Vermeer
EMI mermaid
seamaid
vermeil
EML beamily
EMN beaming
Ben Mann
Desmond
ferment
germane
Germans
Germany
hetmans
Leeming
Lehmann
lemming
seeming
segment
sermons
teeming
tegmina
termini
Vermont
EMO fermion
new moon
EMR Denmark
gemmery
EMS sea moss
EMT fermata
fermate
lemmata
permute
regmata
termite
EMU fermium
Seymour
ENA beanbag
bean-bag
Feynman
hernial
ENB her nibs
ENC Bernice
redneck
re-enact
END Kennedy
ENE Leontes
meander
pennies
re-enter
Régnier
Tenniel
veinlet
vernier□
ENG peonage
teenage
ENI deontic
Jeannie
Resnais
ENL pennill
Reynold
ENM pen name
pen-name
pet name
pet-name
ENN Bernini
Denning
keening
leaning
leonine
meaning
pennant
pennine
regnant
remnant
Tennant
ENO lean-tos
Meinhof
reunion
Réunion
ENR Bernard
deanery
Jean Arp
Leonard
Leonora
re-entry
reynard□
ENS fennish

fewness
newness
peonism
redness
wetness
ENT Bennett
Kenneth
keynote
meant to
neonate
peanuts
pennate
reunite
Sennett
ternate
ENU heinous
ENV beknave
ENZ Neo-Nazi
EOA Deborah
femoral
Jehovah
Kerouac
memo pad
menorah
men-o'-war
nemoral
removal
serosae
serosas
xeromas
EOB redoubt
Secombe
EOC debouch
deforce
devoice
Menorca
rejoice
retouch
EOD Deronda
records
seconde
secondi
EOE beloved❑
betoken
decoder
demoded
deposer
devoted
devotee
get over
meioses
recover
re-cover
rejones
remodel
remoter
removed
remover
reposed
revoked
see over
venomed
EOG regorge
EOH Lesotho
EOI aerobic
Bedouin
be for it
begonia
demonic
demotic
deposit
hedonic
henotic
ketosis
meiosis
meiotic
melodic
metopic
nepotic
reposit
Segovia
Zenobia
EOL Men Only
remould
EON demount
heroine
rebound
recount
redound
remount
repoint
resound
EOO aerosol
decolor
EOR begorra
be yours
devoirs
heronry
memoirs
rejourn
velours
zedoary
EOS delouse
Genoese
Heloise
heroise
heroism
rehouse
remorse
EOT get onto
Menotti
reports
reroute
velouté
EOU decorum
pelorus
EOV devolve
resolve
revolve
EOZ heroize
EPA bespeak
respeak
respray
EPC bespice
henpeck
respect
wet pack
EPE deep-fet
deep-sea
deep-set
keepnet
peopled
peoples
perplex
telpher
temples
templet
tempter
EPF keep off
EPG seepage
Web page
EPI Delphic
despair❑
despoil
get paid
keep fit
keep-fit
Leipzig
Memphis
EPK bespoke
seppuku
EPL leg-pull
Leopold
pep pill
Red Poll
redpoll
EPN despond
dew-pond
helping
keeping
peeping
perpend
reaping
respond
sea pink
seeping
Serpens
serpent❑
terpene
weapons
weeping
EPO heaps of
weep for
EPR besport
deep-fry
helpers
jeepers
lempira
leopard
Newport
peppery
respire
seaport
sexpert
tempera
tempura
vespers
EPS bedpost
deepest
despise
get past
let pass
tempest
EPT despite
respite
EPU bespout
eelpout
helpful
help out
keep mum
keep out
seep out
EQA Newquay
EQI re-equip
ERA beer-mat
betread
decrial
Feargal
get real
hearsay
meercat
meerkat
Meg Ryan
retread
retreat
retrial
tear gas
tear-gas
ERC bedrock
defrock
derrick❑
detract
Herrick
new rich
refract
retrace
retract
secrecy
terrace
verruca
ERD débride
degrade
Derrida
detrude
let ride
ERE bearded
debrief
decreed
decrier
De Vries
Ferrier
hearken
hearted
hearten
henries
learned
learner
Negroes
pearled
pearler
Perrier®
regreet
reorder
serried
terrier
wearied
yearner
ERF petrify
redraft
tear off
terrify
wear off
ERG peerage
ERI detrain
Detroit
Geordie
Georgia
georgic
Georgie
Hebraic
Henry IV
Negroid
pearlin
recruit
refrain
terrain
weirdie
zebroid
ERK heureka
ERL dearnly
febrile
ferrule
heartly
merrily
peartly
wearily
weirdly
ERM begrime
deary me
ERN bearing
Behrens
Behring
dear one
gearing
hearing
herring
jeering
leering
nearing
neurone
peering
Petrine
rear end
rearing
reprint
searing
terrine
veering
wearing❑
ERO bedroom
gearbox
legroom
Pearson
Reardon
reproof

tea room
weirdos
ERP decrypt
ERR Deirdre
Ferrara
Ferrari
Ferrari®
ERS bearish
bed-rest
dearest
defrost
depress
heiress
leg-rest
leprosy
nearest
necrose
peeress
Penrose
redress
re-dress
refresh
regress
repress
re-press
reprise
seeress
tea rose
ERT betroth
ferrate
ferrite
Negrito
Penrith
regrate
regrets
retrate
rewrite
secrete
serrate
ERU bear out
defraud
fearful
ferrous
hear out
leprous
petrous
regroup
tearful
tear out
wear out
ERV deprave
deprive
Henry VI
reprove
Segrave
ERW decrown
Hebrews
ESA beeswax
censual
deiseal
felspar
geishas
hessian

Messiah
Newsday
newsman
Persian
Renshaw
seismal
sensual
Tees Bay
ESC Jessica
seasick
Versace
ESD bedside
leg side
seaside
ESE Deus det
feaster
gessoes
heister
Hershey
keister
leister
measles
Meissen
meister
mens rea
oersted
Perspex®
Pevsner
Webster
ESF densify
versify
ESG message
ESI beastie
cesspit
deasoil
deistic
leg slip
leg spin
let slip
seismic
set sail
wet suit
ESK netsuke
ESL beastly
densely
herself
messily
pensile
sea-salt
sessile
tensely
tensile
tersely
ESM beesome
Newsome
pessima
ESN ceasing
leasing
Lessing
lessons
Messina
peasant
persona

persons
reasons
retsina
teasing
tensing
versant
versing
weasand
ESO Beeston
cession
feast on
gemsbok
pension
seise of
session
tea shop
tension
version
wet snow
ESP Lesseps
ESR bedsore
berserk
censure
dessert
leisure
measure
pessary
sensory
seysure
tessera
ESS persist
EST density
Web site
ESU Celsius
deasiul
Persaud
Perseus
Persius
sea slug
tense up
ESV pensive
zemstva
ETA beltman
Bentham
Bertram
bestead
bestial
best man
central
dextral
dextran
gentian
neutral
oestral
tea tray
textual
Vectian
ventral
vestral
ETC bestick
Lettice
lettuce
restock

ETD peptide
ETE Beatles
Bentley®
bestrew
feather
fettler
genteel
heathen
heather❑
kestrel
leather
Meitner
neither
nettled
seltzer
settled
settler
weather
web-toed
Werther
ETF beatify
beat off
certify
rectify
testify
ETG nest egg
ventage
ventige
vertigo
vestige
ETH gertcha
ETI beatnik
Beatrix
benthic
certain
deltaic
deltoid
deutzia
dextrin
felt-tip
Leitrim
pertain
rectrix
tectrix
Ventris
Yeltsin
ETK pertake
ETL deathly
fertile
gentile
gestalt❑
heftily
meatily
pep talk
pettily
reptile
restyle
Seattle
tenthly
test-fly
testily
textile
ETM bedtime

centime
centimo
meltemi
rectums
septime
ETN beating
Beltane
belting
Bentine
Bettina
betting
dentine
destine
destiny
getting
heating
heptane
jesting
Keating
leptons
meeting
melting
neoteny
Neptune
netting
pentane
petting
renting
reptant
resting
seating
sestina
setting
Sextans
sextant❑
testing
venting
vetting
ETO beat box
benthos
best boy
death on
destroy
festoon
lection
menthol
mention
neutron
rent-boy
section
Ventnor
ETP Gestapo
red tape
ETR century
denture
Dettori
feature
fetters
gesture
hectare
lectern
lecture
leotard

Words marked ❑ can also be spelled with an initial capital letter

letters
nectary
perturb
rectory
restart
restore
sectary
testern
texture
venture
Venturi
vesture
western
ETS dentist
Kentish
leftism
leftist
pectise
pectose
pentose
peptise
pertuse
pettish
ventose
wettish
ETT dentate
gestate
peltate
restate
tektite
testate
ETU beat out
belt out
centaur□
jestful
Nerthus
oestrus
Pentium®
rent out
restful
zestful
ETV centavo
festive
restive
ETW new town
ETZ mestiza
mestizo
pectize
peptize
EUA Ketubah
medusae
medusas
mezuzah
nebulae
nebular
nebulas
perusal
refusal
regulae
regular
secular
tegulae
EUC defunct
felucca
EUE bemused
be quiet
be ruled
cerumen
deduced
deluded
deluder
denuded
deputed
genuses
get used
Lemures
peruser
rebuker
rebuses
reduced
reducer
refugee
refuter
reputed
requiem□
secured
securer
seducer
tenured
EUG remuage
EUI Lemuria
Menuhin
Perugia
petunia
refugia
sequoia
EUL beguile
decuple
medulla
rebuild
rebuilt
sequela
tequila
EUN beguine
genuine
returns
sequent
EUO gen up on
let up on
set upon
tenutos
EUR require
EUS bequest
Debussy
repulse□
request
Senussi
EUT get up to
Jesuits
requite
results
tenuity
EUU jejunum
Réaumur
regulus
remueur
Telugus
tenuous
Zebulun
EUV decurve
recurve
EVA serve as
EVC service
EVD pervade
EVE bevvied
EVG selvage
EVH heave ho!
EVI vervain
EVL heavily
nervily
servile
weevily
EVN cervine
fervent
heavens
heaving
leaving
servant
serving
weaving
EVR nervure
pervert
EVS dervish
Gervase
peevish
EVT heave to
velvety
EVU Delvaux
fervour
heave up
nervous
serve up
EWC Keswick
Lerwick
EWE between
seaweed
EWI gee whiz
EWL Beowulf
get well
sea wolf
sea-wolf
EWN red wine
redwing
EWO redwood□
EWR bedward
bedwarf
bed-work
eelworm
keyword
leeward
legwork
network
new word
redware
seaward
seaware
EWS get wise
EWV new wave
EYA New Year
per year
EYL recycle
EYM kerygma
EYN defying
denying
levying
EYR New York
EZA Merzbau
Penzias
Weizman
EZI benzoic
benzoin
Neozoic
EZM leeze me
EZN benzene
benzine
seizing
Tenzing
EZO Mezzrow
seize of
EZR seizure
EZU seize up
FAL affable
affably
FAR affairs
FBA off beam
off beat
offbeat
off-beat
FBS off base
FDT off duty
off-duty
FEC offence
FED effendi
FEE offerer
FEO offeror
FER affeard
FET effects
FEU offer up
FFR off form
FHN Afghani
offhand
off-hand
FIA African
FIE officer
FKN of a kind
FLA offload
FLC afflict
FLG ufology
FLN off line
off-line
FMN of a mind
FMT sfumato
FNI pfennig□
FOC afforce
FOT of sorts
Y-fronts
FPA off-peak
FRA off-road
FRN affront
FRR a far cry
FSD offside
FSI off-spin
FSR of a sort
FST off-site
of use to
FSU offscum
FSZ of a size
FUG effulge
FWR off-ward
off work
FWT off with
GAH agrapha
GAI oghamic
GAN Igraine
GAO ignaros
GCS egg-cosy
GEI Egreria
GEL H G Wells
GEO agree on
GES ogreish
GET agree to
GEU igneous
GFI egg-flip
GHA egghead
GIE ignited
igniter
GIP Agrippa
GIS against
GKA Aga Khan
GLL agilely
GLS ageless
GLT agility
GNE agonies
GNS agonise
GNZ agonize
GOE ignored
ignorer
GOL ignoble
ignobly
GON aground
GRC W G Grace
GRD aggrade
GRS aggress
GSI Agassiz
GTI ego-trip
GTS egotise
egotism
egotist
GTT agitate
agitato
GTZ egotize
GWS eggwash
GYO Iggy Pop
HAA choanae
phrasal
shy away
HAE cheapen
cheater
phraser
shearer□
sheaved
sheaves
wheaten
HAH sheathe
sheaths

Words marked □ can also be spelled with an initial capital letter

HAI thiamin
HAL Cheadle
cheaply
HAM chiasma
chiasmi
chiasms
HAO ahead of
cheap of
cheat on
Zhdanov
HAR theatre
HAS shiatsu
HAT Chianti
the arts
HAU pH value
HAZ shiatzu
HBA The Boat
HBE shebeen
HBF the buff
HBI Chablis
HBL The Bell
the Bill
HBN shebang
HBO Chabrol
the boot
HBR rhubarb
the Bard
HBS the boss
HBU the blue
HCA Choctaw
HCE checked
checker
chicken
shocked
shocker
thicken
thicket
whacked
whacker
whicker
HCG Chicago
HCI check in
check-in
chuck in
phacoid
rhachis
HCL chuckle
shackle
thickly
HCN chicane
the cane
HCO chochos
the chop
thickos
whackos
HCR chicory
HCU check up
check-up
shack up
HDA Cheddar
chuddar
khaddar
Phidias
the dead
HDE shedder
shudder
the deep
whidder
HDL shadily
HDN chiding
shading
HDO shadoof
HDU rhodium
HDV khediva
khedive
HDW shadows□
shadowy
HEA chaetae
cheetah
HED thready
HEE thieves
Wheeler
whoever
whyever
HEG wheenge
HEH wheesht
HEI cheerio
phoenix□
phrenic
wheelie
HEL chiefly
sheerly
shtetls
wheedle
wheeple
wheezle
HEM phlegmy
HEO cheer on
phaeton
sheepos
threnos
Wheeson
HER Phaedra
HES the East
HET threats
HEU cheer up
HFA the flat
HFC The Face
HFE Chaffee
chaffer
chuffed
Shaffer
HFI the fair
HFL shuffle
The Fall
whiffle
HFN chafing
HFO chiffon
The Fool
HFR shofars
HFU shift up
HFZ the fuzz
HGD the gods
HGE chigger
HGI chagrin
HGL Chagall
shoggle
HGM the game
HGO chignon
thuggos
HHN the hang
HHR the herd
HHT the hots
T H White
HHZ shih tzu
HIE chained
shrivel
HII Shiitic
HIL shrilly
whaisle
whaizle
HIO chrisom
HIT Christo
Christy
thrifty
HKA the Klan
HKD shakudo
HKE chukker
shakoes
HKL shakily
shekels
HKN chi kung
choking
shaking
HKO Chekhov
HKS The Kiss
HKU choke up
shake up
shake-up
HLA challah
Chilean
shellac
the lead
HLC chalice
Ehrlich
Shylock
HLD The Lady
HLE Chaldee
Chelsea
Chelsey
childed
chilled
phellem
Shelley
shelter
shelved
shelves
HLF chylify
HLG Shelagh
HLI cheloid
chillis
ghillie
Phillip
Phyllis
sheltie
HLK the like
HLM thalami
the Lamb
the lump
HLN choline
phalanx
whaling
HLO shallop
shallot
shallow
Sheldon
Shilton
HLR cholera
philtre
HLT chelate
Shalott
HLU chalk up
phallus
thallus
thulium
HLZ chalaza
HME chamber
chamfer
chimley
chimney
chumley
shimmer
Thomsen
whimper
whimsey
Whymper
HMF chymify
HMH Thimphu
HMI chamois
chime in
khamsin
rhombic
HMK Chomsky
HML shamble
thimble
whemmle
HMN rhyming
shamans
shaming
the many
thymine
HMO rhomboi
shampoo
Thomson
HMR chambré
chimera□
the morn
HMS chemise
chemist
rhymist
HMT themata
HMU rhombus
HMZ Shimizu
HNA Chantal
chinwag
Shankar
shine at
HNC phonics
HND Chengdu
Rhondda
HNE chancel
chancer
chances
changed
changer
changes
channel
chanter
Chunnel
chunter
shunned
shunter
thankee
thinker
thinner
thunder□
whangee
whene'er
whinger
HNH Chungho
rhonchi
HNI chinkie□
shindig
HNL Shankly
shingle
shingly
HNM phoneme
HNN shining
whining
HNO chanson
chinook□
phantom
Shannon
shine on
think of
HNR bhangra
chancre
Chandra
chantry
chondri
HNS Chinese
Rhenish
shyness
HNT Cheng-tu
phonate
HNU phone up
rhenium
think up
thin out
HNZ chintzy
HOA chloral
shoot at
The Oval
HOB theorbo
thrombi
HOE chromel
phloxes
shooter
The Omen
theorem
whoopee
whooper
HOG through
HOI chaotic
chloric

Words marked □ can also be spelled with an initial capital letter

chronic
phlomis
shoogie
throw in
throw-in
HOK the Oaks
HOL shoogle
HOO chromos
throw on
HOS shmoose
HOT throaty
HOU shoot up
throw up
whoobub
HOZ shmooze
HPA chapman□
shiplap
Shipman
the play
whipsaw
HPE chaplet
chapped
chapter
chipped
chipper
chopper
Shapley
shipmen
shopper
whipped
whipper
whippet
whopper
HPF chip off
chop off
HPI Chaplin
the pair
HPL Chapala
shapely
Whipple
HPN shaping
HPO Shipton
shop-boy
shop for
HPR Shepard
HPS the push
HPT chapati
the pits
HPU shape up
Thapsus
HQE chequer
HRA chordae
gharial
Pharlap
Shari'ah
shariat
Sharman
Shergar
Sherman
Sherpas
thereat
theriac
thermae
thermal
Thoreau
whereas
whereat
HRB cherubs
thereby
The Robe
whereby
HRC the Rock
HRD charade
HRE charged
charger
charges
Charles
Charley
charmed
charmer
charred
charted
charter
sharpen
sharper
sherbet
shereef
shirker
Shirley
shorten
Shorter
Thurber
thyrses
wharves
whereer
wherret
whirler
whorled
HRF sheriff
thurify
HRG the rage
HRI charlie□
chervil
choroid
gherkin
share in
shortie
therein
thyroid
wherein
HRL charily
chorale
chortle
sharply
shortly
thirdly
HRN Khorana
pharynx
sharing
shoring
The Ring
the ring
the runs
whoring
HRO chariot
cheroot
chorion
gheraos
Kharkov
Kherson
pharaoh□
short of
short on
thereof
Wharton
whereof
HRP therapy
the rope
HRS cherish
Theresa
the rush
whereso
HRT charity□
thereto
thirsty
whereto
HRU chirrup
shore up
Theroux
thorium
HRZ chorizo
HSA Ohm's law
The Star
this day
thus far
HSC physics
the sack
HSE chasten
Chester
shyster
whisked
whisker
whiskey
whisper
HSH who's who
HSI Chassid
chassis
phase in
HSL ghastly
ghostly
thistle
thistly
whistle
HSM the same
HSN chasing
HSO physios
HSU Theseus
the soup
HTA chateau
château
khutbah
Whitlam
Whitman
HTB the tube
HTE chattel
chatter
chitter
chutney
Shatner
shatter
shutter
whateer
whether
whetter
whither
whitter
HTF shut off
shut-off
HTI Chatwin
whatsit
HTL shuttle
whittle□
HTM Khatami
HTN rhatany
whiting
HTO ghettos
shit-hot
what for
what not
whatnot
what now?
whitlow
HTP the tops
HTS whitish
HTU Photius
shotgun
shotput
shut out
shut-out
what's up?
Whitsun
HTY shut-eye
HUB shrubby
HUC thrutch
HUE Chaucer
rheumed
shouter
W H Auden
HUG theurgy
HUH thought
HVI I have it
HVN shaving
HVO Cheviot
chevron
Shavuot
Zhivkov
HVR shivers
shivery
HWA showman
HWE chowder
Shawnee
HWF show off
show-off
HWH showghe
HWI show biz
showbiz
HWL showily
The Wall
HWN showing
thawing
HWR showery
the Word
HWU chew out
shown up
thaw out
HYA they say
HZI rhizoid
whiz kid
HZM rhizome
IAA die away
die-away
pitapat
IAC finance
IAD Miranda
Ricardo
Rivaldo
Vivaldi
IAE citadel
dilated
fixated
Kilauea
limaces
minaret
IAF giraffe□
IAG hidalga
IAH hibachi
piranha
IAI dibasic
DiCanio
filaria
jig-a-jig
Picabia
piratic
Titania
titanic□
vis-à-vis
vitamin
vivaria
IAL citable
disable
disally
finable
finagle
finally
Hinault
hirable
likable
miracle
misally
mixable
sizable
vitally
IAO disavow
girasol
gitanos
mikados
Mina Loy
mirador
picador
tinamou
viragos
IAR bizarre
Pizarro
rivalry
Sinatra

IAS Picasso
IAU Cimabué
Hilarus
Piraeus
IAV bivalve
IBA Siobhán
tie beam
IBC die back
dieback
finback
hit back
lie back
limbeck
sit back
win back
IBE bilboes
nibbler
nibbles
timbrel
yibbles
IBI fimbria
IBL diabolo
piebald
pinball
timbale
IBN Big Bang
disband
fibbing
Gibbons
hip-bone
ribband
ribbing
IBR disbark
filbert
Finbarr
Gilbert
Hilbert
Limburg
Milburn
Tilbury
IBT kibbutz
Lisbeth
Lizbeth
titbits
IBU gibbous
niobium
Rimbaud
ICD zip code
ICE aircrew
biccies
circler
circlet
ciscoes
ditched
filcher
Fischer
hitched
hitcher
kitchen
piccies
pilcher
pinched
pitcher

ICF zincify
ICG discage
ribcage
ICI biscuit
circuit
discoid
pitch in
tie clip
viscoid
ICL Lincoln
miscall
piccolo
vincula
Zincala
Zincali
Zincalo
ICN mincing
Miocene
piscina
piscine
Vincent
ICO air-cool
ICP discept
miscopy
ICR discard
discern
discord
Piccard
pincers
sincere
viscera
ICS diocese
discase
discuss
giocoso
miscast
viscose
ICT big cats
zincite
ICU hitch up
linctus
Mitchum
viscous
winch up
IDA Lindsay
misdeal
misdial
misdraw
wildcat
wild man
wild oat
windbag
IDC viaduct
IDE diddler
Diddley
fiddler
Hindley
kiddies
kindler
kindred
Lindsey
middle C
Mildred

mindset
misdeed
piddler
riddler
tiddler
IDG windage
windigo
IDI Airdrie
disdain
IDL Biddell
giddily
Liddell
Mindelo
windily
IDN bidding
binding
birding
finding
gilding
kidding
minding
Siddons
winding
IDO air-drop
mind you
wild dog
windrow
Windsor
IDR bindery
cinders
cindery
Kildare
Mindoro
IDS kiddush
wild ass
wildish
Yiddish
IDT misdate
IDU died out
find out
giddy-up
mindful
mind out
IDW die down
kip down
lie down
lie-down
mildewy
pin down
sit down
sit-down
tie down
Windows®
IEA bikeway
fireman
give ear
give way
liberal
like mad
literal
mineral
pile-cap
pine tar

sidecar
Tibetan
tideway
time lag
time was
vinegar
virelay
wine-bag
wine bar
wiretap
wire-tap
wise man
Wiseman
IEC licence
silence
IED limeade
videnda
IEE fine leg
Jiménez
Lineker
Nineveh
pie-eyed
ripened
rivered
riveted
sidemen
widener
wizened
Ximenes
IEF dine off
file off
fire off
give off
hive off
live off
time off
IEG diverge
lineage
mileage
IEI dimeric
eidetic
Fidelio
kinesis
kinetic
Liberia
lived-in
mimesis
mimetic
Nigeria
niterie
IEL firefly
fixedly
Giselle
miserly
mixedly
nigella❑
tiredly
vitelli
vixenly
Viyella®
IEM dilemma
pip emma
IEN nice and

IEO aileron
bibelot
Diderot
Dineson
firedog
fixed on
liberos
live for
pine for
Simenon
viceroy
wide boy
IEP dirempt
IER fine art
firearm
sidearm
IES cineast
disease
dis-ease
diverse
finesse
license
sizeism
sizeist
Vitebsk
IET biretta
Bizerta
dinette
given to
liberty
liken to
Linette
Lisette
Ninette
pileate
pimento
pipette
Vicente
IEU ciseaux
dine out
direful
firebug
fire-bug
fired up
fire out
give out
hideous
hide out
hideout
hire out
like fun
liven up
live out
Miletus
mixed up
mixed-up
niveous
piceous
pileous
pipeful
piteous
ride out
silenus❑

Words marked ❑ can also be spelled with an initial capital letter

Time Out
time out
time-out
tire out
wipe out
wipeout
wised up
wise guy
IEV Minerva
IEZ Vicenza
IFE misfeed
piaffer
Wilfred
IFI bid fair
tinfoil
Wilfrid
IFL miffily
misfile
pinfold
pitfall
sixfold
tinfuls
IFN tiffany❑
IFO Bigfoot
fiefdom
IFR difform
disform
Gifford
misfire
misform
Mitford
IFS diffuse
IGA diagram
dingbat
gingham
lingual
Virgoan
IGE Biggles
dingoes
giggler
jingler
jingoes
lingoes
mingled
mingler
niggler
pingoes
ringlet
singlet
wiggler
wing-led
IGI king-hit
kingpin
pilgrim
pinguid
ringgit
IGL gingili
virgule
IGM big game
die game
IGN big guns
Higgins
ridging
rigging
ringing
singing
wigging
winging
IGO hinge on
kingdom
widgeon
IGR figgery
gingery
niggard
piggery
singers
Zingara
Zingare
Zingari
Zingaro
IGS biggest
biggish
disgust
piggish
riggish
IGT fidgets
fidgety
Piggott
IGU kingcup
ring out
sing out
wing nut
IGV misgive
IGW disgown
IHA bighead
high bar
high-hat
high-tar
highway
mishear
Mishnah
Mithras
pinhead
pithead
rich man
IHE Bishkek
fighter
fishnet
high-fed
high-key
highmen
high tea
high-tea
lighted
lighten
lighter
Michael
Richler
Richter
sighted
tighten
IHF fishify
IHI fishgig
nightie
IHL airhole
dishelm
lightly
lithely
Nichola
nightly
pinhole
pithily
rightly
sightly
Sithole
tightly
wightly
IHM dishome
Mishima
IHN fishing
sighing
sithens
wishing
IHO high-top
light on
right-oh
right on
right-on
rightos
sigh for
wish for
IHR bighorn
cithern
Die Hard
diehard
die-hard
dishorn
dithery
fishery
Richard
tinhorn
withers
IHS highest
Sikhism
IHT Wichita
IHU dish out
fish out
light up
lithium
wishful
without
IIA digital
finical
minicab
minicam
minimal
minimax
similar
vicinal
Viminal
IIE cimices
citizen
divided
divider
diviner
filibeg
limited
limiter
limites
Minitel
miniver
similes
vibices
IIG fixings
tidings
IIH rikishi
III divisim
militia
minikin
silicic
IIK finicky
IIL civilly
licitly
lividly
rigidly
risible
timidly
visible
visibly
vividly
IIN ripieni
ripieno
IIO didicoi
didicoy
divisor
liaison
libidos
midiron
pin it on
silicon
similor
Sir Ivor
visitor
IIR biliary
mimicry
riviera
rivière
IIS tiniest
IIT ciliate
dig into
din into
dip into
miniate
rip into
viciate
vitiate
IIU bilious
hit it up
milieus
milieux
minibus
minimum
pitiful
vicious
vidimus
IIV rilievi
rilievo
IJC disject
IJI disjoin
misjoin
IJM jimjams
pig-jump
IKA link man
linkman
milkman
milk pan
sick bay
sick pay
silk-man
Wickham
IKE dinkies
pickeer
pickled
pickler
pinkoes
sickbed
Winkler
IKF kick off
kick-off
pick off
tick off
zinkify
IKG linkage
IKH ricksha
IKI pink gin
IKL kinkily
milkily
riskily
silkily
IKN dickens❑
kirking
licking
linking
milking
nicking
picking
Rifkind
sinking
ticking
winking
IKO hickdom
milksop
misknow
Wicklow
IKR hickory
Sickert
IKT Pickett
rickets
rickety
IKU kick out
pick out
IKX pickaxe
pick-axe
ILA disleaf
disload
Gilliam
Gillian
Jillian
Kiel Bay
Killian
Lillian
mislead
William
ILC airlock
dialect

hillock
killick
killock
misluck
niblick
pillock
rim-lock
Tillich
ILE billies
dialler
fielded
fielder
Nielsen
wielder
willies
yielder
ILF airlift
kill off
ILG biology
pillage
tillage
village
ILI diploid
Millais
mislaid
sirloin
villain
villein
ILK dislike
siclike
ILL sillily
ILM diploma
dislimb
dislimn
ILN aiblins
airline
biplane
dislink
filling
Finland
Gin Lane
hidling
hidlins
killing
Kipling
midland
milling
rifling
sibling
tilling
violent
willing
ILO billion
billy-oh
hill top
hilltop
killjoy
million
Niel Gow
niellos
pill-box
pillion
till now

zillion
ILR Hillary
pillory
titlark
ILS aimless
airless
dialyse
finless
girlish
hit list
lidless
ribless
rimless
sinless
villose
violist
wigless
witless
ILT giblets
violate
yield to
ILU fill out
Gielgud
villous
ILW billowy
willowy
ILZ dialyze
IMC gimmick
titmice
IMD Diomede
IME film set
filmset
IMI airmail
IMK mismake
IMN ailment
diamond□
dimming
figment
fitment
pigment
Riemann
siamang
siemens□
IMO miombos
IMS biomass
dimmish
dismask
dismast
dismiss
kirmess
midmost
Siamese
IMT bismuth
mismate
sigmate
INB his nibs
INC bionics
Kinnock
minnick
pinnace
INE fiancée
Fiennes
pioneer

INF dignify
lignify
signify
INI Tianjin
INL Pianola®
pinnule
INM big name
misname
visnomy
INN sinning
winning
INR kiln-dry
Signora
Signore
signori
signors
INS bigness
dimness
disnest
Finnish
fitness
lioness
lionise
pianist
witness
Zionism
Zionist
INT big-note
dignity
lignite
pinnate
INU Vilnius
INZ lionize
IOA bifocal
bipolar
bitonal
bivouac
dipolar
Filofax®
Nicolas
pivotal
IOC divorce
Minorca
sirocco
IOE bigoted
bilobed
disobey
Limoges
litotes
mitoses
Nilotes
picotee
tip over
widowed
widower
win over
IOH Timothy
IOI ciboria
kilobit
mitosis
mitotic
Nicosia
Nilotic

Sidonie
sinopia
Vitoria
IOL pinocle
ION Livorno
IOO gigolos
kiloton
kimonos
Mikonos
IOR bigotry
IOS Titoism
IOT Minolta®
ricotta
riposte
risotto
IOU linocut
Minogue
IPA display
misplay
IPC nit-pick
six-pack
IPE dimpled
pimpled
rippled
ripplet
tippler
IPI limpkin
silphia
Simpkin
IPL nippily
oil-palm
IPM Air Pump
oil pump
IPN dipping
dispone
Hispano
limping
lisping
nipping
ripping
timpani
IPO Simpson
IPP Limpopo
IPR airport
bit-part
dioptre
dispark
dispart
disport
nippers
IPS dispose
dispost
wimpish
IPT dispute
Tippett
Tirpitz
IPU wimp out
IQE picquet
IRA diurnal
lip-read
misread
IRB disrobe
microbe

IRC pibroch
Tim Rice
vitrics
IRD GI bride
nitride
IRE Citroën
diaries
pierced
tierced
tiercel
IRF midriff
nigrify
nitrify
vitrify
IRH diarchy
IRI air raid
fibroid
milreis
IRL fierily
misrule
IRM diorama
IRN citrine
disrank
microns
migrant
mikrons
vibrant
IRO disroot
hip roof
pierrot□
vibrios
vitriol
IRP digraph
disrupt
IRR library
IRS diarise
diarist
digress
fibrose
tigress
IRT citrate
disrate
librate
migrate
misrate
nitrate
nitrite
titrate
vibrate
vibrato
IRU fibrous
nitrous
vitraux
IRZ diarize
ISA disseat
kinsman
miasmal
Riksdag
sits vac
ISC airsick
dissect
ISD airside
ISE kinsmen

Words marked □ can also be spelled with an initial capital letter

linseed
minster
misstep
Pilsner
tipster
ISF kiss off
kiss-off
piss off
tipsify
ISH kitschy
ISI airship
first in
kidskin
kinship
Kirstin
Liassic
miasmic
missuit
oilskin
pigskin
pissoir
ISL firstly
fissile
himself
missile
rissole
tipsily
ISM lissome
winsome
ISN dissent
ginseng
Gissing
hissing
lip-sync
missend
missing
oil sand
rinsing
sinsyne
ISO air shot
big shot
dies non
fiascos
fission
mission
Nilsson
six-spot
Winston
ISR fissure
piastre
ISS missish
IST hirsute
ISU miss out
ISV fissive
missive
ITA mistral
victual
Vietnam
virtual
ITC diptych
mistico
pin tuck
Riot Act
viatica
ITE Aintree
dirtied
fifteen
fifties
mist-net
sixteen
sixties
vintner
ITF distaff
lift off
lift-off
ITG mintage
vintage
ITI pigtail
pintail
Pistoia
ITK mistake
ITL dirtily
fictile
fifthly
fistula
mistell
mistily
niftily
ninthly
pistole
sixthly
Vistula
wittily
ITM airtime
big time
mistime
ITN distant
distend
fitting
histone
hitting
jilting
lifting
lilting
listing
mistune
rioting
sifting
sitting
tilting
wilting
witting
ITO bistros
cistron
diction
fiction
mistook
ITR bistort
bittern
bitters
cistern
cittern
dietary
diptera
distort
disturb
fixture
gittern
history
jitters
jittery
midterm
misterm
mixture
picture
victory❑
wintery
ITS Pictish
pietism
pietist
ITT dictate
nictate
vittate
ITU fistful
riotous
sistrum
wistful
ITY diethyl
IUA fibular
pilular
situlae
titular
IUE bitumen
diluted
disused
figured
figures
minutes
misused
misuser
rivulet
sinuses
viruses
IUF liquefy
IUG divulge
liturgy
Virunga
IUL piously
IUN diluent
minuend
piquant
Tijuana
IUO fie upon
hit upon
sit upon
win upon
IUT liquate
sinuate
situate
IUU liqueur
sinuous
IVA Kiev Dam
IVE civvies
IVN nirvana❑
Silvana
IVR sievert
silvery
silver-Y
IVU divvy up
IWC Midwich
IWF midwife
IWL oil well
Sitwell
IWN viewing
IWR airward
misword
pinworm
ribwort
viewers
IWT mix with
vie with
IXA biaxial
IXD dioxide
IYA lily pad
IYI Tiny Tim
IYK disyoke
misyoke
IYL bicycle
Sibylla
IYN biryani
minyans
pitying
IYO tiny tot
IYU tidy sum
IZE diazoes
sizzler
IZL dizzily
IZN fizzing
IZO Jinzhou
Liuzhou
IZR gizzard
IZZ pizzazz
JBA Ojibwas
JCI Ajaccio
JCO ejector
JML Djemila
JMO sjambok
KAL skiable
KAN Ukraine
KBN ikebana
KBU sky-blue
KCU Ski Club
KDA Skiddaw
skid pan
KDI skid lid
KDO skid row
KEG skreigh
KFL skiffle
KHG sky-high
KHT Akihito
KJC skyjack
KLE skelder
skelter
skilled
skillet
skulker
KLF ski lift
KLI skaldic
skellie
KLL ukelele
ukulele
KLN skyline
KLO Skelton
KLR skylark
KLU skilful
KME skimmer
KMI skimmia
KMO skimp on
KNE skinned
Skinner
KNU skinful
KNW Okinawa
KOS Okhotsk
KPE skipper
skippet
KPU skepful
KRE skirted
KSI skysail
KTE skitter
KTH sketchy
KTL skittle
KTN skating
KUA Nkrumah
KVN skiving
KWR skyward
KYM Okayama
LAA almanac
cloacae
cloacal
flea-bag
ilkaday
LAC Fleance
pliancy
LAD El Mahdi
LAE Alhazen
aliases
alkanet
Alvarez
bloated
bloater
cleaner
cleared
cleaver
cloaked
floatel
floater
gleaner
pleader
pleased
pleated
LAF alfalfa
LAI Albania
alkalis
fleapit
gliadin
olearia
ulnaria
LAK Almack's
LAL bleakly
cleanly
clearly
pliable
pliably
LAN Oleanna
LAO a load of

clear of
Eleanor
LAS cleanse
illapse
LAT Alma-Ata
LAU clean up
clean-up
clear up
float up
LBA clubman
flyboat
old bean
plebean
LBE blabber
blubber
clobber
clubbed
clubber
ill-bred
slabbed
slabber
slobber
slubbed
slubber
LBF plebify
LBI Aly Bain
globoid
LBL globule
LBM Alabama
LBO flybook
LBS globose
LBT globate
LCA glacial
LCB placebo
LCC Allcock
LCE blacken
blocked
blocker
Blücher
clichéd
cliché'd
clicket
elected
flacker
flacket
flecked
flecker
flicker
glacier
placket
slacken
slacker
slicken
slicker
slocken
LCI block in
clock in
flaccid
placoid
LCL blackly
slackly
slickly
LCN glycine

placing
slicing
LCO clock on
elector
place on
LCR Electra
electro
placard
plectra
LCS glucose
LCT elocute
placate
placita
plicate
LCU block up
clock up
floccus
pluck up
slack up
slice up
LDA old dear
LDE bladder
bludger
fledged
Flodden
gladden
pledged
pledgee
pledger
pledget
plodder
sledger
slidder
LDI slide in
LDN all done
gliding
sliding
LDO pledgor
LDY glad eye
LEA bluecap
blue jay
Blue-tak®
glue ear
illegal
LEB Allenby
LEC fluency
Iliescu
LED Allende
already
LEE alleged
altered
bleeder
bleeper
fleecer
Kleenex®
sleeken
sleeper
sleeved
ulcered
LEG allergy
LEI Albéniz
Algeria
Almeria

blue tit
bluetit
sleep in
sloe gin
LEK blue-sky
LEL alveoli
elderly
fleetly
Floella
sleekly
LEN al segno
fleeing
LEO albedos
sleep on
LER algebra
all ears
allegro
LET Alberta
Alberti
al dente
clients
LEU blue gum
clued up
clued-up
gleeful
LFE bluffer
flaffer
LFL bluffly
LFM ill fame
LFN plafond
LFS fly-fish
LGA elegiac
LGE aligned
blagger
clogged
plagued
plugged
plugger
slogger
LGF slag off
LGL old gold
LGN elegant
LGR Aligarh
old girl
LGS elegise
elegist
oligist
LGT flighty
LGZ elegize
LHE althaea
LHG fly high
LHI Alfheim
LHM alchemy
LHN old hand
LHO ale hoof
LHR alphorn
althorn
LIE claimed
claimer
plaited
plaiter
sleided
LIH alright

sleight
LII fluidic
illicit
LIL plainly
LIO albinos
LIR Algiers
LIS ellipse
LIT slàinte
LKT flokati
LLA flyleaf
LLC ill luck
ill-luck
LLD old lady
LLK elflike
LLN Cleland
ululant
LLT ululate
LMA alumnae
LMD à la mode
alamode
ill-made
LME clamber
clamped
clamper
climber
flamfew
glimmer
Klammer
plumber
plummet
slammer
slimmer
slumber
Slumkey
LMG plumage
LMI Alamgir
old maid
Olympia
Olympic
plum pie
LML plumply
plumula
plumule
slimily
LMN aliment
alimony
alumina
clamant
clement❑
element
Ellmann
flaming
Fleming
Ullmann
LMO climb on
flummox
old moon
plum job
LMS blemish
Flemish
glimpse
plumose
LMT climate

plumate
LMU alumnus
clamour
climb up
glamour
Olympus
Olympus®
plumous
LNA Clannad
plantar
LNC Old Nick
LNE Al Unser
blanket
blended
blender
blinded
blinder
blinker
Blondel
Blunden
blunder
clanger
clinger
clinker❑
flanged
flanker
flannel
flunkey
glandes
klinker
planned
planner
planter
plonker
plunder
plunger
slander
slanted
slender
LNH Blanche
elenchi
LNI Blondie
Blondin
Glennie
Tlingit
LNL alonely
blandly
blankly
blindly
bluntly
slantly
LNN alanine
cloning
LNO Clinton
plan for
LNR plenary
LNS illness
oldness
planish
slyness
LNT alength
cling to
LNV Ulanova

LOA Algo Bay
also-ran
gliomas
LOE all over
all-over
allowed
alloyed
almoner
blooded
bloomer
blooper
flooded
floored
floorer
fly open
flyover
LOG allonge
LOI floosie
floozie
gliosis
LOL aloofly
LOO alcohol
LOR almonry
LOS Alfonso
LOY allonym
LPA slipway
LPE clapper
clipped
clipper
elapsed
flapper
flipper
slipper
LPF slip off
LPI glyptic
LPN sloping
LPO Clapton
LPT Elspeth
LPU flip out
slope up
slop out
LQE cliquey
LQO aliquot
LRB glory be
LRC Aldrich
Clarice
clerics
El Greco
LRD Florida
LRE alarmed
Al Green
blarney❑
blurred
claroes
slurred
LRF clarify
glorify
LRI Florrie
floruit
glory in
LRL alertly
LRM pleroma
LRN blaring
clarini
glaring
LRO Blériot
clarion
LRS florist
old rose
oloroso
LRT alert to
clarity
LRU flare up
flare-up
LSA Alashan
all-star
elysian❑
LSB close by
LSE all-seer
blasted
blaster
blessed
blister
blusher
blushes
bluster
classes
cluster
flasher
flushed
fluster
glisten
glosser
oldster
Olmsted
Plassey
plaster
plusses
slashed
slasher
sloshed
Ulysses
LSI classic
clastic
close in
elastic
elastin
Flossie
Glossic
plasmid
plasmin
plastic
plastid
LSL closely
fleshly
LSM bless me!
LSN all's one
closing
LSO blesbok
blossom
close on
elision
fly-slow
Glasgow
Glashow
Old Spot
plessor
LSR closure
LSS closest
LST close to
LSU alyssum
close up
close-up
Elysium
LSV elusive
plosive
LTA all that
flat cap
flat-cap
flotsam
flytrap
glottal
gluteal
plateau
LTE blather
blatter
blether
blither
blitzed
Blitzen
blotter
clatter
clitter
clothed
clothes
clotted
clotter
clutter
flatlet
flatten
flatter
flitter
flutter
glitter
glutaei
glutted
platter
plotter
slather
slatter
slither
slitter
LTG flotage
LTH blotchy
LTI glottic
glottis
LTL a little
all told
LTM all-time
old-time
LTN blatant
fluting
platane
slating
LTO elation
elytron
glutton
platoon❑
LTR cloture
LTS elitism
elitist
élitist
LTU blot out
elytrum
flat out
gluteus
LUA clausal
pleurae
pleural
LUC flounce
LUD aliunde
LUE albumen
clauses
clouded
flouter
ileuses
ill-used
plouter
LUH claucht
claught
flaught
LUI albumin
alluvia
Claudia
Claudio
plaudit
LUO albugos
blouson
fly upon
LUT flaunty
LUU Plautus
LVA fluvial
pluvial
LVE Olivier
LVF Slavify
LVI Plovdiv
LVL Clavell
LVN flavine
olivine
slaving
Slovene
LVR slavery
LVS slavish
LVT alive to
elevate
LVU flavour
LWA Clew Bay
LWC Alnwick
LWE plowter
LWF alewife
claw off
LWL ill will
ill-will
LWN blowing
flowing
glowing
slowing
LWO plywood
LWR flowers
flowery
LWS all-wise
LWT blewits
LWU blown up
blow out
blow-out
flow out
LXL flexile
LXO flexion
LXR flexure
LXU Alexius
LXV fluxive
LYC play-act
LYE playpen
LYF play off
play-off
LYN cloying
flaying
playing
slaying
LYO playboy❑
LYR players
LYU playful
play out
LZA al-Azhar
LZE glazier
klezmer
LZN blazing
glazing
LZU blaze up
MAA impalas
MAE empanel
impaled
ommatea
smearer
MAG embargo
MAH empathy
MAI Amharic
MAL amiable
amiably
MAN impaint
MAS embassy
impasse
MAT impaste
impasto
MCE smacker
MCI smectic
MCL smickly
MCO omicron
MCT emicate
MDE smidgen
smudger
MDI smidgin
MDU Amadeus
MEA amoebae
amoebas
MEC impeach
MEE ammeter
MEG immerge
MEI amnesia
amnesic
amoebic
imperia
imperil
MEO emperor
MER impearl

MES immense
immerse
MET amnesty
MEU impetus
MGE imagoes
MGL smuggle
MGN imagine□
imaging
MGR imagery
MHR amphora
MIE imbiber
MIG impinge
MII empiric
omnific
MIN ambient
MIT impiety
MIU impious
omnibus
MKL smokily
MKN smoking
MLA amalgam
smell at
smile at
MLC emplace
MLD implode
MLE implied
smaller
smelled
smeller
MLF amplify
MLM emblema
MLN emplane
implant
smiling
MLO a mill of
embloom
smaltos
smell of
smile on
MLR implore
MLS amylase
MLT emulate
implate
MLU emulous
MLZ emblaze
MMN a moment
MMT imamate
MNE Emanuel
MNI amentia
MNN emanant
eminent
MNS amongst
MNT amanita
amenity
emanate
MNU omentum
ominous
MOA immoral
umbonal
MOE ambones
embowel
embower
empower
imbower
Imhotep
imposed
umbones
MOH smoothy
MOI ammonia
emporia
MOL ampoule
MON embound
impound
MOO embosom
imbosom
MOT imposte
MOU embogue
embolus
MRA Umbrian
MRC embrace
MRE smarten
MRG umbrage
MRI ambroid
embroil
smartie
MRL emerald□
smartly
MRN amorini
imprint
MRO embryos
Emerson
MRS Ambrose
amorist
amoroso
empress
impress
imprest
umbrose
MRT emeriti
emirate
MRU amorous
umbrous
MRV improve
MRW embrown
imbrown
MSA Ameslan
Amistad
MSE smashed
smasher
MSN amusing
MSU smash up
smash-up
MTE emptied
empties
omitted
smatter
smitten
smother
umpteen
MTL emptily
MTN Smetana
MTO emotion
emption
MTR amatory
MTT imitate
MTU amateur
MTV amative
emotive
MUE amputee
immured
MUL ampulla
MUN imbuing
MUS impulse
MYM empyema
MZN amazing
NAA Andaman
NAC enhance
in banco
infancy
unlatch
NAD en garde
innards
inwards
onwards
unhandy
NAE Annabel
Antares
encaged
engaged
enraged
inhaler
invader
kneader
on paper
sneaker
uneaten
unfaded
unfazed
unlaced
unnamed
unpaged
unpanel
unpaper
unravel
untaken
untamed
unwaged
unwares
unwater
NAG enlarge
NAH Inkatha
NAI antacid
entasis
inhabit
invalid
Ontario
sneak in
NAL entayle
unmanly
NAN uncanny
unpaint
unsaint
NAP unhappy
NAR ondatra
unmarry
NAS en masse
NAT andante
annatto
inearth
infanta
infante
in haste
on earth
unearth
unhasty
unlaste
NBA ant-bear
NBD anybody
in a body
NBE enabler
NBL knobble
knobbly
knubble
NBR antbird
NCE knacker
knocker
snicker
unscrew
NCH gnocchi
NCL insculp
knuckle
unscale
NCM in a coma
NCO knock on
knock-on
snack on
NCR unicorn□
NCU knock up
knock-up
sneck up
snick up
NDN anodyne
NDS anodise
NDZ anodize
in a daze
NEA enteral
kneecap
knee-cap
sneer at
NEB Entebbe
NEC inherce
in peace
unperch
unteach
NED underdo
unready
NEE angered
anoeses
Dnieper
end even
enterer
entêtée
indexer
indexes
ingener
integer
kneeled
kneeler
sneerer
sneezer
unbeget
unsexed
NEF enfeoff
undeify
NEG inveigh
undergo
NEI anaemia
anaemic
angelic
annelid
antefix
endemic
enteric
inherit
interim
NEL en règle
injelly
NEN antenna
inferno
interne
unbeing
NEO angekok
Angelou
enter on
envelop
envenom
NEP unkempt
NER in tears
unheard
unheart
unlearn
NES incense
intense
inverse
unherst
unleash
unsense
NET Annette
entente
in depth
in-depth
Insecta
unneath
NEU angelus
ingénue
knees-up
NEV innerve
inweave
unnerve
unreave
unreeve
unweave
NFA in a flap
sniff at
NFE on offer
sniffer
snuffer
unified
unifier
unoften
NFI snuff it
NFL snaffle
sniffle
snuffle
NFN knifing

NFR uniform❑
NGA anagram
NGE snagged
snigger
NGG anagogy
NGL sniggle
snuggle
NGM endgame❑
NGN in agony
NHA anthrax
enthral
NHC in shock
uncheck
NHE enwheel
in chief
NHF in a huff
NHG on the go
NHI enchain
on the in
unchain
NHL in a hole
inshell
unchild
unshale
unshell
NHN Anthony
enchant
in thing
in-thing
unshun'd
unthink
NHO unshoot
NHP in shape
unshape
NHQ on the QT
NHR inshore
in short
onshore
on-shore
uncharm
unshorn
NHS enchase
enthuse
in phase
NHU on the up
unshout
NHV anchovy
NHZ in a haze
NIA infimae
intimae
NIB in limbo
NIC Antioch
unhitch
unwitch
NIE Antibes
antigen
enginer
enliven
enticed
enticer
inciter
indices
infidel
insider
insides
insinew
unaided
unfixed
unlined
unmixed
unoiled
unrivet
unsinew
NIG on wings
unhinge
NIH in sight
insight
NII inhibit
insipid
uncivil
NIK unpinkt
NIL Anfield
Enfield
entitle
infield
unfitly
NIM angioma
NIN ancient
Indiana
NIO andiron
angicos
environ
in aid of
incisor
indigos
unvisor
NIR in fieri
in vitro
NIT anxiety
ungirth
NIU antique
anxious
envious
NKL snakily
NKN snaking
unaking
unskan'd
NLA antliae
unclean
unclear
uncloak
NLB englobe
NLC Anglice
inflect
inflict
in place
unblock
unplace
NLD include
NLE on sleep
NLG analogy
NLM inflame
unplumb
unplume
NLN angling
aniline
endlang
endlong
England
enplane
incline
inkling
unblind
unsling
NLO engloom
in blood
in bloom
NLS analyse
analyst
enclasp
enclose
endless
enflesh
English
inclose
in flesh
unbless
unclasp
unclose
unflesh
unflush
NLT anility
inflate
NLU encloud
uncloud
NLV enclave
enslave
NLW unblown
NME f-number
NML animals❑
anomaly
in small
NMN anemone
NMO in a mood
NMR any more
NMS animism
animist
endmost
in a mess
NMT animate
animato
enemata
NMU enamour
NNI in-and-in
in antis
NNL inanely
NNO on and on
NNR ensnare
unsnarl
NNS onanism
onanist
oneness
NNT inanity
NNW unknown
NOA in no way
in total
unmoral
unwoman
NOB in doubt
NOC enforce
in force
in touch
invoice
unvoice
NOD inroads
NOE ancones
annoyed
endowed
incomer
in holes
in power
snooker
snooper
snoozer
unbowed
uncover
unloved
unmoved
unnoted
NOG engorge
NOI anionic
Antonia
Antonio
encomia
inconie
in folio
in for it
NOL ennoble
snoozle
ungodly
unmould
unnoble
NON enround
inbound
ingoing
injoint
in point
ongoing
unbound
undoing
unjoint
unmount
unsound
NOO endozoa
entozoa
on top of
unbosom
NOR Andorra
inboard
indoors
on board
unhoard
NOS endorse
indorse
in-house
in posse
unhorse
unhouse
unloose
unroost
NOT en poste
en route
oncosts
uncouth
NOU in focus
in vogue
one of us
NOV involve
NOY antonym
NPA snipe at
unspeak
NPC in space
inspect
NPE snapper
snipper
snippet
NPF snap off
NPL inaptly
ineptly
knapple
unaptly
unspell
NPN sniping
unspent
NPR inspire
on appro
NQA unequal
NRA angry at
anyroad
entreat
in dread
snarl at
untread
NRC engrace
infract
unbrace
unfrock
untrace
NRD intrude
untride
NRE gnarled
inbreed
in brief
in order
knurled
on order
snarled
snarler
snorkel
snorter
unarmed
undried
unorder
untried
NRF engraft
indraft
NRH anarchy
NRI android
aneroid
engrail
engrain
entrain
inertia
in grain
ingrain

in train
introit
NRL angrily
inertly
on a roll
snirtle
untruly
NRM enframe
Ingrams
NRN enprint
entrant
in front
in print
snaring
NRO in error
NRP encrypt
entropy
NRS ancress
Andress
encrust
engross
entrism
entrist
entrust
incross
incrust
ingress
in gross
intrust
uncross
undress
untruss
NRT encraty
in truth
untruth
unwrite
NRU onerous
snarl up
snarl-up
NRV engrave
on-drive
NRW Andrews
in-crowd
indrawn
ingrown
uncrown
NSA unusual
NSE aniseed
Gnasher
in a stew
Knesset
one-step
unasked
NSI anosmia
E Nesbit
gnostic
Onassis
NSK Anushka
NSL in a sulk
one self
oneself
NSO and so on
in a spot
one-stop
NSR in a sort
NTA and that
gnathal
initial
instead
unstrap
NTC D-notice
in a tick
in stock
unstack
unstick
unstock
unstuck
NTE another
ensteep
knitter
knotted
snotter
unsteel
NTG on stage
on-stage
NTH snatchy
NTI gnathic
on a trip
unstrip
NTL install
in style
NTM anatomy
anytime
enstamp
on a time
one time
one-time
NTN instant
uniting
NTO anattos
unction
NTR in store
in-store
in utero
unitard
unitary
NTS unitise
NTT instate
unstate
NTV unitive
NTZ in a tizz
unitize
NUA angular
annular
infulae
inhuman
insular
ungulae
NUC enounce
injunct
NUE annulet
end-user
ennuied
ensured
incudes
injured
insured
insurer
snouted
uncured
unqueen
unquiet
unsured
untuned
NUF unruffe
NUG indulge
NUI Aneurin
indusia
insulin
NUK unlucky
NUL Anouilh
inbuilt
in-built
unbuild
NUN ensuing
in ruins
in turns
unguent
NUR enguard
enquire
enquiry
inquire
inquiry
on guard
unguard
NUS anguish
inquest
uncurse
unfussy
unpurse
NUT annuity
en suite
insults
unquote
NUU annulus
incubus
NUV incurve
NVC una voce
NVR knavery
NVS knavish
NWA known as
snowcap
snowman
unswear
NWE anywhen
NWI in twain
unswai'd
NWL indwell
inkwell
know-all
snowily
NWN entwine
gnawing
intwine
knowing
untwine
NWO know-how
Snowdon
NWR Antwerp
in a word
unaware
NWS anywise
endwise
entwist
intwist
untwist
NWY endways
NXC inexact
NYA in my way
NYI enzymic
NYN undying
NYO only too
NZL snuzzle
OAA tokamak
OAC Jo March
monarch
noyance
romance
sonance
tobacco
OAD Bogarde
no can do
notanda
Ronaldo
towards
Yolanda
OAE do later
dowager
forager
foramen
forayer
located
po-faced
Rosabel
sofa bed
voyager
OAH gouache
OAI boracic
botanic
cohabit
conaria
do magic
domatia
Goiânia
Horatio
komatik
Koranic
monadic
Moravia
nomadic
not a bit
Novalis
Polaris
potamic
Romania
Rosalie
Rosaria
Rosario
solatia
Somalia
somatic
vocalic
OAL coracle
coralla
do badly
focally
locally
lovable
loyally
modally
morally
movable
movably
nodally
notable
notably
potable
ropable
royally
tonally
totally
towable
vocable
vocally
volable
womanly
OAN cocaine
hoc anno
hosanna
moraine
no' canny
Rosanna
Roxanne
OAO donator
dorados
nonagon
robalos
rotator
solanos
OAR conacre
Conakry
podagra
OAS morassy
soda ash
OAT go Fanti
Hogarth
Jocasta
loyalty
royalty
OAU conatus
go kaput
Romanus
Volapük
OAY sokaiya
OAZ bonanza
OBA forbear
Rotblat
soy bean
OBC hogback
OBD forbade
OBE cobbler
doubled
doublet
doubter
gobbler

low-bred
nobbler
wobbler
yobboes
OBF zombify
OBI con brio
Holbein
howbeit
OBL cowbell
nobbily
tombola
OBM Hobbema
OBN bobbing
bombing
combine
cowbane
do a bunk
robbing
Robbins
sobbing
OBO Joe Blow
logbook
lowbrow
OBR bombard
bombora
Colbert
cowbird
Fosbury
Homburg
Lombard
low-born
robbery
Romberg
Roobarb
OBS bombast
combust
Mombasa
soubise
yobbish
OBT bobbitt
Cobbett
Corbett
OBU comb out
go about
OCA conceal
conchae
ponceau
topcoat
OCC concoct
OCD concede
concedo
OCE botched
botcher
Boucher
conches
moocher
notched
notchel
poacher
pouched
torcher
touched
voucher

wotcher
OCG boscage
OCI conceit
OCL doucely
OCM coxcomb
how come?
non-come
OCN porcine
voicing
volcano□
OCO Foochow
honchos
ponchos
torchon
touch on
OCP concept
concupy
forceps
OCR concern
concert
concord□
dogcart
dog-cart
popcorn
sorcery
OCS concise
concuss
low-cost
OCT boycott□
toccata
OCU botch up
botch-up
co-occur
douceur
notch up
Roscius
touch up
OCV concave
ODA bondman
cold war
cordial
Goldman
good-day
Goodman
Gordian
mondial
roadman
road-map
road tax
roadway
Roedean
rondeau
woodman
wood tar
ODB cordoba
Córdoba
ODC conduce
conduct
Roddick
top deck
ODD howdy-do
ODE Boodle's
coddled

Cowdrey
doodler
fondler
good-den
good-e'en
not deep
roe deer
soldier
toddler
ODF hold off
ODG bondage
condign
cordage
good egg
wordage
ODI boudoir
conduit
hordein
Lord Jim
non-drip
ODL Bob Dole
condole
dowdily
gondola
holdall
hold-all
Mondale
moodily
rowdily
wordily
ODM condemn
ODN bonding
codding
condone
folding
fondant
goading
Golding
good and
holding□
mordant
mordent
nodding
sordini
sordino
tondini
voiding
wording
ODO road-hog
ODR borders□
bordure
doddery
Goddard
goldarn
Hordern
moidore
powdery
rondure
wonders
ODS foodism
goddess
loudish
ODT cordate

cordite
toady to
ODU goldcup
good buy
hold out
hoodlum
woodcut
ODV Moldova
ODW bog down
bow down
hoe-down
jot down
lowdown
low-down
mow down
ODY Goldwyn
goodbye
good-bye
OEA Coleman
Docetae
Donegal
Donegan
forelay
foreman□
foreran
lose way
love-day
mole rat
nosebag
nosegay
notepad
polecat
rodeway
ropeway
someday
someway
to be had
tonepad
tote bag
OEB moved by
OEC cogency
Ionesco
potency
OED Hodeida
morendo
OEE coherer
covered
cozener
foreleg
foremen
foresee
for ever
forever
honeyed
however
lorelei□
lovered
lowered
moneyed
notelet
not ever
pop-eyed
powered

rose-red
some few
towered
OEF come off
cone off
doze off
gone off
OEG foreign
lozenge
OEH none the
OEI coterie
cover in
forelie
godetia
Goneril
Homeric
Jocelin
lobelia
polemic
soredia
tonemic
totemic
zooecia
OEL Corelli
modelli
modello
morello
moselle□
notedly
novella
novelle
Novello
rosella
roseola
soberly
OEN codeine
doyenne
Mole End
someone
OEO a one for
boleros
boredom
comedos
come for
come low
done for
dovecot
foretop
hope for
none too
nose job
pomelos
popedom
Robeson
somehow
Toledos
toreros
vote for
OER bone-dry
forearm
OES Colenso
Donetsk
moreish

nor'-east
poseuse
to tease
OET Colette
dozenth
fouetté
foveate
honesty
Josette
lomenta
Lorentz
Loretta
lorette
modesty
momenta
nonetti
novelty
polenta
poverty
Roberta
Roberts
roseate
Rosetta
rosette
to death
OEU boletus
come out
coteaux
cover up
cover-up
doleful
dole out
forerun
hole out
hopeful❑
lose out
move out
nose out
poke fun
poke out
rose-bug
OEX pole-axe
OEY Jocelyn
OEZ Lorenzo
OFA for fear
golf bag
Hoffman
wolfram
OFC confect
OFD confide
OFE coffret
comfrey
for free
go after
Godfree
Godfrey
hop-flea
pomfret
poufter
toffees❑
Torfaen
woofter
OFI forfeit
OFL boxfuls
goofily
Norfolk
potfuls
souffle
soufflé
topfull
OFN confine
loafing
not find
Rolfing
roofing
OFO hotfoot
mouflon
rooftop
tomfool
OFR bonfire
coffers
comfort
confirm
conform
OFS confess
confuse
dogfish
loafish
wolfish
OFT confute
OFU conflux
OFV Hot Five
OGA congeal
Douglas
Gorgias
loggias
songman
Songnam
top gear
OGE goggles
long leg
mongrel
pongoes
roughen
soignée
toughen
OGF long off
OGG foggage
long ago
OGI do again
Hodgkin
long-oil
rough in
rough it
toughie
OGL foggily
roughly
soggily
toughly
OGN dodging
doggone
forging
Gorgons
hogging
jogging
lodging
longing
nogging
OGO Dodgson
for good
gorgios
longbow
long for
long hop
not good
rough on
sorghos
OGR cowgirl
forgery
gougère
Hoggart
Rodgers
OGS congest
doggish
hoggish
OGT doughty
not go to
OGU cough up
rough up
sorghum
OGV forgave
forgive
OHA bodhran
Cochran
go ahead
go-ahead
godhead❑
hothead
lochial
Lothian
moth-eat
OHB Sotheby
OHC Toshack
OHD cowhide
OHE cochlea
potheen
OHI Lothair
pochoir
to a hair
OHL foxhole
not half
pothole
toehold
top-hole
OHN cowhand
forhent
moshing
nothing
OHO boyhood
OHP Bob Hope
OHR cowherd
foghorn
not harm
not here
nowhere
pochard
so there
yoghurt
OHS sophism
sophist
OHT go white
OHU Jodhpur
OHV not have
OHW goshawk
OIA bolivar
Bolívar
comical
comital
conical
holiday❑
logical
loricae
mohican❑
nominal
Novi Sad
topical
OIC goyisch
oomiack
to-pinch
OIE codices
conifer
Dorigen
fomites
ioniser
ionizer
Mogilev
moniker
motives
nominee
noticed
posited
rotifer
OIG cotinga
Domingo
foliage
OIH moriche
tonight
OII Bolivia
codicil
colitis
conidia
Dominic
dominie
gonidia
hominid
oolitic
politic
robinia
solicit
OIK colicky
Soyinka
OIL foliole
gorilla
rouille
solidly
OIN Coligny
Corinna
Corinne
OIO bog-iron
bonitos
co-pilot
dominos
dosi-dos
Honiton
horizon
monitor
Morisot
zorinos
OIR Honiara
Honiari
hosiery
Molière
poniard
topiary
OIS do first
foliose
go first
OIT Corinth
Corinto
foliate
goliath❑
modiste
society
OIU copious
corious
modicum
noxious
solidus
Zosimus
OJA Don Juan
OJC conject
OJH Don John
OJI conjoin
OJN goujons
OJR conjure
OJV Bon Jovi
OJZ hot jazz
OKA cork oak
lockjaw
workbag
work-day
workman
OKD cockade
OKE booklet
cockney
Hockney
Lockyer
look-see
Monkees
porkies
Rockies
Tolkien
workmen
OKF cook off
work off
OKG corkage
lockage
soakage
OKH workshy
work-shy
OKI cockpit
pockpit
OKK rokkaku
OKL cockily
Rockall

rockily
OKN booking
cooking
docking
Don King
Dorking
forking
Hopkins
looking
mocking
rocking
soaking
working
OKO bowknot
Cookson
kolkhoz
look for
not know
topknot
workbox
work for
worktop
you know
OKR bonkers
cookery
folk art
mockery
rock art
rockery
rookery
workers
Yonkers
OKS bookish
monkish
Yorkist
OKT rockets
OKU book out
conk out
forkful
fork out
lock out
lockout
look out
lookout
soukous
work out
workout
work-out
OKY donkeys
monkeys
monkey's
sockeye
OLA coal gas
coeliac
cool bag
poll tax
roll-bar
toolbag
toolbar
Zoilean
OLB could be
would-be
OLC bollock
collect
cowlick
hoc loco
pollack□
pollock□
pot luck
rollick
rowlock
OLD collide
collude
roulade
OLE boulder□
colleen□
collier
Follies
goolies
Hollies
holloes
moulder
woollen
Woolley
woolsey
OLF boil off
cool off
for life
jollify
mollify
OLG collage
college
zoology
OLH holla-ho!
OLI coal tit
coal-tit
colloid
toolkit
OLK cowlike
godlike
rodlike
OLL jollily
lowlily
worldly
OLM coulomb□
fog lamp
to blame
OLN boiling
bowline
bowling
Coblenz
codling
coiling
Collins
coolant
cooling
Copland
cowling
Dowland
foiling
fooling
fouling
fowling
go along
go blank
gosling
Gotland
holland□
hot line
howling
Koblenz
lowland
polling
Poulenc
rolling
Rollins
Rowland
Rowling
soiling
toiling
topline
towline
Toyland
yowling
OLO cool box
Kowloon
rollmop
toolbox
OLR bollard
foolery
forlorn
foulard
pollard
poulard
poultry
OLS coalise
fogless
foolish
godless
goulash
jobless
joyless
mollusc
rodless
topless
OLT collate
jollity
pollute
OLU bowlful
soulful
OLV for love
OLY volleys
OLZ coalize
OMC dormice
not much
too much
OMD commode
commodo
OME Gormley
Mommsen
OML foamily
formula
hot melt
roomily
OMN booming
Bormann
coaming
command
commend
comment
commons□
commune
dormant
foaming
formant
forming
hormone
looming
Normans
not many
not mind
noumena
roaming
torment
OMO hoummos
OMR Coimbra
woomera
OMS go amiss
koumiss
not miss
topmost
OMT commute
con moto
formate
OMU boom out
holmium
roomful
worm out
ONA corneal
John Gay
John Ray
noonday
poundal
town gas
ONC connect
cornice
OND tornado□
ONE boonies
bouncer
bounded
bounden
bounder
counsel
counter
données
Dornier
founder
go under
hounded
John Dee
jointed
loonier
loonies
lounder
lounger
Moonies
mounted
not need
pointed
pointer
pointes
rounded
roundel
rounder
Toynbee
wounded
younger
ONG coinage
tonnage
ONI council
hobnail
johnnie□
moonlit
mountie□
toenail
ONK Roanoke
ONL bonnily
Cornell
jointly
roundly
soundly
ONN fornent
joining
moaning
morning
Rodnina
ONO coin box
count on
go in for
going on
Johnson
round on
ONR Bonnard
Connery
Connors
country
foundry
joinery
ONS cognise
Cornish
coyness
donnish
donnism
hotness
lowness
roynish
so and so
so-and-so
soonest
Souness
ONT bornite
bound to
cognate
connate
connote
going to
Hornets
point to
ONU count up
horn-bug
moanful
mount up
point up
round up
round-up

worn out
worn-out
wound up
young'un
ONV connive
ONY John Pym
romneya
ONZ cognize
OOA coronae
coronal
coronas
go so far
go to war
Potomac
Sonoran
sororal
so to say
OOB Colombo
no doubt
OOC for once
morocco❑
OOE boloney
colonel
colones
coroner
coronet
coyotes
Dolores
go lower
go to bed
go to sea
ionomer
monomer
no-hoper
poroses
soboles
vocoder
won over
OOG borough
OOH Dorothy
OOI Borodin
colonic
do to wit
go for it
monodic
moronic
oogonia
robotic
rosolio
sorosis
OOK mono-ski
OOL corolla
monocle
OON Bologna
cologne❑
go round
Novotna
to point
OOO Comoros
corozos
go to pot
Molotov
potoroo

Robocop
rococos
Solomon
OOR colours
honours
sojourn
OOS colossi
molossi
soloist
OOT cocotte
cohorts
Toronto
OOU coconut
colobus
OOY homonym
toponym
OPA compear
OPC compact
coppice
hospice
OPD torpedo
OPE compeer
complex
coupled
couplet
Doppler
kouprey
OPF torpefy
OPI complin
dolphin❑
Pompeii
OPK cowpoke
OPL compile
Coppola
Gospels
soapily
soppily
OPN compand
company❑
hopping
looping
pompano
popping
romping
sopping
topping
OPO complot
Compton
morphos
soapbox
soupçon
tompion
OPR compare
compère
comport
coppers
coppery
corpora
foppery
go spare
Gosport
oospore
to spare

OPS compass
compose
compost
foppish
OPT compete
compote
compute
Morpeth
towpath
OPU nonplus
pompous
OQA coequal
rorqual
Torquay
OQE bouquet
conquer
docquet
OQI jonquil❑
ORA Boorman
doorman
doormat
doorway
for real
journal
poor law
Tournai
ORC correct
porrect
touraco
ORD comrade
corrade
corrode
joy-ride
ORE boarder
bourrée
coarsen
coerced
Courbet
courier
courser
courses
Fourier
gourmet
hoarder
hoarsen
journey
Lou Reed
moorhen
mourner
poursew
to order
tourney
worried
worrier
worries
ORF horrify
torrefy
ORG courage
ORI Boursin
do or die
do-or-die
ORK go broke
ORL courtly

Dorrell
hoarily
loo roll
mob rule
mob-rule
sorrily
ORM no-trump
ORN do wrong
Goering
go wrong
louring
mooring
pouring
roaring
soaring
soprani
soprano
souring
top-rank
Torrens
torrent
touring
ORO bourbon❑
bourdon
go crook
godroon
journos
soursop
you're on!
ORP corrupt
towrope
ORS boorish
dog rose
Forrest
Moorish
nourish
poorest
sourish
tourism
tourist
ORT co-write
ORU board up
hoard up
pour out
poursue
ORW do brown
go brown
ORY Holroyd
ORZ go crazy
OSA bobstay
borstal
coastal
dog's-ear
Dog Star
Housman
pop star
Potsdam
rodsman
Sod's law
Woosnam
OSC Conseco
Corsica
Cossack

fossick
nonsuch
OSD go aside
gorsedd
topside
OSE boaster
bobsled
bolster
booster
coaster
conster
corslet
cowshed
dossier
Forster
hoisted
hoister
holster
jouster
lobster
Loesser
mobster
moisten
monster
roasted
roaster
rodster
roister
rooster
Ross Sea
toasted
toaster
tousled
Vorster
Wooster
worsted
OSF toss off
OSG consign
corsage
OSH borscht
Porsche
Porsche®
OSI bolshie
corsair
cowslip
foxship
non-skid
non-slip
nonsuit
poussin❑
souslik
toastie
topsail
topsoil
topspin
worship
OSK forsake
OSL bossily
console
consols
consult
for sale
fossils

Words marked ❑ can also be spelled with an initial capital letter

loosely
lousily
moistly
noisily
nousell
tossily
woosell
OSM consume
noisome
woesome
OSN consent
cousins□
dossing
dousing
godsend
housing
loosing
mousing
pop song
Rossini
rousing
tossing
OSO boast of
forslow
God slot
hoosgow
hotshot
hot spot
Houston
monsoon
non-stop
not spot
not stop
Poisson
pop-shop
pot shot
rouse on
Tolstoy
too soon
torsion
tosspot
OSP gossipy
OSR consort
dossers
for sure
Ronsard
tonsure
OSS consist
possess
Sotsass
OST Forsyth
Fossett
OSU hotspur□
louse up
toss out
OTA boatman
Cocteau
costean
don't say
footman
footpad
footway
FORTRAN

Godthab
not that
Pontian
portray
postman
postwar
rostral
OTC bortsch
contact
low-tech
mortice
portico
Rostock
OTD low tide
tostada
OTE bootleg
bottled
Coetzee
Costner
dottrel
footmen
forties□
loftier
moither
mottled
mottoes
norther
now then!
Poitier
röntgen□
rootlet
sonties
soother
souther
Southey
toothed
OTF fortify
mortify
pontiff
pontify
OTG cortège
cottage
footage
hostage
montage
Montagu
Montego
portage
postage
pottage
voltage
OTI bobtail
contain
footsie□
hoatzin
nostril
postfix
tootsie□
worth it
OTK Roethke
OTL cortili
go stale
hostile

loftily
monthly
mortals
noctule
not tall
soothly
sootily
OTM contemn
costume
zootomy
OTN Boateng
boating
box tent
coating
contend
content
Cortina®
cottony
footing
Fortuna
fortune□
hotting
jolting
jotting
looting
Montana
norteña
portend
portent
Rostand
rotting
routine
sorting
soutane
tontine
OTO coition
control
dogtrot
foxtrot□
fox-trot
jogtrot
pontoon
Porthos
portion
post-bop
root for
soft top
OTR contort
Costard
couture
doctor's
lottery
montero
postern
posture
pottery
to a turn
torture
tottery
OTS coltish
contest
contuse
doltish

goatish
hostess
loutish
mortise
poetess
poetise
sottish
OTU boot out
contour
cost out
nostrum
root out
rostrum
sort out
OTV costive
Poltava
tortive
OTX context
OTY Fonteyn
OTZ poetize
OUA jocular
locular
modular
nodular
popular
torulae
OUB Columba
Columbo
OUC go Dutch
OUD rotunda
OUE boluses
focused
focuses
locules
moguled
voluted
OUL soluble
voluble
volubly
wofully
OUN Corunna
roguing
toluene
OUO colugos
do out of
focus on
OUR roguery
OUS roguish
voguish
OUT coquito
not up to
robusta
tot up to
woe unto
OUU loculus
modulus
Romulus
to sum up
OVA Vouvray
OVC convict
OVE louvred
OVI for vain
Louvain

OVK convoke
OVL Torvill
OVN convene
convent
corvine
solvent
solving
OVR convert
not very
OVS wolvish
OVT not vote
solvate
OWA no sweat
OWC Norwich
OWE hogweed
OWI you wait!
OWL Boswell
OWO boxwood
dogwood
OWR forward
forwarn
godward
hot-wire
lobworm
norward
nor'ward
not work
OWS hogwash
nor'-west
OWT Sopwith
toy with
OXA coaxial
OXN coaxing
OXS coexist
OYA copycat
copy-cat
cotylae
go by car
holydam
holy day
holy war
OYE cotyles
polymer
polypes
OYH Corypha
OYI Kosygin
OYN copying
Holy One
OYO holy Joe
polygon
OYS copyist
fogyish
Toryism
OYU copy out
Toby jug
OZC Wozzeck
OZE sozzled
OZL boozily
Gonzalo
woozily
OZN Boyzone
OZR rozzers
OZU booze-up

PAC splatch
upcatch
PAD upwards
PAE apparel
speaker
speared
sprayer
PAH splashy
PAI aphagia
aphasia
aphasic
apraxia
PAN spraint
PAO speak of
spray-on
PAS upraise
PAT appalti
speak to
PAU speak up
upvalue
PBV up above
PCA epochal
spacial
special
PCE species
PCF specify
PCL speckle
specula
spicily
spicula
spicule
upscale
PCN epicene
spacing
PCP apocope
PCR epicarp
epicure
spectra
spectre
PCT opacity
spicate
PCU spice up
PDE spadger
spadoes
PDR Spiders
spidery
PDU apodous
PEA spaeman
spheral
PEB upset by
PEC appeach
PEE ephebes
speeder
sphered
spieler
PEI aphelia
aphesis
aphetic
apperil
apteria
ephebic
Ophelia
spheric

PEN spleeny
PEO speedos
PEP up-tempo
PES appease
PEU Ephesus
speed up
PEV upheave
PEY apteryx
PGA epigram
PGM apogamy
PGN epigene
epigone
epigoni
PHC upchuck
PHE upcheer
PHL spyhole
PHO upshoot
upthrow
PHR up there
PIA oppidan
optical
optimal
PIE aphides
apsides
spliced
splicer
spoiled
spoiler
upsides
PIG spairge
springe
springy
PIH upright
uptight
PII ophitic
PIO apricot
epsilon
split on
upsilon
PIR a priori
PIT à pointe
PIU optimum
split up
split-up
PKL spikily
PKN Spokane
PLA spelean
PLE applied
spelder
spelled
spelter
spilled
PLG apology
PLI spulzie
PLN opaline
opulent
up-along
PLO apollos
PLT apply to
epilate
Spoleto
PLU applaud
PMU spumous

PNA open day
PNC spinach
PNE spancel
spandex□
spaniel
spanker
spanner
spencer□
spender□
Spenser
spinner
spinney
spondee
sponger
up-ended
PNF spin-off
PNG apanage
PNI open-air
opuntia
PNL spangle
spangly
spindle
spindly
spinule
PNN opening
PNO open-top
opinion
spent on
sponson
sponsor
PNR spin-dry
PNS aptness
Spanish
spinose
PNU open out
spinous
spin out
spun out
PNZ Spinoza
POA up to par
POC splotch
POE opposed
opposer
speoses
spoofer
Spooner
POG splodge
splodgy
POI aphonia
aphotic
POL M People
PON appoint
POO apropos
up to now
POR uphoard
uphoord
POS upcoast
PPA upspeak
upspear
PPI epopeia
PRA spartan□
sporran
upbreak

PRD upgrade
PRE sparrer
spiraea
spurned
spurrey
PRI Ephraim
upbraid
uptrain
PRL sparely
sparkle
sparkly
spirtle
sporule
spurtle
PRN operand
operant
sparing
up front
upfront
up-front
PRO a part of
sparrow
PRS apprise
oppress
PRT epurate
operate
spirits
PRV approve
PSD episode
PSE Opus Dei
PSI spastic
PSK Spassky
PSL apishly
apostle
epistle
Uppsala
PSU opossum
PTA aphthae
spatial
PTE apothem
epithem
epithet
spathed
spatter
spitter
spotted
spotter
sputter
up a tree
PTG upstage
PTI Epstein
spathic
sputnik□
PTL spatula
spittle
PTM epitome
PTO spite of
PTP epitaph
PTR upstare
upstart
PTT apatite
upstate
PTU spit out

PTX epitaxy
PUA spousal
PUG splurge
splurgy
upsurge
PUL upbuild
PUS upburst
PWC Ipswich
PWE spawner
PWN spewing
upswing
PWR up-swarm
PWU spew out
PYL aphylly
PZA epizoan
PZI epizoic
PZO epizoon
QAA squamae
QAB squabby
QAC squacco
QAD squaddy
QAE squarer
QAH squashy
QAI aquaria
aquatic
aquavit
squalid
QAK squawky
QAL equable
equably
equally
squally
QAO equator
squalor
QAT equal to
QEC squelch
QEK squeaky
QER equerry
Squeers
QEU aqueous
QEZ squeeze
squeezy
QIA Aquinas
QIC squinch
QIE aquifer
aquiver
QIF squiffy
QIG squidge
squidgy
QIH squishy
QIM squirmy
QIN squinny
QIO Aquilon
equinox
Iquitos
QIU Iquique
RAC truancy
RAD Orlando
RAE arrayed
breaker
broaden
creased
creaser

Words marked □ can also be spelled with an initial capital letter

dreaded
dreamed
dreamer
dryades
greaten
greater
Greaves
groaner
oreades
treader
treated
treater
wreaker
RAG arraign
arrange
great go
RAH breathe
breathy
preachy
wreathe
wreaths
RAI Arcadia
break in
break-in
creatin
Croatia
erratic
organic
triacid
triadic
RAL broadly
dreadly
friable
greatly
treacle
treacly
treadle
triable
RAN Ariadne
RAO creator□
dream of
treason
RAT breadth
breasts
RAU break up
break-up
dream up
erratum
RAZ organza
RBA Arabian
Brabham
drybeat
RBB crybaby
cry-baby
RBC arabica
Brubeck
try back
RBD tribade
tribady
RBE crabbed
cribbed
driblet
grabbed
grubber
problem
RBL cribble
Drabble
dribble
grabble
prabble
proball
wrybill
RBN armband
prebend
proband
probang
probing
tribune□
RBR bribery
RBS arabise
Arabist
RBT probate
probity
tribute
RBZ arabize
RCA crucial
fractal
Grecian
trochal
Wroclaw
RCD brocade
precede
RCE a rocket
bracken
bracket
cracked
cracker
cricket
crickey
crochet
crocket
erecter
proceed
trachea
tracker
tricked
tricker
trochee
trucker
wracked
wrecked
wrecker
RCF crucify
RCI breccia
crack it
Crackit
cricoid
RCL crackle
crackly
Dracula
erectly
freckle
freckly
grackle
grockle
prickle
prickly
trickle
truckle
RCM drachma
RCN Arachne
bracing
iracund
tracing
RCO crack on
erector
precook
proctor
tractor
RCP precept
triceps
RCR dry-cure
grocery
procure
tracery
tricorn
RCS precast
precess
precise
process
tricksy
RCU crack up
Proclus
RCZ Grecize
RDA Bradman
graddan
gradual
Trudeau
RDC Art Deco
Cradock
predict
produce
product
traduce
RDE Bradlee
Bradley
Bridges
Bridget
bridled
dredger
trodden
RDG prodigy
RDI Freddie
Prydain
trade in
trade-in
RDK Brodsky
RDL crudely
gradely
griddle
RDN erodent
grading
gradini
prudent
trading
trident
uridine
RDO trade on
RDR prudery
RDS iridise
prudish
RDT aridity
credits
crudity
erudite
gradate
predate
RDU iridium
trade up
RDW bradawl
cry down
RDZ iridize
REA arsenal
creedal
freeman
Friedan
Trueman
REC urgency
REE breeder
briefed
creeper
dry-eyed
freebee
freemen
freezer
grieved
griever
ordered
praeses
REI Armenia
arsenic
Artemis
freebie
freesia
troelie
true rib
uraemia
uraemic
REL briefly
cruelly
greenly
orderly
REN freeing
orleans□
Orléans
REO freedom
praetor
treetop
REP pre-empt
RER arrears
RET arietta
ariette
cruelty
Trieste
REU Croesus
dried up
dried-up
fraenum
RFC orifice
preface
prefect
proface
RFD prefade
RFE crofter
draftee
drifter
grafter
proffer
trifler
trifles
RFI griffin□
traffic
trefoil
RFL armfuls
gruffly
profile
truffle
urnfuls
RFM Profumo
RFN profane
RFO dry-foot
griffon
RFR preform
triform
RFS profess
profuse
RFT profits
RGA frogman
grogram
program
trigram
Uruguay
RGD brigade
tragedy
RGE cragged
dragnet
drugged
drugget
trigger
RGF frig off
RGI Brighid
Broglie
druggie
RGL draggle
fragile
gregale
wriggle
wriggly
RGM Mrs Gamp
origami
RGN brigand
oregano
origins
orogeny
progeny
RGO dragoon
E-region
Grigson
RGR Gregory
RGT frigate
RGU drag out
RHA archway
Brahman
Orphean
RHE orphrey

RHI archaic
RHL armhole
dry hole
RHM Grahame
RHN prehend
RHR archery
orchard
try hard
RHU Orpheus
RHV archive
RIA arrival
artisan
orbital
ordinal
RIE arbiter
armiger
braided
brained
broiler
bruised
bruiser
cruiser
drained
drainer
fruiter
grained
groined
orbiter
praises
trailer
trained
trainee
trainer
RIH freight
Mr Right
RII Craigie
druidic
prairie
RIL article
braille□
frailly
O'Reilly
RIO Orbison
train on
traitor
try it on
RIS traipse
RIT artiste
frailty
Orvieto
RIU Troilus
Ursinus
RJC project
traject
RKE trekker
RKI Prakrit
RKN broking
Erskine
RLA Uralian
RLC armlock
frolics
prelacy
prelect
RLD prelude
preludi
RLE Aral Sea
drilled
frilled
trolley
RLF pro-life
RLG orology
trilogy
urology
RLI trellis
RLM prelims
RLN dry land
ere long
erelong
Ireland
praline
proline
prolong
RLO trollop
RLS armless
artless
braless
RLT prelate
RLY trilbys
RMA grammar
gremial
tramway
trumeau
RMB Grimsby
RMC grimace
primacy
RMD bromide
RME Bramley
Bremner
Bromley
crammed
crammer
cramped
crimped
crimper
crumpet
drummer
grommet
grummet
krimmer
premier
trammel
trampet
trimmed
trimmer
trommel
trumpet
RMF from off
RMI Aramaic
Brummie
drumlin
gremlin
kremlin
Tremain
RMK Gromyko
RML bramble□
brambly
crimple
crumble
crumbly
crumple
drumble
frumple
grimily
grumble
grumbly
primely
primula
trample
tremble
trembly
tremolo
Trimble
RMN Art Monk
bromine
crimina
dromond
framing
Grimond
priming
RMO crampon
crimson
RMP Mrs Mopp
RMR primary
RMS premise
premiss
promise
RMT cremate
eremite
primate
promote
RMU brimful
brumous
drum out
frame-up
from out
grampus
premium
trump up
RMV premove
RNA Brendan
Brennan
brinjal
cranial
frontal
grandad
Iranian
Uranian
RNC Cranach
Orinoco
tranect
wryneck
RND Granada
Grenada
grenade
RNE Arundel
branded
brander
Branwen
brinded
bringer
Bronwen
bronzed
Brynner
Cranmer
cringer
drinker
drunken
Erinyes
Frances
fringed
fringes
fronted
grandee
granted
grantee
Grendel
grinder
grunter
orangey
Prancer
printed
printer
pronged
tranced
trinket
wringer
wronged
wronger
RNG Branagh
Bronagh
Iron Age
RNH branchy
bronchi
broncho
crunchy
Frenchy
tranche
RNI araneid
bring in
crinoid
drink in
Francis
Frankie
frantic
grannie
prenzie
Princip
trannie
transit
trenail
RNL brantle
brindle
Brundle
crankle
cringle
crinkle
crinkly
crunkle
frankly
frenula
grandly
granule
gruntle
pronely
trindle
trundle
wrangle
wrinkle
wrinkly
wrongly
RNM grandma
RNN droning
ironing
pruning
urinant
RNO Branson
bring on
broncos
Bronson
drongos
eryngos
front on
fronton
grantor
princox
pronaoi
transom
Trenton
RNP grandpa
RNR granary
iron ore
trinary
urinary
RNS brinish
crinose
dryness
ironise
wryness
RNT bring to
crenate
crinate
crinite
drink to
e re nata
granite
pronate
prone to
pronota
trinity□
uranite
urinate
RNU bren gun□
bring up
cranium
drink up
iron out
pronoun
uranium
urinous
wrong 'un
RNZ ironize
ROA areolae
ortolan
ROE brooder
Brookes

Words marked □ can also be spelled with an initial capital letter

crooked
crooner
cruores
cry over
grooved
proofed
triolet
trooper
ROH brioche
ROI drookit
troolie
ROL croodle
ROO ariosos
arroyos
brood on
ROR armoire
armoury
ROS Brooks's
ROT Ariosto
prior to
RPA cryptal
RPC prepack
RPE Crippen
cropped
cropper
droplet
drop-net
dropped
dropper
grapnel
gripped
gripper
prophet
trapped
trapper
triplet
tripper
wrapped
wrapper
RPF a rip-off
drop off
RPG propage
RPH Arapaho
RPI cryptic
erepsin
graphic
prepaid
trophic
trypsin
tryptic
RPL aripple
cripple
grapple
propyla
Tripoli
tripple
RPN draping
griping
prepone
propane
propend
propone
trepang

RPO cryptos
gryphon□
krypton
trip hop
RPR drapery
drip-dry
gropers
prepare
Tripura
RPS prepose
propose
tropism
RPU crap out
drop out
dropout
drop-out
Gropius
trip out
RPZ trapeze
RQE briquet
croquet
prequel
RQI croquis
RRA orarian
RRG prurigo
RRM trireme
RRO Brer Fox
RRT pro rata
prorate
RSA Brassai
cristae
crustae
crystal□
Frisian
Grisham
trishaw
Tristan
RSC trisect
RSD crusade
preside
prosody
RSE brisken
brisket
brushed
brusher
crashed
cresset
crested
crosier
crushed
crusher
Dresden
dressed
dresser
freshen
fresher
freshet
Fresnel
frisker
frosted
Orestes
Presley
pressed

Prestel®
prosper
tressed
tresses
trussed
trusser
trusted
trustee
truster
wrester
RSF prosify
RSG presage
RSI brassie
Brescia
Crispin
drastic
dress in
eristic
Praslin
pressie
prosaic
prussic
trust in
trysail
RSL briskly
bristle
bristly
crassly
crisply
crossly
dry-salt
freshly
gristle
gristly
grossly
pre-sell
prosily
trestle
wrestle
RSM irksome
presume
trisomy
RSN arising
Krishna
present
RSO aristos
bristol□
Bristow
Cresson
dry-shod
erosion
frescos
frisson
grass on
Grissom
press on
Preston
prestos
RSR erasure
RST irisate
RSU brush up
brush-up
brusque

Crassus
dress up
Erasmus
friseur
frustum
grass up
gross up
press-up
pre-stun
RSV erosive
RTA Brittan
fretsaw
protean□
RTC erotica
protect
RTE Britten
brothel
brother
dratted
Eritrea
fritter
gritter
pretzel
trotter
written
RTF brutify
frutify
gratify
RTG protégé
RTI arctoid
Britain
protein
write in
RTK Gretzky
Trotsky
RTL brattle
brittle
brittly
crotala
irately
prattle
tritely
RTM Tritoma
RTN Aretino
bruting
gratiné
grating
orotund
prating
pretend
tritone
writing
RTO Britpop
grottos
oration
RTR friture
oratory
preterm
urethra
RTS British
brutish
protest
protist

RTT write to
RTU fretful
Grotius
Proteus
tritium
trot out
write up
write-up
RTX pretext
RUA arousal
traumas
RUC frounce
graunch
trounce
RUD grounds
RUE arguses
aroused
grouped
grouper
grouser
trouper
trouser
RUH brought
draught
drought
fraught
grouchy
wrought
RUI groupie
Proudie
RUL proudly
trouble
RUN arguing
RUO croûton
RUP triumph
Triumph®
RUS Irkutsk
RUT arcuate
RUU arduous
RVA drive at
gravlax
trivial
RVC crevice
privacy
RVD bravado
provide
RVE bravoes
preview
RVI drive-in
prevail
travail
RVK provoke
RVL bravely
gravely
privily
travels
RVN craving
crivens
driving
prevene
prevent
provine
Trevino

Words marked □ can also be spelled with an initial capital letter

RVR bravery
bravura
gravure
proverb
RVS previse
Prévost
proviso
provost
RVT brevity
gravity
private
privity
privy to
prove to
RVU trivium
RWA crewman
crowbar
growl at
RWE brawler
browned
browser
crawler
Crawley
crowded
Crowley
drowned
growler
prowler
trawler
RWF draw off
RWI brownie□
RWL cry wolf
grow old
RWN brewing
crowing
drawing
growing
RWO draw hoe
Erewhon
frown on
RWR artwork
brewery
drawers
froward
RWS pre-wash
prowess
RWT drawn to
frowsty
RWU crewcut
crew-cut
drawn up
draw out
grown-up
RXA Wrexham
RXM proximo
RYN army ant
greying
preying
RYO Croydon
RYR Gruyère
prayers
RYS greyish
RYU Dreyfus

preyful
trayful
RZE brazier
crazies
crozier
Frazier
frizzed
grazier
Prizren
RZI prezzie
RZL crazily
drizzle
drizzly
frazzle
frizzle
grizzle
grizzly
RZN Arizona
crazing
grazing
SAA as far as
assagai
Isfahan
Tswanas
SAC askance
SAE ashamed
assayer
escaped
escapee
escaper
V-shaped
Y-shaped
SAI ascarid
Asiatic
askaris
astatic
Islamic
SAL assault
Israeli
Osmanli
usually
SAN ascaunt
SAR Astaire
SAT esparto
SBR Ashbery
SCA asocial
SCI psychic
SCO psychos
SCP usucapt
SCU psych up
SDM isodoma
SDR Isadora
Isadore
Isidora
Isidore
SDW Ashdown
SEA assegai
SEC essence
SEE Essenes
isoetes
SEG asperge
SEI ascesis
ascetic

C S Lewis
usher in
SEL Estella
Estelle
SEM osteoma
SES asperse
SEU osseous
SFO as of now
SFR Ashford
SGA Asa Gray
SGO a sign of
SHA escheat
SHE isohyet
SHL asphalt
SHU ischium
isthmus
SIE assizes
SII ascidia
aspidia
aspirin
SIL ossicle
SIO Eskimos
Ustinov
SIR ostiary
SJK as a joke
SJR Esbjerg
SLE psalter
SLM asylums
SLN asklent
Asplund
SLO T S Eliot
SLS use less
useless
SLT isolate
SME Ishmael
SMR Ostmark
SNC asinico
SNE asunder
SNM isonomy
tsunami
SNN asinine
SNQ p's and q's
SNU using-up
SOC a sconce
SOD Osmonds
SOE ask over
SOI Estonia
osmosis
osmotic
SON astound
Osborne
SOR L S Lowry
SOS espouse
SPE asepses
SPI asepsis
aseptic
SRA a scream
estreat
SRB ascribe
escribe
SRC astrict
ostraca
ostrich

SRD astride
SRE usurper
SRK ostraka
SRL as a rule
SRN astrand
G-string
tsarina
usuring
SRO tsardom
SRP estrepe
SRS tsarism
tsarist
SSA as usual
STA as a team
STP isotope
isotopy
SUA oscular
SUE assumed
assured
assurer
SUG assuage
SUN asquint
SUO escudos
SUR esquire□
estuary
ossuary
T-square
SUT Asquith
SUU osculum
SXA asexual
SYT A S Byatt
TAC attacca
TAE atlases
stealer
steamed
steamer
strayed
strayer
TAG at large
strange
TAH attaché
TAI Athalia
ptyalin
steamie
stearic
stearin
TAL at fault
at table
St Paul's
TAN at pains
attaint
TAO attaboy
ethanol
TAP strappy
TAS Strauss
TAT Atlanta
stealth□
straits
TAU steam up
stratum
stratus
TBE stabber
stubbed

TBI atebrin
TBL stubble
stubbly
TBN stibine
TBO at a blow
TBT Stibitz
TBU stub out
TCA stick at
TCB stick by
TCE stacked
stacker
sticker
TCI stichic
stick in
TCL stickle
TCM Atacama
TCO stichoi
stick-on
stuccos
stuck on
TCT stick to
TCU stack up
stick up
stick-up
stock up
stuck up
stuck-up
TDE studded
studied
studies
TDN student
TDO studios
TDU stadium
TEC at peace
stretch
TEE steeped
steepen
steerer
St Leger
strewer
uttered
TEH Utrecht
TEI St Denis
sthenic
TEK streaky
TEL Othello
steeple
steeply
utterly
TEM it seems
streamy
TEP attempt
TER at heart
TES atheise
atheism
atheist
at least
TET strette
stretti
stretto
strewth
TEZ atheize
TFE staffer

Words marked □ can also be spelled with an initial capital letter

stiffen
stifled
stifler
stuffed
TFI stiffie
stuff it
TFL stiffly
TGA stigmas
Stygian
TGE stagger
TGL stagily
TGN staging
THL at a halt
THN etching
itching
THO itch for
TIA ethical
stoical
strigae
TID St Kilda
TIE at times
attired
stained
stainer
Staines
Steiger
Steinem
Steiner
stoiter
striker
striped
TIG strings
stringy
TII strigil
strip in
TIL a trifle
staidly
utricle
Utrillo
TIM atriums
TIO stridor
TIS at first
TIT striate
TKU stoke up
TLA Italian
stellar
TLE atelier
stalked
stilted
stollen
TLG otology
TLI otalgia
TLL stalely
TLM Ptolemy
TLO Stilton
TLS at a loss
stylise
stylish
stylist
utilise
TLT athlete
otolith
stylite
utility
TLZ stylize
utilize
TMC stomach
TME stammer
stamped
stamper
stemlet
stemmed
stumped
stumper
stymied
TMI ethmoid
TML stimuli
stumble
TMN atamans
etymons
stamens
stamina
TMO stamnoi
stemson
TMS atomise
atomism
itemise
TMT stomata
TMU stump up
TMZ atomize
itemize
TNA Etonian
TNB stand by
stand-by
TNE FT Index
Stanley
Stengel
stinged
stinger
stinker
stinted
stinter
stonker
stunned
stunner
stunted
TNG at one go
TNI stand in
stand-in
stannic
stencil
utensil
TNL atingle
stonily
TNM stone me!
TNN at an end
atoning
stoning
TNO stand on
stingos
TNT stand to
TNU stand up
stand-up
sten gun□
stun gun
TOA ottoman□
TOE stooker
stooped
TOH atrophy
strophe
TOI atropin
etiolin
Otto Dix
St Louis
strobic
TON at point
St John's
TOP stroppy
TOS at worst
TPA stopgap
stop-gap
utopian□
TPE stapler
Stephen
stepper
stopper
TPF step off
stop off
stop-off
stupefy
TPI styptic
TPL stipple
stipule
stopple
TPN stipend
stoping
TPS at a push
TPU step out
TRA eternal□
stare at
sternal
TRC attract
TRD at grade
TRE otaries
starken
starlet
started
starter
starved
stirpes
stirred
stirrer
storied
stories
sturmer□
TRG storage
TRH starchy
TRI starlit
start in
steroid
TRL starkly
startle
sterile
sternly
TRN staring
styrene
uterine
TRO stardom
start on
stereos
TRR stir-fry
TRS at press
TRT attrite
iterate
TRU start up
start-up
sternum
stir out
stirrup
store up
yttrium
TRX ataraxy
TRY storeys
TSA etesian
TSI stushie
TSM stasima
TSO atishoo
TSU at issue
TTC statics
TTE stotter
stutter
TTL stately
TTN statant
TTO station
stetson
TTR Ataturk
Atatürk
stature
TTT statute
TTV stative
TUA strumae
TUC staunch
TUE attuned
stouten
strudel
TUI St Lucia
TUL stoutly
TUT attuite
TVE stovies
TVN Stevens
TVS atavism
TWC at twice
TWG stowage
TWL Attwell
TWN stowing
TWR at a word
athwart
steward
Stewart
TYF stay off
TYU stay out
stay put
UAA curaçao□
cutaway
Gujarat
Mubarak
Puranas
put away
rub away
run away
runaway
UAC surance
UAD mutanda
UAE lunated
mutagen
sugared
UAH nuraghi
UAI lunatic
puparia
Sudanic
tutania
UAK autarky
rusalka
UAL aurally
buyable
curable
ducally
dupable
durable
durably
fugally
humanly
jurally
mutable
mutably
rulable
rurally
tunable
tunably
UAN lucarne
Sukarno
Susanna
UAO bugaboo
curator
Euratom
fugatos
fumados
rubatos
run amok
turacos
UAR Sumatra
UAS Judaise
Judaism
UAT Bugatti
mulatta
mulatto
Suharto
UAU buy a pup
subaqua
UAZ Judaize
UBA bugbear
bum-boat
cudbear
gunboat
outbrag
sunbeam
UBB rum baba
UBC buy back
buy-back
cut back
cutback
jumbuck
Lubbock
outback
put back

Words marked □ can also be spelled with an initial capital letter

UBE bubbles❑
bumbler
fumbler
humbled
jumbled
mumbled
mumbler
tumbled
tumbler
tumbrel
UBG Burbage
lumbago
UBI Cumbria
gumboil
tumbril
UBK sunbake
UBL quibble
sunbelt
UBN Burbank
curbing
gubbins
husband
numbing
rubbing
turband
turbine
turbond
UBO gumboot
pueblos
UBR Bunbury
Hubbard
Humbert
Lubbers
numbers❑
rubbery
Sudbury
sunbird
sunburn
turbary
UBS furbish
kurbash
rubbish
surbase
UBT mudbath
UBU bulbous
UBZ bumbaze
UCA Funchal
UCD suicide
UCE bunched
butcher
hunched
juncoes
lurcher
muncher
muscles
punched
quacker
quicken
succeed
UCI quickie
UCL furcula
out cold
Purcell

quackle
quickly❑
UCM outcome
succumb
UCN buccina
Puccini
Vulcano
UCO nuncios
outcrop
punctos
UCR muscari
Runcorn
UCS nutcase
outcast
put case
success
succuss
UCT furcate
Guscott
Succoth
sulcate
UCU fulcrum
punch-up
Quechua
succour
UCV muscovy
UDA cut dead
quadrat
subdual
sundial
UDC burdock
gun deck
Murdoch
ruddock
subduct
sundeck
UDE curdled
fuddled
huddled
hundred
hurdler
hurdles
muddied
muddled
muddler
rundlet
subdued
UDF mundify
UDI quadric
quids in
UDL Dundalk
muddily
quiddle
ruddily
UDM ducdame
quidams
UDN budding
burdens
duodena
funding
guiding
mundane
pudding

UDO bundook
gumdrop
Muldoon
outdoor
UDR duddery
Kundera
outdare
UDS Kurdish
tun-dish
UDT Luddite
outdate
UDU humdrum
UDV sub divo
UDW cut down
gun down
put down
putdown
put-down
rub down
rub-down
run down
rundown
run-down
sundown
UEA funeral
humeral
Juvenal
Luce Bay
numeral
ruderal
tutelar
tutenag
UEB rudesby
ruled by
UEC pudency
quiesce
tumesce
UED pudenda
UEE murexes
Nureyev
quieten
UEI auxesis
Dunedin
Eugenia
eugenic
Eugenie
Eugénie
Eusebio
numeric
Queenie
subedit
suberic
suberin
UEK Zuleika
UEL aureola
aureole
cure-all
nucelli
queenly
queerly
quietly
rubella
rubeola

UEM museums
UEN lucerne❑
UEO Auberon
dukedom
fuse box
pukekos
rules OK
tupelos
tuxedos
UEP Euterpe
UER Auxerre
UES eupepsy
UET aureate
burette
curette
fumette
fumetti
lunette
puberty
UEU bureaus
bureaux
duteous
humerus
museful
quietus
rule out
tuneful
tune out
UFA Gulf War
mudflap
mudflat
ruffian
UFC outface
suffice
surface❑
UFE muffled
muffler
quaffer
ruffled
UFI buff-tip
funfair
surfeit
UFL buffalo❑
cupfuls
huffily
jugfuls
mugfuls
outfall
puffily
Suffolk
tubfuls
zuffoli
UFN puffing
surfing
UFO buffoon
buy from
outflow
outfoot
UFR gunfire
UFS huffish
subfusc
suffuse
sunfast

sunfish
UFU puff out
turf out
UGA burglar
Jungian
lunge at
UGE bungler
burgher
juggler
outgoes
UGG luggage
UGI fungoid
UGL nutgall
UGN bugging
bulging
fudging
fulgent
Huygens
juggins
mugging
muggins
pugging
pungent
purging
sugging
surging
tugging
UGO burgeon
dudgeon
dungeon
gudgeon
murgeon
outgrow
surgeon
UGR Hungary
surgery
UGS Burgess
suggest
UGT nuggety
Vulgate
UGU budge up
bulghur
fungous
UHA bushman
UHB hushaby
UHE Buchner
Büchner
UHF push off
UHG nurhags
UHI fuchsia
Guthrie
Pushkin
Rushdie
UHL mushily
UHM Duchamp
UHN Cushing
euphony
gushing
Kuching
pushing
ruching
rushing
UHO cushion

push for
push-rod
rush job
UHR futhark
futhork
Kushiro
outhire
run hard
UHS duchess
UHU push out
quahaug
UIA cubical
Guri Dam
Huainan
kufiyah
musical
puritan
rufiyaa
UID Lucinda
UIE culices
jubilee
juniper
Jupiter
Lucifer
murices
quoiter
UIG bubinga
UIH rupiahs
UII bulimia
bulimic
juridic
rub it in
Tunisia
UIL audible
audibly
auricle
cubicle
cuticle
fusible
fusilli
humidly
lucidly
Lucilla
Lucille
luridly
tumidly
tunicle
UIN Juliana
Luciano
UIO auditor
humidor
put it on
rubicon□
UIR Lumière
UIS furioso□
jujitsu
ju-jitsu
UIT buy into
cut into
dubiety
run into
UIU curious
dubious

dutiful
furious
UJA Tudjman
UJB Punjabi
UJC subject
UJI subjoin
UJR suo jure
UJS outjest
UJV sub Jove
UKA buckram
muskrat
UKE buckled
buckler
Buckley
buckoes
huckles
ruckled
suckler
turkies
Turkmen
UKF bunk off
suck off
Turkify
UKL bulkily
cuckold
duskily
huskily
luckily
murkily
muskily
sulkily
UKN ducking
dunking
fucking
hulking
lurking
quaking
Turkana
UKO Lucknow
UKR Dunkirk
hunkers
Quakers
suck dry
UKS puckish
Turkish
UKT Burkitt
Sukkoth
UKU bulk out
luck out
ULA nuclear
outleap
Pullman
ULB Lualaba
lullaby
ULC bullock□
gunlock
mullock
suo loco
ULD nuclide
Our Lady
ULE builder
bullied
dueller

fueller
guilder
Guillem
gullies
outlier
purlieu
queller
quilted
quilter
sullied
wurlies
ULF nullify
pull off
qualify
ULG sullage
ULI build in
built-in
mullein
nucleic
purloin
ULK sunlike
ULL surlily
ULM sublime
ULN bus lane
curling
dulling
dunlins
euglena
furlong
hurling
Jutland
lulling
mulling
outline
pulling
purline
ULO build on
bulldog
bullion
duellos
full-hot
mullion
nucleon
outlook
pull for
ULR butlery
cutlery
dullard
mudlark
ULS Auslese
bugloss
bullish
cutlass
dualism
gutless
hueless
outlast
publish
sunless
ULT bullets
duality
nullity
quality

sublate
ULU build up
build-up
built-up
Bull Run
full-out
nucleus
out loud
pull out
pull-out
ULV outlive
ULY gulleys
pulleys
wurleys
UMC hummock
UMD outmode
UMF mummify
UMG rummage
UMI turmoil
UML bummalo
rummily
UMN augment
humming
hutment
Kunming
mumming
summons
UMR mummery
nummary
summary
summery
UMS Burmese
outmost
quamash
surmise
UMT gummata
summate
UMV outmove
UNA quintal
quintan
quondam
UNC dunnock
furnace
guanaco
UNE Burnley
duendes
funnier
funnies
quintet
turnkey
turn red
UNF turn off
turn-off
UNH Huang Ho
UNI quantic
Quentin
Quintin
UNL funnily
Gunnell
sunnily
UNM outname
surname
UNN burning

cunning
guanine
punning
quinine
quinone
running
turning
UNO burn for
guangos
quangos
Quinton
runnion
turn for
UNR Gunners
gunnery
gurnard
nunnery
quinary
runners
UNS burnish
fulness
furnish
nunnish
Sunnism
UNT Burnett
Kuznets
quinate
ruinate
UNU burnous
quantum
ruinous
turn out
turnout
turn-out
UOA aurorae
auroras
humoral
mucosae
UOE buy over
cut open
out-over
put over
run over
Tupolev
tutored
UOH aurochs
UOI bubonic
bucolic
dulosis
eulogia
Ludovic
out of it
UOP Rudolph
UOR out-owre
rumours
UOS autopsy
UOT put on to
UOU Autocue
UPA outplay
outpray
UPC auspice
mudpack
outpace

suspect
UPE guppies
jump-jet
outpeer
rump-fed
rumpled
UPF bump off
jump off
jump-off
pulpify
pump off
yuppify
UPH Ruapehu
UPI bumpkin
culprit
dumpbin
pumpkin
UPL bumpily
duopoly
jumpily
lumpily
pulpily
UPN cupping
pumping
suspend
vulpine
UPO subplot
UPR guipure
Humphry
Huppert
purport
support
suspire
UPS lumpish
outpost
purpose
run past
suppose
surpass
UPT cuspate
turpeth
UPU lump sum
outpour
pulpous
pump out
sulphur
surplus
UPW Quapaws
UQA cumquat
kumquat
URA quartan
surreal
URC currach
Kubrick
Lucrece
URD outride
URE burrhel
furrier
guarded
hurried
quarrel
quarter
quartet

URF putrefy
URG curragh
outrage
URH hurrahs
URI murrain
quartic
URL burrell
Durrell
puerile
URM supreme
suprême
supremo
URN currant
current
furring
guarani
Guaraní
outrank
purring
URO guerdon
gunroom
murrion
quartos
run riot
sunroof
URP guy-rope
URS bulrush
cuirass
outrush
querist
sub rosa
sucrose
sunrise
tutress
URT burrito
cuprite
cut-rate
outrate
quorate
URU cuprous
hurry up
URZ guereza
USA Dunstan
fur seal
outspan
outstay
Russian
Tuesday
USC tussock
USD outside
subside
subsidy
USE guessed
guesser
Munster
Münster
outstep
punster
pursuer
quashed
quester
USF Russify
USI burst in

Hussain
Hussein
lugsail
outsail
pursuit
quassia
subsoil
USL Bussell
fussily
outsell
Russell
USM fulsome
subsume
USN cuisine
cursing
cussing
Hudson's
nursing
pulsing
USO bus stop
fusspot
fuss-pot
gumshoe
gunshot
mug shot
mugshot
questor
sunspot
USR bursary
cursory
hussars
Husserl
nursery
tussore
USS subsist
UST Hussite
pulsate
russety
USU gussy up
suss out
USV cursive
tussive
USZ outsize
UTA austral
but that
dustman
fustian
lustral
muntjac
muntjak
nuptial
quetzal
quittal
suntrap
UTC buttock
Eustace
futtock
justice
UTD custody
UTE bustier
bustler
cup-tied
curtsey

cuttoes
further
hustler□
lustres
nut-tree
quitter
rustler
Surtees
Surtsey
UTF justify
Mustafa
UTI Austria
curtail
curtain
dustbin
put to it
sustain
UTL cuittle
ductile
dustily
fustily
lustily
mustily
nuttily
pustule
rustily
UTM customs
run time
UTN bunting
butt end
buttons
cutting
dusting
hunting
hurting
Justina
Justine
jutting
munting
mustang□
nutting
ousting
putting
quoting
rusting
subtend
suiting
sultana
tufting
UTO auction
duettos
hunt for
just now
ruction
suction
tuition
UTR austere
bustard□
buttery
culture
custard□
multure
mustard

nurture
outturn
punters
rupture
tuatara
vulture
UTS cultish
cultism
cultist
eustasy
quite so
runtish
ruttish
UTT guttate
UTU hunt out
hunt's-up
hurtful
lustful
putt out
UTV furtive
UTX subtext
UUA augural
jugular
lunular
tubular
tumular
Zulu War
UUB suburbs
UUD Burundi
UUE augurer
fucuses
UUH pupunha
UUI tubulin
UUK Fukuoka
UUL bubukle
UUO Audubon
Kutuzov
lucumos
put upon
put-upon
UUT Augusta
put up to
UUU cumulus
queue up
tumulus
UUY ouguiya
UVE purview
surview
UVL suavely
UVN curving
pulvini
UVR culvert
Guevara
quavery
quivery
subvert
UVT outvote
suavity
UVU fulvous
UVV survive
UWA outwear
UWC outwick
UWE outweep

Words marked □ can also be spelled with an initial capital letter

UWL gunwale
run wild
UWN outwent
outwing
UWR bulwark
lugworm
outward
outwork
outworn
sunward
UWS put wise
sunwise
UWT hum with
out with
outwith
run with
UYA juryman
Ruby Wax
UYE jurymen
UYG quayage
UYI jury rig
UYN buoyant
burying
Guiyang
Luoyang
Lutyens
UZE guzzler
puzzled
puzzler
quizzer
quizzes
UZF buzz off
UZI muezzin
UZL fuzzily
muzzily
UZN buzzing
UZR buzzard
subzero
VAO aviator
VBR Avebury
VCD avocado
VCE evacuee
evicted
VCT evocate
VDC oviduct
VDN evident
VDT avidity
VFR oviform
VGO Avignon
VIA ovoidal
VIE avoided
avoider
TV Times
VLA avellan
VLN Evil One
VLT evolute
ovulate
VLY evil eye
VNE avenger
evangel
eventer
VNN evening
VNO even now
Ivanhoe
VNS evanish
VNU even out
VOI TV movie
VRA ovarian
overeat
overfar
overlap
overlay
overman
overpay
overtax
VRC avarice
overact
VRE overfed
overget
overnet
overred
overren
oversee
overset
oversew
VRG average
over age
over-age
VRI overbid
overhit
overlie
VRL overall
over-all
overfly
overply
overtly
VRO overjoy
oversow
overtop
VRR overarm
VRS overuse
VRT Everett
evirate
VRU overbuy
overdue
overrun
VRW overawe
VSA Avestan
Evesham
VSI Avestic
VSO evasion
VSV evasive
VTO ovation
VTT evitate
WAA swear at
WAB swear by
WAE swearer
sweater
WAI swear in
WAT swear to
WBE swabber
WBL twibill
WBT two bits
WCA Zwickau
WDE two deep
WDL swaddle
twaddle
twaddly
twiddle
twiddly
WDS Swedish
WDW two-down
WEB owned by
WEE sweeper
sweeten
tweeter
WEF sweet FA
WEI sweetie
WEL sweetly
tweedle
WEO sweet on
WFL swiftly
twafald
twofold
WGA own goal
swagman
WGE swagger
twiggen
WGI swaggie
WHL Swahili
WHN two-hand
WIE awaited
WJM Iwo Jima
WKN awaking
WLE dweller
swelled
swelter
swollen
twilled
WLI dwell in
WLK owl-like
WLO dwell on
Gwalior
swallow
WLS awnless
WLT twelfth
WLY Gwillym
WME swamped
swimmer
WND Gwynedd
WNE swanker
Swansea
swinger
twinned
twin-set
WNF swan off
WNG swindge
WNI swing it
WNJ Gwangju
WNL dwindle
swindle
swingle
twinkle
Zwingli
WNN twining
WNO Swindon
WNS swinish
WNT Gwenyth
Gwyneth
owing to
WOH P W Botha
WOO swoop on
WPE swapper
WPN swiping
WRE dwarfed
dwarves
swarded
swerver
twirler
WRH swarthy
WRO aware of
WSE swasher
Swisses
twisted
twister
two-step
WSM awesome
twosome
WTE swathed
swatter
swither
twitter
WTH twitchy
WTI Swithin
WTL twattle
WTM two-time
WTN two-tone
WUL awfully
WUT own up to
WWR awkward
WYN swaying
WZL swizzle
twizzle
XAL axially
XAS exhaust
expanse
XCL exactly
XCN exscind
XCR exocarp
XCT execute
XDA exedrae
XDN exuding
oxidant
XDR exoderm
XDS oxidase
oxidise
XDT exudate
oxidate
XDZ oxidize
XEP excerpt
XES expense
XGM exogamy
XGN exigent
XGT exegete
XIC extinct
XIE excited
exciter
expired
XII exhibit
XIO exciton
excitor
XIT expiate
XLA axillae
axillar
XLD exclude
explode
XLE exalted
exulted
XLI exclaim
explain
exploit
exult in
XLN explant
XLO Axelrod
oxblood
XLR explore
XLT axolotl
XLV exclave
XML example
exempla
XMN examine
XNA Oxonian
XOA exposal
XOE exposed
XON expound
XOT Exmouth
XRA exurban
uxorial
XRC extract
XRD extrude
XRI exordia
exurbia
XRM extreme
XRS express
XRT exarate
excreta
excrete
XTC exotica
XTN oxytone
XUA excusal
XUE excused
XUG expunge
expurge
XVA exuviae
exuvial
YAA Aymaras
lyra-way
pyjamas
YAE by water
hyraces
hyraxes
Nykanen
YAI dynamic
hydatid
Hypatia
pyramid
pyramis
Sybaris
YAL gyrally
YAN tyranny
YAO by way of
dynamos
YAS synapse
YAT dynasty
YAU Pyramus

YAW Myfanwy
YBE bye-byes
YBL eyeball
symbols
YCO Pynchon
YCP syncope
YCR synchro
YDA Wyndham
YDL Tyndale
YDO eye-drop
YEA hymenal
Lyme Bay
Mycenae
YEC Eysenck
YEE typeset
YEG synergy
YEH Ayeesha
YEI mycelia
pyaemia
pyretic
pyrexia
YEK Lysenko
YEM lyceums
YEO hyperon
YER by heart
YET Lynette
YEU hyped up
YHA Pytheas
YHB by the by
YHE mynheer
YHI typhoid
YHL wych-elm
YHO typhoon
YHS mythise
YHU typhous
YHZ mythize
YIA cynical
Lycidas
lyrical
typical
YID myriads
YIE by times
cylices
pyrites
pyxides
YIG syringa
syringe
YIH by right
YII pyxidia
YIL Sybilla
YIN hygiene
YIT by birth
YIY WYSIWYG
YLB syllabi
YLI cycloid
hyaloid
myalgia
myalgic
myeloid
YLM myeloma
YLN cyclone
hyaline
YLP cyclops□
YLS cyclist
eyelash
eyeless
YLT hyalite
YMA pygmean
YMN Wyoming
YNA Myanmar
Nyanjas
YNB by and by
by-and-by
YND cyanide
hymnody
YNI hypnoid
lying-in
YNL dyingly
lyingly
vyingly
YNR gymnura
YNS by a nose
cyanise
gymnast
hymnist
kyanise
YNT cyanite
kyanite
YNZ cyanize
kyanize
YOA Sycorax
xylomas
zygomas
YOC by force
YOE hypogea
pyrogen
tyloses
tyrones
YOI hypoxia
hypoxic
mycosis
mycotic
pyloric
pyrosis
synovia
zygotic
zymotic
YON Cy Young
YOO tylopod
YOU pylorus
YOY hyponym
synonym
YPA lymphad
nymphal
YPE dyspnea
nymphet
YPN tympana
tympani
YPO symptom
YRA Cyprian
YRD hydride
YRI hydroid
pyrrhic□
YRL pyrrole
YRN hydrant
YRO Cypriot
YRR Nyerere
YRS cypress
YRT hydrate
YRU hydrous
YRY Aykroyd
YSA Ayeshah
YSI gym slip
YSO gym shoe
YSR eyesore
YTF mystify
YTI cyathia
Cynthia
YTL systole
YTN cystine
YTR mystery
YUI pyruvic
YUN by turns
YWL Tynwald
YWN eye-wink
YWR Aylward
YWS eyewash
ZES Izhevsk
ZGN tzigany
ZGU azygous
ZKE Ezekiel
ZLR Szilard
ZME tzimmes
ZMT azimuth
ZNS ozonise
ZNZ ozonize
ZRN azurine
czarina
ZTS azotise
ZTZ azotize
ZVE Azov Sea

8 letters – even

AAAA katakana
maharaja
Mahayana
Nataraja
pacarana
Ramayana
Yamagata
AAAD Nagaland
saraband
AAAE carapace
database
malaxate
paravane
Sarasate
AAAH calabash
Karabakh
AAAI calamari
Kalahari
Kawasaki
maharani
Mata Hari
Nagasaki
Varanasi
AAAK databank
AAAL pay a call
AAAM car alarm
AAAN say again
AAAO Fanagalo
Saramago
AAAR Karabair
AAAT cataract
AAAY Malagasy
AABE harambee
AABN Casaubon
AABS Barabbas
AACD balanced
valanced
AACN Jamaican
AACO Masaccio
AACR balancer
AACS Damascus
AADR marauder
AAEA habanera
karateka
Pasadena
AAED far ahead
AAEE Canarese
Gadarene
Japanese
Kanarese
Nazarene
AAEG lay an egg
AAEH Nazareth
AAEM Vanaheim
AAEN fava bean
AAEO jalapeño
Sarajevo
AAES managers
AAET parakeet
AAEX camaïeux
AAEY savagely
savagery
AAFN paraffin
AAGE harangue
AAGR Jahangir
AAHA barathea
AAHH Halakhah
AAHN marathon□
Ramadhan
AAHP rajaship
AAHR Mahathir
AAHS Caiaphas
AAIA Mahavira
AAID salaried
tamarind
AAIE banalise
banalize
calamine
canalise
canalize
faradise
faradize
Japanise
Japanize
laxative
lay aside
macarise
macarize
magazine
mala fide
nasalise
nasalize
Nazarite
paganise
paganize
palatine□

papalise
papalize
paradise□
parasite
sanative
AAIG damaging
garaging
managing
parading
ravaging
vacating
AAIH dahabieh
AAII hara-kiri
Paganini
Sabatini
AAIK tamarisk
AAIL malarial
palatial
AAIM fatalism
paganism
papalism
paradigm
samarium
Satanism
vanadium
AAIN Canadian
halation
Hawaiian
natation
par avion
taxation
vacation
AAIO palamino
AAIR cavalier
Daladier
AAIS Makarios
vagaries
AAIT fatalist
papalist
Satanist
AAIY banality
calamity
capacity
fatality
Macavity
nasality
rapacity
sagacity
salacity
AAKK Habakkuk
AAKN damaskin
AAKR Gavaskar
AAKY malarkey
AALE canaille
AALL parallel
AALN Van Allen
AALS eatables
manacles
AALX parallax
AALY Macaulay
AAMC marasmic
AAMS marasmus
AANH savannah□
AANN Manannan
AAOA Casanova
Maradona
parabola
paranoia
Saratoga
AAOB catacomb
AAOC paranoic
AAOD paranoid
say aloud
vagabond
AAOE Nakasone
parabole
sagamore
AAOG tag along
AAOI macaroni
AAON macaroon
parazoan
talapoin
AAOO Carabobo
Yamamoto
AAOR paramour
vavasour
AAOS lavaboes
AAOT day about
gad about
gadabout
lax about
layabout
mad about
marabout
AAOY lavatory
natatory
paradoxy
AAPR Jabalpur
AARG Taganrog
AARP Malaprop
AARS zamarras
zamarros
AASA Malaysia
AASC banausic
AASD harassed
AASH Manasseh
AASR Makassar
AATA Samantha
AATC basaltic
galactic
tac-au-tac
AATR varactor
AATY vacantly
AAUE Maja Nude
AAUO tapaculo
AAUT catapult
AAUY Paraguay
AAYE catalyse
paralyse
AAYT catalyst
AAZC Karadzic
AAZR kala-azar
ABAX jambeaux
ABAY Ian Brady
ABCE barbecue
ABCN barbican
ABDA Cambodia
ABDS Barbados
gambados
ABDY day by day
ABEK bad break
daybreak
ABEN dabble in
ramble on
ABES has-beens
ABIE war bride
ABIG babbling
baubling
dabbling
gabbling
gambling
garbling
marbling
rambling
ABIN Cambrian
ABKK Habbakuk
ABKN lambskin
ABLA Marbella
ABLC carbolic
ABNC carbonic
rabbinic
ABND rawboned
raw-boned
ABNS bambinos
ABNY lambency
ABOD bad blood
ABOH tarboosh
ABQE barbeque
ABRA Canberra
ABRC barbaric
ABRE jamboree
ABRH Hamburgh
ABRN Van Buren
ABRR jabberer
ABRT carburet
ABRY barberry
hagberry
waxberry
ABSE Barbusse
lambaste
ABSS iambuses
ABTD rabbeted
ABTN rabbit on
rambutan
ABTR rabbiter
ABTY rabbitry
ABUG faubourg
ABUH Vanbrugh
ABUS cambiums
ABZN Barbizon
ACAE calceate
ACAG Nanchang
ACAL catch-all
ACAO Marciano
ACAT bar chart
ACBX matchbox
ACCE fascicle
ACCL farcical
ACDC saccadic
ACDD bar-coded
ACDG watchdog
ACEF Van Cleef
ACEN pancheon
ACEO ranchero
ACES pancreas
ACEY patchery
ACFL fanciful
watchful
ACFR watch for
ACHM catch him
ACIE war crime
ACIG catching
hatching
matching
parching
watching
ACIK dabchick
ACIN sanction
ACIY patchily
sanctify
sanctity
ACLP parcel up
ACLR vascular
ACLS calculus
saccules
sacculus
ACLT Lancelot
ACLY rascally
ACMN fancy man
watchman
ACMS sarcomas
ACNA calcanea
vaccinia
ACNI calcanei
ACNL vaccinal
ACNO mancando
ACNR falconer
parcener
ACNT carcanet
sarcenet
ACNY falconry
nascency
ACOH waxcloth
ACOS tau cross
ACOT Bancroft
catch out
watch out
ACPE manciple
ACPN saucepan
ACRA calcaria
ACRE Sancerre
ACRT baccarat
ACSI Fascisti
narcissi
ACSS Caucasus
Fascists
Las Casas
mancuses
narcosis
ACTA Calcutta
ACTC narcotic
ACTD falcated

Words marked □ can also be spelled with an initial capital letter

ACUE farceuse
ACUG Taichung
ACUT lawcourt
pay court
ACWY hatchway
ADAD hard card
landward
ADAE baldpate
handmade
hard case
hardware
laid bare
landrace
maid-pale
mandrake
ADAH hard cash
ADAK aardvark
hand back
hardback
hardtack
laid back
laid-back
land bank
landmark
sandbank
ADAL handball
handrail
hardball
landfall
land-haul
landrail
ADAS landmass
ADAT handcart
sand-cast
ADAX bandeaux
ADAY landlady
ADBE laudable
mandible
ADBY laudably
ADCE Sadducee
ADCP handicap
ADCS caudices
ADDE hard edge
ADDH lah-di-dah
ADDY candidly
ADEL handbell
ADEM bad dream
daydream
Waldheim
ADEO San Diego
ADER Landseer
ADES baldness
handless
hardness
wardress
ADEY saddlery
ADGD bandaged
ADGN cardigan□
ADHE sandshoe
ADHP hardship
wardship
ADHR Kandahar
ADID yardbird

ADIE hand line
hard line
hardline
hard-line
land mine
land-mine
landside
ADIG dawdling
handling
Maudling
waddling
ADIH dandyish
land-fish
land with
sandwich□
ADIK baldrick
hand-pick
hard disk
ADIL handbill
landfill
land-girl
mandrill
sandhill
ADIM dandyism
ADIY tawdrily
ADKM zaddikim
ADKR Baedeker
ADLA sand flea
ADLE Candolle
hard-a-lee
ADLH Bardolph
Randolph
ADLN Magdalen
mandolin
ADLO gardyloo
ADLP handclap
landslip
ADLS Daedalus
ADLY Mandalay
ADMC pandemic
ADME Van Damme
ADMM cardamom
cardamum
ADMN bandsman
cardamon
handyman
ADMR mal de mer
ADMS mandamus
ADMY randomly
ADNA bandanna
gardenia
Sardinia
ADNC sardonic
ADND hardened
maddened
saddened
ADNE fan dance
pardon me
tap-dance
war dance
ADNL cardinal
eau de nil
ADNM laudanum

ADNO fandango
ADNR gardener
Gardiner
hardener
pardoner
ADNS sardines
ADNT hand-knit
ADNX sardonyx
ADNY maidenly
ADOA mandioca
ADOD hardwood
landlord
ADOE handsome
hard core
hard-core
wardrobe
ADOF aardwolf
hands off
hands-off
ADOI tandoori
ADOK handbook
handwork
hard rock
hard work
ADOM wardroom
ADON bawd-born
hand down
hard porn
laid down
ADOS ear drops
Vandross
ADOT handpost
ADOY hard copy
ADRA caldaria
ADRC sandarac
ADRD laddered
ADRL banderol
falderal
ADRN mandarin□
ADRO pander to
wanderoo
ADRP handgrip
ADRR panderer
wanderer
ADRY panderly
ADSK Gajdusek
ADTD caudated
ADTI banditti
ADTT hard at it
ADTY banditry
ADUE sand-dune
ADUF dandruff
handcuff
ADUG Sandburg
ADUK hard luck
ADUS handfuls
hand-outs
ADVE eau de vie
ADVR hand over
handover
ADVS Maldives
ADXS caudexes
AEAA Kalevala

Lake Tana
AEAD make hard
waveband
AEAE base rate
caretake
catenate
date rape
lacerate
macerate
makebate
make late
make pale
make safe
namesake
nametape
racemate
take care
AEAI Maserati®
AEAK bareback
cakewalk
face pack
pare back
take back
AEAL baseball
hate mail
make sail
AEAM date palm
date-palm
make warm
AEAP base camp
AEAS game laws
Rabelais
AEAT Davenant
make fast
take part
AEAY catenary
make easy
AEBD make a bed
water-bed
AEBE dateable
hateable
Lake Abbe
nameable
rateable
saleable
tameable
AEBG water bag
AEBS water bus
AEBW take a bow
AEBY rateably
saleably
AECA Valencia
AECE face-ache
AEDE Kate Adie
AEDP take a dip
AEDR calendar
calender
lavender
AEED male lead
pale-dead
take heed
AEEE same here
AEEK tape deck

Words marked □ can also be spelled with an initial capital letter

AEEL Bakewell
farewell
harebell
make well
rakehell
AEER cameleer
Kaieteur
AEES bareness
baseless
baseness
bateless
careless
dateless
faceless
fadeless
gameness
haleness
lameness
lateness
make less
maleness
maneless
nameless
paleness
rareness
safeness
sameness
saneness
tameness
vaneless
waveless
AEET basement
casement
easement
make neat
pavement
safe seat
AEFR cater for
eager for
AEFX James Fox
AEGD saw-edged
AEGO Lavengro
AEGS water gas
AEGY make ugly
AEHD Lake Chad
AEHF Zamenhof
AEHN make thin
water-hen
AEHP mateship
take ship
AEHT Take That
AEHW game show
AEIA Katerina
Lake Biwa
AEID cagebird
rare bird
rarefied
AEIE Bakelite®
capeline
facetiae
have life
lakeside
laterite
Madeline
maderise
maderize
make like
make time
mazelike
palewise
racemise
racemize
take fire
take five
take rise
tax exile
water ice
AEIG catering
havering❑
lacewing
Mafeking
make wing
papering
ravening
take wing
tapering
wakening
wavering
AEIH hamewith
make with
AEIK make sick
maverick
AEIL material
matériel
AEIM racemism
AEIN valerian❑
AEIS Galerius
AEIT facelift
maledict
race riot
AEIU Lake Kivu
AEIY Have Pity
make tidy
AEJB have a job
AEKV Malenkov
AELA camellia
AELD labelled
Lake Bled
lapelled
ravelled
AELE lamellae
patellae
AELG waterlog
AELN game plan
Magellan
AELO Waterloo
AELP make a lip
AELS patellas
AELT make flat
AELW make flow
AELY Bareilly
make play
Waverley
AEMN dalesman
salesman
waterman
AENG make snug
AENL maternal
paternal
AENO wade into
AENP take a nap
AENR taverner
AENT hazelnut
Max Ernst
wale knot
AEOD gatefold
make bold
make cold
make good
AEOE barebone
cakehole
gamesome
have done
have to be
make love
racemose
take home
take-home
take note
AEOF taper off
AEOK gamecock
havelock
lacework
laverock
Yale lock
Yale®lock
AEOM saleroom
tapeworm
waveform
AEON Cameroon
Cape Town
careworn
face down
fade down
make down
pare down
take down
wave down
AEOO kakemono
Lake Como
AEOR café noir
AEOS gazeboes
have-nots
ravenous
AEOT banewort
barefoot
gatepost
hanepoot
take root
AEOY category
make holy
AEPF made up of
AEPN panel pin
AEPO face up to
make up to
wake up to
AEQE Palenque
AERA game area
AERE carefree
date-tree
Lake Erie
AERG water rug
AERM safe from
AERP name-drop
AERT water rat
AERW have a row
AERY Jane Grey
Zane Grey
AESF make as if
AESI water-ski
AESN Paterson
AESS Ramesses
AESW panel saw
AETC majestic
AETD lamented
talented
AETE patentee
AETL parental
AETO make it to
AETR gamester
man-eater
patentor
AETV mazel tov
mazeltov
AETX sales tax
AETY have a try
latently
patently
tapestry
AEUE make sure
tape-lure
AEUH Babe Ruth
Kate Bush
AEUK lame duck
AEUL make full
AEUN ramequin
AEUS make cuts
AEVN make even
AEVR have over
made over
make over
makeover
rave over
take over
takeover
AEWY fade away
make away
take away
takeaway
take-away
waterway
AEYE Jane Eyre
Lake Eyre
AEYY panegyry
AFAF half-calf
AFAL gaff sail
taffrail
AFAT half-mast
AFDL daffodil
AFED Garfield
gasfield
AFEM half-term

AFIE	caffeine
	half-life
	half-size
	half-time
AFIG	baffling
	waffling
AFIH	bad faith
AFIS	halflins
AFIT	half-pint
AFKN	calfskin
AFLP	half-slip
AFLY	lawfully
	manfully
AFNH	half-inch
	hawfinch
AFOE	half-done
	half-sole
	half-tone
AFOK	half-cock
AFON	half-moon
AFOR	half-hour
AFOT	half-boot
AFOY	saffrony
AFRD	half-bred
AFRN	fanfaron
	warfarin
AFRR	wayfarer
AFRY	car ferry
	Rafferty
AFTP	half-step
AFUG	far-flung
AFUS	Dan Fouts
AFUT	half-butt
AFVR	hay fever
AFYH	kaffiyeh
AGAD	gangland
	Langland
	vanguard
AGAE	gang rape
	language
	Palgrave
AGAF	langlauf
AGAH	bar graph
AGAK	hang back
AGAL	hangnail
	Sangraal
	Sangrail
AGBE	tangible
AGBY	mangabey
	tangibly
AGDC	Haggadic
AGDH	Haggadah
AGDY	jaggedly
	raggedly
AGEE	bargeese
	cargeese
	gangrene
AGEL	Sangreal
AGES	fangless
AGHN	Langshan
	Tangshan
AGHU	Hangzhou
AGIE	hang fire
	narghile
	sanguine
AGIG	dangling
	gangling
	haggling
	jangling
	laughing
AGIH	Dalglish
	languish
AGIN	ganglion
AGIR	gangliar
AGIY	sanguify
AGLG	gang plug
AGLH	nargileh
AGLN	pangolin
AGLO	Bargello
AGLS	tangelos
AGLY	Caughley
AGND	margined
AGNI	Wanganui
AGNL	marginal
AGNO	hang on to
AGNS	daggings
	hangings
AGNY	garganey
AGOE	Maggiore
	mangrove
AGOF	laugh off
AGON	hang down
AGOS	bang goes
AGPN	gang up on
AGRD	badgered
	gauge rod
AGRN	hanger-on
AGRO	kangaroo
AGRT	Margaret
AGSE	largesse
AGSO	sargasso❑
AGTE	Naughtie
AGTN	Laughton
AGTP	caught up
AGTR	daughter
	gangster
	laughter
	Sangster
AGTY	gadgetry
AGUR	Langmuir
AGVN	Langevin
AGVR	hang over
	hangover
	law-giver
AGYE	gargoyle
	lang syne
AHAD	cash card
AHAH	MacHeath
AHBE	oathable
	washable
AHBT	bad habit
AHDP	washed-up
AHDS	rachides
	raphides
AHEA	Bagheera
AHEE	cashmere
AHEH	hasheesh
AHEK	cash desk
AHEN	Kathleen
AHEO	Tashtego
AHES	cashless
	pathless
	rashness
AHET	Tashkent
AHGN	pathogen
AHIG	yachting
AHII	Kashmiri
AHIM	taghairm
AHLA	parhelia
	Valhalla
AHLC	catholic
	parhelic
AHLN	Sakhalin
	Van Halen
AHLR	bachelor
AHLW	cash flow
AHNN	cash in on
AHNO	pachinko
AHNS	lashings
AHNU	Rathenau
AHOE	bathrobe
AHOM	bathroom
	washroom
AHON	cash down
	wash down
AHOT	sash bolt
AHRD	gathered
AHRE	warhorse
AHRN	gather in
	vacherin
AHRP	cash crop
AHRR	gatherer
AHRT	Bathurst
AHRV	Sakharov
AHRY	fatherly
AHSE	tachisme
	tachiste
AHSO	machismo
AHSS	rachises
AHTC	bathetic
	pathetic
	rachitic
AHTR	catheter
AHTS	rachitis
AHUE	bathcube
	cathouse
	cat-house
	madhouse
	tap-house
AHUH	Kashruth
AHUS	man-hours
AHVN	tax haven
AHWY	wash away
AHXS	cathexes
	cathexis
AIAE	badinage
	cavitate
	fatigate
	kamikaze
	laminate
	Latinate
	marinade
	marinate
	navigate
	paginate
	palisade
	radicate
	saginate
	salivate
	sanitate
	validate
AIAH	calipash
AIAI	capitani
	hari-kari
AIAK	taxi rank
AIAO	palisado
AIAS	habitans
AIAT	habitant
AIAY	lapidary
	salivary
	sanitary
AIBE	satiable
	variable
AIBY	cabin boy
	panic-buy
	variably
AICL	maniacal
AIDR	havildar
AIDT	samizdat
AIDV	Kapil Dev
AIDY	variedly
AIEA	saliceta
AIEE	magic eye
AIEN	Galilean
AIES	caginess
	easiness
	gaminess
	haziness
	laziness
	matiness
	raciness
	wariness
	waviness
	waxiness
	zaniness
AIET	manifest
AIEY	facilely
	natively
AIFL	basinful
AIGN	taking-in
	taking on
	taking-on
AIGP	taking up
	taking-up
AIGR	Basinger
	malinger
	Salinger
AIGY	daringly
	gapingly
	Haringey
	ragingly
	ravingly

savingly
takingly
AIHD banished
famished
ravished
vanished
AIHE Lapithae
Pasiphae
AIHM Havisham
AIHS Laoighis
AIHY garishly
lavishly
rakishly
AIIA basilica
AIID pacified
ramified
ratified
AIIE Catiline
laciniae
Latinise
Latinize
maritime
maximise
maximize
sanitise
sanitize
satirise
satirize
AIIK basilisk□
AIIL familial
AIIM basidium
Hasidism
Latinism
nativism
pacifism
AIIN magician
Maximian
Parisian
pavilion
Tahitian
AIIR familiar
pacifier
AIIS papilios
AIIT Hasidist
Latinist
nativist
pacifist
satirist
AIIY facility
nativity
rabidity
rapidity
salinity
sapidity
validity
vapidity
AILA Daniella
radialia
AILC Cadillac®
Pauillac
AILE Danielle
mamillae
maxillae

papillae
AILM Panislam
AILN carillon
papillon
vanillin
AILR caviller
variolar
AILS bacillus
AILW Ladislaw
AILY facially
labially
racially
radially
AIMN kakiemon□
talisman
AINA hacienda
AIND maligned
AINE patience□
radiance
salience
sapience
valiance
variance
AINL national
rational
AINR maligner
AINS MacInnes
AINY malignly
radiancy
saliency
AIOA Danilova
Manitoba
AIOD manifold
marigold□
AIOE baritone
camisole
varicose
AIOI yakitori
AIOM ramiform
variform
vasiform
AIOS calicoes
manitous
AIOY palimony
AIRE caviarie
AIRM variorum
AISN Taliesin
AISS radiuses
AITA Jacintha
AITC sadistic
AITD satiated
AITE Jacinthe
Mariette
Mariotte
AITL parietal
sagittal
AITN Hamilton
Pakistan
AITR banister
canister
ganister
radiator
varistor

AITS Calixtus
haliotis
AITY papistry
AIUA Caligula
capitula
AIUD fatigued
AIUE latitude
manicure
vaginule
AIUL habitual
AIUN taciturn
AJIT banjoist
AJNG mah-jongg
AJRE Marjorie
AJRM marjoram
AJRS zanjeros
AKAD backhand
backward
backyard
parkland
parkward
AKAE back-date
Jack Cade
AKAH backlash
backwash
Balkhash
AKAK backpack
hark back
talk back
AKAL talk tall
walk tall
AKAS Walkmans
AKBY Hawke Bay
AKCE backache
AKDP tanked up
AKDY markedly
AKED backveld
Bankhead
hawkweed
AKEL back-heel
AKES dankness
darkness
lankness
rankness
AKET backbeat
dark meat
rack-rent
AKGR packager
AKGS packages
AKHP talk shop
AKHT backchat
AKHW talk show
AKIE backbite□
backfire
backside
hawklike
mark time
Parklife
AKIG cackling
darkling
rankling
AKIH bank-high
jack-high

AKIL backfill
AKIT backlist
AKLE dark-blue
AKMN marksman
AKND darkened
AKNN Hakkinen
AKNO talk into
walk into
AKNS markings
AKNW mackinaw
AKOB back-comb
AKOD back-load
Mark Todd
pack-load
AKOE backbone
banknote
AKOK hack-work
AKOL bankroll
AKOM backroom
darkroom
AKON back down
mark down
mark-down
pack down
talk down
AKOR back-door
AKOT jackboot
AKPN backspin
AKPR larkspur
AKRE Valkyrie
AKRL mackerel
AKRO jackaroo
jackeroo
AKRP backdrop
AKTE hackette
AKTN pack it in
AKTP backstop
pack it up
AKTR marketer
AKTY basketry
AKUS sackfuls
tankfuls
AKUT bankrupt
AKVR talk over
walk over
walkover
walk-over
AKWY back away
hark away
pack away
AKYD hawk-eyed
ALAD galliard
halliard
kailyard
railcard
tailband
ALAE fail-safe
malleate
palliate
tailgate
talliate
wayleave
ALAH Paul Nash

ALAI	Cagliari
ALAK	ball park
	ballpark
	call back
	fall back
	fall-back
	hallmark
	tailback
ALAO	Galliano
ALAS	wall bars
ALAX	fabliaux
	Karl Marx
	tableaux
ALAY	hail Mary❑
ALBD	Karlsbad
ALBE	fallible
	sailable
ALBY	fallibly
	Table Bay
ALCO	mallecho
ALCS	ballocks
	halluces
ALCY	garlicky
ALDN	nailed on
	walled in
ALDO	Palladio
ALDS	Ballades
ALDY	pallidly
ALED	nail-head
	railhead
	Wallsend
ALEG	Paul Berg
ALES	tailless
	tallness
ALET	earliest
ALEY	raillery
ALEZ	Karl Benz
ALFL	faultful
	ladleful
ALGG	lallygag
ALGT	daylight
	fanlight
	gaslight
	wax-light
ALHM	Hailsham
ALHO	ballyhoo
ALHP	tall ship
ALHS	tally-hos
ALHT	mailshot
ALID	jailbird
	tail wind
ALIE	MacLaine
	tailpipe
ALIG	dallying
	rallying
	vaulting
ALIH	MacLeish
	sailfish
ALIL	ball-girl
	call girl
	callgirl
	call-girl
ALIM	Gaullism
ALIN	call sign
ALIR	Gaultier
ALIT	Gaullist
	rallyist
ALIY	faultily
	haploidy
ALLE	Paul Klee
ALLT	badly lit
	fall flat
ALMH	gallumph
ALMN	bailsman
	Lac Léman
	tallyman
ALMT	table mat
ALNE	parlance
ALNO	parlando
	sail into
ALNR	Faulkner
ALNS	Rawlings
ALNT	wall knot
ALOD	railroad
ALOE	calliope❑
ALOF	badly off
ALOK	ballcock
ALOM	ballroom
	Karl Böhm
ALON	call down
	fall down
	nail down
ALOT	ladle out
ALPN	call upon
	fall upon
	tailspin
ALPR	calliper
	galloper
	walloper
ALRA	galleria
ALRD	tailored
ALRE	Mallarmé
ALRF	Carl Orff
ALRG	ballyrag
ALRM	hail from
ALRN	cauldron
ALRO	wallaroo
ALRY	Earl Grey
ALSE	Carlisle
ALSR	Walliser
ALSS	galluses
ALSY	Wallasey
ALTA	Valletta
ALTC	balletic
ALTE	Paulette
	raclette
ALTN	tarlatan
ALTO	varletto
ALTY	harlotry
	varletry
ALUG	Carl Jung
ALUI	halloumi
ALVR	call over
	fall over
ALVT	gallivat
ALWD	hallowed
ALWN	wallow in
ALWR	wallower
ALWS	Day-Lewis
	Mawlawis
ALWY	call away
	Calloway
	fall away
	galloway❑
ALYR	parleyer
	waylayer
ALZI	Paolozzi
AMAD	farm-hand
	farmland
	farmyard
AMAE	barm cake
AMAO	Naum Gabo
AMDA	gammadia
AMDC	Talmudic
AMES	calmness
	harmless
	warmness
AMFS	earmuffs
AMHL	Taj Mahal
AMHT	palmchat
AMKR	haymaker
	law-maker
AMLA	yarmulka
AMLE	yarmulke
AMNA	sarmenta
	Tasmania
AMNC	daemonic
	daimonic
	harmonic
AMNO	farm into
AMNS	garments
AMON	calm down
AMOT	warm-boot
AMRA	Mad Maria
AMRD	hammered
AMRL	balmoral
AMRY	gamma ray
AMSN	Parmesan
AMST	marmoset
AMTC	dalmatic
	haematic
	magmatic
	Sarmatic
AMTD	Halmstad
	palmated
AMTE	palmette
AMTN	haematin
AMTR	gas meter
AMUH	badmouth
	bad-mouth
	Falmouth
ANAD	barnyard
	dawn raid
	mainland
ANAE	taeniate
ANAL	mainsail
	rainfall
ANAN	maintain
ANAT	fainéant
	mainmast
	main part
ANAY	balneary
ANBE	damnable
	wannabee
ANBL	cannibal
	Hannibal
ANBS	Barnabas
	cannabis
ANBY	damnably
ANCE	barnacle
ANCT	wainscot
ANDC	maenadic
ANEK	main deck
ANEL	main meal
ANEM	Mannheim
ANES	gainless
	painless
	rainless
	Saunders
	vainness
ANET	faintest
ANEY	vauntery
ANGE	Carnegie
ANHD	launched
ANHN	launch in
ANHP	pawnshop
ANHR	launcher
ANHS	haunches
ANID	rainbird
ANIE	gain time
	jaundice
	MacNeice
	main line
	mainline
ANIG	daunting
	fainting
	haunting
	painting
	tainting
	taunting
	vaunting
ANIH	nannyish
ANIY	daintily
	jauntily
	main city
ANKA	Mauna Kea
ANKN	cannikin
	mannikin
	pannikin
ANKS	larnakes
ANLA	magnolia
	Mauna Loa
ANLE	cannulae
ANLS	cannulas
ANLT	gauntlet
ANLY	Barnsley
	carnally
	tarnally
ANNS	earnings
	fannings
ANNY	cannonry
ANOD	taenioid

Words marked ❑ can also be spelled with an initial capital letter

ANOK nainsook
ANOL tawny owl
ANON sainfoin
ANOS carneous
ANOT raincoat
ANOY rainbowy
ANPN gain upon
ANRD mannered
ANRE pain-free
rain-tree
ANRH far north
ANRK Ragnarok
ANRP raindrop
ANRT banneret
lanneret
ANRY mannerly
ANSA magnesia
ANTC magnetic
ANTO say not to
ANTS fainites
magnetos
ANTY gannetry
mainstay
ANUA carnauba
ANVL carnival□
ANVR Hannover
ANYE Jarndyce
AOAA panorama
sayonara
Vadodara
AOAD Savoyard
AOAE sabotage
Zakopane
AOAM sago-palm
AOAO gado-gado
Pago Pago
AOAY mahogany
AOCE barouche
farouche
pabouche
AOCT razor-cut
AODE caboodle
canoodle
AOEE carotene
La Bohème
AOEN Jacobean
napoleon□
AOER saboteur
AOES baroness
canoness
mayoress
AOEY cajolery
AOGD man of God
AOGE Laforgue
AOGS calor gas®
AOHD caboched
AOHE pahoehoe
AOHN cabochon
AOHS Basothos
AOIA japonica
maiolica
majolica
Salonica
Salonika
AOIE camomile
canonise
canonize
caponise
caponize
Caroline
gasoline
Jacobite
Katowice
Saxonise
Saxonize
valorise
valorize
vaporise
vaporize
AOIG canoeing
AOII Pasolini
AOIL baronial
manorial
AOIM laconism
AOIN Salopian
AOIO palomino□
AOIT canoeist
parodist
AOIY majority
saponify
AOLH masoolah
AOLO Badoglio
AOLT wagon-lit
AOLW canon law
AOMA paroemia
AOMN Calormen
AOND marooned
AOOE Gaborone
AOOR malodour
AOOS canorous
saporous
valorous
vaporous
AOOY cacology
taxonomy
AOPE magot-pie
AORD favoured
laboured
savoured
AORF savour of
AORR favourer
labourer
AORT tabouret
AOSA parousia
AOSE jalousie
Larousse
AOSL carousal
carousel□
AOSN Jacobsen
man of sin
AOSR carouser
AOSS galowses
AOSY famously
Panofsky
Yanofsky
AOTC panoptic
AOTT barostat
AOUA La Coruna
AOWR man-of-war
AOYM paroxysm
APAE warplane
APAT wax plant
APBE palpable
APBY palpably
APCO gazpacho
APDM pappadom
APDO San Pedro
APEE camphene
APEL Campbell
harp seal
harp-seal
APES bad press
dampness
lampreys
APGI Malpighi
APIE campsite
samphire
sapphire
APIG Rampling
sampling
APIM sapphism□
APIN campaign
APIS nauplius
APIT Hay Point
sapphist
war paint
APKR gas poker
APLT pamphlet
APND dampened
APNE jampanee
APNN happen on
APNO happen to
APNR dampener
APNY rampancy
APOA Pamplona
APOE car phone
APOG Haiphong
APON damp down
tamp down
APOT lamppost
APPR bagpiper
wax paper
APPS bagpipes
Pan-pipes
APRA Walpurga
APRC vampiric
APRD hampered
pampered
APRR pamperer
tamperer
APRS pamperos
APRV Kasparov
APRY dapperly
APSE lampasse
APSS campuses
APTN Rasputin
APTP camp it up
APUO São Paulo
APWR manpower
APYR taxpayer
AQAD jacquard
AQEN May queen
AQES lacqueys
marquess
AQIE marquise
AQIH vanquish
AQII daiquiri
ARAD hair-band
ARAE carriage
fair game
laureate
marriage
patriate
ARAH Hal Roach
Max Roach
ARAL fair fall
ARAY Macready
ARCA Patricia
ARCI capricci
ARCS barracks
barricos
Caprices
matrices
ARCT carrycot
carry-cot
ARDE Oak Ridge
ARDN harridan
ARDO car radio
ARDR Labrador
ARDY sacredly
ARES fairness
hairless
AREY farriery
ARGL madrigal
warragal
warrigal
ARGN tarragon
ARGS farragos
ARHN Hanrahan
ARIE hairlike
hairline
pairwise
ARIG carrying
dairying
harrying
marrying
tarrying
ARIH pair with
ARKN larrikin
ARLY fair play
ARMH harrumph
ARMI haeremai
ARMN dairyman
ARNA Tauranga
ARNC hadronic
ARNE Lagrange
Laurence
Lawrence
ARNF patron of
ARNL patronal
ARNN safranin
ARNS madroños

Words marked □ can also be spelled with an initial capital letter

	Marranos
	vagrants
ARNY	matronly
	vagrancy
	warranty
AROA	Catriona
AROE	cabriole
	capriole
AROF	carry off
	marry off
AROS	carry-ons
	hair loss
	nacreous
AROT	carry out
	carry-out
AROY	fair copy
ARPD	macropod
	Sauropod
ARPL	satrapal
ARRA	sacraria
ARRP	hairgrip
ARRS	Carreras
ARSA	Laurasia
ARSE	Fair Isle
	lacrosse
ARSN	garrison
	Harrison
ARSY	sacristy
ARTA	Lauretta
	Sabratha
ARTE	garrotte
	Magritte
ARTR	narrator
	parroter
ARTY	Hanratty
ARUD	pay round
ARUH	Bayreuth
ARUT	Barrault
ARWD	harrowed
	narrowed
ARWY	narrowly
ARXS	matrixes
ASAD	hatstand
ASAE	nauseate
	Ramsgate
	Sam Spade
ASAF	Falstaff
ASAK	haystack
	pass-back
ASAL	Marshall
ASAT	camshaft
	naissant
ASBE	passable
	passible
	raisable
ASBY	False Bay
	passably
	passibly
ASCA	Nausicaa
ASCE	massacre
ASCM	capsicum
ASCS	waesucks
ASDS	passados

ASDY	caused by
ASEL	bad smell
ASFL	Parsifal
ASGO	dal segno
ASGS	marsh gas
	sapsagos
ASIA	Faustina
ASIH	Ian Smith
ASIK	canstick
ASIN	Gaussian
ASIS	warships
ASIY	karstify
ASLF	bass clef
ASLR	capsular
ASLS	Marsalis
	Rasselas
ASLY	causally
	tasselly
ASMC	balsamic
ASMR	ransomer
ASNE	Lausanne
ASNH	Ram Singh
ASNO	Bassanio
	pass into
ASNS	cassinos
	paisanos
ASNT	bassinet
	Massenet
	sarsenet
ASNY	mansonry
ASOA	massoola
ASOD	basswood
	password
ASOE	capstone
	ragstone
ASOK	mass-book
ASON	lasslorn
	pass down
ASOO	maestoso
ASOS	nauseous
	passions
ASOT	passport
ASPN	pass upon
ASRB	false rib
ASRE	caesurae
ASRF	sanserif
ASRM	bass drum
	Hans Gram
ASRS	caesuras
	maestros
ASRT	Sanskrit
ASRU	hausfrau
ASRY	passer-by
	say sorry
ASTE	cassette
ASTO	falsetto
ASTS	passatas
ASUE	danseuse
	masseuse
	Saussure
ASUS	Jan Smuts
ASUY	Lansbury
ASVR	pass over

	Passover
ASWY	causeway
	pass away
ASYR	nay-sayer
ASZD	man-sized
ATAA	Santa Ana
ATAD	Cartland
	eastward
ATAE	Carthage
	castrate
	rag trade
	salt lake
ATAI	canthari
	castrati
	Haft Wadi
	pastrami
ATAK	cast back
	fastback
	fast-talk
ATAL	fastball
ATAO	castrato
	Santiago
ATAP	last-gasp
ATAS	manteaus
	Matthaus
ATAX	manteaux
ATBD	taste bud
ATBE	pantable
	partible
	tastable
ATBN	waste bin
ATCE	canticle
	particle
	pastiche
ATCL	nautical
	tactical
ATDN	mastodon
ATDY	day-to-day
ATEA	cattleya
ATED	masthead
ATEE	xanthene
ATEI	Galtieri
ATEN	pantheon❑
	rattle on
ATER	can't bear
ATES	daftness
	fastness
	gastness
	Matthews
	mattress
	partners
	saltless
	tactless
	tartness
	tautness
	vastness
	waitress
ATET	farthest
	maltreat
ATFE	pantofle
	Tartuffe
ATFL	faithful❑
	tasteful

	wasteful
ATFS	cast-offs
ATGA	Mantegna
ATGN	martagon
	Rattigan
ATID	east wind
ATIE	gantline
	part-time
ATIF	car-thief
ATIG	farthing
	partying
	rattling
ATIH	part with
ATIK	hat trick
	salt lick
ATIM	partyism
	Tantrism
ATIN	Parthian
ATIS	captain's
	Castries
	eastlins
	Matthias
ATIT	wait-list
ATIY	paltrily
ATKA	Lattakia
ATKV	Saltykov
ATKY	kantikoy
ATLA	mantilla
ATLC	dactylic
ATLD	pantiled
ATLE	bastille❑
	pastille
ATLM	tantalum
ATLO	martello
ATLR	Wat Tyler
ATLS	cattalos
	nautilus
	tantalus❑
ATLT	salt flat
ATMN	Earthman
	man to man
	man-to-man
	party man
	Rastaman
ATMS	Gay Times
ATNA	galtonia
ATND	fastened
ATNN	fasten on
	santonin
ATNO	saltando
ATNR	fastener
	fattener
ATNS	Hastings
ATNT	martinet
ATNY	wantonly
ATOA	xanthoma
ATOD	Dartford
	Eastwood
	fast food
	Hartford
	last word
ATOF	malt loaf
ATOK	partwork

ATOM	maltworm
ATON	cast down
	cast-down
	hawthorn
	salt down
	want down
ATOR	Dartmoor
	watt-hour
ATOS	captious
	cast lots
	cautious
	factious
	xanthous
ATOT	faltboat
	saltwort
ATPE	Zantippe
ATPN	wait upon
ATRA	bacteria
	martyria
ATRC	tartaric
ATRD	battered
	raftered
	tattered
ATRE	batterie
	Sauterne
ATRL	pastoral
	pastural
ATRN	cast iron
	cast-iron
ATRR	banterer
	barterer
	capturer
	natterer
ATRS	halteres
	Tartarus
ATRY	easterly
	latterly
	masterly
ATSA	Earthsea
	fantasia□
	mantissa
ATSE	bad taste
ATSN	partisan
	Pattison
ATSS	Baptists
	cactuses
	Hattusas
	saltuses
ATSY	sad to say
ATTM	factotum
ATTS	mastitis
ATUA	sastruga
ATUH	saltbush
ATUI	sastrugi
	zastrugi
ATUK	fast buck
ATUL	fauteuil
ATUS	tantrums
ATUT	pant suit
ATWY	cast away
	castaway
	salt away
ATZD	baptized

AUAE	hamulate
	jaculate
	maculate
	maturate
	radulate
	saturate
	tabulate
	vapulate
AUAS	lacunars
AUAT	saturant
AUAY	lacunary
	salutary
AUBE	valuable
AUBR	raw umber
AUBY	valuably
AUCE	caruncle
AUDR	gazunder
AUDT	valued at
AUDY	Saturday
AUEY	maturely
AUHA	babushka
AUHN	capuchin□
AUIE	fabulise
	fabulize
	paludine
AUIG	manuring
	saluting
AUIM	naturism
AUIN	Danubian
AUIT	fabulist
	naturist
AUIY	caducity
	maturity
AUKH	Hanukkah
AULR	vacuolar
AULS	Catullus
AULY	casually
	casualty
	manually
AUNM	laburnum
AUOE	papulose
	sabulose
AUOS	caducous
	fabulous
	papulous
	sabulous
AUPX	haruspex
AURA	manubria
AURE	Daguerre
AURS	saguaros
	vaqueros
AUTE	baguette
	maquette
AUTR	baluster
AUUE	Sarum use
AVBS	bad vibes
AVDR	Salvador
AVDS	Calvados
AVGL	aasvogel
AVGS	Las Vegas
AVIE	mauveine
AVLE	Banville
	par value

	valvu-lae
AVLO	Malvolio
AVLR	valvular
AVNC	galvanic
AVNE	parvenue
AVOT	carve out
AVSA	Malvasia
AWES	man-weeks
AWMN	day-woman
	laywoman
	madwoman
AWRH	Hayworth
	Tamworth
AWRS	waxworks
AWSE	lay waste
	radwaste
AWTH	Magwitch
AYAA	capybara
AYAD	Maryland
	navy yard
AYAE	easy-care
	easy game
AYAS	man-years
AYAY	Mary Daly
AYED	Mary Read
AYEE	Ganymede
AYET	easy meat
AYGS	larynges
AYHP	Ladyship
AYIA	Latynina
AYID	ladybird
AYIE	ladylike
AYIT	Navy List
AYLE	navy blue
AYMN	lady's man
AYOD	babyhood
	manyfold
AYOE	lady love
	lady-love
	Mary Rose
AYOL	baby doll
AYRS	Babygros
AYSO	say yes to
AYSS	calypsos
AYTD	caryatid
AYUD	many-hued
AYVR	easy over
AYXS	larynxes
AZBR	Zanzibar
AZEA	zarzuela
AZIG	dazzling
AZNA	Tanzania
AZNS	calzones
	canzonas
AZNT	canzonet
AZPN	marzipan
AZRM	mahzorim
AZUG	Salzburg
AZUK	jazz-funk
BAIE	ablative
	abrasive
BAIG	abrading
BAIN	ablation

	abrasion
	oblation
BAND	obtained
BANR	obtainer
BAOY	oblatory
BCRD	obscured
BCSA	abscissa
BCSS	abacuses
BDAI	Abu Dhabi
BDET	obedient
BDOE	a bad move
BDUN	a bad turn
BEAE	abnegate
BEPR	obtemper
BESD	obsessed
BETE	absentee
BETO	object to
BETR	objector
BETY	abjectly
	absently
BEVD	observed
BEVR	observer
BGAD	a big hand
BIAE	abdicate
	obligate
BIAI	obligati
BIAO	obligato
BIAT	obeisant
BIGD	abridged
BIIG	obliging
BIIN	oblivion
	obsidian
BITE	absinthe
BMSM	abomasum
BNAT	abundant
BNDL	Abu Nidal
BNTO	ab initio
BOAE	abrogate
BOBD	absorbed
BOEE	obsolete
BOIE	ebionise
	ebionize
BOML	abnormal
BOUE	absolute□
BOVD	absolved
BQIY	ubiquity
BRAE	aberrate
BRAT	aberrant
BRDR	obtruder
BREN	Aberdeen
	eburnean
BRIE	abortive
BRIG	aborning
	aborting
BRIN	abortion
BTAT	abstract
BTAY	obituary
BTCE	obstacle
BTET	abetment
	abutment
BTIG	abetting
	abutting
BTIT	abstrict

BTOR	abattoir
BTRE	absterge
BTUA	a battuta
BTUE	abstruse
BTUH	a bit much
BTUT	obstruct
BUAE	obdurate
	obturate
BUAY	obduracy
BUDN	abound in
BUDY	absurdly
BUEY	obtusely
BUIN	ablution
BUIY	obtusity
BUTR	abductor
BUTY	abruptly
BVAL	above all
BVPR	above par
BWAE	Ebbw Vale
BYNE	abeyance
CAAA	McNamara
CABE	scrabble
	Scrabble®
	scramble
CACY	scratchy
CAEY	scrape by
CAIA	sciatica
CAIG	scraping
CAIN	occasion
	Oceanian
CAIS	oceanids
CAJT	scramjet
CALD	scrawled
CALR	scrawler
CAON	octaroon
CAPD	scrapped
CATE	scrattle
CATL	octantal
CATS	sceattas
CATY	McCarthy
CBAD	scabbard
CBIK	iceblink
CBOS	scabious
	scabrous
CBUD	icebound
CCEM	ice cream
CCLR	acicular
CDAN	acid rain
CDAZ	acid jazz
CDED	acid-head
CDMA	academia
CDMC	academic
CDNE	ice dance
CDOK	acid rock
CDOS	aciduous
CDRP	acid drop
CDSS	acidosis
CEAA	schemata
CEAE	acierate
CECY	screechy
CEDR	screeder
CEEE	screw eye
CEEO	accede to
CEIG	acceding
	scheming
CEMR	screamer
CEND	screened
CENR	screener
CEOA	scleroma
CEOE	sclerose
CEOO	Ecce Homo
CEOS	Achelous
	echelons
	sclerous
CETC	eclectic
CETD	accepted
CETR	accentor
	acceptor
	scienter
CEUE	schedule
CEYU	screw you
CEZS	scherzos
CFED	Scofield
CFEK	ecofreak
CFIG	scoffing
CFOD	scaffold
CIAE	activate
CIBE	scribble
CIBN	Scriabin
CIBY	scribbly
CIET	accident
	Occident
CIEY	actively
CIGE	scriggle
CIGY	achingly
CIIE	actiniae
	actinide
CIIM	actinium
	activism
CIIS	actinias
CIIT	activist
CIIY	acridity
	activity
CILR	Schiller
CILS	Achilles
	W C Fields
CILY	McKinley
CIOD	echinoid
	schizoid
CIOY	acrimony
CIPD	scrimped
CIPY	scrimply
CITC	ecliptic
CIVD	achieved
CIVR	achiever
CLAE	aculeate
	ocellate
CLBL	eco-label
CLCS	scoleces
	scolices
CLCT	scilicet
CLCY	schlocky
CLDR	occluder
CLDS	scalados
CLEE	McAleese
CLEY	scullery
CLGC	ecologic
CLGL	Schlegel
CLIG	scalding
	scolding
	sculling
CLII	scaldini
CLIN	scallion
CLLY	ice lolly
CLNS	scalenus
CLPY	schleppy
CLRY	ocularly
CLTD	oculated
CLTR	sculptor□
CMIH	scampish
	scomfish
CMLZ	schmaltz
CMOE	schmooze
CMTR	scimitar
CNHS	acanthus
CNIG	scanning
CNIM	scandium
CNIN	scansion
CNIY	scantily
CNMC	economic
CNPS	schnapps
CNRO	scenario
CNWE	acknowne
COAD	McDonald
COAE	accolade
CODE	scrowdge
COEM	ectoderm
COEN	McGovern
COES	echoless
COFL	scoopful
COGD	act of God
COIM	sciolism
COIN	eclosion
	scholion
COIT	sciolist
COLD	schooled
	scrolled
CONE	scrounge
CONR	schooner
CONS	accounts
COON	octoroon
COOS	sciolous
COOT	scoop out
COTC	acrostic
COTE	accoutre
COTR	accouter
COUA	scrofula
COUH	octopush
CPLE	scapulae
CPLO	Acapulco
CPLR	scapular
CPLS	scapulas
CPOD	scaphoid
CPRD	sceptred
CRAE	acerbate
	ochreate
CRCO	scirocco
CRDF	scared of
CRDR	Schröder
CRDT	accredit
CREE	Scorsese
CRET	Scarlett
CREY	scarcely
CRFL	scornful
CRGR	McGregor
CRHD	scorched
CRHR	scorcher
CRHS	scirrhus
CRIN	scorpion□
CRIS	Scorpios
	Scorpius
CRIY	acerbity
	scarcity
	scurvily
CRMT	achromat
CROF	scare off
	score off
CROS	ochreous
CROT	score out
CSAE	ice skate
CSET	ice sheet
CSIN	scission
CSOS	scissors
CSUE	scissure
CTAD	Scotland
CTIE	Scottice
CTIG	scathing
CTIH	Scottish
CTIY	Scottify
CTLA	scutella
CTMN	Scotsman
CTMS	scotomas
CTRE	scot free
	scot-free
CTTC	ecstatic
CTXC	ecotoxic
CTYC	ichthyic
CUAE	accurate
CUAN	Schumann
CUAT	occupant
CUAY	accuracy
CUBD	scrubbed
CUBR	scrubber
CUCY	scrunchy
CUDO	I could go
CUEF	accuse of
CUET	à couvert
	Schubert
CUGN	McGuigan
CUGR	scourger
CUHR	scouther
CUID	occupied
CUIE	sciurine
CUIG	accusing
	scouring
	scouting
CUIR	occupier
CUIT	acquaint
CUIY	scrutiny
CULN	McCullin
CULS	scruples
CULT	octuplet

Words marked □ can also be spelled with an initial capital letter

CULY	actually
CURD	acquired
CUSD	accursed
CUSL	Schüssel
CUTC	acoustic
CUTM	accustom
CUTY	occultly
CVGR	scavager
CVNE	scavenge
CWHR	scowther
CWIG	scowling
CWRN	Schwerin
DACD	advanced
DACS	advances
DAEA	Ndjamena
DAET	adjacent
DAGS	ideal gas
DAIE	idealise
	idealize
DAIM	idealism
DAIT	idealist
DCAE	I declare!
DCBE	educable
	educible
DCIN	eduction
DCOS	edacious
DCTD	educated
DCTR	educator
DEAK	idle talk
DEAS	edgeways
DEDM	addendum
DEEO	adhere to
DEES	edgeless
	idleness
DEET	adherent
DEIE	adhesive
	edgewise
	idée fixe
	idle time
DEIG	adhering
DEIN	adhesion
DELY	Adderley
DEOL	edge tool
DFIG	edifying
DIBR	ad-libber
DIES	admirers
	advisers
	edginess
DIIE	additive
DIIG	admiring
	advising
DIIN	addition
DINE	Adrianne
	Adrienne
DIOY	advisory
DITC	Adriatic
DITD	addicted
	admitted
DLET	Adalbert
DLEY	adultery
DLIE	Adelaide
DLIR	Id al-Fitr
DLIT	idyllist
DLSR	idoliser
DLTR	adulator
	idolater
DLTY	idolatry
DLZD	idolized
DLZR	idolizer
DMEE	Adam Bede
DMIW	a dim view
DMNO	Idomeneo
DMNS	oddments
DMTR	udometer
DMTY	odometry
DMUD	idem quod
DNAE	edentate
DNIY	identify
	identity
DNMS	adenomas
DNOD	odontoid
DNUR	Adenauer
DOAE	advocate
DOAT	advocaat
DOAY	advocacy
DOBX	idiot box
DOET	idiolect
DOEY	ad hocery
DOIH	admonish
DOOY	ideology
DORM	ideogram
DOSY	odiously
DOTN	Edmonton
DOTY	adroitly
DPIE	adaptive
	adoptive
DPIN	adoption
DQAE	adequate
DQAY	adequacy
DRBE	adorable
DRBY	adorably
DRIG	adorning
DRSY	I dare say
	I daresay
DSEN	Odyssean
DSES	Odysseus
DTJY	Ode to Joy
	ode to joy
DUAT	adjutant
	adjuvant
DUTD	adjusted
DUTR	adjuster
DYHH	Eddy Shah
EAAA	Te Kanawa
	vena cava
EAAD	legal aid
EAAE	De La Mare
	Delaware
	legal age
	separate
EAAN	yet again
EAAT	relaxant
	set apart
EAAY	legatary
EABE	bedabble
EACE	démarche
	menarche
EACN	Besançon
EADC	heraldic
EADD	demanded
	regarded
	retarded
EADH	verandah
EADR	demander
	Menander
	regarder
	retarder
	rewarder
EADS	regard as
EADY	heraldry
EAEA	de Valera
	rewarewa
EAED	get ahead
EAEE	legalese
	Nepalese
EAEN	cetacean
	fedayeen
EAEO	relate to
EAES	bejabers
EAET	beta test
	beta-test
	decadent
	red alert
	remanent
EAEY	pedately
	sedately
EAGD	deranged
EAGE	bedaggle
EAGY	get angry
EAHC	seraphic
EAHD	detached
	rehashed
EAHM	seraphim
	teraphim
EAHN	seraphin
EAHR	metaphor
EAIA	hepatica
	velamina
EAIE	gelatine
	get a life
	hematite
	hepatise
	hepatize
	ketamine
	legalise
	legalize
	melamine
	metalize
	negative
	penalise
	penalize
	relative
	sedative
	set aside
	set-aside
	tetanise
	tetanize
	velarise
	velarize
EAIG	berating
	debasing
	decaying
	delaying
	menacing
	relating
	relaxing
	relaying
EAIH	megalith
EAIM	geranium
	legalism
	teratism
	veganism
EAIN	aeration
	delation
	deration
	gelation
	legation
	negation
	relation
	sedation
	venation
	vexation
EAIS	ceramics
	denarius
	Gelasius
	Pelagius
	Vesalius
EAIT	legalist
EAIY	denazify
	feracity
	legality
	regality
	tenacity
	venality
	veracity
EAKD	remarked
EAKN	bedarken
	remark on
EAKR	remarker
EALC	metallic
EALD	detailed
EALO	seraglio
EALP	megaflop
EALR	retailer
EALS	Heracles
EALT	metaplot
	retail at
EAMD	becalmed
EAND	detained
	retained
EANE	detainee
EANH	relaunch
EANM	per annum
EANR	regainer
	retainer
EANY	Delaunay
EAOA	lecanora
	melanoma
	teratoma
EAOB	hecatomb
EAOD	ceratoid
	keratoid

	sesamoid
	teratoid
EAOE	keratose
	let alone
	let-alone
	megapode
	nematode
EAOF	see a wolf
EAOG	get along
EAON	metazoan
EAOR	belabour
EAOS	de Valois❏
	pedaloes
	rebatoes
EAOT	get about
	see about
	set about
EAOY	demagogy
	pedagogy
EAQE	pétanque
	remarque❏
EARD	debarred
EARE	hetaerae
EARI	hetairai
EARM	hexagram
EARN	betatron
	bevatron
EARS	hetairas
EARZ	Veracruz
EASD	relapsed
EASE	Selassie
EASR	relapser
EASS	xeransis
EATA	semantra
EATC	gelastic
	pedantic
	semantic
	Vedantic
EATD	departed
	tenanted
EATE	Lemaître
	repartee
EATR	decanter
	recanter
	redactor
	remaster
EATS	cerastes
EATY	pedantry
	secantly
	tenantry
EAUA	tenacula
EAUD	devalued
EAUE	denature
EAUK	megabuck
EAYE	megabyte
EAYF	be wary of
EAZE	bedazzle
EBAD	keyboard
	lee-board
	Redbeard
	seaboard
EBAE	membrane
	verbiage
EBAK	jet-black
EBDY	red biddy
EBED	tea bread
EBEK	leg break
	tea break
EBEM	sea bream
EBIE	kerbside
EBIK	redbrick
EBLS	cembalos
EBLT	herbelet
EBLY	verbally
EBOD	let blood
	new blood
EBOM	new broom
EBON	new-blown
EBOS	temblors
EBRA	herbaria
EBRD	membered
EBRE	seaborne
EBRH	new birth
EBRS	Cerberus
EBTM	verbatim
EBTN	verboten
EBUK	Delbrück
ECAT	merchant❏
	penchant
ECAX	berceaux
ECBE	fencible
	peccable
ECDN	fenced in
ECDR	red cedar
ECDS	Mercedes
ECDY	deucedly
	tea caddy
ECEE	New Crete
ECER	get clear
ECES	teachers
ECET	nescient
	tea chest
ECFL	merciful
	peaceful
ECHT	beach-hut
ECIE	describe
	perceive
	reactive
ECIF	kerchief
ECIG	belching
	fetching
	reaching
	retching
	teaching
ECII	zecchini
ECIN	reaction
	Reichian
ECIO	zecchino
ECIT	rescript
ECIY	tetchily
ECLA	mea culpa
ECLN	mescalin
	pencil in
ECLS	Hercules
ECMN	henchman
	hench-men
	Newcomen
ECMR	newcomer
ECMS	Newcomes
ECNO	bel canto
ECNT	beech nut
ECNY	peccancy
ECOF	fence off
	fetch off
ECOH	tea cloth
ECOL	deschool
ECOS	Red Cross
ECOT	fetch out
	reach out
ECRC	mercuric
ECSW	bench saw
ECTO	Mercutio
ECTR	Mercator
ECUE	berceuse
ECUY	re-occupy
ECVL	Perceval
	Percival
ECVR	bedcover
ECVS	peccavis
EDAD	headband
	headland
EDAE	headcase
	headrace
	seedcake
EDAF	red dwarf
EDAK	feedback
	send back
EDAL	headsail
EDAP	headlamp
EDBE	beddable
	bendable
	readable
	vendible
	weldable
EDBY	readably
	Teddy boy
	vendibly
EDCE	headache
EDCY	headachy
EDED	deadhead
	dead-head
EDEN	meddle in
EDER	headgear
EDES	deadness
	deedless
	headless
	heedless
	lewdness
	needless
	seedless
	weedless
EDET	dead beat
	dead-beat
	dead cert
	dead heat
	dead-heat
	headrest
EDHP	headship
EDHT	dead shot
EDIA	rendzina
EDIE	bendwise
	deadline
	dendrite
	headline
	lead time
	let drive
	sex drive
EDIG	meddling
	peddling
	seedling
EDIH	send with
EDIK	herdwick
EDIL	head girl
EDLI	New Delhi
EDLM	pendulum
EDLO	verdelho
EDLR	pendular
EDLY	feudally
EDMN	headsman
	herdsman❏
EDMS	Mesdames
EDNA	reddenda
EDND	deadened
	reddened
EDNE	tea dance
EDNO	lead into
	perdendo
	read into
EDNR	deadener
EDNY	leadenly
	tendency
	verdancy
EDOD	dead wood
	dendroid
	head cold
	headword
	send word
EDOE	send home
EDOG	headlong
EDOK	deadlock
	headwork
EDOL	deed poll
EDOM	headroom
EDON	send down
EDOS	dead loss
EDOT	dead bolt
EDOY	dead body
EDPN	read up on
EDPO	lead up to
EDPR	feldspar
EDPT	dead spit
EDRE	gendarme
EDRR	renderer
EDRY	tenderly
EDSC	geodesic
EDTA	vendetta
EDTC	geodetic
EDTH	Redditch
EDTP	dead stop
EDTR	verditer
EDUK	dead duck
	get drunk

Words marked ❏ can also be spelled with an initial capital letter

reedbuck
EDUT head-butt
headhunt
EDWY send away
EEAA demerara
EEAD Hereward
EEAE beverage
defecate
delegate
federate
generate
hebetate
leverage
regelate
relegate
renegade
renegate
serenade
vegetate
venerate
EEAH telepath
EEAK telemark
EEAL femerall
EEAN Telemann
EEAS Menelaus
EEAT benefact
hebetant
pederast
relevant
renevant
revenant
telecast
EEAY delegacy
federacy
federary
EEBE resemble
EEBR December
remember
EEBX jewel-box
EECE tedesche
EECI tedeschi
EECS defences
Seleucus
EEDD defended
EEDN depend on
EEDR defender
EEDS nereides
EEED repetend
reverend
EEEE Genevese
EEEL venereal
EEEN renege on
EEET cerement
deselect
reverent
teletext
tenement
vehement
EEEY cemetery
serenely
severely
EEFN bedeafen
EEFW feverfew
EEGE sea eagle
EEGR Berengar
Meleager
revenger
EEHA petechia
EEHF Meyerhof
EEHN telethon
EEIA Teresina
EEIC celeriac
EEID Dedekind
jeremiad
Wedekind
EEIE benefice
Berenice
pelerine
rere-mice
selenite
televise
Tenerife
vegetive
EEIG receding
renewing
seceding
severing
EEIH feverish
herewith
Hezekiah
Jeremiah
Meredith
Nehemiah
EEII fedelini
EEIK Benedick
EEIL remedial
EEIM selenium
EEIN deletion
Hegelian
redesign
Venetian
EEIS genetics
senecios
EEIT Benedict
derelict
EEIW teleview
EEIY celerity
heredity
serenity
severity
temerity
EEKN Peterkin
EELD bevelled
levelled
newelled
repelled
revealed
EELE reveille
EELN Medellín
EELR jeweller
leveller
repealer
repeller
revealer
reveller
EELY Beverley
Keneally
redeploy
EEMR redeemer□
EEMS tenesmus
EENO hereunto
EENS Cévennes
EEOD Hereford
EEOE Penelope
EEOF level off
werewolf
EEOH behemoth
EEOI peperoni
EEOS feverous
generous
here goes!
Hereroes
venerous
EEOT peter out
teleport
EEOY ceremony
feretory
hegemony
EEPN hereupon
Peter Pan
EEPS receipts
EERC meteoric
EERD deferred
EERE rehearse
terebrae
EERH research
EERL cerebral
deferral
referral
EERM cerebrum
herefrom
telegram
EERR deferrer
veneerer
EERS terebras
EERT sewer rat
sewer-rat
EESD deceased
recessed
released
reversed
EESL demersal
reversal
EESN Peterson
EESR reverser
EESS reversos
EESY Kerensky
EETA dementia
fenestra
EETD cemented
defeated
dejected
demented
deserted
detested
rejected
repeated
selected
EETE nepenthe
resettle
EETF bereft of
EETL pedestal
EETM cementum
EETN Ben Elton
EETR bee-eater
begetter
defector
deserter
detector
receptor
reheater
rejecter
rejector
repeater
repenter
resetter
selector
semester
EETS mementos
EETY decently
recently
EEUE hebetude
EEUN henequin
EEUR reneguer
EEUS revenues
EEUT bejesuit
EEVD bereaved
deceived
deserved
received
reserved
EEVR deceiver
receiver
EEVS reserves
EEWY hereaway
EFAE beefcake
leaf-base
self-made
selfsame
self-same
EFAL leaf-fall
EFCA perfecta
EFCD red-faced
EFCL deifical
EFEL self-heal
EFEP Self-Help
EFES deafness
Jeffreys
leafless
leaflets
selfless
EFID leafbird
EFIL self-will
EFIM reaffirm
EFIY self-pity
EFLS beefalos
EFMD perfumed
EFMR perfumer
EFNT reef knot
EFOD selfhood
serfhood
EFOE self-love

Words marked □ can also be spelled with an initial capital letter

EFON self-sown
EFOT seafront
EFRE perforce
EFRH set forth
EFRR seafarer
EFRY Geoffrey
EFUD new-found
EFUE deaf-mute
self-rule
EFUL leaf-curl
EFXL leaf axil
EFYH keffiyeh
EFYT let fly at
EGAD leg guard
Red Guard
EGAE Belgrade
Redgrave
EGAI Benghazi
EGAP Bergkamp
EGAS eelgrass
EGAT red giant
sergeant
EGEN pea-green
EGER seigneur
EGEY meagrely
EGFL vengeful
EGHG hedgehog
EGHI feng shui
EGHN lengthen
EGHP hedge-hop
EGIF fee-grief
EGIG beagling
feigning
get going
reigning
seagoing
sea-going
set going
weighing
EGIR seignior
EGLE Peggy Lee
EGMD hey-go-mad
EGMM Pergamum
EGMN Pergamon
EGMT bergamot
EGNS leggings
EGNY reagency
EGOD Wedgwood
EGOF weigh off
EGOR peignoir
EGOT weigh out
EGRC Bergerac
EGRD beggared
Belgorod
EGRE kedgeree
EGRW hedgerow
EGRY beggarly
EGSE Peggy Sue
EGSN Ferguson
EGSU Mengistu
EGTD weighted
EGTN Deighton
heighten

EGTY Peggotty
EGUE lee-gauge
EHAE rephrase
EHAK bethwack
EHDC methodic
EHFY get huffy
EHGN Ben Hogan
EHHS Nephthys
EHIE nephrite
EHIS technics
EHLC cephalic
EHLY lethally
sea holly
EHML béchamel
EHNC mechanic
EHNE bechance
EHNL methanal
methanol
EHOE dethrone
EHOK meshwork
mesh-work
EHRD tethered
EHRE recharge
seahorse
EHRY lethargy
EHSS methysis
EHTC mephitic
EHTP get het up
EHTS mephitis
EHUA Gezhouba
EHVH yeshivah
EHVN New Haven
Newhaven
EHWR Peshawar
EIAD Reginald
EIAE celibate
decimate
dedicate
defilade
delicate
depilate
geminate
heritage
hesitate
levigate
levitate
medicate
meditate
resinate
seminate
vesicate
EIAI teriyaki
EIAP pericarp
EIAS genitals
EIAT hesitant
vesicant
EIAY celibacy
delicacy
seminary
EIBE deniable
reliable
EIBY deniably
reliably

EICE mediocre
EICL heliacal
EICS meniscus
EIDC periodic
EIDE rekindle
EIDR bewilder
reminder
EIEE Bedivere
Pekinese
EIEI beriberi
EIEK helideck
EIEL perineal
EIEM perineum
EIEN decide on
Oedipean
reside in
EIEO be wise to
EIES dewiness
eeriness
get ideas
sexiness
EIET pediment
penitent
redirect
regiment
renitent
resident
reticent
sediment
EIEY delivery
refinery
senilely
EIGD besieged
EIGE meringue
EIGN Lewis gun
EIGR rejigger
EIGS meninges
seeing as
EIGY vexingly
EIHD perished
EIHM Lewisham
EIHN lecithin
EIHR decipher
perisher
EIHY Jewishly
newishly
EIID verified
EIIE decisive
definite
derisive
feminine
feminise
feminize
genitive
Leninite
lenitive
lewisite
medicine
regicide
resinise
resinize
Semitise
Semitize

Tebilise
EIIG deciding
defiling
deriving
desiring
devising
refining
retiring
reviling
reviving
EIIH devilish
EIIL remigial
EIIM delirium
feminism
Leninism
EIIN decision
derision
meridian
petition
recision
religion□
revision
sedition
EIIR verifier
EIIS verities
EIIT feminist
Leninist
EIIY debility
felicity□
resinify
revivify
senility
tepidity
EILM vexillum
EILN Sémillon
tefillin
EILS Pericles
vehicles
EILY aerially
genially
medially
mesially
serially
venially
EIML petit mal
EIMS melismas
EIND designed
resigned
EINE defiance
deviance
lenience
reliance
EINH perianth
EINL regional
EINR beginner
designer
resigner
EINY benignly
deviancy
leniency
EIOE lepidote
pericope
Seminole

Words marked □ can also be spelled with an initial capital letter

	semitone
EIOF	demi-wolf
	get it off
EIOI	periboli
EIOM	Benidorm
	reniform
	retiform
EION	demijohn
EIOS	desirous
	perilous
	resinous
EIOT	heliport
EIOY	derisory
	revisory
EIRE	pedigree
EIRM	lexigram
EIRO	senior to
EIRP	let it rip
EIRX	heritrix
EISS	geniuses
EISY	remissly
EITC	semiotic
	veristic
EITE	belittle
	remittee
EITL	remittal
EITM	meristem
	seriatim
EITR	demister
	depicter
	depictor
	mediator□
	register
	remitter
	remittor
	resister
	resistor
EITY	registry
EIUA	vesicula
EIUE	deciduae
	pedicure
	perilune
	refigure
	reticule
EIUI	pediculi
EIUL	residual
EIUM	residuum
EIUN	heniquin
EIUS	deciduas
EIVD	believed
	relieved
EIVL	medieval
EIVR	believer
	desilver
	reliever
EIVS	relievos
EIWL	reviewal
EIWR	reviewer
EJAT	serjeant
EJIE	verjuice
EJMN	Benjamin
	Betjeman
EJRD	perjured
EJRR	perjurer
EKAD	deck hand
	deckhand
	neckband
EKAE	necklace
EKER	neckwear
EKES	feckless
	meekness
	reckless
	weakness
EKIE	neckline
	penknife
	weak side
EKIG	weakling
EKLY	Berkeley
	Ned Kelly
EKND	reckoned
	weakened
EKNN	reckon on
EKNP	reckon up
EKNR	reckoner
	weakener
EKOD	Beckford
EKPT	weak spot
EKSY	Ken Kesey
EKVR	deck over
ELAD	hellward
	well-paid
ELAE	telltale
	tell-tale
	well-made
	wet lease
ELAL	keel-haul
ELAN	feel pain
	Gell-Mann
ELBE	sellable
ELBG	jelly bag
ELCD	pellucid
ELCE	Jellicoe
	pellicle
ELCR	replacer
ELDC	Helladic
ELDD	secluded
ELED	wellhead
	well-head
	well-read
ELEL	pell-mell
ELES	realness
ELET	bell tent
	hell-bent
	well-kept
ELFL	bellyful
ELGA	pellagra
ELGE	negligee
	verligte
ELGT	red light
ELHM	Sealyham
ELHN	fellahin
ELIE	feel like
	hellfire
	hell-kite
	real life
	real-life
	real live
	Verlaine
ELIG	seal ring
ELIH	deal with
	feel with
	well-nigh
ELKN	oerlikon□
ELLE	tell a lie
ELLR	cellular
ELMN	wealsman
ELNC	Hellenic
ELNN	bed linen
	bed-linen
ELNR	recliner
ELNS	dealings
	feelings
	ley lines
	wetlands
ELNT	well-knit
ELOD	feelgood
ELOE	let loose
	set loose
	well done
	well-done
ELON	Gellhorn
	well-born
	well-worn
ELOO	well-to-do
ELOT	keelboat
ELPN	well up on
ELPO	feel up to
ELPP	sell a pup
ELRC	telluric
ELRD	declared
	well-bred
ELRH	keel arch
ELRO	Key Largo
ELRR	declarer
ELSD	well-used
ELTC	perlitic
	zeolitic
ELTD	deflated
	depleted
ELTH	declutch
ELTN	New Latin
ELTR	deflater
	deflator
ELTY	zealotry
ELUN	red lauan
ELUY	bell buoy
	jealousy
ELVL	sea level
	sea-level
ELVN	replevin
ELVR	heel over
	keel over
	well over
ELVS	Mevlevis
ELWD	newly-wed
ELWN	Nell Gwyn
ELWR	beflower
	deflower
	get lower
ELWY	fellowly
	mellowly
ELXY	reflexly
ELYN	Wesleyan
ELZD	realized
ELZR	realizer
EMAE	permeate
	team-mate
EMAL	Heimdall
EMCN	neomycin
	pemmican
EMDL	new-model
EMDN	Bermudan
	hemmed in
EMDS	Bermudas
EMES	germless
	seamless
EMID	helm wind
EMIE	Germaine
	seem like
	teamwise
EMIH	teem with
EMMN	helmsman
EMNA	tegmenta
EMNC	Germanic
EMND	vermined
EMNH	helminth
EMNL	germinal□
	terminal
EMNR	Leo Minor
EMNS	terminus
EMNY	key money
	seamanly
	yeomanly
	yeomanry
EMOE	Hermione
	re-impose
EMOK	teamwork
EMON	team down
EMPN	Belmopan
EMRC	mesmeric
EMRE	germ-free
EMRH	besmirch
	Meg March
EMSE	kermesse
	let me see
EMTC	hermetic
	hermitic
EMTD	helmeted
EMTR	geometer
	seamster
EMTS	fermatas
	new maths
EMTY	geometry
EMUE	sea mouse
EMUH	vermouth□
	Weymouth
ENAK	lean back
	rein back
ENAP	neon lamp
ENCE	vernicle
	Wernicke
ENCS	Les Noces

ENDS Leonidas
ENED Seinfeld
ENEE meunière
ENEG Weinberg
ENER reindeer
ENES keenness
leanness
meanness
ENET re-invent
reinvest
ENFR Jennifer
ENGD teenaged
ENGR teenager
ENHS Jean Rhys
ENHW hernshaw
ENID fernbird
ENIE meantime
ENIF Leontief
ENIG weanling
ENLM Léon Blum
ENLS Reynolds
ENLY vernally
ENNS Jennings
Pennines
remnants
ENNT seine net
ENOE beanpole
ENOK Jean Rook
ENOM reinform
ENON mean-born
ENRE wet nurse
wet-nurse
ENRO Leonardo
ENSN Tennyson
ENTE Jeanette
ENTL neonatal
ENTR Leinster
ENUD reinfund
ENUE ceinture
reinsure
ENUK Dean Rusk
ENUR Jean Muir
ENUT Regnault
ENVR lean over
ENVS Ben Nevis
ENWR reanswer
EOAA xeromata
EOAD Legoland
EOAE decorate
derogate
desolate
detonate
lemonade
pejorate
perorate
relocate
renovate
resonate
zero-rate
EOAH cenotaph□
EOAL reposall
EOAR debonair
EOAT resonant

EOBE redouble
EOCN resorcin
EOCR rejoicer
EODD recorded
EODF devoid of
EODL keloidal
EODN beholden
EODR beholder
recorder
seconder
EODY secondly
EOEE felo de se
Genovese
kerosene
Veronese
EOEL peroneal
EOEM mesoderm
EOEN melodeon
EOEO zero-zero
EOES devotees
EOET De Forest
deforest
deponent
redolent
reforest
remotest
EOEY recovery
remotely
EOFN get off on
EOGO belong to
EOHN Xenophon
EOHR be mother
EOIA semolina
Señorita
veronica□
EOIC demoniac
EOIE aerolite
demonise
demonize
genocide
kerosine
leporine
melodise
melodize
memorise
memorize
peroxide
tenorite
EOIG becoming
beloving
decoding
denoting
reposing
revoking
EOIH aerolith
demolish
xenolith
EOIL memorial
EOIM demonism
hedonism
meconium
nepotism
EOIN demotion

Devonian
devotion
melodion
Neronian
remotion
EOIO Geronimo
EOIS aerobics
Bedouins
hedonics
memories
EOIT hedonist
melodist
nepotist
EOIY detoxify
ferocity
velocity
venosity
EOLR recoiler
EOMD deformed
EOMR reformer
EOND renowned
EONE denounce
renounce
EONN zero in on
EONR dehorner
EOOC Cenozoic
Mesozoic
EOOD be so bold
EOOL aerofoil
EOOM jeroboam
rehoboam
EOOR decolour
zero hour
EOOS decorous
venomous
EOOY oenology
penology
serology
sexology
EOPE decouple
EOPR below par
EORE recourse
resource
EORH begorrah
EORM aerogram
EORR devourer
EORT democrat
EOSE repoussé
EOSW tenon saw
tenon-saw
EOTA lemon tea
EOTD besotted
deported
reported
revolted
EOTE deportee
EOTF get out of
EOTN be soft on
EOTO resort to
EOTR reporter
resorter
revolter
sea otter

EOTY devoutly
EOUE resolute
revolute
EOVD devolved
resolved
EOVR resolver
revolver
EOVY reconvey
EOWR men-of-war
EOYE genotype
serotype
EOYY metonymy
EPAD deep-laid
EPAE helpmate
keep pace
keep safe
keepsake
seaplane
sea-plane
template
wet-plate
EPAK keep back
keep dark
EPAM keep calm
keep warm
neoplasm
EPAN Helpmann
EPAY vespiary
EPBE helpable
EPCI Vespucci
EPCS respects
EPED bespread
resplend
EPEE Bel Paese
bel paese
neoprene
set piece
EPER leap year
reappear
EPES deepness
helpless
EPET helpmeet
EPGI Respighi
EPIE helpline
keep time
semplice
EPIG tempting
EPIH help with
EPIS deep kiss
EPIT key point
set point
EPLE Deep Blue
serpulae
EPLN zeppelin□
EPNC geoponic
EPND weaponed
EPNE response
ten pence
EPNH keypunch
EPNT keep on at
EPNY new penny
weaponry
EPOD keep cold

Words marked □ can also be spelled with an initial capital letter

EPOE	neophobe
	peephole
EPON	deep down
	keep down
EPRD	peppered
EPRG	leap-frog
EPRI	Leopardi
EPRL	temporal
EPRM	keep from
EPRS	Hesperus
EPRY	jeopardy
	tea-party
EPTC	despotic
	herpetic
EPTH	despatch
EPTP	keep step
EPTT	keep at it
EPUY	keep busy
EPVR	leap over
EPWY	keep away
EPYD	deep-dyed
EPYE	neophyte
ERAD	bear hard
	near-hand
	rearward
ERAE	decrease
	degrease
	ferriage
	recreate
ERAH	reproach
ERAN	pearmain
ERAT	Near East
	recreant
	retroact
ERAY	February
	get ready
ERBE	bearable
	hearable
	terrible
	wearable
ERBY	bearably
	terribly
ERCD	terraced
ERCE	verrucae
ERCL	metrical
ERCN	jerrycan
ERCS	verrucas
ERDD	degraded
ERDE	begrudge
ERDF	get rid of
ERDI	perradii
ERDP	geared up
ERDS	Hebrides
ERED	befriend
EREE	dearie me
	defreeze
	derrière
	repreeve
	reprieve
	retrieve
ERER	hear, hear!
	near beer
ERES	dearness
	fearless
	heirless
	nearness
	peerless
	tearless
ERET	reorient
ERFC	terrific
ERFR	yearn for
ERFT	retrofit
ERGN	Kerrigan
	tetragon
ERGS	verrugas
ERGT	set right
ERHN	wear thin
ERHR	searcher
ERIA	Georgina
ERIE	Hebraise
	Hebraize
	nearside
	pearlite
	rearmice
ERIG	decrying
	learning
	wearying
	yearling
	yearning
ERIH	bear with
ERIM	Negroism
ERIN	Georgian
ERIS	Georgics
	near miss
	pearlies
ERIY	heartily
ERKN	bearskin
	deerskin
ERLO	Negrillo
ERLY	neurally
	retrally
ERMD	begrimed
ERMN	Berryman
	ferryman
	merryman
ERMS	neuromas
ERNE	befringe
	Terrance
ERNH	bedrench
	retrench
ERNI	Ferranti
ERNO	tear into
ERNS	bearings
EROE	fearsome
EROG	yearlong
EROK	yearbook
	year-book
EROM	Beerbohm
	heirloom
ERON	bear down
	Dearborn
	gear down
	tear down
	wear down
EROS	ferreous
EROT	rearmost
	weary out
ERPD	tetrapod
ERPE	Henry Pye
ERPN	bear upon
	terrapin
ERPT	decrepit
ERPY	necropsy
ERRA	terraria
ERRE	retrorse
ERRH	Petrarch
ERRP	pear drop
ERSA	Nebraska
ERSL	reprisal
ERSS	necrosis
	neuroses
	neurosis
ERTC	Nearctic
	necrotic
	neurotic
ERTD	serrated
ERTL	decretal
	detrital
ERTN	secretin
ERTS	detritus
	Negritos
	neuritis
ERTY	secretly
ERUD	get round
ERUT	tear duct
ERVD	depraved
	deprived
ERVR	Red River
	reprover
	sea rover
	sea-rover
ERWY	bear away
	tearaway
	wear away
ERYD	betrayed
ERYL	betrayal❑
	defrayal
ERYR	betrayer
	defrayer
ERYT	Peer Gynt
ERZO	terrazzo
ESAE	key stage
	persuade
	seascape
ESAK	redshank
ESAN	Messiaen
	Weismann
ESAP	jew's harp❑
ESAT	newscast
	redstart
ESBE	feasible
	leasable
	sensible
	tensible
ESBY	feasibly
	sensibly
ESCB	Welsh Cob
ESCE	versicle
ESCS	bedsocks
ESDF	seised of
ESDN	versed in
ESDP	messed up
ESDY	feast day
ESED	bedstead
	reascend
ESEK	kenspeck
	newspeak
	Newsweek
ESEL	deisheal
	newsreel
	seashell
ESEP	REM sleep
ESER	menswear
ESES	reassess
ESHL	Herschel
ESHN	less than
ESIE	fess-wise
	let slide
	perspire
	Teesside
ESIG	feasting
	Pershing
ESIT	red shirt
	tee shirt
	tee-shirt
ESIY	beastily
ESLA	sensilla
ESLY	weaselly
ESMN	Welshman
ESMR	Bessemer
ESND	reasoned
	seasoned
ESNE	personae
ESNI	Helsinki
ESNL	personal
	seasonal
ESNR	seasoner
ESNS	personas
ESNY	peasanty
ESOE	gemstone
	keystone
	seashore
ESOG	Rees-Mogg
ESOK	penstock
ESOL	cesspool
ESOM	newsroom
ESON	teaspoon
ESOS	sensuous
	Sessions
ESOT	Sea Scout
ESRA	menstrua
	sensoria
ESRD	leisured
	measured
ESRE	tesserae
ESRL	mensural
ESRN	Mensuren
ESRR	censurer
ESRS	measures
ESRW	bedstraw
	setscrew
ESTM	news item

Words marked ❑ can also be spelled with an initial capital letter

ESUE reassure
red sauce
ESUK get stuck
ESUT Deus vult
ESVS zemstvos
ESWN feast-won
Gershwin
ESYE New Style
ETAD left-hand
leftward
westward
ETAE left face!
Lestrade
test case
ETAH heat rash
ETAK beat back
ETAL meatball
ETAN restrain
ETAT best part
ETAY bestiary
tertiary❑
ETBA vertebra
ETBE beatable
lettable
testable
ETCE denticle
lenticle
pentacle
tentacle
testicle
ETCL vertical
verticil
ETCP death cap
ETCS vertices
ETCY Kentucky
ETDS testudos
ETDY pettedly
ETEE aesthete
get there
ETEK bestreak
ETEN centre on
leathern
settle in
settle on
yestreen
ETEP settle up
ETES deftness
heathens
meatless
neatness
pertness
restless
ETET next best
seat belt
sentient
vestment
ETEY feathery
leathery
ETFC beatific
ETFG pettifog
ETGA vestigia
ETGN heptagon
pentagon

ETGS vestiges
ETIE Beatrice
bestride
dextrine
tentwise
ETIG beetling
left-wing
nestling
nettling
seething
settling
teething
ETIH meet with
rest with
ETIL testrill
ETIM centrism
ETIO neutrino
ETIS westlins
ETIT centrist
restrict
ETIY gentrify
lent-lily
ETLA dentalia
ETLE dentelle
ETLY festally
mentally
rectally
ETMB rent-a-mob
ETNC leptonic
tectonic
Teutonic
ETND destined
ETNE sentence
ETNK Bentinck
ETNL sentinel
ETNO lentando
melt into
ETNS centones
pectines
ETOD bentwood
Hertford
Westwood
ETOE dextrose
ETOF meat loaf
ETOK textbook
ETOM rest room
ETON beat down
meltdown
pelt down
sent down
ETOR next door
next-door
ETOS dextrous
oestrous
ETOT beat to it
beetroot
sea trout
ETPE centuple
septuple
sextuple
Zentippe
ETPN beat up on
ETPS gestapos

ETRA septaria
ETRC neoteric
ETRD festered
fettered
lettered
pestered
restored
textured
ETRE rent-free
sesterce
ETRH heptarch
ETRL gestural
pectoral
sectoral
textural
ETRN deuteron
ETRR lecturer
pesterer
pewterer
restorer
venturer
ETRS dentures
features
lectures
ETRW Heathrow
ETRY westerly
ETSD pertused
ETSN jettison
ETSS centeses
meatuses
ETTE septette
ETTL teetotal
ETTM teetotum
ETTO set to two
ETUE Gertrude
test tube
ETUP heat pump
ETUS Centaurs
centrums
ETUT destruct
ETVL aestival
festival
ETVR left over
leftover
left-over
ETVS centavos
ETWL bestowal
tea towel
ETWY melt away
ETXS vertexes
ETZS mestizas
mestizos
EUAE depurate
peculate
regulate
EUAH bequeath
EUAS Beauvais
mezuzahs
regulars
EUAT débutant
petulant
recusant
EUBA penumbra

EUBD benumbed
EUBS nelumbos
EUCE peduncle
EUDE befuddle
EUDR refunder
EUEN cerulean
EUET feculent
tegument
EUEY demurely
jejunely
reduce by
securely
EUFE kefuffle
EUGT requight
EUHR nenuphar
EUIE delusive
deputise
deputize
nebulise
nebulize
reguline
regulise
regulize
EUIG bemusing
deluding
refusing
securing
EUIL tenurial
EUIM refugium
EUIN delusion
Peruvian
Venusian
EUIO Perugino
EUIR peculiar
EUIS beauties
Vesuvius
EUIY beautify
jejunity
repurify
security
sedulity
EULC republic
EULD beguiled
EULE medullae
sequelae
EULR medullar
EULS medullas
EULY sexually
EUMR remurmur
EUND returned
sequined
EUNE sequence
EUNK refusnik
EUNO return to
EUOD medusoid
EUOH mezuzoth
EUOR Beauvoir
EUOS nebulous
sedulous
EUOT Beaufort
Beaumont
EUOY delusory
EURD required

Words marked ❑ can also be spelled with an initial capital letter

8 _E_U_R

EURL	demurral
EURM	delubrum
EURR	requirer
EUSD	repulsed
EUSN	be nuts on
EUSS	Senussis
EUTD	requited
EUTL	rebuttal
	requital
EUTN	result in
EUTR	rebutter
	requiter
EUYE	requoyle
EVAE	perviate
EVCL	cervical
EVCS	cervices
	services
EVDD	pervaded
EVDE	selvedge
EVDY	fervidly
EVGS	nerve gas
EVLE	Melville
EVLO	Benvolio
EVLT	cervelat
EVND	leavened
EVNS	leavings
	servants
EVNY	fervency
	heavenly
EVOF	leave off
EVOS	pervious
EVOT	leave out
	serve out
EVRE	perverse
EVSS	pelvises
EVTC	Helvetic
EVXS	cervixes
EWAK	eelwrack
	sea wrack
EWED	Verwoerd
EWEE	see where
EWKN	reawaken
EWMN	leg-woman
	penwoman
EWOG	get wrong
EWRD	New World
EWRE	get worse
EWRH	Hepworth
EWRS	bedwards
	seawards
EWTR	seawater
EYAT	very fast
EYAY	very many
EYEE	Terylene®
EYEL	very well
EYHS	lekythos
EYOD	very good
	very loud
EYON	very soon
EYTA	Kenyatta
EYUH	very much
EYYD	dewy-eyed
EZAN	Weizmann
EZBE	seizable
EZIK	Selznick
EZLS	Berzelis
EZNE	Penzance
EZTI	terzetti
FADF	afraid of
FADN	off and on
FBEK	off-break
FDIE	off-drive
FEAL	after all
FEDD	offended
FEDR	offender
FEEE	aftereye
FEET	afferent
	efferent
FEEY	effetely
FEIG	offering
FERT	of secret
FETD	affected
FETR	effector
FETX	after tax
	after-tax
FEUE	of repute
FGAD	off guard
FIAY	efficacy
FIBT	a fair bet
FIES	officers
FIHS	of nights
FIIL	official
FIIY	affinity
FINE	affiance
FLET	affluent
	effluent
FLVA	effluvia
FMTS	sfumatos
FNGT	of a night
FNYO	if only to
FOET	afforest
FORE	of course
FPEE	of a piece
FPIT	offprint
FPSE	off-piste
FRAI	sforzati
FRAO	sforzato
FRGT	affright
FSAE	off-shake
	off-stage
FSLS	off-sales
FSOE	offshore
FSOT	offshoot
FTMS	ofttimes
FTUH	of a truth
FUIE	effusive
FUIN	affusion
	effusion
FUTR	aflutter
FWIE	off-white
FWRS	off-wards
GAIN	agrarian
GAIS	Ignatius
GAOS	ignaroes
GAOT	Agra Fort
GDES	agedness
GEIG	agreeing
GERH	ogee arch
GETC	agrestic
GGOP	age group
GHAS	eggheads
GIEL	ego ideal
GIES	ugliness
GIHY	aguishly
GIIG	igniting
GIIN	ignition
GIMR	aglimmer
GIOA	Agricola
GIOY	agrimony
GITC	egoistic
GITR	aglitter
GLRM	ngultrum
GMNA	egomania
GNZD	agonized
GOAT	ignorant
GOBT	a good bet
GOBY	a good buy
GOFW	a good few
GOIG	ignoring
GOIY	ignominy
GOOY	agronomy
GOTC	agnostic
GOWY	a good way
GPAT	eggplant
GPIN	Egyptian
GPTS	Agapetus
GREE	aggrieve
GRGR	agar-agar
GSEL	eggshell
GSIE	egg-slice
GSII	Agostini
GSON	egg-spoon
GTMR	egg-timer
GTRP	agitprop
GTTD	agitated
GTTR	agitator
GUDI	Agnus Dei
HAAO	The Alamo
HAAT	pheasant
HACY	thearchy
HADM	thraldom
HAER	wheatear
HAHR	thrasher
HAIE	thiamine
HAIG	cheating
	phrasing
	sheading
HAMS	chiasmus
HANL	shrapnel
HANN	Rhiannon
HAOO	whoa-ho-ho
HAPE	the Apple
	thrapple
HAPN	shear pin
HATD	thwarted
HATY	thwartly
HBAA	Jhabvala
HBAO	The Beano
HBAS	the brass
HBAT	the Beast
HBIE	thebaine
HBIY	shabbily
	the briny
HBNS	the bends
HBOD	rhabdoid
HBOH	Shabuoth
HBOX	The Bronx
HBRH	the birch
HBRI	Ghiberti
HBRS	The Birds
HBTE	who but he
HBUS	the blues
HCAE	the craze
HCAK	the Chalk
HCED	the Creed
HCEK	The Clerk
HCES	checkers
HCIG	checking
	shocking
	whacking
HCLD	shackled
HCLS	shackles
HCLY	Shockley
HCNE	chaconne
HCOF	check off
HCOH	the cloth
HCOS	thickoes
	whackoes
HCOT	check out
	checkout
	chuck out
HCPA	chick pea
	chickpea
HCRE	the curse
HCST	thickset
HCWR	Chaco War
HDEL	Shadwell
HDES	Thaddeus
HDEY	shuddery
HDIG	shedding
	thudding
HDIK	Chadwick
	the drink
HDIY	shoddily
HDNY	The Dandy
HDSA	Rhodesia
HDVL	khedival
	the Devil
HDWY	the downy
HEAE	shoelace
HEBW	the elbow
HEDD	shielded
HEDG	sheepdog
HEDN	threaden
HEDP	sheep-dip
HEDR	shredder
HEDY	shrewdly
HEES	shoeless
HEEY	the Enemy
	thievery
HEFL	cheerful
HEGE	The Eagle

HEHN Phaethon
HEHR thresher
HEIG cheering
sheeting
thieving
wheeling
wheezing
HEIH sheepish
shrewish
thievish
HEIL shoebill
HEIN Rhaetian
HEIS cheerios
HEIY cheekily
cheerily
wheezily
HELR wheedler
HEMN three-man
HEOE threnode
HEON shoehorn
HEOY threnody
HEPY three-ply
HERS Phaedrus
HETC phreatic
HETN threaten
HEWY three-way
HEYO cheeky to
HFIG chaffing
shifting
HFIR The Friar
HFIS The Flies
HFIY shiftily
HFLD shuffled
HFLR shuffler
HFNY the fancy
HFOD the Flood
HFOH shofroth
HFOS The Frogs
HFOY chiffony
HFRE the Force
HGAE the grave
HGDS rhagades
HGEN shagreen
HGES the Greys
HGEY thuggery
Whiggery
HGIH thuggish
Whiggish
HGIM Whiggism
HGIY shaggily
HGLA shigella
HGNL shogunal
HGNS the gents
HGOS the goods
The Goons
HHGE The Hague
HHLS the halls
HHNC chthonic
HHSS phthisis
HIAD Thailand
HIAE shiitake
HIBY choirboy
HIET choicest

HIEY choicely
HIID The Iliad
HIIG thriving
HIIS Pheidias
HIIT The Idiot
HIKR shrieker
HILD thrilled
HILR thriller
HIML chrismal
HIMN chairman
HIRA Chris Rea
HISE Chrissie
HISS thripses
HISW chainsaw
HITC theistic
HITE Christie
HITN christen
HITS Christus
HIVL shrieval
HKAK the knack
HKBE shakable
HKOF choke off
shake off
HKOT shake out
shake-out
HLAS Whillans
HLBG philibeg
HLDS pholades
HLES Childers
HLIE phyllite
HLIG childing
chilling
shelling
shelving
shilling
HLIH childish
HLIM phallism
thallium
HLIS chillies
Phillips
HLIY chillily
HLMN Philemon
HLMS thalamus
HLMT the limit
HLNE phalange
HLOD thalloid
HLOE phyllode
HLOL whale oil
HLOS shallows
HLOT chalk out
chill out
shell out
HLPA Philippa
HLPI Philippi
HLPR Sholapur
HLRC choleric
HLRN children
HLSS thyloses
HLTC phyletic
HLUK shelduck
HLZE chalazae
HLZS chalazas
HMCL chemical

HMDA the media
HMEA chimaera□
HMEF themself
HMES Chambers
champers
HMEY shimmery
HMFL shameful
HMHM whim-wham
HMIG thumping
HMII Khomeini
HMIN champion□
HMIY whimsily
HMIZ Chemnitz
HMLS shambles
HMNH The Month
HMNI Khamenei
HMOD rhomboid
HMOK shamrock
HMOS shampoos
HMRC chimeric
HMRL whimbrel
HMRO Chamorro
HMRY chambray
HMSN Thompson
HMSP thumbs up
thumbs-up
HMSR The Miser
HMSS chamises
chamisos
phimosis
shamuses
HMTC thematic
HMTR ohmmeter
HMUN Thom Gunn
HMVR whomever
HNAE chantage
HNAG Shenyang
HNAM phantasm
HNAY phantasy
thingamy
HNDT whinid'st
HNEL Shinwell
HNEN chance on
HNEP change up
HNES channels
chinless
thinners
thinness
HNET chance it
HNEY chancery
thundery
HNFL thankful
HNFT think fit
HNHI shanghai□
HNHL rhonchal
HNHN chin-chin
HNHS rhonchus
HNIG changing
shunning
thinking
thinning
HNIN Ghanaian
HNLE chenille

HNLN Shanklin
HNLR chandler□
HNLS shingles
HNMC phonemic
HNMN Chinaman
HNOE shinbone
HNOT think out
HNRS the narks
HNSA Changsha
HNSE thanks be
HNSO thanks to
HNTA China tea
HNTC phenetic
phonetic
HNTP phone-tap
HNTS rhinitis
Thanatos
HNUG shantung
HNVR whenever
HNYU thank you
thankyou
HOAE chlorate
HOBN thrombin
HOBS theorbos
thrombus
HODD shrouded
HOFR shoot for
HOGD thronged
HOHR the other
HOIE chloride
chlorine
chromite
rhyolite
theorise
theorize
HOIG choosing
shooting
HOIM chromium
HOIT shootist
theorist
HOOA Theodora
HOOD rheocord
HOOE Theodore
HOOF shoot off
throw off
HOOT shoot-out
throw out
HOOY rheology
theology
HOPE thropple
HORT theocrat
HOTE throstle
throttle
HOTT rheostat
HPAD Shephard
Sheppard
shipyard
whip hand
HPAE shipmate
HPAH whiplash
HPAL The Pearl
HPAN chaplain
HPAO The Piano

Words marked □ can also be spelled with an initial capital letter

HPAX	chapeaux
HPBE	shapable
HPED	shepherd
HPEL	Chappell
HPES	shoppers
	the plebs
HPET	shipment
HPHP	chop-chop
HPHT	chip shot
HPID	whipbird
HPIE	ship-tire
HPIG	shipping
	shopping
	whipping
	whopping
HPIL	shop-girl
HPIT	shoplift
	the point
HPOD	shipload
	whipcord
HPOM	shipworm
HPON	chop down
HPOY	rhapsody
HPRN	chaperon
HPSA	ship a sea
HPTI	chapatti
HPTR	whipster
HPTW	Chepstow
HPUK	chipmunk
HPUY	chop suey
HRAB	choriamb
HRAE	shortage
	wharfage
HRAF	Chargaff
HRAY	charlady
	pharmacy
HRBC	cherubic
HRBM	cherubim
HRBN	cherubin
HRBY	Shark Bay
HRCC	thoracic
HRCS	thoraces
HRCT	short cut
	short-cut
HRDM	whoredom
HRDN	Sheridan
HRDO	VHF radio
HRDS	charades
HRDY	Thursday
HRED	sharp end
HREE	Charlene
	The Reeve
HREN	thirteen
HRFR	short for
	therefor
	wherefor
HRHY	churchly
HRIG	charming
	chirping
	shirking
	whirling
	whirring
HRIH	churlish
	sharpish
HRIM	Chartism
	Phormium
HRIN	thermion
HRIS	thirties
	wherries
HRIT	Chartist
HRIY	chirpily
	shirtily
HRKE	Cherokee
HRLG	short leg
HRLY	Charnley
	chorally
HRMN	theramin
	third man
HROK	charlock
HROL	charcoal
	short-oil
HROM	Khartoum
HROT	churn out
	share out
	share-out
HRPD	Theropod
HRRS	Chartres
HRSA	charisma
HRSE	Pharisee
HRST	sharp-set
HRTN	Charlton
	Sheraton
HRUH	thorough
HRUY	chirrupy
HRVR	wherever
HRXN	thyroxin
HRXS	thoraxes
HRZS	chorizos
HSAE	the stage
HSAS	the stars
HSBE	chasuble
HSCL	physical
HSDN	The Sudan
HSEE	phosgene
	this here
HSER	chasseur
HSES	whiskers
HSEY	chastely
	whiskery
HSGR	Thesiger
HSHR	phosphor
HSIE	chastise
	Cheshire
	The Shire
	thuswise
HSIG	The Sting
HSIN	thespian❑
HSIS	the shits
HSIY	chastity
HSLR	whistler❑
HSLS	the sulks
HSMN	chessman
HSNT	chestnut
HSNU	Chisinau
HSOE	Shoshone
	the Smoke
HSOT	phase out
HSQE	physique
HSRP	the strap
HSUI	thesauri
HTAD	Shetland
HTAT	white ant
HTAX	châteaux
HTEE	white-eye
HTEK	what reck?
HTES	chattels
HTET	what next?
HTEY	shattery
HTFT	Photofit®
	what of it?
HTFY	whitefly
HTGR	The Tyger
HTHN	what then?
HTHR	thatcher❑
HTHT	chitchat
	chit-chat
	white-hot
HTHW	chat show
HTIG	shutting
	The Thing
	the thing
HTIH	what with
HTIL	The Trial
HTIR	Whittier
HTIT	Whitgift
HTLE	what else?
	white lie
HTLG	white-leg
HTLR	whittler
HTLW	Whitelaw
HTMC	rhythmic
HTMS	The Times
HTNF	what an if
HTNW	what's new?
HTOD	Thetford
HTOE	Thutmose
HTOM	chat room
HTON	shut down
	shutdown
HTOS	ghettoes
	the trots
HTOT	white out
	white-out
HTPH	chutzpah
HTRC	rhetoric
HTSA	White Sea
HTTE	white tie
HTTL	the total
HTVR	whatever
HTWY	shut away
	thataway
HUAD	thousand
HUDR	shoulder
HUDT	shouldn't
HUHE	shauchle
HUHS	thoughts
HUIG	shouting
HUIH	ghoulish
HUIN	the Union
HUKN	shrunken
HUOF	shrug off
HUOT	shout out
HUTN	thrust in
HUUL	the usual
HVEL	Chevreul
HVLR	shoveler
HVLY	chivalry
HVOF	shove off
HVOH	Shavuoth
HVRE	chivaree
HWAE	showcase
HWEN	chow mein
HWHW	chow-chow
HWIE	the while
HWIL	showgirl
HWIY	show pity
HWLG	show a leg
HWLS	the wells
HWOM	showroom
HWON	showdown
HWOT	Show Boat
HWRD	the world
HWRN	chawdron
HWRS	the works
HWRT	the worst
HWSS	The Wasps
HWVR	chew over
HWVS	The Waves
HYIN	Phrygian
HYLR	Chrysler®
HYNE	Cheyenne
HYUG	the young
HZAG	whizbang
HZBA	rhizobia
HZIG	whizzing
HZKD	whizz kid
HZPD	rhizopod
IAAA	Hinayana
	hiragana
IAAE	divagate
	vicarage
IAAI	Dipavali
IAAT	final act
IAAU	Kinabalu
IABR	Micawber
IACA	sidalcea
IACS	finances
IADN	Girardin
IADT	gin and it
IADY	ribaldry
	wizardly
	wizardry
IAEI	Piranesi
IAEL	Vila Real
IAEN	dilate on
	lima bean
IAET	bivalent
	divalent
	filament
	ligament
	vizament
IAEU	Mirabeau

Words marked ❑ can also be spelled with an initial capital letter

IAGO DiMaggio
IAGS hidalgas
hidalgos
IAHS hibachis
IAIE finalise
finalize
fixative
rivalise
rivalize
vitalise
vitalize
IAIL bilabial
filarial
riparial
vicarial
IAIM titanium
vivarium
IAIN citation
dilation
fixation
libation
ligation
misalign
riparian
IAIT bigamist
finalist
IAIY dicacity
finality
hilarity
vitality
vivacity
IAKR hijacker
IALD disabled
IALT hit a blot
misallot
IALW disallow
IAMD disarmed
IANL disannul
IANX disannex
IAOE girasole
pinafore
viva voce
IAOI rigatoni
IAON picaroon
rigadoon
IAOS bigamous
viragoes
IAOT lie about
IAOY dilatory
minatory
IAPY disapply
misapply
IARE disagree
filagree
IARL binaural
IARX cicatrix
IARY disarray
IASL Limassol
IASY bioassay
final say
IATC didactic
gigantic
IATR disaster
pilaster
IATS ailantos
Gigantes
IAUE disabuse
ligature
picayune
IAUL bimanual
IAUO Pinatubo
IAYE gigabyte
IBAE air brake
rim-brake
IBAN midbrain
IBBE Zimbabwe
IBBT bit by bit
IBCS big bucks
IBEK tie-break
IBEL limbmeal
IBEO liable to
IBES limbless
IBEY Dimbleby
IBIG nibbling
IBIM nimbyism
IBKU Timbuktu
IBLC diabolic
IBLM cimbalom
IBNH disbench
IBRD timbered
IBRE airborne
disburse
Lilburne
IBRK Simbirsk
IBRP limber up
IBRY bilberry
Kimberly
IBSM disbosom
IBSS nimbuses
IBTA ciabatta
IBTC diabetic
IBTS diabetes
IBUH air-brush
IBWL disbowel
ICAD pilchard
ICAK gimcrack
Jim Clark
ICAM disclaim
ICAR Sinclair
ICAT aircraft
pie chart
ICBE miscible
vincible
ICCA viscacha
vizcacha
ICDG ditch-dog
ICEE discrete
ICEL Mitchell
ICET discreet
ICEY witchery
ICGN miscegen
ICHT pinch-hit
ICIF mischief
ICIG birching
circling
ditching
filching
pinching
pitching
ICIN Pitcairn
ICIS biscuits
ICIY biscuity
bitchily
hitchily
zinckify
ICLM vinculum
ICLR circular
miscolor
piacular
ICLS piccolos
ICLY fiscally
zircaloy
Zircoloy®
ICNA Piacenza
ICNE piscinae
ICNI Visconti
ICNL diaconal
ICNS piscinas
ICNY discandy
ICNZ pince-nez
ICOA cinchona
ICOE disclose
ICOH oilcloth
ICON discrown
ICOT piece out
ICPE disciple
mince pie
ICPN linchpin
ICPT sinciput
ICRL visceral
ICRY miscarry
ICSN diocesan
ICSY circussy
ICTR circiter
piscator□
ICUE cincture
tincture
ICUH hiccough
ICUT discount
miscount
viscount
ICVR discover
IDAD hindward
wild card
wind band
IDAE birdcage
IDAH birdbath
IDAL bird call
birdcall
windfall
IDAM wind farm
IDAS windlass
IDAT hind part
IDBE biddable
IDCY diddicoy
IDED bindweed
birdseed
misdread
IDEE Birdseye
mind's eye
IDES kindless
kindness
mildness
mindless
rindless
wildness
windless
IDET Wild West
IDGO lie doggo
IDHT birdshot
IDIE bird-lime
Hinduise
Hinduize
wildfire
wildlife
wild rice
windpipe
IDIG fiddling
hindwing
kindling
middling
piddling
windring
IDIL windmill
IDIM Hinduism
IDLO vindaloo
IDNE riddance
IDNO Mindanao
IDNS findings
IDNY hiddenly
IDOD wildwood
IDOE wind cone
IDOG bird song
IDOK Windhoek
windsock
IDOL wild fowl
wildfowl
IDON wind down
IDOR wild boar
IDOS fiddious
IDOT bird-bolt
hindmost
IDRC Pindaric
IDRM siddurim
wild arum
IDRR hinderer
IDRS wild iris
IDUF windsurf
IDUN windburn
IDUT misdoubt
IDVR bind over
IDWD mildewed
IDWY find a way
IDYE wild type
IEAD hiveward
sideband
sideward
vineyard
wideward
IEAE Airedale
filename
Liberace

	liberate
	literate
	liveware
	siderate
	sine wave
IEAI	literati
IEAK	bite back
	give back
	kite mark□
	sidewalk
	tidemark
	wine rack
IEAL	fireball
	firewall
	give bail
	sidewall
IEAP	fire damp
	firedamp
	time warp
IEAR	fine hair
IEAS	Gil Evans
	sideways
	wideways
IEAT	ci-devant
	disenact
	file past
IEAY	cinerary
	literacy
	literary
	vinegary
IEBE	hireable
	likeable
	liveable
	sizeable
IEBG	mixed bag
IECE	wiseacre
IECO	libeccio
IECR	silencer
IECY	Givenchy
IEDM	videndum
IEDW	disendow
IEED	fireweed
	give head
IEEL	give hell
	live well
	sidereal
IEEN	give rein
	nineteen
IEER	life peer
IEES	fineless
	fineness
	fireless
	lifeless
	likeness
	niceness
	pipeless
	rifeness
	ripeness
	riteless
	timeless
	tireless
	vileness
	wideness
	wireless
IEET	lifebelt
	virement
IEFT	videofit
IEHP	fireship
IEHS	like this
IEHT	like that
IEHW	sideshow
IEID	fine mind
	liveried
IEIE	bitesize
	dimerise
	dimerize
	fireside
	give line
	lifelike
	lifeline
	life-size
	lifetime
	likewise
	live wire
	pipelike
	pipeline
	piperine
	riverine
	sideline
	siderite
	sidewise
	sirenise
	sirenize
IEIG	hireling
	ripening
	riveting
	sideling
	widening
	wiseling
IEIH	liverish
	live with
	pipefish
	side dish
	side with
	tigerish
	viperish
	vixenish
IEIK	limerick□
	sidekick
IEIN	limekiln
	Siberian
IEIS	fivepins
	kinesics
	kinetics
	Liberius
	miseries
	niceties
	ninepins
	nineties
	Sibelius
	Tiberias
	Tiberius
	Tiresias
	Tiselius
IEIT	wine list
IEIW	side view
IEIY	fidelity
	livelily
IEKN	wineskin
IEKY	bi-weekly
IELD	rivelled
IELE	libellee
	live a lie
	Nile blue
IELP	sideslip
IELT	time slot
IELY	lineally
	pipeclay
IEMN	linesman
	sidesman
IENL	hibernal
IENO	give in to
	give into
	give on to
	give onto
	wire into
IENR	Zigeuner
IENY	pigeonry
IEOB	dive-bomb
	fire-bomb
	time bomb
	time-bomb
IEOD	firewood
	fivefold
	Mike Todd
	ninefold
	pinewood
	wifehood
IEOE	cicerone
	fire hose
	literose
	nine-hole
	pine cone
	time code
	time zone
	tiresome
	wife-to-be
	wire rope
IEOG	lifelong
	livelong
	sidelong
IEOI	ciceroni
IEOK	firelock
	firework
	life-work
	pipework
	wirework
IEOL	wire wool
IEOM	wireworm
IEON	live down
	pipe down
	ride down
	timeworn
	time-worn
	tire down
IEOR	fire door
IEOS	viperous
IEOT	diner-out
	lifeboat
	milepost
	mine host
	rise to it
	tired out
	tired-out
	wiped out
IEOY	file copy
IEPL	fire opal
IEPN	give up on
	lifespan
	time span
	wide open
	wide-open
IEPO	live up to
IERL	dihedral
	disenrol
IERM	side drum
	side-drum
IERS	firearms
	pile arms
IERW	fine-draw
	wiredraw
IERY	bi-yearly
	linearly
IESD	diseased
	licensed
IESE	cineaste
	licensee
IESY	diversly
IETD	bisected
	directed
	divested
	pileated
IETN	pile it on
IETO	give it to
IETP	live it up
	mixer tap
	sidestep
	side-step
IETR	bisector
	digester
	director
IETS	pimentos
IETT	direct at
IETY	directly
	silently
IEUE	fine-tune
	sinecure
IEUL	bisexual
IEUO	ritenuto
IEUS	pipefuls
IEUY	lifebuoy
	like fury
IEVR	give over
	tide over
IEWY	fire away
	give away
	giveaway
	give-away
	hide away
	hideaway
	hide-away
	pine away

wire away
IEYD fire-eyed
wide-eyed
IEYO likely to
IFAE airframe
IFAF niffnaff
riff-raff
IFAK hip flask
IFAT diffract
IFBG Jiffy bag®
IFED airfield
midfield
misfield
oilfield
IFES bigfeets
IFGR Hilfiger
IFIG piffling
IFLY fitfully
sinfully
wilfully
IFNA sinfonia
IFOK disfrock
IFOT air frost
IFRD oil-fired
pilfered
IFRE air force
IFRR pilferer
IFRS pifferos
IFSD diffused
IFSR diffuser
IGAE disgrace
wing case
IGAF misgraff
IGAH biograph
IGAK ring-bark
IGAL ringtail
IGAN ring main
IGAS dingbats
ringhals
IGAT misgraft
IGBE diggable
IGDY wingedly
IGER King Lear
IGES kingless
ringlets
wingless
IGET wingbeat
IGEY pinguefy
Tinguely
IGHP kingship
IGIE disguise
kinglike
king-size
misguide
ringside
ring-time
ringwise
IGIG bingeing
giggling
mingling
niggling
tingling
wingding
IGIH kingfish
IGII linguini
IGIK Sidgwick
IGIM jingoism
IGIT jingoist
linguist
IGLM cingulum
IGLR singular
IGLY Kingsley
IGMN liegeman
IGNA Virginia
IGNL diagonal
virginal
IGNS diggings
IGNY virginly
IGOD kingwood
ring road
IGOE diagnose
kid-glove
ringbone
ring-dove
IGOG ding-dong
King Kong
ping pong
ping-pong
singsong
IGOM ringworm
IGON ding doun
King John
IGOS gingkoes
IGOT ring fort
IGPN wingspan
IGRD fingered
jiggered
IGRE disgorge
lingerie
ring true
IGRP ginger up
IGRR lingerer
IGRT ziggurat
IGRY gingerly
IGSS diegesis
IGTN Kingston
IGUE oil gauge
IGVL disgavel
gingival
IGWY ridgeway
IGYI ginglymi
IHAA Mithraea
IHAC Mishnaic
IHAD highland□
misheard
nigh-hand
IHAE fishcake
lichgate
light ale
with ease
IHAF with calf
IHAH mishmash
mish-mash
IHAK fish-hawk
highjack
IHAL fish-tail
highball
hightail
IHAM right arm
IHAN Eichmann
IHAS High Mass
Sikh Wars
IHBE tithable
IHBT dishabit
IHCP nightcap
IHDG night-dog
IHEA Michaela
IHEH high tech
IHEL wish well
IHEN eighteen
IHER high gear
IHES highness
high seas
pithless
richness
IHET rich-left
IHFL rightful
IHFR fight for
IHGE pishogue
IHGN Michigan
IHHS with this
IHHT with that
IHHY eighthly
IHIE fish dive
fish-like
fishwife
high-five
high life
high-rise
high tide
high time
high wire
IHIG fighting
lighting
sighting
IHIH lightish
IHIK high kick
high-risk
IHIS eighties
IHIT rightist
IHIY mightily
IHJB with a job
IHJR nightjar
IHLE Michelle
IHLN Michelin
IHLS Nicholas
IHLT Michelet
IHNE sithence
IHNL diphenyl
IHNR Michener
IHNS Tithonus
IHNV Kishinev
IHNW right now
IHOC dichroic
IHOD Richmond
withhold
IHOE fishbone
high-lone
Nichrome®
wishbone
with hope
IHOF fight off
right off
IHOL with foal
IHON highborn
high-born
High Noon
high noon
IHOT high-cost
right out
IHPN light pen
IHPT high spot
IHRD high-bred
withered
IHRE dishorse
litharge
pilhorse
IHRM pichurim
IHRO hitherto
IHRP higher-up
IHRR ditherer
IHRS Richards
IHRW highbrow
withdraw
IHRY litherly
IHSA dichasia
IHSE sightsee
IHUE dishouse
IHUK with luck
IHUP high jump
IHUY Highbury
IHVL dishevel
IHVR sigh over
IHVS eightvos
IHWD tightwad
IIAA Titicaca
IIAE digitate
litigate
militate
mitigate
sibilate
silicate
tidivate
titivate
vicinage
IIAI biriyani
Kiribati
IIAT dividant
litigant
militant
sibilant
vigilant
visitant
IIAY limitary
military
IIBE pitiable
IIBI cicisbei
sigisbei
IIBY pitiably
IICS hibiscus
IIED dividend
vilipend

IIEP divide up
IIES airiness
citizens
dividers
liminess
oiliness
pitiless
tidiness
tininess
wiliness
wiriness
IIET diligent
liniment
vivisect
IIEY divinely
finitely
IIGN giving in
giving-in
living-in
IIGP giving up
giving-up
lining up
IIGY gibingly
IIHD finished
IIHP finish up
IIHR finisher
IIIA Sigiriya
IIIE civilise
civilize
digitise
digitize
divinise
divinize
divisive
filicide
minimise
minimize
rigidise
rigidize
similise
similize
sinicise
sinicize
IIIG dividing
divining
limiting
visiting
IIIH diminish
IIII piri-piri
IIIK minidisk
IIIL minipill
IIIM nihilism
virilism
IIIN civilian
division
viridian
IIIO Pilipino
vitiligo
IIIR vilifier
IIIS Vigilius
IIIT nihilist
IIIY civility
divinify
divinity
lividity
nihility
rigidify
rigidity
silicify
timidity
vicinity
viridity
virility
IIKR mimicker
IILT air inlet
IILW civil law
IILY filially
IINL visional
IINO pimiento
IINS ripienos
IIOE silicone
IIOF hit it off
IIOH Visigoth
IIOM piliform
pisiform
IIOS visitors
IIRD Winifred
IIRE filigree
IISA Nijinska
IISY Nijinsky
IITD miniated
vitiated
IITR disinter
minister
sinister
vitiator
IITY ministry
IIUE finitude
ridicule
IIWR civil war
IJDE misjudge
IJIT disjoint
IJMS Sid James
IJNT disjunct
IJTU jiu-jitsu
ninjitsu
ninjutsu
IKAD kirkward
milkmaid
IKAE Milk Race
nickname
IKAK kick back
kickback
nick-nack
rick-rack
tick-tack
IKAL Kirkwall
IKAS Nicklaus
rinkhals
IKDY wickedly
IKEN Dick Hern
IKEP pick-me-up
IKES pinkness
sickness
IKEY Nickleby
IKHW kickshaw
rickshaw
IKIE disklike
IKIG tickling
IKIH link with
ticklish
IKIK Pickwick
IKIT sick list
IKIY sicklily
IKJU kinkajou
IKLY Kirkaldy
IKMX pick-'n'-mix
IKND sickened
IKNS pickings
IKNT sink unit
IKNY Kilkenny
IKOD Mirkwood
Pickford
pinkwood
IKOK picklock
silky oak
tick-tock
IKOM silkworm
IKON kickdown
IKOS ginkgoes
IKRL pickerel
IKRR tinkerer
IKRY sickerly
IKTE diskette
IKTR picketer
IKUN kick turn
IKVR tick over
IKWY tick away
ILAD billiard
Hilliard
milliard
ILAE disleave
ILAO villiago
ILAS Williams
ILBB sillabub
ILBE tillable
violable
ILBR millibar
ILBY billy boy
violably
ILCE pirlicue
ILCL biblical
ILCY hillocky
ILDE dislodge
ILDW field-dew
ILDY field day
ILED pillhead
ILEE millième
ILEF Mill Reef
ILEM Niflheim
ILER killdeer
ILGE dialogue
ILGN field gun
Milligan
ILGR pillager
villager
ILGT mislight
ILIE field ice
hillside
kill time
ILIG Fielding
yielding
ILIY villainy
ILKD disliked
ILKN disliken
Millikan
ILKR Jim Laker
ILLT dimly lit
ILMN rifleman
ILMT diplomat
ILNE violence
ILNR airliner
bin-liner
milliner
ILNS hidlings
ILOD bill-fold
girlhood
millpond
ILOE Fillmore
ILOH Billroth
ILOK billhook
ILOS billions
millions
zillions
ILOT hill fort
hill-fort
ILRN dieldrin
ILRO jillaroo
ILSR dialyser
ILSS dialyses
dialysis
ILTE Sillitoe
Villette
ILTR violator
ILWW williwaw
ILYL disloyal
ILZA diplozoa
IMAE firmware
IMAO Kismaayo
IMBE filmable
IMCY gimmicky
IMDS Diomedes
IMES firmness
IMIO Ciampino
IMLY dismally
IMNE diamanté
IMNS fitments
IMON firm down
IMOR filmgoer
film noir
IMRA Tia Maria®
IMRK Bismarck
IMRY mismarry
IMTD mismated
IMTE mismetre
IMTH mismatch
IMTR diameter
film star
pia mater
IMTY biometry
IMUE titmouse
IMUH big mouth

	bigmouth
	big-mouth
IMUT	dismount
IMVR	film over
IMYD	dismayed
INAD	Zionward
INAE	Lion Gate
INBE	winnable
INBR	cinnabar
INCE	binnacle
	pinnacle
INEE	Viennese
INEN	Linnaean
INER	signieur
INES	giantess
	Linnaeus
INGO	Rio Negro
INGT	midnight
INHS	dianthus
INIE	big noise
INIH	fiendish
INIL	biennial
INLI	Minnelli
INLO	signal to
INLY	signally
INMC	bionomic
INME	fisnomie
INMN	cinnamon
INMR	misnomer
INNG	Tir nan-Og
INNS	pianinos
	winnings
INOA	minneola
INOS	ligneous
INOT	signpost
INPG	Winnipeg
INSO	finnesko
INSS	Dionysus
INTE	vignette
INTS	tinnitus
INUL	biannual
INVR	sign over
INWD	winnowed
INWR	winnower
INWY	sign away
INYY	Disneyfy
IOAA	lipomata
IOAE	bilobate
	pilotage
	Pinotage
IOAR	dinosaur
	Minotaur
IOAS	bifocals
IOAT	kilowatt
IOAY	misogamy
IOBD	disorbed
IOCD	divorced
IOCE	divorcee
IOCS	siroccos
IODR	disorder
	misorder
IOEM	linoleum
IOGE	Lilongwe

IOHE	pinochle
IOHI	piroshki
	pirozhki
IOHT	Pinochet
	ricochet
IOIE	limonite
	Minorite
	nicotine
	Timonise
	Timonize
IOIG	piloting
	pivoting
IOIH	vigorish
IOIL	binomial
IOIO	Hirohito
IOIT	rigorist
IOIV	Zinoviev
IOIY	minority
	pilosity
	vinosity
IOND	disowned
IOOE	liposome
	ribosome
IOOO	vigoroso
IOOS	nidorous
	rigorous
	timorous
	vigorous
IOOT	kilovolt
IOOY	kidology
	Sinology
	virology
IORD	Titograd
IORM	kilogram
	lipogram
IORY	kilogray
IOSA	Timor Sea
IOSI	Sikorski
IOSN	Limousin
	Nicolson
IOSY	Sikorsky
	timously
IOTS	ridottos
	risottos
IOTT	hit out at
IOUO	risoluto
IOVX	biconvex
IOYE	kilobyte
	Linotype®
IOYY	misogyny
IPAE	airplane
	displace
	misplace
	tinplate
IPAN	Lippmann
IPAT	displant
IPDY	limpidly
IPED	dispread
	misplead
IPES	limpness
IPIE	misprise
	misprize
IPIG	rippling

IPIT	midpoint
	mid-point
	mispoint
	misprint
	oil paint
	pinpoint
	pin-point
IPIY	simplify
IPNE	dispense
	disponge
	dispunge
	sixpence
IPNY	sixpenny
IPOE	disprove
IPOF	disproof
IPRE	disperse
	dispurse
IPRT	dispirit
IPSD	disposed
IPSL	disposal
IPSN	diapason
IPTD	disputed
IPTH	dispatch
IPTI	rispetti
IPTR	disputer
IPUE	diapause
	displume
IQAN	cinquain
IQIT	disquiet
IQOE	misquote
IRBC	microbic
IRBD	disrobed
IRBS	microbes
IRDT	microdot
IREI	Disraeli
IRES	Mirrlees
IREY	fiercely
IRFE	air rifle
IRGN	nitrogen
IRIE	migraine
IRIG	piercing
IRIZ	Biarritz
IRMS	fibromas
IRMY	gin rummy
IRNY	vibrancy
IROS	vitreous
IRPD	cirriped
IRRH	hierarch
IRSA	vibrissa
IRSS	diereses
	fibrosis
	hidrosis
IRTC	diuretic
	hieratic
IRTE	aigrette
IRTI	libretti
IRTO	libretto
IRTR	migrator
	vibrator
IRTS	vibratos
IRUD	win round
IRUE	misroute
ISAA	Kinshasa

	piassaba
	piassava
ISAE	airspace
	diastase
	dissuade
	misshape
	misstate
	oil shale
ISAF	tipstaff
ISBE	kissable
	missable
ISDS	dipsades
ISED	airspeed
	misspend
ISEG	Ginsberg
ISEK	misspeak
ISEL	misspell
ISEN	Einstein
	Milstein
ISES	hipsters
ISET	misspent
ISIE	disseise
	disseize
	miss fire
ISIG	gin sling
	Riesling
ISIH	tinsmith
ISIK	big stick
	dipstick
	lipstick
	oil slick
ISIL	pigswill
ISIS	midships
ISLE	dissolve
ISLS	missiles
ISLY	tinselly
ISMY	lissomly
ISNH	lip-synch
ISNR	Pilsener
ISOA	diaspora
ISOE	big smoke
	bioscope
	diastole
	oilstone
ISOK	kinsfolk
ISON	piss down
ISOS	big shots
	fiascoes
	miasmous
ISPO	kiss up to
ISRD	fissured
ISRE	dies irae
	disserve
ISRL	minstrel
ISRO	Pissarro
ISRP	airstrip
ISUI	Missouri
ISVR	dissever
ITAA	fistiana
ITAE	filtrate
ITAH	misteach
ITAN	distrain
ITAR	air-to-air

ITAS victuals
ITAT distract
distrait
ITBE bistable
ITCM viaticum
ITCS distichs
misticos
Pittacus
ITDG dirty dog
ITDM birthdom
ITDP lifted up
ITDS pintados
ITDY birthday
giftedly
ITEH fiftieth
sixtieth
ITEO little go
Little Mo
ITES distress
listless
mistress
riftless
ITET fit to eat
littlest
mistreat
ointment
ITFL mirthful
ITGT airtight
sit tight
ITIE diatribe
pint-size
ITIH Dietrich
fiftyish
ITIK misthink
ITIN histrion
ITIS histrios
ITIT district
ITIY filthily
ITKN mistaken
ITLE fistulae
ITLN biathlon
ITLR fistular
ITLS fistulas
ITLY distally
wittolly
ITMC diatomic
ITMD mistimed
ITMR big timer
ITNC diatonic
Miltonic
ITNE distance
pittance
ITNN listen in
ITNO listen to
ITNP listen up
ITNR listener
ITNS fittings
ITNT distinct
ITOA virtuosa
ITOE virtuose
ITOI virtuosi
ITOO virtuoso
ITOS virtuous

ITPT pitty-pat
ITRA listeria
victoria❑
Vittoria
wistaria
wisteria
ITRC historic
ITRD filtered
littered
ITRE Pieterse
ITRL dipteral
littoral
ITRN witter on
ITRP gift-wrap
ITRS fixtures
pictures
ITRY bitterly
sisterly
winterly
ITSE distaste
ITSS cistuses
hiatuses
ITTC dietetic
ITTD dictated
ITTE mistitle
ITTR dictator
ITUE fit to use
ITUT distrust
mistrust
ITVR mist over
ITYT mistryst
IUAE simulate
titubate
IUAT figurant
IUDR sit under
IUDY liquidly
IUEN figure on
IUET virulent
IUEY minutely
IUGD divulged
IUIE disunite
figurine
minutiae
IUIG figuring
IUIL diluvial
fiducial
IUIN dilution
diluvian
disunion
Ligurian
Silurian
IUIY disunity
IULE aiguille
IULS Tibullus
IULY ritually
visually
IUNM viburnum
IUNY piquancy
IUOD sinusoid
IUOS bibulous
IUPD bicuspid
IUSE liquesce
IUTD sinuated

situated
IVNS Silvanus
IVPR pit viper
IVRY silverly
IVUH disvouch
IWAA viewdata
IWAE fin whale
IWBE viewable
IWEL big wheel
pinwheel
IWIE miswrite
IWMN airwoman
IWRS airwards
IWTA Hiawatha
IWVS midwives
IWWY view away
IYAL city hall
IYEK city desk
IYHS Sisyphus
IYNM minyanim
IYOM tiny room
IYOS didymous
IYWY tidy away
IZAS mitzvahs
IZGY zigzaggy
IZIG sizzling
IZOH mitzvoth
IZPM diazepam
IZRA pizzeria
JBUI Djibouti
JCIE ejective
JCIN ejection
JKRA Djakarta
JRNN A J Cronin
KAOA Oklahoma
KBUS Sky blues
KDOD skid road
KGES Skegness
KLCP skullcap
KLGT skylight
KLIG skulking
KLOH skelloch
KLTL skeletal
KLTN skeleton
KMIG skimming
skimping
KMIY skimpily
KNAE skincare
KNDU skene-dhu
KNED skinhead
KNEP skin-deep
KNET skin test
KPAK skipjack
KPIG skipping
KPLT sky pilot
KPNS ski pants
KRIG skirting
KRIH skirmish
KRIK skerrick
KSMO Akosombo
KTHR sketcher
KTIH skittish
KTLS skittles

KVNO Okavango
KVOF skive off
KWAD skewbald
KWES skewness
KWLS ekpweles
KWRH skew arch
KWRS skywards
KYOE okey-doke
LAAE cleavage
floatage
LAAT pleasant
LABA Alhambra
LABY altar boy
LACT clean-cut
clear-cut
LADR oleander
LAEO cleave to
please to
LAET please it
LAFR plead for
LAHD bleached
LAHR bleacher
LAIA Altamira
LAIE alkaline
alkalise
alkalize
flea-bite
fly a kite
LAIG aliasing
allaying
bleating
bloating
cleaning
clearing
floating
gleaming
gleaning
gloaming
gloating
pleading
pleasing
LAII Aldaniti
LAIN Albanian
Alsatian
illation
LAIO Al Pacino
LAIS alkalies
LAIY alkalify
blearily
sleazily
LAOD alkaloid
LAOE Al Capone
Eleanore
LAOF clear off
LAOG all along
LAOL Ullapool
LAOT all about
clean out
clear out
fleawort
LAOY aleatory
LASA all at sea
LASD cleansed

Words marked ❑ can also be spelled with an initial capital letter

LASR cleanser
LATR oleaster
LATY pliantly
LAUE pleasure
LAWY clearway
LBAE glabrate
LBAL club-haul
LBES glibness
LBEY slobbery
LBIG blabbing
clubbing
slubbing
LBIH slobbish
LBIN plebeian
LBIY flabbily
LBLA glabella
LBLN globulin
LBLR globular
LBLT globulet
LBLY globally
LBNM olibanum
LBOA club soda
LBOD ill blood
LBOS glabrous
slyboots
LBOT clubroot
LCAE blockade
blockage
glaciate
LCAT black art
LCBE placable
LCBS placebos
LCBX black box
LCBY placably
LCCP black cap
blackcap
LCDG Black Dog
LCDY placidly
LCED clichéed
LCEE black eye
LCFY blackfly
LCGN glucagon
glycogen
LCID elf-child
LCIE black ice
elective
LCIG blacking
blocking
slacking
LCIH blockish
LCIN election
LCIY alacrity
pluckily
LCLG blackleg
LCMN placeman
placemen
LCMT place mat
LCNA placenta
LCNE Alicante
LCOE floccose
LCOF block off
clock off
pluck off
slack off
LCOS electors
LCOT black out
blackout
block out
clock out
LCRC electric
LCRD Black Rod
LCRE à la carte
LCRL glycerol
LCRM plectrum
LCRN electron
glycerin
LCRS electros
plectres
LCRT black rat
electret
LCSA Black Sea
LCSS glacises
LCTE black tie
LCTR flichter
LCUI flocculi
LDAD glad hand
LDAS glad rags
LDBE eludible
LDEN bludgeon
LDER pledgeor
LDES gladness
LDIG cladding
plodding
sledding
sledging
LDIH cloddish
LDMR Vladimir
LDOE gladsome
LDOI gladioli
LEAE alienate
ulcerate
LEAY blue baby
LEEA aloe vera
LEEL bluebell
LEES blueness
clueless
LEGC allergic
LEGI alberghi
LEGN allergen
LEHP blue-chip
LEID bluebird
LEIE Blue Nile
elsewise
flue pipe
ilmenite
LEIG bleeding
fleeting
sleeping
sleeving
LEIM blue film
LEIR ulterior
LEIY sleepily
LELG blue flag
LELN Fluellen
LELR alveolar
LELS alveolus
LEMN alderman
aldermen
LENN Algernon
LENY Alderney
LEOE blue note
LEOF sleep off
LEOS ulcerous
LEOT Bluecoat
sleep out
LEOY allegory
LERM flee from
LERS allegros
LERY blue-grey
LETS Alcestis
LETY fluently
LEUA alleluia
LEUE flue-cure
LEUK blue funk
LEWY alleyway
LEYE aldehyde
LFAE old flame
LFED Oldfield
LFGY old fogey
LFMD ill-famed
LFOD Clifford
LFSU Blefuscu
LFTD ill-fated
LFUD all found
LGAD old guard
sluggard
LGAT flagrant
LGBE eligible
LGBY eligibly
LGEP slag heap
LGGY plug-ugly
LGHP flagship
LGIG clogging
flagging
flogging
plaguing
plugging
LGIH sluggish
LGIY plaguily
LGLA flagella
LGNE elegance
LGNY elegancy
LGON flag down
LGOY Old Glory
LGRH oligarch
LGTD blighted
plighted
LGTR blighter
slighter
LGTY slightly
LGWY plug away
slog away
LHBT alphabet
LHEN glühwein□
LHRY alpha ray
Old Harry
LHUE alehouse
LHUH although
LIAA ultimata
LIAE alginate
ultimate
LIAL all in all
LIAT claimant
LIAY ultimacy
LIDS Pleiades
LIHY almighty□
LIIE albitise
albitize
fluidise
fluidize
LIIG plaining
LIIM albinism
LIIS fluidics
LIIY fluidify
fluidity
LINE alliance
LIOE all in one
Elsinore
LIOS Illinois
LISS ellipses
ellipsis
LITC elliptic
LITR cloister
slaister
LIUE altitude
LKDM blokedom
LKIE Alekhine
LKIH blokeish
LKOF flake off
LKOT flake out
LLCS elflocks
LMAG slam-bang
LMAO plumbago
LMBE blamable
LMBY blamably
LMEN Alcmaeon
LMES glumness
slimness
LMEU flambeau
LMEY flummery
LMFR plump for
LMID Olympiad
LMIG climbing
plumbing
slamming
slimming
slumming
LMIH blimpish
LMIM plumbism
LMIN Olympian
LMIY clammily
clumsily
flimsily
LMLE plumulae
LMLM flim-flam
LMNE Clemente
LMNK Vlaminck
LMNO flamenco
flamingo
glom on to
LMNS elements
LMNY clemency

Words marked □ can also be spelled with an initial capital letter

LMOE	plimsole
LMOF	climb off
LMOK	glam rock
	slummock
LMOL	plimsoll
LMON	slim down
LMOT	flame out
LMTC	climatic
LMTS	clematis
LMUH	all mouth
	Plymouth
LNAE	elongate
	plantage
LNAN	plantain
LNAT	Alan Tait
LNBY	Blind Bay
LNCL	clinical
LNEM	Blenheim
LNEN	Alan Bean
LNES	blankets
	Flanders
	flannels
	Flinders
	glanders
LNET	Blunkett
	glance at
	plangent
LNEY	blankety
LNHD	blanched
	clenched
	planched
LNHR	clincher
	flincher
LNHS	elenchus
LNHT	planchet
LNIE	Klondike
LNIG	blending
	blinding
	blinking
	clinging
	flanking
	glancing
	glinting
	planking
	planning
	plunging
	slanging
	slanting
LNIH	blandish
	clannish
LNIY	flintify
	flintily
	slangily
LNLE	planulae
LNLY	clonally
LNMN	clansman
	Klansman
LNOD	Alan Bond
LNOR	clangour
LNOT	blank out
	fling out
	plant out
LNPW	Blind Pew
LNRE	Old Norse
LNRS	llaneros
LNTC	elenctic
LNTN	plankton
LNWY	a long way
LNYE	Blantyre
	Klondyke
LNYF	plenty of
LOAA	gliomata
LOAE	allocate
LOAM	pleonasm
LOAO	El Dorado
LOEE	Pliocene
LOES	bloomers
LOFR	allow for
LOID	bloodied
LOIE	fluoride
	fluorine
	fluorite
LOIG	allowing
	blooming
	flooding
	flooring
LOIY	bloodily
	gloomily
LOKN	Algonkin
LOLF	alto clef
LOOO	Aldo Moro
LORD	blood-red
LOSN	Al Jolson
	Ole Olsen
LOTD	allotted
LOWY	floodway
LPAE	slipcase
	slippage
	slipware
LPAG	slap bang
	slap-bang
LPAH	slapdash
	slap-dash
LPAK	flapjack
LPAT	elephant
	flippant
	slip-cast
LPCA	alopecia
LPES	clappers
	clippers
LPEY	slippery
LPHD	slipshod
LPIE	flip side
LPIG	clapping
	clipping
	flapping
	flipping
	flopping
	slapping
	slipping
LPIY	floppily
	sloppily
LPLP	clip-clop
	clop-clop
	flip-flap
	flip-flop
LPNO	slip into
LPNT	slipknot
LPOD	slip road
LPOF	slope off
LPOH	Klaproth
LPON	clip coin
LPPR	flypaper
LPRP	claptrap
LPTH	flypitch
LPVR	flap over
LPWY	slip away
LQET	eloquent
LQIH	cliquish
LRAA	Gloriana
LRAH	clarsach
LRBX	glory box
LRCL	clerical
LRDY	floridly
LRES	clerkess
LRGB	Llaregyb
LRGN	florigen
LRGT	Albright
	all right
	all-right
LRHW	clerihew
LRID	flurried
LRIG	alarming
	glorying
LRIH	clerkish
LRIM	alarmism
	altruism
	ultraism
LRIT	alarmist
	altruist
	ultraist
LRLY	florally
	plurally
LRNA	Clarinda
LRNE	Clarence
	Florence
LRNS	clarinos
LRNT	clarinet
LROE	gloriole
LROS	glareous
	glorious
LROT	blare out
	blurt out
	flare out
LRSA	Clarissa
LRSE	plurisie
LRSO	alfresco
LRSS	all-risks
	olorosos
LRTH	eldritch
LRUD	all round
	all-round
LRZL	Florizel
LSAE	elastase
	glissade
LSAR	Alasdair
	Alastair
	Alistair
LSAS	All Stars
LSAY	glossary
LSDN	closed in
LSEE	glass eye
LSES	Klosters
LSEY	blistery
	blustery
	clustery
	flustery
	plastery
LSFL	blissful
LSGN	flashgun
LSIE	allspice
	glassine
LSIG	blasting
	blessing
	blushing
	clashing
	classing
	flashing
	Flushing
	slashing
LSIH	Eli Smith
LSIS	plastics
LSIY	classify
	flashily
	glassify
	glassily
	glossily
LSMN	Flashman
LSOF	blast off
	blast-off
	close off
LSOT	blast out
	elf-shoot
	flesh out
	glasnost
LSOY	blossomy
	old story
LSRL	plastral
LSRN	klystron
	plastron
LSST	close-set
LSUA	blastula
LSUS	All Souls
LSWR	class war
LSYE	Old Style
	old style
LSYU	bless you
LTAD	flatland
LTAE	flatmate
	flat race
	flat rate
LTAK	flatback
LTAS	flatways
	plateaus
LTAX	plateaux
LTCP	cloth cap
LTDY	elatedly
LTED	flathead
LTEE	all there
LTEN	clothe on
	slattern
LTES	flatness

plotless
plotters
LTET ill-treat
LTEY blithely
flattery
fluttery
glittery
Slattery
slithery
LTFL plateful
slothful
LTHD blotched
LTHR fletcher☐
LTHS clutches
LTIE flatwise
LTIG all-thing
blotting
clothing
clotting
flatling
flitting
fly-tying
plotting
LTIH flatfish
flattish
sluttish
LTIR clothier
LTIY glitzily
LTLA clitella
flotilla
LTLT platelet
LTMD ill-timed
LTMR old-timer
LTNC platinic
platonic☐
plutonic
LTNM platinum
LTNS Plotinus
LTNT flat knot
LTOA plethora
LTOF flat roof
LTOG flatlong
LTOL clotpoll
LTOM flatworm
platform
LTOT flatboat
flatfoot
LTOY gluttony
LTPN flat spin
LTPS platypus
LTRH Plutarch
LTRL clitoral
LTRN flatiron
LTRS clitoris
LTSS flatuses
LTYE flat tyre
LUAE ill-usage
LUDR flounder
LUEO allude to
LUET Flaubert
LUHN plough in
LUHR sloucher
LUIE allusive

Claudine
illumine
illusive
LUIG alluring
LUIH flourish
LUIL alluvial
LUIM alluvium
LUIN allusion
Claudian
illusion
LUIS Claudius
plaudits
LUIT flautist
LUIY cloudily
pleurisy
LUOA glaucoma
LUOE aleurone
LUOS glaucous
LUOY illusory
LUTA claustra
LUTR flaunter
LVBX glove box
LVCE clavicle
LVDN Clevedon
LVKA Slovakia
LVNA Slovenia
LVNC Slavonic
LVNH eleventh
LVNY slovenly
slovenry
LVRR slaverer
LVRY cleverly
LVTD elevated
LVTI Olivetti
LVTR elevator
LWAK claw back
clawback
flow back
LWEL flywheel
LWES flawless
slowness
LWEY clownery
LWIE blowpipe
clew-line
LWIG clowning
LWIH clownish
LWLG glow plug
LWLN Llewelyn
LWMN old woman
LWOM glowworm
glow-worm
slowworm
LWON slow down
slowdown
LWOT blown-out
LWRD Old World
old-world
LWRR flowerer
LWRT floweret
LWVR blow over
flow over
LWVS alewives
LWWY blow away

LXBE flexible
LXBY flexibly
LXIY flax-lily
LXNA gloxinia
LXOE flexuose
LXOS flexuous
LXRL flexural
LXSS plexuses
LXUH flax-bush
LYAE playmate
play safe
LYAK play back
playback
LYAL play ball
LYAR play fair
LYBE playable
LYES cloyless
LYET cloyment
LYIE claypipe
play fine
playtime
LYIH play with
LYIL playbill
LYOE claymore
LYON play down
LYPN play upon
LYPO play up to
LYRA play area
LYUL play full
LYVR play over
LZAD blizzard
LZBL Olazabal
LZNY blazonry
LZRD blazered
MABE emmarble
MAEM ommateum
MAET immanent
MAEY immanely
MAHC empathic
MAIY smearily
MAKN embark on
MAKT empacket
MAMR embalmer
MARD impaired
MARN empatron
MATD impasto'd
MATE embattle
immantle
MATN impact on
MATO impart to
MATS amiantus
impastos
MAUE immature
MAUL Emmanuel
MCAE emaciate
MCBE amicable
MCBY amicably
MCIG smacking
smocking
MDEN smidgeon
MDIY smudgily
MDOT amidmost
MDVT amadavat

MEAE amperage
MEAY Imre Nagy
MEDD embedded
MEIC amnesiac
MEIE Emmeline
emperise
emperize
imbecile
MEIG impeding
MEIL imperial
MEIM imperium
MEIO impetigo
MELR impeller
umbellar
MEOD amberoid
MESD immersed
METL Emmental
MEZE embezzle
MGAA amygdala
MGAE amygdale
emigrate
MGAT emigrant
MGES smugness
MGLR smuggler
MGND imagined
MGNR imaginer
MGNS imagines
MGUE amygdule
MHLS omphalos
MHPD amphipod
MHRC amphoric
MHRE amphorae
MHSS emphases
emphasis
MHTC emphatic
MIET imminent
MIHY impishly
MIIN ambition
MINE ambiance
ambience
MIOE omnivore
MIOY omnivory
MISR Amritsar
MITR embitter
MKBE smokable
MKDY smoke-dry
MKOT smoke out
MLAH empleach
impleach
MLCT implicit
MLDE impledge
MLET smallest
Smollett
MLFY small fry
MLIG smelling
smelting
MLIH smallish
MLIN a million
emulsion
MLIY emulsify
MLNE implunge
MLNK Smolensk
MLON amelcorn

Words marked ☐ can also be spelled with an initial capital letter

MLOT	smell out
MLPX	smallpox
MLTE	omelette
MLTR	emulator
MLVA	impluvia
MLXS	amplexus
MLYD	employed
MLYE	employee
MLYR	employer
MLZN	emblazon
MMRH	Amy March
MNAE	emendate
MNBE	amenable
MNBY	amenably
MNIE	amandine
MNNE	eminence
MNSN	Amundsen
MOAE	immolate
	umbonate
MODN	embolden
MODR	emborder
	empolder
	impolder
MOEN	impose on
MOET	immodest
	immoment
	impotent
MOHE	smoothie
MOHN	smoothen
MOHY	smoothly
MOID	embodied
MOIE	ammonite
	immobile
	impolite
MOIG	imposing
MOIM	ammonium
	embolism
	emporium
MOSD	embossed
MOTD	imported
MOTL	immortal
MOTR	importer
	imposter
	impostor
MRAS	smart ass
	smart-ass
MRCN	American
MRCS	imbrices
MRET	emergent
MRGY	smart guy
MRIE	amortise
	amortize
MRIG	emerging
	smarting
MRIH	smartish
MRIN	emersion
MRIY	smarmily
MRLA	umbrella
MRLO	Amarillo
MRLS	amarylis
MRMS	imprimis
MRNH	amaranth
MROI	G Marconi
MROS	embryons
MRPR	improper
MRSA	ambrosia
MRSN	imprison
MRSS	amorosos
MRTI	amoretti
MRTO	amaretto
MRTS	emeritus
MRVD	improved
MRVR	improver
MSAY	emissary
MSDY	amusedly
MSHT	smash hit
	smash-hit
MSIE	emissive
	omissive
MSIG	smashing
MSIN	emission
	omission
MTBE	imitable
MTCL	emetical
MTCN	emoticon
MTEY	smothery
MTIG	emptying
	omitting
MTIY	smuttily
MTOF	smite off
MTOS	emotions
MTOT	empty out
MTSS	amitosis
MTTC	amitotic
MTTD	imitated
MTTR	imitator
MTYT	amethyst
MUAE	ambulate
	amputate
MUAT	ambulant
MUDR	smoulder
MUEO	immune to
MUET	impudent
MUEY	impurely
MUHD	ambushed
MUIE	immunise
	immunize
	umquhile
MUIY	immunity
	impunity
	impurity
MULE	ampullae
MUMN	Omdurman
MUPE	empurple
MUTO	amount to
MYEL	empyreal
MYEN	empyrean
MZDY	amazedly
MZNA	Amazonia
NAAE	endamage
NAAT	inhalant
NACD	unhatch'd
NACP	sneak-cup
NADD	uncandid
NADE	unsaddle
NADM	in tandem
NADY	inwardly
NAEA	in camera
	on camera
NAED	unnaneld
NAEF	in care of
	in case of
NAEN	engage in
NAEP	unmade-up
NAEY	innately
	insanely
	unsafely
	unsafety
	unwarely
NAFL	unlawful
NAGD	enlarged
NAGE	entangle
	untangle
NAGR	endanger
	enlarger
NAGT	on target
	untaught
NAHD	unwashed
NAHR	ingather
NAHS	uneathes
NAID	unvaried
NAIE	annalise
	annalize
	infamise
	infamize
	invasive
NAIG	engaging
	enraging
	inhaling
	inlaying
	kneading
	sneaking
	sneaping
	uncaging
	uncaring
	unfading
	untaxing
NAIH	enravish
NAIL	uniaxial
NAIN	invasion
NAIO	uno animo
NAIT	annalist
NAIY	insanity
	sneakily
	uneasily
	unwarily
NAKD	unbacked
	unmarked
NAKE	untackle
NAKF	in back of
NAKR	unmasker
NALD	unhailed
NALO	intaglio
NAMD	unharmed
NAND	unearned
	unmanned
NANE	enraunge
NANF	on pain of
NANL	unpannel
NANY	ungainly
NAOD	Anna Ford
NAOF	sneak off
NAOR	in favour
NAOS	infamous
NAPD	untapped
NARD	unbarred
	unmarred
	unpaired
NARY	unfairly
NASA	intarsia
NATD	unwanted
NATE	Ondaatje
	unmantle
NATN	unfasten
NATS	annattos
NATY	infantry
NAUD	unvalued
NAZE	undazzle
NBES	anableps
NBEY	snobbery
NBIG	snubbing
NBIH	snobbish
NBIM	snobbism
NBLC	anabolic
NBOE	one by one
	snub nose
NBTD	unabated
NCBR	snackbar
NCCE	unicycle
NCEN	Anacreon
NCES	knickers
	knockers
NCIE	inactive
	inscribe
NCIG	knocking
NCIN	in action
	inaction
NCLR	unicolor
NCNA	anaconda
NCNC	aniconic
NCNE	ensconce
	insconce
NCOC	anechoic
NCOD	in accord
NCOE	anecdote
NCOF	knock off
NCOL	inscroll
NCOT	knock out
	knockout
	knock-out
NCRA	una corda
NCUE	enacture
NDBE	inedible
NDTD	unedited
NEAD	in demand
	on demand
	on remand
NEAE	antedate
	under age
	under-age
NEAL	in detail
NEAM	underarm

NEAT interact
under-act
untenant
NEBD underbid
NEBE enfeeble
ensemble
NEBY underbuy
NECD unfenced
NECM intercom
NECT intercut
undercut
NEDD intended
undeeded
unheeded
unleaded
unneeded
unseeded
untended
unweeded
NEDG underdog
NEDO intend to
NEDR engender
NEEE antecede
NEEK knee-jerk
NEEM unbeseem
NEEP knee-deep
NEER inner ear
NEET antevert
indecent
inherent
interest
NEFD underfed
NEFR underfur
NEGE in league
inveigle
NEGT in weight
NEHR untether
NEHS unnethes
NEIA angelica❑
Angelina
antefixa
NEIE anserine
NEIF unbelief
NEIG angering
entering
indexing
kneeling
sneering
sneezing
unseeing
NEIH knee-high
NEIN annexion
NEIO Angelico
NEIR anterior
inferior
interior
NEIS in series
NEKK angekkok
NELD unpeeled
unsealed
NELE underlie
NELP underlap
NELS entellus
NELT underlet
NELY interlay
underlay
unreally
NEMC endermic
NEMN inner man
underman
NEMT intermit
NEMX intermix
NEMY unseemly
NEND interned
NENE antennae
enceinte
internee
NENL enkernel
infernal
internal
unkennel
NENS antennas
infernos
NEOC unheroic
NEOD on record
NEOE anaerobe
antelope
envelope
in repose
kneehole
once more
NEOM anteroom
NEOT ante-post
undevout
NEPE unpeople
NEPL Interpol
NEPN underpin
unweapon
NEPR under par
untemper
NEPY underpay
NERD inferred
NERE enhearse
inhearse
unhearse
NERL integral
NERN underrun
NERS an-heires
NERT in secret
unsecret
NESA undersea
NESD incensed
unversed
NESN Andersen
Anderson
in person
in reason
in season
unperson
unreason
NEST Intelsat
underset
NESX intersex
NETD indebted
indented
infected
infested
inserted
invented
inverted
unheated
untested
NETE in ventre
unsettle
NETN intent on
invest in
unbeaten
NETO in debt to
NETR ancestor
anteater
Dniester
enfetter
inserter
inventor
investor
unfetter
NETW undertow
NETY ancestry
intently
ungently
unmeetly
NEUD infecund
NEUE insecure
NEUL unsexual
NEUN in return
NEVD unnerved
NEVL interval
NEVR once-over
NEVT on velvet
NEWY in her way
under way
NFAD unafraid
NFAH in a flash
NFBX snuffbox
NFEH one flesh
NFET in effect
NFIG sniffing
unifying
NFIY sniffily
NFLR sniffler
snuffler
NFOT sniff out
snuff out
NGES snugness
NGEY snuggery
NGTY knightly❑
NGYH anaglyph
NHAE inchoate
NHAH ensheath
NHAL in thrall
NHAR in the air
on the air
NHBG in the bag
NHBT on the bit
NHDT on the dot
NHDW unshadow
NHED enshield
in the end
unthread
NHEL inchmeal
NHES in shreds
NHFY on the fly
NHHP on the hop
NHIE enshrine
NHJB on the job
NHKN unshaken
NHLA anthelia
NHLY enthalpy
NHMA anthemia
NHMP on the map
NHMT on the mat
NHND on the nod
NHOD enshroud
unshroud
NHOE enthrone
unthrone
NHOK in shtook
NHOY in theory
NHPD unshaped
NHPN unshapen
NHPO in the poo
NHRC enchoric
NHRD anchored
in the red
unshared
NHRE in charge
one-horse
uncharge
NHRH unchurch
NHRN on the run
NHRT anchoret
NHRW in the raw
NHRY in a hurry
NHSD enchased
enthused
NHSE unchaste
NHSS anthesis
NHSY on the sly
NHTB on the tab
NHTH unthatch
NHUD unshrubd
NHVN unshaven
NHWY in the way
on the way
NIAD unvizard
NIAE enfilade
ensilage
envisage
indicate
intimate
uncinate
NIAT indicant
NIAY intimacy
NIBE enviable
unviable
NIBR unlimber
NIBY enviably
NICE encircle
NICS in pieces
NIDD unminded
NIDE engirdle
enkindle

Words marked ❑ can also be spelled with an initial capital letter

	unriddle
NIDM	unwisdom
NIDN	unbidden
	unhidden
NIDY	unkindly
NIEA	anti-sera
NIER	engineer
NIES	inkiness
NIET	incident
	indigent
	indigest
	indirect
NIEY	entirely
	entirety
	unlikely
	untimely
	unwisely
NIGD	enridged
	unhinged
NIHD	unwished
NIHN	antiphon
NIHP	unbishop
NIHR	encipher
	uncipher
NIIE	incisive
	infinite
NIIG	enticing
	inciting
	inviting
	ungiving
	untiring
NIIL	unfilial
NIIM	intimism
NIIN	envision
	incision
NIIY	infinity
	untidily
NILD	entitled
	unfilled
	untilled
	untitled
	unwilled
NILY	unwieldy
NIMD	undimmed
NIMN	Indiaman
NIMS	angiomas
NIMY	infirmly
NINA	insignia
NIND	unsigned
NINW	until now
NIOE	antidote
	Antigone
	antinode
	antipope
NIOK	anti-lock
NIOM	unciform
NIOS	environs
	indigoes
NIOY	antibody
	antimony
	antinomy
NIRE	enfierce
NISD	unbiased
NISN	Anfinsen
NITD	unfitted
	unlisted
NITE	enlistee
	indictee
	in little
NITN	insist on
NITR	anointer
NIUE	in disuse
	intitule
NIUF	in lieu of
NIUS	antiques
NIWF	in view of
NIWY	in his way
NJFY	in a jiffy
NLCD	unplaced
NLCN	Anglican
NLCS	in flocks
NLDD	included
NLFR	angle for
NLGE	analogue
NLGT	in-flight
NLIE	unsluice
NLMD	inflamed
NLMS	in flames
NLND	inclined
NLNR	one-liner
NLNY	in plenty
NLRD	antlered
NLSD	enclosed
	unclosed
NLSM	Uncle Sam
NLSR	analyser
NLSS	analyses
	analysis
NLSY	Anglesey
	unfleshy
NLTC	analytic
	enclitic
NLTD	inflated
NLTE	enclothe
	unclothe
NLTH	unclutch
NLTM	Uncle Tom
NLVD	enslaved
NLWD	unblowed
	unflawed
NLWR	enflower
	in flower
NMCL	inimical
NMLC	animalic
NMLY	animally
NMNC	mnemonic
NMOH	unsmooth
NMTD	animated
NMTR	animator
NNAE	inundate
NNAT	inundant
NNGT	unknight
NNHR	unanchor
NNIG	unending
NNOF	on and off
NNRD	ensnared
NNSN	in unison
NOAD	untoward
NOAE	annotate
	innovate
	insolate
	intonate
NOAP	endocarp
NOAY	endogamy
NOBD	uncombed
NOBE	undouble
NOCD	enforced
	unforced
	unvoiced
NODD	unfolded
	unwooded
NODR	unfolder
	unloader
	unsolder
NOEE	oncogene
NOEM	endoderm
NOET	enforest
	indolent
	innocent ❑
	insolent
NOEY	ontogeny
	uncomely
	unlovely
NOGD	engorged
NOGN	end organ
NOGT	unsought
NOIE	indocile
	in no time
	unionise
	unionize
NOIG	annoying
	incoming
	oncoming
	snooping
	snoozing
	unloving
	unmoving
NOIL	unsocial
NOIM	encomium
	enconium
	unionism ❑
NOIN	encomion
	in motion
NOIS	Antonius
NOIT	unionist
NOIW	into view
NOIY	snootily
	unholily
NOKD	uncooked
	unlocked
	unworked
NOKR	onlooker
NOKT	in pocket
	unsocket
NOLD	unpolled
	unsoiled
NOMD	informed
	unformed
NOML	informal
NOMN	in common
	inform on
	uncommon
NOMR	informer
NONA	insomnia
NOND	uncoyned
NONE	announce
NONT	an sonnet
	unbonnet
NOON	endozoon
	entozoon
NOOR	encolour
NOOY	oncology
	ontology
NOPE	uncouple
NORE	in course
NOSD	endorsed
NOSE	endorsee
NOSN	unloosen
	unpoison
NOSR	endorser
NOTC	enzootic
NOTD	unbolted
	unsorted
	unwonted
NOTO	one or two
NOTY	unworthy
NOUE	involute
NOUH	insomuch
NOVD	involved
	unsolved
NOVY	in convoy
NPAE	anaphase
NPAK	knapsack
NPCE	in specie
NPDY	in a paddy
NPED	knapweed
NPEE	ensphere
	insphere
	one-piece
	unsphere
NPEN	snap bean
NPES	snippets
NPET	anapaest
NPEY	snippety
NPHT	snapshot
NPIG	snapping
	snipping
NPIH	snappish
NPIT	unspoilt
NPIY	snappily
NPKN	unspoken
NPLR	unipolar
NPNC	in a panic
NPNP	snip-snap
NPOA	anaphora
NPPR	endpaper
NPRD	inspired
NPRE	ens per se
NPRR	inspirer
NPRT	inspirit
NPRY	one-party
NQEE	in a queue

Words marked ❑ can also be spelled with an initial capital letter

NQEO	unique to
NQEY	uniquely
NQIY	inequity
	iniquity
NRAE	enervate
	increase
	inornate
	uncreate
NRAH	encroach
NRAT	undreamt
NRAY	entreaty
NRBY	Enard Bay
NRCE	entr'acte
NRDE	encradle
	unbridle
NRDG	infra dig
NRDO	inured to
NRDR	intruder
NRDS	intrados
NRDT	in credit
	on credit
NREE	enfreeze
	unfreeze
NREH	unbreech
NRET	unpriest
NRGE	intrigue
NRGN	androgen
	in origin
NRGS	inert gas
NRHC	anarchic
NRIE	energise
	energize
	unpraise
NRIG	knurling
	snarling
	snorting
	unerring
NRIL	inertial
NRIM	entryism
NRIS	entrails
NRIT	entryist
NRIY	enormity
NRKN	unbroken
NRMD	unframed
	unprimed
NRMT	intromit
NRNE	entrance
	infringe
	intrince
NRNH	entrench
	intrench
NRNS	entrants
NROE	engroove
	ingroove
NROS	enormous
NRPC	entropic
NRPD	intrepid
	undraped
NRPT	entrepot
	entrepôt
NRPV	Andropov
NRRD	infrared
NRRE	antrorse
NRSD	unbrused
NRSS	enuresis
NRSY	untrusty
NRTC	enuretic
NRTI	Andretti
NRUE	en croûte
NRVD	unproved
NRVN	unproven
NRVR	engraver
NRVS	in droves
NRWS	Andrewes
	in crowds
NRXA	anorexia
NRXC	anorexic
NRZD	unprized
NSAD	inkstand
NSAE	in a state
NSBE	unusable
NSDD	one-sided
NSEF	one's self
NSET	in a sweat
NSNE	in a sense
NSNL	unisonal
NSRM	angstrom
	Ångström
NSUF	and stuff
NTAE	initiate
NTAK	one-track
NTAS	initials
NTAY	unsteady
NTBE	instable
	unstable
NTDY	unitedly
NTEA	anathema
NTEF	in itself
NTEM	on stream
	on-stream
NTER	knitwear
NTES	instress
NTGS	in stages
NTHR	snatcher
	snitcher
NTHT	snatch at
NTIE	in a trice
	on strike
NTIG	anything
	knitting
	unstring
NTIY	snottily
NTNE	instance
NTNS	Instants
NTNT	instinct
NTNY	instancy
NTOE	one-to-one
NTOS	unctuous
NTOT	unit cost
NTRH	unstarch
NTTD	unstated
NTTH	unstitch
NTUG	unstrung
NTUT	instruct
NTZY	in a tizzy
NUAE	incubate
	indurate
	inhumane
	inhumate
	insulate
	intubate
	undulate
	ungulate
NUAN	Indurain
NUAT	undulant
NUBD	uncurbed
NUBR	encumber
NUDD	unguided
NUDN	unburden
NUDR	in sunder
NUFD	engulfed
NUFE	unmuffle
	unruffle
NUGD	indulged
NUGR	enhunger
NUIE	infusive
NUIG	enduring
	inducing
	infusing
NUIM	aneurism
NUIN	infusion
NUKE	unbuckle
NULA	Anguilla
NULC	in public
NULD	annulled
	unfurled
NULY	annually
NUMD	unsummed
NUNL	inguinal
NUNO	innuendo
NUPE	unsupple
NURO	en cuerpo
	in cuerpo
	in querpo
NURR	enquirer
	inquirer
NURW	unburrow
NUTD	insulted
	unquoted
	unsuited
NUTE	unsubtle
NUTN	unbutton
NUTR	inductor
	inputter
NUTY	industry
	unjustly
NUVD	incurved
NUWY	in our way
NUYM	aneurysm
NUZE	unmuzzle
NVCL	univocal
NVLE	univalve
NVLY	snivelly
NVNY	unevenly
NVRE	universe
NWAL	snowball❑
	snowfall
NWBE	knowable
NWDN	snowed in
NWDP	snowed up
NWEE	anywhere
NWHE	snowshoe
	snow-shoe
NWIE	in a while
	snowline
NWOL	snowy owl
NWRO	answer to
NWRP	snowdrop
NWRS	unawares
NWTE	enswathe
	inswathe
	unswathe
NXES	in excess
NXET	inexpert
NYIN	endymion❑
NYOD	on my word
NYOE	ankylose
NYOK	in my book
NYTD	encysted
NYUT	only just
OAAE	rotavate
OAAI	bonamani
OAAK	tomahawk
OAAL	not at all
OAAS	nowadays
OACA	focaccia
OACE	Comanche
OACR	romancer
OACS	tobaccos
OACY	monarchy
OADR	colander
	pomander
OADY	cowardly
	monandry
OAEA	to camera
OAEE	nota bene
OAEI	Comaneci
OAEL	Moray eel
OAEN	soya bean
OAEP	not a peep
OAER	voyageur
OAFL	god-awful
OAFU	pot-au-feu
OAGO	coraggio
OAGS	botargos
OAHN	Jonathan
	Jonathon
	Monaghan
OAIA	foramina
	Mona Lisa
	sonatina
	Tomasina
OAID	Rosalind
OAIE	bona fide
	botanise
	botanize
	dopamine
	focalise
	focalize
	for a time
	go native
	localise

Words marked ❑ can also be spelled with an initial capital letter

localize
locative
moralise
moralize
nodalise
nodalize
nomadise
nomadize
notarise
notarize
polarise
polarize
Romanise
Romanize
Rosaline
soda lime
sodalite
solarise
solarize
totalise
totalize
vocalise
vocalize
vocative
volatile
womanise
womanize
OAIG donating
locating
rotating
voyaging
OAIH tovarich
tovarish
womanish
OAIL notarial
OAIM localism
moralism
nomadism
rosarium
royalism
solarium
solatium
vocalism
OAIN donation
Horatian
location
Moravian
notation
Novatian
potation
rogation
Romanian
rosarian
Rotarian
rotation
vocation
OAIT botanist
loyalist
moralist
royalist❑
vocalist
votarist
OAIY Iowa City

locality
modality
molarity
morality
polarity
sodality
tonality
totality
voracity
OAKN go back on
OALD so-called
OALE rocaille
OALS movables
OALW Bonar Law
not allow
OAMA toxaemia
OAMC toxaemic
OAMD Mohammed
OANC morainic
OANL domainal
morainal
OAOA Coca Cola®
OAOD Polaroid®
Rosamond
OAOE comatose
con amore
not a hope
OAOL not a soul
OAOS oogamous
pomatoes
potatoes
tomatoes
voragoes
OAOT dot about
how about
sod about
OAOY rotatory
OARL monaural
podagral
OASA Coral Sea
OASI Kowalski
Polanski
OASN Johanson
OASS molasses
OATC cobaltic
monastic
romantic
OATE do battle
Iolanthe
OATR go faster
no matter
OATS corantos
OAUD Rosamund
Zola Budd
OAVN coq au vin
OAVS go halves
OAWR total war
OAYN go easy on
OBAD go aboard
OBAS top brass
OBDF robbed of
OBDY morbidly
OBEE Corbiere

OBEO sombrero
OBEP double up
gobble up
OBES cobblers
Goebbels
OBET no object
OBEY cobblery
sombrely
OBFL doubtful
OBIE bombsite
combwise
OBIG cobbling
doubling
doubting
hobbling
lobbying
nobbling
wobbling
OBIH Gombrich
OBIT lobbyist
OBIY gorblimy
OBLS tombolos
OBLY gor-belly
pot belly
pot-belly
OBND combined
OBOD go abroad
OBOH tolbooth
OBON doubloon
OBPN bobby-pin
OBRI Lombardi
OBRN dobber-in
OBRY cowberry
Dogberry
OBSS sorbuses
OBTL sorbitol
OBUD fogbound
OBUE boob tube
OBUH Tombaugh
OCAE conclave
OCAM non-claim
OCAS top-class
OCAT couchant
OCAX morceaux
ponceaux
OCBE forcible
OCBN log cabin
OCBX voice-box
OCBY forcibly
OCDA coccidia
OCDR conceder
OCDY forcedly
OCEE concrete
OCEP not cheap
OCEY louchely
OCFL forceful
OCFR vouch for
OCGS coccyges
OCIA colchica
OCID godchild
OCIE coactive
conceive
OCIG botching

coaching
couching
poaching
touching
OCIN coaction
OCIY touchily
OCLN Joscelin
OCLS zoccolos
OCLT Poncelet
OCMN coachman
OCNC volcanic
OCNI Korchnoi
OCOE not close
OCOF mooch off
touch off
OCOG souchong
OCOS go across
OCOT force out
OCPI concepti
OCRE Concorde
OCRI concerti
OCRO concerto
OCRR sorcerer
OCRS concerns
OCSN moccasin
OCTA zoocytia
OCTI concetti
OCUE conclude
OCUT Foucault
Goncourt
OCZN hoactzin
ODAA Gondwana
ODAD bondmaid
gold card
hold hard
hold hard!
woodland
Woodward
ODAE bold face
good name
road rage
word game
wordgame
ODAK hold back
woodlark
ODAL Toad Hall
ODAT hold fast
holdfast
ODAX Bordeaux
rondeaux
ODBE foldable
fordable
voidable
ODCA Boadicea
Boudicca
ODCI conducti
Mordecai
ODDS soldados
ODDY sordidly
ODED cold-weld
good deed
ODEF gold leaf
ODEG Goldberg

ODEL	cold meal
ODEM	Sondheim
ODEO	how-d'ye-do
	toodle-oo
ODEP	good help
ODER	Goodyear
	hold dear
ODES	boldness
	coldness
	cordless
	fondness
	goodness
	good news
	lordless
	loudness
	roadless
	soldiers
	top-dress
	voidness
	woodless
	wordless
ODET	road-test
ODFL	wondeful
ODGE	Dordogne
ODHD	woodshed
ODHP	lordship❑
	woodchip
ODIC	gold disc
ODID	woodwind
ODIE	gold mine
	roadside
	woodpile
ODIG	fondling
	toadying
ODIH	food-fish
	goldfish
	hold high
	hold with
	toadyish
ODIK	hoodwink
	hot drink
ODIL	good will
	goodwill
ODIM	rowdyism
	toadyism
ODIN	Mondrian
	road sign
ODIT	word-list
ODIY	non-dairy
ODLA	Cordelia
ODLC	Goidelic
ODLN	Bob Dylan
ODLO	bordello
ODLR	condoler
ODLX	toadflax
ODLY	word play
	wordplay
	word-play
ODMD	moody-mad
ODMN	bondsman
	woodsman
ODMR	Gordimer
ODNE	condense
	Joe Dante
	toe-dance
	voidance
ODNO	hold on to
ODNP	cold snap
ODNS	holdings
	rondinos
	tondinos
ODNY	goldenly
	mordancy
	woodenly
ODOD	cordwood
	good word
	hold good
ODOE	cold sore
	word-lore
ODOK	cold-work
	good book
	woodcock
	woodwork
	wordbook
	word-book
ODOL	gold foil
ODOM	good form
	woodworm
ODON	hold down
ODOS	wondrous
ODOT	foldboat
ODRD	bordered
	powdered
ODRE	foedarie
ODRL	folderol
ODRN	border on
ODRR	borderer
	solderer
	wonderer
ODRS	Honduras
ODRT	wonder at
ODRY	corduroy
ODSS	lordosis
ODTC	lordotic
ODTR	loadstar
	roadster
	Wordstar®
ODUF	woodruff
ODUH	gold rush
ODUK	good luck
	Lord Muck
ODUN	good turn
ODUP	road hump
	wood pulp
ODUS	cold cuts
	doldrums
ODUT	gold dust
ODVD	Joe David
ODVL	rondavel
ODVN	good-even
ODVR	hold over
ODWY	foldaway
	hold sway
	Koldewey
OEAD	forehand
	foreland
	foresaid
	hole card
	homeland
	homeward
	noseband
	Romeward
	to be paid
OEAE	coverage
	foredate
	forename
	home-made
	home page
	lose face
	Lovelace
	moderate
	notecase
	somegate
	tolerate
OEAK	come back
	comeback
	move back
	rope-walk
OEAL	coverall
	dovetail
	foresail
OEAN	forewarn
	rope-yarn
OEAO	moderato
OEAS	someways
OEAT	cosecant
	covenant
	forecast
	foremast
	forepart
	forepast
	move past
	tolerant
OEAY	monetary
	rosemary❑
OEBE	honey bee
	loveable
	moveable
	ropeable
OEBG	money-bag
OEBR	November
OEBX	moneybox
	money-box
OEBY	moveably
OECT	power cut
OEDE	bone idle
	bone-idle
	comeddle
	money due
OEDM	yokeldom
OEDN	Poseidon
OEDR	toreador
OEDW	honeydew
OEEB	nose-herb
OEED	bonehead
	coke-head
	forehead
	foreread
	pokeweed
	rope's end
OEEE	novelese
OEEF	tone-deaf
OEEL	bone meal
	forefeel
	foretell
OEEN	foreseen
OEEP	home help
OEER	come near
	forebear
OEES	boneless
	homeless
	hopeless
	loveless
	noseless
	noteless
	soreness
	toneless
OEET	coherent
	come next
	dome tent
	forefeet
	forehent
	movement
	non-event
OEEY	no remedy
OEFL	powerful
OEFR	cover for
	hoped-for
OEGR	Honegger
OEHN	more than
OEHR	together
OEHS	Josephus
OEHT	gone phut
	somewhat
OEHW	foreshew
	foreshow
OEID	go behind
	lovebird
OEIE	cohesive
	dovelike
	homelike
	Joceline
	lose time
	love life
	monetise
	monetize
	more time
	nosedive
	nose-dive
	novelise
	novelize
	polemise
	polemize
	roselike
	soberise
	soberize
	solecise
	solecize
	sometime
	somewise
OEIG	covering
	coveting

	forewing
	hovering
	lowering
	nose-ring
	sobering
	towering
OEIH	come high
	come with
	cope with
	done with
	fogeyish
	Goderich
	novelish
	tone with
OEIK	homesick
	lovesick
	Roderick
	rose-pink
OEIL	molehill
	soterial
OEIM	nobelium
	solecism
	tokenism
	totemism
OEIN	bohemian❑
	cohesion
	comedian
OEIR	hotelier
OEIS	polemics
OEIT	novelist
	polemist
	totemist
OEIY	homelily
OEKN	foreskin
	moleskin
	Potemkin
OEKR	Honecker
OELE	novellae
OELN	foreplan
OELP	lower lip
OELR	modeller
	yodeller
OELS	modellos
	morellos
	novellas
OELT	coverlet
OELW	coleslaw
	foreslow
OELY	foreplay
	role-play
OEMN	bogeyman
	Doberman
	moneyman
OENA	Roseanna
OENE	Roseanne
OENN	come in on
	home in on
	move in on
OENO	come in to
	come into
OENR	governor
OENT	home unit
OENW	foreknow
OENY	modernly
	solemnly
OEOD	foreword
	go beyond
	rosewood
	solenoid
OEOE	borehole
	come home
	come to be
	dovecote
	forebode
	foregone
	go before
	lonesome
	lose hope
	loved one
	rotenone
	some hope
OEOF	lone wolf
OEOG	love-song
OEOK	forelock
	homework
	notebook
OEOM	foredoom
	tone poem
OEON	come down
	comedown
	forenoon
	home loan
	home town
	lovelorn
	move down
	note down
	tone down
	vote down
OEOS	covetous
OEOT	forefoot
	foremost
OEOY	somebody
OEPE	so help me
OEPN	bone up on
	come upon
	homespun
OEPO	come up to
OERD	dog-eared
	home-bred
	lop-eared
OERE	come true
OERM	come from
OERS	foie gras
OERW	home brew
	home-brew
OERY	too early
OESC	forensic
OESE	Bodensee
OESS	coleuses
OEST	Somerset
OETC	domestic
OETD	forested
OETL	forestal
OETM	momentum
	tomentum
OETR	fomenter
	forester❑
	go better
	go-getter
	lodestar
	molester
	Pole Star
OETS	nonettos
OETY	cogently
	Coventry
	covertly
	forestry
	honestly
	modestly
	momently
	nocently
	potently
OEUD	rose-hued
OEUE	home rule
	molecule
	to be sure
OEUH	nonesuch
OEVR	come over
	moreover
	move over
	pore over
OEWY	come away
	move away
OFAA	golfiana
OFAE	conflate
OFAK	roof rack
	wolf pack
OFAL	golf ball
	korfball
OFAN	Hoffmann
OFAT	bouffant
OFEE	confrère
OFER	coiffeur
OFES	roofless
OFGI	solfeggi
OFGT	dogfight
OFIE	rooflike
	roof tile
OFIS	forfeits
OFIT	conflict
OFLB	golf club
OFLN	gonfalon
	moufflon
OFLY	joyfully
	not fully
	woefully
OFND	confined
OFNS	confines
OFOE	wolf note
OFON	wolf down
OFOO	con fuoco
OFOT	confront
OFRA	conferva
OFSD	confused
OFTI	confetti
OFUD	confound
OFUE	coiffure
OFUT	to a fault
OGAD	longhand
OGAE	Cosgrave
	long face
	low-grade
	roughage
	top-grade
OGAL	long haul
OGAS	congrats
	longways
OGAT	poignant
OGBG	doggy-bag
OGDS	long odds
OGDY	doggedly
	rough-dry
OGEE	Congreve
OGEG	ronggeng
OGEM	long-term
OGER	jongleur
	longueur
OGES	congress❑
OGET	foggiest
OGHP	longship
OGHW	rough-hew
OGID	songbird
OGIE	long time
	longwise
OGIG	tonguing
OGIH	roughish
	toughish
OGLA	Mongolia
OGLM	coagulum
OGLP	long slip
OGNR	congener
OGNS	lodgings
	Longinus
OGNT	doughnut
OGOD	Longford
OGOE	conglobe
	foxglove
	long-gone
	long home
	mongoose
OGOG	Hong Kong
OGOK	songbook
OGOM	long poem
OGON	Longhorn
OGOP	pop group
OGOS	gorgeous
	hot goods
OGOT	gouge out
	longboat
	rough out
	tough out
OGRD	Novgorod
OGRL	doggerel
OGTN	Loaghtan
OGTP	long stop
OGTR	songster
OGTT	forget it
OGUP	long jump
OGVN	forgiven
OHAE	Rochdale
OHAL	mothball
OHAN	Loch Earn

OHAY top-heavy
OHBD to the bad
OHED to the end
OHEE cochleae
OHER cochlear
OHES Loch Ness
OHLD potholed
pot-holed
OHME bonhomie
OHMN non-human
OHNE no chance
OHNS no thanks
Tom Hanks
OHOH pooh-pooh
OHRD bothered
OHRI cothurni
OHRO Lothario
OHRS cothurns
go shares
OHRY Docherty
motherly
OHTE pochette
OHUD foxhound
OHUE cowhouse
Hobhouse
hothouse
OHUS jodhpurs
OHUT yoghourt
OHVM moshavim
OIAE Boniface
cogitate
dominate
loricate
motivate
nominate
solidare
volitate
OIAN Mosimann
OIAT dominant
toxicant
OIAY solitary
vomitary
OIBE sociable
OIBY sociably
OICL zodiacal
OICS Moriscos
to pieces
OIDD so-minded
OIDR louis d'or
louis-d'or
OIDY Robin Day
OIEM coliseum[□]
OIER domineer
OIES bodiless
boniness
cosiness
dopiness
doziness
goriness
holiness
nosiness
ooziness
ropiness
rosiness
OIET lorikeet
OIEY bovinely
docilely
go widely
politely
OIFR to die for
OIGN doting on
OIGP coming up
OIGY boringly
cooingly
dotingly
jokingly
losingly
lovingly
mopingly
movingly
posingly
wooingly
OIHC eolithic[□]
OIHD polished
OIHP polish up
OIHY boyishly
coyishly
modishly
mopishly
popishly
tonishly
toyishly
OIIA Dominica
OIID codified
modified
OIIE domicile
homicide
Ionicise
Ionicize
logicise
logicize
mobilise
mobilize
monitive
positive
volitive
vomitive
OIIG noticing
policing
vomiting
OIIK politick
OIIN dominion
Domitian
logician
monition
nolition
position
volition
OIIR codifier
modifier
OIIS homilies
policies
politics
OIIT homilist
OIIY docility
mobility
motility
motivity
nobility
solicity
solidify
solidity
toxicity
OIJY popinjay
OIKR monicker
OILN bouillon
OILS zorillos
OILW son-in-law
OILY jovially
socially
OINC Polignac
OINL notional
OIOD hominoid
OIOS dominoes
OIOY monitory
vomitory
OIRN positron
OIRY Moriarty
OISN Robinson
OISY kolinsky
OITC aoristic
holistic
logistic
monistic
OITL societal
OITY podiatry
OIUD foribund
moribund
OIUE not in use
solitude
OIUL Solihull
OIUS modicums
OIZR howitzer
OJDE forjudge
OJGL conjugal
OJIT conjoint
OJNS Tom Jones
OJRR conjurer
conjuror
OKAD dockyard
work hard
OKAE bookcase
book-mate
folk tale
folk-tale
lock gate
rock cake
rock-face
workfare
workmate
work rate
OKAK bookmark
look back
pockmark
work back
OKAL cocktail
rockfall
OKAT rock salt
rock-salt
OKBE bookable
lockable
workable
OKCS for kicks
OKDN hooked on
OKDP booked-up
cooked-up
locked up
worked up
worked-up
OKDT polka-dot
OKDY forkedly
workaday
OKED rockweed
OKEE look here!
OKEO folk hero
OKER workwear
OKES for keeps
workless
OKHP bookshop
workshop
OKIE booklice
look like
OKIG rockling
OKIH monkfish
rockfish
work with
OKIK look pink
OKIO Hokkaido
OKIT book list
OKIY cocknify
OKLB book club
OKLE Roskilde
OKNN look in on
OKNO lock on to
look into
look onto
work into
OKNS workings
OKOD monkhood
Rockford
workload
OKOE folklore
look to be
rock dove
rock rose
OKOG folk-song
OKOK cookbook
folk rock
workbook
OKOL rock wool
OKOM bookworm
hookworm
workroom
OKON look down
Yorktown
OKOS God knows
OKOT cockboat
OKPN look upon
work upon
OKPO look up to
OKRL cockerel
OKRN looker-on

OKRW	cockcrow
	cock-crow
OKTD	socketed
OKTO	cockatoo
OKTY	rocketry
OKUE	cocksure
OKUS	forkfuls
OKVR	fork over
	look over
	look-over
	work over
OKWY	lock away
	look awry
	soakaway
	work away
OKYD	cock-eyed
OLAE	coalface
	soul mate
OLAI	kohlrabi
OLAK	woolsack
OLAL	roll-call
OLAS	rouleaus
OLAX	rouleaux
OLAY	Donleavy
OLCE	follicle
OLCP	fool's cap
	foolscap
	World Cup
OLCS	bollocks
	go places
	Horlicks®
	pollices
OLDE	Coolidge
OLDM	hollidam
OLDR	colluder
OLDY	fooled by
OLEN	Moulmein
OLES	coolness
	foulness
	goalless
	soulless
OLEY	colliery
OLGA	collegia
OLGE	Boulogne
	collogue
OLGG	lollygag
OLGN	collagen
	hooligan
OLGR	Holliger
OLGS	noble gas
OLHA	holla-hoa!
OLHD	woolshed
OLIE	coalmine
	goal line
	poultice
OLIG	moulding
OLIH	fool with
OLIK	goal kick
OLIS	woollies
OLLY	doolally
	foul play
OLMN	nobleman
	noblemen
OLNA	pollinia
OLNO	fool into
OLOD	soul food
OLOE	toilsome
OLON	boil down
	cool down
	fool-born
	howl down
OLOT	Coalport
	go all out
	goalpost
OLPE	collapse
OLPP	lollipop
OLQE	colloque
OLQY	colloquy
OLRA	collyria
OLRD	collared
OLRE	toll-free
OLRS	Coelurus
OLRT	noble rot
OLSE	coalesce
	coulisse
OLTD	polluted
OLTE	roulette
OLTH	potlatch
OLTN	Low Latin
OLTR	collator
	pollster
OLTY	toiletry
OLUE	Toulouse
OLUS	Joe Louis
OLVL	low-level
OLVR	boil over
	bowl over
	Rod Laver
	roll over
	roll-over
OLWD	hollowed
OLWG	gollywog
OLWN	follow on
	follow-on
OLWP	follow up
	follow-up
OLWR	follower
	world war
OLWY	boil away
	fool away
	go slowly
	hollowly
OLYR	volleyer
OMAT	wormcast
OMBE	formable
OMDF	formed of
OMDS	Commodus
	dolmades
OMDY	doomsday
OMER	worm gear
OMES	foamless
	formless
	gormless
	zoom lens
OMGN	tommy-gun
OMIE	boom time
OMLE	formulae
OMLN	formalin
OMLS	formulas
OMLY	formally
	normally
OMNE	commence
OMNL	communal
	hormonal
OMNN	zoom in on
OMNO	commando
OMNR	commoner
OMNY	commonly
	dormancy
	Hogmanay
	hot money
OMOD	wormwood
OMOE	wormhole
OMRE	commerce
	commerge
OMRL	non-moral
OMRT	tommyrot
	tommy-rot
OMRY	formerly
OMSS	Formosus
OMTC	cosmetic
	dogmatic
OMTH	not match
OMTL	non-metal
	pot metal
OMTR	commuter
	doomster
OMUE	dormouse
OMUH	Monmouth
OMUS	roomfuls
ONAD	downward
ONAE	John Cage
	moonface
	Poincaré
	poundage
	somniate
ONAH	John Nash
ONAK	moonwalk
ONAL	Cornwall
	downfall
	John Paul
	moon-ball
	town hall
ONAM	point aim
ONAN	fountain
	John Wain
	mountain
ONAS	tonneaus
ONAT	downcast
ONAX	tonneaux
ONAY	boundary
	John Cary
ONAZ	Joan Baez
ONBA	coenobia
ONBD	going bad
ONBL	John Abel
ONBN	loony bin
ONCT	Connacht
ONDS	tornados
ONEE	coinhere
ONEG	Kornberg
ONEL	Cornwell
ONEM	hornbeam
	moonbeam
ONEN	John Venn
	pounce on
ONEP	John Kemp
ONES	countess
	hornfels
	moonless
	pointers
	rounders
ONET	downbeat
	down-beat
ONFC	somnific
ONFO	to and fro
ONGN	roentgen□
ONGT	go and get
	Vonnegut
ONHN	worn thin
ONHP	township
ONHT	moonshot
ONID	downwind
ONIE	coincide
	downside
	downsize
	go on fire
	hornpipe
	moonlike
	noontide
ONIG	bouncing
	counting
	founding
	hounding
	jointing
	lounging
	mounting
	pointing
	pounding
	sounding
	wounding
ONIH	down with
	go in with
	join with
	youngish
ONIL	downhill
	hornbill
ONIO	Joan Miró
ONIS	counties
	Joan Sims
ONIT	John Birt
ONIY	bouncily
	woundily
ONLN	town plan
ONLW	Hounslow
ONLY	Connolly
	downplay
ONMN	cognomen
	townsman
	young man
ONNO	go in unto
ONNS	mornings

Words marked □ can also be spelled with an initial capital letter

ONNT	fornenst
ONNX	John Knox
ONOD	John Ford
	loan-word
ONOE	born to be
	corn pone
	young one
ONOF	going off
	round off
	sound off
ONOK	hornbook
ONON	downtown
	down-town
ONOR	downpour
ONOS	corneous
	John Ross
ONOT	count out
	downmost
	going out
	going-out
	point out
	sound out
ONOY	John Dory
ONRD	cornered
ONRE	Born Free
	Rowntree
ONSE	cognosce
	go and see
ONSN	goings-on
ONSS	zoonoses
ONTH	top notch
	top-notch
ONTI	cornetti
	Mount Tai
ONTS	cornutos
	hornitos
ONUE	John Hume
	jointure
ONUN	downturn
ONUS	John Huss
ONUT	John Hunt
	John Hurt
ONUU	Mount Usu
ONVC	Young Vic
ONVR	conniver
ONYG	John Byng
OOAA	Tomonaga
	toxocara
	Yokohama
OOAD	honorand
OOAE	cohobate
	rotovate
OOAH	coronach
OOAI	Cotopaxi
OOAK	monomark
OOAL	monorail
OOAM	coco-palm
	rotor arm
OOAO	Colorado
OOAP	monocarp
OOAT	colorant
	roborant
	sonorant
OOAY	coronary
	homogamy
	honorary
	monogamy
OOBA	Colombia
OOBS	motor-bus
OOCR	motor car
OOCS	moroccos
OODL	toroidal
OODN	go cold on
OODO	do good to
OODR	do-gooder
	no wonder
OOED	go to seed
	locoweed
OOEE	Holocene
OOEH	Voronezh
OOEK	polo neck
	polo-neck
OOEY	homogeny
	jocosely
	morosely
OOFR	go too far
OOGD	Son of God
OOGN	toboggan
OOGS	so long as
OOHA	Dorothea
OOHE	Donoghue
OOHN	colophon
OOIE	colonise
	colonize
	dolomite
	monoxide
	motorise
	motorize
	polonise
	polonize
	robotise
	sororise
	sororize
OOIH	monolith
OOIK	bobolink
OOIL	colonial❑
	monomial
	sororial
OOIM	polonium
OOIS	go to bits
	Honorius
	Polonius
	robotics
OOIT	colonist
	monodist
	monotint
	motorist
	oologist
	to-do list
OOIY	jocosity
	nodosity
	porosity
	sonority
	sorority
OOKR	coworker
	co-worker
OOLD	monocled
OOLM	Mo Mowlam
OOLO	rosoglio
OOLT	monoglot
OOMN	Son of Man
OONN	go down on
OONO	go down to
OONR	no sooner
OOOE	corocore
	locomote
	monotone
	soporose
OOON	go to town
OOOO	cocobolo
	doloroso
OOOS	dolorous
	sonorous
OOOY	doxology
	homology
	horology
	lobotomy
	monopoly
	Monopoly®
	monotony
	nosology
	posology
	topology
OORA	no-go area
OORD	coloured
	honoured
OORE	coco-tree
OORM	hologram
	logogram
	monogram
	nomogram
	sonogram
OORN	colour in
OORP	colour up
OORT	monocrat
OORW	to borrow
	tomorrow
OOSL	colossal
OOSM	Son of Sam
OOSS	colossus
OOSY	joyously
OOTF	con out of
OOTN	go rotten
	go soft on
	Joe Orton
	not often
OOUL	monohull
OOUO	Yokosuko
OOUU	Honolulu
OOUY	sonobuoy
OOWY	motorway
OOYE	logotype
	monocyte
	monotype
	Monotype®
OOYV	Korolyov
OOYY	monogyny
	toponymy
OPAE	not place
	volplane
OPAN	complain
OPAT	pot plant
OPDM	poppadum
OPDO	Don Pedro
OPDP	cooped up
OPDS	torpedos
OPDU	Pompidou
OPDY	torpidly
OPEE	complete
	morpheme
OPEK	poop deck
OPES	compress
	hot-press
	Morpheus
OPGS	compages
OPIE	compline
	comprise
	co-optive
	hooplike
	low-price
	morphine
	porpoise
	Tom Paine
	zoophile
OPIG	coupling
	morphing
	toppling
OPIN	co-option
OPIT	comprint
	low point
	top point
OPLA	Coppélia
OPLR	compiler
OPNS	hot pants
	jog pants
	pompanos
	volpinos
OPOD	top-proud
OPOE	loophole
	romp home
OPOT	soapwort
OPRL	corporal
OPRN	Couperin
OPRY	non-party
OPSD	composed
OPSN	Tok Pisin
OPSR	composer
OPTA	hospitia
OPTD	not-pated
OPTL	hospital
OPTR	computer
OPUD	compound
OPUS	soapsuds
OPYE	zoophyte
OPYR	non-payer
OPYY	porphyry❑
OQES	bouquets
OQET	conquest
OQIE	not quite
OQIO	mosquito
ORAD	gourmand
	hour hand

Words marked ❑ can also be spelled with an initial capital letter

	moorland
ORAH	sour mash
ORAS	Boer Wars
	journals
ORAT	pot roast
	pot-roast
ORBE	horrible
ORBY	horribly
ORCS	do tricks
	Horrocks
	touracos
ORDD	corroded
ORDE	porridge
ORDR	corridor
	joyrider
ORDS	comrades
ORDY	horridly
	torridly
OREF	yourself
OREL	doorbell
OREN	fourteen
ORER	Tourneur
ORES	dourness
	journeys
	poorness
	sourness
OREY	coarsely
	courtesy
	hoarsely
	sobriety
ORFC	horrific
ORFL	mournful
ORFR	sorry for
ORGN	Morrigan
ORGS	porrigos
ORGT	not right
ORHP	lorry-hop
ORHY	fourthly
ORID	your mind
ORIE	coercive
	Lorraine
ORIG	boarding
	coursing
	courting
	hoarding
	mourning
	sourcing
	worrying
ORIH	sorryish
ORIN	coercion
ORIR	courtier
	Tournier
ORLS	no frills
	no-frills
ORMN	Boardman
ORNE	courante
	Torrance
ORNS	sopranos
ORNY	Courtney
	sovranly
OROD	fourfold
	sour-cold
OROE	foursome
OROG	hourlong
OROK	moorcock
OROL	moorfowl
ORON	poor-John
	pour down
OROT	board out
	doorpost
	four-foot
	worry out
ORSN	Morrison
ORSY	touristy
ORTC	Socratic
ORTP	doorstep
	doorstop
ORTS	botritis
	Socrates
ORUD	go around
ORUS	sourpuss
ORUT	poursuit
ORVA	Monrovia
ORVE	Don Revie
ORVR	pour over
ORWD	borrowed
	sorrowed
ORWR	borrower
	sorrower
OSAA	Botswana
	moussaka
OSAD	not stand
OSAE	constate
	Lonsdale
	Rosslare
OSAK	gobsmack
	hog's back
	hog's-back
OSAN	coxswain
	Torshavn
	Tórshavn
OSAP	not sharp
OSAS	bobstays
	Constans
OSAT	constant❑
	not start
OSAZ	Konstanz
OSBA	Lok Sabha
OSBE	possible
OSBT	house bat
OSBX	loose box
OSBY	houseboy
	possibly
OSCE	God's acre
OSDD	lopsided
	lop-sided
OSDG	house-dog
OSDR	consider
OSEA	monstera
OSED	forspend
	Godspeed
	hogshead
	loose end
	potsherd
OSEK	forspeak
OSEL	Godspell
OSEN	Holstein
OSER	forswear
	Monsieur
OSES	Goossens
OSEU	Cousteau
	Rousseau
OSFL	boastful
OSFY	horsefly
	housefly
OSGG	goosegog
OSHF	sous-chef
OSHT	how's that
OSIE	conspire
	solstice
OSIG	boasting
	boosting
	roasting
	roisting
OSIK	joystick
	non-stick
OSIL	God's will
OSIY	moistify
OSKN	forsaken
OSLR	consoler
	consular
	Koestler
OSLT	corselet
OSLY	dorsally
	Wolseley
OSMD	consumed
OSME	consommé
OSMN	horseman
	horsemen
	houseman
	Norseman
OSMR	consumer
	gossamer
OSMT	mouse mat
OSND	poisoned
OSNE	nonsense
OSNP	loosen up
OSNR	loosener
	poisoner
OSNS	housings
OSOD	Cotswold
OSOE	go ashore
OSOF	worse off
OSOH	forsooth
OSON	doss down
OSOR	voussoir
OSOS	couscous
OSOT	for short
OSOY	dogsbody
	Toy Story
OSRD	house red
	tonsured
OSRE	conserve
	construe
OSRT	bowsprit
OSRY	go astray
OSST	house-sit
OSTD	cosseted
OSTE	noisette
OSTI	Rossetti
OSTP	housetop
OSTY	corsetry
OSUE	moisture
	soy sauce
OSUF	hot stuff
	sob-stuff
OSVN	Hot Seven
OTAB	Godthaab
OTAD	boat-yard
	Portland
	Port Said
	postcard
OTAE	Boat Race
	boat race
	bootlace
	boot sale
	Coltrane
	mortgage
	postdate
	software
OTAH	footpath
OTAK	boot-jack
	footmark
	postmark
	softback
OTAL	football
	footfall
	root-ball
OTAT	contract
	contrast
	portrait
OTAY	contrary
	go steady
	mortuary
OTBE	bootable
	portable
	sortable
OTBK	bontebok
OTCE	monticle
	postiche
	soutache
OTCL	cortical
	poetical
	vortical
OTCS	contacts
	cortices
	porticos
	vortices
OTDY	rootedly
OTED	goatherd
	softhead
	soft-head
	Southend
OTEE	not there
	portière
OTEH	fortieth
OTEK	boat deck
OTEL	Montreal
	soft sell
OTEN	northern
	southern❑
OTEP	bottle up

Words marked ❑ can also be spelled with an initial capital letter

OTER	footwear
	root beer
OTES	bootless
	footless
	fortress
	Poitiers
	rootless
	soft lens
	softness
OTET	footrest
	loftiest
OTEX	Montreux
OTFL	loathful
	mouthful
	youthful
OTGE	Montague
OTGL	Portugal
OTIA	Port-Vila
OTIE	contrite
	contrive
	doctrine
	rootlike
	soft line
	tortoise
	Voltaire
OTIG	footling
	goatling
	loathing
	mottling
	northing
	soothing
	Worthing
OTIH	fortyish
OTIK	bootlick
	con trick
	not thick
	not think
OTIL	foothill
OTIR	worthier
OTIS	Boethius
	worthies
OTIY	fortuity
	toothily
	worthily
OTLA	tortilla
OTLG	footslog
OTLO	Costello
	Portillo
OTLW	soft-slow
OTLY	hostelry
	mortally
	postally
OTMN	routeman
OTMR	costumer
	Mortimer
OTMT	contempt
OTNA	continua
OTND	low-toned
	softened
OTNE	continue
	Oostende
	sortance
OTNL	fontanel
OTNN	cotton on
OTNO	contango
	continuo
OTNP	soften up
OTNR	softener
OTNS	contents
	jottings
	norteñas
	norteños
OTNW	don't know
OTNY	Fontenoy
	moltenly
	rottenly
OTOD	foothold
	soft food
	softwood
OTOE	bolthole
	boothose
	footnote
	footsore
	Montrose
	porthole
	postcode
	postpone
	postpose
	soft-core
OTOF	mouth off
OTOH	dog-tooth
OTOK	footwork
OTOL	soft-boil
OTON	bolt down
	poltroon
	soft loan
OTOO	Nostromo
OTOP	soft soap
	soft-soap
OTOS	controls
	tortuous
OTOT	Montfort
OTPT	got to pot
	soft spot
OTPW	southpaw
OTQE	boutique
OTRD	dog-tired
	tortured
OTRE	cost-free
	nocturne
	post-free
OTRL	doctoral
	dotterel
	postural
OTRP	Northrop
	root crop
OTRR	fosterer
	loiterer
	posturer
	potterer
	torturer
	totterer
OTRS	monteros
OTRY	porterly
OTSA	North Sea
OTSR	mortiser
OTSY	not to say
	soothsay
OTTE	toe to toe
OTTP	footstep
OTUB	Tom Thumb
OTUD	Dortmund
	soft-hued
OTUH	Portrush
OTUS	contours
OTUT	zoot suit
OTXC	non-toxic
OTXS	cortexes
	vortexes
OTYF	worthy of
OUAA	Tokugawa
OUAE	copulate
	modulate
	populace
	populate
OUBA	Columbia
OUBS	Columbus
OUCS	Moluccas
OUDM	corundum
OUDY	jocundly
	rotundly
OUET	document
	monument□
OUGY	go hungry
OUHO	so much so
OUHS	so much as
OUIE	volumise
	volumize
OUIG	focusing
OUIM	botulism
	populism
OUIN	locution
	non-union
	solution
	volution
OUIT	populist
OULC	go public
OUND	columned
OUNL	columnal
OUNR	columnar
OUOE	nodulose
OUOS	nodulous
	populous
OUOU	tohu bohu
OUTE	coquette
	locustae
	moquette
OUTS	coquitos
OUTY	coquetry
	robustly
OUUN	do a U-turn
	To Autumn
OVAI	souvlaki
OVBE	solvable
OVIE	low voice
OVLE	convolve
	convulse
OVNE	convince
OVNR	convener
	convenor
	souvenir
OVNY	solvency
OVRE	converge
	converse
OVRO	go over to
OVTE	corvette
	Corvette®
OVXY	convexly
OVYR	conveyor
OWAY	dog-weary
OWBY	cobwebby
OWEL	cogwheel
	joy-wheel
OWIE	non-white
OWIS	Tom Waits
OWLE	Tom Wolfe
OWNA	Morwenna
OWRS	forwards
	godwards
OWTR	hot water
	low water
	pomwater
OWYN	Norweyan
OXED	coextend
OXES	to excess
OYAE	holydame
OYAH	polymath
OYAL	ponytail
OYAP	Polycarp
OYAY	polygamy
OYDT	copy-edit
OYED	copyread
	Holyhead
OYEE	polygene
OYEK	Holy Week
OYEL	Holywell
OYEN	Tony Benn
OYEY	polysemy
OYHE	coryphee
	coryphée
OYHP	body shop
OYHT	cosy chat
OYID	to my mind
OYIE	bodyline
OYIK	Moby Dick
OYIS	Polybius
OYIY	Holy City
OYLT	polyglot□
OYLW	body blow
OYOE	polysome
OYOK	bodywork
	copybook
OYOS	polypous
OYOT	go by foot
OYOY	roly-poly
OYRT	Holy Writ
	holy writ
OYUT	bodysuit
OYYY	polygyny
OZLS	Gonzales
OZLZ	González
OZRM	momzerim

Words marked □ can also be spelled with an initial capital letter

OZTI	bozzetti
OZUI	bouzouki
PAAE	appanage
PADY	upwardly
PAET	apparent
PAFR	speak for
PAGE	sprangle
PAGN	spraygun
PAHR	upgather
PAIE	optative
PAIG	speaking
	updating
PAIN	apiarian
PAIT	apiarist
PAKE	sprackle
PAKT	up-market
PALD	appalled
PANM	sphagnum
PAOT	speak out
PATC	aplastic
PATE	sprattle
PATR	splatter
PBAT	epiblast
PCAE	space age
	speciate
	spectate
PCAO	spiccato
PCCE	epicycle
PCDA	epicedia
PCDS	epicedes
PCFC	specific
PCIE	apocrine
PCLD	speckled
PCLM	speculum
PCLR	specular
	spicular
PCLX	epicalyx
PCLY	apically
	epically
PCMN	spaceman❑
	specimen
PCOS	spacious
	specious
PCOT	space out
PCRL	spectral
PCRM	spectrum
PCRS	Epicurus
PCTD	spicated
PDCS	spadices
PDFL	spadeful
PDMC	epidemic
PDNS	spadones
PDRL	epidural
PDSS	apodosis
PEAE	a presage
PECT	uppercut
PEDD	splendid
PEDN	spread on
PEDO	spread to
PEDR	spreader
PEDX	appendix
PEEA	ephemera
PEEF	a piece of

PEET	appetent
PEGR	Sprenger
PEIE	aphetise
	aphetize
	appetise
	appetite
	appetize
	spaewife
PEIG	speeding
PEIL	apperill
	splenial
PEIN	aphelion
PEIS	splenius
PEIY	speedily
PELO	appeal to
PELP	upper lip
PEOD	spheroid
PEOS	apterous
PERS	appear as
PESI	après-ski
PESR	appeaser
PETR	upsetter
PEUE	spherule
PEVL	upheaval
PEWY	speedway
PFIG	spiffing
PGAH	epigraph
PGAS	spyglass
PHUT	upthrust
PIAE	oppilate
	optimate
	spoilage
PIED	split end
PIFR	spoil for
PIGD	sprigged
PIGN	spring on
PIGP	spring up
PIGS	sphinges
PIHY	uppishly
PIIE	optimise
	optimize
PIIG	spoiling
	uprising
PIIM	optimism
PIIN	ophidian
	optician
PIIT	optimist
PIKE	sprinkle
PINL	optional
PIOF	split off
PIPA	split pea
PIPN	split pin
PITD	uplifted
PITR	splinter
	splitter
	sprinter
PIUE	aptitude
PIXS	sphinxes
PIZG	spritzig
PIZR	spritzer
PKLE	Spike Lee
PKLT	spikelet
PLAE	spillage

	Spillane
	spoliate
PLEN	spelaean
PLFR	apply for
PLGA	apologia
PLGE	apologue
	epilogue
PLIS	Apuleius
PLKN	spilikin
PLMC	Applemac®
PLNE	opulence
PLOL	apply oil
PLOT	spell out
PLPE	apple pie
PLPY	epilepsy
PLQE	appliqué
PLTN	Appleton
PLTR	epilator
PLUE	applause
PLYN	Apollyon
PMNE	spumante❑
PNAC	spondaic
PNAD	Spaniard
PNAH	upon oath
PNAL	spendall
PNAT	open-cast
PNBE	openable
PNES	openness
	spinneys
PNHP	open shop
PNHR	up-anchor
PNID	open mind
PNIE	open fire
	open side
PNIG	spanking
	spending
	spinning
	sponging
PNIK	spun silk
PNIN	sponsion
PNIS	spinnies
PNIY	spongily
PNLD	spangled
PNLN	open-plan
PNLR	Spengler
PNNO	open on to
	open onto
PNOE	open sore
PNOK	open book
	open work
	openwork
PNOR	open door
PNOS	opinions
PNRL	spandrel
	spandril
PNRS	up in arms
PNSY	epinasty
PNTR	spinster
PNYD	open-eyed
POAE	up to date
	up-to-date
POCY	splotchy
PODR	upholder

POET	opponent
POFL	spoonful
POIE	aphorise
	aphorize
	apposite
	opposite
	up to time
POIG	opposing
	upcoming
POIH	spookish
POIM	aphorism
POIT	aphorist
POIY	spookily
	spoonily
POKD	uplocked
POKP	Spion Kop
POKT	sprocket
POLW	upfollow
POMN	apron-man
PONR	uptowner
POTD	uprooted
POTF	opt out of
POTP	sprout up
PPAE	spy plane
PPAY	epiphany❑
PPEY	apoplexy
PPIG	upspring
PPYE	apophyge
	epiphyte
PQEY	opaquely
PRAH	approach
PRAL	spur-gall
PRAY	spermary
PRBE	operable
	sparable
PRCE	spiracle
PRDA	sporidia
PRDC	sporadic
PRER	spur gear
PRES	spurless
PRET	aperient
PREY	sparsely
PRGP	spark gap
PRIE	appraise
	sportive
PRIG	sparring
	sporting
	spurning
	spurting
PRIY	sparsity
	sportily
PRLA	spirilla
PRLR	sparkler
	sporular
PRLY	spirally
PROF	spark off
PROL	sperm oil
PROS	spurious
PROT	spark out
PRRB	spare rib
	spare-rib
PRSD	apprised
PRSL	apprisal

PRTA	operetta
PRTC	operatic
PRTD	spirated
	spirited
PRTF	aperitif
PRTR	operator
PRUA	opercula
PRUE	aperture
PRVD	approved
PRVL	approval
PRXS	sparaxis
PSAE	apostate
PSAY	apostasy
PSDC	episodic
PSLS	epistles
PSUA	opuscula
PSYE	epistyle
PTAH	spot cash
PTCS	up sticks
PTED	spot-weld
PTEE	Spätlese
PTEM	apothegm
	upstream
PTES	epithems
	spotless
PTEY	sputtery
PTFL	spiteful
PTIE	spitfire□
PTIG	spitting
	spotting
PTIS	upstairs
PTIY	spottily
PTLR	spatular
PTOE	spathose
	upstroke
PTON	spittoon
PTSS	epitases
PTTC	apatetic
PUAE	spousage
PUAS	spousals
PUEP	spruce up
PUEY	sprucely
PUKR	spruiker
PUND	upturned
PUNR	oppugner
PUOF	spout off
PUTR	splutter
PWIG	spawning
PYES	spryness
QAAH	squabash
QABE	squabble
QACR	squad car
QACS	squaccos
QADE	squaddie
QADR	squander
QAEP	square up
QAEY	squarely
QAHD	squashed
QAIE	equalise
	equalize
QAIG	squaring
QAIH	squarish
QAIL	squarial
QAIM	aquarium
QAIN	Aquarian
	equation
QAIS	Aquarius
QAIT	aquatint
QAIY	equality
QAKR	squawker
QALR	squaller
QAMN	squawman
QAOE	squamose
QAOS	squamous
QARN	squadron
QATE	squattle
QATR	squatter
QAUG	aqualung
QECY	squelchy
QEGE	squeegee
QEKR	squeaker
QELN	squeal on
QELR	squealer
QEUT	aqueduct
QEZD	squeezed
QEZR	squeezer
QIAE	equipage
QIEY	squirely
QIGE	squiggle
QIGY	squiggly
QIIE	aquiline
QIIS	equities
QIPD	equipped
QIRL	squirrel
QITR	squinter
	squirter
RAAE	breakage
	great ape
RAAK	great auk
RAAL	try a fall
RABE	preamble
RABG	great big
RABN	breadbin
RADE	organdie
RADG	Great Dog
RADY	trial-day
RAEO	Brian Eno
RAEP	crease up
RAET	armament
	greatest
	ornament
RAEY	arcanely
	creamery
	ornately
	urbanely
RAFL	dreadful
RAGD	arranged
RAGE	triangle□
RAGR	arranger
RAHN	breath in
RAHO	broach to
RAHR	breather
	preacher
RAIE	Arianise
	Arianize
	Aryanise
	Aryanize
	creatine
	creative
	organise
	organize
	treatise
	urbanise
	urbanite
	urbanize
RAIG	breaking
	creaking
	creating
	croaking
	dreaming
	groaning
	treading
	treating
	wreaking
RAIH	freakish
RAIM	organism
RAIN	Arcadian
	creation□
	Croatian
	Orcadian
RAIS	greasies
	treaties
RAIT	organist
	trialist
RAIY	creakily
	croakily
	dreamily
	drearily
	greasily
	urbanity
RANC	Armagnac
RAND	ordained
RANR	ordainer
RAOF	break off
RAOT	break out
	breakout
	freak out
	freak-out
RARN	trial run
RASC	Triassic
RASS	Arkansas
RATA	cream-tea
RATC	orgastic
RATT	great tit
RATY	arrantly
	errantly
	errantry
RAUE	armature
	creature
	treasure
RAUY	treasury
RAVW	break-vow
RBAE	cribbage
	cribrate
RBAH	tribrach
RBBE	bribable
	probable
RBBY	probably
RBDC	tribadic
RBES	drabness
	problems
RBIE	crabwise
RBIG	cribbing
	drubbing
	grabbing
RBIK	grub kick
RBIY	crabbily
RBLA	Arabella
	cribella
RBLY	tribally
RBNL	tribunal
RBOE	cribrose
RBOS	frabjous
RBUG	Fribourg
RCAC	orichalc
	trochaic
RCAE	eructate
	wreckage
RCAM	proclaim
RCAR	armchair
RCBE	crucible
RCBT	brickbat
RCCD	uric acid
RCCE	tricycle
RCDD	brocaded
RCDE	Eric Idle
RCDL	fricadel
RCDT	priced at
RCEE	tracheae
RCEL	bracteal
	tracheal
RCEN	dry-clean
RCES	crackers
	proceeds
RCEY	crockery
	trickery
RCFL	graceful
RCFX	crucifix
RCIA	trichina
RCIE	erectile
	practice
	practise
	procaine
	tractile
	tractive
RCIG	cracking
	pricking
	tracking
	tricking
	trucking
	wrecking
RCIH	brackish
RCIK	trochisk
RCIL	brachial
RCIM	brachium
RCIN	erection
	fraction
	friction
	traction
RCIY	fructify
	trickily
RCLA	trochlea

RCLD	freckled
RCLR	oracular
	truckler
RCLT	bracelet
RCME	drachmae
RCMI	drachmai
RCMN	truch-men
RCMS	drachmas
RCNC	draconic
RCND	arachnid
RCNL	cracknel
RCNO	trecento
RCNR	Bruckner
RCNT	precinct
RCOA	trachoma
RCOD	trichoid
	trochoid
RCOE	fructose
	orecrowe
	trichome
RCOI	broccoli
RCOS	gracious
	precious
RCOT	trick out
RCPS	precepts
RCPT	crackpot
	precepit
RCRD	brick-red
	track rod
RCRE	precurse
	tricorne
RCRR	procurer
RCSN	Ericsson
RCSS	crocuses
RCTG	price tag
RCUE	brochure
	fracture
	preclude
RCWR	price war
RCYE	trachyte
RDAD	graduand
RDAE	eradiate
	graduate
RDBE	credible
	erodible
RDBY	credibly
RDCD	produced
RDCR	producer
	traducer
RDCS	products
RDED	Bridgend
RDEP	dredge up
RDES	aridness
RDET	bridle at
	Fred West
	gradient
RDEY	drudgery
RDFL	prideful
RDGL	prodigal
RDGP	trade gap
RDIG	grudging
	prodding
RDIT	Brad Pitt
RDLA	predella
RDNA	credenda
	uredinia
RDNE	credence
	prudence ❑
RDNS	Eridanus
	uredines
RDOD	Bradford
RDOE	prodnose
	prodrome
RDOF	trade off
	trade-off
RDOK	gridlock
RDOL	crude oil
RDRC	Frederic
RDRN	gridiron
RDTM	gradatim
RDTR	creditor
	predator
RDUY	Bradbury
RDWR	trade war
READ	free hand
	freehand
REAE	freebase
	freeware
REAF	tree calf
REAL	free fall
	free-fall
	treenail
REAT	artefact
REDY	friendly
	-friendly
REEN	free rein
	tree fern
REEP	breeze up
	freeze-up
REES	freeness
	treeless
	trueness
REET	praefect
	pre-elect
REEY	greenery
REFY	greenfly
REGO	arpeggio
REHL	Brueghel
REHS	breeches
REIE	arsenide
	arsenite
	free time
	Graecise
	Graecize
	tree line
REIG	breeding
	briefing
	creeping
	freezing
	greening
	greeting
	grieving
	ordering
	preening
REIH	greenish
REIK	free kick
REIL	arterial
	free will
	praedial
	proemial
REIN	Armenian
	Friesian
REIS	arteries
	greenies
	Ortelius
REIT	free gift
	pre-exist
REIU	prie-dieu
REIY	breezily
	greedily
REKN	Friedkin
REKY	Greek key
RELE	true-blue
REMN	freedman
	freedmen
	Friedman
REOD	freehold
	freeload
REOE	free love
	free vote
	gruesome
	truelove
REOK	Greenock
REOM	free-form
REON	freeborn
	Freetown
REOS	grievous
REOT	freeboot
	Freeport
RERE	greegree
RERG	tree frog
REST	cruet set
RETA	green tea
RETD	oriented
RETL	oriental
RETR	arrester
RETY	ardently
	priestly
	urgently
REVS	F R Leavis
RFAT	Truffaut
RFCA	trifecta
RFCL	trifocal
RFED	urnfield
RFIG	crofting
	drafting
	drifting
	grafting
	trifling
RFIH	Griffith
RFII	graffiti
RFIO	graffito
RFIY	craftily
RFLY	artfully
	irefully
RFNT	drift-net
RFOF	drift off
RFPE	Graf Spee
RFRA	pro forma
	triforia
RFTY	profit by
RFUD	profound
RGAA	bregmata
RGAE	drag race
	prograde
RGAH	trigraph
RGAT	braggart
	fragrant
	pregnant
RGCL	tragical
RGDY	frigidly
RGEA	Drogheda
RGES	preggers
	progress
RGET	fragment
RGEY	priggery
RGIE	dragline
RGIG	bragging
	dragging
	frigging
RGIH	priggish
RGIT	druggist
RGLR	wriggler
RGLY	frugally
RGMN	dragoman
RGNA	Braganza
RGNC	erogenic
	orogenic
	trigonic
RGNL	original
	trigonal
RGNM	origanum
RGNS	oreganos
RGOE	dragrope
RGOS	dragoons
RGPN	tragopan
RGSR	drug user
RGTM	gregatim
RGTN	brighten
	Brighton
	frighten
RGTR	dragster
RGTY	brightly
RGUT	armgaunt
RGYH	triglyph
RHBT	prohibit
RHDX	orthodox
RHEN	Archaean
RHEY	orthoepy
RHIE	archaise
	archaize
	archwise
RHIM	archaism
RHLA	orchella
	orchilla
RHND	orphaned
RHOK	arch-mock
RHSS	orthoses
	orthosis
RHTC	orthotic
RHUE	archduke
RHVL	archival

Words marked ❑ can also be spelled with an initial capital letter

RHVS	archives
RIAD	ordinand
RIAE	drainage
	fruitage
	irrigate
	irritate
	ordinate
	urticate
RIAM	arm-in-arm
RIAT	artifact
	irritant
	urticant
RIAY	ordinary
RIBT	fruit bat
RIBX	brainbox
RIEE	draisene
RIET	arrive at
	orpiment
RIFL	fruitful
RIGR	Grainger
RIGY	erringly
	pryingly
	tryingly
RIHY	graithly
RIIE	arginine
	artifice
	draisine
RIIG	arriving
	broiling
	bruising
	cruising
	draining
	graining
	groining
	praising
	trailing
	training
RIIH	brainish
RIIM	druidism□
RIIN	fruition
RIIS	Arminius
RIKE	Mr Pickle
RILD	articled
RILR	brailler
RILS	articles
RIOF	trail off
RIRS	arrieros
RITA	fruit tea
RITC	artistic
	truistic
RITY	artistry
RJDE	prejudge
RJLO	Trujillo
RJLS	frijoles
RKIA	Praktica®
RKIG	trekking
RKNN	broken in
RKNY	brokenly
RKPD	brake pad
RKTA	Krakatoa
RLBT	drill bit
RLES	trolleys
RLEY	drollery
RLFC	prolific
RLFR	pro-lifer
RLGC	urologic
RLGE	prologue
RLIG	drilling
	grilling
	Trilling
RLIM	trillium
RLIS	frillies
	trilbies
	trollies
RLNA	Sri Lanka
RLOE	Trollope
RLOH	gralloch
RLOS	trilloes
RLOY	trollopy
RLPE	prolapse
RLPN	grill pan
RLRG	drill rig
RLTC	prelatic
RLXY	prolixly
RMAS	Drum Mass
RMAX	trumeaux
RMDC	bromidic
	Tremadoc
RMDY	framed by
RMED	drumhead
RMEE	premiere
	première
RMEH	cromlech
RMEL	Cromwell
RMES	brimless
	grimness
	primness
	trammels
	trimness
RMET	drumbeat
RMEY	trumpery
RMIG	brimming
	cramming
	drumming
	trimming
RMIH	frumpish
RMIN	Grampian
RMIY	arum lily
	grumpily
RMLD	crumpled
	trampled
RMLI	Grimaldi
RMLR	grumbler
	premolar
	trampler
	trembler
RMLS	brambles
	tremolos
RMLY	primally
RMNE	Bramante
RMNL	criminal
RMNO	drum into
RMNS	trominos
RMOE	Mrs Moore
	primrose□
	trombone
RMON	crumhorn
RMOS	cramboes
RMRC	trimeric
RMRI	trimurti□
RMRN	trimaran
RMRY	Cromarty
RMSD	premised
	promised
RMSE	promisee
RMSR	promiser
	promisor
RMSS	premises
RMSW	frame-saw
RMSY	kromesky
RMTB	from A to B
RMTC	aromatic
	dramatic
	eremitic
RMTD	promoted
RMTN	Crompton
RMTR	promoter
	prompter
	trimeter
RMTY	promptly
RMTZ	from A to Z
RMUE	Drambuie®
RMUS	premiums
RMVL	primeval
RMVR	brim over
RNAD	drunkard
	iron hand
RNAE	frontage
	truncate
RNAO	Brentano
RNAT	transact
RNBE	Grenoble
RNCE	Grenache
RNCL	irenical
	ironical
RNDD	granddad
	Trinidad
RNDS	grenades
RNER	grandeur
RNES	Irenaeus
	princess
	trinkets
RNET	cringe at
	transect
	transept
RNEY	orangery
	princely
RNFL	wrongful
RNFR	transfer
RNFX	transfix
RNFY	cranefly
RNGR	Srinagar
RNHD	branched
	drenched
RNHM	Grantham
RNHP	tranship
RNHR	trencher
RNHS	bronchos
	bronchus
RNID	brandied
	crannied
	frenzied
RNIE	Cronkite
	Francine
	Ironside
RNIG	bronzing
	cringing
	drinking
	fronting
	granting
	grinding
	grunting
	prancing
	printing
	wringing
RNIH	brandish
	Frankish
	prankish
RNII	Brindisi
RNIL	prandial
RNIM	francium
RNIR	frontier
RNIY	crankily
	trendily
RNLA	prunella□
RNLD	brindled
	crinkled
	ironclad
	iron-clad
	wrinkled
RNLE	crenelle
RNLN	Franklin
RNLR	granular
	wrangler
RNLT	frontlet
RNLW	bring low
RNML	grand mal
RNMN	front man
	frontman
RNMT	transmit
RNNE	ordnance
RNNW	brand-new
RNOE	frondose
RNOF	bring off
	drink off
	wring off
RNOS	drongoes
	eryngoes
RNOT	bring out
	printout
	wring out
RNRE	dry-nurse
RNRN	print run
RNRY	iron-grey
RNSN	grandson
RNTC	frenetic
	granitic
RNTE	brunette
RNTL	prenatal
RNTR	pronator
RNUE	transude
	transume

Words marked □ can also be spelled with an initial capital letter

wrong use
RNUG iron lung
RNUI Brancusi
RNUL tranquil
RNUO Trinculo
RNUS craniums
ROAE arrogate
ROAT arrogant
ROEA arboreta
ROEL arboreal
ROES prioress
troopers
ROIE cryolite
ergotise
ergotize
trioxide
ROIG brooding
drooping
ROIL armorial
ROIM ergotism
ROIN Triodion
ROIS cryonics
ROIT arsonist
ROIY droopily
priority
ROLN Brooklyn
ROLS criollos
RONR Brookner
ROOE creosote
ROOO Oroonoko
RORD armoured
RORO groo-groo
RORR armourer
ROTT cryostat
RPAE dry-plate
prophase
triptane
RPAK drop back
RPCL tropical
RPDL tripodal
RPED drip-feed
drop-dead
RPEE grapheme
RPEF drop-leaf
RPES prophets
wrappers
RPEY frippery
prophecy
prophesy
RPHT drop-shot
RPID dropsied
RPIE dropwise
eruptive
graphite
trephine
RPIG dripping
dropping
gripping
trapping
wrapping
RPIK drop-kick
RPIM graphium
RPIN eruption

RPIS graphics
RPIT dry-point
Trappist
RPIY preppily
RPLD crippled
RPLN propylon
RPNE prepense
RPNN drop in on
RPOD triploid
RPOE traphole
RPON drop down
RPOR trapdoor
RPPN wrap up in
RPRA troparia
RPRD prepared
RPRY properly
property
RPSD proposed
RPSL proposal
RPSR proposer
RPTS crepitus
RPUD propound
RPUS cropfuls
RPWY drop away
RPYH triptych
RPZA trapezia
RQET frequent
RQIS cry quits
RQOS Iroquois
RRAH Arbroath
RRET prurient
RRGE prorogue
RRGS prurigos
RRSR dry riser
RRTC pruritic
RRTS pruritis
pruritus
RRYL Ark Royal
RSAE Brisbane
dressage
ore-stare
prostate
RSAI Frascati
RSAR fresh air
RSAS trespass
RSBE erasable
RSBR crossbar
RSBW crossbow
RSBX grass box
press box
RSCT crosscut
RSDA presidia
RSDC prosodic
RSDR crusader
RSDS Crusades
crusados
RSEA Oresteia
RSEE cross-eye
Grasmere
triskele
RSEK grosbeak
Irish elk
RSEN drisheen

RSEO Prospero
RSES Brussels
trustees
RSET crescent❑
prospect
RSFL tristful
trustful
RSFR press for
RSGR presager
RSHN groschen❑
RSHT brass hat
RSIA brassica
Cressida
Pristina
RSID prescind
RSIE Aristide
prestige
pristine
RSIG brisling
brushing
crashing
crossing
crushing
dressing
frosting
grasping
pressing
trussing
trusting
RSIN Crispian
Prussian
RSIY brassily
crustily
friskily
frostily
Prussify
trashily
trustily
RSLA Brasília
Griselda
RSLB Arts Club
RSLD bristled
RSLR wrestler
RSLT crosslet
wristlet
RSMC trisomic
RSMD presumed
RSMN freshman
Irishman
pressman
pressmen
RSNE presence
RSNR prisoner
RSNW fresh-new
RSOD frescoed
RSOE dry-stone
RSOF brass off
brush off
brush-off
RSOR frescoer
RSOS bristols
frescoes
griseous

RSOT crash out
cross out
gross out
Prescott
press out
RSPN wrist pin
RSPY gross pay
RSRE preserve
RSRM Tristram
RSRS braseros
grisgris
RSSA Irish Sea
RSTD irisated
RSTE grisette
RSUE pressure
RSUS frustums
RSYE Criseyde
prostyle
RTAE frottage
protease
tritiate
urethane
RTAK brat pack
RTAL pratfall
RTAN Brittain
RTAT protract
RTCL critical
protocol
RTCM triticum
RTCS frutices
RTEA erythema
RTES brothers
trotters
RTFL grateful
truthful
wrathful
RTFY froth-fly
RTGE protégée
RTGR Hrothgar
RTGT try to get
RTHD wretched
RTHS britches
RTHT Cratchit
crotchet
RTIE brattice
critcize
RTIG dratting
frothing
RTIH brattish
RTIS pretties
RTIY frothily
gratuity
prettify
prettily
wrathily
RTLD writhled
RTLR prattler
RTLY brutally
RTNA prytanea
RTNE cretonne
gratinée
pretence
RTNO pro tanto

RTNS	writings
RTOD	Trotwood
RTOF	write off
	write-off
RTOK	fretwork
RTOS	grottoes
RTOT	write out
RTQE	critique
RTRA	criteria
	Pretoria
RTRC	ureteric
RTRE	urethrae
RTRL	ureteral
	urethral
RTRN	brethren
RTRO	oratorio
RTRS	Arcturus
	urethras
RTSS	protases
	protasis
RTTC	erotetic
RTTM	Art Tatum
RTUA	Arethusa
RTUE	protrude
RTWN	try to win
RTZA	protozoa
RUAA	brouhaha
	traumata
RUAE	frautage
RUBE	arguable
RUBS	arquebus
RUBY	arguably
RUDD	grounded
RUEE	trouvère
RUEN	Fräulein
RUER	trouveur
RUES	groupers
	trousers
RUET	argument
RUEY	argutely
	crousely
RUFR	argue for
RUHE	trauchle
RUHL	Breughel
RUHM	brougham
RUHN	Proudhon
RUHS	draughts
RUHY	draughty
RUIE	Ursuline
RUIG	arousing
	grouping
	grouting
RUIN	Freudian
RUIR	croupier
RUIY	triunity
RULD	troubled
RULS	troubles
RUOS	ordurous
	orgulous
RURU	frou-frou
RUVR	triumvir
RVAT	proviant
RVAY	breviary

RVBE	drivable
	provable
RVBY	provably
RVDD	provided
RVDR	provider
RVDS	bravados
	privados
RVES	crivvens
RVHK	Kravchuk
RVKD	provoked
RVKR	provoker
RVLA	Travolta
RVLE	Greville
RVLT	travel at
RVLY	gravelly
	trevally
RVMD	drive mad
RVMN	gravamen
RVNE	province
RVNY	cravenly
RVOS	previous
RVOT	drive out
RVRE	traverse
RVRL	proviral
RVRS	Proverbs
	provirus
RVSE	crevasse
RVSR	provisor
RVSS	provisos
RVSY	travesty
RVTS	gravitas
	privates
RVWY	driveway
RWAE	brown ale
	grow pale
RWAK	draw back
	drawback
RWBG	brown-bag
RWEK	crew neck
RWEL	a raw deal
RWEN	draw rein
RWER	draw near
RWES	grow less
RWET	browbeat
RWFT	brown fat
RWIG	brawling
	browning❑
	browsing
	crawling
	crowning
	growling
	trawling
RWIH	brownish
	crawfish
	grow rich
RWIK	grow pink
RWIY	drowsily
RWNO	draw into
	grow into
RWOD	Crawford
RWOL	brown owl
RWOS	draw lots
RWOT	crowfoot

	drawn-out
RWPN	draw upon
RWRT	brown rat
RWWY	draw away
RXML	proximal
RYEL	grey seal
RYES	greyness
RYIG	grayling
RYIH	crayfish
RYNT	X-ray unit
RYOF	grey wolf
RYRA	grey area
RYRP	tray-trip
RYUS	Dreyfuss
	Grey nuns
	trayfuls
RZDS	cruzados
RZLD	grizzled
RZMN	prizeman
RZNV	Brezhnev
RZNY	brazenly
RZOO	grazioso
SAAE	escalade
	escalate
	escapade
SABL	Istanbul
SACA	estancia
SADM	Aswan Dam
SADR	islander
SADY	as said by
SAGT	escargot
SAHR	Issachar
SAIE	astatine
	Islamise
	Islamize
SAIM	escapism
SAIR	espalier
SAIT	escapist
	essayist
SALP	escallop
SALR	assailer
SAOE	escalope
SAOT	ask about
SARQ	Istabraq
SASN	assassin
SATS	espartos
SAYS	as many as
SBLA	Isabella
SBNS	as a bonus
SBRC	isobaric
SCAY	isocracy
SCOT	Ashcroft
SEAE	asperate
SEBE	assemble
SEBY	assembly❑
SEDR	ascender
SEFR	asked for
SEIK	asterisk
SEIL	especial
SEIM	ascetism
SEIY	asperity
	esterify
SELS	as well as

SEMD	esteemed
SEOD	asteroid
SESR	asperser
	assessor
SETO	assent to
SETS	asbestos
	osteitis
SETY	Oswestry
SFLY	usefully
SFRE	use force
SFRT	ask for it
SFUT	usufruct
SGGC	isagogic
SGOP	as a group
SGOS	isogloss
SHDL	asphodel
SHMA	ischemia
SHMS	R S Thomas
SHNA	asthenia
SHNC	asthenic
SHUH	as though
SHWL	eschewal
SHXA	asphyxia
SIAE	aspirate
	estimate
	oscitate
SIAO	ostinato
SIAT	aspirant
	oscitant
SIEO	aspire to
SIID	ossified
SIIG	aspiring
SIMC	aseismic
SIND	assigned
SINE	assignee
SINR	assignor
SITN	assist in
SIUO	Ishiguro
SLEY	psaltery
SLIT	psalmist
SLOY	psalmody
SLSS	psilosis
SLTD	isolated
SMRC	isomeric
SMRH	isomorph
SNIN	Asunción
SNMN	as one man
SNRY	asynergy
SOAE	assonate
SOBC	ascorbic
SODS	as good as
SOGS	as long as
SOIH	astonish
SOIN	Estonian
SOLR	US dollar
SONS	as soon as
SOSD	espoused
SOSL	espousal
SOTD	assorted
SPEE	isoprene
SPIM	psephism
SRAE	user name
SRET	esurient

SRGL astragal
SRGN Estragon
estrogen
SRIG usurping
SRNE astringe
estrange
SROS usurious
SRSO espresso
SRUD ask round
SRVA tsarevna
SSAY isostasy
SSOE asystole
STDY USA Today
STEE as it were
isothere
STEM isotherm
STNC isotonic
STOY isotropy
STPC isotopic
STRC esoteric
SUAE osculate
SUBY issuably
SUET esculent
SUEY astutely
pseudery
SUHS as much as
SUIG assuming
SUIS Asturias
SUIY astucity
SUNE issuance
SUSE esquisse
SWOE as a whole
SYIN Assyrian
TAAE stearate
Strabane
TAAG stravaig
TAAH stramash
TACT straucht
TADD stranded
TADE straddle
TADM at random
TAEY strategy
TAGE straggle
strangle
TAGR stranger
TAGT straight
straught
TAGY straggly
TAHD attached
TAHO attach to
TAHT straw hat
TAHY Strachey
TAIE ptyalise
ptyalize
stearine
steatite
TAIG steading
stealing
steaming
straying
TAIM strabism
TAIS St David's
TAIY steadily
steamily
stratify
TAKR attacker
TALN St Gallen
TAND strained
TANR strainer
TAOC ethanoic
TAOE stratose
TAPD strapped
TAPR strapper
TATC Atlantic
TATN straiten
TATS Atlantes
Atlantis
TATY stealthy
TAYN steady on!
TBIE stibnite
TBIG stabbing
TBLD stubbled
TBON stubborn
TCAE stackade
stockade
TCAO staccato
TCCR stock car
TCFR stuck for
TCIG sticking
stocking
TCIT stockist
TCIY stickily
stockily
TCLR stickler
TCMN stockman
TCOS stocious
TCOT stick out
TCPT stockpot
TCSF stacks of
TCTN Stockton
TDIG studding
studying
TDIY stodgily
TDNS students
TDOS studious
TDUS stadiums
TEAE steerage
TEBK steenbok
TECY stretchy
TEDD attended
TEDN attend on
TEDO attend to
TEDR attender
TEEA et cetera
etcetera
TEEI et ceteri
TEEL ethereal
TEES St Helens
TEFR steer for
TEGH at length
strength
TEIE athetise
athetize
etherise
etherize
TEIG steeping
steering
uttering
TEIH steepish
TEIN Athenian
TEIR St Helier
TEIS etaerios
TEIY etherify
TEKD streaked
TEKR streaker
TELD steepled
TEMN other man
TEMR streamer
TENT Ethernet
TEOA atheroma
TERD Ethelred
TESD stressed
TESR stressor
TETD attested
TETN Atherton
TETO attest to
TFHM stuff him
TFHR stuff her
TFIG stifling
stuffing
TFIH stiffish
TFIY stuffily
TFOD Stafford
TFYU stuff you
TGAA stigmata
TGAE stagnate
TGAT stagnant
TGES staggers
THBR at the bar
THED at the end
TIDE striddle
TIEN strike in
TIEP strike up
TIET strident
strigent
strike at
TIEY at livery
TIGD stringed
TIGP string up
TIGR stringer
TIIE Atticise
Atticize
ethicise
ethicize
TIIG staining
striking
striving
TIIM Atticism
stoicism
TIIZ Steinitz
TIKE strickle
strinkle
TIKN stricken
TIMR Strimmer®
TIOE strigose
TIOF strip off
TIOT strip out
TIPA Ethiopia
TIPC Ethiopic
TIPD stripped
TIPR stripper
TISN Atkinson
TITD striated
TITR atwitter
TITY strictly
TIUE attitude
TIUI utriculi
TIWY stairway
Steinway
TKOF stake off
TKOT stake out
stake-out
TLAE stellate
stillage
TLAS St Albans
TLAT stalwart
TLDY stolidly
TLEE stilbene
TLHK stulchak
TLIE stelline
TLIG stalking
stalling
stilting
TLIN stallion
TLIY stellify
stultify
TLNA Atalanta
TLOE Stallone
TLOS stalkoes
TLOT STOLport
TLSS styluses
TLTC athletic
TLTO stiletto
TLYU I tell you
TLZR utilizer
TMAA stemmata
TMEE stampede
TMEL stem cell
TMES stemless
TMIE ptomaine
TMIG stamping
TMIY stumpily
TMLS stimulus
TMOB atom bomb
TMOD Stamford
TMOT stamp out
TMSR atomiser
TMTC stomatic
TMTL stomatal
TMZD itemized
TMZR atomizer
TNAC stanzaic
TNAD standard
TNAE Stone Age
TNAK Stenmark
TNAY stannary
TNEZ Stan Getz
TNFR atone for
stand for
TNFY stonefly
TNHL stanchel
Stendhal

TNHR	at anchor
	stancher
TNHY	stanchly
TNIE	stannite
TNIG	standing
	stinging
	stinking
	stinting
	stonking
	stunning
TNIH	Standish
TNIS	utensils
TNIY	stingily
TNLW	stand low
TNMN	stuntman
TNNH	at an inch
TNOE	stanhope□
TNOF	Atansoff
	stand off
	stand-off
TNOS	stannous
TNOT	stand out
	standout
	stink out
TNPT	stand pat
TNRP	Eton crop
TNRY	stingray
TNSS	stenoses
	stenosis
TNTC	stenotic
TOAA	stromata
TOAE	etiolate
TOGR	stronger
TOGY	strongly
TOHC	strophic
TOHE	stooshie
TOIE	at no time
	atropine
	Ottoline
	strobile
TOIG	stooping
TOII	strobili
TOIY	atrocity
	otiosity
TOIZ	St Moritz
TOLN	stroll on!
TOLR	stroller
TONS	at points
TONY	attorney
TOON	Otto John
TOOT	at no cost
TOOY	ethology
TOTM	at bottom
TOYE	atmolyse
	atmolyze
TPAD	Stoppard
TPAE	stoppage
TPAH	stop bath
TPAK	step back
TPAO	Stephano
TPCL	atypical
TPDS	stapedes
TPDY	stupidly

TPES	stopless
TPGP	stop a gap
TPIE	at a price
	stepwise
TPIG	stopping
TPIT	at a point
TPLD	stippled
	stipuled
TPLR	stippler
	stipular
TPNH	at a pinch
TPNO	step into
TPNT	step on it
TPOD	Stepford
TPOK	stopcock
	stop work
TPON	step down
	step-down
	stop down
TPVR	stop over
	stopover
TRAE	star-gaze
	sternage
TRAS	ITAR-Tass
	Itar-Tass
	Star Wars
TRBE	storable
TREN	sturgeon
TRES	starkers
	starless
	starters
	stirless
TRGA	pterygia
TRHD	starched
TRHR	starcher
TRIE	eternise
	eternize
	Itúrbide
	starlike
TRIG	starling
	starting
	starving
	sterling
	Stirling
	stirring
	storming
	Storting
TRIH	starfish
TRIY	eternity
	starrily
	stormily
	sturdily
TRLD	startled
TRLE	pterylae
TRLR	startler
TRMN	storeman
TRNE	iterance
TROF	start off
TROT	stare out
	start out
	starwort
TRPZ	St-Tropez
TRRS	Stari Ras

TRUK	Starbuck
TRUN	star turn
TRUT	stardust
TRUY	star ruby
TRXA	ataraxia
TRXC	ataraxic
TRYR	at prayer
TSAD	it is said
TSAT	at a slant
TSOE	otoscope
TTAY	statuary
TTBE	statable
TTDY	statedly
TTHD	stitched
TTHP	stitch up
TTHR	stitcher
TTNA	Itatinga
	stotinka
TTNI	stotinki
TTOS	stotious
TTSS	statuses
TTTS	statutes
TUGE	struggle
TUGP	strung up
TUIH	stoutish
TUKN	struck on
TUOE	strumose
TUOS	strumous
TUPT	strumpet
TVOF	stave off
TWIS	stowlins
TWWY	stow away
	stowaway
TYAE	ethylate
TYAL	staysail
TYIH	stay with
TYOL	stay cool
TYVR	stay over
UAAA	Surabaya
UAAH	cut a dash
UAAO	Bulawayo
UAAS	nunataks
UACY	autarchy
UADA	hum and ha
UADM	muqaddam
UADT	Turandot
UAEE	Sudanese
UAEI	Sulawesi
UAET	Budapest
UAEY	humanely
UAGM	sugar gum
UAIA	putamina
UAIE	curarise
	curarize
	curative
	humanise
	humanize
	put aside
	putative
	ruralise
	ruralize
UAIG	sugaring
UAII	bucatini

UAIK	run a risk
UAIM	humanism
	sudarium
UAIN	duration
	Eurasian
	mutation
	nutation
	Rumanian
UAIR	Duvalier
UAIT	humanist
	lutanist
	muralist
UAIY	audacity
	fugacity
	humanity
	queasily
	rurality
UAKC	autarkic
UAMD	Muhammad
UANH	Susannah
UAOD	autacoid
	humanoid
UAOE	fumarole
UAOG	cut along
	rub along
	run along
UAON	ducatoon
UAOS	fumadoes
UAOT	put about
	runabout
UAOY	fumatory
	nugatory
	sudatory
UAPA	sugar pea
UARD	eupatrid
UARM	Muharram
UASC	Jurassic
UATR	run after
UAUA	hula-hula
UAUL	Guyaquil
UAYT	rubaiyat
UBAD	cupboard
	outboard
UBAE	outbrave
UBCR	Quebecer
UBDY	turbidly
UBED	outbreed
UBEK	outbreak
UBEN	tumble in
UBEO	tumble to
UBEP	jumble up
	tumble up
UBES	dumbness
	numbness
UBFN	turbofan
UBGS	lumbagos
UBHR	surbahar
UBHW	dumb show
UBID	purblind
	sunblind
UBIE	jumboise
	jumboize
UBIG	bubbling

Words marked □ can also be spelled with an initial capital letter

	bumbling
	fumbling
	humbling
	mumbling
	rumbling
	tumbling
UBJT	jumbo jet
	turbojet
UBLR	quibbler
UBLT	Humboldt
UBLW	furbelow
UBND	turbaned
UBNL	turbinal
UBNS	turbines
UBOK	sunblock
UBON	dumb down
	nut-brown
UBOS	cumbrous
UBRD	numbered
UBRT	outburst
	sunburnt
	sunburst
UBRY	Burberry
	lubberly
	mulberry
UBSY	rubbishy
UBTE	sunbathe
UBUD	outbound
UCAE	purchase
UCAL	pub-crawl
UCAS	outclass
UCAU	nunchaku
UCBE	succubae
UCBS	succubus
UCDL	muscadel
	suicidal
UCDN	muscadin
UCDT	Muscadet
UCEM	Dutch elm
	sun cream
UCEN	luncheon
	muscle in
UCES	butcher's
UCEY	butchery
	quackery
UCFX	quick fix
UCHE	Dutch hoe
UCIG	bunching
	hunching
	lurching
	punching
UCII	zucchini
UCIL	Burchill
UCIN	function
	junction
UCKD	mud-caked
UCLR	furcular
	muscular
UCME	buncombe
UCMN	Dutchman
	Dutchmen
UCMR	dulcimer
UCNC	succinic

UCNT	succinct
UCOE	run close
UCOK	bum-clock
UCOS	luscious
	outcross
UCSE	outcaste
UCSS	cut costs
	outcasts
UCST	quickset
UCTD	sulcated
UCTL	muscatel
UCUE	juncture
	puncture
UCUL	punctual
UCUS	fulcrums
UDAA	gurdwara
UDAE	quadrate
UDAT	quadrant
UDDG	guide dog
UDEA	buddleia
UDEL	outdwell
UDEP	bundle up
	cuddle up
	muddle up
UDES	hundreds
UDGY	Buddy Guy
UDIG	hurdling
	muddling
	puddling
UDIM	Buddhism
UDIT	Buddhist
UDIY	quiddity
UDND	burdened
UDNE	guidance
UDNL	duodenal
	nundinal
UDNM	duodenum
UDNY	suddenly
UDON	quadroon
UDOS	outdoors
UDRD	sundered
UDRR	murderer
UDSC	cul-de-sac
UDTD	outdated
UDUC	quidnunc
UEAD	superadd
	sure card
UEAE	fuselage
	numerate
	suberate
	tutelage
UEAM	lukewarm
UEAN	suzerain
UEAY	funerary
	numeracy
	tutelary
UEBE	queen bee
	tuneable
UEBR	outer bar
UEBY	superbly
UECE	tubercle
UECL	Lupercal
UEDM	pudendum

	queendom
UEEI	Museveni
UEEL	funereal
UEEO	superego
	super-ego
UEER	muleteer
UEES	cuteness
	hugeness
	muteness
	nudeness
	pureness
	rudeness
	ruleless
	sureness
	tubeless
	tuneless
UEID	tumefied
UEIE	juvenile
	suberise
	suberize
	sure-fire
	tubelike
	Yuletide
UEIH	queerish
UEIM	lutecium
	lutetium
UEIN	Sumerian
UEIR	superior❑
UEIS	Aurelius
	eugenics
	Eugenius
	Eusebius
UEIT	lutenist
UELS	nucellus
UEMB	Queen Mab
UEMN	Süleyman
	superman
UENL	supernal
UEOE	suberose
	tuberose
UEOL	fusel-oil
UEOM	tube worm
UEOR	au revoir
UEOS	numerous
	tuberous
	tuxedoes
UEOT	cube root
	ruled out
	tube foot
UERD	pure-bred
UERL	funebral
UERP	June drop
UESA	eupepsia
UESI	Rusedski
UETC	eupeptic
UETN	Nuneaton
UETX	supertax
UEUE	quietude
UEUG	Queequeg
UEUS	tubefuls
UEVR	muse over
UEWN	mute swan
UFAE	subframe

	suffrage
UFAK	outflank
UFAL	puffball
UFCD	surfaced
UFCR	sufficer
	surfacer
UFDP	puffed up
UFED	gulfweed
	outfield
UFGT	gunfight
UFID	puffbird
UFIG	muffling
	ruffling
UFIK	cufflink
UFIS	Dumfries
UFLB	Turf Club
UFLY	ruefully
UFON	outfrown
UFOR	subfloor
UFRD	buffered
UFRH	put forth
UFRR	sufferer
UFRT	run for it
UFSD	suffused
UFUD	dumfound
UFUK	surf duck
UGAD	mudguard
UGAE	outglare
	subgrade
UGAS	cut glass
UGAY	burglary
UGBE	huggable
UGCL	surgical
UGDN	Gunga Din
UGDY	ruggedly
	turgidly
UGEN	mung bean
UGET	judgment
UGIE	quagmire
UGIG	bungling
	gurgling
	juggling
	outgoing
UGIY	hungrily
UGKV	Bulgakov
UGLW	bungalow
UGNN	Bulganin
UGNS	subgenus
UGNV	Turgenev
UGNY	burgundy❑
	fulgency
	pungency
UGOE	bunghole
UGOT	bulge out
	lungwort
UGPN	hung up on
UGRA	Bulgaria
UGRL	fulgural
UGRU	Jungfrau
UGRY	hungerly
	vulgarly
UGSA	Tunguska
UGSS	funguses

Words marked ❑ can also be spelled with an initial capital letter

	Tunguses
UGTN	tungsten
UGUY	hung jury
UGVR	hung over
UHAK	bushwalk
	push back
UHAY	bushbaby
	bush-baby
	euphrasy
UHDN	pushed in
UHED	bushveld
UHES	lushness
	much less
	ruthless
UHET	Cuthbert
UHHT	such that
UHIE	bushfire
	euphuise
	euphuize
	fuchsine
	push-bike
	such like
	suchwise
UHIM	euphuism
UHJB	cushy job
UHMN	subhuman
UHNC	euphonic
UHNE	Duchenne
	Dushanbe
UHNN	Buchanan
UHNO	push into
UHOM	mushroom
UHON	push down
UHOR	rush hour
UHOY	cushiony
UHPN	push open
UHRA	euphoria
UHRC	euphoric
UHRD	out-Herod
UHRN	Bukharin
	Lutheran
UHSE	duchesse
UHTH	nuthatch
UHUE	Mulhouse
	nuthouse
	nut-house
	outhouse
UHUH	hush-hush
UHUK	bushbuck
UHVR	pushover
	push-over
UIAE	dubitate
	fumigate
	jubilate
	mucilage
	mutilate
	ruminate
	supinate
	suricate
	Suriname
UIAI	sukiyaki
UIAO	Lusitano
UIAT	fumigant
	jubilant
	ruminant
UIAY	culinary
	luminary
UIBE	dutiable
UIBX	music box
UIER	mutineer
UIES	business
	puniness
UIET	rudiment
UIEY	futilely
	supinely
UIFR	put in for
UIGN	Tübingen
UIGY	musingly
	pulingly
UIHY	mulishly
UIIA	Curitiba
UIID	purified
UIIE	cutinise
	cutinize
	fugitive
	punitive
	subitise
	subitize
UIIL	judicial
UIIM	pugilism
	rubidium
UIIN	audition
	munition
	musician
UIIR	fusilier
	purifier
UIIS	Lucilius
	nudities
UIIT	pugilist
UIIY	cupidity
	futility
	humidify
	humidity
	humility
	lucidity
	nubility
	tumidity
UIKD	tunicked
UINE	audience
	julienne
UIOI	Fujimori
UIOM	fusiform
	nubiform
	tubiform
UIOS	luminous
	mutinous
	numinous
UIOT	cut it out
UIOY	auditory
	fumitory
UIRO	junior to
UIRS	Hudibras
UISH	Lubitsch
UISS	furiosos
UITC	autistic
	juristic
	puristic
UITY	quaintly
UIUD	furibund
	rubicund
UIZR	Pulitzer
UJCS	subjects
UJRS	sui juris
UKAD	Auckland
	junkyard
UKAE	muck-rake
	suck face
UKAI	Gurkhali
UKAK	rucksack
UKAL	junk mail
UKCP	Turk's cap
UKDP	lucky dip
UKED	bulkhead
	duckweed
UKEO	buckle to
UKEP	muckheap
UKER	musk deer
UKES	luckless
UKHE	buckshee
UKHT	buckshot
UKIG	duckling
	suckling□
UKJM	Lucky Jim
UKKN	buckskin
UKNO	tuck into
UKOE	funkhole
	musk rose
UKOK	punk rock
UKON	buckhorn
UKOP	Duck Soup
UKPO	suck up to
UKRD	puckered
UKRO	buckaroo
UKRP	pucker up
UKRY	Quakerly
UKTR	huckster
UKTY	musketry
UKWY	tuck away
ULAD	full hand
ULAE	full-face
	full-page
	nuclease
	nucleate
	sublease
ULAK	fullback
	pull back
	pull rank
ULAL	full-sail
ULAN	outlearn
ULAY	Dunleary
ULBE	gullible
ULBY	bully boy
	bully-boy
ULCE	curlicue
ULCN	publican
ULCY	publicly
ULDN	Culloden
ULED	bullhead
ULEE	bull's eye
	Bullseye
	bull's-eye
ULEP	bull kelp
ULES	dullness
	fullness
	nullness
	purlieus
ULET	full-pelt
ULFL	guileful
ULFO	full of go
ULGE	duologue
ULGN	Mulligan
ULGT	sunlight
ULHP	bullwhip
ULHT	bullshit
ULIE	full time
	full-time
ULIG	building
	bullying
	outlying
	quelling
	quilting
	sullying
ULIH	qualmish
ULIT	duellist
	full tilt
	full-tilt
ULIY	guiltily
ULKN	Mulliken
ULMN	fugleman
ULNO	bull into
ULNR	sublunar
ULNS	outlines
ULNY	sullenly
ULOE	bulldoze
	cut loose
ULOI	nucleoli
ULOK	full-cock
ULON	full moon
	hull-down
	pull down
ULOS	full toss
ULRG	bullfrog
	bullyrag
ULTN	bulletin
ULTP	full stop
ULUA	pull out a
ULUH	furlough
ULVN	Sullivan
ULVR	Gulliver
	mull over
	pull over
	pullover
	Tulliver
ULWD	outlawed
ULWY	outlawry
	pull away
ULYF	guilty of
UMBE	hummable
UMCY	hummocky
UMDD	outmoded
UMGR	rummager
UMGY	nutmeggy

Words marked □ can also be spelled with an initial capital letter

8 _U_M_I

UMII	duumviri
UMIS	duumvirs
UMKI	Gurmukhi
UMNK	Murmansk
UMNN	our man in
UMNP	summon up
UMNR	summoner
UMNS	cummings
	pulmones
UMRC	turmeric
UMRD	murmured
UMRE	submerge
	submerse
UMRN	dummy run
UMRR	murmurer
UMSD	surmised
UMSR	surmiser
UMTL	gunmetal
UMTO	submit to
UMUT	surmount
UNAE	turn pale
UNAG	quandang
UNAK	turn back
UNAL	turn tail
UNAY	quandary
UNBE	burnable
	runnable
UNCS	huanacos
UNDN	turned on
	turned-on
UNEG	Nürnberg
UNES	Guinness
UNGT	outnight
UNHD	quenched
UNHG	bunny-hug
UNHR	quencher
UNID	quinsied
UNIE	Burnside
	cut no ice
	quantise
	quantize
	turnpike
UNIY	quantify
	quantity
UNLA	quinella
UNLE	burn blue
	quenelle
UNMN	funny man
UNNO	turn into
UNOD	turn cold
UNOE	turnsole
UNOG	quandong
	quantong
UNON	burn down
	turn down
	turn-down
UNOR	turn sour
UNOT	burnt out
	turncoat
UNPN	turn upon
UNRP	runner-up
UNRS	Juan Gris
UNSD	pug-nosed
UNTN	turn it in
UNTP	turn it up
UNUK	turn Turk
UNUX	quincunx
UNVR	turn over
	turnover
UNWY	turn away
UOAA	automata
	Kurosawa
UOAE	auto-da-fé
	automate
	Lucozade®
	tutorage
UOAN	autobahn
UOAP	autoharp
UOAY	autogamy
UODI	dupondii
UOEN	European
UOER	au voleur
UOES	tutoress
UOEY	rugosely
UOFN	rub off on
UOIE	eulogise
	eulogize
	put on ice
	tutorise
	tutorize
UOIG	tutoring
UOIL	sutorial
	tutorial
UOIM	eulogium
	europium
UOIN	sutorian
UOIO	autogiro
UOIS	Ausonius
	eulogies
UOIT	humorist
UOIY	mucosity
	rugosity
UOKY	out of key
UOLV	Yugoslav
UONR	suborner
UOOD	Eurobond
UOOE	autosome
UOOI	sumotori
UOOS	humorous
	tumorous
UOOT	Europort
UOOY	autonomy
	autotomy
UORD	rumoured
UORT	autocrat
	Eurocrat
UOTA	cup of tea
UOTF	run out of
UOTN	run out on
UOTS	culottes
UOWR	tug of war
	tug-of-war
UOYE	autodyne
	autolyse
	autolyze
	autotype
UOYO	autogyro
UPAE	outplace
	sulphate
	sur place
UPAK	humpback
	jump back
UPAL	jump bail
UPAO	sup-peago
UPAT	supplant
UPBE	culpable
UPBY	culpably
UPCS	auspices
UPDP	jumped up
	jumped-up
UPEA	subpoena
UPED	jump lead
UPES	suppress
UPEY	supplely
UPHP	jump ship
UPIE	cut price
	cut-price
	outprice
	outprize
	sulphide
	sulphite
	surplice
	surprise
UPIG	dumpling
UPIH	lumpfish
	purplish
	quippish
UPIN	gumption
UPIR	supplier
UPIS	murphies
	supplies
UPIT	gunpoint
	outpoint
UPNE	suspense
UPNO	bump into
	jump onto
UPNY	tuppenny
UPOD	pulpwood
UPOE	sulphone
UPON	gulp down
UPOT	jump to it!
UPPY	mudpuppy
UPRN	pump iron
UPRS	Humphrys
UPRY	Humphrey
UPSD	purposed
	supposed
UPSR	supposer
UPTR	pulpiter
	quipster
UPTY	puppetry
UPUT	jumpsuit
UPUY	sulphury
UPVR	jump over
UPWR	outpower
UPWY	jump away
UQAH	musquash
URAE	guardage
URAH	Auerbach
	outreach
URBT	surrebut
URDG	guard dog
URDR	outrider
URDY	putridly
URES	quarrels
	quarters
URET	nutrient
URGD	outraged
URGT	outright
	put right
URIA	Guernica
URIE	quartile
URIG	guarding
	querying
URIH	quirkish
URIN	guardian
	outreign
URIY	quirkily
URLA	guerilla
URMS	supremos
URNL	Quirinal
URNS	mucrones
URNY	currency
	guaranty
	Mulroney
URSW	currasow
URSY	guernsey❑
URTA	Lucretia
URTD	turreted
URTN	au gratin
URTS	burritos
URUD	surround
URVL	outrival
URWD	furrowed
USAD	outstand
USAE	outstare
	sunshade
USAL	Ruisdael
	Ruysdael
USAS	Huysmans
USAT	outsmart
	puissant
	pursuant
	questant
USCT	pussy cat
USCY	tussocky
USDE	pulsidge
USDR	outsider
USDY	cursedly
USED	outspend
USEL	nutshell
	outswell
USEP	outsleep
USER	bum steer
	outswear
USHN	Burschen
USIE	outshine
	sunshine
USIG	bursting
	guessing
	nursling
	pursuing

	quashing
	questing
	quisling❑
USIH	gunsmith
USIN	question
USIY	sunshiny
USLR	subsolar
USLS	Huis Clos
USNC	subsonic
USNE	nuisance
USOE	gunstone
	mudstone
USON	outscorn
USOT	burst out
	cut short
	outsport
	run short
USRE	subserve
USRP	outstrip
USTS	bursitis
USUG	Augsburg
	Duisburg
USUL	numskull
USVR	fuss over
UTAE	australe
	lustrate
	must-have
	suitcase
UTAL	hunt ball
UTAN	Bultmann
	quatrain
UTAS	just pass
	nuptials
UTAT	dustcart
	subtract
UTBD	put to bed
UTBE	quotable
	suitable
UTBY	quotably
	suitably
UTCS	buttocks
UTDS	custodes
UTEH	cut teeth
UTEP	rustle up
UTES	buttress
	curtness
	huntress
	justness
UTET	furthest
	quotient
	rust belt
UTEY	subtlety
UTGM	multigym
UTGT	bust a gut
UTIE	buntline
UTIG	bustling
	quitting
	rustling
UTIK	outthink
	out-think
UTIN	Austrian
UTIS	curtains
UTIT	duettist
UTIY	multeity
	sultrily
UTMN	huntsman❑
UTMR	customer
UTNC	subtonic
	sultanic
UTNN	butt in on
UTNP	button up
UTNS	cuttings
	hustings
UTOL	dust bowl
UTON	hunt down
UTOS	lustrous
UTOT	out to out
UTPA	subtopia
UTPE	multiple
UTPY	multiply
UTRD	cultured
	muttered
	ruptured
UTRE	quatorze
UTRL	cultural
	guttural
	nurtural
UTRN	muster in
	putter-on
UTRP	butter up
UTRR	mutterer
	nurturer
UTSA	put to sea
UTSS	kurtosis
UTTC	eustatic
UTTD	guttated
UTTE	subtitle
	surtitle
UTTL	subtotal
	sum total
UTTM	rum-ti-tum
UTUE	put to use
	subtrude
UTUP	tub-thump
UTUS	lustrums
UTVR	cultivar
UUAA	Fukuyama
UUAE	cumulate
	jugulate
	subulate
	tubulate
UUBA	suburbia
UUBN	suburban
UUBR	cucumber
UUCE	furuncle
UUET	purulent
UUIE	autunite
UUIM	futurism❑
UUIT	futurist
UUIY	futurity
UUJB	put-up job
UULS	Lucullus
UULY	mutually
UUNT	Huguenot
UUOS	tubulous
UUQE	tu quoque
UURS	susurrus
UUSN	Aubusson
UUTN	Augustan
UUTS	Augustus
UUTY	augustly
UUUI	durukuli
UVDN	curved in
UVIE	outvoice
UVLE	pulville
UVLI	pulvilli
UVLO	pulvilio
UVNM	outvenom
UVNR	pulvinar
UVNS	pulvinus
UVRL	subviral
UVRR	quaverer
UVRT	subverst
UVSR	sun visor
UVVL	survival
UVVR	survivor
UVYR	purveyor
	surveyor
UWAY	outweary
UWIH	outweigh
UWOY	Dunwoody
UWRH	outworth
UWRS	bulwarks
	outwards
	sunwards
UWTH	outwatch
UWTR	cut-water
UXTC	quixotic
UXTY	quixotry
UYES	busyness
UYHY	eurythmy
UYIE	Eurydice
	quayside
UYIH	busy with
UYNE	buoyance
UYNY	buoyancy
UYOT	ruby port
UYOY	busybody
UYRE	duty-free
UYUY	jury duty
UZAG	zugzwang
UZIG	guzzling
	puzzling
	quizzing
UZIY	quizzify
UZOD	buzz word
UZUG	Würzburg
VAIN	aviation
VAIT	aviarist
VCAE	evacuate
VCAT	evacuant
VCDS	avocados
VCIN	eviction
VCNA	Avicenna
VDBE	evadable
VDCL	oviducal
VDEG	Svedberg
VDNE	evidence
VDVT	avadavat
VEOE	Aviemore
VFUA	avifauna
VGDO	Avogadro
VINR	TV dinner
VLAE	evaluate
	evulgate
VLES	evilness
VLIE	Ovaltine®
VLIG	evolving
VLOR	evildoer
	evil-doer
VLRY	uvularly
VMRA	Ave Maria
VNAE	ovenware
VNAI	Svengali
VNBY	Evans Bay
VNES	evenness
VNFL	eventful
VNHN	even then
VNID	ovenbird
VNIE	Aventine
	eventide
VNIG	avenging
	eventing
VNNS	evenings
VNOG	evensong
VNPN	even up on
VNSE	evanesce
VNUL	eventual
VOIS	avionics
VPRN	Eva Perón
VPST	oviposit
VRAD	overhand
	overland
	overlard
VRAE	overlade
	overname
	overpage
	overrake
	overrate
	overtake
VRAG	overgang
	overhang
VRAK	overrack
	overtalk
	overtask
VRAL	overcall
	overfall
	overgall
	overhaul
	oversail
VRAS	overpass
VRAT	overcast
	overmast
	overpart
	overt act
VRBT	every bit
VRDY	every day
	everyday
VRED	overfeed
	overhead
	overlend
	overread

Words marked ❑ can also be spelled with an initial capital letter

VREF overleaf
VREL oversell
overveil
VREM overteem
VREP overleap
VRER overbear
overhear
overpeer
overseer
overwear
VRES overseas
VRET averment
overheat
VREY aversely
VRHE overshoe
over-shoe
VRHT overshot
VRID overwind
VRIE overlive
overnice
over-nice
override
overripe
overside
oversize
overtime
VRIG overwing
VRIH over with
VRIL overfill
overkill
VRIN aversion
eversion
VRIW overview
VRKP overskip
VRLB over-club
VRLP overslip
VRLS overalls
VRLW overblow
overflow
VRLY overcloy
overplay
VRMN Everyman
VROD overfold
overhold
overload
overlord
VROE ever more
evermore
everyone
overcome
overdone
overdose
overtone
VROG overlong
VROK overbook
overcook
overlock
overlook
overwork
VROS Averroës
VROT overcoat
overdo it
VRRH overarch
VRRP overcrop
VRRW overdraw
overgrow
VRSD overused
VRTP overstep
VRTS ovaritis
VRTY overstay
VRUE overrule
overture
VRUF overruff
VRUH overmuch
VRUK overbulk
VRUL overfull
VRUN overburn
overturn
VRUP overjump
VRUY overbusy
VRWD overawed
VRWM overswim
VRWY everyway
VRYE overtype
VWBE avowable
VWDY avowedly
WAHR a-weather
WAIG swearing
sweating
WAOF swear off
WBON swab down
WDLR twaddler
twiddler
WEAK Zwieback
WEES tweeness
tweezers
WEGD two-edged
WEIG sweeping
tweeting
WEPA sweet pea
WESP sweetsop
WFCD two-faced
WFLT swiftlet
WHOS two hoots
WIGP owning-up
WIIG awaiting
WLBX swell box
WLGT twilight
WLIG dwelling
swelling
WLOT swill out
WMIG swimming
WMUT swimsuit
WNAE Swan Lake
WNEY swannery
WNIE swanlike
WNIG swanking
swinging
twinning
WNIL Swan Hill
WNIS twenties
WNLR swindler
twinkler
WNOG swan song
WNON Gwen John
WPEE two-piece
WPIG swapping
WPNE two pence
twopence
WPNY twopenny
WPUD two pound
WRIG swarming
swerving
swirling
twirling
WRIH dwarfish
WRIM dwarfism
WROP owerloup
WSDD two-sided
WSIA swastika
WSIG twisting
WTCS two ticks
WTEY twittery
WTHN switch on
WTHR twitcher❑
WTHS switches
WTIG swotting
WTMR two-timer
WTPN swot up on
WYAK sway-back
WYIH away with
WYRM away from
XAAE excavate
XADD expanded
XADN expand on
XADR expander
XAIY axiality
XCAE execrate
XCIE exocrine
XCIG exacting
XCIN exaction
XCTD executed
XCTR executer
executor
XDZD oxidized
XDZR oxidizer
XEDD expended
extended
XEIE expedite
XEIR exterior
XEKR ox-pecker
XELD expelled
XELE expellee
XENL external
XERE exhedrae
XESR extensor
XESS expenses
XETD excepted
expected
XETY expertly
XGIY exiguity
XGMC exogamic
XGNY exigency
XGOS exiguous
XGSS exegesis
XGTC exegetic
XHNE exchange
XIAT excitant
XIBE expiable
XIIG exciting
expiring
XIIN excision
XITR expiator
XLAT exultant
XLAY axillary
XLCT explicit
XLDD excluded
exploded
XLIG exalting
exulting
XLIS exploits
XLRR explorer
XMLR exemplar
XMNE examinee
XMNR examiner
XMRN oxymoron
XOET exponent
XOGE ox-tongue
XOLR extoller
XOOY axiology
XOTR exporter
XOUE exposure
XPAY exophagy
XQIL exequial
XQIS exequies
XRDE Oxbridge
XRDR extruder
XRDS extrados
XRIE exercise
exorcise
exorcize
XRIL exordial
XRIM exorcism
exordium
XRIN exertion
XRIT exorcist
XROS uxorious
XRSM extra sum
XRSO expresso
XRTA ex gratia
XSET existent
XSIG existing
XTCC oxytocic
XTCN oxytocin
XTOL exit poll
XUAE exhumate
XUEE excuse me
excuse-me
XUGR expunger
XUIG excusing
XUSS excursus
XVAE exuviate
YAAA Ayia Napa
YADR Lysander
YAES Myra Hess
YAGA hypalgia
YAID myna bird
YAIE dynamise
dynamite
dynamize
lyra-wise
sybarite❑

YAIG gyrating
YAIM cymatium
dynamism
YAIN gyration
YAIS dynamics
Pyramids
YANC tyrannic
YAOE sycamore
YAOY gyratory
YASS synapses
synapsis
YATC dynastic
synaptic
YAUE Syracuse
YAVS by halves
YBDA cymbidia
YBHN Ayub Khan
YBLC symbolic
YBLS cymbalos
YBOT symbiont
YCIE syncline
YCIG lynching
YCLW lynch law
YCNH hyacinth
YCRA dyschroa
YCTA syncytia
YDOE syndrome
YDOS eye drops
YEAE typeface
YEAT typecast
YEEL hymeneal
YEEN hymenean
YEES Pyrenees
YEGC lysergic
YEGT by weight
YEID lyrebird
lyre-bird
YEIH type-high
YEIL mycelial
YEIM mycelium
YEIN by design
Hyperion
YEPC type spec
YERA synedria
YEUF Cynewulf
YEUN by return
YGAS eyeglass
nylghaus
ryegrass
YHAE lychgate
YHBE by the bye
YHCL mythical
YHIE by choice
YHLS syphilis
YHNC pythonic
typhonic
YHNE by chance
YHSS kyphosis
YHTC kyphotic
YHWY by the way
YIDR cylinder
YIGS syringes
YIHS by rights
YIID typified
YIIE pyridine
pyritise
pyritize
YIIM cynicism
lyricism
YIIR typifier
YIIT lyricist
YILC Cyrillic
YINC hygienic
YIPD myriapod
YITF by dint of
YIXS syrinxes
YKAA gymkhana
YLBB syllabub
YLBC syllabic
YLBE syllable
YLBS syllabus
YLCL cyclical
YLDS Cyclades
YLFE Wycliffe
YLMN cyclamen
YLNC cyclonic
YLPS Cyclopes
YLSS cycloses
YLTC pyelitic
YLTS myelitis
pyelitis
YLWY cycleway
YLXA dyslexia
YLXC dyslexic
YMDN myrmidon
YMEN pygmaean
YMTY symmetry
YNFR dying for
YNGN cyanogen
YNHS by inches
YNOK hymn-book
YNOT dying out
dying-out
YNSA gymnasia
YNSD cyanosed
YNSN lyings-in
YNSS cyanosis
hypnosis
YNTC cyanotic
hypnotic
YOAA hypogaea
myxomata
xylomata
zygomata
YOEE hypogene
pyroxene
Tyrolese
YOEL hypogeal
YOEM hypogeum
YOEN hypogean
Tyrolean
YOHC hypothec
YOIE cytokine
cytosine
mylonite
tyrosine
YOOE lysosome
YOOY cytology
mycology
YORM kymogram
YOSS synopses
synopsis
YOTC synoptic
YOUE cynosure
YOYE lysozyme
pyrolyse
pyrolyze
YOYY hyponymy
synonymy
YPDA sympodia
YPEN nymphean
YPNC tympanic
YPNM tympanum
YPOA dyspnoea
lymphoma
YPOD lymphoid
YPOY symphony
YPPY dyspepsy
YPSA symposia
YPTY dyspathy
sympathy
YRDS cyprides
YREA ayurveda
YRGN hydrogen
YRML hydromel
YRXL hydroxyl
YRYE eye rhyme
YRZA hydrozoa
YSGT eyesight
YSIE Ayrshire
hyoscine
YTCL mystical
YTEE eye to eye
YTEF by itself
YTEH eye teeth
YTIE cysteine
YTLC systolic
YTMC systemic
YTOH eye tooth
YTQE mystique
YTRA hysteria
YTRC hysteric
YTTN nystatin
YTTS cystitis
YUGS Lycurgus
YVNA Sylvania
YXYD lynx-eyed
YYIL by my will
YYIS syzygies
YYKM Kyzyl-Kum
ZLJS azulejos
ZNZR ozonizer
ZRVA czarevna
ZTII tzatziki

9 letters – even

AAAA Canada Day
catamaran
maharajah
panama hat
tacamahac
AAAB Maracaibo
AAAD jacaranda
sarabánde
AAAE maharanee
AAAI Barataria
fat as a pig
katabatic
macadamia
pan-Arabic
paralalia
AAAK balalaika
AAAL Caracalla
palatable
palatably
AAAM man-at-arms
AAAO galapagos
Galápagos
AAAR Canada Dry®
AAAT paramatta
AAAU Paranagua
AAAZ paparazzi
paparazzo
AABA canal-boat
AABL carambola
AABN malar bone
nasal bone
AACD cavalcade
AACN balancing
damascene
AACO kalanchoe
AACU Naval Club
AADL farandole
AADN gabardine
marauding
AADU hazardous
AADY salad days
AAEA tapaderas
AAEE Japaneses
parameter
AAEI catalexis
catamenia
paramecia
paramedic

9 _A_A_E

AAEL bagatelle
panatella
AAEO tapaderos
AAES catalepsy
AAET cabalette
Canaletto
Lafayette
lazaretto
AAEU fabaceous
AAFN paraffiny
AAGE haranguer
AAGM Sarah Gamp
AAHN matachina
matachini
AAHS Ramaphosa
AAHT malachite
parachute
AAHU barathrum
AAIA fanatical
paradisal
Samaritan
satanical
AAIE karabiner
parasites
AAIH maharishi
AAII parasitic
pay a visit
AAIL camarilla
sabadilla
tamarillo
AAIN Galatians
AAIO capacitor
caparison
AAIU capacious
malarious
rapacious
sagacious
salacious
AAJN Nagarjuna
AAKE damaskeen
palankeen
AAKN Samarkand
AAKO Dan Aykrod
AAKR ra-ra skirt
AALK lazar-like
AALM Dalai Lama
dalai lama
AALO capable of
AALS cataclysm
AALT Paraclete
AALV balaclava□
dataglove
AALX cataplexy
AAOA parabolas
paranoiac
AAOD vagabonds
AAOE paradores
AAOI catatonia
catatonic
macaronic
macaronis
natatoria
parabolic
parapodia
sanatoria
AAON bat around
pal around
paramount
AAOO cacafogos
tapacolos
AAOS calaboose
Saragossa
AAOT Pavarotti
AAOU catalogue
AAPL macaw-palm
AAQI damasquin
palanquin
AARA catarrhal
hamadryad
AARI maladroit
AARK parabrake
AARP paragraph
AARS calabrese□
AASA Malaysian
AASI Dadaistic
Lamaistic
rajahship
AASN harassing
AASU Carausius
AATA radar trap
Rajasthan
AATL tarantula
AATN galantine
Lamartine
Tarantino
AATS galactose
AATU galanthus
MacArthur
AAUO tapaculos
AAUR Kama Sutra
Kamasutra
AAUT Famagusta
AAVT Sarasvati
AAWL may as well
AAWT Saraswati
AAYE paralysed
paralyser
AAYI catalysis
catalytic
paralysis
paralytic
ABAT Galbraith
ABCL parbuckle
ABDA Barbadian
Cambodian
ABDE gambadoes
ABEL may beetle
ABFO Lamb of God
ABFR day before
lay before
ABHN lag behind
ABIG Cambridge
ABLG garbology
ABLO Cat Ballou
ABLS cabbalism□
cabbalist
ABLY jambalaya
ABND carbonado
ABNE harbinger
ABNL carbuncle
lambently
ABNO garbanzos
ABNS carbonise
ABNT carbonate
rabbinate
ABNZ carbonize
ABOL bamboozle
ABON Sam Browne
ABRA barbarian
ABRE hamburger
Pat Barker
ABRN jabbering
yabbering
ABRS barbarise
barbarism
carburise
ABRT barbarity
carburate
ABRU barbarous
ABRZ barbarize
carburize
ABSE Van Basten
ABSO barbascos
ABTA Ian Botham
rabbet saw
ABTE had better
ABTS sabbatise
ABTZ sabbatize
ABUC Lambrusco
ABUE tabbouleh
ACAA bacchanal□
catch away
ACAI saccharin
ACAK Kamchatka
ACAL catchable
danceable
fanciable
watchable
ACAT bacchants
ACBA sauce boat
ACBC hatchback
ACBE Maccabees
ACBL latch bolt
ACCL calcicole
catch cold
fascicule
fasciculi
ACCR sarcocarp
ACCS watchcase
ACDN cascading
ACDT rancidity
ACEI gaucherie
ACEL parchedly
ACEO rancheros
ACET haecceity
ACFE fancy-free
ACFG calcifuge
ACFL batch file
ACFR catch fire
falciform
watch fire
ACHR March hare
ACIF Radcliffe
ACIN Gascoigne
sanctions
ACIT march into
ACLA batch loaf
caecilian
ACLE canceleer
cancelier
cancelled
ACLM vasculums
ACLN Barcelona
masculine
ACLS matchless
ACLT calculate
laccolith
rascality
ACLU cancel out
Marcellus
parcel out
ACMN catchment
hatchment
parchment
ACMT sarcomata
ACNA Mancunian
ACND gasconade
ACNM carcinoma
ACNR day centre
law centre
ACNS fanciness
gasconism
larcenist
sauciness
ACNT fascinate
lancinate
vaccinate
ACNU calcaneum
calcaneus
larcenous
ACOA Marc Bolan
ACOE watch over
ACOL patchouli
ACOT latch on to
latch onto
ACPL Marco Polo
ACPS march past
march-past
ACPT mancipate
ACRE camcorder
ACRL barcarole
ACRT cancerate
ACRU cancerous
rancorous
saucerful
ACSA Caucasian
ACSC fancy-sick
ACSE Lancaster
ACSI Caucasoid
fascistic
sarcastic
ACSO Marcus Fox

Words marked □ can also be spelled with an initial capital letter

saucisson
ACST bad cess to
marcasite
ACSU narcissus□
ACTS narcotise
narcotism
patch test
ACTZ narcotize
ACUE Vancouver
ACUI catch up in
ACUL raucously
ACUR sanctuary
ACUT match up to
ACWO matchwood
ACWR catchword
fancywork
patchwork
watchword
ACWT march with
match with
ADAD landwards
ADAE bald-faced
laid paper
sandpaper
ADAL bald eagle
card table
ADAN landdamne
ADAO bandwagon
ADBE mandibles
ADBR Magdeburg
ADCA Laodicean
pas de chat
Sadducean
ADCI baldachin
ADCK lardy cake
ADCO bandicoot
ADCP landscape
ADCS Sadducism
ADCT manducate
ADDA padded bag
ADDC candidacy
ADDT candidate
ADDU pas de deux
ADDW hands down
ADEA Candlemas
saddlebag
ADEG sand wedge
ADEO saddlebow
ADFE dandified
ADFO hand of God
land of Nod
ADGA Mardi Gras
ADGL Sandy Gall
ADHA hard wheat
ADHK handshake
ADHL maid-child
ADHN cardphone
ADHO hardihood
ADHR card-sharp
ADIE hardliner
hard lines
Hard Times
hard times

hard-wired
sandpiper
ADIT bandwidth
ADKU Hardaknut
ADLD landslide
ADLE bandoleer
bandolier
sandalled
ADLG paedology
ADLL Sandy Lyle
ADLN bandoline
Bardolino
Magdalena
Magdalene
mandoline
sand-blind
ADLO caudillos
dandelion
Mandelson
ADLS sandblast
vandalise
vandalism
ADLZ vandalize
ADMS randomise
ADMZ randomize
ADNA Sardinian
ADNE card-index
tap-dancer
ADNF harden off
ADNI land snail
ADNK Kandinsky
ADNL fandangle
MacDonald
Macdonald
ADNN gardening
hardening
maddening
saddening
ADNO fandangos
Mandingos
ADNS bawdiness
faddiness
gaudiness
handiness
hardiness
maidenish
randiness
sandiness
tardiness
ADOC mandiocca
ADOE hard money
hard-nosed
Land Rover®
ADON hand round
ADOR cardboard
hardboard
hard court
ADPA dandiprat
ADPK handspike
ADQI baldaquin
ADRA hand organ
ADRB garderobe
ADRC sandarach

ADRF handcraft
wander off
ADRK handbrake
ADRL banderole
dandy-roll
ADRN wandering
ADRO Sanderson
ADRS paederast
panderess
ADSU pas de seul
ADTC yardstick
ADTF candytuft
hard stuff
ADTN bandstand
handstand
Maidstone
sandstone
ADTO faldstool
laudation
ADTR hand's turn
laudatory
mandatory
sand storm
sandstorm
ADTV laudative
ADUA Hasdrubal
ADUE hard-ruled
ADUF handcuffs
ADWE landowner
ADWR handiwork
ADYN hardly any
AEAA cameraman
taken away
AEAD Lake Garda
AEAE barefaced
caretaker
face-saver
fare-payer
lacerated
make water
make waves
name names
pacemaker
ratepayer
safe haven
AEAG make laugh
AEAH camera-shy
AEAI have had it
AEAL laterally
AEAN take pains
AEAO macerator
AEAP make happy
AEAS have cause
naye paise
AEAT bare facts
have faith
make haste
rare earth
AEAU face value
make vague
AEBA water bear
AEBC make a back
paperback

take aback
waterbuck
AEBI Barenboim
AEBL have a ball
AEBM make a bomb
AEBN James Bond
Palembang
AEBR Camembert
water bird
AEBS have a bash
AEBT have a bath
take a bath
water butt
water-butt
AEBU care about
rave about
AECI paperclip
AECL make a call
AECN canescent
AECO James Cook
water-cool
AECR have a care
make a card
water cure
AEDA have ideas
James Dean
make a deal
AEDL calendula
AEDN gaberdine
AEDO eavesdrop
AEDR Pat Eddery
AEDS Cavendish
AEDW water down
AEEA make legal
AEEC make peace
make-peace
AEED Cape Verde
James Eads
make ready
makeready
AEEE make level
AEEI cafeteria
daredevil
dare-devil
AEEM make terms
AEEN have being
madeleine□
AEEO lay eyes on
pademelon
patereros
AEER make merry
take heart
AEES make sense
make tense
AEEU vade-mecum
AEEV take leave
AEFC make a face
AEFE make after
name after
take after
water flea
AEFL Lagerfeld
waterfall

AEFR	Waterford
AEFS	ease of use
	make a fuss
AEFW	waterfowl
AEGA	have a go at
AEGF	make a gift
AEGR	salesgirl
AEGT	water gate
	Watergate
AEHA	Gateshead
AEHF	makeshift
AEHG	James Hogg
AEHI	Lake Ohrid
AEHL	make a hole
	make whole
	waterhole
AEHN	James Hunt
AEHP	game chips
	take shape
	waveshape
AEHR	take short
AEHS	catechise
	catechism
	catechist
AEHT	make white
AEHZ	catechize
AEIB	taken in by
AEID	game birds
AEIE	make fixed
	make tired
	make wider
	take sides
AEIH	make right
	safe light
AEIL	Masefield
	materials
	Wakefield
AEIR	cafetière
AEIT	make dirty
AEIU	facetious
AEIZ	make dizzy
AEJM	water jump
AELA	have a loan
	make clear
	take a leak
AELC	have place
	safe place
	take place
AELD	naked lady
	saleslady
AELI	make plain
AELL	water lily
AELN	James Lind
	labelling
	make blind
	Mayerling
	panelling
	ravelling
	waterline
AELS	made flesh
	make a list
	panellist
	paperless
	waterless
AELT	face-cloth
	face plate
	satellite
AELU	have clout
	lager lout
AELV	wage slave
AEMA	make a meal
AEMI	water main
AEMN	have a mind
	ravelment
AEMR	watermark
AEMS	make a mess
	take amiss
AEMT	make empty
AEMV	make a move
AENG	Lake Onega
AENI	make unfit
AENO	have in tow
	take in tow
AENR	make angry
	pageantry
AENS	eagerness
	mateyness
	nakedness
	satedness
AENT	maternity
	paternity
AENU	cavernous
AENW	made known
	make known
AEOD	have words
	Jane Fonda
AEOE	bare bones
	gate money
	gate-money
	gate-tower
	make money
	paper over
	take cover
	wave power
AEOG	Malebolge
	Wade Boggs
AEOI	categoric
	Macedonia
	paregoric
AEON	game point
	have round
AEOO	kakemonos
AEOP	Lake Poopó
AEOS	bakehouse
	gatehouse
	make worse
	racehorse
	safe house
	take horse
	warehouse
AEOT	have got to
AEOZ	make woozy
AEPL	water polo
AEPM	water pump
AEPO	make up for
AEPP	water pipe
AEPR	davenport❑
	take apart
AEQA	make equal
AERA	make or mar
AERC	race track
	racetrack
	sale price
AERE	care order
	take order
AERI	water rail
AERN	Janet Reno
	make drunk
	name brand
AERS	careerism
	careerist
	gatecrash
	have a rest
	James Ross
	sagebrush
	take a rest
	take a risk
AERT	water rate
AERU	make proud
AERV	make brave
AESA	have a stab
	take a seat
AESC	haversack
AESD	take aside
	waterside
	wave aside
AESE	watershed
AESG	make a sign
AESI	have a shit
	make a slip
	make a stir
AESN	haversine
AESO	have a shot
	make use of
AESU	take issue
AETA	cadential
	have it bad
	later than
AETC	take stock
AETE	gazetteer
AETG	fare stage
	fare-stage
	parentage
AETI	have-at-him
	make a trip
	paper-thin
	wafer-thin
AETL	sales talk
	take it ill
AETM	date-stamp
	vasectomy
AETN	lamenting
	man-eating
	panettone
	panettoni
	parenting
	valentine❑
	Valentino
AETP	take steps
AETR	calenture
	take a turn
AETS	caber toss
AETU	have it out
	Maxentius
AETW	Jamestown
AEUA	cane-sugar
AEUL	balefully
	banefully
	carefully
	fatefully
	hatefully
	wakefully
AEUN	take turns
AEUO	Lake Huron
	make fun of
	mamelucos
AEUR	safeguard
AEVL	water vole
AEWL	take a walk
AEWO	Hazelwood
AEWR	make aware
	navelwort
	panel-work
	paperwork
AEWS	have a wash
	taperwise
AEWT	faced with
	James Watt
	taken with
AEWU	caterwaul
AEWV	water-wave
AEYA	yakety-yak
AEYE	safety net
AEYI	barely win
	panegyric
	safety pin
AEYS	Lake Nyasa
AFAD	half-hardy
AFAE	half-baked
	half-faced
AFAT	half-caste
AFBU	faff about
AFEC	halfpence
AFEL	ramfeezle
AFEN	halfpenny
AFFL	carfuffle
AFGR	lay-figure
AFHE	half-cheek
AFIA	man Friday❑
AFIC	half hitch
	half-hitch
AFIG	halflings
AFIH	half-light
AFIL	half-title
AFIN	man friend
AFLN	half-blind
AFLO	half-blood
AFLT	half-plate
AFNA	Baffin Bay
AFNE	Garfunkel
AFOE	half-dozen
	mayflower❑

safflower
saffroned
wax flower
AFOI far from it
AFRC half-price
half-track
AFRD fanfarade
AFRE half-breed
malformed
AFRN half-drunk
wayfaring
AFRS half-cross
Sanforise
AFRT half-truth
AFRW half-crown
AFRZ Sanforize
AFSE ham-fisted
AFSL raffishly
AFTE hamfatter
AFWK half-awake
AGAL gaugeable
laughable
laughably
AGBU hang about
AGCT large city
AGDU fagged out
AGEO malgré moi
vargueños
AGET larghetto
AGEU malgré lui
AGIE bargainer
AGIL languidly
AGIN ganglions
AGLD hang-glide
AGLF hang a left
AGLN gangplank
AGLO bargellos
AGLR Bangalore
AGMA large meal
AGNE jargoneer
AGNI barging-in
AGNL laggingly
AGNO far gone on
AGNS bagginess
jargonise
jargonist
largeness
manganese
manginess
tanginess
AGNT manganite
marginate
AGNZ jargonize
AGOG hang tough
AGOS hang loose
AGPL bargepole
AGRA pan-German
AGRI sangfroid
sang-froid
AGRL haggardly
AGRN badgering
margarine
tangerine

AGRO hangers-on
AGRS gargarise
AGRT margarita
AGRU dangerous
AGRZ gargarize
AGSL haggishly
waggishly
AGSN Langesund
AGSO sargassos
AGSU sargassum
AGTB Jay Gatsby
AGTI maggot-pie
AGTL haughtily
naughtily
AGTU mange tout
mangetout
AGUA hang out at
AGUC gang-punch
AGUT langouste
AGVN law-giving
AHAD Kathmandu
AHAE fat-headed
AHAI washbasin
AHAT bad health
AHDA cathedral
AHDI Sanhedrim
Sanhedrin
AHDR pachyderm
AHDU washed out
washed-out
AHET pay heed to
AHGN pathogeny
AHHB Bathsheba
AHHI bath chair□
AHHN dachshund
each thing
AHIL Nashville
AHLA mashallah
wash clean
AHLE Pachelbel
AHLG pathology
AHLO lay hold of
parhelion
AHLT batholith
AHMU fathom out
AHNE ham-handed
Nathaniel
AHNL dashingly
manhandle
AHNM taphonomy
AHNR machinery
AHNS machinist
AHNT machinate
AHNU washing-up
AHOE fashioned
fashioner
AHOI machzorim
AHOR dashboard
washboard
AHOS washhouse
AHRA gather way
washerman
Zacharias

AHRE catharses
AHRI catharsis
cathartic
AHRN Catharine
Catherina
Catherine
gathering
Katharina
Katharine
Katherine
AHRS catharise
ratherish
AHRZ catharize
AHSA yachtsman
AHSO Ian Hislop
AHTA Manhattan
AHTE each other
AHTN washstand
AHUA lash out at
AHUL bashfully
AHYA lachrymal
AHZR haphazard
AIAD garibaldi□
AIAE camisades
laminated
patinated
validated
AIAI sanitaria
Tariq Aziz
AIAL basically
capitally
fatigable
habitable
habitably
magically
manically
maritally
maximally
navigable
navigably
radically
vaginally
AIAO camisados
capitanos
navigator
AIAS pari passu
AIBA Caribbean
AIBR Salisbury
AICE cabin crew
AICI mariachis
radicchio
AIEC Taoiseach
AIEE taximeter
AIEL capitella
varicella
AIEM taxidermy
AIET manifesto
Marinetti
satinette
AIFC satisfice
AIFE satisfied
AIFL basinfuls
pay in full

AIFR rapid fire
AIGA radiogram
AIGF laying-off
taking off
AIGT variegate
AIGU paying-out
taking out
AIHA Radiohead
AIHL David Hill
AIHM Basil Hume
David Hume
AIHN cap in hand
famishing
ravishing
vanishing
AIHP David Hope
AIHR David Hare
AIHT caliphate
AIIA fatidical
satirical
vaticidal
AIIE sanitized
sanitizer
AIIR marinière
AIIT laciniate
AIIU malicious
AILA David Lean
AILE Ramillies
AILG hagiology
radiology
AILM papilloma
AILN cabilline
cavilling
Rab Island
AILR capillary
mamillary
maxillary
papillary
AILS labialise
racialism
racialist
radialise
AILT hariolate
papillate
papillote
vacillate
variolate
AILU Ladislaus
AILZ labialize
radialize
AIMC David Mach
AIMN talismans
AIND Tamil Nadu
AINE Gaziantep
AINL patiently
radiantly
rationale
saliently
sapiently
valiantly
AINN malignant
maligning
rationing

Words marked □ can also be spelled with an initial capital letter

AINS	Fabianism
	Fabianist
	rabidness
	rapidness
	tacitness
	vapidness
AINT	malignity
AINU	ration out
AIOE	David Owen
AIOI	halitosis
AIOO	makimonos
AIOT	manicotti
AIPZ	Mario Puzo
AIRG	saxifrage
AIRT	calibrate
AISA	ladies' man
	pay its way
AISL	David Sole
AISO	magic-show
AISR	janissary
AITA	magistral
AITE	varieties
AITL	radiately
AITN	Pakistani
AITO	radiation
	satiation
	variation
AITR	banisters
AITS	macintosh
AITT	sagittate
AIUA	navicular
AIUI	halieutic
	Paricutín
AIUL	variously
AIUN	fatiguing
	marihuana
	marijuana
AIUT	habituate
AIUU	capitulum
AIWO	satinwood
AIWR	magic word
AIWT	bavin wits
AIWV	radio wave
AIYA	family man
	family way
	vanity bag
	yakity-yak
AIYE	easily led
AIYI	salicylic
AIYN	pacifying
AIYU	easily dug
AJLL	banjolele
AKAC	Jack-sauce
AKAD	backwards
	parkwards
AKAE	back water
	backwater
AKAO	Hank Aaron
AKBL	hawksbill
AKBU	lark about
	talk about
	walkabout
AKDF	hacked off
AKDU	packed out
AKEA	back-pedal
AKEE	barkeeper
	bar-keeper
	hackneyed
AKET	back teeth
AKGN	packaging
AKIE	backbiter
	lack-linen
	rank-rider
AKIG	darklings
AKIK	Jacky Ickx
AKKB	Bar Kokhba
AKLD	backslide
AKLE	Dark blues
AKLN	Baekeland
	Jack-a-Lent
AKLR	bank clerk
AKLT	backcloth
	sackcloth
AKLV	Jack-slave
AKMO	Hawksmoor
AKMR	hackamore
AKNF	jackknife
AKNI	Mackenzie
	walk on air
AKNL	balkingly
AKNN	darkening
AKNO	Parkinson
	talking of
	Tarkenton
AKNP	jack-snipe
AKNS	Balkanise
	gawkiness
	lankiness
	tackiness
	wackiness
AKNT	talking-to
AKNU	packing-up
AKNZ	Balkanize
AKOB	Jack Hobbs
AKOC	task force
	task-force
AKOD	backwoods
	tae kwon do
AKOE	banknotes
	Jack Jones
AKON	talk round
AKOR	backboard
	backcourt
AKOS	dark horse
AKOT	Dankworth
AKPC	backspace
AKPE	backspeer
AKPI	backspeir
AKPT	Mark Spitz
AKRC	backtrack
AKRE	Valkyries
AKRI	lack-brain
AKRN	hankering
AKRO	hanker for
AKRS	back-cross
	Jack Frost
AKRU	cankerous
	Valkyriur
AKSL	hawkishly
	mawkishly
AKTA	Jack Straw
AKTE	marketeer
	market-led
	racketeer
AKTG	backstage
AKTL	backstall
AKTN	marketing
AKTO	Saskatoon
	walkathon
AKTU	basketful
AKTV	talkative
AKUO	back out of
	talk out of
	walk out on
AKUS	Pankhurst
AKWI	Mark Twain
AKWN	backswing
AKWT	Mankowitz
ALAA	Carl Sagan
ALAC	dalliance
ALAE	call names
	wallpaper
ALAH	Gaeltacht
ALAK	hallmarks
ALAL	malleable
ALAS	Carl Gauss
	paillasse
	palliasse
ALAT	Karl Barth
ALBL	ballabili
ALBR	early bird
	Jarlsberg
ALBU	day-labour
	fall about
ALCI	Carluccio
ALCS	gaelicise
	Gallicise
ALCT	Paul Scott
ALCZ	gaelicize
	Gallicize
ALDE	balladeer
ALDF	called off
ALDO	called for
	called-for
ALDT	callidity
ALDU	palladium
ALDY	early days
ALEA	sallee-man
ALEE	eagle-eyed
	had liefer
	had liever
ALEI	Carl Lewis
ALEO	earlier on
ALES	Carl Zeiss
ALFI	ball of air
ALFL	ladlefuls
ALGA	Callaghan
ALHL	call a halt
	daily help
ALHR	fall short
ALIA	Paul Dirac
ALIC	tailpiece
ALIE	Earl Hines
	gauleiter
	nail-biter
ALIL	Caulfield
ALIO	Paul Simon
ALLA	maple leaf
ALLG	haplology
ALLN	sailplane
	Sally Lunn
	tableland
	tailplane
ALLR	fallalery
ALLS	faultless
ALLT	sailcloth
	wall plate
ALMI	Daily Mail
ALMN	fall among
ALMR	Haslemere
ALNE	tail-ender
ALNG	gallonage
ALNI	falling-in
ALNL	gallantly
	gallingly
	railingly
	wailingly
ALNR	Carl Andre
	gallantry
ALNS	earliness
	kaolinise
	manliness
	palliness
ALNT	kaolinite
ALNZ	kaolinize
ALOE	ballooned
	fail to get
	Paul Jones
ALOI	fail to hit
ALON	ballpoint
	call round
	haul round
ALOR	sailboard
	tailboard
ALOS	jailhouse
ALOT	call forth
ALPD	gallopade
ALPI	Gallophil
ALPN	galloping
	walloping
ALPR	callipers
	fall apart
ALPU	Fallopius
ALQI	harlequin
ALRA	jailbreak
	sailor-hat
ALRD	Sally Ride
ALRE	galleried
	galleries
	tall order
ALRH	Karlsruhe
ALRN	ballerina

ALRP wall a rope
ALRS tailoress
ALSA Daily Star
ALSI ballistic
ALSL haplessly
lawlessly
table salt
ALSS gallisise
ALST callosity
ALSU Callistus
ALSZ gallisize
ALTC mahlstick
maulstick
tailstock
ALTL Table Talk
ALTN gallstone
hallstand
ALTO ballot-box
maelstrom
ALTR hailstorm
tablature
tall story
ALTS palletise
ALTT Hallstatt
ALTZ palletize
ALUA Paul Dukas
ALUL callously
ALUT call out to
ALVA Pavlovian
ALVK Caslavska
ALVN gallivant
ALWC bailiwick
ALWE gallowses
Hallowe'en
ALWN hallowing
table wine
wallowing
ALWR tableware
ALWS sallowish
tablewise
ALWT dally with
tally with
ALYN parleying
waylaying
ALYO parleyvoo
AMBS Jan Mabuse
AMCH Sammy Cahn
AMCT haemocyte
AMDO gammadion
AMDS Talmudist
AMEA Ian McEwan
AMEC Palm Beach
AMGE San Miguel
AMKN haymaking
law-making
AMLA Macmillan
mammalian
mammillae
AMLD marmalade
AMLS marmelise
AMLT Carmelite
AMLZ marmelize
AMNA Tasman Bay
Tasmanian
AMNC harmonica
harmonics
AMNE harmonies
Tasman Sea
warmonger
AMNL gas mantle
AMNO badminton
AMNS balminess
harmonise
harmonist
mammonish
mammonism
mammonist
AMNT mammonite
AMNU harmonium
sarmentum
AMNZ harmonize
AMOS farmhouse
AMRA marmoreal
AMRB Hammurabi
AMRC barmbrack
AMRE earmarked
AMRL wax myrtle
AMRN Dan Marino
hammering
San Marino
warm front
AMRO hammer-toe
AMRS marmarise
AMRU hammer out
AMRY gamma rays
AMRZ marmarize
AMSA haemostat
AMSE paymaster
Rasmussen
AMSR palmistry
AMTA Dalmatian
farmstead
harmattan
Sarmatian
AMTL palmately
AMTM haematoma
AMTO palmettos
AMTT haematite
AMTV calmative
AMUL harmfully
AMUT harmful to
AMWL Naomi Wolf
ANAC barn dance
fainéance
ANAE gainsayer
ANAG rain gauge
rain-gauge
ANAI bain-marie
ANAK Iain Banks
ANAL paintable
ANAP lagniappe
ANBL paintball
ANBR Sainsbury
ANDS damnedest
ANDU fanned out
ANEE laundered
saunterer
ANEO Launcelot
Launceton
maunder on
ANFE magnifier
ANHA launch pad
ANHE mainsheet
ANHL raunchily
ANHN launching
main thing
ANHO sainthood
ANIE jaundiced
mainliner
ANJA Saint Joan
ANKY Danny Kaye
ANLA carnelian
ANLE pannelled
ANLK saintlike
ANLR vainglory
ANLS carnalise
dauntless
ANLT carnality
ANLU magnalium
rain-cloud
ANLZ carnalize
ANMN Hahnemann
ANND cannonade
ANNI D'Annunzio
ANNL fawningly
yawningly
ANNS canniness
faintness
gauntness
raininess
ANOC main force
ANOE lawnmower
ANON main point
ANPR tawny port
ANQI mannequin
ANRC mainbrace
Patna rice
ANRM mainframe
ANRO rainproof
ANRP raindrops
ANRS laundress
mannerism
mannerist
ANSA magnesian
saint's day
ANSE bannister□
gannister
garnishee
tarnished
varnisher
ANSL earnestly
ANSO Magnusson
ANSR garnishry
ANSU magnesium
Parnassus
ANTD magnitude
ANTK Karnataka
ANTO carnation
damnation
magnetron
ANTR damnatory
garniture
main store
rainstorm
ANTS magnetise
magnetism
ANTT magnetite
ANTZ magnetize
ANUL gainfully
painfully
ANVR carnivore
ANZI Caenozoic
Cainozoic
AOAI panoramic
AOAL razorable
AOAO mako-makos
AOAR Bay of Acre
AOAT mayoralty
AOBA carob bean
AOBL razorbill
AOBU Saxon blue
AOCI capocchia
AODM major-domo
AOEC baronetcy
AOEE barometer
can-opener
gasometer
manometer
AOEI Samoyedic
AOEO cacodemon
AOER manometry
AOET lay open to
majorette
vaporetti
vaporetto
wagonette
AOHA parochial
AOHL Damon Hill
halophile
Max Ophuls
AOHM Kagoshima
AOHN cacophony
saxophone
AOIA Aaronical
canonical
parodical
AOIE tamoxifen
vaporizer
AOII calorific
AOIL sapodilla
AOIO palominos
AOIU laborious
AOLA Damoclean
wagonload
AOLF way of life
AOLT wagon-lits
AOLV Yaroslavl
AONN marooning
AOOI taxonomic
AOOL paso doble
AOOP lagomorph
AOPG Bay of Pigs

Words marked □ can also be spelled with an initial capital letter

AORE Carol Reed
AORL savourily
AORN favouring
labouring
AORP barograph
AORR labourers
AORS vapourish
AORT favourite
AOSE jalousied
Lavoisier
AOSI wagons-lit
AOSN carousing
AOSO Aaron's rod
AOTN cavorting
AOTU raconteur
AOUE caroluses
AOUR manoeuvre
AOWR razor wire
AOYN parodying
APAC Max Planck
APAS wasp waist
APCE jam-packed
Kampuchea
APCO gazpachos
APDS Lampedusa
APER raspberry
APGN rampaging
APHD lampshade
APHR Hampshire
APHU happy hour
APIH lamplight
APLA Las Palmas
APLC lamp-black
APLT pamphlets
APMR Harpo Marx
APNE carpenter
APNL campanile
campanili
campanula
carpingly
gaspingly
rampantly
raspingly
APNN dampening
happening
APNR carpentry
APNS happiness
sappiness
wasp's nest
wasps' nest
APOE harpooner
lampooner
APOI camphoric
panphobia
APQI damp squib
APRE Harper Lee
APRN hampering
pampering
tampering
APRO bad person
damp-proof
lay person
layperson
mad person
pauperdom
APRS jasperise
nappy rash
pauperise
pauperism
vampirise
vampirism
APRT Max Perutz
APRZ jasperize
pauperize
vampirize
APSL waspishly
APTN carpeting
APTT palpitate
APUI tarpaulin
AQAC sasquatch
AQAL Dan Quayle
AQER marquetry
parquetry
AQEU harquebus
AQIE pasquiler
ARAA carry away
ARAC matriarch
patriarch
ARAK Fairbanks
ARBA macrobian
ARBC carry back
ARBR Larry Bird
ARCA patrician
ARCD barracuda
barricade
matricide
parricide
patricide
ARCE barricoes
patricoes
ARCI capriccio□
ARCR Capricorn
ARCS macrocosm
ARCT fabricate
ARCU Fabricius
Patroclus
ARDA Sacred Way
ARDE hag-ridden
ARDO sacred cow
ARDR Laura Dern
AREE Laurie Lee
AREL Gabrielle
ARFC sacrifice
ARFL barrefull
ARGE carrageen
farragoes
ARGN Tarragona
ARGR cairngorm
ARGT Harrogate
ARHR hair shirt
ARIC hairpiece
hair-piece
ARIE fair-sized
ram-raider
ARIT marry into
ARJH Barry John
ARKE parrakeet
ARKS Marrakesh
ARLA patrol car
patrolman
ARLE bas relief
bas-relief
patroller
ARLG macrology
sacrilege
ARLK fairylike
ARLN fairyland□
ARLS sacralise
ARLT garrulity
haircloth
saprolite
ARLU barrelful
garrulous
ARLZ sacralize
ARMI dairymaid
ARMN matrimony
patrimony
sacrament□
ARMR Barrymore
ARMS lacrimoso
lagrimoso
ARNE warranted
warrantee
warranter
ARNG patronage
ARNL jarringly
ARNN safranine
ARNO warrantor
ARNS hairiness
matronise
patroness
patronise
tarriness
ARNZ matronize
patronize
AROA pair-royal
AROE cabriolet
carry over
gadrooned
garryowen
AROI patriotic
ARPA hairspray
ARPR madrepore
ARRE hairdrier
hairdryer
ARRN fairy ring
ARRS hairbrush
ARRU sacrarium
ARSA sacristan
ARSE barrister
ARSI patristic
ARSU Hadrosaur
ARTE garrotter
had rather
ARTL carrytale
fairy tale
fairytale
fairy-tale
hairstyle
ARTO narration
ARTR fairy tern
narratory
tax return
ARTU Mauritius
ARTV narrative
ARWA marrowfat
ARWK marrowsky
ARWN harrowing
narrowing
ARWO barrow-boy
ARWR Maori Wars
ARZI saprozoic
ASAE Carstares
fan-shaped
nauseated
pass water
ASAH Hans Sachs
ASAI pan-Slavic
ASAK Haystacks
ASAL mass rally
raiseable
ranshakle
ASBN waistband
ASCA waistcoat
ASCE ransacked
ransacker
sapsucker
ASCI raise Cain
ASCR false-card
ASDE passadoes
ASDW false dawn
ASEH Hans Bethe
ASEI mass media
sans serif
ASEL haustella
ASEN far-seeing
ASES baksheesh
Parseeism
ASFA pass off as
sassafras
ASFE falsified
falsifier
ASFL days of old
ASFT hats off to
ASGS paysagist
ASHL hawsehole
raise hell
ASHO falsehood
ASHR cause harm
ASHW marsh hawk
ASIE false idea
Pan's pipes
wassailer
ASIL Catskills
Mansfield
ASIO bad sailor
ASLE tasselled
ASLG vassalage
ASLL damselfly
ASLN marshland
waistline
ASLS capsulise

Words marked □ can also be spelled with an initial capital letter

	pauseless
ASLT	causality
ASLU	mausoleum
ASLZ	capsulize
ASMA	hansom-cab
ASML	facsimile
ASMN	parsimony
	passement
	ransoming
ASNA	Pausanias
ASNC	Sassenach
ASNE	passenger
ASNG	parsonage
ASNL	pausingly
ASNM	false name
ASNO	passing on
ASNR	Cassandra
	Sassandra
ASNS	falseness
	gassiness
	harshness
ASOA	batswoman
	oarswoman
	passional
ASOC	Sans Souci
ASOH	Naas Botha
ASOI	haustoria
ASON	pass round
ASOT	false oath
ASPA	marsupial
ASPI	cause pain
	pansophic
ASPP	hawsepipe
ASPU	marsupium
ASRB	Hans Krebs
	passers-by
ASRL	casserole
ASRN	hamstring
	hamstrung
	passerine
ASRO	kaiserdom
ASRT	lapse rate
ASSE	false step
ASSO	false show
ASTB	cause to be
ASTD	lassitude
ASTO	causation
	falsettos
ASTV	causative
ASUE	cassoulet
ASVL	massively
	passively
ASVT	passivate
	passivity
ASWR	cassowary
ATAA	balthazar
	waste away
ATAD	eastwards
ATAE	castrated
	saltwater
ATAL	factually
	martially
	partially
	tactually
	wait table
ATAS	salt marsh
ATAT	partial to
ATAU	lanthanum
ATBD	can't abide
ATBL	cantabile
	earth ball
ATBN	cantabank
ATBU	cast about
ATCA	tactician
ATCE	Baltic Sea
	Nantucket
	particles
ATCT	masticate
ATCU	Santa Cruz
ATEA	Castlebar
	cattleman
ATEE	wattmeter
ATEF	rattle off
ATEG	Eastleigh
ATEI	eat the air
ATEO	panthenol
	Parthenon
ATER	battle cry
	battle-cry
	saltpetre
ATES	pantheism
	pantheist
ATEX	battleaxe
	battle-axe
ATFL	earthfall
	pantoffle
ATGA	D'Artagnan
ATGE	party-goer
ATGN	Cartagena
ATGT	castigate
ATGU	fastigium
ATHE	cartwheel
	fact sheet
ATHR	hartshorn
ATHS	pantihose
ATIC	captaincy
	last-ditch
ATIE	East River
	part-timer
ATIG	cartridge
	eastlings
	partridge❑
ATII	Fantaisie
	gastritis
ATIP	Xanthippe
ATIR	captain RN
ATIT	waltz into
ATKL	Gaitskell
ATKN	partaking
ATKO	partake of
ATLA	castellan
ATLE	cattaloes
ATLG	cartilage
	tautology
ATLN	cantilena
	earthling
	pantiling
	party line
	wasteland
ATLO	battalion
	martellos
	pantaloon
ATLS	cartelise
	faithless
	tantalise
	tasteless
ATLT	tactility
	tantalite
ATLU	cantaloup
	cautelous
ATLZ	cartelize
	tantalize
ATMA	Jan Timman
ATME	bad temper
ATMM	pantomime
ATMN	bad timing
	battement
ATMR	Baltimore
ATNA	Martinmas
ATNC	santonica
ATND	bastinade
	bastinado
ATNE	bartender
	Santander
ATNL	dartingly
	haltingly
	lastingly
	pantingly
	rantingly
ATNN	fastening
	fattening
	hastening
ATNS	Cantonese
	cantonise
	cattiness
	daltonism❑
	fattiness
	hastiness
	nastiness
	nattiness
	pastiness
	saltiness
	tastiness
	tattiness
	wantonise
ATNT	castanets
ATNY	cast an eye
ATNZ	cantonize
	wantonize
ATOA	factional
	xanthomas
ATOI	Bartholin
	wait for it!
ATOK	saltworks
ATON	eastbound
	Hawthorne
ATOO	gastropod
ATOS	cast loose
ATOT	Dartmouth
ATPP	waste pipe
ATRA	bacterial
	Easter Day
	factorial
	lactarian
	latter-day
	Pasternak
	raptorial
	sartorial
ATRC	fast-track
ATRE	patterned
	Sauternes
ATRG	Easter egg
	pasturage
ATRL	dastardly
	pastorale
	pastorali
ATRN	bantering
	bartering
	battering
	faltering
	Hart Crane
	mattering
	pattering
	raftering
	Santorini
ATRO	martyrdom
ATRS	bacterise
	cauterise
	factorise
	lay to rest
	martyrise
	rapturise
	tartarise
ATRT	pastorate
ATRU	bacterium
	masterful
	rapturous
	sartorius
ATRZ	bacterize
	cauterize
	factorize
	martyrize
	rapturize
	rasterize
	tartarize
ATSA	Bantustan
	baptismal
	Cartesian
ATSD	cast aside
ATSI	fantastic
	pants suit
ATSL	cattishly
	saltishly
ATSR	baptistry
ATSS	fantasise
	fantasist
ATSU	Dantesque
ATSZ	fantasize
	party-size
ATTM	factotums
	waste time
ATTN	can't stand

Words marked ❑ can also be spelled with an initial capital letter

ATTO	jactation
	lactation
	mactation
	partition
	saltation
ATTR	saltatory
ATTV	factitive
	partitive
ATUB	Matt Busby
ATUH	cartouche
ATUL	pantoufle
	tactfully
ATVT	captivate
	captivity
	cast a vote
ATWE	part-owner
ATWL	party wall
ATWR	earthwork
	earthworm
ATYA	Bantry Bay
ATYN	Santayana
AUAE	saturated
AUAI	lacunaria
AUAL	naturally
	saturable
	tabularly
AUAO	tabulator
AUBE	valuables
AUCL	majuscule
	ranunculi
AUDF	Raoul Dufy
AUDT	facundity
AUIA	matutinal
	paludinal
AULN	Jaqueline
AULS	casualise
	valueless
AULZ	casualize
AUNA	Saturnian
AUNN	saturnine
AUNS	saturnism
	vagueness
AUPC	haruspicy
AURI	La Guardia
AURT	salubrity
AURU	manubrium
AUSI	casuistic
AUSR	casuistry
	maquisard
AUTE	faculties
AUTO	valuation
AUTU	fatuitous
AUUL	fatuously
	vacuously
AUWT	pal up with
AVNS	Calvinism
	Calvinist
	galvanise
	galvanism
	naïveness
AVNZ	galvanize
AVRE	cap verses
AVSA	Walvis Bay
AVSE	canvasser
	harvester
AVSO	Galveston
AVTE	calvities
AVTO	salvation
AWIH	Ian Wright
AWLE	jaywalker
	Sam Weller
AWLI	rauwolfia
AWLO	Fay Weldon
AWNA	Darwinian
AWNL	Van Winkle
AWNO	bay window
AWNS	Darwinism
	Darwinist
AWRL	waywardly
AWSE	war-wasted
AWYA	Galway Bay
AXOA	Manxwoman
AYAS	lazy-daisy
AYEM	easy terms
AYES	easy-peasy
AYET	baby teeth
AYGA	laryngeal
AYHI	easy chair
AYIA	satyrical
AYIE	many-sided
	many times
AYIT	labyrinth
AYLG	karyology
AYMI	lady's maid
AYMT	Ladysmith
AYOC	easy touch
AYOE	easy money
	lazybones
	lazy-bones
AYON	easygoing
	easy-going
AYOT	baby tooth
AYPE	caryopses
AYRN	Cary Grant
AYRS	Magyarise
AYRZ	Magyarize
AYSB	easy as ABC
AYTD	caryatids
AYTM	many a time
AYTP	karyotype
AYUA	lazy Susan
AYUN	Mary Quant
AZDN	Mao Zedong
AZLO	manzellos
AZNS	gauziness
AZOS	wayzgoose
AZRN	lazzaroni
AZRT	Lanzarote
BAIA	ablatival
BANN	obtaining
BBRW	a bob or two
BCNE	absconder
BCNL	obscenely
BCNT	obscenity
BCRL	obscurely
BCRN	obscurant
BCRT	obscurity
BCSA	abscissae
	abscissas
BCSE	abscisses
BDEC	obedience
BDNL	abidingly
BEBO	absey book
BEDR	objet d'art
BELN	abseiling
BERT	obsecrate
BESL	obversely
BESO	abreast of
	obsession
	obversion
BESV	obsessive
BETF	objectify
BETO	abjection
	objection
BETV	objective
BEUE	obsequies
BEUN	obsequent
BEVN	observant
BGOS	a big noise
BIAC	obeisance
BIAE	obligated
BIAO	obligatos
BIET	obliged to
BIIU	oblivious
BINT	obsignate
BIOE	absit omen
BITO	obviation
BIUL	obliquely
	obviously
BIUT	obliquity
BLGT	obbligato
BLIN	ebullient
BLSE	abolished
BLTO	abolition
BMNT	abominate
BNAC	abundance
BNOE	abandoned
	abandonee
BOAE	abrogated
BOBN	absorbent
	absorbing
BODT	obcordate
BOEC	obsolesce
BOIA	abdominal
	obconical
BOIU	obnoxious
BORN	abhorrent
BPOE	ibuprofen
BRAC	aberrance
	aberrancy
BREH	Abernethy
BRGN	aborigine❑
BRSO	obtrusion
BRSV	obtrusive
BSAL	abysmally
BSEL	abashedly
BSME	Abu Simbel
BSMN	abasement
	abashment
BSNS	obeseness
BSVL	abusively
BTHC	a bit thick
BTIE	abstainer
BTMN	abatement
BTNC	obstinacy
BTNN	abstinent
BTNT	obstinate
BTTI	obstetric
BUCT	obfuscate
BUDN	abounding
BUDT	absurdity
BUES	about east
BUFC	about-face
BUGT	objurgate
BUSI	about-ship
BUTO	abduction
BUTR	about-turn
BVTL	obovately
CABE	scrambled
	scrambler
CABO	scrapbook
CACE	scratched
	scratcher
CAEE	octameter
CAER	octahedra
CAGL	scraggily
CAHR	octachord
CAIE	oceanides
CAIG	scrapings
CAOA	octagonal
CAPI	eclampsia
CAPL	scrappily
CAPN	scrapping
CATE	McCartney
CAYR	scrapyard
CBCE	ice bucket
CCBL	acock-bill
CDLT	acidulate
CDLU	acidulous
CDMC	academics
CDMR	Scudamore
CDMU	Scudamour
CDOS	Acid House
	acid house
	acid-house
CEAI	schematic
CEBL	screwball
CECA	McGeechan
CECE	screecher
CEEU	screwed up
	screwed-up
CELN	Schelling
CELT	scheelite
CEMN	screaming
CENA	octennial
CENF	screen off
CENN	screening
CEOE	scleroses
CEOI	sclerosis
	sclerotia
	sclerotic
	sclerotin

Words marked ❑ can also be spelled with an initial capital letter

CESO accession
CESR accessory
CETA sciential
CETE screw them
CETI eccentric
CETN accepting
CETS scientise
scientism
scientist
CETZ scientize
CEUE scheduled
CHCE ice hockey
ice-hockey
CHRO McPherson
CIAL actinally
CIAO activator
CIBE scribbler
CIEC accidence
CIEE achimenes
scrivener
CIGO acting for
CIIA occipital
CILN schilling
CILO octillion
CIMG scrimmage
CIOR écritoire
CIPL scrimpily
CIPN scrimping
CISA scrimshaw
CITR scripture□
CITS schistose
CLAA scallawag
CLAE aculeated
ocellated
CLCA ochlocrat
CLDN occludent
CLDW scale down
CLGS ecologist
CLIE acclaimed
Schleiden
CLIG scaldings
CLLS scalpless
CLMT acclimate
CLNE Icelander
CLNI Icelandic
CLNS scaliness
CLOE scalloped
CLOI scoliosis
scoliotic
CLRS ocularist
CLSO occlusion
CLSV occlusive
CLTR sculpture
CLVT acclivity
CLVU acclivous
CLYA scallywag
CMEC e-commerce
CMLN scumbling
CMLZ schmaltzy
CMNC ecumenics
CMNS ecumenism
CMNT acuminate
CNES e converso

CNHU acanthous
CNIE Schneider
CNIL scintilla
CNLG iconology
CNLN scantling
CNMC economics
CNMS economise
economist
CNMZ economize
CNNS scantness
CNRE schnorkel
schnorrer
CNRO scenarios
CNRS scenarise
CNRZ scenarize
CNTE schnitzel
CNUE Schnauzer
CNUO ichneumon
CNZL schnozzle
COAI acrobatic
echolalia
octonarii
COAL scholarly
CODN accordant
according
CODO accordion
COEI acroteria
COFL scoopfuls
COIS scholiast
COIU ECHO virus
echo virus
COLA school cap
scroll-saw
COLN schooling
scrolling
COLO schoolboy
COLS ectoblast
ectoplasm
CONE scrounger
COOI acropolis□
COOP ectomorph
COPN accompany
COUE octopuses
COYI acronymic
COYO Scooby Doo
CPEE scuppered
CPEL a cappella
CPGA scapegoat
CPIA sceptical
CPLR scapulary
CRAT Scarlatti
CRBE scarabaei
CRCO scarecrow
sci-roccos
CRCR scorecard
CRET scarpetti
CRFE scarifier
CRHI scirrhoid
CRHN scorching
CRHU scirrhous
CRMN accrument
CRTO accretion
CRTV accretive

CRUI scorbutic
CRWS scarfwise
CSAE ice-skater
CSAS écossaise
CSHR ecosphere
CSSE ecosystem
CTBL acetabula
CTBV a cut above
CTEE scattered
scatterer
CTHG Scotch egg
CTLN acetylene
CTLO ocotillos
CTLU scutellum
CTMT scotomata
CTNS acuteness
CTPN Scots pine
CTSS ecstasise
CTSZ ecstasize
CTYI ichthyoid
CUAC occupancy
CUAO scrutator
CUAT occupants
CUBN scrubbing
CUBR scrub-bird
CUDE scoundrel
CUDS I could use
CUEC acquiesce
CUGN scourging
CUHL scrum half
CUIG scourings
CULN scrubland
CULO a couple of
CULR McCullers
CULS actualise
CULT actuality
CULZ actualize
CUMG scrummage
CUOR scrutoire
CURA actuarial
CURN acquiring
occurrent
occurring
CUTA acquittal
CUTC acoustics
CUTE acquitted
CUTO actuation
CUTS occultism
occultist
CVNE scavenger
CYIS ecdysiast
CZNE scazontes
DACN advancing
DADA Edwardian
DAEC adjacency
DAHM Ideal Home
DAHR adiaphora
DAIE idealized
idealizer
DASA ad nauseam
DATG advantage
DBLT edibility
DBSO Edgbaston

DCAL edictally
DCTO education
DCTR educatory
DCTV educative
DEAA idled away
DEAC idle fancy
DEAI adrenalin
DEBA adverbial
DEEC adherence
DEET adherents
DEHE idle wheel
DEOS idle boast
DEOT Edgeworth
DESL adversely
DESR admeasure
adversary□
DEST adversity
DETN advertent
DETO edged tool
DETR adventure
DETS Adventist
advertise
DETV adjective
DGAT Adi Granth
DIAL admirable
admirably
advisable
advisably
DIAT Admiralty
DIBN ad-libbing
DIEL advisedly
DIGO Eddington
DILN Edwin Land
DIMI Edwin Muir
DISO admission
DITN admitting
DITO addiction
DITR admixture
DITV addictive
DJBA odd-jobman
DJBE odd-jobber
DKBA aduki bean
DLEE adulterer
DLES edelweiss
DLHO adulthood
DLLO Adolf Loos
DLSU odalisque
DLTE odd-lotter
DLTO adulation
DLTR adulatory
DLZN idolizing
DMMT Adam Smith
DMNL adamantly
DMNU odd man out
DMRT adumbrate
DNAG odontalgy
DNIA adenoidal
identical
DNII identikit□
DNKO I don't know
DNME odd number
DNMT adenomata
DNOA odontomas

DNUG Edinburgh
DOAI idiomatic
DOBN adsorbent
DODO Edmondson
DOEU odd one out
DOIE ad hominem
DONN adjoining
DOOU ideologue
DORE adjourned
DORP ideograph
DPAL adaptable
DPIU adoptious
DPNS adeptness
DRHN Adar Sheni
DRMN adornment
DRNL adoringly
DRSE addressee
addresses
DRTO adoration
DRUL odorously
DSBB Adis Abeba
DSUT Eduskunta
DTPA Edith Piaf
DTRA editorial
DUAC adjutancy
DUCL adjunctly
DUGN adjudging
DUIL adducible
DULS odourless
EAAA be bananas
EAAE separated
separates
EAAL debatable
get-at-able
reparable
reparably
repayable
separable
separably
EAAO separator
EACD penal code
EACE debauched
debauchee
EACF decalcify
EACN renascent
EACO sea anchor
EACS legal case
EACT defalcate
demarcate
EADA hem and haw
EADE Depardieu
EADI web and pin
EADN celandine
demanding
Geraldine
regarding
retardant
rewarding
EADT decaudate
EADU nefandous
regardful
EAEA beta decay
temazepam
EAEC decadence
Hexateuch
recalesce
remanence
remanency
EAED Mesa Verde
EAEE hexameter
EAEI Melanesia
menagerie
EAEL belatedly
EAEN ten a penny
EAEO Decameron
female dog
EAER decametre
hexahedra
secateurs
EAET megadeath
megahertz
related to
EAEU ceraceous
sebaceous
setaceous
EAHA selachian
EAHM seraphims
EAHN detaching
megaphone
seraphins
EAHO decathlon
refashion
EAHR hexachord
semaphore
EAHS metaphase
EAIE legalized
relatives
EAIH set alight
EAII hepatitis
keratitis
EAIL Delafield
EAIN menadione
relations
EAIR decalitre
EAIT reradiate
retaliate
EAIU behaviour
feracious
nefarious
tenacious
veracious
vexatious
EALA set afloat
EALE defaulter
EALI metalloid
EALN detailing
EALO default on
Heraklion
medallion
seraglios
EALS Jena glass
medallist
metallise
EALZ metallize
set ablaze
EAMN debarment
repayment
EANE remainder
EANN demanning
regaining
remaining
EANR retainers
EAOA decagonal
hexagonal
melanomas
EAOE keratoses
telamones
teratogen
EAOI demagogic
keratosis
melatonin
metabolic
pedagogic
EAON get around
EAOU Decalogue
demagogue
pedagogue
EAPA sex appeal
EAPN decamping
recapping
EAQE Velázquez
EARA repairman
EARC set a price
EARI Delacroix
EARN debarring
mepacrine
veratrine
EARS get across
EASN relapsing
EASO because of
EATA Sebastian
EATC semantics
EATL hexastyle
EATN departing
Levantine
recasting
EATO redaction
EATR departure
depasture
megastore
recapture
repasture
EATS pedantise
pedantism
Vedantism
EATT devastate
EATZ pedantize
EAUK megabucks
EAUT devaluate
EAUU tenaculum
EAWR metalwork
EAYA legal year
EAYH Netanyahu
EBAC semblance
EBAD Rembrandt
EBAI herb-Paris
EBAL semblably
EBCA get back at
EBCD herbicide
EBCL Benbecula
EBCT get back to
EBES redbreast
EBEZ sea breeze
EBFR leg before
set before
EBGE get bigger
EBHN get behind
EBIG Redbridge
EBLE herbal tea
EBLS herbalism
herbalist
verbalise
verbalism
verbalist
EBLZ verbalize
EBOE temblores
EBOK Mel Brooks
EBRL kerb drill
EBRS herborise
EBRU herbarium
EBRZ herborize
EBSD set beside
EBSL verbosely
EBST verbosity
EBTE get better
EBTN kerbstone
EBUG Zeebrugge
EBUN Melbourne
EBVR herbivore
herbivory
EBVT Leibovitz
ECAC perchance
ECAE Neuchâtel
ECAG sea change
ECAL peaceable
peaceably
reachable
teachable
ECBE fencibles
ECBL beach-ball
ECBY Beach Boys
ECEC nescience
ECEO Percheron
ECET new-create
ECHA beachhead
ECHL bench-hole
ECIE described
describer
ECIO zecchinos
ECLA herculean❑
ECLE get colder
penciller
ECLK leechlike
ECLN vetchling
ECLO Deucalion
ECLS fenceless
merciless
ECLT percolate
ECMN see coming
welcoming
ECMR benchmark
ECNE descender

rescinded
ECNL peccantly
ECNO descend on
ECNR mercenary
ECNS deaconess
ECON re-echoing
ECOU mercy on us
ECPP peace-pipe
ECPT per capita
ECPU teacupful
ECRA cercariae
mercurial
ECRE Descartes
red carpet
ECRO L'Escargot
ECRS mercerise
mercurise
ECRT mercurate
ECRU mercurous
ECRZ mercerize
mercurize
ECSA Reichstag
Wenceslas
ECSE Leicester
ECSL Newcastle
ECTM leucotomy
peacetime
ECUH get caught
ECYU Aeschylus
EDAC dead-march
EDAY hendiadys
EDBE beddy-byes
vendibles
EDCN mendicant
EDCR headscarf
EDCT mendacity
mendicity
re-educate
EDEC headreach
EDEL Leadbelly
EDEO beadledom
EDER seed-pearl
EDES lend-lease
EDGE Heidegger
EDGI verdigris
EDHN lend a hand
EDHW seldshown
EDIE dead tired
headliner
EDIH headlight
EDII dendritic
EDIS head first
EDLA Mendelian
EDLM pendulums
EDLT pendulate
EDLU pendulous
read aloud
EDMD ready-made
EDMN Desdemona
EDMU neodymium
EDNA lend an ear
Leyden jar
EDNI Pendennis
EDNL bendingly
pendently
verdantly
EDNN deadening
Ferdinand
reddening
EDNO reddendos
EDNS headiness
neediness
readiness
seediness
weediness
EDNT tending to
EDNU heading up
EDOC head voice
EDOE seed money
EDOL Dead Souls
EDON dead point
head count
EDOR headboard
EDOS deadhouse
EDOT send forth
EDRE gendarmes
EDRL seed drill
EDRN deodorant
rendering
tendering
EDRO Henderson
EDRS deodorise
headdress
EDRU verdurous
EDRZ deodorize
EDSS geodesist
EDTC feedstock
headstock
EDTL headstall
EDTN headstone
EDTO perdition
rendition
vendition
EDTR head start
EDUL heedfully
needfully
EDUO heedful of
tend out on
EDVL Red devils
EDWO Les Dawson
EDWR send a wire
EDWT get down to
EDXE Ted Dexter
EEAC relevance
relevancy
severance
EEAE delegated
delegates
serenader
venerated
EEAH telepathy
EEAI federarie
generalia
EEAL deferable
delegable
generally
referable
relegable
renewable
severable
severally
vegetable
vegetably
venerable
venerably
EEAO generator
renegados
EEAR Téméraire
EEBC Feuerbach
EEBE Meyerbeer
EEBR Lederberg
EEBS level best
EEBU hereabout
EECA seneschal
EECN senescent
EECO Peter Cook
EECP telescope□
EECS repercuss
EEDH Heyerdahl
EEDN beheading
defendant
defending
dependant
dependent
rereading
EEDR legendary
EEDW level down
EEDY Seven Days
EEEC deference
reference
reverence
vehemence
EEED referenda
EEEE Never Ever
telemeter
EEEH tête-bêche
EEEL cerebella
Gene Kelly
EEEO pedereros
set eyes on
EEER here we are
telemetry
EEFE hereafter
EEFL sevenfold
EEGE beleaguer
EEGN detergent
revenging
EEGT Serengeti
EEGV revengive
EEHA petechiae
petechial
Peterhead
EEHG repechage
EEHL Peter Hall
EEHN telephone
telephony
EEHT telephoto
EEIA genetical
heretical
EEIE beneficed
redeliver
teredines
EEIG Beveridge
EEIT derelicts
EEIU Severinus
EEIV Genevieve
EELG genealogy
teleology
EELI peneplain
EELK rebel-like
EELN leger-line
levelling
rebelling
repealing
repellant
repellent
repelling
revealing
revelling
EELO rebellion
EELR jewellery
EELT cerecloth
EEMN deferment
determent
determine
never mind
redeeming
revetment
EEMR nevermore
EENA decennial
perennial
EENE Aegean Sea
hereunder
EENN demeaning
EENS levelness
EENT perennate
EENU demeanour
EEOD mere words
EEOE developed
developer
EEOI bene vobis
peperomia
EEOO heterodox
EEOR bête noire
EEOY heteronym
EEPN reserpine
EERA rehearsal
EERE rehearser
EERI meteoroid
EERM cerebrums
EERN celebrant
deterrent
deterring
penetrant
peregrine□
veneering
EERO tenebrios
EERP telegraph
EERS tenebrism
tenebrose
EERT celebrate
celebrity

Words marked □ can also be spelled with an initial capital letter

cerebrate
desecrate
meteorite
penetrate
tenebrity
terebrate
EERU Demetrius
tenebrous
EESA petersham
seven seas
EESG Red Ensign
EESL reversely
EESM Release Me
EESN reversing
EESO Peter Snow
recension
recession
reversion
secession
EESR necessary
remeasure
EEST necessity
EESV defensive
recessive
EETA celestial
fenestral
EETE seventeen
seventies
EETL seventhly
EETN besetting
Celestine
cementing
dejecting
Heseltine
relenting
repeating
repentant
EETO deception
defection
dejection
desertion
detection
detention
reception
refection
rejection
resection
retention
selection
EETR debenture
defeature
mesentery
refectory
repertory
retexture
sedentary
EETS defeatism
defeatist
EETT Nefertiti
tête-à-tête
EETU deceitful
resentful
select out
EETV deceptive
defective
detective
receptive
retentive
selective
EEUL Venezuela
EEVI reservoir
EEVN deceiving
deserving
receiving
EEVR decemviri
decemvirs
EEVS reservist
EEWT level with
EEYN remedying
EFAE beefeater□
EFBS self-abuse
EFCE perfected
EFCL perfectly
EFCO perfectos
EFDT perfidity
EFEL leaf cells
EFFL kerfuffle
EFIG Selfridge
EFIN pen-friend
EFLE beefaloes
EFLO bedfellow
gerfalcon
EFMG self-image
EFMN feoffment
EFMR perfumery
EFNN deafening
EFNS beefiness
EFOB self-doubt
EFOI set foot in
EFOT self-worth
EFRD self-pride
EFRE performed
performer
EFRI perfervid
EFRL new for old
EFRN seafaring
self-wrong
EFRO Jefferson
EFRS New Forest
welfarism
welfarist
EFRT perforate
set fire to
EFRV self-drive
EFSL selfishly
EFSO perfusion
EFTA beefsteak
EFWU fee-faw-fum
EGAC sergeancy
vengeance
EGAG Red Grange
EGAH geography
EGAL vengeably
weighable
EGBO Mel Gibson
EGBU neighbour
EGDW weigh down
EGEL feignedly
EGEU weighed-up
EGHL lengthily
EGHN Leigh Hunt
EGIE New Guinea
EGIT weigh into
EGLS Bengalese
EGMO Sedgemoor
EGNE bergander
merganser
EGNL beggingly
EGRE Teagarden
EGRO Ben Gurion
Ben-Gurion
EGTI Neo-Gothic
neo-gothic
EGTL weightily
EGTN weighting
EGTO Bergström
EGUO weigh upon
EGWS wedgewise
EGWT weigh with
EHAC Beth March
déchéance
EHBT Rechabite
EHDN methadone
pethidine
EHDS methodise
Methodism
Methodist
EHDU Methodius
EHDZ methodize
EHEE Bethlehem
EHFL reshuffle
EHGE get higher
Ted Hughes
EHIA technical
EHII nephritic
nephritis
EHIU technique
EHLG nephology
EHLI tephillin
EHLO get hold of
EHLS nephalism
nephalist
EHLT lethality
methylate
EHNA Zephaniah
EHNC mechanics
EHNE redhanded
red-handed
EHNI bethankit
EHNS mechanise
mechanism
EHNT set hand to
EHNZ mechanize
EHOG be through
EHPN reshaping
EHRA Zechariah
EHRH recherché
EHRI Gerhardie
lethargic
EHRU lecherous
EHTO Len Hutton
EHUF réchauffé
EHVT yeshivoth
EHWN reshowing
EIAA perinatal
EIAC heritance
hesitance
hesitancy
EIAD Mélisande
EIAE dedicated
dedicatee
depilated
medicated
EIAI devil a bit
genitalia
Semiramis
EIAL decimally
definable
definably
derivable
derivably
desirable
desirably
Géricault
helically
heritable
heritably
lexically
medicable
medically
revisable
revivable
revivably
seminally
veritable
veritably
EIAN devil a one
EIAO decimator
dedicator
EIAS demitasse
EIAY perikarya
EICE bewitched
EICI meniscoid
EICN dehiscent
desiccant
EICP periscope
EICR debit card
EICT desiccate
EIDA Red Indian
EIDN reminding
EIDU remindful
EIEA mediaeval
EIEB decided by
EIEC penitence
residence
residency
reticence
EIEE deliverer
perimeter
EIEF demi-deify
EIEI peripetia
EIEL decidedly

Words marked □ can also be spelled with an initial capital letter

refinedly
reticella
retiredly
EIER decimetre
EIET delineate
residents
EIEU sericeous
EIFA relief map
EIFU petit four
EIGA Hemingway
meningeal
EIGE Bering Sea
seeing red
EIGN besieging
rejigging
EIGO Lexington
EIGS Pekingese
EIGT redingote
EIHE benighted
delighted
EIHI delight in
EIHN perishing
set in hand
EIHR periphery
EIHS fetichise
fetishise
fetishism
fetishist
EIHZ fetichize
fetishize
EIIA genitival
medicinal
regicidal
veridical
EIIC reminisce
EIIE delimited
feliciter
EIII peridinia
retinitis
semi-rigid
EIIM deliriums
EIIN deficient
recipient
resilient
EIIR decilitre
EIIS religiose
religioso
EIIT feminists
EIIU delicious
delirious
Leviticus
redivivus
religieux
religious
seditious
EIJR petit jury
EIKN Cecil King
EILG aetiology
semiology
EILH megillahs
EILI venial sin
EILO decillion
penillion
EILR vexillary
EILS aerialist
genialise
periclase
serialise
serialism
EILT feuilleté
geniality
legislate
megilloth
EILZ genialize
serialize
EIMN devilment
refitment
remitment
EIMT melismata
EINE Periander
EINL defiantly
leniently
EINN beginning
benignant
designing
EINO reliant on
EINR legionary
EINS Fenianism
fetidness
EINT benignity
designate
gelignite
EIOD demi-monde
EIOE pericones
semivowel
EIOI peridotic
semitonic
EIOO periboloi
semicolon
EIOR Demi Moore
EIPA Lenin Peak
EIPR perisperm
EIRE pedigreed
EIRF denitrify
devitrify
EIRP serigraph
EIRS heritress
EIRT denigrate
denitrate
meliorate
remigrate
seniority
EIRV semibreve
EISA heliostat
EISL peninsula
EISO remission
EISU régisseur
EISV remissive
EITA leviathan❑
registrar
EITC semiotics
EITE belittler
EITI geriatric
EITL mediately
peristyle
seriately
EITN befitting
deviating
mediating
refitting
remittent
resistant
resisting
EITO depiction
deviation
mediation
EITP heliotype
heliotypy
EITR be history
mediatory
registers
EITS mediatise
EITV depictive
mediative
EITZ mediatize
EIUA reliquiae
reticular
retinulae
vehicular
vesiculae
EIUL deviously
seriously
tediously
EIUR reliquary
residuary
EIUU deciduous
de rigueur
reticulum
EIVI believe in
EIVN believing
relieving
EIVR believers
EIWT get in with
EIYN verifying
EJCE bed-jacket
EJNO Ben Jonson
EJRE New Jersey
EKAI Reykjavík
EKBU week about
EKDA peaked cap
EKDU decked out
EKEE beekeeper
EKEI leukaemia
EKFE seek after
EKHR Berkshire
EKIH weeknight
EKLT neckcloth
EKLU berkelium
EKNA Peckinpah
EKNE weak-kneed
weekender
EKNF Pecksniff
EKNN reckoning
weakening
EKNS jerkiness
leakiness
perkiness
EKOE seek votes
EKON desk-bound
weak point
EKRO leakproof
EKTE sex kitten
EKWT Berkowitz
ELAD hellwards
ELAE hell-hated
tell tales
well-baked
well-famed
ELAH bellyache
belly-ache
ELBA jelly bean
ELBB jelly baby
ELBE beslobber
beslubber
ELBR hellebore
ELCE neglected
ELCI tesla coil
ELCO deflector
real McCoy
reflect on
reflector
ELCS bellicose
ELCT replicate
vellicate
ELEI Nellie Kim
ELEN wellbeing
well-being
ELEU Beelzebub
ELFE feel after
ELFO belly-flop
ELFS jellyfish
ELGE jet-lagged
ELGI pellagrin
tell again
ELGN negligent
ELGS geologise
geologist
neologise
neologism
neologist
ELGZ geologize
neologize
ELHA feel cheap
wealth tax
ELHE fellaheen
healthier
ELHL healthily
wealthily
ELHN cellphone
ELHR sell short
ELHU healthful
ELIE declaimer
reclaimer
well-aimed
well-liked
well-oiled
well-timed
ELLC hell-black
ELLI celluloid®
get laldie
ELLK jelly-like

ELLS	cellulose
	realmless
ELLT	cellulite
ELMK	sell smoke
ELML	feel small
ELMU	beglamour
ELNL	feelingly
	healingly
	reelingly
	tellingly
ELNN	declining
	reclining
	red-lining
ELNS	Ceylonese
	Hellenise
	Hellenism
	Hellenist
	replenish
ELNT	reclinate
ELNW	well known
	well-known
ELNZ	Hellenize
ELOE	be all over
	bell tower
	peel-tower
	tell jokes
ELOL	real world
ELON	hellhound
	Neil Young
ELOR	feel sorry
ELPN	well-spent
ELPR	tell apart
ELRA	tellurian
ELRE	well-armed
	Zeller See
ELRG	cellarage
ELRS	tellurise
ELRT	deflorate
	hell-broth
ELRU	tellurium
ELRZ	tellurize
ELSI	realistic
ELSL	hellishly
	reclusely
ELSO	reclusion
	seclusion
ELSV	reclusive
ELTE	realities
	red-letter
ELTF	pelletify
ELTI	neolithic❑
ELTL	tell a tale
ELTN	deflating
ELTO	deflation
	depletion
	fellatios
	reflation
	repletion
ELTP	Sellotape®
ELTR	pellitory
ELTS	pelletise
ELTZ	pelletize
ELUL	jealously
	well-built
	zealously
ELUO	jealous of
ELUT	belly up to
ELVT	declivity
ELVU	declivous
ELWD	newlyweds
ELWE	Yellow Sea
ELWS	yellowish
ELWT	dealt with
ELWU	mellow out
ELXO	reflexion
ELXR	reflex arc
ELXV	reflexive
EMAC	permeance
EMAE	permeated
EMAL	permeable
	permeably
EMCB	set much by
EMCD	germicide
	vermicide
EMFR	vermiform
EMGN	termagant
EMIE	Des Moines
EMIL	vermeille
EMLE	Lee Miller
	red mullet
EMLN	reimplant
EMLO	permalloy
	vermilion
EMME	new member
EMNA	segmental
EMNC	Germanice
EMNE	fermented
EMNL	beamingly
	germanely
	seemingly
EMNN	permanent
EMNO	Lermontov
EMNS	Germanise
	Pelmanism
	seaminess
	sermonise
EMNT	germinate
	terminate
	verminate
EMNU	germanium
	verminous
EMNZ	Germanize
	sermonize
EMOT	Helmholtz
EMRE	newmarket❑
EMRS	mesmerise
	mesmerism
	mesmerist
EMRZ	mesmerize
EMTC	hermetics
EMTE	permitted
EMTG	hermitage❑
EMTI	dermatoid
	geometric
EMTO	gemmation
	new method
EMTS	lemmatise
EMTT	pegmatite
	permutate
EMTZ	lemmatize
EMUS	reimburse
EMXC	New Mexico
ENAD	Bernhardt
	Reinhardt
ENAE	herniated
ENAS	Léon Bakst
ENEE	Bernières
	Jean Genet
	Jennie Lee
ENEI	Jean Genie
ENEL	Sean Kelly
ENER	reindeers
ENES	beanfeast
ENET	Jeannette
ENFR	penniform
ENHL	Benny Hill
	meanwhile
ENIH	neon light
ENLN	Jenny Lind
	Penny Lane
ENLS	penniless
	vernalise
ENLZ	vernalize
ENMT	reanimate
ENNE	Fernandel
ENNL	meaningly
ENNO	Cernunnos
ENOC	re-enforce
	reinforce
ENOI	be in for it
ENRU	meandrous
ENSA	Dennis Law
	Keynesian
	Wednesday
ENSE	Tennessee
ENTI	Bernstein
ENTL	beanstalk
	be in a tale
	reinstall
	re-install
	ternately
ENTO	vernation
ENTT	reinstate
ENUL	Bernoulli
	heinously
ENUO	be one up on
ENWS	penny-wise
ENZS	Neo-Nazism
EOAC	resonance
EOAD	memoranda
EOAE	decorated
	desolater
	zero-rated
EOAL	deposable
	memorable
	memorably
	removable
	removably
	revocable
	revocably
	revokable
EOAO	decorator
	detonator
	renovator
	resonator
EOAS	menopause
EOBN	recombine
	resorbent
EOCE	retoucher
	tenor clef
EOCG	heroic age
EOCI	rejoice in
EOCK	Genoa cake
EOCL	reconcile
EOCN	rejoicing
EOCP	fetoscopy
EOCR	lemon curd
EODN	beyond one
	recording
	rewording
	seconding
EODO	beyond you
	lemon drop
	second job
EODR	secondary
EODT	recondite
EODU	tenor-drum
EODW	bed of down
EOEA	before tax
EOEC	redolence
	redolency
EOEE	pedometer
	recovered
	recoverer
EOEG	set on edge
EOEL	become ill
	devotedly
	reposedly
EOEO	before now
EOET	devoted to
EOEU	reposeful
EOFE	web offset
EOFO	set on foot
EOFR	set on fire
EOGN	belonging
EOGS	decongest
EOHB	xenophobe
	xenophoby
EOHG	oesophagi
EOHL	mesophyll
	oenophile
EOHS	telophase
EOHT	xerophyte
EOIA	genocidal
EOIE	memoriter
	Menominee
EOII	neroli oil
EOIL	memorials
EOIN	defoliant
	devotions
EOIO	depositor
EOIT	defoliate

negotiate
EOIU felonious
ferocious
melodious
Véronique
EOKN reworking
EOLC recollect
EOLD remoulade
rémoulade
EOLM be to blame
EOLN aeroplane
EOLT decollate
décolleté
EOMN recommend
reforming
EOMS reformism
reformist
EOMT Aerosmith
deformity
EONA recountal
EONE denouncer
recounter
rejoinder
renouncer
EONN De Kooning
EONO besognios
EONS recognise
EONZ recognize
EOOI serotonin
EOOP mesomorph
EOOS meno mosso
EOOU Herodotus
EOPC aerospace
EOPE lemon peel
EOPG decoupage
découpage
EOPN recouping
EOPS decompose
EORC democracy
EORE recourses
resources
EORM aerodrome
melodrama
velodrome
EORN devouring
EORS memoirist
EORT Zenocrate
EOSA A E Housman
EOSL lemon sole
EOSN rehousing
EOSS repossess
EOTG reportage
EOTN befortune
remontant
reporting
revolting
EOTO decoction
decontrol
retortion
EOTR decocture
lemon tart
reporters
EOUI ketonuria
EOUL resoluble
EOVN reconvene
resolvent
revolving
EOVR reconvert
EOWL get on well
EOWT get on with
EOYI genotypic
metonymic
EPAC keep watch
EPAE deep water
EPAT keep faith
EPCE henpecked
henpecker
respected
respecter
EPCL bespeckle
EPEA Temple Bar
EPEE perplexed
EPET hey-presto
EPGA Perpignan
EPGE serpigoes
EPIE despoiler
EPII delphinia
EPIL deep field
EPIT key points
EPIU Delphinus
EPLE leg-puller
EPLV keep alive
EPMN Melpomene
EPMT despumate
EPNC geoponics
keep an act
EPNE keep under
EPNL bespangle
weepingly
EPNN deepening
reopening
EPNO responsor
EPNT respond to
EPOE deep-toned
EPOI neophobia
neophobic
EPON keep going
reappoint
EPOR keep hours
EPOS keep house
EPPC deep space
EPPE Red Pepper
red pepper
EPPR keep apart
EPRA Hesperian
EPRD desperado
EPRE Jespersen
EPRN pepperoni
tempering
EPRO new person
per person
EPRR temporary
EPRS new phrase
set phrase
temporise
temptress
EPRT desperate
temperate
EPRZ temporize
EPSA Vespasian
EPSE get pissed
penpusher
pen-pusher
EPTA keep at bay
perpetual
EPTE bespatter
EPTR keep a term
EPTS despotism
EPUE keep quiet
EPUL helpfully
EPUR keep guard
EPVL Deepavali
EQEE becquerel□
ERAC recreance
recreancy
ERAD rearwards
ERAG rearrange
ERAH heartache
ERAI gear ratio
ERAS Béarnaise
ERBA ferry-boat
heartbeat
ERBC Pearl Buck
reprobacy
ERBE sea robber
sea-robber
ERBR heartburn
ERBT reprobate
retribute
ERCD retrocede
ERCE refracted
ERCI Petruchio
ERCO detractor
refractor
retractor
ERCS metricise
reprocess
verrucose
ERCT deprecate
metricate
ERCU verrucous
ERCZ metricize
ERDA heart-dear
Hebridean
ERDC reproduce
ERDE bedridden
bed-ridden
ERDN degrading
ERDS Petri dish
ERDT depredate
EREA retrieval
EREE gear-lever
retriever
EREL beer belly
beer-belly
learnedly
EREO George Fox
ERET georgette□
Henrietta
ERFE petrified
retroflex
terrified
ERFG febrifuge
ERFL heartfelt
heart-felt
ERFO fear of God
ERFR Henry Ford
terraform
ERGA deprogram
pearl-gray
ERGE pearl-grey
ERGL bedraggle
ERGT segregate
ERHB Beersheba
ERHE gearwheel
ERHN bear a hand
near thing
reprehend
searching
ERHO search for
ERHU search out
ERIA negroidal
recruital
ERIE pearlised
pearlized
recruiter
ERIH rear light
ERII pearlitic
ERIN Georgiana
ERJC retroject
ERLG neurology
petrology
tetralogy
ERLI neuralgia
neuralgic
ERLN heartland
heartling
ERLO Negrillos
ERLS beardless
heartless
weariless
ERLT serrulate
ERLU petroleum
pétroleur
ERMN decrement
detriment
merriment
reprimand
year's mind
ERMT neuromata
ERNE derringer
ERNL jeeringly
leeringly
terrenely
veeringly
wearingly
ERNM metronome
ERNS merriness
weariness
weirdness
ERNU Petronius
ERNV Terranova

Words marked □ can also be spelled with an initial capital letter

ERNW dear knows
EROC near touch
ERON bear young
year-round
ERPO bear up for
ERPR tear apart
ERRC Jerry Rice
ERRI bear fruit
ERRS terrorise
terrorism
terrorist
ERRU peer group
terrarium
ERRZ terrorize
ERSA pearl spar
Petrosian
ERSC heartsick
ERSE Beardsley
defroster
depressed
refreshed
refreshen
refresher
repressed
ERSI heuristic
peirastic
ERSK Petrushka
ERSL bearishly
ERSM wearisome
ERSN represent
re-present
ERSO depressor
repressor
ERSR heart-sore
ERTA betrothal
Nemrut Dag
ERTC gear-stick
ERTE betrothed
ERTN rewriting
ERTO detrition
secretion
serration
ERTR secretary
secretory
territory
ERTS necrotise
ERTT Henry Tate
ERTU ferret out
regretful
ERTV secretive
ERTZ necrotize
ERUE defrauder
ERUL fearfully
tearfully
ERUR rearguard
ERUS retroussé
ERVI Henry VIII
ERVN depraving
reproving
ERVO deprive of
ERVR retrovert
ERVT depravity
ERWO heartwood
Henry Wood
zebrawood
ERWR pearlwort
ERYE nearly new
nearly-new
ERYL nearly all
ERZO terrazzos
ESAE newspaper
persuaded
persuader
reistafel
Teeswater
ESAI Messianic
ESAL sensually
ESAN feiseanna
ESBC leaseback
ESBO Jesse Boot
ESBU mess about
ESCE fen-sucked
ESCS Persicise
ESCT persecute
ESCZ Persicize
ESDT sense data
ESEI Deusdedit
Menshevik
news media
ESEN persienne
ESEO penstemon
ESFE versifier
ESFR ceasefire
cease-fire
ESGN newsagent
ESHE news sheet
news-sheet
ESHL leasehold
ESHR geosphere
Welsh harp
ESIA deistical
ESIC hem-stitch
ESIE red spider
ESIR vers libre
ESLA tessellae
ESLK beastlike
ESLN lease-lend
Messalina
ESLS ceaseless
newsflash
senseless
ESLT pensility
tensility
ESME Welsummer
ESML fee simple
ESMN jessamine
ESMO persimmon
ESMS pessimism
pessimist
ESNA yersiniae
yersinias
ESNE messenger
personnel
ESNF personify
ESNG personage
ESNL teasingly
ESNN lessening
reasoning
seasoning
ESNO messing on
ESNR peasantry
ESNS denseness
messiness
newsiness
personise
tenseness
terseness
ESNT pepsinate
personate
ESNZ personize
ESOA sessional
versional
ESOE pensioner
ESON newshound
ESOO get shot of
ESPN Welsh Pony
ESRA bedspread
censorial
menstrual
ESRK keystroke
ESRL berserkly
leisurely
sensorily
ESRN measuring
newsprint
ESRU measure up
newsgroup
sensorium
ESSI persist in
ESTE bedsitter
bed-sitter
ESTL versatile
ESTN news-stand
ESTO cessation
sensation
ESTR tessitura
ESTS sensitise
ESTV sensitive
ESTZ sensitize
ESUE pea-souper
reassured
reassurer
ESUR set square
set-square
ESVL pensively
ESVR persevere
ESWN seesawing
ESWS fesse-wise
ESWY leastways
ETAC test match
ETAD Bert Hardy
leftwards
westwards
ETAE test paper
ETAL centrally
dextrally
meatballs
neutrally
ventrally
ETAN be at pains
restraint
ETAT central to
ETBA vertebrae
vertebral
ETBL vestibule
ETBO death blow
death-blow
ETBU Betty Blue
west-about
ETCA petticoat
ETCD menticide
pesticide
ETCE tentacled
testicles
ETCN fettucine
fettucini
ETCS Pentecost
petty cash
ETCT septicity
ETDA Seated Man
ETDT death duty
ETEA gentleman
ETEC sentience
ETEE feathered
weathered
wet the bed
ETEI aesthetic
ETEL genteelly
ETEO settle for
weather on
ETER leg theory
ETES Zeitgeist
ETET heat death
vestments
Westmeath
ETEU kettleful
ETEX get the axe
ETFE certified
certifier
rectifier
testifier
ETFI next of kin
ETFR tectiform
ETFT testify to
ETFV set to five
ETGA hectogram
pentagram
vestigial
ETGR Kentigern
ETIE rectrices
tectrices
ETIG restringe
see things
settlings
ETIL centriole
certainly
ventricle
ETIO certain of
neutrinos
test pilot
ETIT certainty
pertain to

ETKO get to know
ETLA reptilian
ETLG pestology
ETLK deathlike
death-like
ETLL fertilely
ETLN pestilent
ETLS deathless
fertilise
gentilise
ETLT fertility
gentility
mentality
ventilate
ETLZ fertilize
gentilize
ETME destemper
September
ETMN sentiment
testament
testimony
ETNC tectonics
ETNI letting in
septennia
ETNL jestingly
meltingly
peltingly
pentangle
rectangle
sea tangle
ETNN pertinent
ETNO getting on
ETNR centenary
ETNS heftiness
meatiness
peptonise
pettiness
testiness
Teutonise
ETNT bentonite
festinate
pectinate
ETNU neptunium
setting up
setting-up
ETNZ peptonize
Teutonize
ETOA kept woman
sectional
ETOE Beethoven
best-loved
destroyed
destroyer
mentioned
oestrogen
ETOI geotropic
leitmotif
leitmotiv
ETOL next world
ETON westbound
ETOS dextrorse
penthouse□
West Coast

ETPD centipede
ETPE septuplet
sextuplet
ETRA gesture at
nectarean
rectorial
sectarian
sectorial
tectorial
yesterday
ETRE letterset
perturbed
Ted Turner
westerner
ETRF better off
ETRH heptarchy
ETRI sestertia
ETRN festering
lettering
mentoring
nectarine
pestering
restoring
teetering
vetturini
westering
ETRO centurion
ETRS neoterise
sectorise
texturise
vectorise
ETRT death rate
deuterate
dexterity
rectorate
reiterate
ETRU deuterium
dexterous
nectarous
tetterous
ETRV test drive
ETRZ neoterize
sectorize
texturize
vectorize
ETSA death star
pertussal
ETSI pertussis
ETSL pettishly
ETSM centesimo
leptosome
ETSR dentistry
ETST pertusate
ventosity
ETTA deathtrap
ETTD beatitude
certitude
rectitude
ETTL death toll
ETTM teetotums
ETTN hestitant
ETTO dentition
gestation

sestettos
ETTT destitute
ETTV tentative
ETUI beat music
ETUL restfully
zestfully
ETUU Centaurus
ETVL festively
restively
ETVR leftovers
ETVT aestivate
festivity
ETWL tea towels
ETWN delta-wing
ETWR deathward
set to work
ETWS death wish
ETXD pentoxide
EUAC petulance
petulancy
recusance
recusancy
EUAE Jerusalem
regulated
EUAL deludable
rebukable
refusable
refutable
refutably
regularly
reputable
reputably
resumable
secularly
securable
tegularly
EUAO peculator
regulator
EUAT beaux arts
débutante
EUBA penumbral
EUBN decumbent
recumbent
EUBS refurbish
EUCE requicken
EUCI sea urchin
EUCM set up camp
EUCN demulcent
EUCR sepulchre
EUDA gerundial
EUDE befuddled
EUDN redundant
EUDT fecundate
fecundity
EUDV gerundive
EUEC Ceausescu
feculence
EUEI oecumenic
refusenik
EUEL reputedly
EUEO teruteros
EUET Beau Geste
get used to

EUEU beauteous
EUFC resurface
EUGN refulgent
resurgent
EUIE nebulizer
EUIL deducible
reducible
EUIN delusions
EUIR pecuniary
EUIT repudiate
EUIU beautiful
penurious
EULC gemütlich
genuflect
EULN beguiling
EULR medullary
EULS sexualise
EULT sexuality
EULZ sexualize
EUNE De Quincey
sequentes
EUNG béguinage
EUNI sequentia
EUNL genuinely
EUNN repugnant
returning
EUOD beau monde
EUPU desulphur
EURC resurrect
EURE fenugreek
EURN demurring
recurrent
recurring
requiring
EURO reguerdon
EUSE requested
requester
sequester
EUSF demulsify
EUSO recursion
repulsion
revulsion
set up shop
EUSR sequestra
EUST decussate
requisite
EUSV recursive
repulsive
revulsive
EUTD desuetude
EUTM penultima
EUTN reluctant
resultant
resulting
EUTO deduction
reduction
seduction
EUTR desultory
sepulture
EUTS reductase
EUTT degustate
reluctate
EUTV deductive

Words marked □ can also be spelled with an initial capital letter

9 _E_U_U

reductive
seductive
EUUL tenuously
EUWP Jesus wept
EVCI pelvic fin
EVCN servicing
EVDR belvedere❑
EVDT fervidity
heavy-duty
EVEE heavy-eyed
EVET serviette
EVIT delve into
EVLL servilely
EVLS nerveless
EVLT servility
EVLY Helvellyn
EVNE Cervantes
EVNL fervently
EVNS heaviness
EVNT ben venuto
EVPR leave port
EVRE perverted
EVSA heavy spar
EVSD Heaviside
EVSL peevishly
EVSO pervasion
EVSV pervasive
EVTA Helvetian
EVTD servitude
EVTE velveteen
EVTM serve time
EVUL nervously
EVWR leave work
EWKT be awake to
EWNO get wind of
EWRE networker
EWRH seaworthy
EWRL seawardly
EWSE get washed
EWST get wise to
EWTI get with it
EXDS deoxidise
EXDT deoxidate
EXDZ deoxidize
EXMN re-examine
EXUE be excused
EYAO be by way of
EYHN hedyphane
EYIH Very light
EYLN recycling
EYLU beryllium
EYML very small
EYNL denyingly
EYOS very noisy
EYRA very great
EYRI aepyornis
EYRT dehydrate
rehydrate
EYTF demystify
EZNN mezzanine
EZRM terze rime
EZTN mezzotint
EZTO terzettos
EZVC mezza voce
EZWG Fezziwigg
FADN ifs and ans
FAOI aflatoxin
FCLU off colour
off-colour
FCNR off-centre
FCUS off course
off-course
FEBC Offenbach
FECR aftercare
FEDC after deck
FEDN offending
FEGO afterglow
FEKN after kind
FELF afterlife
after-life
FEMT aftermath
FEND J F Kennedy
FENO afternoon
FENS oftenness
FESV offensive
FETA after that
effectual
FETN affecting
effecting
FETO affection
FETR offertory
FETV affective
effective
FEVC of service
FEWR afterword
FHNE offhanded
FHTL of that ilk
FIAE Afrikaner
FIAI affidavit
FIAN Afrikaans
FIIA officinal
FIIN efficient
officiant
FIIT affiliate
officiate
FIIU officious
FINE affianced
FKLE off kilter
FLCE afflicted
FLEC affluence
effluence
FLGS ufologist
FLMT off limits
off-limits
FLVU effluvium
FLXO effluxion
FNMN of one mind
FOLK if you like
FOUA Afro-Cuban
FOVI of no avail
FRAD sforzandi
sforzando
FRAO sforzatos
FRCT affricate
FRHN aforehand
FRIR a fortiori
FRNE affronted
FRSI aforesaid
FRTM aforetime
FSAO offseason
FSBC a fast buck
FSDL offsaddle
FSRA off-stream
FSRE off-street
FSRN offspring
FTEA off the map
FTEE off the peg
off-the-peg
FTEI off the air
off the bit
FTRE off target
off-target
FUGN effulgent
FUPS of purpose
GAFT sgraffiti
sgraffito
GALR J G Ballard
GAOO iguanodon❑
GATN eglantine
GEAL agreeable
agreeably
GEHE Aguecheek
GEIU egregious
GEMN agreement
GENS Ogden Nash
GEOK Agnes Oaks
GESO egression
GEWT agree with
GIAL ignitable
GIIL ignitible
GIRI ugli® fruit
GMMO Agamemnon
GMNA egomaniac
GNAN agony aunt
GNNU agent noun
GNOR Agincourt
GNRN Egon Krenz
GNZN agonizing
GOAC ignorance
GOAU ignoramus
GODA a good deal
GOMN a good many
GOOI agronomic
GOOT agnolotti
GOSR a good sort
GOTR a good turn
GREE aggrieved
GRGT aggregate
GRSO aggressor
GRVT aggravate
GSAE egg-shaped
GSIE egg slicer
GTES egotheism
GTSI egotistic
GTTN agitating
GTTO agitation
GYSI ugly as sin
HAAA Ahmadabad
HAAT pheasants
HABE wheat beer
HACE the Archer
the Arches
HAEE cheapened
HAGA Chiang Mai
HAGR wheat germ
HAHN sheathing
thrashing
HAHU thrash out
HAJC cheapjack
cheap-jack
HAKN chiacking
HALN shearling
HAMA wheatmeal
HANI The Aeneid
HANS cheapness
HARC theatrics
HART cheap-rate
HATN thwarting
HAWS shoalwise
HAYE chlamydes
chlamyses
HAYI chlamydia
HBAD the boards
HBAN the brains
HBIC dhobi itch
HBIH shibuichi
HBLC Chubb® lock
HBTH who but she
HBTL the bottle
HBYM Shibayama
HBYN the Beyond
HCAA Chickasaw
chuck away
HCAE chickadee
HCAH cha-cha-cha
HCAU the cratur
HCEA Thackeray
HCEE thickened
whichever
HCEI shochetim
HCEP the creeps
HCFL chock-full
HCHA thickhead
HCIE rhachides
rhachises
HCII chuck it in
HCLG phycology
HCLN chuckling
HCLP thick-lips
HCLS checklist
HCLT chocolate
chocolaty
HCMO the common
HCMR Chico Marx
HCMT checkmate
HCNO The Cantos
HCNR chicanery
HCNS thickness
HCOD The Clouds
HCOE check over
HCUC the church
HCWE chickweed

HCWT	thick with
HCWV	shock wave
HDAA	Ehud Barak
HDEA	shudder at
HDER	shed tears
HDLO	shed blood
HDLS	shadeless
HDLT	rhodolite
HDME	the damned
HDMN	rhodamine
HDNI	whodunnit
HDNS	rhodanise
	shadiness
HDNT	rhodonite
HDNZ	rhodanize
HDPH	the depths
HDPI	rhodopsin
HDVA	khedivial
HDVL	The Devils
HDVT	khedivate
HDWN	shadowing
HEAC	wheel arch
HEAE	shoemaker□
HEBN	cheekbone
	sheet bend
HEBS	wheelbase
HECT	sheepcote
HEDC	shielduck
HEDE	three deep
HEDN	shielding
HEEF	cheese off
HEEI	threnetic
HEEO	cheesed of
HEFE	sheet-feed
HEFL	threefold
HEGT	the eights
HEHL	threshold
HEHN	shoeshine
HEII	phlebitis
HELC	sheep-lice
	shtetlach
HELK	thief-like
HELN	wheedling
HELS	cheerless
HEMC	shrewmice
HEMR	wheelmark
HENN	threonine
HENS	sheerness□
HEOE	Chaeronea
HEOI	threnodic
HESI	sheepskin
	wheel spin
HESM	threesome
HETI	chieftain
HEWL	sheepwalk
HEYL	Cheeryble
HFIC	chaffinch
HFIL	Sheffield
HFIN	The Friend
HFLN	shuffling
	whiffling
HFLS	shiftless
HGCT	phagocyte
HGIE	chagrined
HGMI	The Gambia
HGNT	shogunate
HGOE	The Grocer
HHAU	chihuahua□
HHBI	The Hobbit
HHNA	chthonian
HHRL	The Herald
HIDY	chairdays
HIGN	chain gang
HIGR	choirgirl
HIHO	sheikhdom
HIKG	shrinkage
HIKN	shrieking
	shrinking
HILF	chairlift
HILN	thrilling
HIMI	chain mail
HIPN	shrimping
HITA	Christian
	Christmas
HITL	thriftily
HITN	Christina
	Christine
HKAE	shake a leg
HKAL	shakeable
HKBC	choke back
HKDW	choke down
	shake down
HKIH	The Knight
HKNS	shakiness
HKOI	shake on it
HLAA	while away
HLAI	Chaliapin
HLBA	whaleboat
HLBN	whalebone
HLDC	sheldduck
HLDE	the ladies
HLEE	sheltered
	shelterer
HLEG	challenge
HLFL	shelf-fuls
HLFO	wholefood
HLFR	shellfire
HLFS	shellfish
HLGN	phylogeny
HLHO	childhood
HLKO	Sholokhov
HLLF	shelf-life
HLLG	philology
HLLI	chilblain
HLLK	childlike
HLLS	childless
HLMA	chalumeau
	wholemeal
HLMN	childmind
HLNE	phalanger
	phalanges
	phalanxes
	philander
HLNS	childness
	wholeness
HLOL	shallowly
HLOS	philhorse
HLPI	philippic
HLPN	Chile pine
HLRI	choleraic
HLRK	sheldrake
HLRP	phalarope
HLSI	shell suit
	thalassic
HLSL	wholesale
HLSM	wholesome
HLTL	philately
HLTS	the latest
HLUE	thalluses
HLUT	chalk up to
HLVN	the living
HLYH	whillywha
HMAN	champagne
HMEE	chamfered
	whimperer
HMET	champerty
HMIA	whimsical
HMKD	The Mikado
HMKO	thumb knot
HMLE	The Miller
HMLN	shambling
	thumbling
HMLO	chameleon□
HMLS	rhymeless
	shameless
HMLV	champlevé
HMML	chamomile
HMMN	the moment
HMNI	thumbnail
HMNS	shamanism
	shamanist
HMNT	the minute
HMNU	them and us
HMOI	shambolic
	shammosim
HMPR	theme park
HMRO	The Mirror
HMSE	rhymester
	the masses
	Thomas Tew
HMSN	theme song
	Thomasina
HMSR	chemistry
HMSY	Thomas Kyd
HMTC	thumbtack
HMTE	the matter
HMTO	the method
HMTU	shamateur
HMUE	rhombuses
HNAE	thin-faced
HNAI	phantasim
HNAL	thinkable
HNAM	phantasms
HNBC	think back
HNBU	thenabout
HNCA	china clay
HNCL	phone call
HNCU	Changchun
HNEE	whencever
HNEL	chandelle
	thin-belly
HNEN	whingeing
HNES	chanteuse
HNEU	chanceful
	changeful
HNGR	China Girl
HNHA	rhonchial
HNIL	Chantilly
HNIZ	Thin Lizzy
HNKA	Chanukkah
HNKN	Chungking
HNLG	phenology
	phonology
	rhinology
HNLR	chandlery
HNLS	thankless
HNLT	phonolite
HNMC	phonemics
HNMN	phenomena
HNNL	shiningly
	whiningly
HNNO	thin on top
HNNS	phoniness
	shininess
HNOE	think over
	whensoeer
HNOS	Shintoism
	Shintoist
HNQN	Chongqing
HNRF	chondrify
HNRL	Shangri-La
	Shangri-la
HNRU	chancrous
HNTA	chinstrap
HNTC	phenetics
	phonetics
HNTN	whinstone
HNTP	phenotype
	phonotype
HNTS	phonetise
	phonetist
HNTW	Chinatown
HNTZ	phonetize
HNUM	thingummy
HNWN	Rhine wine
HNWT	think with
HNZO	Zhengzhou
HOAA	throw away
	throwaway
	throw-away
HOAI	chromatic
	chromatid
	chromatin
	theomania
	throw a fit
HOBC	throw back
	throwback
HOBN	throbbing
HOBS	thrombose
HOCL	the occult
HODO	the old sod
HODR	throw dirt

Words marked □ can also be spelled with an initial capital letter

HODW	shoot down
	throw down
HOEI	theoretic
HOEL	chlorella
HOEU	shoot-'em-up
HOHR	Oh So Sharp
HOIE	theorizer
HOII	chromidia
	rhyolitic
HOIL	chronicle
HOIU	theorique
	whoop it up
HOOE	throw open
	throw over
HOOH	theosophy
HOOI	Theodoric
HOPN	Phnom Penh
HORC	theocracy
HOTL	throatily
HPAD	The Phaedo
HPAE	ship water
HPAL	shapeable
HPEI	whipper-in
HPHP	shipshape
HPIE	rhaphides
HPLO	shop floor
HPLS	shapeless
HPLT	chipolata
HPNK	whip snake
HPOE	the proles
HPOI	rhapsodic
HPOL	The People
HPON	whip-round
HPOR	chipboard
	shipboard
HPRA	chaparral
HPRC	shipwreck
HPRF	whip-graft
HPRN	chaperone
HPRO	the period
HPTC	whipstock
HPTL	whipstall
HPTT	the potato
HQEE	chequered
HRAA	charlatan
	thereaway
	where away?
HRAI	sherwanis
HRAL	thermally
HRAM	the real me
HRAN	Charmaine
HRAU	Pharsalus
HRBI	Charybdis
HRBL	the rabble
	thornbill
HRBM	cherubims
HRBN	charabanc
HRCA	short-coat
HRCE	character
HRCK	shortcake
HRCO	sharecrop
HRDK	Thorndike
HREA	charge-cap
HREE	chartered
	charterer
	sharpener
	sharp-eyed
	shortened
HREI	Charteris
HREK	Chernenko
HREO	Charleroi
	charnecos
HREU	sharpen up
HRFL	shortfall
HRFO	shirk from
	therefrom
HRFR	short form
	therefore
	wherefore
HRFS	short fuse
HRHA	churchman
	short-head
HRHE	churchmen
HRHL	Churchill
HRHN	shorthand
HRHR	shorthorn□
HRHT	Shere Hite
HRII	there it is
	where it is
	whirligig
HRIT	thereinto
	thirtieth
HRKA	Shere Khan
HRLI	Charolais
HRLN	chortling
	shoreline
HRLS	charmless
	shortlist
	short-list
HRMN	pheromone
HRNA	pharyngal
HRNE	pharynges
	pharynxes
HRNM	chironomy
HRNO	charangos
	Cherenkov
HRNS	chariness
	sharpness
	shortness
HROA	charwoman
HROE	chernozem
HROI	Pharaonic
HROO	the root of
HROR	Cherbourg
HROT	Charlotte
HROY	Chernobyl
HRPD	chiropody
HRPE	therapies
HRPO	whirlpool
HRPS	therapist
HRRT	third-rate
HRSE	cherished
	chorister
HRSI	pharisaic□
	sharkskin
	short slip
HRSO	the rise of
HRTE	the rather
HRTL	thirstily
HRTM	short time
HRTN	thirsting
HRTO	thirst for
HRTR	short-term
HRUO	thereupon
	whereupon
HRUT	whereunto
HRVL	The Rivals
HRWN	whirlwind
HRWR	shareware
	shoreward
HRWT	therewith
	wherewith
HRWV	short wave
HRXN	thyroxine
HRYD	cherryade
HSAA	chase away
HSAE	the shakes
	the States
HSAN	Ghislaine
HSAS	lhasa apso
HSCA	physician
HSCS	physicism
	physicist
HSDY	these days
HSEE	chastened
	whiskered
	whispered
	whisperer
	whosoever
HSHT	phosphate
HSIE	the Shires
HSII	the Spirit
HSIK	the sticks
HSLH	The Sylphs
HSLK	ghostlike
HSMA	the same as
HSRA	The Scream
HSRW	the screws
HSSE	the system
HSTW	ghost town
HSUR	The Squire
HSUU	thesaurus
HSWR	ghost word
HSXC	the sex act
HTBA	whitebeam
HTBE	The Tablet
HTBI	whitebait
HTCP	photocopy
HTCS	rhotacise
HTCZ	rhotacize
HTEE	chatterer
	shattered
HTEV	the Twelve
HTFA	that's flat
	white flag
HTFS	white fish
HTGL	white gold
HTGN	phytogeny
HTHA	whitehead□
	white heat
HTHP	what a hope
	white hope
HTIG	chitlings
HTIL	Whitfield
HTLA	white lead
HTLD	white lady
HTLE	white lies
HTLN	white line
HTLS	photolyse
HTMA	white meat
HTMR	what's more
HTNL	White Nile
HTNN	whitening
HTNS	whiteness
HTNU	chitinous
HTOE	whatsoeer
HTOS	ghettoise
HTOT	Whitworth
HTOZ	ghettoize
HTPR	white port
HTRA	Whitbread
	Whiteread
HTRE	shit creek
HTRO	the Terror
HTRS	rhetorise
HTRZ	rhetorize
HTSA	photostat
	Photostat®
	white-seam
HTSL	white sale
HTTA	that's that
HTTD	what's to do?
HTTE	The Tatler
HTTN	whetstone
HTWA	what's what
HTWN	white wine
HTWO	whitewood
HTWS	whitewash
HTWT	what's with
HUAD	thousands
HUAI	rheumatic
HUBR	shrubbery
HUDW	shout down
HUFU	chauffeur
HUHE	thoughten
HUHO	thought of
HUTN	thrusting
HUTU	thrust out
HVLE	chevalier□
	shoveller
HVLU	shovelful
HVOE	Chevrolet
HVRI	the Virgin
HVRN	shivering
HWAS	show cause
HWEC	show mercy
HWIC	showpiece
HWLC	showplace
HWLU	The Walrus
HWNS	showiness
HWNU	showing up
HWRA	shewbread

Words marked □ can also be spelled with an initial capital letter

HWRG the word go
HYAE whey-faced
HYAI chrysalid
chrysalis
HYTN phlyctena
HZBN whizz-bang
HZCR rhizocarp
HZIA rhizoidal
IAAA Himalayas
IAAU Nicaragua
IABR Digambara
IACA financial
IACE financier
IACN financing
IACO disanchor
IACR disaccord
IADE pin and web
ribaudred
Wig and Pen
IADL girandola
girandole
IADU hit-and-run
tip and run
IAEA bicameral
bilateral
IAEC bivalency
IAEL Pisanello
IAET cigarette
vivamente
IAFC disaffect
IAFR disaffirm
IAFT Eid al-Fitr
IAGN Kisangani
lilangeni
IAHS lie at host
IAIA piratical
IAIE finalized
IAIL cigarillo
IAIM vivariums
IAIT bivariate
vicariate
visagiste
IAIU bifarious
hilarious
minacious
vicarious
vivacious
IAKN hijacking
IALE misallied
IALN disabling
IALS rivalless
IAMN disarming
IAOA disavowal
IAON disanoint
lie around
sit around
IAOS viragoish
IAPA disappear
IARC cicatrice
fix a price
IARL bizarrely
IARS cicatrise
IARZ cicatrize

IASG misassign
IASI sizarship
vicarship
IATC didactics
IATN disattune
IATS gigantism
IATT bipartite
IAUE disabused
IAUH hibakusha
IAVS misadvise
IAWV tidal wave
IBAC disbranch
IBCA hit back at
IBDI sitbodkin
IBEI diablerie
IBEL oil beetle
IBEO liable for
Wimbledon
IBGI kirbigrip□
IBHN lie behind
IBHV misbehave
IBIT fimbriate
IBLE disbelief
misbelief
IBLS diabolise
diabolism
diabolist
IBLT liability
viability
IBLZ diabolize
IBPI limb sprig
IBRA disbursal
IBRE disburden
Kimberley
Limburger
Tinbergen
IBRN timbering
IBRO Tim Burton
IBRS gibberish
IBSO misbestow
IBST gibbosity
IBTI kibbutzim
IBTO hit bottom
IBUL gibbously
ICAC mischance
ICAG discharge
mischarge
ICBC pinchbeck
ICBN aitchbone
ICCC Hitchcock
ICDA circadian
ICDR pitch-dark
ICDT viscidity
ICEE Kitchener
ICEI discredit
ICEN miscreant
ICES big cheese
ICET fiochetti
witchetty
ICFR pitchfork
ICGN miscegene
miscegine
ICHE disc wheel

ICHK hitch-hike
ICHN witch hunt
ICHT zinc white
ICIA discoidal
ICII diacritic
ICIO Mitchison
ICIR circuitry
ICIT pitch into
ICLE discalced
ICLK witchlike
ICLR circulars
ICLT circulate
niccolite
ICLU discolour
miscolour
ICMA mincemeat
piecemeal
ICMI discomfit
ICMO discommon
ICNI discandie
Vincentio
Wisconsin
ICNT diaconate
ICNU zirconium
ICOE air-cooled
air cooler
disclosed
ICOL Discworld
ICPL pitch-pole
pitch-poll
ICPN pitchpine
ICPT sincipita
sinciputs
ICRE discarded
ICRK disc brake
ICRL sincerely
ICRO Kit Carson
ICRT sincerity
viscerate
ICST viscosity
ICTR piscatory
ICTV siccative
ICUE linctuses
ICUS discourse
ICUT viscounty
ICVL piacevole
ICVR discovery□
ICXD zinc oxide
IDAC hindrance
IDAD windwards
IDAG wind gauge
IDAL find fault
find-fault
IDAS wild pansy
IDAT wild party
IDBU wild about
IDCT vindicate
IDEA middle ear
middleman
middle way
IDEG Lindbergh
IDEL fix deeply
IDEO Middleton

IDIE disdained
IDIH hindsight
IDKS Hindu Kush
IDLN bird-alone
IDMA misdemean
IDMT Hindemith
IDNL windingly
IDNS giddiness
windiness
IDNU winding-up
IDOA wild woman
IDOE Eindhoven
wind-hover
IDON windborne
wind-borne
windbound
IDOS bird-house
IDPE big dipper
IDPY vin de pays
IDRA windbreak
IDRC misdirect
IDRI birdbrain
hindbrain
kilderkin
IDRN hinder end
hindering
IDRO tinderbox
windproof
IDRS Pindarise
IDRZ Pindarize
IDSE yiddisher□
IDTE mild steel
IDTR windstorm
IDUL mindfully
IDUO mindful of
IDUS wild guess
IDWN kiddywink
IDWO window box
IDWP windswept
IDYA Six-Day War
IEAA miles away
IEAD hivewards
sidewards
IEAE fire-eater
firewater
fire-water
liberated
life-saver
like water
limewater
rice paper
IEAG tide gauge
wire gauge
IEAI cinematic
cineraria
kinematic
literatim
IEAL disenable
liberally
literally
miserable
miserably
side-table

tide table
timetable
wine vault
IEAO liberator
IEAP River Alph
IEAS give pause
IEAT give way to
IEAZ wire gauze
IEBC give a back
IEBD disembody
IEBL give a bell
IEBN Nigel Benn
IEBR disembark
like a bird
IEBU time about
IEBV rise above
IEBZ give a buzz
IECL limescale
time scale
timescale
IECN silencing
virescent
IECO libeccios
IEDC eider duck
IEDL Rivendell
IEDM give a damn
IEDW eiderdown
IEEB riveted by
IEEC five pence
IEEE diaereses
IEEG Mike Leigh
IEEI diaeresis
IEER life-weary
IEES vice versa
IEEV give leave
IEFA time of day
IEGG disengage
IEGM video game
IEGN divergent
diverging
IEHE time sheet
wire wheel
IEHI side chain
IEHN give a hand
IEHO give the OK
IEHR firethorn
timeshare
IEHS give chase
IEIA vicesimal
vigesimal
IEIC timepiece
IEIE fixed idea
life-sized
IEIH limelight
sidelight
IEII time limit
IEIT give birth
ninetieth
IEIU dioecious
IEKC give a kick
IEKE give a knee
IELA give a lead
IELC fireplace
give place
time clock
IELE like flies
IELF give a lift
IELL Tiger Lily
tiger lily
IELN libellant
vitelline
IELO fixed look
lifeblood
IELR fire alarm
vitellary
IELS riderless
riverless
wine glass
IELT wire cloth
IELU libellous
Vitellius
IELY pineal eye
IEMK like smoke
IEMN lineament
IEMS give a miss
IEMT tiger moth
IENA Hibernian
vicennial
IENI live in sin
live on air
IENL wide-angle
IENM given name
IENR vide infra
IENS fixedness
hibernise
tiredness
IENT hibernate
IENZ hibernize
IEOA bite to eat
wise woman
IEOC life-force
IEOE cicerones
fire-power
fire-robed
give money
IEOH Hideyoshi
IEOI siderosis
IEOK fireworks
IEON fine point
hidebound
hide-bound
IEOR sideboard
IEOT give forth
IEPL pineapple
IEPO Liverpool
misemploy
IERA pipe dream
pipe-dream
time trial
IERC firebrick
sidetrack
wisecrack
IERD give a ride
IERE Nile green
IERL fire drill
IERN firebrand
IERO fireproof
fire-proof
IERS bide tryst
side-dress
winepress
wire brush
wire grass
IERU bite or sup
IERV line-grove
IERZ like crazy
IESD riverside□
IESF diversify
IESL diversely
win easily
IESO dimension
diversion
like a shot
like as not
liver spot
IEST diversity
IESY River Styx
tiger's eye
IETA direct tax
IETC livestock
IETD dipeptide
IETE disesteem
liberties
misesteem
IETF pikestaff
IETG give it a go
IETI directrix
disentail
IETL give a talk
lifestyle
IETM disentomb
IETN directing
diverting
eigentone
Firestone
libertine
like stink
limestone
milestone
minestone
pipestone
IETO bisection
digestion
direction
IETP videotape
IETR directors
directory□
fire-storm
life story
IETV digestive
directive
divertive
IETX videotext
IEUE Nine Muses
IEUL direfully
hideously
piteously
timeously
IEUN sideburns
IEUO dine out on
live out of
ritenutos
IEUR fireguard
lifeguard
vide supra
IEWK wide awake
wide-awake
IEWO tigerwood
IEWP side-swipe
IEWR liverwort
IEYA liveryman
IEYL life-cycle
IEYO Mike Tyson
IFAO misfeasor
IFCL difficult
IFDN diffident
IFGR disfigure
IFLE air filter
oil filter
IFNE Zinfandel
IFRA tit for tat
IFRG pilferage
IFRI hit for six
IFRL fix firmly
IFRN different
differing
pilfering
IFRO Mia Farrow
IFRR pifferari
IFRS disforest
IFSL diffusely
IFSO diffusion
IFSV diffusive
IFVU disfavour
IGAD Rio Grande
IGAE disgraced
kingmaker
IGAG ring gauge
IGAH biography
IGAL lingually
IGBC piggyback
IGBN piggy-bank
IGDU rigged out
IGEC ring-fence
IGEE ringleted
single ten
IGEO singleton
IGEU single out
vingt-et-un
IGGL misguggle
IGHI wing chair
IGIE Diaghilev
disguised
king-sized
misguided
IGLN King's Lynn
singalong
ting-a-ling
IGLR liege lord
IGML Kingsmill
IGNL ringingly
singingly

IGNS dinginess
mininess
IGNT virginity
IGNU biogenous
IGOE diagnoses
kingdomed
IGOI diagnosis
IGOL Ringworld
IGOR king cobra
IGPR Singapore
Singapura
IGRE Siegfried
IGRL ginger ale
niggardly
IGRN fingering
lingering
IGRU ginger nut
gingerous
IGRW king prawn
IGSE disgusted
IGSL piggishly
IGTL ridge-tile
IGTN fidgeting
ridge tent
IGTW Kingstown
IGVN misgiving
IGVR misgovern
IGYU ginglymus
IHAA right away
IHAE big headed
bigheaded
big-headed
dishwater
high water
pigheaded
pig-headed
IHAI Lithuania
IHAL high table
rightable
IHAS Mithraism
tight arse
IHBC fight back
IHBL light bulb
night-bell
IHBM with a bump
IHBO light blow
IHCF Night Café
IHCO night-crow
IHCU nightclub
night-club
IHDO wished-for
IHDW right down
right-down
IHEE high-level
tightened
IHEU lighten up
righteous
IHFC right face!
IHFL eightfold
nightfall
IHFO eightfoot
eight-foot
IHGW nightgown

IHHI high-chair
IHHL with child
IHHN diphthong
right-hand
IHIE high-viced
IHIH highlight
IHIK high jinks
IHIL Lichfield
IHIT eightieth
high birth
IHKI tight-knit
IHLA high altar
IHLC fish slice
tight-lace
IHLE high-flier
high flyer
high-flyer
Michel Ney
Richelieu
IHLF nightlife
IHLG lithology
IHLN nightlong
IHLO dishallow
Michelson
Nicholson
IHLS high-class
sightless
Sinhalese
IHLT dish-cloth
IHLW high-flown
IHMA light meal
IHMR nightmare
IHMT Highsmith
IHMU dishumour
IHNA Tim Henman
IHNH Pichincha
IHNL mishandle
sighingly
IHNN lightning
IHNS dishonest
fishiness
lightness
litheness
pithiness
rightness
tightness
IHNU dishonour
IHOD high words
IHOE dishtowel
high-toned
IHON high point
with young
IHOO wish to God
IHOR High Court
high court
IHOS dichroism
IHPE high-speed
IHPI bishopric
IHPN lithopone
IHRA fisherman
sight-read
IHRD high-grade
IHRI bilharzia

light rain
Richardia
Richard II
IHRL night-rule
IHRM dithyramb
IHRN dithering
withering
IHRO lie hard on
IHRP tightrope
IHRW highbrows
high-grown
withdrawn
IHSD right side
IHSE sightseer
IHSF night safe
IHSI lightship
night-soil
IHSM eightsome
lithesome
IHSN sight-sing
IHSO nightspot
tight spot
IHSU lights out
IHSZ rightsize
IHTM dichotomy
lithotomy
night-time
IHTN withstand
IHUL wishfully
IHUO light upon
IHUR Fishguard
IHWN right wing
right-wing
IHWR rightward
IHYA light-year
IIAC militancy
sibilance
sibilancy
vigilance
IIAD Niki Lauda
IIAE digitated
pixilated
IIAI digitalin
digitalis
militaria
IIAL civically
finically
limitable
similarly
visitable
IIAO divinator
litigator
mitigator
IIAT similar to
vigilante
IICE viliacoes
IIEC diligence
IIEF divide off
IIEL dividedly
limitedly
IIER citizenry
IIET midinette
IIEU divide out

siliceous
IIFC disinfect
IIFR misinform
IIFS disinfest
IIGA bilingual
giving way
IIGF giving-off
IIGO piping hot
IIGU giving-out
Rising Sun
IIHF finish off
IIHM disinhume
IIHN finishing
IIHO pixie hood
IIIA libidinal
IIIE civilised
civilized
digitizer
IIIL dirigible
divisible
divisibly
IIIM dirigisme
IIIN Miliciens
siciliane
IIIO Filipinos
IIIT dimidiate
dirigiste
lixiviate
IIIU litigious
silicious
IIKN mimicking
IIKR mini skirt
miniskirt
IIKT finickety
IILD disillude
IILN Dixieland
IILS civil list
limitless
IILT titillate
IIMN Sigismund
IIMR disimmure
IINO pimientos
IINR visionary
IINS lividness
rigidness
timidness
vividness
IIOI silicosis
IIOR Timisoara
IIRA minibreak
vizierial
IIRI kiwi fruit
IIRT vizierate
IISN Kim Il-sung
IITA sinistral
IITO filiation
vitiation
IITR miniature
ministers
IIUE ridiculer
IIUI bilirubin
IIUL biliously
pitifully

viciously
IIVS disinvest
IIWI lie in wait
IIWT tie in with
visit with
IIYN vilifying
vivifying
IJDE misjudged
IJIE disjoined
IJNI Kim Jong Il
Kim Jong-Il
IKAD Kirkcaldy
Nick Faldo
IKAE Linklater
risk-taker
IKBC pickaback
IKBR Dicky Bird
dicky-bird
Vicksburg
IKBU kick about
IKDN rinky-dink
IKET milk teeth
IKEV sick leave
IKHK milk shake
IKHT milk-white
IKLA kick pleat
IKLN Birkeland
IKLS nickelise
IKLY Pink Floyd
IKLZ nickelize
IKMR Dick Emery
IKNL winkingly
IKNN sickening
IKNO Dickinson
sicken for
IKNS kinkiness
milkiness
riskiness
silkiness
IKON milk round
IKOT milk tooth
IKRN bickering
IKRO pinkerton
IKRS lickerish
IKRV disk drive
IKSL sickishly
IKTA ticket day
IKTI Rick Stein
IKTL ricketily
IKTN kickstand
IKTR kick-start
IKTU milk stout
IKUS pick-purse
IKWK Minkowski
ILAD billiards
ILAE Bill Gates
Bill Haley
ILBD Billy Budd
ILBH Niels Bohr
ILBM Mills bomb
ILBN billabong
ILBO field book
ILCA dialectal
ILCI dialectic
ILCN Millicent
ILCT dislocate
ILDE title deed
ILDI Bill Oddie
ILEP Will Kempe
ILER killdeers
ILFR fieldfare
villiform
ILFS killifish
ILGA field goal
ILGE villagree
ILGN pillaging
ILGS biologist
dialogise
ILGZ dialogize
ILHE mill wheel
ILHN field hand
ILIE Bill Sikes
ILIL hillbilly
ILJA Billy Jean
ILJE Billy Joel
ILLA Billy Liar
ILLR gillflirt
ILMC diplomacy
ILMT diplomate
ILNE Dillinger
uitlander
ILNI filling-in
Finlandia
millennia
ILNL violently
willingly
ILNO fill in for
ILNR millenary
millinery
ILNS hilliness
silliness
violinist
ILNT willing to
ILOB Bill Cosby
ILOE willpower
ILOR billboard
millboard
ILOS fill-horse
ILOT billionth
millionth
ILPD millepede
millipede
ILPE mislippen
ILPG title page
ILPR Villa Park
ILRE Killarney
ILRL title role
ILRS Hitlerism
Hitlerist
pillarist
pillorise
ILRT Hitlerite
ILRZ Girl Crazy
pillorize
ILSA fieldsman
ILSI Gillespie
ILSL aimlessly
girlishly
sinlessly
witlessly
ILTE rillettes
ILTI field trip
ILTN millstone
ILTO violation
ILUD Girl Guide
ILVL Jim Lovell
ILWN billowing
ILWR fieldward
fieldwork
ILWS willowish
ILYN mislaying
IMCN Fiumicino
IMCO film actor
IMCR gimmickry
IMGE diamagnet
IMHG Lismahago
IMLA bismillah
IMLE Niemöller
IMLG gismology
gizmology
IMME dismember
IMMN firmament
IMNE diamonded
pigmented
IMNG mismanage
IMNL dismantle
IMNS filminess
IMRA Cimmerian
IMRL rigmarole
IMSA dismissal
IMSE dismissed
IMTI biometric
diametric
IMYL Rik Mayall
IMYN dismaying
INAC mix 'n' match
INCE picnicker
INDR Diana Dors
INER lion-heart
INFE dignified
INHH Minnehaha
ININ Vientiane
INLA signalman
INLG limnology
INLS pianolist
signalise
INLZ signalize
INMC bionomics
INNL winningly
INNO signing on
INNU signing up
signing-up
INPE Kidnapped
kidnapper
INPP Giant Pope
INRD giant rude
INRE dinner set
INRG Diana Rigg
INRN Signorina
signorine
signorini
INRS Diana Ross
INSA giant star
INSE witnesser
INST Minnesota
INSU Dionysius
INTL pinnately
INTR dignitary
signatory
signature
INUI signeurie
INXT lie next to
INZN lionizing
IOAC Fibonacci
IOAL pivotally
IOAP Tirol Alps
IOBR widow bird
IOCI finocchio
Pinocchio
IOCK Ninotchka
IOCV biconcave
IOEE disobeyed
milometer
tin-opener
IOEI Milosevic
IOER kilometre
IOET kilohertz
Nicolette
pirouette
Rigoletto
IOEU Nicodemus
IOFA pilot flag
IOHM Hiroshima
IOHO widowhood
IOIN disorient
nicotiana
IOLG disoblige
IOLS pilotless
IOMS hit or miss
hit-or-miss
IOMU ginormous
IONI Pinot Noir
IONN disowning
IOOA ribosomal
IOOI filopodia
IOOL kilojoule
IOPI dimorphic
IORC timocracy
IORE Sigourney
IORL minor role
IORN Winogrand
IOSN limousine
IOSY Simon says
IOTL bimonthly
IOUA binocular
IOYL kilocycle
IPAE bit player
displaced
displayed
misplaced
IPAS dispraise
mispraise

IPCE	nit-picker
IPDT	hispidity
	limpidity
IPEI	diapyesis
IPEO	simpleton
IPES	displease
IPIB	Kim Philby
IPIE	simplices
IPIM	silphiums
IPIO	disprison
IPLT	Hippolyta
IPNE	dispenser
	dispondee
IPNL	limpingly
	lispingly
	nippingly
IPNS	nippiness
	Nipponese
	timpanist
IPOL	dispeople
IPRA	dispersal
IPRC	dioptrics
IPRD	hit parade
IPRE	dispersed
	pimpernel
IPRG	diaphragm
	disparage
IPRN	simpering
IPRR	Tipperary
IPRT	disparate
	disparity
IPSL	wimpishly
IPSO	dispose of
IPTC	simpatico
IPTN	disputant
IPUE	dispauper
IPYE	Simply Red
IRAE	lip-reader
IRAL	diurnally
IRBA	microbial
IRCD	microcode
IRCE	ditrochee
IRCL	vibracula
IRCO	misreckon
IRCP	microcopy
IRCS	microcosm
IREE	Vic Reeves
IRFL	microfilm
IRFR	vitriform
IRGR	disregard
IRHE	diarrhoea
IRIN	Giorgione
IRLA	fibrillae
	fibrillar
	Gibraltar
IRLI	fibrillin
IRLR	tirra-lyra
IRLS	disrelish
	fibreless
IRLT	microlith
	misrelate
IRMS	micromesh
IRMT	fibromata
IRNL	vibrantly
IRNS	fieriness
IROI	cirrhosis
	vitriolic
IRPD	cirripede
IRPE	disrupted
	disrupter
IRPI	disrepair
IRPL	micropyle
IRPR	misreport
IRPT	disrepute
IRRA	librarian
IRRH	hierarchy
IRSA	vibrissae
IRSI	Midrashim
IRSL	tigrishly
IRSN	nigrosine
IRTL	vibratile
IRTM	microtome
IRTN	migrating
	vibrating
IRTO	librettos
	migration
	nitration
	titration
	vibration
IRTR	fioritura
	fioriture
	migratory
	vibratory
IRTV	vibrative
IRUS	bierwurst
IRVG	gilravage
IRVU	Vitruvius
IRWV	microwave
IRYH	biorhythm
ISAD	kiss hands
ISAE	Miss Bates
	misshapen
	rijstafel
	tipstaves
	Wiesbaden
ISAF	tipstaffs
ISAI	diastasic
	diastatic
	miasmatic
ISAT	dies fasti
ISBR	first-born
ISBS	first base
ISCE	dissected
ISCK	tipsy cake
ISDF	pissed off
ISDK	Pilsudski
ISDN	dissident
ISET	dies festi
ISFO	first-foot
ISGA	kissagram
	kissogram
ISHL	kitschily
ISHN	firsthand
	first-hand
ISHR	biosphere
ISLD	first lady
ISLI	diesel oil
ISLS	dieselise
ISLT	dissolute
ISLZ	dieselize
ISME	midsummer
ISML	dissemble
	dissimile
	lissomely
	winsomely
ISMV	first move
ISNE	dissenter
	dissunder
	Kissinger
ISNL	hissingly
	missingly
ISNM	first name
ISNN	dissonant
ISNS	sissiness
	tipsiness
ISNU	Nissen hut
ISOA	kinswoman
ISOE	missioner
ISOI	diastolic
ISOU	Dioscorus
ISPR	first part
ISPT	dissipate
ISRA	midstream
ISRE	big screen
ISRT	first rate
	first-rate
ISSE	first step
ISTF	kids' stuff
ISTM	first time
ISTY	miss stays
ISUA	pipsqueak
ISUI	Miss Julie
ISUO	miss out on
ISYA	first-year
ITAC	mint sauce
ITAE	air travel
	Miltiades
ITAL	filtrable
	virtually
ITAN	distraint
ITAT	distraite
ITBA	pinto bean
ITBM	dirty bomb
ITCA	dietician
ITCI	pistachio
ITCM	viaticums
ITCS	witticism
ITDE	gilt-edged
ITDN	histidine
ITDU	fitted out
ITEA	hit the hay
	win the day
ITEI	diathesis
	diathetic
	little bit
ITEM	diathermy
ITEN	little end
	little one
ITEO	little boy
	Little Dog
	mistletoe
ITET	fifteenth
	sixteenth
ITEV	Little Eva
ITEW	little owl
ITFN	DiStefano
ITFR	sixth form
ITGA	histogram
	pictogram
ITGN	histogeny
ITHA	dirt cheap
	dirt-cheap
ITHE	diet sheet
ITHN	lift a hand
ITHR	Wiltshire
ITIE	pint-sized
ITLE	distilled
	distiller
ITLG	histology
ITLO	dirty look
ITLS	mirthless
ITLU	fistulous
ITME	distemper
ITMN	histamine
ITMR	birthmark
	dirty mark
ITMS	victimise
ITMZ	victimize
ITNE	distended
	oil-tanker
ITNF	bitten off
ITNI	Rin Tin Tin
ITNL	distantly
	fittingly
	hintingly
	siftingly
	wittingly
ITNN	listening
ITNO	piston rod
ITNR	listeners
ITNS	dirtiness
	kittenish
	mistiness
	niftiness
	wittiness
ITOA	fictional
ITOE	Einthoven
	gift token
ITOO	virtuosos
ITOT	list costs
ITRA	cisternae
	historian
	pictorial
	Victorian
ITRE	distorted
	disturbed
ITRF	historify
ITRI	filter-tip
	litter bin
ITRN	binturong
	disthrone
	sistering

	tittering
ITRS	Listerise
	winterise
ITRT	micturate
ITRU	dipterous
	jitterbug
ITRZ	Listerize
ITSH	Nietzsche
ITSI	pietistic
ITTA	dietitian
ITTC	dietetics
ITTO	dictation
	nictation
ITTR	dictatory
ITTT	nictitate
ITUE	mint-julep
ITUL	riotously
	wistfully
ITVT	tittivate
ITWK	kittiwake
ITWR	birth-wort
	dirty word
	dirty work
ITWS	widthwise
ITWY	widthways
IUAE	simulated
IUAL	dilutable
	titularly
IUAO	simulator
IUAR	simulacra
IUCL	minuscule
IUCS	simulcast
IUCT	bifurcate
	Sioux City
IUDS	liquidise
IUDT	liquidate
	liquidity
IUDZ	liquidize
IUEC	virulence
IUEE	minutemen
IUEU	figure out
IUFE	liquefied
	liquefier
IUIE	disunited
IUII	sinusitis
IUIR	fiduciary
IULI	visual aid
IULS	ritualise
	ritualism
	ritualist
	visualise
IULZ	ritualize
	visualize
IUNL	piquantly
IUNS	piousness
IURC	liquorice
IUST	sinuosity
IUTL	sinuately
IUTO	sinuation
	situation
IUTR	pituitary
IUUL	sinuously
IUWT	tie up with
IVRO	silver fox
IVRS	silverise
IVRU	Silverius
IVRZ	silverize
IVSR	Silvestra
IVTB	sieve tube
IWCE	hit wicket
	mid-wicket
IWFR	midwifery
IWON	viewpoint
IWRH	airworthy
IWTE	dimwitted
	dim-witted
IWUE	Milwaukee
IYAR	airy-fairy
IYCP	cityscape
IYFO	city of God
IYHT	lily-white
IYLN	sibylline
IYLS	bicyclist
IYNL	pityingly
IYOI	dizygotic
IYWS	vinyl wash
IZCT	pizzicato
IZEU	fizzle out
IZNS	dizziness
JBJN	Ljubljana
JCLT	ejaculate
JIPO	O J Simpson
JNTO	T-junction
JRBR	Bjorn Borg
JTYO	A J P Taylor
KANA	Ukrainian
KDDL	skedaddle
KDVN	sky-diving
KEAE	Akhenaten
KEAO	Akhenaton
KJCE	skyjacker
KJRN	ski-joring
KLEI	skilled in
KLUL	skilfully
KMTV	Akhmatova
KNIE	skin-diver
KNIH	skintight
	skin-tight
KNLN	skinflint
KNLV	skin alive
KNYI	skinny-dip
KOLN	J K Rowling
KOWA	I know what
KRCE	skyrocket
	sky-rocket
KTHL	sketchily
KTHN	sketching
KTHU	sketch out
KTOE	skate over
KVYN	skivvying
KWHF	skew-whiff
KYOE	okey-dokey
LAAA	Allahabad
	clear away
	Elia Kazan
LAAC	clearance
LAAE	alma mater
LAAI	fly agaric
LAAL	cleavable
	floatable
	pleadable
LABR	Alban Berg
LAEC	Pleasence
LAEL	albarelli
LAEO	please you
LAES	ill at ease
LAEU	oleaceous
LAHN	bleaching
LANS	bleakness
	cleanness
	clearness
LAOC	all at once
LAOI	aleatoric
LAON	all around
LARO	clean room
	cloakroom
LARS	albatross
LARV	alla breve
LASN	cleansing
LATI	allantoic
	allantois
LATR	olfactory
LAUE	pleasurer
LAWS	altarwise
LAWT	plead with
LBAL	clubbable
LBIE	Old Bailey
LBLA	glabellae
LBLK	globelike
LBLS	club class
	globalise
LBLZ	globalize
LBNO	à l'abandon
LBOA	clubwoman
LBOS	clubhouse
LBRT	elaborate
LBSE	alabaster
LBTO	globe-trot
LBWR	fly-by-wire
LCAA	slack away
LCAC	ill-chance
LCAE	blockaded
LCAL	electable
LCAT	black arts
LCBA	black bean
	black bear
LCBD	black body
LCBE	placeboes
LCBK	slack-bake
LCBL	blackball
	black belt
	black bile
LCBN	Alice band
LCBR	Black Bart
	blackbird
	Blackburn
LCCC	blackcock
LCCI	alicyclic
LCCR	place card
LCDE	old codger
LCDR	placoderm
LCDT	elucidate
	placidity
LCEE	fleckered
LCET	fléchette
LCEU	slacken up
LCFA	black flag
LCFC	blackface
LCFE	Blackfeet
LCFO	Blackfoot
LCHA	blackhead
	blockhead
LCHL	black hole
LCII	Black Iris
LCIL	flaccidly
LCJC	blackjack
LCKC	place kick
LCLO	black look
LCLS	blacklist
LCMI	blackmail
LCMN	placement
LCMR	all comers
	black mark
LCMS	black mass
LCNA	placentae
	placental
	placentas
LCNI	Placentia
LCNS	blackness
	slackness
	slickness
LCOA	electoral
LCOE	ill-chosen
	place over
LCPO	Blackpool
LCRD	electrode
	glyceride
LCRF	electrify
LCRM	plectrums
LCRN	glycerine
	plectrons
LCRS	electrise
LCRZ	electrize
LCSA	black swan
LCSD	glucoside
	glycoside
LCSO	black spot
LCTL	plicately
LCTN	eliciting
LCTO	elocution
	placation
LCTR	placatory
LCTV	placative
LCUN	fluctuant
LCUR	electuary
LCUT	fluctuate
LCUU	flocculus
LCVT	block vote
LCWL	Blackwell
LCWO	blackwood
LCWR	clockwork
LCWS	clockwise

LDAO	gladiator
LDLN	fledgling
	plod along
LDNL	glidingly
	slidingly
LDOE	gladioles
	slide open
LDOU	gladiolus
LDPT	glide path
LDRL	slide-rule
LDTN	Gladstone
LEAA	Aldebaran
LEAD	allemande
LEAE	alienated
LEAL	alienable
	alterable
	illegally
LEBR	Oldenburg
LECT	altercate
LEDU	all ends up
LEDY	olden days
LEEE	Blue Peter
	blue peter
LEEL	allegedly
LEEO	alter egos
LEER	blueberry
LEFO	fleet-foot
LEHL	blue whale
LEHR	alpenhorn
	elsewhere
LEHS	Alger Hiss
LEIA	Algeciras
LEIL	illegible
	illegibly
LEIM	blue films
LEIN	allegiant
	Blue Vinny
LEIS	blue rinse
LEIT	alleviate
LEKE	blue-skies
LELC	blue-black
LELO	blue blood
LELS	sleepless
LENS	fleetness
	glueyness
	sleekness
LENT	alternate
LEOE	sleep over
LEOI	blue movie
	sleep on it
LERA	Alter-Réal
LERI	algebraic
LERN	blueprint
LERS	bluegrass
LESO	Aldershot
LETL	clientele
	clientèle
LETN	Albertina
LEUE	flue-cured
LEUL	gleefully
LEWO	Fleetwood
LEWT	sleep with
LFFC	cliff face
	cliff-face
LFHN	cliffhang
LFNS	bluffness
LFTE	ill-fitted
LGAA	elegiacal
LGAC	clog dance
	flagrancy
LGAE	flag-waver
	sluggabed
LGCN	Oligocene
LGLU	flagellum
LGMN	alignment
LGNE	sloganeer
LGNL	elegantly
LGNS	sloganise
LGNU	uliginous
LGNZ	sloganize
LGOE	flageolet
LGPL	oligopoly
LGRH	oligarchy
LGTA	flight bag
LGTE	ill-gotten
LGTL	flightily
LGTN	flagstone
	slighting
LGTS	slightest
LGTT	flagitate
LHAT	ill health
	ill-health
LHIE	Alzheimer
LHMS	alchemise
	alchemist
LHMU	ill-humour
LHMZ	alchemize
LHSE	Althusser
LHSR	alphasort
LHTS	alpha test
	alphatest
LHWV	alpha wave
LIAL	claimable
LIAO	alligator
LIAU	ultimatum
LIBC	claim back
LICN	Pleiocene
LIEA	illiberal
LIEE	altimeter
LIGA	Allingham
LIGI	flying jib
LIGO	Aldington
	Ellington
	flying fox
LIHL	allicholy
LIHN	sleighing
LIIE	illimited
LIIL	illicitly
LILM	Aldis lamp
LINS	fluidness
	plainness
LION	cloisonné
LISE	plainsmen
LISI	ellipsoid
LISN	plainsong
LITA	cloistral
LITF	plaintiff
LITR	cloisters
LITV	plaintive
LJDE	ill-judged
LKAO	Plekhanov
LKDU	flaked out
LKMR	Blakemore
LKNS	flakiness
LLMI	El Alamein
LLTO	ululation
LMAL	blameable
	blameably
	climbable
	flammable
LMAO	plumbagos
LMCI	climactic
LMDW	clamp down
	clampdown
	climb down
LMEE	Klemperer
	slumberer
LMEU	clamber up
	flambeaus
	flambeaux
LMLN	plumb line
	plumb-line
LMLS	blameless
LMNA	elemental
LMNI	Alemannic
LMNL	clamantly
	clemently
	flamingly
LMNO	flamencos
	flamingos
LMNS	aluminise
	plumpness
	sliminess
LMNT	eliminate
LMNU	aluminium
	aluminous
LMNZ	aluminize
LMOE	flummoxed
LMOT	climb on to
LMRL	glomeruli
LMRS	glamorise
LMRT	glomerate
LMRU	clamorous
	glamorous
	slumbrous
LMRZ	glamorize
LMSE	blemished
	old master
LMTE	Flamsteed
LMTR	climature
LMTS	climatise
LMTZ	climatize
LMUS	Blomquist
LNAE	Alan Bates
	elongated
LNAL	plantable
LNAO	Ulan Bator
LNAR	glengarry
LNBC	slingback
LNBR	Flensburg
LNCA	clinician
LNDT	blind date
LNDW	fling down
LNEC	plangency
LNEE	blanketed
	blinkered
	blunderer
	plunderer
	slanderer
LNEF	glance off
LNEL	slenderly
LNEN	Llangefni
LNEU	plenteous
LNFL	blindfold
	clingfilm
LNFO	plant food
LNHN	clinching
LNIA	élan vital
LNIE	klondiker
LNIU	plentiful
LNJR	pleno jure
LNLC	blond-lace
	flintlock
	plant-lice
LNLF	plant life
LNLR	Alan Clark
LNMN	Klinsmann
LNNS	aloneness
	blandness
	blankness
	blindness
	bluntness
LNNT	Alan Knott
LNRA	planarian
LNRL	plenarily
LNSA	plantsman
LNSD	alongside
	blind side
LNSE	planisher
LNSO	blind spot
LNTD	plenitude
LNTI	planetoid
LNTR	ill nature
	planetary
LNUA	Alan Sugar
	glandular
LNWS	slantwise
LNWT	along with
LNWY	slantways
LNYE	klondyker
LOAC	allowance
LOAL	allocable
	allowable
	allowably
LOAR	Cleopatra
LOBI	allow bail
LOBN	blood bank
LOBT	bloodbath
	blood-bath
LOCL	blood cell
LOEC	fluoresce
LOEE	ill-omened

Words marked ❑ can also be spelled with an initial capital letter

LOEL	allowedly
LOFO	blood-flow
LOFU	blood-feud
LOGT	floodgate
LOIA	illogical
LOIH	algorithm
LOJH	Elton John
LOKA	Algonkian
LOLS	bloodless
	bloodlust
LOMN	allotment
LONS	aloofness
LOOA	Almodovar
LOOI	alcoholic
LOPA	floor plan
LOQI	Algonquin
LORO	elbow-room
LORP	allotrope
	allotropy
	oleograph
LOSA	fluorspar
LOSE	bloodshed
LOSO	bloodshot
	floor show
LOTD	floodtide
LOTL	almost all
	floor tile
LOTM	ileostomy
LOTO	almost not
LOTP	blood type
LOTR	allottery
LOTS	blood test
LOUU	Cleobulus
LOWL	floodwall
LPAC	flippancy
LPAD	clap hands
LPAE	flap-eared
LPAI	aliphatic
LPAL	flappable
LPAM	slope arms
LPAP	slaphappy
	slap-happy
LPEE	slippered
LPMN	elopement
LPNL	slopingly
LPOL	old people
LPTC	slapstick
LPWS	slopewise
LPWT	elope with
LQEC	eloquence
LQET	plaquette
LRAE	floreated
	floriated
LRBL	alarm-bell
LRBT	Clara Butt
LRCA	altricial
LRDT	floridity
LREL	alarmedly
LRFE	clarifier
LRFR	floriform
LRGL	flirt-gill
LRHL	Clare Hall
	glory hole
LRLS	pluralise
	pluralism
	pluralist
LRLT	plurality
LRLZ	pluralize
LRMA	Alf Ramsay
LRNL	flaringly
	glaringly
LRNS	alertness
LRSA	flare star
LRSI	clerkship
	floristic
LRSR	floristry
LRWT	flirt with
LRYA	clergyman
LRYE	clergymen
LSAA	flush away
LSAD	glissandi
	glissando
LSAE	old stager
	Ullswater
LSAI	plasmatic
LSAO	glossator
LSBC	flashback
LSBL	flashbulb
LSBR	flash burn
LSBT	Elisabeth
LSCL	close call
LSCR	flash card
LSDW	close down
LSEE	blistered
	blusterer
	clustered
	flustered
	plastered
	plasterer
LSEL	blessedly
LSEN	all-seeing
LSFL	glassfuls
LSFN	slush fund
LSHM	blaspheme
	blasphemy
LSHO	old school
LSIA	classical
LSIE	all smiles
	alms-giver
	ill-suited
LSIG	fleshings
LSIO	close in on
LSIT	All Saints
LSIU	plastique
LSKI	close-knit
LSLK	glasslike
LSLS	classless
	fleshless
LSMN	blastment
	fleshment
LSNS	closeness
LSOE	elastomer
	flash-over
	gloss over
LSOI	plasmodia
LSON	plus point
LSOR	plus-fours
LSOS	alms-house
LSRN	all serene
	alms-drink
LSRO	classroom
LSUR	all square
LSUT	close up to
LSVL	elusively
LSWN	blush wine
LSWO	glass wool
LSWR	glassware
	glasswort
LSWT	clash with
	close with
LTBU	flit about
LTCA	plutocrat
LTCN	Slate Cone
LTEA	all the way
LTEE	cluttered
	flatterer
LTEI	clothed in
LTEU	clutter up
LTHA	clutch bag
LTIE	glottides
	glottises
LTIG	all things
	flatlings
LTIT	elutriate
LTLN	flatulent
LTME	ill temper
	ill-temper
LTMN	glutamine
LTMT	glutamate
LTNA	Plutonian
LTNL	blatantly
LTNS	platinise
	Platonise
	Platonism
	Platonist
LTNU	glutenous
	glutinous
	platinous
	plutonium
LTNZ	platinize
	Platonize
LTRA	Ulsterman
LTRC	plate rack
LTRI	plate rail
LTRK	flat broke
LTRS	flat brush
LTTD	platitude
LTTI	Blyth Tait
LTTO	flotation
LTUB	all thumbs
LUBS	cloud base
LUCP	cloud-capt
LUER	Albufeira
LUET	Claudette
LUHA	ploughman
LUHE	flaughter
	ploughmen
	slaughter
LUHN	slouching
LUII	pleuritic
LUIL	plausible
	plausibly
LULS	cloudless
LUNN	cloud nine
LUOE	cloud over
LUTN	flaunting
LUUA	clausulae
LUWT	all up with
LVAA	slave away
LVCR	clavicorn
LVDA	olive drab
LVLN	Cleveland
LVNA	Slovenian
LVNE	elevenses
LVNS	aliveness
	Slavonise
LVNZ	Slavonize
LVRN	slavering
LVRU	flavorous
LVSL	slavishly
LVTK	Blavatsky
LVTN	elevating
LVTO	elevation
	élevation
LVTR	elevatory
LVUE	flavoured
LVVT	slivovitz
LVWT	alive with
LWAC	slow-march
	slow match
LWFS	blow a fuse
LWHE	flow sheet
LWHR	flow chart
LWIH	flyweight
LWIU	slow virus
LWNL	flowingly
	glowingly
LWNU	slowing-up
LWOC	slowcoach
LWRE	flower-bed
LWRN	flowering
	glowering
LWRO	flowerpot
LWRU	flower-bud
LWSE	alewashed
	ill-wisher
LXAE	Alex James
LXGA	Plexiglas®
LXNE	Alexander
LXNR	Alexandra
LXTM	flexitime
LYAE	play games
LYAS	play false
LYBU	play about
LYCO	play actor
	play-actor
LYDU	played out
	played-out
LYHN	plaything
LYLN	play along
LYOK	play hooky
LYOR	clay court

LYOS playhouse❑
LYOT play booty
LYPR play a part
LYRL play a role
LYRU playgroup
LYUL playfully
LYYA play by ear
LZAA blaze away
LZBT Elizabeth
LZOE gloze over
LZOI klezmorim
MAAC imbalance
MAEC immanence
immanency
MAGE embargoed
embargoes
MAHS empathise
MAHZ empathize
MAII ommatidia
MAIL impavidly
MAIN impatiens
impatient
MAKA Imran Khan
MALN emballing
MAOL empanoply
MARN impairing
MARS embarrass
MASI empaestic
MASO impassion
MASV impassive
MATA impartial
MATE embattled
impastoed
MATN imparting
MATO impaction
MATS smear test
MATU amianthus
MCAE emaciated
MCEO smackeroo
MDCU ami de cour
MDHP amidships
MDRI Amy Dorrit
MEAC impedance
MEAO imperator
MEDN impending
MEFC imperfect
MEGI ambergris
MEIC immediacy
MEII imbecilic
MEIO impeticos
impetigos
MEIT immediate
MEIU imperious
MEJC amberjack
MELN impellent
MELS embellish
MELT umbellate
MENG empennage
MERT impetrate
MESL immensely
MESN ampersand
MESO immersion
MEST immensity
META Emmenthal
MEUE impetuses
MEUU impetuous
MEZE embezzler
MGGM a mug's game
MGLN smuggling
MGNN imagining
MGNR imaginary
MGTB image tube
MHBA amphibian
MHBL amphibole
amphiboly
MHSM emphysema
MHSS emphasise
MHSZ emphasize
MHYE emphlyses
MIEC imminence
MIGA Immingham
MIGN impinging
MIIA empirical
umbilical
MIIU ambitious
umbilicus
MIRN immigrant
MIRT immigrate
MIUE omnibuses
MIUL impiously
MIUT ambiguity
MIUU ambiguous
MKBL smoke-ball
MKBM smoke-bomb
MKLS smokeless
MKNS smokiness
MLAA smell a rat
MLAE small area
MLBE small beer
MLCT implicate
MLEL impliedly
MLFE amplified
amplifier
MLIN emollient
MLIT emolliate
MLMN emolument
implement
MLMS emblemise
MLMT emblemata
MLMZ emblemize
MLNE implanted
MLNL smilingly
MLNS ampleness
smallness
MLOI amblyopia
MLRN imploring
MLRU Emile Roux
Émile Roux
MLSD Ambleside
MLSO emblossom
implosion
MLSV implosive
MLTD amplitude
MLTL small talk
MLTM small-time
MLTN emulating
MLTO emulation
MLTW small-town
MLUL emulously
MLWL Amy Lowell
MLYE employees
MLYR employers
MLZL Emile Zola
MNAI amino acid
MNAL amendable
MNMN amendment
MNNL eminently
MNOE Amenhotep
MNRT a minority
MNTE amenities
MNTO emanation
MNUL ominously
MOAL immorally
immovable
immovably
MOAO immolator
MOEC impotence
MOEO imposed on
MOET immodesty
MOHU smooth out
MOII impolitic
MOIM emporiums
MONE impounded
impounder
MOSE E M Forster
MOSN embossing
MOTM impostume
MOTN important
importune
MOTR imposture
MRAD smorzando
MRAE smart alec
MRAS smart arse
MRBT improbity
MRCN Americana
embracing
MRCR smart card
MRCS imprecise
MRCT embrocate
imbricate
imprecate
MRCU americium
MRDN imprudent
MRDU smart drug
MREC emergence
emergency
MREU smarten up
MRGI imbroglio
MRHU amorphous
MRIE embroider
embroiled
MRLI amaryllis
MRLT amorality
MRMT impromptu
MRNS smartness
MROI embryonic
MRSA ambrosial
ambrosian
Amerasian
MRSE impressed
MRSR embrasure
impresari
MRTL umbratile
MRTO amarettos
MRUL amorously
MRVN improving
MRVO improve on
MRVS improvise
MSHT Smash Hits
MSIL omissible
MSIT smash into
MSMN amassment
amusement
MSNL amusingly
MTAC omittance
MTEE smothered
smotherer
MTET umpteenth
MTNS emptiness
MTOA emotional
MTRA amatorial
Amsterdam
MTTL empty talk
MTTN imitating
MTTO imitation
MTTV imitative
MUAC ambulance
MUAL immutable
immutably
imputable
imputably
MUAR ambulacra
MUCD ambuscade
MUEC impudence
MUOI amaurosis
amaurotic
MUSA ombudsman
MUSE Ombudsmen
MUSO impulsion
MUSV impulsive
MZMN amazement
MZNA Amazonian
MZNL amazingly
NAAC on balance
unbalance
NAAE undamaged
NAAL incapable
incapably
uncapable
uneatable
unsavable
unsayable
untamably
NABU unharbour
NACE unlatched
unmatched
unwatched
NACI Antarctic
NACN enhancing
NADL one and all
unhandily
NAEE unwatered

NAEI	engaged in
NAEL	Annabella
	Annabelle
NAEO	engage for
NAET	Ungaretti
NAGE	entangled
NAGN	enlarging
NAGO	enlarge on
NAHO	in fashion
NAIE	inhabited
NAIL	en famille
	invalidly
NAIN	invariant
NAIT	insatiety
NAKN	unmasking
NALK	unwarlike
NALN	engarland
	unfailing
NALO	intaglios
NALS	in ballast
NAMN	in harmony
NANE	undaunted
	untainted
NANL	uncannily
NANS	in earnest
	in harness
	unharness
NANT	incarnate
NAOI	Annapolis
NAON	any amount
NAOR	unsavoury
NAOT	in cahoots
NAPL	unhappily
NAPR	en rapport
	in bad part
	in rapport
NARE	unmarried
NARU	Anna Freud
NASI	encaustic
NASN	en passant
	in passing
NATE	unearthed
NATL	infantile
	unearthly
NATN	andantino
NATO	incaution
NATR	enrapture
	in tatters
NAUA	unnatural
NAUE	unmatured
NAUN	Annapurna
NAUT	infatuate
NAYN	unvarying
NBDA	in a bad way
NBGA	in a big way
NBIN	inebriant
NBIT	inebriate
	inebriety
NBLS	anabolism
NBLT	inability
NBOE	snub-nosed
NBRU	Enobarbus
NBSE	unabashed

NBTU	Knabstrup
NCAL	unactable
NCBC	knock back
	knock-back
NCCL	knock cold
NCCP	knock copy
NCDW	knock down
	knock-down
NCEE	knackered
NCET	enucleate
NCEU	Anacletus
	knocker-up
NCIE	inscriber
NCLM	in a column
NCLT	inoculate
NCLU	unicolour
NCMN	enactment
NCNE	ensconced
NCNS	aniconism
	aniconist
NCOA	anecdotal
NCOE	knock over
NCON	on account
NCRE	in a corner
NCTE	unscathed
NCUE	anacruses
NCUI	anacrusis
NCWO	knock wood
NDAC	in advance
NDIE	unadvised
NDNS	snideness
NDPE	unadopted
NDRE	unadorned
NDTE	in a dither
NEAA	antenatal
NEAE	unrelated
	unrelaxed
NEAI	inter alia
NEAL	enterable
	inferable
	untenable
NEBA	underbear
NEBE	enfeebled
	interbred
	underbred
NEBR	inselberg
NEBS	underbush
NEBT	underbite
NECA	underclad
	undercoat
NECD	intercede
NECK	angel cake
NECM	unwelcome
NECO	intercrop
	undercook
	undercool
NECP	intercept
NECR	undercard
	undercart
NECT	inner city
	inner-city
	intercity
NECU	underclub

NEDA	underdraw
NEDC	interdict
NEDL	unheedily
	unreadily
NEDN	unbending
	underdone
	unheeding
NEDO	intend for
NEDS	angel dust
	interdash
NEEA	in general
	in several
NEEC	indecency
	inference
NEEE	unrenewed
NEEO	Angelenos
NEEV	in reserve
	undeceive
	undeserve
	unreserve
NEFC	interface
NEFE	underfeed
NEFL	interfold
	underfelt
NEFN	underfund
NEFO	interflow
	underflow
	underfoot
NEFR	interfere
	underfire
NEFS	angel-fish
	interfuse
	unselfish
NEGE	inveigled
	inveigler
	unfeigned
	unweighed
NEGI	once again
NEGO	intergrow
NEGR	undergird
NEHN	underhand
	underhung
NEIE	antefixes
	endenizen
	inherited
	undecided
	undefiled
	undefined
	undesired
	unmerited
	unrefined
NEII	enteritis
NEIL	indelible
	indelibly
NEIO	inheritor
NEIT	enter into
NEIU	ingenious
NEIV	unbelieve
NEJC	interject
NEJI	interjoin
NEKI	interknit
NELA	interleaf
NELC	intellect

	interlace
	interlock
NELD	interlude
NELH	unhealthy
NELN	annealing
	index-link
	interline
	interlink
	underline
	underling
	unfeeling
	unveiling
NELP	interlope
NELR	interlard
NELS	unrealise
NELT	in reality
	unreality
NELZ	unrealize
NEMN	interment
	undermine
	unseeming
NEMO	in terms of
NEMS	innermost
	undermost
NEND	internode
NENF	indemnify
NENN	unmeaning
	unpenning
NENS	Inverness
NENT	indemnity
	undernote
NENW	unbeknown
NEOE	enveloped
	envenomed
	unbeloved
NEOI	anaerobic
	unmelodic
NEON	Anne Bonny
NEOT	under oath
NEOU	indecorum
NEPA	interplay
	unbespeak
	underplay
NEPE	interpret
	underpeep
	unpeopled
NEPG	interpage
NEPN	in keeping
	interpone
NEPS	interpose
	underpass
NEPU	unhelpful
NERE	enhearten
	unlearned
	unwearied
NERI	interrail
NERN	Anne Frank
	endearing
	integrand
	unbearing
	under-ring
NERO	unheard of
	unheard-of

NERP interrupt
NERT integrate
integrity
underrate
under-rate
NESA underseal
NESC intersect
NESD underside
NESF intensify
NESG undersign
NESL inner self
intensely
inversely
undersell
NESN incessant
unceasing
NESO en pension
in session
intension
inversion
undershot
NEST insensate
intensity
NESV intensive
NETA ancestral
NETB inner tube
NETC intestacy
NETE unsettled
NETI entertain
uncertain
NETK undertake
NETL infertile
NETN intestine
investing
undertone
unresting
unseating
NETO inception
indention
infection
ingestion
injection
insertion
intention
invention
NETP Intertype®
NETR ancestors
indenture
inventory
NETS invertase
NETT intestate
NETV incentive
inceptive
infective
invective
inventive
NEUE unrebuked
unsecured
NEUL unbeguile
NEUN ungenuine
NEUO enter upon
NEUT ingenuity
NEUU ingenuous
NEVC in service
in-service
NEVE interview
NEVI intervein
NEVN intervene
unnerving
NEVR unpervert
NEVS undervest
NEVT innervate
NEVU endeavour❑
NEWA underwear
NEWE in-between
once a week
NEWL inner wall
NEWN interwind
underwing
NEWO underwood❑
NEWR interwork
underwork
NEYA once a year
NFAL ineffable
ineffably
unifiable
NFEG knife-edge
NFEZ in a frenzy
NFLN sniffling
snuffling
NFRE uniformed
NFRL uniformly
NFRN end for end
NGAI enigmatic
NGEE sniggerer
NGLU snuggle up
NHAH ensheathe
insheathe
unsheathe
NHBA on the beam
on the beat
on the bias
NHBF in the buff
NHBI on the boil
NHBL on the ball
NHBO on the broo
NHBS on the bash
NHCA anthocyan
NHCE unchecked
NHCL unshackle
NHCR in the cart
NHCU in the club
on the club
NHDL on the dole
NHDR in the dark
NHEG on the edge
NHGM on the game
NHHO on the hoof
NHHU on the hour
NHIE enchained
NHIT unthrifty
NHKO in the know
NHLA inshallah
in the lead
NHLD enchilada
NHLE enshelter
innholder
inshelter
NHLG anthology
NHLM in the lump
NHLO anthelion
NHLS anchylose
NHMI in the main
NHMK on the make
NHMN in the mind
on the mend
NHMS in the mass
NHMV on the move
NHNC on thin ice
NHND in the nude
NHNE enchanted
enchanter
unchanged
NHNI on the nail
NHNS on the nose
NHOE in the open
NHPL on the pill
NHPN in the pink
NHPS in the past
NHRA anchorman
enchorial
in the rear
in the road
On the Road
on the road
NHRE uncharnel
uncharted
NHRG anchorage❑
NHRS anchoress
on the rise
NHRT anchorite
NHRU anthurium
NHSA in this way
NHSD on the side
NHSI in the shit
in the swim
NHSO on the spot
on-the-spot
NHSU in the soup
NHTE unshutter
NHTK on the take
NHTO on the trot
NHTR on the turn
NHTW On the Town
NHWN in the wind
on the wane
on the wing
NIAE indicated
NIAH antipathy
NIAL inaidable
NIAO indicator
NIAT antipasto
NIBN in ribbons
NICE encircled
unhitched
NICR insincere
NICU Antiochus
NIDE unriddler
NIDN unbinding
unwinding
NIDU unmindful
NIEA Gneisenau
NIEC incidence
indigence
on-licence
NIEE enlivener
unripened
NIEI antivenin
unlived-in
NIEU antiserum
inside out
NIGA angiogram
NIGS in disgust
NIHE enlighten
unsighted
NIHL Annie Hall
unsightly
NIHN enriching
NIHO in right of
NIIE inhibited
inhibiter
undivided
unlimited
unvisited
NIIL insipidly
invisible
invisibly
uncivilly
NIIN incipient
NIIO inhibitor
NIIU insidious
invidious
NILC inviolacy
NILE infielder
NILK snail-like
NILN anticline
unwilling
NILR ancillary
NILT inviolate
NIMI snail mail
NIMR infirmary
NIMT angio-mata
infirmity
NINC antiknock
NINE Indian red
NINF undignify
NINL anciently
NINN Indian ink
indignant
NINR ancientry
NINS Indianise
unfitness
NINT indignity
NINZ Indianize
NIOA antipodal
NIOE anti-novel
antipodes
NIOI antitoxin
NIOU Antigonus
NIPA on display
NIPS indispose
NIPT in dispute

Words marked ❑ can also be spelled with an initial capital letter

NIRG antitragi
NIRO encierros
NISE unbiassed
NISS gneissose
NITL unwittily
NITN enlisting
insistent
unfitting
unsisting
unwitting
NITO indiction
NIUE undiluted
NIUL antiquely
anxiously
enviously
NIUR antiquary
NIUT antiquate
antiquity
insinuate
NIYN unpitying
NKBR snakebird
NKBT snakebite
NKEE innkeeper
NKIU Inuktitut
NKLE unskilled
NKLK snakelike
NKLU unskilful
NKNS snakiness
NKWE snakeweed
NKWS snakewise
NLAA Anglo-Arab
NLAL uncleanly
unpliable
NLCE inflicter
unblocked
NLCO inflictor
in place of
NLCS anglicise
Anglicism
NLCZ anglicize
NLDE unfledged
NLDI include in
NLDN including
NLEC influence
NLEE unaltered
NLEI analgesia
analgesic
NLEZ influenza
NLGN inelegant
NLGS analogise
NLGU analogous
NLGZ analogize
NLIE unclaimed
NLIO angle iron
NLME unplumbed
NLMN inclement
inflaming
NLNE unplanned
unplanted
NLNN inclining
NLNO inglenook
NLOE unalloyed
NLPI analeptic

NLPR in ill part
NLRE unalarmed
NLSI inelastic
unelastic
NLSL endlessly
NLSN analysand
enclosing
NLSO inclusion
NLSR enclosure
inclosure
NLSV inclusive
NLTE in a lather
unclothed
NLTO inflation
NLUE unclouded
NLUH onslaught
NLWN inflowing
unflowing
NLWS anglewise
NLXO inflexion
NMEE anamneses
unimpeded
NMEI anamnesis
NMEO a number of
NMLA animal fat
NMLE enamelled
NMLN unsmiling
NMLS animalise
animalism
animalist
NMLT animality
NMLU anomalous
NMLZ animalize
NMMN in a moment
NMNE in a manner
NMNT any minute
in a minute
NMRT enumerate
inamorata
inamorato
inumbrate
NMSI animistic
NMST animosity
NMTN animating
NMTO animation
NMUE enamoured
NMUS on impulse
NNAE inundated
unengaged
NNCS in any case
NNHN in any hand
NNIE uninvited
NNIT enunciate
NNMS anonymise
NNMT anonymity
inanimate
unanimity
NNMU anonymous
unanimous
NNMZ anonymize
NNNS inaneness
NNSA on one's way
NNSD on one side

NNSI onanistic
NNSO on one's tod
NNSW on one's own
NNTL uninstall
NNTO inanition
inunction
NNUE uninjured
NNUS in anguish
NNWN unknowing
NOAA in so far as
insofar as
NOAC annoyance
NOAL enjoyable
enjoyably
unmovable
unmovably
unwomanly
NOAO annotator
innovator
NOAT into parts
NOBE undoubted
NOBN uncombine
NOCE untouched
NOCP endoscope
endoscopy
NOCR in concert
unconcern
NODG in bondage
NODM onion dome
NODN unfolding
unloading
NODO any old how
NOEA income tax
in some way
NOEB annoyed by
NOEC Antonescu
indolence
innocence
insolence
NOEE onion-eyed
uncovered
NOEI Indonesia
oncogenic
ontogenic
NOEL unmovedly
NOET in poverty
NOFN unconfine
NOGA uncongeal
NOHG endophagy
NOHT endophyte
NOIA on holiday
NOIE unionized
unnoticed
NOIM encomiums
NOIN Antonioni
NOIS encomiast
NOIU Antoninus
NOJC Union Jack
NOKN onlooking
NOKR onlookers
NOLF enjoy life
NOLL ungodlily
unworldly

NOLN unrolling
NOLS endoplasm
NOMD incommode
NOMN endowment
enjoyment
enrolment
in command
informant
informing
NONA insomniac
NONE announcer
encounter❑
enjoinder
unbounded
uncounted
unfounded
unjointed
unpointed
unrounded
unsounded
NONI in council
NONL unsoundly
NONO in point of
NONT incognito
NOOI ontologic
NOOP endomorph
NOPE uncoupled
NOPI endorphin
NOPN in company
NOPO encolpion
NOPR endosperm
NOPS encompass
NORC incorrect
NORE unworried
NORG encourage
entourage
NORN endocrine
NORP incorrupt
uncorrupt
NOSN endorsing
NOSR in consort
NOTL uncouthly
NOTO in control
NOUA unpopular
NOUE unfocused
NOUL insoluble
insolubly
NOUR involucre
NOUU innocuous
NOVN insolvent
NPAG snap gauge
NPCO inspector
NPEE anopheles
NPIE unspoiled
NPNS inaptness
ineptness
unaptness
NPOE unopposed
NPOI anaphoric
kniphofia
NPRN inspiring
unsparing
NPRU uniparous

NPTE	unspotted
NPTM	in epitome
NPTO	in spite of
NQAL	unequally
NRAC	inerrancy
NRAE	enervated
	increased
	undreamed
	untreated
NRAH	enwreathe
	inbreathe
	inwreathe
	unwreathe
NRAI	inorganic
NRAL	inerrably
NRAO	Andrianov
NRCA	entrechat
NRCC	intricacy
NRCO	infractor
NRCT	entrecôte
	intricate
NRDC	introduce
NRDE	unbridled
	untrodden
NRDN	intruding
NRDU	snare-drum
NREI	energetic
NREO	enfreedom
NRER	in arrears
NRET	in order to
NRGD	André Gide
NRGE	intrigued
	intriguer
NRGN	intrigant
NRHS	anarchise
	anarchism
	anarchist
NRHZ	anarchize
NRIE	energizer
	ingrained
	unpraised
	untrained
NRJC	introject
NRLG	andrology
NRMD	Andromeda
NRME	entrammel
NRMN	increment
	inurement
NRMO	encrimson
NRMT	entremets
NRMU	en primeur
NRNE	entranced
	infringer
	unbranded
NRNG	engrenage
NRNI	in transit
	intrinsic
NRNL	unwrinkle
NRNO	in front of
NRNS	inertness
NRNU	entre nous
NROE	ungroomed
NROT	Andreotti
NRPE	entrapper
NRPR	unprepare
NRSA	András Fay
NRSE	engrossed
	uncrossed
	undressed
NRSL	end result
NRSO	intrusion
NRSV	intrusive
NRTE	unwritten
NRTL	ingrately
NRTN	in writing
NRUH	indraught
	unfraught
NRUL	in trouble
	onerously
NRVC	in privacy
NRVD	unprovide
NRVK	unprovoke
NRVN	engraving
NRVR	introvert
NRVT	in private
NRWE	uncrowded
	uncrowned
NRWN	in drawing
	ingrowing
NRYA	energy gap
NSAA	in as far as
NSAE	unashamed
NSAI	Anastasia
NSAL	unusually
NSEC	in essence
	unessence
NSNN	unisonant
NSNU	unisonous
NSRC	Innsbruck
NSRN	on a string
NSRP	in a scrape
NSXA	unisexual
NTAE	gnateater
NTAL	initially
NTAO	initiator
	instead of
NTDE	unstudied
NTEA	anathemas
NTEE	unuttered
NTET	and twenty
NTGT	instigate
NTHL	snatchily
NTHN	snatching
NTIA	unethical
NTIE	unstained
NTIG	and things
NTLA	Anatolian
NTLT	inutility
NTME	in a temper
NTMS	anatomise
	anatomist
NTMZ	anatomize
NTNB	on standby
	on stand-by
NTNE	instanced
	unstinted
NTNL	instantly
NTOI	gnathonic
NTPE	unstopped
	unstopper
NTRA	Unitarian
NTRC	unit price
NTRE	unstirred
NTRS	knot grass
	knotgrass
	unit trust
NTSD	on its side
NTTT	institute
NTVL	unitively
NUAC	endurance
	insurance
NUAE	insulated
	undulated
NUAI	pneumatic
NUAL	endurable
	endurably
	incurable
	incurably
	inhumanly
	insularly
	insurable
	uncurable
	untunably
NUAO	incubator
	insulator
NUBN	incumbent
NUBR	in numbers
NUCT	inculcate
NUDE	unbundler
	unsubdued
NUEC	intumesce
NUEL	inquietly
	unquietly
NUET	indumenta
NUEU	untuneful
NUFE	unruffled
NUGI	indulge in
NUGN	indulgent
	insurgent
NUGO	endungeon
NUHN	inrushing
	onrushing
NUIA	unmusical
NUIL	inaudible
	inaudibly
	inducible
	infusible
NUIT	infuriate
NUIU	incurious
	injurious
	undutiful
NUKL	unluckily
NULE	unsullied
NULI	in full rig
NULN	annulling
	unfurling
NULR	in full cry
NULS	annualise
NULZ	annualize
NUMI	in turmoil
NUMN	annulment
NUNO	innuendos
NUNS	unfurnish
NUNT	inquinate
NUOE	untutored
NUOI	pneumonia
NUPS	on purpose
NUPT	inculpate
NURE	enquiries
	inquiries
	unguarded
	unhurried
NURN	enquiring
	inquiring
NURT	inquorate
NUSE	anguished
NUSO	incursion
NUSV	incursive
NUTC	injustice
NUTD	in custody
NUTI	encurtain
	uncurtain
NUTM	in due time
NUTN	insulting
NUTO	induction
	intuition
NUTV	inductive
	intuitive
NUUA	inaugural
NUVN	uncurving
NUVT	incurvate
NUZE	unmuzzled
NVLE	sniveller
NVLN	univalent
NVNE	an even bet
NVRA	universal
NVRG	on average
NVRI	I never did!
NVSL	knavishly
NWDL	unswaddle
NWEG	knowledge
NWER	snowberry
NWHT	snow-white
NWIL	snowfield
NWLK	snowflake
NWLN	snow-blind
NWNE	inswinger
	snow under
NWNL	knowingly
NWNS	snowiness
NWON	snowbound
NWOR	snowboard
NWOS	snow goose
NWRF	snowdrift
NWRO	answer for
NWTL	know-it-all
NWTO	in two twos
NWTR	snow storm
	snowstorm
NXCL	inexactly
NXIE	unexcited
NXLE	unexalted

NYAI enzymatic
NYAL untypable
NYIA untypical
NYNL undyingly
NYOC in my voice
NYOI ankylosis
NYRD anhydride
NYRU anhydrous
OAAA go bananas
OAAC soja sauce
soya sauce
OAAE soda water
OAAG for a laugh
OAAL rotatable
OAAT Bonaparte
OABA polar bear
OABL rocambole
OABU royal blue
OACA not a scrap
OACD local code
moral code
OACE tobaccoes
OACL local call
solar cell
OACN romancing
OACS mosaicist
OADC cowardice
OADI Tom and Tib
OADO Box and Cox
OADU go hard but
OAEA forage-cap
OAEI copacetic
kopasetic
OAEL Donatello
OAEO forage for
how are you?
OAEU rosaceous
OAFR royal fern
OAGE botargoes
OAGN cotangent
OAGO coraggios
OAHL notaphily
OAHM not at home
OAHN not a thing
OAHO borachios
womanhood
OAHR Local Hero
OAHS monachism
OAHU Fomalhaut
OAIA botanical
foraminal
OAIC tovarisch
OAIE cohabitee
localized
moralizer
totaliser
totalizer
womanizer
OAIH logarithm
Mogadishu
OAIN donations
OAIT vocalists
OAIU voracious
OAKN womankind
OALK womanlike
OALM Jonah Lomo
OALN coralline
totalling
OALT for all it's
OAMC forasmuch
not as much
OAMN not as many
OAMS royal mast
OANS cocainise
OANZ cocainize
OAOI moratoria
OAON not around
OAOT go cahoots
OAPL royal palm
OAPN go camping
OAPS woman post
OAQE Bosanquet
OARA Nolan Ryan
OASU potassium
OASW Woman's Own
OATA Mozartean
Mozartian
OATE corantoes
OATL moral tale
OATM local time
solar time
OATR for a start
monastery
OAVN vol-au-vent
OAWE coral weed
OAWN solar wind
OAWR go haywire
not at work
OAYA Botany Bay
solar year
OBAL porbeagle
OBAO Bob Beamon
OBCE Gorbachev
OBDA forbiddal
OBDE forbidden
low-budget
OBDT morbidity
OBEC double act
OBEL dor beetle
OBEO sombreros
OBET soubrette
OBGN wobbegong
woebegone
OBHL bombshell
OBIE cor blimey
gorblimey
pot-boiler
OBIH too bright
OBIT lobbyists
OBLA Roubiliac
OBLE corbelled
non-belief
OBLF corbel off
OBLS doubtless
OBLT bombilate
OBLU corbel out
OBNL sobbingly
OBNN combining
top banana
OBNT bombinate
OBOG Joe Bloggs
OBRE pot barley
OBRO bombproof
bomb-proof
OBSI bombastic
OBSL yobbishly
OBSN bombasine
OBTA booby-trap
OBTD woe betide
OBTN combatant
tombstone
OBTS sorbitise
OBTV combative
OBTZ sorbitize
OBYS tomboyish
OCAC how chance?
Tom Clancy
OCAE concealed
concealer
Lon Chaney
moschatel
OCAL touchable
OCBC force back
OCBN concubine
OCCE concocted
concocter
OCCO concoctor
OCCR Joyce Cary
OCDW touch down
OCEG concierge
OCEK Rodchenko
OCET couchette
OCFE force-feed
OCFL pouchfuls
OCHL touch-hole
OCIE conceited
OCIU colchicum
OCLA conciliar
dog-collar
OCLI porcelain
OCLN force-land
touchline
OCLR con calore
OCLS forceless
voiceless
OCMA forcemeat
OCMI coxcombic
OCMO Roscommon
OCNE concenter
volcanoes
OCNL do a candle
OCNN Toscanini
OCNR concentre
OCNS volcanise
OCNZ volcanize
OCOA Conchobar
OCOC for choice
OCOE force open
voice-over
OCON no-account
to account
OCPN porcupine
OCRA concordat
OCRE concerned
concerted
OCRI Concordia
OCRO concertos
OCRS sorceress
OCRU sorcerous
OCSE concussed
Doncaster
Worcester
OCSF vouchsafe
OCSL concisely
OCSO concision
OCTP touch-type
OCTU coach tour
OCUE concluded
OCUO touch upon
OCUS concourse
Tom Cruise
OCVL concavely
OCVT concavity
dolce vita
OCWO touch wood
touchwood
OCWR coachwork
ODAA food canal
ODAD hold hands
ODAE bond paper
Goldwater
goodfaced
hold water
toad-eater
top drawer
top-drawer
ODAL cordially
ODAO Lord Mayor
ODAT good taste
ODAU good value
ODCE woodscrew
ODCL hold a call
ODCO conductor
ODCV conducive
ODDL condiddle
ODEA gold medal
ODEE fondue set
ODEH Dordrecht
ODEI toodle-pip
ODEL soldierly
ODEM good terms
ODEO soldier on
ODER goodyears
ODES good sense
ODEU doodlebug
ODGE to a degree
ODGL condignly
ODHC woodchuck
ODHE good cheer
ODHI food chain
ODHN good thing
ODHP good shape

ODIC goldfinch
ODIH goodnight
hold tight
ODIL goldfield
ODIR wood fibre
ODKI pondokkie
ODLC roadblock
wood block
woodblock
ODLE gondolier
ODLN word-blind
ODLO bordellos
ODLR con dolore
ODLS hold close
ODLT gold plate
gold-plate
ODLV bond-slave
ODME condemned
ODMI Golda Meir
ODMN condiment
ODMT goldsmith❑
wordsmith
ODNE condensed
condenser
fold under
ODNF cordon off
ODNG golden age
ODNL mordantly
noddingly
ODNN condoning
ODNO goldenrod
good on you
ODNS dowdiness
goodiness
hoydenish
hoydenism
Londonise
lordiness
moodiness
rowdiness
woodiness
wordiness
ODNT coadunate
ODNW Lord knows
ODNY GoldenEye
golden-eye
ODNZ Londonize
ODOA bondwoman
ODOD how-d'you-do
ODOI road movie
ODOK good looks
roadworks
ODON gold point
good point
ODOR food court
hold court
ODOS Gold Coast
loud noise
roadhouse
Woodhouse
woodlouse
ODOT hold forth
loudmouth
loud-mouth
ODPL toddy-palm
ODRA cold cream
ODRC gold brick
ODRE good grief
powder keg
word order
ODRF woodcraft
ODRI Hölderlin
ODRM cold frame
ODRN bordering
cold drink
cold front
doddering
pondering
soldering
wondering
ODRS goldcrest
good press
ODRT foederati
ponderate
ODRU ponderous
wonderful
ODRW gold crown
ODSN soi-disant
ODTA hold at bay
roadstead
ODTF foodstuff
ODTN loadstone
ODTO condition
toadstool
ODUA Lord Lucan
ODUO coadjutor
hold out on
ODWA cold sweat
ODYP wood nymph
OEAA cower away
OEAB Morecambe
OEAC rope-dance
tolerance
OEAD homewards
Romewards
OEAE forenamed
lose water
notepaper
pome-water
tolerated
wove paper
OEAL covetable
pole vault
tolerable
tolerably
OEAO dodecagon
moderator
OEAT foretaste
Jose Marti
lose caste
OEBG moneybags
OEBL money belt
note a bill
OEBR bowerbird
Rosenberg
OEBU come about
mope about
move about
OECE Morescoes
OECM honeycomb
OECS boxercise
lower-case
OEDC lower deck
OEDV power dive
OEDW lower down
money down
toned down
OEEC coherence
forereach
OEEG sovereign
OEEI oogenesis
yoke-devil
OEER forebears
lose heart
OEET foreteeth
novelette
OEFC for effect
OEFE come after
OEFG come of age
OEFI come off it!
OEFL womenfolk
OEFO home of God
OEGA Honeyghan
OEGE foreigner
OEGI come again
come again?
Lohengrin
OEGM power game
OEGN ion engine
OEGR cover girl
OEHL love child
love-child
OEHN bone china
forethink
Josephine
Joséphine
something
OEHR come short
foreshore
somewhere
OEIA Gore Vidal
polemical
OEIE fore-cited
home video
sometimes
OEIG Coleridge
coverings
OEIH foresight
sole right
OEIN dope-fiend
OEIS come first
OEIT cover into
Docetists
OEKN womenkind
OEKR foreskirt
OELA come clean
OELE nosebleed
OELN come along
Home Alone
modelling
power line
to be blunt
towelling
OELO lose blood
OELP pole-clipt
OELS coverless
foreclose
powellise
powerless
OELT home plate
OELU go belly up
go belly-up
OELV come alive
OELZ powellize
OEMN Dobermann
OEMO honeymoon
OEMS come amiss
OENA Korean War
OENE come under
gone under
OENF solemnify
OENG come and go
OENN foreanent
governing
hole in one
OENO come in for
OENR governors
OENS gooeyness
governess
modernise
modernism❑
modernist
soberness
solemnise
OENT cover note
modernity
solemnity
OENZ modernize
solemnize
OEOA foreroyal
forewoman
OEOB Morecombe
OEOE foretoken
forewomen
lose power
role model
tower over
OEOG not enough
OEOI home movie
OEON come round
foregoing
forepoint
move round
sore point
OEOO come to you
OEOR forecourt
OEOS gone goose
move house
Wodehouse
OEOT come forth
OEPA forespeak
OEPC not expect

	power pack
OEPL	totem pole
OEPN	forespend
OEPR	come apart
	hoverport
OEPT	homeopath
OERE	to be brief
OERF	homecraft
OERI	forebrain
OERN	forefront
	gone wrong
	to be frank
OERS	co-heiress
	voyeurism
OERT	home truth
OERW	dove-drawn
	home-grown
OESE	nor'-easter
OESI	women's lib
OESL	Dover sole
OESR	go berserk
OESU	rowel-spur
OETA	homestead
	lower than
	potential
OETE	none other
	novelties
	Robert Kee
	some other
OETF	Lowestoft
OETG	forestage
OETL	forestall
OETM	lobectomy
OETN	fomenting
	forestine
	go-getting
	lodestone
	momentany
OETO	dog-eat-dog
	Robertson
OETR	love story
	momentary
OETS	potentise
OETT	nonentity
	potentate
OETU	momentous
OETZ	potentize
OEUA	molecular
	poke fun at
OEUE	boletuses
	homebuyer
OEUG	forejudge
OEUI	come out in
OEUL	dolefully
	hopefully
OEUO	come out of
	move out of
OEUR	home guard
OEVH	yo-heave-ho
OEWE	go between
	go-between
	home-owner
OEWT	cover with
OEYA	come by car
OEYN	no denying
OFAO	for fear of
OFBN	wolfsbane
OFBR	Wolfsburg
OFCA	Confucian
OFCT	forficate
OFCU	Confucius
OFDN	confidant
	confident
	confiding
OFEA	coffee bar
OFEE	Toffeemen
OFEO	coffee pot
OFES	coiffeuse
OFGI	solfeggio
OFGR	configure
OFIE	forfeiter
OFIH	top-flight
OFIK	golf links
OFIN	boyfriend
OFLE	Roy Fuller
OFLN	moufflons
OFLO	vow-fellow
OFNE	Tom Finney
OFNN	confining
OFNT	coffinite
OFOI	hotfoot it
OFON	wolfhound
	wolf-hound
OFRA	cofferdam
	conferral
	confervae
	confervas
OFRE	confirmed
	conformer
	not forget
OFRF	not far off
OFRN	Solferino
OFRO	not for Joe
OFRT	conform to
	Nosferatu
OFSE	confessed
	rodfisher
OFSL	confestly
	wolfishly
OFSN	confusing
OFSO	confessor
	confusion
OFST	confess to
OFTE	godfather
OFTR	confiture
	solfatara
OFUN	confluent
OFWT	go off with
OGAC	long march
	poignancy
OGAE	congealed
	long-faced
OGAL	forgeable
OGBI	hobgoblin
OGCS	roughcast
OGCT	Doug Scott
OGDA	rough-draw
OGDO	cough drop
	cough-drop
OGDW	cough down
OGEC	Long Beach
OGEE	toughened
	toughener
OGEI	tongue-tie
OGEL	mongrelly
OGEN	Joe Greene
OGEO	goggle-box
OGET	lorgnette
OGFL	Fongafale
OGGA	Volgograd
OGHI	Lou Gehrig
OGHR	longshore
OGHW	rough-hewn
OGIE	long-lived
	rough idea
OGIL	long field
OGIS	go against
OGLA	Mongolian
OGLC	tough luck
OGLI	Mongoloid
OGLN	coagulant
OGLS	Mongolise
	mongolism
OGLT	coagulate
OGLV	tough love
OGLZ	Mongolize
OGMT	songsmith
OGNA	congenial
	not go near
OGNC	roughneck
OGNI	gorgoneia
OGNL	longingly
OGNS	bogginess
	fogginess
	gorgonise
	podginess
	roughness
	sogginess
	toughness
OGNZ	gorgonize
OGOE	mongooses
OGPF	rough-puff
OGRA	Low German
OGRE	conger eel
	congeries
OGRI	Podgorniy
OGRR	Tongariro
OGRW	long-drawn
OGSE	congested
OGSL	doggishly
	hoggishly
OGSO	roughshod
OGTD	longitude
OGTE	forgather
	forgotten
OGTL	doughtily
OGTR	long story
OGTU	forgetful
OGTV	forgetive
OGUL	songfully
OGUN	congruent
OGUT	congruity
OGUU	congruous
OGVN	forgiving
OGVT	longevity
OGVU	longevous
	not give up
OGWT	not go with
OGYL	song cycle
OHAE	hotheaded
	hot-headed
	moth-eaten
OHAO	go ahead of
OHBC	to the back
OHBN	to the bone
OHCE	no chicken
	Sophocles
OHCR	to the core
OHCS	gothicise
OHCZ	gothicize
OHEE	Loch Leven
OHET	cochleate
OHFL	to the full
OHFR	to the fore
OHGO	to the good
OHHL	to the hilt
OHLE	job-holder
OHLF	to the life
OHLN	pot-holing
OHMN	Ho Chi Minh
	vox humana
OHMT	Gothamite
OHNA	cochineal
	Lochinvar
OHNE	pot-hunter
OHOA	Loch Morar
OHOG	go through
OHPC	go the pace
OHRA	Rotherham
	to the rear
OHRN	bothering
OHRO	Lotharios
	mothproof
OHSE	Rochester
OHSI	sophistic
	Sophus Lie
OHSL	go whistle
OHSM	do the same
OHSR	sophistry
OHTE	no whither
OHWD	to the wide
OIAC	dominance
OIAE	dominated
	nominated
OIAI	boric acid
	folic acid
OIAL	cogitable
	comically
	conically
	logically
	nominally
	topically

toxically
OIAO motivator
nominator
OIAR solitaire
OIAT Rosinante
OIBM logic bomb
OIBN ionic bond
sonic bang
OIBO sonic boom
OIBR politburo❑
OICE Moriscoes
OICO Robin Cook
OIDA no big deal
OIDE Bo Diddley
OIDN go wilding
OIEA policeman
poriferan
OIEE dosimeter
focimeter
Polixenes
Sosigenes
OIEI homiletic
OIEO police dog
OIER D'Oliveira
Yogi Berra
OIET Donizetti
OIGA coping-saw
OIGO Bonington
OIGU coming out
coming-out
loving-cup
poking out
OIHF polish off
OIHN go fishing
polishing
OIHO Robin Hood
OIHU do without
go without
OIIA Dominican
homicidal
political
OIIE domiciled
mobilizer
OIIL politicly
OIIN boliviano
Louisiana
OIIO politicos
solicitor
OIIR nobiliary
OIIT noviciate
novitiate
OILG sociology
OILO nonillion
OILS socialise
socialism
socialist
OILT joviality
socialite
sociality
OILZ socialize
OINE coriander
Ionian Sea
OINS solidness

OIOU soliloquy
OIPT sociopath
OIRS topiarist
OISA movie star
OISD go airside
OISE Holinshed
not in step
OISN go missing
OISS solipsism
solipsist
OITC logistics
OITO foliation
OITR foliature
OITS sovietise
sovietism
OITZ sovietize
OIUA lodiculae
OIUL copiously
noxiously
OIWN tonic wine
OIWT solid with
OIYN modifying
OJGT conjugate
OJIE conjoined
OJKN not joking
OJRN conjuring
OJRU conjure up
OKAE bookmaker
folk tales
folktales
OKAL workmanly
worktable
OKAU book value
OKCE corkscrew
OKCM cockscomb
OKDA cocked hat
OKDE mockadoes
OKDO looked-for
OKDU booked-out
conked out
zonked out
OKEC workbench
OKEF cockneyfy
OKEU not keep up
OKEV folk-weave
OKFE look after
OKFO cocksfoot
OKFR work of art
OKHE worksheet
OKHL bookshelf
cook-chill
OKHO cock-a-hoop
monkshood
OKHR look sharp
look where
Yorkshire
OKIC workpiece
OKIH cockfight
OKIN Cockaigne
OKLC book block
workplace
OKLK lookalike
look-alike

OKLN rock plant
OKLT bookplate
OKLV look alive
OKML look small
OKMR look smart
OKMT locksmith
OKNL mockingly
soakingly
OKNR look angry
OKNS cockiness
corkiness
rockiness
Tonkinese
OKNU soaking-up
OKOA workwoman
OKOC cockroach
workforce
OKOI folkloric
OKON lock horns
rock-bound
OKOS workhorse
OKPU Yom Kippur
OKRC book price
OKRL Cockerell
rock 'n' roll
OKRO lookers-on
OKRP rock tripe
OKRR rocker arm
OKTD work study
OKTE cockateel
cockatiel
rocketeer
Tom Kitten
OKTI Jock Stein
work ethic
OKTL bookstall
OKTN bookstand
honky-tonk
pocketing
rocketing
OKTU pocketful
OKUI folk music
OKUO look out on
OKWI cockswain
OKYS jockeyism
OKYU monkey nut
OLAD foolhardy
OLAE toolmaker
OLAL mouldable
not liable
OLAN Pollyanna
OLAU colleague
OLBA jollyboat
OLBN World Bank
OLBU fool about
loll about
OLCE collected
OLCO collector
OLCT collocate
OLDH Roald Dahl
OLDN colluding
OLEE poulterer
OLEO no flies on

OLFE mollifier
OLGE bow-legged
OLGN Goolagong
OLGS collagist
zoologist
OLGT colligate
OLHC hollyhock
OLHR Coulthard
OLIA colloidal
OLIE coal-fired
coalminer
OLIL coalfield
OLLC coal-black
OLLN bowl along
roll along
worldling
OLML foul smell
OLMR Collymore
OLMT collimate
OLMW mollymawk
OLNA collinear
OLNE Boulanger
OLNL lollingly
OLNS godliness
jolliness
lowliness
nobleness
OLNT pollinate
OLOE Joel Cohen
OLOT goalmouth
tollbooth
Woolworth
OLPE collapsed
OLQI colloquia
OLRA bowler hat
OLRL forlornly
OLRN collaring
OLRO foolproof
OLRT Hollerith
OLSA Boyle's law
OLSE coalesced
OLSL foolishly
godlessly
joylessly
OLSO collision
collusion
pollusion
OLSV collusive
OLTA popliteal
would that
OLTF cowl-staff
OLTL Doolittle
too little
OLTN pollutant
polluting
OLTO coalition
collation
pollution
OLTP collotype
OLTU voilà tout
OLUE soul-curer
OLUI soul music
OLUL soulfully

9 _O_L_V

OLVE	world-view
OLVR	boulevard
OLWD	worldwide
OLWN	following
OLWO	Bollywood
	Hollywood
OLWR	followers
	World War I
OLWT	go ill with
OLWU	follow out
	hollow out
OMAC	doomwatch
OMAE	worm-eaten
OMAK	form ranks
OMCR	formicary
OMDF	commodify
OMDR	commodore
OMDT	commodity
OMGN	cosmogony
OMHE	worm wheel
OMKI	not make it
OMLG	cosmology
OMLI	formulaic
OMLR	formulary
OMLS	formalise
	formalism
	formalist
	formulise
	normalise
OMLT	formality
	formulate
	normality
OMLZ	formalize
	formulize
	normalize
OMME	non-member
OMNA	commensal
	common law
	non-manual
	Roumanian
OMNE	commander
	commenter
	low-minded
	tormented
OMNI	tormentil
OMNL	commingle
	foamingly
OMNN	communing
OMNO	commandos
	comment on
	communion❑
	tormentor
OMNR	Common Era
	commoners
OMNS	communise
	communism
	communist
	foaminess
	loaminess
	Mormonism
	Normanise
	roominess
OMNT	comminate
	comminute
	community
OMNU	cosmonaut
OMNZ	communize
	Normanize
OMOE	wormholed
OMPR	for my part
OMRE	Bob Marley
OMRN	boomerang
	cormorant
OMSA	commissar
OMSN	Toamasina
OMTA	committal
OMTC	cosmetics
OMTE	committed
	committee
	formatter
	godmother
	not matter
OMTO	commotion
	formation
OMTR	dormitory
OMTS	dogmatise
	dogmatism
	dogmatist
OMTT	commutate
OMTV	formative
	normative
OMTZ	dogmatize
ONAA	going away
ONAC	round arch
ONAD	downwards
ONAE	horn-maker
	moon-faced
	moonraker
ONAL	countable
	not nearly
ONAN	John Wayne
ONAO	going AWOL
	John Cabot
	John Major
	John Mayow
ONBA	connubial
ONBR	doing bird
ONBT	coenobite
ONBU	coenobium
ONCE	connected
	connecter
ONCI	pound coin
ONCK	pound cake
ONCO	connector
	Mount Cook
ONCP	moonscape
	townscape
ONCT	to a nicety
ONDE	go on a diet
	poinadoes
	tornadoes
ONDM	John Adams
ONDW	going down
	going-down
ONEA	lounge bar
	roundelay
ONEB	Bounderby
ONEE	foundered
	young-eyed
ONEF	bounce off
ONEL	pointedly
ONEN	Mount Etna
ONER	John Henry
ONET	John Keats
	John Reith
ONEU	bounteous
	rounded up
ONFJ	Mount Fuji
ONFL	townsfolk
ONFR	Joan of Arc
ONGI	born again
	born-again
ONGO	John Ogdon
ONGR	young girl
ONHN	moonshine
	moonshiny
ONHR	down there
	loan shark
	loan-shark
ONIE	hobnailed
	John Piper
ONIH	downright
	moonlight
ONIL	Corneille
	John Mills
ONIN	poinciana
ONIU	bountiful
ONLA	cornelian
	John Elway
ONLC	point-lace
ONLD	young lady
ONLG	poenology
ONLN	foundling
	John Glenn
	somnolent
ONLR	John Clare
	town clerk
ONLS	boundless
	countless
	pointless
	soundless
ONLT	loincloth
ONLU	Cornelius
	cornflour
ONMI	you name it
ONMN	cognomens
	cognomina
ONMR	Connemara
ONMT	John Smith
ONNA	John Inman
ONNO	go on and on
ONNS	corniness
	downiness
	horniness
	jointness
	roundness
	soundness
ONNU	joining up
ONOA	go on to say
ONOE	born loser
	coin money
	going-over
	young ones
ONOK	boondocks
	John Locke
ONOL	down tools
ONON	John Donne
	John Soane
ONOS	Mount Ossa
	town house
	town-house
ONPK	John Speke
ONRA	Cointreau®
	corn bread
ONRD	downgrade
ONRE	countries
	John Arden
	town crier
ONRI	John Greig
ONRK	corncrake
ONRN	go in front
ONSA	go one's way
ONSD	to one side
ONSE	youngster
ONSG	pound sign
ONSI	do one's bit
ONSL	tonnishly
	to oneself
ONSN	cognisant
ONSO	John Astor
	point shoe
ONSU	do one's nut
	join issue
ONTC	not notice
ONTE	sonneteer
ONTG	downstage
ONTK	go and take
ONTM	doing time
ONTN	Johnstone
	moonstone
ONTO	cognation
	cognition
ONTR	Young Turk
ONTS	cornetist
	sonnetise
ONTT	connotate
ONTV	cognitive
	non-native
ONTZ	sonnetize
ONUH	Connaught
ONUL	moanfully
ONUO	count upon
	John Junor
ONUR	John Curry
ONVN	conniving
ONWN	downswing
ONWR	roundworm
ONWV	sound wave
ONXO	connexion
ONYE	down-gyved
	John Tyler
ONZN	cognizant

Words marked ❑ can also be spelled with an initial capital letter

OOAA go so far as
OOAD go towards
OOAH logomachy
OOAI honoraria
monogamic
monomania
OOAO Rotovator®
OOAS holocaust
polonaise
OOAT go to earth
go to waste
OOAU son of a gun
OOBA motor boat
OOBK motorbike
motor-bike
OOCD motorcade
OOCF motoscafi
OOCK Kokoschka
OOCP horoscope
horoscopy
OOCR donor card
OODR do wonders
OOEC colonelcy
OOEE hodometer
monometer
OOEI monomeric
OOEO Monoceros
OOET do to death
not open to
OOGL pot of gold
OOHA Motorhead
OOHB homophobe
OOHG Lotophagi
OOHM monorhyme
OOHN do nothing
do-nothing
homophone
homophony
OOHR notochord
polo shirt
OOHS molochise
OOHT holophyte
OOHZ molochize
OOIE colonized
colonizer
Dolomites
OOII honorific
soporific
OOIT notoriety
pogoniate
OOIU notorious❑
OOKE mono-skier
OOLE go to sleep
OOLN monocline
monoplane
OOLR corollary
OOLT now of late
OOMC do too much
OOMN do you mind?
no comment
OOND colonnade
OONN cocooning
OONS Bolognese
OONT go round to
OOOA go so low as
OOOC gonococci
OOOE horologer
OOOI horologic
OOOO locofocos
locomotor
OOOP homomorph
OOOR go to court
OOOU homologue
monocoque
monologue
OOPA so to speak
OORA colour bar
colourway
OORC mobocracy
monocracy
OORE sojourner
OORM monotreme
OORN colourant
colouring
honouring
OORP hodograph
holograph
homograph
logograph
monograph
nomograph
rotograph
sonograph
OORS colourise
colourist
go to grass
go to press
motocross
OORU colourful
OORZ colourize
OOSE Zoroaster
OOSN monopsony
OOSU colosseum
OOTC pogo stick
OOTM colostomy
OOTU colostrum
OOUA monocular
OOUE colobuses
OOUU Borobudur
OOVI to no avail
OOWR go forward
OOYI toponymic
OPAN complaint
OPAO to speak of
OPCC poppycock
OPCE compacted
OPCL compactly
OPDE torpedoes
OPDL dog-paddle
OPDT torpidity
OPDU pompadour
OPEA coup d'état
OPEE completed
OPEI morphemic
OPEL complexly
OPIE low-priced
OPIN compliant
OPLE compelled
OPLN corpulent
OPLO hoi polloi
OPLS gospelise
OPLZ gospelize
OPNI compendia
OPNL rompingly
toppingly
OPNN component
OPNO companion
cosponsor
OPNS soapiness
soppiness
OPOE gomphoses
not proven
OPOI non-profit
zoophobia
OPOY pompholyx
OPPE rod puppet
OPPL vox populi
OPPR soap opera
OPRA corporeal
OPRF corporify
OPRI nonpareil
OPRN godparent
OPRO non-person
OPRS do a perish
OPRT cooperate
co-operate
corporate
OPRU non-porous
OPSI go ape-shit
OPSL corpuscle
foppishly
rompishly
OPSO Dos Passos
OPSR composure
OPST composite
pomposity
OPTD torpitude
OPTK soopstake
OPTN competent
competing
soapstone
OPTT hot potato
OPUL pompously
OPUR potpourri
pot-pourri
OPWL go up a wall
OPYN complying
OQAL coequally
OQEE conquered
OQEO conqueror
ORAD your cards
ORAL not really
ORCL correctly
ORCO corrector
ORCS court case
ORDL comradely
ORDN corroding
joy-riding
ORDW worry down
OREA courtesan
OREE journeyer
OREI bourgeois❑
OREL worriedly
OREO tournedos
ORET courgette
OREU courteous
ORFE horrified
torrefied
ORGI Correggio
ORGT corrugate
worryguts
ORIL coercible
coercibly
ORLS four-flush
hourglass
ORLT coprolite
correlate
ORMN Borromini
Jo Grimond
worriment
ORNC doorknock
ORNE do a runner
porringer
ORNL louringly
roaringly
soaringly
ORNN sopranini
sopranino
ORNS hoariness
sorriness
OROA go crook at
OROG sourdough
OROO go crook on
OROR pourboire
OROS poorhouse
OROT poor-mouth
pour forth
ORPE corrupted
corrupter
ORPL corruptly
ORQE sobriquet
ORRA sour cream
ORRO boardroom
courtroom
ORRS hoar-frost
ORSE Forrester
nourisher
ORSI board ship
courtship
touristic
ORSL boorishly
sourishly
ORSM worrisome
ORSO corrosion
court shoe
court-shoe
ORSV corrosive
ORTS Socratise
ORTT coarctate
ORTZ Socratize
ORUD tour guide
ORUT poursuitt

Words marked ❑ can also be spelled with an initial capital letter

ORWN	borrowing
	sorrowing
ORWO	sorrow for
ORWU	sorrowful
ORYI	poorly lit
ORYR	courtyard
OSAA	go as far as
OSAC	Constance
	constancy
OSAE	bow-shaped
OSAH	moustache
OSAL	constable❑
OSAO	hors la loi
OSAP	Tom Sharpe
OSAT	Constanta
OSBA	houseboat
OSBC	horseback
OSBE	possibles
OSBR	mousebird
OSCA	housecoat
OSCD	Morse code
OSCE	top secret
	top-secret
OSDE	mouse-deer
OSEE	howsoever
	roisterer
OSEG	bobsleigh
OSEI	Bolshevik
OSET	poussette
OSEU	bolster up
OSFL	housefuls
OSFO	goosefoot
OSGE	consigned
	consignee
	consigner
OSGO	consignor
	Monsignor
OSGT	moss agate
OSHC	Rorschach
OSHI	horsehair
OSHL	household
OSHN	house-hunt
	mouse-hunt
OSIE	conspirer
OSIU	conscious
OSKN	forsaking
OSLA	loose-leaf
	tonsillar
OSLC	worse luck
OSLN	coastline
	consoling
OSLS	fossilise
	noiseless
OSLT	consolate
	consulate
OSLZ	fossilize
OSMC	not so much
OSMI	housemaid
OSML	noisomely
OSMN	consuming
	not so many
OSMR	consumers
	gossamery
OSNA	sons-in-law
OSNE	goosander
	pop singer
OSNL	rousingly
OSNN	consonant
	loosening
	worsening
OSNS	horsiness
	looseness
	lousiness
	moistness
	mossiness
	mousiness
	noisiness
OSNT	consent to
OSNU	consensus
	poisonous
OSNV	bossa nova
	bossanova
	poison ivy
OSOA	monsoonal
	torsional
OSOC	hopscotch
OSOE	non-smoker
OSOS	dosshouse
	lobscouse
OSOT	jobsworth
OSPA	horseplay
OSPE	gossipper
OSPN	gossiping
OSRA	fossorial
	Monsarrat
	tonsorial
	Yossarian
OSRB	conscribe
OSRC	constrict
	construct
	toast rack
OSRE	moss green
OSRI	consortia
	constrain
OSRN	hot spring
	Roy Strong
OSRO	houseroom
OSRP	conscript
OSRT	God's truth
OSRU	monstrous
OSSE	goose-step
	possessed
OSSF	noises off
OSSI	consist in
OSSO	consist of
	horseshoe
	houseshoe
	possessor
OSTA	mouse-trap
OSTC	joss-stick
OSTE	corsetier
OSTF	toss it off
OSTI	forsythia
	horsetail
OSTN	cosseting
OSVL	Roosevelt
OSWE	Bob Sawyer
	Tom Sawyer
OSWF	housewife
OSWI	horsewhip
OSWN	house wine
OSWR	coastward
	housework
OSWS	coastwise
OSXA	non-sexual
OTAA	Port Natal
	portrayal
	postnatal
	root canal
OTAC	Goa trance
OTAE	bootmaker
	portrayer
OTAH	toothache
OTAK	footmarks
OTAL	footfault
OTAN	hootnanny
OTAO	mortgagor
OTAS	lost cause
OTAT	contralti
	contralto
	Northants
	posthaste
	post-haste
OTAU	Port Salut
OTBM	cost a bomb
OTBN	South Bend
OTCA	mortician
OTCE	porticoes
OTCI	corticoid
OTCL	poeticule
OTCM	forthcome
OTCS	poeticise
	vorticism❑
	vorticist
OTCU	posticous
	youth club
OTCZ	poeticize
OTDN	contadine
	contadini
OTDW	Southdown
OTEA	soft pedal
	soft-pedal
OTEE	voltmeter
OTEI	zoothecia
OTEL	northerly
	southerly
OTEM	so it seems
OTEO	pottle-pot
OTES	north-east
	South-East
	south-east
OTET	top twenty
OTEU	bottled-up
OTFC	volte-face
OTFE	fortified
	fortifier
	for toffee
	mortified
OTFL	most of all
	mouthfuls
OTFO	coltsfoot
OTFV	forty-five
OTGE	Portuguee
OTGN	cottaging
OTGO	contagion
OTGR	Vortigern
OTIA	doctrinal
OTIE	bobtailed
	contained
	container
	contrived
	contriver
	doctrines
	most-liked
	tortrices
OTIG	no strings
OTIH	fortnight
OTIK	con tricks
OTIN	Montaigne
OTIO	Port Limon
OTIS	worthiest
OTLE	hosteller
	monthlies
	Tortelier
OTLG	sortilege
	sortilegy
OTLI	nostalgia
	nostalgic
OTLL	hostilely
OTLN	go it alone
	Mont Blanc
	portolani
	postulant
OTLO	postilion
OTLS	mortalise
	toothless
	worthless
OTLT	footplate
	hostile to
	hostility
	mortality
	postulate
OTLZ	Fortaleza
	mortalize
OTMC	contumacy
OTMD	mouth-made
OTME	Bottomley
	contemper
	costumier
OTML	contumely
OTMN	Boltzmann
OTMU	bottom out
	bottoms up
OTNA	continual
OTNE	contender
	contented
	continued
OTNI	Hortensio
OTNL	joltingly
	poutingly
	routinely
OTNN	continent

Words marked ❑ can also be spelled with an initial capital letter

softening
OTNO contangos
continuos
Hottentot
OTNS dottiness
goutiness
loathness
loftiness
pottiness
routinise
sootiness
OTNT fortunate
sostenuto
OTNU continuum
totting-up
OTNV Porto Novo
OTNZ routinize
OTOA postwoman
OTOC soft touch
soft voice
OTOE contrôlée
footnotes
postponed
soft-cover
soft-toned
OTOI portfolio
Port Louis
OTON foot-pound
OTOR don't worry
OTOS boathouse
boat-house
footloose
posthorse
posthouse
OTOT Fort Worth
OTOU soft focus
OTPC toothpick
OTPL North Pole
north pole
South Pole
south pole
OTPR mouthpart
Southport
OTRA nocturnal
Rotterdam
OTRC cost price
OTRE contorted
couturier
Monterrey
Nocturnes
OTRI soft fruit
OTRK foot brake
OTRN footprint
fostering
loitering
posturing
pottering
root-prune
rostering
soft drink
tottering
OTRO contornos
posterior

OTRT doctorate
posterity
OTRU torturous
OTRY Boothroyd
OTSA contessas
most usual
North Star
South Seas
OTSE contested
contester
poetaster
route-step
OTSL doltishly
loutishly
sottishly
OTSM loathsome
toothsome
OTSN cortisone
OTSO contusion
OTTA bootstrap
OTTC rootstock
OTTD fortitude
OTTL footstalk
OTTO footstool
hortation
OTTR hortatory
OTTV hortative
portative
OTUA Port Sudan
OTUS North Uist
South Uist
OTVC sotto voce
OTVL costively
OTWI boatswain
OTWL Southwell
OTWN kowtowing
north wind
OTWR northward
southward
Southwark
OTWS mouthwash
north-west
South-West
south-west
OTWT forthwith
OTZM Montezuma
OUAE nodulated
populated
OUAL jocularly
popularly
OUAO joculator
modulator
OUBN columbine
OUBU columbium
OUCL go quickly
homuncule
homunculi
OUCN coruscant
OUCT coruscate
loquacity
OUDT jocundity
rotundate
rotundity

OUDU conundrum
OUET documents
OUFR Roquefort
OUHO so much for
OUML Rogue Male
OUNS columnist
OURM docudrama
OURN volucrine
OUSL roguishly
OUTE volunteer
OUTR coculture
voluntary
voluptary
OUUL nocuously
OUWR vogue word
OUWT go out with
OUYO do duty for
OVAI souvlakia
OVCE convicted
OVCO convector
OVLT convolute
OVNE convinced
OVNI Botvinnik
OVRA Hoover Dam
OVRE converted
converter
OVRI go over big
OVRN wolverene
wolverine
OVRO bovver boy
convertor
OVSL wolvishly
OVTN non-voting
not voting
OVTO solvation
OVVA convivial
OVVN bon vivant
OVVU bon viveur
OVXT convexity
OVYG bon voyage
OWGA Norwegian
OWLA boxwallah
OWNA Colwyn Bay
OWNO bow window
OWRL forwardly
OWSE nor'wester
sou'wester
OWTI not with it
OWYA Norway rat
OXAL coaxially
OXNL coaxingly
OYAC cony-catch
OYAE holy water
OYAH polymathy
OYAI polybasic
OYAT body waste
corybants
OYDM Tony Adams
OYEC Toby Belch
OYEO cotyledon
OYER polyhedra
OYHC body-check
OYHE coryphaei

OYHN polyphone
polyphony
polythene
OYIH copyright
OYIL Holy Bible
Holyfield
OYLC body clock
holy place
OYLI polyploid
Tony Blair
OYLN cosy along
OYMD polyamide
OYNR polyandry
OYOA polygonal
OYRE holy-cruel
OYRH polyarchy
OYRI Tony Greig
OYRP polygraph
OYSE polyester
OYTC polyptych
OYTN holystone
OYUE body-curer
OYUI Roxy Music
OYUR bodyguard
OZNS wooziness
PAAE apsarases
PAAL speakable
PAAS ups-a-daisy
PAAU apparatus
PACL spraickle
PADO upwards of
PAFO splay foot
PAFS spearfish
PAHA spearhead
PAHL splashily
PAHN splashing
PAHU splash out
PALN appalling
sprawling
PALU sprawl out
PAMN spearmint
PAOS Appaloosa
PATE L P Hartley
PAUO a plague on
PCAL specially
spectacle
PCAO spectator
spiccatos
PCAT specialty
PCBS spicebush
PCCI epicyclic
PCDA epicedial
epicedian
PCDU spaced out
PCEE epicleses
PCEI epiclesis
PCFC specifics
PCFE specified
PCLG spicilege
PCLS spaceless
speckless
PCLT speculate
spiculate

PCNR	epicentre
PCNS	spiciness
PCPT	apocopate
PCRA	epicurean
PCRC	spice rack
PCRS	epicurise
	epicurism
PCRZ	epicurize
PCSI	spaceship
PCTM	space-time
PCWL	space walk
	space-walk
PCYH	Apocrypha
PDCI	apodictic
PDFL	spadefuls
PDLK	spadelike
PDPI	epedaphic
PDRA	epidermal
	spiderman
PDRI	epidermis
PDUU	Epidaurus
PDWR	spadework
PEBA	speedboat
PEBL	speedball
PEBM	speed bump
PEBR	Spielberg
PECS	upper-case
PEDG	appendage
PEDN	spreading
PEDU	splendour
	spread out
PEEA	ephemerae
	ephemeral
	ephemeras
PEEC	appetence
	appetency
PEEI	apheresis
	ephemeris
	splenetic
PEEO	ephemeron
PEHA	speech day
PEHF	speechify
PEHN	upper hand
PEIA	spherical
PEIE	appetiser
	appetizer
	ephelides
PEII	ipse dixit
	splenitis
PEIN	Ephesians
PELA	Up-Helly-Aa
PELM	upper limb
PELN	appealing
	appellant
PELT	appellate
PEMS	uppermost
PERN	appearing
	ephedrine
PESN	appeasing
PETA	speed trap
PETI	appertain
PETN	upsetting
PEUA	spherular
PEWL	speedwell
PEYE	apteryxes
PGAH	epigraphy
PGET	spaghetti
PGIS	up against
PGMU	apogamous
PHAT	up the ante
PHDF	up the duff
PHNE	up-Channel
	upthunder
PHWL	up the wall
PIAE	optimates
PIAL	optically
	optimally
PICE	sphincter
PIFO	April fool
PIGL	springily
PIGN	springing
PIGO	springbok
PIHE	uplighter
PIHL	sprightly
	uprightly
PIKE	sprinkled
	sprinkler
PILE	ephialtes
PILO	up till now
PISI	spritsail
PITN	splitting
	sprinting
	uplifting
PITR	splintery
PKNO	spoken for
PKNR	spikenard
PKSA	spokesman
PKSE	spokesmen
PKWS	spokewise
PLAC	appliance
PLAO	spoliator
PLBN	spellbind
PLCN	applicant
PLGE	apologies
PLGS	apologise
	apologist
	epilogise
PLGZ	apologize
	epilogize
PLIA	spellican
PLJH	apple-John
PLNE	spelunker
PLNL	opulently
PLOE	spill over
	spillover
PLPI	epileptic
PLTO	epilation
PNAE	spinnaker
PNAL	spendable
PNDW	up and down
	up-and-down
PNEE	spinneret
PNFR	spiniform
PNIE	Apennines
PNLN	spangling
PNLS	spineless
	spinulose
PNLU	spinulous
PNMU	eponymous
PNNE	open-ended
PNNS	spininess
PNNU	opening-up
PNOE	up-and-over
PNON	spin round
PNOR	open court
PNOS	open house
PNPC	open space
PNRF	spindrift
PNSA	Upanishad
PNTM	spend time
	upon a time
PNUA	spun sugar
PNYR	spin a yarn
POAL	opposable
POAT	ipso facto
PODN	upholding
POEC	opponency
POEE	optometer
POER	optometry
POET	opponents
	opposed to
POFE	spoon-feed
POFL	spoonfuls
POGL	splodgily
POHN	optophone
PONE	appointed
	appointee
PONF	up to snuff
PONR	up-country
POOO	apropos of
POPE	up to speed
POSE	upholster
POSL	up for sale
POTN	opportune
	sprouting
	uprooting
POTO	apportion
POWS	spoonwise
POWY	spoonways
PPOI	apiphobia
PPYE	apophyses
	epiphyses
PPYI	apophysis
	epiphysis
PRAI	spermaria
	spermatia
	spermatic
	spermatid
PRAU	Spartacus
PRBH	Aphra Behn
PRBN	sperm bank
PRBT	approbate
PRCI	spark coil
PRCL	spiracula
PRDN	upgrading
PRDT	Aphrodite
PRFO	apart from
PRGR	spirogyra
PRHE	spur wheel
PRHI	apartheid
PRHN	apprehend
PRIA	appraisal
PRIE	appraiser
PRLE	sparklies
	spiralled
PRLN	sparkling
PRLT	sporulate
PRMN	apartment
PRNI	sporangia
PRNL	sparingly
PRNS	spareness
PRPR	spare part
PRPU	spark plug
PRPY	sporophyl
PRRO	spare room
PRSA	sports car
	sportsman
PRSE	oppressed
PRSL	operosely
PRSO	oppressor
PRTA	spiritual
PRTM	spare time
PRTN	operating
PRTO	epuration
	operation
	spiration
PRTR	spare tyre
PRTS	spiritism
	spiritist
	spiritoso
PRTU	spirit gum
PRTV	operative
PRUA	opercular
PRUH	upbrought
	upwrought
PRUU	operculum
PRVN	approving
PRVO	approve of
PRWS	spirewise
PSAE	epistases
PSOA	episcopal
PSOE	a pushover
PSOI	apostolic
	spasmodic
PTAL	spatially
PTAO	apathaton
PTEE	sputterer
PTEI	apathetic
	apothecia
	epithetic
PTHC	spot check
	spot-check
PTIH	spotlight
PTLT	spatulate
PTMS	epitomise
	epitomist
PTMZ	epitomize
PTOS	spit-roast
PTXA	epitaxial
PUET	epaulette
PUNN	oppugnant
PUTR	spluttery

PUWR	Opium Wars
PWNU	spewing up
PYAS	upsy-daisy
PYLU	aphyllous
PZOI	epizootic
QABE	squabbler
QADW	squat down
QAEE	square leg
QAEF	square off
QAEI	aqua regia
QAEL	aquarelle
QAEN	square one
QAHL	squashily
QAIA	aqua vitae
QAIL	squalidly
QAIM	aquariums
QALN	aquaplane
QANS	squatness
QAPR	equal part
QARS	squarrose
QASG	equal sign
QATR	squatters
QATT	a quantity
QECE	squelcher
QEKL	squeakily
QEKN	squeaking
QELN	squealing
QEMS	squeamish
QEZN	squeezing
QIAI	Aquitania
QIAL	equitable
	equitably
QIEI	aquilegia
QIKN	a quick one
QIMN	equipment
QIOA	equivocal
QIOS	equipoise
QIPN	equipping
QITN	squinting
	squirting
RAAA	break away
	breakaway
RAAD	Irrawaddy
RAAL	breakable
	treatable
RAAN	great-aunt
RAAO	Ursa Major
RABA	breakbeat
	broad bean
	dreamboat
	Great Bear
RABL	break bulk
	broadbill
RABN	broadband
RABR	friarbird
RACA	greatcoat
RACM	break camp
RACS	broadcast
RADA	great deal
RADN	Great Dane
RADO	errand-boy
	pro and con
RADS	dry as dust

	Dryasdust
RADW	break down
	breakdown
RAEE	break even
RAEL	organelle
RAET	armaments
	ornaments
RAEU	grease gun
RAFE	break free
RAFR	trial-fire
RAFS	breakfast
RAGE	arraigner
RAGN	arranging
RAHE	Uriah Heep
RAHF	preachify
RAHI	breathe in
RAHL	breathily
	preachily
RAHN	breathing
	preaching
	wreathing
RAHO	breathe on
	triathlon
RAHR	treachery
RAIE	organized
	organizer
RAIL	armadillo
RAIN	irradiant
RAIO	break in on
	Ursa Minor
RAIT	break into
	irradiate
RAIU	ortanique
RAJI	break jail
RAJY	Irian Jaya
RALK	dreamlike
RALN	breadline
RALO	broadloom
RALR	Brian Lara
RALS	dreadless
	dreamless
	triallist
RAML	treadmill
RAMN	treatment
RAMT	urban myth
RANC	breakneck
RANS	broadness
	greatness
RAOE	break open
RAOI	triatomic
RARN	break rank
RASA	Great Seal
RASD	broadside
	cream soda
RASE	break step
RASL	Great Salt
RATC	Friar Tuck
RATI	breastpin
RATM	breaktime
RATV	proactive
RAUE	treasured
	treasurer
RAWN	break wind

RAWR	creamware
RAWS	broadwise
RAWT	break with
	treat with
RAWY	broadways
RAZN	organzine
RBAE	Art Blakey
RBCE	grub screw
	trebuchet
RBCL	trabecula
RBDS	tribadism
RBEL	crabbedly
RBEO	Mrs Beeton
RBIL	crab-sidle
RBLG	tribology
RBLS	tribalism
RBNA	prebendal
RBNS	Trubenise
RBNT	tribunate
	Tribunite
RBPL	crab apple
RBSA	tribesman
RBSE	Frobisher
RBSI	proboscis
RBSU	arabesque
RBTO	probation
RBTR	tributary
RBZN	Trebizond
RCAA	crack a can
RCAL	crucially
	traceable
	traceably
	tractable
	tractably
RCBA	bric-à-brac
RCBL	trackball
RCBT	brickbats
RCCA	frock-coat
	precocial
RCCT	precocity
	procacity
RCDL	crocodile
RCDN	precedent
	preceding
RCDR	procedure
RCDW	crack down
	crackdown
	track down
RCEB	Eric Newby
RCEE	bracketed
	cricketer
RCEN	procreant
RCET	brochette
	procreate
	tracheate
RCFR	cruciform
RCHS	Erica Hess
RCIA	practical
	trichinae
	trichinas
RCIE	practised
RCII	proclitic
	triclinic

RCIT	brachiate
RCIU	fractious
RCLA	trochlear
RCLN	crackling
	prickling
	truckling
	truculent
RCLS	graceless
	priceless
	price list
	traceless
	trackless
RCLT	bracelets
RCLU	tricolour□
RCMN	truchmans
RCNA	draconian□
RCNE	pre-cancel
RCNI	arachnoid
RCNO	precentor
RCNS	erectness
	preconise
RCNT	grace note
	precincts
RCNU	proconsul
RCNZ	preconize
RCOI	trichosis
RCOO	graciosos
RCPC	precipice
RCPO	preceptor
RCPU	Procopius
RCRC	procuracy
RCRE	groceries
	precurrer
	traceried
RCRI	trichroic
RCRO	precursor
RCRS	procuress
RCSA	precisian
RCSE	fricassee
	processed
	trickster
RCSI	crocosmia
	tracksuit
	tricuspid
RCSL	precisely
RCSM	tricksome
RCSN	prick-song
RCSO	crack shot
	precision
	processor
	track shoe
RCTR	precatory
RCTV	fricative
	precative
RCUE	brochures
	fractured
	precluded
RCUT	fructuate
RCUU	fructuous
RCWR	brickwork
RCYI	trachytic
RCYR	brickyard
RDAI	Fred Davis

Words marked □ can also be spelled with an initial capital letter

9 _R_D_A

RDAL	gradually
RDCE	predicted
RDCN	producing
	traducing
RDCT	eradicate
	predicate
RDDW	trade down
RDEA	bridleway
RDER	Fred Perry
RDFI	trade fair
RDGN	Fredegond
RDGS	predigest
RDKN	predikant
RDLC	predilect
RDLS	prideless
RDLT	credulity
RDLU	credulous
RDMR	trademark
RDNA	tridental
RDNL	prudently
RDNM	tradename
RDNS	crudeness
RDOA	prodromal
RDOL	Fred Hoyle
RDOU	prodromus
RDRC	Frederica
	Frederick
RDRN	Gradgrind
RDSA	tradesman
RDSL	prudishly
RDTB	bride-to-be
RDTL	eruditely
RDTO	erudition
	gradation
	tradition
RDTR	predatory
	traditors
RDTV	predative
RDUY	Bradburys
	Bradbury's
RDWN	trade wind
REAA	Greenaway
REAC	freelance
	grievance
REAG	free-range
REAL	freezable
REAO	Freemason
REBA	green bean
REBC	greenback
	order back
REBL	green belt
REBT	breed-bate
REBY	pre-embryo
RECR	green card
RECS	briefcase
REDN	friending
REEE	green-eyed
REEN	truepenny
REEO	grieve for
REER	freeze-dry
REES	free verse
REET	Prue Leith
REEU	freeze out

REGF	Greek gift
REGG	greengage
REGO	arpeggios
REHE	freesheet
	freewheel
	pre-echoes
	tree shrew
REHN	breeching
	freephone
REHR	greenhorn
REIE	tree-lined
REIG	greetings
REII	artemisia
REIL	arteriole
REIT	creep into
REIU	triecious
RELA	Orwellian
RELN	Greenland
	gruelling
RELO	brief look
RELS	briefless
	orderless
RELT	urceolate
REMI	greenmail
RENA	triennial
RENK	tree snake
RENS	briefness
	greenness
REOA	freewoman
REOE	freewomen
	praenomen
REOI	Freedonia
REOS	free house
RERC	Friedrich
RERD	free trade
	free-trade
RERE	greegrees
RERO	Green Room
	green room
	greenroom
RESO	grief-shot
RETE	orienteer
	Priestley
RETL	freestyle
RETN	Argentina
	Argentine
	arresting
	freestone
RETS	priestess
RETT	orientate
REUA	irregular
REUC	free lunch
REUI	praeludia
REWC	Greenwich
REWO	green wood
	greenwood❑
REWS	greenwash
RFAM	oriflamme
RFCA	orificial
RFFI	craft fair
RFGR	prefigure
RFII	traffic in
RFLA	Trafalgar

RFNL	profanely
RFNS	gruffness
RFNT	profanity
RFRE	preferred
	triformed
RFRU	triforium
RFSA	craftsman
RFSE	professed
RFSL	profusely
RFSO	professor
	profusion
RFTE	profiteer
RFTR	prefatory
RFWO	driftwood
RFWR	craftwork
	Kraftwerk
RGAC	fragrance
	fragrancy
	frogmarch
	pregnancy
RGAE	drug taker
RGAH	orography
	urography
RGAI	pragmatic
RGAL	pregnable
RGAM	programme
RGBU	brag about
RGDA	tragedian
RGDE	brigadier
RGDO	Brigadoon
RGDT	frigidity
RGEI	Trygve Lie
RGET	fragments
RGGN	Prigogine
RGLL	fragilely
RGLN	wriggling
RGLT	fragility
	frugality
RGMN	dragomans
RGNL	dragonfly
RGNR	brigandry
	Fragonard
RGNS	dragonise
RGNT	aragonite
	originate
RGNU	erogenous
	trigonous
RGNZ	dragonize
RGOE	prognoses
RGOI	prognosis
RGOT	frogmouth
RGSI	progestin
RGTU	frightful
	tregetour
RGUD	Mrs Grundy
RGUO	drag out of
RHAE	orthoaxes
RHBL	Archibald
RHDX	orthodoxy
RHII	arthritic
	arthritis
RHIN	arch-fiend
RHLE	cry halves

RHMG	Archimago
RHNE	archangel❑
RHNG	orphanage
RHNU	Arrhenius
RHOO	arthropod
RHPI	orthoptic
RHRA	Arthurian
RHRE	Arthur Mee
RHSI	orchestic
RHSR	orchestra
RHTC	architect
	orthotics
RHTP	archetype
RHTS	orthotist
RHUH	archduchy
RHVL	archivolt
RHVS	archivist
RIAA	trail away
RIAC	arrivancy
	ordinance
RIAE	irritated
RIAI	urticaria
RIAL	irrigable
	irritable
	irritably
	trainable
RIBN	trainband
RICK	fruitcake
RIDA	brain-dead
RIEE	fruiterer
RIEU	praiseful
RIFN	train fine
RIGA	frying-pan
RIGO	Orpington
RIGU	drying out
RIHE	freighter
RIHI	ornithoid
RIHK	artichoke
RIIA	druidical
RIIE	artificer
RIIT	arriviste
RILR	armillary
	artillery
RILS	brainless
	fruitless
RILU	orgillous
RINS	frailness
RIOL	traitorly
RIPP	drainpipe
RIRG	arbitrage
RIRI	arris rail
RIRR	arbitrary
RIRS	arbitress
	traitress
RIRT	arbitrate
RISA	Artie Shaw
RISE	brainstem
RISI	orgiastic
RISN	croissant
RISR	Froissart
RITC	armistice
RITL	arris tile
RITR	fruit tart

Words marked ❑ can also be spelled with an initial capital letter

RIUA articular
orbicular
RIWS brainwash
Ernie Wise
RIWV brainwave
RIYA a rainy day
RJCE projected
RJCO projector
RJDC prejudice
RJNA Trojan War
RJPT Prajapati
RKAE frikkadel
RKAI Erik Satie
RKDU brake drum
RKFE Prokofiev
RKRG brokerage
RKSA Drake's Bay
RKSO brake shoe
RLBT trilobite
RLCI prolactin
RLDA preludial
RLGS orologist
prologise
urologist
RLGZ prologize
RLIN brilliant
RLIT drill into
RLMN prolamine
RLNE prolonged
RLPE prolepses
RLPI prolepsis
proleptic
RLPU prolapsus
RLSL artlessly
RLSR prelusory
RLSV prelusive
RLTL prolately
RLTS prelatise
uralitise
RLTZ prelatize
uralitize
RLWE Trelawney
RLXT prolixity
RMAE brummagem
RMAK trim marks
RMCS prime cost
RMDR dromedary
RMEA primaeval
RMEE trumpeted
trumpeter
RMET trampette
RMEU trumped-up
RMGO Cro-Magnon
RMHR from where
krummhorn
RMIG trimmings
RMIN Grampians
RMLA bromeliad
grumble at
RMLI grimalkin
RMLN brambling
Crimplene®
crumbling
grumbling
primuline
trembling
RMLT tremulate
RMLU tremulous
RMLV Primo Levi
RMND promenade
RMNE Preminger
trominoes
RMNL Fremantle
RMNN prominent
RMNS griminess
RMNT criminate
RMOI trampolin
RMOO from now on
RMPC from space
RMPR primipara
RMRK drum brake
RMRL primarily
RMRT prime rate
RMRU trimerous
RMSN promising
RMTC dramatics
drumstick
RMTD trematode
RMTI trematoid
RMTM prime time
RMTN brimstone
frame tent
promoting
prompting
RMTO cremation
promotion
RMTR premature
prompture
RMTS aromatise
dramatise
dramatist
eremitism
RMTV primitive
RMTZ aromatize
dramatize
RMVR Primavera
RMWR framework
RNAD grandaddy
RNAE frontager
truncated
RNAL drinkable
grantable
printable
RNAN grand-aunt
RNBC bring back
prongbuck
RNBP Franz Bopp
RNCL trunk call
RNCN transcend
RNCS crankcase
RNDE grenadier
wrongdoer
RNDK grand duke
RNDN grenadine
RNDW bring down
grind down
RNEA Orangeman
Prince Hal
RNED orangeade
RNEG Bronze Age
RNEI orange-tip
RNEL drunkenly
trancedly
RNEO princedom
Princeton
RNER cranberry
trinketry
RNFC transfect
RNFL trunkfuls
RNFO wrong-foot
RNFR Frankfort
Frankfurt
transform
RNFS transfuse
RNHA branchiae
bronchial
Frenchman
grindhval
RNHE Frenchmen
RNHF branch off
Frenchify
RNHI drink-hail
Trondheim
RNHL Frans Hals
RNHM bring home
transhume
RNHN branching
drenching
trenchant
wrenching
RNHO truncheon
RNHR French fry
pronghorn
RNHS franchise
RNHU branch out
RNIA crinoidal
principal
RNID Brunhilde
RNIE wrong idea
RNII principia
RNIL frangible
franticly
Grenville
principle
RNIN transient
RNIO Grandison
RNIS grandiose
RNLE wrinklies
RNLI franglais
RNLM granuloma
RNLN crinkling
crinoline
front line
wrangling
RNLO prunellos
RNLS frontless
RNLT crenelate
granulate
translate
RNMA trinomial
RNMR Franz Marc
RNMT transmute
RNNE Groningen
RNNL droningly
RNNM brand name
brand-name
RNNS frankness
grandness
proneness
wrongness
RNNT uraninite
RNOE bring over
RNOI francolin
RNOT front onto
RNPG front-page
RNPI Grand Prix
RNPP grandpapa
RNPR transpire
transport
RNPS transpose
RNRI Mrs Norris
RNRO front room
RNSA grand slam
RNSD wrong side
RNSE prankster
RNSI transship
RNSL dronishly
RNSM pranksome
RNTN ironstone
RNTO urination
RNTS granitise
RNTU grand tour
RNTZ granitize
RNUA orang utan
orang-utan
RNUC pronounce
RNVS transvest
RNWC Brunswick
RNWK Bronowski
RNWL Grünewald
RNWR frontward
trunk-work
wrong word
RNWS frontwise
RNWY frontways
RNYS Grundyism
ROAC arrogance
ROAT Argonauts
ROBC crookback
ROCP preoccupy
RODA Arnold Bax
RODI preordain
ROEL crookedly
ROEU arboreous
arboretum
erroneous
ROFC o're-office
ROFN Arnolfini
ROHT bryophyte
ROMO prooemion
ROMU prooemium
ROOE drool over

ROOI ergonomic
RORA proofread
RORO arrowroot
RORP broomrape
ROSA groomsman
ROSI troop-ship
ROTO cry out for
ROWO arrowwood
RPCN drop-scene
drop-scone
RPEI graphemic
prophetic
RPEL Grappelli
RPET gruppetti
RPEU wrapped up
RPGT propagate
RPGU uropygium
RPHF prop shaft
RPIA dropsical
graphical
RPIE trephiner
RPIG droppings
trappings
wrappings
RPII graphitic
RPIL graphicly
RPIT propriety
RPLE propeller
Propylaea
RPLN crapulant
crapulent
crippling
RPLU crapulous
RPNE trepanner
RPNL gripingly
gropingly
RPNN proponent
RPOA cryptogam
RPOG drop-forge
RPON wrapround
RPRE draperies
RPRN preparing
RPTI Kropotkin
pro patria
RPTK Tripitaka
RPTN crepitant
prepotent
RPTT crepitate
RPUO drop out of
RPVN grapevine
RPYU triptyque
RPZA trapezial
RPZI trapezoid
RPZU trapezium
trapezius
RQEC frequency
RQER triquetra
RQET briquette
croquette
RQOA Iroquoian
RREC prurience
RRGT prorogate
RRNT pro re nata
RRPE Dr Crippen
RRSE ore-rested
RRTN ororotund
RRUH ore-raught
RSAB Ernst Abbe
RSAI prismatic
RSAL crossable
crushable
graspable
RSAU Cresta Run
crush a cup
RSBA crossbeam
RSBE crossbred
RSBL crossbill
RSBN brass band
wristband
RSBR Pressburg
RSBT crossbite
frostbite
RSCO trisector
RSCT prosecute
RSDA presidial
RSDN crusading
president
RSDO presidios
RSDS prosodist
RSDU presidium
RSDV crash dive
RSDW dress down
press down
RSED crescendo
RSEE cross-eyed
RSEI brasserie
dressed in
triskelia
RSEO arms depot
brassed of
RSER dry sherry
RSES tristesse
RSET prospects
RSEU freshen up
RSFD cross-fade
RSFN trust fund
RSFR crossfire
RSGE Trésaguet
RSGN presaging
pressgang
press-gang
RSHM press home
RSHO preschool
RSIA eristical
RSIH tristichs
RSIL grisaille
irascible
irascibly
Priscilla
RSIN crescioni
prescient
RSIR brassiere
brassière
RSIT crash into
RSLC preselect
RSLK frostlike
frostwork
RSLN bristling
crashland
grassland
wrestling
RSLS frostless
grassless
RSLT proselyte
wristlets
RSMA prosimian
RSMC Ernst Mach
RSMK dressmake
RSML irksomely
RSMN erasement
presuming
RSMO presume on
RSMS Irish moss
RSMT Grossmith
RSNC brass neck
RSNE presented
presenter
RSNI frost-nail
RSNL presently
RSNS brashness
briskness
crassness
crispness
crossness
freshness
grossness
prosiness
RSOE prise open
RSOL Aristotle
RSON Gros Morne
gros point
RSOS frescoist
RSPE prose poem
RSRA crossroad
RSRB prescribe
proscribe
RSRE preserved
preserver
RSRH Ernst Röhm
RSRI grosgrain
RSRK grass-rake
RSRN Armstrong
pre-shrink
RSRP prescript
RSRT frustrate
prostrate
RSSE Irish stew
RSSI dress suit
RSSU press stud
RSTS crash-test
RSUE Ernst Udet
pressured
RSUL brusquely
RSUO brush up on
RSWC Prestwick
RSWL crosswalk
RSWN crosswind
RSWO brushwood
RSWR brushwork
crossword
RSWS crosswise
RSWY crossways
RSYE presbyter
RTAA write away
RTAI Brittania
Brittanic
RTAL prothalli
RTBA try to beat
RTBC write back
RTCE protected
RTCL graticule
triticale
RTCO Arctic fox
protector
RTCS Briticise
Briticism
criticise
criticism
eroticise
eroticism
RTCZ Briticize
criticize
eroticize
RTDU truth drug
RTDW write down
write-down
RTEI prothesis
prothetic
RTEL brotherly
RTES tritheism
tritheist
RTFC brute fact
RTFE gratified
RTFN try to find
RTHL erstwhile
RTHT crotchety
Pratchett
RTLL brittlely
RTLN Fritz Lang
prattling
RTLS brutalise
brutalism
frothless
RTLT brutality
RTLZ brutalize
RTMN protamine
RTMR Britomart
RTNE pretended
pretender
RTNI arytenoid
Britannia
RTNL gratingly
pratingly
RTNS cretinise
cretinism
triteness
RTNT gratinate
RTNU cretinous
RTNZ cretinize
RTOI trattoria
trattorie
RTRA fraternal

	oratorial
RTRO	criterion
	oratorios
RTRT	preterite
	triturate
RTRU	craterous
RTSA	protest at
RTSE	protester
RTSL	brutishly
RTSO	protestor
RTSU	grotesque
RTTD	gratitude
RTTP	prototype
RTUE	proteuses
RTUL	fretfully
RTUS	bratwurst
RTWK	Grotowski
RTZA	protozoal
	protozoan
RUAI	traumatic
RUCN	trouncing
RUDE	groundsel
RUDN	grounding
RUDO	groundhog
RUDU	groundnut
RUDV	ground ivy
RUHL	grouchily
RUHU	wrought-up
RULN	troubling
RUPA	triumphal
RUPE	proud-pied
	triumpher
RUSA	trousseau
RUSE	fraudster
RUTO	erruption
	irruption
RUTT	proustite
RUTV	irruptive
RUUL	arduously
RUVR	triumviri
	triumvirs
RUWR	groupware
RUWT	argue with
RVAA	drive away
RVAL	driveable
	proveable
	proveably
	trivially
RVBA	gravy boat
RVBC	drive back
RVBL	drive belt
RVDA	Dravidian
	gravadlax
RVDE	bravadoes
	privadoes
RVDN	provident
	providing
RVDT	gravidity
RVHM	drive home
RVIT	drive into
RVKN	provoking
RVLA	travel bag
	Trevelyan
RVLE	groveller
	travelled
	traveller
RVLG	privilege
RVLN	prevalent
	trivalent
RVLO	travel-cot
RVLS	graveless
RVLT	frivolity
RVLU	frivolous
RVMN	brevi manu
	gravamina
RVNA	Provençal
RVNE	provender
	provinces
RVNS	graveness
RVNT	drive nuts
RVPS	drive past
RVRA	traversal
RVRE	traversed
	traverser
RVRG	Mr Average
RVSA	privy seal
RVSE	provisoes
RVSN	Gravesend
RVSO	prevision
	provision
RVSR	provisory
RVTE	privateer
RVTL	privately
RVTO	privation
RVTS	privatise
RVTT	gravitate
RVTV	privative
RVTZ	privatize
RVYR	graveyard
RWBA	brown bear
RWBU	crow about
RWEE	draw level
RWEL	tri-weekly
RWFE	crow's feet
RWFO	crow's foot
RWHE	draw-sheet
RWHT	grow white
RWIE	draw lines
	grow tired
RWIH	Arkwright
	grow light
RWLN	draw blank
RWNI	drawing-in
RWNR	grow angry
RWNS	brownness
	crow's nest
RWNU	growing up
RWRC	brown rice
RWRL	frowardly
RWSI	crowd sail
RWUO	frown upon
	grow out of
RWWR	drawn work
RXMT	proximate
	proximity
RYAG	argy-bargy
RYER	greybeard
RYES	arsy-versy
RYHL	grey whale
RYNI	pray in aid
RYNL	prayingly
RYOL	grey mould
RYON	greyhound□
RYRA	Grey Friar
	prayer mat
RYRU	prayerful
	prayer rug
RZAT	frizzante□
RZDE	cruzadoes
RZIO	cruzeiros
RZLA	Brazilian
RZLN	drizzling
	grizzling
RZLU	brazil nut
RZNS	craziness
RZNU	brazen out
SAAA	Islamabad
SAAE	escalated
SAAL	escapable
SAAO	escalator
SAAU	asparagus
SAEA	estate car
SAEL	ashamedly
SAET	estafette
SAIE	ascarides
SALE	assaulter
SALN	assailant
SALS	establish
SALT	Israelite
SALY	Ismailiya
SANL	espagnole
SANS	usualness
SARC	Osnabrück
SARL	usual rule
SATM	aspartame
SAVC	ask advice
SBLT	usability
SCAI	isocratic
SCCI	isocyclic
SCEU	psyched up
SCIA	isoclinal
SCOD	as accords
SCOE	psychoses
SCOI	psychosis
	psychotic
SDFO	aside from
SEAC	esperance
SEAD	as regards
SEAT	Esperanto
SEBE	assembled
	assembler
SEDN	ascendant
	ascending
SEEI	osmeteria
SEET	usherette
SEFA	Isle of Man
SELG	osteology
SEPT	osteopath
SESO	ascension□
	aspersion
SESR	aspersory
SESV	aspersive
	ostensive
SETA	aspectual
	essential
SETI	ascertain
SETN	assenting
SETO	assertion
SETV	assertive
SEWO	Isherwood
SGIS	as against
SHAI	asthmatic
SHEI	ischaemia
SHLI	asphaltic
SHNA	Esthonian
SIAC	oscitancy
SIAE	estimated
SIAL	estimable
	estimably
SIAO	aspirator
	estimator
	ostinatos
SIBR	W S Gilbert
SIGO	Islington
SILT	oscillate
SING	espionage
SINO	assientos
SIOI	Issigonis
SIOO	Eskimo dog
SIRG	ossifrage
SITN	assistant
	assisting
SIUT	assiduity
SIUU	assiduous
SKAA	Ashkhabad
SKNZ	Ashkenazy
SLEI	psalteria
SLND	esplanade
SLPU	Asclepius
SLSL	uselessly
SLTA	as all that
SLTN	isolating
SLTO	isolation
SMBD	a somebody
SMER	asymmetry
SMII	psammitic
SMRS	isomerise
SMRZ	isomerize
SMTI	isometric
SMTT	asymptote
SNEI	asyndetic
SNEO	asyndeton
SNLS	isinglass
SNNT	asininity
SNRI	asynergia
SOAC	assonance
SOFE	Escoffier
SOIT	associate
SOLW	as follows
SONE	astounded
SOPR	ascospore
SOSL	espousals

SOWR	as you were
SPLU	asepalous
SPRO	ask pardon
SRAI	psoriasis
SRBL	Tsar's Bell
SRCS	ostracise
	ostracism
SRCZ	ostracize
SRDL	astraddle
SRDM	astrodome
SREC	esurience
	esuriency
SREL	usurpedly
SRGT	Ostrogoth
SRKA	astrakhan❑
SRLB	astrolabe
SRLG	astrology
SRNE	a stranger
	estranged
SRNM	astronomy
SRNU	astronaut
SRSL	as a result
SRSO	espressos
SSEE	isosceles
STEL	tsetse-fly
STOE	as it comes
STOI	isotropic
STRO	Esztergom
SUAC	assurance
SUAL	assumable
	assumably
	assurable
SUEL	assumedly
	assuredly
SUGN	assuaging
	assurgent
SULN	Esquiline
SUOO	espumosos
SUOY	pseudonym
SURA	estuarial
SURN	estuarine
SUSV	assuasive
SXAL	asexually
TAAA	steal away
TAAE	stratagem
TAAR	St-Nazaire
TABA	steamboat
	steam-boat
TABR	Strasberg
TABT	steam bath
TADN	stranding
TAEI	strategic
TAEU	steamed up
TAFO	steal from
	stray from
TAFS	steadfast
TAGE	straggler
	strangler
	strangles
TAGL	strangely
TAGR	strangury
TAHN	attaching
	strap-hang
TAHU	steam-haul
TAII	steatitic
TAIO	ottavinos
	steam iron
TALK	strawlike
TALS	strapless
TANE	attainder
TANN	attaining
	straining
TAOE	steam open
TAPD	strappado
TAPL	straw poll
TAPN	strapping
TARE	Stranraer
TARO	steam room
TASI	steamship
TASN	Stralsund
TAVT	straw vote
TBEA	stable lad
	stableman
TBEO	stableboy
TBLS	stabilise
TBLT	stability
TBLZ	stabilize
TCAA	stoccatas
TCAI	stick at it
TCAO	staccatos
	stoccados
TCCB	stock cube
TCEU	stick 'em up!
TCFS	stockfish
TCHL	Stockholm
TCIG	stockings
TCII	stichidia
TCIT	stick into
	stick it to
TCNE	CT scanner
TCPL	stockpile
TCPR	Stockport
TCRO	stockroom
TCTK	stocktake
TCUO	stock up on
TCWT	stick with
TCYR	stockyard
TDEL	studiedly
TDHR	study hard
TDOE	stud poker
TEAC	utterance
TEAI	athematic
TEAL	steerable
	utterable
TEAU	Athenaeum
TEBA	steenbras
TEBN	steel band
TEBR	Ethelbert
TEBU	steel-blue
	ytterbium
TECE	Streicher
	stretched
	stretcher
TEDN	attendant
	attending
TEHL	other half
TEIZ	strelitzi
TEKL	streakily
TEKN	streaking
TELT	Stieglitz
TEMN	streaming
	strewment
TEMS	uttermost
TENR	St Bernard
TENS	otherness
	steepness
	utterness
TERE	St George's
TESA	Athelstan
	steersman
TESD	other side
TESI	atheistic
TESN	Streisand
TESR	at leisure
TESU	stressful
	stress out
TETA	other than
TETN	attestant
TETO	attention
TETV	attentive
TEUT	attenuate
TEUU	strenuous
TEWL	Ethelwulf
TEWO	steel wool
TEWR	steelwork
TEWS	otherwise
TEYA	Steely Dan
TEYR	steelyard
TFEE	stiffener
TFNS	stiffness
TFTE	stuff them
TFWR	stiffware
TGAC	at a glance
	stagnancy
TGAI	stigmatic
TGAT	stag party
TGDO	stage door
TGDV	stage-dive
TGEE	staggered
TGIH	stag night
TGNM	stage name
	stage-name
TGNS	staginess
THAP	Atahualpa
THBC	at the back
THFL	at the full
THFR	at the fore
THHA	at the head
THHL	at the helm
THMS	at the most
THNS	itchiness
THRA	at the rear
THTM	at the time
TIAL	ethically
	stoically
TIBC	Steinbeck
	steinbock
TICS	staircase
TICU	strip club
TIDW	strip down
TIEA	strike pay
TIEC	stridence
	stridency
TIEF	strike off
TIEI	strike oil
TIEO	strive for
TIET	at liberty
TIEU	strike out
TIGI	string tie
TIGL	stringily
TIGN	stringent
TIGU	string out
TILN	stridling
	stripling
TILS	stainless
TINS	staidness
TIPA	Ethiopian
TIPN	stripping
TITM	a thin time
TITO	striation
TITR	stricture
TITS	strictish
TIUA	utricular
TIUE	attitudes
TIWL	stairwell
TIWS	stairwise
TKHL	stokehold
TLAE	etoliated
	stellated
TLBR	stillborn
TLBT	stylobate
TLCS	italicise
TLCZ	italicize
TLDT	stolidity
TLEL	stiltedly
TLFE	stall-feed
TLGS	otologist
TLHN	still-hunt
TLLF	still life
TLLS	stalkless
TLMR	still more
TLMT	stalemate
TLNS	staleness
	Stalinism
	Stalinist
	stillness
TLSI	stylistic
TLSL	stylishly
TLTC	athletics
TLTE	utilities
TLTO	stilettos
TLUA	stellular
TLWB	at a low ebb
TMCA	stomachal
TMCE	stomacher
TMCI	stomachic
TMCT	atomicity
TMDT	stamp duty
TMEE	stammerer
TMIA	ethmoidal
TMLG	etymology
TMLN	stimulant

Words marked ❑ can also be spelled with an initial capital letter

stumbling
TMLO St-Émilion
stumble on
TMLT stimulate
TMML stamp mill
TNAD standards
TNAE stingaree
TNBI stand bail
TNBM Stand By Me
stink bomb
TNBS stone bass
TNCA stonechat
TNCD ethnocide
TNCL stone-cold
TNCO stonecrop
TNCS at any cost
TNCT atonicity
ethnicity
TNDA stone-dead
stone-deaf
TNDW stand down
TNEB stander-by
TNEL stintedly
TNES stand easy
TNFO stand from
TNFR stand fire
stand firm
TNFS stand fast
stonefish
TNGO stand good
TNHN at any hand
TNHO stanchion
TNHR stinkhorn
stone-hard
TNLG ethnology
TNLS atonalism
stingless
stoneless
TNLT atonality
TNMN atonement
TNNL at an angle
atoningly
TNNS stoniness
TNOE stand over
TNPP standpipe
TNRN itinerant
TNRR itinerary
TNRT at any rate
itinerate
TNRW St Andrews
TNSA Stanislaw
TNTM at any time
at one time
TNUO stand upon
TNUT stand up to
TNWE stinkweed
TNWL stand well
stonewall
TNWO stinkwood
TNWR stoneware
stonework
stonewort
TNWT stand with

TOAE etiolated
TOAI stromatic
TOBL stoolball
Stromboli
TOEE atmometer
TOGO strongbox
TOGR strongarm
TOGS strongish
TOHE atrophied
TOIA strobilae
TOIU atrocious
strobilus
TOLN strolling
TONY attorneys
TOSR strossers
TOTR Otto Stern
TOTU strontium
TOYI atmolysis
TPAC stopwatch
TPAI Stephanie
TPDT stupidity
TPFE stupefied
stupefier
TPHE stop thief
TPHL stepchild
TPHR stop short
TPIH stoplight
TPLT stipulate
TPON stop doing
TPRS stop press
TPRU stuporous
TPSN stop using
TPTT stipitate
TQET etiquette
TRAE stargazer
star-gazer
TRAL eternally
TRBC start back
TRBO storybook
story-book
TRBT attribute
TRCE attracted
TRCF storm cuff
TRCI ataractic
TRCR store card
TRDA steradian
TRDO storm door
TRDW stare down
TREL stornelli
TRHL starchily
star shell
TRIA ptarmigan
TRIH starlight
TRIO start in on
TRLN startling
storyline
TRLS sterilise
stormless
TRLT sterility
TRLZ sterilize
TRNL staringly
TRNS star-anise
starkness

sternness
TROA stercoral
Stornoway
TROE start over
TROR starboard
TRRI star fruit
TRRO storeroom
TRSN at present
TRSU pterosaur
TRTO attrition
iteration
TRTV iterative
TRWR sternward
TSAA stash away
TSBU Ctesibius
TSLU it is all up
TSOE it is hoped
TTDM State Duma
TTEE stutterer
TTEN St-Étienne
TTET statuette
TTGR Stuttgart
TTHN stitching
TTHO statehood
TTHR stitchery
TTLL statelily
TTLN state line
TTLS stateless
TTMN statement
TTOE stationer
TTRO stateroom
TTSA statesman
TTSD stateside☐
TTSI statistic
TTSU Status Quo
status quo
TTTR statutory
TUAI strumatic
TUCL staunchly
TUGE struggler
TUGU strung out
TUKF struck off
TULE at full sea
TUNI St-Quentin
TUNS stoutness
TUTN strutting
TUTR structure
TVBK Steve Biko
TVCA Steve Cram
TVDR stevedore
TVNE Stavanger
TVNG Stevenage
TVNO Stevenson
TVOO Stavropol
TVPP stovepipe
TVSI atavistic
TWLN stownlins
TWYO at a why-not
TYHI strychnic
TYIS itsy-bitsy
TYOS stay loose
UAAE dura mater
nunataker

rural area
UABE sugar beet
UABN jugal bone
UABR sugar bird
UABT Bud Abbott
UACB sugar-cube
UACI autarchic
UACN sugar cane
UADA hum and haw
rural dean
UADR cut and dry
hue and cry
UADU cut and run
out and out
out-and-out
UAEI mujahedin
mutagenic
UAES put at ease
UAEU cutaneous
tufaceous
UAFR human form
UAGE Aurangzeb
UAHE out at heel
UAHL Judas-hole
UAHR put ashore
UAIL subacidly
UAIN butadiene
UAIU audacious
fugacious
furacious
UAKN humankind
UAKR hula skirt
UAKS autarkist
UALF human life
UALM sugar-lump
UALS sugarless
UANS humanness
UAOI fumatoria
subatomic
UAON bum around
run around
runaround
UAPL sugar palm
UAPN subalpine
UARC human race
UARE Du Maurier
UARS cut across
put across
put at risk
run across
UASA sugar soap
UATR subaltern
UAUE au naturel
UAUI Duralumin®
UAYT eucalypti
eucaryote
eukaryote
UBAC cumbrance
UBAE cup-bearer
UBAH quebracho
UBBO rugby boot
UBCE Quebecker
UBCI Québecois

Words marked ☐ can also be spelled with an initial capital letter

rudbeckia
UBCO cut back on
UBDE mum-budget
UBDT turbidity
UBEE bumblebee
bumble-bee
humble-bee
UBEI humble pie
UBER tumble-dry
UBEU tumble-bug
UBHL cubbyhole
cubby-hole
UBIG Muybridge
UBKL numbskull
UBLN quibbling
turbulent
UBNE gubbinses
UBNL husbandly
numbingly
UBNR husbandry
UBNS tubbiness
UBNT turbinate
UBON dumbfound
UBPO turboprop
UBRE Number Ten
Sue Barker
sunburned
UBRF number off
UBRN lumbering
numbering
number one
UBRO Dumbarton
UBRS rubberise
UBRW number two
UBRZ rubberize
UBSE furbisher
Kuybyshev
UBSO Luc Besson
UBTE sunbather
UBUL bulbously
UCAE purchaser
UCAG surcharge
UCAO guacharos
UCAT outcrafty
UCBC hunchback
UCBR Dutch barn
UCBW punch bowl
UCEA muscleman
UCEE quickener
succeeder
UCEI succeed in
UCEL butcherly
UCET succeed to
zucchetto
UCFR quick-fire
UCGL Dutch gold
UCIF Sutcliffe
UCII punctilio
zucchinis
UCLA Dutch leaf
UCLN punchline
succulent
UCLO curculios
quick look
UCLS juiceless
sulcalise
UCLZ sulcalize
UCML guacamole
UCMT succumb to
UCNE buccaneer
UCNL surcingle
UCNS butchness
juiciness
quickness
vulcanise
UCNT runcinate
succinate
vulcanite
UCNZ vulcanize
UCOE Dutch oven
UCPT nuncupate
UCRR Tuscarora
UCSE quickstep
UCSN quicksand
UCSO successor
UCTD dulcitude
UCTE nut cutlet
UCTM lunchtime
quick time
UCTO furcation
UCTS succotash
UCTT suscitate
UCUE punctured
succourer
UCUT punctuate
UCVD muscovado
UCVT muscovite❑
UCWR Dutch Wars
UCWT Auschwitz
UDAI quadratic
UDAL subduable
UDAO subdeacon
UDBO guidebook
UDEF bundle off
UDEL quadrella
subduedly
UDET hundredth
UDGR Ruddigore
UDIA quadrigae
UDIE quodlibet
UDII quadrifid
UDIL quadrille
UDLN guideline
UDMN fundament
UDNE humdinger
UDNL mundanely
UDNS muddiness
ruddiness
UDNT mundanity
UDPS guidepost
UDRN juddering
UDRS murderess
UDRU murderous
UDSA Bundesrat
Bundestag
UDUE quadruped
UDUL quadruple
quadruply
UDVD subdivide
UDVL Sundsvall
UDWE sundowner
UDWT put down to
UEAD Audenarde
Butenandt
UEAE mudéjares
UEAL numerable
numerably
superable
superably
UEAN Queen Anne
Queen-Anne
UEAO numerator
UEBR Gutenberg
Luxemburg
Nuremberg
UECE tubercled
UECN pubescent
quiescent
rufescent
tumescent
UECO supercool
UEEE quietened
UEER Juneberry
UEEU subereous
UEFN superfine
UEFR cuneiform
UEFS queer fish
superfuse
UEFU superflux
UEGN aubergine
UEGU superglue
Superglue®
UEHA superheat
UEHN sure thing
UEHR superhero
UEIA numerical
UEII juvenilia
UEIO subeditor
UELK queenlike
UELO pure-blood
UELT rubellite
UEMR Queen Mary
UEMS outermost
UEMT tunesmith
UENS luteinise
mutedness
queerness
quietness
UENV supernova
UENZ luteinize
UEON numero uno
UEPS superpose
UERA funebrial
UESA superstar
UESD supersede
UESI queenship
UESZ queen-size
UETG curettage
UETM tubectomy
UETN humectant
UETT humectate
UEUA nubeculae
UEUL duteously
musefully
tunefully
UEVN supervene
UEVS supervise
UEWA outerwear
UFAA suffragan
UFAL ruffianly
UFBI fur fabric
UFCN surfacing
UFCT suffocate
UFDE puff adder
UFDU puffed out
puffed-out
UFIE surfeited
UFLA duffel bag
UFLE buffaloes
fulfilled
UFML subfamily
UFNA muffin-cap
UFNL puffingly
UFNS huffiness
puffiness
turfiness
UFOE sunflower
UFOR surfboard
UFRN suffering
UFRU furfurous
UFSL huffishly
UFSO suffusion
UFSV suffusive
UFTE Our Father
outfitter
UFTN buffeting
UFWE Guy Fawkes
UFWN guffawing
UGBE fungibles
UGBO Guy Gibson
UGCD fungicide
UGCK fudge cake
UGDS ruggedise
UGDT turgidity
UGDZ ruggedize
UGIG outgoings
UGMN judgement
UGNL bulgingly
fulgently
pungently
tuggingly
UGNO Dungannon
UGNR subgenera
UGNS mugginess
pudginess
UGOE surge over
UGOT outgrowth
UGPR Mungo Park
UGRA Hungarian
vulgarian
UGRE dungarees
UGRL bugger all

Words marked ❑ can also be spelled with an initial capital letter

UGRN hungering
UGRO hunger for
UGRS Bulgarise
vulgarise
vulgarism
UGRT fulgurate
vulgarity
UGRZ Bulgarize
vulgarize
UGSE suggested
UGSI judgeship
UGTO budget for
purgation
UGTR budgetary
purgatory□
UGTV purgative
UHAE Euphrates
rug-headed
UHBR Dukhobors
UHDO pushed for
UHHC bushwhack
UHHR bush shirt
UHLG euchology
UHLI Ruth Ellis
UHLN push along
UHLZ Buthelezi
UHMS euphemise
euphemism
UHMZ euphemize
UHNC euphenics
UHNI authentic
UHNL gushingly
pushingly
UHNS bushiness
euphonise
pushiness
UHNU euphonium
ruthenium
UHNZ euphonize
UHOE cushioned
hush money
much loved
UHRA authorial
UHRN Hugh Grant
wuthering
UHRS authoress
authorise
Bucharest
Eucharist
UHRT authority
UHRZ authorize
UHTA Sukhothai
UHTM eurhythmy
UHTR push-start
UHUL pushfully
ruthfully
UHUR Hugh Munro
UIAC luminance
UIAE mutilated
UIAI Lusitania
put in a bid
Ruritania
UIAL cubically
dubitably
ludically
musically
UIAO fumigator
mutilator
ruminator
subimagos
supinator
UICP auriscope
UICS subincise
UIDM music-demy
UIEC Judi Dench
luminesce
UIET rudiments
UIFN cut it fine
run it fine
UIFO cubic foot
UIGA audiogram
UIGU ruling out
UIHL cut in half
music hall
UIHN punishing
UIIA juridical
municipal
UIIC cubic inch
UIIE Euripides
UIIN humiliant
munitions
UIIR auxiliary
judiciary
UIIT humiliate
UIIU judicious
UIJI put in jail
UILD fusillade
UIMN put in mind
UINS humidness
lucidness
luridness
tumidness
UIOI auditoria
UIPP Lucia Popp
UIRU ludicrous
UISL run itself
UISO Cupid's bow
UIST curiosity
UITA juliet cap
UITP audiotape
UIUA auricular
cuticular
funicular
UIUD Kunigunde
UIUL curiously
dubiously
dutifully
furiously
UIWO tulipwood
UIWR Punic Wars
UIYN purifying
UIYR cubic yard
UJCE outjockey
subjected
UJCN subjacent
UJCT subject to
UJDC sub judice
UJGT subjugate
UKAE muck-raker
UKAS duck's arse
UKBC huckaback
UKBL buckyball
UKBU muck about
UKCS Turkicise
UKCZ Turkicize
UKDR hunky-dory
UKEO musk melon
UKFZ buck's fizz□
UKHA buckwheat
Turk's head
UKHR buckthorn
UKLL cuckoldly
UKLR cuckoldry
UKMN Turkomans
UKNI tucking-in
UKNL quakingly
UKNS bulkiness
duskiness
huskiness
muckiness
murkiness
muskiness
quakiness
sulkiness
UKOT bucktooth
UKRS Quakerish
Quakerism
UKSE sun-kissed
UKSL buckishly
duskishly
UKTE junketeer
musketeer
UKTN junketing
UKTU bucketful
UKUO duck out of
UKYE Turkey red
UKYO buckayros
ULAE full-faced
pull baker
ULAG fuel gauge
ULAK full marks
ULBR pull a bird
ULCA public bar
ULCL full-scale
ULCS publicise
publicist
ULCT duplicate
duplicity
publicity
ULCY public eye
ULCZ publicize
ULDA Euclidean
ULEO guillemot
ULET oubliette
ULFC pull a face
ULFE nullified
nullifier
qualified
qualifier
ULFR Guildford
ULHA pull ahead
ULHL guildhall
ULIC bullfinch
ULIE pull wires
purloined
ULIG buildings
ULIH bullfight
pull tight
ULKA Kubla Khan
ULLE full blues
ULLS full blast
full-blast
guileless
guiltless
ULLT pullulate
ULLW full-blown
ULML sublimely
ULMR Tullamore
ULMS sublimise
ULMT sublimate
sublimity
ULMZ sublimize
ULNA Dublin Bay
ULNB full and by
ULNE outlander
ULNR Dubliners
sublunary
ULNS curliness
surliness
ULOE bulldozer
mullioned
ULOH guilloche
ULOI Guillotin
ULON bull point
full point
pull round
ULOS full house
ULOU nucleolus
ULPE full-speed
ULPI full-split
ULPR nullipore
pull apart
ULRS full dress
ULRW full-grown
ULSE published
sublessee
ULSI dualistic
ULSL bullishly
ULSO sublessor
ULSR outlustre
ULSU burlesque
ULTE qualities
subletter
Wurlitzer®
ULTF pull it off
ULUC outlaunch
ULUG sun lounge
ULUO build upon
pull out of
ULVN fun-loving
UMCS submucosa
UMCU submucous

UMFE mummified
UMGN rummaging
UMLE surmullet
UMLR nummulary
UMNE augmented
summonses
UMNN fulminant
UMNO augmentor
UMNR pulmonary
UMNS gumminess
UMNT culminate
fulminate
UMNU summing-up
UMRE submerged
submersed
UMRL summarily
UMRN murmuring
submarine
UMRS summarise
summarist
UMRU murmurous
UMRZ summarize
UMSN surmising
UMSO mummy's boy
UMTE submitted
submitter
UMTO summation
UMTV summative
UNAE guinea hen
UNAI guinea pig
UNAL turntable
UNBN funny bone
UNBU turn about
turnabout
UNCT pugnacity
UNDF turned off
UNDN quinidine
UNDU turned out
UNEO Juan Perón
UNET quintette
quintetti
UNFR funny farm
UNGI turn again
UNGR Funny Girl
UNHH funny ha-ha
UNHN quenching
UNHT turn white
UNIA quantical
UNLE funnelled
funnel-web
tunneller
UNLN quinoline
UNME outnumber
UNMN buonamani
UNNE turn under
UNNL burningly
cunningly
punningly
runningly
UNNS funniness
sunniness
UNNT turning to
UNON turn round

UNOS turn loose
UNOT turn forth
UNRA subnormal
UNRE nunneries
UNRO quintroon
UNRR vulnerary
UNRU runners-up
UNRW turn brown
UNSD sunny side
turn aside
UNSE burnished
furnished
UNTL turnstile
UNTN turnstone
UNTO ruination
UNTR furniture
UNUL quintuple
ruinously
UNVL Furnivall
UNVR Guinevere
UOAC Tudor arch
UOAE automated
Hugo Capet
UOAI autogamic
automatic
UOAL aurorally
humorally
UOAO automaton
out of a job
UOAR put on airs
UOCR out of curl
UOCS out of cash
UODB out of debt
UODF autos-da-fé
UODT out of date
out-of-date
UOEG put on edge
UOGU humongous
UOHL put on hold
UOHN out of hand
UOIE autotimer
eulogizer
UOII sudorific
UOIM eulogiums
UOIO autogiros
autopilot
UOIT autopista
UOLC out of luck
UOLN out of line
UOLV autoclave
tug-of-love
UOMN out of mind
UOOA autosomal
UOOI autonomic
sumotoris
UOOR Europoort
UOOT autoroute
UOPA out of play
UOPF out of puff
UORC autocracy
UORF autograft
UORN au courant
humouring

UORP autograph
UORS autocross
Tudor rose
UOSD put on side
UOSE out of step
UOSI put on sail
tutorship
UOSN out of sync
UOSO put on show
UOTM out of time
UOTN out of tune
UOTO cut out for
UOTU out of true
UOUO tucotucos
UOWR out of work
UOYI autolysis
UOYO autogyros
UOYU Autolycus
UPCE suspected
UPCO suspicion
UPCT auspicate
UPDT cuspidate
UPEL yuppie flu
UPEO yuppiedom
UPIE surprised
surpriser
UPIN suppliant
UPIT put paid to
UPIU bumptious
UPLV puppy love
UPNE suspended
suspender
UPNS bumpiness
dumpiness
jumpiness
lumpiness
UPOI sulphonic
UPRA Wuppertal
UPRE purported
supported
supporter
UPRT suppurate
UPSL dumpishly
lumpishly
mumpishly
purposely
UPSN supposing
UPSV purposive
UPTD turpitude
UPTE pulpiteer
puppeteer
UPTR bump start
jump start
UPUI sulphuric
UPUR sumptuary
UPUU sumptuous
UPWE gunpowder
UPWL Bud Powell
UPYN supplying
UPYO Humpty Doo
UQOS turquoise
URCA rubrician
URCE Dutrochet

URCL curricula
guard cell
URCN hurricane□
lubricant
URCT lubricate
lubricity
rubricate
URDE outredden
URDT putridity
UREA puerperal
UREI aubrietia
quercetin
UREL guardedly
hurriedly
quarterly
URET quartette
URFE putrefied
URGC surrogacy
URGE outrigger
URGT subrogate
surrogate
URIL guerrilla
Muirfield
URIR Guarnieri
URJI surrejoin
URJN currajong
kurrajong
URLT puerility
URLU querulous
URMC supremacy
URML supremely
URMN nutriment
URNE guaranies
guarantee
gunrunner
surrender
URNL currently
purringly
URNO guarantor
URNS furriness
URNT mucronate
URPI eutrophic
URRI guardrail
URRN guard ring
URRO guardroom
URSA guardsman
URSI hubristic
URSL currishly
URTO nutrition
URTU Lucretius
turret-gun
URTV lucrative
nutritive
URUD surrounds
URUH Burroughs
URVI Dubrovnik
URWN currawong
URZT quartzite
USAC puissance
pursuance
substance
USAE run scared
USAL Dunstable

	guessable
USBU	nuts about
USDI	outside in
USDN	subsiding
USDO	outside of
USDS	subsidise
USDZ	subsidize
USEI	sub specie
USFO	pussyfoot
	pussy-foot
USIL	gumshield
USIN	questions
USIO	burst in on
USIT	outskirts
USIZ	Zugspitze
USLA	vulsellae
USLE	Mussulmen
	ourselves
USLI	subsellia
USLN	Mussolini
	nurseling
USMI	nursemaid
USML	fulsomely
USMN	subsuming
USNA	Hudson Bay
USNN	Dunsinane
USNR	cursenary
USNS	fussiness
	gutsiness
USOE	burst open
	outspoken
USRA	outspread
USRB	subscribe
USRC	substract
	substruct
USRD	Bulstrode
USRE	sunscreen
USRI	outstrain
USRK	outstrike
	sunstroke
USRL	cursorily
USRN	outspring
USRP	subscript
USRS	questrist
USRT	substrata
	substrate
USTL	pulsatile
USTN	nurse-tend
	pulsating
USTO	pulsation
USTR	burst tyre
	pulsatory
USTV	pulsative
USUC	outsource
USUG	sun spurge
USVL	cursively
	suasively
USWR	guesswork
UTAC	quittance
UTAE	australes
	quetzales
	quite a few
	suitcases
UTAI	Australia
UTAL	Aunt Sally
UTBU	just about
UTCI	mustachio
UTCS	rusticise
	rusticism
UTCT	rusticate
	rusticity
UTCZ	rusticize
UTDA	custodial
	custodian
	quotidian
UTED	must needs
UTEI	dust-devil
UTEL	Kurt Weill
UTEO	further on
UTFE	hunt after
	justified
	justifier
	lust after
UTFR	multiform
UTGO	quite good
UTHD	Buxtehude
UTHF	butt-shaft
UTHR	Dusty Hare
UTIE	curtailed
	sustained
	sustainer
UTIG	buy things
UTIO	duettinos
UTLI	quitclaim
UTLS	subtilise
UTLT	ductility
	pustulate
UTLZ	subtilize
UTML	Guatemala
	Sun Temple
UTMR	customary
	customers
UTMS	customise
UTMZ	customize
UTNA	Justinian
UTNE	sun-tanned
UTNI	butting-in
	cutting-in
	rusty nail
UTNL	juttingly
UTNS	dustiness
	fustiness
	gustiness
	lustiness
	mustiness
	nuttiness
	rustiness
UTNT	sultanate
UTNU	cutting up
	outtongue
	Suetonius
UTOA	Multnomah
	tuitional
UTOE	dust cover
	Kurt Gödel
UTOI	subtropic
UTOS	Kurt Jooss
UTPA	subtopian
UTPE	multiplex
UTPR	multipara
UTPS	juxtapose
UTRA	auctorial
	cut-throat
	gutter-man
	suctorial
UTRL	austerely
	butterfly
UTRN	guttering
	muttering
	nurturing
	vulturine
UTRS	guitarist
	suetcrust
	vulturish
UTRT	austerity
UTRU	buttercup
	muster out
	vulturous
UTSE	run to seed
UTSR	Cutty Sark
UTSU	out to stud
UTTD	multitude
UTTO	gustation
	guttation
	quotation
UTTR	dust-storm
	gustatory
UTTV	gustative
UTUL	hurtfully
	lustfully
UTVL	furtively
UTVT	cultivate
UUAA	Guru Nanak
UUAL	suturally
UUBR	Bujumbura
UUEC	purulence
UUGU	humungous
UUHS	eunuchise
UUHZ	eunuchize
UUIN	luxuriant
UUIT	luxuriate
UUIU	luxurious
UUJM	queue-jump
UULF	Nuku'alofa
UULS	mutualise
	mutualism
UULT	mutuality
UULZ	mutualize
UUOE	lucumones
UURT	lucubrate
	susurrate
UUTN	Augustine
UUUO	tucutucos
UUWT	put up with
UVDU	curved out
UVFR	curviform
	vulviform
UVIL	surveille
UVLA	pulvillar
UVLI	pulvillio
UVMC	nux vomica
UVNS	suaveness
UVNT	pulvinate
UVRE	subverter
UVRN	quavering
	quivering
UVRS	pulverise
UVRU	quiverful
UVRZ	pulverize
UVTR	curvature
UVVN	surviving
UVYN	surveying
UWNE	cup-winner
UWRE	outworker
UWRL	outwardly
UWTI	out with it!
UXTS	quixotism
UYOA	jurywoman
UYOE	jurywomen
UYON	duty-bound
UYQI	Guayaquil
UYTE	Sun Yat-Sen
UZEU	puzzle out
UZIA	quizzical
UZNL	buzzingly
UZNS	fuzziness
	muzziness
UZOD	buzz words
VANL	Eve Arnold
VCTO	avocation
	evocation
VCTV	evocative
VDCA	oviductal
VDNL	evidently
VGNT	evaginate
VIAC	avoidance
VIAL	available
	availably
	avoidable
VLAO	evaluator
VLAU	Ivy League
VLNH	avalanche
VLON	evil-doing
VLTO	evolution
	ovulation
VNED	Ivan Lendl
	oven-ready
VNIL	evincible
	evincibly
VNLV	oven glove
VNOE	even money
VNOS	oven-roast
VNRT	eventrate
VNUA	avuncular
VNUI	Ivan Bunin
VNUT	eventuate
VPRT	evaporate
	evaporite
	oviparity
VPRU	oviparous
VRAC	overmatch
	overwatch

VRAE overbaked
overtaxed
VRAN overpaint
VRAT overhasty
VRAU overvalue
VRBD everybody
VRCR overscore
VREC overperch
overreach
overreact
VRED overheads
VREG overweigh
VREL avertedly
VRER overweary
VRFE ever after
VRGI over again
VRHC overcheck
VRHD overshade
VRHE over-shoes
VRHL overwhelm
VRHN overshine
VRHO overshoot
overthrow
VRIC every inch
overpitch
VRIE overrider
overtired
VRIH overnight
oversight
VRIL avertible
eversible
VRLD everglade
VRLE oversleep
VRLO overgloom
VRLS every last
VRLU overcloud
VRLW overblown
VRLZ overglaze
VROE overjoyed
overpower
overtower
VRON overcount
overdoing
overmount
VROO over to you!
VROR overboard
VROS overpoise
VRPL overspill
VRPN overspend
VRRC overprice
VRRD over-trade
VRRE evergreen
overgreen
VRRF overdraft
VRRI overgrain
overtrain
VRRM overtrump
VRRN overprint
VRRS overdress
overgrass
overpress
overwrest
VRRT overwrite
VRRV overdrive
VRRW overcrowd
overdrawn
overgrown
VRRZ overprize
VRSU overissue
VRTE oversteer
VRTF overstaff
VRTM every time
VRTN overstink
VRTR overstare
VRTT overstate
VRUE overtures
VRUH ever such a
VRUL overbuild
VRVT uvarovite
VRWE every week
oversweet
VRWI every whit
VRWL overswell
VRXC over-exact
VRXR overexert
VRYA every year
VSVL evasively
VTRE Eva Turner
VTSE ovotestes
VZNU avizandum
WAEN two a penny
WASI sweatsuit
WAWR swear-word
WBFU two-by-four
WCES ewe-cheese
WCOE twice over
WDLN twaddling
twiddling
WEBC sweepback
WECR sweetcorn
WEDS sweet dish
WEEE sweetened
sweetener
WEIG sweepings
WELR F W De Klerk
F W de Klerk
WEMA sweetmeal
sweetmeat
WENS sweetness
WESI ownership
WESO sweet spot
WETL sweet talk
sweet-talk
WFNS swiftness
WGEE swaggerer
WHNE two-handed
WKNN awakening
WLEO twelvemos
WLIG dwellings
WLOU swallow up
WLTL twelfthly
WMAL swimmable
WMEE swimmeret
WMLN swampland
WNAL Owen Falls
WNBA swingboat
WNBU swan about
WNEN swingeing
WNIE Swan River
WNIT twentieth
WNLA Zwinglian
WNLN dwindling
swindling
twinkling
WNNL twiningly
WNOE Gwendolen
WNSL swinishly
WNUN Swinburne
WNWN swing-wing
WNYN twenty-one
WNYS twentyish
WPBC sweptback
WPCR swipe card
WPWN sweptwing
WRET awarded to
WRFS swordfish❑
WRNS awareness
WROE swarm over
WRPA swordplay
WRSA swordsman
WRWT swarm with
WSAL twistable
WSML awesomely
WSRC awestruck
WSRK awestrike
WSRL Swiss roll
WTEE twitterer
WTHF switch off
WTHN switching
twitching
WTIE Two Tribes
WTMN two-timing
WUNS awfulness
WWRL awkwardly
WZLN Swaziland
XAAE excavated
XAAO excavator
XADN expanding
XAIT expatiate
XAIU Excalibur
XANT excarnate
XASE exhausted
XASO expansion
XASV expansive
XBRN exuberant
XBRT exuberate
XCAL execrable
execrably
XCNS exactness
XCTI executrix
XCTN executant
XCTO execution
XCTR executory
XCTV executive
XDTO exudation
oxidation
XEDN exceeding
expending
XEIN expedient
XELN excellent
excelling
XEMN extermine
XENL externals
XEOE excel over
XEPO excerptor
XEPR extempore
XESL extensile
XESO excelsior
extension
XESV excessive
expensive
extensive
XETL exsertile
XETN excepting
expectant
expecting
XETO except for
exception
XETS expertise
XETV exsertive
XETZ expertize
XEUT extenuate
XFII ex officio
XGMU exogamous
XGNL exigently
XGNS oxygenise
XGNT oxygenate
XGNU exogenous
oxygenous
XGNZ oxygenize
XGTS exegetist
XHNE exchanged
exchanger
XHQE exchequer
XIAC excitancy
XIAL excisable
excitable
XICE extincted
XICT expiscate
exsiccate
XIEA exciseman
XIEL excitedly
XIIE exhibited
XIIO exhibitor
XIPT extirpate
XISE Axminster
XITO expiation
XITR expiatory
XLCT explicate
XLDN excluding
XLEL exaltedly
XLIE exploited
exploiter
XLSO exclusion
explosion
XLSV exclusive
explosive
XLTV expletive
XMLF exemplify
XMLR exemplary
XMNN examinant
XMTO exemption

XNHM exanthema
exanthems
XNMT exanimate
XNRT exonerate
XOAI axiomatic
XOET exposed to
XOIL exponible
XOIO expositor
XOIT excoriate
exfoliate
XOLN extolling
XOMN extolment
XONE expounder
XOTO extortion
XOTR exposture
XRAL uxorially
XRCD uxoricide
XRCO extractor
XRCT extricate
XRDT extradite
XRIE exerciser
exercises
XRIM exordiums
XRML extremely
XRMN excrement
XRMS extremism
extremist
XRMT extremity
XRNI extrinsic
XRPS extrapose
XRSE expressed
XRSL expressly
XRSO extrusion
XRSR extrusory
XRSV extrusive
XRTM extra time
XRTO excretion
XRTR excretory
XRTV excretive
XRUH extraught
XRVR extravert
extrovert
XSEC existence
XSFO exist from
XSHR exosphere
XSOE exostoses
XTCS exoticism
XUAL excusable
excusably
XUEO excuse for
XUGT expurgate
XUPT exculpate
XUSO excursion
expulsion
XUST exquisite
XUSV excursive
expulsive
YABR mynah bird
YACU gynaecium
YAIA pyramidal
YAIE pyramises
YAII pyramidic
sybaritic❑

YALG hypallage
YANS tyrannise
YANU tyrannous
YANZ tyrannize
YAOU synagogue
YATN Byzantine
YATU Byzantium
YBDU cymbidium
YBLE cymbaloes
YBLG symbology
YBLN Cymbeline
YBLS cymbalist
symbolise
symbolism❑
symbolist
YBLZ symbolize
YBOI symbiosis
symbiotic
YCPT syncopate
YCRN synchrony
YDCT syndicate
YDOI syndromic
YEAA Hyderabad
Mycenaean
YEAG tyre gauge
YEAL by default
YEBL hyperbola
hyperbole
YEBR Aylesbury
YECF cybercafé
YECL type scale
YEEA type metal
YEGS synergise
synergism
YEGZ synergize
YEHI tyre chain
YEHU pyrethrum
YELN hyperlink
YENO by means of
YENT cybernate
YEPN cyberpunk
YERE by degrees
YERT typewrite
YETR dysentery
YETX hypertext
YEWL Lymeswold
YFBI myofibril
YFLO gyrfalcon
YGOI myoglobin
YHBO by the book
YHCS mythicise
mythicist
YHCZ mythicize
YHIA typhoidal
YHII typhlitic
typhlitis
YHLG mythology
YHLS syphilise
YHLZ syphilize
YHNK Vyshinsky
YHNS hyphenise
pythoness
YHNT hyphenate

YHNZ hyphenize
YHRE Wycherley
YHWE by the week
YHYR by the yard
YIAL cynically
lyrically
typically
YIAO typical of
YIBN hyoid bone
YIDI cylindric
YIGO Lymington
YIJA Cyril Joad
YINC hygienics
YINE Tyrian red
YINS hygienist
YITK by mistake
YKOR Ayckbourn
YLBF syllabify
YLBR syllabary
YLBS syllabise
YLBZ syllabize
YLGS syllogise
syllogism
YLGZ syllogize
YLIA cycloidal
YLMT cyclamate
YLNS hyalinise
YLNZ hyalinize
YLPA cyclopean
YLPE Cyclopses
syllepses
YLPI syllepsis
sylleptic
YLRM cyclorama
YLTO cyclotron
YMCU Symmachus
YMDN Myrmidons
YMLO Pygmalion
YNAS Lyonnaise
YNDS hymnodist
YNDW dying-down
lying down
YNFA lying flat
YNIA hypnoidal
YNIG Ryan Giggs
YNLG by analogy
hymnology
hypnology
YNOT wyandotte❑
YNSE gymnasien
YNSI gymnastic
YNSL by oneself
YNSU gymnasium
YNTS hypnotise
hypnotism
hypnotist
YNTZ hypnotize
YNYN Pyongyang
YOAI pyromania
zygomatic
YOAS hypocaust
YOAT hyponasty
YOAU gyrovague

YOCP gyroscope
YOCS synoecise
YOCU gynoecium
YOCZ synoecize
YODM myxoedema
YOEE eye-opener
pyrometer
YOEI pyrogenic
YOEM hypoderma
YOEN by no means
YOER pyrometry
YOHN sycophant
xylophone
YOII cytokinin
synovitis
YOIU myxovirus
YOLS cytoplasm
hypoblast
pyroclast
YOOG cynomolgi
YOOI cytotoxic
cytotoxin
hypotonia
hypotonic
mycologic
mycotoxin
YORP kymograph
YORS hypocrisy
YORT hypocrite
YOSS synopsise
YOSZ synopsize
YOTL hypostyle
YOYI pyrolysis
YPAI dysphasia
dysplasia
lymphatic
YPII lyophilic
YPLK sylphlike
sylph-like
YPND lymph node
YPNS tympanist
YPOI lyophobic
symphonic
YPPI dyspepsia
dyspeptic
YPSU symposium
YRCL hydrocele
YRDC by-product
YRDM hybridoma
YRDS hybridise
hybridism
YRDT hybridity
YRDZ hybridize
YRFI hydrofoil
YRHE pyorrhoea
YRLG hydrology
hygrology
YRLS hydrolyse
YRLT hydrolyte
YRLZ hydrolyze
YRNE hydrangea
YRSA hydrostat
hygrostat

YRTO hydration
YRUI hydraulic
YRXD hydroxide
YRZA hydrozoan
YTCI syntactic
YTCS mysticism
YTEE syntheses
YTEI synthesis
synthetic
YTFE mystified
mystifier
YTGI nystagmic
YTGU nystagmus
YTLA ayatollah□
YTLI systaltic
YTLO Lyttelton
YTML Eye Temple
YTMS systemise
YTMZ systemize
YTNE bystander
YTNS syntonise
YTNZ syntonize
YTOH dystrophy
YTRC hysterics
YTRE mysteries
YUBR by numbers
YVSE Sylvester
YVSR Sylvestra
YZNK Wyszynski
ZAON Ezra Pound
ZMTA azimuthal
ZNAI Dzungaria
ZORP azeotrope

10 letters – even

AAACR Madagascar
AAACS calamancos
AAADR salamander
AAAGO Caravaggio
AAAIE macadamise
macadamize
palatalise
palatalize
Tananarive
AAAIM pan-Arabism
AAAIN Panamanian
AAAIO Paramaribo
AAAIY Panama City
AAAKN banana skin
AAAKR parawalker
AAAQE catafalque
AAATD maladapted
AABIF papal brief
AACEE damasceene
AACEM salad cream
AACIE Balanchine
AACIM Lamarckism
AACIO maraschino
AACNA parascenia
AACND damascened
AACOS papal cross
AACOT balance out
AADER far and near
AADIE far and wide
AADWY far and away
AAEAA parabemata
AAEAD garage band
AAEBE damageable
manageable
AAEBY manageably
AAEDS zapateados
AAEEE paraselene
AAEES manageress
parameters
savageness
AAEET management
ravagement
AAEHP karate chop
AAEIE caramelise
caramelize
papaverine
AAEIL managerial
AAEIM Paramecium
AAELB Savage Club
AAELS Bagatelles
AAEOS cadaverous
AAERC parametric
AAERE Karageorge
AAESS Paracelsus
AAETC catalectic
cataleptic
AAETS cabalettas
lazarettos
AAETY malapertly
AAFRE naval force
AAGTE Bazalgette
AAHAE paraphrase
AAHAT paraphrast
AAHES Galashiels
AAHOO Takashi Ono
AAHSS paraphyses
AAHTN Kazakhstan
AAIAC paradisaic
AAIAE capacitate
AAIAK safari park
AAIGY damagingly
AAIIA jamahiriya
AAIIC paradisiac
AAIIE fanaticise
fanaticize
parasitise
parasitize
AAIIG law-abiding
AAIIL natalitial
AAIIM fanaticism
parasitism
AAIIS fatalities
AAIIY capability
ratability
AAILY palatially
AAIOS calamitous
AAIRY cavalierly
AAISS paralipses
paralipsis
AAITC fatalistic
AAIUI canaliculi
AAIUT safari suit
AAKBR karaoke bar
AAKLM damask plum
AAKOE damask rose
AALDR paraglider
AALEE lavallière
AALGA paraplegia
AALGC paraplegic
AALLY parallelly
AALNA Capablanca
Casablanca
AALOE zabaglione
AALRS caballeros
AANSA paramnesia
AANSS paraenesis
AANTA Jagannatha
AAOEE Palaeocene
AAOIE parabolise
parabolize
paralogise
paralogize
AAOIL lavatorial
natatorial
AAOIM catabolism
paralogism
sanatorium
AAOIN Patagonian
AAOIS macaronies
AAOML paranormal
AAONY paramouncy
AAOOC Palaeozoic
AAOOY laparotomy
AAOSY Mayakovsky
AAOTR paradoctor
AAOUE paradoxure
AAOUR cataloguer
AAPNI Rawalpindi
AARAS Hamadryads
AARCN pan-African
AARMN cavalryman
cavalrymen
AAROS paratroops
AARPS malapropos
AARYR say a prayer
AASDY harassedly
AASET harassment
AASFN Marat Safin
AASOE radarscope
AASRY nasal spray
AASUE satay sauce
AATES vacantness
AATLA tarantella
AATNO San Antonio
AAUFN ragamuffin
AAYIG paralysing
AAYPC Paralympic
ABAND fatbrained
madbrained
ABCLY iambically
ABEKR lawbreaker
law-breaker
ABERH Marble Arch
ABGCN garbage can
ABIGY dabblingly
ramblingly
warblingly
ABLAE barbellate
ABNCL rabbinical
ABNDS carbonados
ABNOY carbon copy
carbon-copy
ABNTD carbonated
ABNTS sanbenitos
ABOLD bamboozled
ABOLR bamboozler
ABPMY namby-pamby
ABRAE Barbary ape
ABRHP barbershop
ABRIR halberdier
ABRLI Barbirolli
ABRLR cat burglar
cat-burglar
ABRPM Barbara Pym
ABRSA Barbarossa
ABSIG ear-bussing
ABTCL sabbatical
ABTEN far between
ABTRC barbituric
ABUAE harbourage
ABUIE tambourine
ABXLC carboxylic
ACAAE Bacchanale
ACABR gas chamber
ACAIE saccharide
saccharine
saccharise
saccharize
ACAIY saccharify
ACALS Ray Charles
ACALT hatch a plot
ACAMO lay claim to
ACAOE saccharose
ACARB catch a crab
ACATR Nancy Astor
watch after

Words marked □ can also be spelled with an initial capital letter

ACATS bacchantes
ACBAD patchboard
ACCAN watch chain
ACCLY farcically
ACDES fancy dress
rancidness
ACEES gaucheness
ACEIH Carchemish
ACEJB hatchet job
ACELD satchelled
ACEMN hatchet man
ACETC pancreatic
ACETN pancreatin
ACETR Manchester
ACFLY fancifully
watchfully
ACFRL calciferol
ACGAS watchglass
ACGOS fancy goods
ACHUE ranchhouse
ACIES patchiness
ACIGP patching up
ACIID sanctified
ACIIR sanctifier
ACIND sanctioned
ACIOY sanctimony
ACIUE sanctitude
ACKIE pancake ice
ACLAD parcel-bawd
ACLAE cancellate
ACLBE calculable
ACLBY calculably
ACLGT catch light
ACLIE parcelwise
parcel-wise
rascal-like
ACLNS marchlands
ACLOB parcel bomb
ACLPY narcolepsy
ACLRY vascularly
ACLSS calculuses
ACLTD calculated
ACLTR calculator
ACLVR latch lever
ACMAY bad company
ACMKR matchmaker
watchmaker
ACMNA narcomania
ACNAT marcantant
ACNET malcontent
ACNGN carcinogen
ACNMS carcinomas
ACNTD fascinated
ACNTR vaccinator
ACOAE lanceolate
ACOIS Sanctorius
ACPAI sarcophagi
ACPAM sarcoplasm
ACPNY catchpenny
ACRAD Cancer Ward
ACRLE barcarolle
ACROE mascarpone
saucer dome

ACROS calcareous
ACRUS saucerfuls
ACSGT catch sight
ACSIE Lancashire
ACSIK matchstick
ACSIM narcissism
ACSIT narcissist
ACSRP watchstrap
ACTHR rat-catcher
ACTRH lancet arch
ACTWR watchtower
watch-tower
ACUTO pay court to
ACVOS lascivious
ACWIE Marco White
ACWMN fancy woman
ADAAE hard palate
ADADN handmaiden
ADAGA cardialgia
ADAGR sandbagger
ADAIN Maid Marian
ADAMD MacDiarmid
ADAND hard-earned
ADAOA mandragora
ADAOR hard labour
ADARC paediatric
ADARW hand-barrow
ADATE sandcastle
ADATN sand martin
ADATR bandmaster
ADBLR mandibular
ADBUH dandy-brush
ADCAT handicraft
ADCEN Sadducaean
ADDAE Bagdad Café
ADDES candidness
ADDNY handy-dandy
ADDON handed down
ADDTS candidates
ADEAK saddleback
ADEDD bald-headed
hard-headed
ADEES saddleless
ADEIH saddle with
ADEIK candlewick
ADEMR daydreamer
ADEOE saddle sore
saddle-sore
ADEOF saddle roof
ADEON hand-me-down
ADEOP saddle soap
ADEOT paddle-boat
ADGAE tardigrade
Waldegrave
ADHEE hard cheese
ADHRE dandy-horse
ADHUE bawdy-house
ADIAD sand lizard
ADIAE land-pirate
ADIES tawdriness
ADIGY dawdlingly
ADIKD hand-picked
ADITD hard-fisted

ADITN hard-bitten
ADITR ward sister
ADLBA candelabra
ADLEL Tam Dalyell
ADLIE Baudelaire
ADLOD sandalwood
ADLRS bandoleros
ADMES randomness
ADMIE randomwise
tandemwise
ADMNC pandemonic
ADMSS mandamuses
ADMZR randomizer
ADNAD hand in hand
ADNAE maiden name
ADNAR maidenhair
ADNBE pardonable
ADNBY pardonably
ADNED Maidenhead
ADNEE jardinière
ADNHP wardenship
ADNIE maidenlike
ADNIG tap-dancing
ADNIY garden city
ADNLS fandangles
ADNLY cardinally
ADNNT landing-net
ADNOD maidenhood
ADNOF warding off
ADNOS fandangoes
ADNOT handing out
handing-out
ADNTN Haddington
ADNVR maiden over
ADOAD hand to hand
hand-to-hand
ADOCS land forces
ADODR landholder
ADOED hard to read
ADOEY handsomely
hard done by
ADOGT hard-fought
ADOIA Said Aouita
ADOKD landlocked
ADOLD hard-boiled
ADOLR sand dollar
ADOOY cardiology
ADOPR sand hopper
ADORM cardiogram
ADPIE paedophile
ADPIG handspring
ADRAH balderdash
ADRIG sanderling
ADRIT Vanderbilt
ADRLA banderilla
ADRLT falderal it
ADRNS wanderings
ADROT Van der Post
ADRRM wander from
ADRUE sandgrouse
ADRUT wanderlust
ADSOK hard as rock
ADSRN hard as iron

ADTFS handstaffs
ADTVS handstaves
ADUHD hard-pushed
ADVLE Mandeville
vaudeville
ADWRH Wandsworth
ADYHN hard hyphen
ADYVR hardly ever
AEAAI Lake Malawi
AEAAK taken aback
AEADD barehanded
AEADN case-harden
face-harden
game warden
AEAEF make game of
take care of
AEAEN Lake Vänern
AEAES Gale Sayers
AEAGA gametangia
AEAGR make larger
AEAIG face-saving
lacerating
AEAIN laceration
maceration
racemation
AEAIR make easier
AEAIS Camerarius
AEAIY laterality
AEAKF take rank of
AEAKL Lake Baikal
AEAKR make darker
AEAKT wage packet
wage-packet
AEAMA Lake Saimaa
AEANR wage-earner
AEAOA Lake Ladoga
AEAPE Jane Marple
AEAPN make happen
AEARD make sacred
race hatred
AEARW make narrow
AEASR Lake Nasser
AEATN take part in
AEATR malefactor
AEAUE ease nature
AEBAD James Braid
paperboard
AEBAH water-brash
AEBAS baked beans
AEBEK take a break
AEBIF take a brief
AEBKR James Baker
Janet Baker
AEBON James Brown
AEBRE waterborne
AEBRH paper birch
AEBWE James Bowie
AECAE James Chase
AECAK have a crack
AECAS take a class
AECAT watercraft
AECCD maleic acid
AECCE water cycle

AECEK sales clerk
salesclerk
water clerk
AECES watercress
AECIN take action
AECOK water clock
AECOS paleaceous
AECRS cadet corps
AECYA parenchyma
AEDIO fazendeiro
AEDIS calendries
AEDKO have a dekko
take a dekko
AEDTL sacerdotal
AEDWR James Dewar
AEEDD bareheaded
AEEDF have need of
take heed of
AEEDR make tender
AEEEA Lake Geneva
AEEGD barelegged
AEEGH wavelength
AEEID safe period
AEEIW rave review
AEEKR make weaker
AEELR tale-teller
AEEOD tape-record
AEEOS patereroes
AEEPR gamekeeper
gatekeeper
AEERR talebearer
AEESI Paderewski
AEESY carelessly
fadelessly
namelessly
AEETR make better
AEEUE make secure
AEFAD make afraid
AEFCD paper-faced
AEFET take effect
AEFOK sale of work
AEFON gate of horn
AEFOT waterfront
AEFPT have off pat
AEGAS waterglass
AEGES make a guess
AEGUE paper gauge
taper gauge
water gauge
AEHAR take the air
AEHAT have a heart
AEHDY name the day
AEHMN catechumen
AEHNH have a hunch
AEHOY game theory
AEHRE take charge
AEHRP take the rap
AEHSN take the sun
AEHSS catechesis
AEHTC catechetic
AEHUE Waterhouse
AEHWY pave the way
AEHZR catechizer

AEIBE make liable
AEIES wateriness
AEIET maleficent
AEIEY make lively
AEIGR make bigger
AEIGY taperingly
waveringly
AEIHR make richer
AEILY materially
AEINR have dinner
AEIOY James Ivory
AEIRS Cader Idris
AEITE café filtre
AEIYN take pity on
AEJAS James Jeans
AEJUE James Joule
AEJYE James Joyce
AEKAT sauerkraut
AEKIE paper-knife
AEKIT Lagerkvist
AELAT Dame Pliant
AELCD Lake Placid
AELET Lake Albert
AELGT take flight
AELIH Janet Leigh
AELOY make gloomy
AELTC satellitic
AELTS satellites
AELVL water level
AEMAE James Meade
AEMCE paper-mâché
AEMLN watermelon
AEMNS make amends
AEMNY paper money
AEMOH make smooth
AEMSC Water Music
AEMSN James Mason
AEMUE make impure
AENAD take in hand
AENAH take an oath
AENAL lateen sail
AENAN take in vain
AENAY make uneasy
AENCE tabernacle
AENEL make unwell
AENGT wake a night
AENID have in mind
AENIE have inside
make a noise
AENIW have in view
AENIY make untidy
AENLY maternally
paternally
AENMH water nymph
AENON have on loan
take on loan
AENRS babe in arms
AENRY wave energy
AEOAE face to face
face-to-face
AEOAK take to task
AEOAT made to last
AEODA have no idea

AEODF take hold of
AEODR make colder
make louder
AEODS make no odds
AEOEF take note of
AEOEN make modern
take to mean
AEOEO make love to
AEOET malevolent
AEOGR make longer
AEOIE categorise
categorize
take notice
AEOIH make do with
AEOIL categorial
AEOIN Caledonian
AEOLF take toll of
AEOLR pace-bowler
AEOOD make so bold
AEOOE have no hope
AEOON take to town
AEORE racecourse
AEOSY ravenously
AEOTD barefooted
AEPAE take-up rate
AEPAT water-plant
AEPER make appear
AEPGT James Paget
AEPIH take up with
AEPOF waterproof
AEPRS take up arms
AEPRY have a party
AEPTH sales pitch
AEPWR water power
AERAH have breath
take breath
AERCS make tracks
AERES take orders
AERGT have a right
make bright
take fright
AERZD care-crazed
AESAD make a stand
Wake Island
AESAE water snake
AESAK have a snack
maker's mark
AESAT make a start
AESDE water's edge
AESDO make used to
AESED take as read
AESET watersmeet
AESIR water-skier
AESOE Mateus Rosé
AESOT taken short
waterspout
AESRE take as true
AESUD make a sound
AESUE caper sauce
AETAE have it made
AETAY take it easy
AETBE lamentable
make stable

patentable
water table
AETBN James Tobin
AETBY lamentably
AETES parentless
patentness
AETET latent heat
AETGR paper tiger
AETGT watertight
AETID tapestried
AETIE take strike
AETIF water thief
AETIH make it with
AETLY parentally
AETOD parenthood
AETOG make strong
AETPT talent-spot
AETRD man-entered
AETRL parenteral
AETSA Barents Sea
AETWR water tower
AETWY have it away
AEUAT café au lait
AEUEF make sure of
AEUGS face fungus
AEUHF make much of
AEULC make public
AEURS safeguards
AEUSS have guests
AEUTN Jane Austen
AEUVD make curved
AEWEL water-wheel
AEWMN saleswoman
AEWRS waterworks
AEYAT Safety Last
AEYET safety belt
AEYIE panegyrise
panegyrize
AEYIT panegyrist
AEYST make eyes at
AFAAT malfeasant
AFCON half-a-crown
AFEET bafflement
AFEIG bad feeling
Ian Fleming
AFERY half-yearly
AFESN half nelson
AFIGY bafflingly
AFITD halfwitted
half-witted
AFITR half-sister
AFLES lawfulness
manfulness
AFLIE farfalline
AFLRN half florin
AFOMD half-formed
AFORY half-hourly
AFRUD faff around
AFSEP half-asleep
AFTHD far-fetched
AFUNA half guinea
AFUTR half-hunter
AGAEH Bangladesh

AGAIA margharita
AGAOS Sangradoes
AGBAD barge-board
AGDES jaggedness
raggedness
AGDET ragged left
AGEIE marguerite
AGEOS gangrenous
AGEOT malgré tout
AGETS larghettos
AGIAY sanguinary
AGIEY sanguinely
AGIFR bargain for
AGIGY laughingly
tanglingly
AGIIG bargaining
AGLDR hang-glider
AGLRA Mangalarga
AGNIA Tanganyika
AGNIE bang on time
AGNIL tangential
AGNLA marginalia
AGNLY marginally
AGNUN gargantuan❑
AGOBE say goodbye
AGOOS languorous
AGOSC Panglossic
AGPIH gang up with
AGPIT large print
AGRAT larger part
AGRGT hang a right
AGRHN larger than
AGRNS Tangerines
AGRUD hang around
AGRVR Range Rover®
AGSAE large-scale
AGSEN mangosteen
AGTRY daughterly
AGUFR hang out for
AGWGA Wagga Wagga
AGWIE Large White
AHAIE Rachmanite
AHAIM Rachmanism
AHEIG cashiering
AHERN mashie iron
AHESN each person
AHGAH tachograph
AHGNC pathogenic
AHHLC naphthalic
AHIDR pathfinder
AHIDW sash window
AHIDY bad hair day
AHIIN Cap Haitian
AHLCN catholicon
AHLOO say hello to
AHLVR Bath Oliver
AHMBE fathomable
AHMES fathomless
AHMTR bathometer
fathometer
tachometer
tachymeter
AHMTY bathymetry

AHNAE cachinnate
Nathan Hale
AHNGN machinegun
machine-gun
AHNLR panhandler
AHNSN lay hands on
AHNTN Washington
AHNTR machinator
AHOIG fashioning
AHRAD fatherland
AHRDY Father's Day
AHRES fatherless
AHRHN rather than
AHRIE fatherlike
AHROD fatherhood
AHRWS hash browns
AHUBR Mach number
AHYOE lachrymose
AIABY Halifax Bay
AIAEP Manila hemp
AIAIE capitalise
capitalize
laminarise
laminarize
radicalise
radicalize
AIAIG validating
AIAIM capitalism
radicalism
Vaticanism
AIAIN capitation
cavitation
habitation
lamination
lapidarian
navigation
patination
salivation
sanitarian
sanitation
validation
AIAIT capitalist
maximalist
Vaticanist
AIAIY sanitarily
AIAOH Marita Koch
AIAOS palisadoes
AIAOY habilatory
AIARM Wasim Akram
AIASM capital sum
AIAUE caricature
AIBEO Maria Bueno
AIBUE David Bruce
AIBWE David Bowie
AICLY maniacally
AICOS Latin cross
AICRE Marie Curie
AIDOE palindrome
AIEAD native land
AIEER native bear
AIEES facileness
nativeness
AIELB Savile Club

AIEMC taxidermic
AIEML taxidermal
AIEOK native rock
AIEON native-born
native town
AIETS manifestos
AIETY manifestly
AIEUS salicetums
AIFAL tariff wall
AIFIG satisfying
AIFOT David Frost
AIFVR cabin fever
AIGAE laying bare
AIGAK taking back
AIGAT fading fast
taking part
AIGEN Paris green
Paris-green
AIGIE having life
AIGOE making love
AIGOL caking coal
AIGOO raring to go
AIGOT Racing Post
AIGPO facing up to
AIGRR malingerer
AIGRY Maxim Gorky
AIGSY having a say
AIGTD variegated
AIGUL Raging Bull
AIGWR David Gower
AIGWY taking away
taking-away
AIHBL David Hubel
AIHES garishness
lavishness
Manichaeus
rakishness
AIHET banishment
famishment
ravishment
AIHLE Danish blue
AIHUP parish pump
parish-pump
AIIAE facilitate
habilitate
pacificate
vaticinate
AIIET habiliment
AIIIM pacificism
AIIIN Maximilian
AIIIS facilities
AIIIT pacificist
AIINE Parisienne
AIIOS caliginous
AIIRY familiarly
AIITC nativistic
AIITN Tajikistan
AIJSN David Jason
AILAR facial hair
AILDE David Lodge
AILGC hagiologic
AILLE maxillulae
AILMC Panislamic

AILNA Mario Lanza
AILNH David Lynch
AILTD papillated
AILTY hagiolatry
AIMEL barium meal
AIMJR Canis Major
AIMMT David Mamet
AIMNC talismanic
AIMNO Papiamento
AIMNR Canis Minor
AIMNS habilments
AIMTR variometer
AINAE Samian ware
AINCO San Ignacio
AINIE nationwide
AININ salientian
AINLY nationally
rationally
AINNY malignancy
AINOD nationhood
AINTE marionette
AINVN David Niven
AIOAK Calico Jack
AIOAS varifocals
AIODY manifoldly
AIOIE Capitoline
saxicoline
AIOIL janitorial
AIOIY varicosity
AIONA California
AIOOS facinorous
saxicolous
AIOOY varicotomy
AIOSI Malinowski
AIOUI Jamiroquai
AIPCS Paris Pacts
AIPET palimpsest
AIRVR Taxi Driver
AISEL David Steel
AISNE radiosonde
AISOM ladies' room
AISRE patisserie
AITAE magistrate
AITAY magistracy
AITLY sagittally
varietally
AITMS Radio Times
AIUAE capitulate
manipulate
AIUAY patibulary
AIUBE fatiguable
AIULH Najibullah
AIULY habitually
AIUNY taciturnly
AIUTD habituated
AIUUL pari-mutuel
AIYAE family name
salicylate
vanity case
vanity-case
AIYAL cavity wall
AIYAR Vanity Fair
AIYEN easily seen

Words marked ❑ can also be spelled with an initial capital letter

AIYNT vanity unit
AIYRE family tree
AJAUN San Joaquin
AJCIG carjacking
AJEIG Darjeeling
AJNRM panjandrum
AKABT jack rabbit
AKADD backhanded
back-handed
cack-handed
AKADR back-hander
AKADY backwardly
AKAEY walk lamely
AKAKR backmarker
backpacker
AKAMN backgammon
back-gammon
AKAMR jackhammer
AKANR Jack Warner
AKARD dark-haired
AKATR dark matter
taskmaster
AKDAL masked ball
AKDED fat-kidney'd
AKDIH say Kaddish
AKDON marked-down
AKECB hackney cab
AKEID walk behind
AKEMN Jack Lemmon
AKEQE Kafkaesque
AKETE bark beetle
AKETR rack-renter
AKFAE lack of fame
AKFET Jack of Lent
AKFIE walk of life
AKFIS lack of bias
AKHLD Jack the Lad
AKIDY talk wildly
AKIIG backbiting
back-biting
backfiring
AKLCS back-blocks
AKLDR backslider
AKNAS Balkan Wars
AKNAT walk-on part
AKNBX packing-box
AKNIE walk in line
AKNOF marking off
AKNOH mackintosh❑
AKNOS Parkinson's
AKNOT marking out
AKNOY Mark Antony
AKNPS jackanapes
AKOAK back to back
AKODN Jack London
AKODY talk loudly
AKOEL walk to heel
AKOHO Mark Rothko
AKONO talk down to
AKORS Mark Morris
AKPNH pack a punch
AKPNY hanky-panky
AKPTL Das Kapital

AKRDY cankeredly
AKRUD background
lark around
AKRUY marker buoy
AKTAE basket case
basket-case
AKTAL basketball
racket-tail
AKTBE marketable
AKTEL market-bell
AKTET back street
AKTHP packet-ship
AKTIS backstairs
AKTLY walky-talky
AKTOE backstroke
AKTOK basketwork
basket-work
AKTON market town
AKTOT packet boat
packet-boat
AKTTH backstitch
AKTUS basketfuls
AKTYK yackety-yak
AKUBR back number
AKUKY talk turkey
AKUNR back burner
AKUTE lacklustre
AKUTY bankruptcy
AKWMN markswoman
ALABC galliambic
ALAEI Karl Nägeli
ALAET palliament
parliament
ALAEY Paul Valéry
ALAIE palliative
ALAII tagliarini
ALAIN palliation
ALAKN fall back on
ALARN Earl Warren
ALASY Karl Jansky
ALBED daily bread
ALBLS ballabiles
ALBUH sable brush
ALCAS Gallic Wars
ALCCD gallic acid
ALCEK tally clerk
ALCLE valleculae
ALCOH tablecloth
ALCOS fallacious
ALCTY Paul McStay
ALDES pallidness
ALDLD Valladolid
ALDZN daily dozen
ALEEE Paul Revere
ALEID fall behind
ALEIE earlierise
earlierize
ALEIG Jan Leeming
ALELW Saul Bellow
ALEMN Paul Newman
ALERO fall heir to
ALERR pall-bearer
ALETN Paul Merton

ALFAE hall of fame
ALFIE ball of fire
ALFRH sally forth
ALGAS galloglass
ALGID daily grind
ALHPD ball-shaped
ALIES faultiness
ALIGY rallyingly
ALIIG nail-biting
ALINL call signal
ALLAD Paul Eluard
ALLJH hallelujah
ALLNN table linen
ALLWR wallflower
ALMKN Takla Makan
ALMNA Gallomania
ALMSC early music
ALNES fallenness
ALNGN gatling gun
gatling-gun
ALNIH fall in with
ALNOE fall in love
ALNOF calling-off
falling-off
ALNOT bawling-out
falling-out
ALNRH fallen arch
ALNTC kaolinitic
ALNTN Darlington
ALNYE Ballantyne
ALNZS gallinazos
ALOAL wall-to-wall
ALOBY Paul Dombey
ALOID call to mind
ALOIG ballooning
ALOIH nail polish
ALOIS fall to bits
ALOIT balloonist
ALOIZ Karl Dönitz
ALOLF fall foul of
ALONN fall down on
ALOPR Karl Popper
ALPAE fault plane
ALPIE Gallophile
ALPOE Gallophobe
ALPOL Gallup poll
ALRAE tailor-made
tailormake
ALRCL wax lyrical
ALRGR Paul Kruger
ALRLI Paolo Rolli
ALRNO San Lorenzo
ALROH Lalla Rookh
ALRUD rally round
ALSEO Carlos Belo
ALSEP fall asleep
ALSIS ballistics
ALSON tablespoon
ALSOT Daily Sport
table-sport
ALSRP maple syrup
ALTDY call it a day
ALTET Wall Street

ALTHE ballet shoe
ALWAE tallow-face
ALWER fallow deer
ALWES callowness
sallowness
ALYAD Talleyrand
ALYET galley-west
AMCDM tarmacadam❑
AMCIS naumachias
AMCTE parmacitie
AMDCL Talmudical
AMDON calmed down
AMEDR palm reader
AMESY harmlessly
AMGNI salmagundi
AMGNY salmagundy
AMLSS haemolysis
AMLTC haemolytic
AMNDS Maimonides
Parmenides
AMNES bad manners
AMNLA salmonella
AMNNS Las Meninas
AMNOE sarmentose
AMNOS harmonious
sarmentous
AMNPN warming-pan
AMNZD harmonized
AMNZR salmanazar
AMRED hammerhead
AMREM hammer beam
AMRHN Carmarthen
AMRNO hammer into
AMROK hammerlock
AMRTN Palmerston
AMSEL Dan Maskell
AMTEY Pat Metheny
AMTOS palmettoes
AMTRA haematuria
AMTVH bar mitzvah
bat mitzvah
AMUDY Palm Sunday
ANADR mainlander
ANAIG gainsaying
yawn-making
ANAND maintained
ANANR maintainer
ANASR Tannhäuser
ANATR main matter
ANBLY cannibally
ANBNS Iain M Banks
ANCCD tannic acid
ANCRA Magna Carta
ANEGT gain height
gain weight
ANEIG laundering
maundering
sauntering
ANESY painlessly
ANETN Launceston
ANFCT magnificat❑
ANFIE main office
ANFIG magnifying

ANHAT faint-heart
ANHNO launch into
ANHOE haunch bone
ANHRS dawn chorus
ANIES daintiness
jauntiness
ANIGY hauntingly
tauntingly
vauntingly
ANIIG gaingiving
mainlining
ANILR painkiller
ANLOI cannelloni
ANLRY Fauntleroy
ANLUE main clause
ANMPS magnum opus
ANNAL cannonball
ANNEG darning egg
Tannenberg
ANOET rainforest
ANONS main points
ANORE main course
ANOTR rain-doctor
ANPIE Fanny Price
ANPIG mainspring
ANRDE Bainbridge
ANRKR pawnbroker
ANRMT Laundromat®
ANRNH Dawn French
ANRRW Cannery Row
ANRSR Dawn Fraser
ANRTE laundrette
ANRUD gain ground
ANSES Saint-Saëns
ANSIG tarnishing
varnishing
ANSIL carnassial
ANTAR Barnet fair
ANTEM mainstream
ANTEP cannot help
ANTPE Barnstaple
ANTZR magnetizer
ANUTE Carnoustie
AOABN halocarbon
AOAOA Savonarola
AOAOY laboratory
AOARS Barosaurus
AOBNS bag of bones
AOBRH day of birth
AODRY Harold Urey
AOEAE halogenate
AOEET cajolement
AOEGD razor-edged
AOEHT eat one's hat
AOEIN Hanoverian
AOENC Napoleonic
AOEOD carotenoid
AOEOS halogenous
AOERC barometric
manometric
AOETS salopettes
vaporettos
AOEWY pay one's way
AOFAE camouflage
AOFEM way off beam
AOFET halo effect
AOFNY Bay of Fundy
AOHAE Samothrace
AOHNS lay on hands
AOHRA Ramos-Horta
AOHUE manor-house
AOIIE Jacobinise
Jacobinize
AOIIM gadolinium
AOIOD carotinoid
AOIOM vaporiform
AONIE mayonnaise
AOOIT taxonomist
AOOIY vaporosity
AOOOS malodorous
AOOSY canorously
valorously
vaporously
AORAP labour camp
AORBE favourable
AORBY favourably
AOREN mavourneen
AORES savourless
AORIH labour with
AOROE laboursome
AORPY cacography
AORUE Baton Rouge
AOSAP razor-sharp
AOSES famousness
AOSIL man of skill
AOSRW man of straw
AOTAN wagon train
AOTCL panoptical
AOTET Way Out West
AOTIE La Fontaine
AOTUE raconteuse
AOURR manoeuvrer
AOURS manoeuvres
AOWEL wagon wheel
AOWES Mason Weems
AOWRS can of worms
war of words
AOYLE Saxony blue
AOYML paroxysmal
APASA Caspian Sea
APAUT Malplaquet
APCIO cappuccino
APEAE marprelate
APEET happy event
APEGE harpy eagle
APERY dapple-grey
APGOS rampageous
APILY Ian Paisley
APINR campaigner
APLAY carpellary
APLIN rampallian
APNDR Ralph Nader
APNES Carpenters
APNLS campaniles
APNNO happen into
APNNS happenings
APNON dampen down
APNPN happen upon
APNRS campaneros
APOAE camphorate
APOER harpooneer
APOEY lampoonery
APOGD wasp-tongu'd
APOIT lampoonist
APORE damp-course
APRAD Raj Persaud
APRBT vampire bat
APRES dapperness
APRET sapperment
APRIG dapperling
APRIH tamper with
APRIO Valparaiso
Valparaíso
APRIW pay-per-view
APSAT Maupassant
APSNS campesinos
APSRL campestral
AQAIY bad quality
AQEAE masquerade
AQEIE Jacqueline
AQEIG banqueting
AQELR man-queller
AQIAE pasquinade
AQIAT pasquilant
AQIHD vanquished
AQIHR vanquisher
AQIIS Tarquinius
AQITY say quietly
ARACY matriarchy
patriarchy
ARADN Ray Reardon
ARAIE patrialise
patrialize
ARAIG map-reading
ARAIY patriality
ARARD fair-haired
ARAVN Caernarvon
ARCAE patriciate
ARCAS patricians
ARCDL matricidal
parricidal
patricidal
ARCDS barricados
ARCER Sacre Coeur
ARCIG barracking
ARCIS capriccios
ARCOS capricious
ARCTD fabricated
ARCTR fabricator
ARCUT raw recruit
ARDES sacredness
ARDVS Laura Davis
AREBG carrier bag
AREDD fair-headed
AREMN married man
AREOK Gabriel Oak
ARFCR sacrificer
ARGEN carragheen
ARGNC iatrogenic
saprogenic
ARGRS Cairngorms
ARHLY Caerphilly
ARIDD fair-minded
ARIGN carrying-on
ARIIG ram-raiding
ARIKM fair dinkum
ARLIG patrolling
rag-rolling
ARLOL barrel roll
ARLUS barrelfuls
ARMNO Sacramento
ARMTA parramatta
ARMVD far-removed
ARNES barrenness
ARNET Fahrenheit
ARNIM lawrencium
ARNIS Laurentius
ARNMC patronymic
ARNTN Barrington
Carrington
Warrington
AROIG fair-boding
gadrooning
AROIM patriotism
ARPIG hairspring
ARPKN fair-spoken
ARPRC madreporic
ARPYE saprophyte
ARSES barristers
ARSHA Saurischia
ARSNT sacrosanct
ARSOY fairy story
ARSUG Harrisburg
ARTAE carrot cake
ARTBE narratable
ARTEK hairstreak
ARTIE parrot-like
ARTIG garrotting
ARTNA Mauretania
Mauritania
ARVAA La Traviata
ARWAT narrowcast
ARWES narrowness
ARWIE Barry White
ARWON narrow down
ARWOT narrow boat
narrow-boat
ARYOD fairly good
ASAAE raise a hare
ASAAM false alarm
ASAIG nauseating
ASAIM pan-Slavism
ASAIT pan-Slavist
ASAIY pass easily
ASAKE hamshackle
ramshackle
ranshackle
ASAKT mass market
mass-market
ASALR Fats Waller
marshaller
ASANR CAT scanner

ASAUT raise a dust
ASCAN daisy-chain
ASCIG ransacking
ASDVR passed over
ASDWY passed away
ASEAD Sam Shepard
ASEEO lay siege to
ASEES Cat Stevens
ASEGR Hans Geiger
ASEST Hatshepsut
ASETR tax shelter
ASFCD false-faced
ASFLY pausefully
ASFOE days of yore
ASFOT false front
ASFVR Lassa fever
ASGDG sausage dog
sausage-dog
ASGTD far-sighted
ASGWY passageway
ASHLR day-scholar
ASIDR Fassbinder
ASIIY causticity
ASILS Marseilles
ASLAD easselward
ASLAE easselgate
Hans Sloane
ASLBD Faisalabad
ASLIH damsel fish
damselfish
ASMBE ransomable
ASMES ransomless
ASMLS facsimiles
ASMNY raise money
ASMRL false morel
ASNAI Rafsanjani
ASNER raisonneur
ASNES passengers
ASNHM Walsingham
ASNIY Carson City
ASNOT passing-out
ASNTE maisonette
ASOAE passionate
ASOAH fat stomach
ASOBE sans nombre
ASOEA Cassiopeia
ASOEY days gone by
lay store by
ASOIO Fats Domino
ASOIT bassoonist
ASOSY nauseously
ASOTY Galsworthy
ASPEL mass appeal
ASPIT pansophist
ASRAT manservant
ASRAY Jay's Treaty
ASRCT Maastricht
ASRIE hansardise
hansardize
ASRNE ear syringe
ASRUD pass around
ASSAT false start
ASSIN jam session
ASSIY Kansas City
ASTEH false teeth
ASTON basset horn
ASTRE Basseterre
Basse-Terre
ASUBR mass number
ASUDR mass murder
ASUNT lansquenet
ASUTR bass guitar
pass muster
ASWAT Warsaw Pact
ASWEL daisy-wheel
ASWLY palsy-walsy
ASZBE capsizable
ATAAT martial art
ATAIE carthamine
partialise
partialize
tartrazine
ATAIM Kantianism
martialism
ATAIN castration
ATAIY factuality
partiality
ATALW martial law
ATATR past master
ATBAD pasteboard
ATBET hartebeest
ATBUD earthbound
ATCAS Santa Claus
ATCCD lactic acid
ATCIG Tao-te-ching
ATCLR particular
ATCLY nautically
tactically
ATCOY mastectomy
ATCPE participle
ATCTR masticator
ATDIK malted milk
ATDOS fastidious
ATDRM parted from
ATEAE cattle cake
ATEAL past recall
ATEAN pay the cain
ATECP panther cap
ATEEK eat the leek
ATEET battlement
ATEHP battleship
ATEID wattlebird
ATEIE cattlelike
pantherine
ATEIF past belief
ATEIH battle with
pantherish
ATEIL pay the bill
ATELR saltcellar
ATEOE battle zone
ATEOF pad the hoof
ATEOK wattle-work
ATEOL Hartlepool
ATEON battle-torn
ATERD cattle grid
ATESY tactlessly
ATETD maltreated
ATFCD pasty-faced
ATFDN East of Eden
ATFLO faithful to
ATFLY faithfully
tastefully
wastefully
ATGAE fastigiate
saltigrade
ATGAH pantograph
ATHAT lay to heart
ATHNE last-chance
ATHSY malt whisky
ATIES earthiness
paltriness
ATIFU gastric flu
ATIGS cartridges
partridges
ATIGY tattlingly
ATILN Matt Dillon
ATINY Walt Disney
ATIPR day-tripper
ATIUE last-minute
ATLAE cantillate
ATLAO martellato
ATLEO hasta luego
ATLSS nautiluses
ATLUE cantaloupe
ATLVR cantilever
ATMMC pantomimic
ATMNE haute monde
ATMRA Santa Maria
ATMRO Tantum ergo
ATMUT tantamount
ATMVR earthmover
ATNAE martingale
ATNDS bastinades
ATNEL Martin Bell
ATNES wantonness
ATNET cantonment
ATNHR cast anchor
ATNIE wait in line
ATNMS Martin Amis
ATNOF casting-off
ATNON batten down
ATNOT casting out
ATNQE Martinique
ATNUG Battenburg
ATOAA xanthomata
ATOAY cautionary
ATOHD gap-toothed
saw-toothed
ATOIG fast-moving
ATOIT cartoonist
ATOLR fast bowler
ATOOE gastronome
ATOOY gastronomy
ATORE Eastbourne
ATOSY captiously
cautiously
factiously
ATOUH eat too much
ATPEE party piece
ATPPR waste paper
ATQAE earthquake
ATRAE battercake
masturbate
ATRAK natterjack
ATRAP Walter Camp
ATRBE pasturable
ATRED Walter Reed
ATRES masterless
Walter Hess
ATRET parturient
ATRID mastermind
ATRIE bastardise
bastardize
Eastertide
gas turbine
ATRII factor VIII
ATRIM nasturtium
ATRLI saltarelli
ATRLS pastorales
ATRLY Hattersley
pastorally
ATRMA bacteremia
ATROK masterwork
ATRON batter down
latter-born
Matterhorn
ATRPD gasteropod
ATRUD fart around
ATRUY Canterbury
ATSEL cast a spell
ATSEP fast asleep
ATSEY baptistery
ATSIO fantastico
ATSUA Battistuta
ATSZD fantasized
ATSZR fantasizer
ATTEM fast stream
ATTOS factitious
ATTTN tarte tatin
ATUIE pasteurise
pasteurize
ATUIN Carthusian
Malthusian
ATUSX East Sussex
ATUTR salt-butter
ATVTD captivated
ATWMN Earthwoman
AUAAA tabula rasa
AUADD value added
AUAGS natural gas
AUAIE maturative
naturalise
naturalize
tabularise
tabularize
AUAIL Majuba Hill
AUAIM naturalism❏
AUAIN maculation
maturation
salutation
saturation
tabulation

vapulation
AUAIT naturalist
AUAIY salutarily
AUAOY salutatory
AUBLI casus belli
AUCIT manuscript
AUCLS ranunculus
AUENO mature into
AUESI Jaruzelski
AUFCD Janus-faced
AUIOE lanuginose
AUIOS paludinous
AUITR manumitter
AULAE maquillage
AULES casualness
AULIS casualties
AULOD Samuel Hood
AULOT Samuel Colt
AUNAE calumniate
AUNHM Nahum Nahum
AUNLA saturnalia❑
AUNOS calumnious
AUNTA Jaquenetta
AUOAH naturopath
AUOSY fabulously
AUPCL haruspical
AUPCS haruspices
AUROS salubrious
AUTAE balustrade
AUTIE lacustrine
AVLOS marvellous
AVNAE Marvin Gaye
Max von Laue
AVNRI Paavo Nurmi
AVNYK Jan Van Eyck
Jan van Eyck
AVRER Jan Vermeer
AVSAK canvasback
AVSIG harvesting
AVSMN harvestman
AVVRS parvovirus
AWAID day-wearied
AWLIG jaywalking
AWONM Ian Woosnam
AYAKR baby-walker
AYAST Mary Cassat
AYEES Mary Peters
AYEKY Mary Leakey
AYELY Mary Wesley
AYESN lazy person
AYFEK Mary of Teck
AYGAA satyagraha
AYGTS laryngitis
AYHDS Gary Rhodes
AYHNS many thanks
AYHPL Lady Chapel
AYIBN baby-ribbon
AYILR lady-killer
AYIMN Mary Wigman
AYITR baby-sitter
AYLYR Gary Player
AYNIG Mary Anning
AYOED easy to read
AYOES Gary Sobers
AYOMR baby boomer
AYOOY palynology
papyrology
AYOPR Gary Cooper
AYOST easy does it
AYRWG lawyer's wig
AYSOK lady's smock
AYTDS caryatides
AYTET Easy Street
easy street
AYTPC karyotypic
AZAAZ razzmatazz
AZIGY dazzlingly
AZNLA manzanilla❑
AZNLO Manzanillo
AZNTE canzonette
AZOIO Laszlo Biro
BADLW ebb and flow
BAINL oblational
BANBE obtainable
BANET obtainment
BCNIG absconding
BDETO obedient to
BDETY obediently
BDOGD abode of God
BEAIN abnegation
BEAOE oboe d'amore
BECIE abreactive
BECIN abreaction
BEEMN able seaman
BEOID able-bodied
BETES abjectness
objectless
BETRM absent from
BETVS objectives
BEUOS obsequious
BEVBE observable
BEVBY observably
BEVNE observance
BIAIN abdication
obligation
BIAOY obligatory
BIEAE obliterate
BIGET abridgment
BIIGY obligingly
BIINL obsidional
BLAMN Abel Tasman
BLEEO I believe so
BLINE ebullience
BLINY ebulliency
BMNBE abominable
BMNBY abominably
BNATY abundantly
BNOIG abandoning
BOAIN abrogation
BOBBE absorbable
BOBDN absorbed in
BOBDY absorbedly
BOBNY absorbency
BOEEY obsoletely
BOMLY abnormally
BOPIE absorptive
BOPIN absorption
BORNE abhorrence
BOUEY absolutely
BOUIM absolutism
BOUIN absolution
BOUIT absolutist
BQIAY ubiquitary
BQIOE ubiquinone
BQIOS ubiquitous
BRAIN aberration
BREIE aberdevine
BRESH Übermensch
BRGNL aboriginal
BRIEY abortively
BRNAE obtruncate
BROIN Aberdonian
BRRMY Abercromby
BRVAE abbreviate
BSIIN Abyssinian
BTAIT obituarist
BTATD abstracted
BTATY abstractly
BTEBT a better bet
BTFAL a bit of tail
BTIIG abstaining
BTMOS abstemious
BTNIN abstention
BTNNE abstinence
BTRET abstergent
BTRIE abstersive
BTRIN abstersion
BTTIS obstetrics
BTUEY abstrusely
BTUTD obstructed
BTUTR obstructor
BUAEY obdurately
BUAIN abjuration
BUCTD obfuscated
BUDES absurdness
BUEES obtuseness
BUIAE obnubilate
BUIBY Aboukir Bay
BUSLM Abdus Salam
BUTES abruptness
BVBAD above board
above-board
BVPIE above price
BVWTR above water
CAAIM oceanarium
CAANT act against
CABIG scrambling
CACIG scratching
CACIY scratchily
CACPD scratch pad
CAERL octahedral
CAERN octahedron
CAGIG ocean-going
CAGLN McLaughlin
CAGLR octangular
CAIIY actability
CAINL occasional
CAIPZ Octavio Paz
CAOOY oceanology
CBEKR icebreaker
CBIES scabbiness
CBOSY scabrously
CCHRE a-cockhorse
CCVRD ice-covered
CDNIG ice dancing
CEAIE schematise
schematize
CEAIM schematism
CEAOS eczematous
CECIG screeching
CEEAE accelerate
CEINM ecce signum
CENET screen test
CENLY screenplay
CENNS screenings
CENRD screen grid
CEOAA scleromata
CEOIE sclerotise
sclerotize
CESBE accessible
CESBY accessibly
CESIE access time
CESOD access road
CETAE accentuate
CETAL accept bail
CETBE acceptable
CETBY acceptably
CETDY acceptedly
CETFC scientific
CETNE acceptance
CEZNI scherzandi
CEZNO scherzando
CFIGY scoffingly
CFOAE scaffolage
CFODR scaffolder
CHISS ecthlipses
CHMSS ecchymosis
CHNSS ecphoneses
CIAIN activation
CIEES activeness
CIEIG scrivening
CIEIT active list
CIETL accidental
occidental❑
CIIIS activities
CIKET Schick test
CIMTC schismatic
CINBE actionable
CINBY actionably
CIOAP schizocarp
CIODL schizoidal
CIOEM echinoderm
CISAK scrimshank
CITRA scriptoria
CITRL scriptural
CITRS Scriptures
CIVBE achievable
CLAIN ocellation
CLCAY ochlocracy
CLDON scaled-down
CLEAN Schliemann
CLEFN Schlieffen

CLGCL ecological
CLIGY scoldingly
CLMTR oculomotor
CLNOK McClintock
CLOIN Scillonian
CLSAE Eccles cake
CLTES sculptress
CLTRD sculptured
CLTRL sculptural
CMEIG scampering
CMIHY scampishly
CMNCL ecumenical
CNAIE scandalise
scandalize
CNAOS scandalous
CNCAM iconoclasm❑
CNCAT iconoclast
CNCLY iconically
scenically
CNHRE Scunthorpe
CNIES scantiness
CNLTR iconolater
CNLTY iconolatry
CNMCL economical
CNMZR economizer
CNSGR icing sugar
COAAL McGonagall
COAIS acrobatics
COATC scholastic
CODNE accordance
COEAE act one's age
COEAY acromegaly
COEMC ectodermic
COEML ectodermal
COERN octohedron
COHBA acrophobia
COITC sciolistic
COLAD schoolward
COLAM school-ma'am
schoolmarm
school-marm
COLAS schooldays
COLIE scrollwise
COLIL schoolgirl
COLOK schoolwork
scrollwork
CONAT accountant
CONEG Schoenberg
CONFR account for
CONIG accounting
scrounging
COOPY ectomorphy
COPIE accomplice
COPIH accomplish
CORTC eccoprotic
COSOS across lots
COUHR octopusher
COUOS scrofulous
COYOS octogynous
CPGAE scapegrace
CPIIM scepticism
CRAEY acervately
CRAIA scarlatina
CRBAD scoreboard
CRBED scarabaeid
CRCOS ochraceous
CRDCT scaredy-cat
CRDTD accredited
CREES scarceness
CRFLY scornfully
CRIES scurfiness
scurviness
CRIIY acerbicity
scurrility
CRIOS scurrilous
CRMTC achromatic
CRSIF scare stiff
CSAIG ice-skating
CSHDA icosahedra
CTAGE acute angle
CTBLM acetabulum
CTCCD acetic acid
CTEIG scattering
CTEOL act the fool
CTEOT act the goat
CTHIT Scotch mist
CTHNP Scotch snap
CTIGY scathingly
CTIIE Scotticise
Scotticize
CTLFL scuttleful
CTNLT scot and lot
CTWMN Scotswoman
CTYSS ichthyosis
CTYTC ichthyotic
CUAEY accurately
CUAHR Schumacher
CUAIE accusative
CUAIN accusation
occupation
CUAOY accusatory
CUIDN occupied in
CUIER scrutineer
CUIGY accusingly
CUIIE scrutinise
scrutinize
CUITD acquainted
CUNES McGuinness
CURNE occurrence
CUSDY accursedly
CUTCL acoustical
CUTES occultness
CUTMD accustomed
CUUAE accumulate
CUUOS scrupulous
CVNEY scavengery
CWIGY scowlingly
CWIZR Schweitzer
CWTES Schwitters
DABIN Edna O'Brien
DADER Edward Lear
DADGS Edgar Degas
DADOD Edward Bond
DADOE Edward Coke
Edward Cope
DADYE Edward Eyre
DAETO adjacent to
DAETY adjacently
DAINL ideational
DAITC idealistic
DATGD advantaged
DATGS advantages
DCOSY edaciously
DDTIS add details
DDUSO add drugs to
DEAIE adrenaline
DEIEY adhesively
DEOSP idle gossip
DETNE advertence
DETNY advertency
DETRR adventurer
DETRS adventures
DETSR advertiser
DETSS Adventists
DETVL adjectival
DFIGY edifyingly
DFLOS Oddfellows
DHRSO add herbs to
DIAAA Addis Ababa
DIAIN admiration
DIDOD Edwin Drood
DIIGY admiringly
DIINL additional
DIITR administer
DINPE Adrianople
DIOAE advisorate
DISBE admissible
DITDO addicted to
DITDY admittedly
DITNE admittance
DLEAE adulterate
DLEAT adulterant
DLEES adulteress
DLEIE adulterine
DLEOS adulterous
DLOAE edulcorate
DLPTD addle-pated
DLSET adolescent
DLTES idolatress
DLTIE idolatrise
idolatrize
DLTOS idolatrous
DLZTN idolizaton
DMAPE Adam's apple
DMNEE Adam and Eve
DMNIE adamantine
DMOAS idem sonans
DNAGA odontalgia
DNAGC odontalgic
DNIID identified
DNOAA odontomata
DNOEY odontogeny
DNOOY odontology
DNTIK I don't think
DOBAD idiot board
DOETL idiolectal
DOIIN admonition
DOIOY admonitory
DOOIT ideologist
DOPIN adsorption
DOPOF idiot-proof
DORPY ideography
DOSES odiousness
DOTES adroitness
DPAIN adaptation
DPIEY adaptively
DPOOY edaphology
DQAEY adequately
DRMNS adornments
DSGRO add sugar to
DSUEO add sauce to
DTEAS Edith Evans
DTRHP editorship
DUAIN adjuration
DUDEN Edmund Kean
DUIAE adjudicate
DUIEN adzuki bean
DUMIS à deux mains
DUTBE adjustable
DUTBY adjustably
DUTDO adjusted to
DUTET adjustment
DYECX Eddy Merckx
EAAAI devanagari❑
EAAEY separately
EAAIE reparative
EAAIG separating
EAAIM separatism
EAAIN defamation
relaxation
reparation
separation
EAAIT separatist
EAANT set against
EAAOY defamatory
EAAPL metacarpal
EAAPS metacarpus
EAASL metatarsal
EAASS metatarsus
EAATK Béla Bartók
EACAR sedan-chair
EACEY debauchery
EACIM revanchism
EACIT revanchist
EACNE renascence
EACOY melancholy
EACTD demarcated
EACTR defalcator
EACVE venae cavae
EADBE demandable
rewardable
EADDS regarded as
EADES regardless
rewardless
EADET retardment
EADOD Gerald Ford
EADOE remand home
EAEBE debateable
EAEDF get ahead of
EAEED female lead
EAEES femaleness
sedateness

EAEET debasement
debatement
defacement
regalement
EAEFR be taken for
EAEGE legal eagle
EAEIA Sexagesima
EAEIH debate with
EAEIN Melanesian
EAEOE sea anemone
EAEOS hexamerous
EAERL decahedral
hexahedral
EAERN decahedron
hexahedron
EAESS metalepsis
EAETY decadently
EAGIG be laughing
EAHAE metaphrase
EAHAT metaphrast
EAHBE detachable
EAHCL seraphical
EAHDY detachedly
EAHEE decathlete
EAHET detachment
EAHSS metatheses
metathesis
EAIAE decapitate
delaminate
deracinate
desalinate
gelatinate
EAIEY negatively
relatively
EAIGO relating to
EAIGY debasingly
debatingly
defacingly
delayingly
menacingly
EAIHC megalithic
EAIHD be famished
EAIIE desalinise
desalinize
gelatinise
gelatinize
keratinise
keratinize
relativise
relativize
EAIIM negativism
relativism
EAIIT negativist
relativist
EAIIY negativity
relativity
tenability
EAIKT get a wicket
EAINL relational
venational
EAIOS gelatinous
keratinous
EAITC legalistic
melanistic
EAITR retaliator
EAKBE remarkable
EAKBY remarkably
EALBE recallable
EALET derailment
EALIG defaulting
EALRY metallurgy
EALTS Heraclitus
EAMRL red admiral
EANBE detainable
retainable
EANET detainment
retainment
EANLR penannular
EANRE remain true
EANYD get annoyed
EAOAA melanomata
teratomata
EAOAR megalosaur
EAODF get a load of
EAOEN get a move on
EAOIE devalorise
devalorize
melaconite
metabolise
metabolite
metabolize
revalorise
revalorize
EAOIL senatorial
EAOIM metabolism
pedagogism
EAOIS pedagogics
EAOKT get a look at
EAOOY hepatology
EAOYE melanocyte
EAPET decampment
EAPNE set a sponge
EARAE repatriate
EARNE T E Lawrence
EARVL new arrival
EATBX penalty box
EATET department
EATIE get astride
EATPL Sebastopol
Sevastopol
EATRM depart from
EATSS metastases
metastasis
EATTD devastated
EATTR devastator
EAUAT denaturant
EAUIE denaturise
denaturize
EAUOI Bela Lugosi
EBADR keyboarder
EBAIM lesbianism
EBAKT wet blanket
EBALE Ben Bradlee
EBCDL herbicidal
EBCOS herbaceous
EBCOT Serbo-Croat
EBEAH pebbledash
EBEDR kerb-vendor
EBEES feebleness
EBEGT kerb weight
EBIAN New Britain
EBLON verbal noun
EBODD red-blooded
EBRDR kerb-trader
EBRHP membership
EBRIG set burning
EBRLM Herbert Lom
EBRUS herbariums
EBSIE Derbyshire
EBSUT sea biscuit
EBTAT Melba toast
ECABE descramble
ECAUP fetch a pump
ECBAE red cabbage
ECCEY peacockery
ECCIH peacockish
ECCOE peacock-ore
ECDLO peccadillo
ECEIT geochemist
ECELS Seychelles
ECEUE reschedule
ECFCS beccaficos
ECFLY mercifully
peacefully
ECFRH henceforth
ECIAE deactivate
reactivate
ECIES describe as
tetchiness
ECIEY reactively
ECIPR tea clipper
ECITR descriptor
ECLEE New College
ECLIG pencilling
ECLTR percolator
ECLVR peace-lover
ECMKR peacemaker
ECMLA peach melba
ECNAE percentage
ECNAT descendant
ECNEN wet canteen
ECNIE mercantile
percentile
ECNIG descending
rescinding
ECNRC geocentric
ECOEO get close to
ECOGD peace of God
ECOHS bedclothes
ECOLR deschooler
ECPET percipient
ECPIE perceptive
ECPIN perception
ECPUS teacupfuls
ECRAN net curtain
ECRAT redcurrant
ECRVR Peace River
ECSAS Wenceslaus
ECSIE percussive
ECSIN percussion
rescission
ECTHE seecatchie
ECUTR rencounter
rev counter
ECWMN henchwomen
ECWRH Letchworth
EDATR headmaster
EDCGN hendecagon
EDCNY mendicancy
EDCOS mendacious
EDEAK needle bank
EDEGT dead-weight
EDEIE needle-like
needle time
EDEIH meddle with
EDEOD needlecord
EDEOE meddlesome
EDEOK needlework
EDESD get dressed
EDESN dead person
EDESY heedlessly
needlessly
EDETE dead centre
deadnettle
dead-nettle
EDFAR head of hair
EDFER head of year
EDFIE head office
EDHWY lead the way
EDIES deadliness
EDIGR dead ringer
EDILD tendrilled
EDILR weedkiller
EDLBS Léo Delibes
EDLEG Heidelberg
EDLIG send flying
EDLNE fer-de-lance
EDLSA Weddell Sea
EDLYV Mendeleyev
EDMDL hebdomadal
EDMHN seldom when
EDMNY ready money
EDMXD ready mixed
EDNAE reading age
EDNDY wedding day
EDNIE dead on time
pendentive
EDNLY Headingley
EDNMN leading man
EDNOF fending off
heading off
EDNTS tendinitis
tendonitis
EDOAO seed-potato
EDODR deed holder
EDOED head to head
EDOOY dendrology
EDOTR head doctor
EDQAE headsquare
EDRAD Gelderland
EDRBE perdurable
renderable

EDRBY perdurably
EDRES tenderness❑
EDRET tenderfeet
EDRHP leadership
readership
EDROT tenderfoot
EDRZR deodorizer
EDSRT jeu d'esprit
EDSRY lead astray
EDTOG headstrong
EDTRN ready to run
EDUGD head-lugged
EDULR Gerd Muller
EDUTR headhunter
EDVSA Zend-Avesta
EDWAK Meadowbank
EDZOS rendezvous
EEACR veteran car
EEAHC telepathic
EEAHS Telemachus
EEAIE federalise
federative
Generalife
generalise
generalize
generative
vegetative
EEAIG vegetating
EEAIM federalism
EEAIN defecation
delegation
federation
generation
regelation
relegation
renegation
revelation❑
vegetarian
vegetation
veneration
EEAIT federalist
generalist
EEAIY generality
EEALS vegetables
EEAOE oedematose
EEAON Geneva gown
EEAOS oedematous
EEAOY revelatory
EEATO relevant to
EEATR benefactor
telecaster
EEATY relevantly
EEBAE Peter Blake
EEBIG resembling
EEBOK Peter Brook
EEBRD remembered
EEBUS hereabouts
EECIG beseeching
EECMN defenceman
EECNE senescence
EECPC telescopic
EECPD telescoped
EECTD get excited
EEDBE defendable
dependable
Peter Debye
EEDBY dependably
EEDCE dependacie
EEDNE dependence
EEDNY dependency
EEEAE decelerate
degenerate
regenerate
EEEAY degeneracy
regeneracy
EEEDM referendum
EEEES sereneness
severeness
EEEGR Pete Seeger
EEELD bejewelled
EEELM cerebellum
EEELR cerebellar
EEEOD telerecord
EEEOS pedereroes
EEERC telemetric
EEESA Celebes Sea
EEETL tenemental
EEETY reverently
vehemently
EEFNA Peter Fonda
EEGFL revengeful
EEGUE Betelgeuse
EEHIC genethliac
EEHLE Leverhulme
EEHNC telephonic
EEHOA Tereshkova
EEHSN lederhosen
EEHUE Peterhouse
EEIAE hereticate
EEIAY hereditary
veterinary
EEIBE remediable
EEIBY remediably
EEIDR Gene Wilder
EEIER répétiteur
EEIES remediless
EEIET beneficent
EEIHY feverishly
EEIIE benedicite
meperidine
repetitive
EEIIL beneficial
EEIIN Ceredigion
repetition
television
EEIIT geneticist
hereditist
EEILD bedevilled
EEILY remedially
EEIND redesigned
EEINY Gene Pitney
EEITR deregister
EEITS Benedictus
EEIUL televisual
EEKBR Tel-El-Kebir
EELBE repealable
revealable
EELGT Verey light
EELNE repellence
EELNY repellency
EELOS rebellious
EELRE Peter Lorre
EELRP cereal crop
EEMBE redeemable
EEMBY redeemably
EEMND determined
EEMNR determiner
EENVR never-never
EEOAE here you are
redecorate
EEOAY heterogamy
heterotaxy
EEOET benevolent
EEOIE penelopise
penelopize
EEOIG developing
EEOIL ceremonial
EEOIY generosity
EEOKR teleworker
EEOOE heretofore
EEOOY heterodoxy
heterogony
heterology
heteronomy
selenology
EEORD Pete Conrad
EEOSY generously
temerously
EEOVS werewolves
EEOYE heterodyne
EEPAS Peter Pears
EEPIE redemptive
EEPIN redemption
EEPOY peremptory
redemptory
EEPTH fever pitch
EERBE deferrable
penetrable
referrable
EERBY penetrably
EERDO referred to
EERHR researcher
EERIG rehearsing
EERLA penetralia
EERNE deterrence
EEROS tenebrious
EERPY telegraphy
EERTC meteoritic
EERTD celebrated
EERTR celebrator
desecrater
desecrator
penetrator
EESAM Lebensraum
EESBE defensible
reversible
EESBY defensibly
EESDY reversedly
EESMN defenseman
EESUG Petersburg
Regensburg
EETAE fenestrate
EETAT new entrant
select part
EETBE delectable
detectable
detectible
detestable
rejectable
rejectible
repeatable
revertible
EETBY delectably
detestably
EETCE receptacle
EETDY dejectedly
dementedly
repeatedly
EETEH seventieth
EETEN nepenthean
EETES recentness
relentless
selectness
EETET resentment
EETHP regentship
EETIE repertoire
EETIL fenestrial
EETIN pedestrian
EETIT derestrict
EETLA fenestella
EETNE repentance
EETOS deceptious
EETYU here's to you
EEUAE deregulate
EEUGR vegeburger
EEUOR De Beauvoir
EEVBE receivable
EEVDF bereaved of
EEVDY deceived by
deservedly
reservedly
EEVSS reservists
EEWLS Helen Wills
EEZDY be seized by
EFAGR self-danger
EFATE beef cattle
EFBSR self-abuser
EFCDY Perfect Day
EFCIE perfective
EFCIG perfecting
self-acting
EFCIN perfection
EFDOS perfidious
EFEAD self-regard
EFEET self-deceit
EFEIL self-denial
EFEKR self-seeker
EFETE self-mettle
EFHRT Geoff Hurst
EFHTL Neufchâtel
EFILD self-titled
self-willed

EFLAE perfoliate
EFNBE self-unable
EFNET self-inject
EFNLD newfangled
new-fangled
EFOAO beef tomato
EFOET reafforest
EFOIG self-loving
EFOPR leaf-hopper
EFRAH self-breath
EFRES performers
EFRIE self-praise
EFRIG performing
EFRLI Zeffirelli
EFRTD perforated
EFRVN self-driven
EFSEM self-esteem
EFSIM Neofascism
EFSIT Neofascist
EFTLD self-styled
EFUDR self-murder
EFUGR beefburger
EFUIG self-ruling
EFVNE Deo favente
EGAHR geographer
EGAIS Deo gratias
EGEES meagreness
EGERY Reggie Kray
EGFLY vengefully
EGHAS lengthways
EGHIE lengthwise
EGHND lengthened
EGIEY penguinery
EGIGP weighing up
weighing-up
EGLFR Serge Lifar
EGPEE Ledge Piece
EGRAT ledger-bait
EGRIE ledger-line
EGSIH be ages with
EGTES weightless
EGTND heightened
EHAEA Lech Walesa
EHAIG rephrasing
EHBLE déshabillé
EHBLY Delhi belly
EHDCL methodical
EHEDF be the end of
EHEIM technetium
EHETS Hephaestus
EHIIE technicise
technicize
EHIIN technician
EHLGC nephologic
EHLNA Cephalonia
EHLPD cephalopod
EHLSW keyhole saw
EHNCL mechanical
EHNZD mechanized
EHOIE methionine
EHOOY nephrology
technology
EHORT technocrat
EHOUL Jethro Tull
EHRIE lethargise
lethargize
EHRIG red herring
EHRNS Zephyrinus
EHROT nethermost
EHSLH methuselah❑
EHTHD get hitched
EIAAN begin again
EIAEN meditate on
EIAET medicament
EIAEY delicately
EIAIE decimalise
decimalize
derivative
devitalise
devitalize
medicalise
medicalize
meditative
recitative
revitalize
EIAIG hesitating
EIAII recitativi
EIAIM revivalism
EIAIN decimation
dedication
depilation
derivation
gemination
hesitation
levitation
medication
meditation
recitation
seminarian
vesication
EIAIS Belisarius
EIAIT revivalist
seminarist
EIANN demi-cannon
EIAOY dedicatory
depilatory
vesicatory
EIATY hesitantly
EIAUA retinacula
EIAWR Mexican War
EIAYN perikaryon
EIBND beribboned
EIBOH Felix Bloch
EICCA Lee Iacocca
EICIG bewitching
EICIY mediocrity
EICLY heliacally
EICMC seriocomic
EICNE dehiscence
EICPC periscopic
EICSS meniscuses
EICTD desiccated
EICTR desiccator
EIDAD behindhand
EIDAS behind bars
EIDCL periodical
EIDIE behind time
EIDOR behind-door
EIDOS her indoors
EIDRD bewildered
EIEAA desiderata
EIEAD New Ireland
EIEAE deliberate
desiderate
EIEBE delineable
EIEEA peripeteia
EIEET defilement
definement
refinement
retirement
revilement
EIEIN Celine Dion
perihelion
EIEIY Belize City
EIEKY semi-weekly
EIEOD Venice gold
EIERC perimetric
EIERM retire from
EIETD pedimented
regimented
EIETL regimental
EIETR delineator
EIETY penitently
EIFSR tea infuser
EIGAH heliograph
EIGHT seeing that
EIGNC mediagenic
EIGTS meningitis
EIHAE periphrase
EIHBE perishable
relishable
EIHBY perishably
EIHCA perithecia
EIHES newishness
EIHFL delightful
EIHRL peripheral
EIHRR decipherer
EIIAE debilitate
delimitate
felicitate
legitimate
EIIAY legitimacy
EIIBE verifiable
EIICE semicircle
EIIEY decisively
definitely
derisively
femininely
EIIGY deridingly
repiningly
retiringly
revilingly
rev ivingly
EIIHY devilishly
EIIIE decivilise
decivilize
definitive
legitimise
legitimize
EIIIM recidivism
EIIIN definition
EIIIT recidivist
EIIIY femininity
legibility
EIIKE periwinkle
EIILN penicillin
EIINA definienda
EIINE desipience
recipience
resilience
EIINL meridional
revisional
EIINR petitioner
religioner
EIINY deficiency
recipiency
resiliency
EIIOS felicitous
EIIUE religieuse
EIKEN Felix Klein
EILGA hemiplegia
EILGC hemiplegic
EILNL periclinal
EILOK menial work
EILOT Nevill Mott
EILTR legislator
EIMTC melismatic
EIMTR heliometer
EINBE designable
EINDO resigned to
EINDY designedly
resignedly
EINES benignness
EINHS helianthus
EINLY regionally
EINNS beginnings
EINNY benignancy
EINRM resign from
EINTD designated
EIOAD Heligoland
EIOEL peritoneal
EIOEM peritoneum
EIOIE peridotite
EIOIY Mexico City
EIOOY lexicology
EIORT meritocrat
EIOSY desirously
perilously
resinously
EIOTR helicopter
EIPEE hemisphere
EIPIT petit point
EIPLS Heliopolis
EIQET delinquent
EIQIH relinquish
EIRCA peritricha
EIRCL reciprocal
EIRCS heritrices
EIRNA hemicrania
EIRPY lexigraphy
serigraphy
EIRTR denigrator

Words marked ❑ can also be spelled with an initial capital letter

EIRXS heritrixes
EISAP Cecil Sharp
EISBE remissible
EISEL periosteal
EISEM periosteum
EISES remissness
EISIA mediastina
EISIH Delia Smith
EISLR peninsular
EISOE Felixstowe
set in stone
EISOS petits pois
EISRN periastron
EISUE Nevil Shute
EITBD get into bed
EITBE resistible
EITBY resistibly
EITIG belittling
rebirthing
EITIS geriatrics
EITKN be mistaken
EITNE desistance
remittance
resistance
EITOE heliotrope
EITOY heliotropy
EITPC heliotypic
EITRA sericteria
EITRD registered
EITRM desist from
EITUH get in touch
EIUAE geniculate
reticulate
vesiculate
EIUIG begin using
EIUOS meticulous
EIURX Oedipus Rex
EIUSE deliquesce
EIUTE netiquette
EIUVR semiquaver
EIVBE believable
relievable
EIVLY medievally
EIWBE reviewable
EIWOY review body
review copy
EIWRH Kenilworth
EIYEE mesitylene
EIYIM perimysium
EJGRE Medjugorje
EJHSN Ben Johnson
EKAPE verkrampte
EKAYW Lee Kuan Yew
EKDIE seek advice
EKEIG beekeeping
EKESY fecklessly
recklessly
EKIDD weak-minded
EKIES weakliness
EKILD weak-willed
EKNER Jenkin's Ear
EKNIH reckon with
EKOET weak moment
EKOTD get knotted
get knotted!
EKRUD jerk around
EKSAP Becky Sharp
ELADD well-padded
ELAGL hell's angel
ELAHR belly-acher
ELAND well-earned
ELBLS hell's bells
ELBOD sell abroad
ELCDY pellucidly
ELCEN bell screen
ELCFL neglectful
ELCIE deflective
reflective
ELCIG deflecting
ELCIN deflection
neglection
reflection
ELCLR pellicular
ELDDY secludedly
ELDEM sealed-beam
ELDLY Hello Dolly
ELDNA belladonna
ELDNE belly-dance
ELEDR hellbender
ELEEL jellied eel
mealie meal
ELEHR bell-wether
ELELD well-heeled
ELEMS Leslie Ames
ELENS real tennis
ELESD well-versed
ELETR feel better
ELGAE deflagrate
ELGAH jellygraph
ELGBE negligible
ELGBY negligibly
ELGCL geological
ELGNE negligence
ELGOS pellagrous
ELGTO set light to
ELHAM health farm
ELHAP health camp
ELHCT bell the cat
ELHOD health food
ELHSN well-chosen
ELIAT reclaimant
ELIDD well-minded
ELIHD well-wished
ELIHR well-wisher
ELILR well-willer
ELLCD well-placed
ELLWR bell-flower
ELMUD jelly mould
ELMUH be all mouth
ELNAL Berlin Wall
ELNBE declinable
reclinable
ELNIN declension
ELNKN Hellenikon
ELNLE Berlin blue
ELNOF telling-off
ELNOS Ceylon moss
ELNTE heel and toe
ELNTN Bedlington
wellington❑
ELNUH well enough
ELNVR well I never!
ELNWX sealing-wax
ELOIE well-to-live
ELOMD well-formed
ELPAE Cellophane®
ELPIG wellspring
well-spring
ELPKN well-spoken
ELRBE declarable
deplorable
ELRBY deplorably
ELRCD well-graced
ELRDY declaredly
ELRED real friend
ELRHP dealership
ELRIE Bellarmine
ELROF declare off
ELRWR declare war
ELSAE real estate
ELSCS Nelly Sachs
ELSIY declassify
ELSOI Berlusconi
ELTEH hell's teeth
ELTIE red lattice
red-lattice
ELTIT belletrist
ELTUE sea lettuce
ELUBR real number
ELUGD well-judged
ELUGY Jealous Guy
ELUND well-turned
ELUNR fell-runner
ELUOT feel put out
ELUTD well-suited
ELWAD yellow card
ELWAK Yellow Jack
ELWES mellowness
yellowness
ELWHP fellowship
ELWIE yellow bile
yellow line
ELWRR deflowerer
ELXBE reflexible
ELYAE sell-by date
ELYAL Wesley Hall
ELYET deployment
ELZBE realizable
EMAIE permeative
EMAIN permeation
EMCDL germicidal
EMCIE Sex Machine
EMCLI vermicelli
EMCLR vermicular
EMDRG Bermuda rig
EMDUS desmodiums
EMENR reim-kennar
EMFOT permafrost
EMIES seemliness
EMLIN vermillion
EMMNS few moments
EMNAY segmentary
EMNBE terminable
EMNBY terminably
EMNCS Germanicus
EMNHP penmanship
seamanship
EMNIE seamanlike
EMNIG fermenting
EMNLY terminally
EMNNE permanence
EMNNY permanency
EMNSS terminuses
EMNTD terminated
EMNTR sea monster
EMNTS few minutes
EMNZR sermonizer
EMOLR seam bowler
EMPIH team up with
EMPRT team spirit
EMRET re-emergent
EMRHD besmirched
EMRID get married
EMRZD mesmerized
EMSIE permissive
EMSIN permission
EMTBE permutable
EMTCL hermetical
hermitical
EMTES seamstress
EMTIE geometrise
geometrize
EMTOL Helmut Kohl
EMTRB hermit crab
EMTSS dermatoses
EMTTC pegmatitic
EMTTS dermatitis
ENAAE being awake
ENAIE Jean Racine
penny-a-line
ENBUE Lenny Bruce
ENCAE pernoctate
ENCEY pernickety
ENCLR vernacular
ENCOS pennaceous
pernicious
ENCSY Sean O'Casey
ENDTE Bernadette
ENECI dernier cri
ENEGR Weinberger
ENEIG meandering
ENEOR Jean Renoir
ENHNY Lenny Henry
ENIGT Jean Piaget
ENILT Jean Millet
ENLLB Kennel Club
ENLSI Jean Alessi
ENMTD reanimated
ENMTL terne metal
ENNFL meaningful
ENNRS Jean Ingres
ENOCD reinforced

ENONW keen to know
ENOOY deontology
ENPEE penny-piece
ENPNH penny-pinch
ENPNS Leon Spinks
ENPOT beansprout
ENRIE Bernardine
ENRYL pennyroyal
ENSAE penny share
ENSHE tennis shoe
ENSOK penny stock
ENTLE pennatulae
ENTLS pennatulas
ENWEE get nowhere
ENWEY teeny-weeny
ENWRH pennyworth
EOADM memorandum
EOAEY derogately
desolately
EOAIE decorative
demoralise
demoralize
denotative
depolarise
depolarize
derogative
devocalise
devocalize
pejorative
remoralise
remoralize
EOAIG decorating
resonating
EOAIN decoration
denotation
derogation
desolation
detonation
pejoration
peroration
relocation
renovation
revocation
EOAIS aerobatics
EOAOY derogatory
revocatory
EOARY debonairly
EOASL menopausal
EOATC aeronautic
EOATY resonantly
EOAVN removal van
EOBNE resorbence
EOCIG debouching
EOCLD reconciled
EOCLR reconciler
EOCLY heroically
EOCNL resorcinol
EOCNS rejoicings
EODAD second hand
second-hand
EODAE second-rate
EODEF second self
EODES beyond seas
EODET second-best
EODID second wind
EODOE beyond hope
second home
second role
EOEAD become hard
beforehand
EOEAE become pale
EOEAY become hazy
EOEEF set oneself
EOEEK become weak
EOEEN Jerome Kern
EOEES become less
remoteness
EOEET denotement
denouement
dénouement
devotement
revokement
EOEHN become thin
EOEIE become fine
become ripe
beforetime
demonetise
demonetize
remonetise
remonetize
EOEIG recovering
EOEIH be done with
EOEIM become firm
EOELD remodelled
EOEOD become cold
become void
EOEOG before long
EOEON before noon
EOERM remote from
EOETY redolently
EOEWY get one's way
EOFLA Zeno of Elea
EOFND be confined
EOGNS belongings
EOHBA xenophobia
EOHBC xenophobic
EOHGS oesophagus
EOHIM henotheism
EOHIT henotheist
EOHLS Herophilus
EOHNS Xenophanes
EOIAE demotivate
denominate
detoxicate
EOIAY depositary
EOIBE negotiable
EOIBX deposit box
EOICL demoniacal
EOIEE velocipede
EOIES Menominees
EOIGY becomingly
EOIHC mesolithic❑
EOIHD demolished
EOIHR demolisher
EOIIE demobilise
demobilize
peroxidise
peroxidize
EOIIG memorizing
EOIIN demolition
deposition
reposition
re-position
EOINE désorienté
EOINL devotional
EOIOY depository
repository
EOITC hedonistic
nepotistic
EOITD defoliated
EOITR defoliator
negotiator
EOJPN Sea of Japan
EOJUS de nos jours
EOLAS New Orleans
EOLES recoilless
EOLIG remoulding
EOLRM recoil from
EOLUH be no slouch
EOMBE reformable
EOMDS reformados
EOMDY deformedly
EOMLB Reform Club
EOMNE recommence
EONIG resounding
EONIS bed of nails
EONUE reioyndure
EONZD recognized
EONZR recognizer
EOOAE decolorate
EOOIE decolonise
decolonize
decolorize
EOOIT oenologist
pedologist
penologist
serologist
sexologist
EOOOY demonology
EOOSS meconopses
EOOSY decorously
venomously
EOPEE mesosphere
EOPES decompress
EOPET recoupment
EOPIE resorptive
EOPIN desorption
resorption
zero option
EOPNE recompense
EOPSD decomposed
EOPSR decomposer
EOPUD decompound
EORME aerogramme
EOROA menorrhoea
seborrhoea
EOROS set of rooms
EORPY demography
xerography
EORSS bed of roses
EORTC democratic
EORTS Democritus
Xenocrates
EOSAE repoussage
EOSDR reconsider
EOSFL remorseful
EOSIE Devonshire
EOTBE reportable
EOTDY besottedly
reportedly
EOTES devoutness
EOTET deportment
EOTIG rerouteing
EOTOH venom-tooth
EOUAE demodulate
depopulate
EOUEY resolutely
EOUIN devolution
resolution
revolution
EOVBE resolvable
EOVDO resolved to
EOVDY resolvedly
EPAIN temptation
EPASN keep tabs on
EPCBE despicable
EPCBY despicably
EPCFL respectful
EPCIE respective
EPCIG henpecking
respecting
EPCLD bespeckled
EPEIG perplexing
EPEIY perplexity
EPERT keep secret
EPESR bedpresser
EPESY helplessly
EPETD deep-seated
EPGNS serpigines
EPHOM keep shtoom
EPHOT deep throat
EPHPL keep chapel
EPIDN keep hidden
EPIGY temptingly
EPIIG despairing
despoiling
EPIIM delphinium
EPIKE besprinkle
EPIKT keep wicket
EPITR deep litter
EPLIG leg-pulling
EPLTN Neapolitan
EPNES weaponless
EPNET despondent
respondent
EPNID keep in mind
EPNIE responsive
serpentine
serpentise
serpentize
EPNIH help on with
keep in with

keep on with
EPNLD bespangled
EPNOY responsory
EPODF keep hold of
EPOIG keep moving
EPOTD deep-rooted
keep posted
EPOUT new product
EPPIH keep up with
EPRCT leopard-cat
EPRDS desperados
Hesperides
EPREE deep-freeze
EPRES leopardess
EPRIE jeopardise
jeopardize
EPRIG keep trying
EPRIL pepper mill
peppermill
EPRIT peppermint
EPRLY temporally
EPRMN kempery-man
EPRNE temperance
EPRON peppercorn
EPRTR respirator
EPRZR temporizer
EPSIG pen-pushing
EPSOS Sex Pistols
EPTAE perpetrate
perpetuate
EPTAK keep it dark
EPTIY perpetuity
EPTLY keep a tally
EPUPE Deep Purple
EPYIS geophysics
EQAAE desquamate
EQIIE perquisite
ERAAS Gerry Adams
ERAAT degreasant
ERADE Keir Hardie
ERAEY decrease by
ERAFN be great fun
ERAHR reproacher
ERAIE reorganize
ERAIG decreasing
ERAIM neorealism
ERAIN recreation
re-creation
ERAIT neorealist
ERALY ferro-alloy
ERAOT learn about
ERATY recreantly
ERBEK heartbreak
ERBID jerry-build
ERBIT jerry-built
ERBNE reprobance
ERBTS Henry Bates
ERCAE depreciate
ERCAM meerschaum
ERCAN leprechaun
ERCCL Henry Cecil
ERCHO Verrocchio
ERCIE refractive
retractile
retractive
ERCIN detraction
refraction
retraction
ERCLY metrically
ERCOR retrochoir
ERCOY refractory
ERCTA terracotta
ERCTR deprecator
ERDBE degradable
ERDCD reproduced
ERDCR reproducer
ERDIG begrudging
ERDSE recrudesce
EREAD George Sand
EREAE George Hale
EREET George Best
EREEY Henry Every
EREGD near-legged
EREIG debriefing
heartening
EREII decree nisi
EREKR tear-jerker
ERELF hear tell of
EREON George Town
Georgetown
ERESY fearlessly
peerlessly
EREUH George Bush
EREYG George Byng
ERFGL febrifugal
ERFIG petrifying
terrifying
ERFLY wearifully
ERFNA Henry Fonda
ERFRA terra firma
ERGAE retrograde
ERGES retrogress
ERGET defragment
ERGLD bedraggled
ERGNL tetragonal
ERGTD segregated
ERGYH petroglyph
ERHDA tetrahedra
ERHGL Georg Hegel
ERHNO search into
ERHNS hear things
ERHPD pear-shaped
ERIDW Rear Window
ERIES heartiness
pearliness
ERIGY wearyingly
yearningly
ERIIG recruiting
refraining
ERJMS Henry James
ERJNS Terry Jones
ERLAK petrol tank
ERLOB petrol bomb
ERLTD serrulated
ERLTM petrolatum
ERLUE pétroleuse
ERLUP petrol pump
ERLWS Jerry Lewis
ERMKR merrymaker
ERMNA necromania
ERMNY necromancy
ERMOE Henry Moore
ERMSN Perry Mason
ERMTR tetrameter
ERNAD bear in hand
ERNAE detruncate
ERNER year-on-year
ERNFR near and far
ERNID bear in mind
ERNMC metronomic
metronymic
ERNMT retransmit
ERNOK Herrenvolk
ERNOT wearing out
ERNPN bear in upon
EROEL ne'er-do-well
EROEY fearsomely
EROTE beer bottle
ERPEA neuroptera
ERPIE necrophile
ERPIN decryption
ERPLS metropolis
necropolis
ERPRD be prepared
ERREY retrorsely
ERRUS terrariums
ERRVR Pearl River
ERRYE Henry Royce
ERRZD terrorized
ERSAE heartsease
heart's-ease
ERSAT depressant
ERSEL Ken Russell
pearl-shell
ERSET retrospect
ERSIE depressive
regressive
repressive
ERSIG depressing
refreshing
ERSIH tetrastich
ERSIN depression
regression
repression
ERSLI Georg Solti
ERSLS get results
ERSOY necroscopy
ERTAD near at hand
ERTET Beer Street
ERTIE secretaire
ERTOE Secret Love
ERTRB heart-throb
ERUDO get round to
ERUIG defrauding
regrouping
ERUKR seersucker
ERVDF deprived of
ERVDY depravedly
ERVRE terre verte
ERVRS retrovirus
ERWIE pearl white
Terry Waite
ERYBE defrayable
ERYET defrayment
ERYIG pearly king
ERYIL nearly kill
ESAAE de-escalate
ESAAS leastaways
ESACT Persian cat
ESAES newspapers
ESAFY Hessian fly
ESAHC felspathic
ESAIE Persianise
Persianize
persuasive
sensualise
sensualize
ESAIM Messianism
sensualism
ESAIN persuasion□
ESAIT sensualist
ESAIY sensuality
ESALW sea swallow
ESAMS gensdarmes
ESATR newscaster
ESAWR Persian War
ESAZR Belshazzar
ESBEF sensible of
ESCLR versicular
ESCTD persecuted
ESCTR persecutor
ESEBE reassemble
ESEDR newsreader
ESEIR Weisse Bier
ESEKE kenspeckle
ESETR newsletter
ESEVR bed-swerver
ESFAE persiflage
ESGNY news agency
ESIAD Leo Szilard
ESIAE deaspirate
ESIES measliness
ESIIG perspiring
ESILS Versailles
ESINR leg spinner
ESJMS Jesse James
ESLAE tessellate
ESLCD get spliced
ESMKR verse-maker
ESMNA leishmania
ESMTR densimeter
ESNBE personable
reasonable
seasonable
ESNBY reasonably
seasonably
ESNEG Heisenberg
ESNIH reason with
ESNLY personally
seasonally
ESNOD personhood
ESNTR personator

Words marked □ can also be spelled with an initial capital letter

ESOAY pensionary
ESOES Jesse Owens
pensioners
ESOEY set store by
ESOGN sense organ
sense-organ
ESOGR newsmonger
ESOIZ Dershowitz
ESOOF pension off
ESOOY seismology
ESORM seismogram
ESOSY sensuously
ESOTY newsworthy
ESPLS Persepolis
ESPOE Persephone
ESRAE menstruate
ESRBE censurable
measurable
mensurable
ESRBY censurably
leisurably
measurably
ESRDY measuredly
ESREL mess or mell
ESREN sea surgeon
ESRET Sea Serpent
sea serpent
ESRHN lesser than
ESRHP censorship
ESROF measure off
ESROS censorious
ESROT measure out
ESRTR news-writer
ESRUD mess around
ESRUS menstruums
sensoriums
ESSET persistent
ESSIE persistive
ESSIG persisting
ESSIH verse-smith
ESTIG jet-setting
ESTZD sensitized
ESUFD get stuffed!
ESUIG reassuring
ESUKN get stuck in
ESUSO set spurs to
ESWMN Welshwoman
ESYIE Merseyside
ETADD left-handed
neat-handed
ETADE bestraddle
ETADO westward ho!
ETADY leftwardly
westwardly
ETAFN ventral fin
ETAIE bestialise
bestialize
centralise
centralize
neutralise
neutralize
ETAIG meat-eating
ETAIL oestradiol
ETAIM centralism
neutralism
ETAIT centralist
neutralist
ETAIY bestiality
centrality
dextrality
neutrality
ETAKT test-market
ETALN Betty Allen
ETAND restrained
ETANR restrainer
ETANS restraints
ETBAE vertebrate
ETBLR vestibular
ETCAK Celtic Park
septic tank
ETCCD pectic acid
ETCIE fettuccine
ETCIF Heathcliff
ETCLR lenticular
tentacular
testicular
ETCLY hectically
septically
vertically
ETCOD heptachord
pentachord
ETCOS testaceous
ETDNS testudines
ETDRH tented arch
ETDVS Bette Davis
ETEAE set the pace
ETEAF centre-half
ETEAG get the hang
ETEAH nettlerash
ETEAK centre-back
ETEAY sex therapy
ETEBD feather bed
featherbed
ETEDA get the idea
ETEDN meet head on
meet head-on
ETEEE weather eye
ETEEL Kettlewell
ETEES gentleness
ETEET settlement
ETEGL West Bengal
ETEHP get the chop
ETEID get the bird
left behind
test period
ETEIE centre-line
genteelise
genteelize
heathenise
heathenize
weatherise
weatherize
ETEIG feathering
leathering
weathering
ETEIH heathenish
seethe with
settle with
ETEIM genteelism
heathenism
ETEIS aesthetics
kettle-pins
ETELR bestseller
ETEML geothermal
ETEMN weatherman
ETEMP weather map
ETEOD centrefold
ETEOE kettle hole
mettlesome
ETEOK gentlefolk
ETEON settle down
ETEOT get the boot
weather out
ETEPE meet people
ETERM kettledrum
kettle-drum
ETERP wentletrap
ETESY restlessly
ETETS neutrettos
ETEUH get the push
ETFIE dentifrice
ETFIG rectifying
ETFLY feet of clay
ETFOD Keith Floyd
ETGAE centigrade
ETGAH hectograph
ETGNL heptagonal
pentagonal
ETGNS lentigines
vertigines
ETGUE depth gauge
ETHAR beat the air
ETHDA pentahedra
ETHED heat shield
ETHGN beat the gun
ETHLA Westphalia
ETHRP beat the rap
ETIGN settling-in
ETIGR left-winger
ETIHS best wishes
ETIID gentrified
ETIIL rectricial
ETIOE ventricose
ETIPN felt-tip pen
ETITD restricted
ETIUE centrifuge
ETKEL death-knell
ETLBE ventilable
ETLCI Bertolucci
ETLIN septillion
sextillion
Tertullian
ETLNE pestilence
ETLSR fertiliser
ETLTE centilitre
hectolitre
ETLTR ventilator
ETLTY Leo Tolstoy
ETLUS dentaliums
ETLZR fertilizer
ETMII centumviri
septemviri
ETMIS septemvirs
ETMNE lentamente
ETMNI pentimenti
ETMNO pentimento
ETMNS sentiments
ETMTE centimetre
hectometre
ETMTR heptameter
pentameter
ETNBX nesting-box
ETNIE heat engine
next in line
ETNIL sentential
septennial
ETNIN West Indian
ETNIS West Indies
ETNLD rectangled
ETNNE pertinence
ETNNY pertinency
ETNOF setting-off
ETNOS Peyton Rous
ETNOT setting-out
ETNPT melting-pot
ETNTD pectinated
ETOBE bent double
ETOEE centromere
ETOIE sectionise
sectionize
ETOIG destroying
ETOIM geotropism
ETOLY tea trolley
ETOOY deltiology
ETORO next door to
ETOSS penthouses
ETOSY dextrously
ETPIM pentaprism
ETRAE perturbate
ETRAF better half
ETRBE restorable
ETRED best friend
letterhead
next friend
ETRER yesteryear
ETRET betterment
ETRHC heptarchic
ETRHN better than
ETRHP mentorship
rectorship
ETRIE dexterwise
westernise
westernize
ETRIG perturbing
ETRIH Metternich
ETRIS sestertius
ETRLY pectorally
texturally
ETROB letter bomb
ETROK tenterhook
ETROS nectareous
ETRUH get through

see through
see-through
wet through
ETSED death's-head
ETSEP get to sleep
ETSIO lentissimo
ETSMC leptosomic
ETSND jettisoned
ETSUD death squad
ETSUE pesto sauce
ETSUG Gettysburg
ETTES meet others
ETTIM left atrium
ETTKN death-token
ETTLN heptathlon
pentathlon
ETTLY teetotally
ETTMN pentstemon
ETTNC pentatonic
ETTOE heatstroke
ETTRE set to three
ETTTR restitutor
ETTUH Heptateuch
Pentateuch
ETUAT restaurant
ETUSX West Sussex
ETWRS deathwards
ETWTH deathwatch
death-watch
EUAAM secular arm
EUABY Meaux Abbey
EUADN Leeuwarden
EUADO get-up-and-go
EUAHD bequeathed
EUAHL bequeathal
EUAIE dehumanise
dehumanize
depurative
regularise
regularize
regulative
reputative
secularise
secularize
EUAIG regulating
EUAIM secularism
EUAIN denudation
depuration
deputation
peculation
refutation
regulation
reputation
EUAIT secularist
EUAIY regularity
secularity
EUAOY regulatory
EUATY petulantly
EUBNE decumbence
recumbence
EUBNY decumbency
recumbency
EUBOS penumbrous
EUBUS nelumbiums
EUCAE denunciate
repurchase
EUCIN defunction
EUCLR peduncular
EUCRL sepulchral
EUDBE refundable
EUDET Gesundheit
EUDLA seguidilla
EUDNY redundancy
EUEAE recuperate
rejuvenate
remunerate
EUECT requiescat
EUEEP refuse-heap
EUEES demureness
jejuneness
secureness
EUEIE rejuvenise
rejuvenize
EUEOE peau de soie
EUETY temulently
EUGNE refulgence
resurgence
EUGNY refulgency
EUHUE set up house
EUIAE resupinate
EUIBE repudiable
EUIEY delusively
EUIGY rebukingly
seducingly
EUIIE securitise
securitize
EUIIN beautician
EUIIR beautifier
EUIIS securities
EUIIY dehumidify
EUILY tenurially
EUIOS ceruminous
leguminous
EUIRO peculiar to
EUIRY peculiarly
EUITR repudiator
EULCN republican
EULIG rebuilding
EULRE sexual urge
EUMNS e e cummings
EUNBE returnable
EUNIG sequencing
EUNIL sequential
EUNNE repugnance
EUOAS Beaujolais
EUOSY nebulously
sedulously
EUPIE resumptive
EUPIN resumption
EURDO required to
EURNE recurrence
EURVN menu-driven
EUSEM get up steam
EUSOB Venus's comb
EUTBE rebuttable
requitable
EUTCL jesuitical
EUTES seductress
EUTIS be curtains
EUTNE reluctance
EUTRL sepultural
EUTRM result from
EUYAG Deputy Dawg
EUYED deputy head
EUYPT beauty spot
EVAET nerve agent
EVAMD heavy-armed
EVAOE leave alone
EVCMN serviceman
servicemen
EVCRH pelvic arch
EVDES fervidness
EVFBE nerve fibre
EVLAE re-evaluate
EVLNE Deo volente
EVMTL heavy metal
EVNAD heavenward
EVNET heaven-sent
EVNIH be even with
EVNOT leaving out
leaving-out
EVNRD heaven-bred
EVOSY perviously
EVREY perversely
EVRIG perverting
EVRIN perversion
EVRIY perversity
EVROT Denver boot
EVRWY beaver away
EVSOS see visions
EVWTR heavy water
EWKND reawakened
EWNSR Red Windsor
EWRES leg-warmers
EWTIG bed-wetting
EXDZR deoxidizer
EXEOE feux de joie
EXEOS jeux de mots
EYAEY very rarely
EYIEY very likely
EYLBE recyclable
EYNAS levy in mass
EYRTD dehydrated
EYRTR dehydrater
dehydrator
EYUGY very hungry
EYUHN See You Then
EZAAD New Zealand
EZCIE benzocaine
EZFRE mezzo forte
mezzo-forte
EZPAO mezzo-piano
Renzo Piano
FADUS ifs and buts
FAEBE effaceable
FAEET effacement
FAIIY affability
FBLNE off balance
off-balance
FCOAO aficionado
FEANE offer a knee
FEAOT after a sort
FEBOD after blood
FEBRH afterbirth
FECFL offenceful
FEDDY offended by
offendedly
FEDES offendress
FEEES effeteness
FEIAE after-image
effeminate
FEIAY effeminacy
FEIIE effeminise
effeminize
FESAE aftershave
FESAL offers bail
FESOK aftershock
FETAE effectuate
FETDY affected by
affectedly
FETMS oftentimes
FETOO affettuoso
FETOS affections
FETSE aftertaste
FEVSE effervesce
FEWRS afterwards
of few words
FHCOK of the clock
FHNAS Afghan Wars
FIADR Africander
FIAIE Africanise
Africanize
FIAIY efficacity
FIEOK office-book
FIILY officially
FIINY efficiency
FIITD affiliated
FIITR officiator
FIMNE affirmance
FLCIG afflicting
FLCIN affliction
FLCNE off-licence
FLETY affluently
FLLVS of all loves
FLRSE effloresce
FLUAE effleurage
FNSOD of one's word
FOAKE if you ask me
FODBE affordable
FOENT off one's nut
FOMSA afrormosia
FOTES effortless
FPTIG off-putting
FRADS sforzandos
FRGTN affrighten
FRNEY effrontery
FRNIG affronting
FTEAE off the face
FTEAK off the mark
FTEAL off the wall
off-the-wall
FTEEL off the reel

FTEEM off the beam
FTEOK off the hook
FTEUF off the cuff
off-the-cuff
FUGNE effulgence
FUIEY effusively
FWMNS of two minds
GCDLR egg coddler
GCNRC egocentric
GEBBE aglet babie
GEFTI ignes fatui
GETEL a great deal
GETRS agree terms
GIMRH Ngaio Marsh
GITCL egoistical
GNSDY agonisedly
GNUCE agony uncle
GNZDY agonizedly
GOATY ignorantly
GOIIY ignobility
GOOIS agronomics
GOOIT agronomist
GOTIG a good thing
GPAHR egg poacher
GPNHS agapanthus
GPOOY Egyptology
GRNIE aggrandise
aggrandize
GRSIE aggressive
GRSIN aggression
GRVTD aggravated
GTTDY agitatedly
HAEIG cheapening
HAEOK phrase book
HAGLS The Angelus
HAHIH thrash with
HAHIL sheathbill
HAIVA Rhea Silvia
HANLS The Annales
HAOTF cheat out of
HARCL theatrical
HARNE D H Lawrence
HASAE cheapskate
HATAS thwartways
HATDY thwartedly
HATHP thwartship
HATIE thwartwise
HATQE the antique
HAWTR shearwater
HAYIL chlamydial
HAYVA Rhea Sylvia
HBCHE The Bacchae
HBGAS the big cats
HBGIE the big time
HBHMS The Bahamas
HBIES chubbiness
shabbiness
HBMEI Thabo Mbeki
HBOEH shibboleth
HBRIG rhubarbing
HCANL the Channel
HCBRY Chuck Berry
HCCRA Chick Corea
HCDDS Thucydides
HCEIG thickening
HCEOT chicken out
HCEPX chickenpox
HCERN chicken run
HCETR Chichester
the Creator
HCGON thick-grown
HCHLC chocaholic
chocoholic
HCIGY shockingly
HCLTN Shackleton
HCLTS chocolates
HCLTY chocolatey
HCPIS the cap fits
HCPIT checkpoint
HCUEF the cause of
HCUTY the country
HDEIG shuddering
HDIES shoddiness
HDIGY thuddingly
HDNID The Dunciad
HDVAE khediviate
HDWAT shadowcast
HEAIG shoemaking
HEBLS three balls
HECAP wheel clamp
HECAR wheelchair
HEDAE threadbare
thread-lace
HEDAK thread mark
HEDES shrewdness
HEDOM threadworm
HEEAE cheesecake
HEEOF cheesed off
HEEOT Shreveport
HEFLY cheerfully
HEHKS cheechakos
HEHUE wheelhouse
HEIBN wheelie bin
HEIES cheekiness
cheeriness
wheeziness
HEIHY sheepishly
shrewishly
thievishly
HEIIM phoenixism
HEIIN Phoenician
HEIOE the Evil One
HEMSC sheet music
HEMTC phlegmatic
HEMUE shrewmouse
HEOIL threnodial
HEOIT threnodist
HEOOY phlebotomy
HEPES The Express
HEPNE threepence
HEPNY threepenny
HEPRS three-parts
HERUE Khmer Rouge
HESAK sheepshank
HESDD three-sided
HESOE threescore
HESUY Shrewsbury
HETMS three times
HFAOT shift about
HFCAF chiffchaff
chiff-chaff
HFFEN the Fifteen
HFIES shiftiness
HFIGY chaffingly
HFISX the fair sex
HFLOF shuffle off
HFOIR chiffonier
HGCTC phagocytic
HGEAA Che Guevara
HGIES shagginess
HGIHY Whiggishly
HGRIS The Gorgias
HHAIS the heavies
HHAUN Chihuahuan
HHROS the horrors
HHRWY the hard way
HHSLR The Hustler
HHYAN The Hay Wain
HIEAT choice part
HIEES choiceness
HIEET Chris Evert
HIELD shrivelled
HIFRO the Inferno
HIKAK shrink back
HIKBE shrinkable
HIKRM shrink from
HIKRP shrink-wrap
HILES shrillness
HILOD Chris Lloyd
HISAT the instant
HISIH Chris Smith
HISOE chain-smoke
chain store
HITBL Christabel
HITES thriftless
HITHP thrift shop
HITIG the in thing
HITND christened
HIVLY shrievalty
HIWMN chairwoman
HJGSP the jig is up
HKAOT chukka boot
HKHNS shake hands
HLAUE child abuse
HLBRH childbirth
HLCES thale cress
HLCEY phylactery
HLCOH whole cloth
HLCRE chelicerae
HLDAE shelldrake
HLEAH shillelagh
HLEBN Chelsea bun
HLEGD challenged
HLEGR challenger
HLEHM Cheltenham
HLEOY chalcedony
HLGAN wholegrain
HLIES chalkiness
chilliness
HLIHY childishly
HLIIM phallicism
HLKSF the likes of
HLMAX chalumeaux
HLNIT phalangist
HLOAY phyllotaxy
HLOEA phylloxera
HLPIE Philippise
Philippize
HLPOF childproof
shellproof
HLPOH Philip Roth
HLSAK whale shark
HLSIE philistine
HLSIN thalassian
HLSLR wholesaler
HLSLY child's play
HLSOD Chelmsford
HLSOT whole shoot
HLSPY philosophy
HLTLC philatelic
HLWET wholewheat
HLYHW whillywhaw
HMAHM shammashim
HMAIE thumb a ride
HMAIT thumb a lift
HMAZE chimpanzee
HMCLY chemically
HMEEN Chamaeleon
HMEIG shimmering
whimpering
HMEOS Chamaerops
HMEPT chamberpot
HMETN Chambertin
HMFCD shamefaced
HMFLY shamefully
HMIDX thumb index
thumb-index
HMIES chumminess
whimsiness
HMIGY thumpingly
HMINN champignon
HMLFL thimbleful
HMLIN the million
HMLRG thimblerig
HMOAO Chimborazo
HMOYU shame on you
HMPAO thumb piano
HMPIH chum up with
HMRCL chimerical
HMRYL rhyme royal
rhyme-royal
HMSAN Thomas Mann
HMSDR Thomas Edur
HMSET the mostest
HMSIH The Messiah
HMSIN The Mission
HMSOD Thomas Gold
Thomas Hood
Thomas Lord
HMSOE Thomas More
HMSOK Thomas Cook
HMSON thumbs down

thumbs-down
HMSRE Thomas Arne
HMSRW thumbscrew
HMSRY Thomas Gray
HMTXS chemotaxis
HNAAN think again
HNAIE phantasime
HNAMC phantasmic
HNAML phantasmal
HNAOD think aloud
HNAOT think about
HNBUS thenabouts
HNCLY phonically
HNCRS rhinoceros
HNCYT phenocryst
HNEAE change face
HNEAK change tack
HNEBE changeable
HNEBY changeably
Thunder Bay
HNEER change gear
HNEES changeless
HNEIE channelise
channelize
HNEIG changeling
chundering
thundering
HNEIR chandelier
HNELD channelled
HNELR chancellor
HNENO change into
HNEON change down
HNEOS thunderous
HNEPN chance upon
HNEVR changeover
change-over
HNFLY thankfully
HNHLA chinchilla
HNIAH Chandigarh
HNIGY thinkingly
HNMNL phenomenal
HNMNN phenomenon
HNNOH Shenandoah
HNOVR whensoever
HNPAE china plate
HNSAE think shame
HNSLT thanks a lot
HNSOE rhinestone
HNSOY rhinoscopy
shank's pony
HNSRD Chinese red
HNTIE think twice
HNTPC phenotypic
HNVRS rhinovirus
HNWOG think wrong
HNWRE Shane Warne
HNYES phoneyness
HOAIE shoot a line
HOAOT throw about
HOBSS thromboses
thrombosis
HOBTC thrombotic
HODAS the old days
HODIL the old Bill
HOEIE Shrovetide
HOGOT throughout
HOGPT throughput
HOIAE chloridate
chlorinate
HOIES choosiness
HOIGP throwing up
HOIIE chloridise
chloridize
chlorinise
chlorinize
HOIIY chronicity
HOILD chronicled
HOILR chronicler
HOILS chronicles❑
HOIOT shoot it out
HOITN phlogiston
HOLSD the ould sod
HOMDT throw mud at
HONWY thrown away
HOOHC theosophic
HOOHL chlorophyl
HOOIE theodolite
theologise
theologize
HOOIN theologian
HOOIS Theodosius
HOOIT rheologist
HOOOA chionodoxa
HOOOE chromosome
HOOOM chloroform
HOOOY chronology
HORTC theocratic
HORTS Theocritus
HOSIE Shropshire
HOYSY The Odyssey
HPAES The Planets
HPAIE chaptalise
chaptalize
HPANY chaplaincy
HPATN Shepparton
HPEIS The Poetics
HPEPR shopkeeper
HPEUE The Prelude
HPHCT whip the cat
HPIDW shop window
HPIES whippiness
HPITR shoplifter
HPLAT chapel cart
HPOIE rhapsodise
rhapsodize
HPOIT rhapsodist
HPRGT shipwright
HPRJS chaparajos
chaparejos
HPRUD shop around
HPTTH whip-stitch
HPWYT chip away at
HQEAD cheque card
HRAET thereanent
HRAIE thermalise
thermalize
HRAIT pharmacist
HRAOG thereamong
HRAOT thereabout
whereabout
HRAPE thorn apple
HRATR thereafter
whereafter
whore after
HRBED shortbread
HRBMC cherubimic
HRBRE shard-borne
HRCAS third class
third-class
HRCES characters
HRCIS the Rockies
HRCUT shortcrust
HRDAE the Red Lane
HRDIG The Red King
HRDTD short-dated
HREAD charge hand
HREBE chargeable
HREBY chargeably
HREET Thar Desert
HREFY Charles Fry
HREIG shortening
HRENH thirteenth
HREON charge down
HRESS Cherkesses
HRETN Charleston
HRFDM sheriffdom
HRGOY chirognomy
HRHAD churchward
churchyard
HRHOR churchgoer
HRHRE shire horse
HRHUE whorehouse
HRIBW The Rainbow
HRIDX share index
HRIES chirpiness
HRIGR wharfinger
HRIGS phorminges
HRIGY charmingly
HRIHY churlishly
HRINC thermionic
HRIST where it's at
HRITR thermistor
HRLVD short-lived
HRMNY chiromancy
HRNEL pharyngeal
HRNOT sharing out
HROEE chersonese
HROER charioteer❑
HROIE thermopile
HRONY Chardonnay
HROTT thermostat
HRPRY third party
HRRIE sherardise
sherardize
HRRNE short-range
HRRUE chartreuse
HRSER wheresoeer
HRSES choristers
HRSIG cherishing
HRSIM pharisaism
HRSOY short story
short-story
HRTBE charitable
HRTBY charitably
HRUDR thereunder
whereunder
HRUHY thoroughly
HRUIG chirruping
HRUTL whereuntil
HRWRD Third World
HRWRS shorewards
HRYID whirlybird
HRYIE Cherry Ripe
HRYIK cherry-pick
HRYOD thirtyfold
HRYUO there you go
HSAOS The Seasons
HSASS lhasa apsos
HSAUL The Seagull
HSBAD chessboard
HSCLY physically
HSDIE whist drive
HSEES chasteness
HSEIG chastening
whispering
HSETN Chesterton
HSHRC phosphoric
HSHRS phosphorus
HSIEF this side of
HSIES the shivers
HSIIG chastising
The Shining
HSIUE this minute
HSLFR whistle for
HSLIG chiselling
HSLOF whistle off
HSOOY physiology
HSPAE Chesapeake
HSPLS she's apples
HSRAT The Servant
HSWIE ghost-write
HSYOR whisky sour
HTAOG chittagong❑
HTAOI chittaroni
HTBAD white-beard
HTBAS white brass
HTCLY thetically
HTDAF white dwarf
HTEBX chatterbox
HTEIG chattering
shattering
HTETN Chatterton
HTFIR White Friar
white friar
HTGAH photograph
HTGNC photogenic
HTGOS white goods
HTHRE white horse
Whitehorse
HTHUH what though
HTIES chattiness
HTIGP chatting up

HTIKR The Thinker
HTLGT white light
HTLIE châtelaine
HTLSS photolysis
HTLTC photolytic
HTMCL rhythmical
HTMES The Timaeus
HTMET The Tempest
HTMGC white magic
HTMTL white metal
HTMTR photometer
the Tempter
HTMTY photometry
HTNDA what an idea!
HTNIE white noise
HTNRM The Tin Drum
HTOVR whatsoever
HTPHP shut up shop
HTPPR white paper
HTRAY The Tar Baby
HTRCL rhetorical
HTRES the three B's
the three F's
the three R's
HTSAE white slave
HTSGR white sugar
HTSOE what is more
HTSUE white sauce
HTTON whitethorn
HTTXS phototaxis
HTUDY Whit Sunday
Whitsunday
HTWAE white whale
HTWTR white water
HUADH thousandth
HUAIM rheumatism
HUAOD rheumatoid
HUFOD chaudfroid
HUFUE chauffeuse
HUHFL thoughtful
HUHHV Khrushchev
HUIGY shoutingly
HUIHY ghoulishly
HUIIM chauvinism
HUIIT chauvinist
HVLAE The Village
HVLOS chivalrous
HVLUS shovelfuls
HVOAN chevrotain
HWHCD chew the cud
HWHFT chew the fat
HWHRG chew the rag
HWHWY show the way
HWLIS the willies
HWLOE The Wild One
HWNGM chewing-gum
HWNOF showing off
showing-off
HWOEF the whole of
HWUPR showjumper
HXTOY thixotropy
HYADT the year dot
HYAIS chrysalids
HYOIE chrysolite
HYSUE shoyu sauce
HYTEA phlyctaena
HYTNE phlyctenae
HZIGY whizzingly
HZLWT Chuzzlewit
IAAIN dilatation
divagation
IAANT pit against
IACUE final cause
IADBT aid and abet
IADER win and wear
IADIS hit and miss
hit-and-miss
IADLI Girardelli
IADLO Pirandello
IADNO ritardando
IAEAE dilacerate
IAEQE picaresque
IAFRE vital force
IAFUD vital fluid
IAIAE dilapidate
disanimate
divaricate
IAIFR dig a pit for
IAIIE vitaminise
vitaminize
IAIIN viraginian
IAIIS vitalities
IAIIY disability
IAILS cigarillos
IAIND misaligned
IAIOE Nina Simone
IAIOS viraginous
IAISS filariasis
IALWD disallowed
IAMXM Hiram Maxim
IAOAA pina colada
piña colada
IAOHK Pinakothek
IAOIY dilatorily
IAOSY bigamously
IAPID misapplied
IAPIT disappoint
IAPOE disapprove
IAPRL disapparel
IAPWR tidal power
IARCS cicatrices
IARLY binaurally
IARNE disarrange
misarrange
IARXS cicatrixes
IARYD disarrayed
IASAK vital spark
IATIE sit astride
IATOS disastrous
IATRD pilastered
IATSN bipartisan
IAULY bimanually
IAUNR Tina Turner
IAUOS miraculous
IAYOE binary code
IAYTR binary star
IBAED win by a head
IBBEN Zimbabwean
IBEES liableness
nimbleness
IBEKR tie-breaker
IBIGY nibblingly
IBITD fimbriated
IBLCL diabolical
IBLEE disbelieve
misbelieve
IBNFT disbenefit
IBNIH ribbonfish
IBNOM ribbonworm
IBNRP Ribbentrop
IBOHR Big Brother
IBRET disbarment
IBRHN disburthen
IBRIE kimberlite
IBROF timber wolf
IBTNK kibbutznik
IBTOK pin-buttock
ICAEA disc camera
ICAGD discharged
ICAGR discharger
ICAMR disclaimer
ICAOT bitch about
ICARW disc harrow
ICBAK pitch-black
ICCAT witchcraft
ICDEF minced beef
ICEAT discrepant
ICEEY discretely
ICEFL pitcherful
ICEIN Diocletian
discretion
ICEIT biochemist
ICETA kitchen tea
ICETR Winchester
Winchester®
ICETY discreetly
ICHKR hitchhiker
ICHPD disc-shaped
ICHZL witch hazel
ICIES bitchiness
pitchiness
ICIGY pinchingly
witchingly
ICIOS circuitous
ICLAE disculpate
ICLAY miscellany
ICLER fiscal year
ICLLI piccalilli
ICLRG fiscal drag
ICLRY circularly
ICLUH disc plough
ICMCN lincomycin
ICMED discommend
ICMET circumvent
ICMIE circumcise
ICMLX circumflex
ICMOE circumpose
discommode
discompose
ICMOP nincompoop
ICMOT discomfort
ICMTI Giacometti
ICMTL mischmetal
ICMUE circumduce
circumfuse
circummure
miscompute
ICMUT circumduct
ICNAI Cincinnati
ICNET disconcert
disconnect
discontent
ICNUT misconduct
ICOIE cinchonise
cinchonize
ICOKY disc jockey
ICOUE disclosure
ICPIE discipline
discophile
ICRAE discarnate
ICRAT discordant
ICRET air-current
miscorrect
ICRIE discursive
ICRIG discarding
discerning
ICRNC diachronic
ICSIN discussion
ICSIS Dio Cassius
ICTLB Kitcat Club
ICTNS pitch tents
ICUAE discourage
ICUFD dischuffed
ICUSL miscounsel
ICUSR discourser
ICUTD discounted
ICUTR discounter
ICUTY viscountcy
ICVRD discovered
ICVRR discoverer
ICYTE winceyette
IDACS hindrances
IDALS find faults
IDAMR windjammer
IDBET wildebeest
IDCBE vindicable
IDCEN windscreen
IDCIE vindictive
IDCME Widdecombe
IDCTD vindicated
IDCTR vindicator
IDEAE girdle cake
middle name
IDEAT Middle East
IDEDR mind-bender
mind-reader
IDEIE riddle-like
IDEIH fiddle with
IDEIK kiddiewink
IDERW middlebrow
IDESN wild person
IDESY mindlessly

IDFRY bird of prey
IDGRY hirdy-girdy
IDHED windshield
IDIES kindliness
IDIFL disdainful
IDIGY riddlingly
IDLWR wild flower
windflower
IDNIE wild endive
IDNIS pieds noirs
IDNUG Hindenburg
IDOLR wildfowler
IDPCD giddy-paced
IDPDR bird-spider
IDPIH tied up with
IDRAD hinderland
IDREE Windermere
IDRES wilderness
IDRET rinderpest
IDRHD wild orchid
IDRIE tinder-like
IDRLA Cinderella
IDSAI Hindustani
IDSEM Hildesheim
IDTAD Lindstrand
IDTIE bird strike
IDTRE pied-à-terre
IDUFR windsurfer
IDULY find guilty
IDUNL wind tunnel
IDWAE windowpane
IDWAH window sash
IDWET window seat
IDWHP window-shop
IDWIL windowsill
IDYEL midday meal
IEADE sidesaddle
IEAEO give name to
IEAIE liberalise
liberalize
literalise
literalize
mineralise
mineralize
IEAIG liberating
life-saving
time-saving
IEAIH vinegarish
IEAIM cinerarium
liberalism
literalism
IEAIN liberation
IEAIS kinematics
IEAIT liberalist
literalist
IEAIY liberality
literarily
IEALC bimetallic
IEAOL mineral oil
IEAOR cinema-goer
IEAOY mineralogy
IEAPR dive-dapper
IEARD wire-haired
IEASR fire-raiser
IEATN pine marten
IEAUE literature
IEBED mixed breed
IEBGE disembogue
IEBOL disembroil
IEBSM disembosom
IEBSN river basin
IEBWL disembowel
IECAM like a charm
IECAN disenchain
IECAT disenchant
IECEN firescreen
IECES give access
IECIS libecchios
IECNE virescence
IECOE disenclose
IECSS fixed costs
IECTS Oireachtas
IEDVS Miles Davis
IEEAP aide-de-camp
IEEDE pine needle
IEEDN ride herd on
IEEET vice-regent
IEELR wine cellar
wine-cellar
IEENH nineteenth
IEENL pine kernel
IEEOE time before
IEEPR timekeeper
IEESN wise person
IEESY lifelessly
tirelessly
IEETE pine beetle
IEETO give vent to
IEETR life-renter
like better
IEEVD time-served
IEEVR file server
IEFAH like a flash
IEFET side effect
IEFIE line of life
IEFOK line of work
IEFUE liver fluke
IEGAH mimeograph
IEGGD disengaged
IEGIL mixed grill
IEGNE divergence
IEHAR give the air
IEHBY ride a hobby
IEHND give the nod
IEHWR Eisenhower
IEIAT kinetic art
IEIDD like-minded
IEIDR sidewinder
IEIEO give life to
give rise to
IEIES likeliness
liveliness
timeliness
IEIHY tigerishly
IEIIE piperidine
IEIIG life-giving
pipelining
IEINL time signal
IEIOD likelihood
livelihood
misericord
IEIOO Hideki Tojo
IEIRR side mirror
IEISN Mike Gibson
IEJBO give a jab to
IELOY pineal body
IELTE River Lethe
IEMNS lineaments
IEMSC piped music
IEMTR mileometer
IENBE disennoble
IENIE fire engine
IENOD pigeon-toed
IENOE pigeonhole
pigeon-hole
IENOT pigeon-post
IENSP bite and sup
IENSY video nasty
IENTE ride and tie
ride-and-tie
IEOBR dive-bomber
IEODO give food to
IEOEY tiresomely
IEOHR give bother
IEOIE give notice
IEOIN Ciceronian
IEOKN ride bodkin
IEOLR wine cooler
IEOMO give form to
IEOOE life to come
time to come
IEOOR give colour
IEOOY diseconomy
IEORS sideboards
IEOSY viperously
IEOTE wine bottle
IEOTT siderostat
IEPAE River Plate
IEPED widespread
IEPOE videophone
IEPOK give up work
IEPWR disempower
IERAE give or take
IERCS wisecracks
IERES give orders
IERIT mime artist
IERMS Fidel Ramos
IERUD give ground
IERVR Niger River
IERWR wiredrawer
IESAE disenslave
fire escape
tiger snake
IESAK tiger shark
IESAT give a start
IESEN Eisenstein
IESLS liver salts
IESOS dimensions
IESOT Giles Scott
Nigel Short
IETAE licentiate
IETAL direct mail
IETAN disentrain
IETBE digestible
IETDF divested of
IETDY digestedly
IETES directness
silentness
IETET divestment
IETIE disentwine
IETNE dilettante
IETNI dilettanti
IETNY like a tansy
IETOE minestrone
sidestroke
IETOS directions
licentious
IETRL disenthral
IETTE disentitle
IETTY give it a try
IEUGN Nibelungen
IEULR wire-puller
IEULY bisexually
IEUNN sine qua non
IEURS Life Guards
IEVLE eigenvalue
IEVLP disenvelop
IEVRN disenviron
IEVRO give over to
IEWEL fixed-wheel
IEWOS Tiger Woods
IEWRT liverwurst
IEYED widely read
widely-read
IEYIE side by side
IFAUE disfeature
IFCLY difficulty
IFDNE diffidence
IFEDR midfielder
IFEGT air freight
IFGRD disfigured
IFLES fitfulness
sinfulness
wilfulness
IFRIH disfurnish
IFRNE difference
IFRUE misfortune
IFSBE diffusible
IFSDY diffusedly
IGAEE Singhalese
IGAHC biographic
IGAHR biographer
IGAIG disgracing
IGATR ringmaster
ring-master
IGBIF king's brief
IGBNH King's Bench
IGEBR singles bar
IGEDR ringleader
IGEES singleness
IGEET minglement
IGEIE single file

IGEKD ring-necked
IGEOM Single Form
IGEOT singled out
IGETP single-step
IGGIE King's Guide
IGHLD King Khaled
IGHPD ring-shaped
IGIAE pilgrimage
IGIDR ring binder
IGIES kingliness
IGIGY minglingly
nigglingly
IGIHR kingfisher
IGIIE pilgrimise
pilgrimize
IGIRR wing mirror
IGITC jingoistic
linguistic
IGLRY singularly
IGLVR King Oliver
IGNLY diagonally
virginally
IGNMN singing-man
IGNSS biogenesis
diagenesis
IGNTC biogenetic
IGOLR wing collar
IGOTC diagnostic
IGPED wingspread
IGRAK fingermark
IGRAL fingernail
IGRAP digger-wasp
IGRDO didgeridoo
IGRER ginger beer
IGRES fingerless
IGRHR King Arthur
IGRIE ginger wine
IGRIG fingerling
IGRIH disgarnish
IGRNP gingersnap
IGROL fingerbowl
IGROT finger-post
IGRSY Bing Crosby
IGRVR linger over
IGSAR Ringo Starr
IGSIG disgusting
IGSOT King's Scout
IGTIH fidget with
IGUCN King Duncan
IGUTE disgruntle
IGVNS misgivings
IGVTS gingivitis
IHADD high-handed
IHADR fish-ladder
highlander
IHAGE right angle
right-angle
IHAHR dishwasher
IHAIG high-paying
IHAIN Lithuanian
IHALT hightail it
IHAMN highwayman
IHAOH Mishnayoth
IHAOR with favour
IHAOT right about
IHATD big-hearted
IHATN dishearten
IHAYN lie heavy on
IHBID night-blind
IHBLE dishabille
IHBON light brown
IHBUS Light blues
IHCAE high-octane
IHCAS nightclass
IHCOL high school
IHDAN right-drawn
IHDES nightdress
IHEAD high regard
IHEGT with weight
IHEIF high relief
IHEIG lightening
tightening
IHEIL dish aerial
IHEMN High German
IHEMS Michaelmas
IHEMT pith helmet
IHENH eighteenth
IHESN high season
with reason
IHFLY rightfully
IHGAD right guard
IHGAH lithograph
IHGYH lithoglyph
IHHFN Richthofen
IHHRA diphtheria
IHHRH High Church
IHHUE lighthouse
IHIAE mithridate
IHIDD high-minded
IHIGR fish-finger
IHIHY tightishly
IHIIG high living
IHIOT fight it out
IHITL Mikhail Tal
IHLCS high places
IHLHS Wilhelm His
IHLIA Wilhelmina
IHLIG high-flying
IHLNH light lunch
IHLOX Michel Roux
IHMTR light meter
IHNAL within call
IHNDY high and dry
IHNEI Bishan Bedi
IHNET with intent
IHNKN kith and kin
IHNLW high and low
IHNRD fishing-rod
IHNRE Night Nurse
IHNSY dishonesty
IHODR withholder
IHOEA light opera
IHOEY high comedy
IHOGR fishmonger
IHOOR high colour
IHOTC dichroitic
IHOWY right of way
IHPYE lithophyte
IHRCD high-priced
IHRET high priest
IHRHN higher than
IHRII Richard III
IHROT hithermost
IHROY disharmony
IHRSN Richardson
IHRVN night-raven
IHRWL withdrawal
IHSAE nightshade
IHSEM high esteem
IHSEP light sleep
IHSES air hostess
IHSIT night shift
nightshirt
IHSYF fight shy of
IHTET high street
IHTGT light-tight
IHTIY lithotrity
IHUED without end
IHUGE mishguggle
IHUTE silhouette
IHVRE vinho verde
IHWAE right whale
IHWIS Jim Hawkins
IHWRS rightwards
IHWSY wishy-washy
IHWTR Vichy water
IIAAT Minimal Art
IIAEY digitately
IIAIE digitalise
digitalize
disimagine
militarise
militarize
mitigative
IIAIG mitigating
IIAIM militarism
minimalism
IIAIN divination
limitation
litigation
mitigation
pixilation
sibilation
titivation
visitation
IIAIT militarist
minimalist
IIAIY finicality
militarily
similarity
viviparity
IIAOS viviparous
IIAOY divinatory
mitigatory
IIATY militantly
sibilantly
vigilantly
IICIE disincline
IICOE disinclose
IICOS liliaceous
IICUT civil court
IIEDN biliverdin
IIEES divineness
finiteness
IIEIE citisenize
citizenize
IIEOS piliferous
IIESY pitilessly
IIETR vivisector
IIETY diligently
IIGAE living wage
IIGAK giving back
giving-back
IIGEL living hell
IIGET timing belt
IIGIE firing line
firing-line
IIGOL mixing bowl
IIGOM dining-room
living-room
IIGOT riding-boot
IIGRP riding-crop
IIGTN Livingston
IIGVR giving-over
IIHBT disinhibit
IIHIH finish with
IIHOK finish work
IIHRT disinherit
IIIAE nidificate
IIIDS Militiades
IIIEY divisively
IIIHD diminished
IIIIG civilizing
minimizing
IIIIS civilities
IIIIT libidinist
IIIIY risibility
visibility
IIIMN militiaman
IIINL divisional
IIINS sicilianos
IIIOS libidinous
IIITC nihilistic
IIIUE similitude
IIKOS tie in knots
IILNA bimillenia
IILTD pixillated
IINES visionless
IINHL Lilienthal
IINIH Lilian Gish
IINLY visionally
IIOIL visitorial
IIOOS nidicolous
IIPOE disimprove
misimprove
IISAE lie in state
IITAT ministrant
IITRA ministeria
IITRE Finisterre
IITRI tibiotarsi
IITRO minister to
IITRY sinisterly

IIUIE diminutive
IIUIG ridiculing
IIUIN diminution
IIUNO diminuendo
IIUOS ridiculous
IIUTR filibuster
IIVLE disinvolve
IIZNR Lipizzaner
IJITD disjointed
IKDES wickedness
IKDIH linked with
IKEES fickleness
IKEIK tickle pink
IKEIL sicklebill
IKESN link person
IKIES sickliness
IKIGY tinklingly
IKIHY ticklishly
IKITD sick-listed
IKNED Birkenhead
IKNIN Dickensian
IKNOF ticking-off
IKNTN Pilkington
IKOIG kick boxing
IKOKT pickpocket
pick-pocket
IKONY Nick Hornby
IKOTE milk bottle
IKOTM Nick Bottom
IKPIH link up with
IKPRW kick up a row
IKRAE ticker tape
IKREL Tinkerbell
IKROK wickerwork
IKRUD kick around
IKSDG sick as a dog
IKTBO tickety-boo
IKTSA rickettsia
IKUKS Dick Butkus
IKUPN Dick Turpin
IKWAE minke whale
IKYAE mickey-take
IKYIN Mickey Finn
ILAIG misleading
ILAKR hillwalker
ILBAK Cilla Black
ILBLY silly-billy
ILBNS Billy Bones
ILCIS dialectics
ILCLY biblically
ILCRC dielectric
ILCRS rifle-corps
ILCTD dislocated
ILDAE digladiate
ILDCS diplodocus❑
ILDIG dislodging
ILDLY dilly-dally
ILEDS Bill Deedes
ILEET field event
ILESY willlessly
ILFAE bill of fare
ILFLY tilly-fally
ILGCL biological
ILHGP fill the gap
ILIAE villeinage
ILIGY yieldingly
ILIOS villainous
ILKBE dislikable
ILLBS Villa-Lobos
ILLMN Willy Loman
ILLTE millilitre
ILMDN silly mid-on
ILMTC diplomatic
ILMTD Willemstad
ILMTE millimetre
ILMUE field mouse
fieldmouse
ILNAT violent act
ILNCO bill and coo
ILNDN Hillingdon
ILNHM Gillingham
ILNIL millennial
ILNIM millennium
ILNLE villanelle
ILNLY willy-nilly
ILNUE Villeneuve
ILOIE will to live
ILOSF millions of
ILPIH fill up with
ILPIT yield point
ILRDY girl Friday❑
ILRED girlfriend
ILRSN Bill Bryson
ILRUD mill around
ILSBE dialysable
ILSML millesimal
ILTGW Linlithgow
ILTIL field trial
ILTIN Midlothian
ILTOX billet-doux
ILTYD gimlet-eyed
ILUTN Will Hutton
ILVLY tilly-vally
ILWAE pillowcase
pillow-lace
ILWAK pillow talk
ILWLP pillowslip
ILWLY willy-willy
ILWRS fieldwards
ILYLY disloyally
disloyalty
IMAUE mismeasure
IMBAH Miami Beach
IMESN Liam Neeson
IMLES dismalness
IMNAY pigmentary
IMNGD mismanaged
IMNHM Birmingham
IMNTN Wilmington
IMRHL air-marshal
IMROK Kilmarnock
IMRON simmer down
IMSCT Siamese cat
IMSET litmus test
IMSIE dismissive
IMSOY dismissory
IMTHD mismatched
IMTIS biometrics
IMUHD big-mouthed
IMWAE pigmy whale
IMWIE Jimmy White
INABS Diane Arbus
INAOF vienna loaf
INCIE lignocaine
INEIG pioneering
INFRE pianoforte
INGTY midnightly
INHTI fianchetti
INHTO fianchetto
INIHY fiendishly
INILY biennially
INLAE simnel cake
INLAT Lionel Bart
INLLG signal flag
INNTE mignonette
INPIG kidnapping
INPNA giant panda
INRAY dinner lady
INSAE lion's share
INSBX witness box
INSIO pianissimo
INTIG signet-ring
INTIT vignettist
INTPD pinnatiped
INUGS Cienfuegos
INULY biannually
INURC Finno-Ugric
INYEB Sidney Webb
INYEN kidney bean
INYIH kidney dish
INZMN Jiang Zemin
IOAGR fit of anger
IOAIT misogamist
IOAIY bipolarity
bitonality
IOARC dinosauric
IOBAC Pinot Blanc
IODRD disordered
IODRY disorderly
IOEEF pit oneself
IOEEL Simone Weil
IOHUE pilot house
IOICL simoniacal
IOLGT pilot light
IOLNS cipollinos
IOLVN riboflavin
IOMGS Simon Magus
IOMRS Simon Marks
IONET disownment
IONLI ritornelli
IONLO ritornello
IOOIT kidologist
Sinologist
virologist
IOOSY rigorously
timorously
vigorously
IOPIM dimorphism
IOPOS dimorphous
IORME kilogramme
IORPY lipography
IOSEK widow's peak
IOSRE misobserve
IOSUF bit of stuff
IOSUY pilot study
IOTRE bijouterie
IOUAS binoculars
IOWAE pilot whale
IOYIT misogynist
IOYOS misogynous
IPAOS diaphanous
IPATS Diophantus
IPCIG nit-picking
IPCMI hippocampi
IPDES limpidness
IPDOE hippodrome
IPDOF hipped roof
IPEAK ripple-mark
IPEES simpleness
IPEIE simple time
IPEIH displenish
IPEON tipple down
IPEOT nipplewort
IPESD displeased
IPGIF hippogriff
IPIGY ripplingly
IPIID simplified
IPIIN misprision
IPIIR simplifier
IPIIS Simplicius
IPIIY simplicity
IPITC simplistic
IPITR oil painter
IPLTS Hippolytus
IPMNA hippomania
IPNAY dispensary
IPNOA Hispaniola
IPNOF ripping off
IPOES disprofess
IPOOS diaphonous
IPPIE hippophile
IPRGR disparager
IPRHS Hipparchos
IPRIN dispersion
IPRTD dispirited
IPSBE disposable
IPSDO disposed to
IPSDY disposedly
IPSES dispossess
IPSIN dispassion
IPTBE disputable
IPTBY disputably
IPTHP hippety-hop
IPTIE limpet mine
IPTMY gippy tummy
IPYIS biophysics
IQAIY disqualify
IQEOL cinquefoil
IQITD disquieted
IQITN disquieten
IQITY disquietly
IRAIG lip-reading

misreading
rip-roaring
IRBAD fibreboard
IRCAK microcrack
IRCCD citric acid
nitric acid
IRCCI micrococci
IREES fierceness
IRFBE microfibre
IRFCE microfiche
IRGAS fibreglass
IRGYH hieroglyph
IRHEC diarrhoeic
IRHEL diarrhoeal
IRIGY piercingly
IRIOS migrainous
IRISS giardiasis
IRLAE fibrillate
IRLAY fibrillary
IRLGT microlight
IRLOE fibrillose
IRLOS fibrillous
IRLRA tirra-lirra
IRMEH Vikram Seth
IRMTE micrometre
IRMTR micrometer
IRMTY micrometry
IRNGN fibrinogen
fibronogen
IRNSA Micronesia
IROAE vitriolate
IROIE vitriolise
vitriolize
IRPAT hierophant
IRPIE disruptive
IRPIN disruption
IRPIT microprint
IRPLS Hierapolis
IRPOE microphone
vibraphone
IRRHC hierarchic
IRRIE mirrorlike
mirrorwise
IRSET disrespect
nigrescent
vitrescent
IRSIE digressive
IRSIG digressing
IRSIN digression
IRSOE fibrescope
microscope□
IRSOY microscopy
IRSTS fibrositis
IRTIT librettist
IRTOS vibrations
IRVLE Libreville
IRWVS microwaves
IRZPM nitrazepam
ISAGN Miss Saigon
ISAIE dissuasive
ISAIG piss-taking
ISAIN dissuasion
ISAOS miasmatous
ISAOY dissuasory
ISAPR wit-snapper
ISCAE dissociate
ISCAS first-class
ISCIG dissecting
ISCIN dissection
ISCUE first cause
ISDNE dissidence
ISEAA diastemata
ISEAE Kiss Me Kate
ISEDR big spender
ISEIE dies feriae
ISFIE kiss of life
ISFOR first floor
ISHBS miss the bus
ISHCT miss the cut
ISHRD kiss the rod
ISIMN midshipman
ISLBE dissoluble
ISLGT first light
ISLIG dissolving
ISLUR kieselguhr
ISMLD dissembled
ISMLR dissembler
dissimilar
ISMNA dipsomania
ISNGT first night
ISNIG dissenting
ISNIN dissension
ISNNE dissonance
ISOAL first of all
ISOAY missionary
ISOIE missionise
missionize
ISOSI Kieslowski
ISOTR ripsnorter
six-shooter
ISPAE first place
ISPIE first prize
ISPOF first proof
ISPTD dissipated
ISRIE disservice
lip service
lip-service
ISRIT piss artist
ISRLY minstrelsy
ISRUD piss around
ISTIG first thing
ISTSY dissatisfy
ISWRD First World
ISYAK Kirsty Wark
ITAEE Vietnamese
ITAGT distraught
ITAIN filtration
ITAIY virtuality
ITALR victualler
ITALY rift valley
ITAMR dirt farmer
ITATD distracted
ITAWR Vietnam War
ITBOS dirty books
ITBRH Pittsburgh
ITCFS fisticuffs
ITCIS pistachios
ITCLR rib-tickler
ITCLY biotically
ITCSS witticisms
ITDES giftedness
ITDFD eisteddfod
ITDIH gifted with
ITDIK fit to drink
ITEAD pittie-ward
ITEAK hit the sack
ITEEK hit the deck
ITEEL Little Nell
ITEER Little Bear
ITEIL fit the bill
little girl
ITEIN Little Lion
ITEMS sixteenmos
ITENS little ones
ITENT tie the knot
ITEOD hit the road
ITEOF hit the roof
ITEOK Little Rock
ITEON Little John
ITERO little or no
ITESD distressed
ITESY listlessly
ITFFY fifty-fifty
ITFLY mirthfully
ITGAH pictograph
ITGCR vintage car
ITGET dirty great
ITGNC histogenic
ITHRY Dirty Harry
ITIES filthiness
ITINC histrionic
ITITE Birtwistle
ITIUE distribute
ITKBE mistakable
ITKNY mistakenly
ITLAE distillate
ITLET distilment
ITLEY distillery
ITLGC histologic
ITLHP pistol-whip
ITLNN dirty linen
ITLRP pistol grip
ITLSS histolysis
ITLTC histolytic
ITMES victimless
ITMNY dirty money
ITMRS ditto marks
ITMZD victimized
ITMZR victimizer
ITNEG Wittenberg
ITNIG distancing
piston ring
ITNIN distension
ITNNN listen in on
ITNNO listen in to
ITNTY distinctly
ITOAY dictionary
ITOIE riot police
ITOIY virtuosity
ITOSY virtuously
ITOTN dirt-rotten
ITPAE birthplace
ITPLI Fittipaldi
ITPNE fifty pence
ITPNS birth-pangs
ITPOE dictaphone
ITRAA victoriana□
ITRAD hinterland
Mitterrand
ITRAT disturbant
ITRBE filterable
ITRCL historical
ITRES bitterness
Victor Hess
ITRGT birthright
ITRHR Winterthur
ITRIE wintertime
ITRIG disturbing
ITRIL bitter pill
winterkill
ITRIN Cistercian
distortion
ITROD bitterwood
Mister Toad
sisterhood
ITROS victorious
ITROT litter-lout
ITRTO Tintoretto
ITRUH win through
ITRUO Victor Hugo
ITRYE Mister Hyde
ITSNE sixth sense
ITTIK dirty trick
ITTOS fictitious
ITWEL fifth wheel
ITYIH filthy rich
IUAIE figurative
IUAIN figuration
simulation
titubation
IUAOE Titus Alone
IUCLR minuscular
IUDSR liquidiser
IUDTD liquidated
IUDTR liquidator
IUDZR liquidizer
IUEAE vituperate
IUEAK minute-jack
IUEAT lieutenant
IUEED figurehead
IUEES minuteness
IUEOK figurework
IUETY virulently
IUFIG liquefying
IUFLS Sioux Falls
IUGCL liturgical
IUGNE divulgence
IUGON Titus Groan
IUIAE bituminate
dijudicate
IUIIE bituminise
bituminize

IUILY fiducially
IUIOS bituminous
IULAN Liv Ullmann
IULRS visual arts
IUODL sinusoidal
IUOSY bibulously
IUPAE bisulphate
IVCNE Gil Vicente
IVRIE silverside
IVRIH silverfish
IVRIT silver-gilt
IVRTR Silver Star
IWESY viewlessly
IWFPG View of a Pig
IWIDR viewfinder
IWITE tin whistle
IWNES Wim Wenders
IWRHP misworship
IWSEN Midwestern
IYDTR city editor
IYETE city centre
IYISS pityriasis
IYLBC disyllabic
IYLBE disyllable
IZCTS pizzicatos
IZDIK fizzy drink
IZEAD FitzGerald
Fitzgerald
IZIGY dizzyingly
sizzlingly
JILAS JJ Williams
KEHBE Okeechobee
KHROR Sky Harbour
KISAK skrimshank
KJCIG skyjacking
KLIGY skulkingly
KLRIG skylarking
KMIES skimpiness
KMIGY skimmingly
skimpingly
KNIIG skin-diving
KPIGY skippingly
KRIHR skirmisher
KSRPR skyscraper
KTBAD skateboard
KTHBE sketchable
KTIHY skittishly
KTLOT skittle out
LAAAE Allan-a-Dale
LAAEA Alma-Tadema
LAAIN floatation
LAALO Alvar Aalto
LAAMD clear as mud
LAATR almacantar
LAATY pleasantly
pleasantry
LADBY illaudably
LAELS albarellos
LAEOT cleaned out
LAGAS float glass
LAGNO allargando
LAHUE Bleak House
LAICS flea circus
LAIES bleariness
sleaziness
LAIEY illatively
LAIGY floatingly
gloatingly
pleadingly
pleasingly
LAIIE alkalinise
alkalinize
LAIIY alkalinity
pliability
LAIOS oleaginous
LAITN flea-bitten
LALNS clean lines
LAOBT Olga Korbut
LAOLR flea collar
LAOTF clean out of
LAPEE altarpiece
LASOE float-stone
LASOY clearstory
LATWL a lead towel
LAUAE illaqueate
LAVDR El Salvador
LAVSD ill-advised
LAYYD bleary-eyed
LBBUD I'll be bound
LBEIG blubbering
clobbering
LBHUE glebe-house
LBHVD ill-behaved
LBIES flabbiness
LBILA Klebsiella
LBLRY globularly
LBNGT fly-by-night
LBRTR elaborator
LBSIE plebiscite
LBYHT I'll buy that
LCAIN glaciation
LCBAD Blackbeard
blackboard
blockboard
LCBED black bread
LCBRY blackberry
LCDAH Black Death
LCDES placidness
LCDTR elucidator
LCEIG blackening
flickering
slackening
LCEOF slacken off
LCEOT blacked out
LCGAD blackguard
LCGNC glycogenic
LCHLS Black Hills
LCHUE blockhouse
LCIES pluckiness
LCIEY electively
LCIIY electivity
flaccidity
LCKIE flick knife
flick-knife
LCLSS glycolysis
LCMGC black magic
LCMRA Black Maria
LCOAE electorate
LCPWR Black Power
black power
LCRNC electronic
LCSDC glycosidic
LCSEP black sheep
LCSIH blacksmith
LCSIT Blackshirt
LCSUP black stump
LCTHR flycatcher
LCTON blackthorn
LCTWR clock tower
LCUAE flocculate
LCUET flocculent
LCUTY old country
LCVLE place value
LCWAE black whale
LCWDW black widow
LDADR glad-hander
LDEBE pledgeable
LDEIG fledgeling
gladdening
LDESD ill-dressed
LDFND ill-defined
LDIGY ploddingly
LDOPR clodhopper
LDSAE Clydesdale
LDSIS cladistics
LEAAT illegal act
LEAIE illegalise
illegalize
ulcerative
LEAIG alienating
LEAIN alienation
allegation
alteration
ulceration
LEAIY illegality
LEAKT bluejacket
LEBRY elderberry
LEEAD sleevehand
LEECL blue pencil
blue-pencil
LEEES fleeceless
sleeveless
LEEVT Blue Velvet
LEIAD blue riband
LEIBN blue ribbon
LEIES sleepiness
sleetiness
LEIGY fleeringly
fleetingly
LEINE allegiance
LEIRY ulteriorly
LEISL Elie Wiesel
LELGT klieg light□
LENIN Blue Ensign
LENTM alternatim
LENTR alternator
LEOIE allegorise
allegorize
LEOLE olde-worlde
LEOLR blue-collar
LEOQE Blue Mosque
LEOSS Blue Horses
LEOSY ulcerously
LEOTE bluebottle
LERIT algebraist
LERTO allegretto
LERUH sleep rough
LESOK alpenstock
LETIE Albert Nile
LETMS olden times
LETOX Albert Roux
LETRY Ellen Terry
LEUDR blue murder
LEWIE bleed white
LFEIG ill feeling
ill-feeling
LFIES fluffiness
LFRDY all-firedly
LFRUE ill fortune
ill-fortune
LFSIG fly-fishing
LFSIK cleft stick
LFTIG ill-fitting
LFUDD ill-founded
LGAIE plagiarise
plagiarize
LGAIG flag-waving
LGAIM plagiarism
LGAIT plagiarist
LGATY flagrantly
LGBLS Elagabalus
LGEOE plaguesome
LGIHY sluggishly
LGLAE flagellate
LGLAT flagellant
LGLON flugelhorn
flügelhorn
LGLTC Glagolitic
LGRHC oligarchic
LGTAH flight path
LGTEK flight deck
LGTES flightless
slightness
LGTLN flight plan
LGTOS flagitious
LGTRW flight crew
LGWYT plug away at
LHBTC alphabetic
LHDCY alpha decay
LHIES Alzheimer's
LHNRD Old Hundred
LHRNA alcheringa
LIAEY ultimately
LIAOL claim a foul
LIAOT flail about
LICAT plainchant
LICMU Plaid Cymru
LICOS alliaceous
LIEAE alliterate
illiterate
LIEAY illiteracy
LIEOS oleiferous

LIGEP flying leap
LIGIH Flying Fish
flying fish
LIGOB flying bomb
LIGOT flying boat
LIGUT flying suit
LIHEL sleigh bell
LIIDS Alcibiades
LIONE fluid ounce
LIPOT Alain Prost
LITCL elliptical
LITES cloistress
LITRD cloistered
LITRR cloisterer
LKAKT flak jacket
LKNOT flaking-out
LKOIG all-knowing
LMANR Plum Warner
LMASF all means of
LMCOS glumaceous
LMEIG glimmering
plummeting
slumbering
LMEOS slumberous
LMFLY blamefully
LMIES clamminess
clumpiness
clumsiness
flimsiness
LMIIH old-maidish
LMMUD slime mould
LMNAY alimentary
elementary
LMNBE eliminable
LMNEU Clemenceau
LMNIA Clementina
LMNIE clementine□
LMNOS flamingoes
LMNTD eliminated
LMNTR eliminator
LMOAT flamboyant
LMPOF flameproof
LMTHD ill-matched
LMUBY glamour boy
LMXDP all mixed up
LNABY Cluny Abbey
LNAIL Glyn Daniel
LNAIN elongation
plantation
LNAKR Alan Parker
LNALY blind alley
LNATY flan pastry
LNCLY clinically
LNCOE Glenn Close
LNDUK blind drunk
LNEIE slenderise
LNEIG blundering
plundering
LNENR Alan Lerner
LNEOS slanderous
LNETY plangently
LNEVR glance over
LNGAS flint glass
LNGES blind guess
LNHAT flint-heart
LNHRM flinch from
LNIES clinginess
flintiness
slanginess
LNIGY glancingly
slantingly
LNIHY clannishly
LNMDT fling mud at
sling mud at
LNMNE blancmange
LNMTR clinometer
planimeter
LNODE Glen Hoddle
LNOFT sling off at
LNOHS Glenrothes
LNOLN Llangollen
LNPNC blind panic
LNROE Alanbrooke
LNSIE Flintshire
LNSOE clingstone
LNTNC planktonic
LNTRA planetaria
LNTRD ill-natured
LNTUT blind trust
LNUIG Alan Turing
LNUTE blanquette
LNVRE blank verse
LNWAG slang-whang
LNWMN clanswoman
LNYAG ylang-ylang
LOAIN allocation
LOALD also called
LOAOS gliomatous
LOARS Allosaurus
LOATC pleonastic
LOBAD floorboard
LOCMN klootchmen
LOCOH floorcloth
LOCUT blood count
LODNR blood donor
LODYD almond-eyed
LOEHR altogether
LOEIG all-obeying
LOETC pleonectic
LOFUE blood fluke
LOHLC oleophilic
LOHUD bloodhound
LOIAE fluoridate
fluorinate
LOIES bloodiness
gloominess
LOIIE fluoridise
fluoridize
LOLGT floodlight
LOOIE alcoholise
alcoholize
LOOIM alcoholism
LOQIN Algonquian
LORPC allotropic
LORPY oleography
LOSAN bloodstain
LOSOE bloodstone
LOSOK bloodstock
LOTAI altostrati
LOTDO allotted to
LOTIL almost kill
LOTUE allow to use
LOUIN illocution
LOUUI altocumuli
LOYAY bloody Mary
LPATY flippantly
LPCBE slip a cable
LPEET all-present
LPEIY slipperily
LPEOT clapped-out
LPIES floppiness
slippiness
sloppiness
LPODF clap hold of
LPPEL slap-up meal
LPRET pluperfect
LPROE all-purpose
LPSIG flyposting
LPTEM slipstream
LPTHR flypitcher
LPYIK floppy disk
LPYSN clap eyes on
LQETY eloquently
LQIES cliquiness
LQIKY fly quickly
LRAIN flirtation
LRBNA floribunda
LRBOM Clare Bloom
LRCOS flory cross
oleraceous
LRDES floridness
LRDOL Alfred Jodl
LRDYR Alfred Ayer
LRFCE ultrafiche
LRFIG glorifying
LRGBE Clark Gable
LRIGY alarmingly
flirtingly
LRITC altruistic
LRLGA florilegia
LRNIE florentine□
LROSY gloriously
LRPOY plerophory
LRSAK flare stack
LRSET florescent
LRSNC ultrasonic
LRSOT Clare Short
LRSOY clerestory
LRSUD ultrasound
LRUDR all-rounder
LRVRS ultra vires
LSADS glissandos
LSAIT glossarist
LSARD ill-starred
LSEIG blistering
blustering
glistening
plastering
LSEIN Glaswegian
LSFBE glass fibre
LSFCD glass-faced
LSFLY blissfully
LSFOD flash flood
LSHMR blasphemer
LSHRY flash Harry
LSHUE glasshouse
LSIAE elasticate
LSIES flashiness
fleshiness
glassiness
glossiness
LSIGY blushingly
LSIID classified
LSIIE classicise
classicize
elasticise
elasticize
plasticise
plasticize
LSIIG almsgiving
alms-giving
LSIIM classicism
LSIIT classicist
LSIIY elasticity
plasticity
LSKIE clasp knife
LSLGT flashlight
LSOAR plesiosaur
LSODY close of day
LSOEM plasmodesm
LSOIG blossoming
LSOIL El Escorial
LSOIM plasmodium
LSOKP All Shook Up
LSOOE plasmosome
LSOYE plasmolyse
plasmolyze
LSPIT flash point
LSRDA clostridia
LSRNS close ranks
LSSAE close shave
LSTIG close thing
LSWUD flesh wound
LTAIG flat racing
LTCAY plutocracy
LTEAD platteland
LTEAE all the rage
all the same
LTEAI glitterati
LTEEM fly the beam
LTEES blitheness
LTEET all the best
LTEIE all the time
LTEIG blathering
blethering
blithering
flattening
flattering
fluttering
glittering
LTENY slatternly
LTEOE all the more

Words marked □ can also be spelled with an initial capital letter

blithesome
LTEOT blotted out
flatten out
LTEPN clothe upon
LTERD cloth-eared
LTETD ill-treated
LTFAD plot of land
LTFLY slothfully
LTGAS plate glass
LTIGY plottingly
LTIHY sluttishly
LTITR elutriator
LTKIG blitzkrieg
LTLNE flatulence
LTLNY flatulency
LTMLW all-time low
LTOIE gluttonise
gluttonize
LTOIH gluttonish
LTOOS gluttonous
LTOTD flat-footed
LTPIG fly-tipping
LTPSS platypuses
LTRUH all through
LTUOR plat du jour
LUATR almucantar
LUBRT cloudburst
LUDLS fleur-de-lis
fleur-de-lys
LUEET allurement
LUEIE albumenize
LUEIZ Clausewitz
LUETR Gloucester
LUFCS Klaus Fuchs
LUHAK plough back
LUHBE ploughable
LUHIE ploughwise
LUHNO plough into
LUIAE illuminate
LUIAI illuminati
LUIAT illuminant
LUIES cloudiness
LUIEY allusively
illusively
LUIGY alluringly
floutingly
LUIHD flourished
LUIIE albuminise
albuminize
LUIOY plauditory
LUOIE glauconite
LUTAE illustrate
LVCOD clavichord
LVCOS olivaceous
LVGRH Cleve-Garth
LVHTH clove hitch
LVJMS Clive James
LVLOD Clive Lloyd
LVNHY eleventhly
LVNLS eleven-plus
LVNOF cloven hoof
LVRED Oliver Reed
LVREF cloverleaf
LVRES cleverness
LVRIK clever dick
LVSET flavescent
LVUIG flavouring
LWAMR claw hammer
LWATD slow-gaited
LWESY flawlessly
LWIHY clownishly
LWITD slow-witted
LWLWY flow slowly
LWOIG slow-moving
LWOIN slow-motion
LWRED flower-head
LWRES flowerless
LWYLW blow-by-blow
LXNES alexanders
LXNRA Alexandria
LYAIN claymation
LYCIG play-acting
LYCOL playschool
LYDON played-down
LYELW playfellow
LYHLY allycholly
LYHNH play a hunch
LYIEN clay pigeon
LYOSM play possum
LYOTO play host to
LYRAT play truant
LYRCS play tricks
LYRGT playwright
LYRTR play-writer
LYRUD play around
playground
LYUAT all you want
MAAIE imparadise
MAEET impalement
MAEIL immaterial
MAHTC empathetic
MAIES smeariness
MAIIM ommatidium
MAIIY amiability
MAINE impatience
MAKET embankment
MAKPN embark upon
MAMET embalmment
MAOAY Emma Bovary
MAPBE impalpable
MAPBY impalpably
MARET impairment
MASBE impassable
MASBY impassably
impassibly
MASDR ambassador
MATBE impartible
MATBY impartibly
MATET impartment
MAUAE immaculate
MAUAY immaculacy
MAUEY immaturely
MAUIY immaturity
MCAIG emaciating
MCAIN emaciation
MDIES smudginess
MEAIE imperative
MECBE impeccable
MECBY impeccably
MEIET impediment
impenitent
MEIIY imbecility
MEILY imperially
MELFR umbellifer
MEOIL immemorial
MEOLS Empedocles
MEOSS ampelopses
MESDN immersed in
MESNL impersonal
METEO Umberto Eco
METLR Emmentaler
MEVOS impervious
MGAIN emigration
MGAOD amygdaloid
MGNBE imaginable
MGNBY imaginably
MHBAH amphibrach
MHBLC amphibolic
MHBOS amphibious
MHMCR amphimacer
MHMXS amphimixis
MHSMC emphysemic
MHTRC amphoteric
MHTYN Amphitryon
MIAET ambivalent
MICBE immiscible
MICET omniscient
MIEIE immiserise
immiserize
MIETY imminently
MIEUL ambisexual
MIHES impishness
MIIAE umbilicate
MIIIM empiricism
MIIIT empiricist
MIOET omnipotent
MIOOS omnivorous
MISIH Emmit Smith
MITRD embittered
MJHSN Amy Johnson
MKAAM smoke alarm
MKDID smoke-dried
MKHUE smokehouse
MKSAK smokestack
MLAAE amalgamate
MLCBE implacable
MLCBY implacably
MLCTD implicated
MLCTY implicitly
MLFRH Ampleforth
MLGOP small group
MLHUS small hours
MLIES smelliness
MLIIR emulsifier
MLIUE a multitude
MLMNS emoluments
implements
MLMTC emblematic
MLNEI emalangeni
MLOAE ameliorate
MLPEE small piece
MLPIT small print
MLRTR implorator
MLSAE small-scale
MLYBE employable
MLYDS employed as
MLYDY employed by
MLYET employment
MMNAO a moment ago
MNAIN emendation
MNAOY emendatory
MNESS amanuenses
amanuensis
MNFED a minefield
MNGOP amino group
MNIAE emancipate
MNRHA amenorrhea
MOAIN immolation
MOAIY immorality
MOCUE embouchure
MOEAE immoderate
MOEAY immoderacy
MOEIG empowering
MOEIH impoverish
MOEPN impose upon
MOETY immodestly
impotently
MOHAF smooth calf
MOHES smoothness
MOHVR smooth over
MOIET embodiment
MOIEY impolitely
MOIGY imposingly
MOIIE immobilise
immobilize
MOIIN imposition
MOIIY immobility
MONAE impoundage
MONIG impounding
MOOIE immobolize
MOSBE impossible
MOTLY immortally
MOTNE importance
MOTNR importuner
MOTNY importancy
MRAEK smart aleck
MRBBE improbable
MRBBY improbably
MRDNE imprudence
MREET amercement
MRELE à merveille
MRETY emergently
MRGAE impregnate
MRGIS embroglios
imbroglios
MRGOS umbrageous
MRHRF Omar Sharif
MRIAE emarginate
MRIES smarminess
MRIEY embroidery
MRIGY smirkingly
MRMTR imprimatur

MRNIG imprinting
MRNIN Amerindian
MROOY embryology
MRPRY improperly
MRSIE impressive
MRSIN impression
MRSMA Amarasimha
MRSND imprisoned
MRSRO impresario
MRVBE improvable
MRVBY improvably
MRVSD improvised
MRVSR improviser
MSUAE emasculate
MTCLY emetically
MTEEN smithereen
MTEIG smattering
smothering
MTIES smuttiness
MTSAE empty space
MTUIH amateurish
MTUIM amateurism
MUAIN ambulation
amputation
imputation
MUAOY ambulatory
MUCDS ambuscados
MUEES impureness
MUEOY immune body
MUETY impudently
MUIIN ammunition
MUIIS impurities
MUNBE impugnable
MUNET impugnment
MUOOY immunology
MUSAT impuissant
MUTWD amount owed
MZNIE Amazon-like
NAACD unbalanced
NAAID unsalaried
NAAIE one at a time
unparadise
NAAIN inhalation
NAAIY incapacity
NAALL in parallel
NAASA Andaman Sea
NABET enjambment
NACFL unwatchful
NACIA Antarctica
NACIG unmatching
NACIN infarction
NACIY unsanctify
NADNY one and only
unmaidenly
NADOE unhandsome
NADSE incandesce
NADUS ins and outs
NAEBE untameable
NAEBY untameably
NAEEL Anna Sewell
NAEES innateness
unsafeness
NAEET encasement
engagement
NAEFR uncared-for
NAEIG unwavering
NAELD unlabelled
unravelled
NAENY in name only
NAETD untalented
NAFLY unlawfully
unmanfully
NAGBE intangible
NAGBY intangibly
NAGDY enlargedly
NAGIE ensanguine
NAGIG unlaughing
NAGRF in danger of
NAHET encashment
NAHMD unfathomed
NAHRD unfathered
NAIAE insalivate
invaginate
invalidate
NAIAT inhabitant
NAIAY insanitary
unsanitary
NAIBE insatiable
invariable
unvariable
NAIBY insatiably
invariably
NAIES sneakiness
uneasiness
unwariness
NAIGY engagingly
sneakingly
NAIHY sneakishly
NAIID unratified
NAIIG inhabiting
NAIIR unfamiliar
NAIIY invalidity
NAILY uniaxially
NAITC annalistic
NALBE infallible
unfallible
NALBY infallibly
NALET entailment
NALHT and all that
NALWD unhallowed
NAMNC enharmonic
NANRD unmannered
NANRY unmannerly
NAOHR one another
NAOIE antagonise
antagonize
infamonise
infamonize
NAOIM antagonism
NAOIT antagonist
NAOOR in bad odour
NAORF in favour of
NAOSY infamously
NAPET encampment
NAPRD unhampered
NARES unfairness
NARSN engarrison
NASAE in bad shape
NASBE unpassable
NATFL unfaithful
NATIG a near thing
unearthing
NATND unfastened
NATNS andantinos
NATOS incautious
NATRD enraptured
NATRS in raptures
NATSE in bad taste
NAUAY insalutary
NAUBE invaluable
NAUBY invaluably
NAUIE andalusite
NAUIN Andalusian
NAUTD infatuated
NAYIE unladylike
NBDOD in a bad mood
NBERE knobkerrie
NBETA in absentia
NBEVD unobserved
NBIGD unabridged
NBIGY snubbingly
NBIHY snobbishly
NBITD inebriated
NBOVD unabsolved
NBPIE anabaptise
anabaptize
NBPIM Anabaptism
NBPIT Anabaptist
NBYNE in abeyance
NCABE unscramble
NCAIN on occasion
NCAOT knock about
knockabout
NCBAD unscabbard
NCEOT knocked out
NCEUE enschedule
on schedule
NCIAE inactivate
NCIEY inactively
NCIIY inactivity
NCITD unscripted
NCKAK knick-knack
NCKED knock-kneed
NCLTA anacolutha
NCLTR inoculator
NCMRL unicameral
NCNMC uneconomic
NCOAE anecdotage
NCOIT anecdotist
NCOLD unschooled
NCUAE inaccurate
NCUAY inaccuracy
NCUID unoccupied
NCWRT knackwurst
knockwurst
NDAIM unidealism
NDCBE ineducable
NDCTD uneducated
NDFIG unedifying
NDIIN in addition
NDLTN Enid Blyton
NDQAE inadequate
NDQAY inadequacy
NEADD unheralded
unregarded
unrewarded
NEADF in regard of
NEADO in regard to
NEAFF on behalf of
NEAIG undecaying
NEAIN annexation
indexation
NEAIY inveracity
NEAKD unremarked
NEALD unrecalled
NEBED interbreed
NEBID underbuild
NEBIG enfeebling
inner being
NEBLY underbelly
NEBRE inselberge
NEBUH underbrush
NECAN interchain
NECAS underclass
NECDR interceder
NECET undercrest
NECFL unmerciful
NECIF undercliff
NECOS intercross
NECOT undercroft
NECUE interclude
NECVR under cover
undercover
NECYE Inverclyde
NEDAN underdrain
NEDAY incendiary
NEDBE unbendable
unreadable
NEDDO intended to
NEDDY intendedly
NEDES underdress
NEDIE underdrive
NEEAE ingenerate
intemerate
inveterate
NEEDD undefended
NEEET antecedent
NEEGH knee-length
NEELD unrevealed
NEEMD unredeemed
NEEOS ungenerous
NEEOT sneezewort
NEERD undeterred
NEETD interested
undefeated
undetected
NEETY indecently
inherently
NEEVD undeceived
undeserved
unreserved
NEEVR undeserver

NEFLS Angel Falls
NEFRN interferon
NEFRR interferer
NEGAE intergrade
underglaze
NEGBE unwedgable
NEGIG inveigling
unweighing
NEHLC encephalic
NEHLN encephalon
enkephalin
NEHRD untethered
NEHXA Enver Hoxha
NEIAE indelicate
ingeminate
inseminate
NEIAY indelicacy
NEIBE undeniable
unreliable
NEIBY undeniably
unreliably
NEIET enregiment
NEIGY incedingly
sneeringly
unseeingly
NEIID unverified
NEIIE indecisive
indefinite
unfeminine
NEIIN indecision
NEIIS in deliciis
NEIIY infelicity
NEIND undesigned
NEIRO inferior to
NEIRX inheritrix
NEIRY anteriorly
inferiorly
interiorly
NEITR enregister
NEIVD unrelieved
NEIVR unbeliever
NEKND unreckoned
NELAE interleave
underlease
NELBE unhealable
untellable
NELIE in real life
NELIG underlying
NELNN underlinen
NELPR interloper
NELRD undeclared
NELWD unmellowed
NELZD unrealized
NEMND undermined
NEMNR underminer
NEMRY intermarry
NEMZI intermezzi
NEMZO intermezzo
NENAH underneath
NENET internment
NENLY infernally
internally
NENWY once in a way
NEOAL once for all
NEODD unrecorded
NEOEN Anne Boleyn
NEOIG unbecoming
NEOIM In Memoriam
in memoriam
NEOMD unreformed
NEOOS indecorous
NEOVD unresolved
NEOYF in memory of
NEPAE interphase
NEPAT interplant
underplant
NEPED interplead
NEPIE enterprise
underprice
NEPNS underpants
NEPRD untempered
NEPRY in jeopardy
NEPSA Enver Pasha
NEPSD interposed
NEQOE underquote
NERBE inferrable
unbearable
NERBY unbearably
NERET endearment
NERGA interregna
NERGS interreges
NERIG unwearying
NERLY integrally
NERNE Anne Brontë
NERTD integrated
NESAD understand
NESAE interspace
interstate
understate
NESBE insensible
unfeasible
NESBY insensibly
unsensibly
NESDN unversed in
NESED underspend
NESEE under siege
NESER understeer
NESIE interstice
NESIT underskirt
NESND unlessoned
unreasoned
unseasoned
NESNM in personam
NESNY incessancy
NESOD understood
NESOE underscore
NESOT undershoot
NESUG underslung
NESUY understudy
NESXD undersexed
NESZD undersized
NETBE ingestible
injectable
unbeatable
NETDO indebted to
NETDY invertedly
NETES intentness
NETET insentient
investment
NETIE intertwine
NETIG unsettling
NETIO intertrigo
NETIT intertwist
NETKR undertaker
NETNL intestinal
NETNS intestines
NETOS infectious
intentions
NETRD unfettered
unlettered
NEUBN interurban
NEUET integument
NEUEY insecurely
NEUIG unrecuring
NEUIY insecurity
NEUNE in sequence
NEURD unrequired
NEUTD unrequited
NEVLE inlet valve
intervolve
undervalue
NEVND unleavened
NEVNR intervener
NEVVS inter vivos
NEWAE interweave
NEWAS under wraps
NEWEM underwhelm
NEWIE underwrite
NEWMN inner woman
NEWRD underwired
underworld
NEWTR underwater
NEYED in very deed
NFBOK knife block
NFEGD knife-edged
NFETD unaffected
NFIAY inefficacy
NFIES sniffiness
NFIGY sniffingly
NFIIL unofficial
NFLAE unifoliate
NFOOS uniflorous
NFPET knife pleat
NFRIY uniformity
NFSIN in a fashion
NGAIE enigmatise
enigmatize
NGEIG sniggering
NGJNS Inigo Jones
NGTOD knighthood
NHAET on the alert
NHAEY inchoately
NHAIE anthracite
inchoative
NHAIN inchoation
NHALD enthralled
NHAVL on the anvil
NHBAK in the black
NHBAN on the brain
NHBIK on the blink
NHBNH on the bench
NHBOD in the blood
NHBOK on the block
NHBRO on the buroo
NHCAR in the chair
NHCEP on the cheap
NHCER in the clear
NHCLD unshackled
NHCOS on the cross
NHCRS on the cards
NHDTF on the dot of
NHEDD unshielded
NHEEF on the eve of
NHEET in the event
NHFEH in the flesh
NHFIZ on the fritz
NHFNE on the fence
NHHUE on the house
NHIIG unchaining
NHION on their own
NHITN unchristen
NHIWY in their way
NHKBE unshakable
NHKBY unshakably
NHLCS anthelices
NHLDS enchiladas
NHLGT in the light
NHLOE on the loose
NHLRH in the lurch
NHLVL on the level
NHMDT in the midst
NHMNY in the money
on the money
NHNEY in chancery
NHNFL unthankful
NHNIG enchanting
unchanging
unthinking
NHODD enshrouded
NHOIE enthronise
enthronize
NHOOD anthropoid
NHOTR on the outer
NHPES in the press
NHPOE anthophore
NHPOL on the prowl
NHPYF in the pay of
NHQIT on the quiet
NHRCS on the rocks
NHRDA antheridia
NHREF in charge of
NHRES anchorless
NHRGT in the right
NHRPS on the ropes
NHRTC anchoritic
NHSAE in the shade
on the slate
NHSAM enthusiasm
NHSAT enthusiast
on the slant
NHSEF on the shelf
NHSIY unchastity

NHSOS in the shops
NHSUP on the stump
NHTLS on the tiles
NHTPS on the tapis
NHWGN on the wagon
NHWNS in the wings
NHWOE on the whole
NHWOG in the wrong
NHWRD in the world
NHWTH on the watch
NHWYF in the way of
NHWYO on the way to
NHYNH inch by inch
NIAEO intimate to
NIAEY intimately
NIAIE incitative
indicative
NIAIN incitation
indication
intimation
invitation
NIALD unrivalled
NIAOY indicatory
NIARY in disarray
NIATR antimatter
NIBRD untimbered
NICBE invincible
NICBY invincibly
NICEE indiscrete
NICET indiscreet
NICIG encircling
NICUE encincture
NIDES unkindness
NIDRD unhindered
NIEAE incinerate
NIEAT inside part
NIEBE enticeable
untireable
NIEEE antivenene
NIEES entireness
unlikeness
unripeness
unwiseness
NIEET enticement
incitement
NIEIE anti-semite
indigenise
indigenize
NIEIG enlivening
NIEIH in line with
NIEIY infidelity
NIEOM engine room
NIEOS indigenous
NIESD unlicensed
NIESS antisepsis
NIETC antiseptic
NIETD indigested
undirected
NIETL incidental
NIETY indigently
indirectly
NIEUS antiserums
NIEVR invite over
NIGAE in disgrace
NIGIE in disguise
NIHET enrichment
NIHFL insightful
NIHIG infighting
in-fighting
NIHIT Antichrist
NIHNL antiphonal
NIHSS antitheses
antithesis
NIHTC antithetic
NIIAE annihilate
anticipate
infinitate
intimidate
invigilate
NIIES untidiness
NIIEY incisively
infinitely
NIIGY enticingly
incitingly
invitingly
NIIHD unfinished
NIIIE infinitive
inhibitive
NIIIG inhibiting
NIIIN inhibition
NIIIY incivility
insipidity
uncivility
NIINE incipience
NIINY incipiency
NIIOY inhibitory
NIISS antibiosis
NIITC antibiotic
NIIUE infinitude
NIIUL individual
NIKBE unsinkable
NILBE inviolable
NILBY inviolably
NILDO entitled to
NILIG unyielding
NILIY unwieldily
NILMX anticlimax
NILNL anticlinal
NIMYD undismayed
NINAS Indian Wars
NINEL Indian meal
NINIE Indian file
NINLB Indian club
NINWD unsinnowed
NIOAE invigorate
NIODR in disorder
NIOIE antimonide
NIOIL antisocial
NIOIN antinomian
NIPPR India paper
NIPSD indisposed
NIPTD undisputed
NIREE antifreeze
NIRTN anti-proton
NISBE unmissable
NISDY unbiasedly
NISEM angiosperm
NITAE infiltrate
NITBE indictable
NITEF in virtue of
NITES in distress
NITET anointment
enlistment
indictment
NITNE insistence
NITNT indistinct
NITNY insistency
NITRC unhistoric
NITRS in pictures
NITTC antistatic
NIUAE infibulate
NIUGD undivulged
NIUTD antiquated
insinuated
NIUTR insinuator
NKRVR Snake River
NLAAT unpleasant
NLBTR ankle-biter
NLCIE inflective
NLCIN inflection
infliction
NLDBE includable
includible
NLDDN included in
NLDOT include out
NLECD influenced
NLECR influencer
NLECS influences
NLEIG unsleeping
NLEZL influenzal
NLFUS on all fours
NLGBE ineligible
NLGBY ineligibly
NLGCL analogical
NLGIG unflagging
NLGNE inelegance
NLHNS on all hands
NLIAR en plein air
NLIIH Anglo-Irish
NLINE in alliance
NLITR uncloister
NLMBE unblamable
NLMNY inclemency
NLNDO inclined to
NLNIG unblinking
NLNUL unilingual
NLPOE anglophobe□
anglophone□
NLPRS in all parts
NLRIH angler fish
NLRMS Uncle Remus
NLROS inglorious
NLSDS on all sides
NLSIG unblushing
NLSMN Englishman
NLSXN Anglo-Saxon
NLTBE inflatable
NLTCL analytical
NLTRL unilateral
NLUHD unploughed
NLVNA Uncle Vanya
NLXBE inflexible
NLXBY inflexibly
NMAET enemy agent
NMARD unimpaired
NMAUE in a measure
NMCLY inimically
NMDET animadvert
NMETC anamnestic
NMGND unimagined
NMHTC unemphatic
NMLAK animal park
NMLAM Animal Farm
NMLIE animal life
NMLIG enamelling
NMLUA animalcula
NMLUE animalcule
NMLYD unemployed
NMMTR anemometer
NMNAD one-man band
NMNBE unamenable
NMRCN un-American
NMRDS enamorados
NMRTR enumerator
NMRTS inamoratas
inamoratos
NMRVD unimproved
NMSIS onomastics
NMTBE inimitable
NMTBY inimitably
NMTDY animatedly
NNAIN inundation
NNEDD unintended
NNEET in any event
NNETD unindebted
uninfected
NNGTY unknightly
NNIBE enunciable
unenviable
NNIBY unenviably
NNIGY unendingly
NNIIG uninviting
NNITR enunciator
NNLSD unenclosed
NNOCD unenforced
NNOMD uninformed
NNOVD uninvolved
NNPEE in one piece
NNPRD uninspired
NNSAE on one's game
NNSAK on one's mark
NNSES on one's legs
NNSET on one's feet
NNSID on one's mind
NNSIE in one's time
NNSOD in ones road
NNSOS on one's toes
NNSUN in one's turn
NNSUS in one's cups
NNWBE unknowable
NNWRD unanswered
NOAAR one of a pair

Words marked □ can also be spelled with an initial capital letter

NOADY untowardly
NOAID one of a kind
NOAIE innovative
NOAIN annotation
innovation
insolation
intonation
invocation
on location
NOAIY unmorality
NOAOY innovatory
invocatory
NOATC unromantic
NOBET entombment
NOBOD in hot blood
NOCAT insouciant
NOCDY enforcedly
unforcedly
NOCPC endoscopic
NODAT in good part
NODIE in good time
NODIK in good nick
NODLN Anton Dolin
NODOM in good form
NODRM in good trim
NOEAT intolerant
NOEBY unmoveably
NOEEN unforeseen
NOEET incoherent
NOEFR unhoped-for
NOEHR untogether
NOEIG uncovering
NOEIH in love with
NOEIN Indonesian
NOELE anyone else
NOEND ungoverned
NOEOS endogenous
NOEOT in some sort
NOETD unforested
NOETF innocent of
NOETY indolently
innocently
insolently
NOFIT in conflict
NOFND unconfined
NOGVN unforgiven❑
NOHLA endothelia
NOHTC endophytic
NOIAE innominate
intoxicate
NOIAT intoxicant
NOIBE unsociable
NOIBY unsociably
NOIES snootiness
unholiness
NOIEY unpolitely
NOIGY annoyingly
intoningly
unlovingly
NOIHD unpolished
NOIID unmodified
NOILY unsocially
NOKBE unlockable
unworkable
NOLTD unpolluted
NOMDF informed of
NOMLY informally
NOMNO on commando
NOMNS endowments
NOMNY uncommonly
NONTD unbonneted
NONTE Antoinette
NONTS incognitos
NOOIG unbosoming
NOOII anno Domini❑
NOOIT oncologist
NOOOY entomology
NOORD uncoloured
unhonoured
NOORF in honour of
NOPEE incomplete
NOPIG uncoupling
NORAE in-your-face
NOREY insobriety
NORGD encouraged
NORIE on your bike
NORIG in mourning
NORNC endocrinic
NORNL endocrinal
NOSAT inconstant
unconstant
NOSBE unpossible
NOSLD unhouseled
NOSMD unconsumed
NOSOT endorse out
NOSOY end of story
NOTAT in contrast
NOTDY unwontedly
NOTFR en route for
NOTIE uncontrite
NOTIY unworthily
NOTYF unworthy of
NOUIN involution
NOURL involucral
NOVBE unsolvable
NOVBY insolvably
NOVDN involved in
NOVNY insolvency
NOWTR in hot water
NOYOS antonymous
NOZLD unhouzzled
NPAET unapparent
NPCFC unspecific
NPCIG inspecting
NPCIN inspection
NPETC anapaestic
NPIES snappiness
NPIGY snappingly
NPIHY snappishly
NPIUE inaptitude
ineptitude
NPNOK an open book
NPNOT snap into it
NPOIE inapposite
NPOUT end-product
NPRBE inoperable
NPRBY inoperably
NPRGN snapdragon
NPRIH on a par with
NPRVD unapproved
NPRVL on approval
NPSAE inspissate
NQAIY inequality
NQALD unequalled
NQEES uniqueness
NQIOS iniquitous
NQIPD unequipped
NRAEY inurbanely
NRAGD unarranged
NRAHD unbroached
NRAHR encroacher
NRAIE enervative
uncreative
NRAIG enervating
entreating
increasing
NRAIN enervation
NRAIS entreaties
NRAIY inurbanity
NRAUE untreasure
NRBBE unbribable
NRBIK André Brink
NRCFL ungraceful
NRCIE in practice
NRCIG unfrocking
NRCIN infraction
NRCOS ungracious
NRDBE incredible
NRDBY incredibly
NRDCD introduced
NRDET ingredient
NRDIG ungrudging
NRDSS intradoses
NREDD unfriended
NREDY unfriendly
NREIG inbreeding
NREIM androecium
NRFLY unartfully
NRFND unprofaned
NRGAT intriguant
unpregnant
NRGES in progress
NRGIG intriguing
NRGNE intrigante
NRGNL unoriginal
NRHCL anarchical
NRHDX unorthodox
NRIAE inordinate
NRIAY in ordinary
NRIFL unfruitful
NRIGY snarlingly
snortingly
unerringly
NRIIG energizing
in training
NRITC inartistic
NRKNY unbrokenly
NRLFC unprolific
NRMCE Andromache
NRMQE Andromaque
NRMRL intramural
NRMRS intra muros
NRMTC undramatic
NRMTD unprompted
NRNCS Andronicus
NRNHD entrenched
NRNIE en principe
NRNIG entrancing
NROSY enormously
NRPDY intrepidly
NRPET entrapment
NRPRD unprepared
NRPRY unproperly
NRQET infrequent
NRREY introrsely
NRSAE incrassate
NRSBY inerasably
inerasibly
NRSET introspect
NRSFL untrustful
NRSIG engrossing
untrusting
NRSIN ingression
NRSNC infrasonic
NRSUD infrasound
NRTAE ingratiate
NRTCL uncritical
NRTFL ungrateful
untruthful
NRUBE unarguable
NRUBY unarguably
NRUDD ungrounded
NRULD untroubled
NRVBE unprovable
NRVKD unprovoked
NRVRS intra vires
NRVTM intra vitam
NRWEL Andrew Neil
NRZBE unprizable
NSAIS Anastasius
NSDDY one-sidedly
NSEFR unasked-for
NSFLY unusefully
NSFRH and so forth
NSIGY gnashingly
NSIIE Gnosticise
Gnosticize
NSIIM Gnosticism
NSITD unassisted
NSNLY unisonally
NSOOE anastomose
NSOTD unescorted
NSRPE anastrophe
NSUAE inosculate
NSUHS in as much as
inasmuch as
NSUIG unassuming
NTAHD unattached
NTAIE initialise
initialize
initiative
NTAIG initiating

NTAIM initialism
NTAIN initiation
NTAIY unsteadily
NTAKD unattacked
NTAOY initiatory
NTASN Knut Hamsun
NTDES unitedness
NTDSI Anita Desai
NTEDD unattended
NTEET and the rest
NTEGH in strength
NTEIE and the like
NTEMD unstreamed
NTETD unattested
NTGTR instigator
NTIES knottiness
snottiness
NTIKD unit-linked
NTLET instalment
instilment
NTLIG installing
instilling
NTMCL anatomical
NTMTC Instamatic®
NTNIG unstinting
NTODR unitholder
NTOIY unctuosity
NTOSY unctuously
NTRFR in store for
NTRIG unstirring
NTTHS in stitches
NTTTN Anatotitan
NTTTR instituter
institutor
NTUET instrument
NTUTD instructed
NTUTR instructor
NUAEY inhumanely
undulately
NUAIE incubative
NUAIG insulating
undulating
NUAIN incubation
inhumation
insulation
undulation
NUAIY angularity
annularity
inhumanity
insularity
NUAOY undulatory
NUBNY incumbency
NUBRD encumbered
unnumbered
NUCAE annunciate
NUCIE injunctive
NUCIN injunction
NUCTR inculcator
NUCUL unpunctual
NUDIH endued with
NUEAE innumerate
NUEAY innumeracy
NUEES unsureness
NUEET inducement
NUEIH in tune with
NUEUE inquietude
NUFAE insufflate
NUFET engulfment
NUGNE indulgence
insurgence
NUGNY insurgency
NUIES unruliness
NUIGY enduringly
NUIHD unpunished
NUIID unpurified
NUITD infuriated
NULIW in full view
NULTD unqualited
NUNBE unburnable
NUNOS innuendoes
NUPBE inculpable
NUPBY inculpably
NUPNE in suspense
NUPTD inculpated
NURBE incurrable
NUSIN in question
NUSTR inquisitor
NUTBE unsuitable
NUTBY unsuitably
NUTES unjustness
NUTET insultment
NUTIL industrial
NUTND unbuttoned
NUTNE inductance
NUTRD uncultured
NUUAE inaugurate
NUVYD unsurveyed
NUYIE injury time
NUYML aneurysmal
NVCLY univocally
NVDNE in evidence
NVIIG unavailing
NVLIG snivelling
NVLNE univalence
NVLNY univalency
NVNAK uneven walk
NVNES unevenness
NVNFL uneventful
NVRIY university
NVRWY in every way
NVTBE inevitable
NVTBY inevitably
NWAAL and what all
NWESN a new person
NWETR know better
NWIHR anywhither
NWLKS snowflakes
NWLUH snowplough
NWLWR snowblower
NWMNS in two minds
NWRAK answer back
NWRBE answerable
NWRBY answerably
NWRIG unswerving
NWTCS in two ticks
NWYBE unswayable
NXCIG unexacting
NXCTD unexecuted
NXELD unexcelled
NXESF in excess of
NXETD unexpected
NXETY inexpertly
NXGRS Anaxagoras
NXHNE in exchange
NXIBY inexpiably
NXIIG unexciting
NXLCT inexplicit
NXLDD unexploded
NXLRD unexplored
NXMLD unexampled
NXMNS Anaximenes
NXRBE inexorable
NXRBY inexorably
NXRMS in extremis
NYAHL Andy Warhol
NYINC unhygienic
NYLCL encyclical
NYOAR ankylosaur
NYOOY enzymology
NYPTY in sympathy
NYRIE Andy Irvine
NYWWY in my own way
OAAIY to capacity
OAAOM sonata form
OAASN Joy Adamson
OABQE Mozambique
OABRH royal burgh
OABRY loganberry
OACEL bon accueil
OACIE monarchise
monarchize
OACIM monarchism
OACIT monarchist
OACLY mosaically
OACOT Nouakchott
OACRS vocal cords
OACTA Nova Scotia
OADAL top and tail
OADED Howards End
OADES Rob Andrews
Roy Andrews
OADHN now and then
OADHP cowardship
OADIH go hard with
OADOE dog and bone
OADOS monandrous
Ronald Ross
OADYE Conan Doyle
OAEOD for a second
OAEQE Romanesque
OAFAE solar flare
OAFBE moral fibre
OAFLY womanfully
OAFUH royal flush
OAGAS cor anglais
OAGAU Nova Iguacu
OAGLS Los Angeles
OAHLC notaphilic
OAHNE not a chance
OAHTR woman-hater
OAIAL to cap it all
OAIHY womanishly
OAIIE rosaniline
volatilise
volatilize
OAIIG moralizing
royal icing
vocalizing
womanizing
OAIIY movability
notability
volatility
OAILS tomatillos
OAILY notarially
OAIND non-aligned
OAINE covariance
OAINL notational
vocational
OAIOS foraminous
OAITC moralistic
OAJLY royal jelly
OAKUT go bankrupt
OALHT for all that
OALIE for all time
OALWD not allowed
OAMNH solar month
OANAE domain name
OANBS coram nobis
OAODL homaloidal
OAODR for a wonder
OAOET for a moment
OAOGD woman of God
OAOHR not another
OAOIM moratorium
OAOTS Pocahontas
OAPIT focal point
OAPTT bon appetit
OAPWR total power
OARDO local radio
OASAD No Man's Land
OASAE coral snake
OASNE moral sense
OATOB cobalt bomb
OAUAY vocabulary
OAVLE no par value
OAYHP notaryship
OAYIH go easy with
OAYLB Rotary Club
OBAIG forbearing
OBAMN Don Bradman
OBCCD sorbic acid
OBCLE corbiculae
OBDES morbidness
OBDIG forbidding
OBEAK double back
double-bank
double-park
Double Talk
double talk
double-talk
OBEAS double bass
OBEES sombreness

OBEHN double chin
OBEID double bind
double-gild
OBEIE double time
OBEIL double bill
OBELT double flat
OBEMN gombeen-man
OBEOD double bond
OBEOK double-book
OBEOR double door
OBETR double star
OBFLY doubtfully
OBHRE hobby-horse
OBIES wobbliness
OBIGY doubtingly
hobblingly
OBIUT soubriquet
OBJNS Bobby Jones
OBLID gor-bellied
potbellied
pot-bellied
OBLIG corbelling
top billing
OBLTI bombolotti
OBMOE Bobby Moore
OBODD hot-blooded
OBONE box Brownie®
OBRIE Colbertine
Norbertine
OBRIR bombardier
OBRRB robber-crab
OBSIN combustion
OBSNS Bobby Sands
OBTOE combat zone
OBYUK Bombay duck
OCAAT nonchalant
OCADO touch and go
touch-and-go
OCAIG concealing
OCAOT ponce about
OCCIN concoction
OCDES forcedness
OCEEY concretely
OCEIE concretise
concretize
OCEIN concretion
OCETR Colchester
Dorchester
OCFLY forcefully
OCGAS couch grass
OCIEF conceive of
OCIES touchiness
OCIGY touchingly
OCILE conchiglie
OCILN conchiolin
OCIUS colchicums
OCLAE conciliate
OCLGT torchlight
OCLIS Tom Collins
OCLTE Dolcelatte
OCMNE dolcemente
OCMNT touch-me-not
OCMOF not come off
OCNAK you can talk
OCNBY Volcano Bay
OCNET non-content
OCNIY concinnity
OCNRC concentric
OCNWN you can't win
OCODL conchoidal
OCOOY conchology
OCPIN Concepción
conception❑
OCPIT voiceprint
OCPRY coach party
OCPTH hotchpotch
hotch-potch
OCPUL conceptual
OCRAE coacervate
OCRAN for certain
OCRAT concordant
OCRET concurrent
OCRIA concertina
OCRIG concerning
concurring
OCRIH concur with
OCRIO concertino
OCSIE concessive
OCSIN concession
concussion
OCSOE touchstone❑
OCUIE conclusive
OCUIG concluding
OCUIN conclusion
ODABR Cold Harbor
ODADR woodlander
ODAIE cordialise
cordialize
ODAIG toad-eating
ODAIY cordiality
good family
ODALN Woody Allen
ODALR good sailor
loudhailer
loud-hailer
ODATO hold fast to
ODATR loadmaster
ODAUE good nature
ODAVR woodcarver
ODBIF hold a brief
ODBUS Moody Blues
ODCEN rood screen
ODCIG conducting
ODCIN conduction
ODDES sordidness
ODDYE Roddy Doyle
ODEAN Goldie Hawn
ODEER wood veneer
ODEIE bowdlerise
bowdlerize
ODEKR woodpecker
ODELH good health
ODELS GoodFellas
ODEMF not dream of
ODESY wordlessly
ODFIE hold office
ODGOY goody-goody
ODHSL cold chisel
ODHUE Lord's house
ODIES goodliness
lordliness
ODIGR gold-digger
Goldfinger
ODIHS good wishes
ODIKR hoodwinker
non-drinker
ODLCS goldilocks
ODLMS condylomas
ODLNE condolence
ODLTD gold-plated
ODMIG condemning
ODMNE sordamente
ODNAE condensate
ODNAF golden calf
ODNAL London Wall
ODNAM Golden Palm
ODNBE condonable
ODNBY loading bay
ODNEN golden mean
ODNES soddenness
ODNID Golden Hind
ODNLU cordon bleu
ODNLY hold in play
ODNOE Golden Rose
ODNOK Golden Rock
ODNRY bond energy
ODNSY you don't say!
ODNUE golden rule
ODNUH good enough
ODOKR good-looker
woodworker
ODORL wood sorrel
ODOSY wondrously
ODOTY roadworthy
ODOYU good for you
ODPRT wood spirit
ODPUE nom de plume
nom-de-plume
ODRAD borderland
wonderland❑
ODRAL Wonderwall
ODRDY Good Friday
ODRED good friend
ODRET ponderment
wonderment
ODRIE borderline
ODRLE powder blue
ODRNW powder snow
ODROM powder room
ODRTS foederatus
ODRUE wood grouse
woodgrouse
ODRUF powder puff
ODSED condescend
ODSOD good as gold
ODTBE Lord's Table
ODTFS foodstuffs
ODTOS conditions
ODTVR lord it over
ODUFR hold out for
ODUKY cold turkey
ODUNR roadrunner
ODUOR good humour
ODWMN bondswoman
ODWRH Wordsworth
ODYUO how do you do?
OEAAT poles apart
OEABY Donegal Bay
OEACR rope-dancer
OEADD forehanded
OEAEE Dodecanese
OEAEY moderately
OEAHR forefather
foregather
OEAIG homemaking
lovemaking
love-making
moderating
OEAIM monetarism
OEAIN moderation
Pomeranian
toleration
OEAIT monetarist
OEAKO come back to
OEAKR rope-walker
OEAKT home market
OEAOE tower above
OEAOG mosey along
OEAOR vote Labour
OEAPE for example
OEATE forecastle
OEATR covenanter
covenantor
forecaster
OEATY not exactly
tolerantly
OEBAE power brake
OEBCN Roger Bacon
OEBOD move abroad
OEBOK power block
tower block
OECAS lower-class
OECAT hovercraft
OECKY hokey cokey
hokey-cokey
OECOS come across
OEDIE cover drive
fore-advise
OEDVY lovey-dovey
OEEDD bone-headed
OEEEA Lope de Vega
OEEGT lose weight
OEELE Lorelei Lee
OEELR foreteller
OEELW yoke-fellow
OEEOE come before
not even one
OEERO come near to
OEERR come nearer
OEESY hopelessly
movelessly
tonelessly

Words marked ❑ can also be spelled with an initial capital letter

OEETE rove beetle
OEETR honeyeater
honey-eater
OEETY coherently
OEEWY covered way
OEFAR love affair
OEFCD poker-faced
OEFLS womenfolks
OEFLY powerfully
OEGAD foreign aid
OEGIE honeyguide
OEHDW foreshadow
OEHFR rose-chafer
OEHGN Copenhagen
OEHKR boneshaker
OEHPD cone-shaped
OEHUE lower house
powerhouse
power-house
OEHWN Joseph Swan
OEHWY lose the way
OEIDW rose window
OEIES comeliness
homeliness
loneliness
loveliness
OEIEY cohesively
OEIGR forefinger
OEIGY covetingly
coweringly
hoveringly
loweringly
soberingly
toweringly
OEIHR come-hither
OEIHS sole rights
OEIHY pokerishly
OEIIT polemicist
OEINE comedienne
OEITA rosehip tea
OEITC novelistic
solecistic
OEKBB doner kebab
OELIH go well with
OELNH power lunch
OELSR come closer
OELVL lower-level
OELWY move slowly
OEMKR money-maker
OEMOE Roger Moore
OENAT fore-and-aft
OENAZ modern jazz
OENBE governable
OENCS Copernicus
OENDY home and dry
OENES solemnness
OENET government
OENNE governance
OENOE come undone
OENZD modernized
OENZR modernizer
OEOAD come to hand
OEOAE come to have
OEOAL nose to tail
OEOAS come to pass
OEOCE gobemouche
OEODL solenoidal
OEODR money order
OEOEL come to heel
OEOET come to rest
to be honest
OEOEY dolesomely
lonesomely
OEOID come to mind
OEOIE come to life
OEOIG foreboding
home-coming
home-loving
money owing
OEOIK bone to pick
OEOIN love potion
OEOIS somebodies
OEOMD foredoomed
OEONN come down on
OEONO come down to
OEONT poke-bonnet
OEONW come to know
OEOOR lose colour
OEOSY covetously
OEOTR Cole Porter
OEOTY come to stay
noteworthy
OEPAT power plant
OEPIE Nobel Prize
Nobel prize
OEPIH come up with
OEPIT cover point
power point
vowel point
OEPOL Moser-Proll
OEPTY homeopathy
OERAN foreordain
OERDE rope bridge
OERES more or less
OERKR love-broker
OERUD foreground
move around
nose around
poke around
OESAK honey-stalk
OESDS sobersides
OESIF bored stiff
OESRM Söderström
OESRY gone astray
OESUT somersault
OETAA Robert Capa
OETAE potentiate
OETAK honest talk
OETBE comestible
OETDM Robert Adam
OETEL Robert Peel
OETES covertness
OETET Robert Kett
OETLA potentilla
OETLE Robert E Lee
OETLS money talks
OETOH Robert Koch
OETON forest-born
OETOT Robert Bolt
OETRY Robert Cray
OETUT power trust
OEUHR dope pusher
OEUNR forerunner
OEURS bodegueros
OEUTD fore-quoted
OEVDM Roger Vadim
OEYEK Pobedy Peak
OFADN roof garden
OFAIG God-fearing
OFAIN conflation
OFAIR Joe Frazier
OFAKR do a flanker
OFAZE to a frazzle
OFCIN confection
non-fiction
OFDNE confidante
confidence
OFEEN coffee bean
OFEHP coffee shop
OFEIL coffee mill
OFIUE forfeiture
OFLES joyfulness
woefulness
OFNAL coffin-nail
OFOEY tomfoolery
OFORE golf course
OFPDR wolf spider
OFRET conferment
OFRIG comforting
conferring
confirming
conforming
OFRIM conformism
OFRIT conformist
OFRIY conformity
OFRNE conference❑
OFRNS solferinos
OFROS non-ferrous
OFRRM not far from
OFRUS not for nuts
OFRWY not far away
OFSAE confiscate
OFSDY confusedly
OFSIN confession
OFTRS solfataras
OFUDD confounded
OFUDT confound it
OFUNE confluence
OGAED forge ahead
OGAOS poignadoes
OGARD long-haired
OGATY poignantly
OGDAT rough-draft
OGDES doggedness
OGDON bogged down
OGDUS bongo drums
bongo-drums
OGEAE congregate
OGEAH tongue-lash
OGEGD long-legged
OGEID tongue-tied
OGEIE mongrelise
mongrelize
OGEIG toughening
OGELW Longfellow
OGETS borghettos
OGEYD goggle-eyed
OGFYE Lough Foyle
OGGES rough guess
OGGID rough-grind
OGHUE rough-house
OGHUH song thrush
OGIDD longwinded
long-winded
OGIES doughiness
OGIOT tough it out
OGLAT topgallant
OGLTD coagulated
OGLTR coagulator
OGNAH Lough Neagh
OGNDA zoogonidia
OGNOA Gorgonzola
OGNRC congeneric
OGNTC morganatic
OGNTL congenital
OGOAE conglobate
OGOSY gorgeously
OGPDE hodgepodge
hodge-podge
OGRED loggerhead
OGREY Joe Gargery
OGRTR songwriter
OGRVR Congo River
OGSAD Long Island
OGSET cough sweet
OGSIE congestive
OGSIN congestion
OGSUF rough-stuff
OGTAE rough trade
OGTES songstress
OGTIG forgetting
OGTSE not go to see
OGTTH longstitch
OGUNE congruence
OGUNY congruency
OGVBE forgivable
OHALD mothballed
OHCID Rothschild
OHCRH Gothic arch
OHDAH to the death
OHDYN Moshe Dayan
OHEDF to the end of
OHEFR Bonhoeffer
OHETD cochleated
OHFOR to the floor
OHISN Josh Gibson
OHJBF do the job of
OHLBD not half bad
OHLMT Roche limit
OHNBT nothing but
OHNLR dog-handler
OHNNS to the nines

Words marked ❑ can also be spelled with an initial capital letter

OHNSO do things to
no thanks to
OHNUG Gothenburg
OHOOD Loch Lomond
OHPIG go shopping
OHPIT to the point
OHQIK to the quick
OHRAD motherland
OHRDY bothered by
Mother's Day
OHREE Rothermere
OHREL Motherwell
OHRES motherless
OHRIE motherlike
OHROD motherhood
OHROE bothersome
mother-to-be
OHRTS oophoritis
OHSIS to the skies
OHTIK do the trick
OHWSR no the wiser
OIAEX folie à deux
OIAEY nominately
OIAIE cogitative
dominative
nominalise
nominalize
nominative
not imagine
OIAIG cogitating
dominating
motivating
OIAIM nominalism
OIAIN cogitation
domination
ionisation
ionization
motivation
nomination
solitarian
OIAIT nominalist
OIAIY comicality
logicality
solidarity
solitarily
topicality
OIALR Toni Sailer
OIAPR nominal par
OIATY dominantly
OIBTA Louis Botha
OICOS coriaceous
foliaceous
OIDVS Colin Davis
OIEAE vociferate
OIEBE noticeable
OIEBY noticeably
OIEEM polite term
OIEES motiveless
politeness
OIEET Gobi Desert
OIEIE do likewise
OIEIS homiletics
OIEOE mobile home
OIEOS coniferous
morigerous
vociferous
OIGER coming near
OIGES boringness
OIGNP Moving On Up
OIGOM robing-room
OIGON coming soon
moving down
roping-down
OIGOT rowing boat
OIHBA toxiphobia
OIHES boyishness
modishness
OIHOS Robin Hood's
OIHPN polish up on
OIIAE nobilitate
OIIBE modifiable
notifiable
OIIEY positively
OIIID solidified
OIIIE politicise
politicize
OIIIG soliciting
OIIIM positivism
OIIIN politician
OIIIT positivist
OIINL positional
volitional
OIINS bolivianos
OIIOS politicoes
solicitous
OIISU Ion Iliescu
OIIUE solicitude
OIKER kodiak bear❑
OIKIE bowie knife
OILAI Modigliani
OILES socialness
OILLB social club
OILNS Coriolanus
OILOK social work
OILZR socializer
OIMAP sodium lamp
OIMAS Colin Meads
OIMLE Louis Malle
OIMTR goniometer
OIMTY sociometry
OINES motionless
OINLY notionally
OINRY Dorian Gray
OIOEA comic opera
OIOIG monitoring
OIOIL monitorial
OIOIS Posidonius
OIOOY codicology
toxicology
OIOTL horizontal
OIPTY sociopathy
OISAE solid-state
OISAM tonic spasm
OISIH Dodie Smith
OISLA tonic sol-fa
OISRE rotisserie
OISRP comic strip
OITCL logistical
OITIE goliathise
goliathize
OITIN Corinthian
OITLY societally
OIVLE Louisville
OIWTR tonic water
OJCUE conjecture
OJGLY conjugally
OJIIG conjoining
OJITY conjointly
OJNIS Roy Jenkins
OJNTY conjunctly
OKADN rock garden
work-harden
OKAIG bookmaking
Tom Keating
OKAKD pockmarked
OKAKR bookmarker
OKAKT workbasket
OKAMN rock salmon
OKATE York Castle
OKBRA kookaburra
OKDPO looked up to
OKDWY locked away
OKELR bookseller
OKELW work-fellow
OKEOC mock-heroic
OKEOY folk-memory
OKEPE workpeople
work-people
OKEPR bookkeeper
OKETY cook gently
OKHFR cockchafer
OKHLC workaholic
OKIDR bookbinder
OKIEN rock pigeon
OKIES folksiness
OKIEY look lively
look lively!
OKIGR folk-singer
OKIHT pork-pie hat
OKLEY cocky-leeky
OKLPY look slippy
OKLTC poikilitic
OKNDY working day
OKNEE hook-and-eye
OKNHM Rockingham
OKNMN working man
OKNOT conking-out
working out
working-out
OKNPY look snappy
OKNSY look and say
OKNTN Workington
OKNWT soaking wet
OKODN look good on
OKOIT folklorist
OKONN look down on
OKOOS Doukhobors
OKOPR rock-hopper
OKOTM rock bottom
rock-bottom
OKOUE work to rule
work-to-rule
OKROM locker room
OKSOE Folkestone
OKTIE cockatrice❑
OKTUS pocket-fuls
OKUSN Rock Hudson
OKWGN Volkswagen®
OKYHP jockeyship
OKYOE donkey vote
OKYOK donkeywork
donkey-work
OLAIG toolmaking
OLART poll-parrot
OLBOM Molly Bloom
OLCAS world-class
OLCIE collective
OLCIG rollicking
rollocking
OLCIN collection
OLCLR follicular
OLCNH coelacanth
OLDOD rolled gold
OLDVR bowled over
OLEDD cool-headed
OLEDM Boulder Dam
OLEGD foolbegged
OLEIG mouldering
OLEPR goalkeeper
OLESY soullessly
OLETY boil gently
OLEVL boll-weevil
OLFIG mollifying
OLFIY toploftily
OLGAE collegiate
OLGAH collograph
OLGCL zoological
OLGCP college cap
OLGUS collegiums
OLIES mouldiness
woolliness
OLITR soul sister
OLKAE Molly Keane
OLMFR to blame for
OLMSC world music
OLMTL noble metal
OLMTR collimator
OLNAO not long ago
OLNFN cooling fan
OLNOG Wollongong
OLNPN rolling-pin
OLOAD Noël Coward
OLOEY toilsomely
OLOLR rollcollar
OLONO boil down to
OLPIG collapsing
OLPKN foul-spoken
OLPWR world power
OLQIE colloquise
colloquize
OLQIL colloquial
OLQIM colloquium

OLRDE toll bridge
tollbridge
OLRFS collar of SS
OLRGR Jolly Roger
OLROE collarbone
poultroone
OLROM boiler room
OLRTD collar stud
OLRUD fool around
OLRUS collyriums
OLRUT boiler suit
OLRYE Rolls-Royce®
OLSET coalescent
OLSIE world's mine
OLTDY pollutedly
OLTGD would to God
OLTIS toiletries
OLTNM go platinum
OLTOL toilet roll
OLTRL collateral
OLTUE cos lettuce
OLWES hollowness
OLWIH go slow with
OLWMN noblewoman
noblewomen
OLWOE follow home
OLWPN follow up on
OLWRI World War II
OLWUT follow suit
OLWYD hollow-eyed
OLYAL volleyball
OLYER woolly bear
OMAUE commeasure
OMCCD formic acid
OMCCP not much cop
OMCFR too much for
OMCLY cosmically
OMCOA not much of a
OMCRA formicaria
OMDBE formidable
OMDBY formidably
OMDOS commodious
OMESY formlessly
OMETR form letter
OMLTR formaliter
OMMNY for my money
OMNAA Joe Montana
OMNAD Moominland
OMNAE commentate
OMNAK common talk
OMNAT commandant
OMNAY commentary
OMNED common bend
common herd
OMNEL common seal
OMNER commandeer
OMNES commonness
OMNHW Norman Shaw
OMNIE common time
gormandise
gormandize
OMNIG commanding
commencing
tormenting
OMNIM gormandism
OMNLE common blue
OMNLY commonalty
communally
noumenally
OMNOD common cold
OMNOM common room
OMNON common noun
OMNQE communiqué
OMNRH Norman arch
OMNUT Holman Hunt
OMOHY go smoothly
OMRES Doc Martens®
OMRIL commercial
OMSAE not mistake
OMSIN commission
OMTBE commutable
OMTET commitment
OMTSN commit a sin
OMTTR commutator
OMXUE commixture
ONADY downwardly
ONAIN foundation
ONAIR John Napier
ONAIS boundaries
ONAKS John Backus
ONAKT down-market
ONALS Cornwallis
ONANS John Barnes
ONAOT going about
round about
roundabout
ONATE join battle
ONATN John Dalton
ONATR point after
ONAUT young adult
ONAVN John Calvin
ONBAK point-blank
ONBIG go and bring
ONBIH hobnob with
ONBNE go on a binge
ONBOD young blood
ONBOK Donnybrook
ONBSE Count Basie
ONBTC coenobitic
ONCDM John McAdam
ONCET John Eckert
ONCIE connective
ONCIG connecting
ONCIN connection
ONCPA cornucopia
ONCTR fornicator
ONDEF corned beef
ONDIH John Edrich
ONDOD horned toad
ONDOE Lorna Doone
ONDZN round dozen
ONEAK bounce back
Connie Mack
mountebank
ONEAT counteract
ONEBW John Benbow
ONEIG foundering
ONELR counsellor
ONELY John Wesley
ONENE John Rennie
ONENN John Heenan
John Lennon
ONEOD go on record
ONERY Ronnie Kray
ONESE countersue
ONETA poinsettia
ONEUT lounge suit
ONEVR John Denver
ONFRE pound force
ONHES go on wheels
ONHNR moonshiner
ONHPD moon-shaped
ONIES bounciness
ONIET coincident
ONIGR John Pilger
ONIGY loungingly
soundingly
woundingly
ONIHR John Fisher
ONIIG coinciding
downsizing
ONIKS John Wilkes
ONILR councillor
ONIMT John Wilmot
ONITN John Milton
ONITX council tax
ONIWN John Kirwan
ONKNA Mount Kenya
ONKRN Donna Karan
ONLEE John Cleese
ONLGN Mount Logan
ONLKS cornflakes
ONLNE hornblende
somnolence
ONLNY somnolency
ONLOK John Alcock
ONLWR cornflower
Hornblower
ONNES John Enders
ONNOT down and out
down-and-out
go in and out
ONOAD John Howard
ONOCS join forces
ONOGN John Morgan
ONOLS John Fowles
ONOLY John Bowlby
ONOTN John Morton
ONPIE John Updike
ONPIH join up with
ONPIN conniption
ONPLE Mount Pelée
ONPOF soundproof
sound-proof
ONPRS Count Paris
ONQAE town square
ONRAS cornerways
ONRBN round robin
ONRDN John Dryden
ONRGT John Bright
ONRHN sooner than
ONRHP corner shop
ONRIE cornerwise
John Braine
ONRMN countryman
ONRNO John Cranko
ONRTN John Bruton
ONRTY John Bratby
ONSAD to one's hand
ONSAE to one's face
to one's name
ONSBY cognisably
ONSET do one's best
ONSID do one's kind
ONSNE cognisance
ONSOL joint-stool
ONSOS pound Scots
ONSRE go on a spree
ONTEL down at heel
down-at-heel
ONTEM downstream
ONTIE go on strike
ONTIG do anything
for nothing
ONTIS downstairs
ONTIT cornettist
ONTRL non-natural
ONTUK moonstruck
ONUAN Von Neumann
ONUDR going under
ONUHN John Buchan
ONUKN John Ruskin
ONULP John Dunlop
ONUMR John Gummer
ONUTN John Huston
ONUTR John Hunter
ONUYN John Bunyan
ONVLE Townsville
ONVLN John Evelyn
ONVNE connivance
ONWMN townswoman
young woman
ONYAH Johnny Cash
ONYEP Johnny Depp
ONYON county town
ONZBY cognizably
ONZNE cognizance
OOAAK go for a walk
OOACR go-go dancer
OOAET monovalent
OOAIC monomaniac
OOAID not of a mind
OOAIM honorarium
OOAIN coloration
coronation
OOAIT monogamist
OOAKT go to market
OOAOS homogamous
monogamous
OOAPC monocarpic
OOARS Torosaurus
OOAUA coloratura

OOBOE go for broke
OOBSN Roy Orbison
OOCAH motor-coach
OOCCE motorcycle
motor-cycle
OOCOS monoecious
OOCPC horoscopic
OOCUE to conclude
OOEES jocoseness
moroseness
OOEHN no more than
OOEHR go together
OOEIE homogenise
homogenize
OOELM Tom o' Bedlam
OOENS Holofernes
OOEOS homogenous
OOERL holohedral
OOERN holohedron
OOEUL homosexual
OOGNR tobogganer
OOHAE holophrase
OOHBA homophobia
OOHBC homophobic
OOHBD go to the bad
OOHIM monotheism
OOHIT monotheist
OOHNC homophonic
monophonic
OOHNL Coco Chanel
OOHOC monochroic
OOHOE monochrome
OOHRL tocopherol
OOHSA monochasia
OOHTC holophytic
OOICS go to pieces
OOIHC monolithic
OOIIE dolomitise
dolomitize
sororicide
OOIIN low opinion
OOILY colonially
sororially
OOLGA monoplegia
OOLGC monoplegic
OOLNL monoclinal
monoclonal
OOMUH motormouth
OONDD colonnaded
OONFO go to and fro
OONIH go down with
OONIL go down hill
go downhill
OONLY Mo Connolly
OOOAE homologate
OOOAH homoeopath
OOOCL gonococcal
OOOCS gonococcus
OOOIE homologise
homologize
lobotomise
lobotomize
locomotive
mo-nologise
mo-nologize
monopolise
monopolize
OOOIL nosocomial
OOOIM Horologium
OOOIN locomotion
OOOIT horologist
monopolist
nosologist
OOONN go to town on
OOOOS homologous
monotonous
OOOOY locomotory
OOOSY dolorously
sonorously
OOPEE ionosphere
OORAH colourwash
OORBE honourable
OORBY colourably
honourably
OORES colourless
OOROA gonorrhoea
logorrhoea
OOROE colour code
colour-code
OORPY holography
nomography
nosography
tomography
topography
OORTC monocratic
OORUD go to ground
OOSAS Colossians
OOSES joyousness
porousness
OOSNE no-nonsense
OOSSS colossuses
OOYLC homocyclic
OOYOE homozygote
OOYOS homozygous
monogynous
OOYRD monohybrid
OPAET complacent
OPAIE co-optative
OPAIN co-optation
OPANR complainer
OPANS complaints
OPAOS zoophagous
OPCIN compaction
OPCIY compactify
OPDES torpidness
OPEED comprehend
OPEET complement
not present
OPEEY completely
OPEIE corpse-like
OPEIG completing
OPEIN completion
complexion
OPEIY complexify
complexity
OPESD compressed
OPESR compressor
OPEVR topple over
OPHPD hoop-shaped
OPIAE complicate
OPIET compliment
OPIIY complicity
OPILY Bob Paisley
OPINE compliance
OPLIE compulsive
gospellise
gospellize
OPLIG compelling
OPLIN compulsion
OPLNE corpulence
OPLNY corpulency
OPLOG gospel song
OPLOY compulsory
OPNAE compensate
OPNHR cowpuncher
OPNIE porpentine
OPNIM compendium
OPNMD hopping mad
OPNNS components
OPNOS companions
OPNSM Kompong Som
OPNWT sopping wet
OPODR soap powder
OPOIE compromise
OPOOY morphology
OPRBE comparable
OPRBY comparably
OPRED copperhead
OPRER colporteur
OPRIY corporeity
OPRLY corporally
OPRSN comparison
OPRTR co-operator
OPSDF composed of
OPSDY composedly
OPSIN compassion
OPSSW compass saw
OPSTR compositor
OPTBE compatible
computable
hospitable
OPTBY compatibly
hospitably
OPTHD low-pitched
OPTIT compatriot
OPTNE competence
OPTNY competency
OPTTR competitor
OPUIG nonplusing
OPUSD nonplussed
OPYET non-payment
OPYIH comply with
OPYIS porphyrios
OQAIY low quality
low-quality
OQEAA Torquemada
OQEIG conquering
OQIOE Don Quixote
OQIOS mosquitoes
ORADD four-handed
ORADE door-handle
ORAEE journalese
ORAET tournament
ORAIE journalise
journalize
tourmaline
ORAIM journalism
ORAIT journalist
non-realist
ORAOT worry about
ORBAS worry beads
ORBRE corroboree
ORCIE corrective
ORCIN correction
ORCLI Torricelli
ORDES horridness
torridness
ORDOE torrid zone
ORDUE Konrad Zuse
OREES coarseness
hoarseness
OREIG journeying
OREIH coarse fish
ORELH poor health
OREMN journeyman
ORENH fourteenth
OREOK coursebook
OREPR doorkeeper
door-keeper
ORETE dorr beetle
OREVS yourselves
ORFIG horrifying
ORFLY mournfully
ORGBE corrigible
ORGNA corrigenda
ORGOS courageous
ORGTD corrugated
ORHAE fourth-rate
ORHAL fourth wall
ORIAE coordinate
co-ordinate
ORICE hour-circle
ORIEY coercively
ORIGY mourningly
worryingly
ORIRY courtierly
ORIUT tourniquet
ORLLA coprolalia
ORLRS Poor Clares
ORLTD correlated
job-related
ORNAD four-in-hand
ORNHD four-inched
ORNIG low-ranking
ORNIL torrential
ORNNS sopraninos
ORNOS horrendous
ORNWT pouring wet
ORODR court order
OROOR door-to-door
OROTD four-footed
OROTR four-poster

ORPIE corruptive
ORPIG corrupting
ORPIN corruption
ORQAE four-square
ORRPS sour grapes
ORSIE morris-pike
ORSIG nourishing
ORSOD correspond
ORTUY yours truly
ORWNS borrowings
ORWVR sorrow over
ORYOR four-by-four
OSAET house agent
OSAHD moustached
OSAIG loss-making
OSAKD gobsmacked
OSALP codswallop
OSAOT boast about
rouseabout
OSATA Constantia
OSATN constantan
OSATR non-starter
OSATY constantly
OSBAS horse brass
OSBET not subject
OSBIT consubsist
OSBMS goose bumps
OSBOK horse block
OSBRY gooseberry
OSBUD housebound
OSCAE consecrate
consociate
OSCAT housecraft
OSDRD considered
OSEAT Rod Stewart
OSEBE forseeable
OSEGR Rod Steiger
OSEIE bolshevise
bolshevize
mousseline
OSEIG roistering
OSEIM Bolshevism
OSEIT Bolshevist
OSEOS boisterous
roisterous
OSETS conspectus
OSEUE consuetude
OSFAE loss of face
OSFEH gooseflesh
horseflesh
OSFIE loss of life
OSFLY boastfully
OSFOS goosefoots
OSGAD coastguard
OSGEN Goose Green
OSGET house guest
OSGIY consignify
OSGOI Monsignori
OSGOS Monsignors
OSHRE Worsthorne
OSIAE constipate
OSIAY conspiracy
OSIFL worshipful
OSIIG conspiring
not shining
OSIIL solstitial
OSIIO con spirito
OSIIS low spirits
OSINE conscience
OSINR dog's dinner
OSIPD worshipped
OSIPR worshipper
OSIUE constitute
OSKNY forsakenly
OSLAT consultant
OSLBE consolable
OSLHP consulship
OSLIG consulting
OSLII Rossellini
OSLTE corselette
OSLUL fossil fuel
OSLVR loose-liver
OSLZD fossilized
OSMAE consummate
OSMBE consumable
OSMSC house music
OSMUE house mouse
OSNIG consenting
OSNIL poison pill
OSNLE boys in blue
OSNNE consonance
OSNNY consonancy
OSNUL consensual
OSOGD house of God
OSOIG non-smoking
OSOPR gobstopper
OSORE lob's course
OSPAT house plant
OSPOD house-proud
OSPOE sousaphone
OSPWR horsepower
OSQET consequent
OSRCS how's tricks?
OSRDR horserider
OSRIG conserving
OSRIM consortium
OSRIO con sordino
OSRIT constraint
OSRNE constringe
monstrance
OSRUD boss around
OSSET consistent
OSSIE possessive
OSSIN possession
OSSNE horse sense
OSSOY consistory
OSTAN house-train
OSTRY topsy-turvy
OSTTH moss stitch
OSUIE moisturise
moisturize
OSVUT horse vault
OSWIE house white
OSWMN horsewoman
loose woman
OSWRS coastwards
OSYOO not say no to
OTAAD contraband
OTAAE soft palate
OTAAS contrabass
OTABN Monte Albán
OTABT Port Talbot
OTADR soft sawder
OTAEE contravene
OTAGT go straight
OTAIG bootmaking
OTAIT contradict
OTAIY contrarily
OTALR footballer
OTALW contraflow
OTAOT dotty about
OTASS zoothap-ses
OTATD contracted
contrasted
OTATM postpartum
OTATN contract in
OTATR contractor
postmaster
OTATS contraltos
OTAYO contrary to
OTBAD goatsbeard
OTBUD northbound
southbound
OTBUH toothbrush
OTCIA South China
OTCIT postscript
OTCLI Botticelli
OTCLO Monticello
OTCLS monticulus
OTCLY poetically
vortically
OTCOS post-echoes
OTCRO Monte Carlo
OTDES rootedness
OTDET dotted rest
OTDIE dotted line
OTDLA mortadella
OTDNS contadinas
OTDOE dotted note
OTDVR dotted over
OTEAE not the same
OTEDD soft-headed
OTEEK bottleneck
OTEET most recent
OTEGR bootlegger
OTEHP for the chop
OTEIE röntgenise
röntgenize
toe the line
OTEIL top the bill
OTEIR Montpelier
OTELR Rottweiler
OTENE bow the knee
OTENR northerner ❑
OTENY southernly
OTEOE most remote
OTEPE boat people
OTERT Montserrat
OTERY cost dearly
OTESY bootlessly
Dostoevsky
OTEUP got the hump
OTEUS bottlefuls
OTEWG hop the twig
OTFAL coat of mail
OTFAT Pontefract
OTFCL pontifical
OTFCS pontifices
OTFIE foot of fine
Post Office
OTFIG fortifying
mortifying
OTFIY tooth fairy
OTFLY youthfully
OTFRS coat of arms
coat-of-arms
OTGBY Montego Bay
OTGEE Portuguese
OTGIY contiguity
OTGOS contagious
contiguous
OTGPE cottage pie
OTHIE post chaise
post-chaise
OTIES costliness
portliness
rootsiness
toothiness
worthiness
OTIEY contritely
most likely
OTIGY loathingly
soothingly
OTIHS footlights
OTIIG contriving
OTIIN contrition
OTIKR bootlicker
OTIOS fortuitous
OTITE sow thistle
OTIUE contribute
OTKRA North Korea
South Korea
OTLAE postillate
OTLCE noctilucae
OTLEN portal vein
OTLGR sortileger
OTLIG hostelling
OTLII tortellini
OTLIN postillion
OTLNA Lotte Lenya
OTLNS portolanos
OTLNY postulancy
OTLOE postal code
OTLTD postulated
OTMES bottomless
OTMIE bottom line
OTMNI coatimundi
portamenti
OTMNO portamento
OTMOE hoc tempore
OTMOT bottommost
OTMRH route-march

OTMSC roots music
OTMTR voltameter
OTMUH Portsmouth
OTNAE continuate
OTNAL cottontail
OTNBY Fortune Bay
OTNEN continue in
OTNES contenders
rottenness
OTNET contingent
OTNHM Nottingham
OTNIG contending
continuing
OTNIN contention
OTNIY continuity
OTNLB Cotton Club
OTNLE fontanelle
OTNNE continence
OTNNO cotton on to
cotton onto
OTNOD cottonwood
OTNOL cotton wool
cottonwool
OTNOS coetaneous
continuous
portentous
OTNOT rooting-out
sorting out
OTNRS Fortinbras
OTNUS continuums
OTOAE not too late
OTODR soft sowder
OTOEN most modern
post-modern
OTOET controvert
OTOEY Montgomery
OTOGN mouth-organ
OTOIG postponing
OTOIS portfolios
OTOLD controlled
soft-boiled
OTOLR controller
OTOMN most common
OTOSY tortiously
tortuously
OTOTM post-mortem
OTPAO fortepiano
OTPEE mouthpiece
OTPIN soft option
OTPKN soft-spoken
OTPRS mouthparts
OTPSE toothpaste
OTRAN souterrain
OTRDE footbridge
OTRDY torturedly
OTREE couturière
OTRGT forthright
OTRIE contortive
OTRIN contortion
OTRIR fox-terrier
OTRLP Doctor Slop
OTRNS footprints
OTROB mortar-bomb
OTRTA montbretia
OTRUD root around
OTRUH nod through
OTSAT contestant
OTSED Portishead
OTSID month's mind
OTSIO fortissimo
OTSOY foetoscopy
OTSYR soothsayer
OTTIY hoity-toity
OTTOS voetstoots
OTUAD Pont du Gard
OTUKR goatsucker
OTULS portcullis
OTUOS posthumous
OTVDO Montevideo
OTVRI Monteverdi
OTWEL tooth-wheel
OTWIE worthwhile
OTWNS forty winks
OTWRS northwards
southwards
OTWRY not to worry
OTXUL contextual
OTYHN soft hyphen
OUAIE popularise
popularize
OUAIG copulating
OUAIN copulation
modulation
nodulation
population
OUAIY jocularity
modularity
popularity
OUBLS holus-bolus
OUBRA columbaria
OUCLR homuncular
OUCLS homunculus
OUCOS loquacious
OUDES rotundness
OUELE columellae
OUETD documented
OUETL documental
monumental
OUETR lotus-eater
OUHUK no such luck
OUIES do business
OUIIE solubilise
solubilize
OUIIY solubility
volubility
OUIOM poculiform
OUIOS voluminous
OUISE bonus issue
OUNNH column inch
OUOSY populously
OUOUE go out of use
OUPCS hocus-pocus
OUSTA Lotus Sutra
OUTAY voluptuary
OUTEN locust bean
OUTES robustness
OUTID locust bird
OUTIH coquettish
OUTOS voluptuous
OUTPR not up to par
OVCIE convective
OVCIN convection
conviction
OVLIE convulsive
OVLIN convulsion
OVLSE convalesce
OVLTD convoluted
OVNBE convenable
OVNET convenient
OVNIG convincing
OVNIN convention□
OVNUL conventual□
OVOET non-violent
OVRAT conversant
OVREN converge on
OVRES go overseas
OVRET convergent
OVREY conversely
OVRIN conversion
OVXDY convexedly
OVXRH convex arch
OVYBE conveyable
OVYNE conveyance
OWLIE Boswellise
Boswellize
OWLIG God willing
not willing
OWRIG forwarding
not working
OWYIH do away with
OWYRM go away from
OXETD to expected
OXRMS to extremes
OXSET coexistent
co-existent
OXSIG coexisting
OYAHC polymathic
OYAHR Holy Father
OYAIT polygamist
OYAKR nosy parker
OYAOS polygamous
OYAPC polycarpic
OYATL polydactyl
OYATS corybantes
OYDNM molybdenum
OYEIE polymerise
polymerize
OYEIN Polynesian
OYEOS polysemous
OYERH body-search
OYERL polyhedral
OYERN polyhedron
OYHGA polyphagia
OYHIM polytheism
OYHIT polytheist
OYHMS Polyphemus
OYHNC polyphonic
OYHOE polychrome
OYHOY polychromy
OYILE holy Willie□
OYITR polyhistor
OYKRA Yogyakarta
OYLIY polyploidy
OYLNC polyclinic
OYLTS Polyclitus
OYMNS polyominos
OYNHS polyanthus
OYNNS Houyhnhnms
OYOIL polynomial
OYRES holy orders
OYRTR copywriter
OYSAD Holy Island
OYTMC polyatomic
OYULP Joey Dunlop
OYUTS Tony Curtis
OYYNA Polyhymnia
OZRLA mozzarella
PAAHP speak a ship
PAAOT speak about
PACNC splanchnic
PADES upwardness
PAEAE sphacelate
PAEIE sphalerite
PAETY apparently
PAHON splash down
splashdown
PAIEY optatively
PAIGY speakingly
PAIIN apparition
PAPIT spray-paint
PARDA sphaeridia
PARSS aphaeresis
PAUFR speak up for
PBATC epiblastic
PCAIE specialise
specialize
PCAIM specialism
PCAIN speciation
PCAIT specialist
PCAIY speciality
PCALD spectacled
PCALS spectacles
PCAOS spectators
PCCAT spacecraft
PCCDT space cadet
PCEIM speciesism
PCEIT speciesist
PCFCL specifical
PCGRS Spice Girls
PCLPE apocalypse□
PCLTR speculator
PCLUE apiculture
PCNHC epicanthic
PCNHS epicanthus
PCNRL epicentral
PCOIY speciosity
PCOSY spaciously
speciously
PCPOE space probe
PCRLY spectrally
PCRMT apochromat
PCROS apocarpous

PCWMN spacewoman
PCYHL apocryphal
PDCOS spadiceous
PDDMS epididymis
PDITC apodeictic
epideictic
PDRIE spider mite
PDRRB spider crab
PECAS upper class
upper-class
PECIE apperceive
PECUT upper crust
upper-crust
PEDBE spreadable
PEDCS appendices
PEDDY splendidly
PEDOS splendrous
PEDUS splendours
PEDVR spread over
PEDXS appendixes
PEEES sphereless
PEEIE spherelike
PEFLY speedfully
PEHES speechless
PEHUE upper house
PEIES speediness
PEIGP speeding-up
PEIIG appetising
appetizing
PEIIY sphericity
PELMT speed limit
upper limit
PEODL spheroidal
PERNE appearance
PEROE appear to be
PFIAE spiflicate
PGAHC epigraphic
PGICI I Pagliacci
PGMRE up a gumtree
PGOLW a peg too low
PGOTS epiglottis
PHCEK up the creek
PHSOT up the spout
PIAIE optimalise
optimalize
PICDN Ophiacodon
PIEEA Iphigeneia
PIEON upside down
upside-down
PIGAK spring back
PIGAL springtail
PIGES springless
PIGIE springlike
spring tide
springtide
springtime
PIGOK spring lock
PIGOL spring roll
PIGUK springbuck
PIHES uppishness
PIHIS split hairs
PIITC optimistic
PIITO split in two
PIKIG sprinkling
PILAD uphillward
PILHN up till then
PILVL split-level
PINLY optionally
PINRE optic nerve
PIOEY epeirogeny
PISIT split shift
PISOT spoilsport
PIXIE sphinxlike
PLACS appliances
PLAIN spallation
spoliation
PLAOY spoliatory
PLBUD spellbound
PLCBE applicable
PLCBY applicably
PLCNS applicants
PLCTR applicator
PLGIE epiloguise
epiloguize
PLGTC apologetic
PLIGY spellingly
PLNIG spelunking
PLOOY speleology
PLSET opalescent
PLTCL apolitical
PMSET spumescent
PNADD open-handed
PNAKT open market
PNCES open access
PNDIG up and doing
PNEAE open sesame
sponge cake
spongeware
PNEAH sponge bath
PNEBE spongeable
PNEIE spongelike
PNEON sponge down
PNERT open secret
PNESN open season
PNETR open letter
PNHAR up in the air
PNHGD upon the gad
PNHQE open cheque
PNHSS epentheses
PNHWY open the way
PNIDD open-minded
PNIES sponginess
PNIGY spankingly
PNLOD spinal cord
PNNOT opening-out
PNOAE spaniolate
PNOIE spaniolise
spaniolize
PNOIL sponsorial
PNOLR spin-bowler
PNOTR spin doctor
PNRSN open prison
PNSAS Upanishads
PNSFY Spanish fly
PNTRY spinsterly
PNYOL upon my soul!
POCIY splotchily
POEES opposeless
POEIM spoonerism
POGAS up for grabs
POIEO opposite to
POIES spookiness
POIEY appositely
oppositely
POIIN apposition
opposition
POITC aphoristic
POLAY J P Donleavy
POPIT up to a point
POROS uproarious
POSEY upholstery
POSLS Epsom salts
PPATA epiplastra
PPETC apoplectic
PPTEM apophthegm
PQEES opaqueness
PRAEI spermaceti
PRAHS approaches
PRAIM Spartanism
PRBFA opera buffa
PRBIM opprobrium
PRCAE appreciate
PRCLM spiraculum
PRCUT sperm count
PREES sparseness
PRFLY sportfully
PRGAS opera-glass
PRGNA sporogonia
PRHUE opera house
PRIES sportiness
PRIEY sportively
PRIGY sportingly
PRIHY sparkishly
PRIIE spermicide
PRIIG upbraiding
PRLIG spiralling
PRNIE apprentice
PRNIG upbringing
PRNIM sporangium
PROSY spuriously
PRPYE sporophyte
PRPYL sporophyll
PRSAL sports hall
PRSDF apprised of
PRSER sportswear
PRSIE oppressive
PRSIN oppression
PRSRA opera seria
PRTDY spiritedly
PRTES spiritless
PRTIT operettist
PRTOS operations
spirituous
PRTWY spirit away
PRUAE operculate
PRWAE sperm whale
PSAIE apostasize
apostatise
apostatize
PSEIS epistemics
PSIIY spasticity
PSMTC aposematic
PSOAE episcopate
PSOAY episcopacy
epistolary
PSOIE apostolise
apostolize
episcopise
episcopize
epistolise
epistolize
PSOOY episiotomy
PSRPE apostrophe
epistrophe
PTAIY spatiality
PTAMA ophthalmia
PTAMC ophthalmic
PTEAA epithemata
PTEAY apothecary
PTEDR spot-welder
PTEIL epithelial
PTEIM epithelium
PTESS apotheoses
apotheosis
PTESY spotlessly
PTFLY spitefully
PTHOK spatchcock
spitchcock
PTIES spottiness
PTMZR epitomizer
PTNIG upstanding
PUEES spruceness
PUFRH spout forth
PUGNE upsurgence
PULIG upbuilding
PUNNY oppugnancy
PUTRR splutterer
PXGSS epexegeses
PXRSN epoxy resin
PYXIE Sphynx-like
PZOIS epizootics
QAAIE aquamarine
QABIG squabbling
QADRD squandered
QADRR squanderer
QAEAD square yard
QAEAL square sail
QAEEL square deal
square meal
QAEES squareness
QAEIE square mile
squarewise
QAEIH equate with
square with
QAENH square inch
QAENT square knot
QAEOT square foot
square root
QAEPO square up to
QAEWY square away
QAHBE squashable
QAIIY equability

equanimity
squalidity
QAOIL equatorial
QAOIY squamosity
QAOTS aqua fortis
QARND squadroned
QASAE equal share
QASIN equals sign
QAUOE squamulose
QETIN equestrian
QEZBE squeezable
QEZBX squeeze-box
QEZOT squeeze out
QIAET equivalent
QIAIN equitation
QIEIE squirelike
QIOAE equivocate
QITYD squint-eyed
RAAAS Bryan Adams
RAAAT break apart
RAAET break a jest
RAANT cry against
RAAOE dry as a bone
RABAD breadboard
RABDY treat badly
RABED break bread
RABSD broad-based
RABSN Great Basin
RACUB breadcrumb
RACVR break cover
RADIL errand-girl
RADNE breakdance
RAEAE arcade game
Mrs Average
RAEDN Armageddon
RAEES arcaneness
ornateness
urbaneness
RAEIG broadening
RAEOT broaden out
freaked out
RAETD ornamented
RAETL ornamental
RAETR ornamenter
RAEXS Artaxerxes
RAFIH break faith
RAFLY dreadfully
RAFRH break forth
RAFRY Bryan Ferry
RAFUT breadfruit
RAGFR arrange for
RAGLM Triangulum
RAGLR triangular
RAGTS break gates
RAHAT Great-heart
RAHBE breathable
RAHEE triathlete
RAHES breathless
RAHOT breathe out
RAHVC wreak havoc
RAIAE irradicate
RAIES creaminess
dreaminess
dreariness
freakiness
greasiness
RAIEY creatively
RAIGP breaking-up
RAIGY dreamingly
RAIHY freakishly
RAIIG organizing
RAIIY creativity
friability
RAILS armadillos
RAIMC organismic
RAIML organismal
RAINL irrational
RAKIE bread knife
RALCS dreadlocks
RALKS Great Lakes
RALOE break loose
RAMOE Brian Moore
RANEE great-niece
RANET ordainment
RAODY break of day
RAOOS treasonous
RAPIT break point
RARNE prearrange
RASAE Great Slave
RASER break sheer
Breakspear
RASET broadsheet
RASNS Dream Songs
RASNY Great Sandy
RASOD broadsword
RASUE bread sauce
RATED breastfeed
breast-feed
RATEP breast-deep
RATIH breast-high
RATOE breastbone
RATOK breastwork
RAUCE great-uncle
RAWIE great white
RAWTR breakwater
tread water
RBAHC tribrachic
RBASA Arabian Sea
RBCCE Krebs cycle
RBCLE trabeculae
RBCLR trabecular
RBELF treble clef
RBERP arable crop
RBEUA Crab nebula
RBIES crabbiness
grubbiness
RBMTR tribometer
RBNAY prebendary
RBNCN Brabanöcon
RBODF grab hold of
RBOSY frabjously
RBSUS Arabesques
RBTET Grub Street
RBTEY dry battery
RCAIN eructation
RCAMD proclaimed
RCAMR proclaimer
RCAOE crack a joke
RCARB crack a crib
RCATR trochanter
RCCIT tricyclist
RCCOS ericaceous
precocious
RCDNE precedence
RCDRL procedural
RCDRS procedures
RCEDG tracker dog
RCEET track event
RCEIG crocheting
proceeding
RCETD tracheated
RCETR procreator
RCETS tracheitis
RCFLY gracefully
RCFRS Crockford's
RCGIE precognise
precognize
RCICS trochiscus
RCIES trickiness
RCIGP cracking-up
RCIHY trickishly
RCIIE trichinise
trichinize
RCIIG practising
RCIIY proclivity
RCINL fractional
frictional
tractional
RCIOE trichinose
RCIOS trichinous
RCIPD brachiopod
RCISS trichiasis
RCJNS Grace Jones
RCLNE truculence
RCLRY oracularly
RCLYR bricklayer
RCMET procumbent
RCMRL tricameral
RCNEN dry canteen
RCNET preconcert
RCNEU fricandeau
RCNIT trecentist
RCOIE proctorise
proctorize
RCOIL proctorial
RCOIY preciosity
RCOOY proctology
trichology
trichotomy
RCOSE gracious me
RCOSY graciously
preciously
RCOTF trick out of
RCOTS Eric Coates
RCPIE preceptive
RCRBE procurable
RCRCS tractrices
RCRIE precursive
RCRIM trichroism
RCRMT trichromat
RCROS precarious
RCROY precursory
RCRTR procurator
RCSIG processing
RCSIN precession
procession
RCTEM Erechtheum
RCTES Erechtheus
RCUIE preclusive
RCUIN precaution
preclusion
RCUTS Procrustes
RCWRS brickworks
RDAIM gradualism
RDAIN graduation
RDAIT gradualist
RDAIY graduality
RDAST Fred Basset
RDCAE predecease
RDCBE eradicable
predicable
producible
RDCCE trade cycle
RDCER cri de coeur
RDCIE predictive
productive
RDCIN prediction
production
RDCOS predacious
RDCTR eradicator
RDEBE bridgeable
RDEED bridgehead
RDEOG cradle song
RDEON Bridgetown
RDEOT Bridgeport
RDFLE trade-falne
RDFLY pridefully
RDGLY prodigally
RDGOM bridegroom
RDGOS prodigious
RDIGY drudgingly
grudgingly
RDIMS Fred Titmus
RDIOE prednisone
RDKHO Frida Kahlo
RDMRS trademarks
RDNAE tridentate
RDNES Mrs Danvers
RDNIE Tridentine
RDNIL credential
prudential
RDOKD gridlocked
RDPIE bride-price
trade price
RDRCA Fredericia
RDRUE trade route
RDSAD bridesmaid
RDSET iridescent
RDSIE predestine
RDSIY predestiny
RDSOE predispose
RDSOK tradesfolk

RDTAD credit card
RDTBE creditable
RDTBY creditably
RDTET Bradstreet
RDTOE credit note
RDTOS traditions
RDTRS traditores
RDUIN trade union
RDWTR Bridgwater
READD free-handed
READT green audit
REAKT free-market
REAOT order about
REAPE free sample
REBRT Green Beret
REBYS pre-embryos
proembryos
RECOS Greek cross
REDES friendless
REDHP friendship
REDIS friendlies
REDIY friendlily
REEAT irrelevant
REEBY irremeably
REEET free-select
irreverent
REEON freeze down
REERH green earth
REEVR freeze over
grieve over
REFIE tree of life
REFNH greenfinch
REFRE armed force
REGAE arpeggiate
REHRH Free Church
REHUE greenhouse
REIES breeziness
greediness
REIET pre-eminent
REIGY creepingly
grievingly
REIIM praesidium
REIIN irreligion
REIKR arse-licker
RELGT free flight
green light
RELNS orderlines
RENAL free on rail
REOAL free-for-all
REOAO tree tomato
REODR freeholder
freeloader
REOES praenomens
REOEY gruesomely
REOIA praenomina
REOIE true-to-life
REOIN praetorian
REOIS Praetorius
REOPR tree hopper
REOSY grievously
REOTD free-footed
REOTR freebooter
praeposter
REOUE irresolute
REPAE Greenpeace
REPEH free speech
REPIE pre-emptive
REPIN pre-emption
REPKN free-spoken
REPPR green paper
order paper
REPRT free spirit
REPRY Green Party
green party
REPUD green pound
RERUD arse around
RESAE Greenslade
RESAK greenshank
RETBE arrestable
RETIE priestlike
RETLR freestyler
RETLY orientally
RETOD priesthood
REWMN freedwoman
freedwomen
REYUS greedy guts
RFCET proficient
RFCUE prefecture
RFEIH trifle with
RFIAE profligate
RFIAY profligacy
RFIES craftiness
RFIGY triflingly
RFIJM traffic jam
RFIKR trafficker
RFKIE craft knife
RFLAE trifoliate
RFLES artfulness
RFNIY profundity
RFPPR kraft paper
RFRAE trifurcate
RFRBE preferable
RFRBY preferably
RFRET preferment
RFRNE preference
RFSIN profession
RFTBE profitable
RFTBY profitably
RFTES profitless
RFTRM profit from
RFUDY profoundly
RGAHC urographic
RGAIE pragmatise
pragmatize
RGAIG drag-racing
RGAIM pragmatism
RGAIS pragmatics
RGAIT pragmatist
RGAMD programmed
RGAMR programmer
RGATY fragrantly
pregnantly
RGCLY tragically
RGCMC tragicomic
RGCNH tragacanth
RGDIT drug addict
RGDSE bragadisme
RGEOF trigger off
RGETD fragmented
RGETL fragmental
RGIES cragginess
grogginess
RGIGN dragging on
RGIGY braggingly
RGIHY priggishly
RGLEY art gallery
RGMNL trigeminal
RGMRH frog's-march
RGNAE brigandage
RGNIE brigantine
RGNLY originally
RGNSS orogenesis
RGNTC orogenetic
RGNTL urogenital
RGNTR originator
progenitor
RGOMN Greg Norman
RGOPR frog-hopper
RGOTC prognostic
RGOYE troglodyte
RGRAD krugerrand[❑]
RGROS gregarious
RGTDA bright idea
RGTES brightness
RGTND frightened
RGTNP brighten up
RGTYS Bright Eyes
RGYHC triglyphic
RHAIM Brahmanism
RHBTD prohibited
RHCAE orthoclase
RHCIE pro hac vice
RHECN archdeacon
RHGNA archegonia
RHGNL orthogonal
RHIHP archbishop
RHMDS Archimedes
RHMIK Graham Hick
RHMIL Graham hill
RHMOK Graham Lock
RHNAD Archenland
RHNIE prehensile
RHNIN prehension
RHNVR or whenever
RHPEA orthoptera
RHPIS orthoptics
RHPIT orthoptist
RHRSE Arthur Ashe
RHRVR or wherever
RHSOY prehistory
RHSRL orchestral
RHTAE architrave
RHTMA arrhythmia
RHTMC arrhythmic
RHTPL archetypal
RHTVR or whatever
RIAEY ordinately
RIAIE irritative
RIAIG irritating
RIAIL urticarial
RIAIN irrigation
irritation
ordination
urtication
RIAIY ordinarily
RIATR dreikanter
traik after
RICID brainchild
RIDAH brain death
RIDAN brain drain
RIEIE greisenise
greisenize
RIFLY fruitfully
RIHAE freightage
RIHIE wraith-like
RIHSS ornithosis
RIIDG prairie dog
RIIES braininess
RIIGY praisingly
trailingly
RIIIL artificial
RIJIE fruit juice
RIOOS traitorous
RIPPS drainpipes
RIPWR brainpower
RIRIE Craig Raine
RIRTR arbitrator
RISLD fruit salad
RISOM brainstorm
RIUAE articulate
RIUAY articulacy
RJCIE projectile
RJCIG projecting
RJCIN projection
RJCOY trajectory
RJDCD prejudiced
RJLYY Mrs Jellyby
RKHRD Erik the Red
RKLGT brake light
RKNES brokenness
RKNIL Broken Hill
RKNOE broken home
RKNON broken down
broken-down
RKROE prokaryote
RLBTC trilobitic
RLCOE frolicsome
RLCTR prolocutor
RLDOS preludious
RLEBS trolleybus
RLGCL orological
urological
RLGIE prologuise
prologuize
RLGUE drill gauge
RLIES frilliness
RLINE brilliance
RLINH trillionth
RLINY brilliancy
RLLAC Ural-Altaic
RLNAE prolongate
RLNUL trilingual

RLOIG trolloping
RLTCL prelatical
RLTRL trilateral
RLXOS prolixious
RMAIN grammarian
RMAUE dry measure
from nature
RMAWR Crimean War
RMDCL premedical
RMDNA prima donna
RMDNE prime donne
RMEIG trumpeting
RMELR trammeller
RMFCE prima facie
RMGNT primogenit
RMHIE from choice
RMIES grumpiness
RMIGY trimmingly
RMLAE promulgate
RMLDN trampled on
RMLFR tremble for
RMMRA pro memoria
RMMVR prime mover
RMNAA tramontana
RMNAE tramontane
RMNDR promenader
RMNHY trimonthly
RMNIH from on high
RMNLY criminally
RMNNE prominence
RMNOS gramineous
tremendous
RMNOY promontory
RMNVR Mrs Miniver
RMOIE trampoline
RMOIT trombonist
RMOKD grimlooked
RMOSA framboesia
RMPOE gramophone
RMPRE primiparae
RMPRS primiparas
RMRHC trimorphic
RMRIL primordial
RMRIM primordium
RMRTL premarital
RMSOY promissory
RMTEN Promethean
RMTES Prometheus
promptness
RMTIE prompt side
RMTIM promethium
RMTKR Bram Stoker
RMTRE dramaturge
RMTRY dramaturgy
RMVLY primevally
RNADD iron-handed
RNADN Iron Maiden
iron maiden
RNAEY truncately
RNAIN truncation
RNAOT bring about
prink about
RNATR ironmaster
transactor
RNBTY Grant Batty
RNBUO Bruno Bruno
Frank Bruno
RNCER Bronx cheer
RNCID grandchild
RNCIE transcribe
RNCIT transcript
RNCLY irenically
ironically
RNCOS arenaceous
RNCPA Frank Capra
RNDCR transducer
RNDCY grand duchy
RNDDY granddaddy
RNDIE drink-drive
RNDIG wrongdoing
RNDNS Grenadines
RNEAE grande dame
RNEEE grande jeté
RNEGN Prinz Eugen
RNEIE grangerise
grangerize
orange-wife
trance-like
RNESY princessly
RNETD Oranjestad
RNETL transeptal
RNETR Bronze Star
RNFED Frank Field
RNFLY wrongfully
RNFRE transferee
RNFRH bring forth
RNFRR transferor
RNFSR transfuser
RNFXD transfixed
RNGES transgress
RNGNC transgenic
RNHEN French bean
RNHES branchless
RNHNT French knot
RNHNY trenchancy
RNHOE bronchiole
RNHOF French loaf
French roof
RNHON French horn
RNHOT trench coat
RNHSE franchisee
RNHSR franchiser
RNHTC bronchitic
RNHTL Grand Hotel
RNHTS bronchitis
RNIAD grant-in-aid
RNIAE principate
RNIAI frangipani
RNICN Franciscan
RNIDY frenziedly
RNIES trendiness
RNIGP bringing up
bringing-up
RNIGY cringingly
grindingly
gruntingly
prancingly
prankingly
RNIIE transitive
RNIIN transition
RNILD iron-willed
principled
RNILS principles
RNINE transience
RNINY transiency
RNIOY transitory
RNITD iron-fisted
RNITR transistor
RNJRR grand juror
RNKFA Franz Kafka
RNKIE Franz Kline
RNLAC Brunel Marc
RNLAE crenellate
RNLCD translucid
RNLMS granulomas
RNLNR translunar
RNLRY granularly
RNLSS urinalysis
RNLST Franz Liszt
RNLTD granulated
RNLTR translator
RNMFI grand Mufti
RNMMA grandmamma
RNMNL pronominal
RNMTR transmuter
RNNEE grand-niece
RNNEG Cronenberg
RNNIS pronuncios
RNNSW pruning-saw
RNOAA Frank O'Hara
RNOAR brontosaur
RNOEA grand opera
RNOGR ironmonger
RNOSY wrongously
RNPAO grand piano
RNPAT transplant
RNPSD transposed
RNPSL transposal
RNPSR transposer
RNPTR transputer
RNRDE Ironbridge
RNRUD bring round
RNSAE trans-shape
RNSAT crankshaft
RNSEM Pringsheim
RNSIL crane's bill
cranesbill
RNSLB Drones Club
RNSOE grindstone
RNSRX grands prix
RNTBY Trinity Bay
RNTGD bring to God
RNTMD wrong-timed
RNTTL grand total
RNUAE transudate
RNUCD pronounced
RNUCE grand-uncle
RNUDR bring under
RNUEU Art Nouveau
RNULY tranquilly
RNVLE transvalue
RNVRE transverse
RNWRS frontwards
RNWYP wrong way up
RNYLT granny flat
RNYNP brandy snap
RNYNT granny knot
RNZPA Frank Zappa
ROAIN arrogation
ROATY arrogantly
ROCOS trioecious
ROEIS cryogenics
ROFRM cry off from
ROFYN Errol Flynn
ROIES broodiness
droopiness
ROIGY broodingly
droopingly
ROIIE prioritise
prioritize
ROIIN Ordovician
ROLNS Brooklands
ROOIS ergonomics
ROOIT ergonomist
ROSIK broomstick
RPAMR trip hammer
RPAND preplanned
RPAYX oropharynx
RPBIK drop a brick
RPCID tropicbird
RPCLY tropically
RPCOS drupaceous
RPDAE tripudiate
RPEES prophetess
RPEIE triple time
RPEIS fripperies
RPELM tropaeolum
RPEUP triple jump
RPFUT grapefruit
RPGNA propaganda
RPGTR propagator
RPIAE triplicate
RPICE crop circle
RPIGY trippingly
RPIIE graphitise
graphitize
RPIIY triplicity
RPITR proprietor
RPLAT propellant
RPLEM propylaeum
RPLET propellent
RPLIE propulsive
RPLIN propulsion
RPLNE crapulence
RPNEY prepensely
propensely
RPNHR drop anchor
RPNIG trepanning
RPNIN propension
RPNIY propensity
RPNMS treponemes
RPOHN tryptophan

RPOIE graptolite
RPONN drop down on
RPOOY graphology
RPORM cryptogram
RPPPR crêpe paper
graph paper
RPRAE proper name
RPRDY preparedly
RPRES properness
RPRFR prepare for
RPRID propertied
RPRIE tripartite
RPRIN proportion
RPRIS Propertius
RPRON proper noun
RPRUD wraparound
RPSES prepossess
RPSTR prepositor
RPSUE crepuscule
RPTAE propitiate
RPTNE prepotence
RPTNY prepotency
RPTOG triphthong
RPTOS propitious
RPUDR propounder
RPWTR gripe-water
RPYBE prepayable
RPYET prepayment
RPZUS trapeziums
RQAIY pre-qualify
RQETR frequenter
RQETY frequently
RQEUE craquelure
RRABT Brer Rabbit
RRETY pruriently
RSAED press ahead
RSAEN crustacean
RSAET press agent
RSAIE brush aside
RSASR trespasser
RSBED crispbread
crossbreed
RSBNS crossbones
RSBUD frostbound
RSCAN Ernst Chain
RSCEK crosscheck
cross-check
RSCIN trisection
RSCOS crisscross
criss-cross
RSCTR prosecutor
RSCUT grass court
RSDAY presidiary
RSDFI crise de foi
RSDNY presidency
RSDUS presidiums
RSEDS crescendos
RSEIA Prosperina
RSEIG freshening
RSEIM proscenium
RSEIN triskelion
RSEIY prosperity
RSEOF brassed off
RSEOS prosperous
RSETC crescentic
RSETR prospector
RSETS prospectus
RSFCD brass-faced
RSFEH press flesh
RSFLY trustfully
RSGFL presageful
RSGIY presignify
RSHSS prostheses
prosthesis
RSHTA bruschetta
RSHTC prosthetic
RSHTE bruschette
RSIES brassiness
crustiness
dressiness
friskiness
frostiness
grassiness
grisliness
prissiness
trashiness
trustiness
RSIGY crushingly
friskingly
graspingly
pressingly
trustingly
RSIIM prosaicism
RSINE prescience
RSIPS Aristippus
RSITI prosciutti
RSITO prosciutto
RSIUE crassitude
prostitute
RSMBY presumably
RSMKR dressmaker
RSMTH cross-match
RSNAP prison camp
RSNDY present-day
RSNET prisonment
RSNIG presenting
RSNIM Krishnaism
RSNRE brass nerve
RSOOI Cristofori
RSORT aristocrat
RSOTF fresh out of
RSPEE crosspiece
RSPIA drosophila
RSPLS erysipelas
RSPOE presuppose
RSPOF press proof
RSPTH crosspatch
RSRAS crossroads
RSRBD prescribed
proscribed
RSRBR prescriber
proscriber
RSRFR cross-refer
RSRIE presurmise
RSRTD frustrated
prostrated
RSSAE grass snake
RSSAT fresh start
RSSIT dress-shirt
RSSNE dress sense
RSTCS brass tacks
RSUHE proseuchae
RSUIE pressurise
pressurize
RSUIG pressuring
RSWDW grass widow
RSWMN Irishwoman
presswoman
presswomen
RSWTH wristwatch
RSWTR freshwater
RSYEY presbytery
RSYPA presbyopia
RSYPC presbyopic
RTAIN tritiation
RTALA prothallia
RTALS prothallus
RTATD protracted
RTATR protractor
RTCIE protective
RTCIG protecting
RTCIN protection
RTCLY critically
tritically
RTCOS cretaceous □
RTCRX protectrix
RTCZD criticized
RTELW written law
RTEOD arytaenoid
RTEOF written off
RTETC protreptic
RTFIG gratifying
RTFLY gratefully
truthfully
wrathfully
RTFRE brute force
RTGRO Greta Garbo
RTGRS Protagoras
RTHBR Fritz Haber
RTHDY wretchedly
RTHRE Brett Harte
RTIES frothiness
prettiness
RTIGY wr ithingly
RTIIE fratricide
RTIOS gratuitous
RTKIE Trotskyite
RTKIM Trotskyism
RTKIT Trotskyist
RTLAY fritillary
RTLIN J R R Tolkien
RTLIY gratillity
RTMOE pro tempore
RTMTC arithmetic
RTNAT pretendant
RTNES Pretenders
RTNIN pretension
pre-tension
RTNIY orotundity
RTNOE pratincole
RTNPD writing-pad
RTOIS trattorias
RTOYE proteolyse
RTPAM protoplasm
RTPAT protoplast
RTPIE arctophile
RTRAE Crater Lake
RTRCL oratorical
RTRIE fraternise
fraternize
RTRIY fraternity
protervity
RTRTC urethritic
RTRTR triturator
RTRTS urethritis
RTSAA Bratislava
RTSAT protestant □
RTSIG protesting
RTSIM Britishism
RTSLE try to solve
RTSRM truth serum
RTTPL prototypal
RTUET protrudent
RTUIE protrusive
RTUIG protruding
RTUIN protrusion
RTYAS pretty pass
RTYEL pretty well
RTYUH pretty much
RTZAS protozoans
RUAIE traumatise
traumatize
RUAIM traumatism
RUAOR troubadour
RUDDY groundedly
RUDES groundless
RUDLN groundplan
RUDOK groundwork
RUEOR grouse moor
RUHAE fraughtage
RULDY troubledly
RUOTN Group of Ten
RUPAT triumphant
RUPEY triumphery
RUPIG triumphing
RUSAS trousseaus
RUSAX trousseaux
RUUET fraudulent
RUVRL triumviral
RVAAT drive apart
RVAIE trivialise
trivialize
RVAIY triviality
RVAOG drive along
RVCAY drive crazy
RVDBE providable
RVDFR provide for
RVDNE providence □
RVDRI a rivederci
RVFLE prove false
RVGOS grave goods
RVHAT Braveheart

Words marked □ can also be spelled with an initial capital letter

RVIIG prevailing
RVLES travellers
RVLGD privileged
RVLGE travelogue
RVLIG grovelling
travelling
RVLIK travel sick
travel-sick
RVLNE prevalence
trivalence
RVLNY trivalency
RVLON travel-worn
RVLTR travelator
travolator
RVLVR travel over
RVMKR grave-maker
RVMTR gravimeter
RVMTY gravimetry
RVNES cravenness
RVNET prevenient
RVNIE preventive
RVNIL provincial
RVNIN prevention
RVNNE provenance
RVNRM Trivandrum
RVNUS driven nuts
RVOET graveolent
RVOSO previous to
RVOSY previously
RVPRE Privy Purse
RVRIE travertine
RVRIG traversing
RVRIL proverbial
RVRUN Trevor Nunn
RVSAT drive shaft
RVSOE gravestone
RVSOS provisions
RVTAN gravy train
RVTEE Private Eye
private eye
RVTIK Trevithick
RVTWR private war
RVTZD privatized
RVWEL drive-wheel
RWAGR grow larger
RWAKR grow darker
RWALD grow pallid
RWATR grow fatter
RWBAK draw a blank
RWBED brown bread
RWCUT crown court
RWCVR draw a cover
RWDAF brown dwarf
RWEKR grow weaker
RWEOF browned off
RWEPR crow-keeper
RWERO draw near to
RWETN browbeaten
RWETR browbeater
RWGOS brown goods
RWIES brawniness
drowsiness
RWIGR grow bigger
RWIGY drawlingly
frowningly
growlingly
prowlingly
RWLOK crewelwork
RWNOT drawing out
RWNPN drawing-pin
RWOGR grow longer
RWOIE grow to like
RWPPR brown paper
RWRAH draw breath
RWRDE drawbridge
Trowbridge
RWRUD crowd round
RWSGR brown sugar
RWSIT Brownshirt
RWSOE brownstone
RWSUE brown sauce
RWSUY brown study
RWTID draw it mild
RWTIE draw it fine
RWTIG drawstring
RWTMS draw stumps
RXMLY proximally
RXTLS Praxiteles
RYARD grey-haired
RYATR grey matter
RYEDD grey-headed
RYETS Fray Bentos
RYRAS Grey friars
Greyfriars
RYRFY arty-crafty
RYROK prayer book
prayerbook
prayer-book
RYTLS pray a tales
RYULT grey mullet
RZAOT crazy about
RZLOD brazilwood
RZNES brazenness
RZWMN prizewoman
SAAIE asparagine
SAAIG escalating
SAAIN escalation
SAAOS escaladoes
escapadoes
SAAOY escalatory
SABAD astarboard
SAEET escapement
SAEOD escape road
SAERM escape from
SAEUY estate duty
SAIIE Islamicise
Islamicize
SAIIT Islamicist
SALBE assailable
SALNA escallonia
SAOOY escapology
SAPET escarpment
SARLE espadrille
SASEN Isaac Stern
SAWLE Oscar Wilde
SBEES usableness
SCITY psychiatry
SCOAH psychopath
SCOOY psychology
SCRNL isochronal
SDNMC isodynamic
SEBAE assemblage
SEBAT osteoblast
SEBIS assemblies
SECAT osteoclast
SEDNY ascendancy
SEDRN Iskenderun
SEEAE asseverate
SEGLA aspergilla
SEGNC osteogenic
SEIIM asceticism
SEILY especially
SEIOU Ismet Inönü
SEPTY osteopathy
SESBE assessable
ostensible
SESBY ostensibly
SESET assessment
SESOS aspersions
SETAS essentials
SETSS asbestosis
SEUUL as per usual
SFEIA asafoetida
SFLES usefulness
SFTUH a soft touch
SHXAE asphyxiate
SIAIN aspiration
estimation
oscitation
SIATY oscitantly
SIIAE assibilate
assimilate
SIIGY aspiringly
SIIIM osmiridium
SIITA aspidistra
SILTR oscillator
SIMTC astigmatic
SINBE assignable
SINDO assigned to
SINET assignment
SISED use instead
SITNE assistance
SLCBN psilocybin
SLOIE psalmodise
psalmodize
SLROK ashlar-work
SLUIE isoleucine
SMERC asymmetric
SMRHC isomorphic
SMTIS isometrics
SMTTC asymptotic
SNFRE using force
SNHOY asynchrony
SOCRS as concerns
SOEEF ask oneself
SOETR C S Forester
SOIHD astonished
SOITD associated
SOITS associates
SONIG astounding
SOTET assortment
SOTIE a short time
SOYEE ascomycete
SPIIE asepticise
asepticize
SPLTK Ostpolitik
SPOOY psephology
SRADN Esarhaddon
SRAIN usurpation
SRBBE ascribable
SRBNS escribanos
SRCZD ostracized
SRETY esuriently
SRGLS astragulus
SRIGY usurpingly
SRLGR astrologer
SRMTY astrometry
SRNEO estrangelo
SRNET astringent
SRNIG estranging
SRNMC astronomic
SRNMR astronomer
SROSY usuriously
SRTIE escritoire
SRTUB a sore thumb
SRVTH tsarevitch
SSIMC isoseismic
SSIML isoseismal
STAIE psittacine
STMRY ask to marry
STRAE Ishtar Gate
STTDY as stated by
SUAIN osculation
SUAOY osculatory
SUBUH usquebaugh
SUCEN escutcheon
SUEES astuteness
SUGNY assurgency
SUIGY assumingly
SUOAP pseudocarp
SUPIE assumptive
SUPIN assumption❑
SXAIY asexuality
TAAGR stravaiger
TAAIS Athanasius
TAALN Ethan Allen
TABEK at daybreak
TABRY strawberry
TABUG Strasbourg
TACHN Ethan Cohen
TACII stracchini
TACIO stracchino
TAECN Athabescan
TAEIT strategist
TAGES Stranglers
TAGIG straggling
TAGTN straighten
straight-on
TAGTP straight up
straight-up
TAGTY straightly
TAGUE steam gauge

TAHDO attached to
TAHET attachment
TAHPY strathspey
TAHUE steakhouse
TAIAI Stradivari
TAIES steadiness
steaminess
TAIGY stealingly
TAIID stratified
TAIMC strabismic
TAIML strabismal
TAIMS strabismus
TAINE at variance
TAIOM stratiform
TAISY Stravinsky
TAKBE attackable
TAKIE steak knife
TANBE attainable
TANDY strainedly
TANET attainment
TAOIM stramonium
TAOTN strapontin
TAPDS strappados
TASHT it says that
TATIY stealthily
TATND straitened
TBEAD stable hand
TBEAS stable lass
TBEES stableness
TBIES stubbiness
TBIGY stabbingly
TBLSR stabiliser
TBLZR stabilizer
TBONY stubbornly
TCAOS sticcatoes
TCATC stochastic
TCIES stickiness
stockiness
TCIGD stockinged
TCIOT stick it out
TCSIL stock-still
TCSIT stick shift
TCUFR stick up for
TCUJB stick-up job
TCYAE sticky tape
TDGOP study group
TDIES stodginess
TDOLT studio flat
TDOSY studiously
TDSIH at odds with
TECIG stretching
TECOT stretch out
TEDDO attended to
TEDNE attendance
TEDNS attendants
TEEAN Stresemann
TEELY ethereally
TEGHN strengthen
TEIES steeliness
TEIOO strepitoso
TEIZA strelitzia
TEIZS strelitzes
TEMIE streamline

TEOTS utter oaths
TERNS other ranks
TESES stressless
TETAD streetward
TETAP streetlamp
TETBE attestable
TETIE streetwise
TETLN street plan
TETOS attentions
TETRB street Arab
street arab
TETRD street cred
TETUS streetfuls
TEUTD attenuated
TEWIE otherwhile
TEWMN other woman
TFCRS staff corps
TFEIG stiffening
TFIES stuffiness
TFIGY stiflingly
TFIRF Steffi Graf
TFNRE staff nurse
TGAIE stigmatise
stigmatize
TGAIG stagnating
TGAIM stigmatism
TGAIN stagnation
TGAIT stigmatist
TGATY stagnantly
TGCAH stagecoach
TGCAT stagecraft
TGEIG staggering
TGETE stag beetle
TGTPT a tight spot
THATR Utahraptor
THLAT at the least
THRAY at the ready
THSAT at the start
THSIE at this time
THSOE at the slope
THTIE at that time
THWEL at the wheel
THWRT at the worst
TIAIY ethicality
TIDEG Strindberg
TIEAK strike back
TIEAL strike sail
TIEAS strideways
TIEES stridelegs
TIENO strike into
TIEOD strike gold
TIEOE strike home
TIEON strike down
TIEOT strike root
TIERE strife-free
TIETY stridently
TIEUB strike dumb
TIGAD string band
TIGAS string bass
TIGEN string bean
TIGET string vest
TIGNO stringendo
TIGNY stringency

TIIES stripiness
TIIGY strikingly
strivingly
TIJIT strip joint
TIPDF stripped of
TITAE striptease
TITES strictness
TITRD strictured
TIUAE stridulate
TIUAT stridulant
TIUOS stridulous
TLAAE Italianate
TLADN still and on
TLAEY stellately
TLAIE Italianise
Italianize
TLATY stalwartly
TLAUE at pleasure
TLBRH stillbirth
TLCSS at all costs
TLDES stolidness
TLHUS at all hours
TLIIR stultifier
TLIOM stelliform
TLLFS still lifes
TLMTY stylometry
TLNRD Stalingrad
TLODR a tall order
TLSIS stylistics
TLTMS at all times
TLUAE stellulate
TLZBE utilizable
TMABM stamp album
TMCFL stomachful
TMCIE atomic pile
TMCOB atomic bomb
TMEIG stammering
TMIES stumpiness
TMIGR stem ginger
TMLBE stimulable
TMLTD stimulated
TMLTR stimulator
TMTTH stem stitch
TMTTS stomatitis
TMYTM item by item
TNAOE stand-alone
TNAOT stand about
TNARL Stan Laurel
TNBID stone-blind
TNBOE stony broke
stony-broke
TNCLY ethnically
TNEET stand erect
TNESY standers-by
TNETN Stan Kenton
TNGAD stand guard
TNGAH stenograph
TNHNE Stonehenge
TNHRP stench trap
TNHRT Stonyhurst
TNIAE stand in awe
TNIES stinginess
TNIFR stand in for

TNIGY standing by
stingingly
stintingly
stunningly
TNILR stenciller
TNMSN stonemason
TNOIN stentorian
TNPIE at any price
TNPIT at one point
standpoint
TNPOE ctenophore
TNRCY Stan Tracey
TNRNY itinerancy
TNSAS Stanislaus
TNSIL stand still
standstill
stone-still
TNTET stand treat
TNTIL stand trial
TNTWN stand to win
TNUFR stand up for
TNWMN stuntwoman
TOAIN etiolation
TOAOF stroganoff
TOAOS stromatous
TOEES otioseness
TOEIH at home with
TOELY stroke play
TOGOD stronghold
TOGOM strongroom
TOIAE strobilate
TOIGY stoopingly
TOPEE atmosphere
TORHM Otto Graham
TORSH Otto Frisch
TOSED at top speed
TOSNR Stroessner
TPADR stepladder
TPAET step-parent
TPAHR stepfather
TPAIE stephanite
utopianise
utopianize
TPAIG stop having
TPAIM utopianism❑
TPDES stupidness
TPEFY Stephen Fry
TPEIM at a premium
TPESN Stephenson
TPFIG stupefying
TPHGP stop the gap
TPIGN stepping-in
TPIGP stepping-up
stopping-up
TPLAE stipellate
TPLTD stipulated
TPLTR stipulator
TPNOS stupendous
TPOHR stepmother
TPYTP step by step
step-by-step
TRAAE start a hare
TRAAN start again

TRAIE eternalise
eternalize
TRAIG stargazing
TRAIN starvation
TRBAD storyboard
TRBOD stir abroad
TRBTS attributes
TRBUD stormbound
TRCIE attractive
TRCIN attraction
TRCOD storm cloud
TREAT Sturtevant
TREIG starveling[a]
TRFLY stormfully
TRGAA sterigmata
TRHDY starchedly
TRHUE storehouse
TRIES starriness
storminess
sturdiness
TRIGY startingly
stirringly
TRLZD sterilized
TRLZR sterilizer
TRNKD stark naked
stark-naked
TROAE stercorate
TROOS stertorous
TRORM stereogram
TROYE stereotype
TROYY stereotypy
TRSIL stork's bill
TRUCP stirrup cup
TRUIG start using
TRWRS sternwards
TRYTM star system
TRYYD starry-eyed
TSRTH at a stretch
TTCAT statecraft
TTCLY statically
TTEIG stuttering
TTEQE statuesque
TTHOT stitchwort
TTNET at a tangent
TTOAY stationary
TTOEY stationery
TTOIG stationing
TTSIS statistics
TTSOE statoscope
TTTBY statutably
TTTCP statute cap
TTWRT at its worst
TUEET attunement
TUGEN struggle on
TUGIG struggling
TUHOS struthious
TULET at full pelt
TULIT at full tilt
TUPIT at gunpoint
TUTRD structured
TUTRL structural
TVDVS Steve Davis
TVJNS Steve Jones
TVNOF staving off
TVNOS Steven Jobs
TVNUE at a venture
TVOET Steve Ovett
TVYUG Steve Young
TWRES stewardess
TYEID stay behind
TYFOT stay afloat
TYHIE strychnine
TYHIM strychnism
TYHOM stay shtoom
TYREO stay true to
TYTOE stay-at-home
UAAEK Musala Peak
UAAMA tularaemia
UAAMC tularaemic
UABIG human being
UACIT autarchist
UACLY Judaically
UACNY sugar candy
UADDY sugar daddy
UADEL buy and sell
UADRN Duran Duran
UADWY out and away
UAEBW out at elbow
UAEDN mujaheddin
UAEDO put an end to
UAEEG curate's egg
UAEES humaneness
UAEIE mutagenise
mutagenize
UAIES queasiness
sugariness
UAIIG humanizing
UAIIS humanities
UAIIY curability
dupability
durability
mutability
UAIKF run a risk of
UAINL mutational
nutational
UAITC humanistic
UAIUE cut a figure
UAIXN put a jinx on
UAKCL autarkical
UAMNH lunar month
UAOIM sudatorium
UARDS Rural Rides
UATES mulattress
UATIH au fait with
UATIY Kuwait City
UATNS sugar tongs
UATPO put a stop to
UATRA eubacteria
UAUEY subacutely
UAUOS subaqueous
UAUTC subaquatic
UAYTC eukaryotic
UAYTS eucalyptus
UBAHS quebrachos
UBATR dumb-waiter
UBDES turbidness
UBEAE jumble sale
UBEAH bubble bath
UBEAK bubble pack
UBEED tumbleweed
UBEES humbleness
mumble-news
UBEFL tumblerful
UBEON tumbledown
tumble-down
UBETD outbreath'd
UBEVR bubble over
UBGEY humbuggery
UBIDY purblindly
UBIGN Zurbriggen
UBIGR Rusbridger
UBIGY fumblingly
humblingly
jumblingly
mumblingly
rumblingly
UBJMO mumbo-jumbo
UBLNE outbalance
turbulence
UBNMN husbandman
UBNTD turbinated
UBOSY cumbrously
UBRAD Cumberland
rubber band
UBRAN outbargain
UBREK rubberneck
UBRES Guy Burgess
numberless
UBRIE Humberside
UBROE cumbersome
UBRRE rubber tree
UBRZD rubberized
UBSTP rubbish tip
UBTEN put between
sunbittern
UBTIG sunbathing
UBTUK dumbstruck
UBUTR outbluster
UBYNR Yul Brynner
UCAES purchasers
UCAGD surcharged
UCAGR surcharger
UCAIG purchasing
UCAIN cunctation
subclavian
UCAIT Sun Chariot
UCAKR nutcracker
UCAUE nunciature
UCDLY suicidally
UCDNA succedanea
UCDUK punch-drunk
UCEIG quickening
succeeding
UCENN muscle in on
UCEPY buy cheaply
UCETS zucchettos
UCFED Burchfield
UCHRT Burckhardt
UCIES bunchiness
UCIIS punctilios
UCINL functional
UCLAE auscultate
UCLNE succulence
UCLNY succulency
UCLRY muscularly
UCLUE subculture
UCMIG succumbing
UCMRH quick march
UCNLA Pulcinella
UCNTY succinctly
UCOSY lusciously
UCPIE susceptive
UCRES cut corners
UCSFL successful
UCSIE successive
UCSIK quick-stick
UCSIN succession
UCSNS quicksands
UCSOS successors
UCTET Dutch treat
UCTIK quick trick
UCTON quickthorn
UCUCE Dutch uncle
UCUIG puncturing
UCULY punctually
UCUTD punctuated
UCVDS muscovados
UCWMN Dutchwoman
Dutchwomen
UDAGE quadrangle
UDATL quadrantal
UDATS quadrantes
UDAUE quadrature
UDCML duodecimal
UDCMS duodecimos
UDDDY fuddy-duddy
UDEAE Dundee cake
UDEIY Dundee City
UDEKE Auld Reekie
UDENA quadrennia
UDEOE cuddlesome
UDETN Huddleston
UDEWY muddle away
UDGRY hurdy-gurdy
UDHEE curd cheese
UDHLY Buddy Holly
UDIEE quadrireme
UDIES quadriceps
UDIET quadrisect
UDIIM quadrivium
UDLBY Dundalk Bay
UDLNS guidelines
UDMVE buddy movie
UDNES suddenness
UDNOE burdensome
UDNRS pundonores
UDODR fundholder
UDRAD Sunderland
UDRED dunderhead
UDRES rudderless
UDRID wunderkind
UDRQO quid pro quo

UDRUK dunderfunk
UDULT quadruplet
Ruud Gullit
UDULX quadruplex
UDVDR subdivider
UDYET Sunday best
UDYOT Sunday Post
UEAII iure mariti
UEAIN numeration
UEAMY lukewarmly
UEANY suzerainty
UEARE Oudenaarde
UEBES superbness
UEBUG Luxembourg
UECLA Lupercalia
UECLN tuberculin
UECLR tubercular
UECNE pubescence
quiescence
tumescence
UECNY quiescency
UECRO supercargo
UEEES Eugene Debs
UEEIE euhemerise
euhemerize
UEELY funereally
UEERM Eugene Aram
UEGAS supergrass
UEGAT supergiant
UEGOP supergroup
UEHMN superhuman
UEIEY juvenilely
UEIIO iure divino
jure divino
UEIIY juvenility
UEIOM tuberiform
UEIOS mucedinous
UEIRO superior to
UEIRY superiorly
UELMT outer limit
UEMDL supermodel
UENLY supernally
UENUH sure enough
UENVE supernovae
UENVS supernovas
UEOIE superoxide
UEOIY tuberosity
UEOOY numerology
UEOSY numerously
UEOTD sure-footed
UEPWR superpower
UERYL super-royal
UESAD Queensland
UESAE outer space
UESDD superseded
UESDR superseder
UESLB Queen's Club
UESNC supersonic
UESOE superstore
UETAY quaestuary
UETNC supertonic
UETTE supertitle
UEUAO iure humano
jure humano
UEUBR huge number
UEURT bureaucrat
UEVIE quiet voice
UEVRE Jules Verne
UEVSR supervisor
UEWMN superwoman
UFAIM ruffianism
suffragism
UFAIT suffragist
UFATY puff pastry
UFCAT surfactant
UFCET sufficient
UFCOS tuffaceous
UFEDR outfielder
UFEED bufflehead
UFEIG gut feeling
UFGNE suffigance
UFGTR gunfighter
UFLES ruefulness
UFLET fulfilment
UFLIG fulfilling
UFLOT duffel coat
UFOES Sunflowers
UFOEY buffoonery
UFOIG outflowing
UFRAD put forward
UFRBE sufferable
UFRBY sufferably
UFRFT suffer a fit
UFRIH puffer fish
UFRNE sufferance
UFROE buffer zone
UFRRM suffer from
UFTEM Gulf Stream
UFTIG outfitting
UFTTS Gulf States
UFUDR dumfounder
UFWEL curfew-bell
UGAIE burglarise
burglarize
UGASS sunglasses
UGCDL fungicidal
UGCLY surgically
UGDAE jugged hare
UGDES ruggedness
UGEIH juggle with
UGEOK Jungle Book
UGEOL jungle fowl
UGETE dung beetle
dung-beetle
UGIES hungriness
quagginess
UGIGY bunglingly
jugglingly
UGISM Gus Grissom
UGNEM Guggenheim
UGNOT bulging out
UGNRC subgeneric
UGNRL outgeneral
UGNRS sui generis
UGNSS subgenuses
UGOIG burgeoning
UGRAT juggernaut
UGRDE Muggeridge
UGRGR budgerigar
UGRHA Tungurahua
UGSET turgescent
UGSIE suggestive
UGSIG suggesting
UGSIN suggestion
UGTZL Turgut Ozal
UHAGR bushranger
UHAHR much rather
UHAKR bushwalker
UHAKT bush jacket
UHARE Hugh Laurie
UHASN Hugh Casson
UHESY ruthlessly
UHIDY rush wildly
UHITC euphuistic
UHLIN Cú Chulainn
UHLNS oughtlings
UHNEK Auchinleck
UHNOS euphonious
UHNSA euthanasia
UHOFR push too far
UHOIG cushioning
UHONR much sooner
UHOYE Euphrosyne
UHRAD Sutherland
UHREE Hugh Greene
UHRHP authorship
UHROD rutherford❑
UHRUD push around
UHRZD authorized
UHSAL Hughes Hall
UHSTS such as it is
UHTMC eurhythmic
UHULY Hugh Huxley
UHUTN push-button
UIABX musical box
UIAEN ruminate on
UIAIE puritanise
puritanize
ruminative
UIAIG ruminating
UIAIM puritanism❑
UIAIN fumigation
jubilation
mutilation
rumination
Ruritanian
UIAIY musicality
UIATY jubilantly
ruminantly
UIAUE judicature
UIBIY muliebrity
UIDAA music drama
UIEES supineness
UIEOS auriferous
luciferous
nuciferous
UIETL rudimental
UIGOP music group
UIHBE punishable
UIHES mulishness
UIHET punishment
UIIET munificent
UIIEY fugitively
UIIIR humidifier
UIIIY audibility
fusibility
UIILY judicially
UIINY musicianly
UIIOS cupidinous
fuliginous
rubiginous
UIITC pugilistic
UIITD humiliated
UIITT humidistat
UILIE burial site
UIMTC numismatic
UIMTE cubic metre
UIMTR audiometer
eudiometer
UINOB fusion bomb
UIODR put in order
UIOIM auditorium
UIOIY luminosity
UIOOS nucivorous
UIOOY musicology
UIOSY luminously
mutinously
UIPAE put in place
UIPIE audiophile
UIRNH nudibranch
UISEN Rubinstein
UISOL music stool
UITCL juristical
UITES quaintness
UJCIE subjective
UJCIN subjection
UJCIY subjectify
UJGTD subjugated
UJGTR subjugator
UKAIG muck-raking
UKBEK lucky break
UKCAM lucky charm
UKDWY tucked away
UKEON buckle down
UKESY lucklessly
UKETE musk beetle
UKLIE cuckoldise
cuckoldize
UKNAH quaking ash
UKNIH muck in with
UKOIT cuckoo pint
UKPED muckspread
UKRIL Bunker Hill
UKRPN dukkeripen
UKRUD muck around
UKSVN Turkish Van
UKTET bucket seat
UKTHP bucket shop
UKTON bucket down
UKTUS bucketfuls
UKTYU sucks to you!
UKYRT turkey-trot

ULAAE fully awake
ULAIE nuclearise
nuclearize
ULAIN nucleation
ULALD full-sailed
ULAND full-manned
ULAWR nuclear war
ULBLO hullabaloo
ULBRY hurly-burly
ULCAE public face
ULCTR duplicator
ULDAE curled-pate
ULDIE mulled wine
ULDOK curled dock
ULEDD bull-headed
ULEGH full-length
ULEGT full weight
ULEKD bull-necked
ULESN full nelson
ULEVS bull-beeves
ULFIE full of life
ULFIG nullifying
qualifying
ULFLY guilefully
ULGON fully-grown
ULICE full-circle
ULIES guiltiness
ULIGD full-rigged
full-winged
ULIGP building-up
ULIHN Kublai Khan
ULIHY qualmishly
ULIIG purloining
ULITD dull-witted
ULMNL subliminal
ULMUT full amount
ULNES sullenness
ULNIH outlandish
ULNOF pulling-off
ULNUL sublingual
ULOAT bulldog ant
ULOCD full-voiced
ULOID full-bodied
ULOIE guillotine
nucleoside
nucleotide
ULOIS nucleonics
ULRCE Guy Laroche
ULRWH full growth
ULSIG publishing
ULSUD burlesqued
ULTIG subletting
ULTPS sur le tapis
ULYIE guilty-like
UMAUE outmeasure
UMCSE submucosae
UMCSL submucosal
UMDAT submediant
UMDEN curmudgeon
UMLIG pummelling
UMNAK summon back
UMNBE summonable
UMNTP humming-top

UMNYN put money on
UMRIE summerlike
summer time
summertime
UMRIN submersion
UMRNR submariner
UMRUD cummerbund
UMRZD summarized
UMSBE surmisable
UMSCT Burmese cat
UMSIE submissive
UMSIN submission
UMTES summitless
UMUTD surmounted
UMUTR surmounter
UNALS Juan Carlos
UNAOL guinea fowl
UNCER subnuclear
UNCIE quinacrine
UNCOS pugnacious
UNDIT turn adrift
UNHBE quenchable
UNHES quenchless
UNIID quantified
UNIIR quantifier
UNIIS quantities
UNINL turn signal
UNJNS Burne-Jones
UNLIG tunnelling
UNMNY funny money
UNNHM Cunningham
UNNMN Running Man
UNNOF running off
UNODR turn colder
UNOOR turn colour
UNOUT turn to dust
UNPLA turnip flea
UNRBE vulnerable
UNREN runner bean
UNRUD turn around
turnaround
UNSIG burnishing
furnishing
UNSOY funny story
UNTIE burnettise
burnettize
UNTIK turn a trick
UNUBR burnt umber
UNULT quintuplet
UNUTE turn turtle
UNWMN funny woman
UOAAT put on an act
UOAIB out on a limb
UOAIM automatism
UOAIN automation
UOAIT automatist
UOAOS autogamous
automatons
UOASY cup of assay
UOBTL suborbital
UOCUT out of court
UODOS out of doors
out-of-doors

UOEEF hug oneself
UOEOS autogenous
UOEQE humoresque
Tudoresque
UOFCS out of focus
UOFES Rudolf Hess
UOFIH run off with
UOFNO rub off on to
UOFRM cut off from
UOFTO Rudolf Otto
UOHBA autophobia
UOHHN autochthon
UOHQE Eurocheque
UOIAT autodidact
UOILY tutorially
UOITC eulogistic
UOJIT out of joint
UOLSY autoplasty
UOLVA Yugoslavia
UOODR out of order
UOOIE automobile
automotive
UOOOS autonomous
UOOSY humorously
UOPAE out of phase
out of place
UOPIT out of print
UOPPR put on paper
UORAH out of reach
UORES humourless
UORPY autography
UORTC autocratic
autoerotic
UOSAE out of shape
UOSGT out of sight
UOSNH out of synch
UOSOK out of stock
UOSRS out of sorts
UOTAA autostrada
UOTIL put on trial
UOTUH out of touch
UOUNL Eurotunnel
UOWAK out of whack
UPAIN sulphation
UPAKD hump-backed
UPATR supplanter
UPCIG suspecting
UPCOS auspicious
suspicious
UPCOY lumpectomy
UPDNA suppedanea
UPDTD cuspidated
UPEAE Purple Haze
UPEAN Purple Rain
UPEES suppleness
UPEET supplement
UPEIN suppletion
UPESD suppressed
UPESR suppressor
UPHGN jump the gun
UPIAE supplicate
UPIAT supplicant
UPIIG surprising

UPINE suppliance
UPNES suspenders
UPNIE suspensive
turpentine
UPNIN out-pension
suspension
UPNOY suspensory
UPOAE sulphonate
UPOJY jump for joy
UPOKY jump-jockey
UPPMY rumpy-pumpy
UPRES supperless
supporters
UPRIE supportive
UPRIG purporting
supporting
UPROM outperform
UPSBE supposable
UPSBY supposably
UPSDO supposed to
UPSDY supposedly
UPSFL purposeful
UPSIG surpassing
UPSIN out-passion
UPSOM rumpus room
UPTHW puppet show
UPUAE sulphurate
UPUIE sulphurise
sulphurize
UPUIG outpouring
UPUKR lumpsucker
UPUOS sulphurous
UPYET supplyment
UPYLW Murphy's law
URAIM surrealism□
URAIT surrealist
URCLM curriculum
URCLR curricular
URCLY rubrically
URCOS lubricious
URCTR lubricator
rubricator
UREAE quarterage
UREIG quartering
UREIM puerperium
URELR quarreller
UREON quarteroon
URESW quarter-saw
URFIG putrefying
URGOS outrageous
URHUE guardhouse
URIES quirkiness
URIGY hurryingly
queryingly
URNAM current aim
URNED guaranteed
URNIE quarantine
URNIG gunrunning
URNIS currencies
URNTD mucronated
UROIO Puerto Rico
URPIN subreption
URPLA eutrapelia

URRNL suprarenal
URSET putrescent
URSOE quernstone
URTOS nutritious
URUDD surrounded
URUIE subroutine
URWED furrow-weed
URZTC quartzitic
USAIE Russianise
Russianize
USAIN outstation
substation
USATA Russian tea
USATY puissantly
pursuantly
USCIN subsection
USCTS Duns Scotus
USDAY subsidiary
USDES cussedness
USDNE subsidence
USDZR subsidizer
USETN outsweeten
USETR bus shelter
USFRH burst forth
USHUE guest house
guesthouse
USIAT pursuivant
USIGR gunslinger
mud-slinger
outswinger
USIGY guessingly
pursuingly
questingly
USINR questioner
USIUE substitute
USLAS Mussulmans
USLOF Düsseldorf
USLRE curselarie
USMBE subsumable
USMIE cut some ice
USNBY Hudson's Bay
USNIS outs and ins
USOOA Luis Somoza
USQET subsequent
USRBR subscriber
USRHP bursarship
USRMN nurseryman
USRSS Guns 'n' Roses
USRSY Mussorgsky
USRTH outstretch
USRTL substratal
USRTM substratum
USSET subsistent
USSIE purse-seine
USSIG subsisting
USUUL Luis Buñuel
UTAED subtrahend
UTAIE fustianise
fustianize
UTAIN Australian
lustration
UTAKT dust jacket
UTAOP Australorp

UTATR subtracter
subtractor
UTBET cult object
UTCAY justiciary
UTCIS mustachios
UTCLY rustically
UTCRS quit scores
UTCTD rusticated
UTDAH put to death
UTEAE lustreware
UTEEK turtle-neck
UTEES lustreless
subtleness
UTEHW run the show
UTEIH cuttlefish
UTEIS subtleties
UTEOE turtledove
UTEOL quatrefoil
UTERH run to earth
UTESY hurtlessly
UTFIG justifying
UTGAE multigrade
UTHJB just the job
UTIES sultriness
UTIGY rustlingly
UTIIG sustaining
UTITD lust-dieted
UTLNH out to lunch
UTLQY multiloquy
UTMAE custom-made
UTMDA multimedia
UTMZD customized
UTNAE sustentate
UTNBX hunting-box
UTNCP hunting-cap
UTNDN Huntingdon
UTNDP buttoned up
UTNED muttonhead
UTNEL button cell
UTNHP sultanship
UTNIE just-in-time
UTNLA fustanella
UTNNE sustenance
UTNOD buttonhold
UTNOE buttonhole
UTNOF cutting-off
putting-off
UTNOT cutting-out
jutting out
UTNRE put to nurse
UTOAY auctionary
tuitionary
UTOER auctioneer
UTOSY lustrously
UTPIR multiplier
UTPSD juxtaposed
UTRAN Quatermain
UTRAY quaternary❑
UTRBY Bustard Bay
UTREN butter bean
UTRGS mustard gas
UTRIE muster-file
UTRIH butter dish

UTRIN quaternion
UTRIZ Austerlitz
UTRLY culturally
gutturally
UTROK muster-book
UTROT butterwort
UTRUE subterfuge
UTRUH put through
run through
run-through
UTSAE multi-stage
put to shame
UTSEP put to sleep
UTSIL multiskill
UTTAK multi-track
UTTDS multitudes
UTUKT rust-bucket
UTUPR tub-thumper
UTVBE cultivable
UTVCL multivocal
UTVLE Huntsville
UTVTD cultivated
UTVTR cultivator
UTWSE run to waste
UUAIE cumulative
UUAIN cumulation
UUBSI Lubumbashi
UUCLR furuncular
UUDBS run up debts
UUEES futureless
UUEIE future wife
UUETY luculently
purulently
UUIIN futurition
UUINE luxuriance
UUITC futuristic
UUNLY autumnally
UUOOY futurology
UUROS lugubrious
UURUH cut up rough
UUTAE tumult-uate
UUTES augustness
UUTOS tumultuous
UUWET durum wheat
UVCOS curvaceous
UVDIE curved line
UVLAN outvillain
UVNIN subvention
UVNTD pulvinated
UVRIE subversive
UVRIN subversion
UVRUD curve round
UVRZD pulverized
UVVBE survivable
UVYNE purveyance
UWGOD Ludwig Mond
UWTIG outwitting
UYHIS Eurythmics
UYIVR ruby silver
UYIZE busy Lizzie
busy lizzie
UYSBE busy as a bee
UZATR quizmaster

UZEET puzzlement
UZEVR puzzle over
UZIGY puzzlingly
UZLGC fuzzy logic
UZLRN Buzz Aldrin
UZNIY Quezon City
VCAIN evacuation
VCLUE aviculture
VDNEF evidence of
VDNIL evidential
VGRNR Ava Gardner
VIIGY availingly
VLAIE evaluative
VLAIN evaluation
VLENO evolve into
VLIDD evil-minded
VLPRT evil spirit
VNADD even-handed
VNALV Ivan Pavlov
VNEET avengement
evincement
VNEIE evangelise
evangelize
VNEIM evangelism❑
VNEIT evangelist❑
VNGRE avant-garde
VNHNE even chance
VNHUH even though
VNRLV Ivan Krylov
VNSET evanescent
VNUBR even number
VNUIE aventurine
VNULY eventually
VOEOO avgolemono
VPRBE evaporable
VPRTD evaporated
VPRTR evaporator
VPSTR ovipositor
VRADD overhanded
VRAIG overeating
VRANH overlaunch
VRAOY overcanopy
VRATR overmaster
VRBTF every bit of
VRCAT Ivory Coast
VRCIG overacting
VRCOS avaricious
VREES averseness
VREGT overweight
VREIE over-refine
VREIG overseeing
VREKN overreckon
VRETD overheated
VRFIE overoffice
VRHDW overshadow
VRHRE overcharge
VRHTP over the top
over-the-top
VRHWR overshower
VRHWY over the way
VRIEY overnicely
overwisely
VRIIG ever-living

overriding
VRITR overwinter
VRLDS Everglades
VRLUH overslaugh
VRLVK Sverdlovsk
VRLYD overplayed
VRNOM overinform
VRNOT over and out
VRNUE overinsure
VRODD overloaded
VROEF every one of
VROET overmodest
VROEY overcome by
VROHR every other
VROIG overcoming
VROKD overcooked
overlooked
overworked
VRPAE every place
VRPED overspread
VRRCD overpriced
VRRIE overpraise
VRRUD overground
VRRWH overgrowth
VRTAN overstrain
VRTES overstress
VRTIE overstride
overstrike
VRTIG everything
VRTTD overstated
VRTUG overstrung
VRTWR ivory tower
ivory-tower
VRUDN overburden
VRUIG overruling
VRUND overturned
VRUNY Ivor Gurney
VRUPY oversupply
VRUTE oversubtle
VRWEE everywhere
VRXOE overexpose
VSAGY Yves Tanguy
VSEAE eviscerate
VTMAA Svetambara
VUHET avouchment
WABOD sweat blood
WAGAD sweat gland
WAIOT sweat it out
WASIT sweatshirt
sweat-shirt
WCEHM Twickenham
WDNOG Swedenborg
WEBED sweetbread
WEBIR sweet brier
WEEIG sweetening
WEHAT sweetheart
WEIES tweediness
WEIGY sweepingly
WELDE Tweedledee
WELDM Tweedledum
WESAE sweepstake
WESEL sweet smell
WETDY a week today
WETND sweet-toned
WGBOK swage block
WGEIG swaggering
WIHES owlishness
WLEIG sweltering
WLEOD twelvefold
WLEOE twelve-tone
WLEON twelve noon
WLGTD twilighted
WLIGY swellingly
WLOGN swell organ
WLOIG swallowing
WLTAP Twyla Tharp
WLTMN twelfth man
WMIGY swimmingly
WNDUK swine-drunk
WNFVR swine fever
WNIGY swingingly
twangingly
WNMNY owing money
WNPIG swan-upping
WNRUD swan around
WNYOD twentyfold
WOAID two of a kind
WOIGY swooningly
WOTRE two or three
WRGAD sword-guard
WRIHY dwarfishly
WRRUD swarm round
WSDIL twist drill
WSFAC Swiss franc
WTEIG twittering
WTEIN zwitterion
WTHAK switchback
WTHRM switch from
WTIGY twittingly
WTOIE two-two time
WVLIG swivelling
WWELR two-wheeler
XAAIN excavation
exhalation
XADBE expandable
XAHDA ex cathedra
XARAE expatriate
XASBE expansible
XASBY expansibly
XASIE exhaustive
XASIG exhausting
XASIN exhaustion
XBOOY exobiology
XBRNE exuberance
XCAIE execrative
XCAIN execration
XCAOY execratory
XCIGY exactingly
XCIUE exactitude
XCRAE exacerbate
XCTBE executable
XCTVS executives
XEDBE expendable
extendable
extendible
XEDDY extendedly
XEDVR extend over
XEIAE expeditate
XEIET experiment
XEIEY expeditely
XEIIN expedition
XEINE expedience
experience
XEINY expediency
XEIRY exteriorly
XELNE excellence
XELNY Excellency
XENLY externally
XEPIN excerption
XESBE extensible
XETBE expectable
XETBY expectably
XETDO expected to
XETDY expectedly
XETES exceptless
expertness
XETNY expectancy
XGEAE exaggerate
XGNAK oxygen mask
XGNET oxygen debt
oxygen tent
XGNTR oxygenator
XGOSY exiguously
XGTCL exegetical
XIAAE exhilarate
XIAIE excitative
XIAIN excitation
expiration
XIAOY excitatory
XICIN extinction
XICTD exsiccated
XICUE extincture
XIEET excitement
XIGIH extinguish
XIIGY excitingly
XIIIE exhibitive
XIIIN exhibition
XIPTR extirpator
XLAIN exaltation
exultation
XLATY exultantly
XLCBE explicable
XLCCD oxalic acid
XLCTY explicitly
XLDBE excludable
XLEAE exulcerate
XLIGY exultingly
XLIIE exploitive
XLIIG explaining
XLSOS explosions
XLTVS expletives
XMNBE examinable
XMOSY eximiously
XMRNC oxymoronic
XMTRM exempt from
XNEAE exenterate
XNRTD exonerated
XOCSO ex concesso
XODAS Oxford bags
XODLE Oxford blue
XOIAE excogitate
XOIIN exposition
XOIOY expository
XOITD excoriated
XONIG expounding
XOTBE exportable
XRAIE exurbanite
XRCAE excruciate
XRCBE extricable
XRCDL uxoricidal
XRCIN extraction
XRCVR extra cover
XRIAT exorbitant
XRLRE extra large
extra-large
XRMRL extramural
XRNOS extraneous
XROSY uxoriously
XRSET excrescent
XRSIE expressive
XRSIN expression
XSEAE exasperate
XSHRC exospheric
XTCES exoticness
XTCLY exotically
XTGID axe to grind
XUAIN exhumation
XUCIN expunction
XUFAE exsufflate
XUGTR expurgater
expurgator
XUSSS excursuses
XYDIY oxeye daisy
YAATA pyracantha
YAGSA hypalgesia
YAGSC hypalgesic
YAIIM sybaritism
YAKNE eye askance
YANCL tyrannical
YANZD tyrannized
YARAY My Fair Lady
YATRA dysarthria
YATRL hypaethral
YBDUS cymbidiums
YBEOE Bye Bye Love
YBLCL symbolical
YBLZR symbolizer
YCEIE syncretise
syncretize
YCEIM syncretism
YCEIT syncretist
YCIET by accident
YCPTR syncopator
YCRIL myocardial
YCRIM myocardium
YCRNC synchronic
YCRNL synchronal
YCRSS synchrysis
YCTHR eye-catcher
YDCTR syndicator
YEAMA hyperaemia
YEAMC hyperaemic

YEBLC hyperbolic
YEBTN hyperbaton
YECIT typescript
YEDCE synecdoche
YEETR typesetter
YEGTC synergetic
YEMDA hypermedia
YENTC cybernetic
YERTR typewriter
YESAE cyberspace
YESNC hypersonic
YESNF by reason of
YETNC hypertonic
YGAHA dysgraphia
YGASS eyeglasses
YGZTN Kyrgyzstan
YHACS ayahuas-cos
YHBAE Tycho Brahe
YHCLY mythically
YHCZR mythicizer
YHGRS Pythagoras
YHLTC syphilitic
YHNTD hyphenated
YHSIE by this time
YHTIE by that time
YIAIY typicality
YIDOD myriadfold
YIIIE pyrimidine
YIOIE pyridoxine
YITAA Lysistrata
YITEF by virtue of
YLBSS syllabuses
YLCIN by-election
YLCLY cyclically
YLCOS cyclo-cross
YLMAS by all means
YLPDA cyclopedia
YLSYE cyclostyle
YMSRW pygmy shrew
YMTIE symmetrise
symmetrize
YNIIE hypnoidise
hypnoidize
YNLRE by and large
YNMAS by any means
YNSEM gymnosperm
YNSIE by one's side
YNSIS gymnastics
YNSUS gymnasiums
YNTZD hypnotized
YOAIC pyromaniac
YOALL pyrogallol
YOCPC gyroscopic
YODUK by good luck
YOEAS bygone days
YOEMC hypodermic
YOEMS hypodermis
YOEOS pyrogenous
YOERC pyrometric
YOEUE hypotenuse
YOHBA cynophobia
pyrophobia
YOHNY sycophancy
YOHOE cytochrome
YOHSS hypophyses
hypophysis
hypotheses
hypothesis
YOHTC hypothetic
YOIAE tyrosinase
YOIIE mylonitise
mylonitize
YOOIM hypocorism
YOOIT cytologist
mycologist
YORPY kymography
typography
YOTAT by contrast
YOTSS hypostases
hypostasis
synostoses
YOTTC hypostatic
YOUIE pyrolusite
YOYEE myxomycete
YOYIE synonymise
synonymize
YOYOS synonymous
YPATA hyoplastra
YPEIM dysphemism
YPGAD lymph gland
YPIIE lyophilise
lyophilize
YPNTC tympanitic
YPNTS tympanites
YPOIM dysprosium
YPOYE lymphocyte
YPTIE sympathise
sympathize
YPTMY gyppy tummy
YRCLY hydrically
YREIN Tyrrhenian
YRGAH hygrograph
YRLGC hydrologic
YRLSS hydrolysis
YRLTC hydrolytic
YRMTR hydrometer
hygrometer
YRMTY hydrometry
hygrometry
YRNIG by-drinking
YRPDA cypripedia
YRPNC hydroponic
YRPOE hydrophone
YRPTY hydropathy
YRPWR hydropower
YRPYE hydrophyte
hygrophyte
YRSMS hydrosomes
YRSOE hydroscope
hygroscope
YRUIS hydraulics
YSHNA myasthenia
YSMTR hypsometer
YSMTY hypsometry
YSPIA gypsophila
YTCLY mystically
YTCRI cysticerci
YTEIE synthesise
synthesize
synthetise
synthetize
YTFIG mystifying
YTGAA syntagmata
YTGOD nystagmoid
YTLPA nyctalopia
YTLPC nyctalopic
YTLPS nyctalopes
YTMTC systematic
YTNSS syntenoses
YTOHN dystrophin
YTRCL hysterical
YTROS mysterious
YTRSS hysteresis
YTRTC hysteretic
YUIES syrupiness
YUPIE by surprise
YUVNE Cyrus Vance
YWIKR by a whisker
YWTES eyewitness
eye-witness
ZEITN Uzbekistan
ZMOSA Szymborska
ZNLYR ozone layer
ZORPC azeotropic
ZRAJN Azerbaijan
ZRVTH czarevitch

11 letters– even

AAAAA Panama Canal
AAACE calamancoes
catafalcoes
AAAEI camaraderie
AAAET caravanette
AAAEZ Takada Kenzo
AAAHR Maharashtra
AAAIE Madara Rider
AAALN parasailing
AAAOS Canada goose
AAAPI banana split
AAAST caravan site
AAATR data capture
taratantara
AAATV maladaptive
AABAO radar beacon
AACEC parascience
AACIO maraschinos
AADEC War and Peace
AADEL cap and bells
AADHD paraldehyde
AADLT Camaldolite
AADRE law and order
AADUL hazardously
AAEAO paracetamol
AAEEA paraselenae
AAEEI paragenesia
paragenesis
AAEFC Raman effect
AAEFN managed fund
AAEIA Las Americas
pan-American
paramedical
AAEOE manage to see
AAEPE paraleipses
AAEPI paraleipsis
AAESI managership
AAETN parapenting
AAHAE paraphraser
AAHEI catachresis
AAHIO kalashnikov
AAHRI parathyroid
AAHRT Mahabharata
AAHTS parachutist
AAIAC capacitance
AAIAL fanatically
satanically
AAIBS Jagadis Bose
AAIIA parasitical
AAIIR carabinieri
AAIIT pay a visit to
AAINS vacationist
AAIOA Navarino Bay
AAIUA canalicular
AAIUL capaciously
rapaciously
sagaciously
salaciously
AAIUU canaliculus
AAJSE maladjusted
AALCI catallactic
cataplectic
parallactic
AALDN paragliding
AALLS parallelise
parallelism
AALLZ parallelize
AALNS capableness
AALSA paraglossae
AALSI cataclysmic
AALTE Maja Clothed
AAMNA sal ammoniac
AAMSL garam masala
AANEO Maya Angelou
AAOCP laparoscopy
AAODS vagabondise

AAODZ vagabondize
AAOIA parabolical
paradoxical
AAOIL ratatouille
AAOIM natatoriums
sanatoriums
AAONC paramountcy
AAONL paramountly
AAOON Jana Novotna
AAOUN cataloguing
AAOUS cataloguise
AAOUZ cataloguize
AARAE hamadry-ades
AARIL maladroitly
AAROE paratrooper
AARPI paragraphia
paragraphic
AARPO lay a trap for
AARPS malapropism
AARSN Ramakrishna
AASNL harassingly
AATEI paranthelia
AATOH catastrophe
AATRA day after day
AAUCD parasuicide
AAYHI paratyphoid
ABABR Ray Bradbury
ABAIE Gambia River
ABEBH Max Beerbohm
ABEKN law-breaking
ABENS garbledness
ABEOS rabble-rouse
ABERO gambrel roof
ABLGS garbologist
ABLSI cabbalistic
ABNAE carbon paper
ABNAO dak bungalow
ABNDE carbonadoes
ABNLC carbon black
ABNLT carbonylate
ABNOE garbanzo pea
ABNTE carbon steel
ABNTO carbonation
ABNYL carbon cycle
ABOSL car boot sale
ABRNL jabberingly
ABROK Jabberwocky
ABRTO carburettor
ABRUL barbarously
ABRWR Barbara Ward
ABTRA Sabbatarian
ABTRT barbiturate
ABTUC rabbit punch
ABTWL Lambeth Walk
ABVNT karbovanets
ACAAI bacchanalia
ACAHL catch a chill
ACALZ catch ablaze
ACAPL Ian Chappell
ACBLO Vasco Balboa
ACCLA catch cold at
ACDGM Vasco da Gama
ACENS parchedness
ACFIA Nancy Friday
ACFRU calciferous
ACHGL Marc Chagall
ACHLO catch hold of
ACIAE dance in a net
ACIHA t'ai chi ch'uan
ACIIA war criminal
ACINS marchioness
ACLAE cancellated
ACLAN Marcel Carné
ACLIS rascalliest
ACLNL masculinely
ACLNS masculinise
ACLNT masculinity
ACLNZ masculinize
ACLOA Cab Calloway
ACLRS vascularise
ACLRZ vascularize
ACLSL matchlessly
ACLTI laccolithic
ACLTN calculating
ACLTO calculate on
calculation
ACMKN watchmaking
ACMNE fancy monger
ACMTU sarcomatous
ACNLA baccanalian
ACNMT carcinomata
ACNTN fascinating
ACNTO fascination
vaccination
ACNUL larcenously
ACOAE lanceolated
ACOAI calceolaria
ACOEO cancioneros
ACOIL Pancho Villa
ACPAU sarcophagus
ACPRS catch phrase
ACRTC cancer-stick
ACRUL rancorously
ACSON Carcassonne
ACSRA Lancastrian
ACSRN watchspring
ACSUE narcissuses
ACTEU catch the sun
ACTEY catch the eye
ACUBL sanctus bell
ACUNS raucousness
ACURS sanctuarise
ACURZ sanctuarize
ACUWT catch up with
ADAAI Saudi Arabia
ADADN hard landing
ADANA hardy annual
ADARC paediatrics
ADBLT laudability
ADCEC hard science
ADCES Sadduceeism
ADCNT Hardicanute
ADCPE handicapped
handicapper
ADDTR candidature
ADEES hand release
ADEHE paddle wheel
ADEIH candlelight
ADELT saddlecloth
ADEMN daydreaming
day-dreaming
ADEON hand-me-downs
ADERE hard-hearted
ADERN hard-wearing
ADETC candlestick
ADEVN maidservant
ADFLR hand of glory
ADFOR ward of court
ADFRN vas deferens
ADGAF Van de Graaff
ADGNA Cardigan Bay
ADHRE card-sharper
ADITN hard-hitting
ADIVN Sandy Irvine
ADKEH landsknecht
ADKUA Sandy Koufax
ADLBA candelabras
ADLBU candelabrum
ADLGS paedologist
ADLLT Mar del Plata
ADLRC Max Delbrück
ADMNU pandemonium
ADNAT garden party
ADNBC handing back
ADNFA landing flap
ADNFO hand and foot
ADNFS hard and fast
hard-and-fast
ADNGA landing gear
landing-gear
ADNIE garden tiger
ADNLT cardinalate
ADNLV hand in glove
ADNNL maddeningly
ADNWA Randy Newman
ADOAC hard to catch
ADODN landholding
ADOKN hard working
hardworking
hard-working
ADOOT hand to mouth
hand-to-mouth
ADORP cardiograph
ADPII paedophilia
ADRAR Wanderjahre
ADRBA Bandar Abbas
ADRND hand grenade
ADRNE hard drinker
ADRNL wanderingly
ADRSE hard-pressed
ADRSO Pandora's box
ADRTE handwritten
ADRTN handwriting
ADSAL hard as nails
ADSCO bald as a coot
ADSLN hard as flint
ADSNS faddishness
laddishness
ADSRP candy stripe
ADSTN hard as stone
ADTOO Bardo Thodol
ADUGG hand-luggage
ADUNN hand-running
ADUTI hard put to it
ADWAM lay down arms
ADWPR Sandown Park
AEAAE have had a few
AEAAK baked Alaska
AEAAO Lake Balaton
AEADL Cakes and Ale
AEAEA make faces at
AEAEI cameraderie
AEAEL barefacedly
AEALA baseball cap
AEALE make earlier
AEALN lateral line
AEALR Tate Gallery
AEANN wage-earning
AEANT take pains to
AEAPN rate-capping
AEARA Jane Fairfax
AEASA Rabelaisian
AEATA have had that
AEATI have faith in
AEATO calefaction
malefaction
rarefaction
tabefaction
AEATR malefactory
AEATV rarefactive
take captive
AEAWT wage war with
AEBAE eager beaver
Water Bearer
Water-bearer
AEBDO make a bad job
make a bid for
AEBEL water beetle
AEBET bated breath
AEBIE Karen Blixen
AEBLT rateability
saleability
AEBOO make a booboo
AEBRI James Barrie
AEBTL water bottle
AECAC take a chance
AECBR James Coburn
AECGE James Cagney
AECLU watercolour
AECNO water cannon
AECOE water closet
water-cooled
AECRE catercorner
AECTR Lake Scutari
AECUI cater-cousin
AECUS watercourse
AEDIO fazendeiros
AEDNE make a dinner
AEDOO eavesdrop on
AEDRS calendarise
AEDRZ calendarize
AEDSE haberdasher

AEDTU make a detour
AEECO have mercy on
AEEDA make headway
AEEDW watered-down
AEEEG take revenge
AEEEV game reserve
AEEIH take delight
AEEIV make believe
make-believe
AEELH make healthy
AEEMU Jane Seymour
AEEOI safe-deposit
AEEPN safekeeping
safe-keeping
AEERE pale-hearted
AEESO make sense of
AEESR tape measure
AEETI make certain
AEEVO take leave of
AEEVU make nervous
AEEWT have sex with
AEFAE James Frazer
AEFEC take offence
AEFER vale of years
AEFES take offense
AEFGR make a figure
AEFNE water-finder
AEFOE made of money
AEFOO make a fool of
AEFSO make a fuss of
AEFWT make off with
AEGIO have a grip on
AEGIS make against
take against
AEGLA James Galway
AEGNE have a gander
AEGZN navel-gazing
AEHAE tame cheater
AEHCK take the cake
AEHEG have the edge
AEHLI make a hole in
AEHLO have a hold on
AEHME water hammer
AEHMR save the mark
AEHNE make thinner
AEHOE make whoopee
AEHOG rake through
wade through
AEHOT take the oath
AEHPC make the pace
AEHPL Lake Chapala
AEHPS take the piss
AEHRA take the road
AEHRE make shorter
AEHSA catechismal
AEHSI catechistic
AEHSO make a hash of
AEHTC catechetics
AEHVI take the veil
AEHWL James Howell
take the wall
AEHWR take the word
AEIAE pale-visaged
AEIAI valeric acid
AEIAL malefically
AEIAM Babes in Arms
AEIEC maleficence
AEIEF take time off
AEIGF tapering off
AEIHE make lighter
AEIHO make light of
AEIIL make visible
AEILS materialise
materialism
materialist
AEILT materiality
AEILZ materialize
AEITN have kittens
AEITO malediction
valediction
AEITR make history
maledictory
valedictory
AEIUL facetiously
AEJCE water jacket
AEKLA James Kelman
AELAO have a load on
AELCR lamellicorn
AELDE naked ladies
AELGE waterlogged
AELLE Water Lilies
AELNE have planned
AELNO camerlengos
camerlingos
AELTS satellitise
AELTZ satellitize
AELVL James Lovell
AEMAO make a meal of
water meadow
AEMCA James Mackay
AEMCO make a muck of
AEMLE make smaller
AEMNO James Monroe
AEMRA James Murray
AEMRG take umbrage
AEMSO make a mess of
AEMTO laced mutton
AEMVO make a move on
AENAI Lake Ontario
AENCL bare-knuckle
AENFR make uniform
AENHL baleen whale
AENIU make anxious
AENLA make unclean
make unclear
AENLS paternalism
AENOD make inroads
AENON case in point
AENOR take on board
AENSA have one's say
have one's way
make one's way
take one's way
AENSE paternoster[❑]
AENSL ease oneself
AENSO make one's bow
AENTO make a note of
AENUL cavernously
AENUN take in turns
AEODC safe conduct
safe-conduct
AEODN have you done?
AEOEA take home pay
take-home pay
AEOEC malevolence
AEOEI make holes in
AEOER take to heart
AEOGL make roughly
AEOHT gametophyte
AEOIA categorical
AEOIE categorized
AEOIH have no right
AEOIT café society
AEOJM make you jump
AEOLC take pot luck
AEOLN pace-bowling
take too long
AEOMC have too much
AEOMO have room for
make room for
AEOOB make no doubt
AEOOR take to court
AEORE made to order
make worried
AEORN Lake Torrens
AEOSC make you sick
AEOSL have for sale
AEOSN warehousing
AEOTC make contact
AEOTL make hostile
AEPGI take up again
AEPHR take up short
AEPLA caterpillar
AEPOI make a profit
AEPRO salesperson
AEPSA make a pass at
AEPSO water pistol
AEPTE sales patter
AEPTR made-up story
AEPWL Baden-Powell
AERAE make greater
safe-breaker
AERBC Dave Brubeck
AERCE safecracker
safe-cracker
AERCK Madeira cake
AERDI take pride in
AERED make friends
AERGO Jane Grigson
AERIE harebrained
hare-brained
AEROA take a room at
AERPA pan-European
AERPE name-dropper
AERRA make or break
make-or-break
AERSE gatecrasher
gate-crasher
AERSN Hare Krishna
AESAA have a stab at
AESAE make ashamed
AESBL Vanessa Bell
AESEC make a speech
AESIE water spider
AESIN water-skiing
AESLA Dar es Salaam
AESNI have as an aim
AESNL caressingly
AESOE baker's dozen
have a shower
AESOO make a show of
AESOT water sports
AESOZ have a snooze
AESPL water supply
AETCI take stock in
AETCO caveat actor
take stock of
AETCU talent scout
AETEE parentheses
AETEI parenthesis
parenthetic
AETER have at heart
AETGN patent agent
AETHN latest thing
AETIE make strides
AETLA make it clear
AETLO take a toll of
AETMG latent image
AETNA Palestinian
Valentinian
AETNL lamentingly
AETNN have it in one
AETNO have it in for
AETRS water thrush
AETTO lamentation
AETUO take it out of
take it out on
AEUCL make quickly
AEUEE make quieter
AEUEN Lake Lucerne
AEUKN Lake Turkana
AEUNS balefulness
carefulness
fatefulness
gaseousness
hatefulness
wakefulness
AEUSC pale tussock
AEUSE James Ussher
AEUSL Jane Russell
AEUWT taken up with
AEVEO have a view of
AEVPU water vapour
AEWCE take a wicket
AEWRO make aware of
AEWTO James Watson
AEWWR make awkward
AEXIE make excited
AEYAC safety match
AEYAO safety razor
AEYAV safety valve
safety-valve

AEYIA panegyrical
AEYLS safety glass
AEYOC take by force
AEYSO have eyes for
AEYTR take by storm
AFAAC malfeasance
AFADN half-landing
AFATN half past one
AFATS half-baptise
AFATW half past two
AFATZ half-baptize
AFEIG bad feelings
AFERE half-hearted
AFHCE half-checked
AFHTM half the time
AFIAE caffeinated
AFIDN half-binding
AFLOE half-blooded
AFNEL halfendeale
AFNHL half-and-half
AFNTO malfunction
AFOSI gaff-topsail
AFRND fanfaronade
AFRTE half-brother
AFSNS raffishness
AFTRE half-starved
AGADS vanguardism
AGAON large amount
AGBLT tangibility
AGBUI hang about in
AGDIH ragged right
AGDOI ragged robin
AGEMT Maggie Smith
AGFNE rangefinder
AGHDU bang the drum
AGIEU sanguineous
AGIGA laughing gas
AGIHN languishing
AGINS languidness
AGLCI pan-galactic
AGLDN hang-gliding
AGLUL laugh loudly
AGNAL tangentally
AGNBC hanging-back
AGNFR hanging fire
AGNHR hang in there
AGNLS marginalise
AGNLT marginality
AGNLZ marginalize
AGNME large number
AGNOD hang on words
AGNRN gas gangrene
AGOSA Panglossian
AGOSL hang loosely
AGRNS haggardness
AGROA kangaroo rat
AGROE danger money
AGROO kangaroo-hop
AGROR daggerboard
AGRTE Margaret Mee
AGRUL dangerously
AGSLS Vargas Llosa
AGSNS waggishness
AGSOE Sargasso Sea
AGSPR largest part
AGTNS haughtiness
naughtiness
AGTRS gangsterism
AGUTN langoustine
AGUWT hang out with
AHAEL Machiavelli
AHAHN cash machine
AHAIO Rachmaninov
AHARS Mathias Rust
AHBZU Bashi-Bazouk
AHCLT machicolate
AHCRI tachycardia
AHDRY cathode rays
AHGAH tachygraphy
AHHLN naphthalane
naphthalene
AHHLS naphthalise
AHHLZ naphthalize
AHLAA parheliacal
AHLCS catholicise
Catholicism
AHLCT catholicity
AHLCZ catholicize
AHLEI panhellenic
AHLGS pathologist
AHMGT pay homage to
AHMMR cache memory
AHMTC mathematics
AHMTS mathematise
AHMTZ mathematize
AHNCD machine code
AHNLK machine-like
AHNLN manhandling
AHNMS taphonomist
AHNSI bathing suit
AHNSL wash oneself
AHNTO machination
machine tool
AHOAL fashionable
fashionably
AHPCH Machu Picchu
AHPOI tachophobia
AHRAA Las Hermanas
AHRIA cathartical
AHRNA father-in-law
AHROA washerwoman
AHRON gather round
AHRPE gather speed
AHRRE washer-drier
AHRRW Father Brown
AHSHR bathysphere
AHSOA yachtswoman
AHTFC wash its face
AHUNS bashfulness
AHZRL haphazardly
AIACT Vatican City
AIAEU farinaceous
AIAFO laminar flow
AIAIM sanitariums
AIANS radicalness
AIASG radical sign
AIATC panic attack
AIATV radioactive
AIAUA caricatural
AIAUE caricatured
AIBAC Bahia Blanca
AIBAO David Beaton
radio beacon
AIBAT David Beatty
AIBCA Marie Bichat
AIBIE David Bailey
AIBLE magic bullet
AIBLT satiability
variability
AIBTO panic button
AICLA Maria Callas
AICNT ratiocinate
AICRE magic carpet
AICRO radiocarbon
AIDNA labiodental
AIDOI palindromic
AIDYU day in day out
AIECA matinée coat
AIEET habilements
AIEIU facinerious
AIEMS taxidermise
taxidermist
AIEMZ taxidermize
AIEOT canine tooth
AIETE manifestoes
AIFAL satisfiable
AIGAD daring-hardy
AIGAH Hagiographa
hagiography
radiography
AIGAT laying waste
AIGBN savings bank
AIGHE baking sheet
AIGLX radio galaxy
AIGNH Rajiv Gandhi
AIGNL David Ginola
AIGNW making known
AIGOR saying sorry
waking hours
AIGRC saving grace
AIGRN malingering
AIGTK Basingstoke
AIGTN paving stone
paving-stone
AIGTO variegation
AIGUS paying guest
AIHAE Mariah Carey
AIHES Manichaeism
AIHLR parish clerk
AIHNA Ravi Shankar
AIHNL ravishingly
vanishingly
AIHOE parishioner
AIIAE habilitated
AIIAL fatidically
pacifically
satirically
AIIAO facilitator
AIIGA Kaliningrad
AIINT paripinnate
AIIRS familiarise
AIIRT familiarity
AIIRZ familiarize
AIITO laciniation
AIIUL maliciously
AIJPI Janis Joplin
AILEO Daniel Defoe
AILGS hagiologist
radiologist
AILMS Panislamism
AILON Daniel Boone
AILRT capillarity
AILRU racial group
AILTN vacillating
AILTO hariolation
vacillation
AILUL Daniel Quilp
AILZL lapis lazuli
AIMJR labia majora
AIMLO David Mellor
AIMNR labia minora
AIMRE David Mercer
AINHA radiant heat
AINIS Damien Hirst
AINLS nationalise
nationalism
nationalist
rationalise
rationalism
rationalist
AINLT nationality
rationality
AINLZ nationalize
rationalize
AINNL malignantly
AINOE Marion Jones
AINWT patient with
AIOBA haricot bean
AIOEE salinometer
AIOIE Jamie Oliver
AIONU californium
AIPOI radiophonic
AIRAH papier-mâché
AIRTO calibration
AIRZI David Rizzio
AISAA David Seaman
AISOE Marie Stopes
AISPI Hagia Sophia
AISUR magic square
AITCU Variety Club
AITEA Cat in the Hat
AITOA variational
AITRA magisterial
Sagittarian
AITRS canisterise
AITRU Sagittarius
AITRZ canisterize
AITSO variety show
AIUAL capitularly
manipulable
AIUAO manipulator
AIUDT fatigue-duty

AIUIA latitudinal
AIUNL fatiguingly
AIUNS variousness
AIUNT taciturnity
AIUTO habituation
AIWLI David Wilkie
AIYHC parity check
AIYIL family Bible
AIYLA family altar
AIYOE easily moved
AIYOR family court
AIYPE easily upset
AJNIG Pat Jennings
AKACN Salk vaccine
AKAKN backpacking
Jack Dawkins
AKASG back passage
AKCAC backscratch
AKCON bank account
AKCTE backscatter
AKDBU talked about
AKDUC packed lunch
AKECE backbencher
AKENT Mack Sennett
AKEOA Jack Kerouac
AKEVL walk heavily
AKFWT walk off with
AKGDA package deal
AKGTU package tour
AKKNE dark-skinned
AKLDN backsliding
AKLOE walk all over
AKNAO rat kangaroo
AKNBO walking-boot
AKNCL Nat King Cole
AKNCS packing-case
AKNDW backing-down
AKNFL back and fill
rank and file
AKNIT talking into
AKNPE pack and peel
AKNRD park-and-ride
AKNRI rack and ruin
AKNTP masking tape
AKOAT back to earth
AKOIA bank holiday
AKOMO backroom-boy
AKONR back-country
AKORN back to front
AKPNS walk Spanish
AKRAE backbreaker
AKRBA Jack Brabham
AKRFE hanker after
AKRLK mackerel sky
AKSNS mawkishness
AKTAE market maker
AKTBE back-stabber
AKTEV basketweave
AKTLC marketplace
market-place
AKTRS racket-press
AKTVL talkatively
AKTYC yackety-yack
AKUPR lack support
AKUSL Jack Russell
AKUWT walk out with
ALADE mail handler
ALAEL tagliatelle
ALAGI Paul Gauguin
ALAIL fall rapidly
ALANS nail varnish
ALAPR Karl Jaspers
ALARE mail-carrier
ALATN call waiting
ALBAI Carlo Blasis
ALBLT fallibility
ALBUE day-labourer
ALCEL Carl Scheele
ALCNT hallucinate
ALCOH tablecloths
ALCRS garlic press
ALCSL Pablo Casals
ALDUL daily double
ALEAN Paul Cézanne
ALEFR Carl Seyfert
ALEOG early enough
ALERN ball-bearing
ALETA earlier than
ALETN Paul Keating
ALEVU Paul Delvaux
ALFET wall of death
ALFNE fault-finder
ALFOE cauliflower
ALGAH calligraphy
haplography
ALHLC Paul Ehrlich
ALHLT call a halt to
ALHOG fall through
sail through
ALHRU Paul Theroux
ALHSE Tallahassee
ALHTN call the tune
ALIGR rallying cry
rallying-cry
ALILC Paul Tillich
ALILE Carl Nielsen
ALLDE gall bladder
ALLSL fallalishly
faultlessly
ALLWT fall ill with
ALMUR gallimaufry
ALNAD rallentando
ALNBA sailing boat
ALNBC falling back
ALNDW falling-down
ALNNE fallen angel
ALNOA fallen woman
ALNPK marlinspike
ALNRD Pablo Neruda
ALNSA falling star
falling-star
ALNTA failing that
ALNTC Callanetics
ALNUG bad language
ALNWL Wailing Wall
ALOAC fail to catch
ALOCU Carlton Club
ALOEO Paul Robeson
ALOEZ fail to seize
ALOOG Marlborough
ALORE call to order
ALORS fail to grasp
ALOSN call cousins
ALOTN Paul Boateng
ALRAE jailbreaker
ALRCR Daily Record
ALSAE early stages
ALSED Baily's beads
ALSEE Carlos Menem
ALSEO Ballesteros
ALSHT tables-d'hôte
ALSNS haplessness
lawlessness
ALTNI table tennis
table-tennis
ALTUT call it quits
ALUGM parlour game
ALUNS callousness
ALVAE Vaclav Havel
ALVNE gallivanter
ALVSO cablevision
ALWAC tallow-catch
ALYAE barley water
ALYLV galley slave
galley-slave
ALYRO galley proof
ALYUA barley sugar
AMCAI haemocyanin
AMCMR gamma camera
AMEAD warm regards
AMEDN palm reading
AMERE warm-hearted
AMGAH mammography
AMGOI haemoglobin
AMHNO Ram Mohan Roy
AMLOE warm-blooded
AMMRA war memorial
AMNEE bad-mannered
AMNLA salmonellae
salmonellas
AMNML farm animals
AMNOE Carmen Jones
AMNRU salmon trout
AMNSI mammonistic
AMNUD salmangundi
AMNZN harmonizing
AMPIG Palm Springs
AMPII haemophilia
AMPYI haemoptysis
AMRCU Farmers Club
AMREE lammergeier
lammergeyer
AMRHG haemorrhage
AMRIO Van Morrison
AMRLN farmer's lung
AMRRL hammer drill
AMRTI Hammerstein
AMSAI haemostasis
haemostatic
AMTCI haematocrit
AMTLG haematology
AMTRA raw material
AMTRC basmati rice
AMUMR Naomi Uemura
AMUNS harmfulness
ANAAH Sanni Abacha
ANALO Iain Macleod
ANATR gain mastery
ANBIE Saint Bride's
ANBLS cannibalise
cannibalism
ANBLT damnability
ANBLZ cannibalize
ANBRE Fanny Burney
ANCBR Bannockburn
ANCTN wainscoting
ANDOD banned goods
ANDVT Danny Devito
ANEAC maintenance
ANEET launderette
ANELD painted lady
ANFAL magnifiable
ANFCE magnificoes
ANFCN magnificent
ANHLN Saint Helena
ANHNS paunchiness
raunchiness
ANILN painkilling
ANKML Fanny Kemble
ANLNS saintliness
ANLSL dauntlessly
taintlessly
ANNMT magnanimity
ANNMU magnanimous
ANOLK rainbow-like
ANOOG Farnborough
ANOSI maintopsail
ANPUI saintpaulia
ANRAE Dawn Treader
ANRKN pawnbroking
ANSAL tarnishable
ANSMN garnishment
ANSNS earnestness
mannishness
ANSOL Wayne's World
ANTKN painstaking
ANULN pain-dulling
ANUNS painfulness
ANVRU carnivorous
ANYOE Maundy money
AOAEU saponaceous
AOATN way of acting
AOATO day of action
AOBNA Bay of Bengal
AOBSA Bay of Biscay
AOCAG baton charge
baton-charge
AOCVT La Dolce Vita
AODLY Harold Lloyd
AODVN Harold Evans
AOEFL eat one's fill
AOETN majoretting

AOFAE camouflaged
AOHAL parochially
AOHNE Tam O'Shanter
tam-o'-shanter
AOHNS saxophonist
AOHNU cacophonous
AOHRN nasopharynx
AOIAL canonically
laconically
vaporizable
AOIAO vasodilator
AOIEE calorimeter
camomile tea
AOIGA Carolingian
AOIHN Capodichino
AOIOT Capodimonte
AOIUL laboriously
AOLVN way of living
AOLXR lap of luxury
AOMRE Jacob Marley
AONLL Madonna-lily
AONPE Bay of Naples
AONRE war of nerves
AONTR law of nature
AONWS madonnawise
AOOAI paronomasia
AOOBE baron of beef
AOODR major orders
AOPET Bay of Plenty
AORAN labour pains
AORAR savoir-faire
AORAT Labour Party
AORIR savoir-vivre
AORNA nasofrontal
AORNL vapouringly
AORNS savouriness
AOROC labour force
AORPE cacographer
AORPI cacographic
AORRI vapour trail
AORSI vasopressin
AORTS favouritism
AOSHC Jacob Schick
AOSNE carol-singer
AOSNL carousingly
AOSTF Jacob's staff
AOTIK bag of tricks
AOTOP ma non troppo
AOUDN sago pudding
AOURN manoeuvring
AOYAA Ramón y Cajal
APAPO Hamp Hampton
APASE wasp-waisted
APATC malpractice
APBIL say publicly
APCIO cappuccinos
APECN ear-piercing
APEPR Hampden Park
APIHE lamplighter
APIHR harpsichord
APINN campaigning
APINO campaign for
APLTE pamphleteer
APLUE Ralph Lauren
APMDU happy medium
APNBU harp on about
APNGI happen again
APNII salpingitis
APNLG campanology
APNST camping-site
APOHL Campion Hall
APRDS Sal Paradise
APRON Jasper Johns
APRRO tamperproof
tamper-proof
APSNS dampishness
waspishness
APSRS pampas grass
APTIN Carpathians
APTTN palpitating
APTTO palpitation
AQEAE masquerader
AQETT Jacques Tati
AQIAE pasquinader
AQIHN vanquishing
ARACA matriarchal
patriarchal
ARAEA carriageway
ARAEE marriage-bed
ARAHE Laura Ashley
ARAHN far-reaching
ARAOC carry a torch
ARASN hair-raising
ARBIG Barry Briggs
ARBOI macrobiotic
ARCBN carrick bend
ARCCU Garrick Club
ARCDE barricadoes
ARCIS capriccioso
ARCLT matriculate
ARCRO barrack-room
ARCRU Capricornus
ARCSI macrocosmic
ARCTL dairy cattle
ARCTO fabrication
ARDDL tarradiddle
ARDLC sacred place
ARDRE Labrador Sea
AREAA carried away
ARERE barrier reef
ARETE fair-weather
AREWV carrier wave
ARFCA sacrificial
ARGNU saprogenous
ARHLE Larry Holmes
ARIAA carry it away
ARIBN hairpin bend
ARIGO carryings-on
ARIGU carrying out
carrying-out
ARLAL barrel vault
ARLGS sacrilegist
ARLNA matrilineal
patrilineal
patrilinear
ARLOA patrolwoman
ARLPL jam roly-poly
ARLRA barrel organ
ARLUE Harry Lauder
ARLUL garrulously
ARMNA matrimonial
patrimonial
sacramental
ARMRS marram grass
ARNAL warrantable
warrantably
ARNAN patron saint
ARNOG Darren Gough
ARNZN patronizing
ARPTE Harry Potter
ARPYI saprophytic
ARRDN Laura Riding
ARRGE hair trigger
ARRIE hair-brained
ARRSE hairdresser
ARRTL sabre-rattle
ARSEN Barry Sheene
ARSOI macroscopic
ARSWE Harris tweed®
ARTEA carry the can
carry the day
ARTLS hairstylist
ARTLV Navratilova
ARTOA carry too far
ARTVL narratively
ARVRO Harry Vardon
ARWAG narrow-gauge
ARWIH carry weight
ARWNL harrowingly
ARYAG fairly large
ASAFA Falstaffian
ASAIG raise a siege
ASALN marshalling
ASALO rapscallion
ASASI oarsmanship
ASATN raise a stink
ASBLE false belief
ASBLT passability
ASBTO false bottom
ASCGI passacaglia
ASCNS carsickness
car-sickness
ASCTE daisy-cutter
ASDEC raised beach
ASDON passed round
ASEMS panspermism
panspermist
ASETN mass meeting
ASFAL falsifiable
ASFET jaws of death
ASFRC days of grace
ASGMA sausage meat
ASGRL sausage roll
ASHMR pass the mark
ASHOG pass through
ASHTS pass the test
ASIAL caustically
ASICE Hans Fischer
ASIHE Hans Richter
ASIJR cause injury
ASIKE Hans Winkler
ASINS causticness
ASISD pass airside
ASLAO San Salvador
ASLSL causelessly
pauselessly
ASMLE Daisy Miller
ASMLO marshmallow
ASMTO pass a motion
ASMZO passamezzos
ASNAA passing away
passing-away
ASNER raison d'être
ASNET maisonnette
ASNNS parson's nose
ASNOE passing over
ASNSO passing shot
ASNWC jam sandwich
ASOAH Matsuo Basho
ASOBI Hans Holbein
ASOLS passionless
ASOMO Marston Moor
ASOPA passion play
ASOTD Passiontide
ASOWE Passion week
ASRDC mass-produce
ASRPR false report
ASRRO mansard roof
ASRTS Sanskritist
ASTDO cause to drop
ASTFL cause to fall
ASTON basset-hound
ASTRS cause to rise
ASTRT cassiterite
ASTVL causatively
ASUCA Cassius Clay
ASUCL pass quickly
ASUHE Hans Buchner
ASUOT sansculotte
ASURN pass current
ASVNS massiveness
passiveness
ASYEC Hans Eysenck
ATADL warts and all
ATAIE cantharides
ATAKO say thank you
ATAMN part payment
ATANS factualness
ATAOI want jam on it
ATBMP Natty Bumppo
ATCLR particulars
ATCLT particulate
ATCPA participial
ATCPN participant
ATCPT participate
ATCTO mastication
ATCTR masticatory
ATCWR latticework
lattice-work
ATDJU carte du jour
ATEEG Castlereagh
ATEET battlements

ATEEU lay the venue
ATEHP battleships
ATEIE pay the piper
ATEIL battlefield
ATENK rattlesnake
ATEOA battle royal
ATERS battledress
ATESI pantheistic
partnership
ATETN farthest end
ATETO fast neutron
ATEWR earthenware
ATFIE last offices
ATFRA Rastafarian
ATGAC cast a glance
ATGAE fastigiated
ATGAH cartography
ATGON waste ground
ATGRL panty girdle
ATGTN castigating
ATGTO castigation
ATGTR castigatory
ATHTA Walt Whitman
ATIAA Captain Ahab
ATIDN fact-finding
ATIHO Captain Hook
cast light on
ATIII mastoiditis
ATIPT past dispute
ATISI captainship
ATLAE castellated
ATLEA Bastille Day
ATLGS tautologise
ATLGU tautologous
ATLGZ tautologize
ATLHL mantelshelf
ATLIC mantelpiece
ATLNS earthliness
ATLRA wastel bread
ATLSL faithlessly
tastelessly
ATLZN tantalizing
ATMEE bad-tempered
ATMMN nasty moment
ATMMS pantomimist
ATMNN hasta mañana
ATMOC saltimbocca
ATMRO jam tomorrow
ATMRS tautomerism
ATMTE waste matter
ATNAA wasting away
ATNBL tantony bell
ATNDE bastinadoes
ATNHE Martin Sheen
ATNLS waiting-list
ATNNS lastingness
ATNPT Martin Opitz
ATNRO waiting-room
ATNRV rant and rave
ATNTD wanting to do
ATNTN cast in stone
ATNUE Martin Buber
ATOAN Mastroianni

ATOCP gastroscope
ATOHA East Lothian
ATOIC Matteo Ricci
ATOLF facts of life
ATOLN fast bowling
ATOOE Bartholomew
ATOOI gastronomic
ATOPN part company
ATOSO cartoon show
ATOWR fast-forward
ATPOE party-pooper
ATRAC Sam Torrance
tartar sauce
ATRAD Walter Baade
ATRAE Walter Hagen
Walter Pater
ATRAL sartorially
ATRCD bactericide
ATRCE fast-tracker
ATRCT Walter Scott
ATRDM Walter Adams
ATREI bacteraemia
ATRFR factory farm
ATRHN factory hand
ATRIC Maeterlinck
masterpiece
ATRIT Walter Mitty
ATRJW lantern jaws
ATRKA Walter Skeat
ATRLN pastureland
ATRLO saltarellos
ATRLS pastoralism
pastureless
ATRLT sad to relate
ATRMS easternmost
ATRNL banteringly
falteringly
yatteringly
ATRRC pattern race
ATRSE pastures new
ATRSO factory shop
ATRTM Eastern Time
ATRTO parturition
ATRUA caster sugar
ATRUL masterfully
rapturously
ATRUY canterburys
ATSAL baptismally
ATSEI hatti-sherif
ATSIA fantastical
ATSII party spirit
ATSNS cattishness
saltishness
ATSTM fastest time
ATSUO cast a slur on
ATSZN fantasizing
ATTBS past its best
ATTEO earth-tremor
ATTRA raptatorial
saltatorial
ATTTO jactitation
ATTVL partitively
ATUIE pasteurizer

ATUNS tactfulness
ATVTN captivating
ATVTO captivation
ATYOR pastry board
ATYOT east-by-north
east-by-south
ATYRS pastry brush
AUABR natural-born
AUAIE naturalized
AUAIN salutations
AUANS naturalness
AUATR manufactory
manufacture
AUAUE macula lutea
AUERI nature trail
AUETD nature study
AUETI nature strip
AUHGL value highly
AUISO manumission
AULEC Raquel Welch
AULEY Samuel Pepys
AULOS Samuel Morse
AULTO vacuolation
AUMAG vacuum gauge
AUMLA vacuum-clean
AUMLS vacuum flask
AUMRK vacuum brake
AUMRU Gaius Marius
AUNAO calumniator
AUNLA Saturnalian
AUOAH naturopathy
AUPCT haruspicate
AUSAU harum-scarum
AUSIA casuistical
AUTOA valuational
AUTTV facultative
AUUNS fatuousness
vacuousness
AVBNH Maeve Binchy
AVGAL salvageable
AVLTL sal volatile
AVLUL carvel-built
AVNLI Calvin Klein
AVNSI Calvinistic
AVSMO harvest moon
AVSTM harvest-time
AVUNS calvousness
AVYMT Harvey Smith
AVYOE Harvey-Jones
AWRNS waywardness
AYABT Lady Macbeth
AYAEU papyraceous
AYEAL Mary Renault
AYECL Mary Seacole
AYFNE lady's finger
AYHIO Baryshnikov
AYHLE Mary Shelley
AYIEE Gary Lineker
AYITN baby-sitting
AYJTA Satyajit Ray
AYOPN Mary Poppins
AYPIE caryopsides
AYRFE lady-trifles

AYSNS babyishness
BAAAR abracadabra
BACIT abranchiate
BCDRA abecedarian
BCIAL abactinally
BCRTO obscuration
BDFOE a bed of roses
BEPRT obtemperate
BESOA obsessional
BETES absenteeism
BETOV objet trouvé
BETVL objectively
BETVS objectivise
objectivism
objectivist
BETVT objectivate
objectivity
BETVZ objectivize
BEVNL observantly
observingly
BEVNO observant of
BEVTO observation
BEVTR observatory
BIAIN obligations
BIEAE obliterated
BIGMN abridgement
BIIUL obliviously
BIIUT oblivious to
BIUNS obliqueness
obviousness
BLINL ebulliently
BMNTO abomination
BNOEL abandonedly
BNOMN abandonment
BNOSI abandon ship
BNTPC a bone to pick
BNWLE T-Bone Walker
BOBNL absorbingly
BOECN obsolescent
BOEEI abiogenesis
abiogenetic
BOIAL abdominally
BOIUL obnoxiously
BOMLT abnormality
BORNL abhorrently
BRETE J B Priestley
BRINS abortionist
BRSVL obtrusively
BRSWT Aberystwyth
BRVAE abbreviated
BSVNS abusiveness
BTATO abstraction
BTFLF a bit of fluff
BTIFO abstain from
BTNNL abstinently
BTNTL obstinately
BTRIT obiter dicta
BTTIA obstetrical
BTUTO obstruction
BTUTV obstructive
BUCTO obfuscation
BUCTR obfuscatory
BUDNI abounding in

BUECN obmutescent
BUENL obtuse angle
BUGTO objurgation
BUOAI ablutomania
BVSAE above-stated
CACCR scratchcard
CAERN octahedrons
CAGNS scragginess
CAKVK Tchaikovsky
CALNL scrawlingly
CANNS scrawniness
CANOS Scharnhorst
CAOAL octagonally
CAPNS scrappiness
CATYS McCarthyism
CATYT McCarthyite
CBRLU scaberulous
CDMCA academician
CDMCS academicism
CDNHR acidanthera
CECPR science park
CEDIE screwdriver
CEEAD accelerando
CEEAE accelerated
CEEAO accelerator
CEMNL screamingly
CENAE screen saver
CENAL octennially
CENHE a clean sheet
CENLT a clean slate
CENWE a clean sweep
CEOAA scleromatas
CEOEM scleroderma
CESRE accessories
CESRL accessorily
CESRS accessorise
CESRZ accessorize
CETAL accentually
CETCS eclecticism
CETLG Scientology
CETLM accept blame
CEZNO scherzandos
CFINL eco-friendly
CFODN scaffolding
CIIAL actinically
occipitally
CIIRN accipitrine
CIKTS Schick's test
CILOT octillionth
CILRS schillerise
CILRZ schillerize
CIMTS schismatise
CIMTZ schismatize
CINRU action group
CIOIU acrimonious
CIPNS scrimpiness
CIVMN achievement
CLCAI ochlocratic
CLMTO acclamation
CLMTR acclamatory
CLMTS acclimatise
CLMTZ acclimatize
CLNSA Iceland spar
CLPOI ochlophobia
ochlophobic
CLSNE Schlesinger
CLSOT a colt's tooth
CLVTU acclivitous
CLYSE Scilly Isles
CMNCS ecumenicism
CMNCT ecumenicity
CNBTL scent bottle
CNCOT scenic route
CNFOM a can of worms
CNGAH iconography
CNILT scintillate
CNMTI econometric
CNMZO economize on
CNOSI icon worship
CNSAI iconostasis
CNWEG acknowledge
COASI scholarship
CODNA according as
CODNL accordantly
accordingly
CODNT according to
COEAL acropetally
COEBO a closed book
COEHN a close thing
COEIO octodecimos
COHME echo chamber
COISI scholiastic
COLAD schoolwards
COLHL schoolchild
COLOS schoolhouse
COLSI ectoblastic
ectoplasmic
COMDT accommodate
CONAC accountancy
CONAL accountable
accountably
CONBO account-book
COONE echo-sounder
COOPI ectomorphic
COPNE accompanied
COPNS accompanist
COTSH schottische
COULN A Chorus Line
CPESR acupressure
CPIAL sceptically
CPIAO sceptical of
CPLMN scopolamine
CPLTL act politely
CPNTR acupuncture
CPOEL act properly
CRDNE Schrödinger
CRDTF scared stiff
CREYN scarcely any
CRHNL scorchingly
CRKEE score-keeper
CRMNE scaremonger
CRMSM X-chromosome
Y-chromosome
CRMTS achromatise
achromatism
CRMTZ achromatize
CRNLG eccrinology
CROOG Scarborough
CSHDO icosahedron
CSOWS scissorwise
CTAGE acute-angled
CTEEL scatteredly
CTGTE act together
CTHRT Scotch broth
CTJPI Scott Joplin
CTLCI acatalectic
CTMTU scotomatous
CTYLG ichthyology
CTYSU ichthyosaur
CUAIA accusatival
CUDEL scoundrelly
CUECI acquiesce in
CUECN acquiescent
CUIIE scrutinizer
CUITN acquainting
CUPIU scrumptious
CURAL actuarially
CURMN acquirement
CURNE occurrences
CUSTO acquisition
CUSTV acquisitive
CUTAC acquittance
CUTCA acoustician
CUTRT acculturate
CUTTO occultation
CUUAO accumulator
CWRKP Schwarzkopf
CYIAI acrylic acid
DACMN advancement
DADAI Edward Sapir
DADEC Edward Teach
DADET Edward Heath
DADIN Edward Milne
DADLA Edward Elgar
DADLE Edward Albee
DADOS Edward Doisy
DADRE Edvard Grieg
DADUC Edvard Munch
DADUE Edward Pusey
DADUR Edward Burra
DCBLT educability
DCTOA educational
DEBAL adverbially
DENWR edge in a word
DESRA adversarial
DETNL advertently
DETRA advertorial
DETRS adventuress
adventurism
DETRU adventurous
DETSN advertising
DETVL adjectively
DFCTO edification
DIACR Eddie Arcaro
DIADI Edwin Aldrin
DIASU Admiral's Cup
DIDFA admit defeat
DIHBL Edwin Hubble
DIIUA adminicular
DIIVN Eddie Irvine
DIMRH Eddie Murphy
DINER Adrian Henri
DINOL Adrian Boult
DINUL sdeignfully
DITBI admit to bail
DITCE Adriatic Sea
DLEAE adulterated
DLHAE addle-headed
DLHTE Adolf Hitler
DLIAL idyllically
DLNAO adelantados
DLSEC adolescence
DLSOS A Doll's House
DLVLC Ada Lovelace
DLZTO idolization
DMAOE a dime a dozen
DMRTO adumbration
DNIAL identically
DNIIU ad infinitum
DNOLS odontoblast
DOIAL idiotically
DOOIA ideological
DORMN adjournment
DORPI ideographic
DOSVN idiot savant
DPIOT add poison to
DPPET add pepper to
DPTKN od's-pitikins
DQAEO adequate for
DRFRU odoriferous
DRLST add relish to
DRNAK Adirondacks
DRSBO address book
DRUNS odorousness
DSNED odds and ends
DSNSD odds and sods
DTATM Ode to Autumn
DTCVL Edith Cavell
DTGTE add together
DTIMN edutainment
DTRAL editorially
DUDUK Edmund Burke
DUIAO adjudicator
DVZNU ad avizandum
DWMNU odd woman out
DYURN eddy current
EAAEA Delaware Bay
EAAEF separate off
EAAEU separate out
EAAFO get away from
EAATO legal action
EAAWT get away with
EABLT perambulate
EABNS decarbonise
EABNZ decarbonize
EABTV rebarbative
EACEL debauchedly
EACOI melancholia
melancholic
EACTO defalcation
demarcation
EADON be hard going

EADOR bed and board
EADTO retardation
EADTR retardatory
EADTV retardative
EADUL regardfully
EAEAL behave badly
EAECA hexateuchal
EAECE female screw
EAECN recalescent
EAEIA hexadecimal
sexagesimal
EAENS belatedness
relatedness
EAERN hexahedrons
EAERS hexametrise
EAERZ hexametrize
EAESO pet aversion
EAFAC César Franck
EAGMN derangement
EAGNU pelargonium
EAHAI metaphrasis
EAHFO get a whiff of
EAHSC metaphysics
EAHSS metathesise
EAHSZ metathesize
EAIAL tetanically
venatically
EAIHN be famishing
EAILN De Havilland
EAILS deracialise
EAILZ deracialize
EAINS negationist
EAITO retaliation
EAITR retaliatory
EAITV retaliative
EAIUA behavioural
EAIUL nefariously
tenaciously
veraciously
vexatiously
EALAC mésalliance
EALCE beta-blocker
EALRI metallurgic
EANAI remain valid
EANLR remain alert
EANTS demagnetise
EANTZ demagnetize
EANUH set at nought
EAOAI megalomania
EAOAL hexagonally
EAOEI teratogenic
EAOIA pedagogical
EAONT get around to
EAOOI megalopolis
EAOPI metamorphic
EAOUR demagoguery
EAPRS depauperise
EAPRT depauperate
EAPRZ depauperize
EARLS desacralise
EARLZ desacralize
EARPO set a trap for
EASAC renaissance
EATAE penalty area
EATCS pedanticise
semanticist
EATCZ pedanticize
EATGA penalty goal
EATKC penalty kick
EATMN département
EATNE legal tender
EATRA redactorial
EATSO penalty spot
EATSS metastasise
EATSZ metastasize
EATTN devastating
EATTO devastation
recantation
repartition
EAUNN menaquinone
EAUTO devaluation
EAWRE metalworker
EBADN keyboarding
EBDHS Zen Buddhism
EBGRT verbigerate
EBLZN verbalizing
EBRBB newborn baby
EBRRA Herbert Read
EBRTO verberation
EBRWE kerb-crawler
EBSNS leg-business
verboseness
EBVRU herbivorous
ECADS merchandise
ECADZ merchandize
ECAKN get cracking
ECARS reach across
ECATA merchant man
merchantman
ECATE merchantmen
ECBLT peccability
ECCBU peacock-blue
ECCLK peacock-like
ECCME beachcomber
sea cucumber
ECDLO peccadillos
ECEBC Reichenbach
ECECN Red Crescent
ECEIA geochemical
ECESE teacher's pet
ECFIH mercy flight
ECIAL deictically
describable
perceivable
perceivably
ECIDE men-children
ECINR reactionary
ECITO description
ECITV descriptive
ECLFE get cold feet
ECLKR pencil-skirt
ECLSL mercilessly
ECLTO percolation
ECLVN peace-loving
ECMDW reach-me-down
ECMKN peacemaking
peace-making
ECMNE peace-monger
ECMNL welcomingly
ECNAT descendants
ECNMN rescindment
ECNRL mercenarily
ECOET get closer to
ECOLN deschooling
ECOMN peace of mind
ECPEC percipience
ECPIL perceptible
perceptibly
ECRAL mercurially
ECTET peace treaty
EDABE reed-warbler
EDAKN send packing
EDALO lead balloon
EDBLT bendability
readability
vendibility
weldability
EDCRE headscarves
EDCSL Leeds Castle
EDCTO re-education
EDECE head teacher
headteacher
EDEOA needlewoman
EDEON needlepoint
EDERF needlecraft
EDFIH dead of night
EDFRS Lee De Forest
EDFTT head of state
EDGBE Hedda Gabler
EDHNT lend a hand to
EDHOG read through
EDIGT lend wings to
EDIHO Len Deighton
EDLSH Mendelssohn
EDLUL pendulously
EDLVU mendelevium
EDMDR hebdomadary
EDMIE seldom-times
EDNBC sending back
EDNBO reading-book
EDNCK wedding cake
EDNCR leading card
EDNDS reading-desk
EDNEG leading edge
EDNIU tendentious
EDNLD leading lady
EDNLM reading-lamp
EDNNT leading note
EDNRL leading role
EDNRN wedding ring
EDNRO reading-room
EDNSA wend one's way
EDOAD tend towards
EDOLE send to sleep
EDOLP dendroglyph
EDOWR send forward
EDPIL Mendip Hills
EDPTI feldspathic
EDREI gendarmerie
EDREK Beiderbecke
EDRLS verdureless
EDROT tenderfoots
EDRYN tender-dying
EDSDD dead as a dodo
EDTDO ready to drop
EDTHL Ready-to-Halt
EDTWR ready to work
EDUCL read quickly
EDUNS heedfulness
needfulness
EDUTN headhunting
EDVRE get divorced
EDWII meadow pipit
EDWNE lead-swinger
EDWRS meadow grass
EDWRW meadow brown
EDWTE ready-witted
EDWWE meadowsweet
EDWYO send away for
EDYIH see daylight
EEAAD Geneva bands
EEAAE Gene Sarazen
EEAET lese-majesty
EEAFL severalfold
EEAHS telepathise
telepathist
EEAHZ telepathize
EEAIE generalized
EEAIL Geneva Bible
EEAIN Generation X
EEAIU temerarious
EEAKN telebanking
EEAOI hemeralopia
hemeralopic
EEAOT Rene LaCoste
EEAPA Pete Sampras
EEARS Geneva cross
EEASI generalship
EEATO benefaction
EEATR benefactory
EEBAC remembrance ❑
resemblance
EEBRN remembering
reverberant
EEBRT reverberate
EECLS defenceless
EECPU Telescopium
EECWS Rebecca West
EEDCT revendicate
EEDLS defeudalise
EEDLZ defeudalize
EEDMI legerdemain
EEDNL dependingly
EEDNO dependent on
depending on
EEDPT serendipity
EEEAE degenerated
EEEAL regenerable
EEEAO decelerator
regenerator
EEEDM referendums
EEEDN never ending

never-ending
EEEIU deleterious
EEELM cerebellums
EEEOY see eye to eye
EEERS decerebrise
EEERT decerebrate
EEERZ decerebrize
EEESG Telemessage®
EEETA deferential
referential
reverential
EEETO deselection
venesection
EEEWT get even with
EEGEE beleaguered
EEGIE Peter Grimes
EEGNL revengingly
EEHAE level headed
level-headed
EEHNS telephonist
EEHRP gene therapy
EEIAL generically
genetically
hereditable
heretically
venefically
EEICD genetic code
EEICN Gene Vincent
EEIEC beneficence
EEIEI telekinesis
telekinetic
EEIGO be seeing you
EEIGU petering out
EEIIR beneficiary
EEIIT beneficiate
EEIIU repetitious
EEIMN bedevilment
EEINE Venetian red
EEINM generic name
EEINS Hegelianism
EEIRT deteriorate
EEITN Benedictine
EEITO benediction
dereliction
EEITR benedictory
EEJCB Derek Jacobi
EEJRA Derek Jarman
EELCT beneplacito
EELGS genealogise
genealogist
teleologist
EELGZ genealogize
EELLE Peter Lilley
EELNL repellantly
repellently
repellingly
EEMNL beseemingly
EEMNN determinant
determining
EEMNS determinism
determinist
EEMNT determinate
EEMRE Helen Mirren
EENAL perennially
sexennially
EENFE hereinafter
EEOAI heterotaxis
EEOAL developable
EEOEC benevolence
EEOIT develop into
EEOIU ceremonious
EEOKN teleworking
EEOMN development
EEOMT telecommute
EEONS derecognise
EEONZ derecognize
EEOOI heterotopia
EEOOL Peter O'Toole
EEORF heterograft
EEORP heterotroph
EEOTG telecottage
EEOTR Heteroptera
EEPNA Peter Pindar
EEPRE Peter Porter
EERGT desegregate
EERHN researching
EERLG meteorology
EERNE teleprinter
EERNT peregrinate
referring to
EERPI telegraphic
EERST tenebrosity
EERTN celebrating
desecrating
penetrating
EERTO celebration
cerebration
desecration
penetration
EERTR celebratory
EERTV penetrative
EESEC Peter's pence
EESOA recessional
reversional
EESRA necessarian
EESRE necessaries
EESRL necessarily
EESSD reverse side
EESTE necessitied
necessities
EESTS desensitise
EESTT necessitate
EESTU necessitous
EESTZ desensitize
EESVL defensively
recessively
EESYI never say die
EETAE fenestrated
EETAL celestially
EETCL receptacula
EETET seventeenth
EETMR memento mori
EETNL repentantly
repentingly
resentingly
EETOK perestroika
EETRL sedentarily
EETTO cementation
delectation
detestation
EETUL deceitfully
resentfully
EETVL deceptively
defectively
retentively
selectively
EETVT receptivity
selectivity
EEULS desexualise
EEULZ desexualize
EEVAE reserve area
EEVBN reserve bank
EEVMN bereavement
EEVNL deservingly
EEVTO reservation
EEVTR reservatory
EEWME Peter Wimsey
EEYRN Jeremy Irons
EFAMN self-harming
EFASN self-raising
EFATR self-mastery
EFCIL perfectible
EFCNS perfectness
EFCTO deification
reification
EFDIE self-admirer
EFEEC self-defence
EFEIN self-reliant
EFEKN self-seeking
EFELN self-sealing
EFEPC self-respect
EFETE self-centred
EFEVC self-service
EFEVN self-serving
EFEYN self-denying
EFFWU fee-fi-faw-fum
EFHOG leaf through
EFHRT self-charity
EFIDN self-winding
EFMLS perfumeless
EFMOE self-imposed
EFNNL deafeningly
EFNTR perfunctory
EFNUE self-induced
EFOCI self-conceit
EFOEE self-covered
EFOMN self-command
EFOSN be of consent
EFOTO self-control
EFPNO self-opinion
EFRAC performance
EFRAL performable
EFRDE Jeff Bridges
EFRTO perforation
EFSNS selfishness
EFSPS deaf as a post
EFSUE self-assured
EFTRE self-starter
EFUDE self-subdued
EFUPR self-support
EFUTN leaf-cutting
EFVDN self-evident
EFXRS self-express
EGACO weigh anchor
EGBAC Serge Blanco
EGBIG weighbridge
EGBUL neighbourly
EGCRN bergschrund
EGCTE hedgecutter
EGEDW weighed down
weighed-down
EGEEE dengue fever
EGERA seigneurial
EGHNN lengthening
EGHNS lengthiness
EGIKA Genghis Khan
EGIUK Sergei Bubka
EGIWT weigh in with
EGTAC weight-watch
EGTNN heightening
EGTNS weightiness
EGTRI weight-train
EGYIO Sergey Kirov
EHASH Meghnad Saha
EHDLG methodology
EHELN Heyhoe Flint
EHEMT dephlegmate
EHETM nephrectomy
EHIAL technically
EHLGS nephologist
EHLLI cephalalgia
EHLRU methyl group
EHNCA mechanician
EHNSI mechanistic
EHOHB technophobe
EHOHL technophile
EHORC technocracy
EHRIO Rex Harrison
EHROL nether world
EHRUL lecherously
EHSEE bewhiskered
EHTOE red-hot poker
EIADA pericardiac
pericardial
EIADU pericardium
EIAEI peripatetic
EIAHN devil a thing
EIAIE devitalized
EIAIO recitativos
EIAPA pericarpial
EIARS get it across
EIAWV Mexican wave
EIBAO Cecil Beaton
EIBLT deniability
reliability
EICMN bewitchment
see it coming
EICTO desiccation
EIDCA periodic law
EIDCT periodicity
revindicate
EIDIC period piece

EIDNA periodontal
religiously
seditiously
EIDOO remind you of
EIDRM period drama
EIDRN bewildering
EIEAC deliverance[a]
EIEAI perihepatic
EIEAL deliverable
mediaevally
EIEAO deliberator
EIEAU desideratum
EIECN revivescent
EIEEO delivered of
EIEHI perinephric
EIEMN bedizenment
EIENS decidedness
refinedness
EIESO demi-pension
EIETA penitential
residential
EIETL regimentals
EIETO delineation
redirection
EIETR sedimentary
EIETV delineative
EIGAH heliography
EIGMN besiegement
EIGOA sewing woman
EIHAE Denis Healey
periphrases
EIHAI periphrasis
EIHEL delightedly
EIHNL perishingly
EIHRN deciphering
EIHSI fetishistic
EIIAE debilitated
EIIAL genitivally
levitically
medicinally
veridically
EIICN reminiscent
reviviscent
EIIEA Medicine Hat
medicine man
EIIIA verisimilar
EIIIM peridiniums
EIILT penicillate
EIILU penicillium
EIINI deficient in
EIINL deficiently
resiliently
EIINN petitioning
EIINR petitionary
religionary
revisionary
seditionary
EIINS religionise
revisionism
revisionist
seditionist
EIINZ religionize
EIIST religiosity
EIIUL deliciously
deliriously

EIIYN revivifying
EIKEA Kevin Keegan
EIKLE semi-skilled
EIKSA Bewick's swan
EILCA periglacial
EILOT decillionth
EILTN legislating
EILTO legislation
EILTR legislature
EILTV legislative
EIMAE medium-dated
EIMTO set in motion
EINAR legionnaire
EINLS regionalise
regionalism
EINLZ regionalize
EINNL benignantly
designingly
EINTO designation
resignation
EIOCP retinoscope
retinoscopy
EIODS demigoddess
EIOII peritonitis
EIOIU meritorious
EIORC meritocracy
EIOTR Lepidoptera
EIOWT get it on with
EIPEI hemispheric
EIQEC delinquency
EIRCT reciprocate
reciprocity
EIRNS defibrinise
EIRNT defibrinate
EIRNU pericranium
EIRNZ defibrinize
EIRPE serigrapher
EIRPI lexigraphic
EIRTN denigrating
EIRTO denigration
melioration
EIRTR denigratory
EIRTV meliorative
EISHR heliosphere
EISII periostitic
EISIU mediastinum
EISLG perissology
EISLT peninsulate
EITAL registrable
EITAS Lévi-Strauss
EITDB get into debt
EITFS gefilte fish
EITIE mediatrices
EITLI peristalsis
peristaltic
EITLT peristalith
EITNL befittingly
remittently
resistingly
EITOI heliotropic
EITRA mediatorial

EITRU hemipterous
EITVL resistively
EITVT resistivity
EIUAL reticularly
EIUNS deviousness
seriousness
tediousness
EIUTR sericulture
EIVLS medievalism
medievalist
EIVNL believingly
EIVRS desilverise
EIVRZ desilverize
EIWNE Felix Wankel
EKDHL beaked whale
EKLHN heckelphone
EKNAE Beckenbauer
EKNCO neck and crop
EKNEL weak-kneedly
EKNNC neck and neck
EKNSE Ben Kingsley
EKRHE neckerchief
ELACE well-matched
ELAHN belly-aching
ELAHR aeolian harp
ELAKN fell-walking
ELBTO belly-button
ELCAC reflectance
ELCAL replaceable
ELCDT pellucidity
ELCMN replacement
ELCSL bellicosely
ELCST bellicosity
ELCTO perlocution
replication
ELCUO reflect upon
ELDIE well-advised
ELDNE belly-dancer
ELDSI her ladyship
ELEAE well behaved
well-behaved
ELEAL peelie-wally
ELEEB Nellie Melba
ELEIE well-defined
well-derived
well-desired
ELEOS feel remorse
ELEOU oeil-de-boeuf
ELFUN mellifluent
ELFUU mellifluous
ELGIS tell against
ELGMN realignment
ELGNL negligently
ELGRN belligerent
ELGSI neologistic
ELHNS healthiness
wealthiness
ELHPS sell the pass
ELHTM health stamp
tell the time
ELHUL healthfully
ELIAL reclaimable
reclaimably

ELIMN Neil Diamond
ELINC Neil Kinnock
ELITN well-fitting
ELLNE well-planned
ELLST feel close to
ELMTO declamation
reclamation
ELMTR declamatory
ELNEE well-entered
ELNLK feeling like
ELNLS feelingless
ELNOC feel in touch
ELNOE keeling-over
well-endowed
ELNRC selling race
ELNSA feel one's way
ELNSE replenisher
ELNSI Hellenistic
ELNSL feel oneself
ELNTO declination
ELNWT dealing with
ELOII realpolitik
ELONE well-founded
well-rounded
ELOTM bell-bottoms
ELRAG feeler gauge
ELRDE well-trodden
ELREE well-briefed
well-ordered
ELRIE well-trained
ELRLW Kepler's laws
ELRNL deploringly
ELROE well-groomed
ELRPO Bellerophon
ELRSE well-dressed
ELRTO declaration
deploration
ELRTR declaratory
ELRTV declarative
ELSCE tell a secret
ELSLR ne plus ultra
ELSNS hellishness
leglessness
recluseness
sexlessness
ELTCE well-stacked
well-stocked
ELTLB set little by
ELTNS repleteness
ELTNT deglutinate
ELTUB be all thumbs
ELUHO jealoushood
ELUKN fell-lurking
ELUNN fell-running
ELUNS zealousness
ELVTU declivitous
ELWAT Yellow Earth
ELWEE yellow fever
ELWEL yellow-belly
ELWIC yellow birch
ELWIE Yellow River
ELWLR yellow alert
ELWNF Yellowknife

Words marked [a] can also be spelled with an initial capital letter

ELXLG reflexology
ELXVL reflexively
ELXVT reflexivity
ELYNS Wesleyanism
ELZTO realization
EMAFR germ warfare
EMCLT vermiculate
vermiculite
EMFTL femme fatale
EMGEI geomagnetic
EMGNL termagantly
EMHSS de-emphasise
EMHSZ de-emphasize
EMIHS Germain Hess
EMMSU Terme Museum
EMNAI permanganic
EMNAL fermentable
segmentally
EMNIH German Bight
EMNLG terminology
EMNNL permanently
EMNNS germaneness
EMNPR Belmont Park
EMNTN terminating
EMNTO germination
termination
EMNTT Desmond Tutu
EMNUI hermeneutic
EMNWT teeming with
EMNZN sermonizing
EMOLN seam bowling
EMPRU gemmiparous
EMREC re-emergence
EMRZN mesmerizing
EMSIL permissible
permissibly
EMTCT hermeticity
EMTIA geometrical
EMTLG dermatology
EMTRU termitarium
EMTTO permutation
EMUCA Seymour Cray
ENAAC Jean Lamarck
ENAAL Leoncavallo
ENAET get nearer to
ENAIT Jean Lafitte
ENAMN Léon Gaumont
ENANT reincarnate
ENCEI Sennacherib
ENCEO Dean Acheson
ENECU Leander Club
ENERT reintegrate
ENETA Neanderthal
ENIGA Venn diagram
ENIHE keen-sighted
ENMGR Me and My Girl
ENMTN reanimating
ENMTO reanimation
ENNCU Deinonychus
ENNLS meaningless
ENNOE leaning over
ENNTL be in one tale
ENNUL Jean Anouilh

ENONR Sean Connery
ENOTA Jean Cocteau
ENPTA Jenny Pitman
ENRDC reintroduce
ENREE Keanu Reeves
ENRKT Bernard Katz
ENRTA Leon Brittan
ENRTK Leon Trotsky
ENSLO tennis elbow
ENSMS Dennis Amiss
ENUNS heinousness
ENWIH pennyweight
ENXEI Lennox Lewis
EOABL Deborah Bull
EOADM memorandums
EOAIE demoralized
EOAII memorabilia
EOAIN decorations
EOATC aeronautics
EOBAL redoubtable
EOBSE Le Corbusier
EOCES heroic verse
lemon cheese
EOCLN reconciling
EOCMN debouchment
EOCNL rejoicingly
EODEC beyond reach
EODIH second sight
EODLS second class
second-class
EODOB beyond doubt
EODOD beyond words
EODRL secondarily
EODRT secondary to
EODTO recondition
EODUS second-guess
EOEAE become paler
become rarer
EOEAI become valid
EOEAL recoverable
EOEAN become faint
EOECA wet one's clay
EOEDL become adult
EOEFO recover from
EOEGA get one's goat
EOEHT become white
EOEIE become fixed
become tired
become wider
EOEIH become light
EOELA become clear
EOELF bet one's life
EOELN remodelling
EOENR become angry
EOENS devotedness
reposedness
EOENW become known
EOEOE become bored
EOEOT get one's oats
EOERA remote areas
EOEUL reposefully
EOEUN become sunny
EOEWN get one's wind

EOEWT get over with
EOFTA let off steam
EOGIA Yegor Gaidar
EOGON below ground
EOHGA oesophageal
EOHNT be nothing to
EOHNU bed of honour
EOHRP pelotherapy
EOIAE denominated
EOIAL aerobically
EOIAO denominator
EOIGA Merovingian
EOILA Memorial Day
EOILS memorialise
EOILZ memorialize
EOITO defoliation
negotiation
EOIUL feloniously
ferociously
melodiously
EOKNA be looking at
EOLCE recollected
EOLNI be rolling in
EOLSI xenoglossia
EOLTG décolletage
EOMDE reformadoes
EOMLS renormalise
EOMLZ renormalize
EOMNE recommended
recommender
EOMNO Devon minnow
EOMTO deformation
leg-of-mutton
reformation
EOMTR reformatory
EOMTV reformative
EONIO be borne in on
EONIR reconnoitre
EONMN recountment
EONRA below normal
EONTO recognition
EONUI be bound up in
EOOAI hedonomania
EOOHU xenodochium
EOOIA oenological
penological
serological
EOOPI mesomorphic
EOORS decolourise
EOORZ decolourize
EOOSI hero worship
hero-worship
EOOVR seroconvert
EOPSN decomposing
EORAI menorrhagia
EOREU resourceful
EORNL devouringly
EOROI seborrhoeic
EORPE demographer
EORPI demographic
xerographic
EORTS democratise
EORTZ democratize

EOSAR belowstairs
EOSLS remorseless
EOSNN be consonant
EOSRC deconstruct
reconstruct
EOSRN remonstrant
EOSRT demonstrate
remonstrate
EOSSO repossessor
EOSUS lemon squash
EOTCA gerontocrat
EOTCT decorticate
EOTEE Demosthenes
EOTEI Demosthenic
EOTFE get out of bed
EOTLG gerontology
EOTNL reportingly
revoltingly
EOTTG report stage
EOTTO deportation
EOTTR dehortatory
EOUAO demodulator
EOUSA Belorussian
EOYAE Melody Maker
EOYAI aerodynamic
EOYIA metonymical
EPACO keep watch on
EPAIN Temptations
EPAKN keep walking
EPAOI Neoplatonic
EPCAL respectable
respectably
EPEAE people-eater
EPEDN resplendent
EPEEL perplexedly
EPEHT Hepplewhite
EPEON Temple Mount
EPFWT help off with
EPGNS neopaganise
EPGNZ neopaganize
EPHOG help through
seep through
EPHRN keep the ring
EPHUH deep thought
EPIAL delphically
EPICE deep-pitched
EPIHO keep sight of
EPIHR Terpsichore
EPIIM delphiniums
EPISN deep kissing
EPLAO keep clear of
EPLTC geopolitics
EPNBU keep on about
EPNDR keeping dark
EPNEC despondency
respondence
respondency
EPNHC keep in check
EPNHN helping hand
EPNHO reaping hook
reaping-hook
EPNIH keep in sight
EPNIL responsible

responsibly
EPNLK serpentlike
EPNOC keep in touch
EPNRP weeping-ripe
EPNSE keep one's bed
EPNSL help oneself
EPNTM leaping-time
EPNYO keep an eye on
EPONE keep counsel
EPOPN keep company
EPOWR leap forward
EPRCO keep track of
EPRDE desperadoes
EPRDU hesperidium
EPRMN temperament
EPRMT leopard-moth
EPRNS pepperiness
EPRRE temporaries
EPRRL temporarily
EPRTL desperately
temperately
EPRTO desperation
respiration
EPRTR respiratory
temperature
EPRZN temporizing
EPSCE keep a secret
EPSTS tempest-tost
EPSUU tempestuous
EPSWL deep as a well
EPTAL perpetually
EPTAO perpetrator
perpetuator
EPTEE bespattered
EPTLG herpetology
EPTRA sempiternal
EPTTA despite that
EPUNS helpfulness
EPURO keep guard on
EPYIA geophysical
EPYOT New Plymouth
ERACS rebroadcast
ERADE merry-andrew
ERAGN rearranging
ERAHU reproachful
ERALN tear-falling
ERATC heart attack
ERATV retroactive
retro-active
ERAYO get ready for
ERBEI Henri Breuil
ERBLS detribalise
ERBLT wearability
ERBLZ detribalize
ERBOE heartbroken
heart-broken
ERBOI necrobiosis
necrobiotic
ERBRE pearl barley
ERBRT learn by rote
ERBTO reprobation
retribution
ERBTR reprobatory
ERBTV reprobative
retributive
ERCAL retractable
ERCDN retrocedent
ERCFO detract from
ERCOE Henry Cooper
ERCTN deprecating
ERCTO deprecation
ERCTR deprecatory
ERCTV deprecative
ERCXD ferric oxide
ERDIA rear admiral
ERDTO degradation
depredation
EREAA George Halas
EREAE George Carey
EREAL retrievable
retrievably
EREAO George Gamow
EREBS George W Bush
ERECT George Scott
EREEA George Medal
EREKN tear-jerking
ERELI George Ellis
ERELK George Blake
ERELO George Eliot
ERENS learnedness
EREOA George Cohan
EREOC George Monck
EREOE George Robey
EREOL George Boole
EREOR George Moore
ERERS George Cross
George Grosz
ERERV George Grove
ERERW George Brown
George-Brown
ERETT reorientate
EREUA George Lucas
EREUN George Burns
EREUO George Cukor
EREYO George Byron
ERFEB terrified by
ERFRC year of grace
ERFSL Henri Fuseli
ERFWE Henry Fowler
ERGAH reprography
ERGNU ferruginous
ERGRN refrigerant
ERGRT refrigerate
ERGTN segregating
ERGTO segregation
ERHAT search party
ERHBN near the bone
ERHDA tetrahedral
ERHDO Henry Hudson
tetrahedron
ERHIH searchlight
ERHNL searchingly
ERHOG wear through
ERIAL Hebraically
ERIFO refrain from
ERIHE near-sighted
ERIMN detrainment
recruitment
ERINS bear witness
ERIVN Henry Irving
ERKBE Henrik Ibsen
ERLGS neurologist
ERLKC Georg Lukács
ERLSL heartlessly
wearilessly
ERMKN merrymaking
ERMLE Henry Miller
ERMNA detrimental
ERMNE gerrymander
necromancer
ERMNI necromantic
ERMNT recriminate
ERMRA Henry Morgan
ERMRU heart murmur
ERMTS dedramatise
ERMTV terremotive
ERMTZ dedramatize
ERNAA wearing away
ERNBN herringbone
herring-bone
ERNDW tearing-down
wearing down
wearing-down
ERNIL refrangible
ERNLT retranslate
ERNOE dégringoler
ERNRI bearing rein
ERNTA wear and tear
ERNTI wearing thin
ERNWA tear and wear
EROET near to death
ERPCE Kerry Packer
ERPII necrophilia
necrophilic
ERPLA Henry Pelham
ERPLI necropoleis
ERPOI necrophobia
ERPTD decrepitude
ERPTT decrepitate
ERRCE retro-rocket
ERRHS Petrarchise
ERRHZ Petrarchize
ERRZN terrorizing
ERSED decrescendo
ERSHE Ferris wheel
ERSIL repressible
repressibly
ERSML wearisomely
ERSMN refreshment
ERSOI necroscopic
ERSRA terrestrial
ERTAL regrettable
regrettably
ERTGN secret agent
ERTIE tear-stained
ERTLE deerstalker
ERTLT serratulate
ERTOA Terry-Thomas
ERTRA secretarial
secretariat
territorial❑
ERTRE territories
ERTUL regretfully
ERTVL secretively
ERUNS fearfulness
tearfulness
ERVLN tetravalent
ERVNL depravingly
reprovingly
ERVTO depravation
deprivation
ERVTS reprivatise
ERVTZ reprivatize
ERWLI Weary Willie
ERYAE pearly gates
ERYUE pearly queen
ESAAE Leos Janácek
ESAAL persuadable
ESAEB persuaded by
ESAIL persuasible
ESALM Persian lamb
ESALS re-establish
ESANS Weismannism
ESATN newscasting
ESAWR Persian Wars
ESBLT feasibility
sensibility
ESCNS seasickness
ESCTO persecution
ESEDL Wensleydale
ESEMT Bessie Smith
ESETV perspective
ESEUT perspecuity
ESGIR bersagliere
ESHLE leaseholder
ESIAL deistically
ESIRS verslibrist
ESIUT perspicuity
ESIUU perspicuous
ESJWL Tessa Jowell
ESLAE tessellated
ESLKL least likely
ESLNS beastliness
pensileness
ESLOD weasel words
ESLSL ceaselessly
senselessly
ESLSO Peasblossom
ESMLE Weissmuller
ESMNA leishmaniae
leishmanias
ESMNE verse-monger
ESMSI pessimistic
ESNBR Helsingborg
ESNFE personified
personifier
ESNLN geosyncline
ESNLS personalise
ESNLT personality
seasonality
ESNLZ personalize
ESNSA Peasants' War

ESNTO personation
ESOAL pensionable
sessionally
tensionally
ESOEE tensiometer
ESOFN pension fund
ESOLN Ken Scotland
ESONU teaspoonful
ESOOI seismologic
ESORP seismograph
ESRAT men-servants
ESRBI Welsh rabbit
ESRIE tea strainer
ESRLS measureless
ESRMN measurement
ESRNE get stronger
ESRPI geostrophic
ESRPO leisure pool
ESRTO mensuration
ESRUT measure up to
ESSEC persistence
persistency
ESTLL versatilely
ESTLT versatility
ESTOA sensational
ESTVL sensitively
ESTVT sensitive to
sensitivity
ESUAC reassurance
ESURE red squirrel
ESVNS pensiveness
ESVRA Deus avertat
ESVRI persevere in
ESVRN persevering
ESVRT perseverate
ETABN central bank
ETAFA meet halfway
ETAGN left hanging
ETAIE neutralizer
ETANN restraining
ETANT be at pains to
ETAPR central part
ETARE heat barrier
ETBAL vertebrally
ETBLS destabilise
ETBLZ destabilize
ETCAG depth charge
depth-charge
ETCEI septicaemia
ETCLE peptic ulcer
ETCLI vertical fin
ETCLT denticulate
gesticulate
verticality
ETCMR Deutschmark
Weltschmerz
ETCRF festschrift
ETCRS Celtic cross
ETCSA Pentecostal
ETDCY pentadactyl
ETDFE beg to differ
ETEAL gentlemanly
ETEAO get the law on
ETEBA weather beam
ETEBC leather-back
ETECA leather-coat
ETECC weather-cock
ETECN set the scene
ETEEV get the heave
ETEFE Set Them Free
ETEFN weather-fend
ETEGR weathergirl
ETEHR Bertie Ahern
ETEIC centrepiece
ETEIH see the light
ETEIT gentle birth
ETELD weatherlady
ETELK featherlike
ETELN bestselling
ETENC leather-neck
ETENS genteelness
ETEOA gentlewoman
ETEOL see the world
ETEON get the point
ETEOR centreboard
ETERS next dearest
ETESD weather side
ETETG centre stage
ETEWR weather-worn
ETEWS weather-wise
ETFAL certifiable
certifiably
rectifiable
ETFCT certificate
ETFGE pettifogger
ETFRU pestiferous
ETGAM centigramme
hectogramme
ETGNU lentiginous
vertiginous
ETGTE get together
get-together
ETHAA Teotihuacán
ETHDA pentahedral
ETHDO pentahedron
ETHDU beat the drum
ETIAL centrically
ETIEA centripetal
ETIGA settling day
ETIGS next biggest
ETISE Westminster
ETITO restriction
ETITV restrictive
ETIUA centrifugal
ventricular
ETJSP Keith Joseph
ETLAL reptilianly
ETLGS pestologist
ETLLC mental block
ETLLS dental floss
ETLMG mental image
ETLNA rectilineal
rectilinear
ETLNL pestilently
ETLNS deathliness
de-Stalinise
ETLNZ de-Stalinize
ETLOI lex talionis
ETLPL deathly pale
ETLTE best clothes
ETLTO ventilation
ETLTV ventilative
ETLYL mentally ill
ETLZN fertilizing
ETMDE Bette Midler
ETMDN pentamidine
ETMNA sentimental
testimonial
ETMNE petty-minded
ETMRS pentamerism
ETMRU pentamerous
ETNAA melting away
ETNCT pertinacity
ETNEC rest in peace
ETNFE setting free
ETNIU sententious
ETNNL pertinently
ETNRA centenarian
ETNSO melting snow
ETNTL festinately
pectinately
ETNTO destination
pectination
ETNUA pentangular
rectangular
ETNUE getting used
ETOAE mentholated
ETOAL mentionable
sectionally
ETOBA Berthon-boat
ETOBM neutron bomb
ETOEI mentioned in
oestrogenic
ETOHA West Lothian
ETOIA neotropical
ETONE meat counter
ETOSA neutron star
ETRAL vectorially
ETRBT deattribute
reattribute
ETRCR beat a record
ETREL perturbedly
ETRFL feature film
ETRGT set to rights
ETRIT venture into
ETRLS featureless
ETRMS westernmost
ETRNL pesteringly
venturingly
ETRNM Deuteronomy
ETROK tenterhooks
ETRRL western roll
ETRRS letterpress
ETRSI lectureship
ETRSM venturesome
ETRTB Venturi tube
ETRTO reiteration
restoration
ETRTV reiterative
restorative
ETRUL dexterously
venturously
ETRUR Hector Munro
ETRWL Western Wall
ETSAN Leptis Magna
ETSEK Yevtushenko
ETSIH pentastichs
ETSNN jettisoning
ETSNS pettishness
ETSRK death-stroke
ETTEO get to the top
new to the job
ETTLE teetotaller
ETTLS teetotalism
ETTMN restatement
ETTTO destitute of
destitution
restitution
ETTTR restitutory
ETTTV restitutive
ETTVL tentatively
ETUKF be struck off
ETUNS restfulness
zestfulness
ETUTO destruction
ETUTR restructure
ETUTV destructive
ETVLN pentavalent
ETVNS restiveness
ETVTE festivities
ETVTO aestivation
EUAIN regulations
EUBNL decumbently
recumbently
EUCAO denunciator
EUCLT pedunculate
EUCRS Jesus Christ
EUCRU sepulchrous
EUCTT resuscitate
EUDNL redundantly
EUDRA get under way
EUDTO fecundation
EUEAE remunerated
EUEAL denumerably
recuperable
remunerable
EUEAO rejuvenator
remunerator
EUEEC rejuvenesce
EUEHE Leeuwenhoek
EUEIA oecumenical
EUEMS Requiem Mass
EUENS bemusedness
EUEPE reduce speed
EUERT reduced rate
EUEUL beauteously
rebukefully
EUGTN regurgitant
EUGTT regurgitate
EUIAM get up in arms
EUIAP Tegucigalpa
EUIEO deputize for

EUIRL pecuniarily
EUIRS peculiarise
EUIRT peculiarity
EUIRZ peculiarize
EUITO repudiation
EUITV repudiative
EUIUL beautifully
penuriously
EUIYN beautifying
EULBS sexual abuse
EULCT reduplicate
EULMN beguilement
EULNL beguilingly
EULNO sexual union
EULRV sexual drive
EULXO genuflexion
EUNAC return match
EUNNS genuineness
EUNNT repugnant to
EUOTE Beaufort Sea
EUOTN verumontana
EURCE resurrected
EURCO resurrector
EURMN requirement
EURNL decurrently
recurrently
EUSBU be nuts about
EUSEE sequestered
EUSRT sequestrate
EUSSO request stop
EUSTL decussately
EUSTO requisition
EUSVL decursively
repulsively
EUTMT penultimate
EUTNL reluctantly
EUTRL desultorily
EUTVL deductively
reductively
seductively
EUULS demutualise
EUULZ demutualize
EUUNS tenuousness
EUYAO beauty salon
EUYLE beauty sleep
EUYUE beauty queen
EVALA heavy as lead
EVBHN leave behind
EVCAE service area
EVCAL serviceable
serviceably
EVCBO servicebook
service-book
EVCFA service flat
EVCNR nerve centre
EVFOE heavy-footed
EVHNE heavy-handed
EVLSL nervelessly
EVNAD heavenwards
EVNEK Mervyn Peake
EVNGT Heaven's Gate
EVNLE Lee Van Cleef
EVNMI serving-maid
EVNNW heaven knows
EVNRG Melvyn Bragg
EVRKO weaver's knot
EVRRO Beaverbrook
EVSNS peevishness
EVSVL pervasively
EVTEO heave the log
EVTHN velvet shank
EVTKN leave-taking
EVTNS velvetiness
EVUDN leave undone
EVUNS nervousness
EVWIH heavy weight
heavyweight
EWETM betweentime
EWKNN reawakening
EWKUT be a wake-up to
EWLIM Ted Williams
EXDTO deoxidation
EXEPI jeux d'esprit
EXETN be expecting
EXGNS deoxygenise
EXGNT deoxygenate
EXGNZ deoxygenize
EYASA New Year's Day
EYASV New Year's Eve
EYLNT demyelinate
EYLSL very closely
EYNSL deny oneself
EYNTS dehypnotise
EYNTZ dehypnotize
EYRCT New York City
EYRTO dehydration
rehydration
EYSRE Meryl Streep
EYUAE see you later
EYUCL very quickly
EZBRO Kenzaburo Oë
EZEZO Mezz Mezzrow
EZIAI benzoic acid
EZPEI Led Zeppelin
EZTNO mezzotintos
FADLN eff and blind
FAYOD of many words
FCOAO aficionados
FDATG of advantage
FEEFC after effect
after-effect
FEEIT of benefit to
FEESR if necessary
FEEST of necessity
FESPE aftersupper
FESVL offensively
FETAL effectually
FETNL affectingly
FETTO affectation
FETVL affectively
effectively
FETVT affectivity
FHNEL offhandedly
FHNON Afghan hound
FHNSA Afghanistan
FIAIU efficacious
FIELC office block
FIEOR office hours
FIILO officialdom
FIILS officialese
officialism
FIINL efficiently
FIITO affiliation
FIIUL officiously
FIMNL affirmingly
FIMTO affirmation
FIMTV affirmative
FLCEB afflicted by
FLRPT of ill repute
FOCON of no account
FOEFC off one's face
FOEFE off one's feed
FOEGM off one's game
FOEHA off one's head
FOEOT off one's oats
FONMN of sound mind
FOPES if you please
FOREO of course not
FRNHS affranchise
FSORN offscouring
FTEAL off the rails
FTEAO off the wagon
FTEHL off the shelf
FTEOK off the hooks
FTEON off the point
FTERC off the track
FUGNL effulgently
GADPO egg-and-spoon
GAIAL agnatically
GEIUL egregiously
GIFTU ignis fatuus
GIINE ignition key
GISTM against time
GIUTR agriculture
GLMRT agglomerate
GLTNT agglutinate
GLTRA egalitarian
GMNAA egomaniacal
GNCIL Egon Schiele
GNCLM agony column
GNOAG Agent Orange
GNSNL agonisingly
GNZNL agonizingly
GOATN Ignorantine
GOAUE ignoramuses
GOCEC agroscience
GOEOS P G Wodehouse
GOIIU ignominious
GOLNS ignobleness
GOTCS agnosticism
GPINA Egyptian Mau
GRGTL aggregately
GRGTO aggregation
GRPOI agoraphobia
agoraphobic
GRVTN aggravating
GRVTO aggravation
GSNAE ages and ages
GTSIA egotistical
HAAET The Analects
HAAFO shy away from
HAAVR phrasal verb
HAEGA phraseogram
HAELG phraseology
HAMGT the Almighty
HAOCR chiaroscuro
HAONE the anointed
HAOTM ahead of time
HARCL theatricals
HARCS theatricise
theatricism
HARCZ theatricize
HATHP thwartships
HATNL thwartingly
HBAKR the black art
HBGLE The Big Sleep
HBGMK the Big Smoke
HBGPL the Big Apple
HBGSU The Big Issue
HBMRS the bum's rush
HBOAC rhabdomancy
HBSNS the business
HCALC chock-a-block
HCCMN thick-coming
HCEFE chickenfeed
HCETO The Creation
HCEWR chicken wire
HCHAE thick-headed
HCHRO shock horror
shock-horror
HCLNE the Colonies
HCLPE thick-lipped
HCMCT phycomycete
HCNUS the Conquest
HCRBE thick-ribbed
HCUIL The Crucible
HCYAE Chuck Yeager
HDESM Chad Newsome
HDFAE the defeated
HDIHO shed light on
HDILN Rhode Island
HDLRM the doldrums
HDPRE the departed
HDROS The Dormouse
HDWNS shadowiness
HDWRP shadowgraph
HEACO sheet-anchor
HEBJW cheek by jowl
HEBRE chief barker
HEBRO wheelbarrow
HEDCE three-decker
HEEAE cheeseparer
HEEIA threnetical
HEELT cheesecloth
HEEOR cheese board
HEETA cheese straw
HEETE shoe leather
HEGAE Three Graces
HEHBU thresh about
HEHKE cheechakoes
HELGE The Eclogues
HENOE three-nooked

HEOCS The Exorcist
HEOOI phrenologic
HERPA The European
HERVR Three Rivers
HESAI The Exstasie
HESIE three-suited
HETIC chieftaincy
HETNN threatening
HETRT the entirety
HEWIH wheelwright
HEWNO wheel window
HFAKI The Franklin
HFAON shift around
HFIHU the Faithful
HFLNL shufflingly
HFLSL shiftlessly
HFNLO the final bow
HFONE chiffonnier
HFOUR chef d'oeuvre
chef-d'oeuvre
HFRBR The Firebird
HFUUL theftuously
HGADA The Guardian
HGAUT The Graduate
HGCTS phagocytose
HGDFR rhagadiform
HGENR The Gleaners
HGETS the greatest
HGMIU the game is up
HGOBO the Good Book
HGOLF the good life
HIBRE Chris Barber
HIEBN Chris Eubank
HIELN shrivelling
HIERW choice-drawn
HIHRO Chaim Herzog
HIKNL shriekingly
shrinkingly
HILNL thrillingly
HILTE chain letter
HIMSE choirmaster
HIPLN shrimp plant
HIPRO chairperson
HISOE chain-smoker
HITAL Christianly
HITAS Christmassy
HITLG Christology
HITNN christening
HITNO Christendom
HITNS thriftiness
HITPE Christopher
HITRE the Internet
HKNAD The King and I
HKSER Shakespeare
HLAEE Shalmaneser
HLAFG Phileas Fogg
HLAON whole amount
HLDMD thalidomide
HLEGN challenging
HLEGR challengers
HLENT Phil Bennett
HLEOI chalcedonic
HLFCO chill factor
HLGNU child genius
HLIGA Chillingham
HLLGS philologist
HLMNE childminder
HLNEE philanderer
HLNME whole number
HLNRB the long robe
HLOAI phyllomania
phyllotaxis
HLOKN The Lion King
HLOLD phylloclade
HLOLN Phil Collins
HLONS shallowness
HLPIE Philippines
HLPIN Philippians
HLPLS Philip Glass
HLSCS the last cast
HLSEO cholesterol
HLSGS the last gasp
HLSML wholesomely
HLSPE philosopher
HLSPI philosophic
HLSWR the last word
HLTLS philatelist
HLVSO She Loves You
HMELI chamberlain[❑]
HMEMI chambermaid
HMIAL whimsically
HMINN championing
HMLFL thimblefuls
HMLIE The Maldives
HMLOI chameleonic
HMLSL shamelessly
HMLYA the Milky Way
HMNEE chemin de fer
Shimon Peres
HMNFA The Man of Law
HMNHE the munchies
HMNSI shamanistic
HMOER rhombohedra
HMOLO Champollion
HMOTE shame on them
HMRHN The Merchant
HMSAD Thomas Hardy
HMSAH Thomas Nashe
HMSCA The Music Man
HMSHM rhyme-scheme
HMSLO Thomas Blood
HMSON Thomas Young
HMSRD Thomas Pride
HMSRW Thomas Brown
HNAMT phantasmata
HNBCT think back to
HNBER the noble art
HNDEL think deeply
HNEAD change hands
HNEBL thunderbolt
HNEBR thunderbird
HNECA thunderclap
HNEDR thunderdart
HNEEL chanterelle
HNEHA thunderhead
HNEIE change sides
HNEIT changed into
HNELK thunder-like
HNELN thin red line
HNELR chancellery
chancellory
HNEON change round
HNEOT thenceforth
whenceforth
HNERN change front
HNEUL changefully
HNEUO change out of
HNEVN chance event
HNFLO thankful for
HNGAH phonography
HNIEI chinoiserie
HNILE chanticleer
HNISL when pigs fly
HNKNE thin-skinned
HNLGS phenologist
phonologist
rhinologist
HNLKL think likely
HNLSL thanklessly
HNMCO think much of
HNMCS phonemicise
phonemicist
HNMCZ phonemicize
HNMNS phenomenise
HNMNZ phenomenize
HNNGN shenanigans
HNNLN Chenin Blanc
HNOLM phantom limb
HNPAT rhinoplasty
HNRZI Phanerozoic
HNSOI rhinoscopic
HNSRK thin as a rake
HNTCA phonetician
HNTCS phoneticise
HNTCZ phoneticize
HNTLG thanatology
HNUAI thingumajig
HNWLO think well of
HOAAT throw a party
HOAON throw around
HOBNL throbbingly
HODLC the old block
HODNM the old enemy
HOEIA theoretical
HOEIE choose sides
HOESA whooper swan
HOETE chrome steel
HOGFR throughfare
HOGWT through with
HOHRA the other day
HOIAC chrominance
HOIAI chloric acid
HOIAL chaotically
chronically
HOIGA shooting war
HOIGU throwing out
HOOAI Theodorakis
HOOEE chronometer
HOOHL chlorophyll
HOOHR chromophore
HOOHS theosophise
theosophist
HOOHZ theosophize
HOOIA rheological
theological
HOOLS chloroplast
HOOOA chromosomal
HOOOE chronologer
HOOPI theomorphic
HOORP chronograph
HORMN theobromine
HOSRE The Observer
HOTER chaos theory
HOTEU shoot the sun
HOTIE The Outsider
HOTNS throatiness
HPAAT the peasants
HPADU The Phaedrus
HPEDL Chippendale
HPEDO shepherd boy
HPEDS shepherdess
HPEPN shopkeeping
HPHOR ship the oars
HPICI ship biscuit
HPIGO whipping-boy
HPIRS The Prioress
HPITN shoplifting
HPLNS shapeliness
HPLTE whippletree
HPNSU whip and spur
HPOHT the prophets
HPOIA rhapsodical
HPPLC the populace
HPRCE shipwrecked
HPROE The Pardoner
HPTRE ship it green
HPTWR shop steward
HPULE shipbuilder
HQEWS chequerwise
HRAOI the reason is
HRAOT thereabouts
whereabouts
HRBSD therebeside
HRCAG short-change
HRCMN shortcoming
HRDGE third degree
HRDUE The Red Queen
HREAN Charlemagne
HREBL Charles Bell
HREBS Charles Best
HREIE Charles Ives
HRELM Charles Lamb
HREMY Charles Mayo
HREOS charge-house
HRESA Charles's law
HRESI shorten sail
HRETW Charlestown
HREUS charge nurse
HREWT charged with
HRFRE sharefarmer
HRGAH chirography
HRHAD churchwards

HRHEC church-bench
HRHIE Church Times
HRHLE shareholder
HRHNE shorthanded
short-handed
HRHOA churchwoman
HRHOE church tower
HRHON church-going
HRHOR churchgoers
HRHOS church-mouse
HRIAL thermically
HRICA Charlie Chan
HRIGO Sherrington
HRINC thermionics
HRLRU choral group
HRLSE shortlisted
HRLSL charmlessly
HRMNE whoremonger
HRNII pharyngitis
HRNRI sharon fruit
HRNTN Sharon Stone
HROEE thermometer
HRORP choreograph
HROTO share option
HRPBI The Republic
HRPDS chiropodist
HRPUI therapeutic
HRSAI charismatic
HRSBW The Rose Bowl
HRSEE wheresoever
HRSIA pharisaical
HRSOE short-spoken
HRSPL short supply
HRSRF short shrift
HRTBL charity ball
HRTFR theretofore
HRTME short temper
HRTNS thirstiness
HRWNE short-winded
HRWTA wherewithal
HRWTE sharp-witted
HRYUR there you are
where you are
HSATE the smart set
HSAWE this day week
HSCLS physicalism
HSCLT physicality
HSCRS The Sick Rose
HSEYA this very day
HSHRS phosphorise
HSHRT phosphorate
HSHRU phosphorous
HSHRZ phosphorize
HSHTS phosphatise
HSHTZ phosphatize
HSIEA Cheshire Cat
HSINR Thespian art
HSLAA whistle away
HSLDW thistledown
HSLNL whistlingly
HSLNS ghastliness
ghostliness
HSLSO whistle-stop
HSMOE The Summoner
HSNTA this and that
HSNTN this instant
HSONM physiognomy
HSONN this morning
HSOOI physiologic
HSREO The Sorceror
HSUGR The Sluggard
HSUUE thesauruses
HSVNN this evening
HSWIE ghost writer
HSZOI the size of it
HTAAA Shatt al-Arab
HTAEO what have you
HTAIE that's an idea
HTAOG Chattanooga
HTBTE Rhett Butler
HTCFE white coffee
HTCLA white-collar
HTCOE white clover
HTCPE white copper
HTDNI that's done it
HTECE the Trenches
HTEON whether or no
HTESG White Ensign
HTEWR thitherward
whitherward
HTFIR White friars
HTGAH photography
HTHHL what the hell
HTHIE white-haired
HTHRE white horses
HTHRS Thatcherism
HTHRT Thatcherite
HTIDA The Third Man
HTKIH white knight
HTLAA whittle away
HTLCC shuttlecock
HTLWS shuttlewise
HTMTE white matter
HTMTI photometric
HTNTM whiting-time
HTOEE whatsomever
HTOWR whet forward
HTPAN White Plains
HTPAU what a plague
HTPOI photophobia
HTPPE white pepper
HTRCA rhetorician
HTRMS a hit or a miss
HTSHR photosphere
HTSII white spirit
HTSOA that is to say
HTTAE what it takes
HTTCI phototactic
HTTRA whitethroat
HTTRI that's torn it!
HTUTD Whitsuntide
HTWLU white walnut
HTYBE Whitby Abbey
HUAIK rheumaticky
HUAUG thaumaturge
thaumaturgy
HUBNS shrubbiness
HUDRA shoulder bag
shoulder-bag
HUHLS thoughtless
HUHSC thought-sick
HUIES The Universe
HUMDA thrummed hat
HUMNL thrummingly
HUPSR choux pastry
HUTTG thrust stage
HVLOR shovelboard
HVRIE the very idea
HVRNL shiveringly
HVRSM the very same
HWASI showmanship
HWECT show mercy to
HWFAD show of hands
HWILN show willing
HWINO show signs of
HWLDC The Wild Duck
HWLWO The Wild Wood
HWNSL show oneself
HWNTL show and tell
HWOCR show concern
HWOEI the whole kit
HWOEO the whole lot
HWOLR The Woodlark
HWREO the worse for
HWRRO showerproof
HWSRO the wiser for
HWTPE show-stopper
HWUPN showjumping
show-jumping
HXTOI thixotropic
HYAIE chrysalides
chrysalises
HYINA Phrygian cap
HYOEY chrysoberyl
HYORS chrysoprase
HYTEA phlyctaenae
HZCRI rhizocarpic
HZMTU rhizomatous
IABNT bicarbonate
IABRS Micawberish
IABTL final battle
IACAL financially
IACSO disaccustom
IADMN final demand
IADNO ritardandos
IADRC bib and brace
IAEAL bilaterally
IAECM bid a welcome
IAETR filamentary
IAETU filamentous
IAFCE disaffected
IAFRS disafforest
IAGET vinaigrette
IAHTN rival-hating
IAIAE dilapidated
divaricated
IAIAL piratically
titanically
IAICU Kiwanis Club
IAIET rifacimenti
IAIUL bifariously
hilariously
vicariously
vivaciously
IALAC misalliance
IALMN disablement
IALNN Rila Planina
IALPA miracle play
IAMMN disarmament
IAMRE Silas Marner
IAOBC Rifat Ozbeck
IAOGN vital organs
IAOSE gila monster
IAPAE disappeared
IAPOA disapproval
IAREN disagreeing
IARNE disarranged
IARNS bizarreness
IASAE cigar-shaped
IASML disassemble
disassembly
IATCS didacticism
IATRP misanthrope
misanthropy
IATSU gigantesque
IATUE ailanthuses
IBDVR Sir Bedivere
IBGTE misbegotten
IBHVN misbehaving
IBITO fimbriation
IBLEE disbeliever
IBLTE liabilities
IBNMN disbandment
IBREA Jim Bergerac
IBRHL Silbury Hill
IBRIC timber hitch
IBRLI gibberellin
IBRMT Wilbur Smith
IBROC Wilberforce
IBRRL Gilbert Ryle
IBSNE Kim Basinger
IBSNS big business
IBSRT nimbostrati
ICADA pitch and pay
ICAGN discharging
ICAKN disc parking
ICAMN disclaiming
ICASF misclassify
ICATA aircraftman
ICBED pitchblende
ICBLT miscibility
vincibility
ICDCO witch doctor
ICEAC discrepancy
ICEET kitchenette
ICEIA biochemical
ICEIE discredited
ICEMI kitchenmaid
ICEOE biocoenoses
ICERO pitched roof
ICESN kitchen sink
kitchen-sink

ICETO miscreation
ICEUI kitchen unit
ICEWR kitchenware
ICGAH discography
ICGNT miscegenate
ICIIA diacritical
ICIVU mischievous
ICLRA circular saw
ICLRS circularise
ICLRT circularity
ICLRZ circularize
ICLTN circulating
ICLTO circulation
ICLTR circulatory
ICLUE discoloured
ICMIE discomfited
ICMLC circumflect
ICMOE discomposed
ICMOV circumvolve
ICMPC circumspect
ICNAU Cincinnatus
ICNEV misconceive
ICNIU discontinue
ICNTU misconstrue
ICOCK piece of cake
ICOLN piece of land
ICOWR piece of work
ICPIE disciplined
ICRAC discordance
ICRIG miscarriage
ICRIL discernible
discernibly
ICRMN discernment
ICSAL discussable
ICSIL discussible
ICSWT discuss with
ICTEU discotheque
discothèque
ICTRA piscatorial
piscatorian
ICUAE discouraged
ICUNS viscousness
ICUTN discounting
ICUTS discourtesy
viscountess
ICVRU piscivorous
IDACE bird-fancier
birdwatcher
IDAER pieds-à-terre
IDAHN wind machine
IDANS misdiagnose
IDCTN vindicating
IDCTO vindication
IDCTR vindicatory
IDCTV vindicative
IDEAC Middlemarch
IDEAD kind regards
IDEAT Middle-Earth
IDEBU fiddle about
IDECA fiddler crab
IDEDN mind-bending
mind-reading
IDEHT Middle White
IDEIE middle-sized
IDELS middle class
middle-class
IDENS kindredness
IDERE kind-hearted
IDESI kindredship
IDETC fiddlestick
IDEUO diddle out of
IDHAE windcheater
IDHCR wild chicory
IDHLD find the lady
IDHLL gild the lily
IDHPL gild the pill
IDJBO find a job for
IDLWN mind-blowing
IDMET wisdom teeth
IDMOT wisdom tooth
IDNML wild animals
IDNRI wind and rain
IDNSL find oneself
gird oneself
IDOKO Windsor knot
IDOLN wildfowling
IDOPR Windsor Park
IDORY mind your eye
IDRCE misdirected
IDREE Biedermeier
IDRHN widdershins
IDRIE bird-brained
IDRNL hinderingly
IDSEL fin de siècle
IDSRB misdescribe
IDTCO lie detector
IDUBN mind-numbing
IDUFN windsurfing
IDUNS mindfulness
IDWEG window ledge
IDWHD window shade
IDYIK tiddlywinks
IEAGN wide-ranging
IEAIA kinematical
IEAIE mineralizer
IEAIN tire-valiant
IEALO kite-balloon
IEALS bimetallism
IEAPN wiretapping
IEASL time capsule
IEASN fire-raising
IEAST fixed assets
IEATN Mike Gatting
time-wasting
IEAUE literatured
IEAWE five-day week
IEBDE disembodied
IEBRE disemburden
IEBTE disembitter
IEBZT give a buzz to
IECEC life science
IECME disencumber
IECMR video camera
IECSE Cirencester
IECSR Fidel Castro
IEDCM aides-de-camp
IEDIA vice-admiral
IEDVE Miles Davies
IEEAL fine details
give details
IEEBI give leg bail
IEELA sidereal day
IEENT give means to
IEEOR aide-mémoire
IEERE Nicene Creed
IEERG life peerage
IEERS life peeress
IEESN give lessons
IEETE Lise Meitner
IEETN wire netting
IEEVN time-serving
IEFEC give offence
pipe of peace
IEFIE life of Riley
IEFOE tiger-footed
IEGNE bioengineer
IEGNL divergently
divergingly
IEHBA ride the beam
IEHDS bite the dust
IEHNT give a hand to
IEHOG live through
IEHPE widechapped
IEHPS give the push
IEHRD ride the rods
IEHRE fines herbes
IEHRN time-sharing
IEHSI give the slip
IEHWL give the wall
IEHWN like the wind
IEIAL eidetically
mimetically
IEIEA wine vinegar
IEIHE firelighter
IEIKN like winking
IEILG kinesiology
IEITT give birth to
IEJRA River Jordan
IEKCT give a kick to
IELAE pipe-cleaner
time-pleaser
IELCT divellicate
give place to
IELFE River Liffey
IELFT give a lift to
IELLN pineal gland
IELNS miserliness
IELUL libellously
IELWO Nigel Lawson
IEMGO filet mignon
IEMRO like a mirror
IENCL hibernacula
IENCN mise en scène
mise-en-scène
IENCS hibernicise
Hibernicism
IENCZ hibernicize
IENDN wine and dine
IENFL rise and fall
IENLC mise en place
IENME mixed number
IENMT give a name to
IENOE live-in lover
pigeonholed
IENSE hide-and-seek
IENSI bite one's lip
IENSL give one's all
give oneself
IENSY pipe one's eye
IENTK give and take
give-and-take
IENTN hibernating
IENTO hibernation
IEOBN dive-bombing
IEOCT give voice to
IEOET given over to
give power to
IEOLK like for like
IEPIT finer points
IERAE pipe-dreamer
IERCE firecracker
sidetracked
wisecracker
IERCR video-record
IERGD fire brigade
IERIE fine-grained
IERLN give a ruling
IERNE line printer
IEROT give a room to
IERSE vine-dresser
IERUL give trouble
IERWN wiredrawing
IESAD Line Islands
IESFA sinews of war
IESFE disease-free
diversified
IESNS diverseness
IESOA dimensional
IESOT give a shot to
IESRA like a streak
IESRO give a sermon
IESRU disenshroud
IETAC disentrance
IETAT Dire Straits
dire straits
IETCL diverticula
IETEI direct debit
kinesthetic
IETEL give it welly
IETHL liberty hall
IETIE directrices
IETLT give a talk to
IETMT misestimate
IETNL disentangle
divertingly
give a tinkle
IETNR bicentenary
IETNS libertinism
IETOA directional
IETRA directorial
libertarian
IETRL disenthrall

IETRS give it a rest
IETRT directorate
IETTE disentitled
IETTO fire station
IETVL digestively
IETVT directivity
IEUDN rice pudding
IEULN wire-pulling
IEUNS hideousness
piteousness
IEWEE minesweeper
IEYNW widely known
widely-known
IFAAC misfeasance
IFATO diffraction
IFATV diffractive
IFCLL difficultly
IFDNL diffidently
IFEBC biofeedback
IFEOE Wilfred Owen
IFLOE Eiffel Tower
IFNET sinfonietta
IFNTH Riefenstahl
IFRNE differences
IFRNI differentia
IFRNL differently
pilferingly
IFSNS diffuseness
IFSVL diffusively
IFSVT diffusivity
IGADE Ring Lardner
IGAEU disgraceful
IGAIU disgracious
IGARE ring-carrier
IGDOD winged words
IGDOS Winged Horse
IGECU singles club
IGEGI king penguin
IGERA single cream
IGEWC Giggleswick
IGEWR ring network
IGFID king of birds
IGFIG king of kings
IGFRT ring of truth
IGHSE ring the shed
IGICI ring circuit
IGIEL disguisedly
misguidedly
IGITC linguistics
IGLRS singularise
IGLRT singularity
IGLRZ singularize
IGNIT Virgin Birth
IGNWN wing-and-wing
IGOAL diagnosable
IGOCM kingdom come
IGOTO Siege of Troy
IGRAE Finger Lakes
IGRAN finger-paint
IGRIO disgarrison
IGRNL lingeringly
IGRNO king's ransom
IGROR fingerboard
IGRRA gingerbread
IGRRN fingerprint
IGRRU ginger group
IGRTL fingerstall
IGRVR Diego Rivera
IGSEC King's Speech
IGSEL disgustedly
IGSNS piggishness
IGTNS fidgetiness
IGUTE disgruntled
IGYLO King's-yellow
IHACD Highway Code
IHAEL pigheadedly
IHAGE right-angled
IHAHO high fashion
IHAKN high-ranking
IHARI right as rain
IHARU right atrium
IHATO with caution
IHAUI highfalutin
IHAWL might as well
IHCAO pichiciagos
IHCRE tight corner
IHEFO Michael Foot
IHEJO Michael J Fox
IHENO eighteenmos
IHEOE Michael Owen
IHEPC with respect
IHESO high-tension
IHEST high-density
IHEUL righteously
IHFOE light-footed
IHFSE tight-fisted
IHGAH lithography
IHHAE light-headed
IHHDR dish the dirt
IHHIE light-haired
IHHNA diphthongal
IHHNE right-handed
right-hander
IHIAE Mithridates
IHICE high-pitched
IHIDW High Windows
IHIGA fighting man
IHIGI fighting fit
IHIGL nightingale[❑]
IHIHE highlighter
high-sighted
IHLGS lithologist
IHLKI tightly-knit
IHLNS His Holiness
sightliness
IHLPE tight-lipped
IHLSL sightlessly
IHLTM high old time
IHLWE Wilhelm Wien
IHMFR Light My Fire
IHMNE right-minded
IHMRS nightmarish
IHNAG within range
IHNBO with knobs on
IHNEC within reach
IHNLN fishing-line
mishandling
IHNOE within cooee
IHNRO within cry of
IHNSL dishonestly
IHNUE dishonoured
IHOAI dichromatic
IHODI right of drip
IHODN withholding
IHOEE high-powered
IHOEU with no let-up
IHOIT high society
IHOTG high-voltage
IHOWY right-of-ways
IHPNO high opinion
IHPRT high spirits
IHPWR Bishops' Wars
IHPYA lithophysae
IHPYI lithophytic
IHRAO high treason
IHRBR Richard Bird
Richard Byrd
IHRFL high profile
IHRFT with profits
IHRGR Richard Gere
IHRHN withershins
IHRKH Richard Kuhn
IHRLN Richard Long
IHRNL witheringly
IHRSA Richards Bay
IHSEN sightseeing
IHSFA rights-of-way
IHSHO night school
IHSHR lithosphere
IHSKT high as a kite
IHSOS vichyssoise
IHSRE sight screen
IHSSE night sister
IHSUC light source
IHTIS lithotripsy
IHTMS dichotomise
IHTMU dichotomous
IHTMZ dichotomize
IHTNE withstander
IHTVT right to vote
IHUBO without book
IHUCS without cost
IHUDB without debt
IHUDO without-door
IHUFI without fail
IHUGO high dudgeon
IHUHL without help
IHULT high quality
high-quality
IHUNS wishfulness
IHUWR without work
IHVET with a view to
IHVLE dishevelled
IHWIH lightweight
IHWNE right-winger
IHYOB High Wycombe
IIABN minicabbing
IIAEO militate for
IIAIN limitations
IIAJR Kilimanjaro
IIANS finicalness
IIATS vigilantism
IICIE disinclined
IICNR civic centre
IIECN viridescent
virilescent
IIEDI Jimi Hendrix
IIEEN Divine Being
divine being
IIEIH divine right
IIEKN Citizen Kane
IIENS limitedness
IIESI citizenship
IIETF misidentify
IIETO vivisection
IIFCE disinfected
IIFRE misinformed
IIGAL bilingually
dining-table
IIGET living death
IIGHI dining-chair
IIGHN living thing
IIGIH riding-light
IIGLC hiding-place
IIGMG living image
IIGQA firing squad
IIGTN Livingstone
IIHIS finish first
IIIAI silicic acid
IIIAL mirifically
IIIGO divining rod
IIIHN diminishing
IIINS civilianise
IIINZ civilianize
IIIRD digitigrade
IIIUL litigiously
IIKNS finickiness
IILNS visibleness
IILSL limitlessly
IILSO disillusion
IILTN titillating
IILTO pixillation
titillation
IINEG Vivien Leigh
IINIE vision mixer
IINUH Vivian Fuchs
IIOCI silicon chip
IIPIO disimprison
IIRBD ciliary body
IISRC misinstruct
IISTD vicissitude
IITAL sinistrally
IITEK pie in the sky
IITEL pipistrelle
IITEU nip in the bud
IITOS sinistrorse
IITRA ministerial
IITRS disinterest
miniaturise
miniaturist
IITRZ miniaturize
IIUNO diminuendos

Words marked ❑ can also be spelled with an initial capital letter

IIUNS biliousness
pitifulness
viciousness
IIUTR viniculture
viticulture
IIUWG minimum wage
IJDMN misjudgment
IJNTV disjunctive
IKAGA Dick Gaughan
IKATE Pink Panther
IKDES linked verse
IKEEI sick benefit
IKEPN tickled pink
IKERI tickle-brain
IKESO kirk session
IKGIS kick against
IKHDS lick the dust
IKIEE milk-livered
IKINE Nikkei index
IKLDO nickelodeon
IKMSU Rijksmuseum
IKNFN sinking fund
IKNNL sickeningly
IKNSA pick one's way
IKNSL kick oneself
IKOAD Dirk Bogarde
IKOBR Dick Fosbury
IKOEI pick holes in
IKOGA Kirk Douglas
IKORW pick-your-own
IKPDS kick up a dust
IKPFS kick up a fuss
IKPPE pick up speed
IKPTL lickspittle
IKRBU tinker about
IKRCS tinker's cuss
IKRNI Dick Francis
IKRSL lickerishly
IKSRC Sitka spruce
IKTNS ricketiness
IKTSA rickettsiae
rickettsial
rickettsias
IKTSI lickety-spit
IKYWE sickly sweet
sickly-sweet
ILABR William Byrd
ILAHR William Hare
ILAKD William Kidd
ILAKN hillwalking
ILALN Will Carling
ILALU William Laud
ILAPN William Penn
ILAPT William Pitt
ILATF William Taft
ILATL William Tell
ILBAD Willy Brandt
ILBNE Billy Bunter
ILBTI Billy Butlin
ILCAL dialectally
ILCIA dialectical
ILCOE Jilly Cooper
ILCRE Will Scarlet
ILCTE Willa Cather
ILCTO dislocation
ILDJI fille de joie
ILDMN dislodgment
ILEET field events
ILFOE gillyflower
ILGAA Billy Graham
ILGCR village cart
ILHBL fill the bill
ILHLE title-holder
ILHNL Bill Shankly
ILKAL dislikeable
ILLNO Bill Clinton
ILMDF silly mid-off
ILMTS diplomatise
diplomatist
ILMTZ diplomatize
ILNEL violoncello
ILNEO Sir Lancelot
ILNIM millenniums
ILNNS willingness
ILNRA millenarian
ILNSL kill oneself
ILNUL villanously
ILOAI bibliomania
ILOAR billionaire
millionaire
ILOFL millionfold
ILOHL bibliophile
ILOVE field of view
ILPTA Lilliputian
ILRAN pillar-saint
ILRHL killer whale
ILRSI his lordship
ILSCN millisecond
ILSNS aimlessness
girlishness
sinlessness
ILSOA fieldswoman
ILSOT field sports
ILTDU billets-doux
ILTEI Billy the Kid
ILTTO hill station
ILWAE pillowcases
ILWLE Billy Wilder
ILWRE field worker
fieldworker
ILYCT Ridley Scott
ILYRN air layering
IMCRE Jimmy Carter
IMETN filmsetting
IMGAH filmography
IMGEI diamagnetic
IMHAR film theatre
IMIAL sigmoidally
IMLIM dismal Jimmy
IMNBC diamond-back
IMNBR diamond bird
IMNDV diamond dove
IMNLN dismantling
IMRHN diamorphine
IMRKE Bismarck Sea
IMSAE litmus paper
IMTAL diametrally
IMTIA diametrical
INABT Diane Abbott
INACO Finn mac Cool
INALE fiançailles
INAOI Minneapolis
INERE lion-hearted
INFCN significant
INFRE pianofortes
INGTU midnight sun
INKAO Diane Keaton
INLGS limnologist
INMIA lignum vitae
INNBL piano nobile
INNOE winning over
INNPS winning-post
INRAC dinner-dance
INRAT dinner party
INRHL finner whale
INRUS Wienerwurst
INSNE Minnesinger
INURA Finno-Ugrian
INYSU Disneyesque
INZTO lionization
IOAEI Nico Ladenis
IOAEL Nikola Tesla
IOAOI kilocalorie
IOARE Nicolas Roeg
IOAUN Ninoy Aquino
IOAYE Winona Ryder
IOBIG pivot bridge
IOCFO divorce from
IOEAH Nicole Farhi
IOEIN disobedient
IOENT Tito Menniti
IOETN pirouetting
IOFRA Milos Forman
IOGNS disorganise
IOGNZ disorganize
IOHGE Simon Hughes
IOIAL mitotically
IOINE disoriented
IOLGE Simon Legree
IOLGN disobliging
IOMRI rigor mortis
IONLO ritornellos
IOODR minor orders
IOOIA virological
IORTI lipoprotein
IORTL Simon Rattle
IOSED widow's weeds
IOTME fit of temper
IOTRO fit of terror
IOUAL binocularly
IOULI ribonucleic
IOUTO liposuction
IOWDA Widow Wadman
IPACE Limp Watches
IPAFR oil platform
IPCAE Hippocrates
IPCMU hippocampus
IPEID Simple Minds
IPESN displeasing
IPESR displeasure
IPIIE simpliciter
IPITN oil painting
oil-painting
IPNAL dispensable
dispensably
IPNCS hispanicise
hispanicism
IPNCZ hispanicize
IPNYI sixpenny bit
IPOEI diaphoresis
diaphoretic
IPOET disproperty
IPPOI hippophobia
IPPTM hippopotami
IPPYE diapophyses
IPREL dispersedly
IPREV misperceive
IPRGN disparaging
IPRNL simperingly
IPRSE limp-wristed
IPRTL disparately
IPRTN dispiriting
IPRUD mispersuade
IPSNL disposingly
IPSNS wimpishness
IPSTO disposition
IPSTV diapositive
IPTHO dispatch box
IPTTO disputation
IPYIA biophysical
IQEET cinquecento
IQITD disquietude
IQITN disquieting
IRAEN Sierra Leone
IRCAD Viv Richards
IRCSI microcosmic
IRCXD nitric oxide
IREAL Pierre Bayle
IREAR Kierkegaard
IREUI Pierre Curie
IRFCE microfiches
IRFOP microfloppy
IRGNS nitrogenise
IRGNU nitrogenous
IRGNZ nitrogenize
IRGRE disregarded
IRGYH hieroglyphs
IRIJC microinject
IRLAV mitral valve
IRMME misremember
IRMRA Piers Morgan
IRMTI micrometric
IRNSA Micronesian
IROTC fibre optics
IRPOI microphonic
IRRHS hierarchism
IRRMG mirror image
IRSEC nigrescence
vitrescence
IRSLA nicrosilial
IRSOI microscopic
IRTBL microtubule

IRTIE Niersteiner
IRTOA vibrational
IRUAI nitrous acid
ISADI first aid kit
ISAKN lip-smacking
ISAPN die-stamping
ISASU dies faustus
ISCAE dissociated
ISCAL dissociably
ISCNS airsickness
ISCOC first choice
ISCUI first cousin
ISEAT dies nefasti
ISELN misspelling
ISENA Einsteinian
ISENU einsteinium
ISETE missheathed
ISFEC kiss of peace
ISFET kiss of death
ISHBA miss the boat
ISHBO kiss the book
ISHFE kiss the feet
ISIDN bias binding
ISLAL dissyllable
ISLIA Jim Sullivan
ISLTL dissolutely
ISLTO dissolution
ISMER dissymmetry
ISMLN dissembling
ISMLT dissimilate
dissimulate
ISMNA dipsomaniac
ISMNS winsomeness
ISMNT disseminate
ISNBB bits and bobs
ISNCL pig's knuckle
ISNGT kissing gate
ISNIN dissentient
ISNIU dissentious
ISNLN missing link
ISNNL dissonantly
ISNSI miss one's tip
ISNSL miss oneself
ISNTL Kiss and Tell
kiss-and-tell
ISOAL fissionable
ISOHN miss nothing
ISOTN ripsnorting
ISPRU fissiparous
ISPTO dissipation
ISPTV dissipative
ISRPN Airstrip One
ISRWN bias-drawing
ISSHO first school
ISSIP Mississippi
ISSRK first strike
ISTNS hirsuteness
ISVRN dissevering
ITAKO Milt Jackson
ITATN distracting
ITATO distraction
ITBTE fit to be tied
ITCLM fifth column
ITCLN rib-tickling
ITDFD eisteddfods
ITDHL gifted child
ITEDN mistreading
ITEET die the death
ITENW little known
little-known
ITEOE Little Women
ITERI hit the trail
ITESN distressing
ITESU distressful
ITETL fifteenthly
sixteenthly
ITFOK list of books
ITGAH dittography
pictography
ITGIT nitty-gritty
ITGPR vintage port
ITGTE fit together
mix together
ITGWN vintage wine
ITINC histrionics
ITIUO distributor
ITKNO mistaken for
ITLGS histologist
ITLSL mirthlessly
ITLVI fit to live in
ITNBT Milton Obote
ITNDC sitting duck
ITNIL distensible
ITNNS fittingness
ITNPS distant past
ITNRO sitting-room
ITNTO distinction
ITNTV distinctive
ITNUS distinguish
ITNUT Mistinguett
ITOCE gift voucher
ITODA dirty old man
ITPLC Pitti Palace
ITPRN birth parent
ITRAC disturbance
ITRAL pictorially
ITRCS historicise
historicism
historicist
ITRCT historicity
ITRCZ historicize
ITREB disturbed by
ITREO bitter lemon
ITRES Winterreise
ITRHP Mister Chips
ITRIA air terminal
ITRNA sister-in-law
ITRRE wintergreen
ITRSU picturesque
ITRTO micturition
ITRWE bittersweet
ITSEU distasteful
ITSHA Nietzschean
ITSOU pittosporum
ITTIK dirty tricks
ITTRA dictatorial
ITTTO nictitation
ITUCL list quickly
ITUNS riotousness
wistfulness
ITUTN distrusting
ITUTU distrustful
mistrustful
ITYUR filthy lucre
IUAHA titular head
IUARM simulacrums
IUBRN Vitus Bering
IUCTO bifurcation
IUDTO liquidation
IUEAC lieutenancy
IUEAT Minute Waltz
IUEBS figured bass
IUEFU figure of fun
IUEHL minute-while
IUFAL liquefiable
IUFIL win unfairly
IUINE Ligurian Sea
IULOG Miguel Torga
IULSI ritualistic
IURHA Ziaur Rahman
IUTOA situational
IUUNS sinuousness
IVRAB silver tabby
IVRAE silver paper
IVREA silver medal
IVRHS Silver Ghost
IVRIC silver birch
IVRLT silver plate
IVRMT silversmith
IVRTN Silverstone
IVSRE civvy street
IWFTA midwife toad
IWSAC view askance
IYAHR city fathers
IYIEE lily-livered
IYLBF disyllabify
IYLCE city slicker
IYLCI bicycle clip
IYLPM bicycle pump
IYOLN Tiny Rowland
IYWLE city-dweller
IZIMN Fitzsimmons
JCLTO ejaculation
JCLTR ejaculatory
JCLTV ejaculative
JNAAE Ajanta caves
KABAT J K Galbraith
KAPRN sky-aspiring
KIEMT skaines mate
KLTNE skeleton key
KLTNS skeletonise
KLTNZ skeletonize
KLUGR skulduggery
KLUNS skilfulness
KLUPA skilful plan
KMEML skimmed milk
KNNBN skin-and-bone
KTAON skate around
KTHNS sketchiness
KTLPN skittle-pins
LAAGI plea bargain
plea-bargain
LABRE Allan Border
LABWE clean bowled
LACES Alcaic verse
LAEHO pleaseth you
LAEIA all-American
LAENS bloatedness
LAETO please it you
LAEWT pleased with
LAGIT plead guilty
LAHAE clear-headed
LAIGI floating rib
LALME clean-limbed
LALNS cleanliness
pliableness
LALVN clean-living
LAORD olla-podrida
LAOTV All About Eve
LARMA Allan Ramsay
LASAE clean-shaven
LASRE ill-assorted
LATEA clear the way
LATEI clear the air
LAUAL pleasurable
pleasurably
LBEDN ill-breeding
LBEGS flabbergast
LBEOE slobber over
LBFOE globeflower
LBGRN globigerina
LBIDN all-building
LBINS plebeianise
LBINZ plebeianize
LBRTL elaborately
LBRTO elaborate on
elaboration
LBRTV elaborative
LBSAE globe-shaped
LCACA black as coal
LCBAT Black Beauty
LCBEL click beetle
LCBLT placability
LCBSE blockbuster
LCBTO black bottom
LCBYN black bryony
LCCEG black clergy
LCCER black cherry
LCCFE black coffee
LCCMD black comedy
LCCOE Alice Cooper
LCDTO elucidation
LCDTR elucidatory
LCDTV elucidative
LCESD slickenside
LCETU old chestnut
LCFIR Black friars
Blackfriars
LCFRS Black Forest
LCGOS black grouse
LCHAE blockheaded
LCINE electioneer

LCLTE block letter
LCMAN à la campagne
LCMIE blackmailer
LCMRE black market
black-market
LCOCK slice of cake
LCODT place of duty
LCOWR place of work
LCPIC Black Prince
LCRCA electrician
electric ray
LCRCE electric eel
LCRCR electric arc
LCRCT electricity
electrocute
LCRCY electric eye
LCRLS electrolyse
LCRLT electrolyte
LCRNC electronics
LCRNU electron gun
LCRTP electrotype
LCSLT glycosylate
LCTTO elicitation
LCTWR Alec Stewart
LCUEC flocculence
LCUTN fluctuating
LCUTO fluctuation
LCVLE black velvet
LCWLE Alice Walker
LDBRO Clyde Barrow
LDESN fly-dressing
LDHOG plod through
LDOPN clodhopping
LDOUE gladioluses
LDRNE Blade Runner
LDSOE ill-disposed
LDVSO Vladivostok
LEAON sleep around
LEATS Ilie Nastase
LEAUT older adults
LECTO altercation
LEEOR sleeve board
LEETI all-electric
LEHNE Alleghenies
LEHRE Cleethorpes
LEHTE elsewhither
LEIGA sleeping car
LEITN alleviating
LEITO alleviation
LEITV alleviative
LELNS elderliness
LELOE blue-blooded
LELSL sleeplessly
LENFE glue-sniffer
LENTL alternately
LENTN alternating
LENTO alternation
LENTV alternative
LEOIA allegorical
LESRE Fleet Street
LETAU Albert Camus
LETPE Albert Speer
LEUPE ill-equipped
LEWLE sleepwalker
LEYDO blue-eyed boy
LEYUE Ellery Queen
LFGYS old-fogeyish
LFHNE cliffhanger
cliff-hanger
LFOSA All Fools' Day
LFPLT cleft palate
LFVUE ill-favoured
LGAAL elegiacally
LGACN clog-dancing
LGADS sluggardise
LGADZ sluggardize
LGAIE plagiarized
plagiarizer
LGBLT eligibility
LGIGF slagging off
slagging-off
LGLAO flagellator
LGNPA plug-and-play
LGOET flog to death
LGOLS plagioclase
LGOTM plagiostome
LGTNL blightingly
slightingly
LGTNS flightiness
LHAIM al-Khwarizmi
LHBTS alphabetise
LHBTZ alphabetize
LHMUE ill-humoured
LHRYH alpha rhythm
LIAHL Ultima Thule
LIBTL Klein bottle
LIEAL illiberally
LIFRE ill-informed
LIGAT flying party
LIGOT Illingworth
LIGQA flying squad
LIGTR flying start
LIIAL illimitable
illimitably
LIILN Ellis Island
LIINS illicitness
LILSE plainly seen
LISIA ellipsoidal
LISOE plainspoken
plain-spoken
LITCN Pleistocene
LITVL plaintively
LIVYN clairvoyant
LMCEI climacteric
LMCIA climactical
LMDWO clamp down on
LMIFA Olympic Flag
LMLSL blamelessly
LMNAL elementally
LMNEE ill-mannered
LMNEO all manner of
LMNTO elimination
LMOAC flamboyance
flamboyancy
LMPUK plume-pluckt
LMRUL clamorously
glamorously
slumbrously
LMSBN Flemish bond
LMTLG climatology
LMUDN plum pudding
LMUGR glamour girl
LMUPS glamourpuss
LMWRH blameworthy
LNAAA blind as a bat
LNCEU blank cheque
LNCNE plano-convex
LNCTE plantcutter
LNEBR Glen Seaborg
LNEBS blunderbuss
LNEET flannelette
LNENS slenderness
LNETN clandestine
LNEUL plenteously
LNEWE blanketweed
LNFGR plane figure
LNHAE Alan Shearer
LNHNL flinchingly
LNHPR Alan Shepard
LNIBR Alan Milburn
LNIGF glancing-off
LNIHN blandishing
LNIRD plantigrade
LNIUL plentifully
LNMLE Glenn Miller
LNOGI Alan Hodgkin
LNORE Flann O'Brien
LNPTN plenipotent
LNSHR planisphere
LNSIG plenishings
LNSOA plantswoman
LNTLG planetology
LNTRU planetarium
LNUAL glandularly
LNULC Alan Bullock
LNWTE blunt-witted
LOAAE Ellora caves
LOAIC all of a piece
LOAOI gliomatosis
LOBUH blood-bought
LOCMN klootchmans
LODPN blood doping
LOECN fluorescent
LOEWT all over with
LOGES elbow grease
elbow-grease
LOIAL illogically
LOIHI algorithmic
LOMNE gloom-monger
LONWA also known as
LOOAG blood orange
LOOCP fluoroscope
fluoroscopy
LOOFE alcohol-free
LOSAE blood-soaked
LOSCE bloodsucker
LOSOT blood sports
LOSRA bloodstream
LOSSE blood-sister
LOTAU altostratus
LOTHV allow to have
LOTPS allow to pass
LOUUU altocumulus
LOVSE blood vessel
LPAII blepharitis
LPATI elephantoid
LPATN elephantine
LPATU elephant gun
LPEBT slipper bath
LPEDS slipped disc
LPEWR slipperwort
LPHOG flip through
LPNSI flip one's lid
LPOAI kleptomania
LPSIL all possible
LPWRU all powerful
all-powerful
LRAIU flirtatious
LRCLS clericalism
LRDDE Alfred Adler
LRDIE Alfred Binet
LRDOE Alfred Nobel
LRDOL Alfred Polly
LRFLE ultrafilter
LRFRU floriferous
LRLGU florilegium
LRLSI pluralistic
LRMDR ultra-modern
LRMRN ultramarine
LRPOI plerophoria
LRRBO Flora Robson
LRSEC florescence
LRSNC ultrasonics
LRVOE ultraviolet
LRVTR Il Trovatore
LRYOA clergywoman
LSADN all standing
LSAHN close at hand
LSARI Alastair Sim
LSBOE glass-blower
LSEBM cluster bomb
cluster-bomb
LSECR blister card
LSECS plaster cast
LSEDW plaster down
LSELN ill-smelling
LSENS blessedness
LSEPC blister pack
LSEWR plasterwork
LSEWT blessed with
LSFIN close friend
LSFSE close-fisted
LSGZN glass-gazing
LSHMU blasphemous
LSHNE close-handed
LSHUE close-hauled
LSIAE elasticated
LSIAL classically
elastically
LSIBM plastic bomb
LSIBN elastic band
LSIIE plasticiser

plasticizer
LSIOE plasminogen
LSLPE close-lipped
LSLSL blushlessly
LSMNE close-minded
fleshmonger
LSMSU bless my soul!
LSNDW closing-down
LSOAI glossolalia
LSOBR Glastonbury
LSOCT Glasgow City
LSOEI elastomeric
LSOLS Elastoplast®
LSPCE close-packed
LSRDU clostridium
LSRIU plus or minus
LSSAO close season
LSTEA close the gap
LSTUE closet queen
LSUSA All Souls Day
All Souls' Day
LTAFR Old Trafford
LTASO glottal stop
LTCAI plutocratic
LTEHL all the while
LTEMT clothes moth
LTEOL all the world
LTGTE all together
LTHNS blotchiness
LTIGU blotting out
blotting-out
LTIHU ulotrichous
LTITO elutriation
LTLNL flatulently
LTMEE ill-tempered
LTMHG all-time high
LTNER Blut und Ehre
LTNUL glutinously
LTOGL cloth of gold
LTPEE all to pieces
LTRHN platyrrhine
LTROA Ulsterwoman
LTUFC flat surface
LUACC Fleur Adcock
LUEIO Claude Simon
LUEOE Claude Monet
clouded over
LUESL Glauber salt
LUHEE slaughtered
slaughterer
LUHHR ploughshare
LUHON sleuth-hound
LUIAC illuminance
LUIAE illuminated
LUIAO illuminator
LUIHN flourishing
LUINR illusionary
LUINS illusionism
illusionist
LULSL cloudlessly
LUSEI fleurs-de-lis
LUSEY fleurs-de-lys
LUTAE illustrated
LUTAO illustrator
LUTIU illustrious
LUTNL flauntingly
LUURU Albuquerque
LUYRS fleury cross
LVBAC olive branch
LVDIE slave-driver
LVNCS Slavonicise
LVNCZ Slavonicize
LVNUE Ulf von Euler
LVPPE glove puppet
LVRAB Oliver Tambo
LVRAD Oliver Hardy
LVRLG clever clogs
cleverclogs
LVRNL slaveringly
LVRTN Oliver Stone
LVRWS Oliver Twist
LVSNS slavishness
LVULS flavourless
LVUSM flavoursome
LWAON clown around
LWETN ill-wresting
LWETO slow neutron
LWFOD flow of words
LWGSE blow a gasket
LWHGF blow the gaff
LWMNS old-womanish
LWNBC flowing-back
LWNSO blow one's top
LWOBO blow for blow
LWRHL flower child
LWRNS floweriness
LWROE flower power
LWRTL flower-stalk
LXAMN Alex Salmond
LXBLT flexibility
LXIAL Alexei Sayle
LXIGN Alex Higgins
LXNRA Alexandrian
LXNRN alexandrine
LXNRT alexandrite
LXSOE Alexis Soyer
LYALO Ally Macleod
LYCOS Ally McCoist
LYGOG Lloyd-George
LYHFO play the fool
LYHGM play the game
LYIEA clay mineral
LYJKO play a joke on
LYNAE playing area
LYNCR playing-card
LYNOD play on words
LYNSC play one's ace
LYOLV play for love
LYOTI play footsie
LYOTM play for time
LYPRI play a part in
LYRIE clay-brained
LYRIN player piano
player-piano
LYRLI play a role in
LYTYA play it by ear
LYUNS playfulness
LYWBE Lloyd Webber
LZARI blaze a trail
LZBTA Elizabethan
MAEMN empanelment
MAENN Emma Tennant
MAINL impatiently
MAKTO embarkation
MALNS amiableness
MAODA Emma Goldman
MARSE embarrassed
MASOE impassioned
MASVL impassively
MASVT impassivity
MATAL impartially
MATTO impartation
MCBLT amicability
MDPUL ami du peuple
MDTHA I'm a Dutchman
MEAIL E M Delafield
MECMN impeachment
MEERT impenetrate
MEFCL imperfectly
MEIEC impenitence
impenitency
MEIET impedimenta
MEIIE impetigines
MEILS imperialise
imperialism
imperialist
MEILZ imperialize
MEIMN imperilment
MEITL immediately
MEIUL imperiously
MELSE embellished
MELTL umbellately
MEMAL impermeable
impermeably
MEMNN impermanent
MEOMT emperor moth
MESNS immenseness
MESNT impersonate
METNN impertinent
MEUIU impecunious
MEUST impetuosity
MEUUL impetuously
MGNTO imagination
MGNTV imaginative
MHBLG amphibology
MHBLT amphibolite
MHSAN amphisbaena
MHTMN amphetamine
MIAEC ambivalence
ambivalency
MIAIU omnifarious
MICEC omniscience
MIGMN impingement
MIGUO impinge upon
MIIAL empirically
immitigably
MIIUL ambitiously
MINRT impignorate
MIOEC omnipotence
MIRSN omnipresent
MIRTO immigration
MITRN embittering
MIUNS impiousness
MIUUL ambiguously
MKLSL smokelessly
MKSRE smokescreen
MLAAE amalgamated
MLAON small amount
MLBOT Emily Brontë
MLCAG small change
MLCMN emplacement
MLCRL small circle
MLCTN implicating
MLCTO implication
MLCTV implicative
MLHLE smallholder
MLICE Emil Fischer
MLIGU smelling-out
MLINS emulsionise
MLINZ emulsionize
MLMNA emolumental
implemental
MLMNE implemented
small-minded
MLMTS emblematise
MLMTZ emblematize
MLNME small number
MLOER Emilio Segrè
MLOUC Emilio Pucci
MLRNL imploringly
MLRTO imploration
MLRTR imploratory
MLSPL ample supply
MLSRE small screen
MLUIL implausible
implausibly
MLUNS emulousness
MLWNE small wonder
MNBLT amenability
MNEAE Amin Gemayel
MNIAE emancipated
MNIAO emancipator
MNILD amontillado
MNRHE amenorrhoea
MNUNS ominousness
MODRU imponderous
MOEBE immoveables
MOEMN empowerment
MOHNK smooth snake
MOIIE immobilized
immobilizer
MOIIL impoliticly
MONAL impoundable
MOTLS immortalise
MOTLT immortality
MOTLZ immortalize
MOTMT impostumate
MOTNC importunacy
MOTNL importantly
importunely
MOTNT importunate
importunity

MOTTO importation
MPNFR HMS Pinafore
MRABR smorgasbord
MRBTR improbatory
MRBTV improbative
MRCIA impractical
MRCMN embracement
MRCNI American Pie
MRCNL embracingly
MRCNS Americanise
Americanism
MRCNZ Americanize
MRCSL imprecisely
MRCSO imprecision
MRCSU America's Cup
MRCTL imbricately
MRCTO embrocation
imprecation
MRCTR imprecatory
MRDNL imprudently
MRFRU umbriferous
MRGAE impregnated
MRGAL impregnable
impregnably
MRHUL amorphously
MRHYA Omar Khayyám
MRIEE embroiderer
MRIMN embroilment
MRPIT impropriate
impropriety
MRSAL ambrosially
MRSIL impressible
MRSIN impressions
MRSRO impresarios
MRTLU umbratilous
MRUNS amorousness
MRVDN improvident
MRVMN improvement
MRVNL improvingly
MRYAT smartypants
MRYOT smartyboots
MTBLT imitability
MTEEN smithereens
MTHAE empty-headed
MTHNE empty-handed
MTNSE empty-nester
MTOAL emotionally
MTOLS emotionless
MTRAL amatorially
MTTVL imitatively
MUCDE ambuscadoes
MUDRN smouldering
MUOSA immunoassay
MUPOR amour-propre
MUSAC impuissance
MUSVL impulsively
MYEMT empyreumata
NAAAL unpalatable
unpalatably
NAALV Anna Pavlova
NACLN unmasculine
NACMN enhancement
NACRT incarcerate
NADNS unhandiness
NADNT incardinate
NAELN unravelling
NAERS ansate cross
NAFLC unlawful act
NAGMN enlargement
NAHLC in each place
NAHOE unfashioned
NAHRN ingathering
NAIAC inhabitance
inhabitancy
NAIAE invalidated
NAIAL inhabitable
innavigably
unnavigable
NAIAT inhabitants
NAIFE unsatisfied
NAIIE unsanitized
NAILT en papillote
NAITL insatiately
NALDO uncalled-for
NALNL unfailingly
NALNS unmanliness
NALTR entablature
NANDN incarnadine
NANEL undauntedly
untaintedly
NANLS encarnalise
NANLZ encarnalize
NANNS uncanniness
NANSE untarnished
unvarnished
NANTO incarnation
NAOIE antagonized
NAORL unsavourily
NAPNS unhappiness
NARLE unpatrolled
NARNE unwarranted
NAROI unpatriotic
NASLT encapsulate
incapsulate
NATCD infanticide
NATLS infantilism
NATNN unfastening
NATRE unpatterned
NATRN unfaltering
NATTO incantation
NATTR incantatory
NATVT in captivity
NATYA infantryman
NATYE infantrymen
NAUAE unsaturated
NAUAL unnaturally
NAURT insalubrity
NAUTO infatuation
NAYBU uneasy about
NAYOC an easy touch
NBDIH in a bad light
NBEVN unobservant
NBIGC enabling act
NBITN inebriating
NBITO inebriation
NBNAC in abundance
NBPIT Anabaptists
NBRSV unobtrusive
NBUFN in a blue funk
NCAIN on occasions
NCAON knock around
NCESE snickersnee
NCFRI knock for six
NCIGF knocking off
NCITO inscription
NCITV inscriptive
NCKAK knickknacks
knick-knacks
NCLDW knuckle down
NCLIE unacclaimed
NCLRT unicolorate
NCLRU unicolorous
NCLTI anacoluthia
NCLTO anacoluthon
inoculation
NCLTR insculpture
NCLTV inoculative
NCLUA unicellular
NCLUE unicoloured
NCOAL anecdotally
unscholarly
NCONO on account of
NCOSE snick or snee
NCOWO knock on wood
NCPWL Enoch Powell
NCRNS anachronism
NCUAL inscrutable
inscrutably
NDACO in advance of
NDBLT inedibility
NDETN inadvertent
NDIAL inadvisable
unadvisable
unadvisably
NDIEL unadvisedly
NDRUL inodorously
NEAAE unseparated
NEAAL inseparable
inseparably
ungetatable
unget-at-able
NEADN undemanding
unrewarding
NEAIU unveracious
NEALO in default of
NEALU under a cloud
NEAPN kneecapping
NEARS under arrest
NEATO interaction
on penalty of
NEATV interactive
NECAG interchange
undercharge
NECAL unreachable
unteachable
NECLR intercalary
NECLT intercalate
NECMN unwelcoming
NECNA under canvas
NECNE undescended
NECPO interceptor
NECSA intercostal
NECSO intercessor
NECUS intercourse
NEDCE interdicted
NEDLS unfeudalise
NEDLZ unfeudalize
NEDNL unbendingly
NEDNS in readiness
unreadiness
NEDNT intending to
NEDPN interdepend
NEDRN engendering
NEDRS under duress
NEEDN independent
NEEEC antecedence
NEELN unrevealing
NEEOE undeveloped
NEEPS underexpose
NEERE unrehearsed
NEESO anteversion
NEESR unnecessary
NEETA inferential
NEETN interesting
unrelenting
unrepentant
NEETV unreceptive
unselective
NEEVN undeserving
NEFCA interfacial
NEFCN interfacing
NEFRI interfere in
NEFRN interfering
NEFSL unselfishly
NEFSO interfusion
NEGEL unfeignedly
NEGON underground
NEGOT undergrowth
NEHME antechamber
NEHNS underhonest
unmechanise
NEHNZ unmechanize
NEIAC inheritance
NEIAL angelically
endemically
indefinable
indefinably
inheritable
undefinable
undesirable
undesirably
unmeritable
NEIAO inseminator
NEICN indehiscent
NEIEL undecidedly
unmeritedly
NEIIU unreligious
NEIRS inheritress
NEIRT inferiority
NEISE in medias res
NEITN unbefitting
undeviating

unremitting
unresisting
NEIUE ungenitured
NEIUL ingeniously
NEIVN unbelieving
NEIWR annelid worm
NEJCN interjacent
NELAE interleaves
NELCE interlocked
NELCN interlacing
NELGN intelligent
NELHL unhealthily
NELHU unhealthful
NELNA interlinear
NELNL unfeelingly
NELNN interlining
underlining
NELSI unrealistic
NELUI interleukin
NEMDL intermeddle
NEMNE undermanned
NEMNL intermingle
NEMNN undermining
NEMZO intermezzos
NENCN internecine
NENFE indemnifier
NENLS internalise
NENLZ internalize
NENME index number
NENNL unmeaningly
NEOAE undecorated
NEOAL unmemorable
unremovable
NEOIU unmelodious
NEOMN envelopment
NEONA in her own way
NEPAE in deep water
underplayed
NEPAS underpraise
NEPCO in respect of
NEPEE interpreter
NEPIE enterprises
underpriced
NEPIO under pain of
NEPLT interpolate
NEPRE inter partes
NEPRN untempering
NEPRT intemperate
NEPSN interposing
NEPTU in perpetuum
NERAL unweariable
NERCA interracial
NEREE unretrieved
NEREL unlearnedly
NERGN interrogant
NERGT interrogate
NERGU interregnum
NERLT interrelate
NERNL endearingly
NERPE interrupted
interrupter
NERPO interruptor
NERSE unrepressed
NERTO integration
NERTU unregretful
NERUL unfearfully
NERWC once or twice
NESAE understated
unpersuaded
NESES intersperse
NESFE intensified
intensifier
NESGE undersigned
NESLE underseller
NESNL incessantly
unceasingly
NESNN unreasoning
NESNS intenseness
NESRS under stress
NESRT understrata
NESTL insensately
NESTV insensitive
NESVL intensively
NESXA intersexual
NETAL ancestrally
NETAN unrestraint
NETCD insecticide
NETEE under the lee
NETEI anaesthesia
anaesthesis
anaesthetic
NETEL unsettledly
NETET investments
NETEU under the sun
NETGT investigate
NETIE entertainer
NETIL uncertainly
NETIO intertrigos
NETIT uncertainty
NETKN undertaking
NETLT infertility
NETNL intertangle
unrestingly
NETOA insertional
intentional
NETOE unmentioned
NETRE unperturbed
NETRN unfettering
NETRS underthrust
NETTD incertitude
NETTO indentation
infestation
NETTR investiture
NETUA invert sugar
NETVL inventively
NETVR insectivore
NETVS incentivise
NETVZ incentivize
NEUCR ensepulchre
NEUDT infecundity
unfecundity
NEUSE unrequested
NEUUL ingenuously
NEVEE interviewee
interviewer
NEVLE undervalued
undervaluer
NEVNN intervening
NEWIE underwriter
NEWIH underweight
NEWSO in her wisdom
NFASI in a flat spin
NFCTO unification
NFESV inoffensive
NFETA ineffectual
NFETV ineffective
NFIGU sniffing-out
NFIIN inefficient
NFRNS uniformness
NFWOD in a few words
NGEMN in agreement
NGOHU in a good hour
NGOII anagnorisis
NGOMO in a good mood
NHAED on the agenda
NHALN enthralling
NHAMN enthralment
NHAOI anthracosis
NHBCO on the back of
NHBTE on the batter
NHBTO on the button
NHCAI anthocyanin
NHCAL unshockable
NHCLN unshackling
NHCLR anthochlore
NHCNR in the centre
NHCRE on the carpet
NHCRO in the care of
NHFCO in the face of
NHFML in the family
NHFTR in the future
NHGIO in the grip of
NHGOV in the groove
NHIKN unshrinking
NHIMN enchainment
NHITA unchristian
NHITL unthriftily
NHKAL unshakeable
NHLEE unsheltered
NHLGS anthologise
anthologist
NHLGZ anthologize
NHLSM unwholesome
NHMDL in the middle
NHMKN in the making
NHMNE in the manner
NHMRE on the market
NHNAL unthinkable
NHNCR Anthony Caro
NHNEE Anthony Eden
NHNMN enchantment
NHNMO in the name of
NHNRS enchantress
NHOFN in the offing
NHPOR on shipboard
NHPRO on the part of
NHPRS on the parish
NHRCE in character
NHRCR on the record
NHRDU antheridium
NHREE unchartered
unsharpened
unshortened
NHRMT ink-horn-mate
NHROA anchorwoman
NHRSE uncherished
NHRZI antherozoid
NHRZL on the razzle
NHSCE in the secret
NHSDL in the saddle
NHSDO on the side of
NHSDY in those days
NHSLC in this place
NHSOK on the stocks
NHSRE on the street
NHSRK on the stroke
NHSUR on the square
NHSUS enthusiuasm
NHTCR on that score
NHTDL on the tiddly
NHTMO in the time of
NHTRE in the throes
NHTRN on the throne
NHUHO unthought-of
NHWYU on the way out
NIAHD anticathode
NIAIN indications
NIBLT unviability
NIBSN Annie Besant
NICOE undisclosed
NICRL insincerely
NICRT insincerity
NIDUL unmindfully
NIEAO incinerator
NIEET enticements
NIEIE antihelices
NIEII anti-Semitic
NIEMN enlivenment
NIEON invite round
NIEPS in times past
NIERC inside track
NIERN engineering
NIESR anniversary
NIETA indirect tax
NIETL incidentals
NIETO antineutron
anti-neutron
indigestion
indirection
NIETR inside story
NIEUL untimeously
NIFRN indifferent
NIGAH angiography
NIGIE undisguised
NIGTL ending it all
NIHAI antiphrasis
NIHDO unwished-for
NIHDY an eight days
NIHEE enlightened
NIHEU unrighteous
NIIAE anticipated
intimidated

unmitigated
NIIAL undividable
unmitigably
NIIAO annihilator
anticipator
intimidator
invigilator
NIIEL undividedly
NIIIA infinitival
NIIIE uncivilised
uncivilized
NIIIL indivisible
indivisibly
NIIIN inhibitions
NIINL incipiently
insipiently
NIINS insipidness
NIITR in miniature
NIIUL individuals
insidiously
invidiously
NIIUT individuate
NIKLE Enniskillen
NILMN entitlement
NILNL unwillingly
NILTL inviolately
NINCA Indian Ocean
NINFE undignified
NINNL indignantly
NINTO indignation
NIOAE invigorated
NIOEM Enrico Fermi
NIOLA anti-roll bar
NIOMN environment
NIONA in his own way
NIRBE India rubber
NIRCS in microcosm
NIRIU antirrhinum
NIRPI in disrepair
NISEL unbiassedly
NITAE infiltrated
NITAO infiltrator
NITDA enlisted man
NITNL insistently
unfittingly
unwittingly
NITNO insistent on
NITOH antistrophe
NITRE undistorted
undisturbed
NIUNS anxiousness
enviousness
NIURA antiquarian
NIUTN insinuating
NIUTO insinuation
NIUTR insinuatory
NIUTV insinuative
NIWSO in his wisdom
NIXDN antioxidant
NIYEI antipyretic
NIYLN anticyclone
NLANS uncleanness
unclearness
NLBRT unelaborate
NLCAL ineluctable
ineluctably
NLCEE unblackened
NLCNS Anglicanism
NLEAL inalienable
inalienably
inalterable
inalterably
unalienable
unalienably
unalterable
unalterably
NLETA influential
NLGNL inelegantly
NLGUL analogously
NLIDA Anglo-Indian
NLISM in altissimo
NLMAL inflammable
inflammably
NLMNL inclemently
NLMSE unblemished
NLNET inclinded to
NLNFL unblindfold
NLNHN unblenching
unflinching
NLNRA Anglo-Norman
NLNTO inclination
NLPAE in all places
NLPAL unflappable
unflappably
NLPII anglophilia
NLPOI anglophobia
NLREA in a large way
NLSEE unflustered
NLSHR English horn
NLSNS endlessness
NLSVL inclusively
NLSVO inclusive of
NLTEE uncluttered
NLTNL inflatingly
NLUIL unplausibly
NLUNN on cloud nine
NLVMN enslavement
NMIIU unambitious
NMIUU unambiguous
NMLAT animal waste
NMLSI anomalistic
NMLUE animalcules
NMOTN unimportant
NMRSE unimpressed
NMRTM one more time
NMRTO enumeration
NMSIO onomasticon
NMTNL animatingly
NMTOA unemotional
NMUEO enamoured of
NNAIE uninhabited
NNEHL anencephaly
NNIIE uninhibited
NNITO enunciation
NNMEO any number of
NNMTL inanimately
NNMTO inanimation
NNMUL anonymously
unanimously
NNNLN on an incline
NNNTN in an instant
NNONE unannounced
NNPRN uninspiring
NNRMN ensnarement
NNSAD on one's hands
NNSAK on one's marks
NNSAT on one's way to
NNSHR in one's shirt
NNSIH in one's light
NNSLE in one's sleep
NNSLO in one's blood
NNSLT on one's plate
NNSUR on one's guard
NNTAE uninitiated
NNTHL in a nutshell
NNUAL unendurable
NNWNL unknowingly
NNWNS unknownness
NOAAT Antofagasta
NOBAL undoubtable
NOBEL undoubtedly
NOCAC insouciance
NOCAE unconcealed
NOCAL enforceable
untouchable
NOCMN enforcement
NOCON on no account
NOCRE unconcerned
NOCWT in touch with
NODAD in good hands
NODAT in good faith
NODCV unconducive
NODDU in good odour
NODEM on good terms
NODER in good heart
NODHP in good shape
NODLO in cold blood
NODNE uncondensed
NODOC in good voice
NODRE in good order
NODTO in condition
on condition
NOEAC intolerance
NOEAL intolerable
intolerably
NOEEC incoherence
NOEEI oncogenesis
ontogenesis
ontogenetic
NOERR Enzo Ferrari
NOERU endometrium
NOEUL unhopefully
NOEWT endowed with
NOFRE unconfirmed
NOFSO in confusion
NOGMN engorgement
NOGNA uncongenial
NOGUT incongruity
NOGUU incongruous
NOGVN unforgiving
NOHBU into the blue
NOHLU endothelium
NOHNI into thin air
NOHNS Indo-Chinese
NOHOE into the open
NOIAE intoxicated
unmotivated
NOIAL indomitable
indomitably
NOIIE unsolicited
NOISI encomiastic
NOIUL innoxiously
NOKDO unlooked-for
NOLCE uncollected
NOLMN ennoblement
NOLNS ungodliness
NOLSO in collusion
NOMLT informality
NOMNO in command of
NOMTC informatics
NOMTE in committee
uncommitted
NOMTO information
NOMTV informative
NONAL uncountable
NONCE unconnected
NONEL unboundedly
unfoundedly
NONHL unborn child
NONNS unsoundness
NONSN incognisant
NONZN incognizant
NOOAI antonomasia
NOOIA ontological
NOOPI endomorphic
NOPEE uncompleted
NOPLE uncompelled
NOPRA incorporeal
NOPRI endospermic
NOPRT incorporate
NOPSE encompassed
NOPTN incompetent
NOQEE unconquered
NORCL incorrectly
NORGN encouraging
NORNA Indo-Iranian
NORPE uncorrupted
NORPL incorruptly
NOSAC inconstancy
NOSIU unconscious
NOSMN endorsement
NOSNN inconsonant
NOTAE in most cases
NOTFE unfortified
NOTME uncontemned
NOTNN incontinent
NOTNS uncouthness
NOTNT unfortunate
NOTOO in control of
NOTSE uncontested
NOUAE unpopulated
NOURT involucrate

NOUTR involuntary
NOUUL innocuously
NOVMN involvement
NOVNE unconvinced
NOVRE unconverted
NPAAL unspeakable
unspeakably
NPCAL en spectacle
NPCFE unspecified
NPELN unappealing
NPLRT unipolarity
NPOTN inopportune
NPRNL inspiringly
unsparingly
NPRTA unspiritual
NPRTN inspiriting
NPRTO in operation
inspiration
NPRTR inspiratory
NPRTV inoperative
NPUOI snap out of it
NPYAI anaphylaxis
NQANS unequalness
NQIAL inequitable
inequitably
NQIOA unequivocal
NRAAL increasable
unbreakable
untreatable
NRAAS Andre Agassi
NRAEO undreamed-of
NRAEU increaseful
NRAIE unorganized
NRANE in great need
NRAOI Andrea Doria
NRAPR André Ampère
in great part
NRCAG entry charge
NRCAL intractable
intractably
untraceable
NRCCE intricacies
NRCIA unpractical
NRCIE unpractised
NRCSE unprocessed
NRCSO in process of
NRCTL intricately
NRCUU anfractuous
infructuous
unfructuous
NRDCE unpredicted
NRDCT introduce to
NRDET ingredients
NRDLT incredulity
NRDLU incredulous
NRDRA intradermal
NRDRI André Derain
NRELN snorkelling
NRERT in arrears to
NRFMN engraftment
NRFSO in profusion
NRGAT intriguante
NRGNU androgynous
NRHDX unorthodoxy
NRHSI anarchistic
NRMNA incremental
NRMNT incriminate
NRMSN unpromising
NRNAL unprintable
NRNEA entranceway
NRNEE entrance fee
NRNHN intrenchant
NRNHS enfranchise
NRNIL infrangible
infrangibly
in principle
on principle
NRPDT intrepidity
NRPEI André Previn
NRQEC infrequency
NRSEC in arm's reach
NRSEI engrossed in
NRSMN engrossment
NRSRE unpreserved
NRSVL intrusively
NRTCE unprotected
NRTTD ingratitude
NRUNS onerousness
NRVDN unprovident
NRVNU intravenous
NRVRE introverted
NSAAL inescapable
inescapably
NSAEL unashamedly
NSALA in a small way
NSANS unusualness
NSCLK and suchlike
NSETA inessential
unessential
NSETE one's best bet
NSETV unassertive
NSIAL gnostically
inestimable
inestimably
NSKPO Anish Kapoor
NSLTO in isolation
NSOOE anastomoses
NSRAL uniserially
NSXAL unisexually
NTACP initial caps
NTBLT instability
NTEAL unutterable
unutterably
NTESM and then some
NTETM another time
NTETO inattention
NTETV inattentive
NTGTN instigating
NTGTO instigation
NTGTV instigative
NTHKL in at the kill
NTHNL snatchingly
NTIGU anything but
NTNIT instantiate
NTNTV instinctive
NTORC a nut to crack
NTPAL unstoppable
unstoppably
NTTMN instatement
NTTTO institution
NTUET instruments
NTUTO instruction
NTUTV instructive
NTZTO unitization
NUAFR in human form
NUANS inhumanness
NUAUU incunabulum
NUBAC encumbrance
NUBDT inturbidate
NUBNE unhusbanded
NUBNL incumbently
NUCLE Angus Calder
NUCLT unguiculate
NUCTO inculcation
NUCUS in due course
NUDAL unsubduable
NUDBL infundibula
NUDNN unburdening
NUDVC input device
NUEAL innumerable
innumerably
insuperable
insuperably
NUECN intumescent
NUEET inducements
NUENS unquietness
NUETM indumentums
NUEUL untunefully
NUFLE unfulfilled
NUGAL unbudgeable
NUGNL indulgently
NUGRS unvulgarise
NUGRZ unvulgarize
NUGTT ingurgitate
NUHNI inauthentic
NUIAL indubitable
indubitably
NUIIU injudicious
NUIRD unguligrade
NUIST incuriosity
NUITN infuriating
NUIUL incuriously
injuriously
undutifully
NUKNS unluckiness
NULAL unquellable
NULCT in duplicate
NULFE unqualified
NULLO in full bloom
NULLR on full alert
NULLS in full blast
NULSE unpublished
NULWN in full swing
NUMBA Angus McBean
NUNSE unfurnished
NUONA in our own way
NUPCE unsuspected
NUPRE unsupported
NUPSE unsurpassed
NUPTO inculpation
NUPTR inculpatory
NUREL unguardedly
unhurriedly
NURIT inquire into
NURNL inquiringly
NURNO inquirendos
NUSAC in substance
NUSTO inquisition
NUSTV inquisitive
NUTFE unjustified
NUTIU industrious
NUTMR uncustomary
NUTNL insultingly
NUTOA inductional
intuitional
NUTVL inductively
intuitively
NUUAO inaugurator
NUVTO incurvation
NUWLO Angus Wilson
NVIAL unavailable
unavailably
unavoidable
unavoidably
NVRAL unavertable
universally
NVRHN on every hand
NVRPR in every part
NVSNS knavishness
NWAEE and whatever
NWALN snowballing
NWDNE snowed under
NWEEE unsweetened
NWEPR snow leopard
NWHSH know who's who
NWNCR knowing card
NWNIO angwantibos
NWNNS knowingness
NWOHN know-nothing
NWORE snowboarder
NWRHN answerphone
NWRNS unawareness
NWUTN snow bunting
NWYIH know by sight
NXCAL inexecrable
NXCNS inexactness
NXEIN inexpedient
unexperient
NXESV inexpensive
NXIAL unexcitable
NXLIE unexplained
unexploited
NXMNE Anaximander
NXRSE unexpressed
NXSEC in existence
NXUAL inexcusable
inexcusably
NYOEI encylopedic
NYRGR Andy Gregory
NYUTI only just win
OAACO not a patch on
OAAON total amount

OAASG not a sausage
OAASN royal assent
OAATU Polacanthus
OACEO comancheros
OACIA monarchical
OACLU local colour
OACNL Roman candle
OACNS tobacconist
OADAK Howard Hawks
OADAO Gog and Magog
OADAR dot and carry
OADEA Donald Dewar
OADGI now and again
OADOE Donald Soper
OADOR you and yours
OADOT dos and don'ts
do's and don'ts
OADRO bow and arrow
OADUG Donald Budge
OAEEG solar energy
OAEPR Roman Empire
OAETA no later than
OAETR Bonaventure
OAFEV roman fleuve
OAFIN woman friend
OAHLC to each place
OAHLS notaphilism
notaphilist
OAIAE foraminated
OAIAI boracic acid
OAIAL botanically
nomadically
somatically
OAIAO Totalisator
Totalizator
OAIER polarimetry
OAIHI logarithmic
OAIKF for a kick-off
OAILE tomatilloes
OAILN coral island
OAINS Moravianism
Rotarianism
OAIOI not a bit of it
OAIUL voraciously
OAKAD go backwards
OALCR for all I care
OALHR not all there
OALNS movableness
notableness
womanliness
OALNT focal length
OALOE for all to see
OALSI go ballistic
OALTA Royal Lytham
OAMDL Mohammed Ali
OAMGT God-almighty
OANPC Locarno Pact
OANSA Johannes Rau
OAOAC tomato sauce
OAOFC local office
OAOIL Monaco-Ville
OAOIM moratoriums
OAORD Romano Prodi
OAPAE non-appearer
OAPEU solar plexus
OARCL total recall
OASEC local speech
OASGO so far so good
OASIE bolas spider
OASSE solar system
OATCS monasticism
romanticise
romanticism❑
romanticist
OATCZ romanticize
OATRA monasterial
OAVLE moral values
OAYRS rotary press
OBAAC forbearance
OBDAC forbiddance
OBDEL forbiddenly
OBEAE double-faced
OBEAL double eagle
double fault
double-fault
OBEDE double-edged
OBEEI double helix
OBEEO hobbledehoy
OBEGN double agent
OBEHC double-check
OBEHN doublethink
OBEHR double sharp
OBEIS double first
OBEKR hobble skirt
OBELC double-click
OBELF double bluff
OBELN double-blind
OBENR double-entry
OBEOR wobble board
OBEPA doublespeak
OBEPC double-space
OBERA double cream
OBERS double-cross
OBESO God bless you
OBEUC double Dutch
double-quick
OBLEE nonbeliever
non-believer
OBLSL doubtlessly
OBLTO bombilation
OBNLO go a bundle on
OBNTO bombination
combination
OBNTR combinatory
OBNTV combinative
OBNWT combine with
OBPRO not be part of
OBRBO Bobby Robson
OBRFO Fosbury flop
OBRGU borborygmus
OBRMN bombardment
OBSIL combustible
OBYSL tomboyishly
OCAAC nonchalance
OCACI Bob Cratchit
OCAMN concealment
OCAON ponce around
OCAPA couch a spear
OCAPO Bob Champion
OCBAE torchbearer
OCBLT forcibility
OCBNG concubinage
OCBTO touch bottom
OCEIA non-chemical
OCGNL touch gently
OCIAL conceivable
conceivably
OCIEL conceitedly
OCLAO conciliator
OCLUE tow-coloured
OCMIA coxcombical
OCMLT not complete
OCMTN concomitant
OCNEV not conceive
OCNIE not confined
not consider
OCNLG volcanology
OCNRT concentrate
non-concrete
OCNTL you can't talk
OCOSU hot cross bun
OCPIU conceptious
OCPTT couch potato
OCPUE conceptuses
OCRAC concordance
OCREC concurrence
OCREL concernedly
OCRHL concert-hall
OCRIO concertinos
OCRMN concernment
OCSAE torch-staves
OCSEL Lou Costello
OCSNS conciseness
OCTNT concatenate
OCTPS touch-typist
OCUIN conclusions
OCUTN not counting
OCWTI voice within
ODABE wood warbler
ODAEE gold-layered
ODANR good manners
ODASI woodmanship
ODATG to advantage
ODATV hold captive
ODAUE good-natured
ODAVN woodcarving
ODCAC conductance
ODCEC food science
ODCER Pondicherry
ODCNL conducingly
ODCRS conductress
ODCTO coeducation
ODCVT conducive to
ODEEV gold reserve
ODEFC word-perfect
WordPerfect®
ODEIE bowdlerizer
ODELK soldierlike
ODELN good feeling
ODERE cold-hearted
good-hearted
ODERN load-bearing
ODESN top-dressing
ODETN bold-beating
ODEVN bondservant
good heavens
ODFIE good offices
ODFOT word of mouth
word-of-mouth
ODGER nom de guerre
ODGIS hold against
ODHBL hold the belt
ODHDC load the dice
ODHFR hold the fort
ODHLN hold the line
ODHRA hold the road
Woody Herman
ODHRN hold the ring
ODIGN gold-digging
ODIKN hoodwinking
ODITR word history
ODLDY good old days
ODLMT condylomata
ODLNE condolences
ODLOE cold-blooded
ODLOO wood alcohol
ODLTO rondolettos
ODMAL condemnable
ODMGI Joe DiMaggio
ODMNU condominium
ODNAK Gordon Banks
ODNAL golden eagle
ODNBC holding-back
ODNEL golden hello
ODNER Londonderry
ODNHC hold in check
ODNHR golden share
ODNLB Golden Globe
ODNLI golden oldie
ODNMN wood anemone
ODNOE holding-over
ODNOS golden goose
ODNPO wooden spoon
ODNRD London pride
ODNRW golden brown
Gordon Brown
ODNSA hold one's jaw
ODNSW hold one's own
ODNTO condonation
ODNTU Gordonstoun
ODNVC Bogdanovich
ODNYU golden syrup
ODODN roadholding
ODOFR cold comfort
ODOHL Voodoo Child
ODOKN good-looking
ODONN good-morning
ODOTE loud-mouthed
ODOTN good fortune
ODOWR word for word
word-for-word
ODPAE loudspeaker

ODPNO good opinion
ODPRT good spirits
ODRCN road pricing
ODREE woodcreeper
ODRGN word origins
ODRHL wonder child
ODRNL ponderingly
wonderingly
ODRNO bordering on
ODRNS dodderiness
ODRUL ponderously
wonderfully
ODRVS Lord Provost
ODSLO bold as a lion
ODSPE Lord's Supper
ODSRP nondescript
ODSRS bold as brass
ODTIE not detailed
ODTIR condottiere
condottieri
ODTOA conditional
ODTOE conditioned
conditioner
ODTRG cold storage
ODUHE goddaughter
ODUTN good hunting!
woodcutting
ODVNN good-evening
ODWLO wood-swallow
ODWRH Goldsworthy
OEAHR forefathers
OEAKN home banking
OEAMN forepayment
OEANN forewarning
OEATN forecasting
OEBDE honey badger
OEBLT moveability
OEBSE Moses basket
OECAG cover charge
OECAT Rosencrantz
OECME honeycombed
OECNE rose-scented
OECRA Roger Corman
OECTN not exciting
OEDIE power-driven
OEEAL foreseeable
OEEDN co-dependant
OEEEI lower eyelid
OEEGL sovereignly
OEEGT sovereignty
OEEIE fore-recited
more desired
to be decided
OEEIH Hore-Belisha
OEEIR joie de vivre
OEELN foretelling
OEEMR for evermore
forevermore
OEETA no fewer than
OEETS novelettish
novelettist
OEETV non-elective
OEEWE come between
OEEWL covered walk
OEFNU honey fungus
OEFRA money for jam
OEGBD foreign body
OEGIS vote against
OEGNS foreignness
OEGRL foreign rule
OEGTE come a gutser
OEHAD Joseph Haydn
OEHAK Joseph Banks
OEHBB lose the baby
OEHEY Joseph Beuys
OEHLS none the less
nonetheless
OEHMT Joseph Smith
OEHNR power-hungry
OEHOG come through
OEHRE foreshorten
OEHRO come short of
OEHTA come what may
OEHUH forethought
OEHYN Joseph Lyons
OEIAL polemically
tonetically
OEIHE foresighted
OEIHL move lightly
OEIHO lose sight of
OEILG soteriology
OEILN Coney Island
Gorée Island
OEILV Women in Love
OEINS bohemianism❑
OEIOR Côte d'Ivoire
OEIRN lower in rank
OEITN more distant
more fitting
non-existent
OEIWT to begin with
OEJDR Mohenjo-daro
OEKEE hotel-keeper
OELNE Hohenlinden
moneylender
money-lender
OELSL powerlessly
OELSR foreclosure
OELST come close to
OELYN role-playing
OEMKN moneymaking
money-making
OEMNU coterminous
OEMOE honeymooner
OENAC modern dance
OENEI come on begin
OENES someone else
OENIE Modern Times
OENIS come in first
OENMR more and more
OENMS love-in-a-mist
OENSA lose one's rag
lose one's way
OENSI modernistic
OENSL lose oneself
OENTC come unstuck
OENWN foreknowing
OENZN modernizing
OEOAA poke borak at
OEOAD come towards
move towards
OEOCE forevouched
OEOEM come to terms
OEOHA come to a head
OEOHL come to a halt
OEOIH come to light
OEOIK Wole Soyinka
OEOKN homeworking
OEOLE gone to sleep
OEOLN gone gosling
OEOLW come to blows
OEONN come to an end
OEORE come to grief
OEORP come to grips
OEOSC Jose Conseco
OEOSI fore-topsail
OEOSN ropes of sand
OEOSO come to a stop
OEOTO lose control
OEOTR done to a turn
OEOUI move to music
OEOWR come forward
move forward
OEPAC come-uppance
OEPAD move upwards
OEPEA coleopteran
OEPEO so help me God
OEPER Robespierre
OEPRE fore-spurrer
nosey parker
OEPRN none-sparing
OEPTI homeopathic
OERCO lose track of
OERMI Rose Tremain
OERNT pomegranate
OERSI voyeuristic
OESAI homeostasis
OESCL honeysuckle
OESIE money spider
OESNU no reason but
OESOT boxer shorts
boxer-shorts
cover shorts
OESPL money supply
OETAK Robert Hawke
OETAL potentially
OETBE comestibles
OETCD rodenticide
OETCS domesticise
OETCT domesticate
domesticity
Robert Scott
OETCZ domesticize
OETEE lowest level
OETEI Robert Cecil
OETER Robert Peary
OETLE forestaller
OETLN poverty line
OETLV Robert Clive
OETNO Robert Ensor
OETNU honest Injun
OETOA Robert Cohan
OETOK Robert Hooke
OETOL Robert Boyle
OETON lowest point
OETOO honest-to-God
Robert Solow
OETRC Robert Bruce
OETRL momentarily
OETRS potent cross
Robert Frost
OETTA poverty trap
OETTO fomentation
forestation
molestation
OETUL momentously
OETUN Robert Burns
OEUAL molecularly
OEUCL move quickly
OEUNS dolefulness
hopefulness
OEURE forequarter
OEUWT come out with
OEXCL more exactly
OEXRM more extreme
OEYER lonely heart
lonely-heart
OEYOE more by token
OEYTR Comedy Store
OFAAC non-feasance
OFART conflagrate
OFBLT confabulate
OFCSL Corfe Castle
OFDNL confidently
confidingly
OFDRC confederacy
OFDRT confederate
OFEAL coffee table
coffee-table
OFECK pomfret cake
OFEOE toffee-nosed
OFEOS coffee house
OFEPL toffee apple
OFERA coffee break
OFFRA loaf of bread
OFGRT configurate
OFHSL wolf whistle
OFIAL forfeitable
OFIIN coefficient
OFITN conflicting
OFLNE gonfalonier
OFNLS confineless
OFNMN confinement
OFNSE not finished
OFOTN confronting
OFRAE God-forsaken
OFRAL comfortable
comfortably
confirmable
conformable
conformably
OFRLS comfortless

OFSAO confiscator
OFSEL confessedly
OFSIN confessions
OFSNS wolfishness
OFTOA not fit to eat
OFTTO confutation
OFUDE confound her
OFUDI confound him
OFUDN confounding
OFUDO confound you
OFUNL confluently
OGAAL congealable
OGADN Douglas Dunn
OGAHG Douglas Hogg
OGAHI Douglas Haig
OGAHM Douglas-Home
OGAHR Douglas Hurd
OGAMN congealment
OGATN long-lasting
OGCAE Jorge Chavez
OGDSK for God's sake
OGENI rouge-et-noir
OGESA congressman
OGESR long-measure
OGEVN long-serving
OGFYI Song of my Cid
OGHNL rough-handle
OGIHE long-sighted
OGLTO coagulation
congelation
OGNAL congenially
OGNEA Morgan le Fay
OGOAN Don Giovanni
OGPDL doggy-paddle
OGRED loggerheads
OGSEC rough sketch
OGSNS hoggishness
OGTEO forget-me-not
OGTFE sought after
sought-after
OGTNS doughtiness
OGTUL forgetfully
OGUDE long hundred
OGUNN long-running
OGUUL congruously
OGVNS forgiveness
OGWIE long-awaited
OHAHN Rosh Hashana
OHAKM Joshua Nkomo
OHANC Loch Rannoch
OHAOE Sophia Loren
OHBTO to the bottom
OHCOE Gothic novel
OHDAM Bodhidharma
OHESE Noah Webster
OHGON to the ground
OHIFR Josh Gifford
OHLTE to the letter
OHLWT not hold with
OHMDL to the middle
OHMNT to the minute
OHNGF nothing-gift
OHNII nothing in it
OHNLT nothing loth
OHNNS nothingness
OHNOI to think of it
OHNTI nothing to it
OHRAT mother earth
OHRNA mother-in-law
nowhere near
OHROR motherboard
OHRTO botheration
OHRUD do the rounds
go the rounds
OHSIA sophistical
OHSLC to this place
OHSTV Bodhisattva
OHTNO to the tune of
OHUMS to the utmost
OHWRO do the work of
OIAAO Louis Aragon
OIACM holiday camp
OIAEE Monica Seles
OIAHA nominal head
OIAIA nominatival
OIAMU hog in armour
OIBAE Louis B Mayer
OIBCE Boris Becker
OIBLT sociability
OIBOG Conisbrough
OIEBM go like a bomb
OIEHN mobile phone
OIEIA homiletical
OIEOA policewoman
OIEOC motive force
police force
OIEOE motive power
OIEOR police court
OIERN domineering
OIERS moline cross
OIETL no time at all
OIETT police state
OIETV nociceptive
OIEUG police burgh
OIFSE Jodie Foster
OIGFG coming of age
OIGIE coming times
OIGLS coming close
OIGPR coming apart
joking apart
OIGRK Bolingbroke
OIGTN coping stone
coping-stone
OIHBN go with a bang
OIIAL politically
OIIDA codified law
OIIIR domiciliary
OIIIT domiciliate
OIINN positioning
OIJUE Louis Jouvet
OILAE Louis Leakey
OILGS sociologist
OILLS social class
OILOT nonillionth
OILRE social order
OILZN socializing
OIMTI sociometric
OINCE Louis Necker
OINLS notionalist
OIOSI monitorship
OIOUS soliloquise
soliloquist
OIOUZ soliloquize
OIPTI sociopathic
OIQIZ Louis-Quinze
OIRCA Rosicrucian
OISAC for instance
OISSI solipsistic
OISTI Möbius strip
OITIN Corinthians
OITUI Joliot-Curie
OIUNS copiousness
noxiousness
OIUTO moxibustion
OIVSV non-invasive
OJCUA conjectural
OJGLT conjugality
OJGTO conjugation
OJNTO conjunction
OJNTR conjuncture
OJNTV conjunctiva
conjunctive
OJOEL Jonjo O'Neill
OJRTO conjuration
OKAGR look daggers
OKALB rock wallaby
OKALK workmanlike
OKAPO Rockhampton
OKASI workmanship
OKBLT workability
OKEPN bookkeeping
OKFLE Rockefeller
OKFOD book of words
OKGIS work against
OKHLE rock shelter
OKHLN work the land
OKHOG book through
look through
soak through
work through
OKHPR look the part
OKIDN bookbinding
OKISE York Minster
OKLEE Volkslieder
OKLEI cockaleekie
cock-a-leekie
OKNAI looking as if
OKNBC looking back
OKNBR mockingbird
OKNLK looking like
OKNRL rock and roll
OKNWE working week
OKOAD work towards
OKODR work wonders
OKOHR work too hard
OKONL work jointly
OKROT Cockermouth
OKRSA rock crystal
OKRWN cock-crowing
OKSAC look askance
OKSAD Cook Islands
OKSAL mock-assault
OKSNS bookishness
OKTAG rocket range
OKTIE pocket-sized
OKTNF pocket knife
pocket-knife
OKTOE pocket money
OKTOO rocket motor
OKTTO work station
workstation
OKUFC work surface
OKWLO Jocky Wilson
OKYBU monkey about
OKYTC hockey stick
OLAEO so please you
OLALT not liable to
OLANS pollyannish
OLBAE world-beater
OLBRT collaborate
OLCAE collectanea
OLCAL collectable
OLCDL mollycoddle
OLCEC soil science
OLCEL collectedly
OLCLS folliculose
OLCTL coal scuttle
OLCTO collocation
OLDWE boiled sweet
OLDWT collide with
OLERN fool's errand
soul-fearing
OLFMU world-famous
OLGNS hooliganism
OLILN soul-killing
OLLNS worldliness
OLLWS worldly wise
worldly-wise
OLMNE noble-minded
OLMTO collimation
OLNAS hollandaise
OLNCR cooling card
OLNDW boiling-down
OLNII rolling in it
OLNKO bowline knot
OLNON pollen count
OLNTO pollination
OLNWL Howling Wolf
OLNWT go along with
OLORW roll-your-own
OLOTE foul-mouthed
OLPAE to all places
OLPAL collapsable
OLPIL collapsible
OLPPA lollipop man
OLPYI Coelophysis
OLQIM colloquiums
OLRCR world record
OLRHP forlorn hope
OLRKT roller-skate
OLRLD rollerblade
OLRLN roller blind

OLRNS forlornness
OLRTE soul brother
would rather
OLSEC coalescence
OLSET not listen to
OLSNS foolishness
godlessness
joylessness
OLSOE would sooner
OLSPR worlds apart
OLSVG noble savage
OLSVL collusively
OLTAE toilet paper
toilet water
OLTCM world to come
OLTEA go all the way
OLTOA coalitional
OLUNS soulfulness
OLVRE Dolly Varden
OLVRI cod-liver oil
OMACE doomwatcher
OMAKN Tommy Atkins
OMCCO not much chop
OMCLI Don McCullin
OMCOE Tommy Cooper
OMCTO formication
OMDRE Tommy Dorsey
OMDTE commodities
OMECE form teacher
OMEVC room service
OMHMK Noam Chomsky
OMIEO not my idea of
OMIFU comme il faut
OMIIE room-divider
OMLAS formal cause
OMLGS cosmologist
OMLOS pommel horse
OMLRS formularise
OMLRZ formularize
OMLSI formalistic
OMLTE formalities
OMLTO formulation
OMMRT commemorate
OMNAL commendable
commendably
commensally
OMNAO commentator
OMNCN communicant
OMNCT communicate
OMNEL tormentedly
OMNES common sense
commonsense
common-sense
OMNHR common-shore
OMNHS Gormenghast
OMNIE gormandizer
OMNLC commonplace
OMNLN commingling
OMNLS communalise
OMNLZ communalize
OMNMN commandment
OMNOE common morel
OMNPS command post
OMNSI communistic
OMNTN Norman Stone
OMNTO commination
comminution
OMNWT commune with
OMRIE Bob Mortimer
former times
OMRTA not more than
OMSRT commiserate
OMSTO solmisation
OMTCA cosmetician
OMTCS cosmeticise
OMTCZ cosmeticize
OMTLI non-metallic
OMTOA formational
OMTTO commutation
OMTTV commutative
OMTVL normatively
OMZTO solmization
ONAAA Mount Ararat
ONABR John Lambert
ONACA John Barclay
ONACC John Hancock
ONACL John Mauchly
ONADN John Haldane
ONAEE John Tavener
ONAGN John Sargent
ONAGO John Habgood
ONAIN foundations
ONAIR Point-a-Pitre
ONAKN John Hawkins
John Hawkyns
ONALE sound asleep
ONAMN down payment
Joan Hammond
ONANE fountain pen
mountain dew
mountaineer
ONANO mountain top
ONANS mountain ash
ONANU mountainous
ONAON going around
ONARC Downpatrick
ONASO John Marston
ONATA John Bartram
ONATO joint action
ONBAL connubially
ONBHL lo and behold
ONBTE go one better
Mountbatten
ONBTS coenobitism
ONBUH bonne-bouche
ONCAL connectable
ONCEL connectedly
ONCIL connectible
ONCIN connections
ONCIU Connecticut
ONCNO John McEnroe
ONCPA cornucopian
ONCSL Doune Castle
ONCTO fornication
ONCWT connect with
ONDEM John-a-dreams
ONDPU point d'appui
ONEAC countenance
ONEAR John Le Carré
ONEBF counterbuff
ONEBO counterblow
ONEBR counterbore
Mount Elbert
ONEBU Mount Elbrus
ONEDA counterdraw
ONEDW rounded down
ONEFI counterfeit
counterfoil
ONEFR joint effort
ONEIG Ronnie Biggs
ONEKE Wounded Knee
ONELN counselling
ONEMN countermand
countermine
Mount Egmont
ONEMR countermure
ONENE John Tenniel
ONENS pointedness
ONEOR Pointe Noire
Pointe-Noire
ONEPN counterpane
ONEPO counter-plot
ONEPR counterpart
ONERE downhearted
down-hearted
ONESA counterseal
ONESE John Webster
ONESG countersign
ONESN countersink
ONEUL bounteously
ONEVI countervail
ONEVT counter-vote
ONEWO John Redwood
ONEWR counterwork
ONFAN John of Gaunt
ONFRU somniferous
ONGAH pornography
ONHCU join the club
ONHMN Down the Mine
ONHWN down the wind
ONIEC coincidence
ONIGU pointing-out
ONIHE moonlighter
ONILI John Millais
ONILS pointillism
pointillist
ONILU John Gielgud
ONISU connoisseur
ONITM point in time
ONIUL bountifully
ONKLO John Skelton
ONLLN John Cleland
ONLMN John Fleming
ONLNI hornblendic
ONLNL somnolently
ONLSL pointlessly
soundlessly
ONLSO Sonny Liston
ONLUL sound loudly
ONMNT cognominate
ONMRT connumerate
ONNCA morning coat
ONNGP corn in Egypt
ONNGW town and gown
ONNOT down-and-outs
ONNSA Morning Star
morning star
ONOAT down to earth
down-to-earth
ONOEE go on for ever
ONOEO do one over on
ONOHC John Toshack
ONOJC found object
ONOLN John Collins
John Dowland
ONONI town council
ONOPP corn cob pipe
ONORA John Boorman
ONOSE John Vorster
ONOSL point of sale
ONOTE John Coetzee
ONOVE point of view
ONPOL townspeople
young people
ONPRO young person
ONPRS coin a phrase
ONRCU Country Club
country club
ONRDE downtrodden
down-trodden
ONRDN downgrading
ONREI Bognor Regis
ONRFE countrified
countryfied
ONRFM John Profumo
ONRLF Country Life
ONRSA country seat
John Grisham
ONRSD countryside
ONRTN cornerstone
corner-stone
ONRWD countrywide
country-wide
ONSAT to one's taste
ONSBR John Ashbery
ONSED going steady
ONSET cognoscente
cognoscenti
ONSHN do one's thing
ONSLC do one's block
ONSME Donna Summer
ONSON John Osborne
ONSOS do one's worst
ONSOT hound's-tooth
ONSRN going strong
ONSTF do one's stuff
ONTEA point the way
ONTNS cognateness
ONTTO connotation
ONTTV connotative
ONTVL cognitively
ONUTE John Surtees

ONUUO John Audubon
ONUWT bound up with
ONWGL hornswoggle
ONWLE town-dweller
ONYAC mornay sauce
ONYDA John Wyndham
ONYOR county court
ONZNO cognizant of
OOAEC monovalence
monovalency
OOAHS logomachist
OOAIC son of a bitch
sonofabitch
OOAIM honorariums
OOAIN homo sapiens❑
OOAPU monocarpous
OOARP coronagraph
OOAWT go to law with
OOEET homogeneity
OOEEU homogeneous
OOEGH go to lengths
OOEHN do something for one thing
OOEPR top one's part
OOERS botoné cross
holohedrism
OOESE cotoneaster
OOETE so mote I thee
OOEWT go to bed with
OOFIN bosom friend
OOGNN tobogganing
OOGNS tobogganist
OOHDG go to the dogs
OOHHN monophthong
OOHOI monochromic
OOHRA holothurian
notochordal
OOHTS holophytism
OOHWL go to the wall
OOIEE colorimeter
OOIER colorimetry
OOIGA monolingual
OOIIS Novosibirsk
OOILS colonialism
colonialist
OOIUL notoriously
OOLNU monoclinous
OOLUC motor launch
OOOAH homoeopathy
OOOIA horological
nosological
topological
OOOIE monopolizer
OOOPI homomorphic
monomorphic
OOORE Conor O'Brien
OOORP coronograph
OOOTD rodomontade
OOOUS monologuise
OOOUZ monologuize
OORCN motor racing
OORES honours easy
OORLN colour-blind
OORLS honours list
OOROA gonorrhoeal
OOROE for our money
OORON honour-bound
OORPE monographer
nosographer
topographer
OORPI holographic
monographic
nomographic
nosographic
topographic
OORPP colour a pipe
OORTO colouration
OORUL colourfully
OORVR rotogravure
OOSRA Zoroastrian
OOTMS soroptimist❑
OOTRU homopterous
OOUAT pococurante
OOULA mononuclear
OOUPL coconut palm
coconut-palm
OOUTR monoculture
OOYFO nobody's fool
OPAEC complacence
complacency
OPAKO zooplankton
OPANN complainant
complaining
OPASN complaisant
OPCDS compact disc
compact disk
OPCEL compactedly
OPCNS compactness
OPDBA torpedo boat
OPDIV hooped bivvy
OPENS complexness
OPERC coup de grâce
OPESO compression
OPESV compressive
OPGNT compaginate
OPHCA coup the cran
OPHLO loop the loop
OPHOG romp through
OPHWL go up the wall
OPIAE complicated
OPIAI dolphinaria
OPICE soup kitchen
OPIET compliments
OPINL compliantly
OPIRT top-priority
OPLET compelled to
OPLNL corpulently
OPLTO compilation
OPNDW go up and down
OPNIM compendiums
OPNIU compendious
OPNMK go up in smoke
OPNTO compunction
OPOIE compromised
OPRAC comportance
OPRAL corporeally
OPRIA non-partisan
OPRIL Copperfield
OPRLE comptroller
OPRLT copperplate
OPRMN compartment
comportment
OPRTL corporately
OPRTN co-operating
OPRTO co-operation
corporation
OPRTS corporatism
OPRTV comparative
co-operative
OPRWT compare with
not part with
OPSNS foppishness
OPSTO composition
OPSUA corpuscular
OPSUL Don Pasquale
OPTLE hospitaller
OPTLS hospitalise
OPTLT hospitality
OPTLZ hospitalize
OPTNL competently
OPTRS computerese
computerise
OPTRT computerate
OPTRZ computerize
OPTTO competition
computation
OPTTR competitors
OPTTV competitive
OPTWT compete with
OPUDY compound eye
OPUNS pompousness
OPYIA non-physical
OPYII porphyritic
OQEAL conquerable
OQIOE mosquito net
ORADS gourmandise
gourmandism
ORADZ gourmandize
ORAGN go great guns
ORAIT journalists
ORBRT corroborate
ORCNS correctness
ORCRE not recorded
ORCRO pour scorn on
ORDLC Conrad Black
ORDSI comradeship
ORENS worriedness
OREOC tour de force
OREOT Bournemouth
ORESN journey's end
OREUL courteously
ORFAS hour of cause
ORGNU corrigendum
ORGTO corrugation
ORIAE co-ordinated
coordinates
co-ordinates
ORIAO co-ordinator
ORILO tourbillion
ORLLV courtly love
ORLNS courtliness
ORLTO correlation
ORLTV correlative
ORMME board member
ORMNI non-romantic
ORPIL corruptible
corruptibly
ORPLN horripilant
ORPLT horripilate
ORPNS corruptness
ORRKE Voortrekker
ORSAC morris dance
morris-dance
ORSDN non-resident
ORSGM Forrest Gump
ORSMN nourishment
ORSNN horrisonant
ORSNS boorishness
ORSVL corrosively
ORTPE doorstepper
ORUGO bourguignon
ORULT poor quality
poor-quality
ORWUL sorrowfully
ORYER Hooray Henry
OSADR non-standard
OSAON horse around
OSARA noise abroad
OSARS house arrest
OSATN Constantine
OSATR for starters
OSBLT possibility
OSBOE house-broken
OSCAE consecrated
OSCAG loose change
OSCTO consecution
OSCTV consecutive
OSDRN considering
OSDRT considerate
OSEII non-specific
OSELT constellate
OSENT consternate
OSEOT Lossiemouth
OSERN forswearing
OSFOE pots of money
OSGAL consignable
OSGMN consignment
OSHLE householder
OSHNE house-hunter
OSIAE constipated
OSIAO conspirator
OSIGA roasting pan
OSIIE low-spirited
OSINU Monseigneur
OSIPN worshipping
OSIUL consciously
OSIUN constituent
OSIUO conscious of
OSIUU conspicuous
OSKEE housekeeper
OSLAC consultancy
OSLAE fossil water

Words marked ❑ can also be spelled with an initial capital letter

OSLDT consolidate
OSLGT house lights
OSLIE fossil-fired
OSLII tonsillitis
OSLME loose-limbed
OSLNL consolingly
OSLSL noiselessly
OSLTO consolation
OSLTR consolatory
OSMAE consummated
OSMNS noisomeness
OSMRI house martin
OSMRS consumerism
OSMSE housemaster
toastmaster
OSMTO consumption
OSMTV consumptive
OSNER boysenberry
OSNIA nonsensical
OSNLI cors anglais
OSNNA consonantal
OSNNL consonantly
OSNNU loosening up
OSNTR toss and turn
OSNUL poisonously
OSNUN consanguine
OSOKY House of Keys
OSOPN not stopping
OSOPR Tom Stoppard
OSOTE hog-shouther
OSOUR hors d'oeuvre
OSQEC consequence
OSQIU non sequitur
OSRAC conservancy
OSRAL conservable
OSRAO conservator
OSRCE constricted
constructer
OSRCN horse-racing
OSRCO constrictor
constructor
OSRDN horse-riding
OSRDS horseradish
OSRGD Boys' Brigade
OSRIE constrained
OSRIM consortiums
OSRIT constraints
OSRST monstrosity
OSRUL monstrously
OSSEC consistence
consistency
OSSIN possessions
OSTRG fons et origo
OSUIE moisturizer
OSWFL housewifely
OSWFR housewifery
OTADA Portland Bay
OTADL boots and all
OTADN soft landing
OTAEI bootlace tie
OTAIT contrariety
OTAKO Port Jackson
OTALA Football War
OTAPN foot-tapping
OTAPO Northampton
Southampton
OTARC South Africa
OTATA contract man
contractual
portmanteau
OTATE Port Cartier
OTATN contrasting
OTATO contraction
contraption
OTATR portraiture
OTATU contract out
OTATV contractive
contrastive
OTBES north by east
south by east
OTBIU most obvious
OTBLT portability
OTBRA contubernal
OTBWS north by west
south by west
OTCAL contactable
OTCAV aortic valve
OTCEC soft science
OTCIF Northcliffe
OTCLI torticollis
OTCLN contact lens
OTCLO ponticellos
OTCMN forthcoming
OTCON cost-account
OTDAE tooth-drawer
OTDBA ports de bras
OTDKT North Dakota
South Dakota
OTECL mottled calf
OTEEP contretemps
OTEGN bootlegging
OTEID for the birds
OTEIT mont-de-piété
OTELE Montpellier
OTENS northernise
southernise
OTENZ northernize
southernize
OTEOS for the worse
OTERE soft-hearted
OTESE north-easter
OTESO post-tension
OTETE soft-centred
OTFAL fortifiable
OTFCL pontificals
OTFCT pontificate
OTFIN mouth-friend
OTFNR port of entry
OTFPI Port of Spain
OTFSL soothfastly
OTGLA cottage loaf
OTGRK Cottage Rake
OTGTE not together
OTHBL foot the bill
OTHHL port the helm
OTHSE youth hostel
OTHTA cost what may
OTIAC contrivance
OTIAL containable
doctrinally
OTIAR doctrinaire
OTIHL fortnightly
OTIKN bootlicking
OTILA Fort William
OTILN North Island
South Island
OTIMN containment
OTITN most distant
OTIUO contributor
OTLCN noctilucent
OTLCU noctilucous
OTLFO monthly flow
OTLRE postal order
OTLSL worthlessly
OTLTE hostilities
OTLTO postulation
OTMBL costume ball
OTMCT contumacity
OTMEE hot-tempered
OTMLT contemplate
OTMNN contaminant
OTMNT contaminate
OTMRS bottom-grass
OTNAC continuance
OTNAL continually
OTNAO costing a lot
OTNEC contingency
OTNEL contentedly
continuedly
OTNHL Notting Hill
OTNIR boutonnière
OTNIU contentious
OTNMN contentment
OTNNA continental
OTNNL continently
OTNNS routineness
OTNPC lost in space
OTNPL rotten apple
OTNTL fortunately
fortune-tell
OTNTN rottenstone
OTNWT contend with
OTOEB Port Moresby
OTOEI Montgomerie
OTOES controversy
OTOFE Montgolfier
OTOLN controlling
OTONR poltroonery
OTPCE tooth-picker
OTPER so it appears
OTPTO Monty Python
OTRAL coeternally
nocturnally
OTRBU potter about
OTRES poltergeist
OTRNL loiteringly
potteringly
torturingly
totteringly
OTROL posteriorly
OTROR mortarboard
mortar-board
OTRWT to start with
OTSAA North Sea gas
OTSAL contestable
OTSAT contestants
OTSBL mortise bolt
OTSLC mortise lock
OTSML loathsomely
toothsomely
OTSNS loutishness
OTSUE Montesquieu
OTSUI montes pubis
OTSYN soothsaying
OTTRL hortatorily
OTTVL hortatively
OTUFC soft surface
OTUSR North Utsire
South Utsire
OTUTN cost-cutting
OTUUT Port Augusta
OTVNO Rostov-on-Don
OTWRL northwardly
southwardly
OTWSE north-wester
OTXRM most extreme
OUBRW do number two
OUBTO conurbation
OUCLE bogus caller
OUCTN coruscating
OUCTO coruscation
OUETR documentary
Lotus-eaters
OUHHN no such thing
OUSAD locus standi
OUSNS roguishness
OUTCT do justice to
OUTMC not up to much
OUTNN locum tenens
OUTRL voluntarily
OUTRS voluntarism
OVCAL convictable
OVCIN convictions
OVCTO convocation
OVLAI Convallaria
OVLIN convulsions
OVLTO convolution
OVLUU convolvulus
OVNEB convinced by
OVNEC convenience
OVNEO convinced of
OVNIL conventicle
OVNIN conventions
OVOEC non-violence
OVRAC conversance
OVRAL conversably
OVRAT gouvernante
OVREC convergence
OVRET converted to
OVRIL convertible
convertibly
OVROR go overboard

OVRWL not very well
OVVAL convivially
OVYNE conveyancer
OWILN Don Whillans
OWOWR Bob Woodward
OWRNS forwardness
OXEET voix céleste
OXESV coextensive
OXRIE do exercises
OXSEC coexistence
OYACC Tony Hancock
OYAKI Tony Jacklin
OYAPU polycarpous
OYCNE body scanner
OYEHI polytechnic
OYENT Tony Bennett
OYERN polyhedrons
OYETD polypeptide
OYEVN body servant
OYHBO go by the book
OYHHA go by the head
OYHOI polychromic
OYLCC Tony Allcock
OYLTA polyglottal
OYLTI polyglottic
OYNRU polyandrous
OYNSU body and soul
OYOAL polygonally
OYOII body politic
OYONT Holy Sonnets
OYOPI polymorphic
OYRCI Toby Crackit
OYRIL Tony O'Reilly
OYRME Rory Bremner
OYRTN copy-writing
OYTRN polystyrene
PAACI apparatchik
PAAUE apparatuses
PABLL speak boldly
PADON ups and downs
PAEIO speak evil of
PAFOE splay-footed
PAHUO splash out on
PALNL appallingly
PAOEL speak openly
PASFL speak softly
PASOL speak slowly
PAWLO speak well of
PCACS special case
PCAIE specialized
specializer
PCANS specialness
PCAUA spectacular
PCCAH ipecacuanha
PCERM epicheirema
PCFAL specifiable
PCFCT specificate
specificity
PCLPI apocalyptic
PCLTO speculation
PCLTV speculative
PCMKN epoch-making
PCODT Space Oddity
PCRGA spectrogram
PCRLT spectrality
PCWIE space writer
PDAHN spud-bashing
PDRLN spider plant
PECMR speed camera
PECRL upper circle
PEDAL spread-eagle
PEDHE spreadsheet
PEDNL spreadingly
PEDRU splendorous
PEEEI upper eyelid
PEEIA splenetical
PEEIE ephemerides
PEETM splenectomy
PEHAE speech-maker
PEHFE speechifier
PEHIE Oppenheimer
PEIAL spherically
PELNL appealingly
PELTO appellation
PELTV appellative
PEODS spheroidise
PEODZ spheroidize
PEOEE speedometer
PESMN appeasement
PESNL appeasingly
PESOE upper storey
PETIT appertain to
PFLCT spifflicate
PGISI up against it
PGMUL apogamously
PGNPK a pig in a poke
PHTRE up shit creek
PIADS optical disk
PICEA sphincteral
PICEI sphincteric
PIGIL Springfield
PIGLA spring-clean
PIGMN spring a mine
PIGNO spring onion
PIGNS springiness
PIGNU springing-up
PIGOR springboard
PIGTE Springsteen
PIHNS uprightness
PIOEI epeirogenic
PISCN split second
PISRE split screen
PITEA spy in the cab
PITNL upliftingly
PITNU splitting-up
PIUFO split up from
PKSOA spokeswoman
PKSOE spokeswomen
PLAZN Spallanzani
PLBNE spellbinder
PLCTO application
PLELG spelaeology
PLIAR Apollinaire
PLPEE apple-pie bed
PLSEC opalescence
PLSUR apple-squire
PLWRE spellworker
PNAEN spend a penny
PNAET spontaneity
PNAEU spontaneous
PNBFD spina bifida
PNCMN up and coming
up-and-coming
PNEDC open verdict
PNELK spaniel-like
PNERE open-hearted
PNFEL spend freely
PNFRU spiniferous
PNGRU spinigerous
PNHSU upon the shun
PNHWN upon the wing
PNICI open circuit
PNIGE spanking new
PNLAA spinal canal
PNLHL spindle hole
PNLPE epanalepses
PNLSL spinelessly
PNNMV opening move
PNNPR opening part
PNNSU open-and-shut
PNNTM opening time
PNOAE opinionated
PNOLN spin-bowling
PNOPL opinion poll
PNOSI sponsorship
PNOTE open-mouthed
PNPRN epinephrine
PNSFW Spanish fowl
PNSMI Spanish Main
PNSMS Spanish moss
PNSTW Spanish Town
PNTRF spendthrift
PNTRS spinsterish
PNUIK spondulicks
PNUOE aponeuroses
PNUOI aponeurosis
aponeurotic
PNYII spondylitis
POCAC up to scratch
POERS optometrist
POGNS splodginess
POHHL up to the hilt
POHMR up to the mark
POIHO up to high doh
PONMN appointment
POSEE upholsterer
POTNL opportunely
POTNS opportunism
opportunist
POTNT opportunity
PRAHN approaching
PRAIA spermatical
PRAOO spermatozoa
PRBIU opprobrious
PRBLT operability
PRBTO approbation
PRBTR approbatory
PRCAE appreciated
PRCAL appreciable
appreciably
PRCAT spirochaete
PRDSA aphrodisiac
PRERN spur gearing
PRGSI sphragistic
PRIAL appraisable
PRIIA spermicidal
PRLNL sparklingly
PRLSL sparklessly
PRNIL sporangiola
PRNNS sparingness
PROBL sparrow-bill
PROHT spermophyte
PROHW sparrowhawk
PROOI spermogonia
PRPIT appropriate
PRPYI sporophytic
PRSIL sports field
PRSNE opera singer
PRSOA sportswoman
PRSOI appressoria
PRTAL spiritually
PRTEE spirit level
PRTGE Spiro T Agnew
PRTOA operational
PRTVL operatively
PRVNL approvingly
PRXMT approximate
PSEIR a posteriori
PSIAL spastically
PSOAL episcopally
PSOIA apostolical
spasmodical
PSRPI apostrophic
PTAAI epithalamia
epithalamic
PTAEU spathaceous
PTAMU epithalmium
PTEDC spotted dick
PTEDS spatterdash
PTESS apotheosise
PTESZ apotheosize
PTSUU apatosaurus ❑
PTXAL epitaxially
PUTNN appurtenant
PUTRN spluttering
PWIGE spawning-bed
PWLIM JPR Williams
PYMGA sphygmogram
QADRN squandering
QAEAC square dance
square-dance
QAEER square metre
QAINS squalidness
QALNN aquaplaning
QARGT equal rights
QAUTR aquaculture
QEKNL squeakingly
QEKNS squeakiness
QEMSL squeamishly
QETIN equestrians
QIAAC equibalance
QIAEA equilateral

Words marked ❑ can also be spelled with an initial capital letter

QIAEC equivalence
QIIRS equilibrist
QIIRT equilibrate
QIIRU equilibrium
QIITN equidistant
QINUA equiangular
QIOAL equivocally
QIOAO equivocator
QIOTA equinoctial
QITNL squintingly
QIUTR aquiculture
RAADS Brian Aldiss
RAAOI Ars Amatoria
RABHN tread behind
RABJR Trial by Jury
RABLT preambulate
RABSE bread basket
RABTE Great Bitter
RACES cream cheese
RACOG Brian Clough
RACRL great circle
RACSE broadcaster
RACUC Broad Church
RADNE breakdancer
RAEAN greasepaint
RAEPR greater part
RAERO greaseproof
RAETA greater than
RAETS ornamentist
RAFRE Bryan Forbes
RAFST breakfast TV
RAFTD area of study
RAGLC Fra Angelico
RAGLT triangulate
RAGMN arraignment
arrangement
RAGON break ground
RAHIT breathe into
RAHNS breathiness
preachiness
RAHRU treacherous
RAHUO breathe upon
RAIAL erratically
organically
RAIDW break it down
RAIGF breaking-off
RAINS Creationism
creationist
RAITO irradiation
RALNS friableness
RALSL dreadlessly
dreamlessly
RALTR treacle tart
RAMNE broad-minded
RAMNS preadmonish
RANME great number
RANPE great-nephew
RANUH dreadnought□
RAOAL treasonable
treasonably
RAPRO trial period
RAPTE Brian Patten
RARBO Brian Robson
RARDN Armatrading
RARNE prearranged
RASAR Broadstairs
RASHN Great Sphinx
RASPL great supply
RASRW urban sprawl
RATCE dream ticket
RATEA break the law
RATEC break the ice
RATLT breastplate
RATWS breadthwise
RATWY breadthways
RAUYA treasury tag
RAWNE breadwinner
RAYPO greasy spoon
RBBLT probability
RBCLT trabeculate
RBEAI problematic
RBEFE problem-free
RBENS crabbedness
RBEPG problem page
RBIGA Brobdingnag
RBLGS tribologist
RBLTO tribulation
RBNSI tribuneship
RBSEC erubescence
RBSIE proboscides
proboscises
RBSOA tribeswoman
RBTOE probationer
RBTRL tributarily
RCADI brace and bit
RCANS Grecian nose
RCATN Eric Cantona
RCCEI crack credit
RCDNL precedently
RCDWO crack down on
RCEBL trackerball
RCEET track events
RCEHO crochet hook
RCEIG proceedings
RCENR dry cleaner's
RCETM tracheotomy
RCETO procreation
RCETV procreative
RCFSI trace fossil
RCFXN price-fixing
RCFXO crucifixion□
RCGOC precognosce
RCGRL Bracegirdle
RCHPO Eric Shipton
RCIAL practicable
practicably
practically
RCIDL Eric Liddell
RCIEI practised in
RCIIA preclinical
RCINS fractionise
RCINT fractionate
RCINZ fractionize
RCIOI trichinosis
RCIUL fractiously
RCIYN fructifying
RCLHA prickly heat
RCLNL truculently
RCLNS prickliness
RCLOI brucellosis
RCLPA prickly pear
RCLPO Eric Clapton
RCLSL gracelessly
pricelessly
tracelessly
tracklessly
RCLUE tricoloured
RCLUL oraculously
RCLWR crackleware
RCLYN bricklaying
RCMRA Precambrian
RCNEU fricandeaux
RCNEV preconceive
RCNLG arachnology
RCNRC precontract
RCNUA proconsular
RCODW crack of dawn
RCOFE tractor feed
RCOOA trichomonad
RCOSI proctorship
RCPOR cry cupboard
RCPRS preceptress
RCPTT precipitate
RCPTU precipitous
RCRCR track record
RCRMN procurement
RCRNS prochronism
RCRSO Eric Bristow
RCRTP triceratops□
RCSNS preciseness
RCTEO Erechtheion
RCUIN precautions
RCUTA Procrustean
RCWLI Bruce Willis
RDADO pride and joy
RDBLT credibility
RDCAL predictable
predictably
RDCMN predicament
traducement
RDCNL traducingly
RDCRI bradycardia
RDCSO predecessor
RDCTO eradication
predication
RDCTV eradicative
predicative
RDERS A Red, Red Rose
RDGLS prodigalise
RDGLT prodigality
RDGLZ prodigalize
RDHPL Fred Whipple
RDIGO Bridlington
RDLCE predilected
RDLCK griddle-cake
RDLCO predilecton
RDLOA Mrs Dalloway
RDLUL credulously
RDMNN predominant
RDMNT predominate
RDNIL credentials
RDNPS trading post
RDRCO Fredericton
RDREA Fred Trueman
RDSAR Fred Astaire
RDSCE trade secret
RDSEC iridescence
RDSIE predestined
RDSNO trades union
RDSNS prudishness
RDSOA tradeswoman
RDSOE predisposed
RDTOA gradational
traditional
RDTRL predatorily
REAAL irreparable
irreparably
REAIA free radical
REAOI Freemasonic
REAON order around
REAOR Freemasonry
RECES green cheese
REDWT friends with
REEAC irrelevance
irrelevancy
REEEC irreverence
REELC breeze block
REEOE true-devoted
REERE truehearted
REERM freeze-frame
REETS irredentism
irredentist
REFRE armed forces
REGOE greengrocer
REHIT breech birth
REHNE freethinker
free-thinker
REHUH freethought
REIEC pre-eminence
REIIU irreligious
REIKN arse-licking
REILS arterialise
REILZ arterialize
REKTN free skating
RELNS orderliness
REMNE green monkey
RENAL triennially
RENES free and easy
free-and-easy
RENOR free on board
RENSL free oneself
REOAL irremovable
irremovably
irrevocable
irrevocably
REODN freeloading
REOEE tree-covered
REOTN freebooting
REOUL irresolubly
REPAT green plants
REPPE green pepper
REPTT fried potato

RERBE armed robber
REREE tree-creeper
RESBR free as a bird
RETEA Ernest Renan
RETEI Ernest Bevin
RETFE cruelty-free
RETHL priest's hole
RETLS orientalise
Orientalist
RETLZ orientalize
RETNA Argentinian
RETRL green turtle
RETTO orientation
REUAL irrecusable
irrecusably
irrefutable
irrefutably
irregularly
REUGO tree surgeon
REUGR tree surgery
REUIL irreducible
irreducibly
REWLI green-wellie
REWNO oriel window
RFCEC proficiency
RFDDE draft-dodger
RFGRT prefigurate
RFIAC trefoil arch
RFIKN trafficking
RFNNS profaneness
RFNTO profanation
RFNTR profanatory
RFSEL professedly
RFSNS profuseness
RFSOA craftswoman
RFTRA prefatorial
RFTRL prefatorily
profiterole
RGAOI braggadocio
RGCMD tragicomedy
RGCRN tragic irony
RGDEN tragedienne
RGDOE frigid zones
RGEFS triggerfish
RGESN progressing
RGESO progression
RGESV progressive
RGETR fragmentary
RGNLI original sin
RGNLT originality
RGNTN originating
RGNTO origination
RGNTR progenitors
RGNTV originative
progenitive
RGOYI troglodytic
RGRPC Gregory Peck
RGTBR frigate bird
frigatebird
RGTNN frightening
RGTNR frighteners
RGTUL frightfully
RHBTN prohibiting
RHBTO prohibition
RHBTR prohibitory
RHBTV prohibitive
RHCNR orthocentre
RHEHR Archie Sharp
RHELG archaeology
RHGAH orthography
RHGNU archegonium
RHIAL archaically
RHICS archdiocese
RHIHP archbishops
RHMOC Graham Gooch
RHMWF Graham Swift
RHPEA orthopteran
RHPEI orthopaedic
RHPLG archipelago
RHRIP Arthur Kipps
RHRLS Arthur Bliss
RHROC Arthur Couch
RHRON Arthur Young
RHRPS Arthur's Pass
RHRRW Arthur Brown
RHRTM Arthur's Tomb
RHRVN Arthur Evans
RHSOI orthoscopic
prehistoric
RHSRT orchestrate
RHUHS archduchess
RIAEU urticaceous
RIASI artisanship
RIATR dreikanters
RIAYE ordinary men
RIBAE trailblazer
trail-blazer
train-bearer
RIBRI argie-bargie
RIDMG brain damage
RIDVS pro indiviso
RIEEC arrivederci
RIGHM crying shame
RIHLG ornithology
RILSL brainlessly
fruitlessly
RINTO pre-ignition
RIRGU arbitrageur
RIRME Erwin Rommel
RIRMN arbitrament
RIRRL arbitrarily
RIRTO arbitration
RISCL brainsickly
RISIL Orbitsville
RITAE brainteaser
brain-teaser
RIUAE articulated
orbiculares
RIUAL articulable
orbicularly
RIUAO articulator
RJCIE projectiles
RJDCA prejudicial
RJDCT prejudicate
RJNOE Trojan Women
RJNOS Trojan Horse
RKNHM broken rhyme
RKNUI broken music
RLBRL argle-bargle
RLFCC prolificacy
RLFRT proliferate
RLGMN prolegomena
RLIGI drilling rig
RLINL brilliantly
RLITR oral history
RLMDM troll-my-dame
RLMNR preliminary
RLSNS artlessness
RLSRL prelusorily
RLSVL prelusively
RLTRA proletarian
proletariat
RMAHN drum machine
RMAIA grammatical
RMBUE crème brulée
RMDCA Tremadoc Bay
RMDCT premedicate
RMDNA prima donnas
RMDTT premeditate
RMEAL primaevally
RMECL trumpet call
RMEFL crammed full
RMEOI trompe l'oeil
trompe-l'oeil
RMEOO From Me To You
RMESI premiership
RMESU Dromaeosaur
RMGNA primigenial
RMIHU from without
RMLAO promulgator
RMLNL grumblingly
tremblingly
RMLNS crumbliness
RMLOE trample over
RMLPO Mrs Malaprop
RMLUL tremulously
RMNLA criminal law
RMNLG criminology
RMNLS criminalise
RMNLT criminality
RMNLZ criminalize
RMNME prime number
RMNNL prominently
RMNTO crimination
premonition
RMNTR premonitory
RMOHR from nowhere
RMOMN frame of mind
RMPOI gramophonic
RMRAE Bremerhaven
RMRCL primary cell
RMRHS trimorphism
RMRHU trimorphous
RMSNL promisingly
RMSUT promiscuity
RMSUU promiscuous
RMTOA promotional
RMTRI dramaturgic
RMTRL prematurely
RMTRU crematorium
RMTTD promptitude
RMTVL primitively
RMTVS primitivism
RMUBN Premium Bond
RMXLA premaxillae
RNAAI Gran Canaria
RNADU bring-and-buy
RNALB frontal lobe
RNAPN transalpine
RNATO transaction
RNBHM Grand Bahama
RNBIG Trent Bridge
RNBLE wrong belief
RNCIE transceiver
transcribed
transcriber
RNCYA Grand Cayman
RNDBO Frank Dobson
RNDDA Trinidadian
RNDIE drink-driver
RNEAN orange-tawny
RNEBR Brandenburg
RNECN frondescent
RNEEA bronze medal
RNEIE Orange River
RNENS drunkenness
RNEOT Grangemouth
RNERH Grande Arche
RNESD Princess Ida
RNETA granted that
RNEUI trance music
RNFEL drink freely
RNFGR transfigure
RNFMT bring fame to
RNFNT transfinite
RNFRA transferral
RNFRE frankfurter
transfer fee
transferred
transferrer
transformed
transformer
RNFRI transferrin
RNFRN transfer RNA
RNFSO transfusion
RNFTE grandfather
RNFXO transfixion
RNGAH uranography
RNGNE Grenzgänger
RNGRU crinigerous
RNHAE wrong-headed
RNHAI Granth Sahib
RNHEE trench fever
RNHEV French leave
RNHHL French chalk
RNHMN transhumant
RNHMT bring home to
RNHNL trenchantly
RNHNS crunchiness
RNHOA Frenchwoman
RNHOE Frenchwomen
truncheoner

RNHOS French toast
RNHPE transhipper
RNHRA trencherman
RNHRE French fries
RNHRN French franc
RNHTC French stick
RNHUV French curve
RNIAL frantically
principally
RNICM transit camp
RNINL transiently
RNISL grandiosely
RNIST grandiosity
RNITW Francistown
RNIVS transit visa
RNLAE brand leader
crenellated
RNLCN translucent
RNLCT granulocyte
translocate
RNLMT granulomata
RNLNR translunary
RNLRT granularity
RNLSL frontlessly
RNLTO granulation
translation
RNMNT prenominate
RNMSE Franz Mesmer
Grand Master
grand master
grandmaster
RNMTA transmittal
RNMTE front matter
frontmatter
grandmother
transmitter
RNMTT transmutate
RNNME wrong number
RNNPE grand-nephew
RNOAE Trincomalee
RNODA grand old man
RNOGR ironmongery
RNOHN francophone
RNOTN orang-outang
RNOYI frontolysis
RNPEC transpierce
RNPNE transponder
RNPRE transported
transporter
RNPRN grandparent
transparent
RNPSN transposing
RNRNE front-runner
RNRQA Iran-Iraq War
RNSAC Brands Hatch
RNSAD Aran Islands
RNSDU wrong side up
RNSEV trunksleeve
RNSOL drink slowly
RNSTE trendsetter
RNTBA bring to bear
RNTBO bring to book
RNTHE bring to heel

RNTHL Trinity Hall
RNTLF bring to life
RNTMN bring to mind
RNTPS bring to pass
RNTRA Trinitarian
RNTRU franc-tireur
RNTTR Trinity term
RNUAI transuranic
RNUBR L Ron Hubbard
RNULT tranquility
RNUTI Iron Curtain
RNUWN bring up wind
RNVRA transversal
RNYMT Granny Smith
RNYOD granny bonds
RNZAO Frantz Fanon
ROBCE crookbacked
ROCPE preoccupied
RODIE preordained
ROECN arborescent
ROEHN try one's hand
ROELC try one's luck
ROENS crookedness
ROEUL erroneously
ROEZA Arno Penzias
ROGRE Errol Garner
ROHGU creophagous
ROHRU eriophorous
ROILG cryobiology
RORDA armoured car
RORLT armour-plate
ROSII proof spirit
ROUGR cryosurgery
ROWLE Orson Welles
RPAIL drop rapidly
RPAON grope around
RPAOO propranolol
RPCRS drop a curtsy
RPDTO trepidation
RPDTR trepidatory
RPEAC dropped arch
RPEON triple point
RPERW triple crown
RPEUI wrapped up in
RPGTO propagation
RPGTV propagative
RPIAL cryptically
graphically
RPINS graphicness
RPITR proprietary
proprietors
RPLEC prepollence
prepollency
RPLTS propylitise
RPLTZ propylitize
RPLWT grapple with
RPNSM trypanosome
RPNTO trepanation
RPNUT propinquity
RPOGN drop-forging
RPOHN tryptophane
RPOOI graphologic
RPORP cryptograph

RPOWR prop forward
RPRAS proper-false
RPRIN proportions
RPRNT preparing to
RPRTO preparation
RPRTR preparatory
RPRYA property man
RPSHR troposphere
RPSIC drop a stitch
RPSTO preposition
proposition
RPSUA crepuscular
RPTAL propitiable
RPTAO propitiator
RPTTO crepitation
RPVSG tripe-visag'd
RPYAI prophylaxis
RPZFR trapeziform
RRBNO Mrs Robinson
RRGTO prorogation
RRGTV prerogative
RSALI crystalloid
RSALN crystalline
RSALS crystallise
RSALZ crystallize
RSAON press around
RSASN trespassing
RSBRE cross-border
Pressburger
RSBTE frostbitten
RSCFE Irish coffee
RSCRL dress circle
RSCTA crosscut saw
RSCTE grass-cutter
RSCTO prosecution
RSCUI cross cousin
RSDOE preside over
RSEJH Prester John
RSESI trusteeship
RSETV prospective
RSFLE crestfallen
RSHNE Irish Hunter
RSHPE grasshopper
RSHTA bruschettas
RSHTC prosthetics
RSIAI prussic acid
RSIAL drastically
prosaically
RSIFC cross-infect
RSIIU prestigious
RSINL presciently
RSINS Prussianise
RSINZ Prussianize
RSISM prestissimo
RSITO prosciuttos
RSKLN prusik sling
RSLAI trisyllabic
RSLAL trisyllable
RSLGE cross-legged
RSLNS bristliness
gristliness
RSLTS proselytise
proselytism

RSLTZ proselytize
RSLWR trestlework
RSLWT wrestle with
RSMKN dressmaking
RSMNL presumingly
RSMNS irksomeness
RSMTO presumption
RSMTV presumptive
RSNAL presentable
presentably
RSNAM present arms
RSNMN presentment
RSNTF presanctify
RSNTM present-time
RSOPN Prestonpans
RSORC aristocracy
RSOSI press of sail
RSOTO arms control
RSPOE presupposed
RSRAL preservable
RSRBN prescribing
RSRSE pre-stressed
RSRTN frustrating
RSRTO frustration
prostration
RSRUG Fraserburgh
RSSIC cross-stitch
RSSOD cross swords
RSSOE brisés volés
RSTBA cross to bear
RSTLN fresh talent
RSUDC Iris Murdoch
RSUIE pressurized
RSUNS brusqueness
RSUOO Prosauropod
RSWRH trustworthy
RTAAI prothalamia
RTATL protractile
RTATO protraction
RTBRN protuberant
RTBRT protuberate
RTCCA Arctic Ocean
RTCLS protocolise
protocolist
RTCLT criticality
RTCLZ protocolize
RTCRS protectress
RTCSE criticaster
RTEAA fritter away
RTEDW written down
RTEHO brotherhood
RTESI tritheistic
RTEWS or otherwise
RTFLO grateful for
RTGNS protagonist
tritagonist
RTGNU erotogenous
RTHPE froth-hopper
RTIIA fratricidal
RTITN arm-twisting
RTLAI fritillaria
RTLNS brittleness
RTMTC arithmetics

RTNDS writing-desk
RTNEL pretendedly
RTNIN pretensions
RTNIU pretentious
RTNMT protonemata
RTNTB pretend to be
RTOAE prothoraces
prothoraxes
RTOFO write off for
RTOIT fritto misto
RTPIH troth-plight
RTRAL fraternally
RTRCT erythrocyte
RTRIE fraternizer
RTRMI prothrombin
RTRTO trituration
RTRZI Proterozoic
RTSNS Britishness
brutishness
RTSUL grotesquely
RTSUR grotesquery
RTSWR British warm
RTUNS fretfulness
RTYEN pretty penny
RTYOA Pretty Woman
RTYOL Pretty Polly
RUDEE ground-level
RUDLE ground elder
RUDLU trous-de-loup
RUDOE ground cover
RUDWL ground swell
RUESI trouser suit
RUHCU Groucho Club
RUHIO wrought iron
RUHMR Groucho Marx
RUHNS drouthiness
grouchiness
RUHSA draughtsman
RULFE trouble-free
RULSM troublesome
RULSO trouble spot
RULUL troublously
RUOFV Group of Five
RUPOE triumph over
RUTER group theory
RUTVL irruptively
RUUEC fraudulence
fraudulency
RUUNS arduousness
RUVRT triumvirate
RVANS trivialness
RVBLT drivability
RVCTO provocation
RVCTV provocative
RVDGE grave-digger
RVDNL providently
RVFSE drive faster
RVIOE prevail over
RVIUO prevail upon
RVKNL provokingly
RVLER travel-weary
RVLGN travel agent
RVLLN travel along
RVLNL prevalently
RVLON travel round
RVLUD travel guide
RVLUL frivolously
RVLYA travel by car
RVMTI gravimetric
RVNAL preventable
RVNEC provenience
RVNIL preventible
RVNIO driving iron
RVNMG graven image
RVNRZ driven crazy
RVNSA driving seat
RVNTS driving test
RVRAL traversable
RVRCT prevaricate
RVRHR try very hard
RVROE Trevor-Roper
RVSOA previsional
provisional❑
RVSRL provisorily
RVTFE gravity-feed
RVTNS privateness
RVTTO gravitation
RVTVL privatively
RWAIL grow rapidly
RWAON crowd around
RWBAO draw a bead on
RWCLN crown colony
RWCVR draw a covert
RWEHA crowned head
RWELN crawler lane
RWETN browbeating
RWEWT crowded with
RWHCO draw the crow
RWHLN draw the line
RWJWL crown jewels
RWMLE grow smaller
RWNBC drawing back
RWNOG draw in rough
RWNRO drawing-room
RWOHA draw to a head
RWONN draw to an end
RWPIC crown prince
RWRNS frowardness
RWSIL Brownsville
RWTNS frowstiness
RWUCL grow quickly
RXMTL proximately
RYGIS pray against
RYRHE prayer wheel
RYRUL prayerfully
RZAIL Brazzaville
RZLBA grizzly bear
RZNAE frozen water
RZNLN grazing land
RZNTF frozen-stiff
RZPVN crazy paving
RZWNE prizewinner
prize-winner
SAAIO Isaac Asimov
SACEO estancieros
SADFA Island of Rab
SADVR Oswald Avery
SAEGN estate agent
SAEHE escape wheel
SAEOS a slate loose
SALSE established
establisher
SANWO Isaac Newton
SAPTA Isaac Pitman
SASNT assassinate
SCEEI psychedelia
psychedelic
SCIAL psychically
SCITI psychiatric
SCOAH psychopathy
SCOEI psychogenic
SCORM psychodrama
SCRNS isochronise
SCRNU isochronous
SCRNZ isochronize
SEATS Esperantist
SEFIH Isle of Wight
SEIAL ascetically
SELGS osteologist
SEMYK Issey Miyake
SEPAT osteoplasty
SEPTI osteopathic
SESVL ostensively
SETAI aspect ratio
SETAL essentially
SETNL assentingly
SETOT a sweet tooth
SETTO ostentation
SETVL assertively
SFROE ask for money
ask for votes
SFYAI as if by magic
SHTLG eschatology
SHTRS aspheterise
SHTRZ aspheterize
SIESO as like as not
SIGRC asking price
SIIAE assimilated
SILGA oscillogram
SILTN oscillating
SILTO oscillation
SILTR oscillatory
SIMTS astigmatism
SINTO assignation
SIUUL assiduously
SLIEB as claimed by
SLSNS uselessness
SMLSI esemplastic
SMRHS isomorphism
SMRHU isomorphous
SNDOE Tsung-Dao Lee
SNXML as an example
SOIAL osmotically
SOIHN astonishing
SOITO association
SOITV associative
SOKVK Tsiolkovsky
SOLKI As You Like It
SPOET as opposed to
SPRIL psi particle
SRCLK ostrich-like
SRMGR A Shrimp Girl
SRNEC astringency
SRNET a stranger to
SRNMS astronomise
SRNMZ astronomize
SRPOI astraphobia
SRSLO as a result of
STAOI psittacosis
STAPN as it happens
STCMI ask to come in
STIHB as it might be
STRCS esotericism
SUENM assumed name
SUENS assuredness
SUGMN assuagement
SUIUL astuciously
SUJGT assubjugate
SUOOI pseudopodia
SUOOP pseudomorph
SUWSL use unwisely
SYILG Assyriology
SZAAO Zsa Zsa Gabor
TAAIE Ottawa River
TABIE steam boiler
TAEGN steam engine
TAEIA strategical
TAFSL steadfastly
TAGLT strangulate
TAGNS strangeness
TAGTA straight man
TAGTF straight off
TAGTS straightish
TAGTU straight out
TAHCS attaché case
attaché-case
TAHLD Strathclyde
TAHNE strap-hanger
TAIIU atrabilious
TAJCE steam jacket
TANAG strain gauge
TAOYI steatopygia
TAPCE steam-packet
TARLE steamroller
steam-roller
TATAE strait-laced
TAVSE steam vessel
TAWIH straw-weight
TBOET stab to death
TBTAE Stabat Mater
TCAON stick around
TCBOE stockbroker
TCHUE Stockhausen
TCIGU sticking out
TCISC stick insect
TCJBE stockjobber
TCLBC stickleback
TCMRE stock market
TCOSE stick or snee
TCOTO stick out for
TCPRS stock phrase
TCTKN stocktaking

TCUWT stock up with
TDOOC studio couch
TDSAC at a distance
TDSON at a discount
TDTRE Studs Terkel
TECAL stretchable
TEELS etherealise
TEELZ etherealize
TEKNS streakiness
TELJC steeplejack
TEMIE streamlined
TEMNL streamingly
TEMNS streaminess
TEPAE steel-plated
TESDU stressed out
stressed-out
TESIA atheistical
TETAD streetwards
TETAU street value
TETEE street-level
TETIH streetlight
TETTO attestation
TETUD street guide
TETVL attentively
TEUST strenuosity
TEUTO attenuation
TEUUL strenuously
TEWRE steelworker
TFMME staff member
TFNCE stiff-necked
TFOLF staff of life
TGAIE stigmatized
TGESV St Agnes's Eve
TGFIH stage fright
TGLTO stagflation
TGMNG stage-manage
TGNPS staging post
TGSRC stage-struck
TGSUU stegosaurus❑
THBCO at the back of
THDUL at the double
THFEO at the feet of
THGCS at a high cost
THHAO at the head of
THHNO at the hand of
THLTS at the latest
THMMN at the moment
THNPL itching palm
THOTE at the outset
THRAO at the rear of
THROO at the root of
THSLC at this place
THSON at this point
THSTG at this stage
THTMO at the time of
THTON at that point
THWIO at the whim of
TIANS ethicalness
TIEAD strike hands
TIELT strike plate
TIEOA strike you as
TIEON strikebound
TIEPS strike a pose
TIGIC string piece
TIGLN string along
TIGNL stringently
TIGNS stringiness
TIITM it pitieth me
TILSL stainlessly
TISAC strip search
TISHN at first hand
TIUAO stridulator
TKALI stake a claim
TLAAO stellarator
TLADL still and all
TLADN still and end
TLCAI atelectasis
atelectatic
TLCII stalactitic
TLEAC stilted arch
TLEET at all events
TLENS stiltedness
TLGII stalagmitic
TLIYN stultifying
TLNOD stolen goods
TLNOE stolen money
TLOAU A Tale of a Tub
TLOEN at a loose end
TLOFR St Elmo's fire
TLPIT at all points
TLSNS stylishness
TLTCS athleticism
TLTRA utilitarian
TLTRO utility room
TLZTO stylization
utilization
TMCFL stomachfuls
TMCIA stomachical
TMCLC atomic clock
TMCPM stomach pump
TMLGS etymologise
etymologist
TMLGZ etymologize
TMLNL stumblingly
TMLTN stimulating
TMLTO stimulation
TMLTV stimulative
TMTLG stomatology
TMZTO itemization
TNADS standardise
TNADZ standardize
TNAES stand at ease
TNCRE stone curlew
stone-curlew
TNCRL stone circle
TNCRU ethnic group
TNENS stintedness
stuntedness
TNEVL at intervals
TNGAH ethnography
stenography
TNGON stoneground
TNIGU standing out
TNILN stand in line
stencilling
TNIWT stand in with
TNLGS ethnologist
TNOFS standoffish
stand-offish
TNRND stun grenade
TNRNL itinerantly
TNSLO at one's elbow
TNTGI stand to gain
TNWLE stonewaller
TNWSE stonewashed
TOABR Otto Warburg
TOERS Athole brose
TOGOC strong force
TOGON strong point
TOGRN strong drink
TOIUL atrociously
TOKLK it looks like
TOLSE it would seem
TONWR St John's wort
TOOCP stroboscope
TOPEI atmospheric
TOPGO stool pigeon
TOSED at loose ends
TPAKN stop talking
TPANN stop raining
TPAOI stephanotis
TPCLT atypicality
TPEKN Stephen King
TPEWL Steppenwolf
TPHRO stop short of
TPHSO stop the show
TPIGU stopping-out
TPLTO stipulation
TPLTR stipulatory
TPNIR stipendiary
TPNIT stipendiate
TPODN stop holding
TPOKN stop working
TPOWR step forward
TPRTE stepbrother
TRACT Eternal City
TRALF eternal life
TRBTO attribution
TRBTV attributive
TRCET attracted to
TRCNR storm centre
TRDCY pterodactyl
TRFAI Star of David
TRGRO storage room
TRHME Star Chamber
TRHNS starchiness
TRILN star billing
TRKEE storekeeper
TRLNL startlingly
TROCP stereoscope
stereoscopy
TROEE stereometer
TROER stereometry
TROHN stereophony
TRORP stereograph
TROYE stereotyped
stereotyper
TROYI stereotypic
TRPTE storm petrel
TRRSE star-crossed
TRTDE star-studded
TRTLE storyteller
TRTOA attritional
TRTVL iteratively
TRUAO sternutator
TRUBN stirrup bone
TRUPM stirrup pump
TRWNO storm window
TRYIH Starry Night
TSADE stoss and lee
TSAWN etesian wind
TSEDN Otis Redding
TTFRL state firmly
TTLHM stately home
TTLNS stateliness
TTOCP stethoscope
TTOFU state of flux
TTOMN state of mind
TTOPA state of play
TTSHO state school
TTSML state simply
TTSOA stateswoman
TTTBO statute book
TTTML statute mile
TTTRL statutorily
TUBIG Stourbridge
TUCNS staunchness
TULLS at full blast
TULPE at full speed
TUTNL struttingly
TUTVL attuitively
TVEMT Stevie Smith
TVMRI Steve Martin
TVRTR at every turn
TWRSI stewardship
TYHPC stay the pace
TYLST stay close to
UAACT put a match to
UAAFO run away from
UAAWT run away with
UABIG human beings
UABLS funambulist
UABLT funambulate
UACIA autarchical
UADAE fun and games
UADAT cut and paste
UADBU out and about
UADOE cut and cover
UADRE cut and dried
cut-and-dried
UADTO suraddition
UAFLD Susan Faludi
UAIII Mutabilitie
UAIUL audaciously
UAKAE Tutankhamen
UALAU Human League
UALNS curableness
durableness
UAMDI Muhammad Zia
UAMDL Muhammad Ali
UAMNA gum ammoniac
UANTR human nature

UANVG Suzanne Vega
UAOIM fumatoriums
UAOLA sugar of lead
UAOSI curatorship
UAPIS Judas Priest
UARAL subaerially
UARCO put a price on
UARGT human rights
UARKO put a brake on
UASFE sugar sifter
UASIL human shield
UASML subassemble
UASNA Susan Sontag
UATVT durante vita
UAWNO Judas-window
UBEDN outbreeding
UBEFL tumblerfuls
UBEHO Pumblechook
UBENE bubble under
UBERE tumble-drier
UBETI rumble strip
UBIDN outbuilding
UBJMO mumbo-jumbos
UBLNL quibblingly
turbulently
UBNTB husband-to-be
UBONE dumbfounded
dumbfounder
UBRAL Cumbernauld
UBRGM numbers game
UBRIL D'Urberville
UBRLN rubber plant
UBRLT number plate
UBRPO numbers pool
UBRTM rubber stamp
rubber-stamp
UBSHA rubbish heap
rubbish-heap
UBSIU rumbustious
UBSUU rumbustuous
UBTWY cut both ways
UBYIL Durbeyfield
UCAEA purchase tax
UCAST quick assets
UCBCE bunch-backed
hunchbacked
UCDNU succedaneum
UCEBR butcherbird
UCEOE muscle power
UCEON muscle-bound
UCFEZ quick-freeze
UCFIH quick flight
UCFRU furciferous
UCFUU dulcifluous
UCHUE Münchhausen
UCIIA subclinical
UCIIU punctilious
UCINE function key
UCINN functioning
UCINO junction box
UCINR functionary
UCLAO auscultator
UCLNL succulently
UCLRT muscularity
UCLTR musculature
UCLUA subcultural
UCLUE mud-coloured
UCMVN quick-moving
UCNLG vulcanology
UCNRC subcontract
UCNRR subcontrary
UCPIL susceptible
susceptibly
UCRIG gun carriage
UCRTD pulchritude
UCSIK quick-sticks
UCSLE quacksalver
quicksilver
UCSLS successless
UCULS succourless
UCULT punctuality
UCUTO punctuation
UCWTE quick-witted
UDAHN quadraphony
UDEFL hundredfold
UDEFU bundle of fun
UDENA quadrennial
UDENS subduedness
UDLAA Guadalcanal
UDLJR Guadalajara
UDMNA fundamental
UDMNN subdominant
UDNET sudden death
UDNSA guiding star
UDNTR sudden start
UDODN fundholding
UDOMA outdoor meal
UDRUL murderously
UDSAC outdistance
UDUBR Ruud Lubbers
UDUEA quadrupedal
UDVSO subdivision
UDVSV subdivisive
UDWTR Muddy Waters
UDYPR Sunday Sport
UDYUC Sunday lunch
UEAIN rubefacient
tumefacient
UEAON superabound
UEAPE funeral poem
UEASN funeral song
UEATO rubefaction
tumefaction
UEBRE Jules Bordet
UECAG supercharge
UECFI queer cuffin
UECLS tuberculise
UECLT tuberculate
UECLZ tuberculize
UECNL quiescently
UEDRA Musée d'Orsay
UEECN juvenescent
UEEDW quieten down
UEFCA superficial
UEFCE superficies
UEFHE rule of three
UEFHM rule of thumb
UEFTE superfatted
UEFTT superfetate
UEFUT superfluity
UEFUU superfluous
UEGDE Rumer Godden
UEIAL eugenically
numerically
UEIDC superinduce
UEIFC superinfect
UEIOE queen it over
UEIPS superimpose
UEIRT superiority
UEITN superintend
UELMT outer limits
UELNS queenliness
UELOE pure-blooded
UELTV superlative
UEMIC museum piece
UEMRE supermarket
UEMTE queen mother
UENTN supernatant
UEOOA iure coronae
UERET nuée ardente
UESCU Queen's Scout
UESEC Queen's Bench
UESRB superscribe
UESRC superstruct
UESRE Queer Street
UESRP superscript
UESUD Queen's Guide
UETAR Hubert Parry
UETNE supertanker
UEUNS tunefulness
UEURC bureaucracy
UEVSN supervising
UEVSO supervision
UEVSR supervisors
supervisory
UFAET suffragette
UFATN surfcasting
UFCEC sufficience
sufficiency
UFCMI surface mail
UFCTN suffocating
UFCTO suffocation
UFCTV suffocative
UFMGT suffumigate
UFNPF huff and puff
UFRLN Dunfermline
UFRLO out for blood
UFRTC buffer stock
UFRTT buffer state
UFXTO suffixation
UGDUO Ouagadougou
UGEEE Jungle Fever
jungle fever
UGERE jungle-green
UGEUC jungle juice
UGMNA judgemental
UGMSE burgomaster
UGRAC hunger march
UGRAI Vulgar Latin
UGSEC turgescence
UGSIL suggestible
UGSIN suggestions
UGTRA purgatorial
UGTVL purgatively
UHAIE Hugh Latimer
UHAKN bushwalking
UHAPL Hugh Walpole
UHBIE much obliged
UHBRS Dukhobortsy
UHBUI much about it
UHEDL Ruth Rendell
UHHCE bushwhacker
UHHOG push through
UHHSM much the same
UHLGO euchologion
UHMSI euphemistic
UHNSA push one's way
UHNSC such-and-such
UHNSL push oneself
UHOGL push roughly
UHOMN mushrooming
UHOWR push forward
rush forward
UHRNS Lutheranism
UHRSI eucharistic ❑
UHRTE authorities
UHTMC eurhythmics
UHTMS eurhythmist
UIAAI Yuri Gagarin
UIAIA puritanical
UIAIE subimagines
UIANS musicalness
UIARS put it across
UIATA Surinam toad
UICAG put in charge
UICAN put in chains
UICNR music centre
UIDNE put in danger
UIECN luminescent
UIESA businessman
UIESN business end
UIETN pumice stone
UIETR rudimentary
UIGLS ruling class
UIHDO punished for
UIHNL punishingly
UIIAL juridically
municipally
UIIEC munificence
UIIRE auxiliaries
UIITN humiliating
UIITO humiliation
UIITR humiliatory
UIITV humiliative
UIIUL judiciously
UILAL burial-vault
UILBL Lucille Ball
UILLC burial place
burial-place
UILON burial mound
UILPR Muriel Spark
UIMLL put it mildly

UIMNO put in mind of
UIMTI audiometric
UIMTO put in motion
UIMTS numismatist
UINRA Julian Bream
UINRU Lucien Freud
UIOIM auditoriums
UIPIO put in prison
UIPLA Judit Polgar
UIPPA tulip poplar
UIRGT subirrigate
UIRSI hudibrastic
UIRUL ludicrously
UISHO music school
UISTE curiosities
UITDB run into debt
UITOA cut it too fat
UIUAL auricularly
UIUNS curiousness
dubiousness
dutifulness
furiousness
UIVSA audiovisual
UJCET subjected to
UJCLS subjectless
UJCSI subjectship
UJGTO subjugation
UJNTO subjunction
UJNTV subjunctive
UKENE buckle under
UKNFS Burkina Faso
UKOLC cuckoo clock
UKRUC sucker-punch
UKSBT Turkish bath
UKSLR Turkish lira
ULABM nuclear bomb
ULACE gull-catcher
ULAEA pull faces at
ULAFE nuclear fuel
ULATF bull-mastiff
ULBLO hullaballoo
ULBLT gullibility
ULBSA hurl abuse at
ULCNM Public Enemy
public enemy
ULCOK public works
ULCOS public house
ULCRE full-acorned
ULCTN duplicating
ULCTO duplication
publication
ULCTU duplicitous
ULCUS public purse
ULCZN publicizing
ULERE bull-terrier
ULERS guelder rose
ULFAL qualifiable
ULFDA full of ideas
nullifidian
ULFEL qualifiedly
ULFEN full of beans
ULFER full of years
ULFIT put life into
ULFRO bully for you
ULHAO pull ahead of
ULHOG pull through
ULIAI nucleic acid
ULIHE bullfighter
ULIUE full-figured
ULKHL run like hell
ULLMU Kuala Lumpur
ULLOE full-blooded
ULLSL guilelessly
guiltlessly
ULLTN pullulating
ULLTO pullulation
ULMNS sublimeness
ULMTO sublimation
ULNBC pulling back
ULNDW pulling-down
ULNOE mulling over
mulling-over
pull one over
ULNVI null and void
ULOCI bulldog clip
ULOTE full-mouthed
ULRDE guilt-ridden
ULRIE dull-brained
ULRNA full-frontal
ULRUH full-fraught
ULSNS bullishness
gutlessness
sunlessness
ULTIG pull strings
ULTLS built to last
ULTRO bulletproof
bullet-proof
ULTTM quality time
ULTTV qualitative
ULUPS dual-purpose
ULWIE Curlew River
ULYAT guilty party
ULYOR Dudley Moore
UMBTO tummy-button
UMGSL rummage sale
UMKUO put make-up on
UMLIL submultiple
UMMOU summum bonum
UMNAL augmentable
UMNBR hummingbird
Humming-Bird
UMNNU summoning-up
UMNTN culminating
fulminating
UMNTO culmination
fulmination
UMNTR fulminatory
UMRAL summersault
UMREC submergence
UMRIA submarginal
UMRIL submergible
submersible
UMRNL murmuringly
UMRNS summariness
UMROS summerhouse
UMRTO murmuration
UMRUL murmurously
UMRZN summarizing
UMSDY Burmese Days
UMSIL submissible
UMTOA summational
UMUTN surmounting
UNEPN Juan-les-Pins
UNFPE turn of speed
UNGIS turn against
UNIHG Quintin Hogg
UNLID tunnel diode
UNNAA running away
running-away
turning away
UNNDW running-down
turning-down
UNNHA running head
UNNKO running knot
UNNLT running late
UNNMT running mate
UNNNS cunningness
UNNTX running text
UNOPA turn to speak
UNOTN turn to stone
UNRBI bunny rabbit
UNRIO turn traitor
UNSDU sunny side up
UNSIE Buenos Aires
UNSIG furnishings
UNUJM quantum jump
UNULA quantum leap
UNUNI quinquennia
UNUNS ruinousness
UNURM quinquereme
UNUTB turn out to be
UNUWL turn out well
UNYOE Quincy Jones
UOAPR put on a spurt
UOARC Out of Africa
UOATO out of action
UOBET out of breath
UOBUD out of bounds
UODNE out of danger
UODNT subordinate
UOEES auto-reverse
UOEMN put one's mind
UOEMR put one's mark
UOENS Europeanise
Europeanism
Europeanist
UOENZ Europeanize
UOERE Hugo De Vries
UOETI Eurocentric
UOFEP Rudolf Kempe
UOFON cut-off point
UOFVU out of favour
UOHHN autochthons
UOHMU out of humour
UOHNE autochanger
UOIAL bucolically
UOKLE out of kilter
UOLSI autoplastic
UOLVA Yugoslavian
UONTO subornation
UOOII automobilia
UOPCE out of pocket
UORCR put on record
UORPI autographic
autotrophic
UORTS autoerotism
UORTU Hugo Grotius
UOSAO out of season
UOTAT cut out waste
UOTEA out of the way
out-of-the-way
put on the map
UOTEO put on the dog
UOTER out of the ark
UOTIG sum of things
UOTME out of temper
UOWIH put on weight
UPAAS bumpsadaisy
UPBLT culpability
UPCEL suspectedly
UPCTO auspication
UPEAC purple patch
UPEER Purple Heart
purple heart
purpleheart
UPESN suppressant
UPESO suppression
UPESV suppressive
UPHAE puppy-headed
UPIEL surprisedly
UPINL suppliantly
UPITO Pulp Fiction
UPIUL bumptiously
UPNBA jumping-bean
UPNEU suspenseful
UPNJC jumping-jack
UPRAC supportance
UPRAL supportable
supportably
UPRDV Humphry Davy
UPREL purportedly
UPRIC Humperdinck
UPRLS supportless
UPRMU out-paramour
UPRRC dumper truck
UPRTN suppurating
UPRTO suppuration
UPRTV suppurative
UPSAL surpassable
UPSLS purposeless
UPSNS lumpishness
UPSTO supposition
UPSTR suppository
UPUAO sulphurator
UPUEU sulphureous
UPUST sumptuosity
UPUTF sulphur tuft
UPUUL sumptuously
UPYIE supply-sider
URATO gut reaction
URCLM curriculums
URCNE hurricanoes

URCTO lubrication
rubrication
UREAL puerperally
UREBC quarterback
UREDC quarter deck
quarterdeck
URELN quarrelling
URELU quarrellous
URENS guardedness
hurriedness
URESM quarrelsome
URETN quarter tone
UREWT quarrel with
URFVU curry favour
URGTO subrogation
URILR guerrillero
URLUL querulously
URMCS supremacism
supremacist
URMNA nutrimental
URMNS supremeness
URMTS Suprematism
URNCE cupro-nickel
URNEE surrenderer
URPWE curry powder
URSEC putrescence
URSUR hurry-scurry
URTAH turret lathe
URTOA nutritional
URTVL lucratively
nutritively
URUDN surrounding
URYIL Murrayfield
USABU Russian Blue
USADN outstanding
USADR substandard
USATA substantial
USATN outsmarting
USATV substantive
USCEL put secretly
USDLF outside left
USHWR mum's the word
USIGN mudslinging
mud-slinging
USINN questioning
USIUE substituted
USIUN substituent
USLAE Luis Alvarez
USMNS fulsomeness
USMOD Sursum Corda
USMTO subsumption
USMTV subsumptive
USNET bums on seats
USNHM nursing home
USNOT Puss in Boots
USOEL outspokenly
USQEC subsequence
USRBR subscribers
USRBT subscribe to
USRCO substractor
USRIH put straight
USRIN subservient
USRMI nurserymaid
USRSO put stress on
USRTV substrative
USSEC subsistence
USTMT guesstimate
USUCN outsourcing
USWLO pussy willow
USWRE guest worker
UTADE muntjac deer
UTAEA Punta Arenas
UTAGE Furtwängler
UTAMS nuptial Mass
UTATO subtraction
UTATV subtractive
UTBEO suitable for
UTBLT quotability
suitability
UTBUT just about to
UTCIE mustachioed
UTCSI justiceship
UTCTO rustication
UTEAC furtherance
UTEET just deserts
UTEIO put the lid on
UTEMR furthermore
UTEMS furthermost
UTESM furthersome
UTESN buttressing
UTETA further than
UTETN furthest end
UTEUR run the guard
UTFAL justifiable
justifiably
UTFIH put to flight
UTFUT Tutti Frutti
tutti-frutti
UTGON run to ground
UTGTE put together
run together
UTHGW hunt-the-gowk
UTHOG hunt through
UTHSM just the same
UTIAL sustainable
UTICL curtain call
UTIDT rumti-iddity
UTIEL sustainedly
UTIMN curtailment
sustainment
UTIWL curtain wall
UTLRA fustilarian
fustilirian
UTMOS custom house
UTMRL customarily
UTMUL custom-built
UTNBC cutting back
UTNEG cutting edge
UTNHP mutton chops
UTNHR hunting-horn
UTNSA hunting-seat
UTNSL suit oneself
UTNTN Huntington's
UTOEE dust-covered
rust-covered
UTOIA subtropical
UTONE hunt counter
UTOPM suction pump
UTPEE cut to pieces
multiplexer
UTPRU multiparous
UTPYN multiplying
UTRCA multiracial
UTRCU Culture Club
UTRGT put to rights
UTRLE butterflies
UTRLS gutturalise
UTRLZ gutturalize
UTRNL mutteringly
UTRNO put to ransom
UTRNP guttersnipe
UTRRA butter cream
UTRRS Günter Grass
gutter press
UTRSE Mustard-seed
UTRTR custard tart
UTSOE multistorey
UTUDN suet pudding
UTUNS hurtfulness
lustfulness
UTUPN tub-thumping
UTUSL Kurt Russell
UTVDR Gustave Doré
UTVLM Gustav Klimt
UTVLN multivalent
UTVNS furtiveness
UTVOS Gustav Holst
UTVTO cultivation
UUACR run up a score
UUAIH put up a fight
UUBNS suburbanise
UUBNT suburbanite
UUBNZ suburbanize
UUCLU Aulus Celsus
furunculous
UUDDE cut up didoes
UUILO augur ill for
UUINL luxuriantly
UUITI luxuriate in
UUIUL luxuriously
UURTO susurration
UUTNA Augustinian
UVILN surveillant
UVLNA curvilinear
UVRLN pulverulent
UVRNL quaveringly
quiveringly
UVRNS quaveriness
UWRFR outward form
UWRNS outwardness
UYALN Judy Garland
UYEDN ruby wedding
UYEVC jury service
UYFIE duty officer
UZIAL quizzically
VCTVL evocatively
VDNIR evidentiary
VGNTO evagination
VIDPI avoirdupois
VLNAG Evelyn Waugh
VNEIA evangelical
VNNMA evening meal
VNSEC evanescence
VNULS eventualise
VNULT eventuality
VNULZ eventualize
VPRTN evaporating
VPRTO evaporation
VPRTV evaporative
VPRUL oviparously
VRAAC overbalance
VRADE overhandled
VRAGN overhanging
VRATN everlasting□
VRCIV overachieve
VREEO overdevelop
VREIE overrefined
over-refined
VRELU overzealous
over-zealous
VRENN overweening
VREPE overpeopled
VRERN overbearing
VRESR overmeasure
VRETE overleather
overweather
VRGIS over against
VRGNS averageness
VRHHL over the hill
VRHHM over the hump
VRHLE overwhelmed
VRHMO over the moon
VRHOD over the odds
VRHRE overcharged
VRITR overpicture
VRLWN overflowing
VRNOE over and over
VRNUG overindulge
over-indulge
VROEE overpowered
VROEL Ivor Novello
VROET overmodesty
VROKN overlooking
VRORC overcorrect
VRPRO every person
VRRAH over-breathe
VRRCS overprecise
over-precise
VRRDC overproduce
VRRHN overarching
VRRIH overfreight
VRRSE overdressed
VRRSL overwrestle
VRRSN ever-present
VRRTC overprotect
VRRUH overwrought
VRRWE overcrowded
VRSCN every second
VRSNL every single
VRTEC overstretch
VRUNN overrunning
VRUWT overrun with

Words marked □ can also be spelled with an initial capital letter

VRXIE overexcited
VSVNS evasiveness
VTRAL eviternally
WADIH two and eight
WECCL sweet cicely
WECUS sweet course
WEETD Sweeney Todd
WEPPE sweet pepper
WEPTT sweet potato
sweet-potato
WESAE sweepstakes
WESER sweet sherry
WETME sweet temper
WGTOD Dwight Moody
WLEHA swelled head
WLEOT twelvemonth
WLODV swallow-dive
WLOTI swallow tail
swallowtail
WNACL Ewan MacColl
WNAWO Gwen Harwood
WNBIG swing bridge
WNENL swingeingly
WNLNL twanglingly
WNLTE swingletree
WNOEE swingometer
WNSNS swinishness
WNWLL swing wildly
WNYEC twenty pence
WPNYI twopenny bit
WRBAE sword-bearer
WRHNS swarthiness
WROTM a work of time
WSIRO kwashiorkor
WSMNS awesomeness
WTELN Switzerland
WTHLD switchblade
WTHOR switchboard
WTHRS twitch grass
WVLHI swivel-chair
WWRNS awkwardness
XAAIN excavations
XAITO expatiate on
expatiation
XASIL exhaustible
XASPP exhaust pipe
XASVL expansively
XBRNL exuberantly
XCRAE exacerbated
XCTIE executrices
executrixes
XCTOE executioner
XCTRA executorial
XCTVL executively
XEDNL exceedingly
XEDTR expenditure
XEIIU expeditious
XEINE experienced
experiences
XEINL expediently
XEIRS exteriorise
XEIRZ exteriorize
XELNL excellently
XEMNT exterminate
XENLS externalise
XENLZ externalize
XEPRR extemporary
XEPRS extemporise
XEPRZ extemporize
XESVL excessively
expensively
extensively
XETNL expectantly
expectingly
XETOA exceptional
XETRN expectorant
XETRT expectorate
XETTO expectation
XEUTN extenuating
XEUTO extenuation
XEUTR extenuatory
XEUTV extenuative
XGEAE exaggerated
XGEAO exaggerator
XGNTO oxygenation
XIAAE exhilarated
XICTO exsiccation
XIENS excitedness
XIETR ex-directory
XIPTO extirpation
XIPTR extirpatory
XLCTO explication
XLCTR explicatory
XLCTV explicative
XLENS exaltedness
XLIAA explain away
XLIAL explainable
exploitable
XLMTO exclamation
XLMTR exclamatory
XLNTO explanation
XLNTR explanatory
XLRTO exploration
XLRTR exploratory
XLRTV explorative
XLSVL exclusively
explosively
XLSVO exclusive of
XLSVT exclusivity
XMLRL exemplarily
XMNTO examination
XNHMT exanthemata
XNRTO exoneration
XNRTV exonerative
XOAIA axiomatical
XOCSI ex concessis
XODHR Oxfordshire
XOETA exponential
XOITO excoriation
exfoliation
XOITV exfoliative
XOOIA axiological
XOSVL extorsively
XOTAT ex post facto
XOTCT excorticate
XOTLT expostulate
XOTOE extortioner
XOTTO exhortation
exportation
XOTTR exhortatory
XOTTV exhortative
XRCAG extra charge
XRCAL extractable
XRCTO extrication
XRDTO extradition
XRIAC exorbitance
XRIAL exercisable
XRMNA excremental
XRMTE extremities
XRPIT expropriate
XRPLT extrapolate
XRSEC excrescence
XRSIL expressible
XRSIN expressions
XRVGN extravagant
XRVRE extroverted
XRVRI extra virgin
XRVST extravasate
XSEAE exasperated
XSEEA exoskeletal
XSEEO exoskeleton
XSETA existential
XUGTO expurgation
XUPTO exculpation
XUPTR exculpatory
XUSTL exquisitely
XUSVL excursively
XUTME exeunt omnes
YACLG gynaecology
YAGRT pyrargyrite
YAIAL dynamically
pyramidally
YAIDE Myra Hindley
YAIIA pyramidical
YANSU tyrannosaur
YANUL tyrannously
YAOEE dynamometer
YATOA Dylan Thomas
YATRP lycanthropy
YBLZN symbolizing
YCIOI synclinoria
YCNHN hyacinthine
YCPTO syncopation
YCRII myocarditis
YCRMS synchromesh
YCRNS synchronise
YCRNU synchronous
YCRNZ synchronize
YCRTO synchrotron
YCTHN eye-catching
YDCLS syndicalism
syndicalist
YDCTO syndication
YDSOE syndesmoses
YEATV hyperactive
YEBLS hyperbolise
hyperbolism
YEBLZ hyperbolize
YEBRA hyperborean
YECAG hypercharge
YECII hyper-critic
YEETN typesetting
YEIES Lyme disease
YEMRE hypermarket
YENTC cybernetics
YENWA Tyne and Wear
YEPAI hyperphagia
YERTE typewritten
YERTN typewriting
YESNC hypersonics
YETOH hypertrophy
YFNTO dysfunction
YFRNY eye for an eye
YGARE Syngman Rhee
YHGRA Pythagorean
YHLGE Mythologies
YHLGS mythologise
mythologist
YHLGZ mythologize
YHNMO by the name of
YHNSU Pythonesque
YHNTO hyphenation
YIACS typical case
YIDIA cylindrical
YIOER pyritohedra
YLBCT syllabicate
YLGSI syllogistic
YLPEI cyclopaedia
YMTIA symmetrical
YNCAC by any chance
YNEMU Lynn Seymour
YNLGS hymnologist
YNPEI hypnopaedia
YNPMI hypnopompic
YNTZN hypnotizing
YNYMT Sydney Smith
YOAOI myxomatosis
YOATI hypogastric
YOEEN by some means
YOEIE bygone times
YOESO hypotension
YOESV hypotensive
YOHCT hypothecate
YOHNI sycophantic
YOHNS xylophonist
YOHRI hypothermia
hypothyroid
YOHSA hypophyseal
hypophysial
YOHSS hypothesise
YOHSZ hypothesize
YOHTS hypothetise
YOHTZ hypothetize
YOIAL Byronically
synodically
zymotically
YOLSA mycoplasmas
YOLSI cytoplasmic
hypoblastic
pyroclastic
YONLO Byron Nelson
YOOAI mycodomatia

11 _Y_O_O

YOOIA cytological
mycological
YOOIM hypocorisma
YOOPS gyrocompass
YORPE typographer
YORPI kymographic
typographic
YOTOH hypostrophe
YOTSS hypostasise
YOTSZ hypostasize
YOTTS hypostatise
YOTTZ hypostatize
YOYLI hypocycloid
YPDAL sympodially
YPOAI nymphomania
symptomatic
YPOIU symphonious
YPTEI dyspathetic
sympathetic
YPTIE sympathizer
YRCAI hydrocyanic
YRCRO hydrocarbon
YRGAH hydrography
YRGNO hydrogen ion
YRGNS hydrogenise
YRGNT hydrogenate
YRGNU hydrogenous
YRGNZ hydrogenize
YRLDN pyrrolidine
YRLGS hydrologist
YRMTI hydrometric
hygrometric
YRPII hydrophilic
YRPNC hydroponics
YRPOI hydrophobia
hydrophobic
YRPTI hydropathic
YRPYI hydrophytic
hygrophytic
YRSAI hydrostatic
YRSHR hydrosphere
YRSMT hydrosomata
YRSOI hygroscopic
YSGAH hypsography
YSMTI hypsometric
YSROE syssarcoses
YSYMN hyoscyamine
YTCIA syntactical
YTEIE synthesiser
synthesized
synthesizer
YTMTC systematics
YTMTS systematise
YTMTZ systematize
YTNEN Ayrton Senna
YTPOI nyctophobia
YTRPA mystery play
YTRTU mystery tour
YTTOI nyctitropic
YUIAI pyruvic acid
YVALT Sylvia Plath
ZCMON azo-compound
ZNSHR ozonosphere
ZNZTO ozonization
ZRAJN Azerbaijani
ZREZA Ezer Weizman

12 letters – even

AAAAAA taramasalata
AAAASM Canada balsam
AAAATR mad as a hatter
AAAGAE paralanguage
AAAIIY palatability
AAASRI caravanserai
AACNIG parascending
AACSET balance sheet
AADWAE Layard's whale
AAEOAY Madame Bovary
AAEOER manage to hear
AAEOGA Casare Borgia
AAERCL parametrical
AAETES malapertness
AAETSS paracentesis
AAGRHN Jahangir Khan
AAHOIM parachronism
AAIACL paradisaical
AAIAIN canalization
nasalization
AAIEOD mazarine hood
AAIEOT Paradise Lost
AAIGRN lay a finger on
AAIHCS Ramapithecus
AAIIAY paramilitary
AAIIIS capabilities
AAIMTC paradigmatic
AAINLS Bavarian Alps
AAIOEA paralipomena
AAIOOY parasitology
AAIOSY calamitously
AAIUAE canaliculate
AALLAS parallel bars
AALLIE parallelwise
AANAAA Canaan Banana
AANVRE lasagne verde
AAOFCR naval officer
AAOHSS parapophyses
AAOIHC palaeolithic□
AAOOAY palaeobotany
AAORPY palaeography
AAOTON man about town
man-about-town
AARTIL cavalry twill
AASDOS Sarah Siddons
AASHSA paraesthesia
AASINR salad spinner
AATEAY natal therapy
AATNIN pay attention
AATOHC catastrophic
AAVUHN Sarah Vaughan
AAYTEA parasyntheta
AAYUAN pay-as-you-earn
ABADON Darby and Joan
ABEOSR rabble-rouser
ABGWIE cabbage white
ABHDAE carbohydrate
ABHVOR bad behaviour
ABIGAE gambling game
ABLCCD carbolic acid
ABNAIG carbon dating
ABNCCD carbonic acid
ABNCLY rabbinically
ABNCOS carbonaceous
ABPEOT l'Abbé Prévost
ABPMIS namby-pambies
ABRMLS Barbara Mills
ABROGR barber-monger
ABROII Lamberto Dini
ABTUKR rabbit-sucker
ACAAIN bacchanalian
ACADAD watch and ward
ACCFED Hancock Field
ACCOEY watch closely
ACDCLY saccadically
ACDRNE Cascade Range
ACEFCD hatchet-faced
ACEFED Macclesfield
ACEPIE Satchel Paige
ACEWEL ratchet-wheel
ACFLES fancifulness
watchfulness
ACIGVR watching-over
ACIIDY sanctifiedly
ACINBE sanctionable
ACLAIN cancellation
ACLLWY Malcolm Lowry
ACLQET pauciloquent
ACLRUT Marcel Proust
ACLTDY calculatedly
ACLTOS calculations
ACMNIE parchmentise
parchmentize
ACMODR talcum powder
ACMTOD Nancy Mitford
ACMTSS sarcomatosis
ACNBAE Dancing Brave
ACNETD malcontented
ACNGAH marconigraph
ACNGNC carcinogenic
ACNQEN Dancing Queen
ACNTDY fascinated by
ACOAEY lanceolately
ACOEEF fancy oneself
ACPAMC sarcoplasmic
ACRMTC panchromatic
ACSAVY Marcus Garvey
ACSGTF catch sight of
ACSITC narcissistic
ACTCLY narcotically
ACTIDW lancet window
ACUOIE calcium oxide
ACVOSY lasciviously
ADAHDS Zandra Rhodes
ADAHIG sand-yachting
ADAHON Paddy Ashdown
ADAORD hard-favoured
ADARIG card-carrying
ADBEDH hand's breadth
ADBURE pas de bourrée
ADCLGE eau de Cologne
eau-de-cologne
ADEAKD saddlebacked

ADECIF handkerchief
ADELNS hard feelings
ADESRS hard measures
ADETRD hard-featured
hard-sectored
ADETTH saddle stitch
ADFOOR maid of honour
ADHUDR hard shoulder
ADIGOL paddling-pool
ADLPIG handclapping
ADMAPE random sample
ADMCES random access
ADMRHC paedomorphic
ADNCAT landing craft
landing-craft
ADNCLY sardonically
ADNETE garden centre
ADNFDN Garden of Eden
ADNFED landing-field
ADNGOE hand and glove
ADNLHP cardinalship
ADNSAE landing-stage
ADNSRP landing-strip
ADNUUB garden suburb
ADOEES handsomeness
ADOEHR band together
ADOLAE hard to please
hard-to-please
ADOOEY hard to come by
ADOOIT cardiologist
ADOORD sand-coloured
ADORPY cardiography
ADPRTD hand-operated
ADRATE Cawdor Castle
ADRNEK mandarin neck
ADRNIG hard drinking
ADRNJW wandering Jew
ADRNUK mandarin duck
ADRSLD Waldorf salad
ADTEEL Land o' the Leal
ADTNIG hard-standing
ADURNY hard currency
ADVLIN vaudevillian
ADVRAD hand over hand
ADVRED hand over head
ADVRIT hand over fist
AEAALL make parallel
AEAASD Hafez al-Assad
AEADND case-hardened
AEAGOE Lake Maggiore
AEAIIR make familiar
AEAKAH Lake Balkhash
AEAKUT make bankrupt
AEATIH take part with
AEAUIA camera lucida
AEBAIG take a beating
AEBAMN water boatman
AEBEES saleableness
AEBFAO water buffalo
AEBIIF water bailiff
AEBITR water blister
AEBLSF make a balls of
AEBLWN James Baldwin
AEBSEL James Boswell
AEBSUT water biscuit
AECAEL James Clavell
AECAIN take occasion
AECANL water-channel
AECILE capercaillie
AECIZE capercailzie
AECMRN James Cameron
AECRIR Water-carrier
AECSFR make a case for
AECUHN have a crush on
AEDACS make advances
AEDAOD Jared Diamond
AEDIKR water-drinker
AEDKOT take a dekko at
AEDOPR eavesdropper
AEDSOE kaleidoscope
AEDTLY sacerdotally
AEDVNR water-diviner
AEDYFT make a day of it
AEEDFR make ready for
AEEIIE make definite
AEELAT Bakewell tart
AEEODR tape recorder
AEEORE have recourse
AEERRY James Earl Ray
AEESES carelessness
namelessness
AEESRS take measures
AEETBE gateleg table
AEFUTR have a flutter
AEGOJB make a good job
AEGTWY make a getaway
AEHAIG panel heating
AEHBTF make a habit of
AEHCAR take the chair
AEHEFL make cheerful
AEHFED take the field
AEHFFH take the Fifth
AEHFOR take the floor
AEHGAE make the grade
AEHHAT have the heart
AEHIEF make choice of
AEHJBF have the job of
AEHLWN have the law on
AEHMSC face the music
AEHNGT wake the night
AEHREF have charge of
take charge of
AEHRIS take the reins
AEHTCL catechetical
AEHTIH make a hit with
AEHUEF have the use of
AEHWEL take the wheel
AEHWRE have the worse
AEIAIN racemization
AEIAIT Katerina Witt
AEIDYO take kindly to
AEIEIS Lake Tiberias
AEIGOE watering-hole
AEIHGN Lake Michigan
AEIIAA Lake Titicaca
AEILES materialness
AEINPG Lake Winnipeg
AEITEF make little of
AEITGT make airtight
AEITOS maledictions
AEITRA Lake Victoria
AEJCSN Janet Jackson
AEKLIG make a killing
AELAUE take pleasure
AELBNS make old bones
AELGBE make eligible
AELNFR make plans for
AELOSE have a look-see
AELPAE same old place
AELRUD same old round
AEMDSN James Madison
AEMLOL water milfoil
AEMNHM James Mancham
AEMNHP gamesmanship
salesmanship
AEMSAE make a mistake
AEMXEL James Maxwell
AENCDY have a nice day
AENCLD bare-knuckled
AENDEN have an edge on
AENFAR have an affair
AENFET have an effect
AENFOT make an effort
AENHDY late in the day
AENHHP have on the hip
AENOVD make involved
AENRAD make an errand
AENSAE save one's face
take one's ease
AENSAK make one's mark
AENSEK save one's neck
AENSET make ends meet
take one's seat
AENSIE make one's pile
take one's time
AENSKN save one's skin
AENSOE have one's home
make one's home
AENSOK take one's hook
AENSOL have one's goal
AENSUD safe and sound
AENSUN take one's turn
AENSYH James Nasmyth
AENUHF have enough of
AENWRS take unawares
AEOAIE take for a ride
AEODAH gates of death
AEODIE make good time
AEOEET have none left
AEOEIH have done with
make love with
AEOETY malevolently
AEOGTT have bought it
AEOICS take to pieces
AEOIEF take notice of
AEOILY categorially
AEONPG take down a peg
AEOOIH have to do with
AEOPEE make complete

AEOSBE make possible
AEOSES ravenousness
AEOSLE mademoiselle❑
AEOSMN warehouseman
AEOVRS make converts
AEPAFR make a play for
AEPCFR have space for
make space for
AEPEWY make up leeway
AEPIEN take a pride in
AEPITF make a point of
AEPITR laser printer
AEPOIS paper profits
AEPRIG valet parking
AEPSOY make up a story
AERAGD have arranged
AEREES carefreeness
AEREIG bate-breeding
AEREIH make free with
AERERM make free from
AEREUN sale or return
AERGAT make pregnant
AERGES make progress
AERGTO have a right to
AERGTR make brighter
AERGTT take fright at
AERIFL make fruitful
AERPIG name-dropping
AERSIG gatecrashing
AERSRE game preserve
AESAEN have a share in
AESBSS have as a basis
AESEAT James Stewart
AESEGL Casey Stengel
AESHBY have as a hobby
AESHUH make as though
AESIEO take a shine to
AESINR James Skinner
AESLBE water-soluble
AESMDL take as a model
AESNOL have as an goal
AESOPS habeas corpus
AESOSS safe as houses
AETBIG have its being
AETCLY majestically
AETEID latent period
AETEIE parenthesise
parenthesize
AETFIE Patent Office
AETIDY take it kindly
AETIGF make a thing of
AETITR make stricter
AETKIE palette knife
AETLIG take a telling
AETMTR caveat emptor
AETNPY make it snappy
AETOFR make it hot for
AETOGR make stronger
AETOIG have it coming
AETRLY parenterally
AETRME take it from me
AETRUE water torture
AETTOS Lamentations
AETUBR James Thurber
AEUAON take out a loan
AEUCIN wave function
AEUEIR Lake Superior
AEURIG safeguarding
AEUSIN make question
AEUTBE make suitable
AEVRRM take over from
AEWDEL James Weddell
AEWFCS have two faces
AEWUIG caterwauling
AEWYAE make a wry face
AEWYIH have a way with
make away with
AEWYRM take away from
AEYATR safety factor
AFAAHN half marathon
half-marathon
AFACSO San Francisco
AFAHUE halfway house
AFAPIT halfway point
AFEIKT raffle-ticket
AFESVR half-seas-over
AFIBRD half-timbered
AFNSAD Baffin Island
AFNSRY waif and stray
AFRAIN malformation
AFRETR Jay Forrester
AGAEES languageless
AGBEES tangibleness
AGDCOL ragged school
AGEEHT langue de chat
AGHATD large-hearted
AGIAIY sanguinarily
AGIEES sanguineness
AGIOET sanguinolent
AGLUZL mangel-wurzel
AGNFIY hang in effigy
AGNILY tangentially
AGNLOE hanging loose
marginal note
AGNLOT marginal cost
AGNSED hang one's head
AGOEEF range oneself
AGOEHR hang together
AGOIHS bang to rights
AGOOSY languorously
AGQITY laugh quietly
AGRAIM pan-Germanism
AGRFAH dagger of lath
AGRINL danger signal
AGRTED Margaret Mead
AGRUDN hang around in
AGTSON laugh to scorn
AGTUPA mangetout pea
AHDOAO mashed potato
AHGAHC tachygraphic
AHGAHR tachygrapher
AHGNSS pathogenesis
AHLASN Rachel Carson
AHLCIG Catholic King
AHLEIM Panhellenism
AHLEIT Panhellenist
AHLGCL pathological
AHLROD bachelorhood
AHMLPE eat humble pie
eat humble-pie
AHMTCL mathematical
AHNCRY cash and carry
cash-and-carry
AHNEEY each and every
AHNTNA Washingtonia
AHNTNC Washington DC
AHNTOS machinations
AHOHUE fashion house
AHOMDL fashion model
AHOPAE fashion plate
AHRAIG oath-breaking
AHRILW fathers-in-law
AHRIUE father-figure
AHRMTR katharometer
AHRRAH gather breath
AHRRUD gather ground
AHSAIN yacht station
AHSHSS rachischisis
AHTCLY pathetically
AHYOEY lachrymosely
AIAANR Marina Warner
AIACOS capital cross
AIAFNS capital funds
AIAGIS capital gains
AIAIEN capitalize on
AIAIES sanitariness
AIAIIY habitability
navigability
AIAINL navigational
AIAITC capitalistic
AIAUIT caricaturist
AIAVNE pay in advance
AIBASA Caribbean Sea
AIBCHM David Beckham
AIBEES variableness
AIBETR variable star
AIBLAY David Bellamy
AIBOOY radiobiology
AICLSE Marie Celeste
AICMAS radio compass
AICMEE David Campese
AICUSR cabin cruiser
AIDOIT palindromist
AIEEET radioelement
AIEMKR cabinet-maker
AIETBE manifestable
AIFCIN satisfaction
AIFCOY satisfactory
AIFIGY satisfyingly
AIFRIG habit-forming
AIFRUA magic formula
AIFUNE bad influence
AIGAEF taking care of
AIGAHC hagiographic
radiographic
AIGAHR radiographer
AIGITE having little
AIGLTN having a lot on
AIGNSS palingeneses

AIGOEY Ealing comedy
AIGOIE babingtonite
AIGRIK David Garrick
AIGTIG having a thing
AIGULC making public
AIHATY Danish pastry
AIHCNY David Hockney
AIHDIH ravished with
AIHHRH parish church
AIHLET David Hilbert
AIHOES parishioners
AIIAIN facilitation
gasification
Nazification
pacification
ramification
ratification
sanitization
AIIAOY pacificatory
AIIOOE radioisotope
AIIRAE familiar name
AIIRIH familiar with
AIIRZD familiarized
AIJHSN Magic Johnson
AILCOS capillaceous
AILCRT Camille Corot
AILGCL hagiological
radiological
AILGLI Camillo Golgi
AILISE facial tissue
AILNEN magic lantern
AILNIE radial engine
AILREA Daniel Ortega
AIMMNS Magic Moments
AINAJB patient as Job
AINCES camiknickers
AINCIE radionuclide
AINILY sapientially
AINLAK national bank
national park
AINLAL national call
AINLET national debt
AINLLB National Club
AINLOE national code
AINLRD national grid
AINLZD nationalized
rationalized
AINPIT salient point
AIOAII Marino Marini
AIODES manifoldness
AIOOAE Casino Royale
AIOORD varicoloured
AIOTIK lay in on thick
lay it on thick
AIPOES basic process
AIPOIS radiophonics
AIPOIT radiophonist
AIRCRO David Ricardo
AIRMET Marie Rambert
AISEIA Marius Petipa
AISETR radius vector
AITCLY papistically
AITEAY radiotherapy
AITEON man in the moon
AITIBE David Trimble
AITLOE parietal bone
parietal lobe
AIUAEY paniculately
AIUAIE manipulative
AIUAIN capitulation
manipulation
AIUAOY manipulatory
AIUDES fatigue-dress
AIUGAS Lalique glass
AIUIOS latitudinous
AIULES habitualness
AIUTDO habituated to
AIYICE family circle
AIYOTR family doctor
AIYOVD easily solved
AIYRDT family credit
AIYRKN easily broken
AKADES backwardness
AKADWR Falklands War
AKDIHT marked with a T
AKEAKE walkie-talkie
AKECAH hackney coach
AKFEOD back of beyond
AKFHNE lack of change
AKFNRY lack of energy
AKHCAK walk the chalk
AKHKIE Mack The Knife
AKHLIS Mark Phillips
AKHPAD Jack Sheppard
AKHPAK walk the plank
AKIKAS Jack Nicklaus
AKITES taskmistress
AKLNIE Wankel engine
AKMNHP marksmanship
AKNAOT larking about
AKNFAE walking-frame
AKNFIE jack-in-office
AKNFRH back and forth
AKNGOP backing group
AKNGUE marking gauge
AKNHAS Talking Heads
AKNHBX jack-in-the-box
AKNIBY Mackenzie Bay
AKNLGT parking-light
AKNMTR parking meter
AKNOAR walking on air
AKNOIM parkinsonism
AKNPIT talking point
talking-point
AKNSAK basking shark
AKNSIK walking stick
walking-stick
AKNSOE backing store
AKNVNY walk unevenly
AKNXUE lack an excuse
AKOAIS back to basics
AKOAUE back to nature
back-to-nature
AKODMN backwoodsman
AKONIG back-wounding
AKOORD dark-coloured
AKOSIG Hawk Roosting
AKOSNE talk nonsense
AKOVLE Jacksonville
AKRAIG backbreaking
back-breaking
AKTADN market garden
AKTALD racket-tailed
AKTBIG back-stabbing
AKTEDR market leader
AKTEIG racketeering
AKTHWN Saskatchewan
AKTOCS market forces
AKTQAE market square
AKWYIH walk away with
AKWYRM walk away from
ALADAE early and late
ALADUG Carl Sandburg
ALAGVN Paul Langevin
ALAIIY malleability
ALAKPN fall back upon
ALBHVD badly behaved
badly-behaved
ALCFED Paul Scofield
ALCILR Karl Schiller
ALCNGN hallucinogen
ALCOIG early closing
ALCOSY fallaciously
ALDCNO Paulo DiCanio
ALDESD badly-dressed
ALEDOG fall headlong
ALEGIH Early English
ALELIE Paul Verlaine
ALENCE Carl Wernicke
ALFAUE call of nature
ALFHEE tail of the eye
ALFNIG fault-finding
ALGAHR calligrapher
ALGNEL Sally Gunnell
ALHSOS call the shots
ALIGAL rallying call
ALINES Carl Linnaeus
ALLCNE table licence
ALNAAT falling apart
ALNADS rallentandos
ALNCOS gallinaceous
ALNESI ballon d'essai
ALNOLY call into play
ALNRNE Darling Range
ALNRNO Marlon Brando
ALNUDY Mail on Sunday
ALOEHR call together
ALOICS fall to pieces
ALONPN ballpoint pen
ALOOIE fail to notice
ALORIR Paul Tournier
ALPCSO Pablo Picasso
ALPNTW wallop in a tow
ALQIAE harlequinade
ALRGIR Paule Régnier
ALRWLS Sadler's Wells
ALSELW Naples-yellow
ALSHNC callisthenic
ALTACR ballet dancer

	ballet-dancer
ALTCLY	balletically
ALUCLO	Paolo Uccello
ALWADE	tallow-candle
ALYCMT	Halley's comet
ALYRDE	Bailey bridge
AMESES	harmlessness
AMFIED	balm of Gilead
AMGEHN	Ian McGeechan
AMKSMR	Jammu-Kashmir
AMLAIS	mammillarias
AMNADR	salmon ladder
AMNALL	Carmen Callil
AMNBAC	Raymond Blanc
AMNCEN	harmonic mean
AMNCLY	harmonically
AMNEIG	warmongering
	war-mongering
AMNINS	Hammond Innes
AMNOSY	harmoniously
AMPIIC	haemophiliac
AMRAIG	palm-greasing
AMRGAD	mammary gland
AMRKOD	Hammarskjöld
AMRNOT	hammering-out
AMTLSS	haematolysis
ANANBE	maintainable
ANBEES	damnableness
ANBRDE	Barnaby Rudge
ANBRUH	Gainsborough
ANCAOK	Fanny Cradock
ANCTIG	wainscotting
ANEIGY	saunteringly
ANERUX	E Annie Proulx
ANESES	painlessness
ANEUEY	Saint-Exupéry
ANFCLY	magnifically
ANFCNE	magnificence
ANGEZY	Wayne Gretzky
ANGOGS	Saint George's
ANHATD	faint-hearted
ANHIDW	launch window
ANHNPD	launching-pad
ANIBAK	Paint It Black
ANLAUE	carnal nature
ANLQET	magniloquent
ANLROS	vainglorious
ANMOUS	magnum bonums
ANNHAS	pain in the ass
ANNLGT	warning light
ANOETM	gain momentum
ANOORD	Cain-coloured
ANOTOT	rainbow trout
ANRIES	mannerliness
ANRRSH	Ragnar Frisch
ANRSTR	Barnard's star
ANSALS	Barnes Wallis
ANSEAT	Payne Stewart
ANSOTR	Wayne Shorter
ANTCAE	magnetic tape
ANTCIE	magnetic mine
ANTCIK	magnetic disk
ANTCLX	magnetic flux
ANTCLY	magnetically
ANTCOL	magnet school
ANTCRM	magnetic drum
ANTEGH	gain strength
ANTEIY	paint the lily
ANTGRK	Magnitogorsk
ANTIIN	malnutrition
ANTMTR	magnetometer
ANTMTY	magnetometry
ANTRIL	Jayne Torvill
ANTZBE	magnetizable
ANUIHD	malnourished
AOALOK	man-of-all-work
AOARML	nasolacrymal
AOBRAA	Major Barbara
AOCBAE	savoy cabbage
AOCPAD	Aaron Copland
AOCPTL	paroccipital
AOCUAE	man of courage
AODIMN	Harold Tilman
AODISN	Harold Wilson
AODITR	Harold Pinter
AOEAOS	gamopetalous
AOESEN	Jacob Epstein
AOETRS	eat one's terms
AOEWRS	eat one's words
AOGNRL	major general
	major-general
AOHAIE	parochialise
	parochialize
AOHAIM	parochialism
AOHAIY	parochiality
AOIAIN	canonization
	valorization
	vaporization
AOIGAD	parotid gland
AOILNS	Faroe Islands
AOINID	Favonian wind
AOIYIW	majority view
AOIYUE	majority rule
AOLBRY	cap of liberty
AOLSAT	Manon Lescaut
AOLTES	man of letters
AOOATC	paronomastic
AOOSES	vaporousness
AOPEIE	major premise
AORAIG	labour-saving
AORDIH	favoured with
AORFOE	labour of love
AOSADR	Jacob's ladder
AOSESN	famous person
AOSOKO	Yamoussoukro
AOTEAD	law of the land
AOTEAK	pat on the back
AOTEIE	lay on the line
AOTETE	Savoy Theatre
AOTUIG	raconteuring
AOURBE	manoeuvrable
APALRY	happy as Larry
APAMCN	panpharmacon
APCIPH	Sam Peckinpah
APFENS	Ralph Fiennes
APGBON	Cappagh-brown
APGLCY	happy-go-lucky
APGOSS	salpiglossis
APLCLA	Valpolicella
APNTNE	happenstance
APOARS	Camptosaurus
APOLWR	camp-follower
APREBE	gas-permeable
APRLAE	happy release
APRORN	Jasper Conran
APTOGR	carpetmonger
AQEAES	masquerade as
AQEDVD	Jacques David
AQEMND	Jacques Monod
AQIHBE	vanquishable
AQIHET	vanquishment
ARACAE	patriarchate
ARAEAD	carriage-paid
ARAEBE	marriageable
ARAERE	carriage-free
ARASAL	Hadrian's Wall
ARBEDH	hair's-breadth
ARBOIS	macrobiotics
ARBRSN	Pat Robertson
ARCMOE	Patrick Moore
ARCOSY	capriciously
ARCPAY	macrocephaly
ARCRVL	Maurice Ravel
ARCWIE	Patrick White
AREAOG	carried along
ARECEM	barrier cream
AREFED	Harry Enfield
AREFUE	Gabriel Fauré
ARENOD	Das Rheingold
ARESAE	married state
ARESES	hairlessness
ARETRR	hair restorer
ARFRAD	carry forward
ARLAUK	Darryl Zanuck
ARLGOS	sacrilegious
ARMLUT	lacrimal duct
ARNAAL	Lauren Bacall
ARNETY	Warren Beatty
ARNULA	Barranquilla
AROEBT	carry one's bat
ARPITR	hair-splitter
ARRSIG	hairdressing
ARSCME	Harry Secombe
ARSNOD	Harrison Ford
ARSPOE	sarrusophone
ARSRMN	Harry S Truman
ARTOSY	barratrously
ARTRIR	cairn terrier
ARTRUH	carry through
ARWAPA	marrowfat pea
ARWHGP	narrow the gap
ARWIDD	narrow-minded
ARWSAE	narrow escape
ASAADO	raise a hand to
ASAGTR	manslaughter
ASAIGY	nauseatingly
ASBEES	passableness
ASBSIN	San Sebastian
ASCLBE	cause célèbre

ASCLUS false colours
ASDSLY false display
ASEERE tapsieteerie
ASEFIE laisser-faire
laissez-faire
ASEHMD Nasseem Hamad
ASETNE pass sentence
ASFOIN laws of motion
ASGGAE passage grave
ASGTDY far-sightedly
ASHATD false-hearted
ASILES cause illness
ASLERE tapsalteerie
ASLETE tassel-gentle
ASLTIG ear-splitting
ASMCBE Danse Macabre
ASMNIE haussmannise
haussmannize
ASMNOS parsimonious
ASMNYN raise money on
ASNHEE damson cheese
ASNMAS ways and means
ASNSOD pass one's word
ASOAEY passionately
ASOBLW Hans von Bülow
ASOEHT raise one's hat
ASOFUT passion fruit
ASOSES nauseousness
ASOTES pass to others
ASPCUE false picture
ASPRLA sarsaparilla
ASPROT passe-partout
ASRDCD mass-produced
ASRRFT Yasser Arafat
ASSDES cause sadness
ASTEID raise the wind
ASTENE raise the ante
ASTEOF raise the roof
ASTOBE cause trouble
ASUDRR mass murderer
ASWTES false witness
ATAEEL last farewell
ATAEIY Salt Lake City
ATARHM Martha Graham
ATBACE carte blanche
ATBRAA Santa Barbara
ATCIIE haute cuisine
ATCLIE nautical mile
ATCLRY particularly
ATCNCN pantechnicon
ATCOPI fait accompli
ATCPNS participants
ATCPTR participator
ATCUUE haute couture
ATDMNO Santo Domingo
ATDOSY fastidiously
ATEEDD rattle-headed
ATEEDR cattleherder
ATEFAA Battle of Zama
ATEFEA Battle of Jena
ATEFOS Battle of Loos
ATEHTL maître d'hôtel
ATELMS fan the flames
ATENRT Walther Nerst
ATEPRS Matthew Paris
ATERUD battleground
ATESES tactlessness
ATETET maltreatment
ATEYUH want very much
ATFLES faithfulness
tastefulness
wastefulness
ATFLMN Marty Feldman
ATFPEH part of speech
ATGAHC cartographic
ATGAHR cartographer
ATGPIT vantage point
ATHAIG Faith Healing
faith healing
ATIBIE East Kilbride
ATIFIT Captain Flint
ATIJIE gastric juice
ATIUEO pay tribute to
ATLCLY dactylically
ATLGCL tautological
ATLVSA hasta la vista
ATMACS saltimbancos
ATMEGT bantamweight
ATMMCL pantomimical
ATMUTO tantamount to
ATNAST wasting asset
ATNEGN Jan Tinbergen
ATNEOS cantankerous
ATNKNN Matti Nykanen
ATNSET past one's best
ATNUHR Martin Luther
ATOAIM factionalism
ATOHOC xanthochroic
ATOHOF sawtooth roof
ATONMI gastrocnemii
ATOOIT gastronomist
ATOSAE waste of space
ATOSES captiousness
cautiousness
ATOTRN xanthopterin
ATPIIT cartophilist
ATPOUT waste product
ATRAIN masturbation
ATRANN Walter Cannon
ATRATN Walter Payton
ATRCCD tartaric acid
ATREIN East Friesian
ATRETR gastarbeiter□
ATRFAT matter-of-fact
ATRFOM matter of form
ATRIES masterliness
ATRJWD lantern-jawed
ATRLED pastoral head
ATRNRM battering-ram
ATRONR factory-owner
ATROOY bacteriology
ATRSAD Easter Island
ATRSUE tartare sauce
ATRTOE masterstroke
ATRTRS master-at-arms
ATRUDY Easter Sunday
ATRUIS canterburies
ATSAIG earth-shaking
ATSCOS Maltese cross
ATSELN cast a spell on
ATSIAE fantasticate
ATSINE earth science
ATSIOS fantasticoes
ATSNHP partisanship
ATTOIG partitioning
ATTOIM saltationism
ATTOIT saltationist
ATTOOF partition off
ATTOSY factitiously
ATTPIE past its prime
ATTROS saltatorious
ATUELE Pasteurellae
ATUELS Pasteurellas
ATVTDY captivated by
ATXHNE part-exchange
ATYSIE East Ayrshire
ATYUTR pastry cutter
AUACID natural child
AUAIES salutariness
AUAINL salutational
AUAITC naturalistic
AUALGT natural light
AUAOIY salutatorily
AUATRD manufactured
AUATRR manufacturer
AUBEES valuableness
AUCLSS ranunculuses
AUGETY value greatly
AULAMR Samuel Palmer
AULDRS maquiladoras
AULEAK casual remark
AULELR Samuel Weller
AULHLS Samuel Phelps
AULOKR manual worker
AULUAD Samuel Cunard
AULULR Samuel Butler
AULYAD casualty ward
AUMAKD vacuum-packed
AUNAIG calumniating
AUNAIN calumniation
AUNAOY calumniatory
AUNOSY calumniously
AUOAHC naturopathic
AUOSES fabulousness
AUROSY salubriously
AVDRAI Salvador Dali
AVFCLY salvifically
AVLOSY marvellously
AVNCLY galvanically
AVNKIE carving-knife
AVNMTR galvanometer
AVRAIN malversation
AVRCOS Calvary cross
AVSMUE harvest mouse
AVSOBY Galveston Bay
AVTOIT Salvationist
AWCSIE Warwickshire
AYAPRV Gary Kasparov
AYCLEE Mary McAleese

AYHLOS dasyphyllous
AYIEES ladylikeness
AYIKOD Mary Pickford
AYITIE labyrinthine
AYKNSS karyokinesis
AYNHEE easy on the eye
AYOEAK Baby Come Back
AYOIET easy to digest
AYOISN Mary Robinson
AYOOIT papyrologist
AYOORD many-coloured
AYSIPR lady's slipper
lady's-slipper
AZAROS Jazz Warriors
AZEAZE razzle-dazzle
AZNAMR katzenjammer
BAADRY Abraham Darby
BAIEES abrasiveness
BCRNIM obscurantism
BCRNIT obscurantist
BEDVRU objet de vertu
BESDIH obsessed with
BESOIT obsessionist
BETETE Abbey Theatre
BETIDD absent-minded
BEUOSY obsequiously
BFTEEM abaft the beam
BIAOIY obligatorily
BIEAIE obliterative
BIEAIN obliteration
BIICNE obliviscence
BIIGES obligingness
BIIVDA absit invidia
BLAWTH Abel Magwitch
BLTOIM abolitionism
BLTOIT abolitionist
BOECNE obsolescence
BOEEES obsoleteness
BOHFBY a broth of a boy
BOMLOD abnormal load
BOUEEO absolute zero
BOUEES absoluteness
BOUEUE absolute rule
BQAUAE absquatulate
BQIOSY ubiquitously
BRENIY Aberdeen City
BRGNLY aboriginally
BRINIL abortion pill
BRVAIN abbreviation
BRVAOY abbreviatory
BTATDY abstractedly
BTATES abstractness
BTCEAE obstacle race
BTEEAE obstreperate
BTEEOS obstreperous
BTMOSY abstemiously
BTRITM obiter dictum
BTTIIN obstetrician
BTUEES abstruseness
BTUTOS obstructions
BUENLD obtuse-angled
BVOEEF above oneself
BVTEAT above the salt
BVTEIE above-the-line
CABIGY scramblingly
CACBID scratchbuild
CACIES scratchiness
CACIGY scratchingly
CAEAIG octane rating
CAEBAD scraperboard
CAEUBR octane number
CAINDY occasioned by
CAINLY occasionally
CAOOIT oceanologist
CAORPY oceanography
CBOSES scabrousness
CDMCES academicness
CDMCLY academically
CEEAIG accelerating
CEEAIN acceleration
CEECYA sclerenchyma
CEEEAE Schéhérézade
CEEFOK scheme of work
CENRTR screen writer
screenwriter
CEOEMA sclerodermia
CEOEMC sclerodermic
CETAIN accentuation
CETCLY eclectically
CETIIY eccentricity
CFOIHY act foolishly
CIBIGY scribblingly
CICAUA acciaccatura
CIETLY accidentally
occidentally
CILSEL Achilles' heel
CIMTCL schismatical
CINAIG action-taking
CINAKD action-packed
CINELY action replay
CIOAPC schizocarpic
CIOEML echinodermal
CIOHMA schizothymia
CIOHMC schizothymic
CIOYEE schizomycete
CIPRLI Schiaparelli
CISEDF act instead of
CITRLY scripturally
CITRTR scriptwriter
CIVMNS achievements
CLBLIG eco-labelling
CLDAIG scale drawing
CLGCLY ecologically
CLMTZD acclimatized
CLPOIC ochlophobiac
CLRUCE ocular muscle
CLSATC ecclesiastic
CLSATS Ecclesiastes
CLSOOY ecclesiology
CLTRLY sculpturally
CMIHES scampishness
CMNCLY ecumenically
CNAOSY scandalously
CNCATC iconoclastic
CNHCOS acanthaceous
CNIAIN Scandinavian
CNIRPY scintigraphy
CNMCLY economically
CNMTIS econometrics
CNWEGD acknowledged
COCEET accouchement
CODOIT accordionist
COEAIN octogenarian
COEHUR Schopenhauer
COEOSY acrogenously
COIUAE scrobiculate
COLATR schoolmaster
COLEVR school-leaver
COONIG echo-sounding
COPIHD accomplished
COPIHR accomplisher
COPNIG accompanying
COSHWY across the way
COTCLY acrostically
COTEET accoutrement
COTEOL scoop the pool
COYHLY acronychally
COYLBC octosyllabic
COYLBE octosyllable
CPITME scyphistomae
CPITMS scyphistomas
CPODOE scaphoid bone
CRBESS scarabaeuses
CRDMTA acaridomatia
acarodomatia
CREFVR scarlet fever
CREWMN scarlet woman
CREYVR scarcely ever
CRFLES scornfulness
CRINIH scorpion fish
CRIOSY scurrilously
CRNGAD eccrine gland
CRTDAH scare to death
CSOSIK scissors kick
CTEATF act the part of
CTEBAN scatterbrain
CTEIGY scatteringly
CTIHOD Scottish Fold
CTLEYE acetaldehyde
CTLGCL scatological
CTTCLY ecstatically
CUAEES accurateness
CUAIEY accusatively
CUAINL occupational
CUAOIL accusatorial
CUECNE acquiescence
CUIDIH occupied with
CUIIIG scrutinizing
CUIOSY scrutinously
CUITIH acquaint with
CUITNE acquaintance
CUSTOS acquisitions
CUTCLY acoustically
CUTMDO accustomed to
CUUAIE accumulative
CUUAIN accumulation
CUUOIY scrupulosity
CUUOSY scrupulously
DACGAD advance guard

Words marked ☐ can also be spelled with an initial capital letter

DADAEE	Edgard Varèse
DADELR	Edward Teller
DADENN	Edward Vernon
DADENR	Edward Jenner
DADEOO	Edward De Bono
DADHMS	Edward Thomas
DADIBN	Edward Gibbon
DADISN	Edward Wilson
DADLEN	Edward Alleyn
DADOBS	Edward Forbes
DAIAIN	idealization
DAINLY	ideationally
DATGOS	advantageous
DCTOIT	educationist
DCTTOS	adscititious
DEAGAD	adrenal gland
DEAITE	Edmé Mariotte
DEBAIE	adverbialise
	adverbialize
DEIEAE	adhesive tape
DEIEES	adhesiveness
DETTOS	adventitious
DETVLY	adjectivally
DGOSSO	add glosses to
DIAIIY	advisability
DIATBY	Admiralty Bay
DICCRN	Eddie Cochran
DIEWRS	Eddie Edwards
DIFRET	Edwin Forrest
DIIERE	additive-free
DIINLY	additionally
DIIUAE	adminiculate
DILTES	Edwin Lutyens
DINEIH	Adrienne Rich
DIOYOY	advisory body
DISOFE	admission fee
DLBAND	addle-brained
DLEAIN	adulteration
DLEOSY	adulterously
DLNPTI	Adelina Patti
DLTOSY	idolatrously
DNIIBE	identifiable
DNIYAD	identity card
DNIYIH	identify with
DNOOIT	odontologist
DODALY	Edmond Halley
DOIHET	admonishment
DOYCAY	idiosyncrasy
DPAIIY	adaptability
DQAEES	adequateness
DRBEES	adorableness
DTCESN	Édith Cresson
DTEEIG	Ode to Evening
DTRAIE	editorialise
	editorialize
DTSTEL	Edith Sitwell
DTWATN	Edith Wharton
DUATID	adjutant bird
DUCIEY	adjunctively
DUDALR	Edmund Waller
DUDISN	Edmund Wilson
DUDUBA	Edmund Rubbra
DUIAIN	adjudication

DURMNT	Edouard Manet
EAAEES	separateness
EAAERM	separate from
EAAGAE	metalanguage
EAAIIY	separability
EAAOIY	defamatorily
EAARCS	separatrices
EAAVSR	legal adviser
EABLTR	perambulator
EACMAY	be bad company
EACMNA	decalcomania
EACOIC	melancholiac
EACTAE	recalcitrate
EACTAT	recalcitrant
EACTOS	demarcations
EADANR	Gerald Ratner
EADCLY	heraldically
EADCRE	Gerald Scarfe
EADERU	Gerard Debreu
EADESF	regardless of
EADESY	regardlessly
EADETE	remand centre
EADIHY	regard highly
EADUPR	Gerard Kuiper
EAEAIN	sexagenarian
EAECNE	recalescence
EAEODM	female condom
EAETOS	ménage à trois
EAEUBR	cetane number
EAFIAE	decaffeinate
EAHCLY	seraphically
EAHLDY	legal holiday
EAHOIG	refashioning
EAHRCL	metaphorical
EAHSCL	metaphysical
EAIAIE	decapitalise
	decapitalize
	recapitalise
	recapitalize
EAIAIN	decapitation
	deracination
	desalination
	legalisation
	legalization
	penalization
	velarization
EAIEES	negativeness
	relativeness
EAIEIE	relative size
EAIEIN	negative sign
EAIEOE	negative pole
EAIGEN	get a wiggle on
EAIIAE	rehabilitate
EAIIIT	relativitist
EAIITC	negativistic
	relativistic
EAIJFA	Tel Aviv-Jaffa
EAIKEN	Melanie Klein
EAINHP	relationship
EAINLY	relationally
EAIUAE	recapitulate
EAIUIM	behaviourism
EAIUIT	behaviourist

EALCLY	metallically
EALCOD	metallic bond
EALRIT	metallurgist
EALULT	retail outlet
EANEAS	Geraint Evans
EANNFE	retaining fee
EANTZR	demagnetizer
EAOAIC	megalomaniac
EAOARS	megalosaurus[◻]
EAODOE	sesamoid bone
EAOEOS	keratogenous
EAOGIH	get along with
EAOILY	senatorially
EAOOIT	hepatologist
EAOPIM	metamorphism
EAOPOE	metamorphose
EARAIN	repatriation
EARTAN	Vera Brittain
EASEDM	New Amsterdam
EASHSA	telaesthesia
EATACE	Sebastian Coe
EATAMR	tenant farmer
EATBNH	penalty bench
EATCLY	pedantically
	semantically
EATETL	departmental
EAUAIE	denaturalise
	denaturalize
EAURSY	get a guernsey
EAVNUE	peradventure
EAZEET	bedazzlement
EBEAEA	Wembley Arena
EBECAT	kerb-merchant
EBEEAD	Leo Baekeland
EBEIDD	feeble-minded
EBGSIE	Denbighshire
EBUNCP	Melbourne Cup
EBUSIK	New Brunswick
ECADSR	merchandiser
ECAHMS	Mercian Hymns
ECASCL	neoclassical
ECATAK	merchant bank
ECATAY	merchant navy
ECATBE	merchantable
ECATIE	merchantlike
ECBOSM	peach blossom
ECCMIG	beachcombing
ECCSAL	peacock's tail
ECDLOS	peccadilloes
ECDSEZ	Mercedes-Benz®
ECEITY	geochemistry
ECENDP	get cleaned up
ECFLES	mercifulness
	peacefulness
ECFRAD	henceforward
ECIAIN	deactivation
	reactivation
ECIEES	reactiveness
ECKLIG	mercy killing
ECLDNA	New Caledonia
ECNEAY	tercentenary
ECNIIM	mercantilism
ECNIIT	mercantilist

ECPIEY perceptively
ECPIIY perceptivity
ECPINL perceptional
ECRAIE mercurialise
mercurialize
ECRUCE red corpuscle
ECSIEY percussively
ECSINL percussional
ECTNOS percutaneous
ECVRNS leg-coverings
EDADAS leads and lags
EDALIE dead-ball line
EDBEES readableness
EDCGNL hendecagonal
EDCOSY mendaciously
EDDRIG Wendy Darling
EDEAPE Dead Sea apple
EDEITR head register
EDESDN get dressed in
EDESES heedlessness
needlessness
EDFROE ready for more
EDHEBW bend the elbow
EDHIKR headshrinker
EDITES headmistress
EDLEIM mendeleevium
EDMDLY hebdomadally
EDNAIE dead-and-alive
EDNATR leading actor
EDNDES wedding dress
EDNDWR wedding-dower
EDNEIE pendente lite
EDNEOE Heldentenöre
EDNEOS Helden-tenors
EDNLGT leading light
EDNMRH wedding march
EDNPAT bedding plant
EDNRYR lead in prayer
EDNSAE feed one's face
EDNSAS mend one's ways
EDNTNT herd instinct
EDOOIT dendrologist
EDORSN send to prison
EDOTIS heads or tails
EDRETD tender-hefted
EDRIIM neo-Darwinism
EDRIIN neo-Darwinian
EDRIIT neo-Darwinist
EDRRTR leader-writer
EDSBON reddish-brown
EDSCIE geodesic line
EDSCOE geodesic dome
EDSUTN dead as mutton
EDTCLY geodetically
EDTEFO lend itself to
EDURES headquarters
EDWYRM lead away from
EEAANT rebel against
EEACPY severance pay
EEACUT federal court
EEAEAD Peter Abelard
EEAIEY vegetatively
EEAINL generational
EEAKOD Peter Ackroyd
EEALFT vegetable fat
EEALOL vegetable oil
EEALWX vegetable wax
EEARCS generatrices
EEARTE René Magritte
EEASAF general staff
EEBACR remembrancer
EEBACS remembrances
EEBHES Peter Behrens
EEBRBY rememberably
EEBRTR reverberator
EEBRUH Peterborough
EECIGY beseechingly
EECOHR see each other
EECSIE repercussive
EECSIG Peter Cushing
EECSIN repercussion
EEEAEY degenerately
EEEAIE degenerative
regenerative
EEEAIG degenerating
regenerating
EEEAIN deceleration
degeneration
regeneration
EEEAOY regeneratory
EEEDNO se defendendo
EEEMSE levée en masse
EEEOTY be here to stay
EEFIIG never-failing
EEGADR New Englander
EEGBIL Peter Gabriel
EEGCLY telergically
EEGFLY revengefully
EEHNBX telephone box
EEHPIG teleshopping
EEIAET hereditament
EEIAIY hereditarily
EEIESY remedilessly
EEIETY beneficently
EEIHES feverishness
EEIIEY repetitively
EEIILO beneficial to
EEIILY beneficially
EEIINE beneficience
EEIOSY veneficously
EEIRTD deteriorated
EEIULY televisually
EELGCL genealogical
teleological
EELHLS Beverly Hills
EELMAD Peter Lombard
EELOSY rebelliously
EEMDWR Peter Medawar
EEMLOM Derek Malcolm
EEMNBE determinable
EEMNBY determinably
EEMNDO determined to
EEMNDY determined by
determinedly
EENAIY perenniality
EENTEE here and there
EEOAIN redecoration
EEOAOS heterogamous
EEOATC heterotactic
EEOEIM heterosexism
EEOEIT heterosexist
EEOEOS heteromerous
EEOETY benevolently
EEOEUL heterosexual
EEOHLY heterophylly
EEOILY ceremonially
EEOLSA heteroplasia
EEOLSY heteroplasty
EEOMNS developments
EEOMTR telecommuter
EEOOIT selenologist
EEOOOS heterogonous
heterologous
heteronomous
EEOOPY heteromorphy
EEORPY heterotrophy
selenography
EEOSES generousness
EEOYLC heterocyclic
EEOYOE heterozygote
EEOYOS heterozygous
EEPGIG level pegging
EEPOIY peremptorily
EERCLY meteorically
EERCOS meretricious
EERDAN referred pain
EERGTD desegregated
EERHWR meteor shower
EERMTR Teleprompter
EERNTR peregrinator
EERPEE telegraphese
EERPIT telegraphist
EERTLE terebratulae
EERTLS terebratulas
EESAFR Peter Shaffer
EESAMN Helen Sharman
EESITN Peter Shilton
EESLES Peter Sellers
EESOAY reversionary
EESOIT secessionist
EESRAE level surface
EESTZR desensitizer
EETAIE decentralise
decentralize
EETAIN fenestration
EETAIY defeat easily
EETDES dejectedness
dementedness
EETEAY fever therapy
EETEES nevertheless
EETEGT seventy-eight
EETESY relentlessly
EETLEK pedestal desk
EETNSN besetting sin
EETOIT receptionist
retentionist
EETRHD Desert Orchid
EETTEF defeat itself
repeat itself

EETVLE Celesteville
EEUAIN deregulation
EEUCUE venepuncture
EEUTNV Peter Ustinov
EEVDES reservedness
EEVDIT reserved list
EEVGIG be heavy going
EEVNST receiving-set
EEVPIE reserve price
EEVRHP receivership
EEVTOS reservations
EEWLOT Derek Walcott
EEYAMN Jeremy Paxman
EEYHRE Jeremy Thorpe
EEYSAS Jeremy Isaacs
EEZDIH be seized with
EFAEES selfsameness
EFAEIG self-catering
EFAGAE deaf language
EFBOBD self-absorbed
EFCFFH perfect fifth
EFCIEY perfectively
EFCPTH perfect pitch
EFDEIE self-adhesive
EFDIIG self-admiring
EFDOSY perfidiously
EFEEVR self-deceiver
EFEINE self-reliance
EFERAH self-reproach
EFESES selflessness
EFESIE Renfrewshire
EFETUT self-destruct
EFFAIG self-effacing
EFFETD self-affected
EFITUT self-distrust
EFLAIG self-pleasing
EFLAIN perfoliation
EFLHBT deaf alphabet
EFLROS self-glorious
EFMLYD self-employed
EFNEET self-interest
EFNERD self-endeared
EFNLDY newfangledly
EFNLSS self-analysis
EFNOVD self-involved
EFOORD self-coloured
EFOTAT self-portrait
EFPRVL self-approval
EFRKSN Leif Eriksson
EFRMGC perform magic
EFRSAE welfare state
EFRSIE Bedfordshire
EFRYIL Geoffrey Hill
EFRYOE Geoffrey Howe
EFSIND new-fashioned
EFTRIG self-starting
EFUDAD Newfoundland
EFUTRD get flustered
EFVDNE self-evidence
EFWTYU be off with you
EGAANT weigh against
EGAFAC Belgian franc
EGAHCL geographical
EGATRY Sergeant Troy
EGBUIG neighbouring
EGFLES vengefulness
EGHFAS length of days
EGHFIE length of time
EGIGTN weighing a ton
EGLOHT ten-gallon hat
EGMNOS pergameneous
EGOACA Sergio Garcia
EGTFAD height of land
EGTIMR hedgetrimmer
EGVRAE tergiversate
EGWRLR sedge warbler
EHDCIG method acting
EHDCLY methodically
EHIAIY technicality
EHLGCL nephological
EHLMTR nephelometer
EHLMTY nephelometry
EHMANR Pelham Warner
EHMSIE New Hampshire
EHNCLY mechanically
EHOABE technobabble
EHOEET dethronement
EHOHBA technophobia
EHOHBC technophobic
EHORTC technocratic
EHRADC Netherlandic
EHRADR Netherlander
EHREBE rechargeable
EIADTS pericarditis
EIAEES delicateness
EIAESN delicatessen□
EIAIEY derivatively
meditatively
EIAIGY hesitatingly
EIAIIG revitalizing
EIAIIY definability
desirability
heritability
EIAINL dedicational
derivational
EIAITC revivalistic
EIAKES semi-darkness
EIAPIT decimal point
EIBKON let it be known
EIBRIT Denis Burkitt
EICIGY bewitchingly
EICNRC heliocentric
EICROL Lewis Carroll
EICSNR Kevin Costner
EIDCLY periodically
EIDDRT Denis Diderot
EIDEOE period before
EIDNIS periodontics
EIDNIT periodontist
EIDRET bewilderment
EIEAEY deliberately
EIEAHD semi-detached
EIEAIE deliberative
demineralise
demineralize
desiderative
remineralise
remineralize
EIEAIN deliberation
EIEHIM perinephrium
EIERCL perimetrical
EIETAY penitentiary
residentiary
EIGAHC heliographic
EIGAUE heliogravure
EIGBLS Heliogabalus
EIHATC periphrastic
EIHFLY delightfully
EIHRBE decipherable
EIHRET decipherment
EIIAEY legitimately
EIIAIE delimitative
demilitarise
demilitarize
EIIAIG debilitating
EIIAIN debilitation
delimitation
felicitation
verification
EIIAIT semifinalist
EIIAIY veridicality
EIIAOY verificatory
EIICLR semicircular
EIICNE reminiscence
EIIEAL medicine ball
EIIEES decisiveness
definiteness
derisiveness
feminineness
EIIEIE decitisenize
decitizenize
EIIEOS seminiferous
EIIHES devilishness
EIIIEY definitively
EIINLY meridionally
EIIOSY felicitously
EIJHSN Celia Johnson
EILGCL aetiological
EILILR serial killer
EILUBR serial number
EIMHRY medium sherry
EIMYAE devil-may-care
EINDES resignedness
EINRRG designer drug
EINULY semi-annually
EIOAES devil of a mess
EIODIE demi-mondaine
EIOFIH get it off with
EIORPY lexicography
EIORTC meritocratic
EIOSES perilousness
EIOURZ Benito Juarez
Benito Juárez
EIQETY delinquently
EIRCLY reciprocally
EIRCOS semi-precious
EIRCTR reciprocator
EIRPCL semi-tropical
EISSAD Devil's Island

Words marked □ can also be spelled with an initial capital letter

EITAAE get into a rage
EITAIN registration
EITEAY heliotherapy
EITEET belittlement
EITESY resistlessly
EITGAE redintegrate
EITIIN geriatrician
EITIUE redistribute
EITOIM deviationism
heliotropism
EITOIT deviationist
EITRUH see it through
EITSAE get into shape
EITSUY begin to study
EIUAEY geniculately
reticulately
EIUAIN reticulation
EIUCUE venipuncture
EIUOSY meticulously
EIUSET deliquescent
EJMLDP get jumbled up
EKESES fecklessness
recklessness
EKIDDY weak-mindedly
EKNFIN Pecksniffian
EKNODR pecking order
ELAACD weal-balanced
well balanced
well-balanced
ELAAOT feel bad about
ELANRD well-mannered
ELCDES pellucidness
ELCFLY neglectfully
ELCIEY reflectively
ELCIGY neglectingly
reflectingly
ELCIIY reflectivity
ELCLEE Keble College
ELDACD well-advanced
ELDCAE well I declare!
ELDCTD well-educated
ELDUTD well-adjusted
ELEEVD well-deserved
ELEIND well-designed
ELESDN well-versed in
ELESND well-reasoned
well-seasoned
ELGAIN deflagration
ELGCLY geologically
neologically
ELGRNE belligerence
ELGRNY belligerency
ELHDMY sell the dummy
ELHEOT health resort
ELHETE health centre
ELHIIG health-giving
ELHPNH feel the pinch
ELHTUH tell the truth
ELIELB Hell-fire Club
ELIETD well-directed
ELIETR Red Leicester
ELIPSD well-disposed
ELMUHD mealy-mouthed
ELNDVT feal and divot
ELNLND feel inclined
ELNOMD well-informed
ELNPAE selling plate
ELNPIE selling price
ELNSAS feel one's oats
ELNSES feel one's legs
ELNSET feel one's feet
ELNTGL Berline-Tegel
ELNTNA Wellingtonia
ELOOIE de-alcoholise
de-alcoholize
ELORFR feel sorry for
ELOTMD bell-bottomed
ELRAGD well-arranged
ELRUDD well-grounded
ELRUFT declare unfit
ELRVDD well-provided
ELSVLS Telly Savalas
ELTOAY deflationary
reflationary
ELTOIT deflationist
ELUPID well-supplied
ELVRES sell overseas
ELWAMR yellowhammer
ELWESY yellow jersey
ELWIBN yellow ribbon
ELWOKR fellow worker
fellow-worker
ELWOKT yellow rocket
ELWTEK yellow streak
ELXAEA reflex camera
EMAIIY permeability
EMAUEF be a measure of
EMCLTD vermiculated
EMCLUE permaculture
vermiculture
EMEIHE Fehmgerichte
EMFFIE term of office
EMGEIM geomagnetism
EMMNHP helmsmanship
EMNAAE permanganate
EMNAIE fermentative
EMNAIN fermentation
segmentation
EMNAOE New Mangalore
EMNBNI Hermann Bondi
EMNCLY Germanically
EMNHSE Hermann Hesse
EMNNWY permanent way
EMNUIS hermeneutics
EMNUIT hermeneutist
EMNVGL Hermann Vogel
EMSALN Seamus Mallon
EMSENY Seamus Heaney
EMSIEY permissively
EMTCLY hermetically
EMTGBY Hermitage Bay
EMTIIN geometrician
EMTIIY permittivity
EMTLWR helmet flower
EMUSBE reimbursable
ENCAIN pernoctation
ENCLRY vernacularly
ENCOSN Ben Nicholson
ENCOSY perniciously
ENDBTD being debated
ENEEET Kenny Everett
ENEOEU Jeanne Moreau
ENEROS reindeer moss
ENGOMN Benny Goodman
ENGYAS teenage years
ENHBOS be on the books
ENIEIS Jean Sibelius
ENIGEY Jean Tinguely
ENIHEZ Heinrich Lenz
ENIHOL Heinrich Böll
ENIOAE reinvigorate
ENMIMD her name is mud
ENNCEK Tennant Creek
ENNFLY meaningfully
ENNLGR Fernand Léger
ENNOTS Hernán Cortés
ENNRYE Leonine rhyme
ENOCLT Jean Poncelet
ENOETY means of entry
ENPNHR penny-pincher
ENPRTD mean-spirited
ENRCHN Leonard Cohen
ENREZG Werner Herzog
ENRLVN Bernard Levin
ENRNMY Leonard Nimoy
ENSATN Vernis Martin
ENSILE Dennis Lillie
ENSISN Dennis Nilsen
ENSOPR Dennis Hopper
ENSWMN be one's own man
ENTBKR Kenneth Baker
ENTCAK Kenneth Clark
ENTOSN Kenneth Olsen
ENTUTR peanut butter
ENUIES mean business
ENUUFT Jean Dubuffet
ENYENY teensy-weensy
ENYVNA Pennsylvania
EOAEAE below average
EOAEES desolateness
EOAIEY decoratively
denotatively
derogatively
pejoratively
EOAIIG demoralizing
EOAIIY memorability
removability
revocability
EOAMNS beso las manos
EOAOIY derogatorily
EOARPA Herod Agrippa
EOATCL aeronautical
EOATPS Herod Antipas
EOBEET redoublement
EOCLBE reconcilable
EOCLBY reconcilably
EOCOHS set of clothes
EODALT second ballot
EODAUE second nature

EODDAL recorded mail
EODEAR beyond repair
EODEEY beyond remedy
EODEIF beyond belief
EODEPR record-keeper
EODIDE second fiddle
EODLYR record-player
EODNIM record on film
EODOIG Second Coming
EODOOE second to none
second-to-none
EODOSN second cousin
EODOTD venom'd-mouth'd
EODRWH second growth
EODTIE second strike
EODTIG second string
EOEACD become rancid
EOEAGD become ragged
EOEAGR become larger
EOEAKR become darker
EOEALD become pallid
EOEALR become taller
EOEARW become narrow
EOEATR become fatter
EOEBOS bet one's boots
get one's books
EOECIE become active
EOECPT set one's cap at
EOECRS get one's cards
EOEDRS rejoneadores
EOEEDR become tender
EOEEFO let oneself go
EOEEKR become weaker
EOEELW become mellow
EOEENN become keen on
EOEIEY become lively
EOEIGR become bigger
EOELUY become cloudy
EOELWR become slower
EOEOCN before you can
EOEODR become colder
EOEOGR become longer
EOEOIG become boring
EOEOTN become lost in
become rotten
EOETEH set one's teeth
EOETRA remotest area
EOEULC become public
EOEVRN get one over on
EOFIIM Zeno of Citium
EOFNIE Tet Offensive
EOFRUE recomforture
EOGGIG be tough going
EOGLLE Sea of Galilee
EOGSAT decongestant
EOGSIE decongestive
EOHITC henotheistic
EOIAIN denomination
memorization
EOIATR Velociraptor
EOICLY demoniacally
EOIGES becomingness
EOIIIE depoliticise
depoliticize
EOIINL depositional
EOINLY devotionally
EOITOS negotiations
EOJSIE bed of justice
EOLCIE recollective
EOLCIN recollection
EOMNIG recommending
EOMRAA Sea of Marmara
EOMRCN Mesoamerican
EOMSIN decommission
EONEET denouncement
renouncement
EONIGY resoundingly
EONIRR reconnoitrer
EONSBY recognisably
EONSNE recognisance
EONZBE recognizable
EONZBY recognizably
EONZNE recognizance
EOODSO be so bold as to
EOOHTK Sea of Okhotsk
EOOIIE seropositive
EOOPOS mesomorphous
EOOSES venomousness
EOPESR decompressor
EOPSBE decomposable
EOREES resourceless
EORMTC melodramatic
EOSCAE deconsecrate
EOSFLY remorsefully
EOSIUE reconstitute
EOSRBE demonstrable
EOSRBY demonstrably
EOSRNE remonstrance
EOSRTR demonstrator
remonstrator
EOSSIN repossession
EOTCAY gerontocracy
EOTDES besottedness
EOTEAT below the salt
EOTEET below the belt
EOTEIE below-the-line
EOTIEF get outside of
EOUAIN demodulation
depopulation
EOUEES resoluteness
EOUINR resolutioner
EOVDES resolvedness
EOYAIS aerodynamics
EOYEIE depolymerise
depolymerize
EOYOGR memory-jogger
EPAEIH keep pace with
EPAEMN deepwatermen
EPAFYR deep-fat fryer
EPAOIM Neoplatonism
EPAOIT Neoplatonist
EPARIH keep fair with
EPCALD bespectacled
EPCFLY respectfully
EPCIEY respectively
EPEAIG people-eating
EPEDNE resplendence
EPEDNY resplendency
EPEFEA Temple of Hera
EPEFOT people's front
EPEIGY perplexingly
EPERNE reappearance
re-appearance
EPESES helplessness
EPHFED keep the field
EPHFUE be up the flume
EPHHUE keep the house
EPHPAE keep the peace
EPHRLS keep the rules
EPIIGY despairingly
EPITNE keep distance
EPLAIN despoliation
EPLBOM Leopold Bloom
EPLOOT keep a lookout
EPLTCL geopolitical
EPNEES responseless
EPNEOD keep on record
EPNETY despondently
EPNHUE leaping-house
EPNIEY responsively
serpentinely
EPNIGY despondingly
EPNIIE serpentinise
serpentinize
EPNIOM serpentiform
EPNOIL responsorial
EPNSED keep one's head
EPNSID keep one's mind
EPNSOD keep one's word
EPNSOL keep one's cool
EPNYOT keep an eye out
EPODIE keep good time
EPPOAE keep up to date
EPRGIG leap-frogging
EPRLOE temporal bone
temporal lobe
EPRLTE temperalitie
EPRMAM keep from harm
EPRMTR respirometer
EPRRUE temporary use
EPRTFR desperate for
EPTAIN perpetration
perpetuation
EPTCLY despotically
EPWYRM keep away from
EPYIIT geophysicist
EQAAIE desquamative
EQAAIN desquamation
EQAAOY desquamatory
ERAARG merry as a grig
ERADAD heart and hand
ERADOL heart and soul
ERADPN bear hard upon
ERAHBE reproachable
ERAIGY decreasingly
ERAINL recreational
ERAITC neorealistic
ERBCNR Georg Büchner
ERBEKR heart-breaker

ERBHAT learn by heart
ERCAIE depreciative
ERCAIN depreciation
retractation
ERCAOY depreciatory
ERCCIE tetracycline
ERCHUE terrace house
ERCIEY detractively
retractively
ERCIGY detractingly
ERCIIY refractivity
retractility
ERCOIY refractorily
ERCQIK get-rich-quick
ERCSIE retrocessive
ERCSIG reprocessing
ERCSIN retrocession
ERCUIY bear scrutiny
ERDCBE reproducible
ERDCIE reproductive
ERDCIN reproduction
ERDSAE heart disease
ERDSET recrudescent
EREADL George Handel
EREALP George Gallup
EREATN George Patton
EREAVR George Carver
EREBZT Georges Bizet
EREEDE George Beadle
EREOTR George Porter
ERERBE George Crabbe
EREREL George Orwell
ERERHM George Graham
ERESES fearlessness
peerlessness
ERESOT George C Scott
ERETBS George Stubbs
ERETKS George Stokes
EREUZN George Curzon
ERFCIN petrifaction
ERFCLY terrifically
ERFEIN retroflexion
ERFIGY terrifyingly
ERFLEL Jerry Falwell
ERFLIG Fear of Flying
ERGAHC reprographic
ERGAHR reprographer
ERGLIM Terry Gilliam
ERGNLY tetragonally
ERGRTR refrigerator
ERGRUD merry-go-round
ERHDIE tetrahedrite
ERHDOS tetrahedrons
ERHGIS Henry Higgins
ERHNIE search engine
ERHNIN reprehension
ERHNOY reprehensory
ERHROR Pearl Harbour
ERHTAE near that date
ERIUAE dearticulate
ERLGCL neurological
ERMNII Henry Mancini
ERMNKN Henry Mencken
ERMNTR recriminator
ERMTSE Henri Matisse
ERNAIN detruncation
ERNALN Keiron Fallon
ERNHET retrenchment
ERNOAE dégringolade
ERNSAR tear one's hair
EROHES tear to shreds
EROICS tear to pieces
ERPAOS necrophagous
ERPEAS neuropterans
ERPIIC necrophiliac
ERPLSS metropolises
necropolises
ERPLTN metropolitan
ERPREL Henry Purcell
ERREUN Henry Raeburn
ERRNIG heart-rending
ERRSUE peer pressure
ERSALY Henry Stanley
ERSAMT near as dammit
ERSEDS decrescendos
ERSEIG refreshening
ERSFLY refreshfully
ERSGAE Henry Segrave
ERSIEY regressively
repressively
ERSIGY depressingly
refreshingly
ERSIIY regressivity
ERSMNS refreshments
ERSNIG representing
ERSTUH near as a touch
ERSUIE depressurise
depressurize
ERTCLY neurotically
ERTHAT heart-to-heart
ERTOEU Henry Thoreau
ERTOIE secret police
ERTYTM secret system
ERVRIN retroversion
ERVUHN Henry Vaughan
ERWRIG heartwarming
heart-warming
ESAAIN de-escalation
ESAEMN newspaperman
newspapermen
New Statesman
ESAIEY persuasively
ESATDN get started on
ESBEES sensibleness
ESCEFR be a sucker for
ESCLNE Jessica Lange
ESDACD less advanced
ESDESR Welsh dresser
ESEMDP get steamed up
ESESET reassessment
ESFCTR versificator
ESGAUE key signature
ESIAIN perspiration
ESIAIY perspicacity
ESINIT New Scientist
ESINUS Messeigneurs
ESJCSN Jesse Jackson
ESLAIN tessellation
ESLHDS Les Sylphides
ESLRUE Geissler tube
ESMSEP get some sleep
ESMWEE get somewhere
ESNAOT messing about
ESNDNE Peasant Dance
ESNDOD seasoned wood
ESNERA messenger RNA
ESNESN Nelson Nelson
ESNIKT season ticket
ESNIUT Nelson Piquet
ESNLET personal best
ESNLZD personalized
ESNRDY person Friday
ESOEAE news coverage
ESOEOF pensioned off
ESOHRD Feast of Herod
ESOICM Deus vobiscum
ESONUS teaspoonfuls
ESOOIT seismologist
ESORGT sense of right
ESORPY seismography
ESOSES sensuousness
ESOSGT sense of sight
ESOTSE sense of taste
ESPDIG pease pudding
ESRAIN menstruation
ESRCDP get spruced up
ESRMNS measurements
ESRNJG measuring jug
ESROSY censoriously
ESRRBT welsh rarebit❑
ESRSEG Lee Strasberg
ESRSON dessertspoon
ESSETY persistently
ESSIGY persistingly
ESTMTR sensitometer
ESUIGY reassuringly
ESUKNO get stuck into
ESVRNE perseverance
ETADDY left-handedly
ETAEIA Septuagesima
ETAIIG neutralizing
ETANDY restrainedly
ETAPIT central point
ETBAIN vertebration
ETCEAK Deutsche Mark
Deutsche mark
ETCLAE verticillate
ETCLCS nectocalyces
ETCLES verticalness
ETCLRY lenticularly
ETCPAI leptocephali
ETDAIG death-dealing
ETDCMS sextodecimos
ETEAGF get the hang of
ETEAIT sex therapist
ETEAKF see the back of
ETEALR meat retailer
ETEAOG weather along
ETEBAD weatherboard

ETEBUD weather-bound
ETECAT weather chart
ETEEDE get the needle
ETEFAS centre of mass
ETEFIH kettle of fish
ETEGAS weather glass
ETEHKS get the shakes
ETEIDF get the wind of
ETEIDP get the wind up
ETEIES featheriness
ETEIGR get the finger
ETEIHY heathenishly
ETEIIE aestheticise
aestheticize
ETEIIM Aestheticism
ETEITN get the mitten
ETEPED centre spread
ETEPIH settle up with
ETEPOF weatherproof
ETERWD beetle-browed
ETESES restlessness
ETESOE settle a score
ETESRP weather strip
ETFAUE debt of nature
ETFCLY beatifically
ETFCTD certificated
ETFGEY pettifoggery
ETFGIG pettifogging
ETFIDN Betty Friedan
ETFOOR debt of honour
ETGAHC hectographic
ETGNLY pentagonally
ETHCOK beat the clock
ETHDOS pentahedrons
ETHWTR test the water
ETIGIG teething ring
ETIGNA West Virginia
ETILNS West Midlands
ETILNT certainly not
ETITDY restrictedly
ETITOS restrictions
ETJRET Keith Jarrett
ETLIGN vestal virgin
ETLNIL pestilential
ETMNAY testamentary
ETNAAT setting apart
ETNAET wetting agent
ETNCLY tectonically
Teutonically
ETNCOS pertinacious
ETNDIK meat and drink
ETNHAR left in the air
ETNHUE meeting-house
Westinghouse
ETNILY sententially
septennially
ETNPAE meeting-place
ETNPIT meeting-point
ETNTEE getting there
ETOAIE sectionalise
sectionalize
ETOAIM sectionalism
ETOBID festoon blind
ETOFCR petty officer
ETOFCS depth of focus
ETOFED depth of field
ETOILY meet socially
ETOOIT deltiologist
ETOSES dextrousness
ETPIAE centuplicate
ETPNLY death penalty
ETRAIE sectarianise
sectarianize
ETRAIM sectarianism
ETRAIN perturbation
ETRCLY neoterically
ETREGT welterweight
ETRILS Western Isles
ETRMIH West Bromwich
ETRODN Dexter Gordon
ETRSMA Western Samoa
ETRSOT Venture Scout
ETRTDY reiteratedly
ETRTET beat a retreat
ETRUHO get through to
ETSAET New Testament
ETSEOE testosterone
ETSMLY centesimally
ETSMTC leptosomatic
ETTRIG West Stirling
ETTUHL Pentateuchal
ETUAER restaurateur
ETUEAY test-tube baby
ETUTBE destructible
ETYHNE meet by chance
EUACAS Beaumarchais
EUACSS regular costs
EUADIK regular drink
EUAIEY reputatively
EUBSIG refurbishing
EUCAIE renunciative
EUCAIN denunciation
renunciation
EUCAOY denunciatory
renunciatory
EUCLEE Jesus College
EUCLTD pedunculated
EUCTBE resuscitable
EUCTTD resuscitated
EUCTTR resuscitator
EUDESD get undressed
EUDRIG red underwing
EUEAIE recuperative
remunerative
EUEAIG recuperating
rejuvenating
EUEAIN recuperation
rejuvenation
remuneration
EUEAOY remuneratory
EUECNE detumescence
EUENAK reduce in rank
EUEOOE refuse to vote
EUEPIS beaux esprits
EUIAIN resupination
EUIEES delusiveness
EUIIIR dehumidifier
EUIIIY deducibility
reducibility
EUIYIK security risk
EULAIE denuclearise
denuclearize
EULBSR sexual abuser
EULCIN genuflection
EULEIE sexual desire
EULEIH gefüllte fish
EULRAS sexual organs
EUNFOT return of post
EUNIKT return ticket
EUNILY sequentially
EUOSES nebulousness
sedulousness
EUPIEY resumptively
EUPUAE desulphurate
EUPUIE desulphurise
desulphurize
EURCIN resurrection
EURMNS requirements
EUSRTR sequestrator
EUTAOE requite atone
EUTCLY jesuitically
EUTOIM reductionism
EUTOIT reductionist
EVCIDE pelvic girdle
EVCWMN servicewoman
servicewomen
EVDIKR heavy drinker
EVFRED leave for dead
EVHATD heavy-hearted
EVIRIS leave in ruins
EVISGT heave in sight
EVISUN serve its turn
EVLAIN re-evaluation
EVLBIT heavily built
EVNAOE heavens above
EVNIES heavenliness
EVNOBD heaven forbid
EVNYIY heavenly city
EVNYOY heavenly body
EVOEOD leave one cold
EVQIKY leave quickly
EVQITY leave quietly
EVRCIG nerve-racking
EVREES perverseness
EVRWYT beaver away at
EVTCTR velvet-scoter
EVTEED heave the lead
EVTEOM leave the room
EVTEUN serve the turn
EVTOKY vervet monkey
EVTURS velvet-guards
EWEDCS between-decks
EWETMS between times
betweentimes
EWEUTO between us two
EWLAOE let well alone
EWNWTR Derwent Water
EYTOGY deny strongly
EYURUD see you around

EZLAIS	Denzil Davies
EZSPAO	mezzo-soprano
EZSRIO	senza sordino
FAYITE	of easy virtue
FEBRIG	afterburning
FEEFCS	after effects
	after-effects
FEFRAE	offer for sale
FEIAEY	effeminately
FEISID	after its kind
FENOTA	afternoon tea
FEOEEF	offer oneself
FEPROE	of set purpose
FETAIN	effectuation
FETDES	affectedness
FETEPY	affect deeply
FETOAE	affectionate
FETOGT	afterthought
FEVSET	effervescent
FHESNE	of the essence
FHODRF	of the order of
FIEBED	of mixed breed
FIEERR	office-bearer
FIENMN	Of Mice and Men
FIEODR	office-holder
FIEOKR	office worker
FIHEUE	of high repute
FIILAK	official mark
FIINDS	afficionados
FIITDO	affiliated to
FIIYAD	affinity card
FLRSET	efflorescent
FMOTNE	of importance
FODEUE	of good repute
FOECUP	off one's chump
FOEGAD	off one's guard
FOEHNS	off one's hands
FOEOIN	off one's onion
FOMRCN	Afro-American
FOSRAD	a fool's errand
FOTESY	effortlessly
FRGTDY	affrightedly
FRNIGY	affrontingly
FRTOGT	aforethought
FSITNE	of assistance
FSORNS	offscourings
FTEEOD	off the record
	off-the-record
FTEIGS	off the hinges
FTEOTE	off the bottle
FUIEES	effusiveness
GEAIIY	agreeability
GEIGIH	agreeing with
GIIAIN	uglification
GIINOL	ignition coil
GITCLY	egoistically
GIUIES	agribusiness
GIUTRL	agricultural
GNGNRL	agent-general
GOCNET	age of consent
GOINNS	a good innings
GOUIES	agrobusiness
GPOOIT	Egyptologist

GRIOSY	Igor Sikorsky
GRSIEY	aggressively
GSEEIT	eggs Benedict
GYUKIG	ugly duckling
HAATET	The Apartment
HACEIT	The Alchemist
HAEOGR	phrasemonger
HAGEAE	the aggregate
HAHNOT	thrashing-out
HAOCRS	chiaroscuros
HAOEAD	the aforesaid
HARCLY	theatrically
HARRYL	Theatre Royal
HATRPC	theanthropic
HAVRAY	the Adversary
HBEKES	the bee's knees
HBODCS	the boondocks
HBTEED	the bitter end
HBTKPA	Phi Beta Kappa
HBYRED	The Boy Friend
HCEOTF	chicken out of
HCIWIH	which is which?
HCLTBX	chocolate-box
HCLTLG	chocolate log
HCNURR	the Conqueror
HCRETR	The Carpenter
HCRTKR	The Caretaker
HCSGTD	thick-sighted
HCSIND	thick-skinned
HCTCIS	shock tactics
HCTEAY	shock therapy
HCTOGD	The City of God
HCXNHN	phycoxanthin
HDDNRN	rhododendron
HDEIGY	shudderingly
HDNTIG	the done thing
HDSOSN	Rhodes Boyson
HDWOIG	shadow-boxing
HEADEL	wheel and deal
HEADXE	wheel and axle
HEDFIE	thread of life
HEEAIG	cheeseparing
	cheese-paring
HEELCR	cheese slicer
HEEUGR	cheeseburger
HEFLES	cheerfulness
HEIHES	sheepishness
	thievishness
HEMTCL	phlegmatical
HEOOIE	phlebotomise
	phlebotomize
	phrenologise
	phrenologize
HEOOIT	phrenologist
	The Economist
HEOSAF	chief of staff
HEQATR	three-quarter
HESKRO	Ahmed Sukarno
HESORL	sheep's sorrel
HETMTY	chrestomathy
HEWTHS	Three Witches
HFDEVE	chefs d'oeuvre
HFNLLW	the final blow

HGADUE	The Grand Duke
HGBTEN	The Go-Between
HGCTCL	phagocytical
HGCTSS	phagocytosis
HGDAHR	The Godfather
HGLEAS	The Golden Ass
HGVDIA	Bhagavad Gita
HHMNAE	the human race
HHRSUF	the hard stuff
HHUEOD	the Household
HIELDP	shrivelled up
HIEOGE	chaise-longue
HIIGIE	shriving-time
HILOGD	shrill-gorged
HITABX	Christmas box
HITADY	Christmas Day
HITAEA	Christian era
HITAEE	Christmas Eve
HITAIE	christianise
	christianize
HITAIY	Christianity
HITESY	thriftlessly
HITHRH	Christ Church
	Christchurch
HLADAK	chalk and talk
HLAMNC	philharmonic
HLBAIG	childbearing
	child-bearing
HLBNFT	child benefit
HLBRGT	she'll be right
HLCMAY	shell company
HLCPES	The Lucy Poems
HLDLHA	Philadelphia
HLDLHS	philadelphus
HLGNSS	phylogenesis
HLGNTC	phylogenetic
HLHATD	wholehearted
	whole-hearted
HLIGAD	a helping hand
HLIHES	childishness
HLJDES	Philo Judaeus
HLLGCL	philological
HLNEIG	philandering
HLNHOE	philanthrope
HLNHOY	philanthropy
HLOAIE	whale of a time
HLOATC	phyllotactic
HLOIHC	Chalcolithic
HLOYIE	chalcopyrite
HLPAKN	Philip Larkin
HLPINY	Philip Sidney
HLRCLY	cholerically
HLSAMA	thalassaemia
HLSEEY	the last enemy
HLSIIE	Philistinise
	Philistinize
HLSIIM	philistinism
HLSPIE	philosophise
	philosophize
HLSSRW	the last straw
HLSWRD	The Lost World
HLWLAE	child welfare
HLYHLY	shilly-shally

HMCLOD chemical bond
HMCLRE chemical-free
HMDATR The Mad Hatter
HMEIGY whimperingly
HMEMSC chamber music
HMESAK chimney stack
HMESEP chimney-sweep
HMFCDY shamefacedly
HMFLES shamefulness
HMIAIY whimsicality
HMINHP championship
HMNSAG rhyming slang
HMOERL rhombohedral
HMOERN rhombohedron
HMRCLY chimerically
HMRHAE The March Hare
HMRSON the morn's morn
HMSAEY Thomas Savery
HMSALR Thomas Waller
HMSATN Thomas Warton
HMSDSN Thomas Edison
HMSEKR Thomas Dekker
HMSEKT Thomas Becket
HMSOBS Thomas Hobbes
HMSOLS Themistocles
HMSOSY Thomas Wolsey
HMSRWE Thomas Browne
HMSUHS Thomas Hughes
HMSULY Thomas Huxley
HMSUNR Thomas Murner
HMTCLY thematically
HMTDAH rhyme to death
HMTEAY chemotherapy
HMTRUH thumb through
HMUERP The Mousetrap
HNACEE Chinua Achebe
HNAMLY phantasmally
HNBDYF think badly of
HNCBNT china cabinet
HNCEHD phonic method
HNCMTC phonocamptic
HNCRSS rhinoceroses
HNCRTC rhinocerotic
HNCRTS rhinocerotes
HNCSAY the necessary
HNECOD thundercloud
HNEFAH thunderflash
HNEFID change of mind
HNEFIE change of life
HNEFOE change of tone
HNEHLG change the leg
HNEOOR change colour
HNEORE change course
HNEOSY thunderously
HNEOVR whencesoever
HNESOE thunder-stone
HNESOM thunderstorm
HNFLES thankfulness
HNGTAE The Nightmare
HNIGAK thinking back
HNKDIY The Naked City
HNLEIE thin blue line
HNLGCL phenological
phonological
rhinological
HNLLNN phenylalanin
HNMCLY phonemically
HNMNLY phenomenally
HNNTEE then and there
HNPATC rhinoplastic
HNRGPA Chandragupta
HNSIIG thanksgiving
HNSNIE things inside
HNSWIE Chinese white
HNTCLY phonetically
HNTMNA thanatomania
HNTPCL phenotypical
HNTRUH think through
HNUMBB thingummybob
HNUMJG thingummyjig
HOAIIM chromaticism
HOAIIY chromaticity
HOAOBY throw a wobbly
HODALY the Old Bailey
HOEELW chrome yellow
HOEIIN theoretician
HOGDIH thronged with
HOGOHR through-other
HOHATS Theophrastus
HOHRIE the other side
HOIAIN chlorination
HOIGRN shooting iron
HOIGTR shooting star
shooting-star
HOIGWY throwing-away
HOLGTN throw light on
HOOERC chronometric
HOOOIE chronologise
chronologize
HOOOIT chronologist
HOOPEE chromosphere
HOTERW shoot the crow
HOUPAE thiosulphate
HPBSUT ship's biscuit
HPCRIN whip scorpion
HPEDIG shepherdling
HPEDPE shepherd's pie
HPEPPR The Pied Piper
HPIEIG the prize-ring
HPIGAL shopping mall
HPIGIT shopping list
HPLCRL rhopaloceral
HPLFAE chapel of ease
HPNPPR The Pink Paper
HPSEGR The Passenger
HPULIG shipbuilding
HQIHQI chiquichiqui
HRAAIM charlatanism
HRAANT thereagainst
HRADHN there and then
HRAETC pharmaceutic
HRAMCY the real McCoy
HRAOOY pharmacology
HRATIG the real thing
HRATTV Gherman Titov
HRBCLY cherubically
HRCAGR short-changer
HRCCUT thoracic duct
HRCEIE characterise
characterize
HRCMOS short commons
HRCOPR sharecropper
HRCRUT short circuit
short-circuit
HRDNGT The Red Knight
HREBEE Charles Beebe
HREBRY Charles Barry
HREFRE Charles Forte
HREHLE Charles Hallé
HREHUE charnel house
charterhouse❑
HRENHY thirteenthly
HRERLS Charles Rolls
HRFCUT sheriff court
HRHADN churchwarden
HRHLIG shareholding
HRIATR thereinafter
HRIGAD thyroid gland
HRIHES churlishness
HRLBRY whortleberry
HRLOIG sharp-looking
HRNOOY pharyngology
HRODVS Sharron Davis
HROFAK Thermos® flask
HROOPE thermocouple
HROPEE thermosphere
HRORPY choreography
thermography
HROTTC thermostatic
HRPATC chiropractic
HRPATR chiropractor
HRPUIS therapeutics
HRRAIG third reading
HRSAFD short-staffed
HRSGTD shortsighted
short-sighted
HRSOTR sharpshooter
HRTEIW share the view
HRTEOT share the cost
HRTNUD sharp-tongued
HRTOHN thyrotrophin
HRTRIM short-termism
HRUHAE thoroughfare
HRUHES thoroughness
HRUHRD thoroughbred❑
HRVRIN short version
HRWITR shirtwaister
HRYIKR cherry picker
HRYRNY cherry brandy
HRYWMS thirty-twomos
HSAEOT The Scapegoat
HSAERW The Scarecrow
HSAOIH Shostakovich
HSAOII Thessaloníki
HSASNS thés dansants
HSBSES Ghostbusters
HSCNSX The Second Sex
HSEADS whiskerandos
HSEFED chesterfield❑

HSEIGY whisperingly
HSEOSY whisperously
HSETTR The Spectator
HSHRSE phosphoresce
HSIEET chastisement
HSIYET chastity belt
HSMOIM The Symposium
HSONMC physiognomic
HSOOIT physiologist
HSORPY physiography
HSOYOS the story goes
HSSATR rhesus factor
HSSOKY rhesus monkey
HSVNES the Seven Seas
HSYAOE Whisky Galore
HTADOL Shetland wool
HTADOY Shetland pony
HTAMRL white admiral
HTAMYE that's as may be
HTATRF what matter if
HTCEIT photochemist
HTCMIN white campion
HTCOIG what's cooking?
HTCPIG photocopying
HTDCOY rhytidectomy
HTEONT whether or not
HTEPOF shatterproof
HTETET the treatment
HTEWRS thitherwards
whitherwards
HTFAHR white feather
HTGAHC photographic
HTGAHR photographer
HTGIGN what's going on
HTGNSS phytogenesis
HTHDOF thatched roof
HTHDVL what the devil
HTHRAE what's-her-name
HTHSAE what's-his-name
HTISAE what's-its-name
HTKUKE white-knuckle
HTMCLY rhythmically
HTMODY the time of day
HTNHAM shot in the arm
HTPDIG white pudding
HTRCLY rhetorically
HTRSIN White Russian
HTTEDS what's the odds?
HTTOIM phototropism
HUAOOY rheumatology
HUBELS The Umbrellas
HUDRIH shoulder-high
HUEWRS Shaun Edwards
HUHFLY thoughtfully
HUIHES ghoulishness
HUIITC chauvinistic
HUTCER Chaunticleer
HUTEDS shout the odds
HVHPNY shove ha'penny
HVLOSY chivalrously
HVLYIS The Valkyries
HVOHLS Cheviot Hills
HVRTIG the very thing

HWCEOE the wicked one
HWNEET show interest
HWNHVR The Windhover
HWNSAD show one's hand
HWNSAE show one's face
HWNSED show one's head
HWOGHP the wrong shop
HWRDED the world's end
HWRDSY the world is my
HWRDVR the world over
HWSEAD The Waste Land
HWUIES show business
HYUGNS The Young Ones
HZCROS rhizocarpous
IAAIDE fit as a fiddle
IAAPTH hit a bad patch
IAAWRH Rita Hayworth
IABGAE disambiguate
IACAAD financial aid
IACAIE disaccharide
IACAIT financialist
IACHUE finance house
IAEAIM bicameralism
bilateralism
IAETED cigarette end
IAFCIN disaffection
IAFLAE disaffiliate
IAGEAE disaggregate
IAGNRL vicar-general
IAIAIN dilapidation
divarication
finalization
vitalization
IAINLI Liza Minnelli
IAKNEA Milan Kundera
IALWNE disallowance
IAOIES dilatoriness
IAPAIG disappearing
IAPEED misapprehend
IAPITD disappointed
IAPOEF disapprove of
IAPOIG disapproving
IAREBE disagreeable
IAREBY disagreeably
IAREET disagreement
IAREIH disagree with
IASCAE disassociate
IASHSA kinaesthesia
IASHSS kinaesthesis
IASHTC kinaesthetic
IATCES giganticness
IATCLY didactically
gigantically
IATOIE disauthorise
disauthorize
IATOSY disastrously
IATRPC misanthropic
IATRPS misanthropos
IATRRA disaster area
IAUOSY miraculously
IAVNAE disadvantage
IAVNUE misadventure
IAVSDY misadvisedly

IAYEPN binary weapon
IAYYTM binary system
IBBGIS Bilbo Baggins
IBCWAE finback whale
IBDNIG limbo-dancing
IBEABE bibble-babble
IBEITD nimble-witted
IBEOTD nimble-footed
IBHVOR misbehaviour
IBLCLY diabolically
IBLEIG disbelieving
IBLOAA Kimball O'Hara
IBREET disbursement
IBRRGT Wilbur Wright
IBRWIE Gilbert White
IBSRTS nimbostratus
ICADIK hitch and kick
ICADUT pitch and putt
ICALAE Mircea Eliade
ICATMN aircraftsman
ICCLUE pisciculture
ICEBOM witches' broom
ICECAR kitchen chair
ICEEES discreteness
ICEIEY discretively
ICEIIG discrediting
ICEINL discretional
ICEITY biochemistry
ICETES discreetness
ICEWNH kitchen-wench
ICFRAD pitch forward
ICGAHR discographer
ICICUB biscuit-crumb
ICICUT circuit court
ICIGOT hitching post
ICIIAE discriminate
ICIOSY circuitously
ICITET zinc ointment
ICLAIT miscellanist
ICLGEN Lincoln green
ICLSIE Lincolnshire
ICLUAE miscalculate
ICMAET circumjacent
ICMCIE circumscribe
ICMIIG discomfiting
ICMIIN circumcision
ICMIUE discomfiture
ICMMNU Giacomo Manzú
ICMOOE air-commodore
ICMOUE circumlocute
discomposure
ICMTNE circumstance
ICMUAE circumnutate
ICMUIN circumfusion
ICMYAE circumgyrate
ICNEIG discandering
ICNETD disconcerted
disconnected
discontented
ICNEVD misconceived
ICNIIN air-condition
ICNIUD discontinued
ICNOAE disconsolate

ICNPIE Vincent Price
ICNTUD misconstrued
ICNTUT misconstruct
ICOEGT piece of eight
ICOGOS piece of goods
ICPEHP discipleship
ICPIAY disciplinary
ICRATY discordantly
ICRIEY discursively
ICUAIG discouraging
ICUTAE discount rate
ICUTBE discountable
ICUTHP viscountship
ICUTOS discourteous
ICVRBE discoverable
ICVRBY Discovery Bay
IDACIG bird-watching
IDANSS misdiagnosis
IDBEES biddableness
IDCIEY vindictively
IDEADE fiddle-faddle
IDECOL middle school
IDEEGT middleweight
IDEEIW bird's eye view
IDEIKE kiddiewinkie
IDEODE niddle-noddle
IDEORE middle course
IDERUD fiddle around
middle ground
IDESES mindlessness
IDETCS fiddlesticks
IDFHNE wind of change
IDFODR bird of wonder
IDIEAK wildlife park
IDIFLY disdainfully
IDJNIO Rio de Janeiro
IDLAAT find pleasant
IDLPAA Rio de la Plata
IDMAOR misdemeanour
IDMPDR diadem spider
IDNSES find one's legs
IDNSET find one's feet
winding-sheet
IDOEOT hindforemost
IDOGIG mind-boggling
IDOYUO mind how you go
IDRATN kindergarten
IDRCIN misdirection
IDUAOT find out about
IDURES hindquarters
IDVRIY biodiversity
IDYCNH wild hyacinth
IDYHNE find by chance
IEAAIE Time Magazine
IEAEIE cinéma vérité
cinéma-vérité
IEAIIY mixed-ability
IEAITC liberalistic
IEAOIE mineralogise
mineralogize
IEAOIT mineralogist
IEAPRY Liberal Party
IEASIT fireman's lift

IEAWTR mineral water
IEBEES likeableness
IEBEIH liveable with
IEBLIH disembellish
IEBOTO give a boost to
IEBRAS disembarrass
IECATD disenchanted
IECECS life sciences
IECPTL fixed capital
IEDLHN river dolphin
IEDULS mixed doubles
IEEATD time-bewasted
IEEDNE lite pendente
IEEEVR wide receiver
IEEGMD like hey-go-mad
IEEGTO give weight to
IEELER sidereal year
IEELIE sidereal time
IEENHY nineteenthly
IEEOOY mixed economy
IEESES lifelessness
timelessness
tirelessness
IEETNE life sentence
IEEYUH like very much
IEFCIN line of action
IEFEIG mixed feeling
IEFETO give effect to
IEFHIT life of Christ
IEFRIG mixed farming
IEFTAK line of attack
IEGTIE six-eight time
IEHEBW give the elbow
IEHHAE give the heave
IEHLEO give the lie to
IEHNDO give the nod to
IEHSES side whiskers
IEHTTE give the title
IEHWRS give the works
IEIEES lifelikeness
IEKNEY Nigel Kennedy
IELBOS like old boots
IELFED Mike Oldfield
IELGPO give a leg up to
IELNTC like a lunatic
IELOEO give a loose to
IELSFL wineglassful
IEMDLO give a medal to
IEMNEL Nigel Mansell
IENAAF time and a half
IENAAN time and again
IENAFL give an earful
IENCLY Hibernically
IENDAH life-and-death
IENDEM live in a dream
IENEUN give in return
IENHRE give in charge
IENLAN live and learn
IENLVR live in clover
IENSED hide one's head
IENSIE bide one's time
give one's life
rise and shine

IENSOD fire and sword
give one's word
IENTBR pipe and tabor
IENTIG like anything
IEOAAL ride for a fall
IEOAMS fide non armis
IEODUT like gold dust
IEOEES tiresomeness
IEOEHR live together
IEONSO give points to
IEOONS ride to hounds
IEOORD time-honoured
IEOTES give to others
IEPAEU Tibet Plateau
IEPDIN Liverpudlian
IEPONX River Phoenix
IERCIG sidetracking
IERDTO give credit to
IERESO give orders to
IESFIG diversifying
IESLIR hired soldier
IESOAY diversionary
IESPAE license plate
IESUAE liver sausage
IETAOR direct labour
IETBET direct object
IETBIH disestablish
IETCES direct access
IETCIN direct action
IETCLM diverticulum
IETCLR diverticular
IETELE give it wellie
IETETN Mike Atherton
IETMNI divertimenti
IETMNO divertimento
IETNIH dilettantish
IETNIM dilettantism
IETNLD disentangled
IETOSY licentiously
IETPEH direct speech
IETPIG Silent Spring
IETRAE river-terrace
IETRHP directorship
IETWIL give it a whirl
IEUCAE hire purchase
hire-purchase
IEUDLT Eisen und Blut
IEUDNE give guidance
IEVDNE give evidence
IEVROT pine overcoat
IEWPIG wife-swapping
IEXOUE time exposure
IEYATD timely-parted
IEYTBE livery stable
IFACIE disfranchise
IFAOOD bioflavonoid
IFCLIS difficulties
IFEHNR air-freshener
IFLAUE sinful nature
IFRNIE differentiae
IFRNIL differential
IGAHCL biographical
IGAMTC diagrammatic

IGAOGN	Mid Glamorgan
IGARNA	lingua franca
IGCLEE	King's College
IGCUSL	King's Counsel
IGEADD	single-handed
IGEAET	single parent
IGEAGE	dingle-dangle
	higgle-haggle
	jingle-jangle
	mingle-mangle
IGEEKR	single-decker
IGEGIH	King's English
IGEIDD	single-minded
IGEIUE	single-figure
IGENIY	single entity
IGEOBT	single combat
IGFEAS	king of metals
IGFESS	king of beasts
IGHGWY	King's highway
IGLYMS	Kingsley Amis
IGNAAE	Virginia Wade
IGNAEG	Virginia Leng
IGNAEL	Virginia reel
IGNSIK	digging stick
IGORPY	biogeography
IGPDIG	figgy pudding
IGRFLS	Niagara Falls
IGRIKN	fingerlickin'
IGROES	Ginger Rogers
IGRRNS	fingerprints
IGRUFT	finger buffet
IGRUPT	finger puppet
IGSFLY	disgustfully
IGSIGY	disgustingly
IHADAN	might and main
IHADET	right-and-left
IHAGAE	with bad grace
IHALNI	Withnail and I
IHATND	disheartened
IHAUIG	highfaluting
IHCOHS	nightclothes
IHCUBR	nightclubber
IHEADO	with regard to
IHEBEK	Michael Buerk
IHECIE	Michael Caine
IHEEAD	Richie Benaud
IHEFAE	Michael Foale
IHEGAE	Michael Grade
IHENHY	eighteenthly
IHEPLN	Michael Palin
IHESAE	Richter scale
IHESEN	Lichtenstein
IHFLES	rightfulness
IHFTIG	tight-fitting
IHGAHC	lithographic
IHGAHR	lithographer
IHHADF	with the aid of
IHHATD	light-hearted
IHHNIE	diphthongise
	diphthongize
IHHNMN	right-hand man
IHIAIE	mithridatise
	mithridatize
IHIEIY	high fidelity
IHIGIH	fighting fish
IHIGOK	fighting cock
IHIHIG	highlighting
IHILIG	high-yielding
IHLAUE	with pleasure
IHLGCL	lithological
IHLKHE	Wilhelm Kühne
IHLNEO	Michelangelo
IHLOIE	Michel Fokine
IHLSAE	Nicholas Cage
IHLSED	with all speed
IHLSOE	Nicholas Rowe
IHNCIS	fish and chips
IHNESN	within reason
IHNHLW	within the law
IHNIHN	Sirhan Sirhan
IHNIIS	within limits
IHNNRD	lightning-rod
IHNONS	within bounds
IHNSON	win hands down
IHNUIG	dishonouring
IHNVIE	with one voice
IHOAIM	dichromatism
IHOETY	right of entry
IHOEUT	with no result
IHONIG	high-sounding
IHOORD	high-coloured
IHOPWR	Night of Power
IHPFOE	Bishop of Rome
IHPNRS	with open arms
IHPRTD	high-spirited
IHRAAS	Richard Adams
IHRAIG	sight-reading
IHRMAE	Richard Meade
IHRNAK	higher in rank
IHRNXN	Richard Nixon
IHRNYN	hither and yon
IHROIE	disharmonise
	disharmonize
IHROIY	high-priority
IHRPYR	Richard Pryor
IHRSOT	Richard Scott
IHRSUE	high-pressure
IHRWRM	withdraw from
IHSHRC	lithospheric
IHSIND	light-skinned
IHSPAE	highest place
IHSPIT	highest point
IHTEEM	right the helm
IHTIIE	lithotritise
	lithotritize
IHTITR	lithotripter
	lithotriptor
IHTNIG	withstanding
IHUDLY	without delay
IHUDUT	without doubt
IHUERR	without error
IHUEUL	without equal
IHUFUT	without fault
IHULMT	without limit
IHUMAS	without means
IHUPIE	without price
IHUSGT	without sight
IHVLET	dishevelment
IHWTES	with a witness
IHYAUD	highly valued
IHYTUG	highly-strung
IIAATR	win in a canter
IIAITC	militaristic
IIAOIL	visitatorial
IIAOSY	viviparously
IIBEES	pitiableness
IICNIE	disincentive
IIDFNE	civil defence
IIEAAA	Kiri Te Kanawa
IIECNE	viridescence
	virilescence
IIEITO	divided in two
IIESAD	Citizens' Band
IIESES	pitilessness
IIFCAT	disinfectant
IIFCIN	disinfection
IIGAIM	bilingualism
IIGEED	living legend
IIGERL	diving petrel
IIGHNS	living things
IIGIEO	giving rise to
IIGNOS	disingenuous
IIGRUD	rising ground
IIHDIH	finished with
IIIAIN	civilisation
	civilization
	digitization
	divinization
	minimization
	nidification
	vilification
	vivification
IIIEES	divisiveness
IIIGAL	dividing wall
IIIGIE	dividing-line
IIIHBE	diminishable
IIIHET	diminishment
IIIIAE	vitilitigate
IIIOSY	libidinously
IIIRES	bikini briefs
IIIYAF	divinity calf
IILBRY	civil liberty
IILNUS	bimilleniums
IIOFIH	hit it off with
IIOMOE	pisiform bone
IIOPTR	minicomputer
IIOSOK	visitors' book
IISRAT	civil servant
IISRIE	civil service
IITAIE	ministrative
IITAIN	ministration
IITGAE	disintegrate
IITIAE	disintricate
IITOSL	sinistrorsal
IITOSY	sinistrously
IITRET	disinterment
IITRIE	sinisterwise
IITRRT	misinterpret
IIUIEY	diminutively

IIUNOS	diminuendoes
IIUOSY	ridiculously
IIUTRL	vinicultural
	viticultural
IIUTRR	filibusterer
IIWIFR	lie in wait for
IIYIIY	niminy-piminy
IJDEET	misjudgement
IJITDY	disjointedly
IKEDCE	sick headache
IKEHPD	sickle-shaped
IKEIKE	kickie-wickie
IKHBRE	lick the birse
IKHHBT	kick the habit
IKIHES	ticklishness
IKNAKR	Rickenbacker
IKNHNY	milk and honey
IKNLSS	risk analysis
IKNSIS	lick one's lips
IKNTRD	sick and tired
IKNYAS	Kilkenny cats
IKOEHR	link together
IKOICS	pick to pieces
IKPHTB	pick up the tab
IKPTIS	kick upstairs
IKRRUD	tinker around
IKTEPR	wicket-keeper
IKTIDW	ticket window
IKTSLT	lickety-split
IKYAIG	mickey-taking
IKYATE	Mickey Mantle
IKYONY	Mickey Rooney
ILAATR	William Astor
ILABAE	William Blake
ILABAG	William Bragg
ILABIH	William Bligh
ILABOH	William Booth
ILABRE	William Burke
ILACAK	William Clark
ILACRY	William Carey
ILAHGE	William Hague
ILAIGY	misleadingly
ILAILW	Will Ladislaw
ILAJHS	William Johns
ILAJMS	William James
ILAPLY	William Paley
ILAPOT	William Prout
ILAPPS	uillean pipes
ILASUG	Williamsburg
ILAWLR	William Wyler
ILBENR	Billy Bremner
ILBSIG	Bible-bashing
ILCIIN	dialectician
ILCLUS	field colours
ILCOOY	dialectology
ILCTDY	dislocatedly
ILDEET	dislodgement
ILDGMA	viola da gamba
ILDSUS	fille des rues
ILEASN	Willie Carson
ILEUOT	Bill Beaumont
ILEWTR	Kielder Water
ILFIHS	Bill of Rights
	bill of rights
ILFULE	millefeuille
ILGASS	field glasses
	field-glasses
ILGCLY	biologically
ILHROA	Villahermosa
ILIGES	yieldingness
ILIGOE	dialling code
	dialling tone
ILIOSY	villainously
ILIPNE	mill-sixpence
ILLEEL	Citlaltépetl
ILMNIL	Billy McNeill
ILMRHL	field marshal
ILNELS	violoncellos
ILNIIY	fill untidily
ILOFCR	field officer
ILOMDY	till doomsday
ILOREY	kill-courtesy
ILORPY	bibliography
ILOSUY	field of study
ILPTAS	Lilliputians
ILRLBY	Willard Libby
ILRORD	pillar-box red
ILRSEL	Willy Russell
ILSEAS	Gilles de Rais
ILSMLY	millesimally
ILSOTY	Miklós Horthy
ILTEIP	will-o'-the-wisp
ILYALY	tilley-valley
ILYNHS	kill by inches
ILYOSN	kill by poison
IMCAIS	biomechanics
IMCNOS	Jimmy Connors
IMGEIM	diamagnetism
IMGEVS	Jimmy Greaves
IMMEIG	dismembering
IMNAIN	pigmentation
IMNFED	Sigmund Freud
IMNHLR	Simmenthaler
IMNSAE	diamond snake
IMSIEY	dismissively
IMSTIS	Siamese twins
IMTRUK	Jimmy Tarbuck
INAGAE	sign language
INDSAR	Giant Despair
INFCNE	significance
INFCNY	significancy
INGTAS	Midnight Mass
INIHES	fiendishness
INLGCL	limnological
INLIHE	Lionel Richie
INLOPN	Lionel Jospin
INLOTP	signal to stop
INMIMD	his name is mud
INSSAD	witness stand
INYEHT	Sidney Bechet
IOAGGL	Nikolai Gogol
IOAIAO	Nicola Pisano
IOATOR	kilowatt hour
IOBLVR	Simon Bolivar
	Simón Bolívar
IOCCUT	divorce court
IODNIE	vin ordinaire
IOEEFF	rid oneself of
IOEEFN	dig oneself in
IOEIMN	Nicole Kidman
IOEINE	disobedience
IOESUS	win one's spurs
IOGMNO	risorgimento
IOGNSD	disorganised
IOGNZD	disorganized
IOHNRA	mitochondria
IOICIA	Nixon in China
IOICLY	simoniacally
IOINAE	disorientate
IOKZES	Simon Kuznets
IOLCIG	lino blocking
IONVRS	picornavirus
IOOFCR	pilot officer
IOOFNE	minor offence
IOOSES	rigorousness
	timorousness
	vigorousness
IOTEAD	lie of the land
IOTEET	six of the best
IOTEIE	bit on the side
IOULAE	ribonuclease
IPAEET	displacement
	misplacement
IPAOSY	diaphanously
IPCAIE	Hippocratise
	Hippocratize
IPEAKD	ripple-marked
IPEFET	ripple effect
IPEIDD	simple-minded
IPESDY	displeasedly
IPIIEE	disprivilege
IPLUIN	air pollution
IPNAIN	dispensation
IPNCLY	Hispanically
IPNEIH	dispense with
IPNOIE	hispaniolise
	hispaniolize
IPNTAE	mispunctuate
IPOONE	mispronounce
IPPTMS	hippopotamus
IPRTDY	dispiritedly
IPSESD	dispossessed
IPTHAE	dispatch case
IPTOSY	dispiteously
IPTTOS	disputatious
IPUEIE	dispauperise
	dispauperize
IPYIIT	biophysicist
IQAIID	disqualified
IQIIIN	disquisition
IQOAIN	misquotation
IRAEAA	Sierra Nevada
IRAOII	Pier Pasolini
IRBOOY	microbiology
IRCIAE	microclimate
IRCLRA	vibracularia
IRCMLS	cirrocumulus
IRCRUT	microcircuit
IREADN	Pierre Cardin

IREALS Pierre Laclos
IREOLZ Pierre Boulez
IREUOT Pierre Du Pont
IRGAIY microgravity
IRGRFL disregardful
IRGRIG disregarding
IRGYHC hieroglyphic
IRHBTT microhabitat
IRLAIN fibrillation
IRLGCL hierological
IRNLSN fibrinolysin
IROSES vitreousness
IRPEET misrepresent
IRPIEY disruptively
IRPITD microprinted
IRPOIT vibraphonist
IRPOMN Piers Plowman
IRPTBE disreputable
IRPTBY disreputably
IRRHCL hierarchical
IRSIEY digressively
IRSINL digressional
IRSOIM Microscopium
IRSREN microsurgeon
IRSREY microsurgery
IRSRTS cirrostratus
IRTUCE vibratiuncle
IRUOIE nitrous oxide
IRWVBE microwavable
ISAECE air-sea rescue
ISAIEY dissuasively
ISAIHM Miss Havisham
ISCAIE dissocialise
dissocialize
ISCAIN dissociation
ISCNEN first concern
ISFREE Bias of Priene
ISHASR kirschwasser
ISHPIT miss the point
ISIHFY pigs might fly
ISLNIE diesel engine
ISMEDY Midsummer Day
ISMERC dissymmetric
ISMLNE dissemblance
ISMLRO dissimilar to
ISMLRY dissimilarly
ISMLTR dissimulator
ISMNTR disseminator
ISNHSS biosynthesis
ISNHTC biosynthetic
ISNIGY dissentingly
ISOAIE missionarise
missionarize
ISOAIS missionaries
ISOFCR first officer
ISOSIH Winston Smith
ISOSLM Winston-Salem
ISPTDY dissipatedly
ISRAIG first reading
ISRAIN dissertation
ISRFSI dies profesti
ISRFSL first refusal
ISRPIM diastrophism
ISSOIG first showing
ISTSID dissatisfied
ISUAOR Sir Scudamour
ISVRET disseverment
ITANET distrainment
ITASAE mistranslate
ITASOT air transport
ITATDY distractedly
ITCOHS dirty clothes
ITDFDC eisteddfodic
ITDFDU eisteddfodau
ITDYAE birthday cake
ITEATE tittle-tattle
ITEEPE little people
ITEHES oil the wheels
ITEIGR little finger
ITEILR little Hitler
ITEORT Little Dorrit
ITEOTE hit the bottle
ITESAE Mistress Page
ITESEN Wittgenstein
ITESES listlessness
ITESOD Mistress Ford
ITETET mistreatment
ITFHGB gift of the gab
ITFLES mirthfulness
ITGAHC pictographic
ITGDRE Kitty Godfree
ITGNSS histogenesis
ITGNTC histogenetic
ITHEBW lift the elbow
ITHEDR Pitt the elder
ITHSIT Wilt the Stilt
ITIUIE distributive
ITIUIN distribution
ITKNES mistakenness
ITLAIN distillation
ITLGCL histological
ITLUDY dirty laundry
ITMCOS diatomaceous
ITMEAE distemperate
ITNAUA tintinnabula
ITNCLY diatonically
ITNENS Milton Keynes
ITNTES distinctness
ITOAIE fictionalise
fictionalize
ITODIN Piet Mondrian
ITOSES virtuousness
ITPRET fifty per cent
ITRABY Tintern Abbey
ITRADN winter garden
ITRAEK Victoria Peak
ITRAIE disturbative
ITRAIM Victorianism
ITRAKT litter basket
ITRAOD Victoria Wood
ITRATR mixter-maxter
pitter-patter
ITRCLY historically
ITREOY Victor de Jouy
ITRFBE dietary fibre
ITRHRY winter cherry
ITRHUE picture-house
ITRIES sisterliness
ITRILW sisters-in-law
ITROSE Mister Wopsle
ITROSY victoriously
ITRPRS winter sports
ITRRUD winter-ground
ITRUBE Mister Bumble
ITRYOD bitterly cold
ITSENA hiatus hernia
ITTCLY dietetically
ITTOSY fictitiously
ITTRHP dictatorship
ITWSIG dirty washing
IUAHTS fidus Achates
IUAIEY figuratively
IUDSES liquid assets
IUEAIE vituperative
IUEAIN vituperation
IUEATY lieutenantry
IUEKTR figure skater
IUFCIN liquefaction
IUGCLY liturgically
IUODLY sinusoidally
IUOHBA ailurophobia
IUOSES bibulousness
IUPUIG Linus Pauling
IUTNIY simultaneity
IUTNOS simultaneous
IUTOIM situationism
IUVCOS Dieu avec nous
IVCLUE silviculture
IVESBO Silva Eusebio
IVNIKE Rip Van Winkle
IVRCEN silver screen
IVRIIG silver lining
IVRLTD silver-plated
IVROLR silver dollar
IYFEUE city of refuge
IYLCAN bicycle chain
IZARBN Yitzhak Rabin
IZEODN Lizzie Borden
IZNROE Zinzan Brooke
KAOAIY Oklahoma City
KEGODY skreigh of day
KHSETN G K Chesterton
KLESAE Skelmersdale
KNNBNS skin and bones
KNSASM a king's ransom
KNYIPR skinny-dipper
KPIGOE skipping-rope
KTIHES skittishness
LAAAEL clear as a bell
LAAPLA alla cappella
LAATES pleasantness
LAATIS pleasantries
LACNTI Elias Canetti
LADUDY all and sundry
LAIGAK clearing bank
LAIGAY cleaning lady
LAIGOK floating dock
LAOCOS Eleanor Cross
LAORGY Eleanor Rigby

LASGTD	clear-sighted
LATOIS	olfactronics
LAUERP	pleasure trip
LAVSDY	ill-advisedly
LBEIGY	slubberingly
LBEMUH	blabbermouth
LBGRNE	globigerinae
LBIGEL	all being well
LBOEHR	club together
LBOSES	glabrousness
LBSEIG	ill-beseeming
LBSIAY	plebiscitary
LBTETE	Globe Theatre
LBTOTR	globetrotter
LCADLE	black-and-blue
LCAIIY	electability
LCBEES	placableness
LCBLIG	blackballing
LCBTEN	place between
LCCPTL	block capital
LCCRAT	blackcurrant
LCEEEN	black-eye bean
LCEEPA	black-eyed pea
LCEIDN	cliché-ridden
LCEIGY	flickeringly
LCEOOY	black economy
LCESIL	glockenspiel
LCESYE	blocked style
LCGADY	blackguardly
LCHATD	black-hearted
LCHWWR	Black Hawk War
LCISAS	slack in stays
LCNELD	ill-concealed
LCNEVD	ill-conceived
LCNIBY	Placentia Bay
LCOBRH	place of birth
LCOFAS	block of flats
LCPDIG	black pudding
LCRCLE	electric blue
LCRCLY	electrically
LCRFIG	electrifying
LCRLAE	block release
LCRLSS	electrolysis
LCRLTC	electrolytic
LCRMTR	electrometer
LCRMTY	electrometry
LCRNUE	electron tube
LCROTC	electro-optic
LCRPAE	electroplate
LCRPIE	electrophile
LCRSIN	black Russian
LCRSOE	electroscope
LCRSOK	electroshock
LCSBAH	Black Sabbath
LCSRNS	Alice Springs
LCSTIG	place setting
LCTERL	Ely Cathedral
LCTOAY	elocutionary
LCTOIS	Old Catholics
LCTOIT	elocutionist
LCTRUH	flick through
LCUAIN	flocculation
LCUNES	Alec Guinness
LCWTHR	clock-watcher
LDAOIL	gladiatorial
LDEAMR	sledgehammer
LDEWAK	bladder wrack
	bladderwrack
LDIHES	cloddishness
LDNSAE	sliding scale
LDSNGT	Gladys Knight
LDTNBG	Gladstone bag
LDVUIG	all-devouring
LEAGET	Blaenau Gwent
LEAIIY	alterability
LEAMRL	fleet admiral
LEBAIG	all-embracing
LEFNEN	Bloemfontein
LEIGES	fleetingness
LEIGIL	sleeping pill
	sleeping-pill
LEIIAE	illegitimate
LEIIAY	illegitimacy
LEIIIY	illegibility
LELEET	alder-liefest
LELGTY	sleep lightly
LELYDE	Alderley Edge
LEMNHP	aldermanship
LENFIG	glue-sniffing
LEOYAY	eleemosynary
LETCIG	bluestocking
LETINY	Albert Finney
LETONY	Albert Hornby
LETTMA	Alberto Tomba
LEWLIG	sleepwalking
LEWOMC	Fleetwood Mac
LEYDIL	blue-eyed girl
LEYOLW	Sleepy Hollow
LFHNIG	cliffhanging
	cliff-hanging
LFRCAD	Cliff Richard
LFSIND	old fashioned
	old-fashioned
LGEIDN	plague-ridden
LGIHES	sluggishness
LGLAIN	flagellation
LGRHCL	oligarchical
LGTOHC	oligotrophic
LGTOSY	flagitiously
LGTYAM	slightly warm
LHAISN	Althea Gibson
LHBTCL	alphabetical
LHNMRC	alphanumeric
LICUIE	all-inclusive
LIDAIG	plain-dealing
LIEACL	Blaise Pascal
LIEAEY	illiterately
LIEAIE	alliterative
	illiberalise
	illiberalize
LIEAIN	alliteration
LIEAIY	illiberality
LIEKIG	Alpine skiing
LIGACR	flying saucer
LIGIAD	flying lizard
LIGOTR	flying doctor
LIGOUN	flying column
LIGRDE	flying bridge
LIHIES	almightiness
LIIAIN	fluidization
LIMRLS	Elgin marbles
LIPELY	Elvis Presley
LIPRAT	all-important
LIRSAS	Alain Resnais
LISIIG	plain sailing
LITAAE	fly into a rage
LITCLY	elliptically
LIVYNE	clairvoyance
LIVYNY	clairvoyancy
LMAIIY	flammability
LMEIGY	glimmeringly
	slumberingly
LMEOSY	slumberously
LMIGMS	Olympic Games
LMIGOT	climbing-boot
LMIGRN	climbing iron
LMNAIE	alimentative
LMNAIN	alimentation
LMNBAD	old man's beard
LMNEAE	Clemence Dane
LMNFED	Clement Freud
LMOATY	flamboyantly
LMOLAK	Plimsoll mark
LMOLIE	Plimsoll line
LMSATE	Glamis Castle
LMTRWR	flame-thrower
LMUHOK	Plymouth Rock
LNCNAE	plano-concave
LNDCIE	blanc-de-chine
LNDNIS	Blanc de Noirs
LNEIGY	blunderingly
LNEOSY	slanderously
LNFCIN	plan of action
LNHATD	flint-hearted
LNHLWR	Blanchflower
LNIGAS	slantingways
LNIHES	clannishness
LNIHET	blandishment
LNILTE	Alan Sillitoe
LNMYTM	plenum system
LNOOSY	clangorously
LNPTNE	plenipotence
LNTRDY	ill-naturedly
LNUOSY	glandulously
LOADRN	blood and iron
LOAIHR	all of a dither
LOAODH	all of a doodah
LOATCL	pleonastical
LOAUDN	all of a sudden
LOBOHR	blood-brother
LOEAAN	all over again
LOECNE	fluorescence
LOIAIY	illogicality
LOLTIG	bloodletting
	blood-letting
LONTIG	all-or-nothing
LOOABN	fluorocarbon
LOOAUE	Eleonora Duse
LOOCPC	fluoroscopic

LOOPIM	pleomorphism	LSTEAK	bless the mark	LYNFED	playing-field
LOPCIG	blood packing	LSTGTY	close tightly	LYOMNY	play for money
LOSAND	bloodstained	LSTOGT	close thought	LYTATR	play at waster
LOSCIG	bloodsucking	LTECEM	clotted cream	LZBTFY	Elizabeth Fry
LOSRYS	Alfonso Reyes	LTEIGY	clatteringly	LZNBOD	blazon abroad
LOSULY	Aldous Huxley		flatteringly	MAEILY	immaterially
LOTETR	allow to enter		glitteringly	MAHMSN	Emma Thompson
LOTFOT	all-out effort	LTEOEY	blithesomely	MALNYE	R M Ballantyne
LOTISY	bloodthirsty	LTEPES	flat-bed press	MAQEET	embarquement
LOWDIG	Blood Wedding	LTEPRT	Blithe Spirit	MARSIG	embarrassing
LOYIDD	bloody-minded	LTETET	ill-treatment	MASDES	ambassadress
LPATEL	elephant seal	LTFLES	slothfulness	MATAIY	impartiality
LPATOD	elephant cord	LTIHES	sluttishness	MATCIS	smear tactics
LPEBAD	clapperboard	LTMETA	Clytemnestra	MATEET	embattlement
LPEIES	slipperiness	LTNBAT	Blatant Beast	MAUAEY	immaculately
LPFHPN	slip of the pen	LTNBDN	Blut und Boden	MAUEES	immatureness
LPHCBE	slip the cable	LTNCLY	platonically	MAULAT	Immanuel Kant
LPMOIG	slip a mooring	LTNESN	Blut und Eisen	MCBEES	amicableness
LPNSAS	slip one's ways	LTNMIC	platinum disc	MCSUIE	amicus curiae
LPNSID	slip one's mind	LTOARS	Plateosaurus	MEAIEY	imperatively
LPOAIC	kleptomaniac	LTOMEL	platform heel	MECPET	impercipient
LPORPY	glyptography	LTOMRA	alstroemeria	MECPIE	imperceptive
LPPIGR	klipspringer	LTOOSY	gluttonously	MEERBE	impenetrable
LPRAIE	all-pervasive	LTSAET	Old Testament	MEERBY	impenetrably
LPUWRS	slope upwards	LUCABR	cloud chamber	MEFCIN	imperfection
LQIHES	cliquishness	LUDEGR	flour dredger	MEIETL	impedimental
LRCLEE	Clare College	LUESAT	Glauber's salt	MEIETY	impenitently
LRCLUE	floriculture	LUHEOS	slaughterous	MEIHBE	imperishable
LRDILY	Alfred Sisley	LUHODY	Plough Monday	MEIHBY	imperishably
LRDISY	Alfred Kinsey	LUIAIE	illuminative	MEIIOS	impetiginous
LRDUTN	Alfred Austin	LUIAIG	illuminating	MELNYU	I'm telling you
LREMUT	a large amount	LUIAIN	claudication	MELSIG	embellishing
LRMNAE	ultramontane		illumination	MEMNNE	impermanence
	ultramundane	LUIEES	illusiveness	MEMNNY	impermanency
LRNOSY	ultroneously	LUIIIY	plausibility	MEOILY	immemorially
LRNTIT	clarinettist	LUKSIG	cloud-kissing	MESNLY	impersonally
LROSES	gloriousness	LUOAOS	glaucomatous	MESNTR	impersonator
LROWRS	clerk of works	LUSRIE	all-up service	MESRBE	immeasurable
LRYAKR	slurry tanker	LUTAIE	illustrative	MESRBY	immeasurably
LSAILY	glossarially	LUTAIN	illustration	METNNE	impertinance
LSBOIG	glass-blowing	LUTAOY	illustratory		impertinence
LSBRUH	close borough	LVNHOR	eleventh-hour	MEVOSY	imperviously
LSCIIG	glass ceiling	LVNIES	slovenliness	MEZEET	embezzlement
LSCMAY	close company	LVNOFD	cloven-hoofed	MGBEKR	image-breaker
LSEBAD	plasterboard	LVNOTD	cloven-footed	MHBAHC	amphibrachic
LSEIGY	blusteringly	LVREOS	Oliver de Bois	MHGSRA	amphigastria
	glisteringly	LVRLVR	clever-clever	MHSOOS	amphistomous
LSESIT	plaster saint	LWESES	flawlessness	MHTCLY	emphatically
LSFLES	blissfulness	LWHCAS	blow the coals	MHTETE	amphitheatre
LSFRAD	flash forward	LWIHES	clownishness	MICETY	omnisciently
	flashforward	LWNSID	blow one's mind	MIETOS	ambidextrous
LSFTIG	close-fitting	LWNSOL	blow one's cool	MIIAIN	umbilication
LSGAND	close-grained	LWOICS	blow to pieces	MIOETY	omnipotently
LSHOTE	old school tie	LWREPE	flower people	MIRSNE	omnipresence
	old-school tie	LWVSAE	old wives' tale	MITRET	embitterment
LSHROY	close harmony	LXEGSN	Alex Ferguson	MLAAIN	amalgamation
LSIIBE	classifiable	LXSARL	Alexis Carrel	MLCMNS	emplacements
LSITDY	All Saints' Day	LYBIGS	Lloyd Bridges	MLCTES	implicitness
LSMUHD	close-mouthed	LYELIH	play hell with	MLCTOS	implications
LSOOAA	plasmosomata	LYHDVL	play the devil	MLDVSN	Emily Davison
LSORNH	elasmobranch	LYHFED	play the field	MLFRUE	small fortune
LSSESO	all systems go	LYHWMN	play the woman	MLHLIG	smallholding
LSTDAH	close to death	LYIHIE	play with fire	MLMNAY	emolumentary

MLMTCL emblematical
MLNAIN implantation
MLOAIE ameliorative
MLOAIN amelioration
MLZNET emblazonment
MNBEES amenableness
MNIAIN emancipation
MNILDS amontillados
MOAIIY immovability
MODRBE imponderable
MOEAEY immoderately
MOEAIN immoderation
MOEIHD impoverished
MOHHWY smooth the way
MOHPKN smooth-spoken
MOIEES impoliteness
MOREIE embourgeoise
MOTUAE imposthumate
MRCTOS imprecations
MRGAIN impregnation
MRGOSY umbrageously
MRIAIN amortisation
amortization
MRIEIG embroidering
MROOIT embryologist
MRSEET empressement
MRSIEY impressively
MRSNET imprisonment
MRVDNE improvidence
MSADRB smash-and-grab
MSOEEF amuse oneself
MSUAIN emasculation
MTEIGY smatteringly
smotheringly
MTOAIM emotionalism
MTTCLY amitotically
MTUIHY amateurishly
MUAIEY imputatively
MUAIIY immutability
MUEYTM immune system
MUIAIN immunization
MUOLBN immunoglobin
MUOOIT immunologist
MUSBYR impulse buyer
NAAAIO Antananarivo
NAAEBE unmanageable
NAAEIA Anna Karenina
NAAIAE incapacitate
NAAIIY incapability
NAALLD unparalleled
NAASDT Anwar al-Sadat
NACIID unsanctified
NACIND unsanctioned
NACLBE incalculable
NACLBY incalculably
NACLTD uncalculated
NACRGS in banco regis
NACRTD incarcerated
NADNBE unpardonable
NADOEY unhandsomely
NADSET incandescent
NAEESN insane person
NAEIGY unwaveringly
NAESDT Anwar el-Sadat
NAETWL an oaken towel
NAFLES unlawfulness
NAGEET entanglement
NAGRET endangerment
NAHMBE unfathomable
NAHMBY unfathomably
NAIAIG invalidating
NAIAIN inhabitation
invagination
invalidation
NAIFIG unsatisfying
NAIGTD unvariegated
NAMNOS inharmonious
unharmonious
NANAND unmaintained
NANIES ungainliness
NAOITC antagonistic
NAORBE unfavourable
NAORBY unfavourably
NAQIHD unvanquished
NATCDL infanticidal
NATCLR in particular
NATCOL infant school
NATFLY unfaithfully
NATOSY incautiously
NATRUE enfant trouvé
NAUAIE unnaturalise
unnaturalize
NAUROS insalubrious
NBANBE unobtainable
NBDETY inobediently
NBEVDY unobservedly
NBIGIL enabling bill
NBIHES snobbishness
NBTUTD unobstructed
NCADNE snick and snee
NCESBE inaccessible
NCESBY inaccessibly
NCETBE unacceptable
NCETBY unacceptably
NCETFC unscientific
NCIGHP knocking shop
knocking-shop
NCIGON knocking-down
NCIGOY knocking copy
NCIVBE unachievable
NCLSET in a cold sweat
NCLUDR knuckle under
NCNMCL uneconomical
NCOAIT anecdotalist
NCODIH in accord with
NCODNE in accordance
NCUAEY inaccurately
NCUITD unacquainted
NCULAT in actual fact
NCULIE in actual life
NCUTMD unaccustomed
NCUUOS unscrupulous
NDETNE inadvertence
NDETNY inadvertency
NDETSD unadvertised
NDIINO in addition to
NDISBE inadmissible
NDISBY inadmissibly
NDNIID unidentified
NDQAEY inadequately
NEAATR Angela Carter
NEACOT Anne Bancroft
NEAHEE underachieve
NEAIIY untenability
NEAINO in relation to
NEAIPN Angela Rippon
NEAKBE unremarkable
NEALBE unrecallable
NEARBE unrepairable
NEBAKT underblanket
NEBEET enfeeblement
NEBFRE enter by force
NECAGD interchanged
NECFLY unmercifully
NECMUE intercommune
NECNET interconnect
interconvert
NECNRL under control
NECOHD underclothed
NECOHS underclothes
NECPIE interceptive
NECPIG intercepting
NECPIN interception
NECRET intercurrent
undercurrent
NECSIN intercession
NECSOY intercessory
NEDAIG underdrawing
NEDAIM incendiarism
NEDCIN interdiction
NEDCOY interdictory
NEDESD underdressed
NEDVLP under-develop
NEEAEY intemerately
inveterately
NEEBRD unremembered
NEEDBE undependable
NEEDNE independence[□]
NEEDNY independency
NEEEAE unregenerate
NEEEAY unregeneracy
NEEETY antecedently
NEEIIM ante meridiem
NEEIIN antemeridian
NEEMND undetermined
NEERDY undeterred by
NEERTD uncelebrated
NEESBE indefeasible
indefensible
NEESBY indefeasibly
indefensibly
NEETBE undefeatable
undetectable
unrepeatable
NEETDN interested in
NEETDY interestedly
NEEVBE undeceivable
NEEVDY undeservedly
unreservedly

NEFEIG underfeeding
NEFLAE interfoliate
NEFLVS Anne of Cleves
NEFNIG underfunding
NEFRNE interference
NEGEET inveiglement
NEGRET undergarment
NEHDCL unmethodical
NEHLTS encephalitis
NEIAEY indelicately
NEIAID unseminaried
NEIAIG unhesitating
NEIAIN insemination
NEIALS undesirables
NEICNE indehiscence
NEIIBE unverifiable
NEIIEY indecisively
indefinitely
NEIIIY unfemininity
NEIIOS infelicitous
NEINDY undesignedly
NEINEF in defiance of
NEINTD undesignated
NEITDY unremittedly
NEIUIN antediluvian
NEIVBE unbelievable
NEIVBY unbelievably
NEJCIN interjection
NELCIG interlocking
NELCIN on reflection
NELCTR interlocutor
NELCUL intellectual
NELGBE intelligible
NELGBY intelligibly
NELGNE intelligence
NELNBY indeclinably
NELNIG index-linking
interlinking
NELNWE in weal and woe
NEMDAE intermediate
NEMDAY intermediary
NEMIES unseemliness
NEMNBE interminable
NEMNBY interminably
NEMSIN intermission
NEMTET intermittent
NEMXUE intermixture
NENAAN once and again
NENNIS internuncios
NENWIE once in a while
NEOEHT under one's hat
NEOIGY unbecomingly
NEOISS anaerobiosis
NEONZD unrecognized
NEOOSY indecorously
NEORTC undemocratic
NEOSFL unremorseful
NEOVBE unresolvable
NEPAES in deep waters
NEPAIG underplaying
NEPEIE interpretive
NEPIIG enterprising
NEPLAE interpellate
NEPNIE unresponsive
NEPNIG underpinning
NEPOET under protest
NEPOLD underpeopled
NEPOUE under-produce
NEPRNE intemperance
NEPROM underperform
NEPSIE intempestive
NEPTIY in perpetuity
NEPYET underpayment
NERAHD unreproached
NEREDD unbefriended
NEREHS knee-breeches
NEREIG enheartening
NERGTR interrogator
NERGUS interregnums
NERHBE unsearchable
NERHBY unsearchably
NERLAT integral part
NERLTD interrelated
NEROIG knee-crooking
NERPIE interruptive
NERPIG interrupting
NERPIN interruption
NERSET in retrospect
NESAFD understaffed
NESAIE unsensualise
unsensualize
NESCIG intersecting
NESCIN intersection
NESELR interstellar
NESFIG intensifying
NESIKR underskinker
NESNBE unreasonable
unseasonable
NESNBY unreasonably
unseasonably
NESOIG underscoring
NESRBY unmeasurably
NETAND unrestrained
NETBAE invertebrate
NETDES indebtedness
NETDIH infected with
NETDNB inverted snob
NETEEL under the heel
NETEES ungentleness
NETEIE anaesthetise
anaesthetize
NETEIT anaesthetist
NETGTR investigator
NETIES entertainers
NETIIG entertaining
NETITD unrestricted
NETLTD unventilated
NETOSY infectiously
NETSUD entertissued
NETXUL intertextual
NEUTDY unrequitedly
NEVNET intervenient
NEVNIN intervention
NEVUIG endeavouring
NEWETE interwreathe
NEWIIG underwriting
NEWOGT underwrought
NFAEBE ineffaceable
NFAEBY ineffaceably
NFAIIY ineffability
NFEFED unified field
NFETDY unaffected by
unaffectedly
NFIILY unofficially
NFIINY inefficiency
NFIITD unaffiliated
NFIWYO in a fair way to
NFMLWY in a family way
NFRINB one for his nob
NGEIGY sniggeringly
NGGCLY anagogically
NGLTEH snaggleteeth
NGLTOH snaggletooth
NGOLGT in a good light
NGRSIE unaggressive
NGTRAT knight-errant
NHALDY enthralled by
NHBAKT on the blanket
NHBGIG in the by-going
NHBIKF on the brink of
NHBLNE in the balance
NHBOIS in the boonies
NHBSSF on the basis of
NHDCIE on the decline
NHEETF in the event of
NHETEE in the extreme
NHFSIN in the fashion
NHHBTF in the habit of
NHHESF on the heels of
NHHRZN on the horizon
NHIPOE on the improve
NHISAT on the instant
NHITRM in the interim
NHKOKR on the knocker
NHLEGD unchallenged
NHLGTF in the light of
NHLNRN in the long run
NHLNSF on the lines of
NHLOOT on the lookout
NHMDTF in the midst of
NHMOFR in the mood for
NHMRIG in the morning
NHNBUT Anthony Blunt
NHNEBE unchangeable
NHNEBY unchangeably
NHNIGY enchantingly
unthinkingly
NHNRMS enchondromas
NHNSNG on Shanks's nag
NHODAS in the old days
NHODRF in the order of
NHOEAD on the one hand
NHOEAR in the open air
NHOEET enthronement
NHOODL anthropoidal
NHOOOY anthropology
NHOTIE on the outside
NHPCUE in the picture
NHPITF on the point of

NHPWRF in the power of
NHQIIE on the qui vive
NHREAE one-horse race
NHREON one-horse town
NHRMAE on the rampage
NHRNIG in the running
NHRODR in short order
NHRTBE uncharitable
NHSAEF in the shape of
NHSATC enthusiastic
NHSEAD in this regard
NHSEES unchasteness
NHSEVS on the shelves
NHSGTF in the sight of
NHSMWY in the same way
NHSRAE on the surface
NHSRES on the streets
NHTEHF in the teeth of
NHTIKF in the thick of
NHUADP on the up and up
NHVREF on the verge of
NHWLAY on the wallaby
NHWOEF in the whole of
NHWRAH on the warpath
NIAADI Indira Gandhi
NIAASR antimacassar
NIAHTC antipathetic
NIAIEY indicatively
NIATCE antiparticle
NIBTOS in his buttons
NICEET encirclement
NICEEY indiscretely
NICEIN indiscretion
NICETY indiscreetly
NICPIE indiscipline
NICRIG undiscerning
NICVRD undiscovered
NIEAIN incineration
NIEANR in like manner
NIEETE in fine fettle
NIEIES unlikeliness
untimeliness
NIEIIM anti-Semitism
NIEIIT anti-feminist
NIEIOD unlikelihood
NIEOSY indigenously
NIERVR engine driver
engine-driver
NIETBE indigestible
NIETBY indigestibly
NIETDY undivestedly
NIETES indirectness
NIETIO antineutrino
anti-neutrino
NIETLY incidentally
NIFRNE indifference
NIGNSS angiogenesis
NIGOLR inking roller
NIHEIG enlightening
NIHFLY unrightfully
NIHNLY antiphonally
NIHTCL antithetical
NIIAIG anticipating
intimidating
NIIAIN annihilation
anticipation
intimidation
invigilation
NIIAOY anticipatory
intimidatory
NIICAT anti-aircraft
NIIEES incisiveness
infiniteness
NIIIEY infinitively
NIIIHD undiminished
NIIIIS incivilities
NIIIIY invisibility
NIILIK invisible ink
NIIULY individually
NILIES unwieldiness
NILIGY unyieldingly
NILMTC undiplomatic
NILNIG Anzio Landing
NILRCL anticlerical
NINGEK ancient Greek
NINPLS Indianapolis
NINRMN ancient Roman
NINTMS ancient times
NINUMR Indian summer
NINUNR Indian runner
NIOAIG invigorating
NIOAIN invigoration
NIOAUO Enrico Caruso
NIOILY antisocially
NIPLAE India Pale Ale
NIPTBE indisputable
NIPTBY indisputably
NIPTDY undisputedly
NISDES unbiasedness
NISLBE indissoluble
NISLBY indissolubly
NITAIN infiltration
NITKBE unmistakable
NITKBY unmistakably
NITNTY indistinctly
NITOSY unvirtuously
NIUAIN infibulation
NIYLNC anticyclonic
NKCAMR snake-charmer
NKIEDE on a knife edge
NKRUFE in a kerfuffle
NLAATY unpleasantly
NLAIGY unpleasingly
NLBTAE in all but name
NLCINL inflectional
NLCNRC Anglocentric
NLEITD unalleviated
NLGCLY analogically
NLHBTC analphabetic
NLMAIN inflammation
NLMAOY inflammatory
NLNIGY unblinkingly
NLQETY ineloquently
NLROSY ingloriously
NLSDSF on all sides of
NLSIGY unblushingly
NLSIID unclassified
NLSIIY inelasticity
NLSWMN Englishwoman
NLTCLY analytically
enclitically
NLTEIG unflattering
NLTOAY inflationary
NLTOIM inflationism
NLTOIT inflationist
NLTRLY unilaterally
NMATBE unimpartable
unimpartible
NMGNBE unimaginable
NMGNBY unimaginably
NMLACS animal faeces
NMLIHS animal rights
NMLYBE unemployable
NMLYET in employment
unemployment
NMNCLY gnomonically
NMNTNW any minute now
NMOTNE unimportance
NMRHSS anamorphoses
anamorphosis
NMRSIE unimpressive
NMTDIM animated film
NMTOIS animatronics
NMTPEA onomatopoeia
NMTPEC onomatopoeic
NNACUT on any account
NNEETD uninterested
NNEHLC anencephalic
NNLECD uninfluenced
NNLSBE unanalysable
NNMSAE and no mistake
NNOADN on and on and on
NNSESN on one's person
NNSESS in one's senses
NNSOKT in one's pocket
NNSPES on one's uppers
NNSRCS in one's tracks
NNVLOR in an evil hour
NNVNEL on an even keel
NNWRBE unanswerable
NNWRBY unanswerably
NOADES untowardness
NOADTS endocarditis
NOANET infotainment
NOBIGY undoubtingly
NOCATY insouciantly
NOCEHV Anton Chekhov
NOCUIE inconclusive
NOCUIN in conclusion
NODELH in good health
NOEAIN in moderation
NOEATY intolerantly
NOEDRS encomenderos
NOEETY incoherently
NOEIES unloveliness
NOENBE ungovernable
NOENBY ungovernably
NOENET in government
NOERTS endometritis

NOESOE snooperscope
NOEUTN snooze button
NOFDNE in confidence
NOFNDY unconfinedly
NOFRIY unconformity
NOFRNE in conference
NOGETY enjoy greatly
NOGVBE unforgivable
NOIAIG intoxicating
NOIAIN intoxication
NOIEAL Antonine Wall
NOIEBE unnoticeable
NOIEBY unnoticeably
NOIGUI Antonio Gaudí
NOILTE andouillette
NOIRAD Antoni Artaud
NOKLTL endoskeletal
NOKLTN endoskeleton
NOMDOS incommodious
NOMNES uncommonness
NOMRIL uncommercial
NOMSIN in commission
NOMTBY incommutably
NONEBY Encounter Bay
NONEET announcement
NONLNE insomnolence
NONZBE incognizable
NONZNE incognizance
NOOAIN incoronation
NOOEEF enjoy oneself
NOOHBA entomophobia
NOOOIE entomologise
entomologize
NOOOIT entomologist
NOPEEY incompletely
NOPRBE incomparable
NOPRBY incomparably
NOPRIY incorporeity
NOPRSN in comparison
NOPRTD incorporated
NOPRUT in hot pursuit
NOPSIG encompassing
NOPTBE incompatible
incomputable
inhospitable
NOPTBY incompatibly
inhospitably
NOPTNE incompetence
NOPTNY incompetency
NORELH in poor health
NORGBE incorrigible
NORGBY incorrigibly
NOSATY inconstantly
NOSCAE unconsecrate
NOSDRD unconsidered
NOSIIS in low spirits
NOSLBE inconsolable
NOSLBY inconsolably
NOSMBE unconsumable
NOSMBY inconsumably
NOSQET inconsequent
NOSRIT unconstraint
NOSSET inconsistent
NOSSIG unpossessing
NOTATO in contrast to
NOTDES unwontedness
NOTEIE end of the line
NOTIAE indoctrinate
NOTIES unworthiness
NOTNNE incontinence
NOTNNY incontinency
NOTOLD uncontrolled
NOUAIY unpopularity
NOUIIE insolubilise
insolubilize
NOUIIY insolubility
NOUOEN Indo-European
NOVNET inconvenient
NOVNIG unconvincing
NOVRAT unconversant
NOYEIH Antony Hewish
NPATNR snap-fastener
NPCIGY inspectingly
NPCOAE inspectorate
NPCOIL inspectorial
NPEIES snippetiness
NPEIIG unappetizing
NPELBE inappellable
NPESBE unappeasable
NPIHES snappishness
NPLCBE inapplicable
NPLCBY inapplicably
NPLGTC unapologetic
NPOIEY inappositely
NPOIIN in opposition
NPYATC anaphylactic
NQIOSY iniquitously
NRADLG an arm and a leg
NRAETD unornamented
NRAHET encroachment
NRAIGY entreatingly
increasingly
NRCAMD unproclaimed
NRCOSY ungraciously
NRCTON André Citroën
NRDCBE ineradicable
introducible
NRDCBY ineradicably
NRDCIE unproductive
NRDCIN introduction
NRDCOY introductory
NRDLFE Ann Radcliffe
NREDIY unfriendlily
NRFAIN engraftation
NRFCET unproficient
NRFRNE in preference
NRFTBE unprofitable
NRGIGY intriguingly
NRHCLY anarchically
NRHOSY anarthrously
NRIAEY inordinately
NRIGES unerringness
NRIUAE inarticulate
NRIUAY inarticulacy
NRJDCD unprejudiced
NRKNES unbrokenness
NRMELD untrammelled
NRMLAX André Malraux
NRMNTD incriminated
NRMSIN intromission
NRNEAL entrance hall
entrance-hall
NRNEET infringement
NRNHET entrenchment
NRNIAE intrinsicate
NRNIET intransigent
NRNIIE intransitive
NRNILD unprincipled
NRNUCD unpronounced
NROFEH an arm of flesh
NROSES enormousness
NRPDES intrepidness
NRPEER entrepreneur
intrapreneur
NRPRDY unpreparedly
NRPTOS unpropitious
NRQETD unfrequented
NRQETY infrequently
NRSAIN encrustation
incrustation
NRSBED incrossbreed
NRTAIG ingratiating
NRTAIN ingratiation
NRTCLY uncritically
NRTELW unwritten law
NRTFLY ungratefully
untruthfully
NRTSIG unprotesting
NRUDDY ungroundedly
NRUEIE intrauterine
NRULDY untroubledly
NRVDDY unprovidedly
NRVKDY unprovokedly
NRVRIN introversion
NRWELN Andrew Mellon
NRWISN Andrew Wilson
NRWOIN Andrew Motion
NRWRIE Andrew Irvine
NSALBE unassailable
NSDDES one-sidedness
NSETHT one's best shot
NSOITD unassociated
NSOTIE in a short time
NSRAEY uniseriately
NSUIGY unassumingly
NSUOTA one's cup of tea
NSXAIY unisexuality
NTAIES unsteadiness
NTAKID one-track mind
NTANBE unattainable
NTASHT and that's that
NTDTTS United States
NTEAIE anathematise
anathematize
NTEWRS in other words
NTGTPT in a tight spot
NTHDAH in at the death
NTIGOS Anything Goes
NTIKIG in a twinkling

NTLAIN installation
instillation
NTMCLY anatomically
NTNIGY unstintingly
NTOSES unctuousness
NTRAIM Unitarianism
NTRCIE unattractive
NTRDIK Anita Roddick
NTTTBY unstatutably
NTUETL instrumental
NTUTBE instructible
NTUTES instructress
NTUTOS instructions
NTUTRD unstructured
NUAIGY undulatingly
NUAIIY incurability
NUCAIN Annunciation
NUCIEY injunctively
NUCSFL unsuccessful
NUCSIN in succession
NUCULY unpunctually
NUDBLR infundibular
NUECNE intumescence
NUEOAK induce to talk
NUEVSD unsupervised
NUFCET insufficient
NUFRBE insufferable
NUFRBY insufferably
NUFRNE on sufferance
NUHRZD unauthorized
NUIBVN Aneurin Bevan
NUIIIY inaudibility
NUIILY injudicially
NUISOE end up in smoke
NULCZD unpublicized
NUMNHP one-upmanship
NUMSIE unsubmissive
NUNHBE unquenchable
NUNRBE invulnerable
NUNRBY invulnerably
NUPCIG unsuspecting
NUPCOS inauspicious
unauspicious
unsuspicious
NUPEES unsuppleness
NUPIIG unsurprising
NUPNIN in suspension
NURAOT inquire about
NURATR inquire after
NURCIN insurrection
NURTOS innutritious
NUSIND unquestioned
NUSSET intussuscept
NUTILY industrially
NUTVBE uncultivable
NUTVTD uncultivated
NUUAIN inauguration
NVRAIE universalise
universalize
NVRAIM universalism□
NVRAIT Universalist
NVRAIY universality
NVRIIS universities

NWALRE snowball tree
NWEGBE knowledgable
NWEGBY knowledgably
NWHRPS know the ropes
NWHSOE know the score
NWHTTS know what it is
NWLRIS snow flurries
NWORIG snowboarding
NWRIGY unswervingly
NXCIUE inexactitude
NXEINE inexpedience
inexperience
NXEINY inexpediency
NXETDY unexpectedly
NXETES inexpertness
NXLCBE inexplicable
NXLCBY inexplicably
NXRCBE inextricable
NXRCBY inextricably
NXRSIE inexpressive
unexpressive
NXUGTD unexpurgated
NXUNBY inexpugnably
NYLPDA encyclopedia
NYLPDC encyclopedic
NYOARS Ankylosaurus
NYOOIT enzymologist
NYTMTC unsystematic
OABTEY solar battery
OACHLC non-alcoholic
OACUTF for account of
OADATR Howard Carter
OADCAE bow and scrape
OADEGN Ronald Reagan
OADERE Ronald Searle
OADIDN Donald Sinden
OADIES cowardliness
OADIHE Donald Michie
OADIHR Ronald Fisher
OADLSR Donald Glaser
OADNAD go hand in hand
OADOFT Donald Wolfit
OADOGN Donald Coggan
OADUHS Howard Hughes
OADUTN Royal Doulton
OAEAIN nonagenarian
OAELPE total eclipse
OAEOLO Homage to Clio
OAETOD covalent bond
OAFCIG not affecting
OAIAAU Kota Kinabalu
OAIAIN cohabitation
focalization
localization
moralization
nomadization
polarisation
polarization
Romanization
totalitarian
vocalization
OAIEES volatileness
OAIEIH womanize with

OAIGTS Horatio Gates
OAIHES womanishness
OAINET non-alignment
OAINLY vocationally
OAISAT for an instant
OAITRE Zola Pieterse
OAIYLY morality play
OALBNW so early by now
OALSTC go ballisitic
OANIHE Johann Fichte
OANOTE Johann Goethe
OANRYF Johann Cruyff
OANSUG Johannesburg
OAOAHR potato masher
OAOGIE for a long time
OAOIGR potato finger
OAOLGT potato blight
OAPRBS coram paribus
OARNLN noradrenalin
OASPOT moral support
OASVMI Jonas Savimbi
OATCLY monastically
romantically
OATEIH do battle with
OATNSU Ion Antonescu
OATRHT no matter what
OATTHN not a stitch on
OATWMN woman-to-woman
OAWRAT royal warrant
OAYULC notary public
OAYYLW Rosalyn Yalow
OBAIGY forbearingly
OBDIGY forbiddingly
OBDZLR bobby-dazzler
OBEAGR double dagger
OBEEKR double-decker
OBEELR double-dealer
OBEEOK gobbledegook
OBEHRE double-charge
OBEIIN double vision
OBELKD double fluked
OBELZD double-glazed
OBEOGE double-tongue
OBEOLR double boiler
OBEYOK gobbledygook
OBFCET sorbefacient
OBFLES doubtfulness
OBFSHR Bobby Fischer
OBGILT Robbe-Grillet
OBNDIH combined with
OBRAKT bomber jacket
OBRARS Bomber Harris
OBYEOK gobblydegook
OBYNSN Dombey and Son
OCAATY nonchalantly
OCADER force and fear
OCBEES forcibleness
OCBIDR coachbuilder
OCEEES concreteness
OCFLES forcefulness
OCIGES touchingness
OCIMRT Joachim Murat
OCLAIE porcellanise

	porcellanize
OCLAIN	conciliation
OCLAOY	conciliatory
OCLBAE	concelebrate
OCLEFR	not called for
OCLGTY	touch lightly
OCLIIE	porcelainise
	porcelainize
OCMAAT	non-combatant
OCMITL	non-committal
OCMJUE	force majeure
OCMLTD	not completed
OCNCLY	volcanically
OCNHUE	forcing-house
OCNRTD	concentrated
OCNUTR	non-conductor
OCOEEF	force oneself
OCOEWY	force one's way
OCOOAE	hot chocolate
OCOOIT	conchologist
OCPSET	concupiscent
OCQAIY	voice quality
OCRATY	concordantly
OCRETY	concurrently
OCRPRY	concert party
OCRPTH	concert pitch
OCSOIL	non-custodial
OCTEAE	force the pace
OCTLAE	force to leave
OCTUFR	not cut out for
OCUIEY	conclusively
OCURNE	co-occurrence
ODAAAD	Gondwanaland
ODABID	hoodman-blind
ODAEIH	hold pace with
ODAKRM	hold back from
ODCIIY	conductivity
ODCOSY	mordaciously
ODEGHG	wood hedgehog
ODEPRD	good-tempered
ODESES	wordlessness
ODFIDM	word of wisdom
ODFOOR	word of honour
ODGTRE	Woody Guthrie
ODHFOR	hold the floor
ODHUDR	cold shoulder
	cold-shoulder
ODIHOL	goldfish bowl
ODMAIN	condemnation
ODMAOY	condemnatory
ODNAIN	condensation
ODNARD	golden-haired
ODNATE	golden wattle
ODNEPE	Golden Temple
ODNETR	Gordon setter
ODNGUE	loading gauge
ODNHNS	holding hands
ODNITD	sodden-witted
ODNLEE	golden fleece
ODNLVR	golden plover
ODNMNY	folding money
ODOASM	hold to ransom
ODOEHR	hold together
ODOORD	gold-coloured
ODOSES	wondrousness
ODRCOS	good gracious
ODREIG	good breeding
ODROKR	wonder-worker
ODROKY	powder monkey
ODROLE	Border collie
ODRSNR	hold prisoner
ODRTUK	wonder-struck
ODSNAK	Goodison Park
ODTNAD	gold standard
ODTNIG	good standing
ODTOIG	conditioning
ODUORD	good-humoured
ODWYVR	hold sway over
OEAAAO	José Saramago
OEAALY	Rose Macaulay
OEACFR	do penance for
OEAEES	moderateness
OEAERN	dodecahedron
OEAGAE	tone language
OEAIIY	tolerability
OEARRS	José Carreras
OEAUBE	more valuable
OEAYET	Rosemary West
OEAYNT	monetary unit
OEBEES	moveableness
OECAFE	Roger Chaffee
OECASS	lower classes
OECAUE	nomenclature
OECEPR	honeycreeper
OECOPR	come a cropper
OECOSS	come across as
OEDOIH	fore-admonish
OEDROE	Côtes du Rhône
OEEDNY	co-dependency
OEEFES	tone-deafness
OEEIGY	foreseeingly
OEESES	homelessness
	hopelessness
OEFCIE	non-effective
OEFCIN	to perfection
OEFEIF	code of belief
OEFIIG	mode of living
OEFIUE	power failure
OEFLES	powerfulness
OEFWRT	come off worst
OEGAET	foreign agent
OEGGOS	foreign goods
OEGTAE	foreign trade
OEGUBR	money-grubber
OEHAIN	Joseph Damien
OEHATN	Joseph Paxton
OEHELR	Joseph Heller
OEHIPE	Joseph Niepce
OEHITR	Joseph Lister
OEHMES	Tower Hamlets
OEHNAF	more than half
OEHOKR	Joseph Hooker
OEHORD	Joseph Conrad
OEHPAE	lose the place
OEHRES	togetherness
OEHRGT	Joseph Wright
OEHRIH	together with
OEHTLN	Joseph Stalin
OEHUNR	Joseph Turner
OEHWSR	none the wiser
OEIKES	homesickness
OEITCL	solecistical
OEITNE	non-existence
	some distance
OEJYET	for enjoyment
OELMEE	son et lumière
OELNIG	moneylending
	money-lending
OEMGUH	Roger McGough
OEMOHY	move smoothly
OEMSAE	coded message
OENAOR	vote in favour
OENATR	fore-and-after
OENESS	someone else's
OENETL	governmental
OENIEN	Come on Eileen
OENOAD	come in to land
OENOIW	come into view
OENOLY	come into play
OENRHP	governorship
OENSAR	lose one's hair
OENSED	lose one's head
OENSET	lose one's seat
OENSIE	lose one's life
OENSOL	lose one's cool
OENTEM	come on stream
OENTOG	come on strong
OENWBE	foreknowable
OEOBBL	Tower of Babel
OEOBBY	Morecombe Bay
OEOCET	come to accept
OEODLY	solenoidally
OEOEEF	lower oneself
OEOEES	lonesomeness
OEOEET	forebodement
OEOEHR	come together
OEOICS	come to pieces
OEOIGY	forebodingly
OEOIIN	pole position
OEONFO	move to and fro
OEONIH	come down with
OEONIS	home counties
OEONPN	come down upon
OEOORD	rose-coloured
OEOSES	covetousness
OEOTIY	noteworthily
OEPCFC	to be specific
OEPEIT	coleopterist
OEPEOS	coleopterous
OEPNOE	Roger Penrose
OERAND	foreordained
OERGOS	lower regions
OERMOE	home from home
OERNIG	lower-ranking
OESAIG	power-sharing
OESAIN	power station
OESCLY	forensically
OESHTE	powers that be
OESIHS	women's rights

OESINR moneyspinner
money-spinner
OESNIL non-essential
OESOES nolens volens
OESUTR somersaulter
OETADN Covent Garden
OETAGT vote straight
OETAIR Robert Napier
OETAIY move steadily
potentiality
OETARN Robert Warren
OETCEP domestic help
OETCLY domestically
OETCOK domestic work
OETCTD domesticated
OETEET cover the feet
OETEIO Robert De Niro
OETEIT nonextremist
OETFAK Roberta Flack
OETIKY cover thickly
OETISN Robert Gibson
OETLIG forestalling
OETLMN Robert Altman
OETNUD honey-tongued
OETOEL Robert Lowell
OETREE Robert Greene
OETRKR honest broker
OETRVS Robert Graves
OETRWE Robert Browne
OETTAS bored to tears
OETTOG come it strong
OETUAE Robert Mugabe
Robert Mugawe
OETUBR lowest number
OETUCE Robert Runcie
OETUSN Robert Bunsen
OETYAL forestaysail
OEUAIY molecularity
OEUOTP come out on top
OEVRIN cover version
OEWSIG money-wasting
OEXETD to be expected
OFADUS no ifs and buts
OFAMBE non-flammable
not flammable
OFASOE go off at score
OFCAIM Confucianism
OFCAIT Confucianist
OFCINL non-fictional
OFCINR confectioner
OFDNIL confidential
OFDRTD confederated
OFEEAS Godfrey Evans
OFEUNY low frequency
OFRAIE confirmative
OFRAIN confirmation
conformation
OFRAOY confirmatory
OFRIGY comfortingly
OFRNIG conferencing
OFROEH not for Joseph
OFROIZ Porfirio Díaz
OFSAIN confiscation

OFSAOY confiscatory
OFSINL confessional
OFUDDY confoundedly
OFUDHM confound them
OGAAAS Douglas Adams
OGABDR Douglas Bader
OGADES Porgy and Bess
OGAUAE congratulate
OGBRUH Loughborough
OGDAOD rough diamond
OGEAIN congregation
OGENOD Ron Greenwood
OGEOGE boogie-woogie
OGEWTH toggle switch
OGFRIE song of praise
OGHWBT rough hawkbit
OGJSIE rough justice
OGMXUE cough mixture
OGNAIY congeniality
OGNDNE song and dance
OGNHUE lodging house
OGNSME hoc genus omne
OGNSOT long-and-short
OGNTIG doughnutting
OGNTLY congenitally
OGOEAE conglomerate
OGORPY zoogeography
OGOSES gorgeousness
OGOUAE conglobulate
OGPSAE rough passage
OGRWOT long-drawn-out
OGSELR hot gospeller
OGTDNL longitudinal
OGTEIG forgathering
OGTIGY forgettingly
OGTNIG long-standing
OGUIAE conglutinate
OGVAAN not give a damn
OGWILM Gough Whitlam
OHAHNH Rosh Hashanah
OHAWAE bowhead whale
OHCIGT not hacking it
OHDRYN do the dirty on
OHEODM moshvei ovdim
OHHNUS do the honours
OHMATR Bonham-Carter
OHNDIG nothing doing
OHNINT nothing if not
OHNLAH nothing loath
OHPROE to the purpose
OHRAUE mother nature
OHRCOY oophorectomy
OHRIES motherliness
OHRILW mothers-in-law
OHROGE mother tongue
OHSIAE sophisticate
OHTFET to that effect
OHUBOS jodhpur boots
OHVALE not have a clue
OIAASZ Louis Agassiz
OIAIES solitariness
OIAIEY nominatively
OIAINL motivational

OIAMKR holidaymaker
OIATMY holiday tummy
OIATTE Così Fan Tutte
OIAVLE nominal value
OIBEES sociableness
OIBEIT Louis Blériot
OIBOOY sociobiology
OIBRIR sonic barrier
OIBYOT Rosie Boycott
OICRUT logic circuit
OICUIG not including
OICUIS Robin Cousins
OICWRY Colin Cowdrey
OIEAIN vociferation
OIEDEM go like a dream
OIEIPR bodice-ripper
OIEOSY vociferously
OIGBOD moving abroad
OIGDNV Boris Godunov
OIGIHS voting rights
OIGPAT foliage plant
OIGPRT moving spirit
OIIAIN codification
mobilization
modification
notification
solicitation
OIICEL Joni Mitchell
OIIEES positiveness
OIINLY volitionally
OIIOSY solicitously
OIIVTS solicit votes
OIJCSN Colin Jackson
OIKROF Boris Karloff
OILGCL sociological
OILOKR social worker
OILRCS social graces
OILSIG Doris Lessing
OILTTS social status
OIOHOY domino theory
OIOILY monitorially
OIOOIT toxicologist
OIORSN Toni Morrison
OIOTLY horizontally
OIOUZR soliloquizer
OIPSER Louis Pasteur
OISADS jolies laides
OISASY Boris Spassky
OISCIN conic section
OISIIS low in spirits
OITCLY holistically
OITETE movie theatre
OITFFY go fifty-fifty
OIUIIN vomiturition
OIYLSN Boris Yeltsin
OJNTVL conjunctival
OKBEES workableness
OKCRIN book-scorpion
OKCUCL works council
OKEEKE cockieleekie
OKERIG book-learning
OKFAKR work a flanker
OKFHBY Dock of the Bay

Code	Word
OKHBOS	cook the books
OKHRFG	Yorkshire fog
OKIHIG	cockfighting
OKLMIG	rock-climbing
OKNATR	looking after
	looking-after
OKNCAR	rocking-chair
OKNCAS	working class
	working-class
OKNGAS	looking-glass
OKNHUS	working hours
OKNLNH	working lunch
OKNMDL	working model
OKNODR	working order
OKNPRS	working parts
OKNPRY	working party
OKNWMN	working woman
OKOEHR	lock together
	work together
OKPUWR	Yom Kippur War
OKRRET	worker priest
OKTNIE	rocket engine
OKTRNH	socket-wrench
OKUEES	cocksureness
OKUTWR	lookout tower
OKYAKT	donkey jacket
OKYRCS	monkey tricks
	monkey-tricks
OKYRUD	monkey around
OKYUZE	monkey puzzle
OKYYAS	donkey's years
OLAGAE	foul language
OLANIH	pollyannaish
OLBAIG	world-beating
OLBIIA	Lollobrigida
OLBRTR	collaborator
OLBWRE	could be worse
OLCDLD	mollycoddled
OLCIEY	collectively
OLCIIE	collectivise
	collectivize
OLCIIM	collectivism
OLESES	soullessness
OLGCLY	zoologically
OLITNS	to all intents
OLLNES	Moll Flanders
OLMLIG	foul-smelling
OLMXUE	dolly mixture
OLNAIY	collinearity
OLNAKT	Goblin Market
OLNBOH	polling-booth
OLNEAE	coelenterate
OLNHHY	roll in the hay
OLNHTH	rolling hitch
OLNPIT	boiling point
OLNSOE	rolling stone
OLNTWR	cooling tower
OLOEHR	pool together
OLPODY	Collop Monday
OLPPAY	lollipop lady
OLQILY	colloquially
OLRKTR	roller-skater
OLSAIG	world-shaking
OLSEIG	not listening
OLSWTY	foolish-witty
OLTIEN	borlotti bean
OLTISE	toilet tissue
OLTOIT	coalitionist
OLTRHN	not later than
OLTRIG	soul-stirring
OLTRLY	collaterally
OLUTAE	to illustrate
OLWBLS	collywobbles
OLWDWB	World Wide Web
OLWHSA	follow the sea
OLWOIE	Hollywoodise
	Hollywoodize
OLYARD	woolly-haired
OLYIBR	Colley Cibber
OLYIDD	motley-minded
OLYUID	would you mind?
OMCAOT	not muck about
OMDOSY	commodiously
OMECAT	doom merchant
OMESES	formlessness
OMHNLY	Tommy Handley
OMLCOL	normal school
OMLEYE	formaldehyde
OMLGAT	non-malignant
OMLGCL	cosmological
OMNAIN	commendation
OMNALR	Norman Mailer
OMNALW	common mallow
OMNALY	Norman Manley
OMNAOT	Norman Lamont
OMNAOY	commendatory
OMNCBE	communicable
OMNCBY	communicably
OMNCNS	communicants
OMNCTR	communicator
OMNEBT	Norman Tebbit
OMNEDR	common gender
OMNEET	commencement
OMNELH	commonwealth □
OMNEPE	Common People
	common people
OMNESN	common person
OMNHUE	rooming-house
OMNIDM	Norman Wisdom
OMNIGY	commandingly
	tormentingly
OMNIIG	common-riding
	gormandizing
OMNLEE	dolman sleeve
OMNNCP	common ink cap
OMNOLR	Norman Fowler
OMNOTR	Norman Foster
OMNPPR	command paper
OMNRUD	common ground
OMNSUK	common as muck
OMNUAE	commensurate
OMPLTN	cosmopolitan □
OMRIDW	dormer window
OMRILY	commercially
OMSAIL	commissarial
OMSAIT	commissariat
OMSAOT	not mess about
OMSDIY	boomps-a-daisy
OMSIND	commissioned
OMSINR	commissioner
OMTCLY	cosmetically
	dogmatically
	noematically
OMTHTP	Room at the Top
OMTRET	commuter belt
ONAAEL	sound as a bell
ONAANT	count against
ONABUH	John Vanbrugh
ONACUT	joint account
ONAINL	foundational
ONAISE	point at issue
ONALAO	John Galliano
ONANED	fountainhead
	fountain-head
ONANIE	mountain bike
	mountainside
ONANIH	mountain-high
ONANIN	mountain lion
ONANOT	mountain goat
ONANYE	John Jarndyce
ONAOTY	roundaboutly
ONASAF	John Falstaff
ONAULY	Joanna Lumley
ONBPIT	point by point
ONCATY	John McCarthy
ONCIEY	connectively
ONDAUA	Count Dracula
ONEAET	counter-agent
ONEAKR	Bonnie Parker
	Ronnie Barker
ONEBAE	counterbrace
ONEBAT	counterblast
ONECAM	countercharm
	counter-claim
ONECEK	countercheck
ONEEET	Mount Everest
ONEIAD	lounge-lizard
ONEJMN	John Betjeman
ONEMRH	countermarch
ONEPED	counterplead
ONEPIE	counterpoise
ONEPIT	counterpoint
ONEPRY	counter-parry
ONERMN	John Berryman
ONERUD	lounge around
ONESHL	John Herschel
ONESIG	John Pershing
ONESOS	John Sessions
ONETNR	counter-tenor
ONEWEL	counter-wheel
ONEWIH	counterweigh
	counter-weigh
ONEWTR	go under water
ONFEDN	John of Leyden
ONFLNY	horn of plenty
ONFRAD	going forward
ONGAHC	pornographic
ONGAHR	pornographer
ONHBIK	go on the blink

ONHDAN down the drain
ONHHTH down the hatch
ONHITE John Christie
ONHRLY John Charnley
ONHSAD Younghusband
ONHSAE go on the stage
ONHSOT go on the shout
ONHTIR John Whittier
ONHTIT John Whitgift
ONIBRE John Lilburne
ONIEIH coincide with
ONIETL coincidental
ONIETY coincidently
ONIGEE corno inglese
ONIGEI corni inglesi
ONIHIG moonlighting
ONIHUE council house
ONILAS John Williams
ONIOWR council of war
ONKNEY John F Kennedy
ONLFUS go on all fours
ONLQIE somniloquise
somniloquize
ONLTHR John Fletcher
ONMBRK Hosni Mubarak
ONMUAE somnambulate
ONMUAT somnambulant
ONMUIM somnambulism
ONMUIT somnambulist
ONNATR morning after
ONNDES morning dress
ONNHCB corn on the cob
ONNHUA Born in the USA
ONOEAL go into detail
ONOEHR join together
ONOEID Born to be Wild
ONOFEH pound of flesh
ONOHRD go into the red
ONOHRY John Sotherby
ONOIIG go into hiding
ONOODR point of order
ONOTAE John Coltrane
ONOTMR John Mortimer
ONOTRP John Northrop
ONOYPS Mount Olympus
ONPRTD coin-operated
ONRCSN John Ericsson
ONRDNE country dance
ONRHUE country house
ONRIIR Mount Rainier
ONRLIS Sonny Rollins
ONRMSC country music
ONRRIA Mount Roraima
ONRSOT John Prescott
ONRVLA John Travolta
ONRWMN countrywoman
ONRWOD Joan Crawford
ONRYKL country yokel
ONSALY Mount Stanley
ONSCOS Cornish cross
ONSESN roundsperson
ONSOGE hound's-tongue
ONSPSY Cornish pasty
ONSTOT do one's utmost
ONSWWY go one's own way
ONTEED round the bend
ONTEOT count the cost
ONTNOF John Atansoff
ONTPIT point-to-point
ONTRLY connaturally
ONTRUH going-through
ONUKIG John Suckling
ONUPRS John Humphrys
ONVNUE joint venture
ONVRNW you never know
ONWTOT going-without
ONYATE bouncy castle
ONYGOE Johnny B Goode
ONYLFE John Wycliffe
ONYNTS Johnny Unitas
ONYOTR Rodney Porter
ONYUTR bounty hunter
OOADLS logodaedalus
OOAEEL Popocatepetl
OOAICL monomaniacal
OOAIDO not of a mind to
OOANCY No Woman, No Cry
OOBCCE motor-bicycle
OOCCIT motorcyclist
OOEAIE not operative
OOEBOD Colonel Blood
OOECOS pop one's clogs
OOEERE to some degree
OOEPIS for one's pains
OOEXET to some extent
OOEYTA Jomo Kenyatta
OOFCHT box-office hit
OOGRAE no longer have
OOHDVL go to the devil
OOHITC monotheistic
OOHNIM do-nothingism
OOHPLS go to the polls
OOHWLS go to the walls
OOHWRD go to the world
OOIAET monofilament
OOIAIN colonisation
colonization
motorization
OOIGIT monolinguist
OOILNS Cocos Islands
OOJCIE non-objective
OONRHN no sooner than
OONSED go to one's head
OONSHS so soon as this
OONSOM go down a storm
OONTIG go for nothing
OONUOE motor neurone
OOOAIN homologation
OOOIIG monopolizing
OOOIIY locomobility
locomotivity
OOOILY monopodially
OOOITC monopolistic
OOOOSY monotonously
OOOPIM homomorphism
OOOPOS homomorphous
monomorphous
OOORGN Komodo dragon
OOOSEL solomon's seal[□]
OOOSES sonorousness
OOOTDR rodomontader
OOOTSS homoeostasis
OORCEE colour scheme
OORITR colour filter
OOROWR honours of war
OORPIT monographist
OORRGT honour bright
OOSSIE colossus-wise
OOTERE top of the tree
OOUTRL monocultural
OOVHCE motor vehicle
OOXRMS go to extremes
OOYEIE co-polymerise
co-polymerize
OOYLBC monosyllabic
OOYLBE monosyllable
OOYOSY homonymously
OOZIKV Todor Zhivkov
OPAETY complacently
OPASNE complaisance
OPEEES completeness
OPEIIS complexities
OPESBE compressible
OPESIT Doppler shift
OPIAIM dolphinarium
OPIAIN complication
OPIAIS comprimarios
OPIOOS non-poisonous
OPLAGR doppelgänger
OPLAIT compile a list
OPLIEY compulsively
OPLOIY compulsorily
OPNAIN compensation
OPNAOY compensatory
OPNHAR go up in the air
OPNLMS go up in flames
OPNNIL componential
OPNOST companion set
OPNTOS compunctious
OPOIIG compromising
OPOOIT morphologist
OPRAIE corporealise
corporealize
OPRAIN compurgation
OPRAIY corporeality
OPRATN copper-fasten
OPRBEO comparable to
OPRLRM Corporal Trim
OPRLTA corpora lutea
OPRNTS compare notes
OPROTM copper-bottom
OPRVLA corpora vilia
OPSETS compos mentis
OPSUEM corpus luteum
OPTRAE computer game
OPTRZD computerized
OPTSAE for pete's sake
OPUDIE compound time
OQEGRI bouquet garni

OQEIGY conqueringly
OQITDR conquistador
ORAITC journalistic
non-realistic
ORAYHP your ladyship
ORBEES horribleness
ORBRBE corroborable
ORBRTD corroborated
ORBRTR corroborator
ORCINL correctional
ORCINR correctioner
ORDITN Conrad Hilton
ORDOEZ Konrad Lorenz
OREAOT worried about
OREBTD journey-bated
ORENHY fourteenthly
ORENOE fourpenny one
ORERNE Tour de France
ORETHT your best shot
ORFCIN to prefection
ORFCLY horrifically
ORFIGY horrifyingly
ORFLES mournfulness
ORGOSY courageously
ORHSAE fourth estate
ORIAEY co-ordinately
ORIAIE co-ordinative
ORIAIG co-ordinating
ORIAIN co-ordination
ORIGAD boarding card
ORIGAS boarding pass
ORIRIE courtierlike
ORLGOS non-religious
ORMRIL court martial
court-martial
ORNDUK roaring drunk
ORNILY torrentially
ORNOSY horrendously
ORNYIE Courtney Pine
OROGUE Bourdon gauge
ORORIE four-four time
OROTAE Board of Trade
ORPRTR tour operator
ORRTUK horror-struck
ORRUEM Correr Museum
ORSCAS tourist class
ORSDNE non-residence
ORSIGY nourishingly
ORSNNE horrisonance
ORSODO correspond to
ORSRUE tourist route
ORSSAT non-resistant
ORTCLY Socratically
ORURES Four Quartets
ORWLOE you're welcome
OSAUAY constabulary
OSBEKR housebreaker
house-breaker
OSCAIN consecration
OSDDES lopsidedness
OSDRBE considerable
OSDRBY considerably
OSDTRY topside-turvy
OSDUTR loss adjuster
OSEASN hors de saison
OSEOBT hors de combat
OSEOSY boisterously
OSETIY conspectuity
OSFLES boastfulness
OSFTIG loose-fitting
OSHDLD non-scheduled
OSHNIG house-hunting
OSIAIN constipation
OSIFLY worshipfully
OSIGOK toasting-fork
OSIGUT Boussingault
OSIIGY conspiringly
OSIILY solstitially
OSIIUL non-spiritual
OSINIE conscientise
conscientize
OSIUIN constitution
OSIUNS constituents
OSIUNY constituency
OSJITD loose-jointed
OSKEIG housekeeping
OSKNES forsakenness
OSLAIE consultative
OSLAIN consultation
OSLAOY consultatory
OSLDTD consolidated
OSLDTR consolidator
OSLWVN loosely woven
OSMAEY consummately
OSMAIN consummation
OSMNHP horsemanship
OSNIGY consentingly
OSNINE consentience
OSNULY consensually
OSOCRS house of cards
OSOLNS lots to blanks
OSOLRS House of Lords
OSOURS hors d'oeuvres
OSPMLS goose-pimples
OSPOGR gossip-monger
OSPOUN gossip column
OSQECS consequences
OSQETY consequently
OSRAIE conservative
OSRAIM conservatism
OSRAIN conservation
OSRAOY conservatory
OSRCIE constrictive
constructive
OSRCIN constriction
construction
OSRPIN conscription
OSSETY consistently
OSSIEY possessively
OSSLIR horse soldier
OSSREN house-surgeon
OSSTIG house-sitting
OSTAIG horsetrading
horse-trading
OSTAND house-trained
OSTCAT coast-to-coast
OSTELR forset-seller
fosset-seller
OSTRIY topsy-turvily
OSUEES moistureless
OSWRIG housewarming
house-warming
OSYOSY housey-housey
OTACUT Port Harcourt
OTADAL tooth and nail
OTADLB Portland Club
OTAEIA North America
South America
OTAGRO no stranger to
OTAIES contrariness
OTAIIE contrariwise
OTALOT football boot
OTARAE poet laureate
OTATAS portmanteaus
OTATAX portmanteaux
OTATBE contractable
contractible
OTATDY contractedly
OTATOS contractions
OTAUTL contrapuntal
OTAYIH go steady with
OTBNER porte-bonheur
OTCLUE horticulture
OTCNCL non-technical
OTCSIO Monte Cassino
OTDLAA Ponta Delgada
OTDLIE Port Adelaide
OTDPEA monte di pietà
monti di pietà
OTDPEE monts-de-piété
OTDRHR Morte d'Arthur
OTDSAE Pott's disease
OTEAEF for the sake of
OTEALD soft-pedalled
OTEEDF sow the seed of
OTEEOD for the record
OTEETR for the better
OTEETY most recently
OTEIEF for the time of
OTEIIM post meridiem
OTEIIN postmeridian
OTENLS Southern Alps
OTENOD southernwood
OTENOT northernmost
southernmost
OTEODF for the good of
OTEOET for the moment
OTEPNR bottle opener
OTERNE Fort de France
Fort-de-France
OTESEN north-eastern
south-eastern
OTESES rootlessness
OTESIG for the asking
OTETES soft feathers
OTEWAE toothed whale
OTEWEL toothed wheel
OTFCLY pontifically
OTFCTR pontificater

OTFIIG cost of living
OTFLES loathfulness
youthfulness
OTGEIG Montague Tigg
OTGOGA South Georgia
OTGOSO contiguous to
OTGOSY contagiously
contiguously
OTGSAP postage stamp
OTHERH cost the earth
OTIACS contrivances
OTIEIE containerise
containerize
OTIOSY fortuitously
OTITRA Port Victoria
OTIUEO contribute to
OTIUIE contributive
OTIUIG contributing
OTIUIN contribution
OTIUOY contributory
OTLCNE noctilucence
OTLHAN Lotte Lehmann
OTLOKR postal worker
OTLYTM postal system
OTMCLY zootomically
OTMCOS contumacious
OTMLOS contumelious
OTMLTR contemplator
OTMNBE contaminable
OTMNIN not to mention
OTMNTD contaminated
OTMOAY contemporary
OTMOIE contemporise
contemporize
OTMRWR bottom drawer
OTMTBE contemptible
OTMTBY contemptibly
OTMTOS contemptuous
OTMUIM noctambulism
OTMUIT noctambulist
OTNAHR Cotton Mather
OTNAIN continuation
OTNAOB costing a bomb
OTNCOS bottony cross
OTNETN contingent on
OTNETY contingently
OTNIDR Norton Zinder
OTNIEY most unlikely
OTNMUH foot-and-mouth
OTNOSY continuously
portentously
OTNSOM port in a storm
OTOEET postponement
OTOFEE Gottlob Frege
OTOGAI Boutros-Ghali
OTOIIE postpositive
OTOIIN postposition
OTOLBE controllable
OTOOIH Rostropovich
OTOPNL control panel
OTOPTR host computer
OTOREF do-it-yourself
OTOSES tortuousness
OTOSIK control stick
OTOTWR control tower
OTOWRS lost for words
OTPCFC South Pacific
OTRAAR not turn a hair
OTRAET foster parent
OTRAIG worth reading
OTRASN Doctor Watson
OTRDAE postgraduate
OTREYL Doctor Jekyll
OTRGTY forthrightly
OTRIAE conterminate
OTRIAT conterminant
OTRIOS conterminous
OTRNIL postprandial
OTROEU Doctor Moreau
OTROGR costermonger
OTRWEL potter's wheel
OTSAIN contestation
OTSGUE mortise gauge
OTSIGY contestingly
OTSILS South Shields
OTTMUH mouth-to-mouth
OTUBIN Northumbrian
OTUOSY posthumously
OTURNE Port-au-Prince
OTWSEN north-western
south-western
OTXULY contextually
OTYOTY softly-softly
OUAFOT popular front
OUCOSY loquaciously
OUETLY monumentally
OUIESN do business in
OUIOSY voluminously
OUNAIN columniation
OUOGNM Novum Organum
OUOSGT go out of sight
OUTIHY coquettishly
OUTOSY robustiously
voluptuously
OUTRIM voluntaryism
OUVVNI modus vivendi
OUWLIG not unwilling
OVARCE nouveau riche
OVCINL convectional
OVEIDW louvre window
OVLIEY convulsively
OVLSET convalescent
OVLSIG convalescing
OVLTOS convolutions
OVNAUE solvent abuse
OVNETY conveniently
OVNIGY convincingly
OVNINL conventional
OVRAIN conversation
OVRHTP go over the top
OVVAIY conviviality
OVYNIG conveyancing
OWGASA Norwegian Sea
OWTCML Sopwith Camel
OWTRAK low-watermark
OWYPUE Norway spruce
OYAGAE body language
OYAOSY polygamously
OYAUDY Holy Saturday
OYEOAY cotyledonary
OYEOOS cotyledonous
OYERTS polyneuritis
OYFEPE body of people
OYFOIS holy of holies
OYHBAD go by the board
OYHITC polytheistic
OYHWRE go by the worse
OYIRIG body piercing
OYNHSS polyanthuses
OYOPIM polymorphism
OYOPOS polymorphous
OYRTAE polyurethane
OYTCIG body stocking
OYTYEE polyethylene
OYULIG body-building
OYYLBC polysyllabic
OYYLBE polysyllable
OZEISN Solzhenitsyn
PAACII apparatchiki
PAACIS apparatchiks
PAAHAS Appalachians
PACRIR spear-carrier
PAETES apparentness
PAETIE apparent time
PAHRHY speak harshly
PAPANY speak plainly
PAQITY speak quietly
PATRIM splatter film
PAVLMS speak volumes
PCADPN spick and span
spick-and-span
PCAITC specialistic
PCAOFR special offer
PCAOIL spectatorial
PCARGT special right
PCFCLY specifically
PCLUIT apiculturist
PCMNAE specimen page
PCOSES spaciousness
speciousness
PCRAIM Epicureanism
PCRGAH spectrograph
PCRMTC apochromatic
PCRMTR spectrometer
PCRMTY spectrometry
PCRSOE spectroscope
PCRSOY spectroscopy
PCSAIN space station
PCSUTE space shuttle
PDDMDS epididymides
PDITCL epideictical
PDMCLY epidemically
PDMOOY epidemiology
PDROKY spider monkey
PECASS upper classes
PECPIN apperception
PEDALD spread-eagled
PEDCOY appendectomy
PEDCTS appendicitis

PEDDES	splendidness
PEDOSP	spread gossip
PEDPAE	spread a plate
PEDRUD	spread around
PEEAIY	ephemerality
PEEESN	spiegeleisen
PEEFAE	a piece of cake
PEEFAL	a piece of tail
PEEFIS	a piece of piss
PEHAIG	speech-making
PEHEET	speech defect
PEHESY	speechlessly
PEHFIG	speechifying
PEIAIY	sphericality
PEIIGY	appetisingly
	appetizingly
PESRDL	apfel strudel
PETPNY	a pretty penny
PFIAIN	spiflication
PGAMTC	epigrammatic
PGGCLY	apagogically
PGSTNS	apage Satanas
PIAFBE	optical fibre
PICEIL	sphincterial
PIGOID	spring to mind
PIHFLY	sprightfully
PIIAIN	optimization
PIOAOK	split on a rock
PITEOE	split the vote
PKSEPE	spokespeople
PKSESN	spokesperson
PLAIFL	spill a bibful
PLBNIG	spellbinding
PLCEKR	spellchecker
PLGTCL	apologetical
PLGZFR	apologize for
PLOEEF	apply oneself
PLOOIT	speleologist
PLOSDM	apple of Sodom
PLTCLY	apolitically
PLUIEY	applausively
PLUIGY	applaudingly
PNADIH	open sandwich
PNARAE	open marriage
PNCILR	spine-chiller
PNEIGR	sponge finger
PNERIG	open learning
PNHAET	upon the alert
PNHAVL	upon the anvil
PNHWOE	upon the whole
PNLOUN	spinal column
PNNNGT	opening night
PNNSES	upon one's legs
PNOEAE	open to debate
PNOESN	open to reason
PNOTAK	open to attack
PNRHSS	epanorthoses
PNRNIG	up and running
PNSLEE	up one's sleeve
PNSSES	Spanish Steps
PNSTET	up one's street
PNSTMY	Spanish tummy
PNTROD	spinsterhood
PNUSIN	open question
PNYOOR	upon my honour
POAIIY	opposability
POGAUA	appoggiatura
POHSIE	up to this time
POIEES	appositeness
	oppositeness
POIGIE	opposing side
POIINL	oppositional
PONMNS	appointments
PONSEK	up to one's neck
PONSYS	up to one's eyes
POROSY	uproariously
PPEOEA	epiphenomena
PPETCL	apoplectical
PRAHBE	approachable
PRAOOC	spermatozoic
PRAOOD	spermatozoid
PRAOOL	spermatozoal
PRAOON	spermatozoan
	spermatozoon
PRAOYE	spermatocyte
PRCAIE	appreciative
PRCAIN	appreciation
PRCMQE	opéra comique
PRDCLY	sporadically
PRGASS	opera-glasses
PRGSIS	sphragistics
PRHNIE	apprehensive
PRHNIN	apprehension
PRIEES	sportiveness
PRIEET	appraisement
PRIIEY	appraisively
PROEOK	sport one's oak
PROGAS	sparrow-grass
PROSES	spuriousness
PRPITR	appropriator
PRSAKT	sports jacket
PRSATR	sportscaster
PRSESN	sportsperson
PRSIEY	oppressively
PRSRUD	sports ground
PRTAIE	spiritualise
	spiritualize
PRTAIM	spiritualism
PRTAIT	spiritualist
PRTAIY	spirituality
PRTCLY	operatically
PRTDES	spiritedness
PRTESY	spiritlessly
PRTFAT	spirit of salt
PRTFIE	spirit of wine
PRTOIY	spirituosity
PSDCLY	episodically
PSEOOY	epistemology
PSRPIE	apostrophise
	apostrophize
PTAAIL	epithalamial
PTEAIS	apothecaries
PTEIGY	sputteringly
PTEIMS	epitheliomas
PTESES	spotlessness
PTFLES	spitefulness
PUGHTM	sprung rhythm
PUTNNE	appurtenance
PYMGAH	sphygmograph
PYMMTR	sphygmometer
QAEIGD	square-rigged
QAEIGR	square-rigger
QAEUBR	square number
QAFOIG	equal footing
QAHENS	squash tennis
QAIAIN	equalization
QAIOSY	equanimously
QAOILY	equatorially
QEKCEN	squeaky clean
	squeaky-clean
QETINE	equestrienne
QIAETO	equivalent to
QIAETY	equivalently
QIIRTR	equilibrator
QIITNE	equidistance
QIOAIG	equivocating
QIOAIN	equivocation
QIOAIY	equivocality
RAAAEO	treat as a hero
RAAEOD	break a record
RAATIE	break a strike
RABIAN	Great Britain
RABLID	great-bellied
RABLNE	trial balance
RABLON	trial balloon
RACAKR	cream cracker
RACIPR	bread-chipper
RACSIG	broadcasting
RADAMR	Armand Hammer
RADNIG	breakdancing
	break-dancing
RADPLA	Brian De Palma
RAEOKY	grease monkey
RAESEN	Great Eastern
RAETAT	greatest part
RAETLY	ornamentally
RAETRA	armamentaria
RAFLES	dreadfulness
RAGIDR	organ-grinder
RAGLRY	triangularly
RAGMNS	arrangements
RAHAAN	breathe again
RAHAIG	breathtaking
	breath-taking
RAHESY	breathlessly
RAHLSR	Breathalyser®
RAIAIN	organisation
	organization
	urbanization
RAIEES	creativeness
RAIGON	breaking-down
RAIHES	freakishness
RAINLY	irrationally
RAMLEN	Great Malvern
RANMES	great numbers
RAOFIH	break off with
RAPIIR	preamplifier
RAPOIE	break-promise
RAPRMD	Great Pyramid

RARNWL	urban renewal
RASASM	friar's balsam
RASOIS	Great Smokies
RASRIE	break service
RATEES	break the news
RATRUH	break through
	breakthrough
RATTOE	breaststroke
RAUEUT	treasure hunt
RAUYOE	treasury note
RAWDOK	break wedlock
RAWSEN	Great Western
RAYFOE	Treaty of Rome
RBCLTD	trabeculated
RBEHNE	treble chance
RBLTOS	tribulations
RBNGOP	Tribune group
RBSEBY	Frobisher Bay
RBSEPE	tribespeople
RBTOAY	probationary
RCAAIN	proclamation
RCAAOY	proclamatory
RCAIIY	traceability
	tractability
RCAOTE	crack a bottle
RCATRC	trochanteric
RCBAND	crackbrained
	crack-brained
RCCAWN	Bruce Chatwin
RCCCIT	trick cyclist
RCCNRL	price control
RCCOSY	precociously
RCEAAN	proceed again
RCECEP	bracket-creep
RCEEET	trace element
RCESOY	tracheostomy
RCFEDR	brickfielder
RCFLES	gracefulness
RCGIIE	precognitive
RCGIIN	precognition
RCIAIM	practicalism
RCIAIT	practicalist
RCIAIY	practicality
RCIELE	trichinellae
RCIELS	trichinellas
RCIEOS	fructiferous
RCIGON	tracking-down
RCIHES	brackishness
RCIINR	practitioner
RCINES	frictionless
RCINLY	fractionally
RCINTR	fractionator
RCIOOS	fructivorous
RCIOOY	Trichinopoly
RCMLRN	Bruce McLaren
RCNEAY	tricentenary
RCNEVD	preconceived
RCNIIN	precondition
RCNPOE	arachnophobe
RCNUOS	iracundulous
RCOAIE	oryctolagine
RCOEEF	brace oneself
RCOILY	proctorially
RCOLGT	trick of light
RCOMNY	price of money
RCOOIE	trichotomise
	trichotomize
RCOOIT	proctologist
	trichologist
RCOOOS	trichotomous
RCORPY	fractography
RCOSES	graciousness
	preciousness
RCOTET	trick or treat
RCPOIL	preceptorial
RCPTNE	precipitance
RCPTNY	precipitancy
RCRMTC	trichromatic
RCROSY	precariously
RCSAIT	precisianist
RCSINL	precessional
	processional
RCSOIT	precisionist
RCTEHP	crack the whip
RCTERL	procathedral
RCUIEY	preclusively
RCYLMN	Tracey Ullman
RDBGIS	Frodo Baggins
RDCIEY	predictively
	productively
RDCIIY	productivity
RDDPIN	traded option
RDEHGP	bridge the gap
RDERLY	Bridget Riley
RDGOSY	prodigiously
RDIGES	grudgingness
RDIGON	bridging loan
RDILKR	Freddie Laker
RDISAR	Freddie Starr
RDJUNL	trade journal
RDLCIN	predilection
RDMNNE	predominance
RDNIKE	a rod in pickle
RDNILY	prudentially
RDNSAP	trading stamp
RDOEEF	pride oneself
RDOPAE	pride of place
RDRKTD	Frederikstad
RDSATA	tradescantia
RDSEPE	tradespeople
RDSESN	tradesperson
RDSETY	iridescently
RDSGAE	predesignate
RDSIAE	predestinate
RDTAIG	credit rating
RDTOIT	traditionist
RDTOTY	creditworthy
RDTRIE	predetermine
REAGRO	tree kangaroo
REAIEY	irrelatively
REAOSN	Arne Jacobsen
RECLEE	Green College
	Oriel College
REDIES	friendliness
REDNED	friend in need
REDYAK	friendly talk
REDYIE	friendly fire
REDYIH	friendly with
REEADN	Graeme Garden
REEATY	irrelevantly
REEEGR	Arsene Wenger
REEETY	irreverently
REEIBE	irremediable
REEIBY	irremediably
REELBY	irrepealably
REEMBE	irredeemable
REEMBY	irredeemably
REEPAE	breeze up sale
REESBE	irreversible
REESBY	irreversibly
REFHRE	free of charge
REFNES	green fingers
REGDES	Green Goddess
REGOEY	greengrocery
REHNIG	freethinking
	free-thinking
REIEIS	Arne Tiselius
REIETY	pre-eminently
REIGOD	freezing cold
REISBE	irremissible
REITBE	irresistible
REITBY	irresistibly
RELMSA	pre-eclampsia
RELNSA	Greenland Sea
REOEEF	preen oneself
REOEES	gruesomeness
REOMBE	irreformable
REOMBY	irreformably
REOSES	grievousness
REOUEY	irresolutely
REOUIN	irresolution
REOVBY	irresolvably
REPCIE	irrespective
RERGBE	irrefragable
RERGBY	irrefragably
RERVBY	irreprovably
RETBIH	pre-establish
RETEIG	orienteering
RETNIG	free-standing
REUAIY	irregularity
REUTBE	irrebuttable
REYRWY	creepy-crawly
RFBIAE	prefabricate
RFCETN	proficient in
RFCETY	proficiently
RFCOIL	prefectorial
RFIAEY	profligately
RFRAIN	trifurcation
RFRNIL	preferential
RFSINL	professional
RFSOIL	professorial
RFTAGN	profit margin
RFTAIG	profit-making
RFTEIG	profiteering
RFTESY	profitlessly
RFUDES	profoundness
RGAMBE	programmable
RGAOIS	braggadocios
RGAYUG	Brigham Young

RGCMCL tragicomical
RGEHPY trigger-happy
RGHPEL Greg Chappell
RGIHES priggishness
RGLOTF wriggle out of
RGMGLR drug-smuggler
RGNMTY trigonometry
RGNSET drag one's feet
RGNTES progenitress
RGOTDS proglottides
RGOYIM troglodytism
RGREDL Gregor Mendel
RGRFCS frigorificos
RGROSY gregariously
RGRUKL Art Garfunkel
RGSEOE progesterone
RGTNDY frightened by
RGTNOK Brighton Rock
RGUESI Greg Rusedski
RGYEIE triglyceride
RHDNIS orthodontics
RHDNIT orthodontist
RHEMTY archaeometry
RHGAHC orthographic
RHGAHR orthographer
RHGNLY orthogonally
RHGNSS orthogenesis
RHGNTC orthogenetic
RHLGRY Arshile Gorky
RHMREE Graham Greene
RHNIIY prehensility
RHPEIS orthopaedics
RHPEIT orthopaedist
RHPEOS orthopterous
RHPLGS archipelagos
RHRARS Arthur Harris
RHRILR Arthur Miller
RHROBC orthorhombic
RHSRPT orchestra pit
RHSRTR orchestrator
RHTCUE architecture
RHTPCL archetypical
RIACHL grain alcohol
RIAIES ordinariness
RIAIIY irritability
RIBAIG fruit-bearing
RIEOTY praiseworthy
RIFLES fruitfulness
RIGELN Irving Berlin
RIGUFR crying out for
RIHLNR freightliner
RIHMMS Ornithomimus
RIHSHA Ornithischia
RIHTAN freight-train
RIIGOY orbiting body
RIIILY artificially
RILCOS argillaceous
RIOEFT fry in one's fat
RIOOSY traitorously
RISOTR train-spotter
RITCDY Armistice Day
RITCLY artistically
RITMDL artist's model
RIUAEY articulately
RIUAIN articulation
RIWSIG brainwashing
RJDEET prejudgement
RKRELR broker-dealer
RLCOEY frolicsomely
RLFCES prolificness
RLFCLY prolifically
RLGMNL prolegomenal
RLGMNN prolegomenon
RLINIE brilliantine
RLMDMS troll-my-dames
RLNAIN prolongation
RLTCLY prelatically
RLTRLY trilaterally
RMAIIE grammaticise
grammaticize
RMATDY from day to day
RMCLEE drama college
RMCRML crème caramel
RMDPPR bromide paper
RMDTTD premeditated
RMEAIE Gram-negative
RMFACE crème fraîche
RMGAIA primigravida
RMGFAS fromage frais
RMGNTL primogenital
RMGNTR primogenitor
RMHHAT from the heart
RMHTIE from that time
RMLAIG promulgating
RMLAIN promulgation
RMMOIE primum mobile
RMNAOE Truman Capote
RMNCOS graminaceous
RMNOSY tremendously
RMNTUL premenstrual
RMOEAH primrose path
RMOIIE Gram-positive
RMOIIG trampolining
RMOIIT trampolinist
RMRILY primordially
RMRISE primary issue
RMSDAD promised land
RMSOIY promissorily
RMTAIE promethazine
RMTCLY dramatically
RMTEAY aromatherapy
RMTRIT dramaturgist
RMUTSN from sun to sun
RMVLTM primeval atom
RNAAET drunk as a newt
RNAAOD drunk as a lord
RNABHN Brendan Behan
RNAHRE bring a charge
RNAIDX cranial index
RNATOS transactions
RNCAGS bring charges
RNCNET transcendent
RNDCES grand duchess
RNDIIG drink-driving
RNECNE frondescence
RNELET Prince Albert
RNEOOE Grande Comore
RNEQAH orange squash
RNESEN Frankenstein
RNEUET Prince Rupert
RNEWRS printed works
RNFLES wrongfulness
RNFRAD bring forward
RNFRBE transferable
RNFRIG transforming
RNFRIT transfer list
RNFRNE transference
RNGAHC uranographic
RNGAHR uranographer
RNGESR transgressor
RNGINL Grand Guignol
RNGNTL urinogenital
RNHETR French letter
RNHIDW French window
RNHLUH trench-plough
RNHMNE transhumance
RNHNOT branching out
branching-out
RNHOIH French polish
French-polish
RNHOTR trench mortar
RNHPET transhipment
RNHPIG transhipping
RNHSOE bronchoscope
RNHTRY Arundhati Roy
RNHUAA French Guiana
RNIABY principal boy
RNIAIY principality
RNIBCN Francis Bacon
RNIBIY Francis Baily
RNICIK Francis Crick
RNICNE frankincense
RNIDAE Francis Drake
RNIIEY transitively
RNIIIY frangibility
RNIINL transitional
RNIMUE Francis Maude
RNIOIY transitorily
RNIPEE frontispiece
RNIRMN frontiersman
RNKAMR Franz Klammer
RNKROE Frank Kermode
RNLAIN crenellation
RNLCNE translucence
RNLCNY translucency
RNLDIG iron-cladding
RNLECI Brunelleschi
RNLESR Frank Loesser
RNLTBE translatable
RNMAIM trinomialism
RNMAIT trinomialist
RNMGAE transmigrate
RNMGIY transmogrify
RNMNAE transmontane
RNMNHP brinkmanship
RNMNLY pronominally
RNMSIE transmissive
RNMSIN transmission
RNMTBE transmutable

RNMTBY transmutably
RNNKIE pruning-knife
RNOARS brontosaurus□
RNOENC transoceanic
RNOSUE François Rude
RNOUTR bronco-buster
RNPATR transplanter
RNPCFC transpacific
RNPRBE transpirable
RNPRIG transporting
RNPRNY transparency
RNPSBE transposable
RNRDIA Irina Rodnina
RNSAEN bring shame on
RNSAEO bring shame to
RNSDOT wrong side out
RNSNTA Frank Sinatra
RNSTIG trendsetting
RNTAAT bring to a halt
RNTAED bring to a head
bring to an end
RNTATP bring to a stop
RNTCLY frenetically
RNTHUE Trinity House
RNTLGT bring to light
RNTOUH drink too much
RNTTIL bring to trial
RNTTRS bring to terms
RNUAIN transudation
RNUCDY pronouncedly
RNULES tranquilness
RNULIE tranquillise
tranquillize
RNULIY tranquillity
RNVREY transversely
RNVSIE transvestite
RNVSIM transvestism
RNWITE Frank Whittle
RNYUTR brandy butter
ROCPIG preoccupying
ROCRET proof-correct
RODAMR Arnold Palmer
RODEKR Arnold Wesker
ROEALR Brooke-Taylor
ROECNE arborescence
ROMSAE error message
RORLTD armour-plated
RPCAGR drop a clanger
RPDCIE crêpe de chine
RPEETC propaedeutic
RPEOGE triple-tongue
RPEUND triple-turned
RPGAIN propugnation
RPGNIE propagandise
propagandize
RPGNIT propagandist
RPIAIN triplication
RPINVL graphic novel
RPITES proprietress
RPNEAE preponderate
RPNEAT preponderant
RPOOIT graphologist
RPORPY cryptography
RPRDES preparedness
RPRIIN tripartition
RPRINL proportional
RPROIN proper motion
RPRTOS preparations
RPSEOS preposterous
RPSHRC tropospheric
RPSZTE crêpe suzette
RPTAIE propitiative
RPTAIN propitiation
RPTAOY propitiatory
RPTOGL triphthongal
RPTOSY propitiously
RPYATC prophylactic
RPZHDA trapezohedra
RQETES frequentness
RQITNE cry quittance
RRGTVD prerogatived
RRQIIE prerequisite
RSACER crystal clear
crystal-clear
RSAGZR crystal-gazer
RSAPIT fresh as paint
RSBRIR crash barrier
crush barrier
RSBTOK cross-buttock
RSCAGS press charges
RSCOIL prosectorial
RSCRET cross-current
RSCTBE prosecutable
RSCTIG press cutting
RSCUTY cross-country
RSDAGT Irish Draught
RSDCLY prosodically
RSDNIL presidential
RSDNRS crise de nerfs
RSEAIE cross-examine
RSEOSY prosperously
RSESAE Brussels lace
RSETSS prospectuses
RSEWRS crossed wires
RSFLES trustfulness
RSGAND cross-grained
RSGLEY press gallery
RSHEKL Ernst Haeckel
RSIGES graspingness
RSIGON dressing-down
dressing-gown
RSIGVR crossing over
RSIIIY irascibility
RSIITR prestigiator
RSINAD Kristiansand
RSINLE Prussian blue
RSISMS prestissimos
RSIUIN prostitution
RSLNIG crash-landing
RSLTVK Brest-Litovsk
RSLTZR proselytizer
RSMTOS presumptuous
RSNAIN presentation
RSNIET presentiment
RSNILY presentially
RSNMRI Krishnamurti
RSOEIN Aristotelian
RSOFCR press officer
RSOHNS Aristophanes
RSORTC aristocratic
RSOUVN griseofulvin
RSOYIM praseodymium
RSRAIE preservative
RSRAIN preservation
RSRLAE press release
RSRPIE prescriptive
proscriptive
RSRPIN prescription
proscription
RSSCIN cross section
cross-section
RSSRKS brush strokes
RSSRTS Erasistratus
RSUEOK pressure-cook
RSUIIG pressurizing
RSYEIN presbyterian
RTAAFR write away for
RTAAIN prothalamion
RTATDY protractedly
RTBRNE protuberance
RTCEIE erotic desire
RTCICE Arctic Circle
RTCIEY protectively
RTCIGY protectingly
RTCIIM protactinium
RTCLAS critical mass
RTCLES criticalness
RTCOAE protectorate
RTEILW brother-in-law
RTFIGY gratifyingly
RTFLED Grateful Dead
RTFLES gratefulness
truthfulness
wrathfulness
RTHDES wretchedness
RTIOSY gratuitously
RTLBNS brittle bones
RTLSIG grit blasting
RTNIGY pretendingly
RTNTBE writing-table
RTPAMC protoplasmic
RTPAML protoplasmal
RTPOET write protect
write-protect
RTQIKY write quickly
RTRCAP writer's cramp
RTRCLY oratorically
RTRIIG fraternizing
RTRMCN erythromycin
RTRSOE urethroscope
RTRSOY urethroscopy
RTSAIN protestation
RTSHNS Eratosthenes
RTSIGY protestingly
RTSURE grotesquerie
RTTPCL prototypical
RTUIEY protrusively
RTYAAT Pretty Vacant
RTYRTY pretty-pretty

RUAANT	argue against
RUCPAN	group captain
RUDESY	groundlessly
RUDETE	ground beetle
RUHATD	proud-hearted
RUHBAD	draughtboard
RUHPOF	draught-proof
RUINLP	Freudian slip
RULMKR	troublemaker
RULSOT	troubleshoot
RUOSVN	Group of Seven
RUOWRS	group of words
RUPAIM	triumphalism
RUPAIT	triumphalist
RUPATY	triumphantly
RUQITT	Trout Quintet
RUTEAY	group therapy
RUTEOS	argue the toss
RUUETY	fraudulently
RVAIIS	trivialities
RVAIIY	driveability
RVBNNS	drive bananas
RVCOHS	graveclothes
RVCUCL	Privy Council
RVDNIL	providential
RVIIGY	prevailingly
RVLCOS	travel across
RVLGNY	travel agency
RVLIEY	travel widely
RVLOOK	travel to work
RVNAIE	preventative
RVNFRE	driving force
RVNIEY	preventively
RVNILY	provincially
RVNPWR	driving-power
RVNUIG	prevent using
RVRALY	Trevor Bailey
RVRCTR	prevaricator
RVRILY	proverbially
RVROAD	Trevor Howard
RVSYOE	travesty role
RVTHTL	private hotel
RVTLVS	Private Lives
RVTMAS	private means
RVTPRS	private parts
RVTRUH	drive through
RVTTTR	private tutor
RWCAKR	prawn cracker
RWHAKT	growth market
RWHBAD	draw the board
RWHTBE	draw the table
RWIGIE	Brownie Guide
RWIGIH	crawling with
RWIPIT	brownie point❑
RWNPWR	drawing power
RWOCOE	draw to a close
RWOEHR	draw together
	grow together
RWRYAT	brewer's yeast
RWTRUH	trawl through
RYAGIG	argy-bargying
RYQIRL	grey squirrel
RYRESY	prayerlessly
RYSBON	greyish-brown
RZFGTR	prizefighter
	prize-fighter
RZWNIG	prize-winning
SAABNZ	Isaac Albéniz
SADNSN	Isaac Dineson
SADOLY	Oswald Mosley
SAELUE	escape clause
SAHGDM	Aswan High Dam
SAIAIN	Islamization
SAOOIT	escapologist
SATCCD	aspartic acid
SAYPOY	A Sea Symphony
SCITIT	psychiatrist
SCOABE	psychobabble
SCOAHC	psychopathic
SCOCIE	psychoactive
SCOEUL	psychosexual
SCOOIE	psychologise
	psychologize
SCOOIL	psychosocial
SCOOIT	psychologist
SCORPC	psychotropic
SCRFLY	use carefully
SCRNLY	isochronally
SDAERC	isodiametric
SDMRHC	isodimorphic
SEBYIE	assembly line
SEBYOM	assembly room
SEEAIN	asseveration
SEGLUS	aspergillums
SEGNSS	osteogenesis
SEGNTC	osteogenetic
SELGCL	osteological
SEMIHY	esteem highly
SEMLCA	osteomalacia
SEPATC	osteoplastic
SEPRSS	osteoporosis
SESODY	Ascension Day
SETAHS	Ashes To Ashes
SETIIG	ascertaining
SETTOS	ostentatious
SFEANT	as often as not
SFRIMY	ask for firmly
SHCOZA	eschscholzia
SHXAIN	asphyxiation
SIALBY	A Suitable Boy
SIHELN	Isaiah Berlin
SIIAIE	assimilative
SIIAIN	assimilation
	ossification
SILGAH	oscillograph
SILSOE	oscilloscope
SLAAMD	as clear as mud
SLTDRA	isolated area
SLTOIM	isolationism
SLTOIT	isolationist
SLYOPR	Astley Cooper
SMERCL	asymmetrical
SMTTCL	asymptotical
SNHOIM	asynchronism
SNHOOS	asynchronous
SNNTNE	as an instance
SNTCLA	A Song to Celia
SOBCCD	ascorbic acid
SOCRIG	as concerning
SODSOD	as good as gold
SOEBAN	use one's brain
SOETRW	a stone's throw
SOIHET	astonishment
SOITOS	associations
SOLCCA	I should cocoa
SOLWRY	I should worry!
SONIGY	astoundingly
SPOOIT	psephologist
SPOTRF	a supporter of
SRCTMS	astrocytomas
SRLGCL	astrological
SRNEET	estrangement
SRNETY	astringently
SRNMCL	astronomical
SRNUIS	astronautics
SRPYIS	astrophysics
SRREDY	user-friendly
SSAIGY	use sparingly
STEMLY	isothermally
STIUEO	as a tribute to
STRCLY	esoterically
SUBNPL	Assurbanipal
SUESGN	as sure as a gun
SUIGHT	assuming that
SUOOAS	pseudomonads
SUOOIM	pseudopodium
SUOYOS	pseudonymous
SUOYSS	pseudocyesis
SWDEDY	Ash Wednesday
SZAOGR	Zsuzsa Polgar
TABADD	it may be added
TADEAK	straddleback
TAGEOD	stranglehold
TAGIGY	stragglingly
TAGTAS	straightways
TAGTDE	straightedge
TAGTES	straightness
TAGTND	straightened
TAGTNP	straighten up
TAGTON	straight down
TAGTWY	straight away
	straightaway
TAIAIS	Stradivarius
TAIMCL	strabismical
TAIRPY	stratigraphy
TALAUE	it's a pleasure
TANPIT	strain a point
TANTIG	it was nothing
TAOCCD	ethanoic acid
TAOPEE	stratosphere
TAOROA	steatorrhoea
TAOYOS	steatopygous
TAPAEH	Uttar Pradesh
TATAKT	straitjacket
TATCIY	Atlantic City
TATEHW	steal the show
TATIES	stealthiness
TATRAE	steak tartare
TATRIE	steam turbine

Words marked ❑ can also be spelled with an initial capital letter

TAWITE	steam whistle	TIEMTH	strike a match	TOEFUK	stroke of luck
TBONES	stubbornness	TIETIH	strike it rich	TOERUD	stooge around
TCAANT	stack against	TIGORE	string course	TOGIDD	strong-minded
TCAIIY	stickability	TIITYU	it pitieth you	TOGILD	strong-willed
TCIGAK	stocking mask	TIPRRM	strippergram	TOGIUR	strong liquor
TCITAE	stock-in-trade	TISBUH	at first blush	TOKOTM	at rock bottom
TCLRIE	stickler-like	TISSGT	at first sight	TOOCPC	stroboscopic
TCOYHA	stichomythia	TIUAIN	stridulation	TOPEIS	atmospherics
TCPNST	stockpunisht	TIUAOY	stridulatory	TPAEIE	stoppage time
TCTEAE	stick the pace	TIUATY	stridulantly	TPEBNT	Stephen Benét
TCTIIE	stick-to-it-ive	TIUIIE	attitudinise	TPECAE	Stephen Crane
TCYIKT	sticky wicket		attitudinize	TPFCET	stupefacient
TDIGAL	studdingsail	TKOTET	Stoke-on-Trent	TPFCIE	stupefactive
TDOSES	studiousness	TLADNN	still and anon	TPFCIN	stupefaction
TDUDAL	St Edmund Hall	TLATES	stalwartness	TPFRAD	steps forward
TEBRUH	Attenborough	TLCLIO	Italo Calvino	TPIGON	stepping-down
TECEOT	stretched out	TLEBSH	Stellenbosch	TPIHIG	stop fighting
TECERF	steer clear of	TLMSTR	Ptolemy Soter	TPLTOS	stipulations
TECIES	stretchiness	TLODES	style of dress	TPNHGS	step on the gas
TECMRS	stretch marks	TLOSRL	stilboestrol	TPNOSY	stupendously
TEEOSY	streperously	TLPEIG	still-peering	TRAPIE	star sapphire
TEESAL	St Benet's Hall	TLSRNE	at close range	TRBTBE	attributable
TEESUG	St Petersburg	TLTCLY	athletically	TRCIEY	attractively
TEGHNR	strengthener	TLTOEL	stiletto heel	TRCIGY	attractingly
TEIATY	strepitantly	TLTRAE	at a later date	TRCTSS	athrocytoses
TEIGER	steering gear	TLTRIE	at a later time	TRDPYE	pteridophyte
TELCAE	steeplechase	TLTSOT	athlete's foot	TREMTR	starter motor
TEODAD	at second hand	TMCEGT	atomic weight	TRFXDY	stare fixedly
TEOEEF	steel oneself	TMCHOY	atomic theory	TRIGAE	starting gate
TERYAS	it's early days	TMCUBR	atomic number	TRIGAT	starring part
TETAKR	streetwalker	TMEIGY	stammeringly	TRIGOS	Stirling Moss
	street-walker	TMFNRL	it's my funeral	TRIYIG	eternity ring
TETCCI	streptococci	TMLGCL	etymological	TROCPC	stereoscopic
TETMCN	streptomycin	TNAANT	stand against	TROERC	stereometric
TETOKY	street hockey	TNADAP	standard lamp	TROHNC	stereophonic
TETOTR	Street-Porter	TNADIE	standard time	TROOSY	stertorously
TETRDR	street-trader	TNADZD	standardized	TRORPY	stereography
TETSOR	at death's door	TNADZR	standardizer	TROSMR	stereoisomer
TEWRDY	otherworldly	TNATIE	stand astride	TROYIG	stereotyping
	other-worldly	TNBCFR	stand back for	TRPNLD	star-spangled
TFCLEE	staff college	TNCNRC	ethnocentric	TRSEGH	at arm's length
TFESIT	stuffed shirt	TNEKIE	Stanley knife®	TRTLIG	story-telling
TFNDEG	Stefan Edberg	TNEMRH	Othniel Marsh	TRUAIE	sternutative
TFOEEF	stuff oneself	TNFPIT	at knife-point	TRUAIN	sternutation
TGEIGY	staggeringly	TNGAHC	ethnographic	TRUAOY	sternutatory
TGETOT	at a great cost		stenographic	TRWRIG	start working
TGTONR	a tight corner	TNGAHR	ethnographer		storm warning
TGWIPR	stage whisper		stenographer	TRYERL	stormy petrel
THFOTF	at the front of	TNHATD	stony-hearted	TTEFES	Statue of Zeus
THGPIE	at a high price	TNIAEF	stand in awe of	TTEIGY	stutteringly
THHESF	at the heels of	TNIGAE	standing wave	TTEQEY	statuesquely
THHNSF	at the hands of	TNIGIH	stinking rich	TTNSAD	Staten Island
THMRYF	at the mercy of	TNIGOE	standing joke	TTOCPC	stethoscopic
THODRF	at the order of	TNIGON	standing-down	TTOHUE	station house
THOTIE	at the outside	TNLGCL	ethnological	TTOSEE	state of siege
THPITF	at the point of	TNMSNY	stonemasonry	TTOSOK	state of shock
THSOET	at this moment	TNSASY	Stanislavsky	TTOWGN	station wagon
THTOET	at that moment	TNSINE	ethnoscience	TTPNIN	state pension
TICEIN	at discretion	TNTEAE	stand the pace	TTSESN	statesperson
TICRON	strip cartoon	TNUCMC	stand-up comic	TTSIIN	statistician
TIEEGD	stridelegged	TNUFGT	stand-up fight	TTSYBL	status symbol
TIEGAS	stained glass	TNURGT	stand upright	TUDRGS	Struldbruggs
TIELGT	strike a light!	TOEEHF	Otto Meyerhof	TUFNUG	Stauffenburg

TUGEIH struggle with
TUGIGY strugglingly
TUHATD stout-hearted
TVBCLY Steve Backley
TVEODR Stevie Wonder
TVFSET Steve Fossett
TVMQEN Steve McQueen
TVNORS Steven Norris
TVPPHT stovepipe hat
TYHIIM strychninism
TYNPWR staying power
TYWYRM stay away from
UAAPRN put a damper on
UAATOY Susan Anthony
UACAAH Lucas Cranach
UACUTC lunar caustic
UADHUT cut and thrust
UADLNT sun-and-planet
UAIAIN humanitarian
humanization
ruralization
UAIGRN put a finger on
UAINLY mutationally
UAOIES nugatoriness
UAOKNT put a sock in it
UAOOIE cut a lot of ice
UASCAK Jurassic Park
UASCEY human society
UATEIL sugar the pill
UAYTSS eucalyptuses
UBCAGD turbocharged
UBCAGR turbocharger
UBEEOY bubble memory
UBEUBE hubble-bubble
UBHNYU put behind you
UBLAIN turbellarian
UBREET rubber cement
UBRESY numberlessly
UBRHOY number theory
UBRHQE rubber cheque
UCACIN Dutch auction
UCADUY Punch and Judy
UCAOIM kurchatovium
UCCUAE Dutch courage
UCDAGT Dutch Draught
UCDNOS succedaneous
UCERLY succeed rally
UCESOK butcher's hook
UCIELS Punchinellos
UCIITS Nunc Dimittis
nunc dimittis
UCINES functionless
UCINLY functionally
UCINOD function word
UCLAIN auscultation
UCLAOY auscultatory
UCLBIT quickly built
UCLQET dulciloquent
UCNCCD succinic acid
UCNCOS subconscious
UCNEIG buccaneering
UCNIET subcontinent
UCNTES succinctness
UCOFVS bunch of fives
UCOSES lusciousness
UCSATY successantly
UCSFLY successfully
UCSIEY successively
UCSINL successional
UCSLEY quicksilvery
UCSSOY success story
UCTNOS subcutaneous
UCUTRO run counter to
UDAEIA Quadragesima
UDAGLR quadrangular
UDAGYE Auld Lang Syne
auld lang syne
UDAHNC quadraphonic
UDIAET quadrivalent
UDILGA quadriplegia
UDILGC quadriplegic
UDIOIL quadrinomial
UDLUVR Guadalquivir
UDMNAS fundamentals
UDMTLD muddy-mettled
UDNBSN pudding basin
UDNELH sudden wealth
UDNLGT guiding light
UDOHNC quadrophonic
UDREAS rudder pedals
UDREDD dunderheaded
UDRFED Huddersfield
UDRIDR wunderkinder
UDUAOS quadrumanous
UDVSBE subdivisible
UDWROS put down roots
UDYCOL Sunday school
UDYRVR Sunday driver
UEAIIY numerability
UEANAE superannuate
UEBARX Queen Beatrix
UECAGR supercharger
UECLAY superciliary
UECLOS supercilious
UECLSS tuberculosis
UECLTD tuberculated
UECNUT superconduct
UECROS supercargoes
UEECNE juvenescence
UEENGN Eugene Onegin
UEENIL Eugene O'Neill
UEEURE ruse de guerre
UEFAIE mute of malice
UEFMIM Duke of Omnium
UEHGWY superhighway
UEHMNY superhumanly
UEHRAT rule the roast
UEHROT rule the roost
UEIAIN suberization
UEIEES juvenileness
UEIEOS tuberiferous
UEIOIL subeditorial
UEIPSD superimposed
UELMNL superluminal
UEMIRT Jules Maigret
UEMNAE supermundane
UEMZRN Jules Mazarin
UENCLM supernaculum
UENTRL supernatural
UEOOIT numerologist
UEOSEA Queen of Sheba
UEOSES numerousness
UEOSOT tuberous root
UEOTDY surefootedly
UEOUAE superovulate
UEOWUH Auberon Waugh
UEPLIG sun-expelling
UERGOS outer regions
UESADM superstardom
UESADR Queenslander
UESAKT buyer's market
UESDNE supersedence
UESIIN superstition
UESPEH Queen's Speech
UESRAE outer surface
UESSIN supersession
UETROE Rupert Brooke
UEURTC bureaucratic
UEVNET supervenient
UEVNIN supervention
UFCETY sufficiently
UFCNIE surface noise
UFCTAR surface-to-air
UFCWTR surface water
UFLPNH Suffolk Punch
Suffolk punch
UFOUDR out from under
UFRCOS furfuraceous
UFREET suffer defeat
UGAAAM burglar alarm
UGAILY subglacially
UGCLAK surgical mask
UGFRAD surge forward
UGGLAI Luigi Galvani
UGOSNT surgeon's knot
UGRRUD bugger around
UGRTIE hunger strike
hunger-strike
UGRUGR hugger-mugger
UGSIEY suggestively
UGTNAP tungsten lamp
UHESES ruthlessness
UHHCIG bushwhacking
UHNIAE authenticate
UHNIIY authenticity
UHNOSY euphoniously
UHNSUK push one's luck
UHONFO rush to and fro
UHRPOF author's proof
UHTUHO tu-whit tu-whoo
UIADES Julie Andrews
UIAEGO Jubilate Agno
UIAEVR ruminate over
UIAGOP musical group
UIAIEY dubitatively
ruminatively
UIAIGY ruminatingly
UIAIOS mucilaginous
UIATEL Lucie Attwell

UICMRN	Julia Cameron
UICNUT	jurisconsult
UIDCIE	jurisdictive
UIDCIN	jurisdiction
UIDGEN	Lucinda Green
UIECNE	luminescence
UIESAD	business card
UIESAK	business park
UIESIE	businesslike
	business-like
UIFUAE	subinfeudate
UIIAIE	municipalise
	municipalize
UIIAIN	humification
	purification
UIIAIY	municipality
UIIAOY	purificatory
UIIEES	fugitiveness
UIIETY	munificently
UIILNS	Kuril Islands
UIINHP	musicianship
UIIOSY	fuliginously
UIIRBD	auxiliary bud
UILRUD	burial ground
UIMSIA	Yukio Mishima
UINRPV	Yuri Andropov
UINULY	Julian Huxley
UIOEEE	mud in one's eye
UIOOIT	musicologist
UIOSES	mutinousness
	numinousness
UIOSLX	luminous flux
UIPUET	jurisprudent
UIRBRS	Julia Roberts
UISASR	Julius Caesar
UISORE	run its course
UITCLY	autistically
	cubistically
	juristically
	puristically
UITEAL	put in the mail
UITEAY	music therapy
UITEOT	put in the boot
	put in the post
UITETE	music theatre
UITOUE	subintroduce
UITWRS	put into words
UIWIIG	put in writing
UJCIEY	subjectively
UJCIIE	subjectivise
	subjectivize
UJCIIM	subjectivism
UJCIIT	subjectivist
UKEITN	Turkmenistan
UKLCAO	Lucky Luciano
UKNAOT	mucking about
UKOLWR	cuckoo flower
UKOOLR	cuckoo-roller
UKPEDR	muckspreader
UKYAPT	Turkey carpet
ULACNE	build a sconce
ULAPWR	nuclear power
ULAWSE	nuclear waste

ULCCOL	public school
ULCETR	public sector
ULCIUE	public figure
ULECUH	Quiller-Couch
ULESEN	Guildenstern
ULFAKR	pull a flanker
ULFEGD	fully fledged
	fully-fledged
ULFLES	guilefulness
ULFNRY	full of energy
ULFSOE	pull a fast one
ULGTWY	mulligatawny
ULHOTD	full-throated
ULHWRS	pull the wires
ULIHIG	bullfighting
ULMNLY	subliminally
ULNETR	fuel injector
ULNIHY	outlandishly
ULNTNS	curling tongs
ULOEHR	pull together
ULOICS	pull to pieces
ULOIIG	guillotining
ULPTKS	pull up stakes
ULQIKY	build quickly
ULWATE	Ludlow Castle
ULWYAE	pull a wry face
UMCOAD	Gus Macdonald
UMDENY	curmudgeonly
UMGRTR	nutmeg grater
UMNAIE	augmentative
UMNAIN	augmentation
UMNEVE	outmanoeuvre
UMNYNO	put money into
UMRCOL	summer school
UMSIEY	submissively
UMUTBE	surmountable
UMXLAY	submaxillary
UNAIPN	turn cat in pan
UNAISU	Guinea-Bissau
UNALGT	burn daylight
UNCOSY	pugnaciously
UNDAER	turn a deaf ear
UNESNE	quintessence
UNFEIG	funny feeling
UNFHAE	turn of phrase
UNFVNS	turn of events
UNHESY	quenchlessly
UNHSAE	turn the scale
UNHSRW	turn the screw
UNIAIE	quantitative
UNIAIN	quantization
UNIIBE	quantifiable
UNIIEY	quantitively
UNLHPD	funnel-shaped
UNLIIN	tunnel vision
UNLNTS	cunnilinctus
UNNAIE	turning aside
	turning-aside
UNNAOE	running a home
UNNATR	running after
UNNBAD	running-board
UNNCSS	running costs
UNNFIY	burn in effigy

UNNOAH	turn into cash
UNNOTN	running out on
UNNPIT	turning-point
UNNSAK	turn one's back
UNNSED	turn one's head
UNNSOT	turn one's coat
UNNTAK	running-track
UNNTTE	running title
UNONOD	turn down cold
UNPAAG	Luang Prabang
UNPRMS	turn up trumps
UNRAIY	subnormality
UNRBEO	vulnerable to
UNRYDL	Gunnar Myrdal
UNTRVN	furniture van
UNUNIL	quinquennial
UNUNIM	quinquennium
UNVNUA	Buenaventura
UOAAYE	autocatalyse
	autocatalyze
UOALIK	out of all nick
UOCNRL	out of control
UODAIG	out of drawing
UODSLY	put on display
UOEHNS	rub one's hands
UOENLN	European plan
UOEORN	put one's oar in
UOESIK	cut one's stick
UOETEH	cut one's teeth
UOETUT	autodestruct
UOEVRN	put one over on
UOFANP	Rudolf Carnap
UOFISL	Rudolf Diesel
UOFSIN	out of fashion
UOHHNL	autochthonal
UOHHNS	autochthones
UOIATC	autodidactic
UOIKHW	autorickshaw
UOKEIG	out of keeping
UONWEE	out of nowhere
UOOEIE	put on one side
UOOOSY	autonomously
UOOSES	humorousness
UORAHF	out of reach of
UORNEF	out of range of
UOROGR	rumour-monger
UOSIIS	out of spirits
UOSRIE	out of service
UOTCLY	autoptically
UOTEAK	put on the rack
UOTEIE	put on the line
UOTEIL	run of the mill
	run-of-the-mill
UOTEIZ	put on the Ritz
UOTELE	out of the blue
UOTEOD	out of the road
	out of the wood
UOTEOL	put on the foil
UOTEPT	put on the spot
UOTIAR	out of thin air
UOURNY	Eurocurrency
UPCOSF	suspicious of
UPCOSY	auspiciously

	suspiciously
UPEETL	supplemental
UPESBE	suppressible
UPESDY	suppressedly
UPHBSM	jump the besom
UPHBUY	hump the bluey
UPHQEE	jump the queue
UPIAIG	supplicating
UPIAIN	supplication
UPIAOY	supplicatory
UPIDIY	rumpti-iddity
UPIIGY	surprisingly
UPNGID	bump and grind
UPNIEY	suspensively
UPNSAL	jump one's bail
UPOAIE	sulphonamide
UPRGOP	support group
UPRIEO	supportive to
UPRIEY	supportively
UPRIKL	pumpernickel
UPSBIT	purpose-built
UPSFLY	purposefully
UPSIGY	surpassingly
UPUAIN	sulphuration
UPYUPY	Humpty-Dumpty
	humpty-dumpty
UQAESL	quaquaversal
URAANT	guard against
URAITC	surrealistic
UREBOD	quarter-blood
UREBUD	quarter bound
URELGT	quarterlight
UREMLR	quarter-miler
URFCIE	putrefactive
URFCIN	putrefaction
URGLRY	buy regularly
URGOSY	outrageously
URILRS	guerrilleros
URINHP	guardianship
URMBIG	Supreme Being
	supreme being
URMCUT	Supreme Court
	supreme court
URMIGE	Murrumbidgee
URMNAE	supramundane
URMSUE	supreme sauce
UROBTL	supraorbital
UROEEF	guard oneself
UROOTS	Puerto Cortes
URTAOT	Lucretia Mott
URTOIT	nutritionist
URTOSY	nutritiously
URTRUH	hurry through
URUDDY	surrounded by
URUDNS	surroundings
URYAKR	Murray Walker
USACOS	Russian cross
USASLD	Russian salad
USATAE	substantiate
USATVL	substantival
USDAIY	subsidiarily
	subsidiarity
USDRGT	outside right
USFOIG	pussyfooting
USINAK	question mark
USINBE	questionable
USINBY	questionably
USINES	questionless
USINIE	question time
USIUIE	substitutive
USIUIN	substitution
USLOIY	subsultorily
USNBLS	nuts and bolts
USNDLS	Guys and Dolls
USNUNR	Bunsen burner
USOLES	rub shoulders
USQETO	subsequent to
USQETY	subsequently
USRBBE	subscribable
USRCUE	substructure
USRINE	subservience
USRINY	subserviency
USRNRE	nursery nurse
USRPIN	subscription
USRRYE	nursery rhyme
USRTHD	outstretched
USTRUH	burst through
UTAAIN	Australasian
UTADEM	Kurt Waldheim
UTAIDY	Australia Day
UTAOER	hunt saboteur
UTATRM	subtract from
UTBEES	suitableness
UTEAEN	put the make on
UTEAKE	cut the cackle
UTECDN	put the acid on
UTEIDP	put the wind up
UTEIDW	out the window
UTEIEN	put the bite on
UTEIKF	run the risk of
UTENLS	Burt Reynolds
UTEOTN	put the boot in
UTETAK	furthest back
UTFCTD	multifaceted
UTFCTR	justificator
UTFRIY	multiformity
UTFROS	multifarious
UTGAIA	multigravida
UTGOUE	put to good use
UTIEHT	just like that
UTLNUL	multilingual
UTLQET	multiloquent
UTLQOS	multiloquous
UTLTRL	multilateral
UTMUIN	customs union
UTNAAD	Austen Layard
UTNATR	Justin Martyr
UTNEDD	mutton-headed
UTNGUE	cutting gauge
UTNLDE	hunting-lodge
UTNNIE	cutting no ice
UTNRAS	Austin friars
UTNSOK	suit one's book
UTOEIE	put to one side
UTOEIN	Austronesian
UTONGT	Kurt Vonnegut
UTOORD	rust-coloured
UTPEHP	multiple shop
UTPIAD	multiplicand
UTPIBE	multipliable
UTPIIY	multiplicity
UTPRIE	multipartite
UTPROE	multipurpose
UTRAEN	subterranean
UTRAHD	lust-breathed
UTRAPE	custard apple
UTRCNO	quattrocento
UTRCTH	butterscotch
UTRETN	Buster Keaton
UTRILR	hunter-killer
UTRSOK	culture shock
UTRULN	butter-muslin
UTRULR	butter curler
UTTEON	put to the horn
UTTSIG	multitasking
UTVALR	Gustav Mahler
UTVLNE	multivalence
UUABLS	tubular bells
UUAIEY	cumulatively
UUFRAE	put up for sale
UUHBBE	Jusuf Habibie
UUJMIG	queue-jumping
UUNRCS	autumn crocus
UUOIBS	cumulonimbus
UUROSY	lugubriously
UUTCME	Auguste Comte
UUTEAR	put up the hair
UUTOIS	August Möbius
UUTOSY	tumultuously
UUTRDN	Auguste Rodin
UUTSON	Augustus John
UUWLFR	augur well for
UVILNE	surveillance
UVRZBE	pulverizable
UWGRAD	Ludwig Erhard
UXTCLY	quixotically
UZEODR	muzzle-loader
UZIAIY	quizzicality
VAQEAE	ave atque vale
VDNILY	evidentially
VETAIL	A View to a Kill
VGDOLW	Avogadro's law
VIAIIY	availability
VLEPRD	evil-tempered
VLIDDY	evil-mindedly
VLMLIG	evil-smelling
VLTOAY	evolutionary
VLTOIM	evolutionism
VLTOIT	evolutionist
VNADDY	even-handedly
VNCUIR	avant-courier
VNEALY	Yvonne Cawley
VNEITC	evangelistic
VNEPRD	even-tempered
VNGRIM	avant-gardism
VNGRIT	avant-gardist
VNHRZN	event horizon
VNNDES	evening dress
	evening-dress

VNSETY evanescently
VNUGNV Ivan Turgenev
VNYPED evenly spread
VRADNT overhand knot
VRAIIR overfamiliar
over-familiar
VRBNAT overabundant
VRCOSY avariciously
VRECIN overreaction
VREIAE overdelicate
VRESAE overpersuade
VRFWAS every few days
VRHLIG overwhelming
VRHNIG ever-changing
VRHRIG overcharging
VRIHBG overnight bag
overnight-bag
VRIHRS Ivor Richards
VRLUIH overflourish
VRLWIH overflow with
VRMHSS overemphasis
VRMNAK every man Jack
VRNAOE over and above
VRNSED over one's head
VRODHP overlordship
VROEIG overpowering
VROEIH overcome with
VRPNIG overspending
VRREDY over-friendly
VRRMTC overdramatic
VRRSIG overtrusting
VRRTCL overcritical
VRRWIG overcrowding
VRSIAE overestimate
VRSOTN every so often
VRTAND overstrained
VRTPIG overstepping
VRUDND overburdened
VRULES overfullness
over-fullness
VRUTPY overmultiply
VRXEDD overextended
VRXOUE overexposure
VSEAIN evisceration
WABCES sweat buckets
WEADOR sweet-and-sour
WEAYSM sweet alyssum
WEFCAL sweet fuck all
WENTIG sweet nothing
WESETD sweet-scented
WETLIG sweet-talking
WETOHD sweet-toothed
WEWLIM sweet william
WFCDES two-facedness
WFTAIS Two Fat Ladies
WGEIGY swaggeringly
WGESIK swagger-stick
WGTODN Dwight Gooden
WISIIG awe-inspiring
WLECOK twelve o'clock
WLGTOE twilight zone
WLTNGT Twelfth Night
WMIGAH swimming-bath
WMIGOD swimming-pond
WMIGOL swimming-pool
WMNRMH Kwame Nkrumah
WNCRGR Ewan McGregor
WNLOTF swindle out of
WNTEED swing the lead
WNYWNY twenty-twenty
WPUDON two pound coin
WRIGIH swarming with
WRWNIG award-winning
WSADUN twist and turn
WSBCLR swashbuckler
WSEFIE a waste of time
WTEIGY twitteringly
WTESOH two-toed sloth
WUDTNW I wouldn't know
WZLSIK swizzle-stick
XADDYE expanded type
XAGIAE exsanguinate
XARAIN expatriation
XASIEY exhaustively
XASOAY expansionary
XASOIM expansionism
XASOIT expansionist
XASVLE exhaust valve
XBOOIT exobiologist
XCAIEY execratively
XCRAIN exacerbation
XCTRHP executorship
XEIETL experimental
XEIETR experimenter
XEINIL expediential
experiential
XEMNTD exterminated
XEMNTR exterminator
XEOETR exteroceptor
XEPRZD extemporized
XETTOS expectations
XETYTM expert system
XEVCMN ex-serviceman
XGEAIN exaggeration
XGOSES exiguousness
XGTCLY exegetically
XHNEAE exchange rate
XHNEBE exchangeable
XHNEBY exchangeably
XIAAIE exhilarative
XIAAIG exhilarating
XIAAIN exhilaration
XIAIIY excitability
XIGIHD extinguished
XIGIHR extinguisher
XIIIEY exhibitively
XIIINR exhibitioner
XLCTES explicitness
XLDDIW exploded view
XLIAIE exploitative
XLIAIN exploitation
XLNAIN explantation
XLSOAY exclusionary
XMLFIG exemplifying
XOEOIK expose to risk
XOEOIW expose to view
XOIAIN excogitation
XOIIEY expositively
XOIINL expositional
XOTEET export reject
XOTLTR expostulator
XOTOAE extortionate
XOTOIT extortionist
XOTTOS exhortations
XPTAMA exophthalmia
XPTAMC exophthalmic
XPTAMS exophthalmos
exophthalmus
XRCAIG excruciating
XRCAIN excruciation
XRCOFN extractor fan
XRDTBE extraditable
XRIATY exorbitantly
XRIEIE exercise bike
XRMRTL extramarital
XRNOSY extraneously
XROEEF exert oneself
XROSES uxoriousness
XRPITR expropriator
XRPLTR extrapolator
XRSCAH express coach
XRSIEY expressively
XRSNOY extrasensory
extra-sensory
XRSTAN express train
XRVGNA extravaganza
XRVGNE extravagance
XRVRIN extraversion
extroversion
XSEAIG exasperating
XSEAIN exasperation
XSHRCL exospherical
XTCACR exotic dancer
XTEMLY exothermally
XTRCLY exoterically
XUFAIN exsufflation
XUSOIE excursionise
excursionize
XUSOIT excursionist
YANCLY tyrannically
YAOHSS zygapophyses
YATCLY dynastically
YATRSS synarthroses
YBLCLY symbolically
YCEITC syncretistic
YCRNZR synchronizer
YDALWS Wyndham Lewis
YDTCLY syndetically
YEAIIY hyperacidity
YEBRAS Hyperboreans
YEGCCD lysergic acid
YEIAIN by derivation
YEIIIN by definition
YEOTRN hymenopteran
YEPCMN type specimen
YETCLY synectically
YETEMA hyperthermia
YETEML hyperthermal
YETNIE hypertensive

YETNIN hypertension
YETOHC hypertrophic
YHAVRE Pythian verse
YHLGCL mythological
YIDRED cylinder head
YIEESN Kyrie eleison
YIIAIN typification
YIMNGE Kylie Minogue
YINCLY hygienically
YINUPE Tyrian purple
YITEOL dye in the wool
YITETE Lyric Theatre
YLBCLY syllabically
YLFEAL Wycliffe Hall
YLNCAK by a long chalk
YLPOAE cyclopropane
YLRSIN Byelorussian
YNHDIK Lynn Chadwick
YNTCLY hypnotically
YNTEAY hypnotherapy
YNTZBE hypnotizable
YOANTC gyromagnetic
YOEEIS cytogenetics
YOEHIS pyrotechnics
YOHLMC hypothalamic
YOHLMS hypothalamus
YOHNIE sycophantise
sycophantize
YOHNRA hypochondria
YOHOIE hypochlorite
YOHTCL hypothetical
YOKLTN cytoskeleton
YOKNPE by cock and pie
YOLCMA hypoglycemia
YOLSAA mycoplasmata
YOOITC hypocoristic
YOOPIE pyromorphite
YOPRSN by comparison
YORTCL hypocritical
YOTCLY synoptically
YOTTCL hypostatical
YOUPIE hyposulphite
YOYOSY synonymously
YPOAIE symptomatise
symptomatize
YRCLRC hydrochloric
YRDIOR hybrid vigour
YRDNMC hydrodynamic
YRDZBE hybridizable
YRFRNE by preference
YRFURC hydrofluoric
YRGAHC hydrographic
YRGAHR hydrographer
YRGNOB hydrogen bomb
YRGNOD hydrogen bond
YRKNTC hydrokinetic
YRLGCL hydrological
YRMDSE Hydromedusae
YRPTIT hydropathist
YRQIOE hydroquinone
YRSAIS hydrostatics
YRTEAY hydrotherapy
YRTOIM hydrotropism
YRUIRM hydraulic ram
YRYIEI György Ligeti
YSIEHT Eyes Wide Shut
YSOTED by a short head
YTFIGY mystifyingly
YTMTZD systematized
YTRCLY hysterically
YTRCOY hysterectomy
YTROSY mysteriously
YTTOIM nyctitropism
ZETOTP Aztec two-step
ZRAJNS Azerbaijanis
ZTIPIE azathioprine

13 letters – even

AAATTO maladaptation
AACOMN balance of mind
AACSTE Damascus steel
AADAGG bag and baggage
AADATR gas and gaiters
AADESN salad dressing
AADETE tar and feather
AADUNS hazardousness
AAEBLT damageability
manageability
AAEETE Madame de Staël
AAEIHU manage without
AAEIOS salade niçoise
AAEPMN paraleipomena
AAHRAI paraphernalia
AAIATC salami tactics
AAIHCN ramapithecine
AAIIAL parasitically
AAINIE Canadian River
AAIUAE canaliculated
AAIUNS capaciousness
rapaciousness
sagaciousness
salaciousness
AAJSMN maladjustment
AALCIA parallactical
AALLGA parallelogram
AALLUE parallel ruler
AAMLIU salaam aleikum
AAMNSE maladminister
AAOCLG palaeoecology
AAOIAC parabolic arch
AAOIAL macaronically
parabolically
paradoxically
AAOILG palaeobiology
AAORPE palaeographer
AAOTLG palaeontology
AARCNS pan-Africanism
AARINS maladroitness
AASEAS palais de danse
AATCLN galactic plane
AAYIAL catalytically
AAYSAD Canary Islands
ABEKNL jawbreakingly
ABEOSN rabble-rousing
ABFRHN pay beforehand
ABIECO eat boiled crow
ABLSIA cabbalistical
ABNFRU carboniferous❑
ABNIXD carbon dioxide
ABNSTO carbonisation
ABNZTO carbonization
ABOLMN bamboozlement
ABOUTI bamboo curtain
ABRCSL Barbara Castle
ABRUNS barbarousness
ABTEEL lay by the heels
ABTNPR rabbit and pork
ACAAQE García Márquez
ACAATA catch at a straw
ACAEFT Jascha Heifetz
ACAIEE saccharimeter
ACAIER saccharimetry
ACASRW catch at straws
ACCROA lance-corporal
ACFCTO calcification
ACIGRE watching brief
ACIOIU sanctimonious
ACITEC catch in the act
ACIYNL sanctifyingly
ACKMKU pancake make-up
ACKRIA Nancy Kerrigan
ACLACA Marcel Marceau
ACLSNS matchlessness
ACLTNL calculatingly
ACLUHM Marcel Duchamp
ACMNAE catchment area
ACNCEC bad conscience
ACOEBC watch one's back
ACOESE watch one's step
ACOFUR catch off guard
ACOTEI catch on the hip
ACPAUE sarcophaguses
ACRCNR day care centre
ACRUNS rancorousness
ACSIAL sarcastically
ACSSAD Caicos Islands
ACSUAC bancassurance
ACTELC watch the clock
ACTERF catch the drift
ACTZTO narcotization
ACUAAE catch unawares
ACWIES mad cow disease
ACYUSL Darcey Bussell
ADAARS cardiac arrest

ADACNO Sandra O'Connor
ADARCA paediatrician
ADASIH Hard Day's Night
ADDCIL tax-deductible
ADECIF handkerchiefs
ADEIMN Dandie Dinmont
ADEOGL handle roughly
ADEREL hard-heartedly
ADETAE paddle steamer
paddle-steamer
ADFERN hard of hearing
ADFLWR maid of all work
maid-of-all-work
ADHMRE raid the market
ADLNLG daddy longlegs
daddy-long-legs
ADLRTE Mandelbrot set
ADMRHS paedomorphism
ADMUSI Saddam Hussein
ADMZTO randomization
ADNETR maiden century
ADNHNC harden the neck
ADNIOE maiden-widowed
ADNLON cardinal point
ADNLRS cardinal cross
ADNOGE maiden-tongued
ADOEIV hard to believe
ADOPNL jawdroppingly
ADORCT cardboard city
ADORPE cardiographer
ADRLEO banderilleros
ADTIET eau-de-toilette
ADWTEA lay down the law
ADYHTM hardly the time
AEAAAB Lake Maracaibo
AEABCR camera obscura
AEAEOG have had enough
AEAFMN have half a mind
AEAIAO make capital of
AEAISA have had its day
AEANRW Pamela Andrews
AEATRE calefactories
AEBCAA James Buchanan
AEBCSA take a back seat
AEBDOO make a bad job of
AEBEAU rateable value
AEBETE take a breather
AEBGOT have a big mouth
AEBIAC make obeisance
AEBSNU have a basinful
AECAWC James Chadwick
AECETU water chestnut
AECLEC par excellence
AECONO make account of
take account of
AECPAO parencephalon
AECREE catercornered
AECRSI James Christie
AEDARL have a dual role
AEDCSO make a decision
AEDNTO make a donation
AEDOPN eavesdropping
AEDSOI kaleidoscopic
AEDTLS sacerdotalise
sacerdotalism
sacerdotalist
AEDTLZ sacerdotalize
AEEADO make demands on
AEEAIN race relations
AEECAE Lake Neuchâtel
AEECWT make peace with
AEEESR make necessary
AEEHNC wave mechanics
AEEIHO take me with you
AEEINO have designs on
AEEOAS male menopause
AEEODN tape-recording
AEERSE make depressed
AEETIH pavement light
AEETIO make certain of
AEETOO make mention of
AEEUAL take regularly
AEEUDN make redundant
AEFECA take offence at
AEFESA take offense at
AEFINO make a friend of
AEFMLA materfamilias
paterfamilias
AEFSBC make a fast buck
AEFUTC gate of justice
AEGMWT have a game with
AEGNEA take a gander at
AEGOMA make a good meal
AEGOMN have a good mind
AEGOTM have a good time
AEHBSO make the best of
AEHDAD Gareth Edwards
AEHEFR make the effort
AEHEGO have the edge on
AEHLDF take the lid off
AEHLOO have the look of
AEHMCE take the mickey
AEHMSO make the most of
AEHNAT James Hanratty
AEHNSU make things hum
AEHPEG take the pledge
AEHPRO take the part of
AEHPUG take the plunge
AEHROO have a horror of
AEHRUD make the rounds
AEHSDO take the side of
AEHSIA catechistical
AEHWNO have the wind of
AEHWYO pave the way for
AEIAAU Lake Nicaragua
AEIEAL make miserable
AEIETE take liberties
AEIFCL make difficult
AEIFRN make different
AEILAS material cause
AEILSI materialistic
AEISBS make first base
AEITRA valedictorian
AEIUNS facetiousness
AEKOPL James Knox Polk
AELBAC lamellibranch
AELESE kapellmeister
AELHLN La Belle Hélène
AELKNT take a liking to
AELNNS make a long nose
AELTDS satellite dish
AELTTW satellite town
AEMCEE James Michener
AEMNEO make a monkey of
AEMNSO make amends for
AEMRAT James Moriarty
AEMRGA take umbrage at
AEMRLE James Mirrlees
AEMRYO make a martyr of
AENETL make infertile
AENHAT hale and hearty
AENLEC have influence
AENLSI paternalistic
AENOVN make insolvent
AENPPE cayenne pepper
AENRTR sale and return
AENSAO save one's bacon
AENSEC make one's peace
AENSEV take one's leave
AENSLC take one's place
AENSUP take one's lumps
AENUHI James Naughtie
AENUHO have enough for
AENUIU paper nautilus
AEOATI have no faith in
AEOCIE make conceited
AEOELS make powerless
AEOENO have someone on
AEOEOI make more solid
AEOESR made to measure
made-to-measure
AEOHNO have nothing on
make nothing of
AEOHRA take to the road
AEOIAL categorically
AEOIEO have no time for
AEOLAE make foul water
AEOMCO make too much of
AEOMNO have command of
take communion
AEONSE take to one's bed
AEONSL have to oneself
AEOOEO make no bones of
AEOSAC Lake Constance
AEOTLT make hostile to
AEOTOO have control of
AEPATI water plantain
AEPHWR take up the word
AEPITN laser printing
AEPREC bad experience
AEPRSL make sparks fly
AERCSO make tracks for
AEREAA Kate Greenaway
AERNOI make a run for it
AEROAA make arroganat
AERVSO make provision
AESADN water-standing
AESNSW take as one's own
AESOER save as you earn

AESOTG	take as hostage
AESOTI	Magersfontein
AESTHM	have as its home
AESUNA	take a squint at
AESUTA	take a shufti at
AESUWT	take issue with
AETCUS	take its course
AETEIA	parenthetical
AETEOS	paper the house
AETETE	patent leather
AETFWT	have it off with
AETICN	Cape St Vincent
AETIGO	have a thing for
AETMOI	have a time of it
AETNNF	take it in snuff
AETNSA	have it one's way
AETNUN	take it in turns
AETOPN	parent company
AETOPO	Daley Thompson
AETPTE	talent spotter
AETSES	Babette's Feast
AETTAG	make it strange
AETTLO	take its toll of
	take its toll on
AETUWT	have it out with
AEUTDO	have custody of
AEVIAL	make available
AEVNLE	James Van Allen
AEVRUE	make overtures
AEWITE	James Whistler
AEWRWT	have a word with
AEWYOT	make a wry mouth
AEXETO	take exception
AEXSEC	have existence
AEYEOI	safety-deposit
AEYIAL	panegyrically
AEYNDW	take lying down
AEYUTI	safety curtain
AFEREL	half-heartedly
AFHBTL	half the battle
AFOEEG	half sovereign
AFRNTE	wayfaring-tree
AGAMTS	pangrammatist
AGBIDN	large building
AGBUWT	hang about with
AGHNUG	Kangchenjunga
AGIGTC	laughing-stock
AGIHNL	languishingly
AGNFEL	hanging freely
AGNHWN	hang in the wind
AGNILT	tangentiality
AGNSTO	jargonisation
AGNVLE	hanging valley
AGNZTO	jargonization
AGOVSO	range of vision
AGPNSA	hang up one's hat
AGQATT	large quantity
AGROOR	kangaroo court
AGRORS	kangaroo grass
AGRTOR	Margaret Court
AGRTUO	Margaret Tudor
AGRUNS	dangerousness
AGSEUI	C Auguste Dupin
AGTOTY	Margot Fonteyn
AGTRNA	daughter-in-law
AGYHNC	hang by the neck
AGYHWL	hang by the wall
AGYTRA	hang by a thread
AHADAI	washhand basin
AHAELA	Machiavellian
AHARDS	Madhya Pradesh
AHEILC	mashie niblick
AHGNCT	pathogenicity
AHIILN	Rathlin Island
AHIPNE	cash dispenser
AHLCIE	Catholic Times
AHMOLG	Wadham College
AHMTCA	mathematician
AHMTCS	mathematicise
AHMTCZ	mathematicize
AHNGNE	machine-gunner
AHNPWE	washing powder
AHNSAD	wash one's hands
AHOVCI	fashion victim
AHRAFE	Madhur Jaffrey
AHREAE	Bashir Gemayel
AHRNPR	Catherine Parr
AHROHA	gather to a head
AHRTYO	Zachary Taylor
AHZRNS	haphazardness
AIAAST	capital assets
AIADET	Mario Andretti
AIAEIA	Latin-American
AIAINS	sanitationist
AIALNS	habitableness
AIALNV	Galina Ulanova
AIALTE	capital letter
AIANSU	Halicarnassus
AIAPWR	magical powers
AIATVT	radioactivity
AIAYLN	salivary gland
AIBEOT	variable costs
AIBUKT	David Blunkett
AICMNC	Nadia Comaneci
AICNTO	ratiocination
AICNTV	ratiocinative
AIDMDC	Marie de Médici
AIDMLB	David Dimbleby
AIDRCL	say indirectly
AIEJCE	matinée jacket
AIEONR	native country
AIEPAE	native speaker
AIETTO	manifestation
AIFEWT	satisfied with
AIGAHS	hagiographist
AIGAPR	having rapport
AIGATV	taking captive
AIGFAT	Naming of Parts
AIGITN	having kittens
AIGNOR	taking on board
AIHONI	parish council
AIHSIG	Gavin Hastings
AIISIC	Basic Instinct
AIIUNS	maliciousness
AILBLE	radiolabelled
AILCTO	radiolocation
AILEOD	Daniel Deronda
AILFRU	papilliferous
AILLTR	radial-ply tyre
AILMTU	papillomatous
AILRPO	Daniel arap Moi
AILTNL	vacillatingly
AILVNE	lay in lavender
AIMSRO	magic mushroom
AINEEG	radiant energy
AINLRN	National Front
AINLRS	National Trust
AINLSI	nationalistic
	rationalistic
AINLUR	National Guard
AISAIU	Fabius Maximus
AISEPR	David Sheppard
AISRCE	panic-stricken
AITATS	variety artist
AITERA	Basil the Great
AITRAL	magisterially
AIUAAL	manipulatable
AIUABN	navicular bone
AIWLIE	Maria Walliser
AIYAAE	easily damaged
AIYEIE	easily decided
AIYIAI	salicylic acid
AIYITR	family history
AIYMNO	Marilyn Monroe
AIYOIE	easily noticed
AJRFAE	Marjory Fraser
AKACLT	back-calculate
AKADWT	pack cards with
AKCACE	backscratcher
	back-scratcher
AKDATR	masked battery
AKDIIA	lackadaisical
AKEGRE	Jack Teagarden
AKETWR	Jackie Stewart
AKFELN	lack of feeling
AKFMTO	lack of emotion
AKFNWR	Sack of Antwerp
AKFOCR	lack of concern
AKFUCS	lack of success
AKHRPE	Jack the Ripper
AKIEBO	talk like a book
AKIHLM	walk with a limp
AKIHLO	Jack Nicholson
AKILWS	Sackville-West
AKNOSA	Parkinson's law
AKNPNO	rack and pinion
AKNZTO	Balkanization
AKOMTO	back-formation
AKONSL	talk to oneself
AKPNDW	walk up and down
AKRLHR	mackerel shark
AKTBLT	marketability
AKTCNM	market economy
AKTETE	Tarka the Otter
AKTVNS	talkativeness
AKWWRL	walk awkwardly
ALABIG	railway bridge
ALACIN	Paul Gascoigne
ALAETR	parliamentary

ALALNS	malleableness
ALAVVN	tableau vivant
ALCATE	Paul McCartney
ALCCSL	Harlech Castle
ALCNTN	hallucinating
ALCNTO	hallucination
ALCNTR	hallucinatory
ALENTI	Carl Bernstein
ALFHWL	Call of the Wild
ALFOBL	table football
ALGAHS	calligraphist
ALGRVS	Pär Lagerkvist
ALHVER	walls have ears
ALIDMT	Paul Hindemith
ALIGON	rallying-point
ALIHNN	ball lightning
ALLSNS	faultlessness
ALMNIT	Haile Mengistu
ALMUTI	Table Mountain
ALNARO	Fallen Warrior
ALNOLC	fall into place
ALNSCE	ball and socket
ALNTBT	falling to bits
ALOCON	call to account
ALOETO	fail to mention
ALOFIC	Karl von Frisch
ALOHAE	vault of heaven
ALOSRC	Jailhouse Rock
ALOTLE	Paul Tortelier
ALOTUP	call for trumps
ALRMRC	fall from grace
ALSHNC	callisthenics
ALSLSI	Haile Selassie
ALSONU	tablespoonful
ALTACN	ballet-dancing
ALTIGN	ballot-rigging
ALVRNS	Paolo Veronese
ALWHMU	gallows humour
ALWHPE	Harlow Shapley
AMDAYI	haemodialysis
AMDVSN	Sammy Davis Jnr
AMEREL	warm-heartedly
AMGOUI	gamma globulin
AMNAWL	Tasmanian wolf
AMNBRN	Carmina Burana
AMNCRE	Raymond Carver
AMNGMN	man-management
AMNSAD	Cayman Islands
AMNUHI	Salman Rushdie
AMNZTO	harmonization
AMNZWT	harmonize with
AMRHIA	haemorrhoidal
AMRHNA	Carmarthen Bay
AMTLGS	haematologist
AMUYLO	cadmium yellow
ANADLR	fauna and flora
ANBLSI	cannibalistic
ANBSEI	cannabis resin
ANCEOS	barnacle goose
ANFCNL	magnificently
ANFCTO	damnification
	magnification
ANHEIL	launch vehicle
ANHRCE	main character
ANLQEC	magniloquence
ANLSNS	dauntlessness
ANLVNA	earn a living as
ANNHAS	pain in the arse
ANNHBT	pain in the butt
ANNHNC	pain in the neck
ANNMUL	magnanimously
ANNNEL	darning-needle
ANNSGA	warning signal
ANNSPR	gain one's spurs
ANOCAE	rainbow-chaser
ANOEAE	mains-operated
ANOTOO	gain control of
ANPAKO	nannoplankton
ANSEAI	Iannis Xenakis
ANSIWL	Manny Shinwell
ANTCIL	magnetic field
ANTCOT	magnetic north
ANTCTR	magnetic storm
ANTKNL	painstakingly
ANTMTV	magnetomotive
ANTNWA	Barnett Newman
ANTPEA	Barnstaple Bay
ANTSHR	magnetosphere
ANTZTO	magnetization
ANVRUL	carnivorously
AOAEAE	law of averages
AOANUF	Carol Ann Duffy
AOAOHS	sado-masochism
AOBHVN	way of behaving
AOBSNS	man of business
AODACC	Harold Babcock
AODAWO	Harold Larwood
AODHPA	Harold Shipman
AODOBN	Harold Robbins
AODVLR	Éamon de Valera
AOHANS	parochialness
AOHSAD	man of his hands
AOIATR	carotid artery
AOIEAL	cat-o'-nine-tails
AOIIAL	Jacobinically
AOITRA	major interval
AOIUNS	laboriousness
AOLMNH	Man of La Mancha
AOMTHL	Major Mitchell
AOOIAL	taxonomically
AOREST	vapour density
AORTCM	favours to come
AORTSO	favourite spot
AOSEKN	way of speaking
AOSRNE	Jacob Sprenger
AOTEAC	man of the match
AOTEAL	lay on the table
AOTEIE	lag of the tides
AOTELT	man of the cloth
AOTEOL	man of the world
AOTERS	Way of the Cross
AOTIKN	way of thinking
APBERS	palpable-gross
APFMLE	happy families
APLBCE	campylobacter
APLNIG	happy landings
APNETM	salpingectomy
APNGON	camping-ground
APNLGS	campanologist
APNNSO	happening soon
APOHMN	rapprochement
APRART	Jasper Carrott
APRVDN	tamper-evident
APRZTO	pauperization
APSHAE	waspish-headed
APTWEE	carpet-sweeper
AQECIA	Jacques Chirac
AQENCE	Jacques Necker
AQIDSD	Marquis de Sade
ARAELC	carriage clock
ARCBJR	Maurice Béjart
ARCLTO	matriculation
ARCMNO	Patrick Manson
ARCPAI	macrocephalic
ARCSAZ	Patrick Swayze
ARCWLE	Maurice Wilkes
AREHRA	Harriet Harman
AREOOI	macroeconomic
ARETBA	Harriet Tubman
ARFCAL	sacrificially
ARFOOR	pair of colours
ARLALE	barrel-vaulted
ARLGVN	payroll giving
ARLHSE	barrel-chested
ARLNAL	matrilineally
	patrilineally
ARLUNS	garrulousness
ARMGIA	Barry McGuigan
ARMLCL	macromolecule
ARMNAL	matrimonially
	patrimonially
	sacramentally
ARNADN	Warren Harding
ARNEAE	Lawrence Oates
ARNERG	Lawrence Bragg
ARNFBU	Laurent Fabius
ARNGAE	marrons glacés
ARNSNL	patronisingly
ARNSUR	fair and square
	fair-and-square
ARNZNL	patronizingly
AROIAL	patriotically
AROTET	carry out tests
ARPITN	hair-splitting
ARPOUT	dairy products
ARRTLN	sabre-rattling
ARSNTT	sacrosanctity
ARTAHO	parrot-fashion
ARTECE	Maurits Escher
ARTECS	carry to excess
ARTEOC	carry the torch
ARWATN	narrowcasting
ASAKTN	mass-marketing
ASCUET	Massachusetts
ASDYBO	raised eyebrow
ASEATR	mass departure
ASECSL	Caister Castle
ASEIEC	false evidence
ASEMTS	panspermatism

	panspermatist
ASEPSE	laissez-passer
ASFCTO	falsification
ASGOAM	passage of arms
ASHNAL	Passchendaele
ASHPRE	pass the parcel
ASILPR	Mansfield Park
ASMNEI	passementerie
ASMRGL	marsh marigold
ASONCU	Lansdowne Club
ASOSNA	Passion Sunday
ASOTHT	passport photo
ASPOOD	basso profondo
ASPOUD	basso profundo
ASRMIH	pass from sight
ASRNOO	bad scran to you
ASRPLC	Caesar's Palace
ASRUSI	Nasser Hussain
ASSERN	false swearing
ASSIGA	lapsus linguae
ASSMHN	Faust Symphony
ASSNEC	pass a sentence
ASTEEI	raise the devil
ASTHPE	cause to happen
ASUGMN	pass judgement
ASUOTS	sansculottism
	sansculottist
ATAFRS	Waltham Forest
ATCLAL	nautical table
ATCLRS	particularise
	particularism
ATCLRT	particularity
ATCLRZ	particularize
ATCLUE	particoloured
	parti-coloured
ATCPAL	participially
ATCPNL	participantly
ATCPTI	participate in
ATCPTN	participating
ATCPTO	participation
ATCPTR	participatory
ATEAIU	battle fatigue
ATEANL	Matthew Arnold
ATEAQE	Hattie Jacques
ATECRE	battle-scarred
ATEFAI	Battle of Pavia
ATEFAN	Battle of Varna
ATEFEA	Battle of Sedan
ATEFPE	Battle of Ypres
ATEFRC	Battle of Crécy
ATEFSU	Battle of Issus
ATEHCG	rattle the cage
ATENDU	wattle and daub
ATENPI	castle in Spain
ATEPRE	Matthew Parker
ATERIE	battle-cruiser
	rattle-brained
ATESIA	pantheistical
ATETOE	last-mentioned
ATLGNU	cartilaginous
ATLGUL	tautologously
ATLOOE	martello tower
ATLSNL	tantalisingly
ATLSNS	faithlessness
	tastelessness
ATLZNL	tantalizingly
ATLZTO	tantalization
ATMTEL	earth-motherly
ATMVMN	earth-movement
ATNHNI	Martina Hingis
ATNICU	East India Club
ATNOMN	Martin Bormann
ATNPRE	part and parcel
ATNRNL	Martin Brundle
ATNSAD	Hastings Banda
ATNSIC	bait and switch
ATNSRM	past one's prime
ATNTHV	wanting to have
ATNTVT	cast a nativity
ATNWEL	Daltons Weekly
ATNYOE	cast an eye over
ATONMU	gastrocnemius
ATOTES	east-north-east
	east-south-east
ATPLOE	cast a pall over
ATPLTC	party politics
ATPPRI	wastepaper bin
ATRAEG	Walter Raleigh
ATRAEO	Walter Bagehot
ATRATA	Walter Matthau
ATRIDN	masterminding
ATRIKR	Walter Sickert
ATRODL	Walter Mondale
ATROFL	capture on film
ATROHG	bacteriophage
ATRRPU	Walter Gropius
ATRSRG	part brass rags
ATRULE	master builder
ATRUNS	masterfulness
ATRZTO	cauterization
	factorization
ATSANM	baptismal name
ATSIAL	fantastically
ATSOFR	baptism of fire
ATTENF	war to the knife
ATUMLV	Can't Buy Me Love
AUACUE	natural causes
AUADDA	value-added tax
AUANME	natural number
AUATRN	manufacturing
AUBAFU	Naguib Mahfouz
AUEEEV	nature reserve
AUFROE	value for money
AUHPNZ	Baruch Spinoza
AUIHGR	Kazuo Ishiguro
AULAGE	Samuel Langley
AULCLU	Gaius Lucilius
AULEAL	Manuel de Falla
AULEKT	Samuel Beckett
AULLME	Samuel Slumkey
AULODY	Samuel Goldwyn
AULONO	Samuel Johnson
AUMLAE	vacuum cleaner
AUPCTO	haruspication
AURETP	daguerreotype
AUSIAL	casuistically
AUTTVL	facultatively
AVNONO	Earvin Johnson
AVNSIA	Calvinistical
AVNZTO	galvanization
AVRTTO	laevorotation
AVSLME	canvas-climber
AVSSIE	harvest spider
AVTOAM	Salvation Army
AVYUHN	Harvey Cushing
AWCCSL	Warwick Castle
AWLDNT	say well done to
AWLDVE	Maxwell Davies
AWNOLG	Darwin College
AYADLN	Mary Magdalene
AYFHLT	Lady of Shalott
AYITNN	easy listening
AYNATN	lady-in-waiting
AYNRBS	Satyendra Bose
AYORTO	Mary Lou Retton
AYRCNL	Lady Bracknell
AYSIKN	easy as winking
BAASOO	Abraham's bosom
BECOMN	absence of mind
BESEET	objets de vertu
BESOAL	obsessionally
BESRUE	objets trouvés
BESVNS	obsessiveness
BETFIT	object of virtu
BETNSL	absent oneself
BETOAL	objectionable
	objectionably
BETVNS	objectiveness
BETVSI	objectivistic
BETVTS	objective test
BEVTOA	observational
BGESLS	A Bigger Splash
BIIUNS	obliviousness
BNZROK	Ebenezer Cooke
BOBBLT	absorbability
BOIUNS	obnoxiousness
BOUEIC	absolute pitch
BOUEOE	absolute power
BOUEUE	absolute ruler
BOUEYO	absolutely not
BRENHR	Aberdeenshire
BRENNU	Aberdeen Angus
BRIAIN	abortifacient
BRSVNS	obtrusiveness
BTATES	abstract verse
BTATVL	abstractively
BTNHSD	a bit on the side
BTTIAL	obstetrically
BTUTVL	obstructively
BUTHPE	about to happen
BVOEHA	above one's head
BVRPOC	above reproach
CACARA	act as chairman
CAEFED	schadenfreude
CAEHOG	scrape through
CAELVN	scrape a living
CAINLS	occasionalism
	occasionalist
CAMDAO	act as mediator

CAOOIA oceanological
CAORPI oceanographic
CDFCTO acidification
CEAIAL schematically
CECMSU Science Museum
CELSRE Scheele's green
CENRCS screen process
CEORTI scleroprotein
CESBLT accessibility
CETAEL accept eagerly
CETBLT acceptability
CETIAL eccentrically
CIDESR Schindler's Ark
CIEEVC active service
CIETLS occidentalise
CIETLZ occidentalize
CIETRN accident-prone
CIIABN occipital bone
CIIALB occipital lobe
CIOAIL actinobacilli
CIOAPU schizocarpous
CIOHEI schizophrenia
schizophrenic
CIOIUL acrimoniously
CIOYEI schizomycetic
CIPNSV scrimp and save
CIVBLT achievability
CLCAIA ochlocratical
CLDDRN occluded front
CLTRSU sculpturesque
CMNCLS ecumenicalism
CNAMNE scandalmonger
CNCALA scenic railway
CNILTN scintillating
CNILTO scintillation
CNMTIA econometrical
CNMZTO economization
CNOAOA Scent of a Woman
COAIAL acrobatically
COALNS scholarliness
COATCS scholasticism
COBHLO act on behalf of
COETNR octocentenary
COLAMS school-marmish
COLECE schoolteacher
COLILS schoolgirlish
COMDTN accommodating
COMDTO accommodation
CONIGO accounting for
CONKEE account-keeper
COPNMN accompaniment
COTEET accoutrements
CPNTRS acupuncturist
CPOVRE a copy of verses
CPUOWN a capful of wind
CRAIWT score a hit with
CRDOET scared to death
CRDTTO accreditation
CRELTE scarlet letter
CRERNE scarlet runner
CRETHR Scarlett O'Hara
CRFCTO scarification
CRMTCT achromaticity

CTXCLG ecotoxicology
CTYLGS ichthyologist
CUEASL accuse falsely
CUECNL acquiescently
acquiescingly
CULZTO actualization
CUPIUL scrumptiously
CURDAT acquired taste
CUSTVL acquisitively
CUTNSL acquit oneself
CUTRTO acculturation
CUYNSL occupy oneself
DAAIAL adiabatically
DAALNO Edgar Allan Poe
DACDEE Advanced level
DACNTC advance notice
DACSOL advance slowly
DADANR Edward Barnard
DADEND Edward Kennedy
DADHME Edward Whymper
DADUHE Eduard Buchner
DCTBLT educatability
DCTNRT Educating Rita
DCTOAL educationally
DEACRE adrenal cortex
DETRUL adventurously
DETSMN advertisement
DFAORN add flavouring
DIATAC Admiralty Arch
DIEGIS advise against
DIGAHN adding machine
DIITAO administrator
DIITRN administering
DILNSE Edwin Landseer
DIOYRU advisory group
DISBLT admissibility
DITEAL Eddie The Eagle
DLECMN Adolf Eichmann
DMRTVL adumbratively
DNIANS identicalness
DNOOIA odontological
DOAIAL idiomatically
DODOTN Edmond Rostand
DOTSUU Edmontosaurus
DOYCAI idiosyncratic
DPIFCO edaphic factor
DPSTSU adipose tissue
DRFRUL odoriferously
DUDILR Edmund Hillary
DUDLNE Edmund Blunden
DUDPNE Edmund Spenser
DUDUSR Edmund Husserl
DURLRE Edouard Lartet
DUTBLT adjustability
EAALNS separableness
EAALVK Vera Caslavska
EAATCE beta particles
EABLTO perambulation
EABLTR perambulatory
EACENS debauchedness
EACPCT legal capacity
EACSOE get accustomed
EACTAC recalcitrance

EADAFA Gerald Kaufman
EADDLA Gerald Edelman
EADEDN demand feeding
EADRSE be hard pressed
EADTCO metal detector
EADURL Gerald Durrell
EAEATO delayed action
EAEEUO get an eyeful of
EAEIAL sexagesimally
EAEIBR Yekaterinburg
EAEILS dematerialise
EAEILZ dematerialize
EAEOAD behave towards
EAGAAE get aggravated
EAHMEI Menachem Begin
EAHSCS metaphysicist
EAIBUT Benazir Bhutto
EAIIAO rehabilitator
EAINLS denationalise
EAINLZ denationalize
EAIUAL behaviourally
EAIUNS nefariousness
tenaciousness
vexatiousness
EALRIA metallurgical
EALZTO metallization
EAMLTI Cesar Milstein
EANNWL retaining wall
EAOEEI teratogenesis
EAOIAL pedagogically
EAOPOE Metamorphoses
EAOPOI metamorphosis❑
EAPRNI megasporangia
EARBLS metagrabolise
metagrobolise
EARBLZ metagrabolize
metagrobolize
EASRLA New Australian
EATATO sex attraction
EATCRE penalty corner
EATTNL devastatingly
EAVRAC set at variance
EBCOTA Serbo-Croatian
EBEACC Herbie Hancock
EBEEBE heebie-jeebies
EBGEDW get bogged down
EBGNIG new beginnings
EBLZTO verbalization
EBOEHR Pembrokeshire
EBRFTF member of staff
EBRHBE Jedburgh Abbey
EBRHOE Herbert Hoover
EBRHPE membership fee
EBTEEL set by the heels
EBUVRL membrum virile
ECADAR fetch and carry
ECADSN merchandising
ECAICI fetch a circuit
ECALNS peaceableness
ECAOPS fetch a compass
ECASCS neoclassicism❑
ECDVDN peace dividend
ECEIAL geochemically

ECGANE	Percy Grainger
ECITVL	descriptively
ECITVS	descriptivism
ECLPIO	Hercule Poirot
ECLSNS	mercilessness
ECNENA	tercentennial
ECNMSE	fencing-master
ECNRCS	geocentricism
ECRMSM	sex chromosome
ECRNLG	geochronology
ECSINS	percussionist
EDABUC	dead-cat bounce
EDASEA	dead man's pedal
EDESHE	dead men's shoes
EDESOA	needless to say
EDETAN	head restraint
EDETRO	dead-letter box
EDIEBO	read like a book
EDLEUI	get dolled up in
EDLUNS	pendulousness
EDNBTL	feeding bottle
EDNCON	send an account
EDNIUL	tendentiously
EDNMTE	reading matter
EDNNCH	Ferdinand Cohn
EDNNFC	Ferdinand Foch
EDNNOC	send an invoice
EDNSLI	read oneself in
EDNTOG	feeding trough
EDNUTD	held in custody
EDOHDG	send to the dogs
EDOOIA	dendrological
EDPIPA	head-up display
EDRCOE	ready reckoner
EDRDGS	Reader's Digest
EDREDN	gender-bending
EDREIG	send greetings
EDRERE	tender-hearted
EDRZTO	deodorization
EDSEDG	ready, steady, go
EDSYLO	reddish-yellow
EDTLGA	send a telegram
EDVREL	head over heels
EDWAFO	meadow saffron
EDWLRL	heads will roll
EDYHNS	lead by the nose
EEAEND	Helena Kennedy
EEAFVL	Teresa of Avila
EEAGLS	televangelist
EEAINA	generation gap
EEAINS	revelationist
EEAISM	generalissimo
EEAIUL	temerariously
EEAKTN	telemarketing
EEALBD	Venerable Bede
EEALDE	general ledger
EEALNS	venerableness
EEAPBI	general public
EEBRTN	reverberating
EEBRTO	reverberation
EEBRTR	reverberatory
EEBRTV	reverberative
EECCNA	Terence Conran
EECLSL	defencelessly
EECPAO	mesencephalon
EECSIN	repercussions
EEDBLT	dependability
EEDNSL	defend oneself
EEDPTU	serendipitous
EEECBO	reference book
EEECRE	René Descartes
EEEEUU	René de Réaumur
EEEIUL	deleteriously
EEEOGI	here we go again
EEETAL	deferentially
	referentially
	reverentially
EEGEMN	beleaguerment
EEGLNE	Fêtes Galantes
EEHMER	fête champêtre
EEHNBO	telephone book
EEHTLN	telephoto lens
EEICSL	Peveril Castle
EEIINS	dereligionise
EEIINZ	dereligionize
EEIIUL	repetitiously
	veneficiously
EEINLN	Venetian blind
EEIRTN	deteriorating
EEIRTO	deterioration
EELNSL	reveal oneself
EEMNSI	deterministic
EEMNTL	determinately
EEMNTO	determination
EEMNTV	determinative
EEMUTI	Jewel Mountain
EENNSL	demean oneself
EENSAD	Aegean Islands
EENYNE	here and yonder
EEODHR	Herefordshire
EEOEEI	heterogenesis
	heterogenetic
EEOEET	heterogeneity
EEOEEU	heterogeneous
EEOIUL	ceremoniously
EEOLSI	heteroplastic
EEOMNA	developmental
EEOMTN	telecommuting
EEONTO	derecognition
EEOOIA	selenological
EEOOPI	heteromorphic
EEORPE	selenographer
EEORPI	heterotrophic
	selenographic
EEOTGN	telecottaging
EEOTRU	heteropterous
EEPESO	new expression
	set expression
EEQETO	vexed question
EERBLT	penetrability
EERGTO	desegregation
EERLAS	cerebral palsy
EERLGS	meteorologist
EERNTN	peregrinating
EERNTO	peregrination
EERSIA	cerebrospinal
EERTNL	penetratingly
EERTVL	penetratively
EESBLT	defensibility
	reversibility
EESNLS	depersonalise
EESNLZ	depersonalize
EESNRM	Reye's syndrome
EESOAL	reversionally
EESTRA	necessitarian
EESTUL	necessitously
EESVNS	recessiveness
EETABD	celestial body
EETAIE	decentralized
EETBLT	delectability
	detestability
EETEIE	never the wiser
EETETL	seventeenthly
EETHAE	seventh heaven
EETINS	pedestrianise
EETINZ	pedestrianize
EETITO	derestriction
EETONL	defeat soundly
EETORO	reception room
EETUNS	deceitfulness
	resentfulness
EETVNS	deceptiveness
	defectiveness
	receptiveness
	retentiveness
EEUCTE	revenue cutter
EEUSTO	derequisition
EEVBLT	receivability
EEVIDG	Reservoir Dogs
EEVIRC	reservoir rock
EEVLIT	be heavily into
EEVNLN	receiving-line
EEVSEC	defervescence
	defervescency
EEVWRL	receive warmly
EEYASA	Seven Years' War
EEYETA	Jeremy Bentham
EEYUCT	Jeremy Guscott
EFAIFE	self-satisfied
EFARFC	self-sacrifice
EFBEVN	self-observing
EFBSMN	self-abasement
EFCFUT	perfect fourth
EFCINS	perfectionism
	perfectionist
EFCINT	perfectionate
EFCISC	perfect insect
EFCNME	perfect number
EFDRSE	self-addressed
EFEACE	Jeffrey Archer
EFEESV	self-defensive
EFEETN	self-defeating
EFEETO	self-deception
EFETAN	self-restraint
EFEYNL	self-denyingly
EFIACN	self-financing
EFIETO	self-direction
EFIHEU	self-righteous
EFIMTO	reaffirmation

EFLUHE	self-slaughter
EFMOTN	self-important
EFNLCE	self-inflicted
EFNLSN	self-analysing
EFNTRL	perfunctorily
EFNUGN	self-indulgent
EFNUTO	self-induction
EFOCIE	self-conceited
EFOENN	self-governing
EFOFDN	self-confident
EFOFSE	self-confessed
EFOLCE	self-collected
EFOSIU	self-conscious
EFOSSE	self-possessed
EFOTIE	self-contained
EFPONE	self-appointed
EFPRVN	self-approving
EFROCT	Jefferson City
EFRPLE	self-propelled
EFRTIK	perform tricks
EFSETN	self-asserting
EFSETO	self-assertion
EFSETV	self-assertive
EFSUAC	self-assurance
EFTACU	Beefsteak Club
EFUFCN	self-sufficing
EFXMNN	self-examining
EGAHRF	Peggy Ashcroft
EGATAO	sergeant-major
EGBUHO	neighbourhood
EGEAKO	Reggie Jackson
EGOEBT	hedge one's bets
EGOTRO	Reign of Terror
	reign of terror
EGRONE	Geiger counter
EGTITN	weightlifting
EGTOAE	height to paper
EGVRAO	tergiversator
EHEKNF	Seth Pecksniff
EHIANS	technicalness
EHLCNE	cephalic index
EHLMTI	nephelometric
EHMLAC	béchamel sauce
EHNZTO	mechanization
EHOOIA	technological
EHRADS	Netherlandish
EHRBRE	Gerhard Berger
EHRIAL	lethargically
EHRULO	lecherous look
EHRUNS	lecherousness
EHTSTA	be that as it may
EIAAHA	Lewis Alan Hoad
EIAAIS	Semipalatinsk
EIACNR	medical centre
EIASSE	decimal system
EIATRP	Le Misanthrope
EIBEIL	Cecil B De Mille
EIDCAL	periodic table
EIDNII	periodontitis
EIDRNL	bewilderingly
EIDYEI	Cecil Day-Lewis
EIEAII	perihepatitis
EIEGIS	decide against
EIEHII	perinephritis
EIEHMR	beside the mark
EIELLS	hemicellulose
EIELRA	pedicellariae
EIEMAL	semi-permeable
EIENSL	beside oneself
EIEOTD	decide not to do
EIEPOL	retired people
EIEPRO	retired person
EIERNA	Mediterranean
EIETAL	penitentially
EIETTO	regimentation
	sedimentation
EIGAHN	sewing-machine
EIGCCA	meningococcal
EIGCCI	meningococcic
EIHBAO	Belisha beacon
EIHBLT	perishability
EIHENS	delightedness
EIHNRU	perichondrium
EIIAIN	felicitations
EIIBLT	verifiability
EIICNE	reminiscences
EIICNL	reminiscently
EIIEHM	feminine rhyme
EIIEOA	medicine woman
EIIEYO	definitely not
EIIIAL	verisimilarly
EIINAL	decision table
EIIUBD	religious body
EIIUNS	deliriousness
	religiousness
	seditiousness
EILTRA	legislatorial
EILTVL	legislatively
EILZTO	serialization
EINFEI	Legion of Merit
EINNSL	resign oneself
EINRAE	designer label
EIOCPS	retinoscopist
EIODCO	semiconductor
EIOEWY	set in one's ways
EIOIUL	meritoriously
EIORNR	genito-urinary
EIORPE	lexicographer
EIORPI	lexicographic
EIOSIU	semiconscious
EIOTEC	get in on the act
EIOTRS	lepidopterist
EIOTRU	lepidopterous
EIPEIA	hemispherical
EIRCLT	reciprocality
EIRCTO	reciprocation
EIRCTV	reciprocative
EIREVC	senior service
EIRIAL	demiurgically
EIRIIE	senior citizen
EIRLAO	defibrillator
EIRPIA	lexigraphical
EISBLT	remissibility
EISDCY	perissodactyl
EISDEL	begin suddenly
EISDWC	Nevil Sidgwick
EISLRA	Peninsular War
EITASI	registrarship
EITBLT	resistibility
EITEAO	get in the way of
EITEHR	Pepin the Short
EITGAE	redintegrated
EITGTE	get it together
EITOIA	heliotropical
EITRAL	mediatorially
EITTEC	get into the act
EIUMNE	serious-minded
EIUOAI	semi-automatic
EIUSEC	deliquescence
EIUTRS	sericulturist
EIUUNS	deciduousness
EIYUAD	see if you can do
EJMNMT	Benjamin Smith
EJWRPE	her jaw dropped
EKDEBA	red kidney bean
EKHHNO	seek the hand of
EKNEKU	week in week out
EKNMNE	heck and manger
EKRESO	weaker version
EKROHN	neck or nothing
EKTACE	Becky Thatcher
ELECRA	Leslie Scarman
ELEEOE	well-developed
ELENTE	tell me another
ELEPCE	well-respected
ELEUAE	well-regulated
ELFUNL	mellifluently
ELFUUL	mellifluously
ELGBLT	negligibility
ELGRNL	belligerently
ELGSIA	neological
ELHIIO	health visitor
ELHLSO	feel the loss of
ELHUHO	well-thought-of
ELIEAL	feel miserable
ELLRAI	cellular radio
ELMTRL	declamatorily
ELNSED	tell one's beads
ELNSIA	Hellenistical
ELNSMN	replenishment
ELNSRN	Per Lindstrand
ELODCE	well-conducted
ELOROD	heels o'er gowdy
ELOTFE	well-fortified
ELPONE	well-appointed
ELRAIE	well-organized
ELRBLT	deplorability
ELRMRE	seller's market
	sellers' market
ELROEL	declare openly
ELRSRE	well preserved
	well-preserved
ELRSRN	Neil Armstrong
ELRTCE	well-protected
ELRTRL	declaratorily
ELRTVL	declaratively
ELRUHU	well-brought-up
ELRUSF	declare unsafe
ELRVLE	well-travelled

ELSETE	belles-lettres
ELSEWT	be blessed with
ELSIAL	realistically
ELSVNS	reclusiveness
ELULFE	well-qualified
ELUNDU	well-turned-out
ELWELE	yellow-bellied
ELWELN	fellow feeling
	fellow-feeling
ELWIIE	fellow citizen
ELWTMN	bellows to mend
ELXBLT	reflexibility
ELXLGS	reflexologist
ELXRSE	well-expressed
ELXVNS	reflexiveness
EMDSOT	Bermuda shorts
EMIERE	Germaine Greer
EMNAAC	segmental arch
EMNASA	Selman Waksman
EMNBLT	terminability
EMNESE	German measles
EMNHAI	helminthiasis
EMNMRI	Desmond Morris
EMNNWV	permanent wave
EMNRTE	German Trotter
EMNTNP	Leamington Spa
EMNTVL	terminatively
EMNUIA	hermeneutical
EMPRDT	hermaphrodite
EMRHLG	geomorphology
EMSRBE	Les Miserables
	Les Misérables
EMTBLT	permutability
EMTCMD	Helmut Schmidt
EMTIAL	geometrically
EMTICE	Jemmy Twitcher
EMTLGS	dermatologist
EMUSMN	reimbursement
ENADUE	Leonhard Euler
ENALAA	Jean Paul Marat
ENALET	Jean Paul Getty
ENANTO	reincarnation
ENCLRS	vernacularise
ENCLRZ	vernacularize
ENDEDU	penny dreadful
ENDLLS	Kenny Dalglish
ENFRHN	penny farthing
	penny-farthing
ENHCOE	be in the closet
ENHLIE	Heinz Holliger
ENIHAT	Heinrich Barth
ENIHEN	Heinrich Heine
ENIHET	Heinrich Hertz
ENIOAE	reinvigorated
ENLQIO	vernal equinox
ENLSNS	pennilessness
ENLSTO	vernalisation
ENLZTO	vernalization
ENMEIU	her number is up
ENOACS	means of access
ENOATM	mean solar time
ENOCMN	reinforcement
ENOEHN	mean something
ENOOIA	deontological
ENPNHN	penny-pinching
ENRISR	Jean Froissart
ENRLVL	Bernard Lovell
ENSKNE	Dennis Skinner
ENSOPO	Dennis Compton
ENSUTR	keen as mustard
ENTCAK	Kenneth Clarke
ENTHPE	meant to happen
ENTKUD	Kenneth Kaunda
ENTTMN	reinstatement
ENUGDR	Jean-Luc Godard
EOBNTO	recombination
EOCLMN	reconcilement
EOCNRT	deconcentrate
EOCOPE	heroic couplet
EODEDN	second reading
EODESR	beyond measure
EODHPL	beyond the pale
EODIPT	beyond dispute
EODNSE	beyond one's ken
EODOPN	be good company
EODOPR	beyond compare
EODRCL	secondary cell
EODRNS	secondariness
EODTNS	reconditeness
EOEBCU	get one's back up
	set one's back up
EOEBIU	become obvious
EOEEIU	become tedious
EOEESN	remote sensing
EOEHBA	before the beam
EOEHMS	before the mast
EOEHNE	become thinner
EOEHNI	get one's hand in
EOEHNT	set one's hand to
EOEHRE	become shorter
EOEHWN	before the wind
EOEIIL	become visible
EOEJRM	Jerome K Jerome
EOELME	become plumper
EOELRE	become blurred
EOELWT	become ill with
EOEMLE	become smaller
EOEMNO	set one's mind on
EOEMNT	set one's mind to
EOENAI	become invalid
EOENSA	be someone's man
EOENSL	devote oneself
EOENTC	become unstuck
EOEONA	get one's own way
EOEOTO	remote control
EOEOUA	become popular
EOERAE	become greater
EOERED	become friends
EOESAO	set one's seal on
EOESAT	set one's seal to
EOETTO	deforestation
EOEWRO	become aware of
EOEXIC	become extinct
EOFHHO	let off the hook
EOFYLU	Get Off My Cloud
EOHHLI	xerophthalmia
EOIBLT	negotiability
EOIINN	repositioning
EOIUNS	feloniousness
	ferociousness
	melodiousness
EOLCEL	recollectedly
EOLCIN	recollections
EOMBLT	reformability
EOMNAL	recommendable
	recommendably
EOMUAS	Reform Judaism
EONIRN	reconnoitring
EONUWT	be bound up with
EOOEFE	get on one's feet
EOOEWC	get on one's wick
EOOIAL	serologically
EOPESO	decompression
EOPESV	decompressive
EOPSTO	decomposition
EORMTS	melodramatise
EORMTZ	melodramatize
EOSADR	below standard
EOSIUN	reconstituent
EOSLSL	remorselessly
EOSRCO	reconstructor
EOSRNL	remonstrantly
EOSRNT	below strength
EOSRTN	demonstrating
EOSRTO	demonstration
	remonstration
EOSRTV	demonstrative
	remonstrative
EOSUEE	lemon squeezer
EOTCAI	gerontocratic
EOTERA	Herod the Great
EOTLGS	gerontologist
EOTMNN	decontaminant
EOTMNT	decontaminate
EOUINR	devolutionary
	revolutionary
EOUINS	devolutionist
	revolutionise
	revolutionism
	revolutionist
EOUINZ	revolutionize
EOVAON	revolve around
EOVBLT	resolvability
EOVNDO	revolving door
EOWLWT	get on well with
EOYIAL	genotypically
	metonymically
EOYOII	tenosynovitis
EPACOE	keep watch over
EPATWT	keep faith with
EPEDNL	resplendently
EPEFIN	People's Friend
EPIHRA	terpsichorean
EPLTNC	Neapolitan ice
EPNEEV	keep in reserve
EPNEIC	ten pence piece
EPNHDR	keep in the dark
	leap in the dark
EPNHUH	deep in thought

EPNIEO deep inside you
EPNIMN keeping in mind
EPNIUA perpendicular
EPNOLN tenpin bowling
ten-pin bowling
EPNSLT help oneself to
EPNSNU keep one's end up
EPNUTD keep in custody
EPNWLO weeping willow
EPNYIC tenpenny piece
EPODOR keep good hours
EPONOT keep down costs
EPONSL keep to oneself
EPOOHS deipnosophist
EPOTDW keep costs down
EPOTTO sexploitation
EPPNOS keep open house
EPRCRO keep a record of
EPRITE peppermint tea
EPRMNA temperamental
EPRNSL pepper-and-salt
EPRRNS temporariness
EPRSNL temporisingly
EPRTNS desperateness
temperateness
EPRZNL temporizingly
EPRZTO temporization
EPSBAE tempest-beaten
EPSTSE tempest-tossed
EPSUUL tempestuously
EPTLGS herpetologist
EPTPOI herpetophobia
EPTRAL sempiternally
EPTUTR deep structure
EPUPYN keep supplying
ERAGMN rearrangement
ERAHUL reproachfully
ERATVL retroactively
ERATVT retroactivity
ERBEKN heartbreaking
heart-breaking
ERBRUS Henri Barbusse
ERBSEE Henry Bessemer
ERBTVL retributively
ERCDOS terraced house
ERCEIA petrochemical
ERCNRT ferroconcrete
ERCOEE refractometer
ERCOSN zebra crossing
ERCTNL deprecatingly
ERCTRL deprecatorily
ERDSEC recrudescence
EREABR George Cadbury
EREABT George Macbeth
EREALR George Mallory
EREANN George Canning
EREATA George Eastham
George Eastman
EREBAU Georges Braque
ERECVE Georges Cuvier
EREDNO Georges Danton
EREDWT be friends with
EREEBR George Herbert
EREETA George Bentham
EREHMO George Thomson
EREHPA George Chapman
EREIDL George Biddell
EREIHE George Michael
EREIKA George Wickham
EREISN George Gissing
EREOEA George Foreman
ERESUA Georges Seurat
ERETBT George Stibitz
ERFATI tear off a strip
ERFBOA neurofibromas
ERFCTO petrification
ERFEDN Henry Fielding
ERFETO retroflection
ERGESO retrogression
ERGESV retrogressive
ERGRTO refrigeration
ERGRTR refrigeratory
ERGRTV refrigerative
ERHARN search warrant
ERHDAL tetrahedrally
ERHNIL reprehensible
reprehensibly
ERIGUV learning curve
ERIHEL near-sightedly
ERINST bear witness to
ERIOEF Georgia O'Keefe
ERLEEI Jerry Lee Lewis
ERLEWR neural network
ERLNUS neurolinguist
ERLSNS heartlessness
ERLTTO petrol station
ERMGEI ferromagnetic
ERMLIA Gerry Mulligan
ERMNAL detrimentally
ERMNAT detrimental to
ERMNLS decriminalise
ERMNLZ decriminalize
ERMNTO recrimination
ERMNTR recriminatory
ERMNTV recriminative
ERNERU year in year out
ERNIMN bearing in mind
ERNMKU wearing make-up
EROHAT heart of hearts
EROOOR fear no colours
EROWSO pearl of wisdom
ERPITN genre painting
ERPTTO decrepitation
ERRBNO Henry Robinson
ERRFET Gerry Rafferty
ERRGAL Henri Regnault
ERRSUU Herrerasaurus
ERRWIG Jerry Rawlings
ERRZTO terrorization
ERSALS recrystallise
ERSALZ recrystallize
ERSCNS heart-sickness
ERSDWC Henry Sidgwick
ERSETO retrospection
ERSETV retrospective
ERSIAL heuristically
peirastically
ERSIFL Jerry Seinfeld
ERSIRN heart-stirring
ERSMNH Georg Simon Ohm
ERSMNS wearisomeness
ERSNAL representable
ERSRAL terrestrially
ERSRPF tear a strip off
ERTESG secret message
ERTETN secret meeting
ERTEVC secret service
ERTLMN Georg Telemann
ERTOIT secret society
ERTRAL territorially
ERTRBR secretary bird
ERTRTN secret writing
ERTUNS regretfulness
ERTVNS secretiveness
ESACRE Persian carpet
ESAEOT persuade not to
ESAINR geostationary
ESBUWT mess about with
ESCLUE versicoloured
ESDMNE bedside manner
ESESNE Meistersinger
ESETVL perspectively
ESETVS perspectivism
ESFCTO versification
ESFOTG mess of pottage
ESIABG pe-tsai cabbage
ESIAIU perspicacious
ESIEMT red spider mite
ESIUUL perspicuously
ESLSNS senselessness
ESLTDU Heysel Stadium
ESMNAE leishmaniases
ESMNAI leishmaniasis
ESMNOE leishmanioses
ESMOES let someone use
ESMOTN less important
ESNADL Nelson Mandela
ESNCLM Nelson's Column
ESNFEN person of means
ESNLLR personal alarm
ESOBRE beast of burden
ESOOIA seismological
ESOOOU cessio bonorum
ESORPE seismographer
ESPOTO get support for
ESRAFO menstrual flow
ESRBLT mensurability
ESRCMD Messerschmidt
ESRCMT Messerschmitt
ESRCNR leisure centre
ESRSOD measure swords
ESSIAL least suitable
ESTLNS versatileness
ESTOAL sensationally
ESTVNS sensitiveness
ESTVTE sensitivities
ESTZTO sensitization
ESUHAE New South Wales
ESVRNL perseveringly

ESXAHN deus ex machina
ETAPRO neutral person
ETARGO Central Region
ETAVOE gentian violet
ETCDFE pesticide-free
ETCIAL geotactically
ETCLTO denticulation
gesticulation
ETCYEB Kentucky Derby
ETEALK gentlemanlike
ETEAON weather a point
ETEBAE weather-beaten
ETEESG get the message
ETEEVH get the heave-ho
ETEIAL aesthetically
ETEILE get the willies
ETEITR get the jitters
get the picture
ETEJCE leatherjacket
leather-jacket
ETENCO get the knack of
ETEOIO Berthe Morisot
ETEOSE Bertie Wooster
ETEOWR centre-forward
ETERCA set the price at
ETETIL left ventricle
ETEWIH featherweight
ETEWNO weather window
ETFCTO beatification
certification
rectification
ETFEML certified milk
ETFRUL pestiferously
ETGNUL vertiginously
ETHBUD beat the bounds
ETHCSO meet the cost of
ETHRCR beat the record
ETHWTR test the waters
ETIETR West Side Story
ETIMSL deltoid muscle
ETIOUS ventriloquise
ventriloquism
ventriloquist
ETIOUZ ventriloquize
ETITVL restrictively
ETIUAL centrifugally
ETIVNC Death in Venice
ETLBEH Bertolt Brecht
ETLFRU reptiliferous
ETLHME gentilshommes
ETLITR mental picture
ETLLNS mental illness
ETLMRA West Glamorgan
ETLNAL rectilinearly
ETLOEN be at a loose end
ETLOML dental formula
ETLSNS deathlessness
ETLSTO fertilisation
ETLTDU fertility drug
ETLZTO fertilization
ETMESN September Song
ETMNAL sentimentally
ETNBAE belt-and-braces
ETNBTE getting better
ETNIUL sententiously
ETNOHP beat into shape
ETNOLG Merton College
ETNPOL meeting people
ETNROA septentrional
ETNSAE meet one's maker
ETNUAL rectangularly
ETNUET getting used to
ETODHR Hertfordshire
ETOEFE get to one's feet
ETOIAL geotropically
ETOKHR West Yorkshire
ETOOHN next to nothing
ETOSYL oestrous cycle
ETOTWS west-north-west
west-south-west
ETRARE letter-carrier
ETRBNO Heath-Robinson
ETRCUC Western Church
ETREFC letter-perfect
ETRELO Hector Berlioz
ETRFEC letter of peace
ETRIGT Lester Piggott
ETRKLE helter-skelter
ETRLNT feature-length
ETRLRS pectoral cross
ETRSML venturesomely
ETRTLF restore to life
ETRTVL restoratively
ETRUNS dexterousness
ETRWIE feature-writer
ETSLAI heptasyllabic
ETSNEC death sentence
ETTDNU rectitudinous
ETTEET fed to the teeth
ETTVNS tentativeness
ETUTRN restructuring
ETUTVL destructively
ETXHNE heat exchanger
ETYTDI Merthyr Tydfil
EUATVT refusal to vote
EUBSMN refurbishment
EUCTTO resuscitation
EUCTTV resuscitative
EUEECN rejuvenescent
EUEOSE reduce to ashes
EUEUNS beauteousness
EUGTTO regurgitation
EUIEUI Yehudi Menuhin
EUIGGN reducing agent
EUILNS deducibleness
EUIUNS penuriousness
EUIYLR security alarm
EUIYUR security guard
EULCKI Gemütlichkeit
EULCNS republicanise
republicanism
EULCNZ republicanize
EULCTO reduplication
EULCTV reduplicative
EULSAL sexual assault
EUNILT sequentiality
EUOENS get up one's nose
EUOTCL Beaufort scale
EUOTNM verumontanums
EUSRTO sequestration
EUSTNS requisiteness
EUSVNS repulsiveness
EUTISO be curtains for
EUTRNS desultoriness
EUTVNS reductiveness
seductiveness
EUWLIM Venus Williams
EUYALU beauty parlour
EUYOTS beauty contest
EVCCAG service charge
EVCLMA cervical smear
EVHDOE heavy hydrogen
EVIATA leave it at that
EVIDSR heavy industry
EVLSNS nervelessness
EVNBHN leaving behind
EVNISN heaven-kissing
EVNNAT heaven on earth
EVNYEN heavenly being
EVOEHM leave one's home
EVOETM serve one's time
EVOETR serve one's turn
EVPRIL heavy particle
EVRHEG be over the edge
EVSADN leave standing
EVSFRS Leaves of Grass
EVSVNS pervasiveness
EVTEOG heave the gorge
EVUSSE nervous system
EVWAKN nerve-wracking
EWAIAD see what I can do
EWEWIE betweenwhiles
EWNOLG Selwyn College
EWRHNS seaworthiness
EXATFC feux d'artifice
EXDZTO deoxidization
EXMNTO re-examination
EYHLGS demythologise
EYHLGZ demythologize
EYHRTM very short time
EYLNHD Jekyll and Hyde
EZNNRA Tenzing Norgay
EZSPAO mezzo-sopranos
FAENSL efface oneself
FEAAHO after a fashion
FESMAH offer sympathy
FESVNS offensiveness
FETATM after that time
FETVNS effectiveness
FEVSEC effervescence
FHDRAE of the Dark Ages
FHNENS offhandedness
FHNTRO of the nature of
FHSMKN of the same kind
FHSMMN of the same mind
FIAIUL efficaciously
FIAVOE African violet
FIEOAM officer of arms
FIILTM official stamp

FIITWT affiliate with
FIIUNS officiousness
FIMTVL affirmatively
FLGEWL if all goes well
FLRSEC efflorescence
FNONMN of unsound mind
FOAIBA Afro-Caribbean
FODBLT affordability
FODNMN if you don't mind
FOENTE off one's nutter
FOEONA off one's own bat
FOERCE off one's rocker
FOESRK off one's stroke
FOETTO afforestation
FOSQEC of consequence
FYNHWL a fly on the wall
GCNRCT egocentricity
GEALNS agreeableness
GEIUNS egregiousness
GETDFE agree to differ
GIADGI again and again
GISTEA against the law
GIUTRS agriculturist
GLMRTO agglomeration
GLTNTO agglutination
GLTNTV agglutinative
GNSEEA agents-general
GNSIAL agonistically
GOIIUL ignominiously
GORDAC a good riddance
GRVTNL aggravatingly
GTSIAL egotistically
HAADAT cheap and nasty
HABRHL The Albert Hall
HAGASE Chiang Kai Shek
Chiang Kai-Shek
HAKADG The Awkward Age
HAOEAE the above-named
HAOIAL thrasonically
HARCLS theatricalise
HARCLT theatricality
HARCLZ theatricalize
HATFUU The Art of Fugue
HATGTE the altogether
HBOATS rhabdomantist
HBOOTE The Book of Thel
HBOSLE The Bookseller
HBSOIN The Bostonians
HBTOLN the bottom line
HBYIBU the boys in blue
HCAALN thick as a plank
HCACSR the chances are
HCASRE shock absorber
shock-absorber
HCMOGO the common good
HCMOWA the common weal
HCODOE the clouds open
HCOEHO the cloven hoof
HCPECE thick-pleached
HCWTEL thick-wittedly
HDBSNS shady business
HDCRST rhodochrosite
HDEHNE The Deer Hunter
HDMUTR The Dam Busters
HDRYOE The Dirty Dozen
HDVLOA the devil to pay
HDWAIE shadow cabinet
HDWFET shadow of death
HECREE three-cornered
HEDOCN shield volcano
HEDYVN three-day event
HEEDAE wheeler-dealer
HEEIAL phrenetically
HEFUTM three-four time
HELNWI three-line whip
HELSNS cheerlessness
HEMNSE chief minister
HEMTLG thremmatology
HEOOIA phrenological
HEPNYI threepenny bit
HESINW Chien-Shiung Wu
HETISI chieftainship
HETNNL threateningly
HFIYUE The Fairy Queen
HFLSNS shiftlessness
HFOLGT the footlights
HGIRAE the grim reaper
HGLEBW The Golden Bowl
HGNOIR The Gondoliers
HGOTAK the ghost walks
HGSSAD Chagos Islands
HGYAAO shaggy parasol
HGYIKA shaggy milk cap
HHRADO the here and now
HIBADA Chris Boardman
HIEFOD choice of words
HIOTEO a hair of the dog
HIRATO chain reaction
HITACK Christmas cake
HITACR Christmas card
HITADO Christian Dior
HITADV Christian Duve
HITANM christian name❑
HITARS Christmas rose
HITASN Christmas song
HITATE Christmas tree
HITISE Christminster
HITNLR Christ in Glory
HIWIMN Chaim Weizmann
HJBEWC The Jabberwock
HJNLBO The Jungle Book
HJWFAT The Jew of Malta
HJZSNE The Jazz Singer
HKOEHA shake one's head
HKSERA Shakespearean
Shakespearian
HKSOLF the kiss of life
HLCBOL whole caboodle
HLCNWL thylacine wolf
HLEGNL challengingly
HLENIL Chiltern Hills
HLLKNS childlikeness
HLNETA The Longest Day
HLNEWT philander with
HLNHOI philanthropic
HLNUMN Thelonius Monk
HLOETI phallocentric
HLOUNN phylloquinone
HLPALW Philip Marlowe
HLPEEL Philippe Sella
HLRNHM children's home
HLSMNS wholesomeness
HLSPIA philosophical
HLSPIE philosophizer
HLSSPE The Last Supper
HLSTCO The Last Tycoon
HLTSWR the latest word
HMATEI champ at the bit
HMBNGO The Mabinogion
HMCTRL The Mock Turtle
HMGCLT The Magic Flute
HMICAC the main chance
HMLOLK chameleon-like
HMLSNS shamelessness
HMOENS thumb one's nose
HMOERN rhombohedrons
HMRCPO chemoreceptor
HMRSIH the morn's nicht
HMSAKO Thomas Jackson
HMSALL Thomas Carlyle
HMSAPO Thomas Campion
HMSATU Thomas Malthus
HMSBCE Thomas à Becket
HMSDIO Thomas Addison
HMSECA Thomas Beecham
HMSECU Thomas Peachum
HMSEDE Thomas Beddoes
HMSEFR Thomas Telford
HMSKMI Thomas à Kempis
HMSOWT Thomas Sopwith
HMSQIA Thomas Aquinas
HMSRKN Thomas Erskine
HMSRNE Thomas Arundel
Thomas Cranmer
HMSYCO Thomas Pynchon
HMTEWT the matter with
HNBTEO think better of
HNEBAE thunder-bearer
HNEBLT changeability
HNEDRE thunder-darter
HNEFER change of heart
HNEFEU change of venue
HNEFTT change of state
HNEHVI the noes have it
HNEIGN change-ringing
HNEMSE thunder-master
HNENSL change oneself
HNENSR chance one's arm
HNEOPA chance to speak
HNEOWR thenceforward
HNEPRO changed person
HNESRC thunderstruck
HNESRK thunderstrike
thunder-stroke
HNGTAC The Night Watch
HNHGLO think highly of
HNIGIC changing-piece
HNIGLC changing place
HNKDUC The Naked Lunch

Words marked ❑ can also be spelled with an initial capital letter

HNLLNN phenylalanine
HNLSNS thanklessness
HNLTLO think little of
HNMNLG phenomenology
HNMNLS phenomenalise
phenomenalism
phenomenalist
HNMNLZ phenomenalize
HNNMRO think no more of
HNOWNT when you want to
HNRSKA Chandrasekhar
HNSLAE Chinese leaves
HNSPZL Chinese puzzle
HNTIZN phenothiazine
HNTRCE The Nutcracker
HNYLDN phencyclidine
HOAATU throw a tantrum
HOADMT Theobald Smith
HOAIAL chromatically
HOAOHR chromatophore
HODEPN the old serpent
HODUTO throw doubts on
HOEIAL theoretically
HOESFL The Odessa File
HOEUSA Shrove Tuesday
HOGTEA through the day
HOHROL the other world
HOIGAG shooting range
HOIGOG whooping cough
HOIGTC shooting stick
HOILPA chronicle play
HOITCT phlogisticate
HOOBVR Theodor Boveri
HOOIAL theologically
HOOOIA chronological
HOOOMN theologoumena
HOORPE chronographer
HOPSTO the opposition
HOTEOK shoot the works
HOTGTE throw together
HPBIWA the public weal
HPEDCU shepherd's club
HPEETA the present day
HPIGOR chopping-board
HPISHO the priesthood
HPJMGM The Pajama Game
HPLCRU rhopalocerous
HPLSNS shapelessness
HPNCAG chop and change
HPNOHP whip into shape
HPNYRP the penny drops
HPOETO the property of
HPOIAL rhapsodically
HPRYOE the party's over
HPSITN shop assistant
shop-assistant
HQEEFA chequered flag
HRADWE short and sweet
HRAETC pharmaceutics
HRAEZN Sherpa Tenzing
HRAMCA the real Mackay
HRAOOI pharmacopoeia
HRBAEE charm bracelet
HRCELS characterless
HRCEPR character part
HREBSE Shirley Bassey
HRECNA Charles Conrad
HREDRI Charles Darwin
HREEDH Thor Heyerdahl
HREEFR shortened form
HREGRO Charles Gordon
HREGUO Charles Gounod
HREMCA Charles Mackay
HREMNU Charles Mingus
HREOIN Charles Onions
HRETEA Charles the Fat
HRETML Shirley Temple
HRFCEK sheriff clerks
HRGAHS chirographist
HRGTTF The Right Stuff
HRHNAE Church in Wales
HRIBFR thereinbefore
HRIPRE Charlie Parker
HRLATS Choral Fantasy
HROETN thermosetting
HROLSI thermoplastic
HRORPE choreographer
HRORPI choreographic
HROTTW Charlottetown
HROULA thermonuclear
HROYAI thermodynamic
HRPATC sharp practice
HRRWOO a hard row to hoe
HRSANR shark's manners
HRSHWR sharp's the word
HRSIAL pharisaically
HRSOTN sharpshooting
HRTMEE short-tempered
HRTYOA Oh, Pretty Woman
HRUHON thoroughgoing
HRYIKN cherry-picking
HSALRN the small print
HSAOIN Thessalonians
HSCLEK physical jerks
HSEATU Chester Arthur
HSENMT Chester Nimitz
HSFENO this afternoon
HSHRLT phosphorylate
HSLBOE whistle-blower
HSOHRP physiotherapy
HSONMS physiognomist
HSOOIA physiological
HSORPE physiographer
HSORPI physiographic
HSOYFR The Story of Art
HSPAEA Chesapeake Bay
HSRIBW chase rainbows
HTABDN that can be done
HTABIN Chateaubriand
HTABUO Château Bougon
HTALFT Château Lafite
HTBGFI that's big of him
HTCEIA photochemical
phytochemical
HTEEHN white elephant
HTEETI photoelectric
HTESEE whithersoever
HTGAHR photographers
HTHPAU what the plague
HTHRLN White Hart lane
HTHTRA Khatchaturian
HTISIA what ails him at?
HTLAAA whittle away at
HTLECM that'll teach me
HTLECU that'll teach us
HTNHDR shot in the dark
HTNODA The Tin Woodman
HTOLSE ghetto-blaster
HTOOKO what do you know?
HTPAKO phytoplankton
HTRCPO photoreceptor
HTSPHR white sapphire
HTSYLO whitish-yellow
HTTETF that's the stuff!
HTUBDW the thumbs-down
HUAIAL rheumatically
HUAUGC thaumaturgics
HUAUGS thaumaturgist
HUDRLD shoulder blade
HUDROL The Underworld
HUDRTA shoulder strap
HUHLSL thoughtlessly
HUIGAC shouting match
shouting-match
HUPRRS the upper crust
HUTNSL thrust oneself
HVRIIN The Virginians
HVTEUE shove the queer
HWEADO show regard for
HWFOBT The Wife of Bath
HWHDOT show the door to
HWIEEI The White Devil
HWNLWO The Winslow Boy
HWNSAD show one's cards
HWNSAE show one's paces
HWNSEL show one's heels
HWNSET show one's teeth
HWOEHO the whole shoot
HWOEIH show to be right
HWOEOL the whole world
HWTHOE The Watchtower
HWTNEC show a tendency
HYATEU chrysanthemum
IACAHL financial help
IACARI financial ruin
IACAYA financial year
IADALW pit and gallows
IADCSO final decision
IAETBT cigarette butt
IAFCEL disaffectedly
IAFRAC disaffirmance
IAIMHT titanium white
IAIUNS vivaciousness
IALWRE miracle-worker
IAOATR Rila Monastery
IAOCRS Vicar of Christ
IAOKIL Sihanoukville
IAPAAC disappearance
IAPEIT misappreciate

IAPITN disappointing
IARBLO Hilaire Belloc
IARZTO cicatrization
IASCAE disassociated
IASMLT disassimilate
IATCLT disarticulate
IATRPS misanthropist
IAVNAE disadvantaged
IBADVE Siobhan Davies
IBNTER Big Bang theory
IBRUIC Liebfraumilch
ICAGTB discharge tube
ICAREI Sinclair Lewis
ICATOA aircraftwoman
ICCLUA piscicultural
ICDOLP minced collops
ICEDVL Kitchen Devils®
ICEFIH circle of light
ICEIAL biochemically
discreditable
discreditably
ICEINR discretionary
ICESAE kitchen scales
ICGNTO miscegenation
ICIFAE mischief-maker
ICIIAO discriminator
ICIVUL mischievously
ICLAET miscellaneity
ICLAEU miscellaneous
ICLMAD Vince Lombardi
ICLRTO discoloration
ICMALT circumvallate
ICMCIE circumscribed
ICMEEC circumference
ICMETO circumvention
ICMMIN circumambient
ICMPCL circumspectly
ICMRHN miscomprehend
ICMRSO air-compressor
ICMTNE circumstances
ICNDPU Vincent de Paul
ICNETN disconcerting
ICNETO disconcertion
disconnection
misconception
ICNETR misconjecture
ICNIUN discontinuing
ICNIUT discontinuity
ICNIUU discontinuous
ICNOMT disconformity
ICNORE Vincent O'Brien
ICOAVC piece of advice
ICOGON piece of ground
ICOSHO Jim Crow school
ICPCTT discapacitate
ICPIAL disciplinable
ICTGTE piece together
ICTNTI Liechtenstein
ICTOIO diacatholicon
ICUTOS discount house
ICVRWL discovery well
IDALWT find fault with
IDCTRL vindicatorily
IDEBOG Middlesbrough
IDEMRC Middle America
IDENLN Middle England
IDEREL kind-heartedly
IDESRE fiddler's green
IDFACT bid defiance to
IDFASG bird of passage
IDGAAL biodegradable
IDHEOT lied ohne worte
IDNENN hidden meaning
IDNOAL find enjoyable
IDNSEE find one's level
IDNSOA Bildungsroman
IDNWOL wild and woolly
IDOCAG winds of change
IDOCSL Windsor Castle
IDRISE Kidderminster
IDUORU tic douloureux
IDWAGN window hanging
IDWYON find a way round
IEAADO like cat and dog
IEAEWO Mike Hazelwood
IEAINS liberationism
liberationist
IEAOIA mineralogical
IEAORP cinematograph
kinematograph
IEAYGN literary agent
IEBESN mixed blessing
IEBMTE give a bum steer
IECETS life scientist
IECSET videocassette
IEDISO give admission
IEDNTO give a donation
IEEALO give details of
IEEDRN life-rendering
IEEGTC bioenergetics
IEEIAU River Eridanus
IEEITN fire-resistant
IEELOT sidereal month
IEESNI give lessons in
IEETRN time-bettering
IEFASG rite of passage
IEFCLF give a facelift
IEFECN line of descent
IEFERI give a free rein
IEFETM time after time
IEFHMR wide of the mark
IEGGMN disengagement
IEHBCE give the bucket
IEHBLE bite the bullet
IEHBOT give the boot to
IEHCMO give the come-on
IEHDNT give a hiding to
IEHNUT give a honour to
IEHPST give the push to
IEHSCT give the sack to
IEHUHT give thought to
IEHVTT give the vote to
IEIEEG kinetic energy
IEIELR live like a lord
IEIHNN like lightning
IEILGS kinesiologist
IEINTR time signature
IELCWR like clockwork
IEMATA side-impact bar
IEMRIG mixed marriage
IEMTPO mixed metaphor
IENATE live-in partner
IENATL Gideon Mantell
IENERE pigeon-hearted
IENHSE pigeon-chested
IENLTI Live and Let Die
IENNHC pile in on thick
IENOSO Siméon Poisson
IENOTO given no option
IENPNO give an opinion
IENSHM bite one's thumb
IENUAC fire insurance
life insurance
IENWRT give an award to
IENXML give an example
IEOCOE give a once-over
IEODMN video-on-demand
IEOHBI rise to the bait
IEOHDG give to the dogs
IEOIIN five positions
IEOKAT firework party
IEORGT give courage to
IEOSMN time-consuming
IEOTCM fine-tooth comb
IEPITN side-splitting
IEPLPL Pineapple Poll
IEPLWE pineapple weed
IEPOEC Aix-en-Provence
IEPOMN misemployment
IERATN give a roasting
IERAVE wide-broad view
IERCET give a rocket to
IERCRE video recorder
IERDTO give credit for
IERMET like grim death
IERSDN vice-president
IESECT give a speech to
IESNEC give a sentence
IESRDE disease-ridden
IESUAC life assurance
IESULS viper's bugloss
IETAAU licentia vatum
IETBDC liberty bodice
IETBLT digestibility
IETECE wide-stretched
IETHRN ride at the ring
IETIUI fide et fiducia
IETNHC pile it on thick
IETNLN disentangling
IETNSL divert oneself
IETOAD direct towards
IETOLS directionless
IETURN direct current
IEULBI disequilibria
IEUOMN time out of mind
IEXESO file extension
IEYOPN livery company
IFEEMU Die Fledermaus
IFEROE Wilfred Rhodes

IFGRMN disfigurement
IFGRTO disfiguration
IFLOSI disfellowship
IFRNFO different from
IFRNIT differentiate
IFSBLT diffusibility
IFSVNS diffusiveness
IGAEUL disgracefully
IGEERE single-hearted
IGEIEC King's evidence
IGEIUE single figures
IGERNH lingue franche
IGFERR king of terrors
IGITCA linguistician
IGMRDN Diego Maradona
IGMSEI Gilgamesh Epic
IGNAEC Virginia Beach
IGNAOL Virginia Woolf
IGNNLS pidgin English
IGNSAD Virgin Islands
IGOMNE wing commander
IGOTCA diagnostician
IGRLNS niggardliness
IGRPKR jiggery-pokery
IGTISO Birgit Nilsson
IGVRMN misgovernment
IHADHL with hands held
IHADLN Highland fling
IHADRS Highland dress
IHAEMR high-water mark
IHAENS bigheadedness
big-headedness
pig-headedness
IHATNN disheartening
IHBDRC with a bad grace
IHBLTT dishabilitate
IHCLUE light-coloured
IHCUBN nightclubbing
IHEHWR Michael Howard
IHEJRA Michael Jordan
IHEMNE Michael Manley
IHEOKN Michael of Kent
IHEPCT with respect to
IHEPWL Michael Powell
IHERMA Michael Ramsay
IHEUNS righteousness
IHFETO with affection
IHFNEE light-fingered
IHHHLO with the help of
IHHLSI with whole skin
IHHMNE with the manner
IHHNAL diphthongally
IHHRSL with the result
IHHUEA lighthouseman
IHHVBE might-have-been
IHIDIH with hindsight
IHIGIK Mikhail Glinka
IHIGOE with kid gloves
IHLCMR pinhole camera
IHLFEN Wilhelm Freund
IHLFGN Michela Figini
IHLPCE tightly packed
IHLSCT Nicholas Scott
IHLSNS sightlessness
IHMRSL nightmarishly
IHNACR with one accord
IHNECO within reach of
IHNERT with integrity
IHNESR within measure
IHNMGT high and mighty
high-and-mighty
IHNNCO within an ace of
IHNSAD with one's hands
IHNUAL dishonourable
dishonourably
IHOACN Night of Ascent
IHOACS right of access
IHODRC with good grace
IHOHNO with nothing on
IHONTR light of nature
IHOSAL High Constable
IHRALS with great loss
IHRBIH Richard Bright
IHRBRO Richard Burton
IHRBTE Richard Butler
IHRCBE Richard Cobden
IHRDAO Richard Deacon
IHRETS high priestess
IHRHDE Richard Hadlee
IHRHNA Richard Hannay
IHRHOE Richard Hooker
IHRLAE Richard Leakey
IHRMRI Richard Martin
IHRNYN hither and yond
IHROIU disharmonious
IHRQEC high frequency
IHRRGR Richard Rogers
IHRSEL Richard Steele
IHRTWE Richard Tawney
IHRVRN Right Reverend
IHRWGE Richard Wagner
IHSIIE light-spirited
IHSMRE eightsome reel
IHSSRR with a siserary
IHTIPN night-tripping
IHTMCE high-stomached
IHTMUL dichotomously
IHTNAL withstandable
IHUAOB without a doubt
IHUAON without a sound
IHUARA without a break
IHUCAG without charge
IHUFIL without frills
IHULOC with full force
IHUNME without number
IHURAO without reason
IHUSEC without speech
IHUVSO without vision
IHWTHA night-watchman
IHXLSV high explosive
IIAYEA Military Medal
IIAYRS Military Cross
IIEGNE civil engineer
IIENOW divide into two
IIEQAL divide equally
IIETOA vivisectional
IIGAIE filing cabinet
IIGHFI riding the fair
IIHNPS finishing post
IIHRTN disinheriting
IIIHNL diminishingly
IIIIAC piri-piri sauce
IIIUNS litigiousness
IILMNT disilluminate
IILSNS limitlessness
IILSOE disillusioned
IILTNL titillatingly
IILWIH mini-flyweight
IIMRIG civil marriage
IINRNS visionariness
IITAIN ministrations
IITGAE disintegrated
IITOSL sinistrorsely
IITRAL ministerially
IITRSE disinterested
IIUCRL vicious circle
IIUTRS viniculturist
viticulturist
IIUWIH minimum weight
IJNTVL disjunctively
IJWRPE his jaw dropped
IKEOET tickle to death
IKEOLN Wilkie Collins
IKHBCE kick the bucket
IKHCLT milk chocolate
IKHKIE Mikka Hakkinen
IKHUHE sick-thoughted
IKLLTN nickel-plating
IKNCOS pick and choose
IKNILC Kirkintilloch
IKNOHP lick into shape
IKNSEL kick one's heels
IKNSER pinking shears
pinking-shears
IKOWIH Dickson Wright
IKPSID kick up a shindy
IKSPRO sick as a parrot
IKTFEV ticket of leave
IKUBIH Kirkcudbright
ILABEN William Boeing
ILABFI William Baffin
ILABRE William Barnes
ILACWE William Cowper
ILADNA William Dunbar
ILADRI William Dorrit
ILAEPO William Empson
ILAGDI William Godwin
ILAHOE William Hoover
ILAHRE William Harvey
ILAKLI William Kelvin
ILAMRI William Morris
ILAOTR William of Tyre
ILATLO William Talbot
ILATML William Temple
ILAWLO William Walton
ILCIAL dialectically
ILCNOL Billy Connolly
ILDLYN dilly-dallying
ILEABY viol-de-gamboys

ILEAGR Lillie Langtry
ILECRD Willie McBride
ILEESA Willie Renshaw
ILEOIA Billie Holiday
ILERNI Killiecrankie
ILHSIA field hospital
ILKALV fit like a glove
ILMTCA diplomatic bag
ILNELS violoncellist
ILOBTL field of battle
ILOENI fill someone in
ILOHAO will not hear of
ILOHWS wills-o'-the-wisp
ILOVSO field of vision
ILPNHN Bible-punching
ILTEFR air letter form
ILTEIP will-o'-the-wisps
ILTUPN Bible-thumping
ILWATR willow pattern[❑]
ILWORS field wood rush
IMMEMN dismemberment
IMNGMN mismanagement
IMNHMS Birminghamise
IMNHMZ Birminghamize
IMRJCO film projector
IMTIAL diametrically
INEAWC Dionne Warwick
INEHPO Winnie-the-Pooh
INFCNL significantly
INFCTO signification
INFCTV significative
INGNWK Finnegans Wake
INHPEG sign the pledge
INIESC Gianni Versace
INLAPO Lionel Hampton
INMEIU his number is up
INNADC finnan haddock
INREVC dinner service
INSIAL pianistically
INSISM pianississimo
INTRLS disnaturalise
INTRLZ disnaturalize
INTROS giant tortoise
INTRTN signature tune
INYAHN kidney machine
INYOTE Sidney Poitier
IOASTN Nicolaus Steno
IODNTL disordinately
IOEINL disobediently
IOESRD hit one's stride
IOGMNO risorgimentos
IOHNRA mitochondrial
IOHNRO mitochondrion
IOIIAI nicotinic acid
IOINAE disorientated
IOITRA minor interval
IOLGNL disobligingly
IONANA Dido and Aeneas
IOOAHN Timon of Athens
IOOEOR lie on one's oars
IOTEEC sit on the fence
IPASNL dispraisingly
IPESNL displeasingly
IPNYIC sixpenny piece
IPOOTO disproportion
mispropoportion
IPRGAI diaphragmatic
IPRGMN disparagement
IPRGNL disparagingly
IPRTNL dispiritingly
IPRTNS disparateness
IPSESO dispossession
IPSINT dispassionate
IPSTVL dispositively
IPTHIE dispatch rider
IPTTVL disputatively
IQEPTE cinque-spotted
IQITNL disquietingly
IRAORN Giordano Bruno
IRCBTO hit rock bottom
IRCMUE microcomputer
IRCSET microcassette
IREENE Pierre Vernier
IREONR Pierre Bonnard
IREOOI microeconomic
IRERDA Pierre Trudeau
IRFCTO nitrification
vitrification
IRGNYL nitrogen cycle
IRGYHC hieroglyphics
IRIAMN Giorgio Armani
IRIZUO Giorgiy Zhukov
IRNTIN micronutrient
IROGNS micro-organism
IRPTTO disreputation
IRRASI librarianship
IRSETU disrespectful
IRSIAL dioristically
IRSRIA microsurgical
IRTOLS vibrationless
IRWVAL microwaveable
IRWVOE microwave oven
ISAENS misshapenness
ISDYOE first-day cover
ISEUTR tissue culture
ISLTNS dissoluteness
ISMLNL dissemblingly
ISMLRT dissimilarity
ISMLTD dissimilitude
ISMLTN dissimulating
ISMLTO dissimulation
ISMNSE first minister
ISMNTO dissemination
ISNASU dies infaustus
ISNGAE airs and graces
ISNIKT Wilson Pickett
ISNMKU kiss and make up
ISNPEE bits and pieces
ISNTEE Missing the Sea
ISOFNE first offender
ISOGAA Winston Graham
ISPEED Giuseppe Verdi
ISPEEN Giuseppe Peano
ISPRUL fissiparously
ISRAFS pig's breakfast
ISSLMI Missa Solemnis
ISTSYN dissatisfying
ISWRDA First World War
ITATNL distractingly
ITATVL distractively
ITCNLG biotechnology
ITCREE kitty-cornered
ITDAIG dirty dealings
ITEAKO hit the jackpot
ITEATE tittle-tattler
ITEELN hit the ceiling
ITEIHR Little Bighorn
Little Richard
ITEITM hit the big time
ITERCA fix the price at
ITESNL distressingly
ITESUL distressfully
ITFHRE list of charges
ITHLDF lift the lid off
ITITOR district court
ITITUS district nurse
ITLSNS mirthlessness
ITMZTO victimization
ITNOLG Girton College
ITNTNN sitting tenant
ITNTRE sitting target
ITNTVL distinctively
ITNUSE distinguished
ITOAIE fictionalized
ITORTN Pietro Aretino
ITOWIE fiction writer
ITRAAL Victoria Falls
ITRAGR Mister Jaggers
ITRARS Victoria Cross
ITRCNT winter aconite
ITREMC Mister Wemmick
ITRHOG filter through
ITRPLC picture-palace
ITRSUL picturesquely
ITRUOU victor ludorum
ITRZTO winterization
ITSEUL distastefully
ITSILN sixty shilling
ITTHRN tilt at the ring
ITTRAL dictatorially
ITUTNL mistrustingly
ITUTUL distrustfully
mistrustfully
ITWITE kist o' whistles
IUDRSA liquid crystal
IUDRTN misunderstand
IUDRTO misunderstood
IUEFIH figure of eight
IUEKTN figure skating
IUEUGN figure-hugging
IULZTO ritualization
visualization
IUOSAD Dieu vous garde
IUPDAV bicuspid valve
IUTRBD pituitary body
IUTRLS biculturalism
IVREVC silver service
IVRIRT silver nitrate
IVROGE silver-tongued

IVRUIE silver jubilee
IVUXBE Rievaulx Abbey
IWRHNS airworthiness
IWYSAD Midway Islands
IYFHNL lily of the nile
IYNSLU tidy oneself up
IZASAI Yitzhak Shamir
IZEETI piezoelectric
IZLMND fizzy lemonade
KATERA Akbar the Great
KLEPRO skilled person
KLEWRE skilled worker
KNOLVN A Kind of Loving
KNYIPN skinny-dipping
KOTLVN eke out a living
KRIGOR skirting-board
KRKRSW Akira Kurosawa
KTHSYO Sketches By Boz
KTLOFS a kettle of fish
LAALNS cleavableness
LAEAGR Sloane Rangers
LAEESO old-age pension
LAENSL please oneself
LAIGNI floating on air
LAIGOA cleaning woman
LATEEK clear the decks
LATEIL old as the hills
LATIKN clear-thinking
LBEGSE flabbergasted
LBLAMN global warming
LBLILG global village
LBRTNS elaborateness
LBTOTN globetrotting
globe-trotting
LBYEWR old-boy network
LCAAKV Alicia Markova
LCADHT black and white
black-and-white
LCAPRO glacial period
LCEEBA black-eyed bean
LCEYLC clickety-click
LCNIEE ill-considered
LCOARL electoral roll
LCOOII place of origin
LCOSFT place of safety
LCRCEC electric fence
LCRCIL electric field
LCRCOO electric motor
LCRCRA electric organ
LCRCTO electrocution
LCRCTR electric storm
LCRMGE electromagnet
LCRMTI electrometric
LCRMTV electromotive
LCRNRB electron probe
LCROTC electro-optics
LCRPII electrophilic
LCRPOU electrophorus
LCRSAI electrostatic
LCRSOI electroscopic
LCRVLN electrovalent
LCSIOI Alec Issigonis
LCTGTE place together
LDENSL pledge oneself
LDMRUI Vladimir Putin
LDSYWR Gladys Aylward
LDTMAG Clyde Tombaugh
LDTOBN slide trombone
LEERAO alleged reason
LEERHL Blueberry Hill
LEGNBR Allen Ginsberg
LEIDCN sleep-inducing
LEIGER bleeding heart
LEIGOC sleeping coach
LEIGYS Sleeping Gypsy
LELKAI bleed like a pig
LELKAO sleep like a log
LELSNS sleeplessness
LEMRPR Ellesmere Port
LENTVL alternatively
LEOIAL allegorically
LEONAN Blue Mountains
LEOTOR sleep outdoors
LERIAL algebraically
LETERN Albert Herring
LETGTE sleep together
LFODDT Clifford Odets
LFVUEL ill-favouredly
LGOEBA flageolet bean
LGPLSI oligopolistic
LGTETE flight-feather
LGTFAC flight of fancy
LGTYRN slightly drunk
LHADMG alpha and omega
LHCNAR Alpha Centauri
LHLOSA All Hallows' Day
LHNEUH Alphonse Mucha
LHPRIL alpha particle
LICSEL Elvis Costello
LIFUNE Alain-Fournier
LIGAHN flying machine
LIGFIE flying officer
LIGOOR flying colours
LIGOTM all in good time
LIHOHN sleight of hand
sleight-of-hand
LIOEIC all in one piece
LISEKN plain speaking
plain-speaking
LITVNS plaintiveness
LMCEIA climacterical
LMCIAL climactically
LMIGLN climbing plant
LMIGRM climbing-frame
LMLSNS blamelessness
LMNATE Clement Attlee
LMRUNS clamorousness
LMRZTO glamorization
LMTLGS climatologist
LNAAKO Glenda Jackson
LNALRE Alan Jay Lerner
LNANBR Alan Sainsbury
LNBCSO slingback shoe
LNDBAC Blanc de Blancs
LNEHOG glance through
LNESIC blanket stitch
LNESWO Clint Eastwood
LNETNL clandestinely
LNEUNS plenteousness
LNEYLN blankety-blank
LNHDBI Blanche Du Bois
LNIGAC slanging match
slanging-match
LNIHET blandishments
LNIUNS plentifulness
LNMNBF blind man's buff
LNOEHO sling one's hook
LNRPWR plenary powers
LNTLGS planetologist
LNTRWU fling throw mud
sling throw mud
LNYKOR Alan Ayckbourn
LOAGRN oleomargarine
LOBOHR Blood Brothers
LOCRLN bloodcurdling
LOCVRN floor-covering
LOLGTN floodlighting
LOLSNS bloodlessness
LOOIAL algologically
LOPESR blood pressure
LOTPNO almost upon you
LPAOPS blepharospasm
LPATAI elephantiasis
LPATHE elephant shrew
LPFHNE clap of thunder
LPNHBC slap on the back
LPNHFC slap in the face
LPNTCL slap and tickle
LPRUAS à la Portugaise
LRADAN flora and fauna
LRAIUL flirtatiously
LRATIE Gloria Steinem
LRCTUE Albrecht Dürer
LRDALC Alfred Wallace
LRDENN Alfred Denning
LRDESE Alfred Hershey
LRDLAE Alfred Alvarez
LRDRYU Alfred Dreyfus
LRFCTO clarification
glorification
LRFCTR clarificatory
LRLOIT plural society
LRLZTO pluralization
LRPGOT Clara Peggotty
LRSIAL floristically
LRVRUU ultra-virtuous
LSADLO flesh and blood
LSAFED elysian fields
LSAROK Alistair Cooke
LSESRN Ulysses S Grant
LSFODN flash flooding
LSHMUL blasphemously
LSIBLE plastic bullet
LSITEA flash in the pan
LSITSU elastic tissue
LSMCAE clishmaclaver
LSOEMT plasmodesmata
LSTGTE clasp together
LSUFED elysium fields

LTAKET I'll thank her to
LTAKIT I'll thank him to
LTAKOT I'll thank you to
LTENOD clothe in words
LTMRCR all-time record
LTNCOI Platonic solid
LTNMLC platinum black
LTNMLN platinum-blond
LTNUNS glutinousness
LTOIAL plethorically
LTTDNS platitudinise
LTTDNU platitudinous
LTTDNZ platitudinize
LUEEUS Claude Debussy
LUEHBO Claude Chabrol
LUEHNO Claude Shannon
LUEONE Claude Dornier
LUEORI Claude Lorrain
LUHHOG plough through
LUIABD Claudio Abbado
LUIAIN illuminations
LUIGTC floutingstock
LUIHNL flourishingly
LUILNS plausibleness
LUTIUL illustriously
LVCMAO clavicembalos
LVSNLI Clive Sinclair
LWCCSL Alnwick Castle
LWHLDF blow the lid off
LWICAG glow discharge
LWRAGN blow great guns
LXIOYI Alexei Kosygin
LXNEBO Alexander Blok
LXNEHI Alexander Haig
LXNEPP Alexander Pope
LYADOE play hard to get
LYAOWT play havoc with
LYBUWT play about with
LYHHRE play the horses
LYHPRO play the part of
LYHRLO play the role of
LYHWNO play the wanton
LYNAON playing around
LYNSUC play one's hunch
LYOSFT play for safety
LYPNOD play upon words
LYTATR play at wasters
LYUATK all you can take
LZBTRA Elizabeth Ryan
MACMAG smear campaign
MACSIL immarcescible
MAEILS immaterialise
MAEILT immateriality
MAEILZ immaterialize
MAHZWT empathize with
MAODOS Emma Woodhouse
MAPBLT impalpability
MARSMN embarrassment
MASBLT impassability
MASDRA ambassadorial
MASVNS impassiveness
MATANS impartialness
MCOELP smack one's lips

MECBLT impeccability
MECIAL imperceivable
MECPIL imperceptible
imperceptibly
MEILSI imperialistic
MEITNS immediateness
MEIUNS imperiousness
MELFRU umbelliferous
MELSMN embellishment
MEMNNL impermanently
MEMSIL impermissible
impermissibly
MEOILL immemorial old
MESNLS impersonalise
MESNLT impersonality
MESNLZ impersonalize
MESNTO impersonation
METNNL impertinently
METRAL imperturbable
imperturbably
MEUIST impecuniosity
MEUIUL impecuniously
MEUUNS impetuousness
MGAAEU amygdalaceous
MGNTIG imagine things
MGNTVL imaginatively
MHSMTU emphysematous
MICNEI amniocentesis
MIEULE empire-builder
MIIACR umbilical cord
MIIUNS ambitiousness
MITCLI amniotic fluid
MIUUNS ambiguousness
MKDTCO smoke detector
MKLSZN smokeless zone
MLAAHR Amelia Earhart
MLCBLT implacability
MLCPTL small capitals
MLCTVL implicatively
MLEAON smaller amount
MLFCTO amplification
MLINAN emulsion paint
MLYPOL Smiley's People
MNNDMI eminent domain
MNNERS éminence grise
MOHAKN smooth-talking
MOHOGE smooth-tongued
MOHUNN smooth-running
MOSBLT impossibility
MOTDOD imported goods
MOTNTL importunately
MRBBLT improbability
MRCIAL impracticable
impracticably
impractically
MRCNAL American eagle
MRCNAO American Samoa
MRCNRS American crust
MRCSNS impreciseness
MRECEI emergency exit
MRHUNS amorphousness
MRLARU umbrella group
MRLATN umbrella-stand

MROOIA embryological
MRSBEC Ambrose Bierce
MRSINS Impressionism
impressionist
MRVDNL improvidently
MRVSTO improvisation
MSMNPR amusement park
MSTPEE smash to pieces
MTTVNS imitativeness
MUALNS immutableness
MUOHRP immunotherapy
MUOOIA immunological
MUSBYN impulse buying
MUSVNS impulsiveness
MYEMTS empyreumatise
MYEMTZ empyreumatize
MYWLIM Emlyn Williams
NAAIAE incapacitated
NACRTO incarceration
NADEEU Inland Revenue
NADHSM one and the same
NADMUT unpaid amounts
NADOKN inward-looking
NADSEC incandescence
NAETEI in parenthesis
NAFLOD unlawful goods
NAGBLT intangibility
NAHOAL unfashionable
unfashionably
NAIBLT insatiability
invariability
NAIFAL unsatisfiable
NAIIRT unfamiliarity
NAKMTV Anna Akhmatova
NALBLT infallibility
NAMNWT in harmony with
NANENS undauntedness
untaintedness
NAORNS unsavouriness
NARNAL unwarrantable
unwarrantably
NARNEL unwarrantedly
NASLTO encapsulation
NATESI in partnership
NATLNS unearthliness
NATRNL unfalteringly
NAUANS unnaturalness
NAVGAL unsalvageable
NBDSUS anybody's guess
NBONTD in a brown study
NBRSVL inobtrusively
unobtrusively
NBRVAE unabbreviated
NCBCAE knock back a few
NCEFRI knocked for six
NCETTC in a cleft stick
NCIGNE knocking knees
NCITOA inscriptional
NCITVL inscriptively
NCLDSE knuckleduster
NCLDWT knuckle down to
NCMRLS unicameralism
unicameralist

NCOEFC knock-on effect
NCONAL unaccountable
unaccountably
NCONWT in account with
NCOPNE unaccompanied
NCOTRP knockout drops
NCRNSI anachronistic
NCRNUL anachronously
NCSDWY knock sideways
NCSOSF knock spots off
NCTGTE knock together
NDAMSE Knud Rasmussen
NDCBLT ineducability
NDETNL inadvertently
NDETRU unadventurous
NDIENS unadvisedness
NDLEAE unadulterated
NEAENS unrelatedness
NEAHEE underachiever
NEAIAL indefatigable
indefatigably
NEALNS untenableness
NEARTS enter a protest
NEBAED on her beam-ends
NEBEDN interbreeding
NECAGN interchanging
NECASA underclassman
NECIAL indescribable
indescribably
undescribable
NECLTO intercalation
NECLUA intercellular
NECOHN underclothing
NECREC intercurrence
NECRIG undercarriage
NEDGTT interdigitate
NEDNAL interdentally
NEDNNS unbendingness
NEEDNL independently
NEEEAE unregenerated
NEEMNC indeterminacy
NEEMNL unbeseemingly
NEEMNT indeterminate
NEEOIU unceremonious
NEEPSR underexposure
NEESRL unnecessarily
NEETAL inferentially
NEETMT underestimate
NEETNL interestingly
unrelentingly
NEETVL unselectively
NEEVNL undeservingly
NEFRNL interferingly
NEFRWT interfere with
NEFSNS unselfishness
NEGAUT undergraduate
NEGBUL unneighbourly
NEGLCI intergalactic
NEGRET undergarments
NEHBIE Inner Hebrides
NEHNEL underhandedly
NEIBLT unreliability
NEIEBE undesireables
NEIIAL unmedicinable
NEIRNL interior angle
NEITNL unremittently
unremittingly
unresistingly
NEIUNS ingeniousness
NEIVNL unbelievingly
NEJCLT interjaculate
NELCEG On Wenlock Edge
NELCMN interlacement
NELCTO interlocution
NELCTR interlocutory
NELCUL intellectuals
NELGNL intelligently
NELHDE unhealthy diet
NELHNS unhealthiness
NELHUL unhealthfully
NELMNT interlaminate
NELNNS unfeelingness
NEMLWO Under Milk Wood
NEMNLN intermingling
NEMRIG intermarriage
NEMTEC intermittence
NENFRL once and for all
NENNNS unmeaningness
NENTOA international
NEOCLT interosculate
NEOEAL unrecoverable
NEOEBL under one's belt
NEOEHA enter one's head
NEOEHN under one's hand
NEOENS under one's nose
NEOIAL anaerobically
NEPCAL unrespectable
NEPEAE underprepared
NEPEAL interpretable
NEPESR under pressure
NEPITN underpainting
NEPLTO interpolation
NEPNIG underpinnings
NEPNTM once upon a time
NEPNWT in keeping with
NEPOIA interproximal
NEPROA interpersonal
NEPRTL intemperately
NEPSTO interposition
NERDAL interradially
NERENS unlearnedness
NERGTO interrogation
NERGTR interrogatory
NERGTV interrogative
NERLTO interrelation
NERMNE unreprimanded
NERPEL interruptedly
NESAAL unpersuadable
NESADN understanding
NESAUA interscapular
NESBLT infeasibility
insensibility
NESESO interspersion
NESESU Anders Celsius
NESETV in perspective
NESNNL unreasoningly
NESNNS incessantness
NESRTF interstratify
NESTNS insensateness
NESTVL insensitively
NESTVT insensitivity
NESVCR intensive care
NESVNS intensiveness
NETEAL under the table
ungentlemanly
NETEIE anaesthetized
NETEIT enter the lists
NETENF under the knife
NETENS unsettledness
NETFAL unrectifiable
NETGTN investigating
NETGTO investigation
NETGTR investigatory
NETGTV investigative
NETIMN entertainment
NETMNA unsentimental
NETOAL intentionally
unmentionable
NETRAL inventorially
unperturbable
NETROK on tenterhooks
NETVNS infectiveness
inventiveness
NETVRU insectivorous
NEUETR integumentary
NEUUNS ingenuousness
NEVCAL unserviceable
NEWEMN underwhelming
NEWRIG inner workings
NFALNS ineffableness
NFEDNL unoffendingly
NFESVL inoffensively
NFETAL ineffectually
NFETVL ineffectively
NFIAIU inefficacious
NFIINL inefficiently
NFIIUL inofficiously
NFRHRA one for the road
NGAIAL enigmatically
NGAMTS anagrammatise
NGAMTZ anagrammatize
NGTERN knights-errant
NHARDS Andhra Pradesh
NHASRC in the abstract
NHCAGO in the charge of
NHCNRR on the contrary
NHCUSO in the course of
NHDGOS in the doghouse
NHDLRM in the doldrums
NHFCOI on the face of it
NHICES on the increase
NHIONA in their own way
NHITAL unchristianly
NHITNS unthriftiness
NHITRA in the interval
NHLITI anthelminthic
NHLNSD on the long side
NHLSML unwholesomely
NHMATM in the meantime

NHMDLO	in the middle of
NHMNEO	in the manner of
NHMTEO	in the matter of
NHNDWL	Anthony Dowell
NHNFKE	Anthony Fokker
NHNPWL	Anthony Powell
NHNQAL	Anthony Quayle
NHNRMT	enchondromata
NHNSMR	on Shanks's mare
NHNSPN	on Shanks's pony
NHNTRO	in the nature of
NHOOER	anthropometry
NHOOHG	anthropophagy
NHOOOH	anthroposophy
NHPPLN	in the pipeline
NHPRBA	on the port beam
NHPVMN	on the pavement
NHRGOO	in the region of
NHRPRO	on the report of
NHRSPL	in short supply
NHSALS	in the smallest
NHSCLS	on the sick list
NHSMBA	in the same boat
NHSOTU	in the short run
NHSRKO	on the stroke of
NHSRNT	on the strength
NHTGAH	in photographs
NHVCNT	in the vicinity
NHWNSY	in the wind's eye
NHWSEO	on the wishes of
NIAILO	one in a million
NICBLT	invincibility
NICLTO	in circulation
NICMIE	uncircumcised
NICMPC	uncircumspect
NICPIE	undisciplined
NICREL	undiscernedly
NICRIL	indiscernible
	indiscernibly
	undiscernible
	undiscernibly
NICRUI	antiscorbutic
NICUAE	undiscouraged
NIDUNS	unmindfulness
NIEGNB	in times gone by
NIEHII	antinephritic
NIEIAL	antigenically
NIESNE	anti-personnel
NIETAT	in dire straits
NIETCS	antisepticise
NIETCZ	antisepticize
NIETOT	indirect route
NIFRNL	indifferently
NIGIEL	undisguisedly
NIHEMN	enlightenment
NIHETE	in high feather
NIHEUL	unrighteously
NIHLNS	unsightliness
NIHPRT	in high spirits
NIHUGO	in high dudgeon
NIIAEL	unmitigatedly
NIIEIA	infinitesimal
NIITMN	antihistamine
NIIULS	individualise
	individualism
	individualist
NIIULT	individuality
NIIULZ	individualize
NIIUNS	insidiousness
	invidiousness
NIIUTO	individuation
NILBLT	inviolability
NILCWS	anticlockwise
NILMCI	anticlimactic
NILNNS	unwillingness
NINFCN	insignificant
NIOAIH	antilogarithm
NIOGLN	anticoagulant
NIOILT	antisociality
NIOINS	antinomianism
NIOMNA	environmental
NIPNAL	indispensable
	indispensably
NIPSTO	indisposition
NISAAL	indissuadably
NISMLN	undissembling
NITENO	until the end of
NITNNS	unwittingness
NITNTV	undistinctive
NIUDTO	in liquidation
NIUTNL	insinuatingly
NJTRNE	ink-jet printer
NKLUNS	unskilfulness
NLALNS	uncleanliness
NLAUAL	unpleasurably
NLBRTL	inelaborately
NLCLNA	Anglo-Colonial
NLCTOI	Anglo-Catholic
NLCZTO	anglicization
NLETAL	influentially
NLFINS	in all fairness
NLGBLT	ineligibility
NLGUNS	analogousness
NLMWRH	unblameworthy
NLNDLN	inclined plane
NLNHNL	unflinchingly
NLRSEC	inflorescence
NLRSET	in all respects
NLSDRE	enclosed order
NLTRLS	unilateralism
	unilateralist
NLTRLT	unilaterality
NLUIAE	unilluminated
NLXBLT	inflexibility
NMARSE	unembarrassed
NMASOE	unimpassioned
NMDESO	animadversion
NMECAL	unimpeachable
NMELSE	unembellished
NMGNTV	unimaginative
NMIUUL	unambiguously
NMLUNS	anomalousness
NMNBLT	unamenability
NMRCNS	un-Americanise
NMRCNZ	un-Americanize
NMREGA	Ingmar Bergman
NMSIAL	onomastically
NMTBLT	inimitability
NMTEEN	in smithereens
NMTOAL	unemotionally
NNAIAL	uninhabitable
NNEETN	uninteresting
NNELGN	unintelligent
NNERPE	uninterrupted
NNETOA	unintentional
NNHSCE	in on the secret
NNIDOI	enantiodromia
NNIHEE	unenlightened
NNIIAE	unanticipated
NNLMAL	uninflammable
NNMREC	in an emergency
NNOCAL	unenforceable
NNOCSO	on any occasion
	on one occasion
NNOEBO	in anyone's book
NNOMTV	uninformative
NNSLMN	in one's element
NNSWHO	on one's own hook
NNSWTM	in one's own time
NNTUTV	uninstructive
NOAINS	innovationist
NOALNS	unwomanliness
NOAYOD	in so many words
NOBSIL	incombustible
	incombustibly
NOBUKE	Anton Bruckner
NOCAAL	unconcealable
NOCIAL	inconceivable
	inconceivably
	unconceivably
NOCREL	unconcernedly
NOCRWT	in concert with
NODPRT	in good spirits
NODTOA	unconditional
NODTOE	unconditioned
NOEEAL	unforeseeable
NOEESR	in some measure
NOEIAL	ontogenically
NOEPLC	incomes policy
NOEROI	endometriosis
NOETCT	undomesticate
NOEUPR	income support
NOFRAL	uncomfortable
	uncomfortably
	unconformable
	unconformably
NOGTAL	unforgettable
NOGTFE	unsought-after
NOGUUL	incongruously
NOIBLT	unsociability
NOICNV	Antonio Canova
NOIDOA	Antonín Dvorák
NOIETL	in no time at all
NOISIA	encomiastical
NOIUPU	Antoninus Pius
NOJNTO	in conjunction
NOKALK	unworkmanlike
NOKBLT	unworkability
NOLLNS	unworldliness

NOMDBU informed about
NOMGIS inform against
NOMNCD incommunicado
NOMSMN Anton Mosimann
NOMTOA informational
NONEAC in countenance
NONENS unboundedness
NONOFC in point of fact
NOOIAL ontologically
NOOOIA entomological
NOORON in honour bound
NOPANN uncomplaining
NOPASN uncomplaisant
NOPIAE uncomplicated
NOPNWT in company with
NOPRAL incorporeally
NOPRTO in co-operation
incorporation
NOPRTV unco-operative
NOPSMN encompassment
NOPTNL incompetently
NOPTTO in competition
NOQEAL unconquerable
NORCNS incorrectness
NORGMN encouragement
NORGNL encouragingly
NORIAE uncoordinated
unco-ordinated
NORNLG endocrinology
NORPIL incorruptible
incorruptibly
NOSCAE unconsecrated
NOSDRT inconsiderate
NOSINL inconsciently
NOSIUL unconsciously
NOSIUU inconspicuous
NOSNNL inconsonantly
NOSQEC in consequence
inconsequence
NOSRIE unconstrained
NOSSEC inconsistency
NOTCMN unforthcoming
NOTCWT in contact with
NOTEAT end of the earth
NOTIAL uncontainable
NOTIAO indoctrinator
NOTMCA in contumaciam
NOTNNL incontinently
NOTNTL unfortunately
NOTSAL incontestable
incontestably
NOUTRL involuntarily
NOUUNS innocuousness
NOVNEC inconvenience
NOVRIL inconvertibly
NOXSEC into existence
NOYFAU Antony of Padua
NOYOME Antony Gormley
NPCAUA unspectacular
NPNAEU unspontaneous
NPOIAL anaphorically
NPOTNL inopportunely
NPRBLT inoperability
NPRBTO on approbation
NPRCAE unappreciated
NPRCAL inappreciable
inappreciably
NPRHNE unapprehended
NPRNNS unsparingness
NPRPIT inappropriate
NPRTAL unspiritually
NPRTNL inspiritingly
NPRTOA inspirational
NPRVNL unapprovingly
NPTOTA in spite of that
NPTOTI in spite of this
NQIOAL unequivocally
NRABAE Andreas Baader
NRADMN in great demand
NRADTI in great detail
NRAHNL encroachingly
NRAIAL inorganically
NRCDNE unprecedented
NRCLUA intracellular
NRCTNS intricateness
NRCUUL infructuously
NRDBLT incredibility
NRDCAL unpredictable
unpredictably
NRDEGA Ingrid Bergman
NRDLUL incredulously
NRDTOA untraditional
NREIAL energetically
NRGESV unprogressive
NRGNLT unoriginality
NRIRMK Andrei Gromyko
NRIUOE Andrei Tupolev
NRMAIA ungrammatical
NRMCEI André Michelin
NRMNTN incriminating
NRMNTO incrimination
NRMNTR incriminatory
NRMOEI in gremio legis
NRMSUA intramuscular
NRNIAL intrinsically
NRNIEC intransigence
NRPEES entrepreneuse
NRPRTO in preparation
NRSEOI Andrés Segovia
NRSETO introspection
NRSETV introspective
NRSVNS intrusiveness
NRSWRH untrustworthy
NRTNIU unpretentious
NRVNAL unpreventable
NRWAKO Andrew Jackson
NRWAVL Andrew Marvell
NRWONO Andrew Johnson
NSALSE unestablished
NSOSRN on a shoestring
NSOTHL in a short while
NSTEHL one's other half
NTBOKE Anita Brookner
NTDAIN United Nations
NTDIGO United Kingdom
NTEAIE anathematized
NTETRT in its entirety
NTETVL inattentively
NTFCON unit of account
NTGTNL instigatingly
NTLAIN installations
NTLFAC Anatole France
NTLKRO Anatoly Karpov
NTLSLG on its last legs
NTMZTO anatomization
NTNAET instantaneity
NTNAEU instantaneous
NTNSRW knit one's brows
NTNTAL instinctually
NTNTVL instinctively
NTOIAL gnathonically
NTTTOA institutional
NTTTVL institutively
NTUTOA instructional
NTUTVL instructively
NUAIAL pneumatically
NUAITR pneumatic tyre
NUATEE undulant fever
NUCPIL insusceptibly
unsusceptible
NUCULT unpunctuality
NUDBLT infundibulate
NUDWAL unputdownable
NUEOPA induce to speak
NUEPRO injured person
NUESRE in queer street
NUFCEC insufficiency
NUIIUL injudiciously
NUITNL infuriatingly
NUIUNS incuriousness
injuriousness
NULETE in full feather
NUODNT insubordinate
NUPBLT inculpability
NUPCEL unsuspectedly
NUPCOO on suspicion of
NUPRAL insupportable
insupportably
NUPREL unsupportedly
NUPSAL unsurpassable
NUPSEL unsurpassedly
NURENS unguardedness
unhurriedness
NUSATA insubstantial
unsubstantial
NUSINN unquestioning
NUSTOA inquisitional
NUSTRA inquisitorial
NUSTVL inquisitively
NUTBLT unsuitability
NUTFAL unjustifiable
unjustifiably
NUTIAL unsustainable
NUTILS industrialise
industrialism
industrialist
NUTILZ industrialize
NUTIUL industriously
NUTOCI induction coil

NUTVNS intuitiveness
NVRACR universal cure
NVRANS universalness
NVRDTI in every detail
NVRPRO in every part of
NVRSDO on every side of
NVTBLT inevitability
NWDEOB Ann Widdecombe
NWEATR a new departure
NWEGAL knowledgeable
knowledgeably
NWEGBS knowledge base
NWHTWA know what's what
NWLNNS snow blindness
NWNIEU know inside out
NWNSLC know one's place
NWNSTF know one's stuff
NWRBLT answerability
NXASIL inexhaustible
inexhaustibly
NXEINE inexperienced
NXEINL inexpediently
NXESVL inexpensively
NXETOA unexceptional
NXGEAE unexaggerated
NXHNEO in exchange for
NXLIAL unexplainable
unexplainably
NXRBLT inexorability
NXRSIL inexpressible
inexpressibly
NYHLNL Only the Lonely
NYLPDS encyclopedist
NYLPEI encyclopaedia
NYMTIA unsymmetrical
NYOTTS enhypostatise
NYOTTZ enhypostatize
NYPTEI unsympathetic
OAAKNO Rowan Atkinson
OABRDL Royal Birkdale
OACTOI Roman Catholic
OADALA Donald Maclean
OADATE Roland Barthes
OADLRS Roman de la Rose
OADOGA Donald Douglas
OADOGI Howard Hodgkin
OAGESO non-aggression
OAGESV non-aggressive
OAHNWF Jonathan Swift
OAHRTM for a short time
OAIGEN not a single one
OAIIAL volatilizable
OAINLO Horatio Nelson
OAIUNS voraciousness
OALOCR for all you care
OALOKO for all you know
OAMDNS Mohammedanise
OAMDNZ Mohammedanize
OANTAS Johann Strauss
OAOAUN Corazon Aquino
OAORPI gonadotrophic
gonadotrophin
OAPAAC non-appearance
OAPLNK Roman Polanski
OAPRAC local parlance
OARALO hot-air balloon
OARNLN noradrenaline
OASADR royal standard
OASEAL not answerable
OATCZN romanticizing
OATEES to say the least
OATELG moral theology
OATESI copartnership
OATFCA not artificial
OATNAC non-attendance
OAUEBR Rosa Luxemburg
OBCALO Bobby Charlton
OBEEDN double wedding
OBEELN double dealing
double-dealing
OBEENN double meaning
double-meaning
OBEIUE double figures
OBELZN double-glazing
OBEONE double-jointed
OBEOOU double coconut
OBERSE double-crosser
OBERUT double or quits
OBFRTM not before time
OBLEAC corbelled arch
OBNFRE combine forces
OBNNFR combining form
OBRMSU Hofburg Museum
OBRWEE Norbert Wiener
OBSIAL bombastically
OBTAIU combat fatigue
OBTERE Zorba the Greek
OBTVNS combativeness
OBYETT doubly dentate
OBYSNS tomboyishness
OCASFE non-classified
OCCIAL concyclically
OCDDFA concede defeat
OCGIAL non-cognizable
OCIENS conceitedness
OCIOOD Soichiro Honda
OCLSNS voicelessness
OCMIAL coxcombically
OCMLAC non-compliance
OCMRMS not compromise
OCMTNL concomitantly
OCNOMS nonconformist
non-conformist
OCNOMT nonconformity
non-conformity
OCNRCT concentricity
OCNRTN concentrating
OCNRTO concentrate on
concentration
OCNUTN non-conducting
OCPINA Conception Bay
OCPSEC concupiscence
OCPULR Conceptual Art
OCPULS conceptualise
conceptualism
OCPULZ conceptualize
OCRENS concernedness
OCREWT concerned with
OCSINR concessionary
OCTESU force the issue
OCTNTO concatenation
ODAAIA good Samaritan
ODACNR top dead-centre
ODAOFR Ford Madox Ford
ODAUEL good-naturedly
ODCNLT hold a candle to
ODCTOA coeducational
ODEREL cold-heartedly
ODFENO good afternoon
ODLNNS word-blindness
ODLOEL cold-bloodedly
ODNDNE nodding donkey
ODNEML condensed milk
ODNENT Gordon Bennett
ODNETO golden section
ODNHHL toad in the hole
toad-in-the-hole
ODNRVN wood engraving
ODNSEC hold one's peace
ODNUIE golden jubilee
ODNUTD hold in custody
ODOCON hold to account
ODODTO good condition
ODOENT hold someone to
ODOSNN food poisoning
ODOWLO Woodrow Wilson
ODPOHM hold up to shame
ODRCSO food processor
word processor
ODRERE Border terrier
ODRNIO soldering-iron
ODROKN wonder-working
ODRSDN Lord President
ODRUNS ponderousness
ODRVSA Lord Privy Seal
ODSEDN condescending
ODSESO condescension
ODSHRT cold as charity
ODSOTG hold as hostage
ODSRPL nondescriptly
ODTMOA Lords Temporal
ODTOAL conditionally
ODTOAO conditional on
ODXRMN void excrement
OEAAUG sober as a judge
OEAECL moderate a call
OEAINS tolerationist
OEAKAD move backwards
OEALNS tolerableness
OEAOSI moderatorship
OECIDE women-children
OECNMC home economics
OECNMS home economist
OEDESN power dressing
OEDWEO honeydew melon
OEEADY for ever and aye
OEELNL forefeelingly
OEETOE forementioned
OEFHRC Dome of the Rock

OEFODC	code of conduct
OEGABN	money-grabbing
OEGOFC	foreign office
OEGUBN	money-grubbing
OEHDIO	Joseph Addison
OEHDWN	foreshadowing
OEHEND	Joseph Kennedy
OEHNIU	something is up
OEHNLK	something like
OEHNRW	Joseph Andrews
OEHNTD	something to do
OEHOBA	Joseph Rotblat
OEHRDK	Joseph Brodsky
OEHRES	somewhere else
OEHUFC	Joseph Surface
OEIETO	Some Like It Hot
OELGRN	cobelligerent
OELNWT	come along with
OELSNS	powerlessness
OELUET	Nobel laureate
OEMVMN	bowel movement
OENATI	fore-and-aft rig
OENCRE	hole-and-corner
OENHWL	hole in the wall
OENNBD	governing body
OENOEN	come into being
OENOIE	move unnoticed
OENOIH	come into sight
OENOOC	come into force
OENSEV	lose one's nerve
OENSHR	lose one's shirt
OENSLC	lose one's place
OENWEG	foreknowledge
OENWNL	foreknowingly
OENZTO	modernization
	solemnization
OEOCIA	come to a climax
OEOHBI	come to the boil
OEOHWL	gone to the wall
OEOLNO	Tower of London
OEONAD	move downwards
OEONSL	come to oneself
OEOOHN	come to nothing
OEOSEN	power of seeing
OEPGIS	come up against
OEPLTC	power politics
OEPNDW	move up and down
OERCIE	money received
OERCSL	more precisely
OESERN	power steering
OESHOE	Gödel's theorem
OESRGL	power struggle
OETACA	Robert Barclay
OETAEB	Robert Catesby
OETAPL	Robert Walpole
OETAWL	Robert Maxwell
OETBGI	Roberto Baggio
OETCAB	domestic tabby
OETCTO	domestication
OETEFR	Robert Redford
OETEND	Robert Kennedy
OETERC	Robert Herrick
OETETM	some other time
OETFIE	rodent officer
OETFRT	moment of truth
OETICU	Robert Mitchum
OETISO	Robert Winston
OETLRC	Robert Aldrich
OETODR	Robert Goddard
OETOEE	potentiometer
OETOTE	Robert Southey
OETRDE	Robert Bridges
OETUDO	Robert Muldoon
OETUNS	momentousness
OEULCA	poke mullock at
OEUQOS	bone turquoise
OEUWTI	come out with it
OEYHBO	done by the book
OFAENT	confraternity
OFAGAL	Wolfgang Pauli
OFAKWT	Wolf Mankowitz
OFARTO	conflagration
OFBLTO	confabulation
OFCINR	confectionery
OFDRTO	confederation
OFGRTO	configuration
OFLILN	Norfolk Island
OFLIMN	non-fulfilment
OFLJCE	Norfolk jacket
OFNDOE	confined to bed
OFNTOA	non-functional
OFOTTO	confrontation
OFRETN	not forgetting
OFRMMN	not for a moment
OFTEAL	go off the rails
OFUDNL	confoundingly
OGADED	rough and ready
	rough-and-ready
OGEAGN	tongue-wagging
OGEAHN	tongue-lashing
OGENHE	tongue in cheek
	tongue-in-cheek
OGENLD	Roy Greenslade
OGESOA	congressional
	congresswoman
OGEWSE	tongue-twister
OGFOOO	Song of Solomon
OGIVLE	bougainvillea
OGNANS	congenialness
OGOADL	for good and all
OGOEOG	not good enough
OGOGTE	long-forgotten
OGORPI	zoogeographic
OGOTRT	do a good turn to
OGRMSU	Fogg Art Museum
OGRNPL	jogger's nipple
OGSELN	hot gospelling
OGTEIL	Rouget de Lisle
OGTGTE	not go together
OGTNSL	forget oneself
OGTUNS	forgetfulness
OGUFRN	long-suffering
OHAENS	hot-headedness
OHBCBN	to the backbone
OHCNRR	to the contrary
OHDSAC	go the distance
OHECOC	Sophie's Choice
OHERGO	Sophie Grigson
OHGETN	to a huge extent
OHLNTO	go the length of
OHMNCT	Ho Chi Minh City
OHNPTN	nothing patent
OHOGRA	no through road
OHOGWT	go through with
OHPOIO	to the profit of
OHRFER	mother-of-pearl
OHRHPO	Mother Shipton
OHRHRS	Mother Theresa
OHRONR	mother country
	mother-country
OHRTTR	nowhere to turn
OHSIAE	sophisticated
OHSIAL	sophistically
OHSOPN	do the shopping
OHTLRE	Roy Hattlersey
OHWOEO	go the whole hog
OIACNR	holiday centre
OIAIAL	nominatively
OIBOTT	Josip Broz Tito
OICMBL	Colin Campbell
OICOPN	logic-chopping
OIDGER	Louis Daguerre
OIDLEC	non-indulgence
OIEFIE	police officer
OIEIAL	homiletically
OIEOMN	polite comment
OIETTO	police station
OIGAKA	moving walkway
OIGOWR	moving forward
OIHHFO	go with the flow
OIHMHE	Doris Humphrey
OIHOSA	Robin Hood's Bay
OIIITO	domiciliation
OILBIS	bouillabaisse
OILHPE	Social Chapter
OILLME	social climber
OILOCR	social concern
OILOPC	social compact
OILOTC	social contact
OILSTO	socialisation
OILUCS	social outcast
OILZTO	socialization
OILZWT	socialize with
OIMCEC	Louis MacNeice
OIMEII	poliomyelitis
OIMIRT	sodium nitrate
OINITR	motion picture
OINSAD	Ionian Islands
OIOLZR	monitor lizard
OIOOIA	toxicological
OIOTLA	horizontal bar
OIOTLT	horizontality
OIPIIP	Louis Philippe
	Louis-Philippe
OIPITN	no oil painting
OIQAOZ	Louis-Quatorze
OITBEL	goliath beetle
OITINS	corinthianise
OITINZ	corinthianize

OITLGS	sovietologist
OITNAE	Coniston Water
OIWLIM	Robin Williams
OJCUAL	conjecturally
OJDMNA	non-judgmental
OJNTVL	conjunctively
OJYMMT	Yohji Yamamoto
OKAGRA	look daggers at
OKALRS	cocktail dress
OKALTC	cocktail stick
OKFHLF	cock of the loft
OKFHWL	cock of the walk
OKFOLN	Hook of Holland
OKHOAL	work the oracle
OKIPSR	pork-pie pastry
OKITRC	fork-lift truck
OKMRIN	Rocky Marciano
OKNHFC	look in the face
OKNPRO	working person
OKOHSI	soak to the skin
OKOWRT	look forward to
OKPCAG	cook up a charge
OKPNDW	look up and down
OKRELA	look briefly at
OKRPNE	cocker spaniel
OKTLSL	look at closely
OKTOOG	pocket borough
OKUCLA	look quickly at
OLADNS	foolhardiness
OLAHRN	woolgathering
	wool-gathering
OLAUDE	Roald Amundsen
OLBBTE	could be better
OLBRTN	collaborating
OLBRTO	collaboration
OLBRTV	collaborative
OLBUWT	fool about with
OLCDLN	mollycoddling
OLCENS	collectedness
OLDNON	rolled into one
OLERHN	soul-searching
OLFCTO	jollification
	mollification
OLGOAM	College of Arms
OLLMNE	worldly-minded
OLLNUG	world language
OLLWAT	worldly wealth
OLNAON	fooling around
OLNMNE	howling monkey
OLNSEL	cool one's heels
OLNSOE	Rolling Stones
OLPOEU	nolle prosequi
OLPRDS	fool's paradise
OLQILS	colloquialism
OLRKTN	roller-skating
OLROSE	rollercoaster
OLRZTO	dollarization
OLTEHE	roulette wheel
OLTHAE	would to heaven
OLWHEE	hollow-cheeked
OLWHOG	follow through
	follow-through
OLWLSL	follow closely
OLWREE	to a lower level
OLYALA	Sorley MacLean
OLYIKA	woolly milk cap
OMCTBA	too much to bear
OMDBLT	formidability
OMDCET	Tommy Docherty
OMFDRS	form of address
OMHLIE	Tommy Hilfiger
OMLEDC	formal verdict
OMLZTO	formalization
	normalization
OMMRTO	commemoration
OMMRTV	commemorative
OMNACI	Norman MacCaig
OMNASI	common caustic
OMNCTO	communication
OMNCTV	communicative
OMNERN	commandeering
OMNMDL	command module
OMNOKE	Norman Lockyer
OMNPNO	form an opinion
OMNROE	Norman Brookes
OMNSAI	worm one's way in
OMNSPA	Communism Peak
OMNTHM	community home
OMNTRA	communitarian
OMNTWR	community work
OMNUAL	commensurable
	commensurably
OMNUDC	common burdock
OMRILS	commercialise
	commercialism
OMRILT	commerciality
OMRILZ	commercialize
OMRYSK	for mercy's sake
OMSINN	commissioning
OMSRTN	commiserating
OMSRTO	commiseration
OMTEJR	commit perjury
OMTNSL	commit oneself
OMTRTW	dormitory town
OMTTVL	commutatively
OMTUCD	commit suicide
OMUHHR	Monmouthshire
ONAAWT	doing away with
ONADRS	point-and-press
ONAEIL	John Masefield
ONAKOT	John Dankworth
ONANAG	mountain range
ONANHG	mountains-high
ONCEWT	connected with
ONCIGO	connecting rod
ONCMRO	Mount Cameroon
ONEAKR	mountebankery
ONEAKS	mountebankism
ONEATC	counter-attack
ONEATO	counteraction
ONEATV	counteractive
ONECAG	countercharge
ONECSE	counter-caster
ONEFIE	counterfeiter
ONEFIL	counterfeitly
ONEGNE	sound engineer
ONEHOE	John Lee Hooker
ONEOBT	Ronnie Corbett
ONEOEA	Lonnie Donegan
ONETRA	born yesterday
ONEUNS	bounteousness
ONEWIH	counter-weight
ONFRSN	going for a song
ONGTAL	non-negotiable
ONHRZL	go on the razzle
ONILNE	John Dillinger
ONIUNS	bountifulness
ONLANE	Kornelia Ender
ONLMTE	John Flamsteed
ONLSNS	boundlessness
	countlessness
	pointlessness
	soundlessness
ONMKNE	Mount McKinley
ONNMNI	moaning minnie
ONNSRE	Downing Street
ONODAE	Dornford Yates
ONOEAL	go into details
ONOFNE	young offender
ONOHNU	point of honour
ONOHWR	down to the wire
ONOPSO	John Dos Passos
ONOSAL	John Constable
ONPRIG	doing porridge
ONRCUI	country cousin
ONRPRO	country person
ONRRAE	sooner or later
ONRSMR	Mount Rushmore
ONSELN	pound sterling
ONSHLN	Mount St Helens
ONSNRM	Down's syndrome
ONTELC	round the clock
	round-the-clock
ONTELR	sound the alarm
ONTEWS	round the twist
ONTHPE	bound to happen
ONTIBC	John Steinbeck
ONTPEE	going to pieces
ONTPSO	cornet-à-piston
ONTRLS	connaturalise
ONTRLZ	connaturalize
ONYMRE	Johnny H Mercer
ONYOOG	county borough
OOAOIE	Colorado River
OODBRE	no holds barred
	no-holds-barred
OODUPS	to good purpose
OOEAME	Honoré Daumier
OOEGNE	jow one's ginger
OOEMMR	jog one's memory
OOENSA	go someone's way
OOESOR	coroner's court
OOEUAL	go to regularly
OOEULT	homosexuality
OOEUPS	to some purpose
OOGRNS	no longer in use
OOHBTO	go to the bottom
OOHOAI	monochromatic
OOIIAL	honorifically

	sodomitically
OOIUNS	notoriousness
OOJRWT	to conjure with
OOLSOI	toxoplasmosis
OONELN	co-counselling
OONHTB	go down the tube
OONLNT	go to any length
OONNAU	go down in value
OOOAHN	Solon of Athens
OOOELF	not on one's life
OOOHRA	homoiothermal
OOOHRI	homoeothermic
OOOIAL	homologically
	topologically
OOOPOI	homomorphosis
OOOYEO	monocotyledon
OOOYOE	Monopoly money
OORBLT	honourability
OORHRP	colour therapy
OORMAI	monogrammatic
OORPIA	monographical
	topographical
OORUNS	colourfulness
OORZTO	colourization
OOSRAC	non-observance
OOTEAS	son of the manse
OOTEEL	hot on the heels
OOTEOL	top of the world
OOUATS	pococurantism
OOULOI	mononucleosis
OOUMNE	colobus monkey
OPANNL	complainingly
OPASNL	complaisantly
OPDBLE	corps de ballet
OPEEEC	for preference
OPEEFC	Doppler effect
OPEENS	complexedness
OPEESO	comprehension
OPEESV	comprehensive
OPEETN	complementing
OPEETR	complementary
OPENME	complex number
OPESDI	compressed air
OPIAIM	dolphinariums
OPIETR	complimentary
OPNAEO	compensate for
OPNCES	popping crease
	popping-crease
OPNIUL	compendiously
OPNNPR	component part
OPNOAL	companionable
	companionably
OPNOLS	companionless
OPNOSI	companionship
OPOEEI	morphogenesis
	morphogenetic
OPOHNM	morphophoneme
OPONTU	Compsognathus
OPOOIA	morphological
OPOUTV	non-productive
OPRBLT	comparability
OPRITN	non-persistent
OPRRME	copper trumpet
OPRTVL	comparatively
	co-operatively
OPRTWT	co-operate with
OPRYIE	copper pyrites
OPSHIT	Corpus Christi
OPSINT	compassionate
OPSNRO	composing room
OPSTNS	compositeness
OPSWNO	compass window
OPTBLT	compatibility
OPTRPA	computerspeak
OPTRRM	computer crime
OPTTOA	computational
OQAOAS	Torquato Tasso
OQITDR	conquistadors
ORADZN	gourmandizing
ORAEOE	pour water over
ORASAE	no great shakes
ORBRTO	corroboration
ORBRTV	corroborative
ORDBRI	Rodrido Borgia
OREFGI	yourself again
OREFTD	course of study
OREIHN	coarse fishing
OREUNS	courteousness
OREYIH	courtesy light
OREYIL	courtesy title
ORGBRI	Rodrigo Borgia
ORGRAC	non-regardance
ORGSEE	non-registered
ORIERS	Lorraine cross
ORIGOS	boarding-house
ORLTVL	correlatively
ORMRIL	court martials
ORMTTO	poor imitation
OROACE	Court of Arches
OROAPA	Court of Appeal
OROCAM	court of claims
ORORCR	court of record
ORPLTO	horripilation
ORRPRE	court reporter
ORSACN	morris dancing
ORSATA	courts martial
ORSODN	correspondent
	corresponding
ORSSAC	non-resistance
ORSVNS	corrosiveness
ORTCRN	Socratic irony
ORTEDN	door attendant
ORTRAL	non-returnable
ORWUNS	sorrowfulness
OSACSR	Constance Spry
OSADON	Horse and Hound
OSBEKN	housebreaking
	house-breaking
OSBLTE	possibilities
OSCETU	horse chestnut
OSCLUE	mouse-coloured
OSCTVL	consecutively
OSDRNL	consideringly
OSDRSA	consider usual
OSDRTL	considerately
OSDRTO	consideration
OSDTRE	topside-turvey
OSEILS	non-specialist
OSELTO	constellation
OSENTO	consternation
OSFAHR	horsefeathers
OSFEHR	horseflesh ore
OSFICE	sons of bitches
OSFOTO	loss of control
OSHCTS	Rorschach test
OSHLNM	household name
OSHLWR	household word
OSINIU	conscientious
OSIUNS	consciousness
OSIUUL	conspicuously
OSLDTO	consolidation
OSLDTV	consolidative
OSLETM	tonsillectomy
OSLFRU	fossiliferous
OSLSNS	noiselessness
OSLZTO	fossilization
OSMCEE	horse mackerel
OSMROD	consumer goods
OSMSRO	horse mushroom
OSMSRS	housemistress
	toastmistress
OSMTVL	consumptively
OSMTVT	consumptivity
OSNBOM	mops and brooms
OSNCOC	Hobson's choice
OSNEES	nonsense verse
OSNETT	housing estate
OSNIAL	nonsensically
OSNLVR	Sons and Lovers
OSNSHM	housing scheme
OSNUNS	poisonousness
OSNUNT	consanguinity
OSOFRE	Job's comforter
OSOPAE	house of prayer
OSOSAE	House of States
OSQETA	consequential
OSRAFS	dog's breakfast
OSRAOR	conservatoire
OSRCAL	constructable
OSRCIL	constructible
OSRIEL	constrainedly
OSRNEC	constringency
OSRPEO	boustrophedon
OSRUNS	monstrousness
OSSLIR	horse soldiers
OSSOAC	horseshoe arch
OSSOCA	horseshoe crab
OSWIPN	horsewhipping
OTAADS	contrabandist
OTAASO	contrabassoon
OTADAE	foot-land-raker
OTADOT	North and South
OTAETO	contraception
	contravention
OTAETV	contraceptive
OTAITN	contradicting
OTAITO	contradiction
OTAITR	contradictory
OTAMTE	for that matter

OTAOTN	worth a fortune
OTAPSO	contrappostos
OTARAO	for that reason
OTARHR	North Ayrshire
	South Ayrshire
OTASNC	postman's knock
OTAUTS	contrapuntist
OTCIAE	South China Sea
OTCIEC	poetic licence
OTCLNE	contact lenses
OTCLUA	horticultural
OTCRLN	North Carolina
	South Carolina
OTCUTC	poetic justice
OTECON	for the account
OTEEAL	root vegetable
OTEEDO	sow the seeds of
OTELNS	northerliness
OTENCA	Southern Ocean
OTENRS	Southern Cross
OTENRW	Northern Crown
	Southern Crown
OTEOPS	box the compass
OTERSN	for the present
OTESEL	north-easterly
	south-easterly
OTESWR	north-eastward
	south-eastward
OTETOI	don't mention it
OTFATR	Pott's fracture
OTFCTN	pontificating
OTFCTO	fortification
	mortification
OTFETV	cost-effective
OTFEWN	fortified wine
OTGCES	cottage cheese
OTIEHL	tortoiseshell☐
OTIELA	Fontainebleau
OTIESI	container ship
OTIRAO	for this reason
OTIUAL	contributable
OTIUIN	contributions
OTKPRI	not take part in
OTLEVC	postal service
OTLIAL	nostalgically
OTLSNS	worthlessness
OTLTRN	mortal-staring
OTLZBT	Port Elizabeth
OTMESI	bottomless pit
OTMLTO	contemplation
OTMLTV	contemplative
OTMNTN	contaminating
OTMNTO	contamination
OTMOTN	most important
OTNBAC	root and branch
	root-and-branch
OTNCOI	fortune cookie
OTNENS	contentedness
OTNHHA	soft in the head
OTNHNE	fortune-hunter
OTNHUH	lost in thought
OTNIKN	cotton-picking
OTNIUL	contentiously

OTNIYA	continuity man
OTNOOG	rotten borough
OTNSDL	boot and saddle
OTNTLE	fortune-teller
OTNYBE	Fontenay Abbey
OTOBIG	pontoon bridge
OTOCLM	control column
OTOENS	Post-Modernism
	Post-modernism
OTOESA	controversial
OTOESL	worth one's salt
OTPRTV	post-operative
OTRASU	Doctor Faustus
OTRHVG	Doctor Zhivago
OTRINS	contortionist
OTRRUI	Doctor Proudie
OTRSAT	poste restante
OTRVLE	foot-traveller
OTSEEI	montes veneris
OTSMNS	loathsomeness
OTUPLT	Pontius Pilate
OTWSEL	north-westerly
	south-westerly
OTWSWR	north-westward
OTWTRN	mouthwatering
	mouth-watering
OTXULS	contextualise
OTXULZ	contextualize
OUADAV	to cut and carve
OUBAIE	Columbia River
OUETRL	documentarily
OUETRS	documentarise
OUETRZ	documentarize
OUETTO	documentation
OUOEAD	modus operandi
OUOFCA	bogus official
OUOTEA	go out of the way
OUPSTO	lotus position
OUSALR	rogues' gallery
OUTNNE	locum tenentes
OVLSEC	convalescence
OVNETO	convenient for
OVRAIN	conversazioni
OVRAPO	Wolverhampton
OVRHEG	go over the edge
OVRIWT	go over big with
OVRTCS	convert to cash
OVSETN	to a vast extent
OWRHDM	not worth a damn
OWRHIL	Bosworth Field
OWTRRS	hot-water crust
OYABNT	polycarbonate
OYARMN	Holy Matrimony
	holy matrimony
OYASNE	body mass index
OYFUPR	body of support
OYHOAI	polychromatic
OYHSUU	Corythosaurus
OYIHAL	copyrightable
OYNEWO	Rory Underwood
OYNOET	Holy Innocents
OYOMNO	Holy Communion
OYRPLN	polypropylene

PAHGLO	speak highly of
PAIGLC	speaking clock
PAOEMN	speak one's mind
PAPITN	spray-painting
PATROI	splatter movie
PCABAC	Special Branch
PCAFIN	special friend
PCAOSI	spectatorship
PCASHO	special school
PCAUAL	spectacularly
PCFCTO	specification
PCLPEO	Apocalypse Now
PCLTVL	speculatively
PCRGAH	spectrography
PCRMTI	spectrometric
PDCIAL	apodictically
PEAPUL	appel au peuple
PEDFRU	splendiferous
PEDHOG	spread through
PEDHWR	spread the word
PEDRMU	spread a rumour
PEDUCL	spread quickly
PEDUOR	spread rumours
PEEIAL	splenetically
PEHHRP	speech therapy
PEIANS	sphericalness
PELTVL	appellatively
PEMRHN	speed merchant
PEODCT	spheroidicity
PERFEI	appear often in
PETIMN	appertainment
PEYSMT	Upper Yosemite
PGAMTS	epigrammatise
PGAMTZ	epigrammatize
PIGAAC	spring balance
PIGHCE	spring chicken
PIGQIO	spring equinox
PIHEUL	uprighteously
PIHLNS	sprightliness
PIOEEI	epeirogenesis
PIOEVT	split one's vote
PITAAU	optic thalamus
PITRRO	splinter-proof
PITRRU	splinter group
PKMLIA	Spike Milligan
PKSESN	spokespersons
PLCBLT	applicability
PLDMLN	apple dumpling
PLOHAR	Apollo Theatre
PLOOIA	speleological
PLOTEY	apple of the eye
PLTEEN	spill the beans
PLTNAE	Appleton layer
PMCIAL	apomictically
PNABLE	Spandau Ballet
PNAEUL	spontaneously
PNATAE	spiny anteater
PNCILN	spine-chilling
PNDPOE	epanadiploses
PNETAE	Spencer Tracey
PNEUDN	sponge pudding
PNHBTL	spin the bottle
PNHDOT	open the door to

PNIGEN	spinning-jenny
PNIGHE	spinning-wheel
PNIGOE	spending money
PNLSNS	spinelessness
PNNGMI	opening gambit
PNSIAL	epinastically
PNTMWT	spend time with
POADWL	Epsom and Ewell
POHEBW	up to the elbows
POHMMN	up to the moment
	up-to-the-moment
POHMNT	up to the minute
	up-to-the-minute
POHSON	up to this point
POHTMO	up to the time of
POKTHE	sprocket wheel
POSNLI	Upton Sinclair
POTNNS	opportuneness
POTNSI	opportunistic
POTOMN	apportionment
PPEOEO	epiphenomenon
PRAOHR	spermatophore
PRAOHT	spermatophyte
PRBIUL	opprobriously
PRCPCT	spare capacity
PRHASO	a Parthian shot
PRPITL	appropriately
PRPITO	appropriation
PRPITT	appropriate to
PRSALK	sportsmanlike
PRSASI	sportsmanship
PRTAIE	spiritualizer
PRTANS	spiritualness
PRTOSL	spirits of salt
PRTOWN	spirits of wine
PRTVNS	operativeness
PRXMTL	approximately
PRXMTN	approximating
PRXMTO	approximation
PRXMTT	approximate to
PSLSRE	Apostles' Creed
PSOIAL	apostolically
	spasmodically
PTAMLG	ophthalmology
PTEIAL	apathetically
PTEIMT	epitheliomata
PTEMTS	apothegmatise
PTEMTZ	apothegmatize
PTIGMG	spitting image
PUTNNE	appurtenances
PUTRNL	splutteringly
PYMGAH	sphygmography
QADRNL	squanderingly
QAEACN	square-dancing
QAEAHN	square-bashing
QAERCE	square bracket
QEMSNS	squeamishness
QETINS	equestrianism
QEUHMU	aqueous humour
QEZBLT	squeezability
QIALNS	equitableness
QIITNL	equidistantly
QIODRT	equiponderate
QIOTAL	equinoctially
RAADRO	trial and error
	trial-and-error
RAAESR	tread a measure
RAALNS	breakableness
RABALK	Great Bear Lake
RABLTR	preambulatory
RABRCR	trial by record
RACLUE	cream-coloured
RADSAC	great distance
RADSRC	urban district
RAELNO	Greater London
RAENME	greater number
RAETTO	ornamentation
RAFEFO	break free from
RAGLRT	triangularity
RAGLTL	triangulately
RAGLTO	triangulation
RAHESL	breathe easily
RAHFEL	breathe freely
RAHFRS	breach of trust
RAHNAA	Brian Hanrahan
RAHROK	Brian Horrocks
RAHRUL	treacherously
RAIGAT	breaking faith
RAINLS	irrationalise
RAINLT	irrationality
RAINLZ	irrationalize
RALKDR	treat like dirt
RALKSI	treat like shit
RALUEC	Friar Laurence
RAMLOE	Brian Mulroney
RAMNEL	broadmindedly
RAOEWR	break one's word
RAOIAL	triatomically
RAONTR	freak of nature
RAOTEY	trial of the pyx
RAOTRA	cream of tartar
RASLLK	Great Salt Lake
RATEAL	break the balls
RATHTP	breast the tape
RAUERV	treasure-trove
RAUESI	treasurership
RAUETR	treasure-store
RAUOEG	tread upon eggs
RAUWSE	great unwashed
RAUYEC	Treasury bench
RAVCOI	Great Victoria
RAYFHN	Treaty of Ghent
RAYFOE	Treaty of Dover
RAYROT	Great Yarmouth
RAZMAW	Great Zimbabwe
RBADRB	dribs and drabs
RBANGT	Arabian Nights
RBBLTE	probabilities
RBEAIA	problematical
RBUMRE	cry blue murder
RCALNS	tractableness
RCATIG	Eric Partridge
RCATNT	procrastinate
RCHNCE	Erich Honecker
RCIAJK	practical joke
RCIANS	practicalness
RCIKAE	Eric Linklater
RCINLS	fractionalise
	fractionalist
RCINLZ	fractionalize
RCINTO	fractionation
RCISUU	brachiosaurus ❑
RCIUNS	fractiousness
RCLCAG	trickle-charge
RCLSNS	gracelessness
	pricelessness
RCNETO	preconception
RCNLGS	arachnologist
RCNPOI	arachnophobia
RCODIL	Bruce Oldfield
RCOEOB	Eric Morecombe
RCOOIA	trichological
RCOSEA	precious metal
RCOSTN	precious stone
RCOTAU	fractostratus
RCOTRU	trichopterous
RCOUUU	fractocumulus
RCPTNL	precipitantly
RCPTTL	precipitately
RCPTTO	precipitation
RCPTUL	precipitously
RCRMRU	Erich Remarque
RCRMTS	trichromatism
RCSEBU	procès-verbaux
RCUINR	precautionary
RDCOSN	grade crossing
RDCTVL	predicatively
RDDSON	trade discount
RDEFOT	bridge of boats
RDEHOG	trudge through
RDEREE	fridge-freezer
RDEULE	bridge-builder
RDLUNS	credulousness
RDMNNL	predominantly
RDNETT	trading estate
RDRCJN	Frederick Jane
RDRCPG	Frederick Page
RDRKHV	Frederikshavn
RDTIMH	Arc de Triomphe
RDTOAL	gradationally
	traditionally
RDTQEZ	credit squeeze
RDTRIE	predetermined
RDTRNS	predatoriness
RDUINS	trade unionism
	trade unionist
RDWTRA	Bridgwater Bay
RECNLC	armed conflict
REEACE	irrelevancies
REEETA	irreverential
REEHOG	breeze through
REEONS	Graeme Souness
REHODN	breech-loading
REHUEA	greenhouse gas
REIGON	freezing point
REIINS	irreligionist
REIIUL	irreligiously
REIPSN	true-disposing
RELCAL	irreplaceable

	irreplaceably
RELIAL	irreclaimable
	irreclaimably
RENSER	dree one's weird
REOBTL	order of battle
REOEAL	irrecoverable
	irrecoverably
REOEET	order of events
REOPNO	free companion
REOTEA	order of the day
REPNIL	irresponsible
	irresponsibly
REREAL	irretrievable
	irretrievably
RERNIL	irrefrangibly
RERSIL	irrepressible
	irrepressibly
RESRCE	grief-stricken
RETFRU	argentiferous
RETRTR	order to return
REWTEV	green with envy
RFGRTO	prefiguration
RFIWRE	traffic warden
RFMYEK	Trofim Lysenko
RFRHMO	cry for the moon
RFRHRE	prefer charges
RFSASI	craftsmanship
RFTBLT	profitability
RFTHRN	profit-sharing
RFTRAL	prefatorially
RGAIAL	pragmatically
RGEEDN	drug-dependent
RGEFNE	trigger finger
RGESVL	progressively
RGESVS	progressivism
	progressivist
RGETRL	fragmentarily
RGETTO	fragmentation
RGMGLN	drug-smuggling
RGNSEL	drag one's heels
RGOTCT	prognosticate
RGOYIA	troglodytical
RGRPNU	Gregory Pincus
RGTNNL	frighteningly
RGTUNS	frightfulness
RHBTVL	prohibitively
RHDAOA	archidiaconal
RHELGS	archaeologist
RHEMTI	archaeometric
RHEPEY	archaeopteryx
RHGAHS	orthographist
RHIHPI	archbishopric
RHMHPA	Graham Chapman
RHMNRT	archimandrite
RHMOLC	Graham Pollock
RHPLGE	archipelagoes
RHRAFU	Arthur Balfour
RHRAKA	Arthur Rackham
RHRAOT	or thereabouts
RHRASM	Arthur Ransome
RHRCAK	Arthur C Clarke
RHRIBU	Arthur Rimbaud
RHROPO	Arthur Compton
RHSOIA	prehistorical
RHSRLS	orchestralist
RHSRTO	orchestration
RHTCOI	architectonic
RHTCUA	architectural
RIALNS	irritableness
RIANME	ordinal number
RIAYRD	Ordinary grade
RICAGF	Erwin Chargaff
RICCTI	fruit cocktail
RICIDE	brainchildren
RIEISL	cruise missile□
RIEOTO	cruise control
RIEPRO	trainee period
RIEWIH	cruiserweight
RIHLGS	ornithologist
RIHLSE	Ornitholestes
RIHSHA	ornithischian
RIIGLN	trailing plant
RIIILS	artificialise
RIIILT	artificiality
RIIILZ	artificialize
RILSNS	brainlessness
	fruitlessness
RILWIH	Orville Wright
RIOECA	trail one's coat
RIPNFK	Erwin Panofsky
RIPSIL	fruit pastille
RIRRNS	arbitrariness
RISOMN	brainstorming
RISOTN	Trainspotting
	train-spotting
RJCINS	projectionist
RJDCAL	prejudicially
RJNCLM	Trajan's Column
RKNERE	brokenhearted
	broken-hearted
RLELZR	frilled lizard
RLFRTO	proliferation
RLFRUL	proliferously
RLGMNR	prolegomenary
RLGMNU	prolegomenous
RLMNRE	preliminaries
RLMNRL	preliminarily
RLNULS	trilingualism
RLONAN	Ural Mountains
RLPIAL	proleptically
RLTRLS	trilateralism
	trilateralist
RMAGAS	crème anglaise
RMAIAL	grammatically
RMDCTO	premedication
RMDMNH	crème de menthe
RMDTTO	premeditation
RMDTTV	premeditative
RMEESA	trumpeter swan
RMGAIA	primigravidae
	primigravidas
RMGNTR	primogenitary
	primogeniture
RMGNTV	primogenitive
RMHWRG	from the word go
RMLPAE	from all places
RMLUNS	tremulousness
RMMNSE	prime minister
RMMRDA	prime meridian
RMNAIU	frumentarious
RMNDDC	promenade deck
RMNLGS	criminologist
RMNLOL	criminal world
RMNLOR	criminal court
RMNSAL	trim one's sails
RMNTRL	premonitorily
RMNVRU	graminivorous
RMPUPR	drum up support
RMRILT	primordiality
RMRSHO	primary school
RMRSRS	primary stress
RMSBEC	promise-breach
RMSUUL	promiscuously
RMTCRN	dramatic irony
RMTRIA	dramaturgical
RMTVNS	primitiveness
RMTZTO	dramatization
RNAAIE	drunk as a piper
RNAEBC	Frank Auerbach
RNAEFR	truncated form
RNALNI	transatlantic
RNATND	transactinide
RNCITO	transcription
RNCITV	transcriptive
RNCNEC	transcendence
	transcendency
RNDUHE	granddaughter
RNEARC	Prince Maurice
RNEASE	Prince Nasseem
RNECSL	Arundel Castle
RNEEEI	fringe benefit
RNEFAE	Prince of Wales
RNEFEC	Prince of Peace
RNEHAR	fringe theatre
RNEIEC	Grande Dixence
RNEMTE	printed matter
RNEOOT	grande cocotte
RNEOSR	prince consort
RNESOA	Princess Royal
RNEWLE	fringe-dweller
RNFRAL	transferrable
	transformable
RNFSVL	transfusively
RNFTEL	grandfatherly
RNGESO	transgression
RNGESV	transgressive
RNHAEL	wrong-headedly
RNHAFR	trench warfare
RNHNUT	bring honour to
RNHRCE	French cricket
RNHRTE	French Trotter
RNIAEU	arundinaceous
RNIAPR	principal part
RNIGLO	Francis Galton
RNIGLS	drinking-glass
RNIGRO	printing error
RNIGRS	printing press
RNIHWR	Frankie Howerd
RNIINR	transitionary

RNIJSP	Francis Joseph
RNILUG	transit lounge
RNIOUN	grandiloquent
RNIOUU	grandiloquous
RNITLN	bring in to land
RNITPA	bring into play
RNITRS	transistorise
RNITRZ	transistorize
RNIXVE	Francis Xavier
RNLCDT	translucidity
RNLCNL	translucently
RNLCTO	translocation
RNLTOA	translational
RNLTRT	transliterate
RNMGAO	transmigrator
RNMSIL	transmissible
RNMTAL	transmittable
RNMTEL	grandmotherly
RNMTTO	transmutation
RNNBAI	grin and bear it
RNNEAU	ordnance datum
RNNEEO	ordnance depot
RNNITO	pronunciation
RNNSER	pruning-shears
RNNTOA	Grand National
	transnational
RNOEEI	frontogenesis
RNOFRN	drink offering
RNOUJA	Franjo Tudjman
RNPATN	transplanting
RNPRAC	transportance
RNPRAL	transportable
RNPRCF	transport café
RNPREL	transportedly
RNPRNL	transparently
RNPROA	transpersonal
RNPRTO	transpiration
RNPSTO	transposition
RNSASI	brinksmanship
RNSHBR	Franz Schubert
RNSLCT	bring solace to
RNTALS	bring to a close
RNTGTE	bring together
RNTSNA	Trinity Sunday
RNUCAL	pronounceable
RNUCMN	pronouncement
RNULIE	tranquilliser
	tranquillizer
RNUTDT	bring up to date
	bring up-to-date
RNVRAL	transversally
RNWDKN	Frank Wedekind
RNWLIM	Frank Williams
RNWYON	wrong way round
RNYLSE	granny glasses
RNYSAD	Orkney Islands
ROCPTO	preoccupation
RODENT	Arnold Bennett
RODNTO	preordination
RODONE	Arnold Toynbee
ROEHNA	try one's hand at
ROELCA	try one's luck at
ROEOOG	Brookeborough
ROEUNS	erroneousness
ROILGS	cryobiologist
ROIUTR	arboriculture
ROOIAL	ergonomically
RORFRO	armour of proof
ROTELO	crook the elbow
RPAAYI	cryptanalysis
RPCLTR	tropical storm
RPEIAL	prophetically
RPEINS	propheticness
RPENET	Triple Entente
RPEODO	prophet of doom
RPHAIT	grape hyacinth
RPICPO	proprioceptor
RPITRA	proprietorial
RPLNHO	grappling-hook
RPLNIO	grappling-iron
RPNEAC	preponderance
RPNIAI	propanoic acid
RPOIAI	propionic acid
RPOOIA	graphological
RPORPE	cryptographer
RPORPI	cryptographic
RPRINT	proportionate
RPRTRL	preparatorily
RPRTRT	preparatory to
RPRTVL	preparatively
RPRYGN	property agent
RPSESN	prepossessing
RPSTOA	prepositional
RPSTVL	prepositively
RPZATS	trapeze artist
	trapeze-artist
RQERUL	triquetrously
RQETTV	frequentative
RRGTVL	prerogatively
RRPALT	Pre-Raphaelite
RRQIIE	prerequisites
RSAAAS	fresh as a daisy
RSAATA	grasp at a straw
RSAGZN	crystal-gazing
RSAIAL	prismatically
RSALNI	prostaglandin
RSAPLC	Crystal Palace
RSASRW	grasp at straws
RSBEDN	cross-breeding
RSCAER	trisoctahedra
RSCLUA	cross-cultural
RSCTIE	prosecutrices
	prosecutrixes
RSDESN	cross-dressing
RSECEU	crossed cheque
RSETKL	dressed to kill
RSETVL	prospectively
RSEUTO	arms reduction
RSFRHN	brass farthing
RSGMRC	Ernst Gombrich
RSGREE	cross-gartered
RSHFMN	Ernst Hoffmann
RSIGAL	dressing-table
RSIGLC	trysting-place
RSLBTC	Ernst Lubitsch
RSLNWT	bristling with
RSLTZN	proselytizing
RSMTVL	presumptively
RSNCAT	Arts and Crafts
RSNFIE	prison officer
RSNISL	present itself
RSNRFA	prisoner of war
RSNTEA	Arms and the Man
RSNTEO	Arms and the Boy
RSOCNA	press of canvas
RSOEMN	cross one's mind
RSPGAH	prosopography
RSQETO	cross-question
RSRTNL	frustratingly
RSTELO	cross the floor
RSTELS	press the flesh
RSTGTE	press together
RSUEAG	pressure gauge
RSUEIU	très au sérieux
RSUEON	pressure point
RSUERU	pressure group
RSWRHL	trustworthily
RTBRNL	protuberantly
RTCINS	protectionist
RTCLON	critical point
RTCLTO	graticulation
RTEEAA	frittered away
RTEKEE	brothel-keeper
RTELLV	brotherly love
RTELNS	brotherliness
RTESIA	tritheistical
RTESNA	brothers-in-law
RTFCTO	gratification
RTLZTO	brutalization
RTMTCA	arithmetician
RTNIUL	pretentiously
RTOENM	write one's name
RTRAUA	preternatural
RTRSOI	urethroscopic
RTSATS	Protestantise
	Protestantism
RTSATZ	Protestantize
RTSLUL	protest loudly
RTSMSU	British Museum
RTSUNS	grotesqueness
RUAIAL	traumatically
RUANRS	Ursula Andress
RUDNMC	group dynamics
RUDRAE	groundbreaker
	ground-breaker
RUETTO	argumentation
RUETTV	argumentative
RUHSOA	draughtswoman
RULMKN	troublemaking
RULSML	troublesomely
RUPAAC	triumphal arch
RUPATC	group practice
RUTGTE	group together
RVCTVL	provocatively
RVFUTI	Trevi Fountain
RVLANE	travel-tainted
RVLESO	traveller's joy
RVLEYN	Greville Wynne
RVLHOG	travel through

RVLIGA	travelling bag
RVLOAD	travel towards
RVNILS	provincialise
	provincialism
	provincialist
RVNILT	provinciality
RVNILZ	provincialize
RVNWOL	Brave New World
RVRCTN	prevaricating
RVRCTO	prevarication
RVRILS	proverbialise
RVRILZ	proverbialize
RVSOAL	provisionally
RVTICM	private income
RVTMTE	private matter
RVTPYE	private pay bed
RVTSCO	private sector
RVTSHO	private school
RVTTOA	gravitational
RVTZTO	privatization
RWARMR	Drew Barrymore
RWCCTI	prawn cocktail
RWEEWT	draw level with
RWEHOG	browse through
RWHLNA	draw the line at
RWHOMN	growth hormone
RWIEOS	grow like Topsy
RWIGIE	Brownie Guider
RWIGLR	crowning glory
RWIGON	crowning point
RWIPRA	crown imperial
RWNSLU	draw oneself up
RWPICS	crown princess
RWVIOE	draw a veil over
RYLNBT	Argyll and Bute
RYNMNI	praying mantis
RYRUNS	prayerfulness
RYSRNM	X-ray astronomy
RZFGTN	prizefighting
	prize-fighting
SAAORA	use as a doormat
SADOPN	island-hopping
SAGALF	as large as life
SALAAM	assault at arms
SALCUS	assault course
SALNGP	Israel in Egypt
SALOAM	assault of arms
SALOTN	a small fortune
SALSAL	establishable
SALSMN	establishment ❑
SAPTRO	Oscar Peterson
SASNTO	assassination
SCIPWR	psychic powers
SCOEEI	psychogenesis
	psychogenetic
SCOERC	psychometrics
SCOHRP	psychotherapy
SCONLS	psychoanalyse
	psychoanalyst
SCOOAI	psychosomatic
SCOOIA	psychological
SCOUGR	psychosurgery
SCOYAI	psychodynamic
SCRNUL	isochronously
SDMRHS	isodimorphism
SDMRHU	isodimorphous
SDRDNA	Isadora Duncan
SEMEII	osteomyelitis
SEOSIL	Isles of Scilly
SESBLT	ostensibility
SESRPE	asset-stripper
SETAPR	essential part
SETIAL	ascertainable
SETIMN	ascertainment
SETIWL	Osbert Sitwell
SETNSL	assert oneself
SETOLV	Aspects of Love
SETVNS	assertiveness
SFROSL	ask for noisily
SFRRUL	ask for trouble
SHAIAL	asthmatically
SHCOTI	eschscholtzia
SHNSHR	asthenosphere
SHTLGS	eschatologist
SICITM	a stitch in time
SIEOAD	aspire towards
SIEYSO	as likely as not
SIIAEI	assimilated in
SIUUNS	assiduousness
SMTIAL	isometrically
SNADAC	a song and dance
SNOELA	using one's loaf
SOIHNL	astonishingly
SOITER	a shot in the arm
SOITWT	associate with
SOTIEG	a short time ago
SPOOIA	psephological
SRCTMT	astrocytomata
SRNEFC	user interface
SRPYIA	astrophysical
SRTEOP	esprit de corps
SSAIAL	isostatically
STOLSE	as it would seem
SUOOPI	pseudomorphic
SUSIAL	use unsuitably
SYILGS	Assyriologist
TAAACO	steal a march on
TAEIAL	strategically
TAFSNS	steadfastness
TAGLTO	strangulation
TAGTAE	straight-faced
TAGTIH	straight fight
	straight-pight
TAGTNL	straight angle
TAGTNN	straightening
TAGTNU	straighten out
TAGTOT	straightforth
TAIRPE	stratigrapher
TAIRPI	stratigraphic
TANBLT	attainability
TANNSL	strain oneself
TAOPEI	stratospheric
TAOUUU	stratocumulus
TBLZTO	stabilization
TBNHBC	stab in the back
TCAISM	staccatissimo
TCECAG	stock exchange
TCIGON	sticking-point
TCITEU	stick-in-the-mud
TCOTML	stick out a mile
TCTGTE	stick together
TEAIAL	athematically
TECAON	stretch a point
TECLUE	steel-coloured
TEESRS	St Peter's cross
TEGHNN	strengthening
TEIGHE	steering-wheel
TELCAE	steeplechaser
TESIAL	atheistically
TETAKN	street-walking
TETCCA	streptococcal
TETCCI	streptococcic
TETCCU	streptococcus
TETHAR	street theatre
TETVNS	attentiveness
TEUUNS	strenuousness
TEWYON	other way round
TFODHR	Staffordshire
TFSREN	staff sergeant
TFTRDT	at a future date
TFTRTM	at a future time
TGAIAL	stigmatically
TGLMUS	Stig Blomquist
THBHSO	at the behest of
THBTOO	at the bottom of
THCAFC	at the coalface
THCNRL	at the controls
THKELA	Itzhak Perlman
THMDON	at the midpoint
THRNTC	at short notice
THSAPN	at the sharp end
THSMTM	at the same time
TIAVLE	ethical values
TIEHBA	strike the beam
TIEHOG	strike through
TIGNNS	stringentness
TIGURE	string quartet
TIHAGE	at right angles
TIHOER	stoichiometry
TIITTE	it pitieth them
TILGTN	strip lighting
TILSNS	stainlessness
TIUIIE	attitudinizer
TLAIBN	Stella Gibbons
TLCZTO	italicization
TLSIES	Still's disease
TLTRLC	at a later place
TMLARS	stumble across
TMNFRU	staminiferous
TMSIAL	atomistically
TNADAG	standard gauge
TNADRD	Standard grade
TNADRO	standard error
TNCNRS	ethnocentrism
	ethnocentrist
TNDATG	at an advantage
TNEMLE	Stanley Miller
TNFIWT	stand fair with
TNIGNO	standing in for

Words marked ❑ can also be spelled with an initial capital letter

TNIGOU	standing to sue
TNIGRE	standing order
TNIGTN	standing stone
TNLNUS	ethnolinguist
TNODOR	Stanford Moore
TNOEHN	stand one's hand
TNOFNO	stand off and on
TNOLMR	Stan Collymore
TNSESR	at one's leisure
TNSEVC	at one's service
TNSISN	at one's wits' end
TNSOMN	at one's command
TNTERW	stone the crows
	stone the crows!
TNTGTE	stand together
TNTRAO	stand to reason
TOEOSS	Ettore Sotsass
TOEPRE	Otto Jespersen
TOEUAT	Ettore Bugatti
TOGELN	strong feeling
TOGRED	at loggerheads
TOIUNS	atrociousness
TOLMEE	Otto Klemperer
TONOSL	at point of sale
TOOIAL	ethologically
TOPEIA	atmospherical
TORMNE	Otto Preminger
TOXRCS	at no extra cost
TPAETN	step-parenting
TPEFER	Stephen Frears
TPEFSE	Stephen Foster
TPEHNR	Stephen Hendry
TPIGLC	stopping-place
TPIGTN	stepping-stone
TPNSAC	stop-and-search
TPTOHN	stop at nothing
TPUOLN	step out of line
TPYOOC	staphylococci
TRBTVL	attributively
TRCSUU	Styracosaurus
TREPPI	Sturmer Pippin
TRFRMS	stern-foremost
TRGDVC	storage device
TRGHAE	storage heater
TRHPSU	stir the possum
TRIGAG	Stirling Range
TRIGGI	starting again
TRIGON	starting point
	starting-point
TRIGRC	starting price
TRITNL	stare intently
TRLSTO	sterilisation
TRLZTO	sterilization
TROAEU	stercoraceous
TROEML	star-nosed mole
TROYIA	stereotypical
TSADTL	at a standstill
TSALPC	at a snail's pace
TSLUWT	it is all up with
TTERLE	State Enrolled
TTOHAT	state of health
TTORPI	state of repair
TTOTER	state of the art
	state-of-the-art
TTSALK	statesmanlike
TTSASI	statesmanship
TTSIAL	statistically
TTTBRE	statute-barred
TUTRLS	structuralism
	structuralist
TVDNGU	Steve Donoghue
TVRDRV	Steve Redgrave
TWRILN	Stewart Island
TWTISA	St Swithin's Day
TYHCUS	stay the course
TYTTHN	stay stitching
UADAEE	sugar diabetes
UAHAUO	put a cheat upon
UAIAYU	lunatic asylum
UAICRO	Judas Iscariot
UAIFIG	lunatic fringe
UAIHSI	run a tight ship
UAITRS	human interest
UAIUNS	audaciousness
UALSEO	put a plaster on
UAMDTM	Muhammad's Tomb
UAONAN	Jura Mountains
UAOTRN	put a foot wrong
UARMUO	put a premium on
UASIAL	Judaistically
UBBREE	Busby Berkeley
UBEHME	bubble-chamber
UBENSL	humble oneself
UBFOBL	rugby football
UBHNBR	put behind bars
UBRRCE	numbers racket
UCAGMN	surchargement
UCAIUA	subclavicular
UCASEE	quick-answered
UCCLNA	Dutch Colonial
UCESRO	butcher's broom
UCIELE	Punchinelloes
UCIIUL	punctiliously
UCINLS	functionalism
	functionalist
UCNLGS	vulcanologist
UCNRCO	subcontractor
UCNZTO	vulcanization
UCSLSL	successlessly
UCTIKN	quick-thinking
UCTMEE	quick-tempered
UCWTEL	quick-wittedly
UDAEIA	quadragesimal
UDAERS	quadrate cross
UDAHNC	quadraphonics
UDDISL	guided missile
UDEHOG	muddle through
UDENAL	quadrennially
UDEWIH	hundredweight
UDFCTV	mundificative
UDIAEA	quadrilateral
UDIATT	quadripartite
UDILOT	quadrillionth
UDMNAL	fundamentally
UDNFRO	burden of proof
UDOHNC	quadrophonics
UDRILU	murder will out
UDRUNS	murderousness
UDRYTR	murder mystery
UDULCT	quadruplicate
UDULTM	quadruple time
UDVSOA	subdivisional
UDWTSZ	cut down to size
UEADTO	superaddition
UEAGII	iure sanguinis
UEANAE	superannuated
UEAUDN	superabundant
UECLNE	supercalender
UECLTO	tuberculation
UECMUE	supercomputer
UEEEDW	quietened down
UEEFAO	Eugene of Savoy
UEEGTO	Sune Bergström
UEEOEC	Eugène Ionesco
UEFCAL	superficially
UEFHRA	rule of the road
UEFNSL	sure of oneself
UEFTTO	superfetation
UEFUDT	superfluidity
UEFUUL	superfluously
UEHBIE	Outer Hebrides
UEHMNS	superhumanise
UEHMNZ	superhumanize
UEHTIL	June Whitfield
UEICNI	Duke Vincentio
UEIEOR	juvenile court
UEIKYA	numeric keypad
UEILAI	Queenie Leavis
UEKDBO	Zuleika Dobson
UELFRU	Jules Laforgue
UELIGO	Duke Ellington
UELTVL	superlatively
UEMCEE	Jules Michelet
UEMSEE	Jules Massenet
UENMRR	supernumerary
UENRAL	supernormally
UENSIE	tune one's pipes
UENSML	pure and simple
UENTRA	gubernatorial
UEODNT	superordinate
UEOOIA	numerological
UEOTEA	Queen of the May
UEPAIO	put emphasis on
UEPICR	Jules Poincaré
UEPYIA	superphysical
UERDRC	Duke Frederick
UESADU	Queensland nut
UESIIN	superstitions
UESIIU	superstitious
UESMER	supersymmetry
UESNIL	supersensibly
UESNLS	Queen's English
UESOLG	Queens' College
UESONE	Queen's Counsel
UESTRT	supersaturate
UETEIC	queer the pitch
UETEUG	Hubert de Burgh
UETUDC	Rupert Murdoch
UEURTS	bureaucratise

UEURTZ bureaucratize
UEWKNN rude awakening
UFAETS suffragettism
UFCATV surface-active
UFCETO sufficient for
UFCTNL suffocatingly
UGAIUL burglariously
UGASUY Aung San Suu Kyi
UGEAFR jungle warfare
UGEUPN bungee jumping
UGOBRN burgh of barony
UGRACE hunger-marcher
UGRTIE hunger-striker
UGRZTO vulgarization
UGSINS suggestionise
UGSINZ suggestionize
UGSISL suggest itself
UGTCON budget account
UHATKL Hugh Gaitskell
UHEERP bush telegraph
UHHBTL push the bottle
UHHBTO push the button
UHIGML Hugh Kingsmill
UHILNL rush violently
UHNIAE authenticated
UHNIAL authentically
UHNIAO authenticator
UHOHWL push to the wall
UHOMLU mushroom cloud
UHPASE push up daisies
UHRODU rutherfordium
UHRTRA authoritarian
UHRTTV authoritative
UHRUBN Luther Burbank
UHRZTO authorization
UIACAR musical chairs
UIACMD musical comedy
UIAEAC put in abeyance
UIAIAL puritanically
UIAURL audita querela
UIBRHL Julie Burchill
UIESOA businesswoman
UIETRL rudimentarily
UIGASO ruling passion
UIGVSA Sunil Gavaskar
UIIRVR auxiliary verb
UIIUNS judiciousness
UIJOAD put in jeopardy
UILHME burial chamber
UILNMT pusillanimity
UILNMU pusillanimous
UINECO fusion reactor
UIOOIA musicological
UIOYAA auditory canal
UIOYEV auditory nerve
UIPSTO put in position
UIPUEC jurisprudence
UIRUNS ludicrousness
UISXLO Julius Axelrod
UISYRR Julius Nyerere
UITATO put into action
UITEFC put into effect
UITEHD put in the shade
UITELO run in the blood
UITERN put in the wrong
UITGTE put it together
UITPEE cut into pieces
UIVSAL audiovisually
UJCMTE subject matter
UJNTVL subjunctively
UKHMNE suck the monkey
UKSAGR Turkish Angora
UKSCFE Turkish coffee
UKYUTR turkey vulture
UKYUZR turkey buzzard
ULAEEG nuclear energy
ULAFML nuclear family
ULAFSO nuclear fusion
ULAWAO nuclear weapon
ULAWNE nuclear winter
ULCEVN public servant
ULCFAR public affairs
ULCNUR public inquiry
ULCOIA public holiday
ULCOPN public company
ULCPAE public speaker
ULCTLT public utility
ULCYNW publicly known
ULETNN sublieutenant
ULFCTO nullification
qualification
ULFCTR qualificatory
ULFITR Mull of Kintyre
ULFNSL full of oneself
ULHPUO pull the plug on
ULIGLC building block
ULKAIH out like a light
ULLNFC pull a long face
ULLSNS guilelessness
guiltlessness
ULLVUE full-flavoured
ULNETO fuel-injection
ULOHBI full to the brim
ULSIAL dualistically
ULSONE sur les pointes
ULSUAC full assurance
ULTNOR bulletin board
ULTOLF quality of life
ULTTVL qualitatively
ULWYOT pull a wry mouth
UMCIEU submachine-gun
UMCMAD summa cum laude
UMFCTO mummification
UMGAON rummage around
UMRCAE turmeric paper
UMREMN summer-seeming
UMRUDN summer pudding
UMRZTO summarization
UNBIDY turn a blind eye
UNBSNS funny business
UNETNR quincentenary
UNFHYA turn of the year
UNHCRE turn the corner
UNHHAO turn the heat on
UNHSAE turn the scales
UNHTBE turn the tables
UNILOT quintillionth
UNIMSY Quentin Massys
UNNAAO cunning as a fox
UNNBTL running battle
UNNHHA turn on the heat
UNNIEU turn inside out
turn inside-out
UNNLGT running lights
UNOCON turn to account
UNPCLA funny peculiar
funny-peculiar
UNRBLT vulnerability
UNUCAL quincuncially
UNUENU Quintus Ennius
UNUGSM Quinquagesima
UNULCT quintuplicate
UNUTER quantum theory
UNUVLN quinquevalent
UOAAYI autocatalysis
UOAIAL automatically
UOCEIS autoschediasm
UOCEIZ autoschediaze
UODNTL subordinately
UODNTO subordination
UODNTT subordinate to
UODNTV subordinative
UOEFCO put one's face on
UOEFEU put one's feet up
UOEHLU autocephalous
UOEHNT put one's hand to
UOELSE cut one's losses
UOELVR sue one's livery
UOEMNT put one's mind to
UOETRA cut one's throat
UOFEEL Rudolf Peierls
UOFTIE Rudolf Steiner
UOFUEE Rudolf Nureyev
UOHHNU autochthonous
UOHRSA out of harm's way
UOIGAH autobiography
UOIPAU bubonic plague
UOOEFC put on one's face
UOOEFE out on one's feet
UOOEHA out of one's head
UOOEMN out of one's mind
UOOERA out of one's road
UOOETE out of one's tree
UOPATC out of practice
UOPEIU furor poeticus
UOQETO out of question
UORPBO autograph book
UORTCS autoeroticism
UOSQEC out of sequence
UOTECE put on the screw
UOTEOD out of the woods
UOTERE rub of the green
rub on the green
UOTFIH put out of sight
UOTFLC put out of place
UOTFON put out of joint
UOTFTA run out of steam
UOTORS put out to grass
UOTOUS put out to nurse

UPAIZN sulphadiazine
UPAKHL humpback whale
UPATTO supplantation
UPCOLS suspicionless
UPEETR supplementary
UPEMEO purple emperor
UPESRO put pressure on
UPFCTO yuppification
UPIUNS bumptiousness
UPNEBL suspender belt
suspender-belt
UPNFRO jumping for joy
UPNTEU jumping the gun
UPOIAI sulphonic acid
UPROLT supercollate
UPSLSL purposelessly
UPSNTA supposing that
UPSTOA suppositional
UPSVNS purposiveness
UPTHAR puppet theatre
UPUBTO sulphur-bottom
UPUEUL sulphureously
UPUIAI sulphuric acid
UPUUNS sumptuousness
UPYECE supply teacher
UREDLA quarter dollar
UREHUL quarter-hourly
UREMSE quartermaster
URESML quarrelsomely
URGTSI surrogateship
URINNE guardian angel
URLUNS querulousness
URMMTE supreme matter
URMSVE Supreme Soviet
URNSON run rings round
UROHNU guard of honour
URPIIU subreptitious
surreptitious
URSIAL hubristically
URUDON surround sound
URYEBR Audrey Hepburn
URZFRU quartziferous
URZRSA quartz crystal
USADNL outstandingly
USAETE russia leather□
USATAL substantially
USATVL substantively
USATVS substantivise
USATVZ substantivize
USECSL Dunster Castle
USFCTO Russification
USINAR questionnaire
USINNL questioningly
USITSN burst into song
USIUAL substitutable
USIUEO substitute for
USOENS outspokenness
USRCUA substructural
USRINL subserviently
USRINT subservient to
USRSHO nursery school
USRSOE nursery slopes
USTNSA pulsating star

UTACSE Burt Lancaster
UTCLUA multicellular
multicultural
UTCLUE multicoloured
multi-coloured
UTDASI custodianship
UTEANE cut the painter
UTEETE Just Seventeen
UTEIOI put the lid on it
UTEKDO put the skids on
UTELCO put the black on
UTELMO put the blame on
UTEOEO put the moves on
UTERKO put the brake on
UTESLN ductless gland
UTEUTR cut the mustard
UTFCTO justification
UTFCTR justificatory
UTFCTV justificative
UTGAIA multigravidae
multigravidas
UTHLTE hunt the letter
UTHNOI just think of it
UTHUTC quatch-buttock
UTIGAA put things away
UTINLN Austrian blind
UTIRIE curtain-raiser
UTLEAL hunt illegally
UTLNUS multilinguist
UTLQEC multiloquence
UTLZTO subtilization
UTMLCT Guatemala City
UTMZTO customization
UTNEMT Austin hermits
UTNIHE Burton Richter
UTNNSI button one's lip
UTNOFA Dustin Hoffman
UTNPWE dusting powder
UTNTOA multinational
UTNUWT putting up with
UTOBIG auction bridge
UTOIAL subtropically
UTOTRE Just So Stories
UTPETR multiple store
UTPIAL multiplicable
UTPSIL quite possibly
UTPSTO juxtaposition
UTPSWT juxtapose with
UTPYOD multiply words
UTPYYW multiply by two
UTRIGR butterfingers
UTRLFS butterfly fish
UTRLKS butterfly kiss
UTRMDU culture medium
UTRNEG butter-and-eggs
UTSILN multiskilling
UTTDNU multitudinous
UTTEOC put to the torch
UTTEOS put to the worse
UTTEUC cut to the quick
UTTEWR put to the sword
UTUCEI just succeed in
UTVEFE Gustave Eiffel

UUDRAE put under water
UUEUBN future husband
UUIUNS luxuriousness
UUOPIT put upon points
UUTSUI Augustus Pugin
UVNINR subventionary
UVRZTO pulverization
UVVBLT survivability
UYAEDS Lucy Cavendish
UYNBEL burying beetle
UZEODN muzzle-loading
VCINRE eviction order
VCTVNS evocativeness
VGDORL Avogadro's rule
VITESU avoid the issue
VLNLNI Evelyn Glennie
VLNSFR Evelyn Ashford
VNEIAL evangelically
VNGRIT avant-gardiste
VNUPSN even supposing
VNYACE evenly matched
VRATNL everlastingly
VRBNAC overabundance
VREOAE overdecorated
VRERNL overbearingly
VRESTV oversensitive
over-sensitive
VRFWOR every few hours
VRGPNE average punter
VRGPRO average person
VRHDWN overshadowing
VRHWCE over the wicket
VRIHSA overnight stay
VRLBRT overelaborate
over-elaborate
VRLWNL overflowingly
VRMHSZ overemphasize
VRMIIU overambitious
VRMTOA overemotional
over-emotional
VRNUGN overindulgent
VROFDN overconfident
over-confident
VROUAE overpopulated
VRQEMS over-squeamish
VRRCSO over-precision
VRRMTZ overdramatize
VRSETV over-assertive
VRSIAE overestimated
VRTECE overstretched
VRTTMN overstatement
VRULFE overqualified
VRUSRB oversubscribe
VRWIHA every which way
VSTARN Yves St Laurent
VVVPRU ovoviviparous
WAELBU sweated labour
WALKAI sweat like a pig
WATEEC swear the peace
WECETU sweet chestnut
WENTIG sweet nothings
WEOCPE owner-occupied
owner-occupier

Words marked □ can also be spelled with an initial capital letter

WESELN sweet-smelling
WESUDN sweet-sounding
WETEOR sweep the board
WLEHAE swollen-headed
WLIGLC dwelling-place
WLIGOS dwelling-house
WLOEUI swallowed up in
WMIGAH swimming-baths
WPNEIC two pence piece
WPNYIC twopenny piece
WRALSU Dwarf Allosaur
WRSASI swordsmanship
WSBCLN swashbuckling
WWESOA two weeks today
WYRMTL away from it all
XADDEA expanded metal
XASBLT expansibility
XASOBL expansion bolt
XASOCR expansion card
XASVNS expansiveness
XBOOIA exobiological
XCIELN exocrine gland
XCLKNS exact likeness
XCLOTM exactly on time
XEDBLT expendability
extendability
extendibility
XEIINR expeditionary
XEIIUL expeditiously
XEINEI experienced in
XEIRNL exterior angle
XEMNTN exterminating
XEMNTO extermination
XEPRRL extemporarily
XEPRZN extemporizing
XESAGG excess baggage
XESOAL extensionally
XESUGG excess luggage
XESVNS excessiveness
expensiveness
extensiveness
XETOAL exceptionable
exceptionably
exceptionally
XETRTO expectoration
XEUTNL extenuatingly
XGEAEL exaggeratedly
XHNEIW exchange views
XIALNS excitableness
XIIINS exhibitionism
exhibitionist
XLDNSA exploding star
XLNTRL explanatorily
XLSVNS exclusiveness
explosiveness
XMLFAL exemplifiable
XMLRNS exemplariness
XMNBLT examinability
XOAIAL axiomatically
XOETAL exponentially
XOMNCT excommunicate
XOTBLT exportability
XOTDOD exported goods
XOTLTO expostulation
XOTLTR expostulatory
XOTLTV expostulative
XOUEEE exposure meter
XRCLUA extracellular
XRMHNE extreme hunger
XRNIAL extrinsically
XRODNR extraordinary
XRPITO expropriation
XRPLTO extrapolation
XRPLTR extrapolatory
XRPLTV extrapolative
XRSDUT express doubts
XRSINS expressionism□
Expressionist
XRVGNL extravagantly
XRVSTO extravasation
XSETAL existentially
XTROLG Exeter College
XUENSL excuse oneself
XUSTNS exquisiteness
XUSVNS excursiveness
YACLGS gynaecologist
YAIIAL pyramidically
YAISAE pyramid-shaped
YANSUU tyrannosaurus□
YANZTO tyrannization
YBLCOI symbolic logic
YBLZTO symbolization
YBOIAL symbiotically
YCODOE synchondroses
YCRNCT synchronicity
YCRNUL synchronously
YDNHWO dyed in the wool
dyed-in-the-wool
YEATVT hyperactivity
YECIIA hypercritical
YEMHAR Lyceum Theatre
YEMTIA hypermetrical
YEMTOI hypermetropia
YEOTRU hymenopterous
YEPYIA hyperphysical
YESADS Myles Standish
YETOHE hypertrophied
YFNTOA dysfunctional
YHAECO by the agency of
YHMTNE Lytham St Anne's
YIDIAL cylindrically
YIDRLC cylinder block
YIDRRS cylinder press
YITUNU Cyril Tourneur
YLACUT by all accounts
YLBCTO syllabication
YLNZTO hyalinization
YLPIAL sylleptically
YMNRHE dysmenorrhoea
YMTIAL symmetrically
YNAINO ayuntamientos
YNSIAL gymnastically
YNTLET by instalments
YNYOLC Sydney Pollack
YOAIBN zygomatic bone
YOANTS gyromagnetism
YODFOT by word of mouth
YOHNRA hypochondriac
YOHNRU hypochondrium
YOHSHT hypophosphite
YOLCEI hypoglycaemia
hypoglycaemic
YORPIA typographical
YOYLIA hypocycloidal
YPAIAL lymphatically
YPOAIO symptomatic of
YPPIAL dyspeptically
YRCPAI hydrocephalic
YRCPAU hydrocephalus
YRDNMC hydrodynamics
YRDZTO hybridization
YREETI hydroelectric
YREINE Tyrrhenian Sea
YRGNTO hydrogenation
YRKNTC hydrokinetics
YRMTIA hydrometrical
hygrometrical
YRSAIA hydrostatical
YRSOIA hygroscopical
YRUIAL hydraulically
YSMSRO gypsy mushroom
YTCIAL syntactically
YTEIAL synthetically
YTEIPO Myrtle Simpson
YTFCTO mystification
YTRACE oystercatcher
YVEULE Sylvie Guillem
ZCRPBI Czech Republic
ZNFINL ozone-friendly
ZSAMLS Czeslaw Milosz

14 letters – even

AAAAURS Mahayana Sutras
AAADRIE salamander-like
AAAEULC banana republic
AAASSET lay a false scent
AAATCLY paratactically
AAATRPC palaeanthropic
AABRHRT Sarah Bernhardt
AACOPWR balance of power
AACOTAE balance of trade
AACTERL Kazan Cathedral
AADUEMN Man and Superman
AAEATFR pay a penalty for

AAEBEES manageableness
AAEEAGD Japanese War God
AAEEETA vasa deferentia
AAEIAIM pan-Americanism
AAEIAIN caramelization
AAEOEPR jalapeño pepper
AAEOSES cadaverousness
AAIGITC paralinguistic
AAILIKE Gamaliel Pickle
AAIMTCL paradigmatical
AAINOET Bavarian Forest
AAINOLR Canadian dollar
AAIOOIT parasitologist
AALLLLM parallel slalom
AALLOIN parallel motion
AALYUKN Macaulay Culkin
AAOIHEE macaroni cheese
AAPORAE malappropriate
AARCSIG data processing
AARTCIN data protection
AASCOOY parapsychology
AASEULY harass sexually
AASUHOM satan's mushroom
AATNINO pay attention to
ABAEBOK Max Beaverbrook
ABCNETE Barbican Centre
ABGROFY cabbage-root fly
ABGTEHT cabbage-tree hat
ABIGSIE Cambridgeshire
ABNOOIE carbon monoxide
ABNTOSY rambunctiously
ABRDSAE Marburg disease
ABRHATE Bamburgh Castle
ABRJCSN Barbara Jackson
ABRTNSN Hanbury-Tenison
ABTRAIM Sabbatarianism
ABTRCCD barbituric acid
ABXLCCD carboxylic acid
ACCRFLY watch carefully
ACDESAL fancy dress ball
ACIADLI Marc Girardelli
ACIGRES marching orders
marching-orders
ACIIAIN sanctification
ACILGLY catch illegally
ACLKAAK watch like a hawk
ACLRFID Malcolm Rifkind
ACLRISE vascular tissue
ACLRUDE vascular bundle
ACLSRET Malcolm Sargent
ACLTDIK calculated risk
ACMNPPR parchment paper
ACNETDY malcontentedly
ACNGNSS carcinogenesis
ACOEDAH catch one's death
ACOOZLS Pancho Gonzales
ACRDADD catch red-handed
ACSNHSS narcosynthesis
ACSNOIS Marcus Antonius
ACSUEIS Marcus Aurelius
ACTROIM narcoterrorism
ACUCRIE calcium carbide
ACVNATN Marco Van Basten
ACVOSES lasciviousness
ADAAEET land management
ADAKATR hard taskmaster
ADAMSAE cardiac massage
ADCATMN handicraftsman
ADDNEET landed interest
ADDNEOE padded envelope
ADECIVS handkerchieves
ADEDDES bald-headedness
hard-headedness
ADFEETY say differently
ADIHORE sandwich course
ADLTERY Gandalf the Grey
ADMAIBE random variable
ADNADIH hand in hand with
ADNLEMN Cardinal Newman
ADNLITE cardinal virtue
ADNLUBR cardinal number
ADNNSET land on one's feet
ADNYRNH pardon my French
ADOACLR cardiovascular
ADODOFX Sandford Koufax
ADOEATR wardrobe master
ADOFOIY hands-off policy
ADOTEAL daddy of them all
ADRNOLR mandarin collar
ADWWAOS lay down weapons
ADYHPAE hardly the place
AEAAFED James A Garfield
AEAAUFL have had a gutful
AEAETGT make watertight
AEAGNIA Lake Tanganyika
AEAIAIN lateralization
AEAOEDY have had one's day
AEASAIM Rabelaisianism
AEASSAT sales assistant
AEBAIGN have a bearing on
AEBANAE have a brainwave
AEBGNIG make a beginning
AEBLFRT make a bolt for it
AEBLSPF make a balls-up of
AECEEKV Pavel Cherenkov
AECESBE make accessible
AECLAHN James Callaghan
AECLUIT watercolourist
AECUITD make acquainted
AEDARSD Rajendra Prasad
AEDASTT make a dead set at
AEDCABE valet de chambre
AEDMIWF take a dim view of
AEEAAIN make reparation
AEEEGFR take revenge for
AEEEUIE sales executive
AEENRUD have been around
AEEOERS pâté de foie gras
AEEOREO have recourse to
AEEPNET make despondent
AEESEUE make less secure
AEESNLY take personally
AEETIDW casement window
AEETRIT pavement artist
AEETRUH make wet through
AEEWNEB James Edwin Webb
AEFNRAE rate of increase
AEFRGES rate of progress
AEFXHNE rate of exchange
AEGETID have a great mind
AEGOJBF make a good job of
AEHBGIE make the big time
AEHBSUT take the biscuit
AEHEGOF take the edge off
AEHFRNY Gareth of Orkney
AEHGIEF take the guise of
AEHHTFR have the hots for
AEHLBRY take the liberty
AEHLUHF have the laugh of
AEHMEIG take a hammering
AEHNSAY take things easy
AEHPAEF take the place of
AEHRNIG make the running
AEHTCLY catechetically
AEHUIIM male chauvinism
AEHUIIT male chauvinist
AEIDREE Lake Windermere
AEIGRUD make rings round
AEIGVNS have misgivings
AEILDCT care killed a cat
AEKEHBE Lake Okeechobee
AELAUEN take pleasure in
AELGTHW laser-light show
AELKNFR have a liking for
AELOACS make allowances
AELTSAE satellite state
AEMKOTF take a mike out of
AENESOD make understood
AENFETN have an effect on
AENGTFT make a night of it
AENITNT make indistinct
AENMATN have an impact on
AENNSAD have in one's hand
AENSHIE take one's choice
AENSHNE take one's chance
AENSILF have one's fill of
AENSOEN have one's home in
make one's home in
AENSONS make one's rounds
AENSRAH save one's breath
take one's breath
AENSSAE make one's escape
AENSYSN have one's eyes on
AENTLAE maternity leave
paternity leave
AENTOAY have one too many
AEOADLS Camelopardalis
AEODAEF take good care of
AEOEAEY make more watery
AEOEAOT make jokes about
AEOEEUE make more secure
AEOEIHS have sole rights
AEOENPY make someone pay
AEOEOTY have come to stay
AEOETBE make more stable
AEOFDNE have confidence
AEOGATD take for granted
AEOHBAS take to the boats
AEOIAIN categorisation

categorization
AEOINLB Caledonian Club
AEONSOS take to one's toes
AEOODFR have no words for
AEOOIEF take no notice of
AEORESO make so free as to
AEOSPRY warehouse party
AEOTENE water on the knee
AEOTIKF make you think of
AEOTWNS have forty winks
AEOVRAT make conversant
AEPCUEF take a picture of
AEPGERF make a pig's ear of
AEPNSID make up one's mind
AEPOIIN take up position
AEPOMUH make a poor mouth
AEPQARL take up a quarrel
AEPRISN James Parkinson
AERAHES make breathless
AERCDNE take precedence
AERESRM take orders from
AERGTND make frightened
AERICEK take a raincheck
AERPLET water-repellent
AERSOTF take a rise out of
AERSSAT water-resistant
AERVNEE have a roving eye
AESAEET make a statement
AESERNE Hamersley Range
AESNAOT make a song about
AESNCRE Paterson's curse
AESNSOE have as one's home
AESTPAE have as its place
AESUNRO take a scunner to
AETEIIE patent medicine
AETLLOE have a tile loose
AETOHAS have it both ways
AETROSN have its roots in
AETWYIH have it away with
AEUIAIN valetudinarian
AEUNRBE make vulnerable
AEUOEBT take out one's bat
AEVRTIG have everything
AEWIRUD have a whip-round
AEYUPIE take by surprise
AFADTAS waifs and strays
AFENWRH halfpennyworth
AFNTOIG malfunctioning
AFTHDES far-fetchedness
AGEULVR Maggie Tulliver
AGGCRIR baggage-carrier
AGGHNLR baggage-handler
AGGRCAM baggage reclaim
AGIAIES sanguinariness
AGNITEE hanging in there
AGRHNIE larger than life
AGRTAGR Margaret Sanger
AGRTTOD Margaret Atwood
AGRTULR Margaret Fuller
AGRUDIH hang around with
AGTAGAE target language
AGTRIES daughterliness
AGTRILW daughters-in-law
AHDRYUE cathode-ray tube
AHGAHCL tachygraphical
AHIECLE Daphnis et Chloé
AHLCEAD Catholic Herald
AHLCICE parhelic circle
AHLGCLY pathologically
AHMTCLY mathematically
AHNCSUE bathing costume
bathing-costume
AHNPWRD machine-powered
AHNRKOT Jan Hendrik Oort
AHNWIIG bad handwriting
AHOMNIG fashionmonging
AHRADOS Fathers and Sons
AHRNWEL Catherine wheel
AHROEHR gather together
AHWIWRH Kathy Whitworth
AHYAGAD lachrymal gland
AIADEUE habit and repute
AIAIAIN capitalization
radicalisation
radicalization
AIAMSUS Vatican Museums
AIATOOY radio astronomy
AIBNUIN David Ben-Gurion
AIBROIZ David Berkowitz
AIBUAGR Nadia Boulanger
AICEITY radiochemistry
AICUTAD David Coulthard
AIDLVIA Basil D'Oliveira
AIEAGAE native language
AIEGLLI Galileo Galilei
AIEGWRH Maria Edgeworth
AIEMRCN Native American
AIEODMR Nadine Gordimer
AIETTEF manifest itself
AIFCOIY satisfactorily
AIFEUNY radio frequency
AIGAHCL hagiographical
AIGLTOO having a lot to do
AIGNTIG eating anything
AIGOULS having no qualms
AIGRBES having problems
AIGRSNR taking prisoner
AIHAINS Hamish MacInnes
AIHEITR parish register
AIHNCEM vanishing cream
AIHNPIT vanishing point
AIINCOS papilionaceous
AILADSK Daniel Gajdusek
AILALWS Daniel Day-Lewis
AILEOIY radial velocity
AILETEE Danielle Steele
AILNWRH Ray Illingworth
AILYMTY radial symmetry
AINLNHM national anthem
AINLUBR rational number
AIOEZIK David O Selznick
AIPESYU may it please you
AIRGCOS saxifragaceous
AISIFET Babinski effect
AISNIIE radiosensitise
radiosensitive
radiosensitize
AITETET man in the street
AITLGAH radiotelegraph
AITLSOE radio telescope
AITLUUE sagittal suture
AIUIAIN latitudinarian
AIYEEVD easily deceived
AIYLNIG family planning
AIYRPRD easily prepared
AJREROS Marjorie Proops
AKADDES cack-handedness
AKCACIG backscratching
AKEHRTN Jackie Charlton
AKETRVR back-seat driver
AKFETDY walk affectedly
AKFHBAT mark of the Beast
AKFHDVL talk of the devil
AKFIAIY lack of vitality
AKFNEET lack of interest
AKGHLDY package holiday
AKHSRES walk the streets
AKIHCOS mark with a cross
AKNIRNE Mackenzie Range
AKNIRVR Mackenzie River
AKNSHLS walk one's chalks
AKNSRIS rack one's brains
AKNTAIY walk unsteadily
AKNWUDD walking wounded
AKOENOF hack someone off
AKOEODY talk more loudly
AKOPLOK Jackson Pollock
AKTEERH market research
AKTGTOE walk a tightrope
AKUNNHM Jack Cunningham
ALACUTR Oak-leaf Cluster
ALADCOL kailyard school
ALAEFED Karl Lagerfield
ALAKIUE ballpark figure
ALCNGNC hallucinogenic
ALCOSES fallaciousness
ALCOTAL Gaelic football
ALCSEES Wallace Stevens
ALDOHBR called to the bar
ALDYOIN early day motion
ALFADIH Earl of Sandwich
ALFOEER cauliflower ear
ALNLTES Pauline Letters
ALNNSET fall on one's feet
ALNOCIN call into action
ALNOEIH fall in love with
ALNSMTY Wayland's Smithy
ALNTNGT Sailing Tonight
ALNTRUH falling-through
ALNUSIN call in question
ALOCLEE Balliol College
ALOEEBR fail to remember
ALOGNZD badly organized
ALOLXES Halldór Laxness
ALPATBS Fallopian tubes
ALSONUS tablespoonfuls
ALVIISY Vaslav Nijinsky
AMAAEET farm management
AMCAEEN Karma Chameleon

AMDOEHR jammed together
AMMTHSN Naomi Mitchison
AMNADVL Tasmanian devil
AMNATGR Tasmanian tiger
AMNCOIN harmonic motion
AMNOSES harmoniousness
AMRLATE Balmoral Castle
AMRNTNS hammer and tongs
ANBIEBY Saint Bride's Bay
ANEODLC Launcelot du Lac
ANEOGBO Launcelot Gobbo
ANHATDY faint-heartedly
ANJHPRE Saint-John Perse
ANLQETY magniloquently
ANLROSY vaingloriously
ANMNFED Jayne Mansfield
ANNRDET main ingredient
ANNSIIG earn one's living
ANREDIE banner headline
ANRFIIG manner of living
ANSEDNY gain ascendancy
ANSEODR garnishee order
ANTCEDE magnetic needle
ANTCTIE magnetic stripe
ANTEEPD cannot be helped
AOAISGT panoramic sight
AOAOEET Day of Atonement
AOATIIN war of attrition
AOBCWAE razorback whale
AOBOOSI Jacob Bronowski
AODAEOT Harold Harefoot
AODXNIE Mason-Dixon Line
AOEHAOF eat one's head off
AOEHNSN lay one's hands on
AOENCAS Napoleonic Wars
AOEPAES say one's prayers
AOERCLY barometrically
AOHREAK man on horseback
AOIAARE Carolina Nairne
AOIAHUS canonical hours
AOIIAIN saponification
AOIIVLE calorific value
AOISROA Kaposi's sarcoma
AOOTEAS canon of the mass
AORBEES favourableness
AORTDIK favourite drink
AORXHNE labour exchange
AOTEOET man of the moment
AOTEUGE law of the jungle
APGOSES rampageousness
APNNOTN happening often
APNOEHR happen together
AQEDRIA Jacques Derrida
ARAEUEU marriage bureau
ARAOCFR carry a torch for
ARCOSES capriciousness
ARCPAOS macrocephalous
ARCTETE Garrick Theatre
ARCURLO Maurice Utrillo
ARDFMLA Sagrada Familia
ARENRIG barrier nursing
AREOOIS macroeconomics
ARGDOHR fairy godmother
ARGLWTR Barry Goldwater
ARIDDES fair-mindedness
ARIGFEL harrying of hell
ARLGOSY sacrilegiously
ARLNHRY Laurel and Hardy
ARLPICP Gavrilo Princip
ARMCRSI Lacrima Christi
ARMNAIM sacramentalism
ARMNAIT sacramentalist
ARMUTIS Matra Mountains
Tatra Mountains
ARNEIYN Laurence Binyon
ARNETRE Laurence Sterne
ARNEUDN Laurence Eusden
ARNFOOR matron of honour
ARNOFCR warrant officer
AROEPIT carry one's point
AROIDIG fair to middling
ARSAIIS matresfamilias
patresfamilias
ARSLRDE Harry Selfridge
ARSNTES sacrosanctness
ARTNSIK carrot and stick
ARWIDDY narrow-mindedly
ARWNGAD Garry Winogrand
ASAEERW raise an eyebrow
ASDLKES Hans Adolf Krebs
ASEPTEN paisley pattern
ASFAIIY falsifiability
ASFEIIN Wars of Religion
ASFHRSS Wars of the Roses
ASGTDES farsightedness
far-sightedness
ASMFIED balsam of Gilead
ASMNOSY parsimoniously
ASMOEAK pay someone back
ASNFSIN passing fashion
ASNSLOF pass oneself off
ASNTEUK passing the buck
ASOAEES passionateness
ASOEGAS raise one's glass
ASOEVIE raise one's voice
ASPENNY false pregnancy
ASPOUDS basso profundos
ASRDCIN mass production
mass-production
ASRRRFT Yasser Ar Arafat
ASSAEET false statement
ASSEERS causes célèbres
ASTEAKT raise the market
ASTEIGE cassette single
ASTELYR cassette player
cassette-player
ASTEOSF cause the loss of
ASTSIOY false testimony
ASTUDRO cause to undergo
ASUSOLS danseurs nobles
ASVCAIN mass evacuation
ASVSOIG passive smoking
ATAELON Martha Gellhorn
ATAIHEI Dante Alighieri
ATAOEUA Santiago de Cuba
ATAWNPY Can't Pay, Won't Pay
ATCLOIG tactical voting
ATCLRES particularness
ATDOSES fastidiousness
ATEBABE Matthew Bramble
ATEBESN Cartier-Bresson
ATEFAEY Battle of Naseby
ATEFANE Battle of Cannae
ATEFARM Battle of Wagram
ATEFCIM Battle of Actium
ATEFEDN Battle of Verdun
ATEFHLH Battle of Shiloh
ATEFIKE Battle of Pinkie
ATEFIWY Battle of Midway
ATEFOOO Battle of Kosovo
ATEFRHM Battle of Arnhem
ATEFYAE Battle of Mycale
ATEISAN castles in Spain
ATENHAR castle in the air
ATERCFR pay the price for
ATETEID farthest behind
ATEXBOK battle-axe block
ATFHERH salt of the earth
ATFRAIM Rastafarianism
ATHRSOE cast a horoscope
ATLGCLY tautologically
ATLMUIZ Bartolomeu Diaz
ATMMCLY pantomimically
ATNAAAE Martin Sarasate
ATNABRN Martin Van Buren
ATNCREE Martin Scorsese
ATNEOSY cantankerously
ATNFROS fast and furious
ATNLPOH Martin Klaproth
ATNPEET Past and Present
ATNTLAN wanting to learn
ATOEAOS xanthomelanous
ATOHWNS cast to the winds
ATPAMTC pantopragmatic
ATPLTCL party political
ATRAUDY Easter Saturday
ATREAAE Walter De La Mare
Walter de la Mare
ATREAIN tatterdemalion
ATREATS Sartor Resartus
ATRFATY matter-of-factly
ATRFORE matter of course
ATRIAIN bastardization
ATRIPAN Walter Lippmann
ATRIPAT castor oil plant
ATROOIT bacteriologist
ATROTSS battery of tests
ATRRNIE Walter Cronkite
ATRYNFR past praying for
ATSELPN cast a spell upon
ATSESOS cast aspersions
ATTEDNE wait attendance
ATTOSES factitiousness
ATTTEUL taste to the full
ATUELSS Pasteurelloses
ATUIAIN pasteurisation
pasteurization
AUAAIIY natural ability
AUAATRO Pamulaparti Rao

AUAHSOY natural history
AUAIAIN naturalization
AUAREET Hague Agreement
AUASINE natural science
AUAWSAE natural wastage
AUHNOKY capuchin monkey
AUJDEET value judgement
AULIKIK Samuel Pickwick
AUNWUNA Papua New Guinea
AUPFENS Ranulph Fiennes
AUROSES salubriousness
AUTOSGT faculty of sight
AVGOBAC Sauvignon Blanc
AVLOSES marvellousness
AVNOLDE Calvin Coolidge
AYAHLDY Lady Day Holiday
AYFHNGT lady of the night
AYURSRY say you are sorry
BAALNON Abraham Lincoln
BETAGAE object language
BETIDDY absent-mindedly
BEUOSES obsequiousness
BEVCOEY observe closely
BEVTOCR observation car
BGORADN I beg your pardon?
BIAOIES obligatoriness
BISNPOE obiit sine prole
BNZRRWR Ebenezer Brewer
BTATDES abstractedness
BTEEOSY obstreperously
BTFLRGT a bit of all right
BTMOSES abstemiousness
BTUTOIM obstructionism
BTUTOIT obstructionist
BVADEOD above and beyond
BVMNIND above-mentioned
BVSSIIN above suspicion
CAEOEHR scrape together
CAINLES occasionalness
CAUSNOT à chacun son goût
CBRLTUE iceberg lettuce
CDOSPRY acid-house party
CEAIAIN schematization
CECFCIN science fiction
science-fiction
CENRNIG screen printing
CEPOELR screw propeller
CETBEES acceptableness
CETFCLY scientifically
CIDESIT Schindler's List
CIEMUIY active immunity
CILSEDN Achilles' tendon
CIMTCLY schismatically
CINANIG action painting
CINTTOS action stations
CIOYEOS schizomycetous
CITEAEF act in the name of
CIVMNAE achievement age
CIVSCES achieve success
CLIRAHR Schleiermacher
CLMTZDO acclimatized to
CLSATCL ecclesiastical
CLSATCS Ecclesiasticus
CLSOOIT ecclesiologist
CNAIAIN scandalization
CNOTEAE icing on the cake
CNWEGET acknowledgment
COADORM echocardiogram
COATCLY scholastically
CODOLSA achondroplasia
COLECIG schoolteaching
COLITES schoolmistress
CONAIIY accountability
COPIHBE accomplishable
COPIHET accomplishment
COPNMNS accompaniments
COSHBAD across-the-board
CRANESN a certain person
CRAONOL score an own goal
CRIOSES scurrilousness
CRMNEIG scaremongering
CRMTCLY achromatically
CRPITOF score points off
CTEBAND scatterbrained
scatter-brained
CTEDARM scatter diagram
CTYLGCL ichthyological
CUIGODR scouring powder
CUIIAIN scrutinization
CUIIIGY scrutinisingly
scrutinizingly
CUITDIH acquainted with
CURSILN acquire skill in
CUTCUTR acoustic guitar
CUTMDES accustomedness
CUUAIEY accumulatively
CUUOSES scrupulousness
CWREEGR Schwarzenegger
DACFCOY advance factory
DACNYAS advancing years
DACTWRS advance towards
DADAABN Edward Casaubon
DADHEDR Edward the Elder
DADPLTN Edward Appleton
DAITCLY idealistically
DASEESN Adlai Stevenson
DATGOSY advantageously
DBEOMUE edible dormouse
DCTOAIT educationalist
DCTTOSY adscititiously
DETTOSY adventitiously
DIINLIE additional time
DIITAIE administrative
DIITAIN administration
DISBEES admissibleness
DLBTNNT Adolf Butenandt
DLHTETE Adelphi Theatre
DLOSIPR idol-worshipper
DLVNAYR Adolf von Baeyer
DNBLEEO I don't believe so
DNIIAIN identification
DNIYRSS identity crisis
DOAHCLY idiopathically
DUDRNIE Edmund Ironside
DVDAIGR J David Salinger
EACMOIE metal composite
EADADNR Gerald Gardiner
EADCEIE heraldic device
EADCLEE Herald's College
EADESES regardlessness
EADYPTY tea and sympathy
EAEUGAD sebaceous gland
EAGDESN deranged person
EAHRCLY metaphorically
semaphorically
EAHSCLY metaphysically
EAIEQIY negative equity
EAIEUBR negative number
EAIIAIE rehabilitative
EAIIAIN denazification
desalinisation
desalinization
gelatinization
keratinization
rehabilitation
EAINLZD denationalized
EAITCLY legalistically
EAIUAIE recapitulative
EAIUAIN recapitulation
EAIUAOY recapitulatory
EAKBEES remarkableness
EANOPSD remain composed
EANTEWN Leda and the Swan
EAOOSMS Heraion of Samos
EAPOAFR get approval for
EASCOOY metapsychology
EASNFVR relapsing fever
EASRIUE penal servitude
EATACBT Sebastian Cabot
EATETLY departmentally
EATHSIE depart this life
EAUOUAA Ieyasu Tokugawa
EBADPCS herbs and spices
EBCTEIO Lee Buck Trevino
EBEIDDY feeble-mindedly
EBESAIM Wembley Stadium
EBRAQIH Herbert Asquith
EBRMRUE Herbert Marcuse
EBRSECR Herbert Spencer
ECAEIIN reach a decision
ECLNAIM neocolonialism
ECLNAIT neocolonialist
ECLSETE Hercules beetle
ECNIEAK percentile rank
ECNRCLY geocentrically
ECOURCT Peace of Utrecht
ECPIEES perceptiveness
ECPIIIY perceptibility
ECSESIE Leicestershire
ECTEALS fence the tables
ECTNOSY percutaneously
EDADHAS heads and thraws
EDASADE dead man's handle
EDEAANT dead set against
EDEOEES meddlesomeness
EDESRLS Dead Sea Scrolls
EDETIHS send best wishes
EDFOEAT deed of covenant
EDFRFGT ready for a fight

EDHROAT	read the riot act
EDILRNZ	Hendrik Lorentz
EDMIELS	Mesdemoiselles
EDNATES	leading actress
EDNIWRS	bending inwards
EDNLBAY	lending library
EDNMCIE	reading-machine
	vending machine
EDNNSET	dead on one's feet
EDNSECS	mend one's fences
EDNYEOY	read only memory
EDODIHS	send good wishes
EDOHATR	lead to the altar
EDOHWRD	dead to the world
EDOOETY	send to Coventry
EDPSNEL	lead apes in hell
EDROEET	Teddy Roosevelt
EDRPCFC	gender-specific
EDSAEET	send a statement
EDSHRIG	dead as a herring
EDUOSAE	bend out of shape
EEACUCL	general council
EEAHCLY	telepathically
EEAIAIN	federalization
	generalization
EEAIEES	generativeness
	vegetativeness
EEAILAS	Serena Williams
EEAISMS	generalissimos
EEAPROE	general-purpose
EEBRTOS	reverberations
EECPCLY	telescopically
EEEAEES	degenerateness
EEEAIEY	regeneratively
EEECPIT	reference-point
EEETAIN	defenestration
EEETCOE	Benedetto Croce
EEGENWY	Peter Greenaway
EEGFLES	revengefulness
EEGOEEF	revenge oneself
EEHICLY	genethliacally
EEHMSED	Hemel Hempstead
EEHNBOH	telephone booth
EEHNCLY	telephonically
EEHNYUK	Peter Henry Buck
EEIAIES	hereditariness
EEIAIIY	hereditability
EEIIEES	repetitiveness
EEIPRNS	genetic parents
EEISCEY	benefit society
EEITAIN	deregistration
EEITROD	Benedict Arnold
EELGCLY	genealogically
	teleologically
EELNSUA	Leaellynasaura
EELOSES	rebelliousness
EELRRUE	jeweller's rouge
EELUDNY	reveal suddenly
EEMNESN	Peter Mandelson
EEMNSEY	Belém Monastery
EEMTCLY	telesmatically
EENVRAD	Never-Never Land
	never-never land
EEOEIEY	Penelope Lively
EEOHLOS	heterophyllous
EEOHOOS	heterochromous
EEPNOLR	Peter Pan collar
EEPOIES	peremptoriness
EEPYHSS	metempsychoses
	metempsychosis
EERCOSY	meretriciously
EERLGCL	meteorological
EERLOTX	cerebral cortex
EESNLGT	reversing light
EESTLFE	Peter Sutcliffe
EESUAOE	Peter Scudamore
EETBEES	delectableness
	detestableness
EETESES	relentlessness
EETOCAS	reception class
EETOODR	reception order
EETRTBE	refectory table
EETVSOY	detective story
EEVBEES	receivableness
EEVDIDM	received wisdom
EEVEGRY	receive eagerly
EEVNHUE	receiving-house
EFBEAIG	self-abnegating
EFBEAIN	self-abnegation
EFBOPIN	self-absorption
EFCCDNE	perfect cadence
EFCEAPE	perfect example
EFCIAIG	self-activating
EFCIIIY	perfectibility
EFCUAIN	self-accusation
EFDETSR	self-advertiser
EFDIAIN	self-admiration
EFDOSES	perfidiousness
EFEPCIG	self-respecting
EFERDML	Les Fleurs du Mal
EFETAND	self-restrained
EFEUAIG	self-regulating
EFFAEET	self-effacement
EFFRGTD	self-affrighted
EFICPIE	self-discipline
EFLTEIG	self-flattering
EFMLYET	self-employment
EFMOAIN	self-immolation
EFMOTNE	self-importance
EFNEETD	self-interested
EFNLDES	newfangledness
EFNUGNE	self-indulgence
EFOENET	self-government
EFOFDNE	self-confidence
EFOGTIG	self-forgetting
EFOPRSN	self-comparison
EFOSQET	self-consequent
EFOSSIN	self-possession
EFOTOLD	self-controlled
EFRACAT	performance art
EFRCAMD	self-proclaimed
EFRIGRS	performing arts
EFRPLIG	self-propelling
EFRYALR	Geoffrey Taylor
EFRYIHR	Geoffrey Fisher
EFUFCET	self-sufficient
EFUFLET	self-fulfilment
EFUFLIG	self-fulfilling
EFUIHET	self-punishment
EFUPRIG	self-supporting
EFUTFIG	self-justifying
EFUTIIG	self-sustaining
EFUTNNE	self-sustenance
EFXLAIN	self-exaltation
EFXLIIG	self-explaining
EFXRSIN	self-expression
EGAHCLY	geographically
EGIOOYV	Sergei Korolyov
EGOTCLY	geognostically
EGSLTEY	Fergus Slattery
EGTESES	weightlessness
EGTRIIG	weight-training
EGTTEEM	weigh to the beam
EGVRAIN	tergiversation
EHBTEFR	be the better for
EHDCLES	methodicalness
EHDLGCL	methodological
EHIAHTH	technical hitch
EHITAIE	dechristianise
	dechristianize
EHLSREY	keyhole surgery
EHMAUEF	be the measure of
EHSOHLS	Mephistopheles
EIAETLY	medicamentally
EIAIAIN	decimalization
	devitalization
	revitalization
EIAOFCR	Medical Officer
	medical officer
EIASINE	medical science
EIBUGOS	petit bourgeois
EIDCEUE	behind schedule
EIDHTMS	behind the times
EIDHWEL	behind the wheel
EIDNSAK	behind one's back
EIEAEES	deliberateness
EIEAEPN	deliberate upon
EIEAIEY	deliberatively
EIEAPEH	deliver a speech
EIEEETA	senile dementia
EIEETOE	retirement home
EIEHPIT	beside the point
EIEIUVR	demisemiquaver
EIEOZLZ	Felipe González
EIEVRIN	Revised Version
EIEYESN	delivery-person
EIFIILY	semi-officially
EIFRNIG	relief printing
EIGAHCL	heliographical
EIGESIS	men in grey suits
EIHAEDR	Jewish calendar
EIHFLES	delightfulness
EIIAEES	legitimateness
EIICLRY	semicircularly
EIIEOET	decisive moment
EIIIAIN	legitimisation
	legitimization
	resinification
	revivification

EIIIEES definitiveness
EIIIIUE verisimilitude
EIINAIG decision-making
EIITEEK get it in the neck
EIIUDOD semi-liquid food
EIIUGOP religious group
EIIUHUE religious house
EIMNGGI Beniamino Gigli
EINLFIE regional office
EINNIER design engineer
EIODCIG semiconducting
EIORPIT lexicographist
EIPRISN Cecil Parkinson
EIQIHET relinquishment
EIRETRR senior lecturer
EIRIIES senior citizens
EIRLAIN defibrillation
EISDOAE devil's advocate
EITIUIN redistribution
EITRDAL registered mail
EITRDOT registered post
EITRFIE register office
EITUHIH get in touch with
EIUCMLX Oedipus complex
EIUDIKR serious drinker
EIUOSES meticulousness
EIVOEEF relieve oneself
EIWOGIH get in wrong with
EJMNULR Benjamin Butler
EJROEEF perjure oneself
EKFHWOS neck of the woods
EKIDDES weak-mindedness
EKTHKES weak at the knees
EKTPASN Hesketh Pearson
ELCBDYN reflect badly on
ELCFLES neglectfulness
ELCIEES reflectiveness
ELCTERL Wells Cathedral
ELCTOAY perlocutionary
ELEERHD well-researched
ELEOSFR feel remorse for
ELETLTD well-ventilated
ELFPRVL seal of approval
ELGCLEE Kellogg College
ELGCLIE geological time
ELHDAGT feel the draught
ELHDMYO sell the dummy to
ELHLOIG healthy-looking
ELHUHOT well-thought-out
ELIAANT declaim against
ELNADAL Decline and Fall
ELNNYAS declining years
ELNTNOT wellington boot
ELOIEAD bells of Ireland
ELOLAHR hell for leather
ELRBEES deplorableness
ELTIETS tell it like it is
ELTONAE tell its own tale
ELTUTRD well-structured
ELVNSOE Ken Livingstone
ELWAINL fellow national
ELWSBON yellowish brown
yellowish-brown
ELWSWIE yellowish-white
ELYNHMS Henley-on-Thames
EMCTERL Reims Cathedral
EMITETE Mermaid Theatre
EMNAIIY fermentability
EMNBEES terminableness
EMNEVLE Herman Melville
EMNGEIG Hermann Goering
EMNHPED German Shepherd
EMNLGCL terminological
EMPRDTC hermaphroditic
EMSIEES permissiveness
EMSIIIY permissibility
ENACLEE Newnham College
ENADUTR Leonhard Hutter
ENALATE Jean-Paul Sartre
ENCEIES pernicketiness
ENCOSES perniciousness
ENDATIH being dealt with
ENDMSIE Léonide Massine
ENDRVHK Leonid Kravchuk
ENDRZNV Leonid Brezhnev
ENDSUSD being discussed
ENDYNYV Gennady Yanayev
ENERFBE Jean Henri Fabre
ENERSOT dernier ressort
ENHHBTF be in the habit of
ENIHLES Heinrich Olbers
ENIHORR Heinrich Rohrer
ENIOAIG reinvigorating
ENIOAIN reinvigoration
ENLSUBR Reynolds number
ENMNFLF being mindful of
ENNFLES meaningfulness
ENNOEOO Fernando de Soto
Hernando de Soto
ENORLAE means of release
ENOSPOT means of support
ENRDCIN reintroduction
ENRHIIK Bernard Haitink
ENRHNUT Bernard Hinault
ENRMLMD Bernard Malamud
ENRMNIG Bernard Manning
ENRWOLY Leonard Woolley
ENSEGAP Dennis Bergkamp
ENTBAAH Kenneth Branagh
ENTGAAE Kenneth Grahame
ENTLAIN reinstallation
ENUDHEE Jean-Luc Dehaene
ENXEKLY Lennox Berkeley
EOAEETL set on a pedestal
EOAESYE Decorated style
EOAIAIN demoralization
depolarization
EOAIEES decorativeness
EOAOIES derogatoriness
EOATCLY aeronautically
EOBNNDA recombinant DNA
EOCLAIN reconciliation
EOCLAOY reconciliatory
EODERAH beyond reproach
EODHUHS second thoughts
EODOLWR Second World War
EODRAIG record-breaking
EODTOIG reconditioning
EODUSIN beyond question
EOEAIIY recoverability
EOEBODP get one's blood up
EOEBOEE become obsolete
EOEDSRS get one's deserts
EOEEDWY get one's end away
EOEEIIE become definite
EOEESBE become sensible
EOEHATN set one's heart on
EOEHBIR become chubbier
EOEHFOD before the flood
EOEHNSN get one's hands on
EOEIBRE become airborne
EOELGVR get one's leg over
EOENSIE before one's time
EOEOETY remote job entry
EOEONAK get one's own back
EOEOPIN zero-zero option
EOEPAET become apparent
EOERGAT become pregnant
EOESOSD become espoused
EOETGAT become stagnant
EOEWITE wet one's whistle
EOEXIIG become exciting
EOFNSIE get off one's bike
EOIACUT deposit account
EOIAIEY denominatively
EOIAINL denominational
EOIIAIN demobilization
detoxification
EOITCLY aerobiotically
EOLCIEY recollectively
EOMNAIN recommendation
EOMNAOY recommendatory
EOMNEET recommencement
EOMSINR decommissioner
EOMTOIT reformationist
EONISNE reconnaissance
EONLADR Hero and Leander
EOOIAIN decolonization
EOOPNOD zero-coupon bond
EOPUDBE decompoundable
EORTCLY democratically
EOSCAIN deconsecration
EOSFLES remorsefulness
EOSIUIN reconstitution
EOSRCIE reconstructive
EOSRCIN deconstruction
reconstruction
EOTDPEH reported speech
EOTLGCL gerontological
EOTMNTD decontaminated
EOTMNTR decontaminator
EOVNPWR resolving power
EOVNSAE revolving stage
EPALHUS keep early hours
EPCAIIE respectabilise
respectabilize
EPCAIIY respectability
EPCFLES respectfulness
EPCLSUH keep a calm sough

EPEFMNA Temple of Amon-Ra
EPEFPLO Temple of Apollo
EPEFTEA Temple of Athena
EPGOHUE keep a good house
EPLTCLY geopolitically
EPNEWAS keep under wraps
EPNIEES responsiveness
EPNIIGY serpentiningly
EPNIIIY responsibility
EPNILFR responsible for
EPNSADN keep one's hand in
EPNSARN keep one's hair on
EPNSHNP keep one's chin up
EPNSIDN keep one's mind on
EPNSOLN keep one's wool on
EPOIEIH be opposite with
EPRTZNS temperate zones
EPRVLIG keep travelling
EPTACEK perpetual check
EPTGTEN keep a tight rein
EPUOSGT keep out of sight
EQIEAIN sesquipedalian
EQIEAIY sesquipedality
ERAIAIN reorganization
ERAMDVR Pedro Almodovar
ERASSUE Béarnaise sauce
ERBATMS neuroblastomas
ERCAIGY depreciatingly
ERCEITY petrochemistry
ERCOIES refractoriness
ERCSEAA Bedrich Smetana
ERCVNIH Henry Cavendish
ERDCIEY reproductively
ERDCIIY reproductivity
ERDTOHT Henri Dutrochet
EREARSN George Harrison
EREASAL George Marshall
EREASUY George Lansbury
EREBOUE decree absolute
ERECOEN George McGovern
EREEEIH George Meredith
EREEFES George Jeffreys
EREEKLY George Berkeley
EREESWN George Gershwin
ERENGTY George Knightly
ERESMNN Georges Simenon
ERETHYR Georgette Heyer
ERETMRA Henrietta Maria
ERFBOAA neurofibromata
ERFTEEL bear off the bell
ERGAAIN retrogradation
ERGAMTN Tetragrammaton
ERGTOIT segregationist
ERHKUKE near the knuckle
ERHNIEY reprehensively
ERHTUBR near that number
ERITCLY Hebraistically
ERIWIRR rear-view mirror
ERJHHIZ Henry John Heinz
ERKSIGR Henry Kissinger
ERLGCLY neurologically
petrologically
ERLUJLY petroleum jelly

ERMGEIM ferromagnetism
ERNIIIY refrangibility
ERNMCBE Le Grand Macabre
ERNSLOT wear oneself out
ERNTEHT wear another hat
EROEAIE retro-operative
ERONETR Dear John letter
EROPRSN bear comparison
ERPACET Terry Pratchett
ERRTIKN terror-stricken
ERSACIG heart-searching
ERSIEES regressiveness
ERSIIUL Negro spiritual
ERSNAIE representative
ERSNAIN representation
ERSOEEF refresh oneself
ERTAGAE secret language
ERTRAIE territorialise
territorialize
ERTRAIY territoriality
ERTWLIG terry towelling
ERUHTBD be brought to bed
ERVOSGT deprive of sight
ESAEWMN newspaperwoman
newspaperwomen
ESAIEES persuasiveness
ESAIIIY persuasibility
ESESNES Meistersingers
ESFHWRD News of the World
ESHNOIE less than no time
ESMOEAE let someone have
ESMOENW let someone know
ESMOEON get someone down
ESMOETT get someone at it
ESMSUEE get some shut-eye
ESNBEES personableness
reasonableness
seasonableness
ESNLOUN personal column
ESNLTRO personal stereo
ESNOESN person-to-person
ESNWDIG Peasant Wedding
ESOEAIG cease operating
ESOEFET keystone effect
ESOFRNE news conference
ESOPROE sense of purpose
ESRACCE menstrual cycle
ESROSES censoriousness
ESRPRUT leisure pursuit
ESRUDIH mess around with
ESSNESN Tessa Sanderson
ESTOAIM sensationalism
ESTOAIT sensationalist
ESTVPAT sensitive plant
ESYRTOD Betsey Trotwood
ETAEAIN septuagenarian
ETAHAIG central heating
ETAIAIN centralization
neutralization
ETALCIG central locking
ETBOHOD Betty Boothroyd
ETBRIOE pentobarbitone
ETCLICE vertical circle

ETCLNLS vertical angles
ETCNTBE petty constable
ETCSAIM Pentecostalism
ETCSAIT Pentecostalist
ETDNEET vested interest
ETDXHNE heated exchange
ETEBAND feather-brained
ETECNFR set the scene for
ETEETRF get the better of
ETEHSOE settle the score
ETEIEON let the side down
ETEOEAE best-before date
ETEPOHT weather prophet
ETEREEP get the breeze up
ETESAIN weather station
ETFCIIN beatific vision
ETFRTAE get to first base
ETGISIH get to grips with
ETHRTET beat the retreat
ETIANIY certain annuity
ETIIAIN gentrification
ETITDES restrictedness
ETITDRA restricted area
ETIUAIE centrifugalise
centrifugalize
ETLADCP mental handicap
ETLIODR mental disorder
ETLNAIY rectilinearity
ETLNILY pestilentially
ETLOPTL mental hospital
ETLTIUE mental attitude
ETMNAIE sentimentalise
sentimentalize
testimonialise
testimonialize
ETMNAIM sentimentalism
ETMNAIT sentimentalist
ETMNAIY sentimentality
testamentarily
ETNCAUG Weltanschauung
ETNCOSY pertinaciously
ETNHLRH left in the lurch
ETNNSAS rest on one's oars
ETNSRAT beat one's breast
ETNSRIS beat one's brains
ETNTRUH getting-through
ETNUAIY rectangularity
ETOOAOY dextrorotatory
ETOTEIE Death on the Nile
ETPATSD death-practised
ETRCPTL venture capital
ETREEOE lector benevole
ETRFHLW letter of the law
ETRFRDT letter of credit
ETRIAIN westernization
ETRTOIM restorationism
ETRTWRS gesture towards
ETRUOIE deuterium oxide
ETRWIIG feature-writing
ETSEDOH death's-head moth
EUAECOS Jerusalem cross
EUAIAIN secularization
EUAPYET regular payment

EUAVSTR regular visitor
EUEAERM recuperate from
EUEECNE rejuvenescence
EUHDEZR nebuchadnezzar□
EUHPTTS serum hepatitis
EUIIAIN beautification
EUIYAEA security camera
EULPEIE sexual appetite
EULSNIE tequila sunrise
EULULVR Lemuel Gulliver
EUSTOAY requisitionary
EUSTOIT requisitionist
EVBETIG heavy breathing
EVCAIIY serviceability
EVCSAIN service station
EVNEFCS leave no effects
EVNYOIS heavenly bodies
EVOASNE leave of absence
EVSDLYR Heaviside layer
EVUTNIN nervous tension
EWRILNS Leeward Islands
EZDAEIE benzodiazepine
EZGOOSI Jerzy Grotowski
FARFOOR affair of honour
FAROSAE affairs of state
FEATUGE after a struggle
FEIAEES effeminateness
FEIOEER a flea in one's ear
FETOAEY affectionately
FETTOGY affect strongly
FEVSIGY effervescingly
FIINCUE efficient cause
FINFCNE of significance
FLIDJSA Afsluitdijk Sea
FOETOLY off one's trolley
FOIEAOE of no fixed abode
FOITEOR a foot in the door
FOTESES effortlessness
FRAATCE of great article
FRMNIND aforementioned
FSTRNIG offset printing
FTEAKOT off the back foot
FTEHUDR off the shoulder
GEOTATE Egremont Castle
GETITNE a great distance
GETUBRF a great number of
GISTEED against the head
GISTEOL against the wool
GIUTRLY agriculturally
GLTRAIM egalitarianism
GRNIEET aggrandizement
GRSIEES aggressiveness
GRTAISY Igor Stravinsky
GTAHITE Agatha Christie
HABSAOS The Ambassadors
HAEFESN The Age of Reason
HAEFRNE The Age of Bronze
HAELGCL phraseological
HATOIIS the authorities
HBYETOR the boy next door
HCEHATD chicken-hearted
HCELVRD chicken-livered
HCENOAO the clean potato
HCMEIIN the competition
HCMIMNS The Commitments
HCNSNOT chacun à son goût
HCOTESN checkout person
HCRLSAD The Coral Island
HCRPAES The Card Players
HCTETET shock treatment
HCTPJMS the cat's pyjamas
HCUTYIE The Country Wife
HDILNRD Rhode Island Red
HDVLNAL the devil and all
HECAATR chief character
HECNTBE chief constable
HECRTIK three-card trick
HEDNTRM thread and thrum
HEEDAIG wheeler-dealing
HEEEUIE chief executive
HEEHNMN The Elephant Man
HEIILNS Phoenix Islands
HEITETE Phoenix Theatre
HELGTIG sheet lightning
HEMTCLY phlegmatically
HEOFRUE wheel of Fortune
wheel of fortune
HEPITUN three-point turn
HERCMLX Phaedra complex
HERHHKR the Earthshaker
HETESOH three-toed sloth
HETTECO cheer to the echo
HEWITIG sheep-whistling
HFRYEAA The Forsyte Saga
HFUSAOS The Four Seasons
HGETASY The Great Gatsby
HGETEOD the Great Beyond
HGLEBUH The Golden Bough
HGNLCAT the gentle craft
HGNRLEL the general weal
HGOODAS the good old days
HGSETUH the gospel truth
HGTSFEL The Gates of Hell
HHNRDAS the Hundred Days
HIBNNTN Chris Bonington
HIDPNET The Independent
HILDOIS thrilled to bits
HIOCMAD chain of command
HITADWT Christian de Wet
HITASED Christian Stead
HITCLEE Christ's College
HITESES thriftlessness
HITPEFY Christopher Fry
HITPELE Christopher Lee
HITPESY Christopher Sly
HITPGUK Christoph Gluck
HKAEWKS The Kraken Wakes
HKHNSIH shake hands with
HKNOKNS The King of Kings
HKOESDS shake one's sides
HKVOETY shake violently
HLBNSOT whole bang shoot
HLBNWAE whalebone whale
HLDKLES The Ladykillers
HLFADOL the life and soul
HLFOJSS The Life of Jesus
HLFORLY the life of Riley
HLHATDY wholeheartedly
whole-heartedly
HLIOCRE chilli con carne
HLLGCLY philologically
HLNFPRA Chilon of Sparta
HLNGOBE The Long Goodbye
HLNHOIT philanthropist
HLOATCL phyllotactical
HLOGAHW Sheldon Glashow
HLPEEAN Philippe Pétain
HLPHRDN Philip Sheridan
HLPUUTS Philip Augustus
HLRNCUT children's court
HLRSOES the Lord's tokens
HLRSRYR the Lord's Prayer
HLRSSAT child-resistant
HLSEPRR The Last Emperor
HLTLWMN the little woman
HLTSAES The Lotus-Eaters
HLYHLIR shilly-shallier
HMCLOLT chemical toilet
HMECUCL chamber council
HMFCDES shamefacedness
HMSAALY Thomas Macaulay
HMSCOES The Music Lovers
HMSECMN Thomas Newcomen
HMSEELY Thomas Keneally
HMSHDEL Thomas Shadwell
HMSRMEL Thomas Cromwell
HNAMGRA phantasmagoria
HNAMGRC phantasmagoric
HNBRIOE phenobarbitone
HNEBEES changeableness
HNEESES changelessness
HNEHPIG channel hopping
HNEILNS Channel Islands
HNELRHP chancellorship
HNENSAS change one's ways
HNENSID change one's mind
HNENSUE change one's tune
HNENSUK chance one's luck
HNESRIG channel surfing
HNEYFIE Chancery Office
HNFLFUT A Handful of Dust
HNHRNHE chincherinchee
HNIGLCS changing places
HNIGORE changing course
HNLCEIS phenolic resins
HNMTCLY phonematically
HNNCSAY think necessary
HNNTIGF think nothing of
HNODGSE chanson de geste
HNSCBAE Chinese cabbage
HNSLNEN Chinese lantern
HNSNWER Chinese New Year
HNTELNS The Netherlands
HNWOKOT The New York Post
HOAISAE chromatic scale
HOAOPEE chromatosphere
HOAORPY chromatography
HOECSIN whoopee cushion
HOGTEOE through the nose

HOIODEG Whoopi Goldberg
HOIOELT throw in one's lot
HONOEHR thrown together
thrown-together
HOOEEFN throw oneself on
HOOEEFT throw oneself at
HOOERCL chronometrical
HOOHCLY theosophically
HOOMMSN Theodor Mommsen
HOOSHAN Theodor Schwann
HORTCLY theocratically
HOTEOKT throw the book at
HOTEREE shoot the breeze
HOTEWTH throw the switch
HOTTEOS throw to the dogs
HOUOECP throw up one's cap
HPEDPRE shepherd's purse
HPEETIE the present time
HPESAPR whippersnapper
HPIGETE shopping centre
HPOEAIT the proletariat
HPOIASN The Prodigal Son
HPOYNLE Rhapsody in Blue
HPWRFOE The Power of Love
HQENPAE the queen's peace
HRAEFOD shortage of food
HRAETCL pharmaceutical
HRAIAIG thermal imaging
HRAIGAE the roaring game
HRAOOIT pharmacologist
HRAPITR thermal printer
HRARATR thermal reactor
HRCEATR character actor
HRCEITC characteristic
HRDMNIN third dimension
HREBBAE Charles Babbage
HREBODN Charles Blondin
HREBOSN Charles Bronson
HREBUBN Charles Bourbon
HREBYOT Charles Boycott
HRECULY Charles Causley
HREDCES Charles Dickens
HREDDSN Charles Dodgson
HREHUHY Charles Haughey
HREKNEY Charles Kennedy
HRELCAO Charles Luciano
HREPREL Charles Parnell
HREPROS Charles Parsons
HRESRAE Charles Surface
HRETEAD Charles the Bald
HRETFAY Charles Tiffany
HRFDPTS sheriff deputes
HRFOFCR sheriff officer
HRGTOMN The Rights of Man
HRHLFLS Churchill Falls
HRHSEBY Church Assembly
HRICALN Charlie Chaplin
HRKBVNS The Rokeby Venus
HRLPEUE chorale prelude
HRLYPOY Choral Symphony
HRNADIE the rank and file
HROFNIE charm offensive
HROKOMS Sherlock Holmes

HROLCRC thermoelectric
HROSFIE Chariots of Fire
HROTRSE charlotte russe
HROTYNE Charlotte Yonge
HROYAIS thermodynamics
HRPATCS sharp practices
HRSGTDY short-sightedly
HRTBEES charitableness
HRTNETN Charlton Heston
HRTNIDR Thornton Wilder
HRTUNHR thirst-quencher
HRYERWR Thirty Years' War
HSCEAET The Secret Agent
HSCLAUE physical nature
HSEIGOE whispering dome
HSHRCCD phosphoric acid
HSHRSET phosphorescent
HSLIHEE The Selfish Gene
HSODAES chest of drawers
chest-of-drawers
HSONMCL physiognomical
HSTERGN chase the dragon
HSXONIS the Six Counties
HTAILNS Chatham Islands
HTASENW What Maisie Knew
HTBODEL white blood cell
HTBTNYU what's biting you?
HTCEITY photochemistry
HTCRUCE white corpuscle
HTEGAIG photoengraving
HTEHUTN Whitney Houston
HTETNYU what's eating you?
HTHDCES what the dickens
HTHMUHF shut the mouth of
HTIDERE the third degree
HTIDSAE the third estate
HTIWATE whittie-whattie
HTLECHM that'll teach him
HTLECHR that'll teach her
HTLECYU that'll teach you
HTLEHDY That'll Be The Day
HTLMNSE photoluminesce
HTMMCIE The Time Machine
HTMNBUS rhythm and blues
HTNSYSO shut one's eyes to
HTODSRE what you deserve
HTOOSYO what do you say to?
HTPROIM photoperiodism
HTPTOOY phytopathology
HTSNHSS photosynthesis
HTSNHTC photosynthetic
HTSNIIE photosensitise
photosensitize
HTTEAAE what's the damage?
HTTEIKT that's the ticket
HTUWTYU what's up with you?
HTVNENE what a vengeance
HTYUALT what-d'you-call-it
HUAIFVR rheumatic fever
HUAOOIT rheumatologist
HUDRDRH shouldered arch
HUDREGT shoulder-height
HUHFLES thoughtfulness

HVHLPNY shove-halfpenny
HVLEGOE the velvet glove
HVLOSES chivalrousness
HVUDFIE chevaux-de-frise
HWIEABT The White Rabbit
HWNESAE The Winter's Tale
HWOEWDE the wooden wedge
HWOLNES The Woodlanders
HWRDOOE the world to come
HWRMYUN the worm may turn
HWTRAIS The Water-Babies
HYAOGAE the Year of Grace
IAAOTLC vicar-apostolic
IABGAIN disambiguation
IACASAE financial state
IACATMS Financial Times
IACCMAY finance company
IACMOAE disaccommodate
IAFLAIN disaffiliation
IAFRAIN disaffirmation
IAITCLY vitalistically
IAJAIDV Nihanj Kapil Dev
IAKOLDE disacknowledge
IAPEITD misappreciated
IAPIAIN misapplication
IAPITET disappointment
IAPOAIE disapprobative
IAPOAIN disapprobation
IAPOAOY disapprobatory
IAPOIGY disapprovingly
IAPORAE disappropriate
misappropriate
IARCLEE Linacre College
IARNEET disarrangement
IASAEET final statement
IASCAIN disassociation
IATCLTD disarticulated
IATIUIN disattribution
IATROWR Disasters of War
IAUOSES miraculousness
IBEIGRD nimble-fingered
IBIEBCE Bix Beiderbecke
IBLTRIR pit bull terrier
IBRILNS Gilbert Islands
IBRSEDN Gilbert Sheldon
ICATWMN aircraftswoman
ICCLUIT pisciculturist
ICECBNT kitchen cabinet
ICEINLY discretionally
ICIBEKR circuit-breaker
ICIIAEY discriminately
ICIIAIE discriminative
ICIIAIG discriminating
ICIIAIN discrimination
ICIIAOY discriminatory
ICIOSES circuitousness
ICKIDUH his cake is dough
ICLCLEE Lincoln College
ICLUAIN discolouration
miscalculation
ICMAIAE circumnavigate
ICMMUAE circumambulate
ICMOEAE discomboberate

ICMOUAE discombobulate
ICMOUIN circumlocution
ICMOUOY circumlocutory
ICMPCII Giacomo Puccini
ICMPCIN circumspection
ICMTNIL circumstantial
ICMYAIN circumgyration
ICNETDY disconnectedly
discontentedly
ICNETET discontentment
ICNIIND air-conditioned
ICNIINR air-conditioner
ICNIUNE discontinuance
ICNOAEY disconsolately
ICNOAIN disconsolation
ICNVNOH Vincent Van Gogh
ICPIAIN disciplinarian
ICRIEES discursiveness
ICRNCLY diachronically
ICUAEET discouragement
ICUAIGY discouragingly
ICUTNNE discountenance
ICUTOSY discourteously
IDCIEES vindictiveness
IDEITNE middle distance
IDFAAIE Bird of Paradise
bird of paradise
IDGAAIN biodegradation
IDIFLES disdainfulness
IDNRAUE hidden treasure
IDNTUET wind instrument
IDOAEIA Birds of America
IDOSCAE wild-goose chase
IDTPOLM find it a problem
IDTRCIE find attractive
IDWHPIG window-shopping
IDWRSIG window dressing
window-dressing
IDWYRUD find a way around
IEAAAIO Cinema Paradiso
IEAIAIN liberalization
mineralization
IEAORPY cinematography
IEASODR nine days' wonder
IEAYEIW Literary Review
IEBDAEO give a bad name to
IEBGADO give a big hand to
IEBGEET disemboguement
IEBRAIN disembarkation
IEBWLET disembowelment
IECATET disenchantment
IECMLIT file a complaint
IEDRYOK give a dirty look
IEECPEE five pence piece
IEEMSIN give permission
IEESNFR give reasons for
IEESORS nine men's morris
IEFACIE disenfranchise
IEFCIIY hive of activity
IEFEDAH life after death
IEFEUNY eigen-frequency
IEFUIES line of business
IEGIGVR give a going-over
IEGNEIG bioengineering
IEHEBWO give the elbow to
IEHGAED give the go-ahead
IEHHAEO give the heave-ho
IEHLWON give the low-down
IEHMEIG give a hammering
IEHRISO give the reins to
IEIDDES like-mindedness
IEJDEET give a judgement
IELAUEO give pleasure to
IEMEOIL time immemorial
IENBETE live and breathe
IENHAOY pile on the agony
IENHCEP live on the cheap
IENLTIE live and let live
IENRATD pigeon-breasted
IENSOKT line one's pocket
IENXHNE give in exchange
IEOENOF ride someone off
IEONSET rise to one's feet
IEOPSAE rites of passage
IEPHAOY pile up the agony
IEPHGOT give up the ghost
IEPNSIE give up one's life
IEPNSOT give up one's post
IERAOFR give a reason for
IERCRIG video recording
IERDNEO give credence to
IEREENO give free rein to
IESBIYO give a subsidy to
IESMAYF give a summary of
IESTLIE fixed satellite
IETAOIY silent majority
IETCLTS diverticulitis
IETEGHO give strength to
IETLIGO give a talking-to
IETOSES licentiousness
IETRAIM libertarianism
IETRCAR director's chair
IETRLIG direct drilling
IETRUPT like it or lump it
IETSEET divertissement
IETVTAT digestive tract
IEUFAEO give suffrage to
IEULBAE disequilibrate
IEURNYO give currency to
IEWTRSE Cider with Rosie
IEXEINE wide experience
IEXETNY life expectancy
IFRNILY differentially
IFRNITR differentiator
IGAHCLY biographically
IGAMTCL diagrammatical
IGEADDY single-handedly
IGEIDDY single-mindedly
IGEOPET single hoop tent
IGERATD single-breasted
IGHCAGS ring the changes
IGITCLY jingoistically
linguistically
IGOOLAS Siege of Orléans
IGPRSIG singapore sling
IGRONIG finger-pointing
IGRSLUE big girl's blouse
IGUTEET disgruntlement
IGVLZUZ Diego Velázquez
IHAARVT right as a trivet
IHACNIN right ascension
IHADATE Highland cattle
IHADDES high-handedness
IHADETE right and centre
IHAOTAE right about face!
IHATDES big-heartedness
IHBIDES night-blindness
IHEAINO with relation to
IHEBNIE Michael Bentine
IHECLIS Michael Collins
IHEDULS Michael Douglas
IHEFRDY Michael Faraday
IHEHLIG Michael Holding
IHEHLOD Michael Holroyd
IHEHREN Michael Hordern
IHEJCSN Michael Jackson
IHEJHSN Michael Johnson
IHEMAHR Michael Meacher
IHEMSEM Michaelmas term
IHETPET Michael Tippett
IHEVNRS Michael Ventris
IHFAORD highy-flavoured
IHFYEGT light-flyweight
IHGOGAE with a good grace
IHHATDY light-heartedly
IHHNWMN right-hand woman
IHHPOIO with the proviso
IHHPROE with the purpose
IHIBKNN Mikhail Bakunin
IHIDDES high-mindedness
IHIEOIL with time to kill
IHIFCLY with difficulty
IHIGHNE fighting chance
IHIGPIE lighting-up time
IHLHVEL Michel Chevreul
IHLOCUT Michel Foucault
IHLRNGN Wilhelm Röntgen
IHLSILY Nicholas Ridley
IHMRABY Nightmare Abbey
IHNCNET with one consent
IHNLGAE with an ill grace
IHNNNHF within an inch of
IHNPNID with an open mind
IHNUINE with an audience
IHOFHBT right off the bat
IHOMSIN High Commission
IHPLUIN light pollution
IHRASED fisherman's bend
IHRASNT fisherman's knot
IHRBASN Richard Branson
IHRBRAE Richard Burbage
IHRDWIS Richard Dawkins
IHRELAN Richard Ellmann
IHRFYMN Richard Feynman
IHRHGAT Richard Hoggart
IHRHKUT Richard Hakluyt
IHRIGAS Richard Ingrams
IHRNILD high-principled
IHRNVLE Richard Neville

IHRRDES Richard Rodgers
IHRSRUS Richard Strauss
IHTETAK high-street bank
IHUAGIG without arguing
IHUBEIH without blemish
IHUDSUE without dispute
IHUFEIG without feeling
IHUMAUE without measure
IHUOWTR fish out of water
IHURSIE without respite
IHURSRE without reserve
IHUTIKR wishful thinker
IHUWRIG without warning
IHVNENE with a vengeance
IHVNRCE right ventricle
IHWNMLS fight windmills
IHYEADD highly regarded
highly-regarded
IHYERWR Eighty Years' War
IHYESND highly seasoned
highly-seasoned
IHYHLIG eighty shilling
IHYSEMD highly esteemed
IIAIAIN militarization
IIAOMDA Divina Commedia
IIAOSES viviparousness
IIAYOIE Military Police
military police
IICIAIN disinclination
IICREAE disincarcerate
IICROAE disincorporate
IIECMAY limited company
IIEEIIN limited edition
IIESRET citizen's arrest
IIETOIT vivisectionist
IIFRAIN disinformation
misinformation
IIGHSAG riding the stang
IIGNOSY disingenuously
IIGURES living quarters
IIHRTNE disinheritance
IIIGATR limiting factor
IIIGCEN dividing screen
IIIIAIN divinification
silicification
vitilitigation
IIIOSES libidinousness
IIJDEET sit in judgement
IILEPRS visible exports
IILIPRS visible imports
IILSOIE disillusionise
disillusionize
IIOEBOS die in one's boots
IIOEHES dig in one's heels
IIOESOS die in one's shoes
IIOOFCR liaison officer
IIOSMOE pin it on someone
IIPNLPI Filippino Lippi
IIRDOTY Winifred Holtby
IIRGLRY visit regularly
IITGAIG disintegrating
IITGAIN disintegration
IITOSLY sinistrorsally

IITRRTD misinterpreted
IIUIEES diminutiveness
IIUOSES ridiculousness
IJITDES disjointedness
IKEHRIG pickled herring
IKFHBNH pick of the bunch
IKNHPNS kick in the pants
IKNHTEH kick in the teeth
IKNMCIE milking machine
IKNSONS lick one's wounds
IKNTRDF sick and tired of
IKNUSIG Vidkun Quisling
IKTKIAI Rikki-Tikki-Tavi
IKYPLAE Mickey Spillane
ILABCLY William Buckley
ILABENN William Brennan
ILABLNE field ambulance
ILABRNZ William Barentz
ILABTSN William Bateson
ILACAGE William Craigie
ILACBET William Cobbett
ILADMIR William Dampier
ILAGLET William Gilbert
ILAGLIG William Golding
ILAHGRH William Hogarth
ILAHONY William H Bonney
ILAHZIT William Hazlitt
ILARNIE William Rankine
ILASANR William Shatner
ILASEES William Siemens
ILASEMN William Sherman
ILASONR William Spooner
ILATLEY field artillery
ILATNAE William Tyndale
ILAWAIG Gillian Wearing
ILAWLAE William Wallace
ILBLEIG Bible-believing
ILCOOIT dialectologist
ILEENIG Billie Jean King
ILEHTLW Willie Whitelaw
ILFXHNE bill of exchange
ILMTCLY diplomatically
ILNFRFR fill in a form for
ILNHCOS kill on the cross
ILNIAIN Finlandisation
Finlandization
ILNOEEF killing oneself
ILNRAIM millenarianism
ILNSEHD Billings method
ILUTETE Gielgud Theatre
IMNJBLE diamond jubilee
IMNRMEG Sigmund Romberg
IMNWDIG diamond wedding
INACMAL Finn mac Cumhail
INFHCOS sign of the cross
INGTOBY Midnight Cowboy
INLRLIG Lionel Trilling
INSASWY Giant's Causeway
INYIAIN Disneyfication
IOAILNS Nicobar Islands
IOAPUSN Nicolas Poussin
IOAVVLV Nikolai Vavilov
IOBROHA Simon Bar Kokhba

IOCTERL Ripon Cathedral
IODLNLS Ninon de Lenclos
IODRIES disorderliness
IOEFIHN pin one's faith on
IOEHESN dig one's heels in
IOEHPSN pin one's hopes on
IOINAIN disorientation
IOOEHNS sit on one's hands
IOTEEDE dip of the needle
IOTEELT Simon the Zealot
IOTEHOE sit on the throne
IOTEPIE sit on the splice
IPAOSES diaphanousness
IPEETNE simple sentence
IPENEET simple interest
IPERCIN simple fraction
IPERCUE simple fracture
IPIIAIN simplification
IPITCLY simplistically
IPNAIEY dispensatively
IPNAOIY dispensatorily
IPRTDES dispiritedness
IPTHPEY hippety-hoppety
IPTTOSY disputatiously
IQIIINL disquisitional
IRAEFEO Tierra del Fuego
IRBOOIT microbiologist
IREAOSE Pierre Larousse
IREEEMT Pierre de Fermat
IREOOIS microeconomics
IRERUHN Pierre Proudhon
IRGRFLY disregardfully
IRGYEIE nitroglycerine
IRGYHCL hieroglyphical
IRIVSRB Giorgio Vasarib
IRLGCLY micrologically
IROGNSS micro-organisms
IROSUOR vitreous humour
IRPEETD misrepresented
IRPOESR microprocessor
IRRBNIG library binding
IRREIIN library edition
IRRHCLY hierarchically
IRRYMTY mirror symmetry
IRSOAGA microsporangia
IRUGNRI Pier Luigi Nervi
ISAEAPE Miss Jane Marple
ISCAERM dissociate from
ISCAIIY dissociability
ISENRDE Miss Jean Brodie
ISMERCL dissymmetrical
ISMNIND first-mentioned
ISMOEON pin someone down
ISNHGEN wigs on the green
ISNNELS pins and needles
ISOENOF piss someone off
ISPEISI Giuseppe Giusti
ISRCRIG first recording
ISYOSKV Rimsky-Korsakov
ITARAIY virtual reality
ITASAIN mistranslation
ITCLMIT fifth columnist
ITDOEHR fitted together

ITENLRE Little and Large
ITEREMN little green men
ITESINL distress signal
ITEXHNE win the exchange
ITEYITE little by little
ITFOTNS list of contents
ITGLATE Tintagel Castle
ITGNCLY histogenically
ITHYUGR Pitt the younger
ITINCLY histrionically
ITIUIEY distributively
ITKNEIF mistaken belief
ITKOEMN mistake one's man
ITLGCLY histologically
ITLTCLY histolytically
ITNAUAE tintinnabulate
ITNMDNA Sistine Madonna
ITNOESN listen to reason
ITNREMN Milton Friedman
ITNUSIG distinguishing
ITOAALO Pietro Badaglio
ITOSICE virtuous circle
ITRAPNE Victoria sponge
ITRASAD Victoria Island
ITRMAUL Victor Emmanuel
ITROCNI Viktor Korchnoi
ITROEIA Vittorio De Sica
ITRORPY historiography
ITROSES victoriousness
ITROSIE winter solstice
ITRREHL Pieter Brueghel
ITRRUHL Pieter Breughel
ITSHAIM Nietzscheanism
IUAIEES figurativeness
IUDAAFN liquid paraffin
IUEAIEY vituperatively
IUEFPEH figure of speech
IUIOSOL bituminous coal
IULNUAN Miguel Indurain
IULSUIS Miguel Asturias
IUTNOSY simultaneously
IUTODOT Dieu et mon droit
IUTRGAD pituitary gland
IVCMRHL air-vice-marshal
IVNIIAO Giovanni Pisano
IYIEYLB City Livery Club
IYLNBOS Sibylline Books
IZGLEPE Dizzy Gillespie
KTOTIIE skate on thin ice
LAAAEPN clean as a new pin
LAADAGR cloak-and-dagger
LAEAPNH pleased as Punch
LAIGECN floating beacon
LAIGSAD floating island
LAIOSES oleaginousness
LAIZEAD Ella Fitzgerald
LAMUTIS Altai Mountains
LANTULY plead not guilty
LAOEEFP clean oneself up
LAOGRAE a load of garbage
LAORBIH a load of rubbish
LARILNS Aldabra Islands
LATEAFR clear the way for
LATERUD clear the ground
LAUEEKR pleasure-seeker
LAUEOIG pleasure-loving
LAUERUD pleasure ground
LAUOEAT clean up one's act
LBATCOE globe artichoke
LBEGSIG flabbergasting
LCADAKE block and tackle
LCDDMNO Plácido Domingo
LCEESSN black-eyed Susan
black-eyed susan
LCINEIG electioneering
LCITEAE black in the face
LCLGTRM block light from
LCMREER black-marketeer
LCNRISS Black Narcissus
LCOTEAE slice of the cake
LCOWRHP place of worship
LCRBOOY electrobiology
LCRCEIT electrochemist
LCRCIDW electric window
LCRCMLX Electra complex
LCRCUTR electric guitar
LCRNCAL electronic mail
LCRNCLY electronically
LCROMSS electro-osmosis
LCROTCL electro-optical
LCRPAIG electroplating
LCRSAIS electrostatics
LCRTEAY electrotherapy
LCRVLNY electrovalency
LCUCUAE pluck up courage
LDECMIN bladder campion
LDPOETR slide projector
LDUEOOY Old Deuteronomy
LEATAFC illegal traffic
LEDSATD already started
LEDTETE Almeida Theatre
LEIGALT sleeping tablet
LEIIAEY illegitimately
LESAEMN elder statesman
LETENLS Albert Reynolds
LETEOIL Albert Memorial
LETISEN Albert Einstein
LETMRVA Alberto Moravia
LFOELNS fluff one's lines
LGDAHRE flog a dead horse
LGLTCAS Glagolitic Mass
LGPOITC oligopsonistic
LGTEGIS ill-gotten gains
LGTNIER flight engineer
LGTOSES flagitiousness
LHBTCLY alphabetically
LHMRCLY alphamerically
LHNMRCL alphanumerical
LHPRILS alpha particles
LIAASOK all in a day's work
LIAZEMR Alois Alzheimer
LIERCLY altimetrically
LIGQIRL flying squirrel
LIGUCMN Flying Dutchman
LIGUTES flying buttress
LIOEIUE ultimogeniture
LITEAEF fly in the face of
LMIIHES old-maidishness
LMNAIES elementariness
LMNFHSA old man of the sea
LMOEEFN plume oneself on
LMRSSAT flame-resistant
LMRTRAT flame-retardant
LMTLGCL climatological
LNCRRDE blank cartridge
LNEMAAE Blenheim Palace
LNESAGS Flinders Ranges
LNESERE Flinders Petrie
LNESOIZ Alan Dershowitz
LNSINIT plant scientist
LNUAFVR glandular fever
LNUBIGR Alan Rusbridger
LOAHCLY allopathically
LOATCLY pleonastically
LOCNUIG blood-consuming
LOEECSS floor exercises
LOETEHP all over the shop
LOOEWYN elbow one's way in
LOSCIIE blood-sacrifice
LOTISIY bloodthirstily
LOTSCED allow to succeed
LPAOLSY blepharoplasty
LPATCVS Elephanta caves
LPNHWIT slap on the wrist
LPOLSOE old people's home
LPYHHES clap by the heels
LRCEIAE ultracrepidate
LRCLOLR clerical collar
LRDENSN Alfred Tennyson
LREUBRF a large number of
LRITCLY altruistically
LRMNAIT ultramontanist
LRNEARW Clarence Darrow
LROTENW glory of the snow
LRSNCLY ultrasonically
LRSRCUE ultrastructure
LRUDAEA all-round camera
LRYASNE clergyman's knee
LSAHRSS plasmapheresis
LSARUNT Alastair Burnet
LSBIDES flash blindness
LSBTVLE Elisabethville
LSCNCOS class-conscious
LSECUTR close encounter
LSEOPRS plaster of Paris
LSFRSEL Blashford-Snell
LSIADOE all skin and bone
LSIIAIN classification
LSIIAOY classificatory
LSISREN plastic surgeon
LSISREY plastic surgery
LSLRLTD closely related
LSMCAES clash-ma-clavers
LSNRMRS closing remarks
LSOBRTR Glastonbury Tor
LSTEEOD close the record
LSTEORO close the door to
LSTTEOE close to the bone
LTAKHMO I'll thank them to

LTENIES slatternliness
LTEOEEF flatter oneself
LTHTSRW clutch at a straw
LTHTTAS clutch at straws
LTIGATR clotting factor
LTNNSAK flat on one's back
LTOTDES flat-footedness
LTRANIE all-terrain bike
LTRDCOY clitoridectomy
LTSPNAE flat as a pancake
LTTCOIS plate tectonics
LUAOHSS pleurapophyses
LUHEHUE slaughterhouse
LUHEOSY slaughterously
LUHHSNS plough the sands
LUTAIEY illustratively
LUTAINL illustrational
LUTOHBA claustrophobia
LUTOHBC claustrophobic
LVETETE Olivier Theatre
LVNCACS Slavonic Dances
LVRRMEL Oliver Cromwell
LWCTETE Aldwych Theatre
LWHWITE blow the whistle
LXLIAIN blaxploitation
LXNEKRA Alexander Korda
LXNEMNO Alexander Monro
LXNRDMS Alexandre Dumas
LXNRPRN Alexandr Oparin
LYFAANT play off against
LYHNYHN Lloyd Honeyghan
LYRUDIH play around with
LZBTDVD Elizabeth David
LZBTFIK Elizabeth Frink
LZBTKNY Elizabeth Kenny
LZDOITE Eliza Doolittle
MASBEES impassableness
MASDRHP ambassadorship
MAUAEES immaculateness
MAULAKR Emmanuel Lasker
MDOVGDO Amedeo Avogadro
MEAIEES imperativeness
MEFCIEY imperfectively
MEHDCLY immethodically
MEILAAE Imperial Palace
MELSIGY embellishingly
MEMAIIY impermeability
MEOPNUN emperor penguin
MEVOSES imperviousness
MGCNETR image converter
MHBLGCL amphibological
MHTIEIH emphathize with
MIETOSY ambidextrously
MIEULIG empire-building
MIMAHRM omnium-gatherum
MIUEIIN omnibus edition
MLAOAAO Emiliano Zapato
MLCBEES implacableness
MLDCISN Emily Dickinson
MLIIAIN emulsification
MLITSIE small intestine
MLMNAIN implementation
MLMTCLY emblematically
MLOBHIG Emil von Behring
MLOTEAP smell of the lamp
MLRGTAK I'm all right, Jack
MLUIIIY implausibility
MOEAEES immoderateness
MOEIHET impoverishment
MOHPAIG smooth-speaking
MOIIAIN immobilization
MRCIAIY impracticality
MRCNEUY American Beauty
MRCNNIN American Indian
MRCTDOF imbricated roof
MRGAIIY impregnability
MRLDESD smartly dressed
MRORNFR embryo transfer
MRSGETY impress greatly
MRSIEES impressiveness
MRSINBE impressionable
MTUIHES amateurishness
MUEEPNE immune response
MUIINUP ammunition dump
MUOUPES immunosuppress
NAAIAIG incapacitating
NAAIAIN incapacitation
NACIOEN Antarctic Ocean
NACNIIN in bad condition
NADOEET onward movement
NAEETOK engagement book
NAGNMES in large numbers
NAIAIES insanitariness
NAIBEES insatiableness
NAIFCOY unsatisfactory
NAIIRIH unfamiliar with
NALHTAZ and all that jazz
NAMDADT one-armed bandit
NAMNCLY enharmonically
NAMNOSY inharmoniously
NANANBE unmaintainable
NANRIES unmannerliness
NAOADHW Anna Howard Shaw
NAOIAIN antagonization
NAOITCO antagonistic to
NARESAE unmarried state
NATERBE enfant terrible
NATFLES unfaithfulness
NATOSES incautiousness
NAUROSY insalubriously
NAUTDIH infatuated with
NAYIEES unladylikeness
NCEBCES knickerbockers
NCITEOE an ace in the hole
NCITRLY unscripturally
NCNWEGD unacknowledged
NCONEFR unaccounted-for
NCOPIHD unaccomplished
NCOTEED knock on the head
NCRNCLY anachronically
NCUAIIY inscrutability
NCUTMDO unaccustomed to
NCUUOSY unscrupulously
NDIAIIY inadvisability
NDNIIBE unidentifiable
NDRCINL unidirectional
NEAAIIY inseparability
NEABLCA interambulacra
NECFLES unmercifulness
NECMGET unwelcome guest
NECNETD interconnected
NECSINL intercessional
NECSOIL intercessorial
NECVROK undercover work
NEDAYOB incendiary bomb
NEDBEES unreadableness
NEDPNET interdependent
NEDVLPD underdeveloped
NEEMNBE indeterminable
NEEMNBY indeterminably
NEEOSES ungenerousness
NEETMTD underestimated
NEEVDES unreservedness
NEFRMTR interferometer
NEGAANT inveigh against
NEHDCLY unmethodically
NEIACTX inheritance tax
NEIAIGY unhesitatingly
NEIBEES undeniableness
NEIHRBE indecipherable
NEIIEES indecisiveness
indefiniteness
NEILGLY enter illegally
NEIREIN interior design
NEIUILY antediluvially
NEJCINL interjectional
NELCULY intellectually
NELGNSA intelligentsia
NELNAIN interlineation
NELNULY interlingually
NEMDAEY intermediately
NEMDAIN intermediation
NEMNIND undermentioned
NEMTETY intermittently
NENLRAS internal organs
NENNMES in penny numbers
NENUIHD undernourished
NEOCLBE unreconcilable
NEOETUB under one's thumb
NEOIGES unbecomingness
NEONZBE unrecognizable
NEOOSES indecorousness
NEOSFLY unremorsefully
NEOSRBE indemonstrable
undemonstrable
NEOSRBY indemonstrably
NEPAEAY interplanetary
NEPEAIE interpretative
NEPEAIN interpretation
NEPEIEY interpretively
NEPIEOE enterprise zone
NEPIIGY enterprisingly
NEPLAIN interpellation
NEPNLYF under penalty of
NEPNTAE interpenetrate
interpunctuate
NEPPLTD underpopulated
NEPSIEY intempestively
NERDTET Anne Bradstreet

NERPIEY interruptively
NESADBE understandable
NESAEET understatement
NESAILY interspatially
NESCEAY under-secretary
NESCINL intersectional
NESNSRM Anders Ångström
NESRCUE understructure
NETANBE unrestrainable
NETANDY unrestrainedly
NETDOMS inverted commas
NETEAEE en ventre sa mère
NETEAEF under the name of
NETEAMR under the hammer
NETERGN Enter the Dragon
NETIIGY entertainingly
NETOALS unmentionables
NETOSES infectiousness
NETUTBE indestructible
NETUTBY indestructibly
NEUEAIE unremunerative
NEVLAIN undervaluation
NFETAIY ineffectuality
NFETDES unaffectedness
NFRIAIN uniformitarian
NGTAHLR knight bachelor
knight-bachelor
NGTTMLR Knights Templar
NHASNEF in the absence of
NHBEDIE on the breadline
NHBGNIG in the beginning
NHBODCS in the boondocks
NHCAIIY unshockability
NHCNRLF in the control of
NHCRISS onchocerciasis
NHCWSRE In Which We Serve
NHFMLWY in the family way
NHFRFOT in the forefront
NHFRIEF on the far side of
NHHGRPS on the high ropes
NHISAIM Anaheim Stadium
NHITAIE unchristianise
unchristianize
NHKOAOT in the know about
NHMAWIE in the meanwhile
NHMREFR in the market for
NHNBRES Anthony Burgess
NHNFLES unthankfulness
NHNHPIS Anthony Hopkins
NHNIGES unthinkingness
NHNOPDA Anthony of Padua
NHNPRIS Anthony Perkins
NHOHRAD on the other hand
NHOOERC anthropometric
NHOOOIT anthropologist
NHPOESF in the process of
NHRGTAK on the right tack
NHSBETF on the subject of
NHSMCNE in the same canoe
NHSMWYS in the same way as
NHSOFOR on the shop floor
NHSOTIE on the short side
NHSRPEP on the scrap heap

NHTGTIE on the tight side
NHTPLGT in the top flight
NHUHFLY unthoughtfully
NHWNYIE on the windy side
NHWOGAK on the wrong tack
NIAHTCL antipathetical
NIAHUAD one in a thousand
NIAINUE indication rule
NIAREET in disagreement
NICIIAE indiscriminate
NICMIIN uncircumcision
NICRTBE indiscerptible
NIEDAIG insider dealing
NIERSAT antidepressant
NIESIAT antiperspirant
anti-perspirant
NIETBET indirect object
NIETCLY antiseptically
NIETPEH indirect speech
NIEUCAE on hire purchase
NIFCLIS in difficulties
NIHNCLY antiphonically
NIHTCLY antithetically
NIIAIEY anticipatively
NIIAOIY anticipatorily
NIIGEOY in living memory
NIIIIIY indivisibility
NILBEES inviolableness
NILIOIZ Annie Leibovitz
NINFCNE insignificance
NINHSOY ancient history
NINIIWR Indian Civil War
NINLPAT Indian elephant
NINPIIG Indian Uprising
NIOVLAT anticonvulsant
NITNTES indistinctness
NJMAEDF one jump ahead of
NJTRNIG ink-jet printing
NLAATES unpleasantness
NLEAIIY inalienability
inalterability
NLGEINL analogue signal
NLIEGIH in plain English
NLMAIIY inflammability
NLPAIIY unflappability
NLROSES ingloriousness
NLSIIBE unclassifiable
NLTLWIE in a little while
NLTMCBN Uncle Tom's Cabin
NLXBEES inflexibleness
NMATEOR enemy at the door
NMDESOS animadversions
NMETCLY anamnestically
NMLRCES Animal Crackers
NMMNOTO in a moment or two
NMNTOTO in a minute or two
NMTBEES inimitableness
NNDAWRD in an ideal world
NNELCUL unintellectual
NNELGBE unintelligible
NNELGNE unintelligence
NNEPIIG unenterprising
NNFLSOP in one fell swoop

NNHSATC unenthusiastic
NNIEGET uninvited guest
NNIIAIN in anticipation
NNSATES on one's last legs
NNSEDET on one's head be it
NNSEMNS on one's beam ends
on one's beam-ends
NNSETBD on one's deathbed
NNSIDEE in one's mind's eye
NNSONAS in one's born days
NNSORTP on one's doorstep
NNSWRGT in one's own right
NNTEPAE in another place
NOAHUAD one of a thousand
NOAIEES innovativeness
NOCNRTD unconcentrated
NOCTLGE union catalogue
NOCUIEY inconclusively
NOEAIIY intolerability
NOEGPRS in foreign parts
NOENSAL on someone's tail
NOENSET in someone's debt
NOESDES in sober sadness
NOETCTD undomesticated
NOGNAIY uncongeniality
NOHBRAN into the bargain
NOIAEOE innominate bone
NOIAIIY indomitability
NOIBEES unsociableness
NOISLEI Antonio Salieri
NOIVVLI Antonio Vivaldi
NOKBEES unworkableness
NOKNODR in working order
NOMDOSY incommodiously
NOMNCBE incommunicable
NOMNCBY incommunicably
NOMNUAE incommensurate
NOMTCLY endosmotically
NONEGOP encounter group
NONNMES in round numbers
NONWTEU Antoine Watteau
NOOAETS in loco parentis
NOPEEES incompleteness
NOPOIIG uncompromising
NOPRAIY incorporeality
NORBRTD uncorroborated
NORIEOK indoor firework
NORLVLA Andorra-la-Vella
NORNGAD endocrine gland
NOSDRBE inconsiderable
NOSDRBY inconsiderably
NOSINBE unconscionable
NOSINBY unconscionably
NOSQETY inconsequently
NOSSETY inconsistently
NOTEEAS one of these days
NOTGOSY incontiguously
NOTIAIN indoctrination
NOTMNTD uncontaminated
NOTOLBE uncontrollable
NOTOLBY incontrollably
uncontrollably
NOTOLDY uncontrolledly

NOTTEUL enjoy to the full
NOVNECD inconvenienced
NOVNEEN Anton von Webern
NOVNETY inconveniently
NOVNINL unconventional
NPCAOFR on special offer
NPCOMRE Inspector Morse
NPIGUTE snapping turtle
snapping-turtle
NPOIEES inappositeness
NPOIINO in opposition to
NPRAHBE unapproachable
NPRAHBY inapproachably
unapproachably
NPRBEES inoperableness
NPRCAIE unappreciative
NPRCIES ens per accidens
NPRHNIE unapprehensive
NPRPITD unappropriated
NPRTAIE unspiritualise
unspiritualize
NRAALDO Andrea Palladio
NRAATGA Andrea Mantegna
NRAEAHR Increase Mather
NRAENIE increase in size
NRAESRO Andrea del Sarto
NRANMES in great numbers
NRCAIIY intractability
NRCOSES ungraciousness
NRDBEES incredibleness
NRDCOIY introductorily
NRDEPNE inbred response
NREAANT unarmed against
NREDIES unfriendliness
NRFRNEO in preference to
NRFSINL unprofessional
NRIAEES inordinateness
NRIAHRV Andrei Sakharov
NRIFLES unfruitfulness
NRIIILY inartificially
NRISLIG inertia selling
NRITCLY inartistically
NRIUAEY inarticulately
NRMDTTD unpremeditated
NRNFRBE untransferable
NRNIETY intransigently
NRNIIEY intransitively
NRNMTBE intransmutable
NRPRDES unpreparedness
NRPRINO in proportion to
NRSRCUE infrastructure
NRTAIGY ingratiatingly
NRTCLES uncriticalness
NRTFLES ungratefulness
untruthfulness
NRTNIGY unpretendingly
NRWANGE Andrew Carnegie
NRWOALW Andrew Bonar Law
NSAAIIY inescapability
NSAEATY one-stage pastry
NSAEFLX in a state of flux
NSETRAF one's better half
NSETTOS unostentatious
NSLTEOD in a split second
NSOGRSS one's gorge rises
NSUIGES unassumingness
NTIGEDE knitting needle
NTLETLN instalment plan
NTUETLY instrumentally
NUAELPE annular eclipse
NUAIGAE insulating tape
NUCPIEY insusceptively
NUCSFLY unsuccessfully
NUEAIIY innumerability
insuperability
NUFCETY insufficiently
NUIAIIY indubitability
NUMRBLS annus mirabilis
NUMUTBE insurmountable
unsurmountable
NUMUTBY insurmountably
NUOOISS pneumoconiosis
NUPCIGY unsuspectingly
NUPCOSY inauspiciously
unsuspiciously
NUPESBE insuppressible
unsuppressible
NUPESBY insuppressibly
NUSINBE unquestionable
NUSINBY unquestionably
NUTBEES unsuitableness
NUTOMTR induction motor
NVIAIIY unavailability
unavoidability
NVNFLES uneventfulness
NVRAJIT universal joint
NVRIAIN universitarian
NVRRSET in every respect
NVTBEES inevitableness
NWAHVYU and what have you
NWMVOTO know a move or two
NWNSNOS know one's onions
NWRAKOE answer back code
NWTAOHR one with another
NXETDES unexpectedness
NXIAIIY inexcitability
unexcitability
NXRSILS inexpressibles
NYCRNZD unsynchronized
NYODOTY Andy Goldworthy
NYPTYIH in sympathy with
NYTMTZD unsystematized
OAATOIY local authority
OACRANY moral certainty
OADAPEL Donald Campbell
OADELNS no hard feelings
OADOASN Donald Johanson
OADOHRD hot and bothered
OADSADI Mohandas Gandhi
OAIIAIN volatilization
OAINUDY Rogation Sunday
OALHWRD for all the world
OALNBTF not a blind bit of
OAMDIED Mohammed Aideed
OANSELR Johannes Kepler
OANSRHS Johannes Brahms
OANSUGR Johannes Fugger
OANSULR Johannes Müller
OANTIGF to say nothing of
OAOCUAE woman of courage
OAOHROD not another word
OAOLTES woman of letters
OAORMNE Donato Bramante
OAOTEON woman of the town
OARSDNE royal residence
OASADRS moral standards
OATCOEY romantic comedy
OAWRETR Royal Worcester
OBDEFUT forbidden fruit
OBDHBNS forbid the banns
OBDIGES forbiddingness
OBEACPN double saucepan
OBEEAIE double negative
OBEELTH double-declutch
OBEEOIH hobbledehoyish
OBEILAS Robbie Williams
OBENEDE double entendre
OBEOCRO double concerto
OBEOEHR cobble together
OBERATD double-breasted
OBERSIG double-crossing
OBETNAD double standard
OBEXOUE double exposure
OBFASLS Tomb of Mausolus
OBHVNAY not be having any
OBIGATE Doubting-Castle
OBIGHMS doubting Thomas
OBLIEET nonbelligerent
OBNDFOT combined effort
OBSIIIY combustibility
OBTEAOT not bother about
OBTKNNY not be taken in by
OBTNYLD not bat an eyelid
OCAOEEF conceal oneself
OCBEEBE forcible feeble
OCEEOTY concrete poetry
OCEEUGE concrete jungle
OCFRINE dolce far niente
OCIAIIY conceivability
OCKFSHR Joschka Fischer
OCMDGNC non-comedogenic
OCMITLY non-committally
OCMUIAT non-communicant
OCNRCLY concentrically
OCNRSIG Toucan crossing
OCNTITR boa constrictor
OCOEWYN force one's way in
OCROEEF concern oneself
OCRORSO concerto grosso
OCSESIE Worcestershire
OCSESUE Worcester sauce
OCSINIE concessionaire
OCUIEES conclusiveness
ODADAIS lords and ladies
lords-and-ladies
ODAKATR cold dark matter
ODAOBON Ford Madox Brown
ODCOEEF conduct oneself
ODDUSIN loaded question

ODEIAIN bowdlerization
ODELWHP good fellowship
ODFHFIS Lord of the Flies
ODFRWUE goods for own use
ODGOIES goody-goodiness
ODHFRFR hold the fort for
ODHNELR Lord Chancellor
ODHUDRD cold shouldered
ODIHSAE wood nightshade
ODIRTOS Good Vibrations
ODIUEAT Lord Lieutenant
ODNAAHN London Marathon
ODNAIIN Golden Pavilion
ODNBYNE hold in abeyance
ODNCMAY holding company
ODNHAAT golden pheasant
ODNIHRS Gordon Richards
ODNOSAE Gordon Lonsdale
ODNOTMT hold in contempt
ODNPTEN holding pattern
ODNSHST hold one's whisht
ODNSOGE hold one's tongue
ODNSOSS hold one's horses
ODNSRUD hold one's ground
ODNVROT wooden overcoat
ODONTIG good-for-nothing
ODOREFR hold no brief for
ODOSINE good conscience
ODOTIES roadworthiness
ODPLBUD hold spellbound
ODPNSED hold up one's head
ODRCSIG word-processing
ODRTIKN wonder-stricken
ODRUWRD Wonderful World
ODSEDPN condescend upon
ODSIIUL Lords Spiritual
ODSMTIG not do something
ODSNSOD good as one's word
ODTOAIY conditionality
ODUAANT hold out against
ODUORDY good-humouredly
OEAAEAS go separate ways
OEAALNA José Capablanca
OEADHKR mover and shaker
OEADUIT Romeo and Juliet
OEAHWIS Coleman Hawkins
OEAOHRA José Ramos-Horta
OEBEKAT power breakfast
OEBNITR Roger Bannister
OECETBE more acceptable
OEDCABE robes-de-chambre
OEEADDY for ever and a day
OEEADVR for ever and ever
OEEGSAE sovereign state
OEFRCIE code of practice
OEGAAIN vowel gradation
OEGPOUT foreign product
OEHCATY Joseph McCarthy
OEHNBKR Josephine Baker
OEHNLKA something like a
OEHNNUH more than enough
OEHOBES Joseph Goebbels
OEHONRE Joseph Rowntree
OEHREIG foreshortening
OEHRMLI Joseph Grimaldi
OEHUIZR Joseph Pulitzer
OEIGETR covering letter
OEIKADM Roderick Random
OEILGCL soteriological
OEINOET Bohemian Forest
OEITCLY solecistically
OEIUEEI Yoweri Museveni
OELOEHR go well together
OENANES Modern Painters
OENATND come unfastened
OENHCIE mose in the chine
OENHHAT hole in the heart
OENHRCS Love on the Rocks
OENHSEE come on the scene
OENOFET come into effect
OENOOHR someone or other
OENSEPR lose one's temper
OENSOEN poke one's nose in
OENSOGE lose one's tongue
OENSOTE lose one's bottle
OENTAIY move unsteadily
OEOAUIY come to maturity
OEOAUTN gone for a Burton
OEOEEFN model oneself on
OEOGIAE Love Songs in Age
OEOGLAT fore-topgallant
OEOHFOT come to the front
OEONADN come down hard on
OEONSAD come to one's hand
OEOOOHR somehow or other
OEOTEES power of the keys
OEOTIES noteworthiness
OEPESOE con espressione
OEPLUSI Józef Pilsudski
OERBLIN Boxer Rebellion
OERIAIN foreordination
OERMEID come from behind
OESFEAL powers of recall
OESOEET women's movement
OETAEEL Robert Bakewell
OETATIY move stealthily
OETCAAA Robert McNamara
OETCUAN Robert Schumann
OETEANY Robert Delaunay
OETEPAN Robert Helpmann
OETEUKE cover the buckle
OETFHLW lowest of the low
OETHBUE Robert the Bruce
OETICIN Robert Pitcairn
OETILKN Robert Millikan
OETODWY Robert Koldewey
OETRWIG Robert Browning
OETULKN Robert Mulliken
OEULICE come full circle
OEURCLM core curriculum
OFDNILY confidentially
OFNTOIG non-functioning
not functioning
OFOCLEE Wolfson College
OFRAIIY conformability
OFRHWRD not for the world
OFRNEAL conference hall
OFRSAIN comfort station
OFTSMOS Bob Fitzsimmons
OGADUBE rough-and-tumble
OGAJRIE Douglas Jardine
OGALAET Long Parliament
OGALAHR tough as leather
OGAUAIE congratulative
OGAUAIN congratulation
OGAUAOY congratulatory
OGBETIG rough breathing
OGEAINL congregational
OGEIDES tongue-tiedness
OGETERE to a great degree
OGETXET to a great extent
OGFIWTA Song of Hiawatha
OGIDDES long-windedness
OGIVLAA bougainvillaea
OGNHTOH long in the tooth
OGNTCLY morganatically
OGOEAIN conglomeration
OGOMAUE for good measure
OGONETE longhorn beetle
OGONIVR Long John Silver
OGOVNAE coign of vantage
OGTDNLY longitudinally
OGTEOUN dodge the column
OHAENLS Joshua Reynolds
OHAESAE for heaven's sake
OHEDFIE to the end of time
OHMTNLB Roehampton Club
OHMUONE roche moutonnée
OHNSEIL nothing special
OHNSOTF nothing short of
OHNTSYO nothing to say to
OHRATAS Lothar Matthaus
OHRCOIE oophorectomise
oophorectomize
OHRUEIR mother superior
OHSIAIN sophistication
OHSMTIG do the same thing
OIAINLY motivationally
OIAMTOG Louis Armstrong
OIATUSR Louis Althusser
OIBAEOE Colin Blakemore
OIBEESN sociable person
OICERLT Louis Chevrolet
OIEOCKS go like hot cakes
OIEOSES vociferousness
OIFAMBE non-inflammable
OIFMLAE forisfamiliate
OIGIDES loving-kindness
OIGNOIW coming into view
OIGNSAR losing one's hair
OIHHWRE go with the worse
OIIAVES political views
OIIEEUT positive result
OIIEUBR positive number
OIIIAIN politicization
solidification
OIIOSES solicitousness
OILEORT social democrat
OILEUIY social security

OILIIIN social division
OILNIER social engineer
OILOTAT social contract
OILSFET Coriolis effect
OILTNIG social standing
OIMHOIE sodium chloride
OINESES motionlessness
OINIKES motion sickness
OIOEAIN not in operation
OIOEEII Cosimo de' Medici
OIPSENK Boris Pasternak
OIRHNHU holier-than-thou
OIRUIIC Louis Roubiliac
OISMLET Tobias Smollett
OISNRSE Robinson Crusoe
OISTAIN no-win situation
OITEAGR dog in the manger
OITILNS Society Islands
OITOJSS Society of Jesus
OITREIG non-interfering
OITRSIG not interesting
OIUIAIN solitudinarian
OIVLEET non-involvement
OIYUCIN bodily function
OJDEETL non-judgemental
OJNTVTS conjunctivitis
OKCMITE works committee
OKDOLDO cock-a-doodle-doo
OKEOCLY mock-heroically
OKLOEFR look all over for
OKLTEMC poikilothermic
OKMUTIS Rocky Mountains
OKNCASS working classes
OKNCPTL working capital
OKNDAIG working drawing
OKNFRAD looking forward
OKOTOBE look for trouble
OKSATES work as partners
OKTEASS mocks the pauses
OKTNNUT pocket an insult
OKUTEOP mock turtle soup
OKXEINE work experience
OKYUIES monkey business
OLAAGBA Boolean algebra
OLADARY hooly and fairly
OLADSAE coeliac disease
OLCEWRS collected works
OLCIEAM collective farm
OLCIEON collective noun
OLCOEEF collect oneself
OLCOSTM collector's item
OLEDDES cool-headedness
OLETHRE could eat a horse
OLETOIG soul-destroying
OLFAIGR not lift a finger
OLIFRNE goal difference
OLLWSMN Worldly Wiseman
OLNTERF would not hear of
OLNWTYU go along with you
OLOFRIG soul-confirming
OLPAIIY collapsability
OLPIIIY collapsibility
OLREXET to a large extent
OLRUDIH fool around with
OLSEBIE noblesse oblige
OLSRCUE Colles' fracture
OLTNCAT Wollstonecraft
OLVOMNY for love or money
OLWAIES world-weariness
OLWHCOD follow the crowd
OLWHRLS follow the rules
OLWNSOE follow one's nose
OMDBEES formidableness
OMDFARS homme d'affaires
OMDOSES commodiousness
OMNAIWF command a view of
OMNAORR common labourer
OMNCTOS communications
OMNEOOY command economy
OMNESCL commonsensical
OMNODLX common toadflax
OMNRADN common or garden
common-or-garden
OMNUAEY commensurately
OMPCUEF form a picture of
OMSINIE commissionaire
OMTESAE committee stage
OMTHMUH foam at the mouth
OMTOEOY commit to memory
ONAADES going-away dress
ONADRIG toing and froing
ONANABY Fountains Abbey
ONANEIG mountaineering
ONANEVR mountain beaver
ONANIIG mountain biking
ONAOGIH going along with
ONAOTDY roundaboutedly
ONAOTES roundaboutness
ONARLOE Joanna Trollope
ONASOTY John Galsworthy
ONAUTOD young adulthood
ONBTEOK going by the book
ONCAGLN John McLaughlin
ONEBLNE counterbalance
ONECLUE counter-culture
ONEFIIG counterfeiting
ONEMAUE countermeasure
ONEMNIG countermanding
ONERPSE counter-riposte
ONESSES Pointer Sisters
ONFHCOS John of the Cross
ONHBPIT John the Baptist
ONHCLUS join the colours
ONHRMAE go on the rampage
ONHYOTM John Chrysostom
ONIETLY coincidentally
ONIGAHR founding father
ONIMTXS Ioannis Metaxas
ONIOSAE Council of State
ONLUNPS Cornelius Nepos
ONMUAIN somnambulation
ONNCLEE Downing College
ONNHDMS down in the dumps
ONNHMUH down in the mouth
ONNNSUK down on one's luck
ONNOAOT go on and on about
ONNPAES morning prayers
ONNSRIE morning service
ONOCAAS John Couch Adams
ONOCNAT point of contact
ONODULP John Boyd Dunlop
ONOFAZE worn to a frazzle
ONOIBID John Logie Baird
ONONILR town councillor
ONONUAN John Von Neumann
ONRBMKN country bumpkin
ONSOEOK do one's homework
ONSUIES do one's business
ONSWTIG do one's own thing
ONTATIL John Stuart Mill
ONTEIKT round the wicket
ONTEONR round the corner
ONTEOTF count the cost of
ONTEPAE to another place
ONTPSOS cornet-à-pistons
ONTTEAL going to the wall
ONUHRAD Joan Sutherland
ONUHROD John Rutherford
ONUSCTS John Duns Scotus
ONYEBNH Johnny Lee Bench
OOACAIE monosaccharide
OOAOELS Corona Borealis
OOAOETE Colorado beetle
OOAYREY coronary artery
OOAYYAS coronary bypass
OOEEAZC Honoré de Balzac
OOEGDAI Colonel Gaddafi
OOEGPRS to foreign parts
OOEHNFR do something for
OOEIAIN homogenization
OOENPOD do someone proud
OOENRGT do someone right
OOENWOG do someone wrong
OOEONAD for one's own hand
OOFHPES hot off the press
OOGRPKN no longer spoken
OOHAROE Dorothea Brooke
OOHCUTY go to the country
OOHHDKN Dorothy Hodgkin
OOHHNIE monophthongise
monophthongize
OOHLAES Dorothy L Sayers
OOIEOSY soporiferously
OOIGAIM monolingualism
OOLLNTS go to all lengths
OONHDAN go down the drain
OONHTBS go down the tubes
OONLNTS go to any lengths
OOOILNS Solomon Islands
OOOTNEE nolo contendere
OORBEES honourableness
OORQETY go to frequently
OOSRAIM Zoroastrianism
OOTEOTR go for the doctor
OOUATIM pococuranteism
OPEEODD not prerecorded
OPEESBE comprehensible
OPEESBY comprehensibly
OPNHWRD go up in the world

OPNNPRS component parts
OPNOEEF topping oneself
OPNPNIN company pension
OPNTOSY compunctiously
OPOBRET Compton-Burnett
OPOREAY non-proprietary
OPRCLOA corpora callosa
OPROEEF comport oneself
OPROORD copper-coloured
OPROTMD copper-bottomed
OPRTOTX corporation tax
OPRTSAE corporate state
OPRUPAE copper sulphate
OPSALSM corpus callosum
OPTAANT compete against
OPTBEES hospitableness
OPTBEIH compatible with
OPTLOTR hospital doctor
OPTRAIG computer dating
OQITDRS conquistadores
ORDDNUR Konrad Adenauer
OREFCIN course of action
OREFNOE source of income
ORERMLS your heart melts
ORETROD four-letter word
ORETRUH journey through
ORGOSES courageousness
ORGTDRN corrugated iron
ORHEDIE four-wheel drive
ORLVLAT Hoare-Laval Pact
ORNOSES horrendousness
OROAPAS court of appeals
OROBSUT Bourbon biscuit
ORODELH your good health
OROJSIE court of justice
OROSSIN Court of Session
ORPIIIY corruptibility
ORRTIKN horror-stricken
ORSNEEY yours sincerely
ORSODIH correspond with
ORSODNE correspondence
ORSODNS correspondents
ORSOSBE not responsible
ORSRCIE non-restrictive
ORTCMAD yours to command
ORTLIGE you're telling me
ORTRVLE non-return valve
OSDRIHY consider highly
OSDROML consider normal
OSEADUP hop, step and jump
OSEOSES boisterousness
OSEUIAY consuetudinary
OSEYTEE not see eye to eye
OSHLGOS household goods
OSIADUP hop, skip and jump
OSIAOIL conspiratorial
OSIFLES worshipfulness
OSILEOS boys will be boys
OSIUINL constitutional
OSLGNRL consuls general
OSLIGOM consulting room
OSLTTDS horse latitudes
OSMISNE housemaid's knee
OSNEAII Bolson de Mapimi
OSNIAIY nonsensicality
OSNUNOS consanguineous
OSOAEOD do as you are told
OSOBLNE torsion-balance
OSOCMOS House of Commons
OSOILAE house of ill fame
OSOTEOS jobs for the boys
OSOWRHP house of worship
OSPLUIN noise pollution
OSPYIIN house-physician
OSRAIEY conservatively
OSRAINL conservational
OSRCIEY constructively
OSRCIIM Constructivism
OSRCINL constructional
OSSETIH consistent with
OSSIEES possessiveness
OSTRIES topsy-turviness
OSVTEAK God save the mark
OSWCUTY God's own country
OTAAOTS contrafagottos
OTADALY motte and bailey
OTAEAKD non-trademarked
OTAIINL nontraditional
OTAKOBY Port Jackson Bay
OTANIAE contraindicate
OTANIAT contraindicant
OTAOIIN contraposition
OTAORBE most favourable
OTASRLA South Australia
OTATRDE contract bridge
OTCLUIT horticulturist
OTCONAT cost-accountant
OTCONIG cost-accounting
OTCSEOD corticosteroid
OTEADIS how the land lies
OTEATIE for the last time
OTEELFT for the hell of it
OTEIDIS how the wind lies
OTEIEFE for the life of me
OTEIHUP for the high jump
OTEMWOG don't get me wrong
OTEOEFT for the love of it
OTEOTAT for the most part
OTEREON Port Georgetown
OTESWRS north-eastwards
OTEUAIN for the duration
OTEULUD not the full quid
OTEUSIN pop the question
OTFATAE Pontefract cake
OTFOEEF fortify oneself
OTGAOGN South Glamorgan
OTHSELR youth hosteller
OTIOSES fortuitousness
OTMCOSY contumaciously
OTMLOSY contumeliously
OTMTOSY contemptuously
OTMUAIN noctambulation
OTNHNIG fortune-hunting
OTNIYIL continuity girl
OTNMGOE Fontana Magiore
OTNOSES continuousness
portentousness
OTNRHAT north-north-east
OTNRHET north-north-west
OTNTLIG fortune-telling
OTNUTBE most unsuitable
OTOETBE controvertible
OTOETBY controvertibly
OTOEWIE worth one's while
OTOIEBE most noticeable
OTOIIEY postpositively
OTONFRE foot-pound force
OTOOEEF control oneself
OTOSIND soft-conscienc'd
OTRDCIN post-production
OTRGTES forthrightness
OTSUHAT south-south-east
OTSUHET south-south-west
OTUBRAD Northumberland
OTWISIE boatswain's pipe
OTWSWRS north-westwards
south-westwards
OTYRSIE North Yorkshire
South Yorkshire
OUAIAIN popularization
OUCASCS locus classicus
OUCOSES loquaciousness
OUERCLY volumetrically
OUETEDR document reader
OUIBIFY to put it briefly
OUIOSES voluminousness
OUOOEWY go out of one's way
OUOTEON go out on the town
OUTIHES coquettishness
OUTOSES voluptuousness
OUTSRTH not up to scratch
OUUEEEO Mobutu Seze Seko
OVAXIHS nouveaux riches
OVNINLY conventionally
OVRAINL conversational
OVRAINS conversaziones
OVRATIH conversant with
OVRIIIY convertibility
OWNTLAE not want to leave
OWRHHCS not worth shucks
OWRHHDY woe worth the day
OWRLOIG forward-looking
OWTROTE hot-water bottle
OYACAIE polysaccharide
OYCITRS holy Scriptures
OYEIAIN polymerisation
polymerization
OYULOIE polynucleotide
PABTEAD speak by the card
PADOIIY upward mobility
PAENHSN a place in the sun
PAITNUS speak in tongues
PASAPYO speak sharply to
PAUCERY speak unclearly
PCAIAIN specialization
PCAITRA specialist area
PCALCNE special licence
PCAMNIN special mention
PCAOSOT spectator sport

PCAUAIY spectacularity
PCFCTOS specifications
PCRGAHC spectrographic
PCTAELR space traveller
PDITCLY apodeictically
PDMOOIT epidemiologist
PEDCCOY appendicectomy
PEDUWRS spread outwards
PEHESES speechlessness
PERUDNY appear suddenly
PIAIAIN optimalization
PIEONAE upside-down cake
PIGATES spring mattress
PIGLAIG spring-cleaning
PIITCLY optimistically
PIOESDS split one's sides
PIOEVTS split one's votes
PLCALTE apple charlotte
PLEPYIS applied physics
PLGTCLY apologetically
PLODSOD apple of discord
PLOEEFO apply oneself to
PLOOEEE apple of one's eye
PLSNPAS apples and pears
PNADDES open-handedness
PNFIILY open officially
PNHHESF upon the heels of
PNIDDES open-mindedness
PNLKWTR spend like water
PNLSAKD spindle-shanked
PNOAIEY opinionatively
PNOUSIN open to question
POHPEET up to the present
POHTCEK a prophetic week
POIERMT opposite prompt
POIEUBR opposite number
POITCLY aphoristically
PONSRCS up to one's tricks
POROSES uproariousness
PPETCLY apoplectically
PPTEMTC apophthegmatic
PRAOHTC spermatophytic
PRAOOIM spermatogonium
PRCAIEY appreciatively
PRHNIEY apprehensively
PRIGHNE sporting chance
PRNIEHP apprenticeship
PRNIEOD apprenticehood
PRSIEES oppressiveness
PRTAITC spiritualistic
PRTESES spiritlessness
PRTNCSS operating costs
PRTNTBE operating table
PRTOSES spirituousness
PSEOOIT epistemologist
PTAMSOE ophthalmoscope
PWIGRUD spawning-ground
PXGTCLY epexegetically
QARNEDR squadron leader
QINUAIY equiangularity
QIODRNE equiponderance
QIRLOKY squirrel monkey
RADFROO Orlando Furioso
RAETFOT greatest effort
RAETMUT greatest amount
RAETRUS armamentariums
RAETXET greatest extent
RAFCIIY area of activity
RAFIHIH break faith with
RAFNEET area of interest
RAFOFIT area of conflict
RAGEHPD triangle-shaped
RAGERLA urban guerrilla
RAGIPIS arrange in pairs
RAHESES breathlessness
RAHFHLW breach of the law
RAHNSAE breathing space
breathing-space
RAHVCIH wreak havoc with
RAIAINL organizational
RAIECIE organized crime
RAIEFCS pro aris et focis
RAIEPRT creative spirit
RAINLER irrational fear
RAIOFIH break it off with
RAITEEM broad in the beam
RALOERM break loose from
RANONXS Ariadne on Naxos
RANSURS break no squares
RANWRUD break new ground
RAOEHAT break one's heart
RARNEET prearrangement
RASAEAE Great Slave Lake
RATEAKF break the back of
RATEEOD break the record
RAUESAD Treasure Island
RAWIEOE great white hope
RAYFMES Treaty of Amiens
RBIGAIN Brobdingnagian
RBNPBIO pro bono publico
RCATNTR procrastinator
RCCOSES precociousness
RCDLTAS crocodile tears
RCIAIIS practicalities
RCIAIIY practicability
RCIAJKR practical joker
RCIAJKS practical jokes
RCIIAIN fructification
RCINNIE traction engine
RCLANRE trochlear nerve
RCLTRUH trickle through
RCLUMTC proceleusmatic
RCNETDY preconcertedly
RCNLGCL arachnological
RCNLSOS try conclusions
RCOOISS trichomoniasis
RCOOOSY trichotomously
RCROSES precariousness
RCRTRHP procuratorship
RCSIVLE tricuspid valve
RCYTCLY procryptically
RDBLTGP credibility gap
RDCAIIY predictability
RDCIEES productiveness
RDCINIE production line
RDCQIKY produce quickly
RDCRSLS produce results
RDCRUHY produce roughly
RDENTHR cradle-snatcher
RDETOGT grudge a thought
RDEULIG bridge-building
RDGOMOE bridegroom-to-be
RDIMRUY Freddie Mercury
RDJFASN Fridtjof Nansen
RDOEEFN pride oneself on
RDRCHPN Frédéric Chopin
RDRCLEE Frederick Loewe
RDRCSDY Frederick Soddy
RDRCSUG Fredericksburg
RDSIAIN predestination
RDSOIIN predisposition
RDTOAIM traditionalism
RDTOAIT traditionalist
RDTOAIY traditionality
RDTRIAE predeterminate
RDTRNFR credit transfer
REAAIIY irreparability
READDES free-handedness
READETD tried and tested
RECOSOE Green Cross Code
REDESES friendlessness
REDYEAK friendly remark
REECUTR Brief Encounter
REERATR breeder reactor
REHEIEY breech delivery
REIGRUD breeding-ground
RELNWAE Greenland whale
RENEPIE free enterprise
free-enterprise
REOAIIY irremovability
irrevocability
REOCLBE irreconcilable
REOCLBY irreconcilably
REOFGTR freedom fighter
freedomfighter
REOTEAH Order of the Bath
REOUEES irresoluteness
REPCIEF irrespective of
REPCIEY irrespectively
REPKNES free-spokenness
REPNIEY irresponsively
RERAHBE irreproachable
RERAHBY irreproachably
RERCKUP Friedrich Krupp
RETANBE irrestrainable
RETCLMN Ornette Coleman
REUAIIY irrefutability
REUCTBY irresuscitably
RFBIAIN prefabrication
RFIHONR Griffith-Joyner
RFNEGPT Gräfenberg spot
RFRNILY preferentially
RFSINLY professionally
RFSOILY professorially
RFTBEES profitableness
RGAMMSC programme music
RGCMCLY tragicomically
RGEYPOY Prague Symphony
RGOSCEY dregs of society

RGOTCTR prognosticator
RGRONSA Gregory of Nyssa
RGROSES gregariousness
RGROTUS Gregory of Tours
RGTDSAE Bright's disease
RGTEADT Brigitte Bardot
RGTNERY bright and early
RHBTOAY prohibitionary
RHBTOIT prohibitionist
RHCRMTC orthochromatic
RHDXHRH Orthodox Church
RHEICPL archiepiscopal
RHELGCL archaeological
RHGAHCL orthographical
RHROEGR Arthur Honegger
RHRONEG Arthur Kornberg
RHROSLR Arthur Koestler
RHRRFIH Arthur Griffith
RHRULVN Arthur Sullivan
RHTCOIS architectonics
RIAYEMN ordinary seaman
RIAYESN ordinary person
RIAYPOY Eroica Symphony
RIEOTIY praiseworthily
RIEUDNY arrive suddenly
RIGAGUR Irving Langmuir
RIHLGCL ornithological
RIIGRUD training ground
RILOFIH article of faith
RIOOSES traitorousness
RIOTOGT train of thought
RITFEES Mr Mistoffelees
RIUAEES articulateness
RKSRGES A Rake's Progress
RLTRAIE proletarianise
proletarianize
RMACEKR grammar checker
RMAKOAK from bank to bank
RMATWRE from bad to worse
RMBLEIA prima ballerina
RMDLCEE crème de la crème
RMDTTDY premeditatedly
RMETNUD trumpet-tongued
RMHSIEN from this time on
RMIEOIE from side to side
from time to time
RMNOSES tremendousness
RMRBTEY primary battery
RMRCLUS primary colours
RMSBEKR promise-breaker
RMSCAMD promise-crammed
RMSKEIG promise-keeping
RMSOYOE promissory note
RMTCRIT dramatic artist
RMTCRWH dramatic growth
RMTEAIT aromatherapist
RNACAMO bring acclaim to
RNAEADR Franz Alexander
RNCNETL transcendental
RNCNETY transcendently
RNCUCIL Frank Churchill
RNECRUT printed circuit
RNEEEIS fringe benefits
RNEHRIG Prince Charming
RNERSUE cranberry sauce
RNFRAIE transformative
RNFRAIN transformation
RNGAHCL uranographical
RNHBESD Bran the Blessed
RNHNCES French knickers
RNHRSIG French dressing
RNIAPRS principal parts
RNIDTOI Frankie Dettori
RNIGFRH bringings forth
RNIGPIE drinking-up time
RNIINLY transitionally
RNILHCS Granville Hicks
RNIOIES transitoriness
RNIOUNE grandiloquence
RNIPCBA Francis Picabia
RNIPUEC Francis Poulenc
RNIRWMN frontierswoman
RNITBIG bring into being
RNITEED wrong in the head
RNITFCS bring into focus
RNLKAIH drink like a fish
RNLNIRE Franklin Pierce
RNLTRTR transliterator
RNMGAIN transmigration
RNMGAOY transmigratory
RNMSIEY transmissively
RNMSIIY transmissivity
RNMSINL transmissional
RNNEUVY Ordnance Survey
RNNIMNO pronunciamento
RNOEEFO bring oneself to
RNOSILN François Villon
RNOSSGN Françoise Sagan
RNPATBE transplantable
RNPCOSY transpicuously
RNPRAIN transportation
RNPRIGY transportingly
RNSBRAD Grand St Bernard
RNSHEDR Vreni Schneider
RNTACUT bring to account
RNTCLEE Trinity College
RNTJSIE bring to justice
RNTRAIM Trinitarianism
RNTRETN Frank Tarkenton
RNTTEOE bring to the fore
RNTTEOL bring to the boil
RNULIIG tranquillizing
RNUTEER bring up the rear
RNVREAE transverse wave
RNVREYO bring variety to
RNVSIIM transvestitism
ROEEEOT cry one's eyes out
ROIUTRL arboricultural
ROOOEON A Room of One's Own
ROOOSAD Oroonoko Island
ROSOISN Brooks Robinson
ROTOEOE cry out to be done
ROTOESD cry out to be used
ROWTAIW A Room with a View
RPCFACR Tropic of Cancer
RPCLOET tropical forest
RPGNIIG propagandizing
RPIFRUA graphic formula
RPISALT graphics tablet
RPITRHP proprietorship
RPLESAT propeller shaft
RPLGCLY tropologically
RPNEATY preponderantly
RPNHOEN drop in the ocean
RPNSUDE drop one's bundle
RPORPDR trapdoor spider
RPRINBY proportionably
RPRINLY proportionally
RPROEEF prepare oneself
RPRRCIN proper fraction
RPSATAE Krapp's Last Tape
RPSEOSY preposterously
RPSUETS crêpes suzettes
RPTAOIY propitiatorily
RPTOSES propitiousness
RPZHDOS trapezohedrons
RSADCNA Tristan da Cunha
RSAILNS Frisian Islands
RSBTEIS cross batteries
RSEIMRH proscenium arch
RSESPOT brussels sprout❑
RSETHPD crescent-shaped
RSFRIIE cross-fertilize
RSIIAIN arms limitation
RSMTOSY presumptuously
RSNAAIM present as a film
RSNAALY present as a play
RSNEFID presence of mind
RSNFRAE present for sale
RSNOEEF present oneself
RSOEHAT cross one's heart
RSPLIAE cross-pollinate
RSPOIIN presupposition
RSRFRNE cross-reference
RSRMHNY Tristram Shandy
RSRPIEY prescriptively
proscriptively
RSRPIIM prescriptivism
RSSCINL cross-sectional
RSSMOEP grass someone up
RSTEETE grasp the nettle
RSTEUTN press the button
RSTTEIL grist to the mill
RSUEOKR pressure cooker
RSWLHUD Irish wolfhound
RSYEILY presbyterially
RTAIMTL Brittania metal
RTARNLN Aretha Franklin
RTCIEES protectiveness
RTCLOET critical moment
RTDTOUH try to do too much
RTECDAL Brother Cadfael
RTGYIKE Mrs Tiggy-Winkle
RTIIAIN prettification
RTMTCLY arithmetically
RTNIMTL Britannia metal
RTPAMTC protoplasmatic
RTRIAIN fraternisation
fraternization

RTRIEIH fraternize with
RTSCOEA British cholera
RTYRTIS pretty-pretties
RUAIAIN traumatization
RUDESES groundlessness
RUDRAIG ground-breaking
RUETCUA argumenti causa
RUHFRAD brought forward
RULSOTR troubleshooter
RVAIAIN trivialization
RVAPRUT Trivial Pursuit®
RVBCWRS drive backwards
RVDNILY providentially
RVIIGID prevailing wind
RVLESLB Travellers Club
RVLIGOK travelling folk
RVLIKES travel sickness
RVNLCNE driving licence
RVNOEEF prevent oneself
RVRCOAD Trevor McDonald
RVTBPIM private baptism
RVTCMAY private company
RVTDSAR drive to despair
RVTSLIR private soldier
RVTTEAL drive to the wall
RVUTEAL drive up the wall
RWADNHR crown and anchor
RWCUTMD grow accustomed
RWHCRAN draw the curtain
RWHLNBW draw the long bow
RWHNUTY growth industry
RWHTEHF draw the teeth of
RYIEAUE grey literature
RYNNSID prey on one's mind
RYONDRY Greyhound Derby
RZNHUDR frozen shoulder
SADPNLR Oswald Spengler
SAEEOIY escape velocity
SAEGNRL Estates General
SAKKSHA Oskar Kokoschka
SALECAT Ismail Merchant
SALUBRF a small number of
SARSNEG Isaac Rosenberg
SBDAGAE use bad language
SBLEDAI Isabelle Adjani
SBLTPRN Isabelita Perón
SCOERSS psychoneuroses
SCONLSR psychoanalyser
SCONLSS psychoanalysis
SCONLTC psychoanalytic
SCOYAIS psychodynamics
SDAERCL isodiametrical
SDFEETY ask differently
SEATRSS osteoarthrosis
SEATRTS osteoarthritis
SEDNARA ascending aorta
SEEAIGY asseveratingly
SEFNLSY Isle of Anglesey
SEIIAIN esterification
SESRPIG asset-stripping
SETSEET asbestos cement
SETTOSY ostentatiously
SFRIEES ask forgiveness

SHCOFIS as the crow flies
SHSOLSY as who should say
SHTLGCL eschatological
SIAAIDE as fit as a fiddle
SIFPELP a stiff upper lip
SIFRAIN ask information
SIMTCLY astigmatically
SMERCAS asymmetric bars
SMERCLY asymmetrically
SMTTCLY asymptotically
SNHOOSY asynchronously
SNOEHNS using one's hands
SOEUAIN osmoregulation
SOITDIH associated with
SPOEBRS a sop to Cerberus
SPRNRHP as a partnership
SRLGCLY astrologically
SRNMCLY astronomically
SRNSOAH a strong stomach
SRPHRLD A Shropshire Lad
SRPYIIT astrophysicist
STCMRUD ask to come round
STMOAIY use temporarily
SUANUEM usque ad nauseam
SUOOPIM pseudomorphism
SUOYOSY pseudonymously
TAAARAE steal a marriage
TABRYAK strawberry mark
TABRYRE strawberry tree
TAGMEIG Strange Meeting
TAGRDAN at daggers drawn
TAGTSDE straight as a die
TAHLBLO attach a label to
TAIIAIN stratification
TAIRPIT stratigraphist
TAITEID straw in the wind
TAKTOGY attack strongly
TAMUTIS Atlas Mountains
TANBEES attainableness
TANOREY strain courtesy
TCADARL stock and barrel
TCANTIG stick at nothing
TCCRAIG stock-car racing
TCIGILR stocking filler
TCOEORN stick one's oar in
TCTNNES Stockton-on-Tees
TCYIGRD sticky-fingered
TDITNEY study intensely
TDNTAHR student teacher
TDOTEID study of the mind
TEGHFID strength of mind
TEGHFIL strength of will
TEIGOUN steering column
steering-column
TEPNRGN Uther Pendragon
TERECOS St George's cross
TERSNEG Ethel Rosenberg
TETAEDF streets ahead of
TETUIIN street-musician
TFODRPS Stafford Cripps
TGAIAIN stigmatization
TGPROMR stage performer
THBDIGF at the bidding of

THBGNIG at the beginning
THCAKAE at the chalkface
THCMADF at the command of
THEPNEF at the expense of
THRGTIE at the right time
THRQETF at the request of
TIEBLNE strike a balance
TIEBRAN strike a bargain
TIHIMTY stoicheiometry
TIHOERC stoichiometric
TILSSEL stainless steel
TITDUCE striated muscle
TIUIIIG attitudinizing
TKSYATE Stokesay Castle
TLIIAIN stultification
TLRNOOY otolaryngology
TLTRAIE utilitarianise
utilitarianize
TLTRAIM utilitarianism
TMCASNT atomic mass unit
TMCLETR stamp collector
TMCTRIG stomach-turning
TMIGRUD stamping-ground
TMLGCLY etymologically
TMLNBOK stumbling-block
TMODRDE Stamford Bridge
TNADERR standard-bearer
TNCLSBR stone-cold sober
TNCNESD stand confessed
TNEBLWN Stanley Baldwin
TNECLEE St Anne's College
TNEKBIK Stanley Kubrick
TNESECR Stanley Spencer
TNFLSOP at one fell swoop
TNGADVR stand guard over
TNGAHCL ethnographical
TNIGETE stinging nettle
TNITEAE stand in the gate
TNITEAL sting in the tail
TNLGCLY ethnologically
TNODSIY Stone of Destiny
TNRWCOS St Andrew's cross
TNSIPSL at one's disposal
TNSRTFR stand surety for
TNUAANT stand up against
TNUOTRS stand upon terms
TOEFEIS stroke of genius
TOEIHIG strobe lighting
TOGAGAE strong language
TOGMLIG strong-smelling
TOIINHL Otto Lilienthal
TONCLEE St John's College
TPEDDLS Stephen Dedalus
TPEDREL Stephen Dorrell
TPEHWIG Stephen Hawking
TPELNTN Stephen Langton
TPESEDR Stephen Spender
TPHMUHF stop the mouth of
TPNHJIE step on the juice
TPNOSES stupendousness
TPYOOCL staphylococcal
TPYOOCS staphylococcus
TRAIAIN eternalization

TRATIUG Sturmabteilung
TRCIEES attractiveness
TRGBTEY storage battery
TRIAECP storm in a teacup
TRIGATE Stirling Castle
TRIGTLS starting stalls
TRITEAE stare in the face
TRITSAE stare into space
TRNSTMS stir one's stumps
TROERCL stereometrical
TROOSES stertorousness
TROSMRC stereoisomeric
TRSCLEE St Cross College
TRTOKOS at a rate of knots
TTEQEES statuesqueness
TTHRIAE State Hermitage
TTIENVS at it like knives
TTOAFIS state of affairs
TTOUDES state of undress
TUHATDY stout-heartedly
TUHCLEE St Hugh's College
TUHFHSN a touch of the sun
TUHNRUH stouth and routh
TULHOTE at full throttle
TUOESUF strut one's stuff
TVNENEG Steven Weinberg
TWLKAIE A Town Like Alice
TYEELCL ethylene glycol
TYUFNRL it's your funeral
UAALNOD put a call on hold
UAMDHRF Muhammad Sharif
UANLNLN Suzanne Lenglen
UAODAEN put a good face on
UARSUCS human resources
UAUSINO put a question to
UAVNEDN Lucas van Leyden
UBCTFOT put back to front
UBEOSAT Hubble constant
UBIGARL tumbling-barrel
UBIGWLS Tunbridge Wells
UBNADIE husband and wife
UBRHMET Humbert Humbert
UBRRNHR number-cruncher
UBRUCUE lumbar puncture
UCETATR juice extractor
UCNCOSY subconsciously
UCNLGCL vulcanological
UCOTERW quick on the draw
UCPIIIY susceptibility
UCSFLES successfulness
UCSIEES successiveness
UCSINES successionless
UCSINLY successionally
UCSLEIG quicksilvering
UCTNOSY subcutaneously
UDAEAIN quadragenarian
UDAGLRY quadrangularly
UDEEDDY muddleheadedly
UDEFAGS bundle of laughs
UDEFEVS bundle of nerves
UDEOEHR huddle together
UDMNAIM fundamentalism❑
UDMNAIT fundamentalist
UDMNAIY fundamentality
UDNNRAE sudden increase
UDNOEES burdensomeness
UEANAIN superannuation
UEAOAIN funeral oration
UEAPROR funeral parlour
UEAUDNE superabundance
UECLOSY superciliously
UECNIET supercontinent
UECNUTR superconductor
UECROHP supercargoship
UEEEAIN superelevation
UEEIAEH Queen Elizabeth
UEEIETY supereminently
UEEOAIN supererogation
UEEOAOY supererogatory
UEEOSES Eugene Goossens
UEFCAIE superficialise
superficialize
UEFCAIY superficiality
UEFYEGT super-flyweight
UEHOSUE Jude the Obscure
UEINTIS Eudemian Ethics
UEITNET superintendent
UEMFODN Museum of London
UENTRLY supernaturally
UEOALLS cure for all ills
UEOTEUE ruse contre ruse
UEPNIUE cut expenditure
UEPOPAE superphosphate
UESNCLY supersonically
UESRCUE superstructure
UESRPIN superscription
UESVDNE Queen's evidence
UETUPRY Hubert Humphrey
UEUEHNE bureau de change
UFCITSY suffice it to say
UFCONAT turf accountant
UFCTNIN surface tension
UFRHCUT out for the count
UFRNSIE run for one's life
UFRSIUE suffer a seizure
UGAEAGS Musgrave Ranges
UGCLPRT surgical spirit
UGIGESN outgoing person
UGNRCLY subgenerically
UGOGNRL surgeon general
UGRRCIN vulgar fraction
UGSIEES suggestiveness
UGSIIIY suggestibility
UHADAMD Hugh MacDiarmid
UHHBAOT push the boat out
UHITCLY euphuistically
UHNIAIN authentication
UHNSECS rush one's fences
UHOHLMT push to the limit
UHRADOS Luther Vandross
UIAALGT put in a bad light
UIAUSEL put in a nutshell
UIDCINL jurisdictional
UIESEPE businesspeople
UIIACUT municipal court
UIIIAIN humidification
UIINROA bulimia nervosa
UIIOSES cupidinousness
UIITCLY pugilistically
UIMTCLY numismatically
UINAEDR Julian calendar
UISEEID Julius Dedekind
UISOSCS Julius von Sachs
UISPLIS Lucius Apuleius
UITEAIY run in the family
UJCHAIG subject heading
UJCIEES subjectiveness
UJCIITC subjectivistic
UKESHNE Buckley's chance
UKSDLGT Turkish delight
UKTNSAE bucket and spade
ULAFSIN nuclear fission
ULAIAIN nuclearization
ULAPWRD nuclear-powered
ULAPYIS nuclear physics
ULARATR nuclear reactor
ULCMGLD Public Image Ltd
ULCPAIG public speaking
ULCPNIG public spending
ULCPRTD public-spirited
ULCUSNE public nuisance
ULDVLPD fully-developed
ULEDDES bull-headedness
ULEEIDW bull's eye window
ULFCTOS qualifications
ULFSIND fully-fashioned
ULFSOEN pull a fast one on
ULHLNBW pull the long bow
ULHSRNS pull the strings
ULNHMLB Hurlingham Club
ULNIHES outlandishness
ULNSEGT pull one's weight
ULOUSIG full to bursting
ULRCVRD fully recovered
ULSEWRS published works
ULSRTHD fully stretched
ULTAAED full steam ahead
ULTCNRL quality control
UMAGDAI Muammar Gaddafi
UMGTRUH rummage through
UMNHLDY busman's holiday
UMNRVLE pulmonary valve
UMRIIIY submergibility
submersibility
UMROFNE summary offence
UMROSIE summer solstice
UMSIEES submissiveness
UNDAERO turn a deaf ear to
UNESNIL quintessential
UNETNIL quincentennial
UNHARLE turn the air blue
UNHBLNE turn the balance
UNHSOAH turn the stomach
UNIAIEY quantitatively
UNIIAIN quantification
UNNNSEL turn on one's heel
UNNRPIS running repairs
UNNSADO turn one's hand to
UNNSAGT burn one's faggot

14 _U_N_N

UNNSAKN	turn one's back on
UNNSLOT	burn oneself out
UNPIEON	turn upside down
	turn upside-down
UNPNSOS	turn up one's toes
UNRBEES	vulnerableness
UNTAIDR	burnt to a cinder
UNTHSAE	burn at the stake
UNUNILY	quinquennially
UOAEETL	put on a pedestal
UOAIPLT	automatic pilot
UOAOELS	aurora borealis
UOCAATR	out of character
UOCNIIN	out of condition
UOEEEVR	run one's eye over
UOESITN	put one's shirt on
UOETEHN	cut one's teeth on
UOFNSET	run off one's feet
UOFOLBN	Rudolf von Laban
UOFUTAN	Rudolf Bultmann
UOIGAHR	autobiographer
UOIKNEY	Ludovic Kennedy
UOITCLY	eulogistically
UOOEDPH	out of one's depth
UOOEGAD	put on one's guard
UORESES	humourlessness
UORPABM	autograph album
UORTCLY	autocratically
UOSEBAE	mucous membrane
UOSRBNI	furor scribendi
UOTEAKT	put on the market
UOTEIDW	out of the window
UOTFCIN	put out of action
UOTIWRD	out of this world
UOTRIOY	Yukon Territory
UOUGSIN	auto-suggestion
UPAIAIE	sulphanilamide
UPAKRDE	humpback bridge
UPALAET	Rump Parliament
UPCOSES	auspiciousness
	suspiciousness
UPEIHAE	purple with rage
UPIAIGY	supplicatingly
UPIETAK	surprise attack
UPIIGES	surprisingness
UPNIERE	turpentine tree
UPRCIKR	Humphry Clinker
UPROEEF	support oneself
UPRYOAT	Humphrey Bogart
UPSFLES	purposefulness
UPSTTOS	supposititious
UPUDOIE	sulphur dioxide
UPUOSCD	sulphurous acid
UQAESLY	quaquaversally
UREAFVR	puerperal fever
URGOSES	outrageousness
URMNOSY	querimoniously
URNACUT	current account
URNEVLE	surrender value
URNSREX	au grand sérieux
URNSRUD	run rings around
URPIAIN	eutrophication
URTOSES	nutritiousness
URUSINR	Burrhus Skinner
URYELAN	Murray Gell-Mann
USAIAIN	Russianization
USATAIE	substantialise
	substantialize
USATAIG	substantiating
USATAIM	substantialism
USATAIN	substantiation
USATAIT	substantialist
USATAIY	substantiality
USATVLY	substantivally
USINFAT	question of fact
USITTAS	burst into tears
USIUIEY	substitutively
USMOEIE	put someone wise
USMTIGT	put something at
USNOFCR	nursing officer
USNSUES	cups and saucers
USRPINV	subscription TV
UTAINLS	Australian Alps
UTCAIAS	rustic capitals
UTCINUE	eustachian tube❑
UTCWTES	Kurt Schwitters
UTEABOE	Curtley Ambrose
UTECESN	put the screws on
UTEHMYN	put the whammy on
UTEIHTN	put the tin hat on
UTEILDN	put the tin lid on
UTEIOHN	put the kibosh on
UTELGOT	put the flags out
UTEOTOK	further outlook
UTERKSN	put the brakes on
UTERNWY	rub the wrong way
UTERORE	run their course
UTFAIIY	justifiability
UTFROSY	multifariously
UTHRVRE	just the reverse
UTIAIIY	sustainability
UTNTDAH	putting to death
UTNTEHT	putting the shot
UTNUHOM	button mushroom
UTPEHIE	multiple-choice
UTPEJNS	Bustopher Jones
UTPIAIN	multiplication
UTRAHRR	hunter-gatherer
UTRCAIM	multiracialism
UTRCNIM	quattrocentism
UTRCNIT	quattrocentist
UTRECAT	gutter-merchant
UTRIGRD	butter-fingered
UTRLETE	cultural centre
UTRVLUE	culture vulture
UTSMTIG	quite something
UTTANIY	curtate annuity
UTUIHET	just punishment
UTVCUBT	Gustave Courbet
UULNUTR	mutual inductor
UUROSES	lugubriousness
UUTCLGL	August Schlegel
UUTESAN	August Weismann
UUTLMEE	Auguste Lumière
UUTNAIM	Augustinianism
UUTOSES	tumultuousness
UUTPCAD	Auguste Piccard
UUTSNIO	Augusto Sandino
UVCOSES	curvaceousness
UWEESHN	auf Wiedersehen
UWRLOIG	outward-looking
UYEOUIN	July Revolution
UYHHTHT	bury the hatchet
UYRKPIG	Rudyard Kipling
VIGIGER	avoid going near
VIOEEFF	avail oneself of
VNADDES	even-handedness
VNEIAIM	evangelicalism
VNEIAIN	evangelization
VNNSRIE	evening service
VPRTDIK	evaporated milk
VRAIAIE	overcapitalise
	overcapitalize
VRAOEEF	overtax oneself
VRATCLR	overparticular
	over-particular
VRATDOS	overfastidious
	over-fastidious
VRCOSES	avariciousness
VRCUUOS	overscrupulous
VREIEET	over-refinement
VREIUOS	over-meticulous
VRHLIGY	overwhelmingly
VRIPIID	oversimplified
VRNUGNE	overindulgence
VROEIGY	overpoweringly
VROFDNE	overconfidence
	over-confidence
VROPNAE	overcompensate
VRPIITC	over-optimistic
VRRTCIE	overprotective
	over-protective
VRSCNDY	every second day
VRSEAOS	Évariste Galois
VRSIAIN	overestimation
VRYEDOY	over my dead body
VRYRTES	Everly Brothers
WDMNINL	two-dimensional
WEOCPNY	owner-occupancy
WEOSNAS	a week of Sundays
WFRIHES	two for his heels
WIIGCIN	awaiting action
WMIGRNS	swimming trunks
WNESELX	twin-lens reflex
WOSAEIE	swoopstake-like
	swoop-stake-like
WRRCPIN	a warm reception
WSAMKIE	Swiss army knife
WSEFFOT	a waste of effort
WSTIGOO	a wise thing to do
XASOBAD	expansion board
XASOJIT	expansion joint
XCRECNE	exacerbescence
XEDDAIY	extended family
XEIETLY	experimentally
XEINILY	expedientially
	experientially
XEPRNOS	extemporaneous
XESACUT	expense account

Words marked ❑ can also be spelled with an initial capital letter

XEVCWMN ex-servicewoman
XGNYIDR oxygen cylinder
XIAAIGY exhilaratingly
XIGIHBE extinguishable
XIIINRA exhibition area
XLSOODR exclusion order
XLSVRGT exclusive right
XMNCOEY examine closely
XMNICIF examine-in-chief
XODOEET Oxford Movement
XOEOAGR expose to danger
XOMNCTR excommunicator
XOTOAEY extortionately
XRCAIGY excruciatingly
XRCAIIY extractability
XRCROEL extracorporeal
XRMLFNY extremely funny
XRMLLRE extremely large
XRMLSAL extremely small
XRMUCIN extreme unction
XRNOSES extraneousness
XRSIEES expressiveness
XRSINAK expression mark
XRSINES expressionless
XRSOEEF express oneself
XRSVLMS express volumes
XRVHCLR extravehicular
XSETAIM existentialism
XSETAIT existentialist
XSFYMTY axis of symmetry
XTEMCLY exothermically
XUEYRNH excuse my French
YACLGCL gynaecological
YAIDSAE hydatid disease
YAISLIG pyramid selling
YCRNCLY synchronically
YDNJHSN Lyndon B Johnson
YEASHSA hyperaesthesia
YEBLCLY hyperbolically
YEBTCLY hyperbatically
YECIIIE hypercriticise
hypercriticize
YECIIIM hypercriticism
YEGYAMA hyperglycaemia
YEIFAIN hyperinflation
YESNIIE hypersensitise
hypersensitive
hypersensitize
YEVNIAE hyperventilate
YHGRAIM Pythagoreanism
YHLGCLY mythologically
YHSMTKN by the same token
YIABLAS Lyrical Ballads
YIAQAIY typical quality
YILBDOD Sybille Bedford
YIRMPOA Cyril Ramaphosa
YITONIE Sybil Thorndike
YLPREOD cycle per second
YNCBLMN cyanocobalamin
YOEMCLY hypodermically
YOHNIHY sycophantishly
YOHNRAT hypochondriast
YOHRIIM hypothyroidism
YOHTCLY hypothetically
YOOITCL hypocoristical
YORTCLY hypocritically
YOTTCLY hypostatically
YPOAOOY symptomatology
YPTIEIH sympathize with
YRCPAOS hydrocephalous
YRDNMCL hydrodynamical
YRDOPTR hybrid computer
YRIVCOY Pyrrhic victory
YRLGCLY hydrologically
YRPNCLY hydroponically
YRPOIIY hydrophobicity
YRSOIIY hygroscopicity
YRUIBAE hydraulic brake
YRUIPES hydraulic press
YTCIRSS cystic fibrosis
YTMFELH system of wealth
YTMTCLY systematically
YTMULIG system building
YTNASLS Wynton Marsalis
YTNTAHY Lytton Strachey
YTRCOIE hysterectomise
hysterectomize
YTROSES mysteriousness
YTRUHOM oyster mushroom
ZDTYIIE azidothymidine
ZRMUTIS Ozark Mountains

15 letters – even

AAALLER Jawaharlal Nehru
AAARLPU Parasaurolophus
AACONTR balance of nature
AAEEOTI Japanese Bobtail
AAEUFLE La Cage aux Folles
AAEUTRL Madame Butterfly
AAIGITC paralinguistics
AAINSAD Hawaiian Islands
AAIYOHA capacity for heat
AAODVLE Papa Doc Duvalier
AAOMSRO parasol mushroom
AAOTLGS palaeontologist
AAUZMNO Lazarus Zamenhof
ABATESN Barbra Streisand
ABRCRLN Barbara Cartland
ABRHPOT Barbara Hepworth
ABUORFG harbour of refuge
ABUPROS harbour porpoise
ACALMSO catch a glimpse of
ACATNAC dance attendance
ACDESAT fancy-dress party
ACETCUC pancreatic juice
ACIGOWR marching forward
ACIOIUL sanctimoniously
ACLBABR Malcolm Bradbury
ACLCMBL Malcolm Campbell
ACLRIES vascular disease
ACLTINL Pascal's triangle
ACOEBET catch one's breath
ACOTERS Pasch of the Cross
ACPOESN batch processing
ADCTFLO hard act to follow
ADENHWN Candle in the Wind
ADERENS hard-heartedness
ADFAMPR Cardiff Arms Park
ADFNSIT land of one's birth
ADIHSAD Sandwich Islands
ADLNOLG Magdalen College
ADNSHEH haud one's wheesht
ADOTEAL cards on the table
ADOUMNR cardiopulmonary
ADTOOEN hand it to someone
ADWOEAM lay down one's arms
AEAEDCP camera-ready copy
AEAFMNT have half a mind to
AEARETE make fair weather
AEATEOT water at the mouth
AEATIKN lateral thinking
AEATNRC take part in a race
AEBCWIE Paperback Writer
AEBEIEO make a beeline for
AEBEKOI make a break for it
AEBGHNO make a big thing of
AEBNTPC have a bone to pick
AEBTHRA take a butcher's at
AECAIGO have a craving for
AECAINO have occasion for
AECENRA make a clean break
AECENWE make a clean sweep
AECLETO have a collection
AECNETO make a connection
AECPCTO have a capacity of
AECUAIN make accusations
AEDATGO take advantage of
AEDFEEC make a difference
AEDSUSO have a discussion
AEDUTET make adjustments
AEEEECT make reference to
AEEGACO take vengeance on
AEENEVC have seen service
AEESXRM make less extreme
AEFLMRA Vale of Glamorgan
AEGODNE make a good dinner
AEGOFSO make a good fist of
AEGOMNT have a good mind to
AEHADCT have the audacity
AEHCILF take the chill off
AEHICUS take their course
AEHNSOS make things worse
AEHRWRO make short work of
AEHSIEF take the shine off

AEHTTAE have what it takes
AEHWASF take the wraps off
AEHWIHO take the weight of
AEHWOGA take the wrong way
AEICMAO make mincemeat of
AEIEELO make life hell for
AEILZTO materialization
AEKLCAE Haleakala Crater
AELEAIN make allegations
AELNIGO have a longing for
AEMNANT make a mental note
AENMIVI take a name in vain
AENNETR make an inventory
AENNSAD have in one's hands
AENOCON take into account
AENODIT make inroads into
AENOSIU make unconscious
AENOUTD take into custody
AENSABE have one's marbles
AENSEAA make one's getaway
AENSEVO take one's leave of
AENSNAA have one's end away
AENSNFI have one's knife in
AENSOTI have one's roots in
AENXETO make an exception
AENXMLO make an example of
AEOBSBU have doubts about
AEOCONO take no account of
AEOCSIN make concessions
AEODTOA make conditional
AEOEETN take some beating
AEOENSA make someone's day
AEOENUO take someone up on
AEOFRAL make comfortable
AEOHGON raze to the ground
AEOMNAS make common cause
AEONSEL take to one's heels
AEONSER take to one's heart
AEORCWT have no truck with
AEOSIUO make conscious of
AEOTCWT make contact with
AEOTERI water on the brain
AEPEIEC take up residence
AEPNNSL take upon oneself
AERAPAO make great play of
AERCSAD Balearic Islands
AERCUIN take precautions
AEREDWT make friends with
AERNHEV take French leave
AERSSAC sales resistance
AESASOO take a snapshot of
AESHSUC have as the source
AESRDRV Vanessa Redgrave
AESRSOS have as a response
AESRWOS have a screw loose
AESTOII have as its origin
AESTSUC have as its source
AETDATG take at advantage
AETEIAL parenthetically
AETNHCI take it on the chin
AETOIII have its origin in
AETREVI take it or leave it
take-it-or-leave-it
AETRMHR take it from there
AEUGSIN make suggestions
AEULSBU have qualms about
AEURMCS male supremacist
AEVRBRE have over a barrel
AEVREFR make every effort
AEVRUET make overtures to
AEWYIHN have a way with one
AEWYYOC take away by force
AEXETOT take exception to
AEYHTRA have by the throat
AFACSOA San Francisco Bay
AFESMHN Manfred Symphony
AFREUAL pay for regularly
AFRHCUS par for the course
AGADADW laugh and lay down
AGADIDW laugh and lie down
AGAIAAK Marghanita Laski
AGAWLIM Vaughan Williams
AGETTRB lay great store by
AGLKARI laugh like a drain
AGROLSR kangaroo closure
AGRTEKT Margaret Beckett
AGRTFNO Margaret of Anjou
AGRTOSE Margaret Forster
AGRTRBL Margaret Drabble
AGTNBWE caught and bowled
AHELAMT Dashiell Hammett
AHENERE Kathleen Ferrier
AHEUARE Daphne Du Maurier
AHIADHO Daphnis and Chloe
AHLHTRA Rachel Whiteread
AHMASJL Dag Hammarskjöld
AHNAHDA Aachen Cathedral
AHNEEYN each and every one
AHNEGEN Nathanael Greene
AHNLNUG machine language
AHNNSHP cash in one's chips
AHNSADO wash one's hands of
AHNULQI washing-up liquid
AHOALNS fashionableness
AHOBSNS fashion business
AHRHITA Father Christmas
AHRNHWR Catherine Howard
AHTCALC pathetic fallacy
AIAGISA capital gains tax
AIAHTRA Fatima Whitbread
AIATIET Marie Antoinette
AICOEBR David Cronenberg
AIDPESV manic-depressive
AIEMNSE cabinet minister
AIESOPS Mariner's Compass
AIFARCU David Frabricius
AIGDATG taking advantage
AIGHBSO making the best of
AIGNFAD laying-on of hands
AIGOERN having no bearing
AIGSNSW taking as one's own
AIHEDRO Hamish Henderson
AIIOAIE Galilieo Galilei
AIIRZTO familiarization
AIIRZWT familiarize with
AILAEBI Daniel Barenboim
AILENUL Daniel Bernoulli
AILPSAR Camille Pissarro
AILRATO capillary action
AILRJDC racial prejudice
AIMCOHN radio microphone
AINFRRT Valiant-for-Truth
AINGIED Patient Griselda
AINLALR National Gallery
AINLEVC national service
AINLHAR National Theatre
AINLOTR National Lottery
AINLZTO nationalization
rationalization
AINNGOT malignant growth
AIPICPE basic principles
AISLTNN Larissa Latynina
AISNATN ladies-in-waiting
AIYADNK Wasily Kandinsky
AIYLOAC family allowance
AJCSNNA Sam Jackson Snead
AKADOKN backward-looking
AKADSAD Falkland Islands
AKDIIAL lackadaisically
AKECRIG hackney carriage
hackney-carriage
AKEEPRS hackneyed phrase
AKFLTAE jack-of-all-trades❑
AKGISTM talk against time
AKNNSEL back on one's heels
AKODQER Wackford Squeers
AKODTOE cask-conditioned
AKOHFTR Back to the Future
AKOQAEN back to square one
ALAETRA parliamentarian
ALAETRL parliamentarily
ALAETRS parliamentarism
ALERHWN sail near the wind
ALGTOBR daylight robbery
ALIRERC Paul Pierre Broca
ALNDERC Marlene Dietrich
ALNNSNE fall on one's knees
ALNTPEE falling to pieces
ALONNAU fall down in value
ALONSNE fall to one's knees
ALPNTTE wallop in a tether
ALSNFTN Wallis and Futuna
ALTETOT call attention to
ALTLVSO cable television
ALUHJNK Karl Guthe Jansky
ALVNIAE badly ventilated
ALVRNSL fall over oneself
AMDMLOC Palma de Mallorca
AMERENS warm-heartedness
AMNCADE Raymond Chandler
AMNPICR Raymond Poincaré
AMNWLIM Raymond Williams
AMRHNHR Carmarthenshire
AMRNSCL Hammer and Sickle
hammer and sickle
ANASNDG rain cats and dogs
ANATROE gain mastery over
ANFIGLS magnifying glass
ANLNWEG carnal knowledge

Words marked ❑ can also be spelled with an initial capital letter

ANNMSRO darning mushroom
ANNMUNS magnanimousness
ANNWEGO gain knowledge of
ANOCLUE rainbow-coloured
ANRSIAL manneristically
ANSANSO Magnus Magnusson
ANTCOPS magnetic compass
ANTCQAO magnetic equator
ANTEONE paint the town red
ANTKNNS painstakingness
ANUSIES Raynaud's disease
AOAICMR panoramic camera
AOAKRDI Radovan Karadzic
AOBRKAD Jacob Burckhardt
AODAMLA Harold Macmillan
AODIHLO Harold Nicholson
AOEFNEO lay one's finger on
AOEHATU eat one's heart out
AOEPESN way of expressing
AOFLSOE pay off old scores
AOLVEFR Jaroslav Seifert
AOMSATO law of mass action
AONADHL Madonna and Child
AONDLRT Madonna del Prato
AOOSRCO vasoconstrictor
AOTEAII War of the Pacific
AOTMIBC Aaron Temkin Beck
AOULNAU Carolus Linnaeus
AOURBLT manoeuvrability
APAAADO happy as a sandboy
APAECOB Ralph Abercromby
APATTOE malpractitioner
APINGIS campaign against
APLADAE Tadpole and Taper
APNNSRN harp on one string
APRADUE Harpers and Queen
APRATOI Caspar Bartholin
APRCADO Ralph Richardson
APRRERC Caspar Friedrich
APSHMCE Ralph Schumacher
AQECUTA Jacques Cousteau
AQEIEUR Jacqueline du Pré
ARAEATE marriage partner
ARAEEVC marriage service
ARAELMD Marriage à la Mode
ARAENPI carriage and pair
ARAEOTO marriage portion
ARCNITO carry conviction
ARCSIAL macrocosmically
ARECNOL Maureen Connolly
ARMNOIE Sacramento River
ARNELVE Laurence Olivier
ARNEURL Lawrence Durrell
AROFHBL carry off the bell
AROTNSA carry out one's bat
ARSOIAL macroscopically
ARSONAN Taurus Mountains
Zagros Mountains
ARSOSAH walrus moustache
ARWNOHL harrowing of hell
ARWNUNS Barrow-in-Furness
ASAILAU Hanseatic League
ASALSAD Marshall Islands
ASBTENS cause bitterness
ASECEBC Hans Reichenbach
ASETUTO mass destruction
ASIPESO false impression
ASLLOTE Wassily Leontief
ASLNGEE Hansel and Gretel
ASNCULR Carson McCullers
ASNEPGO passenger pigeon
ASNSUHN lapsang souchong
ASOEHNT raise one's hand to
ASOESGT raise one's sights
ASONTEA pass round the hat
ASRSNMN cause resentment
ASSNQAO causa sine qua non
ASTLSFC cause to lose face
ASTTEEC raise to the bench
ASTTKPR cause to take part
ASUGMNO pass judgement on
ASVIMNT passive immunity
ASVRSSE passive resister
ASYADNL Ramsay MacDonald
ATADIUE facts and figures
ATAFATO partial fraction
ATAVNYR Martha's Vineyard
ATCEHSC particle physics
ATDNFSE catted and fished
ATEAIWR say the magic word
ATEFAAI Battle of Salamis
ATEFABA Battle of Cambrai
ATEFAEG Battle of Marengo
ATEFAEN Battle of Salerno
ATEFEAT Battle of Lepanto
ATEFECR Battle of Leuctra
ATEFHNL Battle of the Nile
ATEFHNV Battle of the Neva
ATEFHPU Battle of Thapsus
ATEFIDR Matthew Flinders
ATEFLDE Battle of Flodden
ATEFLSE Battle of Plassey
ATEFOES Battle of Colenso
ATEFOUN Battle of Corunna
ATEFRAC past performance
ATEFRSE Battle of Dresden
ATEFRTI Battle of Britain
ATEFULN Battle of Jutland
ATEFWJM Battle of Iwo Jima
ATEITEI castles in the air
ATEOEEI parthenogenesis
parthenogenetic
ATEONWT can't be doing with
ATEOTBU Battles of Tobruk
ATERTEA Walther Rathenau
ATIASLT Captain Absolute
ATIMCET Captain MacHeath
ATNEDGE Martin Heidegger
ATNFROO Waiting For Godot
ATNIMLE Martin Niemöller
ATNRBSE Martin Frobisher
ATNSYOE cast one's eye over
ATNVRMC wanting very much
ATOAYAE Cautionary Tales
ATOEBET waste one's breath
ATONEII gastroenteritis
gastro-enteritis
ATOOEFI Bartholomew Fair
ATOPNWT part company with
ATPRAHN fast approaching
ATREELO Easter Rebellion
ATRFSIA Lantern Festival
ATRLETR Pastoral Letters
ATROEAE battery-operated
ATROOIA bacteriological
ATRUYAE Canterbury Tales
ATSAOOE cast a shadow over
ATSATRN earth-shattering
ATSFOBL fantasy football
ATSIVYG Fantastic Voyage
ATVGTRA lactovegetarian
AUAIMNT natural immunity
AUAINON saturation point
AUALNUG natural language
AUARSOS natural response
AUATELG natural theology
AULANMN Samuel Hahnemann
AVDRLED Salvador Allende
AVSFSIA harvest festival
AVYIETN Harvey Firestone
AYODVLE Baby Doc Duvalier
AYOEOWT easy to get on with
AYPEDUE many-splendoured
AZNFHAE Tarzan of the Apes
AZNHAEA Tarzan the Ape Man
BDOTEEI abode of the devil
BETFCTO objectification
BEVTOAL observationally
BEVTOPS observation post
BNZRCOG Ebenezer Scrooge
BTUTVNS obstructiveness
BULHBAI Abdullah Ibrahim
BUOEPRO about one's person
BVALESR above all measure
BVTEETE above the weather
CACAROA act as chairwoman
CAINLAL occasional table
CAORPIA oceanographical
CAPAEAE act as peacemaker
CETIPRO eccentric person
CEUECSE scheduled castes
CIDFUTM A Child of our Time
CIEESAS scrivener's palsy
CIIYOIA activity holiday
CINOETA action potential
CINOMTE action committee
CIOEMTU echinodermatous
CITSMAI schistosomiasis
CLMTZTO acclimatization
CLNTINL scalene triangle
CLSATCS ecclesiasticism
CLSOOIA ecclesiological
CNMCEUE economic refugee
CNWEGMN acknowledgement
COAGESO act of aggression
CODOLSI achondroplastic
CODOPET accordion pleats
COKNNSO a crook in one's lot
COLFHUH school of thought

COMDTNL accommodatingly
CONALNS accountableness
COPRIMN Act of Parliament
COSHTAK across the tracks
CPOFIAU Scipio Africanus
CRSMSAO A Christmas Carol
CSFDORA Acts of Adjournal
CTEIDGA act the giddy goat
CTIHERE Scottish terrier
CTIHODR Scottish Borders
CTXCLGS ecotoxicologist
CUSTVNS acquisitiveness
CUTCOPE acoustic coupler
DACDNER advanced in years
DACPSTO advance position
DADHMRY Edward the Martyr
DADOHSE Edward Rochester
DADPOOZ Eduardo Paolozzi
DADRBNO Edward G Robinson
DETRUNS adventurousness
DIAGASE Admiral Graf Spee
DINDODO Adrian Edmondson
DINOIET Adriano Olivetti
DLOSIPN idol-worshipping
DLSFHKN Idylls of the King
DNIYLMN identity element
DNIYNMR identifying mark
DNUGCSL Edinburgh Castle
DOITECA a drop in the ocean
DOMLNHL Ode on Melancholy
DORPIAL ideographically
DRFRUNS odoriferousness
DURDLDE Edouard Daladier
Édouard Daladier
EABNZTO decarbonization
EABRZTO decarburization
EACFCTO decalcification
EACMLTL relax completely
EACTOLN demarcation line
EADEADE Gérard Depardieu
EADHDAO Bel and the Dragon
EADNAMN demand in payment
EADRAFS bed and breakfast
EADSHSM regard as the same
EAEOLSL behave foolishly
EAERVLE New Age traveller
EAHOOHN hexachlorophene
EAIEEST relative density
EAIGATC delaying tactics
EALTAEU get all steamed up
EANTZTO demagnetization
EAOUSNS pedagoguishness
EATAFUK Sebastian Faulks
EATETLS departmentalise
departmentalism
EATETLZ departmentalize
EATETTR department store
EBCTNRA get back to normal
EBFRWCE leg before wicket
EBLIRHE verbal diarrhoea
EBOEOLG Pembroke College
EBRMRIO Herbert Morrison
ECATEVC merchant service
ECCNIGA Merce Cunningham
ECFLEES merciful release
ECINHRP reichian therapy❑
ECITVNS descriptiveness
ECMADET Ten Commandments
ECRCBTO reach rock bottom
ECRNLGS geochronologist
EDCSLAI hendecasyllabic
EDCSLAL hendecasyllable
EDESIGR dead men's fingers
EDFCESO deed of accession
EDIVROR Hendrik Verwoerd
EDMRYAC lead a merry dance
EDNMLPR leading male part
EDNMLRL leading male role
EDNNMRO Ferdinand Marcos
EDNOTAD bending outwards
EDNPSTO leading position
EDNQETO leading question
EDNRSMT Weedon Grossmith
EDNSEAD send one's regards
EDNVRMC needing very much
EDODLNE send condolences
EDOHGBE send to the gibbet
EDONTEA send round the hat
EDSDONI dead as a doornail
dead as a door-nail
EDVREFO get divorced from
EDYEERP send by telegraph
EEAASML General Assembly
EEABLRN General Belgrano
EEADHWK Hereward the Wake
EEADHWL Peter and the Wolf
EEAEETO general election
EEALEEG renewable energy
EEALSEO Seve Ballesteros
EEALVTK Helena Blavatsky
EEAPATC general practice
EEBFRSE never before seen
EECLSNS defencelessness
EECPCIH telescopic sight
EECRTIA Terence Rattigan
EECSIAO Seleucus Nicator
EEDNCAS dependent clause
EEDPTUL serendipitously
EEGRFOR Berengar of Tours
EEHAENS level-headedness
EEHNNME telephone number
EEHTGAH telephotography
EEIIUNS repetitiousness
EEIOCEG benefit of clergy
EEIOELN Federico Fellini
EEITERW jewel in the crown
EEOEEUL heterogeneously
EEOEULT heterosexuality
EEOHOAI heterochromatic
EEOIUNS ceremoniousness
EEOMNAE development area
EEOMNAL developmentally
EEPURBN Peter Paul Rubens
EERADAI Père Armand David
EERDAMN deferred payment
EERDNUT deferred annuity
EERNFLO peregrine falcon
EERNPCL Peregrine Pickle
EERPIAL telegraphically
EERTVNS penetrativeness
EESTKOE reverse takeover
EESTZTO desensitization
EETASHR celestial sphere
EETOCNR detention centre
reception centre
EETOMTE select committee
EETSILN seventy shilling
EEVCREC reserve currency
EEVDNLS Received English
EEYOADH Gene Myron Amdahl
EFARFCN self-sacrificing
EFBEVTO self-observation
EFCINSI perfectionistic
EFCITRA perfect interval
EFEEMNN self-determining
EFEILTN self-legislating
EFERAHU self-reproachful
EFERCTN self-deprecating
EFERCTO self-deprecation
EFETENS self-centredness
EFETUTO self-destruction
EFEVCCF self-service café
EFICPIE self-disciplined
EFMLAWT get familiar with
EFNTRNS perfunctoriness
EFOEEGT self-sovereignty
EFOETTO reafforestation
EFOSQEC self-consequence
EFPNOAE self-opinionated
EFPRBTO self-approbation
EFRYHUE Geoffrey Chaucer
EFRYOCT Geoffrey Boycott
EFTAFNU beefsteak fungus
EFTMLTO self-stimulation
EFUFCEC self-sufficiency
EFURCRO perfluorocarbon
EFUSATA self-substantial
EFUTIMN self-sustainment
EFXLNTR self-explanatory
EFXMNTO self-examination
EGBULNS neighbourliness
EGETTRB set great store by
EGIIGIE Sergei Diaghilev
EGIRKFE Sergei Prokofiev
EHIVRAL Cepheid variable
EHLNETO lethal injection
EHMHTMN methamphetamine
EHNSIAL mechanistically
EHOITCT dephlogisticate
EHOOIAL technologically
EHREOWL Lee Harvey Oswald
EHRSHOE Gerhard Schröder
EHSOHLA Mephistophelian
EIACOSN pelican crossing
EIACREC decimal currency
EIAEHMS meditate the muse
EIAFATO decimal fraction
EIALAGU let it all hang out
EIDHSEE behind the scenes

EIEAEDC deliver a verdict
EIEAHTE beside each other
EIEHREI Meriwether Lewis
EIETAAE residential area
EIETAHM residential home
EIETEOD deliver the goods
EIEYFIE delivery officer
EIHRBLT decipherability
EIIAERM legitimate drama
EIIEOMN definite comment
EIIFNTH Leni Riefenstahl
EIIMRMN delirium tremens
EIJMSHR Cecil James Sharp
EILBOHR Neville Brothers
EINLSTO regionalisation
EINLZTO regionalization
EINTOFO resignation from
EIOADIH Heligoland Bight
EIOEBNE bee in one's bonnet
EIOIUNS meritoriousness
EIORPIA lexicographical
EIOUSLN Benito Mussolini
EITOIAL heliotropically
EIUDIKN serious drinking
EJMNRTE Benjamin Britten
EKNOMTO seek information
ELDSOEE newly discovered
ELEHREI Leslie Charteris
ELEUSOA feel revulsion at
ELFUUNS mellifluousness
ELGREEA feel aggrieved at
ELIHUCL deal with quickly
ELITRBU feel bitter about
ELNNSOE feel in one's bones
ELNNTVT declining to vote
ELNSIAL Hellenistically
ELNSWTL tell one's own tale
ELPOSEE well-upholstered
ELRINCN declare innocent
ELRLMRO Jelly Roll Morton
ELSAEGN real-estate agent
ELSALSE well-established
ELWRCRA yellow brick road
ELWRVLE fellow-traveller
ELWUMRN Yellow Submarine
ELYHCNL sell by the candle
EMDTINL Bermuda Triangle
EMNAHLC German Catholics
EMNAIAI permanganic acid
EMNNMGE permanent magnet
EMNOLRT Herman Hollerith
EMNUIAL hermeneutically
EMPRDTS hermaphroditism
EMRHLGS geomorphologist
EMSINOE permission to see
EMTGMSU Hermitage Museum
ENADIMN Bernhard Riemann
ENCNIEE being considered
ENETOBM Meindert Hobbema
ENETRNI Jeannette Rankin
ENEVNRU Wernher von Braun
ENHMOLO Jean Champollion
ENHSFSD be on the safe side
ENLUEIL Jean Claude Killy
ENNLSNS meaninglessness
ENOAPOC means of approach
ENRHBOS Leonard Hobhouse
ENROAIC Leonardo da Vinci
ENTWLIM Kenneth Williams
ENUTILS deindustrialise
ENUTILZ deindustrialize
ENYOTSE keenly contested
EOAEWNO decorated window
EOAOGRL hen on a hot girdle
EOCLBLT reconcilability
EODHLHO second childhood
EODNOMN second-in-command
EODNUAC beyond endurance
EODRCLU secondary colour
EODRCUE secondary causes
EODRSHO secondary school
EOEALNS recoverableness
EOEBAIG get one's bearings
EOEDNEU get one's dander up
EOEHIDW let one's hair down
EOEIFRN become different
EOELEAE become alienated
EOELUCE peroneal muscles
EOEMCAE become emaciated
EOEMMEO become a member of
EOEMNEU get one's monkey up
EOENINN become indignant
EOENOVN become insolvent
EOEOAAT Jérôme Bonaparte
EOEOEOI become more solid
EOEOKOI before you know it
EOEOTLT become hostile to
EOEPRTV become operative
EOESAEO get one's skates on
EOESGTO set one's sights on
EOESITU get one's shirt out
EOESRNE become estranged
EOETETO devote attention
EOEULFO remove guilt from
EOEVIAL become available
EOFHGON get off the ground
EOFNSHS get off one's chest
EOILEVC memorial service
EOITEOL get on in the world
EOMLSTO renormalisation
EOMLZTO renormalization
EOMNAIN recommendations
EOMSINN decommissioning
EOOEBET below one's breath
EOOENRE get on one's nerves
EOREUNS resourcefulness
EORTZTO democratization
EOSDRTO reconsideration
EOSIERA Devonshire cream
EOSLSNS remorselessness
EOSRTVL demonstratively
EOSRTWT remonstrate with
EOTEUFC below the surface
EOTMMXM Deo Optimo Maximo
EOTMNTO decontamination
EOTMNTV decontaminative
EOUINRE revolutionaries
EOVNCEI revolving credit
EOYAIAL aerodynamically
EPEASML People's Assembly
EPECNRS People's Congress
EPEFAHO Temple of Hathoor
EPEFOOO Temple of Solomon
EPEFREI Temple of Artemis
EPLOOTO keep a lookout for
EPLVNAK Leopold von Ranke
EPLWRFL keep a low profile
EPNIUAL perpendicularly
EPNODRE keep in good order
EPNSHMO keep one's thumb on
EPNSHRO keep one's shirt on
EPOHNBC keep nothing back
EPOPNWT keep company with
EPRCEPR jeepers creepers
EPRITRA peppermint cream
EPRMNAL temperamentally
EPSFEIG deepest feelings
EPSUUNS tempestuousness
EPTAMTO perpetual motion
EQIETNR sesquicentenary
ERAEUCL decrease quickly
ERAHUNS reproachfulness
ERBLZTO detribalization
ERCIENE refractive index
EREACUE George Vancouver
EREATYN George Santayana
EREEAHT wear several hats
EREFREO degree of freedom
ERELMIR Georges Lemaître
EREOETO George Robertson
EREOHVS George von Hevesy
EREPMIO Georges Pompidou
ERERNIL George Grenville
ERERSMT George Grossmith
ERERVLA George Trevelyan
EREUARE George Du Maurier
EREVLUO bear heavily upon
ERGESVL retrogressively
ERHBECE wear the breeches
ERHTOSR wear the trousers
ERIGUPR learning support
ERKTLWL Henry Kettlewell
ERLNUSI neurolinguistic
ERMNIAL necromantically
ERNCLAS nearing collapse
ERNDSAC hearing distance
ERNSARU tear one's hair out
ERNSITE beer and skittles
ERNTEOS fearing the worst
ERONSER dear to one's heart
near to one's heart
ERPLTNS metropolitanise
ERPLTNZ metropolitanize
ERRFIIG bearer of tidings
ERSETVL retrospectively
ERSIEEC near as ninepence
ERSNAIE representatives
ERTRAAM Territorial Army
ERVOVSO deprive of vision

ERVTZTO reprivatization
ERWYHBL bear away the bell
ERXMNTO bear examination
ESALSMN re-establishment
ESGOCRS message of Christ
ESIAIUL perspicaciously
ESIUUNS perspicuousness
ESMOEGA get someone's goat
ESMOEIH see someone right
ESMRRCS Bessemer process
ESMSIAL pessimistically
ESNFCTO personification
ESNFORG person of courage
ESNLESO personal pension
ESNLFET personal effects
ESNLRNU personal pronoun
ESNLTCL personality cult
ESNLZTO personalization
ESNNNRT persona non grata
ESOEAIN cease operations
ESOIETT sense of identity
ESOTUPT feast of trumpets
ESRATVT leisure activity
ESREADN lesser celandine
ESRNSSE measuring system
ESRSRNT measure strength
ESUBYIL Tess Durbeyfield
ETADIRS Perth and Kinross
ETADUSL Bertrand Russell
ETBACLM vertebral column
ETBLREV vestibular nerve
ETCEMSU Deutsches Museum
ETEAFRE gentleman farmer
ETEALNS gentlemanliness
ETEAYHA wet the baby's head
ETEBADN weatherboarding
ETEBSNS genteel business
ETEFNRI centre of inertia
ETEFRAC best performance
ETEFRCS weather forecast
ETEFRVT centre of gravity
ETEIGRU get the finger out
ETELSOE settle old scores
ETEOENS feather one's nest
ETEOSOI get the worst of it
ETEOWLO leather on willow
ETERNIE get the wrong idea
ETERPNN get the drop on one
ETETETR weather the storm
ETEUAON get the runaround
ETFECEU certified cheque
ETFIILR heath fritillary
ETGNUNS vertiginousness
ETIGMVN get things moving
ETLBLTE mental abilities
ETLCECN Fertile Crescent
ETLHMSR mental chemistry
ETLRADW mental breakdown
ETNIUNS sententiousness
ETNPTTE meat and potatoes
ETNUEMR Weston-super-Mare
ETOAHTE next to each other
ETODOLG Hertford College
ETOENTI beat someone to it
ETOIGNE destroying angel
ETPRTLO Neath Port Talbot
ETPYHLG depth psychology
ETRLSAO pectoralis major
ETRLSIO pectoralis minor
ETUTBLT destructibility
ETUTVNS destructiveness
ETWNWRO get to windward of
ETWTROS Keith Waterhouse
EUACSOE regular customer
EUAICSL Beaumaris Castle
EUBNFGR Recumbent Figure
EUIYLNE security blanket
EUIYONI Security Council
EULEAIN sexual relations
EULNTNT sexual instincts
EULYSAL sexually assault
EUNFHJD Return of the Jedi
EUOTORS be put out to grass
EURCINR resurrectionary
EURCINS resurrectionise
resurrectionist
EURCINZ resurrectionize
EUTMSHE get up to mischief
EUTTAIE Gewürztraminer
EVCALNS serviceableness
EVCIDSR service industry
EVHGADR leave high and dry
EVIAEAC leave in abeyance
EVITEUC leave in the lurch
EVNFEVN heaven of heavens
EVSECLS leave speechless
EVUDSRE nervous disorder
EWEYUNM between you and me
EYBIBIG Beryl Bainbridge
EYTFCTO demystification
FEDDCIN after deductions
FEUOELF offer up one's life
FHFRTAE of the first water
FHMDLAE of the Middle Ages
FIAEEHN African elephant
FIAIUNS efficaciousness
FIEOTEA officer of the day
FIHRULT of higher quality
FLETOIT affluent society
FNEITEI a finger in the pie
FNSWACR of one's own accord
FOOSQEC of no consequence
FRWLTAM A Farewell to Arms
FSOTFAE a fish out of water
GADPORC egg-and-spoon race
GISTELC against the clock
GISTERI against the grain
GIUTRLS agriculturalist
GODSRTO age of discretion
GSNONHN eggs in moonshine
HAEFNIT The Age of Anxiety
HAHTEWR sheathe the sword
HANNITO The Annunciation
HAOOETM ahead of one's time
HAOSHDL ahead of schedule
HAOTEIE ahead of the times
HARCNUE The African Queen
HATEALW cheat the gallows
HATUDDE The Artful Dodger
HBCCEHE The Bicycle Thief
HBCOBYN the back of beyond
HBGASPR The Beggar's Opera
HBIHLGT the bright lights
HBRHFEU The Birth of Venus
HBTEPRO the better part of
HBTHODS the bitch goddess
HCATSLA the coast is clear
HCLTELI chocolate éclair
HCMOPOL the common people
HCOEPOL the chosen people
HCTWIKR the cat's whiskers
HCWRLLO The Cowardly Lion
HDAHFAA The Death of Marat
HDNEFET The Dance of Death
HDVLTTO the devil's tattoo
HDVNCMD The Divine Comedy
HEAIACL wheel animalcule
HEDFHRA the end of the road
HEEFTGE The Eve of St Agnes
HEMNNBA Three Men in a Boat
HEPNYIC threepenny piece
HESYOEI The Essays of Elia
HETMSHE three times three
HFAELTO The Flagellation
HFEIQEN The Faerie Queene
HFFRNSL shift for oneself
HFMLENC The Female Eunuch
HFOEGON shift one's ground
HFTLITR the fatal sisters
HGEKAED the Greek calends
HGFOTEA the gift of the gab
HGOEAEF the gloves are off
HGOSEHR the Good Shepherd
HGREOEE The Garden of Eden
HHWNTEH the how and the why
HIEACMT The Iceman Cometh
HIKNVOE shrinking violet
HILOAAO The Isle of Avalon
HITACCU Christmas cactus
HITADDV Christian de Duve
HITAILN Christmas Island
HITDLHA Christadelphian
HITNAET Christ in Majesty
HITPEDA Christopher Dean
HITPEWE Christopher Wren
HIVSBEA The Invisible Man
HJBJUAT Thojib N J Suharto
HKNOCMD The King of Comedy
HLANLUS Thelma and Louise
HLCLIEO cholecalciferol
HLDVNSE The Lady Vanishes
HLEATCU Chelsea Arts Club
HLEFHLN the lie of the land
HLIGHDO chalking the door
HLIOECA a hole in one's coat
HLNHOIA philanthropical
HLRNCRE Children's Corner
HLSFIEU Thales of Miletus
HLSFTSA child-safety seat

HLSOHRP thalassotherapy
HLSPIAL philosophically
HLTLPIC The Little Prince
HLYHLYN shilly-shallying
HMCLAFR chemical warfare
HMCLLMN chemical element
HMNINOS the Mansion House
HMNISEC thumbnail sketch
HMOSAEL Thomson's gazelle
HMRBOHR The Marx Brothers
HMRIGFE the morning after
HMRSONN the morn's morning
HMSEFRO Thomas Jefferson
HMSEUNE Thomas De Quincey
HMSIDEO Thomas Middleton
HMSRDRN Thomas Gradgrind
HNBECEC the noble science
HNEFDRS change of address
HNLEOUI phenylketonuria
phenylketonuric
HNLHHLI phenolphthalein
HNMNLGS phenomenologist
HNNHGON thin on the ground
HNOOEFE think on one's feet
HNOTGTE think of together
HNSCEUR Chinese chequers
HNSCLNA Chinese calendar
HNSWIPR Chinese whispers
HNTEOLO think the world of
HNWOKIE The New York Times
HOFOTEI shoot from the hip
HOGTEIH through the night
HOIGALR shooting gallery
HOIOEHN throw in one's hand
HOITEAD throw in the cards
HOITEOE throw in the towel
HOITRLE throw into relief
HOOBLRT Theodor Billroth
HOOEOTK Theodore Roethke
HOOFAAC throw off balance
HOOOIAL chronologically
HOOSEBR Theodor Svedberg
HOTTEID throw to the winds
HOTTEIN throw to the lions
HOUTEAD throw up the cards
HPALIHR The Pearl Fishers
HPEADES chapter and verse
HPFHDSR ship of the desert
HPOECUS shape one's course
HPRSOMN the Paris Commune
HPTTETR The Potato Eaters
HPWRTAB the powers that be
HRCEITC characteristics
HRCESEC character sketch
HREAFIE chargé d'affaires
HREDGUL Charles de Gaulle
HREERGE Charles Earl Grey
HREGEDR Where Eagles Dare
HREGEIL Charles Greville
HREGOYA Charles Goodyear
HREJMSO Charles James Fox
HREKNSE Charles Kingsley
HRELUHO Charles Laughton
HREMCAN Shirley MacLaine
HREPRIL charged particle
HREWLIM Shirley Williams
HREYNFK Charles Yanofsky
HRFOMDS The Raft of Medusa
HRHFNLN Church of England
HRIIBEL whirligig beetle
HRINCAV thermionic valve
HRIOESD thorn in one's side
HRITELS thorn in the flesh
HRNFEIG sharing feelings
HRNTOGT sharing thoughts
HRNTORC a hard nut to crack
HROTAAI Charlotte Amalie
HROTBOT Charlotte Brontë
HROTCRA Charlotte Corday
HROTSIL Charlottesville
HRPOERP The Rape of Europa
HRPUIAL therapeutically
HRSAPHC short sharp shock
HRSIANS pharisaicalness
HRSOELN there's no telling
HRTOSRN The Rite of Spring
HRTUNHN thirst-quenching
HSCEGRE The Secret Garden
HSCNCMN The Second Coming
HSELSRE Chester-le-Street
HSHRSEC phosphorescence
HSLADLT whistle and flute
HSLFRWN whistle for a wind
HSMODTR the same old story
HSOHRPS physiotherapist
HSOOIAL physiologically
HSORPIA physiographical
HSPRAUA the supernatural
HSUDFUI The Sound of Music
HSYTEII the sky's the limit
HTADSAD Shetland Islands
HTCAECR Whitechapel cart
HTDEUCR whited sepulchre
HTLECTE that'll teach them
HTMLILE photomultiplier
HTMNBRE white man's burden
HTMRLKI that's more like it
HTREICE The Three Witches
HTREIEE the Three Wise Men
HTREITR The Three Sisters
HTRHNHT whiter than white
HTRIOEO white rhinoceros
HTVRHCS whatever the cost
HTVRTAE whatever it takes
HTWRFAE The Tower of Babel
HUAOOIA rheumatological
HUBUMRE shout blue murder
HUDRHTE shoulder-shotten
HUDRLPE shoulder-clapper
HUHHGLO thought highly of
HUHLSNS thoughtlessness
HUTOHWL thrust to the wall
HVOATVT a hive of activity
HVOIDSR a hive of industry
HVRYIBR shiver my timbers
HWAEVSE the weaker vessel
HWCNETO show a connection
HWIDITR the Weird Sisters
HWMNNHT The Woman in White
HWNSVRE show one's ivories
HWODATG show to advantage
HWOEHBN the whole shebang
HWOTMTO show contempt for
HWREOWA the worse for wear
IAALBLT bioavailability
IACASSE financial system
IAEQEOE picaresque novel
IAFCENS disaffectedness
IAFRSMN disafforestment
IAIBOPE vitamin B complex
IAPEESO misapprehension
IAPEESV misapprehensive
IAPROCL final port of call
IAREBLT disagreeability
IASAITC vital statistics
IAVNAEU disadvantageous
IBAHRHA win by a short head
IBCOEER pin back one's ears
IBLWHBL hit below the belt
IBRECES limburger cheese
ICATARE aircraft carrier
ICEINRL discretionarily
ICIFASA air-chief-marshal
ICINSAD Pitcairn Islands
ICIOSOT circuitous route
ICITANN circuit training
ICIVUNS mischievousness
ICLAEUL miscellaneously
ICLMMRA Lincoln Memorial
ICLPGNN Niccolò Paganini
ICMAECE circumjacencies
ICMAIAO circumnavigator
ICMAOTN Giacomo Agostini
ICMCITO circumscription
ICMLOAD Giacomo Leopardi
ICMTNIT circumstantiate
ICNIINN air-conditioning
ICNIUTO discontinuation
ICNIUUL discontinuously
ICNOELN Vincenzo Bellini
ICNTUTO misconstruction
ICOOEMN piece of one's mind
ICRDSAN Giscard d'Estaing
ICROSUD discord of sounds
ICSINRU discussion group
ICUTNNE discountenanced
IDADSAD Windward Islands
IDCENIE windscreen-wiper
IDEFHRA middle-of-the-road
IDEFOHR middle of nowhere
IDERENS kind-heartedness
IDHASET find the answer to
IDMFOOO Wisdom of Solomon
IDNEETN find interesting
IDNSANR mind one's manners
IDNSCON find one's account
IDNSSNQ mind one's p's and q's
IDOAETE birds of a feather
IDPNSON gird up one's loins

IDRSIUU Diodorus Siculus
IDSONAN Pindus Mountains
IDWADNN window gardening
IEADMCA Liberal Democrat
IEAEERE Airedale terrier
IEAGUTR like gangbusters
IEALCTI bimetallic strip
IEAORPE cinematographer
IEAORPI cinematographic
IECNEEC videoconference
IEDGDNE like a dog's dinner
IEDNTOT give a donation to
IEEEEGT give new energy to
IEEJSII fides et justitia
IEEPESO fixed expression
IEFCLFT give a facelift to
IEFRLSL win effortlessly
IEGILNT give a grilling to
IEHBUHF give the brush-off
IEHCAPR like the clappers
IEHETNN life-threatening
IEHGMAA give the game away
IEHIPRO vice-chairperson
IEHNELT give the needle to
IEHOCOE give the once-over
IEHRTMT give a hard time to
IEHSOAA give the show away
IEHTUBU give the thumbs-up
IEHWRDO give the world for
IEITNTO fine distinction
IENHBIL bite on the bridle
IENHBLE bite on the bullet
IENNSEL fire in one's belly
IENSAKN give one's backing
IENSLAA give oneself away
IENSLAR give oneself airs
IENSOKT line one's pockets
IENSOSN give one's consent
IENSPNO give one's opinion
IENSUAC give an assurance
IENSUPR give one's support
IENVTOT give an ovation to
IEOEAIU time-zone fatigue
IEOEIES time-zone disease
IEOENFV give someone five
IEOENHL give someone hell
IEOTEOT Lives of the Poets
IEPHTRN give up the throne
IESFAYO Rivers of Babylon
IESFCTO diversification
IESTFDA fixed set of ideas
IETAKTN direct marketing
IETDVLI Ninette De Valois
Ninette de Valois
IETNLMN disentanglement
IETOOEN give it to someone
IEUGSIN give suggestions
IEUHRTT give authority to
IFCLTFN difficult to find
IFETEIE Wilfred Thesiger
IFRCRSI Linford Christie
IFRNITN differentiating
IFRNITO differentiation
IGALDEU ring-tailed lemur
IGFHCSL king of the castle
IGFHFRS king of the forest
IGLRZTO singularization
IGNAREE Virginia creeper
IGNTESN sing another song
IGNTETN sing another tune
IGOMFKN Siege of Mafeking
IGRERLN ginger beer plant
IHACOPO Richmal Crompton
IHADJIE with hands joined
IHAEBET with bated breath
IHAPNST wish happiness to
IHCNHOU Pithecanthropus
IHDFEEC with a difference
IHEEECT with reference to
IHEFOTO with self-control
IHEODAJ Michael Ondaatje
IHEOEBL tighten one's belt
IHEPRIL Michael Portillo
IHEPRTR high temperature
IHERDRV Michael Redgrave
IHFSENS tight-fistedness
IHHAENS light-headedness
IHHNPRO right-hand person
IHHNUAL Right Honourable
IHIBLAO Mikhail Bulgakov
IHIEOPR with time to spare
IHINVOO Nizhniy Novgorod
IHISLYO Michail Saltykov
IHLSENT Wilhelm Steinitz
IHLSIEA Nicholas Wiseman
IHMNENS light-mindedness
right-mindedness
IHNNSRK lightning strike
IHNRSEC within arm's reach
IHOECRE fight ones corner
IHOETBR with money to burn
IHOFHRE right off the reel
IHOHNII with nothing in it
IHOHNTD with nothing to do
IHOWRHR Wish You Were Here
IHPADON with ups and downs
IHRDCTO higher education
IHRDEFS Richard Dreyfuss
IHRDMLB Richard Dimbleby
IHRDNOD Richard Dunwoody
IHRHMLO Richard Hamilton
IHRLVLC Richard Lovelace
IHRNYNE hither and yonder
IHRPWLE tight-rope walker
IHRVLLN high-gravel-blind
IHSRWOS with a screw loose
IHTTEOE fight to the ropes
IHUAATE without a partner
IHUACAC without a scratch
IHUARAI without a break in
IHUCEKN without checking
IHUCRMN without ceremony
IHUPANN without planning
IHUPRLE without parallel
IHUQETO without question
IHUTIKN wishful thinking
without thinking
IHYEEOE highly-developed
IIAEGIS militate against
IIAYOOR military honours
IIAYWSE military two-step
IIEESNE divine messenger
IIESHAR Citizen's Theatre
IIHNSRK finishing stroke
IIIIGOR digitizing board
IILSETU visible spectrum
IILSOMN disillusionment
IIOETRA lie in one's throat
IISTDNU vicissitudinous
IITRFTT Minister of State
IITRSEL disinterestedly
IITRZTO miniaturization
IKAHRPE pick gather speed
IKESEEI sickness benefit
IKNMCWE Wilkins Micawber
IKPHPEE pick up the pieces
IKPNSEL kick up one's heels
ILABAMN William Beaumont
ILABCFR William Beckford
ILABNIC William Bentinck
ILACNRV William Congreve
ILACOIG William Coolidge
ILACSRV William Cosgrave
ILADVNN William Davenant
ILAFIDI William Friedkin
ILAFUKE William Faulkner
ILAHRCE William Herschel
ILAHRIO William Harrison
ILAIOSD William Ironside
ILALNLN William Langland
ILAMKNE William McKinley
ILAMRDT William Meredith
ILAOOAG William of Orange
ILAOOKA William of Ockham
ILAREMG William Rees-Mogg
ILASEHR Gillian Shepherd
ILASOKE William Shockley
ILAWIEA William Whitelaw
ILEAAIE girlie magazines
ILEHEAE Willie Shoemaker
ILGCLLC biological clock
ILIGOCM till kingdom come
ILMEONN Willem De Kooning
ILMITOE Willem Einthoven
ILMNSEC bioluminescence
ILMTCOP diplomatic corps
ILNMSFL Killing Me Softly
ILONROT Giulio Andreotti
ILRFLMR Millard Fillmore
ILTCAOR Violeta Chamorro
ILTECPR wield the sceptre
INERENS lion-heartedness
INGTXRS Midnight Express
INLARMR Lionel Barrymore
INRCNTE Wiener schnitzel
IOABKAI Nikolay Bukharin
IOABLAI Nikolai Bulganin
IOAOADN Girolamo Cardano
IOASESE Nikolaus Pevsner

IODMNFR Simon de Montfort
IOGNZTO disorganization
IOILHOE binomial theorem
IOTECBR tip of the iceberg
IOTEOIO dip of the horizon
IOULIAI ribonucleic acid
IPAEPRO displaced person
IPCAIOT Hippocratic oath
IPOOTOE misproportioned
IPRAPIO dispersal prison
IPSINTL dispassionately
IRCCDYL citric acid cycle
IREEOSR Pierre de Ronsard
IREETOI microelectronic
IREONIL Pierre Corneille
IRERSGE Pierre Trésaguet
IRIMLNO Giorgiy Malenkov
IRNERSA Tigran Petrosian
IRNMSOC Hieronymus Bosch
IRSETUL disrespectfully
IRSOIAL microscopically
ISAPAAC first appearance
ISCALNS dissociableness
ISLETNN first-lieutenant
ISMOEPL oil someone's palm
ISNWITE pigs and whistles
ISOENSS kiss someone's ass
ISPICPE first principles
ISTSATO dissatisfaction
ITDYOOR birthday honours
ITEEDIE hit the headlines
ITEELRN Little Nell Trent
ITEIHPT hit the high spots
ITENLNE little Englander
ITERYEL little grey cells
ITESUCL Mistress Quickly
ITHMELI Wilt Chamberlain
ITNAEUL listen carefully
ITNNDVC listening device
ITNTVNS distinctiveness
ITNUSAL distinguishable
ITNUSMN distinguishment
ITPNEIC fifty pence piece
ITRCLOE historical novel
ITREZWG Mister Fezziwigg
ITRORPE historiographer
ITRORPI historiographic
ITRPSCR picture postcard
ITRSUNS picturesqueness
ITTRANS dictatorialness
IUADOIU Titus Andronicus
IUENCOD Figure and Clouds
IULSIAL ritualistically
IUTOCMD situation comedy
IUTOEHC situation ethics
IVNIASN Giovanni Cassini
IVNIELN Giovanni Bellini
IVNIIAU Giovanni Cimabué
IYFHVLE lily of the valley
lily-of-the-valley
JNOENAD Django Reinhardt
LAAAHSL clean as a whistle
LAEESOE old-age pensioner
LAHNPWE bleaching powder
LAIGAIA floating capital
LALWSME al-hallown summer
LAOETRA clear one's throat
LAQAEMI Allan Quatermain
LAUEEKN pleasure-seeking
LBETGBE flibbertigibbet
LBLRLSE globular cluster
LCAODRO place an order for
LCNGTHD black nightshade
LCOBSNS place of business
LCOEVSO block one's vision
LCOGAHM Alec Douglas-Home
LCRAOSI electroacoustic
LCRCATR electric battery
LCRCEIA electrochemical
LCRCLNE electric blanket
LCRCLTR electrical storm
LCRCOEE electric-powered
LCRCURN electric current
LCRDNMC electrodynamics
LCRFCTO electrification
LCRIOEO black rhinoceros
LCRMGEI electromagnetic
LCRMTIA electrometrical
LCRNCLS electronic flash
LCRNCUI electronic music
LCRNGTV electronegative
LCRPOEI electrophoresis
electrophoretic
LCRTCNC electrotechnics
LCSDBSD place side by side
LCWTREE blackwater fever
LDMRAOO Vladimir Nabokov
LECMASN all-encompassing
LEGNRTO older generation
LEIGATE sleeping partner
LEMRILN Ellesmere Island
LENTVVT Alternative Vote
LEOTDOB blue-footed booby
LETFJMR Alberto Fujimori
LETIHLO Albert Michelson
LETNMSU Albertina Museum
LGNSUSU slog one's guts out
LGTNOGP Flight into Egypt
LGTNSRT plight one's troth
LGTTEDN flight attendant
LIGHLNE flying phalanger
LIIALNS illimitableness
LISEHNO Elsie Stephenson
LITRRWE Aleister Crowley
LMNAYAA alimentary canal
LMNBETN Clemens Brentano
LMWRHNS blameworthiness
LNCLATS clinical baptism
LNKCNTN Planck's constant
LNOMSAR Glencoe Massacre
LNPTNIR plenipotentiary
LNTEIEO along the lines of
LNTTEID fling to the winds
LOCRLNL bloodcurdlingly
LOETELC all over the place
LOFHHNL fly off the handle
LPFHTNU slip of the tongue
LPOOTOE ill-proportioned
LPWRUNS all-powerfulness
LRCNRFG ultracentrifuge
LRDADTN Old Red Sandstone
LRDHTHA Alfred Whitehead
LRDICCC Alfred Hitchcock
LRDTELT Alfred Stieglitz
LRMCOCP ultramicroscope
ultramicroscopy
LROTEOK clerk of the works
LROTEOR clerk of the court
LROTERN Clermont-Ferrand
LRSAALW Clarissa Harlowe
LSADOOT Alessandro Volta
LSARALA Alistair Maclean
LSARALN Alistair Darling
LSFSENS close-fistedness
LSHNENS close-handedness
LSIADOE all skin and bones
LSIGEDW Flushing Meadows
LSLTGTE closely together
LSOEEET close one's eyes to
LSTTEHS close to the chest
LSUSOLG All Souls College
LTEAARS all the way across
LTEAEOO all the same to you
LTEIDSR clothes industry
LTOBEOT I'll trouble you to
LUCCOLN Cloudcuckooland
cloud-cuckoo-land
LUETRHR Gloucestershire
LUHASUC ploughman's lunch
LUHFEPN slough of despond
LUINSAD Aleutian Islands
LUISONE Claudius Dornier
LUTIUNS illustriousness
LVADIKN alive and kicking
LVEMSIE Olivier Messiaen
LVHWRBL Clive Howard Bell
LVREVSD Oliver Heaviside
LVRODMT Oliver Goldsmith
LVUJSPU Flavius Josephus
LWAPERE blow raspberries
LWNHUTK slow on the uptake
LWNNHWN Blowin' in the Wind
LWNSHNE blow one's chances
LWNSWHR blow one's own horn
LWRHNSA slower than usual
LWYUSRL slowly but surely
LXNECLE Alexander Calder
LXNEDBE Alexander Dubcek
LXNEIVN Alexander Irvine
LXNENVK Alexander Nevski
Alexander Nevsky
LXNSUCE flex one's muscles
LYDYHBO played by the book
LYISFDL play first fiddle
LYNTEIL playing the field
LYOTIWT play footsie with
LZBTBNE Elizabeth Bennet
LZBTBSO Elizabeth Bishop
LZBTTYO Elizabeth Taylor

MARSEHI embarras de choix
MARSUHI embarras du choix
MAULOLG Emmanuel College
MEERBLT impenetrability
MEIHBLT imperishability
MEIKUIU emperick qutique
MEOCNET Emperor Concerto
MESOHAE immersion heater
MEUIUNS impecuniousness
MGNRNME imaginary number
MGNTVNS imaginativeness
MIIETOA omnidirectional
MKOTEAE Smoke on the Water
MLIGFOE smelling of roses
MLMNENS small-mindedness
MNHFUDY a month of Sundays
MOTDRDC imported product
MOTLZTO immortalization
MRCNRTE American Trotter
MRGVSUC Amerigo Vespucci
MRSBRSD Ambrose Burnside
MRSINSI impressionistic
MSMNACD amusement arcade
MUOOIAL immunologically
NACLBLT incalculability
NAHMBLT unfathomability
NALAETR unparliamentary
NAREAIU unfair behaviour
NAYCAIN on many occasions
NBETOAL unobjectionable
unobjectionably
NBRSVNS unobtrusiveness
NCALFHA knock all of a heap
NCESBLT inaccessibility
NCETBLT unacceptability
NCLSNWC knuckle sandwich
NCOMDTN unaccommodating
NCTEOKO knock the socks of
NDFEETA in a different way
NDISBLT inadmissibility
NEAASNM under a false name
NECAGAL interchangeable
interchangeably
NECAGMN interchangement
NECMUSO under compulsion
NECNETN interconnecting
NECNETO interconnection
NECRETO under correction
NECVRGN undercover agent
NEDPNEC interdependence
NEDSUSO under discussion
NEEBACO in remembrance of
NEEDNEA Independence Day
NEEMNTL indeterminately
NEEOIUL unceremoniously
NEEPOMN underemployment
NEESBLT indefeasibility
indefensibility
NEESRNS unnecessariness
NEETHAE in seventh heaven
NEETMTO underestimation
NEETNNS unrelentingness
NEETSAL indecent assault
NEEUTMT antepenultimate
NEFCHAT in perfect health
NEFOSIU unselfconscious
NEHNENS underhandedness
NEIALNS undesirableness
NEIRHME anterior chamber
NEITNNS unremittingness
NELCADE under lock and key
NELCULS intellectualise
intellectualism
NELCULT intellectuality
NELCULZ intellectualize
NELGBLT intelligibility
NENBUMO once in a blue moon
NENFCTO indemnification
NENLEIN infernal regions
NENLZTO internalization
NENTOAL internationally
NEOCLAL unreconciliable
NEOEBET under one's breath
NEOLGTO under obligation
NEONTOO in recognition of
NEOSRTV undemonstrative
NEPEESI interpretership
NEPIIEE underprivileged
NERCGRL Anne Bracegirdle
NERGTVL interrogatively
NESADNL understandingly
NESFCTO intensification
NESHLSI interscholastic
NETCRIL entente cordiale
NETEAOO under the baton of
NETEEIO under the aegis of
NETEETE under the weather
NETEIAL anaesthetically
NETEOCN Under the Volcano
NETEONE under the counter
under-the-counter
NETETRS investment trust
NETROSI ancestor-worship
NETXULT intertextuality
NEVNINS interventionism
interventionist
NEWEWIE in between whiles
NFESVNS inoffensiveness
NFETANS ineffectualness
NFETVNS ineffectiveness
NFIAIUL inefficaciously
NGEMNWT in agreement with
NGTFHPS knight of the post
NGTFHRA knight of the road
NGTFHWI knight of the whip
NHACNAC in the ascendancy
NHATGTE in the altogether
NHBCBRE on the back burner
NHBCGON in the background
NHDNELS on the danger list
NHFRTLC in the first place
NHFRTLS in the first flush
NHIEMLD Unchained Melody
NHITRSO in the interest of
NHLEGAL unchallengeable
NHLSMNS unwholesomeness
NHLSRSR in the last resort
NHMLIGO in the melting-pot
NHNAFTR in the near future
NHNCOTM in the nick of time
NHNEBLT unchangeability
NHNMOLV In the Name of Love
NHNRDOR one hundred hours
NHNTOLP Anthony Trollope
NHNVREE on the never-never
NHOOETI anthropocentric
NHOOHGT anthropophagite
NHOOOHS anthroposophist
NHOOOIA anthropological
NHOOOPI anthropomorphic
NHPEECO in the presence of
NHRGTRC on the right track
NHSAADG in this day and age
NHSMBET in the same breath
NHSRNTO on the strength of
NHVCNTO in the vicinity of
NHWTRRN On the Waterfront
NIETBLT indigestibility
NIETLUI incidental music
NIGTORU Annie Get Your Gun
NIHEUNS unrighteousness
NIIEIAL infinitesimally
NIIIENS uncivilizedness
NIIULSI individualistic
NILRCLS anticlericalism
NINFCNL insignificantly
NINMNMN ancient monument
NISLBLT indissolubility
NISNSAT in fits and starts
NITNUSE undistinguished
NKITERS snake in the grass
NKLEWRE unskilled worker
NLCADHT in black and white
NLCNCEC in all conscience
NLDRCIN in all directions
NLEALNS inalterableness
unalterableness
NLLKLHO in all likelihood
NMIUUNS unambiguousness
NMLANTS animal magnetism
NMLSIAL anomalistically
NMLXRMN animal excrement
NMTDATO animated cartoon
NNEETNL uninterestingly
NNERPEL uninterruptedly
NNETOAL unintentionally
NNSATBE on one's pantables
NNSIHMN in one's right mind
NNSIHOS on one's high horse
NNSPRTM in one's spare time
NNWQATT unknown quantity
NODODTO in good condition
NODTOAL unconditionally
NODTOTA on condition that
NOEALNS intolerableness
NOEEIAL ontogenetically
NOEGCIE in foreign climes
NOENBLT ungovernability
NOENSET in someone's teeth

NOENSOE in someone's power
NOETEIH one over the eight
NOFOTTO in confrontation
NOGUUNS incongruousness
NOGVNNS unforgivingness
NOHSIAE unsophisticated
NOIALNS indomitableness
NOISIAL encomiastically
NOLBRTO in collaboration
NOMNCTV uncommunicative
NOMNUAL incommensurable
NOOOIAL entomologically
NOOTEOL on top of the world
NOPEEDN uncomprehending
NOPEESO incomprehension
NOPIETR uncomplimentary
NOPRBLT incomparability
NOPSINT uncompassionate
NOPTBLT incompatibility
NORBNTI Anton Rubinstein
NORGBLT incorrigibility
NORGTTL encourage to talk
NORNLGS endocrinologist
NOSDRTL inconsiderately
NOSDRTO inconsideration
NOSIUNS unconsciousness
NOSIUSL unconscious self
NOSIUUL inconspicuously
NOSLBLT inconsolability
NOSQECO in consequence of
NOSQETA inconsequential
NOTENRW one of the in-crowd
NPAIGEM on speaking terms
NPGMGTL and pigs might fly
NPLCBLT inapplicability
NPLPERE in apple-pie order
NPOTNNS inopportuneness
NPRETOL in a perfect world
NPRHNIL inapprehensible
NPRNFML one-parent family
NPRPITL inappropriately
NPRTOAL inspirationally
NQIALNS inequitableness
NQIOANS unequivocalness
NRAEUCL increase quickly
NRAVSLU Andreas Vesalius
NRBADRB in dribs and drabs
NRCDNEL unprecedentedly
NRDLUNS incredulousness
NREDYEM on friendly terms
NRETTMN untrue statement
NRIYHNK Andrei Vyshinsky
NRLTOSI in a relationship
NRMDNBL Andromeda nebula
NRNHSMN enfranchisement
NRPEERA entrepreneurial
NRPSESN unprepossessing
NRSIGDE engrossing a deed
NRTNIUL unpretentiously
NRTSATS unprotestantise
NRTSATZ unprotestantize
NRXAEVS anorexia nervosa
NSAIEET one's native heath
NSAISMZ Anastasio Somoza
NSALBLT unassailability
NSETIAL unascertainable
NSETVNS unassertiveness
NSRIHLN in a straight line
NSYIOWR a nasty bit of work
NTECPFE another cup of tea
NTERSET in other respects
NTETVNS inattentiveness
NTNAEUL instantaneously
NTUETAE instrument panel
NTUETLS instrumentalist
NTUETLT instrumentality
NTUETTO instrumentation
NTUTOBO instruction book
NTUTVNS instructiveness
NUEALNS innumerableness
NUHNIAE unauthenticated
NUHRIII annus horribilis
NUIALNS indubitableness
NUIIUNS injudiciousness
NUNRBLT invulnerability
NUODNTL insubordinately
NUODNTO insubordination
NUOIPAU pneumonic plague
NUPCENS unsuspectedness
NURCINR insurrectionary
NURCINS insurrectionist
NUSATAE unsubstantiated
NUSATAL insubstantially
NUSINNL unquestioningly
NUSSETO intussusception
NUSTRAL inquisitorially
NUSTVNS inquisitiveness
NUTIUNS industriousness
NVIALNS unavoidableness
NVRARMD universal remedy
NWAPSTO in a weak position
NWDNEWT snowed under with
NWNSWMN know one's own mind
NWTIGRW know a thing or two
NWYRNTE one way or another
NXEINEI inexperienced in
NXESVNS inexpensiveness
NXETOAL unexceptionable
unexceptionably
NXETTOO in expectation of
NXLCBLT inexplicability
OABDBRE total body burden
OABRIGO Jonah Barrington
OACMISO Royal Commission
royal commission
OADLAAC Donald Pleasance
OADMNRG coram domino rege
OAGVRMN local government
OAHNDAD Jonathan Edwards
OAIAINS totalitarianism
OAIHIAL logarithmically
OANAHLE Johann Pachelbel
OANOHRE Johann von Herder
OANSCHR Johannes Eckhart
OAOTELT woman of the cloth
OAOTEOL woman of the world
OAPICPE moral principles
OAPIOOH moral philosophy
OASASAD Coral Sea Islands
OATCITO romantic fiction
OATCZTO romanticization
OBDCIEB not be deceived by
OBDEPAE Forbidden Planet
OBEEOHO hobbledehoyhood
OBENENT Double Indemnity
OBENUOI double pneumonia
OBESHMR God bless the mark
OBETGTE cobbled together
OBETRED to absent friends
OBNTOLC combination lock
OBNWLWT combine well with
OBSILNS combustibleness
OBYNIDA cowboy and Indian
OCITALC force into a place
OCMNITI not coming into it
OCMOMNI non compos mentis
OCPOUTO voice production
OCREATO concerted action
ODCIIHE Mordecai Richler
ODDAEOS bonded warehouse
ODEEWME Lord Peter Wimsey
ODEPNIL hold responsible
ODERENS cold-heartedness
ODHMELI Lord Chamberlain
ODIHDIA Lord High Admiral
ODLOENS cold-bloodedness
ODMTBEL goldsmith beetle
ODNAAHT golden parachute
ODNADHK golden handshake
ODNADUF golden handcuffs
ODNALDU London Palladium
ODNALIL Holden Caulfield
ODNEEEC hold in reverence
ODNEIIU Golden Delicious
golden delicious
ODNEREE golden retriever
ODNGTHD woody nightshade
ODNOEAC nodding ogee arch
ODNTEEN holding the reins
ODNTGTE holding together
ODOAPOA goods on approval
ODOAYHN good for anything
ODOFRFR Cold Comfort Farm
ODOPSTO cold composition
ODSEDNL condescendingly
ODUDIEC road fund licence
ODVRBRE hold over a barrel
OEAENCL moderate in a call
OEANRHN come rain or shine
OEATFOK covenant of works
OEATFRC covenant of grace
OEFEAIU code of behaviour
OEFLYUL powerfully built
OEFRLRP money for old rope
OEFROHN Money for Nothing
OEGECAG foreign exchange
OEGISHP hope against hope
OEHECAG lose the exchange
OEHHTOT Joseph Whitworth

OEHPNSF bore the pants off
OEHRETE Joseph Priestley
OEHRTLV somewhere to live
OEHRWRW come the raw prawn
OEHULOI Joseph Guillotin
OEHWREO none the worse for
OEIHHWN Gone With the Wind
Gone with the Wind
OEIRNTA lower in rank than
OEMIOIE Moses Maimonides
OEMNGMN money management
OENHMRE come on the market
OENONSW come into one's own
OENOOTC come into contact
OENREEA governor-general
OENSAAC lose one's balance
OENSABE lose one's marbles
OENSERT lose one's heart to
OENSOTN lose one's footing
OEOATRE power of attorney
OEODCSO come to a decision
OEOEMWT come to terms with
OEOENSA come someone's way
OEOEOOS come home to roost
OEOETAK cover one's tracks
OEOHMNO come to the mind of
OEOINAE money-orientated
OEONEVO come down heavy on
OEONOWT to be going on with
OEORPWT come to grips with
OEOSRNT tower of strength
OEPHLDE move up the ladder
OEPOCAC come up to scratch
OEPTIAL homeopathically
OESHSUU Roget's Thesaurus
OESLAON Love is All Around
OESNTTT Women's Institute
OESTAGA Somerset Maugham
OETAEEG potential energy
OETCATR domestic matters
OETCCEC domestic science
OETCEET Roberto Clemente
OETNOLG Homerton College
OETOTWL Robert Southwell
OETSRCE poverty stricken
poverty-stricken
OEYFANR comedy of manners
OEZGIET Lorenzo Ghiberti
OFAAAGN go off at a tangent
OFAHLCC go off at half cock
OFDNERC confidence trick
OFDNILT confidentiality
OFEALBO coffee-table book
OFGRTOA configurational
OFTEEPN go off the deep end
OFTEUJC go off the subject
OGAODOT tough as old boots
OGAOPAN lodge a complaint
OGAUAIN congratulations
OGCRBEL longicorn beetle
OGEEALR Borghese Gallery
OGISIES Hodgkin's disease
OGLIBRE Jorge Luis Borges
OGNDNEC song-and-dance act
OGNTESU dodging the issue
OGONSSK for goodness sake
OGOTBTU too good to be true
OGSALSE long-established
OGTNSIE forget one's lines
OGVRMNA non-governmental
OHAEEBR Joshua Lederberg
OHESOSE Loch Ness monster
OHFLETN to the full extent
OHLGTOS To the Lighthouse
OHMNEBR to the manner born
OHNFRTU nothing for it but
OHNLSTA nothing less than
OHRGTBU to the right about
OHTHTOO do a hatchet job on
OHVEOGO not have enough of
OHVNEOG not having enough
OIAAACT Louisa May Alcott
OIDGADU folie de grandeur
OIEOREI Louise Bourgeois
OIGOFLO Robin Goodfellow
OIGOOHN coming to nothing
OIGTICS moving staircase
OIHAHTE go with each other
OIHHSRA go with the stream
OIHONEB Josiah Bounderby
OIHUSYN go without saying
OIIAAYU political asylum
OIIEETN positive vetting
OIINHAR Dominion Theatre
OILEORC social democracy
OILERTR social secretary
OILLASN social cleansing
OILNUAC social insurance
OILSIAL socialistically
OILWRNS social awareness
OIMABNT sodium carbonate
OIMYRXD sodium hydroxide
OIOOIAL toxicologically
OIPATTO ion implantation
OISNOLG Robinson College
OITREEC non-interference
OITRETO non-intervention
OIYFAIN comity of nations
OKAKNNE Look Back in Anger
OKDIHNN forked lightning
OKDOHSI soaked to the skin
OKHOHRA look the other way
OKHRRPE Yorkshire Ripper
OKHSAKN look who's talking
OKIETOA work like a Trojan
OKNMJRT working majority
OKNSASG work one's passage
OKNSUSU work one's guts out
OKNTGTE working together
OKOBEIE work double tides
OKTCETS rocket scientist
OKTNFRN pocket an affront
OKTNSRD pocket one's pride
OKUTEOA work out the total
OLCOSIC collector's piece
OLESESR poulters' measure
OLGLCUE college lecturer
OLIHSOE Rollright Stones
OLMIEOE bowl a maiden over
OLNCRLS couldn't care less
OLRILMC dollar diplomacy
OLSATRN world-shattering
OLSCCME cool as a cucumber
OLSEDGE to a lesser degree
OLSEETN to a lesser extent
OLSOCUS collision course
OLUEATE Toulouse-Lautrec
OLWTOTN world without end
OMCTEIE not much the wiser
OMCTLOA not much to look at
OMCTOON Too Much Too Young
OMEPRTR room temperature
OMNASOS common-law spouse
OMNCTVL communicatively
OMNCTWT communicate with
OMNELHA Commonwealth Day
OMNFATR common of pasture
OMNNHSI common in the soil
OMNNWEG common knowledge
OMNTCAG community charge
OMNTCNR community centre
OMNTMNE community-minded
OMNTSHO community school
OMOWNAA room to swing a cat
OMRAEOS Donmar Warehouse
OMRILRA commercial break
OMSNDMA Cosmas and Damian
OMSRTWT commiserate with
OMTCUGR cosmetic surgery
OMTEMME committee member
ONAINTN foundation stone
ONAOTOT roundabout route
ONAVYOE John Harvey-Jones
ONBTETA go one better than
ONCLSNE John Schlesinger
ONEAGMN counter-argument
ONENTAE John Bennet Lawes
ONERENS downheartedness
ONERNWA John Henry Newman
ONHLPOS John Philip Sousa
ONHSRIE join the services
ONIKSOT John Wilkes Booth
ONIOERP Council of Europe
ONIOSAE Council of States
ONLUJNE Cornelius Jansen
ONNARMN join in matrimony
ONNHPRL born in the purple
ONNSCNS morning sickness
ONNSOMN soundness of mind
ONOAIEM horns of a dilemma
ONOEONA going one's own way
ONONRTR point of no return
ONOOMTE go into committee
ONOTELA horns of the altar
ONPCELN go on a picket line
ONRARDN Joan Armatrading
ONRNLTO loan-translation
ONROOII country of origin
ONSANDS do one's damnedest

ONSEEBS do one's level best
ONSNWEG to one's knowledge
ONTOEHA going to one's head
ONUNYDM John Quincy Adams
OOAHRTM go for a short time
OOAKNRI go to rack and ruin
OOAOPIG Colorado Springs
OOASMSU Holocaust Museum
OOAUTAI Corona Australis
OODIESK for old time's sake
OOEGCIE to foreign climes
OOENSET to someone's teeth
OOETRAO not open to reason
OOEWLOT sow one's wild oats
OOHPTIO Dorothy Pattison
OONADON go round and round
OONSCON go to one's account
OOOCCTI Molotov cocktail
OOOENLI not on one's nellie
OOOOAAI locomotor ataxia
OORPIAL topographically
OOTEELO hot on the heels of
OOTEUUA go for the jugular
OOWYANS motorway madness
OPEENUT complete annuity
OPEESVL comprehensively
OPEESVS comprehensivise
OPEESVZ comprehensivize
OPEETDE complete studies
OPEETRL complementarily
OPESBLT compressibility
OPESNEC complex sentence
OPIGHCE no spring chicken
OPNIUNS compendiousness
OPNOWLE Company of Wolves
OPOESOA non-professional
OPOIMKN non-profit-making
OPOOIET doppio movimento
OPPLVXE vox populi vox Dei
OPRIASI non-partisanship
OPRTRIE corporate raider
OPSINTL compassionately
OPTLZTO hospitalization
OPTRCEC computer science
OPTRZTO computerization
OPTTVNS competitiveness
OPYTETO not pay attention
ORAOMTO poor man of mutton
ORCIGLI correcting fluid
OREFTDE course of studies
OREONAN Mourne Mountains
ORFIHUL yours faithfully
ORHIESO fourth dimension
ORLTOPO Worrall Thompson
ORODAEO pour cold water on
ORODRNS hours of darkness
ORSODNL correspondingly
ORSODNT corresponding to
OSADATC horse and hattock
OSATABR Constant Lambert
OSBTNIT consubstantiate
OSCTVNS consecutiveness
OSDRNTA considering that
OSDRTNS considerateness
OSEIEAC mousseline sauce
OSEREAI Monsieur de Paris
OSERNSL forswear oneself
OSIIENS low-spiritedness
OSINEOE conscience money
OSINERO conscience-proof
OSINIUL conscientiously
OSIUNPR constituent part
OSIUUNS conspicuousness
OSLUQOS fossil turquoise
OSMMPII noisomemephitic
OSMROIT consumer society
OSMTVNS consumptiveness
OSNIANS nonsensicalness
OSNIGDL consenting adult
OSNTEAE tossing the caber
OSOASML House of Assembly
OSPOUNS gossip columnist
OSQETAL consequentially
OSRAINS conservationist
OTAADFA contraband of war
OTADADE boots and saddles
OTAEEAG don't make me laugh
OTAGRBE Northanger Abbey
OTAITRL contradictorily
OTANMCE Mont-Saint-Michel
OTASEAL non-transferable
OTBNCNR South Bank Centre
OTCROAL Monte Carlo Rally
OTEEEIO for the benefit of
OTEIDLW how the wind blows
OTEIEEN for the time being
OTEIEFE for the life of her
OTEIEFI for the life of him
OTEODOI not the word for it
OTEOEHL bottlenose whale
OTERENS soft-heartedness
OTGIDSR cottage industry
OTHVAHS not to have a ghost
OTIBAME Gottlieb Daimler
OTIEBGE don't give a bugger
OTIMNHU month in month out
OTINFCN most significant
OTKKNLT not take kindly to
OTMLTVL contemplatively
OTMOAET contemporaneity
OTMOAEU contemporaneous
OTMRHEE Mortimer Wheeler
OTMTBLT contemptibility
OTMTFOR contempt of court
OTNHMHR Nottinghamshire
OTNIUNS contentiousness
OTNLETA most influential
OTNTEAT costing the earth
OTOESAL controversially
OTOEYLF Montgomery Clift
OTOILNT montmorillonite
OTOLBLT controllability
OTOMDTE soft commodities
OTRAMRN Götterdämmerung
OTRESME Gottfried Semper
OTRMHBU bolt from the blue
OTSALPC go at a snail's pace
OTTEHSL worth the whistle
OTUNSIG soft furnishings
OTYCRNS post-synchronise
OTYCRNZ post-synchronize
OTYPIHE softly-sprighted
OULKAIH go out like a light
OUOBSNS go out of business
OUOEMNO focus one's mind on
OUTRMSL voluntary muscle
OVGTEHR you've got me there
OVLEUSN nouvelle cuisine
OVNECFO convenience food
OVNINLS conventionalise
conventionalism
conventionalist
OVNINLT conventionality
OVNINLZ conventionalize
OVRALNS conversableness
OVSNFSE loaves and fishes
OWLINMT Joe Willie Namath
OWRMVMN forward movement
OWRPANN forward planning
OWRTIKN forward-thinking
OWTSADN notwithstanding
OYHNSPN go by shanks's pony
OYNAUAE polyunsaturated
OYOAEPR Holy Roman Empire
OYUEAKN now you're talking
PAIDRCL speak indirectly
PAOBHLO speak on behalf of
PAOFHCF speak off the cuff
PAOTGIS speak out against
PATCNEI aplastic anaemia
PATTEER speak to the heart
PCADLVR special delivery
PCADPNE spick and span new
PCAIEAE specialized area
PCAPEDN special pleading
PCFCRVT specific gravity
PCLPIAL apocalyptically
PCLTVNS speculativeness
PCTCNLG space technology
PDMOOIA epidemiological
PEAMSHR upper atmosphere
PECSLTE upper-case letter
PEDHGSE spread the gospel
PEDNSIG spread one's wings
PEDONAD spread downwards
PEHHRPS speech therapist
PIAILSO optical illusion
PIGRPNE springer spaniel
PIIFNTV split infinitive
PIKESSE sprinkler system
PLIGITK spelling mistake
PNAEUNS spontaneousness
PNAOTNO spend a fortune on
PNEPREA Spencer Perceval
PNOAENS opinionatedness
PNOEBET spend one's breath
PNSCVLA Spanish Civil War
POIEXRM opposite extreme
PONMNBO appointment book

POTNTCS opportunity cost
PPTEMTZ apophthegmatize
PRAHBLT approachability
PRAOEEI spermatogenesis
spermatogenetic
PRFHMMN spur of the moment
spur-of-the-moment
PRICABR Ephraim Chambers
PRIGATE sparring partner
PRPITNS appropriateness
PRTFMOI spirit of ammonia
PRTNSSE operating system
PRXMTCS approximate cost
PRXMTNS approximateness
PSAEONI A Passage to India
PSEOOIA epistemological
PSOAINS episcopalianism
PTAMLGS ophthalmologist
PTAMSOI ophthalmoscopic
PYRAHDA Speyer Cathedral
QAEEUPR square leg umpire
QAEIOER square kilometre
QIANPIC Aquila and Prisca
QIERLWE Squire Trelawney
RAAACWT break a lance with
RABTELK Great Bitter Lake
RABUIEA Mr Tambourine Man
RAEHWEL grease the wheels
RAEQATT greater quantity
RAHFRMS breach of promise
RAHOELS breathe one's last
RAHRUNS treacherousness
RAISFAI Treaties of Paris
RAITPEE break into pieces
RALAEDC broad-leaved dock
RAMNENS broad-mindedness
RANROHM Dr Barnardo's home
RAOALNS treasonableness
RAOSRNT trial of strength
RBEAIAL problematically
RBIGAIN Brobdingnagians
RBSIMNE proboscis monkey
RCATNTN procrastinating
RCATNTO procrastination
RCCLETO Frick Collection
RCDLDNE Crocodile Dundee
RCETGTE bracket together
RCIALNS practicableness
RCIGTTO tracking station
RCPTTNS precipitateness
RCPTUNS precipitousness
RCSIGLN processing plant
RCUOEER prick up one's ears
RDRCAHE Frederic Raphael
RDRCAHO Frederick Ashton
RDRCBAD Frederick Blanda
RDRCDLU Frederick Delius
RDRCSNE Frederick Sanger
RDRCTEE Frederick Treves
RDRCTYO Frederick Taylor
RDTRIAL predeterminable
REDYOIT friendly society
REESBLT irreversibility
REFNWEG tree of knowledge
REIIUNS irreligiousness
REISBLT irremissibility
REITBLT irresistibility
REOFOPI freedom from pain
REOINUR praetorian guard
RERCEGL Friedrich Engels
RERGBLT irrefragability
RERHNIL irreprehensible
RESOITO free association
RETEIGA Ernest Hemingway
RETTEET armed to the teeth
RFLPOIP Fra Filippo Lippi
RFSINLS professionalise
professionalism
RFSINLZ professionalize
RGESVNS progressiveness
RGETRNS fragmentariness
RGFDITO drug of addiction
RGMNLEV trigeminal nerve
RGOTCTO prognostication
RGTNBEZ bright and breezy
RGTSBTO bright as a button
RHBLGRO Archibald Garrod
RHBTDOD prohibited goods
RHBTVNS prohibitiveness
RHRDIGO Arthur Eddington
RHREDNI Arthur Pendennis
RHSOIAL prehistorically
RHTCUAL architecturally
RIAYIIE ordinary citizen
RIHRYCU ornithorhynchus
RIIGOLG training-college
RKNCIDR Erskine Childers
RLXMNTO oral examination
RMADOOT from hand to mouth
RMEUCAG trumped-up charge
RMHSOLE from the shoulder
RMISTLS from first to last
RMLNPPA trembling poplar
RMNLSTO criminalisation
RMNLZTO criminalization
RMOTBTO from top to bottom
RMPOIAL gramophonically
RMSSLML promise solemnly
RMTESON Prometheus Bound
RNADUSL bring and buy sale
RNBCTLF bring back to life
RNCITOA transcriptional
RNDWTSZ bring down to size
RNEBRGT Brandenburg Gate
RNFGRMN transfigurement
RNFGRTO transfiguration□
RNFRAMI Frankfurt am Main
RNFRBLT transferability
RNGESOA transgressional
RNHAENS wrong-headedness
RNHOYEI French Polynesia
RNIBAFR Francis Beaufort
RNIBAMN Francis Beaumont
RNICDGY Francisco de Goya
RNICFAC Francisco Franco
RNIGAHN printing-machine
RNIGOIH bringing to light
RNILMNT transilluminate
RNIMNTT grant immunity to
RNIOASS Francis of Assisi
RNIOUNL grandiloquently
RNIPLRV Francis Palgrave
RNLTDUA granulated sugar
RNLTRTO transliteration
RNMTBLT transmutability
RNMTTOA transmutational
RNOSARA François Mauriac
RNOSEEO François Fénelon
RNOSOCE François Boucher
RNOTEOS front of the house
RNPATTO transplantation
RNPRNNS transparentness
RNPSTOA transpositional
RNTMTRT bring to maturity
RNTOOUN trinitrotoluene
RNWOLOT Frank W Woolworth
RNYLXNE brandy Alexander
ROEHATU cry one's heart out
ROIUTRS arboriculturist
ROOHSUU Cryolophosaurus
ROOIETT proof of identity
ROOPRHS proof of purchase
ROPIOFO arrow-poison frog
RORCPTT cryoprecipitate
RORDEIL armoured vehicle
RPIDSGE graphic designer
RPITRNM proprietary name
RPNSICE drop one's aitches
RPNSMAI trypanosomiasis
RPRINTL proportionately
RPSAOST propose a toast to
RPSTOAL prepositionally
RPZUMSL trapezius muscle
RSALGAH crystallography
RSALSTO crystallisation
RSALZTO crystallization
RSCNEEC press conference
RSCUTYU cross-country run
RSETGTE pressed together
RSETVWF prospective wife
RSHARCU Arts Theatre Club
RSHPEMN grasshopper mind
RSIIIAO prestidigitator
RSIKNFS cry stinking fish
RSLTZTO proselytization
RSOSGOG Cross of St George
RSRAINS preservationist
RSRBDOD proscribed goods
RSSMOEF brass someone off
RSSODWT cross swords with
RSTEUIO cross the Rubicon
RSWLEMY Ernst Walter Mayr
RSWRHNS trustworthiness
RSWRPZL crossword puzzle
RSYEINS Presbyterianise
Presbyterianism
RSYEINZ Presbyterianize
RTCINOE protection money
RTECEPR brothel-creepers

Words marked □ can also be spelled with an initial capital letter

RTEPESO trite expression
RTNIUNS pretentiousness
RTNNTOE pretend not to see
RTRAUAL preternaturally
RTSCLMI British Columbia
RTSLNHI British longhair
RTYANUC pretty damn quick
RUETTVL argumentatively
RUHSASI draughtsmanship
RULSMNS troublesomeness
RULSOTN troubleshooting
RUOOCNN Arturo Toscanini
RURBNTI Artur Rubinstein
RVCUCLO Privy Councillor
RVLGDLS privileged class
RVLONFO travel to and from
RVLOUET travel documents
RVNETRN prevent entering
RVNRAHN prevent reaching
RVRLVLN Grover Cleveland
RVTPAFR gravity platform
RVTSLIR private soldiers
RVTTOAL gravitationally
RWNNSON draw in one's horns
RWSMOEU drown someone out
RWTETOT draw attention to
RXMCNAR Proxima Centauri
RYNNVCU Army and Navy Club
RYONRCN greyhound-racing
RYRASOB Greyfriars Bobby
RYRFZRA Prayer of Azariah
SAAOCAS escalator clause
SALSEWR established work
SALSXAL assault sexually
SAOTERS a slap on the wrist
SBLEUPR Isabelle Huppert
SCOAHLG psychopathology
SCOHRPS psychotherapist
SCOOIAL psychologically
SDRSARB Isidor Isaac Rabi
SEDHTRN ascend the throne
SETACSE Osbert Lancaster
SETAFCO essential factor
SHCAALN as thick as a plank
SHRCICL Escherichia coli
SLATEIL as old as the hills
SMLAMSU Ashmolean Museum
SMTEOFC as a matter of fact
SNLENTV as an alternative
SOIPESR osmotic pressure
SOMNTAU a storm in a teacup
SONAAOC as sound as a roach
SOTEHRF I Shot the Sheriff
SPOLTGV ask people to give
SRNVGTO astro-navigation
SSMOEOA ask someone to pay
STOLAPA as it would appear
SUATTMN issue a statement
TAETNSA St Valentine's Day
TAGTOWR straightforward
TAPDOCS strapped for cash
TAREONR it's a free country
TBONSML stubborn as a mule
TCIFVUO stack in favour of
TCIGLSE sticking-plaster
TCIOECA stick in one's craw
TCOENSI stick one's nose in
TCSNSOE stocks and stones
TCTOEGN stick to one's guns
TCTTEUE stick to the rules
TEARMCO Athena Promachos
TECOELG stretch one's legs
TECTERT stretch the truth
TEIGLAO steering clear of
TEOCEOI atherosclerosis
TESFETE stress of weather
TFNYZNK Stefan Wyszynski
THDOOAA at the drop of a hat
THFRTLS at the first blush
THISACO at the instance of
THLSMNT at the last minute
THSMMMN at the same moment
THSMTMA at the same time as
THTILTG at the trial stage
TIEBDAC strike a bad patch
TIETIUE strike attitudes
TITADEI St Kitts and Nevis
TLACATE Stella McCartney
TLNSDRT stilpnosiderite
TLOSEKN style of speaking
TLSALOC still small voice
TLSFROD at a loss for words
TLSQATR at close quarters
TMCTUTR atomic structure
TMOAPOA stamp of approval
TNADNLS Standard English
TNADZTO standardization
TNALETM at an earlier time
TNCLASN ethnic cleansing
TNEKWLK Stanley Kowalski
TNEMTHW Stanley Matthews
TNIGAAO stinking parasol
TNIGVTO standing ovation
TNLNUSI ethnolinguistic
TNMSCLG ethnomusicology
TNOCRMN stand on ceremony
TNOECRE stand one's corner
TNOEGON stand one's ground
TNTOEGN stand to one's guns
TNUOPIT stand upon points
TOEFALC stroke of bad luck
TOPEIAL atmospherically
TOSNADN a thousand and one
TOSOMTE it does not matter
TPEJYOL Stephen Jay Gould
TPEPRRL stop temporarily
TPESNHI Stephen Sondheim
TPPHLDE step up the ladder
TRADTIE Stars and Stripes
TRATINL eternal triangle
TRGCPCT storage capacity
TROHMSR stereochemistry
TROOELF story of one's life
TROSMRS stereoisomerism
TRTWRHR start to work hard
TRWTAOA story with a moral
TSNMOTN it is unimportant
TTEFIET Statue of Liberty
TTLSPRO stateless person
TTRGSEE State Registered
TVNPEBR Steven Spielberg
UAAIHAD Guiana Highlands
UAATNOE put a fast one over
UADOEGI cut and come again
UADUSAC sum and substance
UAEPRTR run a temperature
UAIAINS humanitarianism
UAIKGIS put a tick against
UAIMTNI mutatis mutandis
UAMCAAU Judas Maccabaeus
UARVFCO put a brave face on
UARYENR Sugar Ray Leonard
UBCTELC put back the clock
UBCTGTE put back together
UBECNTN Hubble's constant
UBENSUA bubble and squeak
bubble-and-squeak
UBRADAC Cumberland sauce
UBRRNHN number-crunching
UCCNEVN quick-conceiving
UCEIESL succeed in easily
UCEMIES Dutch elm disease
UCENOCE luncheon voucher
UCIIUNS punctiliousness
UCINLRU functional group
UCLPEAE quickly prepared
UCPILNS susceptibleness
UCRLSON run circles round
UCRTDNU pulchritudinous
UCWTENS quick-wittedness
UDEYASA Hundred Years' War
UDMNAUI fundamental unit
UDMUASN Guy de Maupassant
UDULCTO quadruplication
UEADRCO funeral director
UEAUDNL superabundantly
UECNUTV superconductive
UEEEARI Eugène Delacroix
UEFCANS superficialness
UEFUUNS superfluousness
UEHTRDN superheterodyne
UEIEOMN juvenile hormone
UEIPSTO superimposition
UEITNEC superintendence
superintendency
UEMFAKN Museum of Mankind
UEMNEIE Süleyman Demirel
UENTRLS supernaturalise
supernaturalism
supernaturalist
UENTRLZ supernaturalize
UEOPDIG queen of puddings
UESIIUL superstitiously
UESRCUA superstructural
UFEDOLG Nuffield College
UGNLNMN Jurgen Klinsmann
UGORGLT burgh of regality
UGPRNEL Luigi Pirandello
UHFMCNS much of a muchness

UHMAHDA Durham Cathedral
UHMSIAL euphemistically
UHNSOTN push one's fortune
UHNVSOT Luchino Visconti
UHRODAE Rutherford Hayes
UHRTTVL authoritatively
UHRVROE Hugh Trevor-Roper
UIADRCO musical director
UIAODRO put in an order for
UICNIER cubic centimetre
UIESMHN Jupiter Symphony
UIETRNS rudimentariness
UIHGEMN Munich Agreement
UILNMUL pusillanimously
UINFOWC Julian of Norwich
UIOHROD put in other words
UIPUETA jurisprudential
UIRLWIH junior-flyweight
UISOEBR Julius Rosenberg
UISTECE Julius Streicher
UITEITR put in the picture
UITOEER music to one's ears
UITPATC put into practice
UITTEHD put into the shade
UIUCNRT musique concrète
UKEERFN Huckleberry Finn
UKNHMHR Buckinghamshire
ULAMDCN nuclear medicine
ULAMMRN nuclear membrane
ULARAEA dual carriageway
ULARATO nuclear reaction
ULCEAIN public relations
ULCTETO public attention
ULEAJCE Full Metal Jacket
ULFEPRO qualified person
ULFIGON qualifying round
ULIGOIT building society
ULNNSON pull in one's horns
ULNSUCE pull one's punches
ULOENSE pull someone's leg
ULOEWNO mullioned window
ULOTEHA built on the cheap
ULPNSOK pull up one's socks
UMNDYEL Summoned by Bells
UMRIHNN summer lightning
UMTAFIN Our Mutual Friend
UNAKORN turn back to front
UNBIDYT turn a blind eye to
UNIHASO burn with passion
UNLESIE funnel-web spider
UNNNNSL turn in on oneself
UNNNSRV turn in one's grave
UNNSTMC turn one's stomach
UNODATG turn to advantage
UNTARZL burnt to a frazzle
UNULCTO quintuplication
UOAIGAH autoradiography
UOARVFC put on a brave face
UOAUTAI aurora australis
UOCMISO out of commission
UODFIUT out of difficulty
UOEBCIT put one's back into
UOEEEOE run one's eyes over
UOEFNEO put one's finger on
UOEFODW put one's foot down
UOEFOII put one's foot in it
UOENMDW put one's name down
UOENONI European Council
UOENZTO Europeanization
UOEOEKE put over one's knee
UOIOROT Ludovico Ariosto
UOOELAU out of one's league
UOOESNE out of one's senses
UOPOOTO out of proportion
UOTEARL put on the payroll
UOTEONR out of the country
UOTEUNN out of the running
UOUOCIU Eudoxus of Cnidus
UOWOELT out of whole cloth
UPAKDHL humpbacked whale
UPEETRE supplementaries
UPEETTO supplementation
UPNAKLS Jumpin' Jack Flash
UPNECON suspense account
UPSLSNS purposelessness
UPSTOAL suppositionally
UPTNSRN Puppet on a String
URCLMIA curriculum vitae
URESMNS quarrelsomeness
URFVUWT curry favour with
URGTMTE surrogate mother
URNHTRA burr in the throat
URPIIUL surreptitiously
URSIDSR sunrise industry
URUDNAE surrounding area
URYERSE Aubrey Beardsley
USACVLA Russian Civil War
USARUET Russian roulette
USATVNS substantiveness
USITFAE burst into flames
USIUINR substitutionary
USLIAON rub salt in a wound
USMLFIT put some life into
USNHCRE puss in the corner
USNONAN Hudson Mountains
USOSOLN curse of Scotland
USSECWG subsistence wage
USTOLVR Sunset Boulevard
USXETNE put six feet under
UTAAEOE just manage to get
UTAINUE Australian Rules
UTDAPRN custodial parent
UTELCBC put the clock back
UTENBSL hustle and bustle
UTEOKRO put the mockers on
UTEREOO buy the freedom of
UTEYSUO put the eyes out of
UTFALNS justifiableness
UTHOPST just the opposite
UTIIGEA sustaining pedal
UTLNULS multilingualism
UTLTRLS multilateralism
multilateralist
UTNODIL Sutton Coldfield
UTNPNRN Burton-upon-Trent
UTNTETN putting the stone
UTNTGTE putting together
UTPATTR Mustapha Atatürk
UTPSTOA juxtapositional
UTRADRS mustard and cress
UTRLSRK butterfly stroke
UTROENU butter someone up
UTSOLEI Justus von Liebig
UTTDNUL multitudinously
UTTEEES quite the reverse
UTVFABR Gustave Flaubert
UUBNZTO suburbanization
UUNLQIO autumnal equinox
UUTMRET Auguste Mariette
UUTNRSE Augustin Fresnel
UUTPNCE Augusto Pinochet
UWGEEBC Ludwig Feuerbach
UWGOKCE Ludwig von Köchel
UWGOTMN Ludwig Boltzmann
VNEOLGN Yvonne Goolagong
VNERHNU Svante Arrhenius
VNHTRIL Ivan the Terrible
VNNPIRS evening primrose
VNNSADR Evening Standard
VRAIIRT overfamiliarity
over-familiarity
VRATNLF everlasting life
VRATNNS everlastingness
VREDNER over head and ears
VREEOMN overdevelopment
VRIDVDA every individual
VRINHRP aversion therapy
VRLWNWT overflowing with
VRMTESO every mother's son
VRNDNWT over and done with
VRNWNTE every now and then
VRSCNWE every second week
WAOOEBO sweat of one's brow
WDWEICE a widow bewitched
WEFNYDM sweet Fanny Adams
WHNRDOR two hundred hours
WMIGOTM swimming costume
WMIHHTD swim with the tide
WNHMELI Owen Chamberlain
WRODMCE sword of Damocles
WROETUB twirl one's thumbs
WTIGLTE swathing-clothes
WUDTHNO I wouldn't think of
WUEPREC awful experience
XEIETLS experimentalise
experimentalism
experimentalist
XEIETLZ experimentalize
XEIETTO experimentation
XEIIUNS expeditiousness
XEINILS experientialism
experientialist
XEIRZTO exteriorization
XENLUFC external surface
XENLZTO externalization
XEPRRNS extemporariness
XEPRZTO extemporization
XESFCTO extensification
XHNEBLT exchangeability

XHNEECE exchange teacher
XHNEETR exchange letters
XHNEIWO exchange views on
XHNENMR Exchange and Mart
XHNEOTO exchange control
XHNETDN exchange student
XIIINSI exhibitionistic
XLMTOMR exclamation mark
XLSVRGT exclusive rights
XMLFCTO exemplification
XOMNCTO excommunication
XOTDRDC exported product
XRIEIYL exercise bicycle
XRILSRT extra-illustrate
XRMNIIU excrementitious
XRMRTLE extramarital sex
XRODNRL extraordinarily
XRSDLVR express delivery
XRSINSI expressionistic
XRSSMAH express sympathy
XTRAHDA Exeter Cathedral
YADOOPI gynandromorphic
YAIOCEP Pyramid of Cheops
YAIOTEU Pyramid of the Sun
YCRNZTO synchronization
YDRHLAI Fyodor Chaliapin
YECIIAL hypercritically
YEHMCOE Sydenham's chorea
YETYODS hyperthyroidism
YHISRAT by a hair's breadth
YHSOTAR by the short hairs
YHSRNHN by the strong hand
YIDRIGO Cyril Darlington
YISNSAT by fits and starts
YLBFCTO syllabification
YLGSIAL syllogistically
YLIMMRN hyaloid membrane
YMLADML by small and small
YNTZBLT hypnotizability
YOHNIAL sycophantically
YOHNRAA hypochondriacal
YOHNRAI hypochondriasis
YOKRYRO by hook or by crook
YOMNOSN by common consent
YORPIAL typographically
YOTCOPL Synoptic Gospels
YPAISSE lymphatic system
YPOAIAL symptomatically
YPTEIAL sympathetically
YRAADRO by trial and error
YRCAIAI hydrocyanic acid
YRDNMCS hydrodynamicist
YRPTIAL hydropathically
YRYOLKC György von Lukacs
YTMAAYI systems analysis
YTMTZTO systematization

Words arranged according to ODD LETTERS

4 letters – odd

AA à bas
ACAS
Adam
Adar
afar
agar
Ahab
ajar
Ajax
alae
Alan
alas
anas
ana's
Arab
arak
Aral
Aram
Aran
ASAP
asap
åsar
atap
away
ayah
azan

AB abba□
Abbe
abbé□
Abby
ambo

AC AOCB
arch
arco
asci

AD AC/DC
Addy
Aida
aide
AIDS
Aids
Andy
Audi®

AE abed
Abel
abet
acer
Aden
a few
aged
agee
ages
ahem
ajee
Alec
Aled
alee
alef
Alex
amen
Ames
Amex
anew
APEX
apex
area
areg
Ares
aret
Aten
AUEW
aver
aves
awed
axed
axel
axes
Ayer

AG Aggy
alga
Algo
Algy
Angy
Argo

AH ache
achy
Ashe
ashy

AI a bit
acid
Adie
agin
akin
alif
amid
Amin
Amis
anil□
anis
Apia
Apis
aria
arid
Asia
as if
as is
at it
avid
axil
axis
ayin
Aziz

AK ankh

AL able
ably
ally□
auld
axle

AM acme
aims
Alma
alms
ammo
arms
army

AN acne
Agni
aîné
ain't
anna□
Anne
a one
Arne
aunt

AO Abos
ados
aeon
agog
ahoy
aloe
a lot
alow
amok
Amos
arow
a-row
as of
atom
atop
Avon
avow
AWOL
axon
Azov

AP Alps

AR Aare
acre□
Afra
Afro
Agra
airs
airt
airy
aura
AWRE
awry

AS also
apse
arse

AT ABTA
acts
ACTT
alto
ante
anti
arts
arty
asta
Asti
as to
auto

AU abut
a due
ague
alum
Alun
Amur
anus
Apus
arum
Arun

AV advt
arvo

AY aryl
azym

AZ adze

BA Baal
BEAB
bead
beak
beam
bean□
bear
beat
beau
bias□
blab
blae
blag
blah
blat
boak
boar
boat
brad
brae
brag
Bram
bran□
brat
braw
bray

BB baba
babe□
Babs
baby
BBBC
bubo

BC Bach
back
beck□
BRCS
buck□

BD Bede
Bedi
bide
bode
body
Budd

BE Baer
Baez
beef
been
beep
beer□
beet
bien
bier
bleb
bled□
blet
blew
Boer
bren
brew
BTEC
byes

BF baff
baft
BBFC
biff
BIFU
BNFL
boff
buff

BG BAgr
bags
bogy
bugs

BH baht
Behn
Böhm
Bohr
buhl

BI bail
Bain
bait
bein
blip
boil
Brie
brig
brim
brio
brit□

BK bake
Baku
bike
Biko
boke
boko

BL bald
bale
Bali
balk
ball□
balm
bell□
Belo
belt
bile
bilk
bill□
bold
bole
boll
Böll
bolt□
bulb
bulk
bull□

BM bomb
bumf
bump

BN band
bane
bang
bani
bank
Bann
bant
bend
BEng
Benn
bent
Benz
bind
bint
bond□
bone
bong
Bonn
bony
Brno
bund
bung
bunk
bunt
Byng

BO BAOR
BCom
Biot
blob
bloc
Blok
blot
blow
boob
book
boom
boon
boor
boot□
brog
Bros
brow
buoy
BYOB

BP BFPO
Bopp
BUPA

BR barb□
bard
bare
barf
Bari
bark
barm
barn
bars
Bart
berg□
berk
berm
Bern
Bert
bird□
birl
Biro
Biro®
birr
Birt
bora
bore
Borg
born□
Boro
Bors
brrr
burk
burl
burn
burp
burr
bury□
Byrd
byre

BS base
BASF
bash
bask
bass
bast□
BASW
Bess
best□

4 B_T_

bise
Bose
bosh
boss
bush❑
busk
bust
busy
BT bate
bath❑
bats
beta
Beth
bite
bits
bitt
both
bott
butt❑
byte
BU baud
blub
blue
Blum
blur❑
BMus
boun
bout
brut
BV bevy
blvd
BW bawd
bawl
Biwa
bowl
bows
BY bays
boyo
Bryn
BZ buzz
CA Chad
Chan
chap
char
chat❑
Chay
ciao
clad
clag
clam
clan
clap
claw
clay❑
CNAA
coal
coat
coax
CPAG
crab❑
crad
crag
cram❑
crap
craw
Cray
cyan
czar
CB Cebu
Ciba
Cobb
Cuba
cube
CC ceca
CICB
coca
cock
coco
CD Cade
cadi
cede
cedi
cide
coda
code
CE Caen
chef
Cher
chew
chez
clef
Clem
Cleo
clew❑
cred
Cree
crew
CSEU
CF cafe
café
C of E
coff
cuff
CG cage❑
cagy
CEGB
CH Cahn
Cohn
CI Cain
ceil
chic❑
chin
chip
chit
chiv
Clio
clip
coif
coil
coin
coir
crib
crit
CK cake
coke
Coke®
CL calf
Cali
calk
call
calm
calx
cell
Celt
CGLI
cola
cold
cole❑
Coll
Colm
colt❑
Colt®
cull
culm
cult
CM came
camp❑
coma
comb
come
Como
comp
cyma
cyme
CN cane
Cano
cant
can't
cent
C-in-C
cine
cone
conk
conn
Cono
cony
CO choc
chon
chop
chow
CIOB
clod
clog
clop
clot
cloy
cook❑
cool
coom
coop
co-op
coot
crop
crow❑
CTOL
CP Capa
cape
capi
CIPA
cope❑
cops
Copt
copy
CR Cara
card
care
Carl
Caro
carp
cars
cart
Cary
cere
Ceri
cert
Cora
cord
core
cork❑
corm
corn
CPRE
curb
curd
cure❑
curé
curl
curr
curt
CS case
cash❑
cask
Cass
cast
CBSO
cist
cosh
cost
cosy
CPSA
cush
cusp
cuss
cyst
CT Cato
Cats
CCTV
cete
cite
cito
city
cote
cute
CU caul
chub
chug
chum
chut
club
clue
coup
crud
crus
crux❑
CV Cava
cave
cavy
cove
CW cowl
cows
CX Ci-xi
coxa
CY CSYS
CZ coze
DA D-Day
dead❑
deaf
deal❑
dean❑
dear
dhai
dhal
dial
Dian
Diaz
Díaz
doab
doat
drab
drag
dram
drap
drat
draw
dray
dual
dwam
DB Debs
debt
do by
DC dace
deck
dice
dich
dick❑
DOCG
dock
duce
duck
duct
DD Dada
dado
Didi
dido❑
Dodd
dodo
dude
duds
DE deed
deek
deem
deep
deer
died
dies
diet❑
doer
dree
drew❑
drey
duel
dues
duet
DF daff
DAFS
daft
deft
defy
doff
duff
Dufy
DG digs
doge
DH dahl❑
Doha
dohs
DI Dáil
dais
do in
drip
DK dike
duke
dyke
DL dale
Dali
Daly
dele
delf
deli
dell
dill
dole❑
doll
dolt
dull❑
duly
DVLA
DM dame
damn
damp
DCMG
deme
demo
demy
dime
dome
Duma
dumb
dump
DN Dana
Dane
dang
dank
Danu
dent
deny
dine
DIng
ding
Dini
dink
dint
Doña
done
dong
Dons
don't
dune
dung
dunk
Dunn
dunt
dyne
DO dhow
Dion
Dior
doom
door
drop
drop-
duos
DP Depp
dopa
dope
dopy
dupe
DR dare
dark
darn
dart
d'art
Dern
derv
dire
dirk❑
dirl
dirt
Dora
Doré
dork
dorm
dorp
Dors
dort
dory
Dury
DS dash
desk
DHSS
disc
dish
disk
diss
dose
dosh
doss
dost
Duse
dush
dusk
dust

Words marked ❑ can also be spelled with an initial capital letter

DT data
date
dite
dote
doth
do to
duty
DU daub
daud
daut
DMus
douc
Doug
do up
dour
dout
drub
drug
drum
Druz
DV Dave
Davy
DCVO
Devi
Devo
diva□
dive
dove□
Duve
DW dawd
dawn□
dawt
dewy
dowl
down
DY Daya
days□
DZ daze
doze
dozy
EA ecad
Edam
egal
élan
Elat
Esau
et al
Evan
Ewan
exam
eyas
EB Elba
Elbe
EC each
ecce
eech
etch
Eyck
ED Eads
Edda
eddy□
EE Eden
enew
épée
even
ever
Ewen
ewer
exes
eyes
EG edge
edgy
eggs
eggy
Eigg
ergo
ergs
euge
EH eche
echo□
echt
EI Edie
edit
emir
emit
Enid
epic
Eric
Erie
Erin
Evie
evil
exit
EK EOKA
EL Ella
Elle
EM Elma
Emma
Emmy
EN Edna
EPNS
erne
EO eaon
Egon
enow
EPOS
epos
Eros
Eton
evoe
exon
exor
eyot
EP espy
expo
ER earl
earn
Ebro
ecru
Eire
ESRC
euro□
Eyre
Ezra
ES ease
east
easy
ECSC
else
ENSA
Erse
erst
esse
Esso
ET eats
EFTA
Efta
EFTS
EU Edur
Elul
EV envy
EW Euwe
FA fear
feat
fiar
fiat
Fiat®
flab
flag□
flak
flan
flap
flat
flaw
flax
flay
foal
foam
frab
frag
frap
Frau
fray
FB fibs
FC face
fact
fico
Foch
foci
FRCP
FRCS
fuci
FD fade
FIDE
FE feed
feel
fees
feet
fief
flea
flee
fleg
flew
flex
fley
foes
Fred
free
fret
Frey
fuel
FF faff
FIFA
fife□
FIFO
fuff
FG fegs
figo
fogy
FH Fahd
föhn
fthm
FI faik
fail
fain
fair
faix
flic
flip
flit
foil
frig
frit
friz
FJ Fiji
Fuji®
FK fake
fike
FL fall
fell□
felt
file
fill
film
filo
fils
fold
folk
full
FM fame
fume
fumy
FN fane
fang
fank
fans
fend
feni
find
fine
fink
Finn
fino
fond
font
fund
funk
FO floe
flog
flop
flor
flow
food
fool□
foot□
frog□
from
FR fard
fare
farm
faro□
fern
fire
firk
firm
fora
ford□
Ford®
fore
fork
form
fort
furl
fury□
FS fash
fast
fess
fest
fish□
fist
foss
FRSE
fuse
fuss
fust
FT fate
feta□
fête
FU faun
feud
flue
flux
foul
four
FV five
FW fawn
fowl
FX foxy
FY Faye
FZ faze
fizz
fuzz
GA gean
gear
ghat
glad
glam
G-man
gnar
gnat
gnaw
goad
goal
go at
goat□
grab
Graf
gram□
gran
GRAS
Gray
Graz
Guam
guan
GB Gabi
Gabo
gibe
GmbH
Gobi
go by
goby
go-by
gybe
GC geck
GD Gide
gods
GE Gaea
Gael
geek
geep
ghee
glee
glei
glen□
gley
goer
goes
goey
gree
grew
grey□
Gwen
GF GIFT
gift
Gifu
guff
GG gaga
gage
gags
giga
Gigi
GIGO
GH GCHQ
GI Gaia
Gail
gain
gait
glia
glib
go in
go it
grid
grig
grim
grin
grip
Gris
grit
GL gala
gale□
gall□
geld
gelt
gila
gild
gill□
gilt
gold□
golf□
gulf
gull
gulp
GM Gama
game
gamp
gamy
GCMG
gems□
gimp
gump
gymp
GN gang
gant
Gdns
gene□
gent□
Gina
gink
gone
gong
gunk
Gunn
guns
GO gaol
geos
gios
glob
glom
glop
glow
good
goof
go on
goop
grog
grot
grow
Györ
GP gape
GR garb
Gary
Gere
germ
Gers
Gert
gird
girl
girn
giro
girt
gore□

gorm
gory
gurl
guru
gyre
GS gash
gasp
GCSE
Gish
gist
gosh
gush
gust
GT gate
GATT
geta
Getz
Gita
gite
gîte
Goth
go to
guts
GU gaud
Gaul
gaum
gaup
geum
glue
glug
glum
glut
gnus
go up
gout
grub
grue
Grus
GV gave
GCVO
give
GNVQ
Govt
gyve
GW gawd
gawk
gawp
GMWU
gowf
gowl
gown
GY Gaye
Glyn
Goya
goys
Gwyn
GZ gaze
Gozo
HA haar
head
heal
heap
hear

heat
Hoad
hoar
hoas
hoax
HB hebe□
hobo
HC hack
hech
heck
hick□
hock
huck
HD hade
hadj
hide
HE haem
heed
heel
hued
Huey
hyen
HF haft
heft
hi-fi
huff
HG high
Hogg
huge
Hugh
Hugo
HH ha-ha
he-he
hohs
HI Haig
haik
hail
hain
hair□
heil!
heir
hoik
huis
HJ haji
hajj
HK haka
hake
hike
hoke
HL hale□
half
hall□
halm
halo
Hals
halt
held
hele
hell□
he'll
helm
help
hila

hili
hill□
hilt
hold
hole
Holi
holm
hols
holt
holy
HTLV
hula
hulk
hull□
HM hame
heme
hemp
home□
homo
Homs
homy
HTML
Hume
hump
hymn
HN hand
hang
hank□
hind
hint
hone
honk
hung
hunk
hunt□
HO hood□
hoof
hook□
hoop
hoot
HP hips
hope□
Hopi
hype
hypo
HR hard
hare□
hark
harl
harm
haro
harp□
hart
Hera
herb
herd
here
herl
Hern
hero□
hers
hire
horn

hors
Hurd
hurl
hurt□
HS hash
hasp
hast
Hess
hisn
his'n
hiss□
hist
HMSO
hose
host
hush
husk
Huss
HT hate
hath
HDTV
heth
Hite
hits
http
HU haud
haul
hour
HV have
hive
Hova
Hove
HW hawk
hawm
Hawn
Howe
howf
howk
howl□
HY hiya
HZ haze
hazy
hizz
IA IAAF
ICAO
IFAD
ikat
imam
Iran
Iraq
I say!
Ivan
Iyar
IB ICBM
inby
IRBM
ISBN
IC Inca
inch
IPCC
IPCS
itch
IUCD

ID Indy
ISDN
IE IAEA
ibex
iced
Icel
idea
idem
Ides
ilea
ilex
Ines
Inez
item
Ives
IF iffy
info
IG Iago
Inga
Inge
II Iain
ibid
ibis
ilia
inia
in it
iris□
ISIS
Isis
ixia
IK Ickx
inky
IL idle□
idly
INLA
inly
Isla
isle
it'll
IM iamb
Irma
IN Iona
isn't
IO Ibos
icon
idol
Ifor
ikon
in on
Ipoh
iron
Ivon
Ivor
IP IPPF
I-spy
IR IBRD
IMRO
in re
inro
iure
IS Iasi
inst
IT IATA

into
iota
IW Iowa
IY idyl
JA jean□
jiao
Joad
Joan
JB jibe
jobe
Jobs
jube
JC jack□
Jock
JD jade□
Jodi
Jodl
Jody
Jude
judo
Judy
JE jeel
jeep□
jeer
Jeez
Joel
joes
joey□
JF Jeff
jiff
JG juga
JH Jehu
john□
JI jail
Jain
join
JJ juju
ju-ju
JK Jake
joke
juke
JL jell
jill□
jilt
jolt
July
JM jamb
Jima
jump
JN Jane
jann
jink
jinn
jinx
Joni
June
Jung
junk
Juno
JO jook
JP jape
JR jerk
Jura

jure
jury
JS jess□
jest
josh□
Joss
just
JT jato
jeté
jute□
JU jaup
jouk
Jouy
JV Java
jive
Jove
JW jaws□
jowl
JX Jixi
JZ jazz
jizz
KA kcal
Kean
khan□
khat
knag
knap
knar
koan
Kray
KWAC
kyat
KB Kaba
kibe
Kobe
KC keck
kick
Koch
KD kadi
Kidd
kids
kudu
KE keek
keel
keen
keep
Kiel
kier
Kiev
Klee
knee
knew
KG kagu
KH kohl□
Kuhn
KI kail
knit
kris
KWIC
KK kaka
kaki
keks
KL kale

kali❑
kelp
kelt❑
kill
kiln
kilo❑
kilt
kola
Köln
kyle
KM Kama
kame
KCMG
Kemi
Kemp
KN kana
Kano
Kant
KANU
Kent
kina
kind
kine
king❑
kink
kino
kuna
KO kaon
knob
knot
know
Knox
kook
KWOC
KP kaph
kepi
kept
koph
KR kara❑
kark
Karl
kart
kerb
kerf
kern❑
kirk❑
kora
Kurd
kuri
Kurt
KS kesh
kiss❑
kist
KT kata
Kate
Kath
Katy
Katz
keta
Kett
kite
Kota
koto
KU knub
knur
Knut
KV kava
KCVO
Kivu
KW kiwi
KY Kaye
kayo
KZ kazi
LA lead
leaf
Leah
leak
leam
lean❑
leap
Lear
Liam
Lian
liar
Lias
load
loaf
loam
loan
LRAM
luau
lyam
LB lobe
lobi
lobo
LC lace
lack
lacy
lech
lice
lick
loch
loci
lock❑
LRCP
LRCS
Luce
luck
Lucy
LD Lada®
lade
lady
Leda
lido
lode
Lódz
Lüda
ludo
LE leek
leep
leer
lees
leet
lied
lien
lies
lieu
lues
lwei
LF left
life
LIFO
lift
loft
luff
LG legs
loge
Logi
logo
luge
Lugh
LI laic
laid
lain
lair
Leix
loid
loin
Lois
LK lake
like
Loki
Luke
LL la-la
lill
lilo❑
lilt
lily❑
Lola
loll
lull
Lulu
Lyle
LM lamb❑
lame
lamé
lamp
Lima
limb
lime
limn
limo
limp
limy
Lomé
Lomo
lump
Lyme
LN land❑
lane
Lang
lank
Lena
lend
Leng
lens
lent❑
Lenz
Lind
line
ling
link
linn
lino
lint
Linz
lone
long❑
Lund
lung
lunt
Lynn
lynx❑
LO Laos
León
lion❑
look
loom
loon
loop
Loos
loot❑
Lvov
LP Lapp
lips
lope
LR Lara
lard
lari
lark
larn
lira
lire
lirk
lord❑
lore
lory
lure
lurk
Lyra
lyre
LS lash
lass
last
less
lest
Lisa
Lise
LISP
lisp
list
lose
loss
lost
lush
lust
lyse
LT late
lath
lats
Leto
LETS
lite
loth
loti
lots
lute
lutz
LU laud❑
Laue
loud
loup
lour
lout
LV lava
lave
leva
leve
Levi
levy
live
Livy
love
LW lawk
lawn
laws
lewd
lown
LZ laze
lazy
lezz
Liza
MA ma'am
Maat
mead❑
meal
mean
meat
moan
moat
M-way
MC mace❑
Mach
mack❑
mica
mice
Mick
mico
MICR
mock
MRCP
much
muck❑
MD made
MIDI
midi
mode
modi
ME Maev
meek
meet
mien
Mmes
MF MAFF
miff
muff
MG mage
magi
mega
Msgr
MH Mahe
MI Maia
maid
mail
maim
main
mein
Meir
Muir
MJ Mojo
MK make
mako
mike❑
moke
ML male
Malé
Mali
mall
malm
malt
meld
mell
melt
mild
mile
milk
mill❑
milt
Mlle
Mold
mole❑
moll❑
mule
mull❑
MM mama
MDMA
memo
mime
mump
MN mane
Mann
Manx
many
mend
mene
menu
mina
mind❑
mine
Ming
mini
Mini®
mink
mint
minx
mona❑
Mond
monk❑
mono
Mons
mRNA
myna
MO meow
mhos
mood
Moog®
moon
moop
moor❑
moot
muon
MP MIPS
mips
mope
mopy
MR marc❑
mare
marg
mark❑
marl
marm
Mars
mart
Marx
Mary
merc
Merc®
mere
mfrs
Mira
mire
miri
mirk
Miró
mirs
MIRV
miry
mora
more❑
MORI
morn
Moro
mure
murk
murl
Myra
MS mase
mash
mask
mass❑
mast
mesa
mesh
mess
mish
miso
miss
mist
mose
moss❑
most

Words marked ❑ can also be spelled with an initial capital letter

MusB
MusD
muse❑
mush
musk
muso
muss
must
MT mate
matt❑
maty
mete
Metz
mite
mitt
moth❑
Mott
motu
mute
muti
mutt
myth
MU Maud
Maui
maul
maun
moue
moup
MV move
MW mewl
mews
MX maxi
moxa
MY Maya
Mayo
Mayr
MZ maze
mazy
moze
NA naan
Neal
neap
near
neat
Noah
Noam
NB nobs
NZBC
NC NCCL
neck
nice❑
nick❑
nock
ND NEDC
nidi
node
nodi
nude
NE need
neep
ne'er
NFER
noel❑

Noël
noes
NF naff
niff
NPFA
NG Nagy
nigh
no go
NH Naha
NAHT
NI naif
naïf
nail
Neil
NK Nike
NL Nell
Nile
nole
null
NVLA
NM name
noma
numb
NN nana❑
Nina
nine
none
nong
no-no
non-U
Nunn
NO neon
nook
noon
NP napa
nape
nipa
nope
NUPE
NR Nara
nard
nark
nary
NERC
nerd
Nero
NIRC
nirl
Nora
nori
norm
nurd
nurl
NS Nash
ness
nest
NFSC
NFSE
nisi
nose
nosh
nosy
NT NATO

Nato
nett
Nita
note
nuts
NU neum
noun
nous
NV nave
navy
NCVQ
Neva
névé
nova
NW news
newt
NFWI
nowl
nowt
NX next
NZ naze
Nazi
OA Oban
ogam
okay
Olav
Oman
Omar
opah
opal
oral
Oran
ou ay
oval
Ozal
OC OECD
once
OSCE
ouch
OD odds
OE obey
odea
Oder
Odes
OEEC
ogee
oleo
omen
OPEC
Opel®
open
oven
over
owed
Owen
ower
oxen
oyes
oyez
OF oafs
Offa
Orff
OG Olga

orgy
OH Oahu
oche
Otho
OI Odie
Odin
Ohio
olio
omit
otic
Otis
Ovid
OK Oaks
OL ogle
oils
oily
olla
only
orle
Oslo
Oulu
Owls
OM Ogma
OHMS
ON oink
oint
OO oboe
obol
Obon
obos
ohos
OP OAPs
oops
oppo
ouph
OR ogre
okra
Oort
owre
OS oast
Omsk
onst
or so
ossa
Ouse
oust
OT oath
oats
Oita
on to
onto
otto❑
OU onus
opus
ovum
Oxus
OY onyx
oryx
OZ ooze
oozy
ouzo
Ozzy
PA PCAS

peak
peal
pear
peas
peat
Piaf
plan
plap
play
pram
prat
prau
pray
Ptah
PB PABX
PSBR
PC paca
pace
pack
pact
pacy
pech
peck❑
Pécs
pica
pice
pick
pics
Pict
pock
poco
puce
puck❑
PD PNdB
pods
PE peek
peel❑
peen
peep
peer
phew
pied
pier
plea
pleb
poem
poet
pree
prep
prey
puer
PF PTFE
puff
PG page❑
pegh
Pegu
pigs❑
pogo
PI paid
paik
pail
pain
pair

pein
Phil
phiz
plié
plim
prig
prim
PK Peke
pika
pike
poke
poky
puke
PL pale
Pali
pall
palm
palp
Pele
pelf
pelt
pila
pile
pili
pill
Pils
pole❑
Polk
poll❑
polo❑
Polo®
poly
pula❑
pule
pull
pulp❑
puly
PM pimp
pome
pomp
puma
pump
PN pane
pang
pant
Penn
pine❑
ping
pink
pins
pint
pint-
piny
pond
pone
pong
pons
pony
punk
puns
punt
puny
PO peon

phon
pion
pioy
plod
plop
plot
ploy
poof
pooh❑
pook
pool
poop
poor
proa
prob
prod❑
prof
prog
PROM
prom
proo
prop
pros
prow
PP papa❑
pepo
pipa
pipe
pipy
pope❑
Popp
pupa
PR para
pard
pare
park❑
parp
parr❑
part
peri
perk
perm❑
PERT
pert
Peru
perv
pore
pork
porn
port
pure
puri
purl
purr
pyre
PS pash
pass
past
PDSA
peso
pest
Pisa
pish

pose
posh
post
posy
psst
push
puss
PT pate
paté
pâté
path
Pete
pita
pith
Pitt
pity
pote
pots
pott
putt
PU Paul
phut
Pius
plug
plum
plus
pouf
pouk
pour
pout
Prue
pruh
PV pave
Pavo
PW pawl
pawn
PX pixy
poxy
PY Phyl
Pu Yi
PZ Puzo
QA quad
quag
quat
quay
QD qadi
QE quep
QI quid
quin
quip
quit
quiz
QO quod
QP qoph
RA RAAF
RCAF
read❑
real
reap
rear
rial
RIAM
RNAS
road
roam
roan
roar
Ryan
RB rabi❑
RIBA
robe
ruby❑
RC race
rack
racy
reck
rice❑
rich❑
rick❑
RICS
ricy
RNCM
rock
ruck
RD RADA
RADC
redd
redo
Reds
ride❑
rode
rudd
rude❑
Ryde
RE RAEC
RAeS
reed❑
reef
reek
reel
rhea❑
Rhee
riel
roed
Roeg
RF raft
rife
riff
rift
ruff
RG raga
rage
ragg
regt
Riga
Rigg
RH Röhm
Ruhr
RI raid
raik
rail
rain
Rais
rait
rein
RNIB
RNID
roil
ruin
RJ raja
RK rake
raki
raku
roke
RL rale
râle
rely
rile
rill
RNLI
role
rôle
Rolf
roll
rule
ruly
Ryle
RM Rama
RAMC
ram i
ramp
Rams
RCMP
REME
rime
rimu
rimy
roma
Rome
romp
rume
rump
RN Rana
rand❑
rang
rani
rank
rant
rend
Rene
René
Reno
rent❑
rind
ring
rink
Rona
rone
RSNC
RSNO
rune
rung
runs
runt
RO RAOC
RCOG
rhos
riot
rood
roof
rook❑
room
roop
root
ryot
RP rape
rapt
repo
repp
rept
RIPA
ripe
rope
ropy
RSPB
RR rare
rore
ro-ro
rort
Rory
rurp
RS rase
rash
rasp
resh
rest
RISC
rise
risk
risp
Rosa
rose❑
rosé
Ross
rosy
RSSA
rusa
ruse❑
rush❑
rusk❑
rust❑
RT rate
rats
retd
rete
Rita
rite
ritt
rota
rote
Roth
roti
Ruth
RU Rhun
roué
roup
Rous
rout
roux❑
RV rave
Ravi
RCVS
Revd
rive
rivo
RNVR
rove
RSVP
RW Rowe
rows
RY rays
Rhyl
Rhys
RZ raze
razz
riza
SA Saar
scab
scad
scag
scam
scan
scar
scat
seal
seam
Sean
SEAQ
sear
seas
seat
Sfax
shad
shag
shah❑
sham
Shaw
sial
Sian
skag
skat
slab
slag
slam
slap
slat
Slav
slay
snab
snag
snap
soak
soap
soar
so as
Soay
SPAB
spae
spam❑
span
spar
spat
spay
stab
stag
star
stay
swab
swad
swag
swam
swan❑
swap
swat
sway
SC sack
SCCL
sech
sect
sick
SNCF
soca
sock
SPCK
SRCh
such
suck
SD sade❑
side
SIDS
soda
suds
SE seed
seek
seel
seem
seen
seep
seer
shea
shed
she'd
Shem
Shep
shes
she's
sien
skep
sker
skew
sled
slew
smee❑
smew
sned
spec
Spee
spew
Spey
stem
step❑
stet
stew
suer
suet
Suez
swee
syen
SF safe
Safi
sift
sofa
S. of
S.
soft
Sufi
SG saga
sage
sago
sego
sigh
sign
SH Saha
soho
so-ho
SYHA
SI said
sail
SCID
seil
Shia
Shi'a
shim
shin
ship
shit
skid
skim
skin
skip
skis
skit
slid
slim
slip
slit
snib
snig
snip
soil
spin
spit
spiv
stir
suit
swig
swim
swiz
SK sake
saki❑
Sekt
sika
Sikh
Suke
sukh
Suky
SL sale
SALT
salt
SDLP
self

sell
sild
sile
silk
sill
silo
silt
sola
sold
sole□
soli
solo
sols
St-Lô
sulk
sulu
SM same
semi
semi-
sima
Sims
SMMT
soma□
some
sumo
sump
SN San'a
sand□
sane
sang
sank
sans
send
sent
sind
sine
sing
sink
song
sung
sunk
sync
synd
syne
SO Scot
scow
shoe
shog
shoo
shop
shot
show
Sion
skol
slob
sloe
slog
slop
slot
slow
smog
snob
snod

snog
snot
snow□
sook
soon
soop
soot
spot
stoa
STOL
stop
stot
stow
swop
swot
SP SCPS
sept
sipe
sype
SQ seqq
SR Sara
sard
sari
Sark
sera
Serb
SERC
sere
serf
serr
Shri
sire
sorb
sore
sori
sorn
sort
spry□
sura
surd
sure
surf
SWRI
SS sa sa
sasa
sash
sass
sist
so so
so-so
soss
SSSI
Susa
suss
Susy
ST SATB
sate
sati
seta
Seth
Seti
sett
Sita

site
sith
Soto
SU Saul
scud□
scum
scur
scut
shul
shun
shut
skua
skug
slub
slue
slug
slum
slur
slut
smug
smur
smut
snub
snug□
souk
soul□
soum
soup
sour
SPUC
spud
spun
spur
stub
STUC
stud
stum
stun
swum
SV save
Siva
Suva
SW sawn
sewn
shwa
sowf
sown
SX sext
sexy
SY SAYE
Skye
soya
stye
SZ size
Suzy
TA Taal
teak
teal
team
tear
teat
Thai
than

Thar
that
thaw
toad□
to a T
trad
tram
trap
tray
tsar
TB tabu
to be
Toby
tuba
tube
TC tack
taco
tact
tech
tice
tich
tick
tock
tuck□
TD tide
tidy
Todd
to-do
tody
TE teem
teen
teer
Tees
Thea
thee
them
then
Theo
thew
they
tied
tier
ties
tree
tref
trek
très
T Rex
trey
TVEI
twee
TF Tafe
Taff
Taft
teff
TEFL
tiff
tift
toff
tofu
tufa
tuff
tuft

TG Tigg
toga
Togo
togs
TH taha
toho
TI tail
Tait
thig
thin
this
toil
trig
trim□
trio
trip
Trix
twig
twin
twit
TJ Tojo
TK taka
take
toke
tyke
TL tala
talc
tale
tali
talk
tall
tell
tile
till
tilt
told
tole
toll
tolu
Tula
Tull
TM tame
tamp
Tema
temp
time□
tomb
tome
tump
TN Tana
tane
tang
tanh
tank
tend
tent
Tina
tind
tine
ting
tink
tint
tiny

tone
tong
Toni
tonk
tons
Tony
tRNA
tuna
tune
tynd
tyn'd
Tyne
TO Thor
thou
took
tool
toom
toot
trod
trog
trot□
trow
troy□
TP tape
tips
tope
topi
tops
tsps
Tupí
type
typo
TR tarn
taro
tart
term
tern
thro
thro'
tire
tirl
tiro
tirr
torc
tore
tori
torn
torr
tort
Tory
turd
turf
Turk
turn
tyre□
tyro
TS tash
task
Tass
tbsp
TESL
Tess
test

tose
tosh
toss
tush
tusk
TT ta-ta
Tate
tath
Tati
tats
tatt
teth
titi
Tito
tits
tote
Toto
tutu□
TU taut
thud
thug
Thun
thus
tour
tout
true
trug
TW taws
TGWU
town
towy□
TX taxa
taxi
text
TZ tizz
toze
UA UCAS
unau
up at
USAF
Utah
UB umbo
unbe
upby
UC UCCA
unci
unco
UD undo
Urdu
UE Udet
urea
Urey
used
user
Utes
UF UEFA
UG urge
UI unit
UNIX
Unix
UNIX®
uric
USIA

utis
Uzis
UL ugly
UN ulna
UO udos
UFOs
up on
upon
US USSR
UT up to
UU Uruk
UV uPVC
VA Vaal
veal
vial
VRAM
VC vice
VD Veda
vide
VE veer
vier
view
VG vagi
Vega
Vigo
VI vain
veil
vein
void
VL vale
Vela
veld
vile
vole
volt
vuln
vvll
VM vamp
VN vane
vang
vant
vena
vend
Venn
vent
vina

vine
vino
vint
viny
VO viol
VSOP
VTOL
VQ VDQS
VR vary
Vera
verb
very
vire
VS Vasa
vase
vast
vest
visa
Voss
VT vatu
veto
Vita
vite
vote
VV viva
vive
VW vows
WA WAAC
Waac
WAAF
weak
weal
wean
wear
wham□
whap
what
woad
WRAC
WRAF
wrap
WB Webb
WC Waco
wick□
WD wadd
wade□

wadi
wads
wady
wide
WE weed
week
weel
weep
weet
whee
when
whe'r
whet
whew
whey
Wien
wren□
WF waft
weft
wife
WG wage
WH Wuhu
WI waif
wail
wain□
wait
Weil
weir
whid
Whig
whim
whin
whip
whir
whit□
whiz
writ
WK wake
woke
WL wald
wale
walk
wall
Walt
waly
weld

welk
well□
we'll
welt
wild
wile
will□
wilt
wily
wold
wolf□
wull
WM WIMP
wimp
womb
WN wand
wane
Wang
wank
want
wany
wend
went
wind
wine
wing
wink
wino
winy
wont
won't
WRNS
wynd
wynn
WO whoa
who'd
whom
whop
who's
whow
wood□
woof
wool
woot
woo't
WP wept

wipe
WR ward□
ware
Wark
warm
warn
warp
wart
wary
were
we're
wire
wiry
word
wore
work
WORM
worm
worn
wort
WS wash
wasp
wast
west□
wise□
wish
wisp
wist
wuss
WT watt□
WFTU
wite
with
wits
Witt
WU wauk
waul
WV wave
wavy
we've
WRVS
WW wawl
WX waxy
Wuxi
WY ways
XA Xi'an

Xmas
X-ray
YA yeah
year
yuan
YC yack
yech
YMCA
yuck
YWCA
YD yodh
YE ylem
Yves
YF yaff
YG yoga
yogh
yogi
YH yo-ho
YK yike
yoke
yuke
yuko
YL Yale
Yalu
yell
yelm
yelp
yolk
Yule
YM yomp
yump
YN yank□
yont
YO yoop
YP yapp
YR yard
yare
yarn
yerk
yird
York
yurt
YS yes's
YT yeti
YU you'd
your

YW yawl
yawn
yawp
yaws
yowl
YY yo-yo
ZA zeal
ZB zebu
Zibo
ZC Zach
Zack
ZF ziff
ZIFT
Zift
ZI zein
zoic
ZL Zola
Zulu
ZM Zama
ZN ZANU
zany
Zena
zinc
zine
zing
zone
zonk
Zuni
Zuñi
ZO Zion
zoom
ZP ZAPU
ZR Zara
zero
ZS zest
Zuse
ZT zati
ZETA
zeta□
ziti
ZU Zeus
zouk
ZZ zizz

5 letters – odd

AAA abaca
abaya
Adana
Agana
Aqaba
asana
AAD Åland
award
AAE abase
abate

adage
agape
agate
agave
alate
amate
amaze
apace
apage
awake

aware
AAH abash
awash□
AAI abaci
acari
agami
Amati
AAK aback
abask
AAL at all

avail
AAM alarm
AAN again
Al Ayn
AAO Alamo
AAS Adams
a mass
amass
Anaïs
AWACS

AAT abaft
adapt
apart
avast
await
AAY ataxy
ABE Albee
amble
ABM album
ABN Alban

ABR Akbar
amber□
arbor
ABS ambos
Arbus
ABT abbot
ambit
ABY abbey
ACA Accra
aecia

5 A_C_I

ACI ASCII
ACN ancon
ACS Alcis
ascus
ACT Ascot
ACY Archy
ADC asdic□
ADD added
ADE Addie
addle
Andre
ADL Abdul
ADN add in
add-on
Aidan
Aiden
Arden
Auden
ADO addio
add to
audio
ADP add up
ADR adder
alder
ADS aides
Andes
ADT audit
AEA Adela
Akela
areca
arena
AED ahead
amend
an-end
AEE Adèle
aleye
anele
Aoede
arête
AEH aleph
AEK apeak
apeek
a-week
AEL aweel
AEM abeam
adeem
AEN Ahern
ASEAN
Asean
AEP ayelp
AET adept
agent
aleft
alert
anent
aren't
arett
avert
AEX à deux
AEY apery
Avery
AFE Alfie
AFL awful
AFR as for
AFX affix
AGD algid
AGE Aggie
algae
Angie
angle□
argue
aygre
AGL ALGOL
Algol
angel□
argal
argil
argol
AGN argon
Argun
AGO aggro
AGR Aegir
anger
auger
augur
AGS aegis
Angus
Argos
Argus
AGT angst
argot
aught
AGY angry
AHA Aphra
AHC ad hoc
AHD aphid
AHN ashen
AHR abhor
Asher
AHS aphis
Århus
ashes
Athos
AHT ashet
AHW as how
AIA anima
Anita
Arica
Arita
Ávila
AID ahind
AIE abide
Adige
afire
agile
Alice
alike
aline
alive
amide
amine
anise
arise
aside
A-side
avine
axile
azide
azine
AIG aging
aping
a-wing
AIH Amish
apish
AII acini
Aditi
alibi
amici
AIL ariel□
axial
AIM axiom
AIN alien□
align
anion
apian
Arian
Asian
avian
AIO amigo
amino
AIS adios
adiós
agios
alias
amiss□
Aries
Arius
AIT agist
ahint
ariot
atilt
AIU adieu
AIY acidy
amity
AKE alkie
ankle
Arkle
AKW askew
ALA Ailsa
ALB ad lib
ad-lib
ALE aglee
Allie
ALF all of
ASLEF
ALH Allah
ALI auloi
ALJ aflaj
ALN Allan
Allen
all in
all-in
Aslan
ALO Aalto
all to
all-to
ALR Adler
ALS Arles
atlas□
ALT aglet
allot
ALW ablow
aglow
allow
ALY agley
allay
alley
alloy
AMD Ahmad
Ahmed
armed
AMN adman
admin
Amman
ammon
atman
AMT admit
aim at
AMX admix
ANA amnia
AND awned
ANE aînée
Annie
ANL annul
ANN Adnan
ANO amnio
ANP a snip
ANR Arnor
ANS Agnes
ANW Agnew
as new
as now
ANX annex
ANY annoy
aunty
AOA agora
aloha
aroma
AOC azoic
AOD abord
acold
agood
ahold
aloud
A-road
avoid
AOE abode
above
adobe
adore
alone
alowe
amove
anode
as one
at one
atone
AOF Adolf
aloof
AOG along
among
AOI aioli
aïoli
AOK acock
AOL aboil
afoul
atoll
AON acorn
adorn
AOO ab ovo
AOP apoop
AOR amour
AOT abort
about
adopt
afoot
a hoot
aloft
aport
ayont
AOY a'body
agony
anomy
atomy
atony
APA alpha□
APC aspic
APE ample
apple
API appui
APL appal
APN aspen□
APO appro
APR as per
at par
APY amply
apply
appuy
ARA aorta
atria
ARC auric
ARD acrid
ARE agree
aurae
ARH arrah
ARI aurei
ARL April
aural
Avril
ARM Abram
abrim
ad rem
Akram
ARN Aaron
abrin
apron
Arran
ARP atrip
ARR airer
ARS acres
après
arras□
arris
auras
ART afrit
ARW arrow□
ARY array
ASA Aisha
Aosta
at sea
Aysha
ASD Assad
ASE aisle
ASI assai
ASM Aksum
Assam
ASN arson
ASP Aesop
ASR aesir
ASS apsis
asses
AST asset
ASY assay
ATA antra
Astra®
ATC antic
artic
attic□
Aztec
ATE antae
ATH aitch
ATL artal
ATN actin
act on
ATO apt to
ATP act up
ATR actor
after
altar□
alter
antar
aster
astir
Astor
attar
ATS act as
actus
altos
autos
ATY aptly
AUA Abuja
alula
AUE abuse
acute
amuse
azure
AUI aguti
AUK amuck
AUL ahull
AUT adult
AUZ abuzz
AVL anvil
AVS arvos
AVZ Ahvaz
AWN Aswan
AWR Anwar
at war
AWS as was

AWY asway
AXN auxin
AYA adyta
AYE azyme
AYN Aryan
AYS abyss
AYT as yet
as-yet
AZC Anzac
AZO Anzio
BAC Blanc
BAD beard
bland
blaud
board
braid❑
brand
BAE Baade
blade
Blake
blame
blare
blasé
blaze
brace
Brahe
brake
brave
braze
BAG bhang
Bragg
BAH beach
brash
BAK black❑
blank
BAL brail
brawl
BAN blain
Boann
brain
Braun
brawn
BAO beano
bravo❑
BAR Blair
by air
BAS beads
beams
brass
BAT beast
beaut
blast
boast
bract
Byatt
BAX beaux
BAY beady
beaky
Brady
BBA Bubka
BBE bible❑
BBL babel❑
BBP bebop
bob up
BBR Babur
Buber
BBY bobby❑
BCE Boche
BCN bacon❑
BCS Buck's
BCY baccy
Becky
BDD bedad
BDE badge
bedye
bodge
budge❑
BDL bedel
BDM bedim
BDN Baden
bid in
BDP bid up
BDR Bader
BDS budos
BDT bidet
BDW bedew
BDY baddy
badly
biddy❑
buddy
BEA Breda
BED bield
bleed
blend
bread
breed
BEE Beebe
breve
BEH beech
BEK bleak
break
Buerk
BEM bream❑
BEO Bueno
BEP bleep
BER blear
BES beefs
bless
BMEWS
BET bleat
Brent
Brest
Brett
BEY beefy
beery
BFA BAFTA
Bafta
buffa
BFD bifid
BFE buffe
BFG befog
BFI buffi
BFO buffo
BFR by far
BFT befit
BGD begad
BGE bigae
bogie
bugle
BGI bags I
BGL bagel
BGM begem
begum
BGN began
begin❑
begun
BGR begar
BGS Biggs
Boggs
bogus
BGT beget
bight
bigot
BGY baggy
biggy
bogey
boggy
buggy
BHI Bahai
Baha'i
BHL BPhil
BHN Behan
BHR Behar
Bihar
BIA Beira
BID Baird
blind❑
build
BIE baize
beige
Boise
bribe
bride
brine
BIF brief
BIG being
boing
bring
BIH Bligh
BII blini
BIK blink
brick
brink❑
brisk
Buick®
BIL brill
BIN bairn
Brian
BIP blimp❑
BIR briar
brier
BIS bliss❑
BIT BLitt
built
buist
BIY Baily
blimy
briny
BIZ blitz
BJA bajra
BJN Bajan
BJU bijou
BKD baked
BKR baker❑
biker
BKS bokos
BKT Bakst
BLA balsa
Bella
bulla
BLE belee
belie
belle❑
bilge
bulge❑
BLH belch❑
BLI balti
BLM Belém
BLN Bolan
BLO Baloo
BLR baler
Balor
BLS balls
bells
bills
bolas
bolos
bolts
bolus
bulls
BLW below
Bülow
by law
by-law
BLY bally
balmy
belay
belly
billy❑
bulgy
bulky
bully
BME bombe
BMH bumph
BMI Bambi
BMO bimbo
BMS bombs
BMY bumpy
BNA Banda
BNB b and b
BND boned
BNE Bände
binge
bonce
bunce
BNF Banff
BNH bench❑
bunch
BNI Benxi
Bondi
BNL banal
binal
BNN Benin
Bunin
BNO banjo
bingo
bongo
bunco
bunko
BNR boner
BNS bangs
Banks
banns
bonds
bones❑
bonus
BNT benet
Benét
Binet
BNU Bantu
BNW by now
BNY bandy
bendy
benny❑
bonny❑
bunny
Bunty
BOA biota
Broca
BOD blond
blood❑
broad
brood
BOE biome
bloke
Boole
Boone
booze
broke
brose
BOF be off
BOH Bloch
booth❑
broch
broth
BOI Baoji
BOK block
brook❑
BOL broil
BOM BComm
bloom❑
broom
BON blown
brown❑
BOP bloop
BOS blows
boobs
books
boots
BOT bloat
boost
BOY blowy
booby
boody
booty
boozy
BPD biped
BRA Barra
Berra
Burma
Burra
bursa❑
BRC boric
BRD bored
BRE barge
barre
Berne
borne
Burke
BRH BArch
Barth
berth
birch
birth
burgh❑
BRK Barak
borak
BRL beryl❑
BRN baron
boron
buran
burin
Byron
BRO burro
BRQ bar-b-q
BRR borer
BRS birds
Biros
Boris
Burns
Byrds
BRT beret
burnt
burst
BRX borax
BRY barmy
Barry
berry❑
burly
BSA Basra
basta
Bosra
by sea
BSC BASIC
basic❑
BSD based
BSE Basie
Basle
baste
BSH Bosch
BSI bassi
BSL basal
basil❑
BSM besom
bosom
BSN basin
bison
boson

bosun
Busan
BSO basho□
BSS bases
basis
buses
BST beset
besot
BSU bussu
BSY Bessy
bosky
bossy
busby□
bushy
busty
BTA Botha
BTE bathe
Bethe
bitte
butte
BTH batch
bitch
botch
butch□
BTK batik
BTL betel
BTN baton
bet on
BTO be two
BTR biter
BTS Bates
baths
batts
bitos
BTT butut
BTU battu
BTY batty□
Betsy
Betty
bitty
bothy
butty
BUB blurb
BUD bound
BUE bouge
bouse
Bruce
brûlé
brute
BUF bluff
BUH blush
bough
brush
BUK baulk
blunk
BUN bourn
BUO Bruno
BUS Beuys
blues□
BUT blunt□
blurt
boult□
bruit
brunt
BUY bluey
BVL bevel
BVN Bevan
Bevin
BVY bevvy
bivvy
BWD bowed
BWE Bowie
bowne
BWG bewig
BWL bowel
BWN bow in
BWO bow to
BWR bower
BWS bowls
BWT bewet
BWY bawdy
byway
BXM buxom
BXN box in
BXR boxer□
BYE Bayle
Boyle
Boyne
BYH Blyth
BYN Bayan
Bryan
buy in
BYP buy up
BYR buyer
BYU bayou
BZA Bazza
BZL bezel
BZS bozos
BZT Bizet
CAA Clara
CAD chard
Claud
CAE cease
chafe
chase□
Clare
coate
crake
crane□
crape
crate
crave
craze
CAF chaff
CAG clang
Craig
CAH clash□
coach
crash□
CAI coati
CAK chack
chalk
chark
clack
clank
Clark
crack
crank
CAL crawl
CAM Chaim
charm
chasm
claim
CAN chain□
CAP champ
clamp
clasp
cramp
CAR chair
charr
CAS chaos
chaps
ciaos
class
claws
craps
crass
CAT chant
chart
clart
claut
coact
coapt
coast
craft
CAY chary
clary
crazy
CBA cobra
CBC Caboc
cubic
CBE cable
CBL cabal
COBOL
CBN cabin
Cuban
CBR caber
CBT Cabot
cubit
CBY cabby
CCA cocoa
CCD cycad
CCE cache
cycle
CCI cacti
cocci
CCL Cecil
CCO cacao
CCS cocos
CCY cocky
CDE cadge
cadre
CDN codon
CDR cedar
cider
cyder
CDS cedis
CDT cadet
CDX codex
CDY caddy
CDZ Cádiz
CEA caeca
chela
CED creed
CEE crème
crepe
crèpe
crêpe
Crete
Crewe
CEH Czech
CEK check
cheek
cleck
cleek
clerk
creak
creek□
CEL creel
CEM cream
CEN clean
Cleon
Creon
CEO credo
CEP cheap
cheep
creep
CER cheer
clear
CES chess□
cress
CET cheat
chert
chest
cleat
cleft
crept
crest
CEY chevy
chewy
Crécy
crêpy
CFD CAFOD
CFO cuffo
CFS cuffs
CGD caged
CGR cigar□
CGS CS gas
CGY cagey
ciggy
CHE COHSE
CHN Cohan
Cohen
CHS cohos
CIA Chiba
chica
china□
Chita
CIB climb
CID child
CIE Caine
chide
Chile
chime
chine
chive
clime
cline
clipe
Clive
crime
crine
CIF chief
cliff
CIG cling
CII ceili
CIK chick
chink□
chirk
click
clink
crick□
CIL chill
chirl
CIM chirm
CIN cairn
CIO Cairo
chiao
chimo
chino
CIP chirp
crimp
crisp
CIR chirr
crier
CIS Chios
coins
cries
CIT chirt
Clift
clint□
CIY chivy
CIZ chizz
CKR Cukor
CLA calla
Celia
cilia
CLC colic
CLE calve
Chloe
CLF calif
CLM Calum
celom
Colum
CLN Colin
colon
Colón
CLO cello
CLS calfs
CLX calyx
CLY coley
colly
CMA CAMRA
comma
CMC comic
CME comae
combe
Comte
CML camel
CMN Cimon
cumin
CMO cameo
combo
CMR comer
CMS camas
Camus
Comus
CMT comet□
CMY campy
comfy
CNA conga
CNC conic
cynic
CND contd
CNE canoe
cense
congé
CNH cinch
conch
CNL canal
CNN canon
Canon®
Cynon
CNO can do
canto
Congo
CNR Conor
CNT canst
CNW C and W
CNY candy□
canny
Cindy
coney
Conwy
COB coomb
COD chord
cloud
crowd
COE choke
chore
chose
clone
close□
cloye
cooee
Cooke
Croce
crome
crone
COF choof
COH cloth
COK chock
cloak
clock□
clonk
croak
crock
crook

CON clown
croon
crown
COO choko
COP chomp
clomp
croup
COR choir
clour
COS chops
cross
COT cloot
clout
coopt
co-opt
Croat
croft
COX choux
COY choky
crony
CPA Capra
CIPFA
copra
cuppa
CPC copec
CPD cupid□
CPE copse
CPI Capri
cippi
CPL cupel
CPN capon
Copán
CPR caper
coper
CPS capos
CPT Capet
capot
caput
CRA Carla
circa
Corea
CRB Carib
carob
CRD cored
cured
CRE Carné
Carré
carve
cerge
cerne
Circe
curie□
curse
curve
CRI carpi
cerci
cirri
CORGI
corgi
corni
cursi
CRL carol□
coral□

Cyril
CRM CD-ROM
coram
CRN Corin
CRO cargo
curio
CRR carer
corer
CRS Ceres
Chris
cords
corms
corps
curbs
Cyrus
CRT carat
caret
Corot
CRU Corfu
CRY Carey
Carly
carny
carry
corky
corny
curly
curry□
curvy
CSA COSLA
costa
CSE caste
cesse
CSO Cosmo
CSS cases
costs
CSY cissy□
Cosby
cushy
CTA cotta
CTD cited
CTH catch
CTN cut in
CTP cut up
CTR cater
CTS Cetus
CITES
cutis
CTT cut it
CTY Cathy
catty
CUB crumb
CUE cause
chute
coupe
coupé
crude
CUF chuff
CUH couch□
cough
crush
CUK caulk
chuck□
chunk

cluck
clunk
CUL churl
cruel
CUN churn
CUP chump
clump
crump
CUR churr
cruor
CUS clubs
clues
CUT count
court□
cruet
crust
CUY crudy
CVC civic
CVL cavil
civil
CVN Cavan
coven
CVR caver
cover
CVT civet
covet
CVY civvy
covey
CWD Clwyd
cowed
CWR cower
CWS Cowes
CWY cowry
CXE coxae
CYE chyle
chyme
Clyde
clype
CYN cry on
CYP cry up
CYT crypt
CYU coypu
CYY coyly
CZN cozen
CZO Cuzco
DAA Dhaka
Diana
drama
Duala
DAE deave
Diane
drake□
drape
Duane
dwale
Dwane
DAF draff
dwarf
DAH death
DAK D-mark
drank
DAL do-all
drail

drawl
DAN drain
drawn
DAO Draco
DAS dials
DRAMs
DAT dealt
draft
drant
DAY diary
DBA Debra
dobra
DBE Debye
DBG debag
debug
DBI Dubai
DBR debar
DBS debts
debus
DBT debit
debut
début
DBY debby□
DCA Dacca
dacha
dicta
DCL ducal
DCO decko
DCR décor
DCT dicht
ducat
DCY decay
decoy
decry
dicey
dicky□
duchy
DDE dodge
DDS dados
didos
dodos
DDY daddy
diddy
dodgy
DED dread
DEE deeve
diene
DEF die of
DEL dwell
DEM dream
DEO due to
DER drear
DES deeds
dregs
dress
duets
DET duett
DFD Dyfed
DFE Defoe
DFR defer
do for
DFT defat
DFY daffy

Duffy
DGA Dagda
dagga
dogma
DGM degum
DGN dig in
DGO doggo
DGP dig up
DGS dagos
degas□
DGT digit
DGY daggy
doggy
DID dried
DIE de-ice
drive
dwine
DIG doing
dying
DIK drink
DIL drill
DIM deism
DIN deign
djinn
DIR drier
DIT deist
DLitt
drift
DIY daily
dairy
daisy□
deify
deity□
doily
Doisy
drily
DJN Dijon
DJS dojos
DKO dekko
DKR Dakar
daker
DKS Dukas
DKU Dukou
DKY dykey
DLA Delia
Della
delta□
dolia
dolma
DLE delve
dolce
dulse
DLH delph
DLI Delhi
DLK Dalek
DLN Dolin
Dylan
DLP Dilip
DLS Dales
delfs
Delos
Dilys
DLT Dalit

delft□
DLY dally
delay
dilly
dolly□
dully
DMB demob
DMD domed
DME damme
DML domal
DMN daman
Damon
deman
demon
DMO dumbo□
DMP dam up
DMR demur
dimer
DMS demos
Dumas
dumps
DMT demit
DMY dimly
dumky
dummy
dumpy
DNA donga
Donna
DNB Deneb
DNC D and C
dinic
DNE Danae
dance
Dante
dense
dinge
donee
Donne
dunce
DNH Dench
Dinah
dunch
dunsh
DNL Donal
DNM denim
DNO dingo
DNR dinar
diner
donor
DNS Denis
Denys
DNT denet
DNU Donau
DNY dandy
Danny
Denny
dingy
dinky□
DOA doona
DOD Drood
DOE diode
Doone
drone

Words marked □ can also be spelled with an initial capital letter

drove
DOI dhobi
dhoti
duomi
DOK drook
drouk
DOL droll
drool
DON drown
DOO duomo
DOP droop
DOS dooms
Doors
dross
DOT do out
droit
DPD doped
duped
DPE duple
DPH depth
DPN dip in
Dupin
DPO dipso
DPT depot
DPY dippy
dopey
duply
DRA darga
derma
Doria
dorsa
Durga
DRC Dirac
Doric
Duroc
DRE dirge
DRG derig
DRK Derek
DRM durum
DRR Dürer
DRS darts
Doris
duros
DRY Darby
Darcy
derby□
dirty
dormy
DSE disme
DSI Desai
DSO disco
DSX desex
DSY dishy
dusky
dusty
DTD dated
DTH ditch
Dutch
DTM datum
DTO ditto
DTR deter
DTX detox
DTY ditsy
ditty
ditzy
dotty
DUD druid□
DUE daube
deuce
douse
drupe
Druse
Druze
DUH dough
DUK drunk
DUO Douro
DUS drugs
DUT daunt
doubt
DVD David
DVE Davie
DVL devil
DVN daven
Devon
divan
DVO Davao
DVR diver
Dover
DVS Davis
Davos
Dives
DVT davit
divot
duvet
DVY divvy
DWE dowle
dowse
DWL dowel
DWR Dewar
dower
DWS downs□
DWY dowdy
downy
dowry
DXE dixie
DYD dryad
DYE Doyle
DYN Dayan
doyen
DYP dry up
dry-up
DYR DIYer
dryer
DYY dryly
DZD dazed
DZN dozen
DZY dizzy
EAD eland
Enard
EAE elate
erase
evade
EAL email
e-mail□
EAO Erato
EAS Evans
EAT enact
epact
exact
exalt
EBD embed
EBG embog
EBR embar
ember
EBS embus
EBW elbow
EBX embox
EBY embay
ECD El Cid
ECE emcee
ECL excel
ECT escot
EDD ended
EDE Eddie
endue
EDM ek dum
EDN Emden
end-on
EDP end up
EDR eider
elder
Ender
EDW endow
EEA enema
EED emend
EEI elemi
Eyeti
EEP eye up
EES evens
EET egest
eject
elect
erect
event
evert□
ewest
exeat
exert
EEY elegy
emery□
enemy
every□
EFE Effie
EFN elfin
EFX enfix
EGD edged
EGE eagle□
eagre
eigne
EGN egg on
EGR eager
Edgar
edger
eggar
egger
Eiger
Elgar
EGS edges
EGT eight
ergot
EHC ethic
EHD ephod
EHL Ethel
ethyl
EHR ether
EHS ethos
EHW ewhow
EIA Eliza
erica□
Evita
EID eliad
EIE elide
elite
élite
exile
EIH Edith
EIS exits
EIT edict
Eliot
evict
exist
EIY edify
Emily
EJY enjoy
EKR esker
ELE Ellie
ELN Ellen
Emlyn
ELR Euler
ELS Ellis
ELT éclat
Eilat
EME Emmie
EMR emmer
EMS Emmys
EMW emmew
enmew
ENE Ernie
ENI ennui
ENT Ernst
EOA Epona
EOE elope
emote
epode
erode
erose
evoke
EOH Enoch
epoch
EOI E. coli
EOY ebony
epoxy
EPL expel
EPS expos
EPT expat
ex-pat
EPY empty
ERD eared
Edred
ERE eerie
eyrie
ERH earth□
ERL enrol
Errol
ERM EPROM
ERR error
ERS Emrys
euros
ERT egret
ERY early
Elroy
ESC EPSRC
ESE Elsie
ensue
Essie
ESL easel
ESM Epsom
ESN eosin
Essen
ESR Ensor
ESX Essex
ESY ensky
essay
ETA entia
extra
ETE ettle
Eytie
ETL extol
ETN eaten
eat in
Elton
ETP eat up
estop
ETR eater
enter
ester
ETY entry
EUB exurb
EUE educe
elude
elute
emule
emure
étude
exude
EUL equal
EUP equip
EUS Equus
EUT eruct
erupt
exult
EVN elvan
erven
EVR elver
EVS eaves
elves
Elvis
EVY envoy
EWN Edwin
Elwyn
EWY Elway
EYA etyma
EYT Egypt
EZD Enzed
FAC franc
FAD fraud
FAE flake
flame
flare
Foale
frame
FAF flaff
FAH flash
FAI frati
FAK Flack
flank
flask
frank□
FAL flail
frail
FAR flair
FAS feats
frass
FAT feast
fract
FAY flaky
foamy
FBE fable
Fabre
fibre
FBO fibro
FCA facia
FCD faced
FCE fiche
FCL focal
FCR facer
FCS facts
ficos
focus
Fuchs
fucus
FCT facet
FDD faded
FDE fidge
fudge
FDP fed up
FDS fados
Fides
FDY faddy
FEA Freda
frena
Freya
FED field□
fiend
freed
Freud
FEE feese
feeze
fleme
Frege
FEH flesh
fresh
FEK fleck
freak
FEN foehn
FER fleer
Fleur
freer

FET fleet□
FEY fiery
FFH fifth
FFR fifer
FFY fifty
FGE fugle
fugue
FGL fugal
FGP fog up
FGS figos
FGT fight
FGY fogey
foggy
fuggy
FID fried
FIE flite
FIG fling
Frigg
FIH faith□
FIK flick
flisk
Frink
frisk
FIL frill
FIN feign
Ffion
FIP flimp
FIR flier
friar
frier
FIS fains
flies
FIT faint
feint
flint
flirt
foist
FIY fairy
FIZ fritz
frizz
FKD faked
FKR faker
fakir
FLA Falla
fella
folia
FLC folic
FLD filed
FLE false□
FLH filch
filth
FLN felon
FLO Faldo
folio
FLR filar
filer
FLS falls
files
films
folks
FLT filet
FLX Felix
FLY felly
filly
filmy
folly
fully
FMD famed
FME femme
FMR femur
FMS fumes
FMT fumet
FNA Fonda
FNE fence
FNH finch
FNI fingi
fundi
fungi
FNL fanal
final
FNN Fanon
Funen
FNR finer
FNS fenks
fines
finis
finos
funds
FNY fancy
Fanny
fenny
finny
fonly
Fundy
funky
funny
FOA Fiona
flora□
FOD fiord
fjord
flood
Floyd
frond
FOE Frome
frore
froze
FOF feoff
FOG flong
FOH froth
FOK flock
frock
FON flown
frown
FOO Flo-Jo
FOR floor
flour
FOS floss
foots
FOT float
flout
front
frost□
FOY footy
FRD farad
fired
FRE farce
farse
force
forge
forme
forte□
furze
FRH Farah
firth
forth□
furth
FRI Farhi
Farsi
fermi□
FRL feral
FRM forum□
FRO forgo
FRQ Faruq
FRR firer
FRT first
FRY ferly
ferny
ferry□
foray
forby
forty
furry
FSA fossa
FSD fused
FSE fesse
Feste
fosse
fusee
FSI fasci
FSL fusil
FSY fishy
fussy
fusty
FTA fatwa
fetta
fetwa
FTD fated
fetid
FTH fetch
fitch
FTL fatal
fetal
FTN fit in
fit on
futon
FTO fatso
FTP fit up
fit-up
FTR fetor
FTS fetus
FTU Fitou
FTY fatly
fatty
fitly
FUA fauna□
FUD fluid
found
FUE Fauré
Fiume
fluke
flume
flute□
FUF fluff
FUH faugh
flush
frush
FUK flunk
FUP flump
frump
FUR fluor
FUS Fouts
FUT fault
Faust
fount
fruit
FUY fluky
fluty
FVA fovea
FVR fever□
fiver
FVS fives
FWR fewer
FWS fowls
FXD fixed
foxed
FXN fix on
Fuxin
FXP fix up
FXR fixer
FXS Foxes
FYE flype
flyte
FYN Flynn
FYP fly up
fry-up
FYR flyer
foyer
fryer
FYT fly at
FYY fly-by
FZD fazed
FZS fezes
FZY fizzy
fuzzy
GAA Ghana
guana
guava
GAD gland
go and
grand
guard
GAE glacé
glade
glare
glaze
go ape
GRACE
grace□
grade□
grape
grate
grave
graze
GAF graff
GAH gnash
graph
GAL gnarl
grail□
GAM glaum
GAN ghayn
grain
GAO GRAPO
Grapo
guano
GAP grasp
GAR glair
glaur
gnarr
GAS gears
Ghats
glass□
goals
grass□
GAT giant□
graft
grant□
GAY gravy
GBD go bad
GBE gable□
GBI gobbi
GBN Gabon
GBO Gobbo
GBR Gabor
giber
GBS gobos
GBY gabby□
GCO gecko
GDL Gödel
GDY giddy
godly
go dry
GEA Geeta
Greta
GED greed□
GEE geese
glebe
grebe
GEG Greig
GEK gleek
Greek
GEM gleam
GEN glean
Glenn
green□
GEO Greco
GEP gee up
GER Greer
GES guess
GET Ghent
gleet
glent
great□
greet
guest
Gwent
GEY geeky
GFE gaffe
GFR go far
gofer
go for
GFS gifts
GGE gigue
GGI Gigli
GGL Gogol
GGS Giggs
GGT gigot
GID grind
guild
GIE glide
glike
grice
grike
grime
gripe
grise
guide
guile
guise
GIF grief
griff
GIG going
Grieg
GIL glial
grill
GIP guimp
GIS gains
grits
GIT glint
grist
guilt
GIY gaily
grimy
GIZ glitz
GJS gajos
GLA Galba
Golda
GLD gelid
GLE Galle
GLF G-clef
GLG gulag
GLH galah
gulch
GLI Golgi
GLM golem
GLN Galen
GLP galop
GLS Giles
gules
GLT gilet
GLY gally
gelly
golly
gully
GMA gamma
gemma□
GMD go mad
GME gimme

GML gimel
Gomel
GMN gamin
GMO gumbo
GMP gum up
GMS games
GMT gamut
gemot
GMW Gamow
GMY gamey
gammy
gummy
GNA ganja
genoa❑
gonia
gonna
GNC genic
GND gonad
GNE genie
genre
gunge
GNH ganch
GNI genii
GNO gonzo
GNP gen up
GNR goner
GNS gents
genus
GNT G and T
genet❑
GNY Ginny
gungy
gunny
gynny
GOD geoid
GOE geode
globe
glove
gnome
goose
grope
grove❑
GOF Geoff
go off
GOH Gooch
GOL ghoul
growl
GOM gloom
groom
GON groan
groin
grown
GOO good-o
GOP gloop
group
GOS gloss
goods
gross
GOT ghost❑
gloat
go out
groat
grout
GOY glory
goody
gooey
goofy❑
GOZ Grosz
GPK gopak
GPL Gopal
GPR gaper
GPS gapós
GPT g-spot
GPY gappy
Gipsy
guppy
gypsy❑
GRA garda❑
Gerda
GRD go red
GRE gerbe
gorge
gorse
GRH girth
GRI garni
GRL gyral
GRM garum
GRO garbo❑
GRS germs
giros
gyrus
GRY Garry
Gerry
girly
Gorky
gorsy
GSE gosse
GSO gesso
gismo
gusto
GSS gases
GSY gassy
gushy
gusty
GTA gotta
gutta
GTD gated
GTN get in
get on
GTO get to
GTP get up
get-up
GTS Gates
getas
GTT get at
get it
GTY get by
Getty
gutsy
GUA Gouda
GUD glued
Gould
gourd
GUE gauge
gauze
glume
gouge
grume
GUF gruff
GUH Gough
GUI Gaudí
Gauri
GUK Gluck
GUL gruel
GUN gluon
GUP grump
GUS gauds
gauss❑
GUT gaunt
grunt
g-suit❑
GUY gaudy
gauzy
gluey
gouty
GVE Gavle
GVL gavel
GVN Gavin
given
GVR giver
GVS gyves
GWR Gower
GWY gawky
GYE Gayle
GYH glyph
GYL ghyll
GYM goyim
GYN geyan
GZA Gazza
GZO gizmo
GZR gazar
HAD heald
heard
hoard
HAE heave
HAH heath❑
HAI Huari
HAS heaps
Hyads
HAT heart
hoast
HAY heady
heavy
hoary
HBL Hubel
HBR Haber
HBS Hobbs
hobos
HBT habit
HBY hobby
hubby
HCS hacks
Hicks
hocus
hucks
HCT hecht
HDA hydra❑
HDE hedge
HDI hadji
HDO hydro
HDS Hades
HDT hadn't
hadst
HEA hyena
HEE heeze
HES hiems
HFI Hefei
HFY hefty
huffy
HGE Hague
HGL Hegel
HGN Hagen
Hogan
HGT hight
hog it
HHM ho-hum
HHT hi-hat
Hohot
HIA Haifa
HIE Heine
HIH haith
heigh
HII Haiti
Heidi
HIK hoick
HIS heirs
HIT heist
hoist
HIU haiku
HIY hairy
HIZ Heinz
HJB hejab
hijab
HJI hajji
HKA Hekla
HKM hakam
hakim
HKR hiker
HKU hokku
HLA halma
halva
Helga
Hilda
holla
HLD holed
HLE Halle
Hallé
halse
halve
helve
HLH hilch
HLL halal
HLM hilum
HLN halon
Helen
HLO hallo
hello❑
hollo
hullo
HLS Halas
halfs
halos
HLT helot
Holst
HLX helix
HLY Haley
hilly
holey
holly❑
HMC humic
HMD Hamad
humid
HMH humph❑
HML hemal
HMN he-man
hem in
human
hymen
HMP ham up
HMR Homer
HMS homes
humus
HMT ham it
HMY hammy
homey
humpy
HNA henna
Honda
HNC h and c
HNE hence
henge
hinge
HNH hunch
HNI Hanoi
Henri
Hindi
HNN Honan
HNO Hanno
HNR Honor
HNS hands
Hanks
Hants
Hines
hints
HNU Hindu
HNY handy
hanky
henry❑
hinny
honey
hunky
HOA hoo-ha
hooka
HOB H-bomb
HOD hyoid
HOE Hooke
HOH hooch
hoosh
HOO hoo-oo
HOS hoofs
Hoops
HOY hooey
hooky
hooly
HPA hypha
HPO hippo
HPR hyper
HPS hypos
HPT hop it
HPY haply
happy
hippy
hoppy
HRA hurra
HRD Herod
hired
HRE Harte
heroe
horde
horse
HRH harsh
HRM harem
HRN heron
Huron
HRR hirer
HRS haros
herbs
herds
herms
Horus
HRT Hirst
horst
hurst❑
HRX hyrax
HRY hardy❑
harpy
harry❑
horny
horsy
hurry
HRZ hertz❑
HSA hasta
Hosea
hosta
HSD Hasid
HSE haste
Hesse
HSI Husni
HSN Hasan
hosen
HSS hoses
hosts
husks
husos
HST hasn't
HSY hasty
husky
hussy
HTA Hatra
HTC hi-tec
HTD hated
HTE hithe
HTH hatch
hitch
hotch
hutch
HTL hotel❑

Words marked ❑ can also be spelled with an initial capital letter

HOTOL
HTN hit on
hot on
HTP het up
hot up
HTT hit at
hit it
HTY Hatty
Hetty
hotly
HUA Hausa
HUD hound
HUE house❑
HUI houri
HUM haulm
HUT haunt
HVC havoc
HVL Havel
hovel
HVN haven
HVR haver
hover
HVS haves
hives
Hovas
HWE Hawke
HWH hewgh
HWL Hywel
HWS Hawks
HXA Hoxha
HXD hexad
HYE Hoyle
HYN Haydn
HYR Heyer
HYS Hayes
HZA huzza
HZL hazel❑
IAA Ivana
IAC Isaac
IAE image
inane
irade
irate
IAI Imari
Iraqi
Iwaki
IAL in all
IAM inarm
IAO Idaho
imago
IAT in alt
inapt
IAY Italy
IBD imbed
in bud
IBE imbue
inbye
ICN Incan
ICR in-car
incur
ICS incus
ICY itchy
IDA India
Indra
IDC Indic
IDE indie
indue
IDI indri
IDS Indus
IDX index
IEA Irena
IEC ileac
IEE Irene
IEL ideal
IEM I-beam
ileum
IEP ice up
IES ideas
items
IET inept
inert
IFA infra
IFN in fun
IFR infer
in for
IFU ICFTU
IFW in few
IFX infix
IGT ingot
IIA Ibiza
IIC iliac
IIG icing
IIH Irish
IIM idiom
ilium
IIO Inigo
IIT idiot
IIY icily
IKD irked
IKE inkle
IKN ink in
ILM Islam
ILO igloo
ILR idler
ILT inlet
islet
ILY inlay
Islay
IMD Iomud
IMI iambi
IMN Inman
IMR Izmir
IMW immew
INC ionic❑
INI I-and-I
INR inner
INS Innes
INT if not
INW I know
IOA Idola
Ilona
Imola
IOB inorb
IOD Isold
IOE I hope
in one
IOF in-off
IOS irons❑
IOU Inönü
IOY irony
ivory❑
IPL impel
IPP in pup
IPS impis
IPT input
IPY imply
IRM in rem
IRS Idris
IRX Ibrox
ISE issue
ISI imshi
ISM in sum
ISN Ibsen
ISS Issus
IST INSET
inset
ISY imshy
ITE istle
ixtle
ITL intil
ITO intro
in two
ITR inter
ITS ictus
ITW in tow
IUE IMunE
inure
in use
IUN Idunn
Ieuan
inurn
IUT Inuit
IVR Invar®
IYL idyll
JAS jeans❑
JBT jabot
JCB Jacob
JCS jacks
JDA Jedda
JDD jaded
JDE Jodie
judge❑
JDH Judah
JDS Judas
JEE Jeeze
JEY Joely
JFA Jaffa
JFY jiffy
JGR jäger
JGY jaggy
JHD jehad
jihad
JHS Johns
JIE juice
JIT joint
joist
JIY juicy
JKR joker
JKS jakes
jokes
JKY jokey
JLA Julia
JLE Julie
JLN Jilin
JLP julep
JLY jelly
jolly
JMA Jemma
Jumna
JME Jamie
JML Jamal
Jamil
JMO jambo
jumbo
JMR jumar
JMS James
JMY jammy
jemmy
Jimmy
jumpy
JNA Jenna
junta
JNH Jonah
JNI jinni
JNN Jinan
JNO jingo❑
junto
JNR Junor
JNS Janis
Janus
Jones
JNT Janet
JNY jenny❑
Jinny
junky
JOS Jools
Jooss
JPN japan❑
jupon
JPR japer
JRD Jared
JRR juror
JRT jurat
JRY jerky
jerry❑
JSE jaspe
Jesse
Josie
JSN Jason
JSS Jesus
jésus
JSY Jessy
JTN jeton
JTS jatos
JTY jetty
jutty
JUE joule❑
JUT jaunt
joust
JVR jiver
JWL jewel
JWY Jewry
jowly
JYE Joyce
JZY jazzy
KAA Ka'aba
koala
KAE Keane
knave
KAG kiang
klang
KAI khadi
khaki
KAK knack
Kraak
KAL kraal
KAS Keats
krans
kvass
KAT kraft
krait
KAZ kranz
KBB kebab
KBL Kabul
KCI Kochi
KCS kecks
kicks
KDE kedge
KDK Kodak®
KDS kudos
KDU kudzu
KDY kiddy
KEA Kiera
KED knead
kneed
knee'd
KEE keeve
KEH keech
KEK Klerk
KEL kneel
knell
KEN Klein
Kreon
KES Krebs
KET knelt
KEZ Krenz
KFA Kafka
kofta
KFC Kufic
KGS kagos
KHE Kühne
KHO Kahlo
KIE Kline
knife
koine❑
KIH Keith
knish
KIL krill
KIT Klimt
KKI kukri
KLE kylie❑
kyloe
KLF kalif
KLK kulak
KLM kelim
kilim
KLO Kelso
KLS kilos
kolos
KLY Kelly
kelpy
kiley
Killy
kilty
KME kamme
Kempe
KMK kamik
KML Kamal
KMO kimbo
KMR Khmer
Kumar
KMT kempt
KMU kombu
KNA kanga❑
Kenya
kinda
Konya
KNF kenaf
KNI kanji
KNK Kanak
KNN kinin
KNO kendo
Kenzo
KNR kunar
KNS Kings
Kinks
kinos
KNY Kandy
Kenny
kindy
kinky
KOA krona
KOE knowe
krone
KOF kloof
KOI koori
KOK kiosk
knock
KOL knoll
KON known
kroon
KOO Kyoto
KOP knosp
KOS knobs
KOT Knott
knout
KOY kooky
KPA kappa
KPE kopje
KPK kapok
kopek
KPS Kipps
KPT kaput
KRA Karla
karma
Korda
korma
KRI karri

KRJ Karaj
KRK Kursk
KRN Karan
Karen
Karin
Koran
KRO Karoo
KRR Koror
KRT karst
KRV Kirov
KRY karsy
karzy
Kerry
Korky
KSA kasha
KSM Kasim
KSY Kesey
KTA Katya
KTE Katie
kithe
Kitwe
kythe
KTH ketch
KTJ Kitaj
KTS kotos
KTW kotow
KTY Kathy
kitty□
KUE Klute
KUI kauri
KUL knurl
KUP Krupp
KUR knurr
KVN Kevin
KVR Kavir
KYD keyed
KYE kbyte
KYK kayak
KYN key in
KYS kayos
KZK Kazak
KZN Kazan
KZO kazoo
LAA Lhasa
liana□
llama
LAE lease
leave
liane
loave
LAH leach
leash
loach
loath
LAN learn
LAS loads
LAT least
LAY leafy
leaky
loamy
LBA labra
Libra
Libya
LBD lobed
LBL label
libel
LBN Laban
LBR lobar
LBY Libby
lobby
LCA Lucia
Lycra®
LCD laced
Le Cid
lucid
LCE Locke
lucre
LCL local
LCM locum
LCN Lucan
LCS locks
locos
locus
Lucas
luces
LCT licit
LCY lucky□
LDA Lydia
LDC ludic
LDE ladle
ledge
lodge□
LDN laden
loden
LDS lidos
ludos
LEE leese
liege
Liège
lieve
Loewe
LEH leech
LES Leeds
loess
LEY leery
LFA luffa
LFE LIFFE
LFR Lifar
lifer
LFY lofty
LGC logic
LGE legge
LGL legal
LGN lug in
LGP leg-up
LGR lager
Léger
liger
Luger
Luger®
LGS Lagos
logos
LGT leg it
legit
light
LGY leggy
LIA Laika
Leica®
Leila
LID laird
LIE Loire
LIG Laing
Luing
lying
LIH laigh
Leigh
Leith
LIS Laius
LIY laity
LKD liked
LKN lakin
liken
LKR Laker
LLA Lalla
LLC lilac
LLE Lille
LLY lolly
Lully
LMA LAMDA
lamia□
lemma
LME lumme
LMH lymph
LMI Limbi
LMN leman
lemon
Loman
lumen
LMO limbo□
LMR lemur
LMT limit
LMY limey
lummy
lumpy
LNA Lanza
Lenya
Linda
Lynda
LND lined
LNE lance□
Lange
lunge
Lynne
LNH lunch
lynch□
LNI Lanai
lenti
lungi
LNL Lendl
LNN Lenin
linen
LNO Lando
lento
lingo
LNR liner
loner
lunar
LNS lands
lenes
lenis
lenos
lines
links
linos
Linus
LNY lanky
Lenny
Lindy
linty
Lundy
LOA Leona
loofa
LOD Lloyd
LOE leone
loose
LOI Lao Zi
LOS Laois
loofs
looks
Lyons
LOY loony
loopy
LPA lepta
LPD lepid
lipid
LPE lapse
LPI Lippi
LPL lapel
LPN lupin
LPP lap up
LPR leper
LPS lapis
Lepus
lupus□
LPY lippy
LPZ La Paz
LRA larva
Lorca
Lorna
LRC lyric
LRD lurid
LRE large
Larne
Lorre
LRH larch
lurch
LRI lurgi
LRN loran□
Loren
LRO largo
LRS Lares
larks
liras
lords□
loris
LRX Lurex®
LRY lardy
Larry
Leroy
lorry
lurgy
LSE lisle
LSI Laski
LSO lasso
lesbo
LSR laser
loser
LSS lysis
LST Liszt
LSY lusty
LTD lated
LTE lathe
latte
let be
lithe
litre
LTH latch
letch
LTI lathi
LTN laten
Latin
let in
let on
Luton
LTO let go
litho
lotto
LTP let up
let-up
lit up
LTR later
LTS laths
litas
lotos
lotus
LTX latex
LTY Letty
LUA Lauda
Laura
LUD laund
LUE Louie
loupe
louse
LUH laugh
lough
Louth
LUS lauds
louis□
LUY lousy
LVA Livia
LVD livid
loved
LVE levee
LVL level
LVN Levin
liven
LVR laver□
lever
liver
lover
LVS lavas
Levis®
lives
LVT lovat
LVY luvvy
LWE lowne
lowse
LWN low on
LWR lower
LWS Lawes
lawks
Lewes
lewis□
LWY lowly
Lowry
LXR Luxor
LXS lexis
luxes
LXY laxly
LYA Layla
LYL loyal
LYN lay in
lay on
LYP lay up
LYR layer
LYY lay by
LZI lazzi
LZN Luzon
LZR lazar
LZY lezzy
MAE Meade
meane
MAH Meath
MAI Miami
MAL miaul
MAS Meads
meals
means
MAT meant
MAW miaow
MAY mealy
meany
meaty
MBG Mr Big
MBL Mabel
MCA Macha
mecca□
micra
mocha
Mucha
MCD mucid
MCE miche
Moche
MCH Micah
MCN Mâcon
MCO Macao
macho
macro
micro
MCS micas
micos
mucus
MCW macaw
MCY McCoy
Micky
mucky
MDA Medea

Words marked □ can also be spelled with an initial capital letter

media
MDC medic
Médoc
MDE Madge
Médée
midge
MDI modii
MDL medal
modal
model
MDM madam
modem
MDN mad on
Medan
mid-on
MDS Midas
MSDOS
MS-DOS
MS-DOS®
MDT midst
MDX Middx
MDY madly
middy
muddy
MEE Maeve
Mneme
MEI Mbeki
MFA Mafia
MFI ma foi
mufti
MFY miffy
MGA Magda
magma
MGC magic
MGL mogul
MGN Megan
MGP mug up
MGS magus
MGT magot
might
MGY moggy
muggy
MHI Mahdi
MHL mohel
MPhil
MHT my hat!
MIA Moira
MIE Maine
maize
moire
moiré
MIO maiko
MIT moist
MIZ Mainz
MJR major□
MJS mojos
MKA mikra
MKR maker□
MKS makos
mokos
MLA Malta
Melba
MLE Malle
melee
mêlée
Milne
MLH milch
mulch
MLL molal
MLN Malin
melon
Milan
MLO Malmo
Malmö
molto
MLR miler
molar
MLS Melos
miles□
Mills
milos
Mlles
molas
Myles
MLT mulct
MLX malax
MLY Malay
malty
milky
Molly
MMA mamba
mamma
momma
MMC mimic
MME Mamie
MMO mambo
MMR mimer
Mimir
MMS memos
mumps
MMT Mamet
MMY mommy
mummy
mumsy
MNA Manga
mania
manna
manta
many a
Mensa
Monza
MNC manic
MND maned
monad
Monod
MNE mange
manse
mense
mince
monte
MNH month
munch□
mynah
MNK Minsk
Monck
MNM Menem
minim
MNO mango
mondo
Monro
Mungo
Munro
MNR manor
minar
miner
minor
MNS Manes
manos
manus
minas
Minos
minus
monos
MNT manat
Manet
Monet
MNU Manzú
MNY -mancy
Mandy
mangy
manky
manly
Manny
mingy
money□
MNZ Muntz
MOE Moore
moose
MOH mooch
MOI Maori
mooli
MOY moody□
moony
MPD moped
MPE maple
MPI Mopti
MPP mop up
mop-up
MPR moper
MRA Maria
marka
Moria
Morna
Myrna
MRD Murad
MRE marge
Marie
Marne
merge
Morse
MRG Morag
MRH march□
marsh□
mirth
morph
myrrh
MRK Merak
MRL Meryl
moral
morel
mural
MRN mirin
moron
Myron
MRO Margo
Murdo
MRS marks□
MIRAS
mores
Moros
MRT Marat
merit
Murat
MRY mardy
Marey
marly
marry
Marty
mercy□
merry
moray□
murky
MSA Mosca
Musca
musha
MSC music
MSE massé
Moshe
MSH musth
MSI Masai
MSL Mosel
Mosul
MSN Masan
mason□
meson
MSO misdo
MSR maser
miser
MSS misos
Moses
musos
MST musit
MSY messy
missy
misty
mosey
mossy
mushy
musky
mussy
musty
MTA Mitla
MTD mated
muted
MTE metre
mitre
motte
MTF metif
motif
MTH match
mitch
MTL metal
metol□
motel
MTN moten
MTO matlo
matzo
me-too
metro
motto
MTR mater
meter
motor
MTS maths
meths
Métis
moths
Motus
myths
MTT motet
MTY matey
Mitty
MUD mould
mound
MUE Maude
mauve
Meuse
mouse
MUH mouch
mouth
MUN mourn
MUT moult
mount
MUY mousy
MVD moved
MVE movie
MVN maven
mavin
MVR mover
MVS mavis□
moves
MWR mower
MXD mixed
MXM maxim□
MXN mix in
MXP mix up
mix-up
MXR mixer
MXT mix it
MYE maybe
MYN Mayon
MYR Mayer
mayor
Meyer
MYW Mayow
MZO mezzo
MZY muzzy
NAA Nuada
Nuala
NVALA
nyala
Nyasa
NAD NSAID
NAE neafe
Neale
NAF nyaff
NAH neath
Niamh
NAI NAAFI
NAL Niall
NAO ngaio□
NAW NUAAW
NBA nabla
NBB nabob
NBC NHBRC
NBE noble
NBL Nobel
NBY nobly
NCA nucha
NCD nicad
NCE nache
nacre
niche
NCM Nicam
NCO NACRO
Nacro
NCR nicer
NCS NUCPS
NCY Nicky
NDA Nadia
NDE nudge
nudie
NDL nidal
nodal
NDO nod to
NDR Nader
nadir
NDY neddy□
noddy
NED no end
NEE neese
neeze
niece
NEI naevi
NES needs
NEY needy
NFA NAFTA
Nafta
NFY niffy
nifty
NGL Nigel
NGO Negro
NGR Niger
NGT night
NGW NUGMW
NHM Nahum
NHS ne has
NHU Nehru
NIA naira
NID naiad
NIE naive
naïve
n mile
noise
NIH neigh
NIY noisy
NKA nakfa
NKD naked

Words marked □ can also be spelled with an initial capital letter

5 N_K_N

NKN Nikon®
NKU nikau
NLN nylon
NLO NALGO
NLS nelis
NLT Nilot
NLY nelly❑
NMB Namib
NMD named
nomad
NMH nymph
NMI nimbi
nomoi
NMN Neman
numen
NMO Nampo
NMR Namur
NMS Nîmes
NMY NIMBY
Nimby
Nimoy
NNA Nanna
ninja
NNE Nance
nonce
NNH ninth
NNN ninon
NNS nones
no-nos
no-no's
NNT nonet
NNY nancy❑
nanny
ninny
NOA Ndola
NOD Njord
NOE Niobe
no one
no-one
noose
NOO Nkomo
NPA nappa
NPC NSPCC
NPE nappe
NPL Nepal
NPO napoo
NPS Nepos
Nupes
NPY nappy
nippy
NRA nary a
nerka
Nerva
noria
Norma
NRE nerve
Norse
nurse❑
NRH Norah
north❑
NRI Nervi
Nurmi
NRO narco
NRS narcs
nares
NRX NIREX
NRY narky
nerdy
nervy
NSA Nesta
NSD nosed
NSE Nashe
NSI nisei
NSL nasal
NSN Nisan
NSY nasty
nosey
NTA Netta
NTD nitid
noted
NTE nitre
NTH natch
notch
NTL natal❑
NTN not on
NTP not up
NTS nates
notes
NTY natty
Netty
nitty
nutty
NUE neume
NUI Nguni
NUU Nauru
NUY nouny
NVE novae
NVL naval
navel
nevel
novel
NVM novum
NVN Niven
NVR never
NVS novas
NVY navvy
NWB nawab
NWE ngwee
NWL newel
NWS ne was
NWY Newby
newly
newsy
no way
noway
NXE nixie
NXN Nixon
NXS Naxos
nexus
NZM nizam
OAA O'Hara
Omaha
omasa
Osaka
OAE of age
O'Hare
orate
ovate
OAH Omagh
OAI okapi
OAS okays
OAT Op Art
OAY oracy
ovary
OBE ombre
ombré
OBS ombus
ombús
OBT orbit
OBY oh boy!
OCE on cue
OCM OCCAM
occam
OCR occur
oncer
oscar❑
ODA oidia
ODE Oddie
oldie
ODN Ogdon
olden
ODR older
order
ODS Ordos
ODY oddly
OEA omega
Onega
opera
OEC oleic
OED on end
oread
OEE obese
OEH obeah
OEI obeli
OEM oleum
OEN ocean
odeon
olein
OEP one up
OES Odets
oleos
Owens
OET overt
Ovett
OFL offal
OFM OXFAM
OFO off to
OFR offer
OGA orgia
OGN oggin
organ
OGS OFGAS
Ofgas
OGT ought
OHE ochre
OHM ogham
OHR other
OHY ochry
OIA Omiya
OIE ogive
olive❑
on ice
opine
ovine
oxide
OIG owing
OII oribi
OIL oriel
OIM odium
opium
OIN onion
Orion
OIR osier
OIS olios
OIZ Opitz
OJA Oujda
OJT objet
OKM oakum
OKN oaken
of kin
OKR ocker
OLD oiled
OLE Ollie
OLP orlop
oxlip
OLR oiler
OLT OFLOT
Oflot
owlet
OLY Otley
OMC ogmic
OMH oomph
OMR ormer
ONE ounce
ONP own up
ONR owner
OOD of old
ovoid
OOE Obote
ohone
ozone
OOF on-off
OOI oboli
ovoli
OOO ovolo
OOR odour
OOY ology
OPE ouphe
OPN orpin
OPS oppos
ORA ocrea
ORD oared
Ohrid
ORH Oprah
ORS orris
ORY o'erby
OSA ossia
OSL ousel
OSN Oisin
Olsen
Orson
OSS oases
oasis❑
odsos
Ossis
OST onset
OTA Ostia
OTC optic❑
OTD octad
OTE outré
OTF out of
OTL octal
OFTEL
Oftel
OTN oaten
often
Orton
OTO outdo
outgo
out to
OTP on tap
OTR otter
outer
oxter
OTS Oates
oaths
OTT octet
OTY outby
OUE of use
ovule
OUI oculi
OVS oaves
OWN Olwen
Olwin
Olwyn
OWT OFWAT
Ofwat
OYL Oryol
OZE Ozzie
OZL ouzel
OZS ouzos
PAA playa
plaza
Praia
prana
PAC PPARC
PAD plaid
PAE peace
Peake
phage
phase
place
plane
plate
poake
prate
PAG phang
prang
PAH peach
plash
Plath
poach
PAK plank
prank
PAL pearl❑
PAM plasm
psalm
PAN plain
prawn
PAO Peano
piano❑
Plato
Prado
PAS Pears
plans
PAT plait
plant
PAU prahu
PAY peaky
Peary
peaty
peavy
PBS pubis
PCE pecke
PCI Pucci
PCN pecan
PCR pacer
PCS pacos
Pecos
PCT picot
PCY pacey
piccy
picky
PDA Padua
podia
PDE padre
PDL pedal
PDO Pedro
PDY paddy❑
podgy
pudgy
PEA pieta❑
pietà❑
PED piel'd
plead
pseud
PEE peepe
peeve
phese
piece
prese
PEN paean
paeon
preen
PES peers
Piers
plebs
poems
press
PET pleat
PEY peeoy
peery
piety
poesy
predy
PFY puffy
PGL pygal

Words marked ❑ can also be spelled with an initial capital letter

PGN pagan
Pugin
PGR pager
PGT Paget
PGY Peggy
piggy❑
pigmy
pygmy
PHW pshaw
PIA Prima
PID poind
PIE Paige
Paine
paire
poise
price❑
pride❑
prime
prise
prize
PIK plink
prick
prink
PIL phial
prial
prill
PIM Priam
prism
PIO primo
PIP primp
PIR plier
prior
PIS pains
pairs
plies
PIT paint
point
print
PIY pricy
primy
privy
PKA pukka
PKE pekoe
PKN pekan
PKR poker
PLA Palma
pilea
polka
PLD piled
PLE pulse
PLI palpi
pilei
PLN Palin
pylon
PLO Pilao
polio
PLP polyp
PLR polar
puler
PLS piles
polos
polys
PLT pilot

PLU Palau
pilau
PLW pilaw
pilow
PLX phlox
PLY Paley
pally
palmy
palsy
Polly
pulpy
PMS pumas
PNA panda
Penda
penna
Penza
pinna
pinta❑
Pinza
punka
PNC panic
Punic
PNE panne
pence
penne
ponce
PNH pinch
punch❑
PNL panel
penal
PNN pen in
pin on
PNO panto
pingo
pinto❑
pongo❑
PNP pin up
pin-up
PNS pangs
pants
penis
PNY pandy
pansy❑
penny❑
poncy
pongy
POA pooka
Poona
POD proud
POE phone
Poole
probe
proke
prole
prone
prore
prose
prove
POF proof
POG prong
POH pooch
POI paoli
Prodi

POK plonk
plook
plouk
pronk
POL prowl
POM pro-am
proem
POO photo
Poopó
promo
Provo
POS pious
psoas
POT Prost
Prout
POY peony
prosy
proxy
PPA Pippa
PPE pupae
PPI Pepsi®
PPL papal
pipal
pipul
pupal
pupil
PPN Pepin
pop in
PPP pep up
pop up
pop-up
PPR paper
piper❑
PPS pepos
Pepys
pipes
pupas
PPT pipit
PPW papaw
PPY pappy
peppy
pippy
poppy
popsy
puppy
PQE pique
piqué
PRA parka
Parma
PRE parge
parse
perse
perve
porge
purée
purge
purse
PRH parch
perch
Perth
porch
PRI pardi
Parsi

PRL peril
PRM Purim
PRN Perón
purin
PRO pareo
porno
PRS Paris
Paros
parts
Peres
PRU pareu
PRY pardy
parky
parry❑
party
Percy
perdy
perky
perry❑
Porgy
porky
pursy
PSA pasha
pasta
PSD posed
PSE passé
paste
piste
PSH Pasch
Pesah
PSM pashm
PSN Pusan
PSO pesto
PSR poser
PSS pesos
PST posit
PSY pasty
pesky
Pusey
pushy
pussy
PTA Patna
Petra
pitta
PTH patch
pitch
PTI Patti
putti
PTL petal
PTN paten
piton
potin
pot on
put in
Putin
put on
put-on
PTO patio
potoo
potto
put to
putto
PTP pot up
put up
PTR pater❑
petar
peter❑
PTS paths
Patos
PTY patly
patsy❑
patty❑
petty
pithy
potty
put by
putty
PUA Paula
PUB plumb
PUD pound❑
PUE pause
plume
pouke
poupe
prude
prune
PUF pluff
PUH plush
pouch
PUI Pauli
PUK pluck
plunk
PUO Pluto
PUP plump
PUT poult
poupt
PUY plumy
pouty
PVA Pavia
PVD paved
PVN pavan
PVT pivot
PWR power
PWS Powys
PWT pewit
PWW pawaw
PWY pawky
PXE pixie
PXL pixel
PXS pyxis❑
PYA phyla
PYE payee
PYH psych
PYL Pwyll
PYN pay in
pry in
PYP pay up
PYR payer
Pryor
PYV pay TV
PZA pizza
PZO Pozzo
QAE quake
QAF quaff
QAH quash
QAI quasi
quasi-
QAK quack
quark
QAL quail
QAM qualm
QAT quant❑
quart
QAY quaky
QBA qibla
QEE queue
QEL quell
QEN queen❑
quern
QER queer
QET quest
QEY query
QHP Q-ship
QIE quire
quite
QIF quiff
QIK quick
quirk
QIL quill
QIO Quito
QIP Quilp
QIS quids
quits
QIT quiet
quilt
quint
quirt
QOA quota
QOE quote
QOK quonk
QON quoin
QOT Q-boat
quoit
QRN Qoran
Quran
Qur'an
QTR Qatar
RAD Roald
RAE roate
RAH reach
roach❑
RAM realm
rearm
RAS reaks
roads
RAT react
reast
roast
RAY ready
RBC rebec
RBD rabid
rebid
RBI rabbi
RBL rebel
RBN Rabin
robin❑
Robyn
rub in
RBP rub up

RBR re-bar
RBS rebus
robes
RBT Rabat
rebut
robot
RBY Robey
RCA recta
RCE recce
ruche
RCI recti
Ricci
RCL recal
RCN racon
RCO recto
RCP recap
RCR racer
recur
RCS races
rocks
RCT récit
recpt
RCY reccy
ricey
Ricky
rocky❑
RDE ridge
Rudge
RDI radii
RDN radon
Rodin
RDO radio
rodeo❑
RDR radar
rider
Ryder
RDX radix
RDY reddy
redly
Roddy
ruddy
REE reeve❑
REM rheum
RES RMetS
RET reest
REY reedy
RFE rifle
RFR refer
RSFSR
RFS Rufus
RFT refit
RGA ragga
RGD rigid
RGE ragde
rogue
RGL regal
RGN Regan
Rogun
RGP rig up
RGR rager
Roger
RGT right
RGY raggy
rugby❑
RHB rehab
RHN Rohan
RIA raita
RIE Raine
raise
Rhine
RIH Reich
Reith
RIN reign
Rhian
RIO rhino
RIS rails
Reims
reins
ruins
RIT reist
roist
RIY rainy
reify
RJG rejig
re-jig
RJH rajah
RJN rejón
RJV Rajiv
RKE rakee
RKR raker
RLC relic
RLD riled
ruled
RLE Rilke
RLH Ralph
RLI Rolli
RLR ruler
RLS Rolls
Rolls®
rules
RLX relax❑
RLY rally
relay
Riley
RMA rumba
RME ramie
rimae
RML ramal
RMN Raman
ramen
ramin
roman❑
rumen
RMO romeo❑
RMS Ramos
ramus
Remus
romas
RMT remit
RMX remex
RMY rumly
rummy
RNB R and B
RNC runic
RNE rance
ranee
range
Ranke
Renée
rinse
RNG renig
RNH ranch
RNL renal
RNN Renan
renin
run in
run-in
run on
RNO rondo
roneo
run to
RNP run up
run-up
RNS rands
rings
RNW renew
RNY randy❑
rangy
runny
ROA Rhoda
Rhona
rioja❑
ROB rhomb
ROE Rhône
roose
ROS roofs
rooms
roots❑
ROT roost
ROY rhody
rooky
roomy
RPA repla
RSPCA
RPD rapid
roped
RPE rupee
RPH RIPHH
RPL repel
RPN ripen
Ripon
RPO repro
RPP rip up
RPR ryper
RPS repos
RPT repot
RPY repay
reply
ropey
RRC roric
RRD rorid
RRL roral
rural
RRN rerun
RRS ro-ros
RRY rorty
RSA RoSPA
RSE Rosie
RSN resin
rosin
RSR riser
RSS Roses
RST reset
resit
roset
RSY raspy
resay
risky
rusty
RTH retch
RTL ratel
RTN ratan
rat on
RTO ratio
retro
RTR rotor
RTS rates
rotis
rotls
RTY ratty❑
retry
ritzy
rutty
RUB rhumb
RUD round
RUE reuse
re-use
rouge
rouse
route
RUH rough
RUN Rouen
RUT roust
RVE Revie
revue
RVL ravel❑
revel
rival
rivel
RVN raven
ravin
RVR raver
river
rover
RVS rivos
RVT revet
rivet
RWL rowel
RWN rowan❑
RWR rower
RWY rawly
rowdy
RYA rhyta
RYE rhyme
Royce
royne
RYL riyal
royal
RYN rayon
RYS Reyes
RYT royst
RZE razee
RZO razoo
RZR razor
SAA scapa
SAD scald
shard
skald
staid
stand
sward
SAE Saame
scale
scape
scare
seame
sease
seaze
shade
shake
shale
shame
Shane
shape❑
share
shave
skate
slade❑
slake
slate
slave
snake
snare
Soane
Soave
space
spade❑
spane
spare
spate
stage
stake
stale
stare
state
stave
suave
swage
swale
SAF scarf
Shaef
staff
swarf
SAG slang
spang
SAH slash
smash
snash
stash
swash
swath
SAI scapi
spahi
swami
Swazi
SAK shack
shank
shark❑
skank
slack
smack
snack
spank
spark❑
stack
stalk
stark
SWALK
swank
SAL scail
shall
shawl
skail
small
snail
snarl
spall
Staël
stall
swayl
SAM shawm
smarm
spasm
swarm
SAN Shaun
Shawn
slain
Spain
spawn
stain
swain
SAO SEATO
shako
SWAPO
Swapo
SAP scalp
scamp
scarp
scaup
sharp❑
stamp
swamp
SAR scaur
stair
Starr
SAS scads
scats
seats
snags
stars
stays
swabs
SAT scant
scart
shaft
shan't
slant

smalt
smart□
spalt
START
start
SAU snafu
SAY scaly
scary
seamy
shady
shaky
shaly
slaty
snaky
soapy
Stacy
stagy
SAZ spazz
SBA sabra
SBE sable
sabre
SBL Sabal
sibyl□
Sybil
SBM sebum
SBR sober
suber
SBT sabot
SCA Sacha
sacra
SCE socle
sucre□
SCI Sochi
succi
SCM SECAM
SCS Sachs
socks
sucks!
SDD sided
SDE sadhe
Sadie
sedge
sidle
SDM sedum
Sodom
SDN sedan□
Sidon
SDR Seder
sudor
SDT Sadat
SDU sadhu
SDY sadly
sedgy
Soddy
sudsy
SEA scena
Sheba
Siena
SED sherd
Snead
speed
speld
spend
stead□
steed
stend
SEE scene
siege
sieve
Speke
stele
stere
Steve
suede
swede□
SEF sheaf
shelf
swerf
SEH sieth
SEK sheik
sleek
sneak
sneck
speak
speck
steak
steek
SEL sheal
sheel
shell
she'll
smell
speel
spell
steal
steel□
stell
sweal
sweel
swell
SEM sperm
steam
SEN sheen□
skean
skein
spean
stean
steen
stein□
stern□
SEO see to
Steno
SEP sheep
skelp
sleep
sneap
steep
sweep
SER shear
sheer
smear
sneer
spear
Speer
speir
steer
swear
SES see as
skeos
specs
steps
SET scent
sheet
Skeat
skeet
sleet
slept
smelt
spelt
spent
stent
sweat
sweet
swept
SEY seedy
seepy
stewy
SFA Sofia
SFN Safin
SFR so far
SFS Sufis
SFY softy
SGA sigla
sigma
SGE Segrè
segue
SGN Sagan
SGR sugar□
SGS segos
signs
SGT sight
SOGAT
SGY saggy
soggy
SHA schwa
SHB sahib
SIA saiga
shiva□
spica□
Suita
SIB stilb
SIE seine□
seize
shine
shire□
skite
skive
slice
slide
slime
slive
Smike
smile
smite
snide
snipe
spice
spike
spile
spine
spire
spite
stile
stipe
stive
suite
swine
swipe
SIF skiff
sniff
stiff
SIG sling
sting
swing
SIH saith
Shiah
slish
smith□
stich
swish
SII sci-fi
SIK shirk
skink
slick
slink
smirk
snick
spick
stick
stink
SIL shiel
shill
skill
skirl
spiel
spill
still
swill
swirl
SIM seism
SIN scion
SIO Sligo
SIP skimp
SIR shirr
skier
skirr
SIS Sails
shies
ships
skies
skios
snips
spies
sties
Swiss
swits
SIT saint
shift
shirt
skint
skirt
snift
spilt
spirt
stilt
stint
swift□
SIY shily
shiny
slily
slimy
spicy
spiky
spiny
SIZ spitz□
SJU sajou
SKE Sukie
SKI Sakai
Sakti
SKR saker
SKS Sikes
SLA salsa
Sella
selva
sol-fa
Sulla
SLC Salic
SLD salad
solid
SLE salve
solve
SLH sylph
SLI salmi
soldi
Solti
sulci
SLM Salam
Salem
Selim
SLN salon
Solon
SLO salto
salvo
SLP shlep
SLR solar
SLS salts
Seles
selfs
sells
Silas
silos
soles
solos
sulks
SLT splat
split□
SLW Solow
SLX silex
SLY sally□
salty
silky
silly
Solly
splay
sulky
sully□
SMA samba
Samoa
SMC sumac
SME Somme
SMN semen
Simon
SMO sambo
SMP sum up
SMS Samos
somas
sumos
SMT Samit
SMU samfu
SMY samey
Sammy
SNA senna□
sensa
senza
Sonia
Sonya
Sunna
Sun Ra
SNC sonic
SND synod
SNE sense
since
singe
sonde
Synge
SNF son of
SNH synch
synth
SNI Sunni
SNL Sunil
SNM S and M
SNP sun-up
SNR Señor
sonar
SNS sands□
sinus
SNW sinew
SNY sandy□
Sindy
Sindy®
sonny
sonsy
sunny
SOA Shona
stoma
SOC stoic
SOD scold
snood
stood
sword
SOE scone
scope
score
shone
shore
shove
slope□
smoke

smore
snoke
snore
spode❑
spoke
spore
stoae
stoke
stole
stone❑
stope
store
stove
Stowe
SOF scoff
spoof
SOH slosh
sloth❑
sooth
SOI shogi
shoji
stoai
SOK shock
shook
smock
snoek
snook
snowk
spook
stock
stonk
stook
stork
SOL scowl
Seoul
shoal
shool
skoal
snool
spoil
spool
stool
SOM sloom
spoom
storm
SON scorn
shorn
shown
spoon
swoon
sworn
SOP scoop❑
scoup
scowp
sloop
snoop
stoep
stomp
stoop
stoup
swoop
SOR scour
smoor

spoor
SOS Scots
shoes
slops
spots
stoas
SOT scoot
Scott
scout
shoot
short❑
shout
smolt
smoot
snoot
snort
snout❑
sport
spout
stoat
stoit
stout
SOU shoyu
SOX Sioux
SOY showy
slopy
smoky
snowy❑
sooty
stony
story
SPA sepia
sopra
supra
SPD sapid
sepad
SPL sepal
SPR Sapir
sapor
Soper
sopor
super
SPY sappy
sepoy
Sophy
soppy
SRA stria
surra
Surya
Syria
SRB scrub
shrub
SRD sarod
shred
strad
SRE saree
sarge
scree
serge
serre
serve
spree
sprue

surge
SRF serif
SRG scrag
shrug
sprag
sprig
sprog
strig
SRH Sarah
surah
Syrah
SRL sural
SRM scram
scrim
scrum
serum
strum
SRN serin
siren❑
SRO Sarto
servo
SRP scrap
scrip
strap
strep
strip
strop
syrup
SRS saros
serfs
SERPS
Serps
sorus
SRT sprat
sprit
strut
Surat
SRW screw
shrew
shrow
straw❑
strew
SRY sarky
serry
sorry
spray
stray
surfy
surly
SSA Sasha
sessa
SSE Susie
SSI sushi
SSL sisal
SSN Susan
SSY sassy
sesey
sissy
STA Sitra
sutra
STD sated
STE Satie
setae

sithe
STM shtum
STN Satan
satin
set in
set on
sit in
sit-in
sit on
STO set to
set-to
STP set up
set-up
shtup
sit up
STR satyr
sitar
Soter
STS situs
STT sit at
STY satay
set by
sit by
SUA sauna
scuba
scuta
Shula
Sousa
sputa
stupa
SUB slubb
squab
squib
Stubb
SUD sound
squad
squid
SUE sauce
sauté
scuse
scute
shule
Shute
souce
souse
spume
stupe
SUF scuff
scurf
snuff
stuff
SUG stung
swung
SUH shush
slush
sough
south❑
SUI scudi
SUK shuck
skulk
skunk
spunk
stuck

SUL scull
skull
SUM stumm
SUN shuln
spurn
SUP slump
slurp
stump
SUS shuls
slugs
Smuts
Spurs
SUT shunt
souct
spurt
squat
squit
stunt
Sturt
SUW squaw
SUY saucy
saury
soupy
spumy
study
SVD saved
SVN savin
seven
Sivan
SVR saver
sever
SVY savey
savoy
savvy
SWD sawed
sewed
sowed
sownd
SWE sowse
SWF sowff
SWH sowth
SWN Suwon
SWP sew up
SWR sewer
SXD sexed
SXE sixte
SXH sixth
SXN Saxon
SXR sixer
SXY sixty
SYD sayid
SYE Sayle
skyre
skyte
slype
style
styme
styre
styte
SYI says I
styli
SYN seyen
spy on

SYO say no
say-so
SYR sayer
skyer
Soyer
SYS styes
SYY shyly
slyly
SZD sized
SZR sizer
TAA tiara
tra-la
TAE tease
thane❑
toaze
trace
trade
trape
TAG twang
TAH teach❑
trash
TAI tragi
TAK thank
track
traik
TAL trail
trawl
TAN train
Twain
TAP Tharp
tramp
TAS teals
tears
TAT toast
tract
trait
trant
TAY teary
toady
Tracy
TBA tabla
tibia
TBD tubed
TBE table❑
tubae
TBL tubal
TBN Tobin
TBO taboo
TBR tabor
Tiber
tuber
TBS tabes
tabus
tubas
TBT Tobit
TBY tabby
Tibby
tubby
TCE tache
TCS tacos
Ticos
tocos
TCT tacet

Words marked ❑ can also be spelled with an initial capital letter

tacit
TCY tacky
TDL tidal
TDR Tudor
TDS to-dos
TDY teddy□
today
toddy
TEA theca
Thera
theta
trefa
TED teend
they'd
tread
trend
tweed□
TEE theme
there
these
TEH teeth
TEK tweak
TEL t-cell
TEM therm
TEN tie in
tie-in
treen
TEP tee up
tie up
tie-up
twerp
TER their
tweer
TES teens
trees
tress
trews
TET theft
treat
Trent
tweet
TEU Taegu
TEY teeny
TFE tuffe
TFS toffs
TFY Taffy
tufty
TGD toga'd
TGN tigon
TGP tog up
TGR tiger
TGS Tagus
TGT tight
THE te-hee
THS tohos
TIA taiga
Thira
Trina
TID teind
third
triad
tried
TIE Taizé

toile
tribe
trice
trine
tripe
trite
twice
twine
twire
twite
TIF thief
TIG thing
TIH thigh
Trish
TIK thick
thilk
think□
trick
twink
TIL thirl
trial
trill
twill
twirl
TIO Taino
TIP twirp
TIR trier□
TIS trios
twins□
TIT taint
twist□
TIY Trixy
twiny
TKA tikka
TKL Tikal
TKN taken
token
TKO Tokyo
TKR taker
TKS tokos
TLA telia
Tulsa
TLD tiled
TLE telae
tilde
tulle
TLH tilth
TLN talon
TLP tulip
TLR tiler
tolar
Tyler
Tylor
TLS tales
talks
talus
TLT to let
TLX telex
TLY tally
telly
Tilly
TMA Tampa
Tomba

TMD tamed
timid
tumid
TME temse
TMI tempi
TMK Tomsk
TML Tamil
TMN Timon
TMO Tambo
tempo
TMR tamer
timer
Timor
Timur
TMS times
timps
tombs
TMT tempt
TMY tammy□
Timmy
tommy□
tummy
TNA tanga□
Tania
tanka
Tanya
tinea
Tonga
TNC tonic
tunic
TND tined
tuned
tyned
TNE tenge
tense
tinge
tonne
tynde
TNH tench
tenth
TNI tondi
TNL tonal
TNN tenon
TNO tango□
tanto
tondo
TNP ton-up
TNR tenor
tuner
TNS tents
tongs
Tonys
tunas
Tunis
TNT tenet
tinct
TNY tangy
tansy
tinny
tunny
TOA Thora
TOE thole
those

trope
TOG thong
TOH Thoth
tooth
troth
TOI tholi
TOL troll
TON thorn
Troon
TOP tromp
troop
two-up
TOS thous
tools
TOT troat
trout
TPC topic
TPD tepid
TPE tepee
topee
TPI tophi
topoi
TPK tupik
TPO typto
TPP top up
TPR taper
tapir
toper
TPS tapas
tapes
typos
TPY tipsy
Topsy
TPZ topaz
TQE toque
tuque
TRA Tarka
terga
Torga
TRB throb
TRC toric□
TRD tired
TRE targe
terce
terne
terse
three
throe
Tiree
torte
TRH Torah
torch
TRI tarsi
torii
Turki
TRM thrum
TRN Turin
TRO torso□
turbo
TRP thrip
TRQ Tariq
TRS taros
teras

terms
torus
turfs
TRT tarot
TRU Turku
TRW thraw
threw
throw
TRY tardy
tarry
tarty
terry□
turfy
TSA tesla□
TESSA
Tessa
testa
Tosca
TSE taste
Tysse
TSN Tyson
TSO Tasso
TSS tbsps
tests
TSY tasty
testy
tossy
tusky
TTA tetra
TTE tithe
title
tutee
TTH titch
TTI tutti
TTL total
TTM Tatum
totem
TTN titan□
TTP titup
tot up
TTR Tatar
tutor
TTS Titus
TTV Titov
TTY tatty
tutty
TUB thumb
TUE taupe
Thule
touse
touze
truce
TUH touch
tough
truth
TUK truck
trunk
TUO Truro
TUP thump
trump
TUS Tours
truss
TUT taunt

trust
TUY Trudy
truly
TVT Tevet
TWE tawse
towse
towze
TWL towel
TWR tawer
tower
TWT to wit
TWY tawny
towny
TXC toxic
TXD taxed
TXL Texel
TXN taxon
toxin
TXS taxes
taxis
Texas
TYE thyme
TYI thymi
TYN try on
try-on
TYR toyer
twyer
TYT tryst
TZE tazze
TZY tizzy
UAA UKAEA
Urawa
UAE ukase
urate
usage
UAM unarm
UAS Urals
UAT UCATT
unapt
UBA umbra
UBD unbed
UBE upbye
UBG unbag
UBK Uzbek
UBL umbel
UBN urban□
UBR umber
unbar
UBS umbos
UBX unbox
UCE uncle
UCP uncap
UCR ulcer
UCS uncos
UCT uncut
UDD undid
UDE undue
UDR udder
under
UDW USDAW
UEA ulema
UEC ureic
UED U-bend

Words marked □ can also be spelled with an initial capital letter

upend
up-end
UEH uneth
UEI uteri
UEL ureal
UEP use up
UES users
UET urent
UFR up for
UFT unfit
UFX unfix
UGD ungod
UGM ungum
UGR urger
UGT unget
UHH uh-huh
UHP unhip
UHR UNHCR
usher
UHT unhat
UIA UNITA
Utica
UIE unite
urine
utile
UIG using
UIK umiak
UIL urial
UIN union
UIO UNIDO
UIS units
UIT UMIST
Uniat
UWIST
UIY unify
unity❑
UJT upjet
ULD unlid
ULN uhlan
ULT unlit
ULY unlay
uplay
UML Uxmal
UMN unman
urman
UMT unmet
UMW unmew
UNE ulnae
UNR ulnar
UOT U-boat
UPN unpen
unpin
UPR upper
UPY unpay
URA UNRWA
URG unrig
URP unrip
USN Ulsan
USR Unser
UST unset
upset
USW unsew
USX unsex
USY unsay
UTA ultra
ultra-
UTE untie
uptie
UTL until
UTN untin
UTP up top
UTR utter
UTX untax
UUA uvula
UUE usure
UUL usual
UUN U-turn
UUP usurp
UUU uhuru
Uluru
UUY usury
UWD unwed
UWT unwit
UZP unzip
VAA Vaasa
VAC vraic
VBS vibes
VBX vibex
VCA vacua
VCB vocab
VCL vocal
VCR vicar
VCS voces
VDA Vedda
vodka
VDC Vedic
VDL Vidal
VDM Vadim
VDO video
VDR Vidar
VDS Vedas
VDY VE day
VDZ Vaduz
VGE vague
vegie
vogue❑
VGL vagal
vigil
Vogel
VGN vegan
VIA voila
voilà
VIE voice
voile
VIG vying
VII voici
VIN V-sign
VIY veily
veiny
VJY Vijay
VLA villa❑
Volga
Volta
vulva
VLD valid
VLE valse
value
valve
volae
volte
VLI villi
VLM velum
VLO Volvo®
vulgo
VLR velar
volar
VLT valet
veldt
VMR vomer
VMT vomit
VNA V and A
VND vaned
VNE Vance
venae
venge
venue
VNL venal
vinyl
VNM venom
VNS Venus
vinos
VNW vinew
VNY veney
VOA viola❑
VOM vroom
VPD vapid
VPR viper
VRA Varna
virga
VRC varec
VRD virid
VRE varve
verge
Verne
verse
verve
VRI Verdi
VRL viral
VRO verso
vireo
Virgo
VRS varus
vires
virus
VRU vertu
virtu
VRX varix
VSA vesta❑
vista
VSE visie
VSL vasal
VSR visor
VST visit
VTA vitta
VTC vatic
VTH vetch
VTL vital
VTR voter
VTS vitas
Vitus
VUH vouch
VUT vault
vaunt
VVD vivid
VVT vivat
VWL vowel
VXD vexed
VXN vixen❑
VZR vizor
WAD weald
WAE weave
whale❑
WAF wharf
WAG whang
WAH wrath
WAK whack
wrack
WAP whaup
WAY weary
WBR weber❑
WCO wacko
WCY wacky
WDE wedge
wodge
WDH width
WDN w iden
widen
Woden
WDR wader
WDW widow
WDY waddy
wedgy
widdy
WED wield
WEE where
WEK whelk
wreak
wreck
WEL wheel
WEP whelp
WES Weems
WET wheat
wrest
WEY weedy
weeny
weepy
WFR wafer
WGD waged
WGN wagon
Wigan
WGR wager
WGS wages
WGT Wight
WHN Wuhan
WHO wahoo
WID weird
WIE Waite
waive
while
whine
white❑
write
WIF whiff
WIG wring
WIH weigh
which
Which?
whish
WIK whisk
wrick
WIL Weill
whirl
WIP whisp
WIR whirr
WIS Waits
whiss
WIT waist
whist
wrist
WIY whiny
WIZ whizz
WKN waken
woken
WLA walla
Wilma
WLE Wilde
Wolfe
WLH Welch
welsh❑
WLO Waldo
wilco
WLR Waler
Wyler
WLS Wales
Wells
wilds
wiles
Wills
WLT welkt
WLY wally❑
welly
willy❑
WLZ waltz
WMN woman❑
women
WMY Wimpy
womby
WNA Wanda
wonga
WNE wince
winze
Wynne
WNH wench
winch
WNI wongi
WNN win on
WNS wings❑
winos
WNY waney
wanly
Wendy
windy
winey
wonky
WOD woold
WOE whole
whore
whose
wrote
WOF Woolf
WOG wrong
WOH woosh
wroth
WOL whorl
WOP whoop
WOR wooer
WOS woods❑
WOY woody
woozy
WPR wiper
WRD wired❑
world❑
WRE Warne
worse
WRH worth
WRR wirer
WRS -wards
wares
words
works
Worms
WRT worst
wurst
WRY warty
wordy
wormy
worry
WSE waste
WSM Wasim
WSR Weser
WSY washy
waspy
wispy
WTE withe
WTH watch
witch
WTN Wotan
WTR water
WTY wetly
withy
witty
WUD would
wound
WUH Waugh
WUK waulk
WVD waved
wived
WVR waver
WVS waves
wives
WWE wowee
WXD waxed
WXN waxen
WXP wax up
WYE Wayne
WYN way in
WYY wryly
WZN wizen

Words marked ❑ can also be spelled with an initial capital letter

WZR wazir
XAA xoana
XBC xebec
XLL xylol
XLM xylem
XNA xenia
XNN xenon
XOA Xhosa
XRC xeric
XRX xerox
Xerox®
XSI xyst i
XXS x-axis
YAN yearn
YAS years
Yeats
YAT yeast
YBO yobbo
YCA yucca
YCT yacht
YCY yucky
YDE yodle
YDL yodel
YED yield
YGC yogic
YGN yogin
YHO yahoo
YIK yoick
YKD yoked
YKL yokel
yokul
YKN Yukon
YKS yikes
YKT Yakut
YKY yukky
YLW Yalow
YMN Yemen
YMY yummy
YNE Yonge
YNS yonks
YPY yappy
yuppy
YRA yerba
Yerma
YRS Ypres
YSS yeses
YTS Yates
YUE you're
you've
YUG young❑
YUH youth
YUL you'll
YUS yours
YXS y-axis
ZBA zabra
zebra
ZBS zobos
ZHR Zohar
ZIE zaire❑
ZIS Zeiss
ZKT zakat
ZLA Zelda
ZLH zilch
ZMI zombi
ZNA zanja
zonda
ZNB zineb
ZNE zonae
ZNL zonal
ZNO zinco
ZNY zingy
ZOS zoons
ZOY zloty
ZPA Zappa
ZPP zap up
zip up
ZPY zappy
zippy
ZRA Zarqa
zirna
Zorba
zurna
ZRS zeros
zoris
ZSY zesty
ZTP ZZ Top
ZUE Zhu De
ZWE zowie
ZYN zayin

6 letters – odd

AAA Abadan
agapae
anabas
Arafat
ataman
avatar
AAD Amanda
AAE abased
agazed
Amabel
amazed
awaken
azalea
AAH Abacha
Agatha
Agatho
apache❑
apathy
AAI abatis
acacia
adagio
Agadir
agamid
agaric
Alaric
arabic❑
aralia
Aramis
ataxia
AAK Alaska
AAL anally
arable
AAN avaunt
AAO a fan of
amazon❑
Aragon
Avalon
AAS Agassi
araise
arayse
as also
AAT anatto
avanti
AAU abacus
Avarua
ABC abbacy
ABD Abbado
aubade
ABE Aubrey
ABI albeit
ABM albums
ABN Albany
albino
ABO Albion
ABR Albert
auburn
ABS abbess
ambush
at best
ABT Abbott
ABU arbour
ABY abbeys
ACC Adcock
Alcock
ACD accede
arcade
ACE Aachen
arched
archer❑
ACI Alcuin
Archie
archil
arctic❑
ACL archly
ACN accent
Ancona
arcana
arcane
ascend
ascent
ACO anchor
ACP accept
ACR accord
ancora
Arcaro
ACS access
accost
accuse
ACT accite
Alcott
ACU accrue
ACV alcove
ADB abdabs
ADC abduce
abduct
addict
adduce
adduct
ADE addled
Aideed
Andrea
Andrew
Audrey
ADH Amdahl
ADI aldrin❑
ADL aedile
and all
audile
ADN adding
add-ins
add-ons
aiding
ardent
ADO addios
and how
Andros
audios
ADS Aldiss
ADU ardour
ADW at dawn
AEA apeman
axeman
AEC agency
amerce
AED agenda
amends
AEE Alexei
apexes
AEG abeigh
avenge
aweigh
AEH Aretha
Ayesha
AEI acedia
acetic
alevin
alexia❑
Alexis
Amelia
anetic
Averil
AEL age-old
areola
AEN ageing
AEO awetos
AEP Aleppo
a tempo
AER afeard
Aveira
AES ageism
ageist
Alessi
at ease
averse
AET amenta
aneath
Avesta
AEU a leg up
avenue
AEY acetyl
aye-aye
AEZ Arezzo
AFA affray
AFC affect
AFE Alfred
AFI affair
au fait
AFN al fine
AFO as from
AFR affirm
afford
AGA Aegean
Afghan
AGE angled
angler
arguer
AGF argufy
AGL Angela
Angelo
Angola
argali
arguli
argyle
AGN angina
AGO Anglos
AGR Al Gore
angora❑
Asgard
augury
AGS august❑
AHA ashlar
ashram
AHB Achebe
AHD aphids
a shade
AHE ashler
Ashley
awheel
a wheen
AHH aphtha
AHL a while
AHM at home
at-home
AHN aching
at hand
Athene
Athens
a'thing
AHO Ashdod
Ashton
athrob
AHR adhere
ashore
a'where
AHS aghast
AIA animal
apical
AIB akimbo
AIC a cinch
a piece
apiece
AIE apices
Aviles
axises
AIH alight
anight
aright
AII acidic
Alicia
avidin
AIL acidly
afield
aridly
arilli
avidly
AIN Amiens
AIO a bit of
Alison
amigos
Asimov
avisos
AIR apiary
aviary
AIS ahimsa
amidst
ariosi
arioso
AIT arista
aviate
AIU acinus
adieus
adieux
animus
AJC abject
AJI adjoin
AJN Adjani
AJR abjure
adjure

Words marked ❑ can also be spelled with an initial capital letter

AJS adjust
AKC ack-ack
AKD aikido
AKE anklet
AKL alkali
Ankole
AKN aikona
alkane
alkene
alkyne
askant
AKO ask for
AKR Ankara
AKS arkose
ALA afloat
agleam
ALD allude
ALE Aileen
allied
allies
all set
asleep
ALG allege
anlage
ALI Aglaia
ALL allele
ALM aflame
aplomb
ALN ablins
ailing
all one
allons
aslant
ALO abloom
all for
ALP aslope
ALR allure
ALS ablush
at last
ALT ablate
ALU ablaut
all but
allium
all out
all-out
ALY Alleyn
alleys
ALZ ablaze
AMC as much
AMD armada
Armado
AME armies
armlet
AMF aim off
AMG Armagh
AMI armpit
AML Akmola
AMN almond
Armani
AMO aim for
AMR admire
Asmara
Aymara
AMS almost
at most
AMU armful
armour
ANA Aeneas
anneal
annual
ANB Annaba
ANC Annecy
arnica
ANE apnoea
Arnhem
ANI agnail
auntie❑
ANK Anneka
Annika
ANL annals
annuli
Arnold
ANN Anning
awning
ANO amnion
ANT agnate
ANX annexe
AOA amoral
anodal
anorak
apodal
atonal
avowal
azonal
AOB amoeba
AOC at once
a touch
avouch
AOD at odds
AOE Abomey
adored
adorer
apogee
apozem
avocet
avowed
avower
Azores
AOI Adonis
anodic
anomie
anoxia
anoxic
atocia
atomic
AOL apollo❑
AON abound
amount
anoint
aroint
around
aroynt
AOO agorot
a lot of
a pox of
a pox on
AOR aboard
AOS Alonso
arouse
AOT agouti
at outs
AOU Aeolus
AOY anonym
APA appeal
appear
APC alpaca
aspect
aspick
APE alpeen
apples
API au pair
APN alpine
append
APR ampere
Ampère
aspire
APS appose
AQI acquit
ARA abroad
Adrian
aerial
air bag
airbag
airman
airway
arrear
Arrian
atrial
ARB aerobe
ARC Africa
arrack
ARD abrade
ARE agreed
Auriel
ARF adrift
aurify
ARG abrégé
Auriga
ARI abraid
adroit
afraid
aortic
ARL airily
ARN afront
airing
arrant
ARO Auriol
ARP abrupt
ARR air-dry
aurora❑
Aurore
ARS across
afresh
aorist
arrest
at rest
at risk
ART aerate
amrita
ARU Aarhus
Airbus®
airgun
Atreus
atrium
aureus
aurous
ARV arrive
ARW acrawl
ASA Anshan
ASC Alsace
as such
ASE answer
Austen
ASG assign
ASI abseil
assail
assoil
Aussie
Austin
ASL Anselm
ASM assume
ASN absent
arsine
assent
ASR absorb
absurd
adsorb
assart
assert
assort
assure
ASS assess
assist
AST ansate
assets
ASU at stud
ASZ assize
ATA actual
Altman
a steal
astral
astray
at that
ATC antics
attach
attack
ATE aether
Althea
Anthea
anthem
anther
antler
as then
Attlee
ATI act big
Altaic
Antlia
Astrid
attain
ATL Attila
ATM asthma
autumn
ATN acting
Antony
attend
attent
attune
ATO act for
action
author
ATR actors
acture
afters
artery
astern
attire
attorn
ATS artist
attest
autism
ATT astute
ATU Actium
act out
antrum
Artaud
artful
Arthur
astrut
auteur
ATV active
AUA aoudad
AUE abused
abuser
acumen
amulet
amused
AUI abulia
Anubis
anuria
AUL Aquila
AUN alumna
alumni
Aquino
AUR Amun-Re
AUS aburst
avulse
AUT acuity
Aouita
AVC advice
AVN advent❑
AVR adverb
advert
AVS advise
AWE atweel
AWL as well
AWN An Wang
AWO Atwood
AWR aswarm
aswirl
at work
ayword
AWX atwixt
AWY always
AYA any day
anyway
AYL any old
AYN any one
anyone
AYO anyhow
AYU asylum
BAA bharal
braxas
BAB Bratby
BAC Bianca
blanch❑
Blanco
branch
BAD Blanda
boards
braide
Brando
Brandt
brandy
BAE Baader
beaded
beaked
beaker
beamer
bearer
beaten
beater
beaver
bhagee
biased
Blakey
blazer
blazes
boater
bracer
braces
brazen
BAI Baalim
beanie
beat it
Blasis
boatie
Brazil
BAK blanky
BAL beadle❑
beagle❑
brawly
BAM Brahma
Brahms
BAN Beaune
Braine
brains
brainy
branny
brawny
BAO beacon
Beamon
beanos
bear on
Beaton
blazon
Brasov
bravos
BAR braird

BAS Blaise
braise
brassy
Bratsk
BAT beasts
Beatty
beauty
bhakti
bratty
BAU bear up
beat up
beat-up
Braque
BBA bobcat
BBE babies
bibber
buboes
BBI bobbin
BBL babble
bobble
bobbly
bubble
bubbly
BBO baboon
Byblos
BCA Bichat
buccal
Buchan
BCE backer
Bechet
Becker
Becket
bicker
bucket
BCL Bacall
becall
becalm
buckle
BCM became
become
BCO back of
beckon
BCP biceps
BCR becurl
BCU back up
backup
back-up
Backus
Bochum
buck up
BDA bedlam
bedpan
BDC bedeck
beduck
bodice
BDE badger❑
bidder
bodies
budget
BDG bodega
BDH Buddha
BDI bedsit
bed-sit
bodkin
budgie
BDL bodily
buddle
BDN be done
bedung
BDO bedrop
BDS badass
bedash
bedust
BDU bedaub
bedbug
bed out
BDZ bedaze
BEA bye-law
BEC Bierce
bleach
blench
breach
breech
BED blende
Brenda
BEE Baeyer
beeper
beeves
Bremen
brewed
brewer❑
BEH Brecht
BEI Breuil
BEL beetle
Beetle®
BEN blenny
Boeing
brenne
BEO Beeton
Breton
BER bleary
BES be easy
breast
BET breath
BEU beef up
beer-up
brew up
BEY bye-bye
BEZ breeze
breezy
BFE buffer
buffet
BFI Baffin
boffin
BFL baffle
befall
BFO befool
Buffon
BFR before
BFU beflum
befoul
buff up
BGA beggar
begnaw
big cat
bogman
BGE bigger
bogies
bugged
bugger
bugler
BGF begift
BGI Baggio
bagnio
BAgric
beguin
biggie
big hit
bigwig
BGL begild
boggle
BGM bigamy
BGN begone
begunk
big end
bygone
BGO bags of
big pot
big top
BGR Bogart
bog-ore
BGT Bogotá
BGU bagful
big gun
BGY bogeys
BHA behead
BHL behalf
behold
by half
BHN behind
by hand
BHS behest
BHV behave
behove
BHW behowl
BIA Baikal
Bairam
bridal
BID bhindi
blinds
BIE bailer
bailey❑
beigel
blimey
Blixen
boiled
boiler
briber
BIF briefs
BIG bridge
Briggs
BIH blight
blithe
bright❑
BII be in it
blinis
Bridie
Brigid
Brigit
BIK brisky
BIL bridle
BIN Briony
BIO Briton
BIR briard
briars
briery
BIU Beirut
brigue
BJR Béjart
BJU bijoux
BJV by Jove
BKN baking
B B King
biking
bikini❑
BKR bakery
BKS bekiss
BLA balk at
ballad
balsam
Balzac
Belial
Bilbao
bullae
BLC belace
BLD bolide
BLE Balder
baleen
ballet
belief
belted
belter
bilker
billet
buller
bullet
BLG beluga
BLI Baltic
BLL baldly
boldly
BLN belong
byline
BLO balboa❑
ballon
ballot
ballow
Belloc
bellow❑
bilbos
billow
Bolton
BLR belfry
beltry
bolero❑
Boléro
BLT boleti
BLU ball up
belaud
belt up
bulbul
bulgur
BLX Biloxi
BLY billy-o
Boleyn
BLZ Belize
BMA bemean
bemoan
Bombay
bum bag
BMD be made
BME bombed
bomber
bummer
bumper
BMI bemoil
BMK Bamako
BML bumalo
bumble❑
bummle
BMO bamboo
bimbos
bombos
bumbos
BMP Bumppo
BMS bemuse
BMU bump up
BNA bandar
banian
banjax
bantam
banyan
banzai
Bengal
bin-bag
binman
bonsai
Bunyan
BNE banded
banger
banker
banned
banner
banter
bended
bender
Bennet
binder
bonnet
Bonney
bunker
Bunsen
Bunter
Buñuel
BNG benign
BNH Binchy
bunchy
BNI bandit
Benoît
Bonnie
bunyip
BNL bangle
bingle
bundle
bungle
BNM bename
benumb
byname
BNN banana
BNO bandog
bang on
Bangor
banjos
bank on
Benbow
bent on
Benton
bingos
Binyon
bonbon
bongos
bon mot
bon ton
buncos
bunion
bunkos
BNP Bengpu
BNR Bantry
binary
bon gré
BNS banish
BNT binate
BNU Bangui
bang up
Banjul
Banquo
Benaud
Ben-Hur
bind up
bone up
bung up
bunkum
BOA baobab
Bhopal
biogas
BOC blotch
broach
bronco
brooch
BOD blonde
bloody
broads
broody
BOE blokey
blower
booked
bootee
Boötes
boozer
broken
broker
BOG brolga
BOI bionic
biopic
biotic
biotin
blow in
blow it
B-movie

boogie
bookie
book in
Brodie
BOK Brooke
Brooks
BOL boodle
Bootle
brolly
BON Browne
browny
BOO Baotou
booboo
boo-boo
boohoo
boo-hoo
BOS biopsy
blouse
blowsy
browse
BOT blotto
Brontë
BOU blot up
blow up
Blow-Up
blow-up
brogue
buoy up
BOZ blowzy
bronze
bronzy
BPA by-play
BPE bopper
BPS bypass
BPT bypath
BRA bark at
barman
Birman
boreal
Boreas
bureau
burial
burlap
bursae
bursar
by road
byroad
BRC Baruch
borsch
BRE barbed
barbel
barber□
barbet
bargee
barker□
barley
Barnes
Barnet
barney□
barred
barrel
barren
barter
Berber
Bergen
Berger
berley
birder
Borden
border□
Bordet
Borges
Borneo
burden
burgee
burger
burhel
buried
burley
burned
burnet□
Burney
burrel
BRF bereft
BRG borage
BRH bertha□
BRI barbie□
Barbie®
bardic
Barkis
Barrie
Berlin
Bernie
Bertie
birdie
Borgia
born in
burn in
by rail
BRL barely
Barolo
birsle
burble
burgle
BRN barony
Bering
boring
BRO Bardot
barrow□
Bartók
baryon
borgos
borrow
borzoi
burbot
Burgos
burros
burrow
burton□
byroom
BRT barite
berate
borate
by rote
BRU barium
barque
burn up
BSA Bassae
Biscay
Bissau
Biswas
BSC basics
be sick
bisect
BSD beside
BSE basher
basket
basset
Bassey
baster
beseem
Bisset
bister
bossed
bosses
bushed
bushel
bushes
busker
busses
BSI Bessie
bestir
BSL basalt
basely
busily
bustle
BSM bosomy
BSN Besant
BSO bash on
bassos
bastos
bespot
Besson
bestow
bishop□
bisson
Boston
BSR besort
be sure
bistre
bistro
BSU basque□
besmut
bestud
bisque
bust up
bust-up
BTA bateau
batman
betray
Botham
BTD betide
BTE bather
battel
batten
batter
beteem
bethel
better
bitten
bitter
bother
bo tree
butler□
butter
by then
BTH bitchy
botchy
BTI betoil
betrim
bite in
Butlin
butt in
BTK betake
BTL battle
botfly
bottle
buttle
BTM Batumi
betime
BTN bating
biting
botany□
butane
BTO bathos
bettor
bottom□
but for
button
BTS betoss
BTU Butkus
BUA Bhutan
brumal
brutal
BUB Brumby
BUC bounce
bouncy
brunch
BUD bounds
BUE boules
Boulez
Bruges
Brunei
Brunel
BUG bludge
blunge
Brugge
BUH bought
BUI Baucis
be up in
bougie
BUL bauble
bluely
bouclé
boulle
BUO Bruton
BUR blurry
BUS bluesy
bluish
bourse
bruise
BUT Bhutto
bounty□
BUU Brutus
BVE bovver
BVN bovine
BVR Bovary
Boveri
BWA bewray
BWB Bowlby
BWE beweep
bowled
bowler
bowser
BWI bewail
bow-tie
BWL bowels
BWO bow-boy
BWR beware
bowery
byword
BWU bow out
BXE Bexley
BXN boxing
BXO Buxton
BYF buy off
BYN beyond
bryony□
buying
BYO Blyton
Boyson
Bryson
buy for
BYR buyers
BYS boyish
BYU boyaux
buy out
buyout
buy-out
BZA bazaar
BZE buzzer
BZN bezant
CAA chadar
chalan
cravat
CAB Crabbe
crabby
CAC chance
chancy
Clancy
clatch
cranch
CAD Claude
CAE chafed
chafer
chalet
Chanel
Chaney
chapel
chaser
claret
claver
claves
clayey
coaler
coated
Coates
coaxer
crases
crater□
craven
crazed
CAG change
Changi
charge
craggy
CAH cha-cha
CAI Chadic
Chasid
cram in
crania
cyanin
CAK chalky
charka
Clarke
Cranko
cranky
CAL cradle
CAM clammy
CAN chains
cranny
CAO chador
Charon
clap on
claros
Cracow
craton
crayon
CAP crappy
CAR chairs
chakra
Claire
CAS chaise
chassé
classy
clause
coarse
CAT chaste
chatty
coaita
crafty
crants
CAU chat up
clam up
claque
CBE Cibber
cobber
Cobden
cobweb□
CBI cabbie
cuboid
CBL cabala
cobalt
cobble
Cybele
CBR Coburn
CBS Cubism
Cubist

Words marked □ can also be spelled with an initial capital letter

CBU cobnut
CCD cicada
CCE cachet
cocker
CCI Cochin
cyclic
CCL cackle
Cecily
cicala
cicely□
cockle
CCO coccos
cocoon
cuckoo
cyclos
CCR Cicero
CCU cactus
coccus
cock up
cock-up
CCY coccyx
CDE cadger
codger
cudgel
CDF codify
CDI caddie
caddis
Cedric
CDL coddle
cuddle
cuddly
CDN cadent
ceding
CDU Cadmus
CEA caecal
caesar□
chelae
coeval
credal
CEC clench
coerce
CEE clever
crenel
crewel
cyeses
CEG clergy
CEH crèche
CEI chemic
Cherie
chesil
cleric
credit
cretin
CEK checks
cheeky
creaky
CEL creole□
CEM creamy
CEO coelom
credos
CEP cheapo
creeps
creepy
CER cheers
cheery
cherry□
CES cheese
cheesy
Cleese
crease
creasy
creese
creesh
CET chesty
create
CEU caecum
cheque
cherub
chew up
clew up
CEV cleave
CFA caftan
CFE coffee
coffer
CFI coffin
CGA Coggan
cognac
CGE Cagney
cygnet
CGI cage in
CGL cagily
coggle
coggly
CGN cogent
CGU Cygnus
CHE cohoes
CHI co-heir
CHN cohune
CHR cohere
cohort
CHS co-host
CIA caiman
Chirac
climax
cnidae
coital
crinal
CIC chiack
clinch
CIE chider
chisel
chives
coiled
coiner
crikey
cripes
crises
cuiter
CIG clingy
cringe
CIH chichi
cliché
CII chip in
chitin
clinic
coin it
crisis
critic
CIK chicks
chinks
cricky
CIL chicly
chilli
chilly
CIN Cairns
client
CIO chigoe
Chilon
chinos
Chiron
CIP chippy
chirpy
Cripps
crispy
CIR chirre
CIS crissa
CIT chintz
chitty
CIU caique
chin up
clique
coitus
crinum
CIV chivvy
CJI cojoin
CJL cajole
CKN caking
CLA Callao
Callas
cellae
cellar
collar
CLB call by
colobi
CLC calico
CLE calces
Calder
called
caller
callet
calver
calves
calxes
Culdee
CLF calefy
CLG colugo
CLI Calais
callid
Callil
call in
Calvin
Celtic
collie
Culkin
cultic
CLL calmly
coldly
CLM calami
column
CLN Celina
colons
colony
CLO call on
callow
cellos
CLP caliph
CLR celery
CLU Callum
call up
call-up
callus
calque
Celsus
cilium
coleus
colour
CLY Colwyn
CMA combat
come at
cymbal
CMB come by
CMD comedo
comedy
CME camber
Camden
camper
comber
compel
cumber
CMI cambia
come in
comfit
commie
commis
commit
commix
cummin
Cymric
CML camply
comely
comply
cumuli
CMN cement
coming
Comino
CMO cameos
camp on
Campos
combos
come of
come on
come-on
common
commos
compos
CMR camera
comart
CMS camash
camass
cymose
CMT came to
come to
comity
CMU campus
come up
CNA cancan
can-can
Cannae
canvas
confab
con man
Conrad
Conran
CND Canada
CNE cancel
cancer□
canker
canned
Cannes
canter
censer
cinder
confer
conger
conjee
conker
convex
convey
CNH canthi
concha
conche
conchs
conchy
CNI candid
confit
confix
Connie
CNL candle
cangle
cantle
CNM cinema
CNN canine
caning
CNO cannon□
cannot
canton□
cantor
cantos
canyon
censor
centos
condom
condor
Connor
con-rod
contos
convoy
CNP canapé
canopy
CNR canard
canary
centra
centre
contra
Cunard
CNT Canute
CNU cantus
census
concur
consul
CNV Canova
COA chop at
choral
clonal
COB coombe
Crosby
COC choice
cloaca
crotch
crouch
COD cloudy
crowds
COE choked
choker
choler
chorea
chosen
cloned
closed
closet
Cloten
cloven
clover
cloves
cooked
cooker
cooler
cooper□
COG chough
cloggy
Clough
COH cloche
clothe
cloths
COI chop in
Chopin
choria
Clovis
cookie
cool it
Cronin
COJ Chonju
COK croaky
COL clodly
coolly
COO chokos
COP choppy
croupy
COS choose
choosy
chouse
crosse
crouse
COT clouts
COU chop up
chorus
clog up
cook up

coop up
crocus
Cronus
crop up
CPC copeck
CPE cipher
copied
copier
copper
cupped
cypher
CPI Coptic
cupric
CPL copula
cupola
CPN Capone
coping
CPO captor
CPR capers
CPT capita
Capote
CPU cippus
cop out
cop-out
copy up
cupful
Cyprus
CQE coquet
CRA carnal
Carnap
carpal
cercal
cereal
Corday
Corman
corral
CRC caract
curacy
CRE career
caries
Carmel
Carmen
carney
carpel
carper
carpet
carrel□
cartel
Carter
carvel
carver□
cermet
corbel
corded
corked
corker
cornea
corned
corner
cornet
corset
Cortes
Cortés

cortex
corves
curbed
curfew
curled
curler
curlew
cursed
curved
curvet
CRF carafe
CRI Cardin
Carrie
cervix
corbie
corkir
corrie
Curtis
CRL Carola
Carole
caroli
circle
curdle
curtly
CRM chrome
corymb
CRN caring
corona
curing
Cyrene
CRO carbon
carboy
care of
carlot
Carlow
carrot
Carson
carton
cordon
corsos
curios
cursor
Curzon
CRR curare
CRS caress
Caruso
cerise
chrism
Christ
corpse
curtsy
CRT curate
CRU carpus
cerium
circus
cirque
cirrus
corium
cornua
corpus
Corvus
curium
curl up

CRZ corozo
CSA casbah□
Caspar
Cassat
casual
Cosmas
costae
costal
co-star
cushat
CSE cashew
casket
casted
caster
cosher
cosier
cosset
coster
cussed
Custer
CSI casein
cash in
Cassie
Cassio
cassis
Cissie
cosmic
cystic
CSL Casals
castle□
cosily
costly
CSN casing
casino
cosine
CSO cascos
Casson
cast on
castor□
ciscos
cosmos
C P Snow
custom
CSR casern
Castro
cesura
CSU cash up
cast up
cestus
cosy up
cuscus
CTA catnap
cottar
CTE Cather
cither
cities
cotter
cutler
cutlet
cutter
CTF citify
cityfy
cut off

cut-off
CTH catchy
CTI catkin
catnip
citric
citrin
cytoid
CTL cattle
cutely
CTN cetane
CTO cation
citron
cotton
CTS cotise
cytisi
CTU catgut
citrus
cut out
cut-out
CUA caudal
causal
cougar
crural
CUB chubby
crumbs
crumby
CUC church□
clutch
crunch
crutch
CUD Cluedo®
cruddy
CUE caules
cautel
cauves
cruces
cruxes
CUF Cruyff
CUH caught
CUI clue in
coulis
cousin
CUK chukka
chunky
clunky
CUL caudle
couple
CUM chummy
crummy
CUO coupon
Crusoe
CUP clumpy
CUS clumsy
course
cruise□
CUT county
courts
crusts
crusty
CUU caucus
clue up
CVA caveat
caviar

CVC civics
CVE Cuvier
CVI cave in
cave-in
CVL Cavell
CVN caving
coving
CVR cavern
cavort
covary
covers
covert
CVT cavity
CWA cowman
cowpat
CWE Cawley
cowpea
Cowper
CWI cowrie
CWO cowboy
cowpox
CWR coward□
CYA cayman
CYC chyack
CYF cry off
CYG Cayuga
CYN crying
CYO Ceylon
CYT coyote
CYU cry out
CZE cozier
CZR cizers
DAB drag by
DAE deaden
deafen
dealer
diadem
diaper
dragée
Drake's
draper
drawer
DAF dwarfs
DAH drachm
DAI deal in
deasil
diacid
draw in
DAL deadly
deafly
dearly
doable
drably
dually
DAM dear me
dharma
DAN Deanna
Deanne
Dianne
draunt
DAO deacon□
dead on
dead-on

diatom
diazos
drag on
dragon□
Dralon®
draw on
DAT dearth
DAU drag up
draw up
DBE Debreu
debted
debtee
dibber
dobber
dubbed
Dubcek
DBI Debbie
debris
débris
dobbin
dubbin
Dublin
Du Bois
DBL dabble
dibble
DBN De Bono
debunk
DBO debtor
Dobson
DBR debark
do bird
DBS debase
deboss
DBT debate
DBU de-blur
dybbuk
DCA Deccan
Declan
DCC decoct
DCD decade
decide
decode
DCE dacker
decked
decree
Dicken
dicker
dickey
docket
DCF decaff
DCI dacoit
deceit
dickie□
DCK decoke
DCL deckle
docile
DCM decamp
DCN decane
decant
decent
DCO Dacron®
deckos
Dickon

Words marked □ can also be spelled with an initial capital letter

doctor
DCP da capo
DCR decarb
decern
DCU dictum
DCY dactyl
DDC deduce
deduct
DDE dadoes
didder
didoes
dodder
dodger
dodoes
dudeen
Dudley
DDL daddle
diddle
doddle
DDM Dodoma
DDO DVD-ROM
DDU dude up
DDW do down
DEA deejay
dee-jay
DEC drench
DEE Deedes
deepen
diesel□
dieses
dieter
DEF die off
DEG dredge
DEI diesis
DEL deeply
DEM dreamt
dreamy
DEN duenna
DEO daemon
die for
DEP Dieppe
DER dreary
DES dressy
DET Dnestr
duetti
duetts
DEU die out
DFA defeat
defrag
defray
DFC deface
defect
DFD Dafydd
DFE defier
deflex
differ
duffel
duffer
DFI daftie
DFL daftly
defile
deftly
duffle
DFM defame
DFN defend
define
DFO daft on
DFR deform
DFS defuse
DGB dagoba
DGE dagger
degree
digger
dogged
dogger□
dog-leg
DGI Duggie
DGL daggle
DGN dog end
dog-end
dugong
DGO dig for
DGS digest
DGU dig out
dugout
DHI dahlia
DHR dehorn
dehort
DIE daiker
de-icer
drivel
driven
driver
duiker
DIG doings
DII deific
DIK drinks
DIL daidle
DIN djinni
DIO daimon
DIR Deidre
DIT dainty
DJC deject
DJR de jure
DJV déjà vu
DKA diktat
DKE Dekker
DKI dakoit
dik-dik
DKO dekkos
DKT Dakota
DLA Dalian
Dallas
dollar
dolmas
DLD delude
DLE delves
dolmen
dulcet
dulled
Dulles
DLG deluge
DLH delphs
DLI Dulcie
DLO dalton□
Delroy
Dillon
dollop
DLP delope
DLS dalasi
DLT daleth
delate
delete
dilate
dilute
Duluth
DLU Delius
doll up
dolour
DLX de luxe
deluxe
de-luxe
DMA Damian
Dammam
demean
DMD démodé
DME Damien
damned□
dampen
damper
damsel
demies
dimmer
Dombey
dumped
dumper
DMG damage
DMI dammit
dimwit
domain
DML damply
dimple
dumbly
DMN demand
dement
domino□
DMO damson
dump on
DMR demark
demure
DMS damask
demise
demist
dumose
DMT demote
dimity
DMU dim out
dim-out
dim sum
dumdum
dumous
DNA Danaan
denial
dental
Dunbar
Duncan
DNB Danube
DND denude
DNE dancer□
dander
danger
Daniel
denier
dented
Denver
dinges
dinner
donder
donkey
Donner
donnés
Dundee
DNH dinghy
DNI Danzig
Dennis
dentil
dentin
Denzil
done in
Donnie
dunlin
DNL dandle
dangle
dingle
dinnle
Donald
DNM denims
dynamo
DNN doning
DNO danios
Danton
dine on
donjon
Dunlop
DNR denary
De Niro
DNS Danish
Denise
dynast
DNT denote
donate
Dönitz
DNU dengue
dinkum
done up
DNV de novo
DOA deodar
doodah
Dvorák
DOB drop by
DOE doomed
do over
drover
droves
DOG drongo
DOI dioxin
Dromio
drop in
drop-in
DOL doodle
drolly
DON Dionne
DOO doo-wop
dromoi
drop on
duomos
DOP droopy□
DOS dropsy
drossy
drowse
drowsy
DOT dhooti
drouth
DOU drogue
DPC depict
DPE dapper
dipper
duplex
DPH depths
DPL dapple
dipole
DPN daphne□
depend
depone
doping
duping
Du Pont
DPO deploy
dipsos
DPR depart
deport
DPS depose
DPT depute
deputy
DQN Daqing
DRA dermal
dirham
dorsal
Durban
Durham
DRC direct
DRD deride
dirndl
dorado
DRE Darién
darken
darned
darnel
darner
Darren
darter
Doreen
dormer
Dorset
Dorsey
Durres
DRI Darwin
derail
Derain
dermic
dermis
derris
dormie
Dorrit
DRL darkle
darkly
dernly
Dervla
dor-fly
DRN daring
during
DRO Darrow
Dermot
DRS dorise
duress
DRT derate
DRU Darius
dorsum
DRV derive
DRY darcys
DRZ dorize
DSA disbar
dismal
disman
dismay
distal
dossal
DSC De Sica
DSE dashed
Dasher
des res
dished
dishes
Disney
dispel
dossel
dosser
dusken
duster
DSG design
dosage
DSI dassie
desmid
distil
Dustin
DSL desalt
duskly
DSO despot
discos
DSR descry
desert
desire
desorb
disarm
DSS desist
disuse
DSU disbud
discus
dish up
dust-up
DSW disown
DTC detach
detect
DTE dither
dotted
duties
DTG dotage

DTI detail
detain
Dottie
DTM do time
DTN dating
Datong
detune
dotant
doting
DTO de trop
dittos
dote on
DTR datura
dotard
DTS detest
DTU detour
DTV dative
DUA Dougal
DUE dauber
dauner
deuced
doused
DUG drudge
druggy
DUH douche
doughy
DUL Douala
double
double-
doubly
dourly
DUU drum up
DVC device
DVD divide
DVE Davies
devvel
DVI devoid
DVL devall
Divali
DVN Davina
divine
diving
DVO dive on
DVR divers
divert
DVS devest
devise
divest
dovish
DVT DeVito
devote
duvets
DVU devour
devout
DWA dewlap
DWE dawner
downer
dowser
DWL dawdle
dewily
Diwali
do well
Dowell
DWO dawn on
Dawson
DWR dawbry
DWT dewitt
do with
DXE dexter□
DYC dry ice
DYD Dryads
DYE day bed
daybed
Dryden
DYF day off
DYL dayglo
day-old
dry-fly
DYN day one
drying
DYO day-boy
Dayton
DYU day out
dry out
dry run
DZL dazzle
DZN dozens
dozing
EAC elance
enarch
eparch
EAE elated
E-layer
enamel
eraser
evader
EAI Elaeis
EAL enable
EAN Elaine
Evadne
EAO etalon
EAS elapse
EAT écarté
EBD embody
EBE emblem
Euboea
EBL embale
emball
embalm
EBN ebbing
embank
Eubank
EBO en bloc
EBR Edberg
Egbert
embark
embers
EBS embase
emboss
EBU embrue
erbium
EBY embryo
ECD encode
escudo
ECE Escher
eschew
etcher
exceed
ECG encage
ECI EBCDIC
Euclid
ECM encamp
excamb
ECN Eocene
ECO escrow
ECP escape
except
ECR encore
escarp
escort
Escort®
euchre
ECS encase
encash
encyst
excess
excise
excuse
ECT excite
ECV encave
EDA endear
Esdras
EDL eidola
EDN ending
EDR Eddery
endart
Enders
endure
EDS eldest
EDV endive
EEA enemas
even as
EEE eleven
Exeter
eyelet
EEG emerge
energy
EEI Edenic
emesis
emetic
eremic
even if
Eyetie
EEL evenly
EEN exeunt
EEO ere now
erenow
even on
EEP exempt
EES even so
ever so
EET egesta
events
EEU eke out
even up
eyeful
EEY Evelyn
EFC efface
effect
enface
EFE Eiffel
enfree
EFG effigy
EFL enfold
EFR effort
EFS effuse
elfish
EFT effete
en fête
EFU efflux
EGE Eagles
eaglet
EGG engage
engagé
EGL Engels
engild
engulf
EGN edging
engine
Eugene
EGO eggnog
engaol
EGR engird
engore
EGT eighth
eighty
EGU eggcup
englut
EGZ El Giza
EHB ephebi
EHC ethics
EHE echoes
EHI echoic
ethnic
EHL enhalo
exhale
EHM exhume
EHN ethane
ethene
ethyne
EHR Erhard
exhort
EIA Elijah
EIC evince
EID Eliade
EIE exiled
EIH Elisha
EII elicit
elixir
Emilia
EIL edible
enisle
evilly
EIM enigma
EIO Edison
editor
Elinor
epizoa
EIR émigré
EIY Erinys
EJI enjoin
EJM enjamb
EKC Ed Koch
EKM Eskimo
EKR Eckert
ELC enlace
enlock
ELE Eileen
ELG eulogy
ELI éclair
ELN Ealing
enlink
ELR enlard
ELS eclose
enlist
ELT eolith
EME Emmies
EMN Eamonn
Edmund
Egmont
ermine
EMO Exmoor
EMS emmesh
enmesh
EMT enmity
ENC Eunice
eunuch
ENN El Niño
ENS eonism
Ernest
ENU Ennius
ENY ennuyé
EOE eloper
enoses
epopee
eposes
eroded
Exocet®
EOG enough
EOI enosis
erotic
exotic
EON Evonne
EOS egoism
egoist
Eloisa
Eloise
EOU econut
exodus□
EOV evolve
EOY eponym
EPC expect
EPG expugn
EPI esprit
EPL empale
EPN expand
expend
EPO EEPROM
employ
Empson
emptor
EPR empire□
expert
expire
expiry
export
EPS El Paso
expose
exposé
ERB enrobe
ERC Edrich
enrich
ERE earned
earner
ERG enrage
ERH Eartha
earthy
ERI earwig
ERK eureka
ERL eerily
ERM Euro-MP
ERN enring
errand
errant
erring
ERO earcon
enroot
ERP enrapt
Europa
Europe
ERS egress
ERT errata
ERU earful
Evreux
ESA enseam
ensear
ESC exsect
ESE eassel
Easter
Elspet
Eusden
ESG ensign
ESI ease in
eassil
ESL easily
ensile
ESN easing
Essene
ESR ensure
exsert
EST ersatz
ESU ease up
ensoul
ETA entrap
estray
extras
ETC entice
ETE either
entrée
esteem
Esther
ETF eat off
ETI entail
entoil
ETL eathly
ETM entame
entomb

ETN eating
extant
extend
extent
ETO EFTPOS
ETP ectopy
ETR eatery
entera
entire
extort
ETS eftest
ETT entêté
entity
estate
ETU eat out
EUE Études
EUL ekuele
EUN eluant
eluent
equine
EUP équipe
EUR Eluard
EUS evulse
EUT eluate
equate
equity
EVR Elvira
EVS elvish
EWA enwrap
EWL enwall
EWM enwomb
EWN Edwina
enwind
EWR Edward
EYE emydes
EYO etymon
EYR Eeyore
elytra
EZM eczema
enzyme
EZN enzone
FAA fracas
FAB flabby
flambé
FAC fiancé
fiasco
France
Franck
Franco
FAE feared
flames
flared
flares
flawed
flaxen
flayer
F-layer
framer
Fraser
frater
frayed
Frazer
FAG flange
FAH flashy
FAI Flavia
flavin
frazil
FAL featly
flatly
FAN flaunt
fraena
FAO flacon
flagon
FAP flappy
frappé
FAR fiacre
FAS fraise
FAT fealty
FAU flatus
FBA Fabian
FBE fabled
fabler
fables
fibber
fibred
FBF fob off
fub off
FBI fabric
fibril
fibrin
FBL fibula
FBO fibros
FBU Fabius
FCA facial
FCD facade
façade□
FCE facies
FCI fucoid
FCL facile
fickle
fo'c'sle
FCN facing
fecund
FCO factor
FCT Fichte
FCU fuck up
FDE fidget
fodder
FDI fade in
fade-in
FDL faddle
fiddle
fiddly
fuddle
FDN fading
fi donc!
FDR fedora□
FDU fade up
FEA faecal
foetal
FEC fierce
fleece
fleech
fleecy
flench
fletch
French
fresco
FED fields□
Freddy
FEE faeces
feeder
feeler
flewed
FEG fledge
FEH flèche
fleshy
FEI feed in
foetid
FEJ Freyja
FEK freaky
FEL feeble
feebly
freely
FEN Fresno
Freund
FEO feed on
flexor
fueros
FER Frears
FES flense
FET fiesta
Fiesta®
FEU feed up
foetus
frenum
FEZ freeze
frenzy
FFI Fafnir
FGE fagged
fogies
Fugger
FGN fag end
fag-end
Figini
FGO faggot
FGR figure
FGT fugato
FGU fag out
FGY fogeys
FHE Führer
FIA Faisal
Friday
FIC flinch
flitch
Frisch
FID Frieda
FIE failed
foiled
FIG fridge
fringe
fringy
FIH flight
fricht
fright
FII fail in
frigid
FIK flicks
frisky
FIL fainly
fairly
foible
frills
frilly
FIN friend
FIO frijol
frivol
FIR friary
FIS flimsy
FIT feisty
flinty
flirty
FIZ frieze
frizzy
FKE Fokker
FKN faking
Fokine
FLA fallal
fellah
filial
foliar
fulmar
FLD Faludi
FLE falces
fallen
falter
feller
filled
filler
fillet
filter
folded
folder
Fuller
FLH filthy
FLI fall in
fill in
fill-in
fillip
filmic
fold in
folkie
fulfil
fulvid
FLL fa la la
FLN feline
felony
filing
FLO falcon
fall on
Fallon
fallow
fellow
folios
follow
full of
fylfot
FLR fulcra
FLS folksy
FLT fall to
folate
FLU fill up
fold up
full up
FML family
female
fumble
FMN famine
foment
fuming
FMR femora
femurs
FMS famish
FMU famous
fumous
FNA Fenian
fenman
Finbar
Fingal
finial
Finlay
finnan
Fintan
fontal
fungal
FNE fanged
fan-jet
fencer
fender□
fennec
fennel
finder
finger□
Finley
finned
Finney
funded
funder
funnel
FNI Fangio
FNL fankle
finale
finely
fondle
fondly
FNO fangos
fanion
fink on
fond of
FNR finery
FNS finest
finish
FNT finite
FNU fan out
fondue
fundus
fungus
fun run
FOA florae
floral
floras
FOC flocci
FOD floods
FOE Flores
floret
flotel
flower
footed
footer
frozen
FOG froggy□
FOH frothy
FOI florid
florin
foodie
footie
foot it
frolic
FOK flocks
FOL footle
foozle
FOP floppy
FOR floury
footra
FOS flossy
flouse
floush
frowst
frowsy
FOT floats
floaty
frosty
FOZ floozy
frowzy
FPL fipple
FRA ferial
Fermat
fire at
firman
formal
Forman
format
forrad
furcal
FRE farmed
farmer
Faroes
ferret
Forbes
forced
forcer
forces
forfex
forged
forger
forget
forked
forker
formed
former
fortes
Furies
FRF far-off
FRG forage
forego
FRI ferric
fervid
firkin

forbid
formic
forrit
fortis
FRL ferule
firmly
for all
FRM forums
FRN far end
farina
ferine
firing
forint
for one
FRO farrow❑
fire on
forgot
forhow
for now
furrow
FRR far cry
furore
FRS forest
FRT ferity
FRU Farouk
far out
far-out
Fergus
fire up
firm up
for fun
fork up
fureur
furfur
FRY for aye
forbye
FSA festal
fiscal
fossae
FSE fasces
fasten
fester
fisher❑
Fishes
foster❑
fusser
FSI fascia
fisgig
fossil
fustic
FSL fissle
Fuseli
FSN fusing
FSO fossor
fusion
FSU fescue
fish up
Fushun
FTA fat cat
fatwah
FTE fat hen
father❑
fatten

fetter
fitted
fitter
fother
FTI fatsia
FTL fettle
futile
FTM Fatima
FTO fathom
fatsos
FTR future
FTS fetish
FTU fitful
fit out
FUA faunae
faunal
faunas
feudal
frugal
FUE fauces
faucet
flukey
fluted
fouter
FUF fluffy
FUH fought
FUK Faulks
flunky
FUL foully
FUN fluent
FUP frumpy
FUR flurry
foutra
FUT faulty
fourth
fousty
fruits
fruity
frusta
FUU Faunus
foul up
foul-up
FVA foveae
foveal
FVL favela
FVU favour
FWE Fawkes
fawner
fowler❑
Fowles
FWO fawn on
FWS fewest
FXA fox-bat
FXN fixing
foxing
FXR fixure
FXT fixate
fixity
FYA Faysal
flyway
FYN flying
fu yung
FYS fly ash

FYU fly out
FZE fezzes
fizzer
FZI fizgig
FZL fizzle
fuzzle
FZO Fuzhou
GAA gnaw at
go away
grab at
Graham
GAB grabby
GAC glance
GAE Glaser
glazed
goaded
goatee
graced
grader
grater
gravel
graven
graver
graves❑
grazed
grazer
GAG grange❑
GAI glacis
goalie
Gracie
gratin
gratis
gravid
GAL gladly
gnarly
GAM Graeme
gramme
Grammy
GAN grains
grainy
granny
GAO glad of
Glagol
go AWOL
guacos
guanos
GAP grappa
GAR glaury
go awry
GAS Gdansk
glassy
grassy
GAT graith
Granta
Granth
GAU gear up
GAY Gladys
GBC go back
GBE gabber
gabled
gibber
gibbet
gobbet

goblet
goboes
GBI go bail
goblin
GBL gabble
gobble
GBN gibing
go bang
Gobind
GBO gibbon❑
Gibson
GBR gabbro
GBS go bush
go bust
GCL go cold
GCO geckos
GCR go-cart
GDA giddap
goddam
GDE gadget
Godden
GDI gadoid
geddit
Godwin
godwit
GDL gadfly
guddle
GDO gadsos
Gideon
godson
GDR Godard
GDU giddup
Gudrun
GDW go down
godown
GEA gherao
GEC Greece
GED Glenda
greedy
Gwenda
GEE gee-gee
geezer
gleyed
GEG gledge
greige
GEH Goethe
GEI Gaelic
GEL greyly
GEN Greene
greens
greeny
GEO gregos
guenon
GEP Guelph
GES gneiss
go easy
grease❑
greasy
GET ghetto
guests
GEV greave
GEY Glenys
GFA guffaw

GFE gaffer
gifted
goffer
GFS go fast
GGI giggit
GGL gaggle
giggle
giggly
gigolo
goggle
guggle
GHI Gehrig
GHM go home
GHN go hang
GHR go hard
GIA Gaidar
guitar
GIC glitch
GIE gaiter
Geiger
glider
Goidel
grices
grivet
guinea❑
guiser
GIF griffe
GIH geisha
GII gaijin
GIK Glinka
GIL gainly
glibly
grille
grimly
grisly
GIM glioma
GIO gain on
guiros
GIR goitre
GIS gainst
grilse
GIT gaiety
go in to
go into
gritty
guilty
GIV grieve
GIZ glitzy
GJA Gujrat
GKR go-kart
GLA Galway
Gilman
golias
gollar
GLE galled
gallet
galley
gilded
gilder
gillet
golden
golfer
gulden

gullet
gulley
GLG galago
GLI Gallic
Galois
gillie
Goldie
Gullit
GLN galena
GLO Galdós
galiot
gallon
gallop
gallow
galoot
Galton
gollop
GLR galore
GLS galosh
golosh
GLT gelati
GLU Gallup
gallus
GLV go live
GLX galaxy
GMA gemmae
GME gemmen
gimlet
gummed
Gummer
GMI gambir
gambit
GML gamble
gamely
GMN gamine
gaming
Gemini
geminy
GMO gambol
gammon
gimmor
gumbos
GMR Gemara
GMT gamete
gomuti
GNA genial
gunman
gunyah
GNB gone by
GNE gander
ganger
Ganges
gannet
gansey
gender
gentes
ginger❑
gunnel
gunner
gynney
GNG ginkgo
GNH Gandhi
gung-ho

gun-shy
GNI ganoid
GNK gingko
GNL gangly
gentle
gently
Ginola
GNM genome
GNO gentoo
Gondor
gun dog
gun for
GNR gantry
genera
gentry
GNS Ganesa
GNU gangue
genius□
GNV Geneva
GOA global
gnomae
go on at
GOC grouch
GOE gaoler
glover
gloves
glower
gnomes
gnoses
Gooden
gooses
go over
grocer
groper
grovel
grower
GOG George
groggy
GOI globin
gloria□
gnomic
goof it
goolie
Gromit
GOL goodly
google
googly
growly
GOM gloomy
GON ground
groyne
Grozny
GOO gnomon
good-oh
googol
grow on
GOS glossy
grouse
GOT Giotto
groats
grotto
grotty
growth
grow to
GOU grow up
GOV groove
groovy
GPA gape at
GPE gopher
GPN gaping
GPO gippos
GPS go past
GPU gypsum
GRA gardai
garial
garran
german□
GRE garden□
garner□
garnet
garret
garter
Garvey
girder
girner
gorged
gorger
gorget
Gurney
GRG garage
GRH Gurkha
GRI Garcia
garlic
gerbil
Gertie
girlie
gorgio
GRL garble
gargle
Gerald
girdle
gorily
gurgle
GRM Göreme
GRN gerund
GRO garbos
garçon
Garrod
garron
garrot
Gordon
gorgon□
GRR Gerard
GRS garish
GRT Gareth
gyrate
GSA gasbag
gas jar
GSE gas jet
gasket
gasper
gospel
gusher
gusset
GSF gasify
GSI gossip
Gussie
GSL gashly
GSO gascon
gismos
go slow
go-slow
GSU go sour
GTA gateau
gâteau
guttae
GTB Gatsby
GTE gather
getter
gutted
gutter
GTF get off
GTI Gothic
GTL guttle
GTN gating
GTO gutrot
GTU get out
get-out
GUB grubby
GUC gaunch
GUD gourde
GUE glutei
gluten
GUG grudge
grunge
grungy
GUH gauche
gaucho
GUL Gaulle
glumly
grumly
GUO Gounod
GUP grumph
grumps
grumpy
GUR gru-gru
GUT Giusti
giusto
go up to
goutte
GVA gavial
GVI give in
give it
GVM give me
GVN giving
Govind
GVO give on
GVR govern
GVU give up
GWA gewgaw
GWE gawper
GWI Gawain
GWL go well
GWS go west
GWT go with
GYE geyser
GYI Gdynia
Glynis
GYN Guyana
GYO Gaynor
glycol
GYS goyish
GZA gaze at
GZB gazebo
GZE gizzen
GZL guzzle
GZM gazump
GZN gazing
GZO gizmos
HAE headed
header
healed
healer
Healey
Heaney
heaped
hearer
heated
heater
heaven□
heaver
hoaxer
Hyades
HAH heathy
HAI heamic
HAN hyaena
HAO head-on
HAS hearse
hoarse
HAT health
hearth
hearty
HAU head up
heap up
heat up
hiatus
HBA hobday
hub-cap
HBE Hebrew
Hibees
Hobbes
hoboes
HBI hobbit
hubbie
hubris
hybrid
HBL hobble
Hubble
HBN hebona
HBO Hebron
hobjob
hobnob
HBR Hobart
Hubert
HBT habits
HBU hubbub
HCB Hecuba
HCE hacker
hicker
hockey
HCI hack it
hectic
HCL hackle
hackly
heckle
huckle
HCO hector□
HCT Hecate
HCU hack up
hiccup
HDA Hadean
HDE Hadlee
hedger
hidden
HDI hydria
hydric
HDL heddle
Hoddle
huddle
HDN hiding
HDO hadron
Hudson
hydros
HDT Hadith
HDU huddup
Hydrus
HEA haemal
heehaw
Heenan
hiemal
hyetal
HEE heeled
HEI haemic
heel in
HGA Haggai
Hoggar
HGE higher□
hogget
Hughes
HGI haggis
Hughie
HGL haggle
higgle
highly
hugely
HGN Hegang
HGR hegira□
HGU high up
high-up
HIA Hainan
Heimat
HID hairdo
HIE haired
heifer
HIH height
HIK hoicks
HJC hijack
HJR Hejira
HKU hike up
HLA hallal
Hellas
HLB hold by
Holtby
HLD halide
HLE Haller
Halley
haloes
halted
halter
halved
halves
Heller
helmet
helper
Hillel
holder
holler
Holmes
HLI haloid
held in
hele in
hold in
hold it!
HLL holily
HLN Helena
holing
HLO halloa
halloo
hallos
hallow
Helios
hellos
Hilton
hold of
hold on
hollos
hollow
hullos
HLR Hilary
HLS holism
holist
HLT halite
hold to
HLU hallux
helium
hold up
hold-up
hole up
HMA hamman
hymnal
HMC humect
HME hamlet□
hammer□
hamper
hempen
Humber
hummel
humped
HMF humify
HMG homage
HMI home in
HMJ Himeji
hamble
hamuli
homely
homily
humble
humbly

HMN homing
humane
humans
HMO himbos
HMR humeri
HMS Hamish
hamose
HMT hamate
HMU hamous
Hamsun
humbug
hummus
humour
humous
HNA Handan
hangar
Hannah
Hannay
Henman
hint at
HNE handed
Handel
hanger
hanker
Henley
hinder
hinged
hinted
honied
hunger
Hun Sen
hunter□
HNH honcho
Honshu
HNI hand in
hang in
hankie
Hingis
honkie
hunt in
HNL handle
HNO hand on
hang on
hansom
HNR Hendry
Honora
hungry
HNS honest
HNU hang up
hang-up
honour□
hung up
hung-up
hunt up
HNY henrys
Henry V
HOA hoo-hah
hookah
hooray
HOC hootch
HOE hooded
hoofed
hoofer

hooked
hooker□
hooley
hooter
Hoover
hooves
HOI hoof it
hook it
HOL hoop-la
HOO hoodoo
hoopoe
hooroo
HOU hook up
hook-up
HPA heptad
hyphae
hyphal
HPE happen
hipped
hopper□
hyphen
HPI haptic
hippic
hippie
hypnic
hypoid
HPL hopple
HPN hoping
HPO hip-hop
hippos
HRA Harman
hartal
herbal
hermae
Herman
hurrah
hurray
HRB hereby
Hornby
HRC Horace
HRE harden
hareem
harken
Harlem
harmed
harper
Harvey
herder□
Hermes
heroes
herpes
Herren
hirsel
hordes
horned
hornet
horses
horsey
hurley
HRH Horthy
HRI Harbin
Hardie
Harris

Herbie
herein
Hermia
hermit
hernia
heroic
heroin
horn in
horrid
HRL Harald
hardly
hareld
Harold
herald
hirple
hirsle
hurdle
hurtle
HRN hiring
HRO harlot
Harlow
harp on
harrow□
hereof
hereon
Herzog
horror
horson
HRR Harare
HRS harass
heresy
HRT hereto
HRU hard up
hard-up
Haroun
HSA Hassan
hussar
HSE haslet
hasten
Hester
hosier
hostel
hushed
HSI Hassid
hispid
Husain
HSL hassle
hustle
HSO Hesiod
Heston
Hislop
Huston
hyssop
HSU hush up
HTA hetman
hit man
hit-man
hot war
HTC hi-tech
HTE hatred
hatter
hither
Hitler

hotbed
hotter
Hutter
HTF hit off
HTI hatpin
Hattie
hot air
HTO hatbox
Hathor
hot dog
hot-dog
hotpot
hot rod
Hutton
HTR hetero
HTU hit out
HUA houdah
houdan
HUC haunch
HUE housel
houses
HUL hourly
HUU haul up
houmus
HVA have at
HVI have it
HVN Havana
haven't
having
HVO have on
HVS Hevesy
HVT have to
HVU have up
HWA haw-haw
howdah
Howrah
howzat
HWE hawker
hawser
howler
HWI Hawaii
HWL Howell
HWO how now
HWR Howard
Howerd
HWS Hewish
HXE Huxley
HXN hexane
HXS hexose
HYA heyday
HYE Hayden
Hayley
hoyden
HYN hryvna
HYO haybox
Haydon
haymow
hey for
HZL hazily
HZR hazard
IAA Ibadan
in a jam
in a way

Isaiah
IAC Isaacs
IAE Isabel
IAI Icaria
in a fix
italic
IAM in arms
IAO imagos
in a row
IAP Itaipu
IAU Icarus
in a rut
IBB imbibe
IBE imbued
inbred
IBL Imbolc
IBN in banc
IBR imbark
in bird
inborn
IBS imbase
IBT in bits
IBU imbrue
ICI ischia
ICL in calf
ICM income
ICN incony
ICO Inchon
ICP incept
ICR in care
ICS incase
in cash
incise
incuse
ICT incite
ICV incave
incavi
IDA Indian
IDB indaba
in debt
IDC indict
induce
induct
IDD iodide
IDE in deed
indeed
IDG indigo
IDI indris
IDN indent
iodine
IDO indoor
IDR indart
Indira
Indore
IDS iodise
IDU indium
IDZ iodize
IEA icecap
IED Imelda
IEE ibexes
ilexes
IEG ice age
IEI irenic

IEL ideals
Iseult
IES in esse
IET ideate
IEU ice out
ireful
iterum
IEX ice axe
IFA in foal
IFC in fact
infect
IFF infeft
IFL infill
infold
in full
IFM infame
infamy
IFN infant
IFO inflow
IFR in fere
infirm
inform
IFS infest
infuse
IFU influx
IGE ingoes
Ingres
IGI Ingrid
IGL ingulf
IGS ingest
IHE Ishbel
IHL inhale
IHM inhume
IHN I Ching
in hand
IHO inhoop
IHR inhere
IIC idiocy
IIE ibices
ibidem
ilices
irides
irised
irises
IIL icicle
inisle
IJC inject
IJK in-joke
IJR injera
injure
injury
IJS in jest
IKA ink cap
ink-cap
IKN in kind
irking
ILA illiad
I'll say!
ILC inlock
in luck
ILD illude
ILF ill off
ILI inlaid

ILM illume
ILN inland
in line
island
ILS ill-use
ILV in love
ILW in-laws
IMI iambic
Ismail
IMN immune
IMR immure
IMS immask
immesh
in mass
inmesh
inmost
IMT inmate
IMU iambus
INA Ionian
INE in need
INI Innuit
INM ignomy
in name
INR ignore
INS ionise
INT ignite
innate
INZ ionize
IOA isobar
IOD Isolda
Isolde
IOE Imogen
Isobel
isohel
isomer
IOI iconic
ironic
IOL if only
IOO irokos
IPA in play
IPC impact
IPD impede
IPE impies
IPG impugn
IPI impair
in pain
IPL impala
impale
IPN impend
impone
IPR impart
import
impure
in part
IPS impish
impose
impost
IPT impute
IPV impave
IRA inroad
IRE Israel
IRG in rags
IRP irrupt

IRS inrush
IRX in rixa
ISA inspan
instar
ISC insect
ISD inside
ISE inseem
in step
instep
ISI inship
instil
ISL insole
insult
itself
ISN insane
in sync
ISR insert
in sort
insure
ISS insist
IST in situ
ISU insoul
ISY it says
ITA in that
in-tray
ITC intact
ITI in trim
intuit
ITK intake
ITM in time
ITN intend
intent
intone
in tune
ITO intron
intros
in twos
ITR intern
in turn
ITS Irtysh
ITT in toto
IUE inured
IUI inulin
IUN iguana
IVD invade
IVE in view
IVI in vain
IVK invoke
IVN invent
Irvine
Irving
IVR invert
IVS invest
invis'd
IVT invite
IVV in vivo
IWA inwrap
IWC inwick
IWL inwall
IWN in want
inwind
IWR inward
in word

in work
inwork
IWT in with
inwith
JAE Juárez
JAI Jeanie
Joanie
JAN Joanna
Joanne
JBE jabber
jobber
JBL jabble
JBO job-lot
JBR jabiru
JBT jubate
JCA jackal
JCB Jacobi
JCE jacket
jockey
JCI jack in
JCN jacana
jocund
JCO jockos
JCS jacksy
jocose
JCU jack up
JDA Jeddah
Jiddah
JDE judder
judged
Judges
JDG judogi
JDI Judaic
JDT Judith
JEA jeer at
JEE jeerer
Jeeves
JEI jeelie
JEL Joelle
JFN Jaffna
JGA jaguar
Jaguar®
jigsaw
jig-saw
JGE jagged
jigger
jogger
JGL jiggle
joggle
juggle
JGO jig-jog
JGT jugate
JGU jugful
JIE jailed
jailer
joined
joiner
JII join in
JIO jailor
JIU Jaipur
join up
JJB jojoba
jujube

JJN jejune
JKL Jekyll
JKN joking
JLA Julian
JLE jilted
Joleen
Juliet
JLN Jolene
JLO jellos
Jolson
Jolyon
JLP jalopy
JLU Julius
JMA jampan
jump at
JME jammed
jumper
JMI Jamnia
JML Jamila
jimply
jumble
jymold
JMM Jemima
JMO jambok
jambos
jumbos
jump on
JMU jump up
jump-up
JNA Jinnah
Juneau
JNC Janice
JNE Jansen
Jenner
jennet
jinnee
jinxed
junket
JNI Jancis
junkie
JNK Jansky
JNL jangle
jangly
jingle
jingly
jungle
jungly
JNN Janina
Janine
JNO Jonson
juncos
junior
juntos
JNU Jan Hus
JPI Joplin
JPN japing
JPT jupati
JQE Jaques
JRA Jarman
Jordan
JRE jersey❑
JRI Jarvis
jerkin

Jervis
JRL jirble
JRM Jeremy
Jerome
JRO jargon
Jarrow
jerboa
JRR jurors
JRU jerque
JSE jasper❑
jessed
jester
josher
JSI jessie❑
Jesuit
Jospin
Justin
JSL jostle
justle
justly
JSO jissom
JSP Joseph
JSS just so
JSU Joshua
JTA jet-lag
jetsam
JTE jet set
jitter
jotter
JTK jataka
JTO jetton
JTR Jethro
JTU jut out
JUC jaunce
jounce
JUE Jouvet
JUN journo
JUS jaunse
JUT jaunty
JUV J-curve
JVA jovial
JWE jowled
JWL jewels
Jowell
JWS Jewish
JYO joy-pop
JYU joyful
joyous
JZU jazz up
KAE kraken
KAG khanga
knaggy
KAH kwacha
KAI Khalid
khalif
KAO Keaton
klaxon
Kraków
KAR kia-ora
KAS Khalsa
KAT krantz
KAZ kwanza
KBA kiblah

KBK kabuki
KBL kabala
Kabyle
kibble
kobold
KBS kibosh
kybosh
KCE kicker
Köchel
KCH kaccha
KCI kick in
KCL keckle
KDA Kidman
kidnap
Kodiak
KDE kidder
kidney
KDO kid-fox
KDR Kid Ory
KEA Keegan
keep at
Kieran
KEC kvetch
KEE keeled
keener
keeper
KEI keelie
keep in
KEL keenly
KEO keen on
keep on
Kieron
KES kreese
KET keen to
keep to
KEU keep up
KFA kaftan
KFE Kaffer
keffel
KGL Kigali
KIE kaiser❑
knives
krises
Kuiper
KIH knight❑
KKP kakapo
KLA kalian
kalpak
Kelman
KLE kelper❑
kelter
killed
killer
kilted
kilter
KLG Kaluga
KLI kalmia
keloid
kelpie
Keltic
kelvin❑
Killie
kiltie

KLM Kolyma
KLN kalong
KLO kelson
KLU kill up
KMD Komodo
KME kameez
kemper
kümmel
KMH kimchi
KMI Kempis
KML kamala❑
Kemble
KMN kimono
KMR kumara
KMS kumiss
KNA Kansas
Kendal
KNC Konica®
KNE kennel
Kinsey
KNF kung fu
KNH kangha
KNI kanjis
kentia
king it
KNK Kanaka
KNL Kandla
kindle
kindly
kingly
KNM kinema
KNO Ken Hom
Kenton
kind of
KNU Kanpur
KOA know as
KOB knobby
KOE kronen
kroner
KOI kaolin
kookie
KOL kgotla
KOO koodoo
kronor
Kronos
KOT knotty
KOU krónur
KPC kopeck
KPE Kepler
kipper
KPI koppie
KPO Kapoor
KRA kirpan
Kirwan
Kurgan
KRB Kariba
Kirkby
KRC kirsch
KRE karsey
karter
kermes
kernel
kersey
KRI karmic
kermis
kerria
korkir
KRL Kerala
kirtle
KRN Karina
koruna
KRO Karpov
Karroo
KRS kaross
KRT karate
Kirsty
KRU Kirkuk
Korbut
KSA kasbah❑
Kaspar
KSC Kosice
KSE Kassel
Kislev
kismet❑
kisser
kosher
KSV Kosovo
KTA kitbag
KTC kitsch
KTE kitten
KTL kettle
kittle
KTN katana
ketone
kiting
KTP katipo
KTU kit out
kittul
KUA Kaunas
Koufax
KUD Kaunda
KUE Kruger
KUG kludge
KUH Kyushu
KUL knurly
KUN Khulna
KWA kowhai
KWI Kuwait
KWO kowtow
KYA key man
keypad
keyway
KYE kayoed
kayoes
Keynes
KYO Krylov
KZK Kazakh
LAA leap at
LAD Luanda
LAE laager
leaden
leader
leafed
Leakey
leaser
leaved
leaven
leaves
loaded❑
loader
loafer
loaves
LAH loathe
LAI lead in
lead-in
Leavis
LAL leally
leanly
liable
LAN Leanne
Lianna
Lianne
LAO lead on
lean on
leasow
llanos
LAS liaise
LAT lead to
lean-to
LAU league
leap up
LBA labial
Libyan
LBC Lübeck
LBD libido
LBE libber
libken
lubber
LBI Lublin
LBL labile
lobule
lobuli
LBR libero
LBT lobate
Lobito
LBU labium
labour
LCA lochan
Lucian
LCE laches
lackey
lecher
lichee
lichen
locked
locker
locket
lychee
LCI lactic
lectin
lock in
LCL locale
loculi
LCM locums
LCN lacing
lacuna
lucent
LCO Laclos
lector
lictor
lock on
LCS locust
LCT locate
LCU lace-up
lock up
lock-up
Lucius
lyceum
LCW lechwe
LDD la-di-da
LDE ladder
ladies
ledger
lidded
lodger
LDF ladify
ladyfy
LDG Ladoga
LDI laddie
LDN lading
LDO Ludlow
LEA leeway
LEE lieder
LEI Liebig
luetic
LEO lie low
LFE Liffey
lifted
lofted
LFI leftie
LFU lift up
LGA leg-man
log-jam
LGC legacy
LGE legged
Legree
ligger
lugger
LGI lignin
loggia
loggie
LGM legume
LGN lag-end
legend
ligand
Lugano
LGO lagoon
legion
loglog
LGS ligase
Lugosi
LGT legate
legato
ligate
Ligeti
lights
LGU lignum
LGY leg bye
LHR Lahore
LIE Leiden
loipen
loiter
LIU laid up
LKC Lukacs
Lukács
LKL likely
LKN liking
LKT Lakota
LLA Lilian
LLE Lilley
loller
LLI Lillie
LLO lollop
LLT Lilith
Lolita
L-plate
LMA Lammas
lemmas
lumbar
LMD lambda
lamedh
LME limber
limner
limpet
lumber
Lumley
lumpen
LMI limpid
LML lamely
limply
LMN lament
lamina
Lamont
Le Mans
lemans
lemony
liming
lumens
lumina
lumine
LMO Lemmon
Lemnos
limbos
lummox
LMR lemurs
LMT limits
LNA landau
lineal
linear
LNC lunacy
LNE lancer
lances
lancet❑
landed
Länder
lender
lenses
Lenten
linden
linger
linked
linnet❑
lintel
longer
Lynsey
lynxes
LNF lenify
LNG lanugo
LNI lentic
lentil
Lyncis
LNL lankly
lonely
longly
lunula
LNN lining
LNO Lennon
lentos
London
long on
LNR Lanark
LNS linish
LNT lanate
length
lenity
lunate
LNU langue
langur
line up
line-up
link up
link-up
LOA loofah
look at
LOE Lionel
lionet
looker
looped
looper
loosen
looter
looves
LOI Leonie
look in
look-in
LOO look on
LOS Lhotse
LOT look to
LOU look up
loom up
LOZ Lao-tzu
LPE lapper
lappet
lapsed
lipped
lippen
lopper
LPF lop off
LPI lipoid
LPN lupine
LPO laptop
lepton
LPT Laputa
LQA loquat
LQI liquid
LQO liquor
LRA lariat
larvae

Words marked ❑ can also be spelled with an initial capital letter

larval
LRC lyrics
LRE larder
largen
larger
Lartet
Lerner
Lorien
LRI Larkin
LRL lordly
LRN larynx
Lorenz
luring
LRO lardon
largos
LRT lyrate
LRU larrup
LSA lascar
LSE lashed
Lasker
Lesley
lessee
lessen
lesser
Lester
Lisbet
lisper
lisses
listen
Lister
LSI lassie□
Leslie
LSK Lusaka
LSL lastly
lushly
LSN losing
lysine
LSO lassos
Lesbos
lesion
lesson
lessor
Lisbon
lissom
Liston
LSR lustra
lustre
LST lost to
LTA lethal
LTB let-a-be
LTE lateen
lather
latten
latter
lethee
letter
lither
litter
Luther
LTF let off
let-off
LTH litchi
LTI Latvia
let rip
Lettie
lithia
lithic
Lottie
lutein
LTL lately
let fly
little
LTN latent
Latina
litany
LTO lithos
lotion
lots of
lottos
LTS latest
latish
lutist
LTU let out
let-out
litmus
LUC launce
launch
LUE Lauder
laurel□
Lauren
Leuven
louden
louses
LUG lounge
LUH laughs
LUI Laurie
leucin
LUL loudly
LUR LAUTRO
louvre□
LUS Louisa
Louise
LVB live by
LVG lovage
LVI live in
live-in
luvvie
LVL lavolt
lively□
Lovell
lovely
LVN levant□
living
loving
LVO live on
LVR levers
livery
lovers
LVS lavish
LVT levity
live to
LWA low-tar
LWE lawyer
low-key
LWI Lawrie
LWL lewdly
Lowell
LWN lowing
LWO Lawson
lowboy
LWS lowest
LWU lawful
low-cut
LXM lexeme
LXR luxury
LXT laxity
luxate
LYA layman
LYE Leyden
LYF lay off
lay-off
LYO lay low
LYR Layard
LYU lay out
layout
LYY lay-bys
LZI Lizzie
LZL lazily
LZN lazing
LZR lizard□
MAA McAdam
MAE moaner
moated
MAI mealie
meanie
MAL meanly
measle
measly
MAM miasma
miasms
MAO meadow
MAR meagre
MAU meatus
MBA McBean
mob-cap
MBE mobbed
mobled
MBL mobile□
MBS Mabuse
MBT Mobutu
MBU Möbius
MCA Mackay
much as
MCE mocker
mucker
MCI Maceio
Michie
muck in
MCL mackle
macula
muckle
Mycale
MCO machos
macron
macros
micron
micros
mucros
MCR macera
MCS mucosa
MCT micate
MCU mock up
mock-up
muck up
mucous
MDA madcap
madman
Mad Max
madras□
mediae
medial
median
medlar
midday
midway□
MDC Medici
medico
MDE madden
madder
medley
midden
midget
mid-leg
Midler
Modred
MDF mid-off
modify
MDG mid-age
MDI Madrid
midrib
MDL meddle
middle
module
moduli
modulo
muddle
MDM Madame
madams
MDN Medina
MDO mod con
MDR modern
MDS Medise
medusa□
modest
modish
MDU made up
made-up
Madhur
medium
MDZ Medize
MEA maenad
McEwan
Moerae
MEE meeken
MEI myelin
MEL meekly
meetly
muesli
MEU Meerut
meet up
MFE miffed
MFI muffin
Muftis
MFL muffle
MFO muflon
my foot!
MGA magian
magmas
Magyar
MGB Mugabe
MGE maglev
magnet
mugger
MGI Maggie
magpie
megrim
moggie
MGL magilp
megilp
mygale
MGO maggot
mignon
MGR Megara
MGT mighty
MGU magnum
Magnus
mugful
MHA mihrab
MHE Mahler
Mehmet
MHI mohair
MHO mahzor
MHU Mahmud
mahout
MHW Mohawk
MIA Moirai
MIE maiden
mailed
Mailer
maimed
moider
MII Maisie
MIL mainly
MIO maikos
MIR maigre
MIT moiety
MJE mojoes
MJI Majlis
MJR Majuro
MKA make at
MKD make do
make-do
mikado□
MKE Meknès
Mukden
MKG make go
MKI make it
MKL Makalu
MKN making
Mekong
MKO make of
make on
MKU make up
make-up
MLA Malian
malmag
Millay
mullah
Multan
MLB Malabo
MLC malice
MLD malady
melody□
milady
my lady
MLE mallet
malted
melted
milden
mildew
milieu
milker
miller□
millet□
molten
Muller
Müller
mullet
MLG Malaga
malign
MLI Melvin
Millie
MLK Moltke
MLL mildly
MLN Malang
MLO Mallon
mallow
Mellon
Mellor
mellow
Milton
MLR mal gré
malgré
milord
My Lord
MLS Milosz
molest
mulish
MLT Melete
Mel Ott
MLW Malawi
MLY Melvyn
MMA mammae
mammal
MME mammer
mammet
member
mummer
MMI memoir
MML mumble
MMN moment
MMO mambos
mammon
Memnon
MMR memory
MMS mimosa
MNA man-day
maniac

Man Ray
manual
menial
mental
Minoan
Monday
MNC menace
Monaco
Monica
Munich
MND monody
MNE manger
mangey
Manley
manned
manner
mantel
mended
Mendel
mender
meneer
menses
mincer
minded
minder
minuet
monger
monied
monies
monkey
MNF minify
munify
MNG manage
manège
ménage
MNI mantic
mantis
menhir
Minnie
muntin
MNK manuka
MNL mangle
manila❑
mantle❑
mingle
MNM Manama
minima
MNN mañana
MNO manioc
Manson
mantos
mentor
mentos
minion
minnow
Minton
Monroe
mungos
Munros
MNR mantra
manure
monera
MNS monism
monist
MNT minute
munite
MNU Manaus
manful
manqué
mantua❑
Mingus
MNY moneys
MOA moolah
MOE mooner
moored
MOI Maoris
muonic
myopia
myopic
myosin
MOS Maoism
Maoist
MPE mapper
mopper
moppet
MPN moping
MPT Maputo
MPU map out
MQI maquis
MRA Marian
marram
merman
Miriam
Moreau
Morgan
mornay❑
morsal
mortal
mortar
Murray
Myrdal
myriad
Myriam
MRC maraca
MRE Marcel
marked
marker
market
Marley
Marner
marred
martel
marten
marvel
marver
mercer❑
merged
merger
Meriel
Mersey
Mirren
morsel
murder
Muriel
Murner
MRG mirage
MRH Marsha
marshy
Martha
Murphy
MRI Marcia
margin
marlin
martin❑
Marvin
merlin❑
Mersin
morbid
Morris
Morris®
Murcia
MRK markka
Merckx
MRL marble
marbly
Marple
merely
morale
morall
morals
Myrtle
MRN marina❑
marine
Marini
Marino
merino
Moroni
murine
MRO Marcos
Marion
Marlon
marmot
maroon
marrow
merlon
Merlot
Merton
mirror
Mordor
Mormon
morros
Morton
MRS morass
more so
morish
morose
MRT merits
miriti
MRU maraud
Marcus
Marius
mark up
mark-up
marque
morgue
murmur
MRY Martyn
martyr
Mervyn
MSA McStay
mescal
mesial
mishap
mislay
missal
moshav
MOSSAD
muscat❑
MSE masher
masked
masker
massed
masses
masted
master
meshed❑
Mesmer
mestee
misken
miskey
misled
missed
missee
misses
misset
mister
Moslem
Mosley
musket
mussel
muster
MSI mashie
massif
mastic
misaim
misfit
mishit
missis
mosaic❑
mossie
Muslim
muslin
mystic
MSL masala
mostly
muscle
muscly
myself
MSN Mishna
musing
MSO mascot
Moscow
Mrs Mop
muse on
musk ox
MSR Maseru
Messrs
misère
misery
Mysore
MSS misuse
MSU masque
mess up
miscue
missus
mist up
mosque
museum
MSY Massys
MTA met man
mutual
MTE Mather
matted
matter
métier
mither
mitten
mother
motley
mutter
MTG metage
MTI matrix
Mattie
metric
mythic
MTL matily
mettle
motile
mottle
mutely
MTN mating
matins
mutant
mutine
mutiny
MTO matlos
matlow
matron
matzos
meteor
method
métros
motion❑
motmot
mutton
MTP metope
MTR mature
MTS mutism
MTT mutate
MTV motive
MUD maundy
mouldy
MUE Mauser
mouser
mousey
MUH mouths
mouthy
MUI mauvin
MUL mousle
MUS mousse
MUT mounty❑
MUU muu-muu
MVE movies
MVI move in
MVN moving
MVO move on
MVU move up
move-up
MWA Mowlam
MWE mewses
MWL Mowgli
MWR my word
MXC Mexico
MXM maxima
myxoma
MXN Maxine
mixing
MYA May Day
mayday❑
MYE mayhem
MYK Miyake
MYL Mayall
mayfly
MYU may bug
MZE mizzen
MZI mozzie
MZL mazily
mizzle
muzzle
MZO mezzos
MZR Mozart
NAA nyalas
NAB near by
nearby
near-by
NAC nuance
NAE neaten
Niamey
NAF neaffe
NAI neanic
niacin
NAJ Nyanja
NAL nearly
neatly
NAO ngaios
NBA Nubian
NBD nobody
NBE nabber
nobles
NBL nebula
nibble
no ball
nobble
nubble
nubile
NBR Nyborg
NBS nebish
NBU Nablus
nobbut
NCA nectar
nuchae
nuchal
NCE Necker
niched
nicked
nickel
nicker
nuclei

NCL Nacala
nicely
Nicola
Nicole
NCO nachos
Nichol
NCT nicety
NDF nidify
nod off
NDL noddle
nodule
nudely
NDN Nadine
NDO nid-nod
NDS nodose
nudism
nudist
NDT nudity
NDU nodous
NEC Niepce
NEE needed
NEI noesis
noetic
NEL needle
needly
nielli
niello
Noelle
NEO Neeson
NEU naevus
NFA no fear
NFE niffer
NFL naffly
NGE nugget
NGI noggin
NGK nogaku
NGL Nägeli
niggle
nighly
NGN nagana
Nagano
NGO nigh on
no good
no-good
NGR nagari
NGT negate
nights
nighty
NGU Nagpur
NGY Nagoya
NID Naiads
NIE nailer
NIN Nairne
NIU nail up
NJK no joke
NKO nekton
NLA nilgai
nilgau
NLE nelies
Nilsen
NLO nelson❑
NLS no less
NLT Nilote

NMA numbat
NME numbed
number
NMH Nymphs
NML namely
nimble
nimbly
numbly
NMN naming
nomina
numina
NMO nem con
NMR no more
NMT Namath
Nimitz
NMU nimbus
NNA Ninian
ninjas
non-fat
NNB Ningbo
NNE Nansen
Nantes
no-noes
NNG nonage
non-ego
NNI nuncio
NNL nuncle
NNN nonane
NNO non-com
NNR nonary
NNT ninety
NOI nookie
NOK Nootka
NOL noodle
NPA Nuphar
NPE Napier
Naples
napped
nephew
nipper❑
NPI napkin
NPL napalm
Nepali
nipple
NPO Nippon
NPR napery
NPU Nippur
NRA narial
nark at
normal
Norman
Norway
NRD Neruda
NRE narked
nerved
nerves
Noreen
nor yet
NRI nark it!
Narnia
Narvik
nereid
Nordic

Norris
NRL neroli
nurdle
nursle
NRN narine
nerine
NRO narcos
nardoo
narrow
NRS Nernst
NSA Nassau
NSB Naseby
NSD no-side
NSE Nasser
nisses
NSH naskhi
NSI Nesbit
NSL nestle
nosily
NSN nosing
NSO Nestor
no-show
nostoc
NSU nose up
nosh-up
NSW NAS/UWT
NTA Nathan
net pay
not bad
not far
NTC notice
NTE natter
nether
netted
not let
not see
nutmeg
nutter
NTF notify
NTH notchy
NTI nitric
nitwit
nut oil
nutria
NTL nettle
NTM no time
NTN not any
noting
not one
nutant
NTO nation
natron
notion
nuts on
NTR nature❑
nitery
notary
NTT notate
nutate
NTU not out
not-out
NTV native
NUA neural

nougat
nounal
NUE nausea❑
neuter
Nouméa
NUH naught
nought
NUI Ngunis
NUL nousle
NUO neuron
NVC novice
NVD Nevada
NVE navies
NVH Navaho
NVJ Navajo
NVL novels
NVN novena
NVR never a
NWA Newham
new man
Newman
new-sad
NWG New Age
NWO new sol
newton❑
NWR Newark
NWS newest
newish
nowise
NWY noways
NXL nextly
NXT next to
NZF Nazify
NZL nozzle
nuzzle
NZS Nazism
OAA on a par
OAC Osasco
OAE O'Casey
onager
OAG orange❑
OAI ogamic
okapis
Oparin
oxalic
oxalis
Ozalid®
OAK Ozarks
OAL oracle❑
orally
ovally
OAO orator
OAU omasum
opaque
OBC Ozbeck
OBR Olbers
Osbert
OCE orchel
OCI orcein
orchid
orchil
OCL occult
on call

oscula
OCM occamy
OCN oscine
OCP occupy
OCS oncost
OCT Olcott
oocyte
ODA oh dear!
Oldham
old hat
old-hat
old lag
old man
ordeal
ODE oldies
oodles
ODG old age
ODI Old Vic
ordain
ODM oedema
ODN Ondine
ODO odd bod
odd lot
odds-on
old boy
ODR orders
ordure
ODS oddish
oldest
oldish
ODT oddity
on-dits
on duty
OEA one day
one-man
one-way
OEB overby
owerby
OED Oreads
overdo
OEE omened
oneyer
opened
opener
ox-eyed
OEF O'Keefe
one-off
OEG on edge
OEH obeche
OEI olefin
Onegin
OEL ocelli
O'Neill
openly
Otello
overly
OEM odeums
OEN oceans
OEO Oberon
ocelot
Oregon
OER oneyre
OES Odense

Odessa
or else
OET Odette
oleate
omenta
omertà
OEU obelus
open up
OEW one-two
OFA off pat
OFC office
olfact
OFE off-key
offset
OFL Offaly
onfall
on file
OFN offend
offing
OFO onflow
on foot
OFR on fire
Oxford
OFS oafish
offish
OFU offcut
OGM oogamy
OGN organa
organs
OGS orgasm
OHE ochrea
OHG on high
OHL on hold
Ophuls
OHN ochone
on hand
OHR on hire
others
OHT ophite
OIA ogival
OID Oviedo
OIE obiter
Oliver
orifex
Origen
OII Olivia
origin
Osiris
otitis
OIL oriole
OIN Onions
oniony
Oriana
orient
OIO orison
OIS Orissa
otiose
OIT opiate
OIU odious
OIW Ojibwa
OJC object
OJR objure
OJT objets

OKE Orkney
OLA oilman
OLC o'clock
OLG oblige
oology
OLI oil rig
OLL oilily
OLN oblong
on-lend
on-line
oolong
oulong
OLS oblast
owlish
OLT oblate
of late
oolite
OMA oomiac
oomiak
oompah
OMG ohmage
OML Ormeli
ormolu
OMO Ogmios
OMS osmose
OMU osmium
ONR owners
ONT of note
ornate
ONU omnium☐
OOD oroide
OOE orogen
OOL O'Toole
OOS oboist
OOT on oath
Oporto
OOU obolus
OPA orphan
OPE osprey
OPG oppugn
OPI Orphic
OPN orpine
OPS oppose
ORA ocreae
oorial
ORD O-grade
ORE O'Brien
ORR orrery
ORS ogress
ogrish
onrush
OSA Ossian
OSD onside
OSE OFSTED
Ofsted
on spec
or snee
ouster
oyster
OSF ossify
OSG obsign
OSI oxslip
OSL on sale
OSN on song
Orsino
OSO on show
OSS obsess
OST on-site
OTA osteal
outgas
outlaw
outlay
outman
OTC on tick
optics
OTE ostler
outlet
outred
outset
OTG Ortega
outage
OTI obtain
outbid
outfit
outsit
outwit
oxtail
OTM on time
optima
OTN octane
Octans
octant☐
opting
Ostend
ostent
outing
OTO octroi
opt for
option
orthos
out for
outfox
outtop
OTP octopi
OTR outcry
OTS obtest
obtuse
out-ask
OTU opt out
opt-out
outgun
output
outrun
outsum
OTV octave
octavo
OTW Ottawa
OTY outbye
OUA ocular
ovular
OUE opuses
OUR oeuvre
OUU oculus
OVE on view
OVR obvert
OWL Orwell
Oswald
OWN Olwyne
OWR onward
OYE oxygen
OYR of yore
OZL oozily
OZN oozing
PAA plagal
planar
platan
play at
Prasad
PAC Pearce
plaice
planch
Planck
prance
PAE peahen
peaked
peavey
phases
Piaget
placer
places
placet
planer
planet
plated
platen
plater
plates
played
player☐
prayer
PAF piaffe
PAG pa'anga
PAI placid
play it
praxis
PAK planks
pranks
PAL pearls
pearly
prawle
PAM plasma
Psalms
PAN plaint
PAO peapod
peason
pharos
pianos
play on
PAS praise
PAT plants
Pratt's
pray to
PAU peanut
plague
plaque
play up
Prague
PAZ piazza
PBI public
PBL pebble
pebbly
PCA pick at
PCE packed
packer☐
packet
pecker
pecten
picked
picker
picket
pocket
pucker
PCF pacify
PCI pack in
pectin
picnic
PCL pickle☐
PCN Pacino
picene
PCO pick on
Pictor
PCU pack up
pick up
pick-up
PDA pedlar
PDE padded
PDI pidgin
PDL paddle
pedalo
peddle
piddle
puddle
PDN Padang
pedant
PDO podsol
podzol
PDT pedate
PDU padauk
pad out
podium
PEA peer at
pleiad
prefab
prepay
pre-tax
PEB plebby
PEC pierce☐
pleach
preach
PED pseudo
PEE peeler
peeved
piecen
pieces
prefer
premed
preses
preset
PEG peenge
pledge
PEI peewit
poetic
précis
prefix
prelim
Previn
pteria
pyemia
PEL paella
Puebla
pueblo☐
PEM pneuma
PEN paeony
PEO phenol
plexor
prey on
pye-dog
PEP Phelps
preppy
PER Phèdre
Pierre
pleura
poetry
PES pheese
please
PET plenty☐
presto
pretty
PEU peepul
plenum
plexus
PEY phenyl
prewyn
PEZ pheeze
PFE puffed
puffer
PFI puffin
PFL piffle
PFO puff on
PFU puff up
PGD pagoda
PGE piglet☐
Pogues
PGI piggie
piggin
PGL puggle
PGO pigeon
pogrom
PGT pigsty
PGU peg out
pignut
pig out
PHN Pahang
PIA plicae
primal
PIB Philby
PIC paiock
prince☐
Prisca
PIE pained
paired
poised
prices
pricey
primed
primer
privet
prized
prizes
PIH plight
PII Philip
PIL primly
PIN pliant☐
puisne
PIO phizog
Poirot
poison
primos
prison
PIR pliers
priory
PIS plissé
priest
prissy
PIT painty
plinth
points
PIU paid-up
pair up
Primus
PIV prieve
PJC pajock
PKE pokies
PKI pyknic
PKK pukeko
PKN Peking
puking
PKR pakora
PKY pokeys
PLA paleae
pallae
palmar
palpal
pelham☐
pillar
Polgar
pollan
pulsar
PLC palace
police☐
policy
PLE pallet
palmer☐
palter
pellet
pelmet
pelves
phloem
pilfer
Pilger
Pilsen
polder
pollen
pollex
pullet
pulley
PLF pilaff
PLG pelage

phlegm
PLI pallia
pallid
pelvic
pelvis
pull in
pulpit
pulvil
PLL palely
palolo
pilule
PLM Paloma
PLN paling
piling
Poland
polony
puling
pylons
PLO pall on
pallor
pillow
polios
Pol Pot
pull on
PLP polypi
polyps
PLR paltry
peltry
PLS palish
pilose
polish□
PLT palate
pelite
pelota
Pilate
polite
polity
PLU palpus
pileum
pile up
pile-up
pileus
Pollux
pull up
pulque
PMA pampas
PMC pomace
pumice
PMD pomade
PME pamper
Pompey
pummel
PML Pamela
pimple
pimply
pomelo
PMN Pomona
PMO pompom
PMU pump up
PNA penman
pennae
pen-pal
pentad
Pentax®
Pindar
pinnae
Punjab
punkah
PND panada
PNE pander
Pángea
panzer
penned
pincer
pinger
pinked
Pinter
ponder
pongee
pontes
punnet
punter
PNH poncho
punchy
PNI pencil
Pinkie
Pinyin
pundit
PNL penile
penult
pingle
pinole
pintle
punily
PNM panama□
PNN Penang
pining
PNO panton
pantos
pennon
pingos
pinion
pinkos
pintos
pondok
pongos
puntos
PNR panary
pantry
penury
Pinero
PNS punish
PNT pineta
puncta
PNU panful
pannus
pan out
pent-up
Pincus
POA phocae
phocas
POB phoebe□
POD ploidy
POE phoney
phooey
pioned
pioner
plover
pooled
pooped
prober
proles
propel
proper
protea
pro tem
proved
proven
ptoses
pyoner
POF proofs
POG plough
POI phobia
phobic
phonic
photic
profit
prolix
prosit
POL people
poodle
poorly
Proulx
POO photon
photos
plod on
poo-poo
PROLOG
promos
proton
Provos
POP prompt
Proops
POS Proust
POT pronto
POU prop up
POY propyl
PPA poplar
PPC papacy
PPE pepper
popper□
poppet
puppet
PPF pop off
PPI papain
pepsin
peptic
pipkin
pippin
poplin
poprin
PPL papula
papule
popple
pupils
PPN pepino
piping
PPO Paphos
popjoy
PPR papers
papery
papyri
Pop Art
PPT pupate
PPU pappus
peplum
pipe up
PPY papaya
PQE piqued
piquet□
PQO Pequod
PRA Parcae
pariah
Parian
parlay
portal
purdah
PRC piracy
PRD parade□
parody
PRE parcel
parget
parked
Parker
parley
parpen
parsec
Parsee
parser
parted
permed
porker
porter□
purler
purser
purvey
PRF purify
PRH Pyrrho
PRI pardie
parkie
parkin
partim
parvis
perdie
pereia
perkin
permit
Portia
purlin
PRK peruke
PRL parole
partly
pertly
portly
purely
purfle
purple
PRN Paraná
parent
paring
piraña
purine
pyrene
PRO pardon
pardon?
parrot
parson
part of
period
perron
person
PRP paraph
pyrope
PRS parish
perish
peruse
phrase
purism□
purist
PRT parity
periti
Perutz
pirate
purity
pyrite
PRU park up
perk up
porous
pursue
PSA PASCAL
pascal□
pasear
pass as
pose as
postal
PSB pass by
PSC Pesach
PSD pesade
PSE pastel
pester
Pisces
pissed
posset
posted
poster
pushed
pusher
pussel
PSI passim
pastis
past it
pistil
postie
postil
push in
PSL pestle
poshly
PSN Pisano
posing
PSO pass on
pastor
pistol□
piston
PSR pastry
PST Pashto
peseta
Pushto
Pushtu
PSU pass up
poseur
possum
push up
PSW pesewa
peshwa
PTA Pathan
pitman□
pit-pat
PTC pataca
putsch
PTE patten□
patter
petrel
petted
Pitney
pitted
pitter
poteen
pother
potted
potter
puttee
putter
putzes
PTF put off
put-off
PTG potage
PTH patchy
pitchy
potche
PTI patois
Pétain
Petrie
pet-sit
putrid
Pythia
PTL pettle
Petula
PTN patent
patina
potent
PTO pathos
patios
Patmos
patrol
patron
Patton
petrol
pithoi
potion
pottos
put for
python
PTP Petipa
PTR petard
Peters
PTS potash
Potosí
PTT petite

potato
PTU potful
put out
put-put
PUA plural
PUC paunch
pounce
PUD pounds
PUE pauper
pauser
Phuket
plumed
pluses
poules
pourer
pouter
pruner
PUF pouffe
PUG plunge
PUH plushy
pouchy
PUI piupiu
plug in
PUK plucky
PUM plummy
PUN pruine
PVN pavane
paving
PVO pavior
Pavlov
PWA pawpaw
powwaw
PWE pawnee□
pawner
pewter
powder
powter
PWL Powell
PWO powwow
PWR powers
PXA Paxman
PXO Paxton
PYE pay bed
PYF pay off
pay-off
PYH psyche
psycho
PYI physic
physio
PYL payola
phyllo
PYN paying
prying
PYO pay for
Payton
PYT peyote
PYU pay out
phylum
pry out
PZA Poznan
PZL puzzle
PZZ pazazz
pizazz
QAA Quapaw
quasar
QAC quaich
QAE Quaker
quaver
QAG quagga
quaggy
quango
QAI qualia
QAL Quayle
QAM qualms
QAN quaint
QAO quahog
QAR quaere
quarry
QAT quanta
quarte
quarto
quartz
QEC quelch
quench
QEE Q-fever
Quebec
QEN Queens
QES queasy
QET QWERTY
qwerty
QGN qi gong
QIC quince□
QIE quiver
QIH quiche
QIK quirky
QIO quinol
QIS quinsy
QIT quinta
quinte
QNA QANTAS
Qantas
QOA quotas
QOE quoted
QOH quotha
QOK quokka
QOT quoits
QOU quorum
QRN QARANC
QARNNS
QWA qawwal
RAA Reagan
RAD Rwanda
RAE reader
reaper
roamer
roarer
RAI read in
roadie
RAL really
rearly
RAM realms
RAO realos
reason
RAU read up
road up
RBC reback
RBE rabbed
rabbet
rabies
ribbed
robbed
robber
rubber
RBF rebuff
rubefy
RBI rabbis
rabbit□
Robbie
rubric
RBK rebuke
RBL rabble
ribald
Ribble
rubble
RBN rebind
riband
Ribena®
Rubens
Rubina
RBO reboot
ribbon□
Rob Roy
Robson
RBR rebore
reborn
Robert
Rubbra
RBS ribose
robust
RBT rebate
rebato
rebite
rubati
rubato
RBU rub out
RCA racial
rectal
ric-rac
rictal
RCC rococo□
RCD recede
re-cede
RCE Rachel
racked
racker
racket
recces
richen
riches
ricker
rochet
rocker
rocket
rucked
RCF Recife
RCI rachis
rechie
recoil
recoin
Richie
RCL racily
recall
richly
ruckle
RCM raceme
RCN Racine
racing
recant
recent
RCO racoon
reccos
reckon
rector
rectos
RCP recipe
RCR record
recure
RCS racism
racist
recast
recess
recuse
RCT recite
RCU recoup
rectum
rectus
rictus
ruckus
RDA radial
radian
redcap
red-cap
Redcar
rediae
red rag
rid way
rodman
RDC redact
reduce
RDE redden
redeem
Red Sea
ridden
ridged
Ridley
Rodney
rudder
RDL raddle
radula
reddle
riddle
ruddle
rudely
Rudolf
RDM radome
RDN riding□
rodent
RDO radios
red hot
red-hot
ride on
rodeos
RDR rudery
RDS radish
RDU radium
radius
red mud
red out
Red Rum
ride up
RDY red-eye
REE reefer
Reeves
REH re-echo
REM Rheims
rheumy
REO reebok
rhebok
REU rhesus
rueful
RFA reflag
RFC refect
RFE rafter
reflet
reflex
rifler
ruffed
RFG refuge
RFI raffia
RFL rafale
raffle
refill
ruffle
RFN refine
refund
RFO reffos
reflow
RFR reform
re-form
RFS refuse
RFT refute
RFU reflux
rufous
RGA ragbag
raglan□
ragtag
reggae
regnal
RGE ragged
reglet
regret
rigger
rugged
rugger
RGI regain
Reggie
Reggio
RGL raggle
regale
RGM regime
régime
RGN raging
regent
Regina
RGO region
RGR regard
Rogers
RGS rugose
RGT righto
rights
rugate
RGU ragout
rigour
rig out
rig-out
rugous
RHA Rahman
rehear
reheat
RHE Rohrer
RHS rehash
RIA rail at
rhinal
RIE raider
raised
raiser
ruined
ruiner
RII rain in
raisin
rein in
Roisin
RIO rhinos
RIU Raipur
RJA Rajkat
RJC reject
RJI rejoin
RJK Rijeka
RJU Rajput
RKI rake in
RKR rakery
RKS rakish
RKU rake up
RLA reload
RLC relics
relict
RLE relief
relier
rillet
rolled
roller□
RLI roll in
RLN relent
reline
Roland
ruling
RLO rely on
roll on
roll-on
rule OK
RLS relish
RLT relate
RLU roll up
roll-up
RLV relive
RMA Rameau
Ramsay
RMD remedy

Words marked □ can also be spelled with an initial capital letter

RME ramjet
rammer
ramper
rimmed
Rommel
romper
rummer
RMF ramify
RMG romage
RMI remain
RMJ romaji
RMK remake
re-make
RML ramble
ramuli
remble
rumble
rumple
RMN remand
remind
Rimini
Romani
Romans
Romany
rumina
RMO ramrod
Romeos
rumbos
RMR remark
remora
RMS ramose
remise
remiss
Romish
RMT ramate
remote
RMU ramous
rumour
rumpus
RMV remove
RNA Randal
rental
runway
RNE randem
ranger
ranker
ranter
render
Rennes
rennet
renter
rinded
ringed
ringer
rinser
rondel
runnel
runner
RNF run off
run-off
RNG renege
RNH Ranchi
RNI rancid
Rankin
Rennie
rennin
Renoir
ring in
Runcie
Runrig
RNL rankle
rankly
Ranulf
Ronald
runkle
RNM rename
RNO random❑
randon
ransom
rondos
ronyon
run low
RNR run dry
RNT Renata
RNU ring up
run out
RNW renown❑
ROA ryokan
ROB rhombi
ROD Rhonda
ROE reopen
Rhodes
rioter
roofed
roofer
roomed
roomer
Rooney
rooted
rooter
ROI rhodie
rookie
ROS rootsy
RPA repeal
repeat
replay
ripsaw
rupiah
RPD rapids
RPE rapier
rappel
rapper
ripped
RPF rip off
rip-off
RPG repugn
RPI raphia❑
repair
rope in
RPL raptly
ripely
ripple
ripply
ropily
RPN rapine
repand
repent
repine
repone
RPO raptor
repros
Rippon
RPR report
repure
Rupert
RPS rapist
repass
repast
repose
RPT repute
RQE Raquel
roquet
RQI requit
RRA reread
RRE rorter
RRF rarefy
RRI rerail
RRL rarely
RRN raring
RRT rarity
RSA rascal
Roseau
rush at
RSC resect
rosace
RSSPCC
RSD reside
RSE rasher
raster
rested
restem
rester
roster
rushed
russet
rusted
RSG resign
re-sign
RSI roscid
Ruskin
Russia
rustic
RSK Russki
Russky
RSL rashly
resale
resile
result
rosily
rustle
RSM resume
résumé
RSN resent
rising
rosiny
RSO reshow
rest on
RSR resorb
resort
rosary
rostra
RSS resist
RSU rescue
rise up
risqué
RTA ratbag
rattan
retial
ritual
RTE rather
Ratner
ratten
ratter
rother
rotten
rotter
rutted
RTF ratify
RTI retail
retain
RTK retake
Rothko
RTL rattle❑
retell
rutile
RTN rating
retina
retund
rotund
RTO ration
ratios
ratoon
retros
Retton
RTR retard
retire
retort
return
re-turn
rotary
RTS retuse
RTT rotate
RTU retour
rotgut
RUB rhumba
RUC raunch
RUD rounds
RUE Reuben
Reuter
roused
rouser
routed
RUL rouble
RUO roucou
RVA reveal
RVE review
RVG ravage
RVK revoke
RVL revels
revile
revolt
rivals
RVM revamp
RVN ravine
raving
roving
RVR reverb
revere❑
revers
revert
Rivera
rivery
Rovere
RVS ravish
revest
revise
RVU rave-up
RVV revive
RWN Rowena
rowing
RWR reward
reword
rework
RXN Roxana
Roxane
RYD Riyadh
RYE rhymed
rhymer
RYH rhythm
RZA rizzar
RZE rizzer
rozzer
RZI Rizzio
RZL razzle
RZN razing
rezone
RZO rizzor
SAA scalae
scalar
scarab
sea cap
seaman❑
Seamas
sea rat
shaman
stalag
stay at
SAB scabby
shabby
SAC scarce
séance
search
snatch
stance
stanch
starch
swatch
SAD shandy❑
swaddy
SAE scales❑
scamel
scared
scarer
sealed
sealer
seamer
seared
seated
shaded
shaken
shaker
shakes
shamed
shaped
shaper
shared
sharer
shares
shaved
shaven
shaver
skater
slated
slaver
slayer
snared
snarer
soaked
soaker
spaced
spacer
spader
spared
Stacey
staged
stager
stagey
stakes
stamen
stapes
stated
stater
staves
stayer
swayed
SAF Scarfe
scarfs
Staffa
Staffs
SAG shaggy
slangy
snaggy
sparge
Swarga
SAH scathe
spathe
swathe
SAI Shamir
sharia
Sharif
Slavic
spadix
spavin
stadia
Stalin
stasis
static
statim

stay in
swan in
SAK slacks
snacks
sparks
sparky
stacks
swanky
SAL Searle
smalls
snarly
stable
stably
stalls
staple
suable
suably
SAM shammy
smarmy
swarms
SAN shanny
SAO sea boy
sea cow
sea dog
season
shadow
shakos
shalom
shalot
Sharon
slalom
spados
stator
stay on
SAP scampi
scarpa
Sharpe
snappy
swampy
SAR slairg
sparry
stairs
starry
SAS sparse
SAT scaith
scanty
scatty
Shakti
shanty
skaith
smalti
smarty
so as to
Sparta
SAU Seamus
shaduf
shamus□
slap-up
snap up
soak up
soakup
statue
status

swan up
SAV starve
swarve
SAZ snazzy
stanza
stanze
stanzo
Swayze
SBA subway
SBC subact
SBE Sibley
subfeu
sublet
subsea
subset
syboes
SBI so be it
submit
SBL subtle□
subtly
SBN Sabina
Sabine
SBO Seb Coe
sub for
SBR Sobers
suborn
suburb
SBT subito
SBU subdue
SBW sybows
SCA sacral
social
such as
SCD secede
SCE sachem
sachet
sacked
sacred
secret
sicken
soccer
socket
sucker
SCI sickie
suck in
SCL Sicily
sickle
sickly
suckle
SCN secant
second
secund
SCO seccos
sector
sick of
sickos
SCR secern
secure
SCU sacrum
suck up
SDC seduce
SDE sadden
Sidney

sodden
sudden
Sydney
SDH saddhu
SDL saddle
sedile
sod all
SDN siding
SDO side-on
SDS sadism
sadist
SDT sedate
sudate
SDU sodium
SEA seesaw
Shevat
stelae
stelar
SEC sheuch
sketch
speech
stench
SED speedo
speedy
steady
SEE scenes
seeded
Seeger
seeker
see red
shekel
skewed
skewer
sleded
soever
spewer
stereo
Steven
stewed
Sweden
Szeged
SEG sledge
sleigh
SEH seethe
SEI scenic
see fit
sherif
specie
step in
steric
SEK sheikh
sneaky
specky
SEL seemly
Sheela
sheila□
shells
skelly
smelly
snelly
Steele
steely
Stella

swells
SEM smegma
steamy
stemma
stemme
SEN seeing
Sheena
Sheene
sheeny
sienna
Sterne
SEO see you
step on
sterol
SEP Sherpa
sleepy
steppe
SER shears
sherry□
sierra□
skerry
smeary
sperre
SES speiss
SET seek to
sheath
sheets
Shelta
shelty
siesta
sleety
sleuth
smeath
smeeth
svelte
sweaty
sweets
sweety
SEU step up
step-up
SEV sheave
shelve
sleave
sleeve
steeve
swerve
SEY Sheryl
SEZ sleaze
sleazy
sneeze
sneezy
SFE sifter
soften
suffer
SFI soffit
softie
suffix
SFL safely
siffle
softly
SFO soft on
SFR safari
SFS Sufism

SFT safety
SGA saggar
signal
SGE sagger
signer
signet
SGI sagoin
saguin
SGL sagely
SGO segnos
sign of
sign on
Signor
SGR sugary
SGU sign up
SHC Schick
SHE schlep
SHM schema
scheme
SHN sphinx□
SHO school
SHR Sahara
sphere
SHS schism
schist
schuss
SHZ schizo
SIA Saimaa
Shiraz
smilax
spicae
spicas
spinal
spiral
SIB slip by
SIC smirch
snitch
stitch
switch□
SID shindy
skiddy
SIE sailed
sailer□
shiner
shiver
skiver
slicer
slider
sliver
smiler
smilet
smiley
smiter
sniper
snipes
snivel
soiled
soirée
spiced
spider
spiked
spinel
spinet

spirea
stipel
stipes
St Ives
suited
swivel
SIF sniffy
stiffy
SIG stingy
swinge
SIH slight
Smiths
smithy
spight
SII Scipio
skip it!
slip in
spirit
SIK slinky
Spinks
sticks
sticky
SIL scilla
shield
skilly
slimly
stifle
SIM stigma
SIN scions
shinny
skiing
skinny
soigné
SIO Saigon
sailor
Shiloh
skibob
skidoo
Skiros
slip on
slip-on
spigot
suitor
SIP skimpy
slippy
stirps
SIR sbirri
SIS Shiism
SIT Saints
shifty
Shiite
Shinto
shinty
shirty
spilth
SIU shin up
skin up
slip up
slip-up
stir up
SIV skivvy
spivvy
SJH St John

SJN sejant
SKI Sikkim
SKO Sukkot
SLA salaam
Salian
salpae
salpas
selvas
silvan
sulcal
sultan
sylvae
sylvan
SLC select
silica
solace
splice
SLD solidi
SLE salted
salued
salver
seller
selves
silken
silver□
solder
solver
spleen
sullen
SLF salify
sclaff
spliff
SLG silage
SLH sulpha
SLI salmis
salvia
Silvia
Sylvia
SLK saluki
SLL Salala
saltly
solely
SLM salami
Salome
solemn
SLN salina
saline
Selene
Selina
Sileni
silent
so long
so long!
so-long
spline
splint
SLO sallow
salmon
saloon
saltos
salvos
seldom
sold on
SLR salary
sclera
sultry
SLS splash
splosh
SLT salute
solito
solute
splits
SLU saltus
sell up
silt up
soleus
sulcus
SLV saliva
SMA sambar
Samian
sampan
simian
summae
SMC so much
sumach
SME samiel
Samuel
Semper
Semtex®
shmoes
simmer
simnel
simper
summer□
SMI semeia
summit
SMK samekh
SML sample
semble
Semele
simile
simple
simply
Somali
St-Malo
SMM sememe
SMN Simone
simony
so many
SMO sambos
samfoo
Samson
Simeon
simoom
simoon
summon
symbol
SMR samara□
sempre
sombre
SMS samosa
SMT somata
SMU sambur
Samsun
SMZ Somoza
SNA sandal
Sangay
Sanjay
sanpan
Sendai
Sinéad
Sontag
sundae
Sunday
sunhat
Sunnah
suntan
syntax
SNC Seneca
sonics
SNE sanded
sander
Sanger
sanies
sender
sennet
senses
Sinden
singer□
sinker
sinner
sinter
sonnet
sunbed
sunder
sundew
sunken
sunset
SNF sanify
SNI sink in
sunlit
syndic
SNL sanely
senile
single
singly
SNN sonant
SNO sankos
Santos
send on
senior
sensor
sunbow
sun-god
synroc
SNR Sandra
Señora
sentry
sundry
SNT sanity
senate□
sonata
SNU send up
send-up
sinful
SNW sinews
sinewy
SOA scopae
Scopas
shop at
shoran
slogan
slog at
Slovak
soon at
stop at
storax
SOB slobby
snobby
stop by
SOC sconce
scorch
scotch□
slouch
smooch
smouch
SOD shoddy
SOE scored
scorer
scores
scoter
shovel
shover
showed
shower
sloken
sloven
smoked
smoker
snorer
soogee
sooner
spoken
stoker□
stokes□
stolen
stoned
stoner
stones
Stopes
stored
stores
storey
stower
SOG slough□
smoggy
sponge
spongy
stodge
stodgy
stooge
stop-go
SOH soothe
SOI scolia
scoria
shojis
shoo-in
skolia
stolid
stop in
SOJ Skopje
SOK spooky
stocks
stocky
SOL shoals
shoole
should
slowly
spoils
spoilt
stools
SOM storms
stormy
SON Sloane
stound
SOO smokos
spot on
spot-on
stolon
SOP sloppy
snoopy□
stoope
SOS scorse
Scouse
skoosh
sloosh
spouse
stoush
swoosh
SOT shorts
shorty
smooth
snooty
snotty
snouty
soon to
sports
sporty
spotty
SOU SCONUL
shogun
show up
slow up
stop up
swot up
SOY storys
SOZ snooze
snoozy
SPE sapped
sapper□
sepses
septet
sipper
sippet
supper
sypher
SPG sapego
SPH Sappho
SPI sepsis
septic
Sophia
Sophie
SPL sapele
sapple
sipple
supple
supply
SPN supine
SPO siphon
syphon
SPR superb
SPU septum
St Paul
SQE sequel
SQI sequin
SRA screak
scream
serial
serrae
serras
serval
Sirhan
spread
streak
stream
striae
stroam
surtax
Syriac
Syrian
SRB scribe
shrubs
Strabo
strobe
SRC Sirach
spruce
strict
struck
SRD shreds
stride
SRE sarsen
screed
screen
series
server
shriek
Sir Ken
sorbet
Sorley
sorrel
sorted
sorter
streek
streel
Streep
street
surfer
surrey□
survey
syrtes
SRF scruff
shrift
shroff
strafe
straff
strife
SRG striga
SRI Sardis

sarnie
Serlio
sordid
sortie
sprain
spruik
straik
strain
strait
SRK shrike
strake
strike
stroke
SRL scroll
shrill
sorely
spryly
stroll
surely
SRM scrimp
scrump
serums
shrimp
skrimp
skrump
stramp
stroma
struma
SRN sarong
Serena
serene
serine
shrank
shrine
shrink
shrunk
Sirens
spring□
sprint
sprung
strand
string
strond
strong□
strung
strunt
syrinx□
SRO Sargon
sartor
scroop
sermon
sorgos
sorrow
sort of
sure of
SRP scrape
scraps
script
serape
seraph
straps
stripe
stripy

syrupy
SRR Sartre
SRS sprush
stress
SRT scruto
sprite
spritz
strata
strath
Strato
surety
SRU serous
shroud
Sirius
sprout
Stroud
strout
SRV scrive
shrive
strive
SRW scrawl
scrawm
screws
screwy
shrewd
shrowd
sprawl
strawy
SSA sashay
SSB Sasebo
SSE sestet
Sisley
sister
system
SSI Saskia
siskin
suslik
SSM sesame
SSO so soon
SSR sistra
SSU sus out
STA satrap
so that
STE sateen
settee
setter
sithen
sithes
sitter
so then
suttee
sythes
STF set off
set-off
STL settle
suttle
suttly
STM shtumm
STN satang
satiny
siting
STO set-tos
set-to's

shtook
shtoom
sitcom
Sutton
STR satire
satori
Saturn
Satyrs
suture
STS setose
STU set out
sit out
STW Sittwe
SUA scutal
Seumas
Seurat
squeak
squeal
SUB slubby
snubby
Stubbs
stubby
SUC scutch
sluice
smutch
source
stucco
SUD squids
sturdy
SUE saucer
sautés
soured
soused
souses
souter
squier
SUF scurfy
snuffy
squiff
stuffy
SUG scunge
sludge
sludgy
smudge
smudgy
snudge
spurge
SUH slushy
SUI shut in
shut-in
SI unit
squail
studio
stupid
SUK shucks
spunky
SUL smugly
snugly
souple
sourly
squall
squill
SUM scummy

slummy
squama
SUN squint
squiny
SUO spur on
stupor
SUP sculpt
slumpy
stumps
stumpy
SUR scurry
slurry
spurry
square
squire
squirm
squirr
squirt
Stuart
SUS Sousse
squash
squish
SUT shufti
shufty
smutty
stunts
SUU scutum
shut up
soup up
sputum
SUV scurvy
SUW squawk
SUZ scuzzy
SVE savvey
Sèvres
soviet□
SVG savage
SVN savant
savine
saving
SVR Savery
severe
Severn
SVT savate
SVU save up
save us
savour
SWA so what?
SWE sawder
sawyer□
SWG sewage
SWL sawfly
Sewell
SWN sewing
SWS sowsse
SWT Soweto
SWU sewn up
SXA sexual
SXE sextet
SXO sexpot
sexton
SXS sexism
sexist

SXU six-gun
Sixtus
SYA Skylab
SYE styled
SYH says he
say why
scyphi
scythe
SYI sayyid
stymie
SYL Scylla
SYN saying
Smyrna
spying
SYO stylos
SYR Sayers
SYS skyish
SYU spy out
stylus
SZL sizzle
sozzle
SZN sizing
SZO Suzhou
SZS sizism
SZU size up
TAA tea bag
tear at
to a man
Trajan
TAC thatch
trance
TAE teasel
teaser
teazel
thaler
Thales
Thames
thawed
to a tee
tracer
traces
Tracey
trader
Tralee
trapes
travel
Tuareg
TAH trashy
TAI tear in
Thalia
that is
tragic
TAK thanks
tracks
TAL teagle
teazle
thalli
TAM trauma
TAN tranny
TAO teapot
TAP tramps
TAT traits
TAU teacup

team up
tear up
tragus
TBA tibiae
tibial
tibias
Tobias
Tubman
TBE tabbed
tablet
tubber
TBF tabefy
TBG Tobago
TBI Tabriz
Tebbit
TBL tubule
Tybalt
TBN tubing
TBO taboos
to boot
TBR tabard
TBT to bits
tubate
TBU Tobruk
tubful
Tubruq
TCB Ty Cobb
TCE ticker
ticket
tocher
tucked
tucket
TCI tactic
tocsin
tuck in
TCL tackle
tickle
TCM Tacoma
to come
to-come
TCN techno
TCO tack on
Tucson
tycoon
TCU tuck up
TDE tedder
TDI tidbit
TDL tiddle
tiddly
tidily
toddle
TDT to date
TDU Te Deum
tedium
tidy up
tidyup
TDY today's
TEA thecae
thecal
the day
the Law
thenar
toecap

toerag
trepan
TEC thence
tierce
trench
TED trendy
tweedy
TEE tee-hee
teepee
teeter
Thebes
the few
the leg
the Met
the Net
the net
the red
theses
the Web
tmeses
Treves
TEH teethe
The Who
TEI taenia
The Kid
thesis
The Wiz
tiepin
TEL The Fly
they'll
treble
trebly
tweely
TEM Thelma
TEN the end
theine
the one
TEO Taejon
the box
the lot
the mob
the now
the Son
tremor
Trevor
TER the dry
theirs
theory
they're
TES teensy
theism
theist
tressy
tsetse
TET treaty
Trento
twenty
TEU the sum
The Sun
tied up
TEV they've
twelve
TEW the two
TEX the axe
TEZ tweeze
TFE toffee
tuffet
tufted
TFI tiffin
TFO Teflon®
TFR tofore
TGE tegmen
Tigger
togaed
tugger
TGI Tigris
tugrik
TGL toggle
TGO tiglon
TGR Tagore
TGT tights
THA Tehran
THC tchick
THN tahini
to hand
THR T-shirt
THT Tahiti
TIA Tainan
taipan
Taiwan
tribal
trinal
TIB Thisbe
trilby❑
TIC twitch
TID triode
TIE tailed
Taipei
toiler
toilet
trimer
trivet
twined
twiner
TIG things
thingy
twiggy
twinge
TIH thighs
Trisha
TII Tricia
trifid
trivia
Trixie
twilit
TIK tricks
tricky
TIL taigle
thinly
trials
trifle
trigly
trimly
triple
triply
twirly
TIN triune
TIO tailor
Tainos
tricot
trigon
tripod
tripos
triton❑
TIP trippy
TIS thirst
TIT thirty
twisty
TIU trip up
TIV thieve
TIY Taimyr
TKH takahe
TKI take in
take it
TKN taking
token'd
TKO take on
TKS tykish
TKT take to
TKU take up
take-up
TLA taleae
talk at
tele-ad
Tilman
tulwar
TLD Toledo
TLE talker
teller❑
tiller
tilted
tolter
TLG Telugu
TLI talkie
Tilsit
TLN talent
tiling
TLO Talbot
talion
talk of
tallow
tell on
telson
TLT talk to
TLU talcum
talk up
Talmud
TMA tambac
tam-tam
Timman
tombac
tombak
tomcat
tympan
TME tamper
temper
timber
Tim Yeo
TMF tumefy
TMI Tamsin
Timmie
tomtit
tom-tit
TML tamale❑
tamely
temple❑
timely
tumble
tumuli
tumult
TMN timing
TMO Tambov
tampon
tempos
timbós
tomboy
tom-tom
TMR Tamara
tamari
Timaru
timbre
TMT tomato
TMU Tammuz
tumour
tum-tum
TNA tankas
tin hat
TNE tandem
tanker
tanned
tanner
tender
tenner
tenrec
tensed
tenter
tenues
tinder
tinker
tinned
tinsel
Tonies
tunnel
TNI tannic
tannin
tennis
tenpin
tonsil
tune in
TNL tangle
tangly
tingle
tinily
tinkle
tinkly
TNM toneme
TNN tenant
tuning
TNO tangos
tannoy❑
tendon
tin god
tinpot
tondos
tons of
TNR tantra❑
tenure
tundra
TNT tenets
tenuto
TNU Tanguy
tank up
tinful
tone up
tongue
tune up
Tungus
TOA Thomas
thorax
too bad
trocar
Trojan
two-way
TOE too few
trowel
TOG though
troggs
trough
TOH toothy
troche
trophy
TOI trofie
tropic
two-bit
TOK troika
TOL tootle
troely
trolly
two-ply
TON thorny
TOO tholoi
too-too
trogon
TOP Thorpe
trompe
troops
troppo
troupe
TOS Taoism
Taoist
tootsy
TOT trouts
TPA Top Cat
top hat
top-hat
TPE tappet
tipped
tippet
Tophet
topper
TPF tepefy
tip off
tip-off
top off
typify
TPK Topeka
TPL tipple
topple
tupelo
TPN typing
TPO tiptoe
tiptop
top dog
Typhon
TPR tephra
TPS typist
TPT tapeta
TPU tip out
Top Gun
top out
typhus
TRA tarmac
tarnal
tarsal
tartan
tartar❑
Tarzan
terrae
thread
threap
threat
throat
Tor Bay
Torbay
turban
Tyrian
TRC thrice
turaco
TRD teredo
tirade
TRE target
tercel
tercet
Terkel
termed
threep
throes
torten
tortes
tureen
turfed
turkey❑
turned
turner❑
turret
turves
TRF tariff
thrift
Torify
Toryfy
TRI tirrit
toroid
torpid
torrid
turbid
turbit
turgid
Turkic

turn in
turnip
Turpin
TRK Tersky
TRL tartly
termly
thrall
thrill
toruli
turtle
TRN threne
throne
throng
Tirana
tiring
Turing
tyrant
Tyrone
TRO terror
torpor
torsos
turbos
turbot
Turcos
turgor
turion
turn on
turn-on
TRP thrips
TRR torero
TRS Teresa
thrash
thresh
thrush
thrust
TRT terata
turn to
TRU targum❑
tarsus❑
tart up
tergum
torque
turn up
turn-up
TRV thrive
TRW Tarawa
thrawn
thrown
TSA Tasman
Tuscan
TSC tisick
TSE tassel
taster
tested
testee
tester
to seek
tusker
tusser
TSH tusche
TSI tussis
TSL to sell
tussle
TSN tisane
TSO toss of
TSR Tishri
TSU tissue
toss up
toss-up
TTA tetrad
titian❑
to-tear
tutsan
TTE tatler
tatter
tether
tetter
titfer
titled
titter
tother
t'other
totter
TTH tetchy
titchy
TTI tattie
titbit
TTL tattle
tittle
titule
TTN Titans
TTO tattoo
TTP Titipu
TTU Titmus
tittup
tut-tut
TUA toucan
Truman
TUE tauten
toupee
tourer
touter
TUG trudge
TUH taught
touché
touchy
TUK trunks
TUL tautly
tousle
touzle
TUN truant
TUO Teuton
Toulon
TUS Thurso
truism
TUT true to
trusty
TUU Taurus
TVL Tuvalu
TVR tavern
TWA towbar
TWC thwack
TWE Tawney
townee
TWG towage
TWI townie
TWN towing
Tswana
TWO tu-whoo
TWR tawdry
thwart
TXE taxies
Tex-Mex
TXI toxoid
TXN taxing
TYM Toyama
TYN toying
try and
trying
TYO Taylor
thymol
toy boy
toyboy
try for
TYR tuyère
TYS thyrsi
TYT Toyota
Toyota®
TYU thymus
try out
try-out
TYY Taymyr
TZA tazzas
UAC usance
UAD Uganda
UAG Ubangi
UAI Ugarit
uracil
Uralic
Urania
uranic
UAL unable
usable
usably
UAT Ubasti
UAU Uranus
UBA umbrae
umbral
umbras
unbear
unbias
upbear
upbeat
UBE umbles
UBL unbelt
unbolt
UBN unbend
unbent
unbind
upbind
urbane
UBO upblow
UBR unbare
unbark
unborn
unbury
UBT unbitt
UCA uncial
unclad
UNCTAD
UCC uncock
UCG uncage
UCI uncoil
upcoil
urchin
UCL uncolt
UCN uncini
UCO unclog
uncool
UCP uncape
uncope
UCR uncord
uncork
uncurl
UCS uncase
upcast
UCT uncate
UNCSTD
UCW uncowl
UDA undead
undeaf
undraw
UDC undeck
undock
UDE undies
UDK Updike
UDL unduly
UDN undine
undone
UDT undate
update
UEC UNESCO
UED ureide
UEE uneven
ureter
UEG unedge
UEI uredia
UES unease
uneasy
UET uneath
used to
UEU used up
useful
uterus
UFI unfair
UFL unfold
UFO unfool
upflow
UFR unform
unfurl
UFZ Uffizi
UGA ungear
ungual
UGE ungues
UGI unguis
UGL ungula
UGN urgent
urging
UGO upgrow
UGR ungird
ungord
Utgard
UGU unglue
UGW ungown
UHA unhead
UHI unhair
UHL unhele
unhelm
unholy
uphill
uphold
UHN unhand
UHO unhook
unhoop
UHR unhurt
UHS unhasp
unhusk
UHU uphaud
UHV unhive
UIA Unitas
urinal
UIE UNICEF
uniped
unisex
united❑
uniter
UII unific
UIO unipod
UNISON
unison
UIT ubiety
Uniate
UIU ubique
unique
UJS unjust
UKE upkeep
UKI unknit
upknit
UKN unkind
unking
UKO unknot
UKR uakari
UKS unkiss
ULA Ullman
unlead
unload
uplead
upload
ULC unlace
unlock
uplock
ULD unlade
ULF uglify
uplift
ULG ullage
ULK unlike
ULL uglily
ULM unlime
ULN unline
unlink
upland
ULO uplook
ULR unlord
ULS unlash
unlast
unless
ULU umlaut
ULV unlive
unlove
UMD unmade
UMK unmake
UMO unmoor
UMR Uemura
UMS unmask
upmost
utmost
UNI unnail
UNS unnest
UOI utopia❑
UPA unpray
UPC unpack
unpick
UPI unpaid
UPN upping
UPP unpope
UPR umpire
UPS uppish
UPT uppity
UPU unplug
URA unread
unreal
uprear
uproar
URB unrobe
URC Ulrica
URE unreel
URI unrein
URK unrake
URL unroll
unrule
unruly
uproll
URO unroof
unroot
uproot
URP unripe
unrope
URS unrest
uprise
uprist
uprose
URT uprate
USA unseal
unseam
unseat
unspar
upsway
USD upside
USE ulster
unseel
unseen
unstep
Ussher
USF unsafe
USI unsaid
unship
unsuit
USL unself

Words marked ❑ can also be spelled with an initial capital letter

Ursula
USN unsung
ursine
USO unshod
unshoe
unstop
unstow
upshot
USR unsure
USU unshut
unsoul
USW unsown
UTA unteam
unthaw
uptear
UTC untack
untuck
urtica
UTD untidy
UTE untied
UTI untrim
up to it
UTK uptake
UTL untile
untold
UTM ultima
ultimo
untame
untomb
UTN untent
untune
UTO ultion
UTR unturf
unturn
upturn
Ust'-Urt
UTU untrue
UTW up town
uptown
UUA uvulae
uvular
uvulas
UUE unused
uruses
usurer
UUQ Urumqi
UVI unveil
UWA unwrap
UWL unwell
unwill
UWN unwind
upwind
up-wind
UWP unwept
UWR unware
unwary
unwire
unwork
upward
usward
UWS unwise
unwish
UWT up with
UWV unwive
UYK unyoke
VAD viands
VAL viable
VBR Viborg
VCI victim
VCN vacant
vicuna
vicuña
VCO vector
victor❑
VCT vacate
VCU vacuum
VDO videos
VDS Vedist
VDT veduta
vedute
veduti
VEA view as
VEE viewer
VEN Vienna
VGN vagina
VGO vagrom
VGR vagary
vigoro
VGU vigour
VHR vihara
VIE veiled
veined
voiced
VIL vainly
VKA Vikram
VKN viking❑
VLA Vulcan
vulgar
VLC veloce
VLE valley
valued
valuer
values
valved
Velsen
velvet
volley
VLF vilify
VLL vildly
vilely
VLM volume
VLN valine
volant
VLO Villon
VLR Valera
Valéry
Velcro®
velure
VLS valise
VLT valeta
valuta
veleta
volute
VLU Valium®
vallum
valour
vellum
velour
villus
VMN vimana
VMS vamose
VNA vandal❑
venial
VNC Venice
VNE vendee
vender
veneer
venter
VNI ventil
VNL venule
VNO vendor
VNR Vänern
vinery
VNS vanish
venose
VNT vanity
venite
VNU venous
vinous
VNW venewe
VOE violet❑
VOI violin
VOO voodoo
VPU vapour
VRA Vargas
verbal
vernal
VRC varech
VRE Varden
varied
verger
vermes
versed
verser
vertex
vervet
vortex
VRF verify
VRG virago
VRI vermil
vermin
vermis
Virgil
virgin❑
VRL verily
virile
VRN Varuna
Verona
virent
VRO Vardon
Vernon
versos
vireos
VRS Varèse
verism
verist
VRT verity❑
VRU Verdun
versus
virtue
VSA vassal
vestal
vestas
visual
VSC vesica
VSE vessel
vested
Vosges
VSG visage
VSI viscid
VSL vastly
VSN Vishnu
VSO vision
VSR vestry
VSU viscus
VTA Vatman
vittae
VTE vetoed
vetoes
VTI vote in
VTL vitals
VTN voting
VTR votary
voters
VTV votive
VUA Vauban
VUO vaudoo
VVA Vivian
VVC vivace
VVE Vivien
VVF vivify
VVL vively
VWR vaward
VWS vowess
VXN vexing
VXO vox pop
VYG voyage
VYU voyeur
VZE vizier
VZL vizsla
VZR vizard
WAE weaken
weaner
wearer
weasel
weaver❑
whaler
WAF wharfs
WAH what ho
WAI what if
WAK wealk'd
whacko
WAL weakly
wraxle
WAM whammy
WAO weapon
wear on
what of
WAS whatso
wrasse
WAT wealth
wraith
WAU wrap up
WBE webbed
WBL wobble
wobbly
WBR Webern
WBS Wabash
WCE wicked
wicker
wicket
WDA Wadman
WDE wadset
wedded
wedged
widget
Widnes
WDI wade in
WDL waddle
wedeln
widdle
widely
WDO wide of
WDS widish
WDT wideth
WEA whenas
WEC wheech
whence
wrench
wretch
WED wieldy
WEE weeder
weeper
weever
wee-wee
Wiener
Wiesel
WEG wheugh
WEI weepie
weevil
WEL weekly
wheels
WEO whet on
WER wherry
WET wreath
WEU woeful
WEZ wheeze
wheezy
WFL waffle
wifely
WFR wafery
WGA Wagram
Wigman
wigwag
wigwam
WGE Wagner
wigged
WGL waggle
waggly
wiggle
wiggly
woggle
WGO waggon
wigeon
WHA wah-wah
WHH wo ha ho
WHN wahine
WIA Weimar
whidah
WIB Whitby
WID weirdo
WIE wailer
waiter
waiver
whiles
whiner
whiten
whites
White's
writer
WIF whiffy
WIG whinge
WIH weight
whisht
wright❑
writhe
WII whip in
WIK whisky
WIL whilly
WIN whinny
WIO wait on
WIP whippy
WIR whirry
WIS whilst
whimsy
WIT wristy
WIU wait up
whip up
WKN waking
Woking
WKT wake to
WKU wake up
WLA wallah
WLD will do
WLE Walden
walker❑
walled
Waller
wallet
Walter
welder
Weller
Welles
welter
Wilder
Wilkes
willed
willet
wilted
Wolsey
wolves
WLI walk it
wall in
Wallis
Walvis
welkin
wellie
Wilkie

Willie
Willis
Wolfit
WLL wildly
wilily
WLN Weland
WLO walk on
walk-on
wallop
wallow
Walton
Weldon
weldor
willow
Wilson
Wilton
WLS Walesa
WLU wall up
walnut
walrus
well up
wilful
WMA wombat
WME Wimsey
WML wamble
wimble
wimple
WMN woman'd
WMO Wim Kok
WMR womera
WNA want ad
wink at
WNE wander
Wankel
wanted
wanter
Wenger
wincer
winded
winder
winged
winger
winker
winner
winter
wonder□
wonted
WNI want in
wing it
Winnie
WNL wangle
winkle
wintle
WNN waning
Winona
WNO wandoo
wanion
wanton
window
winnow
WNR winery
wintry
WNT wont to
WNU want up
wind up
wind-up
win out
WOE wooded
wooden
woosel
WOL wholly
woolly
WON wooing
WOP whoops
WOS whoosh
WOT wroath
WPE wapper
WPL Wopsle
WPT wapiti
WPU wipe up
WRA Warsaw
work as
work at
WRD worlds
WRE warden
warder
warner□
warped
warper
warren□
warrey
worked
worker
wormer
worsen
worser
WRG word go
WRH worthy
WRI wire in
work in
work-in
worrit
WRL warble
warily
warmly
wirily
wordly
WRN wiring
WRO wardog
Warhol
warn of
Warton
wary of
work on
WRR War Cry
war cry
warcry
WRT warmth
warm to
WRU warm up
warm-up
work up
WSE washed
washer
wasted
waster
Wesker
Wesley
wester
wisher
WSI Wessis
Westie
WSL wisely
wistly
WSO wisdom□
wish on
WSS wisest
WST wise to
WSU wash up
wise up
WTE wether
wither
witter
wuther
WTI within
with it
WTL wattle
WTO Watson
wet rot
WTR Waters
watery
WTU wet out
WUH waught
WVL wavily
WVN waving
WVR wivern
wyvern
WVT wave to
WWE wowser
WXE wax-red
WXL waxily
WYA waylay
whydah
WYU way out
way-out
WZI wiz kid
WZL wuzzle
WZR wizard
XAE Xiamen
XLI xyloid
XLN xylene
XNA xenial
XND Xanadu
XNH Xanthe
XNN Xining
XOA Xhosan
XRE Xerxes
XVE Xavier
XZO Xuzhou
YAE Yeager
YAL yearly
YAT yeasty
YBE yabber
YBO yobbos
YCU Yichun
YET Yvette
YFL yaffle
YGE yagger
YGN yogini
YGR yogurt
YHE Yahweh
YHH yo-ho-ho
YHO Yahoos
YIK yoicks
YKE yikker
YKZ yakuza
YLA yell at
YLE yelper
YLO Y-alloy
yellow□
YME yammer
YMU yum-yum
YNE Yankee
yonder
YNO Yangon
yen for
YOA yeoman
YOE yeomen
YOI Yeovil
YON Yvonne
YOO yoo-hoo
YPE yapper
yippee
YPI yuppie
YRB Yoruba
YRC Yorick
YRE yorker
YRH yarpha
YRI Yardie
yorkie□
YRO yarrow
YRS Y-cross
YSA yes-man
YSE yesses
YSI Yasmin
YTE yatter
YUE you bet
YUH youths
YYM Yo-Yo Ma
ZAO zealot
ZCO zoccos
ZDA zodiac□
ZDN Zidane
ZEI zoetic
ZFE zaffer
ZFL zufoli
ZFR zaffre
ZGA zigzag
ZGE Zagreb
ZGT zygote
ZIA Zainab
ZLS zeloso
ZMI Zambia
zombie
ZMO zambos
ZMS zymase
ZNC Zanuck
ZNE Zinder
zinger
zonked
ZNI zinnia
ZNN zenana
ZNO zincos
ZNT zenith
ZOI zoom in
ZOO zoozoo
ZOY zlotys
ZPE zapper
zipper
ZPT Zapata
ZPY zephyr
ZRB zareba
ZRC Zurich
ZRI zero in
ZRO zircon
zorros
ZRT zeroth
ZSE zester
zoster
ZTE zither
ZUM zeugma
ZUO Zhukov
ZYA Zaynab

7 letters – odd

AAAA Alabama
Atacama
AAAC Aramaic
AAAE apanage
AAAO Arapaho
AAAS atamans
AAAT adamant
at a halt
AAAY ataraxy
AACO Ajaccio
AACY a far cry
anarchy
AADN Abaddon
abandon
AAED araneid
at an end
AAEE academe
AAEF aware of
AAEG a bad egg
AAEM as a team
AAER amateur
AAES Amadeus
AAEY academy
AAGM amalgam
AAGR Alamgir
AAHD abashed
AAHE Arachne
AAHN Aga Khan
Alashan
AAHR al-Azhar
AAHT a bad hat
AAIA amanita
arabica
AAIE alanine
amative
apatite
arabise
arabize
avarice
AAIG abating
amazing
awaking
AAIM atavism
AAIN Acadian
Arabian
AAIS acacias
adagios
AAIT Arabist
AALW at a blow
AAMA anaemia
AAMC anaemic
AAMD alarmed
AANT against
AAOD at a word
AAOE abalone

à la mode
alamode
as a joke
AAOS at a loss
AAOY amatory
anagogy
analogy
anatomy
AARM anagram
AARY Asa Gray
AASA Aral Sea
AASN Adamson
AASZ Agassiz
AATA acantha
AATD adapted
awaited
AATF a part of
AATR adapter
adaptor
AATS abattis
anattos
AAUE abature
as a rule
AAUH at a push
AAUK Ataturk
Atatürk
AAYE analyse
AAYT analyst
ABAT A S Byatt
ABDS albedos
ABET ambient
ABGS albugos
ABIS aiblins
ABMN albumen
albumin
ABNA Albania
ABNS albinos
ambones
ABNZ Albéniz
ABOD ambroid
ABOE Ambrose
ABRA Alberta
ABRI Alberti
ABRN Auberon
ABTR arbiter
ACAC archaic
ACAE arcuate
ACAM acclaim
ACAT accoast
ACDA aecidia
Arcadia
ascidia
ACDE accidie
ACEE accrete
ACEM a scream
ACES ancress
ACET ancient
ACEY alchemy
archery
ACHL alcohol
ACIE archive
ascribe
ACIN auction

ACNE accinge
a sconce
ACNS ancones
ACOD arctoid
ACOY anchovy
ACRD ascarid
ACRE accurse
ACSD accused
ACSR accuser
ACSS ascesis
ACTC ascetic
ACUL accrual
ACUT account
ascaunt
ACWY archway
ADBE audible
ADBN Audubon
ADBY audibly
ADDO added to
ADES address
Andress
Andrews
ADHT and that
ADIH Aldrich
ADMN abdomen
Andaman
ADNA addenda
ADNE al dente
andante
ADOD android
ADON and so on
ADOS arduous
ADPO add up to
ADRA Andorra
ADRN andiron
ADSN Addison
ADTR auditor
AEAD Abelard
AEAE acetate
average
AEBC acerbic
AEDF ahead of
AEES ageless
AEFN Aberfan
AEGH alength
AEGR avenger
AEHH Ayeshah
AEIE adenine
alewife
AEIO Aretino
AEIR atelier
AEIS Alexius
AEIY acetify
amenity
AELE areolae
AELN Ameslan
avellan
AEOD aneroid
AEOE acetone
anemone
awesome
AEOF ale hoof
AEOS acetous

AERD Axelrod
AERN Aneurin
atebrin
AESA Ayeesha
AESS asepses
asepsis
AETA amentia
AETC aseptic
Avestic
AETN Avestan
AETO alert to
AETR abetter
abettor
AETY adeptly
alertly
AEUL asexual
AEUY Avebury
AFAD affeard
AFBE affable
AFBY affably
AFED Anfield
AFEM Alfheim
AFIS affairs
AFIT afflict
AFLA alfalfa
AFLY awfully
AFNO Alfonso
AFOT affront
AFRE afforce
AFRS as far as
AFRT at first
AFUT at fault
AGAE aggrade
at grade
AGAI Afghani
AGBA algebra
AGBY Algo Bay
AGCS angicos
AGEN Al Green
AGES aggress
Algiers
AGET augment
AGIE Anglice
AGIG angling
arguing
AGIH anguish
AGIY angrily
AGKK angekok
AGLC angelic
AGLR angular
AGLS angelus
AGLU Angelou
AGOA angioma
AGRA Algeria
AGRD angered
AGRL augural
AGRR augurer
AGSA Augusta
AGSS arguses
AGYT angry at
AHAT at heart
athwart
AHBT adhibit

AHDS aphides
AHEE achieve
athlete
AHEY Ashbery
AHFR ache for
AHGA aphagia
AHHE aphthae
AHIE atheise
atheize
AHIM atheism
AHIT atheist
AHLA aphelia
Athalia
AHLY aphylly
AHMD ashamed
AHNA aphonia
AHOD Ashford
AHON Ashdown
AHRC Amharic
AHRN Acheron
AHSA aphasia
AHSC aphasic
AHSN Acheson
AHSS aphesis
AHTC aphetic
aphotic
AHVL à cheval
AHZN Alhazen
AIAE agitate
animate
AIAH Aligarh
AIAL abigail□
AIAO agitato
animato
AIAS animals□
AIBE amiable
AIBY amiably
AIDE Ariadne
AIED aniseed
AIEO alive to
AIET aliment
AIEY abide by
agilely
AIGE atingle
AIHO atishoo
AIHY apishly
AIIE aniline
asinine
AIIG abiding
arising
AIIM animism
AIIO Akihito
asinico
AIIT animist
AIIY ability
acidify
acidity
agility
anility
aridity
avidity
AIJN Abidjan
AILE axillae

AILF a mill of
AILR axillar
AILY axially
AINC anionic
AIND aligned
AINE aliunde
AINF a sign of
AINN Avignon
AIOA Arizona
AIOE adipose
AIOF a bit off
a rip-off
AIOY alimony
AIPE aripple
AISE at issue
AISO Ariosto
AISS aliases
ariosos
AITA arietta
AITC Asiatic
AITD Amistad
AITE a little
ariette
AITR aviator
AITS aristos
AIUH azimuth
AIUT aliquot
AJDE adjudge
AJIT abjoint
AJNT adjunct
AJUN adjourn
AKAD awkward
AKET asklent
AKLS alkalis
AKMA ack-emma
AKNE askance
AKNT alkanet
AKOD Ackroyd
Aykroyd
AKRS askaris
AKVR ask over
ALAD Aylward
ALAS all ears
ALAT at least
ALER all-seer
ALET ailment
ALGD alleged
ALGO allegro
ALHT all that
ALIE all-time
all-wise
ALNA Atlanta
ALNE Allende
allonge
ALNM allonym
ALNY Allenby
ALOD all told
ALOE all done
all's one
ALOG Aalborg
ALOK Allcock
ALRE at large
ALRN aileron

Words marked □ can also be spelled with an initial capital letter

ALRY allergy
ALSS atlases
ALTR all-star
ALVA alluvia
ALVR all over
all-over
ALWD allowed
ALYD alloyed
AMAA Alma-Ata
AMAD armband
AMAT army ant
AMCS Almack's
AMES aimless
armless
AMGR armiger
AMIE armoire
AMLE A A Milne
AMNA ammonia
Armenia
AMNC almanac
AMNR almoner
AMNY almonry
AMOE armhole
AMOK armlock
AMRA Almeria
AMRD admired
AMRL admiral
AMRR admirer
AMRS Aymaras
AMTR ammeter
AMUS armfuls
AMUY armoury
ANBL Annabel
ANES awnless
ANFR a one for
ANIK Alnwick
ANIY annuity
ANLD annelid
ANLR annular
ANLS annulus
ANLT annulet
ANRE Aintree
ANSA amnesia
ANSC amnesic
ANSY amnesty
ANTE Annette
ANTO annatto
ANYD annoyed
AOAA abomasa
AOAO avocado
AOAY anomaly
apogamy
AOBC amoebic
AOBE amoebae
AOBS amoebas
AODD avoided
AODE a doddle
AODF a load of
AODR avoider
AOEO at one go
AOET a moment
AOEY alonely
AOFY aloofly
AOGT amongst
AOHM apothem
AOHR another
AOIE aconite
adonise
adonize
agonise
agonize
anodise
anodize
atomise
atomize
azotise
azotize
AOIG adoring
atoning
AOIH abolish
Anouilh
AOII amorini
AOIL asocial
AOIM atomism
AOIN aeolian
AOIS agonies
AOIT amorist
AOKR Aboukir
AOKT a rocket
AOLA aboulia
AOLS apollos
AOMA anosmia
AOND adorned
AONE à pointe
AONW as of now
AOOE apocope
AOOL axolotl
AOOO amoroso
AOOS amorous
apodous
AOOY apology
AOPE a couple
AOSA Azov Sea
AOSD aroused
AOSL arousal
AOSS anoeses
AOTD adopted
AOTE apostle
AOYE acolyte
anodyne
APAD applaud
APAE appease
at peace
APAH appeach
APAT asphalt
APDA aspidia
APES adpress
at press
APID applied
APIE apprise
APIS at pains
APIT appoint
at point
APIY amplify
APLA ampulla
APLI appalti
APOA amphora
APOE approve
APON alphorn
APRE asperge
asperse
APRL apparel
apperil
APRN aspirin
APTE amputee
APUD Asplund
APUE ampoule
APYO apply to
AQIE acquire
AQIH Asquith
AQIT asquint
ARAA Adriana
ARAD air raid
airward
ARAE acreage
aureate
ARAL airmail
ARAS arrears
ARAT abreact
abreast
ARAY already
ARBC aerobic
ARBT acrobat
ARCE auricle
ARCN African
ARCS aurochs
ARCT apricot
ARDD abraded
ARDE abridge
AREN agree on
AREO agree to
ARES airless
ARFE a trifle
ARGT alright
ARHM Abraham
ARHP airship
ARHT air shot
ARIE airline
airside
airtime
ARIK airsick
ARIN arraign
ARIT airlift
ARLC acrylic
ARLY aurally
ARMA acromia
ARNC Aaronic
ARNE arrange
ARNL adrenal
ARNM acronym
AROA aureola
AROE abrooke
airhole
aureole
AROI a priori
AROK airlock
AROL air-cool
AROT airport
ARPA agrapha
Agrippa
ARPN atropin
ARPS apropos
ARPY atrophy
ARRE Airdrie
aurorae
ARRP air-drop
ARRS auroras
ARRW aircrew
ARSL aerosol
ARTD aerated
ARUD aground
ARUP Air Pump
ARUS atriums
ARVL arrival
ARXA apraxia
ARXS abraxas
ARYD arrayed
ARYS arroyos
ARZS abrazos
ASAE assuage
ASAN abstain
ASDS apsides
ASEE Auslese
austere
ASES abscess
ASGI assagai
assegai
ASGO al segno
ASID abscind
ASIE abscise
auspice
ASLE absolve
ASLM Absalom
ASMD assumed
ASNC arsenic
ASNE absence
ASNH absinth
ASNL arsenal
ASOD abscond
ASRA Austria
ASRD assured
ASRL austral
ASRN also-ran
ASRR assurer
ASUT assault
ASYR assayer
ASZS assizes
ATAA althaea
ATAD astrand
ATAE actuate
ATAT attract
ATAY actuary
ATBE actable
at table
ATBS Antibes
ATBY attaboy
ATCA attacca
ATCD antacid
ATCE article
attaché
Autocue
ATEL Attwell
ATEN Actaeon
ATEO Art Deco
ATEP Antwerp
ATER ant-bear
ATES actress
aptness
artless
ATFX antefix
ATGN antigen
ATID antbird
ATIE antliae
Astaire
astride
attrite
attuite
at twice
ATIO act dido
ATIT astrict
attaint
ATMS Artemis
at times
ATMT attempt
ATNA antenna
Antonia
ATND attuned
ATNM antonym
ATNO Antonio
ATOH Antioch
ATOK Art Monk
artwork
ATON althorn
ATOS actions
ATOY Anthony
ATPN act upon
ATPO act up to
ATPY autopsy
ATQE antique
ATRA apteria
ATRD altered
attired
ATRS Antares
ATRX anthrax
apteryx
ATRY autarky
ATSE artiste
ATSN artisan
ATTC astatic
ATUD astound
AUAE adulate
AUDL Arundel
AUDR asunder
AUEA Abu Mena
AUEY acutely
AUFR aquifer
AUHA Anushka
AUIA alumina
AUIE abusive
azurine
AUIG amusing
AULN Aquilon
AUNE alumnae
AUNS alumnus
Aquinas

AUOS aqueous
AURA aquaria
AUSR Al Unser
AUTC aquatic
AUUL as usual
AUVR aquiver
AUVT aquavit
AVNE advance
AVOI alveoli
AVRE adverse
AVRZ Alvarez
AVSD advised
AVSR adviser
advisor
AWRT at worst
AXEY anxiety
AXOS anxious
AXRE Auxerre
AXSS auxesis
AYAE amylase
AYAN Aly Bain
AYHN anywhen
AYIE anytime
anywise
AYML abysmal
AYOD anyroad
AYOE any more
AYOS azygous
AYOY anybody
AYSM alyssum
AYUS asylums
BAAH Branagh
BAAL bradawl
BAAO bravado
BAAT blatant
BABE bramble❑
BABG beanbag
bean-bag
BABK Baalbek
BABR blabber
BABX beat box
BABY brambly
BACE Blanche
BACY branchy
BADD bearded
braided
branded
BADP board up
BADR bladder
boarder
brander
BADY blandly
by and by
by-and-by
BAEG Boateng
BAEP blaze up
BAES braless
BAEY bravely
bravery
BAGA bhangra
BAGR blagger
BAHD beached
BAHM Brabham
BAHR blather
BAIG beading
beaming
bearing
beating
blaring
blazing
boating
bracing
BAIH bearish
BAIL biaxial
BAIR brazier
BAIY beamily
beatify
BAKN blacken
bracken
BAKT blanket
bracket
BAKY blackly
blankly
BALE Bradlee
braille❑
BALR beagler
brawler
BALS Beatles
BALY Bradley
Bramley
BAMN boatman
Bradman
Brahman
BAND brained
BANK beatnik
BANY blarney❑
BAOE by a nose
BAOF beat off
BAOS bravoes
BAOT be about
bear out
beat out
BARX Beatrix
BASE brassie
BASI Brassai
BASN Branson
BATD blasted
BATE beastie
brantle
brattle
BATF boast of
BATR blaster
blatter
boaster
BATY beastly
BAUA bravura
BAWN Branwen
BBAE Babbage
BBAL bobtail
BBGN be big on
BBIG bobbing
BBIH babyish
BBIS Babrius
BBIT Babbitt
bobbitt
BBKE bubukle
BBLD bobsled
BBLN Babylon
BBLR babbler
BBLS bubbles❑
BBLT bibelot
BBNA bubinga
BBNC bubonic
BBOE Bob Dole
Bob Hope
BBOK Babcock
BBRH by birth
BBST babysit
baby-sit
BBSU babassu
BBTY bobstay
BCAA baclava
BCAE baccare
backare
BCAM becharm
BCCE bicycle
BCES backers
BCET Beckett
BCHI bacchii
BCHM Beckham
BCHS Bacchus
BCIA buccina
BCIG backing
BCIS biccies
BCLC bucolic
BCLD buckled
BCLG backlog
BCLI bacilli
BCLR buckler
BCLY Backley
Buckley
BCNR Buchner
Büchner
BCOD becloud
BCOF back off
BCOS buckoes
BCOT back out
BCRM buckram
BCUE because
BDAD bedward
BDAF bedwarf
BDAR bid fair
BDEL Biddell
BDEP budge up
BDES badness
bad news
BDET bad debt
bed-rest
BDGT bedight
BDIE bedside
bedtime
BDIG bedding
bidding
budding
BDJZ Badajoz
BDOD bad mood
Bedford
BDOE bedsore
BDOK bedrock
bed-work
BDOM bad form
bedroom
BDON bed down
BDOS Beddoes
BDOT bedpost
BDRN bodhran
BDRP bad trip
BDUK bad luck
BDUN bad turn
Bedouin
BDVL bedevil
BDZN bedizen
BEAO beefalo
BEBK blesbok
BECA breccia
Brescia
BEDD blended
BEDH breadth
BEDN Brendan
BEDR bleeder
blender
breeder
BEES Bee Gees
BEEY brewery
BEFX Brer Fox
BEGN bren gun❑
BEHM Beecham
BEHR blether
BEIE beehive
beeline
BEIG beefing
brewing
BEIH blemish
BEIS blewits
BEIT Blériot
BEIY brevity
BEKN break in
break-in
BEKP break up
break-up
BEKR breaker
BEKY bleakly
BEMT beer-mat
BENN Brennan
BENR Bremner
BEOE beesome
BEPR bleeper
BESD blessed
BESE bless me!
BESS breasts
BETE breathe
BETN Beeston
BETY breathy
BEWX beeswax
BEYS bye-byes
BFAO buffalo❑
BFCL bifocal
BFLD baffled
BFON buffoon
BFRE by force
BFRT be for it
BFTP buff-tip
BGAE baggage
big game
big name
BGAG Big Bang
BGAS big cats
BGAY bag lady
beggary
BGBO bugaboo
BGDD Baghdad
BGED bighead
BGER bugbear
BGES bigness
BGET biggest
BGHT Bagehot
big shot
BGIE bagpipe
begrime
beguile
beguine
big time
BGIG begging
bugging
BGIH biggish
BGIS Baggins
bagnios
baguios
BGIY baggily
BGLS Biggles
BGNA begonia
BGOE big-note
BGOM begloom
BGON bighorn
bog down
BGOS bugloss
BGOT Bigfoot
BGRA begorra
BGRE Bogarde
BGRN bog-iron
BGTD bigoted
BGTI Bugatti
BGTY bigotry
BGUS bagfuls
Bagpuss
big guns
BHAN Bahrain
BHAT by heart
BHES Behrens
BHIG Behring
BHIM Bahaism
Baha'ism
BHIT Bahaist
BHMS Bahamas
BIAD brigand
BIAE brigade
BIAN Britain
BICE brioche
BIDD blinded
brinded
BIDE brindle
BIDN build in
build on
BIDP build up
build-up

BIDR blinder
builder
BIDY blindly
BIEY bribery
BIFD briefed
BIFL brimful
BIFY briefly
BIGN bring in
bring on
BIGO bring to
BIGP bring up
BIGR bringer
BIGS Bridges
BIGT Bridget
BIHD Brighid
BIHR blither
BIIF bailiff
BIIG baiting
Beijing
boiling
BIIH brinish
British
BIJL brinjal
BIKN brisken
BIKR blinker
BIKT brisket
BIKY briskly
BILD bridled
BIOF boil off
BIOT bail out
BIPP Britpop
BITE bristle
brittle
BITL bristol❑
BITN Brittan
Britten
built-in
BITP built-up
BITR blister
BITW Bristow
BITY bristly
brittly
BIUT briquet
BIZD blitzed
BIZN Blitzen
BJWL bejewel
BKAA baklava
BKAE beknave
BKNN Bakunin
BKWY bikeway
BLAD Ballard
bollard
BLAE ballade
Beltane
BLAK bulwark
BLAT ballast
Belfast
BLAY Bellamy
biliary
BLBD bilobed
BLBY ball-boy
bell-boy
BLDG bulldog

BLEE believe
BLEK Belleek
BLEL balneal
BLES beliefs
bullets
BLFL baleful
BLGA Bologna
BLHE bolshie
BLHP bell-hop
BLHR bulghur
BLID bullied
BLIG balding
balking
belting
bulging
BLIH bullish
BLII Bellini
BLIM Belgium
BLIN Belgian
billion
bullion
BLIS billies
BLIY balmily
bulkily
BLMA bulimia
BLMC bulimic
BLMN beltman
BLNA Belinda
BLNE balance
BLNY baloney
boloney
BLOA Bellona
BLOK bollock
bullock❑
BLON balloon
BLOR Balfour
BLOS bellows
bilboes
bilious
bulbous
BLOT bale out
belt out
bulk out
BLOY balcony
billowy
BLRC baldric
BLRN Bull Run
BLRS Belarus
boleros
BLSA Belisha
BLSP balls up
balls-up
BLSS boluses
BLTD belated
BLTN Balaton
BLTR bolster
BLTS boletus
BLUH bulrush
BLVA Bolivia
BLVD beloved❑
BLVR bolivar
Bolívar
BLWN Baldwin

BLYH billy-oh
BMAD bombard
BMAE bumbaze
BMAO bummalo
BMAT bombast
BMDL bemedal
BMIG bombing
BMII bambini
BMIY bumpily
BMKN bumpkin
BMLR bumbler
BMOA bombora
BMOF bump off
BMOT bum-boat
BMSD bemused
BNAA bandana
BNAD Band-aid®
Bonnard
BNAE bandage
bondage
BNAH beneath
BNAI Bengali
BNAN Ben Mann
BNDY bone-dry
BNEE benzene
BNES bonkers
BNET Bennett
BNEU bandeau
BNEY bindery
BNFL baneful
BNFT benefit
BNGT benight
BNHC benthic
BNHD bunched
BNHE banshee
BNHM Bentham
BNHR bencher
BNHS benthos
BNIE Bentine
benzine
bonfire
BNIG banging
banking
Banting
bending
binding
bonding
bunting
BNIO Bendigo
BNIS bandits
BNIY bonnily
BNKK Bangkok
BNLR bungler
BNLX Benelux
BNLY banally
Bentley®
BNMN bondman
BNNA bonanza
BNNS bananas
BNOC benzoic
BNOF bang off
bunk off
BNOI Bon Jovi

BNOK bannock
bundook
BNON benzoin
BNOS banjoes
BNOT bang out
BNRS Banares
Benares
BNSA banksia
BNSN benison
BNSW band-saw
BNTS bonitos
BNUG Bandung
BNUN Ben Gunn
BNUT banquet
BNUY Banbury
Bunbury
BOAE brocade
BOAH Bronagh
BOAS biomass
BOAT buoyant
BOCI bronchi
BOCO broncho
BOCS broncos
BOCY blotchy
BODD blooded
BODE Blondie
BODL Blondel
BODN Blondin
broaden
brood on
BODR brooder
BODY broadly
BOEP booze-up
BOGT brought
BOHL brothel
BOHR brother
BOIE bromide
bromine
BOIG blowing
booking
booming
broking
BOIH bookish
boorish
BOIS bionics
boonies
BOIY boozily
BOKD blocked
BOKN block in
BOKP block up
BOKR blocker
BOKS Brookes
Brooks's
BOLE Broglie
BOLG bootleg
BOLR broiler
BOLS Boodle's
BOLT booklet
BOLY Bromley
BOMN Boorman
BOMR bloomer
BOND browned
BONE brownie❑

BONP blown up
BOOT blot out
blow out
blow-out
book out
boom out
boot out
BOOY biology
BOPR blooper
BOSM blossom
BOSN blouson
Bronson
BOSR browser
BOSY Brodsky
BOTD bloated
BOTR bloater
blotter
booster
BOUF Beowulf
BOWN Bronwen
BOZD bronzed
BPAE biplane
BPIE baptise
baptize
BPIM baptism
BPIT baptist
BPLR bipolar
BQET bequest
BQIT be quiet
BRAA Barbara
Bergama
BRAD barmaid
Barnard
Bernard
BRAE barrage
bereave
Burbage
BRAI biryani
BRAK barrack
Burbank
BRAN bargain
Bormann
BRAO Bergamo
BRAS bureaus
BRAX bureaux
BRAY Barnaby
bursary
BRCC boracic
BRCT borscht
BRDM boredom
BRDN Borodin
BREA Berbera
BREE Burmese
BREK berserk
BREL burrell
BREN barge in
burgeon
BRES borders❑
burdens
Burgess
BRET Burnett
BRFR burn for
BRGT by right

BRHL burrhel
BRHR burgher
BRHS Barthes
BRIE Bernice
bornite
BRIG barfing
barring
birding
burning
burying
BRIH burnish
BRII Bernini
BRIO burrito
BRIR barrier
BRIS barrios
Bergius
BRIT Burkitt
BRIZ Berlioz
BRLD be ruled
BRLR burglar
BRLY Barclay
Burnley
BRMN Bergman
BRNI Burundi
BRNS Barents
BRNT baronet
BRNZ Barentz
BROD barwood
BROE bar code
bar none
BROK burdock
BROL barn owl
BROM bar-room
BROS burnous
BRQE baroque❑
BRRM Bartram
Bertram
BRSH bortsch
BRTA biretta
BRTE burette
BRTL borstal
BRTN burst in
BRTS barytes
BRUA Bermuda
BRUE barbule
bordure
BRUH borough
BSAD bastard
bustard❑
BSAE beslave
boscage
bus lane
BSBY best boy
BSDA basidia
BSDN based on
BSDS besides
BSED bestead
BSEE besiege
BSEH beseech
BSEK bespeak
BSEL Boswell
Bussell
BSER besmear
BSFL bashful
BSIE bespice
BSIG bashing
basking
basting
BSIK bestick
BSIL bestial
BSIN bastion
BSIR bustier
BSIS Beskids
BSIT bassist
BSIY bossily
BSKK Bishkek
BSLR basilar
bustler
BSMN best man
bushman
BSOE bespoke
BSON bassoon
BSOT base out
besport
bespout
bistort
BSRS bistros
BSRW bestrew
BSTP bus stop
BSUE bascule
BSUH bismuth
BSUT biscuit
BTAT bit-part
BTAX bateaux
BTAY Bethany
BTBN Bath bun
BTED betread
butt end
BTEE beteeme
be there
BTEN between
bittern
BTES bitters
BTEY battery
butlery
buttery
by the by
BTHD botched
BTHP botch up
botch-up
BTHR botcher
butcher
BTHT but that
BTIA Bettina
BTIG batting
betting
BTIK bethink
BTKN betoken
BTLD bottled
BTLR battler
BTLS battles
BTMN batsman
bitumen
BTMS betimes
by times
BTNC botanic
BTNL bitonal
BTOH betroth
BTOK buttock
BTOS buttons
BTRS by turns
BTSA Batista
BTSN Bateson
BTTB bathtub
BTTE betitle
BTUB bethumb
BTUP bethump
BUBN bourbon❑
BUBR blubber
BUCP bluecap
BUCR bouncer
BUDD bounded
BUDE Brundle
BUDN Blunden
bounden
bourdon
BUDO bound to
BUDR blunder
boulder❑
bounder
BUEK Brubeck
BUFR bluffer
BUFY bluffly
BUGM blue gum
BUGR bludger
BUHD brushed
BUHE bauchle
BUHP brush up
brush-up
BUHR Blücher
blusher
Boucher
brusher
BUHS blushes
BUIE bauxite
BUIG bruting
BUIH brutish
BUIY brutify
BUJY blue jay
BULS baubles
BUME Brummie
BUOR boudoir
BUOS brumous
BUQE brusque
BURD blurred
BURE bourrée
BUSD bruised
BUSN Boursin
BUSR bruiser
BUSY blue-sky
BUTK Blue-tak®
BUTR bluster
BUTT blue tit
bluetit
BUTY bluntly
BUUT bouquet
BVID bevvied
BVLE bivalve
BVUC bivouac
BWFL bowlful
BWIE bowline
BWIG bowling
BWIY bawdily
BWNT bowknot
BWOE bewhore
BWON bow down
BWOT bawl out
BWTH bewitch
BWTR by water
BWYF by way of
BXET box tent
BXIL Bexhill
BXOD boxwood
BXUS boxfuls
BYAK buy back
buy-back
BYBE buyable
BYNO buy into
BYNR Brynner
BYNT bayonet
BYOD boyhood
BYOE Boyzone
BYOT boycott❑
BYPP buy a pup
BYRM buy from
BYUS be yours
BYVR buy over
BZAD buzzard
BZIG buzzing
BZOA bazooka
BZOF buzz off
BZQE bezique
BZRA Bizerta
BZRE bizarre
BZUI bazouki
CAAA chalaza
Chapala
CAAE charade
CAAH Cranach
CAAI chapati
CAAL Chagall
CAAT clamant
CABD crabbed
CABE chambré
CABR chamber
clamber
CACE chancre
CACL chancel
CACR chancer
Chaucer
CACS chances
CACT claucht
CADA Chandra
Claudia
CADE Chaldee
CADO Claudio
CAEL Clavell
CAEU chateau
château
CAFE Chaffee
CAFR chaffer
chamfer
CAGD changed
charged
cragged
CAGE Craigie
CAGR changer
charger
clanger
CAGS changes
charges
coal gas
CAGT claught
CAHA cyathia
CAHD crashed
CAIA czarina
CAIE chalice
Clarice
coalise
coalize
cyanide
cyanise
cyanite
cyanize
CAIG ceasing
chafing
chasing
coaming
coating
coaxing
craving
crazing
CAII clarini
CAIL coaxial
cranial
CAIM cranium
CAIN clarion
CAIS crazies
CAIT chariot
CAIY charily
charity❑
clarify
clarity
crazily
CAKD cracked
CAKE crackle
crankle
CAKN crack on
CAKP chalk up
crack up
CAKR cracker
CAKT crack it
Crackit
CAKY crackly
CALE charlie❑
CALH challah
CALN Chaplin
CALR crawler
CALS Chablis
Charles
CALT chaplet
CALY Charley
Crawley
CAMD charmed
claimed

crammed
CAMN chapman❑
CAMR charmer
claimer
crammer
Cranmer
CAND chained
Clannad
CANL channel
CAOF claw off
CAOK Cradock
CAOR clamour
CAOS chamois
claroes
CAOT crap out
CAPD chapped
clamped
cramped
CAPN crampon
CAPR clamper
clapper
CARD charred
CARL Chabrol
CARN chagrin
CASC classic
CASD Chassid
CASL clausal
CASN chanson
coarsen
CASS chassis
classes
clauses
Crassus
CASY crassly
CATC chaotic
clastic
CATD charted
CATE chaetae
CATL Chantal
chattel
coastal
CATN chasten
Clapton
CATR chanter
chapter
charter
chatter
clatter
coaster
CATT coal tit
coal-tit
CATY chantry
CAWN Chatwin
CBAA cabbala
CBAE cabbage
CBCE cubicle
CBCL cubical
CBET Cobbett
CBEV cable TV
CBEZ Coblenz
CBLE Caballé
CBLR cobbler
CBNA Cabinda
CBNS cabanos
CBNT cabinet
CBRA ciboria
CBRT cabaret❑
CCAE cockade
CCEU Cocteau
CCIE cocaine
CCIT cyclist
CCIY cockily
CCLA Cecilia
cochlea
CCNT coconut
CCNY ca' canny
cockney
CCOD cuckold
cycloid
CCOE cyclone
CCOS cyclops❑
CCPT cockpit
CCRN Cochran
CCTE cocotte
CDAL Cadfael
CDAX cadeaux
CDCI caducei
CDCL codicil
CDCS codices
CDER cudbear
CDIE codeine
CDIG cadging
codding
codling
CDIH caddish
CDIM cadmium
CDLA cedilla
CDLD coddled
CDLE cadelle
CDNA cadenza
CDNE cadence
CDUY Cadbury
CDVR cadaver
CDYS caddyss
CEAD Cleland
CEAE chelate
cremate
crenate
CEBY Clew Bay
CECD coerced
CECT crewcut
crew-cut
CEDE Cheadle
CEDL creedal
CEDR Cheddar
CEET clement❑
CEGU Chengdu
Cheng-tu
CEHV Chekhov
CEIC coeliac
CEIE chemise
crevice
CEIH cherish
CEIM caesium
CEIN Caelian
CEIS clerics
credits
CEIT chemist
Cheviot
coexist
CEKD checked
CEKN check in
check-in
CEKP check up
check-up
CEKR checker
CEMN Caedmon
crewman
CENE cleanse
CENP clean up
clean-up
CENR cleaner
CENY cleanly
CEOD cheloid
CEOT cheroot
chew out
CEPF cheap of
CEPN cheapen
CEPR creeper
CEPY cheaply
CERD cleared
CERF clear of
CERN cheer on
chevron
CERO cheerio
CERP cheer up
clear up
CERY clearly
CESA Chelsea
CESD creased
CESN Cresson
CESR creaser
CEST cresset
CESY Chelsey
CETD crested
CETH cheetah
CETN cheat on
creatin
CETR cheater
Chester
creator❑
CEUA caesura
CEUL coequal
CEUR chequer
CEUS cherubs
CEVL chervil
CEVR cleaver
CEZE Coetzee
CFES coffers
CFRT coffret
CGAE cognate
CGIE cognise
cognize
CGNY cogency
CGUE cagoule
CHBT cohabit
CHOS cahoots
CHRR coherer
CHRS cohorts
CIAE chicane
climate
coinage
crinate
CIAO Chicago
CIAS cuirass
CIBA Coimbra
CIBD cribbed
CIBE cribble
CIBN climb on
CIBP climb up
CIBR climber
CIBX coin box
CIDD childed
CIEA chimera❑
CIEE Chinese
CIEN Chilean
chime in
CIES crivens
CIFN chiffon
CIFY chiefly
CIGE cringle
CIGO cling to
CIGR chigger
clinger
cringer
CIHD clichéd
cliché'd
CIIA crimina
CIIE crinite
cuisine
CIIF caitiff
CIIG ceiling
chiding
coiling
CIIH ceilidh
CIIN coition
CIKE chinkie❑
crinkle
CIKN chicken
CIKR clinker❑
CIKT clicket
cricket
CIKY crickey
crinkly
CILD chilled
CILN Caitlín
CILS chillis
CILY chimley
CINI Chianti
CINN chignon
CINS clients
CINY chimney
CIOD cricoid
crinoid
CIOE crinose
CIOF chip off
CIOK chinook❑
CIOY chicory
CIPD chipped
clipped
crimped
CIPE crimple
cripple
CIPN Crippen
Crispin
CIPR chipper
clipper
crimper
CIPY crisply
CIRP chirrup
CISA chiasma
CISI chiasmi
CISN caisson
crimson
CISS chiasms
CITE cristae
cuittle
CITN Clinton
CITR chitter
clitter
CITY chintzy
CIUG chi kung
CIUY cliquey
CIWG chinwag
CJLR cajoler
CLAE ciliate
collage
collate
CLAT calmant
CLAY Calgary
CLBE calibre
CLBN Caliban
CLBR Calabar
CLBS Celebes
colobus
CLCS calices
calicos
calyces
culices
cylices
CLCT Calicut
CLCY colicky
CLDN celadon
CLEA caldera❑
CLEE college
CLEN colleen❑
CLES callers
CLET Colbert
collect
culvert
CLFR call for
CLGE cologne❑
CLGS colugos
CLGY Coligny
CLIE calcine
calcite
collide
CLIG calling
calming
CLIH coltish
cultish
CLII Cellini
CLIM calcium
cultism
CLIO Calvino

CLIR collier
CLIS Celsius
Collins
CLIT cellist
cultist
CLIY calcify
CLMA Columba
CLMN Coleman
CLMO Colombo
Columbo
CLMS calamus
CLMT calumet
CLMY calumny
CLNC colonic
CLNL colonel
CLNO calando
Colenso
CLNS calends
colones
CLOD colloid
CLOE calzone
CLOF call off
CLOI calzoni
CLOS callous
CLOT call out
CLPE calipee
CLPO calypso❑
CLRC chloric
CLRE calorie
CLRL chloral
CLRN caldron
CLRT culprit
CLSA celesta
CLSE celeste
CLSI colossi
CLTE Colette
CLTI calathi
CLTS colitis
CLUE cellule
collude
culture
CLUI calculi
CLUS colours
CLVR caliver
CLWR cold war
CLWS C S Lewis
CLXS calyxes
CMAD command
compand
CMAE compare
comrade
CMAI cembali
CMAS compass
CMAT compact
CMAY company❑
CMBD camp-bed
CMBE Cimabué
CMCL comical
CMCS cimices
CMDS comedos
CMED commend
CMEE Campese
compère

compete
CMER compear
compeer
CMET comment
CMFR come for
CMHR camphor
CMIE combine
compile
CMIM cambium
CMIN campion❑
CMLA Camilla
CMLN complin
CMLS cumulus
CMLT Camelot
complot
CMLW come low
CMLX complex
CMOD Camford
camwood
CMOE commode
compose
compote
CMOF come off
CMOO commodo
CMOS commons❑
CMOT camp out
comb out
come out
comfort
comport
compost
CMRA Cumbria
CMRC cambric
CMRE camerae
CMRI Cambrai
CMRN camaron
Cameron
CMRS cameras
Comoros
CMRY comfrey
CMTL comital
CMTN Compton
CMUE commune
commute
compute
CMUT combust
cumquat
CNAA cantata
CNAE Candace
concave
connate
CNAN contain
CNAO centavo
CNAR centaur❑
CNAS canvass
CNAT cineast
contact
CNCE conacre
CNCL conical
cynical
CNDA conidia
CNEA candela
CNED contend

CNEE concede
convene
CNEL conceal
congeal
CNEN canteen
concern
condemn
contemn
CNEO concedo
Conseco
CNES cinders
confess
CNET conceit
concept
concert
confect
congest
conject
connect
consent
content
contest
context
convent
convert
CNEY cindery
Connery
CNFR conifer
CNHA Cynthia
CNHE conchae
CNHS conches
CNIA candida❑
CNID candied
CNIE Candice
Candide
centime
concise
confide
confine
connive
CNIG Canning
canting
cunning
CNIM confirm
CNIN condign
consign
CNIO centimo
CNIS candies
CNIT consist
convict
CNIY cannily
CNKN canakin
canikin
CNKY Conakry
CNLX conflux
CNOA Cantona
CNOD concord❑
CNOE condole
condone
connote
console
convoke
CNOF cone off

CNOI canzoni
CNOK candock
CNOM conform
CNON conjoin
CNOO con moto
CNOR candour
contour
CNOS cannons
Connors
consols
CNOT concoct
conk out
consort
contort
CNPS Canopus
CNRA conaria
CNRL central
control
CNRO con brio
CNRT cane rat
CNSA canasta
CNTI Canetti
CNTR conster
CNTS conatus
CNUA cannula
CNUE censure
conduce
confuse
confute
conjure
consume
contuse
CNUL censual
CNUR conquer
CNUS canfuls
concuss
CNUT conduct
conduit
consult
CNUY century
concupy
COAA crotala
COAE chorale
COAT coolant
COBG cool bag
COBR clobber
crowbar
COBX cool box
COCE cloacae
COCL cloacal
COCR co-occur
CODD clouded
crowded
CODE chordae
croodle
CODI chondri
CODN Croydon
CODR chowder
COEA cholera
COEN close in
close on
COEO close to
COEP choke up

close up
close-up
COET closest
COEY close by
closely
cookery
COGD clogged
COHD clothed
COHS chochos
clothes
COHT crochet
COIE choline
COIG choking
cloning
closing
cloying
cooking
cooling
crowing
COIN chorion
COIO chorizo
COIR crosier
crozier
COKD cloaked
crooked
COKN clock in
clock on
COKP clock up
COKT crocket
COLY Crowley
CONE choanae
CONR crooner
COOD choroid
COOF chop off
cook off
cool off
COPD cropped
COPR chopper
cropper
COSN Cookson
COSS Croesus
COSY Chomsky
crossly
COTA Croatia
COTD clotted
COTE chortle
COTN croûton
COTR clotter
crofter
COTW Choctaw
COUE closure
cloture
COUS croquis
COUT croquet
CPAD Copland
CPAN captain
CPBE capable
CPBY capably
CPCE capuche
CPCT copycat
copy-cat
CPES Cepheus
coppers

cypress
CPEY coppery
CPID cup-tied
CPIE caprice
caprine
capsize
captive
coppice
cuprite
CPIG capping
copying
cupping
CPIN caption
Cyprian
CPIT copyist
Cypriot
CPIY caprify
CPLA Capella
CPLT Capulet
co-pilot
CPOA Coppola
CPOS copious
cuprous
CPOT copy out
CPPE cap-a-pie
cap-à-pie
CPTL capital❑
CPTN capstan
CPUE capsule
capture
CPUS cupfuls
CQIO coquito
CRAE carcase
carnage
cordage
cordate
corkage
corrade
corsage
CRAH currach
curragh
CRAK carjack
CRAL cure-all
curtail
CRAN certain
curtain
CRAO Cardano
CRAR corsair
CRAS carcass
cereals
CRAT currant
CRBA cerebra
CRBD carabid
CRBE curable
CRBU caribou
CRCE coracle
CRCL caracal
caracol
caracul
CRCM CARICOM
CRCO curaçao❑
CRCS Caracas
carices
CREE cortège
CREL carrell
corneal
Cornell
CREP carve up
carve-up
CRES carneys
CRET Corbett
correct
current
CREY carvery
CRFL careful
CRFR care for
CRIA Corsica
Cortina®
CRIC cardiac
CRIE carbide
carbine
carmine
cervine
cordite
cornice
corvine
cursive
CRIF Cardiff
CRIG carding
Carling
carping
carving
curbing
curling
cursing
curving
CRIH Cornish
CRII cortili
CRIK carsick
car-sick
CRIL cordial
CRIN carrion
CRIR carrier
CRIY carnify
certify
CRLA coralla
corolla
CRLD curdled
CRLI Corelli
CRLN Carolyn
CRLR circler
CRLT circlet
corslet
CRMA caramba
CRMC ceramic
CRML caramel
chromel
CRMN cerumen
CRMS chromos
CRNA Corinna
Corunna
CRNC chronic
CRNE Corinne
coronae
CRNH Corinth
CRNL coronal
CRNO Corinto
CRNR coroner
CRNS coronas
CRNT coronet
CROA cordoba
Córdoba
corpora
CROB car bomb
CROE carnose
corrode
CROF cart off
CROK cork oak
CROL Carroll
CRON cartoon
CROS cargoes
carious
cereous
corious
curious
CROT car port
carport
Carrott
CROY carroty
cursory
CRPA Corypha
CRSM chrisom
CRSO Christo
CRSY Christy
curtsey
CRTD carotid
CRTE curette
CRTN carotin
CRTR curator
CRTS caritas
CRUE carouse
CRUS carduus
CRUT circuit
corrupt
CRVL caravel
CRVN caravan
CRWY caraway
CRYE Carlyle
CRYN carry on
carry-on❑
CRYP carry up
CRYS carpyus
CRYT carry it
CRZS corozos
CSAA cassava
CSAD Costard
custard❑
CSAE cascade
cuspate
CSAK Cossack
CSAX ciseaux
CSBX cash box
CSEN cistern
costean
CSIE costive
cystine
CSIG casting
Cushing
cussing
CSII Cassini
CSIN Caspian
cession
cushion
CSIR cashier
CSIS Cassius
CSIT casuist
CSNR Costner
CSNS casinos
CSOF cast off
cast-off
CSOK cassock
CSOS caseous
ciscoes
customs
CSOT cast out
cost out
CSOY custody
CSPT cesspit
CSRN cistron
CSUE costume
CTAE citrate
cottage
cut-rate
CTAI Cathari
CTAK catwalk
cut back
cutback
CTAL catcall
CTAS Cathars
cutlass
CTAX coteaux
CTBE citable
CTCE cuticle
CTDL citadel
CTED cut dead
CTEE cat's eye
CTEN cithern
cittern
CTEY cattery
cutlery
CTHE catch me
CTHN catch on
CTHP catch up
CTHR catcher
CTHS catches
CTHT catch at
catch it
CTIE catlike
citrine
CTIG cutting
CTIH catfish
CTIT catmint
CTIY cattily
CTLE cotylae
CTLN Catalan
CTLS cotyles
CTNA Catania
cotinga
CTNE catenae
CTNO cut into
CTNS catenas
CTOE cathode
CTON Citroën
cut down
CTOS cuttoes
CTOT catboat
CTOY cottony
CTPN cut open
CTPW cat's paw
cat's-paw
CTRE coterie
CTRH catarrh
CTRO cater to
CTRR caterer
CTSY Catesby
CTUT catsuit
CTWY cutaway
CTZN citizen
CUAE caudate
courage
crusade
CUBD clubbed
CUBE crumble
CUBR clubber
CUBT Courbet
CUBY crumbly
CUCL council
CUCY crunchy
CUDE could be
CUDP clued up
clued-up
CUDR chuddar
CUEY crudely
CUFD chuffed
CUGO Chungho
CUHD crushed
CUHP cough up
CUHR crusher
CUIE cauline
CUIG causing
CUIL crucial
CUIN caution
CUIR courier
CUIS cousins❑
CUIY crucify
crudity
CUKE chuckle
crunkle
CUKN chuck in
CUKR chukker
CULD coupled
CULT couplet
CULY Causley
chumley
cruelly
cruelty
CUMN clubman
CUNL Chunnel
CUNY chutney
CUOB coulomb❑
CUPE crumple
CUPT crumpet
CURS cruores
CUSL counsel
CUSR courser

cruiser
CUSS courses
CUTC caustic
CUTE crustae
CUTN count on
CUTP count up
CUTR chunter
cluster
clutter
counter
CUTY country
courtly
CUUE couture
CVAE caviare
CVAT cave art
CVDN caved-in
CVIS civvies
CVLY cavalry
civilly
CVMN caveman
CVRD covered
CVRN cover in
CVRP cover up
cover-up
CVTI cavetti
CVTO cavetto
CWAD cowhand
CWAE cowbane
CWED cowherd
CWEL cowbell
CWHD cowshed
CWID cowbird
CWIE cowhide
cowlike
co-write
CWIG cowling
CWIK cowlick
CWIL cowgirl
CWLP cowslip
CWOE cowpoke
CWRY Cowdrey
CXOB coxcomb
CYAS caymans
CYAY crybaby
cry-baby
CYES coyness
CYIY chylify
chymify
CYNE cayenne□
CYOF cry wolf
CYON cry down
CYTC cryptic
CYTL cryptal
crystal□
CYTS coyotes
cryptos
CYUG Cy Young
CYVR cry over
CZNE Cézanne
CZNR cozener
DAAN do again
DABE Drabble
DACY diarchy
DAED dead end
DAEE dead-eye
DAES drawers
DAET dearest
dialect
DAEY deanery
drapery
DAFD dwarfed
DAGE draggle
DAGT draught
DAHA drachma
DAHE draw hoe
DAHN death on
DAHY deathly
DAIE diarise
diarize
DAIG dealing
draping
drawing
DAIL deasiul
DAIM dualism
DAIS diaries
DAIT diarist
DAIY duality
DALR dialler
DAND drained
DANO drawn to
DANP drawn up
DANR drainer
DANT dragnet
DANY dearnly
DAOD diamond□
DAOE dear one
DAOF draw off
DAOL deasoil
DAON dragoon
DAOO diabolo
DAOS diazoes
DAOT deal out
drag out
draw out
DAPN deadpan
dead-pan
DARM diagram
DASA Dead Sea
DAST dead set
DATC drastic
DATD dratted
DATE draftee
DAUA Dracula
DAUK do a bunk
DAVS dwarves
DAYE deary me
dialyse
dialyze
DBAD dab hand
DBCE debacle
débâcle
DBDY do badly
DBEY dubiety
DBIE débride
DBIF debrief
DBLR dabbler
DBON do brown
DBOS dubious
DBRH Deborah
DBSC dibasic
DBSD debased
DBSR debaser
DBSY Debussy
DBTD debated
DBTR debater
debitor
DBUH debauch
debouch
DCAE decease
declare
dictate
ducdame
DCAM declaim
DCAP Duchamp
DCAS declass
DCBL decibel
DCDD decided
DCDR decider
decoder
DCED decreed
DCES dickens□
duchess
DCGN decagon
DCIE deceive
decline
ductile
DCIG decking
docking
ducking
DCIL decrial
DCIN diction
DCIR decrier
DCIY dacoity
DCLR decolor
DCLY ducally
DCML decimal
DCNL decanal
DCNO DiCanio
DCNY decency
DCOD d'accord
DCON decrown
DCOS doctor's
DCOT deck out
DCPD decapod
DCPE decuple
DCRE decurve
DCRM decorum
DCTE Docetae
DCUT docquet
DCYD decayed
DCYT decrypt
DDCD deduced
DDCI didicoi
DDCY didicoy
DDEN dudgeon
DDEY doddery
duddery
DDIG dodging
DDIM Dadaism
DDIT Dadaist
DDLR diddler
DDLS Dedalus
DDLY Diddley
DDRT Diderot
DDSN Dodgson
DEAD Die Hard
diehard
die-hard
DEAE die game
DEAK die back
dieback
DEAY dietary
DEDD dreaded
DEDN Dresden
DEDS duendes
DEDY dreadly
DEET deepest
DEFS Dreyfus
DEFT deep-fet
DEFY deep-fry
DEGR dredger
DEHL diethyl
DEIA Djemila
DEIY deedily
DELN dwell in
dwell on
DELR dueller
dweller
DELS duellos
DEMD dreamed
DEMF dream of
DEMP dream up
DEMR dreamer
DENN dies non
DEON die down
DEOT died out
DESA deep-sea
DESD dressed
DESN dress in
DESP dress up
DESR dresser
DEST deep-set
DETS duettos
DEWY die away
die-away
DFAD defraud
DFAE deflate
DFAT defiant
DFCD defaced
DFCO de facto
DFCR defacer
DFCT deficit
DFET deflect
DFIG defying
DFLD defiled
DFMD defamed
DFMR defamer
DFND defined
DFNE defence
DFNR definer
DFNT defunct
DFOK defrock
DFOM difform
DFOT defrost
DFRE deforce
DFRO defer to
DFRT do first
DFUE diffuse
DFUT default
DGAE degrade
DGAH digraph
DGAT dogcart
dog-cart
DGER dog's-ear
DGES daggers
digress
DGIH dogfish
doggish
DGIY dignify
dignity
DGNO dig into
DGOD dogwood
DGOE doggone
dog rose
DGRT dogtrot
DGTL digital
DGTR Dog Star
DGUS degauss
DHEE Dehaene
DHSE dehisce
DIBE dribble
DIDE Deirdre
dwindle
DIDP dried up
dried-up
DIDY drip-dry
DIEL deiseal
DIEN drive-in
DIET drive at
DIGY dyingly
DIIG driving
DIIS daimios
DIKN drink in
DIKO drink to
DIKP drink up
DIKR drinker
DILD drilled
DILR Daimler
Daimler®
DILT driblet
DIOM deiform
DIPR Dnieper
DITC deistic
DITR drifter
DIZE drizzle
DIZY drizzly
DKDM dukedom
DKEK De Klerk
DLAC deltaic
DLAD dullard
DLAX Delvaux
DLBS Delibes
DLDD deluded
DLDR deluder
DLEL Dalyell

DLET diluent
DLFL doleful
DLGT delight
DLHC Delphic
DLHN dolphin□
DLIG dulling
DLIH doltish
DLIR dallier
DLLH Delilah
DLMA dilemma
DLMT delimit
DLOD deltoid
DLOT dole out
DLRA deliria
DLRS Dolores
DLSS dulosis
DLTD dilated
diluted
DLTR do later
DLUE delouse
DLVR deliver
DLYD delayed
DLYR delayer
DMAL damn all
DMBN dumpbin
DMDD demoded
DMES dimness
DMGC do magic
DMGD damaged
demigod
DMGS damages
DMIG damning
dimming
DMIH dampish
dimmish
DMIR Dampier
DMIY damnify
DMLD dimpled
DMLE de Mille□
DMNC demonic
Dominic
DMNE dominie
DMNO Domingo
DMNS dominos
DMOL damfool
DMRC dimeric
DMRE demerge
DMRL Demirel
DMSC demi-sec
DMSS Damasus
DMTA domatia
DMTC demotic
DMTR Demeter
DMUT demount
DNAE dentate
DNAK Denmark
Dundalk
DNBT dingbat
DNDD denuded
DNDN Dunedin
DNEA Daniela
DNEN Dantean
dungeon

DNER danseur
DNES Danvers
donkeys
données
DNEY densely
DNFR done for
DNGL Donegal
DNGN Donegan
DNIE dentine
DNIG dancing
Denning
denying
Don King
dunking
DNIH dankish
donnish
DNIK Dunkirk
DNIM donnism
DNIS dinkies
dunlins
DNIT dentist
DNIY dandify
dandily
densify
density
DNKR Dansker
DNLW Danelaw
DNMC dynamic
DNMS dynamos
DNNO din into
DNOF dine off
DNOK dunnock
DNON Don John
DNOS dingoes
DNOT dine out
DNRI denarii
DNRN dendron
DNSN Dineson
DNSY don't say
dynasty
DNTE dinette
DNTK Donetsk
DNTN Dunstan
DNTR donator
DNUE Deneuve
denture
DNUN Don Juan
DNZN denizen
DOAA diorama
DODE do or die
do-or-die
DOEA duodena
DOEE diocese
Diomede
DOGS drongos
DOGT drought
DOIE dioxide
D-notice
DOIG droning
DOKT drookit
DOLR doodler
DOLT droplet
DOMN doorman

DOMT doormat
DOND drowned
DONT drop-net
DOOD dromond
DOOF drop off
DOOT drop out
dropout
drop-out
DOOY duopoly
DOPD dropped
DOPR dropper
DOTC deontic
DOTE dioptre
DOTF do out of
DOWY doorway
DPAE deplane
deprave
DPBE dupable
DPEA diptera
DPEE deplete
DPES depress
DPIE deprive
DPIG dipping
DPLA De Palma
DPLD dappled
DPLR dipolar
Doppler
DPNA daphnia
DPNO dip into
DPNS Daphnis
DPOA diploma
DPOD diploid
DPOE deplore
DPSR deposer
DPST deposit
DPTD deputed
DPUE deplume
DPYH diptych
DRAT dormant
DRBE durable
DRBY durably
DRDR derider
DRDS dorados
DREL Dorrell
Durrell
DRFL dareful
direful
DRGN Dorigen
DRHN darshan
DRIA Derrida
DRID dirtied
DRIE dormice
DRIG darling□
darning
Dorking
DRIH darkish
dervish
DRIK derrick□
DRIR Dornier
DRIS darbies
darcies
DRIY dirtily
DRMT dirempt

DRNA Deronda
DRNE derange
DROE dariole
DROO Dario Fo
DRTY Dorothy
DRVD derived
DSAD dastard
disband
discard
DSAE descale
discage
discase
disease
dis-ease
disrate
DSAF distaff
DSAK disbark
dismask
dispark
disrank
DSAN disdain
DSAR despair□
DSAT descant
dismast
dispart
distant
DSBE disable
DSBN dustbin
DSBY disobey
DSDS dosi-dos
DSED descend
distend
DSEF disleaf
DSEI dasheki
DSEM dishelm
DSEN dasheen
discern
DSES dossers
DSET descent
dessert
discept
disject
disnest
disseat
dissect
dissent
DSIB dislimb
DSIE despise
despite
destine
dislike
DSIG dashing
dossing
dusting
DSII dashiki
DSIK dislink
DSIL deskill
DSIN dislimn
DSIR dossier
DSIS dismiss
DSIY destiny
duskily
dustily

DSLY disally
display
DSMN dustman
DSNA dyspnea
DSOD Desmond
despond
discoid
discord
disload
DSOE dishome
dispone
dispose
disrobe
disyoke
DSOF dash off
DSOL despoil
DSOM disform
DSON disgown
dishorn
disjoin
DSOT dash out
dish out
disport
dispost
disroot
distort
DSRD desired
DSRE deserve
Désirée
DSRS deserts
DSRY destroy
DSSD disused
DSTP desktop
DSUB disturb
DSUE dispute
DSUS discuss
DSUT disgust
disrupt
DSVW disavow
DTAN detrain
DTAT detract
DTBE datable
DTEY dithery
DTFL dutiful
DTHD ditched
DTIS details
DTNE détente
DTOI Dettori
DTOS duteous
DTOT Detroit
DTRE deterge
DTRL dottrel
DTUE detrude
DTWT do to wit
DUBE drumble
DUDC druidic
DUDR daunder
DUDT Deus det
DUER douceur
DUEY doucely
DUGD drugged
DUGE druggie
DUGT drugget

DUHY doughty
DUIG dousing
DUIR Daumier
DUKN drunken
DULD doubled
DULN drumlin
DULS Douglas
DULT doublet
DUMR drummer
DUNL diurnal
DUOT drum out
DUTD daunted
DUTN daunton
DUTR doubter
DUZA deutzia
DVAE deviate
DVAT deviant
DVCT dovecot
DVDD divided
DVDR divider
DVIE devoice
DVIS devoirs
De Vries
DVLE devalue
devolve
divulge
DVLP develop
DVLY devilry
DVNR diviner
DVOS devious
DVRE diverge
diverse
divorce
DVSE devisee
DVSL devisal
DVSM divisim
DVSN Davison
DVSR deviser
devisor
divisor
DVTD devoted
DVTE devotee
DVYP divvy up
DVZS Devizes
DWAD Dowland
DWGR dowager
DWIG dawning
DWIS Dawkins
DWIY dowdily
DWLR dawdler
DWOD dew-pond
DWOG do wrong
DWOK dawcock
DWRN Dawn Run
DWTR dewater
DXRL dextral
DXRN dextran
dextrin
DYAD dry land
DYAE day care
DYAT dry-salt
DYBY Daya Bay
DYDS dryades

DYES dryness
DYET drybeat
DYHD dry-shod
DYIE daytime
DYIL day-girl
DYIY day-lily
DYNE doyenne
DYOA Daytona
DYOE dry hole
DYOG daylong
DYOK daybook
day-book
DYOM day room
day-room
DYOT dry-foot
DYRP day trip
DYTR daystar
DYUE dry-cure
DYYD dry-eyed
DZDY dazedly
DZIY dizzily
DZLD dazzled
DZLR dazzler
DZNH dozenth
DZOF doze off
EAAE emanate
exarate
EAAT emanant
EACE ébauche
EAGL evangel
EAHC edaphic
EAIE evasive
examine
EAIH evanish
EAIN elation
evasion
EAIY edacity
EALR enabler
EAMS Erasmus
EAOR enamour
EAPE example
EASD elapsed
EATC elastic
EATD exalted
EATN elastin
EATY exactly
EAUE erasure
evacuee
EAUL Emanuel
EBAE emblaze
embrace
EBEA emblema
EBEG Esbjerg
EBGE embogue
EBIE ebb tide
ebbtide
EBLS embolus
EBOL embroil
EBOM embloom
EBON embrown
EBRO embargo
EBSM embosom
EBSY embassy

EBUD embound
EBWL embowel
EBWR embower
EBWY ebb away
EBYS embryos
ECAE enchase
enclave
exclave
ECAM exclaim
ECAN enchain
ECAP enclasp
ECAT enchant
ECAY encraty
ECDS escudos
ECEA excreta
ECEE excrete
ECET escheat
ECGD encaged
ECIE eccrine
escribe
ECIG etching
ECMA encomia
ECOD encloud
ECOE each one
enclose
ECPD escaped
ECPE escapee
ECPR escaper
ECRT excerpt
ECSD excused
ECSL excusal
ECTD excited
ECTN exciton
ECTR exciter
excitor
ECUE exclude
ECUT encrust
ECWY each way
ECYT encrypt
EDAE endgame[□]
EDAG endlang
EDAS endways
EDES endless
EDIE endwise
EDMC endemic
EDOG endlong
EDOT endmost
EDRE endorse
EDRY elderly
EDSR end-user
EDSS ecdysis
EDTC eidetic
EDVN end even
EDWD endowed
EDZA endozoa
EEAA enemata
e re nata
EEAD emerald[□]
EEAE elevate
EEAH eyelash
eyewash
EEAL eyeball
EEAT elegant

EEBT E Nesbit
EECI elenchi
EEEE exegete
EEES eyeless
EEET element
Everett
EEHM Evesham
EEHN Erewhon
EEIC elegiac
EEIE elegise
elegize
eremite
EEIG evening
EEII emeriti
EEIK eye-wink
EEIL Ezekiel
EEIN E-region
etesian
EEIT elegist
EEMN Edelman
EENL eternal[□]
EENR Eleanor
EENW even now
EEOE eyesore
EEOG ere long
erelong
EEOT even out
EEPA exempla
EERE exedrae
EERP eye-drop
EESN Emerson
erepsin
EETA Electra
EETD elected
EETO electro
EETR ejector
elector
erecter
erector
eventer
EETY erectly
EEUE execute
EFAE enframe
EFCS effects
EFED Enfield
EFEH enflesh
EFIE elflike
EFLE effulge
EFNI effendi
EFOF enfeoff
EFRE enforce
EGAD England
enguard
EGAE engrace
engrave
EGAH eggwash
EGAL engrail
EGAN engrain
EGAT engraft
EGEA euglena
EGED egghead
EGEO El Greco
EGGD engaged

EGIH English
EGLP egg-flip
EGNA Eugenia
EGNC eugenic
EGNE Eugenie
Eugénie
EGNR enginer
EGOE englobe
EGOM engloom
EGOS engross
EGOT edge out
EGOY egg-cosy
EGRE en garde
engorge
EGRO eager to
EGRY eagerly
EHAM Ephraim
EHBC ephebic
EHBS ephebes
EHBT exhibit
EHCL ethical
EHDA echidna
EHIE echoise
echoize
EHIG echoing
EHLN echelon
EHNE enhance
EHNL ethanol
EHNS echinus
EHOD ethmoid
EHPE échappé
EHSS Ephesus
EHUT exhaust
EIAE emicate
emirate
epilate
evirate
evitate
EIAH epitaph
EIAP epicarp
EIAY epitaxy
EIEE epicene
epigene
evil eye
EIET eminent
evident
exigent
EIHM epithem
EIHT epithet
EIIE edifice
EIIG editing
EIIM elitism
EIIN edition
elision
EIIT elitist
élitist
EILN etiolin
EILS edibles
EIOC epizoic
EIOE epigone
episode
epitome
Evil One

EIOI epigoni
EION epizoan
epizoon
EIOT edit out
EIRA Eritrea
EIRM epigram
EITC eristic
EITD evicted
EITE epistle
EITL edictal
EIUE epicure
EIYS Erinyes
EKAT Eckhart
EKMS Eskimos
ELAN Ellmann
ELGA eulogia
ELGE eclogue
ELOM eelworm
ELOT eelpout
ELPE eclipse□
ellipse
ELRE enlarge
ELVN enliven
EMHI El Mahdi
EMSE en masse
EMSS Ed Moses
EMUH Exmouth
ENBE ennoble
ENID ennuied
EOAE evocate
EOAP exocarp
EOAY exogamy
EODA exordia
EOEA epopeia
EOEM exoderm
EOET erodent
EOHL epochal
EOIA erotica
exotica
EOIE ebonise
ebonite
ebonize
ecocide
egotise
egotize
emotive
erosive
EOIM egotism
EOIN emotion
erosion
Etonian
EOIT egotist
EONE enounce
EOOY ecology
economy
EORP ego-trip
EOTA e contra
EOUE elocute
evolute
EOYE ecotype
EPAE emplace
emplane
enplane
expiate
EPAN explain
EPAT explant
EPEA empyema
EPES empress
express
EPID emptied
EPIN emption
EPIS empties
EPIT enprint
EPIY emptily
EPNE expanse
expense
expunge
EPNL empanel
EPOE explode
explore
EPOT exploit
EPOY euphony
EPPY eupepsy
EPRA emporia
EPRC empiric
EPRD expired
EPRE expurge
EPRO esparto
EPRR emperor
EPSD exposed
EPSE en poste
EPSL exposal
EPTY empathy
EPUD expound
EPUE espouse
EPWR empower
EQIE enquire
esquire□
EQIY enquiry
ERAK earmark
ERAT Earhart
ERDM earldom
ERET earnest
ERGD enraged
ERGE en règle
ERHN earthen
ERHT earshot
ERHY earthly
ERIG earning
earring
ERIH Ehrlich
ERIR earlier
EROT earn out
ERRA Egreria
ERRM eardrum
ERTC erratic
ERTM erratum
Euratom
ERUD enround
ERUE en route
ESAE enslave
ensnare
Eustace
ESAP enstamp
ESAY ecstasy□
eustasy
ESBO Eusebio
ESED East End
ESEH Elspeth
ESEN eastern□
Epstein
ESEP ensteep
ESFL easeful
ESHM Eastham
ESID exscind
ESIE en suite
Erskine
ESIG easting
ensuing
ESLN epsilon
ESMN Eastman
ESNE essence
ESNK Eysenck
ESNS Essenes
ESOF ease off
ESRD ensured
ETAN entrain
ETAT entrant
extract
ETAY estuary
ETBE eatable
Entebbe
ETCD enticed
ETCR enticer
ETEE estrepe
extreme
ETET entreat
estreat
ETIE entwine
ETIM entrism
ETIT eat dirt
entrist
entwist
ETLA Estella
ETLE Estelle
ETNA Estonia
ETNE entente
ETNO eat into
ETNT extinct
ETOY entropy
ETPA ectopia
ETPC ectopic
ETRC enteric
ETRE Euterpe
ETRL enteral
enthral
ETRN enter on
ETRR enterer
ETRW eat crow
ETSS ectases
entasis
ETTE entêtée
entitle
ETUE enthuse
extrude
ETUT entrust
ETWY eat away
ETYE entayle
ETZA ectozoa
entozoa
EUAE educate
emulate
epurate
exudate
EUBA exurbia
EUBE equable
EUBN exurban
EUBY equably
EUDR Ecuador
EUIE elusive
erudite
exuviae
EUIG exuding
EUIL exuvial
EULO equal to
EULY equally
EUNX equinox
EUOS emulous
EURY equerry
EUTD exulted
EUTN exult in
EUTR equator
EVLP envelop
EVNM envenom
EVOS envious
EVRN environ
EWEL enwheel
EWRS Edwards
EYGS eryngos
EYIM Elysium
EYIN elysian□
EYOS etymons
EYRM elytrum
EYRN elytron
EZMC enzymic
FACD flaccid
FACE fiancée
FACP flat cap
flat-cap
FACS fiascos
Frances
Francis
FAEP flare up
flare-up
frame-up
FAFL fearful
FAFR flaffer
FAFW flamfew
FAGD flanged
FAGL Feargal
FAGT flaught
fraught
FAHR feather
flasher
FAIE flavine
fragile
FAIG flaming
flaying
foaming
framing
FAIR Frazier
FAIY foamily
FAKE Frankie
FAKR flacker
flanker
FAKT flacket
FAKY frankly
FALT flatlet
FALY frailly
frailty
FANL flannel
FANM fraenum
FANY flaunty
FAOR flavour
FAOT flat out
FAPR flapper
FATC frantic
FATL fractal
FATN feast on
flatten
FATR feaster
flatter
FAUE feature
FAZE frazzle
FBIE febrile
FBIG fibbing
FBLR fibular
FBOD fibroid
FBOE fibrose
FBOS fibrous
FCIE factive
fictile
FCIG fucking
FCIN faction
fiction
FCLE faculae
FCLY faculty
focally
FCOD factoid
FCOF face-off
FCOS factors
FCOT face out
FCOY factory
FCSA fuchsia
FCSD focused
FCSN focus on
FCSS focuses
fucuses
FCUL factual
FDDY fadedly
FDES fidgets
FDEY fidgety
FDIG fudging
FDIH faddish
FDLD fuddled
FDLO Fidelio
FDLR fiddler
FDOT fade out
fade-out
FDRE fedarie
FDRL federal
FDYE fedayee
FEAM fee-farm
FEBD feel-bad
FEBE freebee

freebie
FEBG flea-bag
FECR fleecer
FECS frescos
FECY Frenchy
FEDD fielded
FEDE Freddie
FEDM fiefdom
freedom
FEDR fielder
FEFL fretful
FEFR feel for
FEGD fledged
FEGT freight
FEHN freshen
FEHR fresher
FEHT freshet
FEHY fleshly
freshly
FEIE flexile
FEIG feeding
feeling
fleeing
Fleming
freeing
FEIH Flemish
FEIN flexion
FEIY fierily
FEKD flecked
FEKE freckle
FEKR flecker
FEKY freckly
FELR fueller
FEMN freeman
freemen
FENE Fleance
FENL Fresnel
FENS Fiennes
FEPN fie upon
FEPT fleapit
FESA freesia
FESD feel sad
FESW fretsaw
FETY fleetly
FEUA frenula
FEUE flexure
FEZR freezer
FFEN fifteen
FFHY fifthly
FFIS fifties
FGAE foggage
FGAP fog lamp
FGES fogless
FGET figment
FGEY figgery
FGIH fogyish
FGIY foggily
FGLY fugally
FGON foghorn
FGRD figured
FGRS figures
FGTI fagotti
FGTR fighter
FGTS fugatos
FIAE frigate
FIBE friable
FIDN Friedan
FIDS fair do's
FIDX FT Index
FIER friseur
FIFX Fairfax
FIGD fringed
FIGS fringes
FIHY flighty
FIIG failing
fairing
foiling
FIIH fairish
FIIN Frisian
FIIY fairily
FIKR flicker
frisker
FILD frilled
FIND feigned
FINE faience
faïence
FINR feigner
FIOF frig off
FIOT flip out
FIPR flipper
FISN frisson
FITD fainted
FITR flitter
fritter
FITY faintly
FIUE failure
friture
FIWY fairway
FIZD frizzed
FIZE frizzle
FJTS fajitas
FKOA Fukuoka
FLAA falbala
FLAE falcate
fellate
foliage
foliate
FLAS fellahs
FLAT folk art
FLAY fallacy
FLBG filibeg
FLCA felicia□
felucca
FLDE fall due
FLEL Falwell
FLES fulness
FLET filbert
fulgent
FLEY falsely
FLFL falafel
felafel
FLFR fall for
FLFX Filofax®
FLGY fall guy
FLHR filcher
FLHT full-hot
FLIG falling
filling
folding
FLII Fellini
FLIK Falkirk
FLIS falsies
Follies
FLIY falsify
falsity
FLMN Feldman
FLOE foliole
foliose
fulsome
FLOF fall off
fall-off
file off
FLOS fellows
fulvous
FLOT fall out
fallout
fill out
full-out
FLPR felspar
FLRA filaria
FLRM fulcrum
FLST film set
filmset
FLTP felt-tip
FMDM Femidom®
FMDS fumados
FMLR fumbler
FMRA fimbria
FMRL femoral
FMTE fumette
FMTI fumetti
FMTS fomites
FNAD Finland
FNAE fanfare
FNAK finback
FNAL fantail
FNAR Finbarr
funfair
FNAT fine art
fondant
FNAY fantasy
FNBE finable
FNCL finical
FNCY finicky
FNEN fence in
Fonteyn
FNES finless
FNET fan belt
FNGE finagle
FNHL Funchal
FNID fancied
FNIE fanwise
fanzine
FNIG fencing
finding
funding
FNIH fennish
Finnish
FNIR fancier
funnier
FNIS funnies
FNIY funnily
FNLA Fenella
FNLD fangled
FNLG fine leg
FNLN Fénelon
FNLR fondler
FNLY finally
FNNE finance
FNOD fanfold
fungoid
FNOF fend off
FNOS fungous
FNOT find out
FNRL funeral
FNSE finesse
FNTC fanatic
FOAD froward
FOAE flotage
footage
FOAI flokati
FOCS floccus
FODD flooded
FODN Flodden
FOES flowers
FOEY flowery
foolery
FOFE feoffee
FOFR feoffer
feoffor
FOHW Foochow
FOIA Florida
FOIG flowing
fooling
footing
FOIH foolish
FOIM foodism
FOIS frolics
FOIT florist
FOLA Floella
FOMN footman
footmen
frogman
FONE flounce
frounce
FONN frown on
FOOF from off
FOOT flow out
from out
FOPD footpad
FORD floored
FORE Florrie
FORR floorer
FOSE floosie
Flossie
footsie□
FOSM flotsam
FOSY frowsty
FOTD fronted
frosted
FOTL floatel
frontal
FOTN front on
fronton
FOTP float up
FOTR floater
flouter
FOUT floruit
FOWY footway
FOZE floozie
FPEY foppery
FPIH foppish
FRAA fermata
Ferrara
FRAD forward
FRAE fermate
ferrate
forbade
forgave
formate
forsake
for sale
furcate
furnace
FRAI Ferrari
Ferrari®
FRAM firearm
forearm
FRAN for vain
forwarn
FRAO farrago
FRAT formant
FRBG firebug
fire-bug
FRDC faradic
FRDG firedog
FRDP fired up
FRDY faraday□
FREE Farnese
FREL for real
fur seal
FRER farceur
forbear
for fear
FRES farness
forceps
FRET far be it
ferment
fervent
forfeit
forhent
fornent
Forrest
FREY forgery
FRFL forkful
FRFY firefly
FRGR forager
FRHM Fareham
FRHR farther
further
FRIE ferrite
fertile
forgive
for life
furtive

FRIG farming
farting
forging
forking
forming
furring
FRIH furbish
furnish
FRIM fermium
FRIN fermion
foreign
FRIR farrier
Ferrier
furrier
FRIS forties❑
FRIY farcify
fortify
FRLE forelie
FRLG foreleg
FRLK fartlek
FRLW forslow
FRLY forelay
FRMN fireman
foramen
foreman❑
foremen
FRNE for once
FROD for good
FROE far gone
for love
FROF fire off
FROG furlong
FRON forlorn
FROO furioso❑
FROR fervour
FROS ferrous
furious
FROT farmost
farm out
fire out
fork out
FRRE for free
FRRN foreran
forerun
FORTRAN
FRSE foresee
FRTN first in
FRTP foretop
FRTR Forster
FRTY firstly
FRUA formula
Fortuna
furcula
FRUE ferrule
for sure
fortune❑
FRVR for ever
forever
FRWY faraway
far-away
FRYH Forsyth
FRYR forayer
FSBE fusible
FSBX fuse box
FSET Fossett
FSEY fishery
FSFL fistful
FSGG fishgig
FSHR Fischer
FSIE fascine
festive
fissile
fissive
FSIG fasting
fishing
FSIH fastish
FSIK fossick
FSIL fascial
FSIM fascism
FSIN fashion
fission
fustian
FSIS fossils
FSIT fascist
FSIY fishify
fussily
fustily
FSLI fusilli
FSNT Fastnet
fishnet
FSOE fast one
FSON festoon
FSOT fish out
FSPT fusspot
fuss-pot
FSUA fistula
FSUE fissure
FSUY Fosbury
FTAK futhark
FTED fat head
fathead
fat-head
FTES fatness
fetters
fitness
FTET fitment
FTFL fateful
FTGE fatigue
FTHP fetch up
FTIG fitting
FTIH fattish
FTIY fatuity
FTLR fettler
FTLY fatally
FTOK fetlock
futhork
futtock
FTOS fathoms
fatsoes
fatuous
FUAD foulard
FUAI faux ami
FUBR f-number
FUDC fluidic
FUDR founder
FUDY foundry
FUHD flushed
FUIE fluxive
FUIG feuding
fluting
fouling
FUIL fluvial
FUIM Fauvism
FUIR Fourier
FUIT Fauvist
FUIY frutify
FUKY flunkey
FUMX flummox
FUNY fluency
FUPE frumple
FUPS faux pas
FUTE fouetté
FUTM frustum
FUTR fluster
flutter
fruiter
FVAE foveate
FVRD fevered
FWES fewness
FWET Fawcett
FWIG fawning
fowling
FXDN fixed on
FXDY fixedly
FXHP foxship
FXNS fixings
FXOE foxhole
FXRT foxtrot❑
fox-trot
FXTD fixated
FXUE fixture
FYEF flyleaf
FYIH fly-fish
fly high
FYLW fly-slow
FYMN Feynman
FYOK flybook
FYOT flyboat
FYPN fly open
fly upon
FYRP flytrap
FYVR flyover
FZIG fizzing
FZIY fuzzily
FZNA fazenda
GAAA Granada
GAAE gradate
Grahame
GAAI guarani
Guaraní
GAAO guanaco
GAAY granary
GABD grabbed
GABE grabble
GABX gearbox
GADA grandma
grandpa
GADD grandad
guarded
GADE grandee
GADN gladden
graddan
GADS glandes
GADY grandly
GAED go ahead
go-ahead
GAEE glad eye
GAEY gradely
gravely
GAGS guangos
GAGU Gwangju
GAGW Glasgow
GAHC gnathic
graphic
GAHL gnathal
GAHR Gnasher
GAHW Glashow
GAIE go aside
granite
gratiné
guanine
GAIG gearing
glaring
glazing
gnawing
goading
grading
grating
grazing
GAIH goatish
GAII gradini
GAIL gharial
glacial
GAIR glacier
glazier
grazier
Gwalior
GAIS go amiss
GAIY gratify
gravity
GAKE grackle
GALD gnarled
GALX gravlax
GAMR grammar
GAND grained
GANE grannie
GANH graunch
GANL grapnel
GAOG go along
GAOR glamour
GAOT go about
GAPE grapple
GAPS grampus
GASN grass on
GASP grass up
GATD granted
GATE grantee
GATR go after
grafter
grantor
GATY ghastly
GAUE granule
gravure
GAUL gradual
GBAH gabnash
GBAK go blank
GBCR go by car
GBES giblets
GBET gabfest
GBIE GI bride
GBIL Gabriel
GBIS gubbins
GBLR gabbler
gobbler
GBOE go broke
GBON go brown
GBOS Gibbons
gibbous
GBRS gabbros
GCAY go crazy
GCOK go crook
GCOS geckoes
GDAD Goddard
godward
GDAI Gaddafi
GDAL gadwall
GDED godhead❑
godsend
GDEN gudgeon
GDES goddess
godless
GDHB Godthab
GDIE godlike
GDIY giddily
GDLT God slot
GDON gadroon
godroon
GDRE Godfree
GDRY Godfrey
GDTA godetia
GDTH go Dutch
GDYP giddy-up
GEAA Grenada
Guevara
GEAE gregale
grenade
GEAS gheraos
GEDL Grendel
GEDM Gaeldom
GEDN guerdon
GEEA guereza
GEFL gleeful
GEGD Gielgud
GEHZ gee whiz
GEIE Grecize
GEIG Goering
greying
GEIH greyish
GEIL gremial
GEIN Grecian
GEKN gherkin
GELN gremlin
GENE Glennie
GENR gleaner
GENY greenly

GEOG Geelong
GEOY Gregory
GESD guessed
GESR guesser
GETN greaten
GETO great go
GETR greater
GETS ghettos
GETY greatly
GEVS Greaves
GEYH Gwenyth
GEZY Gretzky
GFNI go Fanti
GFOD Gifford
GFRT go first
go for it
GGIG gagging
GGLR giggler
GGLS gigolos
goggles
GGRN Gagarin
GGTR gagster
GHNA Gehenna
GIAE grimace
GIAG Guiyang
GIDE griddle
GIDN gliadin
GIDR grinder
guilder
GIFL gainful
GIFN griffin□
griffon
GIFR go in for
GIGN going on
GIGO going to
GIHM Grisham
GIHS geishas
GIIG gaining
gliding
griping
guiding
GIIY grimily
GILE ghillie
GILM Guillem
Gwillym
GIMR glimmer
GIMS gliomas
GINA Goiânia
GIOD Grimond
GIPD gripped
GIPE glimpse
GIPR gripper
GISM Grissom
GISN Grigson
GISS gliosis
GISY gainsay
Grimsby
GITE gristle
GITN glisten
GITR glitter
gritter
GITY gristly
GIUE guipure

GIVD grieved
GIVR griever
GIZE grizzle
GIZY grizzly
GJRT Gujarat
GKPT go kaput
GLAH goliath□
GLAI Galvani
GLAN goldarn
GLAT gallant
GLBG golf bag
GLCP goldcup
GLDY gala day
gelidly
GLEN galleon
GLES gulleys
GLET Gilbert
GLEY gallery
GLGS galagos
GLHD Galahad
GLIE Gallice
gallise
gallize
GLIG galling
gilding
Golding
GLIM gallium
Gilliam
GLIN Gillian
GLIS Gallios
gullies
GLIT galliot
GLLE Galilee
GLLI Galilei
GLLO Galileo
GLMH galumph
GLMN Goldman
GLNT gallnut
GLON galloon
GLOS gallows
GLTA Galatea
GLTE galette
GLTN gelatin
GLWN Goldwyn
GLWR go lower
Gulf War
GMAA gummata
GMAT gymnast
GMBK gemsbok
GMEY gemmery
GMHE gumshoe
gym shoe
GMIK gimmick
GMIR gambier
GMLP gym slip
GMLR gambler
GMNS Geminis
GMOE gamboge
GMOK gammock
GMOL gumboil
GMOT gumboot
GMRL gambrel
GMRP gumdrop

GMTC gametic
GMUA gymnura
GMYL Gemayel
GNAE Gin Lane
gunwale
GNAF Gandalf
GNAO Gonzalo
GNDA gonidia
GNEE Genoese
GNEG ginseng
GNEK gun deck
GNEL genteel
Gunnell
GNES Gunners
GNEY gingery
gunnery
GNHM gingham
GNHT gunshot
GNIE gentile
genuine
gunfire
GNII gingili
GNIN gentian
GNLA ganglia
GNOA gondola
GNOF gone off
GNOK gunlock
GNOM gunroom
GNON gun down
GNOT gunboat
GNPN gen up on
GNRC generic
GNRL gangrel
general
Goneril
GNSA Ganesha
gangsta
genista
GNSS geneses
genesis□
genuses
GNSW gang saw
GNTC genetic
GNTE genette
GNTL genital
GNVN Genevan
GNWY gangway
GOAD good and
GOAE globate
GOBE goodbye
good-bye
GOBY good buy
GOCI gnocchi
GOCY grouchy
GODE Geordie
GODN good-den
GODY good-day
GOEG good egg
GOEN good-e'en
GOES gropers
GOEY geodesy
grocery
GOGA Georgia

GOGC georgic
GOGE Georgie
GOIG glowing
growing
GOIS goolies
Gropius
Grotius
GOIY glorify
goofily
GOKE grockle
GOLR growler
GOLT growl at
GOMN Goodman
GOMT grommet
GOND groined
GONP grown-up
GONR groaner
GONS grounds
GOOD globoid
grow old
GOOE globose
GOOO giocoso
GOOY geology
GOPD grouped
GOPE groupie
GOPR grouper
GORM grogram
GOSC Glossic
GOSP gross up
GOSR glosser
grouser
GOSY grossly
GOTC glottic
gnostic
GOTL glottal
GOTS glottis
grottos
GOTY ghostly
GOUE globule
GOVD grooved
GOYE glory be
GOYN glory in
GOYO Gromyko
GPIE gap site
GPIS guppies
GRAD garland□
gurnard
GRAE garbage
germane
Gervase
GRAS Germans
GRAY Germany
GRCA gertcha
GRDM Guri Dam
GRED gorsedd
GRES gardens
GRET garment
GREY Gargery
GRFE giraffe□
GRIE garpike
GRIH garfish
garnish
girlish

GRIK Garrick
GRIN Gordian
GRIS Gorgias
gorgios
GRIT Geraint
GRLA gorilla
GRLD garbled
GRLY Gormley
gyrally
GRMA Garamba
GRNE Garonne
GRNR Gardner
GROS Gorgons
GRSL girasol
GRTE garotte
GRUD go round
GSAE gestate
go spare
go stale
GSAK gas mask
gas tank
goshawk
GSAN gas main
GSAO Gestapo
GSAT gestalt□
GSEL Gaskell
GSES Gospels
GSFR go so far
GSHL gasohol
GSIG gasping
gas ring
gassing
Gissing
gosling
gushing
GSIY gossipy
GSLE Giselle
GSOS gaseous
gessoes
GSOT Gosport
Guscott
GSRC gastric
GSRN gastrin
GSUE gesture
GSYP gussy up
GTAD get paid
Gotland
GTAE guttate
GTAK get back
GTAS gateaus
GTAT get past
GTAX gâteaux
GTBD go to bed
GTEE get here
GTEL get real
get well
GTEN gittern
GTES get less
gutless
GTIE get wise
GTIG Gatting
getting
G-string

Words marked □ can also be spelled with an initial capital letter

GTIK Gatwick
GTNN get in on
GTNO get in to
get into
get onto
GTNS gitanos
GTOD get cold
GTON get down
GTOT get lost
get lost!
GTPO get up to
GTPT go to pot
GTRE Guthrie
GTSA go to sea
GTSD get used
GTTN get it on
GTVN get even
GTVR get over
GTWR go to war
GTWY gateway
get away
getaway
GUAH goulash
GUAI glutaei
GUBE grumble
GUBR grubber
GUBY grumbly
GUCE gouache
GUDR go under
GUEE gougère
Gruyère
GUEL gluteal
GUER glue ear
GUES gluteus
GUEY gaudery
GUFR gauffer
GUFY gruffly
GUHN Gaughan
GUHS gauchos
GUIG gauging
GUIH Gaulish
GUIR Gautier
GUIY gaudily
GUMT gourmet
grummet
GUOE glucose
GUOS goujons
GUOT Gaumont
GUTD glutted
GUTE gruntle
GUTN glutton
GUTR grunter
GUTY gauntly
GUUN Gauguin
GVER give ear
GVNO given to
GVOF give off
GVOT give out
GVTE gavotte
GVWY give way
GWAS gewgaws
GWIE go white
GWOG go wrong
GYED Gwynedd
GYEH Gwyneth
GYES gayness
GYHN gryphon□
GYIE glycine
GYOE guy-rope
GYSH goyisch
GYTC glyptic
GZAD gizzard
GZBS gazebos
GZLE gazelle
GZLR guzzler
GZTE gazette
HABY head boy
HADP hoard up
HADR hoarder
HAEO heave ho!
heave to
HAEP heave up
HAES heavens
HAFR head for
HAGO Huang Ho
HAHN heathen
HAHR heather□
HAIE hyaline
hyalite
HAIG heading
healing
hearing
heating
heaving
HAIY headily
heavily
hoarily
HAKN hearken
HAMN headman
HANN Huainan
HAOD hyaloid
HAOF head off
HAOT hear out
HASF heaps of
HASN hoarsen
HAST headset
HASY hearsay
HATD hearted
HATN hearten
HATY healthy
heartly
HAWY headway
HAZN hoatzin
HBAC Hebraic
HBAD Hubbard
HBAL hobnail
HBAS habdabs
HBBE Habibie
HBCI hibachi
HBEA Hobbema
HBES Hebrews
HBNN hebenon
HBOD Habgood
HBTE habitué
HBTS H E Bates
HBTT habitat
HCAE hectare
HCDM hickdom
HCEY hackery
HCIG hacking
HCLR hackler
heckler
HCLS huckles
HCNO hoc anno
HCNY hackney□
Hockney
HCOF hack off
HCOO hoc loco
HCOY hickory
HCSW hacksaw
HCUE hachure
HDAE hydrate
HDAT hydrant
HDEN hedge in
HDET had best
HDIA Hodeida
HDIE hydride
HDIG hedging
hidling
HDIN Hadrian
HDIS hidlins
HDKN Hodgkin
HDLA hidalga
HDLD huddled
HDNC hedonic
HDOD hydroid
HDOK haddock
HDOS hideous
Hudson's
hydrous
HDOT hide out
hideout
HDTD hydatid
HEES hueless
HEFL heedful
HEIG heeding
HEKL Haeckel
HEON hoe-down
HFIH huffish
HFIM hafnium
HFIY heftily
huffily
HFMN Hoffman
HGAD haggard□
HGAH hogwash
HGAK hogback
HGAT Hoggart
HGBR high bar
HGED hogweed
HGEE hygiene
HGET highest
HGFD high-fed
HGHT high-hat
HGIE hag-ride
HGIG hogging
HGIH hagfish
haggish
hoggish
HGIS Higgins
HGKY high-key
HGLR haggler
HGMN highmen
HGRH Hogarth
HGTA high tea
high-tea
HGTP high-top
HGTR high-tar
HGWY highway
HHIM hahnium
HICT haircut
HIDS hairdos
HIES heiress
HIEZ Heifetz
HIHO heigh-ho
HIIK Haitink
HIIN Haitian
HINT hairnet
HIOS heinous
HIPN hairpin
HITD hoisted
HITR heister
hoister
HIUK haiduck
HKUT Hakluyt
HLAD halyard
holland□
HLAE Haldane
HLAL holdall
hold-all
HLAO holla-ho!
HLAY Hillary
HLBT halibut
HLCA Halacha
HLCL helical
HLCP half-cap
HLCS helices
HLCT half-cut
hell-cat
HLDM holydam
HLDY half-day
holiday□
holy day
HLED halberd
HLEE Hellene
HLEN Holbein
HLES halvers
helpers
HLET halbert
Hilbert
HLFL helpful
HLFX Halifax
HLGN halogen
HLIE Heloise
HLIG halting
helping
holding□
hulking
HLIH hellish
HLIM holmium
HLIN hellion
HLIS Hollies
HLJE holy Joe
HLKH Halakah
HLOA hellova
HLOD helcoid
Holroyd
HLOE half one
Holy One
HLOF hold off
HLOK hillock
HLOS holloes
HLOT help out
hold out
hole out
HLPD helipad
HLRS Hilarus
HLTO half two
HLTP hill top
hilltop
HLTR holster
HLWR holy war
HLWT halfwit
half-wit
HLWY halfway
hallway
HLXS helixes
HLYN halcyon
HMDR humidor
HMDY humidly
HMEF himself
HMES Hammers
HMET Hammett
Hamnett
Humbert
HMHY Humphry
HMIG humming
HMIH hum with
HMIT hymnist
HMIY hammily
HMLD humbled
HMLR hamular
HMLS hamulus
HMND hominid
HMNL hymenal
HMNM homonym
HMNY humanly
HMOD Hammond
HMOK hammock
hemlock
hummock
HMOY hymnody
HMRC Homeric
HMRL humeral
humoral
HMRM humdrum
HMRS humerus
HMTC Hamitic
HMTN Hampton
HMTR hamster
HMUG Hamburg
Hamhung
Homburg
HNAA Honiara
HNAD Hansard
HNAE handaxe

Words marked □ can also be spelled with an initial capital letter

henbane
HNAI Honiari
HNAP Hans Arp
HNAY Hungary
HNBG handbag
HNDG hangdog
HNEK henpeck
HNEN hinge on
HNES hunkers
HNFL handful
HNFR hunt for
HNGN handgun
HNHD hunched
HNHS honchos
HNIG hanging
hunting
HNIS henries
HNIY handily
HNLD handled
HNLR handler
HNLY Handley
Hindley
HNMN hangman
hanuman□
HNOF hang off
HNOK Hancock
HNOT hand out
handout
hand-out
hang out
hangout
hang-out
hunt out
HNRD hundred
HNRX Hendrix
HNSL handsel
HNSN hands on
hands-on
HNSP hands up
hunt's-up
HNST handset
HNSW handsaw
HNSY honesty
HNTC henotic
HNTN Honiton
HNUS honours
HNUT Hinault
HNVR Hanover
HNYD honeyed
HNYI Henry VI
HNYV Henry IV
HOGW hoosgow
HOLM hoodlum
HPAE heptane
HPDP hyped up
HPES hapless
HPET Huppert
HPFL hopeful□
HPFR hope for
HPGA hypogea
HPIG hopping
HPIS Hopkins
HPIY happily
HPLA hop-flea
HPNM hyponym
HPNY ha'penny
HPOD haploid
hypnoid
HPOE hip-bone
HPOF hip roof
HPRH hap'orth
HPRN heparin
hyperon
HPTA Hypatia
HPTC hepatic
HPUN Hepburn
HPXA hypoxia
HPXC hypoxic
HRAD Harvard
HRAE herbage
HRAS hurrahs
HRBE hirable
HRBG horn-bug
HRBY herdboy
HRCS hyraces
HRCT haricot
HREF herself
HREN hordein
Hordern
HRES harness
herdess
Hornets
HRET hardest
harvest
Herbert
HRFL harmful
hurtful
HRHN harshen
HRHT hard hat
hard-hit
HRHY harshly
Hershey
HRID harried
hurried
HRIE heroine
heroise
heroize
HRIG Harding
herding
herring
hurling
hurting
HRIH Harwich
HRIK Herrick
HRIL hernial
HRIM heroism
HRIR harrier
HRIS Harpies
her nibs
HRIT harpist
Harriet
herbist
HRIY hardily
horrify
HRLP hare lip
HRLR hurdler
HRLS hurdles
HRLT herblet
HRLY Hartley
HRNY heronry
HROD Harwood
HROE hardoke
Harlowe
hormone
HRON harpoon
HROR harbour
HROT hire out
HROY harmony
HRPT hard put
HRRS Hereros
HRSO here's to
HRTC heretic
HRTD Harstad
HRTO Horatio
HRTR heritor
HRUE hirsute
HRXS hyraxes
HRYP hurry up
HRZN horizon
HSAD husband
HSAE hastate
hostage
HSAN Hussain
HSAO Hispano
HSAS hussars
HSAY hushaby
HSDC Hasidic
HSDM Hasidim
HSEL Husserl
HSEN has-been
Hussein
HSES hostess
HSEY hosiery
HSIE hospice
hostile
Hussite
HSIG hissing
HSIH hashish
HSIN hessian
HSIS his nibs
HSIY hastily
huskily
HSLD hassled
HSLR hustler□
HSNA hosanna
HSOE histone
HSOK hassock
HSOY history
HSVN Heshvan
HTAD hatband
HTAK hit back
HTAS hetmans
HTAZ hot jazz
HTBE hatable
HTEA hetaera
HTED hothead
HTES hatless
hotness
HTET hot melt
hutment
HTFL hateful
HTHD hitched
HTHL hatchel
HTHP hitch up
HTHR hitcher
HTHT hatchet
hotshot
HTIA hetaira
HTIE Hot Five
hot line
hot-wire
HTIG hitting
hotting
HTIT hit list
HTOT hotfoot
HTPN hit upon
HTPR hotspur□
HTPT hot spot
HTRS heteros
HTTP hit it up
HTUS hatfuls
HUAE haulage
HUBY hautboy
HUDD hounded
HUEA heureka
HUEK hauberk
HUER hauteur
HUHY Haughey
haughty
HUIG housing
HUIR haulier
HUMN Housman
HUMS hoummos
HUOF haul off
HUOT haul out
HUTD haunted
HUTN Houston
HUTR haunter
HVAO have a go
have-a-go
HVFN have fun
HVGT have got
HVNT have-not
HVOF hive off
HVRR haverer
HVSX have sex
HVWY have way
HWET howbeit
HWIG hawking□
howling
HWIH hawkish
HWIS Hawkins
HWLS H G Wells
HWOE how come?
HWVR however
HWYO howdy-do
HWYS Hawkyns
HXGN hexagon
HXPD hexapod
HYED hayseed
HYES Huygens
HYIE haywire
HYIK hayrick
HYOK haycock
hay fork
hayfork
HYUE Hey Jude
HZIT Hazlitt
IAAE imamate
in a daze
in a haze
IADF in aid of
IADN in-and-in
IAES in a mess
IAET I have it
IAEY imagery
inanely
irately
IAHE Ivanhoe
IAIE imagine□
IAIG imaging
IAIK in a tick
IAIN Iranian
Italian
IAIY inanity
IAIZ in a tizz
IALP in a flap
IAOA in a coma
Isadora
IAOD in a mood
in a word
IAOE in a hole
Isadore
IAOS imagoes
IAOT in a sort
IAOY in a body
in agony
IAPT in a spot
IATS in antis
IATW in a stew
IATY inaptly
IAUD iracund
IAUF in a huff
IAUK in a sulk
IBAD inboard
IBBR imbiber
IBED inbreed
IBIF in brief
IBIG imbuing
IBIT inbuilt
in-built
IBNO in banco
IBOD in blood
IBOM in bloom
IBON imbrown
IBSM imbosom
IBUD inbound
IBWR imbower
ICBS incubus
ICCA Iacocca
ICDS incudes
ICFR itch for
ICIE incline
ICIF in chief
ICIG itching

ICIM ischium
ICMR incomer
ICNE incense
inconie
ICOD in-crowd
ICOE inclose
ICOS incross
ICRE incurve
ICSR incisor
ICTR inciter
ICUE include
ICUT incrust
IDAA Indiana
IDAN indrawn
IDAT indraft
IDCS indices
IDED in dread
IDEL indwell
IDGS indigos
IDLE indulge
IDOS indoors
IDPH in depth
in-depth
IDRE indorse
IDSA indusia
IDUT in doubt
IDXR indexer
IDXS indexes
IEAA ikebana
IEAD Iceland
Ireland
IEAE iterate
IEAT inexact
IEEG iceberg
IEIE itemise
itemize
IEIK ice pick
IEIN Iberian
IELE ice floe
IELY ideally
IEOD ice-cold
IERH inearth
IERR in error
IESS ileuses
IETA inertia
IETY ineptly
inertly
IEUE ice cube
IEVR ice over
IFAE inflame
inflate
IFAT infract
IFCS in focus
IFDL infidel
IFED infield
IFEH in flesh
IFEI in fieri
IFET inflect
IFHN Isfahan
IFIT inflict
IFLE infulae
IFLO in folio
IFME infimae

IFNA infanta
IFNE infante
IFNY infancy
IFOT in front
IFRE in force
IFRO inferno
IFRT in for it
IGAN in grain
ingrain
IGAS Ingrams
IGES ingress
IGIG ingoing
IGNE ingénue
IGNR ingener
IGON ingrown
IGOS in gross
IGPP Iggy Pop
IHAL Ishmael
IHBD ichabod
IHBT inhabit
inhibit
IHLR inhaler
IHLS in holes
IHMN inhuman
IHRE inherce
IHRT inherit
IHSE in haste
IHTP Imhotep
IHUE in-house
IHVK Izhevsk
IIAE imitate
irisate
IIES iciness
IIIE iridise
iridize
IIIL initial
IIIM iridium
IIMN Idi Amin
IIOA Isidora
IIOE Isidore
IISU Iliescu
IITC idiotic
IJIT injoint
IJLY injelly
IJNT injunct
IJRD injured
IKDY ilkaday
IKEL inkwell
IKIG inkling
IKOE irksome
IKTA Inkatha
IKTK Irkutsk
ILAE ill fame
ill-made
ILCT illicit
ILES illness
ILGL illegal
ILIL ill will
ill-will
ILMC Islamic
ILMO in limbo
ILPE illapse
ILRD ill-bred

ILSD ill-used
ILUK ill luck
ill-luck
IMIS iambics
IMNE immense
IMRD immured
IMRE immerge
immerse
IMRL immoral
IMWY in my way
INBE ignoble
INBY ignobly
INMR ionomer
INOS igneous
INRD ignored
INRE innerve
INRR ignorer
INRS ignaros
innards
INSO Ionesco
INSR ioniser
INTD ignited
INTR igniter
INUH Ian Rush
INUY Ian Dury
INWY in no way
INZR ionizer
IOAE Iron Age
isolate
IODR in order
IOIA Iwo Jima
IOIE iconise
iconize
idolise
idolize
ironise
ironize
IOIG ironing
IOIM idolism
IOIT idolist
IOIY iconify
IOOA isodoma
IOOE iron ore
isotope
IOOT iron out
IOOY isonomy
isotopy
IOTS isoetes
IOYT isohyet
IPAE implate
in peace
in phase
in place
IPAH impeach
IPAL impearl
IPAT implant
IPES impress
IPET imprest
IPEY impiety
IPID implied
IPIT impaint
imprint
in point

in print
IPLD impaled
IPLE impulse
IPLS impalas
IPNE impinge
IPOE implode
implore
improve
IPOS impious
IPRA imperia
IPRL imperil
IPSD imposed
IPSE impasse
impaste
imposte
in posse
IPSO impasto
IPTS impetus
IPUD impound
IPWR in power
IQET inquest
IQIE inquire
IQIY inquiry
IRAS inroads
IREI Israeli
IRHM Ibrahim
IRIE Igraine
IRIS in ruins
ISAE in shape
in space
instate
ISAL in small
install
ISAT instant
ISCA Insecta
ISDR insider
ISDS insides
ISED instead
ISEL inshell
ISES it seems
ISET inspect
ISGT in sight
insight
ISIE inspire
ISIH Ipswich
ISLN insulin
ISLR insular
ISLS insults
ISNW insinew
ISOE inshore
in store
in-store
ISOK in shock
in stock
ISOT in short
ISPD insipid
ISRD insured
ISRR insurer
ISUP insculp
ISYE in style
ISYU I ask you!
ITAN in train
in twain

ITAS in tears
ITGR integer
ITIE intwine
ITIG in thing
in-thing
ITIT intwist
ITME intimae
ITMS isthmus
ITNE intense
ITNS Ictinus
ITOT introit
ITRE interne
ITRM interim
ITRS in turns
ITSS ictuses
ITTL in total
ITUE intrude
ITUH in touch
in truth
ITUT intrust
IUEO in utero
IUQE Iquique
IUTS Iquitos
IVDR invader
IVGE in vogue
IVIE invoice
IVIH inveigh
IVLD invalid
IVLE involve
IVRE inverse
IVTO in vitro
IWAE inweave
IWRS inwards
IYLC idyllic
JAAP Jean Arp
JANE Jeannie
JAOS jealous
JBES jobless
JBLE jubilee
JCAS jackass
JCDW jackdaw
JCLN Jacklin
Jocelin
Jocelyn
JCLR jocular
JCMR jacamar
JCNA Jacinta
JCNH jacinth□
JCNT jaconet
JCOF jack off
JCPT jackpot
JCSA Jocasta
JCSN Jackson
JCTR Jack Tar
Jack tar
JCUS Jacques
JCZI Jacuzzi®
JDDY jadedly
JDIE jadeite
Judaise
Judaize
JDIM Judaism
JDPR Jodhpur

JDUE j'adoube
JEES jeepers
JEIG jeering
JELW Joe Blow
JFRY Jaffrey
Jeffrey
JGES Jaggers
JGIG jogging
JGIS juggins
JGJG jig-a-jig
JGLR juggler
jugular
JGRT jogtrot
JGUS jugfuls
JHDE John Dee
JHGY John Gay
JHNE johnnie❑
JHPM John Pym
JHRY John Ray
JHSN Johnson
JHVH Jehovah
JIEY joinery
JIIG joining
JIIM Jainism
JITD jointed
JITY jointly
JJNM jejunum
JJTU jujitsu
ju-jitsu
JKRA Jakarta
JLAA Juliana
JLID jellied
JLIG jilting
jolting
JLIN Jillian
JLIY jellify
jollify
jollily
jollity
JLPY jaloppy
JLUE jalouse
JLYY Jellyby
JMAI jampani
JMAS jimjams
JMAT jam tart
JMEX jambeux
JMIA Jamaica
jambiya
JMIY jumpily
JMJT jump-jet
JMLD jumbled
JMNZ Jiménez
JMOF jump off
jump-off
JMOL jam roll
JMRH Jo March
JMSN Jameson
JMUK jumbuck
JNAY January
JNCK Janácek
JNES jankers
JNHU Jinzhou
JNIN Jungian
JNIS Jenkins
JNKS janskys
JNLR jingler
JNOK jannock
JNOS jingoes
juncoes
JNPR juniper
JNTA Janetta
JNTE Janette
JNTR janitor
JNUL jonquil❑
JPEH Japheth
JPTA Jephtha
JPTR Jupiter
JRCO Jericho
JRDC juridic
JRET Jarrett
JRIE Jardine
JRIG jarring
JRIY jerkily
JRLY jurally
JRMN juryman
jurymen
JROF jerk off
JRON jargoon
JRRG jury rig
JRUS jarfuls
JSES Jaspers
JSFL jestful
JSIA Jessica
Justina
JSIE jasmine❑
justice
Justine
JSIG jesting
JSIS Jesuits
JSIY justify
JSNW just now
JSTE Josette
JTAD Jutland
JTES jitters
JTEY jittery
JTIG jotting
jutting
JTON jot down
JUNL journal
JUNS journos
JUNY journey
JUTR jouster
JVLN javelin
JVMN Java Man
JVNL Juvenal
JVSA Java Sea
JWOE jawbone
JYAK jaywalk
JYES joyless
JYIE joy-ride
JZBL Jezebel
JZIY jazzily
KAAI Khatami
KADR khaddar
KAEY knavery
KAIE kyanise
kyanite
kyanize
KAIG Keating
KAIH knavish
KAKR knacker
KAKV Kharkov
KAMR Klammer
KAPE knapple
KASN khamsin
KBAA kabbala
KBEZ Koblenz
KBIK Kubrick
KBUZ kibbutz
KCIG Kuching
KCOF kick off
kick-off
KCOT kick out
KDIG kidding
KDIH Kaddish
KDIS kiddies
KDKN kidskin
KDUH kiddush
KEBY Kiel Bay
KECP kneecap
knee-cap
KEDM Kiev Dam
KEDR kneader
KEFT keep fit
keep-fit
KEIA khediva
KEIE khedive
KEIG keening
keeping
KELD kneeled
KELN kremlin
KELR kneeler
KEMM keep mum
KEMR klezmer
KENT keepnet
KENX Kleenex®
KEOF keep off
KEOT keep out
KESN keelson
Kherson
KESP knees-up
KEST Knesset
KFYH kufiyah
KGER keg beer
KGUE kagoule
KIHA Krishna
KIIE kainite
KIIG knifing
KIKR klinker
KIMR krimmer
KITR keister
knitter
KKPS kakapos
KLAE Kildare
KLBT kilobit
KLDY kiln-dry
KLHZ kolkhoz
KLIG killing
KLIK killick
KLIN Killian
KLJY killjoy
KLNN Kalinin
KLNS kalends
KLOF kill off
KLOK killock
KLTN kiloton
KLUA Kilauea
KMAA Kampala
KMNS kimonos
KMOG kampong
KMRD kamerad
KMTK komatik
KMUT kumquat
KNCP kingcup
KNDM kingdom
KNEA Kundera
KNEH Kenneth
KNEY Kennedy
KNHP kinship
KNHT king-hit
KNIG Kunming
KNIH Kentish
KNIM Kantism
KNIN Kantian
KNIT Kantist
KNIY kinkily
KNLR kindler
KNMN kinsman
kinsmen
KNOD Ken Dodd
KNOK Kinnock
KNPN kingpin
KNRD kindred
KNSS kinesis
KNTA Kenitra
KNTC kinetic
KOAA Khorana
KOAL know-all
KOBE knobble
KOBY knobbly
KOHW know-how
KOIE kaoline
KOIG knowing
KOKN knock on
knock-on
KOKP knock up
knock-up
KOKR knocker
KONS known as
KOTD knotted
KPIG Kipling
KPON kip down
KRAH kurbash
KRCI Karachi
KRES kirmess
KRGA kerygma
KRIG karting
kirking
KRIH Kurdish
KRJN Karajan
KRKL karakul
KRKM Kara Kum
KRNC Koranic
KROE karaoke
Kermode
KROF Karloff
KRSA Kara Sea
KRTN keratin
Kirstin
KRUC Kerouac
KSGN Kosygin
KSIK Keswick
KSIO Kushiro
KSOF kiss off
kiss-off
KSRL kestrel
KSRS kashrus❑
KSRT kashrut❑
KTBH Ketubah
KTCY kitschy
KTHN kitchen
KTHP ketchup
KTIA Katrina
KTRN Kathryn
KTSS ketosis
KTZV Kutuzov
KUBE knubble
KUBH khutbah
KUIS koumiss
KUKE knuckle
KULD knurled
KUMN Kaufman
KURY kouprey
KWON Kowloon
KYAD key card
KYDP keyed up
keyed-up
KYEI Kayseri
KYES keyless
KYIG kayoing
KYOD key-cold
keyword
KYOE keyhole
keynote
KYTN krypton
KZES Kuznets
LAAA Lualaba
LAAE leafage
leakage
LAES leaders
LAHR leather
LAIG leading
leaking
leaning
leasing
leaving
loafing
LAIH loafish
LALT leaflet
LAND learned
LANR learner
LAOF lead off
LAOT lead out
leak out
LASC Liassic

LASN liaison
LATS lean-tos
LAUR leaguer
LBAE labiate
librate
LBAY library
LBDS libidos
LBES Lubbers
LBLA labella
lobelia
LBNN Lebanon
LBOK Lubbock
LBOM lobworm
LBRA Liberia
LBRL liberal
LBRM labarum
LBRS liberos
LBRY liberty
LBTR lobster
LCAE lactate
lockage
LCAO Luciano
LCBY Luce Bay
LCDS Lycidas
LCDY lucidly
LCEE Lucrece
LCEL lacteal
LCEN lectern
LCES lackeys
LCEY lechery
LCFR Lucifer
LCIG lacking
licking
LCIL lochial
LCIN lection
LCIY luckily
LCJW lockjaw
LCLA Lucilla
LCLE Lucille
LCLN Lachlan
LCLR locular
LCLS locules
loculus
LCLY locally
LCMS lucumos
LCNA Lucinda
LCNC laconic
LCNE lacunae
licence
license
LCNW Lucknow
LCOE lactose
LCOT lock out
lockout
luck out
LCOX Lacroix
LCRA Lacerta
LCRE Le Carré
lucarne
lucerne❑
LCSE LaCoste
LCTD located
LCTY licitly

LCUE lecture
LCUR lacquer
LCUS lyceums
LCYR Lockyer
LDDY Lady Day
LDEL Liddell
LDES ledgers
lidless
LDIE Luddite
LDIG lodging
LDIH laddish
LDNS Ladenis
Ladinos
LDVC Ludovic
LEAD leeward
LEAE lee-gage
LEAK lie back
LEDR Laender
LEEE leeze me
LEEM lee beam
LEIG Leeming
leering
LEON lie down
lie-down
LESR Loesser
LETS Laertes
LFIG lifting
LFIM leftism
LFIR loftier
LFIT leftist
LFIY loftily
LFOF lift off
lift-off
LFTE Lafitte
LFVR Le Fever
LGAD laggard
LGAE luggage
LGAL lugsail
LGBE legible
LGBY legibly
LGCL logical
LGDR L'Age d'Or
LGES legless
LGET leg-rest
LGIE leg side
lignite
LGIG lagging
LGIS loggias
LGIY lignify
LGLP leg slip
LGLY legally
LGNA Lagonda®
LGNS legends
LGOK legwork
logbook
LGOM legroom
lugworm
LGON leghorn❑
LGOS legions
LGPN leg spin
LGRN leg-iron
LGTD lighted
LGTE legatee

LGTN lighten
light on
LGTP light up
LGTR lighter
LGTS legatos
LGTY lightly
LGUL leg-pull
LHAN Lehmann
LHVE Le Havre
LIGN lying-in
LIGY lyingly
LILW laid low
LINZ Leibniz
LIOF laid off
LIRM Leitrim
LITR leister
LIUE leisure
LIZG Leipzig
LKBE likable
LKFN like fun
LKHI Lakshmi
LKMD like mad
LKNO liken to
LKVN Lake Van
LLAS Lallans
LLAY lullaby
LLIG lilting
lulling
LLIN Lillian
LLPD lily pad
LLWY L S Lowry
LMAA lambada
lemmata
LMAD Lombard
LMAE limeade
LMAO lumbago
LMAT lambast
LMBY Lyme Bay
LMCS limaces
LMEE Lumière
LMEH Lambeth
LMEK limbeck
LMET lambent
lambert❑
LMGS Limoges
LMHD lymphad
LMIA lempira
LMIG lamming
lemming
limping
LMIH lumpish
LMIM Lamaism
LMIT Lamaist
LMIY lumpily
LMKN limpkin
LMLA lamella
LMNA lomenta
LMNE laminae
LMNR laminar
LMON lampoon
LMOO Limpopo
LMRA Lemuria
LMRK Lamarck

LMRS Lemures
LMRY lamprey
LMSM lump sum
LMTD limited
LMTR limiter
LMTS limites
LMUG Limburg
LNAD laniard
lanyard
LNAE lineage
linkage
LNAO long ago
LNBW longbow
LNCT linocut
LNED linseed
LNEN lantern
LNES lancers❑
LNET lenient
lunge at
LNFR long for
LNGS lanugos
LNHP long hop
LNHU Lanzhou
LNIG landing
lending
linking
longing
LNIY lankily
LNKR Lineker
LNLG long leg
LNLN lanolin
Lenglen
LNLR lunular
LNLS Lenclos
LNLY Langley
LNMN link man
linkman
LNOF long off
LNOL long-oil
LNON Lincoln
LNOR langour
LNOS lingoes
LNSY Lindsay
Lindsey
LNTC lunatic
LNTD lunated
LNTE Linette
lunette
Lynette
LNTN Langton
LNTS lengths
linctus
LNTY Langtry
lengthy
LNUD languid
LNUL lingual
LNUR languor
LOAD Leonard
leopard
leotard
LOAG Luoyang
LOES lioness
LOEY loosely

LOFR look for
LOIE leonine
lionise
lionize
LOIG looking
looming
looping
loosing
looting
LOIR loonier
LOIS loonies
LOOA Leonora
LOOD Leopold
LOOL loo roll
LOON Laocoon
LOOT look out
lookout
LOSE look-see
LOTS Leontes
LPAA La Plata
LPAE Laplace
LPAG lapsang
LPDS Lepidus
LPED lip-read
LPIG lapping
lapwing
LPNO Lepanto
LPOS leprous
leptons
LPOY leprosy
LPTS Lapiths
LPYC lip-sync
LQAE liquate
LQER liqueur
LQEY liquefy
LRAA Larnaca
LRCE Laroche
loricae
LRCL lyrical
LRDY luridly
LRES largess
LRET largest
LREY larceny
largely
LRHR lurcher
LRIG lurking
LRIH largish
LRIK Lerwick
LRJM Lord Jim
LRLI lorelei❑
LRNO Lorenzo
LRNR Lardner
LRNZ Lorentz
LROD Larwood
LRON lardoon
LRTA Loretta
LRTE lorette
LRVR L-driver
LRWY lyra-way
LSAT last act
LSEH Lisbeth
LSES Lesseps
LSFL lustful

LSGA lasagna
LSGE lasagne
LSIG lashing
lasting
Lessing
lisping
listing
LSIN lesbian
LSIY lustily
LSMN last man
LSNO Lysenko
LSOE lissome
LSOS lassoes
lessons
LSOT lash out
last out
lose out
LSRL lustral
LSRS lustres
LSTE Lisette
LSTO Lesotho
LSWY lose way
LTAL let fall
LTAR Lothair
LTAS let pass
LTCS latices
LTEN lethean
LTES letters
Lutyens
LTEY lathery
lithely
lottery
LTID lethied
LTIE latrine
lattice
let ride
Lettice
LTIM lithium
LTIN Latvian
Lothian
LTKA Latakia
LTLP let slip
LTMR Latimer
LTNN let in on
LTNO let into
LTNS Latinus
LTNW let know
LTNY latency
LTOF let go of
LTON let down
let-down
LTPN let up on
LTRL lateral
literal
LTRN later on
LTRP let drop
LTRY liturgy
LTTA Letitia
LTTO let it go
LTTS litotes
LTUE lettuce
LTXS latexes
LUAN Louvain
LUDR launder
lounder
LUDY laundry
LUED Lou Reed
LUEP louse up
LUES laurels
LUGR lounger
LUHT laugh at
LUHU Liuzhou
LUIE leucine
LUIG louring
LUIH loudish
loutish
LUIY lousily
LUOA leucoma
LURD louvred
LUTA Leuctra
LVBE lovable
LVBS lavabos
LVDN lived-in
LVDY lividly
love-day
LVFR live for
LVIG levying
LVLA lavolta
LVLP level up
LVLT level at
LVNA Lavinia
LVNP liven up
LVOF live off
LVOT live out
LVRD lovered
LVRO Livorno
LVRT leveret
LVTR levator
LWAD lowland
LWEH low-tech
LWES lawless
lawyers
lowness
LWIE low tide
LWIY lowlily
LWOD Law Lord
LWON low-born
lowdown
low-down
LWOT low-cost
LWRD low-bred
lowered
LWRW lowbrow
LWSA lewisia
LWUT lawsuit
LXCL lexical
LXCN lexicon
LXES laxness❑
LYAE lay bare
LYDS lay odds
LYLY loyally
loyalty
LYMN Layamon
LYNO lay into
LYON lay down
LYPN lay open
LYRD layered
LYTE layette
LYTN lay it on
LZEH Lizbeth
LZNE lozenge
LZRS Lazarus
LZRT lazaret
MAAE Mbabane
MADR meander
MAFL moanful
MAGA myalgia
MAGC myalgic
MAHR Meacher
MAIG meaning
moaning
MAIY meatily
MALS measles
MAMC miasmic
MAML miasmal
MAMR Myanmar
MAOK meacock
MAOS meadows
MAOY meadowy
MATO meant to
MAUE measure
MBIE McBride
MBRK Mubarak
MBTR mobster
MBUE mob rule
mob-rule
MCAE macramé
MCAG MacCaig
MCAL Michael
MCBE macabre
MCCS macacos
MCDM macadam
MCED MacLeod
Macleod
MCEE machete
MCEH Macbeth
MCEN MacLean
Maclean
MCEY mockery
MCIE machine
MCIG mocking
MCIT McCoist
MCLA mycelia
MCLE maculae
MCLN Mechlin
MCLR macular
MCNE Mycenae
MCOE microbe
MCOL MacColl
MCOS microns
MCQE macaque
MCSE mucosae
MCSS mycosis
MCTC mycotic
MCUF Macduff
MDAD midland
MDAE mediate
MDAH mudbath
MDAK mudlark
mudpack
MDAT mediant
MDCL medical
MDCM modicum
MDCS medicos
MDEM midterm
MDES madness
MDIA Madeira
MDID muddied
MDIE midwife
MDIF midriff
MDIH Midwich
MDIY muddily
MDLA medulla
MDLC middle C
MDLD muddled
MDLI modelli
MDLO modello
MDLP mudflap
MDLR meddler
modular
muddler
MDLS modulus
MDLT mudflat
MDLY modally
MDNA Madonna
MDOT midmost
MDRD mad-bred
MDRI Madurai
MDRN midiron
MDSE medusae
modiste
MDSN Madison
MDSS medusas
MDSY modesty
MDUS mediums
MDWR Medawar
MEAS Maenads
MECT meercat
MEET Mae West
MEIG meeting
MEKT meerkat
MEOA myeloma
MEOD myeloid
MEPE M People
MERE McEnroe
METI maestri
METO maestro
MEZN muezzin
MFIK maffick
MFIY miffily
MFLD muffled
MFLR muffler
MFNY Myfanwy
MFOI Mafiosi
MFOO mafioso❑
MGAA magmata
MGAE magnate
migrate
MGAT migrant
MGCL magical
MGEO magneto
MGHT mug shot
mugshot
MGIG mugging
MGIS Magpies
muggins
MGIY magnify
MGLD moguled
MGLV Mogilev
MGNA magenta
MGOY maggoty
MGTN megaton
MGUH McGough
MGUS magnums
mugfuls
MGYN Meg Ryan
MHCN mohican❑
MHIT Mahdist
MHMT Mahomet
MHOG mah-jong
MHOZ Mahfouz
MHTA mahatma❑
MIHF Meinhof
MIHR moither
MIIG maiming
MIMN mailman
MINR Meitner
MIOE moidore
MIRT Maigret
MISN Meissen
MISS meioses
meiosis
MITC meiotic
MITN moisten
MITR meister
MITY moistly
MJRA Majorca
MJRN major in
MJSY majesty
MKBE makable
MKDS mikados
MKFR make for
MKLW make law
MKNS Mikonos
MKOF make off
MKOS mikrons
MKOT make out
MKWR make war
MKWT make wet
MKWY make way
MLAD mallard
MLAE maltase
mileage
MLAS Millais
MLAX Malraux
MLCI Malachi
MLCO malicho
MLDC melodic
MLED Mole End
MLEE Maltese
Molière
MLEI meltemi
MLEN Malvern
mullein
MLES malleus

milieus
milreis
MLEX milieux
MLEY mildewy
MLHS Malthus
MLIE malaise
MLIG malting
melting
milking
milling
mulling
MLIN million
mullion
MLIY milkily
mollify
MLMD Malamud
MLMN milkman
MLNE melange
mélange
Melanie
MLNN melanin
MLNS melanos
MLOA Moldova
MLOE maltose
MLOK mullock
MLOM Malcolm
malform
MLON Muldoon
MLOS Mellors
MLOY Mallory
MLPN milk pan
MLRA malaria
MLRD Mildred
MLRN McLaren
MLRT mole rat
MLRY malarky
MLSA Melissa
MLSI molossi
MLSN malison
MLSP milksop
MLSY malmsey
MLTA militia
mulatta
MLTO mulatto
MLTS Miletus
MLTV Molotov
MLUC mollusc
MLUE multure
MLUN Milburn
MMAA Mombasa
MMAS mammals
MMAY mammary
MMCY mimicry
MMES mamzers
members
MMEY mummery
MMHS Memphis
MMIG mumming
MMIS memoirs
MMIY mummify
MMLA mamilla
MMLD mumbled
MMLR mumbler

MMNA momenta
MMNO memento
MMOH mammoth
MMPD memo pad
MMRL membral
MMSN Mommsen
MMSS mimesis
MMTC mimetic
MNAA mandala
Montana
MNAD mansard
MNAE mandate
man-made
miniate
mintage
Mondale
montage
mundane
MNAK man jack
manjack
MNAS man-days
manoaos
minyans
MNAU Montagu
MNBS minibus
MNCB minicab
MNCE manacle
monocle
MNCM minicam
MNCR menacer
MNCS menaces
MNCT Manx cat
MNDC monadic
monodic
MNEA Mandela
MNED minuend
MNEL Mansell
Mantell
MNEO Mindelo
Montego
montero
MNER mynheer
MNES manners
Monkees
monkeys
monkey's
MNFL mindful
MNGA Managua
MNGE Minogue
MNGR manager
MNHC manihoc
MNHL menthol
MNHM Mancham
MNHN Menuhin
MNHR muncher
MNHT manchet
MNHY monthly
MNIC mandioc
MNID mankind
MNIE manlike
man-like
man-size
MNIG Manning

mending
mincing
minding
munting
MNIH mannish
monkish
MNII Mancini
MNIK minnick
MNIL McNeill
mondial
MNIN mansion
mention
MNIS Mencius
MNIY mundify
MNJC muntjac
MNJK muntjak
MNKN manakin
manikin
Mencken
minikin
MNKR moniker
MNLA manilla
Minolta®
MNLD mangled
mingled
MNLR mangler
mingler
MNLY Mina Loy
MNML minimal
MNMM minimum
MNMN Manxman
MNMR monomer
MNMT manumit
MNMX minimax
MNNY Men Only
MNOA Mendoza
MNOD manhood
MNOE manhole
MNOI Manzoni
MNOK menfolk
MNON monsoon
MNOO Mindoro
MNOR man-hour
MNOS mangoes
mantoes
MNOT mind out
MNPR Manipur
MNRA Menorca
mens rea
Minerva
Minorca
MNRH menorah
monarch
MNRL mandrel
mandril
mineral
mongrel
MNRM mantram
MNRP mantrap
MNRR manurer
MNRT minaret
MNSI menisci
mono-ski

MNST mindset
MNTE manatee
MNTI Menotti
MNTL Minitel
MNTR minster
monitor
monster
Munster
Münster
MNTS minutes
MNUT manhunt
MNVR miniver
MNWR man-o'-war
men-o'-war
MNYD moneyed
MNYU mind you
MOBS miombos
MOEE Miocene
MOHN moorhen
MOHR moocher
MOIG mooring
MOIH Moorish
MOIS Moonies
MOIY moodily
MOLT moonlit
MPEY mappery
MPIE mapwise
MPIG mapping
MQEN McQueen
MRAA Mariana
Marmara
Marsala
MRAD mermaid
MRAE Margate
MRAN murrain
MRAO marcato
MRAS mortals
myriads
MRAT mordant
MRAX Margaux
MRBU marabou
Merzbau
MRCE miracle
moriche
MRCO morocco□
MRCS maracas
murices
MRCY Maracay
MRDR mirador
MREE Marlene
MREH Morpeth
MREL Marvell
MREN murgeon
MRES marvels
MRET Martext
mordent
MREU Marceau
MREY Margery
MRGT Mr Right
MRHL marshal
MRHR marcher
MRHS marches
morphos

MRIA Martina
MRID married
MRIE marline
marmite□
Martine
moraine
mortice
mortise
MRIG marking
merging
morning
MRIH moreish
MRII martini
MRIL martial□
MRIM Marxism
MRIN Marcian
Marmion
Martian
murrion
MRIS margins
MRIT Marxist
MRIY mercify
merrily
mortify
murkily
MRKA markkaa
MRKS markkas
MRLD marbled
MRLN Marilyn
MRLO morello
MRLS marbles
MRLT martlet
MRLY morally
MRMA marimba
MRNA Miranda
MRNC moronic
MRNO Marengo
morendo
MRNR mariner
MRNS Marinus
merinos
MROA Markova
MROE Marlowe
MROF mark off
MROH Murdoch
MROI Marconi
MROT mark out
MROY Marjory
marrowy
MRST Morisot
MRSY morassy
MRTD merited
MRTL marital
MRTN Marston
MRUE Marcuse
marquee
MRUG Marburg
MRUS marquis
MRUY mercury□
MRUZ Márquez
MRVA Moravia
MRXS murexes
MRYT Marryat

MRYY martyry
MSAA mascara
mastaba
Mustafa
MSAD mislaid
mustard
MSAE massage
message
misdate
mismake
mismate
misname
misrate
mistake
MSAG mustang□
MSAI muscari
MSAL miscall
MSAP Mrs Gamp
MSAT miscast
MSCL musical
MSED misdeed
misfeed
mislead
misread
missend
MSEL Maskell
misdeal
mistell
MSEM misterm
MSER masseur
mishear
MSEY mastery
mystery
MSFL museful
MSHD Mashhad
MSIA Messina
mestiza
Mishima
MSIE Massine
massive
misfile
misfire
misgive
missile
missive
mistime
MSIF mastiff
MSIG missing
moshing
MSIH Messiah
missish
MSIL misdial
MSIN mission
MSIO mestizo
mistico
MSIY messily
mistily
mushily
muskily
mustily
mystify
MSLE moselle□
MSLN mesclun
MSLS muscles
MSLY mesally
misally
misplay
MSNC masonic□
MSNH Mishnah
MSNT mist-net
MSNW misknow
MSNY masonry
MSOD mastoid
misword
MSOE misyoke
MSOK mistook
MSOM misform
MSON misjoin
MSOP Mrs Mopp
MSOT miss out
MSOY miscopy
muscovy
MSRL mistral
MSRT muskrat
MSRW misdraw
MSRY miserly
MSSD misused
MSSR misuser
MSTP misstep
MSUE misrule
mistune
MSUK misluck
MSUS museums
MSUT missuit
MTAE methane
MTAS matrass
matzahs
MTBE mutable
MTBY mutably
MTCL metical
MTCS maticos
MTDR matador
MTES matters
MTET moth-eat
MTEY Metheny
MTGN mutagen
MTHD matched
MTHM Mitchum
MTHP match up
MTHS matches
MTHU Matthau
MTHW Matthew
MTIE mythise
mythize
MTIG matting
MTLA Matilda
MTLD mottled
MTLT matelot
MTNA mutanda
MTNE matinee
matinée
MTNL matinal
MTOD Mitford
MTOH matzoth
MTOK Matlock
mattock
MTOS matlows
methods
mottoes
MTOT mete out
MTPC metopic
MTRS Mithras
MTSE Matisse
Métisse
MTSS mitoses
mitosis
MTTC mitotic
MTUO Matsudo
MTVS motives
MTXS Metaxas
MUDR maunder
moulder
MUEN Maureen
mauvein
MUHM Maugham
MUHY Mauchly
MUIC Mauriac
MUIE Maurice
mauvine
MUIG mauling
mousing
MULN maudlin
mouflon
MUNR mourner
MUTD mounted
MUTE mountie□
MUTP mount up
MVBE movable
MVBY movably
MVDY moved by
MVOT move out
MWIH mawkish
MWON mow down
MXBE mixable
MXCN Mexican
MXDP mixed up
mixed-up
MXDY mixedly
MXEL maxwell□
MXIH mix with
MXLA maxilla
MXML maximal
MXMM maximum
MXMN maximin
MXON Max Born
MXUE Max Euwe
mixture
MYAD may I add
MYAK may I ask
MYAR Mayfair
MYED mayweed
MYIY may-lily
MYOE maypole
MYRL mayoral
MZIY muzzily
MZPA Mazeppa
MZRA mazurka
MZRN Mazarin
MZRW Mezzrow
MZZH mezuzah
NAET nearest
NAIG nearing
NAJS Nyanjas
NATE naartje
NBCO Nabucco
NBIG nabbing
NBIH nebbich
nebbish
NBIK niblick
NBIY nobbily
NBKV Nabokov
NBLE nebulae
NBLR nebular
nibbler
nobbler
NBLS nebulas
nibbles
NCAD nice and
NCAE nictate
NCAY nectary
NCEC nucleic
NCEN nucleon
NCER nuclear
NCES nucleus
NCIE nuclide
NCIG necking
nicking
NCLE nacelle
NCLI nucelli
NCLS Nicolas
NCLT necklet
NCNO no can do
NCNY no' canny
NCOA Nichola
NCOE necrose
NCSA Nicosia
NCTE necktie
NCUE noctule
NCUT NBC suit
NDIG nodding
NDLR nodular
NDLY nodally
NDUT no doubt
NEEE Nyerere
NEFL needful
NEGW Niel Gow
NEIG needing
NEIY needily
NELD needled
NELS niellos
NEOD naevoid
NESN Nielsen
NFIG naffing
NFIY niftily
NGAD niggard
NGET neglect
NGEY nuggety
NGIG nagging
nogging
NGIO Negrito
NGIY nigrify
NGLA nigella□
NGLR niggler
NGOD Negroid
NGOS Negroes
NGRA Nigeria
NGTE nightie
NGTY nightly
NHPR no-hoper
NIAL Naipaul
NIBD nail-bed
NIDS naiades
NIEE naïveté
NIEY nailery
naively
naïvely
naivety
naïvety
NIGN nail gun
NIHR neither
NIIY noisily
NIOE noisome
NIOI Nairobi
NKDY nakedly
NKNN Nykanen
NLIY nullify
nullity
NLSN Nilsson
NLTC Nilotic
NLTS Nilotes
NMAY nummary
NMBA Namibia
NMBE namable
NMDC nomadic
NMES numbers□
NMFR name for
NMHL nymphal
NMHT nymphet
NMIG numbing
NMNE nominee
NMNL nominal
NMRC numeric
NMRL nemoral
numeral
NMSA nemesia
NMSS Nemeses
nemesis□
NNEN nankeen
NNEY nunnery
NNGN nonagon
NNHY ninthly
NNIG Nanjing
Nanking
Nanning
NNIH nunnish
NNIS Nancies
nannies
nuncios
NNKD non-skid
NNLP non-slip
NNLS nonplus
NNOE non-come
NNRP non-drip
NNTE Nanette
Ninette

none the
NNTI nonetti
NNTO none too
NNTP non-stop
NNUH nonsuch
NNUT nonsuit
NNVH Nineveh
NOAE neonate
NOAI Neo-Nazi
NODY noonday
NOEY neoteny
NOIH neolith
NOIM niobium
NOOC Neozoic
NPES nippers
NPIG napping
nipping
NPIL nuptial
NPIS napkins
nappies
NPIY nippily
NPLS Nepalis
NPRN nephron
NPTA naphtha
NPTC nepotic
NPUE Neptune
NRAA nirvana□
NRAD norward
nor'ward
NRAE narrate
NRAS Normans
nurhags
NRAT nor'-east
NREA norteña
NRET nor'-west
NREY nursery
NRGI nuraghi
NRHL narwhal
NRHR norther
NRHS Nerthus
NRHX narthex
NRIE nargile
NRIG nursing
NRIH Norwich
NRIS Nereids
NRIY nervily
NRJE nartjie
NRMH Nkrumah
NROK Norfolk
NROS narrows
nervous
NRUE nervure
nurture
NRYV Nureyev
NSAE Nastase
NSBG nosebag
NSEG nest egg
NSET nascent
no sweat
NSGY nosegay
NSIY nastily
NSJB nose job
NSLY nasally
NSOT nose out
NSRL nostril
NSRM nostrum
NSYH Nasmyth
NTAE net game
nitrate
not have
nutcase
NTAF not half
NTAL netball
not tall
nutgall
NTAM not harm
NTAY not many
NTBE notable
NTBT not a bit
NTBY notably
NTCD noticed
NTDY notedly
NTED not need
NTEE not here
NTEP not deep
NTEY not very
NTHD notched
NTHL notchel
NTHP notch up
NTHT not that
NTHZ Natchez
NTID not find
not mind
NTIE nitride
nitrite
NTIG netting
nothing
nutting
NTIK nit-pick
NTIS not miss
NTIY nattily
nitrify
nuttily
NTLA Natalia
NTLD nettled
NTLE Natalie
NTLT notelet
NTNA notanda
NTNW not know
NTOD not good
NTOE not vote
NTOK network
not work
NTOO not go to
NTOS nations
nitrous
NTPD notepad
NTPO not up to
NTPT not spot
NTRE niterie
nut-tree
NTRL natural
NTSA Natasha
NTTP not stop
NTUE netsuke
NTUH not much
NTUP no-trump
NTVR not ever
NTVS natives
NUEA noumena
NUEL nousell
NUHY naughty
NUIH nourish
NUII nautili
NULI nauplii
NUOE neurone
NURL neutral
NURN neutron
NVHS Navahos
NVJS Navajos
NVLA novella
NVLE Neville
novelle
NVLO Novello
NVLS Novalis
NVLY novelty
NVOS niveous
NVRN navarin
NVSD Novi Sad
NVTA Novotna
NWAD new-laid
NWAE new wave
NWAL New Hall
NWAN new dawn
NWDY Newsday
NWEE nowhere
NWEF new leaf
NWER New Year
NWES newness
NWET New Left
NWHM new chum
NWHN now then!
NWIH new rich
NWMN newsman
NWOD new word
NWOE Newsome
NWOK new look
New York
NWON newborn
new moon
new town
NWOT Newport
NWUY Newbury
Newquay
NXOS noxious
NYAD nayward
NYNE noyance
NYOD nayword
OAAA Okayama
OADN on and on
OAGA otalgia
OAGY orangey
OAIA ocarina
OAID of a kind
of a mind
OAIE of a size
on a time
opaline
OAIH Obadiah
OAIK odalisk
OAIM onanism
OAIN orarian
oration
ovarian
ovation
OAIS otaries
OAIT onanist
OAIY opacity
OAOL on a roll
OAOT of a sort
OAOY oratory
OAPO on appro
OARP on a trip
OASS Onassis
OBAD on board
OBOD oxblood
OBRE Osborne
OBSN Orbison
OBTL orbital
OBTR orbiter
OCAD orchard
OCLM osculum
OCLR oscular
OCNC obconic
OCPT occiput
OCRO occur to
OCSS oncosts
OCUE occlude
ODAD old hand
old maid
ODAL oddball
ODAY old lady
ODEN old bean
ODER old dear
ODES oddness
oldness
ODET oddment
ODIE old-time
on-drive
ODIH odd fish
ODIK Old Nick
ODIL old girl
ODNL ordinal
ODOD old gold
ODOE old rose
ODON old moon
ODOT odd sort
ODPL oedipal□
ODPS Oedipus
ODPT Old Spot
ODRD ordered
ODRY orderly
ODTA ondatra
ODTR oldster
ODVN odd-even
OEAD operand
OEAE operate
over age
over-age
overawe
OEAL overall
over-all
OEAM overarm
OEAO oregano
OEAR open-air
OEAT operant
overact
OEBD overbid
OEBY overbuy
OEDE overdue
OEDS oreades
OEDY open day
OEEF one self
oneself
OEES oneness
OEET overeat
OEFD overfed
OEFR overfar
OEFS one of us
OEFY overfly
OEGT overget
OEHT overhit
OEIE obelise
obelize
one time
one-time
OEIG opening
OEIK obelisk
OEIY obesity
OEJY overjoy
OELE overlie
OELP overlap
OELR ocellar
OELS ocellus
OELY O'Reilly
overlay
OEMN overman
OENA Oleanna
OENC oceanic
OENS Oceanus
OENT overnet
OEOS onerous
OEOT open out
OEPY overpay
overply
OERA olearia
OERD overred
OERH on earth
OERN overren
overrun
OESE oversee
OEST overset
OESW oversew
oversow
OETM omentum
OETP one-step
one-stop
open-top
overtop
OETS Orestes
OETX overtax
OETY overtly
OEUE overuse
OFAD offhand
off-hand

Words marked □ can also be spelled with an initial capital letter

off-ward
OFAE off base
OFCM offscum
OFCR officer
OFEK off-peak
OFEM off beam
OFET off beat
offbeat
off-beat
OFIE off line
off-line
offside
off-site
OFIH off with
OFNE offence
OFOD offload
off-road
OFOK off work
OFOM off form
OFPN off-spin
OFRP offer up
OFRR offerer
offeror
OFUY off duty
off-duty
OGAD on guard
OGIA ouguiya
OGIG ongoing
OGNA oogonia
organza
OGNC organic
OHEE ochreae
OHLA Ophelia
OHLO Othello
OHMC oghamic
OHOS ochrous
OHTC ophitic
OHTK Okhotsk
OIAA Okinawa
OIAE oxidase
oxidate
OIAI origami
OIAT oxidant
OIGO owing to
OIIE olivine
orifice
oxidise
oxidize
OIIN opinion
OIIR Olivier
OIIS origins
OIIT oligist
OIOM oviform
OIOO Orinoco
OIOS ominous
OIRN omicron
OITD omitted
OIUT oviduct
OIWS Ojibwas
OJCS objects
OKAD Oakland
OKAL oak-gall
OKOS oak moss

OLAD oil sand
OLAM oil-palm
OLAS orleans□
Orléans
OLEL oil well
OLGD obliged
OLIE owl-like
OLKN oilskin
OLNO Orlando
OLQE oblique
OLQY obloquy
OLTC oolitic
OLTO only too
OLUP oil pump
OMAK oomiack
OMLW Ohm's law
OMNI Osmanli
OMNS Osmonds
OMSS osmosis
OMTA ommatea
OMTC osmotic
OMTD Olmsted
ONBS omnibus
ONDY owned by
ONFC omnific
ONOL own goal
ONPO own up to
OOAE obovate
OOAY obolary
OODL ovoidal
OODR on order
OOEY orogeny
OOFR on offer
OOIE ozonise
ozonize
OOIH otolith
OOIN Oxonian
OONR O'Connor
OOOO oloroso
OOOS odorous
OOOY orology
otology
OOSM opossum
OOUD orotund
OPDN oppidan
OPEN Orphean
OPES oppress
Orpheus
OPPR on paper
OPRY orphrey
OPSD opposed
OPSR opposer
ORAG o'ergang
ORAY Our Lady
ORED oarweed
ORES oarless
ORIH ogreish
ORMN oarsman
ORTD oersted
OSAE on stage
on-stage
OSAY ossuary
OSCE ossicle

OSEE obscene
OSEP on sleep
OSIG ousting
OSOE onshore
on-shore
oospore
OSOS osseous
OSQY obsequy
OSRE observe
OSRL oestral
OSRS oestrus
of sorts
OSUE obscure
OTAA ostraca
ostraka
OTAD outward
OTAE oatcake
outdare
outdate
outface
outname
outpace
outrage
outrate
OTAK Ostmark
outback
outrank
OTAL outfall
outsail
OTAT outcast
outlast
OTAY ostiary
OTBR October
OTCL optical
OTDC octadic
OTDX Otto Dix
OTEL oatmeal
outsell
OTEN on the in
OTEO on the go
OTEP on the up
outleap
outweep
OTER outpeer
outwear
OTET on the QT
outjest
outwent
OTFT out of it
OTGN octagon
OTIE outhire
outline
outlive
outride
outside
outsize
OTIG outwing
OTIH ostrich
out with
outwith
OTIK outwick
OTIR outlier
OTLN ortolan

OTLW outflow
OTLY outplay
OTML optimal
OTMM optimum
OTMN ottoman□
OTOA osteoma
OTOD out cold
out loud
OTOE outcome
outmode
outmove
outvote
OTOK outlook
outwork
OTON outworn
OTOR outdoor
outpour
OTOS outgoes
OTOT outfoot
outmost
outpost
OTPE octuple
OTPF on top of
OTPN outspan
OTPS octopus
OTRG outbrag
OTRO Ontario
OTRP outcrop
OTRW outgrow
OTRY outpray
OTTE octette
OTTP outstep
OTTY outstay
OTUE obtrude
OTUH outrush
OTUN outturn
OTVA Octavia
OTVR out-over
OTVS octavos
OTWE out-owre
OUAE oculate
ovulate
OUDI Opus Dei
OUEO of use to
OUET opulent
OUIT oculist
OUTA opuntia
OVAE obviate
OVEO Orvieto
OVOS obvious
OVRE obverse
OWNS on wings
OWRS onwards
OYOE oxytone
OYPA Olympia
OYPC Olympic
OYPS Olympus
Olympus®
OYSY odyssey
PAAD placard
PAAE placate
platane
PAAH pharaoh□

PAAT peasant
play-act
PAAX phalanx
PABE prabble
PABY playboy□
PACR Prancer
PADA Phaedra
PADS p's and q's
PADT plaudit
PAEN phase in
place on
PAEO placebo
PAES players
prayers
PAEU plateau
PAFL playful
PAFR piaffer
plan for
PAHM Peachum
PAHR poacher
PAIA placita
PAIE praline
PAIG placing
playing
prating
PAIH planish
PAIT pianist
PAKT placket
PALD pearled
PALN pearlin
Praslin
PALP Pharlap
PALR pearler
PALS phallus
PAMA pyaemia
PAMD plasmid
PAMN plasmin
PAND planned
PANR planner
PANY plainly
PAOA Pianola®
PAOD phacoid
placoid
plafond
PAOF play off
play-off
PAOK peacock□
PAOL peafowl
PAON platoon□
PAOT play out
PAPN playpen
PARE prairie
PART Prakrit
PASN Pearson
PASS praeses
praises
PASY Plassey
PATC plastic
PATD plaited
plastid
PATE piastre
prattle
PATM phantom

PATN phaeton
PATR plaiter
plantar
planter
plaster
platter
praetor
psalter
PATS Plautus
PATY peartly
PAUD plagued
PAUS peanuts
PAYX pharynx
PBIH publish
PBLD pebbled
PBLM pabulum
PBLS pebbles
PBOH pibroch
PBRY puberty
PBTA P W Botha
PCAD Piccard
pochard
PCAE package
pickaxe
pick-axe
PCAI peccavi
PCAT peccant
PCAY peccary
PCBA Picabia
PCDR picador
PCER pickeer
PCES packets
PCET Pickett
PCFC pacific❑
PCIE pack ice
pectise
pectize
PCIG packing
picking
PCIH peckish
Pictish
puckish
PCII pachisi
Puccini
PCIN paction
PCIS piccies
PCLD pickled
PCLR pickler
PCMN packman
PCOA Pechora
PCOE pectose
PCOF pack off
pick off
PCOO piccolo
PCOR pochoir
PCOS piceous
PCOT pace out
pick out
PCPT pockpit
PCRT pack rat
pack-rat
PCSO Picasso
PCTE picotee
PCUE picture
PCUT picquet
PDCB pedicab
PDCE pedicle
PDCL pedicel
PDGA podagra
PDIG padding
pudding
PDLR peddler
piddler
PDLS pedalos
PDNA pudenda
PDNY pudency
PDOE padrone
PDOI padroni
PDOK paddock
padlock
PEAD piebald
prepaid
PEAE peerage
predate
preface
prefade
prelate
prepare
presage
PEAH pre-wash
PEAK prepack
PEAL prevail
PEAT precast
PEAY plenary
prelacy
PECD pierced
PECY preachy
PEDR pleader
PEED prebend
prehend
pretend
PEEE precede
prevene
PEEL pre-sell
PEEM preterm
PEEN plebean
PEES peeress
poetess
precess
PEET precept
prefect
prelect
present
pretext
prevent
PEFL preyful
PEGD pledged
PEGE pledgee
PEGR pledger
pledgor
PEGT pledget
PEIE poetise
poetize
precise
premise
preside
previse
puerile
PEIG peeling
peeping
peering
preying
PEIH peevish
PEIM pietism
premium
PEIR premier
PEIS prelims
premiss
PEIT pietist
predict
PEIW preview
PEIY plebify
PELM phellem
PELS Peebles
pueblos
PELY Presley
PEMT pre-empt
PENG pfennig❑
PEOA pleroma
PEOE premove
prepone
prepose
PEOF peel off
PEOK precook
PEOM preform
PEOT Prévost
PERE pleurae
PERL pleural
PERT pierrot❑
PESD pleased
pressed
PESE pressie
PESN press on
PESP press-up
PESR plessor
PETA plectra
PETD pleated
PETL Prestel®
PETN Preston
pre-stun
PETS prestos
PEUE prelude
presume
PEUI preludi
PEUL prequel
PEYD pie-eyed
PEZE prenzie
prezzie
PEZL pretzel
PFCD po-faced
PFIG puffing
PFIY puffily
PFOT puff out
PGAK peg back
PGAL pigtail
PGAT pageant
PGBY pageboy
PGEN pygmean
PGET pigment
PGEY piggery
PGIG pugging
PGIH piggish
PGKN pigskin
PGON peg down
PGOT Piggott
PGSS Pegasus
PGUP pig-jump
PGWY peg away
PIAE plicate
primate
private
PIAO paisano
PIAY primacy
primary
privacy
PIBE pliable
PIBY pliably
PICE paiocke
PICP Princip
PICX princox
PIEY primely
PIFL pailful
painful
PIIG pairing
priming
PIIR Poitier
PIIS Phidias
PIIY privily
privity
PIKE prickle
PIKY prickly
PILP Phillip
PILY paisley❑
PINY pliancy
PIOF pair off
PIRN Prizren
PIRO prior to
PISN Poisson
PITD painted
pointed
printed
PITE philtre
PITO point to
PITP point up
PITR painter
pointer
printer
PITS pointes
PIUA primula
PIYO privy to
PJCE pajocke
PJMS P D James
pyjamas
PKFN poke fun
PKKS pukekos
PKOT poke out
PKPO pakapoo
PLAA Poltava
PLAD pollard
PLAE pale ale
palmate
palpate
peltate
pileate
pillage
pole-axe
pulsate
PLAK pollack❑
PLBX pill-box
PLCN pelican❑
PLCP pile-cap
PLCT polecat
PLDL paludal
PLDN paladin
PLES pellets
pulleys
PLFR pull for
PLGC pelagic
PLGN polygon
PLGY phlegmy
PLHR pilcher
PLID palsied
PLIG polling
pulling
pulsing
PLII pulvini
PLIM pallium
PLIN pillion
PLIT palmist
PLIY pulpify
pulpily
PLKR Palikir
PLLR pilular
PLLS palolos
PLMC polemic
PLME palamae
PLMN Pullman
PLMR polymer
PLMS phlomis
PLNA polenta
PLNR Pilsner
PLOA palooka
PLOF palm off
pull off
PLOK pillock
pollock❑
PLOS pileous
pulpous
PLOT pull out
pull-out
PLOY pillory
PLPS polypes
PLRC pyloric
PLRM pilgrim
PLRO Palermo
PLRS pelorus
Polaris
pylorus
PLSE pelisse
PLTC pelitic
politic
PLTE palette
PLTL palatal
PLTP palmtop
PLTX poll tax

PLUE pollute
PLVR palaver
PLXS phloxes
PLYA palmyra
PLZI palazzi
PLZO palazzo
PMAO pompano
PMCN pemican
PMEI Pompeii
PMEO pampero
PMIG pumping
PMKN pumpkin
PMLD pimpled
PMLS pomelos
PMNO pimento
PMOF pump off
PMOS pompous
PMOT pump out
PMRT pomfret
PNAA Pangaea
PNAD poniard
PNAE pancake
pen name
pen-name
pennate
pentane
pinnace
pinnate
PNAI Panjabi
Punjabi
PNAL pinball
pintail
PNAT pendant
pennant
PNCA panacea
panocha
PNCE panache
panicle
pinocle
PNCY panicky
PNED pinhead
PNEN Pandean
PNES pincers
punters
PNET pendent
pungent
PNEU ponceau
PNFR pant for
pine for
PNGN pink gin
PNHD pinched
punched
PNHN Pynchon
PNHP punch-up
PNHR panther
PNHS ponchos
PNHX panchax
PNIE pantile
pennine
pensile
pensive
PNIF pontiff
PNIG panging
panting
pending
punning
PNIH Penrith
PNIL pennill
PNIM Pentium®
PNIN pension
Pontian
PNIR pannier
PNIS panties
pennies
Penzias
PNIY pontify
PNLR pantler
PNLV pan-Slav
PNLY penally
penalty
PNNE penance
PNOA Pandora
PNOD penfold
pinfold
PNOE pannose
Penrose
pentose
pinhole
PNOM pinworm
PNON pin down
pontoon
PNOS pingoes
pinkoes
pongoes
PNPY panoply
PNRB pan-Arab
PNRM pangram
PNTN pin it on
PNTR pine tar
punster
PNTS Penates
punctos
PNUD pinguid
PNUE pinnule
PNUK pin tuck
PNUN penguin
PNUS panfuls
POAA pro rata
POAC prosaic
POAD proband
POAE peonage
phonate
probate
proface
profane
pronate
propage
propane
prorate
POAG probang
POAI pronaoi
POAL proball
PODE Proudie
PODR plodder
PODV Plovdiv
PODY proudly
POEB proverb
POED proceed
propend
POEE phoneme
protégé
POEN protean❑
protein
POEO prone to
prove to
POEP phone up
POER pioneer
POES process
profess
Proteus
prowess
POET poorest
project
protect
protest
POEY progeny
pronely
Ptolemy
POFD proofed
POFR proffer
POGD pronged
POHT prophet
POIE plosive
profile
pro-life
proline
promise
provide
provine
POIG probing
POIM peonism
POIO proviso
proximo
POIS phonics
Photius
profits
POIT protist
POIY probity
prodigy
prosify
prosily
POKR plonker
POLD peopled
POLM problem
POLR prowler
POLS peoples
Proclus
POLW poor law
PONX phoenix❑
POOA pronota
POOE promote
propone
propose
provoke
POOG prolong
POON pronoun
POOT provost
POOY prosody
POPR prosper
PORM program
POSY piously
POTR plotter
plouter
plowter
proctor
POUE procure
produce
profuse
POUO Profumo
POUT product
POYA propyla
PPAK pep talk
PPDM popedom
PPEE Papeete
PPEY peppery
PPFL pipeful
PPHP pop-shop
PPIA paprika
PPIE peptide
peptise
peptize
PPIG popping
PPIL pep pill
PPLA papilla
PPLE papulae
PPLR papular
popular
PPLS papules
PPLY papally
PPMA pip emma
PPNA pupunha
PPOE papoose
pappose
PPOG pop song
PPON popcorn
PPOS pappous
PPRA puparia
PPRR paperer
PPRS papyrus
PPTE pipette
PPTR pop star
PPYD pop-eyed
PQAT piquant
PRAD Persaud
PRAE partake
pertake
pervade
portage
PRAI Parvati
PRAN pertain
PRAS perhaps
PRAT parfait
periapt
PRBE parable
PRCE paracme
Porsche
Porsche®
PRDC parodic
PRDP Paradip
PRDS parados
PRDT peridot
PRDX paradox
PRED per head
perpend
portend
PREL Parnell
Purcell
PRER per year
PRES parcels
Perseus
Piraeus
PRET per cent
percept
perfect
pervert
porrect
portent
PREU parvenu
PRGA Perugia
PRGE perigee
PRGN paragon
pyrogen
PRHC pyrrhic❑
PRHD parched
PRHS Porthos
PRIA partita
Perdita
pereira
PRIE partite
parvise
perlite
porcine
purline
PRIG parting
purging
purring
PRIL partial
PRIN Permian
Persian
portion
PRIO portico
PRIR Perrier®
PRIS parties
Perkins
Persius
porkies
PRIT persist
PRIU purlieu
PRIW purview
PRIY perfidy
perkily
PRLX perplex
PRLY parsley
PRMD pyramid
PRMN Perlman
PRMS paramos
pyramis
Pyramus
PRNA piranha
PRNC phrenic
PRNM paranym
paronym
PRNP parsnip
PRNR partner
PRNS parents

Puranas
PROA pergola
persona
PROD percoid
PROE purpose
pyrrole
PROF part-off
PROK parrock
PROL parboil
PROM perform
PRON purloin
PROR parlour
PROS parlous
Parsons
persons
PROT purport
PRPT parapet
PRPX Perspex®
PRQE perique
PRRA parerga
PRRD para-red
PRRY portray
PRSL parasol
perusal
phrasal
PRSN parison
PRSR peruser
phraser
PRSS paresis
poroses
pyrosis
PRTA paratha
PRTC paretic
piratic
pyretic
PRTD parotid
PRTN puritan
PRTR paritor
PRTS pyrites
PRUB perturb
PRUE perdure
perfume
perfuse
perjure
permute
pertuse
PRUR pursuer
PRUS percuss
PRUT parquet
pursuit
PRUY perfumy
perjury
PRVC pyruvic
PRWG periwig
PRWY part way
PRXA pyrexia
PRYO party to
PRZA Parazoa
PSAA passata
PSAE Pascale
passade
passage
postage
PSAT passant
PSAY pessary
PSBP post-bop
PSEL pas seul
PSEN pastern
postern
PSEP paste-up
PSER Pasteur
PSES pastels
possess
PSFR pass for
push for
PSFX postfix
PSHL paschal□
PSIA pessima
piscina
PSIE passive
pastime
piscine
PSIG passing
pasting
pushing
PSIN passion□
PSIY peskily
PSKN Pushkin
PSKY passkey
PSMN postman
PSNE pesante
PSOA Pistoia
PSOE pistole
PSOF pass off
piss off
push off
PSOR pissoir
PSOT pass out
push out
PSRD push-rod
PSTD posited
PSUE pasture
poseuse
posture
pustule
PSUL Pasquil
PSWR postwar
PSWS pesewas
PTAE pet hate
pet name
pet-name
pottage
put case
PTAH Pat Cash
PTAK put back
PTAL pitfall
PTBE potable
PTDM Potsdam
PTED pithead
PTEN pattern
potheen
PTES Pytheas
PTET patient
PTEY pottery
putrefy
PTFL pitiful
PTGA patagia
PTHN pitch in
PTHP patch up
patch-up
PTHR pitcher
PTHT pot shot
PTIE Petrine
put wise
PTIG petting
pitying
putting
PTIH pettish
PTIK Patrick
PTIL patrial
PTIT patriot
PTIY petrify
pettily
pithily
PTLA patella
PTMC potamic
Potomac
PTNA petunia
PTNO put on to
PTNY potency
PTOE petiole
pothole
PTON put down
putdown
put-down
PTOS patrons
petrous
piteous
PTOT put to it
putt out
PTPN put upon
put-upon
PTPO put up to
PTPT pitapat
PTRE paterae
PTRO potoroo
PTTN put it on
PTUK pot luck
PTUS potfuls
PTVR put over
PTWY pathway
put away
PUAD poulard
PUAE plumage
plumate
PUBR plumber
PUCY paunchy
PUDL poundal
PUDR plunder
PUEC Poulenc
PUET prudent
PUEY prudery
PUGD plugged
PUGR plugger
plunger
PUHD pouched
PUIA Paulina
PUIE Pauline
PUIG Pauling
pausing
pouring
pruning
PUIH prudish
PUIL pluvial
PUIO prurigo
PUIY paucity
PUJB plum job
PUKP pluck up
PUMT plummet
PUOE plumose
PUOS plumous
PUOT pour out
PUPE plum pie
PUPY Paul Pry
plumply
PUSC prussic
PUSE poursue
PUSN poussin□
PUSS plusses
PUSW poursew
PUTR poufter
PUTY poultry
PUUA plumula
PUUE plumule
PVLE pH value
PVNR Pevsner
PVOA pavlova□
PVRY poverty
PVTL pivotal
PWEY powdery
PWIY pawkily
PWRD powered
PXDA pyxidia
PXDS pyxides
PXUA paxiuba
PYAE paysage
PYAK pay back
PYAN pay cain
Prydain
PYBE payable
PYED pay heed
PYET payment
PYHC psychic
PYHP psych up
PYHS psychos
PYIS physics
physios
PYLN ptyalin
PYLS Phyllis
PYOD payload
pay-load
plywood
PYOE pay home
PYOL payroll
PZAZ pazzazz
pizzazz
PZLD puzzled
PZLR puzzler
PZRO Pizarro
QAAE quayage
QAAG quahaug
QAAH quamash
QAAS Quapaws
QAES Quakers
QAEY quavery
QAFR quaffer
QAGS quangos
QAHD quashed
QAIG quaking
QAIY qualify
quality
QAKE quackle
QAKR quacker
QARC quadric
QARL quarrel
QART quadrat
QASA quassia
QATC quantic
quartic
QATM quantum
QATN quartan
QATR quarter
QATS quartos
QATT quartet
QDIH Qaddish
QEEP queue up
QEHA Quechua
QEIT querist
QELR queller
QENE Queenie
QENY queenly
QERY queerly
QETN Quentin
QETR quester
questor
QEZL quetzal
QIAE quinate
QIAS quidams
QIAY quinary
QIBE quibble
QIDE quiddle
QIEO quite so
QIEY quivery
QIIE quinine
QIKE quickie
QIKN quicken
QIKY quickly□
QIOE quinone
QISE quiesce
QISN quids in
QITD quilted
QITL quintal
quittal
QITN quieten
quintan
Quintin
Quinton
QITR quilter
quitter
QITS quietus
QITT quintet
QITY quietly
QIZR quizzer

Words marked □ can also be spelled with an initial capital letter

QIZS quizzes
QOAE quorate
QODM quondam
QOIG quoting
QOTR quoiter
QWAI qawwali
RAAE real ale
RAAY rhatany
RADN Reardon
RAED rear end
RAET reagent
RAEU Ruapehu
RAGR realgar
RAHG road-hog
RAHS reaches
rhachis
RAIE realise
realize
RAIG reading□
reaping
rearing
roaming
roaring
RAIM realism□
RAIN realign
RAIS readies
RAIT realist
RAIY readily
reality
RAMN roadman
RAMP road-map
RAMR Réaumur
RAOE Roanoke
RAOF read off
RAOS reasons
RAOT read out
RATD roasted
RATO react to
RATR realtor
roaster
RATX road tax
RAWY roadway
RAYO ready to
RBAD ribband
RBAE ribcage
RBCA Rebecca
RBCN rubicon□
RBCP Robocop
RBDE rebadge
RBDY rabidly
RBES ribless
RBEY robbery
rubbery
RBID rebuild
RBIG ribbing
robbing
rubbing
RBIH rubbish
RBIS rabbins
Robbins
RBIT rebuilt
RBIY rabbity
RBKH Rebekah
RBKR rebuker
RBLA rubella
RBLS robalos
RBNA robinia
RBOA rubeola
RBON rub down
rub-down
RBOT ribwort
RBRA Roberta
RBRH rebirth
RBRS Roberts
RBSA robusta
RBSN Robeson
RBSS rebuses
RBTC robotic
RBTE rabatte
RBTN rub it in
RBTS rubatos
RBUD rebound
RBWX Ruby Wax
RBWY rub away
RCAD Richard
RCAE rechate
RCAL Rachael
Rockall
RCAM reclaim
RCAT rock art
RCCE recycle
RCCS rococos
RCES rackets
rickets
rockets
RCET recheat
RCEY rickety
rockery
RCHM Rackham
RCIE receive
recline
RCIG racking
rocking
ruching
RCIN ruction
RCIS Rockies
RCIT receipt
RCIY rectify
rockily
RCLD ruckled
RCLR Richler
RCMC racemic
RCMD racemed
RCMN rich man
RCNE recense
RCNY recency
RCON raccoon
RCOY rectory
RCPS recipes
RCRE recurve
RCRO Ricardo
RCRS records
RCRX rectrix
RCSA ricksha
RCTA ricotta
RCTL recital
RCTR reciter
Richter
RCUE recluse
RCUS rectums
RCUT racquet
recount
recruit
RCVR recover
re-cover
RDAD red card
RDAE radiale
radiate
red tape
redware
RDAK redback
RDAT radiant
redraft
RDCD reduced
RDCE radicle
RDCL radical
RDCR reducer
RDCS radices
RDED redhead
red lead
RDEK redneck
RDER red deer
RDES redness
redress
re-dress
Rodgers
rodless
RDET red cent
red heat
red meat
RDIA Rodnina
RDIE red-line
red wine
rodlike
RDIG Redding
redwing
ridging
RDIH reddish
RDIK Roddick
RDIY ruddily
RDLD raddled
RDLE radulae
RDLG red flag
RDLH Rudolph
RDLR radular
riddler
RDMN rodsman
RDOD Redford
redwood□
RDOK ruddock
RDOL Red Poll
redpoll
RDOT redcoat
ride out
RDRL ruderal
RDSY rudesby
RDTR rodster
RDUD redound
RDUT redoubt
RDWY rodeway
REAN Riemann
REAT re-enact
REEN Roedean
REER roe deer
REET re-elect
REHE reechie
Roethke
REIG reeking
reeling
REIH Rhenish
REIM rhenium
REIY re-edify
REMD rheumed
REOF reel off
RETR re-enter
RETY re-entry
REUN Raeburn
REUP re-equip
RFAE reflate
RFAN refrain
RFAT refract
RFEH refresh
RFES rafters
RFET reflect
RFGA refugia
RFGE refugee
RFID Rifkind
RFIG rifling
RFIH raffish
RFIN ruffian
RFLD ruffled
RFLR raffler
RFLS Raffles
RFND refined
RFNR refiner
RFRE referee
RFRO refer to
RFSL refusal
RFTR refuter
RFYA rufiyaa
RGAA regmata
RGAE regrate
RGAT regnant
RGDY rigidly
RGED ragweed
RGES regress
regrets
RGET regreet
RGEY raggedy
roguery
RGIE ragtime
RGIG ragging
rigging
roguing
RGIH riggish
roguish
RGIR Régnier
RGLA regalia
RGLE regulae
RGLR regular
RGLS regulus
RGLY regally
RGMN regimen
RGNY regency□
RGOK rag-book
ragwork
RGOL rag-doll
RGOM ragworm
RGOP regroup
RGOT ragbolt
ragwort
RGRE regorge
RGRS regards
RGTA regatta
RGTH right-oh
RGTN right on
right-on
RGTS rightos
RGTY rightly
RHUE rehouse
RIAE Reigate
ruinate
RIBW rainbow
RIET raiment
RIIG raiding
railing
raining
raising
RIIR Rainier
RIMN Rain Man
RIOD rhizoid
RIOE rhizome
RIOS ruinous
RITR roister
RIWY railway
RJIE rejoice
RJNS rejones
RJOT Rajpoot
RJUN rejourn
RKAU rokkaku
RKDG Riksdag
RKHS rakshas
RKOF rake-off
RKSI rikishi
RLAE release
RLAN relearn
RLAT reliant
RLBE rulable
RLBR roll-bar
RLDY ruled by
RLEE relieve
RLEI rilievi
RLEO relievo
rilievo
RLIG R D Laing
Rolfing
rolling
RLIH Raleigh
Raleigh®
RLIK rollick
RLIR rallier
RLIS Rollins
RLMP rollmop
RLOT rule out
RLPE relapse

Words marked □ can also be spelled with an initial capital letter

RLSK rules OK
RLTD related
RLTR relater
RLVR reliver
RLXD relaxed
RLXN relax in
relaxin
RMAA rum baba
RMAD ram-raid
Rimbaud
RMAE rampage
remuage
rummage
RMAT rampant
rampart
remnant
RMDL remodel
RMDN Ramadan
RMEA romneya
RMEG Romberg
RMER remueur
RMES rimless
RMET Rambert
RMFD rump-fed
RMGS remiges
RMIG ramping
romping
RMIN rampion
RMIS remains
RMIY rummily
RMKN ramakin
ramekin
RMLD rumpled
RMLR rambler
RMLS ramulus
Romulus
RMNA ramenta
Romania
RMNE romance
RMNS Romanus
RMOK rim-lock
RMRE remerge
remorse
RMTH rematch
RMTM ramstam
RMTR remoter
RMUD remould
RMUS rumours
RMUT remount
RMVD removed
RMVL removal
RMVR remover
RNAD Ronsard
run hard
RNAK ransack
RNAL Randall
RNAT run past
RNBY rent-boy
RNEL Rendell
RNES runners
RNEU rondeau
RNGE renague
renegue
RNGN röntgen❑
RNGR reneger
RNGT ringgit
RNHR rancher
RNHS ranchos
RNHW Renshaw
RNID run wild
RNIE Rankine
run time
RNIG ranging
ranking
ranting
rending
renting
ringing
rinsing
running
RNIH runtish
run with
RNIN runnion
RNIT run riot
RNLD rankled
RNLH Ranulph
RNLO Ronaldo
RNLT ringlet
rundlet
RNMK run amok
RNNO run into
RNOE Ransome
RNOF Randolf
RNOH Rannoch
RNON Rangoon
Runcorn
run down
rundown
run-down
RNOR rancour
RNOT rent out
ring out
RNUE rondure
RNUT Renault
RNVR run over
RNWD renewed
RNWL renewal
RNWR renewer
RNWY run away
runaway
ROAB Roobarb
ROAT Riot Act
ROBC rhombic
ROBI rhomboi
ROBS rhombus
ROCI rhonchi
RODA Rhondda
RODR reorder
ROEY rookery
ROFL roomful
ROFR root for
ROIG rioting
roofing
ROIM rhodium
ROIY roomily
ROLT rootlet
ROOS riotous
ROOT root out
ROTP rooftop
ROTR rooster
RPAE replace
RPAL Raphael
RPAS rupiahs
RPAT replant
reptant
RPBE ropable
RPDY rapidly
RPEE replete
RPEI ripieni
RPEO ripieno
RPES repress
re-press
RPEY replevy
RPIA replica
RPIE reprise
reptile
RPIG ripping
RPIR replier
RPIS repairs
RPIT repaint
repoint
reprint
RPLD rippled
RPLE repulse❑
RPLT ripplet
RPND ripened
RPNO rip into
RPOE reprove
RPOF reproof
RPOT rapport
RPQE repique
RPRS reports
RPSD reposed
RPSE riposte
RPST reposit
RPTD reputed
RPUE rapture
rupture
RPWY ropeway
RPYO reply to
RQET request
RQIE require
requite
RQIM requiem❑
RRBT rarebit
RRDS reredos
RRGS rare gas
RRLY rurally
RRUE reroute
RRUL rorqual
RSAD Rostand
RSAE rescale
re-scale
reshape
restate
roseate
RSAS réseaus
Resnais
RSAT restart
RSAX réseaux
RSBE risible
RSBG rose-bug
RSBL Rosabel
RSDA residua
RSDE residue
Rushdie
RSDR resider
RSEK respeak
RSEL Russell
RSET respect
RSEY russety
RSFL restful
RSID rescind
RSIE respire
respite
restive
RSIG rasping
resting
rushing
rusting
RSII Rossini
RSIL reskill
RSIN Russian
RSIS Roscius
RSIY riskily
Russify
rustily
RSJB rush job
RSLA rosella
rusalka
RSLE resolve
Rosalie
RSLO rosolio
RSLR rustler
RSLS results
RSNA Rosanna
RSOA roseola
RSOD respond
RSOE rescore
restore
rissole
RSOK restock
Rostock
RSRA Rosaria
RSRD rose-red
RSRE reserve
RSRL rostral
RSRM rostrum
RSRO Rosario
RSRY respray
RSSA Ross Sea
RSTA Rosetta
RSTE rosette
RSTO risotto
RSUD resound
RSUR rescuer
RSYE restyle
RTAE rat race
retrace
retrate
RTAK ratpack
RTAT retract
RTAY retiary
RTBE ratable
retable
RTBY ratably
RTCE reticle
RTCP rate-cap
RTED retread
RTET retreat
RTFA ratafia
RTFR rotifer
RTHT ratchet
RTIA retsina
RTIG rotting
RTIH ruttish
RTIK rethink
RTIL retrial
RTKR retaker
RTLT Rotblat
RTNA rotunda
RTNE retinae
retinue
RTNL retinal
retinol
RTNS ratings
retinas
RTOS rations
RTRD retired
RTRL retiral
RTRS returns
RTTR rotator
RTUH retouch
RUAB rhubarb
RUAE roulade
RUCY raunchy
RUDD rounded
RUDL roundel
RUDN round on
RUDP round up
round-up
RUDR rounder
RUDY roundly
RUEN rouse on
RUHN roughen
rough in
rough on
RUHP rough up
RUHT rough it
RUHY roughly
RUIE reunite
routine
RUIG rousing
RUIN reunion
Réunion
RULE rouille
RUOS raucous
RVEA riviera
RVEE rivière
RVES reviews
RVGD ravaged
RVGR ravager
RVGS ravages
RVKD revoked
RVLE revalue

revolve
RVLN ravelin
revel in
RVLO Rivaldo
RVLR reviler
RVLT rivulet
RVLY revelry
rivalry
RVNA Ravenna
RVNE revenge
revenue
RVOI ravioli
RVRD revered
rivered
RVRE reverie
reverse
RVRR reverer
RVSL revisal
RVSR reviser
RVST revisit
RVTD riveted
RVVD revived
RVVL revival
RVVR reviver
RWAD Rowland
RWES rawness
RWIE rawhide
rewrite
RWIG Rowling
RWIY rowdily
RWOK rowlock
RWRS rewards
RXNE Roxanne
RYAD reynard❑
RYIG rhyming
RYIH roynish
RYIT rhymist
RYLY royally
royalty
RYOD Raymond
Reynold
RZES rozzers
SAAD seamaid
seaward
SAAE sea lace
seaware
soakage
SAAG siamang
SAAS sea bass
shamans
SAAT sealant
sea-salt
statant
SABD slabbed
SABE scabble
scamble
shamble
SABK sjambok
SABR slabber
stabber
swabber
SABX soapbox
SACL spancel
SACY snatchy
starchy
SADC scaldic
skaldic
SADD swarded
SADE swaddle
SADL scandal
SADM stardom
SADN stand in
stand-in
stand on
SADO so and so
so-and-so
stand to
SADP stand up
stand-up
SADR scalder
slander
SADX spandex❑
SADY staidly
stand by
stand-by
SAED seaweed
SAEE scalene
Siamese
SAEI scaleni
SAEL Scafell
SAEN share in
SAEP scale up
scare up
shake up
shake-up
shape up
SAES sea legs
stamens
SAET stare at
SAEY shapely
slavery
sparely
stalely
stately
suavely
SAFE scaffie
snaffle
SAFR Shaffer
staffer
SAGD snagged
SAGE spangle
swaggie
SAGR spadger
stagger
swagger
SAGY spangly
SAHC spathic
SAHD slashed
smashed
spathed
swathed
SAHP smash up
smash-up
SAHR slasher
slather
smasher
swasher
SAIA stamina
stasima
SAIE sea-like
seaside
stative
SAIG scaling
scaring
searing
seating
shading
shaking
shaming
shaping
sharing
shaving
skating
slating
slaving
slaying
snaking
snaring
soaking
soaring
spacing
sparing
staging
staring
swaying
SAIH Shari'ah
slavish
Spanish
SAII Swahili
SAIK sea pink
seasick
SAIL spacial
spaniel
spatial
SAIM stadium
SAIN sea lion
station
SAIS scabies
statics
SAIT sea-girt
shariat
SAIY scarify
shadily
shakily
Slavify
snakily
soapily
stagily
suavity
SAKD stacked
stalked
SAKE shackle
sparkle
SAKN slacken
snack on
starken
SAKP shack up
slack up
stack up
SAKR Shankar
slacker
smacker
spanker
stacker
swanker
SAKY Shankly
slackly
sparkly
starkly
SALD snarled
SALG sea slug
SALP scallop
shallop
snarl up
snarl-up
SALR smaller
snarler
stapler
SALT scarlet❑
shallot
snarl at
starlet
starlit
SALW shallow
swallow
SALY Shapley
Stanley
SAMN Scarman
Sharman
spaeman
swagman
SAMR slammer
stammer
SANC stannic
SAND stained
SANE Shawnee
slàinte
SANH staunch
SANI stamnoi
SANN Shannon
SANR scanner
Shatner
spanner
spawner
stainer
SANS Staines
SAOD seafood
SAOE Seacole
SAOF seal off
sea wolf
sea-wolf
shadoof
slag off
snap off
stay off
swan off
SAOG Seaborg
SAOH sea-loch
SAON sea gown
SAOS scazons
sea moss
shadows❑
shakoes
spadoes
SAOT Sea Goat
seaport
Shalott
stay out
SAOY shadowy
SAPD stamped
swamped
SAPE scapple
SAPL scalpel
SAPN sharpen
SAPO shampoo
SAPR scamper
scarper
sharper
snapper
stamper
swapper
SAPT stay put
SAPY sharply
SARD scabrid
scarred
SARE spairge
SARR sparrer
SARW sparrow
SASA Swansea
SASY Spassky
SATC spastic
SATD slanted
started
SATE scantle
Seattle
smartie
startle
SATN smarten
spartan❑
start in
start on
SATP start up
start-up
SATR scatter
shatter
slatter
smatter
spatter
starter
swatter
SATS smaltos
SATY scantly
slantly
smartly
swarthy
SAUA scapula
spatula
SAUE stature
statute
SAUL seagull
SAUO shakudo
SAUT Shavuot
SAVD starved
SAVS scarves
SBAE sublate

SBAH Sabbath
SBDT subedit
SBED subtend
SBEO subzero
SBET subject
subtext
subvert
SBHN Sabahan
SBIA Sabrina
SBIE sublime
subside
SBIG sibling
sobbing
SBIO sub divo
SBIT subsist
SBIY subsidy
SBLA Sibylla
Sybilla
SBLS soboles
SBLT subplot
SBOA sub rosa
SBOE sub Jove
SBOL subsoil
SBON subjoin
SBQA subaqua
SBRC suberic
SBRN suberin
SBRS suburbs
Sybaris
SBRY soberly
SBUC subfusc
SBUD subdued
SBUE subsume
SBUL subdual
SBUT subduct
SBYN sabayon
SCAE saccade
saccate
SCAY sectary
SCBD sickbed
SCBT sackbut
SCBY sick bay
SCDR seceder
SCDY suck dry
SCED succeed
SCEE secrete
sockeye
SCES success
SCET Sickert
SCEY secrecy
society
SCFL sackful
SCIE siclike
SCIG sacking
SCIN section
suction
SCIT sacrist
SCLA sacella
SCLR secular
suckler
SCME Secombe
SCNE seconde
SCNI secondi

SCOE sucrose
SCOF suck off
SCOH Succoth
SCOR succour
SCPY sick pay
SCRD secured
SCRR securer
SCRX Sycorax
SCUB succumb
SCUE saccule
seclude
SCUI sacculi
SCUS succuss
SDAH soda ash
SDAM sidearm
SDCR seducer
sidecar
SDES sadness
SDIE Sedaine
SDLR saddler
SDLW Sod's law
SDMN sidemen
SDNC Sudanic
SDNE Sidonie
SDNS St Denis
SDOS Siddons
SDUY Sudbury
SEAA Smetana
SEAD Shepard
steward
SEAE seepage
SEAG shebang
SEAH Shelagh
SEAT Stewart
SEBD seedbed
SEBT sherbet
SECL stencil
SECR spencer□
SECY sketchy
SEDD sleided
SEDN Sheldon
SEDP speed up
SEDR shedder
skelder
slender
speeder
spelder
spender□
SEDS speedos
SEEF shereef
SEEN shebeen
spelean
SEES seeress
shekels
siemens□
stereos
Stevens
SEET sievert
SEEY scenery
SEFL skepful
SEFR seek for
SEGL Stengel
SEGN sten gun□

SEGR Shergar
sledger
Steiger
SEGT sleight
SEHN Stephen
SEIE see life
sterile
SEIF sheriff
SEIG seeking
seeming
seeping
spewing
SEIH Swedish
SEIL special
SEIS species
SEIY seedily
specify
SEKE speckle
SEKF speak of
SEKN sleeken
sneak in
SEKO speak to
SEKP sneck up
speak up
SEKR sneaker
speaker
SEKY sleekly
SELC shellac
SELD smelled
spelled
swelled
SELE skellie
SELF smell of
SELH stealth□
SELR smeller
stealer
stellar
SELT smell at
stemlet
SELY Shelley
SEMD steamed
stemmed
SEME steamie
SEMN Sherman
SEMP steam up
SEMR steamer
SENL sternal
SENM Steinem
sternum
SENR Steiner
SENY sternly
SEOD steroid
SEOF step off
SEOT seek out
seep out
spew out
step out
SEPD steeped
SEPE steeple
SEPN sleep in
sleep on
steepen
SEPR sleeper

stepper
sweeper
SEPS sheepos
Sherpas
SEPY steeply
SERC stearic
SERD speared
SERN stearin
swear in
SERO swear to
SERR shearer□
smearer
sneerer
steerer
swearer
SERT sneer at
swear at
SERY sheerly
swear by
SESN stemson
stetson
SESR Spenser
SESS speoses
SETA spectra
sweet FA
SETC sceptic
smectic
SETD scented
SETE sceptre□
sheathe
sheltie
spectre
sweetie
SETN Skelton
spent on
sweeten
sweet on
SETR shelter
skelter
spelter
sweater
swelter
SETS sheaths
SETY sweetly
SEUA specula
SEVD sheaved
shelved
sleeved
SEVR see over
swerver
SEVS sheaves
shelves
SEZR sneezer
SFBD sofa bed
SFBT safe bet
SFIE suffice
SFIG sifting
SFIN saffian
SFOK Suffolk
SFRN saffron□
SFRS Seferis
SFTP soft top
SFUE suffuse

SGAE Segrave
sigmate
SGAO saguaro
SGET segment
suggest
SGFR sigh for
SGIG sagging
sighing
sugging
SGIY signify
soggily
SGOA Signora
SGOE Signore
SGOI signori
SGOS signors
SGRD sugared
SGTA Sagitta
SGTD sighted
SGTY sightly
SGUN sagouin
SGVA Segovia
SHAN Schwann
SHAS schnaps
SHEE Scheele
Schiele
SHEL schnell
SHEP schlepp
SHIH schlich
SHIT Schmidt
SHLA scholia
SHLR scholar
SHMR schemer
SHNC sthenic
SHOE schoole
SHOK schlock
schtook
SHOM schtoom
SHOR schnorr
SHOS schloss□
schmoes
schools
SHPE schappe
SHPL Schipol
SHRC spheric
SHRD sphered
SHRI scherzi
SHRL spheral
SHRN Saharan
SHRO scherzo
Suharto
SHUK schmuck
SHZS schizos
SIAA spiraea
SIAD Szilard
SIAE spicate
SIAH spinach
SIBE skiable
SIDE spindle
swindge
swindle
SIDG shindig
SIDN Swindon
SIDR slidder

Words marked □ can also be spelled with an initial capital letter

SIDW Skiddaw
SIDY spindly
spin-dry
SIED stipend
SIEF seise of
seize of
spite of
SIEN shine on
slide in
smile on
SIEP seize up
slice up
spice up
SIES shivers
Spiders
SIET Seifert
shine at
smile at
snipe at
SIEY shivery
spidery
SIFE skiffle
sniffle
stiffie
SIFL skilful
skinful
SIFN stiffen
SIFR sniffer
SIFT sniff at
SIFY stiffly
stir-fry
SIGD stinged
SIGE shingle
sniggle
swingle
SIGN smidgen
smidgin
SIGR snigger
stinger
swinger
SIGS stingos
SIGT swing it
SIGY shingly
SIHC stichic
SIHI stichoi
SIHN Swithin
SIHR slither
swither
SIHT shit-hot
SIIE stibine
suicide
SIIG sailing
seizing
shining
skiving
slicing
sliding
smiling
sniping
soiling
suiting
swiping
SIIH swinish

SIII saimiri
SIIS spirits
SIIT ski lift
SIIU Shimizu
SIIY slimily
spicily
spikily
SIIZ Stibitz
SIKE stickle
SIKN slicken
stick in
stick-on
SIKO stick to
SIKP snick up
stick up
stick-up
SIKR shirker
slicker
snicker
sticker
stinker
SIKT stick at
SIKY slickly
smickly
stick by
SILB Ski Club
SILD skid lid
skilled
spilled
stifled
SILO sciolto
SILP shiplap
SILR spieler
stifler
SILT skillet
SILY Shirley
SIMA skimmia
SIMC seismic
SIML seismal
SIMN Shipman
shipmen
SIMR shimmer
skimmer
slimmer
swimmer
SIMS stigmas
SIND skinned
SINE science❑
soignée
SINR Skinner
spinner
SINY spinney
SIOA Spinoza
SIOE spinose
SIOF slip off
spin-off
SIOS spinous
SIOT spin out
spit out
stir out
SIPE stipple
SIPN skid pan
skimp on

SIPR skipper
slipper
snipper
SIPS stirpes
SIPT skippet
snippet
SIRD stirred
SIRP stirrup
SIRR stirrer
SIRW skid row
SISR scissor
SISS Swisses
SITC sciatic
Shiitic
SITD sainted
skirted
stilted
stinted
SITE skittle
snirtle
spirtle
spittle
SITN Shilton
Shipton
smitten
Stilton
SITP shift up
SITR skitter
slitter
spitter
stinter
SITU shiatsu
shiatzu
shih tzu
SITY saintly
swiftly
SIUA spicula
SIUE seizure
spicule
spinule
stipule
SIUI stimuli
SIWY slipway
SIZE swizzle
SJHS St John's
SJUN sojourn
SKIA sokaiya
SKIM Sikhism
SKLA St Kilda
SKMT Sekhmet
SKOH Sukkoth
SKRO Sukarno
SKRT sakeret
SLAA Silvana
sultana
SLAE saltate
salvage
selvage
solvate
sulcate
sullage
SLAI syllabi
SLAO saltato

SLAT saltant
SLBE soluble
SLBY salably
SLCA St Lucia
SLCC silicic
SLCD spliced
SLCN salicin
silicon
SLCR splicer
SLCS salices
SLCT solicit
SLDE splodge
SLDS solidus
SLDY solidly
splodgy
SLEE salvete
SLEI Salieri
SLEN Salween
SLES Sellers
SLET salient
solvent
SLEY silvery
silver-Y
spleeny
SLFR sell for
SLGR St Leger
SLHA silphia
SLHR sulphur
SLHW salchow
SLID sullied
SLIE saltire❑
SLIG salting
selling
solving
SLIH saltish
selfish
SLIK Selkirk
SLIR saltier
soldier
SLIT soloist
SLIX salpinx
SLIY salsify
saltily
silkily
sillily
sulkily
SLMN silk-man
Solomon
SLMS Salamis
SLNA Selenga
SLNC selenic
SLNE silence
SLNS silenus❑
solanos
SLOD Salford
Salmond
SLOF sell off
SLOS salmons
salvoes
SLOT salt out
sell out
sell-out
SLOY sallowy

SLPN salt pan
SLRE splurge
SLRO Salerno
SLRY splurgy
SLSW self-sow
SLSY splashy
SLTA solatia
SLTH splatch
splotch
SLTN split on
SLTP split up
split-up
SLTR saluter
SLUS St Louis
SLUT Sallust
SLZR seltzer
SMAE summate
SMAN Samhain
SMAY summary
SMDY someday
SMEY summery
SMFW some few
SMHW somehow
SMKN Simpkin
SMLA Somalia
SMLR sampler
similar
similor
SMLS similes
SMNL seminal
SMNN Simenon
SMNR seminar
SMOE shmoose
shmooze
someone
SMOS summons
symbols
SMRA Samaria
SMRI samurai
SMRS Sampras
SMSN samisen
Simpson
SMSS samosas
SMTA Sumatra
SMTC sematic
Semitic
somatic
SMTM symptom
SMVR samovar
SMWY someway
SMYD Samoyed
SNAA Sankara
SNAD sunward
SNAE Santa Fe
sinuate
sunbake
SNAT sunfast
SNBG sandbag
SNBR sand bar
sandbar
SNBX sandbox
SNBY sandboy
SNEE sincere

SNEK sundeck
SNEL sand eel
SNEM sunbeam
SNEO San Remo
SNES singers
sinless
sunless
SNET Sennett
sunbelt
SNFR send for
SNFY sandfly
SNGL Senegal
Sénégal
SNHO synchro
SNHS sanchos
SNID sunbird
SNIE sunlike
sunrise
sunwise
SNIG sending
singing
sinking
sinning
SNIH sunfish
SNIL sundial
SNIM Sunnism
SNIO Sandino
San Siro
SNIS sonties
SNIY sunnily
SNLT singlet
SNMN songman
SNNE sonance
SNNM Songnam
synonym
SNOE San José
syncope
SNOF send off
send-off
sunroof
SNON Sandown
sundown
SNOS sanious
sinuous
SNOT send out
sing out
SNOY sensory
SNPA sinopia
SNPE synapse
SNPT sandpit
sunspot
SNRA sangria
SNRI senarii
SNRN Sonoran
SNRP suntrap
SNRY synergy
SNSI Senussi
SNSS sinuses
SNTA Sinatra
SNTM sanctum
SNTR senator
SNTS Sanctus
SNUL sensual
SNUN San Juan
sunburn
SNVA synovia
SNYE sinsyne
SOAA stomata
SOAE Spokane
storage
stowage
SOAH stomach
SOAS shofars
SOBR slobber
SOBY shop-boy
SOBZ show biz
showbiz
SOCL stoical
SOCP snowcap
SODE spondee
SODN Snowdon
SODR scolder
scowder
SOEE Slovene
stone me!
SOEO Spoleto
SOEP shore up
slope up
stoke up
store up
SOES storeys
SOET soonest
SOEY showery
SOFR scoffer
shop for
spoofer
SOFT scoff at
SOGE shoggle
shoogie
shoogle
showghe
SOGN shotgun
sloe gin
SOGP stopgap
stop-gap
SOGR slogger
sponger
SOHD sloshed
SOHN Siobhán
SOHR smother
soother
SOHY soothly
SOID storied
SOIE scoriae
Scotice
SOIG shoring
showing
sloping
slowing
smoking
stoning
stoping
stowing
SOIS stories
stovies
SOIY scorify
Scotify
showily
smokily
snowily
sootily
stonily
SOKD shocked
SOKL snorkel
SOKN slocken
SOKP stock up
SOKR shocker
snooker
stonker
stooker
SOLD spoiled
SOLN stollen
swollen
SOLR spoiler
SOMN showman
snowman
SONP shown up
SONR scorner
Spooner
SOOA scotoma
SOOE Sao Tomé
São Tomé
SOOF show off
show-off
stop off
stop-off
SOOO suo loco
SOOT slop out
SOPD scooped
stooped
SOPE stopple
SOPN swoop on
SOPO Scorpio
SOPP scoop up
SOPR scooper
shopper
snooper
stopper
SOPT shotput
SORE scourge
SORN sporran
SORR scourer
SOSL spousal
SOSN sponson
SOSR sponsor
SOTD snouted
spotted
SOTE Scottie
shortie
SOTF short of
SOTN shorten
short on
stouten
SOTP shoot up
SOTR scooter
Scouter
shooter
Shorter
shouter
snorter
snotter
spotter
stoiter
stotter
SOTT shoot at
SOTY shortly
smoothy
stoutly
SOUE sporule
suo jure
SOUS São Luis
SOVC SCOTVEC
Scotvec
SOZE snoozle
SOZR snoozer
SPAI soprani
SPAO soprano
SPEA saphena
SPEE supreme
suprême
SPEO supremo
SPET sapient
SPHC Sapphic
SPIE septime
SPIG sapling
sapping
sopping
SPIH Sopwith
SPIM sophism
SPIT sophist
SPIY soppily
SPJU sapajou
SPNN saponin
SPOD sapwood
SPOE suppose
SPOO Sapporo
SPOT support
SPUS St Paul's
SPUU seppuku
SQEA sequela
SQET sequent
SQOA sequoia
SRAE seriate
serrate
striate
surbase
surface□
surname
SRAM sarcasm
SRAS surpass
SRAT servant
SRAY streaky
streamy
SRBC strobic
SRBL scribal
SRBP scrub up
SRBR scriber
SRBY shrubby
SRCN Saracen
sericin
SRCO sirocco
SRDA soredia
SRDL strudel
SRDM serfdom
SRDR stridor
SREE screeve
scrieve
SREH screech
SREL surreal
SREN surgeon
SREP serve up
SRES Serpens
serve as
Surtees
SRET Sargent
serpent□
surfeit
SREY sorcery
surgery
SRFY scruffy
SRGE strigae
SRGL strigil
SRGY scraggy
SRHM sorghum
SRHS sorghos
SRID serried
SRIE sardine
service
servile
surmise
survive
SRIG sarking
serving
sorting
surfing
surging
SRIH scraich
scraigh
skreigh
SRII sordini
SRIN Serbian
SRIO sordino
SRIS sardius
Sergius
straits
SRIT spraint
SRIW surview
SRIY sorrily
surlily
SRKR striker
SRLS surplus
SRLY shrilly
SRME strumae
SRMY scrimpy
scrummy
scrumpy
SRNA syringa
SRNE springe
strange
surance
syringe
SRNH scranch
scrunch
SRNS strings
SRNY springy

Words marked □ can also be spelled with an initial capital letter

stringy
SROA sarcoma
SROE Scrooge
SRON sirloin
SROS sarcous
serious
sermons
SROT sort out
SRPD scraped
striped
SRPE scrapie
scruple
strophe
SRPN strip in
SRPR scraper
SRPS seraphs
SRPY scrappy
strappy
stroppy
SRRL sororal
SRSE serosae
SRSS serosas
sorosis
SRSY Surtsey
SRTE strette
SRTH scratch
scritch
stretch
SRTI stretti
SRTM scrotum
stratum
SRTO stretto
SRTS scrutos
stratus
SRTV Saratov
SRUE scrouge
SRUH scraugh
SRUS Strauss
SRVL shrivel
SRVR Sir Ivor
SRWH strewth
SRWP screw up
screw-up
SRWR screwer
strewer
SRWT screw it
SRWY scrawly
scrawny
SRYD strayed
SRYN spray-on
SRYR sprayer
strayer
SRZN Sarazen
SSAN sustain
SSAY sassaby
SSED suspend
SSET suspect
SSIA sestina
SSIE sessile
suspire
SSII sashimi
SSIN session
SSNA Susanna
SSOE systole
SSON Sassoon
SSOT suss out
SSRM sistrum
STAE satiate
situate
STAK set back
setback
sit back
STAL set sail
STAR set fair
STAS Sotsass
STAY satrapy
STEE so there
STEL Sitwell
STES sithens
STEY satiety
Sotheby
STHL satchel
STHO Satchmo
STIE setline
STIG setting
sitting
STIH sottish
STLD settled
STLE situlae
STLR settler
STNC satanic
STNT satinet
STOE Sithole
STOK set book
STON set down
sit down
sit-down
STPN set upon
sit upon
STRC satiric
satyric
STRD satyrid
STRE set free
STSY satisfy
so to say
STTS shtetls
STUA satsuma❑
STVC sits vac
SUAE sausage
scutate
soutane
SUAI Scutari
SUAO sfumato
SUAY squeaky
SUBD slubbed
stubbed
SUBE scumble
stubble
stumble
SUBG scumbag
SUBR slubber
slumber
SUBY squabby
stubbly
SUCN soupçon
SUCO squacco
SUCS stuccos
SUDD studded
SUDE scuddle
squidge
SUDR scudder
shudder
SUDY soundly
squaddy
squidgy
SUEE shut-eye
squeeze
SUES sautées
Souness
Squeers
SUET student
SUEY squeezy
stupefy
SUFD stuffed
SUFE scuffle
shuffle
snuffle
souffle
soufflé
SUFL soulful
SUFR snuffer
SUFT snuff it
stuff it
SUFY squiffy
SUGE smuggle
snuggle
SUGN stun gun
SUGR smudger
SUHE stushie
SUHR souther
SUHY Southey
SUID studied
SUIE soubise
SUIG souring
SUIH sourish
SUIN saurian
SUIS studies
studios
SUIY saucily
SUKN stuck on
SUKP stuck up
stuck-up
SUKR skulker
SUKY Slumkey
SULD squalid
SULH squelch
SULK souslik
SULR sculler
squalor
SULY squally
SUME squamae
SUMR scummer
sturmer❑
SUND shunned
spurned
stunned
SUNH squinch
SUNK sputnik❑
SUNR scunner
stunner
SUNY squinny
SUOF shut off
shut-off
SUOS soukous
spumous
SUOT shut out
shut-out
spun out
stub out
SUPD stumped
SUPP stump up
SUPR scupper
stumper
SURD slurred
SURR squarer
SURY spurrey
squirmy
SUSP soursop
SUSY squashy
squishy
SUTD stunted
SUTE scuttle
shuttle
spurtle
SUTR saunter
scutter
shunter
shutter
sputter
stutter
SUWY squawky
SUZE snuzzle
spulzie
SVBE savable
SVLE Seville
SVLS Savalas
SVLY saveloy
SVMI Savimbi
SVNA savanna
SVNH seventh
SVNS savings
SVNY seventy
SVOR saviour❑
SVRD severed
SVRL several
SVRS Severus
SVUY savoury
SVYU save you
SWIE sawlike
SXAK six-pack
SXAS Sextans
SXAT sextant❑
SXEN sixteen
SXES sexless
SXET sexpert
SXHY sixthly
SXIS sixties
SXOB sex bomb
SXOD sixfold
SXON saxhorn
SXPT six-spot
SYAA scybala
SYAD skyward
SYAK skyjack
skylark
SYAL skysail
SYBE sayable
SYEE styrene
SYEN soy bean
SYES shyness
slyness
SYET Seyfert
SYHN say when
SYID stymied
SYIE skyline
stylise
stylite
stylize
SYIH sky-high
stylish
SYIN Stygian
SYIT stylist
SYLE sky-blue
SYNA Soyinka
SYNS sayings
SYOE spyhole
SYOK Shylock
SYOO say no to
SYOR Seymour
SYTC styptic
SYTR shyster
SYUE seysure
SYWY shy away
SYYU says you
SZBE sizable
SZIM sizeism
SZIT sizeist
SZLD sozzled
SZLR sizzler
SZRC Sazerac®
TAAA tuatara
TAAD twafald
TAAE teacake
TAAI thalami
TAAL travail
TAAR to a hair
TACD tranced
TACE tranche
TADE twaddle
TADM tsardom
TADY twaddly
TAEE trapeze
TAEF tea leaf
TAEN trade in
trade-in
trade on
TAEP trade up
TAES travels
TAET traject
tranect
TAEY tracery
tragedy
TAFC traffic
TAFL tearful
trayful

TAGS tear gas
tear-gas
TAHA trachea
TAHN teach-in
TAHP tea shop
TAHR teacher
TAIA tsarina
TAIG teasing
thawing
tracing
trading
TAIM tsarism
TAIT tsarist
TAJN Tianjin
TAKE thankee
TAKR tracker
TALR trailer
trawler
TALS thallus
TAML trammel
TAMS traumas
TAND trained
TANE trainee
trannie
TANN train on
TANR trainer
TAOE tea rose
TAOF tear off
TAOM tea room
TAOT tear out
thaw out
TAOY tea cosy
TAPD trapped
TAPE traipse
trample
TAPR trapper
TAPT trampet
TARY tea tray
TASM transom
TASS Thapsus
TAST transit
TATD toasted
TATE toastie
twattle
TATR toaster
tractor
traitor
TAUE traduce
TAUN to a turn
TAWY tramway
TAYO toady to
TBAE to blame
TBCO tobacco
TBEU tableau
TBHD to be had
TBIG tabling
TBJG Toby jug
TBLE tabulae
TBLN tubulin
TBLR tabular
tubular
TBOD tabloid
TBRT tabaret
TBSO Tabasco®
TBTA Tabitha
TBTN Tibetan
TBUS tubfuls
TCAA toccata
TCFL tactful
TCIE tactile
TCIG ticking
TCIM tachism
TCIS tactics
TCIT tachist
TCIY tackily
techily
TCLR tackler
TCNC technic
TCOF tick off
TCRX tectrix
TCTS Tacitus
TCTY tacitly
TDAH to death
TDLR tiddler
toddler
TDMN Tudjman
TDNS tidings
TDOE tadpole
TDOS tedious
TDSA tedesca
TDSM tidy sum
TDWY tideway
TEAA themata
TEAB the Lamb
TEAD the Bard
TEAE teenage
the cane
The Face
the game
the rage
the same
TEAG the hang
trepang
TEAK the sack
TEAL The Fall
The Wall
toenail
trenail
TEAN Tremain
TEAR the fair
the pair
TEAS the Oaks
TEAT the East
TEAY The Lady
the many
therapy
TEBE tremble
TEBY Tees Bay
trembly
TECD tierced
TECE treacle
TECL tiercel
TECY treacly
TEDE treadle
tweedle
TEDR treader
TEDY Tuesday
TEEA Theresa
TEED the dead
the herd
the lead
TEEF thereof
TEEL The Bell
TEEM tie beam
TEEN therein
TEEO thereto
TEEP the deep
TEES Theseus
TEET thereat
TEEY thereby
TEFH twelfth
TEHP the chop
TEIC theriac
TEIE taeniae
the like
TEIG teeming
The Ring
the ring
TEIL the Bill
TEIO Trevino
TEIS taenias
The Kiss
the pits
TEIT T S Eliot
TEKR trekker
TELE the blue
TELN the Klan
TELP tie clip
TELS trellis
TELT the flat
TELY the play
TEME thermae
TEML thermal
TEMN The Omen
TEOD the Word
toehold
TEOE The Robe
the rope
TEOK the Rock
TEOL The Fool
trefoil
TEON the morn
tie down
TEOO tremolo
TEOP the soup
TEOS the boss
the gods
the hots
the tops
TEOT The Boat
the boot
TEOX Theroux
TERM theorem
TERO theorbo
TERS the arts
TERY theurgy
TESD tressed
TESN treason
TESS tresses
TESY they say
TETD treated
TETE theatre
trestle
TETN Trenton
TETP treetop
TETR The Star
treater
tweeter
TEUE the tube
TEUF the buff
TEUH the push
the rush
TEUP the lump
TEUS the runs
TEUZ the fuzz
TEVL The Oval
TFAY tiffany□
TFEA taffeta
TFES toffees□
TFIG tufting
TGAA tagmata
TGES tigress
TGIA tegmina
TGIG tugging
TGLE tegulae
TGLG Tagálog
TGTN tighten
TGTS tagetes
TGTY tightly
THRN Teheran
TIAE tribade
TIAY tribady
trinary
tzigany
TIBE thimble
triable
Trimble
TIBS trilbys
TICD triacid
TICY twitchy
TIDC triadic
TIDE trindle
twiddle
TIDY thirdly
this day
twiddly
TIED tail end
tail-end
TIEE trireme
TIES triceps
TIET trident
trisect
TIEY tritely
TIFN tail fin
TIGN twiggen
TIGR trigger
TIGT Tlingit
TIHP trip hop
TIHW trishaw
TIIG tailing
toiling
twining
TIII Tbilisi
TIIL trivial
twibill
TIIM tritium
trivium
TIIN tuition
TIIY trinity□
TIKD tricked
TIKE trickle
twinkle
TIKF think of
TIKN thicken
TIKP think up
TIKR thinker
tricker
TIKS thickos
TIKT thicket
trinket
TIKY thickly
tricksy
TILD twilled
TILR trifler
twirler
TILS tailles
trifles
TILT triolet
triplet
TIMD trimmed
TIMH triumph
Triumph®
TIMN thiamin
TIMR trimmer
TIMS tzimmes
TIND twinned
TINR thinner
TIOA Tritoma
TIOE tritone
TIOF tail off
TIOI Tripoli
TIOM triform
TION tricorn
TIOT thin out
trip out
TIOY trilogy
trisomy
TIPE tripple
TIPR tripper
TIPU Thimphu
TIRM trigram
TISE Trieste
TIST twin-set
TISY thirsty
TITD tainted
twisted
TITE thistle
TITN Tristan
TITR twister
twitter
TITY thistly
TIUA Tripura
TIUE tribune□
tribute
TIUN Taiyuan

TIVS thieves
TIZE twizzle
TJAA Tijuana
TKAM take aim
TKAR take air
TKFR take for
TKIE tektite
TKMK tokamak
TKNN taken in
TKNP taken up
TKNS takings
TKOF take off
take-off
TKOT take out
TLAE tallage
tillage
TLAL tell all
TLBG talk big
TLBY tallboy
TLDS Toledos
TLEE toluene
TLET tallent
TLFX telefax
TLGS Telugus
TLHR telpher
TLIG talking
telling
tilling
tilting
TLIH tallith
Tillich
TLIN Tallinn
Tolkien
TLIS tallies
TLMN telamon
TLNW till now
TLOD Telford
TLOF tell off
TLOT talk out
TLPD tylopod
TLPS talipes
TLPT talipat
talipot
TLSS tyloses
TLTY Tolstoy
TLUY Tilbury
TLVV Tel Aviv
TLYO tally-ho
TMAA tympana
TMAE timbale
TMAI timpani
tympani
TMBE tamable
TMDY timidly
tumidly
TMEA tempera
TMET tempest
TMIE Tim Rice
TMIN tampion
tompion
TMIO Tampico
TMLD tumbled
TMLG time lag
TMLR tumbler
tumular
TMLS temples
tumulus
TMLT templet
TMOA tombola
TMOF time off
TMOL tomfool
TMOR tambour
TMOT Time Out
time out
time-out
TMRL timbrel
tumbrel
tumbril
TMRN tamarin
TMSE tumesce
TMTR tempter
TMTY Timothy
TMUA tambura
tempura
TMVE TV movie
TMWS time was
TNAA tantara
TNAD tankard
Tynwald
TNAE tonnage
Tyndale
TNAT Tennant
TNBE tenable
tunable
TNBY tunably
TNCE tunicle
TNEO tangelo
TNEP tense up
TNET tangent
tiniest
TNEY tannery
tensely
TNFL tankful
tuneful
TNGR tanager
TNGT tonight
TNHY tenthly
TNIE tensile
tontine
TNIG tanning
tending
tensing
Tenzing
TNIH tun-dish
TNII tondini
TNIL Tenniel
TNIN tension
TNIR Tangier
TNIY tenuity
TNLD tangled
TNLY tonally
TNMC tonemic
TNMU tinamou
TNNY tenancy
TNOD tenfold
TNOL tinfoil
TNON tinhorn
TNOS tenuous
TNOT tune out
TNPD tonepad
TNRC Tantric
TNRD Tancred
tenured
TNRL tendril
TNRM tangram
tantrum
TNRN tendron
TNSA Tunisia
TNTM Tiny Tim
TNTP tank top
TNTS tenutos
TNTT tiny tot
TNUE tonsure
TNUS tinfuls
TOAD two-hand
TOBE trouble
TOBG toolbag
TOBR toolbar
TOBX toolbox
TODN trodden
TODR to order
TOEP two deep
TOEU Thoreau
TOGT thought
TOHC trophic
TOHD toothed
TOHE trochee
TOHL trochal
TOIE two-time
TOIM thorium
tropism
TOIS two bits
TOKT toolkit
TOLE troelie
troolie
TOLP trollop
TOLS Troilus
TOLY trolley
TOML trommel
TONE trounce
TOOD twofold
TOOE twosome
two-tone
TOON too soon
two-down
TOOT trot out
TOPR trooper
trouper
TOSE tootsie□
TOSN Thomsen
Thomson
TOSR trouser
TOSY Trotsky
TOTP two-step
TOTR trotter
TOUH too much
TPAK top-rank
TPAL topsail
TPAY topiary
TPCL topical
typical
TPDY tepidly
TPEK top deck
TPER top gear
TPES topless
TPET Tippett
TPIE tappice
topline
topside
TPIG tapping
topping
TPIT to point
TPIY tipsify
tipsily
TPLR tippler
TPLS tupelos
TPLV Tupolev
TPNH to-pinch
TPNM toponym
TPNT topknot
TPOA tapioca
TPOD typhoid
TPOE top-hole
TPOL topsoil
TPOM taproom
TPON typhoon
TPOS typhous
TPOT topcoat
topmost
TPPN topspin
TPRD tapered
TPST typeset
TPTM tapetum
TPTR tipster
TPUL topfull
TPVR tip over
TQAE T-square
TQIA tequila
TRAA Turkana
TRAD turband
TRAE tartane
ternate
terrace
TRAN terrain
Torfaen
TRAO tornado□
TRAS threats
TRAY thready
throaty
turbary
TRCS turacos
TRDS teredos
TRDY tiredly
TREA Tarpeia
TREE terpene
TREH turpeth
TREL tar-seal
TREO torpedo
TRES Targets
Torrens
TRET torment
torrent
TREY tersely
torpefy
torrefy
TRFR turn for
TRFY thrifty
TRHN torchon
TRHR torcher
TRIE termite
terrine
tortive
turbine
TRIG turning
TRIH tarnish
Turkish
TRII termini
TRIL Torvill
TRIM terbium
Toryism
TRIN torsion
TRIR tarrier
tarsier
terrier
TRIS tercios
turkies
TRIY tardily
terrify
Turkify
TRIZ Tirpitz
TRKY turnkey
TRLE torulae
TRLT tartlet
TRMI thrombi
TRMN Turkmen
TRNE Terence
TRNO Taranto
Toronto
TRNS threnos
tyrones
TRNY tyranny
TROD turbond
TROF turn off
turn-off
TROL turmoil
TROT tire out
turf out
turn out
turnout
turn-out
TRRD turn red
TRRS toreros
TRTH thrutch
TRUE torture
TRUH through
TRUK Tarbuck
TRUN Tarquin
TRUS Targums
TRUY Torquay
TRWN throw in
throw-in
throw on
TRWP throw up
TSAA tostada
TSAE testate

to spare
TSAK Toshack
TSEA tessera
TSEN testern
TSFY test-fly
TSIE tussive
TSIG tasting
testing
tossing
TSIY tastily
testify
testily
tossily
TSMP to sum up
TSOE tussore
TSOF toss off
TSOK tussock
TSOT toss out
TSPT tosspot
TTAE titrate
to tease
TTAK titlark
TTBG tote bag
TTES tatters
tutress
TTEY tottery
TTIE titmice
TTIG tatting
TTIM Titoism
TTIS titbits
TTIY tattily
TTLR tattler
titular
tutelar
TTLY totally
TTMC totemic
TTMS TV Times
TTNA Titania
tutania
TTNC titanic❑
TTNG tutenag
TTNS tetanus
TTPO tot up to
TTRD tutored
TUAI tsunami
TUAO touraco
TUBR Thurber
TUDE trundle
TUDR thunder❑
TUEN Taurean
TUEU Trudeau
trumeau
TUFE truffle
TUFR thus far
TUGS thuggos
TUHD touched
TUHE toughie
TUHN touch on
toughen
TUHP touch up
TUHY toughly
TUIG touring
TUIM thulium

tourism
TUIT tourist
TUIY thurify
TUKE truckle
TUKR trucker
TULD tousled
TUMN Trueman
TUNI Tournai
TUNY tourney
truancy
TUPP trump up
TUPT trumpet
TURB true rib
TUSD trussed
TUSR trusser
TUTD trusted
TUTE trustee
TUTN Taunton
trust in
TUTR truster
TVNR Tavener
TVRA taverna
TWAH towpath
TWBE towable
TWGS town gas
TWIE T H White
towline
TWNS Tswanas
TWOE towrope
TWRD towered
TWRS towards
TXBE taxable
TXBY taxably
TXCB taxicab
TXDS tuxedos
TXIC tax disc
TXIE textile
TXRE tax-free
TXUE texture
TXUL textual
TYAD Toyland
try hard
TYAK try back
TYAL trysail
TYBE Toynbee
TYIE Tayside
thymine
TYIH toy with
TYOD thyroid
TYSN trypsin
TYSS thyrses
TYTC tryptic
TYTN try it on
UAAE unaware
UAAI Ucayali
UADD unaided
UAIE uranite
UAIG unaking
UAIM uranium
UAIN Uralian
Uranian
UAKD unasked
UAMA uraemia

UAMC uraemic
UAMD unarmed
UAOA Ulanova
UAOE una voce
up above
UAOG up-along
UARE up a tree
UATY unaptly
UBAD upbraid
UBAE umbrage
unbrace
UBEK upbreak
UBES unbless
UBGT unbeget
UBID unblind
unbuild
upbuild
UBIG unbeing
UBIN Umbrian
UBNL umbonal
UBNS umbones
UBOE umbrose
UBOK unblock
UBON unblown
UBOS umbrous
UBRT upburst
UBSM unbosom
UBUD unbound
UBWD unbowed
UCAM uncharm
UCAN unchain
UCAP unclasp
UCAT upcoast
UCEK uncheck
UCEN unclean
UCER unclear
upcheer
UCID unchild
UCIN unction
UCLO Uccello
UCNY uncanny
UCOD uncloud
UCOE unclose
UCOK uncloak
UCON uncrown
UCOS uncross
UCRD ulcered
uncured
UCRE uncurse
UCTH upcatch
UCUH uncouth
UCUK upchuck
UCVL uncivil
UCVR uncover
UDES undress
UDID undried
UDIG undoing
undying
UDIY undeify
UDRO underdo
undergo
UEDD up-ended
UEEE ukelele

UEES use less
useless
UEHA urethra
UEIE uterine
UERH unearth
UESL utensil
UETN uneaten
UEUL unequal
UFDD unfaded
UFEH unflesh
UFOK unfrock
UFOT up front
upfront
up-front
UFSY unfussy
UFTY unfitly
UFUH unflush
UFXD unfixed
UFZD unfazed
UGAD unguard
UGAE upgrade
UGDY ungodly
UGET unguent
UGLE ungulae
UGNY urgency
UGRH ungirth
UHAD unheard
unhoard
uphoard
UHAE upheave
UHAT unheart
UHNE unhinge
UHNY unhandy
UHOD uphoord
UHPY unhappy
UHRE unhorse
UHRN usher in
UHRT unherst
UHSY unhasty
UHTH unhitch
UHUE unhouse
UIAD unitard
UIAE urinate
UIAT urinant
UIAY unitary
urinary
UIGP using-up
UIID unified
UIIE unitise
unitive
unitize
uridine
utilise
utilize
UIIG uniting
UIIR unifier
UIIY utility
UIOM uniform❑
UION unicorn❑
UIOS urinous
UJIT unjoint
UKMT unkempt
UKON unknown

ULAH unleash
ULAN Ullmann
unlearn
ULCD unlaced
ULCY unlucky
ULND unlined
ULOE unloose
ULSE unlaste
ULTH unlatch
ULVD unloved
UMNY unmanly
UMRL unmoral
UMRY unmarry
UMUD unmould
UMUT unmount
UMVD unmoved
UMXD unmixed
UNAH unneath
UNBE unnoble
UNMD unnamed
UNRA ulnaria
UNRE unnerve
UNTD unnoted
UNUS urnfuls
UODR unorder
UOIL uxorial
UOIN utopian❑
UOLD unoiled
UOOY ufology
urology
UOTN unoften
UPAA Uppsala
UPAE unplace
UPEN umpteen
UPGD unpaged
UPIT unpaint
UPNL unpanel
UPNT unpinkt
UPPR unpaper
UPRE unpurse
UPRH unperch
UPUB unplumb
UPUE unplume
UQEN unqueen
UQIT unquiet
UQOE unquote
URAE unreave
URAY unready
URCE utricle
URCT Utrecht
UREE unreeve
URFE unruffe
URGT upright
URIE Ukraine
upraise
URLO Utrillo
UROT unroost
URVL unravel
URVT unrivet
USAD unskan'd
unswai'd
USAE unscale
unshale

unshape
unstate
upscale
upstage
upstare
upstate
USAK unstack
USAL unsnarl
USAM up-swarm
USAT upstart
USDS upsides
USEK unspeak
upspeak
USEL unshell
unspell
unsteel
USER unswear
upspear
USET unspent
USIG unsling
upswing
USIK unstick
USIT unsaint
USLN upsilon
USNE unsense
USNS Ursinus
USNW unsinew
USOK unstock
USON unshorn
USOT unshoot
unshout
upshoot
USRD unsured
USRE upsurge
USRP unstrap
unstrip
USRW unscrew
USTY upset by
USUD unshun'd
unsound
USUK unstuck
USXD unsexed
UTAE untrace
UTAH unteach
UTAN uptrain
UTED untread
UTEE up there
UTGT uptight
UTID untried
UTIE untride
untwine
UTIK unthink
UTIT untwist
UTKN untaken
UTMD untamed
UTMO up-tempo
UTND untuned
UTNV Ustinov
UTNW up to now
UTPR up to par
UTRD uttered
UTRW upthrow
UTRY utterly
UTUH untruth
UTUS untruss
UTUY untruly
UUAE ululate
UUAT ululant
usucapt
UUEE ukulele
UUIG usuring
UULY usually
UUPR usurper
UUUL unusual
UUUY Uruguay
UVIE unvoice
UVLE upvalue
UVSR unvisor
UWAE unweave
UWGD unwaged
UWIE unwrite
UWMN unwoman
UWRS unwares
upwards
UWTH unwitch
UWTR unwater
UYSS Ulysses
VAIA viatica
VAUT viaduct
VBAE vibrate
VBAO vibrato
VBAT vibrant
VBCS vibices
VBIS vibrios
VCAE viciate
VCBE vocable
VCDR vocoder
VCIE vaccine
VCIN Vectian
VCIY vacuity
VCLC vocalic
VCLY vocally
VCNA Vicenza
VCNE Vicente
VCNL vicinal
VCNY vacancy
VCOE vacuole
VCOS vacuous
vicious
VCOY victory❑
VCRY viceroy
VCUL victual
VCUS vacuums
VDLA vedalia
VDMS vidimus
VDNA Vedanta
videnda
VEES viewers
VEIG veering
viewing
VEIH vie with
VENM Vietnam
VGAT vagrant
VGEY vaguely
VGIH voguish
VGTL vegetal
VHCE vehicle
VHPD V-shaped
VIGY vyingly
VIIG veiling
voicing
voiding
VILT veinlet
VLAE valuate
valvate
village
voltage
Vulgate
VLAN villain
VLAO volcano❑
Vulcano
VLAT valiant
VLBE volable
voluble
VLBY volubly
VLDY validly
VLEN villein
VLES valleys
volleys
VLEY velvety
VLIE vulpine
VLIG valuing
VLIS Vilnius
VLMN velamen
VLNA valonia
VLNE valance
VLNY valency
VLOE villose
VLOS villous
VLPK Volapük
VLRA velaria
VLRE Valerie
VLTA Valetta
VLTD voluted
VLUE velouté
vulture
VLUS velours
VMIE vampire
VMIH vampish
VMNL Viminal
VMOE vamoose
VNAD vanward
VNAE vantage
vendace
ventage
vintage
VNAU Vanuatu
VNET Vincent
VNGR vinegar
VNIE V-engine
ventige
VNIG vending
venting
VNLA vanilla
VNLY venally
VNMD venomed
VNNR Ventnor
vintner
VNOE ventose
VNOH Van Gogh
VNRL ventral
VNRR venerer
VNRS Ventris
VNSA Vanessa
VNSN venison
VNTA Venetia
VNTR venator
VNTS vanitas
VNUA vincula
VNUE venture
VNUI Venturi
VNYE vandyke❑
VNYK Van Eyck
VOAE violate
VOET violent
VOIT violist
VPDY vapidly
VPUY vapoury
VQEO vaquero
VRAE variate
Versace
VRAN vervain
VRAT variant
verdant
versant
VRCS varices
VREA verbena
VREL vermeil
VREN verge on
VRER Vermeer
VREY variety
VRGS viragos
VRIG varying
verging
versing
VRIH varnish
VRIN vermian
version
VRIO vertigo
VRIR vernier❑
VRIT verdict
VRIY varsity
verbify
versify
VRLS verglas
VRLY virelay
VRNA veranda
Virunga
VROA variola
VROE verbose
VRON Virgoan
VROS various
VROT Vermont
VRSS viruses
VRTR Vorster
VRUA verruca
VRUE verdure
virgule
VRUL virtual
VSBE visible
VSBY visibly
VSCE vesicae
vesicle
VSCL vesical
VSEA viscera
VSES vespers
VSIE vestige
VSOD viscoid
VSOE viscose
VSOS viscous
VSOY visnomy
VSRB Vasarib
VSRL vestral
VSTR visitor
VSUA vascula
Vistula
VSUE vesture
VSVS vis-à-vis
VTAE vitiate
vittate
VTAX vitraux
VTBK Vitebsk
VTCN Vatican
VTFR vote for
VTIG vetting
VTIL vitriol
VTIS vitrics
VTIY vitrify
VTLI vitelli
VTLY vitally
VTMN vitamin
VTRA Vitoria
VTRN veteran
VTUS vatfuls
VUHN Vaughan
VUHR voucher
VUOS Vaudois
VUOX vaudoux
VURY Vouvray
VUTR vaunter
VVDY vividly
VVLI Vivaldi
VVLV Vavilov
VVRA vivaria
VXDY vexedly
VXLA vexilla
VXNY vixenly
VYGR voyager
VYLA Viyella®
WAAD weasand
WADN W H Auden
WAER whateer
WAFR what for
WAGE whangee
wrangle
WAHR weather
WAID wearied
WAIG wearing❑
weaving
whaling
WAIY wearily
WAKD whacked
wracked
WAKR whacker
WAKS whackos

WANT what not
whatnot
WANW what now?
WAOF wear off
WAOS weapons
WAOT wear out
WAPD wrapped
WAPR wrapper
WASE whaisle
WASP what's up?
WAST whatsit
WATN Wharton
WATY wealthy
WAVS wharves
WAZE whaizle
WBAE Web page
WBIE Web site
WBIG webbing
WBLR wobbler
WBOD web-toed
WBOT webfoot
WBTR Webster
WCEM wych-elm
WCHM Wickham
WCIA Wichita
WCLW Wicklow
WDBY wide boy
WDEL Weddell
WDEN widgeon
WDIG wadding
wedding
WDLR waddler
WDNR widener
WDOK wedlock
WDWD widowed
WDWR widower
WEDE wheedle
WEDR wielder
WEDY weekday
WEED weekend
WEEF whereof
WEEN wherein
WEEO whereso
whereto
WEER whene'er
whereer
WEES whereas
WEET whereat
WEEY whereby
WEFR weep for
WEHM Wrexham
WEHR whether
WEIG weeding
weeping
WEIY weevily
WEKD wrecked
WEKR wreaker
wrecker
WELE wheelie
WELR Wheeler
WEME whemmle
WENE wheenge
WENO woe unto

WEOE woesome
WEOT weed out
WEPE wheeple
WERT wherret
WESN Wheeson
WEST wheesht
WETE wreathe
wrestle
WETN wheaten
WETR whetter
wrester
WETS wreaths
WEZE wheezle
WFIG wafting
WFLY wofully
WFUE wafture
WGAE W G Grace
WGAL wagtail
WGES wigless
WGEY waggery
WGIG wigging
WGIH waggish
WGLR wiggler
WGNR wagoner
WGRR wagerer
WGTY wightly
WGWR wage war
WIAD Weiland
WIDE weirdie
WIDR whidder
WIDS weirdos
WIDY weirdly
WIEA weigela
WIEN write in
WIEO write to
WIEP write up
write-up
WIFE whiffle
WIFR wait for
WIGE wriggle
WIGR whinger
wringer
WIGY wriggly
WIHN weigh in
weigh-in
WIHP weigh up
WIHR weigher
whither
WIHY weighty
WIIG wailing
waiting
waiving
whining
whiting
writing
WIIH whitish
WIKD whisked
whiz kid
WIKE wrinkle
WIKR whicker
whisker
WIKY whiskey
wrinkly

WILM Whitlam
WILR whirler
WILW whitlow
WIMN Weizman
Whitman
WIOF wait off
WIPD whipped
WIPE Whipple
WIPR whimper
whipper
whisper
WIPT whippet
WISN Whitsun
WISW whipsaw
WISY whimsey
WITD waisted
WITE whistle
whittle❑
WITN written
WITR whitter
WKFL wakeful
WKMN Waksman
WKND wakened
WKNO waken to
WLAE Wallace
welfare
WLAL Walsall
WLAS wild ass
WLAY wallaby
WLCT wildcat
WLDG wild dog
WLIG walking
welding
welling
willing
wilting
WLIH wildish
wolfish
wolvish
WLIM William
WLIS wallies
willies
WLLT well-lit
WLMN wild man
WLOE Walpole
welcome
WLOF walk off
wall off
well off
well-off
WLON Walloon
WLOT Walcott
walk out
walk-out
wild oat
WLOY willowy
WLRD Wilfred
Wilfrid
WLRM wolfram
WLRN well-run
WLWY walkway
WLZR waltzer
WMIH wampish

wimpish
WMIK Wemmick
WMNY womanly
WMOT wimp out
WNAE wannabe
windage
WNAK win back
WNBG windbag
wine-bag
WNBR wine bar
WNES wanness
Wenders
wonders
WNEY wintery
WNHM Wyndham
WNHP winch up
WNIG wanking
wanting
winding
winging
winking
winning
WNIO windigo
WNIY windily
WNLD wing-led
WNLR wangler
Winkler
WNNT wing nut
WNOE winsome
WNOS Windows®
WNOT want out
WNPN win upon
WNRW windrow
WNSR Windsor
WNTN Winston
WNVR win over
won over
WOBB whoobub
WOCT woodcut
WOEA woomera
WOEL woosell
WOGD wronged
WOGN wrong 'un
WOGR wronger
WOGT wrought
WOGY wrongly
WOIG whoring
Wyoming
WOIY woozily
WOLD whorled
WOLN woollen
WOLW Wroclaw
WOLY Woolley
WOMN woodman
WONM Woosnam
WOPE whoopee
WOPR whooper
whopper
WOSY woolsey
WOTR wood tar
woofter
Wooster
WOVR whoever

WOWO who's who
WPED wappend
WPOT wipe out
wipeout
WRAE warfare
war game
wordage
WRAH warpath
WRAT warrant
WRAY war baby
WRBG workbag
WRBX workbox
WRDY work-day
worldly
WRED warhead
WRES workers
wurleys
WRFR work for
WRHG warthog
WRHP warship
worship
WRHR Werther
WRHT worth it
WRID worried
WRIE warlike
wartime
WRIG warning
warring
wording
working
WRIH warmish
WRIK Warwick
WRIR warrior
worrier
WRIS worries
wurlies
WRIY wordily
WRLR warbler
WRMN workman
workmen
WROD warlord
WROE war zone
WROF ward off
warn off
work off
WROG war song
war-song
WROK warlock
WRON war-torn
war-worn
WROT work out
workout
work-out
worm out
worn out
worn-out
WRSY workshy
work-shy
WRTD worsted
WRTH waratah
WRTP wiretap
wire-tap
worktop

WRUG Warburg
WSAE wastage
WSAL wassail
WSDP wised up
WSDY washday
WSEN western
WSFL wishful
wistful
WSFR wish for
WSGY wise guy
WSIG washing
wasting
wishing
WSIH waspish
WSMN wise man
Wiseman
WSOT wash out
washout
wash-out
WSRL wastrel
WSWG WYSIWYG
WTAD wetland
WTAE wattage
WTAK wet pack
WTES wetness
withers
witless
witness
WTEU Watteau
WTHD watched
WTHN watch in
WTHP watch up
WTHR watcher
wotcher
WTHT watch it!
WTIG witting
WTIH wettish
WTIY wittily
WTLD wattled
WTNW wet snow
WTOD Watford
WTOT without
WTRD watered
WTRR waterer
WTUT wet suit
WUDD wounded
WUDE would-be
WUDP wound up
WVLT wavelet
WVOF wave off
WVRR waverer
WXAM wax palm
WXEN wax bean
WXIG waxwing
WXIL waxbill
WXOD Wexford
WXOK waxwork
WXRE wax tree
WYAD Wayland
wayward
WYAK waymark
WYAS W B Yeats
WYEK wryneck
WYES wryness
WYIE wayside
WYIL waybill
wrybill
WYOE waygone
WYON wayworn
WYOT waypost
WYPR Whymper
WYVR whyever
WZEK Wozzeck
WZND wizened
XLMS xylomas
XMNS Ximenes
XNHC xanthic
XNKS Xenakis
XRMS xeromas
YANR yearner
YBIH yobbish
YBLS yibbles
YBOS yobboes
YDIH Yiddish
YEDO yield to
YEDR yielder
YGUT yoghurt
YHPD Y-shaped
YLIG yelling
YLNA Yolanda
YLOH yelloch
YLOY yellowy
YLSN Yeltsin
YNES Yonkers
YNSI Yenisei
YNTE Yangtze
YNYV Yanayev
YONE Yaoundé
YPIY yuppify
YRAE yardage
YRAG yardang
YRAM yard-arm
YRIT Yorkist
YRNA yaranga
YRNS Y-fronts
YRVN Yerevan
YSIA yeshiva
YSMK yashmak
YTGN yatagan
YTIM yttrium
YUAT you wait!
YUEN you're on!
YUGN young'un
YUGR younger
YUNW you know
YWIG yawning
yowling
ZAAD Zealand
ZAOS zealous
ZBLN Zebulun
ZBOD zebroid
ZCAY Zachary
ZDAY zedoary
ZDIS zaddiks
ZDNV Zhdanov
ZFOI zuffoli
ZGMS zygomas
ZGTC zygotic
ZIEN Zairean
Zoilean
ZIGI Zwingli
ZIKU Zwickau
ZIKV Zhivkov
ZKSI zakuski
ZLIA Zuleika
ZLIN zillion
ZLWR Zulu War
ZMEI Zambezi
ZMIN Zambian
ZMIY zombify
ZMOE zampone
ZMOI zamponi
ZMTA zemstva
ZMTC zymotic
ZNAA Zincala
Zingara
ZNAE Zingare
ZNAI Zincali
Zingari
ZNAO Zincalo
Zingaro
ZNBA Zenobia
ZNIE zincite
ZNIM zanyism
ZNIY zincify
zinkify
ZOCA zooecia
ZOIE zeolite
ZOIM Zionism
ZOIT Zionist
ZOOY zoology
zootomy
ZPOE zip code
ZPTP zap it up
ZRNS zorinos
ZSFL zestful
ZSMS Zosimus
ZTTC zetetic

8 letters – odd

AAAA agar-agar
amadavat
avadavat
AAAI ataraxia
ataraxic
AAAS anapaest
AAAT à la carte
amaranth
Atalanta
AABA Alan Bean
AABD Adam Bede
AABN Alan Bond
AABR Adalbert
AACI anarchic
AACO at anchor
AADA a raw deal
AADI Alasdair
AADN amandine
AAEI academia
academic
apatetic
AAEL amazedly
Arabella
AAET amaretto
AAEU Agapetus
AAFO away from
AAHI arachnid
AAHL as a whole
AAHM anathema
AAHR anaphora
AAHS anaphase
AAIC at an inch
at a pinch
AAIL Amarillo
AALN at a slant
AALP anableps
anaglyph
AAMN alarming
AAMS alarmism
alarmist
AAMV a bad move
AAOD anaconda
AAOI Amazonia
anabolic
AAON at a point
AAOU analogue
as a bonus
AARB anaerobe
AARC at a price
AARE a fair bet
AARO Anacreon
AART alacrity
AARU as a group
AASF Atansoff
AATI abattoir
Alan Tait
Alastair
AATN awaiting
AATR a bad turn
AATT a battuta
AATU acanthus
AATV adaptive
AAUC Acapulco
AAUE abacuses
AAWT away with
AAYE analyser
analyses
AAYI amarylis
analysis
analytic
ABAC ambiance
ABEC ambience
ABIH Albright
ABLN ambulant
ABLT ambulate
ABNA Albanian
ABNS albinism
ABOI ambrosia
ABOT Arbroath
ABRA arboreal
ABRH alberghi
ABRI amberoid
ABRT arboreta
ABSE ambushed
ABSO asbestos
Aubusson
ABTO ambition
at bottom

ABTS	albitise
ABTZ	albitize
ACAA	Archaean
ACAO	Alcmaeon
ACAS	archaise
	archaism
ACAZ	archaize
ACDA	Arcadian
ACDK	archduke
ACDN	acceding
	accident
ACDT	accede to
ACEI	accredit
ACIA	archival
ACIE	archives
ACLD	accolade
ACLN	Auckland
ACMC	arch-mock
ACNE	ascender
ACNL	arcanely
ACNO	accentor
ACOE	anchored
	anchoret
ACOI	A J Cronin
ACPE	accepted
ACPN	Al Capone
ACPO	acceptor
ACRC	accuracy
ACRE	accursed
ACRI	ascorbic
ACRT	accurate
ACSI	Alcestis
ACSN	accusing
ACSO	accuse of
	accustom
	ancestor
ACSR	ancestry
ACTS	ascetism
ACUE	accouter
ACUR	accoutre
ACUT	accounts
ACUU	Arcturus
ACWS	archwise
ADCE	addicted
ADCO	abductor
ADCT	abdicate
	audacity
ADEC	audience
ADEE	Andrewes
ADET	Andretti
ADHD	aldehyde
ADMR	Aldo Moro
ADNL	ardently
ADNT	Aldaniti
ADNU	addendum
ADOE	androgen
ADOO	Andropov
ADRA	alderman
ADRE	Adderley
	aldermen
	Alderney
	Andersen
ADRO	Anderson
ADTF	and stuff
ADTO	addition
	audition
ADTR	auditory
ADTV	additive
AEAC	abeyance
AEAD	Adelaide
AEAE	Adenauer
AEAI	Ave Maria
AEAL	amenable
	amenably
AEBC	Auerbach
AEBT	acerbate
	acerbity
AECR	amelcorn
AEDE	Aberdeen
AEDT	anecdote
AEGN	avenging
AEHI	anechoic
AEHN	Alekhine
AEHS	amethyst
	Arethusa
AEIA	American
AEIE	alewives
AEII	aperitif
AEIN	aperient
AEMN	abetment
	averment
AENS	agedness
AEOA	adenomas
AEOS	alehouse
AERE	Averroës
AERN	aberrant
	aleurone
AERS	aneurism
	aneurysm
AERT	aberrate
AERU	age group
AESI	aseismic
AESL	aversely
AESO	aversion
AETE	a-weather
AETN	abetting
	Aventine
AETR	aleatory
	aperture
AEUC	adequacy
AEUT	adequate
AFAC	affiance
AFCE	affected
AFEC	alfresco
AFIH	affright
AFNE	Anfinsen
AFNT	affinity
AFRN	afferent
AFRS	afforest
AFSO	affusion
AFUN	affluent
AGAI	au gratin
AGAL	arguable
	arguably
AGBR	Augsburg
AGEE	Anglesey
AGEO	angle for
	argue for
AGET	aigrette
AGIA	Anglican
AGIL	aiguille
	Anguilla
AGIV	aggrieve
AGKO	angekkok
AGLC	angelica□
	Angelico
AGLN	Angelina
AGMN	argument
AGNI	Algonkin
AGNN	arginine
AGNT	alginate
AGOA	angiomas
	as good as
AGRN	angering
AGRO	Algernon
AGSA	Augustan
AGSL	augustly
AGSU	Augustus
AGTL	argutely
AGTO	angstrom
	Ångström
AHCR	ad hocery
AHEE	achieved
	achiever
AHEI	athletic
AHIE	an-heires
AHLE	Achilles
AHLO	aphelion
AHLU	Achelous
AHMR	Alhambra
AHNA	Athenian
AHNL	achingly
AHOA	achromat
AHRF	Ashcroft
AHRM	atheroma
AHRN	adherent
	adhering
AHRO	Atherton
AHRS	aphorise
	aphorism
	aphorist
AHRT	adhere to
AHRZ	aphorize
AHSO	adhesion
AHSV	adhesive
AHTS	aphetise
	athetise
AHTZ	aphetize
	athetize
AIAE	agitated
	animated
AIAI	animalic
AIAL	amicable
	amicably
	animally
	apically
AIAN	avifauna
AIAO	agitator
	animator
AIAT	Alicante
AICO	a piece of
AIDO	acid drop
AIEN	Avicenna
AIHA	acid-head
AIHN	a big hand
AIII	ab initio
AIJZ	acid jazz
AILG	axiology
AILO	a million
AILR	axillary
AILT	axiality
AIMC	a bit much
AIMR	Aviemore
AIMS	amidmost
AINC	avionics
AINP	Ayia Napa
AINS	Arianise
	aridness
AINT	alienate
AINU	amiantus
AINZ	Arianize
AIOI	acidosis
	amitosis
	amitotic
	aniconic
AIPO	agitprop
AIRA	apiarian
AIRC	acid rock
AIRI	acid rain
AIRS	apiarist
	aviarist
AIRT	acierate
AISN	aliasing
AITD	Aristide
AITI	Alistair
AITO	aviation
AIUA	acicular
AIUU	aciduous
AIVE	a dim view
AIWR	as it were
AJCL	abjectly
AJCN	adjacent
AJLO	Al Jolson
AJSE	adjusted
	adjuster
AJTN	adjutant
AJVN	adjuvant
AKBU	ask about
AKDO	asked for
AKLE	alkalies
AKLF	alkalify
AKLI	alkaloid
AKLN	alkaline
AKLS	alkalise
	ankylose
AKLZ	alkalize
AKNA	Arkansas
AKNO	Atkinson
AKOA	Ark Royal
AKOI	ask for it
AKON	acknowne
	ask round

Words marked □ can also be spelled with an initial capital letter

ALAC	alliance
ALBE	ad-libber
ALBU	all about
ALCT	allocate
ALDT	allude to
ALGO	allegros
ALGR	allegory
ALHN	all-thing
ALHR	all there
ALIH	all right
	all-right
ALIK	all-risks
ALLI	alleluia
ALLN	all along
ALME	aglimmer
ALNA	as long as
ALNE	Atlantes
ALNI	Atlantic
	Atlantis
ALNL	all in all
ALNN	all in one
ALNO	ailantos
ALNT	at length
ALOL	All Souls
ALON	all found
	all round
	all-round
ALOT	all mouth
ALPC	allspice
ALRE	allergen
ALRI	allergic
ALRN	alluring
ALSI	aplastic
ALSO	allusion
ALSV	allusive
ALTE	aflutter
	aglitter
	all at sea
	allotted
ALTO	ablation
	ablution
ALTR	All Stars
ALTV	ablative
ALVA	alluvial
ALVR	at livery
ALVU	alluvium
ALWN	allowing
ALWO	allow for
ALYA	alleyway
ALYN	allaying
AMAN	armgaunt
AMCA	as much as
AMGA	Armagnac
AMGT	almighty❑
AMHI	armchair
AMLS	atmolyse
AMLZ	atmolyze
AMMN	armament
AMNA	Armenian
	as many as
AMNR	arm-in-arm
AMNS	admonish
AMNT	ammonite

AMNU	ammonium
	Arminius
AMRA	armorial
AMRN	admiring
AMRR	admirers
AMTE	admitted
AMTR	armature
AMUE	armoured
	armourer
ANAL	annually
ANCS	at no cost
ANFR	Anna Ford
ANGT	abnegate
ANLE	annulled
ANLS	annalise
	annalist
ANLZ	annalize
ANRA	abnormal
ANSA	amnesiac
ANSE	Agnus Dei
ANSI	agnostic
ANTM	at no time
ANTO	annattos
ANTT	annotate
ANUC	announce
ANXO	annexion
ANYN	annoying
AOAI	aromatic
AOAL	adorable
	adorably
	avowable
AOAO	avocados
AOAR	Avogadro
AOAU	abomasum
AOBM	atom bomb
AODA	a good way
AODE	a good bet
	a good few
AODU	a good buy
AOEA	above par
	as one man
AOEI	alopecia
	anorexia
	anorexic
AOEL	above all
	avowedly
AOEO	atone for
AOET	amoretti
AOGA	a long way
AOHG	apophyge
	apothegm
AOIE	agonized
	atomiser
	atomizer
AOLO	Apollyon
AOLX	apoplexy
AONE	anointer
AONI	abound in
AONN	aborning
	adorning
AONT	amount to
AOOB	Akosombo
AOOI	apodosis

	apologia
AOOO	amorosos
AOOU	apologue
AORN	apocrine
AOSI	acoustic
AOSN	arousing
AOTN	aborting
	Agostini
AOTO	abortion
	adoption
AOTS	amortise
	apostasy
AOTT	apostate
AOTV	abortive
	adoptive
AOTZ	amortize
AOVR	à couvert
	aloe vera
APAA	alpha ray
	appear as
APAE	alphabet
	appeaser
	at prayer
APAS	applause
	appraise
APAT	appeal to
APCN	Al Pacino
APEA	Applemac®
APEI	apple pie
APEO	Appleton
APEU	amplexus
APGI	arpeggio
APIA	apprisal
APIE	apprised
APIO	amphipod
APIT	at points
APIU	appliqué
APLA	ampullae
APLE	appalled
APNG	appanage
APNI	appendix
APOA	amphorae
	approval
APOC	approach
APOE	approved
	asphodel
APOI	amphoric
APRE	asperser
APRG	amperage
APRL	apperill
APRN	apparent
	aspirant
	aspiring
APRT	asperate
	asperity
	aspirate
	aspire to
APST	apposite
APTN	appetent
APTS	appetise
APTT	amputate
	appetite
APTZ	appetize

APYI	apply oil
	asphyxia
APYO	apply for
AQAN	acquaint
AQEU	arquebus
AQIE	acquired
ARAD	airwards
ARAI	Adriatic
ARAL	aerially
ARAN	Adrianne
ARBC	aerobics
ARCL	Agricola
ARCT	atrocity
ARDE	abridged
ARDL	Airedale
ARDN	abrading
ARDT	acridity
AREN	Adrienne
	agreeing
AREO	arrieros
ARFI	aerofoil
ARFR	Agra Fort
ARGA	aerogram
ARGN	arrogant
ARGT	abrogate
	arrogate
ARHR	Ayrshire
ARIE	airliner
ARIH	airtight
ARIL	adroitly
	airfield
	air rifle
ARIO	afraid of
ARLN	airplane
ARLT	aerolite
	aerolith
ARLU	Aurelius
ARMN	acrimony
	agrimony
ARNA	apron-man
ARNE	air inlet
	arranged
	arranger
ARNL	arrantly
ARNM	agronomy
ARNO	at random
ARNS	airiness
AROA	airwoman
AROC	air force
AROI	air-to-air
ARON	airborne
ARPC	airspace
ARPE	airspeed
ARPL	abruptly
ARPN	atropine
ARRA	agrarian
ARRF	aircraft
ARRK	air brake
ARRM	airframe
ARRS	air-brush
	air frost
ARSE	arrester
ARSG	a presage

Words marked ❑ can also be spelled with an initial capital letter

ARSI	acrostic
	agrestic
	aoristic
ARSK	après-ski
ARSO	abrasion
ARSV	abrasive
ARTA	Amritsar
ARTI	airstrip
ARTO	aeration
ARVA	arrive at
ARVI	au revoir
ARVN	arriving
ARVR	aardvark
ARWL	aardwolf
ASEG	absterge
ASET	answer to
ASGE	assigned
	assignee
ASGO	assignor
ASHT	aesthete
ASIA	aestival
ASIB	as said by
ASIE	assailer
	auspices
ASIS	abscissa
ASLE	absolved
ASLT	absolute□
ASML	assemble
	assembly□
ASMN	assuming
ASND	arsenide
ASNE	absentee
	an sonnet
ASNH	absinthe
ASNL	absently
ASNS	arsonist
ASNT	arsenite
	assent to
	assonate
ASNU	Ausonius
ASOA	as soon as
ASOE	aasvogel
ASRA	Assyrian
	Austrian
ASRC	abstract
	abstrict
ASRE	absorbed
	assorted
ASRL	absurdly
	australe
ASRN	anserine
ASRS	abstruse
ASSI	assassin
	assist in
ASSO	assessor
ASTA	Alsatian
ATAA	astragal
ATAE	anteater
ATAL	actually
ATAU	Art Tatum
ATBD	antibody
ATBH	autobahn
ATCA	autocrat
ATCD	antecede
ATCE	alto clef
	articled
	articles
	attached
	attacker
ATCI	autacoid
ATCS	Atticise
	Atticism
ATCT	astucity
	attach to
ATCU	Arts Club
ATCZ	Atticize
ATDF	auto-da-fé
ATDN	autodyne
ATDT	antedate
	antidote
ATEA	at the bar
ATEE	antlered
ATEI	anthelia
	anthemia
	anthesis
	asthenia
	asthenic
ATEN	at the end
ATFC	artefact
	artifact
	artifice
ATFO	act of God
ATFX	antefixa
ATGM	autogamy
ATGN	Antigone
ATGR	autogiro
	autogyro
ATHR	autoharp
ATIG	astringe
ATLC	anti-lock
ATLP	antelope
ATLS	autolyse
ATLZ	autolyze
ATMN	antimony
ATMR	Altamira
ATMT	automata
	automate
ATNA	actiniae
	actinias
	antennae
	antennas
ATND	actinide
	antinode
ATNE	attended
	attender
ATNM	antinomy
	autonomy
ATNO	attend on
ATNS	astonish
ATNT	attend to
	autunite
ATNU	actinium
	Antonius
ATOG	although
	as though
ATOS	antrorse
ATPO	antiphon
ATPP	antipope
ATPS	ante-post
ATQE	antiques
ATRA	after tax
	after-tax
	arterial
	Asturias
ATRE	arteries
	attorney
ATRH	autarchy
ATRI	asteroid
	autarkic
ATRL	after all
ATRO	altar boy
	anterior
	anteroom
ATRS	asterisk
ATRU	apterous
ATRY	aftereye
ATSE	attested
ATSI	artistic
	autistic
ATSM	autosome
ATSR	anti-sera
	artistry
ATST	attest to
ATTD	altitude
	aptitude
	attitude
ATTL	astutely
ATTM	autotomy
ATTN	astatine
ATTP	autotype
ATUL	artfully
ATUS	altruism
	altruist
ATVL	actively
ATVR	antevert
ATVS	activism
	activist
ATVT	activate
	activity
AUAO	adulator
AUCO	Asunción
AUDC	aqueduct
AUDE	Amundsen
AUDN	abundant
AUEL	amusedly
AUEO	azulejos
AUET	aculeate
AUEU	Apuleius
AUHB	Abu Dhabi
AUIA	Abu Nidal
AUKA	Ayub Khan
AULL	arum lily
AULN	aqualung
	aquiline
AUMN	abutment
AURA	Aquarian
AURU	aquarium
	Aquarius
AUSL	aguishly
AUTN	abutting
	aquatint
AUTR	adultery
AUVD	ayurveda
AVCA	advocaat
AVCC	advocacy
AVCT	advocate
AVLU	au voleur
AVNE	advanced
	advances
AVOA	alveolar
AVOU	alveolus
AVSN	advising
AVSR	advisers
	advisory
AWLA	as well as
AWNA	Aswan Dam
AWTE	atwitter
AYAC	Amy March
AYDL	amygdala
	amygdale
	amygdule
AYEG	asynergy
AYHN	anything
AYHR	anywhere
AYIA	atypical
AYNS	Aryanise
AYNZ	Aryanize
AYTL	asystole
BAAA	bear away
BAAL	bearable
	bearably
	beatable
	blamable
	blamably
BAAO	bravados
BAAT	Bramante
BAAZ	Braganza
BABC	beat back
BABE	brambles
BABN	blabbing
BABR	Bradbury
BACE	blanched
	branched
BACS	Brancusi
BADA	Boardman
BADC	boat deck
BADE	brandied
	brand-new
BADN	boarding
BADS	blandish
	brandish
BADU	board out
BADW	bear down
	beat down
BAEA	brake pad
BAEE	blazered
	bracelet
BAEL	brazenly
BAEO	braseros
BAEU	blare out
BAFR	Beaufort
	Bradford

BAGN	bragging
BAGR	braggart
BAHA	brachial
BAHO	biathlon
BAHR	bear hard
BAHU	beach-hut
	brachium
BAIE	Boadicea
BAIG	bearings
BAII	beatific
	Brasília
BAKA	black cap
	blackcap
	black rat
BAKC	black ice
BAKE	blackleg
	Black Sea
BAKI	black tie
BAKL	blackfly
BAKN	blacking
BAKO	black box
	Black Dog
	Black Rod
BAKR	black art
BAKS	brackish
BAKT	blankets
	blankety
BAKU	black out
	blackout
	blank out
BAKY	black eye
BALE	brailler
BALN	beagling
	brawling
BAMN	Beaumont
BANA	biannual
BANO	brainbox
BANS	brainish
BAOR	blazonry
BAPC	brat pack
BAPL	beanpole
BAPT	Brad Pitt
BARC	Beatrice
	Boat Race
	boat race
BART	Biarritz
BASA	brass hat
BASC	brassica
BASF	brass off
BASI	bearskin
BASL	brassily
BATA	bracteal
BATC	brattice
BATE	beauties
BATF	beautify
	blast off
	blast-off
BATI	beat to it
BATL	beastily
	blastula
BATN	blasting
	boasting
BATR	Blantyre
BATS	brattish
BATU	blast out
	boastful
BAUO	bear upon
	beat up on
BAVI	Beauvais
	Beauvoir
BAWT	bear with
BAYR	boat-yard
BBDL	baby doll
BBGO	Babygros
BBHO	babyhood
BBIA	biblical
BBLN	babbling
	bobolink
	bubbling
BBLU	bibulous
BBRT	Babe Ruth
BBSK	babushka
BBTY	bobstays
BBYA	Bob Dylan
BBYI	bobby-pin
BCAA	baccarat
	back away
	Buchanan
BCAC	bechance
	by chance
BCAE	béchamel
BCAH	backache
BCAO	buckaroo
BCBA	backbeat
BCBN	backbone
BCBT	backbite❑
BCCA	backchat
BCCM	back-comb
BCDO	back-door
	backdrop
BCDT	back-date
BCDW	back down
BCEI	bacteria
BCEO	bachelor
BCFL	backfill
BCFR	backfire
	Beckford
BCHE	back-heel
BCHN	backhand
BCHR	buckhorn
BCLA	back-load
BCLE	becalmed
BCLS	backlash
	backlist
BCLT	buckle to
BCLU	bacillus
BCMN	becoming
BCNE	biconvex
BCOC	by choice
BCPC	backpack
BCRO	backroom
BCSD	backside
BCSE	buckshee
BCSI	backspin
	bicuspid
	buckskin
BCSO	backstop
	buckshot
BCTN	bucatini
BCVL	backveld
BCWR	backward
BCWS	backwash
BCYR	backyard
BDAD	bedwards
BDAE	bedeafen
BDAI	bad habit
BDAL	beddable
	biddable
BDAT	bad faith
	bad taste
BDBL	bedabble
BDBO	body blow
BDEC	bedrench
BDEE	badgered
BDGI	Badoglio
BDGL	bedaggle
BDHS	Buddhism
	Buddhist
BDIE	bad vibes
	bed linen
	bed-linen
BDLI	buddleia
BDLN	bodyline
BDLO	bad blood
BDLS	bodiless
BDML	bad smell
BDNE	Bodensee
BDNG	badinage
BDNO	by dint of
BDOE	bedcover
BDOK	bedsocks
BDOT	badmouth
	bad-mouth
BDPS	Budapest
BDRA	bad break
	bad dream
BDRE	bedarken
BDRS	bad press
BDSG	by design
BDSI	bodysuit
BDSO	body shop
BDTA	bedstead
	bedstraw
BDUN	Bedouins
BDVR	Bedivere
BDWR	bodywork
BDYF	badly off
BDYI	badly lit
BDYU	Buddy Guy
BDZL	bedazzle
BEAE	bee-eater
BEAO	beefalos
BEBH	Beerbohm
BECE	bleached
	bleacher
	breeches
BECK	beefcake
BEDI	breadbin
BEDN	bleeding
	blending
	breeding
BEEE	Baedeker
BEGE	Breughel
BEHE	brethren
	Brezhnev
BEHI	Blenheim
BEHU	beech nut
	Boethius
BEIR	breviary
BEKF	break off
BEKG	breakage
BEKN	breaking
BEKO	break-vow
BEKU	break out
	breakout
BELN	beetling
BEMT	bregmata
BENA	biennial
BERL	blearily
BERO	beetroot
BESN	blessing
BESO	bless you
BETE	breather
BETI	breath in
BETN	bleating
	Brentano
BEUC	Blefuscu
BEWR	Boer Wars
BEZL	breezily
BEZU	breeze up
BFCL	bifocals
BFDL	befuddle
BFEE	buffered
BFIG	befringe
BFIN	befriend
BFLN	baffling
BFOE	beflower
BGAE	beggared
BGAL	beggarly
BGER	Bagheera
BGET	baguette
	bigfeets
BGHE	big wheel
BGHT	big shots
BGIE	bagpiper
	bagpipes
	begrimed
	beguiled
	big timer
BGMK	big smoke
BGMS	bigamist
BGMU	bigamous
BGNE	beginner
BGOS	big noise
BGOT	big mouth
	bigmouth
	big-mouth
BGRA	begorrah
BGTC	big stick
BGTE	begetter
BGUG	begrudge
BGUK	big bucks

BGYA	bogeyman
BHLE	beholden
	beholder
	by halves
BHMA	bohemian❑
BHMT	behemoth
BIAA	boil away
BIAL	bribable
BIBN	Brisbane
BICE	britches
	by inches
BIDA	Blind Bay
BIDE	Blind Pew
	brindled
BIDN	blinding
	building
BIDS	Brindisi
BIDW	boil down
BIFN	briefing
BIGF	bring off
BIGN	Bridgend
BIGO	bring low
BIGU	bring out
BIHE	blighted
	blighter
	brighten
BIHL	blithely
	brightly
BIHO	Brighton
BIKA	brickbat
BIKE	brick-red
BIKN	blinking
BILA	bridle at
BILN	brisling
BILS	brimless
BIMN	brimming
BINN	Brian Eno
BIOE	boil over
	brim over
BIPS	blimpish
BISA	bailsman
BISL	by itself
BISU	blissful
BITE	bristled
BITI	Brittain
BITL	bristols
BITR	blistery
BIZR	blizzard
BJBR	bejabers
BJSI	bejesuit
BKAI	Bukharin
BKLT	Bakelite®
BKWL	Bakewell
BLAE	Ballades
BLAI	balsamic
	Bulganin
	Bulgaria
BLAK	bulwarks
BLAO	Bulgakov
BLAS	Bel Paese
	bel paese
BLAT	bel canto
BLBA	bilabial
BLBO	bell buoy
BLBT	bilobate
BLBU	belabour
BLCC	ballcock
BLDW	bolt down
BLDZ	bulldoze
BLEE	believed
	believer
BLEI	balletic
	bulletin
BLER	balneary
	bilberry
BLEU	bulge out
BLFC	bold face
BLFL	bill-fold
BLFO	bullfrog
BLGR	ball-girl
BLHA	bulkhead
	bullhead
BLHL	bolthole
BLHN	belching
BLHO	billhook
BLHS	Balkhash
BLIN	billions
BLIR	billiard
BLIT	bull into
BLKL	bull kelp
BLMN	Bultmann
BLNE	balanced
	balancer
BLNS	baldness
	boldness
BLNT	belong to
BLOA	balmoral
	Belmopan
BLOK	ballocks
	bollocks
BLOO	Belgorod
BLPR	ball park
	ballpark
BLPT	baldpate
BLRC	baldrick
BLRD	Belgrade
BLRO	ballroom
BLRT	Billroth
BLSE	baluster
BLSI	bullshit
BLSY	bull's eye
	Bullseye
	bull's-eye
BLTL	belittle
BLTN	bell tent
BLVN	beloving
BLWA	below par
BLWI	bullwhip
BLWY	Bulawayo
BLYA	ballyrag
	bullyrag
BLYN	bullying
BLYO	ballyhoo
	billy boy
	bully boy
	bully-boy
BLYU	bellyful
BMIO	bambinos
BMIT	bump into
BMLC	bum-clock
BMLN	bumbling
BMNA	bimanual
BMSN	bemusing
BMST	bombsite
BMTE	be mother
	bum steer
BMWL	by my will
BNAE	bandaged
BNAI	Benjamin
BNAL	bendable
	binnacle
BNAN	bandanna
BNAO	bungalow
BNDC	Benedick
	Benedict
BNDR	Benidorm
BNEE	banneret
	banterer
BNEI	Ben Nevis
BNEN	bingeing
BNEO	banderol
	bontebok
BNEU	bandeaux
BNFC	benefact
	benefice
	Boniface
BNFD	bona fide
BNGE	bang goes
BNGL	benignly
BNHA	Bankhead
	bench saw
	bonehead
BNHG	bank-high
BNHL	bunghole
BNHN	bunching
BNHZ	Benghazi
BNIC	Bentinck
BNIE	bin-liner
BNIL	Banville
	bone idle
	bone-idle
BNIR	banditry
BNIT	banditti
BNLN	bungling
	buntline
BNLO	Ben Elton
BNLS	banalise
	boneless
BNLT	banality
BNLU	bundle up
BNLZ	banalize
BNMA	binomial
	bone meal
BNME	benumbed
BNMI	bondmaid
BNMN	bonamani
BNNS	boniness
BNNT	banknote
BNOA	Ben Hogan
BNOB	buncombe
BNOE	bind over
BNOI	Benvolio
	bonhomie
BNOS	banjoist
BNRA	Bonar Law
BNRF	Bancroft
BNRL	bankroll
BNRP	bankrupt
BNSA	bandsman
	bondsman
BNSE	banished
	banister
BNTO	be nuts on
BNUA	binaural
BNUI	banausic
BNUO	bone up on
BNWE	bindweed
BNWO	bentwood
BNWR	banewort
BNWS	bendwise
BNYU	bunny-hug
BOAA	blow away
BOAC	buoyance
	buoyancy
BOAE	brocaded
BOAL	bookable
	bootable
BOBA	browbeat
BOCE	blotched
BOCL	broccoli
BOCO	bronchos
BOCP	bioscope
BOCS	bookcase
BOCT	broach to
BOCU	book club
	bronchus
BODE	bloodied
	blood-red
BODL	bloodily
BODN	brooding
BOEI	broken in
BOEL	brokenly
BOEO	blokedom
BOER	biometry
BOES	blokeish
BOEU	booked-up
BOGA	brougham
BOHH	brouhaha
BOHR	brochure
	brothers
BOHS	boothose
BOII	bromidic
BOJC	boot-jack
BOKD	blockade
BOKE	Brookner
BOKF	block off
BOKG	blockage
BOKN	blocking
BOKS	blockish
BOKU	block out
BOKY	Brooklyn
BOLC	booklice

	bootlace
	bootlick
BOLN	broiling
BOLS	book list
	bootless
BOMN	blooming
BOMR	bloomers
	bookmark
BOMT	book-mate
BONA	brown-bag
	brown fat
	brown rat
BONL	brown ale
BONN	browning❑
BONS	brownish
BONU	blown-out
BONW	brown owl
BOOE	blow over
BOOI	bionomic
BOPP	blowpipe
BORP	biograph
BOSA	bioassay
BOSL	boot sale
BOSM	blossomy
BOSN	browsing
BOSO	bookshop
BOTB	boob tube
BOTM	boom time
BOTN	bloating
	blotting
	boosting
BOWR	bookworm
BOZN	bronzing
BPIE	baptized
BPIT	Baptists
BQET	bequeath
BRAA	Barnabas
BRAE	bereaved
BRAI	barbaric
BRAK	barracks
BRAL	barnacle
	Barrault
	burnable
BRAO	Barbados
	bergamot
BRBA	Barabbas
BRBC	bareback
BRBL	bird-bolt
BRBN	barebone
BRBR	beriberi
BRBT	birdbath
BRBU	burn blue
BRCE	Burschen
BRCG	birdcage
BRCK	barm cake
BRCL	bird call
	birdcall
BRDW	burn down
BREA	Bergerac
BREE	barterer
	Berkeley
	bordered
	borderer
	burdened
BREI	Berzelis
BREL	Bargello
	bordello
BREO	border on
BRER	barberry
	Burberry
BRES	bargeese
	berceuse
BREU	barbecue
	barbeque
	berceaux
	Bordeaux
BRFE	Born Free
BRFO	barefoot
	bereft of
BRGT	by rights
BRHA	birthday
BRHL	borehole
	Burchill
BRHN	birching
BRHO	birthdom
BRHR	bar chart
BRIA	barbican
BRII	bursitis
BRIL	Bareilly
BRIO	Barbizon
	barricos
	burritos
BRKM	Bergkamp
BRLM	bird-lime
BRLR	burglary
BRNA	baronial
	Berengar
BRNC	Berenice
BRNL	boringly
BRNS	bareness
	baroness
BROE	bar-coded
	borrowed
	borrower
BROP	Bardolph
BRRP	bar graph
BRSA	barostat
BRSD	Burnside
BRSE	Barnsley
	birdseed
BRSN	bird song
BRSO	birdshot
BRSY	Birdseye
BRTB	born to be
BRTE	barathea
BRTN	baritone
	berating
	bursting
BRTR	by return
BRTU	burnt out
	burst out
BRUA	Bermudan
	Bermudas
BRUD	burgundy❑
BRUH	barouche
BRUS	Barbusse
BRYA	Berryman
BRYN	biriyani
BRYR	barnyard
BSAC	Bismarck
BSAI	Bassanio
BSAL	bistable
BSAU	bust a gut
BSBB	bushbaby
	bush-baby
BSBC	bushbuck
BSBD	busybody
BSBL	baseball
	be so bold
BSCE	bass clef
	bisected
BSCM	base camp
BSCO	bisector
BSDU	basidium
	bass drum
BSEE	besieged
	Bessemer
BSER	basketry
BSFO	be soft on
BSFR	bushfire
BSIC	besmirch
BSIE	bassinet
BSIL	bastille❑
BSIR	bestiary
BSLC	basilica
BSLI	basaltic
BSLN	bustling
BSLS	baseless
	basilisk❑
BSMN	basement
BSNE	Basinger
BSNO	Besançon
BSNS	baseness
	business
	busyness
BSNU	basinful
BSOA	bestowal
BSPR	best part
BSRA	bespread
	bestreak
BSRD	bestride
BSRT	base rate
BSTE	besotted
BSTO	Basothos
BSUT	biscuits
	biscuity
BSVL	bushveld
BSWL	bushwalk
BSWO	basswood
BSWT	busy with
BSXA	bisexual
BTAA	betrayal❑
BTAE	betrayed
	betrayer
BTBC	bite back
BTCB	bathcube
BTEA	Betjeman
	by the way
BTEE	battered
	bothered
BTEI	bathetic
	batterie
BTEL	bitterly
BTEU	butter up
BTEY	by the bye
BTHL	bitchily
BTHN	botching
BTHR	butcher's
	butchery
BTII	botritis
BTIO	butt in on
BTLS	bateless
	botulism
BTLU	bottle up
BTNS	botanise
	botanist
BTNZ	botanize
BTOK	buttocks
BTOU	button up
BTRB	bathrobe
BTRO	bathroom
	botargos
BTRS	buttress
BTSZ	bitesize
BTTO	betatron
BTTS	beta test
	beta-test
BTUS	Bathurst
BTWC	bethwack
BTWN	Botswana
BTYI	bit by bit
BUAL	brutally
BUBB	blue baby
BUBL	bluebell
BUBR	bluebird
BUCA	Bluecoat
BUCI	blue-chip
BUCL	bouncily
BUCN	bouncing
BUDR	boundary
BUET	brunette
BUFA	blue flag
BUFL	blue film
BUFN	blue funk
	bouffant
BUGE	blue-grey
	Brueghel
BUGO	bludgeon
BUHF	brush off
	brush-off
BUHN	blushing
	brushing
BUIC	Boudicca
BUIU	boutique
BUKE	Bruckner
BUKT	Blunkett
BULN	baubling
BULO	bouillon
BUNL	Blue Nile
BUNS	blueness
BUNT	blue note
BUOK	bouzouki

BUON Boulogne
BUSL Brussels
BUSN bruising
BUTR blustery
BUTU blurt out
BUUT bouquets
BVLE bevelled
BVLN bivalent
BVNL bovinely
BVRE Beverley
BVRG beverage
BVTO bevatron
BWBR bawd-born
BWEL bi-weekly
BWIH by weight
BWLE bewilder
BWOE bowl over
BWPI bowsprit
BWRO be wary of
BWST be wise to
BYAL bi-yearly
BYET Bayreuth
BYSL boyishly
BZET bozzetti
BZWR buzz word
CAAA chalazae
chalazas
CAAE charades
CAAT chapatti
ciabatta
CABA chambray
CABC claw back
clawback
CABE cramboes
CABL crabbily
CABR Chambers
CACA charcoal
CACI chance it
Cratchit
CACO chance on
CACR chancery
CADA Claudian
CADE chandler❑
CADN cladding
Claudine
CADO chawdron
CADU Claudius
CAEC Clarence
coalesce
CAEL cranefly
cravenly
CAEN czarevna
CAEO chaperon
CAEU chapeaux
châteaux
CAFC coalface
CAFN chaffing
CAFR Crawford
CAFS crawfish
crayfish
CAGF Chargaff
CAGH Changsha
CAGN changing
CAGU change up
clangour
CAHA coachman
CAHN clashing
coaching
crashing
CAHU crash out
CAID Clarinda
CAIE chamises
clarinet
CAIL clavicle
CAIM charisma
craniums
CAIO chamisos
clarinos
CAIS Clarissa
CAKE cracknel
CAKL crankily
CAKN cracking
CAKO crackpot
CAKR crackers
CAKU chalk out
CALC charlock
CALD charlady
CALI chaplain
CALN Charlene
crawling
CALO Charlton
CAML clammily
CAMN charming
claimant
coalmine
cramming
CAMR claymore
CANA chainsaw
CANE Charnley
crannied
CANL channels
CANS clannish
CAOA Chaco War
CAOE cyanogen
cyanosed
CAOI cyanosis
cyanotic
CAON chaconne
CAOR Chamorro
CAPL Chappell
CAPN Ciampino
clapping
CAPO champion❑
CAPP claypipe
CAPR champers
clappers
Coalport
CARA chairman
CARO chat room
CASA clansman
class war
CASC clarsach
CASF classify
CASL coarsely
CASN classing
CASO chat show
CASR claustra
CASU chasseur
CATA claptrap
CATE Chartres
CATG chantage
CATL chastely
chattels
craftily
CATO coaction
CATS Chartism
Chartist
chastise
CATT chastity
CATV coactive
CAUL chasuble
CAUU coagulum
CAWC Chadwick
CAWS crabwise
CBCE caboched
CBCO cabochon
CBEB cobwebby
CBIL cabriole
CBLI cobaltic
CBLN cobbling
CBLR cobblers
cobblery
CBNO cabin boy
CBOL caboodle
CBRO cube root
CCAE Cyclades
cyclamen
CCAO cockatoo
CCBA cockboat
CCBL cocobolo
CCCL Coca Cola®
CCCO cockcrow
cock-crow
CCEA cycleway
CCEE cockerel
cock-eyed
CCIA cyclical
CCII coccidia
CCLA cochleae
cochlear
CCLG cacology
CCLN cackling
CCME cucumber
CCNF cocknify
CCOE Cyclopes
cycloses
CCOI cyclonic
CCPL coco-palm
CCRN cicerone
ciceroni
CCSE cicisbei
CCSR cocksure
CCTE coco-tree
CCTI cicatrix
cocktail
CCUE cactuses
CCYE coccyges
CDCT caducity
CDCU caducous
CDFE codified
codifier
CDLA Cadillac®
CDLU cuddle up
CDVN ci-devant
CEAI clematis
CEAS crevasse
CECE clenched
CECN crescent❑
CECO coercion
CECV coercive
CEEC clemency
credence
CEED credenda
CEEL cleverly
crenelle
CEEN Cheyenne
CEEO Clevedon
CEET Clemente
CEHR Cheshire
CEIA chemical
clerical
CEIE clerihew
CEIL chenille
credible
credibly
CEIO creditor
CEIU crepitus
CEKF check off
CEKL cheekily
creakily
CEKN checking
creaking
CEKR checkers
CEKS clerkess
clerkish
CEKT cheeky to
CEKU check out
checkout
CELN clew-line
CEME cream-tea
CEMR creamery
CENC crew neck
CENE cleansed
cleanser
CENN cleaning
CENT Chemnitz
CENU clean-cut
clean out
CEOE Cherokee
chew over
CEOI coenobia
CEON cretonne
CEPN creeping
CERA clearway
CERF clear off
CERL cheerily
CERN cheering
clearing
CERO cheerios
CERU cheerful
Chevreul
clear-cut

clear out
CESA chessman
CESD Cressida
CESO Chepstow
CEST creosote
CESU crease up
CETN cheating
coextend
creatine
creating
CETO creation□
CETR creature
CETU chestnut
CETV creative
CEUA caesurae
caesuras
CEUI cherubic
cherubim
cherubin
CEUU Coelurus
CEVG cleavage
CEVT cleave to
CFEN caffeine
CFLN cufflink
CFNI café noir
CGBR cagebird
CGHE cogwheel
CGIR Cagliari
CGNL cogently
CGNS caginess
CGOC cognosce
CGOE cognomen
CGTT cogitate
CHBT cohobate
CHRN coherent
CHSO cohesion
CHSV cohesive
CIAA Chinaman
CIAE China tea
chivaree
CIAI climatic
CIAR chimaera□
chivalry
CIBF climb off
CIBG cribbage
CIBN climbing
cribbing
CICA chitchat
chit-chat
CICD coincide
CICE clincher
CICI chin-chin
clip coin
CICO clip-clop
CICZ critcize
CIDE children
CIDN childing
CIDR Childers
CIDS childish
CIED Criseyde
CIEI chimeric
criteria
CIEL clitella

cribella
CIFN chiffony
CIFR Clifford
coiffure
CIFU coiffeur
CIGA cringe at
CIGN clinging
cringing
CIHE clichéed
CIHR coinhere
CIIA Chisinau
clinical
criminal
critical
CIIU critique
CIKE chick pea
chickpea
crinkled
CILE chillies
CILL chillily
CILN chilling
CILO criollos
CILS chinless
CILU chill out
CIMN chipmunk
CIOA clitoral
CIOI clitoris
CIPA Caiaphas
Crispian
CIPE crippled
CIPL chirpily
CIPN chirping
clipping
CIPR clippers
CIRP chirrupy
CIRS cribrose
CIRT cribrate
CISO chip shot
CISU chiasmus
CITR ceinture
CIUS cliquish
CIVN crivvens
CJLR cajolery
CKHA coke-head
CKHL cakehole
CKWL cakewalk
CLAA call away
CLAE calcanea
calcanei
collagen
collared
CLAI calcaria
caldaria
CLAL culpable
culpably
CLAO Calvados
collator
CLAS collapse
CLBC call back
celibacy
CLBS calabash
CLBT celibate
CLCE calicoes

CLCT cold cuts
CLDW call down
calm down
CLEA cul-de-sac
CLEI collegia
CLET calceate
CLGL Caligula
CLGR call girl
callgirl
call-girl
CLHC colchica
CLIA cultivar
CLIE calliper
CLIP calliope□
CLIR colliery
CLMA cold meal
columnal
columnar
CLME columned
CLMI Colombia
Columbia
CLMN calamine
CLMR calamari
CLMT calamity
CLMU Columbus
CLNA calendar
colonial□
CLNE calender
colander
cylinder
CLNR culinary
CLNS calmness
coldness
colonise
colonist
CLNZ colonize
CLOA Calloway
CLOE call over
calzones
Culloden
CLOU collogue
colloque
colloquy
CLPO calypsos
colophon
CLPS calipash
CLRA calor gas®
celeriac
CLRD chloride
Colorado
CLRE Calormen
CLRN chlorine
colorant
Coltrane
CLRT celerity
chlorate
CLSA cold snap
coleslaw
colossal
CLSG call sign
CLSI calfskin
CLSR cold sore
CLSU coliseum□

colossus
CLTE culottes
CLUA cellular
cultural
CLUE coleuses
colluder
coloured
cultured
CLUI colour in
CLUO call upon
CLUT Calcutta
CLUU calculus
colour up
CLWL cold-weld
CLWR cold-work
CLXU Calixtus
CLYI collyria
CMAA come away
CMAD commando
CMAE compages
comrades
CMAG campaign
CMAO cembalos
cimbalom
cymbalos
CMBC come back
comeback
CMBL Campbell
CMDA comedian
CMDL comeddle
CMDW come down
comedown
CMEC commence
commerce
CMEG commerge
CMFO come from
CMHF camshaft
CMHG come high
CMHM come home
CMHN camphene
CMIE combined
compiler
CMIG cummings
CMII cymbidia
CMIM cambiums
CMIO come in on
CMIT come in to
come into
CMIU camaïeux
camp it up
CMLE cameleer
CMLI camellia
complain
CMLN compline
CMLT complete
cumulate
CMML camomile
CMNA come near
CMNC Comaneci
CMNE cemented
CMNH Comanche
CMNU cementum
coming up

CMNX	come next
CMOE	come over
	commoner
	composed
	composer
CMOI	Cambodia
CMOL	commonly
CMON	compound
CMOU	Commodus
CMRA	Cambrian
CMRN	comprint
CMRO	Cameroon
CMRS	compress
	comprise
CMRU	cumbrous
CMSL	camisole
CMST	campsite
CMTB	come to be
CMTR	cemetery
CMTS	comatose
CMTU	come true
	cymatium
CMUA	communal
CMUE	campuses
	commuter
	computer
CMUO	come upon
CMUT	come up to
CMWS	combwise
CMWT	come with
CNAA	cinnabar
CNAG	contango
CNAH	Connacht
CNAI	cannabis
CNAO	centavos
	cinnamon
CNAR	Centaurs
CNAT	cineaste
	contacts
CNBA	can't bear
CNCS	cynicism
CNDA	Canadian
CNEE	centeses
	conceder
	congener
	convener
CNEG	converge
CNEL	convexly
CNEN	canoeing
	concerns
CNEO	convenor
	conveyor
CNEP	contempt
CNER	Canberra
CNES	canoeist
	condense
	converse
CNET	concepti
	concerti
	concerto
	concetti
	confetti
	contents
CNEV	conceive
	conferva
	conserve
CNHN	cinchona
CNHR	canthari
CNIA	cannibal
CNIC	convince
CNIE	confined
	confines
	conniver
	consider
CNII	cannikin
CNIL	canaille
	candidly
	canticle
CNIU	continua
	continue
	continuo
CNLB	conglobe
CNLC	conflict
CNLD	conclude
CNLS	canalise
CNLT	conflate
CNLV	conclave
CNLZ	canalize
CNMR	con amore
CNNA	canon law
CNNS	canoness
	canonise
CNNZ	canonize
CNOA	canzonas
CNOD	Concorde
CNOE	canzonet
	centones
	condoler
	consoler
CNOL	Candolle
	canoodle
	Connolly
CNOM	consommé
CNON	confound
	conjoint
CNOR	cannonry
	contours
CNOV	convolve
CNPR	conspire
CNRC	contract
	con trick
CNRL	controls
CNRM	centrums
CNRN	confront
CNRO	centre on
CNRR	cinerary
	confrère
	contrary
CNRS	Canarese
	centrism
	centrist
	congress❑
	contrast
CNRT	concrete
	congrats
	contrite
CNRU	canorous
CNRV	Congreve
	contrive
CNSE	canister
CNSR	cynosure
CNTC	canstick
CNTN	Constans
	constant❑
CNTP	cenotaph❑
CNTR	cincture
CNTT	constate
CNTU	construe
CNUA	cannulae
	cannulas
	conjugal
	consular
CNUC	con fuoco
CNUE	censurer
	confused
	conjurer
	consumed
	consumer
CNUI	cinquain
CNUL	centuple
CNUO	conjuror
	con out of
CNUS	conquest
	convulse
CNUT	conducti
CNUU	cingulum
CNWL	Cynewulf
CNZI	Cenozoic
COAL	chorally
	clonally
COAT	Cromarty
COBO	cookbook
COCE	crotchet
COCL	choicely
COCO	chop-chop
	chow-chow
	clop-clop
COCS	choicest
CODL	cloudily
CODS	cloddish
CODW	chop down
	cool down
COEE	close-set
COEF	choke off
	close off
COEI	choleric
	closed in
COEU	cooked-up
	cooped up
COFL	cropfuls
COFO	crowfoot
COGN	clogging
COHA	cloth cap
COHE	clothier
COHN	clothing
COHO	clothe on
COIG	Coolidge
COIM	choriamb
COIO	chorizos
COKF	clock off
COKL	croakily
COKN	croaking
COKR	crockery
COKT	Cronkite
COKU	clock out
COLC	cromlech
COLS	cloyless
COMI	chow mein
COMN	cloyment
CONL	cooingly
CONN	clowning
	crowning
CONR	clownery
CONS	clownish
	coolness
COPE	croupier
COPL	clotpoll
COPO	Crompton
CORO	choirboy
COSA	crossbar
COSE	chop suey
	cloister
	crosslet
COSL	crousely
COSN	choosing
	crossing
COSO	crossbow
COSU	crosscut
	cross out
COSY	cross-eye
COTA	Croatian
COTN	clotting
	crofting
COTO	co-option
COTV	co-optive
COUE	crocuses
COWL	Cromwell
CPAI	cephalic
CPAN	captain's
CPBO	copybook
CPBR	capybara
CPCI	capuchin❑
CPCT	capacity
CPDT	cupidity
CPEI	Coppélia
	copy-edit
CPFE	cup of tea
CPIC	capricci
CPIE	Caprices
	cyprides
CPIL	capriole
CPIU	capsicum
	captious
CPLN	capeline
CPLT	copulate
CPNS	caponise
CPNZ	caponize
CPOR	cupboard
CPRA	copyread
CPTL	capitula
CPTN	capitani
	capstone

Words marked ❑ can also be spelled with an initial capital letter

CPTW Cape Town
CPUA capsular
CPUE capturer
CPWT cope with
CQER coquetry
CQET coquette
CQIO coquitos
CQUI coq au vin
CRAB carnauba
CRAE carcanet
CRAI car radio
caryatid
CRAL carnally
CRAN curtains
CRAO cardamom
cardamon
currasow
CRAU cardamum
CRBA cerebral
CRBB Carabobo
CRBU cerebrum
CRCR corocore
CREA Carreras
cervelat
CREC currency
CREE cornered
corselet
cortexes
CREI Carnegie
Cordelia
curved in
CREL cursedly
CRER car ferry
corsetry
CRES cargeese
CRET cornetti
corvette
Corvette®
CREU carneous
carve out
Cerberus
corneous
CRFE carefree
CRGI coraggio
CRHE car-thief
CRHG Carthage
CRHN car phone
CRIA cardigan❑
cardinal
carnival❑
cervical
cortical
CRIE cervices
cervixes
circiter
cirriped
cortices
CRIG carriage
CRIL Carlisle
CRIO corridor
CRIR Corbiere
CRIU curlicue
CRJN Carl Jung
CRLA cerulean
CRLE Coral Sea
CRLI Cyrillic
CRLN Caroline
Cartland
circling
CRLO carillon
CRLR car alarm
CRLS careless
cordless
CRMC ceramics
CRMN cerement
ceremony
CRMT chromite
CRMU chromium
CRNC coronach
CRNL caruncle
CRNO corantos
CRNR coronary
CRNS curtness
CRNU corundum
CROA corporal
CROE corroded
CROF Carl Orff
CROI carbolic
carbonic
CRPC carapace
CRPE coryphee
coryphée
CRPN corn pone
CRRS curarise
CRRZ curarize
CRSA chrismal
CRSE cerastes
Chris Rea
christen
Chrysler®
CRSI Chrissie
Christie
CRSU Christus
CRTB Curitiba
CRTI ceratoid
CRTK caretake
CRTN carotene
CRTV curative
CRUA carousal
circular
CRUE carburet
carousel❑
carouser
CRUO corduroy
cornutos
CRUS circussy
CRWL Cornwall
Cornwell
CRWO cordwood
CRWR careworn
CRYF carry off
CRYN carrying
carry-ons
CRYO carrycot
carry-cot
CRYU carry out
carry-out
CSAA cast away
castaway
CSAL casually
CSAT casualty
CSBC cast back
CSCA cosy chat
CSCN cosecant
CSCO cash crop
CSCR cash card
CSDS cash desk
CSDW cash down
cast down
cast-down
CSEE cosseted
CSEI cosmetic
CSEL Costello
CSEN cysteine
CSET cassette
CSFE cost-free
CSFO cash flow
CSII cystitis
CSIN cushiony
CSIO cash in on
cassinos
cast iron
cast-iron
CSLS cashless
CSLT cast lots
CSMN casement
CSMR cashmere
CSNS cosiness
CSNV Casanova
CSOE custodes
customer
CSOF cast-offs
CSPO cesspool
CSRE Castries
CSRT castrate
castrati
castrato
CSRV Cosgrave
CSUE cistuses
costumer
CSUO Casaubon
CSYO cushy job
CTAE cut-water
CTAO cattalos
CTBR Cuthbert
CTCA cetacean
CTCM catacomb
CTDS city desk
cut a dash
CTEE catheter
cathexes
CTEI cathexis
CTET cut teeth
CTGR category
CTHI catch him
CTHL catch-all
city hall
CTHN catching
CTHR cut short
CTHU catch out
CTIG cuttings
CTIN Catriona
CTKN cytokine
CTLG cytology
CTLN Catiline
cut along
CTLS catalyse
catalyst
cut glass
CTLU Catullus
CTLY cattleya
CTNR catenary
CTNS cuteness
cutinise
CTNT catenate
CTNZ cutinize
CTOC cut no ice
CTOI catholic
chthonic
CTOO cotton on
CTOS cathouse
cat-house
cut loose
CTOT cut costs
CTPL catapult
CTPX Cotopaxi
CTRC cataract
cut price
cut-price
CTRN catering
CTRO cater for
CTSN cytosine
CTTO citation
CTTU cut it out
CTUN cothurni
cothurns
CTWL Cotswold
CTZN citizens
CUAE caudated
crusader
Crusades
CUAL causally
CUAO crusados
cruzados
CUAT courante
CUAU Caucasus
CUBN clubbing
CUCE clutches
CUCL churchly
CUCU couscous
CUDO cauldron
CUEA causeway
CUEB caused by
CUEE caudexes
CUEI Couperin
crude oil
CUHE Caughley
CUHN couchant
couching
crushing
CUHR crumhorn
CUHU caught up

	club-haul
CUIE	caudices
CUII	crucifix
CUIL	crucible
CUIS	coulisse
CUIU	cautious
CUKU	chuck out
CULN	coupling
CULS	churlish
	clueless
CUNU	churn out
CUPE	crumpled
CURO	clubroot
CUSD	club soda
CUSL	clumsily
CUSN	coursing
	cruising
CUTA	Cousteau
CUTE	counties
	courtier
	Courtney
	cruet set
CUTL	crustily
CUTN	counting
	courting
CUTR	clustery
CUTS	countess
	courtesy
CUTU	count out
CUZA	chutzpah
CVAI	caviarie
CVLA	civilian
	civil law
	civil war
CVLE	cavalier
	caviller
CVLS	civilise
CVLT	civility
CVLZ	civilize
CVNE	Cévennes
CVNN	covenant
CVNR	Coventry
CVRE	coverlet
CVRG	coverage
CVRL	coverall
	covertly
CVRN	covering
CVRO	cover for
CVTN	coveting
CVTT	cavitate
CVTU	covetous
CWER	cowberry
CWOS	cowhouse
CWRE	coworker
	co-worker
CWRL	cowardly
CXWI	coxswain
CYLT	cryolite
CYNC	cryonics
CYSA	cryostat
CYSL	coyishly
CYUT	cry quits
DAAA	draw away
DAAI	dramatic
DAAO	diapason
DAAS	diapause
DAAT	diamanté
	Djakarta
DABA	dead beat
	dead-beat
DABC	draw back
	drawback
DABD	dead body
DABI	Drambuie®
DABL	dead bolt
DABR	Dearborn
DACR	dead cert
DADC	dead duck
DAEA	diazepam
DAEE	deadened
	deadener
	diabetes
	diameter
DAEI	diabetic
DAFS	dwarfish
	dwarfism
DAGN	dragging
DAGT	draughts
	draughty
DAHA	deadhead
	dead-head
	dead heat
	dead-heat
	death cap
	drachmae
	drachmai
	drachmas
DAIG	dealings
DAIM	dearie me
DAIT	draw into
DALC	deadlock
DALN	deadline
	dragline
DALS	dead loss
DALT	draw lots
DAMT	deaf-mute
DANA	draw near
DANG	drainage
DANN	draining
DANS	deadness
	deafness
	dearness
	diagnose
	drabness
DANU	drawn-out
DAOA	diaconal
	diagonal
	dragoman
DAOI	diabolic
	diatomic
	diatonic
	draconic
DAON	dragoons
DAOU	dialogue
DAPR	diaspora
DARB	diatribe
DARC	drag race
DARI	draw rein
DARP	dragrope
DARS	Dean Rusk
DASE	dragster
DASI	dead spit
DASN	draisene
	draisine
DASO	dead shot
	dead stop
DATL	diastole
DATN	drafting
	dratting
DATR	do a U-turn
DATS	diastase
DATU	dianthus
DAUO	draw upon
DAWO	dead wood
DAWT	deal with
DAYE	dialyser
	dialyses
DAYI	dialysis
DBEI	dobber-in
DBHC	dabchick
DBLI	dabble in
DBLN	dabbling
DBLT	debility
DBNI	debonair
DBRA	Doberman
DBRE	debarred
DBSN	debasing
DBTL	do battle
DBTN	débutant
DBTT	dubitate
DCAE	deceased
	declared
	declarer
	dictated
DCAI	dichasia
DCAO	dictator
DCCT	dicacity
DCDA	deciduae
	deciduas
DCDN	decadent
	deciding
	decoding
DCDO	decide on
DCEA	decretal
DCEI	decrepit
DCEN	Duchenne
DCES	decrease
	duchesse
DCET	Docherty
DCHN	deck hand
	deckhand
DCHR	Dick Hern
DCIE	deceived
	deceiver
DCLL	docilely
DCLN	duckling
DCLT	docility
DCLU	decolour
DCME	December
DCMN	document
DCMT	decimate
DCNE	decanter
DCNL	decently
DCOA	doctoral
DCOE	deck over
DCPE	decipher
DCRI	dichroic
DCRN	doctrine
DCRT	decorate
DCRU	decorous
DCSO	decision
DCSU	Duck Soup
DCSV	decisive
DCTO	ducatoon
DCUC	declutch
DCUL	decouple
DCWE	duckweed
DCYI	dactylic
DCYN	decaying
	decrying
DCYR	dockyard
DDCI	didactic
DDCT	dedicate
DDIO	diddicoy
DDKN	Dedekind
DDMU	didymous
DEAU	Daedalus
DEBU	Deep Blue
DECE	drenched
DEDE	deep-dyed
DEDI	dieldrin
DEDU	dreadful
DEDW	deep down
DEEE	diereses
DEEI	diegesis
	dietetic
DEFS	Dreyfuss
DEGU	dredge up
DEIA	dies irae
DEKS	deep kiss
DELI	deep-laid
DELN	dwelling
DELS	deedless
	duellist
DEML	dreamily
DEMN	dreaming
DENS	deepness
DEOI	daemonic
DEPL	deed poll
DERC	Dietrich
DERL	drearily
DESG	dressage
DESI	deerskin
DESN	dressing
DETS	duettist
DFAA	defrayal
DFAC	defiance
DFAE	defeated
	deflated
	deflater
	defrayer
DFAO	deflator

DFCO	defector
DFCT	defecate
DFEZ	defreeze
DFLD	defilade
DFLN	defiling
DFNE	defences
	defended
	defender
DFNS	daftness
	deftness
DFNT	definite
DFOE	deflower
DFOI	daffodil
DFRA	deferral
DFRC	diffract
DFRE	deferred
	deferrer
	deformed
DFRS	De Forest
	deforest
DFUE	diffused
	diffuser
DGAE	degraded
	dog-eared
DGAI	dogmatic
DGAL	diggable
DGBD	dogsbody
DGEE	doggerel
DGEL	doggedly
DGER	Daguerre
	Dogberry
	dog-weary
DGES	degrease
DGIE	dog-tired
DGIG	daggings
	diggings
DGIH	dogfight
DGOE	do-gooder
DGOT	do good to
	dog-tooth
DGSE	digester
DGTS	digitise
DGTT	digitate
DGTZ	digitize
DGYA	doggy-bag
DHBE	dahabieh
DHDA	dihedral
DHRE	dehorner
DIAL	drivable
DIBR	Duisburg
DIEA	drive mad
	driveway
DIEU	drive out
DIFE	drip-feed
DIGO	dying for
DIGU	dying out
	dying-out
DIHA	deisheal
DIHE	drisheen
DIHO	Deighton
DIIA	deifical
DIKF	drink off
DIKN	drinking
DILI	drill bit
	drill rig
DILN	drilling
DIOI	daimonic
DIOT	Djibouti
DIPN	dripping
DISE	Dniester
DITE	drift-net
DITF	drift off
DITL	daintily
DITN	drifting
DIUR	daiquiri
DIYA	dairyman
DIYN	dairying
DJCE	dejected
DLAE	dolmades
DLAI	dalmatic
DLBU	delubrum
DLCC	delicacy
DLCT	delicate
DLDE	Daladier
DLDN	deluding
DLEN	dal segno
DLGC	delegacy
DLGN	diligent
DLGT	delegate
DLIE	dulcimer
DLLS	Dalglish
DLMR	De La Mare
DLMT	dolomite
DLNS	dullness
DLRC	Delbrück
DLRM	doldrums
DLRS	doloroso
DLRU	delirium
	dolorous
DLSA	dalesman
DLSO	delusion
DLSR	delusory
DLSV	delusive
DLTO	delation
	deletion
	dilate on
	dilation
	dilution
DLTR	dilatory
DLUA	Delaunay
DLVA	diluvial
	diluvian
DLVR	delivery
DLWR	Delaware
DLYN	dallying
	delaying
DMAL	damnable
	damnably
DMCA	democrat
DMCL	domicile
DMDW	damp down
	dumb down
DMEE	dampened
	dampener
DMGG	demagogy
DMGI	DiMaggio
DMGN	damaging
DMIA	domainal
DMJH	demijohn
DMLB	Dimbleby
DMLN	dumpling
DMLS	demolish
DMNA	demoniac
DMNC	Dominica
DMNE	demanded
	demander
	demented
	domineer
	dominoes
DMNI	dementia
DMNN	dominant
DMNO	dominion
DMNS	dampness
	demonise
	demonism
	diminish
	dumbness
DMNT	dominate
DMNZ	demonize
DMON	dumfound
DMRA	demersal
	demurral
DMRE	Dumfries
DMRH	démarche
DMRL	demurely
DMRR	demerara
DMRS	dimerise
DMRZ	dimerize
DMSE	demister
DMSI	damaskin
	domestic
DMSO	dumb show
DMSU	Damascus
DMTA	Domitian
DMTN	dome tent
DMTO	demotion
DMWL	demi-wolf
DMYI	dimly lit
DMYU	dummy run
DNAI	dentalia
DNAL	deniable
	deniably
DNBA	Danubian
DNBT	dingbats
DNDN	ding-dong
DNDU	ding doun
DNEI	Don Revie
DNEL	Daniella
	Danielle
	dentelle
DNER	Don Pedro
	Dunleary
DNES	danseuse
DNEV	Donleavy
DNGU	Donoghue
DNIL	denticle
DNKO	don't know
DNLN	dangling
DNLV	Danilova
DNMC	dynamics
DNMS	dynamise
	dynamism
DNMT	dynamite
DNMZ	dynamize
DNNS	dankness
DNOD	Dunwoody
DNOT	Dan Fouts
DNRF	dandruff
DNRI	dendroid
DNRT	dendrite
DNRU	denarius
	diner-out
DNSI	dynastic
DNSU	dinosaur
DNTN	denoting
	donating
DNTO	donation
DNTR	denature
DNUC	denounce
DNUE	dentures
DNWT	done with
DNYS	dandyish
	dandyism
DNZF	denazify
DOAA	drop away
DOAL	doolally
DOBC	drop back
DOBL	doorbell
DODA	drop-dead
DODW	drop down
DOEA	diocesan
	duodenal
DOEE	Diomedes
DOEU	duodenum
DOGE	drongoes
DOHD	Drogheda
DOIO	drop in on
DOKC	drop-kick
DOLA	drop-leaf
DOLR	drollery
DOOU	duologue
DOPL	droopily
DOPN	drooping
	dropping
DOPS	doorpost
DOSA	doomsday
DOSE	doomster
	doorstep
	dropsied
DOSL	drowsily
DOSO	doorstop
	drop-shot
DOWS	dropwise
DOYU	Dionysus
DPAE	depraved
	dipsades
DPCE	depicter
DPCO	depictor
DPEA	dipteral
DPEE	depleted
DPEL	dapperly
DPEY	diphenyl

DPIE	deprived
DPLT	depilate
DPMN	dopamine
DPNI	dupondii
DPNN	deponent
DPNO	depend on
DPNS	dopiness
DPOA	diplomat
DPOO	diplozoa
DPRE	departed
	deported
	deportee
DPRT	depurate
DPTC	dipstick
DPTS	deputise
DPTZ	deputize
DPVL	Dipavali
DRAC	dormancy
DRAL	dorsally
DRBU	dark-blue
DRCA	direct at
DRCE	directed
DRCL	directly
DRCO	director
DREE	darkened
DRFR	Dartford
DRGT	derogate
DRIR	derrière
DRKL	durukuli
DRLC	derelict
DRLN	darkling
DRMA	dark meat
DRMN	Dortmund
DRMO	Dartmoor
DRNE	deranged
DRNL	daringly
DRNS	darkness
DRON	Dordogne
DROS	dormouse
DRRO	darkroom
DRSO	derision
DRSR	derisory
DRSV	derisive
DRTE	Dorothea
DRTO	deration
	duration
DRVN	deriving
DRYO	dirty dog
DSAB	Dushanbe
DSAC	despatch
	dispatch
	distance
DSAD	discandy
DSAE	diseased
	disgavel
	dismayed
DSAH	dyspathy
DSAI	dishabit
DSAL	dismally
	Disraeli
	distally
DSAT	distaste
DSBE	disabled
DSBS	disabuse
DSBW	dust bowl
DSCR	dustcart
DSDW	doss down
DSEC	disbench
DSEE	dishevel
	dissever
DSEF	Disneyfy
DSEI	dyslexia
	dyslexic
DSES	dispense
	disperse
	disseise
	dyspepsy
DSET	diskette
DSEV	disleave
	disserve
DSEZ	disseize
DSGE	designed
	designer
	disagree
DSHO	deschool
	dyschroa
DSIC	distinct
DSIE	destined
	disliked
	disliken
DSIH	distichs
DSII	dispirit
DSIL	disciple
DSLC	deselect
	displace
DSLE	desilver
DSLI	disclaim
DSLK	disklike
DSLM	displume
DSLN	displant
DSLO	disallow
DSLS	disclose
DSLT	desolate
DSNC	disenact
DSNE	disannex
	disinter
	dyspnoea
DSNO	disendow
	disenrol
	disunion
DSNT	disunite
	disunity
DSNU	disannul
DSOA	disloyal
	disposal
DSOC	disvouch
DSOE	disbowel
	discover
	disposed
	disrobed
DSOG	disgorge
	dislodge
	disponge
DSOI	despotic
DSON	discount
	disjoint
	dismount
DSOO	disbosom
DSOS	dishorse
	dishouse
DSOV	dissolve
DSPL	disapply
DSRA	disarray
	dispread
DSRB	describe
DSRC	destruct
	disfrock
	disgrace
	distract
	district
DSRE	deserted
	deserter
	deserved
	disarmed
	discreet
	disorbed
	disorder
DSRI	distrain
	distrait
DSRN	desiring
DSRO	disproof
DSRS	distress
	distrust
DSRT	discrete
DSRU	desirous
DSRV	disprove
DSRW	discrown
DSSE	disaster
DSUC	disjunct
DSUD	dissuade
DSUE	disputed
	disputer
	disquiet
DSUG	dispunge
DSUS	disburse
	disguise
	dispurse
DSWE	disowned
DTAL	dateable
	dutiable
DTBN	databank
DTBS	database
DTBU	dot about
DTCE	detached
DTCO	detector
DTEE	ditherer
	dotterel
DTFE	duty-free
DTHA	Dutchman
DTHE	Dutchmen
DTHL	Dutch elm
DTHN	ditching
DTHO	ditch-dog
	Dutch hoe
DTIA	detrital
DTIE	detailed
	detained
	detainee
DTIK	do tricks
DTIU	detritus
DTLS	dateless
DTNL	dotingly
DTNO	doting on
DTNT	detonate
DTPL	date palm
	date-palm
DTRN	dethrone
DTRP	date rape
DTSE	detested
DTTE	date-tree
DTXF	detoxify
DUBA	drumbeat
DUBN	drubbing
DUDS	druidism□
DUEI	diuretic
DUEL	deucedly
DUEO	deuteron
DUGR	drudgery
DUGS	druggist
DUHA	drumhead
DUHE	daughter
DUHU	doughnut
DUIT	drum into
DUKR	drunkard
DULN	doubling
DULO	doubloon
DULU	double up
DUMN	drumming
DUMS	Drum Mass
DUNS	dourness
DUTN	daunting
	doubting
DUTU	doubtful
DUUE	drug user
DUVL	Deus vult
DUVR	duumviri
	duumvirs
DVAC	deviance
	deviancy
DVBM	dive-bomb
DVCT	dovecote
DVDN	dividant
	dividend
	dividing
DVDR	dividers
DVDU	divide up
DVGT	divagate
DVIO	devoid of
DVLE	devalued
	devolved
	divulged
	Duvalier
DVLI	de Valois□
DVLK	dovelike
DVLN	divalent
DVLR	de Valera
DVLS	devilish
DVNA	Devonian
DVNF	divinify
DVNL	divinely
DVNN	Davenant
	divining

DVNS	divinise
DVNT	divinity
DVNZ	divinize
DVRE	divorced
	divorcee
DVRL	diversly
DVSE	divested
DVSN	devising
DVSO	division
DVSV	divisive
DVTE	devotees
DVTI	dovetail
DVTO	devotion
DVUE	devourer
DVUL	devoutly
DWBA	downbeat
	down-beat
DWCS	downcast
DWEE	dewy-eyed
DWFL	downfall
DWHL	downhill
DWLN	dawdling
DWMS	downmost
DWNS	dewiness
DWPA	downplay
DWPU	downpour
DWRI	dawn raid
DWSD	downside
DWSZ	downsize
DWTR	downturn
DWTW	downtown
	down-town
DWWN	downwind
DWWR	downward
DWWT	down with
DXLG	doxology
DXRN	dextrine
DXRS	dextrose
DXRU	dextrous
DYBU	day about
DYEI	Day-Lewis
DYIE	dry riser
DYIH	daylight
DYLA	dry-clean
DYLT	dry-plate
DYOA	day-to-day
	day-woman
DYON	dry-point
DYRA	daybreak
	daydream
DYTN	dry-stone
DYUS	dry-nurse
DYYA	day by day
DZLN	dazzling
DZNS	doziness
EAAL	erasable
	evadable
EADA	Enard Bay
EAEC	evanesce
EAEL	elatedly
EAEO	Eva Perón
EAIE	examinee
	examiner
EAIT	emaciate
	eradiate
EAIU	edacious
EARO	etaerios
EASA	Evans Bay
EATN	exacting
	exalting
EATO	exaction
EATR	enacture
EATS	elastase
EAUN	evacuant
EAUT	evacuate
	evaluate
EBAO	emblazon
EBDE	embedded
	embodied
EBLE	embalmer
	embolden
EBLS	embolism
EBRE	emborder
EBRO	embark on
EBSE	embossed
EBTE	embitter
EBTL	embattle
EBVL	Ebbw Vale
EBYN	embryons
EBZL	embezzle
ECAE	enchased
ECAG	exchange
ECAL	encradle
ECEA	eschewal
ECEP	en cuerpo
ECHM	Ecce Homo
ECII	enclitic
ECIT	enceinte
ECLD	escalade
ECLN	esculent
ECLO	escallop
ECLP	escalope
ECLT	escalate
ECLU	encolour
ECME	encumber
ECMN	Eichmann
ECMO	encomion
ECMU	encomium
ECNU	enconium
ECOC	encroach
ECOE	enclosed
ECOH	enclothe
ECOI	enchoric
ECOT	en croûte
ECPD	escapade
ECPE	encipher
	excepted
ECPS	escapism
	escapist
ECRL	encircle
ECRO	escargot
ECRU	excursus
ECSE	encysted
ECSM	excuse me
	excuse-me
ECSN	excusing
ECSO	excision
ECTN	excitant
	exciting
ECTR	et cetera
	etcetera
	et ceteri
ECUE	excluded
ECVT	excavate
EDAE	endpaper
EDCR	endocarp
EDDR	endoderm
EDGM	endogamy
EDIC	eldritch
EDMG	endamage
EDMO	endymion❑
EDNE	endanger
EDRA	end organ
EDRD	El Dorado
EDRE	endorsed
	endorsee
	endorser
EDRI	endermic
EDRN	enduring
EDSA	Eddy Shah
EDZO	endozoon
EEAC	elegance
	elegancy
EEAE	elevated
EEAO	elevator
EECI	elenctic
EECS	exercise
EECU	elenchus
EEDT	emendate
EEEI	exegesis
	exegetic
EEET	elements
	eleventh
	eye teeth
EEGN	emergent
	emerging
EEGS	energise
EEGZ	energize
EEHM	eye rhyme
EEHN	elephant
EEIA	emetical
EEIG	evenings
EEIH	eyesight
EEII	eremitic
EEIU	emeritus
EELS	eyeglass
EEMR	ever more
	evermore
EENR	Eleanore
EENS	eternise
	evenness
EENT	eternity
EENZ	eternize
EEOT	eye tooth
EEOY	eye to eye
EEPA	exemplar
EERP	eye drops
EERT	execrate
EESN	evensong
EESO	emersion
	eversion
EETA	eventual
EETD	eventide
EETE	electret
	even then
EETI	electric
EETL	erectile
EETN	eventing
EETO	ejection
	election
	electron
	electros
	erection
	exertion
EETR	electors
EETT	edentate
EETU	eventful
EETV	ejective
	elective
EEUA	exequial
EEUE	executed
	executer
	exequies
EEUO	even up on
	executor
EEVT	enervate
EEYA	every day
	everyday
	Everyman
	everyway
EEYI	every bit
EEYN	everyone
EFCC	efficacy
EFCO	effector
EFEC	enfierce
EFEL	enfeeble
EFEZ	enfreeze
EFHL	elf-child
EFHO	elf-shoot
EFLD	enfilade
EFOE	enflower
EFOK	elflocks
EFRE	enforced
EFRN	efferent
EFRS	enforest
EFSO	effusion
EFSV	effusive
EFTE	enfetter
EFTL	effetely
EFUI	effluvia
EFUN	effluent
EGAE	engraver
EGAI	ex gratia
EGED	eggheads
EGGI	engage in
EGGN	engaging
EGHL	eggshell
EGIE	egg-timer
EGLC	egg-slice
EGLE	engulfed
EGLN	eggplant
EGLS	edgeless

Words marked ❑ can also be spelled with an initial capital letter

EGNC	eugenics
EGNE	engender
	engineer
EGNS	edginess
EGNU	Eugenius
EGOV	engroove
EGPO	egg-spoon
EGRE	engorged
EGRL	engirdle
EGRO	eager for
EGTE	eighteen
	eighties
EGTL	eighthly
EGTO	edge tool
	eightvos
EGTS	ergotise
	ergotism
EGTZ	ergotize
EGWS	edgewise
EGWY	edgeways
EHAS	enhearse
EHCS	ethicise
EHCZ	ethicize
EHDA	exhedrae
EHLE	Ethelred
EHLG	ethology
EHLN	echelons
EHLS	echoless
EHLT	ethylate
EHMR	ephemera
EHMT	exhumate
EHNE	enhunger
EHNI	echinoid
	ethanoic
EHOI	Ethiopia
	Ethiopic
EHRA	ethereal
EHRE	Ethernet
EHRF	etherify
EHRS	etherise
EHRZ	etherize
EIAE	epitases
EIAL	epically
EIAO	epilator
EIAT	epinasty
EIAU	Eridanus
EIAY	epicalyx
EIDE	evildoer
	evil-doer
EIEC	eminence
	evidence
	exigency
EIEE	epicedes
EIEI	epicedia
	epidemic
EIES	epilepsy
EIHM	epithems
EIHN	epiphany❑
EIHT	epiphyte
EIIL	eligible
	eligibly
	Eric Idle
EILS	epiblast
EILT	etiolate
EIMT	Eli Smith
EINS	ebionise
	evilness
EINZ	ebionize
EIOI	episodic
EIOU	epilogue
EIPL	exit poll
EIRN	emigrant
EIRP	epigraph
EIRT	emigrate
EISO	emission
	Ericsson
EISR	emissary
EISV	emissive
EITE	epistles
EITL	epistyle
EITN	existent
	existing
EITO	eviction
EIUA	epidural
EIUT	exiguity
EIUU	Epicurus
	exiguous
EIYL	epicycle
EIYN	edifying
EKNL	enkindle
EKRE	enkernel
ELCI	eclectic
ELGE	eulogies
ELGS	eulogise
ELGU	eulogium
ELGZ	eulogize
ELPE	ellipses
ELPI	ecliptic
	ellipsis
	elliptic
ELRC	eelwrack
ELRE	enlarged
	enlarger
ELRS	eelgrass
ELSE	enlistee
ELSO	eclosion
ELTI	eolithic❑
EMLN	Emmeline
EMNA	Emmental
EMNE	Emmanuel
EMNO	Edmonton
EMRL	emmarble
ENTI	Einstein
EOAE	eco-label
EOAI	egomania
	exogamic
EOCO	Eton crop
EOCS	exorcise
	exorcism
	exorcist
EOCZ	exorcize
EODA	ego ideal
	exordial
EODU	exordium
EOEI	erogenic
	erotetic
	esoteric
EOGT	elongate
EOHG	exophagy
EOIL	erodible
EOIN	emotions
EOIO	emoticon
EOMT	enormity
EOMU	enormous
EOOI	ecologic
	economic
	ecotoxic
EORA	ecofreak
EORN	exocrine
EOSI	egoistic
EOUN	eloquent
EOVN	evolving
EPAE	emphases
EPAI	emphasis
	emphatic
EPAL	expiable
EPAO	expiator
EPCA	especial
EPCE	empacket
	expected
EPDT	expedite
EPEC	empleach
EPEE	ekpweles
EPES	espresso
	expresso
EPII	explicit
EPLE	empolder
	espalier
	expelled
	expellee
EPNE	expanded
	expander
	expended
	expenses
	expunger
EPNN	exponent
EPNO	expand on
EPOE	employed
	employee
	employer
	exploded
	explorer
EPOI	euphonic
	euphoria
	euphoric
EPOT	exploits
EPPI	eupepsia
	eupeptic
EPRA	empyreal
	empyrean
EPRE	exporter
EPRL	empurple
	expertly
EPRN	expiring
EPRO	espartos
EPRS	emperise
	euphrasy
EPRU	emporium
EPRZ	emperize
EPSR	exposure
EPTI	empathic
	eupatrid
EPTO	empatron
EPUA	espousal
EPUE	espoused
EPUS	euphuise
	euphuism
EPUZ	euphuize
EPYN	emptying
EPYU	empty out
EQIE	enquirer
EQIS	esquisse
ERBN	Eurobond
ERCA	Eurocrat
ERDC	Eurydice
ERDE	enridged
ERGE	Earl Grey
ERGN	enraging
ERHA	Earthman
ERHE	Earthsea
ERIG	earnings
ERIS	earliest
ERNL	errantly
	erringly
ERNR	errantry
ERNS	eeriness
ERPA	European
ERPR	Europort
ERPU	europium
ERRP	ear drops
ERSA	Eurasian
ERTM	eurythmy
ERUF	earmuffs
ERUG	enraunge
ERVS	enravish
ESAE	enslaved
	ensnared
ESAH	enswathe
ESAI	ecstatic
	eustatic
ESBU	Eusebius
ESCR	easy-care
ESEL	easterly
ESES	ens per se
ESET	ensheath
ESGM	easy game
ESHR	ensphere
ESIL	enshield
ESLG	ensilage
ESLN	eastlins
ESMA	easy meat
ESML	ensemble
ESMN	easement
ESNR	Elsinore
ESNS	easiness
ESOC	ensconce
ESOE	easy over
ESRN	enshrine
ESRU	enshroud
ESWN	east wind
ESWO	Eastwood
ESWR	eastward

Words marked ❑ can also be spelled with an initial capital letter

ESWS	elsewise
ESYS	essayist
ETAC	entrance
ETAG	estrange
ETAL	entrails
ETAO	Estragon
	extrados
ETAP	enthalpy
ETAT	entr'acte
	entrants
ETAU	extra sum
ETBE	eatables
ETCN	enticing
ETDR	ectoderm
ETEC	entrench
ETEE	esteemed
ETEO	entrepot
	entrepôt
ETET	entreaty
ETLE	extoller
ETLU	entellus
ETMT	estimate
ETNA	Estonian
ETNE	extended
ETNI	estancia
ETNL	entangle
ETNO	extensor
ETOE	estrogen
ETOI	entropic
ETRA	external
ETRF	esterify
ETRL	entirely
ETRN	entering
	enthrone
ETRO	exterior
ETRT	entirety
ETTE	entitled
ETUE	enthused
	extruder
ETYS	entryism
	entryist
ETZO	entozoon
EUAE	educated
EUAL	educable
EUAO	educator
	emulator
EUEI	eau de nil
	eau de vie
	enuresis
	enuretic
EUGT	evulgate
EUIL	educible
	eludible
EUIN	esurient
EUIT	exuviate
EULS	equalise
EULT	equality
EULZ	equalize
EUNA	eburnean
EUPE	equipped
EUPG	equipage
EUSF	emulsify
EUSO	emulsion
EUTE	equities
EUTN	exultant
	exulting
EUTO	eduction
	equation
	eruption
EUTT	eructate
EUTV	eruptive
EVAL	enviable
	enviably
EVLP	envelope
EVRN	environs
EVSG	envisage
EVSO	envision
EYGE	eryngoes
EYHM	erythema
EYTA	Egyptian
EZOI	enzootic
FABA	flambeau
	flatboat
FABC	flatback
FABL	flabbily
FABR	Flaubert
FABS	flax-bush
FACE	fiascoes
FACN	Francine
FACT	Frascati
FACU	francium
FADR	Flanders
FADW	flag down
FAEA	frame-saw
FAEB	framed by
FAEC	flamenco
FAEF	flake off
FAEL	flagella
FAEU	flake out
	flame out
	flare out
FAFO	flatfoot
FAFS	flatfish
FAGN	flagging
FAHA	Flashman
	flathead
FAHL	flashily
FAHN	flashing
FAHR	feathery
FAHU	flashgun
FAIG	flamingo
FAIL	feasible
	feasibly
FAIO	flatiron
FAJC	flapjack
FAJU	frabjous
FAKI	Franklin
FAKN	flanking
FAKO	flat knot
FAKS	Frankish
FALI	Fräulein
FALL	flax-lily
FALN	flatland
	flatling
	flatlong
FALS	fearless
	flawless
	foamless
FAMN	fragment
FAMT	flatmate
FANE	flaunter
FANL	flannels
FANS	flatness
FAOE	flap over
FAPN	flapping
FARC	flat race
FARN	flagrant
	fragrant
FARO	flat roof
FART	flat rate
FASI	flagship
	flat spin
FASM	fearsome
FATA	feast day
FATG	frautage
FATN	feasting
FATO	feast-won
	fraction
FATR	flattery
	flat tyre
	fracture
FATS	flattish
	flautist
FAUE	features
	flatuses
FAWR	flatworm
FAWS	flatwise
FAWY	flatways
FBIU	fabliaux
FBLS	fabulise
	fabulist
FBLU	fabulous
FBLZ	fabulize
FBOA	fibromas
FBOI	fibrosis
FBUR	February
FCAH	face-ache
FCAL	facially
FCCI	focaccia
FCDW	face down
FCIU	factious
FCLF	facelift
FCLL	facilely
FCLN	feculent
FCLS	faceless
	feckless
	focalise
FCLT	facility
FCLZ	focalize
FCOU	factotum
FCPC	face pack
FCSN	focusing
	fuchsine
FCTA	facetiae
FCUT	face up to
FDAA	fade away
FDCA	fiducial
FDDW	fade down
FDIU	fiddious
FDLN	fedelini
	fiddling
FDLS	fadeless
FDLT	fidelity
FDRC	federacy
FDRR	federary
FDRT	federate
FDYE	fedayeen
FEAI	foedarie
FEBC	feedback
FEBO	freeboot
FEBR	freeborn
FEBS	freebase
FEBT	flea-bite
FECE	fletcher❑
	frescoed
	frescoer
	frescoes
FECL	fiercely
FEDA	field day
	freedman
	Freudian
FEDC	field ice
FEDE	field-dew
	freedmen
FEDN	Fielding
FEDS	fiendish
FEDU	field gun
FEEI	Frederic
	frenetic
FEFL	free fall
	free-fall
FEFO	flee from
FEFR	free-form
FEGF	free gift
FEGO	feelgood
FEHA	freshman
FEHE	fresh-new
FEHI	fresh air
FEHL	freehold
FEHN	free hand
	freehand
FEHU	flesh out
FEIG	feelings
FEIL	flexible
	flexibly
FEKC	free kick
FEKE	freckled
FEKS	freakish
FEKU	freak out
	freak-out
FELA	freeload
FELK	feel like
FELV	free love
FENS	freeness
FEPI	feel pain
FEPR	Freeport
FERE	fee-grief
FERI	free rein
FETM	free time
FETN	fleeting
FETW	Freetown
FEUA	flexural

Words marked ❑ can also be spelled with an initial capital letter

FEUN	frequent
FEUS	flexuose
FEUT	feel up to
FEUU	flexuous
FEVT	free vote
FEWL	free will
FEWR	fleawort
	freeware
	fretwork
FEWS	Fred West
FEWT	feel with
FEZE	frenzied
FEZN	freezing
FEZU	freeze-up
FFIT	fiftieth
FFYS	fiftyish
FGCT	fugacity
FGEA	fugleman
FGIS	foggiest
FGON	fogbound
FGRN	figurant
	figurine
	figuring
FGRO	figure on
FGTF	fight off
FGTN	fighting
FGTO	fight for
FGTV	fugitive
FGYS	fogeyish
FIAE	fricadel
FICE	flincher
FICP	fair copy
FIDA	Friedman
FIDI	Friedkin
FIDR	Flinders
FIEN	fainéant
FIFA	flim-flam
	flip-flap
FIFL	fair fall
FIFO	flip-flop
FIGA	foie gras
FIGM	fair game
FIGN	frigging
FIGU	fling out
FIHE	flichter
	frighten
FIHU	faithful□
FIIE	fainites
FIIL	Fair Isle
	frigidly
FIKL	friskily
FILE	frillies
FINL	friendly
	-friendly
FINN	feigning
FINS	fairness
FIOE	frijoles
FIOR	Fribourg
FIPA	fair play
FIPN	flippant
	flipping
FIPR	frippery
FISA	Friesian
FISD	flip side
FISF	fail-safe
FISL	flimsily
FITF	flintify
FITL	flintily
FITN	fainting
	flitting
FITO	friction
FITS	faintest
FJMR	Fujimori
FKYM	Fukuyama
FLAA	fall away
	foldaway
FLAE	falcated
FLAI	fellahin
	F R Leavis
FLAL	filially
	filmable
	foldable
FLBA	faltboat
	foldboat
FLBC	fall back
	fall-back
	fullback
FLCC	full-cock
FLCD	filicide
FLCP	file copy
FLCT	felicity□
FLDS	felo de se
FLDW	fall down
FLEA	falderal
	False Bay
FLEC	fulgency
FLEE	filtered
FLEI	false rib
FLEO	folderol
FLET	falsetto
FLFA	fall flat
FLFC	full-face
FLGE	filagree
	filigree
	filmgoer
FLHL	filthily
FLHN	filching
	full hand
FLHR	folk hero
FLIL	fallible
	fallibly
	follicle
FLLR	folklore
FLMN	filament
FLMO	full moon
FLMR	Fillmore
FLNI	film noir
FLNM	filename
FLNS	fullness
FLOE	falconer
	fall over
	film over
	follower
FLOG	full of go
FLOL	fellowly
FLOO	follow on
	follow-on
FLOR	falconry
FLOT	Falmouth
FLOU	follow up
	follow-up
FLPG	full-page
FLPL	full-pelt
FLPS	file past
FLRA	filarial
FLRC	folk rock
FLRM	fulcrums
FLRT	filtrate
FLSA	feldspar
	film star
FLSI	full-sail
FLSN	folk-song
FLSO	full stop
FLTF	Falstaff
FLTL	folk tale
	folk-tale
	full tilt
	full-tilt
FLTM	full time
	full-time
FLTS	full toss
FLUA	fulgural
FLUO	fall upon
FMDE	fumadoes
FMGN	fumigant
FMGT	fumigate
FMLA	familial
	familiar
FMLN	fumbling
FMNE	fomenter
FMNN	feminine
FMNS	feminise
	feminism
	feminist
FMNZ	feminize
FMRL	femerall
	fumarole
FMSE	famished
FMTR	fumatory
	fumitory
FMUL	famously
FNAA	find a way
FNAC	fan dance
FNAE	fontanel
FNAG	fandango
FNAI	fantasia□
FNAO	fanfaron
FNBA	funebral
FNDA	fine-draw
FNEE	fingered
FNEF	fence off
FNEI	fenced in
FNEK	finnesko
FNEO	Fontenoy
FNGL	Fanagalo
FNHI	fine hair
FNHL	fin whale
	funkhole
FNIG	fannings
	findings
FNIH	fanlight
FNIL	fencible
FNIU	fanciful
FNLA	final say
FNLC	final act
FNLN	fondling
FNLS	fangless
	finalise
	finalist
	fineless
FNLT	finality
FNLZ	finalize
FNMN	fine mind
FNNE	finances
FNNS	fineness
	fondness
FNRA	funereal
FNRR	funerary
FNSE	finished
	finisher
FNSR	fenestra
FNSU	feng shui
	finish up
FNTD	finitude
FNTL	finitely
FNTN	fine-tune
FNTO	function
FNUE	funguses
FNYA	fancy man
	funny man
FOAA	fool away
FOAL	florally
FOAO	from A to B
	from A to Z
FOBC	flow back
FOBL	football
FOBR	fool-born
FOCL	flocculi
FOCS	floccose
FODA	floodway
FODN	flooding
FODS	frondose
FOEB	fooled by
FOEC	Florence
FOEE	flowerer
	floweret
FOFL	footfall
FOFO	frou-frou
FOFS	food-fish
FOGN	flogging
FOHL	foothill
	foothold
	froth-fly
	frothily
FOHN	frothing
FOIE	florigen
	Florizel
FOIL	floridly
	flotilla
FOIT	fool into
FOLN	footling
FOLS	footless

FOMR	footmark
FONE	flounder
FONT	footnote
FOOE	flow over
FOPL	floppily
FOPN	flopping
FOPT	footpath
FORN	flooring
FORS	flourish
	footrest
FOSA	fool's cap
	foolscap
FOSE	footstep
FOSO	footslog
FOSR	footsore
FOTA	front man
	frontman
FOTE	frontier
	frontlet
FOTG	floatage
	frontage
	frottage
FOTL	frostily
FOTN	floating
	fronting
	frosting
FOWA	footwear
FOWR	footwork
FOWT	fool with
FRAA	fermatas
	fire away
FRAD	forwards
FRAE	forsaken
FRAI	formalin
FRAL	fordable
	formable
	formally
FRAM	firearms
FRAO	farragos
FRAT	Ferranti
FRBA	forebear
FRBD	forebode
FRBL	fireball
FRBM	fire-bomb
FRBN	foribund
	furibund
FRBR	fernbird
FRCS	forecast
FRCT	feracity
	ferocity
FRDM	fire damp
	firedamp
FRDO	fire door
	foredoom
FRDS	faradise
FRDT	foredate
FRDW	firm down
FRDZ	faradize
FREC	fervency
FREE	fire-eyed
FREI	forget it
FREL	forcedly
	forkedly
	formerly
FREO	formed of
	furbelow
FREP	for keeps
FRES	farceuse
	fornenst
FRET	forfeits
FREU	ferreous
	forceful
	force out
FRFE	forefeel
	forefeet
FRFL	forkfuls
FRFO	forefoot
FRGN	foregone
FRHA	far ahead
	forehead
FRHN	farm-hand
	farthing
	forehand
	forehent
FRHR	for short
FRHS	farthest
	fire hose
	furthest
FRIA	farcical
FRIE	forgiven
FRIG	ferriage
FRIK	for kicks
FRIL	fervidly
	forcible
	forcibly
FRIR	farriery
FRIT	farm into
	fortieth
FRKO	foreknow
FRLC	firelock
	forelock
FRLN	far-flung
	farmland
	foreland
FRLS	fireless
	formless
FRMN	foramina
FRMS	foremast
	foremost
FRNI	forensic
FRNL	furuncle
FRNM	forename
FRNO	forenoon
FRNS	firmness
FROA	fire opal
FROE	fork over
	furrowed
FROG	furlough
FROO	furiosos
FROT	far north
	forsooth
FROU	Formosus
FRPA	foreplan
	foreplay
	forspeak
FRPN	forspend
FRPR	forepart
FRPS	forepast
FRRA	foreread
FRRS	fortress
FRSA	forestal
FRSD	fireside
FRSE	foreseen
	foreshew
	forested
	forester❑
FRSI	fireship
	foresaid
	foresail
	foreskin
FRSO	foreshow
	foreslow
FRSR	forestry
FRTL	foretell
FRTM	for a time
FRTR	feretory
FRUA	formulae
	formulas
	furcular
FRUG	forjudge
FRUH	farouche
FRUO	Ferguson
FRUT	fortuity
FRWA	forswear
FRWE	fireweed
FRWL	farewell
	firewall
FRWN	forewing
FRWO	firewood
FRWR	firework
	firmware
	forewarn
	foreword
FRYA	ferryman
FRYR	farmyard
FRYS	fortyish
FSAL	festally
	fiscally
FSBC	fastback
	fast buck
FSBL	fastball
FSBN	fishbone
FSCK	fishcake
FSDV	fish dive
FSEE	fastened
	fastener
	festered
	fosterer
FSEO	fasten on
FSFO	fast food
FSFR	fusiform
FSHW	fish-hawk
FSIA	festival
FSIL	fascicle
FSIN	fistiana
FSIT	Fascisti
	Fascists
FSLE	fusilier
FSLG	fuselage
FSLI	fusel-oil
FSLK	fish-like
FSNS	fastness
FSOE	fuss over
FSOI	fisnomie
FSTI	fish-tail
FSTL	fast-talk
FSUA	fistulae
	fistular
	fistulas
FSUE	fissured
FSWF	fishwife
FSWS	fess-wise
FTEE	fattener
	fettered
FTEL	fatherly
FTET	fitments
FTGE	fatigued
FTGT	fatigate
FTHF	fetch off
FTHN	fetching
FTHU	fetch out
FTIG	fittings
FTLL	futilely
FTLS	fatalism
	fatalist
FTLT	fatality
	futility
FTOA	fit to eat
FTOS	fit to use
FTRS	futurism❑
	futurist
FTRT	futurity
FTUL	fitfully
FUAL	feudally
	Foucault
	frugally
FUCR	flue-cure
FUDC	fluidics
FUDF	fluidify
FUDN	founding
FUDS	fluidise
FUDT	fluidity
FUDZ	fluidize
FUEI	fauteuil
FUFL	fourfold
FUFO	four-foot
FUHN	Flushing
FUIE	frutices
FUKE	Faulkner
FULE	Fluellen
FUMR	flummery
FUNL	fluently
FUNS	foulness
FUOR	faubourg
FUPA	foul play
FUPP	flue pipe
FUPS	frumpish
FURD	fluoride
FURE	flurried
FURN	fluorine
FURT	fluorite
FUSM	foursome

FUTA fruit bat
FUTE fourteen
fruit tea
FUTF fructify
FUTG fruitage
FUTI fountain
FUTL faultily
fourthly
FUTM frustums
FUTN Faustina
FUTO fruition
FUTR flustery
fluttery
FUTS fructose
FUTU faultful
fruitful
FVBA fava bean
FVFL fivefold
FVPN fivepins
FVRE feverfew
FVRS feverish
FVRU feverous
FVUE favoured
favourer
FXLV foxglove
FXON foxhound
FXTO fixation
FXTV fixative
FXUE fixtures
FYAE flypaper
FYHE flywheel
FYIC flypitch
FYKT fly a kite
FYYN fly-tying
GAAA Ghanaian
GAAE gravamen
GAAI gradatim
GAAT guaranty
GABN grabbing
GACA glance at
GACM glaucoma
GACN glancing
G Marconi
GACS Graecise
GACU glaucous
GACZ Graecize
GADA granddad
grand mal
guardian
GADE go and get
go and see
GADG guardage
GADN guarding
GADO grandson
guard dog
GADR glanders
GADU grandeur
GADW gear down
GAEL glabella
gravelly
GAEU geared up
glareous
graceful
grateful
GAFT graffiti
graffito
GAHC graphics
GAHM grapheme
GAHN glad hand
GAHR go ashore
goatherd
GAHT graphite
GAHU graphium
GAIA gravitas
GAIE glacises
gratinée
GAII granitic
GAIL gladioli
GAIN gradient
GAIS grazioso
GAIT glaciate
GAIU gracious
GAKC goal kick
GALC gralloch
GALN goal line
goatling
grayling
GALS goalless
GALU go all out
GAMR Grasmere
GANE Grainger
GANN graining
GANS gladness
glasnost
GAON go around
GAOR go aboard
GAPA Grampian
GAPN grasping
GAPS goalpost
GARA go abroad
GARC glam rock
GARG glad rags
GARS go across
GART glabrate
GARU glabrous
GASE Graf Spee
GASF glassify
GASL glassily
GASM gladsome
GASN glassine
GASO grass box
GASY glass eye
GATA go astray
Grantham
GATL graithly
GATN grafting
granting
GATS giantess
GAUA granular
GAUN graduand
GAUT graduate
gratuity
GBCO go back on
GBFO go by foot
GBFR go before
GBHN go behind
GBLN gabbling
GBLU gobble up
GBMC gobsmack
GBNL gibingly
GBRN Gaborone
GBTE go better
GBYN go beyond
GCLO go cold on
GDAD godwards
GDAR God's acre
GDBU gad about
gadabout
GDER gadgetry
GDGD gado-gado
GDHA Godthaab
GDHL godchild
GDNW God knows
GDPE Godspeed
GDPL Godspell
GDRC Goderich
GDRN Gadarene
GDWL God's will
GDWO go down on
GDWT go down to
GDWU god-awful
GEAE grenades
grey area
GEAH Grenache
GEAI gregatim
GEBL Goebbels
GEDL greedily
GEGE greegree
GEIL Greville
guerilla
GEJH Gwen John
GEKE Greek key
GEMN gleaming
GENC Greenock
Guernica
GENE greenies
green tea
guernsey□
GENL greenfly
GENN gleaning
greening
Grey nuns
GENR greenery
GENS greenish
greyness
GEOL Grenoble
GESA grey seal
GESE greasies
GESL greasily
GESN guessing
GESO go easy on
GETE ghettoes
GETI great big
great tit
GETN greeting
GETO Great Dog
GETP great ape
GETS greatest
GETU great auk
GEWL grey wolf
GFEL giftedly
GFSE go faster
GFSI gaff sail
GFWA gift-wrap
GGBT gigabyte
GGLN giggling
GGNE Gigantes
GGNI gigantic
GGTE go-getter
GHLE go halves
GHNR go hungry
GIAC guidance
GIAD Grimaldi
GIDN grinding
GIED Griselda
GIEI Goidelic
GIEO guide dog
GIET Ghiberti
grisette
GIEU griseous
guileful
GIFT Griffith
GIGA going bad
GIGF going off
GIGI grisgris
GIGO goings-on
GIGU going out
going-out
GIIO gridiron
GILA grill pan
GILC gridlock
GILN grilling
GILS gainless
GIMT gliomata
GINS glibness
grimness
Guinness
GIPN gripping
GISD glissade
GITL guiltily
GITM gain time
GITN glinting
GITO guilty of
GITR glittery
GIUO gain upon
GIUT go in unto
GIVN grieving
GIVU grievous
GIWT go in with
GIZE grizzled
GIZL glitzily
GJUE Gajdusek
GLAI galvanic
GLBL golf ball
GLBR Goldberg
GLCI galactic
GLCR gold card
GLCU golf club
GLDS gold disc
gold dust
GLDW gulp down
GLEI galleria

GLEL goldenly
GLFI gold foil
GLFS goldfish
GLHR Gellhorn
GLIA gallivat
GLIE Gulliver
GLIL gullible
GLIN Galliano
golfiana
GLIR galliard
Galtieri
GLLA Galilean
gold leaf
GLMN Gell-Mann
gold mine
GLOA galloway□
GLOE galloper
GLOI galtonia
GLRS gold rush
GLRU Galerius
GLSI gelastic
GLSU Gelasius
GLTN gelatine
GLTO gelation
GLUE galluses
GLUP gallumph
GLVN Gil Evans
GLWE galowses
gulfweed
GLYO gollywog
GMAA gamma ray
GMAE game area
GMAI gammadia
gymnasia
GMAO gambados
GMCC gamecock
GMHN gymkhana
GMIK gimmicky
GMLN gambling
GMLW game laws
GMNS gameness
gaminess
GMNT geminate
GMPA game plan
GMRC gimcrack
Gombrich
GMSE gamester
GMSM gamesome
GMSO game show
GMTN gemstone
GMTO gumption
GNAE Gonzales
González
GNAI Gunga Din
GNAL genially
GNAM gendarme
GNAO gonfalon
GNBR Ginsberg
GNCD genocide
GNEA gunmetal
GNEL gingerly
GNER gannetry
GNEU ginger up

GNGE ginkgoes
GNIA gingival
GNIH gunfight
GNKE gingkoes
GNLA gangliar
GNLM ginglymi
GNLN gangland
gangling
gantline
gin sling
GNLO ganglion
GNMD Ganymede
GNMT gunsmith
GNNI gin and it
GNON gunpoint
GNOR Goncourt
GNPU gang plug
gone phut
GNRF gentrify
GNRN gangrene
GNRP gang rape
GNRT generate
GNRU generous
GNSE gangster
ganister
GNTC genetics
GNTL genitals
GNTN gunstone
GNTP genotype
GNTV genitive
go native
GNUE geniuses
GNUM gin rummy
GNUO gang up on
GNVS Genevese
Genovese
GNWN Gondwana
GOAL globally
GOBA grosbeak
GOBO good book
GOCE groschen□
GODE good deed
GOEE geometer
good-even
GOEI geodesic
geodetic
GOEO glove box
goosegog
GOER geometry
GOET go over to
GOFE Geoffrey
GOFR good form
go on fire
GOGA Georgian
GOGC Georgics
GOGN Georgina
GOGO groo-groo
GOHL good help
GOII gloxinia
GOIL gloriole
GOIN Gloriana
GOIT grow into
GOIU glorious

GOLC good luck
GOLN growling
GOLS ghoulish
grow less
GOML gloomily
GOMN gloaming
GONE grounded
GONM good name
GONN groaning
groining
GONS goodness
GONW good news
GOOI geoponic
GOOT glom on to
GOPL grow pale
GOPN grouping
grow pink
GOPR groupers
GOPU glow plug
GORC grow rich
GOSA gross pay
GOSL glossily
GOSN Goossens
GOSR glossary
GOSU gross out
GOTE grottoes
GOTN gloating
grouting
GOTR good turn
GOUA globular
GOUE globulet
GOUI globulin
GOWL good will
goodwill
GOWR glowworm
glow-worm
good word
GOYA Goodyear
GOYN glorying
GOYO glory box
GPAE go places
GPBI go public
GPNL gapingly
GRAE garganey
GRAI Germanic
GRAN Germaine
GREE gardener
GREI gardenia
GREL gor-belly
GRET garments
GREU gorgeous
GRFE germ-free
GRGN garaging
GRHI Gershwin
GRHL Gurkhali
GRHO girlhood
GRIA germinal□
GRIE Gardiner
Gordimer
GRIK garlicky
GRIL Garfield
GRIO garrison
GRLM gorblimy

GRLN garbling
gurgling
GRLS germless
gormless
GRNM Geronimo
GRNS goriness
GRNU geranium
GROL gargoyle
GROT garrotte
GRRD Gertrude
GRRI Girardin
GRSL garishly
girasole
GRTE go rotten
GRTN gyrating
GRTO gyration
GRTR gyratory
GRUH Gurmukhi
GRWR gurdwara
GRYO gardyloo
GSAE go shares
gossamer
GSAO gestapos
GSED go steady
GSEE gas meter
GSFO go soft on
GSIH gaslight
GSIL gasfield
GSLN gasoline
GSNS gastness
GSOE gas poker
GSOL go slowly
GSUA gestural
GTAE guttated
GTBT go to bits
GTBU get about
GTDA get ideas
GTED get ready
GTEE gathered
gatherer
GTEI gather in
GTEU get het up
GTFL gatefold
GTFO get off on
GTHA get ahead
GTHR get there
GTIO get rid of
GTLA get clear
GTLF get a life
GTLN get along
GTNR get angry
GTOA go too far
GTOE get lower
GTON get going
get round
GTOO got to pot
GTOS get worse
GTPS gatepost
GTRN get drunk
get wrong
GTSE go to seed
GTTC get stuck
GTTF get it off

GTTW	go to town
GTUA	guttural
GTUF	get huffy
GTUO	get out of
GUAO	glucagon
GUBE	grumbler
GUEO	gauge rod
GUEU	gouge out
GUGN	grudging
GUKC	grub kick
GULS	Gaullism
	Gaullist
GUMN	gourmand
GUNS	glumness
GUPL	grumpily
GUSA	Gaussian
GUSM	gruesome
GUTE	Gaultier
	gauntlet
GUTN	gluttony
	grunting
GUWI	glühwein□
GVAA	give away
	giveaway
	give-away
GVBC	give back
GVBI	give bail
GVHA	give head
GVHL	give hell
GVIT	give in to
	give into
	give it to
GVLN	give line
GVNH	Givenchy
GVNI	giving in
	giving-in
GVNU	giving up
	giving-up
GVOE	give over
GVOT	give on to
	give onto
GVRI	give rein
GVRO	governor
GVSA	Gavaskar
GVUO	give up on
GWDL	go widely
GYEI	glycerin
GYEO	glycerol
GYIE	Gay Times
GYOE	glycogen
GYQI	Guyaquil
GZAH	gazpacho
GZBE	gazeboes
GZLN	guzzling
GZNE	gazunder
GZOB	Gezhouba
HAAH	headache
	headachy
	Hiawatha
HAAL	hearable
HAAO	huanacos
HABN	headband
HABT	head-butt
HACL	head cold
HACS	headcase
HADN	hoarding
HAEL	heavenly
HAGA	headgear
HAGR	head girl
HAHA	hear, hear!
HAHN	headhunt
	heathens
HAHO	Heathrow
HAIT	hyacinth
HALM	headlamp
HALN	headland
	headline
	headlong
HALS	headless
HAPM	heat pump
HARC	headrace
HARO	headroom
HARS	headrest
	heat rash
HASA	headsman
HASI	headsail
	headship
HASL	hoarsely
HATI	hoactzin
HATL	heartily
HAUE	hiatuses
HAWR	headword
	headwork
HBAS	Hebraise
HBAU	Habbakuk
HBAZ	Hebraize
HBCI	hibachis
HBIE	Hebrides
HBKU	Habakkuk
HBLN	hobbling
HBNR	habanera
HBOS	Hobhouse
HBRA	hibernal
HBSU	hibiscus
HBTA	habitual
HBTD	hebetude
HBTN	habitans
	habitant
	hebetant
HBTT	hebetate
HCED	hacienda
HCET	hackette
HCOG	hiccough
HCSE	huckster
HCTM	hecatomb
HCWR	hack-work
HDAA	hide away
	hideaway
	hide-away
HDBA	Hudibras
HDEL	hiddenly
HDEO	hedgehog
	hedge-hop
	hedgerow
HDIG	hidlings
HDLA	hidalgas
HDLO	hidalgos
HDNC	hedonics
HDNS	hedonism
	hedonist
HDOE	hydrogen
	hydromel
HDOI	hadronic
	hidrosis
HDOO	hydrozoa
HDOY	hydroxyl
HEAC	hierarch
HEAI	haematic
	haematin
	hieratic
HEEA	haeremai
HELS	heedless
HEOE	heel over
HFMN	Hoffmann
HFWD	Haft Wadi
HGAA	Haggadah
	Hogmanay
HGAI	Haggadic
HGAL	huggable
HGBC	hog's back
	hog's-back
HGBE	high-bred
HGBL	highball
HGBO	highbrow
HGBR	highborn
	high-born
	Highbury
HGCS	high-cost
HGEI	hygienic
HGEO	Huguenot
HGER	hagberry
HGEU	higher-up
HGFV	high-five
HGGA	high gear
HGHA	hogshead
HGJC	highjack
HGJM	high jump
HGKC	high kick
HGLA	Hegelian
HGLF	high life
HGLN	haggling
	highland□
	high-lone
HGMN	hegemony
HGMS	High Mass
HGNO	High Noon
	high noon
HGNS	highness
	hugeness
HGRS	high-rise
	high-risk
HGSA	high seas
HGSO	high spot
HGTC	high tech
HGTD	high tide
HGTI	hightail
HGTM	high time
HGWR	high wire
HIBN	hair-band
HICO	Huis Clos
HIDL	Heimdall
HIFO	hail from
HIGI	hairgrip
HIHE	heighten
HIHN	Haiphong
HILK	hairlike
HILN	hairline
HILO	heirloom
HILS	hairless
	hair loss
	heirless
HIMR	hail Mary□
HISA	Hailsham
HJCE	hijacker
HKAD	Hokkaido
HKIE	Hakkinen
HLAA	heliacal
HLAI	Helladic
HLAL	helpable
HLAO	holla-hoa!
HLBC	hold back
HLBE	half-bred
HLBN	hell-bent
HLBO	half-boot
HLBT	half-butt
HLCC	half-cock
HLCL	half-calf
HLCN	Holocene
HLCR	hole card
HLCT	Holy City
HLDA	hold dear
HLDC	helideck
HLDM	holydame
HLDN	half-done
HLDW	hold down
	hull-down
HLEE	halteres
	helmeted
HLEI	Hellenic
	Helvetic
HLFR	hellfire
	hill fort
	hill-fort
HLFS	hold fast
	holdfast
HLGA	hologram
HLGO	hold good
HLHA	Holyhead
HLHG	hold high
HLHL	hula-hula
HLHR	hold hard
	hold hard!
HLHU	half-hour
HLIA	hollidam
HLIC	half-inch
HLIE	Hilfiger
	Holliger
HLIG	holdings
HLIK	Helsinki
HLIR	halliard
	Hilliard
HLIT	helminth

Words marked □ can also be spelled with an initial capital letter

HLKA Halakhah
HLKT hell-kite
HLLF half-life
HLLN halflins
helpline
HLLS helpless
HLME helpmeet
HLMN Helpmann
HLMO half-moon
HLMR hallmark
HLMS half-mast
HLMT helpmate
HLNS haleness
holiness
HLOC Hal Roach
HLOE hallowed
hold over
hollowed
HLOI haliotis
HLOK hillocky
HLOL hollowly
HLOM halloumi
HLOT hold on to
HLPN half-pint
HLPR heliport
HLRT hilarity
HLSA Halmstad
helmsman
hold sway
HLSD hillside
HLSE half-step
HLSI half-slip
holistic
HLSL half-sole
HLSZ half-size
HLTI Holstein
HLTM half-time
HLTN half-tone
HLTO halation
HLTR half-term
HLUE halluces
HLWE Holy Week
HLWI Holy Writ
holy writ
HLWL Holywell
HLWN helm wind
HLWR hellward
HLWT help with
hold with
HMAL hummable
HMBC humpback
HMBE home-bred
home brew
home-brew
HMBO hymn-book
HMCD homicide
HMDF humidify
HMDT humidity
HMEE hammered
hampered
HMEI hemmed in
HMGM homogamy
HMGN homogeny
HMHE Humphrey
HMHL home help
HMHY Humphrys
HMIO home in on
HMLA home loan
HMLE homilies
HMLG homology
HMLK homelike
HMLL homelily
HMLN homeland
humbling
HMLO Hamilton
HMLS homeless
homilist
HMLT hamulate
humility
HMMD home-made
HMNA hymeneal
hymenean
HMNH hum and ha
HMNI hominoid
humanoid
HMNL humanely
HMNS humanise
humanism
humanist
HMNT humanity
HMNZ humanize
HMOD Humboldt
HMOK hummocky
HMPG home page
HMRL home rule
HMRS humorist
HMRU humorous
HMSC homesick
HMSU homespun
HMTT hematite
HMTW home town
HMUG Hamburgh
HMUI home unit
HMWR homeward
homework
HMWT hamewith
HNAA Hanrahan
HNAT Hanratty
HNBC hand back
hang back
HNBL handball
handbell
handbill
hunt ball
HNBO handbook
HNCA handclap
HNCE Honecker
HNCF handcuff
HNCR handcart
HNDW hand down
hang down
hunt down
HNEE hinderer
HNEL hungerly
HNEO hanger-on
HNFL handfuls
HNFR hang fire
HNGA Hans Gram
HNGE Honegger
HNGI handgrip
HNHA henchman
HNHE hench-men
HNHN hunching
HNIA handicap
Hannibal
HNIG hangings
HNJR hung jury
HNKA Hanukkah
HNKI hand-knit
HNKN Hong Kong
HNLL Honolulu
HNLN hand line
handling
HNLS handless
HNMD handmade
HNMS hindmost
HNNI hangnail
HNOE hand over
handover
hang over
hangover
Hannover
hung over
HNOT hand-outs
hang on to
HNPC hand-pick
HNPO hanepoot
HNPR hind part
HNPS handpost
HNQI henequin
heniquin
HNRD hundreds
HNRI handrail
HNRL hungrily
HNRN honorand
HNRR honorary
HNRS huntress
HNRU Honorius
HNSA huntsman□
HNSF hands off
hands-off
HNSL honestly
HNSM handsome
HNUA Honduras
HNUE honoured
HNUO hung up on
HNUS Hinduise
Hinduism
HNUZ Hinduize
HNWN hindwing
HNWR handwork
hindward
HNYA handyman
HNYE honey bee
honeydew
HNYN Hinayana
HNYY Henry Pye
HNZO Hangzhou
HOCN hyoscine
HOEO hooked on
HOHA Hrothgar
HOIA hooligan
HOLK hooplike
HOWN hoodwink
HOWR hookworm
HPAC heptarch
HPAO heptagon
HPDO hoped-for
HPEO happen on
HPET happen to
HPGA hypogeal
hypogean
HPGE hypogaea
HPGN hypogene
HPGU hypogeum
HPLI hypalgia
HPLS hip flask
hopeless
HPNM hyponymy
HPOD haploidy
HPOI hypnosis
hypnotic
HPOT Hepworth
HPRO Hyperion
HPTC hepatica
HPTE hypothec
HPTR hipsters
HPTS hepatise
HPTZ hepatize
HRAA hark away
hereaway
HRAE hard-a-lee
HRAI hard at it
herbaria
HRAL hireable
HRBA hornbeam
HRBC hardback
hark back
HRBL hardball
harebell
hornbill
HRBO hornbook
HRCE Heracles
Herschel
HRCP hard copy
HRCR hard card
hard core
hard-core
HRCS hard case
hard cash
HRDS hard disk
HRDT heredity
HREA horseman
HREE hardened
hardener
herbelet
horsemen
HREG hard edge
HREI hermetic
herpetic
HREL horsefly
HRFL hornfels

HRFO herefrom
HRFR Hartford
Hereford
Hertford
HRGE here goes!
HRGN hiragana
HRHT Hirohito
HRIA harridan
HRII hermitic
horrific
HRIK Horlicks®
HRIL horrible
horribly
horridly
HRIN Hermione
HRIO Harrison
hornitos
HRKR hara-kiri
hari-kari
HRLC hard luck
HRLG horology
HRLI heraldic
HRLN hard line
hardline
hard-line
hireling
hurdling
HRLR heraldry
HRLS harmless
HRME harambee
HRNE Haringey
HRNS hardness
HRNU harangue
HROA hormonal
HROE harrowed
HROI harmonic
HROK Horrocks
HROR harlotry
HRPP hornpipe
HRPR hard porn
HRRC hard rock
HRRE Hereroes
HRSA harp seal
harp-seal
herdsman□
hernshaw
HRSE harassed
haruspex
HRSI hardship
HRTA Horatian
HRTC hardtack
HRTG heritage
HRTI heritrix
HRUE Hercules
HRUO hereupon
HRUP harrumph
HRUT hereunto
HRWC herdwick
HRWO hardwood
HRWR hardware
hard work
Hereward
HRWT herewith

HRYN harrying
HSDS Hasidism
Hasidist
HSEI hysteria
hysteric
HSEN has-beens
HSER hostelry
HSES hasheesh
HSEU Hesperus
HSHS hush-hush
HSIA hospital
HSIG Hastings
hustings
HSII hospitia
HSOI historic
HSRO histrion
histrios
HSTN hesitant
HSTT hesitate
HTAE hot water
HTAL hateable
HTAT hot pants
HTBO hit a blot
HTEA hetaerae
HTEE Hot Seven
HTET hitherto
HTHA hatchway
HTHL hitchily
HTHN hatching
HTIA hetairai
hetairas
HTLE hotelier
HTMI hate mail
HTOD hot goods
HTOE hot money
HTOS hothouse
HTRC hat trick
HTRN hot drink
HTRS hot-press
HTTF hit it off
hot stuff
HTTN hatstand
HTUA Hattusas
hit out at
HUCE haunches
HUDN hounding
HUEA house bat
houseman
HUEE house red
HUEI house-sit
HUEL housefly
HUEO houseboy
house-dog
housetop
HUFA hausfrau
HUHN hour hand
HUIG housings
HULN hourlong
HUSO Hounslow
HUTN haunting
HVAO have a job
have a row
HVAR have a try

HVDN have done
HVLA havildar
HVLC havelock
HVLF have life
HVNT have-nots
HVOE have over
HVPT Have Pity
HVRN havering□
hovering
HVSA Havisham
HVTB have to be
HVWR hiveward
HWBU how about
HWDW howl down
HWEA Hawke Bay
HWEE hawk-eyed
HWHR hawthorn
HWIA Hawaiian
HWIC hawfinch
HWLK hawklike
HWTA how's that
HWTE howitzer
HWWE hawkweed
HWYD how-d'ye-do
HXGA hexagram
HYAE haymaker
HYEE hay fever
HYMN Huysmans
HYOA hey-go-mad
HYON Hay Point
HYOT Hayworth
HYTC haystack
HZKA Hezekiah
HZLU hazelnut
HZNS haziness
IAAD in a paddy
IAAI in a panic
IACR in accord
IAEA I dare say
I daresay
IAEL Isabella
IAES in a sense
IAFT Id al-Fitr
IAHL in a while
IAIE imagined
imaginer
imagines
IAIF in a jiffy
IAIG Itatinga
IAIZ in a tizzy
IALS in a flash
IAOI isagogic
IARC in a trice
IATO in action
inaction
IATS ITAR-Tass
Itar-Tass
IATT in a state
IATV inactive
IAUR in a hurry
IAUU in a queue
IAWA in a sweat
IBCL imbecile

IBCO in back of
IBIE imbrices
ICAG in charge
ICBT incubate
ICDN incident
ICEI in credit
ischemia
ICEP in cuerpo
ICES increase
ICIE inclined
ICMA inchmeal
ICMN incoming
ICMO in common
ICMR in camera
ICNE incensed
ICNO in convoy
ICOD in crowds
ICOT inchoate
ICRE incurved
ICRO in care of
ICSO in case of
incision
ICSV incisive
ICTN inciting
ICUE included
ICUS in course
IDAA Indiaman
IDBE indebted
IDBT in debt to
IDCE indictee
IDCL indocile
IDCN indecent
indicant
inducing
IDCO inductor
IDCT indicate
IDGE indigoes
IDGN indigent
IDGS indigest
IDLE indulged
IDLN indolent
IDMN in demand
IDNE indented
IDOE in droves
IDRC indirect
IDRI Indurain
IDRT indurate
IDSR industry
IDSS in disuse
IDTI in detail
IDXN indexing
IEAC ice dance
iterance
IEAU Irenaeus
IECS in excess
IEFC in effect
IEFX idée fixe
IEGA ideogram
IEHE ice sheet
IEIA irenical
IEIE itemized
IEIL inedible
IEKT ice skate

IELA ideal gas
IELG ideology
IELN iceblink
IELO I tell you
IELR I declare!
IELS idealise
idealism
idealist
IELZ idealize
IEOL ice lolly
IEON icebound
IEPR inexpert
IEQO idem quod
IERA ice cream
IETA inert gas
inertial
IETF identify
IETT identity
IEUL irefully
IEUT inequity
IFAE inflamed
in flames
inflated
infrared
IFAI infra dig
IFCE infected
IFCN infecund
IFIG infringe
IFIH in-flight
IFMS infamise
IFMU infamous
IFMZ infamize
IFNR infantry
IFNT infinite
infinity
IFOE in flower
IFOK in flocks
IFRA infernal
informal
IFRE inferred
informed
informer
IFRL infirmly
IFRO inferior
infernos
inform on
IFSE infested
IFSN infusing
IFSO infusion
IFSV infusive
IFVU in favour
IGIA inguinal
IGOV ingroove
IGTE ingather
IHAS inhearse
IHGR Ishiguro
IHHI ichthyic
IHLN inhalant
inhaling
IHMN inhumane
IHMT inhumate
IHRA in her way
IHRN inherent

IHSA in his way
IIAE imitated
irisated
IIAL imitable
IIAO imitator
IIHA Irishman
IIHE Irish Sea
IIHL Irish elk
IIIA inimical
IIIL initials
IIIT initiate
IILC idiolect
IISI it is said
IISL in itself
IITO idiot box
IIUT iniquity
IKNS inkiness
IKTN inkstand
ILAE ill-famed
ill-fated
ILAU in league
ILEO in lieu of
ILIE ill-timed
ILLO ill blood
ILMN illumine
ILMS Islamise
ILMZ Islamize
ILNE islander
ILNH Iolanthe
ILNI Illinois
ILNS idleness
ILRA ill-treat
ILSG ill-usage
ILSO illusion
ILSR illusory
ILSV illusive
ILTL idle talk
in little
ILTM idle time
ILTO illation
ILYN inlaying
IMBL immobile
IMBO in my book
IMDS immodest
IMLT immolate
IMMN immoment
IMNL immanely
immantle
IMNN immanent
imminent
IMNS immunise
IMNT ilmenite
immune to
immunity
IMNZ immunize
IMRA immortal
IMRE immersed
IMTO in motion
IMTR immature
IMUE iambuses
INCN innocent□
INCS Ionicise
INCZ Ionicize

INED innuendo
INMN ignominy
INMT Ian Smith
INRA inner ear
inner man
INRD Ian Brady
INRE ignaroes
INRN ignorant
ignoring
INTL innately
INTM in no time
INTN igniting
INTO ignition
INTU Ignatius
INVT innovate
IOAE idolater
isolated
IOAI isobaric
IOAR idolatry
IOCA ironclad
iron-clad
IOEE Idomeneo
IOEI isomeric
IOGE iron-grey
IOHN iron hand
IOHR isothere
isotherm
IOIA ironical
IOIE idoliser
idolized
idolizer
IOII in origin
IOLG I could go
IOLN iron lung
IOLS isogloss
IOLT if only to
IONT inornate
IOOI isotonic
isotopic
IOOP isomorph
IORA in our way
IORC isocracy
IORN isoprene
IORP isotropy
IOSD Ironside
IOTS isostasy
IOUI Iroquois
IPBI in public
IPCE in pocket
IPCO impact on
IPDN impeding
impudent
IPEC impleach
IPEE in pieces
IPEG impledge
IPET in plenty
IPIE impaired
IPII implicit
imprimis
IPIO imprison
IPLE impeller
impolder
IPLT impolite

IPNT impunity
IPOE improper
improved
improver
IPRA imperial
IPRE imported
importer
IPRL impurely
IPRO in person
IPRT impart to
impurity
IPRU imperium
IPSE imposter
IPSL impishly
IPSN imposing
IPSO impasto'd
impastos
impose on
impostor
IPTE inputter
IPTG impetigo
IPTN impotent
IPUG implunge
IPUI impluvia
IQEP in querpo
IQIE inquirer
IRAO in reason
IRGT irrigate
IRNG Imre Nagy
IRPS in repose
IRTN irritant
IRTR in return
IRTT irritate
ISAC instance
instancy
issuance
ISAE in stages
ISAH inswathe
ISAL instable
issuably
ISAO in season
ISAT Instants
ISCA Issachar
ISCE in secret
ISCR insecure
ISEI in specie
ISGI insignia
ISHR insphere
ISIC instinct
ISIE inspired
inspirer
ISII inspirit
ISLE insulted
ISLN insolent
ISLT insolate
insulate
ISMC insomuch
ISMI insomnia
ISNE in sunder
ISNL insanely
ISNT insanity
ISOC insconce
ISRB inscribe

ISRC	instruct
ISRD	in shreds
ISRE	in series
	inserted
	inserter
ISRL	inscroll
ISRS	instress
ISSO	insist on
ISTO	in shtook
ITAO	intrados
ITBA	Istabraq
ITBT	intubate
ITEA	in the bag
	in the raw
	in the way
ITEC	intrench
ITEE	in the red
ITEI	in the air
	intrepid
ITEN	in the end
ITEO	in the poo
ITER	in theory
ITGA	integral
ITGI	intaglio
ITIC	intrince
ITIU	intrigue
ITLA	Intelsat
ITMC	intimacy
ITMS	intimism
ITMT	intimate
ITNE	in tandem
	intended
ITNL	intently
ITNO	intent on
ITNT	intend to
	intonate
ITNU	Istanbul
ITOI	intromit
ITRA	interlay
	internal
	interval
ITRC	interact
ITRE	interned
	internee
	intersex
ITRI	intarsia
	intermit
	intermix
ITRL	in thrall
ITRO	intercom
	interior
	Interpol
ITRS	interest
ITRU	intercut
ITTL	intitule
ITUE	intruder
ITVE	into view
IUBD	Itúrbide
IUDN	inundant
IUDT	inundate
IUET	inured to
IUIO	in unison
IVEO	in view of

IVIL	inveigle
IVLE	involved
IVLT	involute
IVNE	invented
IVNO	inventor
IVNR	in ventre
IVRE	inverted
IVSI	invest in
IVSO	invasion
	investor
IVSV	invasive
IVTN	inviting
IWCT	Iowa City
IWIH	in weight
IWRL	inwardly
IYLS	idyllist
JABE	Joan Baez
JAET	Jeanette
JAGI	Juan Gris
JAMI	Jean Muir
JAMR	Joan Miró
JAOS	jealousy
JARO	Jean Rook
JARY	Jean Rhys
JASM	Joan Sims
JAVL	Jhabvala
JBEE	jabberer
JBLN	jubilant
JBLT	jubilate
JBLU	Jabalpur
JCAO	jackaroo
JCBA	Jacobean
JCBE	Jacobsen
JCBO	jackboot
JCBT	Jacobite
JCCD	Jack Cade
JCEO	jackeroo
JCHG	jack-high
JCLN	Joceline
JCLT	jaculate
JCNH	Jacintha
	Jacinthe
JCNL	jocundly
JCSL	jocosely
JCST	jocosity
JCUR	jacquard
JDCA	judicial
JDMN	judgment
JDPR	jodhpurs
JEAI	Joe David
JEAT	Joe Dante
JEOI	Joe Louis
JERO	Joe Orton
JFRY	Jeffreys
JFYA	Jiffy bag®
JGAT	jog pants
JGEE	jiggered
JGEL	jaggedly
JGLN	juggling
JGLT	jugulate
JHAE	John Abel
JHBN	John Byng
JHBR	John Birt

JHCG	John Cage
JHCR	John Cary
JHDR	John Dory
JHFR	John Ford
JHHM	John Hume
JHHN	John Hunt
JHHR	John Hurt
JHHS	John Huss
JHKM	John Kemp
JHKO	John Knox
JHNI	Jahangir
JHNO	Johanson
JHNS	John Nash
JHPU	John Paul
JHRS	John Ross
JHVN	John Venn
JHWI	John Wain
JIBR	jailbird
JITN	jointing
JITR	jointure
JIWT	join with
JJNL	jejunely
JJNT	jejunity
JKNL	jokingly
JLAO	jillaroo
JLEN	julienne
JLIO	Jellicoe
JLPN	jalapeño
JLUI	jalousie
JLYA	jelly bag
JMAA	jump away
JMAE	jampanee
	Jim Laker
JMBC	jump back
JMBI	jump bail
JMEU	jambeaux
	jumped up
	jumped-up
JMIA	Jamaican
JMLA	jump lead
JMLR	Jim Clark
JMLU	jumble up
JMOE	jamboree
	jumbo jet
	jump over
JMOS	jumboise
JMOT	jump onto
JMOZ	jumboize
JMSI	jump ship
	jumpsuit
JMSO	James Fox
JMTI	jump to it!
JNDO	June drop
JNER	Jane Eyre
JNFA	Jungfrau
JNGE	Jane Grey
JNIE	Jennifer
JNIG	Jennings
JNLN	jangling
JNLU	jongleur
JNMI	junk mail
JNMT	Jan Smuts
JNOS	jingoism

	jingoist
JNOT	junior to
JNTA	Jonathan
JNTO	Jonathon
	junction
JNTR	juncture
JNYR	junkyard
JOAD	jeopardy
JPNC	japonica
JPNS	Japanese
	Japanise
JPNZ	Japanize
JRBA	jeroboam
JRDC	Jarndyce
JRDT	jury duty
JRMA	jeremiad
	Jeremiah
JRSI	Jurassic
	juristic
JRYA	jerrycan
JSEI	Joscelin
JSNS	justness
JSPS	just pass
JSPU	Josephus
JTIG	jottings
JTIO	jettison
JTLC	jet-black
JUDC	jaundice
JUIS	jiu-jitsu
JUNL	journals
JUNY	journeys
JUTL	jauntily
JVAL	jovially
JVNL	juvenile
JWHR	jew's harp❑
JWLE	jeweller
JWLO	jewel-box
JWSL	Jewishly
JYHE	joy-wheel
JYIE	joyrider
JYTC	joystick
JYUL	joyfully
	joyously
JZFN	jazz-funk
KAAO	Krakatoa
KACU	Kravchuk
KAEE	Khamenei
KART	Klaproth
KASA	Klansman
KASC	knapsack
KATU	Khartoum
KAWE	knapweed
KCBC	kick back
	kickback
KCDW	kickdown
KCSA	kickshaw
KCTR	kick turn
KDEE	kedgeree
KDLG	kidology
KDLV	kid-glove
KEAA	keep away
KEAC	keel arch
KEAI	keep at it

Words marked ❑ can also be spelled with an initial capital letter

KEBA	keelboat
KEBC	keep back
KEBS	keep busy
KECL	keep calm
	keep cold
KEDE	knee-deep
KEDN	kneading
KEDR	keep dark
KEDW	keep down
KEFO	keep from
KEHG	knee-high
KEHL	kneehole
KEHU	keel-haul
KEIA	khedival
KEJR	knee-jerk
KELN	kneeling
KENS	keenness
KEOA	keep on at
KEOE	keel over
KEPC	keep pace
KESE	keep step
KESF	keep safe
KESK	keepsake
KETE	Koestler
KETM	keep time
KEWR	keep warm
KFFL	kefuffle
KFIE	kaffiyeh
	keffiyeh
KHRB	kohlrabi
KIHL	knightly❑
KIKR	knickers
KITN	knitting
KITU	Kaieteur
KIWA	knitwear
KIYR	kailyard
KKEO	kakiemon❑
KKMN	kakemono
KLAA	kala-azar
KLBT	kilobyte
KLDE	killdeer
KLEE	Koldewey
KLEN	Kilkenny
KLGA	kilogram
	kilogray
KLHR	Kalahari
KLIA	keloidal
KLNK	kolinsky
KLTM	kill time
KLVL	Kalevala
	kilovolt
KLWT	kilowatt
KMEL	Kimberly
KMGA	kymogram
KMKZ	kamikaze
KNAA	Kandahar
KNAL	Keneally
KNAO	kangaroo
	kinkajou
KNAT	Kenyatta
KNBL	Kinabalu
KNEE	Ken Kesey
KNFL	kinsfolk

KNFS	kingfish
KNHS	Kinshasa
KNIO	kantikoy
KNJH	King John
KNKN	King Kong
KNLA	King Lear
KNLK	kinglike
KNLN	kindling
KNLS	kindless
	kingless
KNNS	kindness
KNPC	kenspeck
KNRS	Kanarese
KNSC	kinesics
KNSE	Kingsley
KNSI	kingship
KNSO	Kingston
KNSZ	king-size
KNTC	kinetics
KNTN	Konstanz
KNUK	Kentucky
KNWO	kingwood
KOAL	knowable
KODK	Klondike
	Klondyke
KOEK	kromesky
KOEN	Khomeini
KOKF	knock off
KOKN	knocking
KOKR	knockers
KOKU	knock out
	knockout
	knock-out
KOTR	Klosters
KPLE	Kapil Dev
KPOI	kyphosis
	kyphotic
KRAD	Kirkaldy
KRBH	Karl Böhm
KRBI	Karabair
KRBK	Karabakh
KRBL	korfball
KRBN	Karl Benz
KRBR	Kornberg
KRBT	Kiribati
KRDI	Karadzic
KRES	kermesse
KRHE	kerchief
KRHO	Korchnoi
KRIA	Kerrigan
KRLO	Korolyov
KRMR	Karl Marx
KRNK	Kerensky
KROI	kurtosis
KRSA	Karlsbad
KRSD	kerbside
KRSN	kerosene
	kerosine
KRSW	Kurosawa
KRTF	karstify
KRTI	keratoid
KRTK	karateka
KRTS	keratose

KRWL	Kirkwall
KRWR	kirkward
KSAL	kissable
KSAO	Kasparov
KSAY	Kismaayo
KSIE	Kishinev
KSMR	Kashmiri
KSRT	Kashruth
KSUT	kiss up to
KTAI	Kate Adie
KTBS	Kate Bush
KTKN	katakana
KTLE	Kathleen
KTMN	ketamine
KTMR	kite mark❑
KTRN	Katerina
KTWC	Katowice
KULN	knurling
KWLK	Kowalski
KWSK	Kawasaki
KYAG	Key Largo
KYOE	key money
KYON	key point
KYOR	keyboard
KYTG	key stage
KYTN	keystone
KYTO	klystron
KYUC	keypunch
KZLU	Kyzyl-Kum
LAAI	leaf axil
LAAL	leasable
LABC	lean back
LABR	leafbird
LABS	leaf-base
LACR	leaf-curl
LAEE	leavened
LAEF	leave off
LAEL	leadenly
LAEO	llaneros
LAEU	leave out
LAEY	Llaregyb
LAFL	leaf-fall
LAFO	leap-frog
LAHA	Loaghtan
LAHN	loathing
LAHR	leathern
	leathery
LAHU	loathful
LAIG	leavings
LAIT	lead into
LALS	leafless
LALT	leaflets
	liable to
LANN	learning
LANS	leanness
LAOE	lean over
	leap over
LASA	loadstar
LATM	lead time
LAUT	lead up to
LAWR	loan-word
LAYA	leap year
LBAL	labially

LBAO	Labrador
LBCI	libeccio
LBEL	lubberly
LBET	libretti
	libretto
LBHM	La Bohème
LBLE	labelled
	libellee
LBRC	Liberace
LBRT	liberate
LBRU	laburnum
	Liberius
LBTC	Lubitsch
LBTM	lobotomy
LBTO	libation
LBUE	laboured
	labourer
LBYN	lobbying
LBYS	lobbyist
LCAA	lock away
LCAL	lockable
LCDT	lucidity
LCEA	Lac Léman
LCEI	Lucretia
LCER	Loch Earn
LCEU	locked up
LCGT	lichgate
	lock gate
	lychgate
LCLS	localise
	localism
	luckless
LCLT	locality
LCLU	Lucilius
	Lucullus
LCLZ	localize
LCMT	locomote
LCNA	laciniae
LCNE	licensed
	licensee
LCNR	lacunars
	lacunary
	lecanora
LCNS	laconism
	Loch Ness
LCOS	lacrosse
LCOT	lock on to
LCRN	La Coruna
LCRT	lacerate
LCRU	Lycurgus
LCSA	locustae
LCTI	lecithin
LCTN	locating
LCTO	location
	locution
LCTV	locative
LCUE	lecturer
	lectures
LCUY	lacqueys
LCWE	locoweed
LCWN	lacewing
LCWR	lacework
LCYI	lucky dip

Words marked ❑ can also be spelled with an initial capital letter

	Lucky Jim
LCZD	Lucozade®
LDBR	ladybird
LDEE	laddered
LDEU	ladleful
	ladle out
LDIG	lodgings
LDLK	ladylike
LDLV	lady love
	lady-love
LDSA	Ladislaw
	lady's man
	lodestar
LDSI	Ladyship
LEAG	lee-gauge
LEBU	lie about
LEEA	liegeman
LEEY	Llewelyn
LEOG	lie doggo
LEOR	lee-board
LFBA	lifeboat
LFBL	lifebelt
LFBO	lifebuoy
LFEU	lifted up
LFFC	left face!
LFHN	left-hand
LFIS	loftiest
LFLK	lifelike
LFLN	lifeline
	lifelong
LFLS	lifeless
LFOE	left over
	leftover
	left-over
LFPE	life peer
LFRU	Laforgue
LFSA	lifespan
LFSZ	life-size
LFTM	lifetime
LFWN	left-wing
LFWR	leftward
	life-work
LGAG	Lagrange
LGAI	log cabin
LGCA	logician
LGCS	logicise
LGCZ	logicize
LGEU	ligneous
LGGA	logogram
LGIG	leggings
LGLG	legal age
LGLI	legal aid
LGLN	Legoland
LGLS	legalese
	legalise
	legalism
	legalist
LGLT	legality
LGLZ	legalize
LGMN	ligament
LGOA	leg-woman
LGRA	leg break
	Ligurian

LGSI	logistic
LGTE	light pen
LGTL	light ale
LGTN	lighting
LGTO	legation
	ligation
LGTP	logotype
LGTR	legatary
	ligature
LGTS	lightish
LGUR	leg guard
LHIA	lah-di-dah
LIBC	laid back
	laid-back
LIBR	laid bare
LIDW	laid down
LIEE	loiterer
LIGI	lyings-in
LISE	Leinster
LIUE	leisured
LKAB	Lake Abbe
LKAH	Lok Sabha
LKAL	likeable
LKBE	Lake Bled
LKBW	Lake Biwa
LKCA	Lake Chad
LKCM	Lake Como
LKEI	Lake Erie
LKER	Lake Eyre
LKFR	like fury
LKKV	Lake Kivu
LKLT	likely to
LKNS	likeness
LKSD	lakeside
LKTA	like that
LKTI	like this
LKTN	Lake Tana
LKTO	lekythos
LKWR	lukewarm
LKWS	likewise
LLIO	lollipop
LLNW	Lilongwe
LLUN	Lilburne
LLYA	lallygag
	lollygag
LMAD	Lombardi
LMAO	lumbagos
LMAS	lampasse
LMAT	lambaste
LMBA	lima bean
LMDC	lame duck
LMEC	lambency
LMEU	limber up
LMFS	lumpfish
LMHI	lymphoid
LMHM	lymphoma
LMIL	limpidly
LMIR	Lemaître
LMKL	limekiln
LMLA	lamellae
LMLS	limbless
LMMA	limbmeal
LMND	lemonade

LMNE	lamented
	lemon tea
LMNR	luminary
LMNS	lameness
	liminess
	limpness
LMNT	laminate
	limonite
LMNU	luminous
LMPS	lamppost
LMRC	limerick□
LMRY	lampreys
LMSI	lambskin
LMSO	Limassol
LMTN	limiting
LMTR	limitary
LMUI	Limousin
LNAA	Linnaean
LNAD	lentando
LNAL	lineally
	linearly
LNAU	Linnaeus
LNBA	longboat
LNBN	land bank
LNBR	Lansbury
LNDL	Lonsdale
LNEC	lenience
	leniency
LNEE	lanneret
	lingerer
	lynx-eyed
LNEI	Langevin
	lingerie
LNEO	Lancelot
LNFC	long face
LNFL	landfall
	landfill
LNFR	Longford
LNFS	land-fish
LNGN	long-gone
LNGR	land-girl
LNHA	lynch law
LNHI	linchpin
LNHM	long home
LNHN	longhand
	lynching
LNHO	luncheon
LNHR	Longhorn
LNHU	land-haul
	long haul
LNIL	lenticle
LNIU	Longinus
LNJM	long jump
LNLD	landlady
LNLL	lent-lily
LNLN	Langland
LNLR	landlord
LNLU	langlauf
	linoleum
LNMI	Langmuir
LNMN	land mine
	land-mine
	liniment

LNMR	landmark
LNMS	landmass
LNNS	lankness
	Leninism
	Leninist
LNNT	Leninite
LNNU	lining up
LNOD	long odds
LNPE	long poem
LNRC	landrace
LNRI	landrail
LNSA	Langshan
	linesman
LNSD	landside
LNSE	Landseer
LNSI	landslip
	longship
	long slip
LNSM	lonesome
LNSN	lang syne
LNSO	long stop
LNTE	lengthen
LNTM	long time
LNTP	Linotype®
LNTR	long-term
LNTV	lenitive
LNUG	language
LNUN	linguini
LNUS	languish
	linguist
LNUU	longueur
LNWL	lone wolf
LNWR	landward
	lungwort
LNWS	longwise
LNWT	land with
	link with
LNWY	longways
LOAD	Leonardo
	Leopardi
LOAR	look awry
LOBC	look back
LOBU	Léon Blum
LODW	look down
LOEE	loosener
LOEN	loose end
LOEO	looker-on
	loose box
LOEU	loosen up
LOGI	Laoighis
LOGT	Lion Gate
LOHL	loophole
LOHR	look here!
LOIA	Leonidas
LOIO	Leo Minor
	look in on
LOIT	look into
LOLK	look like
LOOE	look over
	look-over
LOOT	look onto
LOPN	look pink
LOTB	look to be

Code	Word
LOTE	Leontief
LOUO	look upon
LOUT	look up to
LOYI	loony bin
LPAE	lop-eared
LPDR	lapidary
LPDT	lepidote
LPGA	lipogram
LPIE	lopsided
	lop-sided
LPLE	lapelled
LPMN	Lippmann
LPMT	lipomata
LPOI	leptonic
LPRA	Lupercal
LPRN	leporine
LPSM	liposome
LPTA	Lapithae
LPTC	lipstick
LPYC	lip-synch
LQEC	liquesce
LQIL	liquidly
LRAE	larnakes
LRAN	Lorraine
LRBR	lyrebird
	lyre-bird
LRCS	lyricism
	lyricist
LRCT	loricate
LRES	largesse
LRHN	lurching
LRII	larrikin
LRKE	lorikeet
LRLS	lordless
LRMC	Lord Muck
LRNE	larynges
	larynxes
LROI	lordosis
	lordotic
LRSI	lordship□
LRSU	larkspur
LRUS	Larousse
LRWS	lyra-wise
LRYO	lorry-hop
LSAA	Las Casas
LSEA	Las Vegas
LSEE	listener
LSEI	listen in
	listeria
LSET	listen to
LSEU	listen up
LSFC	lose face
LSGS	last-gasp
LSHP	lose hope
LSIG	lashings
LSIU	luscious
LSLR	lasslorn
LSLS	listless
LSNE	Lysander
LSNL	losingly
LSNS	lushness
LSOE	Les Noces
LSOL	lissomly
LSRD	Lestrade
LSRI	lysergic
LSRM	lustrums
LSRT	lustrate
LSRU	lustrous
LSSM	lysosome
LSTA	less than
LSTM	lose time
LSTN	Lusitano
LSWR	last word
LSZM	lysozyme
LTAG	lethargy
	litharge
LTAI	Lattakia
	Lothario
LTAL	lethally
	lettable
LTCU	lutecium
LTEA	Lutheran
LTEE	let me see
	lettered
	littered
LTEL	latterly
	litherly
LTGN	litigant
LTGT	litigate
LTLA	let fly at
LTLD	let slide
LTLG	little go
LTLM	Little Mo
LTLN	let alone
	let-alone
LTLO	let blood
LTLS	littlest
LTNL	latently
LTNN	Latynina
LTNS	lateness
	Latinise
	Latinism
	Latinist
	lutanist
	lutenist
LTNT	Latinate
LTNZ	Latinize
LTOA	littoral
LTOS	let loose
LTRC	literacy
LTRR	literary
LTRS	literose
LTRT	laterite
	literate
	literati
LTRV	let drive
LTTD	latitude
LTTI	let it rip
LTTU	lutetium
LUAI	Laurasia
LUAL	laudable
	laudably
LUAN	Lausanne
LUAU	laudanum
LUCE	launched
	launcher
LUCI	launch in
LUEC	Laurence
LUET	laureate
	Lauretta
LUGN	lounging
LUHE	laughter
LUHF	laugh off
LUHL	louchely
LUHN	laughing
LUHO	Laughton
LUNS	loudness
LUSO	louis d'or
	louis-d'or
LVAI	live a lie
LVAL	liveable
	loveable
LVBE	lavaboes
LVBR	lovebird
LVDN	loved one
LVDT	lividity
LVDW	live down
LVGT	levigate
LVIU	live it up
LVLC	Lovelace
LVLE	levelled
	leveller
LVLF	level off
	love life
LVLL	livelily
LVLN	livelong
LVLR	lovelorn
LVLS	loveless
LVNE	lavender
LVNI	living-in
LVNL	lovingly
LVNR	Lavengro
LVRC	laverock
LVRE	liveried
LVRG	leverage
LVRS	liverish
LVSC	lovesick
LVSL	lavishly
LVSN	love-song
LVTR	lavatory
LVTT	levitate
LVUT	live up to
LVWL	live well
LVWR	liveware
	live wire
LVWT	live with
LWAE	law-maker
	low water
LWAI	Low Latin
LWEC	Lawrence
LWEE	low-level
LWIE	law-giver
LWNS	lewdness
LWOC	low voice
LWOE	low-toned
LWON	low point
LWOR	lawcourt
LWRC	low-price
LWRD	low-grade
LWRI	lower lip
LWRN	lowering
LWSA	Lewisham
LWST	lewisite
LWSU	Lewis gun
LWUL	lawfully
LXBU	lax about
LXGA	lexigram
LXTV	laxative
LYAT	lay waste
LYBU	layabout
LYIE	ley lines
LYLS	loyalist
LYNG	lay an egg
LYOA	laywoman
LYSD	lay aside
LZNS	laziness
MABL	meatball
MABR	mean-born
MAES	McAleese
MALA	meat loaf
MALS	meatless
MAMU	miasmous
MANS	meanness
MARL	meagrely
MATM	meantime
MAUE	measured
	measures
	meatuses
MAUP	mea culpa
MBDC	Moby Dick
MBLS	mobilise
MBLT	mobility
MBLZ	mobilize
MCAI	mechanic
	moccasin
MCAL	Michaela
MCAN	MacLaine
MCEC	MacNeice
MCED	Macready
MCEE	mackerel
	Michelet
	Michener
MCEI	Michelin
MCEL	Michelle
MCES	MacLeish
MCET	MacHeath
MCHA	muckheap
MCIA	mackinaw
	Michigan
MCIM	machismo
MCLA	mycelial
MCLG	mucilage
	mycology
MCLI	McCullin
MCLS	much less
MCLT	maculate
MCLU	mycelium
MCNE	MacInnes
MCNU	meconium
MCOE	microbes
	mucrones
MCOI	microbic

Words marked □ can also be spelled with an initial capital letter

MCOO	macropod
	microdot
MCRH	McCarthy
MCRK	muck-rake
MCRN	macaroni
MCRO	macaroon
MCRS	macarise
MCRT	macerate
MCRZ	macarize
MCST	mucosity
MCUA	Macaulay
MCVT	Macavity
MCWE	Micawber
MDAE	mud-caked
MDAI	Mad Maria
MDAL	medially
MDAO	mediator❑
MDBU	mad about
MDCM	modicums
MDCN	medicine
MDCT	medicate
MDEA	medieval
MDEE	maddened
MDFE	modified
	modifier
MDHP	midships
MDIA	madrigal
MDIE	midwives
MDIH	midnight
MDIL	midfield
MDLA	medullae
	medullar
	medullas
MDLE	modeller
MDLI	meddle in
	Medellín
MDLN	Madeline
	meddling
	middling
	muddling
MDLO	modellos
MDLT	modality
	modulate
MDLU	muddle up
MDNL	McDonald
MDOA	madwoman
MDOE	made over
MDON	midpoint
	mid-point
MDOO	madroños
MDOR	mediocre
MDOS	madhouse
MDRI	midbrain
MDRL	modernly
MDRS	maderise
MDRT	moderate
	moderato
MDRZ	maderize
MDSI	medusoid
MDSL	modestly
	modishly
MDTN	mudstone
MDTT	meditate
MDUO	made up of
MDUP	mudpuppy
MDUR	mudguard
MEAI	maenadic
MEII	myelitis
MENS	meekness
MEOI	mnemonic
METO	maestros
METS	maestoso
MEWT	meet with
MFKN	Mafeking
MFLN	muffling
MGAC	Meg March
MGAE	Magdalen
MGAI	magmatic
MGAN	migraine
MGAO	migrator
MGBC	megabuck
MGBT	megabyte
MGCA	magician
MGCY	magic eye
MGEI	magnesia
	magnetic
MGEO	magnetos
	McGregor
MGFO	megaflop
MGIA	McGuigan
MGIC	Magwitch
MGIR	Maggiore
MGIT	Magritte
MGLA	Magellan
MGLT	megalith
MGOI	magnolia
MGPD	megapode
MGTI	magot-pie
MGTL	mightily
MGVR	McGovern
MGZN	magazine
MHGN	mahogany
MHMA	Muhammad
MHME	Mohammed
MHOG	mah-jongg
MHOI	mahzorim
MHRA	Muharram
MHRJ	maharaja
MHRN	maharani
MHTI	Mahathir
MHVR	Mahavira
MHYN	Mahayana
MICT	main city
MIDC	main deck
MIEL	maidenly
MILC	maiolica
MILN	mainland
	main line
	mainline
MIMA	main meal
MIMS	mainmast
MIPL	maid-pale
MIPR	main part
MISA	mainstay
MISI	mainsail
MISO	mailshot
MITF	moistify
MITI	maintain
MITR	moisture
MJLC	majolica
MJND	Maja Nude
MJRT	majority
MJSI	majestic
MKAA	make away
MKAE	make a bed
MKAI	make a lip
	make as if
MKBL	make bold
MKBT	makebate
MKCL	make cold
MKCT	make cuts
MKDW	make down
MKEE	make even
MKES	make easy
MKFA	make flat
MKFL	make full
MKFO	make flow
MKFS	make fast
MKGO	make good
MKHL	make holy
MKHR	make hard
MKIT	make it to
MKLK	make like
MKLS	make less
MKLT	make late
MKLV	make love
MKNA	make neat
MKNE	McKinley
MKOE	make over
	makeover
MKPA	make play
MKPL	make pale
MKRO	Makarios
MKSA	Makassar
MKSC	make sick
MKSF	make safe
MKSI	make sail
MKSR	make sure
MKSU	make snug
MKTD	make tidy
	Mike Todd
MKTI	make thin
MKTM	make time
MKUL	make ugly
MKUT	make up to
MKWL	make well
MKWN	make wing
MKWR	make warm
MKWT	make with
MLAA	melt away
MLAE	Meleager
MLAI	Malvasia
MLAM	Mallarmé
MLCA	Moluccas
MLCL	molecule
MLDC	maledict
MLDO	melodeon
	melodion
MLDS	melodise
	melodist
MLDU	malodour
MLDW	meltdown
MLDZ	melodize
MLEE	mal de mer
	mildewed
MLEH	mallecho
MLEL	moltenly
MLER	mulberry
MLET	malleate
	multeity
MLFD	mala fide
MLGE	maligned
	maligner
MLGL	malignly
MLGS	Malagasy
MLHL	molehill
MLIA	millibar
	Milligan
	Millikan
	Mulligan
MLIE	Maldives
	milliner
	Mulliken
MLIH	Malpighi
MLIL	Melville
	multiple
	multiply
MLIM	millième
MLIN	millions
MLIR	milliard
MLIT	melt into
MLIY	multigym
MLLA	male lead
	malt loaf
MLMI	milkmaid
MLMN	melamine
MLNE	malinger
MLNM	melanoma
MLNO	Malenkov
MLNS	maleness
	mildness
MLNT	mylonite
MLOE	mull over
	Mulroney
MLOI	Malvolio
	Miltonic
MLOL	mellowly
MLOS	Mulhouse
MLPN	millpond
MLPO	Malaprop
MLPS	milepost
MLRA	malarial
	maltreat
MLRC	Milk Race
MLRE	malarkey
	Mill Reef
MLRT	molarity
MLSA	melismas
MLSE	molasses
	molester
MLSI	moleskin
MLSL	mulishly

Words marked ❑ can also be spelled with an initial capital letter

Code	Word
MLTE	muleteer
MLTI	Milstein
MLTN	militant
MLTR	military
MLTT	militate
MLWR	maltworm
MLXT	malaxate
MLYI	Malaysia
MMCE	mimicker
MMEE	membered
MMEI	momzerim
MMLA	mamillae
MMLN	mumbling
MMNL	momently
MMNO	mementos
MMNU	momentum
MMRA	memorial
MMRE	memories
MMRN	membrane
MMRS	memorise
MMRZ	memorize
MMWA	Mo Mowlam
MNAA	Mandalay
	maniacal
	Mindanao
MNAD	mancando
MNAE	man-eater
	mangabey
	miniated
MNAI	mandarin□
	minyanim
MNAL	manually
	mentally
MNAU	mandamus
	Montague
MNBA	mung bean
MNBI	manubria
MNBR	myna bird
MNCA	monocrat
MNCE	manacles
	monicker
	monocled
MNCN	menacing
MNCR	manicure
	monocarp
MNCT	monocyte
MNDS	minidisk
	monodist
MNEE	mannered
MNEI	mince pie
MNEK	man-weeks
MNEL	mannerly
	Minnelli
	minneola
MNEN	Mantegna
MNEO	monteros
MNER	man-years
MNEU	manteaus
	manteaux
MNFA	man-of-war
	men-of-war
MNFI	man of sin
MNFL	manifold
	manyfold
MNFO	man of God
MNFR	Montfort
MNFS	manifest
	monkfish
MNGA	Monaghan
	monogram
MNGM	monogamy
MNGN	managing
	monogyny
MNGO	monoglot
MNGR	managers
MNHE	many-hued
MNHI	Mannheim
MNHL	monohull
MNHO	monkhood
MNHS	mine host
MNIC	mandioca
MNIE	man-sized
MNII	mannikin
MNIL	manciple
	mandible
	mantilla
	monticle
MNIS	mantissa
MNIT	Mengistu
MNIU	Monsieur
MNLN	mingling
MNLS	maneless
	mindless
	Mona Lisa
MNLT	monolith
MNLU	Menelaus
MNMA	monomial
MNMN	monument□
MNMR	McNamara
	monomark
MNMS	minimise
MNMZ	minimize
MNNA	Manannan
MNNE	Menander
	meninges
MNNR	monandry
MNOA	man to man
	man-to-man
MNOE	manpower
MNOI	mandolin
	Mongolia
	Monrovia
MNOR	man-hours
	mansonry
MNOS	mongoose
MNOT	Monmouth
MNPL	minipill
	monopoly
	Monopoly®
MNRA	manorial
	Mondrian
	Montreal
MNRH	menarche
	monarchy
MNRI	monorail
MNRK	mandrake
MNRL	mandrill
MNRN	manuring
MNRS	Montrose
MNRT	Minorite
	minority
MNRU	Montreux
MNRV	mangrove
MNSE	Manasseh
	minister
MNSI	monastic
	monistic
MNSR	ministry
MNSU	meniscus
MNSY	mind's eye
MNTA	minutiae
MNTB	Manitoba
MNTE	minstrel
MNTL	minutely
MNTN	monotint
	monotone
	monotony
MNTO	monition
	munition
MNTP	monotype
	Monotype®
MNTR	minatory
	monetary
	monitory
	monstera
MNTS	monetise
MNTU	manitous
	menstrua
	Minotaur
MNTV	monitive
MNTZ	monetize
MNUA	mensural
	monaural
MNUE	mancuses
	Mensuren
MNUL	manfully
MNWA	menswear
MNXD	monoxide
MNYA	money-bag
	moneyman
MNYO	moneybox
	money-box
MNYU	money due
MOBA	moonbeam
MOBL	moon-ball
MOCC	moorcock
MOFC	moonface
MOFW	moorfowl
MOHF	mooch off
MOLK	moonlike
MOLN	moorland
MOLS	moonless
MOSO	moonshot
MOWL	moonwalk
MOYA	moody-mad
MPCL	Mr Pickle
MPII	mephitic
	mephitis
MPNL	mopingly
MPSL	mopishly
MQDA	muqaddam
MQET	maquette
	moquette
MRAC	mordancy
MRAE	Margaret
MRAI	Marsalis
MRAL	mortally
MRAO	Marranos
	martagon
	Mercator
	myriapod
MRAS	Murmansk
MRAT	Moriarty
MRBA	Mirabeau
MRBN	moribund
MRBU	marabout
MRCO	moroccos
MRDA	meridian
MRDL	Mary Daly
MRDN	Maradona
MRDT	Meredith
MRDW	mark down
	mark-down
MREA	Mordecai
MREE	marketer
	Mercedes
	murderer
MREL	Marbella
	markedly
	martello
MREN	Morwenna
MRET	Mariette
MREU	morceaux
MRGG	mortgage
MRGL	marigold□
MRHA	marsh gas
MRHE	murphies
MRHL	Marshall
MRHM	morpheme
MRHN	merchant□
	morphine
	morphing
MRHS	Myra Hess
MRHU	mirthful
	Morpheus
MRIA	marginal
	marzipan
	morainal
	Morrigan
MRIE	margined
	martinet
	Mortimer
	mortiser
MRIG	markings
	marriage
	mornings
MRII	morainic
MRIL	morbidly
MRIN	Marciano
MRIO	Morrison
	myrmidon
MRIU	merciful

Words marked □ can also be spelled with an initial capital letter

Code	Word
MRLE	Mirrlees
MRLN	marbling
	Maryland
MRLO	morellos
MRLS	moralise
	moralism
	moralist
	muralist
MRLT	morality
MRLZ	moralize
MRND	marinade
MRNT	marinate
MRNU	meringue
MROA	marjoram
MROE	marmoset
	marooned
	moreover
MROI	Marjorie
MROT	Mariotte
MRRA	Mary Read
MRRS	Mary Rose
MRSA	marksman
MRSE	meristem
MRSI	marasmic
MRSL	morosely
MRSO	Moriscos
MRSU	marasmus
MRTA	more than
MRTD	Mark Todd
MRTM	maritime
	mark time
	more time
MRTO	marathon□
MRUE	marauder
	murmured
	murmurer
MRUI	mercuric
	Mercutio
MRUR	mortuary
MRUS	marquess
	marquise
MRVA	Moravian
MRWO	Mirkwood
MRYA	merryman
MRYE	Moray eel
MRYF	marry off
MRYI	martyria
MRYN	marrying
MSAC	mismatch
MSAE	Mesdames
	mismated
	mistaken
	muscadel
	Muscadet
	muscatel
MSAI	mescalin
	moshavim
	muscadin
MSAL	mesially
	missable
MSAR	massacre
	miscarry
	mismarry

Code	Word
MSBO	mass-book
MSCA	musician
MSCI	Masaccio
MSCO	music box
MSDE	musk deer
MSDR	mesoderm
MSEC	misteach
MSEE	Massenet
	miscegen
MSEI	mesmeric
	muster in
MSEL	masterly
MSER	misheard
	mismetre
	musketry
MSES	masseuse
MSEU	messed up
MSFR	miss fire
MSGM	misogamy
MSGN	misogyny
MSHA	masthead
MSHE	mischief
MSHN	misthink
MSHP	misshape
MSHV	must-have
MSIA	mestizas
	mystical
MSIE	Messiaen
	missiles
	mistimed
MSIH	mislight
MSII	mastitis
MSIL	miscible
	misfield
	mistitle
MSIO	mestizos
	misticos
MSIU	mystique
MSLA	misplead
MSLC	misplace
MSLG	misalign
MSLI	muscle in
MSLO	misallot
MSMN	Mosimann
MSMS	mishmash
	mish-mash
MSNI	Mishnaic
MSNL	musingly
MSOA	masoolah
MSOB	misdoubt
MSOE	misnomer
	mist over
	muse over
MSOL	massoola
MSON	miscount
	mispoint
MSOO	mastodon
	miscolor
MSOR	Missouri
	Mrs Moore
MSOT	misroute
MSPA	misspeak
MSPL	misapply

Code	Word
	misspell
MSPN	misspend
	misspent
MSRA	misdread
	mistreat
MSRE	miseries
	misorder
MSRF	misgraff
	misgraft
MSRN	misprint
MSRO	mushroom
MSRS	misprise
	mistress
	mistrust
	mistryst
	musk rose
MSRT	Maserati®
	miswrite
MSRZ	misprize
MSTT	misstate
MSUA	muscular
MSUD	misguide
MSUG	misjudge
MSUS	musquash
MSUT	misquote
	mosquito
MSVN	Museveni
MSWR	meshwork
	mesh-work
MSZI	Mesozoic
MTAA	methanal
MTAL	mutually
MTAO	methanol
MTBL	mothball
MTEE	muttered
	mutterer
MTEL	motherly
MTGT	mitigate
MTHA	Matthias
MTHL	Mitchell
MTHN	matching
MTHO	matchbox
MTHR	Mata Hari
MTHU	Matthaus
MTHW	Matthews
MTIA	metrical
	mythical
MTIE	matrices
	matrixes
MTLI	metallic
MTLN	mottling
MTLT	motility
	mutilate
MTLZ	metalize
MTNE	mutineer
MTNM	metonymy
MTNS	matiness
	muteness
MTNU	mutinous
MTOI	meteoric
	methodic
MTOL	matronly
MTPO	metaphor

Code	Word
	metaplot
MTRA	material
	maternal
	motor car
	motorway
MTRE	matériel
	Mithraea
MTRL	maturely
MTRS	mattress
	motorise
	motorist
MTRT	maturate
	maturity
MTRU	motor-bus
MTRZ	motorize
MTSA	mute swan
MTSI	mateship
MTTO	mutation
MTVH	mitzvahs
MTVT	mitzvoth
	motivate
	motivity
MTYI	methysis
MTZA	metazoan
MUAE	Mauna Kea
MUAO	Mauna Loa
MUDN	moulding
MUEA	mouse mat
MUEN	mauveine
MUFO	moufflon
MUHF	mouth off
MUHU	mouthful
MUIR	meunière
MULN	Maudling
MUMI	Moulmein
MUNN	mourning
MUNU	mournful
MUSK	moussaka
MUTA	Mount Tai
MUTI	mountain
MUTN	mounting
MUTS	Mount Usu
MVAA	move away
MVAL	moveable
	moveably
MVBC	move back
MVBE	movables
MVDW	move down
MVEI	Mevlevis
MVIO	move in on
MVMN	movement
MVNL	movingly
MVOE	move over
MVPS	move past
MVRC	maverick
MWAI	Mawlawis
MXDA	mixed bag
MXLA	maxillae
MXMA	Maximian
MXMS	maximise
MXMT	myxomata
MXMZ	maximize
MXOC	Max Roach

Words marked □ can also be spelled with an initial capital letter

MXRA	mixer tap
MXRS	Max Ernst
MYRO	Meyerhof
MYRS	mayoress
MYUE	May queen
MZLK	mazelike
MZLO	mazel tov
	mazeltov
MZZH	mezuzahs
MZZT	mezuzoth
NABE	near beer
NACI	Nearctic
NAES	Near East
NAHN	near-hand
NAMS	near miss
NANS	nearness
	neatness
NASD	nearside
NBAK	Nebraska
NBEA	noble gas
	nobleman
NBEE	noblemen
NBEO	noble rot
NBFR	nubiform
NBLN	nibbling
	nobbling
NBLS	nebulise
NBLT	nobility
	nubility
NBLU	nebulous
	nobelium
NBLZ	nebulize
NCAC	no chance
NCBN	neckband
NCEL	nucleoli
NCES	nuclease
NCET	nucleate
NCEU	nacreous
NCLB	Nickleby
NCLC	necklace
NCLN	neckline
NCLO	Nicolson
NCLU	Nicklaus
	nucellus
NCNC	nick-nack
NCNL	nocently
NCNM	nickname
NCNS	niceness
NCOA	Nicholas
NCOI	necrosis
	necrotic
NCOS	necropsy
NCRM	Nichrome®
NCTE	niceties
NCTN	nicotine
NCUN	nocturne
NCWA	neckwear
NDEL	Ned Kelly
NDLS	nodalise
	nodulose
NDLU	nodulous
NDLZ	nodalize
NDNS	nudeness
NDRU	nidorous
NDST	nodosity
NDTE	nudities
NELS	needless
NFHI	Niflheim
NFIL	no frills
	no-frills
NFNF	niffnaff
NGAE	no-go area
NGHN	nigh-hand
NGIE	negligee
NGIL	Negrillo
NGIO	Negritos
NGLN	Nagaland
	niggling
NGOS	Negroism
NGSK	Nagasaki
NGTA	nightcap
	nightjar
NGTO	negation
	night-dog
NGTR	nugatory
NGTV	negative
NHLS	nihilism
	nihilist
NHLT	nihility
NHMA	Nehemiah
NIAC	nuisance
NIDW	nail down
NIEO	nailed on
NIET	noisette
NIHA	nail-head
NISN	naissant
NISO	nainsook
NJMN	Ndjamena
NJNK	Nijinska
	Nijinsky
NKSN	Nakasone
NLBU	Nile blue
NLGY	Nell Gwyn
NLHU	nylghaus
NLMO	nelumbos
NLNS	nullness
NLTO	nolition
NMAL	nameable
NMDO	name-drop
NMDS	nomadise
	nomadism
NMDZ	nomadize
NMEE	numbered
NMGA	nomogram
NMHA	nymphean
NMKL	numskull
NMLS	nameless
NMNS	numbness
NMNT	nominate
NMNU	numinous
NMRC	numeracy
NMRT	numerate
NMRU	numerous
NMSK	namesake
NMTD	nematode
NMTE	no matter
NMTP	nametape
NMUE	nimbuses
NMYS	nimbyism
NNAE	non-payer
NNAO	Nuneaton
NNAR	non-dairy
NNAT	non-party
NNEA	non-metal
NNES	nonsense
NNFL	ninefold
NNHK	nunchaku
NNHL	nine-hole
NNHN	Nanchang
NNHT	non-white
NNIA	nundinal
NNIS	ninjitsu
NNLI	non-claim
NNNO	non-union
NNOA	non-moral
NNOI	non-toxic
NNPA	nenuphar
NNPN	ninepins
NNSC	nonesuch
NNTC	non-stick
NNTE	nineteen
	nineties
NNTK	nunataks
NNTO	nonettos
NNUA	non-human
NNUS	ninjutsu
NNVN	non-event
NNYS	nannyish
NOAA	neonatal
NOEI	neoteric
NOHB	neophobe
NOHT	neophyte
NOJC	no object
NOLM	neon lamp
NOLS	neoplasm
NORN	neoprene
NOTD	noontide
NOYI	neomycin
NPIL	nuptials
NPLO	napoleon❑
NPLS	Nepalese
NPNH	nepenthe
NPRT	nephrite
NPTS	nepotism
	nepotist
NPTY	Nephthys
NRAL	normally
NRAO	narrator
NRBR	Nürnberg
NREA	nerve gas
	Norseman
	norteñas
	Norweyan
NREO	norteños
NRHE	North Sea
NRHL	narghile
NRHN	northing
NRHO	Northrop
NRHR	northern
NRIE	nargileh
	nereides
NRIS	narcissi
NRLN	nursling
NRMD	no remedy
NRNA	Neronian
NROE	narrowed
NROI	narcosis
	narcotic
NROL	narrowly
NRUA	nurtural
NRUE	nurturer
NSAI	nystatin
NSBN	noseband
NSDV	nosedive
	nose-dive
NSEC	nascency
NSHR	nose-herb
NSIN	nescient
NSLG	nosology
NSLN	nestling
NSLS	nasalise
	noseless
NSLT	nasality
NSLZ	nasalize
NSNS	nosiness
NSOE	no sooner
NSRM	Nostromo
NSRN	nose-ring
NTAC	not match
	nuthatch
NTAE	not-pated
NTAK	no thanks
NTBN	nota bene
NTBO	notebook
NTCN	noticing
NTCS	notecase
NTDW	note down
NTEE	natterer
NTEG	nutmeggy
NTFE	not often
NTHA	not cheap
NTHC	not thick
NTHL	nutshell
NTHN	not think
NTHP	not a hope
NTHR	not sharp
	not there
NTIH	not right
NTIN	nutrient
NTLC	not place
NTLN	nettling
NTLO	not allow
NTLS	not close
	noteless
NTNS	not in use
NTOA	national
	notional
	not to say
NTOE	nitrogen
NTOS	nuthouse
	nut-house
NTPE	not a peep

Words marked ❑ can also be spelled with an initial capital letter

NTRA	notarial
NTRJ	Nataraja
NTRS	naturism
	naturist
	notarise
NTRW	nut-brown
NTRZ	notarize
NTSU	not a soul
NTTL	not at all
NTTN	not stand
NTTO	natation
	notation
	nutation
NTTR	natatory
	not start
NTUL	not fully
NTUT	not quite
NTVL	natively
NTVS	nativism
	nativist
NTVT	nativity
NUAL	neurally
NUET	nauseate
NUEU	nauseous
NUGB	Naum Gabo
NUHI	Naughtie
NUIA	Nausicaa
	nautical
NUII	neuritis
NUIU	nautilus
NULU	nauplius
NUOA	neuromas
NUOE	neuroses
NUOI	neurosis
	neurotic
NURN	neutrino
NUTU	ngultrum
NVBU	navy blue
NVGT	navigate
NVLA	novellae
	novellas
NVLS	Navy List
	novelese
	novelise
	novelish
	novelist
NVLZ	novelize
NVME	November
NVOO	Novgorod
NVTA	Novatian
NVYR	navy yard
NWAE	New Haven
	Newhaven
NWAH	new maths
NWAI	New Latin
NWCS	newscast
NWDY	nowadays
NWEH	New Delhi
NWEN	new penny
NWIE	news item
NWIT	new birth
NWLE	newelled
NWLO	new blood

NWLW	new-blown
NWNE	no wonder
NWOE	Newcomen
	newcomer
	Newcomes
	new-model
NWOL	New World
NWON	new-found
NWPA	newspeak
NWRE	newsreel
NWRO	new broom
	newsroom
NWRT	New Crete
NWSL	newishly
NWTL	New Style
NWWE	Newsweek
NWYE	newly-wed
NXBS	next best
NXDO	next door
	next-door
NYAE	nay-sayer
NZRN	Nazarene
NZRT	Nazareth
	Nazarite
OAAA	Olazabal
OAAG	Okavango
OADF	on and off
OAGR	orangery
OAIC	of a piece
OAIH	of a night
OAII	ovaritis
OAOI	oratorio
OART	of a truth
OATN	Ovaltine®
OAUA	oracular
OAUL	opaquely
OBIG	Oxbridge
OCDA	Orcadian
OCDN	Occident
OCEI	on credit
OCEL	orchella
OCGN	oncogene
OCIL	orchilla
OCLG	oncology
OCLL	occultly
OCLT	osculate
OCMN	oncoming
OCMR	on camera
	once more
OCOE	once-over
OCPE	occupied
	occupier
OCPN	occupant
OCSO	occasion
OCTN	oscitant
OCTT	oscitate
OCUE	occluder
OCUS	of course
ODAC	ordnance
ODAJ	Ondaatje
ODAR	Old Harry
ODET	oddments
ODIE	old-timer

	ordained
	ordainer
ODIL	Oldfield
ODLM	old flame
ODLR	Old Glory
ODMN	on demand
ODNN	ordinand
ODNR	ordinary
ODNT	ordinate
ODOA	old woman
ODOE	old fogey
ODOL	Old World
	old-world
ODOS	Old Norse
ODPA	Oedipean
ODRA	Omdurman
ODRC	obduracy
ODRN	ordering
ODRT	obdurate
ODRU	ordurous
ODTL	Old Style
	old style
ODTR	old story
ODUR	old guard
OEAC	ogee arch
	overarch
OEAE	overawed
OEAI	operatic
OEAL	openable
	operable
	overalls
OEAO	operator
	oreganos
OEAT	one-party
OEBA	overbear
OEBL	overbulk
OEBO	open book
	overblow
	overbook
OEBR	ovenbird
	overburn
OEBS	overbusy
OECA	overcoat
OECL	opercula
	overcall
OECM	overcome
OECO	overcloy
	overcook
	overcrop
OECS	open-cast
	overcast
OECU	over-club
OEDA	overdraw
OEDI	overdo it
OEDK	okey-doke
OEDN	overdone
OEDO	open door
OEDS	overdose
OEEE	open-eyed
OEET	omelette
	operetta
OEFE	overfeed
OEFL	overfall

	overfill
	overfold
	overfull
OEFO	overflow
OEFR	open fire
OEGL	overgall
OEGN	overgang
OEGO	overgrow
OEHA	overhead
	overhear
	overheat
OEHL	overhold
OEHN	overhand
	overhang
OEHU	overhaul
OEIC	one-piece
OEIE	one-liner
	one-sided
OEIN	obedient
OEJM	overjump
OEKL	overkill
OELA	overleaf
	overleap
	overload
OELC	overlock
OELD	overlade
OELE	Ole Olsen
OELN	overland
	overlend
	overlong
OELO	overlook
OELR	overlard
	overlord
OELS	one flesh
OELT	ocellate
OELU	owerloup
OELV	overlive
OEMC	overmuch
OEMN	open mind
OEMS	overmast
OENA	Oceanian
OENC	overnice
	over-nice
OEND	oceanids
OENE	oleander
OENM	overname
OENS	openness
OEON	one-to-one
OEOO	Ode to Joy
	ode to joy
OEOS	one-horse
OEOT	open on to
	open onto
OEPA	open-plan
	overplay
OEPE	overpeer
OEPG	overpage
OEPR	overpart
OEPS	overpass
OERA	overread
OERC	one-track
	overrack
OERD	override

Code	Word
OERF	overruff
OERK	overrake
OERL	overrule
OERP	overripe
OERT	overrate
OERW	one or two
	orecrowe
OESA	overseas
	overstay
OESD	open side
	overside
OESE	oleaster
	overseer
	overstep
OESI	oversail
	overskip
	overslip
	overswim
OESL	one's self
	oversell
OESN	obeisant
OESO	open shop
	overshoe
	over-shoe
	overshot
OESR	open sore
OESZ	oversize
OETC	overt act
OETE	overteem
OETI	Oresteia
OETK	overtake
OETL	overtalk
OETM	overtime
OETN	overtone
OETP	overtype
OETR	ore-stare
	overture
	overturn
OETS	overtask
OEUE	overused
OEVE	overview
OEVI	overveil
OEWA	overwear
OEWN	overwind
	overwing
OEWR	open work
	openwork
	ovenware
	overwork
OEWT	over with
OEYN	one by one
OFAD	off-wards
OFAE	off-sales
OFCA	official
OFCR	officers
OFHK	off-shake
OFHO	offshoot
OFHR	offshore
OFHT	off-white
OFIT	off-piste
OFNE	offended
	offender
OFNO	off and on
OFRA	off-break
OFRN	offering
	offprint
OFRV	off-drive
OFTG	off-stage
OFUR	off guard
OGLU	orgulous
OGMU	oogamous
OGNI	organdie
OGNS	organise
	organism
	organist
OGNZ	organize
OGSI	orgastic
OHDA	ophidian
OHET	ochreate
OHEU	ochreous
OHRA	other man
OIAC	oligarch
OIAU	olibanum
	origanum
OIET	Olivetti
OIHL	orichalc
OIIA	original
OIIE	oxidized
	oxidizer
OIIN	opinions
OINA	oriental
OINE	oriented
OIOI	oviposit
OISO	omission
OIST	otiosity
OISV	omissive
OITN	omitting
OIUA	oviducal
OIUL	odiously
OIUR	obituary
OJCO	objector
OJCT	object to
OKIG	Oak Ridge
OLAG	oil gauge
OLAN	oil paint
OLGN	obliging
OLGS	oologist
OLGT	obligate
	obligati
	obligato
OLHL	oil shale
OLHM	Oklahoma
OLIE	oil-fired
OLIL	oilfield
OLJS	only just
OLLC	oil slick
OLLT	oilcloth
OLNS	oiliness
OLOE	onlooker
OLTN	oilstone
OLTO	oblation
OLTR	oblatory
OLVO	oblivion
OMEE	ohmmeter
OMTU	ommateum
OMWR	on my word
ONGT	of nights
ONLG	oenology
ONMN	ointment
	ornament
ONNU	owning-up
ONTL	ornately
ONVR	omnivore
	omnivory
OOCP	otoscope
OOEI	orogenic
OOER	odometry
OOIE	ozonizer
OONK	Oroonoko
OOOO	olorosos
OOTI	odontoid
OPAE	orphaned
OPAO	omphalos
OPCE	ox-pecker
OPGE	oppugner
OPIO	on pain of
OPLT	oppilate
OPMN	orpiment
OPNN	opponent
OPSN	opposing
OPST	opposite
ORAI	our man in
ORCR	on record
ORIO	oerlikon□
ORMN	on remand
ORPT	of repute
OSAL	obstacle
OSCE	of secret
OSDA	obsidian
OSED	Oostende
OSFE	ossified
OSLT	obsolete
OSRA	on stream
	on-stream
OSRC	obstruct
OSRE	observed
	observer
OSRK	on strike
OSRU	oestrous
OSSE	obsessed
OSUE	obscured
OTAC	outwatch
OTAD	outwards
OTAE	outdated
	outlawed
	outraged
OTAL	oathable
OTAR	outlawry
OTAT	outcaste
	outcasts
OTCA	optician
OTCR	outscorn
OTEA	on the map
	on the mat
	on the tab
	on the way
OTEC	outreach
OTEG	outreign
	outweigh
OTEI	on the air
	on the bit
OTEL	on the fly
	on the sly
OTEO	on the dot
	on the hop
	on the job
	on the nod
	out-Herod
	outvenom
OTER	outlearn
	outweary
OTEU	on the run
OTFE	out of key
OTGN	ontogeny
OTHN	outshine
	outthink
	out-think
OTIA	outrival
OTIE	obtained
	obtainer
	ofttimes
	outlines
	outrider
	outsider
OTIH	outnight
	outright
OTII	osteitis
OTIL	outfield
OTJH	Otto John
OTLC	outplace
OTLE	outsleep
OTLG	ontology
OTLN	Ottoline
	outflank
OTLR	outglare
OTLS	outclass
OTLU	Ortelius
OTME	obtemper
OTMR	outsmart
OTMS	optimise
	optimism
	optimist
OTMT	optimate
OTMZ	optimize
OTNA	octantal
OTNT	ostinato
OTNU	ox-tongue
OTOA	optional
OTOC	outvoice
OTOE	orthoses
	outmoded
	outpower
OTOI	orthosis
	orthotic
OTON	outbound
	outgoing
	outpoint
OTOO	orthodox
OTOP	orthoepy
OTOR	outboard
	outdoors
OTOS	outhouse

Words marked □ can also be spelled with an initial capital letter

OTOT outworth
OTOU out to out
OTPE octuplet
OTPN outspend
OTPR outsport
OTPS octopush
OTRA outbreak
outer bar
OTRC outprice
OTRE on target
outbreed
OTRO octaroon
octoroon
OTRS outcross
OTRT obturate
OTRV outbrave
OTRW outfrown
OTRZ outprize
OTSL obtusely
OTST obtusity
OTTI outstrip
OTTN outstand
OTTR outstare
OTTV optative
OTUE obtruder
OTUO opt out of
OTUS outburst
OTWA outswear
OTWL outdwell
outswell
OTYN outlying
OUAE oculated
OUAL ocularly
OUCL opuscula
OUEC opulence
OVLE on velvet
OWSR Oswestry
OYOI oxytocic
oxytocin
OYOO oxymoron
OYPA Olympiad
Olympian
OYSA Odyssean
OYSU Odysseus
OZNS ooziness
PAAE pia mater
play area
PAAG phalange
PAAL placable
placably
playable
PAAT peasanty
PABC play back
playback
PABL play ball
playbill
PACE planched
planchet
PACN prancing
PADA praedial
prandial
PADO pear drop
PADT plaudits
PADU Phaedrus
PADW play down
PAEA placeman
place mat
PAEE placemen
platelet
PAEO placebos
PAET placenta
PAEU peaceful
phase out
plateaus
plateaux
plateful
PAEZ Piacenza
PAFC praefect
PAFI play fair
PAFL play full
pratfall
PAFN play fine
PAFR platform
PAGN plangent
PAHN poaching
PAIE Pharisee
PAII platinic
PAIL placidly
PAIO pianinos
PAIU platinum
PAKN planking
PAKO plankton
PAKS prankish
PALE pearlies
PALS phallism
PALT pearlite
PAMC pharmacy
PAMD psalmody
PAMI pearmain
PAMS psalmist
PAMT playmate
PANN plaining
planning
PAOE play over
PAOI platonic[□]
PARE pea-green
PASB piassaba
PASF play safe
PASN praising
PASV piassava
PATA plastral
PATC plastics
practice
Praktica®
PATE prattler
PATG plantage
PATI plantain
PATM playtime
PATO Phaethon
plastron
PATR plastery
psaltery
PATS phantasm
phantasy
practise
PATU plant out
PAUA piacular
planulae
PAUL plaguily
PAUN plaguing
PAUO play upon
PAUT play up to
PAWT play with
PAYU platypus
PBIA publican
PBIL publicly
PBRW pub-crawl
PBUH pabouche
PCAA pack away
PCAC peccancy
PCAE packager
packages
PCAI peccavis
PCAL peccable
PCDW pack down
PCEE pickerel
picketer
puckered
PCET pochette
PCEU pucker up
PCFE pacified
pacifier
PCFR Pickford
PCFS pacifism
pacifist
PCIE pectines
PCIG pickings
PCII pack it in
PCIK pachinko
PCIU pack it up
PCLA pack-load
peculiar
PCLC picklock
PCLT peculate
PCMR pockmark
PCMU pick-me-up
PCNI pick-'n'-mix
PCOA pectoral
PCOO piccolos
PCRN pacarana
PCRO picaroon
PCUE pictures
PCUI pichurim
PCWC Pickwick
PCYN picayune
PDAR podiatry
PDCL pediculi
PDCR pedicure
PDGA podagral
PDGE pedigree
PDGG pedagogy
PDLE pedaloes
PDLN peddling
piddling
puddling
PDMN pediment
PDNI pedantic
PDNL peduncle
PDNR pedantry
PDNU pudendum
PDRS pederast
PDSA pedestal
PDTL pedately
PEAA prenatal
PEAE Pleiades
prepared
presager
PEAI prelatic
PEAO predator
PECE preacher
PECN piercing
prescind
PECT Prescott
PEDA Pheidias
PEDN pleading
PEDO plead for
PEDR pseudery
PEEA plebeian
PEEC presence
pretence
PEEI phenetic
precepit
PEEL predella
PEES Pieterse
prepense
PEET precepts
PEEU piece out
PEEV preserve
PEGN Peer Gynt
PEGO pledgeor
PEGR preggers
PEHL peephole
PEHR pie chart
plethora
PEHS psephism
PEIA poetical
PEIC precinct
PEIE premised
premises
PEII presidia
pyelitic
pyelitis
PEIM premiums
PEIR premiere
première
PEIU precious
previous
PELC pre-elect
PELD preclude
PELS peerless
PEML preamble
PENN preening
pregnant
PENS pleonasm
PEOA premolar
PEOI Pretoria
PEPL preppily
PERS pleurisy
PESA pressman
PESE pressmen
PESI please it
PESN pheasant

Words marked [□] can also be spelled with an initial capital letter

Code	Word
	pleasant
	pleasing
	pressing
PESO	press box
	press for
PESR	pleasure
	pressure
PEST	please to
PESU	press out
PETE	plectres
	pretties
PETF	prettify
PETG	prestige
PETL	prettily
PETO	plenty of
PETU	plectrum
PEUE	plexuses
	presumed
PEUG	prejudge
PEUS	precurse
PEXS	pre-exist
PEYA	pterylae
PEYI	pterygia
PFBL	puffball
PFBR	puffbird
PFEO	pifferos
PFEU	puffed up
PFLN	piffling
PGAA	pygmaean
PGLS	pugilism
	pugilist
PGNN	Paganini
PGNS	paganise
	paganism
PGNT	paginate
PGNZ	paganize
PGOE	pug-nosed
PGOR	pigeonry
PGOT	Peggotty
PGPG	Pago Pago
PGWL	pigswill
PGYE	Peggy Lee
PGYU	Peggy Sue
PHEO	pahoehoe
PIAE	privates
PIAL	primally
PIAO	paisanos
	privados
PICL	princely
PICN	Pliocene
PICR	Poincaré
PICS	princess
PIDE	prie-dieu
PIEA	priced at
	price tag
	price war
	primeval
	prizeman
PIEO	Philemon
PIEU	prideful
PIFE	pain-free
PIGR	priggery
PIGS	priggish
PIHE	plighted
PIIE	philibeg
PIIP	Philippa
	Philippi
PIIR	Poitiers
PIKN	pricking
PILP	Phillips
PILS	painless
PINI	peignoir
PINL	pliantly
PINN	poignant
PINS	primness
PIOE	poisoned
	poisoner
	prisoner
PIOI	phimosis
	psilosis
PIRS	primrose❑
	prioress
PIRT	priority
PISL	plimsole
	plimsoll
	priestly
PISN	puissant
PITI	point aim
PITN	painting
	pointing
	printing
	Pristina
	pristine
PITR	pointers
PITU	point out
	printout
	print run
PIWS	pairwise
PIWT	pair with
PJRT	pejorate
PKNS	Pekinese
PKSA	Pakistan
PKWE	pokeweed
PLAA	pull away
PLAE	palmated
	pileated
	pillager
PLAI	Palladio
PLAL	palpable
	palpably
PLAM	pile arms
PLAO	polka-dot
PLAR	pellagra
PLBC	pull back
PLBU	Polybius
PLCA	palmchat
PLCE	policies
PLCN	policing
PLCR	Polycarp
PLDA	pale-dead
PLDN	paludine
PLDW	pelt down
	pull down
PLEE	pilfered
	pilferer
	Pilsener
PLET	palmette
PLFR	piliform
PLGA	Polignac
PLGM	polygamy
PLGN	polygene
	polygyny
PLGO	polyglot❑
PLGU	Pelagius
PLHA	pillhead
PLHR	pilchard
PLIA	pulvinar
PLIE	pelvises
	pollices
	pulpiter
PLIG	pulsidge
PLII	pollinia
	pulvilio
PLIL	pallidly
	pellicle
	pulville
	pulvilli
PLIO	pile it on
PLIT	palliate
PLIU	pulvinus
PLMC	polemics
PLML	pell-mell
PLMN	palamino
	palimony
	palomino❑
PLMS	polemise
	polemist
PLMT	polymath
PLMZ	polemize
PLNC	polo neck
	polo-neck
PLNK	Polanski
PLNL	pulingly
PLNS	paleness
	polonise
PLNU	Palenque
	polonium
	Polonius
PLNZ	polonize
PLOE	pull over
	pullover
	pulmones
PLOS	pilhorse
PLOT	pull out a
PLPN	Pilipino
PLPU	polypous
PLRI	Polaroid®
PLRL	paltrily
PLRN	pelerine
	pull rank
PLRO	poltroon
PLRS	polarise
PLRT	polarity
PLRV	Palgrave
PLRZ	polarize
PLSA	Pole Star
PLSD	palisade
	palisado
PLSE	pilaster
	polished
	pollster
PLSM	polysemy
	polysome
PLST	pilosity
PLSU	polish up
PLTA	palatial
PLTC	politick
	politics
PLTE	Pulitzer
PLTG	pilotage
PLTL	politely
PLTN	palatine❑
	piloting
PLUE	polluted
PLUI	pellucid
PLWO	pulpwood
PLWS	palewise
PMAE	pomwater
PMAO	pompanos
PMEE	pampered
	pamperer
PMEO	pamperos
PMET	pimiento
PMHE	pamphlet
PMIA	pemmican
PMIO	Pompidou
	pump iron
PMLN	Pamplona
PMNE	pomander
PMNO	pimentos
PMTE	pomatoes
PNAA	pine away
PNAC	Penzance
PNAI	Pindaric
PNAL	pantable
	pentacle
	pinnacle
PNAO	pentagon
	pintados
PNCE	Pinochet
PNCL	pinochle
PNCN	pine cone
PNCU	panic-buy
PNEC	pungency
PNEE	panderer
	pince-nez
	Poncelet
PNEI	pandemic
PNEL	panderly
PNET	pander to
PNEU	ponceaux
PNFK	Panofsky
PNFR	pinafore
PNGR	panegyry
PNHE	pinwheel
PNHI	pinch-hit
PNHN	penchant
	pinching
	punching
PNHO	pancheon
	pantheon❑
PNIE	Pan-pipes

Words marked ❑ can also be spelled with an initial capital letter

Code	Word
	pantiled
	Pennines
PNII	pannikin
	pencil in
PNLA	panel saw
PNLG	penology
PNLI	panel pin
PNLP	Penelope
PNLS	penalise
PNLZ	penalize
PNMR	penumbra
PNNF	penknife
PNNS	pinkness
	puniness
PNOA	penwoman
PNOI	pangolin
PNOL	pantofle
PNON	pinpoint
	pin-point
PNPI	panoptic
PNPN	ping pong
	ping-pong
PNRA	pancreas
PNRC	punk rock
PNRM	panorama
PNSA	Panislam
PNSI	pant suit
PNSZ	pint-size
PNTA	punctual
PNTB	Pinatubo
PNTC	penstock
PNTG	Pinotage
PNTI	ponytail
PNTN	penitent
PNTR	puncture
PNTV	punitive
PNUA	pendular
PNUF	pinguefy
PNUU	pendulum
PNWO	pinewood
	pinkwood
POAE	pholades
	protases
POAI	protasis
POAL	probable
	probably
	provable
	provably
POAN	procaine
	ptomaine
POAO	pronator
POAS	prolapse
POAT	pro tanto
PODC	poop deck
PODN	plodding
	prodding
PODO	Proudhon
POEA	phone-tap
POEB	Proverbs
POED	proceeds
POEE	protégée
POEI	phonemic
	phonetic
POEL	properly
POES	protease
POET	property
POGI	plough in
POGN	phosgene
POHC	prophecy
POHS	prophase
	prophesy
POHT	prophets
POIA	prodigal
	proviral
	proximal
POIB	profit by
POIC	province
POIE	pro-lifer
	promised
	promisee
	promiser
	provided
	provider
POII	prohibit
	prolific
POIL	prolixly
POIN	proviant
POIO	promisor
	provisor
	provisos
POIU	Plotinus
	provirus
POJH	poor-John
POLI	proclaim
POLM	problems
POLS	plotless
POMA	proemial
POMU	Phormium
PONS	poorness
	prodnose
POOA	proposal
POOE	promoted
	promoter
	proposed
	proposer
	provoked
	provoker
POOI	Photofit®
	prosodic
POOM	pro forma
POON	profound
	propound
POOO	protocol
	protozoa
POOU	prologue
	prorogue
POOZ	Paolozzi
POPC	prospect
POPE	prompter
POPL	promptly
POPO	phosphor
	pooh-pooh
POPR	Prospero
PORC	protract
PORD	prograde
	protrude
PORM	prodrome
PORS	progress
POTL	prostyle
POTN	plotting
POTR	plotters
POTT	prostate
POUE	procurer
	produced
	producer
POUT	products
POYO	propylon
PPAO	pappadom
PPAU	poppadum
PPCA	pipeclay
PPDW	pipe down
PPEE	peppered
PPER	puppetry
PPFL	pipefuls
PPFS	pipefish
PPLA	papillae
PPLC	populace
PPLK	pipelike
PPLN	pipeline
PPLO	papilios
	papillon
PPLS	papalise
	papalism
	papalist
	papulose
	pipeless
	populism
	populist
PPLT	populate
PPLU	papulous
	populous
PPLZ	papalize
PPNA	popinjay
PPRN	papering
	peperoni
	piperine
PPRU	pop group
PPSL	popishly
PPSR	papistry
PPWR	pipework
PQAC	piquancy
PRAC	parlance
PRAD	parlando
PRAE	pervaded
PRAI	perradii
	phreatic
PRAL	portable
PRAO	Pergamon
PRAT	perianth
PRAU	par value
	Pergamum
PRBC	pare back
PRBE	pure-bred
PRBL	parabola
	parabole
	periboli
PRCE	Pericles
PRCP	pericope
PRCR	pericarp
PRDG	paradigm
PRDN	parading
	pyridine
PRDS	paradise❑
	parodist
PRDW	pare down
PRDX	paradoxy
PREA	parietal
	Parmesan
	Perceval
PRED	perdendo
PREE	parcener
	parleyer
PREI	parhelia
	parhelic
	paroemia
PREL	porterly
PREO	purveyor
PRES	perverse
PRET	perfecta
	permeate
PREU	parcel up
	parvenue
PREV	perceive
PRFE	purified
	purifier
PRFI	paraffin
PRGA	Paraguay
	Phrygian
PRGN	Perugino
PRHA	Parthian
PRHL	porthole
PRHN	parching
	Pershing
PRHR	porphyry❑
PRHS	purchase
PRIA	Parsifal
	partisan
	Percival
PRIG	porridge
PRII	perlitic
PRIL	partible
	particle
	Portillo
PRIO	porrigos
	porticos
PRIR	portière
PRIT	perviate
PRIU	pervious
	pirlicue
	purlieus
PRKE	parakeet
PRLA	parallax
PRLE	parallel
PRLF	Parklife
PRLN	parkland
	perilune
	Portland
	purblind
	purulent
PRLS	paralyse
	purplish
	pyrolyse

Words marked ❑ can also be spelled with an initial capital letter

PRLU	perilous
PRLZ	pyrolyze
PRMD	Pyramids
PRMU	paramour
PRNA	parental
	perineal
	peroneal
PRNE	Pyrenees
PRNI	paranoia
	paranoic
	paranoid
PRNR	partners
PRNS	pertness
	Piranesi
	pureness
PRNU	per annum
	perineum
PROA	personae
	personal
	personas
PROC	perforce
PROE	pardoner
	parroter
	pore over
	purposed
PROI	periodic
PROM	pardon me
PROS	porpoise
PRPR	perspire
	piri-piri
PRRI	portrait
PRRS	Portrush
PRRT	perorate
PRSA	Parisian
PRSE	perished
	perisher
PRSI	Port Said
	puristic
PRSK	piroshki
PRSN	phrasing
PRST	parasite
	porosity
PRTM	part-time
PRTS	pyritise
PRTZ	pyritize
PRUA	Portugal
PRUD	persuade
PRUE	perfumed
	perfumer
	perjured
	perjurer
	pertused
PRUI	parousia
PRUN	pursuant
	pursuing
PRVA	Peruvian
PRVL	Port-Vila
PRVN	paravane
PRVO	par avion
PRWR	parkward
	partwork
PRWT	part with
PRXD	peroxide
PRXN	pyroxene
PRXS	paroxysm
PRYA	party man
PRYN	partying
PRYS	partyism
PRZA	parazoan
PRZK	pirozhki
PSAA	passatas
	pass away
	Peshawar
PSAL	passable
	passably
	postally
PSAO	passados
	piscator□
PSAR	Pissarro
PSBC	pass-back
	push back
PSBK	push-bike
PSCD	postcode
PSCR	postcard
PSDN	Pasadena
PSDT	postdate
PSDW	pass down
	piss down
	push down
PSEB	passer-by
PSEE	pestered
	pesterer
PSEI	pushed in
PSFE	post-free
PSFR	pisiform
PSIA	piscinae
	piscinas
PSIH	pastiche
	postiche
PSIL	passible
	passibly
	pastille
	possible
	possibly
PSIN	passions
PSIO	Poseidon
PSIT	pass into
	push into
PSLG	posology
PSLN	Pasolini
PSMR	postmark
PSNL	posingly
PSOA	pastoral
PSOE	pass over
	Passover
	push open
	pushover
	push-over
PSOU	pishogue
PSPA	Pasiphae
PSPN	postpone
PSPR	passport
PSPS	postpose
PSRM	pastrami
PSTO	position
	positron
PSTV	positive
PSUA	pastural
	postural
PSUE	posturer
PSUO	pass upon
PSWR	password
PSYA	pussy cat
PTAC	Petrarch
	pittance
	potlatch
PTAL	pitiable
	pitiably
PTAR	Pitcairn
PTAU	Pittacus
PTBU	put about
PTCI	petechia
PTEA	pot metal
PTEC	patience□
PTEE	potterer
PTEI	pathetic
PTEL	pettedly
	pot belly
	pot-belly
PTEO	putter-on
PTHL	patchily
PTHN	pitching
PTHR	patchery
	potsherd
PTIE	pit viper
PTIH	put right
PTII	Patricia
	phthisis
PTIL	putridly
PTIO	Pattison
	pettifog
PTIT	patriate
PTLA	patellae
	patellas
PTLN	petulant
	pot plant
PTLS	pathless
	pithless
	pitiless
PTMI	Potemkin
PTMN	putamina
PTNC	put on ice
PTNE	patentee
PTNL	patently
	potently
PTNO	patentor
	put in for
PTNU	pétanque
PTOA	patronal
PTOE	pathogen
	potholed
	pot-holed
	put to bed
	put to sea
PTOI	pythonic
PTOO	patron of
PTOS	pot roast
	pot-roast
	put to use
PTOT	put forth
PTPO	put-up job
PTRA	paternal
	Peter Pan
PTRI	Peterkin
PTRO	Paterson
	Peterson
PTRU	peter out
PTSD	put aside
PTTA	petit mal
PTTE	potatoes
PTTO	petition
	potation
PTTV	putative
PTUE	pot-au-feu
PTYA	pitty-pat
PUAA	plug away
PUAC	Plutarch
PUAL	plurally
PUBG	plumbago
PUBN	plumbing
PUBR	Paul Berg
PUBS	plumbism
PUCO	pounce on
PUDG	poundage
PUDN	pounding
PUDW	pour down
PUEC	prudence□
PUEL	prunella□
PUET	Paulette
PUGN	plugging
	plunging
PUII	plurisie
	pruritic
	pruritis
PUIN	prurient
PUIO	prurigos
PUIU	pruritus
PUKE	Paul Klee
PUKF	pluck off
PUKL	pluckily
PULA	Pauillac
PUNS	Paul Nash
PUOE	pour over
PUOI	plutonic
PUPO	plump for
PUSA	Prussian
PUSF	Prussify
PUSI	poursuit
PUTC	poultice
PUUA	plumulae
PUUL	plug-ugly
PVLO	pavilion
PVMN	pavement
PVTN	pivoting
PWEE	pewterer
	powdered
PWRU	power cut
	powerful
PWSO	pawnshop
PYAE	prytanea
PYCL	pay a call
PYEI	phyletic

Words marked □ can also be spelled with an initial capital letter

Code	Word
PYIA	physical
PYIU	physique
PYLD	phyllode
PYLS	ptyalise
PYLT	phyllite
PYLZ	ptyalize
PYNL	pryingly
PYON	pay round
PYOR	pay court
PYOT	Plymouth
PZEI	pizzeria
PZLN	puzzling
QADN	quandang
	quandong
QADR	quandary
QAEE	quaverer
QAEL	Quakerly
QAHN	quashing
QAKR	quackery
QAMR	quagmire
QAMS	qualmish
QANL	quaintly
QAOZ	quatorze
QARI	quatrain
QARL	quarrels
QARN	quadrant
QARO	quadroon
QART	quadrate
QASD	quayside
QATF	quantify
QATL	quartile
QATN	quantong
QATR	quarters
QATS	quantise
QATT	quantity
QATZ	quantize
QECE	quenched
	quencher
QEEE	Quebecer
QEEL	quenelle
QELN	quelling
QENA	Queen Mab
QENE	queen bee
QENO	queendom
QEQE	Queequeg
QERS	queerish
QESL	queasily
QETN	questant
	questing
QETO	question
QEYN	querying
QIBE	quibbler
QICN	quincunx
QIDT	quiddity
QIEL	quinella
QIIA	Quirinal
QIKE	quickset
QIKI	quick fix
QIKL	quirkily
QIKS	quirkish
QILN	quisling❑
QINN	quidnunc
QIOI	quixotic
QIOR	quixotry
QIPS	quippish
QISE	quinsied
	quipster
QITD	quietude
QITN	quilting
	quitting
QIZF	quizzify
QIZN	quizzing
QOAL	quotable
	quotably
QOIN	quotient
RAAE	reawaken
	rhagades
RAAL	readable
	readably
RACN	reascend
RADI	rhabdoid
RAEC	reagency
RAFR	reaffirm
RAHM	road hump
RAHN	reaching
RAHU	reach out
RAIE	realized
	realizer
RAIT	read into
RALF	real life
	real-life
RALS	roadless
RALV	real live
RAMC	rearmice
RAMS	rearmost
RANS	realness
RAOE	reasoned
RAPA	reappear
RARG	road rage
RASD	rhapsody
	roadside
RASE	reanswer
	roadster
RASG	road sign
RASR	reassure
RASS	reassess
RATA	Rhaetian
RATN	roasting
RATO	reaction
RATS	road-test
RATV	reactive
RAUO	read up on
RAWR	rearward
RBCN	rubicund
RBDT	rabidity
RBDU	rubidium
RBEE	rabbeted
RBEO	robbed of
RBFO	rub off on
RBIA	rubaiyat
RBIE	rabbiter
RBIH	rubbishy
RBII	rabbinic
RBIO	rabbit on
RBIR	rabbitry
RBLI	Rabelais
RBLN	rub along
RBLR	ribaldry
RBNA	Robin Day
RBNO	Robinson
RBPR	ruby port
RBRN	roborant
RBSL	robustly
RBSM	ribosome
RBTA	rebuttal
RBTC	robotics
RBTE	rebatoes
	rebutter
RBTS	robotise
RCAD	Richards
RCAG	recharge
RCAL	racially
	rectally
RCCE	ricochet
RCCK	rock cake
RCDL	Rochdale
RCDN	receding
RCDV	rock dove
RCEN	recreant
RCER	rocketry
RCET	raclette
	recreate
RCFC	rock-face
RCFL	rockfall
RCFR	Rockford
RCFS	rockfish
RCIE	rachides
	rachises
	received
	receiver
	recliner
	recoiler
RCII	rachitic
	rachitis
RCIL	rocaille
RCIT	receipts
RCLF	rich-left
RCLN	rockling
RCLS	reckless
RCMN	Richmond
RCMS	racemise
	racemism
	racemose
RCMT	racemate
RCMZ	racemize
RCNE	recanter
	reconvey
RCNL	recently
RCNS	raciness
	richness
RCOE	reckoned
	reckoner
RCOO	reckon on
RCOU	reckon up
RCPO	receptor
RCRC	rick-rack
RCRE	recorded
	recorder
RCRN	rack-rent
RCRO	race riot
RCRS	rock rose
RCSA	rickshaw
RCSC	rucksack
RCSE	recessed
RCSL	rock salt
	rock-salt
RCSN	recusant
RCSO	recision
RCUS	recourse
RCVR	recovery
RCWE	rockweed
RCWO	rock wool
RDAA	red lauan
RDAC	radiance
	radiancy
	red sauce
	riddance
RDAE	red-faced
	Rod Laver
RDAI	radialia
RDAL	radially
RDAO	radiator
RDAT	radwaste
RDCB	reduce by
RDCL	ridicule
RDCO	redactor
RDCT	radicate
RDDW	ride down
RDEA	red cedar
	ridgeway
RDED	reddenda
RDEE	reddened
	redeemer❑
RDER	Redbeard
RDHN	redshank
RDHR	red shirt
RDIC	Redditch
RDID	red biddy
RDIE	Red River
RDIH	red light
RDIN	red giant
RDLN	redolent
RDLR	red alert
RDLT	radulate
RDMN	rudiment
RDNS	rudeness
RDPO	redeploy
RDRC	redbrick
	redirect
	Roderick
RDRS	Red Cross
RDRV	Redgrave
RDSG	redesign
RDTO	ridottos
RDTR	redstart
RDUE	radiuses
RDUL	redouble
RDUR	Red Guard
RDWR	red dwarf
REBC	reedbuck
RECR	rheocord
REKO	reef knot

Words marked ❑ can also be spelled with an initial capital letter

Code	Word
RELG	rheology
RELN	Riesling
REMG	Rees-Mogg
REOI	rhetoric
RERS	ryegrass
RESA	rheostat
RETE	roentgen❑
REUL	ruefully
RFEA	rifleman
RFEE	raftered
RFEL	reflexly
RFET	Rafferty
RFGR	refigure
RFGU	refugium
RFLN	ruffling
RFLS	riftless
RFNE	refunder
RFNN	refining
RFNR	refinery
RFNS	rifeness
RFRA	referral
RFRE	reformer
RFRF	riff-raff
RFRS	reforest
RFSI	refusnik
RFSN	refusing
RGAL	Regnault
RGAO	Ragnarok
RGCD	regicide
RGDF	rigidify
RGDO	rigadoon
RGDS	rigidise
RGDT	rigidity
RGDZ	rigidize
RGEL	raggedly
	ruggedly
RGIE	regainer
RGLN	reguline
RGLR	regulars
RGLS	regulise
RGLT	regality
	regelate
	regulate
RGLZ	regulize
RGMN	regiment
RGNL	ragingly
	Reginald
RGOA	regional
RGRA	regard as
RGRD	rag trade
RGRE	regarded
	regarder
RGRS	rigorist
RGRU	rigorous
RGSE	register
RGSL	rugosely
RGSR	registry
RGST	rugosity
RGTF	right off
RGTN	ragstone
	rigatoni
RGTO	right now
	rogation
RGTR	right arm
RGTS	rightist
RGTU	rightful
	right out
RHAE	reheater
RHAS	rehearse
RHBA	rehoboam
RHSE	rehashed
RIAL	raisable
RIBC	rein back
RIBR	rainbird
RIBW	rainbowy
RICA	raincoat
RICR	railcard
RIDE	reindeer
	Ruisdael
RIDO	raindrop
RIFL	rainfall
RIFN	reinfund
RIFR	reinform
RIHA	railhead
	Reichian
RIII	rhinitis
RILR	raillery
RILS	rainless
RINN	reigning
RINO	Rhiannon
RIOI	rhizobia
RIOO	rhizopod
RIPS	re-impose
RIRA	railroad
RISR	reinsure
RITE	rain-tree
RITN	roisting
RIVN	re-invent
RIVS	reinvest
RJCE	rejected
	rejecter
RJCO	rejector
RJGE	rejigger
RJIE	rejoicer
RJSI	rajaship
RKHL	rakehell
RKNL	rekindle
RKSL	rakishly
RLAC	reliance
RLAE	released
RLAL	reliable
	reliably
RLCL	roll-call
RLCT	relocate
RLDU	ruled out
RLEE	relieved
	reliever
RLEO	relievos
RLGO	religion❑
RLGT	relegate
RLLS	ruleless
RLOE	roll over
	roll-over
RLPA	role-play
RLPE	relapsed
	relapser
RLPL	roly-poly
RLTN	relating
RLTO	relation
RLTT	relate to
RLTV	relative
RLUC	relaunch
RLVN	relevant
RLXN	relaxant
	relaxing
RLYN	rallying
	relaying
RLYS	rallyist
RMAC	rampancy
RMAE	rummager
RMAT	remnants
RMDA	Ramadhan
	remedial
RMFE	ramified
RMFR	ramiform
RMGA	remigial
RMGT	Ramsgate
RMHM	romp home
RMIG	Ram Singh
RMIU	rum-ti-tum
RMLE	REM sleep
RMLN	rambling
	Rampling
	rumbling
RMLO	ramble on
RMME	remember
RMNA	Romanian
	Rumanian
RMNE	reminder
	romancer
RMNI	romantic
RMNN	remanent
	ruminant
RMNS	Romanise
RMNT	ruminate
RMNZ	Romanize
RMQI	ramequin
RMRE	remarked
	remarker
RMRK	rim-brake
RMRO	remark on
RMRU	remarque❑
	remurmur
RMSE	Ramesses
	remaster
RMSL	remissly
RMTA	remittal
RMTE	remittee
	remitter
RMTL	remotely
RMTO	remittor
	remotion
RMTS	remotest
RMUA	rambutan
RMUE	rumoured
RMWR	Romeward
RMYN	Ramayana
RNAE	rondavel
RNAL	runnable
RNAO	rent-a-mob
RNBN	ringbone
RNBR	ring-bark
RNBU	runabout
RNDV	ring-dove
RNEE	renderer
RNEU	rondeaux
	runner-up
RNFE	rent-free
	run after
RNFR	reniform
	ring fort
RNGD	renegade
RNGE	reneguer
RNGN	ronggeng
RNGO	renege on
RNGT	renegate
RNHL	ringhals
	rinkhals
RNHR	ranchero
	run short
RNIO	rondinos
RNLN	rankling
	run along
RNLS	rindless
	run close
RNLT	ringlets
RNMI	ring main
RNNS	rankness
RNOE	ransomer
RNOI	run for it
RNOL	randomly
RNOP	Randolph
RNRA	ring road
RNRS	run a risk
RNSD	ringside
RNTI	ringtail
RNTM	ring-time
RNTN	renitent
RNTU	ring true
RNUC	renounce
RNUO	run out of
	run out on
RNVN	renevant
RNVT	renovate
RNWE	renowned
RNWN	renewing
RNWR	ringworm
RNWS	ringwise
RNZN	rendzina
ROBE	root beer
ROBI	rhomboid
ROBL	root-ball
ROCA	rhonchal
ROCO	root crop
ROCP	re-occupy
ROCU	rhonchus
ROEI	Rhodesia
ROEL	rootedly
ROER	Rio Negro
ROFL	roomfuls
ROIN	reorient
ROLK	rooflike

Words marked ❑ can also be spelled with an initial capital letter

Code	Word
	rootlike
ROLS	roofless
	rootless
RORC	roof rack
ROTL	roof tile
RPAE	repealer
	repeated
	repeater
	replacer
RPAL	ropeable
RPBI	republic
RPCT	rapacity
RPDT	rapidity
RPEI	replevin
RPEO	ripienos
RPEV	repreeve
RPIA	reprisal
RPIE	raphides
RPIV	reprieve
RPLE	repelled
	repeller
	repulsed
RPLN	rippling
RPNE	repenter
RPNN	ripening
RPNS	ripeness
	ropiness
RPOC	reproach
RPOE	reprover
RPRA	riparial
	riparian
RPRE	repartee
	reported
	reporter
RPRF	repurify
RPRS	rephrase
RPSL	reposall
RPSN	reposing
	rope's end
RPTN	repetend
RPUE	ruptured
RPUS	repoussé
RPWL	rope-walk
RPYR	rope-yarn
RQIA	requital
RQIE	required
	requirer
	requited
	requiter
RQIH	requight
RQOL	requoyle
RRBR	rare bird
RRFE	rarefied
RRLS	ruralise
RRLT	rurality
RRLZ	ruralize
RRMC	rere-mice
RRNS	rareness
RSAA	Rastaman
RSAC	research
RSAL	rascally
RSAN	Roseanna
	Roseanne
RSBL	rust belt
RSDA	residual
RSDI	reside in
RSDK	Rusedski
RSDN	resident
RSDU	residuum
RSEA	Rasselas
RSET	respects
	rispetti
	Rossetti
RSGE	resigned
	resigner
RSGI	rosoglio
RSHE	rose-hued
RSHU	rush hour
RSID	Roskilde
RSIH	Respighi
RSLE	resolved
	resolver
RSLI	result in
RSLK	roselike
RSLN	resplend
	Rosalind
	Rosaline
	rustling
RSLR	Rosslare
RSLS	restless
RSLT	resolute
	risoluto
RSLU	rustle up
RSML	resemble
RSMN	Rosamond
	Rosamund
RSMR	rosemary□
RSNF	resinify
RSNN	resonant
RSNS	rashness
	resinise
	rosiness
RSNT	resinate
	resonate
RSNU	resinous
RSNZ	resinize
RSOE	restored
	restorer
RSOS	response
RSPN	rose-pink
RSRA	rosarian
RSRC	restrict
RSRE	reserved
	reserves
	resorter
RSRI	resorcin
	restrain
RSRO	rest room
RSRP	rescript
RSRT	resort to
RSRU	rosarium
RSSE	resister
RSSO	resistor
RSTE	resetter
RSTI	rise to it
RSTL	resettle
RSTO	risottos
RSUC	resource
RSUI	Rasputin
RSWO	rosewood
RSWT	rest with
RTAL	rateable
	rateably
	retrally
	ritually
RTCL	reticule
RTCN	reticent
RTEA	Rathenau
RTEC	retrench
RTEL	rottenly
RTFE	ratified
RTFR	retiform
RTHN	retching
RTIA	Rattigan
	retail at
RTIE	retailer
	retained
	retainer
RTIV	retrieve
RTLN	rattling
RTLO	rattle on
RTLS	riteless
	ruthless
RTNL	rotundly
RTNN	rotenone
RTNT	ritenuto
RTOA	rational
	R S Thomas
RTOC	retroact
RTOI	retrofit
RTOS	retrorse
RTRA	Rotarian
RTRE	retarded
	retarder
	returned
RTRN	retiring
RTRR	rotor arm
RTRT	return to
RTTN	rotating
RTTO	rotation
RTTR	rotatory
RTVT	rotavate
	rotovate
RUDF	round off
RUDR	rounders
RUEA	routeman
RUET	roulette
RUEU	rouleaus
	rouleaux
RUHE	rough-hew
RUHG	roughage
RUHR	rough-dry
RUHS	roughish
RUHU	rough out
RUSA	Rousseau
RVAE	revealed
	revealer
RVEA	reviewal
RVEE	reviewer
RVGN	ravaging
RVIL	reveille
RVKN	revoking
RVLE	ravelled
	reveller
	revolted
	revolter
	revolver
	rivelled
RVLN	reviling
RVLS	rivalise
RVLT	revolute
RVLZ	rivalize
RVNE	revenger
	revenues
RVNL	ravingly
RVNN	ravening
	revenant
RVNU	ravenous
RVOE	rave over
RVRA	reversal
RVRE	reversed
	reverser
RVRN	reverend
	reverent
	riverine
RVRO	reversos
RVSE	ravished
RVSO	revision
RVSR	revisory
RVTN	riveting
RVVF	revivify
RVVN	reviving
RWIG	Rawlings
RWME	raw umber
RWOE	rawboned
	raw-boned
RWRE	rewarder
RWRW	rewarewa
RWTE	Rowntree
RWYS	rowdyism
RYDE	Ruysdael
RYHI	rhythmic
RYLS	royalism
	royalist□
RYLT	rhyolite
RYOD	Reynolds
RZRU	razor-cut
SAAA	soakaway
SAAD	seawards
SAAE	scavager
	seafarer
	seawater
SAAI	sparaxis
SAAL	sea eagle
	seamanly
	shakable
	shapable
	sparable
	statable
SAAO	scalados
SABA	snap bean
SABC	Starbuck

Code	Word
	sway-back
SABE	shambles
SABL	seat belt
	shabbily
SABN	slam-bang
	slap bang
	slap-bang
	stabbing
	St Albans
SABR	scabbard
SACA	snatch at
SACE	searcher
	snatcher
	stanchel
	stancher
	starched
	starcher
SACL	scarcely
	shauchle
	stanchly
SACO	stay cool
SACP	seascape
SACT	scarcity
	staccato
SACU	Sea Scout
SADA	stand pat
SADE	spandrel
SADF	stand off
	stand-off
SADI	spandril
SADN	scalding
	scaldini
	standing
SADO	stand for
	stand low
SADR	standard
SADS	slapdash
	slap-dash
	Standish
	stardust
SADU	scandium
	stand out
	standout
SADW	swab down
SAEA	spaceman□
SAEE	sea level
	sea-level
	slaverer
	stapedes
SAEF	scare off
	shake off
	stake off
	stave off
SAEG	scavenge
	space age
SAEI	spare rib
	spare-rib
SAEL	statedly
SAEO	scared of
SAEU	scalenus
	shake out
	shake-out
	shameful
	share out
	share-out
	space out
	spadeful
	stake out
	stake-out
	stare out
SAFL	scaffold
SAFR	Stafford
	Stamford
SAFS	starfish
SAGA	shanghai□
SAGE	spangled
SAGL	shaggily
	slangily
SAGN	slanging
SAGR	staggers
SAGT	Stan Getz
SAGZ	star-gaze
SAHA	slag heap
SAHI	scaphoid
	smash hit
	smash-hit
SAHL	seashell
	Swan Hill
SAHN	scathing
	slashing
	smashing
SAHP	stanhope□
SAHR	seashore
SAHS	spathose
SAIA	Stari Ras
SAIE	spadices
SAIM	stadiums
SAIR	Spaniard
SAIU	scabious
	spacious
SAKA	Shark Bay
	snackbar
	spark gap
SAKD	stackade
SAKE	shackled
	shackles
	sparkler
	stalkoes
SAKF	slack off
	spark off
SAKI	Shanklin
SAKN	slacking
	smacking
	spanking
	stalking
	swanking
SAKO	stacks of
SAKR	starkers
SAKU	spark out
SALK	starlike
	Swan Lake
	swanlike
SALN	seaplane
	sea-plane
	snarling
	stalling
	Stallone
	starling
SALO	scallion
	smallpox
	stallion
SALR	small fry
SALS	seamless
	smallest
	smallish
	Spätlese
	starless
SALT	Scarlett
SALW	shallows
SAML	smarmily
SAMN	slamming
	swarming
SANN	scanning
	spawning
	stagnant
	staining
SANR	stannary
	swannery
SANT	stagnate
	stannite
SANU	stannous
SAOA	seasonal
SAOE	sea rover
	sea-rover
	seasoned
	seasoner
	spadones
	stay over
SAOI	Slavonic
SAOL	sea holly
SAON	seaborne
	seagoing
	sea-going
SAOR	seaboard
SAOS	seahorse
	sea mouse
SAPD	stampede
SAPE	sharp-set
SAPL	snappily
SAPN	sharp end
	slapping
	snapping
	stamping
	swapping
SAPO	shampoos
SAPS	scampish
	sharpish
	snappish
SAPU	stamp out
SARA	sea bream
	stairway
SARB	star ruby
SARC	sea wrack
	shamrock
SARE	shagreen
SARL	starrily
SARN	seafront
	seal ring
	sparring
SARU	scabrous
	sea trout
SASD	soapsuds
SASE	seamster
	slaister
SASI	staysail
SASL	sparsely
SASN	swan song
SASO	scansion
	snapshot
SAST	sparsity
SATE	sea otter
	startled
	startler
SATF	start off
SATK	swastika
SATL	scantily
SATN	shantung
	slanting
	smarting
	starting
SATR	shattery
	slattern
	Slattery
	starters
	star turn
SATS	smart ass
	smart-ass
	smartish
SATU	smart guy
	start out
SAUA	scapulae
	scapular
	scapulas
	spatular
SAUE	shamuses
	statuses
	statutes
SAUR	statuary
SAUT	Shabuoth
	Shavuoth
SAVN	starving
SAWF	spaewife
SAWL	Shadwell
SAWR	soapwort
	stalwart
	Star Wars
	starwort
SAWT	stay with
SAYA	Sealyham
SAZI	stanzaic
SBAH	Sabratha
SBEG	submerge
SBES	sublease
	submerse
	subverst
SBET	subjects
SBEU	subgenus
SBEV	subserve
SBIA	subviral
SBIL	subtitle
SBIT	sobriety
	submit to

Code	Word
SBLN	sibilant
SBLO	subfloor
SBLS	sabulose
SBLT	sibilate
	subtlety
	subulate
SBLU	sabulous
	Sibelius
SBOA	subsolar
	subtotal
SBOI	subsonic
	subtonic
	subtopia
SBON	subpoena
SBRA	Siberian
	suburban
SBRC	subtract
SBRD	subgrade
	subtrude
SBRE	suborner
SBRI	suburbia
SBRM	subframe
SBRN	sobering
SBRS	soberise
	suberise
	suberose
SBRT	suberate
	sybarite[❑]
SBRZ	soberize
	suberize
SBTF	sob-stuff
SBTG	sabotage
SBTN	Sabatini
SBTS	subitise
SBTU	saboteur
SBTZ	subitize
SBUA	subhuman
	sublunar
SCAE	Socrates
SCAI	saccadic
	sacraria
	Socratic
SCAL	sociable
	sociably
	socially
SCDN	seceding
SCEA	societal
SCEE	sickened
	socketed
SCEI	secretin
SCEL	sacredly
	secretly
	sickerly
SCFC	suck face
SCFL	sackfuls
SCIC	succinct
SCII	succinic
SCIT	sacristy
SCLE	so-called
SCLK	such like
SCLL	sicklily
SCLN	suckling[❑]
SCLS	sick list
SCMR	sycamore
SCNE	seconder
SCNL	secantly
	secondly
SCNS	sickness
SCOA	sectoral
SCRL	securely
SCRN	securing
SCRT	security
SCTA	such that
SCUA	succubae
SCUE	saccules
	secluded
SCUT	suck up to
SCUU	sacculus
	succubus
SCWS	suchwise
SDAE	Sid James
SDBN	sideband
SDBU	sod about
SDDS	side dish
SDDU	side drum
	side-drum
SDEE	saddened
SDEL	suddenly
SDKC	sidekick
SDLE	sidalcea
SDLM	soda lime
SDLN	sideline
	sideling
	sidelong
SDLR	saddlery
SDLT	sedulity
	sodalite
	sodality
SDLU	sedulous
SDMN	sediment
SDNS	Sudanese
SDOA	sad to say
SDRA	sidereal
SDRT	siderate
	siderite
SDRU	sudarium
SDSA	sidesman
SDSE	sidestep
	side-step
SDSI	sadistic
	sideslip
SDSO	sideshow
SDTL	sedately
SDTO	sedation
	sedition
SDTR	sudatory
SDTV	sedative
SDUE	Sadducee
SDUI	siddurim
SDVD	St David's
SDVE	side view
SDWC	Sidgwick
SDWL	sidewalk
	sidewall
SDWR	sideward
SDWS	sidewise
SDWT	side with
SDWY	sideways
SEAA	spelaean
SEAC	skew arch
SEAI	scenario
SEAO	Sheraton
SEBC	step back
SEBL	skewbald
SEBR	Svedberg
SEBU	see about
SECE	sketcher
SECK	seedcake
SECL	stem cell
SEDA	speedway
	Stendhal
SEDC	shelduck
SEDL	speedily
	spendall
	steadily
SEDN	sheading
	shedding
	sledding
	speeding
	spending
	steading
SEDO	steady on!
SEDW	step down
	step-down
SEEA	skeletal
SEEH	skene-dhu
SEEO	skeleton
SEFR	Stepford
SEGE	Spengler
SEGL	Svengali
SEGN	sledging
SEHN	seething
	Stephano
SEHR	see where
	Shephard
	shepherd
SEIA	Sheridan
SEIE	specimen
SEII	specific
SEIT	speciate
	step into
SEIU	specious
SEKE	speckled
SEKF	sneak off
SEKL	sneakily
SEKN	sneaking
	speaking
SEKO	speak for
SEKU	sneak-cup
	speak out
SELC	skelloch
SELF	stellify
SELH	stealthy
SELK	seem like
SELN	seedling
	shelling
	Shetland
	smelling
	stealing
	stelline
	sterling
	swelling
SELO	swell box
SELS	seedless
	stemless
SELT	stellate
SELU	shell out
	smell out
	spell out
SEMI	sperm oil
SEML	steamily
SEMN	steaming
SEMR	spermary
	Stenmark
SEMT	stemmata
SENA	seeing as
	Steinway
SENG	sternage
SENO	steenbok
SENS	Skegness
	skewness
SENT	Steinitz
SEOE	stenoses
SEOI	stenosis
	stenotic
	step on it
SEPE	steepled
SEPF	sleep off
SEPI	sheep-dip
SEPL	sleepily
SEPN	sleeping
	sneaping
	steeping
	sweeping
SEPO	sheepdog
SEPR	Sheppard
SEPS	sheepish
	steepish
SEPU	sleep out
SERC	skerrick
SERF	swear off
SERG	steerage
SERI	shear pin
SERL	smearily
SERN	sneering
	stearine
	steering
	swearing
SERO	steer for
SERT	stearate
SETA	sceattas
	spectral
SETE	sceptred
	sweet pea
SETN	sheeting
	smelting
	sweating
SETO	sweetsop
SETT	spectate
	steatite
SETU	spectrum
SEUA	specular

SEUU speculum
SEVN shelving
sleeving
swerving
SEWL see a wolf
SEWS stepwise
SEYN Shenyang
SEZL sleazily
SEZN sneezing
SFAI safranin
SFBC softback
SFBI soft-boil
SFCR soft-core
SFEE softened
softener
sufferer
SFEU soften up
SFFO safe from
soft food
SFHA softhead
soft-head
SFHE soft-hued
SFIE sufficer
SFLA soft loan
SFLN soft lens
soft line
SFNS safeness
softness
SFRG suffrage
SFRN saffrony
SFSA safe seat
soft soap
soft-soap
SFSL soft sell
SFSO soft-slow
soft spot
SFUE suffused
SFWO softwood
SFWR software
SGAA sign away
SGAL signally
SGAO saguaros
SGAT signal to
SGCT sagacity
SGIU signieur
SGLE St Gallen
SGMR sagamore
SGNT saginate
SGOE sigh over
sign over
SGPL sago-palm
SGPS signpost
SGRE sugar pea
SGRN sugaring
SGRU sugar gum
SGRY Sigiriya
SGSE sigisbei
SGTA sagittal
SGTE sightsee
SGTN sighting
SHAP schnapps
SHAT schmaltz
SHBR Schubert

SHDL schedule
SHEE Schlegel
SHEI Schwerin
SHEP schleppy
SHGU sphagnum
SHLE Schiller
St Helier
SHLM so help me
SHLN St Helens
SHLO scholion
SHMN scheming
Schumann
SHMT schemata
SHNE sphinges
sphinxes
SHOE schooled
schooner
Schröder
SHOK schlocky
SHOZ schmooze
SHRI spheroid
SHRL spherule
SHRO scherzos
SHSE Schüssel
SHZI schizoid
SIAA slip away
Srinagar
SIAE ship a sea
spicated
spirated
SIAK Sri Lanka
SIAL sailable
seizable
spiracle
spirally
suitable
suitably
SIAT ski pants
SIBN shinbone
stilbene
SICE snitcher
stitched
stitcher
switches
SICO switch on
SICR skincare
SICS slipcase
slip-cast
suitcase
SICT spiccato
SICU stitch up
SIDE skin-deep
swindler
SIDW slim down
SIEE seine net
Spike Lee
spikelet
SIEF skive off
smite off
SIEL shigella
snivelly
SIEO seised of
SIET stiletto

SIEU spiteful
SIFE sniffler
SIFI sainfoin
SIFL Seinfeld
sniffily
SIFN sniffing
spiffing
SIFR spitfire□
SIFS sailfish
stiffish
SIFU sniff out
SIGA stingray
SIGE shingles
SIGL stingily
SIGN stinging
swinging
SIGO smidgeon
SIHA skinhead
SIHE slighter
SIHL slightly
SIHR slithery
SIIA scimitar
suicidal
SIIE scilicet
spirited
SIII spilikin
SIIL spirilla
SIIT sail into
slip into
SIJC skipjack
SIKE stickler
SIKL stickily
SIKN shirking
sticking
stinking
SIKO slipknot
SIKU stick out
stink out
SILA shipload
SILE shielded
SILG spillage
stillage
SILN shilling
Spillane
stifling
Stirling
swirling
SILS sciolism
sciolist
stirless
SILU sciolous
swill out
SIMN shipment
skimming
slimming
swimming
SIMR shimmery
SIMS skirmish
SIMT shipmate
stigmata
SINE scienter
spinnies
SINN spinning

SINO seignior
Spion Kop
SINS slimness
SINT stibnite
SINU seigneur
SINY spinneys
SIOC scirocco
SIPE stippled
stippler
SIPG slippage
SIPL skimpily
SIPN shipping
skimping
skipping
slipping
snipping
SIPR slippery
SIPT snippets
snippety
SIRA skid road
slip road
SIRN sciurine
stirring
SIRU scirrhus
SISA snip-snap
SISE spinster
SISI swimsuit
SISO scission
slipshod
SISR scissors
scissure
SITC sciatica
SITE skittles
swiftlet
SITK shiitake
SITL shiftily
shirtily
SITN shifting
skirting
spitting
stilting
stinting
SITO spittoon
SITR ship-tire
SITS skin test
skittish
SIUA spicular
stipular
SIUE stipuled
SIUI sui juris
SIUU stimulus
SIWL Shinwell
SIWR shipworm
slipware
SIYR shipyard
SKAI Sakhalin
SKAO Sakharov
SKRK Sikorski
Sikorsky
SKWR Sikh Wars
SKYK sukiyaki
SLAA salt away
SLAD saltando

Words marked □ can also be spelled with an initial capital letter

Code	Word
SLAE	sulcated
SLAI	sultanic
	syllabic
	Sylvania
SLAL	saleable
	saleably
	sellable
	solvable
	syllable
SLAO	Salvador
	soldados
SLAU	sell a pup
	sillabub
	Silvanus
	syllabub
	syllabus
SLBR	Salzburg
SLBS	saltbush
SLCE	selected
SLCF	silicify
SLCN	silicone
SLCO	selector
SLCS	solecise
	solecism
SLCT	salacity
	saliceta
	silicate
	solicity
SLCZ	solecize
SLDF	solidify
SLDR	solidare
SLDT	solidity
SLDW	salt down
SLEC	salience
	saliency
	solvency
SLEE	solderer
SLEG	selvedge
	solfeggi
SLEL	silverly
	sullenly
SLFA	salt flat
SLHA	self-heal
SLHD	sulphide
SLHL	Self-Help
	Solihull
SLHN	sulphone
SLHO	selfhood
SLHR	sulphury
SLHT	sulphate
	sulphite
SLIA	Sullivan
SLIO	Sillitoe
SLIR	soldiers
SLLC	salt lick
SLLK	salt lake
SLLS	saltless
	selfless
SLLV	self-love
SLMD	self-made
SLML	solemnly
SLNA	so long as
	splenial
SLNC	Salonica
	Selznick
SLNE	Salinger
	silencer
	splinter
SLNI	solenoid
	splendid
SLNK	Salonika
SLNL	silently
SLNT	salinity
	selenite
SLNU	selenium
	splenius
SLPA	Salopian
SLPT	self-pity
SLRA	Silurian
SLRE	salaried
SLRL	self-rule
	sultrily
SLRM	scleroma
SLRO	saleroom
SLRS	sclerose
	solarise
SLRU	sclerous
	solarium
SLRZ	solarize
SLSA	salesman
	sales tax
SLSI	Selassie
SLSM	selfsame
	self-same
SLSW	self-sown
SLTC	solstice
SLTD	solitude
SLTE	splatter
	split pea
	splitter
	splutter
SLTF	split off
SLTH	splotchy
SLTI	split pin
SLTN	saluting
	split end
SLTO	solution
SLTR	salutary
	solitary
SLTU	solatium
SLUE	saltuses
SLUU	Seleucus
SLVR	salivary
SLVT	salivate
SLWL	self-will
SLWR	saltwort
	silkworm
SLWS	Sulawesi
SLYA	silky oak
	Süleyman
SLYN	sullying
SLYO	Saltykov
SMAH	sympathy
SMBD	somebody
SMCA	so much as
SMCS	so much so
SMER	symmetry
SMGT	somegate
SMHN	symphony
SMHP	some hope
SMHR	same here
	samphire
SMII	somnific
SMIN	symbiont
SMIS	Simbirsk
SMIT	somniate
SMLC	semplice
SMLF	simplify
SMLN	sampling
	semolina
SMLO	Sémillon
SMLS	similise
SMLT	simulate
SMLZ	similize
SMNE	so-minded
SMNH	Samantha
SMNI	semantic
SMNL	Seminole
SMNR	semantra
	seminary
SMNS	sameness
SMNT	seminate
SMOA	sum total
SMOE	summoner
SMOI	semiotic
	symbolic
	sympodia
	symposia
SMOU	summon up
SMPD	Sam Spade
SMRA	Sumerian
SMRE	Somerset
SMRL	sombrely
SMRR	sombrero
SMRT	St Moritz
SMRU	samarium
SMSE	semester
SMTM	sometime
SMTN	semitone
SMTR	sumotori
SMTS	Semitise
SMTZ	Semitize
SMWA	somewhat
SMWS	somewise
SMWY	someways
SMZA	samizdat
SNAA	sandarac
	send away
SNAD	sunwards
SNAE	sinuated
SNAH	sunbathe
SNAN	Santa Ana
SNBC	send back
SNBN	sandbank
SNBO	songbook
	sonobuoy
SNBR	Sandburg
	songbird
SNCO	senecios
SNCR	sinecure
SNCS	sand-cast
	sinicise
SNCZ	sinicize
SNDI	synedria
SNDN	sand-dune
SNDW	send down
	sent down
SNEC	sentence
SNEE	sundered
SNEI	sanserif
SNER	Sancerre
	San Pedro
SNFA	Son of Man
	Son of Sam
SNFE	sand flea
SNFO	Son of God
SNGA	sonogram
SNHD	sunshade
SNHI	Sondheim
SNHL	sandhill
SNHM	send home
SNHN	sunshine
	sunshiny
SNIE	sentinel
SNIG	San Diego
	Santiago
SNIH	sunlight
SNIL	sensible
	sensibly
	sensilla
SNIN	sentient
SNIO	sun visor
SNIU	sinciput
SNKI	Sanskrit
SNLC	sunblock
SNLG	Sinology
SNLI	Sinclair
SNLL	senilely
SNLN	sunblind
	syncline
SNLT	senility
SNNA	son-in-law
SNNM	synonymy
SNNS	saneness
SNOI	santonin
	sensoria
	sinfonia
SNOT	senior to
SNPE	synapses
	synopses
SNPI	synapsis
	synaptic
	synopsis
	synoptic
SNRA	Sangraal
	Sangreal
	sun cream
SNRI	Sangrail
SNRM	syndrome
SNRN	sonorant
SNRT	Señorita
	sonority

Code	Word
SNRU	sonorous
SNSE	Sangster
	sinister
	songster
SNSI	Senussis
	sinusoid
SNSN	singsong
SNSO	sandshoe
SNTF	sanctify
SNTN	sonatina
SNTO	sanction
SNTR	sanitary
SNTS	sanitise
SNTT	sanctity
	sanitate
SNTV	sanative
SNTZ	sanitize
SNUA	singular
SNUF	sanguify
SNUI	sink unit
SNUL	sinfully
SNUN	sanguine
	sunburnt
SNUS	sunburst
SNUU	sensuous
SNWC	sandwich□
SNWR	send word
SNWT	send with
SNWV	sine wave
SNYI	syncytia
SOAA	slog away
	stomatal
	stop a gap
	stow away
	stowaway
SOAE	show a leg
SOAI	Slovakia
	sporadic
	stomatic
SOAL	São Paulo
	smokable
	storable
SOAU	Sholapur
SOBA	Show Boat
SOBL	shoebill
	snowball□
SOBR	slobbery
	snobbery
SOBS	slobbish
	snobbish
	snobbism
SOBT	stop bath
SOCC	stopcock
SOCE	scorched
	scorcher
	sloucher
SOCS	showcase
	spot cash
	stoicism
SODI	spondaic
SODL	shoddily
SODN	scolding
SODO	snowdrop
SODW	showdown
	slow down
	slowdown
	stop down
SOEA	storeman
SOEE	scoleces
	shoveler
SOEF	score off
	shove off
	slope off
SOEG	Stone Age
SOEI	Slovenia
	snowed in
SOEL	slovenly
	stonefly
SOER	slovenry
	smoke-dry
SOES	Smolensk
SOEU	score out
	smoke out
	snowed up
SOFE	scot free
	scot-free
SOFL	snowfall
SOFN	scoffing
SOFS	scomfish
SOGL	spongily
	stodgily
SOGN	sponging
SOGR	shop-girl
	showgirl
SOHA	soothsay
SOHN	Shoshone
	soothing
SOHR	shoehorn
	smothery
SOHU	slothful
SOIE	scolices
SOII	sporidia
SOIK	stotinka
	stotinki
SOIL	Scofield
	stolidly
SOIT	spoliate
SOIU	stocious
	stotious
SOKA	stock car
	stockman
SOKD	stockade
SOKE	Shockley
SOKL	spookily
	stockily
SOKN	shocking
	smocking
	stocking
	stonking
SOKO	stockpot
	Stockton
SOKS	spookish
	stockist
SOLC	shoelace
SOLE	shoulder
	smoulder
SOLF	shoplift
SOLG	spoilage
SOLN	Scotland
	scowling
	shouldn't
	snowline
	spoiling
	stowlins
SOLO	spoil for
SOLS	shoeless
	spotless
	stopless
SOLT	Smollett
SOML	stormily
SOMN	storming
SONL	spoonily
SONS	slowness
SONU	scornful
	spoonful
SOOA	scotomas
SOOE	stop over
	stopover
SOPG	stoppage
SOPL	sloppily
SOPN	shopping
	snooping
	stooping
	stopping
SOPO	scorpion□
	Scorpios
SOPR	shoppers
	STOLport
	Stoppard
SOPT	show pity
SOPU	scoopful
	scoop out
	Scorpius
SORE	scourger
SORN	scouring
SORO	showroom
SORT	shofroth
SOSA	Scotsman
SOSG	spousage
SOSI	stooshie
SOSL	spousals
SOSO	snowshoe
	snow-shoe
	sponsion
SOSS	Scorsese
SOTC	Scottice
SOTE	scouther
	scowther
	short leg
	smoothen
SOTF	Scottify
	shoot off
	spout off
SOTG	shortage
SOTI	short-oil
	smoothie
SOTL	smoothly
	snootily
	snottily
	sportily
	spottily
SOTN	scouting
	shooting
	shouting
	snorting
	sporting
	spotting
	Storting
	swotting
SOTO	shoot for
	short for
SOTS	Scottish
	shootist
	stoutish
SOTU	shoot-out
	short cut
	short-cut
	shout out
SOTV	sportive
SOUA	shogunal
	sporular
SOUO	swot up on
SOWL	spot-weld
SOWR	slowworm
	stop work
SOYW	snowy owl
SOZN	snoozing
SOZT	sforzati
	sforzato
SPAI	septaria
SPAO	sapsagos
	sopranos
SPDT	sapidity
SPEC	sapience
SPEG	sup-peago
SPEO	supremos
SPET	septette
SPHR	sapphire
SPHS	sapphism□
	sapphist
SPII	syphilis
SPLE	supplier
	supplies
SPLL	supplely
SPLN	supplant
SPNF	saponify
SPNL	supinely
SPNT	supinate
SPOE	supposed
	supposer
SPRA	superman
	supernal
	supertax
SPRD	superadd
SPRG	superego
	super-ego
SPRL	superbly
SPRO	superior□
SPRS	soporose
	suppress
SPRT	separate
SPRU	saporous

Words marked □ can also be spelled with an initial capital letter

Code	Word
SPUL	septuple
SQEA	sequelae
SQEC	sequence
SQIE	sequined
SRAA	surbahar
SRAC	sortance
SRAE	screamer
	serrated
	spreader
	streaked
	streaker
	streamer
	striated
	surfaced
	surfacer
SRAI	Sarmatic
	Scriabin
	seriatim
SRAL	serially
	sortable
SRAO	spread on
SRAS	sargasso□
SRAT	servants
	spread to
SRBE	scrubbed
	scrubber
SRBL	scrabble□
	Scrabble®
	scribble
	scribbly
	strobile
	strobili
SRBN	saraband
	Strabane
SRBS	strabism
SRBY	Surabaya
SRCE	sprocket
	Strachey
	stricken
SRCL	sprackle
	sprucely
	strickle
	strictly
SRCO	siroccos
	struck on
SRCR	sure card
SRCS	Syracuse
SRCT	suricate
SRCU	spruce up
SRDC	surf duck
SRDE	shredder
SRDL	straddle
	striddle
SRDN	strident
SREA	shrieval
SREE	sarcenet
	sarsenet
	screeder
	screened
	screener
	shrieker
	sorcerer
SREH	screechy
SREN	sergeant
	serjeant
SREO	surveyor
SRET	sarmenta
SREU	serve out
	surrebut
SRFL	scrofula
SRFR	sure-fire
SRGE	sprigged
SRGF	shrug off
SRGI	seraglio
SRGL	scriggle
	straggle
	straggly
	struggle
SRGN	strigent
SRGS	strigose
SRHO	serfhood
SRIA	surgical
	survival
SRIE	sardines
	services
	spruiker
	strained
	strainer
	straiten
	surmised
	surmiser
SRIH	straight
SRII	Sardinia
SRIL	sordidly
	surtitle
SRIO	sorbitol
	survivor
SRJV	Sarajevo
SRKA	strike at
SRKI	strike in
SRKN	striking
SRKU	strike up
SRLC	sur place
	surplice
SRLE	scrolled
	stroller
SRLG	serology
SRLO	stroll on!
SRME	scramjet
	scrimped
	Strimmer®
	strumpet
SRMG	Saramago
SRML	scramble
	scrimply
SRMS	Sarum use
	stramash
	strumose
SRMT	stromata
SRMU	strumous
SRND	serenade
SRNE	shrunken
	Sprenger
	sprinter
	stranded
	stranger
	stringed
	stringer
	stronger
	syringes
	syrinxes
SRNH	scrunchy
SRNL	serenely
	sprangle
	sprinkle
	strangle
	strinkle
	strongly
SRNM	Suriname
SRNO	spring on
SRNS	sirenise
	soreness
	spryness
	sureness
SRNT	serenity
	strength
SRNU	spring up
	string up
	strung up
SRNZ	sirenize
SROA	sarcomas
SROE	sorrowed
	sorrower
SROI	sardonic
SRON	surmount
	surround
SROY	sardonyx
SRPB	scrape by
SRPE	scrapped
	scruples
	shrapnel
	strapped
	strapper
	stripped
	stripper
SRPF	strip off
SRPI	seraphic
	seraphim
	seraphin
	strophic
SRPN	scraping
SRPU	strip out
SRRA	sororial
SRRS	sororise
	surprise
SRRT	sorority
SRRZ	sororize
SRSE	stressed
SRSO	stressor
SRST	Sarasate
SRTE	spritzer
SRTF	stratify
SRTG	Saratoga
	strategy
SRTH	scratchy
	stretchy
SRTI	spritzig
SRTL	scrattle
	sprattle
SRTN	scrutiny
SRTP	serotype
SRTS	stratose
SRUA	serpulae
SRUE	shrouded
	sorbuses
SRUG	scrounge
SRUH	straucht
	straught
SRUU	sprout up
SRVI	stravaig
SRVN	striving
SRWA	straw hat
SRWE	scrawled
	scrawler
SRWG	scrowdge
SRWL	shrewdly
SRWO	screw you
SRWS	shrewish
SRWY	screw eye
SRYN	straying
SRYO	sorry for
SRYS	sorryish
SRYU	spraygun
SSBL	sash bolt
SSEC	sesterce
SSEI	systemic
SSEL	sisterly
SSES	suspense
SSIN	Sessions
SSMI	sesamoid
SSNA	Susannah
SSOI	systolic
SSPU	Sisyphus
SSRG	sastruga
	sastrugi
SSRU	susurrus
STAA	satrapal
STAE	satiated
	situated
STAL	satiable
STBU	set about
STCE	setscrew
STEC	sithence
STIC	set piece
STIH	set right
	sit tight
STLI	settle in
STLN	settling
STLO	settle on
STLU	settle up
STNE	sit under
STNS	Satanism
	Satanist
STOE	St-Tropez
STON	set going
	set point
STOS	set loose
STOT	set forth
STOW	set to two
STPR	set apart
STRA	Saturday
	soterial

Code	Word
	sutorial
	sutorian
STRN	saturant
STRS	satirise
	satirist
STRT	saturate
STRZ	satirize
STSD	set aside
	set-aside
SUAA	shut away
SUAE	squeaker
	squealer
SUAH	soutache
SUAO	sfumatos
	squeal on
SUAT	spumante❑
SUBE	stubbled
SUBL	squabble
SUBN	slubbing
	snubbing
SUBR	stubborn
SUBS	squabash
SUCA	stulchak
SUCE	sous-chef
SUCL	sour-cold
SUCN	sourcing
SUCO	squaccos
SUDA	squad car
SUDF	sound off
SUDI	squaddie
SUDL	sturdily
SUDN	sounding
	studding
SUDO	squadron
SUDR	Saunders
	shuddery
SUDU	sound out
SUDW	shut down
	shutdown
SUEA	saucepan
SUEE	squeegee
	squeezed
	squeezer
SUEI	souvenir
SUEL	scutella
SUEN	Sauterne
SUET	students
SUFE	shuffled
	shuffler
	snuffler
	stuff her
SUFI	stuff him
SUFL	stuffily
SUFN	stuffing
SUFO	snuffbox
	soul food
	stuff you
SUFU	snuff out
SUGA	spur gear
SUGE	smuggler
SUGL	smudgily
	spur-gall
	squiggle
	squiggly
SUGO	sturgeon
SUGR	sluggard
	snuggery
SUGS	sluggish
SUHA	southpaw
SUHN	souchong
	Southend
SUHR	southern❑
SUIL	stupidly
SUIU	spurious
	studious
SUKN	skulking
SUKO	stuck for
SULA	skullcap
SULE	squaller
SULH	squelchy
SULK	souvlaki
SULN	sculling
SULR	scullery
SULS	soulless
	spurless
SUMC	slummock
SUMN	slumming
SUMS	sour mash
	squamose
SUMT	soul mate
SUMU	squamous
SUNE	squander
	squinter
SUNN	shunning
	spurning
	stunning
SUNS	smugness
	snub nose
	snugness
	sourness
SUOO	Sauropod
SUPL	stumpily
SUPO	sculptor❑
SUPS	sourpuss
SURA	squarial
SURE	squirrel
	squirter
SURL	squarely
	squirely
SURN	squaring
SURS	squarish
SURU	square up
SUSE	squashed
SUSL	spun silk
SUSR	Saussure
SUTA	stuntman
SUTE	squatter
SUTF	stultify
SUTL	smuttily
	squattle
SUTN	shutting
	spurting
SUTR	sputtery
SUTS	sluttish
SUVL	scurvily
SUWA	squawman
SUWE	squawker
SUYN	studying
SVAL	sovranly
SVGL	savagely
SVGR	savagery
SVNA	savannah❑
SVNL	savingly
SVRL	severely
SVRN	severing
SVRT	severity
SVUE	savoured
SVUO	savour of
SVYR	Savoyard
SWDE	saw-edged
SWRA	sewer rat
	sewer-rat
SXAL	sexually
SXEC	sixpence
SXEN	sixpenny
SXIT	sixtieth
SXLG	sexology
SXNS	Saxonise
	sexiness
SXNZ	Saxonize
SXRV	sex drive
SXUL	sextuple
SYAC	soy sauce
SYAD	skywards
SYBA	soya bean
SYET	say yes to
SYGI	say again
SYIH	skylight
SYIO	sky pilot
SYLE	Sky blues
SYLN	spy plane
SYLS	spyglass
SYLU	say aloud
SYNR	sayonara
SYOR	say sorry
SYOT	say not to
	slyboots
SYUE	styluses
SZAL	sizeable
SZGE	syzygies
SZLN	sizzling
SZRI	suzerain
TAAA	tearaway
	thataway
TAAC	tea dance
TAAD	tea caddy
TAAI	Tia Maria®
TAAL	to a fault
TAAO	Thanatos
TAAT	tea-party
TAAU	thalamus
TACE	thatcher❑
TACL	trauchle
TADC	tear duct
TADE	twaddler
TADO	trapdoor
TADR	to and fro
TADU	Thaddeus
TADW	team down
	tear down
TAEA	trade gap
	trade war
	travel at
TAEF	trade off
	trade-off
TAEI	trapezia
TAEN	tsarevna
TAES	traverse
TAET	travesty
TAFA	toadflax
TAFL	trayfuls
TAHA	tracheae
	tracheal
TAHL	Toad Hall
	traphole
	trashily
TAHM	trachoma
TAHN	teaching
TAHR	teachers
TAHS	tea chest
TAHT	trachyte
TAIA	tragical
TAIT	tear into
TAKB	thanks be
TAKN	tracking
TAKO	thank you
	thankyou
	track rod
TAKT	thanks to
TAKU	thankful
TALF	trail off
TALI	thalloid
TALN	Thailand
	trailing
	trawling
TALS	tearless
TALT	tea cloth
TALU	thallium
TAML	trammels
TAMT	team-mate
	traumata
TANN	training
TAOA	tragopan
TAOE	tea towel
TAOT	Travolta
TAPE	trampled
	trampler
TAPN	trapping
TAPO	teaspoon
TAPS	Trappist
TAQI	tranquil
TARA	tea bread
	tea break
TASC	transact
	transect
TASD	transude
TASE	transfer
TASI	transfix
	tranship
	transmit
TASM	transume
TASP	transept

Words marked ❑ can also be spelled with an initial capital letter

TATI	tray-trip
TATL	tractile
TATM	To Autumn
TATO	traction
TATV	tractive
TAUE	traducer
TAWR	teamwork
TAWS	teamwise
TAYN	toadying
TAYS	toadyish
	toadyism
TAZK	tzatziki
TBCO	tobaccos
TBEA	Table Bay
	table mat
TBEU	tableaux
TBFL	tubefuls
TBFO	tube foot
TBFR	tubiform
TBGA	toboggan
TBHM	tub-thump
TBLK	tubelike
TBLS	Tebilise
	tubeless
TBLT	tabulate
	tubulate
TBLU	Tibullus
	tubulous
TBNE	Tübingen
TBPI	to be paid
TBRA	Tiberias
TBRL	tubercle
TBRO	to borrow
TBRS	tuberose
TBRU	Tiberius
	tuberous
TBSR	to be sure
TBUE	tabouret
TBWR	tube worm
TCAA	tick away
	tuck away
TCIA	tactical
TCIM	tachisme
TCIT	tachiste
	tuck into
TCLN	tickling
TCLS	tactless
	ticklish
TCMR	to camera
TCNC	technics
TCOE	tick over
TCOI	tectonic
TCTC	tick-tack
	tick-tock
TCTR	taciturn
TCUA	tac-au-tac
TDAA	tidy away
TDEO	to die for
TDLS	to-do list
TDMR	tidemark
TDNE	TV dinner
TDNS	tidiness
TDOE	tide over
TDSH	tedesche
	tedeschi
TDVT	tidivate
TDYO	Teddy boy
TEAC	the fancy
	toe-dance
TEAD	The Dandy
TEAE	teenaged
	teenager
	The Waves
TEAI	thematic
	theramin
TEAK	the narks
TEAL	The Eagle
	the halls
	trevally
TEAN	thebaine
TEAO	Tremadoc
TEAP	The Wasps
TEAR	thesauri
TEAU	The Hague
TEBE	trembler
TECA	theocrat
TECE	trencher
TECL	tree calf
TECS	to excess
TEDL	trendily
TEDN	treading
TEDO	The Idiot
TEDR	Theodora
	Theodore
TEED	the bends
TEEI	the Devil
	the media
TEEL	the wells
TEEN	The Beano
TEEO	therefor
TEER	The Pearl
TEES	the Beast
TEET	the gents
	trecento
TEEV	The Reeve
TEFO	tree frog
TEFR	Thetford
	tree fern
TEHL	the Chalk
	the while
TEHN	teething
	The Thing
	the thing
	trephine
TEHR	tee shirt
	tee-shirt
	The Shire
TEHT	the shits
TEIC	the birch
TEID	The Birds
TEIE	The Miser
	Thesiger
	The Times
TEII	taenioid
	the limit
TEIN	The Piano
TEIT	taeniate
TEKN	trekking
TELA	The Iliad
TELB	the plebs
TELE	the blues
	The Flies
TELG	theology
TELM	The Alamo
TELN	tree line
TELO	the elbow
	the Flood
TELR	The Clerk
TELS	treeless
TELT	the cloth
TEMK	the Smoke
TEMO	thermion
TENC	the knack
TENI	treenail
TENM	the Enemy
TENO	the Union
TENS	tweeness
TEOA	teetotal
	the total
TEOC	the Force
TEOD	the goods
TEOK	the works
TEOL	the world
TEON	the downy
	The Goons
	the point
	the young
TEOO	Theropod
	toe to toe
	tremolos
TEOS	the worst
TEOT	The Month
TEOU	teetotum
TEPA	thespian❑
TEPL	the Apple
TEPS	trespass
TERA	The Friar
	The Trial
	tie-break
TERE	the Creed
TERG	The Frogs
TERH	thearchy
TERN	the briny
	The Bronx
	the drink
TERO	theorbos
TERS	the brass
	theorise
	theorist
TERT	the trots
TERV	the grave
TERY	the Greys
TERZ	the craze
	theorize
TESA	the usual
TESD	Teesside
TESI	theistic
TESL	themself
TESR	treasure
	treasury
TETA	the strap
TETE	the other
	treaties
	twenties
TETG	the stage
TETN	The Sting
	treating
	tweeting
TETR	the stars
TETS	treatise
TEUA	The Sudan
TEUK	the sulks
TEUS	the curse
TEWT	teem with
TEYE	The Tyger
TEZR	tweezers
TFLI	tefillin
TFRI	taffrail
TGAR	taghairm
TGET	tegmenta
TGFA	tug of war
	tug-of-war
TGLN	tag along
TGMN	tegument
TGNO	Taganrog
TGRS	tigerish
TGTA	tightwad
TGTE	together
THBH	tohu bohu
THTA	Tahitian
TIAA	trimaran
TIAI	tribadic
TIAL	tribally
TIBC	tailback
TIBE	trilbies
TIBN	tailband
TICE	twitcher❑
TICL	Trinculo
TIDA	third man
TIDE	twiddler
TIDO	Triodion
TIEE	trimeter
TIEI	trimeric
TIER	toiletry
TIET	trifecta
TIGM	thingamy
TIGT	tailgate
TIHI	trichoid
TIHM	trichome
TIHN	Taichung
	trichina
TIHR	this here
TIIA	Trinidad
TIIH	twilight
TIIT	tritiate
TIIU	triticum
TIKE	thickoes
	thickset
	twinkler
TIKI	think fit
TIKL	trickily
	triskele

TIKN thinking
tricking
TIKR trickery
TIKT trinkets
TIKU think out
trick out
TILA trial-day
TILE trilloes
TILI triploid
TILN trifling
Trilling
twirling
TILP triglyph
TILS tailless
trialist
TILU trial run
trillium
TIMI triumvir
TIMN thiamine
trimming
TINL triangle❑
TINN thinning
twinning
TINR thinners
TINS thinness
trimness
TINT triunity
TIOA trifocal
trigonal
tripodal
TIOE tailored
TIOI triforia
trigonic
trisomic
TION tricorne
TIPP tailpipe
TIRC tribrach
TIRP trigraph
TISI tailspin
Triassic
TISM toilsome
TITA Tristram
TITC triptych
TITE thirteen
thirties
TITN tainting
triptane
twisting
TITR twittery
TITU tristful
TIUA tribunal
TIUT trimurti❑
TIVN thieving
TIVR thievery
TIVS thievish
TIWN tail wind
TIXD trioxide
TIYL tricycle
TJAA Taj Mahal
TKAA take a nap
take away
takeaway
take-away

TKAI take a dip
TKAO take a bow
TKBC take back
TKCR take care
TKDW take down
TKFR take fire
TKFV take five
TKGW Tokugawa
TKHE take heed
TKHM take home
take-home
TKII Tok Pisin
TKNI taking-in
TKNL takingly
TKNO taking on
taking-on
TKNS tokenism
TKNT take note
TKNU taking up
taking-up
TKNW Te Kanawa
TKOE take over
takeover
TKPR take part
TKRO take root
TKRS take rise
TKSI take ship
TKTA Take That
TKWN take wing
TLAI tell a lie
TLAL tillable
TLBC talk back
TLCS telecast
TLDW talk down
TLEI Taliesin
TLFE toll-free
TLGA telegram
TLIE Tulliver
TLIT talk into
talliate
TLMN Telemann
TLMR telemark
TLNE talented
TLNS tallness
TLOE talk over
TLOT tolbooth
TLPI talapoin
TLPR teleport
TLPT telepath
TLRN tolerant
TLRT tolerate
TLSA talisman
TLSI tall ship
TLSO talk shop
talk show
TLTL talk tall
telltale
tell-tale
TLTO telethon
TLTX teletext
TLUI Talmudic
telluric
TLVE teleview

TLVS televise
TLYA tallyman
TLYO tally-hos
TMAG Tombaugh
TMAI tympanic
TMAK Tom Hanks
TMAL tameable
TMAN Tom Paine
TMAT Tom Waits
TMAU tympanum
TMBM time bomb
time-bomb
TMCD time code
TMDT timidity
tumidity
TMDW tamp down
TMEE tamperer
timbered
TMFE tumefied
TMHM Tom Thumb
TMHW tomahawk
TMLI tumble in
TMLN tumbling
TMLR temblors
TMLS timeless
TMLT template
tumble to
TMLU tumble up
TMMN to my mind
TMNG Tomonaga
TMNS tameness
Timonise
TMNU tomentum
TMNZ Timonize
TMOA temporal
TMOE Tom Jones
TMOF Tom Wolfe
TMOO tombolos
TMOT Tamworth
TMRE Timor Sea
TMRN tamarind
TMRO tomorrow
TMRS tamarisk
TMRT temerity
TMRU timorous
tumorous
TMSA time span
TMSN Tomasina
TMSO time slot
TMTE tomatoes
TMTN tempting
TMUL timously
TMUT Timbuktu
TMWR time warp
timeworn
time-worn
TMYO tommyrot
tommy-rot
TMYU tommy-gun
TMZN time zone
TNAI Tanzania
TNAL tentacle
tuneable

TNAU tantalum
tantalus❑
TNBN Tony Benn
TNCE tunicked
TNCL tenacula
TNCT tenacity
TNDA tone-deaf
TNDW tone down
TNEC tendency
ten pence
TNEE tinkerer
TNEL tenderly
tinselly
TNEO tangelos
TNEU tanked up
tonneaus
tonneaux
TNFL tankfuls
TNIL tangible
tangibly
tensible
TNIO tondinos
TNIU tinnitus
TNLN tingling
TNLS toneless
tuneless
TNLT tinplate
tonality
TNMN tenement
TNMT tinsmith
TNNA tenon saw
tenon-saw
TNNE tenanted
TNNR tenantry
TNNS tininess
TNOR tandoori
TNPE tone poem
TNRA tenurial
TNRF Tenerife
TNRM tantrums
TNRO tiny room
TNRS Tantrism
TNRT tenorite
TNSA Tangshan
TNSE tungsten
TNSL tonishly
TNSU tenesmus
TNTR tincture
TNUE tonsured
Tunguses
TNUK Tunguska
TNUL Tinguely
TNUN tonguing
TNWS tentwise
TNWT tone with
TNYO Tennyson
TOAE thoraces
thoraxes
two-faced
TOAI thoracic
troparia
TOAL too early
TOBE troubled

Words marked ❑ can also be spelled with an initial capital letter

8 T_O_B

troubles
TOBN trombone
TODE two-edged
TOEC two pence
twopence
TOEN twopenny
TOGN Thom Gunn
TOGT thoughts
TOHE trochlea
TOHI trochaic
trochoid
TOHL toothily
TOHS trochisk
TOIA tropical
TOIC two-piece
TOIE two-sided
two-timer
TOIK two ticks
TOIO trominos
TOLE trollies
TOLO toodle-oo
TOLP Trollope
trollopy
TOLY trolleys
TOOG thorough
TOON two pound
TOOT two hoots
TOPO Thompson
TOPR troopers
TOSN thousand
TOSR trousers
TOTR trotters
TOVR trouvère
TOVU trouveur
TOWO Trotwood
TPAC tap-dance
TPCL tapaculo
TPCS typecast
TPDC tape deck
TPDT tepidity
TPEE to pieces
TPEN tuppenny
TPEV top-heavy
TPFC typeface
TPFE typified
typifier
TPHG type-high
TPLG topology
TPLN toppling
TPLR tape-lure
TPLS top-class
TPNM toponymy
TPOC top notch
top-notch
TPOI typhonic
TPON top point
TPOS tap-house
TPRD top-grade
TPRF taper off
TPRN tapering
TPRS top brass
top-dress
TPRU top-proud

TPSE type spec
TPSR tapestry
TPTF tipstaff
TPWR tapeworm
TQOU tu quoque
TRAA tarlatan
turn away
TRAC Terrance
Torrance
TRAE terraced
threaden
threaten
turbaned
TRAI tartaric
terrapin
terraria
TRAL tarnally
TRAO tarragon
Tir nan-Og
toreador
tornados
TRAU Tartarus
TRAZ terrazzo
TRBA terebrae
terebras
TRBC turn back
TRCA turncoat
TRCL turn cold
TRCU Turf Club
TRDU tired out
tired-out
TRDW tire down
turn down
turn-down
TREA three-man
three-way
TREE Turgenev
turreted
TREI turmeric
TREL three-ply
TREO torpedos
turned on
turned-on
TRET terzetti
TRHV Torshavn
Tórshavn
TRIA terminal
toroidal
turbinal
TRIE turbines
TRII terrific
turn it in
TRIL terrible
terribly
torpidly
torridly
tortilla
turbidly
turgidly
TRIR tertiary❑
TRIT turn into
TRIU terminus
turn it up

TRLA Tyrolean
TRLE thrilled
thriller
TRLN Terylene®
TRLO thraldom
TRLS tireless
Tyrolese
TRMI thrombin
TRMU thrombus
TRND threnode
threnody
TRNE thronged
TRNI tyrannic
TRNO Turandot
TRNS tartness
TROA turbofan
TROE turbojet
turn over
turnover
TROS tarboosh
tortoise
TRPE thripses
TRPI teraphim
TRPK turnpike
TRPL thrapple
thropple
turn pale
TRSA Tiresias
Turk's cap
TRSE thrasher
thresher
TRSI thrust in
TRSL throstle
turnsole
TRSM tiresome
TRSN Teresina
tyrosine
TRSU turn sour
TRTI teratoid
turn tail
TRTL throttle
TRTM teratoma
TRTR turn Turk
TRTS teratism
TRUE tortured
torturer
TRUF Tartuffe
TRUO turn upon
TRUU tortuous
TRVN thriving
TRWF throw off
TRWU throw out
TRYK teriyaki
TRYN tarrying
TSAI Tasmania
TSAL tastable
testable
TSCS test case
TSEA tesserae
TSEL tasselly
TSEU taste bud
tasteful
TSIL testicle

TSKN Tashkent
TSLU Tiselius
TSOK tussocky
TSRL testrill
TSTB test tube
TSTG Tashtego
TSUO testudos
TTAL tithable
TTAO tetragon
tetrapod
TTBT titubate
TTCC Titicaca
TTEA to the bad
TTEE tattered
tethered
totterer
TTEN to the end
TTGA Titograd
TTHL tetchily
TTLA total war
TTLG tutelage
TTLR tutelary
TTLS totalise
TTLT totality
TTLZ totalize
TTMS totemism
totemist
TTNS tetanise
TTNU titanium
TTNZ tetanize
TTOS titmouse
TTOU Tithonus
TTRA tutorial
TTRG tutorage
TTRN tutoring
TTRS tutoress
tutorise
TTRZ tutorize
TTVT titivate
TUAG Tauranga
TUAO touracos
TUBU thumbs up
thumbs-up
true-blue
TUCT truncate
TUDN thudding
TUDR thundery
TUEU trumeaux
TUFU Truffaut
TUGR thuggery
TUGS thuggish
TUHE truch-men
TUHF touch off
TUHL touchily
TUHN touching
TUHS toughish
TUHU tough out
truthful
TUIL Trujillo
TUIT touristy
TUKE truckler
TUKN trucking
TULV truelove

Words marked ❑ can also be spelled with an initial capital letter

TUMS Thutmose
TUNE Tournier
TUNS tautness
trueness
TUNU Tourneur
TUOI Teutonic
TUOS Toulouse
TUPN thumping
TUPR trumpery
TURS tau cross
TUSA Thursday
TUSI truistic
TUSN trussing
TUTE trustees
TUTL trustily
TUTN taunting
trusting
TUTU trustful
TUWS thuswise
TVRC tovarich
TVRE taverner
TVRS tovarish
TWHL town hall
TWPA town plan
TWRE thwarted
TWRL tawdrily
thwartly
TWRN towering
TWSA townsman
TWSI township
TWYW tawny owl
TXAE tax haven
taxpayer
TXBO textbook
TXCN toxicant
TXCR toxocara
TXCT toxicity
TXDE tuxedoes
TXEI toxaemia
toxaemic
TXNM taxonomy
TXRN taxi rank
TXTO taxation
TXUA textural
TXUE textured
TXXL tax exile
TYFL try a fall
TYNL tryingly
TYOE thyloses
try to get
TYOI thyroxin
try to win
TYSL toyishly
TYTR Toy Story
UAAE unabated
unawares
UACO unanchor
up-anchor
UAOA USA Today
UAOD una corda
UARI unafraid
UBAE unbeaten
unbiased

UBCE unbacked
UBCL unbuckle
UBDE unbidden
UBEC unbreech
UBEL umbrella
UBIL unbridle
UBLA umbellar
UBLE unbelief
unbolted
UBNE unbonnet
UBNL urbanely
UBNS urbanise
UBNT umbonate
urbanite
urbanity
UBNZ urbanize
UBOE unblowed
unbroken
UBRE unbarred
unburden
UBRO unburrow
UBSE unbeseem
UBSO unbishop
UBTO unbutton
UBUE unbrused
UCAG uncharge
UCAT unchaste
UCEA Uncle Sam
UCEO Uncle Tom
UCET uncreate
UCFR unciform
UCGN uncaging
UCME uncombed
UCML uncomely
UCMN upcoming
UCMO uncommon
UCNI uncandid
UCNT uncinate
UCOE unclosed
uncooked
UCOH unclothe
UCPE uncipher
UCRE uncurbed
UCRN uncaring
UCRT ulcerate
UCRU ulcerous
UCUC unchurch
unclutch
UCUL uncouple
UCUU unctuous
UCYE uncoyned
UDAE undraped
UDEE undeeded
UDEM undreamt
UDLA US dollar
UDLN undulant
UDLT undulate
UDME undimmed
UDRA underlap
underlay
underman
under par
underpay

under way
UDRC under-act
UDRE underfed
underlet
undersea
underset
UDRG under age
under-age
UDRI underbid
underlie
underpin
UDRO underdog
undertow
UDRR underarm
UDRU underbuy
undercut
underfur
underrun
UDTN updating
UDUL undouble
UDVU undevout
UDZL undazzle
UEDN unending
UEEA ureteral
UEEI ureteric
UEEL unevenly
UEHA urethrae
urethral
urethras
UEHN urethane
UEIE unedited
uredines
UEII uredinia
UENM user name
UEOC use force
UERE unearned
UERN unerring
UESL uneasily
utensils
UETE uneathes
UEUL usefully
UFAE unflawed
unframed
UFDN unfading
UFEH unfleshy
UFEZ unfreeze
UFIL unfairly
UFLA unfilial
UFLE unfilled
unfolded
unfolder
UFLO upfollow
UFNE unfenced
UFRE unforced
unformed
unfurled
UFSE unfasten
UFTE unfetter
unfitted
UGIE unguided
UGIL ungainly
UGLT ungulate
UGNL ungently

urgently
UGTE upgather
UGVN ungiving
UHAA upheaval
UHAE unheated
UHAS unhearse
UHDE unhidden
UHEE unheeded
UHIE unhailed
UHLE upholder
UHLL unholily
UHNE unhinged
UHRE unharmed
UHRI unheroic
UHTH unhatch'd
UIAI uric acid
UIAM up in arms
UIAV univalve
UICS unit cost
UIEL unitedly
UIES universe
UIIE utilizer
UINS unionise
unionism❑
unionist
UINZ unionize
UIOA unipolar
unisonal
univocal
UIOO unicolor
UIUL uniquely
UIUT ubiquity
unique to
UIXA uniaxial
UIYL unicycle
UIYN unifying
UJSL unjustly
UKIH unknight
UKNE unkennel
UKNL unkindly
ULAE unleaded
unloader
ULCE unlocked
uplocked
ULFE uplifted
ULKL unlikely
ULME unlimber
ULNS ugliness
ULOE unloosen
ULPO Ullapool
ULSE unlisted
ULVL unlovely
ULVN unloving
ULWU unlawful
UMDU unmade-up
UMEL unmeetly
UMFL unmuffle
UMNE unmanned
unminded
UMNL unmantle
UMRE unmarked
unmarred
up-market

UMSE	unmasker
UMVN	unmoving
UMZL	unmuzzle
UNEE	unneeded
UNIL	urnfield
UNNL	unnaneld
UNRE	unnerved
UNTE	unnethes
UOEE	udometer
UOIU	uxorious
UONM	uno animo
UOOI	urologic
UOOT	upon oath
UPAE	unplaced
UPAS	unpraise
UPEE	unpeeled
UPIE	unpaired
	unprimed
	unprized
UPIO	unpoison
UPIS	unpriest
UPLE	unpolled
UPNE	unpannel
UPOE	unproved
	unproven
UPOL	unpeople
UPRI	upper lip
UPRO	unperson
UPRU	uppercut
UPSL	uppishly
UQHL	umquhile
UQOE	unquoted
URAL	unreally
URAO	unreason
URCL	utriculi
URDL	unriddle
URFL	unruffle
UROE	uprooted
URSN	uprising
USAC	unstarch
USAE	unsealed
	unshaken
	unshaped
	unshapen
	unshared
	unshaven
	unstated
USAH	unswathe
USAL	unstable
USAO	unshadow
USAR	upstairs
USBL	unsubtle
USCA	unsocial
USCE	unsecret
	unsocket
USDL	unsaddle
USED	unsteady
USEE	unseeded
USEL	unseemly
USEN	unseeing
USFL	unsafely
USFT	unsafety
USGE	unsigned
USHR	unsphere
USIC	unstitch
USIE	unsoiled
	unsuited
USIK	up sticks
USLE	unsolder
	unsolved
USLN	Ursuline
USME	unsummed
USOE	unspoken
USOL	unspoilt
USOT	unsmooth
USPL	unsupple
USRA	upstream
USRB	unshrubd
USRE	unsorted
USRK	upstroke
USRN	unstring
	unstrung
	upspring
USRU	unshroud
USTE	upsetter
USTL	unsettle
USUC	unsluice
USUH	unsought
USXA	unsexual
UTAC	unthatch
UTAS	ultraism
	ultraist
UTCL	untackle
UTCN	urticant
UTCT	urticate
UTDL	untidily
UTDT	up to date
	up-to-date
UTLE	untilled
UTLO	until now
UTMC	ultimacy
UTME	untemper
UTML	untimely
UTMT	ultimata
	ultimate
UTNE	untended
UTNL	untangle
UTNN	untenant
UTPE	untapped
UTRA	unthread
UTRE	upturned
UTRN	unthrone
	untiring
	uttering
UTRO	ulterior
UTRS	upthrust
UTSE	untested
UTTE	untether
	untitled
UTTM	up to time
UTUH	untaught
UTUT	untrusty
UTWE	uptowner
UTWR	untoward
UTXN	untaxing
UUAL	unusable
	uvularly
UUIU	usurious
UUPN	usurping
UURC	usufruct
UVAL	unviable
UVIE	unvoiced
UVLE	unvalued
UVRE	unvaried
	unversed
UVZR	unvizard
UWAO	unweapon
UWED	unwieldy
UWEE	unweeded
UWLE	unwilled
UWNE	unwanted
	unwonted
UWOE	unwooded
UWRE	unworked
UWRH	unworthy
UWRL	unwarely
	unwarily
	upwardly
UWSE	unwashed
	unwished
UWSL	unwisely
UWSO	unwisdom
VAIC	Vlaminck
VAII	Vladimir
VAIU	viaticum
VBAC	vibrancy
VBAO	vibrator
	vibratos
VBIS	vibrissa
VBRU	viburnum
VCEI	vacherin
VCIA	vaccinal
VCII	vaccinia
VCLS	vocalise
	vocalism
	vocalist
VCLZ	vocalize
VCNG	vicinage
VCNL	vacantly
VCNT	vicinity
VCOA	vacuolar
VCOI	victoria□
VCRA	vicarial
VCRG	vicarage
VCTN	vacating
VCTO	vacation
	vocation
VCTV	vocative
VCUL	victuals
VDDR	Vadodara
VDNI	Vedantic
VDNU	videndum
VDOI	videofit
VEAA	view away
VEAL	viewable
VEDT	viewdata
VENS	Viennese
VFAI	VHF radio
VGAC	vagrancy
VGAT	vagrants
VGBN	vagabond
VGET	vignette
VGLN	vigilant
VGLU	Vigilius
VGNL	vaginule
VGNS	veganism
VGRE	vagaries
VGRS	vigorish
	vigoroso
VGRU	vigorous
VGTT	vegetate
VGTV	vegetive
VHCE	vehicles
VHMN	vehement
VIAC	voidance
VIAL	voidable
VIEO	voice-box
VINS	vainness
	voidness
VLAC	valiance
VLAE	villager
VLAI	volcanic
VLAL	Valhalla
	valuable
	valuably
	vulgarly
VLAN	villainy
VLAR	Voltaire
VLCT	velocity
VLDT	validate
	validity
VLEA	valued at
VLEE	volleyer
VLET	Valletta
	Villette
VLFE	vilifier
VLIG	villiago
VLIO	volpinos
VLLN	volplane
VLMN	velamina
VLMS	volumise
VLMZ	volumize
VLNE	valanced
VLNI	Valencia
VLNS	vileness
VLPN	vilipend
VLRA	valerian□
	Vila Real
VLRS	valorise
	velarise
VLRU	valorous
VLRZ	valorize
	velarize
VLTL	volatile
VLTO	volition
	volution
VLTT	volitate
VLTV	volitive
VLUA	valvu-lae
	valvular
VLYI	Valkyrie
VMII	vampiric

Words marked □ can also be spelled with an initial capital letter

VMTN	vomiting
VMTR	vomitary
	vomitory
VMTV	vomitive
VNAE	Van Halen
VNAL	venially
VNAM	Van Damme
VNAO	vindaloo
VNCV	vena cava
VNDU	vanadium
VNEE	veneerer
VNET	vendetta
VNEU	vengeful
	Vonnegut
VNGR	vinegary
VNHI	Vanaheim
VNIL	vendible
	vendibly
	vincible
VNLE	Van Allen
	Van Cleef
VNLI	vanillin
VNLS	vaneless
VNLT	venality
VNMU	venomous
VNRA	venereal
VNRG	Vanbrugh
VNRS	Vandross
VNRT	venerate
VNRU	venerous
VNSA	Venusian
VNSE	vanished
VNST	venosity
	vinosity
VNTA	Venetian
VNTO	venation
VNUE	Van Buren
	venturer
VNUR	vanguard
VNUS	vanquish
VNUU	vinculum
VNYR	vineyard
VOAL	violable
	violably
VOAO	violator
VOEC	violence
VPDT	vapidity
VPLT	vapulate
VPRS	vaporise
	viperish
VPRU	vaporous
	viperous
VPRZ	vaporize
VQEO	vaqueros
VRAC	variance
	verdancy
VRAI	verbatim
VRAL	variable
	variably
	verbally
	vernally
VRAN	Verlaine
VRCO	varactor

VRCS	varicose
VRCT	veracity
	voracity
VRCU	Veracruz
VRDA	viridian
VRDT	viridity
VREE	vertexes
	vortexes
VREH	verdelho
VREI	versed in
VREL	variedly
VRER	varletry
	vertebra
VRET	varletto
VRFE	verified
	verifier
VRFR	variform
VRFS	very fast
VRGE	viragoes
	voragoes
VRGO	very good
VRIA	vertical
	virginal
	vortical
VRIE	verditer
	vermined
	vertices
	vortices
VRIG	verbiage
VRII	verticil
	Virginia
VRIL	vernicle
	versicle
	virginly
VRIT	verligte
VRLG	virology
VRLN	virulent
VRLS	virilism
VRLT	virility
VRLU	very loud
VRMC	very much
VRMN	very many
	virement
VRNA	verandah
VRNC	veronica❑
VRNS	Varanasi
	Veronese
VRNZ	Voronezh
VROA	variolar
VROE	verboten
VROR	Verwoerd
VROT	vermouth❑
VROU	variorum
VRSI	veristic
VRSO	varistor
	very soon
VRTE	verities
VRUA	verrucae
	verrucas
	verrugas
VRUC	verjuice
VRUS	virtuosa
	virtuose

	virtuosi
	virtuoso
VRUU	virtuous
VRWL	very well
VSAH	viscacha
VSAL	visually
VSCL	vesicula
VSCN	vesicant
VSCT	vesicate
VSEA	visceral
VSFR	vasiform
VSGT	Visigoth
VSIE	vestiges
VSII	vestigia
VSIR	vespiary
VSLU	Vesalius
VSMN	vestment
VSNS	vastness
VSOA	visional
VSON	viscount
VSOT	Visconti
VSTN	visitant
	visiting
VSTR	visitors
VSUA	vascular
VSUC	Vespucci
VSVU	Vesuvius
VTAE	vitiated
VTAO	vitiator
VTDW	vote down
VTEU	vitreous
VTLG	vitiligo
VTLS	vitalise
VTLT	vitality
VTLZ	vitalize
VTOI	Vittoria
VTRS	votarist
VUHO	vouch for
VUSI	voussoir
VUTN	vaulting
	vaunting
VUTR	vauntery
VVCT	vivacity
VVRU	vivarium
VVSC	vivisect
VVSU	vavasour
VVVC	viva voce
VXLU	vexillum
VXNL	vexingly
VXNS	vixenish
VXTO	vexation
VYGN	voyaging
VYGU	voyageur
VZAH	vizcacha
VZMN	vizament
WAAA	wear away
WAAI	what an if
WAAL	wearable
WADW	wear down
WAEE	weakened
	weakener
	whatever
WAEI	whale oil

WAEL	weaselly
WAES	what else?
WAFG	wharfage
WAGE	wrangler
WAHL	wrathily
WAHU	wrathful
WAKE	whackoes
WAKN	whacking
WALN	weakling
	weanling
WANS	weakness
WANX	what next?
WAOE	weaponed
WAOI	what of it?
WAOR	weaponry
WAPN	wrapping
WAPR	wrappers
WARC	what reck?
WASA	wealsman
WASD	weak side
WASE	what's new?
WASO	weak spot
WATE	what then?
WATI	wear thin
WAUI	wrap up in
WAWT	what with
WAYN	wearying
WAYU	weary out
WBLN	wobbling
WCEL	wickedly
WCIF	Wycliffe
WDEE	wide-eyed
WDIT	wade into
WDKN	Wedekind
WDLN	waddling
WDNN	widening
WDNS	wideness
WDOE	wide open
	wide-open
WDWO	Wedgwood
WDWR	wideward
WDWY	wideways
WECE	wretched
WEDE	wheedler
WEEE	whenever
	wherever
WEEO	wherefor
WEKG	wreckage
WEKN	wreaking
	wrecking
WELN	wheeling
WELS	weedless
WERE	wherries
WETA	wheatear
WETE	wrestler
WEUK	waesucks
WEUL	woefully
WEZL	wheezily
WEZN	wheezing
WFED	W C Fields
WFHO	wifehood
WFLN	waffling
WFTB	wife-to-be

WGNI	wagon-lit
WIBE	whimbrel
WIBN	whizbang
WIBR	Weinberg
	whipbird
WICR	whipcord
WIEA	Whitelaw
WIEE	white-leg
	White Sea
WIEF	write off
	write-off
WIEI	white lie
	white tie
WIEL	whitefly
WIEN	white ant
WIEO	white-hot
WIEU	white out
	white-out
	write out
WIEY	white-eye
WIGE	wriggler
WIGF	Whitgift
	wring off
WIGN	wringing
WIGR	Whiggery
WIGS	Whiggish
	Whiggism
WIGU	wring out
WIHE	weighted
	writhled
WIHF	weigh off
WIHN	weighing
	whip hand
WIHU	weigh out
WIIG	writings
WIIS	whinid'st
WIKE	wrinkled
WIKR	whiskers
	whiskery
WILN	Whillans
	whirling
WILS	wait-list
	whiplash
WIMN	Weismann
	Weizmann
WIPN	whipping
WIRN	whirring
WIRS	waitress
WISE	whipster
WISL	whimsily
WISO	wainscot
WITE	whistler❑
	Whittier
	whittler
	wristlet
WITI	wrist pin
WIUO	wait upon
WIWA	whim-wham
WIZI	whizz kid
WIZN	whizzing
WKNN	wakening
WKUT	wake up to
WLAE	Wallasey
WLAL	weldable
WLAO	wallaroo
WLAU	wild arum
WLBA	wild boar
WLBE	well-bred
WLBR	wall bars
	well-born
WLCR	wild card
WLDN	well done
	well-done
WLDW	wolf down
WLEE	Wolseley
WLEI	walled in
WLFR	wildfire
WLFW	wild fowl
	wildfowl
WLHA	wellhead
	well-head
	Welshman
WLHI	Waldheim
WLHO	Welsh Cob
WLIA	williwaw
WLIE	Walliser
WLII	wild iris
WLIM	Williams
WLIT	walk into
WLKI	well-knit
WLKO	wale knot
	wall knot
WLKP	well-kept
WLLF	wildlife
WLMD	well-made
WLMN	Walkmans
WLNG	well-nigh
WLNS	wildness
	wiliness
WLNT	wolf note
WLOE	walk over
	walkover
	walk-over
	walloper
	wallower
	well over
WLOI	wallow in
WLPC	wolf pack
WLPI	well-paid
WLRA	well-read
WLRC	wild rice
WLSN	Wallsend
WLTD	well-to-do
WLTL	walk tall
WLTP	wild type
WLUE	well-used
WLUG	Walpurga
WLUL	wilfully
WLUO	well up on
WLWO	wildwood
WLWR	well-worn
WLWS	Wild West
WMNS	womanise
	womanish
WMNZ	womanize
WNAE	wannabee
WNAL	winnable
WNAU	Wanganui
WNBA	wingbeat
WNBN	wind band
WNBR	windburn
WNCN	wind cone
WNCS	wing case
WNDN	wingding
WNDW	want down
	wind down
WNEA	wonder at
WNEE	wanderer
	wonderer
WNEL	wingedly
	winterly
WNEO	wanderoo
WNEU	wondeful
WNFE	Winifred
WNFL	windfall
WNFR	wind farm
WNHE	Windhoek
WNIE	Winnipeg
WNIG	winnings
WNLS	windlass
	windless
	wine list
	wingless
WNML	windmill
WNOE	winnowed
	winnower
WNOL	wantonly
WNON	win round
WNPP	windpipe
WNRC	wine rack
WNRN	windring
WNRU	wondrous
WNSA	wingspan
WNSC	windsock
WNSI	wineskin
WNSR	windsurf
WOCC	woodcock
WOCI	woodchip
WOEE	whomever
WOEL	woodenly
WOEO	whoredom
WOGS	wrong use
WOGU	wrongful
WOHH	whoa-ho-ho
WOLE	woollies
WOLN	woodland
WOLR	woodlark
WOLS	woodless
WONL	wooingly
WOPL	woodpile
	wood pulp
WOPN	whopping
WORF	woodruff
WOSA	woodsman
WOSC	woolsack
WOSE	woodshed
	woolshed
WOUH	who but he
WOWN	woodwind
WOWR	Woodward
	woodwork
	woodworm
WPDU	wiped out
WRAA	warragal
	wire away
	workaday
	work away
WRAC	war dance
WRAI	warfarin
WRAL	workable
WRAN	war paint
WRAT	warranty
WRBC	work back
WRBO	warm-boot
	wordbook
	word-book
	workbook
WRBR	Würzburg
WRCS	wormcast
WRDA	wiredraw
	world war
WRDU	World Cup
WREF	worse off
WREU	worked up
	worked-up
WRFR	workfare
WRGA	worm gear
WRGM	word game
	wordgame
WRHE	worthier
	worthies
WRHL	wormhole
	worthily
WRHN	Worthing
WRHO	worthy of
WRHP	warships
WRHR	work hard
WRIA	warrigal
WRIG	workings
WRIK	Wernicke
WRIT	wire into
	work into
WRLA	workload
WRLN	warplane
WRLR	word-lore
WRLS	wireless
	wordless
	word-list
	workless
WRMT	workmate
WRNS	wariness
	warmness
	wiriness
WROE	work over
WROS	warhorse
WRPA	word play
	wordplay
	word-play
WRRB	wardrobe
WRRD	war bride
WRRM	war crime
WRRO	wardroom

workroom
WRRP wire rope
WRRS wardress
WRRT work rate
WRSA Wordstar®
WRSI wardship
WRSO workshop
WRTI worn thin
WRUO work upon
WRWA workwear
WRWL werewolf
WRWO wire wool
wormwood
WRWR wirework
wireworm
WRWT work with
WRYN worrying
WRYU worry out
WSAA wash away
WSAI wistaria
WSAL washable
WSAR wiseacre
WSBN wishbone
WSDW wash down
WSEA Wesleyan
WSEI waste bin
wisteria
WSEL westerly
WSEU washed-up
wasteful
WSLN westlins
wiseling
WSRO washroom
WSWL wish well
WSWO Westwood
WSWR westward
WTAD wetlands
WTAO with a job
WTCL with calf
WTDA withdraw
WTEE withered
WTEO witter on
WTES wet lease
with ease
WTFA with foal
WTHA watchman
WTHL withhold
WTHN watching
WTHO watchdog
watch for
WTHP with hope
WTHR witchery
WTHU watchful
watch out
watt-hour
WTLC with luck
WTLT wet-plate
WTOL wittolly
WTRA water bag
water gas
waterman
water rat
waterway
WTRC water ice
WTRE water-bed
water-hen
WTRK water-ski
WTRO waterlog
Waterloo
WTRU water bus
water rug
WTTA with that
WTTI with this
WTUS wet nurse
wet-nurse
WTYE Wat Tyler
WUDL woundily
WUDN wounding
WVBN waveband
WVDW wave down
WVFR waveform
WVLS waveless
WVNS waviness
WVRE Waverley
WVRN wavering
WXAE wax paper
WXER waxberry
WXIH wax-light
WXLN wax plant
WXLT waxcloth
WXNS waxiness
WXOK waxworks
WYAE wayfarer
waylayer
WYEV wayleave
WYOT Weymouth
WZRL wizardly
WZRR wizardry
XAUI X-ray unit
XLMT xylomata
XNHM xanthoma
XNHN xanthene
XNHU xanthous
XNLT xenolith
XNPO Xenophon
XRMT xeromata
XRNI xeransis
YABO yearbook
year-book
YALN yearling
yearlong
YANN yearning
YANO yearn for
YCTN yachting
YDLE yodeller
YEDN yielding
YGOR yoghourt
YGSA Yugoslav
YKHM Yokohama
YKLO yokeldom
YKSK Yokosuko
YKTR yakitori
YLLC Yale lock
Yale® lock
YLTD Yuletide
YMGT Yamagata
YMMT Yamamoto
YNFK Yanofsky
YOAL yeomanly
YOAR yeomanry
YRBR yardbird
YRTW Yorktown
YRUK yarmulka
yarmulke
YSIA yeshivah
YSRE yestreen
YTGI yet again
YUGA young man
YUGI Young Vic
YUGN young one
YUGS youngish
YUHU youthful
YUMN your mind
YUSL yourself
ZAOR zealotry
ZCHN zecchini
zecchino
zucchini
ZCOO zoccolos
ZDAA zodiacal
ZDII zaddikim
ZGAG zigzaggy
ZGMT zygomata
ZGUA ziggurat
ZGUE Zigeuner
ZGWN zugzwang
ZIBC Zwieback
ZKPN Zakopane
ZLBD Zola Budd
ZLIN zillions
ZMAW Zimbabwe
ZMNO Zamenhof
ZMRA zamarras
ZMRO zamarros
ZMTO zemstvos
ZNEO zanjeros
ZNGE Zane Grey
ZNIA Zanzibar
ZNIP Zantippe
Zentippe
ZNKF zinckify
ZNNS zaniness
ZNVE Zinoviev
ZOHL zoophile
ZOHT zoophyte
ZOII zeolitic
ZOIO zoom in on
ZOLN zoom lens
ZOOE zoonoses
ZOSI zoot suit
ZOWR Zionward
ZOYI zoocytia
ZPEI zeppelin□
ZRAO zircaloy
ZRHU zero hour
ZRIO zero in on
ZRLO zorillos
ZROO Zircoloy®
ZRRT zero-rate
ZRUL zarzuela
ZRZR zero-zero
ZSRG zastrugi

9 letters – odd

AAACE avalanche
AAADN à l'abandon
AAAGE at an angle
AAANT as against
AAATC ataractic
AAATR alabaster
AAATY adamantly
AABTS Alan Bates
AACAK Alan Clark
AACIE anarchise
anarchize
AACIM anarchism
AACIT anarchist
AACRS as accords
AADDO awarded to
AADND abandoned
AADNE abandonee
AAEES awareness
AAEET abasement
abatement
amazement
AAEIG awakening
AAEIS academics
AAENN Agamemnon
AAEQE arabesque
AAETC analeptic
AAETS amarettos
AAEUT as a result
AAGSA analgesia
AAGSC analgesic
AAHDY abashedly
AAHET abashment
AAHMS anathemas
AAHNT at a why-not
AAHOD arachnoid
AAHRC anaphoric
AAHTC apathetic
AAHTN apathaton
AAIGY amazingly
AAITC atavistic

Words marked □ can also be spelled with an initial capital letter

Code	Word
AAKOT	Alan Knott
AALBE	available
AALBY	availably
AALHT	as all that
AALNE	at a glance
AALTS	Anacletus
AAMDY	alarmedly
AAMEL	alarm-bell
AANDY	a rainy day
AANSS	anamneses
	anamnesis
AAOEB	at a low ebb
AAOIE	analogise
	analogize
	anatomise
	anatomize
	aragonite
AAOIL	amatorial
AAOIM	anabolism
AAOIN	Amazonian
	Anatolian
AAOIT	anatomist
AAOLH	ayatollah❑
AAOOS	analogous
AAPLA	a cappella
AARBC	anaerobic
AARSS	amaurosis
	anacruses
	anacrusis
AARTC	amaurotic
AASEI	Adar Sheni
AASET	amassment
AASGR	Alan Sugar
AASIH	Adam Smith
AATBE	adaptable
AATED	apartheid
AATET	apartment
AATOS	acanthous
AATRM	apart from
AATSA	Anastasia
AATUK	a fast buck
AAULA	Atahualpa
AAYAD	analysand
	at any hand
AAYAE	at any rate
AAYIE	at any time
AAYLS	amaryllis
AAYOT	at any cost
ABEIE	Ambleside
ABFIA	Albufeira
ABGIY	ambiguity
ABGOS	ambiguous
ABITA	aubrietia
ABLCA	ambulacra
ABLNE	ambulance
ABNEG	Alban Berg
ABOIL	ambrosial
ABOIN	ambrosian
ABRAK	amberjack
ABRIA	Albertina
ABRIE	aubergine
ABRLI	albarelli
ABROS	arboreous
ABRRS	ambergris
ABRTM	arboretum
ABSAE	ambuscade
ABTAE	arbitrage
	arbitrate
ABTAY	arbitrary
ABTES	arbitress
ABTOS	albatross
	ambitious
ABYPA	amblyopia
ACAGL	archangel❑
ACAMD	acclaimed
ACBUN	Ayckbourn
ACDCY	archduchy
ACDNE	accidence
ACEIE	accretive
	alchemise
	alchemize
ACEIN	accretion
ACEIS	Asclepius
ACEIT	alchemist
ACETY	anciently
	ancientry
ACEYE	archetype
ACFED	arch-fiend
ACHLC	alcoholic
ACIAD	Archibald
ACIAE	acclimate
ACIAO	Archimago
ACIET	architect
ACIFX	Arctic fox
ACIIT	archivist
ACIIY	acclivity
ACIOS	acclivous
ACIOT	archivolt
ACLAY	ancillary
ACMAY	accompany
ACNAT	ascendant
ACNIG	ascending
ACNIN	ascension❑
ACOAE	anchorage❑
ACOES	anchoress
ACOIE	anchorite
ACOIL	auctorial
ACOMN	anchorman
ACPIG	accepting
ACRAN	ascertain
ACRAT	accordant
ACRDS	ascarides
ACRIG	according
ACRIN	accordion
ACSIN	accession
ACSOE	ascospore
ACSOS	ancestors
ACSOY	accessory
ACSRL	ancestral
ACUAT	au courant
ACUET	accrument
ACYOE	anchylose
ADAFY	András Fay
ADBRN	Aldebaran
ADCBE	adducible
ADCIE	addictive
ADCIN	abduction
	addiction
ADCOS	audacious
ADEIE	André Gide
ADESE	addressee
ADESS	addresses
ADETI	Andreotti
ADHNS	and things
ADINV	Andrianov
ADMNL	abdominal
ADNIO	andantino
ADNRE	Audenarde
ADNTN	Aldington
ADOAE	audiotape
ADOEA	Andromeda
ADOOY	andrology
ADORM	audiogram
ADOSY	arduously
ADRHT	Aldershot
ADSAP	Aldis lamp
ADTRA	auditoria
ADWNY	and twenty
AEADA	Alexandra
AEADR	Alexander
AEAHD	alewashed
AEAIN	Amerasian
AEANC	Alemannic
AEAOS	asepalous
AEAUA	acetabula
AEDBE	amendable
AEDET	amendment
AEDTL	anecdotal
AEEBT	an even bet
AEHTP	Amenhotep
AEIAA	Americana
AEIIM	americium
AEIIS	amenities
AEJMS	Alex James
AENNS	Apennines
AENTY	Abernethy
AEOAA	adenomata
AEODL	adenoidal
AEOEY	awesomely
AERNE	aberrance
AERNY	aberrancy
AETBE	avertible
AETDY	avertedly
AETES	adeptness
	alertness
AETIE	awestrike
AETOE	azeotrope
AETON	agent noun
AETRC	aleatoric
AETUK	awestruck
AEULY	asexually
AEYEE	acetylene
AFACD	affianced
AFASY	Alf Ramsay
AFCIE	affective
AFCIG	affecting
AFCIN	affection
AFDVT	affidavit
AFIAE	affricate
AFITD	afflicted
AFLAE	affiliate
AFLES	awfulness
AFLOS	as follows
AFLSA	at full sea
AFOTD	affronted
AFUNE	affluence
AGAAE	aggravate
AGASA	Aegean Sea
AGBAC	algebraic
AGBRY	argy-bargy
AGCRS	Algeciras
AGEAE	aggregate
AGEIE	anglewise
AGEIH	argue with
AGERN	angle iron
AGESR	aggressor
AGETD	augmented
AGETR	augmentor
AGIHD	anguished
AGIIE	anglicise
	anglicize
AGIIM	Anglicism
AGIVD	aggrieved
AGLAE	angel cake
AGLIH	angel-fish
AGLNS	Angelenos
AGLUT	angel dust
AGNIA	Argentina
AGNIE	Argentine
AGNIN	Algonkian
AGNUN	Algonquin
AGNUS	Argonauts
AGOAA	angio-mata
AGORB	Anglo-Arab
AGORM	angiogram
AGRIS	Alger Hiss
AGRTM	algorithm
AGSIE	Augustine
AHAEN	Aphra Behn
AHAOA	Akhmatova
AHDIE	anhydride
AHDOS	anhydrous
AHEAY	Ashkenazy
AHEIS	athletics
AHHBD	Ashkhabad
AHITC	atheistic
AHLOS	aphyllous
AHLTN	Athelstan
AHMDY	ashamedly
AHMNM	ad hominem
AHMNS	achimenes
AHMTC	athematic
AHNEM	Athenaeum
AHNIE	a thin time
AHNTN	Akhenaten
	Akhenaton
AHOIE	Aphrodite
AHRET	abhorrent
AHRNE	adherence
AHRNS	adherents
AHRSS	apheresis
AHUMN	A E Housman

Words marked ❑ can also be spelled with an initial capital letter

AIADM avizandum
AIAEA Adis Abeba
AIAFT animal fat
AIAIE animalise
animalize
AIAIG agitating
animating
AIAIM animalism
AIAIN agitation
animation
AIAIT animalist
AIAIY animality
AICMS as it comes
AICUT Agincourt
AIEAD Alice band
AIEES aliveness
AIEIH alive with
AIEOR ami de cour
AIERM aside from
AIHBA apiphobia
AIHTC aliphatic
AIHUE Acid House
acid house
acid-house
AIIGY abidingly
AIIIY asininity
AIITC animistic
AIMTC axiomatic
AINBE alienable
AINET alignment
AINHS amianthus
AINIE a big noise
AINTD alienated
AIOCD amino acid
AIOIM aniconism
AIOIT aniconist
AIOIY a minority
animosity
AIPOA adiaphora
AIRNH Adi Granth
AISIS amidships
AITIK a bit thick
AITTE Aristotle
AIUAE acidulate
AIUHL azimuthal
AIUOS acidulous
AIYLC alicyclic
AJCIE adjective
AJCIN abjection
AJCNY adjacency
AJDIG adjudging
AJIIG adjoining
AJNTY adjunctly
AJTNY adjutancy
AJUND adjourned
AKADN ask pardon
AKADY awkwardly
AKDIE ask advice
AKLSS ankylosis
AKRGT Arkwright
ALANS All Saints
ALBEE alla breve
ALBIG ad-libbing

ALBRY at liberty
ALCBE allocable
ALCOY allicholy
ALEEE all serene
ALEIG all-seeing
ALGAT allegiant
ALGDY allegedly
ALGEN a plague on
ALGTR alligator
ALHBD Allahabad
ALHMS all thumbs
ALHNS all things
ALHWY all the way
ALIUE at leisure
ALMLS all smiles
ALMNE allemande
ALNHM Allingham
ALNOC allantoic
ALNOS allantois
ALNSP all ends up
ALOES all comers
ALPIH all up with
ALQAE all square
ALRUD all around
ALSUY Aylesbury
ALTET allotment
ALTEY allottery
ALTNE all at once
ALTOE allotrope
ALTOY allotropy
ALTVL ablatival
ALTXN aflatoxin
ALVAE alleviate
ALWAL allow bail
ALWBE allowable
ALWBY allowably
ALWDY allowedly
ALWNE allowance
AMAUE admeasure
AMDBD Ahmadabad
AMDIK alms-drink
AMDLO armadillo
AMDPT arms depot
AMDVR Almodovar
AMESY aimlessly
AMGVR alms-giver
AMHUE alms-house
AMLAY armillary
AMLSS atmolysis
AMMNS armaments
AMMTR alma mater
atmometer
AMNTR Axminster
AMRBE admirable
AMRBY admirably
AMRLY Admiralty
AMSAL almost all
AMSIE armistice
AMSIN admission
AMSNT almost not
AMTIG admitting
AMTOG Armstrong
AMXUE admixture

ANAIE annualise
annualize
ANAIG annealing
ANBLA Annabella
ANBLE Annabelle
ANBNY Anne Bonny
ANEAL Annie Hall
ANFAK Anne Frank
ANFED Anna Freud
ANLBX Arnold Bax
ANLET annulment
ANLIG annulling
ANLII Arnolfini
ANLTI agnolotti
ANPLS Annapolis
ANPRA Annapurna
ANSAS Agnes Oaks
ANSLY Aunt Sally
ANTRL au naturel
ANTTR annotator
ANUCR announcer
ANUEM ad nauseam
ANYDY annoyed by
ANYNE annoyance
AOAIE aromatise
aromatize
AOAIM atonalism
AOAIN adoration
avocation
AOAIY amorality
atonality
AOAOS anomalous
apogamous
AODAY a good many
AODBE avoidable
AODEL a good deal
AODNE avoidance
AODOT a good sort
AODUN a good turn
AOEAD aforehand
aforesaid
AOEES aloneness
AOEET atonement
AOEIE aforetime
at one time
AOEOY a somebody
AOFES aloofness
AOFOS Adolf Loos
AOGIE alongside
AOGIH along with
AOHCA apothecia
AOHLS anopheles
AOHSS apophyses
apophysis
AOIAE abominate
AOIGY adoringly
atoningly
AOIHD abolished
AOIIE aborigine❑
AOIIG agonizing
AOIIN abolition
AOIIY atomicity
atonicity

AOITC apodictic
AOKIL acock-bill
AONET adornment
AONIG abounding
AOOAE apocopate
AOOIE apologise
apologize
AOOIS apologies
AOOIT apologist
AOOSY amorously
AOOTO a bob or two
AOPEF a couple of
AOPOS amorphous
AORPA Apocrypha
AOSIS acoustics
AOTAE about-face
AOTAT about east
AOTHP about-ship
AOTLC apostolic
AOTOI a fortiori
AOTOS adoptious
AOTUN about-turn
AOYIE anonymise
anonymize
AOYIY anonymity
AOYOS anonymous
AOYUT agony aunt
APAAE alpha wave
APAET alpha test
alphatest
APAIG appealing
appearing
appeasing
APALR A J P Taylor
APAOT alphasort
APASL appraisal
APASR appraiser
APATC asphaltic
APCUL aspectual
APEED apprehend
APEES ampleness
APEET at present
APEON apple-John
APGIS arpeggios
APIAT applicant
APIID amplified
APIIN amphibian
APIIR amplifier
APINE appliance
APIOE amphibole
APIOY amphiboly
APITD appointed
APITE appointee
APIUE amplitude
APLAE appellate
APLAT appellant
APLIG appalling
APLOA Appaloosa
APNAE appendage
APNON alpenhorn
APOAE approbate
APOEF approve of
APOIG approving

Words marked ❑ can also be spelled with an initial capital letter

APONS	aepyornis
APRAD	ampersand
APRAE	aspartame
APRAN	appertain
APRGS	asparagus
APRIE	aspersive
APRIN	apportion
	aspersion
APROY	aspersory
APRTR	aspirator
APRTS	apparatus
APTNE	appetence
APTNY	appetency
APTSR	appetiser
APTZR	appetizer
AQIIG	acquiring
AQISE	acquiesce
AQITD	acquitted
AQITL	acquittal
ARAIT	aerialist
ARATF	abreast of
ARBTC	acrobatic
ARCBN	Afro-Cuban
ARCLR	auricular
ARCOS	atrocious
ARDOE	aerodrome
AREBE	agreeable
AREBY	agreeably
AREET	agreement
AREIH	agree with
AREIS	Arrhenius
ARFIY	airy-fairy
ARGNE	arrogance
ARGRS	as regards
ARGTD	abrogated
ARINR	arraigner
ARITR	air filter
ARKAS	Afrikaans
ARKNR	Afrikaner
ARLOL	April fool
ARNCL	Aaronical
ARNIG	arranging
ARNLN	adrenalin
ARNMC	acronymic
	agronomic
ARNRD	Aaron's rod
ARNZB	Aurangzeb
AROLD	air-cooled
AROLR	air cooler
AROTY	airworthy
ARPAE	aeroplane
ARPID	atrophied
ARPLS	acropolis□
ARPSF	apropos of
ARRLY	aurorally
ARRVL	air travel
ARSAE	aerospace
ARSAL	arris rail
ARSIE	arris tile
ARSIG	arresting
ARSIH	Aerosmith
ARSOE	auriscope
ARTRA	acroteria

ARVNY	arrivancy
ARVSE	arriviste
ARWOD	arrowwood
ARWOT	arrowroot
ASAIE	assuasive
ASAIG	assuaging
ASANR	abstainer
ASCAE	associate
ASDIY	assiduity
ASDOS	assiduous
ASEDM	Amsterdam
ASEEY	austerely
ASEFR	answer for
ASEIY	austerity
ASETS	assientos
ASHIZ	Auschwitz
ASHLS	Aeschylus
ASHTC	aesthetic
ASIAE	aestivate
	auspicate
ASIAT	assailant
ASIET	abstinent
ASIIG	abseiling
ASISE	abscissae
ASISS	abscissas
	abscisses
ASMBE	assumable
ASMBY	assumably
ASMDY	assumedly
ASMLD	assembled
ASMLR	assembler
ASNIG	assenting
ASNNE	assonance
ASODR	absconder
ASRBE	assurable
ASRDY	assuredly
ASRET	absorbent
	adsorbent
	assurgent
ASRIE	assertive
ASRIG	absorbing
ASRIN	assertion
ASRIY	absurdity
ASRLA	Australia
ASRLS	australes
ASRNE	assurance
ASRSS	apsarases
ASSAT	assistant
ASSIG	assisting
ASTMN	absit omen
ASUTR	assaulter
ASVRY	arsy-versy
ASYOK	absey book
ATADE	astraddle
ATAGR	a stranger
ATAHN	astrakhan□
ATAIE	actualise
	actualize
ATAIL	actuarial
ATAIN	actuation
ATAIY	actuality
ATATD	attracted
ATCAE	autoclave

ATCAY	autocracy
ATCIE	anticline
ATCIG	attaching
ATCLR	articular
ATCOE	artichoke
ATCOS	autocross
ATEAK	at the back
ATEED	at the head
ATEEM	at the helm
ATEER	at the rear
ATEHW	Artie Shaw
ATEIE	at the time
ATEIN	anthelion
ATEOE	at the fore
ATEOT	at the most
ATESY	artlessly
ATETC	authentic
ATEUL	at the full
ATFCR	artificer
ATFXS	antefixes
ATGAH	autograph
ATGAT	autograft
ATGMC	autogamic
ATGNS	Antigonus
ATGRS	autogiros
	autogyros
ATHOE	aitchbone
ATIDR	attainder
ATIIG	attaining
ATIIL	altricial
ATIIN	attrition
ATIUE	attribute
ATKOK	antiknock
ATLCS	Autolycus
ATLEY	artillery
ATLKY	Art Blakey
ATLSS	autolysis
ATMSA	artemisia
ATMTC	asthmatic
	automatic
ATMTD	automated
ATMTN	automaton
ATMTR	altimeter
ATNAE	attenuate
ATNAT	attendant
ATNFR	acting for
ATNIE	attentive
ATNIG	attending
ATNIN	attention
ATNLY	actinally
ATNMC	autonomic
ATNNS	Antoninus
ATNOI	Antonioni
ATNSU	Antonescu
ATNTL	antenatal
ATNVL	anti-novel
ATOAE	astrolabe
ATOAT	astronaut
ATOES	authoress
ATOHS	Antiochus
ATOIE	authorise
	authorize
ATOIL	authorial

ATOIY	authority
ATOOE	astrodome
ATOOY	aetiology
	anthology
	astrology
	astronomy
ATOYN	anthocyan
ATPDL	antipodal
ATPDS	antipodes
ATPLT	autopilot
ATPSA	autopista
ATPSO	antipasto
ATPTY	antipathy
ATQAE	antiquate
ATQAY	antiquary
ATQEY	antiquely
ATQIY	antiquity
ATRAE	aftercare
	altercate
	alternate
ATRAH	aftermath
ATRBE	alterable
ATREK	after deck
ATREL	Alter-Réal
ATRES	attorneys
ATRGS	alter egos
ATRHC	autarchic
ATRHT	after that
ATRID	after kind
ATRIE	afterlife
	after-life
	altarwise
ATRIT	autarkist
ATRLW	afterglow
ATROD	afterword
ATROE	arteriole
ATRON	afternoon
ATRPD	arthropod
ATRTC	Antarctic
	arthritic
ATRTS	arthritis
ATRUE	autoroute
ATRXS	apteryxes
ATSAE	autos-da-fé
ATSAT	attestant
ATSML	autosomal
ATSRM	antiserum
ATTAI	antitragi
ATTDS	attitudes
ATTMR	autotimer
ATTXN	antitoxin
ATUDD	astounded
ATUIM	anthurium
ATUIN	Arthurian
ATUME	Arthur Mee
ATUSR	Althusser
ATVNN	antivenin
ATVTR	activator
AUAIN	adulation
AUAOE	a cut above
AUAOY	adulatory
AUBAE	adumbrate
AUBRF	a number of

AUCEK Aguecheek
AUCLR avuncular
AUCOE a quick one
AUDNE abundance
AUEES acuteness
AUEET amusement
AUETD aculeated
AUHVR a pushover
AUIAE acuminate
AUIBL Abu Simbel
AUIEN aduki bean
AUIEY abusively
AUIGY amusingly
AUIIE aluminise
aluminize
AUIIM aluminium
AUIOS aluminous
AULGA aquilegia
AUNIY a quantity
AUPAE aquaplane
AURGA aqua regia
AURLE aquarelle
AURUS aquariums
AUSAE a mug's game
AUTNA Aquitania
AUTOD adulthood
AUTRR adulterer
AUVTE aqua vitae
AVNAE advantage
AVNIG advancing
AVNIT Adventist
AVNUE adventure
AVRAY adversary□
AVRET advertent
AVREY adversely
AVRIE advertise
AVRIL adverbial
AVRIY adversity
AVSBE advisable
AVSBY advisably
AVSDY advisedly
AXLAY auxiliary
AXOSY anxiously
AYDTC asyndetic
AYDTN asyndeton
AYEGA asynergia
AYEOD arytenoid
AYIUE any minute
AYLHW any old how
AYMLY abysmally
AYMTY asymmetry
AYMUT any amount
AYOEL Amy Lowell
AYORT Amy Dorrit
AYPOE asymptote
AYUEE as you were
AZEMR Alzheimer
BAAAD bear a hand
BAAEO be awake to
BAAOS bravadoes
BAAOT brag about
BAAOY by analogy
BAASY Blavatsky
BAATY blatantly
BABIG brambling
BABRS Bradburys
Bradbury's
BACIE branchiae
BACIG branching
BACOF branch off
BACOT branch out
BADAE brand name
brand-name
BADES beardless
blandness
BADHP board ship
BADLY Beardsley
BADOM boardroom
BAEBE blameable
BAEBY blameably
BAEES blameless
bracelets
BAEHE brake shoe
BAEOE Blakemore
BAEOT brazen out
BAERM brake drum
BAEWY blaze away
BAFAT beanfeast
BAFUT bear fruit
BAGSE Beau Geste
BAHAE brachiate
BAHAL beach-ball
BAHED beachhead
BAHES brashness
BAHOS Beach Boys
BAHUE boathouse
boat-house
BAIGY beamingly
BAIHY bearishly
BAIIN Brazilian
BAINT brazil nut
BAIUE beatitude
BAKAE blackface
BAKAK blackjack
black mark
BAKAL blackball
blackmail
BAKAS black mass
BAKAT Black Bart
BAKED blackhead
BAKEL Blackwell
BAKEN black bean
BAKER black bear
BAKES blackness
blankness
BAKET black belt
Blackfeet
BAKID blackbird
BAKIE black bile
BAKIT blacklist
BAKLG black flag
BAKOD blackwood
BAKOE black hole
BAKOK blackcock
black look
BAKOL Blackpool
BAKOT Blackfoot
BAKOY black body
BAKPT black spot
BAKRS black arts
Black Iris
BAKTD blanketed
bracketed
BAKUN Blackburn
BAKWN black swan
BALDM beadledom
BALVR be all over
BAMNE beau monde
BAMSC beat music
BANAE brainwave
BANAH brainwash
BANED brain-dead
BANES brainless
BANIE Béarnaise
BANTM brainstem
BAPEE blaspheme
BAPEY blasphemy
BAPIS be at pains
BASAD brass band
BASAK beanstalk
BASAN boatswain
BASDF brassed of
BASEE brassiere
brassière
BASEK brass neck
BASRE brasserie
BATET blastment
BATFL beautiful
BATIE beastlike
BATOS beauteous
BAUFR bear up for
BAWRT bratwurst
BAXRS beaux arts
BAYUG bear young
BBALD bobtailed
BBALY Bob Marley
BBAYR Bob Sawyer
BBEMN Bob Beamon
BBLIH bobsleigh
BBNNS be bananas
BBTEH baby teeth
BBTOH baby tooth
BBWYF be by way of
BCAER buccaneer
BCAET Bucharest
BCARS buckayros
BCBAD backboard
BCBTR backbiter
BCCIT bicyclist
BCCOH backcloth
BCCOS back-cross
BCCUT backcourt
BCEFL bucketful
BCEIE bacterise
bacterize
BCEIG bickering
BCEIL bacterial
BCEIM bacterium
BCHNL bacchanal□
BCHNS bacchants
BCIHY buckishly
BCMIL become ill
BCMRL bicameral
BCNAE biconcave
BCOTF back out of
BCPDL back-pedal
BCSAE backspace
backstage
BCSAL backstall
BCSER backspeer
backspeir
BCSIE backslide
BCSIG backswing
BCSIZ buck's fizz□
BCTAK backtrack
BCTEH back teeth
BCTOH bucktooth
BCTON buckthorn
BCUEF because of
BCURL becquerel□
BCWET buckwheat
BCWOS backwoods
BCWRS backwards
BCWTR back water
backwater
BCYAL buckyball
BDAGE bedraggle
BDAKT bed-jacket
BDALR bad sailor
BDBOT Bud Abbott
BDCEK body-check
BDCOK body clock
BDCRR body-curer
BDDLY Bo Diddley
BDEAY budgetary
BDEFR budget for
BDEIG badgering
BDELH bad health
BDELW bedfellow
BDEPR bad temper
BDESN bad person
BDESO bad cess to
BDFON bed of down
BDFUT by default
BDGAD bodyguard
BDGES by degrees
BDIDN bedridden
bed-ridden
BDIIG bad timing
BDITN badminton
BDITR bedsitter
bed-sitter
BDOEL Bud Powell
BDPED bedspread
BDTYT bide tryst
BDWSE body waste
BDYYS beddy-byes
BEAOS beefaloes
BEBLY beer belly
beer-belly
BECIG bleaching
breeching

BECSD	be excused
BEDAE	breed-bate
BEDIE	breadline
BEEAD	Baekeland
BEEPR	beekeeper
BEETR	beefeater□
BEHVN	Beethoven
BEIAU	brevi manu
BEIES	beefiness
BEIHD	blemished
BEKAK	break rank
BEKAL	break jail
BEKAP	break camp
BEKAT	breakfast
BEKBE	breakable
BEKEK	breakneck
BEKES	bleakness
BEKET	breakbeat
BEKID	break wind
BEKIE	breaktime
BEKIH	break with
BEKNN	break in on
BEKNO	break into
BEKON	break down
	breakdown
BEKPN	break open
BEKRE	break free
BEKTP	break step
BEKUK	break bulk
BEKVN	break even
BEKWY	break away
	breakaway
BESDY	blessedly
BESEA	Beersheba
BESEK	beefsteak
BESPN	breastpin
BETEN	breathe in
	breathe on
BETIG	breathing
BETIY	breathily
BEWRT	bierwurst
BEZBB	Beelzebub
BFAOS	buffaloes
BFDLD	befuddled
BFEIG	buffeting
BFIBY	Baffin Bay
BFRAE	bifurcate
BFRNW	before now
BFROS	bifarious
BFRTX	before tax
BFRUE	befortune
BFTIG	befitting
BGAOR	beglamour
BGCEN	big screen
BGEAL	bugger all
BGEDD	big headed
	bigheaded
	big-headed
BGHEE	big cheese
BGIAE	béguinage
BGIES	bagginess
	bogginess
BGIGY	beggingly
BGIIG	beguiling
BGIPR	big dipper
BGNIG	beginning
BGTLE	bagatelle
BHAIG	beheading
BHSOY	be history
BHVOR	behaviour
BIAAE	be in a tale
BIADY	brigandry
BIAIR	brigadier
BIANA	Britannia
BIAON	Brigadoon
BIARC	bric-à-brac
BIDAE	blind date
BIDES	blindness
BIDIE	blind side
BIDNS	buildings
BIDOD	blindfold
BIDPN	build upon
BIDPT	blind spot
BIEOE	bride-to-be
BIFAE	briefcase
BIFES	briefless
	briefness
BIFOK	brief look
BIFRT	be in for it
BIGAK	bring back
BIGOE	bring home
BIGON	bring down
BIGVR	bring over
BIIIE	Briticise
	Briticize
BIIIK	bailiwick
BIIIM	Briticism
BIKAD	brickyard
BIKAS	brickbats
BIKES	briskness
BIKOK	brickwork
BIKRD	blinkered
BILAT	brilliant
BILWY	bridleway
BIMRE	bain-marie
BINAA	Brian Lara
BIOAT	Britomart
BISOE	brimstone
BITEY	brittlely
BITIG	bristling
BITNA	Brittania
BITNC	Brittanic
BITRD	blistered
BIUTE	briquette
BJMUA	Bujumbura
BKHEH	baksheesh
BKHUE	bakehouse
BLAER	balladeer
BLAHN	baldachin
BLAIE	Balkanise
	Balkanize
	Bulgarise
	Bulgarize
BLAII	ballabili
BLAOG	billabong
BLAUN	baldaquin
BLAUR	beleaguer
BLAZA	bilharzia
BLBAD	billboard
BLCAA	balaclava□
BLCSY	Bill Cosby
BLDZR	bulldozer
BLEEE	belvedere□
BLEEN	believe in
BLEES	believers
BLEGE	bald eagle
BLEIA	ballerina
BLEIG	believing
BLFCD	bald-faced
BLFGT	bullfight
BLFLY	balefully
BLFNH	bullfinch
BLGEE	Bolognese
BLGTS	Bill Gates
BLHLY	Bill Haley
BLHVK	Bolshevik
BLHZR	balthazar
BLIES	balminess
	bulkiness
BLIGY	balkingly
	bulgingly
BLIHY	bullishly
BLINH	billionth
BLIOE	Baltimore
	bellicose
BLIRS	billiards
BLISA	Baltic Sea
BLITC	ballistic
BLLIA	balalaika
BLNIG	balancing
	belonging
BLNUL	bilingual
BLOAR	ball of air
BLOBX	ballot-box
BLODE	Bill Oddie
BLOIG	billowing
BLOND	ballooned
BLOSY	biliously
	bulbously
BLPIT	ballpoint
	bull point
BLRBN	bilirubin
BLSKS	Bill Sikes
BLTDY	belatedly
BLTLR	belittler
BLTOE	Bulstrode
BLTRL	bilateral
BLTRP	bolster up
BLTSS	boletuses
BLTWR	bell tower
BLVAO	boliviano
BLYCE	bellyache
	belly-ache
BLYEN	Billy Jean
BLYIR	Billy Liar
BLYLP	belly-flop
BLYOD	Bollywood
BLYOL	Billy Joel
BLYPO	belly up to
BLYUD	Billy Budd
BLZAN	Boltzmann
BMAIE	bombasine
BMASF	by means of
BMATC	bombastic
BMIAE	bombilate
	bombinate
BMIES	bumpiness
BMLBE	bumblebee
	bumble-bee
BMNHY	bimonthly
BMOZE	bamboozle
BMPOF	bombproof
	bomb-proof
BMRUD	bum around
BMSAE	by mistake
BMSAT	bump start
BMSEL	bombshell
BMTOS	bumptious
BNAEE	Bengalese
BNAOE	Bangalore
BNCEK	bank clerk
BNCIA	bone china
BNCLR	binocular
BNEIG	bantering
BNEOE	banderole
BNERT	Bundesrat
BNETG	Bundestag
BNEUA	Benbecula
BNEUO	ben venuto
BNFCD	beneficed
BNFLY	banefully
BNGAT	benignant
BNGIY	benignity
BNGTD	benighted
BNHAK	benchmark
BNHOE	bench-hole
BNIAT	bon vivant
BNIER	bon viveur
BNIGY	bendingly
BNIOT	bandicoot
BNITR	bannister□
BNLOF	bundle off
BNMAS	by no means
BNMES	by numbers
BNNTN	Bonington
BNNTS	banknotes
BNOAE	bon voyage
BNOEE	banjolele
BNOER	bandoleer
BNOIE	bandoline
	bentonite
BNOIR	bandolier
BNOSN	Ben Jonson
BNPPR	bond paper
BNPRE	Bonaparte
BNRBY	Bantry Bay
BNSAD	bandstand
BNSAE	bond-slave
BNSES	banisters
BNUIN	Ben Gurion
	Ben-Gurion
BNUOG	binturong

Words marked □ can also be spelled with an initial capital letter

BNUTN Bantustan
BNVBS bene vobis
BNWDH bandwidth
BNWGN bandwagon
BNWMN bondwoman
BNYIL Benny Hill
BOAAI buonamani
BOAUE blow a fuse
BOBOK book block
BOCIL bronchial
BODAD broadband
BODAE blond-lace
BODAH bloodbath
blood-bath
BODAK blood bank
BODAS broadways
BODAT broadcast
BODCS boondocks
BODED blood-feud
BODEL blood cell
BODEN broad bean
BODES bloodless
broadness
BODET blood test
BODHD bloodshed
BODHT bloodshot
BODIE broadside
broadwise
BODIL broadbill
BODLW blood-flow
BODOM broadloom
BODUT bloodlust
BODYE blood type
BOEAE brokerage
BOEAG boomerang
BOEEF by oneself
BOEID bromeliad
BOEOS biogenous
BOEOT booked-out
BOEPN be one up on
BOERC biometric
BOHOD Boothroyd
BOHRS brochures
BOHRY brotherly
BOHTE brochette
BOHTM biorhythm
BOIHY boorishly
BOKDD blockaded
BOKED blockhead
BOKOE block vote
BOMAE broomrape
BOMKR bookmaker
bootmaker
BONER brown bear
BONES brownness
BONIE brown rice
BONOG Bjorn Borg
BOOIS bionomics
BOOIT biologist
BOOSI Bronowski
BOPAE bookplate
BOPEE biosphere
BOPIE book price
BOQIT Blomquist
BORPY biography
BOSAD bookstand
BOSAL bookstall
BOSEF bookshelf
BOSRP bootstrap
BOVLE book value
BOYRP booby-trap
BOZAE Bronze Age
BPIML baptismal
BPITY baptistry
BPOUT by-product
BPRIE bipartite
BRAAN born again
born-again
BRACS barbascos
BRADR bergander
BRAIE barbarise
barbarize
BRAIM barbarism
BRAIN Barbadian
barbarian
BRAIY barbarity
BRANR bargainer
BRAOE barcarole
bird-alone
BRAOS barbarous
BRAUA barracuda
BRBAK barmbrack
BRBAN birdbrain
BRBDR Borobudur
BRBNS bare bones
BRCCD boric acid
BRCIS borachios
BRDNE barn dance
BREAD Birkeland
BREDR bartender
BREFL barrelful
BREIG bartering
bordering
BREIM berkelium
BREKY berserkly
BRELS bargellos
bordellos
BREOA Barcelona
BREOE bargepole
BREPR barkeeper
bar-keeper
BREQE burlesque
BREUL barrefull
BRFCD barefaced
BRFCS bare facts
BRGAH barograph
BRHAK birthmark
BRHLN Bartholin
BRHOT birth-wort
BRHRT Bernhardt
BRHRY Bert Hardy
BRHUE bird-house
BRIAE barricade
BRIGN barging-in
BRIGY burningly
BRIHD burnished
BRIOS barricoes
BRIRS Bernières
BRITR barrister
BRLIM beryllium
BRLSR born loser
BRLWN barely win
BRMTR barometer
BRNOM Barenboim
BRNSA Bering Sea
BRNTY baronetcy
BROBY barrow-boy
BROGS Burroughs
BROHA Bar Kokhba
BROIG borrowing
BROII Borromini
BROIO Bardolino
BROIZ Berkowitz
BROLI Bernoulli
BRSEN Bernstein
BRSIE Berkshire
BRSRM Bergström
BRTNN burst in on
BRTPN burst open
BRTRA Barataria
BRTRM barathrum
BRTYE burst tyre
BRYOE Barrymore
BRYON Barry John
BSADR bystander
BSAGE bespangle
BSAOA bossa nova
bossanova
BSATR bespatter
BSCIN bisection
BSCLY basically
BSEFL basketful
BSEIF bas relief
bas-relief
BSEIG besieging
BSEKE bespeckle
BSFLY bashfully
BSGIS besognios
BSIAE bastinade
BSIAO bastinado
BSIES bushiness
BSILH bismillah
BSLUE Basil Hume
BSLVD best-loved
BSNUS basinfuls
BSNUT Bosanquet
BSOBR beslobber
BSORC bishopric
BSSIT bush shirt
BSTIG besetting
BSUBR beslubber
BSWAK bushwhack
BTAIN battalion
BTAKT bethankit
BTBAE be to blame
BTCAR bath chair❑
BTDCY beta decay
BTDEE butadiene
BTEAD by the yard
BTECP buttercup
BTEEI Buthelezi
BTEEK by the week
BTEET battement
BTEFY butterfly
BTEIG battering
bothering
BTEOF better off
bitten off
BTEOK by the book
BTHES butchness
BTHIE batch file
BTHOF batch loaf
BTHRY butcherly
BTIGN butting-in
BTINK Botvinnik
BTLAE battleaxe
battle-axe
BTLCY battle cry
battle-cry
BTLDP bottled-up
BTLHM Bethlehem
BTLYR bit player
BTMRH Beth March
BTNBY Botany Bay
BTNCL botanical
BTNIE bête noire
BTNNT Butenandt
BTOHD betrothed
BTOHL betrothal
BTOIH batholith
BTOLY Bottomley
BTOOT bottom out
BTOSP bite or sup
bottoms up
BTROS botargoes
BTRUD bat around
BTRUH be through
BTSAT butt-shaft
BTSEA Bathsheba
BTTET bite to eat
BTWMN batswoman
BTYLE Betty Blue
BUAGR Boulanger
BUAIE brutalise
brutalize
BUAIM brutalism
BUAIY brutality
BUBAK blue-black
BUBOD blue blood
BUBRY blueberry
BUCOF bounce off
BUDES boundless
BUDRR blunderer
BUDRY Bounderby
BUEAD boulevard
BUEAT brute fact
BUFES bluffness
BUFLS blue films
BUGAS bluegrass
BUGOS bourgeois❑
BUHIE blush wine
BUHLE Brunhilde

BUHOD	brushwood
BUHOK	brushwork
BUHPN	brush up on
BUIHY	brutishly
BUMGM	brummagem
BUMVE	blue movie
BUPIT	blueprint
BUPTR	Blue Peter
	blue peter
BUQEY	brusquely
BURNE	blue rinse
BUSIK	Brunswick
BUSIS	blue-skies
BUTES	bluntness
BUTFL	bountiful
BUTOS	bounteous
BUTRR	blusterer
BUVNY	Blue Vinny
BUWAE	blue whale
BVEBY	bovver boy
BVLNY	bivalency
BVNIS	bavin wits
BVRAE	bivariate
BVRDE	Beveridge
BWAOG	bowl along
BWEGD	bow-legged
BWEHT	bowler hat
BWHPD	bow-shaped
BWIDW	bow window
BWIES	bawdiness
BWRID	bowerbird
BWTHD	bewitched
BXALH	boxwallah
BXEUE	Buxtehude
BXNCX	Box and Cox
BXRIE	boxercise
BYELW	Boyle's law
BYFCE	Bay of Acre
BYFIS	Bay of Pigs
BYHAT	Blyth Tait
BYHNS	buy things
BYIDW	bay window
BYNOE	beyond one
BYNYU	beyond you
BYPYE	bryophyte
BYRED	boyfriend
BZIGY	buzzingly
BZNIE	Byzantine
BZNIM	Byzantium
BZREY	bizarrely
BZWRS	buzz words
CAAAC	charabanc
CAAGS	charangos
CAAPE	crab apple
CAARL	chaparral
CAATR	character
CAATY	clamantly
CAAUT	Clara Butt
CABAK	coal-black
CABDY	crabbedly
CABRP	clamber up
CABRY	cranberry
CACAE	coarctate
CACFL	chanceful
CACOS	chancrous
CACUT	clay court
CADEY	chandlery
CADLE	chandelle
CADTE	Claudette
CAEAL	Clare Hall
CAECD	coalesced
CAEEN	chameleon❑
CAEES	ceaseless
CAEIE	ceasefire
	cease-fire
CAEOE	chaperone
CAEOS	craterous
CAEWY	chase away
CAFED	coalfield
CAFER	chauffeur
CAFNH	chaffinch
CAFRD	chamfered
	coal-fired
CAGCP	charge-cap
CAGFL	changeful
CAGHN	Changchun
CAHAD	crashland
CAHCA	cha-cha-cha
CAHET	crash-test
CAHIE	crash dive
CAHIH	clash with
CAHNO	crash into
CAHNS	clap hands
CAHOK	coachwork
CAHOR	coach tour
CAIES	chariness
	craziness
CAIGY	coaxingly
CAIIN	coalition
CAIIR	clarifier
CAILY	coaxially
CAION	clavicorn
CAIPN	Chaliapin
CAJTR	coadjutor
CAKAE	crankcase
CAKCN	crack a can
CAKHT	crack shot
CAKIG	crackling
CAKON	crack down
	crackdown
CAKPO	chalk up to
CALNE	challenge
CALRI	Charleroi
CALTE	Charlotte
CALTN	charlatan
CAMAK	claim back
CAMBE	claimable
CAMES	charmless
CAMIE	Charmaine
CAMNR	coalminer
CANAG	chain gang
CANAL	chain mail
CANCS	charnecos
CAOAS	Charolais
CAOIE	chamomile
CAOOS	clamorous
CAPEE	champlevé
CAPGE	champagne
CAPON	clamp down
	clampdown
CAPRY	champerty
CARAS	chairdays
CARIT	chairlift
CARNA	Chaeronea
CARND	chagrined
CASCL	classical
CASDE	crab-sidle
CASES	classless
	crassness
CASLE	clausulae
CASOM	classroom
CASSU	Ceausescu
CATAD	coastward
CATAR	craft fair
CATIE	coastline
	coastwise
CATLY	Chantilly
CATMN	craftsman
CATND	chastened
CATOK	craftwork
CATRD	chartered
CATRR	charterer
	chatterer
CATRS	Charteris
CATUE	chanteuse
CAUAE	coadunate
	coagulate
CAUAT	coagulant
	crapulant
CAUET	crapulent
CAUEU	chalumeau
CAUKH	Chanukkah
CAUOS	crapulous
CAWMN	charwoman
CAYDS	Charybdis
CBAIM	cabbalism❑
CBAIT	cabbalist
CBCAD	cubic yard
CBCLY	cubically
CBCNH	cubic inch
CBCOT	cubic foot
CBILT	cabriolet
CBLIE	cabilline
CBLTE	cabalette
CBNRW	cabin crew
CBRAE	cybercafé
	cybernate
CBROS	caber toss
CBRUK	cyberpunk
CBYOE	cubbyhole
	cubby-hole
CCAAE	cyclamate
CCAEL	cockateel
CCAGE	Cockaigne
CCAIL	cockatiel
CCAOP	cock-a-hoop
CCDMN	cacodemon
CCEEL	Cockerell
CCEHT	cocked hat
CCFGS	cacafogos
CCFGT	cockfight
CCIEL	cochineal
CCIES	cockiness
CCIIE	cocainise
	cocainize
CCLAE	cochleate
CCLIG	Cecil King
CCLUE	coculture
CCNYY	cockneyfy
CCOAA	cyclorama
CCODL	cycloidal
CCODY	cuckoldly
	cuckoldry
CCOEN	cyclopean
CCOIG	cocooning
CCORN	cyclotron
CCOSS	Cyclopses
CCPOY	cacophony
CCRAH	cockroach
CCRNS	cicerones
CCSAN	cockswain
CCSOB	cockscomb
CCSOT	cocksfoot
CCTIE	cicatrice
	cicatrise
	cicatrize
CDNIL	cadential
CEAIN	cremation
CEAIR	chevalier❑
CEBLS	Cleobulus
CEBUG	Cherbourg
CECBE	coercible
CECBY	coercibly
CECNO	crescendo
CECOI	crescioni
CEEAD	Cleveland
CEEAE	crenelate
CEEKV	Cherenkov
CEETY	clemently
CEGMN	clergyman
	clergymen
CEIAE	crepitate
CEIAT	crepitant
CEIHD	cherished
CEIIE	cretinise
	cretinize
CEIIM	cretinism
CEIIN	caecilian
CEIIS	Ctesibius
CEIOS	cretinous
CEITY	chemistry
CEKAE	checkmate
CEKHP	clerkship
CEKIT	checklist
CEKOE	cheekbone
CEKVR	check over
CEMAE	creamware
CEMOA	cream soda
CENBL	Chernobyl
CENES	cleanness
CENIG	cleansing
CENNO	Chernenko

Words marked ❑ can also be spelled with an initial capital letter

Code	Word
CENOM	clean room
CENZM	chernozem
CEOIE	coenobite
CEOIM	coenobium
CEOOC	Caenozoic
CEPAE	cheap-rate
CEPAK	cheapjack
	cheap-jack
CEPES	cheapness
CEPND	cheapened
CEPNO	creep into
CEPTA	Cleopatra
CERAE	cherryade
CERBE	Cheeryble
CERES	cheerless
	clearness
CERLT	Chevrolet
CERNE	clearance
CERWY	clear away
CESDF	cheesed of
CESOF	cheese off
CETRN	Cresta Run
CEUIS	cherubims
CEUIY	credulity
CEULY	coequally
CEUOS	credulous
CEURD	chequered
CEVBE	cleavable
CFEBR	coffee bar
CFEDM	cofferdam
CFEPT	coffee pot
CFIIE	coffinite
CFTEE	cafetière
CFTRA	cafeteria
CGAIN	cognation
CGIAT	cognisant
	cognizant
CGIIE	cognitive
CGIIN	cognition
CGOES	cognomens
CGOIA	cognomina
CGRLO	cigarillo
CGRTE	cigarette
CGTBE	cogitable
CHBTE	cohabitee
CHIES	co-heiress
CHRNE	coherence
CIAEY	chicanery
CIAIE	climatise
	climatize
CIAIL	China Girl
CIALY	china clay
CIAON	Chinatown
CIATC	climactic
CIAUE	climature
CIBAD	chipboard
CIBAN	chilblain
CIBBE	climbable
CIBNO	climb on to
CIBON	climb down
CICIG	chiacking
	clinching
CIDES	childless
	childness
CIDID	childmind
CIDIE	childlike
CIDOD	childhood
CIEIE	Chile pine
CIEIN	criterion
CIFAE	cliff face
	cliff-face
CIFAG	cliffhang
CIFAN	chieftain
CIFUE	coiffeuse
CIGIM	clingfilm
CIIAE	criminate
CIIIE	criticise
	criticize
CIIIM	criticism
CIIIN	clinician
CIIOS	chitinous
CIKDE	chickadee
CIKED	chickweed
CIKIG	crinkling
CIKSW	Chickasaw
CIKTR	cricketer
CILNS	chitlings
CIMNY	coin money
CINEE	clientele
	clientèle
CINMI	Chiang Mai
CINOM	cairngorm
CIOAA	chipolata
CIOAX	Chico Marx
CIODL	crinoidal
CIOIE	crinoline
CIOOC	Cainozoic
CIOOY	chironomy
	chiropody
CIPEE	Crimplene®
CIPES	crispness
CIPIG	crippling
CISRP	chinstrap
CITEU	Cointreau®
CIUHA	chihuahua❑
CLAAE	cellarage
CLAAT	call a halt
CLAEM	calcaneum
CLAES	calcaneus
CLAHN	Callaghan
CLAIE	calmative
CLAIG	collaring
CLAIN	collation
CLAIT	collagist
CLASD	collapsed
CLBAE	calibrate
	celebrate
CLBAT	celebrant
CLBEE	calabrese❑
CLBIY	celebrity
CLBOE	calaboose
CLBSS	colobuses
CLCEM	cold cream
CLDIK	cold drink
CLEFR	called for
	called-for
CLEGE	colleague
CLEOF	called off
CLETD	collected
CLETR	collector
CLFAE	cold frame
CLFOT	cold front
CLFRH	call forth
CLHCM	colchicum
CLIAE	colligate
	collimate
	culminate
	cultivate
CLIER	collinear
CLIES	callipers
CLIIM	Calvinism
CLIIN	collision
CLIIS	calvities
CLIIT	Calvinist
CLIIY	callidity
CLIOE	calcicole
CLITS	Callistus
CLIUE	calcifuge
CLMDA	chlamydia
CLMDS	chlamydes
CLMIE	columbine
CLMIM	columbium
CLMIT	columnist
CLMSS	chlamyses
CLNAE	colonnade
CLNIE	celandine
CLNLY	colonelcy
CLNMS	call names
CLNRC	cylindric
CLNUA	calendula
CLNUE	calenture
CLNZD	colonized
CLNZR	colonizer
CLOAE	collocate
CLODL	colloidal
CLOIY	callosity
CLOSY	callously
CLOTO	call out to
CLOUA	colloquia
CLOYE	collotype
CLPAE	caliphate
CLPOE	cellphone
CLRDE	Coleridge
CLRFC	calorific
CLRLA	chlorella
CLRUD	call round
CLSEM	colosseum
CLSET	cold sweat
CLSIE	Celestine
CLSIL	celestial
CLSOT	coltsfoot
CLSOY	colostomy
CLSRM	colostrum
CLUAE	calculate
CLUAT	colourant
CLUBR	colour bar
CLUFL	colourful
CLUIE	cellulite
	collusive
	colourise
	colourize
CLUIG	colluding
	colouring
CLUIN	collusion
CLUIT	colourist
CLUOD	celluloid®
CLUOE	cellulose
CLUWY	colourway
CLYBY	Colwyn Bay
CLYOE	Collymore
CMAAN	come again
	come again?
CMAAT	combatant
	come apart
CMADO	come and go
CMADR	commander
CMADS	commandos
CMAEY	comradely
CMAIE	campanile
	combative
	come alive
CMAII	campanili
CMAIN	companion
CMAIS	come amiss
CMAIT	cymbalist
CMAOG	come along
CMAOS	cymbaloes
CMAOT	come about
CMATD	compacted
CMATR	come after
CMATY	compactly
CMAUA	campanula
CMBCR	come by car
CMCEN	come clean
CMCLY	comically
CMEDA	compendia
CMEET	competent
CMEIE	Cymbeline
CMEIG	competing
CMEIN	Cimmerian
CMELD	compelled
CMESL	commensal
CMETN	comment on
CMETR	commenter
CMFRH	come forth
CMFRT	come first
CMHRC	camphoric
CMIAE	comminate
CMIFR	come in for
CMIGE	commingle
CMIIG	combining
CMIIM	cymbidium
CMISR	commissar
CMITD	committed
CMITE	committee
CMITL	committal
CMIUE	comminute
CMLAT	compliant
CMLIG	complying
CMLIT	complaint
CMLTD	completed
CMLXY	complexly

Words marked ❑ can also be spelled with an initial capital letter

CMMET Camembert
CMNIG cementing
CMNOT coming out
coming-out
CMOAE come of age
CMODR camcorder
CMOEA Common Era
CMOES commoners
CMOET component
CMOFT come off it!
CMOIE composite
CMOIN Cambodian
commotion
CMOIY commodify
commodity
CMOLW common law
CMOOE commodore
CMOTF come out of
CMOTN come out in
CMOUE composure
CMRDE Cambridge
CMRLA camarilla
CMRMN cameraman
CMRNE cumbrance
CMRSY camera-shy
CMRUD come round
CMSDS camisades
camisados
CMSOT come short
CMTYU come to you
CMUAE commutate
CMUDR come under
CMUIE communise
communize
CMUIG communing
CMUIM communism
CMUIN communion□
CMUIT communist
CMUIY community
CNAAK cantabank
CNAEY concavely
CNAGS contangos
CNAGT Connaught
CNAIE can't abide
cantabile
contadine
CNAII contadini
CNAIN contagion
CNAIY concavity
CNAND contained
CNANR container
CNAOE con calore
CNAOP cantaloup
CNARS Centaurus
CNASR canvasser
CNCIE conscribe
CNCIT conscript
CNCLY conically
cynically
CNCOS conscious
CNCTH cony-catch
CNDDY Canada Day
Canada Dry®

CNEAA Connemara
CNEAE cancerate
CNEAY centenary
CNEDR contender
CNEEL conger eel
CNEER canceleer
CNEIL congenial
CNEIN connexion
CNEIO centesimo
CNEIR cancelier
CNEIS congeries
CNEIY convexity
CNELD cancelled
concealed
congealed
CNELR concealer
CNEND concerned
condemned
CNEOS cancerous
cankerous
CNEOT cancel out
conked out
CNEPR contemper
CNERL conferral
CNESD condensed
confessed
CNESO confess to
CNESR condenser
confessor
CNESS consensus
contessas
CNETD conceited
concerted
congested
connected
contented
contested
converted
CNETE concentre
CNETO consent to
CNETR concenter
connecter
connector
contester
convector
converter
convertor
CNETS concertos
CNETY confestly
CNEVE confervae
CNEVS confervas
CNHBR Conchobar
CNIAE candidate
CNIAT confidant
CNIAY candidacy
CNICD convinced
CNIDE condiddle
CNIEA cantilena
CNIEE centipede
CNIES canniness
CNIET condiment
confident
continent

CNIEY concisely
CNIGY cunningly
CNIIG confiding
confining
conniving
CNIIL convivial
CNIIN concision
condition
CNIIR conciliar
CNIMD confirmed
CNIND consigned
CNINE consignee
CNINR consigner
consignor
CNINY condignly
CNIOM cuneiform
CNIRE concierge
CNITD convicted
CNITF consist of
CNITN consist in
CNIUD continued
CNIUE configure
confiture
CNIUL continual
CNIUM continuum
CNIUS continuos
CNLDD concluded
CNLET confluent
CNLMS Candlemas
CNLOT canal-boat
CNLTO Canaletto
CNMLI cynomolgi
CNMTC cinematic
CNNCL canonical
CNNRM conundrum
CNOAE cannonade
connotate
consolate
CNOAT consonant
CNODA Concordia
CNODT concordat
CNOEE Cantonese
CNOIE cantonise
cantonize
CNOIG condoning
consoling
CNOIL censorial
CNOMO conform to
CNOMR conformer
CNOND conjoined
CNONS contornos
CNOOE con dolore
CNORE concourse
CNOTA consortia
CNOTD concocted
contorted
CNOTR concocter
concoctor
CNOUE convolute
CNPNR can-opener
CNPRR conspirer
CNRCS con tricks
CNRET congruent

CNRIY congruity
CNRLE contrôlée
CNRLI contralti
CNRLO central to
contralto
CNRLY centrally
CNROE centriole
CNROS congruous
CNRRA cineraria
CNRVD contrived
CNRVR contriver
CNSAD can't stand
CNSET canescent
CNSGR cane-sugar
CNTAN constrain
CNTBE constable□
CNTIT constrict
CNTNA Constanta
CNTNE Constance
CNTNY constancy
CNTUT construct
CNUAE conjugate
consulate
CNUAY contumacy
CNUEP conjure up
CNUES consumers
CNUEY contumely
CNUIE concubine
conducive
CNUIG confusing
conjuring
consuming
CNUIL connubial
CNUIN centurion
Confucian
confusion
contusion
CNUIS Confucius
CNURD conquered
CNURR conqueror
CNUSD concussed
CNUTR conductor
CNYUT candytuft
COANN Cro-Magnon
COAOT crow about
COCEY crotchety
COCIL cook-chill
CODAE cloud base
CODAL crowd sail
CODAT cloud-capt
CODES cloudless
CODIE cloud nine
CODIY chondrify
CODNE clog dance
CODVR cloud over
COEAC choleraic
COEAE cooperate
co-operate
COEAK choke back
COEAL close call
COEES closeness
COEIH close with
COENN close in on

COENT close-knit
COEON choke down
close down
COEPO close up to
COGIG Chongqing
COHDN clothed in
COITR chorister
COKAK crookback
COKDY crookedly
COKIE clockwise
COKOK clockwork
COKOM cloakroom
COKUL chock-full
COOAE chocolate
COOAY chocolaty
COOIE crocodile
COOMA crocosmia
CORIL choirgirl
COSAE cross-fade
COSAK crosswalk
COSAS crossways
COSAT croissant
COSBE crossable
COSEM crossbeam
COSES cloisters
crossness
COSET crow's feet
crow's nest
COSID crosswind
COSIE crossbite
crossfire
crosswise
COSIL crossbill
COSNE cloisonné
COSOD crossroad
crossword
COSOT crow's foot
COSRD crossbred
COSRL cloistral
COSYD cross-eyed
COTIG chortling
COUTE croquette
CPANN captain RN
CPANY captaincy
CPBEF capable of
CPCHA capocchia
CPCOS capacious
CPCTC copacetic
CPCTR capacitor
CPDBW Cupid's bow
CPERR cup-bearer
CPESS cap verses
CPIAE captivate
CPICO capriccio❑
CPIIY captivity
CPINR cup-winner
CPION Capricorn
CPLAY capillary
CPNAD cap in hand
CPNSW coping-saw
CPOIE coprolite
CPOSY copiously
CPRGT copyright
CPRSN caparison
CPTLA capitella
CPTLM capitulum
CPTLY capitally
CPTNS capitanos
CPUIE capsulise
capsulize
CPVRE Cape Verde
CRADE Carl Andre
CRADR coriander
CRAEA Cartagena
CRAEN carrageen
CRAIE carnalise
carnalize
cercariae
CRAIN carnation
circadian
CRAIS caryatids
CRAIY carnality
CRALD curtailed
CRANF certain of
CRANY certainly
certainty
CRAOG currajong
currawong
CRAOT care about
CRATS Cervantes
CRAUE curvature
CRBAD cardboard
CRBAE cerebrate
CRBED corn bread
CRBEN Caribbean
carob bean
CRBLA cerebella
CRBNS corybants
CRBUS cerebrums
CRCAE corncrake
CRCLA Caracalla
CRCOH cerecloth
CRCOS ceraceous
CREAE correlate
CREAY cursenary
CREGO Correggio
CREIE Carmelite
cartelise
cartelize
CREIG carpeting
CREIM careerism
CREIN carnelian
Cartesian
cornelian
CREIR corsetier
CREIS Cornelius
CREIT careerist
cornetist
CRELD corbelled
CRELE Corneille
CREOF corbel off
CREOT corbel out
curved out
CRETR carpenter
corrector
CRETY carpentry
correctly
currently
CRFLY carefully
CRFOR cornflour
CRGAT Cary Grant
CRGIS coraggios
CRGUS Carl Gauss
CRHSS cirrhosis
CRIAE cartilage
CRIDX card-index
CRIEE cirripede
CRIES corkiness
corniness
curliness
CRIEY cursively
CRIGY carpingly
CRIHY currishly
CRIID certified
CRIIR certifier
CRILY cordially
CRIOA carcinoma
CRIOD corticoid
CRIOE carnivore
cortisone
CRIOM curviform
CRIUA curricula
CRIUE certitude
CRLAY corollary
CRLED Carol Reed
coral weed
CRLIE coralline
CRLMY cor blimey
CRLOD Cyril Joad
CRLSS caroluses
CRLWS Carl Lewis
CRMDA chromidia
CRMOA carambola
CRMTC chromatic
CRMTD chromatid
CRMTN chromatin
CRNCE chronicle
CRNOS corantoes
CROAE carbonate
corporate
CROAO carbonado
CROAT cormorant
CROCE cartouche
CRODR care order
CROEL corporeal
CROIE carbonise
carbonize
corrosive
CROIG corroding
CROIN corrosion
CROIY corporify
curiosity
cursorily
CROOF cordon off
CROSS caryopses
CROSY curiously
CRPAI coryphaei
CRPOE cardphone
CRRDE cartridge
CRSAE coruscate
CRSAP card-sharp
CRSAT coruscant
CRSGN Carl Sagan
CRSIA Christina
CRSIE Christine
CRSIN Christian
CRSLD chrysalid
CRSLS chrysalis
CRSMS Christmas
CRSRW corkscrew
CRTAE curettage
CRTBE card table
CRTKR caretaker
CRTRS Carstares
CRUAE carburate
circulate
corrugate
CRUAS circulars
CRUCE carbuncle
corpuscle
CRUCO Carluccio
CRUET corpulent
CRUFE carfuffle
CRUIE carburise
carburize
CRUIG carousing
CRUIS Carausius
curculios
CRUNS Cernunnos
CRUTD corrupted
CRUTR corrupter
CRUTY circuitry
corruptly
CRWEL cartwheel
CRYAE carrytale
CRYAK carry back
CRYVR carry over
CRYWY carry away
CRZIS Carl Zeiss
CSADA Cassandra
CSAEE cast an eye
CSAES castanets
CSAIE cast aside
casualise
casualize
CSAIG cascading
CSAIN cessation
CSANR CT scanner
CSAOB cost a bomb
CSAOE cast a vote
CSAOG cosy along
CSAOT cast about
CSASA Caslavska
CSEIG cosseting
CSEIS cosmetics
CSELN castellan
CSENE cisternae
CSEOE casserole
CSIAE castigate
cuspidate
CSIEY costively
CSIND cushioned

CSITC casuistic
CSITY casuistry
CSLBR Castlebar
CSLOE cast loose
CSOAT cosmonaut
CSOAY cassowary
customary
CSOES customers
CSOIE customise
customize
CSOIL custodial
CSOIN custodian
CSOLT cassoulet
CSOOY cosmogony
cosmology
CSOSR cosponsor
CSPIE cost price
CSRTD castrated
CSUIR costumier
CTAIE Catharine
catharise
catharize
CTAIG cottaging
CTAKN cut back on
CTALU Cat Ballou
CTAOS cattaloes
CTASS catharses
catharsis
CTATC cathartic
CTCIE catechise
catechize
CTCIM catechism
CTCIT catechist
CTCLR cuticular
CTCOS cut across
CTCYM cataclysm
CTEIA Catherina
CTEIE Catherine
CTERL cathedral
CTGRC categoric
CTHBE catchable
CTHET catchment
CTHIE catch fire
CTHOD catch cold
catchword
CTHOT cut-throat
CTHPN catch up in
CTHWY catch away
CTIES cattiness
CTIGN cutting-in
CTIGP cutting up
CTIHY cattishly
CTKLS Catskills
CTKNN cytokinin
CTLDN cotyledon
CTLGE catalogue
CTLMN cattleman
CTLPY catalepsy
CTLSS catalysis
CTLTC catalytic
CTLXS catalexis
CTMNA catamenia
CTMRN catamaran

CTNAF cut in half
CTNDY cut and dry
CTNET cotangent
CTNOS cutaneous
CTNRN cut and run
CTOGD city of God
CTOIN chthonian
CTPAM cytoplasm
CTPEY cataplexy
CTRAL caterwaul
CTRHL catarrhal
CTSAE cityscape
CTTIE cut it fine
CTTNA catatonia
CTTNC catatonic
CTTXC cytotoxic
CTTXN cytotoxin
CTUFR cut out for
CTYAK Cutty Sark
CTZNY citizenry
CUAIE causative
CUAIG crusading
CUAIN Caucasian
causation
CUAIY causality
CUAOD Caucasoid
CUAOS cruzadoes
CUBBE clubbable
CUBIG crumbling
CUBOK Chubb® lock
CUCAS club class
CUCBG clutch bag
CUCIL Churchill
CUCMN churchman
churchmen
CUDTT coup d'état
CUEAM cause harm
CUEAN cause pain
CUEES crudeness
CUEIE cauterise
cauterize
CUEOE cause to be
CUEOS cautelous
CUERS cruzeiros
CUFED Caulfield
CUGIG Chungking
CUGTE courgette
CUHBE crushable
CUHCP crush a cup
CUHON cough down
CUHRP cough drop
cough-drop
CUHTE couchette
CUHUE clubhouse
CUILS caudillos
CUILY crucially
CUIOM cruciform
CUKIG chuckling
CUKTN chuck it in
CUKWY chuck away
CUTAD Coulthard
courtyard
CUTAE court case

CUTBE countable
CUTES countless
CUTHE court shoe
court-shoe
CUTHP courtship
CUTIS countries
CUTOM courtroom
CUTOS courteous
CUTPN count upon
CUTRD clustered
cluttered
CUTRP clutter up
CUTSN courtesan
CUUIR couturier
CUWMN clubwoman
CVCLY civically
CVLAE cavalcade
CVLIG cavilling
CVLIT civil list
CVLSD civilised
CVLZD civilized
CVNIH Cavendish
CVRES coverless
CVRIG cavorting
CVRIH cover with
CVRIL cover girl
CVRNO cover into
CVRNS coverings
CVROE cover note
CVROS cavernous
CVTBE covetable
CWRIE cowardice
CWRWY cower away
CWSAF cowl-staff
CXOBC coxcombic
CYAVS cry halves
CYOEE Ceylonese
CYTGM cryptogam
CYUFR cry out for
DAADE do a candle
DAAIE dramatise
dramatize
DAAIG Diana Rigg
DAAIS dramatics
DAAIT dramatist
DAANT diamagnet
DAAOS Diana Dors
Diana Ross
DABAK draw blank
DAEBY Drake's Bay
DAEIG deadening
deafening
DAEIH do a perish
DAEIS draperies
DAERC diametric
DAETC dialectic
DAETL dialectal
DAHAD deathward
DAHAE death rate
DAHAM diaphragm
DAHES deathless
DAHIE deathlike
death-like

DAHIH death wish
DAHLV Diaghilev
DAHLW death blow
death-blow
DAHOL death toll
DAHRP deathtrap
DAHRY diathermy
DAHSS diathesis
DAHTC diathetic
DAHTR death star
DAHUE deadhouse
DAHUY death duty
DAIGN drawing-in
DAIIN Dravidian
DAITC dualistic
DAKOS dear knows
DALNS draw lines
DALRE diablerie
DALVL draw level
DAMRH dead-march
DANIE drainpipe
DANOK drawn work
DANSS diagnoses
diagnosis
DAOAE diaconate
DAOAS dragomans
DAODD diamonded
DAOES deaconess
DAOFY dragonfly
DAOIE diabolise
diabolize
dialogise
dialogize
dragonise
dragonize
DAOIM diabolism
DAOIN draconian❑
DAOIT diabolist
DAOTF drag out of
DAPIT dead point
DAROA diarrhoea
DARSS diaereses
diaeresis
DARTC diacritic
DASET draw-sheet
DASUS Dead Souls
DATIH dealt with
DATLC diastolic
DATRD dead tired
DATSC diastasic
DATTC diastatic
DAUNR do a runner
DAYSS diapyesis
DBIBY Dublin Bay
DBIES Dubliners
DBNUE debenture
DBONK Dubrovnik
DBOSY dubiously
DBRAN Dobermann
DBRET debarment
DBRIG debarring
DBTAD debit card
DBTBE debatable

DBTBY	dubitably
DBTNE	débutante
DBUHD	debauched
DBUHE	debauchee
DCAIN	dictation
DCAMR	declaimer
DCAOY	dictatory
DCCIN	decoction
DCCUE	decocture
DCDAA	docudrama
DCDDY	decided by
	decidedly
DCDNE	decadence
DCDOS	deciduous
DCEET	decrement
DCEEY	Dick Emery
DCENE	déchéance
DCEOT	decked out
DCGNL	decagonal
DCIFL	deceitful
DCIIG	deceiving
	declining
DCIIY	declivity
	ductility
DCIOS	declivous
DCIPN	Dr Crippen
DCISN	Dickinson
DCLAE	decollate
DCLEE	décolleté
DCLGE	Decalogue
DCLIN	decillion
DCLIY	decalcify
DCLTE	decalitre
	decilitre
DCMET	decumbent
DCMIG	decamping
DCMII	decemviri
DCMIS	decemvirs
DCMLY	decimally
DCMNS	documents
DCMOE	decompose
DCMRN	Decameron
DCMTE	decametre
	decimetre
DCMTR	decimator
DCNET	decongest
DCNIL	decennial
DCNRL	decontrol
DCOAE	doctorate
DCOOY	dichotomy
DCOTF	duck out of
DCPIE	deceptive
DCPIN	deception
DCRIM	dichroism
DCRNL	doctrinal
DCRNS	doctrines
DCRTD	decorated
DCRTR	decorator
DCSAE	decussate
DCSRE	duck's arse
DCSUD	dachshund
DCTLN	decathlon
DCTSS	Docetists

DCUAE	decaudate
	decoupage
	découpage
DCYID	Dicky Bird
	dicky-bird
DDCBE	deducible
DDCGN	dodecagon
DDCIE	deductive
DDCIN	deduction
DDCIS	didactics
DDCTD	dedicated
DDCTE	dedicatee
DDCTR	dedicator
DDEIG	doddering
DDITC	Dadaistic
DDTFR	do duty for
DEAAI	Deepavali
DECIG	drenching
DEDES	dreadless
DEEIE	dieselise
	dieselize
DEEIG	deepening
DEEIS	dietetics
DEEOL	diesel oil
DEFED	deep field
DEFSI	dies fasti
	dies festi
DEIIN	dietician
	dietitian
DELNS	dwellings
DEMES	dreamless
DEMIE	dreamlike
DEMOT	dreamboat
DESAE	deep space
	dressmake
DESDN	dressed in
DESET	diet sheet
DESON	dress down
DESUT	dress suit
DETND	deep-toned
DETNS	duettinos
DEWTR	deep water
DFADR	defrauder
DFAIG	deflating
DFAIM	defeatism
DFAIN	deflation
DFAIT	defeatist
DFATY	defiantly
DFAUE	defeature
DFCET	deficient
DFCIE	defective
DFCIN	defection
DFEBG	duffel bag
DFEET	different
DFEIG	differing
DFETR	deflector
DFIET	diffident
DFIUT	difficult
DFLAE	defalcate
	defoliate
DFLAT	defoliant
DFNAT	defendant
DFNBE	definable

DFNBY	definably
DFNIE	defensive
DFNIG	defending
DFOAE	deflorate
DFOTR	defroster
DFRBE	deferable
DFRET	deferment
DFRIY	deformity
DFRNE	deference
DFUEY	diffusely
DFUIE	diffusive
DFUIN	diffusion
DFUTN	default on
DFUTR	defaulter
DGADE	dog-paddle
DGADG	dog-eat-dog
DGAIE	dogmatise
	dogmatize
DGAIG	degrading
DGAIM	dogmatism
DGAIT	dogmatist
DGIAY	dignitary
DGIHY	doggishly
DGIID	dignified
DGMAA	Digambara
DGOLR	dog-collar
DGSAE	degustate
DGSIE	digestive
DGSIN	digestion
DGTLN	digitalin
DGTLS	digitalis
DGTTD	digitated
DGTZR	digitizer
DHDAE	dehydrate
DHSET	dehiscent
DIDIG	dwindling
DIEAK	drive back
DIEAT	drive past
DIEBE	driveable
DIEET	drive belt
DIENO	drive into
DIEOE	drive home
DIEUS	drive nuts
DIEWY	drive away
DIGID	doing bird
DIGIE	doing time
DIGON	dying-down
DIKAL	drink-hail
DIKBE	drinkable
DILNO	drill into
DITCL	deistical
DITOD	driftwood
DIYAD	dairymaid
DIYAL	Daily Mail
DIYEP	daily help
DIYTR	Daily Star
DIZIG	drizzling
DJCIG	dejecting
DJCIN	dejection
DKOIG	De Kooning
DKOOS	Dukhobors
DLAIG	delta-wing
DLAIN	Dalmatian

DLCOS	delicious
DLCOX	Delacroix
DLDBE	deludable
DLEIA	dolce vita
DLENO	delve into
DLFED	Delafield
DLFLY	dolefully
DLGBE	delegable
DLGNE	diligence
DLGTD	delegated
	delighted
DLGTN	delight in
DLGTS	delegates
DLHNA	delphinia
DLHNS	Delphinus
DLIAA	Dalai Lama
	dalai lama
DLIGR	Dillinger
DLIHY	doltishly
DLINE	dalliance
DLIUE	dulcitude
DLMTD	delimited
DLMTS	Dolomites
DLNAE	delineate
DLOIM	daltonism❑
DLROS	delirious
DLRUS	deliriums
DLSOS	delusions
DLTBE	dilutable
DLVIA	D'Oliveira
DLVRR	deliverer
DLYIH	dally with
DMAIG	demeaning
DMAIN	damnation
DMAOR	demeanour
DMAOY	damnatory
DMATN	Dumbarton
DMCAY	democracy
DMCEN	Damoclean
DMCLD	domiciled
DMDAE	dimidiate
DMDIY	demi-deify
DMEET	damnedest
DMEFY	damselfly
DMEIG	dampening
DMFUD	dumbfound
DMGGC	demagogic
DMGGE	demagogue
DMIES	dumpiness
DMIHY	dumpishly
DMITD	dimwitted
	dim-witted
DMLET	demulcent
DMLIY	demulsify
DMMNE	demi-monde
DMMOE	Demi Moore
DMNCN	Dominican
DMNIG	demanding
	demanning
DMNIL	Damon Hill
DMNIN	dimension
DMNNE	dominance
DMNTD	dominated

Words marked ❑ can also be spelled with an initial capital letter

Code	Word
DMPOF	damp-proof
DMRAE	demarcate
DMRHC	dimorphic
DMRIG	demurring
DMSEE	damascene
DMSEN	damaskeen
DMSIY	demystify
DMSUB	damp squib
DMSUN	damasquin
DMTIS	Demetrius
DMTSE	demitasse
DMUIR	Du Maurier
DNAES	dungarees
DNAIO	Dan Marino
DNANN	Dungannon
DNATR	Doncaster
DNEBE	danceable
DNEES	denseness
DNEIN	dandelion
DNEOS	dangerous
DNEQE	Dantesque
DNEST	dinner set
DNGAE	denigrate
DNIAE	Dunsinane
DNIES	dinginess
DNIGY	denyingly
DNIID	dandified
DNIIN	dentition
DNILW	Dennis Law
DNIRT	dandiprat
DNITY	dentistry
DNOTN	dine out on
DNRAD	donor card
DNRTC	dendritic
DNTAE	denitrate
DNTBE	Dunstable
DNTIG	do nothing
	do-nothing
DNTIY	denitrify
DNTLO	Donatello
DNTOS	donations
DNUCR	denouncer
DNUYE	Dan Quayle
DNUZO	D'Annunzio
DNWRH	Dankworth
DNWRY	don't worry
DNYAE	Danny Kaye
DNYOL	dandy-roll
DNYRD	Dan Aykrod
DNZTI	Donizetti
DOCOS	dioecious
DOCRS	Dioscorus
DOEAY	dromedary
DOEBT	do one's bit
DOENT	do one's nut
DOFRE	drop-forge
DOIAE	deoxidate
DOIGY	droningly
DOIHY	dronishly
DOIIE	deoxidise
	deoxidize
DOITE	Doolittle
DOITH	dhobi itch
DOKOK	doorknock
DOLBG	doodlebug
DOLVR	drool over
DOOAT	deodorant
DOOIE	deodorise
	deodorize
DOOTF	drop out of
DOPNS	droppings
DOSCL	dropsical
DOSEE	drop-scene
DOSOE	drop-scone
DOTIS	dioptrics
DOWTH	doomwatch
DOYIS	Dionysius
DPAIG	depraving
DPAIY	depravity
DPCIE	depictive
DPCIN	depiction
DPEAE	deprecate
	depredate
DPEIN	depletion
DPEOS	dipterous
DPESD	depressed
DPESR	depressor
DPFED	dope-fiend
DPIAE	duplicate
DPIEF	deprive of
DPIIY	duplicity
DPLTD	depilated
DPNAT	dependant
DPNET	dependent
DPOAE	diplomate
DPOAY	diplomacy
DPORM	deprogram
DPPIE	dipeptide
DPRIG	departing
DPRIU	Depardieu
DPRUE	departure
DPSBE	deposable
DPSTR	depositor
DPSUE	depasture
DPTOG	diphthong
DQICY	De Quincey
DRANN	D'Artagnan
DRAOD	dermatoid
DRBUS	Dark blues
DRCEP	dirt cheap
	dirt-cheap
DRCIE	directive
DRCIG	directing
DRCIN	direction
DRCOS	directors
DRCOY	directory❑
DRCRX	directrix
DRCTX	direct tax
DRDVL	daredevil
	dare-devil
DREIG	darkening
DRETE	dor beetle
DRFLY	direfully
DRGBE	dirigible
DRGER	de rigueur
DRGSE	dirigisme
	dirigiste
DRHRE	dark horse
DRIES	dirtiness
DRIGR	derringer
DRIGY	dartingly
DRIIM	Darwinism
DRIIN	Darwinian
DRIIT	Darwinist
DRIOY	dormitory
DRLCS	derelicts
DRLMN	Duralumin®
DRLNS	darklings
DRMTR	dura mater
DRMUH	Dartmouth
DRRCT	Dordrecht
DRVBE	derivable
DRVBY	derivably
DRYAK	dirty mark
DRYOB	dirty bomb
DRYOD	dirty word
DRYOK	dirty look
	dirty work
DSAAE	disparage
	disparate
DSACD	discalced
DSADD	discarded
DSADE	discandie
DSADY	dastardly
DSAIG	dismaying
DSAIY	disparity
DSALW	dishallow
DSAND	disdained
DSAOR	disfavour
DSAPR	dispauper
DSASS	Dos Passos
DSATE	dismantle
DSATS	Descartes
DSATY	distantly
DSBAD	dashboard
DSBAE	disc brake
DSBIE	disoblige
DSBIG	disabling
DSBSD	disabused
DSBUD	desk-bound
DSBYD	disobeyed
DSCAE	desecrate
	desiccate
DSCAT	desiccant
DSCOD	disaccord
DSCOH	dish-cloth
DSCVR	dust cover
DSDIE	disk drive
DSDVL	dust-devil
DSEAD	disregard
DSEAE	desperate
DSEAO	desperado
	DiStefano
DSEAR	disrepair
DSEBE	dissemble
DSEBR	dismember
DSEDD	distended
DSEDN	descend on
DSEDR	descender
DSEIF	disbelief
DSEIH	disrelish
DSEOA	Desdemona
DSEPE	dispeople
DSEPR	destemper
	distemper
DSESA	dyspepsia
DSESD	dispersed
DSESL	dispersal
DSESR	dispenser
DSETC	dyspeptic
DSETD	dissected
DSETR	dissenter
DSEUE	desuetude
	disrepute
DSFET	disaffect
DSFIM	disaffirm
DSGAE	designate
DSGIG	designing
DSHOE	disthrone
DSHRE	discharge
DSHSA	dysphasia
DSHUE	dosshouse
DSIAE	dissipate
DSIES	duskiness
	dustiness
DSIET	dissident
DSIGY	dashingly
DSIHY	duskishly
DSIIE	dissimile
DSILD	distilled
DSILR	distiller
DSISD	dismissed
DSISL	dismissal
DSIUE	destitute
	disfigure
DSLAE	displease
DSLCD	displaced
DSLHR	desulphur
DSLOY	desultory
DSLSA	dysplasia
DSLSD	disclosed
DSLTR	desolater
DSLUE	disillude
DSLYD	displayed
DSMAK	disembark
DSMOY	disembody
DSMTR	dosimeter
DSMUE	disimmure
DSNAE	disengage
DSNAL	disentail
DSNBE	disenable
DSNET	disinfect
	disinfest
	disinvest
DSNEY	dysentery
DSNHR	disanchor
DSNIT	disanoint
DSNOB	disentomb
DSNTD	disunited
DSNUE	disinhume
DSOAE	dislocate
DSOAT	dissonant

Words marked ❑ can also be spelled with an initial capital letter

DSODE dispondee
DSODL discoidal
DSOEF dispose of
DSOET disforest
dishonest
DSOEY discovery□
DSOFT discomfit
DSOIM despotism
DSOLR despoiler
DSOMN discommon
DSOND disjoined
DSONS Des Moines
DSOOR discolour
dishonour
DSORE discourse
DSOTD distorted
DSOUE dissolute
DSPER disappear
DSRBD described
DSRBE desirable
DSRBR describer
DSRBY desirably
DSRCD disgraced
DSRDT discredit
DSRET disorient
DSRIE dispraise
distraite
DSRIG deserving
disarming
DSRIN desertion
DSRIT distraint
DSRNH disbranch
DSRPY dystrophy
DSRSN disprison
DSRYD destroyed
DSRYR destroyer
DSSEM disesteem
DSSOM dust-storm
DSTUE disattune
DSTWL dishtowel
DSUAE despumate
DSUAT disputant
DSUBD disturbed
DSUDN disburden
DSUDR dissunder
DSUOR dishumour
DSUSD disguised
DSUSL disbursal
DSUTD disgusted
disrupted
DSUTR disrupter
DSVWL disavowal
DSWEL disc wheel
DSWIG disowning
DSWRD Discworld
DSWTR dishwater
DSYAE Dusty Hare
DTATR detractor
DTBUD duty-bound
DTCIE detective
DTCIG detaching
DTCIN detection
DTDAH do to death

DTEAE do the same
DTEIG dithering
DTFLY dutifully
DTGOE dataglove
DTHAN Dutch barn
DTHAS Dutch Wars
DTHEF Dutch leaf
DTHOD Dutch gold
DTHVN Dutch oven
DTIES dottiness
DTIET detriment
DTIIG detailing
DTIIN detrition
DTNIN detention
DTNTR detonator
DTOHE ditrochee
DTOHT Dutrochet
DTOSY duteously
DTOUH do too much
DTRET detergent
determent
deterrent
DTRIE determine
DTRIG deterring
DTSAP date-stamp
DTYAB dithyramb
DUAIN Deucalion
DUBAE drum brake
DUDCL druidical
DUDDT Deusdedit
DUEAE deuterate
DUEIM deuterium
DUGRA Dzungaria
DUHIY doughtily
DUKNY drunkenly
DULAT double act
DUNLY diurnally
DUSIK drumstick
DUSOT Doug Scott
DUTES dauntless
doubtless
DUTKR drug taker
DVAIG deviating
DVAIN deviation
DVDAE David Hare
DVDAH David Mach
DVDAN dove-drawn
DVDDY dividedly
DVDEN David Lean
DVDIL David Hill
DVDOE David Hope
David Sole
DVDOF divide off
DVDOT divide out
DVDUE David Hume
DVDWN David Owen
DVLAE devaluate
DVLBT devil a bit
DVLET devilment
DVLOE devil a one
DVLPD developed
DVLPR developer
DVNOT davenport□

DVNTR divinator
DVOSY deviously
DVRET divergent
DVREY diversely
DVRIE divertive
DVRIG diverging
diverting
DVRIN diversion
DVRIY diversify
diversity
DVROE Dover sole
DVSAE devastate
DVSBE divisible
DVSBY divisibly
DVTDO devoted to
DVTDY devotedly
DVTIY devitrify
DVTOS devotions
DVUIG devouring
DWGAE downgrade
DWGVD down-gyved
DWIES dowdiness
downiness
DWNES do wonders
DWRGT downright
DWSAE downstage
DWSIG downswing
DWTEE down there
DWTOS down tools
DWTOT do without
DWWRS downwards
DXEAD Dixieland
DXEIY dexterity
DXEOS dexterous
DXRLY dextrally
DXRRE dextrorse
DYAOR day-labour
DYEOE day before
DYETE day centre
DYHRY dry sherry
DYNOT drying out
DYOOD days of old
DYSUT dry as dust
Dryasdust
DYUID do you mind?
DZGTC dizygotic
DZIES dizziness
EAAEN El Alamein
EAAIN emanation
EAEET erasement
EAELD enamelled
EAIAE eradicate
evaginate
exanimate
EAIAT examinant
EAIEY evasively
EAITD emaciated
EALTE epaulette
EAOAE elaborate
evaporate
EAOIE evaporite
EAORD enamoured
EATDY exaltedly

EATEA exanthema
EATES exactness
exanthems
EATET enactment
EATMR elastomer
EAUAE ejaculate
EAUNR Eva Turner
EAUTR evaluator
EAVTL élan vital
EBAIG embracing
EBAUE embrasure
EBEAA emblemata
EBEIE emblemise
emblemize
EBLIG emballing
EBLIH embellish
EBOAE embrocate
EBODR embroider
EBOLD embroiled
EBOSM emblossom
EBRAS embarrass
EBROD embargoed
EBROS embargoes
EBSIG embossing
EBTLD embattled
EBWOM elbow-room
EBYNC embryonic
EBZLR embezzler
ECAGD exchanged
ECAGR exchanger
ECAIT Eucharist
ECAND enchained
ECATD enchanted
ECATR enchanter
ECEET excrement
ECEIE excretive
ECEIG exceeding
ECEIN excretion
ECEOY excretory
ECERS encierros
ECEUR exchequer
ECFIR Escoffier
ECIAA enchilada
ECIEN Euclidean
ECISN encrimson
ECLAE exculpate
ECLBR Excalibur
ECLET excellent
ECLIG excelling
ECLIN encolpion
ECLIR excelsior
ECLPI eucalypti
ECLTD escalated
ECLTR escalator
ECLVR excel over
ECMAS encompass
ECMAT encomiast
ECMUS encomiums
ECNRC eccentric
ECOHR each other
ECOIG enclosing
ECOIL enchorial
ECOOY euchology

Words marked □ can also be spelled with an initial capital letter

ECOUE enclosure
ECPBE escapable
ECPFR except for
ECPIG excepting
ECPIN exception
ECRAE excarnate
excoriate
ECRAN encurtain
ECRIE excursive
ECRIN excursion
ECRLD encircled
ECROE eucaryote
ECRTR excerptor
ECSBE excisable
excusable
ECSBY excusably
ECSFR excuse for
ECSIE excessive
ECSMN exciseman
ECTBE excitable
ECTDY excitedly
ECTIG each thing
ECTNY excitancy
ECUAE encourage
ECUIE exclusive
ECUIG excluding
ECUIN exclusion
ECUTC encaustic
ECUTR encounter□
ECVTD excavated
ECVTR excavator
EDAIG endearing
EDAOR endeavour□
EDCIE endocrine
EDESY endlessly
EDEUT end result
EDLIR Eid al-Fitr
EDMRH endomorph
EDNEN endungeon
EDNTN Eddington
EDNZN endenizen
EDOED end for end
EDPAM endoplasm
EDPAY endophagy
EDPYE endophyte
EDRBE endurable
EDRBY endurably
EDRHN endorphin
EDRIG endorsing
EDRNE endurance
EDRON eiderdown
EDRUK eider duck
EDSAT ecdysiast
EDSEM endosperm
EDSOE endoscope
EDSOY endoscopy
EDWET endowment
EEAHC epedaphic
EEAIG elevating
EEAIN elevation
élevation
EEAOY elevatory
EEATR ever after

EEATY elegantly
EECSR exerciser
EECSS exercises
EEEIT exegetist
EEEPE Eye Temple
EEESS elevenses
EEETL elemental
EEGAE everglade
EEGEN evergreen
EEGGP energy gap
EEGNE emergence
EEGNY emergency
EEGTC energetic
EEGZR energizer
EEHEE ewe-cheese
EEICL elegiacal
EEIIM eremitism
EEMNY even money
EENLY eternally
EEPAY exemplary
EEPIN exemption
EEPIY exemplify
EEPNR eye-opener
EERBE execrable
EERBY execrably
EEROD Eve Arnold
EESBE eversible
EESCA ever such a
EETAE eventrate
eventuate
EETAY electuary
EETBE electable
EETES erectness
EETIE electrise
electrize
EETIY electrify
EETOE electrode
EETRL electoral
EEUAT executant
EEUIE executive
EEUIN execution
EEUOY executory
EEURX executrix
EEVTD enervated
EEWIS edelweiss
EEYAT every last
EEYEK every week
EEYER every year
EEYHT every whit
EEYIE every time
EEYNH every inch
EEYOY everybody
EFCET efficient
EFCIE effective
EFCIG effecting
EFCUL effectual
EFEDM enfreedom
EFELD enfeebled
EFLAE exfoliate
EFLET effulgent
EFMLE en famille
EFRTR E M Forster
EFUIM effluvium

EFUIN effluxion
EFUNE effluence
EGAIG engraving
EGATN Edgbaston
EGDOL edged tool
EGEAE engrenage
EGEYD eagle-eyed
EGGDN engaged in
EGGFR engage for
EGHPD egg-shaped
EGLCR egg slicer
EGNMC ergonomic
EGNOE eigentone
EGOSD engrossed
EGRAD engarland
EGRES eagerness
EGTEH eightieth
EGTOD eightfold
EGTOE eightsome
EGTOT eightfoot
eight-foot
EGWRH Edgeworth
EHATN enhearten
EHATS ephialtes
EHBTD exhibited
EHBTR exhibitor
EHCLY ethically
EHDIE ephedrine
EHIIY ethnicity
EHLDS ephelides
EHLET Ethelbert
EHLLA echolalia
EHLUF Ethelwulf
EHMRE ephemerae
EHMRL ephemeral
EHMRN ephemeron
EHMRS ephemeras
ephemeris
EHNIG enhancing
EHODL ethmoidal
EHOIE ethnocide
EHOIN Ethiopian
EHOOY ethnology
EHSAS Ephesians
EHUTD exhausted
EHVRS ECHO virus
echo virus
EIAEH Elisabeth
Elizabeth
EIAES Erica Hess
EIAIL epitaxial
EIAIN epilation
EIARS Epidaurus
EIBRH Edinburgh
EICBE evincible
EICBY evincibly
EICPL episcopal
EIDIG evil-doing
EIEIL epicedial
EIEIN epicedian
EIEML epidermal
EIEMS epidermis
EIEOA Emile Zola

EIEOX Emile Roux
Émile Roux
EIETC epileptic
EIETE epicentre
EIETY eminently
evidently
exigently
EIHIF Edith Piaf
EIHSS epiphyses
epiphysis
EIHTC epithetic
EIIAE eliminate
EIIIG eliciting
EIIIY edibility
EIKZN Elia Kazan
EILSS epicleses
epiclesis
EILTD etiolated
EIMTC enigmatic
EINWY Eric Newby
EIOIE epilogise
epilogize
epitomise
epitomize
EIOIL editorial
EIOIT epitomist
EIOTC epizootic
EIRPY epigraphy
EISTE Erik Satie
EITCL eristical
EITLY edictally
EITNE existence
EITRM exist from
EITSS epistases
EIUEN epicurean
EIUIE epicurise
epicurize
EIUIM epicurism
EIUTE etiquette
EIYLC epicyclic
EJIDR enjoinder
EJYBE enjoyable
EJYBY enjoyably
EJYET enjoyment
EJYIE enjoy life
EKMDG Eskimo dog
EKROE eukaryote
ELGTN enlighten
ELGUS eulogiums
ELGZR eulogizer
ELMSA eclampsia
ELNIE eglantine
ELNTN Ellington
ELPOD ellipsoid
ELREN enlarge on
ELRIG enlarging
ELSIG enlisting
ELVNR enlivener
EMNHL Emmenthal
EMNSN Edmondson
ENCIE eunuchise
eunuchize
ENEIE Ernie Wise

Code	Word
ENHVN	Eindhoven
	Einthoven
ENTAH	Ernst Mach
ENTBE	Ernst Abbe
ENTDT	Ernst Udet
ENTOM	Ernst Röhm
EOABS	Enobarbus
EOAIC	egomaniac
EOAIE	evocative
EOAIN	evocation
EOAOS	exogamous
EODUS	exordiums
EOEAE	exonerate
EOEET	elopement
EOEIH	elope with
EOEOS	erogenous
	exogenous
EOFCO	ex officio
EOGTD	elongated
EOHIM	egotheism
EOIIE	eroticise
	eroticize
EOIIM	eroticism
	exoticism
EOINL	emotional
EOITC	egotistic
EOITD	etoliated
EOKEZ	Egon Krenz
EOLAE	emolliate
EOLET	emollient
EOMRE	e-commerce
EOOIE	economise
	economize
EOOIS	economics
EOOIT	ecologist
	economist
EOPEE	ecosphere
	exosphere
EOSIE	écossaise
EOTSS	exostoses
EOUET	emolument
EOUIN	elocution
	evolution
EOUNE	eloquence
EOVRO	e converso
EOYOS	eponymous
EOYTM	ecosystem
EPAAE	esplanade
EPAIE	emphasise
	emphasize
EPAIN	expiation
EPAOY	expiatory
EPCAT	expectant
EPCIG	expecting
EPDET	expedient
EPEIE	euphemise
	euphemize
	expletive
EPEIM	euphemism
EPEIS	euphenics
EPESD	expressed
EPESS	espressos
EPESY	expressly
EPETC	empaestic
EPGOE	espagnole
EPIAE	explicate
EPIER	en primeur
EPIES	emptiness
EPLIE	expulsive
EPLIN	expulsion
EPLSS	emphlyses
EPMSS	espumosos
EPNAE	empennage
EPNBE	exponible
EPNIE	expansive
	expensive
EPNIG	expanding
	expending
EPNIN	en pension
	expansion
EPNPY	empanoply
EPOAE	espionage
EPOES	employees
	employers
EPOIE	euphonise
	euphonize
	explosive
EPOIM	euphonium
EPOIN	explosion
EPOTD	exploited
EPOTR	exploiter
EPRAE	expurgate
EPRCL	empirical
EPRIE	expertise
	expertize
EPRNE	esperance
EPRNO	Esperanto
EPRTS	Euphrates
EPRUS	emporiums
EPSAE	expiscate
EPSAT	en passant
EPSDO	exposed to
EPSTR	expositor
EPSUE	exposture
EPTAE	expatiate
EPTIE	empathise
	empathize
EPUAS	espousals
EPUDR	expounder
EPYAK	empty talk
EPYEA	emphysema
EQIIE	Esquiline
	exquisite
EQIIG	enquiring
EQIIS	enquiries
ERAKD	earmarked
ERCIG	enriching
ERETY	earnestly
ERGOS	egregious
ERHAL	earth ball
	earthfall
ERHIG	earthling
ERHNS	Earl Hines
ERHOK	earthwork
ERHOM	earthworm
ERIES	earliness
ERIRN	earlier on
ERLET	enrolment
ERNBY	errand-boy
ERNOS	erroneous
ERPDS	Euripides
ERPIN	erruption
ERPOT	en rapport
	Europoort
ERPUD	Ezra Pound
ERPUE	enrapture
ERSIN	egression
ERTIE	écritoire
ERYAS	early days
ERYHY	eurhythmy
ERYID	early bird
ESAAC	easy as ABC
ESAIE	ecstasise
	ecstasize
ESBUD	eastbound
ESCAE	exsiccate
ESCAR	easy chair
ESEDY	Easter Day
ESEEG	Easter egg
ESETE	ensheathe
ESETR	enshelter
ESGIG	easygoing
	easy-going
ESLDG	easily dug
ESLIH	Eastleigh
ESLLD	easily led
ESLNS	eastlings
ESMNY	easy money
ESNIL	essential
ESOCD	ensconced
ESOUE	ease of use
ESPAY	easy-peasy
ESRIE	exsertile
	exsertive
ESRVR	East River
ESTRS	easy terms
ESTUH	easy touch
ESWEE	elsewhere
ESWIE	erstwhile
ESWRS	eastwards
ETACD	entranced
ETAET	extravert
ETAGD	estranged
ETAGT	extraught
ETAIE	estuarine
	extradite
	extra time
ETAIL	estuarial
ETAML	entrammel
ETAOE	extrapose
ETAPR	entrapper
ETATR	extractor
ETBAT	ectoblast
ETBIH	establish
ETEES	entremets
ETEEY	extremely
ETEHT	entrechat
ETEIM	extremism
ETEIT	extremist
ETEIY	extremity
ETEOE	entrecôte
ETEOS	entre nous
ETFTE	estafette
ETHAR	eat the air
ETIAE	extricate
ETISC	extrinsic
ETLET	extolment
ETLIG	extolling
ETMBE	estimable
ETMBY	estimably
ETMOE	extempore
ETMRH	ectomorph
ETMTD	estimated
ETMTR	estimator
ETNAE	extenuate
ETNIE	extensile
	extensive
ETNIN	extension
ETNLD	entangled
ETNON	Elton John
ETNTD	extincted
ETOET	extrovert
ETOHC	eutrophic
ETOIN	Esthonian
ETPAM	ectoplasm
ETRAE	extirpate
ETRAN	entertain
ETRAS	externals
ETRBE	enterable
ETRIE	extermine
ETRIN	extortion
ETRNO	enter into
ETRPN	enter upon
ETRTS	enteritis
ETTCR	estate car
ETUAE	entourage
ETUIE	extrusive
ETUIN	extrusion
ETUOY	extrusory
EUAIE	educative
EUAIG	emulating
EUAIN	education
	emulation
	epuration
	exudation
EUAOY	educatory
EUBRK	Ehud Barak
EUCAE	enunciate
EUEAE	enumerate
	exuberate
EUEAT	exuberant
EUEIM	ecumenism
EUEIS	ecumenics
EUIAE	elucidate
EUIEY	elusively
	eruditely
EUIIN	erudition
EUINE	esurience
EUINY	esuriency
EUKNA	Eduskunta
EULAE	enucleate
EULAT	equal part

EULET ebullient
EULIN equal sign
EUOSY emulously
EUPET equipment
EUPIE equipoise
EUPIG equipping
EURAE elutriate
EUTBE equitable
EUTBY equitably
EUVCL equivocal
EVLPD enveloped
EVNMD envenomed
EVOSY enviously
EVSRP eavesdrop
EWETE enwreathe
EWNAD Edwin Land
EWNUR Edwin Muir
EWRIN Edwardian
EYOOY etymology
EZEGM Esztergom
EZMTC enzymatic
FABAS flambeaus
FABAX flambeaux
FABOE flat broke
FABUH flat brush
FACDY flaccidly
FACIE franchise
FACLN francolin
FADTR fraudster
FAECS flamencos
FAEET frame tent
FAELM flagellum
FAELT flageolet
FAENL fraternal
FAEOK framework
FAEOT flaked out
FAERD flap-eared
FAETR flare star
FAFLY fearfully
FAGAS franglais
FAGBE frangible
FAGTR flaughter
FAHAD flash card
FAHAK flashback
FAHRD feathered
FAHUB flashbulb
FAHUN flash burn
FAHVR flash-over
FAIAE flagitate
FAIES flakiness
foaminess
FAIEY fragilely
FAIGS flamingos
FAIGY flamingly
flaringly
foamingly
FAIIY fragility
FAKES frankness
FAKOT Frankfort
FAKUT Frankfurt
FALES frailness
FALNS flatlings
FAMBE flammable
FAMNS fragments
FANIG flaunting
FAOAD Fragonard
FAOGD fear of God
FAOOS flavorous
FAORD flavoured
FAPBE flappable
FARNE fragrance
FARNY flagrancy
fragrancy
FASAS Frans Hals
FASED Flamsteed
FASOE flagstone
FATCY franticly
FATOS fractious
FATRD fractured
FATRR flatterer
FAUET flatulent
FAWVR flag-waver
FAZAC Franz Marc
FAZOP Franz Bopp
FBAIM Fabianism
FBAIT Fabianist
FBCOS fabaceous
FBEES fibreless
FBIAE fabricate
FBIIS Fabricius
FBILE fibrillae
FBILN fibrillin
FBILR fibrillar
FBIUE febrifuge
FBNCI Fibonacci
FBOAA fibromata
FCCOH face-cloth
FCDIH faced with
FCIIE facsimile
factitive
FCINL factional
fictional
FCLIS faculties
FCLNE feculence
FCMTR focimeter
FCNAE fecundate
FCNIY facundity
fecundity
FCOIE factorise
factorize
FCOIL factorial
FCOUS factotums
FCPAE face plate
FCSET fact sheet
FCSVR face-saver
FCTOS facetious
FCULY factually
FCVLE face value
FDCAY fiduciary
FDEAE fudge cake
FDEIG fidgeting
FDIES faddiness
FDKEK F W De Klerk
F W de Klerk
FDRRE federarie
FEAFM fee-faw-fum
FEATE Fremantle
FEATR feel after
FECEP feel cheap
FECFY French fry
FECIT frescoist
FECIY Frenchify
FECMN Frenchman
Frenchmen
FEDAD field hand
fieldward
FEDAE fieldfare
FEDMN fieldsman
FEDNA Freedonia
FEDOK field book
fieldwork
FEDOL field goal
FEDRP field trip
FEDVS Fred Davis
FEEAI foederati
FEEIA Frederica
FEEIK Frederick
FEEOD Fredegond
FEFLY fretfully
FEGIG fledgling
FEGTR freighter
FEGUE fuel gauge
FEHES fleshless
freshness
FEHET fleshment
FEHNP freshen up
FEHNS fleshings
FEHTE fléchette
FEHUE free house
FEHYE Fred Hoyle
FEIES fieriness
FEIGY feelingly
FEIIE flexitime
FEIPE fee simple
FEKRD fleckered
FELNE freelance
FELNH free lunch
FEMSN Freemason
FEPOE freephone
FEPRY Fred Perry
FERNE free-range
FESAL feel small
FESET freesheet
FESOE freestone
FESOK feedstock
FESRY feel sorry
FESUG Flensburg
FESYE freestyle
FETAE free trade
free-trade
FETES fleetness
FETOD Fleetwood
FETOT fleet-foot
FEUNY frequency
FEVRE free verse
FEWEL freewheel
FEWMN freewoman
freewomen
FEZBE freezable
FEZDY freeze-dry
FEZOT freeze out
FFAOT faff about
FFENH fifteenth
FGCOS fugacious
FGEOT fagged out
FGIES fogginess
FGROT figure out
FGTAK fight back
FIAIE fricative
FIAOT flit about
FIASE fricassee
FIBNS Fairbanks
FIDIH Friedrich
FIENA feiseanna
FIENE fainéance
FIGON fling down
FIHBG flight bag
FIHES faithless
FIHFL frightful
FIHIY flightily
FIIIY frigidity
FIKDL frikkadel
FINDY feignedly
FINIG friending
FIOIY frivolity
FIOOS frivolous
FIPNY flippancy
FIRID friarbird
FIRUK Friar Tuck
FISZD fair-sized
FITES faintness
FITGT fail to get
FITHT fail to hit
FITIH flirt with
FITIL flirt-gill
FITOK flintlock
FIYAD fairyland□
FIYAE fairy tale
fairytale
fairy-tale
FIYEN fairy tern
FIYIE fairylike
FIYIG fairy ring
FIZAG Fritz Lang
FIZNE frizzante□
FLAAT fall apart
FLADY full and by
FLAEN fellaheen
FLAEY fallalery
FLAIN filiation
foliation
FLAIS fellatios
FLAOG fall among
FLAOT fall about
FLATR film actor
FLAUE foliature
FLBAT full blast
full-blast
FLBON full-blown
FLBUS full blues
FLCCD folic acid
FLCTR feliciter

FLDES full dress
FLEAD false-card
FLEAE false name
FLEAH false oath
FLEAN false dawn
FLEDA false idea
FLEES falseness
FLEHW false show
FLEIG faltering
FLEOD falsehood
FLETP false step
filter-tip
FLETS falsettos
FLETY fulgently
FLFCD full-faced
FLGON full-grown
FLHRE fill-horse
FLHUE full house
FLIAE fulminate
FLIAT fulminant
FLIES filminess
FLIFR fill in for
FLIGN falling-in
filling-in
FLIID falsified
FLIIR falsifier
FLILD fulfilled
FLIOM falciform
FLLRC folkloric
FLMRS full marks
FLMSC folk music
FLNOS felonious
FLOES followers
FLOEY fulsomely
FLOIG following
FLOIS Fallopius
FLOOT follow out
FLPDA filopodia
FLPIT full point
FLPNS Filipinos
FLRBE filtrable
FLSAE full-scale
FLSED full-speed
FLSLT full-split
FLSOL faldstool
FLSOT fall short
FLTLS folk tales
folktales
FLUAE fulgurate
FLUDR fold under
FLWAE folk-weave
FMGSA Famagusta
FMGTR fumigator
FMLAT Fomalhaut
FMLDG female dog
FMLMN family man
FMLWY family way
FMNIG fomenting
FMNSS feminists
FMRAE fimbriate
FMSIG famishing
FMTRA fumatoria
FNAAE fanfarade
Fongafale
FNADA Finlandia
FNAET fundament
FNAGE fandangle
FNAGS fandangos
FNAIE fantasise
fantasize
FNAIM Fenianism
FNAIT fantasist
FNASE Fantaisie
FNATC fantastic
FNBIL funebrial
FNCEY finickety
FNCHO finocchio
FNCLR funicular
FNCLY finically
FNEES fenceless
FNEIG fingering
FNELD funnelled
FNEOT fanned out
FNEWB funnel-web
FNFUT find fault
find-fault
FNGEK fenugreek
FNHPD fan-shaped
FNIBE fanciable
FNIES fanciness
funniness
FNIIE fungicide
FNILS fencibles
fungibles
FNLZD finalized
FNNIG financing
FNNIL financial
FNNIR financier
FNOIG fun-loving
FNPIT fine point
FNSIG finishing
FNSOF finish off
FNSRL fenestral
FNTCL fanatical
FNUKD fen-sucked
FNUST fondue set
FNYAA funny ha-ha
FNYAM funny farm
FNYIK fancy-sick
FNYIL Funny Girl
FNYOE funny bone
FNYOK fancywork
FNYRE fancy-free
FOADY frowardly
FOAIN flotation
FOAOT fool about
FOBAE foot brake
FOCAN food chain
FOCAT flow chart
FOCLS flocculus
FOCNL food canal
FOCUT food court
FODAE floodgate
FODAL floodwall
FODIE floodtide
FOEBD flower-bed
flower-bud
FOEIG flowering
FOEPT flowerpot
FOETD floreated
FOFET feoffment
FOFUT footfault
FOHES frothless
FOHRY foolhardy
FOHTI fiochetti
FOIGY flowingly
FOIHR Frobisher
FOIHY foolishly
FOIIY floridity
FOIOM floriform
FOITC floristic
FOITD floriated
FOITY floristry
FOIUA fioritura
FOIUE fioriture
FOKOT frock-coat
FOLOE footloose
FOMRH frogmarch
FOMRS footmarks
FOMUH frogmouth
FONPN frown upon
FONTS footnotes
FONWN from now on
FOPAE footplate
FOPIT footprint
FOPOF foolproof
FOPUD foot-pound
FORHW floor show
FORIE floor tile
FORLN floor plan
FOSAE from space
FOSAK footstalk
FOSAT Froissart
FOSET flow sheet
FOSOL footstool
FOSUF foodstuff
FOTAD frontward
FOTAE front-page
FOTAL frost-nail
FOTAS frontways
FOTBE floatable
FOTES frontless
frostless
FOTGR frontager
FOTIE front line
frontwise
frostbite
frostlike
FOTNO front onto
FOTOK frostwork
FOTOM front room
FOWEE from where
FPIHY foppishly
FRAAM fire alarm
FRADL Fernandel
FRADY forwardly
FRAEA Fortaleza
FRAET firmament
foreanent
FRAHR forgather
FRAIE formalise
formalize
formative
FRAIG forsaking
FRAIM formalism
FRAIN formation
furcation
FRAIT formalist
FRAIY formality
FRAOS farragoes
FRARC fur fabric
FRATR formatter
FRBAD firebrand
FRBAN forebrain
FRBAS forebears
FRBIK firebrick
FRCOE foreclose
FRCOS feracious
ferocious
furacious
FRCTD fore-cited
FRCUT forecourt
FRDIL fire drill
FREAD force-land
FREAK force back
FREBE forgeable
FREED force-feed
FREES forceless
FREET forcemeat
FREFL forgetful
FREIE forgetive
FREIG far-seeing
FREOT ferret out
FREPN force open
FRERF for fear of
FRETD fermented
FRETR fire-eater
forfeiter
Forrester
FRETY fervently
FRFET for effect
FRFOT forefront
FRGAD fireguard
FRGCP forage-cap
FRGFR forage for
FRGIG foregoing
FRHIE for choice
FRHIH forthwith
FRHOE forthcome
FRHRN further on
FRHUE farmhouse
FRIAD Ferdinand
FRIAE forficate
FRIAL Furnivall
FRIAY formicary
FRIDL forbiddal
FRIDN forbidden
FRIES furriness
FRIEY fertilely
furtively
FRIHD furnished

Code	Word
FRIHR	furbisher
FRIID	fortified
FRIIE	fertilise
	fertilize
FRIIG	forgiving
FRIIR	fortifier
FRIIY	fertility
	fervidity
FRINR	foreigner
FRIUE	fortitude
	furniture
FRJDE	forejudge
FRLIS	for all it's
FRLUH	for a laugh
FRMNL	foraminal
FRNGT	fortnight
FRNMD	forenamed
FRNOE	farandole
FROEN	far gone on
FROFE	for toffee
FRONY	forlornly
FROSY	furiously
FROTN	forgotten
FRPAE	fireplace
FRPIT	forepoint
FRPOF	fireproof
	fire-proof
FRPWR	fire-power
FRPYR	fare-payer
FRRAH	forereach
FRRBD	fire-robed
FRRMT	far from it
FRRNS	form ranks
FRRYL	foreroyal
FRSAE	fare stage
	fare-stage
	forestage
FRSAL	forestall
FRSAT	for a start
FRSED	farmstead
	forespend
FRSEK	forespeak
FRSGT	foresight
FRSIE	forestine
FRSIT	foreskirt
FRSOE	Firestone
	foreshore
FRSOM	fire-storm
FRSUH	forasmuch
FRTAD	firsthand
	first-hand
FRTAE	first base
	first name
	first rate
	first-rate
FRTAT	first part
FRTAY	first lady
FRTEH	foreteeth
FRTER	first-year
FRTIE	first time
FRTIK	forethink
FRTKN	foretoken
FRTOE	first move
FRTON	firethorn
	first-born
FRTOT	first-foot
FRTSE	foretaste
FRTTP	first step
FRUAC	formulaic
FRUAE	formulate
	fortunate
FRUAY	formulary
FRUIE	formulise
	formulize
FRUOS	furfurous
FRWMN	forewoman
	forewomen
FRWRH	Fort Worth
FRWRS	fireworks
FRWTR	firewater
	fire-water
FRYAT	for my part
FRYHA	forsythia
FRYIE	forty-five
FRYOT	ferry-boat
FSEIE	fesse-wise
FSEIG	fastening
	festering
	fostering
FSEMN	fisherman
FSGAD	Fishguard
FSIAE	fascinate
	festinate
FSIES	fishiness
	fussiness
	fustiness
FSIEY	festively
FSIIE	fossilise
	fossilize
FSIIM	fastigium
FSIIY	festivity
FSIND	fashioned
FSINR	fashioner
FSITC	fascistic
FSIUE	fascicule
FSIUI	fasciculi
FSLAE	fusillade
FSOIL	fossorial
FSSIE	fish slice
FSTAK	fast-track
FSUOS	fistulous
FTCIE	fetichise
	fetichize
FTDCL	fatidical
FTDES	fetidness
FTEDD	fat-headed
FTEIG	fattening
FTEOT	fitted out
FTFLY	fatefully
FTGBE	fatigable
FTGIG	fatiguing
FTIES	fattiness
FTIGY	fittingly
FTIOS	fatuitous
FTOOT	fathom out
FTOSY	fatuously
FTSIE	fetishise
	fetishize
FTSIM	fetishism
FTSIT	fetishist
FTSOY	fetoscopy
FTSPG	fat as a pig
FTUIE	fettucine
FTUII	fettucini
FUAIY	frugality
FUCRD	flue-cured
FUDES	fluidness
FUDIG	foundling
FUDRD	foundered
FUFUH	four-flush
FUHWY	flush away
FUIIO	Fiumicino
FULEE	feuilleté
FUMXD	flummoxed
FURAH	Feuerbach
FURPR	fluorspar
FURSE	fluoresce
FUSEL	foul smell
FUTAE	fluctuate
	fructuate
	fruitcake
	frustrate
FUTAT	fluctuant
	fruit tart
FUTES	faultless
	fruitless
FUTOS	fructuous
FUTRD	flustered
FUTRR	fruiterer
FVPNE	five pence
FVUIE	favourite
FVUIG	favouring
FWIGY	fawningly
FXDDA	fixed idea
FXDES	fixedness
FXDOK	fixed look
FXEPY	fix deeply
FXIMY	fix firmly
FXPIE	fix a price
FYEDN	Fay Weldon
FYEGT	flyweight
FYGRC	fly agaric
FYNFX	flying fox
FYNJB	flying jib
FYNPN	frying-pan
FYYIE	fly-by-wire
FZIES	fuzziness
FZIIG	Fezziwigg
FZLOT	fizzle out
GAAIA	gravamina
GAAIN	gradation
GAAIS	guaranies
GAALX	gravadlax
GAANT	go against
GAAOE	guacamole
GAATE	guarantee
GAATR	guarantor
GAAUL	Guayaquil
GACOF	glance off
GADAA	grandpapa
GADAE	go and take
GADAL	guardrail
GADDY	grandaddy
	guardedly
GADEL	guard cell
GADES	grandness
GADIG	guard ring
GADLM	grand slam
GADLR	glandular
GADMN	guardsman
GADOE	grandiose
GADOM	guardroom
GADOR	grand tour
GADRX	Grand Prix
GADSN	Grandison
GADUE	grand duke
GADUT	grand-aunt
GAEAA	Guatemala
GAEAD	graveyard
GAEDF	go ahead of
GAEED	Gravesend
GAEES	graceless
	graveless
	graveness
GAEHT	go ape-shit
GAEIE	grapevine
GAELE	glabellae
GAEOE	grace note
GAETR	gnateater
GAFRS	go as far as
GAGID	Gradgrind
GAHCL	graphical
GAHCY	graphicly
GAHMC	graphemic
GAHNC	gnathonic
GAHRS	guacharos
GAHTC	graphitic
GAIAE	gratinate
	gravitate
GAIGY	glaringly
	gratingly
GAIID	gratified
GAIIE	granitise
	granitize
GAIIY	gravidity
GAILS	gladioles
	gladiolus
GAISS	graciosos
GAITR	gladiator
GAIUE	graticule
	gratitude
GALVR	gear-lever
GAMUH	goalmouth
GANEI	Guarnieri
GAOIE	glamorise
	glamorize
GAOOS	glamorous
GAPAS	Grampians
GAPBE	graspable
GAPLI	Grappelli
GARIE	go airside
GARNE	Goa trance

GARTO	gear ratio
GASAD	grassland
GASAE	glassware
	grass-rake
GASES	grassless
GASIE	glasslike
GASIK	gear-stick
GASOE	Gladstone
GASOL	glass wool
GASOT	glasswort
GASUS	glassfuls
GATBE	grantable
GATOE	Giant Pope
GATTR	giant star
GATUE	giant rude
GAUAE	granulate
GAULY	gradually
GAUOA	granuloma
GAWEL	gearwheel
GAYOT	gravy boat
GBATR	Gibraltar
GBEIH	gibberish
GBILE	Gabrielle
GBISS	gubbinses
GBLYP	go belly up
	go belly-up
GBNNS	go bananas
GBOIY	gibbosity
GBOSY	gibbously
GBREK	go berserk
GBRIE	gabardine
	gaberdine
GBTEN	go between
	go-between
GCHOS	go cahoots
GCMIG	go camping
GCOKN	go crook on
GCOKT	go crook at
GDAET	godparent
GDAHR	godfather
GDESY	godlessly
GDIES	giddiness
	godliness
GDOHR	godmother
GDOND	gadrooned
GDTUH	God's truth
GEAIE	grenadine
GEAIR	grenadier
GEBAD	greybeard
GEDLN	Gwendolen
GEFIR	Grey Friar
GEFLY	gleefully
GEGES	greegrees
GEGRY	glengarry
GEHUD	greyhound□
GEIIE	gaelicise
	gaelicize
GEKIT	Greek gift
GEMUD	grey mould
GENAD	green card
	Greenland
GENAE	greengage
GENAH	greenwash
GENAK	greenback
GENAL	greenmail
GENEN	green bean
GENES	greenness
GENET	green belt
GENIH	Greenwich
GENOD	green wood
	greenwood□
GENOM	Green Room
	green room
	greenroom
GENON	greenhorn
GENWY	Greenaway
GENYD	green-eyed
GERLA	guerrilla
GESBE	guessable
GESGN	grease gun
GESNU	Gneisenau
GESOE	gneissose
GESOK	guesswork
GETAE	Great Dane
GETAT	Great Salt
GETCT	Gaeltacht
GETEL	great deal
	Great Seal
GETER	Great Bear
GETES	greatness
GETIE	ghettoise
	ghettoize
GETNS	greetings
GETOT	greatcoat
GETUT	great-aunt
GEVLE	Grenville
GEWAE	grey whale
GFAIG	guffawing
GFRAD	go forward
GFSIG	go fishing
GFTKN	gift token
GGLBX	goggle-box
GGNIM	gigantism
GGTIG	go-getting
GHRBT	go hard but
GHYIE	go haywire
GIAIT	guitarist
GIAKN	grimalkin
GIALE	grisaille
GIAOE	go it alone
GIDAL	guildhall
GIDOD	Guildford
GIDON	grind down
GIDVL	grindhval
GIEAH	glide path
GIEEE	Guinevere
GIEES	guileless
GIEHN	guinea hen
GIEIE	guideline
GIEOK	guidebook
GIEOT	guidepost
GIEPG	guinea pig
GIFHT	grief-shot
GIFLY	gainfully
GIFOT	go in front
GIGON	going down
	going-down
GIGVR	going-over
GIGWL	going AWOL
GIGWY	going away
GIIES	griminess
GIIGY	glidingly
	gripingly
GILCE	guilloche
GILIE	Ghislaine
GILIH	go ill with
GILMT	guillemot
GILTN	Guillotin
GISEL	Gaitskell
GISNI	glissandi
GISNO	glissando
GISYR	gainsayer
GITES	guiltless
GIVFR	grieve for
GIVNE	grievance
GIZIG	grizzling
GLAAE	gilravage
GLABY	Galway Bay
GLAER	Golda Meir
GLAIE	galvanise
	galvanize
GLAIM	galvanism
GLATY	gallantly
	gallantry
GLBIK	gold brick
GLCAT	Gold Coast
GLCET	goldcrest
GLCOE	galactose
GLCON	gold crown
GLEAE	golden age
GLEEE	GoldenEye
	golden-eye
GLEGD	gilt-edged
GLEID	galleried
GLEIS	galleries
GLEPE	Gillespie
GLERD	goldenrod
GLETN	Galveston
GLFED	goldfield
GLFIT	gillflirt
GLFNH	goldfinch
GLGIE	gelignite
GLIAT	gallivant
GLIGY	gallingly
GLIIE	Gallicise
	Gallicize
	gallisise
	gallisize
GLLNS	golf links
GLMDL	gold medal
GLNHS	galanthus
GLNIE	galantine
GLOAE	gallonage
	gallopade
GLOHL	Gallophil
GLOIG	galloping
GLOSS	gallowses
GLPAE	gold plate
	gold-plate
GLPGS	galapagos
	Galápagos
GLPIT	gold point
GLRIH	Galbraith
GLSIH	goldsmith□
GLSOE	gallstone
GLTAS	Galatians
GLWTR	Goldwater
GMAAS	gamma rays
GMAIM	gymnasium
GMAIN	gammadion
	gemmation
	gymnasien
GMAOS	gambadoes
GMATC	gymnastic
GMBRS	game birds
GMCIS	game chips
GMHED	gumshield
GMHSS	gomphoses
GMIES	gumminess
GMIKY	gimmickry
GMPIT	game point
GMSIG	go missing
GMTIH	gemütlich
GNAAE	Genoa cake
GNAIE	genialise
	genialize
GNAIY	geniality
GNAMS	gendarmes
GNAOY	genealogy
GNCCI	gonococci
GNCDL	genocidal
GNEAE	ginger ale
GNEIM	gynaecium
	gynoecium
GNELY	genteelly
GNENT	ginger nut
GNEOS	gingerous
GNFET	genuflect
GNGOE	gone goose
GNIEY	genuinely
GNIIE	gentilise
	gentilize
GNIIY	gentility
GNITR	gannister
GNKLY	Gene Kelly
GNLMN	gentleman
GNLMS	ginglymus
GNLOS	ganglions
GNODR	gunpowder
GNOIR	gondolier
GNPAK	gangplank
GNPNH	gang-punch
GNRLA	generalia
GNRLY	generally
GNROS	ginormous
GNRTR	generator
GNTCL	genetical
GNTLA	genitalia
GNTPC	genotypic
GNTVL	genitival
GNUDR	gone under
GNUNR	gunrunner

Code	Word
GNVEE	Genevieve
GNWOG	gone wrong
GOADN	go on and on
GOADR	goosander
GOAGY	grow angry
GOAIE	globalise
	globalize
GOAIT	go on a diet
GOAOG	Goolagong
GOCER	good cheer
GOCIY	grouchily
GOEAE	glomerate
GOEBG	go over big
GOEIE	globelike
GOEIG	glowering
GOEIS	groceries
GOEIT	geodesist
GOELR	groveller
GOEOT	goosefoot
GOEQE	grotesque
GOERC	geometric
GOERT	globe-trot
GOETP	goose-step
GOEUI	glomeruli
GOEVR	gloze over
GOEWY	go one's way
GOFCD	goodfaced
GOFIH	go off with
GOGAA	Georgiana
GOGAN	grosgrain
GOGFX	George Fox
GOGIF	good grief
GOGOE	Giorgione
GOGTE	georgette□
GOIES	goodiness
GOIGN	Groningen
GOIGP	growing up
GOIGY	glowingly
	gropingly
GOLGT	grow light
GOLOS	good looks
GOMMN	groomsman
GOMRE	Gros Morne
GONGT	goodnight
GONHG	groundhog
GONIG	grounding
GONIY	ground ivy
GONNT	groundnut
GONSL	groundsel
GOOIE	geologise
	geologize
GOOIS	geoponics
GOOIT	geologist
GOOSI	Grotowski
GOOTF	grow out of
GOOYU	good on you
GOPAE	groupware
GOPEE	geosphere
GOPES	good press
GOPIT	good point
	gros point
GORPC	geotropic
GORPY	geography
GOSAE	good shape
GOSES	grossness
GOSIH	Grossmith
GOSNE	good sense
GOSTR	glossator
GOSVR	gloss over
GOTDS	glottides
GOTIE	ghostlike
GOTIG	good thing
GOTIH	go out with
GOTOD	ghost word
GOTON	ghost town
GOTRD	grow tired
GOTRS	good terms
GOTSE	good taste
GOTSS	glottises
GOTSY	go on to say
GOVLE	good value
GOWIE	grow white
GOYAS	goodyears
GOYES	gooeyness
GOYOE	glory hole
GQIKY	go quickly
GRACN	gerfalcon
	gyrfalcon
GRADE	Gerhardie
GRAEY	germanely
GRAHV	Gorbachev
GRAIE	gargarise
	gargarize
	Germanice
	Germanise
	Germanize
GRAIM	germanium
GRARC	geriatric
GRAZS	garbanzos
GRBLI	garibaldi□
GRCAY	Girl Crazy
GRCUT	Géricault
GREIG	gardening
GREOE	garderobe
GRGIE	Girl Guide
GRIAE	germinate
GRIHE	garnishee
GRIHY	garnishry
	girlishly
GRIIE	germicide
GRIUE	garniture
GRLIE	Geraldine
GRLMY	gorblimey
GRNIE	gerundive
GRNIL	gerundial
GRNNK	Guru Nanak
GRNOA	girandola
GRNOE	girandole
GROEA	gorgoneia
GROIE	gorgonise
	gorgonize
GROOY	garbology
GROTR	garrotter
GRSOE	gyroscope
GRUDO	go round to
GRUIY	garrulity
GRUKL	Garfunkel
GRUOS	garrulous
GRVDL	Gore Vidal
GRVGE	gyrovague
GRYWN	garryowen
GSAEY	gossamery
GSAIE	gustative
GSAIN	gestation
	gustation
GSAOY	gustatory
GSATE	gas mantle
GSEIE	gospelise
	gospelize
GSFRS	go so far as
GSIES	gassiness
	gustiness
GSIGY	gaspingly
	gushingly
GSIIG	gossiping
GSIPR	gossipper
GSLWS	go so low as
GSMTR	gasometer
GSOAE	gasconade
GSOGE	Gascoigne
GSOIM	gasconism
GSOOY	gismology
GSRPD	gastropod
GSRTS	gastritis
GSUET	gesture at
GTADE	get laldie
GTAGT	get caught
GTAHD	get washed
GTAIE	Gothamite
GTAIN	guttation
GTAKO	get back to
GTAKT	get back at
GTCAH	gatecrash
GTCOS	get across
GTCUT	go to court
GTEAE	go the pace
GTEID	get behind
GTEIG	gathering
	guttering
GTEMN	gutter-man
GTERH	go to earth
GTETR	get better
GTEWY	gather way
GTGAS	go to grass
GTHAE	get the axe
GTHTF	get shot of
GTHUE	gatehouse
GTIDF	get wind of
GTIEO	get wise to
GTIES	gutsiness
GTIGN	getting on
GTIGR	get bigger
GTIHR	get higher
GTIHT	get with it
GTIIE	gothicise
	gothicize
GTISD	get pissed
GTMNY	gate money
	gate-money
GTNEG	Gutenberg
GTNEL	get on well
GTNIH	get in with
	get on with
GTODF	get hold of
GTODR	get colder
GTONO	get down to
GTONW	get to know
GTPES	go to press
GTRUD	get around
GTRUH	go through
GTSDO	get used to
GTSED	Gateshead
GTSEP	go to sleep
GTTBE	get-at-able
GTTWR	gate-tower
GTWRS	go towards
GTWSE	go to waste
GUAAE	glutamate
GUAAL	go up a wall
GUAIE	glutamine
GUBET	grumble at
GUBIG	grumbling
GUDIM	Grundyism
GUEAD	Grünewald
GUEBE	gaugeable
GUEOS	glutenous
GUETR	gauleiter
GUFES	gruffness
GUHRE	gaucherie
GUIES	gaudiness
	gauziness
	goutiness
GUIOS	glutinous
GULIG	gruelling
GUOIE	glucoside
GUPTI	gruppetti
GUSRW	grub screw
GUTES	gauntness
GUYES	glueyness
GVAAD	give a hand
GVAAK	give a back
	give a talk
GVAAN	give a damn
GVAED	give a lead
GVAEL	give a bell
GVAIE	give a ride
GVAIK	give a kick
GVAIS	give a miss
GVAIT	give a lift
GVANE	give a knee
GVAUZ	give a buzz
GVBRH	give birth
GVCAE	give chase
GVFRH	give forth
GVIAO	give it a go
GVLAE	give leave
GVMNY	give money
GVNAE	given name
GVNOF	giving-off
GVNOT	giving-out
GVNWY	giving way
GVPAE	give place

Words marked □ can also be spelled with an initial capital letter

Code	Word
GVPUE	give pause
GVRES	governess
GVRIG	governing
GVROS	governors
GVTEK	give the OK
GVWYO	give way to
GWIES	gawkiness
GWITE	go whistle
GWLIG	go wilding
GWTOT	go without
GYAKS	Guy Fawkes
GYEIE	glyceride
	glycerine
GYISN	Guy Gibson
GYOIE	glycoside
GZAHS	gazpachos
GZATP	Gaziantep
GZOOY	gizmology
GZTER	gazetteer
HABAD	headboard
HACUT	head count
HADAH	heat death
HADES	headdress
HAFOT	hoar-frost
HAFRT	head first
HAIES	headiness
	heaviness
	hoariness
HAIGP	heading up
HAIGY	healingly
HAIIE	Heaviside
	hyalinise
	hyalinize
HALGT	headlight
HALNR	headliner
HARAH	headreach
HASAF	headscarf
HASAL	headstall
HASAT	head start
HASOE	headstone
HASOK	headstock
HATAD	heartland
HATCE	heartache
HATER	heart-dear
HATES	heartless
HATET	heartbeat
	heartfelt
	heart-felt
HATFL	healthful
HATIG	heartling
HATIK	heartsick
HATIR	healthier
HATIY	healthily
HATOD	heartwood
HATOE	heart-sore
HATUN	heartburn
HAVIE	head voice
HAYPR	heavy spar
HAYUY	heavy-duty
HAYYD	heavy-eyed
HBALD	hobnailed
HBIEN	Hebridean
HBIIE	hybridise
	hybridize
HBIIM	hybridism
HBIIY	hybridity
HBIOA	hybridoma
HBITC	hubristic
HBKSA	hibakusha
HBOLN	hobgoblin
HBRAE	hibernate
HBRIE	hibernise
	hibernize
HBRIN	Hibernian
HBTAE	habituate
HBTBE	habitable
HBTBY	habitably
HCAAK	huckaback
HCAOE	hackamore
HCEOF	hacked off
HCIIH	Ho Chi Minh
HCNYD	hackneyed
HCORM	hectogram
HDAGA	hydrangea
HDAHR	had rather
HDAIN	hydration
HDALC	hydraulic
HDBUD	hidebound
	hide-bound
HDETR	had better
HDGAH	hodograph
HDIFR	had liefer
HDIVR	had liever
HDMTR	hodometer
HDOAR	Hadrosaur
HDOBY	Hudson Bay
HDOEE	hydrocele
HDOIE	hydroxide
HDOOL	hydrofoil
HDOON	hydrozoan
HDOOY	hydrology
HDOSY	hideously
HDOTT	hydrostat
HDOYE	hydrolyse
	hydrolyte
	hydrolyze
HDPAE	hedyphane
HDRBD	Hyderabad
HDYSI	Hideyoshi
HEACY	hierarchy
HEAIE	haematite
HEAOA	haematoma
HECIY	haecceity
HEFLF	heedful of
HEFLY	heedfully
HENCY	hue and cry
HEOTT	haemostat
HEOYE	haemocyte
HFIES	heftiness
	huffiness
HFIHY	huffishly
HGADY	haggardly
HGATR	high altar
HGBOS	highbrows
HGBRH	high birth
HGCAR	high-chair
HGCAS	high-class
HGCPT	Hugo Capet
HGCUT	High Court
	high court
HGEIS	hygienics
HGEIT	hygienist
HGFIR	high-flier
HGFON	high-flown
HGFYR	high flyer
	high-flyer
HGGAE	high-grade
HGGAT	Hugh Grant
HGGON	high-grown
HGIDN	hag-ridden
HGIHY	haggishly
	hoggishly
HGJNS	high jinks
HGLGT	highlight
HGLVL	high-level
HGMNO	Hugh Munro
HGOOY	hagiology
	hygrology
HGOTT	hygrostat
HGPIT	high point
HGSED	high-speed
HGSIH	Highsmith
HGTBE	high table
HGTND	high-toned
HGVCD	high-viced
HGWRS	high words
HGWTR	high water
HHEAN	Hahnemann
HIBUH	hairbrush
HICOH	haircloth
HIDIR	hairdrier
HIDYR	hairdryer
HIEGR	Heidegger
HIIES	hairiness
HIOLI	hoi polloi
HIOSY	heinously
HIPEE	hairpiece
	hair-piece
HISIT	hair shirt
HISOM	hailstorm
HISRY	hairspray
HISYE	hairstyle
HJCIG	hijacking
HLAAE	half-awake
HLAAL	hold a call
HLABY	hold at bay
HLBAK	hell-black
HLBBE	Holy Bible
HLBED	half-breed
HLBID	half-blind
HLBKD	half-baked
HLBLY	hillbilly
HLBOD	half-blood
HLBOH	hell-broth
HLCEK	half-cheek
HLCLY	helically
HLCOE	hold close
HLCON	half-crown
HLCOS	half-cross
HLCSE	half-caste
HLCUL	holy-cruel
HLCUT	hold court
	holocaust
HLDUK	half-drunk
HLDZN	half-dozen
HLEIE	Hellenise
	Hellenize
HLEIH	Hollerith
HLEIM	Hellenism
HLEIN	Helvetian
HLEIT	Hellenist
HLELN	Helvellyn
	Hölderlin
HLEOE	hellebore
HLETC	halieutic
HLFCD	half-faced
HLFED	Holyfield
HLFLY	helpfully
HLFRH	hold forth
HLGAH	holograph
HLHLZ	Helmholtz
HLHNS	hold hands
HLHRY	half-hardy
HLHTD	hell-hated
HLHTH	half hitch
	half-hitch
HLHUD	hellhound
HLIES	hilliness
HLIGY	haltingly
HLIHY	hellishly
HLIOE	hole in one
HLLGT	half-light
HLLNS	halflings
HLMRS	hallmarks
HLNHD	Holinshed
HLOEN	Hallowe'en
HLOIG	hallowing
HLOOT	hollow out
HLOTN	hold out on
HLOTT	heliostat
HLOYE	heliotype
HLOYY	heliotypy
HLPAE	half-plate
	holy place
HLPIE	half-price
	halophile
HLPNE	halfpence
HLPNY	halfpenny
HLPYE	holophyte
HLROS	hilarious
HLSAD	hallstand
HLSAT	Hallstatt
HLSIT	hula skirt
HLSOE	holystone
HLTAK	half-track
HLTGT	hold tight
HLTSS	halitosis
HLTTE	half-title
HLTUH	half-truth
HLWRS	hellwards
HLWTR	hold water
	holy water

HLYOD	Hollywood
HLYOK	hollyhock
HMADD	ham-handed
HMAOE	Home Alone
HMATR	hamfatter
HMBYR	homebuyer
HMCAE	humectate
HMCAT	homecraft
	humectant
HMCDL	homicidal
HMDES	humidness
HMDYD	hamadryad
HMEIG	hammering
	hampering
HMEOT	hammer out
HMETE	hammer-toe
HMGAD	home guard
HMGAH	homograph
HMGON	home-grown
HMIGR	humdinger
HMITD	ham-fisted
HMLAE	humiliate
HMLAT	humiliant
HMLBE	humble-bee
HMLGE	homologue
HMLPE	humble pie
HMLTC	homiletic
HMLYS	Himalayas
HMMRH	homomorph
HMMVE	home movie
HMNAE	human race
HMNES	humanness
HMNHW	hem and haw
	hum and haw
HMNID	humankind
HMNIE	human life
HMNOM	human form
HMNOS	humongous
	humungous
HMNUE	homuncule
HMNUI	homunculi
HMNWY	Hemingway
HMOAH	homeopath
HMOGD	home of God
HMOIT	hymnodist
HMONR	home-owner
HMOOY	hymnology
HMPAE	home plate
HMPOE	homophobe
	homophone
HMPOY	homophony
HMRLY	humorally
HMSED	homestead
HMSIE	Hampshire
HMTDO	Humpty Doo
HMTIG	hamstring
HMTTH	hem-stitch
HMTUG	hamstrung
HMTUH	home truth
HMUAI	Hammurabi
HMUGR	hamburger
HMUIG	humouring
HMVDO	home video
HMWRS	homewards
HNAET	hang a left
HNAIN	Hungarian
HNAOT	hang about
HNARN	Hank Aaron
HNATR	hunt after
HNBAE	handbrake
HNBAN	hindbrain
HNBTE	Hans Bethe
HNCAT	handcraft
HNCFS	handcuffs
HNEED	hinder end
HNEFR	hanker for
	hunger for
HNEIG	hankering
	hindering
	hungering
HNEIH	Hindemith
HNEKD	henpecked
HNEKR	henpecker
HNESN	hangers-on
	Henderson
HNGIE	hang-glide
HNHAK	hunchback
HNIDS	hendiadys
HNIES	handiness
HNIGY	hintingly
HNIOK	handiwork
HNITA	Henrietta
HNKES	Hans Krebs
HNLOE	hang loose
HNOCB	hansom-cab
HNOGD	hand of God
HNOGN	hand organ
HNOTT	hang out at
HNRDH	hundredth
HNRFC	honorific
HNRNE	hindrance
HNRRA	honoraria
HNRUD	hand round
HNSAD	handstand
HNSAE	handshake
HNSCS	Hans Sachs
HNSGT	hindsight
HNSIE	handspike
HNSON	hands down
HNSUN	hand's turn
HNTUH	hang tough
HNUIG	honouring
HNUUH	Hindu Kush
HNYAE	Henry Tate
HNYHN	Honeyghan
HNYII	Henry VIII
HNYOB	honeycomb
HNYOD	Henry Ford
	Henry Wood
HNYOK	honky-tonk
HNYON	honeymoon
HNYOY	hunky-dory
HODOE	hyoid bone
HOEDM	Hoover Dam
HONNY	hootnanny
HPAAD	haphazard
HPACY	heptarchy
HPBAT	hypoblast
HPCIE	hypocrite
HPCIY	hypocrisy
HPCTH	hopscotch
HPCUT	hypocaust
HPDRA	hypoderma
HPEAE	hyphenate
HPEIE	hyphenise
	hyphenize
HPEIG	happening
HPESY	haplessly
HPFLY	hopefully
HPIES	happiness
HPLAE	hypallage
HPNSY	hyponasty
HPODL	hypnoidal
HPOIE	hypnotise
	hypnotize
HPOIM	hypnotism
HPOIT	hypnotist
HPOOY	haplology
	hypnology
HPOYA	Hippolyta
HPRET	hypertext
HPRIK	hyperlink
HPROA	hyperbola
HPROE	hyperbole
HPSYE	hypostyle
HPTNA	hypotonia
HPTNC	hypotonic
HPTTS	hepatitis
HPYOR	happy hour
HRAIE	hortative
HRAIM	herbalism
	herbarium
HRAIN	hortation
HRAIT	herbalist
HRANT	Hardaknut
HRAOT	hereabout
HRAOY	hortatory
HRATA	herbal tea
HRATN	harmattan
HRATR	hereafter
HRBAD	hardboard
HRCAE	Hart Crane
HRCUT	hard court
HRDTS	Herodotus
HREAK	horseback
HREAL	horsetail
HREAR	horsehair
HREHE	horseshoe
HREHP	horsewhip
HREIG	hardening
HREIS	hermetics
HRELE	Harper Lee
HRELY	horseplay
HREOF	harden off
HRESO	Hortensio
HRETR	harvester
HREUN	harlequin
HRFLO	harmful to
HRFLY	harmfully
	hurtfully
HRHES	harshness
HRIAE	hermitage□
	heroic age
	hurricane□
HRIDY	hurriedly
HRIES	hardiness
	horniness
	horsiness
HRIGR	harbinger
HRIID	horrified
HRIIE	herbicide
HRIOD	hardihood
HRIOE	herbivore
HRIOY	herbivory
HRITD	herniated
HRKIN	Heraklion
HRLAY	hardly any
HRLGC	horologic
HRLGR	horologer
HRLLI	hors la loi
HRLNR	hardliner
HRLNS	hard lines
HRMKR	horn-maker
HRMNY	hard money
HRNSD	hard-nosed
HRNUR	haranguer
HROAE	hariolate
	Harrogate
HROAX	Harpo Marx
HROIA	harmonica
HROIE	harmonise
	harmonize
	herborise
	herborize
HROIG	harrowing
HROIM	harmonium
HROIS	harmonics
	harmonies
HROIT	harmonist
HRONR	harpooner
HRPRS	herb-Paris
HRRLD	hard-ruled
HRSIA	Hiroshima
HRSIG	harassing
HRSIY	haruspicy
HRSOE	horoscope
HRSON	hartshorn
HRSOY	horoscopy
HRSUF	hard stuff
HRTBE	heritable
HRTBY	heritably
HRTCL	heretical
HRTES	heritress
HRTMS	Hard Times
	hard times
HRTNE	heritance
HRUBS	harquebus
HRUDR	hereunder
HRUEN	herculean□
HRWAE	here we are
HRWET	hard wheat
HRWRD	hard-wired

Words marked □ can also be spelled with an initial capital letter

Code	Entry
HSADY	husbandly
	husbandry
HSAIE	histamine
HSEEE	Haslemere
HSEIG	hastening
HSEIN	Hesperian
HSEIS	hysterics
HSELR	hosteller
HSIAT	hestitant
HSIEO	hostile to
HSIES	hastiness
	huskiness
HSIEY	hostilely
HSIGY	hissingly
HSIIE	histidine
HSIIY	hispidity
	hostility
HSLIE	Heseltine
HSMNY	hush money
HSOEY	histogeny
HSOIN	historian
HSOIY	historify
HSOOY	histology
HSORM	histogram
HSRBL	Hasdrubal
HSTNE	hesitance
HSTNY	hesitancy
HTAAE	hit parade
HTAKT	hit back at
HTEDD	hotheaded
	hot-headed
HTEIE	Hitlerite
HTEIM	Hitlerism
HTEIT	Hitlerist
HTETT	Hottentot
HTFLY	hatefully
HTHAK	hatchback
HTHET	hatchment
HTHHY	hit the hay
HTHIE	hitch-hike
HTHOK	Hitchcock
HTIKT	hit wicket
HTNRN	hit-and-run
HTOAO	hot potato
HTOFO	hats off to
HTOSX	hit for six
HTOTM	hit bottom
HTOTT	hotfoot it
HTPIG	hot spring
HTRDX	heterodox
HTRIS	hit or miss
	hit-or-miss
HTRNM	heteronym
HUEAD	housemaid
HUEHE	houseshoe
HUEIE	housewife
	house wine
HUEOD	household
HUEOK	housework
HUEOM	houseroom
HUEOT	houseboat
	housecoat
HUEUS	housefuls
HUEUT	house-hunt
HUGAS	hourglass
HUHIY	haughtily
HUITC	heuristic
HURUD	haul round
HUTLA	haustella
HUTRA	haustoria
HVAAE	have a care
HVAAH	have a bash
	have a bath
	have a wash
HVAAL	have a ball
HVAET	have a rest
HVAHM	have-at-him
HVAHT	have a shit
	have a shot
HVAID	have a mind
HVAON	have a loan
HVAOT	have a go at
HVATB	have a stab
HVBIG	have being
HVCOT	have clout
HVCUE	have cause
HVFIH	have faith
HVGTO	have got to
HVHDT	have had it
HVIBD	have it bad
HVIES	have ideas
HVIOT	have it out
HVITW	have in tow
HVPAE	have place
HVRAK	haversack
HVRIE	haversine
HVROT	hoverport
HVRUD	have round
HVWRS	have words
	hivewards
HWEIE	hawsepipe
HWEOE	hawsehole
HWHNE	how chance?
HWHRE	Hawthorne
HWIHY	hawkishly
HWOVR	howsoever
HWRYU	how are you?
HWSIL	hawksbill
HWSOR	Hawksmoor
HWYUO	how-d'you-do
HXCOD	hexachord
HXGNL	hexagonal
HXHDA	hexahedra
HXMTR	hexameter
HXSYE	hexastyle
HXTUH	Hexateuch
HYAIG	haymaking
HYEIH	hoydenish
HYEIM	hoydenism
HYRAL	Heyerdahl
HYRSO	hey-presto
HYTCS	Haystacks
HZLOD	Hazelwood
HZROS	hazardous
IAAHR	in a lather
IAANR	in a manner
IAAWY	in a bad way
IABNN	Ivan Bunin
IACAE	in a scrape
IACBE	irascible
IACBY	irascibly
IADBE	inaidable
	inaudible
IADBY	inaudibly
IAEES	inaneness
IAEPR	in a temper
IAEUE	image tube
IAFRS	in as far as
IAGIH	in anguish
IAGRL	inaugural
IAIAE	inanimate
IAIAY	imaginary
IAIHR	in a dither
IAIIE	italicise
	italicize
IAIIG	imagining
IAIIN	inanition
IAIIY	inability
IAIUE	in a minute
IAIWY	in a big way
IALNL	Ivan Lendl
IAOAA	inamorata
IAOAO	inamorato
IAOET	in a moment
IAONR	in a corner
IAOUN	in a column
IARAS	in arrears
IARNY	in a frenzy
IATES	inaptness
IAVNE	in advance
IAYAD	in any hand
IAYAE	in any case
IBCLC	imbecilic
IBDAT	in bad part
IBETE	inbreathe
IBIAE	imbricate
IBLAT	in ballast
IBLNE	imbalance
IBNAE	in bondage
IBOLO	imbroglio
IBTEN	in-between
ICAMA	ischaemia
ICBTR	incubator
ICDNE	incidence
ICEET	inclement
	increment
ICESD	increased
ICGIO	incognito
ICHOS	in cahoots
ICIES	itchiness
ICIIG	inclining
ICLAE	inculcate
	inculpate
ICMAD	in command
ICMAY	in company
ICMET	incumbent
ICMOE	incommode
ICMTX	income tax
ICNET	in concert
ICNIE	incentive
ICNOT	in consort
ICNRL	in control
ICOUE	inclosure
ICPBE	incapable
ICPBY	incapably
ICPET	incipient
ICPIE	inceptive
ICPIN	inception
ICRAE	incarnate
	incurvate
ICRBE	incurable
ICRBY	incurably
ICRET	incorrect
ICRIE	incursive
ICRIN	incursion
ICROS	incurious
ICRUT	incorrupt
ICSAT	incessant
ICSOY	in custody
ICUCL	in council
ICUEN	include in
ICUIE	inclusive
ICUIG	including
ICUIN	incaution
	inclusion
IDAGT	indraught
IDAIE	Indianise
	Indianize
IDAIG	in drawing
IDAIK	Indian ink
IDARD	Indian red
IDCBE	inducible
IDCIE	inductive
IDCIN	indiction
	induction
IDCNY	indecency
IDCRM	indecorum
IDCTD	indicated
IDCTR	indicator
IDEIE	in due time
IDGAT	indignant
IDGIY	indignity
IDGNE	indigence
IDLBE	indelible
IDLBY	indelibly
IDLEN	indulge in
IDLET	indulgent
IDLNE	indolence
IDMIY	indemnify
	indemnity
IDMNA	indumenta
IDNIN	indention
IDNSA	Indonesia
IDNUE	indenture
IDSOE	indispose
IDSUE	in dispute
IDSUT	in disgust
IDXIK	index-link
IEADC	Icelandic
IEADR	Icelander
IEAIE	iterative
IEAIN	iteration

IEATC inelastic
IEATY inexactly
IEEAT inelegant
IEEDD I never did!
IEFBE ineffable
IEFBY ineffably
IEGAH ideograph
IEIOE in epitome
IEKTR ice-skater
IELGE ideologue
IELOE Ideal Home
IELZD idealized
IELZR idealizer
IEOKY ice hockey
ice-hockey
IERAE inebriate
IERAT inebriant
IERBY inerrably
IERET in earnest
IEREY inebriety
IERNY inerrancy
IESNE in essence
IESOY ileostomy
IETCL identical
IETES ineptness
inertness
IETKT identikit□
IEUKT ice bucket
IFAIG inflaming
IFAIN inflation
IFATR infractor
IFCIE infective
IFCIN infection
IFEDR infielder
IFEIN inflexion
IFIGR infringer
IFITR inflicter
inflictor
IFLCY in full cry
IFLRG in full rig
IFNIE infantile
IFOIG inflowing
IFOTF in front of
IFRAE infuriate
IFRAT informant
IFRAY infirmary
IFRBE inferable
IFRIE infertile
IFRIG informing
IFRIY infirmity
IFRNE inference
IFSBE infusible
IFSIN in fashion
IFTAE infatuate
IFUNA influenza
IFUNE influence
IGAEY ingrately
IGAND ingrained
IGEOK inglenook
IGNIY ingenuity
IGNOS ingenious
ingenuous
IGNRL in general
IGOIG ingrowing
IGSIN ingestion
IHBTD inhabited
inhibited
IHBTR inhibiter
inhibitor
IHEMN ichneumon
IHHOD ichthyoid
IHMNY inhumanly
IHRES in harness
IHROD Isherwood
IHROY in harmony
IHRTD inherited
IHRTR inheritor
IIAIE imitative
IIAIG imitating
IIAIN imitation
IIALP it is all up
IIBNS Iain Banks
IIEAE itinerate
IIEAT itinerant
IIEAY itinerary
IIGAS isinglass
IIHOS Irish moss
IIHPD it is hoped
IIHTW Irish stew
IIILY initially
IIITR initiator
IILAT in ill part
IIMTC idiomatic
IINAA Irian Jaya
IJCIN injection
IJROS injurious
IJSIE injustice
IKEIG in keeping
IKOEY irksomely
ILAUE ill nature
ILBAT idle boast
ILBRL illiberal
ILCTY illicitly
ILDWY idled away
ILELH ill health
ill-health
ILEPR ill temper
ill-temper
ILFNY idle fancy
ILGBE illegible
ILGBY illegibly
ILGCL illogical
ILGLY illegally
ILHNE ill-chance
ILHSN ill-chosen
ILIHR ill-wisher
ILITD ill-fitted
ILMBD Islamabad
ILMND ill-omened
ILMTD illimited
ILNTN Islington
ILOMN Isle of Man
ILOTN ill-gotten
ILTAE ill at ease
ILUGD ill-judged
ILUOR ill-humour
ILUTD ill-suited
ILWEL idle wheel
IMDAE immediate
IMDAY immediacy
IMDSY immodesty
IMGAE immigrate
IMGAT immigrant
IMIIA Ismailiya
IMLTR immolator
IMNEY immensely
IMNHM Immingham
IMNIY immensity
IMNNE immanence
imminence
IMNNY immanency
IMRIN immersion
IMRLY immorally
IMTBE immutable
IMTBY immutably
IMVBE immovable
IMVBY immovably
IMVIE in my voice
INASA Ionian Sea
INBUK Innsbruck
INCNE innocence
INCOD ionic bond
INCOS innocuous
INCWN Ian McEwan
INEDS innuendos
INEPR innkeeper
INILP Ian Hislop
INMES in numbers
INNIE ion engine
INODR innholder
INOHM Ian Botham
INRAE innervate
INRAL inner wall
INREF inner self
INRGT Ian Wright
INRIY inner city
inner-city
INRMS ignoramus
INRNE ignorance
INROT innermost
INRUE inner tube
INTBE ignitable
ignitible
INVTR innovator
INWHT I know what
IOAIG isolating
IOAIN isolation
IOCLS isosceles
IODRO in order to
IOEIE isomerise
isomerize
IOERC isometric
IOGNC inorganic
IOIIG idolizing
IOLNL isoclinal
IOLUE I could use
IOOOY iconology
IORPC isotropic
IORTC isocratic
IOSOE ironstone
IOTNW I don't know
IOUAE inoculate
IOUIN Iroquoian
IOYLC isocyclic
IPAEF in place of
IPATD implanted
IPCIN impaction
IPDNE impedance
impudence
IPEAE imprecate
IPEAI impresari
IPEET implement
IPEIE imprecise
IPESD impressed
IPIAE implicate
in private
IPIAY in privacy
IPIDY impliedly
IPIIG impairing
IPITF in point of
IPLET impellent
IPLIE impulsive
IPLIN impulsion
IPLTC impolitic
IPNIG impending
impinging
IPOEN improve on
IPOIE implosive
improvise
IPOIG imploring
improving
IPOIN implosion
IPOIY improbity
IPOPU impromptu
IPOSY impiously
IPRAT important
IPRET imperfect
IPRIG imparting
IPRIL impartial
IPROS imperious
IPRTR imperator
IPRUE importune
IPSDN imposed on
IPSIE impassive
IPSIG in passing
IPSIN impassion
IPSOD impastoed
IPSUE impostume
imposture
IPTAE impetrate
IPTBE imputable
IPTBY imputably
IPTCS impeticos
IPTES impatiens
IPTET impatient
IPTGS impetigos
IPTNE impotence
IPTOS impetuous
IPTSS impetuses
IPUDD impounded
IPUDR impounder
IPUET imprudent

Words marked □ can also be spelled with an initial capital letter

IPVDY impavidly
IPVRY in poverty
IQIAE inquinate
IQIIG inquiring
IQIIS inquiries
IQITY inquietly
IQOAE inquorate
IRAIY in reality
IRBOS in ribbons
IRDAE irradiate
IRDAT irradiant
IREIE Israelite
IRGBE irrigable
IRGLR irregular
IRGTF in right of
IRNHN Imran Khan
IRPIE irruptive
IRPIN irruption
IRPOT in rapport
IRSIG inrushing
IRSRE in reserve
IRTBE irritable
IRTBY irritably
IRTTD irritated
IRWDY Irrawaddy
ISACD instanced
ISALH inshallah
ISATY instantly
ISBTY itsy-bitsy
ISDOS insidious
ISDOT inside out
ISDXT ipse dixit
ISEDF instead of
ISETE insheathe
ISETR inshelter
inspector
ISFCO ipso facto
ISFRS in so far as
insofar as
ISGNS Issigonis
ISIAE instigate
ISIEF in spite of
ISIGR inswinger
ISIIG inspiring
ISIUE institute
ISLBE insoluble
ISLBY insolubly
ISLEG inselberg
ISLET insolvent
ISLIG insulting
ISLNE insolence
ISLRY insularly
ISLTD insulated
ISLTR insulator
ISMIC insomniac
ISMWY in some way
ISNAE insensate
insinuate
ISNAS ifs and ans
ISNEE insincere
ISPDY insipidly
ISRBE insurable
ISRBR inscriber
ISRET insurgent
ISRIE in service
in-service
ISRIN insertion
ISRNE insurance
ISSET insistent
ISSIN in session
ISTEY insatiety
ISVRL in several
ITAST in transit
ITEAK in the dark
ITEAN in the main
ITEAS in the mass
ITEAT in the cart
in the past
ITEED in the lead
ITEER in the rear
ITEHT in the shit
ITEID in the mind
in the wind
ITEIK in the pink
ITELB in the club
ITENW in the know
ITEOD in the road
ITEOP in the soup
ITEPN in the open
ITEUE in the nude
ITEUF in the buff
ITEUP in the lump
ITEWM in the swim
ITGAD integrand
ITGAE integrate
ITGIS intaglios
ITGIY integrity
ITIAE intricate
ITIAT intrigant
ITIAY intricacy
ITIIE intuitive
ITIIN intuition
ITISC intrinsic
ITIUD intrigued
ITIUR intriguer
ITIWY in this way
ITLET intellect
ITMSE intumesce
ITNEY intensely
ITNFR intend for
ITNIE intensive
ITNIN intension
intention
ITNIY intensify
intensity
ITOBE in trouble
ITOET introject
introvert
ITOUE introduce
ITOWS in two twos
ITPRS into parts
ITRAD interlard
ITRAE interface
interlace
interpage
ITRAH interdash
ITRAL interrail
ITREE intercede
interfere
intervene
ITREF interleaf
ITREN intervein
ITRET intercept
interject
interment
intersect
ITRID interwind
ITRIE interline
ITRIK interlink
ITRIT interdict
ITRIW interview
ITRIY intercity
ITRLA inter alia
ITRLW interflow
ITRLY interplay
ITRNT interknit
ITROD interfold
ITROE interlope
internode
interpone
interpose
ITROK interlock
interwork
ITROL in turmoil
ITRON interjoin
ITRRD interbred
ITRRP intercrop
ITRRT interpret
ITRRW intergrow
ITRSF in terms of
ITRUE interfuse
interlude
ITRUT interrupt
ITRYE Intertype®
ITSAE intestate
ITSAY intestacy
ITSIE intestine
ITTES in tatters
ITUIE intrusive
ITUIG intruding
ITUIN intrusion
IUBAE inumbrate
IUCIN inunction
IUDTD inundated
IUEET inurement
IUIIY inutility
IUNDN iguanodon❑
IURFN ibuprofen
IUTTT Inuktitut
IVCIE invective
IVDOS invidious
IVILD inveigled
IVILR inveigler
IVLCE involucre
IVLDY invalidly
IVNIE inventive
IVNIN invention
IVNOY inventory
IVOAE inviolate
IVOAY inviolacy
IVRAE invertase
IVRAT invariant
IVRES Inverness
IVREY inversely
IVRIN inversion
IVSBE invisible
IVSBY invisibly
IVSIG investing
IWETE inwreathe
IWIIG in writing
IYEGE Ivy League
IYUIE if you like
JAGNE Jean Genie
JAGNT Jean Genet
JANTE Jeannette
JAOAC Joan of Arc
JAOSF jealous of
JAOSY jealously
JAPRN Juan Perón
JBEIG jabbering
JBLAD J G Ballard
JBODR job-holder
JBWRH jobsworth
JCAET Jack-a-Lent
JCAIN jactation
JCEIM jockeyism
JCFOT Jack Frost
JCHBS Jack Hobbs
JCJNS Jack Jones
JCKIE jackknife
JCLRY jocularly
JCLTR joculator
JCNIY jocundity
JCRNA jacaranda
JCSAE Jack-slave
JCSEN Jock Stein
JCSIE jack-snipe
JCSRW Jack Straw
JCSUE Jack-sauce
JCYCX Jacky Ickx
JDCAY judiciary
JDCOS judicious
JDDNH Judi Dench
JDEET judgement
JDEHP judgeship
JDEIG juddering
JDSOE Judas-hole
JECHN Joel Cohen
JEIGY jeeringly
JELGS Joe Bloggs
JEREE Joe Greene
JFESN Jefferson
JGIOD Jo Grimond
JGLOE jugal bone
JHAAS John Adams
JHADN John Arden
JHATR John Astor
JHCAE John Clare
JHCBT John Cabot
JHCRY John Curry
JHDNE John Donne
JHEWY John Elway

JHGEG John Greig
JHGEN John Glenn
JHHNY John Henry
JHIMN John Inman
JHJNR John Junor
JHKAS John Keats
JHLCE John Locke
JHMJR John Major
JHMLS John Mills
JHMYW John Mayow
JHODN John Ogdon
JHPPR John Piper
JHRIH John Reith
JHSAE John Soane
JHSEE John Speke
JHSIH John Smith
JHSOE Johnstone
JHTLR John Tyler
JHWYE John Wayne
JIBEK jailbreak
JIEES juiceless
JIHUE jailhouse
JIIES juiciness
JIIGP joining up
JIISE join issue
JITES jointness
JKNEY J F Kennedy
JLECP juliet cap
JLIES jolliness
JLIGY joltingly
JLUID jalousied
JLYAY jelly baby
JLYEN jelly bean
JLYIE jelly-like
JLYIH jellyfish
JLYOT jollyboat
JMAAA jambalaya
JMAKD jam-packed
JMIES jumpiness
JMOEL Jim Lovell
JMSAS James Eads
JMSAT James Watt
jump start
JMSEN James Dean
JMSID James Lind
JMSOD James Bond
JMSOG James Hogg
JMSOK James Cook
JMSON Jamestown
JMSOS James Ross
JMSUT James Hunt
JNAUE Jan Mabuse
JNBRY Juneberry
JNEER junketeer
JNEIG junketing
JNFNA Jane Fonda
JNGAS Jena glass
JNHOO Jonah Lomo
JNILE Jennie Lee
JNIMN Jan Timman
JNSAY janissary
JNTEO Janet Reno
JNYID Jenny Lind
JPNSS Japaneses
JQEIE Jaqueline
JRDCL juridical
JRIES jerkiness
JRIGY jarringly
JROER jargoneer
JROIE jargonise
jargonize
JROIT jargonist
JRSEG Jarlsberg
JRSLM Jerusalem
JRWIG J K Rowling
JRWMN jurywoman
jurywomen
JRYIE Jerry Rice
JSAIE jessamine
JSAOT just about
JSEIE jasperise
jasperize
JSEOT Jesse Boot
JSESN Jespersen
JSIGY jestingly
JSIID justified
JSIIN Justinian
JSIIR justifier
JSMRI Jose Marti
JSPIE Josephine
Joséphine
JSSET Jesus wept
JSSIK joss-stick
JTAGD jet-lagged
JTEBG jitterbug
JTIGY juttingly
JUDCD jaundiced
JUNYR journeyer
JVAIY joviality
JVNLA juvenilia
JWLEY jewellery
JXAOE juxtapose
JYAKR jaywalker
JYASY Jay Gatsby
JYEAY Joyce Cary
JYESY joylessly
JYIIG joy-riding
KAIHY knavishly
KAKRD knackered
KASRP Knabstrup
KATEK Kraftwerk
KBAHN Kubla Khan
KBUZM kibbutzim
KCAOT kick about
KCPET kick pleat
KCSAD kickstand
KCSAT kick-start
KDAPD Kidnapped
KDAPR kidnapper
KDSUF kids' stuff
KDYIK kiddywink
KEAAT keep an act
keep apart
KEABY keep at bay
KEAEM keep a term
KEAIE keep alive
KEFIH keep faith
KEGAD keep guard
KEGIG keep going
KEHUE keep house
KEHUS keep hours
KEIAE khedivate
KEIIL khedivial
KEMRM klezmorim
KEPRR Klemperer
KEQIT keep quiet
KEUDR keep under
KEWTH keep watch
KGSIA Kagoshima
KIEDE knife-edge
KIEDM kaiserdom
KIHFA kniphofia
KISAN Klinsmann
KKMNS kakemonos
KKSHA Kokoschka
KLANY Killarney
KLCCE kilocycle
KLDES killdeers
KLEKN kilderkin
KLHRZ kilohertz
KLIIH killifish
KLJUE kilojoule
KLMTE kilometre
KLNHE kalanchoe
KMELY Kimberley
KMGAH kymograph
KMHLY Kim Philby
KMHTA Kamchatka
KMLUG Kim Il-sung
KMOGL Kim Jong Il
Kim Jong-Il
KMSTA Kama Sutra
Kamasutra
KMUHA Kampuchea
KNCBA king cobra
KNDMD kingdomed
KNGNE Kunigunde
KNIEN Kentigern
KNIES kinkiness
KNISY Kandinsky
KNMKR kingmaker
KNMTC kinematic
KNPAN king prawn
KNSIL Kingsmill
KNSON Kingstown
KNSYN King's Lynn
KNSZD king-sized
KNWMN kinswoman
KODKR klondiker
klondyker
KOGAS knot grass
knotgrass
KOIAL know-it-all
KOIGY knowingly
KOIIE kaolinise
kaolinite
kaolinize
KOKAK knock back
knock-back
KOKOD knock cold
knock wood
KOKON knock down
knock-down
KOKOY knock copy
KOKRP knocker-up
KOKVR knock over
KOLDE knowledge
KOOKN Kropotkin
KPSTC kopasetic
KPWMN kept woman
KRAAA Karnataka
KRAOG kurrajong
KRAWR Korean War
KRBNR karabiner
KRBRH Karl Barth
KRCLY Kirkcaldy
KRDIL kerb drill
KRGDL Kurt Gödel
KRIRP kirbigrip❑
KRJOS Kurt Jooss
KROOY karyology
KROYE karyotype
KRSOE kerbstone
KRSUE Karlsruhe
KRTSS keratoses
keratosis
KRTTS keratitis
KRUFE kerfuffle
KRWIL Kurt Weill
KSARM kissagram
KSHNS kiss hands
KSIGR Kissinger
KSNAI Kisangani
KSORM kissogram
KTAIA Katharina
KTAIE Katharine
KTASN Kit Carson
KTBTC katabatic
KTCIY kitschily
KTEIE Katherine
KTEIH kittenish
KTHNR Kitchener
KTIAE kittiwake
KTLFL kettleful
KTMNU Kathmandu
KTNRA ketonuria
KUMON krummhorn
KWFUT kiwi fruit
KWOIG kowtowing
KYEIN Keynesian
KYONS key points
KYTOE keystroke
KYYHV Kuybyshev
LAAPO lhasa apso
LABLY Leadbelly
LACLS leaf cells
LAEAK leaseback
LAEED lease-lend
LAEOD leasehold
LAEOK leave work
LAEOT leave port
LAGFI Llangefni

LAHES loathness
LAHOE loathsome
LAIES leakiness
loaminess
LAIIY liability
LALFR liable for
LANDY learnedly
LAPOF leakproof
LASAK loan shark
loan-shark
LASOE loadstone
LATAS leastways
LBAIE labialise
labialize
LBAIN librarian
LBCIS libeccios
LBCOY lobectomy
LBCUE lobscouse
LBDNL libidinal
LBETS librettos
LBIAE lubricate
LBIAT lubricant
LBIIY lubricity
LBLAT libellant
LBLIG labelling
LBLOS libellous
LBRIE libertine
LBRIS liberties
LBRLY liberally
LBRNH labyrinth
LBROS laborious
LBRTD liberated
LBRTR liberator
LBUES labourers
LBUIG labouring
LBYSS lobbyists
LCAIE lucrative
LCAIN lactarian
lactation
LCAOP Lucia Popp
LCBAE lucubrate
LCBAN lack-brain
LCDES lucidness
LCEIH lickerish
LCEIS Lucretius
LCEOS lecherous
LCESN Luc Besson
LCFCS locofocos
LCFED Lichfield
LCHRS lock horns
LCIOO lacrimoso
LCIVR Lochinvar
LCLAL local call
LCLEO Local Hero
LCLIE local time
LCLNN lack-linen
LCLOE local code
LCLVN Loch Leven
LCLZD localized
LCMNS lucumones
LCMRR Loch Morar
LCMTR locomotor
LCNAE laciniate
LCNRA lacunaria
LCOIH laccolith
LCRML lachrymal
LCRTD lacerated
LCSIH locksmith
LDCLE lodiculae
LDCLY ludically
LDCOS ludicrous
LDEMN ladies' man
LDEUS ladlefuls
LDREG Lederberg
LDSAD lady's maid
LDSAS Ladislaus
LDSIH Ladysmith
LDSOE lodestone
LEADN lie hard on
LEEID lie behind
LEEOD liege lord
LEETO lie next to
LEHIE leechlike
LEIGY leeringly
LEILR Lee Miller
LENAT lie in wait
LERUD lie around
LETOT lie at host
LFAAD lift a hand
LFBOD lifeblood
LFCCE life-cycle
LFFRE life-force
LFGAD lifeguard
LFIES loftiness
LFOES leftovers
LFSOY life story
LFSVR life-saver
LFSYE lifestyle
LFSZD life-sized
LFWAY life-weary
LFWRS leftwards
LFYTE Lafayette
LGADA La Guardia
LGCLY logically
LGCOB logic bomb
LGEID lag behind
LGEOE leg before
LGGAH logograph
LGHOY leg theory
LGIGY laggingly
LGIOO lagrimoso
LGIPE lagniappe
LGLAE legal case
LGLER legal year
LGLZD legalized
LGMCY logomachy
LGMRH lagomorph
LGNAY legendary
LGOAY legionary
LGRED Lagerfeld
LGRIE leger-line
LGROT lager lout
LGRTM logarithm
LGSAE legislate
LGSIS logistics
LGTAN light rain
LGTEL light meal
LGTER light-year
LGTES lightness
LGTHP lightship
LGTIG lightning
LGTLW light blow
LGTNP lighten up
LGTOT lights out
LGTPN light upon
LGTUB light bulb
LGULR leg-puller
LHNRN Lohengrin
LHRLY L P Hartley
LICOH loincloth
LIEIG loitering
LIETR Leicester
LIGLT lying flat
LIGON lying down
LIHUT Leigh Hunt
LIMTF leitmotif
LIMTV leitmotiv
LIOIZ Leibovitz
LIPPR laid paper
LIUEY leisurely
LKAHT like a shot
LKAID like a bird
LKANT like as not
LKCAY like crazy
LKFIS like flies
LKGRA Lake Garda
LKHRN Lake Huron
LKNAA Lake Nyasa
LKOEA Lake Onega
LKORD Lake Ohrid
LKPOO Lake Poopó
LKSIK like stink
LKSOE like smoke
LKWTR like water
LLAOT loll about
LLIGY lollingly
LLNEI lilangeni
LLWIE lily-white
LMAIE lemmatise
lemmatize
LMBAK lamp-black
LMEIG lumbering
LMETY lambently
LMEUA Lampedusa
LMHOE lymph node
LMHTC lymphatic
LMIES lumpiness
LMIGY limpingly
LMIHY lumpishly
LMIIY limpidity
LMITC Lamaistic
LMLGT lamplight
limelight
LMNAT lemon tart
LMNEL lemon peel
LMNIG lamenting
LMNNE luminance
LMNOE lemon sole
LMNRP lemon drop
LMNSE luminesce
LMNTD laminated
LMNTN Lymington
LMNUD lemon curd
LMOGD Lamb of God
LMONR lampooner
LMOOY limnology
LMRIE Lamartine
LMRSO Lambrusco
LMSAE lampshade
limescale
LMSOD Lymeswold
LMSOE limestone
LMSRG limb sprig
LMTBE limitable
LMTDY limitedly
LMTES limitless
LMUGR Limburger
LMUIE limousine
LMWTR limewater
LNAAD lend a hand
LNAER lend an ear
LNAET lineament
LNAOE Lanzarote
LNATR Lancaster
LNBAH Long Beach
LNBRH Lindbergh
LNDAN long-drawn
LNDME landdamne
LNEIG lingering
LNEIY longevity
LNEOS longevous
LNETY leniently
LNEUD Langesund
LNFCD long-faced
LNFED long field
LNGOE line-grove
LNHIE lunchtime
LNHNM lanthanum
LNHNY Lon Chaney
LNIAE lancinate
LNIES lankiness
LNIGY longingly
LNIUE longitude
LNLAE lend-lease
LNLTR Linklater
LNLVD long-lived
LNMRH long march
LNNEK Lenin Peak
LNOIE Londonise
Londonize
LNOND land of Nod
LNONR landowner
LNOSE langouste
LNRVR Land Rover®
LNSAE landscape
LNSAL land snail
LNSIE landslide
LNSOE longshore
LNSOY long story
LNTIY lengthily
LNTSS linctuses
LNUDY languidly

LNULY lingually
LNUTN Len Hutton
LNWRS landwards
LOAGY look angry
LOAIE lookalike
look-alike
look alive
LOATR look after
LOBKT Léon Bakst
LOEEF loose-leaf
LOEES looseness
LOEFR looked-for
LOEIG loosening
LOESN lookers-on
LOHAT lion-heart
LOHBC lyophobic
LOHLC lyophilic
LOIEN Laodicean
LOIIG lionizing
LONIE Lyonnaise
LOOTN look out on
LOSAL look small
LOSAP look sharp
LOSAT look smart
LOWEE look where
LPEAE lapse rate
LPEDR lip-reader
LPOOE leptosome
LQAIY loquacity
LQEID liquefied
LQEIR liquefier
LQIAE liquidate
LQIIE liquidise
liquidize
LQIIY liquidity
LQOIE liquorice
LRAOT lark about
LRCLY lyrically
LRDES luridness
LREEL large meal
LREES largeness
LREIT larcenist
LREIY large city
LREOS larcenous
LRHTO larghetto
LRIES lordiness
LRKOS Lord knows
LRLCN Lord Lucan
LRMYR Lord Mayor
LRNEL laryngeal
LRNTE lorgnette
LROTV Lermontov
LRYAE lardy cake
LRYID Larry Bird
LSAAO Lismahago
LSAGT L'Escargot
LSAMS Las Palmas
LSASN Les Dawson
LSATR lust after
LSBOD lose blood
LSCSE lose caste
LSCSS list costs
LSCUE lost cause
LSDTH last-ditch
LSEES listeners
LSEIE Listerise
Listerize
LSEIG lessening
listening
LSFLY lustfully
LSHAT lose heart
LSIES lustiness
LSIGY lastingly
lispingly
LSIUE lassitude
LSOEY lissomely
LSOTT lash out at
LSPWR lose power
LSTNA Lusitania
LSWTR lose water
LTAGC lethargic
LTAIS Lotharios
LTAIY lethality
LTEBN litter bin
LTEDY latter-day
LTEES litheness
LTEIG lettering
LTEOE lithesome
LTEST letterset
LTETN Lyttelton
LTGOS litigious
LTGTR litigator
LTHNO latch on to
latch onto
LTHOT latch bolt
LTIGN letting in
LTIIE luteinise
luteinize
LTLBT little bit
LTLBY little boy
LTLDG Little Dog
LTLEA Little Eva
LTLED little end
LTLOE little one
LTLOL little owl
LTOOE lithopone
LTOOY lithology
lithotomy
LTPAI Lotophagi
LTRHN later than
LTRLY laterally
literally
LTRTM literatim
LTUNA Lithuania
LUAEN Laura Dern
LUAIE laudative
LUAIN laudation
LUAMA leukaemia
LUAOY laudatory
LUCIG launching
LUCLT Launcelot
LUCPD launch pad
LUCTN Launceton
LUDES laundress
LUDRD laundered
LUERG Lou Gehrig
LUGBR lounge bar
LUHBE laughable
LUHBY laughably
LUIES lousiness
LUIGY louringly
LUIHY loutishly
LUILE Laurie Lee
LULAA Ljubljana
LUMUH loudmouth
loud-mouth
LUNIE loud noise
LUOOY leucotomy
LUSAA Louisiana
LVAHN leviathan□
LVCID love child
love-child
LVDES lividness
LVIIR Lavoisier
LVISN live in sin
LVLES levelness
LVLET level best
LVLIG levelling
LVLIH level with
LVLON level down
LVNCP loving-cup
LVNIE Levantine
LVOAR live on air
LVOTF live out of
LVRMN liveryman
LVROL Liverpool
LVROT liverwort
LVRPT liver spot
LVSOK livestock
LVSOY love story
LVTCS Leviticus
LWAIG law-making
LWEMN Low German
LWESY lawlessly
LWETE law centre
LWIDD low-minded
LWIES lowliness
LWIIG law-giving
LWMWR lawnmower
LWRAE lower-case
LWRCD low-priced
LWREK lower deck
LWRHN lower than
LWRON lower down
LWSOT Lowestoft
LWUGT low-budget
LXCLY lexically
LXMUG Luxemburg
LXNTN Lexington
LXRAE luxuriate
LXRAT luxuriant
LXROS luxurious
LXVAE lixiviate
LYEJR Leyden jar
LYEOE lay before
LYESN lay person
layperson
LYIUE lay-figure
LYNOF laying-off
LYODF lay hold of
LYOET lay to rest
LYPNO lay open to
LYYSN lay eyes on
LZAOI lazzaroni
LZBNS lazybones
lazy-bones
LZDIY lazy-daisy
LZRIE lazar-like
LZRTO lazaretto
LZSSN lazy Susan
MAARW Mia Farrow
MABLS meatballs
MADOS meandrous
MAEAE Mr Average
MAFLY moanfully
MAIES meatiness
MAIGY meaningly
MAMTC miasmatic
MAUEP measure up
MAUIG measuring
MAWIE meanwhile
MBCAY mobocracy
MBLZR mobilizer
MCAES Maccabees
MCAIE mechanise
mechanize
MCAIM mechanism
MCAIN mactation
MCAIS mechanics
MCAOS mockadoes
MCAOT muck about
MCDMA macadamia
MCDNA Macedonia
MCENY Michel Ney
MCESN Michelson
MCEZE Mackenzie
MCIAE machinate
MCIES muckiness
MCIEY machinery
MCIGY mockingly
MCIIT machinist
MCILN Macmillan
MCLES McCullers
MCLGC mycologic
MCLVD much loved
MCNEN Mycenaean
MCNOH macintosh
MCOAD MacDonald
Macdonald
MCOAE microwave
mucronate
MCOEH micromesh
MCOIH microlith
MCOIL microbial
MCOIM microfilm
MCOIN macrobian
MCOOE microcode
microtome
MCOOM macrocosm
microcosm
MCOOY macrology
microcopy

Words marked □ can also be spelled with an initial capital letter

Code	Word
MCOYE	micropyle
MCRHR	MacArthur
MCRKR	muck-raker
MCRNC	macaronic
MCRNS	macaronis
MCRNY	McCartney
MCRTR	macerator
MCTXN	mycotoxin
MCUAE	micturate
MCWAM	macaw-palm
MCZRM	machzorim
MDAEY	mediately
MDAHM	Midrashim
MDAIE	mediatise
	mediative
	mediatize
MDAIG	mediating
MDAIN	mediation
MDAOY	mediatory
MDAVL	mediaeval
MDCBE	medicable
MDCLY	medically
MDCNL	medicinal
MDCTD	medicated
MDEIG	maddening
MDEOE	madrepore
MDESN	mad person
MDFEH	made flesh
MDFIG	modifying
MDIES	muddiness
MDIEY	midwifery
MDIKT	mid-wicket
MDJRS	mudéjares
MDKON	made known
MDLAY	medullary
MDLER	middle ear
MDLIE	madeleine❑
MDLIG	modelling
MDLIN	medallion
MDLIT	medallist
MDLMN	middleman
MDLTN	Middleton
MDLTR	modulator
MDLWY	middle way
MDNTE	midinette
MDRIE	modernise
	modernize
MDRIM	modernism❑
MDRIT	modernist
MDRIY	modernity
MDRTR	moderator
MDTEM	midstream
MDUMR	midsummer
MESRM	maelstrom
MFICP	muffin-cap
MGAEA	Magdalena
MGAEE	Magdalene
MGAIE	Magyarise
	Magyarize
MGAIG	migrating
MGAIM	magnalium
MGAIN	migration
MGAOY	migratory
MGBCS	megabucks
MGCHW	magic-show
MGCLY	magically
MGCOD	magic word
MGDAH	megadeath
MGDSU	Mogadishu
MGEHN	McGeechan
MGEIE	magnetise
	magnetite
	magnetize
MGEIM	magnesium
	magnetism
MGEIN	magnesian
MGERN	magnetron
MGEUG	Magdeburg
MGHRZ	megahertz
MGIES	mugginess
MGIIR	magnifier
MGIUE	magnitude
MGLAS	megillahs
MGLOH	megilloth
MGOPE	maggot-pie
MGPOE	megaphone
MGSOE	megastore
MGSRL	magistral
MGUSN	Magnusson
MHRJH	maharajah
MHRNE	maharanee
MHRSI	maharishi
MHSIK	mahlstick
MIBAE	mainbrace
MICID	maid-child
MIEIH	maidenish
MIFAE	mainframe
MIFED	Muirfield
MIFRE	main force
MILNR	mainliner
MIPIT	main point
MISET	mainsheet
MISOE	Maidstone
	main store
MITES	moistness
MITIG	main thing
MJHDN	mujahedin
MJROO	major-domo
MJRTE	majorette
MJSUE	majuscule
MKAAD	make a card
MKAAE	make a face
	make aware
MKAAK	make a back
MKAAL	make a call
MKAEL	make a deal
	make a meal
MKAES	make a mess
MKAGY	make angry
MKAIN	make a sign
MKAIT	make a gift
	make a list
MKALP	make a slip
MKAOB	make a bomb
MKAOE	make a hole
	make a move
MKARP	make a trip
MKATR	make after
	make a stir
MKAUS	make a fuss
MKBAE	make brave
MKBID	make blind
MKCER	make clear
MKDRY	make dirty
MKDUK	make drunk
MKDZY	make dizzy
MKEPY	make empty
MKEUL	make equal
MKFNF	make fun of
MKFXD	make fixed
MKHPY	make happy
MKHSE	make haste
MKKON	make known
MKLGL	make legal
MKLIH	Mike Leigh
MKLUH	make laugh
MKLVL	make level
MKMKS	mako-makos
MKMNS	makimonos
MKMNY	make money
MKMRY	make merry
MKOMR	make or mar
MKPAE	make peace
	make-peace
MKPAN	make plain
MKPOD	make proud
MKRAY	make ready
	makeready
MKRGT	make right
MKSIT	makeshift
MKSNE	make sense
MKTNE	make tense
MKTRD	make tired
MKTRS	make terms
MKTSN	Mike Tyson
MKUEF	make use of
MKUFR	make up for
MKUFT	make unfit
MKVGE	make vague
MKWDR	make wider
MKWIE	make white
MKWOE	make whole
MKWOY	make woozy
MKWRE	make worse
MKWTR	make water
MKWVS	make waves
MLAKE	Milwaukee
MLBAD	millboard
MLBLE	Malebolge
MLCES	Miliciens
MLCIE	malachite
	molochise
	molochize
MLCLR	molecular
MLCOS	malicious
MLDAA	melodrama
MLDOS	melodious
MLDOT	maladroit
MLEAY	millenary
MLEBE	malleable
MLEEE	millepede
MLENA	millennia
MLGAT	malignant
MLGIG	maligning
MLGIY	malignity
MLIAA	multipara
MLIDS	Miltiades
MLIEE	millipede
MLIES	milkiness
MLIET	Millicent
MLIEY	millinery
MLIGY	meltingly
MLIIR	mollifier
MLILX	multiplex
MLIND	mullioned
MLINH	millionth
MLIOM	multiform
MLISN	Mel Gibson
MLIUE	multitude
MLMTR	milometer
MLNMH	Multnomah
MLNMS	melanomas
MLNSA	Melanesia
MLOAE	meliorate
MLOEE	Melpomene
MLOMD	malformed
MLOOT	mellow out
MLORE	Melbourne
MLRLI	malgré lui
MLRMI	malgré moi
MLROE	malar bone
MLROS	malarious
	Mel Brooks
MLRUD	milk round
MLSAA	melismata
MLSAE	milk shake
MLSEL	mild steel
MLSNE	Mélisande
MLSOB	Mills bomb
MLSOE	milestone
	millstone
MLSOT	milk stout
MLSVC	Milosevic
MLSWY	miles away
MLTEH	milk teeth
MLTNN	melatonin
MLTNY	militancy
MLTOH	milk tooth
MLTRA	militaria
MLWEL	mill wheel
MLWIE	milk-white
MLYAK	mollymawk
MLYIN	Malaysian
MMAIN	mammalian
MMCIG	mimicking
MMIHY	mumpishly
MMIID	mummified
MMIIT	memoirist
MMILE	mammillae
MMLAY	mamillary
MMLCS	mamelucos
MMNAY	momentany

9 M_M_N

momentary
MMNOS momentous
MMOIE mammonite
MMOIH mammonish
MMOIM mammonism
MMOIT mammonist
MMRAS memorials
MMRBE memorable
MMRBY memorably
MMRNA memoranda
MMRTR memoriter
MMUGT mum-budget
MMYBY mummy's boy
MNADE manhandle
MNAEE manganese
MNAEY mundanely
MNAGE Montaigne
MNAIE manganite
many a time
MNAIG man-eating
MNAIY mendacity
mentality
mundanity
MNAOY mandatory
MNART Monsarrat
MNATN Manhattan
MNAUE miniature
MNBAC Mont Blanc
MNBEK minibreak
MNBIM manubrium
MNCAY monocracy
MNCIE monocline
MNCIM monachism
MNCLR monocular
MNCLY manically
MNCOS minacious
MNCPL municipal
MNCQE monocoque
MNCRS Monoceros
MNCTI manicotti
MNDOE menadione
MNEAA Minnehaha
MNEET mincemeat
MNEIM mannerism
MNEIN Mendelian
MNEIT mannerist
MNELS manzellos
MNENT monkey nut
MNEOA Minnesota
MNEOT mange tout
mangetout
MNERY Monterrey
MNESN Mandelson
MNEUA Montezuma
MNEUN mannequin
MNEVE manoeuvre
MNFED Mansfield
MNFLF mindful of
MNFLY mindfully
MNFSO manifesto
MNGAH monograph
MNGMC monogamic
MNGRE menagerie
MNHID mynah bird
MNHIS monthlies
MNHVK Menshevik
MNIAE mancipate
MNIAT mendicant
MNICA mandiocca
MNIES manginess
manliness
minginess
MNIGS Mandingos
MNIIE menticide
MNIIY mendicity
MNILS mandibles
MNIND mentioned
MNINR Monsignor
MNJLP mint-julep
MNLGE monologue
MNMNA monomania
MNMNE Menominee
MNMRC monomeric
MNMSO meno mosso
MNMTR manometer
monometer
MNMTY manometry
MNNEL meningeal
MNOAK Mungo Park
MNOIE mandoline
Mongolise
Mongolize
MNOIG mentoring
MNOIM mongolism
MNOIN Mongolian
MNOIZ Mankowitz
MNONL monsoonal
MNOOD Mongoloid
MNOSI Minkowski
MNOSS mongooses
MNPAE monoplane
MNPOY monopsony
MNPUE menopause
MNRDY man Friday❑
MNRED man friend
MNRLY mongrelly
MNROE minor role
MNRYE monorhyme
MNSDD many-sided
MNSES ministers
MNSEY monastery
MNSIR mono-skier
MNSIT mini skirt
miniskirt
MNSOD meniscoid
monkshood
MNSOE minestone
MNSUE mint sauce
minuscule
MNTEE monotreme
MNTMN minutemen
MNTMS many times
MNTOS monstrous
munitions
MNTRS man-at-arms
MNTUL menstrual
MNUAE manducate
MNUIN Mancunian
MNWMN Manxwoman
MNYAS moneybags
MNYET money belt
MNYON money down
MOEOG Mao Zedong
MOFCD moon-faced
MOIAS Maori Wars
MOIES moodiness
MOIRL myofibril
MOLBN myoglobin
MOLGT moonlight
MORKR moonraker
MOSAE moonscape
MOSIE moonshine
MOSIY moonshiny
MOSOE moonstone
MPAOT mope about
MPCIE mepacrine
MPEEF maple leaf
MPESN McPherson
MQIAD maquisard
MRAAE marmalade
MRAEH Marrakesh
MRAHS mariachis
MRAIA margarita
MRAIE marcasite
margarine
marmarise
marmarize
mortalise
mortalize
MRAIY mortality
MRASR merganser
MRATY mordantly
MRBLN Marc Bolan
MRCIO Maracaibo
MRCME Morecambe
Morecombe
MREAY mercenary
MREER marketeer
MREES murderess
MREIE marmelise
marmelize
mercerise
mercerize
MREIG marketing
MRELD market-led
MRELS Marcellus
martellos
MREOE Morse code
MREOS murderous
MRGGR mortgagor
MRHAA marihuana
MRHAD marshland
MRHAE March hare
MRHAK marsh hawk
MRHAT march past
march-past
MRHES mirthless
MRHIH march with
MRHMC morphemic
MRHNO march into
MRIAE marginate
MRIES merciless
merriness
murkiness
MRIET merriment
MRIID mortified
MRIIN mortician
MRIIY morbidity
MRILY martially
MRIMS Martinmas
MRIOS Myrmidons
MRIRS Mardi Gras
MRJAA marijuana
MRLAE moral tale
MRLOE moral code
MRLZR moralizer
MRNEE marinière
MRNTI Marinetti
MROEL marmoreal
MROFT marrowfat
MROIG marooning
MROIM Mormonism
MROOO Marco Polo
MROSY marrowsky
MROUO Mario Puzo
MRQAT Mary Quant
MRSIZ Mark Spitz
MRSOS Morescoes
Moriscoes
MRTAN Mark Twain
MRTLY maritally
MRTRA moratoria
MRUAE mercurate
MRUFX Marcus Fox
MRUIE mercurise
mercurize
MRUIG marauding
murmuring
MRUIL marsupial
mercurial
MRUIM marsupium
MRUOS mercurous
murmurous
MRUTY marquetry
MRWRS mere words
MRYDM martyrdom
MRYIE martyrise
martyrize
MRYNO marry into
MRYNS mercy on us
MSAAE mismanage
moss agate
MSADE mishandle
MSAHO mustachio
MSAIA Messalina
MSAIG mislaying
MSALH mashallah
MSAOT mess about
MSBTS Miss Bates
MSCAL music hall
MSCEY music-demy
MSCLY musically

Words marked ❑ can also be spelled with an initial capital letter

Code	Word
MSDIE	misadvise
MSEAE	misbehave
	misrelate
MSEEE	miscegene
MSEEN	misdemean
MSEER	musketeer
MSEFL	masterful
MSEGR	messenger
MSEIE	mesmerise
	mesmerize
	miscegine
MSEIF	misbelief
MSEIM	mesmerism
MSEIS	mysteries
MSEIT	mesmerist
MSEKN	misreckon
MSEOT	misreport
	muster out
MSESR	misfeasor
MSETN	Mrs Beeton
MSETW	misbestow
MSFED	Masefield
MSFLY	musefully
MSGEN	moss green
MSHNE	mischance
MSHPN	misshapen
MSHRE	mischarge
MSHTL	moschatel
MSIAE	masticate
MSIES	messiness
	mistiness
	mossiness
	muskiness
	mustiness
MSIET	misdirect
MSIEY	massively
MSIGN	messing on
MSIGY	missingly
MSIID	mystified
MSIIG	misgiving
MSIIM	mysticism
MSIIR	mystifier
MSIIT	mosaicist
MSINC	Messianic
MSINR	missioner
MSIPN	mislippen
MSJLE	Miss Julie
MSLCD	misplaced
MSLID	misallied
MSLKD	most-liked
MSLMN	muscleman
MSLTE	mistletoe
MSMDA	mass media
MSMLN	musk melon
MSMLY	misemploy
MSMRH	mesomorph
MSNES	must needs
MSNEY	mesentery
MSNOM	misinform
MSOAL	most of all
MSOAO	muscovado
MSOEN	misgovern
MSOIE	muscovite❑
MSOII	Mussolini
MSOOR	miscolour
MSORS	Mrs Norris
MSOTN	miss out on
MSPYL	mesophyll
MSRAT	miscreant
MSRBE	miserable
MSRBY	miserably
MSRIE	mispraise
MSRLY	mass rally
MSRNY	Mrs Grundy
MSSAS	miss stays
MSSEM	misesteem
MSSIN	misassign
MSUDD	misguided
MSUGD	misjudged
MSUGE	misguggle
MSUIE	masculine
MSUMN	Mussulmen
MSUUL	most usual
MSVRE	Mesa Verde
MTAIE	mutualise
	mutualize
MTAIM	mutualism
MTAIY	mutuality
MTAOE	methadone
MTBLC	metabolic
MTBSY	Matt Busby
MTCIA	matachina
MTCII	matachini
MTCOS	motocross
MTDES	mutedness
MTEIG	mattering
	muttering
MTETN	moth-eaten
MTGNC	mutagenic
MTGTR	mitigator
MTHES	matchless
MTHIH	match with
MTHOD	matchwood
MTHPO	match up to
MTHSN	Mitchison
MTIAE	metricate
MTIIE	matricide
	metricise
	metricize
	mythicise
	mythicize
MTIIT	mythicist
MTIOY	matrimony
MTIRH	matriarch
MTLIE	metallise
	metallize
MTLOD	metalloid
MTLOK	metalwork
MTLTD	mutilated
MTLTR	mutilator
MTNMC	metonymic
MTOIE	matronise
	matronize
	meteorite
	methodise
	methodize
MTOIM	Methodism
MTOIS	Methodius
MTOIT	Methodist
MTOOD	meteoroid
MTOOE	metronome
MTOOY	mythology
MTPAE	metaphase
MTPOF	mothproof
MTRAE	motorcade
MTRAS	materials
MTRED	Motorhead
MTRIE	motorbike
	motor-bike
MTRIM	Mithraism
MTRIY	maternity
MTROT	motor boat
MTSAI	motoscafi
MTTNL	matutinal
MTVTR	motivator
MTYAE	methylate
MTYES	mateyness
MUDBE	mouldable
MUDRN	maunder on
MUEER	mouse-deer
MUEID	mousebird
MUERP	mouse-trap
MUEUT	mouse-hunt
MUFOS	moufflons
MUHAE	mouth-made
MUHAH	mouthwash
MUHAT	mouthpart
MUHUS	mouthfuls
MUIES	mousiness
MUIIS	Mauritius
MUOEM	mausoleum
MUSIK	maulstick
MUTCE	moustache
MUTOK	Mount Cook
MUTSA	Mount Ossa
MUTTA	Mount Etna
MUTUI	Mount Fuji
MVAOT	move about
MVETR	movie star
MVHUE	move house
MVOTF	move out of
MVRUD	move round
MWIHY	mawkishly
MXEEA	myxoedema
MXEUZ	Max Perutz
MXLAY	maxillary
MXLNK	Max Planck
MXMLY	maximally
MXMTH	mix 'n' match
MXNIS	Maxentius
MXPUS	Max Ophuls
MXVRS	myxovirus
MYETE	may beetle
MYLWR	mayflower❑
MYRDE	Muybridge
MYRER	Meyerbeer
MYRIG	Mayerling
MYRLY	mayoralty
MYSEL	may as well
MZAIE	mezzanine
MZAOE	mezza voce
MZIES	muzziness
MZOIT	mezzotint
MZREN	Mozartean
MZRIN	Mozartian
NABTA	Naas Botha
NACUT	no-account
NALAL	nearly all
NALNW	nearly new
	nearly-new
NATIG	near thing
NATUH	near touch
NBCLE	nubeculae
NBEES	nobleness
NBGEL	no big deal
NBLAY	nobiliary
NBLZR	nebulizer
NCAEN	nectarean
NCAIE	nectarine
NCAIN	nictation
NCAOS	nectarous
NCCOH	neckcloth
NCDMS	Nicodemus
NCEIE	nickelise
	nickelize
NCELS	nucleolus
NCFLO	Nick Faldo
NCIAE	nictitate
NCIKN	no chicken
NCLTE	Nicolette
NCMET	no comment
NCOIE	necrotise
	necrotize
	niccolite
NCOSN	Nicholson
NCOSY	nocuously
NCRGA	Nicaragua
NCSAY	necessary
NCSIY	necessity
NCTAA	nicotiana
NCUNL	nocturnal
NCUNS	Nocturnes
NDIGY	noddingly
NDLTD	nodulated
NDNIG	no denying
NEFLY	needfully
NEIES	neediness
NEOLR	Niemöller
NESOR	Niels Bohr
NEZCE	Nietzsche
NFIES	niftiness
NFISN	no flies on
NFNOS	nefandous
NFRII	Nefertiti
NFROS	nefarious
NGADY	niggardly
NGETD	neglected
NGIET	negligent
NGILS	Negrillos
NGLEN	Nigel Benn
NGODL	negroidal
NGOIE	nigrosine

Words marked ❑ can also be spelled with an initial capital letter

9 N_G_R

NGRUA	Nagarjuna
NGTAE	negotiate
	Night Café
	nightmare
	night safe
NGTAL	nightfall
NGTEL	night-bell
NGTIE	nightlife
	night-time
NGTLB	nightclub
	night-club
NGTOG	nightlong
NGTOL	night-soil
NGTON	nightgown
NGTPT	nightspot
NGTRW	night-crow
NGTUE	night-rule
NIBTR	nail-biter
NIEES	naïveness
	noiseless
NIEOF	noises off
NIHOR	neighbour
NIIES	noisiness
NIOEY	noisomely
NIYUG	Neil Young
NKAOA	Nuku'alofa
NKDAY	naked lady
NKDES	nakedness
NKLUA	Niki Lauda
NLGEN	Nile green
NLIID	nullified
NLIIR	nullifier
NLIKM	Nellie Kim
NLIOE	nullipore
NLNYN	Nolan Ryan
NMATR	name after
NMBAD	name brand
NMEIG	numbering
NMEOE	number one
NMEOF	number off
NMETN	Number Ten
NMETO	number two
NMGAH	nomograph
NMIGY	numbingly
NMNLY	nominally
NMNMS	name names
NMNTD	nominated
NMNTR	nominator
NMRBE	numerable
NMRBY	numerably
NMRCL	numerical
NMRTR	numerator
NMRUO	numero uno
NMSUL	numbskull
NMUAY	nummulary
NMUDG	Nemrut Dag
NNAEL	nonpareil
NNAIE	non-native
NNAUL	non-manual
NNEBR	non-member
NNEIF	non-belief
NNEIS	nunneries
NNESN	non-person
NNEUL	non-sexual
NNLIN	nonillion
NNMKR	non-smoker
NNMSS	Nine Muses
NNNIY	nonentity
NNOHR	none other
NNOIG	non-voting
NNOOS	non-porous
NNRFT	non-profit
NNTEH	ninetieth
NNTHA	Ninotchka
NNTKR	nunataker
NNUAE	nuncupate
NNUKT	Nantucket
NOAIM	Neo-Nazism
NOEIE	neoterise
	neoterize
NOHBA	neophobia
NOHBC	neophobic
NOIHC	neolithic❑
NOIOF	Naomi Wolf
NOLGT	neon light
NOOHC	Neo-Gothic
	neo-gothic
NOOIE	neologise
	neologize
NOOIM	neologism
NOOIT	neologist
NOYIM	neodymium
NPAIM	nephalism
NPAIT	nephalist
NPIES	nippiness
NPIGY	nippingly
NPOEE	Nipponese
NPOOY	nephology
NPRTC	nephritic
NPRTS	nephritis
NPUIM	neptunium
NPYAH	nappy rash
NRAIE	narrative
	normalise
	normalize
	Normanise
	Normanize
	normative
NRAIN	narration
NRAIY	normality
NRAOY	narratory
NRART	Norway rat
NRATR	nor'-easter
NREAD	nursemaid
NREED	nurse-tend
NREES	nerveless
NREIG	nurseling
NREIN	Norwegian
NRETR	nor'wester
NRHAD	northward
NRHAT	north-east
NRHET	north-west
NRHID	north wind
NRHIT	North Uist
NRHNS	Northants
NRHOE	North Pole
	north pole
NRHRY	northerly
NRHTR	North Star
NRISS	narcissus❑
NRLOL	neroli oil
NRMEG	Nuremberg
NROIE	narcotise
	narcotize
NROIG	narrowing
NROIM	narcotism
NROSY	nervously
NRUIG	nurturing
NSAGA	nostalgia
NSAGC	nostalgic
NSAMC	nystagmic
NSAMS	nystagmus
NSBED	nosebleed
NSEAU	Nosferatu
NSEHT	Nissen hut
NSIES	nastiness
NSINE	nescience
NSLOE	nasal bone
NSRNS	no strings
NSVLE	Nashville
NTAET	not make it
NTAIL	Nathaniel
	note a bill
NTAIN	nitration
NTAOF	not far off
NTAOT	nuts about
NTATR	not matter
NTCOD	notochord
NTELY	not really
NTEPP	not keep up
NTERY	not nearly
NTIBE	not liable
NTIEP	not give up
NTIES	nattiness
	nuttiness
NTIET	nutriment
NTIHT	not with it
NTIIE	nutritive
NTIIN	nutrition
NTIKR	nit-picker
NTNAU	Netanyahu
NTNTP	not in step
NTNUH	not enough
NTOAY	not so many
NTOER	not go near
NTOGT	not forget
NTOIE	not notice
NTOIG	not joking
	not voting
NTOIH	not go with
NTOJE	not for Joe
NTOKR	networker
NTOUH	not so much
NTPIY	notaphily
NTPNO	not open to
NTPPR	notepaper
NTREY	notoriety
NTRLY	naturally
NTROS	notorious❑
NTRUD	not around
NTRVN	not proven
NTSAY	not as many
NTSRP	not a scrap
NTSUH	not as much
NTTIG	not a thing
NTTOE	not at home
NTTOK	not at work
NTTRA	natatoria
NTULT	nut cutlet
NTXET	not expect
NUAGA	neuralgia
NUAGC	neuralgic
NUETD	nauseated
NUHIY	naughtily
NUHTL	Neuchâtel
NUIHR	nourisher
NUOAA	neuromata
NUOOY	neurology
NURLY	neutrally
NURNS	neutrinos
NVCAE	noviciate
NVCLR	navicular
NVGBE	navigable
NVGBY	navigably
NVGTR	navigator
NVLIS	novelties
NVLLB	Naval Club
NVLOT	navelwort
NVLTE	novelette
NVRID	never mind
NVROE	nevermore
NVRVR	Never Ever
NVTAE	novitiate
NWAET	newsagent
NWAKT	newmarket❑
NWATE	Newcastle
NWEBR	new member
NWEHD	new method
NWEIO	New Mexico
NWESN	new person
NWESY	New Jersey
NWFAE	now of late
NWFAH	newsflash
NWGOP	newsgroup
NWHAE	new phrase
NWHUD	newshound
NWIES	newsiness
NWIHR	no whither
NWMDA	news media
NWOET	New Forest
NWOOD	new for old
NWPIT	newsprint
NWPPR	newspaper
NWRAE	new-create
NWSAD	news-stand
NWSET	news sheet
	news-sheet
NWUNA	New Guinea
NWYES	newlyweds
NXOIA	nux vomica
NXOKN	next of kin
NXOSY	noxiously

Words marked ❑ can also be spelled with an initial capital letter

NXWRD	next world
NYPIE	naye paise
OACUT	on account
OAEAE	on average
OAGAE	orangeade
OAGMN	Orangeman
OAGTN	orang utan
	orang-utan
OAGTP	orange-tip
OAIQE	odalisque
OAITC	onanistic
OAOIL	oratorial
OAOIS	oratorios
OATIG	on a string
OBCLR	orbicular
OBDMN	ombudsman
	Ombudsmen
OBIAO	obbligato
OBITE	oubliette
OBLNE	on balance
OCAAN	once again
OCAEK	once a week
OCAER	once a year
OCETA	orchestra
OCETC	orchestic
OCGNC	oncogenic
OCLAE	oscillate
OCLIM	occultism
OCLIT	occultist
OCMNC	oecumenic
OCNCL	obconical
OCPNS	occupants
OCPNY	occupancy
OCPTL	occipital
OCRAE	obcordate
OCRET	occurrent
OCRIG	occurring
OCTNY	oscitancy
OCUET	occludent
OCUIE	occlusive
OCUIN	occlusion
ODALY	Old Bailey
ODAOT	odd man out
ODATR	old master
ODCOL	old school
ODEPE	old people
ODNAH	Ogden Nash
ODNAS	olden days
ODNNE	ordinance
ODNOT	odd one out
ODNUG	Oldenburg
ODOBR	odd-jobber
ODOGR	old codger
ODOMN	odd-jobman
ODOTR	odd-lotter
ODRAK	order back
ODRES	orderless
ODSLY	on display
ODTGR	old stager
ODUBR	odd number
OEAAN	over again
OEAGT	ore-raught
OEAIE	operative
OEAIG	operating
OEAIN	operation
OEBAD	overboard
OEBID	overbuild
OEBKD	overbaked
OEBON	overblown
OECEK	overcheck
OECLM	operculum
OECLR	opercular
OECOD	overcloud
	overcrowd
OECOS	oleaceous
OECUT	open court
	overcount
OEDAN	overdrawn
OEDAT	overdraft
OEDES	overdress
OEDIE	overdrive
OEDIG	overdoing
OEDKY	okey-dokey
OEEAT	over-exact
OEEDD	open-ended
OEEES	obeseness
OEEET	overexert
OEETD	ore-rested
OEFIE	o're-office
OEFLS	Owen Falls
OEGAE	overglaze
OEGAH	oleograph
OEGAN	overgrain
OEGAS	overgrass
OEGEN	overgreen
OEGOE	oven glove
OEGOM	overgloom
OEGON	overgrown
OEHAS	overheads
OEHSY	overhasty
OEHUE	open house
OEIGP	opening-up
OEINE	obedience
OEISE	overissue
OEJYD	overjoyed
OELTD	ocellated
OEMTH	overmatch
OEMUT	overmount
OENAL	one and all
OENDS	oceanides
OENGT	overnight
OEOEY	operosely
OEOSY	onerously
OEPES	overpress
OEPIE	overpoise
	overprice
	overprize
OEPIT	overpaint
	overprint
OEPRH	overperch
OEPTH	overpitch
OEPWR	overpower
OERAH	overreach
OERAT	oven-roast
	overreact
OERAY	oven-ready
OERDR	overrider
OESAE	open space
	overshade
	overstare
	overstate
OESAF	overstaff
OESED	overspend
OESEL	overswell
OESEP	oversleep
OESER	oversteer
OESET	oversweet
OESGT	oversight
OESIE	overshine
OESIK	overstink
OESIL	overspill
OESNE	obeisance
OESOE	overscore
OESOS	over-shoes
OESOT	overshoot
OETAE	over-trade
OETAN	overtrain
OETRD	overtired
OETRS	overtures
OETRW	overthrow
OETUP	overtrump
OETWR	overtower
OETXD	overtaxed
OETYU	over to you!
OEVLE	overvalue
OEWAY	overweary
OEWEM	overwhelm
OEWET	overwrest
OEWIE	overwrite
OEWIH	overweigh
OEWTH	overwatch
OFADD	offhanded
OFADE	offsaddle
OFAGT	off target
	off-target
OFCAE	officiate
OFCAT	officiant
OFCNL	officinal
OFCOS	officious
OFCOY	olfactory
OFESN	offseason
OFETE	off-centre
OFHAR	off the air
OFHBT	off the bit
OFHMP	off the map
OFHPG	off the peg
	off-the-peg
OFIIS	off limits
	off-limits
OFITR	off kilter
OFNAH	Offenbach
OFNIE	offensive
OFNIG	offending
OFOOR	off colour
	off-colour
OFORE	off course
	off-course
OFPIG	offspring
OFROY	offertory
OFSAE	obfuscate
OFTEM	off-stream
OFTET	off-street
OGATC	orgiastic
OGLOS	orgillous
OGNIE	organzine
OGNLE	organelle
OGNSS	oogenesis
OGNZD	organized
OGNZR	organizer
OHLDY	on holiday
OHORT	ochlocrat
OHRAF	other half
OHRES	otherness
OHRHN	other than
OHRIE	other side
	otherwise
OIACY	oligarchy
OIAIN	oxidation
OIAIY	oviparity
OIAOS	oviparous
OIERB	olive drab
OIIAE	originate
OIIIL	orificial
OILME	oriflamme
OIMAS	Opium Wars
OINAE	orientate
OINER	orienteer
OINOE	onion dome
OINYD	onion-eyed
OIOEE	Oligocene
OIOOY	oligopoly
OIOSY	ominously
OIPLE	on impulse
OISBE	omissible
OISIE	on its side
OITNE	omittance
OIUTL	oviductal
OJCIE	objective
OJCIN	objection
OJCIY	objectify
OJRAE	objurgate
OJTAT	objet d'art
OLAKR	oil-tanker
OLCNE	on-licence
OLETE	oil beetle
OLGDO	obliged to
OLGTD	obligated
OLGTS	obligatos
OLITR	oil filter
OLOES	onlookers
OLOIG	onlooking
OLQEY	obliquely
OLQIY	obliquity
OLVOS	oblivious
OMTDA	ommatidia
OMTRA	osmeteria
ONAAL	of no avail
ONBSS	omnibuses
ONBUK	Osnabrück
ONMNS	ornaments
ONPIE	oenophile
ONRHP	ownership

ONTOD ornithoid
ONXOS obnoxious
OOAEY obovately
OOEID of one mind
OOEIE on one side
OOEON on one's own
OOETD on one's tod
OOETS ovotestes
OOEWY on one's way
OOILS ocotillos
OOOIT orologist
otologist
OOOSY odorously
OOOUD ororotund
OORES odourless
OORPY orography
OOTLY odontalgy
OOTMS odontomas
OPAAE orphanage
OPESD oppressed
OPESR oppressor
OPGAT oppugnant
OPNNS opponents
OPNNY opponency
OPNTN Orpington
OPROE of purpose
on purpose
OPRUE opportune
OPSBE opposable
OPSDO opposed to
ORAHR Our Father
OREVS ourselves
ORSIG onrushing
ORWMN oarswoman
OSADY on standby
on stand-by
OSAGT onslaught
OSCAE obsecrate
OSEEY obscenely
OSEIY obscenity
OSERC obstetric
OSFAE ossifrage
OSGAE obsignate
OSIAE obstinate
OSIAY obstinacy
OSLSE obsolesce
OSMSN O J Simpson
OSPAI oesophagi
OSQET obsequent
OSQIS obsequies
OSRAT observant
OSRGN oestrogen
OSRIE of service
OSSAP Oh So Sharp
OSSIE obsessive
OSSIN obsession
OSUAT obscurant
OSUEY obscurely
OSUIY obscurity
OTADR outlander
OTADY outwardly
OTAIE ostracise
ostracize
OTAIK of that ilk
OTAIM ostracism
OTANH outlaunch
OTCLY optically
OTCOD octachord
OTEAE on the game
on the make
on the take
on the wane
OTEAH on the bash
OTEAL on the ball
on the nail
OTEDE on the edge
OTEDN outredden
OTEED on the mend
OTEEM on the beam
OTEET on the beat
OTEIE on the rise
on the side
OTEIG on the wing
OTEIL on the pill
OTEIS on the bias
OTELB on the club
OTEOD On the Road
on the road
OTEOE on the dole
on the move
on the nose
OTEOF on the hoof
OTEOL on the boil
OTEON On the Town
OTEOR on the hour
OTEPT on the spot
on-the-spot
OTERO on the broo
OTERT on the trot
OTEUN on the turn
OTFAD out of hand
OTFAE out of date
out-of-date
OTFAH out of cash
OTFET out of debt
OTFID out of mind
OTFIE out of line
out of time
OTFJB out of a job
OTFLY out of play
OTFOK out of work
OTFRE out of true
OTFTP out of step
OTFUE out of tune
OTFUF out of puff
OTFUK out of luck
OTFUL out of curl
OTFYC out of sync
OTGNC ontogenic
OTGNL octagonal
OTHDA octahedra
OTIEF outside of
OTIEN outside in
OTIGR outrigger
OTIHT out with it!
OTIIE on thin ice
OTIIG obtaining
OTITR outfitter
OTKRS outskirts
OTLGC ontologic
OTLIN octillion
OTMLY optimally
OTMTR octameter
optometer
OTMTS optimates
OTMTY optometry
OTNES oftenness
OTNIE ostensive
OTNIL octennial
OTNOT out and out
out-and-out
OTNQE ortanique
OTNRI octonarii
OTNTS ostinatos
OTOAH osteopath
OTOGE outtongue
OTOIS orthotics
OTOIT orthotist
OTOKR outworker
OTOKY outjockey
OTONS outgoings
OTOOH Ostrogoth
OTOOY orthodoxy
osteology
OTORE outsource
OTOTC orthoptic
OTOTD out to stud
OTOXS orthoaxes
OTPED outspread
OTPIG outspring
OTPKN outspoken
OTPOE optophone
OTPSS octopuses
OTRER outerwear
OTRFY outcrafty
OTROT outermost
OTRWH outgrowth
OTSEN Otto Stern
OTTAN outstrain
OTTEL out at heel
OTTIE outstrike
OTUBR outnumber
OTUIE obtrusive
OTUIN obtrusion
OTUTE outlustre
OTVNS ottavinos
OUAIN ovulation
OUAIT ocularist
OUETY opulently
OVAIN obviation
OVOSY obviously
OVREY obversely
OVRIN obversion
OWLIN Orwellian
OYEAE oxygenate
OYEIE oxygenise
oxygenize
OYEOS oxygenous
PAAAI Prajapati
PAAAT play a part
PAAGR phalanger
PAAGS phalanges
PAAIE placative
PAAIN placation
planarian
PAANC Pharaonic
PAAOE phalarope
play a role
PAAOG play along
PAAOT play about
PAAOY placatory
PAATR play actor
play-actor
PAATY peasantry
PAAXS phalanxes
PABER play by ear
PABOY play booty
PACET Pratchett
PAEAD place card
PAEAK plate rack
PAEAL plate rail
PAEAY planetary
PAEBE peaceable
PAEBY peaceably
PAECP peaked cap
PAEET placement
PAEFL prayerful
PAEIE peace-pipe
peacetime
PAEIK place kick
PAEMT prayer mat
PAEOD planetoid
PAEOE piacevole
PAEOS placeboes
PAEOT played out
played-out
PAERG prayer rug
PAETA Placentia
PAETE placentae
PAETL placental
PAETS placentas
PAEVR place over
PAFLE play false
PAFLY playfully
PAGMS play games
PAGNY plangency
PAGOP playgroup
PAHOY play hooky
PAHUE playhouse❑
PAIAC pharisaic❑
PAIAD pray in aid
PAIGY pratingly
prayingly
PAIHR planisher
PAIIE platinise
platinize
PAIIY placidity
PAIOS platinous
PAIUE platitude
PAKOE pranksome
PAKTR prankster
PALDA praeludia

PALOT	pearlwort
PALPR	pearl spar
PALRY	pearl-gray
	pearl-grey
PALSD	pearlised
PALTC	pearlitic
PALUK	Pearl Buck
PALZD	pearlized
PAMDA	plasmodia
PAMGN	ptarmigan
PAMTC	plasmatic
	pragmatic
	psammitic
PANES	plainness
PANIE	plaintive
PANIF	plaintiff
PANMN	plainsmen
	praenomen
PANOG	plainsong
PAOEM	placoderm
PAOIE	Platonise
	Platonize
PAOIM	Platonism
PAOIT	pianolist
	Platonist
PAOPR	pea-souper
PAOYE	phagocyte
PASBE	plausible
PASBY	plausibly
PASFL	praiseful
PASLS	Pharsalus
PATBE	plantable
PATCL	practical
PATIE	plant-lice
	plant life
PATIG	plaything
	prattling
PATMN	plantsman
PATOD	plant food
PATQE	plastique
PATRA	psalteria
PATRD	plastered
PATRR	plasterer
PATSD	practised
PATSM	phantasim
PATSS	phantasms
PAUTE	plaquette
PAYGL	pharyngal
PAYGS	pharynges
PAYXS	pharynxes
PBIBR	public bar
PBIEE	public eye
PBIHD	published
PBIIE	publicise
	publicize
PBIIT	publicist
PBIIY	publicity
PBSET	pubescent
PCAAK	pickaback
PCAIG	packaging
PCATY	peccantly
PCEBL	Pachelbel
PCEFL	pocketful
PCEIG	pocketing
PCEOT	packed out
PCFIG	pacifying
PCIAE	pectinate
PCICA	Pichincha
PCIGP	packing-up
PCIKR	picnicker
PCIPH	Peckinpah
PCLTR	peculator
PCMKR	pacemaker
PCNAY	pecuniary
PCOIL	pictorial
PCORM	pictogram
PCPRE	pick-purse
PCSIF	Pecksniff
PCYEM	pachyderm
PDEBG	padded bag
PDGED	pedigreed
PDGGC	pedagogic
PDGGE	pedagogue
PDIES	podginess
	pudginess
PDMLN	pademelon
PDMTR	pedometer
PDNIE	pedantise
	pedantize
PDNIM	pedantism
PDONY	Podgorniy
PDRRS	pedereros
PEACL	pre-cancel
PEAET	prevalent
PEAIE	precative
	predative
	prelatise
	prelatize
PEAIG	preparing
	presaging
PEAIY	plenarily
PEAOY	precatory
	predatory
	prefatory
PEATR	poetaster
PEAUE	premature
PEBTR	presbyter
PECET	prescient
PECIE	prescribe
PECIG	preaching
PECIT	prescript
PECIY	preachify
	preachily
PECOL	preschool
PECOS	pre-echoes
PECUY	preoccupy
PEDBE	pleadable
PEDIH	plead with
PEDNM	pseudonym
PEEAT	paederast
PEEDD	pretended
PEEDL	prebendal
PEEDR	pretender
PEEEL	piecemeal
PEEET	precedent
	preselect
PEEIE	preterite
PEEIG	preceding
PEEIS	phenetics
PEERD	preferred
PEETD	presented
PEETR	precentor
	preceptor
	presenter
PEETY	presently
PEEVD	preserved
PEEVR	preserver
PEGOP	peer group
PEHIK	pre-shrink
PEHNV	Plekhanov
PEIAE	predicate
PEIAT	predikant
PEICS	precincts
PEIET	predigest
	predilect
	president
PEIEY	precisely
PEIGR	Preminger
PEIHY	peevishly
PEIIE	poeticise
	poeticize
	precipice
PEIIL	presidial
PEIIM	presidium
PEIIN	precisian
	precision
	prevision
PEIIS	presidios
PEIIY	puerility
PEILS	Plexiglas®
PEITC	pietistic
PEITD	predicted
PEIUE	plenitude
	poeticule
	prefigure
PELDD	precluded
PEMNA	pneumonia
PEMRO	pre-embryo
PEMTC	pneumatic
PENBE	pregnable
PENNY	pregnancy
PEOAR	pterosaur
PEOEA	phenomena
PEOEE	Pleiocene
PEOET	prepotent
PEOIE	preconise
	preconize
PEOIL	precocial
PEOIY	precocity
PEOOE	pheromone
PEOOY	paedology
	phenology
	poenology
PEOUE	pleno jure
PEOYE	phenotype
PEPRL	puerperal
PERAN	preordain
PERTC	pleuritic
PESAG	pressgang
	press-gang
PESNE	Pleasence
PESNS	pheasants
PESOE	press home
PESON	press down
PESRD	pressured
PESRR	pleasurer
PESTD	press stud
PESUG	Pressburg
PESYU	please you
PETFL	plentiful
PETIK	Prestwick
PETOS	plectrons
	plenteous
PETUS	plectrums
PETWR	peel-tower
PEUEN	presume on
PEUIE	prejudice
	prelusive
PEUIG	presuming
PEUIL	preludial
PEUOY	prelusory
PEURR	precurrer
PEUSR	precursor
PFADR	puff adder
PFEAI	pifferari
PFEOT	puffed out
	puffed-out
PFIES	puffiness
PFIGY	puffingly
PGAIE	pegmatite
PGAIN	Pygmalion
PGAIY	pugnacity
PGATY	pageantry
PGEDD	pigheaded
	pig-headed
PGETD	pigmented
PGIHY	piggishly
PGNAE	pogoniate
PGSIK	pogo stick
PGYAK	piggyback
	piggy-bank
PIADR	philander
PIAEA	Primavera
PIAER	privateer
PIAEY	philately
	plicately
	privately
PIAIE	privatise
	privative
	privatize
PIAIN	privation
PIAIY	primarily
PIAOS	poinadoes
	privadoes
PIATC	peirastic
PIAVL	primaeval
PICAA	poinciana
PICDM	princedom
PICHL	Prince Hal
PICLA	Priscilla
PICPA	principia
PICPE	principle

PICPL principal
PICTN Princeton
PIEAE prime rate
PIEES priceless
prideless
PIEIE prime time
PIEIT price list
PIEOT prime cost
PIEPN prise open
PIFLY painfully
PIHRE philhorse
PIIAA primipara
PIIEE privilege
PIIIE primitive
PIIPC philippic
PIKIG prickling
PIKOG prick-song
PILSE paillasse
PIMTC prismatic
PINNY poignancy
PIOEI Primo Levi
PIOIE Prigogine
PIOIY poison ivy
PIOOS poisonous
PIOOY philology
PIRYL pair-royal
PISES priestess
PISLY Priestley
PISNE puissance
PITAE point-lace
PITAL paintball
PITBE paintable
printable
PITDY pointedly
PITES pointless
PITHE point shoe
PIUIE primuline
PIYEL privy seal
PKFNT poke fun at
PKNEE Pekingese
PKNOT poking out
PKSAF pikestaff
PKSAI Pakistani
PLAAE pull a face
PLAAT pull apart
PLACY polyarchy
PLADY polyandry
PLAED pull ahead
PLAEY palmately
PLAID pull a bird
PLAIE polyamide
pulsatile
pulsative
PLAIG pillaging
pulsating
PLAIM palladium
Pelmanism
PLAIN pulsation
PLAIT pillarist
PLAOY pulsatory
PLARN pellagrin
PLBAH Palm Beach
PLBKR pull baker
PLBSC polybasic
PLBTS phlebitis
PLCDG police dog
PLCEA phlyctena
PLCIT pole-clipt
PLCMN policeman
PLDNL paludinal
PLEAE pilferage
PLEIE palletise
palletize
pelletise
pelletize
pulverise
pulverize
PLEIG pilfering
PLEIY pelletify
PLETR polyester
PLETS palmettos
PLGAH polygraph
PLGNL polygonal
PLHDA polyhedra
PLIAE palpitate
pollinate
pulvinate
PLIER pulpiteer
PLIES palliness
PLIFN pelvic fin
PLIGY peltingly
PLILO pulvillio
PLILR pulvillar
PLIOF pull it off
PLIOY pellitory
PLISE palliasse
PLITY palmistry
PLMAG Palembang
PLMCL polemical
PLMNS palominos
PLMTY polymathy
PLNEN palankeen
PLNIE polonaise
PLNUN palanquin
PLOAY pulmonary
PLOIE pillorise
pillorize
PLOTF pull out of
PLPIH pal up with
PLPOD polyploid
PLPOE polyphone
PLPOY polyphony
PLPYH polyptych
PLRER polar bear
PLRUD pal around
pull round
PLSIG polishing
PLSIT polo shirt
PLSOF polish off
PLTBE palatable
PLTBY palatably
PLTCL political
PLTCS politicos
PLTCY politicly
PLTEE polythene
PLTES pilotless
PLTGT pull tight
PLTLG pilot flag
PLTUO politburo□
PLUAE pullulate
PLUAT pollutant
PLUIG polluting
PLUIN pollusion
pollution
PLUSI Pilsudski
PLVUT pole vault
PLWRS pull wires
PLXNS Polixenes
PLYNA Pollyanna
PMAOR pompadour
PMEIG pampering
PMENL pimpernel
PMETS pimientos
PMHES pamphlets
PMHLX pompholyx
PMOIY pomposity
PMOSY pompously
PMWTR pome-water
PNAEE pineal eye
PNAEY pinnately
PNAGE pentangle
PNAIE Pindarise
Pindarize
PNAON pantaloon
PNAPE pineapple
PNARM pentagram
PNCAS Punic Wars
PNCHO Pinocchio
PNEAE ponderate
PNEES panderess
PNEIG pondering
PNELD pannelled
PNEMN pan-German
PNENS Pendennis
PNEOS ponderous
PNEOT Pentecost
PNETN pinkerton
PNETY pendently
pungently
PNFOD Pink Floyd
PNGRC panegyric
PNHBA panphobia
PNHEK pinchbeck
PNHIE punchline
PNHIM pantheism
PNHIT pantheist
PNHNL panthenol
PNHOL punch bowl
PNHRT Pankhurst
PNHUE penthouse□
PNIES penniless
PNIEY pensively
PNIGY pantingly
punningly
PNIIG pantiling
PNIIY pensility
PNILR penciller
PNINR pensioner
PNIOE pantihose
PNIOM penniform
PNLIA penultima
PNLIG panelling
PNLIN penillion
PNLIT panellist
PNLOE penal code
PNLOK panel-work
PNLVC pan-Slavic
PNMEH Phnom Penh
PNMHT panama hat
PNMRL penumbral
PNNUA peninsula
PNNWB pin and web
PNOEN pinto bean
PNOFE pantoffle
pantoufle
PNOHC pansophic
PNOIE pantomime
pentoxide
PNOKE pondokkie
PNPAN peneplain
PNPPS Pan's pipes
PNRBC pan-Arabic
PNRED pen-friend
PNRMC panoramic
PNROS penurious
PNSIG punishing
PNSUT pants suit
PNSZD pint-sized
PNTAE penetrate
punctuate
PNTAT penetrant
PNTLA panatella
PNTLO punctilio
PNTMN penstemon
PNTNE penitence
PNTOE panettone
PNTOI panettoni
PNTOR Pinot Noir
PNTRD punctured
PNUAE pendulate
PNUHR penpusher
pen-pusher
PNUOS pendulous
PNUUS pendulums
PNYAE Penny Lane
PNYIE penny-wise
POAAE propagate
POAEY profanely
prolately
POAIE prolamine
protamine
POAIN probation
POAIY procacity
profanity
POAOG plod along
POARA pro patria
POASS prolapsus
POATN prolactin
POCIE proactive
proscribe
PODID proud-pied
POEAA pro re nata

POEAE promenade
POEAL phone call
POEBE proveable
POEBY proveably
POECL Provençal
POEDR provender
POEES proneness
POEIE phonetise
phonetize
POEIM prooemium
POEIN prooemion
POEIS phonemics
phonetics
POEIT phonetist
POELR propeller
POEOM prose poem
POESD processed
professed
POESR processor
professor
POESS prolepses
prolepsis
proteuses
POETC proleptic
POETD projected
protected
POETN progestin
POETR projector
protector
protester
protestor
POETT protest at
POEUE procedure
prosecute
POEYE proselyte
POFED proofread
POGAG Pyongyang
POGMN ploughman
ploughmen
POGON pronghorn
POGUK prongbuck
POHLI prothalli
POHSS prothesis
POHTC prophetic
prothetic
POHUE poorhouse
POIAE proximate
POICS provinces
POIER profiteer
POIES phoniness
prosiness
POIET prominent
provident
POIIG promising
providing
POIIN prosimian
provision
POIIY prolixity
proximity
POIOS provisoes
POIOY provisory
POISS psoriasis
POLLT poorly lit
POLTC proclitic
POMUH poor-mouth
PONCN pro and con
PONSS prognoses
prognosis
POOAE prorogate
POOCS proboscis
POOET proponent
POOGD prolonged
POOIE phonolite
prologise
prologize
POOIG promoting
provoking
POOIN promotion
POOIS Procopius
POOIT prosodist
POOIV Prokofiev
POONE pronounce
POOOL protozoal
POOON protozoan
POOOY phonology
photocopy
POOSL proconsul
POOTT photostat
Photostat®
POOYE phonotype
photolyse
prototype
POPAE phosphate
POPCS prospects
POPIG prompting
POPUE prompture
PORAE procreate
PORAT procreant
POREY propriety
PORME programme
PORML prodromal
PORMS prodromus
POROA pyorrhoea
POSAT prop shaft
POSES piousness
POSIE proustite
POTAE prostrate
POUAY procuracy
POUES procuress
POUEY profusely
POUIG producing
POUIN profusion
POYAA Propylaea
PPDEM pipe dream
pipe-dream
PPEER puppeteer
PPEOI pepperoni
PPIAE pepsinate
PPIEL popliteal
PPIGR pop singer
PPLAE papillate
PPLAY papillary
PPLOA papilloma
PPLOE papillote
PPLRY popularly
PPLTD populated
PPNHT piping hot
PPOIE peptonise
peptonize
PPQEK pipsqueak
PPRAK paperback
PPRES paperless
PPRHN paper-thin
PPRLP paperclip
PPRMA peperomia
PPROK paperwork
PPRVR paper over
PPRZI paparazzi
PPRZO paparazzo
PPSOE pipestone
PPYOE puppy love
PPYOK poppycock
PQATY piquantly
PRADR Periander
PRAEF partake of
PRAET parrakeet
permanent
PRAIA per capita
PRAIE pervasive
portative
purgative
PRAIG partaking
PRAIN pervasion
purgation
PRALY permalloy
PRANO pertain to
PRAOY purgatory❑
PRASS Parnassus
PRBAE parabrake
PRBLC parabolic
PRBLI periboloi
PRBLS parabolas
PRBOD pure-blood
PRCAE periclase
PRCAT pyroclast
PRCEE Paraclete
PRCIL parochial
PRCNS pericones
PRCTN Paricutín
PRCUE parachute
PRDCL parodical
PRDIG parodying
PRDNA peridinia
PRDRS paradores
PRDSL paradisal
PRDTC peridotic
PREAN porcelain
PREBE permeable
PREBY permeably
PREEE persevere
PREGE porbeagle
PREIG parleying
PREIM Parseeism
PREIN parhelion
PRENE permeance
PREOT parcel out
PRESN per person
PRETD perfected
permeated
perverted
PRETS perfectos
PRETY perfectly
PREUE persecute
PREUL perpetual
PREVD perfervid
PREVO parleyvoo
PRFIG purifying
PRFIY paraffiny
PRFLO portfolio
PRFRN poriferan
PRGAH paragraph
PRGIE peregrine❑
PRGNC pyrogenic
PRGRC paregoric
PRHDY parchedly
PRHET parchment
PRHNE perchance
PRHNN Parthenon
PRHRN Percheron
PRHSR purchaser
PRIES perkiness
PRIET pertinent
PRIGR porringer
PRIGY purringly
PRIIE parricide
partitive
Persicise
Persicize
PRIIN partition
perdition
PRIIY perfidity
PRILO partial to
PRILS particles
PRILY partially
PRIMN persimmon
PRINE persienne
PRINN Perpignan
PRIOS porticoes
PRIOY parsimony
PRISN Parkinson
PRITD permitted
PRITN persist in
PRKRA perikarya
PRLLA paralalia
PRLMN Port Limon
PRLNE purulence
PRLSD paralysed
PRLSR paralyser
PRLSS paralysis
pyrolysis
PRLTC paralytic
PRLUS Port Louis
PRLXD perplexed
PRMCA paramecia
PRMDC paramedic
pyramidic
PRMDL pyramidal
PRMNA pyromania
PRMSS pyramises
PRMTA paramatta
PRMTR parameter
perimeter

Words marked ❑ can also be spelled with an initial capital letter

pyrometer
PRMTY pyrometry
PRMUT paramount
PRNAE parentage
perennate
PRNGA Paranagua
PRNIC paranoiac
PRNIG parenting
PRNIL perennial
PRNTL perinatal
Port Natal
PROAE parsonage
percolate
perforate
personage
personate
PROAI portolani
PROEY purposely
PROIE personise
personize
purposive
PROIY personify
PROMD performed
PROMR performer
PROND purloined
PRONL personnel
PRONR part-owner
PROOO Porto Novo
PROTD purported
PRPDA parapodia
PRPEY periphery
PRPSU pari passu
PRPTA peripetia
PRRDE partridge□
PRRYL portrayal
PRRYR portrayer
PRSDN Port Sudan
PRSEM perisperm
PRSIG perishing
PRSLT Port Salut
PRSOE periscope
PRSTC parasitic
PRSTS parasites
PRSYE peristyle
PRTCL piratical
PRTMR part-timer
PRTRM pyrethrum
PRUAE permutate
pertusate
PRUBD perturbed
PRUDD persuaded
PRUDR persuader
PRUEY perfumery
PRUIE porcupine
PRUIN perfusion
PRUKE parbuckle
PRUNE pursuance
PRUSL pertussal
PRUSS pertussis
PRUTE pirouette
PRUTY parquetry
PRUUE Portuguee
PRWRS parkwards
PRYAL party wall
PRYIE party line
party-size
PRYOR party-goer
PSAHO pistachio
PSAOG push along
PSAOS passadoes
PSAOY piscatory
PSDBE paso doble
PSEEL pas de seul
PSEET passement
PSEEX pas de deux
PSEFR pushed for
PSEGR passenger
PSEHT pas de chat
PSEIE passerine
PSEIG pestering
PSEIR posterior
PSEIY posterity
PSENK Pasternak
PSEOF pissed off
PSESD possessed
PSESR possessor
PSESY passers-by
PSFLY pushfully
PSHRE posthorse
PSHSE posthaste
post-haste
PSHUE posthouse
PSIAE passivate
PSIES pastiness
pushiness
PSIET pestilent
PSIEY passively
PSIGN passing on
PSIGY pushingly
PSIIE pesticide
PSIIM pessimism
PSIIN postilion
PSIIT pessimist
PSIIY passivity
PSILS possibles
PSINL passional
PSIOS posticous
PSNLO Pisanello
PSNTL postnatal
PSOAE pastorale
pastorate
PSOAI pastorali
PSOFS pass off as
PSOOY pestology
PSORD piston rod
PSPND postponed
PSRUD pass round
PSSAT push-start
PSUAE pasturage
postulate
pustulate
PSUAT postulant
PSUIG posturing
PSULR pasquiler
PSWMN postwoman
PSWTR pass water
PSYOT pussyfoot
pussy-foot
PTADO put paid to
PTAIE Patna rice
PTAKR Pat Barker
PTALY pot barley
PTCIE petechiae
PTCIL petechial
PTCOS put across
PTDEY Pat Eddery
PTEID putrefied
PTEIG pattering
pottering
PTEND patterned
PTETY patiently
PTFLY pitifully
PTFOD pot of gold
PTHAK pitch-dark
PTHET patch test
PTHIE pitchpine
PTHNO pitch into
PTHOE pitch-pole
PTHOK patchwork
pitchfork
PTHOL pitch-poll
PTHUI patchouli
PTIAY pituitary
PTIES pettiness
pithiness
pottiness
PTIGY pityingly
PTIHY pettishly
PTIID petrified
PTIIE patricide
pethidine
PTIIH Petri dish
PTIIN patrician
PTIIY putridity
PTIOS patricoes
PTIOT petticoat
PTIOY patrimony
PTIRH patriarch
PTITC patriotic
patristic
PTLNE petulance
PTLNY petulancy
PTLPT pottle-pot
PTNAE potentate
PTNAL put in jail
put on sail
PTNBD put in a bid
PTNDE put on edge
PTNHW put on show
PTNID put in mind
PTNIE potentise
potentize
put on side
PTNIL potential
PTNIS put on airs
PTNOD put on hold
PTNTD patinated
PTOAE patronage
PTOCR patrol car
PTOEM petroleum
PTOER pétroleur
PTOES patroness
pythoness
PTOEY pathogeny
PTOIE patronise
patronize
PTOIG pot-holing
PTOIN Petrosian
PTOIS Petronius
PTOLR patroller
pot-boiler
PTOLS Patroclus
PTOMN patrolman
PTONO put down to
PTOOY pathology
petrology
PTORI potpourri
pot-pourri
PTOSY piteously
PTPIH put up with
PTRAL Peter Hall
PTRED Peterhead
PTRHM petersham
PTRIY paternity
PTRNW Peter Snow
PTROK Peter Cook
PTRRS patereros
PTSIM potassium
PTSOE put ashore
PTTAE put at ease
PTTIK put at risk
PTTOR petit four
PTTUY petit jury
PTUHA Petrushka
PTUHO Petruchio
PTUTR pot-hunter
PTYAH petty cash
PUAIE pluralise
pluralize
PUAIM pluralism
PUAIS Pausanias
PUAIT pluralist
PUAIY plurality
PUBGS plumbagos
PUBIE plumb line
plumb-line
pourboire
PUDAE pound cake
PUDIN pound sign
PUDKS Paul Dukas
PUDON pound coin
PUDRC Paul Dirac
PUDRR plunderer
PUEDM pauperdom
PUEES pauseless
PUEIE pauperise
pauperize
PUEIM pauperism
PUELS prunellos
PUETY prudently
PUFRH pour forth
PUFUS plus-fours

PUHUS pouchfuls
PUIGY pausingly
poutingly
PUIHY prudishly
PUINE prurience
PUJNS Paul Jones
PULIH Prue Leith
PUOIM plutonium
PUOIN Plutonian
PUORT plutocrat
PUPES plumpness
PUPIT plus point
PUSIT poursuitt
PUSMN Paul Simon
PUSOT Paul Scott
PUSTE poussette
PUTRR poulterer
PVOIN Pavlovian
PVRTI Pavarotti
PVTLY pivotally
PWEKG powder keg
PWLIE powellise
powellize
PWRAE power game
PWRAK power pack
PWRES powerless
PWRIE power dive
power line
PXEOD pixie hood
PXLTD pixilated
PYAIT paysagist
PYATR paymaster
PYEDO pay heed to
PYHDP psyched up
PYHSS psychoses
psychosis
PYHTC psychotic
PYIIM physicism
PYIIN physician
PYIIT physicist
PYNOT paying-out
PYNUL pay in full
PYOEY phylogeny
phytogeny
PYOOY phycology
PYTWY pay its way
PYVST pay a visit
PZIAO pizzicato
PZLOT puzzle out
QAEIG quavering
QAEIH Quakerish
QAEIM Quakerism
QAIES quakiness
QAIGY quakingly
QAIID qualified
QAIIR qualifier
QAIIS qualities
QARFD quadrifid
QARGE quadrigae
QARLA quadrella
QARLE quadrille
QARPD quadruped
QARPE quadruple
QARPY quadruply
QARTC quadratic
QATCL quantical
QATIE quartzite
QATRY quarterly
QATTE quartette
QECIG quenching
QECTN quercetin
QEEKR Quebecker
QEEOS Québecois
QEEUP queue-jump
QENAY Queen Mary
QENHP queenship
QENIE queenlike
queen-size
QENNE Queen Anne
Queen-Anne
QERCO quebracho
QERES queerness
QERIH queer fish
QETIT questrist
QETOS questions
QEUOS querulous
QEZLS quetzales
QIBIG quibbling
QICAM quitclaim
QIEFL quiverful
QIEFW quite a few
QIEIG quivering
QIEOD quite good
QIIIE quinidine
QIKAD quicksand
QIKES quickness
QIKIE quick-fire
quick time
QIKNR quickener
QIKOK quick look
QIKTP quickstep
QIOIE quinoline
QIOIM quixotism
QISET quiescent
QITES quietness
QITND quietened
QITNE quittance
QITON quintroon
QITPE quintuple
QITTE quintette
QITTI quintetti
QIZCL quizzical
QOAIN quotation
QOIIN quotidian
QOLBT quodlibet
RAAOD read aloud
RABOK roadblock
RADAL Roald Dahl
RAGAD rearguard
RAGGS Ryan Giggs
RAHBE reachable
RAHDS rhachides
rhaphides
RAHSS rhachises
RAHUE roadhouse
RAIAE reanimate
RAIES readiness
RAIGY roaringly
RAIIS realities
RAITC realistic
RALGT rear light
RAMCY real McCoy
RAMES realmless
RAMVE road movie
RAOIG reasoning
RAPIT reappoint
RARNE rearrange
RASDC rhapsodic
RASED roadstead
RASRD reassured
RASRR reassurer
RAWRD real world
RAWRS rearwards
roadworks
RAYAE ready-made
RBDES rabidness
RBEIE rubberise
rubberize
RBESW rabbet saw
RBIAE rabbinate
rubricate
RBIIN rubrician
RBKBE rebukable
RBLIE rebel-like
rubellite
RBLIG rebelling
RBLIN rebellion
RBNOD Robin Hood
RBNOK Robin Cook
RBRKE Robert Kee
RBRSN Robertson
RBSAD Rab Island
RBSML ribosomal
RBURD ribaudred
RCADA Richardia
RCADI Richard II
RCAFE réchauffé
RCAGE rectangle
RCAIE Rechabite
RCAIM racialism
RCAIT racialist
RCAMR reclaimer
RCBUD rock-bound
RCCIG recycling
RCEAM rocker arm
RCECE recherché
RCEER racketeer
rocketeer
RCEIG rocketing
RCEIU Richelieu
RCEIY ricketily
RCENE recreance
RCENY recreancy
RCETR Rochester
RCGIE recognise
recognize
RCHRE racehorse
RCIAE reclinate
RCIES rockiness
RCIIG receiving
reclining
RCIIR rectifier
RCIUE rectitude
RCLET recollect
RCLSE recalesce
RCMED recommend
RCMET recumbent
RCMIE recombine
RCMOE rocambole
RCNEE reconvene
RCNER raconteur
RCNET reconvert
RCNIE reconcile
recondite
RCNIN recension
RCNOL rock 'n' roll
RCOAE rectorate
RCOIG reckoning
RCOIL rectorial
RCPAT rock plant
RCPET recipient
RCPIE receptive
RCPIG recapping
RCPIN reception
RCPPR rice paper
RCPUE recapture
RCRCS rectrices
RCRET recurrent
RCRIE recursive
RCRIG recording
recurring
RCRIN recursion
RCSEN Rick Stein
RCSIE recessive
RCSIG recasting
RCSIN recession
RCSNE recusance
RCSNY recusancy
RCTAK race track
racetrack
RCTIE rock tripe
RCUEY reclusely
RCUIE reclusive
RCUIG recouping
RCUIN reclusion
RCUSS recourses
RCUTL recountal
recruital
RCUTR recounter
recruiter
RCVRD recovered
RCVRR recoverer
RDADD redhanded
red-handed
RDAEY radiately
RDAIE radialise
radialize
RDAIN radiation
RDAPT red carpet
RDATY radiantly
RDCAE reductase
RDCBE reducible

RDCHO radicchio
RDCIE reductive
RDCIN redaction
reduction
RDCLR ridiculer
RDCLY radically
RDEDS reddendos
RDEET ridge tent
RDEIE ridge-tile
RDEIG reddening
redeeming
RDEIS Red devils
RDEKA rudbeckia
RDEPR Red Pepper
red pepper
RDETR red-letter
RDHNO Rodchenko
RDIES ruddiness
RDIHR rodfisher
RDIIG red-lining
RDIOE Ruddigore
RDLFE Radcliffe
RDLNE redolence
RDLNY redolency
RDLVR redeliver
RDMNS rudiments
RDNAT redundant
RDNIN Red Ensign
Red Indian
RDNOE redingote
RDOAE radio wave
RDOED Radiohead
RDOOY radiology
RDORM radiogram
RDPDR red spider
RDRAT redbreast
RDRDE Redbridge
RDRES riderless
RDRNE Red Grange
RDRRP radar trap
RDULT red mullet
RDUPT rod puppet
RDVVS redivivus
REAIE re-examine
REFRE re-enforce
REHIG re-echoing
REIGY reelingly
REMTC rheumatic
REOIE rhetorise
rhetorize
REUAE re-educate
RFAIN reflation
RFATD refracted
RFATR refractor
RFCIN refection
RFCOY refectory
RFEAC reflex arc
RFEHD refreshed
RFEHN refreshen
RFEHR refresher
RFEIE reflexive
RFEIG raftering
RFEIN reflexion

RFETN reflect on
RFETR reflector
RFIHY raffishly
RFINY ruffianly
RFLET refulgent
RFNDY refinedly
RFRBE referable
RFRIG reforming
RFRIH refurbish
RFRIM reformism
RFRIT reformist
RFRNA referenda
RFRNE reference
RFSBE refusable
RFSET rufescent
RFSIN refashion
RFSNK refusenik
RFTBE refutable
RFTBY refutably
RFTET refitment
RFTIG refitting
RGAOE rigmarole
RGCDL regicidal
RGDES rigidness
RGEAE Rogue Male
RGEDD rug-headed
RGEDN reguerdon
RGEFL regretful
RGEIE ruggedise
ruggedize
RGEOT rigged out
RGIHY roguishly
RGIIG regaining
RGLRY regularly
RGLTD regulated
RGLTO Rigoletto
RGLTR regulator
RGRFL regardful
RGRIG regarding
RGSER régisseur
RGSES registers
RGSRR registrar
RGTAD right-hand
rightward
RGTAE right face!
RGTBE rightable
RGTES rightness
RGTIE right side
rightsize
RGTIG right wing
right-wing
RGTON right down
right-down
RGTOS righteous
RGTWY right away
RGYOT rugby boot
RHASL rehearsal
RHASR rehearser
RHDAE rehydrate
RHUIG rehousing
RIAIN ruination
RIBRE reimburse
RICOD rain-cloud

RIDES reindeers
RIDOS raindrops
RIEAE reiterate
RIEAN raise Cain
RIEBE raiseable
RIEEL raise hell
RIEIE Rhine wine
RIFRE reinforce
RIGUE rain gauge
rain-gauge
RIHRT Reinhardt
RIHTG Reichstag
RIIES raininess
RIIGY railingly
RIOAP rhizocarp
RIODL rhizoidal
RIOOY rhinology
RIOSY ruinously
RIPAT reimplant
RIPOF rainproof
RISAE reinstate
RISAL reinstall
re-install
RISOM rainstorm
RITFL reistafel
RITRR roisterer
RJCIN rejection
RJGIG rejigging
RJHHP rajahship
RJIDR rejoinder
RJIEN rejoice in
RJIIG rejoicing
RJSHN Rajasthan
RJTFL rijstafel
RKAAL Rik Mayall
RLAEE Release Me
RLAOG roll along
RLATN reliant on
RLCAE reluctate
RLCAT reluctant
RLEIG relieving
RLEMP relief map
RLETS rillettes
RLGBE relegable
RLGEX religieux
RLGOE religiose
RLGOO religioso
RLGOS religious
RLMDL role model
RLNIG relenting
RLNOT ruling out
RLPIG relapsing
RLQAY reliquary
RLQIE reliquiae
RLTDO related to
RLTOS relations
RLTVS relatives
RLVNE relevance
RLVNY relevancy
RMADR ram-raider
RMAIG rampaging
rummaging
RMATY rampantly

RMAUE remeasure
RMDIG remedying
RMEZE ramfeezle
RMGAE remigrate
RMIDR remainder
RMIGY rompingly
RMIHY rompishly
RMIIG remaining
RMLIS Ramillies
RMNAT remontant
RMNFL remindful
RMNIG reminding
romancing
RMNNE remanence
RMNNY remanency
RMNSE reminisce
RMNTR ruminator
RMPOA Ramaphosa
RMRNT Rembrandt
RMSIE remissive
RMSIN remission
RMTET remitment
remittent
RMUAE remoulade
rémoulade
RMVBE removable
RMVBY removably
RMWRS Romewards
RNAKD ransacked
RNAKR ransacker
RNCOS run across
RNCRD run scared
RNEIG rendering
RNESP runners-up
RNFNE ring-fence
RNGDS renegados
RNGUE ring gauge
RNHKE ranshakle
RNHRS rancheros
RNIAE runcinate
RNIES randiness
RNIGY rantingly
ringingly
runningly
RNIIN rendition
RNIIY rancidity
RNITN Rin Tin Tin
RNLTD ringleted
RNNUI ranunculi
RNOED run to seed
RNOIE randomise
randomize
RNOIG ransoming
RNOOS rancorous
RNRDR rank-rider
RNRUD run around
runaround
RNSET renascent
RNTEF run itself
RNTIE run it fine
RNUCR renouncer
RNVTR renovator
RNWBE renewable

RNWRD	Ringworld
RNYIK	rinky-dink
ROAIE	rhodamine
	rhodanise
	rhodanize
	rhotacise
	rhotacize
ROBSS	rhombuses
ROCIL	rhonchial
ROCNL	root canal
ROEET	Roosevelt
ROEIG	reopening
ROIES	roominess
ROLUY	Raoul Dufy
ROOIE	rhodolite
	rhodonite
ROOSN	rhodopsin
ROOSY	riotously
ROPUE	root-prune
RORNE	Rio Grande
ROSOK	rootstock
RPAIG	repealing
	repeating
RPCAE	repechage
RPCOS	rapacious
RPDAE	repudiate
RPDES	rapidness
RPDIE	rapid fire
RPDNE	rope-dance
RPEED	reprehend
RPEET	represent
	re-present
RPEIH	replenish
RPEIN	repletion
RPESD	repressed
RPESR	repressor
RPGAT	repugnant
RPIAD	reprimand
RPIAE	replicate
RPIIN	reptilian
RPIMN	repairman
RPLAT	repellant
RPLET	repellent
RPLIE	repulsive
RPLIG	repelling
RPLIN	repulsion
RPNAT	repentant
RPOAE	reprobate
RPOAY	reprobacy
RPOES	reprocess
RPOIG	reproving
RPOIL	raptorial
RPOUE	reproduce
RPRAE	reportage
RPRBE	reparable
RPRBY	reparably
RPRES	reporters
RPRIG	reporting
RPROY	repertory
RPRUS	repercuss
RPSDY	reposedly
RPSES	repossess
RPSFL	reposeful
RPSUE	repasture
RPTBE	reputable
RPTBY	reputably
RPTDY	reputedly
RPUIE	rapturise
	rapturize
RPUOS	rapturous
RPYBE	repayable
RPYET	repayment
RQEOT	Roquefort
RQETD	requested
RQETR	requester
RQIIE	requisite
RQIIG	requiring
RQIKN	requicken
RRAIG	rereading
RRCAH	Rorschach
RRDAE	reradiate
RRERH	rare earth
RRLEN	rural dean
RRLRA	rural area
RRSIT	ra-ra skirt
RRTNA	Ruritania
RSAIG	reshaping
RSAIY	rascality
RSAOE	rise above
RSBRY	raspberry
RSCIN	resection
RSCOS	rosaceous
RSDAY	residuary
RSDNE	residence
RSDNS	residents
RSDNY	residency
RSEIE	rasterize
RSEIG	rostering
RSETD	respected
RSETR	respecter
RSFLY	restfully
RSIAE	rusticate
RSIDD	rescinded
RSIES	riskiness
	rustiness
RSIEY	restively
RSIGY	raspingly
RSIIE	rusticise
	rusticize
RSIIM	rusticism
RSIIY	rusticity
RSLAT	resultant
RSLBE	resoluble
RSLET	resilient
	resolvent
RSLIG	resulting
RSMBE	resumable
RSNEG	Rosenberg
RSNFL	resentful
RSNNE	resonance
	Rosinante
RSNSN	Rising Sun
RSNTR	resonator
RSODO	respond to
RSOIG	reshowing
	restoring
RSOMN	Roscommon
RSOSR	responsor
RSRAE	resurface
RSRET	resorbent
	resurgent
	resurrect
RSRIE	reserpine
RSRIT	reservist
	restraint
RSRNE	restringe
RSROR	reservoir
RSSAT	resistant
RSSIG	resisting
RSTKR	risk-taker
RSUCS	resources
RSUFE	reshuffle
RSUSN	Rasmussen
RSYAL	rusty nail
RTAIE	ritualise
	ritualize
RTAIM	ritualism
RTAIT	ritualist
RTATR	retractor
RTCLA	reticella
RTCLM	reticulum
RTCLR	reticular
RTCNE	reticence
RTEDM	Rotterdam
RTEHM	Rotherham
RTEIH	ratherish
RTEIM	ruthenium
RTELS	Ruth Ellis
RTFLY	ruthfully
RTGAH	rotograph
RTIES	retainers
RTIUE	retribute
RTIVL	retrieval
RTIVR	retriever
RTLAE	retaliate
RTLOF	rattle off
RTNAE	rotundate
RTNIE	retentive
RTNIN	retention
RTNIY	rotundity
RTNLE	retinulae
RTNTS	retinitis
	ritenutos
RTOAE	rationale
RTOEE	retrocede
RTOET	retroject
	retrovert
RTOIG	rationing
RTOLX	retroflex
RTOOT	ration out
RTOSE	retroussé
RTPYR	ratepayer
RTRAT	retardant
RTRDY	retiredly
RTRIG	returning
RTRIN	retortion
RTTBE	rotatable
RTUHR	retoucher
RTVTR	Rotovator®
RTXUE	retexture
RUAIN	Roumanian
RUCIY	raunchily
RUDDP	rounded up
RUDES	roundness
RUDLY	roundelay
RUDOM	roundworm
RUDRH	round arch
RUETP	route-step
RUHAT	roughcast
RUHDA	rough idea
RUHEK	roughneck
RUHEN	rough-hewn
RUHES	roughness
RUHHD	roughshod
RUHRW	rough-draw
RUHUF	rough-puff
RUIEY	routinely
RUIGY	rousingly
RUIIC	Roubiliac
RUIIE	routinise
	routinize
RUOFA	rauwolfia
RUOSY	raucously
RVAIG	revealing
RVAOT	rave about
RVCBE	revocable
RVCBY	revocably
RVKBE	revokable
RVLES	rivalless
RVLET	ravelment
RVLIE	revulsive
RVLIG	ravelling
	revelling
	revolting
	revolving
RVLIN	revulsion
RVNEL	Rivendell
RVNIE	revengive
RVNIG	revenging
RVRES	riverless
RVREY	reversely
RVRIE	riverside❑
RVRIG	reversing
RVRIN	reversion
RVRLH	River Alph
RVRNE	reverence
RVRTX	River Styx
RVSBE	revisable
RVSIG	ravishing
RVTDY	riveted by
RVTET	revetment
RVVBE	revivable
RVVBY	revivably
RWIES	rowdiness
RWIIG	rewriting
RWLPR	rowel-spur
RWRIG	rewarding
	rewording
	reworking
RXMSC	Roxy Music
RYEES	rhymeless
RYETR	rhymester

Words marked ❑ can also be spelled with an initial capital letter

RYJVK Reykjavík
RYLAM royal palm
RYLAT royal mast
RYLEN royal fern
RYLLE royal blue
RYLTC rhyolitic
RYTOG Roy Strong
RYULR Roy Fuller
RZRBE razorable
RZRIE razor wire
RZRIL razorbill
SAAAI scarabaei
SAADY seawardly
SAAER shamateur
SAAGE sea tangle
SAAGR Stavanger
SAAIE star-anise
SAAIG seafaring
SAAIM shamanism
SAAIT shamanist
SAAOT swan about
SABAD starboard
SABIG shambling
SABLC shambolic
SACFR search for
SACIG searching
snatching
SACIN stanchion
SACIY snatchily
starchily
SACOT search out
SACTS staccatos
SADAL stand bail
SADAT stand fast
SADAY stand easy
SADEL stand well
SADES staidness
St Andrews
SADIE stand fire
standpipe
SADIH stand with
SADIM stand firm
SADNS scaldings
SADOD stand good
SADON stand down
SADPN stand upon
SADPO stand up to
SADRM stand from
SADRR slanderer
SADRS standards
SADRY stander-by
SADVR stand over
SADYE Stand By Me
SAEAE shareware
stage name
stage-name
stalemate
SAEAK space walk
space-walk
SAEAT spare part
SAEBE shakeable
shapeable
SAEED snakeweed
SAEES shadeless
shameless
shapeless
spaceless
spareness
staleness
stateless
suaveness
SAEET statement
SAEGR scavenger
SAEHP spaceship
SAEID snakebird
SAEIE snakebite
snakelike
snakewise
space-time
spadelike
spare time
stage-dive
state line
stateside[□]
SAEIG slavering
SAEIY statelily
SAELG shake a leg
SAEMN Seated Man
statesman
SAENT shake on it
SAEOD statehood
SAEOE Slate Cone
SAEOK spadework
SAEOM spare room
stateroom
SAEON scale down
shake down
stare down
SAEOR stage door
SAEOT scapegoat
spaced out
SAERM snare-drum
SAERP sharecrop
SAERW scarecrow
SAEUA State Duma
SAEUS spadefuls
SAEVR skate over
SAEWY slave away
SAEYE spare tyre
SAFIE scarfwise
SAFUT star fruit
SAGIA Shangri-La
Shangri-la
SAGIG spangling
SAGRD staggered
SAGRR swaggerer
SAGTR slaughter
SAGUE snap gauge
SAGZR stargazer
star-gazer
SAHIS Smash Hits
SAHNE sea change
SAHNO smash into
SAHPY slaphappy
slap-happy
SAHTI spaghetti
SAHWY stash away
SAIAD Swaziland
SAIES scaliness
seaminess
shadiness
shakiness
snakiness
soapiness
staginess
SAIEY suasively
SAIGP soaking-up
SAIGY soakingly
soaringly
sparingly
staringly
SAIHY slavishly
SAIIE stabilise
stabilize
SAIIM Stalinism
SAIIR scarifier
SAIIT Stalinist
SAIIY stability
SAILW Stanislaw
SAILY spatially
SAINR stationer
SAITC statistic
SAKAE slack-bake
SAKES slackness
stalkless
starkness
SAKIG sparkling
SAKIS sparklies
SAKKN sharkskin
SAKLG spark plug
SAKLY Sean Kelly
SAKNP slacken up
SAKOL spark coil
SAKRO smackeroo
SAKWY slack away
SALAK small talk
SALAL snail mail
SALBY stableboy
SALED stall-feed
SALER small beer
SALES smallness
SALGT starlight
SALIE small-time
snail-like
SALLD stable lad
SALMN stableman
SALOE stay loose
SALON small-town
SALPD scalloped
SALRA small area
SALTI Scarlatti
SALWG scallawag
scallywag
SALWP swallow up
SALWY shallowly
SAMDC spasmodic
SAMIH swarm with
SAMRR stammerer
SAMSM shammosim
SAMVR swarm over
SANES stainless
SANGT stag night
SANHR sea anchor
SANHY staunchly
SANNY stagnancy
SAOBR sea robber
sea-robber
SAOEA soap opera
SAOIE Slavonise
Slavonize
SAOIG seasoning
shadowing
SAOTS scazontes
SAOTY seaworthy
SAPAD swampland
SAPES scalpless
sharpness
SAPIL stamp mill
SAPNP sharpen up
SAPNR sharpener
SAPRY stag party
SAPTI scarpetti
SAPUY stamp duty
SAPYD sharp-eyed
SARAE staircase
SAREE sea breeze
SAREL stairwell
SARHN sea urchin
SARIE stairwise
SARPL Stavropol
SARVR Swan River
SASEL star shell
SASIK slapstick
SASOE soapstone
SATAD smart card
SATAK start back
SATAS slantways
SATCS Spartacus
SATES scantness
smartness
SATIE slantwise
SATIG scantling
startling
SATLC smart alec
SATNN start in on
SATNP smarten up
SATRD scattered
shattered
SATRE smart arse
SATRG smart drug
SATRR scatterer
SATVR start over
SAUAE spatulate
SAUAY scapulary
SAUOY statutory
SAUQO Status Quo
status quo
SAUTE statuette
SBAET subjacent
SBAIE sabbatise
sabbatize
submarine

SBAIY subfamily
SBCDY subacidly
SBCIE subscribe
SBCIT subscript
SBCOS sebaceous
SBDLA sabadilla
SBDTR subeditor
SBECN subdeacon
SBEEA subgenera
SBEGD submerged
SBELA subsellia
SBESD submersed
SBESE sublessee
SBESR sublessor
SBETD subjected
SBETO subject to
SBETR subletter
subverter
SBIAE sublimate
SBIEY sublimely
SBIGY sobbingly
SBIIE subdivide
sublimise
sublimize
subsidise
subsidize
subtilise
subtilize
SBIIG subsiding
SBIIY sublimity
SBITD submitted
SBITR submitter
SBIUT sobriquet
SBLEN subaltern
SBLIE sibylline
subalpine
SBLNE sibilance
SBLNY sibilancy
SBMGS subimagos
SBNIE subincise
SBOAE subrogate
SBOIN subtopian
SBOML subnormal
SBPCE sub specie
SBRAD St Bernard
SBRES soberness
SBROS subereous
SBRPC subtropic
SBRTC sybaritic❑
SBSIN Sebastian
SBTAA substrata
SBTAE substrate
SBTAT substract
SBTMC subatomic
SBTNE substance
SBTUT substruct
SBUAE subjugate
SBUAY sublunary
SBUBE subduable
SBUDY subduedly
SBUIE sub judice
SBUIG subsuming
SBUOA submucosa
SBUOS submucous
SCAET sacrament❑
SCAIE sacralise
sacralize
siccative
socialise
socialite
socialize
Socratise
Socratize
SCAIM sacrarium
socialism
SCAIN sectarian
SCAIT socialist
SCAIY sociality
SCCOH sackcloth
SCEAY secretary
SCECW sacred cow
SCEDN succeed in
SCEDO succeed to
SCEDR succeeder
SCEFR sicken for
SCEIE secretive
SCEIG sickening
SCEIN secretion
SCEOY secretory
SCESR successor
SCEWY Sacred Way
SCHRN saccharin
SCIAE succinate
SCIEE sacrilege
SCIHY sickishly
SCIIE sacrifice
SCINL sectional
SCITN sacristan
SCLAE siciliane
sick leave
SCLRY secularly
SCNAY secondary
SCNIG seconding
SCNJB second job
SCOAH sociopath
succotash
SCOIE sectorise
sectorize
SCOIL sectorial
suctorial
SCOOY sociology
SCORR succourer
SCPAT sycophant
SCRBE securable
SCSIN secession
SCTUS secateurs
SCUBO succumb to
SCUET succulent
SCUIN seclusion
SDBAD sideboard
SDBRS sideburns
SDCAN side chain
SDCIE seductive
SDCIN seduction
SDDES side-dress
SDEIG saddening
SDEOR Sedgemoor
SDLBG saddlebag
SDLBW saddlebow
SDLGT sidelight
SDNAY sedentary
SDRFC sudorific
SDRSS siderosis
SDSIE side-swipe
SDTAK sidetrack
SDTBE side-table
SDTOS seditious
SDUEN Sadducean
SDUIM Sadducism
SDWRS sidewards
SDWTR soda water
SEADE skedaddle
SEAIE scenarise
scenarize
SEAIG seesawing
SEAIN steradian
SEAIS scenarios
SEAKR Sue Barker
SEATR seek after
SEBED shewbread
SEBOD shed blood
SECDY speech day
SECID stepchild
SECIG sketching
SECIY sketchily
speechify
SECOT sketch out
SECRL stercoral
SECUT suetcrust
SEDAE sheldrake
SEDAL speedball
SEDAT steadfast
SEDBE spendable
SEDEL speedwell
SEDIE spend time
SEDIL seed drill
SEDOT speedboat
SEDRP speed trap
SEDRY slenderly
SEDUK sheldduck
SEDUP speed bump
SEEAE Stevenage
SEEHN Shere Khan
SEEIE Shere Hite
SEEIO Steve Biko
SEEOE stevedore
SEERM Steve Cram
SEESN Stevenson
SEEUE sieve tube
SEFED Sheffield
SEFID Siegfried
SEFIE shelf-life
SEFUS shelf-fuls
SEGIG sleighing
SEHNE Stephanie
SEHNS see things
SEIES seediness
SEIGP spewing up
SEIGY seemingly
SEIID specified
SEIIE sterilise
sterilize
SEIIN St-Émilion
SEIIS specifics
SEIIY sterility
SEILY specially
specialty
SEINE St-Étienne
SEKBE speakable
SEKDM sheikhdom
SEKES sleekness
speckless
SELAD steel band
steelyard
SELCN spellican
SELDN Steely Dan
SELID spellbind
SELIE shellfire
SELIH shellfish
SELLE steel-blue
SELLR stellular
SELOK steelwork
SELOL steel wool
SELRM steal from
SELRT smell a rat
SELTD stellated
SELUT shell suit
SELWY steal away
SEMAH steam bath
SEMAK sperm bank
SEMAL steam-haul
SEMDP steamed up
SEMHP steamship
SEMNY seed money
SEMOM steam room
SEMOT steamboat
steam-boat
SEMPN steam open
SEMRA spermaria
SEMRN steam iron
SEMTA spermatia
SEMTC spermatic
SEMTD spermatid
SENAD sternward
SENEK Steinbeck
SENES sternness
SENOK steinbock
SENRD seeing red
SENRS steenbras
SEOIG see coming
SEOIS Suetonius
SEPAK sheepwalk
sweepback
SEPAL seed-pearl
SEPES sleepless
steepness
SEPIE sheep-lice
SEPIH sleep with
SEPKN sheepskin
SEPNS sweepings
SEPNT sleep on it
SEPOE sheepcote

SEPVR	sleep over
SERBE	steerable
SERED	spearhead
SERES	sheerness❑
SERET	smear test
SERIG	shearling
SERIH	spearfish
SERIT	spearmint
SERMN	steersman
SEROD	swear-word
SETAK	sweet talk
	sweet-talk
	sweptback
SETAS	shed tears
SETCE	spectacle
SETCL	sceptical
SETED	sheet bend
	sheet-feed
SETEL	sweetmeal
SETES	sweetness
SETET	sweetmeat
SETIG	sheathing
	sweptwing
SETIH	sweet dish
SETND	sweetened
SETNR	sweetener
SETON	sweetcorn
SETPT	sweet spot
SETRD	sheltered
SETRR	shelterer
SETTC	steatitic
SETTR	spectator
SETUT	sweatsuit
SEUAE	speculate
SEUKR	spelunker
SEVTS	seek votes
SEWIF	skew-whiff
SEWNS	sherwanis
SFAIE	safranine
SFCVR	soft-cover
SFDIK	soft drink
SFEIG	softening
	suffering
SFFCS	soft focus
SFFUT	soft fruit
SFGAD	safeguard
SFHUE	safe house
SFHVN	safe haven
SFIGY	siftingly
SFLGT	safe light
SFLWR	safflower
SFOAE	suffocate
SFPAE	safe place
SFPDL	soft pedal
	soft-pedal
SFRGN	suffragan
SFRND	saffroned
SFTND	soft-toned
SFTNT	safety net
SFTPN	safety pin
SFTUH	soft touch
SFUIE	suffusive
SFUIN	suffusion
SFVIE	soft voice
SGAIE	signalise
	signalize
SGAMN	signalman
SGAOY	signatory
SGAUE	signature
SGBUH	sagebrush
SGCOS	sagacious
SGEAE	segregate
SGERE	signeurie
SGETD	suggested
SGETL	segmental
SGIES	sogginess
SGIGN	signing on
SGIGP	signing up
	signing-up
SGIGY	sighingly
SGOGS	St George's
SGOIA	Signorina
SGOIE	signorine
SGOII	signorini
SGRAE	sugar cane
SGRAM	sugar palm
SGRES	sugarless
SGRET	sugar beet
SGRID	sugar bird
SGROP	sugar soap
SGRUE	sugar-cube
SGRUP	sugar-lump
SGSUD	Sigismund
SGTAE	sagittate
SGTED	sight-read
SGTER	sightseer
SGTES	sightless
SGTIG	sight-sing
SGUNY	Sigourney
SHATY	schmaltzy
SHAZR	Schnauzer
SHDLD	scheduled
SHEDN	Schleiden
SHEDR	Schneider
SHEIE	scheelite
SHIZL	schnitzel
SHLAT	scholiast
SHLIG	Schelling
	schilling
SHLRY	scholarly
SHMTC	schematic
SHNTR	sphincter
SHOBY	schoolboy
SHOCP	school cap
SHOIG	schooling
SHOKL	schnorkel
SHORR	schnorrer
SHOZE	schnozzle
SHRCL	spherical
SHRLR	spherular
SHSOE	schistose
SIAAA	Shibayama
SIAAN	spin a yarn
SIAIE	skin alive
SIAIN	spiration
SIALD	spiralled
SIAUA	spiracula
SIBAD	sailboard
	shipboard
SIBRE	Swinburne
SICEK	shit creek
SICEY	stitchery
SICIG	stitching
	switching
SICOF	switch off
SICOH	sailcloth
SICSS	suitcases
SICTS	spiccatos
SIDIG	swindling
SIDIT	spindrift
SIDVR	skin-diver
SIEAD	spikenard
	swipe card
SIEAK	spice rack
SIEES	snideness
	spineless
SIEIE	spirewise
SIEIG	shivering
SIELR	sniveller
SIEMN	spiderman
SIEPN	slide open
SIETS	stilettos
SIEUE	slide-rule
SIEUH	spicebush
SIFAE	stiffware
SIFES	stiffness
SIFIG	sniffling
SIFIT	skinflint
SIFLY	skilfully
SIFNR	stiffener
SIGAK	slingback
SIGES	stingless
SIGIG	swingeing
	swing-wing
SIGIZ	Stieglitz
SIGOT	swingboat
SIGRE	stingaree
SIGRR	sniggerer
SIHDA	stichidia
SIHET	slightest
SIHIG	slighting
SIIAE	stipitate
SIIAT	soi-disant
SIIEE	spicilege
SIIES	shininess
	sliminess
	spiciness
	spininess
SIIGM	spirit gum
SIIGY	shiningly
	slidingly
	smilingly
SIIHY	swinishly
SIIIM	spiritism
SIIIT	spiritist
SIIOM	spiniform
SIIOO	spiritoso
SIIUL	spiritual
SIKED	stinkweed
SIKES	slickness
SIKIH	stick with
SIKMP	stick 'em up!
SIKNO	stick into
SIKOB	stink bomb
SIKOD	stinkwood
SIKON	stinkhorn
SIKRM	shirk from
SIKTO	stick it to
SIKTT	stick at it
SILDN	skilled in
SILEG	Spielberg
SILES	stillness
SILIE	still life
SILIG	shielding
SILOE	still more
SILON	stillborn
SILUK	shielduck
SILUT	still-hunt
SILVR	spill over
	spillover
SIMBE	swimmable
SIMRT	swimmeret
SIMTC	stigmatic
SINDP	skinny-dip
SINIE	scientise
	scientize
SINIL	sciential
SINIM	scientism
SINIT	scientist
SINKR	spinnaker
SINRT	spinneret
SIOCS	sci-roccos
SIOHT	sailor-hat
SIOIG	ski-joring
SIOIZ	slivovitz
SIOYA	spirogyra
SIPAE	sailplane
SIPRD	slippered
SIRAT	spit-roast
SIROD	scirrhoid
SIROS	scirrhous
SIRUD	spin round
SISAE	shipshape
SISES	so it seems
SISOL	Swiss roll
SISUY	Sainsbury
SITDY	saint's day
	stiltedly
	stintedly
SITES	shiftless
	swiftness
SITGT	skintight
	skin-tight
SITIE	saintlike
SITIM	Shintoism
SITIT	Shintoist
SITLA	scintilla
SITOD	sainthood
SITON	Saint Joan
SIUAE	spiculate
	stimulate
	stipulate

Words marked ❑ can also be spelled with an initial capital letter

SIUAT stimulant
SIUCI shibuichi
SIUOE spinulose
SIUOS spinulous
SIVIG skivvying
SIWEK shipwreck
SIWTR ship water
SJSUE soja sauce
SJUNR sojourner
SKOHI Sukhothai
SLAAA solfatara
SLAAE sultanate
SLAAY syllabary
SLAIE sulcalise
sulcalize
syllabise
syllabize
SLAIN saltation
salvation
solvation
SLAIY syllabify
SLAOY saltatory
SLAUE self-abuse
SLBIY salubrity
SLCIE selective
SLCIN selachian
selection
SLCLC salicylic
SLCOS salacious
siliceous
silicious
SLCOT select out
SLCSS silicosis
SLCTR solicitor
SLDAS salad days
SLDES solidness
SLDIE self-drive
SLDIH solid with
SLDIY splodgily
SLDUT self-doubt
SLEFX silver fox
SLEGO solfeggio
SLEIE silverise
silverize
SLEIG soldering
SLEIO Solferino
SLEIS Silverius
SLEMN sallee-man
SLESS syllepses
syllepsis
SLETA Silvestra
Sylvestra
SLETC sylleptic
SLETR Sylvester
SLETY saliently
SLHIE sylphlike
sylph-like
SLHNC sulphonic
SLHRC sulphuric
SLHUS silphiums
SLIAE self-image
SLIES saltiness
silkiness
silliness
sulkiness
SLIHY saltishly
selfishly
SLIRN soldier on
SLIRY soldierly
SLLQY soliloquy
SLMIE solemnise
solemnize
SLMIY solemnify
solemnity
SLMRH salt marsh
SLNEY splintery
SLNIG silencing
SLNOR splendour
SLNTC splenetic
SLNTS splenitis
SLOAE Sellotape®
SLOIE syllogise
syllogize
SLOIH sallowish
SLOIM syllogism
SLPIE sale price
self-pride
SLPIM solipsism
SLPIT solipsist
SLPTE saltpetre
SLRDE Selfridge
SLREL solar cell
SLRER solar year
SLRGT sole right
SLRID solar wind
SLRIE solar time
SLRSS scleroses
sclerosis
SLRTA sclerotia
SLRTC sclerotic
SLRTN sclerotin
SLSAK sales talk
SLSAY saleslady
SLSIG splashing
SLSIL salesgirl
SLSIY splashily
SLSOE sell smoke
SLSON seldshown
SLSOT sell short
splash out
SLSUY Salisbury
SLTEY spluttery
SLTIE solitaire
SLTIG splitting
SLWOG self-wrong
SLWRH self-worth
SLWRS saltworks
SLWTR saltwater
SLYIE Sally Ride
SLYOT splay foot
SLYUN Sally Lunn
SMAHS Symmachus
SMAIE summarise
summarize
summative
SMAIN summation
SMAIO simpatico
SMAIT summarist
SMAIY summarily
SMBEE semibreve
SMCFR so much for
SMCLN semicolon
SMEIG simpering
SMELR Sam Weller
SMHNC symphonic
SMIGP summing-up
SMISS symbiosis
SMITC symbiotic
SMLAT simulcast
SMLBY semblably
SMLCA simulacra
SMLCS simplices
SMLNE semblance
SMLRD Simply Red
SMLRO similar to
SMLRY similarly
SMLTD simulated
SMLTN simpleton
SMLTR simulator
SMNAS Simon says
SMNIS semantics
SMNLY seminally
SMOET somnolent
SMOHR some other
SMOIE symbolise
symbolize
SMOIM symbolism❑
symposium
SMOIS semiotics
SMOIT symbolist
SMOOY semiology
symbology
SMOSS summonses
SMPOE semaphore
SMRAD Samarkand
SMRGD semi-rigid
SMRMS Semiramis
SMRRS sombreros
SMRTN Samaritan
SMRWE Sam Browne
SMTAY sumptuary
SMTIG something
SMTMS sometimes
SMTNC semitonic
SMTOS sumptuous
SMTRS sumotoris
SMVWL semivowel
SMWEE somewhere
SMYAN Sammy Cahn
SMYDC Samoyedic
SNAAA Santayana
SNAAH sandarach
SNADR Santander
SNAEE Sinhalese
SNAEY sinuately
SNAHR sunbather
SNAIE send a wire
SNAIN sensation
sinuation
SNAIO San Marino
SNALD sandalled
SNAND sun-tanned
SNAOE Singapore
SNAOG singalong
SNARZ Santa Cruz
SNASN Sun Yat-Sen
SNATC syntactic
SNAUA Singapura
SNBAT sandblast
SNBID sand-blind
SNCAG sonic bang
SNCCE song cycle
SNCEN sunscreen
SNCOM sonic boom
SNEAA sense data
SNEER sonneteer
SNEES senseless
SNEEY sincerely
SNEIE sonnetise
sonnetize
synoecise
synoecize
SNEIY sincerity
SNEPE Sun Temple
SNERM Sanhedrim
SNERN Sanhedrin
SNESN Sanderson
SNESY sinlessly
SNFGN son of a gun
SNFLY songfully
SNFOD sangfroid
sang-froid
SNFRH send forth
SNGAH sonograph
SNGGE synagogue
SNHOY synchrony
SNHSS syntheses
synthesis
SNHTC synthetic
SNIAE syndicate
SNIES sandiness
sunniness
SNIET sentiment
SNIGY singingly
SNIIA sincipita
SNIIE sensitise
sensitive
sensitize
SNILW sons-in-law
SNINE sentience
SNISD sun-kissed
SNIUL San Miguel
SNIUS sinciputs
SNLOT single out
SNLTN single ten
singleton
SNLWR sunflower
SNOAE syncopate
SNOIA santonica
SNOIE Sanforise
Sanforize
syntonise

	syntonize
SNOII	Santorini
SNOIM	sensorium
SNOIY	seniority
	sensorily
	sinuosity
SNONE	sun lounge
SNONR	sundowner
SNOSY	sinuously
SNPIE	synopsise
	synopsize
SNPPR	sandpaper
	sandpiper
SNPRE	sun spurge
SNRIE	synergise
	synergize
SNRIM	synergism
SNRMC	syndromic
SNSAL	Sundsvall
SNSET	senescent
SNSHL	seneschal
SNSIH	songsmith
SNSOE	sandstone
SNSOM	sand storm
	sandstorm
SNSRF	sans serif
SNSRL	sinistral
SNSTS	sinusitis
SNSUI	Sans Souci
SNTAY	sanctuary
SNTOE	sunstroke
SNTOS	sanctions
SNTRA	sanatoria
	sanitaria
SNTZD	sanitized
SNTZR	sanitizer
SNULY	sensually
SNUND	sunburned
SNVTS	synovitis
SNWDE	sand wedge
SNYAL	Sandy Gall
SNYIE	sunny side
SNYYE	Sandy Lyle
SNZIE	St-Nazaire
SOAER	sloganeer
SOAGA	sporangia
SOAHC	stomachic
SOAHL	stomachal
SOAHR	stomacher
SOAIE	sloganise
	sloganize
SOBAD	snowboard
SOBDO	Scooby Doo
SOBID	snow-blind
SOBRY	snowberry
SOBTC	scorbutic
SOBUD	snowbound
SOCAH	slowcoach
SOCDS	stoccados
SOCEG	Scotch egg
SOCEK	spot check
	spot-check
SOCIG	scorching
	slouching
SOCLY	stoically
SOCTS	stoccatas
SOCUE	show cause
SODIG	stop doing
SODIH	swordfish❑
SODIT	snowdrift
SODLY	swordplay
SODMN	swordsman
SOEAD	scorecard
	shoreward
	stone-hard
	store card
SOEAE	stoneware
SOEAL	smoke-ball
	stonewall
SOEAS	stone bass
SOEED	stone-dead
SOEEF	stone-deaf
SOEES	smokeless
	stoneless
SOEFL	shovelful
SOEFR	spoken for
SOEHT	stonechat
SOEIE	shoreline
	slopewise
	spokewise
	stovepipe
SOEIH	stonefish
SOEIN	Slovenian
SOELR	shoveller
SOEMN	spokesman
	spokesmen
SOEOB	smoke-bomb
SOEOD	stokehold
	stone-cold
SOEOK	stonework
SOEOM	storeroom
SOEOT	stonewort
SOERP	stonecrop
SOERS	slope arms
SOFAE	snowflake
SOFED	snowfield
SOFOR	shop floor
SOGOE	snow goose
SOHRD	smothered
SOHRR	smotherer
SOHTM	shochetim
SOIES	showiness
	smokiness
	snowiness
	sootiness
	stoniness
SOIGP	showing up
	slowing-up
SOIGY	slopingly
SOIIY	stolidity
SOISS	scoliosis
SOITC	scoliotic
SOITR	spoliator
SOKAD	stockyard
SOKAE	shock wave
	stocktake
SOKIE	stockpile
SOKIH	stockfish
SOKNS	stockings
SOKOM	Stockholm
	stockroom
SOKOT	Stockport
SOKPN	stock up on
SOKUE	stock cube
SOLAL	stoolball
SOLGT	spotlight
	stoplight
SOLIE	shoalwise
SOMES	stormless
SOMKR	shoemaker❑
SOMOR	storm door
SOMRH	slow-march
SOMRY	show mercy
SOMTH	slow match
SOMUF	storm cuff
SONAS	spoonways
SONED	spoon-feed
SONIE	spoonwise
SONIS	stownlins
SONLI	stornelli
SONRL	scoundrel
SONUS	spoonfuls
SONWY	Stornoway
SOOAA	scotomata
SOOHL	sporophyl
SOOHV	Sholokhov
SOPAE	showplace
SOPEE	showpiece
SOPES	stop press
SOPUS	scoopfuls
SORIG	scourging
SORNS	scourings
SOSAE	soopstake
SOSIE	Scots pine
	shoeshine
SOSOM	snow storm
	snowstorm
SOSOT	stop short
SOTAD	shorthand
SOTAE	shortcake
	short wave
SOTAL	shortfall
SOTCR	sports car
SOTED	short-head
SOTEM	short-term
SOTES	shortness
	stoutness
SOTIE	short time
SOTIF	stop thief
SOTIT	shortlist
	short-list
SOTLP	short slip
SOTMN	sportsman
SOTMP	shoot-'em-up
SOTND	shortened
SOTOM	short form
SOTON	shoot down
	shorthorn❑
	shout down
SOTOT	short-coat
	smooth out
SOTUE	short fuse
SOUAE	shogunate
	sporulate
SOUDR	snow under
SOUIG	stop using
SOVRS	slow virus
SOWIE	snow-white
SOWTH	stopwatch
SOXIY	Sioux City
SOYIE	storyline
SOYOK	storybook
	story-book
SOZNI	sforzandi
SOZNO	sforzando
	smorzando
SOZTS	sforzatos
SPAII	sopranini
SPAIO	sopranino
SPDLA	sapodilla
SPEAY	supremacy
SPEBR	September
SPEEY	supremely
SPENA	septennia
SPETY	sapiently
SPIES	sappiness
	soppiness
SPIIE	syphilise
	syphilize
SPIIY	septicity
SPITC	sophistic
SPITY	sophistry
SPLAT	suppliant
SPLHE	sepulchre
SPLIG	supplying
SPLUE	sepulture
SPNTR	supinator
SPOIE	saprolite
SPOIG	supposing
SPOLS	Sophocles
SPOOC	saprozoic
SPOTD	supported
SPOTR	supporter
SPRBE	separable
	superable
SPRBY	separably
	superably
SPREE	supersede
	supervene
SPREO	superhero
SPRET	superheat
SPRFC	soporific
SPRIE	superfine
	supervise
SPRLE	superglue
	Superglue®
SPRLX	superflux
SPROA	supernova
SPROE	superpose
SPROL	supercool
SPRTD	separated
SPRTR	separator

Words marked ❑ can also be spelled with an initial capital letter

superstar
SPRTS separates
SPRUE superfuse
SPUAE suppurate
SPUKR sapsucker
SPULE Sophus Lie
SPULT septuplet
SQETA sequentia
sequestra
SQETN St-Quentin
SQETR sequester
SQETS sequentes
SRAEY seriately
SRAIE serialise
serialize
SRAIG screaming
spreading
streaking
streaming
surfacing
SRAIM serialism
SRAIN Sarmatian
serration
striation
SRAIY streakily
SRAOT spread out
SRASM sargassum
SRASS sargassos
SRATC sarcastic
SRBAD scrubland
surfboard
SRBEY shrubbery
SRBID scrub-bird
SRBIG scrubbing
SRBLE strobilae
SRBLR scribbler
SRBLS strobilus
SRBNE sarabande
SRCIH strictish
SRCNC strychnic
SRCOF struck off
SRCOS sericeous
SRCUE stricture
structure
SRDIG stridling
SRDNE stridence
SRDNY stridency
SREDR surrender
SREES sorceress
SREHR screecher
SREIE serve time
SREIG screening
shrieking
surveying
SRELE surveille
SRENY sergeancy
SREOF screen off
SREON surrejoin
SREOS sorcerous
SRETD surfeited
SRETM sarmentum
SREVR surge over
SRFII sgraffiti
SRFIO sgraffito
SRGAH serigraph
SRGIS seraglios
SRGIY scraggily
SRGLR straggler
struggler
SRGSA Saragossa
SRGTY sprightly
SRHAP Sarah Gamp
SRHRE surcharge
SRIAD Streisand
SRIEE sortilege
SRIES sorriness
surliness
SRIEY servilely
sortilegy
SRIGE surcingle
SRIHR Streicher
SRIIE sorbitise
sorbitize
SRIIG servicing
straining
surmising
surviving
SRIIN Sardinian
SRIIY servility
SRIKE spraickle
SRIOS serpigoes
SRITE serviette
SRIUE servitude
SRKOF strike off
SRKOL strike oil
SRKOT strike out
SRKPY strike pay
SRLIG scrolling
strolling
SRLSW scroll-saw
SRLTI strelitzi
SRLUD Stralsund
SRMAE scrimmage
scrummage
SRMAF scrum half
SRMHW scrimshaw
SRMIG scrimping
shrimping
SRMIY scrimpily
SRMLD scrambled
SRMLR scrambler
SRMOI Stromboli
SRMTC stromatic
strumatic
SRNAE shrinkage
SRNAM strongarm
SRNAR Stranraer
SRNBK springbok
SRNBX strongbox
SRNDR serenader
SRNEI Serengeti
SRNET stringent
SRNEY strangely
SRNIG shrinking
springing
sprinting
stranding
SRNIH strongish
SRNIM strontium
SRNIY springily
stringily
SRNLD sprinkled
SRNLR sprinkler
strangler
SRNLS strangles
SRNOS strenuous
SRNOT string out
strung out
SRNTE string tie
SRNUY strangury
SROAA sarcomata
SROAE surrogate
SROAP sarcocarp
SROAY surrogacy
SROFL sorrowful
SROFR sorrow for
SROIE sermonise
sermonize
SROIG sorrowing
SROIL sartorial
SROIS sartorius
SRONS surrounds
SROSY seriously
SRPAD scrapyard
SRPAG strap-hang
SRPAO strappado
SRPES strapless
SRPIG scrapping
strapping
stripling
stripping
SRPIS seraphims
seraphins
SRPIT sore point
SRPIY scrappily
SRPLB strip club
SRPNS scrapings
SRPOK scrapbook
SRPON strip down
SRPUE scripture❑
SRRSD surprised
SRRSR surpriser
SRSAI Sarasvati
Saraswati
SRSEG Strasberg
SRSES strossers
SRSFL stressful
SRSOT stress out
SRTAL spritsail
SRTGC strategic
SRTGM stratagem
SRTHD scratched
stretched
SRTHR scratcher
stretcher
SRTIE scrutoire
SRTIG strutting
sure thing
SRTNN serotonin
SRTTR scrutator
SRUAE serrulate
SRUGR scrounger
SRUIG sprouting
SRULT surmullet
SRVFR strive for
SRVNR scrivener
SRWAL screwball
SRWDP screwed up
screwed-up
SRWET strewment
SRWHM screw them
SRWIE shrewmice
strawlike
SRWIG sprawling
SRWOE straw vote
SRWOL straw poll
SRWOT sprawl out
SRYRM stray from
SSADA Sassandra
SSAND sustained
SSANR sustainer
SSAON Saskatoon
SSARS sassafras
SSATC systaltic
SSEAH Sassenach
SSEDD suspended
SSEDR suspender
SSEIE systemise
systemize
SSEIG sistering
SSETA sestertia
SSETD suspected
SSETS sestettos
SSEUO sostenuto
SSGNS Sosigenes
SSIAE suscitate
SSIES sissiness
SSIIN suspicion
SSINL sessional
SSRAE susurrate
SSUTH sasquatch
STADO set hand to
STAIN satiation
situation
STBAE set ablaze
STCOS setaceous
STDES satedness
STEIE set beside
STEOE set before
STFOT set afloat
STHAE set phrase
STIEO set fire to
STIGP setting up
setting-up
STIHY sottishly
STLFE Sutcliffe
STLFR settle for
STLGT set alight
STLIE satellite
STLNS settlings
STNAD set in hand
STNCL satanical

STNDE	set on edge
STNIE	set on fire
STNOD	satinwood
STNOT	set on foot
STNTE	satinette
STOIE	set to five
STOKN	sitbodkin
STOOE	sotto voce
STOOK	set to work
STOTN	set foot in
STPAP	set up camp
STPHP	set up shop
STPIE	set a price
STQAE	set square
	set-square
STRBE	saturable
STRCL	satirical
	satyrical
STRIE	saturnine
STRIM	saturnism
STRIN	Saturnian
STRLY	suturally
STRTD	saturated
STRUD	sit around
STSEK	so to speak
STSID	satisfied
STSIE	satisfice
STTAH	shtetlach
STUHY	set much by
STYSN	set eyes on
SUAIG	squeaking
	squealing
SUAIH	squeamish
SUAIY	squeakily
SUAOE	Scudamore
SUAOR	Scudamour
SUBEN	stumble on
SUBIG	scumbling
	stumbling
SUBLR	squabbler
SUBOS	slumbrous
SUBRR	slumberer
SUCEM	sour cream
SUCRR	soul-curer
SUDAE	sound wave
SUDES	soundless
	soundness
SUDRT	shudder at
SUDUH	sourdough
SUEFL	saucerful
SUEID	stupefied
SUEIG	squeezing
SUEIR	stupefier
SUELM	scutellum
SUENS	Sauternes
SUEOT	sauce boat
SUETR	sou'wester
SUFHM	stuff them
SUFIG	shuffling
	snuffling
SUFLY	soulfully
SUGBD	sluggabed
SUGEP	snuggle up

SUGIG	smuggling
SUHAD	southward
SUHAK	Southwark
SUHAT	South-East
	south-east
SUHED	South Bend
SUHEL	Southwell
SUHES	South Seas
SUHET	South-West
	south-west
SUHIT	South Uist
SUHOE	South Pole
	south pole
SUHON	Southdown
SUHOT	Southport
SUHRY	southerly
SUHUD	slush fund
SUIDY	studiedly
SUIES	sauciness
SUIHY	sourishly
SUIIY	stupidity
SUISN	saucisson
SULDY	squalidly
SULHR	squelcher
SULKA	souvlakia
SUMSC	soul music
SUNIG	squinting
SUNSD	snub-nosed
SUOOS	stuporous
SUPKR	stud poker
SUPRD	scuppered
SUPUE	sculpture
SURIG	squirting
SURLG	square leg
SUROE	square one
	squarrose
SUROF	square off
SURTE	soubrette
SUSGR	spun sugar
SUSIY	squashily
SUTAT	Stuttgart
SUTES	squatness
	squatters
SUTON	squat down
SUTRR	saunterer
	sputterer
	stutterer
SUWEL	spur wheel
SUYAD	study hard
SVEIE	sovietise
	sovietize
SVEIM	sovietism
SVNAS	Seven Days
SVNEN	seventeen
SVNES	seven seas
SVNHY	seventhly
SVNIS	seventies
SVNOD	sevenfold
SVRBE	severable
SVRIN	sovereign
SVRLY	severally
SVRNE	severance
SVRNS	Severinus

SVUIY	savourily
SXAIE	sexualise
	sexualize
SXAIY	sexuality
SXAWR	Six-Day War
SXENH	sixteenth
SXFAE	saxifrage
SXHOM	sixth form
SXITN	sex kitten
SXNLE	Saxon blue
SXPEL	sex appeal
SXPOE	saxophone
SXULT	sextuplet
SYAKR	skyjacker
SYIHY	stylishly
SYIIG	sky-diving
SYITC	stylistic
SYOAE	stylobate
SYOKT	skyrocket
	sky-rocket
SYSUE	soya sauce
SZRHP	sizarship
TAAAT	tear apart
TAADN	Teagarden
TAAGR	Trafalgar
TAAIA	Toamasina
TAASC	thalassic
TACDY	trancedly
TACUT	to account
TADIG	twaddling
TAEAE	tradename
TAEAK	trademark
TAEAR	trade fair
TAEBE	traceable
TAEBG	travel bag
TAEBY	traceably
TAECT	travel-cot
TAEES	traceless
TAEID	traceried
	trade wind
TAEIL	trapezial
TAEIM	trapezium
TAEIN	tragedian
TAEIS	trapezius
TAELD	travelled
TAELR	traveller
TAEMN	tradesman
TAEOD	trapezoid
TAEON	trade down
TAERE	to a degree
TAESD	traversed
TAESL	traversal
TAESR	traverser
TAETR	toad-eater
TAEUA	trabecula
TAFCN	traffic in
TAFLY	tearfully
TAHAE	tracheate
TAHBE	teachable
TAHTC	trachytic
TAIEY	to a nicety
TAIGY	teasingly
TAIIN	tradition

TAIOS	traditors
TAKAL	trackball
TAKES	thankless
	trackless
TAKHE	track shoe
TAKON	track down
TAKRY	Thackeray
TAKUT	tracksuit
TALSS	thalluses
TALWY	trail away
TAMTC	traumatic
TANAD	trainband
TANBE	trainable
TANIE	train fine
TAOES	tea towels
TAPLN	trampolin
TAPNS	trappings
TAPTE	trampette
TASAE	translate
TASED	transcend
TASEL	Tsar's Bell
TASET	transfect
	transient
	transvest
TASHP	transship
TASHT	that's that
TASIE	transpire
TASLT	that's flat
TASOE	transpose
TASOL	toadstool
TASOM	transform
TASOT	transport
TASUE	transfuse
	transhume
	transmute
TATAK	toast rack
TATBE	tractable
TATBY	tractably
TATES	traitress
TATRA	trattoria
TATRE	trattorie
TATRY	traitorly
TAUFL	teacupful
TAUIG	traducing
TBAUE	tablature
TBBIF	to be brief
TBBLH	Toby Belch
TBBUT	to be blunt
TBCOS	tobaccoes
TBCOY	tubectomy
TBEAD	tableland
TBEAE	tableware
TBEAK	Table Talk
TBEAT	table salt
TBEIE	table wine
	tablewise
TBFAK	to be frank
TBIES	tubbiness
TBLRY	tabularly
TBLTR	tabulator
TBOLH	tabbouleh
TBRLD	tubercled
TCEDY	ticket day

TCFLY tactfully
TCIES tackiness
TCIGN tucking-in
TCIIN tactician
TCIIY tactility
TCIOM tectiform
TCMHC tacamahac
TCNCL technical
TCNQE technique
TCOIL tectorial
TCOIS tectonics
TCRCS tectrices
TCTCS tucotucos
tucutucos
TCTES tacitness
TCULY tactually
TDETR Ted Dexter
TDGUE tide gauge
TDLAE tidal wave
TDOSY tediously
TDROE Tudor rose
TDRRH Tudor arch
TDTBE tide table
TDUHS Ted Hughes
TDUNR Ted Turner
TDYAM toddy-palm
TEABA The Gambia
TEABE the rabble
TEADS them and us
TEAES the same as
TEAET the latest
TEAHR the rather
TEAIS the ladies
therapies
TEAIT therapist
TEALR The Tatler
TEALT The Tablet
TEAND the damned
TEANR trepanner
TEANY Trelawney
TEAOD trematoid
TEAOE trematode
TEAOT thenabout
TEARS thesaurus
The Walrus
TEASS the masses
TEATR the matter
TEATS The Cantos
TEAUT Trésaguet
TEBIG trembling
TECAT trenchant
TECAY theocracy
TECEM The Scream
TECES the screws
TECEY treachery
TECUT the occult
TEDIL treadmill
TEDRC Theodoric
TEEAD The Herald
TEEAK theme park
TEEAS these days
TEEAT the sex act
TEEED The Aeneid
TEEHD the method
TEEID the period
TEEIG teetering
TEEIH therewith
TEEIS The Devils
TEELE the real me
TEENO thereinto
TEEOD the Beyond
TEEOE therefore
TEEOG theme song
TEEOR tregetour
TEEPE The People
TEEPN thereupon
TEERM therefrom
TEERR the Terror
TEETS the depths
there it is
TEEWY thereaway
TEEYN Trevelyan
TEFHY twelfthly
TEHEO The Phaedo
TEHKS the shakes
TEHNR trephiner
TEHRH the church
TEHRS the Shires
TEIAO The Mikado
TEIAS The Rivals
TEIEF the rise of
TEIGN the Virgin
TEIHS the eights
TEIIG the living
TEILR The Miller
TEIOD Trebizond
TEIRR The Mirror
TEIUE the minute
TELND tree-lined
TELSD the old sod
TELUS The Clouds
TEMLY thermally
TEMNA theomania
TENGT The Knight
TENIH tie in with
TEOAO the potato
TEOBT The Hobbit
TEODO the word go
TEOET the moment
TEOMN the common
TEORS the boards
TEOTE the bottle
TEOTF the root of
TEOUS teetotums
TEPIH tie up with
TEPRT the Spirit
TEQIE The Squire
TERCR The Grocer
TERED The Friend
TERES the creeps
TERHR the Archer
TERHS the Arches
TERIS the brains
TERLS the proles
TERQE theorique
TERTC theoretic
TERTR the cratur
TERZR theorizer
TESAE tree snake
TESFY tsetse-fly
TESPY theosophy
TESRD treasured
TESRR treasurer
TESRW tree shrew
TETBE treatable
TETCS the sticks
TETEH twentieth
TETET treatment
TETIH treat with
twentyish
TETIS theatrics
TETOE twenty-one
TETTS the States
TEUAE tremulate
TEUHT trebuchet
TEUOS tremulous
TEVMS twelvemos
TEWLE the Twelve
TEWNO tae kwon do
TEWTR Teeswater
TEYPS The Sylphs
TEYTM the system
TFCOS tufaceous
TFEMN Toffeemen
TGFOE tug-of-love
TGIGY tuggingly
TGIHY tigrishly
TGLRY tegularly
TGREE tiger's eye
TGRIY Tiger Lily
tiger lily
TGROD tigerwood
TGROH tiger moth
TGTAE tight-lace
TGTES tightness
TGTND tightened
TGTNT tight-knit
TGTOE tightrope
TGTPT tight spot
TGTRE tight arse
TIAET trivalent
TIAIM tribadism
tribalism
TIBAD tailboard
TIBLY thin-belly
TICIG twitching
TICOS triecious
TIDAE third-rate
TIDIG twiddling
TIEDR tail-ender
TIEES triteness
TIEKY tri-weekly
TIEMN tribesman
TIEOS trimerous
TIETL tridental
TIETR trisector
TIEVR twice over
TIFCD thin-faced
TIFIE thief-like
TIGMY thingummy
TIHIM tritheism
TIHIT tritheist
TIHNE trichinae
TIHNS trichinas
TIHOC trichroic
TIHSS trichosis
TIIAA Tripitaka
TIIAE triticale
TIIGY twiningly
TIILY trivially
TIINL tuitional
TIKAK think back
TIKBE thinkable
TIKED thickhead
TIKES thickness
TIKIG twinkling
TIKIH thick with
think with
TIKIS thick-lips
TIKLA triskelia
TIKND thickened
TIKOE tricksome
TIKTR trickster
TIKTY trinketry
TIKVR think over
TILIE trial-fire
TILIT triallist
TILNC triclinic
TILZY Thin Lizzy
TIMHL triumphal
TIMHR triumpher
TIMII triumviri
TIMIS triumvirs
TIMNS trimmings
TIMRS trim marks
TINIL triennial
TIOES tailoress
TIOIE trilobite
TIOIL trinomial
TIOIM triforium
TIOMD triformed
TIOOR tricolour❑
TIOOS trigonous
TIOOY tribology
TIOTP thin on top
TIPAE tailplane
TIPEE tailpiece
TISFR thirst for
TISIG thirsting
TISIY thirstily
TISOK tailstock
TITBE twistable
TITCS tristichs
TITEH thirtieth
TITLN triathlon
TITMC triatomic
TITQE triptyque
TITRR twitterer
TITSE tristesse
TIUAE tribunate
triturate
TIUAY tributary

TIUIE Tribunite
TIUPD tricuspid
TIUTA triquetra
TKAAH take a bath
TKAAK take aback
take a walk
TKAAT take apart
TKAEK take a leak
TKAET take a rest
take a seat
TKAIE take aside
TKAIK take a risk
TKAIS take amiss
TKATR take after
TKAUN take a turn
TKCVR take cover
TKHAT take heart
TKHRE take horse
TKIIL take it ill
TKISE take issue
TKITW take in tow
TKLAE take leave
TKNIH taken with
TKNNY taken in by
TKNOF taking off
TKNOT taking out
TKNWY taken away
TKODR take order
TKPAE take place
TKPIS take pains
TKSAE take shape
TKSDS take sides
TKSES take steps
TKSOK take stock
TKSOT take short
TKTRS take turns
TLAAE tell a tale
TLAAN tell again
TLAAT tell apart
TLAIE talkative
TLAOE Tullamore
TLAOT talk about
TLBOH tollbooth
TLGAH telegraph
TLIGF talking of
TLIGO talking-to
TLIGY tellingly
TLJKS tell jokes
TLMNS telamones
TLMTR telemeter
TLMTY telemetry
TLODR tall order
TLOOY teleology
TLOTF talk out of
TLPAE telophase
TLPOD tulipwood
TLPOE telephone
TLPOO telephoto
TLPOY telephony
TLPTY telepathy
TLRBE tolerable
TLRBY tolerably
TLRNE tolerance
TLRTD tolerated
TLRUD talk round
TLSAS talismans
TLSOE telescope❑
TLSOY tall story
TLTLS tell tales
TLUIE tellurise
tellurize
TLUIM tellurium
TLUIN tellurian
TLUIT Talmudist
TLYIH tally with
TMAIT timpanist
tympanist
TMAOT time about
TMAYR Tom Sawyer
TMCAY timocracy
TMCOK time clock
TMDES timidness
tumidness
TMEAE temperate
TMEIG tampering
tempering
timbering
TMEMN Tim Henman
TMHRE Tom Sharpe
TMINY Tom Finney
TMITN Tom Kitten
TMLAU Tamil Nadu
TMLBG tumble-bug
TMLBR Temple Bar
TMLDY tumble-dry
TMLMT time limit
TMLNY Tom Clancy
TMLRS temblores
TMNTB Tom and Tib
TMOAY temporary
TMODY time of day
TMOIE temporise
temporize
TMOIH tomboyish
TMOSY timeously
TMPEE timepiece
TMRIE Téméraire
Tom Cruise
TMRLO tamarillo
TMSAA Timisoara
TMSAE time scale
timescale
timeshare
TMSET time sheet
tumescent
TMSOE tombstone
TMTBE timetable
TMTES temptress
TMTIL time trial
TMUTN Tim Burton
TMXFN tamoxifen
TMZPM temazepam
TNAAL to no avail
TNAAS Tony Adams
TNAIE tantalise
tantalite
tantalize
tentative
TNAIG ting-a-ling
TNAIO Tongariro
TNALD tentacled
TNBAR Tony Blair
TNBIM tenebrism
TNBIS tenebrios
TNBIY tenebrity
TNBOE tenebrose
TNBOS tenebrous
TNCIE tonic wine
TNCLM tenaculum
TNCOS tenacious
TNDON toned down
TNEBX tinderbox
TNEES tenseness
TNEGN Tinbergen
TNEIE tangerine
TNEIG tendering
TNELR tunneller
TNESE Tennessee
TNFLY tunefully
TNGEG Tony Greig
TNIEE Tonkinese
TNIES tanginess
TNIGO tending to
TNIHY tonnishly
TNIIY tensility
TNILR tonsillar
TNOIL tonsorial
TNOSY tenuously
TNOTN tend out on
TNPNR tin-opener
TNPNY ten a penny
TNRLF tenor clef
TNRRM tenor-drum
TNSIH tunesmith
TNUTE tongue-tie
TOADD two-handed
TOAIA Thomasina
TOAKD Thomas Kyd
TOATW Thomas Tew
TOAWR Trojan War
TOBIG troubling
TODEM Trondheim
TOEEF to oneself
TOEIE to one side
TOGTF thought of
TOGTN thoughten
TOHCE toothache
TOHER trochlear
TOHES toothless
TOHIK toothpick
TOHOE toothsome
TOIIG two-timing
TOIOS trominoes
TOITE too little
TOLPP toodle-pip
TOMKR toolmaker
TONIE Thorndike
TONIG trouncing
TONIL thornbill
TOPHP troop-ship
TOPNY two a penny
TORBS Two Tribes
TORGT too bright
TOSAH Taoiseach
TOSEU trousseau
TOSNS thousands
TOYOR two-by-four
TPAAA top banana
TPACR tap-dancer
TPAIT topiarist
TPCLF typical of
TPCLS tapacolos
tapaculos
TPCLY topically
typically
TPDRS tapaderas
tapaderos
TPEAY Tipperary
TPERT top secret
top-secret
TPIES tipsiness
TPIGY toppingly
TPILN tephillin
TPLGT top-flight
TPLTC typhlitic
TPLTS typhlitis
TPMTL type metal
TPNMC toponymic
TPNRN tip and run
TPODL typhoidal
TPOOY taphonomy
TPRIE taperwise
TPRWR top drawer
top-drawer
TPSAE type scale
TPTFS tipstaffs
TPTVS tipstaves
TPWIE typewrite
TPWNY top twenty
TPYAE tipsy cake
TRAAN turn again
TRAAT termagant
TRAEY ternately
TRAIE tartarise
tartarize
turn aside
TRAIM terrarium
TRAIY throatily
TRALN tarpaulin
TRAOA Tarragona
Terranova
TRAOM terraform
TRAOS tornadoes
TRAOT turn about
turnabout
TRARD Tyrian red
TRAYA tirra-lyra
TRAZS terrazzos
TRBAE terebrate
TRBIG throbbing
TRBON turn brown
TRCAN tyre chain

Words marked ❑ can also be spelled with an initial capital letter

TRDES	tiredness
TRDNS	teredines
TREEP	three deep
TREES	terseness
TREEY	terrenely
TREGN	turret-gun
TREID	torrefied
TREIE	terze rime
TREIR	Tortelier
TREOD	threefold
TREOE	threesome
TREOF	turned off
TREOS	torpedoes
TREOT	turned out
TRERD	Turkey red
TRETD	tormented
TRETL	tormentil
TRETN	Tarkenton
TRETR	tormentor
TRETS	terzettos
TRFIY	thriftily
TRFRH	turn forth
TRGUE	tyre gauge
TRIAE	terminate
	turbinate
TRIES	tardiness
	tarriness
	turfiness
TRIGO	turning to
TRIHD	tarnished
TRIID	terrified
TRIIE	Turkicise
	Turkicize
TRIIY	torpidity
	turbidity
	turgidity
TRINL	torsional
TRIOY	territory
TRIUE	torpitude
	turpitude
TRLIG	thrilling
TRLLS	Tirol Alps
TRLOE	turn loose
TRMOE	thrombose
TRNDC	threnodic
TRNIE	tyrannise
	tyrannize
TRNIO	Tarantino
TRNOS	tyrannous
TRNTC	threnetic
TRNUA	tarantula
TROAS	Turkomans
TROIE	terrorise
	terrorize
	threonine
TROIM	terrorism
TROIT	terrorist
TRORP	turboprop
TRQZZ	Tariq Aziz
TRRCS	tortrices
TRRUD	turn round
TRSED	Turk's head
TRSIE	turnstile
TRSIG	thrashing
	thrusting
TRSOD	threshold
TRSOE	turnstone
TRSOT	thrash out
	thrust out
TRTBE	turntable
TRTGN	teratogen
TRTRS	teruteros
TRUDR	turn under
TRUET	turbulent
TRUIE	turquoise
TRUOS	torturous
TRWAK	throw back
	throwback
TRWFT	throw a fit
TRWIE	turn white
TRWIT	throw dirt
TRWON	throw down
TRWPN	throw open
TRWVR	throw over
TRWWY	throw away
	throwaway
	throw-away
TSABY	Tasman Bay
TSAET	testament
TSAII	Toscanini
TSAIN	Tasmanian
TSAOA	Tuscarora
TSAOL	tesla coil
TSASA	Tasman Sea
TSDIE	test drive
TSEES	tasteless
TSEKF	to speak of
TSELD	tasselled
TSELE	tessellae
TSFRE	task force
	task-force
TSIES	tastiness
	testiness
TSIIR	testifier
TSILS	testicles
TSIOF	toss it off
TSIOY	testimony
TSIUA	tessitura
TSIYO	testify to
TSMTH	test match
TSPLT	test pilot
TSPPR	test paper
TTAEE	tête-à-tête
TTAIN	titration
TTAOY	tetralogy
TTBCE	tête-bêche
TTEAE	title page
TTEAK	to the back
TTEED	title deed
TTEER	to the rear
TTEIE	to the life
	to the wide
TTEIG	tittering
	tottering
TTEIT	to the hilt
TTEOD	to the good
TTEOE	title role
	to the bone
	to the core
	to the fore
TTEOS	tetterous
TTEUL	to the full
TTIAE	tittivate
TTIES	tattiness
TTIGP	totting-up
TTLAE	titillate
TTLIG	totalling
TTLRY	titularly
TTLSR	totaliser
TTLZR	totalizer
TTMOE	totem pole
TTOTT	tit for tat
TTRHP	tutorship
TUBAK	thumbtack
TUBAL	thumbnail
TUBIG	thumbling
TUBNT	thumb knot
TUCEN	truncheon
TUCIN	T-junction
TUCTD	truncated
TUEIE	Trubenise
TUGIE	tour guide
TUHAS	truchmans
TUHBE	touchable
TUHES	toughness
TUHIE	touchline
TUHND	toughened
TUHNR	toughener
TUHOD	touch wood
	touchwood
TUHOE	touch-hole
	tough love
TUHON	touch down
TUHPN	touch upon
TUHRG	truth drug
TUHUK	tough luck
TUHYE	touch-type
TUITC	touristic
TUKAL	trunk call
TUKIG	truckling
TUKOK	trunk-work
TUKUS	trunkfuls
TUNDS	tournedos
TUOIE	Teutonise
	Teutonize
TUOOY	tautology
TUPDP	trumped-up
TUPNY	truepenny
TUPTD	trumpeted
TUPTR	trumpeter
TUTUD	trust fund
TUUET	truculent
TVRSH	tovarisch
TWCEK	town clerk
TWCIR	town crier
TWHUE	town house
	town-house
TWLIG	towelling
TWRIG	thwarting
TWRVR	tower over
TWSAE	townscape
TWSOK	townsfolk
TWYOT	tawny port
TXCLY	toxically
TXDRY	taxidermy
TXEUN	tax return
TXMTR	taximeter
TXNMC	taxonomic
TXUIE	texturise
	texturize
TYOET	try to beat
TYOID	try to find
TYOIE	thyroxine
TYVLE	Trygve Lie
UAAHD	unabashed
UAAMD	unalarmed
UAANT	up against
UABTR	Ulan Bator
UADON	up and down
	up-and-down
UADVR	up-and-over
UAHMD	unashamed
UAIHD	Upanishad
UAIIE	uralitise
	uralitize
	uraninite
UAIIY	unanimity
	usability
UAIOS	unanimous
UALYD	unalloyed
UAOIE	uvarovite
UAOND	unadorned
UAOTD	unadopted
UATBE	unactable
UATES	unaptness
UATRD	unaltered
UAVSD	unadvised
UBADD	unbranded
UBAIE	umbratile
UBAIG	unbearing
UBASD	unbiassed
UBGIE	unbeguile
UBILD	unbridled
UBKON	unbeknown
UBLAE	umbellate
UBLCL	umbilical
UBLCS	umbilicus
UBLEE	unbelieve
UBLNE	unbalance
UBLVD	unbeloved
UBNIG	unbending
	unbinding
UBNLR	unbundler
UBNYH	urban myth
UBOGT	upbrought
UBOKD	unblocked
UBSEK	unbespeak
UBUDD	unbounded
UCAGD	unchanged
UCAIG	unceasing
UCAMD	unclaimed
UCANL	uncharnel

	up-Channel
UCATD	uncharted
UCEKD	unchecked
UCENY	uncleanly
UCMIE	uncombine
UCNEL	uncongeal
UCNEN	unconcern
UCNIE	unconfine
UCNIY	uncannily
UCOAE	urceolate
UCODD	unclouded
	uncrowded
UCOHD	unclothed
UCOND	uncrowned
UCOSD	uncrossed
UCPBE	uncapable
UCRAN	uncertain
	uncurtain
UCRBE	uncurable
UCRIG	uncurving
UCRUT	uncorrupt
UCUHY	uncouthly
UCULD	uncoupled
UCUTD	uncounted
UCUTY	up-country
UCVLY	uncivilly
UCVRD	uncovered
UDCDD	undecided
UDCIE	undeceive
UDEMD	undreamed
UDESD	undressed
UDFLD	undefiled
UDFND	undefined
UDGIY	undignify
UDIGY	undyingly
UDLTD	undiluted
	undulated
UDMGD	undamaged
UDRAD	undercard
	underhand
UDRAE	underrate
	under-rate
	undertake
UDRAH	under oath
UDRAS	underpass
UDRAT	undercart
UDRED	underfeed
UDREL	underseal
	undersell
UDREP	underpeep
UDRER	underbear
	underwear
UDRET	underfelt
	undervest
UDRHT	undershot
UDRID	undergird
UDRIE	underbite
	underfire
	underline
	undermine
	underside
UDRIG	underling
	under-ring
	underwing
UDRIN	undersign
UDRLB	underclub
UDRLD	underclad
UDRLW	underflow
UDRLY	underplay
UDROD	underwood□
UDROE	underdone
	undernote
	undertone
UDROK	undercook
	underwork
UDROL	undercool
UDROT	undercoat
	underfoot
	undermost
UDRRD	underbred
UDRRW	underdraw
UDRUD	underfund
UDRUG	underhung
UDRUH	underbush
UDSRD	undesired
UDSRE	undeserve
UDTFL	undutiful
UDUTD	undaunted
	undoubted
UDVDD	undivided
UEATC	unelastic
UEATD	unexalted
UECTD	unexcited
UEESY	uselessly
UEGGD	unengaged
UEHCL	unethical
UERHD	unearthed
UERHY	unearthly
UESNE	unessence
UETBE	uneatable
UEULY	unequally
UFAGT	unfraught
UFCSD	unfocused
UFEGD	unfledged
UFEIG	unfeeling
UFIIG	unfailing
UFIND	unfeigned
UFLIG	unfolding
UFOIG	unflowing
UFRAE	up for sale
UFRIG	unfurling
UFRIH	unfurnish
UFTES	unfitness
UFTIG	unfitting
UFUDD	unfounded
UGADD	unguarded
UGAIG	upgrading
UGDIY	ungodlily
UGNIE	ungenuine
UGOMD	ungroomed
UGRTI	Ungaretti
UHADF	unheard of
	unheard-of
UHATY	unhealthy
UHEIG	unheeding
UHEIY	unheedily
UHLFL	unhelpful
UHLIG	upholding
UHLTR	upholster
UHLYA	Up-Helly-Aa
UHNIY	unhandily
UHPIY	unhappily
UHRES	unharness
UHRID	unhurried
UHROR	unharbour
UHRTE	usherette
UHTHD	unhitched
UIAET	univalent
UIAIN	Unitarian
	urination
UIAOS	uniparous
UIESL	universal
UIEUL	unisexual
UIHEP	Uriah Heep
UIIBE	unifiable
UIIEY	unitively
UIIIS	utilities
UIIOS	uliginous
UIJRD	uninjured
UINAK	Union Jack
UINZD	unionized
UIOAT	unisonant
UIOMD	uniformed
UIOMY	uniformly
UIOOR	unicolour
UIOOS	unisonous
UIPDD	unimpeded
UIPIE	unit price
UISAL	uninstall
UITUT	unit trust
UIVTD	uninvited
UJITD	unjointed
UKOIG	unknowing
ULAIG	unloading
ULAND	unlearned
ULASN	ugly as sin
ULCIY	unluckily
ULFIG	uplifting
ULFUT	ugli® fruit
ULGTR	uplighter
ULMTD	unlimited
ULTHD	unlatched
ULVDN	unlived-in
ULWTR	Ullswater
UMAIG	unmeaning
UMLDC	unmelodic
UMNFL	unmindful
UMRID	unmarried
UMRTD	unmerited
UMSCL	unmusical
UMSIG	unmasking
UMTHD	unmatched
UMTRD	unmatured
UMVBE	unmovable
UMVBY	unmovably
UMVDY	unmovedly
UMZLD	unmuzzled
UNRIG	unnerving
UNTCD	unnoticed
UNTRL	unnatural
UOAIE	upon a time
UOIIE	uxoricide
UOILY	uxorially
UOOIT	ufologist
	urologist
UOPSD	unopposed
UORPY	urography
UOYIM	uropygium
UPAND	unplanned
UPASD	unpraised
UPATD	unplanted
UPEAE	unprepare
UPENH	umpteenth
UPIBE	unpliable
UPITD	unpointed
UPNIG	unpenning
UPOIE	unprovide
UPOLD	unpeopled
UPOOE	unprovoke
UPPLR	unpopular
UPRAD	upper hand
UPRAE	upper-case
UPRET	unpervert
UPRIB	upper limb
UPROT	uppermost
UPTIG	unpitying
UPUBD	unplumbed
UQITY	unquietly
URAIE	unrealise
	unrealize
URAIY	unreadily
	unreality
URBKD	unrebuked
URCLR	utricular
URDLR	unriddler
URFLD	unruffled
URFND	unrefined
URGTY	uprightly
URIIN	Ukrainian
URLIG	unrolling
URLTD	unrelated
URLXD	unrelaxed
URNWD	unrenewed
UROIG	uprooting
URPND	unripened
URSIG	unresting
URSRE	unreserve
URUDD	unrounded
USADE	unswaddle
USAHD	unscathed
USAIG	unseating
	unsparing
USAKE	unshackle
USAND	unstained
USBUD	unsubdued
USCRD	unsecured
USDIY	ups-a-daisy
	upsy-daisy
USEIG	unseeming
USEMN	Ulsterman
USETE	unsheathe
USGTD	unsighted

Words marked □ can also be spelled with an initial capital letter

USGTY	unsightly
USIFL	unskilful
USIIG	unsmiling
USILD	unskilled
USIRD	unstirred
USITD	unstinted
USLID	unsullied
USLIH	unselfish
USMJR	Ursa Major
USMNR	Ursa Minor
USOLD	unspoiled
USOPD	unstopped
USOPR	unstopper
USOTD	unspotted
USSIG	unsisting
USTIG	upsetting
USTLD	unsettled
USUDD	unsounded
USUDY	unsoundly
USUID	unstudied
USUTR	unshutter
USVBE	unsavable
USVUY	unsavoury
USYBE	unsayable
UTADR	uitlander
UTAND	untrained
UTCRA	urticaria
UTEAL	up the wall
UTENE	up the ante
UTETD	untreated
UTEUF	up the duff
UTITD	untainted
UTLNW	up till now
UTMBY	untamably
UTMTM	ultimatum
UTNBE	untenable
UTNBY	untunably
UTNFL	untuneful
UTODN	untrodden
UTPBE	untypable
UTPCL	untypical
UTRBE	utterable
UTRES	utterness
UTRFY	unthrifty
UTRNE	utterance
UTROT	uttermost
UTSED	up to speed
UTSUF	up to snuff
UTTRD	untutored
UTUDR	upthunder
UTUHD	untouched
UUAIN	ululation
UULES	usualness
UULUE	usual rule
UUPDY	usurpedly
UUTRD	unuttered
UUULY	unusually
UVIIG	unveiling
UVRIG	unvarying
UVSTD	unvisited
UWAID	unwearied
UWETE	unwreathe
UWIHD	unweighed
UWIKE	unwrinkle
UWITN	unwritten
UWLIG	unwilling
UWLOE	unwelcome
UWMNY	unwomanly
UWNIG	unwinding
UWOGT	upwrought
UWRDY	unworldly
UWRID	unworried
UWRIE	unwarlike
UWRSF	upwards of
UWTHD	unwatched
UWTIG	unwitting
UWTIY	unwittily
UWTRD	unwatered
VAIIY	viability
VAIUS	viaticums
VBAIE	vibratile
	vibrative
VBAIG	vibrating
VBAIN	vibration
VBAOY	vibratory
VBATY	vibrantly
VBAUA	vibracula
VBISE	vibrissae
VCEVS	Vic Reeves
VCIAE	vaccinate
VCIIE	victimise
	victimize
VCLAE	vacillate
VCLSS	vocalists
VCNIL	vicennial
VCOIE	vectorise
	vectorize
VCOIN	Victorian
VCOSY	vacuously
	viciously
VCRAE	vicariate
VCRHP	vicarship
VCROS	vicarious
VCSML	vicesimal
VCSUG	Vicksburg
VCVRA	vice versa
VDIFA	vide infra
VDMCM	vade-mecum
VDNIM	Vedantism
VDOAE	video game
	videotape
VDOET	videotext
VDSPA	vide supra
VEIGY	veeringly
VEPIT	viewpoint
VETAE	Vientiane
VGBNS	vagabonds
VGEES	vagueness
VGEOD	vogue word
VGLNE	vigilance
	vigilante
VGNLY	vaginally
VGSML	vigesimal
VGTBE	vegetable
VGTBY	vegetably
VHCLR	vehicular
VHMNE	vehemence
VIAOT	voilà tout
VIEES	voiceless
VIEVR	voice-over
VIGOY	vainglory
VLAAK	Villa Park
VLAIE	volcanise
	volcanize
	vulcanise
	vulcanite
	vulcanize
	vulgarise
	vulgarize
VLAIM	vulgarism
VLAIN	valuation
	vulgarian
VLAIY	vulgarity
VLALS	valuables
VLAOS	viliacoes
	volcanoes
VLARE	villagree
VLATY	valiantly
VLCIE	volucrine
VLDOE	velodrome
VLDTD	validated
VLEAE	volte-face
VLEAY	vulnerary
VLEEN	velveteen
VLEES	valueless
VLELE	vulsellae
VLFIG	vilifying
VLIAE	vellicate
VLIOM	villiform
	vulviform
VLMTR	voltmeter
VLNAY	voluntary
VLNER	volunteer
VLNIE	valentine❑
VLNIO	Valentino
VLORD	Volgograd
VLPAY	voluptary
VLUET	vol-au-vent
VLUIE	vulturine
VLUIH	vulturish
VLUOS	vulturous
VLYIR	Valkyriur
VLYIS	Valkyries
VLZUZ	Velázquez
VMIIE	vampirise
	vampirize
VMIIM	vampirism
VNAIE	vandalise
	vandalize
VNAIM	vandalism
VNASN	venial sin
VNATN	Van Basten
VNEAS	vin de pays
VNEBY	vengeably
VNEIG	veneering
VNENE	vengeance
VNETO	Vincentio
VNIAE	ventilate
	vindicate
VNIIN	vendition
VNIKE	Van Winkle
VNILS	vendibles
VNLAH	vinyl wash
VNOIY	ventosity
VNOVR	Vancouver
VNRBE	venerable
VNRBY	venerably
VNRCE	ventricle
VNRLY	ventrally
VNRTD	venerated
VNSIG	vanishing
VNTBG	vanity bag
VNTTN	vingt-et-un
VNZEA	Venezuela
VOAIN	violation
VOETY	violently
VOIIT	violinist
VPDES	vapidness
VPRTI	vaporetti
VPRTO	vaporetto
VPRZR	vaporizer
VPUIH	vapourish
VRAIE	verbalise
	verbalize
	vernalise
	vernalize
	versatile
VRAIM	verbalism
VRAIN	variation
	vernation
VRAIT	verbalist
VRATY	verdantly
VRCLA	varicella
VRCOS	veracious
	voracious
VRDCL	veridical
VREAE	variegate
VREIS	varieties
VRELE	vermeille
VRERE	vertebrae
VRERL	vertebral
VRFIG	verifying
VRGET	very great
VRGIH	viragoish
VRIAE	verminate
VRIEN	Vortigern
VRIHR	varnisher
VRIIE	vermicide
VRIIM	vorticism❑
VRIIN	vermilion
VRIIR	versifier
VRIIT	vorticist
VRIIY	virginity
VRINL	versional
VRIOM	vermiform
VRIOS	verminous
VRIRS	verdigris
VRLBE	vers libre
VRLGT	Very light
VRLNE	virulence
VRNIY	very noisy
VRNQE	Véronique

Words marked ❑ can also be spelled with an initial capital letter

VROAE	variolate
VROEY	verbosely
VROIY	verbosity
VROSY	variously
VRSAL	very small
VRSET	virescent
VRTBE	veritable
VRTBY	veritably
VRTIE	veratrine
VRULY	virtually
VRUNS	vargueños
VRUOE	verrucose
VRUOS	verdurous
	verrucous
VRUSS	virtuosos
VSAAD	visual aid
VSAAE	vassalage
VSAIE	visualise
	visualize
VSAIN	Vespasian
VSCLE	vesiculae
VSCOY	vasectomy
VSEAE	viscerate
VSGSE	visagiste
VSIIL	vestigial
VSIIY	viscidity
VSISY	Vyshinsky
VSIUE	vestibule
VSMNS	vestments
VSOAY	visionary
VSOIY	viscosity
VSONY	viscounty
VSTBE	visitable
VSTIH	visit with
VSUUS	vasculums
VTAIN	vitiation
VTCDL	vaticidal
VTHIG	vetchling
VTILC	vitriolic
VTIOM	vitriform
VTLAY	vitellary
VTLIE	vitelline
VTLIS	Vitellius
VTUII	vetturini
VTUIS	Vitruvius
VUHAE	vouchsafe
VVCOS	vivacious
VVDES	vividness
VVFIG	vivifying
VVMNE	vivamente
VVRUS	vivariums
VWELW	vow-fellow
VXLAY	vexillary
VXOUI	vox populi
VXTOS	vexatious
VXUAA	vox humana
VYUIM	voyeurism
VZEAE	vizierate
VZEIL	vizierial
WAAOE	what a hope
WADTE	wyandotte❑
WAEIG	weakening
WAEOE	whalebone
WAEOT	whaleboat
WAGIG	wrangling
WAHRD	weathered
WAHRN	weather on
WAIES	weariless
	weariness
WAIGY	wearingly
WAIOE	wearisome
WAKED	weak-kneed
WAPDP	wrapped up
WAPIT	weak point
WAPNS	wrappings
WARUD	wrapround
WASER	whatsoeer
WASHT	what's what
WASIH	what's with
WASOE	what's more
WASOO	what's to do?
WATIY	wealthily
WATTX	wealth tax
WBEOG	wobbegong
WBFST	web offset
WBNPN	web and pin
WCELY	Wycherley
WCIES	wackiness
WDAAE	wide awake
	wide-awake
WDAGE	wide-angle
WDBGS	Wade Boggs
WDEDY	Wednesday
WDEIE	wedgewise
WDHAS	widthways
WDHIE	widthwise
WDHUE	Wodehouse
WDWID	widow bird
WDWOD	widowhood
WEAOT	week about
WEBDN	Wiesbaden
WECIG	wrenching
WECVR	whencever
WEDIG	wheedling
WEEDR	weekender
WEEIE	woe betide
WEEIH	wherewith
WEENO	whereunto
WEEOE	wherefore
	woebegone
WEEPN	whereupon
WEETS	where it is
WEEWY	where away?
WEFCD	whey-faced
WEIES	weediness
WEIGY	weepingly
WELAE	wheelbase
WELAK	wheelmark
WELPN	wheel spin
WELRH	wheel arch
WENGT	weeknight
WESER	whensoeer
WESOE	whetstone
WETEL	wheatmeal
WETEM	wheat germ
WETER	wheat beer
WETIG	wreathing
	wrestling
WFRHN	wafer-thin
WGIHY	waggishly
WGLET	W S Gilbert
WGNIS	wagon-lits
WGNLT	wagons-lit
WGNOD	wagonload
WGNPN	Wig and Pen
WGNTE	wagonette
WGSAE	wage slave
WIBED	Whitbread
WIDES	weirdness
WIEAE	white sale
WIEAH	whitewash
WIEAK	write back
WIEAT	whitebait
WIEAY	white lady
WIEED	whitehead❑
	white lead
	Whiteread
WIEEM	whitebeam
	white-seam
WIEES	whiteness
WIEET	white heat
	white meat
WIEIE	white line
	White Nile
	white wine
WIEIG	whitening
WIEIH	white fish
WIEIS	white lies
WIELG	white flag
WIEOD	white gold
	whitewood
WIEOE	white hope
WIEON	write down
	write-down
WIEOT	white port
WIEWY	while away
	write away
WIFED	Whitfield
WIFIG	whiffling
WIFRT	wait for it!
WIGAT	whip-graft
WIGIG	whingeing
	wriggling
WIHBE	weighable
WIHDP	weighed-up
WIHIG	weighting
WIHIH	weigh with
WIHIY	weightily
WIHNO	weigh into
WIHON	weigh down
WIHPN	weigh upon
WIHVR	whichever
WIIGY	wailingly
	whiningly
WIKIS	wrinklies
WIKRD	whiskered
WILGG	whirligig
WILID	whirlwind
WILOL	whirlpool
WILWA	whillywha
WIPRD	whispered
WIPRN	whipper-in
WIPRR	whimperer
	whisperer
WIRUD	whip-round
WISAE	whip snake
WISAL	whipstall
WISCL	whimsical
WISOE	whinstone
WISOK	whipstock
WITAD	waistband
	wristband
WITBE	wait table
WITES	wristlets
WITIE	waistline
WITOT	waistcoat
WIWRH	Whitworth
WIZAG	whizz-bang
WKFED	Wakefield
WKFLY	wakefully
WLAHN	walkathon
WLAIM	welfarism
WLAIT	welfarist
WLAMD	well-aimed
	well-armed
WLAOE	wall a rope
WLAOT	walkabout
	wild about
WLBIG	wellbeing
	well-being
WLBIT	well-built
WLBKD	well-baked
WLEEE	wolverene
WLEIE	wolverine
WLFMD	well-famed
WLGES	wild guess
WLHAP	Welsh harp
WLHOY	Welsh Pony
WLHUD	wolfhound
	wolf-hound
WLIBY	Walvis Bay
WLIGO	willing to
WLIGY	willingly
WLIHY	wolfishly
	wolvishly
WLKME	Will Kempe
WLKON	well known
	well-known
WLLKD	well-liked
WLOAR	walk on air
WLOIG	walloping
	wallowing
	welcoming
WLOIH	willowish
WLOLD	well-oiled
WLOTN	walk out on
WLPAE	wall plate
WLPNY	wild pansy
WLPPR	wallpaper
WLPRY	wild party
WLPWR	willpower
WLSAE	wolfsbane

Words marked ❑ can also be spelled with an initial capital letter

WLSET well-spent
WLSIE Wiltshire
WLSUG Wolfsburg
WLTMD well-timed
WLUMR Welsummer
WLWMN wild woman
WLZNO waltz into
WMIHY wimpishly
WMLDN Wimbledon
WMNID womankind
womenkind
WMNIE womanlike
WMNLB women's lib
WMNOD womanhood
WMNOK womenfolk
WMNON Woman's Own
WMNOT woman post
WMNZR womanizer
WNAIY win easily
WNBEK windbreak
WNBRE windborne
wind-borne
WNBUD windbound
WNCAR wing chair
WNEFL wonderful
WNEIE winterise
WNEIG wandering
wondering
WNELS Wenceslas
WNEOF wander off
WNGAD Winogrand
WNGAS wine glass
WNGUE wind gauge
WNHDY win the day
WNHVR wind-hover
WNIES windiness
WNIGP winding-up
WNIGY windingly
winkingly
winningly
WNOBX window box
WNOEY winsomely
WNOIE wantonise
wantonize
WNPES winepress
WNPOF windproof
WNSET windswept
WNSOM windstorm
WNVUT wine vault
WNWRS windwards
WOBOK wood block
woodblock
WOCAT woodcraft
WOCUK woodchuck
WOEAE wholesale
WOEEL wholemeal
WOEES wholeness
WOEOD wholefood
WOEOE wholesome
WOFBE wood fibre
WOGDA wrong idea
WOGES wrongness
WOGIE wrong side
WOGOD wrong word
WOGOR wrongdoer
WOGOT wrong-foot
WOGTP wrought-up
WOHUE Woodhouse
WOIES woodiness
wooziness
WOLUE woodlouse
WONMH wood nymph
WOOVR whosoever
WOPTP whoop it up
WOSRW woodscrew
WOUNT whodunnit
WOUSE who but she
WOWRH Woolworth
WPETL Wuppertal
WRATD warranted
war-wasted
WRATE warrantee
WRATR warranter
warrantor
WRBID word-blind
WRBNH workbench
WRBUH wire brush
WRCOH wire cloth
WRDAI World War I
WRDAK World Bank
WRDIE worldwide
WRDIG worldling
WRDIW world-view
WREHC work ethic
WREIG worsening
WRETN worm-eaten
WRETR Worcester
WREUK worse luck
WRFOT warm front
WRFRE workforce
WRGAS wire grass
WRGUE wire gauge
wire gauze
WRHES worthless
WRHET worthiest
WRHLD wormholed
WRHRE workhorse
WRHUE warehouse
WRIDY worriedly
WRIES wordiness
WRIET worriment
WRIOE worrisome
WRIZR Wurlitzer®
WRMNY workmanly
WROAT work of art
WRODR word order
WROGR warmonger
WRPAE workplace
WRPEE workpiece
WRSET worksheet
WRSIH wordsmith
WRSUY work study
WRTBE worktable
WRWEL wire wheel
worm wheel
WRWMN workwoman
WRYON worry down
WRYUS worryguts
WSALR wassailer
WSAOT west-about
WSBAD washboard
WSBSN washbasin
WSBUD westbound
WSCAK wisecrack
WSCAT West Coast
WSCEN wash clean
WSEAD wasteland
WSEFR wished-for
WSEIE waste pipe
waste time
WSEIG westering
WSEMN washerman
WSENR westerner
WSEOT washed out
washed-out
WSEWY waste away
WSFLY wishfully
wistfully
WSHUE washhouse
WSIGP washing-up
WSIHY waspishly
WSMAH Westmeath
WSOSN Wisconsin
WSSAD washstand
WSSET wasp's nest
wasps' nest
WSTGD wish to God
WSWIT wasp waist
WSWMN wise woman
WSWRS westwards
WSYSI Wyszynski
WTAUP with a bump
WTCID with child
WTDAN withdrawn
WTEIG withering
wuthering
WTESR witnesser
WTESY witlessly
WTHAE watchcase
WTHBD wet the bed
WTHBE watchable
WTHIE watch fire
witchlike
WTHOD watchword
WTHTY witchetty
WTHUT witch hunt
WTHVR watch over
WTIES wittiness
WTIGY wittingly
WTIIM witticism
WTMTR wattmeter
WTRAE water gate
Watergate
water rate
water-wave
WTRAK watermark
WTRAL waterfall
water rail
WTRAN water main
WTRER water bear
WTRES waterless
WTRHD watershed
WTRID water bird
WTRIE waterline
water pipe
waterside
WTRIY water lily
WTRLA water flea
WTROD Waterford
WTROE waterhole
water vole
WTROL water-cool
waterfowl
WTRON water down
WTROO water polo
WTRUE water cure
WTRUK waterbuck
WTRUP water jump
water pump
WTRUT water butt
water-butt
WTSAD withstand
WTYUG with young
WUDHT would that
WVAIE wave aside
WVPPR wove paper
WVPWR wave power
WVSAE waveshape
WXLWR wax flower
WXYTE wax myrtle
WYADY waywardly
WYAIG wayfaring
waylaying
WYFIE way of life
WYGOE wayzgoose
XLPOE xylophone
XNHMS xanthomas
XNHPE Xanthippe
XNPOE xenophobe
XNPOY xenophoby
XRPYE xerophyte
YARUD year-round
YASID year's mind
YBEIG yabbering
YBIHY yobbishly
YCTMN yachtsman
YDIHR yiddisher❑
YGBRA Yogi Berra
YHAEO yo-heave-ho
YKDVL yoke-devil
YKTYK yakety-yak
yakity-yak
YLOIH yellowish
YLOSA Yellow Sea
YMIPR Yom Kippur
YPIDM yuppiedom
YPIFU yuppie flu
YRIIE yersiniae
YRIIS yersinias
YRSAL Yaroslavl
YRSIE Yorkshire
YRSIK yardstick

9 Y_S_A

YSAIN Yossarian
YSEDY yesterday
YSIOH yeshivoth
YTRIM ytterbium
YUAET you name it
YUCRS your cards
YUGAY young lady
YUGIL young girl
YUGNS young ones
YUGTR youngster
YUGUK Young Turk
YUGYD young-eyed
YUHLB youth club
YWIGY yawningly
ZAOSY zealously
ZBAOD zebrawood
ZCAIH Zechariah
ZCAIS Zacharias
ZCHNS zecchinos
zucchinis
ZCHTO zucchetto
ZEGHU Zhengzhou
ZERGE Zeebrugge
ZGMTC zygomatic
ZGPTE Zugspitze
ZIGIN Zwinglian
ZIGIT Zeitgeist
ZLESE Zeller See
ZNADL Zinfandel
ZNCAE Zenocrate
ZNEOT zonked out
ZNOIE zinc oxide
ZNWIE zinc white
ZOHBA zoophobia
ZOHCA zoothecia
ZOOIT zoologist
ZPAIH Zephaniah
ZRATR Zoroaster
ZROIM zirconium
ZRRTD zero-rated
ZSFLY zestfully

10 letters – odd

AAADE Ava Gardner
AAADV Adam and Eve
AAAGN at a tangent
AAAIH Amarasimha
AAAOA Anaxagoras
AAASI anapaestic
AAATN adamantine
AAATS anabaptise
Anabaptism
Anabaptist
AAATU agapanthus
AAATZ anabaptize
AABOK Alanbrooke
AACIA anarchical
AADNN abandoning
AAEQE Arabesques
AAERS amateurish
amateurism
AAETR at a venture
AAGMT amalgamate
AAIEE Anaximenes
AAIIU avaricious
AAINE Arabian Sea
AALCO arable crop
AALIE at all times
AALNL availingly
AALOR at all hours
AALOT at all costs
AALRE Alan Lerner
a tall order
AAMNL alarmingly
AANRS Alain Prost
AANSI anamnestic
AAOIA analogical
anatomical
Anatotitan
AAOLK Amazon-like
AAOTD asafoetida
AAOUH anacolutha
AAPRE Alan Parker
AARMU at a premium
AASPL Adam's apple
AATAD avant-garde
AATEC at a stretch
AATMS anastomose
AATOH anastrophe
AATRN Alan Turing
AATSU Anastasius
AATTO adaptation
AATVL adaptively
AAUNE amanuenses
AAUNI amanuensis
AAUSO ayahuas-cos
AAYIA analytical
AAYRC at any price
ABEIT abbreviate
ABLTO ambulation
ABLTR ambulatory
ABMNS albuminise
ABMNZ albumenize
albuminize
ABRLO albarellos
ABRNL Albert Nile
ABRRU Albert Roux
ABSAO ambassador
ambuscados
ABSOI asbestosis
ABSXA ambisexual
ABTAO arbitrator
ABVLN ambivalent
ACBAE Alcibiades
ACBSO archbishop
ACDAO archdeacon
ACDGM arcade game
ACDNA accidental
ACEIE accredited
ACEIG alcheringa
ACELN Archenland
ACEOI archegonia
ACEYA archetypal
ACHLS alcoholise
alcoholism
ACHLZ alcoholize
ACIAL ascribable
ACIEE Archimedes
ACILC Auchinleck
ACINE auctioneer
ACINR auctionary
ACIRV architrave
ACLRT accelerate
ACMCT ascomycete
ACMLC accomplice
ACMLS accomplish
ACMLT accumulate
ACNAC ascendancy
ACNEN as concerns
ACNNS arcaneness
ACNUT accentuate
ACOHL arctophile
ACOII anchoritic
ACOLS anchorless
ACPAC acceptance
ACPAL acceptable
acceptably
ACPBI accept bail
ACPEL acceptedly
ACRAC accordance
ACREL accursedly
ACRTL accurately
ACSIL accessible
accessibly
ACSNL accusingly
ACSOE accustomed
ACSRA access road
ACSTM access time
ACSTO accusation
ACSTR accusatory
ACSTV accusative
ACTCS asceticism
ACUTN accountant
accounting
ACUTO account for
ADACT add sauce to
ADBLT audibility
ADCET addicted to
ADCTO abdication
ADDCM aide-de-camp
ADEAE addle-pated
ADEAL add details
ADEBT add herbs to
ADENI Andrew Neil
ADERN André Brink
ADHLK and the like
ADHRS and the rest
ADHTL and what all
ADIVN Andy Irvine
ADLSA Andalusian
ADLST andalusite
ADLTA and all that
ADMNE Andaman Sea
ADNAE aid and abet
ADNIO andantinos
ADOAH Andromache
ADOAU Andromaque
ADOCU androecium
ADOEE audiometer
ADOHL audiophile
ADOIU Andronicus
ADOOT and so forth
ADRGT add drugs to
ADSAA Abdus Salam
ADSBB Addis Ababa
ADTOA additional
ADTRU auditorium
ADUAT add sugar to
ADWRO Andy Warhol
ADYRA at daybreak
AEADI Alexandria
AEADR alexanders
AEAEU arenaceous
AEAUU acetabulum
AEBCT acerbicity
AEBIA Azerbaijan
AECMN amercement
AECOB Abercromby
AEDNA Aberdonian
AEDOE a lead towel
AEDTG anecdotage
AEDTS anecdotist
AEDVN aberdevine
AEGMN avengement
AEIAI acetic acid
AEIDA Amerindian
AEIRT ameliorate
AEKOA a week today
AEOEE anemometer
AEORE amenorrhea
AEORN axe to grind
AEPRO a new person
AERHN a near thing
AERSA aneurysmal
AERTO aberration
AESNS averseness
AETCS asepticise
AETCZ asepticize
AETOI azeotropic
AETOO a peg too low
AETRE a better bet

AETRN aventurine
AETSA Abel Tasman
AEULT asexuality
AEUTL adequately
AEVIL à merveille
AEVTL acervately
AEXAN à deux mains
AFBLT affability
AFCEB affected by
AFCEL affectedly
AFCIN affections
AFEAE Alfred Ayer
AFEJD Alfred Jodl
AFIHE affrighten
AFITN afflicting
AFITO affliction
AFIWT au fait with
AFLAE affiliated
AFLPL at full pelt
AFLTL at full tilt
AFOTN affronting
AFRAC affirmance
AFRAL affordable
AFTUS affettuoso
AFUNL affluently
AGAAE aggravated
AGADS aggrandise
AGADZ aggrandize
AGAWR Afghan Wars
AGBAS algebraist
AGEFS angler fish
AGESO aggression
AGESV aggressive
AGLAL Angel Falls
AGLMN avgolemono
AGLRT angularity
AGNON at gunpoint
AGNUA Algonquian
AGOAO Anglo-Saxon
AGOHB anglophobe❑
AGOHN anglophone❑
AGOPR angiosperm
AGORS Anglo-Irish
AGSNS augustness
AHAWR ashlar-work
AHBSA Athabescan
AHEAL achievable
AHEEI aphaeresis
AHMWT at home with
AHNSU Athanasius
AHOAI achromatic
AHREC abhorrence
AHRSI aphoristic
AHRTM a short time
AHSVL adhesively
AIACL animalcula
animalcule
AIAEA Anita Desai
AIAEL agitatedly
animatedly
AIAFR Animal Farm
AIALF animal life
AIAPR animal park

AIAVR animadvert
AIBLT amiability
AIEEC a rivederci
AIEIL a minefield
AIETR alimentary
AIHEI arithmetic
AIHSO a tight spot
AIIND aficionado
AINTN alienating
AINTO alienation
AIORU amino group
AIOTI a bit of tail
AISOS at its worst
AITCA aristocrat
AITPU Aristippus
AIUTR apiculture
aviculture
AJCIA adjectival
AJCNL adjacently
AJCNS abjectness
AJCNT adjacent to
AJDCT adjudicate
AJRTO abjuration
adjuration
AJSAL adjustable
adjustably
AJSET adjusted to
AJSMN adjustment
AKEIE ankle-biter
AKLNS alkalinise
AKLNT alkalinity
AKLNZ alkalinize
AKLSU ankylosaur
AKNSL ask oneself
AKOAR ask to marry
ALAEU alliaceous
ALBDE able-bodied
ALBYN all-obeying
ALCOL allycholly
ALCTO allocation
ALENO all means of
ALGAC allegiance
ALGET allegretto
ALGRS allegorise
ALGRZ allegorize
ALGTO allegation
ALHBS all the best
ALHMR all the more
ALHOG all through
ALHOU All Shook Up
ALHRG all the rage
ALHSM all the same
ALHTM all the time
ALIEL all-firedly
ALIEO all-time low
ALIEU all mixed up
ALNDL Allan-a-Dale
ALNWN all-knowing
ALONE all-rounder
ALOWN all you want
ALRAD allargando
ALREI Auld Reekie
ALRMN allurement

ALRNL alluringly
ALRSN all-present
ALSAA able seaman
ALSUU Allosaurus
ALSVL allusively
ALTAI aglet babie
ALTET allotted to
ALTOI allotropic
ALTRT alliterate
ALUPS all-purpose
ALWOS allow to use
AMCNA almacantar
almucantar
AMDLO armadillos
AMDOC armed force
AMGDO Armageddon
AMGVN almsgiving
alms-giving
AMNEE almond-eyed
AMNSE administer
AMNTO admonition
ammunition
AMNTR admonitory
AMRNL admiringly
AMRTO admiration
AMSHR atmosphere
AMSIL admissible
AMSKL almost kill
AMTAC admittance
AMTDM Alma-Tadema
AMTEL admittedly
ANBLY Anne Boleyn
ANBOT Anne Brontë
ANDMN anno Domini❑
ANGTO abnegation
ANHLT annihilate
ANLRT annularity
ANLSI annalistic
ANNIT annunciate
ANRAL abnormally
ANSWL Anna Sewell
ANTTO annotation
ANXTO annexation
ANYNL annoyingly
AOAPU apocarpous
AOAYS apocalypse❑
AOCMN avouchment
AODHN a good thing
AODWT at odds with
AOEAE above water
AOEAI aposematic
AOEBO an open book
AOECI apodeictic
AOECN adolescent
AOEFO abode of God
AOEHM a sore thumb
AOEON at one point
AOEOR above board
above-board
AOERC above price
AOETG a moment ago
AOHCR apothecary
AOHHG apophthegm

AOHOA apochromat
AOHOE apotheoses
AOHOI apotheosis
AOIAL abominable
abominably
AOIBM atomic bomb
AOIEL agonisedly
agonizedly
AOIIA aboriginal
apolitical
AOIPL atomic pile
AOKOS a-cockhorse
AOKRA Aboukir Bay
AOLCI apoplectic
AONET adornments
AONMN anointment
AONOE amount owed
AOOEI apologetic
AORPA apocryphal
AOSIA acoustical
AOTLS apostolise
AOTLZ apostolize
AOTOC a soft touch
AOTOH apostrophe
AOTSZ apostasize
AOTTS apostatise
AOTTZ apostatize
AOTVL abortively
AOYNL agony uncle
APAAC appearance
APAEA alpha decay
APAEI alphabetic
APATB appear to be
APDSR aspidistra
APEIT appreciate
APEOT Ampleforth
APESR at pleasure
APETC apprentice
APGIT arpeggiate
APIAE amphimacer
APIAL applicable
applicably
APIAO applicator
APIAT applicants
APIEO apprised of
APIII amphimixis
APIIU amphibious
APINE appliances
APIOI amphibolic
APIRC amphibrach
APIRO Amphitryon
APLPE ampelopses
APNIE appendices
appendixes
APNTC alpenstock
APOCE approaches
APOEI amphoteric
APREV apperceive
APRGN asparagine
APRIL aspergilla
APRIN aspersions
APRNL apparently
aspiringly

Words marked ❑ can also be spelled with an initial capital letter

APRSA	as per usual
APRTO	apparition
	aspiration
APSTL	appositely
APSTO	apposition
APTSN	appetising
APTTO	amputation
APTZN	appetizing
APYIT	asphyxiate
AQANE	acquainted
ARADA	a great deal
ARAOL	Adrianople
ARASA	air-marshal
ARATO	abreaction
ARATV	abreactive
ARBTC	acrobatics
	aerobatics
ARCNE	Africander
ARCNS	Africanise
ARCNZ	Africanize
ARDMN	abridgment
AREEM	agree terms
ARFRU	auriferous
ARGAM	aerogramme
ARGNL	arrogantly
ARGTO	abrogation
	arrogation
ARINS	adroitness
ARMGL	acromegaly
ARNEO	arrange for
ARNLN	adrenaline
ARNMC	agronomics
ARNMS	agronomist
ARNUI	aeronautic
AROTS	air hostess
ARPNS	abruptness
ARPOI	acrophobia
ARRIH	air freight
ARROI	afrormosia
ARSAL	arrestable
ARSLT	across lots
ARURN	air-current
ARYHI	arrhythmia
	arrhythmic
ASAEB	as stated by
ASANN	abstaining
ASAON	arse around
ASBLT	assibilate
ASCAE	associated
	associates
ASCLE	also called
ASEAL	answerable
	answerably
ASEBC	answer back
ASEGN	abstergent
ASEIU	abstemious
ASELT	Austerlitz
ASESO	abstersion
ASESV	abstersive
ASETO	abstention
ASGAL	assignable
ASGET	assigned to
ASGMN	assignment
ASHTC	aesthetics
ASIAL	assailable
ASIEC	abstinence
ASIIU	auspicious
ASLCE	arse-licker
ASLTL	absolutely
ASLTO	absolution
ASLTS	absolutism
	absolutist
ASMLE	assemblies
ASMLG	assemblage
ASMLT	assimilate
ASMNL	assumingly
ASMTO	assumption□
ASMTV	assumptive
ASNFO	absent from
ASODN	absconding
ASRAL	absorbable
ASRCE	abstracted
ASRCL	abstractly
ASREC	absorbency
	assurgency
ASREI	absorbed in
ASREL	absorbedly
ASRLA	Australian
ASRLR	Australorp
ASRMN	assortment
ASRNS	absurdness
ASRSL	abstrusely
ASRTO	absorption
	adsorption
ASRTV	absorptive
ASSAC	assistance
ASSAL	assessable
ASSMN	assessment
ASUTT	auscultate
ASVRT	asseverate
ATALR	art gallery
ATATM	at that time
ATATO	attraction
ATATV	attractive
ATAUU	astragulus
ATBLT	actability
ATBOI	antibiosis
	antibiotic
ATCAI	autocratic
ATCAL	attackable
ATCAT	arty-crafty
ATCDN	antecedent
ATCET	attached to
ATCIA	anticlimax
	anticlinal
ATCLC	articulacy
ATCLT	articulate
ATCML	altocumuli
ATCMN	attachment
ATCPT	anticipate
ATCRS	Antichrist
ATCTO	autochthon
ATDDC	autodidact
ATEED	at the ready
ATEES	at the least
ATEHE	at the wheel
ATEIE	anthelices
ATEII	antheridia
ATELP	at the slope
ATEOI	autoerotic
ATEOS	at the worst
ATETR	at the start
ATFCA	artificial
ATFEZ	antifreeze
ATGAH	autography
ATGAI	astigmatic
ATGIS	act against
ATGMU	autogamous
ATGNS	antagonise
	antagonism
	antagonist
ATGNU	autogenous
ATGNZ	antagonize
ATGTE	altogether
ATHFO	act the fool
ATHGA	act the goat
ATIAL	attainable
ATIET	Antoinette
ATIGN	astringent
ATIMN	attainment
ATITM	at this time
ATIUE	attributes
ATMAL	autumnally
ATMBL	automobile
ATMND	antimonide
ATMTE	antimatter
ATMTN	automatons
ATMTO	automation
ATMTS	automatism
	automatist
ATMTV	automotive
ATNAC	attendance
ATNAE	attenuated
ATNAT	attendants
ATNET	attended to
ATNIN	attentions
ATNMA	antinomian
ATNMN	attunement
ATNMU	antonymous
	autonomous
ATNOI	Anton Dolin
ATNSE	astonished
ATNSG	act one's age
ATOAL	actionable
	actionably
ATOER	astrometry
ATOHR	anthophore
ATOIE	authorized
ATOOE	astrologer
	astronomer
ATOOI	astronomic
ATOSI	authorship
ATOVA	Art Nouveau
ATPAT	autoplasty
ATPOA	antiphonal
ATPOI	autophobia
ATPOO	anti-proton
ATPPE	at top speed
ATQAE	antiquated
ATRAD	afterwards
ATRAI	alternatim
ATRAO	alternator
ATRAT	aftertaste
ATRCT	anthracite
ATRHC	aftershock
ATRHS	autarchist
ATRHV	aftershave
ATRIA	autarkical
ATRIC	altarpiece
ATRIT	afterbirth
ATRLO	after blood
ATRMG	after-image
ATROL	anteriorly
ATROR	astarboard
ATRPI	anthropoid
ATRSR	after a sort
ATRTC	Antarctica
ATRTO	alteration
ATSAI	antistatic
ATSAL	attestable
ATSCA	antisocial
ATSMT	anti-semite
ATSPI	antisepsis
	antiseptic
ATSRD	autostrada
ATSRM	antiserums
ATSRT	altostrati
ATTEE	antitheses
ATTEI	antithesis
	antithetic
ATTNS	astuteness
ATUAH	Arthur Ashe
ATUDN	astounding
ATUNS	artfulness
ATUSI	altruistic
ATVLS	active list
ATVNN	antivenene
ATVNS	activeness
ATVTE	activities
ATVTO	activation
ATXRE	Artaxerxes
AUDNL	abundantly
AUENL	acute angle
AUFRI	aqua fortis
AUMRN	aquamarine
AUTRN	adulterant
	adulterine
AUTRS	adulteress
AUTRT	adulterate
AUTRU	adulterous
AUTTD	a multitude
AVNAE	advantaged
	advantages
AVNIT	Adventists
AVNUE	adventurer
	adventures
AVRAC	at variance
AVRAT	Alvar Aalto
AVREC	advertence
	advertency
AVRIE	advertiser
AVSRT	advisorate

Words marked □ can also be spelled with an initial capital letter

AYANI arytaenoid
AYCRN asynchrony
AYDLI amygdaloid
AYHTE anywhither
AYMTI asymmetric
AYNES anyone else
AYONO Amy Johnson
AYPOI asymptotic
AYSNA Abyssinian
AZEMR Alzheimer's
AZKBA adzuki bean
BAAIM bragadisme
BAAOO Brabanôcon
BACAG blancmange
BACDN by accident
BACLS branchless
BADAG by and large
BADSA brandy snap
BAEAA beaver away
BAEER Braveheart
BAEIH brake light
BAENS brazenness
BAEUL blamefully
BAEWT be ages with
BAGNL braggingly
BAHOO brachiopod
BAHRN blathering
BAHSE by a whisker
BAIHN bear in hand
BAILV Bratislava
BAIMN bear in mind
BAIUO bear in upon
BAIWO brazilwood
BAJLI Beaujolais
BAKAI black magic
Black Maria
BAKDU blacked out
BAKER Blackbeard
blackberry
BAKES blank verse
BAKET Black Death
BAKHE black sheep
BAKHL black whale
BAKHR Blackshirt
blackthorn
BAKIL Black Hills
BAKIO black widow
BAKMT blacksmith
BAKNN blackening
BAKOE Black Power
black power
BAKOR blackboard
BAKRA black bread
BAKTM black stump
BAKUR blackguard
BALEN by all means
BALOT be all mouth
BAMNS Brahmanism
BANAL biannually
BANET brain death
BANHL brainchild
BANNS braininess
brawniness
BANOE brainpower
BANRI brain drain
BANTR brainstorm
BAPEE blasphemer
BAPOL boat people
BAQET blanquette
BASAE brass-faced
BASAK brass tacks
BASDF brassed off
BASEV brass nerve
BASNS brassiness
BASOE Bram Stoker
BASRE Bradstreet
BASRU beansprout
BATBU boast about
BATCA beautician
BATEA beat the rap
BATEI beat the air
BATEU beat the gun
BATFE beautifier
BATSO beauty spot
BATUL boastfully
BAYEN by any means
BBASE Bob Paisley
BBBOE baby boomer
BBIAL biblically
BBIAM babe in arms
BBLBT bubble bath
BBLOE bubble over
BBLPC bubble pack
BBLUL bibulously
BBRBO baby-ribbon
BBSTE baby-sitter
BBWLE baby-walker
BBYAD Bobby Sands
BBYOE Bobby Jones
BBYOR Bobby Moore
BCAIO beccaficos
BCBOK back-blocks
BCBRE back burner
BCBTN backbiting
back-biting
BCEDW bucket down
BCEEI bacteremia
BCEFL bucketfuls
BCESA bucket seat
BCESO bucket shop
BCFRN backfiring
BCGMO backgammon
back-gammon
BCGON background
BCHNE bacchantes
backhanded
back-handed
back-hander
BCHNL Bacchanale
BCLDW buckle down
BCMCL become cold
BCMFN become fine
BCMFR become firm
BCMHR become hard
BCMHZ become hazy
BCMLS become less
BCMNL becomingly
BCMPL become pale
BCMRE backmarker
BCMRP become ripe
BCMTI become thin
BCMVI become void
BCMWA become weak
BCNIE be confined
BCNME back number
BCNRS by contrast
BCPCE backpacker
BCRAN be curtains
BCSAR backstairs
BCSIC backstitch
BCSIE backslider
BCSRE back street
BCSRK backstroke
BCTBC back to back
BCWRL backwardly
BCYHR Becky Sharp
BDAGE bedraggled
BDANR bad manners
BDARA bad hair day
BDEIA budgerigar
BDELN bad feeling
BDETN bed-wetting
BDFAL bed of nails
BDFOE bed of roses
BDGEO bodegueros
BDIGO Bedlington
BDIKN by-drinking
BDLTE bedclothes
BDNWT be done with
BDOPN bad company
BDRSE bedpresser
BDSAC body-search
BDULT bad quality
BDVLE bedevilled
BDWRE bed-swerver
BDYOI buddy movie
BDYOL Buddy Holly
BEBRE beefburger
BEBTL beer bottle
BECTL beef cattle
BEDAC bread sauce
BEDHT bleed white
BEDNF bread knife
BEDOR breadboard
BEDRI breadfruit
BEDRM breadcrumb
BEEPN beekeeping
BEETO by-election
BEEWT be even with
BEHRN blethering
BEKAC breakdance
BEKAE break gates
breakwater
BEKAT break faith
BEKFA break of day
BEKHE break sheer
BEKJS break a jest
BEKNU breaking-up
BEKOE break cover
BEKON break point
BEKOS Bleak House
break loose
BEKOT break forth
BEKPA Breakspear
BEKPR break apart
BEKRA break bread
BENAL biennially
BERBI Brer Rabbit
BEREE bleary-eyed
BERNS bleariness
BESBN breastbone
BESDE breast-deep
BESFE breastfeed
breast-feed
BESHG breast-high
BESRE Beer Street
BESWR breastwork
BETAL breathable
BETAT Brett Harte
BETEU breathe out
BETLS breathless
BETMT beef tomato
BEYLV Bye Bye Love
BEZNS breeziness
BFEZN buffer zone
BFLHA bufflehead
BFLMN bafflement
BFLNL bafflingly
BFMSE be famished
BFONR buffoonery
BFRHN beforehand
BFRLN before long
BFRNO before noon
BFRTM beforetime
BGACF Bagdad Café
BGEDW bogged down
BGERE big-hearted
BGETU be great fun
BGFOE bag of bones
BGMUL bigamously
BGNDY bygone days
BGNGI begin again
BGNIG beginnings
BGNSN begin using
BGOLC by good luck
BGOTE big-mouthed
BGPNE big spender
BGRTE Big Brother
BGTLE Bagatelles
BGUGN begrudging
BHNBR behind bars
BHNDO behind-door
BHNHN behindhand
BHNTM behind time
BIADG brigandage
BIATN brigantine
BIBIG Bainbridge
BIDAI blind panic
BIDLE blind alley
BIDNU building-up
BIDRN blind drunk
BIDRS blind trust

BIDUS blind guess
BIDWT boil down to
BIEMI bridesmaid
BIERC bride-price
BIERO boiler room
bridegroom
BIESI boiler suit
BIGAE Bridgwater
BIGAL bridgeable
BIGBU bring about
BIGHA bridgehead
BIGNE bring under
BIGNL boil gently
BIGNU bringing up
bringing-up
BIGON bring round
BIGOO bring to God
BIGOT bring forth
BIGPR Bridgeport
BIGTW Bridgetown
BIGWK being awake
BIHEE Bright Eyes
BIHEU brighten up
BIHIE bright idea
BIHNS blitheness
brightness
BIHRN blithering
BIHSM blithesome
BIIHS Britishism
BIKAE bricklayer
BIKOK brickworks
BILAC brilliance
brilliancy
BINOR Brian Moore
BISUL blissfully
BITRN blistering
BITRU boisterous
BIZRE blitzkrieg
BJUEI bijouterie
BJWLE bejewelled
BKDEN baked beans
BLADO bill and coo
BLAIE ballabiles
BLAMN Bellarmine
BLAON belladonna
BLATN Ballantyne
BLAWR Balkan Wars
BLBEE bull-beeves
BLBRO Béla Bartók
BLBYO Bill Bryson
BLDEE Bill Deedes
BLDGN bulldog ant
BLEAL believable
BLEDS balderdash
BLEDU billet-doux
BLERS belletrist
BLESO ballet shoe
BLFOE bell-flower
BLHAE bald-headed
bull-headed
BLHVS bolshevise
Bolshevism
Bolshevist
BLHVZ bolshevize
BLHZA Belshazzar
BLIGU bulging out
BLITC ballistics
BLLGS Bela Lugosi
BLNCE bull-necked
BLNEU balance out
BLNHN Balanchine
BLNIG belongings
BLOFR ball of fire
bill of fare
BLONN ballooning
BLONS balloonist
BLSAE ball-shaped
BLSRD balustrade
BLSRE bell screen
BLSRU Belisarius
BLTEA bell the cat
BLTLN belittling
BLUHN be laughing
BLVAO bolivianos
BLVRI biliverdin
BLWEI boll-weevil
BLWTE bell-wether
BLYAC belly-dance
BLYCE belly-acher
BLYOE Billy Bones
BLZCT Belize City
BMADC Bombay duck
BMADE bombardier
BMLEI bimillenia
BMNAL bimanually
BMOOT bombolotti
BMOZE bamboozled
bamboozler
BMSAE be mistaken
BMTLI bimetallic
BNCLR binoculars
BNCOB Bing Crosby
BNCUI bon accueil
BNDCT benedicite
BNDCU Benedictus
BNDUL bent double
BNEEG bond energy
BNEHL Bunker Hill
BNEIL banderilla
BNFCA beneficial
BNFCN beneficent
BNFCO benefactor
BNGAC benignancy
BNGNS benignness
BNHAE bone-headed
BNHNS bunchiness
BNLDS Bangladesh
BNLNL bunglingly
BNMSE bandmaster
BNNSI banana skin
BNOAN benzocaine
BNOEO bandoleros
BNOFE Bonhoeffer
BNONO Ben Johnson
BNORM bongo drums
bongo-drums
BNOTM bang on time
BNPEI bon appetit
BNRCD binary code
BNRDE Ben Bradlee
BNRPC bankruptcy
BNRSA binary star
BNSAE boneshaker
BNSMN banishment
BNSOA bondswoman
BNSOC be no slouch
BNSSU bonus issue
BNTPC bone to pick
BNUAL binaurally
BNUTN banqueting
BNVLN benevolent
BOBAE browbeaten
browbeater
BOBBO blow-by-blow
BOBNE bookbinder
BOCII bronchitic
bronchitis
BOCIL bronchiole
BODAE broad-based
BODHE broadsheet
BODLK blood fluke
BODMR bloody Mary
BODNL broodingly
BODNN broadening
BODNS bloodiness
broodiness
BODNU broaden out
BODON blood count
bloodhound
BODOO blood donor
BODTC bloodstock
BODTI bloodstain
BODTN bloodstone
BODWR broadsword
BOEDW broken down
broken-down
BOEEI biogenesis
biogenetic
BOEHL Broken Hill
BOEHM broken home
BOENS brokenness
BOERC biometrics
BOESD by one's side
BOHMS biochemist
BOHSC biophysics
BOIAL biotically
BOKAD Brooklands
BOKEE bookkeeper
BOKOR blockboard
BOKOS blockhouse
BOLCE bootlicker
BOLGE bootlegger
BOLSL bootlessly
BOMKN bookmaking
bootmaking
BOMRE bookmarker
BOMTC broomstick
BONAC brown sauce
BONAE brown paper
BONDF browned off
BONHR Brownshirt
BONOD brown goods
BONRA brown bread
BONTD brown study
BONTN brownstone
BONUA brown sugar
BONWR brown dwarf
BOOIA biological
BORPE biographer
BORPI biographic
BOSLE bookseller
BOSMN blossoming
BOTDU blotted out
BOTSU brontosaur
BOXHE Bronx cheer
BOZSA Bronze Star
BPEAE be prepared
BPITR baptistery
BPLRT bipolarity
BPRIA bipartisan
BQETA bequeathal
BQETE bequeathed
BRAAY Barbara Pym
BRACA bureaucrat
BRADN Bernardine
BRAEO bereaved of
BRAET Bernadette
BRAKN barracking
BRANN bargaining
BRANO bargain for
BRAOL barcarolle
BRAOO by reason of
BRAOS Barbarossa
BRASI bursarship
BRAST burial site
BRAYP Barbary ape
BRBEL bark beetle
BRBOE beribboned
BRDTF bored stiff
BREEA Burmese cat
BREFI Barnet fair
BREFL barrelfuls
BREHA Birkenhead
BRELN borderland
borderline
BRELT barbellate
BRENN burgeoning
BRENS barrenness
BREOE Burne-Jones
BREOR barge-board
BREQE burlesqued
BRERL barrel roll
BRESM burdensome
BRESO barbershop
BRETS burnettise
BRETZ burnettize
BRFOE barefooted
BRHAE bareheaded
BRHAG birth-pangs
BRHIH birthright
BRHIL Burchfield
BRHLC birthplace

BRHNE	barehanded
BRHTO	borghettos
BRIAO	barricados
BRIBU	Berlin blue
BRIGA	Birmingham
BRIGO	Barrington
BRIHN	burnishing
BRIOL	Barbirolli
BRITR	barristers
BRIUI	barbituric
BRIWL	Berlin Wall
BRIZA	bar mitzvah
BRKAD	Burckhardt
BRLGE	barelegged
BRLRS	burglarise
BRLRZ	burglarize
BRMTI	barometric
BRNNS	boringness
BRNSE	Barents Sea
BROIG	borrowings
BROPE	bird of prey
BROUC	Bertolucci
BRSAL	Barnstaple
BRSIE	bird-spider
BRSRK	bird strike
BRSUU	Barosaurus
BRTME	burnt umber
BRTOT	burst forth
BRUAI	Bermuda rig
BRUCN	Berlusconi
BRUMA	barium meal
BRWSL	Birtwistle
BRYHT	Barry White
BSAAE	busy as a bee
BSABD	Bishan Bedi
BSADA	Bustard Bay
BSADS	bastardise
BSADZ	bastardize
BSAGE	bespangled
BSAON	boss around
BSEBL	basketball
BSECS	basket case
	basket-case
BSEER	Basseterre
	Basse-Terre
BSEFL	basketfuls
BSEHN	beseeching
BSEHR	basset horn
BSEKE	bespeckled
BSELS	Boswellise
BSELZ	Boswellize
BSEWR	basketwork
	basket-work
BSFIN	best friend
BSGIA	bass guitar
BSHLE	bus shelter
BSIAE	bastinades
BSICE	besmirched
BSIEB	be seized by
BSILS	bestialise
BSILT	bestiality
BSILZ	bestialize
BSJCE	bush jacket
BSLHT	bisulphate
BSLZI	busy Lizzie
	busy lizzie
BSONS	bassoonist
BSRDL	bestraddle
BSRNE	bushranger
BSRNL	besprinkle
BSRRS	by surprise
BSSLE	bestseller
BSTEL	besottedly
BSWLE	bushwalker
BSWSE	best wishes
BSXAL	bisexually
BTADU	bite and sup
BTATM	by that time
BTEAI	Bette Davis
BTEBA	butter bean
BTEBR	Battenburg
BTECK	battercake
BTEDS	butter dish
BTEDW	batten down
	batter down
BTEEB	bothered by
BTEHL	better half
BTEMN	betterment
BTENO	be the end of
BTENS	bitterness
BTEPL	bitter pill
BTESM	bothersome
BTETA	better than
BTEWO	bitterwood
BTEWR	butterwort
BTFTF	bit of stuff
BTHBU	bitch about
BTHNS	bitchiness
BTIEL	Botticelli
BTITM	by this time
BTITT	Battistuta
BTIZA	bat mitzvah
BTKNO	be taken for
BTLES	Betelgeuse
BTLFL	bottlefuls
BTLMN	battlement
BTLNC	bottleneck
BTLSI	battleship
BTLTR	battle-torn
BTLWT	battle with
BTLZN	battle zone
BTMNS	bituminise
BTMNT	bituminate
BTMNU	bituminous
BTMNZ	bituminize
BTNLT	bitonality
BTNOG	Baton Rouge
BTOCL	button cell
BTOEE	bathometer
BTOEU	buttoned up
BTOHL	buttonhold
	buttonhole
BTOIE	Bath Oliver
BTOLN	bottom line
BTOLS	bottomless
BTOMS	bottommost
BTYER	bathymetry
BTYLE	Betty Allen
BUBRN	blubbering
BUBTL	bluebottle
BUCBC	bounce back
BUCET	bruschetta
	bruschette
BUCLA	blue-collar
BUCNS	bounciness
BUDRA	Boulder Dam
BUDRE	boundaries
BUDRN	blundering
BUEAR	Baudelaire
BUEMR	Brunel Marc
BUEOC	brute force
BUESG	Blue Ensign
BUHNL	blushingly
BUHRE	Blue Horses
BUHSD	brush aside
BUJCE	bluejacket
BUMRE	blue murder
BUMSU	Blue Mosque
BUORN	Bruno Bruno
BUPNI	blue pencil
	blue-pencil
BURBN	blue riband
BURBO	blue ribbon
BUTRN	blustering
BUVLE	Blue Velvet
BVRUO	by virtue of
BWENF	bowie knife
BWEOE	bowled over
BWHKE	bow the knee
BWIGU	bawling-out
BWLEE	bewildered
BWLRS	bowdlerise
BWLRZ	bowdlerize
BWTHN	bewitching
BWYOS	bawdy-house
BXRWI	box Brownie®
BYFUD	Bay of Fundy
BYHAL	buy cheaply
BYIBU	boys in blue
BYNDM	Bryan Adams
BYNER	Bryan Ferry
BYNHP	beyond hope
BYNSA	beyond seas
BYNSL	buy and sell
BYSNS	boyishness
BZADI	Buzz Aldrin
BZLET	Bazalgette
CAAAO	chaparajos
CAAEO	chaparejos
CAALO	Chamaeleon
CAARP	Chamaerops
CAATR	characters
CABNS	crabbiness
CABRI	Chambertin
CABRO	chamberpot
CACDN	chalcedony
CACLO	chancellor
CACUO	chance upon
CADGR	Chandigarh
CADLE	chandelier
CADNA	Chardonnay
CADRI	chaudfroid
CAEAN	châtelaine
CAEBL	crane's bill
	cranesbill
CAECN	coalescent
CAECR	chapel cart
CAEEO	clap eyes on
CAEHR	Clare Short
CAEIC	czarevitch
CAELK	Crater Lake
CAELO	Clare Bloom
CAENS	cravenness
CAEVT	coacervate
CAFES	chauffeuse
CAFNL	chaffingly
CAGAL	changeable
	changeably
	chargeable
	chargeably
CAGAN	Craig Raine
CAGDW	change down
	charge down
CAGFC	change face
CAGGA	change gear
CAGHN	charge hand
CAGIT	change into
CAGLN	changeling
CAGLS	changeless
CAGNS	cragginess
CAGOE	changeover
	change-over
CAGTC	change tack
CAHAT	coach party
CAHLO	clap hold of
CAHME	claw hammer
CAIAL	charitable
	charitably
CAIHR	clavichord
CAITC	cladistics
CAITE	charioteer❑
CAIUD	coatimundi
CAKAL	Clark Gable
CAKCI	crack a crib
CAKHF	crankshaft
CAKJK	crack a joke
CAKNS	chalkiness
CAKNU	cracking-up
CALIC	chaplaincy
CALNE	challenged
	challenger
CALSN	cradle song
CALSO	Charleston
CALSR	Charles Fry
CAMFU	claim a foul
CAMNL	charmingly
CAMNS	clamminess
CAMTO	claymation
CANBL	Crab nebula
CANLE	channelled
CANLS	channelise
CANLZ	channelize

Words marked ❑ can also be spelled with an initial capital letter

CANMK	chain-smoke
CANSL	clannishly
CANTR	chain store
CAOAM	coat of arms
	coat-of-arms
CAOMI	coat of mail
CAPDU	clapped-out
CAPGO	champignon
	clay pigeon
CAPNF	clasp knife
CAROA	chairwoman
CASCS	classicise
	classicism
	classicist
CASCZ	classicize
CASFE	classified
CASFS	coarse fish
CASNS	coarseness
CASOA	clanswoman
CASTD	crassitude
CASWT	Clausewitz
CATAD	coastwards
CATES	chartreuse
CATLS	chaptalise
CATLZ	chaptalize
CATNF	craft knife
CATNN	chastening
CATNS	chasteness
	chattiness
	craftiness
CATNU	chatting up
CATRN	chattering
CATRO	chatterbox
	Chatterton
CATSN	chastising
CATUR	coastguard
CAUAE	coagulated
CAUAO	coagulator
CAUEC	crapulence
CAUEU	chalumeaux
CAULR	craquelure
CAVNS	chauvinism
	chauvinist
CAYBU	crazy about
CBCER	cubic metre
CBLBM	cobalt bomb
CBLEO	caballeros
CBLTA	cabalettas
CBNEE	cabin fever
CBREI	cybernetic
CBRPC	cyberspace
CCARC	cockatrice□
CCCAE	cockchafer
	Coco Chanel
CCGAH	cacography
CCHNE	cack-handed
CCIAL	cyclically
CCINT	cachinnate
CCLAE	cochleated
CCLHR	Cecil Sharp
CCODS	cuckoldise
CCODZ	cuckoldize
CCOEI	cyclopedia

CCOPN	cuckoo pint
CCORS	cyclo-cross
CCOTL	cyclostyle
CCRNA	Ciceronian
CCTIE	cicatrices
	cicatrixes
CCUAN	Cú Chulainn
CCYEK	cocky-leeky
CDCLG	codicology
CDLSM	cuddlesome
CDRDI	Cader Idris
CDTOP	cadet corps
CDVRU	cadaverous
CDWLO	codswallop
CEAAT	coelacanth
CEAEK	Chesapeake
CEAEU	coetaneous
	cretaceous□
CECAO	cheechakos
CECNI	crescentic
CECNO	crescendos
CECVL	coercively
CEEAE	crêpe paper
CEEAT	Cleve-Garth
CEECA	Clemenceau
CEEDC	clever dick
CEELT	crenellate
CEENS	cleverness
CEETA	credential
CEETN	Clementina
	clementine□
CEETR	clerestory
CEEWR	crewelwork
CEFEO	Cienfuegos
CEIAL	chemically
	creditable
	creditably
CEICR	credit card
CEIEA	chelicerae
CEIGU	chewing-gum
CEIHN	cherishing
CEINT	credit note
CEITN	coexistent
	co-existent
	coexisting
CEKNS	cheekiness
CEKON	checkpoint
CEKSE	Cherkesses
CEMFR	Chelmsford
CEMNS	creaminess
CENDU	cleaned out
CENIE	clean lines
CENRO	Caernarvon
CENUO	clean out of
CEOAI	chemotaxis
CEOHR	ctenophore
CEOII	coenobitic
CEPIL	Caerphilly
CEPKT	cheapskate
CEPNL	creepingly
CEPNN	cheapening
CERNS	cheeriness
CERPC	cherry-pick

CERRP	Cherry Ripe
CERSU	clear as mud
CERTI	chevrotain
CERTR	clearstory
CERUL	cheerfully
CESAU	Chelsea bun
CESCK	cheesecake
CESDF	cheesed off
CESNS	chersonese
CESOR	chessboard
CETEA	chew the fat
	chew the rag
CETEU	chew the cud
CETNA	Cheltenham
CETRO	Chesterton
CETTC	cleft stick
CETUO	cheat out of
CETVL	creatively
CETVT	creativity
CEUCL	crepuscule
CEUCR	cheque card
CEUII	cherubimic
CEUVR	Che Guevara
CFALI	café au lait
CFEBA	coffee bean
CFEML	coffee mill
CFESO	coffee shop
CFFLR	café filtre
CFINI	coffin-nail
CFRSE	C S Forester
CGIAC	cognisance
	cognizance
CGIAL	cognisably
	cognizably
CGRLO	cigarillos
CGTTN	cogitating
CGTTO	cogitation
CGTTV	cogitative
CHRNL	coherently
CHSVL	cohesively
CIAAA	chip away at
CIALT	china plate
CIARU	chivalrous
CIBRZ	Chimborazo
CICDN	coincident
	coinciding
CICIL	chinchilla
CIDBS	child abuse
CIDIT	childbirth
CIDPA	child's play
CIDRO	childproof
CIDSL	childishly
CIEAE	Clive James
CIEEE	Chinese red
CIEEO	crise de foi
CIEIA	chimerical
CIELN	chiselling
CIELY	Clive Lloyd
CIENA	Crimean War
CIEOU	cri de coeur
CIFHF	chiffchaff
	chiff-chaff
CIFNE	chiffonier

CIGNL	cringingly
CIGNS	clinginess
CIGTN	clingstone
CIHSE	Chichester
CIIAL	clinically
	criminally
	critically
CIIIE	criticized
CIKNO	chickenpox
CIKNU	chicken out
	chicken run
CIKOE	Chick Corea
CILNS	chilliness
CINDX	chionodoxa
CINOM	Cairngorms
CIOAC	chiromancy
CIOEE	clinometer
CIONM	chirognomy
CIPNE	chimpanzee
CIPNS	chirpiness
CIPRA	crispbread
CIRPN	chirruping
CISRS	crisscross
	criss-cross
CITFR	Cristofori
CITGN	chittagong□
CITRN	chittaroni
CIUHA	Chihuahuan
CIUNS	cliquiness
CJLMN	cajolement
CKNCA	caking coal
CLABN	collarbone
CLAEA	collateral
CLAEU	calcareous
CLALC	Cilla Black
CLAOS	collar of SS
CLASN	collapsing
CLASU	collar stud
CLBAE	celebrated
CLBAO	celebrator
CLBSE	Celebes Sea
CLCIE	cold chisel
CLCJC	Calico Jack
CLDNA	Caledonian
CLEDW	calmed down
CLEEA	college cap
CLEIM	collegiums
CLEIT	collegiate
CLETN	Colbertine
CLETO	collection
CLETV	collective
CLFRI	California
CLGNU	caliginous
CLHCM	colchicums
CLHRO	Cold Harbor
CLHSE	Colchester
CLIAA	call it a day
CLIAE	cultivated
CLIAL	cultivable
CLIAO	collimator
	cultivator
CLIEO	calciferol
CLIGF	calling-off

CLIPR	Celtic Park
CLMAI	columbaria
CLMDA	chlamydial
CLMIC	column inch
CLMIT	calumniate
CLMIU	calumnious
CLMLA	columellae
CLMNO	calamancos
CLMTU	calamitous
CLNAE	colonnaded
CLNAI	Colin Davis
CLNAL	colonially
CLNDO	Celine Dion
CLNED	Colin Meads
CLNRE	calendries
CLOHN	Cellophane®
CLOJC	cult object
CLONS	callowness
CLORP	collograph
CLOTU	colporteur
CLOUA	colloquial
CLOUS	colloquise
CLOUU	colloquium
CLOUZ	colloquize
CLPRE	Cole Porter
CLRDS	chloridise
CLRDT	chloridate
CLRDZ	chloridize
CLRFR	chloroform
CLRNS	chlorinise
CLRNT	chlorinate
CLRNZ	chlorinize
CLRPY	chlorophyl
CLRTO	coloration
CLRTR	coloratura
CLSGA	call signal
CLSIN	Colossians
CLSUE	colossuses
CLTMN	call to mind
CLTRE	cold turkey
CLUAE	calculated
CLUAL	calculable
	calculably
	colourably
	culturally
CLUAO	calculator
CLUCD	colour code
	colour-code
CLULS	colourless
CLUUE	calculuses
CLUWS	colourwash
CLYIM	collyriums
CMAAL	comparable
	comparably
CMADE	commandeer
CMADN	commandant
	commanding
CMAEO	campaneros
CMAGE	campaigner
CMAIE	campaniles
CMAIL	compatible
	compatibly
CMAIN	companions
CMAIO	comparison
CMARO	compatriot
CMARS	come across
CMASA	compass saw
CMASO	compassion
CMATF	compactify
CMATO	compaction
CMAZN	combat zone
CMBCT	come back to
CMBFR	come before
CMCLT	comicality
CMCOE	come closer
CMCPR	comic opera
CMCTI	comic strip
CMDEN	comedienne
CMDWO	come down on
CMDWT	come down to
CMEBN	cummerbund
CMECA	commercial
CMECN	commencing
CMEDU	compendium
CMEEC	competence
	competency
CMEIO	campesinos
	competitor
CMELN	compelling
	Cumberland
CMESM	cumbersome
CMESR	commeasure
CMEST	compensate
CMETA	campestral
CMETR	commentary
CMETT	commentate
CMHRT	camphorate
CMHTE	come-hither
CMIAI	commit a sin
CMIIM	cymbidiums
CMIMN	commitment
CMISO	commission
CMITR	commixture
CMLAC	compliance
CMLCN	complacent
CMLCT	complicate
	complicity
CMLIE	complainer
CMLIT	complaints
CMLMN	complement
	compliment
CMLNS	comeliness
CMLTL	completely
CMLTN	completing
CMLTO	completion
	cumulation
CMLTV	cumulative
CMLWT	comply with
CMLXF	complexify
CMLXO	complexion
CMLXT	complexity
CMNAE	come nearer
CMNAT	come near to
CMNNA	coming near
CMNSO	coming soon
CMOAT	commonalty
CMOBN	common bend
CMOBU	common blue
CMOCL	common cold
CMOEL	composedly
CMOEO	composed of
CMOET	components
CMOHR	common herd
CMOIO	compositor
CMOIU	commodious
CMONS	commonness
CMONU	common noun
CMORO	common room
CMOSA	common seal
CMOTL	common talk
CMOTM	common time
CMOTN	comforting
CMRHN	comprehend
CMRMS	compromise
CMRRU	Camerarius
CMRSE	compressed
CMRSO	compressor
CMRUL	cumbrously
CMSIL	comestible
CMTHE	come to heel
CMTHN	come to hand
CMTHV	come to have
CMTKO	come to know
CMTLF	come to life
CMTMN	come to mind
CMTPS	come to pass
CMTRS	come to rest
CMTSA	come to stay
CMUAL	communally
	commutable
	computable
CMUAO	commutator
CMUDN	come undone
CMUIU	communiqué
CMULG	camouflage
CMUSO	compulsion
CMUSR	compulsory
CMUSV	compulsive
CMUTO	combustion
CMUWT	come up with
CNABC	canvasback
CNAEC	convalesce
CNAIA	contadinas
CNAIU	contagious
CNAOP	cantaloupe
CNCEC	conscience
CNEAC	convex arch
	conveyance
CNEAL	convenable
	conveyable
CNEAR	candelabra
CNEBR	Canterbury
CNECN	condescend
CNECO	Concepción
CNEDN	contending
CNEDR	contenders
CNEEC	conference□
CNEEI	congeneric
CNEEL	cankeredly
	Cinderella
	convexedly
CNEGN	convergent
CNEGO	converge on
CNEIA	congenital
CNEIN	convenient
CNELN	cannelloni
	concealing
CNELT	cancellate
CNEMN	conferment
CNENN	concerning
	condemning
CNERN	conferring
CNERT	consecrate
CNESA	consensual
CNESL	conversely
CNESN	conversant
CNESO	concession
	confession
	conversion
CNEST	condensate
CNESV	concessive
CNETA	conceptual
	contextual
	conventual□
CNETI	concentric
CNETN	concertina
	concertino
	connecting
	consenting
	contestant
CNETO	conception□
	confection
	congestion
	connection
	contention
	convection
	convention□
CNETR	conjecture
CNETV	congestive
	connective
	convective
CNEUN	consequent
CNEVN	conserving
CNEVO	conceive of
CNEWR	Cancer Ward
CNEYO	Cannery Row
CNFOM	can of worms
CNFRU	coniferous
CNHGI	conchiglie
CNHIA	conchoidal
CNHLG	conchology
CNHNS	cinchonise
CNHNZ	cinchonize
CNHOI	conchiolin
CNIAC	connivance
CNIAE	candidates
CNIAL	cannibally
CNIAT	confidante
CNICN	convincing
CNICT	confiscate
CNIEC	confidence
	continence

Words marked □ can also be spelled with an initial capital letter

CNIEE	cantilever
	considered
CNIER	centimetre
CNIGA	Cunningham
CNIGN	contingent
CNIGU	conking-out
CNIIN	conditions
CNIIR	centilitre
CNIIT	conciliate
CNILT	cantillate
CNIMC	Connie Mack
CNIMN	confirming
CNINF	consignify
CNINS	candidness
CNINT	Cincinnati
	concinnity
CNIRD	centigrade
CNITN	consistent
CNITO	conniption
	conviction
CNITR	consistory
CNIUI	continue in
CNIUM	continuums
CNIUN	continuing
CNIUT	contiguity
	continuate
	continuity
CNIUU	contiguous
	continuous
CNLBT	conglobate
CNLCL	canaliculi
CNLDN	concluding
CNLEC	confluence
CNLSO	conclusion
CNLSV	conclusive
CNLTO	conflation
CNLWC	candlewick
CNMGE	cinema-goer
CNNOL	Conan Doyle
CNOAC	consonance
	consonancy
CNOAL	condonable
	consolable
CNOBL	cannonball
CNODN	concordant
	con sordino
CNOEC	condolence
CNOET	canzonette
CNOHL	cannot help
CNOIE	Congo River
CNOIT	consociate
CNOIU	censorious
CNOMN	cantonment
	conforming
CNOMS	conformism
	conformist
CNOMT	conformity
CNONE	confounded
CNONI	confound it
CNONL	conjointly
CNONN	conjoining
CNOSI	censorship
CNOTO	concoction
	contortion
CNOTU	consortium
CNOTV	contortive
CNOUE	convoluted
CNPCU	conspectus
CNPOI	cynophobia
CNPRC	conspiracy
CNPRN	conspiring
CNPRT	con spirito
CNRBC	centre-back
CNRBN	contraband
CNRBS	contrabass
CNRBT	contribute
CNRCE	contracted
CNRCI	contract in
CNRCO	contractor
CNRDC	contradict
CNREC	congruence
	congruency
CNRFG	centrifuge
CNRFL	centrefold
CNRFO	contraflow
CNRGT	congregate
CNRHL	centre-half
CNRLE	controlled
	controller
CNRLN	centre-line
CNRLO	contraltos
CNRLS	centralise
	centralism
	centralist
CNRLT	centrality
CNRLZ	centralize
CNRMR	centromere
CNRRL	contrarily
CNRRT	contrary to
CNRRU	cinerarium
CNRSE	contrasted
CNRTL	concretely
	contritely
CNRTO	concretion
	contrition
CNRTS	concretise
CNRTZ	concretize
CNRUL	canorously
CNRVN	contravene
	contriving
CNRVR	controvert
CNSAE	cone-shaped
CNSAO	Canis Major
CNSIO	Canis Minor
CNTAN	constraint
CNTIG	constringe
CNTNA	constantan
CNTNI	Constantia
CNTNL	constantly
CNTPT	constipate
CNTTO	cunctation
CNTTT	constitute
CNUAL	censurable
	censurably
	conjugally
	consumable
CNUCL	conjunctly
CNUEL	confusedly
CNUFI	cinquefoil
CNUMT	consummate
CNURN	concurrent
	concurring
	conquering
CNUSI	consulship
CNUSO	concussion
	convulsion
CNUSS	consubsist
CNUSV	convulsive
CNUTD	consuetude
CNUTN	conducting
	consultant
	consulting
CNUTO	conduction
CNUVR	centumviri
CNUWT	concur with
CNYOA	condylomas
COAOI	chocaholic
COBRN	clobbering
COCNS	choiceness
COCPR	choice part
COCRL	crop circle
CODNS	cloudiness
CODNT	coordinate
	co-ordinate
CODON	crowd round
CODUS	cloudburst
COEAK	close ranks
COEAO	co-operator
COEBR	Cronenberg
COEFA	close of day
COEHN	close thing
COEHO	cloven hoof
COEHV	close shave
COEIC	clove hitch
COELA	cloverleaf
COGNL	cook gently
COHAE	cloth-eared
	cool-headed
COHPE	clodhopper
COHTN	crocheting
COHUO	clothe upon
COIGA	cooling fan
COITR	choristers
COKEE	crow-keeper
COKOD	Crockford's
COKOE	clock tower
CONOR	crown court
CONSL	clownishly
COOAE	chocolates
	chocolatey
COOOI	chocoholic
COSAC	cross-match
	crosspatch
COSEE	cloistered
	cloisterer
	cross-refer
COSHC	crosscheck
	cross-check
COSIC	crosspiece
COSNS	choosiness
COSOD	crossroads
COSOE	crossbones
COSRE	crossbreed
COSRS	cloistress
COTII	clostridia
COTTO	co-optation
COTTV	co-optative
CPAOI	Cephalonia
CPAOO	cephalopod
CPATA	Cap Haitian
CPBAC	Capablanca
CPBLT	capability
CPCTT	capacitate
CPDNU	cupidinous
CPEHA	copperhead
CPFSA	cup of assay
CPIAE	captivated
CPIAL	capsizable
CPICO	capriccios
CPIEI	cypripedia
CPIIU	capricious
CPIUL	captiously
CPLIO	cipollinos
CPLTN	copulating
CPLTO	copulation
CPNAE	Copenhagen
CPOAI	coprolalia
CPRAC	caper sauce
CPRIU	Copernicus
CPTLN	Capitoline
CPTLS	capitalise
	capitalism
	capitalist
CPTLT	capitulate
CPTLU	capital sum
CPTLZ	capitalize
CPTTO	capitation
CPUCN	cappuccino
CPWIE	copywriter
CQETS	coquettish
CRACO	cereal crop
CRAEU	coriaceous
	curvaceous
CRAHE	carragheen
CRAIE	caryatides
CRAKN	carjacking
CRASA	carnassial
CRATE	Carmarthen
CRBLA	cerebellar
CRBLT	curability
CRBLU	cerebellum
CRBNE	corybantes
CRCAE	care-crazed
CRCES	curd cheese
CRCTR	caricature
CRDGO	Ceredigion
CREAE	correlated
CREAI	curselarie
CREBE	corned beef
CREBL	curfew-bell
CRECE	currencies
CREDC	curled dock

CREET corselette
CRELN corbelling
curved line
CRELR carpellary
CREON curve round
CREPN correspond
CREPT curled-pate
CRESO corner shop
CRETI current aim
CRETO correction
CRETR Carpenters
CRETS cornettist
CRETV corrective
CREWS cornerwise
CREWY cornerways
CRFAE cornflakes
CRFOE cornflower
CRHMN carthamine
CRHMS Carchemish
CRHSA Carthusian
CRIAL cardinally
CRIED corrigenda
CRIGA cardiogram
CRIGO Carrington
CRIIL corrigible
CRILG cardiology
CRILI cardialgia
CRILS cordialise
CRILT cordiality
CRILZ cordialize
CRIOA carcinomas
CRIOE carcinogen
CRIRA carrier bag
CRIUA corbiculae
curricular
CRIUU curriculum
CRLNK coral snake
CRLSL carelessly
CRMLS caramelise
CRMLZ caramelize
CRMNA ceremonial
CRMNU ceruminous
CRMOI coram nobis
CRMSM chromosome
CRNCE chronicled
chronicler
chronicles❑
CRNCT chronicity
CRNHA Corinthian
CRNLG chronology
CRNLI cor anglais
CRNTO coronation
CROAE carbonated
CROAL corporally
CROAO carbonados
CROAU Coriolanus
CROBE cordon bleu
CROBL Carlos Belo
CROCK carrot cake
CROCP carbon copy
carbon-copy
CROCT Carson City
CROET corporeity
CRONS cartoonist
CROOE corroboree
CROSI Carnoustie
CROYI carboxylic
CRRDE cartridges
CRSAC Cyrus Vance
CRSAE Christabel
CRSEE christened
CRSLD chrysalids
CRSLK corpse-like
CRSLT chrysolite
CRSLY Chris Lloyd
CRSMT Chris Smith
CRSVR Chris Evert
CRTNI carotenoid
carotinoid
CRTSG curate's egg
CRUAE corrugated
CRUAL circularly
CRUCS circumcise
CRUDC circumduce
circumduct
CRUEC corpulence
corpulency
CRUFE circumflex
CRUFS circumfuse
CRUGO curmudgeon
CRUMR circummure
CRUOI cornucopia
CRUPS circumpose
CRUTN corrupting
CRUTO corruption
CRUTU circuitous
CRUTV corruptive
CRUVN circumvent
CRVGI Caravaggio
CRWLI Cornwallis
CRYNO carrying-on
CSACO cast anchor
CSANS casualness
CSAPL cast a spell
CSATE casualties
CSBAC Casablanca
CSDAL cost dearly
CSECA Cistercian
CSENS cussedness
CSETC cos lettuce
CSHRE case-harden
CSIAE cuspidated
CSIAL cosmically
CSIEC cysticerci
CSIGF casting-off
CSIGU casting out
CSINE Caspian Sea
CSINN cushioning
CSIPI Cassiopeia
CSIRN cashiering
CSLNS costliness
CSOIE customized
CSOMD custom-made
CSRTO castration
CSSEL casus belli
CTAEI cottage pie
CTBLS catabolism
CTCEI catechesis
catechetic
CTCIE catechizer
CTCNE CAT scanner
CTCNR city centre
CTCRM cytochrome
CTCUE catechumen
CTEIO city editor
CTFFO cut off from
CTFGR cut a figure
CTFLU catafalque
CTGRA categorial
CTGRS categorise
CTGRZ categorize
CTHCA catch a crab
CTHEN catchpenny
CTHIH catch light
catch sight
CTIAI citric acid
CTIGF cutting-off
CTIGU cutting-out
CTLCI catalectic
CTLCK cattle cake
CTLFS cuttlefish
CTLGE cataloguer
CTLGI cattle grid
CTLGS cytologist
CTLLK cattlelike
CTLPI cataleptic
CTOCU Cotton Club
CTOEC cut some ice
CTOIO catholicon
CTONR cut corners
CTOOT cotton on to
cotton onto
CTOTI cottontail
CTOWO cottonwood
cotton wool
cottonwool
CTPOG cut up rough
CTSNZ citisenize
CTTVN Cat Stevens
CTUGA cat burglar
cat-burglar
CTZNZ citizenize
CUAEU courageous
CUBNS chubbiness
CUCGE churchgoer
CUCLA council tax
CUCLO councillor
CUCWR churchward
CUCYR churchyard
CUDRN chundering
CUHNL crushingly
CUHRS couch grass
CUHWE cough sweet
CUINR cautionary
CUIUL cautiously
CUKBO chukka boot
CUKER Chuck Berry
CULSL churlishly
CUMNS chumminess
CUPNS clumpiness
CUSBO coursebook
CUSLO counsellor
CUSNS clumsiness
CUTAI Count Basie
Count Paris
CUTCA crustacean
CUTCT causticity
CUTEL courtierly
CUTNS crustiness
CUTRC counteract
CUTRE court order
CUTRU countersue
CUTTW county town
CUTYA countryman
CUUIR couturière
CUUWT chum up with
CUYBE Cluny Abbey
CUZEI Chuzzlewit
CVLEL cavalierly
CVLOR civil court
CVLTE civilities
CVLYA cavalryman
CVLYE cavalrymen
CVLZN civilizing
CVNNE covenanter
CVNNO covenantor
CVRAC covariance
CVRDA covered way
CVRNS covertness
CVRON cover point
CVRRV cover drive
CVTNL covetingly
CVTTO cavitation
CVTUL covetously
CVTWL cavity wall
CWRNL coweringly
CWRSI cowardship
CWUCE cowpuncher
CYEDL Clydesdale
CYFFO cry off from
CYGIS cry against
CYGNC cryogenics
CYOMS Ceylon moss
CYTGA cryptogram
DAALN draw a blank
DAAOE draw a cover
DAAUG dramaturge
dramaturgy
DAAWT do away with
DABET draw breath
DABIG drawbridge
DACNR dead centre
DAEEI diagenesis
DAERU Diane Arbus
DAESI dealership
DAETC dialectics
DAFSL dwarfishly
DAGNO dragging on
DAHAC deathwatch
death-watch
DAHAD deathwards
DAHHA death's-head

Words marked ❑ can also be spelled with an initial capital letter

DAHNL death-knell
DAHNU diaphanous
diaphonous
DAHOE death-token
DAHOI diachronic
DAHQA death squad
DAIFN draw it fine
DAIGI drawing-pin
DAIGU drawing out
DAIML draw it mild
DALNE do a flanker
DALNL drawlingly
DALNS deadliness
DANAT draw near to
DANIE drainpipes
DANSI diagnostic
DANTL deadnettle
dead-nettle
DAOAL diagonally
DAOIA diabolical
DAOTM dead on time
DAPRO dead person
DAPRT deaspirate
DARCN drag-racing
DARNE dead ringer
DAROA diarrhoeal
DAROI diarrhoeic
DASRN drawstring
DASUP draw stumps
DATMT diastemata
DATVT deactivate
DAWIH dead-weight
DAYAL dialysable
DAYHN do anything
DBAVI De Beauvoir
DBIFN debriefing
DBLNL dabblingly
DBLTT debilitate
DBNIL debonairly
DBSMN debasement
DBSNL debasingly
DBSNS do business
DBTAL debateable
DBTMN debatement
DBTNL debatingly
DBTWT debate with
DBUHN debouching
DBUHR debauchery
DCAAL declarable
DCAEA declare war
DCAEF declare off
DCAEL declaredly
DCAHN dictaphone
DCASF declassify
DCATN Doc Martens®
DCBTU Dick Butkus
DCDNL decadently
DCENS decree nisi
DCESA Dickensian
DCESB decrease by
DCESN decreasing
DCESO declension
DCHDA decahedral
DCHDO decahedron
DCIAL declinable
DCIEB deceived by
DCINR dictionary
DCLNS decolonise
DCLNZ decolonize
DCLRT decelerate
decolorate
DCLRZ decolorize
DCMEC decumbence
decumbency
DCMLS decimalise
DCMLZ decimalize
DCMMN decampment
DCMNA documental
DCMNE documented
DCMOE decomposed
decomposer
DCMON decompound
DCMRS decompress
DCMTO decimation
DCOSO Doctor Slop
DCPEE decipherer
DCPIU deceptious
DCPTT decapitate
DCRII dichroitic
DCRTN decorating
DCRTO decoration
DCRTV decorative
DCRUL decorously
DCSVL decisively
DCTLT decathlete
DCTRI Dick Turpin
DCVLS decivilise
DCVLZ decivilize
DCYTO decryption
DDCNS Dodecanese
DDCTO dedication
DDCTR dedicatory
DDEIO didgeridoo
DDEMT Dodie Smith
DECLT de-escalate
DEDOK dreadlocks
DEDUL dreadfully
DEETI dielectric
DEFEZ deep-freeze
DEFRA dies feriae
DEHLE deed holder
DEKNE dreikanter
DELTE deep litter
DEMNL dreamingly
DEMNS dreaminess
DEMOG Dream Songs
DEPRL Deep Purple
DERNS dreariness
DEROE deep-rooted
DESAE deep-seated
dressmaker
DESES dress sense
DESHR dress-shirt
DESNS dressiness
DETRA deep throat
DFAAL defrayable
DFADN defrauding
DFAMN defragment
defrayment
DFART deflagrate
DFCEC deficiency
DFCMN defacement
DFCNL defacingly
DFCTO defecation
DFECA duffel coat
DFEEC difference
DFETN deflecting
DFETO deflection
DFETV deflective
DFIEC diffidence
DFIUT difficulty
DFLAE defoliated
DFLAO defalcator
defoliator
DFLMN defilement
DFMTO defamation
DFMTR defamatory
DFNAL defendable
DFNEA defenceman
defenseman
DFNED definienda
DFNIL defensible
defensibly
DFNMN definement
DFNTL definitely
DFNTO definition
defunction
DFNTV definitive
DFOEE deflowerer
DFRAL deferrable
DFREL deformedly
DFUEL diffusedly
DFUIL diffusible
DFUTN defaulting
DGAAL degradable
DGADE dog-handler
DGAIT digladiate
DGDNE dog's dinner
DGENS doggedness
DGESN degreasant
digressing
DGESO digression
DGESV digressive
DGEWS digger-wasp
DGNBN dog and bone
DGNRC degeneracy
DGNRT degenerate
DGPTO dig a pit for
DGSEL digestedly
DGSIL digestible
DGTLS digitalise
DGTLZ digitalize
DGTTL digitately
DHDAE dehydrated
dehydrater
DHDAO dehydrator
DHMDF dehumidify
DHMNS dehumanise
DHMNZ dehumanize
DHSEC dehiscence
DIEHE drive-wheel
DIEHF drive shaft
DIELN drive along
DIENT driven nuts
DIEPR drive apart
DIERZ drive crazy
DIKRV drink-drive
DILAG drill gauge
DITNS daintiness
DIYHE daisy-wheel
DIYHI daisy-chain
DIYOE daily dozen
DIYPR Daily Sport
DIYRA daily bread
DIYRN daily grind
DJCEL dejectedly
DJDCT dijudicate
DKEIE dukkeripen
DLAMT Delia Smith
DLBRT deliberate
DLCAL delectable
delectably
DLCRT dilacerate
DLCTL delicately
DLEAT Dolcelatte
DLEET dolcemente
DLGNL diligently
DLGTO delegation
DLGTU delightful
DLHNU delphinium
DLIEL Delhi belly
DLILG deltiology
DLKWS do likewise
DLMNT delaminate
DLMTS dolomitise
DLMTT delimitate
DLMTZ dolomitize
DLNAL delineable
DLNAO delineator
DLNUN delinquent
DLPDT dilapidate
DLQEC deliquesce
DLRUL dolorously
DLSML dolesomely
DLSVL delusively
DLTAT dilettante
dilettanti
DLTRL dilatorily
DLTTO dilatation
DLWEC D H Lawrence
DLWTE dull-witted
DLYAL dilly-dally
DLYNL delayingly
DMBLS demobilise
DMBLZ demobilize
DMCAI democratic
DMCIU Democritus
DMCNO demi-cannon
DMCUS damp-course
DMDLT demodulate
DMEDW dampen down
DMEFS damsel fish

	damselfish
DMGAH	demography
DMGAL	damageable
DMGNL	damagingly
DMINM	domain name
DMLSE	demolished
	demolisher
DMLTO	demolition
DMNAA	demoniacal
DMNAL	demandable
DMNED	diminuendo
DMNEL	dementedly
DMNIN	dimensions
DMNLG	demonology
DMNNL	dominantly
DMNSE	diminished
DMNTN	dominating
DMNTO	diminution
	domination
DMNTS	demonetise
DMNTV	diminutive
	dominative
DMNTZ	demonetize
DMONE	dumfounder
DMPIN	Dame Pliant
DMRAE	demarcated
DMRHS	dimorphism
DMRHU	dimorphous
DMRLS	demoralise
DMRLZ	demoralize
DMRNS	demureness
DMSEE	damascened
DMSEN	damasceene
DMSPU	damask plum
DMSRC	dumbstruck
DMSRS	damask rose
DMTVT	demotivate
DMWIE	dumb-waiter
DNAAA	Donna Karan
DNAIM	dentaliums
DNAKA	Dundalk Bay
DNAKL	Dan Maskell
DNBEL	dung beetle
	dung-beetle
DNDTO	denudation
DNEBO	Denver boot
DNECK	Dundee cake
DNECT	Dundee City
DNEFN	dunderfunk
DNEHA	dunderhead
DNELD	dinner lady
DNEVT	donkey vote
DNEWR	donkeywork
	donkey-work
DNGAO	denigrator
DNGLA	Donegal Bay
DNIEE	densimeter
DNIRC	dentifrice
DNMNT	denominate
DNNIT	denunciate
DNNRO	dining-room
DNRDA	Don Bradman
DNREA	doner kebab
DNRLG	dendrology
DNSBU	Danish blue
DNSOR	de nos jours
DNSOU	Duns Scotus
DNSUI	dinosauric
DNTMN	denotement
DNTRN	denaturant
DNTRS	denaturise
DNTRZ	denaturize
DNTTO	denotation
DNTTV	denotative
DNUMN	denouement
	dénouement
DNUXT	Don Quixote
DNYOS	dandy-horse
DNYRO	Donnybrook
DNYRS	dandy-brush
DOACO	drop anchor
DOAET	Deo favente
DOARC	drop a brick
DOASU	Dio Cassius
DODWO	drop down on
DOEBS	do one's best
DOECU	Drones Club
DOEIA	duodecimal
DOEIO	duodecimos
DOEKN	do one's kind
DOHNL	door-handle
DOHNU	Diophantus
DOIIE	deoxidizer
DOKEE	doorkeeper
	door-keeper
DOLTA	Diocletian
DOOET	Deo volente
DOOHL	drosophila
DOOIE	deodorizer
DOPNL	droopingly
DOPNS	droopiness
DORTA	Deo gratias
DOSNS	drowsiness
DOTDO	door-to-door
DOTLG	deontology
DPAEL	depravedly
DPBLT	dupability
DPEAO	deprecator
DPEIT	depreciate
DPELN	dapperling
DPENS	dapperness
DPESN	depressant
	depressing
DPESO	depression
DPESV	depressive
DPHAG	depth gauge
DPIAO	duplicator
DPIEO	deprived of
DPLGE	dapple-grey
DPLRS	depolarise
DPLRZ	depolarize
DPLTO	depilation
DPLTR	depilatory
DPNAI	dependacie
DPNAL	dependable
	dependably
DPNEC	dependence
	dependency
DPOAI	diplomatic
	dipsomania
DPOAL	deplorable
	deplorably
DPOMN	deployment
DPOOU	diplodocus❑
DPPLT	depopulate
DPPSE	dope pusher
DPRFO	depart from
DPRMN	department
	deportment
DPRTO	depuration
DPRTV	depurative
DPSTO	deposit box
	deposition
DPSTR	depositary
	depository
DPTDW	Deputy Dawg
DPTEI	diphtheria
DPTHA	deputy head
DPTTO	deputation
DRAGA	Dorian Gray
DRAII	dermatitis
DRAOE	dermatoses
DRBEL	dorr beetle
DRBLT	durability
DRCIN	directions
DRCMI	direct mail
DRCNS	directness
DRCNT	deracinate
DRDNL	deridingly
DRELN	Darjeeling
DRFRE	dirt farmer
DRGLT	deregulate
DRGSE	deregister
DRGTL	derogately
DRGTO	derogation
DRGTR	derogatory
DRGTV	derogative
DRHIE	dark-haired
DRHSE	Dorchester
DRHWT	Dershowitz
DRIGG	darning egg
DRIGO	Darlington
DRIMN	derailment
DRIRR	dernier cri
DRMHA	durum wheat
DRMTE	dark matter
DRNUA	Duran Duran
DRRTE	dirt-rotten
DRSRC	derestrict
DRSVL	derisively
DRVTO	derivation
DRVTV	derivative
DRYAR	Dirty Harry
DRYHR	Derbyshire
DRYIE	dirty linen
DRYOE	dirty money
DRYOK	dirty books
DRYRA	dirty great
DRYRC	dirty trick
DSAAE	disparager
DSACN	distancing
DSADN	discarding
DSAIA	Das Kapital
DSAIF	dissatisfy
DSAIL	déshabillé
	dishabille
DSAMN	disbarment
	disharmony
DSANS	disgarnish
	dismalness
DSANT	discarnate
DSANU	disdainful
DSARA	dish aerial
DSARN	despairing
DSASO	dispassion
DSBLT	disability
DSCAE	desecrater
	desiccated
DSCAO	desecrator
	desiccator
DSCMR	disc camera
DSCNM	diseconomy
DSDRT	desiderata
	desiderate
DSEAO	desperados
DSEBE	dissembled
	dissembler
DSEDN	descendant
	descending
DSEDR	Düsseldorf
DSEEI	disbenefit
DSEIV	disbelieve
DSENN	discerning
DSEPC	disrespect
DSERE	dishearten
DSESO	dispersion
	dissension
	distension
DSESR	dispensary
DSETN	dissecting
	dissenting
DSETO	dissection
DSETR	disfeature
DSEVC	disservice
DSGAE	designated
DSGAL	designable
DSGEL	designedly
DSHFE	dischuffed
DSHMS	dysphemism
DSHOE	deschooler
DSHRE	discharged
	discharger
DSHRO	disc harrow
DSIAE	dissipated
DSIAL	despicable
	despicably
	dislikable
DSICL	distinctly
DSIEC	dissidence
DSIIA	dissimilar
DSIIE	dispirited
DSILN	discipline

Words marked ❑ can also be spelled with an initial capital letter

DSILR	distillery
DSILT	distillate
DSIMN	distilment
DSISR	dismissory
DSISV	dismissive
DSIUE	disfigured
DSJCE	disc jockey
	dust jacket
DSLAE	displeased
DSLAI	disyllabic
DSLAL	disyllable
DSLIE	disclaimer
DSLNS	desalinise
	displenish
DSLNT	desalinate
DSLNZ	desalinize
DSLOE	disallowed
DSLSR	disclosure
DSLTL	desolately
DSLTO	desolation
DSMGN	disimagine
DSMOE	disembowel
	disempower
DSMOO	disembosom
DSMOU	disembogue
DSMRI	disembroil
DSMRV	disimprove
DSNAE	disengaged
DSNEI	disinherit
DSNEO	disenvelop
DSNHA	disenthral
DSNHI	disenchain
DSNHN	disenchant
DSNII	disinhibit
DSNIL	disentitle
DSNIO	disenviron
DSNLN	disincline
DSNLS	disenclose
	disinclose
DSNLV	disenslave
DSNMT	disanimate
DSNOL	disennoble
DSNOV	disinvolve
DSNRI	disentrain
DSNWN	disentwine
DSOAC	dissonance
DSOAE	dislocated
DSOAL	disloyally
	disposable
DSOAT	disloyalty
DSOCR	disconcert
DSODN	despondent
	discordant
DSOEE	discovered
	discoverer
DSOEL	disposedly
DSOET	dishonesty
	disposed to
DSOFR	discomfort
DSOGN	dislodging
DSOHL	discophile
DSOIM	desmodiums
DSOIT	dissociate
DSOLN	despoiling
DSOMD	discommode
DSOMN	discommend
DSONC	disconnect
DSONE	discounted
	discounter
	disjointed
DSOPS	discompose
DSORE	discourser
DSORG	discourage
DSOSS	dispossess
DSOTN	discontent
DSOTO	distortion
DSOUL	dissoluble
DSOVK	Dostoevsky
DSOVN	dissolving
DSPAE	disapparel
DSPEC	desipience
DSPOG	disc plough
DSPON	disappoint
DSPRV	disapprove
DSRAE	disarrayed
DSRAG	disarrange
DSRBA	describe as
DSRBT	distribute
DSRCE	distracted
DSRCN	disgracing
DSREE	disordered
DSREL	deservedly
	discreetly
	disorderly
DSRET	désorienté
DSRFS	disprofess
DSRHI	dysarthria
DSRML	descramble
DSRNL	disgruntle
DSRPI	dysgraphia
	dystrophin
DSRPN	discrepant
DSRPO	descriptor
DSRSE	distressed
DSRSU	dysprosium
DSRTL	discretely
DSRTO	desorption
	discretion
DSRUH	distraught
DSRUL	desirously
DSRYN	destroying
DSSAC	desistance
DSSAE	disc-shaped
DSSFO	desist from
DSSRU	disastrous
DSUAL	disputable
	disputably
DSUBN	disturbant
	disturbing
DSUEE	disquieted
	disquieten
DSUEL	disquietly
DSULF	disqualify
DSUMT	desquamate
DSUNS	disfurnish
DSUPT	disculpate
DSUSO	discussion
	dissuasion
DSUSR	dissuasory
DSUSV	discursive
	dissuasive
DSUTE	disburthen
DSUTN	disgusting
DSUTO	disruption
DSUTV	disruptive
DSWMN	disownment
DSWSE	dishwasher
DTATO	detraction
DTCAL	detachable
	detectable
DTCEL	detachedly
DTCIL	detectible
DTCMN	detachment
DTELN	dotted line
DTENT	dotted note
DTEOE	dotted over
DTEOO	do the job of
DTERC	do the trick
DTERS	dotted rest
DTHNL	Dutch uncle
DTHOA	Dutchwoman
DTHOE	Dutchwomen
DTHRA	Dutch treat
DTIAL	detainable
DTIGT	do things to
DTIMN	detainment
DTNTO	detonation
DTOAK	ditto marks
DTREC	deterrence
DTRIE	determined
	determiner
DTSAL	detestable
	detestably
DTUCT	detruncate
DTXCT	detoxicate
DTYBU	dotty about
DUADC	drug addict
DUAEU	drupaceous
DUGNL	drudgingly
DUHBR	Doukhobors
DUHEL	daughterly
DUHNS	doughiness
DULBC	double back
DULBL	double bill
DULBN	double-bank
	double bind
	double bond
DULBO	double-book
DULBS	double bass
DULCI	double chin
DULDO	double door
DULFA	double flat
DULGL	double-gild
DULPR	double-park
DULSA	double star
DULTL	Double Talk
	double talk
	double-talk
DULTM	double time
DUTNL	doubtingly
DUTUL	doubtfully
DVBME	dive-bomber
DVCLS	devocalise
DVCLZ	devocalize
DVDAE	David Mamet
DVDAO	David Jason
DVDIE	David Niven
DVDOE	David Gower
DVDOG	David Lodge
DVDOI	David Bowie
DVDPE	dive-dapper
DVDRC	David Bruce
DVDRS	David Frost
DVDTE	David Steel
DVDUE	David Hubel
DVDYC	David Lynch
DVGTO	divagation
DVLEC	divulgence
DVLPN	developing
DVLRS	devalorise
DVLRZ	devalorize
DVLSL	devilishly
DVLTO	devolution
DVNGR	devanagari□
DVNHR	Devonshire
DVNNS	divineness
DVNTO	divination
DVNTR	divinatory
DVRCT	divaricate
DVREC	divergence
DVSAE	devastated
DVSAO	devastator
DVSEO	divested of
DVSMN	divestment
DVSOA	divisional
DVSVL	divisively
DVTLS	devitalise
DVTLZ	devitalize
DVTMN	devotement
DVTOA	devotional
DVUNS	devoutness
DWADU	down and out
	down-and-out
DWAHE	down at heel
	down-at-heel
DWCOU	dawn chorus
DWFAE	Dawn Fraser
DWFEC	Dawn French
DWLNL	dawdlingly
DWMRE	down-market
DWSAR	downstairs
DWSRA	downstream
DWSZN	downsizing
DWWRL	downwardly
DXEWS	dexterwise
DXRLT	dextrality
DXRUL	dextrously
DYATE	dry canteen
DYATR	dry battery
DYCOA	day-scholar
DYERE	day-wearied
DYESR	dry measure

DYFIT	day of birth
DYGNB	days gone by
DYOYR	days of yore
DYRAE	daydreamer
DYRPE	day-tripper
DYSBN	dry as a bone
DZLNL	dazzlingly
DZYNL	dizzyingly
EAAAU	Elagabalus
EAAGN	emalangeni
EACLT	emasculate
EACPT	emancipate
EAEBT	exacerbate
EAECN	evanescent
EAELN	enamelling
EAGLS	evangelise
	evangelism❑
	evangelist❑
EAGLZ	evangelize
EAGNT	emarginate
EAGRT	exaggerate
EAHDO	Esarhaddon
EAHLG	edaphology
EAIAL	eradicable
	examinable
EAIAO	eradicator
EAITN	emaciating
EAITO	emaciation
EAIUL	edaciously
EAOAE	evaporated
EAOAL	evaporable
EAOAO	elaborator
	enamorados
	evaporator
EAPRT	exasperate
EATCS	elasticise
EATCT	elasticate
	elasticity
EATCZ	elasticize
EATNL	exactingly
EATTD	exactitude
EATTO	exaltation
EAUTO	evacuation
	evaluation
EAUTV	evaluative
EBCEI	eubacteria
EBDMN	embodiment
EBEAI	emblematic
EBLMN	embalmment
EBNFO	ebb and flow
EBNMN	embankment
EBODR	embroidery
EBOLO	embroglios
EBRUO	embark upon
EBTEE	embittered
EBUHR	embouchure
EBYLG	embryology
ECATN	enchanting
ECCIA	encyclical
ECECK	Eccles cake
ECECN	excrescent
ECGTT	excogitate
ECIAA	enchiladas
ECIAO	escribanos
ECIOR	escritoire
ECLDE	escaladoes
ECLEC	excellence
	Excellency
ECLOI	escallonia
ECLPU	eucalyptus
ECLTN	escalating
ECLTO	escalation
ECLTR	escalatory
ECMEE	encumbered
ECMIG	e e cummings
ECMMN	encampment
ECNES	ex concesso
ECNTR	encincture
ECOCE	encroacher
ECPAI	encephalic
ECPAO	encephalon
ECPDE	escapadoes
ECPFO	escape from
ECPLG	escapology
ECPLS	exceptless
ECPMN	escapement
ECPOI	eccoprotic
ECPRA	escape road
ECPRO	each person
ECRAE	excoriated
ECRLN	encircling
ECRMN	escarpment
ECRTO	excerption
ECRUE	excursuses
ECSGU	ecce signum
ECSMN	encasement
	encashment
ECTER	ex cathedra
ECTHO	escutcheon
ECTMN	excitement
ECTNL	excitingly
ECTTO	excitation
ECTTR	excitatory
ECTTV	excitative
ECUAE	encouraged
ECUAL	excludable
ECUIT	excruciate
ECVTO	excavation
ECYOI	ecchymosis
EDAMN	endearment
EDCIA	endocrinal
EDCII	endocrinic
EDEWT	endued with
EDFTR	end of story
EDGNU	endogenous
EDMRK	Eddy Merckx
EDOEE	eudiometer
EDPYI	endophytic
EDRDC	end-product
EDRER	elderberry
EDREU	endorse out
EDRNL	enduringly
EDSOI	endoscopic
EDTEI	endothelia
EDWET	endowments
EEACE	eye-catcher
EECAC	even chance
EECRA	El Escorial
EEDTO	emendation
EEDTR	emendatory
EEEEE	epexegeses
EEEIA	exegetical
EEEPU	eleven-plus
EEETL	eleventhly
EEETR	elementary
EEGAE	Everglades
EEGNL	emergently
EEGZN	energizing
EEHHU	Erechtheum
	Erechtheus
EEHNE	even-handed
EEIAL	emetically
EEINS	eyewitness
	eye-witness
EELSE	eyeglasses
EELVN	ever-living
EENLS	eternalise
EENLZ	eternalize
EENME	even number
EEPFO	exempt from
EERGN	epeirogeny
EERTO	execration
EERTR	execratory
EERTV	execrative
EESAC	eye askance
EETAL	eventually
EETEE	epentheses
EETOG	even though
EETOI	electronic
EETRT	electorate
	exenterate
EETVL	electively
EETVT	electivity
EEUAL	executable
EEUIE	executives
EEVTN	enervating
EEVTO	enervation
EEVTV	enervative
EEYGN	enemy agent
EEYHN	everything
EEYHR	everywhere
EEYIO	every bit of
EEYLC	every place
EEYNO	every one of
EEYTE	every other
EFCAL	effaceable
EFCCT	efficacity
EFCEC	efficiency
EFCMN	effacement
EFCUT	effectuate
EFELN	enfeebling
EFERG	effleurage
EFLEC	effulgence
EFMNC	effeminacy
EFMNS	effeminise
EFMNT	effeminate
EFMNZ	effeminize
EFOEC	effloresce
EFOTR	effrontery
EFREC	effervesce
EFREL	enforcedly
EFRLS	effortless
EFSVL	effusively
EFTNS	effeteness
EGGMN	engagement
EGGNL	engagingly
EGIHA	Englishman
EGLMN	engulfment
EGNAA	Eugene Aram
EGNAU	eigenvalue
EGNDB	Eugene Debs
EGNMC	ergonomics
EGNMS	ergonomist
EGNRO	engine room
EGOCE	egg poacher
EGODE	egg coddler
EGOSN	engrossing
EGREA	Edgar Degas
EGRIO	engarrison
EGTET	eighteenth
EHBTO	exhibition
EHBTV	exhibitive
EHCLT	ethicality
EHIAL	ethnically
EHLRT	exhilarate
EHLTO	exhalation
EHMRS	euhemerise
EHMRZ	euhemerize
EHMTO	exhumation
EHNDR	echinoderm
EHNLE	Ethan Allen
EHNOE	Ethan Cohen
EHRAL	ethereally
EHROI	enharmonic
EHUTN	exhausting
EHUTO	exhaustion
EHUTV	exhaustive
EIAEU	ericaceous
EIATI	epicanthic
EIATU	epicanthus
EIBYO	Enid Blyton
EICAE	Eric Coates
EICMN	evincement
EICPC	episcopacy
EICPS	episcopise
EICPT	episcopate
EICPZ	episcopize
EICRT	eviscerate
EIECI	epideictic
EIECO	evidence of
EIETA	epicentral
	evidential
EIHLA	epithelial
EIHLU	epithelium
EIHMT	epithemata
EIHVN	Edith Evans
EIIAE	eliminated
EIIAL	eliminable
EIIAO	eliminator
EIITM	episiotomy
EIIUL	eximiously
EIIYI	epididymis

EILSI epiblastic
EILSR epiplastra
EILTI epiglottis
EILTO etiolation
EIMNE evil-minded
EIMTS enigmatise
EIMTZ enigmatize
EIOIE epitomizer
EIOSI editorship
EIOTC epizootics
EIOUS epiloguise
EIOUZ epiloguize
EIRPI epigraphic
EIRTO emigration
EISII evil spirit
EITEE Erik the Red
EITLR epistolary
EITLS epistolise
EITLZ epistolize
EITMC epistemics
EITOH epistrophe
EIUUL exiguously
EIWEE Elie Wiesel
EIYNL edifyingly
EJMMN enjambment
EKPAI enkephalin
EKROI eukaryotic
ELGSI eulogistic
ELNER Ellen Terry
ELPIA elliptical
ELREL enlargedly
ELSMN enlistment
ELVNN enlivening
EMBVR Emma Bovary
EMNAE Emmentaler
EMNKA Edmund Kean
EMTMT Emmit Smith
ENORE Edna O'Brien
ENTHI Ernst Chain
EOBTN exorbitant
EOEAE exonerated
EOETI egocentric
EOGTO elongation
EOIAL exotically
EOILG exobiology
EOINS exoticness
EOMUL enormously
EOOIA ecological
economical
EOOIE economizer
EOPEI exospheric
EOSIA egoistical
EOUET emoluments
EOUNL eloquently
EOVIT evolve into
EOYEI epoxy resin
EPANN explaining
EPCAC expectancy
EPCAL especially
expectable
expectably
EPCEL expectedly
EPCET expected to

EPDCE Empedocles
EPDEC expedience
expediency
EPDIL espadrille
EPDTL expeditely
EPDTO expedition
EPDTT expeditate
EPEIE expletives
EPENI en plein air
EPESO expression
EPESV expressive
EPIAL explicable
EPICP en principe
EPIIL explicitly
EPNAL expandable
expendable
EPNIL expansible
expansibly
EPNTO expunction
EPOAL employable
EPOEA employed as
EPOEB employed by
EPOEE ecphoneses
EPOIN explosions
EPOIU euphonious
EPOMN employment
EPOTV exploitive
EPRAE expurgater
EPRAL exportable
EPRAO expurgator
EPRCS empiricism
empiricist
EPREC experience
EPRMN experiment
EPRNS expertness
EPRSN Euphrosyne
EPRTO expiration
EPSTO exposition
EPSTR expository
EPTEI empathetic
EPTIT expatriate
EPUDN expounding
EPUSI euphuistic
EPWRN empowering
EPYEI emphysemic
EPYPC empty space
ERCEU Eurocheque
ERCMN enrichment
ERGMN enregiment
ERGSE enregister
ERHNS earthiness
ERHOA Earthwoman
ERHOE earthmover
ERHON earthbound
ERHUK earthquake
ERIRS earlierise
ERIRZ earlierize
ERLLN Errol Flynn
ERNGR errand-girl
ERPUE enraptured
ERTMC Eurythmics
ERTNE Eurotunnel
ERUEO en route for

ERUSN ear-bussing
ERWRE Earl Warren
ERYHI eurhythmic
ERYIG ear syringe
ERYUI early music
ESBUN Eastbourne
ESCAE exsiccated
ESDEI easy does it
ESEDO eisteddfod
ESEGT easselgate
ESETD Eastertide
ESEWR easselward
ESFLT exsufflate
ESHDL enschedule
ESLAO El Salvador
ESLSE easily seen
ESMAT Epsom salts
ESNIL essentials
ESNOE Eisenhower
ESNTI Eisenstein
ESNTR ease nature
ESNUN ensanguine
ESOEE East of Eden
ESRUE enshrouded
ESSRE Easy Street
easy street
ESSSE East Sussex
ESTRA easy to read
ETAAG extra large
extra-large
ETAAI euthanasia
ETACN entrancing
ETAEI eutrapelia
ETAEU extraneous
ETAGL estrangelo
ETAGN estranging
ETAMN entrapment
ETAOE extra cover
ETATO extraction
ETAUA extramural
ETCAL enticeable
ETCMN enticement
ETCNL enticingly
ETDRA ectodermal
ETDRI ectodermic
ETECE entrenched
ETETE entreaties
ETETN entreating
ETHLE eat the leek
ETIAL extricable
ETIMN entailment
ETLPE ecthlipses
ETMLG entomology
ETMMN entombment
ETMRH ectomorphy
ETMTO estimation
ETNAL extendable
ETNEL extendedly
ETNIL extendible
extensible
ETNOE extend over
ETNSA eat one's hat
ETNTO extinction

ETNTR extincture
ETNUS extinguish
ETOMC eat too much
ETRAL externally
ETRAO extirpator
ETRLE enthralled
ETRNS enthronise
entireness
ETRNZ enthronize
ETROL exteriorly
ETRRS enterprise
ETTDT estate duty
ETTET entitled to
ETUIS enthusiasm
enthusiast
EUBLT equability
EUBNT exurbanite
EUCAL enunciable
EUCAO enunciator
EUCRT edulcorate
exulcerate
EUEAC exuberance
EUEAO enumerator
EUEIA ecumenical
EUIAO elucidator
EUINL esuriently
EULEC ebullience
ebulliency
EULHR equal share
EULSG equals sign
EUNMT equanimity
EURAO elutriator
EUSFE emulsifier
EUSRA equestrian
EUTNL exultantly
exultingly
EUTRA equatorial
EUTTO equitation
eructation
exultation
EUTWT equate with
EUVCT equivocate
EUVLN equivalent
EVRAH Enver Pasha
EVROH Enver Hoxha
EWNRO Edwin Drood
EWRBN Edward Bond
EWRCK Edward Coke
EWRCP Edward Cope
EWRER Edward Eyre
EWRLA Edward Lear
EYIEA erysipelas
EYTLG Egyptology
EZMLG enzymology
EZMTU eczematous
FABEI framboesia
FABNO Fray Bentos
FABNS flabbiness
FABYN flamboyant
FACDT flaccidity
FACET fianchetti
fianchetto
FACIE franchisee

franchiser
FACSA Franciscan
FADLN fraudulent
FAECN flavescent
FAELN flagellant
FAELT flagellate
FAENS fraternise
FAENT fraternity
FAENZ fraternize
FAERO flameproof
FAETC flare stack
FAFOE flat-footed
FAGPN frangipani
FAGTG fraughtage
FAHAR flash Harry
FAHIH flashlight
FAHLO flash flood
FAHNS flashiness
FAHON flash point
FAHRE feather bed
featherbed
FAHRN feathering
FAIGE flamingoes
FAIGU flaking-out
FAIIU flagitious
FAJCE flak jacket
FAJUL frabjously
FAKAP Frank Zappa
FAKAR Frank Capra
FAKHR Frank O'Hara
FAKIL Frank Field
FAKRN Frank Bruno
FALBU flail about
FALSL fearlessly
flawlessly
FAMNA fragmental
FAMNE fragmented
FAORN flavouring
FAPSR flan pastry
FARCD fratricide
FARCN flat racing
FARNL flagrantly
fragrantly
FASML fearsomely
FATNN flattening
FATNU flatten out
FATOA fractional
FATRN flattering
FAUEC flatulence
flatulency
FAWVN flag-waving
FAZAK Franz Kafka
FAZIZ Franz Liszt
FAZLN Franz Kline
FBECP fibrescope
FBELS fibreglass
FBEOR fibreboard
FBIAE fabricated
FBIAO fabricator
FBILR fibrillary
FBILS fibrillose
FBILT fibrillate
FBILU fibrillous
FBIOE fibrinogen
FBIUA febrifugal
FBLUL fabulously
FBOII fibrositis
FBOOE fibronogen
FCAHI facial hair
FCFNU face fungus
FCHRE face-harden
FCIIE facsimiles
FCIIU factitious
fictitious
FCIUL factiously
FCLNS facileness
fickleness
FCLON focal point
FCLSL fecklessly
FCLTE facilities
FCLTT facilitate
FCNRU facinorous
FCNUT facing up to
FCOVI factor VIII
FCSVN face-saving
FCTFC face to face
face-to-face
FCULT factuality
FDCAL fiducially
FDEWT fidget with
FDLAO Fidel Ramos
FDLSL fadelessly
FDLWT fiddle with
FDNFS fading fast
FDRLS federalise
federalism
federalist
FDRTO federation
FDRTV federative
FDYUD fuddy-duddy
FEBOE freebooter
FEBSE Fred Basset
FEBTE feel better
flea-bitten
FECBA French bean
FECHR French horn
FECKO French knot
FECLA flea collar
French loaf
FECLS fleeceless
FECNS fierceness
FECRO French roof
FECRU flea circus
FECUC Free Church
FEDAD fieldwards
FEDOA freedwoman
FEDOE freedwomen
FEDOS field mouse
fieldmouse
FEDRA field trial
FEDSL fiendishly
FEDVN field event
FEEAU foederatus
FEEII Fredericia
FEFIH free flight
FEFOE free-footed
FEFRL free-for-all
FEGLN fledgeling
FEGTG freightage
FEHAE freshwater
FEHLE freeholder
FEHNE free-handed
FEHNN freshening
FEHNS fleshiness
FEHON flesh wound
FEHTR fresh start
FEHUO fresh out of
FEKDU freaked out
FEKNS freakiness
FEKSL freakishly
FELAE freeloader
FELNS feebleness
FEMRE free-market
FEOCA feet of clay
FEOCP foetoscopy
FEORI free on rail
FEPTU feel put out
FEREI fleur-de-lis
FEREY fleur-de-lys
FERNL fleeringly
FESEC free speech
FESII free spirit
FESLC free-select
FESML free sample
FESOE free-spoken
FESYE freestyler
FETNL fleetingly
FETTU Fred Titmus
FEUNE frequenter
FEUNL frequently
FEZDW freeze down
FEZEL frenziedly
FEZOE freeze over
FFAON faff around
FFHHE fifth wheel
FFYEC fifty pence
FFYIT fifty-fifty
FGRHA figurehead
FGRTO figuration
FGRTV figurative
FGRWR figurework
FGTHO fight shy of
FGTTU fight it out
FGTVL fugitively
FHEHI Fahrenheit
FIAAA Faisalabad
FIAAL Frida Kahlo
FIADA fricandeau
FIBDN fair-boding
FIBLT friability
FICFO flinch from
FIDNU fair dinkum
FIGUA fling mud at
FIHAE fair-headed
FIHCE flight crew
FIHDC flight deck
FIHEE frightened
FIHIE fair-haired
FIHLS flightless
FIHPA flight plan
FIHPT flight path
FIHUL faithfully
FIHUT faithful to
FIILR fritillary
FIKNF flick knife
flick-knife
FIKNL friskingly
FIKNS friskiness
FIKRN flickering
FILGO fairly good
FILNS frilliness
FIMNE fair-minded
FINLE friendlies
FINLL friendlily
FINLS friendless
FINSI friendship
FIPNL flippantly
FIPRE fripperies
FISNS flimsiness
FISOE fair-spoken
FITER faint-heart
flint-heart
FITHR Flintshire
FITLS flint glass
FITNL flirtingly
FITNS flintiness
FITOA frictional
FITTO flirtation
FIYTR fairy story
FIZAE Fritz Haber
FLAEU foliaceous
FLAIU fallacious
FLALE fall asleep
FLAON full amount
FLBCO fall back on
FLBDE full-bodied
FLBHN fall behind
FLBSE filibuster
FLCRL full-circle
FLCTT felicitate
FLCTU felicitous
FLDWO fall down on
FLEAC fallen arch
FLEAE false-faced
FLEAI falderal it
FLEAL filterable
FLEDU folie à deux
FLEET false teeth
FLELR false alarm
FLENS fallenness
FLEOE false morel
FLERN false front
FLETN Folkestone
FLETR false start
FLFUO fall foul of
FLGNU fuliginous
FLGOT full growth
FLHIT fall heir to
FLHNS filthiness
FLHRC filthy rich
FLIGF falling-off
FLIGU falling-out

FLILN	fulfilling
FLILV	fall in love
FLIMN	fulfilment
FLIUA	follicular
FLIWT	fall in with
FLLNT	full-length
FLLRS	folklorist
FLMMR	folk-memory
FLMNE	full-manned
FLNLO	full nelson
FLODE	fallow deer
FLOHM	follow home
FLOLF	full of life
FLOSI	fellowship
	follow suit
FLOUO	follow up on
FLPTI	felspathic
FLRAI	filariasis
FLRGE	full-rigged
FLRNE	fell-runner
FLRTO	filtration
FLSIE	full-sailed
FLSNE	folk-singer
FLSNS	folksiness
FLSRE	file server
FLTBT	fall to bits
FLTEA	fill the gap
FLTPE	felt-tip pen
FLUWT	fill up with
FLVIE	full-voiced
FLWIH	full weight
FLWNE	full-winged
FLXLC	Felix Bloch
FLXLI	Felix Klein
FLXTW	Felixstowe
FLYRW	fully-grown
FLYWK	fully awake
FMGTO	fumigation
FMLAL	familiarly
FMLLA	female lead
FMLNL	fumblingly
FMLNM	family name
FMLNS	femaleness
FMLTE	family tree
FMNNL	femininely
FMNNT	femininity
FMRAE	fimbriated
FMSMN	famishment
FMUNS	famousness
FNAEL	fontanelle
FNAGE	fandangles
	fandangoes
FNAIE	fantasized
	fantasizer
FNATC	fantastico
FNCLT	finicality
FNEBW	fingerbowl
FNELN	fingerling
FNELS	fingerless
FNEMR	fingermark
FNENI	fingernail
FNEPS	finger-post
FNFUT	find faults
FNGIT	find guilty
FNHLE	fundholder
FNIGF	fending off
FNIIA	fungicidal
FNIUL	fancifully
FNLAS	final cause
FNOGI	Finno-Ugric
FNRAL	funereally
FNSEL	fenestella
FNSER	Finisterre
FNSRA	fenestrial
FNSRT	fenestrate
FNSWR	finish work
FNSWT	finish with
FNTCS	fanaticise
	fanaticism
FNTCZ	fanaticize
FNTNS	finiteness
FNTOA	functional
FNYOA	fancy woman
	funny woman
FNYOD	fancy goods
FNYOE	funny money
FNYRC	Fanny Price
FNYRS	fancy dress
FNYTR	funny story
FOAON	fool around
FOBGE	foolbegged
FOBIG	footbridge
FOBLE	footballer
FOCLN	flocculent
FOCLT	flocculate
FOCOC	from choice
FODIH	floodlight
FOECN	florescent
FOEHA	flower-head
FOELS	flowerless
FOETN	florentine❑
FOHNS	frothiness
FOHPE	frog-hopper
FOIEI	florilegia
FOINS	floridness
FOISM	frolicsome
FOIUD	floribunda
FOLGT	footlights
FONNL	frowningly
FONTR	from nature
FOOFN	foot of fine
FOOHG	from on high
FOPDS	floppy disk
FOPIT	footprints
FOPNS	floppiness
FORLT	floorcloth
FOROR	floorboard
FORSE	flourished
FOSAC	frog's-march
FOSOL	flow slowly
FOSUF	foodstuffs
FOTAD	frontwards
FOTLS	float glass
FOTNL	floatingly
	floutingly
FOTNS	frostiness
FOTON	frostbound
FOTTN	float-stone
FOTTO	floatation
FOYRS	flory cross
FRADF	fore-and-aft
FRADN	forwarding
FRAEL	forsakenly
FRAIE	formaliter
FRALN	farfalline
FRAON	fart around
FRAVS	fore-advise
FRBDN	foreboding
FRCSE	forecaster
FRCSL	forecastle
FRDOE	foredoomed
FREAC	fer-de-lance
FREAL	forseeable
FRECE	far-fetched
FRECP	fire escape
FREGN	fire engine
FREHA	forge ahead
FREIN	fortepiano
FRENS	forcedness
FREOE	far-removed
FRERN	forbearing
FRETI	for certain
FRETN	fermenting
	forgetting
FRETR	forfeiture
FREUL	forcefully
FREWE	far between
FRFNE	forefinger
FRFTE	forefather
FRGON	foreground
FRGTE	foregather
FRHCO	for the chop
FRHIH	forthright
FRHNE	forehanded
FRIAI	formic acid
	formicaria
FRIAL	farcically
	forgivable
	formidable
	formidably
FRIAO	fornicator
FRIBA	Fortinbras
FRIDN	forbidding
FRIHE	far-sighted
FRIHN	furnishing
FRIIE	fertiliser
	fertilizer
FRINI	foreign aid
FRINS	fervidness
FRISM	fortissimo
FRIYN	fortifying
FRLSL	formlessly
FRLTA	for all that
FRLTE	form letter
FRLTM	for all time
FRMMN	for a moment
FRMNU	foraminous
FRNAA	far and away
FRNLN	firing line
	firing-line
FRNNA	far and near
FRNUA	furuncular
FRNWD	far and wide
FRODI	foreordain
FROHN	for nothing
FROLO	ferro-alloy
FROWE	furrow-weed
FRQOE	fore-quoted
FRRIE	fire-raiser
FRRNE	forerunner
FRSAO	foreshadow
FRSBR	forest-born
FRSCN	for a second
FRSRE	firescreen
FRTAS	first cause
FRTFL	first of all
FRTHN	first thing
FRTIH	first light
	first night
FRTLC	first place
FRTLE	foreteller
FRTLO	first floor
FRTLS	first-class
FRTOL	First World
FRTRO	first proof
FRTRZ	first prize
FRUEA	Fortune Bay
FRUTU	fortuitous
FRWNE	for a wonder
FRXML	for example
FRYIK	forty winks
FRYOE	for my money
FSADA	fiscal drag
FSAEL	fustanella
FSALE	fast asleep
FSAYA	fiscal year
FSBLT	fusibility
FSBNE	Fassbinder
FSBWE	fast bowler
FSFNE	fish-finger
FSIAE	fascinated
FSIFE	fossil fuel
FSIGO	fishing-rod
FSIIE	fossilized
FSIIT	fastigiate
FSIIU	fastidious
FSINN	fashioning
FSINS	fustianise
FSINZ	fustianize
FSIUF	fisticuffs
FSLDE	fish-ladder
FSMNE	fishmonger
FSMVN	fast-moving
FSOBM	fusion bomb
FSSRA	fast stream
FTDMN	Fats Domino
FTEHO	fatherhood
FTELK	fatherlike
FTELN	fatherland
FTELS	fatherless
FTESA	Father's Day
FTFNE	fit of anger

Words marked ❑ can also be spelled with an initial capital letter

FTGAL fatiguable
FTGRL FitzGerald
Fitzgerald
FTHBL fit the bill
FTHPM fetch a pump
FTIAD Fittipaldi
FTINY fat-kidney'd
FTLSI fatalistic
FTLTE fatalities
FTOAL fathomable
FTOEE fathometer
FTOLS fathomless
FTORN fit to drink
FTRIE fatbrained
FTRLG futurology
FTRLS futureless
FTRSI futuristic
FTRTO futurition
FTRWF future wife
FTTMC fat stomach
FTUCN fettuccine
FTUNS fitfulness
FTWLE Fats Waller
FUBFU four-by-four
FUDJI feux de joie
FUDRN foundering
FUDTO foundation
FUDUC fluid ounce
FUEHR flugelhorn
flügelhorn
FUFNS fluffiness
FUFOE four-footed
FUHNE four-handed
FUICE four-inched
FUIHN four-in-hand
FUPSE four-poster
FURDS fluoridise
FURDT fluoridate
FURDZ fluoridize
FURNT fluorinate
FUSOE foul-spoken
FUSUR four-square
FUTAA fruit salad
FUTAE frustrated
FUTEO Fauntleroy
FUTET fourteenth
FUTLN fault plane
FUTNS faultiness
FUTRN fluttering
FUTRT fourth-rate
FUTUC fruit juice
FUTUL fruitfully
FUTWL fourth wall
FVRIC fever pitch
FVRSL feverishly
FVUAL favourable
favourably
FWIUE few minutes
FWOET few moments
FXDHE fixed-wheel
FXDOT fixed costs
FXERE fox-terrier
FYACE flycatcher
FYHBA fly the beam
FYICE flypitcher
FYIHN fly-fishing
FYIPN fly-tipping
FYNBA flying boat
FYNBM flying bomb
FYNFS Flying Fish
flying fish
FYNLA flying leap
FYNSI flying suit
FYOTN flyposting
FYUCL fly quickly
FYYIH fly-by-night
FZNER fazendeiro
FZYOI fuzzy logic
FZYRN fizzy drink
GAAFO go away from
GAAHC Graham Hick
GAAHL Graham hill
GAALC Graham Lock
GAATE guaranteed
GACNL glancingly
GACNT glauconite
GACOE glance over
GADAD granddaddy
GADAI giardiasis
GADAM grandmamma
GADDM grande dame
GADHL grandchild
GADIC grand-niece
GADIN grand piano
GADJT grande jeté
GADNL grand-uncle
GADNN gladdening
GADOA grand total
GADOE Grand Hotel
GADOS guardhouse
GADPI grands prix
GADPR grand opera
GADRN go and bring
GADUH grand duchy
GADUO grand juror
GADUT grand Mufti
GAEAE grave-maker
GAELN graveolent
GAEOD grave goods
GAEOE Grace Jones
GAERI grapefruit
GAETN gravestone
GAEUL gracefully
gratefully
GAGRS grangerise
GAGRZ grangerize
GAHAE graph paper
GAHLG graphology
GAHLO grab hold of
GAHNE glad-hander
GAHNL gnashingly
GAHTS graphitise
GAHTZ graphitize
GAIEE gravimeter
GAIER gravimetry
GAIEU gramineous
GAILT gratillity
GAITO glaciation
GAIUL graciously
GAIUM gracious me
GAIYN gratifying
GAKEE goalkeeper
GAMRA grammarian
GANFA granny flat
GANKO granny knot
GAOET Giacometti
GAOHN gramophone
GAOII Glagolitic
GAORO glamour boy
GAPNL graspingly
GASAE glass-faced
GASCE goatsucker
GASER goatsbeard
GASIO grass widow
GASIR glass fibre
GASNK grass snake
GASNS glassiness
grassiness
GASOR grass court
GASOS glasshouse
GATAD giant panda
GATAT Grant Batty
GATLT graptolite
GATNI grant-in-aid
GAUAE granulated
GAUAL granularly
GAULS gradualism
gradualist
GAULT graduality
GAUOA granulomas
GAUTO graduation
GAUTU gratuitous
GAWGA Glaswegian
GAYRI gravy train
GBDSR Gobi Desert
GBILA Gabriel Oak
GBMCE gobsmacked
GBMUH gobemouche
GBNRP go bankrupt
GBTPE gobstopper
GDERN God-fearing
GDILN God willing
GDLNU gadolinium
GDONN gadrooning
GDWHL go down hill
go downhill
GDWWT go down with
GDYAE giddy-paced
GEAAB Greta Garbo
GEAIE Grenadines
GEAIU gregarious
GEDGT greedy guts
GEDNS greediness
GEEOS glebe-house
GEFIR Grey friars
Greyfriars
GEHAE grey-headed
GEHDL Glen Hoddle
GEHIE grey-haired
GEKRS Greek cross
GEMLE grey mullet
GEMTE grey matter
GENAE green paper
GENAT green earth
Green Party
green party
GENEC Greenpeace
GENEE Green Beret
GENHN greenshank
GENIC greenfinch
GENIH green light
GENLD Greenslade
GENLS Glenn Close
GENON green pound
GENOS greenhouse
GENRA Greg Norman
GENUI green audit
GERTE Glenrothes
GESNL guessingly
GESNS greasiness
greisenise
GESNZ greisenize
GESWT go easy with
GETAD Great Sandy
GETAE Great Lakes
GETAI Great Basin
GETER Great-heart
GETHT great white
GETIC great-niece
GETLV Great Slave
GETNL great-uncle
GETOS guest house
guesthouse
GFENS giftedness
GFEWT gifted with
GFRRK go for broke
GFRWL go for a walk
GGDNE go-go dancer
GGEHI Guggenheim
GGLEE goggle-eyed
GHRWT go hard with
GIADU go in and out
GIDNL grindingly
GIDTN grindstone
GIEAE gripe-water
GIEFW guinea fowl
GIEIE guidelines
GIEUL guilefully
GIGBU going about
GIGNE going under
GIGON gain ground
GIGVN gaingiving
GIHIH gain height
GILCE gridlocked
GILNS grisliness
GILOE grimlooked
GILTN guillotine
GIMRN glimmering
GIMTU gliomatous
GISNO glissandos
GISYN gainsaying
GITLK guilty-like

GITNN glistening
GITNS guiltiness
GITRN glittering
GITRT glitterati
GIVNL grievingly
GIVOE grieve over
GIVUL grievously
GIWIH gain weight
GLAHS goliathise
GLAHZ goliathize
GLCUS golf course
GLDGE gold-digger
GLECL golden calf
GLEHN Golden Hind
GLELN Gelderland
GLEMA golden mean
GLEPL Golden Palm
GLERC Golden Rock
GLERL golden rule
GLERS Golden Rose
GLEWS galley-west
GLFNE Goldfinger
GLIAI gallic acid
GLIAO gallinazos
GLIET Gil Vicente
GLIGA Gillingham
GLIHW Goldie Hawn
GLIMI galliambic
GLIOK goldilocks
GLIWR Gallic Wars
GLOAI Gallomania
GLOHB Gallophobe
GLOHL Gallophile
GLOLS galloglass
GLPAE gold-plated
GLSAE Gulf States
GLSCT Giles Scott
GLSIL Galashiels
GLSRA Gulf Stream
GLSYR Gale Sayers
GLTNS gelatinise
GLTNT gelatinate
GLTNU gelatinous
GLTNZ gelatinize
GLUPL Gallup poll
GLWRH Galsworthy
GMAIM gymnasiums
GMATC gymnastics
GMEEE gimlet-eyed
GMENA gombeen-man
GMKEE gamekeeper
GMNTO gemination
GMOPR gymnosperm
GMTER game theory
GMTNI gametangia
GMWRE game warden
GNATA gone astray
GNCCA gonococcal
GNCCU gonococcus
GNCLT geniculate
GNDRE gensdarmes
GNEBE ginger beer
GNELS genteelise
genteelism
GNELZ genteelize
GNESA gingersnap
GNEWN ginger wine
GNIHE gunfighter
GNIII gingivitis
GNLFL gentlefolk
GNLNE gunslinger
GNLNS gentleness
GNNOE Guns 'n' Roses
GNOEE goniometer
GNPTE Gene Pitney
GNRFE gentrified
GNRHE gonorrhoea
GNRLF Generalife
GNRLS generalise
generalist
GNRLT generality
GNRLZ generalize
GNRNU gangrenous
GNRST generosity
GNRTO generation
GNRTV generative
GNRUL generously
GNTCS geneticist
GNTLA genethliac
GNUNN gunrunning
GNUWT gang up with
GNVGW Geneva gown
GNWLE Gene Wilder
GOAGL good as gold
GOAIG go on a binge
GOAPE go on a spree
GOBGE grow bigger
GOCSE Gloucester
GODRE grow darker
GOEER gooseberry
GOELN grovelling
GOELS gooseflesh
GOEOG good enough
GOEOT goosefoots
GOERE Goose Green
GOERS geometrise
GOERZ geometrize
GOESA go overseas
GOETI geocentric
GOEUP goose bumps
GOFIA Good Friday
GOFIN good friend
GOFLA GoodFellas
GOFML good family
GOFRO good for you
GOFTE grow fatter
GOFUS Geoff Hurst
GOGBN George Byng
GOGBS George Best
George Bush
GOGEE Georg Hegel
GOGHL George Hale
GOGNS grogginess
GOGOT Georg Solti
GOGSN George Sand
GOGTW George Town
Georgetown
GOHAT good health
GOHMS geochemist
GOHMU good humour
GOHRA geothermal
GOHSC geophysics
GOIUL gloriously
GOIYN glorifying
GOLNE grow longer
GOLNL growlingly
GOLNS goodliness
GOLOE good-looker
GOLRE grow larger
GOLSL ghoulishly
GOMNS gloominess
GONEL groundedly
GONLS groundless
GONPA groundplan
GONTR good nature
GONWR groundwork
GOOIA geological
GOPFE Group of Ten
GOPLI grow pallid
GORCR go on record
GORPE geographer
GORPS geotropism
GOSIO good sailor
GOSMO grouse moor
GOSNS glossiness
GOSRK go on strike
GOSRS glossarist
GOTCS Gnosticise
Gnosticism
GOTCZ Gnosticize
GOTFS go out of use
GOTLK grow to like
GOTNL gloatingly
GOTRT ghost-write
GOUAL globularly
GOWAE grow weaker
GOWEL go on wheels
GOWSE good wishes
GOYOD goody-goody
GPAIU go platinum
GPOHL gypsophila
GPOTE gap-toothed
GPYUM gippy tummy
gyppy tummy
GRADS gormandise
gormandism
GRADZ gormandize
GRAEA garbage can
GRAIU Germanicus
GRARC geriatrics
GRATA gargantuan❑
GRCOE Gary Cooper
GRECT garden city
GRELE gor-bellied
GREUL gorgeously
GRFIA girl Friday❑
GRFIN girlfriend
GRGBN garage band
GRIIA germicidal
GRLCK girdle cake
GRLFR Gerald Ford
GRMLE Gerd Muller
GROTN garrotting
GROZL Gorgonzola
GRPAE Gary Player
GRREL Girardelli
GRROE Gary Rhodes
GRSBR Gary Sobers
GRSNS garishness
GRSOI gyroscopic
GRYDM Gerry Adams
GSELS gospellise
GSELZ gospellize
GSEOO gasteropod
GSESN gospel song
GSHME gas chamber
GSNHI Gesundheit
GSOPN go shopping
GSOTL go smoothly
GSOWT go slow with
GSRCL gastric flu
GSRIH go straight
GSRNM gastronome
gastronomy
GSRSO Gus Grissom
GSUBN gas turbine
GTADR go to and fro
GTARE get married
GTEBR Gothenburg
GTELN gut feeling
GTEUT get results
GTGON go to ground
GTGTE go together
GTHAO get ahead of
GTHBO get the boot
GTHBR get the bird
GTHCO get the chop
GTHHM got the hump
GTHHN get the hang
GTHIE get the idea
GTHOG get through
GTHPS get the push
GTIAC Gothic arch
GTICE get hitched
GTIGU gatling gun
gatling-gun
GTKEE gatekeeper
GTLAO get a load of
GTLOA get a look at
GTLST get close to
GTMRE go to market
GTMVO get a move on
GTNOC get in touch
GTNOE get annoyed
get into bed
GTNSA get one's way
GTNTE get knotted
get knotted!
GTOHR gate of horn
get nowhere
GTOLE get to sleep
GTONT get round to

GTPEE	go to pieces
GTPIE	get spliced
GTPNG	get-up-and-go
GTPTA	get up steam
GTRSE	get dressed
GTSRD	get astride
GTTCI	get stuck in
GTTEA	go to the bad
GTTFE	get stuffed!
GTTWO	go to town on
GTUAL	gutturally
GTWCE	get a wicket
GTXIE	get excited
GTYBR	Gettysburg
GUAEU	glumaceous
GUBNS	grubbiness
GUGNL	grudgingly
GUHNS	gaucheness
GUPNS	grumpiness
GUSML	gruesomely
GUSRE	Grub Street
GUTNL	gruntingly
GUTNS	gluttonise
	gluttonish
GUTNU	gluttonous
GUTNZ	gluttonize
GVAAT	give a jab to
GVACS	give access
GVATR	give a start
GVBTE	give bother
GVCLU	give colour
GVFOT	give food to
GVFRT	give form to
GVGON	give ground
GVIAR	give it a try
GVLFT	give life to
GVNBC	giving back
	giving-back
GVNMT	give name to
GVNOE	giving-over
GVNTC	give notice
GVODR	give orders
GVOET	give over to
GVOTK	give or take
GVRAC	governance
GVRAL	governable
GVRMN	government
GVRST	give rise to
GVTEI	give the air
GVTEO	give the nod
GVUWR	give up work
GVVNT	give vent to
GWLWT	go well with
GYAOH	Guy Laroche
GYDNE	Glyn Daniel
GYOEI	glycogenic
GYOII	glycosidic
GYOYI	glycolysis
GYUGS	Guy Burgess
HADCO	head doctor
HAEBE	heaven-bred
HAEGN	heat engine
HAESN	heaven-sent
HAEWR	heavenward
HAHLF	Heathcliff
HAHNE	headhunter
HAHNS	heathenise
	heathenish
	heathenism
HAHNZ	heathenize
HAIGE	Headingley
HAIGF	heading off
HALGE	head-lugged
HAMSE	headmaster
HAOFC	head office
HAOHI	head of hair
HAOYA	head of year
HASIL	heat shield
HASNS	hoarseness
HASRK	heatstroke
HASRN	headstrong
HASUR	headsquare
HATCM	health camp
HATES	heartsease
	heart's-ease
HATFO	health food
HATFR	health farm
HATHA	head to head
HATHO	heart-throb
HATIG	hear things
HATLO	hear tell of
HATNN	heartening
HATNS	heartiness
HATRA	heartbreak
HAYAE	heavy water
HAYEA	heavy metal
HAYRE	heavy-armed
HBLET	habilments
HBLMN	habiliment
HBLNL	hobblingly
HBLTR	habilatory
HBLTT	habilitate
HBOAA	hebdomadal
HBOWT	hobnob with
HBTAE	habituated
HBTAL	habitually
HBTTO	habitation
HBYOS	hobby-horse
HCEPR	hoc tempore
HCIAL	hectically
HCNYA	hackney cab
HCOER	hectometre
HCOIR	hectolitre
HCORP	hectograph
HCSOU	hocus-pocus
HDALC	hydraulics
HDEOG	hodgepodge
	hodge-podge
HDIAL	hydrically
HDIGO	Haddington
HDKTJ	Hideki Tojo
HDLSO	Huddleston
HDNSI	hedonistic
HDOAH	hydropathy
HDOCP	hydroscope
HDOEE	hydrometer
HDOER	hydrometry
HDOHN	hydrophone
HDOHT	hydrophyte
HDOOE	hydropower
	hydrosomes
HDOOI	hydrologic
	hydroponic
HDOSA	Hudson's Bay
HDOYI	hydrolysis
	hydrolytic
HEACI	hierarchic
HEADO	heel and toe
HEAOI	Hierapolis
HEAUI	haematuria
HELSL	heedlessly
HEOHN	hierophant
HEOLP	hieroglyph
HEOYI	haemolysis
	haemolytic
HGADO	high and low
HGADR	high and dry
HGCLU	high colour
HGCMD	high comedy
HGCSO	Hugh Casson
HGCUC	High Church
HGEHL	Hughes Hall
HGETA	higher than
HGETE	high esteem
HGFYN	high-flying
HGGEN	Hugh Greene
HGGRA	High German
HGHNE	high-handed
HGHXE	Hugh Huxley
HGLNE	highlander
HGLUI	Hugh Laurie
HGLVN	high living
HGMNE	high-minded
HGNME	huge number
HGNSL	hug oneself
HGOAR	hagiolatry
HGOCP	hygroscope
HGOEE	hygrometer
HGOER	hygrometry
HGOHT	hygrophyte
HGOOI	hagiologic
HGORP	hygrograph
HGOTN	high-octane
HGPAE	high places
HGPIE	high-priced
HGPIS	high priest
HGPYN	high-paying
HGRGR	high regard
HGRLE	high relief
HGSAO	high season
HGSHO	high school
HGSRE	high street
HGTII	hightail it
HGWYA	highwayman
HIEBR	Heidelberg
	Heisenberg
HIHEE	heightened
HISRA	hairstreak
HISRN	hairspring
HIYOT	hoity-toity
HKYOE	hokey cokey
	hokey-cokey
HLAAL	heliacally
HLAAO	hullabaloo
HLAHN	Holman Hunt
HLALE	half-asleep
HLARE	hold a brief
HLARW	half-a-crown
HLATU	helianthus
HLBNE	hellbender
HLCPE	helicopter
HLCRO	halocarbon
HLEDE	halberdier
HLEFC	halo effect
HLEHI	Hildesheim
HLEIO	Hellenikon
HLEUA	hallelujah
HLFOI	half florin
HLFRE	half-formed
	Holofernes
HLFST	hold fast to
HLFTE	Holy Father
HLFXA	Halifax Bay
HLGAH	holography
HLGIE	half guinea
HLGLN	Heligoland
HLGNT	halogenate
HLGNU	halogenous
HLHDA	holohedral
HLHDO	holohedron
HLHNE	half-hunter
HLHUL	half-hourly
HLIGO	Hillingdon
HLILN	Holy Island
HLIPA	hold in play
HLLSL	helplessly
HLNIL	Helen Wills
HLNLO	half nelson
HLODR	holy orders
HLOEE	heliometer
	hollow-eyed
HLOFC	hold office
HLOFM	hall of fame
HLONS	hollowness
HLOOI	Heliopolis
HLOOL	Hello Dolly
HLORP	heliograph
	heliotrope
	heliotropy
HLOTO	hold out for
HLOWT	help on with
HLOYI	heliotypic
HLPRS	holophrase
HLPYI	holophytic
HLSEL	hell's bells
HLSET	hell's teeth
HLSNE	hell's angel
HLSOU	holus-bolus
HLSSE	half-sister
HLUKH	Helmut Kohl
HLWLE	hillwalker
HLWLI	holy Willie❏

Words marked ❏ can also be spelled with an initial capital letter

Code	Word
HLWTE	halfwitted
	half-witted
HLYAL	half-yearly
HMADR	home and dry
HMBCE	hump-backed
HMCAI	hemicrania
HMCCI	homocyclic
HMCMN	home-coming
HMDFE	humidifier
HMDSA	humidistat
HMDYD	Hamadryads
HMEBA	hammer beam
HMEHA	hammerhead
HMEIT	hammer into
HMELC	hammerlock
HMEPT	homoeopath
HMESD	Humberside
HMGMU	homogamous
HMGNS	homogenise
HMGNU	homogenous
HMGNZ	homogenize
HMHCL	hamshackle
HMIGO	humming-top
HMLAE	humiliated
HMLGS	homologise
HMLGT	homologate
HMLGU	homologous
HMLGZ	homologize
HMLIA	homaloidal
HMLNL	humblingly
HMLNS	homeliness
	humbleness
HMLTC	homiletics
HMLVN	home-loving
HMMKN	homemaking
HMMRE	home market
HMNEN	human being
HMNNS	humaneness
HMNSI	humanistic
HMNTE	humanities
HMNUA	homuncular
HMNUU	homunculus
HMNZN	humanizing
HMOAH	homeopathy
HMPEI	hemiplegia
	hemiplegic
HMPOI	homophobia
	homophobic
	homophonic
HMRSU	humoresque
HMRUL	humorously
HMSHR	hemisphere
HMSXA	homosexual
HMUGR	humbuggery
HMULS	humourless
HMZGT	homozygote
HMZGU	homozygous
HNADS	hansardise
HNADZ	hansardize
HNAIH	hang a right
HNAON	hang around
HNBRO	hand-barrow
HNEAO	hendecagon
HNEBR	Hindenburg
HNEDW	handed down
HNEKN	henpecking
HNELN	hinderland
	hinterland
HNEOT	henceforth
HNGIE	hang-glider
	Hans Geiger
HNHOE	henchwomen
HNIGA	hunting-cap
HNIGO	hunting-box
	Huntingdon
HNIGU	handing out
	handing-out
HNIHN	hand in hand
HNIRF	handicraft
HNMDW	hand-me-down
HNMIE	handmaiden
HNOTO	hang out for
HNPCE	hand-picked
HNRNE	hindrances
HNRNS	hungriness
HNRRU	honorarium
HNSAE	handstaves
HNSAF	handstaffs
HNSIL	Huntsville
HNSML	handsomely
HNSON	Hans Sloane
HNSRN	handspring
HNSTL	honest talk
HNTES	henotheism
	henotheist
HNTHN	hand to hand
	hand-to-hand
HNUAL	honourable
	honourably
HNUTN	Hindustani
HNVRA	Hanoverian
HNYAD	handy-dandy
HNYAE	Henry Bates
	Henry James
	honeyeater
	honey-eater
HNYAK	hanky-panky
HNYEI	Henry Cecil
HNYOC	Henry Royce
HNYOD	Henry Fonda
HNYOR	Henry Moore
HNYTL	honey-stalk
HNYUD	honeyguide
HNYVR	Henry Every
HOADY	hook-and-eye
HOLSR	hyoplastra
HOSAE	hoop-shaped
HOWNE	hoodwinker
HPACI	heptarchic
HPACO	Hipparchos
HPAEC	Heptateuch
HPAEE	heptameter
HPAHO	heptathlon
HPAHR	heptachord
HPAOA	heptagonal
HPASU	Hephaestus
HPCRS	hypocorism
HPDRI	hypodermic
	hypodermis
HPEAE	hyphenated
HPEHA	hypaethral
HPEIG	happenings
HPEIT	happen into
HPERO	hipped roof
HPEUO	happen upon
HPEYO	hippety-hop
HPHTI	hop the twig
HPIGA	hopping mad
HPLEI	hypalgesia
	hypalgesic
HPLSL	hopelessly
HPOAI	hippomania
HPOAP	hippocampi
HPODS	hypnoidise
HPODZ	hypnoidize
HPOEE	hypsometer
HPOER	hypsometry
HPOHL	hippophile
HPOIE	hypnotized
HPORF	hippogriff
HPORM	hippodrome
HPOYU	Hippolytus
HPPYE	hypophyses
HPPYI	hypophysis
HPRAO	hyperbaton
HPREI	hyperaemia
	hyperaemic
	hypermedia
HPROI	hyperbolic
	hypersonic
	hypertonic
HPSAE	hypostases
HPSAI	hypostasis
	hypostatic
HPTEE	hypotheses
HPTEI	hypothesis
	hypothetic
HPTLG	hepatology
HPTNS	hypotenuse
HPYVN	happy event
HRAEU	herbaceous
HRAIM	herbariums
HRAIO	hard as iron
HRAOT	hereabouts
HRARC	hard as rock
HRBED	hornblende
HRBIE	hard-boiled
HRBOE	Hornblower
HRBTE	hard-bitten
HRCES	hard cheese
HRCIU	Heraclitus
HRDNB	hard done by
HRDTR	hereditary
HRDTS	hereditist
HREAL	horse vault
HREDU	horrendous
HREES	hartebeest
	horse sense
HREIA	hermetical
HREIE	horserider
HRELC	horse block
HRELS	horseflesh
HREOA	horsewoman
HREOE	horsepower
HRERE	hard-earned
HRERS	horse brass
HRETA	harvestman
	horned toad
HRETN	harvesting
HRETO	Herbert Lom
HREVL	Herrenvolk
HRFSE	hard-fisted
HRFUH	hard-fought
HRHAE	hard-headed
HRHPE	hard hyphen
HRIAL	heroically
HRIBR	Harrisburg
HRICA	hermit crab
HRIIA	herbicidal
	hermitical
HRINS	horridness
HRIYN	horrifying
HRLBU	hard labour
HRLEE	hardly ever
HRLGS	horologist
HRLGU	Horologium
HRLPO	Hartlepool
HRLSL	harmlessly
	hurtlessly
HRLUE	Harold Urey
HRMAI	Hiram Maxim
HRNOR	her indoors
HROIE	harmonized
HROIU	harmonious
HRONE	harpooneer
HRORG	harbourage
HRPIU	Herophilus
HRPLT	hard palate
HRPSE	hard-pushed
HRSEL	harassedly
HRSIA	haruspical
HRSIE	haruspices
HRSMN	harassment
HRSOI	horoscopic
HRSOO	here's to you
HRTCT	hereticate
HRTFR	heretofore
HRTIE	heritrices
	heritrixes
HRTRA	hard to read
HRYAL	harpy eagle
HRYID	hirdy-girdy
HRYNL	hurryingly
HRYUD	hurdy-gurdy
HRYUL	hurly-burly
HRYUR	here you are
HRZNA	horizontal
HSADA	husbandman
HSAIL	Hispaniola
HSAUG	hasta luego
HSBON	hash browns
HSEEI	hysteresis

Words marked ❑ can also be spelled with an initial capital letter

Code	Word
	hysteretic
HSEIA	hysterical
HSEIE	Hesperides
HSELN	hostelling
HSIAL	hospitable
	hospitably
HSINL	Hessian fly
HSOEI	histogenic
HSOIA	historical
HSOOI	histologic
HSOYI	histolysis
	histolytic
HSROI	histrionic
HSTNL	hesitantly
HSTTN	hesitating
HSTTO	hesitation
HTEMS	hithermost
HTESE	Hattersley
HTHDC	hit the deck
HTHIE	hitchhiker
HTHOC	hotchpotch
	hotch-potch
HTHPO	hatch a plot
HTHPU	Hatshepsut
HTHRA	hit the road
HTHRO	hit the roof
HTHSC	hit the sack
HTHTA	hatchet man
HTHTO	hatchet job
HTLOE	hot-blooded
HTNMS	hit and miss
	hit-and-miss
HTRDN	heterodyne
HTRDX	heterodoxy
HTRGM	heterogamy
HTRGN	heterogony
HTRLG	heterology
HTRNM	heteronomy
HTRTX	heterotaxy
HUCBN	haunch bone
HUCRL	hour-circle
HUEFO	house of God
HUEGN	house agent
HUEHT	house white
HUELN	house plant
HUEOD	haute monde
HUEON	housebound
HUEOS	house mouse
HUERF	housecraft
HUERI	house-train
HUERU	house-proud
HUEUI	house music
HUEUS	house guest
HUHHM	Houyhnhnms
HUTNL	hauntingly
HVAAT	have a party
HVAEK	have a dekko
HVAER	have a heart
HVAIH	have a right
HVANC	have a snack
HVARC	have a crack
HVAUC	have a hunch
HVBET	have breath
HVDNE	have dinner
HVGET	have guests
HVIAA	have it away
HVIMD	have it made
HVIMN	have in mind
HVISD	have inside
HVIVE	have in view
HVNAA	having a say
HVNEO	have need of
HVNHP	have no hope
HVNIE	have no idea
HVNLF	having life
HVOFA	have off pat
HVOLA	have on loan
HVRNL	hoveringly
HVRRF	hovercraft
HWOOD	how do you do?
HWRSN	Howards End
HWTIK	how's tricks?
HXHDA	hexahedral
HXHDO	hexahedron
HXMRU	hexamerous
IAAHO	in a fashion
IAAMO	in a bad mood
IACRC	inaccuracy
IACRT	inaccurate
IACTR	Isaac Stern
IADTO	in addition
IAEAC	in abeyance
IAESR	in a measure
IAEUC	inadequacy
IAEUT	inadequate
IAGRT	inaugurate
IAIAL	imaginable
	imaginably
IAINS	Italianise
IAINT	Italianate
IAINZ	Italianize
IAKYO	Ivan Krylov
IALAC	in alliance
	I Pagliacci
IALAT	in all parts
IAMCA	in as much as
	inasmuch as
IAOAA	inamoratas
IAOAO	inamoratos
IAPST	inapposite
IAPVO	Ivan Pavlov
IASNI	in absentia
IATSI	inartistic
IATTD	inaptitude
IATVL	inactively
IATVT	inactivate
	inactivity
IAYVN	in any event
IBCLT	imbecility
IBDAT	in bad taste
IBDDU	in bad odour
IBDHP	in bad shape
IBEDN	inbreeding
IBOLO	imbroglios
ICACR	in chancery
ICAGO	in charge of
ICAST	incrassate
ICBIC	inch by inch
ICBTO	incubation
ICBTV	incubative
ICDNA	incidental
ICDNL	incedingly
ICEEC	inclemency
ICEIL	incredible
	incredibly
ICESN	increasing
ICGIO	incognitos
ICHRN	incoherent
ICIET	inclined to
ICLAE	inculpated
ICLAL	inculpable
	inculpably
ICLAO	inculcator
ICMEC	incumbency
ICMLT	incomplete
ICNEC	incandesce
ICNIR	incendiary
ICNLC	in conflict
ICNRS	in contrast
ICNRT	incinerate
ICNTN	inconstant
ICOTL	inchoately
ICOTO	inchoation
ICOTV	inchoative
ICPCT	incapacity
ICPEC	incipience
	incipiency
ICRAL	incurrable
ICSAC	incessancy
ICSVL	incisively
ICTMN	incitement
ICTNL	incitingly
ICTTO	incitation
ICTTV	incitative
ICUAL	includable
ICUEI	included in
ICUEU	include out
ICUIL	includible
ICUIU	incautious
ICVLT	incivility
IDAAE	India paper
IDACU	Indian club
IDAFL	Indian file
IDAMA	Indian meal
IDAWR	Indian Wars
IDBET	indebted to
IDCAC	inductance
IDCAL	indictable
IDCMN	indictment
	inducement
IDCNL	indecently
IDCRU	indecorous
IDCSO	indecision
IDCSV	indecisive
IDCTO	indication
IDCTR	indicatory
IDCTV	indicative
IDFNT	indefinite
IDGNL	indigently
IDGNS	indigenise
IDGNU	indigenous
IDGNZ	indigenize
IDGSE	indigested
IDLCC	indelicacy
IDLCI	in deliciis
IDLCT	indelicate
IDLEC	indulgence
IDLNL	indolently
IDNEO	in danger of
IDNSA	Indonesian
IDRCL	indirectly
IDSIC	indistinct
IDSOE	indisposed
IDSRA	in disarray
	industrial
IDSRC	in disgrace
IDSRE	indiscreet
	in disorder
IDSRS	in distress
IDSRT	indiscrete
IDSUS	in disguise
IDVDA	individual
IDXTO	indexation
IEAAL	inerasably
IEACN	ice dancing
IEAIL	inerasibly
IEBIE	item by item
IECAG	in exchange
IECSO	in excess of
IEEAC	inelegance
IEEYA	in every way
IEFCC	inefficacy
IEGAH	ideography
IEIAL	inevitable
	inevitably
	irenically
IEIEC	in evidence
IEIIL	ineligible
	ineligibly
IEIVS	I believe so
IEKTN	ice-skating
IELGS	ideologist
IELSI	idealistic
IEOAL	inexorable
	inexorably
IEOEE	ice-covered
IEPAL	inexpiably
IEPII	inexplicit
IEPRL	inexpertly
IERAE	icebreaker
	inebriated
IESNN	idem sonans
IETEI	in extremis
IETFE	identified
IETOA	ideational
IETTD	ineptitude
IEUAL	ineducable
IEULT	inequality
IFAAL	inflatable
IFAOI	infrasonic
IFAON	infrasound
IFATO	infraction

Code	Word
IFBLT	infibulate
IFCIU	infectious
IFDLT	infidelity
IFEIL	inflexible
	inflexibly
IFETO	inflection
IFETV	inflective
IFEUN	infrequent
IFGTN	infighting
	in-fighting
IFITO	infliction
IFLCT	infelicity
IFLIL	infallible
	infallibly
IFLRT	infiltrate
IFLVE	in full view
IFMNS	infamonise
IFMNZ	infamonize
IFMUL	infamously
IFNTD	infinitude
IFNTL	infinitely
IFNTT	infinitate
IFNTV	infinitive
IFRAE	infuriated
IFRAL	infernally
	inferrable
	informally
IFREO	informed of
IFROL	inferiorly
IFROT	inferior to
IFRTO	infarction
IFTAE	infatuated
IFUNA	influenzal
IFUNE	influenced
	influencer
	influences
IFVUO	in favour of
IGAIT	ingratiate
IGEIN	ingredient
IGESO	ingression
IGMNT	ingeminate
IGNRT	ingenerate
IGOFR	in good form
IGOIU	inglorious
IGONC	in good nick
IGOPR	in good part
IGOTI	in good trim
IGOTM	in good time
IGSIL	ingestible
IHAGT	Ishtar Gate
IHBTN	inhabitant
	inhabiting
	inhibiting
IHBTO	inhibition
IHBTR	inhibitory
IHBTV	inhibitive
IHGNI	Iphigeneia
IHHOI	ichthyosis
	ichthyotic
IHLTO	inhalation
IHMNL	inhumanely
IHMNT	inhumanity
IHMTO	inhumation
IHNUO	in honour of
IHRNL	inherently
IHRTI	inheritrix
IHTAE	in hot water
IHTLO	in hot blood
IIEAC	itinerancy
IIECN	iridescent
IIGUA	icing sugar
IIHOA	Irishwoman
IIIAL	inimically
	inimitable
	inimitably
IIILS	initialise
	initialism
IIILZ	initialize
IIITN	initiating
IIITO	initiation
IIITR	initiatory
IIITV	initiative
IILCA	idiolectal
IIMAK	Iain M Banks
IIOOE	Inigo Jones
IITOR	idiot board
IITRO	idiot-proof
IIUTU	iniquitous
IJCAL	injectable
IJNTO	injunction
IJNTV	injunctive
IJOAD	in jeopardy
IJRTM	injury time
IKNEU	Iskenderun
ILACE	ill-matched
ILAUE	ill-natured
ILCTO	illocution
ILDIE	ill-advised
ILEAE	ill-behaved
ILEIE	ill-defined
ILELN	ill feeling
	ill-feeling
ILEON	I'll be bound
ILGLC	illegal act
ILGLS	illegalise
ILGLT	illegality
ILGLZ	illegalize
ILGSI	idle gossip
ILITN	ill-fitting
ILMCS	Islamicise
	Islamicist
ILMCZ	Islamicize
ILMNN	illuminant
ILMNT	illuminate
	illuminati
ILNWT	in line with
ILONE	ill-founded
ILOTN	ill fortune
	ill-fortune
ILQET	illaqueate
ILRAE	ill-treated
ILRSE	ill-dressed
ILSRT	illustrate
ILSVL	illusively
ILTAV	inlet valve
ILTRC	illiteracy
ILTRE	ill-starred
ILTRT	illiterate
ILTVL	illatively
ILUAL	illaudably
ILUTA	I'll buy that
ILVWT	in love with
IMBLS	immobilise
IMBLT	immobility
IMBLZ	immobilize
	immobolize
IMCLC	immaculacy
IMCLT	immaculate
IMDRC	immoderacy
IMDRT	immoderate
IMDSL	immodestly
IMIAL	iambically
IMLTO	immolation
IMMRA	immemorial
	In Memoriam
	in memoriam
IMMRO	in memory of
IMNBD	immune body
IMNLG	immunology
IMNNL	imminently
IMONA	in my own way
IMRAL	immortally
IMREI	immersed in
IMRLT	immorality
IMSIL	immiscible
IMSRS	immiserise
IMSRZ	immiserize
IMTNN	Ismet Inönü
IMTRA	immaterial
IMTRL	immaturely
IMTRT	immaturity
IMUNN	in mourning
INASE	Ian Paisley
INBLT	ignobility
INCNL	innocently
INCNO	innocent of
INEDE	innuendoes
INLEC	Ion Iliescu
INLMN	Ian Fleming
INMNT	innominate
INMOL	in name only
INMRC	innumeracy
INMRT	innumerate
INOSA	Ian Woosnam
INREN	inner being
INRNL	ignorantly
INROA	inner woman
INSAU	ignes fatui
INSHR	ionosphere
INSTO	ionisation
INTNS	innateness
INVTO	innovation
INVTR	innovatory
INVTV	innovative
INZTO	ionization
IOAER	icosahedra
IOARS	idolatress
	idolatrise
IOARU	idolatrous
IOARZ	idolatrize
IOBIG	Ironbridge
IOCLT	inosculate
IODNR	in ordinary
IODNT	inordinate
IOEAL	inoperable
	inoperably
IOECN	isoleucine
IOECP	in one's cups
IOEIC	in one piece
IOERA	in ones road
IOERC	isometrics
IOESA	isoseismal
IOESI	isoseismic
IOETM	in one's time
IOETR	in one's turn
IOFSE	iron-fisted
IOGRE	Ivor Gurney
IOHNE	iron-handed
IOHOA	isochronal
IOIAL	iconically
	ironically
IOIAO	idolizaton
IOMIE	Iron Maiden
	iron maiden
IOMNE	ironmonger
IOMSE	ironmaster
IOOAE	iconolater
IOOAR	iconolatry
IOOLS	iconoclasm□
	iconoclast
IOOPI	isomorphic
IOTHN	I don't think
IOUAO	inoculator
IOWLE	iron-willed
IOYAI	isodynamic
IOYOE	ivory tower
	ivory-tower
IOYOS	Ivory Coast
IPAAL	implacable
	implacably
IPATC	in practice
IPCAL	impeccable
	impeccably
IPCUE	in pictures
IPDMN	impediment
IPDNL	impudently
IPEAI	impresario
IPEET	implements
IPENT	impregnate
IPESO	impression
IPESV	impressive
IPGAL	impugnable
IPGMN	impugnment
IPIAE	implicated
IPIAU	imprimatur
IPIIL	implicitly
IPIMN	impairment
IPIOE	imprisoned
IPISN	impuissant
IPITN	imprinting
IPLAL	impalpable
	impalpably

Words marked □ can also be spelled with an initial capital letter

IPLMN impalement
IPLTL impolitely
IPNTN impenitent
IPOAL improbable
improbably
improvable
improvably
IPOAO implorator
IPOEL improperly
IPOIE improvised
improviser
IPORS in progress
IPRAC importance
importancy
IPRAL imperially
IPRDS imparadise
IPRIL impartible
impartibly
IPRIU impervious
IPRLE in parallel
IPRMN impartment
IPRNS impureness
IPROA impersonal
in personam
IPRTE impurities
IPRTV imperative
IPRUE importuner
IPSAL impassable
impassably
IPSIL impassibly
impossible
IPSNL imposingly
IPSNS impishness
IPSTO imposition
IPSUO impose upon
IPTEC impatience
IPTNL impotently
IPTTO imputation
IPUDG impoundage
IPUDN impounding
IPUEC imprudence
IPVRS impoverish
IQETO in question
IQIIO inquisitor
IQITD inquietude
IRALF in real life
IRDCT irradicate
IRDVN iure divino
IRGRO in regard of
IRGRT in regard to
IRGTO irrigation
IRHMN iure humano
IRLGO irreligion
IRLVN irrelevant
IRMAL irremeably
IRMRT iure mariti
IRPUE in raptures
IRSLT irresolute
IRTOA irrational
IRTTN irritating
IRTTO irritation
IRTTV irritative
IRVRN irreverent

ISAAI Instamatic®
ISALN installing
ISAMN instalment
ISBIT insobriety
ISCRL insecurely
ISCRT insecurity
ISDPR inside part
ISETN inspecting
ISETO inspection
ISFLT insufflate
ISGTU insightful
ISIAO instigator
ISICE in stitches
ISILN instilling
ISIMN instilment
ISIST inspissate
ISIUE instituter
ISIUO institutor
ISLAL insolvably
ISLEC insolvency
ISLEG inselberge
ISLMN insultment
ISLNL insolently
ISLRT insularity
ISLTN insulating
ISLTO insolation
insulation
ISLTR insalutary
ISLVT insalivate
ISMAH in sympathy
ISMNT inseminate
ISMSR in some sort
ISNAE insinuated
ISNAO insinuator
ISNBT ifs and buts
ISNIL insensible
insensibly
ISNIN insentient
ISNOT ins and outs
ISNTR insanitary
ISOEO in store for
ISPDT insipidity
ISQEC in sequence
ISRCE instructed
ISRCO instructor
ISREC insurgence
insurgency
ISRMN instrument
ISRNT in strength
ISSEC insistence
insistency
ISSES in suspense
ISTAL insatiable
insatiably
ISUIN insouciant
ISYTA it says that
ITAIA intra vitam
ITAIE intra vires
ITANN in training
ITAOE intradoses
ITAUA intramural
ITAUO intra muros
ITEAO in the pay of

in the way of
ITEHD in the shade
ITEHI in the chair
ITEHP in the shops
ITEIG in the wings
ITEIH in the light
in the right
ITEIL intrepidly
ITEIS in the midst
ITELA in the clear
ITELC in the black
ITELO in the blood
ITELS in the flesh
ITEOE in the money
ITEOL in the world
ITERA in their way
ITERN in the wrong
ITERS in the press
ITEUC in the lurch
ITEVN in the event
ITGAE integrated
ITGAL integrally
ITGMN integument
ITIAT intrigante
ITIUN intriguant
intriguing
ITLRN intolerant
ITMDT intimidate
ITMRT intemerate
ITMTL intimately
ITMTO intimation
ITMTT intimate to
ITNEL intendedly
ITNET intended to
ITNIL intangible
intangibly
ITNIN intentions
ITNNL intoningly
ITNNS intentness
ITNTO intonation
ITNWT in tune with
ITOEI iatrogenic
ITOID in two minds
ITOIK in two ticks
ITOPC introspect
ITOSL introrsely
ITOUE introduced
ITRAL internally
ITRAR intermarry
ITREE interceder
interferer
interreges
intervener
ITREN interregna
ITREO interferon
ITREV interleave
interweave
ITREZ intermezzi
intermezzo
ITRHI interchain
ITRHS interphase
ITRIO inter vivos
ITRLA interplead

ITRLD interclude
ITRLN interplant
ITRMN internment
ITROE interloper
interposed
ITROL interiorly
ITROV intervolve
ITRPC interspace
ITRRA interurban
ITRRD intergrade
ITRRE interbreed
ITRRG intertrigo
ITRRS intercross
ITRSE interested
ITRTC interstice
ITRTT interstate
ITRWN intertwine
ITRWS intertwist
ITSIA intestinal
ITSIE intestines
ITXCN intoxicant
ITXCT intoxicate
IUBNL inurbanely
IUBNT inurbanity
IUDTO inundation
IVCTO invocation
IVCTR invocatory
IVGLT invigilate
IVGNT invaginate
IVGRT invigorate
IVILN inveigling
IVLAL invaluable
invaluably
IVLCA involucral
IVLDT invalidate
invalidity
IVLEI involved in
IVLTO involution
IVNIL invincible
invincibly
IVOAL inviolable
inviolably
IVRAL invariable
invariably
IVRCT inveracity
IVRDE in very deed
IVREL invertedly
IVRLD Inverclyde
IVRUO in virtue of
IVSMN investment
IVTNL invitingly
IVTOE invite over
IVTRT inveterate
IVTTO invitation
IYUFC in-your-face
IYUSM if you ask me
JAAES Jean Alessi
JACRO Juan Carlos
JAGEI Jiang Zemin
JAIGE Jean Ingres
JAMLE Jean Millet
JAOSU Jealous Guy
JAPAE Jean Piaget

JARCN Jean Racine
JARNI Jean Renoir
JBEAE job-related
JBLNL jubilantly
JBLTO jubilation
JCAAE jackanapes
JCBNS Jacobinise
JCBNZ Jacobinize
JCESI jockeyship
JCHME jackhammer
JCLMO Jack Lemmon
JCLNO Jack London
JCLRT jocularity
JCOLN Jack of Lent
JCRBI jack rabbit
JCSNS jocoseness
JCTEA Jack the Lad
JCULN Jacqueline
JCWRE Jack Warner
JDCAL judicially
JDCTR judicature
JDIAL Judaically
JDNEV J P Donleavy
JEAGR Joe Gargery
JEDNO Joey Dunlop
JEOTN Joe Montana
JERZE Joe Frazier
JGEHR jugged hare
JGENS jaggedness
JGENU juggernaut
JGLNL jugglingly
JGLWT juggle with
JGNAH Jagannatha
JHACC John Alcock
JHBAB John Bratby
JHBAN John Braine
JHBCA John Buchan
JHBCU John Backus
JHBIH John Bright
JHBNA John Bunyan
JHBNO John Benbow
JHBRE John Barnes
JHBUO John Bruton
JHBWB John Bowlby
JHCAK John Cranko
JHCES John Cleese
JHCLI John Calvin
JHDLO John Dalton
JHDNE John Denver
JHDNO John Dunlop
JHDYE John Dryden
JHEDR John Enders
JHEEY John Evelyn
JHEKR John Eckert
JHERC John Edrich
JHFSE John Fisher
JHFWE John Fowles
JHGME John Gummer
JHHEA John Heenan
JHHNE John Hunter
JHHSO John Huston
JHHWR John Howard
JHKRA John Kirwan

JHLNO John Lennon
JHMAA John McAdam
JHMLO John Milton
JHMRA John Morgan
JHMRO John Morton
JHNCS Johnny Cash
JHNDP Johnny Depp
JHNPE John Napier
JHPLE John Pilger
JHRNI John Rennie
JHRSI John Ruskin
JHUDK John Updike
JHWLE John Wilkes
JHWLO John Wilmot
JHWSE John Wesley
JIBTL join battle
JIFRE join forces
JITTO joint-stool
JIUWT join up with
JJNNS jejuneness
JLIDE jellied eel
JLSEN Jules Verne
JLYOE Jolly Roger
JLYOL jelly mould
JLYRP jellygraph
JMAKN Jim Hawkins
JMESO jam session
JMFRO jump for joy
JMHRY jamahiriya
JMJCE jump-jockey
JMLNL jumblingly
JMLSL jumble sale
JMRQA Jamiroquai
JMSAE James Baker
James Paget
JMSAO James Mason
JMSEA James Dewar
JMSED James Meade
JMSEN James Jeans
JMSHS James Chase
JMSOC James Joyce
JMSOI James Bowie
James Tobin
JMSOL James Joule
JMSRI James Braid
JMSRW James Brown
JMSVR James Ivory
JMTEU jump the gun
JMYHT Jimmy White
JNAEC Jan Van Eyck
Jan van Eyck
JNASE Jane Austen
JNEME Jan Vermeer
JNEMN Jan Leeming
JNISA Jenkin's Ear
JNLBO Jungle Book
JNLFW jungle fowl
JNMRL Jane Marple
JNOSI jingoistic
JNSAE Janus-faced
JNTAE Janet Baker
JNTEG Janet Leigh
JNTRA janitorial

JOADS jeopardise
JOADZ jeopardize
JQEET Jaquenetta
JRAON jerk around
JRDVN jure divino
JRHMN jure humano
JRIIR jardinière
JRMKR Jerome Kern
JROKE J R R Tolkien
JRSIA juristical
JRYEI Jerry Lewis
JRYUL jerry-build
jerry-built
JRZLK Jaruzelski
JSEAE Jesse James
JSEWN Jesse Owens
JSGBO Josh Gibson
JSIIA jesuitical
JSIIR justiciary
JSITM just-in-time
JSIYN justifying
JSPSA Joseph Swan
JSTEO just the job
JTETN jet-setting
JTIGU jutting out
JTIOE jettisoned
JTRTL Jethro Tull
JUDMT jeux de mots
JUEPI jeu d'esprit
JUNLS journalese
journalise
journalism
journalist
JUNLZ journalize
JUNYA journeyman
JUNYN journeying
JUTNS jauntiness
JVNLL juvenilely
JVNLT juvenility
JWLIM JJ Williams
JXAOE juxtaposed
JYAKN jaywalking
JYDMO Joy Adamson
JYTET Jay's Treaty
JYUNS joyfulness
joyousness
KAKUS knackwurst
KASUH Klaus Fuchs
KATAE kraft paper
KBAKA Kublai Khan
KBUZI kibbutznik
KCAON kick around
KCBXN kick boxing
KCUAO kick up a row
KDABA kodiak bear □
KDAPN kidnapping
KDEBA kidney bean
KDEDS kidney dish
KDIWN kiddiewink
KDLGS kidologist
KEAAL keep a tally
KECAE keep chapel
KEEGH kieselguhr

KEHDE keep hidden
KEHLO keep hold of
KEIDR keep it dark
KEIIT khediviate
KEIMN keep in mind
KEIWT keep in with
KELNT knee-length
KELWK Kieslowski
KEMVN keep moving
KEOWT keep on with
KEPSE keep posted
KESCE keep secret
KESEL Klebsiella
KESTO keep shtoom
KESYL Krebs cycle
KETBO keep tabs on
KETKO keen to know
KETYN keep trying
KEUWT keep up with
KEWCE keep wicket
KFASU Kafkaesque
KIEDE knife-edged
KIELA knife pleat
KIELC knife block
KIGIH klieg light □
KIHAS Krishnaism
KIHHO knighthood
KIHLY Keith Floyd
KIHRI Keir Hardie
KIKNC knick-knack
KLANC Kilmarnock
KLGAM kilogramme
KMELT kimberlite
KMEYA kempery-man
KMGAH kymography
KMOGO Kompong Som
KMROG Khmer Rouge
KNACT Kansas City
KNATU King Arthur
KNAZS Konrad Zuse
KNDNA King Duncan
KNECU Kennel Club
KNFSE kingfisher
KNINS Kantianism
KNKAE King Khaled
KNLNS kindliness
kingliness
KNLOT Kenilworth
KNMTC kinematics
KNOIE King Oliver
KNPCL kenspeckle
KNSCU King's Scout
KNSEC King's Bench
KNSRE king's brief
KNSUD King's Guide
KNTCR kinetic art
KNUSL Ken Russell
KOAUR kookaburra
KOBTE know better
KOIII kaolinitic
KOKBU knock about
knockabout
KOKDU knocked out

Words marked □ can also be spelled with an initial capital letter

Code	Word
KOKNE	knock-kneed
KOKRI	knobkerrie
KOKUS	knockwurst
KOTHE	klootchmen
KOTNS	knottiness
KRDNT	Karl Dönitz
KRGOG	Karageorge
KRJNK	Karl Jansky
KRNGL	Karl Nägeli
KROEA	karaoke bar
KROYI	karyotypic
KRPPE	Karl Popper
KRSCE	Khrushchev
KRTAE	kerb-trader
KRTCO	karate chop
KRTNS	keratinise
KRTNU	keratinous
KRTNZ	keratinize
KRTWR	Kirsty Wark
KRVNO	kerb-vendor
KRWIH	kerb weight
KRYSA	Kyrgyzstan
KSMKT	Kiss Me Kate
KSOLF	kiss of life
KSTEO	kiss the rod
KTACU	Kitcat Club
KTADI	kith and kin
KTHNE	kitchen tea
KTLDU	kettledrum
	kettle-drum
KTLHL	kettle hole
KTLPN	kettle-pins
KTLWL	Kettlewell
KUERN	krugerrand☐
KUHMU	Knut Hamsun
KWICT	Kuwait City
KYOEA	keyhole saw
KYORE	keyboarder
KZKSA	Kazakhstan
LAAPO	lhasa apsos
LAATA	lead astray
LAELN	leave alone
LAESI	leadership
LAGLE	Llangollen
LAHNL	loathingly
LAHPE	leaf-hopper
LAHRN	leathering
LAIGA	leading man
	loading bay
LAIGU	leaving out
	leaving-out
LALNS	liableness
LAMSE	loadmaster
LANBU	learn about
LANEO	Liam Neeson
LATEA	lead the way
LATWY	leastaways
LBCHO	libecchios
LBCUS	lob's course
LBDNS	libidinist
LBDNU	libidinous
LBEIL	Libreville
LBETS	librettist
LBIAO	lubricator
LBIIU	lubricious
LBMAH	Lubumbashi
LBNRU	Lebensraum
LBRLS	liberalise
	liberalism
	liberalist
LBRLT	liberality
LBRLZ	liberalize
LBRTN	liberating
LBRTO	liberation
LBRTR	laboratory
LBTMS	lobotomise
LBTMZ	lobotomize
LBUCM	labour camp
LBUSM	laboursome
LBUWT	labour with
LCEAA	locked away
LCERO	locker room
LCFRU	luciferous
LCIAI	lactic acid
LCLAI	local radio
LCLMN	Loch Lomond
LCLNL	luculently
LCLSL	lucklessly
LCLSR	lacklustre
LCMTO	locomotion
LCMTR	locomotory
LCMTV	locomotive
LCNIT	licentiate
LCNIU	licentious
LCOBA	lack of bias
LCOFM	lack of fame
LCRMS	lachrymose
LCRTN	lacerating
LCRTO	laceration
LCSBA	locust bean
LCSBR	locust bird
LCSRN	lacustrine
LCWLS	Lech Walesa
LCYHR	lucky charm
LCYRA	lucky break
LDCAE	Lady Chapel
LDEBI	ledger-bait
LDEIC	Ledge Piece
LDELN	ledger-line
LDERO	ladies' room
LDIMN	Ludwig Mond
LDKLE	lady-killer
LDROE	lederhosen
LDSMC	lady's smock
LEAOC	Lee Iacocca
LEEVO	lie heavy on
LENTT	lie in state
LETNN	lieutenant
LEUNE	Lee Kuan Yew
LEWRE	Leeuwarden
LFARU	left atrium
LFBHN	left behind
LFGAD	Life Guards
LFGVN	life-giving
LFHNE	left-handed
LFLSL	lifelessly
LFNAN	La Fontaine
LFRNE	life-renter
LFSVN	life-saving
LFTCM	life to come
LFWNE	left-winger
LFWRL	leftwardly
LGAMR	leg-warmers
LGBIU	lugubrious
LGBLT	legibility
LGCLT	logicality
LGEHA	loggerhead
LGLAL	legal eagle
LGLSI	legalistic
LGMNU	leguminous
LGNER	loganberry
LGOAN	lignocaine
LGPNE	leg spinner
LGRHE	logorrhoea
LGRVS	Lagerkvist
LGSAO	legislator
LGSIA	logistical
LGTEE	light meter
LGTIH	light-tight
LGTLE	Light blues
	light sleep
LGTMC	legitimacy
LGTMS	legitimise
LGTMT	legitimate
LGTMZ	legitimize
LGTNN	lightening
LGTOS	lighthouse
LGTPR	light opera
LGTRW	light brown
LGTUC	light lunch
LGULN	leg-pulling
LIBNE	Luis Buñuel
LIHAI	leishmania
LISMZ	Luis Somoza
LIUAL	leisurably
LKAAS	like a tansy
LKABR	Lake Albert
LKAHR	like a charm
LKALS	like a flash
LKBIA	Lake Baikal
LKBTE	like better
LKGNV	Lake Geneva
LKLDG	Lake Ladoga
LKLHO	likelihood
LKLNS	likeliness
LKMLW	Lake Malawi
LKMNE	like-minded
LKNSE	Lake Nasser
LKPAI	Lake Placid
LKSIA	Lake Saimaa
LKVNR	Lake Vänern
LKWRL	lukewarmly
LLAEU	liliaceous
LLAGS	Lilian Gish
LLAOK	Lalla Rookh
LLETA	Lilienthal
LMEMN	limpet mine
LMETM	lumpectomy
LMHCT	lymphocyte
LMHLN	lymph gland
LMINS	limpidness
LMNAL	lamentable
	lamentably
LMNRS	laminarise
LMNRZ	laminarize
LMNST	luminosity
LMNTO	lamination
LMNUL	luminously
LMONR	lampoonery
LMONS	lampoonist
LMRKS	Lamarckism
LMSCE	lumpsucker
LMTTO	limitation
LNAET	lentamente
	lineaments
LNAHR	Lancashire
LNEAC	lancet arch
LNELT	lanceolate
LNEOE	linger over
LNEWT	linked with
LNFLO	Longfellow
LNFRE	land forces
LNGNS	lanuginose
LNHIE	long-haired
LNHLE	landholder
LNIGE	landing-net
LNIHO	Linlithgow
LNIIE	lentigines
LNILN	Long Island
LNISM	lentissimo
LNIUA	lenticular
LNLCE	landlocked
LNLGE	long-legged
LNLNS	loneliness
LNOLF	line of life
LNOWL	London Wall
LNOWR	line of work
LNOYI	lincomycin
LNPRO	link person
LNPRT	land-pirate
LNQEE	lansquenet
LNROT	lunar month
LNSIC	longstitch
LNSML	lonesomely
LNSRN	Lindstrand
LNTEE	lengthened
LNTWS	lengthwise
LNTWY	lengthways
LNURU	languorous
LNUSI	linguistic
LNUWT	link up with
LNWNE	longwinded
	long-winded
LNYER	Lenny Henry
LNYRC	Lenny Bruce
LOADA	leopard-cat
	look and say
LOADS	leopardess
LODWO	look down on
LOEBR	Lionel Bart
LOEIE	Léo Delibes
	loose-liver

Words marked ☐ can also be spelled with an initial capital letter

LOEOA loose woman
LOEUT looked up to
LOGOO look good on
LOHLS lyophilise
LOHLZ lyophilize
LOLVL look lively
look lively!
LOOSO Leo Tolstoy
LOSAP look snappy
LOSHR lion's share
LOSIK Leon Spinks
LOSIP look slippy
LOZLR Leo Szilard
LPDRA lapidarian
LPDVG Lope de Vega
LPEDN lip-reading
LPEHU leprechaun
LPEVC lip service
lip-service
LPGAH lipography
LPOOI leptosomic
LPRAI Lupercalia
LPRTM laparotomy
LPZAE Lipizzaner
LQAIU loquacious
LQEYN liquefying
LQIAE liquidated
LQIAO liquidator
LQIIE liquidiser
liquidizer
LRAON lark around
Lorna Doone
LRECL large-scale
LREHT Large White
LREPR larger part
LRERN large print
LRETA larger than
LRHTO larghettos
LRIOE lord it over
LRLIE Lorelei Lee
LRLNS lordliness
LRNII laryngitis
LRSAL Lord's Table
LRSOS Lord's house
LSAEE Lassa fever
LSCAC last-chance
LSCLU lose colour
LSDEE lust-dieted
LSEIA Las Meninas
LSEIO listen in on
LSEIT listen in to
LSETA lesser than
LSIAE Leslie Ames
LSIIU lascivious
LSINS lesbianism
LSIUL lusciously
LSLBR Laszlo Biro
LSLSL listlessly
LSMKN loss-making
LSMNT last-minute
LSNEE Los Angeles
LSOFC loss of face
LSOLF loss of life

LSRLS lustreless
LSRTO lustration
LSRUL lustrously
LSRWR lustreware
LSSRT Lysistrata
LSTEA lose the way
LSWIH lose weight
LTAGS lethargise
LTAGZ lethargize
LTAIT La Traviata
LTEBM letter bomb
LTEBR latter-born
LTEEY Lotte Lenya
LTEHA letterhead
LTELU litter-lout
LTESI lateen sail
LTGTO litigation
LTHEE latch lever
LTHOT Letchworth
LTLBA Little Bear
LTLGR little girl
LTLJH Little John
LTLLO Little Lion
LTLNL Little Nell
LTLOE little ones
LTLON little or no
LTLRC Little Rock
LTNHA latent heat
LTNRS Latin cross
LTOHT lithophyte
LTOLP lithoglyph
LTORP lithograph
LTORT lithotrity
LTRIA liturgical
LTRLS literalise
literalism
literalist
LTRLT laterality
LTRLZ literalize
LTRRL literarily
LTRTR literature
LTSAE lotus-eater
LTSUR Lotus Sutra
LTUNA Lithuanian
LTUTS litmus test
LUAAI Laura Davis
LUCIT launch into
LUCSO Launceston
LUDET laundrette
LUDOA Laundromat®
LUDRN laundering
LUETU Laurentius
LUGNL loungingly
LUGSI lounge suit
LUHEG Lough Neagh
LUHIE loudhailer
loud-hailer
LUHNL laughingly
LUHOL Lough Foyle
LUSAL Louis Malle
LUSIL Louisville
LUSOH Louis Botha
LVAFI love affair

LVBOE love-broker
LVIMS levy in mass
LVLHO livelihood
LVLIR lavallière
LVLMN Liv Ullmann
LVLNS liveliness
loveliness
LVMKN lovemaking
love-making
LVNHL living hell
LVNRO living-room
LVNSO Livingston
LVNWG living wage
LVPTO love potion
LVRAT liver salts
LVRLK liver fluke
LVRUM Leverhulme
LVRUS liverwurst
LVSNS lavishness
LVTRA lavatorial
LVTTO levitation
LVYOE lovey-dovey
LWAKN low-ranking
LWBDN law-abiding
LWECU lawrencium
LWESI lawyer's wig
LWICE low-pitched
LWPNO low opinion
LWPRT low spirits
LWRAE lawbreaker
law-breaker
LWREE lower-level
LWRLS lower-class
LWRNL loweringly
LWROS lower house
LWULT low quality
low-quality
LWUNS lawfulness
LXCLG lexicology
LXGAH lexigraphy
LXMOR Luxembourg
LXRAC luxuriance
LYADO lay hands on
LYIGT lay siege to
LYLIT lay claim to
LYNAD lay on hands
LYNBR laying bare
LYOER lay to heart
LYTRB lay store by
LZPRO lazy person
LZRTO lazarettos
MADRN meandering
MAETN meat-eating
MAIEC Miami Beach
MAIGU meaningful
MAIMA mealie meal
MALNS measliness
MAMTU miasmatous
MAOBN Meadowbank
MARNS meagreness
MATEI myasthenia
MATIH Maastricht
MAUAL measurable

measurably
MAUEF measure off
MAUEL measuredly
MAUEU measure out
MAXBE Meaux Abbey
MBLHM mobile home
MCAIA mechanical
MCAIE mechanized
MCALA Michaelmas
MCAON muck around
MCDMS macadamise
MCDMZ macadamize
MCDNU mucedinous
MCEFN Mickey Finn
MCERU Michel Roux
MCETK mickey-take
MCHRI mock-heroic
MCIAO machinator
MCIEU machinegun
machine-gun
MCIRI MacDiarmid
MCITC McClintock
MCITS mackintosh❑
MCIWT muck in with
MCLGS mycologist
MCLTO maculation
MCNME Mach number
MCNOL Mo Connolly
MCNPE meconopses
MCOAE microwaves
mucronated
MCOCP microscope❑
microscopy
MCOEE micrometer
MCOEI Micronesia
MCOER micrometre
micrometry
MCOHN microphone
MCOIH microfiche
microlight
MCOIR microfibre
MCOOC micrococci
MCORC microcrack
MCORN microprint
MCRKN muck-raking
MCRNE macaronies
MCRTE much rather
MCRTO maceration
MCSOE much sooner
MCSRA muckspread
MDAEI mediagenic
MDAMA midday meal
MDATN mediastina
MDCLS medicalise
MDCLZ medicalize
MDCMN medicament
MDCTO medication
MDEAL medievally
MDEOI madreporic
MDETR Midwestern
MDFAL modifiable
MDGIN Modigliani
MDGSA Madagascar

Code	Word
MDHPA	midshipman
MDIHL	midnightly
MDILE	midfielder
MDLAA	muddle away
MDLBO	middlebrow
MDLES	Middle East
MDLNE	mud-slinger
MDLNM	middle name
MDLRT	modularity
MDLSM	meddlesome
MDLTO	modulation
MDLWT	meddle with
MDOHA	Midlothian
MDORT	mediocrity
MDRIE	madbrained
	modernized
	modernizer
MDRJZ	modern jazz
MDRTL	moderately
MDRTN	moderating
MDRTO	moderation
MDSNS	modishness
MDTLS	made to last
MDTTO	meditate on
	meditation
MDTTV	meditative
MDUOJ	Medjugorje
MEHAO	meet head on
	meet head-on
MEOHR	meet others
MEPOL	meet people
MESHU	meerschaum
MFILD	My Fair Lady
MGAAT	Magna Carta
MGANU	migrainous
MGEIE	magnetizer
MGEIG	Muggeridge
MGIIA	magnificat□
MGINS	McGuinness
MGIYN	magnifying
MGLSU	megalosaur
MGLTI	megalithic
MGNGL	McGonagall
MGOET	mignonette
MGSRC	magistracy
MGSRT	magistrate
MGUOU	magnum opus
MICAS	main clause
MICUS	main course
MIEHA	Maidenhead
MIEHI	maidenhair
MIEHO	maidenhood
MIELK	maidenlike
MIENM	maiden name
MIEOE	maiden over
MILNE	mainlander
MILNN	mainlining
MIMRA	Maid Marian
MIMTE	main matter
MIOET	maisonette
MIOFC	main office
MIOIE	Maimonides
MIPIT	main points
MISRA	mainstream
MISRN	mainspring
MITIE	maintained
	maintainer
MITRS	moisturise
MITRZ	moisturize
MJBHL	Majuba Hill
MJHDI	mujaheddin
MKAED	make amends
MKALA	Mikhail Tal
MKAON	make a sound
MKAOS	make a noise
MKAPA	make appear
MKARI	make afraid
MKATN	make a stand
MKATR	make a start
MKAUS	make a guess
MKBGE	make bigger
MKBIH	make bright
MKBTE	make better
MKCLE	make colder
MKCRE	make curved
MKDRE	make darker
MKDWT	make do with
MKEEA	make eyes at
MKESE	make easier
MKGBO	Mike Gibson
MKGMO	make game of
MKGOM	make gloomy
MKHPE	make happen
MKIPR	make impure
MKIWT	make it with
MKLAL	make liable
MKLNE	make longer
MKLRE	make larger
MKLUE	make louder
MKLVL	make lively
MKLVT	make love to
MKMCO	make much of
MKMDR	make modern
MKNLV	making love
MKNOD	make no odds
MKNRO	make narrow
MKPBI	make public
MKRCE	make richer
MKRMR	maker's mark
MKSAL	make stable
MKSBL	make so bold
MKSCE	make sacred
MKSCR	make secure
MKSOT	make smooth
MKSRN	make strong
MKSRO	make sure of
MKTAK	make tracks
MKTNE	make tender
MKUES	make uneasy
MKUET	make used to
MKUTD	make untidy
MKUWL	make unwell
MKWAE	make weaker
MLAON	mill around
MLAOS	Melba toast
MLBEU	molybdenum
MLBTL	milk bottle
MLCNT	melaconite
MLDPE	maladapted
MLDRU	malodorous
MLEIA	millesimal
MLEML	malted milk
MLENA	millennial
MLENU	millennium
MLERT	muliebrity
MLESN	malfeasant
MLEWN	mulled wine
MLFCN	maleficent
MLFCO	malefactor
MLGAC	malignancy
MLHSA	Malthusian
MLIAI	maleic acid
MLIEI	multimedia
MLIER	millimetre
MLIGO	melting-pot
MLIIR	millilitre
MLIKL	multiskill
MLILE	multiplier
MLINO	millions of
MLIOA	multivocal
MLIOU	multiloquy
MLIRC	multi-track
MLIRD	multigrade
MLITG	multi-stage
MLIUE	multitudes
MLIYN	mollifying
MLLQE	Malplaquet
MLNCT	melanocyte
MLNEE	malingerer
MLNHL	melancholy
MLNMT	melanomata
MLNSA	Melanesian
MLNSI	melanistic
MLNTS	mylonitise
MLNTZ	mylonitize
MLNWK	Malinowski
MLOEE	mileometer
MLONS	mellowness
MLOTN	malcontent
MLPOO	malapropos
MLPRL	malapertly
MLRAE	maltreated
MLRTU	malgré tout
MLSAI	melismatic
	Miles Davis
MLSNS	mulishness
MLTAA	militiaman
MLTAE	Militiades
MLTNL	militantly
MLTRL	militarily
MLTRS	militarise
	militarism
	militarist
	mulattress
MLTRZ	militarize
MLUHI	McLaughlin
MLVLN	malevolent
MLWIK	malt whisky
MLYEN	Molly Keane
MLYLO	Molly Bloom
MMATS	mime artist
MMESI	membership
MMLNL	mumblingly
MMLNW	mumble-news
MMORP	mimeograph
MMOUB	mumbo-jumbo
MMRNU	memorandum
MMRZN	memorizing
MNAAG	Mangalarga
MNAAL	maniacally
MNAIL	manzanilla□
	Manzanillo
MNAIU	mendacious
MNAUE	mandamuses
MNAWR	menial work
MNBEI	montbretia
MNBNE	mind-bender
MNCAI	monochasia
	monocratic
MNCAU	Manichaeus
MNCIA	monoclinal
MNCNL	menacingly
MNCOA	monoclonal
MNCRI	monocarpic
	monochroic
MNCRM	monochrome
MNDIE	menu-driven
MNEAL	Monte Carlo
MNEBE	minced beef
MNEED	Monteverdi
MNEEE	Mendeleyev
MNEHL	minke whale
MNEIE	Montevideo
MNEIL	Mandeville
MNEIU	monoecious
MNELA	Monte Albán
MNEOA	Montego Bay
MNEVE	manoeuvrer
	manoeuvres
MNEVN	manservant
MNFCN	munificent
MNFKL	man of skill
MNFLL	manifoldly
MNFSL	manifestly
MNFSO	manifestos
MNFTA	man of straw
MNGAL	manageable
	manageably
MNGMN	management
MNGMR	Montgomery
MNGMS	monogamist
MNGMU	monogamous
MNGNU	monogynous
MNGRA	managerial
MNGRS	manageress
MNHBI	monohybrid
MNHMN	month's mind
MNHSE	Manchester
MNIAC	mendicancy
MNIEL	Monticello
MNINR	Monsignori
	Monsignors

Words marked □ can also be spelled with an initial capital letter

10 M_N_I

Code	Word
MNIUA	mandibular
MNIUU	monticulus
MNLGS	mo-nologise
MNLGZ	mo-nologize
MNLHM	Manila hemp
MNLMN	minglement
MNLNL	minglingly
MNLSL	mindlessly
MNLTI	monolithic
MNMLR	Minimal Art
MNMLS	minimalism
	minimalist
MNMNA	monomaniac
	monumental
MNMNE	Menominees
MNMTE	manumitter
MNMTI	manometric
MNMZN	minimizing
MNNEE	man-entered
MNNII	meningitis
MNNRU	monandrous
MNOSI	mentorship
MNOTE	mangosteen
MNPEI	monoplegia
	monoplegic
MNPLE	Montpelier
MNPLS	monopolise
	monopolist
MNPLT	manipulate
MNPLZ	monopolize
MNPOI	monophonic
MNPUA	menopausal
MNRAE	mind-reader
MNRGR	mandragora
MNRHE	menorrhoea
MNRHS	monarchise
	monarchism
	monarchist
MNRHZ	monarchize
MNRLG	mineralogy
MNRLI	mineral oil
MNRLS	mineralise
	mongrelise
MNRLZ	mineralize
	mongrelize
MNROS	manor-house
MNSEI	ministeria
MNSET	minister to
MNSRA	Montserrat
MNSRN	minestrone
	ministrant
MNSRP	manuscript
MNSUA	minuscular
MNSUE	meniscuses
MNTAC	monstrance
MNTAK	many thanks
MNTES	minstrelsy
	monotheism
	monotheist
MNTJC	minute-jack
MNTNS	minuteness
MNTNU	monotonous
MNTRA	monitorial
MNTRN	monitoring
MNTRS	monetarism
	monetarist
MNTUM	menstruums
MNTUT	menstruate
MNUAL	mensurable
MNULE	man-queller
MNUNS	manfulness
MNVLN	monovalent
MNYAE	money-maker
MNYAK	money talks
MNYRE	money order
MNYWN	money owing
MOADA	myocardial
MOADU	myocardium
MOILN	Moominland
MOSAE	moon-shaped
MOSIE	moonshiner
MOSRC	moonstruck
MOYLE	Moody Blues
MPEDN	map-reading
MPEYU	maple syrup
MPRDN	meperidine
MQILG	maquillage
MRAAI	morganatic
MRABM	mortar-bomb
MRAEL	mortadella
MRAFL	myriadfold
MRANN	Mary Anning
MRATL	mercantile
MRATN	marcantant
	Mark Antony
MRAUN	Maria Bueno
MRCLU	miraculous
MRCSA	Mary Cassat
MRDOA	meridional
MREAL	marketable
MREBL	market-bell
MREBO	marker buoy
MREDW	marked-down
MRELE	Marseilles
MRELT	martellato
MRELU	marvellous
MRESD	Merseyside
MRETW	market town
MREUI	Marie Curie
MRGRU	morigerous
MRHAD	marchlands
MRHLE	marshaller
MRHLG	morphology
MRHRT	margharita
MRHSA	Murphy's law
MRHUL	mirthfully
MRIAI	marginalia
	Martin Amis
MRIAL	marginally
MRIBL	Martin Bell
MRIDA	married man
MRIGF	marking off
MRIGL	martingale
MRIGU	marking out
MRIGY	Marvin Gaye
MRIIU	Martinique
MRILA	martial law
MRILR	martial art
MRILS	martialism
MRINS	morbidness
MRIPK	morris-pike
MRIUL	mercifully
MRIYN	mortifying
MRLAC	Marble Arch
MRLAE	Mary Leakey
MRLES	moral sense
MRLIR	moral fibre
MRLSI	moralistic
MRLZN	moralizing
MRMRI	Mark Morris
MROAZ	Mario Lanza
MROET	marionette
MROHT	Marco White
MROLK	mirrorlike
MROLS	more or less
MROTC	Mary of Teck
MROWS	mirrorwise
MRPTR	Mary Peters
MRRLT	marprelate
MRRTK	Mark Rothko
MRSHN	maraschino
MRSNS	moroseness
MRSOA	markswoman
MRTAI	Marat Safin
MRTCA	meritocrat
MRTKC	Marita Koch
MRTRU	moratorium
MRURT	marguerite
MRWGA	Mary Wigman
MRWSE	Mary Wesley
MRYAE	merrymaker
MSAAE	mismanaged
MSAAL	mistakable
MSACE	mismatched
MSADA	mustard gas
MSAEL	mistakenly
MSAHO	mustachios
MSAON	mess around
MSAPA	mass appeal
MSAPN	mascarpone
MSAVR	Mrs Danvers
MSBEL	musk beetle
MSBEV	misobserve
MSCAL	musicianly
MSCLG	musicology
MSCLO	musical box
MSCLT	musicality
MSCMO	most common
MSCRM	music drama
MSCRU	music group
MSCTO	music stool
MSEAA	Moshe Dayan
MSEBL	masked ball
MSEBO	muster-book
MSEDN	misleading
	misreading
MSEFL	muster-file
MSEHD	Mister Hyde
MSEIE	mesmerized
MSEIU	mysterious
MSEIV	misbelieve
MSELB	Mrs Jellyby
MSELN	miscellany
MSELS	masterless
MSEMN	mastermind
MSESR	mismeasure
MSETA	Mister Toad
MSETM	mastectomy
MSEWR	masterwork
MSGGL	mishguggle
MSGMS	misogamist
MSGNS	misogynist
MSGNU	misogynous
MSHEA	mischmetal
MSIAL	mosaically
	mystically
MSIAO	masticator
MSIIE	Mrs Miniver
MSIIG	misgivings
MSIIO	mashie iron
MSINR	missionary
MSINS	Messianism
	missionise
MSINZ	missionize
MSIYN	mystifying
MSLGE	misaligned
MSLIO	muscle in on
MSLKL	most likely
MSLPA	Musala Peak
MSLTI	mesolithic□
MSMDR	most modern
MSMRE	mass market
	mass-market
	mass murder
MSMRV	misimprove
MSNEM	Mason Weems
MSNME	mass number
MSNYT	Mishnayoth
MSOAO	muscovados
MSODC	misconduct
MSOGK	Mussorgsky
MSOML	mess or mell
MSONE	miscounsel
MSOPT	miscompute
MSORC	miscorrect
MSOSI	misworship
MSOTN	misfortune
MSPLE	misapplied
MSRAG	misarrange
MSRCN	most recent
MSRCR	misericord
MSRMT	most remote
MSRRL	Moser-Proll
MSRSO	misprision
MSSHR	mesosphere
MSSIC	moss stitch
MSSIO	Miss Saigon
MSTEU	miss the bus
	miss the cut
MSTLN	mesitylene
MSUAL	muscularly
MSUBT	masturbate

Words marked □ can also be spelled with an initial capital letter

MSUMN Mussulmans
MSURD masquerade
MSUTE mosquitoes
MSVRG Mrs Average
MSYLN mosey along
MTBLE mothballed
MTBLS metabolise
metabolism
MTBLT metabolite
mutability
MTBLZ metabolize
MTCLU meticulous
MTCRA metacarpal
MTCRU metacarpus
MTDLO Matt Dillon
MTEHO motherhood
MTEHR Matterhorn
MTELK motherlike
MTELN motherland
MTELS motherless
MTENC Metternich
MTERN Mitterrand
MTESA Mother's Day
MTETB mother-to-be
MTEWL Motherwell
MTGNS mutagenise
MTGNZ mutagenize
MTGTN mitigating
MTGTO mitigation
MTGTR mitigatory
MTGTV mitigative
MTHAE matchmaker
MTHTC matchstick
MTIAL metrically
mythically
MTIIA matricidal
MTIIE mythicizer
MTINN methionine
MTIRH matriarchy
MTLPI metalepsis
MTLSM mettlesome
MTLTO mutilation
MTLUG metallurgy
MTNUL mutinously
MTOHA muttonhead
MTOIA methodical
MTOII meteoritic
MTOLS motionless
MTOOI metronomic
metropolis
MTOYI metronymic
MTPRS metaphrase
metaphrast
MTRAL materially
maternally
MTRDT mithridate
MTRIT mature into
MTROC motor-coach
MTROT motormouth
MTRTO maturation
MTRTV maturative
MTRYL motorcycle
motor-cycle
MTSAE metastases
MTSAI metastasis
MTTEE metatheses
MTTEI metathesis
MTTOA mutational
MTTRA metatarsal
MTTRU metatarsus
MTUEA methuselah❑
MTURS Mateus Rosé
MTVLS motiveless
MTVTN motivating
MTVTO motivation
MUASN Maupassant
MUDNS mouldiness
MUDRN maundering
mouldering
MUEAI Mauretania
MUHAT mouthparts
MUHIC mouthpiece
MUHRA mouth-organ
MUIAI Mauritania
MUNNL mourningly
MUNUL mournfully
MUSLN mousseline
MUTBN mountebank
MUTCE moustached
MUTEE Mount Pelée
MUTEY Mount Kenya
MUTOA Mount Logan
MVAON move around
MVARA move abroad
MVBLT movability
MVLSL movelessly
MVNDW moving down
MVNOU Moving On Up
MVSOL move slowly
MVUNE mavourneen
MXCCT Mexico City
MXCNA Mexican War
MXDRE mixed breed
MXDRL mixed grill
MXLUA maxillulae
MXMCT myxomycete
MXMLA Maximilian
MXMLS maximalist
MXMOK Maxim Gorky
MXNBW mixing bowl
MXOLU Max von Laue
MYKVK Mayakovsky
MYNAS mayonnaise
MZAEL mozzarella
MZMIU Mozambique
MZOIN mezzo-piano
MZOOT mezzo forte
mezzo-forte
NAADA near and far
NAAHN near at hand
NAHNE neat-handed
NALGE near-legged
NALKL nearly kill
NAOAS Ngaio Marsh
NAOIA Neapolitan
NBEEA noble metal
NBEOA noblewoman
NBEOE noblewomen
NBLNE Nibelungen
NBLNL nibblingly
NBLRZ Nobel Prize
Nobel prize
NBLTT nobilitate
NBLUL nebulously
NCAEU nectareous
NCAOE nyctalopes
NCAOI nyctalopia
nyctalopic
NCBTO Nick Bottom
NCENC nucleonics
NCERA nuclear war
NCERS nuclearise
NCERZ nuclearize
NCESD nucleoside
NCETD nucleotide
NCETO nucleation
NCFRU nuciferous
NCHRB Nick Hornby
NCIUA noctilucae
NCOAC necromancy
NCOAI necromania
NCOCP necroscopy
NCOHL necrophile
NCOOI necropolis
NCVRU nucivorous
NDBAC nudibranch
NDCLU nidicolous
NDFCT nidificate
NDHOG nod through
NDLTO nodulation
NECWR Noël Coward
NEDWL ne'er-do-well
NELBN needle bank
NELCR needlecord
NELLK needle-like
NELSL needlessly
NELTM needle time
NELWR needlework
NGECN nigrescent
NGETO neglection
NGETU neglectful
NGIEC negligence
NGIIL negligible
negligibly
NGLHR Nigel Short
NGLNL nigglingly
NGRIE Niger River
NGTAE night-raven
NGTAL negotiable
NGTAO negotiator
NGTHD nightshade
NGTHF night shift
NGTHR nightshirt
NGTLN night-blind
NGTLS nightclass
NGTRS nightdress
NGTUS Night Nurse
NGTVL negatively
NGTVS negativism
negativist
NGTVT negativity
NHLSI nihilistic
NHMAU Nahum Nahum
NIBTN nail-biting
NIPLS nail polish
NJBLA Najibullah
NLIYN nullifying
NLMIM nelumbiums
NLYAH Nelly Sachs
NMELM nom de plume
nom-de-plume
NMELS numberless
NMGAH nomography
NMLNS nimbleness
NMLSL namelessly
NMNLA nominal par
NMNLN No Man's Land
NMNLS nominalise
nominalism
nominalist
NMNLZ nominalize
NMNTL nominately
NMNTO nomination
NMNTV nominative
NMRLG numerology
NMRTA no more than
NMRTO numeration
NMRUL numerously
NMSAI numismatic
NMTEA name the day
NMYAB namby-pamby
NNAMN non-payment
NNAUA non-natural
NNELS non-realist
NNERU non-ferrous
NNHLN nonchalant
NNILN non-violent
NNITO non-fiction
NNITR nunciature
NNLGE non-aligned
NNLSE nonplussed
NNLSN nonplusing
NNMKN non-smoking
NNNES no-nonsense
NNOPO nincompoop
NNOTN non-content
NNRNE non-drinker
NNSMN Nina Simone
NNTET nineteenth
NNTRE non-starter
NNYSO Nancy Astor
NOACS Neofascism
Neofascist
NOELS neorealism
neorealist
NPLOI Napoleonic
NPLWR nipplewort
NPNHA nepenthean
NPOOI nephologic
NPRAU no par value
NPRLG nephrology
NPTAI naphthalic

Words marked ❑ can also be spelled with an initial capital letter

NPTSI	nepotistic
NRAAC	Norman arch
NRAAL	narratable
NRASA	Norman Shaw
NREGN	nerve agent
NREIR	nerve fibre
NRETN	Norbertine
NREYA	nurseryman
NRHAD	northwards
NRHOE	North Korea
NRHON	northbound
NRHRE	northerner□
NRISS	narcissism
	narcissist
NROAI	narcomania
NROBA	narrow boat
	narrow-boat
NROCS	narrowcast
NRODW	narrow down
NROES	narcolepsy
NRONS	narrowness
NSAMI	nystagmoid
NSAON	nose around
NSCLC	no such luck
NSCMA	nosocomial
NSGAH	nosography
NSIGO	nesting-box
NSLGS	nosologist
NSLPA	nasal spray
NSPRE	nosy parker
NSTTI	nose to tail
NSUTU	nasturtium
NTAAA	not far away
NTAEA	nitrazepam
NTAFA	not half bad
NTAFO	not far from
NTAHL	Nathan Hale
NTAKT	no thanks to
NTANT	not say no to
NTBLT	notability
NTCAC	not a chance
NTCAL	noticeable
	noticeably
NTEIE	no the wiser
NTEJC	natterjack
NTEMS	nethermost
NTFAL	notifiable
NTFMN	not of a mind
NTHNN	not shining
NTHSM	not the same
NTIAI	nitric acid
NTIGA	Nottingham
NTIGU	nothing but
NTIIU	nutritious
NTIKN	nit-picking
NTILN	not willing
NTITK	not mistake
NTLOE	not allowed
NTLRS	nettlerash
NTLTA	natalitial
NTMGN	not imagine
NTNTE	not another
NTOAL	nationally
	notionally
NTOEF	not come off
NTOGG	not long ago
NTOHO	nationhood
NTOKN	not working
NTOLT	not too late
NTONT	not for nuts
NTOOE	not go to see
NTOOR	not to worry
NTOWD	nationwide
NTPII	notaphilic
NTPOA	not up to par
NTQET	netiquette
NTRAL	notarially
NTRAO	not dream of
NTRCE	nutcracker
NTRLA	natural gas
NTRLS	naturalise
	naturalism□
	naturalist
NTRLZ	naturalize
NTRPT	naturopath
NTRSI	notaryship
NTRSN	not present
NTTOA	notational
	nutational
NTTRA	natatorial
NTUHF	not much of a
NTUHO	not much cop
NTUJC	not subject
NTUTI	net curtain
NTVBA	native bear
NTVBR	native-born
NTVLN	native land
NTVNN	not even one
NTVNS	nativeness
NTVRC	native rock
NTVSI	nativistic
NTVTW	native town
NTWRH	noteworthy
NTXCL	not exactly
NUAHA	naumachias
NUCAE	Neufchâtel
NUEAL	noumenally
NUETN	nauseating
NUEUL	nauseously
NUIAL	nautically
NUIHN	nourishing
NUIUE	nautiluses
NUKHT	Nouakchott
NUOTR	neuroptera
NURLS	neutralise
	neutralism
	neutralist
NURLT	neutrality
NURLZ	neutralize
NURTO	neutrettos
NVGTO	navigation
NVIUC	Nova Iguacu
NVLHT	Nevil Shute
NVLMT	Nevill Mott
NVLOC	naval force
NVLSI	novelistic
NVREE	never-never
NVSOI	Nova Scotia
NWAEC	news agency
NWAGE	newfangled
	new-fangled
NWCSE	newscaster
NWELN	New Zealand
NWLTE	newsletter
NWMNE	newsmonger
NWNRN	new entrant
NWNTE	now and then
NWOLG	New College
NWPPR	newspapers
NWRAE	newsreader
NWRDC	new product
NWREN	New Orleans
NWRIA	new arrival
NWRLN	New Ireland
NWRTI	New Britain
NWSNS	newishness
NWWIE	news-writer
NWWRH	newsworthy
NXDOT	next door to
NXFIN	next friend
NXILN	next in line
OAAWT	on a par with
OAECN	opalescent
OAGWF	orange-wife
OAIAI	oxalic acid
OAJSA	Oranjestad
OALAD	on all hands
OALIE	on all sides
OALOE	of all loves
OALOR	on all fours
OAOIA	oratorical
OAPOA	on approval
OASAI	Omar Sharif
OAUAL	oracularly
OAUNS	opaqueness
OBHLO	on behalf of
OCDNA	occidental□
OCETA	orchestral
OCFRL	once for all
OCIAA	once in a way
OCLAO	oscillator
OCLGS	oncologist
OCLNS	occultness
OCLTO	osculation
OCLTR	osculatory
OCMAD	on commando
OCPEI	occupied in
OCPTO	occupation
OCREC	occurrence
OCRID	Oscar Wilde
OCSOA	occasional
OCTNL	oscitantly
OCTTO	oscitation
ODADS	old-maidish
ODELW	Oddfellows
ODIMN	ordainment
ODMTS	oedematose
ODMTU	oedematous
ODNAD	Oudenaarde
ODNIE	olden times
ODNRL	ordinarily
ODNTL	ordinately
ODNTO	ordination
ODONR	old country
ODPSE	Oedipus Rex
ODRAE	order paper
ODRBU	order about
ODRIE	orderlines
ODRTL	obdurately
ODUDE	Old Hundred
ODVCA	Ordovician
ODWRD	olde-worlde
OEABN	one-man band
OEACS	open access
OEADU	over and out
OEAEI	opera seria
OEAEU	oleraceous
OEAIN	operations
OEALS	opera-glass
OEAOS	opera house
OEATN	overacting
OEAUF	opera buffa
OEBRE	overburden
OECAG	overcharge
OECEU	open cheque
OECLT	operculate
OECMB	overcome by
OECMN	overcoming
OECNP	overcanopy
OECOE	Okeechobee
	overcooked
OEEAS	oxeye daisy
OEEPS	overexpose
OEETN	overeating
OEETS	operettist
OEFKN	one of a kind
OEFPI	one of a pair
OEFRU	oleiferous
OEGAH	oleography
OEGNU	oleaginous
OEGON	overground
OEGOT	overgrowth
OEHAE	overheated
OEHNE	open-handed
	overhanded
OEIEL	one-sidedly
OEIFR	overinform
OEIGU	opening-out
OEINL	obediently
OEINT	obedient to
OEISR	overinsure
OELAE	overloaded
OELOE	overlooked
OELTE	open letter
OELTO	ocellation
OELUC	overlaunch
OEMDS	overmodest
OEMNE	open-minded
OEMRE	open market
OEMSE	overmaster
OENCL	overnicely
OENLG	oceanology

Words marked □ can also be spelled with an initial capital letter

OENOL	one and only
OENON	ocean-going
OENRU	oceanarium
OENTE	one another
OEOFC	overoffice
OEPAE	overplayed
OEPAS	overpraise
OEPIE	overpriced
OEPII	oleophilic
OEPIO	open prison
OERCO	overreckon
OERDN	overriding
OERFN	over-refine
OERLN	overruling
OESAE	overstated
OESAG	overslaugh
OESAO	open season
	overshadow
OESBL	oversubtle
OESCE	open secret
OESEN	overseeing
OESOE	overshower
OESPL	oversupply
OESRA	overspread
OESRD	overstride
OESRI	overstrain
OESRK	overstrike
OESRN	overstrung
OESRS	overstress
OESSM	open sesame
OETEA	open the way
	over the way
OETEO	over the top
	over-the-top
OETRE	overturned
OETTM	one at a time
OEWIH	overweight
OEWNE	overwinter
OEWRE	overworked
OEWSL	overwisely
OFAAC	off balance
	off-balance
OFCAL	officially
OFCAO	officiator
OFCBO	office-book
OFHBA	off the beam
OFHCF	off the cuff
	off-the-cuff
OFHFC	off the face
OFHHO	off the hook
OFHMR	off the mark
OFHRE	off the reel
OFHWL	off the wall
	off-the-wall
OFIEC	off-licence
OFNEB	offended by
OFNEL	offendedly
OFNEU	offenceful
OFNRS	offendress
OFNSU	off one's nut
OFRBG	Oxford bags
OFRBI	offers bail
OFRBU	Oxford blue
OFRKE	offer a knee
OFSAE	obfuscated
OFUTN	off-putting
OFWOD	of few words
OGKRU	Olga Korbut
OGNSA	organismal
OGNSI	organismic
OGNZN	organizing
OGTIG	oughtlings
OHAEU	ochraceous
OHAOO	Ophiacodon
OHHLI	ophthalmia
	ophthalmic
OHORC	ochlocracy
OHRAK	other ranks
OHRHL	otherwhile
OHROA	other woman
OIACI	oligarchic
OIAEU	olivaceous
OIERE	Oliver Reed
OIGOE	owing money
OIIAL	originally
OIIAO	originator
OINAL	orientally
OIOIO	ovipositor
OISNS	otioseness
OIUNS	odiousness
OIURS	obituarist
OJCIE	objectives
OJCLS	objectless
OLANE	oil painter
OLCTO	on location
OLGNL	obligingly
OLGTO	obligation
OLGTR	obligatory
OLSNS	owlishness
OLTOA	oblational
OLTRT	obliterate
OMRDU	osmiridium
OMTDU	ommatidium
ONBLT	obnubilate
ONLGS	oenologist
ONMNA	ornamental
ONMNE	ornamented
	ornamenter
ONPTN	omnipotent
ONSIN	omniscient
ONTNS	ornateness
ONTOI	ornithosis
ONVRU	omnivorous
OOATC	onomastics
OOCSO	on occasion
OODMR	oboe d'amore
OOEAE	ozone layer
OOEEI	orogenesis
	orogenetic
OOEFE	on one's feet
OOEGM	on one's game
OOELG	on one's legs
OOEMN	on one's mind
OOEMR	on one's mark
OOETE	on one's toes
OOEWR	of one's word
OOHRN	oropharynx
OOOIA	orological
OOTGN	odontogeny
OOTLG	odontology
OOTLI	odontalgia
	odontalgic
OOTMT	odontomata
OOUDT	orotundity
OPESO	oppression
OPESV	oppressive
OPGAC	oppugnancy
OPOII	oophoritis
OPORU	opprobrium
OPSLS	opposeless
OPSTL	oppositely
OPSTO	opposition
OPSTT	opposite to
ORAHA	Oireachtas
OSDOA	obsidional
OSERC	obstetrics
OSHDL	on schedule
OSLTL	obsoletely
OSPAU	oesophagus
OSQIU	obsequious
OSRAC	observance
OSRAL	observable
	observably
OSRCE	obstructed
OSRCO	obstructor
OSRDO	oestradiol
OTAAC	outbalance
OTADN	outs and ins
OTADS	outlandish
OTAEU	outrageous
OTAGI	outbargain
OTAIE	ostracized
OTASO	out-passion
OTCEV	optic nerve
OTEAC	on the watch
OTEAD	on the cards
OTEAI	on the tapis
OTEAO	on the wagon
OTEAT	on the way to
OTEEA	outgeneral
OTEEC	on the bench
	on the fence
OTEEE	on the level
OTEFR	outperform
OTEHA	on the cheap
OTEHL	on the shelf
	on the whole
OTEIE	on the tiles
OTELC	of the clock
	on the block
OTELN	on the blink
	on the slant
OTELR	on the alert
OTELT	on the slate
OTENI	on the anvil
OTEOE	on the money
	on the ropes
OTEOK	on the rocks
OTEOO	on the dot of
OTEOS	on the house
	on the loose
OTERI	on the brain
OTERS	on the cross
OTERT	on the fritz
OTERW	on their own
	on the prowl
OTESO	out-pension
OTESR	outmeasure
OTETM	on the stump
OTEUE	on the outer
	on the quiet
OTEUO	on the buroo
OTEVO	on the eve of
OTFEC	out of reach
OTFHC	out of whack
OTFHP	out of shape
OTFHS	out of phase
OTFIC	Otto Frisch
OTFIH	out of sight
OTFLC	out of place
OTFOC	out of touch
OTFON	out of joint
OTFOR	out of court
	out of doors
	out-of-doors
OTFOT	out of sorts
OTFOU	out of focus
OTFRE	out of order
OTFRN	out of print
OTFTC	out of stock
OTFYC	out of synch
OTGAA	Otto Graham
OTGNU	octogynous
OTHDA	octahedral
OTHDO	octahedron
	octohedron
OTIAL	obtainable
OTILE	outfielder
OTILI	outvillain
OTIMN	obtainment
OTITN	outfitting
	outwitting
OTLSE	outbluster
OTLWN	outflowing
OTMLS	optimalise
OTMLZ	optimalize
OTMSI	optimistic
OTNAA	out and away
OTNIE	oftentimes
OTNIL	ostensible
	ostensibly
OTNLM	out on a limb
OTNUA	octangular
OTOAH	osteopathy
OTOAL	optionally
OTOEI	osteogenic
OTOID	of two minds
OTOII	Ostpolitik
OTOLS	orthoclase
	osteoblast
	osteoclast
OTOOA	orthogonal

OTORN outpouring
OTOTC orthoptics
OTOTR orthoptera
OTOTS orthoptist
OTOUC out to lunch
OTPSE octopusher
OTRAH outbreath'd
OTRII outer limit
OTRPC outer space
OTSNS obtuseness
OTTEC outstretch
OTTLO out at elbow
OTTTO outstation
OTTVL optatively
OTUCT obtruncate
OTVOA Octavio Paz
OTWEE outsweeten
OTWNE outswinger
OUOOO oculomotor
OWAEE or whatever
OWEEE or whenever
or wherever
OYEAO oxygenator
OYEDB oxygen debt
OYEMS oxygen mask
OYETN oxygen tent
OYOOI oxymoronic
OYUBK on your bike
PAAAE pray a tales
PAAGS phalangist
PAAON play around
PAATN play-acting
PAAUC play a hunch
PACNL prancingly
PADJU plat du jour
PADSI peau de soie
PADTR plauditory
PADYR Plaid Cymru
PAEAE peacemaker
PAEAI planetaria
PAEAU place value
PAEBO prayer book
prayerbook
prayer-book
PAEDW played-down
PAEFO peace of God
PAEIE Peace River
PAELS plate glass
PAEOE peace-lover
PAEUL peacefully
PAFLO playfellow
PAGNL plangently
PAGON playground
PAHEB peach melba
PAHST play host to
PAIAS pharisaism
PAICL pratincole
PAIEE planimeter
Praxiteles
PAINS placidness
PAIRS plagiarise
plagiarism
plagiarist
PAIRZ plagiarize
PAISM pianissimo
PAKNL prankingly
PAKOI planktonic
PALCS phallicism
PALHL pearl-shell
PALHT pearl white
PALIE Pearl River
PALKN pearly king
PALNS pearliness
PAMCS pharmacist
PAMDS plasmodesm
psalmodise
PAMDU plasmodium
PAMDZ psalmodize
PAMLS plasmolyse
PAMLZ plasmolyze
PAMSM plasmosome
PAMTC pragmatics
PAMTS pragmatise
pragmatism
pragmatist
PAMTZ pragmatize
PANHN plainchant
PANMN praenomens
praenomina
PAOKR peacockery
peacock-ore
PAOKS peacockish
PAOOT pianoforte
PAOUM Paavo Nurmi
PAOYI phagocytic
PAPSE praeposter
PAPSU play possum
PAREO prairie dog
PASAE pear-shaped
PASDU praesidium
PASHO playschool
PASNL praisingly
PATCS plasticise
PATCT plasticity
PATCZ plasticize
PATIK play tricks
PATLN platteland
PATRA praetorian
PATRN plastering
PATRU Praetorius
PATSA phantasmal
PATSI phantasmic
PATSM phantasime
PATSN practising
PATTO plantation
PATUN play truant
PAUSM plaguesome
PAWIE play-writer
PAWIH playwright
PAYGA pharyngeal
PAYUE platypuses
PBDPA Pobedy Peak
PBIFC public face
PBIHN publishing
PBLDS pebbledash
PBSEC pubescence
PCAIL peccadillo
piccalilli
PCAUC pack a punch
PCBWE pace-bowler
PCEBA packet boat
packet-boat
PCEFL pocket-fuls
PCESI packet-ship
PCFCS pacificism
pacificist
PCFCT pacificate
PCHNA Pocahontas
PCIAE pectinated
PCIAI pectic acid
PCIGO packing-box
PCLAL peculiarly
PCLAT peculiar to
PCLFR poculiform
PCLTO peculation
PCMRE pockmarked
PCOAL pectorally
PCORP pictograph
PCPCE pickpocket
pick-pocket
PCRSU picaresque
PDGGC pedagogics
PDGGS pedagogism
PDHHO pad the hoof
PDLBA paddle-boat
PDLGS pedologist
PDMNE pedimented
PDNUA peduncular
PDRRE pedereroes
PDRWK Paderewski
PDSRA pedestrian
PEAAL prepayable
PEAEC prevalence
PEAEL preparedly
PEAEO prepare for
PEAER pied-à-terre
PEAEU presageful
PEAIA prelatical
premarital
PEAIU precarious
predacious
PEALN prevailing
PEAMN prepayment
PEATO precaution
PEBOI presbyopia
presbyopic
PEBTR presbytery
PECEC prescience
PECIE prescribed
prescriber
PECNL piercingly
PEDCR pseudocarp
PEDNL pleadingly
PEEAL preferable
preferably
PEEDN pretendant
PEEDR prebendary
Pretenders
PEEEC precedence
preference
PEEES predecease
PEEIA premedical
PEEIN prevenient
PEEMN preferment
PEESL prehensile
prepensely
PEESO precession
prehension
pretension
pre-tension
PEETA present-day
PEETN predestine
predestiny
presenting
PEETO prevention
PEETR prefecture
PEETV preceptive
preventive
PEGAL pledgeable
PEHLG psephology
PEIAL poetically
predicable
PEICT plebiscite
PEIEC presidency
PEIIM presidiums
PEIIR presidiary
PEINF presignify
PEIPS predispose
PEIST preciosity
PEISU plesiosaur
PEITI paediatric
PEITO prediction
PEITR prehistory
PEITV predictive
PEIUL preciously
previously
PEIUT previous to
PELNE preplanned
PELSL peerlessly
PELSO preclusion
PELSV preclusive
PEMNN pre-eminent
PEMRO pre-embryos
PEMTO pre-emption
PEMTV pre-emptive
PENCI pleonectic
PENNL pregnantly
PENSI pleonastic
PENSN prednisone
PEOCR preconcert
PEOEA phenomenal
PEOEC prepotence
prepotency
PEOEO phenomenon
PEOHL paedophile
PEOHR plerophory
PEOIO prepositor
PEOIU precocious
PEONS precognise
PEONZ precognize
PEORS phenocryst
PEOSS prepossess

PEOYI phenotypic
PEPRU puerperium
PERAG prearrange
PESGN press agent
PESHA press ahead
PESLS press flesh
PESNL pleasantly
pleasingly
pressingly
PESNR pleasantry
PESOA presswoman
PESOE presswomen
PESOR pieds noirs
PESRN pressuring
PESRO press proof
PESRS pressurise
PESRZ pressurize
PETMC pretty much
PETNS prettiness
PETPS pretty pass
PETRC Puerto Rico
PETWL pretty well
PEUAL presumably
PEUIE prejudiced
PEUIU preludious
PEULF pre-qualify
PEUMS presurmise
PEUPS presuppose
PEUSR precursory
PEUSV precursive
PFEFS puffer fish
PFPSR puff pastry
PGAII pegmatitic
PGAIU pugnacious
PGETR pigmentary
PGLSI pugilistic
PGOHL pigeonhole
pigeon-hole
PGOPS pigeon-post
PGOTE pigeon-toed
PGYHE pygmy shrew
PGYHL pigmy whale
PIAAI prima facie
PIAEA private war
PIAEI philatelic
PIAEY Private Eye
private eye
PIAIE privatized
PIAON prima donna
PIBLT pliability
PICPE principled
principles
PICPT principate
PICSL princessly
PIEAL primevally
PIEOA prizewoman
PIEOE prime mover
PIEON prime donne
PIEUL pridefully
PIGHI Pringsheim
PIGSL priggishly
PIIAA primiparae
primiparas
PIIEE privileged
PIIII poikilitic
PIIPS Philippise
PIIPZ Philippize
PIIRT Philip Roth
PIITN philistine
PIKBU prink about
PIKLE painkiller
PILSL painlessly
PINDE poignadoes
PINNL poignantly
PIOCM prison camp
PIODA primordial
PIODU primordium
PIOEI primogenit
PIOMN prisonment
PIOOH philosophy
PIOPL poison pill
PIOYI psilocybin
PIRTS prioritise
PIRTZ prioritize
PISHO priesthood
PISLK priestlike
PISNL puissantly
PISNS prissiness
PISTI poinsettia
PITCN psittacine
PITFE point after
PITLN point-blank
PIYUS Privy Purse
PIZUE Prinz Eugen
PJRTO pejoration
PJRTV pejorative
PKAON poke around
PKBNE poke-bonnet
PKRAE poker-faced
PKRSL pokerishly
PLAEU paleaceous
PLAOI polyatomic
PLARU pellagrous
PLATU polyanthus
PLBAE pall-bearer
PLBTM phlebotomy
PLCAN phlyctaena
PLCEA phlyctenae
PLCII polyclinic
PLCIU Polyclitus
PLCRI polycarpic
PLCRM polychrome
polychromy
PLDCY polydactyl
PLDNU paludinous
PLECN Palaeocene
PLEIE pulverized
PLESO Palmerston
PLETE palmettoes
PLEZI Palaeozoic
PLFRU piliferous
PLGAI phlegmatic
PLGMS polygamist
PLGMU polygamous
PLGSO phlogiston
PLHDA polyhedral
PLHDO polyhedron
PLHMI Polyhymnia
PLHSO polyhistor
PLIAC pelvic arch
PLIAE pulvinated
PLIEL Pulcinella
PLIGF pulling-off
PLIGO Pilkington
PLIMN palliament
PLINS pallidness
PLITO palliation
PLITV palliative
PLIUA pellicular
PLMCS polemicist
PLMRS polymerise
PLMRZ polymerize
PLMSS palimpsest
PLMTI polymathic
PLNLG palynology
PLNMA polynomial
PLNRM palindrome
PLNSA Polynesian
PLOCS pillowcase
PLOIO polyominos
PLOLC pillow-lace
PLOSI pillowslip
PLOTL pillow talk
PLPAI polyphagia
PLPEU Polyphemus
PLPOD polyploidy
PLPOI polyphonic
PLPRO poll-parrot
PLRAE palm reader
PLRMG pilgrimage
PLRMS pilgrimise
PLRMZ pilgrimize
PLRNS paltriness
PLSDE palisadoes
PLSEE pilastered
PLSMU polysemous
PLSNA Palm Sunday
PLSPR poles apart
PLSUO polish up on
PLTAL palatially
PLTCA politician
PLTCE politicoes
PLTCS politicise
PLTCZ politicize
PLTES polytheism
polytheist
PLTHL pilot whale
PLTIH pilot light
PLTLS palatalise
PLTLZ palatalize
PLTNS politeness
PLTOS pilot house
PLTTD pilot study
PLTTR polite term
PLUEL pollutedly
PLUIL pellucidly
PLYAS palsy-walsy
PMELN pummelling
PMRNA Pomeranian
PNABD pineal body
PNADE panhandler
PNADU panjandrum
PNAEC pancake ice
Pentateuch
PNAEE pentameter
PNAER pentahedra
PNAEU pennaceous
PNAHO pentathlon
PNAHR pentachord
PNAIE pinnatiped
PNAOA pentagonal
PNAOI pentatonic
PNARS pentaprism
PNASI penmanship
PNAUA pennatulae
pennatulas
PNBEL pine beetle
PNCLD pina colada
piña colada
PNCLI penicillin
PNDGR Pont du Gard
PNEBU ponce about
PNEMN ponderment
PNEOI pandemonic
PNERC Pontefract
PNETV pendentive
PNFIA pan-African
PNGRS panegyrise
panegyrist
PNGRZ panegyrize
PNHNL pinchingly
PNHRA panther cap
PNHRN pantherine
punch-drunk
PNHRS pantherish
PNHUE penthouses
PNIET pentimenti
pentimento
PNIIA pontifical
PNIIE pontifices
PNILN pencilling
PNINF pension off
PNINR pensionary
pensioners
PNKRE pine kernel
PNKTE Pinakothek
PNLGS penologist
PNLPS penelopise
PNLPZ penelopize
PNLSI Panglossic
PNLVS pan-Slavism
pan-Slavist
PNLYO penalty box
PNMCT Panama City
PNMNA Panamanian
PNMRE pine marten
PNMRU penumbrous
PNNEL pine needle
PNNUA penannular
peninsular
PNOHS pansophist
PNOII pantomimic

Code	Word
PNOOE	pundonores
PNORP	pantograph
PNPIA	panoptical
PNRAI	pancreatic
	pancreatin
PNRBS	pan-Arabism
PNSAI	Panislamic
PNSAL	punishable
PNSEO	pentstemon
PNSMN	punishment
PNTAE	punctuated
PNTAI	penetralia
PNTAL	penetrable
	penetrably
	punctually
PNTAO	penetrator
PNTLN	Pinot Blanc
PNTLO	punctilios
PNTNL	penitently
PNTRN	puncturing
PNUHN	pen-pushing
PNUNR	penguinery
PNUTC	pin-buttock
PNYHR	penny share
PNYIC	penny-piece
	penny-pinch
PNYLN	penny-a-line
PNYOA	pennyroyal
PNYOT	pennyworth
PNYTC	penny stock
POAAD	propaganda
POAAO	propagator
POACS	prosaicism
POAOA	Protagoras
POAVC	pro hac vice
POAYT	prokaryote
POCAE	Poor Clares
POCIE	proscribed
	proscriber
POCNU	proscenium
POCUT	prosciutti
	prosciutto
PODNL	ploddingly
POEAC	provenance
POEAE	promenader
POEAS	prove false
POEBA	proverbial
POECA	proseuchae
POEDN	proceeding
POEHA	Promethean
POEHU	Prometheus
	promethium
POEIO	progenitor
POELN	propellant
	propellent
POELS	proteolyse
POENM	proper name
POENS	phoneyness
	properness
POENU	proper noun
POEOI	pro memoria
POEPR	pro tempore
POERN	pioneering
POESL	propensely
POESN	processing
POESO	procession
	profession
	propension
POEST	propensity
POETE	propertied
POETI	protectrix
POETL	projectile
POETN	projecting
	protecting
	protestant❑
	protesting
POETO	projection
	protection
POETU	Propertius
POETV	protective
POEUA	procedural
POEUE	procedures
POEUO	prosecutor
POEVT	protervity
POGAL	ploughable
POGBC	plough back
POGIT	plough into
POGWS	ploughwise
POHAT	poor health
POHLI	prothallia
POHLU	prothallus
POHTS	prophetess
POIAL	phonically
	prodigally
	profitable
	profitably
	providable
	proximally
POICA	provincial
POIEC	prominence
	providence❑
POIEO	provide for
POIFO	profit from
POIIE	prohibited
POIIN	proficient
	provisions
POIIT	propitiate
POIIU	prodigious
	prolixious
	propitious
POILS	profitless
POISR	promissory
POLGC	profligacy
POLGT	profligate
POLIE	proclaimed
	proclaimer
POLNL	prowlingly
POLVT	proclivity
POMNE	phorminges
POMRO	proembryos
PONCA	Phoenician
PONSI	prognostic
PONXS	phoenixism
POOAI	phototaxis
POOEE	photometer
POOEI	photogenic
POOER	photometry
POOGT	prolongate
POOIA	pronominal
POOLN	plot of land
POOLS	protoplasm
	protoplast
POONE	pronounced
	propounder
POONL	profoundly
POOOL	Paolo Rolli
POOON	protozoans
POORP	photograph
POOTO	proportion
POOTR	promontory
POOUO	prolocutor
POOUS	prologuise
POOUZ	prologuize
POOYA	prototypal
POOYI	photolysis
	photolytic
POPCO	prospector
POPCU	prospectus
POPNS	promptness
POPOI	phosphoric
POPOU	phosphorus
POPRN	Prosperina
POPRT	prosperity
POPRU	prosperous
POPSD	prompt side
PORAO	procreator
PORCE	protracted
PORCO	protractor
PORDN	protrudent
	protruding
POREO	proprietor
PORME	programmed
	programmer
PORPI	protreptic
PORSE	Procrustes
PORSO	protrusion
PORSV	protrusive
POTAE	prostrated
POTEE	prostheses
POTEI	prosthesis
	prosthetic
POTLG	proctology
POTNL	plottingly
POTRA	proctorial
POTRS	proctorise
POTRZ	proctorize
POTTT	prostitute
POUAL	procurable
POUAO	procurator
POUBN	procumbent
POUCO	pronuncios
POUDT	profundity
POUGT	promulgate
POUIL	producible
POUSO	propulsion
POUSV	propulsive
POUTO	production
POUTV	productive
POYAU	propylaeum
PPAET	Papiamento
PPDUI	piped music
PPECR	peppercorn
PPEML	pepper mill
	peppermill
PPEMN	peppermint
PPESO	puppet show
PPLAE	papillated
PPLNN	pipelining
PPLRE	papal brief
PPLRS	papal cross
	popularise
PPLRT	popularity
PPLRZ	popularize
PPLTO	population
PPLUL	populously
PPRAE	paper-faced
PPRAG	paper gauge
PPRAH	paper-mâché
PPRDN	piperidine
PPRIC	paper birch
PPRIE	paper tiger
PPRLG	papyrology
PPRNF	paper-knife
PPROE	paper money
PPROR	paperboard
PPVRN	papaverine
PRAAT	parramatta
PRAEC	permanence
	permanency
PRAET	portamenti
	portamento
PRAII	parmacitie
PRARS	permafrost
PRATO	periastron
PRAVI	portal vein
PRBLS	parabolise
PRBLZ	parabolize
PRBMT	parabemata
PRCIA	periclinal
PRCLI	portcullis
PRCLU	Paracelsus
PRCNH	pyracantha
PRDCO	paradoctor
PRDSA	paradisiac
PRDSI	paradisaic
PRDTT	peridotite
PRDXN	pyridoxine
PRDXR	paradoxure
PREAC	purveyance
PREBM	parcel bomb
PREBW	parcel-bawd
PREEI	paraenesis
PREEN	purse-seine
PREFO	parted from
PREHN	Persephone
PREIE	Parmenides
PREOI	Persepolis
PRERT	perpetrate
PRESL	perversely
PRESO	perversion
PREST	perversity
PRETA	Perfect Day

Code	Word
PRETG	percentage
PRETL	percentile
PRETN	perfecting
	perverting
	porpentine
PRETO	perception
	perfection
	permeation
PRETU	portentous
PRETV	perceptive
	perfective
	permeative
PREUE	persecuted
PREUO	persecutor
PREUT	perpetuate
	perpetuity
PREWS	parcelwise
	parcel-wise
PRFLO	portfolios
PRGIE	paraglider
PRGLO	pyrogallol
PRGNU	pyrogenous
PRHLO	perihelion
PRHRO	porphyrios
PRHSN	purchasing
PRHSR	purchasers
PRIEC	pertinence
	pertinency
PRIHA	Portishead
PRIIA	parricidal
PRIIL	participle
PRIIN	percipient
PRIIU	perfidious
	pernicious
PRIKT	pernickety
PRILG	persiflage
PRILS	partialise
PRILT	partiality
PRILZ	partialize
PRIMN	parliament
PRINA	Persian cat
	Persian War
PRINS	Persianise
PRINZ	Persianize
PRISN	Parkinson's
PRISO	permission
PRISV	permissive
PRITN	persistent
	persisting
PRITV	persistive
PRIUA	particular
PRIUL	perviously
PRKRO	perikaryon
PRLEL	parallelly
PRLGS	paralogise
	paralogism
PRLGZ	paralogize
PRLHZ	Purple Haze
PRLMI	Paralympic
PRLNL	purblindly
	purulently
PRLNS	portliness
PRLPE	paralipses
PRLPI	paralipsis
PRLRI	Purple Rain
PRLSN	paralysing
PRLST	pyrolusite
PRLUL	perilously
PRLXN	perplexing
PRLXT	perplexity
PRMCU	Paramecium
PRMDN	pyrimidine
PRMEI	paramnesia
PRMNA	pyromaniac
PRMRB	Paramaribo
PRMSU	perimysium
PRMTE	pari-mutuel
PRMTI	parametric
	perimetric
	pyrometric
PRMTR	parameters
	peremptory
PRMUC	paramouncy
PRNAL	parentally
PRNEA	parenteral
PRNEL	Pirandello
PRNHM	parenchyma
PRNHO	parenthood
PRNLS	parentless
PRNRA	paranormal
PROAE	perforated
PROAL	pardonable
	pardonably
	personable
	personally
PROAO	percolator
	personator
	portolanos
PROEU	purposeful
PROHO	personhood
PROIA	periodical
PROIT	perfoliate
PROIU	parvovirus
PROLK	parrot-like
PROMN	performing
PROMR	performers
PRONN	purloining
PROTA	periosteal
PROTN	purporting
PROTT	pernoctate
PROTU	periosteum
PRPEA	peripheral
	pork-pie hat
PRPEI	paraplegia
	paraplegic
PRPOI	pyrophobia
PRPRN	perspiring
PRPRS	paraphrase
	paraphrast
	periphrase
PRPTI	peripeteia
PRPYE	paraphyses
PRRDE	partridges
PRRTO	peroration
PRSAL	perishable
	perishably
PRSAT	Paris Pacts
PRSBO	phrase book
PRSEI	parascenia
PRSEN	Parisienne
PRSLN	paraselene
PRSOI	periscopic
PRSOT	Portsmouth
PRSPM	parish pump
	parish-pump
PRSRE	Paris green
	Paris-green
PRSTS	parasitise
	parasitism
PRSTZ	parasitize
PRTEI	perithecia
PRTIH	peritricha
PRTLO	Port Talbot
PRTNA	peritoneal
PRTNS	puritanise
	puritanism□
PRTNU	peritoneum
PRTNZ	puritanize
PRTOP	paratroops
PRUAL	perdurable
	perdurably
	permutable
PRUBN	perturbing
PRUBT	perturbate
PRUIN	parturient
PRUNL	pursuantly
	pursuingly
PRUNS	porousness
PRUSO	percussion
	persuasion□
PRUST	perquisite
PRUSV	percussive
	persuasive
PRUUS	Portuguese
PRUVN	pursuivant
PRWLE	parawalker
PRWNL	periwinkle
PRXDS	peroxidise
PRXDZ	peroxidize
PRXSA	paroxysmal
PRYAO	Perry Mason
PRYIC	party piece
PSACD	postal code
PSAEA	passageway
PSAHO	pistachios
PSAON	pass around
	piss around
	push around
PSATS	piss artist
PSBLE	past belief
PSBTO	push-button
PSCAS	post chaise
	post-chaise
PSDNU	Posidonius
PSEAA	passed away
PSEGR	passengers
PSEHE	post-echoes
PSEOE	passed over
PSEOR	pasteboard
PSERS	pasteurise
PSERZ	pasteurize
PSESL	pass easily
PSESO	possession
PSESV	possessive
PSHMU	posthumous
PSIEC	pestilence
PSIGU	passing-out
PSILO	postillion
PSILT	postillate
PSINT	passionate
PSMDR	post-modern
PSMRE	post-mortem
PSMSE	pass muster
	past master
	postmaster
PSOAC	pesto sauce
PSOAE	pastorales
PSOAL	pastorally
PSOFC	Post Office
PSOGI	pistol grip
PSORN	piston ring
PSOWI	pistol-whip
PSPNN	postponing
PSPRU	postpartum
PSRCL	past recall
PSSRP	postscript
PSTKN	piss-taking
PSTOA	positional
	push too far
PSTVL	positively
PSTVS	positivism
	positivist
PSUAC	postulancy
PSUAE	postulated
PSUAL	pasturable
PSULN	pasquilant
PSUND	pasquinade
PSYAE	pasty-faced
PTAOA	Pythagoras
PTBLR	patibulary
PTCNA	Pete Conrad
PTECN	putrescent
PTEHN	Pat Metheny
PTELE	potbellied
	pot-bellied
PTEWE	put between
PTEYN	putrefying
PTFNE	pathfinder
PTGIS	pit against
PTGNA	Patagonian
PTHET	pitch tents
PTHLC	pitch-black
PTHLE	pith helmet
PTHNS	patchiness
	pitchiness
PTHNU	patching up
PTHOG	put through
PTHOR	patchboard
PTHRU	pitcherful
PTIGF	putting-off
PTIIA	patricidal
PTIIN	patricians

Words marked □ can also be spelled with an initial capital letter

PTIIT patriciate
PTILS patrialise
PTILT patriality
PTILZ patrialize
PTIRH patriarchy
PTITS patriotism
PTIWR pittie-ward
PTIYN petrifying
PTJNO put a jinx on
PTLNL petulantly
PTLSL pitilessly
PTNAE put on paper
PTNAL patentable
PTNIL potentilla
PTNIT potentiate
PTNLC put in place
PTNNC put on an act
PTNNS patentness
PTNNT put an end to
PTNRA put on trial
PTNRE put in order
PTNSL pit oneself
PTNTO patination
PTOAU petrolatum
PTOBM petrol bomb
PTOEI pathogenic
PTOEO put money on
PTOES pétroleuse
PTOET put to death
PTOHM put to shame
PTOLE put to sleep
PTOLN patrolling
PTOLP petroglyph
PTOPM petrol pump
PTOTN petrol tank
PTOUS put to nurse
PTOWR put forward
PTOYI patronymic
PTRAI pityriasis
PTRAL paternally
PTRBR Petersburg
PTRER Peter Pears
PTREY Peter Debye
PTRLK Peter Blake
PTROD Peter Fonda
PTROR Peter Lorre
PTROS Peterhouse
PTRRE patereroes
PTRRO Peter Brook
PTSEE Pete Seeger
PTSEI patisserie
PTSOT put a stop to
PTSUG Pittsburgh
PTTOE petitioner
PTTON petit point
PTTPI petits pois
PUAAA plug away at
PUDCT pound Scots
PUDME Paul Dombey
PUDOC pound force
PUDRN plundering
PUEFC pluperfect
PUETA prudential
PUEUL pausefully
PUEUR Paul Eluard
PUIGA pruning-saw
PUIGE pouring wet
PUINL pruriently
PUKNS pluckiness
PUKUE Paul Kruger
PUMRO Paul Merton
PUMSA Paul McStay
PUMTN plummeting
PUNWA Paul Newman
PUORC plutocracy
PURVR Paul Revere
PUTON poultroone
PUVLR Paul Valéry
PUWRE Plum Warner
PVTEA pave the way
PWBOE pawnbroker
PWEBU powder blue
PWEPF powder puff
PWERO powder room
PWESO powder snow
PWRLC power block
PWRLN power plant
PWRON power point
PWROS powerhouse
power-house
PWRRK power brake
PWRRS power trust
PWRUC power lunch
PWRUL powerfully
PXLAE pixillated
PXLTO pixilation
PYATR phylactery
PYEVE pay-per-view
PYHAR psychiatry
PYHBL pay the bill
PYHCI pay the cain
PYHLG psychology
PYHPT psychopath
PYIAL physically
PYILG physiology
PYLTX phyllotaxy
PYLXR phylloxera
PYNSA pay one's way
PYORT pay court to
PYORU Peyton Rous
PZIAO pizzicatos
PZLMN puzzlement
PZLNL puzzlingly
PZLOE puzzle over
QAATN quarantine
QAEMI Quatermain
QAENO quaternion
QAENR quaternary❑
QAGNS quagginess
QAIGS quaking ash
QAIYN qualifying
QAMSL qualmishly
QANNS quaintness
QARCP quadriceps
QARFI quatrefoil
QARLE quarreller
QARNA quadrantal
QARNE quadrantes
QARNI quadrennia
QARNL quadrangle
QARPE quadruplet
quadruplex
QARRM quadrireme
QARSC quadrisect
QARTR quadrature
QARVU quadrivium
QASUR quaestuary
QATFE quantified
quantifier
QATII quartzitic
QATRA quarter-saw
QATRG quarterage
QATRN quartering
QATRO quarteroon
QATTE quantities
QECAL quenchable
QECLS quenchless
QENCU Queen's Club
QENLN Queensland
QENTN quernstone
QEOCT Quezon City
QERCO quebrachos
QESNS queasiness
QETNL questingly
QETOE questioner
QEYNL queryingly
QIARN quinacrine
QIKAC quick march
QIKAD quicksands
QIKHR quickthorn
QIKNN quickening
QIKNS quirkiness
QIKRC quick trick
QIKTC quick-stick
QIMSE quizmaster
QIPOU quid pro quo
QISEC quiescence
quiescency
QISOE quit scores
QITOC quiet voice
QITPE quintuplet
RAAEE reawakened
RAESI readership
RAETT real estate
RAFIN real friend
RAFRS reafforest
RAIAE reanimated
RAIAL realizable
RAIGG reading age
RANME real number
RAOAL reasonable
reasonably
RAOWT reason with
RARNE roadrunner
RASDS rhapsodise
rhapsodist
RASDZ rhapsodize
RASML reassemble
RASRN reassuring
RATNI real tennis
RATVL reactively
RATVT reactivate
RAWNO Rear Window
RAWRH roadworthy
RAYIE ready mixed
RAYOE ready money
RAYOU ready to run
RBEBN rubber band
RBECA robber-crab
RBEIE rubberized
RBENC rubberneck
RBETE rubber tree
RBETO Ribbentrop
RBFAI riboflavin
RBFOT rub off on to
RBGNU rubiginous
RBIAL rubrically
RBIAO rubricator
RBIDN rebuilding
RBIHI rubbish tip
RBIIA rabbinical
RBIKE rib-tickler
RBKNL rebukingly
RBLIU rebellious
RBNOD Robin Hood's
RBNRO robing-room
RBNRW Rob Andrews
RBNTI Rubinstein
RBOFS ribbonfish
RBOWR ribbonworm
RBRAA Robert Adam
RBRBL Robert Bolt
RBRCA Robert Cray
RBRCP Robert Capa
RBREE Robert E Lee
RBRHN rebirthing
RBRKC Robert Koch
RBRKT Robert Kett
RBRPE Robert Peel
RBSLE ruby silver
RBSNS robustness
RBTAL rebuttable
RCADI Richard III
RCADO Richardson
RCAGE rectangled
RCAMN reclaimant
RCBTO rock bottom
rock-bottom
RCCAL recyclable
RCCUS racecourse
RCDVS recidivism
recidivist
RCEII Roche limit
RCENL recreantly
RCETI racket-tail
rickettsia
RCETO recreation
re-creation
RCGIE recognized
recognizer
RCGRE rock garden
RCHDO Rock Hudson

RCHPE rock-hopper
RCHTE race hatred
RCIAL receivable
reclinable
RCIFO recoil from
RCIGA Rockingham
RCILS recoilless
RCIYN rectifying
RCLAL recallable
RCLSL recklessly
RCMEC recommence
recumbence
recumbency
RCMES recompense
RCMNS Rachmanism
RCMNT Rachmanite
RCMTO racemation
RCNES raconteuse
RCNIE reconciled
reconciler
reconsider
RCNNS recentness
RCNPS Racing Post
RCOSI rectorship
RCOWT reckon with
RCPAL receptacle
RCPEC recipience
recipiency
RCPGO rock pigeon
RCPOA reciprocal
RCPRT recuperate
RCRCA rectricial
RCREC recurrence
RCRNE rack-renter
RCSLO rock salmon
RCTOE Richthofen
RCTTO recitation
RCTTV recitative
recitativi
RCUEC recrudesce
RCUMN recoupment
RCUTN recruiting
RCVRN recovering
RDABG red cabbage
RDADI ride and tie
ride-and-tie
RDAOB ride a hobby
RDATC red lattice
red-lattice
RDBDI ride bodkin
RDCLN ridiculing
RDCLS radicalise
radicalism
RDCLU ridiculous
RDCLZ radicalize
RDCRT redecorate
RDDIA red admiral
RDEAL redeemable
redeemably
RDELS rudderless
RDERN red herring
RDHRO ride herd on
RDIDO Red Windsor

RDLHS Rudolf Hess
RDLLK riddle-like
RDLNL redolently
riddlingly
RDLOE red-blooded
RDLOT Rudolf Otto
RDMNA rudimental
RDMTO redemption
RDMTR redemptory
RDMTV redemptive
RDNAC redundancy
RDNBO riding-boot
RDNCO riding-crop
RDOIE Radio Times
RDOOD radiosonde
RDRCP radarscope
RDSGE redesigned
RDTIE Rod Steiger
RDTWR Rod Stewart
RDURN redcurrant
RDYOL Roddy Doyle
REAUT re-evaluate
REEGN re-emergent
RELGS rheologist
REMTI rheumatoid
REMTS rheumatism
REOIA rhetorical
RESLI Rhea Silvia
Rhea Sylvia
REUNS ruefulness
RFAJN Rafsanjani
RFANN refraining
RFATO refraction
RFATR refractory
RFATV refractive
RFEHN refreshing
RFEIL reflexible
RFEOP rifle-corps
RFETO reflection
RFETV reflective
RFINS ruffianism
RFLEC refulgence
refulgency
RFNAL refundable
RFNMN refinement
RFRAL referrable
reformable
RFRAO reformados
RFRCU Reform Club
RFRET referred to
RFRNU referendum
RFSHA refuse-heap
RFTTO refutation
RFVLE rift valley
RGELF ragged left
RGENS raggedness
ruggedness
RGESO regression
RGESV regressive
RGIKA Reggie Kray
RGLMN regalement
RGLRS regularise
RGLRT regularity

RGLRZ regularize
RGLTN regulating
RGLTO regelation
regulation
RGLTR regulatory
RGLTV regulative
RGMFI ragamuffin
RGMNA regimental
RGMNE regimented
RGNBL Raging Bull
RGNBR Regensburg
RGNRC regeneracy
RGNRT regenerate
RGNSI regentship
RGOAL regionally
RGOLN rag-rolling
RGOPN regrouping
RGRAI Roger Vadim
RGRAO Roger Bacon
RGREA regarded as
RGRLS regardless
RGROR Roger Moore
RGRUL rigorously
RGSEE registered
RGTAD rightwards
RGTBU right about
RGTFA right of way
RGTHL right whale
RGTNL right angle
right-angle
RGTRW right-drawn
RGTUL rightfully
RGTUR right guard
RHASN rehearsing
RIDCO rain-doctor
RIEDS raise a dust
RIEHR raise a hare
RIEOE raise money
RIETN rhinestone
RIFRE reinforced
RIFRS rainforest
RIKNA reim-kennar
RIOCP rhinoscopy
RIOEO rhinoceros
RIOIU rhinovirus
RIONU raisonneur
RITRN roistering
RITRU roisterous
RIYDR reioyndure
RJCAL rejectable
RJCIL rejectible
RJESU Raj Persaud
RJIIG rejoicings
RJVNS rejuvenise
RJVNT rejuvenate
RJVNZ rejuvenize
RKSNS rakishness
RLCAC reluctance
RLCLA rollcollar
RLCTO relocation
RLEAL relievable
RLEGL rolled gold
RLGES religieuse

RLGOE religioner
RLGTO relegation
RLHAE Ralph Nader
RLIGI rolling-pin
RLIKN rollicking
RLNLS relentless
RLNUS relinquish
RLOKN rollocking
RLSAL relishable
RLSOC Rolls-Royce®
RLTNT relating to
RLTOA relational
RLTVL relatively
RLTVS relativise
relativism
relativist
RLTVT relativity
RLTVZ relativize
RLVNL relevantly
RLVNT relevant to
RLXTO relaxation
RLYNL rallyingly
RLYON rally round
RMADN ram-raiding
RMAEU rampageous
RMALA rampallian
RMDAL remediable
remediably
remedially
RMDLE remodelled
RMDLS remediless
RMHCL ramshackle
RMITU remain true
RMLNL ramblingly
rumblingly
RMMEE remembered
RMNHM remand home
RMNNL ruminantly
RMNRT remunerate
RMNSU Romanesque
RMNTN ruminating
RMNTO ruminate on
rumination
RMNTS remonetise
RMNTV ruminative
RMNTZ remonetize
RMRAL remarkable
remarkably
RMREU remorseful
RMRLS remoralise
RMRLZ remoralize
RMSIL remissible
RMSNS remissness
RMSOT Ramos-Horta
RMTAC remittance
RMTFO remote from
RMTNS remoteness
RMUDN remoulding
RMURO rumpus room
RMVLA removal van
RMYUP rumpy-pumpy
RNAKN ransacking
RNBNE ring binder

RNEAL	renderable
RNEBA	runner bean
RNEOE	Range Rover®
RNEPS	rinderpest
RNEVU	rendezvous
RNFWT	run off with
RNGNS	röntgenise
RNGNZ	röntgenize
RNGTO	renegation
RNHCL	ranshackle
RNHOG	run through
	run-through
RNHOS	ranchhouse
RNHSO	run the show
RNIGA	Running Man
RNIGF	running off
RNIKA	Ronnie Kray
RNINS	rancidness
RNLAE	ringleader
RNLRS	Ronald Ross
RNMSE	ringmaster
	ring-master
RNNCE	ring-necked
RNNUU	ranunculus
RNOAL	ransomable
RNOAT	run to earth
	run to waste
RNOIE	randomizer
RNOIN	Renzo Piano
RNOLS	ransomless
RNONE	rencounter
RNONS	randomness
RNOTR	Ringo Starr
RNOWS	randomwise
RNPET	run up debts
RNRSO	run a risk of
RNSAE	ring-shaped
RNSEC	renascence
RNVTO	renovation
ROAON	root around
ROENS	rootedness
ROGNZ	reorganize
ROGRE	roof garden
ROIGU	rooting-out
ROPLC	riot police
ROSNS	rootsiness
ROSRE	rood screen
ROSUI	roots music
RPAAL	repealable
	repeatable
RPAEL	repeatedly
RPBIA	republican
RPBIG	rope bridge
RPDAL	repudiable
RPDAO	repudiator
RPDNE	rope-dancer
RPESO	repression
RPESV	repressive
RPGAC	repugnance
RPIGF	ripping off
RPLEC	repellence
	repellency
RPLMR	ripple-mark
RPLNL	ripplingly
RPNAC	repentance
RPNDW	roping-down
RPNNL	repiningly
RPNRE	ripsnorter
RPOAC	reprobance
RPOCE	reproacher
RPORN	rip-roaring
RPOUE	reproduced
	reproducer
RPRAL	reportable
RPREL	reportedly
RPRHS	repurchase
RPROR	repertoire
RPRSN	rephrasing
RPRTO	reparation
RPRTV	reparative
RPSTO	reposition
	re-position
RPSTR	repository
RPTIT	repatriate
RPTTO	repetition
	reputation
RPTTU	répétiteur
RPTTV	repetitive
	reputative
RPUSG	repoussage
RPWLE	rope-walker
RQIAL	requitable
RQIET	required to
RQISA	requiescat
RRLIE	Rural Rides
RRNTG	raring to go
RRTNA	Ruritanian
RRUEN	rerouteing
RSACE	researcher
RSALK	rascal-like
RSARN	restaurant
RSBCE	rust-bucket
RSBLT	risibility
RSCAE	rose-chafer
RSELN	Rossellini
RSETN	respecting
RSETU	respectful
RSETV	respective
RSGEL	resignedly
RSGET	resigned to
RSGFO	resign from
RSHDL	reschedule
RSHPE	rosehip tea
RSIAE	rusticated
RSIAL	rustically
RSIAO	respirator
RSIDN	rescinding
RSINE	Russian tea
RSINS	Russianise
RSINZ	Russianize
RSISO	rescission
RSIUO	restitutor
RSLAL	resolvable
RSLEC	resilience
	resiliency
RSLEL	resolvedly
RSLET	resolved to
RSLFO	result from
RSLNL	rustlingly
RSLSL	restlessly
RSLTL	resolutely
RSLTO	resolution
RSMLN	resembling
RSMTO	resumption
RSMTV	resumptive
RSNLN	rosaniline
RSNMN	resentment
RSNNL	resonantly
RSNTN	resonating
RSNUL	resinously
RSOAL	restorable
RSODN	respondent
RSOSR	responsory
RSOSV	responsive
RSPNT	resupinate
RSRCE	restricted
RSRDE	Rusbridger
RSREC	resorbence
	resurgence
RSREL	reservedly
RSRIE	restrained
	restrainer
RSRIO	resorcinol
RSRIT	reservists
	restraints
RSRTO	resorption
RSRTV	resorptive
RSSAC	resistance
RSSIL	resistible
	resistibly
RSUDN	resounding
RSWLL	rush wildly
RSWNO	rose window
RTACE	rat-catcher
RTASI	retransmit
RTATL	retractile
RTATO	retraction
RTATV	retractive
RTBLT	ratability
RTCLT	reticulate
RTEFR	rutherford❑
RTEMR	Rothermere
RTENS	rottenness
RTETA	rather than
RTIAL	retainable
RTIMN	retainment
RTLAO	retaliator
RTLSL	ruthlessly
RTNCL	retinacula
RTNNS	rotundness
RTOAL	rationally
RTOHI	retrochoir
RTOIU	retrovirus
RTOPC	retrospect
RTORD	retrograde
RTORS	retrogress
RTOSL	retrorsely
RTRAD	ritardando
RTRAL	returnable
RTRCU	Rotary Club
RTREL	ritornelli
	ritornello
RTRFO	retire from
RTRMN	retardment
	retirement
RTRNL	retiringly
RTSEI	rotisserie
RTSHL	Rothschild
RTWIE	Rottweiler
RUABN	rhubarbing
RUDBU	round about
	roundabout
RUDOE	round dozen
RUDOI	round robin
RUEAC	route-march
RUEBU	rouseabout
RUGLI	Ruud Gullit
RUHOS	rough-house
RUHRD	rough trade
RUHRF	rough-draft
RUHRN	rough-grind
RUHTF	rough-stuff
RUHUS	rough guess
RVAAL	revealable
RVBEL	rove beetle
RVCTO	revocation
RVCTR	revocatory
RVEAL	reviewable
RVEBD	review body
RVECP	review copy
RVGMN	ravagement
RVKMN	revokement
RVLMN	revilement
RVLNL	revilingly
RVLRS	revalorise
RVLRZ	revalorize
RVLTO	revelation❑
	revolution
RVLTR	revelatory
RVNEU	revengeful
RVNHS	revanchism
	revanchist
RVNUL	ravenously
RVONE	rev counter
RVRAI	river basin
RVREH	River Lethe
RVREL	reversedly
RVRIL	reversible
	revertible
RVRLT	River Plate
RVRNL	reverently
RVRVE	rave review
RVSMN	ravishment
RVSOA	revisional
RVTLZ	revitalize
RVVLS	revivalism
	revivalist
RVVNL	rev ivingly
RWERI	raw recruit
RWLID	Rawalpindi
RWNBA	rowing boat
RWRAL	rewardable

Words marked ❑ can also be spelled with an initial capital letter

RWRLS rewardless
RYEKN Roy Jenkins
RYEOA rhyme royal
rhyme-royal
RYERO Ray Reardon
RYHIA rhythmical
RYHRE Ray Charles
RYLCN royal icing
RYLEL royal jelly
RYLLS royal flush
RYLUG royal burgh
RYNRW Roy Andrews
RYRIO Roy Orbison
RZMTZ razzmatazz
RZRDE razor-edged
RZRHR razor-sharp
SAAAI scarabaeid
SAAHM stay-at-home
SAALA stay afloat
SAALK seamanlike
SAAON swan around
SAASI seamanship
SABEL stag beetle
SABHN stay behind
SABNL stabbingly
SABNS scabbiness
shabbiness
SABWE seam bowler
SACCC spatchcock
SACEL starchedly
SACIT search into
SACNS scarceness
SADAO snapdragon
SADBU stand about
SADLN stand-alone
SADLS scandalise
SADLU scandalous
SADLZ scandalize
SADNB standing by
SADNO stand in for
SADNW stand in awe
SADOI stand to win
SADON shard-borne
standpoint
SADPO stand up for
SADRA stand treat
stand trial
SADRB standers-by
SADRC stand erect
SADRU slanderous
SADTL stand still
standstill
SADUR stand guard
SAEAD shake hands
SAEAE shamefaced
space cadet
SAEAN Shane Warne
SAEBA sealed-beam
SAEDW scaled-down
SAEEA Siamese cat
SAEGR scavengery
SAEIE Snake River
SAELC swage block

SAENE share index
SAENO shame on you
SAEOA spacewoman
SAEOC stagecoach
SAEOR skateboard
SAEPN Sea Serpent
sea serpent
SAERB space probe
SAERC scapegrace
SAERF spacecraft
stagecraft
statecraft
SAETC sea lettuce
SAETF scare stiff
SAEUL shamefully
SAEYA scaredy-cat
SAFAA Sea of Japan
SAFLE scaffolder
SAFLG scaffolage
SAFOP staff corps
SAFUS staff nurse
SAGHN slang-whang
SAGNS shagginess
slanginess
SAGRN staggering
swaggering
SAGZN stargazing
SAHNL scathingly
SAIAL statically
SAICI sea biscuit
SAIEU spadiceous
SAIGA sealing-wax
Stalingrad
SAIGE soaking wet
SAIGF staving off
SAIGU sharing out
SAIHL Spanish fly
SAIIE stabiliser
stabilizer
SAILS spaniolise
SAILT spaniolate
spatiality
SAILU Stanislaus
SAILZ spaniolize
SAINN stationing
SAINR stationary
stationery
SAITC statistics
SAITI snap into it
SAIUL spaciously
SAKAE stark naked
stark-naked
SAKEO Shackleton
SAKNF slacken off
SAKNL spankingly
SAKNN slackening
SAKNO Stan Kenton
SAKPN shank's pony
SAKSL sparkishly
SALCL small-scale
SALHN stable hand
SALIC small piece
SALLS stable lass

SALNL snarlingly
SALNS stableness
SALOR small hours
SALRN small print
SALRU small group
SALTN scarlatina
SALTO spallation
SALUE Stan Laurel
SALWN swallowing
SAMNS smarminess
SAMON swarm round
SAMRN stammering
SAMSI shammashim
SANMN sea anemone
SANNL stagnantly
SANTN stagnating
SANTO stagnation
SAOAE Sean O'Casey
SAOAL seasonable
seasonably
seasonally
SAOCP statoscope
SAOCS shadowcast
SAOSE sea monster
SAPLU stamp album
SAPNL snappingly
SAPNS snappiness
SAPRN scampering
SAPSL scampishly
snappishly
SAPWE soap powder
SAREE starry-eyed
SARNS starriness
SARUL scabrously
SASNS sparseness
SASRS seamstress
SASSE star system
SASTO stay shtoom
SATAE Stan Tracey
SATCT spasticity
SATGI start again
SATHR start a hare
SATLC smart aleck
SATNL slantingly
startingly
SATNS scantiness
Spartanism
SATRL slatternly
SATRN scattering
shattering
smattering
SATSN start using
SATUT stay true to
SAUAL statutably
SAUEA statute cap
SAUGO sea surgeon
SAUMA slap-up meal
SAUPN swan-upping
SAUSU statuesque
SAVLN starveling❑
SAVTO starvation
SAWLO sea swallow
SAWRL stalwartly

SBAIA sabbatical
SBAIE submariner
SBCIE subscriber
SBCTL subacutely
SBEEI subgeneric
SBEFG subterfuge
SBEIN submediant
SBERS sable brush
SBESO submersion
subversion
SBESV subversive
SBETF subjectify
SBETN subletting
SBETO subjection
subreption
subsection
subvention
SBETV subjective
SBEUE subgenuses
SBEUN subsequent
SBIEC subsidence
SBIGA sublingual
SBIIA subliminal
SBIIE subdivider
subsidizer
SBIIR subsidiary
SBISO submission
SBISV submissive
SBITN subsistent
subsisting
SBLNL sibilantly
SBLNS subtleness
SBLTE subtleties
SBLTO sibilation
SBLVA subclavian
SBOTN subroutine
SBQAI subaquatic
SBQEU subaqueous
SBRCE subtracter
SBRCO subtractor
SBRHE seborrhoea
SBRHN subtrahend
SBRIA suborbital
SBRIE sobersides
SBRNL soberingly
SBRTS sybaritism
SBSOO Sebastopol
SBTAA substratal
SBTAU substratum
SBTTO substation
SBTTT substitute
SBUAE subjugated
SBUAL subsumable
SBUAO subjugator
SBULA subnuclear
SBUOA submucosae
submucosal
SBUTR subculture
SCAAO sick as a dog
SCACU social club
SCAET Sacramento
SCAIE socializer
SCAII such as it is

Words marked ❑ can also be spelled with an initial capital letter

Code	Word
SCANS	socialness
SCAWR	social work
SCEAE	succedanea
SCEAL	societally
SCEAR	secretaire
SCEDN	succeeding
SCELV	Secret Love
SCENS	sacredness
SCEOU	Sacre Coeur
SCESO	succession
SCESR	successors
SCESU	successful
SCESV	successive
SCHRD	saccharide
SCHRF	saccharify
SCHRN	saccharine
SCHRS	saccharise
	saccharose
SCHRZ	saccharize
SCICL	succinctly
SCIIE	sacrificer
SCINS	sectionise
SCINZ	sectionize
SCLAO	sicilianos
SCLBL	sicklebill
SCLNS	sickliness
SCLRR	secular arm
SCLRS	secularise
	secularism
	secularist
SCLRT	secularity
SCLRZ	secularize
SCLSE	sick-listed
SCNBS	second-best
SCNHM	second home
SCNHN	second hand
	second-hand
SCNRL	second role
SCNRT	second-rate
SCNSL	second self
SCNWN	second wind
SCOAC	sacrosanct
SCOAH	sociopathy
SCOER	sociometry
SCPAC	sycophancy
SCRNS	secureness
SCROA	sacerdotal
SCRTE	securities
SCRTS	securitise
SCRTZ	securitize
SCSOO	sucks to you!
SCUBN	succumbing
SCUEC	succulence
	succulency
SCUEL	secludedly
SDBAD	sideboards
SDBSD	side by side
SDCNL	seducingly
SDCRS	seductress
SDEFC	side effect
SDENS	soddenness
	suddenness
SDEWB	Sidney Webb
SDLBC	saddleback
SDLLS	saddleless
SDLRO	saddle roof
SDLSA	saddle soap
SDLSR	saddle sore
	saddle-sore
SDLUL	sedulously
SDLWT	saddle with
SDMRO	side mirror
SDNHI	sedan-chair
SDRSA	siderostat
SDRTO	Söderström
SDSDL	sidesaddle
SDSRK	sidestroke
SDTNS	sedateness
SDTRU	sudatorium
SDUAA	Sadducaean
SDULM	sodium lamp
SDWNE	sidewinder
SEABR	Svetambara
SEACI	seecatchie
SEADA	Shenandoah
SEADS	sherardise
	stewardess
SEADZ	sherardize
SEAPE	she's apples
SEAVC	seek advice
SEBSE	step by step
	step-by-step
SECAL	sketchable
SECLE	stenciller
SECLS	speechless
SECRT	stercorate
SECTA	stench trap
SEDII	speed limit
SEDNS	speediness
	steadiness
SEDNU	speeding-up
SEDOS	Sverdlovsk
SEDRS	slenderise
SEDUL	speedfully
SEEAI	Steve Davis
SEEBR	Swedenborg
SEEGA	stereogram
SEEJB	Steven Jobs
SEELG	speleology
SEEOE	Steve Jones
SEEON	Steve Young
SEETP	stereotype
	stereotypy
SEEVT	Steve Ovett
SEFGA	Steffi Graf
SEFTE	stepfather
SEGBL	sleigh bell
SEGNE	stem ginger
SEHNO	Stephenson
SEHNR	Stephen Fry
SEHNT	stephanite
SEHOG	see through
	see-through
SEHWT	seethe with
SEIAL	scenically
SEIFO	sheriffdom
SEIIA	specifical
SEIIE	sterilized
	sterilizer
SEIIN	see visions
SEILS	specialise
	specialism
	specialist
SEILT	speciality
SEILZ	specialize
SEIMT	sterigmata
SEISS	speciesism
	speciesist
SEIST	speciosity
SEITO	speciation
SEIUL	speciously
SEKBU	speak about
SEKNF	steak knife
SEKNL	sneakingly
	speakingly
SEKNS	sneakiness
SEKOS	steakhouse
SEKPO	speak up for
SEKSI	speak a ship
SEKSL	sneakishly
SELDE	stepladder
SELFR	stelliform
SELHL	stealthily
SELLT	stellulate
SELNL	spellingly
	stealingly
	swellingly
SELNS	seemliness
	smelliness
	steeliness
SELON	spellbound
SELRA	swell organ
SELRK	shelldrake
SELRO	shellproof
SELTL	stellately
SEMAG	steam gauge
SEMCD	spermicide
SEMCT	spermaceti
SEMHL	sperm whale
SEMNS	steaminess
SEMON	sperm count
SEMTE	stepmother
SENAD	sternwards
SENTA	seeing that
SEORP	stenograph
SEOTE	See You Then
SEPHN	sheepshank
SEPNI	stepping-in
SEPNL	sweepingly
SEPNS	sleepiness
SEPNU	stepping-up
SEPOG	sleep rough
SEPRN	step-parent
SEPRO	Shepparton
SEPSL	sheepishly
SEPTK	sweepstake
SEPTT	seed-potato
SERAE	shearwater
SERNL	sneeringly
SERNS	smeariness
SESCE	seersucker
SESIC	stem stitch
SETAL	spectrally
SETBL	sheathbill
SETCE	spectacled
	spectacles
SETCS	scepticism
SETER	sweetheart
SETHR	sweatshirt
	sweat-shirt
SETLN	sweat gland
SETLO	sweat blood
SETML	sweet smell
SETNN	sweetening
SETNS	sleetiness
SETOE	sweet-toned
SETRA	stentorian
	sweetbread
SETRE	sweet brier
SETRN	sweltering
SETRU	stertorous
SETTR	spectators
SETTU	sweat it out
SETUI	sheet music
SEUAO	speculator
SEUKN	spelunking
SEVHN	sleevehand
SEVLS	sleeveless
SEZNS	sleaziness
SEZWR	sneezewort
SFBIE	soft-boiled
SFEAC	sufferance
SFEAI	suffer a fit
SFEAL	sufferable
	sufferably
SFEFO	suffer from
SFGAD	safeguards
SFHAE	soft-headed
SFHPE	soft hyphen
SFIAC	suffigance
SFIIN	sufficient
SFOTO	soft option
SFPLT	soft palate
SFPRO	safe period
SFRGS	suffragism
	suffragist
SFRPR	safari park
SFRSI	safari suit
SFSOE	soft-spoken
SFSWE	soft sawder
	soft sowder
SFTBL	safety belt
SFTLS	Safety Last
SGAFA	signal flag
SGEAE	segregated
SGERN	signet-ring
SGETN	suggesting
SGETO	suggestion
SGETR	segmentary
SGETV	suggestive
SGIIL	seguidilla
SGRAD	sugar candy

Code	Word
	sugar daddy
SGRNS	sugariness
SGROG	sugar tongs
SGTAL	sagittally
SHCLT	sphacelate
SHCTS	Schick test
SHEBR	Schoenberg
SHEII	sphaeridia
SHETE	Schweitzer
SHIFE	Schlieffen
SHIMN	Schliemann
SHITR	Schwitters
SHLRT	sphalerite
SHLSI	scholastic
SHMCE	Schumacher
SHMTS	schematise
	schematism
SHMTZ	schematize
SHNLK	sphinxlike
	Sphynx-like
SHODY	schooldays
SHOGR	schoolgirl
SHOMA	school-ma'am
SHOMR	schoolmarm
	school-marm
SHOWR	schoolward
	schoolwork
SHRAD	scherzandi
	scherzando
SHRCT	sphericity
SHRIA	spheroidal
SHRLK	spherelike
SHRLS	sphereless
SHSAI	schismatic
SHZCR	schizocarp
SHZIA	schizoidal
SIAAL	slip a cable
SIACR	spinal cord
SIALN	spiralling
SIARA	stir abroad
SIAUT	Said Aouita
SIAUU	spiraculum
SIBLT	shibboleth
SIBWE	spin-bowler
SICBC	switchback
SICCC	spitchcock
SICFO	switch from
SICTE	sticcatoes
SICWR	stitchwort
SIDCO	spin doctor
SIDVN	skin-diving
SIECA	spider crab
SIEEE	swine fever
SIEEI	sui generis
SIEIL	Spice Girls
SIELN	snivelling
	swivelling
SIELT	stipellate
SIEMT	spider mite
SIEOL	slime mould
SIEOS	shire horse
SIERN	swine-drunk
SIEUL	spitefully
SIFNL	sniffingly
SIFNN	stiffening
SIFNS	sniffiness
SIGFA	sling off at
SIGNL	stingingly
	swingingly
SIGNS	stinginess
SIGRN	sniggering
SIGUA	sling mud at
SIHNS	slightness
SIHRE	smithereen
SIIAA	spirit away
SIIAL	suicidally
SIIEL	spiritedly
SIILS	spiritless
SIIUU	spirituous
SIKHF	stick shift
SIKNL	smirkingly
SIKNS	stickiness
SIKPO	stick up for
	stick-up job
SIKTP	sticky tape
SIKTU	stick it out
SILCT	spiflicate
SILIE	still lifes
SILIT	stillbirth
SILLG	shillelagh
SILNA	Scillonian
SILNL	stiflingly
SILNO	still and on
SILSI	sciolistic
SIMGA	seismogram
SIMLG	seismology
SIMNL	skimmingly
	swimmingly
SIMRN	shimmering
SIMSE	skirmisher
SIMTS	stigmatise
	stigmatism
	stigmatist
SIMTZ	stigmatize
SINII	scientific
SIPNL	skimpingly
	skippingly
SIPNS	skimpiness
	slippiness
SIPRL	slipperily
SIRNL	stirringly
SIRPU	stirrup cup
SISEL	spinsterly
SISRA	slipstream
SISRN	Swiss franc
SITAN	Saint-Saëns
SITBU	shift about
SITEU	skittle out
SITNL	stintingly
SITNS	shiftiness
SITSL	skittishly
SIUAE	stimulated
	stipulated
SIUAL	stimulable
SIUAO	stimulator
	stipulator
SIWIH	shipwright
SLAAA	salmanazar
	solfataras
SLAEL	saltarelli
SLARA	sell abroad
SLASI	sultanship
SLATN	self-acting
SLAUD	salmagundi
	salmagundy
SLAUE	self-abuser
	syllabuses
SLBDT	sell-by date
SLBET	self-breath
SLBIU	salubrious
SLBLS	solubilise
SLBLT	solubility
SLBLZ	solubilize
SLBTE	salt-butter
SLCLA	saltcellar
SLCLT	salicylate
SLCNS	selectness
SLCPR	select part
SLCSI	solecistic
SLCTD	solicitude
SLCTM	salicetums
SLCTN	soliciting
SLCTU	solicitous
SLDCI	self-deceit
SLDFE	solidified
SLDIE	self-driven
SLDNA	self-denial
SLDNE	self-danger
SLDRA	salad cream
SLDRT	solidarity
SLDTT	solid-state
SLEFS	silverfish
SLEGL	silver-gilt
SLEIO	solferinos
SLENS	sullenness
SLESA	Silver Star
SLESD	silverside
SLETA	salientian
SLETE	self-esteem
SLHNT	sulphonate
SLHRS	sulphurise
SLHRT	sulphurate
SLHRU	sulphurous
SLHRZ	sulphurize
SLHTO	sulphation
SLIJC	self-inject
SLIRD	saltigrade
SLLVN	self-loving
SLMNE	salamander
SLMNS	solemnness
SLMRE	self-murder
SLMTL	self-mettle
SLNHI	splanchnic
SLNIA	solenoidal
SLNIL	splendidly
SLNLG	selenology
SLNNS	silentness
SLNOR	splendours
SLNRU	splendrous
SLOEL	salmonella
SLOET	silhouette
SLONS	sallowness
SLOWE	seldom when
SLOWR	sale of work
SLPAS	self-praise
SLPTE	salopettes
SLRGR	self-regard
SLRGT	sole rights
SLRLN	self-ruling
SLRLR	solar flare
SLRMT	scleromata
SLRNS	sultriness
SLROT	solar month
SLRTS	sclerotise
SLRTZ	sclerotize
SLSDW	splash down
	splashdown
SLSEE	self-seeker
SLSIC	sales pitch
SLSLR	sales clerk
	salesclerk
SLSOA	saleswoman
SLSYE	self-styled
SLTAR	split hairs
SLTEE	split-level
	splutterer
SLTHF	split shift
SLTHL	splotchily
SLTNW	split in two
SLTRA	solitarian
SLTRL	salutarily
	solitarily
SLTTA	solstitial
SLTTE	self-titled
SLTTO	salutation
SLTTR	salutatory
SLUAL	self-unable
SLVTO	salivation
SLWLE	self-willed
SLYIL	silly-billy
SLYIO	silly mid-on
SLYOT	sally forth
SMAHS	sympathise
SMAHZ	sympathize
SMAIE	summarized
SMAWR	Samian ware
SMBDE	somebodies
SMCRL	semicircle
SMECK	simnel cake
SMECL	Samuel Colt
SMEDW	simmer down
SMEHO	Samuel Hood
SMELK	summerlike
SMERS	symmetrise
SMERZ	symmetrize
SMETM	summer time
	summertime
SMHPR	Sam Shepard
SMILS	summitless
SMLCT	simplicity
SMLCU	Simplicius
SMLFE	simplified

simplifier
SMLNS simpleness
SMLRT similarity
SMLSI simplistic
SMLTD similitude
SMLTM simple time
SMLTO simulation
SMNAA simoniacal
SMNAK Simon Marks
SMNAU Simon Magus
SMNRA seminarian
SMNRS seminarist
SMNWI Simone Weil
SMOAL summonable
SMOBC summon back
SMOEC somnolence
somnolency
SMOIA symbolical
SMOIE symbolizer
SMQAE semiquaver
SMRAL somersault
SMRNS sombreness
SMTRC Samothrace
SMWEL semi-weekly
SNAAI Santa Maria
SNABS Sunday best
SNAHN sunbathing
SNALU Santa Claus
SNAMT syntagmata
SNAPS Sunday Post
SNAWO sandalwood
SNBGE sandbagger
SNCOH synecdoche
SNCSL sandcastle
SNDLA sand dollar
SNEIO sanbenitos
SNELN sanderling
Sunderland
SNEOE syntenoses
SNERA sense organ
sense-organ
SNETA sentential
SNFYN send flying
SNGAI San Ignacio
SNGOS sandgrouse
SNHLS Singhalese
SNHOA synchronal
SNHOI synchronic
SNHPE sand hopper
SNHRO Sun Chariot
SNHSS synthesise
SNHSZ synthesize
SNHTS synthetise
SNHTZ synthetize
SNHYI synchrysis
SNIAO syndicator
SNIET sentiments
SNIGA singing-man
SNIIE sensitized
SNILO sensible of
SNITR sunbittern
SNLDU singled out
SNLFL single file
SNLFR Single Form
SNLGS Sinologist
SNLNS singleness
SNLSA singles bar
SNLSE single-step
sunglasses
SNLWR Sunflowers
SNLZR sand lizard
SNMRI sand martin
SNNMR sans nombre
SNNMS synonymise
SNNMU synonymous
SNNMZ synonymize
SNNOI San Antonio
SNOAO syncopator
SNOEZ San Lorenzo
SNOIM sensoriums
SNOQI San Joaquin
SNQAO sine qua non
SNRDE Sangradoes
SNREI synergetic
SNRTS syncretise
syncretism
syncretist
SNRTZ syncretize
SNRUL sonorously
SNSEC senescence
SNSEL sinisterly
SNSIA sinusoidal
SNSOE synostoses
SNSRS songstress
SNTFE sanctified
sanctifier
SNTFR sonata form
SNTMN sanctimony
SNTOE sanctioned
SNTRA sanitarian
senatorial
SNTRL sanitarily
SNTRS song thrush
SNTRU sanatorium
Sanctorius
SNTTD sanctitude
SNTTO sanitation
SNUAL singularly
SNULS sensualise
sensualism
sensualist
SNULT sensuality
SNULZ sensualize
SNUNL sanguinely
SNUNR sanguinary
SNUNS sinfulness
SNUUL sensuously
SNWIE songwriter
SOADO scot and lot
SOAGU sporangium
SOAHU stomachful
SOAII stomatitis
SOAON shop around
SOBOE snowblower
SOBSL snobbishly
SOCMS Scotch mist
SOCSA Scotch snap
SODNL scoldingly
SODNS shoddiness
SODUR sword-guard
SOEAD shorewards
SOEAO stonemason
SOEEG Stonehenge
SOEFL shovelfuls
SOELN stone-blind
SOELR smoke alarm
SOEOR scoreboard
SOEOS smokehouse
storehouse
SOERE smoke-dried
SOETA sooner than
SOETC smokestack
SOETL stone-still
SOFAE snowflakes
SOFNL scoffingly
SOGAL spongeable
SOGBT sponge bath
SOGCK sponge cake
SOGDW sponge down
SOGIE slow-gaited
SOGLK spongelike
SOGNS sponginess
stodginess
SOGWR spongeware
SOHAE soothsayer
SOHNL soothingly
SOHRN smothering
SOHSI stochastic
SOHUL slothfully
SOHVN stop having
SOIGF showing off
showing-off
SOINS stolidness
SOITO spoliation
SOITR spoliatory
SOJME showjumper
SOKBL stork's bill
SOKEE shopkeeper
SOKNE stockinged
SOKNL shockingly
SOKNS spookiness
stockiness
SOKTL stock-still
SOLFE shoplifter
SOLNL scowlingly
SOLPR spoilsport
SOLSL spotlessly
SOMKN shoemaking
SOMLU storm cloud
SOMNS storminess
SOMON stormbound
SOMTO slow-motion
SOMUL stormfully
SOMVN slow-moving
SONNL swooningly
SONRS spoonerism
SONUL scornfully
SOOHL sporophyll
SOOHT sporophyte
SOOOI sporogonia
SOPNL stoopingly
SOPNS sloppiness
SOPNU stopping-up
SOPOG snowplough
SOSOA Scotswoman
SOSRA sponsorial
SOTAE short-dated
SOTAG short-range
SOTCL smooth calf
SOTCS Scotticise
SOTCZ Scotticize
SOTEA show the way
stop the gap
SOTHL sports hall
SOTIE short-lived
SOTLN shoot a line
SOTNL shoutingly
snortingly
sportingly
SOTNN shortening
SOTNS smoothness
snootiness
snottiness
sportiness
spottiness
SOTOE smooth over
SOTOT spout forth
SOTRA shortbread
SOTRS shortcrust
SOTTR short story
short-story
SOTTU shoot it out
SOTUL sportfully
SOTVL sportively
SOTWA sportswear
SOUAC shoyu sauce
SOWLE spot-welder
SOWNO shop window
SOWTE slow-witted
SOXAL Sioux Falls
SOYOR storyboard
SOYRK stony broke
stony-broke
SOYUS Stonyhurst
SOZNO sforzandos
SPAEA suprarenal
SPAIO sopraninos
SPEAE suppedanea
SPELS supperless
SPEMN sapperment
SPENA septennial
SPEVR septemviri
septemvirs
SPIAL septically
SPIGE sopping wet
SPIII syphilitic
SPILO septillion
SPITN septic tank
SPLAC suppliance
SPLCN supplicant
SPLCT supplicate
SPLHA sepulchral

Code	Word
SPLMN	supplement
	supplyment
SPLNE	supplanter
SPLNS	suppleness
SPLTO	suppletion
SPLUA	sepultural
SPNNS	supineness
SPOAL	supposable
	supposably
SPOEI	saprogenic
SPOEL	supposedly
SPOET	supposed to
SPOHT	saprophyte
SPOTN	supporting
SPOTR	supporters
SPOTV	supportive
SPRAG	supercargo
SPRAL	supernally
SPREE	superseded
	superseder
SPRIL	supertitle
SPRIN	supergiant
SPRIO	supervisor
SPRNS	superbness
SPROA	supernovae
	supernovas
	super-royal
	superwoman
SPROE	supermodel
	superpower
SPROI	supersonic
	supertonic
SPROL	superiorly
SPROT	superior to
SPRRS	supergrass
SPRRU	supergroup
SPRSE	suppressed
SPRSO	suppressor
SPRTL	separately
SPRTN	separating
SPRTO	separation
SPRTR	superstore
SPRTS	separatism
	separatist
SPRUA	superhuman
SPRXD	superoxide
SQECN	sequencing
SQETA	sequential
SRAAL	spreadable
SRAET	sordamente
SRALN	streamline
SRAOE	spread over
SRASN	surpassing
SRATN	surfactant
SRBLT	strobilate
SRBSA	strabismal
SRBSI	strabismic
SRBSU	strabismus
SRCEI	sericteria
SRCHN	stracchini
	stracchino
SRCNN	strychnine
SRCNS	spruceness
	strictness
	strychnism
SRCUA	structural
SRCUE	strictured
	structured
SRDLG	stridelegs
SRDLN	stridulant
SRDLT	stridulate
SRDLU	stridulous
SRDNL	stridently
SRDVR	Stradivari
SRDWY	strideways
SREAA	street Arab
	street arab
SREAI	sur le tapis
SREAT	shrievalty
SRECE	street cred
SREFL	streetfuls
SREGI	screen grid
SREHN	screeching
SREIA	Serge Lifar
SREIG	screenings
SRELM	streetlamp
SRELS	surrealism□
	surrealist
SREOG	sure enough
SREPA	screenplay
	street plan
SRESE	Stroessner
SRETN	serpentine
SRETS	sarmentose
	screen test
	serpentise
SRETU	sarmentous
SRETZ	serpentize
SREWR	streetward
SREWS	streetwise
SRFFE	strife-free
SRFLU	scrofulous
SRFOE	sure-footed
SRGAH	serigraphy
SRGLN	straggling
	struggling
SRGLO	struggle on
SRGNF	stroganoff
SRHRE	surcharged
	surcharger
SRIAI	sorbic acid
SRIAL	surgically
	surmisable
	survivable
SRIEA	serviceman
SRIEE	servicemen
	sortileger
	straitened
SRIEL	strainedly
SRIGU	sorting out
SRIHE	straighten
SRIHL	straightly
SRIHO	straight-on
SRIHU	straight up
	straight-up
SRIIE	serpigines
SRINS	sordidness
SRKBC	strike back
SRKDM	strike dumb
SRKDW	strike down
SRKGL	strike gold
SRKHM	strike home
SRKIT	strike into
SRKNL	strikingly
SRKPA	stroke play
SRKRO	strike root
SRKSI	strike sail
SRLGS	serologist
SRLNS	shrillness
SRLTE	strelitzes
SRLTI	strelitzia
SRLWR	scrollwork
SRLWS	scrollwise
SRMHN	scrimshank
	skrimshank
SRMLN	scrambling
SRMNU	stramonium
SRMTU	stromatous
SRNAL	shrinkable
SRNBA	string bean
SRNBC	shrink back
	spring back
	springbuck
SRNBN	string band
SRNBR	Strindberg
SRNBS	string bass
SRNEC	stringency
SRNED	stringendo
SRNFO	shrink from
SRNHL	stronghold
SRNLC	spring lock
SRNLK	springlike
SRNLN	sprinkling
SRNLR	Stranglers
SRNLS	springless
SRNNS	sereneness
SRNRL	spring roll
SRNRO	strongroom
SRNTD	spring tide
	springtide
SRNTE	strengthen
SRNTI	springtail
SRNTM	springtime
SRNVS	string vest
SRNWA	shrink-wrap
SROHG	sarcophagi
SROIE	sermonizer
SROLS	sarcoplasm
SRONE	surmounted
	surmounter
	surrounded
SROOE	sorrow over
SROOI	seriocomic
SRORA	Serbo-Croat
SRPAO	strappados
SRPEO	stripped of
SRPES	striptease
SRPHR	Shropshire
SRPIA	seraphical
SRPLU	scrupulous
SRPNI	strapontin
SRPNS	stripiness
	syrupiness
SRPOI	scriptoria
SRPON	strip joint
SRPTS	strepitoso
SRPUA	scriptural
SRPUE	Scriptures
SRRAL	sororially
SRRCD	sororicide
SRRSN	surprising
SRSLS	stressless
SRSMN	Stresemann
SRSOR	Strasbourg
SRTFE	stratified
SRTFR	stratiform
SRTGS	strategist
SRTHA	scratch pad
SRTHL	scratchily
SRTHN	scratching
	stretching
SRTHU	stretch out
SRTIU	struthious
SRTNE	scrutineer
SRTNS	scrutinise
SRTNZ	scrutinize
SRTSE	strathspey
SRUAE	serrulated
SRUGN	scrounging
SRVIE	stravaiger
SRVLE	shrivelled
SRVNK	Stravinsky
SRVNL	strivingly
SRVNN	scrivening
SRVPR	Shreveport
SRVTD	Shrovetide
SRWBR	Shrewsbury
SRWER	strawberry
SRWNS	shrewdness
SRWOS	shrewmouse
SRWSL	shrewishly
SRYAN	spray-paint
SSANN	sustaining
SSEAC	sustenance
SSEAI	systematic
SSEDR	suspenders
SSEHO	sisterhood
SSESO	suspension
SSESR	suspensory
SSESV	suspensive
SSETN	suspecting
SSETT	sustentate
SSETU	sestertius
SSETV	susceptive
SSIIU	suspicious
SSWNO	sash window
STARH	satyagraha
STELN	Sutherland
STFOM	set of rooms
STGIS	set against
STHLE	satchelled
STHPC	set the pace

Words marked □ can also be spelled with an initial capital letter

STIGF	setting-off
STIGU	setting-out
STIHT	set light to
STLDW	settle down
STLIE	satellites
STLII	satellitic
STLMN	settlement
STLNI	settling-in
STLWT	settle with
STNSL	set oneself
STNTN	set in stone
STOHE	set to three
STPOS	set up house
STPRT	set spurs to
STRAI	saturnalia□
STRTO	saturation
STSOG	set a sponge
STSRD	sit astride
STSYN	satisfying
STTRB	set store by
STUNN	set burning
STYAC	satay sauce
SUAEO	sausage dog
	sausage-dog
SUAHN	sousaphone
SUBLN	squabbling
SUBLO	Saul Bellow
SUBNL	snubbingly
SUBNS	stubbiness
SUBRL	stubbornly
SUBRN	slumbering
SUBRU	slumberous
SUDNL	soundingly
SUDNS	sturdiness
SUDOE	squadroned
SUDRN	shuddering
SUDRO	soundproof
	sound-proof
SUEAL	squeezable
SUECN	spumescent
SUEDM	saucer dome
SUEDU	stupendous
SUEEO	squeeze-box
SUEEU	squeeze out
SUEFL	saucerfuls
SUERI	souterrain
SUEYN	stupefying
SUFEF	shuffle off
SUFNS	scurfiness
	stuffiness
SUGAE	sour grapes
SUGNS	smudginess
SUGSL	sluggishly
SUHAD	southwards
SUHHN	South China
SUHOE	South Korea
SUHON	southbound
SUHRL	southernly
SUICI	Saurischia
SUIFA	studio flat
SUINS	stupidness
SUIUL	spuriously
	studiously
SUKNL	skulkingly
SULDT	squalidity
SULSL	soullessly
SUMLS	squamulose
SUMST	squamosity
SUNEE	squandered
	squanderer
	squint-eyed
SUNNL	stunningly
SUPNS	stumpiness
SUPRS	sculptress
SUPUA	sculptural
SUPUE	sculptured
SURAA	square away
SURDA	square deal
SURFO	square foot
SURIC	square inch
SURKO	square knot
SURLK	squirelike
SURLT	scurrility
SURLU	scurrilous
SURMA	square meal
SURML	square mile
SURNS	squareness
SURQE	soubriquet
SURRO	square root
SURRU	sauerkraut
SURSI	square sail
SURUT	square up to
SURWS	squarewise
SURWT	square with
SURYR	square yard
SUSAL	squashable
SUSSE	soul sister
SUTEU	scuttleful
SUTFE	stultifier
SUTNS	smuttiness
SUTOA	stuntwoman
SUTOP	Scunthorpe
SUTRN	sauntering
	stuttering
SUTSL	sluttishly
SUTVN	Sturtevant
SUUSO	shut up shop
SUVNS	scurviness
SUYRU	study group
SVGCU	Savage Club
SVGNS	savageness
SVLCU	Savile Club
SVNIT	seventieth
SVNRL	Savonarola
SVRNS	severeness
SVSOO	Sevastopol
SVULS	savourless
SWHSL	sow thistle
SWOTE	saw-toothed
SXAHN	Sex Machine
SXAUG	sexual urge
SXCLN	saxicoline
SXCLU	saxicolous
SXENO	sixteenmos
SXGSM	Sexagesima
SXHES	sixth sense
SXHOE	six-shooter
SXHRP	sex therapy
SXILO	sextillion
SXITL	Sex Pistols
SXLGS	sexologist
SXNBU	Saxony blue
SYABU	Sky Harbour
SYADS	say Kaddish
SYAKN	skyjacking
	skylarking
SYBRK	Szymborska
SYCAE	skyscraper
SYELT	say hello to
SYHLE	Seychelles
SYITC	stylistics
SYODY	say goodbye
SYOER	stylometry
SYPAE	say a prayer
SYUEL	say quietly
SZLNL	sizzlingly
SZRIT	suzerainty
TAAAT	tragacanth
TAASA	thalassian
TACLK	trance-like
TADSR	Thar Desert
TAEAK	trademarks
TAEAN	trade-falne
TAEAO	travelator
TAEFL	tradesfolk
TAEIC	tsarevitch
TAEIM	trapeziums
TAELN	travelling
TAELR	travellers
TAENO	trade union
TAEOE	travel over
TAEOT	trade route
TAEOU	travelogue
TAERC	trade price
TAERS	thale cress
TAESC	travel sick
	travel-sick
TAESN	traversing
TAETN	toad-eating
	travertine
TAETR	trajectory
TAEUA	trabeculae
	trabecular
TAEWR	travel-worn
TAEYL	trade cycle
TAFCA	traffic jam
TAFCE	trafficker
TAGNL	twangingly
TAHAE	tracheated
TAHII	tracheitis
TAHNS	trashiness
TAIAL	tragically
TAIIN	traditions
TAIOE	traditores
TAIOI	tragicomic
TAJRE	tear-jerker
TAKAO	thanks a lot
TAKFE	traik after
TAKRO	tracker dog
TAKUL	thankfully
TAKVN	track event
TALNL	trailingly
TALPE	tea clipper
TAMLE	trammeller
TAMTS	traumatise
	traumatism
TAMTZ	traumatize
TANUE	tea infuser
TAOAO	travolator
TAOBK	Thabo Mbeki
TAOTN	tramontana
	tramontane
TAPEO	trampled on
TAPLN	trampoline
TAQIL	tranquilly
TARLE	tea trolley
TARZL	to a frazzle
TASAO	translator
TASAU	transvalue
TASCO	transactor
TASDT	transudate
TASEC	transience
	transiency
TASEE	transferee
TASEI	transgenic
TASEO	transferor
TASES	transverse
TASHP	trans-shape
TASIE	transfixed
TASII	team spirit
TASLN	transplant
TASOA	transposal
TASOE	transposed
	transposer
TASPA	transeptal
TASRB	transcribe
TASRP	transcript
TASRS	transgress
TASSO	transistor
TASTO	transition
TASTR	transitory
TASTV	transitive
TASUA	translunar
TASUE	transducer
	transfuser
	transmuter
	transputer
TASUI	translucid
TATIE	tractrices
TATOA	tractional
TATRA	trattorias
TATRU	traitorous
TAUFL	teacupfuls
TAUWT	team up with
TBAEO	to blame for
TBEIE	table linen
TBELT	tablecloth
TBEPO	tablespoon
TBEPR	table-sport
TBGAE	tobogganer
TBHME	tub-thumper
TBHNS	to be honest

Words marked □ can also be spelled with an initial capital letter

Code	Word
TBLRS	tabula rasa
	tabularise
TBLRZ	tabularize
TBLTO	tabulation
TBOAS	tibiotarsi
TBRAL	tabernacle
TBRFR	tuberiform
TBRST	tuberosity
TBRUA	tubercular
TBRUI	tuberculin
TCEAA	tucked away
TCETP	ticker tape
TCEYO	tickety-boo
TCIAL	tactically
TCIGF	ticking-off
TCLPN	tickle pink
TCLSL	tactlessly
	ticklishly
TCNCA	technician
	technocrat
TCNCS	technicise
TCNCZ	technicize
TCNLD	to conclude
TCNLG	technology
TCNTU	technetium
TCOEE	tachometer
TCORH	Tycho Brahe
TCORP	tachograph
TCPCT	to capacity
TCPEO	tocopherol
TCPTL	to cap it all
TCTRL	taciturnly
TCYEE	tachymeter
TDLOE	tidal power
TDRSU	Tudoresque
TEAAA	The Bahamas
TEABB	The Tar Baby
TEACA	The Bacchae
TEADA	the hard way
TEAFT	the cap fits
TEANN	trepanning
TEANO	The Rainbow
TEAOT	thenabouts
TEARE	the fair sex
TEASO	the cause of
TEAWI	The Hay Wain
TEBEO	tremble for
TECAC	trenchancy
TECAI	theocratic
TECCA	trench coat
TECIU	Theocritus
TEDAE	tread water
TEDEE	Tweedledee
TEDEU	Tweedledum
TEDLT	theodolite
TEDNS	trendiness
	tweediness
TEDSE	The Odyssey
TEDSU	Theodosius
TEEBU	thereabout
TEEDU	tremendous
TEEFE	thereafter
TEEGL	The Seagull
TEEKN	The Red King
TEELN	the Red Lane
TEEMN	thereamong
TEENE	thereunder
TEENN	thereanent
TEEOG	there you go
TEEPE	the Tempter
TEEPS	The Tempest
TEERO	the year dot
TEESA	The Messiah
TEESN	The Seasons
TEETS	trecentist
TEEVE	the heavies
TEEVN	The Servant
TEFHA	twelfth man
TEHEB	the three B's
TEHEF	the three F's
TEHER	the three R's
TEHKO	tie the knot
TEHLN	toe the line
TEHLO	the whole of
TEHNE	the Channel
	The Thinker
TEHNN	The Shining
TEHPE	tree hopper
TEHVR	the shivers
TEIAL	thetically
TEIAU	The Timaeus
TEICT	the big cats
TEIDN	The Wild One
TEIDU	The Tin Drum
TEIEO	the likes of
TEIHC	Trevithick
TEIIU	the jig is up
TEILE	the willies
TEILG	The Village
TEILO	the million
TEISO	The Mission
TEITE	the Fifteen
TEITM	the big time
TELBL	the old Bill
TELCE	treble clef
TELDY	the old days
TELGA	theologian
TELGS	theologise
TELGZ	theologize
TELNT	The Planets
TEMLS	thermalise
TEMLZ	thermalize
TEMOI	thermionic
TEMPL	thermopile
TEMSA	thermostat
TEMSO	thermistor
TENAE	The Annales
TENEN	the Inferno
TENEU	The Angelus
TENHN	the in thing
TENIU	the antique
TENNT	tie in knots
TENTN	the instant
TEOAL	teetotally
TEOEE	treponemes
TEOGA	The Gorgias
TEOKE	the Rockies
TEOLF	tree of life
TEONN	Trevor Nunn
TEONR	the country
TEORR	the horrors
TEOTC	The Poetics
TEOTS	the mostest
TEPCE	to expected
TEPSE	trespasser
TERAE	tie-breaker
TERAO	the Creator
TERLD	The Prelude
TESNU	treasonous
TESPI	theosophic
TETAL	treat badly
TETEE	to extremes
TETFL	twentyfold
TETIA	theatrical
TETMT	tree tomato
TEUCA	The Dunciad
TEUDO	the ould sod
TEUTE	The Hustler
TEUWT	tied up with
TEVFL	twelvefold
TEVLN	the Evil One
TEVNO	twelve noon
TEVTN	twelve-tone
TEXRS	The Express
TEYEN	teeny-weeny
TFAEU	tuffaceous
TGIRN	tagliarini
TGRHR	tiger shark
TGRNK	tiger snake
TGROD	Tiger Woods
TGRSL	tigerishly
TGTNN	tightening
TGTSL	tightishly
TIADU	Trivandrum
TIAEA	tricameral
	trilateral
TIAEC	trivalence
	trivalency
TIATT	tripartite
TIBEI	thimblerig
TIBEU	thimbleful
TIDAT	third party
TIDLS	third class
	third-class
TIDOL	Third World
TIEIA	trigeminal
TIEIU	trioecious
TIERE	toiletries
TIERL	toilet roll
TIETN	Tridentine
TIETO	trisection
TIETT	tridentate
TIGRF	trigger off
TIHAI	trichiasis
TIHHN	triphthong
TIHLG	trichology
TIHME	trip hammer
TIHNS	trichinise
	trichinose
TIHNU	trichinous
TIHNZ	trichinize
TIHOA	trichromat
TIHOS	trichroism
TIHTM	trichotomy
TIIAL	tritically
TIIGA	trilingual
TIIHE	twilighted
TIILS	trivialise
TIILT	triviality
TIILZ	trivialize
TIINR	tuitionary
TIITO	tritiation
TIIYA	Trinity Bay
TIKBU	think about
TIKGI	think again
TIKHM	think shame
TIKLO	triskelion
TIKLU	think aloud
TIKNA	Twickenham
TIKNL	thinkingly
TIKNN	thickening
TIKNS	trickiness
TIKRN	think wrong
TIKRW	thick-grown
TIKSL	trickishly
TIKUO	trick out of
TIKWC	think twice
TILCT	triplicate
	triplicity
TILJM	triple jump
TILNL	triflingly
TILOT	trillionth
TILPI	triglyphic
TILTM	triple time
TILWT	trifle with
TIMHN	triumphant
	triumphing
TIMHR	triumphery
TIMIA	triumviral
TIMNL	trimmingly
TIMNT	this minute
TINUA	triangular
TINUU	Triangulum
TIOEE	tribometer
TIOII	trilobitic
TIOIT	trifoliate
TIOMD	tailor-made
TIOMK	tailormake
TIOPI	trimorphic
TIORP	thixotropy
TIOTL	trimonthly
TIPNL	trippingly
TIRCI	tribrachic
TISDO	this side of
TISML	toilsomely
TITET	thirteenth
TITFL	thirtyfold
TITLT	triathlete
TITNL	twittingly
TITRL	twist drill
TITRN	twittering
TIUAO	triturator

Code	Word
TIUCT	trifurcate
TIUIT	tripudiate
TIVSL	thievishly
TIYLS	tricyclist
TJKSA	Tajikistan
TKAAA	Takla Makan
TKAEK	take a dekko
TKALS	take a class
TKAOT	take an oath
TKARA	take a break
	take as read
TKARE	take a brief
TKATO	take action
TKATU	take as true
TKBET	take breath
TKCAG	take charge
TKCRO	take care of
TKEFC	take effect
TKFIH	take flight
	take fright
TKHEO	take heed of
TKHLO	take hold of
TKIES	take it easy
TKIHN	take in hand
TKIVI	take in vain
TKNAA	taking away
	taking-away
TKNBC	taken aback
	taking back
TKNHR	taken short
TKNPR	taking part
TKNTC	take notice
TKNTO	take note of
TKODR	take orders
TKOLA	take on loan
TKPRI	take part in
TKPTO	take pity on
TKRNO	take rank of
TKSIN	Takashi Ono
TKSRK	take strike
TKTEA	take the rap
TKTEI	take the air
TKTEU	take the sun
TKTLO	take toll of
TKTMA	take to mean
TKTTS	take to task
TKTTW	take to town
TKUAM	take up arms
TKURT	take-up rate
TKUWT	take up with
TLBAE	talebearer
TLBIG	toll bridge
	tollbridge
TLCSE	telecaster
TLDWT	talk down to
TLERN	Talleyrand
TLGAH	telegraphy
TLIGF	telling-off
TLLEI	Tel-El-Kebir
TLLUL	talk loudly
TLMCU	Telemachus
TLMTI	telemetric
TLNSO	talent-spot
TLOFC	tallow-face
TLPOI	telephonic
TLPTI	telepathic
TLRCR	telerecord
TLREI	tularaemia
	tularaemic
TLRNL	tolerantly
TLRTO	toleration
TLSAI	talismanic
TLSOE	telescoped
TLSOI	telescopic
TLTLE	tale-teller
TLTRE	talk turkey
TLUIA	Talmudical
TLVSA	televisual
TLVSO	television
TLWEC	T E Lawrence
TLWLL	talk wildly
TLWRE	teleworker
TLYAL	tilly-fally
	tilly-vally
TLYLR	tally clerk
TMAIE	tympanites
TMAII	tympanitic
TMAYL	Tam Dalyell
TMBDA	Tom o' Bedlam
TMBFR	time before
TMEAC	temperance
TMETN	Tom Keating
TMEWL	timber wolf
TMEWT	tamper with
TMGAH	tomography
TMKEE	timekeeper
TMLDW	tumbledown
	tumble-down
TMLNL	temulently
TMLNS	timeliness
TMLRU	tumblerful
TMLUT	tumult-uate
TMLUU	tumultuous
TMLWE	tumbleweed
TMNBL	timing belt
TMOAL	temporally
TMOIE	temporizer
TMOLN	Tom Collins
TMOLR	tomfoolery
TMORN	tambourine
TMRUL	temerously
	timorously
TMSEC	tumescence
TMSGA	time signal
TMSRE	time-served
TMSVN	time-saving
TMTCM	time to come
TMTLO	tomatillos
TMTNL	temptingly
TMTTO	temptation
TNAON	tantamount
TNAUA	tentacular
TNAYK	Tanganyika
TNBIU	tenebrious
TNBLT	tenability
TNCAE	tonic water
TNCOF	tonic sol-fa
TNCPS	tonic spasm
TNCRI	Tony Curtis
TNEAC	tented arch
TNEBL	Tinkerbell
TNEBR	Tannenberg
TNEFE	tenderfeet
TNEFO	tenderfoot
TNEHO	tenterhook
TNEIE	Tangerines
TNELK	tinder-like
TNELN	tunnelling
TNENS	tenderness❑
TNETA	tangential
TNEWS	tandemwise
TNHSL	tin whistle
TNHUE	Tannhäuser
TNIAI	tannic acid
TNIII	tendinitis
TNISO	tennis shoe
TNLNL	tanglingly
	tinklingly
TNLSL	tonelessly
TNMNA	tenemental
TNNRV	Tananarive
TNOET	Tintoretto
TNOII	tendonitis
TNRAL	tenurially
TNRLE	tendrilled
TNSIE	Toni Sailer
TNTRE	Tina Turner
TNUAU	Tungurahua
TNUEG	Tantum ergo
TNULS	tongue-lash
TNUTE	tongue-tied
TOAAN	Thomas Arne
TOACO	Thomas Cook
TOAEU	Thomas Edur
TOAGA	Thomas Gray
TOAGL	Thomas Gold
TOAHO	Thomas Hood
TOALR	Thomas Lord
TOAMN	Thomas Mann
TOAMR	Thomas More
TOAOU	tropaeolum
TOBDU	troubadour
TOBEL	troubledly
TOBIG	Trowbridge
TOBNS	trombonist
TOEFC	to one's face
TOEHN	Tao-te-ching
	to one's hand
TOENM	to one's name
TOFKN	two of a kind
TOGTU	thoughtful
TOHAR	tooth fairy
TOHAT	toothpaste
TOHEE	two-wheeler
TOHHE	tooth-wheel
TOHNE	trochanter
TOHNS	toothiness
TOHRS	toothbrush
TOHSU	trochiscus
TOIAL	tropically
TOIBR	tropicbird
TOLDT	troglodyte
TOLPN	trolloping
TOLYU	trolleybus
TOMKN	toolmaking
TONPL	thorn apple
TOOGL	thoroughly
TORHE	two or three
TOSEU	trousseaus
	trousseaux
TOSNT	thousandth
TOSYS	Trotskyism
	Trotskyist
TOSYT	Trotskyite
TOUHO	too much for
TOWTM	two-two time
TPACN	tap-dancing
TPALN	topgallant
TPCLT	topicality
	typicality
TPGAH	topography
	typography
TPHBL	top the bill
TPILN	top billing
TPLDW	tipple down
TPLOE	topple over
TPNTI	top and tail
TPOTL	toploftily
TPRAG	taper gauge
TPRCR	tape-record
TPRNL	taperingly
TPSRE	tapestried
TPSRP	typescript
TPSTE	typesetter
TPWIE	typewriter
TPYUV	topsy-turvy
TRAAA	tarmacadam❑
TRABR	threadbare
TRAIM	terra firma
	terrariums
TRAIR	tirra-lirra
TRALC	thread-lace
TRAMR	thread mark
TRAON	turn around
	turnaround
TRAOT	terracotta
TRARC	turn a trick
TRARF	turn adrift
TRAWR	threadworm
TRCLE	turn colder
TRCLU	turn colour
TREAI	tarte tatin
TREAL	three balls
TREAT	three-parts
TRECN	turgescent
TRECR	threescore
TREEA	terne metal
TREEC	threepence
TREEN	threepenny
TREET	terre verte
TREIE	three-sided
	three times

Words marked ❑ can also be spelled with an initial capital letter

TRELN tortellini
TRETA torrential
TRETN tormenting
turpentine
TRETO turkey-trot
TRFLS thriftless
TRFSO thrift shop
TRFWL tariff wall
TRHIH torchlight
TRHNA Tyrrhenian
TRIAE terminated
turbinated
TRIAL terminable
terminably
terminally
TRIEL Torricelli
TRIFE turnip flea
TRIHA Turkish Van
TRIHN tarnishing
TRINS torpidness
torridness
turbidness
TRIRD tardigrade
TRIUE terminuses
TRIUL tortiously
TRIYN terrifying
TRIZN torrid zone
TRLDV turtledove
TRLNC turtle-neck
TRLSL tirelessly
TRMOE thromboses
TRMOI thrombosis
thrombotic
TRNDA threnodial
TRNDS threnodist
TRNEL tarantella
TRNIA tyrannical
TRNIE tyrannized
TROIE terrorized
TRRZN tartrazine
TRSGA turn signal
TRSKV Tereshkova
TRSML tiresomely
TRSNS tyrosinase
TRSUU Torosaurus
TRSWT thrash with
TRTDS turn to dust
TRTMT teratomata
TRTRL turn turtle
TRUEC turbulence
TRUEL torturedly
TRUHU throughout
throughput
TRULA Tertullian
TRUMD Torquemada
TRUNU Tarquinius
TRUOA Turgut Ozal
TRUUL tortuously
TRWAA thrown away
TRWBU throw about
TRWNU throwing up
TRWUA throw mud at
TRYAT Terry Waite
TRYOE Terry Jones
TSAEU testaceous
TSELT tessellate
TSEUL tastefully
TSIUA testicular
TSMRE test-market
TSMSE taskmaster
TSPRO test period
TSUIE testudines
TTAEE tetrameter
TTAER tetrahedra
TTAOA tetragonal
TTATC tetrastich
TTBTO titubation
TTEET to the death
TTEIE to the nines
TTEKE to the skies
TTELO to the floor
TTENO to the end of
TTEON to the point
TTEUC to the quick
TTHNS tetchiness
TTLNL tattlingly
TTLOE total power
TTRAL tutorially
TTSLN Titus Alone
TTSRA Titus Groan
TTVTO titivation
TUBCE thumbscrew
TUBDW thumbs down
thumbs-down
TUBIN thumb piano
TUBLF thumb a lift
TUBNE thumb index
thumb-index
TUBRD thumb a ride
TUCTL truncately
TUCTO truncation
TUDNL thuddingly
TUDRA Thunder Bay
TUDRN thundering
TUDRU thunderous
TUHEO touch-me-not
TUHEU truth serum
TUHNG touch and go
touch-and-go
TUHNL touchingly
TUHNN toughening
TUHNS touchiness
TUHTN touchstone❑
TUHTU tough it out
TUHUL truthfully
TUMLN tourmaline
TUNMN tournament
TUNQE tourniquet
TUPNL thumpingly
TUPTN trumpeting
TUTLF true-to-life
TUTNL tauntingly
trustingly
TUTNS trustiness
TUTUL trustfully
TUUEC truculence
TUYIE Thucydides
TWRBV tower above
TWREL thwartedly
TWRLC tower block
TWRNL toweringly
TWRNS tawdriness
TWRSI thwartship
TWRWS thwartwise
TWRWY thwartways
TWSIL Townsville
TWSOA townswoman
TWSUR town square
TXCLG toxicology
TXDIE Taxi Driver
TXDRA taxidermal
TXDRI taxidermic
TXHLE tax shelter
TXNMS taxonomist
TXPOI toxiphobia
TXUAL texturally
TYAHR Twyla Tharp
TYOOV try to solve
TYTPA tryptophan
UAALN unavailing
UAATI Ural-Altaic
UADON up and doing
UAEAL unamenable
UAEIA un-American
UAFCE unaffected
UAGAL unarguable
unarguably
UAIHD Upanishads
UAKDO unasked-for
UALNS usableness
UAPOE unapproved
UAPRN unapparent
UARDE unabridged
UARNE unarranged
UARPO Utahraptor
UASEE unanswered
UASLE unabsolved
UASMN unassuming
UASSE unassisted
UATCE unattached
unattacked
UATNE unattended
UATSE unattested
UATUL unartfully
UAUTE up a gumtree
UBAAL unbearable
unbearably
unbeatable
unblamable
UBADN upbraiding
UBAEL unbiasedly
UBAEU umbrageous
UBCMN unbecoming
UBIAL unbribable
UBIDN upbuilding
UBIGN upbringing
UBIKN unblinking
UBKSA Uzbekistan
UBLCT umbilicate
UBLEE unbeliever
UBLIE umbellifer
UBLNE unbalanced
UBNAL unbendable
UBNEE unbonneted
UBNNS urbaneness
UBOCE unbroached
UBOEL unbrokenly
UBRAL unburnable
UBROC Umberto Eco
UBSMN unbosoming
UBTOE unbuttoned
UBUHN unblushing
UCAGN unchanging
UCANN unchaining
UCATT unchastity
UCEAY Uncle Vanya
UCEEU Uncle Remus
UCETV uncreative
UCIIA uncritical
UCLUE uncoloured
uncultured
UCMOL uncommonly
UCNIE unconfined
UCNRT uncontrite
UCNTN unconstant
UCNUE unconsumed
UCOSE uncloister
UCRDO uncared-for
UCRSE unchristen
UCRTO ulceration
UCRTV ulcerative
UCRUL ulcerously
UCULN uncoupling
UCUST unctuosity
UCUUL unctuously
UCVLT uncivility
UCVRN uncovering
UDAAI undramatic
UDCAE undeclared
UDCIE undeceived
UDCYN undecaying
UDFAE undefeated
UDFNE undefended
UDLTL undulately
UDLTN undulating
UDLTO undulation
UDLTR undulatory
UDNAL undeniable
undeniably
UDRAE undertaker
underwater
UDRAT underpants
UDRAU undervalue
UDRCE undirected
UDRCR underscore
UDREE undersexed
UDREL underbelly
UDRES underlease
UDRET underneath
UDRHL underwhelm
UDRHO undershoot
UDRIE underlinen

Words marked ❑ can also be spelled with an initial capital letter

	undermined
	underminer
	undersized
	underwired
UDRIG	under siege
UDRKR	underskirt
UDRLF	undercliff
UDRLN	underplant
	underslung
UDRLS	underclass
UDRLZ	underglaze
UDROE	under cover
	undercover
UDROL	underworld
UDRPN	underspend
UDRRC	underprice
UDRRF	undercroft
UDRRI	underdrain
UDRRP	under wraps
UDRRS	underbrush
	undercrest
	underdress
UDRRT	underwrite
UDRRV	underdrive
UDRTD	understudy
UDRTE	understeer
UDRTN	understand
UDRTO	understood
UDRTT	understate
UDRUL	underbuild
UDRUT	underquote
UDRYN	underlying
UDSAE	undismayed
UDSGE	undesigned
UDSRE	undeserved
	undeserver
UDSUE	undisputed
UDTCE	undetected
UDTRE	undeterred
UDVLE	undivulged
UEAPE	unexampled
UEATN	unexacting
UECLE	unexcelled
UECOE	unenclosed
UECRE	unescorted
UECTN	unexciting
UEDNL	unendingly
UEENS	unevenness
UEETU	uneventful
UEEUE	unexecuted
UEEWL	uneven walk
UEFRE	unenforced
UEHII	urethritic
	urethritis
UEIYN	unedifying
UEMNC	Übermensch
UENTA	use instead
UEOOI	uneconomic
UEPAI	unemphatic
UEPCE	unexpected
UEPOE	unemployed
	unexploded
	unexplored

UERHN	unearthing
UERNL	unerringly
UESNS	uneasiness
UEUAE	uneducated
UEULE	unequalled
UEUNS	usefulness
UEUPE	unequipped
UEVAL	unenviable
	unenviably
UFAGN	unflagging
UFAIL	unfeasible
UFIHU	unfaithful
UFINE	unfriended
UFINL	unfriendly
UFINS	unfairness
UFLIL	unfallible
UFMLA	unfamiliar
UFMNN	unfeminine
UFNSE	unfinished
UFOKN	unfrocking
UFREL	unforcedly
UFRIE	unforgiven □
UFRRB	up for grabs
UFRSE	unforeseen
	unforested
UFSEE	unfastened
UFTEE	unfathered
	unfettered
UFTOE	unfathomed
UFUTU	unfruitful
UGAEU	ungraceful
	ungrateful
UGAIU	ungracious
UGNRU	ungenerous
UGONE	ungrounded
UGUGN	ungrudging
UGVRE	ungoverned
UHAAL	unhealable
UHGEI	unhygienic
UHLNS	unholiness
UHLOE	unhallowed
UHLTR	upholstery
UHLWR	uphillward
UHMEE	unhampered
UHNEE	unhindered
UHNSM	unhandsome
UHNUE	unhonoured
UHPDO	unhoped-for
UHRLE	unheralded
UHSOI	unhistoric
UHUEE	unhouseled
UHUZE	unhouzzled
UIAEA	unicameral
	unilateral
UIAEC	univalence
	univalency
UIAIE	unimagined
UIAYI	urinalysis
UIDBE	unindebted
UIELS	unidealism
UIENS	unitedness
UIEST	university
UIFCE	uninfected

UIFRE	uninformed
UIGOC	using force
UIHLE	unitholder
UIIAL	utilizable
UIIGA	unilingual
UILNE	unit-linked
UILRU	uniflorous
UIOAL	unisonally
	univocally
UIOIT	unifoliate
UIOMT	uniformity
UIPIE	unimpaired
UIPOE	unimproved
UISIE	uninspired
UITEI	up in the air
UITNE	unintended
UIUNN	ubiquinone
UIUNS	uniqueness
UIUTR	ubiquitary
UIUTU	ubiquitous
UIVLE	uninvolved
UIVTN	uninviting
UIXAL	uniaxially
UJSNS	unjustness
UKIHL	unknightly
UKNNS	unkindness
UKOAL	unknowable
ULAEE	unleavened
ULBLE	unlabelled
ULCAL	unlockable
ULCNE	unlicensed
ULDLK	unladylike
ULKNS	unlikeness
ULSOE	unlessoned
ULTEE	unlettered
ULUHN	unlaughing
ULVNL	unlovingly
ULWUL	unlawfully
UMDFE	unmodified
UMIEL	unmaidenly
UMLOE	unmellowed
UMNEE	unmannered
UMNEL	unmannerly
UMNUL	unmanfully
UMRIU	unmerciful
UMRLT	unmorality
UMSAL	unmissable
UMTHN	unmatching
UMVAL	unmoveably
UNMEE	unnumbered
UOCPE	unoccupied
UOEIA	urogenital
UOFCA	unofficial
UOIIA	unoriginal
	uxoricidal
UOINS	utopianise
	utopianism □
UOINZ	utopianize
UOIUL	uxoriously
UOMSU	upon my soul!
UOOIA	urological
UORPI	urographic
UOSRE	unobserved

UOTEA	upon the gad
UOTOO	unorthodox
UPEAE	unprepared
UPENN	unpregnant
UPESN	unpleasant
UPIAL	unprizable
UPLSE	unpolished
UPLTL	unpolitely
UPLUE	unpolluted
UPNSE	unpunished
UPNTA	unpunctual
UPOAE	unprofaned
UPOAL	unprovable
UPOEL	unproperly
UPOGE	unploughed
UPOII	unprolific
UPOOE	unprovoked
UPOPE	unprompted
UPRDS	unparadise
UPRFE	unpurified
UPRII	upper limit
UPRLS	upper class
	upper-class
UPROS	upper house
UPRRS	upper crust
	upper-crust
UPSAL	unpassable
UPSIL	unpossible
UPSNS	uppishness
UQAIE	unqualited
UQEAG	usquebaugh
URAAL	unreadable
URAIE	unrealized
URAIU	uproarious
URAOE	unreasoned
URCLE	unrecalled
URCOE	unreckoned
URCRE	unrecorded
URCRN	unrecuring
URDEE	unredeemed
URFRE	unreformed
URGRE	unregarded
URLAL	unreliable
	unreliably
URLEE	unrelieved
URLNS	unruliness
URMNI	unromantic
URMRE	unremarked
URPNS	unripeness
URQIE	unrequired
	unrequited
URSLE	unresolved
URSRE	unreserved
URTFE	unratified
URVAE	unrevealed
URVLE	unravelled
	unrivalled
URWRE	unrewarded
USAAL	unshakable
	unshakably
	unswayable
USABR	unscabbard
USADN	upstanding

Words marked □ can also be spelled with an initial capital letter

Code	Word
USAKE	unshackled
USAOE	unseasoned
USCAL	unsociable
	unsociably
	unsocially
USDDW	upside down
	upside-down
USEDL	unsteadily
USEII	unspecific
USENL	unseeingly
USEPN	unsleeping
USEVN	unswerving
USFNS	unsafeness
USHOE	unschooled
USIAL	unsuitable
	unsuitably
USILE	unshielded
USIRN	unstirring
USITN	unstinting
USLAL	unsolvable
USLRE	unsalaried
USNAL	unsinkable
USNIL	unsensibly
USNOE	unsinnowed
USNTF	unsanctify
USNTR	unsanitary
USRAE	unstreamed
USREC	upsurgence
USREE	unsurveyed
USRML	unscramble
USRNS	unsureness
USRPE	unscripted
USTLN	unsettling
UTAIE	ultra vires
UTAIH	ultrafiche
UTAKU	unthankful
UTAOI	ultrasonic
UTAON	ultrasound
	up to a point
UTCRA	urticarial
UTCTO	urtication
UTDNS	untidiness
UTEPU	up the spout
UTERE	up the creek
UTESR	untreasure
UTGTE	untogether
UTIKN	unthinking
UTLAL	untellable
UTLNE	untalented
UTLTE	up till then
UTMAL	untameable
	untameably
UTMEE	untempered
	untimbered
UTMTL	ultimately
UTOBE	untroubled
UTRAH	utter oaths
UTRAL	untireable
UTROL	ulteriorly
UTTEE	untethered
UTUHU	untruthful
UTUTN	untrusting
UTUTU	untrustful
UTWRL	untowardly
UUEUL	unusefully
UUIUL	usuriously
UUPNL	usurpingly
UUPTO	usurpation
UVRAL	unvariable
UVREI	unversed in
UVRFE	unverified
UWAYN	unwearying
UWDAL	unwedgable
UWEDL	unwieldily
UWIHN	unweighing
UWNEL	unwontedly
UWRAL	unworkable
UWRHL	unworthily
UWRHO	unworthy of
UWRNS	unwariness
	upwardness
UWSNS	unwiseness
UWTHU	unwatchful
UWVRN	unwavering
UYEDN	unyielding
VBAHN	vibraphone
VBAIN	vibrations
VCBLR	vocabulary
VCFRT	vociferate
VCFRU	vociferous
VCIAO	vaccinator
VCIIE	victimized
	victimizer
VCILS	victimless
VCLOD	vocal cords
VCLZN	vocalizing
VCNNS	vacantness
VCOHG	Victor Hugo
VCOHS	Victor Hess
VCOIN	victoriana❑
VCOIU	victorious
VCRGN	vice-regent
VCTOA	vocational
VCULE	victualler
VCYAE	Vichy water
VDOAT	video nasty
VDOHN	videophone
VEFNE	viewfinder
VELSL	viewlessly
VENLA	vienna loaf
VENMA	Vietnam War
VENMS	Vietnamese
VEOAI	View of a Pig
VESOT	voetstoots
VGBRE	vegeburger
VGETS	vignettist
VGLNL	vigilantly
VGRUL	vigorously
VGTBE	vegetables
VGTRA	vegetarian
VGTTN	vegetating
VGTTO	vegetation
VGTTV	vegetative
VHMNL	vehemently
VIERN	voiceprint
VKAST	Vikram Seth
VLAAS	Valparaiso
	Valparaíso
VLAEE	voltameter
VLAEL	villanelle
VLANU	villainous
VLAOA	Volcano Bay
VLAOI	Valladolid
VLAOO	Villa-Lobos
VLBLT	volubility
VLCPD	velocipede
VLDTN	validating
VLDTO	validation
VLEAL	vulnerable
VLEBL	volleyball
VLEDE	value added
VLEEV	Villeneuve
VLENG	villeinage
VLEUA	valleculae
VLMNU	voluminous
VLPUR	voluptuary
VLPUU	voluptuous
VLRUL	valorously
VLSAE	Volkswagen®
VLTLS	volatilise
VLTLT	volatility
VLTLZ	volatilize
VLTOA	volitional
VMIEA	vampire bat
VNAEA	vintage car
VNCGL	Venice gold
VNEAA	venae cavae
VNEBL	Vanderbilt
VNEMN	Von Neumann
VNEPS	Van der Post
VNEUL	vengefully
VNGRS	vinegarish
VNIAE	vindicated
VNIAL	ventilable
	vindicable
VNIAO	ventilator
	vindicator
VNITV	vindictive
VNMOT	venom-tooth
VNMUL	venomously
VNOED	vinho verde
VNRCS	ventricose
VNRLI	ventral fin
VNRTO	veneration
VNSCM	Venus's comb
VNTCS	vanity case
	vanity-case
VNTFI	Vanity Fair
VNTOA	venational
VNTUI	vanity unit
VNUSE	vanquished
	vanquisher
VOETC	violent act
VPLTO	vapulation
VPRFR	vaporiform
VPRST	vaporosity
VPRTO	vaporettos
VPRUL	vaporously
	viperously
VRALE	Versailles
VRANU	verbal noun
VRAUA	vernacular
VRCST	varicosity
VRCTM	varicotomy
VREAE	variegated
	verse-maker
VREAL	varietally
VREMT	verse-smith
VRERT	vertebrate
VRFAL	verifiable
VRFCL	varifocals
VRGNA	viraginian
VRGNU	viraginous
VRHNR	very hungry
VRIAL	vertically
	virginally
	vortically
VRIEL	vermicelli
VRIHN	varnishing
VRIIE	vertigines
VRILO	vermillion
VRIUA	vermicular
	versicular
VRLGS	virologist
VRLKL	very likely
VRLNL	virulently
VROCI	Verrocchio
VROEE	variometer
VRRMT	verkrampte
VRRRL	very rarely
VRSEC	virescence
VRULT	virtuality
VRUST	virtuosity
VRUUL	virtuously
VRYIH	Verey light
VSAAT	visual arts
VSBLT	visibility
VSCLT	vesiculate
VSCTO	vesication
VSCTR	vesicatory
VSIUA	vestibular
VSOAL	visionally
VSOLS	visionless
VSONC	viscountcy
VSTRA	visitorial
VSTTO	visitation
VSUAL	vascularly
VTCNS	Vaticanism
	Vaticanist
VTCNT	vaticinate
VTECN	vitrescent
VTILS	vitriolise
VTILT	vitriolate
VTILZ	vitriolize
VTLBU	vote Labour
VTLLI	vital fluid
VTLOC	vital force
VTLPR	vital spark
VTLTE	vitalities
VTMNS	vitaminise
VTMNZ	vitaminize
VTPRT	vituperate

Words marked ❑ can also be spelled with an initial capital letter

Code	Word
VTRNA	veteran car
VTRNR	veterinary
VUEIL	vaudeville
VUTNL	vauntingly
VVPRT	viviparity
VVPRU	viviparous
VVSCO	vivisector
VWLON	vowel point
WAAIE	what an idea!
WAAON	wraparound
WAEHR	whale shark
WAFNE	wharfinger
WAHRA	weatherman
	weather map
WAHRN	weathering
WAHRS	weatherise
WAHRU	weather out
WAHRY	weather eye
WAHRZ	weatherize
WAHUL	wrathfully
WAIGU	wearing out
WAIMR	what is more
WAIUL	wearifully
WALNS	weakliness
WAMMN	weak moment
WAMNE	weak-minded
WAOLS	weaponless
WASEE	whatsoever
WATLK	wraith-like
WATOG	what though
WAWLE	weak-willed
WAYNL	wearyingly
WBLNS	wobbliness
WCENS	wickedness
WCEWR	wickerwork
WDELE	Weddell Sea
WDEOB	Widdecombe
WDIGA	wedding day
WDLRA	widely read
	widely-read
WDSRA	widespread
WDWPA	widow's peak
WECEL	wretchedly
WEEBU	whereabout
WEEFE	whereafter
WEENE	whereunder
WEENI	whereuntil
WEEOE	wheresoeer
WEETA	where it's at
WEKAO	wreak havoc
WEKLE	weedkiller
WELEI	wheelie bin
WELHI	wheelchair
WELLM	wheel clamp
WELOS	wheelhouse
WESEE	whensoever
WEUNS	woefulness
WEZNS	wheeziness
WGAAG	Wagga Wagga
WGERE	wage-earner
WGNHE	wagon wheel
WGNRI	wagon train
WGPCE	wage packet
	wage-packet
WIBRE	Weinberger
WIEAC	white sauce
WIEAE	white paper
	white water
WIEAI	white magic
WIEEA	white metal
WIEER	white-beard
WIEHL	white whale
WIEHR	whitethorn
WIEIH	white light
WIELV	white slave
WIEOD	white goods
WIEOS	white horse
	Whitehorse
	white noise
WIERA	White Friar
	white friar
WIERS	white brass
WIEUA	white sugar
WIEWR	white dwarf
WIGSL	Whiggishly
WIHLS	weightless
WIHNL	wr ithingly
WIHNU	weighing up
	weighing-up
WIIGA	writing-pad
WIILN	wait in line
WIKSU	whisky sour
WILBR	whirlybird
WILWA	whillywhaw
WIPNS	whippiness
WIPRN	whimpering
	whispering
WISBE	Weisse Bier
WISIC	whip-stitch
WISNA	Whit Sunday
	Whitsunday
WISNS	whimsiness
WITAC	wristwatch
WITEA	whip the cat
WITEF	whistle off
WITEO	whistle for
WITNA	written law
WITNF	written off
WITRV	whist drive
WIZNL	whizzingly
WKAIH	wake a night
WKILN	Wake Island
WLBHN	walk behind
WLCOE	well-chosen
WLDSE	Walt Disney
WLECM	Walter Camp
WLEDV	wild endive
WLEES	wildebeest
WLEHS	Walter Hess
WLEMI	Wilhelm His
WLEMN	Wilhelmina
WLENS	wilderness
WLEOG	well enough
WLERE	Walter Reed
	well-earned
WLERV	Waldegrave
WLESA	Willemstad
WLFOE	wallflower
	wild flower
WLFRE	well-formed
WLFWE	wildfowler
WLGAE	well-graced
WLHEE	well-heeled
WLHOA	Welshwoman
WLHTO	Will Hutton
WLIEE	well I never!
WLIGA	Walsingham
WLIGO	wellington□
	Wilmington
WLILN	walk in line
WLJDE	well-judged
WLLML	walk lamely
WLLSL	willlessly
WLMNE	well-minded
WLOCI	wild orchid
WLOGN	Wollongong
WLOLF	walk of life
WLOPR	walk-on part
WLPAE	well-placed
WLPDE	well-padded
WLPRO	wild person
WLSIE	well-suited
	wolf spider
WLSOE	well-spoken
WLSRE	Wall Street
WLSRN	wellspring
	well-spring
WLTHE	walk to heel
WLTLV	well-to-live
	will to live
WLTRE	well-turned
WLTWL	wall-to-wall
WLUNS	wilfulness
WLVRE	well-versed
WLWLE	well-willer
WLWSE	well-wished
	well-wisher
WLYAK	walky-talky
WLYIL	willy-nilly
	willy-willy
WLYOA	Willy Loman
WMEDR	Wim Wenders
WMNAE	woman-hater
WMNFO	woman of God
WMNOK	womenfolks
WMNSL	womanishly
WMNUL	womanfully
WMNZN	womanizing
WNBTL	wine bottle
WNCLA	wine cellar
	wine-cellar
	wing collar
WNCOE	wine cooler
WNEET	winceyette
WNEFO	wander from
WNEIG	wanderings
WNEKL	winterkill
WNEKN	wunderkind
WNELN	wonderland□
WNELS	wanderlust
WNELU	Wenceslaus
WNEMN	wonderment
WNEMR	Windermere
WNETM	wintertime
WNETU	Winterthur
WNEWL	Wonderwall
WNFOE	windflower
WNHOG	win through
WNHSE	Winchester
	Winchester®
WNJME	windjammer
WNLTA	wentletrap
WNMRO	wing mirror
WNNWA	win and wear
WNONS	wantonness
WNOPN	windowpane
WNOSA	window seat
WNOSL	windowsill
WNOSO	window-shop
WNOSS	window sash
WNRUL	wondrously
WNSIL	windshield
WNSOT	Wandsworth
WNSRA	wingspread
WNSRE	windscreen
	windsurfer
WNTNE	wind tunnel
WNYHA	win by a head
WOCRE	woodcarver
WOEAE	wholesaler
WOEFE	whore after
WOEHA	wholewheat
WOEHO	whole shoot
WOELT	whole cloth
WOEOS	whorehouse
WOERI	wholegrain
WOGAU	wrong way up
WOGIE	wrong-timed
WOGON	wrongdoing
WOGOS	wood grouse
	woodgrouse
WOGUL	wrongfully
	wrongously
WOLBA	woolly bear
WOLNE	woodlander
WOLNS	woolliness
WOPCE	woodpecker
WOSII	wood spirit
WOSRE	wood sorrel
WOVNE	wood veneer
WOWRE	woodworker
WOYLE	Woody Allen
WRAOI	workaholic
WRAPC	Warsaw Pact
WRBSE	workbasket
WRDAE	wiredrawer
WRDAI	World War II
WRDLS	world-class
WRDMN	world's mine
WRDOE	world power
WRDUI	world music
WRESI	wardenship

WRFLO	work-fellow
WRFOD	war of words
WRHHL	worthwhile
WRHIE	wire-haired
WRHNS	worthiness
WRHPE	worshipped
	worshipper
WRHPU	worshipful
WRHRE	work-harden
WRIGA	warming-pan
	working day
	working man
WRIGF	warding off
WRIGO	Warrington
	Workington
WRIGU	working out
	working-out
WRLNL	warblingly
WRLSL	wordlessly
WRPLE	wire-puller
WRPOL	workpeople
	work-people
WRSOT	Wordsworth
WRSSE	ward sister
WRTON	Worsthorne
WRTRL	work to rule
	work-to-rule
WRWLE	werewolves
WRYBU	worry about
WRYED	worry beads
WRYNL	worryingly
WSBNA	West Bengal
WSCAK	wisecracks
WSEAE	waste paper
WSEHL	Wesley Hall
WSENS	westernise
WSENZ	westernize
WSEUL	wastefully
WSIDA	West Indian
WSIDE	West Indies
WSIGO	Washington

WSMKA	Wasim Akram
WSPAI	Westphalia
WSPRO	wise person
WSSSE	West Sussex
WSTNU	wasp-tongu'd
WSWRH	westward ho!
WSWRL	westwardly
WSYAH	wishy-washy
WTATE	wet canteen
WTDAA	withdrawal
WTEBR	Wittenberg
WTESO	witness box
WTFVU	with favour
WTHAE	watchmaker
	witch hazel
WTHFE	watch after
WTHHI	watch chain
WTHLE	withholder
WTHLS	watchglass
WTHNL	witchingly
WTHOE	watchtower
	watch-tower
WTHOG	wet through
WTHRF	witchcraft
WTHTA	watchstrap
WTHUL	watchfully
WTICL	within call
WTIIM	witticisms
WTITN	with intent
WTLBR	wattlebird
WTLNE	wet blanket
WTLWR	wattle-work
WTNPE	wit-snapper
WTOTN	without end
WTRAG	water gauge
WTRAL	water table
WTRAO	with reason
WTREE	water level
WTREG	water's edge
WTREO	watermelon
WTRHE	water thief

	water-wheel
WTRIH	watertight
WTRKE	water-skier
WTRLC	water clock
WTRLN	water-plant
WTRLR	water clerk
WTRLS	waterglass
WTRME	watersmeet
WTRNK	water snake
WTRNS	wateriness
WTROE	water power
	water tower
WTROK	waterworks
WTRON	waterborne
WTROS	Waterhouse
WTRPU	waterspout
WTRRF	watercraft
WTRRN	waterfront
WTRRO	waterproof
WTRRS	water-brash
	watercress
WTRUI	Water Music
WTRYL	water cycle
WTRYP	water nymph
WTWIH	with weight
WUDNL	woundingly
WUDOO	would to God
WVEEG	wave energy
WVLNT	wavelength
WVRNL	waveringly
WXYIA	wax lyrical
WYFBA	way off beam
WYUWS	Way Out West
XNCAE	Xenocrates
XNHMT	xanthomata
XNPAE	Xenophanes
XNPOI	xenophobia
	xenophobic
XRGAH	xerography
YAGLN	ylang-ylang
YANNL	yearningly

YAOYA	year-on-year
YCEYA	yackety-yak
YEDNL	yieldingly
YEDON	yield point
YETNU	Yves Tanguy
YGAAT	Yogyakarta
YGSAI	Yugoslavia
YKFLO	yoke-fellow
YLOBL	yellow bile
YLOCR	yellow card
YLOJC	Yellow Jack
YLOLN	yellow line
YLONS	yellowness
YLRNE	Yul Brynner
YRCSL	York Castle
YSEYA	yesteryear
YUATI	you can't win
YUATL	you can talk
YUGDL	young adult
YUGLO	young blood
YUGOA	young woman
YUHUL	youthfully
YUOTA	you don't say!
YUSLE	yourselves
YUSRL	yours truly
YWMKN	yawn-making
ZBGIN	zabaglione
ZCHTO	zucchettos
ZFIEL	Zeffirelli
ZITRO	zwitterion
ZMAWA	Zimbabwean
ZNAET	Zend-Avesta
ZNOEE	Zeno of Elea
ZOHGU	zoophagous
ZOHPE	zoothap-ses
ZOOIA	zoological
ZOOII	zoogonidia
ZPTAO	zapateados
ZPYIU	Zephyrinus
ZROTO	zero option
ZRRGE	Zurbriggen

11 letters – odd

AAAETC	acatalectic
AAAPGE	à la campagne
AAATSS	Anabaptists
AABLOK	Alan Bullock
AACITC	anarchistic
AADNDY	abandonedly
AADNET	abandonment
AADNHP	abandon ship
AAEAPE	as an example
AAEFTB	A Tale of a Tub
AAEIIM	academicism
AAEIIN	academician
AAEUTF	as a result of
AAGMTD	amalgamated
AAHDKN	Alan Hodgkin

AAHLXS	anaphylaxis
AAHOIM	anachronism
AAHOOY	arachnology
AAIADM	ad avizandum
AAIADR	Anaximander
AAICUT	at a discount
AAIHOT	at a high cost
AAILNS	Aran Islands
AAITNE	at a distance
AALONS	at all points
AALVNS	at all events
AAMLUN	Alan Milburn
AANRSS	anagnorisis
AANTIE	against time
AAOARS	apatosaurus❑

AAOEAE	Ada Lovelace
AAOILY	amatorially
AAOOSY	analogously
AAOSED	at a loose end
AAOUHA	anacoluthia
AAOUHN	anacoluthon
AAOWRS	a can of worms
AASEAD	Alan Shepard
AASERR	Alan Shearer
AASHSA	anaesthesia
AASHSS	anaesthesis
AASHTC	anaesthetic
AATCVS	Ajanta caves
AATISM	Alastair Sim
AATMSS	anastomoses

AATNLY	abactinally
ABEITD	abbreviated
ABGOSY	ambiguously
ABOILY	ambrosially
ABQEQE	Albuquerque
ABRCMS	Albert Camus
ABRSER	Albert Speer
ABRSET	arborescent
ABSAOS	ambuscadoes
ABTAER	arbitrageur
ABTAET	arbitrament
ABTAIN	arbitration
ABTAIY	arbitrarily
ABTOSY	ambitiously
ABVLNE	ambivalence
ABVLNY	ambivalency
ACAAIN	acclamation
ACAAOY	acclamatory
ACACLY	archaically
ACAMDY	as claimed by
ACAOOY	archaeology
ACBSOS	archbishops
ACDCES	archduchess
ACDOEE	archdiocese
ACEOIM	archegonium
ACHLRE	alcohol-free
ACIAIE	acclimatise
	acclimatize
ACIEAO	archipelago
ACIIOS	acclivitous
ACIOEN	Arctic Ocean
ACISAP	Archie Sharp
ACIVRE	Alcaic verse
ACLRNO	accelerando
ACLRTD	accelerated
ACLRTR	accelerator
ACLUAE	acculturate
ACMAID	accompanied
ACMAIT	accompanist
ACMLTR	accumulator
ACMOAE	accommodate
ACNULY	accentually
ACOWMN	anchorwoman
ACPBAE	accept blame
ACPTIE	accipitrine
ACRATY	accordantly
ACRIGO	according to
ACRIGS	according as
ACRIGY	accordingly
ACSOIE	accessorise
	accessorize
ACSOIS	accessories
ACSOIY	accessorily
ACSRLY	ancestrally
ACSTVL	accusatival
ACTCLY	ascetically
ACUTBE	accountable
ACUTBY	accountably
ACUTNY	accountancy
ACUTOK	account-book
ADCOSY	audaciously
ADEDRA	Andrea Doria
ADEEAN	André Derain
ADEEDD	addle-headed
ADEGSI	Andre Agassi
ADEIHO	add relish to
ADEMEE	André Ampère
ADEPRO	add pepper to
ADERVN	André Previn
ADESOK	address book
ADGEOY	Andy Gregory
ADHNOE	and then some
ADHTVR	and whatever
ADMMIE	aide-mémoire
ADMNLY	abdominally
ADOEHR	add together
ADOERC	audiometric
ADOIUL	audiovisual
ADOSES	arduousness
ADOSNO	add poison to
ADOYOS	androgynous
ADSEAP	aides-de-camp
ADTRUS	auditoriums
ADUHIE	and suchlike
AEADGS	ages and ages
AEADIE	alexandrine
	alexandrite
AEADIN	Alexandrian
AEAEES	averageness
AEAIIY	amenability
AEATDS	adelantados
AEBIAI	Azerbaijani
AECPAY	anencephaly
AEDFIE	ahead of time
AEDTLY	anecdotally
AEEAIN	abecedarian
AEESYE	Alexei Sayle
AEETSS	atelectasis
AEETTC	atelectatic
AEEYUN	at every turn
AEGTAS	an eight days
AEHGIS	Alex Higgins
AEIACP	America's Cup
AEIAIE	Americanise
	Americanize
AEIAIM	Americanism
AEIAPE	American Pie
AEISYR	Alexis Soyer
AEOEES	awesomeness
AEOROA	amenorrhoea
AEORSS	a bed of roses
AEOSUY	area of study
AERDOE	A Red, Red Rose
AESEAT	Alec Stewart
AESLOD	Alex Salmond
AESTUH	an easy touch
AETRNE	Agent Orange
AEUTFR	adequate for
AEYTYH	Aberystwyth
AFACIE	affranchise
AFATOS	anfractuous
AFCAIN	affectation
AFCIEY	affectively
AFCIGY	affectingly
AFCIIY	affectivity
AFEALR	Alfred Adler
AFEBNT	Alfred Binet
AFENBL	Alfred Nobel
AFEPLY	Alfred Polly
AFITDY	afflicted by
AFLAIN	affiliation
AFLBAT	at full blast
AFLSED	at full speed
AFRAIE	affirmative
AFRAIN	affirmation
AFRIGY	affirmingly
AFRTAD	at first hand
AGAAIG	aggravating
AGAAIN	aggravation
AGAHUD	Afghan hound
AGAITN	Afghanistan
AGATBS	angwantibos
AGEAEY	aggregately
AGEAGE	argie-bargie
	argle-bargle
AGEAIN	aggregation
AGETBE	augmentable
AGIAIM	Anglicanism
AGLCLY	angelically
AGNIIN	Argentinian
AGOEAE	agglomerate
AGOHBA	anglophobia
AGOHLA	anglophilia
AGONIN	Anglo-Indian
AGOOMN	Anglo-Norman
AGORPY	angiography
AGRLFR	augur ill for
AGRTMC	algorithmic
AGSADR	Angus Calder
AGSCEN	Angus McBean
AGSIIN	Augustinian
AGSISN	Angus Wilson
AGUIAE	agglutinate
AHEEET	achievement
AHEIIM	athleticism
AHIPIL	A Shrimp Girl
AHITCL	atheistical
AHLBOE	Athole brose
AHOAIE	achromatise
	achromatize
AHOAIM	achromatism
AHOIIC	aphrodisiac
AHRETY	abhorrently
AHRSIE	A Chorus Line
AIACLS	animalcules
AIAIGY	animatingly
AIAIIY	amicability
AIATEA	acidanthera
AIAWSE	animal waste
AIBEES	amiableness
AIBMGC	as if by magic
AIEAKR	Alice Walker
AIEDZN	a dime a dozen
AIEOPR	Alice Cooper
AIFNTM	ad infinitum
AIGMYL	Amin Gemayel
AIGNSS	abiogenesis
AIGNTC	abiogenetic
AIHAOR	Anish Kapoor

AIHEIS arithmetics
AIHPES as it happens
AIIAOE a pig in a poke
AIINDS aficionados
AILGCL axiological
AIMGTE as it might be
AIMTCL axiomatical
AIOAIS a hit or a miss
AIODCS Adirondacks
AIOFUF a bit of fluff
AITCAY aristocracy
AITRAS at intervals
AIUEPE ami du peuple
AJCIEY adjectively
AJDCTR adjudicator
AJUNET adjournment
AKADES awkwardness
AKNPIE asking price
AKOLDE acknowledge
AKOMNY ask for money
AKOOEN ask to come in
AKOVTS ask for votes
AKWRZI al-Khwarizmi
ALANRF all manner of
ALASAE a clean slate
ALASEP a clean sweep
ALASET a clean sheet
ALBUEE All About Eve
ALFPEE all of a piece
ALGEIS Alleghenies
ALGRCL allegorical
ALHWIE all the while
ALHWRD all the world
ALIEIH all-time high
ALKANT as like as not
ALLCRC all-electric
ALMCED Ally Macleod
ALMCIT Ally McCoist
ALMRCN all-American
ALNASY Allan Ramsay
ALNHSS ailanthuses
ALNODR Allan Border
ALOEFL all powerful
all-powerful
ALOEHR all together
ALOENS at loose ends
ALOICS all to pieces
ALOLDY All Fools' Day
All Souls Day
All Souls' Day
ALOSBE all possible
ALSDOK a closed book
ALSESS Aulus Celsus
ALSTIG a close thing
ALTLOE a slate loose
ALTMNA ablutomania
ALTNIG all standing
ALULIG all-building
ALVAIE alleviative
ALVAIG alleviating
ALVAIN alleviation
ALVRIH all over with
ALWOAE allow to have
ALWOAS allow to pass
AMCNRL arms control
AMDOBR armed robber
AMDOCS armed forces
AMESES aimlessness
AMNCLR adminicular
AMRLCP Admiral's Cup
AMSHRC atmospheric
AMTAIG Armatrading
AMTEET admit defeat
AMTOAL admit to bail
AMUECR armoured car
AMUPAE armour-plate
AMWSIG arm-twisting
ANEEAT Annie Besant
ANHLTR annihilator
ANLDOM annelid worm
ANPNIS Arno Penzias
ANPVOA Anna Pavlova
ANRAIY abnormality
ANSIIM agnosticism
ANTCLY agnatically
ANVRAY anniversary
AOAHBA agoraphobia
AOAHBC agoraphobic
AOAITC anomalistic
AOAOSY apogamously
AOAYTC apocalyptic
AOECNE adolescence
AOEEBW at one's elbow
AOEOIK a bone to pick
AOERSS aponeuroses
aponeurosis
AOERTC aponeurotic
AOETTD above-stated
AOFILR Adolf Hitler
AOHOIE apotheosise
apotheosize
AOHRIE another time
AOIAIN abomination
AOICOK atomic clock
AOIIGY agonisingly
agonizingly
AOINAP aeolian harp
AOKFIE a work of time
AOLHUE A Doll's House
AOLNIE Apollinaire
AONIGN abounding in
AOOPUD azo-compound
AOOSES amorousness
AOPOSY amorphously
AOPSDO as opposed to
AORRPE amour-propre
AORUOS avoirdupois
AOSIIN acoustician
AOTLAO amontillado
AOTLCL apostolical
AOTOHC apostrophic
AOTOIT abortionist
AOTROI a posteriori
AOTTOH a colt's tooth
AOYOSY anonymously
AOYOUN agony column
APAEET appeasement
APAEIE alphabetise
alphabetize
APAHTM alpha rhythm
APAIGY appealingly
appeasingly
APASBE appraisable
APCRTO aspect ratio
APEAIE amphetamine
APEEIE aspheterise
aspheterize
APEIBD apple-pie bed
APEIBE appreciable
APEIBY appreciably
APEITD appreciated
APEQIE apple-squire
APESRA appressoria
APEUPY ample supply
APIAIN application
APIBEA amphisbaena
APIOIE amphibolite
APIOOY amphibology
APITET appointment
APLAIE appellative
APLAIN appellation
APLIGY appallingly
APOAIN approbation
APOAOY approbatory
APOCIG approaching
APOIAE approximate
APOIGY approvingly
APORAE appropriate
APRANO appertain to
APREAT appurtenant
APRTHK apparatchik
APRTSS apparatuses
AQANIG acquainting
AQIEET acquirement
AQIIIE acquisitive
AQIIIN acquisition
AQISEN acquiesce in
AQISET acquiescent
AQITNE acquittance
ARABUT Adrian Boult
ARAEIG air layering
ARAHNI Adrian Henri
ARAISA Adriatic Sea
ARBCLY aerobically
ARBLOS atrabilious
ARCDBA abracadabra
ARCLRY auricularly
ARCLUE agriculture
ARCOSY atrociously
ARDEET abridgement
ARDNMC aerodynamic
AREMNL air terminal
ARIKES airsickness
ARINET arraignment
ARIVLE aortic valve
ARLCCD acrylic acid
ARMNOS acrimonious
ARNEET arrangement
ARNHAE abranchiate

ARNUIS aeronautics
AROSNA Ayrton Senna
ARPTLY acropetally
ARRFMN aircraftman
ARSINE agroscience
ARTIOE Airstrip One
ARVDRI arrivederci
ASAEET assuagement
ASANRM abstain from
ASBUAE assubjugate
ASCAIE associative
ASCAIN association
ASDOSY assiduously
ASEPOE answerphone
ASGAIN assignation
ASIAIN aestivation
auspication
ASIETY abstinently
ASKONS also known as
ASLCIG arse-licking
ASMDAE assumed name
ASMLTD assimilated
ASMTRA Ars Amatoria
ASNEIM absenteeism
ASNIGY assentingly
ASRCIN abstraction
ASRDES assuredness
ASRIEY assertively
ASRIGY absorbingly
ASROOY Assyriology
ASSIAE assassinate
ASTCOS ansate cross
ASUTTR auscultator
ATAGRO a stranger to
ATAHBA astraphobia
ATAILY actuarially
ATAPIT at that point
ATATDO attracted to
ATCABR antechamber
ATCAGR autochanger
ATCCOE anticyclone
ATCDNE antecedence
ATCEAE attaché case
attaché-case
ATCLBE articulable
ATCLTD articulated
ATCLTR articulator
ATCMLS altocumulus
ATCOSY astuciously
ATCPTD anticipated
ATCPTR anticipator
ATCTOE anticathode
ATCTOS autochthons
ATEADF at the hand of
ATEAET at the latest
ATEAKF at the back of
ATEEDF at the head of
ATEERF at the rear of
ATEETF at the feet of
ATEHMF at the whim of
ATEIEF at the time of
ATEIIM antheridium
ATEOBE at the double
ATEOET at the moment
ATEOIM autoerotism
ATEOOD antherozoid
ATEOTF at the root of
ATESES artlessness
ATEUST at the outset
ATFGSA Antofagasta
ATGAHC autographic
ATGAIM astigmatism
ATGNZD antagonized
ATHLCS antihelices
ATIGNY astringency
ATIIEY attuitively
ATIINL attritional
ATIPAE at this place
ATIPIT at this point
ATISAE at this stage
ATIUIE attributive
ATIUIN attribution
ATMBLA automobilia
ATNAIN attenuation
ATNCLY actinically
ATNIEY attentively
ATNMSA antonomasia
ATNSIG astonishing
ATNURN antineutron
anti-neutron
ATOEHR act together
ATOGOP action group
ATOHOE anthochlore
ATOIAT antioxidant
ATOIEY act politely
ATOIIS authorities
ATOOIE anthologise
anthologize
astronomise
astronomize
ATOOIT anthologist
ATOYAO Anthony Caro
ATOYDN Anthony Eden
ATOYNN anthocyanin
ATPATC autoplastic
ATPRSS antiphrasis
ATPRTC antipyretic
ATQAIN antiquarian
ATRAEY alternately
ATRAIE alternative
arterialise
arterialize
ATRAIG alternating
ATRAIN altercation
alternation
ATRCSS anthracosis
ATRFET after effect
after-effect
ATRHCL autarchical
ATRHNM antirrhinum
ATRLBR anti-roll bar
ATRPRY act properly
ATRUPR aftersupper
ATRVRE auto-reverse
ATSAIN attestation
ATSMTC anti-Semitic
ATSNHP artisanship
ATSRPE antistrophe
ATSRTS altostratus
ATTOHC autotrophic
ATUBIS Arthur Bliss
ATUBON Arthur Brown
ATUCUH Arthur Couch
ATUEAS Arthur Evans
ATUKPS Arthur Kipps
ATUSAS Arthur's Pass
ATUSOB Arthur's Tomb
ATUYUG Arthur Young
ATVRIN anteversion
AUBAIN adumbration
AUCLUE aquaculture
aquiculture
AUENLD acute-angled
AUIEES abusiveness
AUPAIG aquaplaning
AURSUE acupressure
AUTCAK a nut to crack
AUTRTD adulterated
AUUCUE acupuncture
AVNEET advancement
AVNUES adventuress
AVNUIM adventurism
AVNUOS adventurous
AVRAIL adversarial
AVRETY advertently
AVRIIG advertising
AVRILY adverbially
AVROIL advertorial
AWETOH a sweet tooth
AXLAIS auxiliaries
AXOSES anxiousness
AYHNBT anything but
AYIAIY atypicality
AYUBRF any number of
AYUIET As You Like It
BAAEOD beat a record
BAAEPO be a wake-up to
BABNIG bias binding
BADAIG bias-drawing
BADEBR board member
BADEDR brand leader
BADHTH Brands Hatch
BADNUG Brandenburg
BADSIG blandishing
BAEBOK Beaverbrook
BAEESY blamelessly
BAEIDE Bracegirdle
BAENBT brace and bit
BAEOTY blameworthy
BAETAL blaze a trail
BAEUNR Blade Runner
BAEWAE beaked whale
BAFRSA Beaufort Sea
BAGDCO braggadocio
BAHOBR beachcomber
BAIGEN bearing rein
BAKAKT black market
black-market
BAKALR blackmailer

BAKEUY Black Beauty
BAKEVT black velvet
BAKHQE blank cheque
BAKHRY black cherry
BAKLRY black clergy
BAKOET Black Forest
BAKOEY black comedy
BAKOFE black coffee
BAKOTM black bottom
BAKRAS Black friars
Blackfriars
BAKRNE Black Prince
BAKROY black bryony
BAKRUE black grouse
BAKSOL black as coal
BAKTED blanketweed
BALHMS be all thumbs
BANAAE brain damage
BANESR brainteaser
brain-teaser
BANESY brainlessly
BANIKY brainsickly
BAPEOS blasphemous
BAPISO be at pains to
BATERM beat the drum
BATFIG beautifying
BATFLY beautifully
BATIES beastliness
BATOSY beauteously
BATQEN beauty queen
BATSEP beauty sleep
BATSLN beauty salon
BAWTES bear witness
BAYADA bradycardia
BAYHNE by any chance
BAZVLE Brazzaville
BBHMIN Bob Champion
BBIHES babyishness
BBIMNA bibliomania
BBIPIE bibliophile
BBLUDR bubble under
BBNBAE bib and brace
BBODAD Bob Woodward
BBOTMR Bob Mortimer
BBRENN be borne in on
BBRTHT Bob Cratchit
BBSNRS Babes in Arms
BBSTIG baby-sitting
BBUDPN be bound up in
BBYOSN Bobby Robson
BCAAIN baccanalian
BCADIL back and fill
BCBEKR backbreaker
BCBNHR backbencher
BCCELP bicycle clip
BCCEUP bicycle pump
BCCUTY back-country
BCEAMA bacteraemia
BCEBUR Beckenbauer
BCEIIE bactericide
BCHNLA bacchanalia
BCIGON backing-down
BCLCLY bucolically
BCLUDR buckle under
BCMAGY become angry
BCMAUT become adult
BCMBRD become bored
BCMCER become clear
BCMFIT become faint
BCMFXD become fixed
BCMKON become known
BCMLGT become light
BCMPLR become paler
BCMRRR become rarer
BCMSNY become sunny
BCMTRD become tired
BCMVLD become valid
BCMWDR become wider
BCMWIE become white
BCNEAY bicentenary
BCNOAT be consonant
BCPCIG backpacking
BCPSAE back passage
BCROAE bicarbonate
BCROBY backroom-boy
BCSABR back-stabber
BCSATR backscatter
BCSIIG backsliding
BCSRTH backscratch
BCTERH back to earth
BCTFOT back to front
BDADOL body and soul
BDAGAE bad language
BDANRD bad-mannered
BDELNS bad feelings
BDEPRD bad-tempered
BDFOOR bed of honour
BDIATA Bodhisattva
BDIHRA Bodhidharma
BDNBAD bed and board
BDNOEL Baden-Powell
BDPLTC body politic
BDSANR body scanner
BDSRAT body servant
BDVLET bedevilment
BDWLOE bid a welcome
BDZNET bedizenment
BECBRH breech birth
BEDAKT bread basket
BEDHAS breadthways
BEDHIE breadthwise
BEDINR breadwinner
BEEHVN Bremerhaven
BEEMIR Biedermeier
BEHRTS blepharitis
BEKACR breakdancer
BEKATV breakfast TV
BEKHIE break the ice
BEKHLW break the law
BEKNOF breaking-off
BEKRUD break ground
BEKTON break it down
BEOARS Buenos Aires
BEPCIG be expecting
BESDES blessedness
BESDIH blessed with
BESPAE breastplate
BESYOL bless my soul!
BETENO breathe into
BETEPN breathe upon
BETIES breathiness
BEZBOK breeze block
BFESAE buffer state
BFESOK buffer stock
BFMSIG be famishing
BFRAIN bifurcation
BFROSY bifariously
BFTIGY befittingly
BGAOIH Bogdanovich
BGFRCS bag of tricks
BGIEET beguilement
BGIIGY beguilingly
BGNTMS bygone times
BGOIFR beg to differ
BGORGS Bognor Regis
BGSALR bogus caller
BGUIES big business
BHALNA Bahia Blanca
BHMAIM bohemianism□
BHRGIG be hard going
BHVBDY behave badly
BHVORL behavioural
BIDSBT blind as a bat
BIEBCE Beiderbecke
BIESET boiled sweet
BIEVLS brisés volés
BIGAEO bring fame to
BIGNBY bring-and-buy
BIGOAS bring to pass
BIGOEL bring to heel
BIGOEO bring home to
BIGOER bring to bear
BIGOID bring to mind
BIGOIE bring to life
BIGOOK bring to book
BIGPID bring up wind
BIHIGY blightingly
BIIGON boiling-down
BIIHAM British warm
BIIHES Britishness
BIKAIG bricklaying
BILATY brilliantly
BILNTN Bridlington
BINATN Brian Patten
BINLIS Brian Aldiss
BINLUH Brian Clough
BINOSN Brian Robson
BIOEAE be in one tale
BITEES brittleness
BITIES bristliness
BITOAT built to last
BITRAD blister card
BITRAK blister pack
BIYBAS Baily's beads
BKDLSA baked Alaska
BKNSET baking sheet
BKRDZN baker's dozen
BLAAIN bold as a lion
BLAAOT bald as a coot

Words marked □ can also be spelled with an initial capital letter

BLABAS bold as brass
BLAURD beleaguered
BLBAIG ball-bearing
bold-beating
BLBTOS bell-bottoms
BLCITN Bill Clinton
BLDGLP bulldog clip
BLEIGY believingly
BLEOHN Bellerophon
BLEPOF bulletproof
bullet-proof
BLESOX billets-doux
BLETRS Ballesteros
BLEWAE baleen whale
BLFGTR bullfighter
BLFLES balefulness
BLIEET belligerent
BLIHES bullishness
BLINIE billionaire
BLIOEY bellicosely
BLIOIY bellicosity
BLMSIF bull-mastiff
BLNBOE Bolingbroke
BLNULY bilingually
BLOIGT be looking at
BLOSES biliousness
BLOTAK Belmont Park
BLRSIN Belorussian
BLSAKY Bill Shankly
BLSPDR bolas spider
BLTDES belatedness
BLTRIR bull-terrier
BLTRLY bilaterally
BLWOML below normal
BLWRUD below ground
BLWTIS belowstairs
BLYACR belly-dancer
BLYCIG belly-aching
BLYHKD Billy the Kid
BLYIDR Billy Wilder
BLYOYU bully for you
BLYRHM Billy Graham
BLYULN Billy Butlin
BLYUTN belly-button
BLYUTR Billy Bunter
BMADET bombardment
BMIAIN bombilation
bombination
BMOSAS bums on seats
BMSDES bemusedness
BMSDIY bumpsadaisy
BMTLIM bimetallism
BMTOSY bumptiously
BNAABS Bandar Abbas
BNACUT bank account
BNAIIY bendability
BNCLRY binocularly
BNDCIE Benedictine
BNDCIN benediction
BNDCOY benedictory
BNEGOS banned goods
BNEIGY banteringly
BNEOCE bonne-bouche

BNFCAE beneficiate
BNFCAY beneficiary
BNFCIN benefaction
BNFCNE beneficence
BNFCOY benefactory
BNGATY benignantly
BNHAKD bunch-backed
BNHLDY bank holiday
BNIGLY Ben Kingsley
BNLOFN bundle of fun
BNNSLT banana split
BNOCCD benzoic acid
BNOKUN Bannockburn
BNPAIO beneplacito
BNSRAT bondservant
BNTAOT be nuts about
BNTERM bang the drum
BNTIGO be nothing to
BNVLNE benevolence
BNVNUE Bonaventure
BNYABT bunny rabbit
BOAAKT blow a gasket
BOBAIG browbeating
BOBNIG bookbinding
BOCIES blotchiness
BOCNET be of consent
BODATR broadcaster
BODESL blood vessel
BODHRH Broad Church
BODIDD broad-minded
BODITR blood-sister
BODNNG Brobdingnag
BODOGT blood-bought
BODOIG blood doping
BODOKD blood-soaked
BODPRS blood sports
BODRNE blood orange
BODTEM bloodstream
BODTIS Broadstairs
BODUKR bloodsucker
BOEDAK biofeedback
BOEMSC broken music
BOERYE broken rhyme
BOFRLW blow for blow
BOHMCL biochemical
BOHROD brotherhood
BOHSCL biophysical
BOIHES bookishness
boorishness
BOKEDD blockheaded
BOKEIG bookkeeping
BOKETR block letter
BOKUTR blockbuster
BOLCIG bootlicking
BOLCTE bootlace tie
BOLGIG bootlegging
BONIER bioengineer
BONVLE Brownsville
BOOETP blow one's top
BOONSS biocoenoses
BOOWRS book of words
BOSNAL boots and all
BOTDES bloatedness

BOTEAF blow the gaff
BOTNOT blotting out
blotting-out
BOTRUH book through
BOZMDL bronze medal
BPIMLY baptismally
BRAAAD Barbara Ward
BRACAY bureaucracy
BRADAZ Bernard Katz
BRAEET bereavement
BRAKOM barrack-room
BRALEE bersagliere
BRAMUD burial mound
BRAOSY barbarously
BRAPAE burial place
burial-place
BRAVUT burial-vault
BRBAND bird-brained
BRCCCD boracic acid
BREEAS Burmese Days
BREIGN bordering on
BREOGN barrel organ
BRESGR barley sugar
BREVUT barrel vault
BREWTR barley water
BRFCDY barefacedly
BRFNIR bird-fancier
BRHAET birth parent
BRHLMW Bartholomew
BRHNOT Berthon-boat
BRIAAO Burkina Faso
BRIAEN Bertie Ahern
BRIAOS barricadoes
BRIREF barrier reef
BRIUAE barbiturate
BRKUKE bare-knuckle
BRLIGN be rolling in
BRNCLY Byronically
BRNESN Byron Nelson
BRNFEF baron of beef
BROATR burgomaster
BROHDL Bardo Thodol
BROYMS borborygmus
BRSEKR Boris Becker
BRSHUD bergschrund
BRSNKV Baryshnikov
BRWTHR birdwatcher
BRYHEE Barry Sheene
BRYRGS Barry Briggs
BSACSA Bismarck Sea
BSAIIE basmati rice
BSATRD bespattered
BSBLCP baseball cap
BSCOHS best clothes
BSEEET besiegement
BSEHUD basset-hound
BSEIGY beseemingly
BSENYU be seeing you
BSEWAE basketweave
BSFLES bashfulness
BSIAOK Bashi-Bazouk
BSIAOS bastinadoes
BSILDY Bastille Day

BSISIH Bessie Smith
BSMMAS by some means
BSMRED bosom friend
BSNSED business end
BSNSMN businessman
BSNSOE Basingstoke
BSOSAS Bishops' Wars
BSRCOF be struck off
BSSLIG bestselling
BSWAKR bushwhacker
BSWLIG bushwalking
BTADOS bits and bobs
BTBOKR beta-blocker
BTDRAH bated breath
BTEAEF by the name of
BTEAIN botheration
BTECEM butter cream
BTEFIS butterflies
BTEILR Bette Midler
BTELMN bitter lemon
BTENIE betweentime
BTESET bittersweet
BTHRID butcherbird
BTIGUT bathing suit
BTLDES battledress
BTLFED battlefield
BTLMNS battlements
BTLRYL battle royal
BTLSIS battleships
BTNCLY botanically
BTNCOS botoné cross
BTNHRE baton charge
baton-charge
BTNSIE bet one's life
BTOELP bite one's lip
BTOGAS bottom-grass
BTRSIG buttressing
BTTEUT bite the dust
BTYPEE bathysphere
BUBODD blue-blooded
BUCETS bruschettas
BUDPIH bound up with
BUDRUS blunderbuss
BUEEBY blue-eyed boy
BUEILS Bruce Willis
BUELSS brucellosis
BUGINN bourguignon
BUHESY blushlessly
BUIHES brutishness
BUNMUH Bournemouth
BUONEE boutonnière
BUQEES brusqueness
BUTFLY bountifully
BUTITD blunt-witted
BUTOSY bounteously
BUUDHE Blut und Ehre
BWCSWN Bewick's swan
BWIENT bowline knot
BWIKRD bewhiskered
BWLEIG bewildering
BWLRZR bowdlerizer
BWNARW bow and arrow
BWTHET bewitchment

BXRHRS boxer shorts
boxer-shorts
BYBIAE Boys' Brigade
BYEBRY boysenberry
BYFALS Bay of Naples
BYFEGL Bay of Bengal
BYFICY Bay of Biscay
BYFLNY Bay of Plenty
BYNDUT beyond doubt
BYNOBS Bryan Forbes
BYNRAH beyond reach
BYNWRS beyond words
BZREES bizarreness
CABAND clay-brained
CABDES crabbedness
CABRAD chambermaid
CABRAN chamberlain❑
CACDNC chalcedonic
CACEET chance event
CACLEY chancellery
CACLOY chancellory
CADMNT Claude Monet
CADSIE clandestine
CADSMN Claude Simon
CAECNE coalescence
CAEENC chameleonic
CAEESY ceaselessly
CAGDIH charged with
CAGDNO changed into
CAGFLY changefully
CAGFOT change front
CAGHNS change hands
CAGHUE charge-house
CAGNRE charge nurse
CAGOTF change out of
CAGRUD change round
CAGSDS change sides
CAIINL coalitional
CAIMTC charismatic
CAIYAL charity ball
CAKEAE crackleware
CAKFAN crack of dawn
CAKONN crack down on
CAKRDT crack credit
CALEHN Charlie Chan
CALMGE Charlemagne
CALNES challengers
CALNIG challenging
CALRAE crawler lane
CALSAB Charles Lamb
CALSAO Charles Mayo
CALSEL Charles Bell
CALSET Charles Best
CALSLW Charles's law
CALSON Charlestown
CALSVS Charles Ives
CAMDUL crammed full
CAMESY charmlessly
CAMEZG Chaim Herzog
CAMNRL clay mineral
CANETR chain letter
CANMKR chain-smoker
CANWOE Chad Newsome

CAOOSY clamorously
CAPLIN Champollion
CAPOIG championing
CAPONN clamp down on
CARESN chairperson
CAROAT clairvoyant
CASCLY classically
CASHOY chaos theory
CASUTE coal scuttle
CATCER chanticleer
CATCLY chaotically
CATNOA Chattanooga
CATRLE chanterelle
CATWMN craftswoman
CAUAIN coagulation
CAYAIG crazy paving
CBAITC cabbalistic
CBALWY Cab Calloway
CBEIIN cablevision
CBREIS cybernetics
CCAEKE cockaleekie
cock-a-leekie
CCCOIG cock-crowing
CCEEOY cache memory
CCEMUH Cockermouth
CCGAHC cacographic
CCGAHR cacographer
CCLETN Cecil Beaton
CCNTAM coconut palm
coconut-palm
CCOADA cyclopaedia
CCOCOK cuckoo clock
CCPOOS cacophonous
CDFELW codified law
CDIEOL cod-liver oil
CDPNAT co-dependant
CEAOIM crematorium
CECAOS cheechakoes
CEDEVE chef d'oeuvre
chef-d'oeuvre
CEECOS clever clogs
cleverclogs
CEELTD crenellated
CEENLY coeternally
CEERLE crème brulée
CEETAS credentials
CEFCET coefficient
CEGWMN clergywoman
CEHRCT Cheshire Cat
CEIAIM clericalism
CEIAIN crepitation
CEIBAC Chenin Blanc
CEIDFR chemin de fer
CEIIIY credibility
CEITNE coexistence
CEKYOL cheek by jowl
CEMHEE cream cheese
CENHVN clean-shaven
CENIBD clean-limbed
CENIES cleanliness
CENIIG clean-living
CENOLD clean bowled
CEOHSS Coelophysis

Words marked ❑ can also be spelled with an initial capital letter

CEOIIM coenobitism
CEPAOS creophagous
CEREDD clear-headed
CERHAR clear the air
CERHWY clear the way
CESBAD cheese board
CESCOH cheesecloth
CESPRR cheeseparer
CESSRW cheese straw
CETAAE cleft palate
CETALN crestfallen
CETNIE coextensive
CETOIM Creationism
CETOIT creationist
CETOPS Cleethorpes
CEUAIN coeducation
CEUCLR crepuscular
CEUOSY credulously
CEURIE chequerwise
CFEBEK coffee break
CFEHUE coffee house
CFENTD caffeinated
CFETBE coffee table
coffee-table
CFSCEY café society
CGAEES cognateness
CGIATF cognizant of
CGIIEY cognitively
CGOCNE cognoscente
CGOCNI cognoscenti
CGOIAE cognominate
CGRHPD cigar-shaped
CIAHAE coin a phrase
CIAOOY climatology
CIATCL climactical
CIATRC climacteric
CICDNE coincidence
CIDEIS child genius
CIDIDR childminder
CIFAGR cliffhanger
cliff-hanger
CIFAKR chief barker
CIFANY chieftaincy
CIFNIR chiffonnier
CIIAIE criminalise
criminalize
CIIAIN crimination
CIIAIY criminality
criticality
CIIALW criminal law
CIIATR criticaster
CIIEOS crinigerous
CIIOOY criminology
CIKETE click beetle
CIKNED chickenfeed
CIKNIE chicken wire
CILATR chill factor
CILNHM Chillingham
CIOOIT chiropodist
CIORPY chirography
CIOSRE chinoiserie
CIPNAE Chippendale
CIRSUO chiaroscuro
CKSNAE Cakes and Ale
CLAATO call a halt to
CLAEIS Callanetics
CLAIIY culpability
CLAOAE collaborate
CLASBE collapsable
collapsible
CLAYOY ciliary body
CLBAIG celebrating
CLBAIN calibration
celebration
CLBAOY celebratory
CLBODD cold-blooded
CLCMOT cold comfort
CLCUIS call cousins
CLELRA calceolaria
CLETBE collectable
CLETDY collectedly
CLETNA collectanea
CLFCIN calefaction
CLFRIM californium
CLHATD cold-hearted
CLIAIG culminating
CLIAIN collimation
culmination
cultivation
CLICOS Celtic cross
CLIEIH collide with
CLIEOS calciferous
CLIITC Calvinistic
CLIKEN Calvin Klein
CLIQIS call it quits
CLIRPY calligraphy
CLMITR calumniator
CLMNOS calamancoes
CLNAIE calendarise
calendarize
CLNAIM colonialism
CLNAIT colonialist
CLNRCL cylindrical
CLOAIN collocation
CLOSES callousness
calvousness
CLOTRN coleopteran
CLOUUS colloquiums
CLRCCD chloric acid
CLRMTR calorimeter
colorimeter
CLRMTY colorimetry
CLRPAT chloroplast
CLRPYL chlorophyll
CLSILY celestially
CLSOAE cold storage
CLTEUE call the tune
CLTODR call to order
CLUAEN calculate on
CLUAIE colour a pipe
CLUAIG calculating
CLUAIN calculation
colouration
CLUBID colour-blind
CLUELB Culture Club
CLUFLY colourfully
CLUIEY collusively
CLWIIG call waiting
CMAAIE comparative
CMADET commandment
CMADOT command post
CMAEHP comradeship
CMAEIH compare with
CMAGFR campaign for
CMAGIG campaigning
CMAIAE compaginate
CMAOOY campanology
CMATDY compactedly
CMATES compactness
CMATET compartment
CMATIC compact disc
CMATIK compact disk
CMAUSR come a gutser
CMBTEN come between
CMCOEO come close to
CMDSOE Comedy Store
CMEDBE commendable
CMEDBY commendably
CMEDOS compendious
CMEDUS compendiums
CMEEIH compete with
CMEETY competently
CMEIIE competitive
CMEIIN competition
CMEIOS competitors
CMELAT comme il faut
CMELDO compelled to
CMENUD Cumbernauld
CMEOAE commemorate
CMESLY commensally
CMETTR commentator
CMFRAD come forward
CMIAIE combinative
CMIAIN combination
commination
compilation
CMIAOY combinatory
CMIEAE commiserate
CMIEIH combine with
CMIFRT come in first
CMIGIE camping-site
CMIGIG commingling
CMINAL Campion Hall
CMIUIN comminution
CMLATY compliantly
CMLCNE complacence
CMLCNY complacency
CMLCTD complicated
CMLIAT complainant
complaisant
CMLIIG complaining
CMLMNS compliments
CMLOIE Camaldolite
CMLXES complexness
CMMLTA camomile tea
CMNAAT coming apart
CMNAIN cementation
CMNCOE coming close
CMNHRS comancheros

CMNOAE	coming of age
CMNTMS	coming times
CMOBGN	come on begin
CMOIIN	composition
CMOIIS	commodities
CMOMRL	common morel
CMONEE	compound eye
CMOPAE	commonplace
CMOSNE	common sense
	commonsense
	common-sense
CMOSOE	common-shore
CMOTBE	comfortable
CMOTBY	comfortably
CMOTES	comfortless
CMOTET	comportment
CMOTIH	come out with
CMOTNE	comportance
CMRDRE	camaraderie
	cameraderie
CMREGS	camerlengos
CMRIGS	camerlingos
CMRMSD	compromised
CMRSIE	compressive
CMRSIN	compression
CMSILS	comestibles
CMSOTF	come short of
CMTAAT	come to a halt
CMTAED	come to a head
	come to an end
CMTATP	come to a stop
CMTBOS	come to blows
CMTGIF	come to grief
CMTGIS	come to grips
CMTLGT	come to light
CMTOLR	comptroller
CMTRUH	come through
CMTTRS	come to terms
CMTWRS	come towards
CMUAIE	communalise
	communalize
	commutative
CMUAIN	commutation
	computation
CMUCIN	compunction
CMUEAE	computerate
CMUEEE	computerese
CMUEIE	computerise
	computerize
CMUEIH	commune with
CMUIAE	communicate
CMUIAT	communicant
CMUITC	communistic
CMULGD	camouflaged
CMUPNE	come-uppance
CMUSUK	come unstuck
CMUTBE	combustible
CMWAMY	come what may
CNABAK	Conrad Black
CNAEAE	concatenate
CNAGIE	consanguine
CNAIAE	contaminate
CNAIAT	contaminant
CNALRA	Convallaria
CNANBE	containable
CNANET	containment
CNATBE	contactable
CNATES	contact lens
CNAUAE	confabulate
CNCOSF	conscious of
CNCOSY	consciously
CNDGOE	Canada goose
CNEACR	conveyancer
CNEAIN	centenarian
	congelation
CNEARM	candelabrum
CNEARS	candelabras
CNEBRS	canterburys
CNEDIH	contend with
CNEEAE	confederate
CNEEAY	confederacy
CNEGNE	convergence
CNEILY	congenially
CNEINE	convenience
CNELBE	congealable
CNELET	concealment
	congealment
CNELTD	cancellated
CNENBE	condemnable
CNENDY	concernedly
CNENET	concernment
CNEPAE	contemplate
CNERTD	consecrated
CNESBY	conversably
CNESDY	confessedly
CNESIK	cancer-stick
CNESNE	conversance
CNESOS	confessions
CNETAE	concentrate
CNETAL	concert-hall
CNETBE	connectable
	connectible
	contestable
	convertible
CNETBY	convertibly
CNETCE	conventicle
CNETCT	Connecticut
CNETDO	converted to
CNETDY	conceitedly
	connectedly
	contentedly
CNETET	contentment
CNETIH	connect with
CNETNS	concertinos
	contestants
CNETOS	conceptious
	connections
	contentious
	conventions
CNETRL	conjectural
CNETSS	conceptuses
CNEUIE	consecutive
CNEUIN	consecution
CNEUNE	consequence
CNEVBE	conceivable
	conservable
CNEVBY	conceivably
CNEVNY	conservancy
CNEVTR	conservator
CNHRDS	cantharides
CNIAIE	cannibalise
	cannibalize
CNIAIM	cannibalism
CNIAUE	candidature
CNICDF	convinced of
CNICDY	convinced by
CNICTR	confiscator
CNIEAE	considerate
CNIEES	conciseness
	confineless
CNIEET	confinement
CNIEIG	considering
CNIETL	continental
CNIETY	confidently
	continently
CNIGES	cunningness
CNIGNY	contingency
CNIIGY	confidingly
CNIILY	convivially
CNIIND	conditioned
CNIINL	conditional
CNIINR	conditioner
CNIITR	conciliator
CNIMBE	confirmable
CNINBE	consignable
CNINET	consignment
CNINRS	cancioneros
CNINTS	Cincinnatus
CNIRME	centigramme
CNITBE	convictable
CNITNE	consistence
CNITNY	consistency
CNITOS	convictions
CNIUAE	configurate
CNIUDY	continuedly
CNIULY	continually
CNIUNE	continuance
CNLCIG	conflicting
CNLCLR	canalicular
CNLCLS	canaliculus
CNLETY	confluently
CNLGAE	conflagrate
CNLLGT	candlelight
CNLSIK	candlestick
CNLSOS	conclusions
CNNCLY	canonically
CNNTOH	canine tooth
CNOAIE	connotative
CNOAIN	condonation
	connotation
	consolation
	convocation
CNOAOY	consolatory
CNOATL	consonantal
CNOATY	consonantly
CNODNE	concordance
CNOECS	condolences
CNOIAE	consolidate
CNOIAT	concomitant

CNOIGY consolingly
CNOIIM condominium
CNOMBE conformable
CNOMBY conformably
CNONHM confound him
CNONHR confound her
CNONIG confounding
CNONYU confound you
CNOSER connoisseur
CNOTEE condottiere
CNOTEI condottieri
CNOTUS consortiums
CNOUIN convolution
CNOVLS convolvulus
CNPCOS conspicuous
CNPRTR conspirator
CNRAIN conurbation
CNRBAD centreboard
CNRBIN Conor O'Brien
CNRBTR contributor
CNRCIE contractive
CNRCIN contraction
CNRCLY centrically
CNRCMN contract man
CNRCOT contract out
CNRCUL contractual
CNRFGL centrifugal
CNRLAK central bank
CNRLAT central part
CNRLIG controlling
CNRNIG confronting
CNROSY congruously
CNRPEE centrepiece
CNRPIN contraption
CNRPTL centripetal
CNRREY contrariety
CNRSAE centre stage
CNRSIE contrastive
CNRSIG contrasting
CNRSMN congressman
CNRTMS contretemps
CNRVNE contrivance
CNRVRY controversy
CNSEIE canisterise
canisterize
CNSRUH Conisbrough
CNTAND constrained
CNTANS constraints
CNTITD constricted
CNTITR constrictor
CNTLAE constellate
CNTNIE Constantine
CNTPTD constipated
CNTRAE consternate
CNTTET constituent
CNTUTR constructer
constructor
CNUAIN confutation
conjugation
conjuration
CNUAIY conjugality
contumacity
CNUCIA conjunctiva
CNUCIE conjunctive
CNUCIN conjunction
CNUCNO cinquecento
CNUCUE conjuncture
CNUEAE connumerate
CNUEIM consumerism
CNUENL contubernal
CNUIAE concubinage
CNUIEO conducive to
CNUIGY conducingly
CNUILY connubially
CNUMTD consummated
CNUPIE consumptive
CNUPIN consumption
CNURBE conquerable
CNURNE concurrence
CNUSOS convulsions
CNUTES conductress
CNUTNE conductance
CNUTNY consultancy
CNYOAA condylomata
CNYSAD Coney Island
CNYTIE candy stripe
COAGOP choral group
COCDAN choice-drawn
CODDIH crowded with
CODDVR clouded over
CODESY cloudlessly
CODNIG clog-dancing
CODNTD co-ordinated
CODNTR co-ordinator
CODNTS coordinates
co-ordinates
CODRUD crowd around
COEADD close-handed
COEAIE co-operative
COEAIG co-operating
COEAIN co-operation
COEAKD close-packed
COEALD close-hauled
COEESN close season
COEGAH choreograph
COEHGP close the gap
COEIDD close-minded
COEIPD close-lipped
COEITD close-fisted
COEQEN closet queen
COERED close friend
COETAD close at hand
COETRL cholesterol
COHFOD cloth of gold
COHPIG clodhopping
COHSOH clothes moth
COHTOK crochet hook
COIGAD cooling card
COIGON closing-down
COILNS Cook Islands
COKAKD crookbacked
COKBOK chock-a-block
COKDES crookedness
CONDED crowned head
CONEES crown jewels
CONOOY crown colony
CONRNE crown prince
CONRUD clown around
CORATR choirmaster
COSEGD cross-legged
COSNET cross-infect
COSODR cross-border
COSOER cross to bear
COSOSN cross cousin
COSSDS choose sides
COSTTH cross-stitch
COSUSW crosscut saw
COSWRS cross swords
COTIIM clostridium
COXATY choux pastry
CPAAGA cephalalgia
CPANHB Captain Ahab
CPANHP captainship
CPANOK Captain Hook
CPBEES capableness
CPCOSY capaciously
CPCTNE capacitance
CPDCIO Capodichino
CPDMNE Capodimonte
CPEFED Copperfield
CPEPAE copperplate
CPIAIG captivating
CPIAIN captivation
CPICOO capriccioso
CPIONS Capricornus
CPLAIY capillarity
CPNBLS cap and bells
CPNSOE coping stone
coping-stone
CPOIKL cupro-nickel
CPOSES copiousness
CPTLRY capitularly
CPUCNS cappuccinos
CPWIIG copy-writing
CRAGAS cors anglais
CRAHAS Carpathians
CRALET curtailment
CRANAL curtain call
curtain wall
CRASNE Carcassonne
CRBAIN cerebration
CRBEES curableness
CRBLUS cerebellums
CRBNEI carabinieri
CRCBIE corn cob pipe
CRCTRD caricatured
CRCTRL caricatural
CREAIE correlative
CREAIN correlation
CREATE Corfe Castle
CREBIT carvel-built
CREJNS Carmen Jones
CRERVR Curlew River
CRESOE cornerstone
corner-stone
CRETES correctness
CREUOR carte du jour
CRFLES carefulness
CRIAAE cardinalate

CRIABY Cardigan Bay
CRIDWY carried away
CRIEDM corrigendum
CRIEYT corn in Egypt
CRIGAH cardiograph
CRIGWY carriageway
CRIIAE certificate
CRIIBE certifiable
CRIIBY certifiably
CRIIER curvilinear
CRIKED carrick bend
CRIKES carsickness
car-sickness
CRIOAA carcinomata
CRIOOS carnivorous
CRIRAE carrier wave
CRIUUS curriculums
CRLIGR carol-singer
CRLNIN Carolingian
CRLSAD coral island
CRMNNE chrominance
CRMNOS ceremonious
CRMPOE chromophore
CRMSEL chrome steel
CRMSML chromosomal
CRNCLY chronically
CRNESN Carl Nielsen
CRNETR Cirencester
CRNGAH chronograph
coronagraph
coronograph
CRNHAS Corinthians
CRNLGR chronologer
CRNMTR chronometer
CROAEY corporately
CROAIM corporatism
CROAIN carbonation
corporation
CROAOS carbonadoes
CROBAK carbon black
CROCCE carbon cycle
CROELY corporeally
CROIEY corrosively
CROIIS curiosities
CROLSS Carlo Blasis
CROMNM Carlos Menem
CRONHW cartoon show
CROOAE corroborate
CROPPR carbon paper
CRORPY cartography
CROSDS caryopsides
CROSEL carbon steel
CROSES curiousness
CROTAE car boot sale
CROYAE carbonylate
CRSABR Chris Barber
CRSAIG coruscating
CRSAIN coruscation
CRSAPR card-sharper
CRSBRL chrysoberyl
CRSEDM Christendom
CRSEIG christening
CRSHEE Carl Scheele
CRSIGY caressingly
CRSINY Christianly
CRSLDS chrysalides
CRSLSS chrysalises
CRSMSY Christmassy
CRSOHR Christopher
CRSOOY Christology
CRSPAE chrysoprase
CRSUAK Chris Eubank
CRSYET Carl Seyfert
CRTNLB Carlton Club
CRTRHP curatorship
CRUAIE circularise
circularize
CRUAIG circulating
CRUAIN circulation
corrugation
CRUAIY circularity
CRUAOY circulatory
CRUASW circular saw
CRUCLR corpuscular
CRUETR carburettor
CRUETY corpulently
CRUFET circumflect
CRUIGY carousingly
CRUOIN cornucopian
CRUSET circumspect
CRUTBE corruptible
CRUTBY corruptibly
CRUTES corruptness
CRUVLE circumvolve
CRVNIE caravan site
CRVNTE caravanette
CRYAOR curry favour
CRYEGT carry weight
CRYHCN carry the can
CRYHDY carry the day
CRYNOT carrying out
carrying-out
CRYNSN carryings-on
CRYODR curry powder
CRYOFR carry too far
CRYTRH carry a torch
CRYTWY carry it away
CSACUT cost-account
CSADAT custard tart
CSALNE cast a glance
CSALRN cast a slur on
CSCTIG cost-cutting
CSEIIE cosmeticise
cosmeticize
CSEIIN cosmetician
CSELTD castellated
CSESGR caster sugar
CSIAIG castigating
CSIAIN castigation
CSIAOY castigatory
CSIEIE cassiterite
CSIGLT costing a lot
CSIPIT case in point
CSISLY Cassius Clay
CSISOE cast in stone
CSITCL casuistical
CSLGTN cast light on
CSLRAH Castlereagh
CSMCIE cash machine
CSOAIY customarily
CSOBIT custom-built
CSOHUE custom house
CSOOIT cosmologist
CSRRNK César Franck
CSUEAL costume ball
CSWAMY cost what may
CTAEAE Cottage Rake
CTAEOF cottage loaf
CTATCL cathartical
CTCEIS catechetics
CTCIML catechismal
CTCITC catechistic
CTCRSS catachresis
CTCYMC cataclysmic
CTDELR city-dweller
CTDVIE Côte d'Ivoire
CTFLOS catafalcoes
CTFPIT cut-off point
CTFTES city fathers
CTGRCL categorical
CTGRZD categorized
CTHBAE catch ablaze
CTHCIL catch a chill
CTHHAE catch phrase
CTHHEE catch the eye
CTHHSN catch the sun
CTHODF catch hold of
CTHODT catch cold at
CTHPIH catch up with
CTIGAK cutting back
CTIGDE cutting edge
CTIHES cattishness
CTLATC catallactic
CTLGCL cytological
CTLGIE cataloguise
cataloguize
CTLGIG cataloguing
CTNATR cotoneaster
CTNCVR cut and cover
CTNDID cut and dried
cut-and-dried
CTNHHT Cat in the Hat
CTNPSE cut and paste
CTOEAS cathode rays
CTOHAS cut both ways
CTOICS cut to pieces
CTOIIE catholicise
catholicize
CTOIIM Catholicism
CTOIIY catholicity
CTPAMC cytoplasmic
CTPETC cataplectic
CTPIOS cut up didoes
CTRILR caterpillar
CTRIOS coterminous
CTRONR catercorner
CTROSN cater-cousin
CTSIKR city slicker
CTSRPE catastrophe

CTTOFT	cut it too fat
CTUWSE	cut out waste
CTZNAE	Citizen Kane
CTZNHP	citizenship
CUAIEY	causatively
CUBIES	crumbliness
CUCBNH	church-bench
CUCGES	churchgoers
CUCGIG	church-going
CUCIES	crunchiness
CUCMUE	church-mouse
CUCTMS	Church Times
CUCTWR	church tower
CUCWMN	churchwoman
CUCWRS	churchwards
CUDGAE	coup de grâce
CUEESY	causelessly
CUENUY	cause injury
CUEOAL	cause to fall
CUEOIE	cause to rise
CUEORP	cause to drop
CUHOAO	couch potato
CUHSER	couch a spear
CUIIIN	crucifixion❑
CUILWR	cauliflower
CUKEGR	Chuck Yeager
CULYRE	cruelty-free
CUSLIG	counselling
CUTCES	causticness
CUTCLY	caustically
CUTCUT	county court
CUTERN	coup the cran
CUTIES	courtliness
CUTIID	countrified
CUTNNE	countenance
CUTOSY	courteously
CUTRAD	countermand
CUTRAE	counterpane
CUTRAL	countervail
CUTRAT	counterpart
CUTREL	counterseal
CUTRET	counterfeit
CUTRIE	countermine
CUTRIK	countersink
CUTRIN	countersign
CUTRLT	counter-plot
CUTRLW	counterblow
CUTROB	cluster bomb
	cluster-bomb
CUTROE	counterbore
	counter-vote
CUTROK	counterwork
CUTROL	counterfoil
CUTRRW	counterdraw
CUTRUE	countermure
CUTRUF	counterbuff
CUTYET	country seat
CUTYID	countryfied
CUTYIE	Country Life
	countryside
	countrywide
	country-wide
CUTYLB	Country Club
	country club
CUTYOE	courtly love
CVAATR	caveat actor
CVCETE	civic centre
CVLAIE	civilianise
	civilianize
CVRDAK	covered walk
CVRHRE	cover charge
CVRHRS	cover shorts
CVROSY	cavernously
CVYTET	civvy street
CXOBCL	coxcombical
CYBOOY	cryobiology
CYEARW	Clyde Barrow
CYNSAE	crying shame
CYSREY	cryosurgery
CYTCLY	cryptically
CYTGAH	cryptograph
CYTLIE	crystalline
	crystallise
	crystallize
CYTLOD	crystalloid
CYUBAD	cry cupboard
DAAAOO	dead as a dodo
DAAAOT	deaf as a post
DAAEDN	draw a bead on
DAAHSN	Dean Acheson
DAANTC	diamagnetic
DAAOET	draw a covert
DAAUGC	dramaturgic
DAEBOT	Diane Abbott
DAEETN	Diane Keaton
DAEIGY	deafeningly
DAERCL	diametrical
DAERLY	diametrally
DAETCL	dialectical
DAETLY	dialectally
DAGTMN	draughtsman
DAHIES	deathliness
DAHRSS	diaphoresis
DAHRTC	diaphoretic
DAHTOE	death-stroke
DAHYAE	deathly pale
DAIGAK	drawing back
DAIGIH	dealing with
DAIGOM	drawing-room
DAIRUH	draw in rough
DANSBE	diagnosable
DAODAK	diamond-back
DAODID	diamond bird
DAODOE	diamond dove
DAOHSS	diapophyses
DAOIIE	diapositive
DAONGT	dead of night
DAOPIE	diamorphine
DAPROE	dual-purpose
DARTCL	diacritical
DATAED	draw to a head
	draw to an end
DATCLY	drastically
DATEIE	draw the line
DATERW	draw the crow
DATIUE	deattribute
DATOGR	draft-dodger
DBLTTD	debilitated
DBOSES	dubiousness
DBRHUL	Deborah Bull
DBUHDY	debauchedly
DBUHET	debouchment
DCAAIE	declarative
DCAAIN	declamation
	declaration
DCAAOY	declamatory
	declaratory
DCAOIL	dictatorial
DCDDES	decidedness
DCECNO	decrescendo
DCEIAE	decrepitate
DCEIUE	decrepitude
DCFACS	Dick Francis
DCFSUY	Dick Fosbury
DCGUHN	Dick Gaughan
DCIAIN	declination
DCIFLY	deceitfully
DCIIOS	declivitous
DCLEAE	décolletage
DCLINH	decillionth
DCLRTR	decelerator
DCLUIE	decolourise
	decolourize
DCMETY	decumbently
DCMNAY	documentary
DCMOIG	decomposing
DCNTUT	deconstruct
DCOOIE	dichotomise
	dichotomize
DCOOOS	dichotomous
DCPEIG	deciphering
DCPIEY	deceptively
DCRBAE	decerebrate
DCRBIE	decerebrise
	decerebrize
DCRETY	decurrently
DCRIAE	decorticate
DCRIEY	decursively
DCRMTC	dichromatic
DCRNIE	doctrinaire
DCRNLY	doctrinally
DCROIE	decarbonise
	decarbonize
DCRTOS	decorations
DCSAEY	decussately
DDAAIE	dedramatise
	dedramatize
DDCIEY	deductively
DDCIIM	didacticism
DDEIES	dodderiness
DDEMOE	Dudley Moore
DDLOTF	diddle out of
DEAAEL	deep as a well
DEDESY	dreadlessly
DEDOGT	dreadnought❑
DEECSS	do exercises
DEFUTS	dies faustus
DEHDAH	die the death
DEKNES	dreikanters

Words marked ❑ can also be spelled with an initial capital letter

DEKSIG deep kissing
DEMESY dreamlessly
DEMIKT dream ticket
DENFSI dies nefasti
DEOIEA Diego Rivera
DEPAIE de-emphasise
de-emphasize
DEPTHD deep-pitched
DESAIG dressmaking
DESAKR deerstalker
DESICE dress circle
DETMIG die-stamping
DETOGT deep thought
DFBIAE defibrinate
DFBIIE defibrinise
defibrinize
DFCETN deficient in
DFCETY deficiently
DFCIEY defectively
DFEECS differences
DFEETA differentia
DFEETY differently
DFIETY diffidently
DFIUTY difficultly
DFLAIN defalcation
defoliation
DFNEES defenceless
DFNIEY defensively
DFRAIN deformation
DFRCIE diffractive
DFRCIN diffraction
DFRNIL deferential
DFUAIE defeudalise
defeudalize
DFUEES diffuseness
DFUIEY diffusively
DFUIIY diffusivity
DGAAIN degradation
DGEBAD daggerboard
DGIGLR dégringoler
DGNRTD degenerated
DGSIEY digestively
DGTGAE digitigrade
DGUIAE deglutinate
DGYADE doggy-paddle
DHDAIN dehydration
DHPOIE dehypnotise
dehypnotize
DHRAOY dehortatory
DHVLAD De Havilland
DIAIIY drivability
DIEATR drive faster
DIECAY driven crazy
DIHMOY Dwight Moody
DIIAIN deification
DIIGET driving seat
driving test
DIIGRN driving iron
DIKLWY drink slowly
DIKREY drink freely
DIKRVR drink-driver
DILNRG drilling rig
DIOYHS Deinonychus
DITCLY deictically
deistically
DIYATE dairy cattle
DIYEOD Daily Record
DIYILR Daisy Miller
DIYOBE daily double
DIYUTR daisy-cutter
DJSIEO do justice to
DKOOTY Dukhobortsy
DKUGLW dak bungalow
DLBAND dull-brained
DLBRTR deliberator
DLCAIN delectation
DLCOSY deliciously
DLFLES dolefulness
DLGTDY delightedly
DLHCLY delphically
DLHNRA dolphinaria
DLHNUS delphiniums
DLILOS dulcifluous
DLNAIE delineative
DLNAIN delineation
DLNHMS Dylan Thomas
DLNUNY delinquency
DLPDTD dilapidated
DLROSY deliriously
DLTROS deleterious
DLVRBE deliverable
DLVRDF delivered of
DLVRNE deliverance□
DLWRBY Delaware Bay
DLYADN Dolly Varden
DMAIIY damnability
DMCAIE democratise
democratize
DMCLAE domiciliate
DMCLAY domiciliary
DMDLTR demodulator
DMEHRT Damien Hirst
DMEIAE demyelinate
DMETUK dumper truck
DMFUDD dumbfounded
DMFUDR dumbfounder
DMGAHC demographic
DMGAHR demographer
DMGDES demigoddess
DMGEIE demagnetise
demagnetize
DMGGEY demagoguery
DMIHES dampishness
DMNEDS diminuendos
DMNEIG domineering
DMNINL dimensional
DMNSIG diminishing
DMNTAE demonstrate
DMPNIN demi-pension
DMRAIN demarcation
DMRLZD demoralized
DMSHNC Demosthenic
DMSHNS Demosthenes
DMSIAE domesticate
DMSIIE domesticise
domesticize
DMSIIY domesticity
DMTAIE demutualise
demutualize
DNAFOS dental floss
DNAIIY deniability
DNAQAE Don Pasquale
DNAUMR Donna Summer
DNCULN Don McCullin
DNEBOE Daniel Boone
DNEDFE Daniel Defoe
DNEDNE dinner-dance
DNEMIE Dunfermline
DNEMNY danger money
DNENNT dance in a net
DNEOSY dangerously
DNEPRY dinner party
DNEQIP Daniel Quilp
DNGAIG denigrating
DNGAIN denigration
DNGAOY denigratory
DNHLAS Don Whillans
DNIAIS Dennis Amiss
DNIUAE denticulate
DNIVNI Don Giovanni
DNLBDE Donald Budge
DNLDWR Donald Dewar
DNLSPR Donald Soper
DNMCLY dynamically
DNMETO do number two
DNMMTR dynamometer
DNMNTD denominated
DNMNTR denominator
DNMRBY denumerably
DNNCAR dining-chair
DNNITR denunciator
DNNTBE dining-table
DNOEEF deny oneself
DNRGYH dendroglyph
DNSELY Denis Healey
DNTAUN done to a turn
DNUFVR dengue fever
DNYEIO Danny Devito
DOAOAR Dromaeosaur
DOATTH drop a stitch
DOAUTY drop a curtsy
DOEBOK do one's block
DOESUF do one's stuff
DOETIG do one's thing
DOEVRN do one over on
DOEWRT do one's worst
DOFRIG drop-forging
DOIAIN deoxidation
DOPDRH dropped arch
DORPDY drop rapidly
DOSEPR doorstepper
DOTIES drouthiness
DOWTHR doomwatcher
DOYEAE deoxygenate
DOYEIE deoxygenise
deoxygenize
DPAAIN depravation
DPAIGY depravingly
DPEAIE deprecative

DPEAIG deprecating
DPEAIN deprecation
depredation
DPEAOY deprecatory
DPHHRE depth charge
depth-charge
DPIAIG duplicating
DPIAIN deprivation
duplication
DPIIOS duplicitous
DPLGAE dephlegmate
DPNETN dependent on
DPNIGN depending on
DPNIGY dependingly
DPOAIC dipsomaniac
DPOAIE diplomatise
diplomatize
DPOAIN deploration
DPOAIT diplomatist
DPOIGY deploringly
DPRAIN deportation
DPREET département
DPTOGL diphthongal
DPTZFR deputize for
DPUEAE depauperate
DPUEIE depauperise
depauperize
DRAOOY dermatology
DRBEES durableness
DRBGRE Dirk Bogarde
DRCAIE deracialise
deracialize
DRCDBT direct debit
DRCGIE derecognise
derecognize
DRCIIY directivity
DRCINL directional
DRCOAE directorate
DRCOIL directorial
DRCRCS directrices
DREFED Durbeyfield
DREGUH Darren Gough
DREVLE D'Urberville
DRKAMN Derek Jarman
DRKAOI Derek Jacobi
DRLCIN dereliction
DRNEET derangement
DRNEIA durante vita
DRNHRY daring-hardy
DRSAAM Dar es Salaam
DRSIND dark-skinned
DRSRIS Dire Straits
dire straits
DRYLMN dirty old man
DRYRCS dirty tricks
DSAAEY disparately
DSAAIG disparaging
DSACBX dispatch box
DSADET disbandment
DSAERE disease-free
DSAHTC dyspathetic
DSAIIE destabilise
destabilize
de-Stalinise
de-Stalinize
DSAJMY dismal Jimmy
DSARSN disgarrison
DSATAT distant past
DSATFL distasteful
DSATIG dismantling
DSBDET disobedient
DSBEET disablement
DSBIIG disobliging
DSCAIE desacralise
desacralize
DSCAIG desecrating
DSCAIN desecration
desiccation
DSCUTM disaccustom
DSCVRD dust-covered
DSDRTM desideratum
DSEADD disregarded
DSEAEY desperately
DSEAIN desperation
DSEAOS desperadoes
DSEBIG dissembling
DSEDNS descendants
DSEEIG dissevering
DSEELD dishevelled
DSEEQE Disneyesque
DSEIAE disseminate
DSEIVR disbeliever
DSENBE discernible
DSENBY discernibly
DSENET discernment
DSESBE dispensable
distensible
DSESBY dispensably
DSESDY dispersedly
DSETET dissentient
DSETOS dissentious
DSFETD disaffected
DSFOET disafforest
DSGAIN designation
DSGEAE desegregate
DSGEIG disagreeing
DSGIGY designingly
DSHOIG deschooling
DSHRIG discharging
DSIAIE dissipative
DSIAIN destination
dissipation
DSICIE distinctive
DSICIN distinction
DSIEBE dislikeable
DSIEHT despite that
DSIGIH distinguish
DSIIAE dissimilate
DSIIIG dispiriting
DSILND disciplined
DSIUAE dissimulate
DSIUEF destitute of
DSIUIN destitution
DSLAIG displeasing
DSLAIY disyllabify
DSLAUE displeasure
DSLCIN deselection
DSLEIE desilverise
desilverize
DSLIIG disclaiming
DSLOIY desultorily
DSLUIN disillusion
DSMITR disembitter
DSMOID disembodied
DSMRSN disimprison
DSMTIG do something
DSMUDN disemburden
DSNAGE disentangle
DSNDNS dos and don'ts
do's and don'ts
DSNEET disinterest
DSNETD disinfected
DSNHAL disenthrall
DSNHOD disenshroud
DSNIIE desensitise
desensitize
DSNILD disentitled
DSNLND disinclined
DSNRNE disentrance
DSNUBR disencumber
DSOAIN dislocation
DSOATY dissonantly
DSODNE discordance
DSODNY despondency
DSODUU Desmond Tutu
DSOETY dishonestly
DSOFTD discomfited
DSOGET dislodgment
DSOHQE discotheque
discothèque
DSOIBY dissociably
DSOIGY disposingly
DSOIIN disposition
DSOITD dissociated
DSONIG discounting
DSOORD discoloured
dishonoured
DSOPSD discomposed
DSOREY discourtesy
DSORGD discouraged
DSORPY discography
DSOTNE discontinue
DSOUEY dissolutely
DSOUIN dissolution
DSPERD disappeared
DSPRIG disc parking
DSPRVL disapproval
DSRAET disarmament
DSRAGD disarranged
DSRAIE disorganise
disorganize
DSRBBE describable
DSRBTR distributor
DSRCFL disgraceful
DSRCIE destructive
DSRCIG distracting
DSRCIN destruction
distraction
DSRCOS disgracious

DSRDTD discredited
DSRETD disoriented
DSRIGY deservingly
DSRNLD disgruntled
DSRPIE descriptive
DSRPIN description
DSRPNY discrepancy
DSRPRY disproperty
DSRSFL distressful
distrustful
DSRSIG distressing
distrusting
DSSEBE disassemble
DSSEBY disassembly
DSTEIT dish the dirt
DSUAIN disputation
DSUBDY disturbed by
DSUBNE disturbance
DSUCIE disjunctive
DSUCIN dysfunction
DSUEIG disquieting
DSUEUE disquietude
DSUSBE discussable
discussible
DSUSDY disguisedly
DSUSIH discuss with
DSUTDY disgustedly
DSXAIE desexualise
desexualize
DSYLBE dissyllable
DSYMTY dissymmetry
DTANET detrainment
DTATRM detract from
DTCPUE data capture
DTEOKF do the work of
DTEONS do the rounds
DTFLES dutifulness
DTIAIE detribalise
detribalize
DTIETL detrimental
DTNCRY dot and carry
DTOFCR duty officer
DTORPY dittography
DTRIAE determinate
DTRIAT determinant
DTRIIG determining
DTRIIM determinism
DTRIIT determinist
DTROAE deteriorate
DTSAIN detestation
DUAETT Deus avertat
DUEATE Doune Castle
DUEOOY Deuteronomy
DUHIES doughtiness
DUKNES drunkenness
DULAET double agent
DULBID double-blind
DULBUF double bluff
DULCEK double-check
DULCEM double cream
DULCIK double-click
DULCOS double-cross
DULDTH double Dutch
DULEGD double-edged
DULEGE double eagle
DULETY double-entry
DULFCD double-faced
DULFRT double first
DULFUT double fault
double-fault
DULHLX double helix
DULQIK double-quick
DULSAE double-space
DULSAG Douglas Haig
DULSAP double sharp
DULSEK doublespeak
DULSOE Douglas-Home
DULSOG Douglas Hogg
DULSUD Douglas Hurd
DULSUN Douglas Dunn
DULTIK doublethink
DUMCIE drum machine
DUSHAK Deutschmark
DUTESY dauntlessly
doubtlessly
DVBMIG dive-bombing
DVBUEK Dave Brubeck
DVDALY David Bailey
DVDECR David Mercer
DVDELR David Mellor
DVDEMN David Seaman
DVDETN David Beaton
DVDETY David Beatty
DVDIKE David Wilkie
DVDIOA David Ginola
DVDIZO David Rizzio
DVLAIN devaluation
DVLIAE divellicate
DVLPBE developable
DVLPET development
DVLPNO develop into
DVLTIG devil a thing
DVNBIG Divine Being
divine being
DVNINW Devon minnow
DVNNRD divining rod
DVNRGT divine right
DVOSES deviousness
DVRCTD divaricated
DVREES diverseness
DVRERM divorce from
DVRETY divergently
DVRIGY divergingly
divertingly
DVRIID diversified
DVRIUA diverticula
DVSAIG devastating
DVSAIN devastation
DVTDES devotedness
DVTLZD devitalized
DVUIGY devouringly
DWADUS down-and-outs
DWGAIG downgrading
DWHATD downhearted
down-hearted
DWPTIK Downpatrick
DWPYET down payment
DWTEDR Dawn Treader
DWTEID down the wind
DWTEIE Down the Mine
DWTERH down to earth
down-to-earth
DWTODN downtrodden
down-trodden
DXEOSY dexterously
DYAORR day-labourer
DYFCIN day of action
DYFEDY day after day
DYLAES dry cleaner's
DYNAOT day in day out
DYOGAE days of grace
DYRAIG daydreaming
day-dreaming
EAAESS epanalepses
EACPTD emancipated
EACPTR emancipator
EAEBTD exacerbated
EAECNE evanescence
EAGLCL evangelical
EAGRTD exaggerated
EAGRTR exaggerator
EAIAIE eradicative
EAIAIN egalitarian
eradication
evagination
examination
EAIEES evasiveness
EALNAT enabling act
EAMCOL Ewan MacColl
EAOAEN elaborate on
EAOAEY elaborately
EAOAIE elaborative
evaporative
EAOAIG evaporating
EAOAIN elaboration
evaporation
EAORDF enamoured of
EAPRTD exasperated
EATCAD elastic band
EATCLY elastically
EATCTD elasticated
EATDES exaltedness
EATEAA exanthemata
EATMRC elastomeric
EATPAT Elastoplast®
EAUAIE ejaculative
EAUAIN ejaculation
EAUAOY ejaculatory
EBAEET embracement
EBAIGY embracingly
EBEAIE emblematise
emblematize
EBLIHD embellished
EBOAIN embrocation
EBODRR embroiderer
EBOLET embroilment
EBRAIN embarkation
EBRASD embarrassed
EBTEIG embittering

11 E_B_W

EBWRAE elbow grease
elbow-grease
ECAAIN exclamation
ECAAOY exclamatory
ECAITC eucharistic□
ECANET enchainment
ECAOOY eschatology
ECATES enchantress
ECATET enchantment
ECECNE excrescence
ECEETL excremental
ECEIGY exceedingly
ECIOOY eccrinology
ECLAIN exculpation
ECLAOY exculpatory
ECLETY excellently
ECLPDC encylopedic
ECMASD encompassed
ECMATC encomiastic
ECMRNE encumbrance
ECNESS ex concessis
ECOOIN euchologion
ECPINL exceptional
ECPUAE encapsulate
ECPWEL escape wheel
ECRAIE encarnalise
encarnalize
ECRAIN excoriation
ECRIAE excorticate
ECRIEY excursively
ECSIEY excessively
ECTDES excitedness
ECUAIG encouraging
ECUIEF exclusive of
ECUIEY exclusively
ECUIIY exclusivity
ECVTOS excavations
EDAIGY endearingly
EDCRET eddy current
EDERAO Eddie Arcaro
EDERIE Eddie Irvine
EDESES endlessness
EDEUPY Eddie Murphy
EDLFED E M Delafield
EDMCLY endemically
EDMRHC endomorphic
EDMTIM endometrium
EDNIAL ending it all
EDRCOY ex-directory
EDREET endorsement
EDRIES elderliness
EDSEMC endospermic
EDTCLY eidetically
EDTEIM endothelium
EDWDIH endowed with
EEACIG eye-catching
EECSBE exercisable
EEETLY elementally
EEHHIN Erechtheion
EEHNGN elephant gun
EEHNIE elephantine
EEHNOD elephantoid
EEICLY elegiacally
EEIGEL evening meal
EEINID etesian wind
EELSIG everlasting□
EENLIE eternal life
EENLIY Eternal City
EENONS exeunt omnes
EEOAEE eye for an eye
EEPAIY exemplarily
EEPATC esemplastic
EEPEET ever-present
EERGNC epeirogenic
EETAIE eventualise
eventualize
EETAIY eventuality
EETIAC electric arc
EETIEE electric eye
EETIEL electric eel
EETIIN electrician
EETIIY electricity
EETIRY electric ray
EETOER electioneer
EETOGN electron gun
EETOIS electronics
EETOUE electrocute
EETOYE electrolyse
electrolyte
electrotype
EEUIEY executively
EEUINR executioner
EEUOIL executorial
EEURCS executrices
EEURXS executrixes
EEWIMN Ezer Weizman
EEYEOD every second
EEYESN every person
EEYIGE every single
EEYWUH Evelyn Waugh
EFACIE enfranchise
EFCCOS efficacious
EFCETY efficiently
EFCIEY effectively
EFCULY effectually
EFETWR Eiffel Tower
EFLAIE exfoliative
EFLAIN exfoliation
EFLETY effulgently
EFNBID eff and blind
EFREBE enforceable
EFREET enforcement
EGATET engraftment
EGIAOD edge in a word
EGIHON English horn
EGNCLY eugenically
EGNEIG engendering
engineering
EGNSON egg-and-spoon
EGOSDN engrossed in
EGOSET engrossment
EGREET engorgement
EGREVR eager beaver
EGTEMS eighteenmos
EHCABR echo chamber
EHCLES ethicalness
EHIGOP ethnic group
EHLRTD exhilarated
EHMRDS ephemerides
EHNEET enhancement
EHOOIT ethnologist
EHORPY ethnography
EHRAIE etherealise
etherealize
exhortative
EHRAIN exhortation
EHRAOY exhortatory
EHSUDR echo-sounder
EHUTBE exhaustible
EHUTIE exhaust pipe
EIAEHN Elizabethan
EIAILY epitaxially
EIBITW Eric Bristow
EICATN Eric Clapton
EICNOA Eric Cantona
EICPLY episcopally
EIEHIE epinephrine
EIENLY eviternally
EIETAY evidentiary
EIFSHR Emil Fischer
EIHAEL Edith Cavell
EIHIEA epicheirema
EIHLIM epithalmium
EIHLMA epithalamia
EIHLMC epithalamic
EIIAIN edification
elicitation
elimination
EIIIIY eligibility
EIIPCI Emilio Pucci
EIISGE Emilio Segrè
EILDEL Eric Liddell
EIOILY editorially
EIPOOS eriophorous
EISITN Eric Shipton
EITNIL existential
EIYRNE Emily Brontë
ELCIIM eclecticism
ELGTND enlightened
ELPODL ellipsoidal
ELRCVS Ellora caves
ELREET enlargement
ELRQEN Ellery Queen
ELSEMN enlisted man
ELSSAD Ellis Island
ELVNET enlivenment
EMGLMN Emma Goldman
EMNBRE Edmund Burke
EMTNAT Emma Tennant
ENBEET ennoblement
ENSBVN Ernest Bevin
ENSILN Enniskillen
ENSRNN Ernest Renan
ENTIIM einsteinium
ENTIIN Einsteinian
EOAICL egomaniacal
EOAIEY evocatively
EOBTNE exorbitance
EOEAIE exonerative

Words marked □ can also be spelled with an initial capital letter

EOEAIN exoneration
EOEIIM esotericism
EOHAIG epoch-making
EOHOEL Enoch Powell
EOINES emotionless
EOINLY emotionally
EOITCL egotistical
EOKLTL exoskeletal
EOKLTN exoskeleton
EOOEOS erotogenous
EOOERC econometric
EOOIEN economize on
EOREDY eco-friendly
EOSHEE Egon Schiele
EOUETL emolumental
EPAAIN explanation
EPAAOY explanatory
EPAEET emplacement
EPANBE explainable
EPANWY explain away
EPCAIN expectation
EPCATY expectantly
EPCIGY expectingly
EPCOAE expectorate
EPCOAT expectorant
EPDETY expediently
EPDTOS expeditious
EPEITC euphemistic
EPESBE expressible
EPESOS expressions
EPIAIE explicative
EPIAIN explication
EPIAOY explicatory
EPNIEY expansively
expensively
EPNIUE expenditure
EPNLET empanelment
EPNNIL exponential
EPOAIE explorative
EPOAIN exploration
EPOAOY exploratory
EPOIEY explosively
EPORAE expropriate
EPOTBE exploitable
EPPLOE en papillote
EPRAIN exportation
expurgation
EPRCLY empirically
EPRECD experienced
EPRECS experiences
EPRNIT Esperantist
EPRROH emperor moth
EPRUAA empyreumata
EPSFCO ex post facto
EPSUAE expostulate
EPTAEN expatiate on
EPTAIN expatiation
EPWRET empowerment
EPYADD empty-handed
EPYEDD empty-headed
EPYETR empty-nester
EQIIEY exquisitely
ERCFRI Enrico Fermi

ERCNRC Eurocentric
ERETES earnestness
ERGOSY egregiously
ERHIES earthliness
ERHNAE earthenware
ERHRMR earth-tremor
ERIRHN earlier than
ERIRIG ear-piercing
ERLANR Errol Garner
ERNOSY erroneously
ERPAIE Europeanise
Europeanize
ERPAIM Europeanism
ERPAIT Europeanist
ERTCLY erratically
ERYHIS eurhythmics
ERYHIT eurhythmist
ERYNUH early enough
ERYTGS early stages
ESAEET enslavement
ensnarement
ESBNRH east-by-north
ESBSUH east-by-south
ESCAIN exsiccation
ESEDOS eisteddfods
ESENIE Eastern Time
ESENOT easternmost
ESETCE en spectacle
ESLMVD easily moved
ESLTIN East Lothian
ESLUST easily upset
ESNILY essentially
ESOEEF ease oneself
ESPLHE ensepulchre
ESWIHR elsewhither
ETAAAE extravasate
ETAAAT extravagant
ETACFE entrance fee
ETACWY entranceway
ETAHRE extra charge
ETAIGN extra virgin
ETAIIN extradition
ETAOAE extrapolate
ETATBE extractable
ETBATC ectoblastic
ETBAUE entablature
ETBIHD established
ETBIHR establisher
ETCMNS enticements
ETEIIS extremities
ETIAIN extrication
ETMOAY extemporary
ETMOIE extemporise
extemporize
ETMRHC ectomorphic
ETNAIE extenuative
ETNAIG extenuating
ETNAIN extenuation
ETNAOY extenuatory
ETNIEY extensively
ETNIRS estancieros
ETNSIL eat one's fill
ETOETD extroverted

ETPAMC ectoplasmic
ETRAIE externalise
externalize
ETRAIN extirpation
ETRANR entertainer
ETRAOY extirpatory
ETRIAE exterminate
ETRIEY extorsively
ETRINR extortioner
ETRLET enthralment
ETRLIG enthralling
ETROIE exteriorise
exteriorize
ETRRSS enterprises
ETTAET estate agent
ETTEET entitlement
ETUIAM enthusiuasm
ETYHRE entry charge
EUAGLR equiangular
EUAIIY educability
EUAINL educational
EUANET edutainment
EUBLNE equibalance
EUCAIN enunciation
EUDSAT equidistant
EUEAIN enumeration
EUEATY exuberantly
EUECNE erubescence
EUEIIM ecumenicism
EUEIIY ecumenicity
EUIAIE elucidative
EUIAIN elucidation
EUIAOY elucidatory
EULBAE equilibrate
EULBIM equilibrium
EULBIT equilibrist
EULETY ebulliently
EULIHS equal rights
EULTRL equilateral
EUNCIL equinoctial
EUOSES emulousness
EURAIN elutriation
EUSOIE emulsionise
emulsionize
EUSRAS equestrians
EUVCLY equivocally
EUVCTR equivocator
EUVLNE equivalence
EVLPET envelopment
EVOSES enviousness
EVRGIG Edvard Grieg
EVRMNH Edvard Munch
EVRNET environment
EVSRPN eavesdrop on
EWNLRN Edwin Aldrin
EWNOML Erwin Rommel
EWNUBE Edwin Hubble
EWRABE Edward Albee
EWRBRA Edward Burra
EWRDIY Edward Doisy
EWREGR Edward Elgar
EWRHAH Edward Heath
EWRMLE Edward Milne

EWRPSY Edward Pusey
EWRSPR Edward Sapir
EWRTAH Edward Teach
EYHOYE erythrocyte
EYOOIE etymologise
etymologize
EYOOIT etymologist
EYTAMU Egyptian Mau
EZFRAI Enzo Ferrari
FABRAT flabbergast
FABYNE flamboyance
FABYNY flamboyancy
FACIER franc-tireur
FACILS fiançailles
FACPOE francophone
FACSON Francistown
FADLNE fraudulence
FADLNY fraudulency
FAEBRH Fraserburgh
FAEFID frame of mind
FAELTR flagellator
FAENLY fraternally
FAENZR fraternizer
FAFLES fearfulness
FAHRIE featherlike
FAIIIY feasibility
FAKOSN Frank Dobson
FAKUTR frankfurter
FAMNAY fragmentary
FANBIN Flann O'Brien
FANEIO Fra Angelico
FANIGY flauntingly
FANLTE flannelette
FAORES flavourless
FAOROE flavoursome
FARCDL fratricidal
FASRAE flat surface
FATCLY frantically
FATFNN Frantz Fanon
FATOAE fractionate
FATOIE fractionise
fractionize
FATOSY fractiously
FAUEES featureless
FAUEIM feature film
FAUETY flatulently
FAZEMR Franz Mesmer
FBEPIS fibre optics
FBIAIN fabrication
FCFNIG fact-finding
FCLAIE facultative
FCLEGH focal length
FCLTTR facilitator
FCNAIN fecundation
FCNROS facinerious
FCOYAD factory hand
FCOYAM factory farm
FCOYHP factory shop
FCSFIE facts of life
FCTOSY facetiously
FCULES factualness
FDEIES fidgetiness
FDIHES faddishness
FDLAOT fiddle about
FDLATO Fidel Castro
FDLRRB fiddler crab
FDLSIK fiddlestick
FEAAID free as a bird
FEADAY free and easy
free-and-easy
FEATIE Fred Astaire
FEBOIG freebooting
FECCAK French chalk
FECCRE French curve
FECFAC French franc
FECFIS French fries
FECLAE French leave
FECOEO feel close to
FECSIK French stick
FECTAT French toast
FECWMN Frenchwoman
Frenchwomen
FEDFIW field of view
FEDOKR field worker
fieldworker
FEDPRS field sports
FEDVNS field events
FEDWMN fieldswoman
FEEGUE feeler gauge
FEEITN Fredericton
FEFLES fretfulness
FEHAET fresh talent
FEHOGR fleshmonger
FEIAFM fee-fi-faw-fum
FEIGES feelingless
FEIGIE feeling like
FEIHOD Flemish bond
FEIIIY flexibility
FEITUH feel in touch
FELAIG freeloading
FEMSNC Freemasonic
FEMSNY Freemasonry
FEOBAD free on board
FEOEEF feel oneself
free oneself
FEOEWY feel one's way
FERCOS fleury cross
FERDCL free radical
FERDLS fleurs-de-lis
fleurs-de-lys
FERDOK Fleur Adcock
FERMRE feel remorse
FESAIG free skating
FETIKR freethinker
free-thinker
FETOGT freethought
FETTET Fleet Street
FETUMN Fred Trueman
FEWIPE Fred Whipple
FEZFAE freeze-frame
FFENHY fifteenthly
FFHOUN fifth column
FGRDAS figured bass
FGROFN figure of fun
FGTNFT fighting fit
FGTNMN fighting man
FIADAX fricandeaux
FIAEID frigate bird
frigatebird
FIBEES friableness
FICIGY flinchingly
FIDOAO fried potato
FIHEES frighteners
FIHEIG frightening
FIHESY faithlessly
FIHFLY frightfully
FIHIES flightiness
FIIGHT failing that
FIILRA fritillaria
FIIZNS frigid zones
FILLRE fairly large
FINSIH friends with
FIOELD flip one's lid
FIOOSY frivolously
FITCTH fail to catch
FITGAP fail to grasp
FITMSO fritto misto
FITRUH flip through
FITRWY fritter away
FITSIE fail to seize
FITTOS flirtatious
FIWAHR fair-weather
FLAIHY fallalishly
FLAOND full-acorned
FLBODD full-blooded
FLEAGL fallen angel
FLEEIF false belief
FLEEOE fille de joie
FLEEOT false report
FLEIGY falteringly
FLEOTM false bottom
FLEWMN fallen woman
FLFAGT full-fraught
FLFGRD full-figured
FLFOTL full-frontal
FLHLCE filthy lucre
FLIAIG fulminating
FLIAIN fulmination
FLIAOY fulminatory
FLIGAK falling back
FLIGON falling-down
FLIGTR falling star
falling-star
FLIIBE falsifiable
FLIIIY fallibility
FLILIH fall ill with
FLIUOE folliculose
FLLRIG fell-lurking
FLMNAY filamentary
FLMNOS filamentous
FLMUHD full-mouthed
FLNOSY feloniously
FLOBAS full of beans
FLOEES fulsomeness
FLOIES full of ideas
FLORPY filmography
FLOYAS full of years
FLRNIG fell-running
FLRPDY fall rapidly

FLSAHC feldspathic
FLSTIG filmsetting
FLTEIL fill the bill
FLTETE film theatre
FLTFIN Falstaffian
FLTINN filet mignon
FLTRUH fall through
FLWLIG fell-walking
FLXAKL Felix Wankel
FMEAAE femme fatale
FMLAIE familiarise
familiarize
FMLAIY familiarity
FMLATR family altar
FMLBBE family Bible
FMLCUT family court
FMLSRW female screw
FMNAIN fomentation
FMRAIN fimbriation
FMTRUS fumatoriums
FNAETL fundamental
FNAIIG fantasizing
FNAOAE fanfaronade
FNAOFR find a job for
FNATCL fantastical
FNCIES finickiness
FNCLES finicalness
FNDTIS fine details
FNEBAD fingerboard
FNEICE fin de siècle
FNELKS Finger Lakes
FNEOIO fons et origo
FNEPIT finger-paint
fingerprint
FNESAL fingerstall
FNEWAE finner whale
FNGAND fine-grained
FNHLIG fundholding
FNLATE final battle
FNLEAD final demand
FNMCOL Finn mac Cool
FNMUAE funambulate
FNMUIT funambulist
FNNGMS fun and games
FNNILY financially
FNOEEF find oneself
FNOGIN Finno-Ugrian
FNRLOG funeral song
FNRLOM funeral poem
FNRONS finer points
FNSEBS fines herbes
FNSFRT finish first
FNSRTD fenestrated
FNTCLY fanatically
FNTEAY find the lady
FNTOAY functionary
FNTOIG functioning
FNTOKY function key
FNYEBE Fanny Kemble
FNYOGR fancy monger
FNYUNY Fanny Burney
FOADES frowardness
FOAOSN Flora Robson
FOBLWR Football War
FOCLNE flocculence
FODSET frondescent
FOECID flower child
FOECNE florescence
FOEIES floweriness
FOEPWR flower power
FOESAK flower-stalk
FOESIF frozen-stiff
FOEWTR frozen water
FOHOPR froth-hopper
FOIEIM florilegium
FOIEOS floriferous
FOIGAK flowing-back
FOIHES foolishness
FOMTYU From Me To You
FONWEE from nowhere
FOOWRS flow of words
FORSIG flourishing
FOSIES frowstiness
FOSINE food science
FOSRAD fool's errand
FOTATR front matter
frontmatter
FOTDAH flog to death
FOTEIL foot the bill
FOTESY frontlessly
FOTITN frostbitten
FOTLOE frontal lobe
FOTLSS frontolysis
FOTNRB floating rib
FOTPIG foot-tapping
FOTUNR front-runner
FOWTOT from without
FPIHES foppishness
FRACUE formal cause
FRADES forwardness
FRAIAS farm animals
FRAIIS formalities
FRAINL formational
FRAITC formalistic
FRBIAE fire brigade
FRBRUH Farnborough
FRCAKR firecracker
FRCOSY ferociously
FRCOUE foreclosure
FRCSIG forecasting
FRECIG far-reaching
FREFLY forgetfully
FREMNT forget-me-not
FRERNE forbearance
FRESLB Farmers Club
FRESUG farmer's lung
FRETBE fermentable
forfeitable
FRETMS former times
FRETUP Forrest Gump
FRFTES forefathers
FRHBRS for the birds
FRHOIG forthcoming
FRHRHN further than
FRHRNE furtherance
FRHROE furthermore
furthersome
FRHROT furthermost
FRHSED farthest end
furthest end
FRHWRE for the worse
FRIAIN formication
fornication
FRIDNE forbiddance
FRIDNY forbiddenly
FRIEES forgiveness
furtiveness
FRIEOS furciferous
FRIHNS furnishings
FRIIBE fortifiable
FRIIIG fertilizing
FRIIIY forcibility
FRINES foreignness
FRINOY foreign body
FRINUE foreign rule
FRIOIE ferric oxide
FRIWEL Ferris wheel
FRKCOF for a kick-off
FRKOIG foreknowing
FRLGTR firelighter
FRLIAE for all I care
FRLTSE for all to see
FRMNTD foraminated
FRNCOS farinaceous
FRNGTY fortnightly
FRNSUD firing squad
FRNTIG for one thing
FRNTNE for instance
FRNUOS furunculous
FRONES forlornness
FRONOE forlorn hope
FROSAE for God's sake
FROSES furiousness
FRPYET forepayment
FRQATR forequarter
FRRCTD fore-recited
FRRIIG fire-raising
FRSAIN fire station
forestation
FRSALR forestaller
FRSEBE foreseeable
FRSGTD foresighted
FRSOTN foreshorten
FRSURR fore-spurrer
FRTAHR form teacher
FRTCOL first school
FRTHIE first choice
FRTIKT first aid kit
FRTLIG foretelling
FRTOGT forethought
FRTOSN first cousin
FRTPAL fore-topsail
FRTRES for starters
FRTTIE first strike
FRUAEY fortunately
FRUAIE formularise
formularize
FRUAIN formulation
FRUEEL fortune-tell

FRUIOS ferruginous
FRUMNY for our money
FRVROE for evermore
forevermore
FRVUHD forevouched
FRWAIG forswearing
FRWLIM Fort William
FRWNLR Furtwängler
FRWRIG forewarning
FSBWIG fast bowling
FSETIE fastest time
FSFRAD fast-forward
FSIAEY festinately
FSIAIG fascinating
FSIAIN fascination
fustilarian
FSIAOS fissiparous
FSIFRD fossil-fired
FSIGIE fishing-line
FSIIIN fustilirian
FSIIIS festivities
FSIITD fastigiated
FSINBE fashionable
fissionable
FSINBY fashionably
FSIWTR fossil water
FSNURN fast neutron
FSSHIT festschrift
FSTAKR fast-tracker
FSUYLP Fosbury flop
FTDCLY fatidically
FTEBON Father Brown
FTEILW father-in-law
FTFEPR fit of temper
FTFERR fit of terror
FTFLES fatefulness
FTGEUY fatigue-duty
FTGIGY fatiguingly
FTIGES fittingness
FTOEHR fit together
FTOEID fit to be tied
FTOIEN fit to live in
FTOSES fatuousness
FTSITC fetishistic
FTSMOS Fitzsimmons
FUDBET found object
FUDTOS foundations
FUMUHD foul-mouthed
FURSET fluorescent
FURSOE fluoroscope
FURSOY fluoroscopy
FUTAIG fluctuating
frustrating
FUTAIN fluctuation
frustration
FUTESY faultlessly
fruitlessly
FUTFIG fructifying
FUTIDR fault-finder
FUTIPN fountain pen
FVDYEK five-day week
FVUIIM favouritism
FXDSES fixed assets
FYNPRY flying party
FYNSAT flying start
FYNSUD flying squad
FYRSIG fly-dressing
FZNERS fazendeiros
GAAAAA Guadalajara
GAACNL Guadalcanal
GAAGOH Graham Gooch
GAAINL gradational
GAASIT Graham Swift
GABRAT Glauber salt
GACNOF glancing-off
GACNRA Gran Canaria
GADAAA Grand Bahama
GADACE Grande Arche
GADAET grandparent
GADAHR grandfather
GADAMN Grand Cayman
GADATR Grand Master
grand master
grandmaster
GADDES guardedness
GADEHW grand-nephew
GADLMN grand old man
GADLRY glandularly
GADOEY grandiosely
GADOHR grandmother
GADOIY grandiosity
GAEESY gracelessly
GAEIAE graven image
GAEIGR grave-digger
GAEUFR grateful for
GAGMUH Grangemouth
GAGWIY Glasgow City
GAHCES graphicness
GAHCLY graphically
GAHLGC graphologic
GAIAIN gravitation
GAIERC gravimetric
GAIGAD grazing land
GAILSS gladioluses
GAIYED gravity-feed
GALHWY go all the way
GAMTCL grammatical
GANBNS granny bonds
GANSIH Granny Smith
GAOGIH go along with
GAOHNC gramophonic
GAOOSY glamorously
GAORIL glamour girl
GAORUS glamourpuss
GAPEIH grapple with
GASAIG glass-gazing
GASLWR glass-blower
GASOPR grasshopper
GASUTR grass-cutter
GATDHT granted that
GATIES ghastliness
GATNUY Glastonbury
GATSHB Granth Sahib
GAUAIN granulation
GAUAIY granularity
GAUDEN go a bundle on
GAUOAA granulomata
GAUOYE granulocyte
GBCWRS go backwards
GBEELN gibberellin
GBLITC go ballistic
GBTEED go by the head
GBTEOK go by the book
GDAGTR goddaughter
GDESES godlessness
GDLIHY God-almighty
GDLSYU God bless you
GDOSKN God-forsaken
GEDROE guelder rose
GEHROD Gwen Harwood
GEINOE Grecian nose
GENELE green-wellie
GENEPR green pepper
GENHEE green cheese
GENILR Glenn Miller
GENLNS green plants
GENOKY green monkey
GENRCR greengrocer
GENUTE green turtle
GEOYEK Gregory Peck
GERLEO guerrillero
GESAOG Glen Seaborg
GESIAE guesstimate
GESPIT greasepaint
GESPOF greaseproof
GESSON greasy spoon
GETEHW great-nephew
GETICE great circle
GETITR Great Bitter
GETOKR guest worker
GETPIX Great Sphinx
GETRAT greater part
GETRHN greater than
GETUBR great number
GETUPY great supply
GEZAGR Grenzgänger
GFECID gifted child
GFLEIH gefilte fish
GFTPAL gaff-topsail
GFVUHR gift voucher
GGETUS go great guns
GGLSIK Giggleswick
GGNEQE gigantesque
GGNMGG Gog and Magog
GIDEAE griddle-cake
GIEESY guilelessly
GIGRUD going around
GIGTAY going steady
GIGTOG going strong
GIIGTR guiding star
GIMSEY gain mastery
GIMTSS gliomatosis
GISAIS Gaius Marius
GITESY guiltlessly
GITIDN guilt-ridden
GITIES gristliness
GITPRY guilty party
GIZYER grizzly bear
GLBADR gall bladder

GLCTHR gull-catcher
GLDGIG gold-digging
GLEBON golden brown
GLEEGE golden eagle
GLEGOE Golden Globe
golden goose
GLEHLO golden hello
GLEODE golden oldie
GLEPOF galley proof
GLESAE galley slave
galley-slave
golden share
GLESRP golden syrup
GLETYE Gilbert Ryle
GLIAFY gallimaufry
GLIATR gallivanter
GLIIIY gullibility
GLKAOB go like a bomb
GLLYRD gold-layered
GLMNTR gila monster
GLRSRE gold reserve
GLSOTY Goldsworthy
GLTEIL gild the pill
GLTEIY gild the lily
GLYLWR gillyflower
GMAAEA gamma camera
GMIAOS gemmiparous
GMIRVR Gambia River
GMMOIC gum ammoniac
GMRLOF gambrel roof
GMRSRE game reserve
GMTPYE gametophyte
GNAMRE gendarmerie
GNAOIE genealogise
genealogize
GNAOIR gonfalonier
GNAOIT genealogist
GNARAE gun carriage
GNEBED gingerbread
GNEGAS Günter Grass
GNEGOP ginger group
GNELES genteelness
GNEOOY gynaecology
GNFEIN genuflexion
GNGSIG gone gosling
GNHSHN Genghis Khan
GNIEES genuineness
GNLBRH gentle birth
GNLMNY gentlemanly
GNLWMN gentlewoman
GNRCAE generic name
GNRCLY generically
GNRHEL gonorrhoeal
GNRLHP generalship
GNRLZD generalized
GNRTOX Generation X
GNSEIM gangsterism
GNSRZN Gene Sarazen
GNTCLY genetically
GNTCOE genetic code
GNTEAY gene therapy
GNTSEP gone to sleep
GNTVLY genitivally

GNVBBE Geneva Bible
GNVBNS Geneva bands
GNVCOS Geneva cross
GNVNET Gene Vincent
GOANTC geomagnetic
GOCIES grouchiness
GOCOAX Groucho Marx
GOCOLB Groucho Club
GOEBAD go overboard
GOEEIG good-evening
GOEETR go one better
GOEHPD globe-shaped
GOELWR globeflower
GOEQEY grotesquely
grotesquery
GOERCL geometrical
GOERUD grope around
GOEUPT glove puppet
GOFEIG good feeling
GOFRUE good fortune
GOFRVR go on for ever
GOGBAE George Blake
GOGBOE George Boole
GOGBON George Brown
George-Brown
GOGBRN George Byron
GOGBRS George Burns
GOGCHN George Cohan
GOGCKR George Cukor
GOGCOS George Cross
GOGCRY George Carey
GOGEIT George Eliot
GOGELS George Ellis
GOGGMW George Gamow
GOGGOE George Grove
GOGGOZ George Grosz
GOGHLS George Halas
GOGLCS George Lucas
GOGMDL George Medal
GOGMNK George Monck
GOGMOE George Moore
GOGRBY George Robey
GOGSOT George Scott
GOGUAS Georg Lukács
GOGWUH George W Bush
GOHAES good heavens
GOHATD good-hearted
GOHMCL geochemical
GOHNIG good hunting!
GOHSCL geophysical
GOIEIA globigerina
GOLOIG good-looking
GOMNES good manners
GOMOGR gloom-monger
GOMRIG good-morning
GONCVR ground cover
GONEDR ground elder
GONLVL ground-level
GONSEL ground swell
GONTRD good-natured
GOODAS good old days
GOOFCS good offices
GOOIIN good opinion

GOOIIS geopolitics
GOPFIE Group of Five
GOPHOY group theory
GOQIKY grow quickly
GORPDY grow rapidly
GOSALR grow smaller
GOSIIS good spirits
GOSLLA glossolalia
GOTCLY gnostically
GOTIES ghostliness
GOTLTP glottal stop
GOTOHC geostrophic
GOTRTR ghost writer
GOYCIE geosyncline
GRABGT German Bight
GRADZR gormandizer
GRAEES germaneness
GRANES Germain Hess
GRAZPA garbanzo pea
GRCMAS gyrocompass
GREGAT Gormenghast
GREPRY garden party
GRESAD Gorée Island
GRETGR garden tiger
GRIAIN germination
GRIHES girlishness
GRIHET garnishment
GRIKLB Garrick Club
GRIPES garlic press
GRLDES garbledness
GRLNKR Gary Lineker
GRMAAA garam masala
GRNOOY gerontology
GRNORT gerontocrat
GROBNS Gordon Banks
GROBON Gordon Brown
GROEEF gird oneself
GROOIT garbologist
GROSON Gordonstoun
GRUOSY garrulously
GRWRAE germ warfare
GRYADR gerrymander
GSAEOE Gustave Doré
GSAGEE gas gangrene
GSAHLT Gustav Holst
GSAKIT Gustav Klimt
GSIUAE gesticulate
GSOSES gaseousness
GSRNMC gastronomic
GSRSOE gastroscope
GTBDIH go to bed with
GTCAHR gatecrasher
gate-crasher
GTECIN gut reaction
GTEDFR get ready for
GTEONS go the rounds
GTEPES gutter press
GTERRO get nearer to
GTERUD gather round
GTESED gather speed
GTESES gutlessness
GTESIE guttersnipe
GTHHAE get the heave

GTHLWN get the law on
GTHPIT get the point
GTIGSD getting used
GTINVL Gothic novel
GTIOCD get divorced
GTLNTS go to lengths
GTLSRO get closer to
GTLWIH go to law with
GTNEWY get under way
GTNOET get into debt
GTNSAS get one's oats
GTNSID get one's wind
GTNSOT get one's goat
GTODET get cold feet
GTOEHR get together
get-together
GTOHTP get to the top
GTPNRS get up in arms
GTRCIG get cracking
GTRUDO get around to
GTTCOS get it across
GTTEAL go to the wall
GTTEOS go to the dogs
GTTNIH get it on with
GTTOGR get stronger
GTUAIE gutturalise
gutturalize
GTUOBD get out of bed
GTVNIH get even with
GTVRIH get over with
GTWIFF get a whiff of
GTWYIH get away with
GTWYRM get away from
GUADON go up and down
GUBIGY grumblingly
GUENNE gouvernante
GUIOSY glutinously
GUISOE go up in smoke
GUMNIE gourmandise
gourmandize
GUMNIM gourmandism
GUSIFR glue-sniffer
GUTEAL go up the wall
GVAADO give a hand to
GVAAEO give a name to
GVAAKO give a talk to
GVADAE give and take
give-and-take
GVAEMN give a sermon
GVAHTO give a shot to
GVAIKE give a tinkle
GVAIKO give a kick to
GVAITO give a lift to
GVAOMO give a room to
GVAUIG give a ruling
GVAUZO give a buzz to
GVBRHO give birth to
GVDTIS give details
GVIAET give it a rest
GVIWLY give it welly
GVLGAL give leg bail
GVLSOS give lessons
GVMASO give means to
GVNVRO given over to
GVOEAL give one's all
GVOEEF give oneself
GVOFNE give offence
GVPAEO give place to
GVPWRO give power to
GVTEAL give the wall
GVTELP give the slip
GVTEUH give the push
GVTOBE give trouble
GVVIEO give voice to
GWTAAG go with a bang
GYOYAE glycosylate
HABRIR heat barrier
HAEHLG heave the log
HAEKOS heaven knows
HAESAE Heaven's Gate
HAEWRS heavenwards
HAHNIG headhunting
HAITIE hyacinthine
HAOSAE head of state
HASAVS headscarves
HATAHR head teacher
headteacher
HATESY heartlessly
HATFLY healthfully
HATIES healthiness
HATRKN heartbroken
heart-broken
HATSAP health stamp
HATTAK heart attack
HATUMR heart murmur
HAYADD heavy-handed
HAYEGT heavy weight
heavyweight
HAYOTD heavy-footed
HAYSED heavy as lead
HBACLY Hebraically
HBLDHY hobbledehoy
HBLMNS habilements
HBLSIT hobble skirt
HBLTTD habilitated
HBOAAY hebdomadary
HBRAHR haberdasher
HBRAIG hibernating
HBRAIN hibernation
HBRAUA hibernacula
HBRIIE hibernicise
hibernicize
HBRIIM Hibernicism
HBRPRY Hubert Parry
HBTAIN habituation
HCEPOE heckelphone
HCESIK hockey stick
HCOMNO Hector Munro
HCORME hectogramme
HDAALR Hedda Gabler
HDADEK hide-and-seek
HDBATC hudibrastic
HDEUTR hedgecutter
HDNMNA hedonomania
HDNPAE hiding-place
HDOABN hydrocarbon
HDOAHC hydropathic
HDOEAE hydrogenate
HDOEIE hydrogenise
hydrogenize
HDOEIN hydrogen ion
HDOEOS hydrogenous
HDOERC hydrometric
HDOHBA hydrophobia
HDOHBC hydrophobic
HDOHLC hydrophilic
HDOHTC hydrophytic
HDOOAA hydrosomata
HDOOIS hydroponics
HDOOIT hydrologist
HDOPEE hydrosphere
HDORPY hydrography
HDOSES hideousness
HDOTTC hydrostatic
HDOYNC hydrocyanic
HEACIM hierarchism
HEAOOY haematology
HEAORT haematocrit
HEFLES heedfulness
HEOHLA haemophilia
HEOLBN haemoglobin
HEOLPS hieroglyphs
HEORAE haemorrhage
HEOTSS haemoptysis
haemostasis
HEOTTC haemostatic
HEOYNN haemocyanin
HFADUF huff and puff
HGAAIE high as a kite
HGADES haggardness
HGAOHA Hagia Sophia
HGDDEN high dudgeon
HGDNIY high-density
HGDVIS Hugo De Vries
HGFLTN highfalutin
HGFSIN high fashion
HGGOIS Hugo Grotius
HGHUHR hog-shouther
HGIHES hoggishness
HGLAIM Hegelianism
HGLGTR highlighter
HGLTMR Hugh Latimer
HGNROR hog in armour
HGOCPC hygroscopic
HGODIE high old time
HGOERC hygrometric
HGOHTC hygrophytic
HGOIIN high opinion
HGOOIT hagiologist
HGORPA Hagiographa
HGORPY hagiography
HGPOIE high profile
HGPTHD high-pitched
HGPWRD high-powered
HGQAIY high quality
high-quality
HGRNIG high-ranking
HGSCEY high society
HGSGTD high-sighted

HGSIIS high spirits
HGTESN high treason
HGTNIN high-tension
HGVLAE high-voltage
HGWCME High Wycombe
HGWLOE Hugh Walpole
HGWNOS High Windows
HGWYOE Highway Code
HHNIDN Hohenlinden
HIBAND hair-brained
HIDESR hairdresser
HIHEIG heightening
HIOSES heinousness
HIPNED hairpin bend
HIRIIG hair-raising
HISYIT hairstylist
HITIGR hair trigger
HLAALO hullaballoo
HLAANT hold against
HLADAF half-and-half
HLADIE hollandaise
HLBNIG half-binding
HLBODD half-blooded
HLBOHR half-brother
HLBPIE half-baptise
half-baptize
HLCEKD half-checked
HLCPIE hold captive
HLDYAP holiday camp
HLEDAE halfendeale
HLEITC Hellenistic
HLFLES helpfulness
HLGAHC holographic
HLHATD half-hearted
HLHDIM holohedrism
HLICEK hold in check
HLIGAD helping hand
HLIGAK holding-back
HLIGOG Helsingborg
HLIGVR holding-over
HLIHES hellishness
HLLNIG half-landing
HLNIRN Helen Mirren
HLOEEF help oneself
HLOEJW hold one's jaw
HLOEON hold one's own
HLOFIH help off with
HLOPEE heliosphere
HLORPC heliotropic
HLORPY heliography
HLPSOE half past one
HLPSTO half past two
HLPYIM holophytism
HLROSY hilariously
HLSAIN hill station
HLSAVD half-starved
HLSNES Holy Sonnets
HLTEET hold the belt
HLTEIE half the time
hold the line
HLTEIG hold the ring
HLTEOD hold the road
HLTEOT hold the fort

HLTRUH help through
HLTUIN holothurian
HLUIAE hallucinate
HLWLIG hillwalking
HMBNIG home banking
HMDNAK Hampden Park
HMDYDS hamadry-ades
HMEDIL hammer drill
HMEDNK Humperdinck
HMEPTY homoeopathy
HMESEN Hammerstein
HMGNIY homogeneity
HMGNOS homogeneous
HMHMTN Hamp Hampton
HMHYAY Humphry Davy
HMIGID hummingbird
Humming-Bird
HMLAIE humiliative
HMLAIG humiliating
HMLAIN humiliation
HMLAOY humiliatory
HMLTCL homiletical
HMMRHC homomorphic
HMNAUE human nature
HMNEGE Human League
HMNENS human beings
HMNHED human shield
HMNIHS human rights
HMOAHC homeopathic
HMOOIT hymnologist
HMOTSS homeostasis
HMPEOS hemipterous
homopterous
HMRLPA hemeralopia
HMRLPC hemeralopic
HMSHRC hemispheric
HMSPES homo sapiens❑
HMWRIG homeworking
HNADOT hand and foot
HNAOTN hang about in
HNBCNR Hans Buchner
HNCUTR hunt counter
HNEATR hanker after
HNEIGY hinderingly
HNEMRH hunger march
HNESNK Hans Eysenck
HNFSHR Hans Fischer
HNGEAE hand grenade
HNGIIG hang-gliding
HNHAKD hunchbacked
HNHLEN Hans Holbein
HNIAPD handicapped
HNIAPR handicapper
HNIGAK handing back
hanging-back
HNIGET hunting-seat
HNIGIE hanging fire
HNIGOE hand in glove
HNIGON hunting-horn
HNIGOS Huntington's
HNIISN Henrik Ibsen
HNIRUL Henri Breuil
HNITEE hang in there

HNIUEI Henri Fuseli
HNLGAE hand-luggage
HNLOEY hang loosely
HNMDWS hand-me-downs
HNOGOY hand of glory
HNOTIH hang out with
HNOWRS hang on words
HNRCTR Hans Richter
HNRDOD hundredfold
HNRLAE hand release
HNRNIG hand-running
HNRRUS honorariums
HNSIJN honest Injun
HNSTGD honest-to-God
HNTEOK hunt-the-gowk
HNTMUH hand to mouth
hand-to-mouth
HNTRUH hunt through
HNUBUD honour-bound
HNUSAY honours easy
HNUSIT honours list
HNWIIG handwriting
HNWITN handwritten
HNWNLR Hans Winkler
HNYAGR honey badger
HNYEHM Henry Pelham
HNYILR Henry Miller
HNYOBD honeycombed
HNYOGN Henry Morgan
HNYOLR Henry Fowler
HNYONR honeymooner
HNYOPR Henry Cooper
HNYRIG Henry Irving
HNYUGS honey fungus
HNYUKE honeysuckle
HNYUSN Henry Hudson
HOAHNY Hooray Henry
HOCAIE hyoscyamine
HOEBVY hooped bivvy
HOIAIM hooliganism
HOWNIG hoodwinking
HPAADY haphazardly
HPBATC hypoblastic
HPCCOD hypocycloid
HPCRSA hypocorisma
HPEAAN happen again
HPEAIN hyphenation
HPESES haplessness
HPFLES hopefulness
HPGSRC hypogastric
HPLWIE Hepplewhite
HPOADA hypnopaedia
HPOAPS hippocampus
HPOERC hypsometric
HPOHBA hippophobia
HPOIIG hypnotizing
HPOOAI hippopotami
HPOOPC hypnopompic
HPORPY haplography
hypsography
HPORTS Hippocrates
HPPYEL hypophyseal
HPPYIL hypophysial

Words marked ❑ can also be spelled with an initial capital letter

Code	Word
HPRAKT	hypermarket
HPRCIE	hyperactive
HPRHGA	hyperphagia
HPRHRE	hypercharge
HPROEN	hyperborean
HPROIE	hyperbolise
	hyperbolize
HPROIM	hyperbolism
HPROIS	hypersonics
HPRRPY	hypertrophy
HPRRTC	hyper-critic
HPSAIE	hypostasise
	hypostasize
	hypostatise
	hypostatize
HPSRPE	hypostrophe
HPTEAE	hypothecate
HPTEIE	hypothesise
	hypothesize
	hypothetise
	hypothetize
HPTEMA	hypothermia
HPTNIE	hypotensive
HPTNIN	hypotension
HPTYOD	hypothyroid
HPYEIM	happy medium
HRADAT	hard and fast
	hard-and-fast
HRAFIT	hard as flint
HRAIEY	hortatively
HRANIS	hard as nails
HRAOIY	hortatorily
HRASOE	hard as stone
HRAUET	hurl abuse at
HRAYHP	her ladyship
HRBAND	harebrained
	hare-brained
HRBEDC	hornblendic
HRBLSA	Hore-Belisha
HRCTEN	haricot bean
HRDEVE	hors d'oeuvre
HRDIKR	hard drinker
HRDTBE	hereditable
HREAIG	horse-racing
HREAIH	horseradish
HREETC	hermeneutic
HREIIG	horse-riding
HREIIY	hermeticity
HREJNS	Harvey-Jones
HREOOY	herpetology
HRERUD	horse around
HRESIH	Harvey Smith
HRETED	Herbert Read
HRETIE	harvest-time
HRETON	harvest moon
HRFLES	harmfulness
	hurtfulness
HRHATD	hard-hearted
HRHTIG	hard-hitting
HRIAOS	hurricanoes
HRIATR	hereinafter
HRIAUE	Hardicanute
HRIDES	hurriedness
HRIGOE	herringbone
	herring-bone
HRIIAE	horripilate
HRIIAT	horripilant
HRIOAT	horrisonant
HRIOOS	herbivorous
HRITED	Harris tweed®
HRIVRE	heroic verse
HRKIHA	Hare Krishna
HRLEAS	Harold Evans
HRLGCL	horological
HRLLOD	Harold Lloyd
HRLNIG	hard landing
HRMCRM	harum-scarum
HROAIN	hariolation
HROAOT	harp on about
HROIGY	harrowingly
HROIIG	harmonizing
HRPESD	hard-pressed
HRPTOT	hard put to it
HRSCOD	harpsichord
HRSIAE	haruspicate
HRSIGY	harassingly
HRSINE	hard science
HRSOGE	hornswoggle
HRTCLY	heretically
HRTCTH	hard to catch
HRUEES	hirsuteness
HRWAIG	hard-wearing
HRWRHP	hero worship
	hero-worship
HRWRIG	hard working
	hardworking
	hard-working
HRYADN	Harry Vardon
HRYADR	Harry Lauder
HRYCRY	hurry-scurry
HRYNUL	hardy annual
HRYOTR	Harry Potter
HSAAAA	hasta mañana
HSADOE	husband-to-be
HSAIIE	hispanicise
	hispanicize
HSAIIM	hispanicism
HSEIIM	hesperidium
HSIAIE	hospitalise
	hospitalize
HSIAIY	hospitality
HSIALR	hospitaller
HSIAOE	HMS Pinafore
HSIIIS	hostilities
HSODHP	his lordship
HSOIES	His Holiness
HSOIIE	historicise
	historicize
HSOIIM	historicism
HSOIIT	historicist
HSOIIY	historicity
HSOOIT	histologist
HSROIS	histrionics
HTEPRD	hot-tempered
HTFLES	hatefulness
HTHTAL	hit the trail
HTIHRF	hatti-sherif
HTLEPR	hotel-keeper
HTRGAT	heterograft
HTRPEA	Heteroptera
HTRSBN	hot cross bun
HTRTOH	heterotroph
HTRTPA	heterotopia
HTRTXS	heterotaxis
HUDTOH	hound's-tooth
HUEATN	house martin
HUEATR	housemaster
HUEEPR	housekeeper
HUEFES	House of Keys
HUEIEY	housewifely
	housewifery
HUEIHS	house lights
HUEODR	householder
HUERET	house arrest
HUERKN	house-broken
HUEUTR	house-hunter
HUHIES	haughtiness
HUOCUE	hour of cause
HVAAAM	have as an aim
HVAADR	have a gander
HVAHAT	have at heart
HVAHWR	have a shower
HVAIWF	have a view of
HVANOE	have a snooze
HVAODN	have a hold on
	have a load on
HVARPN	have a grip on
HVATBT	have a stab at
HVEEFR	have eyes for
HVFIHN	have faith in
HVFRAE	have for sale
HVHDFW	have had a few
HVHDHT	have had that
HVIIFR	have it in for
HVIIOE	have it in one
HVKTES	have kittens
HVMRYN	have mercy on
HVNRGT	have no right
HVOESY	have one's say
HVOEWY	have one's way
HVPAND	have planned
HVROFR	have room for
HVSXIH	have sex with
HVTEDE	have the edge
HVTOUH	have too much
HVYUOE	have you done?
HWIGOF	Howling Wolf
HWRHWS	Howard Hawks
HXDCML	hexadecimal
HXGNLY	hexagonally
HXHDOS	hexahedrons
HXMTIE	hexametrise
	hexametrize
HXTUHL	hexateuchal
HYOFIT	Heyhoe Flint
HZROSY	hazardously
IAAGWY	in a large way
IAALGT	in a bad light
IACETN	Isaac Newton

IACIMN Isaac Pitman
IACSMV Isaac Asimov
IAEWRS in a few words
IAGRTR inaugurator
IAIAEY inanimately
IAIAIE imaginative
IAIAIN imagination
inanimation
IAIAWR Iran-Iraq War
IAINBE inalienable
IAINBY inalienably
IAISAT in an instant
IALEUK in a blue funk
IALLCS in all places
IALTPN in a flat spin
IAMLWY in a small way
IAMRAH in arm's reach
IAODOD in a good mood
IAODOR in a good hour
IARASO in arrears to
IAREET in agreement
IATEIL in at the kill
IATETC inauthentic
IATNIE inattentive
IATNIN inattention
IATRBE inalterable
IATRBY inalterably
IATSIO in altissimo
IAUCMN I'm a Dutchman
IAUDNE in abundance
IAUSEL in a nutshell
IAVNEF in advance of
IAVRET inadvertent
IAVSBE inadvisable
IBIAEY imbricately
ICAATR in character
ICDNAS incidentals
ICEETL incremental
ICEETY inclemently
ICESBE increasable
ICESFL increaseful
ICEUIY incredulity
ICEUOS incredulous
ICGIAT incognisant
incognizant
ICHRNE incoherence
ICIAIN inclination
ICIDDO inclinded to
ICIGAM itching palm
ICIIAE incriminate
ICLAIN inculcation
inculpation
ICLAOY inculpatory
ICLBOD in cold blood
ICLUIN in collusion
ICMADF in command of
ICMEET incompetent
ICMETY incumbently
ICMITE in committee
ICNAIN incantation
ICNAOY incantatory
ICNBLM incunabulum
ICNIET incontinent
ICNIIE incentivise
incentivize
ICNIIN in condition
ICNOAT inconsonant
ICNRIY incongruity
ICNRLF in control of
ICNROS incongruous
ICNRTR incinerator
ICNTNY inconstancy
ICNUIN in confusion
ICPETY incipiently
ICPIIY in captivity
ICPUAE incapsulate
ICRAIE incarnadine
ICRAIN incarnation
incurvation
ICREAE incarcerate
ICRETY incorrectly
ICRIAE incardinate
ICRIUE incertitude
ICROAE incorporate
ICROEL incorporeal
ICROIY incuriosity
ICROSY incuriously
ICRUTY incorruptly
ICSATY incessantly
ICUIEF inclusive of
ICUIEY inclusively
IDAOEN Indian Ocean
IDAUBR India rubber
IDBTBE indubitable
IDBTBY indubitably
IDCIEE Indo-Chinese
IDCIEY inductively
IDCINL inductional
IDCMNS inducements
IDCTOS indications
IDEORE in due course
IDEWTR in deep water
IDFEET indifferent
IDFNBE indefinable
IDFNBY indefinably
IDFUTF in default of
IDGAIN indignation
IDGATY indignantly
IDGSIN indigestion
IDHSET indehiscent
IDIAIN Indo-Iranian
IDLETY indulgently
IDMIIR indemnifier
IDMNUS indumentums
IDMTBE indomitable
IDMTBY indomitably
IDNAIN indentation
IDPIAE in duplicate
IDPNET independent
IDRCIN indirection
IDRCTX indirect tax
IDSEAR in disrepair
IDSROS industrious
IDVDAE individuate
IDVDAS individuals
IDVSBE indivisible
IDVSBY indivisibly
IDXUBR index number
IEADPR Iceland spar
IEAIEY iteratively
IEATES inexactness
IEAUNA ipecacuanha
IECPAE in each place
IECPBE inescapable
IECPBY inescapably
IECSBE inexcusable
IECSBY inexcusably
IEEATY inelegantly
IEERBE inexecrable
IEEYAT in every part
IEFCET inefficient
IEFCIE ineffective
IEFCUL ineffectual
IEGAHC ideographic
IEIAIN itemization
IEIIIY inedibility
IEITNE in existence
IELGCL ideological
IEPDET inexpedient
IEPNIE inexpensive
IERAIG inebriating
IERAIN inebriation
IESNIL inessential
IETCLY identically
IETMBE inestimable
IETMBY inestimably
IEUTBE ineluctable
inequitable
IEUTBY ineluctably
inequitably
IFAGBE infrangible
IFAGBY infrangibly
IFAIGY inflatingly
IFAMBE inflammable
IFAMBY inflammably
IFCNIY infecundity
IFEUNY infrequency
IFLBAT in full blast
IFLBOM in full bloom
IFLRTD infiltrated
IFLRTR infiltrator
IFLSIG in full swing
IFNIIE infanticide
IFNIIM infantilism
IFNIUA infundibula
IFNRMN infantryman
infantrymen
IFNTVL infinitival
IFRAIE informative
IFRAIG infuriating
IFRAIN information
IFRAIS informatics
IFRAIY informality
IFRIIY infertility
IFRNIL inferential
IFROIY inferiority
IFSAIN infestation
IFTAIN infatuation
IFUNIL influential

IFUTOS infructuous
IGAIUE ingratitude
IGEINS ingredients
IGETAT in great part
IGETED in great need
IGNOSY ingeniously
ingenuously
IGOFIH in good faith
IGOHAT in good heart
IGOHNS in good hands
IGOODR in good order
IGOOOR in good odour
IGOSAE in good shape
IGOVIE in good voice
IGRIAE ingurgitate
IGTEIG ingathering
IHBTBE inhabitable
IHBTNE inhabitance
IHBTNS inhabitants
IHBTNY inhabitancy
IHBTOS inhibitions
IHHOAR ichthyosaur
IHHOOY ichthyology
IHMNES inhumanness
IHMNOM in human form
IHRIDM in her wisdom
IHRTBE inheritable
IHRTES inheritress
IHRTNE inheritance
IHRWWY in her own way
IHSIDM in his wisdom
IHSWWY in his own way
IIAIEY imitatively
IIAIIY imitability
IIEATY itinerantly
IIECNE iridescence
IIHOFE Irish coffee
IIHUTR Irish Hunter
IIILAS initial caps
IIMCED Iain Macleod
IIMROH Iris Murdoch
IINSAE Ilie Nastase
IIOAIN in isolation
IITAAT idiot savant
IITCLY idiotically
IJDCOS injudicious
IJROSY injuriously
IKOEES irksomeness
IKONAE ink-horn-mate
ILANRD ill-mannered
ILAORD ill-favoured
ILBRLY illiberally
ILCTES illicitness
ILEPRD ill-tempered
ILGCLY illogically
ILIPSD ill-disposed
ILMLIG ill-smelling
ILMNNE illuminance
ILMNTD illuminated
ILMNTR illuminator
ILMTBE illimitable
ILMTBY illimitably
ILNOMD ill-informed
ILNORB Island of Rab
ILNWRH Illingworth
ILOSIE it looks like
ILOWGT Isle of Wight
ILQIPD ill-equipped
ILREIG ill-breeding
ILRSIG ill-wresting
ILSOAY illusionary
ILSOIM illusionism
ILSOIT illusionist
ILSOTD ill-assorted
ILSROS illustrious
ILSRTD illustrated
ILSRTR illustrator
ILUORD ill-humoured
IMBLZD immobilized
IMBLZR immobilizer
IMCOOM in microcosm
IMDAEY immediately
IMDARS in medias res
IMGAIN immigration
IMNASY immunoassay
IMNAUE in miniature
IMNEES immenseness
IMRAIE immortalise
immortalize
IMRAIY immortality
IMSCSS in most cases
IMTGBY immitigably
IMVALS immoveables
INBEES ignobleness
INCOSY innocuously
INCSAY if necessary
INHPEL Ian Chappell
INMNOS ignominious
INMRBE innumerable
INMRBY innumerably
INRMSS ignoramuses
INRNIE Ignorantine
INSAUS ignis fatuus
INTOKY ignition key
INVGBY innavigably
INXOSY innoxiously
IOAERN icosahedron
IOCRAN Iron Curtain
IOEAIE inoperative
IOEAIN in operation
IOEBOD in one's blood
IOELGT in one's light
IOESEP in one's sleep
IOESIT in one's shirt
IOFNIE inoffensive
IOHOIE isochronise
isochronize
IOHOOS isochronous
IOIAIN idolization
IOMNEY ironmongery
IONVLO Ivor Novello
IOOOSY inodorously
IOOPIM isomorphism
IOOPOS isomorphous
IOORPY iconography
IOOTSS iconostasis
IOPRUE inopportune
IORWWY in our own way
IOUAIE inoculative
IOUAIN inoculation
IOWRHP icon worship
IPAHET impeachment
IPASBE implausible
IPASBY implausibly
IPATCL impractical
IPCNOS impecunious
IPDMNA impedimenta
IPEAIN imprecation
IPEAIS impresarios
IPEAOY imprecatory
IPEETD implemented
IPEETL implemental
IPEIEY imprecisely
IPEIIN imprecision
IPENBE impregnable
IPENBY impregnably
IPENTD impregnated
IPESBE impressible
IPESOS impressions
IPGOAE impignorate
IPIAIE implicative
IPIAIG implicating
IPIAIN implication
IPICPE in principle
IPISNE impuissance
IPLIEY impulsively
IPLTCY impolitically
IPNEET impingement
IPNEOS imponderous
IPNEPN impinge upon
IPNTAE impenetrate
IPNTNE impenitence
IPNTNY impenitency
IPOAIE improbative
IPOAIN imploration
IPOAOY imploratory
improbatory
IPOEET improvement
IPOESF in process of
IPOIET improvident
IPOIGY imploringly
improvingly
IPORAE impropriate
IPOREY impropriety
IPOSES impiousness
IPOUIN in profusion
IPRAET impermanent
IPRAIE imperialise
imperialize
IPRAIM imperialism
IPRAIN impartation
importation
IPRAIT imperialist
IPRATY importantly
IPREBE impermeable
IPREBY impermeably
IPRETY imperfectly
IPREUM in perpetuum
IPRIET impertinent

IPRILY impartially
IPRLET imperilment
IPROAE impersonate
IPROSY imperiously
IPRUAE importunate
IPRUAY importunacy
IPRUEY importunely
IPRUIY importunity
IPSIEY impassively
IPSIIY impassivity
IPSIND impassioned
IPSUAE impostumate
IPTEHE it pitieth me
IPTEIE input device
IPTETY impatiently
IPTGNS impetigines
IPTOIY impetuosity
IPTOSY impetuously
IPUDBE impoundable
IPUETY imprudently
IQIEDS inquirendos
IQIENO inquire into
IQIIGY inquiringly
IQIIIE inquisitive
IQIIIN inquisition
IRAIES in readiness
IRCRNE iure coronae
IRCSBE irrecusable
IRCSBY irrecusably
IRDAIN irradiation
IRDCBE irreducible
IRDCBY irreducibly
IRDNIM irredentism
IRDNIT irredentist
IRFTBE irrefutable
IRFTBY irrefutably
IRGLRY irregularly
IRLGOS irreligious
IRLVNE irrelevance
IRLVNY irrelevancy
IRMVBE irremovable
IRMVBY irremovably
IRPIEY irruptively
IRPRBE irreparable
IRPRBY irreparably
IRSETF in respect of
IRSLBY irresolubly
IRVCBE irrevocable
IRVCBY irrevocably
IRVRNE irreverence
ISAEET instatement
ISAIIY instability
ISATAE instantiate
ISBTNE in substance
ISCIIE insecticide
ISCIOE insectivore
ISDOSY insidiously
ISDSOY inside story
ISDTAK inside track
ISIAIE instigative
ISIAIG instigating
ISIAIN inspiration
instigation

ISIAOY inspiratory
ISICIE instinctive
ISIIGY inspiringly
ISIIIG inspiriting
ISIUIN institution
ISLBIY insalubrity
ISLIGY insultingly
ISMNTR inseminator
ISNAEY insensately
ISNAIE insinuative
ISNAIG insinuating
ISNAIN insinuation
ISNAOY insinuatory
ISNEEY insincerely
ISNEIY insincerity
ISNIIE insensitive
ISPDES insipidness
ISPETY insipiently
ISPRBE inseparable
insuperable
ISPRBY inseparably
insuperably
ISRCIE instructive
ISRCIN instruction
ISRINL insertional
ISRMNS instruments
ISRPIE inscriptive
ISRPIN inscription
ISRTBE inscrutable
ISRTBY inscrutably
ISSETN insistent on
ISSETY insistently
ISTAEY insatiately
ISUINE insouciance
ISUPUE insculpture
ISYIAE Issey Miyake
ITAEML intradermal
ITAEOS intravenous
ITATBE intractable
ITATBY intractably
ITEADE in the saddle
ITEAEF in the care of
in the face of
in the name of
ITEAIG in the making
ITEAIY in the family
ITEANR in the manner
ITECAT intrenchant
ITEERT in the secret
ITEETE in the centre
ITEFIG in the offing
ITEHOS in the throes
ITEIDE in the middle
ITEIEF in the time of
ITEIIY intrepidity
ITEROE in the groove
ITERPF in the grip of
ITEUUE in the future
ITGAIN integration
ITIAEY intricately
ITIAIS intricacies
ITIIEY intuitively
ITIINL intuitional

ITIPAE in this place
ITIUNE intriguante
ITLIET intelligent
ITLRBE intolerable
ITLRBY intolerably
ITLRNE intolerance
ITMDTD intimidated
ITMDTR intimidator
ITMEAE intemperate
ITMSAT in times past
ITMSET intumescent
ITNEES intenseness
ITNIEY intensively
ITNIGO intending to
ITNIID intensified
ITNIIR intensifier
ITNINL intentional
ITOAOE Il Trovatore
ITOEAS in those days
ITOETD introverted
ITOUEO introduce to
ITRAAE intercalate
ITRAAY intercalary
ITRAET interjacent
ITRAGE intertangle
ITRAIE internalise
internalize
ITRAIG interfacing
interlacing
ITRAIL interfacial
interracial
ITRATS inter partes
ITRCIE interactive
ITRCIN interaction
ITREAE interrelate
ITREDE intermeddle
ITREED interdepend
ITREEN interfere in
ITREIE internecine
ITREIG interfering
intervening
ITREKN interleukin
ITRENM interregnum
ITRESR intercessor
ITRETR interceptor
ITREUL intersexual
ITREVS interleaves
ITREZS intermezzos
ITRHNE interchange
ITRIAE inturbidate
ITRIER interlinear
ITRIGE intermingle
ITRIIG interlining
ITRITD interdicted
ITRIWE interviewee
ITRIWR interviewer
ITROAE interpolate
interrogate
ITROAT interrogant
ITROIG interposing
ITROKD interlocked
ITRORE intercourse
ITROTL intercostal

ITRPRE	intersperse
ITRRGS	intertrigos
ITRRTR	interpreter
ITRSIG	interesting
ITRUIN	interfusion
ITRUTD	interrupted
ITRUTR	interrupter
	interruptor
ITTELE	into the blue
ITTEPN	into the open
ITTIAR	into thin air
ITUHIH	in touch with
ITUIEY	intrusively
ITXCTD	intoxicated
IVDOSY	invidiously
IVGLTR	invigilator
IVGRTD	invigorated
IVLCAE	involucrate
IVLDTD	invalidated
IVLEET	involvement
IVLNAY	involuntary
IVNIEY	inventively
IVOAEY	inviolately
IVRSGR	invert sugar
IVSIAE	investigate
IVSIUE	investiture
IVSMNS	investments
IVTRUD	invite round
IWUDEM	it would seem
IYLCLY	idyllically
IYULAE	if you please
JAAOIH	Jean Anouilh
JACCEU	Jean Cocteau
JAHMOD	Joan Hammond
JALFTE	Jean Lafitte
JALMRK	Jean Lamarck
JALSIS	Juan-les-Pins
JAOSOD	jealoushood
JBEIGY	jabberingly
JBEWCY	Jabberwocky
JCBAHM	Jack Brabham
JCBALY	Jacob Marley
JCBCIK	Jacob Schick
JCBSAF	Jacob's staff
JCDWIS	Jack Dawkins
JCIAIN	jactitation
JCKRUC	Jack Kerouac
JCRSEL	Jack Russell
JCUSAI	Jacques Tati
JCYISN	Jocky Wilson
JDCOSY	judiciously
JDEETL	judgemental
JDEOTR	Jodie Foster
JDGRAD	Judy Garland
JDSIDW	Judas-window
JDSRET	Judas Priest
JDTOGR	Judit Polgar
JEIAGO	Joe DiMaggio
JFBIGS	Jeff Bridges
JGDSOE	Jagadis Bose
JGLRIH	J K Galbraith
JHADBN	John Audubon
JHAHEY	John Ashbery
JHARAS	John-a-dreams
JHBOMN	John Boorman
JHBRLY	John Barclay
JHBRRM	John Bartram
JHCEAD	John Cleland
JHCEZE	John Coetzee
JHCLIS	John Collins
JHDWAD	John Dowland
JHFEIG	John Fleming
JHGEGD	John Gielgud
JHGIHM	John Grisham
JHHBOD	John Habgood
JHHLAE	John Haldane
JHHNOK	John Hancock
JHHWIS	John Hawkins
JHHWYS	John Hawkyns
JHLCRE	John Le Carré
JHLMET	John Lambert
JHMERE	John McEnroe
JHMLAS	John Millais
JHMRTN	John Marston
JHMUHY	John Mauchly
JHNERU	Johannes Rau
JHOBRE	John Osborne
JHOGUT	John of Gaunt
JHPOUO	John Profumo
JHRDOD	John Redwood
JHSETN	John Skelton
JHSRES	John Surtees
JHSRET	John Sargent
JHTNIL	John Tenniel
JHTSAK	John Toshack
JHTVNR	John Tavener
JHVRTR	John Vorster
JHWBTR	John Webster
JHWNHM	John Wyndham
JIBEKR	jailbreaker
JIDVVE	joie de vivre
JITCIN	joint action
JITELB	join the club
JITFOT	joint effort
JKNAAT	joking apart
JLABEM	Julian Bream
JLOCRE	Joliot-Curie
JLSODT	Jules Bordet
JLYOPR	Jilly Cooper
JMADIH	jam sandwich
JMEGRC	Jim Bergerac
JMELVR	Jamie Oliver
JMHNRX	Jimi Hendrix
JMIGAK	jumping-jack
JMIGEN	jumping-bean
JMOORW	jam tomorrow
JMOYOY	jam roly-poly
JMSAKY	James Mackay
JMSANY	James Cagney
JMSARE	James Barrie
JMSASN	James Watson
JMSAWY	James Galway
JMSEMN	James Kelman
JMSOEL	James Howell
	James Lovell
JMSORE	James Monroe
JMSOUN	James Coburn
JMSRZR	James Frazer
JMSSHR	James Ussher
JMSURY	James Murray
JMULVN	Jim Sullivan
JMYATR	Jimmy Carter
JNFIFX	Jane Fairfax
JNGISN	Jane Grigson
JNLFVR	Jungle Fever
	jungle fever
JNLGEN	jungle-green
JNLJIE	jungle juice
JNNVTA	Jana Novotna
JNONIL	Jonjo O'Neill
JNRSEL	Jane Russell
JNSOLN	Janis Joplin
JNSYOR	Jane Seymour
JNTOBX	junction box
JNYIMN	Jenny Pitman
JPISLY	J B Priestley
JRDCLY	juridically
JREHVZ	Jorge Chavez
JRILAS	JPR Williams
JRMIOS	Jeremy Irons
JRSRIE	jury service
JSAOTO	just about to
JSCNEO	Jose Conseco
JSDSRS	just deserts
JSEJHS	Jasper Johns
JSGFOD	Josh Gifford
JSIEHP	justiceship
JSIIBE	justifiable
JSIIBY	justifiably
JSPBNS	Joseph Banks
JSPBUS	Joseph Beuys
JSPHYN	Joseph Haydn
JSPLOS	Joseph Lyons
JSPSIH	Joseph Smith
JSSHIT	Jesus Christ
JSTEAE	just the same
JSUNOO	Joshua Nkomo
JTIOIG	jettisoning
JUDSRT	jeux d'esprit
JUNLSS	journalists
JUNYED	journey's end
JVNSET	juvenescent
JWODAH	jaws of death
JYESES	joylessness
KAAUPR	Kuala Lumpur
KAHOKR	kwashiorkor
KAIHES	knavishness
KAUEVS	Keanu Reeves
KCAANT	kick against
KCOEEF	kick oneself
KCUAUS	kick up a fuss
KCUAUT	kick up a dust
KEAEEN	keep an eye on
KEAERT	keep a secret
KECERF	keep clear of
KECMAY	keep company
KECPIG	kneecapping
KECUSL	keep counsel
KEGADN	keep guard on

KEICEK keep in check
KEIGAK keeping dark
KEIGVR keeling-over
KEISGT keep in sight
KEITUH keep in touch
KEKGAD Kierkegaard
KENOTE Klein bottle
KEOAOT keep on about
KEOEBD keep one's bed
KESGTD keen-sighted
KESGTF keep sight of
KETAKF keep track of
KETEIG keep the ring
KETMNA kleptomania
KEWLIG keep walking
KEWTHN keep watch on
KIHOEH Keith Joseph
KIKNCS knickknacks
knick-knacks
KLCLRE kilocalorie
KLEWAE killer whale
KLMNAO Kilimanjaro
KLNNRD Kaliningrad
KLOEEF kill oneself
KLSNKV kalashnikov
KMAIGR Kim Basinger
KMGAHC kymographic
KNAOHP kangaroo-hop
KNAORT kangaroo rat
KNAUOE Kenzaburo Oë
KNCTAD Ken Scotland
KNDMOE kingdom come
KNHATD kind-hearted
KNMTCL kinematical
KNOBRS king of birds
KNOKNS king of kings
KNPNUN king penguin
KNRDES kindredness
KNRDHP kindredship
KNRGRS kind regards
KNSASM king's ransom
KNSELW King's-yellow
KNSHTC kinesthetic
KNSOOY kinesiology
KNSPEH King's Speech
KOBSGT know by sight
KOIGAD knowing card
KOIGES knowingness
KOKNOD knock on wood
KOKNOF knocking off
KOKOSX knock for six
KOKRUD knock around
KONTIG know-nothing
KOTHAS klootchmans
KOWOWO know who's who
KPESAS Kepler's laws
KRCALR kerb-crawler
KRDULS Kirk Douglas
KRJSES Karl Jaspers
KRNLXN Karen Blixen
KROAES karbovanets
KRRSEL Kurt Russell
KRSSIN kirk session

KRYAKR Kerry Packer
KSADEL Kiss and Tell
kiss-and-tell
KSIGAE kissing gate
KSODAH kiss of death
KSOPAE kiss of peace
KSTEET kiss the feet
KSTEOK kiss the book
KTBLON kite-balloon
KTHNAD kitchenmaid
KTHNAE kitchenware
KTHNIK kitchen sink
kitchen-sink
KTHNNT kitchen unit
KTHNTE kitchenette
KUKEON knuckle down
KVNEGN Kevin Keegan
KWNSLB Kiwanis Club
KYORIG keyboarding
LABAIG load-bearing
LABLON lead balloon
LACTIG leaf-cutting
LADEOD lo and behold
LADRLB Leander Club
LAEAIG leave-taking
LAEEID leave behind
LAENOE leave undone
LAEODR leaseholder
LAFRAD leap forward
LAHOEY loathsomely
LAHRAK leather-back
LAHREK leather-neck
LAHROT leather-coat
LAIGAD leading card
LAIGAY leading lady
LAIGDE leading edge
LAIGIE leaping-time
LAIGOE leading note
leading role
LAIGVR leaning over
LAIIIS liabilities
LANDES learnedness
LANYOE learn by rote
LAOBED loaf of bread
LASIGR lead-swinger
LATEIE load the dice
LATIEY least likely
LATRUH leaf through
LBAAOA labia majora
LBAIOA labia minora
LBAOSA Labrador Sea
LBIAIN lubrication
LBLOSY libellously
LBOETL labiodental
LBRAIN libertarian
LBRIIM libertinism
LBROSY laboriously
LBRYAL liberty hall
LBUFRE labour force
LBUPIS labour pains
LBUPRY Labour Party
LCAIEY lucratively
LCDUTN laced mutton

LCEFED Lucien Freud
LCEIHY lickerishly
LCEOSY lecherously
LCEYPT lickety-spit
LCLEAL Lucille Ball
LCLFIE local office
LCLOOR local colour
LCLPEH local speech
LCMEES locum tenens
LCNAIN laciniation
LCNCLY laconically
LCNHOY lycanthropy
LCOIHC laccolithic
LCRNOH Loch Rannoch
LCROAT Locarno Pact
LCRUIR Le Corbusier
LCSITE lickspittle
LCSPOT lack support
LCSTNI locus standi
LCTEUT lick the dust
LCUEHP lectureship
LDCOSY ludicrously
LDEPLN Led Zeppelin
LDIHES laddishness
LDLEIA La Dolce Vita
LDMCEH Lady Macbeth
LDSIGR lady's finger
LDTILS lady-trifles
LEACEF Lee Van Cleef
LEEETR lie detector
LEEOET Lee De Forest
LESATE Leeds Castle
LETNNY lieutenancy
LEWNOK Leeuwenhoek
LFHNIG left hanging
LFORLY life of Riley
LFPEAE life peerage
LFPEES life peeress
LFSINE life science
LGEHAS loggerheads
LGESES leglessness
LGFUTN leg-of-mutton
LGLCIN legal action
LGLEDR legal tender
LGMCIT logomachist
LGONIE legionnaire
LGRASA Ligurian Sea
LGREAN legerdemain
LGRTMC logarithmic
LGSAIE legislative
LGSAIG legislating
LGSAIN legislation
LGSAUE legislature
LGTARD light-haired
LGTEDD light-headed
LGTEGT lightweight
LGTORE light source
LGTOTD light-footed
LGTYIE Light My Fire
LGUIES leg-business
LGUVTE lignum vitae
LIAVRZ Luis Alvarez
LIEIGY loiteringly

LIHAIE leishmaniae
LIHAIS leishmanias
LIUEOL leisure pool
LKAIRR like a mirror
LKATEK like a streak
LKBLTN Lake Balaton
LKCAAA Lake Chapala
LKFRIE like for like
LKLCRE Lake Lucerne
LKOTRO Lake Ontario
LKSUAI Lake Scutari
LKTEID like the wind
LKTRAA Lake Turkana
LKTRES Lake Torrens
LKWNIG like winking
LLIOMN lollipop man
LLIUIN Lilliputian
LLLVRD lily-livered
LMDSAE Lyme disease
LMEGIR lammergeier
LMEGYR lammergeyer
LMEHAK Lambeth Walk
LMIHES lumpishness
LMLGTR lamplighter
LMLION lamellicorn
LMNAIN lamentation
LMNHEE lemon cheese
LMNIGY lamentingly
LMNQAH lemon squash
LMNRLW laminar flow
LMNSET luminescent
LMOOIT limnologist
LMTDES limitedness
LMTESY limitlessly
LMTTOS limitations
LMWITD limp-wristed
LMWTHS Limp Watches
LNAADO lend a hand to
LNAATD long-awaited
LNATIN Lancastrian
LNEGTN Len Deighton
LNEIGY lingeringly
LNELTD lanceolated
LNENAS lantern jaws
LNEVRE linked verse
LNHLIG landholding
LNHNRD long hundred
LNIGER landing gear
landing-gear
LNIGLP landing flap
LNIIOS lentiginous
LNILNS Line Islands
LNLHAT lonely heart
lonely-heart
LNLSIG long-lasting
LNMAUE long-measure
LNODRY Londonderry
LNOLWS Lennox Lewis
LNOPIE London pride
LNOSIE langoustine
LNPITR line printer
LNRNIG long-running
LNSGTD long-sighted
LNSNCT landsknecht
LNSRIG long-serving
LNSYOR Lynn Seymour
LNTEIG lengthening
LNTIES lengthiness
LNUDES languidness
LNUSIG languishing
LNUSIS linguistics
LNWNSO lend wings to
LOADOH leopard-moth
LOAKNE look askance
LOBITN Leon Brittan
LOCVLO Leoncavallo
LODEBR Lloyd Webber
LODERE Lloyd-George
LODGES look daggers
LOEHNE loose change
LOEIBD loose-limbed
LOEIGP loosening up
LOGUOT Léon Gaumont
LOHATD lion-hearted
LOHBAD L Ron Hubbard
LOIAIN lionization
LOIGAK looking back
LOIGIE looking like
LOIGSF looking as if
LOJNCK Leos Janácek
LOTEAT look the part
LOTEOP loop the loop
LOTOSY Leon Trotsky
LOTRUH look through
LPDPEA Lepidoptera
LPFUUY lap of luxury
LPIMGA Leptis Magna
LPMCIG lip-smacking
LPPOEN lipoprotein
LPRSOY laparoscopy
LPSAUI lapis lazuli
LPSCIN liposuction
LQEIBE liquefiable
LQIAIN liquidation
LREMUT large amount
LREOSY larcenously
LRETAT largest part
LREUBR large number
LRPOOT Lord Provost
LRSUPR Lord's Supper
LRYOMS Larry Holmes
LSCNRL lose control
LSEMNS Las Hermanas
LSFLES lustfulness
LSIGES lastingness
LSIMUH Lossiemouth
LSISAE lost in space
LSMINR Lise Meitner
LSMJSY lese-majesty
LSMRCS Las Americas
LSOBOS list of books
LSOEEF lose oneself
LSOERG lose one's rag
LSOEWY lose one's way
LSOFCS last offices
LSQIKY list quickly
LSSGTF lose sight of
LSTAKF lose track of
LSTEAY lose the baby
LTEAIM Lutheranism
LTEPES letterpress
LTFSEM let off steam
LTGOSY litigiously
LTIEOK latticework
lattice-work
LTLKON little known
little-known
LTLWMN Little Women
LTNIAE latent image
LTOHSE lithophysae
LTOHTC lithophytic
LTOOIT lithologist
LTOPEE lithosphere
LTORPY lithography
lithotripsy
LTRLIE lateral line
LTRTRD literatured
LTSAES Lotus-eaters
LTSTIG latest thing
LTTDNL latitudinal
LTUPPR litmus paper
LUAIIG Laura Riding
LUAIIY laudability
LUASLY Laura Ashley
LUDRTE launderette
LUHNGS laughing gas
LUHODY laugh loudly
LUIHES loutishness
LUMUHD loud-mouthed
LUOTLO Lou Costello
LUSEKR loudspeaker
Louis Necker
LUSEKY Louis Leakey
LUSMYR Louis B Mayer
LUSOVT Louis Jouvet
LUSRGN Louis Aragon
LUSUNE Louis-Quinze
LVIAIT love-in-a-mist
LVILVR live-in lover
LVLEDD level headed
level-headed
LVNDAH living death
LVNIAE living image
LVNSOE Livingstone
LVNTIG living thing
LVSRUS Lévi-Strauss
LVTCLY levitically
LVTRUH live through
LWESES lawlessness
LWFAUE law of nature
LWNODR law and order
LWPRTD low-spirited
LWRAIG law-breaking
LWRNAK lower in rank
LWRYLD lower eyelid
LWSLVL lowest level
LWSPIT lowest point
LXAINS lex talionis
LXGAHC lexigraphic

LXRAEN	luxuriate in
LXRATY	luxuriantly
LXROSY	luxuriously
LYHVNE	lay the venue
LYNWSE	laying waste
LYONRS	lay down arms
LYTAFR	lay a trap for
MACUTR	meat counter
MADYIL	Me and My Girl
MAIGES	meaningless
MAOBON	meadow brown
MAOGAS	meadow grass
MAOPPT	meadow pipit
MAOSET	meadowsweet
MAUEES	measureless
MAUEET	measurement
MAUEPO	measure up to
MBLPOE	mobile phone
MBUSRP	Möbius strip
MCAIIN	mechanician
MCAITC	mechanistic
MCALFX	Michael J Fox
MCALOT	Michael Foot
MCALWN	Michael Owen
MCAOTT	much about it
MCASUT	mock-assault
MCDMTA	mycodomatia
MCEESY	mackerel sky
MCIAIN	machination
MCIEIE	machine-like
MCIEOE	machine code
MCIEOL	machine tool
MCIGID	mockingbird
MCIOAE	machicolate
MCIVLI	Machiavelli
MCLGCL	mycological
MCLLTA	macula lutea
MCOCPC	macroscopic
	microscopic
MCOEIN	Micronesian
MCOERC	micrometric
MCOHNC	microphonic
MCOIHS	microfiches
MCOITC	macrobiotic
MCOLGD	much obliged
MCOLPY	microfloppy
MCONET	microinject
MCOOMC	macrocosmic
	microcosmic
MCOUUE	microtubule
MCPAMS	mycoplasmas
MCRHIE	McCarthyite
MCRHIM	McCarthyism
MCSNET	Mack Sennett
MCTEAE	much the same
MCUICU	Machu Picchu
MCUIIN	micturition
MCWEIH	Micawberish
MDAOIL	mediatorial
MDARCS	mediatrices
MDATNM	mediastinum
MDAVLY	mediaevally
MDCNHT	Medicine Hat
MDCNLY	medicinally
MDCNMN	medicine man
MDEAIM	medievalism
MDEAIT	medievalist
MDEIGY	maddeningly
MDIAAE	Madeira cake
MDIEOD	midwife toad
MDIHSN	midnight sun
MDLCAS	middle class
	middle-class
MDLERH	Middle-Earth
MDLMRH	Middlemarch
MDLNIG	mudslinging
	mud-slinging
MDLSZD	middle-sized
MDLWIE	Middle White
MDNAIE	madonnawise
MDNAIY	Madonna-lily
MDOMNY	made of money
MDOORD	mud-coloured
MDRDNE	modern dance
MDRIIG	modernizing
MDRITC	modernistic
MDRRDR	Madara Rider
MDRTMS	Modern Times
MDTODR	made to order
MDUDTD	medium-dated
MDUSOY	made-up story
MDYAES	Muddy Waters
MEEICY	Maeve Binchy
MEELNK	Maeterlinck
MEHLWY	meet halfway
MGAIIY	magnanimity
MGAIOS	magnanimous
MGCAPT	magic carpet
MGCQAE	magic square
MGCULT	magic bullet
MGETRA	Miguel Torga
MGIIBE	magnifiable
MGIIET	magnificent
MGIIOS	magnificoes
MGISIH	Maggie Smith
MGLMNA	megalomania
MGLPLS	megalopolis
MGNDAA	Meghnad Saha
MGSEIL	magisterial
MGTSEL	might as well
MHBAAA	Mahabharata
MHMAAI	Muhammad Ali
MHMAZA	Muhammad Zia
MHMEAI	Mohammed Ali
MHNOAO	Mohenjo-daro
MHRSTA	Maharashtra
MICRIR	mail-carrier
MIHNLR	mail handler
MIONTE	maisonnette
MISRAT	maidservant
MITNNE	maintenance
MITPAL	maintopsail
MITRZR	moisturizer
MJCOHD	Maja Clothed
MJRRES	major orders
MJRTIG	majoretting
MKAAEF	make aware of
MKAAHF	make a hash of
MKAAJB	make a bad job
MKAANT	make against
MKAAST	make a pass at
MKAELF	make a meal of
MKAEOR	make a detour
MKAESF	make a mess of
MKAHMD	make ashamed
MKAHWF	make a show of
MKAIFR	make a bid for
MKAINR	make a dinner
MKAIUE	make a figure
MKAKAD	make awkward
MKAOBO	make a booboo
MKAOEF	make a note of
MKAOEN	make a hole in
	make a move on
MKAOLF	make a fool of
MKAPEH	make a speech
MKARFT	make a profit
MKAUKF	make a muck of
MKAUSF	make a fuss of
MKAXOS	make anxious
MKBLEE	make believe
	make-believe
MKCNAT	make contact
MKCRAN	make certain
MKECTD	make excited
MKERIR	make earlier
MKFCST	make faces at
MKFINS	make friends
MKGETR	make greater
MKGTIG	Mike Gatting
MKHATY	make healthy
MKHAWY	make headway
MKHLSN	make holes in
MKHSIE	make hostile
MKHSOY	make history
MKICER	make it clear
MKIRAS	make inroads
MKLGTF	make light of
MKLGTR	make lighter
MKNDUT	make no doubt
MKNKON	making known
MKNROS	make nervous
MKOBEK	make or break
	make-or-break
MKOEBW	make one's bow
MKOEWY	make one's way
MKOFIH	make off with
MKQIKY	make quickly
MKQITR	make quieter
MKROFR	make room for
MKRUHY	make roughly
MKSALR	make smaller
MKSNEF	make sense of
MKSOTR	make shorter
MKSRDS	make strides
MKTEAE	make the pace
MKTINR	make thinner
MKUCEN	make unclean
MKUCER	make unclear

MKUIOM make uniform
MKVSBE make visible
MKWOPE make whoopee
MKWRID make worried
MKYUIK make you sick
MKYUUP make you jump
MLCLRY molecularly
MLCOSY maliciously
MLDCIN malediction
MLDCOY maledictory
MLDMKR Melody Maker
MLDOSY melodiously
MLDOTY maladroitly
MLDPIE maladaptive
MLDUTD maladjusted
MLEAIN millenarian
MLENUS millenniums
MLESNE malfeasance
MLFCIN malefaction
MLFCLY malefically
MLFCNE maleficence
MLFCOY malefactory
MLGATY malignantly
MLIAET multivalent
MLIAIL multiracial
MLIAOS multiparous
MLIEOD millisecond
MLIGNW melting snow
MLIGVR mulling over
mulling-over
MLIGWY melting away
MLILET mellifluent
MLILIG multiplying
MLILOS mellifluous
MLILXR multiplexer
MLINIE millionaire
MLINOD millionfold
MLITRY multistorey
MLJCSN Milt Jackson
MLLVRD milk-livered
MLNCOS moline cross
MLNEIG malingering
MLNHLA melancholia
MLNHLC melancholic
MLOAIE meliorative
MLOAIN melioration
MLOOOE Milton Obote
MLPOIM malapropism
MLRCIE malpractice
MLSAIN molestation
MLSAIS Miles Davies
MLSOMN Milos Forman
MLTTFR militate for
MLUCIN malfunction
MLVLNE malevolence
MLYBAG Melvyn Bragg
MLYODE mollycoddle
MMNAIY momentarily
MMNOOI memento mori
MMNOSY momentously
MMOITC mammonistic
MMORPY mammography
MMOUBS mumbo-jumbos
MMRADY Memorial Day
MMRAIE memorialise
memorialize
MMRBLA memorabilia
MMRNUS memorandums
MMTCLY mimetically
MMTEOD mum's the word
MNABOK mental block
MNADIG manhandling
MNADOF mansard roof
MNAIAE mental image
MNALIL mentally ill
MNAUIE miniaturise
miniaturize
MNAUIT miniaturist
MNBNIG mind-bending
MNBOIG mind-blowing
MNCAIM Manichaeism
MNCBIG minicabbing
MNCIOS monoclinous
MNCLUE monoculture
MNCPLY municipally
MNCRMC monochromic
MNCROS monocarpous
MNCSLS Monica Seles
MNCVLE Monaco-Ville
MNDPEE mont-de-piété
MNEAOT monkey about
MNEEIM mendelevium
MNEGER Monseigneur
MNEIGR Minnesinger
MNEPBS montes pubis
MNEPEE mantelpiece
MNEPLS Minneapolis
MNEQIU Montesquieu
MNESEF mantelshelf
MNESON Mendelssohn
MNEVIG manoeuvring
MNEVNS men-servants
MNFCNE munificence
MNFCOY manufactory
MNFCUE manufacture
MNFLES mindfulness
MNFSOS manifestoes
MNGAHC monographic
MNGAHR monographer
MNGDUD managed fund
MNGLIR Montgolfier
MNGMRE Montgomerie
MNGRHP managership
MNGTSE manage to see
MNHASN Münchhausen
MNHLRN men-children
MNHLTD mentholated
MNHYLW monthly flow
MNIHES mannishness
MNIHLS Mendip Hills
MNINBE mentionable
MNINDN mentioned in
MNJCER muntjac deer
MNLGIE monologuise
monologuize
MNLNUL monolingual
MNMMAE minimum wage
MNMRHC monomorphic
MNMSIN manumission
MNNCER mononuclear
MNNMIG mind-numbing
MNNRPO ma non troppo
MNPLBE manipulable
MNPLIR Montpellier
MNPLTR manipulator
MNPLZR monopolizer
MNPTOG monophthong
MNQIOE menaquinone
MNRAIG mind-reading
MNRHCL monarchical
MNRHGA menorrhagia
MNRLZR mineralizer
MNRRES minor orders
MNSEIL ministerial
monasterial
MNSEPR minesweeper
MNSIIM monasticism
MNTOIY monstrosity
MNTOSY monstrously
MNTRHP monitorship
MNTWIE minute-while
MNTWLZ Minute Waltz
MNUAIN mensuration
MNVLNE monovalence
MNVLNY monovalency
MNYAIG moneymaking
money-making
MNYEDR moneylender
money-lender
MNYOJM money for jam
MNYPDR money spider
MNYUEE mind your eye
MNYUPY money supply
MNYYHN Monty Python
MOADTS myocarditis
MOLGTR moonlighter
MRAALS Maria Callas
MRABAD mortarboard
mortar-board
MRACRY Mariah Carey
MRADOE more and more
MRAEME Margaret Mee
MRAFED Murrayfield
MRAGAS marram grass
MRALFY Morgan le Fay
MRASUE mornay sauce
MRBRUH Marlborough
MRBTKN more by token
MRCAAL Marc Chagall
MRCELY miracle play
MRDSAT more distant
MRDSRD more desired
MREAIY mercenarily
MREATY more exactly
MRECRE Marcel Carné
MREIHT Marie Bichat
MREMKR market maker
MREOSY murderously
MREPAA Mar del Plata

MREPAE marketplace
market-place
MRESAK Muriel Spark
MRETEE more extreme
MRETPS Marie Stopes
MRFCLY mirifically
MRFTIG more fitting
MRHALW marshmallow
MRHESY mirthlessly
MRHLIG marshalling
MRHNIE merchandise
merchandize
MRHNLY Myra Hindley
MRHNMN merchant man
merchantman
merchantmen
MRHOES marchioness
MRIAIE marginalise
marginalize
MRIAIY marginality
MRIBBR Martin Buber
MRIDNE morris dance
morris-dance
MRIEOK mortise lock
MRIEOT mortise bolt
MRIESY mercilessly
MRIGBD marriage-bed
MRIGOT morning coat
MRIGTR Morning Star
morning star
MRIOIZ Martin Opitz
MRISEN Martin Sheen
MRISIE marlinspike
MRLAUS moral values
MRLTEP Meryl Streep
MROIAE mirror image
MROJNS Marion Jones
MRPPIS Mary Poppins
MRRNUT Mary Renault
MRSAOE Mary Seacole
MRSELY Mary Shelley
MRSHNS maraschinos
MRTCAY meritocracy
MRTNOR Marston Moor
MRTROS meritorious
MRTRUS moratoriums
MRUAIN murmuration
MRUIGY murmuringly
MRUILY mercurially
MRUOSY murmurously
MRVAIM Moravianism
MRVNIN Merovingian
MRYAIG merrymaking
MRYLGT mercy flight
MRYNRW merry-andrew
MRYPAE Mervyn Peake
MSAARP Mrs Malaprop
MSADED Mustard-seed
MSADIG mishandling
MSAEFR mistaken for
MSAHOD mustachioed
MSALWY Mrs Dalloway
MSARAE miscarriage

MSCCOL music school
MSCETE music centre
MSCLES musicalness
MSDNIY misidentify
MSDSAT most distant
MSEAIG misbehaving
MSECIE misdescribe
misperceive
MSECIS Mister Chips
MSEEAE miscegenate
MSEEBR misremember
MSEFLY masterfully
MSEIIG mesmerizing
MSEOSY Musée d'Orsay
MSEOTN misbegotten
MSEPAE mise en place
MSEPEE masterpiece
MSESAE mispersuade
MSESEE mise en scène
mise-en-scène
MSESNE misfeasance
MSETEE most extreme
MSEYLY mystery play
MSEYOR mystery tour
MSHAHD missheathed
MSHEOS mischievous
MSIAIN mastication
MSIAOY masticatory
MSIEES massiveness
MSIETD misdirected
MSIGAE masking tape
MSIGET Mistinguett
MSIGIK missing link
MSIGOE misdiagnose
MSIIIY miscibility
MSISPI Mississippi
MSLBUD muscle-bound
MSLINE mésalliance
misalliance
MSLPWR muscle power
MSLSIY misclassify
MSMEIG mass meeting
MSMRHC mesomorphic
MSNHOE misanthrope
MSNHOY misanthropy
MSNOMD misinformed
MSNTIG miss nothing
MSNTUT misinstruct
MSOCIE misconceive
MSODTS mastoiditis
MSOEEF miss oneself
MSOETP miss one's tip
MSOISN Mrs Robinson
MSOSRE misconstrue
MSOVOS most obvious
MSPLIG misspelling
MSPOUE mass-produce
MSRAIG mistreading
MSRAIN miscreation
MSRIES miserliness
MSRINI Mastroianni
MSROIG mushrooming
MSRSFL mistrustful

MSSAKT Moses basket
MSSIAE misestimate
MSTEOT miss the boat
MSUAIY muscularity
MSUAUE musculature
MSUDDY misguidedly
MSUGET misjudgment
MSUIEY masculinely
MSUIIE masculinise
masculinize
MSUIIY masculinity
MSUPEE museum piece
MSURDR masquerader
MSUTNT mosquito net
MTAVLE mitral valve
MTBLTE Mutabilitie
MTEAIE mathematise
mathematize
MTEAIS mathematics
MTEBAD motherboard
MTEERH mother earth
MTEIGY mutteringly
MTEILW mother-in-law
MTERCI Matteo Ricci
MTHESY matchlessly
MTIIEL matrilineal
MTIOIL matrimonial
MTIRHL matriarchal
MTISUT Mathias Rust
MTIUAE matriculate
MTLDAF mottled calf
MTLOKR metalworker
MTLUGC metallurgic
MTMRHC metamorphic
MTNEOT matinée coat
MTNMCL metonymical
MTOCOS mutton chops
MTOOIE mythologise
mythologize
MTOOIS Mythologies
MTOOIT mythologist
MTOOOY meteorology
methodology
MTPRSS metaphrasis
MTPYIS metaphysics
MTRAIE materialise
materialize
MTRAIG motor racing
MTRAIM materialism
MTRAIT materialist
MTRAIY materiality
MTRANH motor launch
MTRDTS Mithridates
MTSAIE metastasise
metastasize
MTTCLY mitotically
MTTEIE metathesise
metathesize
MTUBSO Matsuo Basho
MTVFRE motive force
MTVPWR motive power
MTYGOP methyl group
MUDMNY Maundy money

MUHRED	mouth-friend
MUTATN	Mountbatten
MUTGOT	Mount Egmont
MUTIAH	mountain ash
MUTIDW	mountain dew
MUTIER	mountaineer
MUTIOS	mountainous
MUTITP	mountain top
MUTLET	Mount Elbert
MUTLRS	Mount Elbrus
MUTRRT	Mount Ararat
MVAIIY	moveability
MVBEES	movableness
MVFRAD	move forward
MVLGTY	move lightly
MVQIKY	move quickly
MVTMSC	move to music
MVTWRS	move towards
MVUWRS	move upwards
MWIHES	mawkishness
MXBSIN	moxibustion
MXCNAE	Mexican wave
MXDUBR	mixed number
MXEBUK	Max Delbrück
MXEROM	Max Beerbohm
MXMTSS	myxomatosis
MXOEHR	mix together
MYAGLU	Maya Angelou
MZMZRW	Mezz Mezzrow
MZOITS	mezzotintos
NACOSY	Noam Chomsky
NADRHL	Neanderthal
NASGTD	near-sighted
NATDAH	near to death
NATEOE	near the bone
NAWBTR	Noah Webster
NBDSOL	nobody's fool
NBEAAE	noble savage
NBEIDD	noble-minded
NCADEK	neck and neck
NCADRP	neck and crop
NCCPIE	nociceptive
NCECCD	nucleic acid
NCECIF	neckerchief
NCEOEN	nickelodeon
NCEROB	nuclear bomb
NCERUL	nuclear fuel
NCIAIN	nictitation
NCIRPC	nyctitropic
NCIUET	noctilucent
NCIUOS	noctilucous
NCLDNS	Nico Ladenis
NCLFRI	Nicole Farhi
NCLSOG	Nicolas Roeg
NCNCED	Nicene Creed
NCOACR	necromancer
NCOATC	necromantic
NCOCPC	necroscopic
NCOHBA	necrophobia
	nyctophobia
NCOHLA	necrophilia
NCOHLC	necrophilic
NCOIIL	nicrosilial
NCOISS	necrobiosis
NCOITC	necrobiotic
NCOOES	necropoleis
NCSAIN	necessarian
NCSAIS	necessaries
NCSAIY	necessarily
NCSIAE	necessitate
NCSIID	necessitied
NCSIIS	necessities
NCSIOS	necessitous
NCUNLY	nocturnally
NEADNE	nuée ardente
NEFLES	needfulness
NELCAT	needlecraft
NELPIT	needlepoint
NELWMN	needlewoman
NESENR	Niersteiner
NEZCEN	Nietzschean
NFROSY	nefariously
NFWRHN	no fewer than
NGECNE	nigrescence
NGIETY	negligently
NGLASN	Nigel Lawson
NGTAIH	nightmarish
NGTAIN	negotiation
NGTCOL	night school
NGTITR	night sister
NGTNAE	nightingale❑
NGTOIT	negationist
NIDAOD	Neil Diamond
NIEBOD	noise abroad
NIEESY	noiselessly
NIHORY	neighbourly
NIKNOK	Neil Kinnock
NIOEES	noisomeness
NIVRIH	nail varnish
NKDAIS	naked ladies
NKEIDX	Nikkei index
NKLTSA	Nikola Tesla
NLADOD	null and void
NLIIIN	nullifidian
NLIMLA	Nellie Melba
NLTRHN	no later than
NMDCLY	nomadically
NMDOPR	name-dropper
NMEPAE	number plate
NMESAE	numbers game
NMESOL	numbers pool
NMEURE	nom de guerre
NMGAHC	nomographic
NMHMNA	nymphomania
NMNLED	nominal head
NMNTVL	nominatival
NMOTAI	nimbostrati
NMRCLY	numerically
NMSAIT	numismatist
NNATSN	non-partisan
NNEALC	non-metallic
NNECIT	nondescript
NNEIET	non-resident
NNEIVR	nonbeliever
	non-believer
NNESCL	nonsensical
NNESNE	non-feasance
NNEUTR	non sequitur
NNHLNE	nonchalance
NNHMCL	non-chemical
NNHSCL	non-physical
NNILNE	non-violence
NNLCIE	non-elective
NNLINH	nonillionth
NNNAIE	non-invasive
NNOATC	non-romantic
NNOCEE	non-concrete
NNPCFC	non-specific
NNPERR	non-appearer
NNSAIG	none-sparing
NNTEES	none the less
	nonetheless
NNTNAD	non-standard
NNXSET	non-existent
NNYQIO	Ninoy Aquino
NNYRDY	Nancy Friday
NOAAIE	neopaganise
	neopaganize
NOIEUA	Naomi Uemura
NOLTNC	Neoplatonic
NOOITC	neologistic
NORPCL	neotropical
NPILAS	nuptial Mass
NPNHBD	nip in the bud
NPOOIT	nephologist
NPRCOY	nephrectomy
NPTAAE	naphthalane
NPTAEE	naphthalene
NPTAIE	naphthalise
	naphthalize
NPUUTA	ne plus ultra
NRAIEY	narratively
	normatively
NRAOBT	no reason but
NRASOE	Norman Stone
NREESY	nervelessly
NREETE	nerve centre
NREYAD	nurserymaid
NRHADY	northwardly
NRHAOA	North Dakota
NRHATR	north-easter
NRHEGS	North Sea gas
NRHETR	north-wester
NRHLFE	Northcliffe
NRHMTN	Northampton
NRHRIE	northernise
	northernize
NRHSAD	North Island
NRHTIE	North Utsire
NRHYAT	north by east
NRHYET	north by west
NRIGOE	nursing home
NRISSS	narcissuses
NROGUE	narrow-gauge
NROSES	nervousness
NSCTIG	no such thing
NSFOTL	nasofrontal
NSGAHC	nosographic
NSGAHR	nosographer

Words marked ❑ can also be spelled with an initial capital letter

NSLGCL nosological
NSPAYX nasopharynx
NSYAKR nosey parker
NSYOET nasty moment
NTATIH not part with
NTBEES notableness
NTBTFT not a bit of it
NTCODL notochordal
NTEALD not detailed
NTEATF not be part of
NTEODD not recorded
NTEWRD nether world
NTEYEL not very well
NTIBEO not liable to
NTIETL nutrimental
NTIGES nothingness
NTIGIL Notting Hill
NTIGIT nothing-gift
NTIGNT nothing in it
NTIGOE Nat King Cole
NTIGOH nothing loth
NTIGOT nothing to it
NTIIEY nutritively
NTIIHD not finished
NTIINL nutritional
NTIOIE nitric oxide
NTITET not fit to eat
NTITNO not listen to
NTLTEE not all there
NTMAAL no time at all
NTOAIE nationalise
nationalize
NTOAIM nationalism
NTOAIT nationalist
notionalist
NTOAIY nationality
NTOCIE not conceive
NTODIH not hold with
NTOEHN not more than
NTOEHR not together
NTOEIE nitrogenise
nitrogenize
NTOEOS nitrogenous
NTOFND not confined
NTONIG not counting
NTOPEE not complete
NTOSCD nitrous acid
NTOSDR not consider
NTPIIM notaphilism
NTPIIT notaphilist
NTPOUH not up to much
NTPTHN not a patch on
NTRLES naturalness
NTRLON natural-born
NTRLZD naturalized
NTROSY notoriously
NTRPTY naturopathy
NTRSRP nature strip
NTRSUY nature study
NTRTAL nature trail
NTSUAE not a sausage
NTTPIG not stopping
NTTRUS natatoriums
NTUHHP not much chop
NTXIIG not exciting
NTYDAF not my idea of
NTYRTY nitty-gritty
NTYUPO Natty Bumppo
NUHIES naughtiness
NUIHET nourishment
NUOOIT neurologist
NURLZR neutralizer
NURNOB neutron bomb
NURNTR neutron star
NVAIOA Navratilova
NVLAIG navel-gazing
NVLTIH novelettish
NVLTIT novelettist
NVRADE never say die
NVRNBY Navarino Bay
NVRNIG never ending
never-ending
NVSBRK Novosibirsk
NWCSIG newscasting
NWEEER nowhere near
NWERDY New Year's Day
NWEREE New Year's Eve
NWLMUH New Plymouth
NWNAAN now and again
NWOHJB new to the job
NWOKIY New York City
NWONAY newborn baby
NXBGET next biggest
NXDAET next dearest
NXOSES noxiousness
OAAOGU Ouagadougou
OACUTF on account of
OAECNE opalescence
OAGRVR Orange River
OAGTWY orange-tawny
OAGUAG orang-outang
OAHSOY oral history
OAICIE on an incline
OAKAYM Omar Khayyám
OAUOSY oraculously
OAVNAE of advantage
OBCLRS orbiculares
OBCLRY orbicularly
OBNFTO of benefit to
OBTVLE Orbitsville
OCETAE orchestrate
OCGNSS oncogenesis
OCLAIG oscillating
OCLAIN occultation
oscillation
OCLAOY oscillatory
OCLORM oscillogram
OCMNCL oecumenical
OCNIIN on condition
OCODIE on cloud nine
OCOTIE once or twice
OCPTLY occipitally
OCRECS occurrences
OCUSNT of course not
ODADNS odds and ends
ODADOS odds and sods
ODHSNT old chestnut
ODNRMN ordinary men
ODOAIH old-womanish
ODOAOT odd woman out
ODOEIH old-fogeyish
ODRDLS older adults
ODRFOD Old Trafford
ODRIES orderliness
ODRRUD order around
OEAANT over against
OEACIG overarching
OEADHT open-and-shut
OEADVR over and over
OEAHEE overachieve
OEAIEY operatively
OEAIGR opera singer
OEAIIY operability
OEAINL operational
OEBAIG overbearing
OEBETE over-breathe
OEBLNE overbalance
OEBSBT one's best bet
OECAGD overcharged
OECODD overcrowded
OECRET overcorrect
OECRUT open circuit
OEDESD overdressed
OEDVLP overdevelop
OEECTD overexcited
OEEYAD on every hand
OEFEGT overfreight
OEFOIG overflowing
OEHATD open-hearted
OEHNIG overhanging
OEHNLD overhandled
OEIDLE overindulge
over-indulge
OEIGAT opening part
OEIGIE opening time
OEIGOE opening move
OELAHR overleather
OELOIG overlooking
OEMAUE overmeasure
OEMDSY overmodesty
OEMUHD open-mouthed
OEOEIE one more time
OEOSES onerousness
OEOUUN Ode to Autumn
OEPCUE overpicture
OEPEIE overprecise
over-precise
OEPOET overprotect
OEPOLD overpeopled
OEPOUE overproduce
OEPWRD overpowered
OERFND overrefined
over-refined
OERNIG overrunning
OERNIH overrun with
OESRTH overstretch
OETEDS over the odds
OETEIL over the hill
OETEON over the moon

OETEUP over the hump
OEVRIT open verdict
OEWAHR overweather
OEWEIG overweening
OEWEMD overwhelmed
OEWETE overwrestle
OEWOGT overwrought
OEZAOS overzealous
over-zealous
OFADDY offhandedly
OFCADM officialdom
OFCAEE officialese
OFCAIM officialism
OFCBOK office block
OFCHUS office hours
OFCOSY officiously
OFCUIG offscouring
OFHHOS off the hooks
OFHPIT off the point
OFHRIS off the rails
OFHSEF off the shelf
OFHTAK off the track
OFHWGN off the wagon
OFLAET on full alert
OFNIEY offensively
OFNSAE off one's face
off one's game
OFNSAS off one's oats
OFNSED off one's feed
off one's head
OFRSIE Oxfordshire
OFSAIN obfuscation
OFSAOY obfuscatory
OGNCLY organically
OGOTRS on good terms
OHOHBA ochlophobia
OHOHBC ochlophobic
OHORTC ochlocratic
OIAOSY oviparously
OIDBEF oeil-de-boeuf
OIEDCA obiter dicta
OIEHRY Oliver Hardy
OIERNH olive branch
OIESOE Oliver Stone
OIETIT Oliver Twist
OIETMO Oliver Tambo
OIIAIE originative
OIIAIG originating
OIIAIN origination
OIIAIY originality
OIIASN original sin
OIINOL opinion poll
OIINTD opinionated
OILEUE of ill repute
OILIDW oriel window
OINAIE orientalise
orientalize
OINAIN orientation
OINAIT Orientalist
OIOSES ominousness
OIRDIG Otis Redding
OJCIAE objectivate
OJCIEY objectively
OJCIIE objectivise
objectivize
OJCIIM objectivism
OJCIIT objectivist
OJCIIY objectivity
OJRAIN objurgation
OJTRUE objet trouvé
OLANIG oil painting
oil-painting
OLGTOS obligations
OLJSWN only just win
OLLTOM oil platform
OLPDIA olla-podrida
OLQEES obliqueness
OLTRTD obliterated
OLVOSO oblivious to
OLVOSY obliviously
OMNWRS of many words
OMTCLY osmotically
OMTSET obmutescent
ONACUT of no account
on no account
ONCSIY of necessity
ONFROS omnifarious
ONLGCL oenological
ONMNIT ornamentist
ONPEET omnipresent
ONPTNE omnipotence
ONSINE omniscience
ONTOOY ornithology
ONXOSY obnoxiously
OOATCN onomasticon
OOCSOS on occasions
OOEGAD on one's guard
OOEHNS on one's hands
OOEMRS on one's marks
OOEPAE on one's plate
OOEWYO on one's way to
OOHRIE or otherwise
OOIAIN ozonization
OOIEOS odoriferous
OOOPEE ozonosphere
OOOSES odorousness
OOTBAT odontoblast
OPICPE on principle
OPNEMR Oppenheimer
OPNLYF on penalty of
OPOROS opprobrious
OPRUEY opportunely
OPRUIM opportunism
OPRUIT opportunist
OPRUIY opportunity
ORMNHP oarsmanship
OSERCL obstetrical
OSIAEY obstinately
OSIBAD on shipboard
OSIIIS od's-pitikins
OSLSET obsolescent
OSNELS Orson Welles
OSPAEL oesophageal
OSRAIN observation
OSRAOY observatory
OSRATF observant of
OSRATY observantly
OSRCIE obstructive
OSRCIN obstruction
OSRGNC oestrogenic
OSRIGY observingly
OSSINL obsessional
OSUAIN obscuration
OSUDID of sound mind
OTAAOR out-paramour
OTADES outwardness
OTADOM outward form
OTASOE on that score
OTCLIK optical disk
OTDCMS octodecimos
OTEAIH on the parish
OTEAKF on the back of
OTEAKT on the market
OTEAOT on the way out
OTEAPT on the carpet
OTEATF on the part of
OTEATR on the batter
OTEAZE on the razzle
OTEEOD on the record
OTEGNA on the agenda
OTEHOE on the throne
OTEIDY on the tiddly
OTEIEF on the side of
OTEQAE on the square
OTETCS on the stocks
OTETET on the street
OTETOE on the stroke
OTEUTN on the button
OTFAGR out of danger
OTFAOR out of favour
OTFCIN out of action
OTFEPR out of temper
OTFESN out of season
OTFFIA Out of Africa
OTFHAK out of the ark
OTFHWY out of the way
out-of-the-way
OTFITR out of kilter
OTFOKT out of pocket
OTFONS out of bounds
OTFRAH out of breath
OTFUOR out of humour
OTGNLY octagonally
OTGNSS ontogenesis
OTGNTC ontogenetic
OTHDOS octahedrons
OTIEET outside left
OTIHIE ostrich-like
OTITNE outdistance
OTLGCL ontological
OTLINH octillionth
OTMEAE obtemperate
OTMRIG outsmarting
OTMTIT optometrist
OTNAIN ostentation
OTNAOT out and about
OTNIEY ostensively
OTNILY octennially
OTOADC orthopaedic

OTOAHC osteopathic
OTOBOD out for blood
OTOCPC orthoscopic
OTOETE orthocentre
OTOLSY osteoplasty
OTOOIT osteologist
OTOREL outdoor meal
OTORIG outsourcing
OTORPY orthography
OTOTRN orthopteran
OTPKNY outspokenly
OTREIG outbreeding
OTRIIS outer limits
OTSAGE obtuse angle
OTTNIG outstanding
OTUIEY obtrusively
OTULIG outbuilding
OTWRUG Otto Warburg
OTWRVR Ottawa River
OVOSES obviousness
OWLAEY Oswald Avery
OYEAIN oxygenation
OYPCLG Olympic Flag
PAAANT pray against
PAAATN play a part in
PAAIIY placability
PAAOEN play a joke on
play a role in
PAATWR Peasants' War
PABOSM Peasblossom
PAEAIG peacemaking
peace-making
PAEAIM planetarium
PAEFID peace of mind
PAEFLY prayerfully
PAEFOK place of work
PAEFUY place of duty
PAEIUE plane figure
PAEOGR peace-monger
PAEOIG peace-loving
PAEOOC Phanerozoic
PAEOOY planetology
PAEPAO player piano
player-piano
PAERAY peace treaty
PAEWEL prayer wheel
PAFLES playfulness
PAFOSE play footsie
PAFRIE play for time
PAFROE play for love
PAIACL pharisaical
PAIBER play it by ear
PAICAE plagioclase
PAIGAD playing-card
PAIGRA playing area
PAIPEE planisphere
PAIRZD plagiarized
PAIRZR plagiarizer
PAISOE plagiostome
PALALY pearl barley
PALGTS pearly gates
PALQEN pearly queen
PAMNGN plasminogen
PANIEY plaintively
PANPKN plainspoken
plain-spoken
PANYEN plainly seen
PAOEAE play one's ace
PAOKIE peacock-like
PAOKLE peacock-blue
PAOOIE piano nobile
PAOOTS pianofortes
PAOOVX plano-convex
PAOWRS play on words
PAOYOE phagocytose
PATCBE practicable
PATCBY practicably
PATCLY practically
PATCOB plastic bomb
PATCSR plasticiser
PATCZR plasticizer
PATEAE play the game
PATEOL play the fool
PATGAE plantigrade
PATMIB phantom limb
PATRAT plaster cast
PATROK plasterwork
PATRON plaster down
PATSAA phantasmata
PATSDN practised in
PATUTR plantcutter
PATWMN plantswoman
PAYGTS pharyngitis
PAYRIE platyrrhine
PBIAIN publication
PBIEEY Public Enemy
public enemy
PBIHUE public house
PBIIIG publicizing
PBIPRE public purse
PBIWRS public works
PBOAAS Pablo Casals
PBOEUA Pablo Neruda
PCADEL pack and peel
PCAEEL package deal
PCAEOR package tour
PCAIIY peccability
PCAILS peccadillos
PCBWIG pace-bowling
PCCRNE pococurante
PCEKIE pocket knife
pocket-knife
PCELNH packed lunch
PCEMNY pocket money
PCESZD pocket-sized
PCFCLY pacifically
PCHLSN pick holes in
PCIAEY pectinately
PCIAIN pectination
PCIGAE packing-case
PCIIGS pichiciagos
PCLAIE peculiarise
peculiarize
PCLAIY peculiarity
PCNAIY pecuniarily
PCOEWY pick one's way
PCOILY pictorially
PCORPY pictography
PCUEQE picturesque
PCUSED pick up speed
PCYUON pick-your-own
PDGGCL pedagogical
PDLWEL paddle wheel
PDNIIE pedanticise
pedanticize
PDNUAE pedunculate
PEAAIN preparation
PEAAOY preparatory
PEABIN Precambrian
PEACIY presanctify
PEAETY prevalently
PEAIAE prevaricate
PEAIGO preparing to
PEAILE premaxillae
PEALPN prevail upon
PEALVR prevail over
PEAOIL prefatorial
PEAOIY predatorily
prefatorily
PEATOS precautions
PEAUEY prematurely
PEBRAN plea bargain
plea-bargain
PECETY presciently
PECIES preachiness
PECIIG prescribing
PECUID preoccupied
PEDMRH pseudomorph
PEDOIH preadmonish
PEDPDA pseudopodia
PEDULY plead guilty
PEEAIE plebeianise
plebeianize
PEEDDY pretendedly
PEEDOE pretend to be
PEEESR predecessor
PEEETY precedently
PEEFAD piece of land
PEEFAE piece of cake
PEEFOK piece of work
PEEIAE premedicate
premeditate
PEESOS pretensions
PEETBE presentable
preventable
preventible
PEETBY presentably
PEETES preceptress
PEETET presentment
PEETIE present-time
PEETND predestined
PEETOS pretentious
PEETRS present arms
PEEVBE preservable
PEGIIN pre-ignition
PEIAET predicament
PEIAIE predicative
PEIAIN predication
PEIEES preciseness

PEIETD	predilected
PEIETN	predilecton
PEIEVR	preside over
PEIHES	peevishness
PEIHNS	plenishings
PEIIAE	precipitate
PEIIAY	preliminary
PEIINL	previsional
PEIIOS	precipitous
PEIMOD	Premium Bond
PEIOET	plenipotent
PEIPSD	predisposed
PEIRHP	premiership
PEITBE	predictable
PEITBY	predictably
PEITIS	paediatrics
PEITRC	prehistoric
PEIUAE	prefigurate
PEIWLY	peelie-wally
PELNCL	preclinical
PEMNNE	pre-eminence
PEMUAE	preambulate
PENHSY	pie in the sky
PEOAIE	prerogative
PEOATL	pterodactyl
PEOCIE	preconceive
PEOEIE	phenomenise
	phenomenize
PEOHLA	paedophilia
PEOHRA	plerophoria
PEOIAE	predominate
	prenominate
PEOIAT	predominant
PEOIIN	premonition
	preposition
PEOIOY	premonitory
PEOLNE	prepollence
PEOLNY	prepollency
PEONSE	precognosce
PEOOIT	paedologist
	phenologist
PEOTAT	precontract
PEPRLY	puerperally
PERAGD	prearranged
PERAND	preordained
PERBYE	Pierre Bayle
PERCRE	Pierre Curie
PESDIH	pleased with
PESFAL	press of sail
PESIYU	please it you
PESOEE	Pleistocene
PESOGN	Piers Morgan
PESRBE	pleasurable
PESRBY	pleasurably
PESRUD	press around
PESRZD	pressurized
PESTRE	pieds-à-terre
PESTYU	pleaseth you
PESUGR	Pressburger
PETESD	pre-stressed
PETFLY	plentifully
PETGOS	prestigious
PETNAS	Prestonpans
PETOSY	plenteously
PETPLY	Pretty Polly
PETPNY	pretty penny
PETRON	Prester John
PETSIO	prestissimo
PETWMN	Pretty Woman
PEUIAE	prejudicate
PEUIEY	prelusively
PEUIGY	presumingly
PEUIIL	prejudicial
PEUOIY	prelusorily
PEUPIE	presumptive
PEUPIN	presumption
PEUPSD	presupposed
PGEDDY	pigheadedly
PGIHES	piggishness
PGKUKE	pig's knuckle
PGOHLD	pigeonholed
PIADRR	philanderer
PIAEES	privateness
PIAEIT	philatelist
PIAIEY	privatively
PIAONS	prima donnas
PIATCE	psi particle
PIAVLY	primaevally
PIAYEL	primary cell
PIBEES	pliableness
PIBNET	Phil Bennett
PICLIS	Phil Collins
PICPLY	principally
PICSIA	Princess Ida
PIDLIG	pain-dulling
PIEESY	pricelessly
PIEIIG	price-fixing
PIEINR	prizewinner
	prize-winner
PIENJY	pride and joy
PIESOG	Phileas Fogg
PIEUBR	prime number
PIFLES	painfulness
PIIEIL	primigenial
PIIGAS	Philip Glass
PIIIEY	primitively
PIIIIM	primitivism
PIIPAS	Philippians
PIIPNS	Philippines
PIKIES	prickliness
PIKLIG	painkilling
PIKYER	prickly pear
PIKYET	prickly heat
PIOOHC	philosophic
PIOOHR	philosopher
PIOOIT	philologist
PIOOSY	poisonously
PISAIG	painstaking
PISSOE	priest's hole
PITAPI	point d'appui
PITCSS	psittacosis
PITDAY	painted lady
PITDES	pointedness
PITESY	pointlessly
PITFAE	point of sale
PITFIW	point of view
PITHWY	point the way
PITLIM	pointillism
PITLIT	pointillist
PITNIE	Pointe Noire
	Pointe-Noire
	point in time
PITNOT	pointing-out
PITPTE	Point-a-Pitre
PKBRKT	poke borak at
PLADOS	polyandrous
PLAEDF	pull ahead of
PLASIT	pillar-saint
PLCANE	phlyctaenae
PLCBRH	police burgh
PLCCUT	police court
PLCFRE	police force
PLCNHS	Polacanthus
PLCRMC	polychromic
PLCROS	polycarpous
PLCSAE	police state
PLCWMN	policewoman
PLECUT	pollen count
PLEGIT	poltergeist
PLEIGY	pilferingly
PLEUET	pulverulent
PLFCIN	Pulp Fiction
PLFCST	pull faces at
PLGNLY	polygonally
PLGOTC	polyglottic
PLGOTL	polyglottal
PLHATD	pale-hearted
PLHDOS	polyhedrons
PLHIUE	pulchritude
PLIAIG	palpitating
PLIAIN	palpitation
	pollination
PLIGAK	pulling back
PLIGON	pulling-down
PLMCLY	polemically
PLMRHC	polymorphic
PLNRMC	palindromic
PLOCSS	pillowcases
PLOEVR	pull one over
PLPPIE	polypeptide
PLRAIG	palm reading
PLRMTY	polarimetry
PLROEY	poltroonery
PLROIM	pelargonium
PLSIIN	Palestinian
PLSRNS	Palm Springs
	pull strings
PLSYEE	polystyrene
PLTCLY	politically
PLTCNC	polytechnic
PLTEAY	pelotherapy
PLTRUH	pull through
PLTSOK	pale tussock
PLUAIG	pullulating
PLUAIN	pullulation
PLUIIY	pellucidity
PLVSGD	pale-visaged
PLYNIH	pollyannish
PMAGAS	pampas grass

PMCSOE pumice stone
PMEHRE pommel horse
PMGAAE pomegranate
PMHEER pamphleteer
PMLCOK Pumblechook
PMOSES pompousness
PMRTAE pomfret cake
PNAAET pentavalent
PNAATC pan-galactic
PNAATL pentadactyl
PNAEIM pentamerism
PNAEOS pentamerous
PNAERL pentahedral
PNAERN pentahedron
PNAGAD pineal gland
PNAGLR pentangular
PNAIIE pentamidine
PNARNS Punta Arenas
PNATCS pentastichs
PNCLAE penicillate
PNCLIM penicillium
PNCTAK panic attack
PNCUTN panic button
PNEIGY ponderingly
PNELNC panhellenic
PNEOIM pandemonium
PNEOSY ponderously
PNEOTL Pentecostal
PNERUD ponce around
PNGRCL panegyrical
PNHITC pantheistic
PNHVLA Pancho Villa
PNIEES pensileness
pensiveness
PNIELS ponticellos
PNIHRY Pondicherry
PNIIAE pontificate
PNIIAS pontificals
PNINBE pensionable
PNINUD pension fund
PNISIT pencil-skirt
PNLGCL penological
PNLIAE penultimate
PNLSIN Panglossian
PNLYIK penalty kick
PNLYOL penalty goal
PNLYPT penalty spot
PNLYRA penalty area
PNMCNL Panama Canal
PNMRCN pan-American
PNNUAE peninsulate
PNOABX Pandora's box
PNOIIT pantomimist
PNPNHR Pink Panther
PNPRIM panspermism
PNPRIT panspermist
PNROSY penuriously
PNSAIM Panislamism
PNSEFR punished for
PNSIGY punishingly
PNTAIE penetrative
PNTAIG penetrating
PNTAIN penetration
punctuation
PNTAIY punctuality
PNTLOS punctilious
PNTNIL penitential
PNUOEN pan-European
PNUOSY pendulously
PNYEGT pennyweight
PNYIDE panty girdle
POAAIE propagative
POAAIN profanation
propagation
POAAOY profanatory
POACLY prosaically
POAEES profaneness
POAIIY probability
POAINR probationer
POAOIT protagonist
POARPD Prosauropod
POCUTS prosciuttos
POEAIN proletarian
POEAIT proletariat
POEDNS proceedings
POEFLE proper-false
POEIIE phonemicise
phonemicize
phoneticise
phoneticize
progenitive
POEIIN phonetician
POEIIT phonemicist
POEINE provenience
POEIOS progenitors
POEOEA prolegomena
POEOOC Proterozoic
POESDY professedly
POETES protectress
POETLS projectiles
POETMN property man
POEUIN prosecution
POEYIE proselytise
proselytize
POEYIM proselytism
POFPRT proof spirit
POFRAD prop forward
POGSAE ploughshare
POHLMA prothalamia
POHLXS prophylaxis
POHOBN prothrombin
POHOIM prochronism
POHRCS prothoraces
POHRXS prothoraxes
POIAEY proximately
POIAIE prodigalise
prodigalize
POIAIY prodigality
POICIY promiscuity
POICOS promiscuous
POIEAE proliferate
POIEOE profiterole
POIETY prominently
providently
POIIAY prolificacy
POIIBE propitiable
POIIGY promisingly
POIIIE prohibitive
POIIIG prohibiting
POIIIN prohibition
POIINL provisional[□]
POIINY proficiency
POIIOY prohibitory
POIITR propitiator
POIOIY provisorily
POIQIY propinquity
POLETR people-eater
POLMAE problem page
POLMRE problem-free
POLMTC problematic
PONIIO pro indiviso
POOAIE provocative
POOAIN prorogation
provocation
POOATC phototactic
POOCDS proboscides
POOCSS proboscises
POOEAA protonemata
POOERC photometric
POOHBA photophobia
POOIGY provokingly
POOIIN proposition
POOINL promotional
POOOIE protocolise
protocolize
POOOIT phonologist
protocolist
POOPEE photosphere
POORPY phonography
photography
POOSLR proconsular
POOTOS proportions
POPAIE phosphatise
phosphatize
POPCIE prospective
POPIUE promptitude
POPOAE phosphorate
POPOIE phosphorise
phosphorize
POPOOS phosphorous
POQAIY poor quality
poor-quality
PORAIE procreative
PORAIN procreation
PORCIE protractile
PORCIN protraction
POREAY proprietary
POREOS proprietors
PORNLL propranolol
PORSEN Procrustean
PORSIE progressive
PORSIG progressing
PORSIN progression
POTAIN prostration
POTEIS prosthetics
POTRHP proctorship
POTRUH plod through
POUEAE protuberate
POUEAT protuberant

Words marked □ can also be spelled with an initial capital letter

Code	Word
POUEES	profuseness
POUEET	procurement
POUGTR	promulgator
POYIIE	propylitise
	propylitize
PPCENR	pipe-cleaner
PPDEMR	pipe-dreamer
PPEIES	pepperiness
PPEMCE	papier-mâché
PPIUCR	peptic ulcer
PPOEEE	pipe one's eye
PPOPAE	pipe of peace
PPRCOS	papyraceous
PPSRLE	pipistrelle
PPYEDD	puppy-headed
PRADIE	park-and-ride
PRAETY	permanently
PRAGNC	permanganic
PRAGSA	Port Augusta
PRAIEY	pervasively
	purgatively
PRAIIY	portability
PRAOIL	purgatorial
PRBLCL	parabolical
PRBODD	pure-blooded
PRCAIM	pericranium
PRCATC	pyroclastic
PRCILY	parochially
PRCMAY	part company
PRCRIC	pericardiac
PRCRIL	pericardial
	pericarpial
PRCRIM	pericardium
PRCRIR	Port Cartier
PRCTML	paracetamol
PRCUIT	parachutist
PRDNUS	peridiniums
PRDXCL	paradoxical
PREEAE	perseverate
PREEEN	persevere in
PREEIG	persevering
PREICL	parheliacal
PRERTR	perpetrator
PRETBE	perceptible
	perfectible
PRETBY	perceptibly
PRETES	perfectness
PREUIN	persecution
PREULY	perpetually
PREUTR	perpetuator
PREVBE	perceivable
PREVBY	perceivably
PRGACP	Phrygian cap
PRGAHA	paragraphia
PRGAHC	paragraphic
PRGAIL	periglacial
PRGIAE	peregrinate
PRGIIG	paragliding
PRGNSA	paragenesia
PRGNSS	paragenesis
PRGOSE	paraglossae
PRHDES	parchedness
PRHPTC	perihepatic
PRHRTC	porphyritic
PRHSTX	purchase tax
PRIAIY	pertinacity
PRIETY	pertinently
PRIIAE	participate
PRIIAT	participant
PRIIEY	partitively
PRIIIL	participial
PRIINE	percipience
PRINAB	Persian lamb
PRINAS	Persian Wars
PRISBE	permissible
PRISBY	permissibly
PRITNE	persistence
PRITNY	persistency
PRIUAE	particulate
PRIUAS	particulars
PRJCSN	Port Jackson
PRLATC	parallactic
PRLEIE	parallelise
	parallelize
PRLEIM	parallelism
PRLEYE	paraldehyde
PRLHAT	Purple Heart
	purple heart
	purpleheart
PRLISS	paraleipses
	paraleipsis
PRLNBY	Portland Bay
PRLPTH	purple patch
PRLXDY	perplexedly
PRMDCL	paramedical
	pyramidical
PRMDLY	pyramidally
PRMNEU	portmanteau
PRMRSY	Port Moresby
PRMUAE	perambulate
PRMUTY	paramountcy
	paramountly
PRNHLA	paranthelia
PRNHSS	parentheses
	parenthesis
PRNHTC	parenthetic
PRNILY	perennially
PRNLGC	phrenologic
PRNMSA	paronomasia
PRNPRC	perinephric
PRNRHP	partnership
PROAIE	personalise
	personalize
PROAIN	percolation
	perforation
	personation
PROAIY	personality
PRODAA	period drama
PROEES	purposeless
PROETY	port of entry
PROIID	personified
PROIIE	pyrrolidine
PROIIR	personifier
PROIIY	periodicity
PROILW	periodic law
PROMBE	performable
PROMNE	performance
PROOTL	periodontal
PROPEE	period piece
PRORAE	parlour game
PRORPY	pornography
PROSAN	Port of Spain
PROSOE	parson's nose
PROTDY	purportedly
PROTTC	periostitic
PROUIN	perlocution
PRPCIE	perspective
PRPCIY	perspecuity
	perspicuity
PRPCOS	perspicuous
PRPNAE	paripinnate
PRPNIG	parapenting
PRPRSR	paraphraser
PRPRSS	periphrases
	periphrasis
PRPTTC	peripatetic
PRPYET	part payment
PRRIUE	portraiture
PRRYIE	pyrargyrite
PRSAIH	peristalith
PRSASS	peristalsis
PRSATC	peristaltic
PRSCEK	parish clerk
PRSERS	ports de bras
PRSIGY	perishingly
PRSIIE	parasuicide
PRSIIG	parasailing
PRSINE	parascience
PRSINR	parishioner
PRSLEB	phrasal verb
PRSLNE	paraselenae
PRSOOY	perissology
	phraseology
PRSORM	phraseogram
PRSRIA	perestroika
PRSTCL	parasitical
PRTCEK	parity check
PRTCLY	piratically
PRTEEM	port the helm
PRTHDA	pyritohedra
PRTNCL	puritanical
PRTNTS	peritonitis
PRTOPR	paratrooper
PRTPOD	paratyphoid
PRTYOD	parathyroid
PRUAIN	permutation
PRUBDY	perturbedly
PRUCOY	perfunctory
PRUDBE	persuadable
PRUDDY	persuaded by
PRUEES	perfumeless
PRUIIN	parturition
PRUSBE	persuasible
PRUTIG	pirouetting
PRVCCD	pyruvic acid
PRYOPR	party-pooper
PRYPRT	party spirit
PSAALA	passacaglia
PSAEZS	passamezzos

PSAIIY passability
PSAODR postal order
PSAOIL piscatorial
PSAOIN pass a motion
piscatorian
PSARIE pass airside
PSCRET pass current
PSDSUE past dispute
PSEIGY pesteringly
PSEIRY posteriorly
PSERUD passed round
PSERZR pasteurizer
PSESOS possessions
PSFRAD push forward
PSIBOS Puss in Boots
PSIEES passiveness
PSIEOS pestiferous
PSIETY pestilently
PSIGHT passing shot
PSIGVR passing over
PSIGWY passing away
passing-away
PSIIIY possibility
PSIITC pessimistic
PSINEK Passion week
PSINES passionless
PSINIE Passiontide
PSINLY passion play
PSIOOS piscivorous
PSISET past its best
PSOAIM pastoralism
PSOEEF push oneself
PSOEWY push one's way
PSOOIT pestologist
PSQIKY pass quickly
PSRBAD pastry board
PSRBUH pastry brush
PSRUHY push roughly
PSTEAK pass the mark
PSTEET pass the test
PSTNIN post-tension
PSTOIG positioning
PSTRUH pass through
push through
PSUAIN postulation
PSUEAD pastureland
PSUEES pastureless
PSUENW pastures new
PSUNDR pasquinader
PSYILW pussy willow
PTACIE Petrarchise
Petrarchize
PTAEPN put make-up on
PTAOEN Pythagorean
PTBAEN put a brake on
PTEAOT potter about
PTECNE putrescence
PTEIGY potteringly
PTENAE pattern race
PTENNS Pat Jennings
PTERTY put secretly
PTETIH patient with
PTFLES pitifulness
PTHDOF pitched roof
PTHLDN put the lid on
PTHLNE pitchblende
PTHNPY pitch and pay
PTIAAE Pitti Palace
PTIENO put life into
PTIHES pettishness
PTIIEL patrilineal
PTIIER patrilinear
PTIOGR pettifogger
PTIOIL patrimonial
PTIRHL patriarchal
PTMTHO put a match to
PTNAET patent agent
PTNAGR put in danger
PTNCOS potent cross
PTNEGT put on weight
PTNEOD put on record
PTNHDG put on the dog
PTNHIS put in chains
PTNHMP put on the map
PTNHRE put in charge
PTNIDF put in mind of
PTNILY potentially
PTNOIN put in motion
PTNRSN put in prison
PTNSAK put one's mark
PTNSID put one's mind
PTNSUT put on a spurt
PTOASM put to ransom
PTOEHR put together
PTOEQE Pythonesque
PTOIHS put to rights
PTOIIG patronizing
PTOLGT put to flight
PTOMNY pots of money
PTOOIT pathologist
PTOPRM pittosporum
PTOSES piteousness
PTOSIT patron saint
PTOWMN patrolwoman
PTPFGT put up a fight
PTPIEN put a price on
PTRAIM paternalism
PTRIDR Peter Pindar
PTRILY Peter Lilley
PTRISY Peter Wimsey
PTRNOT petering out
PTROTR paternoster[□]
Peter Porter
PTRPNE Peter's pence
PTRRMS Peter Grimes
PTRTOE Peter O'Toole
PTSMRS Pete Sampras
PTTAGT put straight
PTTCOS put it across
PTTESN put stress on
PTTIDY put it mildly
PTTOAY petitionary
PTTOIG petitioning
PTVRIN pet aversion
PTYIDD petty-minded
PUADLY plug-and-play
PUAITC pluralistic
PUBAEG Paul Boateng
PUCIES paunchiness
PUCZNE Paul Cézanne
PUDLAX Paul Delvaux
PUEESY pauselessly
PUELCT plume-pluckt
PUERIH Paul Ehrlich
PUGUUN Paul Gauguin
PUIHES prudishness
PUISIG prusik sling
PUKAIG Paul Keating
PUOMNS plus or minus
PUORTC plutocratic
PUPDIG plum pudding
PURBSN Paul Robeson
PUSAIE Prussianise
Prussianize
PUSCCD prussic acid
PUSONN pour scorn on
PUTEOX Paul Theroux
PUTLIH Paul Tillich
PVNSOE paving stone
paving-stone
PVRYIE poverty line
PVRYRP poverty trap
PVTRDE pivot bridge
PWBOIG pawnbroking
PWDHUE P G Wodehouse
PWRESY powerlessly
PWRRVN power-driven
PWRUGY power-hungry
PXLAIN pixillation
PYHARC psychiatric
PYHCLY psychically
PYHDAA psychodrama
PYHDLA psychedelia
PYHDLC psychedelic
PYHGNC psychogenic
PYHPPR pay the piper
PYHPTY psychopathy
PYIAIM physicalism
PYIAIY physicality
PYIGOY physiognomy
PYILGC physiologic
PYLCAE phylloclade
PYLMNA phyllomania
PYLTXS phyllotaxis
PYNGET paying guest
PYOAEO pay homage to
PYOYEE phycomycete
PYVSTO pay a visit to
QAEIES quaveriness
QAEIGY quaveringly
QAIAIE qualitative
QAIIBE qualifiable
QAIIDY qualifiedly
QAIYIE quality time
QAKAVR quacksalver
QARLIG quarrelling
QARLIH quarrel with
QARLOE quarrelsome
QARLOS quarrellous

Words marked [□] can also be spelled with an initial capital letter

QARNIL	quadrennial
QARPDL	quadrupedal
QARPOY	quadraphony
QATMEP	quantum leap
QATMUP	quantum jump
QATRAK	quarterback
QATREK	quarter deck
	quarterdeck
QATROE	quarter tone
QENBNH	Queen's Bench
QENGIE	Queen's Guide
QENIES	queenliness
QENOHR	queen mother
QENSOT	Queen's Scout
QENTVR	queen it over
QERTET	Queer Street
QERUFN	queer cuffin
QETOIG	questioning
QEUOSY	querulously
QIBIGY	quibblingly
QICJNS	Quincy Jones
QIEIGY	quiveringly
QIKITD	quick-witted
QIKIVR	quicksilver
QIKLGT	quick flight
QIKOIG	quick-moving
QIKREE	quick-freeze
QIKSES	quick assets
QIKTCS	quick-sticks
QIQEEE	quinquereme
QIQENA	quinquennia
QISETY	quiescently
QITNOG	Quintin Hogg
QITNON	quieten down
QIZCLY	quizzically
QOAIIY	quotability
RAAEIG	reawakening
RAAIIY	readability
RAAIOM	rhagadiform
RAAMRL	rear admiral
RADMNY	rhabdomancy
RAHCOS	reach across
RAHEON	reach-me-down
RAHLIG	roadholding
RAIAIG	reanimating
RAIAIN	realization
	reanimation
RAIGAP	reading-lamp
RAIGEK	reading-desk
RAIGOK	reading-book
	reaping hook
	reaping-hook
RAIGOM	reading-room
RAINET	realignment
RAPIIG	road pricing
RAPLTK	realpolitik
RAQIKY	read quickly
RARNIG	rearranging
RASDCL	rhapsodical
RASRNE	reassurance
RATIUE	reattribute
RATNPN	roasting pan
RATOAY	reactionary
RATRUH	read through
RAYITD	ready-witted
RAYOAT	Ready-to-Halt
RAYOOK	ready to work
RAYORP	ready to drop
RBCAET	Rebecca West
RBEPAT	rubber plant
RBESAP	rubber stamp
	rubber-stamp
RBFCET	rubefacient
RBFCIN	rubefaction
RBIAIN	rubrication
RBIHEP	rubbish heap
	rubbish-heap
RBIKIG	rib-tickling
RBIPNH	rabbit punch
RBKFLY	rebukefully
RBLIIN	Rabelaisian
RBLRUE	rabble-rouse
RBNCEC	ribonucleic
RBODAT	rebroadcast
RBRAIE	rebarbative
RBRBRS	Robert Burns
RBRBUE	Robert Bruce
RBRBYE	Robert Boyle
RBRCCL	Robert Cecil
RBRCHN	Robert Cohan
RBRCIE	Robert Clive
RBRESR	Robert Ensor
RBRFOT	Robert Frost
RBRHOE	Robert Hooke
RBRHWE	Robert Hawke
RBRPAY	Robert Peary
RBRSLW	Robert Solow
RBRSOT	Robert Scott
RBSIRE	Robespierre
RBWDIG	ruby wedding
RCAAIN	reclamation
RCADBY	Richards Bay
RCADEE	Richard Gere
RCADID	Richard Bird
RCADOG	Richard Long
RCADOL	rock and roll
RCADUN	rack and ruin
	Richard Kuhn
RCADYD	Richard Byrd
RCAGLR	rectangular
RCAGOP	racial group
RCAMBE	reclaimable
RCAMBY	reclaimably
RCCYTL	rock crystal
RCEELR	Rockefeller
RCEIES	ricketiness
RCEMTR	rocket motor
RCEPES	racket-press
RCERNE	rocket range
RCETIE	rickettsiae
RCETIL	rickettsial
RCETIS	rickettsias
RCGIIN	recognition
RCHMTN	Rockhampton
RCIIAE	recriminate
RCIIBE	rectifiable
RCIIEL	rectilineal
RCIIER	rectilinear
RCLETD	recollected
RCLSET	recalescent
RCMEDD	recommended
RCMEDR	recommender
RCMETY	recumbently
RCMNNV	Rachmaninov
RCNAIN	recantation
RCNIIG	reconciling
RCNIIN	recondition
RCNOTE	reconnoitre
RCNTUT	reconstruct
RCPAUA	receptacula
RCPDIG	rice pudding
RCPIIY	receptivity
RCPOAE	reciprocate
RCPOIY	reciprocity
RCPRBE	recuperable
RCRETY	recurrently
RCSETR	rock shelter
RCSIEY	recessively
RCSINL	recessional
RCTTVS	recitativos
RCUEES	recluseness
RCUTET	recountment
	recruitment
RCVRBE	recoverable
RCVRRM	recover from
RCWLAY	rock wallaby
RDATET	radiant heat
RDCDAE	reduced rate
RDCIEY	reductively
RDCLES	radicalness
RDCLIN	radical sign
RDCOIL	redactorial
RDCSED	reduce speed
RDESOT	Ridley Scott
RDLKME	Rudolf Kempe
RDMNAE	rodomontade
RDMNAY	rudimentary
RDNATY	redundantly
RDNIIE	rodenticide
RDNLGT	riding-light
RDOAAY	radio galaxy
RDOABN	radiocarbon
RDOCIE	radioactive
RDOECN	radio beacon
RDOHNC	radiophonic
RDOOIT	radiologist
RDOPKR	red-hot poker
RDORPY	radiography
RDPIAE	reduplicate
RDQIRL	red squirrel
RDRCIN	redirection
RDRECN	radar beacon
RDRSET	Red Crescent
RDTEEM	ride the beam
RDTEOS	ride the rods
RDUTBE	redoubtable
REEGNE	re-emergence
REESAL	Riefenstahl
RELGCL	rheological

REMTCY rheumaticky
REOIIN rhetorician
RETBIH re-establish
RETULR Rhett Butler
REUAIN re-education
REWRLR reed-warbler
RFAGBE refrangible
RFANRM refrain from
RFCMNI rifacimenti
RFEHET refreshment
RFEIEY reflexively
RFEIIY reflexivity
RFEOOY reflexology
RFETNE reflectance
RFETPN reflect upon
RFIEAE refrigerate
RFIEAT refrigerant
RFIHES raffishness
RFNDES refinedness
RFRAIE reformative
RFRAIN reformation
RFRAOS reformadoes
RFRAOY reformatory
RFRIGO referring to
RFRNIL referential
RFRNUS referendums
RFTZEK Rifat Ozbeck
RGEFLY regretfully
RGERBN ragged robin
RGERGT ragged right
RGETBE regrettable
RGETBY regrettably
RGIHES roguishness
RGLTOS regulations
RGMNAS regimentals
RGNRBE regenerable
RGNRTR regenerator
RGOAIE regionalise
regionalize
RGOAIM regionalism
RGRFLY regardfully
RGRIAE regurgitate
RGRIAT regurgitant
RGROMN Roger Corman
RGROTS rigor mortis
RGSRBE registrable
RGTADD right-handed
RGTADR right-hander
RGTFAS right-of-ways
RGTFRP right of drip
RGTIDD right-minded
RGTIGR right-winger
RGTNLD right-angled
RGTOOE right to vote
RGTOSY righteously
RGTOWY rights-of-way
RGTSAN right as rain
RGTTIM right atrium
RHDAIN rehydration
RIBWIE rainbow-like
RICRAE reincarnate
RIEAIE reiterative
RIEAIN reiteration
RIEBAH raised beach
RIESEE raise a siege
RIESIK raise a stink
RIHNAH Reichenbach
RIIAIN reification
RIOAOS rhizomatous
RIOAPC rhizocarpic
RIOCPC rhinoscopic
RIODTE raison d'être
RIOLSY rhinoplasty
RIOOIT rhinologist
RIOSES ruinousness
RITGAE reintegrate
RITOUE reintroduce
RJIIGY rejoicingly
RJSUEM Rijksmuseum
RJVADI Rajiv Gandhi
RJVNSE rejuvenesce
RJVNTR rejuvenator
RKTRUH rake through
RLAIIY reliability
RLCATY reluctantly
RLEBAE rollerblade
RLEBID roller blind
RLESAE roller-skate
RLETNO rallentando
RLGOAY religionary
RLGOIE religionise
religionize
RLGOIY religiosity
RLGOSY religiously
RLHARN Ralph Lauren
RLIGNT rolling in it
RLNCAS ruling class
RLOTRE rule of three
RLOTUB rule of thumb
RLPAIA Rila Planina
RLPAIG role-playing
RLTDES relatedness
RLYNCY rallying cry
rallying-cry
RLYUON roll-your-own
RMAEAE rummage sale
RMDLIG remodelling
RMIAET remain alert
RMIDIY rumti-iddity
RMIVLD remain valid
RMKIHA Ramakrishna
RMLSRP rumble strip
RMMEIG remembering
RMMRNE remembrance❑
RMNADE Roman candle
RMNCJL Ramón y Cajal
RMNFET Raman effect
RMNIIE romanticise
romanticize
RMNIIM romanticism❑
RMNIIT romanticist
RMNLUE roman fleuve
RMNMIE Roman Empire
RMNPOI Rómano Prodi
RMNRBE remunerable
RMNRTD remunerated
RMNRTR remunerator
RMNSET reminiscent
RMNTAE remonstrate
RMNTAT remonstrant
RMNYUF remind you of
RMOARY Ram Mohan Roy
RMREES remorseless
RMRODN Rumer Godden
RMTAES remote areas
RMTETY remittently
RMTRUH romp through
RMUTOS rumbustious
rumbustuous
RNADAE rant and rave
RNADIE rank and file
RNCRIR ring-carrier
RNCRUT ring circuit
RNEIDR rangefinder
RNHGAD run the guard
RNIBGS Ronnie Biggs
RNIEEL run like hell
RNIGAE running late
running mate
RNIGED running head
RNIGET running text
RNIGNT running knot
RNIGON running-down
RNIGWY running away
running-away
RNISNE renaissance
RNLCSE Rene LaCoste
RNLRNR Ring Lardner
RNNOET run into debt
RNNTOK ring network
RNOEHR run together
RNOETS rondolettos
RNOOSY rancorously
RNORUD run to ground
RNOTUH ring of truth
RNPSOE run up a score
RNRAIE renormalise
renormalize
RNTEHD ring the shed
RNWYIH run away with
RNWYRM run away from
RNYEMN Randy Newman
ROBHDA rhombohedra
RODVDR room-divider
ROESAD Rhode Island
ROINAE reorientate
ROOSES riotousness
ROSRIE room service
RPAEBE replaceable
RPAEET replacement
RPAOIL raptatorial
RPCLIN rapscallion
RPCOSY rapaciously
RPDAIE repudiative
RPDAIN repudiation
RPEEES repleteness
RPEIHR replenisher
RPESBE repressible
RPESBY repressibly

Words marked ❑ can also be spelled with an initial capital letter

RPGATO repugnant to
RPIAIE reprivatise
reprivatize
RPIAIN replication
RPIINY reptilianly
RPLATY repellantly
RPLETY repellently
RPLIEY repulsively
RPLIGY repellingly
RPNATY repentantly
RPNIGY repentingly
RPNRIG ripsnorting
RPOAIE reprobative
RPOAIN reprobation
RPOAOY reprobatory
RPOCFL reproachful
RPOIGY reprovingly
RPORPY reprography
RPRIGY reportingly
RPRIIN repartition
RPRSAE report stage
RPSDES reposedness
RPSESR repossessor
RPSFAD ropes of sand
RPSFLY reposefully
RPTTOS repetitious
RPUOSY rapturously
RQETTP request stop
RQEWLH Raquel Welch
RQIEET requirement
RQIIIN requisition
RQIMAS Requiem Mass
RRBENR Rory Bremner
RRFCIE rarefactive
RRFCIN rarefaction
RSAAIN Rastafarian
RSACIG researching
RSADAL rise and fall
RSAEET restatement
RSALET rascalliest
RSCUIN Rosicrucian
RSCVRD rust-covered
RSDNIL residential
RSETBE respectable
RSETBY respectably
RSFLES restfulness
RSFRAD rush forward
RSGAIN resignation
RSHSAA Rosh Hashana
RSIAIN respiration
rustication
RSIAOY respiratory
RSIDET rescindment
RSIEES restiveness
RSINLE Russian Blue
RSIPAE rest in peace
RSIUIE restitutive
RSIUIN restitution
RSIUOY restitutory
RSLETY resiliently
RSLNET resplendent
RSMLNE resemblance
RSNFLY resentfully
RSNIGY resentingly
RSNRNZ Rosencrantz
RSOAIE restorative
RSOAIN restoration
RSODNE respondence
RSODNY respondency
RSOODN Rostov-on-Don
RSOSBE responsible
RSOSBY responsibly
RSRAIN reservation
RSRAOY reservatory
RSRCIE restrictive
RSRCIN restriction
RSRCUE restructure
RSREAK reserve bank
RSRERA reserve area
RSRETD resurrected
RSRETR resurrector
RSRIIG restraining
RSSETD rose-scented
RSSIAE resuscitate
RSSIEY resistively
RSSIGY resistingly
RSSIIY resistivity
RSTEAN Rose Tremain
RSUCFL resourceful
RTAGRO rat kangaroo
RTAIIY rateability
RTAITC ritualistic
RTASAE retranslate
RTATBE retractable
RTCLRY reticularly
RTCPIG rate-capping
RTEAPE rotten apple
RTESOE rottenstone
RTGAUE rotogravure
RTIUIE retributive
RTIUIN retribution
RTIVBE retrievable
RTIVBY retrievably
RTLAIE retaliative
RTLAIN retaliation
RTLAOY retaliatory
RTLSAE rattlesnake
RTNIEY retentively
RTNSOE retinoscope
RTNSOY retinoscopy
RTOAIE rationalise
rationalize
RTOAIM rationalism
RTOAIT rationalist
RTOAIY rationality
RTOCIE retroactive
retro-active
RTOEET retrocedent
RTOIAE ratiocinate
RTOOKT retro-rocket
RTRADS ritardandos
RTRAIE retardative
RTRAIM Rotarianism
RTRAIN retardation
RTRAOY retardatory
RTRELS ritornellos
RTRMTH return match
RTRNEL Ruth Rendell
RTRPES rotary press
RTTULE ratatouille
RUCIES raunchiness
RUDDON rounded down
RUETOR rouge-et-noir
RUHADE rough-handle
RUHKTH rough sketch
RUIEES routineness
RULBES Ruud Lubbers
RUOSES raucousness
RVLAIG rival-hating
RVLIGY revoltingly
RVNIAE revendicate
revindicate
RVNIGY revengingly
RVREAE reverberate
RVREAT reverberant
RVREIE reverse side
RVRIFY River Liffey
RVRINL reversional
RVRNIL reverential
RVRODN River Jordan
RVSAKR Ravi Shankar
RVSIGY ravishingly
RVSOAY revisionary
RVSOIM revisionism
RVSOIT revisionist
RVVFIG revivifying
RVVSET revivescent
reviviscent
RWAEIL raw material
RXARSN Rex Harrison
RYECEE rhyme-scheme
RYLSET royal assent
RYLYHM Royal Lytham
RYRDUY Ray Bradbury
SAAITC shamanistic
SAAMTC stalagmitic
SAAMTR Stabat Mater
SAATTC stalactitic
SABLIG star billing
SABRUH Scarborough
SABWIG seam bowling
SACABR Star Chamber
SACIES starchiness
SACIGY searchingly
snatchingly
SACLAY scarcely any
SACLGT searchlight
SACNEY Sean Connery
SACOEO stay close to
SACOSD star-crossed
SACPRY search party
SADFIH standoffish
stand-offish
SADNIE stand in line
SADNIH stand in with
SADNOT standing out
SADOAN stand to gain
SADRIE standardise
standardize

SADTAE stand at ease
SAEAAE stage-manage
SAEAMR sharefarmer
SAECAM stake a claim
SAECOL state school
SAEDIY Space Oddity
SAEESY shamelessly
SAEFID state of mind
SAEFLX state of flux
SAEFLY state of play
SAEIES shapeliness
stateliness
SAEIGY slaveringly
SAEIMY state firmly
SAEIPY state simply
SAENHM shame on them
SAEODR shareholder
SAEOGR scaremonger
SAEPAE Shakespeare
SAEPIN share option
SAERGT stage fright
SAERTR space writer
SAERUD skate around
SAERVR slave-driver
SAESIF scared stiff
SAETUK stage-struck
SAEUOS scaberulous
SAEWMN stateswoman
SAEYOE stately home
SAFAIN stagflation
SAFEBR staff member
SAFFIE staff of life
SAFLIG scaffolding
SAGNOF slagging off
slagging-off
SAGTRD slaughtered
SAGTRR slaughterer
SAHCOS spathaceous
SAIGES sparingness
SAIGOT staging post
SAIHAN Spanish Main
SAIHES slavishness
SAIHOL Spanish fowl
SAIHON Spanish Town
SAIHOS Spanish moss
SAIKES seasickness
SAILIE spaniel-like
SAKESY sparklessly
SAKIGY sparklingly
SAKNNW spanking new
SALCEN small screen
SALHNE small change
SALICE small circle
SALIDD small-minded
SALMUT small amount
SALNAI Spallanzani
SALODR smallholder
small wonder
SALUBR small number
SALWAL swallow tail
swallowtail
SALWES shallowness
SALWIE swallow-dive

SAMDCL spasmodical
SAMNSR Shalmaneser
SANESY stainlessly
SANHES staunchness
SANNBD spawning-bed
SANSAE skaines mate
SANSEE St Agnes's Eve
SAOAIY seasonality
SAODVD Star of David
SAOFUT sharon fruit
SAOGAH shadowgraph
SAOIES shadowiness
SAOIIE Slavonicise
Slavonicize
SAOSOE Sharon Stone
SAOTFT snap out of it
SAPITD sharp-witted
SARNGT Starry Night
SARWAK sparrowhawk
SARWIL sparrow-bill
SASUDD star-studded
SATBOS smartyboots
SATCLY spastically
SATDAH stab to death
SATEAE stay the pace
SATIES swarthiness
SATIGY startlingly
SATLRB Shatt al-Arab
SATPNS smartypants
SATRAH spatterdash
SATRDY scatteredly
SATRUH soak through
SAUEIE statute mile
SAUEOK statute book
SAUOIY statutorily
SAUUBR sea cucumber
SBAAIN Sabbatarian
SBAGNL submarginal
SBCIEO subscribe to
SBCIES subscribers
SBEATE sabre-rattle
SBEGBE submergible
SBEGNE submergence
SBEILY subaerially
SBESBE submersible
SBETDO subjected to
SBETES subjectless
SBETHP subjectship
SBEUNE subsequence
SBEVET subservient
SBIAIN sublimation
SBIEES sublimeness
SBIIIE subdivisive
SBIIIN subdivision
SBISBE submissible
SBITNE subsistence
SBLNCL subclinical
SBMGNS subimagines
SBOAIN subrogation
SBOIAT subdominant
SBOTAT subcontract
SBOTAY subcontrary
SBRAIE suburbanise

suburbanite
suburbanize
SBRAIN subornation
SBRCIE subtractive
SBRCIN subtraction
SBRHEC seborrhoeic
SBRIAE subirrigate
subordinate
SBRPCL subtropical
SBSEBE subassemble
SBTAIE substrative
SBTATR substractor
SBTNAD substandard
SBTNIE substantive
SBTNIL substantial
SBTTET substituent
SBTTTD substituted
SBUAIN subjugation
SBUCIE subjunctive
SBUCIN subjunction
SBUDES subduedness
SBUPIE subsumptive
SBUPIN subsumption
SBUTPE submultiple
SBUTRL subcultural
SCACAS social class
SCADUH such-and-such
SCAETL sacramental
SCAIIG socializing
SCAIIY sociability
SCAODR social order
SCBNFT sick benefit
SCEAEM succedaneum
SCEAET secret agent
SCEAIL secretarial
SCEAIT secretariat
SCEIEY secretively
SCEIGY sickeningly
SCEPAE sacred place
SCEPNH sucker-punch
SCESES successless
SCIEIT sacrilegist
SCIIIL sacrificial
SCINLY sectionally
SCINUP suction pump
SCLSET sickly sweet
sickly-sweet
SCNAIY secondarily
SCNAYO secondary to
SCNCAS second class
second-class
SCNGES second-guess
SCNSGT second sight
SCOAHC sociopathic
SCOERC sociometric
SCOOIT sociologist
SCORES succourless
SCPATC sycophantic
SCUETY succulently
SDCIEY seductively
SDEDAH sudden death
SDESAT sudden start
SDESIH Sydney Smith

SDLCOH saddlecloth
SDMNAY sedimentary
SDNAIY sedentarily
SDOEAE sad to relate
SDRADY sidereal day
SDTAKD sidetracked
SDTOAY seditionary
SDTOIT seditionist
SDTOSY seditiously
SDUEIM Sadduceeism
SEADHP stewardship
SEAIAS shenanigans
SEALGT see daylight
SEAOOY spelaeology
SEBOHR stepbrother
SECIES sketchiness
SECIIR speechifier
SECLIG stencilling
SECMKR speech-maker
SEDAEA speed camera
SEDATY steadfastly
SEDHIT spendthrift
SEDMTR speedometer
SEDPNY spend a penny
SEDRES slenderness
SEDREY spend freely
SEEATN Steve Martin
SEEFRY Siege of Troy
SEEGAH stereograph
SEEMTR stereometer
SEEMTY stereometry
SEEOIE skeletonise
skeletonize
SEEOKY skeleton key
SEEPOY stereophony
SEESOE stereoscope
SEESOY stereoscopy
SEETPC stereotypic
SEETPD stereotyped
SEETPR stereotyper
SEFRAD step forward
SEGFLY sdeignfully
SEHLGT see the light
SEHNIG Stephen King
SEHNTS stephanotis
SEHRBY shepherd boy
SEHRES shepherdess
SEHSOE stethoscope
SEHWRD see the world
SEIIAE specificate
SEIIBE specifiable
SEIIIY specificity
SEILAE special case
SEILES specialness
SEILZD specialized
SEILZR specializer
SEIRUE scenic route
SEISIH Stevie Smith
SEKELF speak well of
SEKLWY speak slowly
SEKODY speak boldly
SEKOTY speak softly
SEKPNY speak openly
SEKVLF speak evil of
SELDED swelled head
SELGTN shed light on
SELIDR spellbinder
SELLTD steel-plated
SELNOT smelling-out
SELOKR spellworker
steelworker
SELRTR stellarator
SEMAKT steam jacket
steam-packet
SEMCDL spermicidal
SEMESL steam vessel
SEMGNA spermogonia
SEMNIE steam engine
SEMOLR steam boiler
steamroller
steam-roller
SEMPYE spermophyte
SEMSIE St Elmo's fire
SEMTCL spermatical
SEMTZA spermatozoa
SENTTR sternutator
SENYOD Sweeney Todd
SEOARS stegosaurus❑
SEOEYU She Loves You
SEOLTR see you later
SEORPY stenography
SEPAKR sleepwalker
SEPDIG suet pudding
SEPEAK steeplejack
SEPESY sleeplessly
SEPNCR sleeping car
SEPNOF Steppenwolf
SEPRUD sleep around
SEPTKS sweepstakes
SERLOE Sierra Leone
SERNTN Sherrington
SETAIY spectrality
SETCLF sceptical of
SETCLR spectacular
SETCLY sceptically
SETEPR sweet pepper
sweet temper
SETHRY sweet sherry
SETHUD sleuth-hound
SETIEY sweet cicely
SETNHR sheet-anchor
SETOAO sweet potato
sweet-potato
SETOIG see it coming
SETORE sweet course
SETORM spectrogram
SETOTE scent bottle
SETPGA steatopygia
SETRUH seep through
SEUAIE speculative
SEUAIN speculation
SEVBAD sleeve board
SEYTEE see eye to eye
SFBEKR safe-breaker
SFCAKR safecracker
safe-cracker
SFCNRD soft-centred
SFCNUT safe conduct
safe-conduct
SFDPST safe-deposit
SFHATD soft-hearted
SFIAIN suffixation
SFIINE sufficience
SFIINY sufficiency
SFKEIG safekeeping
safe-keeping
SFLNIG soft landing
SFOAIE suffocative
SFOAIG suffocating
SFOAIN suffocation
SFRGTE suffragette
SFROOD so far so good
SFSINE soft science
SFSRAE soft surface
SFTGAS safety glass
SFTMTH safety match
SFTRZR safety razor
SFTVLE safety valve
safety-valve
SFUIAE suffumigate
SGCOSY sagaciously
SGEAIG segregating
SGEAIN segregation
SGETBE suggestible
SGETLY segmentally
SGETOS suggestions
SGIIAT significant
SGODLY sigmoidally
SGPDIG sago pudding
SGRFED sugar of lead
SGRITR sugar sifter
SGTAIN Sagittarian
SGTAIS Sagittarius
SGTCEN sight screen
SGTEIG sightseeing
SGTESY sightlessly
SGTIES sightliness
SHAITC sphragistic
SHAZOF Schwarzkopf
SHCSET Schick's test
SHEIGR Schlesinger
SHGORM sphygmogram
SHLATC scholiastic
SHLEIE schillerise
schillerize
SHLMGD so help me God
SHLRHP scholarship
SHNTRC sphincteric
SHNTRL sphincteral
SHOCID schoolchild
SHOHUE schoolhouse
SHOIGR Schrödinger
SHOWRS schoolwards
SHRADS scherzandos
SHRCLY spherically
SHRHRT Scharnhorst
SHRIIE spheroidise
spheroidize
SHSAIE schismatise

Words marked ❑ can also be spelled with an initial capital letter

	schismatize
SHTICE	schottische
SIACNL	spinal canal
SIADOE	skin-and-bone
SIAIIA	spina bifida
SIAIIY	suitability
SIALFR	suitable for
SIAPAS	so it appears
SIBIDR	shipbuilder
SIBSUT	ship biscuit
SIBWIG	spin-bowling
SICBAD	switchboard
SICBAE	switchblade
SIDEOE	spindle hole
SIECAR	swivel-chair
SIEDAE	stipendiate
SIEDAY	stipendiary
SIEESY	spinelessly
SIEFAE	slice of cake
SIEIGY	shiveringly
SIEPAT	spider plant
SIFEKD	stiff-necked
SIFIAE	spifflicate
SIFLES	skilfulness
SIFLLN	skilful plan
SIFNOT	sniffing-out
SIGERE	swingletree
SIGIDY	swing wildly
SIGIGY	swingeingly
SIGMTR	swingometer
SIGRDE	swing bridge
SIHIGY	slightingly
SIHRES	smithereens
SIIEOS	spiniferous
	spinigerous
SIIGEN	ship it green
SIIGOT	sailing boat
SIIHES	swinishness
SIILVL	spirit level
SIIULY	spiritually
SIKEAK	stickleback
SIKNET	stick insect
SIKNIE	slickenside
SIKNOT	sticking out
SIKRNE	snickersnee
	snick or snee
	stick or snee
SIKRUD	stick around
SIKUFR	stick out for
SILILS	Scilly Isles
SILNAL	still and all
SILNED	still and end
SIMDIK	skimmed milk
SIMGAH	seismograph
SIMLGC	seismologic
SIMTZD	stigmatized
SINEAK	science park
SINOOY	Scientology
SINUIL	seigneurial
SIOANW	Spiro T Agnew
SIOEEF	suit oneself
SIOHEE	spirochaete
SIOPRS	Shimon Peres
SIPDIC	slipped disc
SIPRAH	slipper bath
SIPROT	slipperwort
SIRPOE	stirrup bone
SIRPUP	stirrup pump
SISEIH	spinsterish
SISINE	soil science
SISRIE	scissorwise
SITALA	saintpaulia
SITDES	stiltedness
	stintedness
SITDRH	stilted arch
SITEAS	ship the oars
SITEEA	Saint Helena
SITEIS	skittle-pins
SITESY	shiftlessly
SITIES	saintliness
SITLAE	scintillate
SITRDS	Saint Bride's
SITRUD	shift around
SITRUH	sail through
SIUAIE	stimulative
SIUAIG	stimulating
SIUAIN	stimulation
	stipulation
SIUAOY	stipulatory
SIWEKD	shipwrecked
SIZRAD	Switzerland
SJHSOT	St John's wort
SLAAIE	Sal Paradise
SLAEBE	salvageable
SLAELS	saltarellos
SLAGNI	salmangundi
SLAIAE	syllabicate
SLAIIY	saleability
SLAMRR	self-admirer
SLAOIL	saltatorial
SLASRD	self-assured
SLCAIY	self-charity
SLCCCD	silicic acid
SLCIEY	selectively
SLCIIY	selectivity
SLCMAD	self-command
SLCNET	self-conceit
SLCNHP	silicon chip
SLCNRD	self-centred
SLCNRL	self-control
SLCOSY	salaciously
SLCVRD	self-covered
SLDFNE	self-defence
SLDIES	splodginess
SLDNIG	self-denying
SLEBRH	silver birch
SLEGOT	Silver Ghost
SLEIET	self-evident
SLEMDL	silver medal
SLEPAE	silver plate
SLEPES	self-express
SLEPPR	silver paper
SLESIH	silversmith
SLESOE	Silverstone
SLETBY	silver tabby
SLHRIG	self-harming
SLHROS	sulphureous
SLHRTR	sulphurator
SLHRUT	sulphur tuft
SLIAIN	solmisation
	solmization
SLIBCA	saltimbocca
SLIDCD	self-induced
SLIGAE	selling race
SLIGTS	salpingitis
SLIHES	saltishness
	selfishness
SLIPAH	Sylvia Plath
SLIPSD	self-imposed
SLIRIE	soldierlike
SLLQIE	soliloquise
	soliloquize
SLLQIT	soliloquist
SLMOIC	sal ammoniac
SLMSEY	self-mastery
SLNCOY	splenectomy
SLNMTR	salinometer
SLNOOS	splendorous
SLNTCL	splenetical
SLOAIE	sal volatile
SLOELE	salmonellae
SLOELS	salmonellas
SLOIIN	self-opinion
SLOITC	syllogistic
SLOTMS	seldom-times
SLOTOT	salmon trout
SLPITC	solipsistic
SLRDRA	scleroderma
SLRIIG	self-raising
SLRLAT	self-reliant
SLRLXS	solar plexus
SLRMTS	scleromatas
SLRNRY	solar energy
SLRSET	self-respect
SLRYTM	solar system
SLSAIG	self-sealing
SLSANR	Silas Marner
SLSATR	sales patter
	self-starter
SLSBUD	self-subdued
SLSEIG	self-seeking
SLSESN	salesperson
SLSOTN	splash out on
SLSPOT	self-support
SLSRIE	self-service
SLSRIG	self-serving
SLTCEN	split screen
SLTEAS	sell the pass
SLTEIG	spluttering
SLTEOD	split second
SLTIGP	splitting-up
SLTPRM	split up from
SLTTOS	salutations
SLUYIL	Silbury Hill
SLVCIE	Salk vaccine
SLWNIG	self-winding
SLYIOF	silly mid-off
SLYOTD	splay-footed
SMAHTC	sympathetic

SMAHZR sympathizer
SMAIES summariness
SMAIIG summarizing
SMAINL summational
SMEHUE summerhouse
SMEIGY simperingly
SMEMRE Samuel Morse
SMEPPS Samuel Pepys
SMERCL symmetrical
SMESUT summersault
SMFHNS sum of things
SMHNOS symphonious
SMIENL sempiternal
SMIEOS somniferous
SMLCTR simpliciter
SMLCUS simulacrums
SMLMNS Simple Minds
SMNATE Simon Rattle
SMNERE Simon Legree
SMNIIT semanticist
SMNUHS Simon Hughes
SMOELE someone else
SMOETY somnolently
SMOIGP summoning-up
SMOIIG symbolizing
SMOILY sympodially
SMORNE Sam Torrance
SMSILD semi-skilled
SMTCLY somatically
SMTIHE so mote I thee
SMTMTC symptomatic
SMTOIY sumptuosity
SMTOSY sumptuously
SMUBNM summum bonum
SNAAFR send away for
SNAHRB Sennacherib
SNAINL sensational
SNALNH Sunday lunch
SNASOT Sunday Sport
SNATCL syntactical
SNAVDR San Salvador
SNCLTE sansculotte
SNDCLY synodically
SNEESY senselessly
SNEMSS syndesmoses
SNESES sinlessness
sunlessness
SNETOS sententious
SNFBTH son of a bitch
sonofabitch
SNFRAD send forward
SNHOEH synchromesh
SNHOIE synchronise
synchronize
SNHOOS synchronous
SNHORN synchrotron
SNHSSR synthesiser
SNHSZD synthesized
SNHSZR synthesizer
SNIAIM syndicalism
SNIAIN syndication
SNIAIT syndicalist
SNIBCA Sanni Abacha
SNIETL sentimental
SNIGAK sending back
SNIGUD sinking fund
SNIIEO sensitive to
SNIIEY sensitively
SNIIIY sensibility
sensitivity
SNKIIT Sanskritist
SNLCEM single cream
SNLNRA synclinoria
SNLSLB singles club
SNMNHE Syngman Rhee
SNOAIN syncopation
SNOITA sinfonietta
SNOMCD Song of my Cid
SNONAK Sandown Park
SNOSES sinuousness
SNPCIG send packing
SNSRLY sinistrally
SNSRRE sinistrorse
SNTAIE sanctuarise
sanctuarize
SNTRUS sanatoriums
sanitariums
SNTSEL sanctus bell
SNTSEP send to sleep
SNUAIE singularise
singularize
SNUAIY singularity
SNUNOS sanguineous
SNWOWR sinews of war
SNYIEP sunny side up
SNYITN Sonny Liston
SNYOFX Sandy Koufax
SNYRIE Sandy Irvine
SOADEL show and tell
SOAEOM storage room
SOAGOA sporangiola
SOAHCL stomachical
SOAHUP stomach pump
SOAHUS stomachfuls
SOAOOY stomatology
SOBADR snowboarder
SOBLIG snowballing
SOBNIG snow bunting
SOBRVR slobber over
SOCBOH Scotch broth
SOCIGY scorchingly
SOCNEN show concern
SODERR sword-bearer
SODLCS spondulicks
SODLTS spondylitis
SOEAHD stonewashed
SOEALR stonewaller
SOEBAD shovelboard
SOECEN smokescreen
SOEEPR score-keeper
storekeeper
SOEESY smokelessly
SOEGOS stolen goods
SOEICE stone circle
SOEMNY stolen money
SOEPOF showerproof
SOERUD stoneground
SOEUDR snowed under
SOEULW stone curlew
stone-curlew
SOEWMN spokeswoman
spokeswomen
SOGSOD smorgasbord
SOHAIG soothsaying
SOHATY soothfastly
SOHLIG stop holding
SOJMIG showjumping
show-jumping
SOKAIG stocktaking
SOKAKT stock market
SOKASN Stockhausen
SOKEIG shopkeeping
SOKHAE stock phrase
SOKLIG snorkelling
SOKOBR stockjobber
SOKORR shock horror
shock-horror
SOKPIH stock up with
SOKRKR stockbroker
SOLAHR shoe leather
SOLEBG shoulder bag
shoulder-bag
SOLEIG smouldering
SOLFIG shoplifting
SOLIEN stool pigeon
SOLOAD snow leopard
SOMERL storm petrel
SOMETE storm centre
SOMIDW storm window
SOMNHP showmanship
SOMRYO show mercy to
SONRLY scoundrelly
SONURN slow neutron
SOOAIE scopolamine
SOOAOS scotomatous
SOOEEF show oneself
SOOHNS show of hands
SOOHTC sporophytic
SOPNOT stopping-out
SORIIG stop raining
SORRDE Stourbridge
SOSEAD shop steward
SOSGSF show signs of
SOSNLE stoss and lee
SOSOPR show-stopper
SOSOTF stop short of
SOSRHP sponsorship
SOTADD shorthanded
short-handed
SOTDIK spotted dick
SOTEHW stop the show
SOTEPR short temper
SOTFED sports field
SOTHIT short shrift
SOTHNE short-change
SOTHSN shoot the sun
SOTIDD short-winded
SOTITD shortlisted
SOTLIG stop talking

SOTNAL shorten sail
SOTNIY spontaneity
SOTNOS spontaneous
SOTNWR shooting war
SOTOIG shortcoming
SOTOLN Scott Joplin
SOTPKN short-spoken
SOTSAE smooth snake
SOTUPY short supply
SOTWMN sportswoman
SOWLIG show willing
SOWRIG stop working
SOYELR storyteller
SPEAIM supremacism
Suprematism
SPEAIT supremacist
SPEEES supremeness
SPESYU so please you
SPIAMA septicaemia
SPILRN Sophia Loren
SPITCL sophistical
SPLATY suppliantly
SPLHOS sepulchrous
SPLSDR supply-sider
SPNCOS saponaceous
SPOEOS saprogenous
SPOHTC saprophytic
SPOIIN supposition
SPOIOY suppository
SPOTBE supportable
SPOTBY supportably
SPOTES supportless
SPOTNE supportance
SPRAAT supernatant
SPRAIE superlative
SPRAKR supertanker
SPRAKT supermarket
SPRATD superfatted
SPRBUD superabound
SPRCIE superscribe
SPRCIT superscript
SPREAE superfetate
SPRHRE supercharge
SPRIIG supervising
SPRIIL superficial
SPRIIN supervision
SPRIIS superficies
SPRIOS supervisors
SPRIOY supervisory
SPRLIY superfluity
SPRLOS superfluous
SPRMOE superimpose
SPRNED superintend
SPRNET superinfect
SPRNUE superinduce
SPROIY superiority
SPRSAT suppressant
SPRSIE suppressive
SPRSIN suppression
SPRTOF separate off
SPRTOT separate out
SPRTUT superstruct
SPUAIE suppurative
SPUAIG suppurating
SPUAIN suppuration
SQETAE sequestrate
SQETRD sequestered
SRACLT Sir Lancelot
SRAEAL surface mail
SRAEGE spread-eagle
SRAIES streakiness
streaminess
SRAIGY screamingly
spreadingly
streamingly
SRALND streamlined
SRASBE surpassable
SRASET spreadsheet
SRASSA Sargasso Sea
SRAUAE serratulate
SRBIES shrubbiness
SRBSOE stroboscope
SRCLUE sericulture
SRCNET seroconvert
SRCSIG surfcasting
SRDIIN suraddition
SRDLTR stridulator
SREBBA Sergei Bubka
SREDRR surrenderer
SREGIE street guide
SREIEE Sir Bedivere
SREIGY shriekingly
SREKRV Sergey Kirov
SRELAT surveillant
SRELGT streetlight
SRELNO Serge Blanco
SRELVL street-level
SRESVR screen saver
SRETIE serpentlike
SREVLE street value
SREWRS streetwards
SRGAHR serigrapher
SRGIES scragginess
SRIEBE serviceable
SRIEBY serviceably
SRIELT service flat
SRIEOK servicebook
service-book
SRIERA service area
SRIGAD serving-maid
SRIGUE strain gauge
SRIHIH straightish
SRIHMN straight man
SRIHOF straight off
SRIHOT straight out
SRILCD strait-laced
SRKAOE strike a pose
SRKBUD strikebound
SRKHNS strike hands
SRKPAE strike plate
SRKYUS strike you as
SRLGCL serological
SRMIES scrimpiness
SRMPAT shrimp plant
SRMTOS scrumptious
SRNAIE spring a mine
SRNAOG string along
SRNBAD springboard
SRNCEN spring-clean
SRNDIK strong drink
SRNEES strangeness
SRNETY stringently
SRNFED Springfield
SRNFRE strong force
SRNIES springiness
stringiness
SRNIGP springing-up
SRNIGY shrinkingly
SRNIIY serendipity
SRNMOD Surinam toad
SRNOIN spring onion
SRNOIY strenuosity
SRNOSY strenuously
SRNPEE string piece
SRNPIT strong point
SRNSEN Springsteen
SRNUAE strangulate
SROAOS sarcomatous
SROFLY sorrowfully
SROHGS sarcophagus
SROIIG sermonizing
SROILY sartorially
SRONIG surmounting
surrounding
SROSES seriousness
SRPAGR strap-hanger
SRPERH strip search
SRPIES scrappiness
SRPIIT soroptimist❑
SRRSDY surprisedly
SRSEOT stressed out
stressed-out
SRTCYE Strathclyde
SRTGCL strategical
SRTHAD scratchcard
SRTHBE stretchable
SRTIGY struttingly
SRTNZR scrutinizer
SRUCRA Sursum Corda
SRVLIG shrivelling
SRWEGT straw-weight
SRWIES scrawniness
SRWIGY scrawlingly
SRWRVR screwdriver
SSACSS syssarcoses
SSANBE sustainable
SSANDY sustainedly
SSANET sustainment
SSEAIE systematise
systematize
SSEAIS systematics
SSEILW sister-in-law
SSESFL suspenseful
SSETBE susceptible
SSETBY susceptibly
SSETDY suspectedly
SSINLY sessionally
SSNAUI Susan Faludi
SSNOTG Susan Sontag

SSRAIN susurration
STAIIY satiability
STAINL situational
STAIRY Satyajit Ray
STAPUE Sitka spruce
STHMRE Set Them Free
STHSEE set the scene
STIGOM sitting-room
STIGRE setting free
STIGUK sitting duck
STITEY set little by
STLIIE satellitise
satellitize
STLNDY settling day
STNCLY satanically
STNOIN set in motion
STOIHS set to rights
STRAIN Saturnalian
STRCLY satirically
STROOY soteriology
STSIBE satisfiable
STTAFR set a trap for
STTOGT set at nought
SUAEET sausage meat
SUAEOL sausage roll
SUAIES squeakiness
SUAIGY squeakingly
SUAIHY squeamishly
SUBIGY stumblingly
SUBOHR soul brother
SUBOSY slumbrously
SUBSIG spud-bashing
SUDESY soundlessly
SUDGEY skulduggery
SUDODY sound loudly
SUDSEP sound asleep
SUFAIG soul-fearing
SUFIGY shufflingly
SUFLES soulfulness
SUGAIG spur gearing
SUGEAE stun grenade
SUGRIE sluggardise
sluggardize
SUHADY southwardly
SUHAOA South Dakota
SUHATR sought after
sought-after
SUHFIA South Africa
SUHMTN Southampton
SUHRIE southernise
southernize
SUHSAD South Island
SUHTIE South Utsire
SUHYAT south by east
SUHYET south by west
SUICUH studio couch
SUIRBA Saudi Arabia
SUKLIG soul-killing
SUKTHN soup kitchen
SULDES squalidness
SUNEIG squandering
SUNIGY squintingly
SURDNE square dance
square-dance
SURMTE square metre
SUSEKL Studs Terkel
SUTDES stuntedness
SUTEIE shuttlewise
SUTEOK shuttlecock
SUTFIG stultifying
SVIFIE savoir-faire
SVIVVE savoir-vivre
SVNENH seventeenth
SVNGAE saving grace
SVNSAK savings bank
SVRINY sovereignly
sovereignty
SVRLOD severalfold
SVTEAK save the mark
SVUIES savouriness
SWNWMN sewing woman
SXAAUE sexual abuse
SXADIE sexual drive
SXAUIN sexual union
SXENBT sixpenny bit
SXENHY sixteenthly
SXESES sexlessness
SXGSML sexagesimal
SXNILY sexennially
SXPOIT saxophonist
SYHNYU say thank you
SYIAIN stylization
SYIHES stylishness
SYNHCB spy in the cab
SYNSRY saying sorry
SYORRY Seymour Cray
SYSIIG sky-aspiring
SYULCY say publicly
SYWYRM shy away from
SZNEEA Suzanne Vega
TAADER tear and wear
TAAOOY thanatology
TACEIE Thatcherite
TACEIM Thatcherism
TACMSC trance music
TAEAET travel agent
TAEAOG travel along
TAEBCR travel by car
TAEERT trade secret
TAEESY tracelessly
TAEGIE travel guide
TAEINE tragedienne
TAEIOM trapeziform
TAEOSL trace fossil
TAERUD travel round
TAESBE traversable
TAEUAE trabeculate
TAEUIN trades union
TAEWAY travel-weary
TAEWMN tradeswoman
TAFCIG trafficking
TAFLES tearfulness
TAFLIG tear-falling
TAGIGY twanglingly
TAHOOY tracheotomy
TAHRPT teacher's pet
TAIGON tearing-down
TAIGOT trading post
TAIINL traditional
TAIIOY tragic irony
TAIOEY tragicomedy
TAIOIE thalidomide
TAITSY that is to say
TAJRIG tear-jerking
TAKEOD track record
TAKESY thanklessly
tracklessly
TAKRAL trackerball
TAKUFR thankful for
TAKVNS track events
TALLCS to all places
TALLZR trailblazer
trail-blazer
TAMTRE thaumaturge
TAMTRY thaumaturgy
TANERR train-bearer
TAPEVR trample over
TAPOFL teaspoonful
TAQIIY tranquility
TASAET transparent
TASAIN translation
TASAND tear-stained
TASCIN transaction
TASEFE transfer fee
TASERA transfer RNA
TASERD transferred
TASERL transferral
TASERN transferrin
TASERR transferrer
TASESL transversal
TASETY transiently
TASEVR transceiver
TASIIE transfinite
TASIIN transfixion
TASIPR transhipper
TASIRE transpierce
TASITL transmittal
TASITR transmitter
TASIUE transfigure
TASLIE transalpine
TASNDA that's an idea
TASOAE translocate
TASODR transponder
TASOET that's done it
TASOIG transposing
TASOMD transformed
TASOMR transformer
TASONT that's torn it!
TASOTD transported
TASOTR transporter
TASRBD transcribed
TASRBR transcriber
TASRNC transuranic
TASTAP transit camp
TASTIA transit visa
TASUAE transmutate
TASUAT transhumant
TASUAY translunary
TASUET translucent

TASUIN transfusion
TATANR tea strainer
TATATR toastmaster
TATRED tractor feed
TAUEET traducement
TAUIGY traducingly
TAVNAE to advantage
TBCAKT Toby Crackit
TBCOIT tobacconist
TBDCDD to be decided
TBEDOE tables-d'hôte
TBEENS table tennis
table-tennis
TBELTS tablecloths
TBFCIN tabefaction
TBGAIG tobogganing
TBGAIT tobogganist
TBGNIH to begin with
TBHMIG tub-thumping
TBRUAE tuberculate
TBRUIE tuberculise
tuberculize
TCFLES tactfulness
TCLBAN tickle-brain
TCLDIK tickled pink
TCNCAY technocracy
TCNCLY technically
TCNPIE technophile
TCNPOE technophobe
TCOHBA tachophobia
TCTRIY taciturnity
TCYADA tachycardia
TCYRPY tachygraphy
TDILAS Ted Williams
TDLWNS tiddlywinks
TDOSES tediousness
TEAAIN trepanation
TEADNR The Pardoner
TEADVS The Maldives
TEAESP the game is up
TEAETC therapeutic
TEAOBY Tremadoc Bay
TEAOLW The Man of Law
TEARSS thesauruses
TEATAP the last gasp
TEATAT the last cast
TEATFL the Faithful
TEATOD the last word
TEBEVR The Observer
TEBIGY tremblingly
TEBOIE theobromine
TECATY trenchantly
TECEAT treacle tart
TECEMN trencherman
TECEOS treacherous
TECEPR tree-creeper
TECFRH thenceforth
TECFVR trench fever
TECOUS The Eclogues
TECPAE to each place
TECVRD tree-covered
TEDEID tread behind
TEDETR trendsetter
TEDRKS Theodorakis
TEEATD the departed
TEEBUS thereabouts
TEECAT The Merchant
TEEEIE therebeside
TEEETD the defeated
TEEOAE there you are
TEEOOE theretofore
TEEQEN The Red Queen
TEESNS the peasants
the reason is
TEEULC The Republic
TEEYAE the very same
TEEYDA the very idea
TEHERS The Phaedrus
TEHLKT the whole kit
TEHLLT the whole lot
TEHRMN The Third Man
TEIABW the final bow
TEIAIN trepidation
TEIAOY trepidatory
TEIAPE the Big Apple
TEIDOD The Wild Wood
TEIDUK The Wild Duck
TEIEFR the wiser for
TEIEFT the size of it
TEIEID The Firebird
TEIGIH teeming with
TEIGNI The King and I
TEIISE The Big Issue
TEIKOE The Sick Rose
TEIKWY the Milky Way
TEINIG The Lion King
TEISEP The Big Sleep
TEISOE the Big Smoke
TELAES The Gleaners
TELBOK the old block
TELCAT the black art
TELEEY the old enemy
TELGAD The Sluggard
TELGCL theological
TELIHY the Almighty
TEMCLY thermically
TEMMTR thermometer
TEMOIS thermionics
TEMRHC theomorphic
TEMRST the smart set
TENENT the Internet
TENIEY the entirety
TENITD the anointed
TENLCS The Analects
TENVRE The Universe
TEOAIM teetotalism
TEOALR teetotaller
TEOCRR The Sorceror
TEODAK The Woodlark
TEODIE the good life
TEODOK the Good Book
TEODUS the doldrums
TEOEOL The Rose Bowl
TEOGOE the long robe
TEOLAT the noble art
TEOLRH trefoil arch
TEOMUE The Dormouse
TEOOIS the Colonies
TEOQET the Conquest
TEORPR Trevor-Roper
TEOSFR the worse for
TEOUAE the populace
TEPAAT Thespian art
TEPSIG trespassing
TERAET the greatest
TERAIN The Creation
TERCBE The Crucible
TERDAE The Graduate
TERNHS the Trenches
TERNLN The Franklin
TEROES The Prioress
TERPES the prophets
TERTCL theoretical
TESNBE treasonable
TESNBY treasonably
TESPIE theosophise
theosophize
TESPIT theosophist
TESREN tree surgeon
TESREY tree surgery
TESRTG treasury tag
TETEDY the other day
TETEOK trestlework
TETIAS theatricals
TETIIE theatricise
theatricize
TETIIM theatricism
TETOSY theftuously
TETPNE twenty pence
TETRDE Trent Bridge
TEUCIS the munchies
TEUIES the business
TEUIMN The Music Man
TEUMNR The Summoner
TEUOEN The European
TEUOSY tremulously
TEURIN The Guardian
TEUSDR The Outsider
TEUSUH the bum's rush
TEVMNH twelvemonth
TEXRIT The Exorcist
TEXTSE The Exstasie
TFEAPE toffee apple
TFENSD toffee-nosed
TGCGLA Tegucigalpa
TGITLE tagliatelle
TGROTD tiger-footed
TGTIPD tight-lipped
TGTITD tight-fisted
TGTONR tight corner
TGTYNT tightly-knit
THIOSY Tchaikovsky
TIAAAE thin as a rake
TIADHT this and that
TIAOIT tritagonist
TIBEUS thimblefuls
TICGAS twitch grass
TICMLE Trincomalee
TIDERE third degree

TIDYEK this day week
TIEAOS triceratops□
TIEEIG this evening
TIEIAD tripe-visag'd
TIEPPR toilet paper
TIEWMN tribeswoman
TIEWTR toilet water
TIGMJG thingumajig
TIGRIH triggerfish
TIHCUN t'ai chi ch'uan
TIHITC tritheistic
TIHMND trichomonad
TIHNSS trichinosis
TIHRAD thitherward
TIIAIN Trinidadian
Trinitarian
TIILES trivialness
TIISAT this instant
TIIYAL Trinity Hall
TIIYEM Trinity term
TIKAKO think back to
TIKEDD thick-headed
TIKELF think well of
TIKEPY think deeply
TIKIBD thick-ribbed
TIKIEY think likely
TIKIPD thick-lipped
TIKOIG thick-coming
TIKUHF think much of
TILCON triple crown
TILEID trial period
TILOSY Tsiolkovsky
TILPIT triple point
TILYUY Trial by Jury
TIMHVR triumph over
TIMIAE triumvirate
TIMRIG this morning
TINILY triennially
TINUAE triangulate
TIOOIT tribologist
TIOORD tricoloured
TIOPIM trimorphism
TIOPOS trimorphous
TIORPC thixotropic
TIRDIE thin red line
TISIES thirstiness
TISIND thin-skinned
TITEON thistledown
TITESY taintlessly
TIUAIN tribulation
trituration
TIUAIY tributarily
TIUEHP tribuneship
TIVRDY this very day
TIYLBC trisyllabic
TIYLBE trisyllable
TKAANT take against
TKAHNE take a chance
TKAIKT take a wicket
TKAOLF take a toll of
TKAOMT take a room at
TKBFRE take by force
TKBSOM take by storm
TKCPIE take captive
TKDKNO Takada Kenzo
TKDLGT take delight
TKHMPY take home pay
take-home pay
TKIOTF take it out of
TKIOTN take it out on
TKITRS take in turns
TKLAEF take leave of
TKNPIH taken up with
TKOBAD take on board
TKOEWY take one's way
TKOFNE take offence
take offense
TKPIEN take pride in
TKPISO take pains to
TKPTUK take pot luck
TKRVNE take revenge
TKSOKF take stock of
TKSOKN take stock in
TKTCUT take to court
TKTEAE take the cake
TKTEAH take the oath
TKTEAL take the wall
TKTEEL take the veil
TKTEIS take the piss
TKTEOD take the road
take the word
TKTHAT take to heart
TKTMOF take time off
TKTOOG take too long
TKUAAN take up again
TKUBAE take umbrage
TKUSOT take up short
TLAANT tell against
TLAASE Tallahassee
TLAERT tell a secret
TLAIEY talkatively
TLBNIG telebanking
TLCMUE telecommute
TLCTAE telecottage
TLEAOT talked about
TLGAHC telegraphic
TLIGNO talking into
TLKNSS telekinesis
TLKNTC telekinetic
TLMSAE Telemessage®
TLNSOT talent scout
TLOCTH tallow-catch
TLOOIT teleologist
TLPITR teleprinter
TLPOIT telephonist
TLPOLR tulip poplar
TLPTIE telepathise
telepathize
TLPTIT telepathist
TLSOIM Telescopium
TLTEIE tell the time
TLWRIG teleworking
TMCETR tame cheater
TMCPUE time capsule
TMEAET temperament
TMEAEY temperately
TMEAUE temperature
TMEHTH timber hitch
TMEPOF tamperproof
tamper-proof
TMETOS tempestuous
TMETOT tempest-tost
TMFCET tumefacient
TMFCIN tumefaction
TMLDIR tumble-drier
TMLMUT Temple Mount
TMLRUS tumblerfuls
TMOAIS temporaries
TMOAIY temporarily
TMOIHY tomboyishly
TMOIIG temporizing
TMPESR time-pleaser
TMRROS temerarious
TMSAIG time-sharing
TMSATR Tam O'Shanter
tam-o'-shanter
TMSRIG time-serving
TMTLOS tomatilloes
TMTPAD Tom Stoppard
TMTSUE tomato sauce
TMTTOS Temptations
TMWSIG time-wasting
TMYOPR Tommy Cooper
TMYOSY Tommy Dorsey
TMYTIS Tommy Atkins
TMYUTN tummy-button
TNADER Tyne and Wear
TNAIEY tentatively
TNAIIG tantalizing
TNALOK Tony Allcock
TNBNET Tony Bennett
TNBOIY tenebrosity
TNCOSY tenaciously
TNEAOT tinker about
TNEDIG tender-dying
TNEDOE tunnel diode
TNEFOS tenderfoots
TNEHOS tenterhooks
TNESUS tinker's cuss
TNETLY tangentally
TNETOS tendentious
TNFLES tunefulness
TNHNOK Tony Hancock
TNIEBW tennis elbow
TNIIIY tangibility
TNILTS tonsillitis
TNIMTR tensiometer
TNINLY tensionally
TNJCLN Tony Jacklin
TNOELY Tony O'Reilly
TNOSES tenuousness
TNOYEL tantony bell
TNRWAD Tiny Rowland
TNTCLY tonetically
TNTWRS tend towards
TOABOD Thomas Blood
TOABON Thomas Brown
TOAHRE Trojan Horse
TOAHRY Thomas Hardy

Words marked □ can also be spelled with an initial capital letter

TOANSE Thomas Nashe
TOAPIE Thomas Pride
TOAWMN Trojan Women
TOAYUG Thomas Young
TOBEOE troublesome
TOBEPT trouble spot
TOBERE trouble-free
TOBOSY troublously
TOEAKR T-Bone Walker
TOENBT twopenny bit
TOETSE to one's taste
TOGTES thoughtless
TOGTIK thought-sick
TOHIKR tooth-picker
TOHLGT troth-plight
TOHOEY toothsomely
TOHRWR tooth-drawer
TOIUCN Teotihuacán
TOLDTC troglodytic
TOLYAE troll-my-dame
TONEGT two and eight
TOOPEE troposphere
TOPLEL trompe l'oeil
trompe-l'oeil
TOSEOP trous-de-loup
TOSRUT trouser suit
TPCLAE typical case
TPGAHC topographic
typographic
TPGAHR topographer
typographer
TPLGCL topological
TPMAUE tape measure
TPNSAT top one's part
TPOOIT taphonomist
TPRNOF tapering off
TPROIY top-priority
TPRSIG top-dressing
TPSTIG typesetting
TPWIIG typewriting
TPWITN typewritten
TRAANT turn against
TRAATY termagantly
TRAEIG threatening
TRAIDE tarradiddle
TRAIES throatiness
TRASUE tartar sauce
TRBIGY throbbingly
TRECNE turgescence
TREEKR three-decker
TREIES Three Rivers
TRELTE turret lathe
TREOIE terremotive
TREOKD three-nooked
TREOOT torpedo boat
TRERCS Three Graces
TRETDY tormentedly
TRETIL terrestrial
TREUEM Terme Museum
TREUTD three-suited
TRFIES thriftiness
TRHERR torchbearer
TRHTVS torch-staves
TRIAIG terminating
TRIAIM termitarium
TRIAIN termination
TRIGON turning-down
TRIGWY turning away
TRIHAH Turkish bath
TRIHBE tarnishable
TRIHIA Turkish lira
TRIIDY terrified by
TRIOIL territorial❑
TRIOIS territories
TRIOLS torticollis
TRIOOY terminology
TRLIGY thrillingly
TRMEHT thrummed hat
TRMIGY thrummingly
TRNOAR tyrannosaur
TRNOSY tyrannously
TRNTCL threnetical
TROIIG terrorizing
TROSED turn of speed
TROTEL turn out well
TROTOE turn out to be
TRSAOT thresh about
TRSCOE Terpsichore
TRSSAE thrust stage
TRTATR turn traitor
TRTGNC teratogenic
TRTNAA taratantara
TRTSEK turn to speak
TRTSOE turn to stone
TRUETY turbulently
TRUHAE throughfare
TRUHIH through with
TRUIGY torturingly
TRVLAT tire-valiant
TRWNOT throwing out
TRWPRY throw a party
TRWRUD throw around
TRYHMS Terry-Thomas
TSADUN toss and turn
TSAOEL Tessa Jowell
TSATIH to start with
TSEESY tastelessly
TSELTD tessellated
TSIOIL testimonial
TTAAET tetravalent
TTAERL tetrahedral
TTAERN tetrahedron
TTEETR to the letter
TTEIDE to the middle
TTEIGY totteringly
TTEIUE to the minute
TTEODR title-holder
TTEOTM to the bottom
TTERUD to the ground
TTETOT to the utmost
TTEUEF to the tune of
TTGLEY Tate Gallery
TTIKFT to think of it
TTIPAE to this place
TTIRTI Tutti Frutti
tutti-frutti
TTLAIG titillating
TTLAIN titillation
TTLEAL total recall
TTLMUT total amount
TTLRED titular head
TTLSTR Totalisator
TTLZTR Totalizator
TTMNII Tito Menniti
TTNCLY tetanically
titanically
TTNHMN Tutankhamen
TUBLIN tourbillion
TUCENR truncheoner
TUDFRE tour de force
TUDRAT thunderdart
TUDRED thunderhead
TUDRID thunderbird
TUDRIE thunder-like
TUDRLP thunderclap
TUDROT thunderbolt
TUDVTD true-devoted
TUGALE Tsung-Dao Lee
TUHATD truehearted
TUHETY touch gently
TUHOTM touch bottom
TUHYIT touch-typist
TUKLEE trunksleeve
TUOEIM tautomerism
TUOOIE tautologise
tautologize
TUOOOS tautologous
TUPTAL trumpet call
TUTEHP trusteeship
TUTOTY trustworthy
TUUETY truculently
TWADON town and gown
TWCUCL town council
TWDELR town-dweller
TWOORD tow-coloured
TWRIGY thwartingly
TWRSIS thwartships
TWSEPE townspeople
TXDRIE taxidermise
taxidermize
TXDRIT taxidermist
TYAOOE trypanosome
TYEYAD try very hard
TYNSAD try one's hand
TYNSUK try one's luck
TYTPAE tryptophane
UAAEES unawareness
UAALBE unavailable
UAALBY unavailably
UAANTT up against it
UABGOS unambiguous
UABTOS unambitious
UACAMD unacclaimed
UADOIG up and coming
up-and-coming
UAETBE unavertable
UAHMDY unashamedly
UAINBE unalienable
UAINBY unalienably

UAIOSY unanimously
UANUCD unannounced
UAODBE unavoidable
UAODBY unavoidably
UAORPY uranography
UAPAIG unappealing
UASRIE unassertive
UATRBE unalterable
UATRBY unalterably
UAVSBE unadvisable
UAVSBY unadvisably
UAVSDY unadvisedly
UBAIOS umbratilous
UBAKND unblackened
UBASDY unbiassedly
UBDEBE unbudgeable
UBECIG unblenching
UBEIHD unblemished
UBEKBE unbreakable
UBFTIG unbefitting
UBIDOD unblindfold
UBIEOS umbriferous
UBLAEY umbellately
UBLEIG unbelieving
UBNIGY unbendingly
UBNPAL urban sprawl
UBRCID unborn child
UBREIG unburdening
UBUDDY unboundedly
UCAIGY unceasingly
UCATRD unchartered
UCEIHD uncherished
UCENES uncleanness
UCERES unclearness
UCLEFR uncalled-for
UCLETD uncollected
UCMELD uncompelled
UCMITD uncommitted
UCMLTD uncompleted
UCNCOS unconscious
UCNEIL uncongenial
UCNELD unconcealed
UCNEND unconcerned
uncontemned
UCNESD uncondensed
UCNETD unconnected
uncontested
unconverted
UCNICD unconvinced
UCNIES uncanniness
UCNIMD unconfirmed
UCNUIE unconducive
UCNURD unconquered
UCRANY uncertainly
uncertainty
UCRSIN unchristian
UCRUTD uncorrupted
UCSOAY uncustomary
UCUHES uncouthness
UCUTBE uncountable
UCUTRD uncluttered
UCVLSD uncivilised
UCVLZD uncivilized

UDCDDY undecidedly
UDCRTD undecorated
UDEMDF undreamed-of
UDFNBE undefinable
UDGIID undignified
UDMNIG undemanding
UDRAIG undertaking
UDRAND undermanned
UDRANF under pain of
UDRAUD undervalued
UDRAUR undervaluer
UDRAVS under canvas
UDRCOD under a cloud
UDREGT underweight
UDRELR underseller
UDRHLE under the lee
UDRHRE undercharge
UDRHSN under the sun
UDRHUT underthrust
UDRIIG underlining
undermining
UDRIND undersigned
UDRLYD underplayed
UDROET underhonest
UDRRCD underpriced
UDRRET under arrest
UDRRIE underpraise
UDRRTR underwriter
UDRRUD underground
UDRRWH undergrowth
UDRTAA understrata
UDRTES under stress
UDRTTD understated
UDRUES under duress
UDRXOE underexpose
UDSEDD undescended
UDSLSD undisclosed
UDSOTD undistorted
UDSRBE undesirable
UDSRBY undesirably
UDSRIG undeserving
UDSUBD undisturbed
UDSUSD undisguised
UDTFLY undutifully
UDUTBE undoubtable
UDUTDY undauntedly
undoubtedly
UDVAIG undeviating
UDVDBE undividable
UDVDDY undividedly
UDVLPD undeveloped
UEAOAE unelaborate
UECTBE unexcitable
UEDRBE unendurable
UEESES uselessness
UENIEY use unwisely
UEOINL unemotional
UEPAND unexplained
UEPESD unexpressed
UEPOTD unexploited
UEPRET unexperient
UESAOT uneasy about
UESNIL unessential

UEULES unequalness
UEUVCL unequivocal
UFAFLY unfearfully
UFAPBE unflappable
UFAPBY unflappably
UFCNIY unfecundity
UFEIGY unfeelingly
UFICIG unflinching
UFIIGY unfailingly
UFINDY unfeignedly
UFLEIG unfaltering
UFLILD unfulfilled
UFOELR Ulf von Euler
UFRIHD unfurnished
UFRIID unfortified
UFRIIG unforgiving
UFRUAE unfortunate
UFSEIG unfastening
UFSIND unfashioned
UFTEIG unfettering
UFTIGY unfittingly
UFUAIE unfeudalise
unfeudalize
UFUDDY unfoundedly
UFUTOS unfructuous
UFUTRD unflustered
UGADDY unguardedly
UGDIES ungodliness
UGIUAE unguiculate
UGLGAE unguligrade
UGNTRD ungenitured
UGTTBE ungetatable
unget-at-able
UHATFL unhealthful
UHATIY unhealthily
UHLTRR upholsterer
UHNIES unhandiness
UHPFLY unhopefully
UHPIES unhappiness
UHRIDY unhurriedly
UHSADD unhusbanded
UIEILY uniserially
UIELLR unicellular
UIESLY universally
UIEULY unisexually
UIHBTD uninhabited
uninhibited
UIIAIN unification
unitization
utilitarian
utilization
UIIITD uninitiated
UIIYOM utility room
UIOAIY unipolarity
UIOMES uniformness
UIOOAE unicolorate
UIOOOS unicolorous
UIOORD unicoloured
UIPESD unimpressed
UIPRAT unimportant
UISIIG uninspiring
UJSIID unjustified
UKOIGY unknowingly

UKONES unknownness
ULANDY unlearnedly
ULCIES unluckiness
ULFIGY upliftingly
ULOEFR unlooked-for
ULWUAT unlawful act
UMAIGY unmeaningly
UMCAIE unmechanise
unmechanize
UMLDOS unmelodious
UMMRBE unmemorable
UMNFLY unmindfully
UMNIES unmanliness
UMNIND unmentioned
UMRTBE unmeritable
UMRTDY unmeritedly
UMSUIE unmasculine
UMTGBY unmitigably
UMTGTD unmitigated
UMTVTD unmotivated
UNCSAY unnecessary
UNTRLY unnaturally
UNVGBE unnavigable
UOGNZD unorganized
UORCOS ulotrichous
UOSRAT unobservant
UOTEHN upon the shun
UOTEIG upon the wing
UOTOOY unorthodoxy
UOTUIE unobtrusive
UPASBY unplausibly
UPATCL unpractical
UPATSD unpractised
UPBIHD unpublished
UPEEVD unpreserved
UPEITD unpredicted
UPITBE unprintable
UPLTBE unpalatable
UPLTBY unpalatably
UPOESD unprocessed
UPOETD unprotected
UPOIET unprovident
UPOIIG unpromising
UPPLTD unpopulated
UPRICE upper circle
UPRTRY upper storey
UPRUBD unperturbed
UPRUDD unpersuaded
UPRYLD upper eyelid
UPTEND unpatterned
UPTITC unpatriotic
UPTOLD unpatrolled
UQAIID unqualified
UQELBE unquellable
UQITES unquietness
URAHBE unreachable
URAIES unreadiness
URAITC unrealistic
URAOIG unreasoning
URCPIE unreceptive
URGEFL unregretful
URGTES uprightness
URGTOS unrighteous
URHASD unrehearsed
URLGOS unreligious
URLNIG unrelenting
URMTIG unremitting
URMVBE unremovable
URPESD unrepressed
URPNAT unrepentant
URQETD unrequested
URSIGY unrestingly
URSRIT unrestraint
URSSIG unresisting
URTIVD unretrieved
URVAIG unrevealing
URVLIG unravelling
URWRIG unrewarding
USAEBE unshakeable
USAIGY unsparingly
USAKIG unshackling
USAPND unsharpened
USBUBE unsubduable
USEIID unspecified
USEKBE unspeakable
USEKBY unspeakably
USETND unsweetened
USETRD unsheltered
USEWMN Ulsterwoman
USHLRY unscholarly
USICEK up shit creek
USIIUL unspiritual
USLCIE unselective
USLCTD unsolicited
USLIHY unselfishly
USNDWS ups and downs
USNTZD unsanitized
USOKBE unshockable
USOPBE unstoppable
USOPBY unstoppably
USOTND unshortened
USPOTD unsupported
USPRTD unseparated
USRASD unsurpassed
USRNIG unshrinking
USSETD unsuspected
USTLDY unsettledly
USTRTD unsaturated
USTSID unsatisfied
USUDES unsoundness
USVUIY unsavourily
UTAAIE ultramarine
UTAEBE untraceable
UTAHBE unteachable
UTAILT ultraviolet
UTAITR ultrafilter
UTAOEN ultra-modern
UTAOIS ultrasonics
UTCCOS urticaceous
UTETBE untreatable
UTHGDH up to high doh
UTIKBE unthinkable
UTITDY untaintedly
UTMEIG untempering
UTMOSY untimeously
UTMTUE Ultima Thule
UTNFLY untunefully
UTOGTF unthought-of
UTRFIY unthriftily
UTRIHD untarnished
UTSRTH up to scratch
UTTEAK up to the mark
UTTEIT up to the hilt
UTUHBE untouchable
UUTRBE unutterable
UUTRBY unutterably
UUULES unusualness
UVAIIY unviability
UVLAIE unvulgarise
unvulgarize
UVRCOS unveracious
UVRIHD unvarnished
UWAIBE unweariable
UWLIGY unwillingly
UWLOIG unwelcoming
UWOEOE unwholesome
UWRATD unwarranted
UWSEFR unwished-for
UWTIGY unwittingly
VAIOTK Vladivostok
VBAINL vibrational
VCAHVL Vaclav Havel
VCAMRL vice-admiral
VCIAIN vaccination
VCLAIG vacillating
VCLAIN vacillation
VCOAIN vacuolation
VCOILY vectorially
VCOSES vacuousness
viciousness
VCROSY vicariously
VCSIUE vicissitude
VCTOIT vacationist
VCUBAE vacuum brake
VCUCEN vacuum-clean
VCUFAK vacuum flask
VCUGUE vacuum gauge
VCYSIE vichyssoise
VDOAEA video camera
VDOEOD video-record
VEAKNE view askance
VGBNIE vagabondise
vagabondize
VGLNIM vigilantism
VICLSE voix céleste
VIEIHN voice within
VLAEAT village cart
VLAINL valuational
VLALTN Vulgar Latin
VLAOOY volcanology
vulcanology
VLAOSY villanously
VLDCIN valediction
VLDCOY valedictory
VLEIES velvetiness
VLEIHY value highly
VLESAK velvet shank
VLNAIM voluntarism
VLNAIY voluntarily

VLNIIN Valentinian
VLOYAS vale of years
VLRCCD valeric acid
VLSIDR Volkslieder
VNAEIE vintage wine
VNAEOT vintage port
VNCLUE viniculture
VNDARM Venn diagram
VNDESR vine-dresser
VNERAF Van de Graaff
VNFCLY venefically
VNIAIE ventilative
vindicative
VNIAIG vindicating
VNIAIN ventilation
vindication
VNIAOY vindicatory
VNIIIY vendibility
vincibility
VNIRTE vinaigrette
VNORSN Van Morrison
VNRCLR ventricular
VNSAEL Vanessa Bell
VNSCIN venesection
VNSIGY vanishingly
VNTARD Venetian red
VNTCLY venatically
VNUENO venture into
VNUEOE venturesome
VNUIGY venturingly
VNUIUE Venturi tube
VNUOSY venturously
VNURIM vanguardism
VNUSIG vanquishing
VOOCID Voodoo Child
VOOCLO violoncello
VOTEKR Voortrekker
VPRZBE vaporizable
VPUIGY vapouringly
VPUTAL vapour trail
VRAIEY versatilely
VRAIIG verbalizing
VRAIIY variability
versatility
VRAINL variational
VRALOA Vargas Llosa
VRCOEY very closely
VRCOSY veraciously
voraciously
VRDCLY veridically
VRDSET viridescent
VREAIN variegation
verberation
VREOGR verse-monger
VRERLY vertebrally
VREYHW variety show
VREYLB Variety Club
VRIAFN vertical fin
VRIAIY verticality
VRIBRH Virgin Birth
VRIEAE verbigerate
VRIIOS vertiginous
VRIUAE vermiculate
VRIUIE vermiculite
VRLBIT verslibrist
VRLGCL virological
VRLSET virilescent
VRMNAA verumontana
VROEES verboseness
VROSES variousness
VRQIKY very quickly
VRSMLR verisimilar
VRUEES verdureless
VSBEES visibleness
VSDLTR vasodilator
VSEEES vas deferens
VSOAAA Vasco da Gama
VSOABA Vasco Balboa
VSOMXR vision mixer
VSONES viscountess
VSOSES viscousness
VSPESN vasopressin
VSUAIE vascularise
vascularize
VTAANT vote against
VTCLUE viticulture
VTCNIY Vatican City
VTECNE vitrescence
VTLRAS vital organs
VTSEIG Vitus Bering
VVAFCS Vivian Fuchs
VVCOSY vivaciously
VVELIH Vivien Leigh
VVIHRS Viv Richards
VVSCIN vivisection
VXTOSY vexatiously
VYUITC voyeuristic
WAADER wear and tear
WAAIIY wearability
WAALGE what a plague
WAESNT weaver's knot
WAEWRS weasel words
WAHRAY weatherlady
WAHRED weather-fend
WAHREM weather beam
WAHRIE weather side
weather-wise
WAHRIL weathergirl
WAHROK weather-cock
WAHRON weather-worn
WAHVYU what have you
WAIESY wearilessly
WAIGHN wearing thin
WAIGON wearing down
wearing-down
WAIGWY wearing away
WAIOEY wearisomely
WAITKS what it takes
WAKEDY weak-kneedly
WAPDPN wrapped up in
WASMVR whatsomever
WATEEL what the hell
WATIES wealthiness
WATRUH wear through
WAYILE Weary Willie
WBLBAD wobble board
WDCAPD widechapped
WDESIS widdershins
WDIGAE wedding cake
WDIGIG wedding ring
WDLKON widely known
widely-known
WDRNIG wide-ranging
WDTRUH wade through
WDWAMN Widow Wadman
WDWWES widow's weeds
WECFRH whenceforth
WEEBUS whereabouts
WEEIHL wherewithal
WEEOAE where you are
WEEOVR wheresoever
WEEWRT Wienerwurst
WEFRAD whet forward
WEHRRO whether or no
WEIGIE weeping-ripe
WELARW wheelbarrow
WELIDW wheel window
WELRGT wheelwright
WEPGFY when pigs fly
WETEIH wrestle with
WGERIG wage-earning
WGIHES waggishness
WGWRIH wage war with
WIADPR whip and spur
WIBABY Whitby Abbey
WIEANT white walnut
WIEARD white-haired
WIEATR white matter
WIEEPR white pepper
WIEFFR write off for
WIEHOT whitethroat
WIELIS White Plains
WIELVR white clover
WIENGT white knight
WIENIN White Ensign
WIEOFE white coffee
WIEOLR white-collar
WIEOPR white copper
WIEOSS white horses
WIEPRT white spirit
WIERAS White friars
WIHDON weighed down
weighed-down
WIHIES weightiness
WIHNHR weigh anchor
WIHNIH weigh in with
WIHRAD whitherward
WIHRDE weighbridge
WIHTAN weight-train
WIHWTH weight-watch
WIIGAL Wailing Wall
WIIGEK writing-desk
WIIGIE whiting-time
WIIGIT waiting-list
WIIGOM waiting-room
WIMNIM Weismannism
WIPERE whippletree
WIPNBY whipping-boy
WISCLY whimsically

WISNIE Whitsuntide
WISOIG wainscoting
WISULR Weissmuller
WITETP whistle-stop
WITEWY whistle away
whittle away
WITIGY whistlingly
WITNON written down
WKFLES wakefulness
WKNHUS waking hours
WLAAHR Willa Cather
WLAIAS wild animals
WLAIIY weldability
WLALVR walk all over
WLAVSD well-advised
WLBHVD well behaved
well-behaved
WLBIFD well-briefed
WLCIOY wild chicory
WLCRIG Will Carling
WLDESD well-dressed
WLDFND well-defined
WLDRVD well-derived
WLDSRD well-desired
WLEAAS Walter Adams
WLEBAE Walter Baade
WLEDWD well-endowed
WLEFRE Wilberforce
WLEHGN Walter Hagen
WLEMIN Wilhelm Wien
WLEMTY Walter Mitty
WLEPTR Walter Pater
WLESET Walter Skeat
WLESOT Walter Scott
WLETRD well-entered
WLFTIG well-fitting
WLFUDD well-founded
WLFWIG wildfowling
WLGOMD well-groomed
WLHABT Welsh rabbit
WLHAIY walk heavily
WLIGES willingness
WLIGOT walking-boot
WLIHES wolfishness
WLIMAD William Laud
WLIMAE William Hare
WLIMAT William Taft
WLIMEL William Tell
WLIMEN William Penn
WLIMID William Kidd
WLIMIT William Pitt
WLIMYD William Byrd
WLMTHD well-matched
WLODAH wall of death
WLODRD well-ordered
WLOFIH walk off with
WLOIGY welcomingly
WLOTIH walk out with
WLPAND well-planned
WLRDWN Wilfred Owen
WLRUDD well-rounded
WLSAIH walk Spanish
WLSAKD well-stacked
WLSALT Will Scarlet
WLSHEZ Weltschmerz
WLSOKD well-stocked
WLSYNA Wole Soyinka
WLTAND well-trained
WLTODN well-trodden
WLUSIH Wilbur Smith
WLWIMN Walt Whitman
WLWITE wolf whistle
WLYRNT Willy Brandt
WMIHES wimpishness
WMNIES womanliness
WMNNOE Women in Love
WMNRED woman friend
WNADAN wind and rain
WNADIE wine and dine
WNADIG wing-and-wing
WNCETR windcheater
WNECID wonder child
WNEFLY wonderfully
WNEGEN wintergreen
WNEHRE Winged Horse
WNEIGY wanderingly
wonderingly
WNEJHE Wanderjahre
WNERIE Winterreise
WNEWRS winged words
WNIGOO wanting to do
WNIGOT winning-post
WNIGVR winning over
WNJMNT want jam on it
WNLYAE Wensleydale
WNMCIE wind machine
WNNARY win unfairly
WNNRDR Winona Ryder
WNOEES winsomeness
WNOEWY wend one's way
WNOLDE window ledge
WNOSAE window shade
WNSRAK Windsor Park
WNSRIG windsurfing
WNSRNT Windsor knot
WNVNGR wine vinegar
WOACHL wood alcohol
WOAEOE wood anemone
WOCEPR woodcreeper
WOCRIG woodcarving
WOCTIG woodcutting
WOEMUT whole amount
WOEOEY wholesomely
WOEOGR whoremonger
WOESON wooden spoon
WOEUBR whole number
WOGEDD wrong-headed
WOGEIF wrong belief
WOGIEP wrong side up
WOGTRN wrought iron
WOGUBR wrong number
WOMNHP woodmanship
WOPRWN whooper swan
WOSALW wood-swallow
WOWRLR wood warbler
WOYEMN Woody Herman
WRAANT work against
WRAIIY workability
WRATBE warrantable
WRATBY warrantably
WRBODD warm-blooded
WRDAAT worlds apart
WRDAIG wiredrawing
WRDAOS world-famous
WRDEOD world record
WRDETR world-beater
WRDIES worldliness
WRDOOE world to come
WRDYIE worldly wise
worldly-wise
WREOIL war memorial
WRFEVS war of nerves
WRFROD word for word
word-for-word
WRHATD warm-hearted
WRHESY worthlessly
WRHPIG worshipping
WRHSOY word history
WRHUIG warehousing
WRIDES worriedness
WRIGEK working week
WRJITY work jointly
WRMNHP workmanship
WRMNIE workmanlike
WRNPAE War and Peace
WRNTIG wire netting
WROCUT ward of court
WROIIS word origins
WROMUH word of mouth
word-of-mouth
WRPLIG wire-pulling
WRPRET word-perfect
WordPerfect®
WRRGRS warm regards
WRRMNL war criminal
WRSAIN work station
workstation
WRSNAL warts and all
WRSRAE work surface
WRTEAD work the land
WRTOAD work too hard
WRTPIG wiretapping
WRTRUH work through
WRTWRS work towards
WRWNES work wonders
WSCAKR wisecracker
WSEAIM Wesleyanism
WSEATR waste matter
WSEBED wastel bread
WSEDIR washer-drier
WSENAL Western Wall
WSENOL western roll
WSENOT westernmost
WSERUD waste ground
WSEWMN washerwoman
WSFLES wishfulness
wistfulness
WSIGWY wasting away
WSIHES waspishness

11 W_S_I

WSISAE	wash its face
WSLTIN	West Lothian
WSMNTR	Westminster
WSOEEF	wash oneself
WSOTEH	wisdom teeth
WSOTOH	wisdom tooth
WSWITD	wasp-waisted
WTAIWO	with a view to
WTCUIN	with caution
WTEIGY	witheringly
WTESIS	withershins
WTHAIG	watchmaking
WTHLIG	withholding
WTHOTR	witch doctor
WTHPIG	watchspring
WTICOE	within cooee
WTICYF	within cry of
WTIRAH	within reach
WTIRNE	within range
WTKOSN	with knobs on
WTNLTP	with no let-up
WTNSLY	wet one's clay
WTOTAL	without fail
WTOTEP	without help
WTOTET	without debt
WTOTOK	without book
	without work
WTOTOR	without-door
WTOTOT	without cost
WTPOIS	with profits
WTRAKT	water jacket
WTRAMR	water hammer
WTRANN	water cannon
WTRAOR	water vapour
WTRDON	watered-down
WTREDW	water meadow
WTRERR	Water Bearer
	Water-bearer
WTRETE	water beetle
WTRHUH	water thrush
WTRIDR	water-finder
WTRIIS	Water Lilies
WTRITL	water pistol
WTRKIG	water-skiing
WTRLST	water closet
WTROGD	waterlogged
WTROLD	water-cooled
WTROOR	watercolour
WTRORE	watercourse
WTROTE	water bottle
WTRPDR	water spider
WTRPRS	water sports
WTRSET	with respect
WTRUPY	water supply
WTSADR	withstander
WUDAHR	would rather
WUDDNE	Wounded Knee
WUDONR	would sooner
WYADES	waywardness
WYEWRD	Wayne's World
WYFCIG	way of acting
WYFIIG	way of living
XHOOOE	X-chromosome
XLPOIT	xylophonist
XNDCIM	xenodochium
XNGOSA	xenoglossia
XRGAHC	xerographic
YAOGAE	year of grace
YCEYAK	yackety-yack
YCTWMN	yachtswoman
YGRADR	Yegor Gaidar
YGSAIN	Yugoslavian
YHOOOE	Y-chromosome
YLOAET	yellow alert
YLOBLY	yellow-belly
YLOBRH	yellow birch
YLOERH	Yellow Earth
YLOFVR	yellow fever
YLOKIE	Yellowknife
YLORVR	Yellow River
YRGGRN	Yuri Gagarin
YRMNTR	York Minster
YTEIGY	yatteringly
YUATAK	you can't talk
YUGEPE	young people
YUGESN	young person
YUHOTL	youth hostel
YUNYUS	you and yours
YVUHNO	Yevtushenko
ZAOSES	zealousness
ZARAMN	Ziaur Rahman
ZASGBR	Zsa Zsa Gabor
ZMTCLY	zymotically
ZNUDIM	Zen Buddhism
ZOLNTN	zooplankton
ZRATIN	Zoroastrian
ZSFLES	zestfulness

12 letters – odd

AAAEDT	at a later date
AAAETM	at a later time
AACIAL	anarchically
AADINN	award-winning
AAEAAA	apage Satanas
AAEIAL	academically
AAEINS	academicness
AAERSL	amateurishly
AAGAON	a large amount
AAGMTO	amalgamation
AAHLCI	anaphylactic
AAHMTS	anathematise
AAHMTZ	anathematize
AAHOHB	arachnophobe
AAHORN	azathioprine
AAIHRC	at a high price
AAIIUL	avariciously
AAIOAI	acaridomatia
AAISAC	as an instance
AALBLT	availability
AAMFLS	an arm of flesh
AAMLNT	at arm's length
AAMNAE	an arm and a leg
AANENI	Alain Resnais
AAOIAL	anagogically
	analogically
	anatomically
	apagogically
AAOOAI	acarodomatia
AAOPOE	anamorphoses
AAOPOI	anamorphosis
AAPAEI	analphabetic
AARACS	at a great cost
AARBOI	anaerobiosis
AARBTT	as a tribute to
AASHTS	anaesthetise
	anaesthetist
AASHTZ	anaesthetize
AASLIO	Alan Sillitoe
AATADS	avant-gardism
	avant-gardist
AATAEU	acanthaceous
AATBLT	adaptability
AATHBA	abaft the beam
AATORE	avant-courier
AATOTM	a waste of time
AATRUL	anarthrously
AAYIAL	analytically
ABDXRU	ambidextrous
ABEITO	abbreviation
ABEITR	abbreviatory
ABRFNE	Albert Finney
ABRHRB	Albert Hornby
ABRNAG	Auberon Waugh
ABROOB	Alberto Tomba
ABRSEC	arborescence
ABSARS	ambassadress
ABYHAR	Abbey Theatre
ACACTR	acciaccatura
ACAOER	archaeometry
ACDNAL	accidentally
ACERSU	as clear as mud
ACETIE	ancient times
ACETOA	ancient Roman
ACETRE	ancient Greek
ACEYIA	archetypical
ACIAIE	acclimatized
ACICRL	Arctic Circle
ACIEAO	archipelagos
ACIETR	architecture
ACLRTN	accelerating
ACLRTO	acceleration
ACMAYN	accompanying
ACMLSE	accomplished
	accomplisher

Words marked ❑ can also be spelled with an initial capital letter

ACMLTO accumulation
ACMLTV accumulative
ACNENN as concerning
ACNINA Ascension Day
ACNUTO accentuation
ACOEAG at close range
ACRANN ascertaining
ACRIAI ascorbic acid
ACRINS accordionist
ACRTNS accurateness
ACSOET accustomed to
ACSTRA accusatorial
ACSTVL accusatively
ACUHMN accouchement
ACURMN accoutrement
ADAHDO at death's door
ADEARU André Malraux
ADEIRE André Citroën
ADEIVN Andrew Irvine
ADEMLO Andrew Mellon
ADEMTO Andrew Motion
ADERIE addle-brained
ADEWLO Andrew Wilson
ADHTTA and that's that
ADLSET add glosses to
ADOITK and no mistake
ADRASI aldermanship
ADREEG Alderley Edge
ADRIFS alder-liefest
ADSRTO at discretion
ADTOAL additionally
ADTVFE additive-free
ADUHXE Aldous Huxley
ADULET andouillette
AEADHD acetaldehyde
AEALNS amenableness
AEBIAI Azerbaijanis
AECPAI anencephalic
AEDECT Aberdeen City
AEDTLS anecdotalist
AEFOSN age of consent
AEFRUO Alex Ferguson
AEGINS Alec Guinness
AEIAAT Adelina Patti
AEICRE Alexis Carrel
AEIRTO amelioration
AEIRTV ameliorative
AEMGIC Abel Magwitch
AENPRN awe-inspiring
AEPNHN a helping hand
AERNEA Aneurin Bevan
AESMHN A Sea Symphony
AETEEA agent-general
AETUVL ave atque vale
AEUTNS adequateness
AFCDEL affect deeply
AFCENS affectedness
AFCINT affectionate
AFCOAO afficionados
AFEASI Alfred Austin
AFEKNE Alfred Kinsey
AFESSE Alfred Sisley
AFIHEL affrightedly
AFLAET affiliated to
AFLTUE apfel strudel
AFNOEE Alfonso Reyes
AFNTCR affinity card
AFOTNL affrontingly
AFRTIH at first sight
AFRTLS at first blush
AGBRYN argy-bargying
AGEGIS argue against
AGEHTS argue the toss
AGESVL aggressively
AGETTO augmentation
AGETTV augmentative
AGLAEU argillaceous
AGLCRE Angela Carter
AGLRPO Angela Rippon
AGOAGL as good as gold
AGOEEI angiogenesis
AGOETI Anglocentric
AGRELO augur well for
AGSEOI Auguste Rodin
AGSEOT Auguste Comte
AGSMBU August Möbius
AGSUJH Augustus John
AHEEET achievements
AHEEFO athlete's foot
AHEIAL athletically
AHENSA Ash Wednesday
AHLEHE Achilles' heel
AHOYOE athrocytoses
AHSOSE Ashes To Ashes
AHSVNS adhesiveness
AHSVTP adhesive tape
AIAEFL animated film
AIAFEE animal faeces
AIALNS amicableness
AIAODC Anita Roddick
AIARGT animal rights
AIARNC animatronics
AICOCK a piece of cake
AICOPS a piece of piss
AICOTI a piece of tail
AIEPIG Alice Springs
AIETTO alimentation
AIETTV alimentative
AIGRNO a king's ransom
AIHCRE a tight corner
AIOIAL amitotically
AITCAI aristocratic
AITPAE Aristophanes
AITTLA Aristotelian
AIUCRA amicus curiae
AIUTRS apiculturist
AIWOKL A View to a Kill
AJCIAL adjectivally
AJDCTO adjudication
AJNTVL adjunctively
AJTNBR adjutant bird
AKIEON at knife-point
AKLSUU Ankylosaurus
AKOFRL ask for firmly
AKOLDE acknowledged
ALANSA All Saints' Day
ALCPEL alla cappella
ALENWL all being well
ALEORN all-devouring
ALEVSV all-pervasive
ALFDOA all of a doodah
ALFDTE all of a dither
ALFSDE all of a sudden
ALLNSN Auld Lang Syne
auld lang syne
ALMOTN all-important
ALMRCN all-embracing
ALNICT Atlantic City
ALNLSV all-inclusive
ALNSNR all and sundry
ALPEVC all-up service
ALROHN all-or-nothing
ALRPOI ailurophobia
ALTRTO alliteration
ALTRTV alliterative
ALUEFR all-out effort
ALVRGI all over again
ALWONE allow to enter
ALYTMG all systems go
AMDUAN Ahmed Sukarno
AMGTNS almightiness
AMMNAI armamentaria
AMNCLT adminiculate
AMNHME Armand Hammer
AMNSMN admonishment
AMRLYA Admiralty Bay
AMSHRC atmospherics
AMSIEA Armistice Day
AMSINE admission fee
AMUPAE armour-plated
ANACIF Ann Radcliffe
ANBNRF Anne Bancroft
ANHLTO annihilation
ANJCBE Arne Jacobsen
ANKRNN Anna Karenina
ANLPLE Arnold Palmer
ANLWSE Arnold Wesker
ANNITO Annunciation
ANOCEE Anne of Cleves
ANRALA abnormal load
ANTSLU Arne Tiselius
ANUCMN announcement
AOAHRP aromatherapy
AOALNS adorableness
AOARSA Avogadro's law
AODNIG a good innings
AOEHLN above-the-line
AOEHSL above the salt
AOEHUH aforethought
AOENSL above oneself
AOGOEI A Song to Celia
AOHCRE apothecaries
AOHOAI apochromatic
AOIIAL aboriginally
apolitically
AOIINS abolitionism
abolitionist
AOINME atomic number
AOIPCL a rod in pickle

Letters	Word
AOITER	atomic theory
AOIWIH	atomic weight
AOKNOE	an oaken towel
AOLCIA	apoplectical
AOLERN	a fool's errand
AOOEIA	apologetical
AOOIEO	apologize for
AOSIAL	acoustically
AOTLAO	amontillados
AOTNSO	as often as not
AOTOHS	apostrophise
AOTOHZ	apostrophize
AOTOPL	abortion pill
AOTSTO	amortisation
AOTZTO	amortization
APADNL	applaudingly
APAEIA	alphabetical
APASMN	appraisement
APASVL	applausively
	appraisively
APAUEI	alphanumeric
APEESO	apprehension
APEESV	apprehensive
APEFOO	apple of Sodom
APEITO	appreciation
APEITV	appreciative
APGITR	appoggiatura
APIATI	amphigastria
APIHAR	amphitheatre
APIRCI	amphibrachic
APITET	appointments
APITMU	amphistomous
APLCIN	Appalachians
APNETM	appendectomy
APNIII	appendicitis
APNSIN	Alpine skiing
APOCAL	approachable
APORAO	appropriator
APREAC	appurtenance
APRETO	apperception
APRIAI	aspartic acid
APRILM	aspergillums
APRNNS	apparentness
APRNTM	apparent time
APRTHK	apparatchiki
	apparatchiks
APSTNS	appositeness
APTSNL	appetisingly
APTZNL	appetizingly
APYITO	asphyxiation
APYNSL	apply oneself
AQANAC	acquaintance
AQANWT	acquaint with
AQIIIN	acquisitions
AQISEC	acquiescence
ARAEIA	Afro-American
ARBSNS	agribusiness
	agrobusiness
ARCBTO	at rock bottom
ARCLUA	agricultural
ARDNMC	aerodynamics
AREBLT	agreeability
ARENRC	Adrienne Rich
ARENWT	agreeing with
ARERSU	air-sea rescue
ARGNUL	acrogenously
ARHMAB	Abraham Darby
ARNCAL	acronychally
ARNEET	arrangements
ARNLLN	adrenal gland
ARNOLN	Aaron Copland
ARNUIA	aeronautical
ARODTO	air-condition
AROLTO	air pollution
AROMDR	air-commodore
ARRFSA	aircraftsman
ARRNPR	air transport
ARRSEE	air-freshener
ARSIAL	acrostically
ARSTEA	across the way
ARSVNS	abrasiveness
ARTOAO	a broth of a boy
ARTYEN	a pretty penny
ASCAIN	associations
ASCNHN	at second hand
ASEIUL	abstemiously
ASELYR	Austen Layard
ASHTCS	aestheticise
	Aestheticism
ASHTCZ	aestheticize
ASIEOK	Arshile Gorky
ASIFIR	Austin friars
ASIIIU	adscititious
ASIIUL	auspiciously
ASLTNS	absoluteness
ASLTRL	absolute rule
ASLTZR	absolute zero
ASMLLN	assembly line
ASMLRO	assembly room
ASMLTO	assimilation
ASMLTV	assimilative
ASMNTA	assuming that
ASNMNE	absent-minded
ASNWNE	Arsene Wenger
ASRAAU	as sure as a gun
ASRAIA	Assurbanipal
ASRCEL	abstractedly
ASRCNS	abstractness
ASREEI	alstroemeria
ASRLAA	Australia Day
ASRLSA	Australasian
ASRNSA	Austronesian
ASRSNS	abstruseness
ASTNII	absit invidia
ASUTLT	absquatulate
ASUTTO	auscultation
ASUTTR	auscultatory
ASVRTO	asseveration
ATAFNE	Art Garfunkel
ATAMMN	at that moment
ATARRF	anti-aircraft
ATATNL	attractingly
ATATVL	attractively
ATCCOI	anticyclonic
ATCDNL	antecedently
ATCEIA	anticlerical
ATCLTL	articulately
ATCLTO	articulation
ATCPTN	anticipating
ATCPTO	anticipation
ATCPTR	anticipatory
ATCTLS	autocatalyse
ATCTLZ	autocatalyze
ATCTOA	autochthonal
ATCTOE	autochthones
ATCWSE	Aztec two-step
ATDDCI	autodidactic
ATDLVA	antediluvian
ATDSRC	autodestruct
ATEADO	at the hands of
ATECOE	Astley Cooper
ATEECO	at the mercy of
ATEELO	at the heels of
ATEGBO	Althea Gibson
ATEONO	at the point of
ATEREO	at the order of
ATERNO	at the front of
ATETCT	authenticate
	authenticity
ATEUSD	at the outside
ATFCAL	artificially
ATFMNS	anti-feminist
ATGNSI	antagonistic
ATHPRO	act the part of
ATIGNL	astringently
ATIMMN	at this moment
ATIUAL	attributable
ATMCOU	autumn crocus
ATMCSA	antimacassar
ATMRDA	antemeridian
ATMRDE	ante meridiem
ATNATU	Antoni Artaud
ATNHKO	Anton Chekhov
ATNHWS	Antony Hewish
ATNMUL	autonomously
ATNNRV	Antananarivo
ATNNWL	Antonine Wall
ATNOAD	Antonio Gaudí
ATNOOG	Attenborough
ATNSHO	a stone's throw
ATNSMN	astonishment
ATNTAO	act instead of
ATNURN	antineutrino
	anti-neutrino
ATOATC	astronautics
ATOHSC	astrophysics
ATOLSL	act foolishly
ATOOIA	aetiological
	astrological
	astronomical
ATOPCE	action-packed
ATORPA	action replay
ATOSRO	author's proof
ATOTKN	action-taking
ATOYLN	Anthony Blunt
ATOYOA	astrocytomas
ATPIAL	autoptically
ATPOAL	antiphonally
ATPRIL	antiparticle

ATPTEI antipathetic
ATRBLT alterability
ATRCSA autorickshaw
ATRFET after effects
after-effects
ATRHUH afterthought
ATRONE afternoon tea
ATRPIA anthropoidal
ATRPLG anthropology
ATRTKN after its kind
ATRUNN afterburning
ATSCAL antisocially
ATSIAL artistically
autistically
ATSMTS anti-Semitism
ATSSOE artist's model
ATTDNS attitudinise
ATTDNZ attitudinize
ATTEIA antithetical
ATUDNL astoundingly
ATUHRI Arthur Harris
ATUMLE Arthur Miller
AUDAIO Arundhati Roy
AUENSL amuse oneself
AUPREO a supporter of
AUTBEO A Suitable Boy
AUTRTO adulteration
AUTRUL adulterously
AVNAEU advantageous
AVNEUR advance guard
AVNIIU adventitious
AVRILS adverbialise
AVRILZ adverbialize
AVSBLT advisability
AVSRBD advisory body
AWNIHA Aswan High Dam
AWRLAA Anwar al-Sadat
Anwar el-Sadat
AXLAYU auxiliary bud
AYCRNS asynchronism
AYCRNU asynchronous
AYHNGE Anything Goes
AYIUEO any minute now
AYMTIA asymmetrical
AYPOIA asymptotical
AZOADN Anzio Landing
BAAAGT Bhagavad Gita
BAAERA beat a retreat
BAATES Blatant Beast
BABROT blabbermouth
BACEHN blanc-de-chine
BACEOR Blanc de Noirs
BACFOE Blanchflower
BACIGU branching out
branching-out
BADBTE brandy butter
BADFRD Board of Trade
BADNCR boarding card
BADNPS boarding pass
BADRRC bladder wrack
bladderwrack
BADSMN blandishment
BAEAAA beaver away at
BAENSL brace oneself
BAESRO be a measure of
BAGDCO braggadocios
BAHOBN beachcombing
BAHRHA by a short head
BAHRUO bear hard upon
BAIIAL beatifically
BAKABT Black Sabbath
BAKAKA Black Hawk War
BAKALN blackballing
BAKCNM black economy
BAKERE black-hearted
BAKNBU black-and-blue
BAKSNS brackishness
BAKTRE bracket-creep
BAKUDN black pudding
BAKURL blackguardly
BAKURN blackcurrant
BAKUSA black Russian
BAKYBA black-eye bean
BAKYDE black-eyed pea
BAMRHI Beaumarchais
BANAHN brainwashing
BANUWN Blaenau Gwent
BAOARA blazon abroad
BAOGHL by a long chalk
BAOPIN Bias of Priene
BASPSA Blaise Pascal
BASRTN bear scrutiny
BATELC beat the clock
BATUNS boastfulness
BAUKRO be a sucker for
BAXSRT beaux esprits
BBCMBC Baby Come Back
BBDOPN be bad company
BBEAHN Bible-bashing
BBIGAH bibliography
BBLBBL bibble-babble
BBLMMR bubble memory
BBLUNS bibulousness
BBNTNT babingtonite
BBYAZE bobby-dazzler
BBYICE Bobby Fischer
BCADOT back and forth
BCAERN buccaneering
BCBEKN backbreaking
back-breaking
BCCADI by cock and pie
BCCEHI bicycle chain
BCEILG bacteriology
BCEOHO bachelorhood
BCHNLA bacchanalian
BCIGRU backing group
BCIGTR backing store
BCMAIO by comparison
BCMATV become active
BCMBGE become bigger
BCMBRN become boring
BCMCLE become colder
BCMCOD become cloudy
BCMDRE become darker
BCMFTE become fatter
BCMKEO become keen on
BCMLNE become longer
BCMLRE become larger
BCMLSI become lost in
BCMLVL become lively
BCMMLO become mellow
BCMNNS becomingness
BCMNRO become narrow
BCMPBI become public
BCMPLI become pallid
BCMRGE become ragged
BCMRLS bicameralism
BCMRNI become rancid
BCMRTE become rotten
BCMSOE become slower
BCMTLE become taller
BCMTNE become tender
BCMWAE become weaker
BCOBYN back of beyond
BCSABN back-stabbing
BCTBSC back to basics
BCTNTR back to nature
back-to-nature
BCWOSA backwoodsman
BCWRNS backwardness
BCWUDN back-wounding
BDALNS biddableness
BDBIDN body-building
BDCRPE bodice-ripper
BDEAIU bad behaviour
BDFNTO by definition
BDFUTC bed of justice
BDIGLN bedding plant
BDLNUG body language
BDNLEC bad influence
BDODHR Bedfordshire
BDOETM bide one's time
BDOPOL body of people
BDPECN body piercing
BDRVTO by derivation
BDSOKN body stocking
BDYEAE badly behaved
badly-behaved
BDYRSE badly-dressed
BDZLMN bedazzlement
BEAETR Buenaventura
BEDHPE bread-chipper
BEDNEA Brendan Behan
BEESES brewer's yeast
BEKACN breakdancing
break-dancing
BEKELC break wedlock
BEKEVC break service
BEKFWT break off with
BEKHNW break the news
BEKHOG break through
breakthrough
BEKNDW breaking-down
BEKRCR break a record
BEKRMS break-promise
BEKSRK break a strike
BELBOE beetle-browed
BEOUSA Byelorussian
BESHMR bless the mark

BESSRK breaststroke
BETAYE Breathalyser®
BETEGI breathe again
BETIOS Brest-Litovsk
BETLSL breathlessly
BETTKN breathtaking
breath-taking
BEZUSL breeze up sale
BFIILN Baffin Island
BFRYUA before you can
BGEAON bugger around
BGNOTD begin to study
BHAYON be heavy going
BHRTSA be here to stay
BHVORS behaviourism
behaviourist
BIDSOC build a sconce
BIDUCL build quickly
BIEBIG Bailey bridge
BIGCAG bring a charge
BIGEAE being debated
BIGHMO bring shame on
BIGHMT bring shame to
BIGHRE bring charges
BIGNLA bridging loan
BIGOEM bring to terms
BIGOHA bring to a head
BIGOHL bring to a halt
BIGOIH bring to light
BIGONN bring to an end
BIGORA bring to trial
BIGOSO bring to a stop
BIGOWR bring forward
BIGTEA bridge the gap
BIGTIE Bridget Riley
BIHMON Brigham Young
BIHORC Brighton Rock
BIHSII Blithe Spirit
BIHSML blithesomely
BIIGON boiling point
BIKASI brinkmanship
BIKILE brickfielder
BILATN brilliantine
BINEAM Brian De Palma
BISUNS blissfulness
BITEOE brittle bones
BITRUL boisterously
BKNBIF bikini briefs
BKWLTR Bakewell tart
BLBAMN Bill Beaumont
BLBTOE bell-bottomed
BLEDNE ballet dancer
ballet-dancer
BLEIAL balletically
BLFGTN bullfighting
BLIEEC belligerence
belligerency
BLINRN Belgian franc
BLNEHE balance sheet
BLNULS bilingualism
BLOAGN Bilbo Baggins
BLODSA ballon d'essai
BLOGLA balm of Gilead
BLORGT Bill of Rights
bill of rights
BLPITE ballpoint pen
BLTLMN belittlement
BLTRLS bilateralism
BLWHBL below the belt
BLWHLN below-the-line
BLWHSL below the salt
BLWVRG below average
BLYCEL Billy McNeill
BLYRME Billy Bremner
BMADRN bump and grind
BMEHRI Bomber Harris
BMEJCE bomber jacket
BMLEIM bimilleniums
BNACRE Bonham-Carter
BNAWIH bantamweight
BNEBRE Bunsen burner
BNFCAL beneficially
BNFCAT beneficial to
BNFCEC beneficience
BNFCNL beneficently
BNHFIE bunch of fives
BNIHLO Ben Nicholson
BNIPRE Bonnie Parker
BNRSSE binary system
BNRWAO binary weapon
BNTELO bend the elbow
BNTGTE band together
BNTJAE Benito Juarez
Benito Juárez
BNTRGT bang to rights
BNVLNL benevolently
BNYODA Benny Goodman
BOCBSE bronco-buster
BOCOCP bronchoscope
BODAKN blood packing
BODATN broadcasting
BODEDN Blood Wedding
BODETN bloodletting
blood-letting
BODHRT bloodthirsty
BODMNE bloody-minded
BODNIO blood and iron
BODRTE blood-brother
BODTIE bloodstained
BODUKN bloodsucking
BOEDAE broker-dealer
BOEGAH biogeography
BOEHNC biomechanics
BOEONA be one's own man
BOFIHO be off with you
BOHMSR biochemistry
BOHRNA brother-in-law
BOHSCS biophysicist
BOIEAE bromide paper
BOIEST biodiversity
BOIWOI boogie-woogie
BOKAIA block capital
BOKDTL blocked style
BOKEES block release
BOKFLT block of flats
BOKTYO Brooke-Taylor
BOLANN book-learning
BOLVNI bioflavonoid
BOMOTI Bloemfontein
BONEON brownie point❑
BONEUD Brownie Guide
BOOECO blow one's cool
BOOEMN blow one's mind
BOOIAL biologically
BOPAAS boomps-a-daisy
BORPIA biographical
BOSOPO book-scorpion
BOTEOK be on the books
BOTEOL blow the coals
BOTPEE blow to pieces
BOTSUU brontosaurus❑
BOYTEI biosynthesis
biosynthetic
BPEEEC by preference
BRAAIL Barbara Mills
BRACAI bureaucratic
BRADEI Bernard Levin
BRADSA Barnard's star
BRAGON burial ground
BRAQIL Barranquilla
BRARUL barratrously
BRAYUG Barnaby Rudge
BRDOER bored to tears
BRDYIH burn daylight
BRECLI Border collie
BREMNE barber-monger
BREWLI Barnes Wallis
BRHACK birthday cake
BRIEEE Berline-Tegel
BRIEFG burn in effigy
BRIRRA barrier cream
BRITES Born in the USA
BRKUKE bare-knuckled
BRLRLR burglar alarm
BROTBA borlotti bean
BROWNE bird of wonder
BRRYOD Burt Reynolds
BRSALF Boris Karloff
BRSETI Boris Yeltsin
BRSOUO Boris Godunov
BRSPSK Boris Spassky
BRSYVE bird's eye view
BRTBWL Born to be Wild
BRTHOG burst through
BRWTHN bird-watching
BSBLAT be so bold as to
BSCRCS basic process
BSEHNL beseechingly
BSEKAO Buster Keaton
BSETCE bespectacled
BSIEWT be seized with
BSIGHR basking shark
BSLSAO beso las manos
BSNSCR business card
BSNSLK businesslike
business-like
BSNSPR business park
BSOORM Bishop of Rome
BSTENS besottedness

BSTIGI besetting sin
BSUTRM biscuit-crumb
BSWAKN bushwhacking
BTBEDN bate-breeding
BTECRE butter curler
BTEIGA battering-ram
BTELCL bitterly cold
BTEMSI butter-muslin
BTENEK between-decks
BTENIE between times
betweentimes
BTENSW between us two
BTESOC butterscotch
BTHRHO butcher's hook
BTLGON battleground
BTLOEE bottle opener
BTLOJN Battle of Jena
BTLOLO Battle of Loos
BTLOZM Battle of Zama
BTNHSD bit on the side
BTNSOT bet one's boots
BTODAE bottom drawer
BTOYRS bottony cross
BTUHON be tough going
BTYREA Betty Friedan
BUCCSL bouncy castle
BUDNAG Bourdon gauge
BUDRNL blunderingly
BUECAE Bruce McLaren
BUEEGR blue-eyed girl
BUEHTI Bruce Chatwin
BUELSH Brunelleschi
BUHTOE brush strokes
BURSHL Boutros-Ghali
BUSLLC Brussels lace
BUSNAL Boussingault
BUSOKN bluestocking
BUTELM be up the flume
BUTHNE bounty hunter
BUTRNL blusteringly
BUUDIE Blut und Eisen
BUUDOE Blut und Boden
BUUTAN bouquet garni
BVRAAP Bavarian Alps
BVRYIL Beverly Hills
BWEDHL bowhead whale
BWLEMN bewilderment
BWNSRP bow and scrape
BWTHNL bewitchingly
BXFIEI box-office hit
BYEUAL buy regularly
BYNBLE beyond belief
BYNRMD beyond remedy
BYNRPI beyond repair
BYRMRE buyer's market
CAATRS characterise
CAATRZ characterize
CABRUI chamber music
CACLTI Chalcolithic
CACPRT chalcopyrite
CADAUT Chandragupta
CADCTO claudication
CAEOES chapel of ease

CAEOLG Clare College
CAGCLU change colour
CAGCUS change course
CAGOLF change of life
CAGOMN change of mind
CAGOTN change of tone
CAGRUL clangorously
CAGTEE change the leg
CAHADN crash-landing
CAHARE crash barrier
CAHULE coachbuilder
CAIETS clarinettist
CAIINS coalitionist
CAILNE cranial index
CAKBTL crack a bottle
CAKHWI crack the whip
CAKNTL chalk and talk
CAKRIE crackbrained
crack-brained
CALNWT crawling with
CALSAL Charles Hallé
CALSAR Charles Barry
CALSEB Charles Beebe
CALSOL Charles Rolls
CALSOT Charles Forte
CALTNS charlatanism
CANILE Chaunticleer
CANLOS charnel house
CANSNS clannishness
CAPOSI championship
CAPROR clapperboard
CAROAC clairvoyance
clairvoyancy
CASFAL classifiable
CASLNU chaise-longue
CATOOS coast-to-coast
CATRNL clatteringly
CATROS charterhouse❑
CATSMN chastisement
CATTBL chastity belt
CAVNSI chauvinistic
CBAEHT cabbage white
CBNRIE cabin cruiser
CBNTAE cabinet-maker
CBSIAL cubistically
CCFGTN cockfighting
CCILEI cockieleekie
CCOFOE cuckoo flower
CCORLE cuckoo-roller
CCORPN cyclopropane
CCSRNS cocksureness
CCSSAD Cocos Islands
CDDESG coded message
CDFCTO codification
CDOBLE code of belief
CDPNEC co-dependency
CEEAAE crème caramel
CEECDN Clemence Dane
CEECEE clever-clever
CEEEHN crêpe de chine
CEELTO crenellation
CEERIH crème fraîche
CEETRT coelenterate

CEETRU Clement Freud
CEEUET crêpe suzette
CEIABN chemical bond
CEIAFE chemical-free
CEIRTN credit rating
CEITIL Cheviot Hills
CEIWRH creditworthy
CEKFOK clerk of works
CEMRCE cream cracker
CENNLD cleaning lady
CEOHRP chemotherapy
CEPCAL creepy-crawly
CERBAD cherry brandy
CERIHE clear-sighted
CERNBN clearing bank
CERPCE cherry picker
CERSBL clear as a bell
CERUNS cheerfulness
CESBRE cheeseburger
CESOUR chefs d'oeuvre
CESPRN cheeseparing
cheese-paring
CESSIE cheese slicer
CETRIL chesterfield❑
CETVNS creativeness
CEUIAL cherubically
CGRTEN cigarette end
CHBTTO cohabitation
CIAAIE china cabinet
CIARUL chivalrously
CIBNBO climbing-boot
CIBNIO climbing iron
CICDNA coincidental
CICDNL coincidently
CICDWT coincide with
CICLUE Cain-coloured
CIDEEI child benefit
CIDEFR child welfare
CIDERN childbearing
child-bearing
CIDSNS childishness
CIEEEF crise de nerfs
CIEEHT Chinese white
CIEIAL chimerically
CIFAGN cliffhanging
cliff-hanging
CIFFTF chief of staff
CIFIHR Cliff Richard
CIHRDE cliché-ridden
CIIAMS critical mass
CIIANS criticalness
CIKNUO chicken out of
CINERE cairn terrier
CINYTC chimney stack
CINYWE chimney-sweep
CIOEAE coin-operated
CIORCI chiropractic
CIORCO chiropractor
CIRSUO chiaroscuros
CIUAHB Chinua Achebe
CIUCIU chiquichiqui
CIUSNS cliquishness
CLAEAL collaterally

Words marked ❑ can also be spelled with an initial capital letter

CLAOAO collaborator
CLAONO Celia Johnson
CLAYRS Calvary cross
CLECBE Colley Cibber
CLETVL collectively
CLETVS collectivise
collectivism
CLETVZ collectivize
CLIERT collinearity
CLIMXD calcium oxide
CLIRPE calligrapher
CLITEI callisthenic
CLITPA call into play
CLMITN calumniating
CLMITO calumniation
columniation
CLMITR calumniatory
CLMIUL calumniously
CLMTUL calamitously
CLNAKO Colin Jackson
CLNEHA cylinder head
CLNLLO Colonel Blood
CLNODE Colin Cowdrey
CLNSTO colonisation
CLNZTO colonization
CLOMNA Collop Monday
CLONTR call of nature
CLOTRS coleopterist
CLOTRU coleopterous
CLOUAL colloquially
CLRNTO chlorination
CLSEIL Celesteville
CLSOLE cold shoulder
cold-shoulder
CLSUWS colossus-wise
CLTEHT call the shots
CLTGTE call together
CLUAEL calculatedly
CLUAIN calculations
CLUEHC culture shock
CLUFLE colour filter
CLUSHM colour scheme
CLYOBE collywobbles
CMAALT comparable to
CMADAE command paper
CMADNL commandingly
CMAEOE compare notes
CMAINE companion set
CMARPE come a cropper
CMARSA come across as
CMDWUO come down upon
CMDWWT come down with
CMECAL commercially
CMECMN commencement
CMEDTO commendation
CMEDTR commendatory
CMESRT commensurate
CMESTO compensation
CMESTR compensatory
CMFLOE camp-follower
CMIELS compile a list
CMIEWT combined with
CMISOE commissioned
commissioner
CMISRA commissarial
commissariat
CMISRN come it strong
CMITLN come in to land
CMITPA come into play
CMITVE come into view
CMKIKR camiknickers
CMLCNL complacently
CMLCTO complication
CMLEOO Camille Corot
CMLIAC complaisance
CMLNMU cumulonimbus
CMLOOG Camillo Golgi
CMLTNS completeness
CMLTVL cumulatively
CMLXTE complexities
CMOAMC common as muck
CMOELE Come on Eileen
CMOETA componential
CMOFOS come off worst
CMOGNE common gender
CMOGON common ground
CMOIKA common ink cap
CMOIUL commodiously
CMOMLO common mallow
CMOMNI compos mentis
CMONTM compound time
CMOPOL Common People
common people
CMOPRO common person
CMORDN common-riding
CMOSRA come on stream
CMOSRN come on strong
CMOTNL comfortingly
CMOTNO come out on top
CMOWAT commonwealth❑
CMRLCD camera lucida
CMRMRO comprimarios
CMRMSN compromising
CMRSIL compressible
CMTACP come to accept
CMTGTE come together
CMTPEE come to pieces
CMTSUU Camptosaurus
CMUCIU compunctious
CMUEBL commuter belt
CMUEGM computer game
CMUEIE computerized
CMUGTO compurgation
CMUIAL communicable
communicably
CMUIAO communicator
CMUIAT communicants
CMUSRL compulsorily
CMUSVL compulsively
CNABNN Canaan Banana
CNAECN convalescent
convalescing
CNAHLO Conrad Hilton
CNAIAE contaminated
CNAIAL contaminable
CNAIUL contagiously
CNAKRU cantankerous
CNANRS containerise
CNANRZ containerize
CNAUAL connaturally
CNCETO conic section
CNCETS conscientise
CNCETZ conscientize
CNCITO conscription
CNDBLA Canada balsam
CNEACN conveyancing
CNEBRE canterburies
CNEEAE confederated
CNEECN conferencing
CNEERT concelebrate
CNEIAL centesimally
congenitally
CNEILT congeniality
CNEINL conveniently
CNELTO cancellation
CNEMNN conterminant
CNEMNT conterminate
CNEMNU conterminous
CNENTO condemnation
CNENTR condemnatory
CNEPAO contemplator
CNEPIL contemptible
contemptibly
CNEPRR contemporary
CNEPRS contemporise
CNEPRZ contemporize
CNEPUU contemptuous
CNERTO consecration
CNESAL consensually
CNESOA confessional
CNESTO condensation
conversation
CNETAE concentrated
CNETAL contextually
CNETAT concert party
CNETEC consentience
CNETIC concert pitch
CNETNL consentingly
contestingly
CNETOA convectional
conventional
CNETOE confectioner
CNETTO contestation
CNETVL connectively
CNEUNE consequences
CNEUNL consequently
CNEVTO conservation
CNEVTR conservatory
CNEVTS conservatism
CNEVTV conservative
CNHLGS conchologist
CNICNL convincingly
CNICTO confiscation
CNICTR confiscatory
CNIEAL considerable
considerably
CNIETA confidential
CNIGNL contingently
CNIGNO contingent on

Words marked ❑ can also be spelled with an initial capital letter

CNIICU cunnilinctus
CNIILT conviviality
CNIINN conditioning
CNIITO conciliation
CNIITR conciliatory
CNIMTO confirmation
CNIMTR confirmatory
CNIMTV confirmative
CNITNL consistently
CNIUTO continuation
CNIUUL contiguously
continuously
CNIUUT contiguous to
CNLBLT conglobulate
CNLCLT canaliculate
CNLMRT conglomerate
CNLSVL conclusively
CNLTNT conglutinate
CNLZTO canalization
CNMVRT cinéma vérité
cinéma-vérité
CNNZTO canonization
CNODNL concordantly
CNOIAE consolidated
CNOIAO consolidator
CNOIUL censoriously
CNOMTO conformation
CNONEL confoundedly
CNONTE confound them
CNOUIN convolutions
CNPCUT conspectuity
CNPRNL conspiringly
CNRBTN contributing
CNRBTO contribution
CNRBTR contributory
CNRBTT contribute to
CNRBTV contributive
CNRCAL contractable
CNRCEL contractedly
CNRCIL contractible
CNRCIN contractions
CNRGTO congregation
CNRLAE control panel
CNRLAL controllable
CNRLOE control tower
CNRLON central point
CNRLTC control stick
CNROMS centre of mass
CNRPNA contrapuntal
CNRRNS contrariness
CNRRWS contrariwise
CNRSRA centre spread
CNRTLT congratulate
CNRTNS concreteness
CNRVNE contrivances
CNTBLR constabulary
CNTITO constriction
CNTITV constrictive
CNTPTO constipation
CNTTEC constituency
CNTTET constituents
CNTTTO constitution
CNTUTO construction
CNTUTV constructive
CNUAIU contumacious
CNUCIA conjunctival
CNUEIU contumelious
CNUICN concupiscent
CNUINS Confucianism
Confucianist
CNULCT centuplicate
CNUMTL consummately
CNUMTO consummation
CNURNL concurrently
conqueringly
CNUSAO conquistador
CNUSVL convulsively
CNUTTO consultation
CNUTTR consultatory
CNUTTV consultative
CNUTVT conductivity
COCREC co-occurrence
CODHME cloud chamber
CODISN cloud-kissing
CODNTL co-ordinately
CODNTN co-ordinating
CODNTO co-ordination
CODNTV co-ordinative
CODSNS cloddishness
COEAMN close harmony
COEFOE cloven-footed
COEGAH choreography
COEHOE cloven-hoofed
COEHUH close thought
COEIAL cholerically
COEIHL close tightly
COEITN close-fitting
COEOET close to death
COEOOG close borough
COEOPN close company
COEOTE close-mouthed
COERIE close-grained
COIGOE cooling tower
COKACE clock-watcher
CONSNS clownishness
COOAEO chocolate-box
chocolate log
COSDIE crossed wires
COSETO cross section
cross-section
COSNOE crossing over
COSONR cross-country
COSRIE cross-grained
COSURN cross-current
COSUTC cross-buttock
COSXMN cross-examine
COTDRA clotted cream
COTEOK cook the books
CPAHRW Cappagh-brown
CPANLN Captain Flint
CPBLTE capabilities
CPEBTO copper-bottom
CPEFSE copper-fasten
CPFIET cap of liberty
CPIAEB captivated by
CPIIUL capriciously
CPIUNS captiousness
CPLAEU capillaceous
CPLMRS co-polymerise
CPLMRZ co-polymerize
CPRALI capercaillie
capercailzie
CPTLAN capital gains
CPTLRS capital cross
CPTLSI capitalistic
CPTLTO capitulation
CPTLUD capital funds
CPTLZO capitalize on
CQETSL coquettishly
CRANTR carnal nature
CRANYO certainly not
CRBENE Caribbean Sea
CRCRYN card-carrying
CRCTRS caricaturist
CRECLI Carmen Callil
CRELNH carte blanche
CREMNE carpetmonger
CREMSU Correr Museum
CREPNT correspond to
CRETOA correctional
CRETOE correctioner
CRFENS carefreeness
CRIASI cardinalship
CRIDLN carried along
CRIGAH cardiography
CRIGFE carriage-free
CRIGNF carving-knife
CRIGOG curling tongs
CRIGPI carriage-paid
CRIHAT Cornish pasty
CRIHRS Cornish cross
CRIIAE certificated
CRILGS cardiologist
CRINLS corni inglesi
CRIOEI carcinogenic
CRLNAU Carl Linnaeus
CRLSNS carelessness
CRMAIU coram paribus
CRMNAL ceremonially
CRMSHR chromosphere
CRMTCS chromaticism
CRMTCT chromaticity
CRMYLO chrome yellow
CRNLGS chronologise
chronologist
CRNLGZ chronologize
CRNMTI chronometric
CROAEU carbonaceous
CROAII corpora vilia
CROATI Corporal Trim
CROAUE corpora lutea
CRODTN carbon dating
CROELS corporealise
CROELT corporeality
CROELZ corporealize
CROHLS cartophilist
CROIAI carbolic acid
carbonic acid
CRONLS corno inglese

CROOAE corroborated
CROOAL corroborable
CROOAO corroborator
CRORPE cartographer
CRORPI cartographic
CROTAU cirrostratus
CROTEO corn on the cob
CROUUU cirrocumulus
CROYRT carbohydrate
CRSCUC Christ Church
Christchurch
CRSINR Christian era
CRSINS christianise
CRSINT Christianity
CRSINZ christianize
CRSMSA Christmas Day
CRSMSO Christmas box
CRSMSV Christmas Eve
CRSNBR Carl Sandburg
CRSOAH chrestomathy
CRUCSO circumcision
CRUFSO circumfusion
CRUGOL curmudgeonly
CRUGRT circumgyrate
CRUJCN circumjacent
CRULCT circumlocute
CRULTU corpus luteum
CRUNTT circumnutate
CRUSAC circumstance
CRUSRB circumscribe
CRUTOR circuit court
CRUTUL circuitously
CRVNEA caravanserai
CRWRIK Carl Wernicke
CRYHOG carry through
CRYNSA carry one's bat
CRYOWR carry forward
CSADAR cash and carry
cash-and-carry
CSADPL custard apple
CSAEAG Cascade Range
CSAPLO cast a spell on
CSARMR casual remark
CSATWR casualty ward
CSEIAL cosmetically
CSEMNE costermonger
CSFNUT Così Fan Tutte
CSHREE case-hardened
CSIGBM costing a bomb
CSNRYL Casino Royale
CSOLVN cost of living
CSOOIA cosmological
cosmopolitan[□]
CSOSNO customs union
CSRBRI Casare Borgia
CSTEAT cost the earth
CSYTNE Casey Stengel
CTATPT Citlaltépetl
CTCEIA catechetical
CTGNTC cytogenetics
CTGRAL categorially
CTHCCL cut the cackle
CTHIHO catch sight of
CTIGAG cutting gauge
CTIGOC cutting no ice
CTLDNR cotyledonary
CTLDNU cotyledonous
CTLHRE cattleherder
CTLTFC cut a lot of ice
CTNNME cetane number
CTNSET cut one's teeth
CTNSTC cut one's stick
CTNTRS cut and thrust
CTOIKN Catholic King
CTOMTE Cotton Mather
CTORFG city of refuge
CTRALN caterwauling
CTSEEO cytoskeleton
CTSRPI catastrophic
CTSUHN Côtes du Rhône
CTZNBN Citizens' Band
CUAEUL courageously
CUCLFA council of war
CUCLOS council house
CUCWRE churchwarden
CUDEOS could be worse
CUEANS cause sadness
CUEEER cause célèbre
CUELNS cause illness
CUERUL cause trouble
CUHARE crush barrier
CUHITR cough mixture
CUIUNS cautiousness
CULSNS churlishness
CUTATA court martial
court-martial
CUTELK courtierlike
CUTEPN Courtney Pine
CUTGIS count against
CUTGTE club together
CUTHCS count the cost
CUTRAC countermarch
CUTRAR counter-parry
CUTRCL Count Dracula
CUTREG counterweigh
counter-weigh
CUTREO counter-tenor
CUTRGN counter-agent
CUTRHC countercheck
CUTRHE counter-wheel
CUTRHR countercharm
CUTRLA counterplead
CUTRLI counter-claim
CUTRLS counterblast
CUTRON counterpoint
CUTROS counterpoise
CUTRRC counterbrace
CUTYAC country dance
CUTYOA countrywoman
CUTYOE country yokel
CUTYOS country house
CUTYUI country music
CVAEPO caveat emptor
CVLEEC civil defence
CVLEVC civil service
CVLEVN civil servant
CVLIET civil liberty
CVLNBN covalent bond
CVLSTO civilisation
CVLYWL cavalry twill
CVLZTO civilization
CVNGRE Covent Garden
CVRESO cover version
CVRHCL cover thickly
CVRHFE cover the feet
CVTUNS covetousness
CWOCSL Cawdor Castle
CWRLNS cowardliness
CYENSR Clytemnestra
CYNOTO crying out for
CYTGAH cryptography
CYTLAE crystal-gazer
CYTLLA crystal clear
crystal-clear
CYUTAC cry quittance
DAADLV dead-and-alive
DAAIAL dramatically
DAAMTO dead as mutton
DAANTS diamagnetism
DAAOLG drama college
DAAPAE deaf alphabet
DAAUGS dramaturgist
DABLLN dead-ball line
DACHLS de-alcoholise
DACHLZ de-alcoholize
DAESIE diadem spider
DAETCA dialectician
DAETLG dialectology
DAGTOR draughtboard
DAGTRO draught-proof
DAHEAT death penalty
DAHELN death-dealing
DAHNUL diaphanously
DAIGOE drawing power
DALNCD dialling code
DALNTN dialling tone
DALNUG deaf language
DAOAEU diatomaceous
DAODNK diamond snake
DAOEFE drag one's feet
DAOIAL diabolically
diatonically
DARMAI diagrammatic
DASAPL Dead Sea apple
DATALS draw to a close
DATCLT dearticulate
DATEAL draw the table
DATEOR draw the board
DATGTE draw together
DATOHS diastrophism
DATVTO deactivation
DBLTTN debilitating
DBLTTO debilitation
DBOHNU debt of honour
DBONTR debt of nature
DBSNSI do business in
DBTLWT do battle with
DBTTVL dubitatively
DCAENI declare unfit

DCAOSI dictatorship
DCECNO decrescendos
DCESNL decreasingly
DCFENT decaffeinate
DCLOAI decalcomania
DCLRTO deceleration
DCMISO decommission
DCMLON decimal point
DCMOAL decomposable
DCMRSO decompressor
DCNERT deconsecrate
DCNETN decongestant
DCNETV decongestive
DCNRLS decentralise
DCNRLZ decentralize
DCOJKL Doctor Jekyll
DCOMRA Doctor Moreau
DCOTEA Dock of the Bay
DCOWTO Doctor Watson
DCPEAL decipherable
DCPEMN decipherment
DCPTLS decapitalise
DCPTLZ decapitalize
DCPTTO decapitation
DCRMTS dichromatism
DCRTVL decoratively
DCSVNS decisiveness
DCTSNZ decitisenize
DCTZNZ decitizenize
DCYIAL dactylically
DDCBLT deducibility
DDCHDO dodecahedron
DDCIAL didactically
DDCTOA dedicational
DEAENU Dieu avec nous
DEAYIR dietary fibre
DECLTO de-escalation
DEDUNS dreadfulness
DEEEGN diesel engine
DEEIAL dietetically
DEFTRE deep-fat fryer
DENHWO dye in the wool
DEPOET dies profesti
DESNDW dressing-down
DESNGW dressing-gown
DEWTRE deepwatermen
DFAESL defeat easily
DFAINR deflationary
DFAINS deflationist
DFAISL defeat itself
DFARTO deflagration
DFEETA differentiae
differential
DFIUTE difficulties
DFMTRL defamatorily
DFNBLT definability
DFNTNS definiteness
DFNTVL definitively
DGAIAL dogmatically
DGEOLT dagger of lath
DGESOA digressional
DGESVL digressively
DGIGLD dégringolade
DGIGTC digging stick
DGNRTL degenerately
DGNRTN degenerating
DGNRTO degeneration
DGNRTV degenerative
DGNSLI dig oneself in
DGTZTO digitization
DHMDFE dehumidifier
DIEAAA drive bananas
DIEBLT driveability
DIEHOG drive through
DIHGOE Dwight Gooden
DIIGOC driving force
DIIGOE driving-power
DIKOMC drink too much
DIKRVN drink-driving
DIYUSL do-it-yourself
DJCENS dejectedness
DKOONU Duke of Omnium
DLASEV dolman sleeve
DLBRTL deliberately
DLBRTO deliberation
DLBRTV deliberative
DLCTNS delicateness
DLCTSE delicatessen❑
DLGTUL delightfully
DLHNRU dolphinarium
DLILGS deltiologist
DLIOUN dulciloquent
DLMTTO delimitation
DLMTTV delimitative
DLNUNL delinquently
DLPDTO dilapidation
DLQECN deliquescent
DLSVNS delusiveness
DLTATS dilettantish
dilettantism
DLTRNS dilatoriness
DLYITR dolly mixture
DMALNS damnableness
DMDLTO demodulation
DMEADO Dombey and Son
DMGEIE demagnetizer
DMLTRS demilitarise
DMLTRZ demilitarize
DMMNAN demi-mondaine
DMNAAL demoniacally
DMNEDE diminuendoes
DMNENS dementedness
DMNRLS demineralise
DMNRLZ demineralize
DMNSAL diminishable
DMNSMN diminishment
DMNTAL demonstrable
demonstrably
DMNTAO demonstrator
DMNTER domino theory
DMNTVL diminutively
DMOCES damson cheese
DMRAIN demarcations
DMRLZN demoralizing
DMSIAE domesticated
DMSIAL domestically
DMSIHL domestic help
DMSIWR domestic work
DNCERS denuclearise
DNCERZ denuclearize
DNEAAR Danse Macabre
DNEHAE dunderheaded
DNEJCE donkey jacket
DNEOTG Daniel Ortega
DNESER donkey's years
DNESGA danger signal
DNIDVE Denzil Davies
DNIGRV Dancing Brave
DNIGUE Dancing Queen
DNIHHR Denbighshire
DNIHPE Dennis Hopper
DNILLI Dennis Lillie
DNINLE Dennis Nilsen
DNLCGA Donald Coggan
DNLDNL dingle-dangle
DNLGAE Donald Glaser
DNLMCI Donald Michie
DNLSNE Donald Sinden
DNLWLI Donald Wolfit
DNMNTO denomination
DNNITO denunciation
DNNITR denunciatory
DNRLGS dendrologist
DNSIAL dynastically
DNSIEO Denis Diderot
DNSPSR Danish pastry
DNSRNL deny strongly
DNSUKT Denis Burkitt
DNTIGS do-nothingism
DNTRLS denaturalise
DNTRLZ denaturalize
DNTTVL denotatively
DNUCMN denouncement
DOALNE drop a clanger
DOEUMS do one's utmost
DOMRHN doom merchant
DPEGNE doppelgänger
DPEITO depreciation
DPEITR depreciatory
DPEITV depreciative
DPESNL depressingly
DPESRS depressurise
DPESRZ depressurize
DPHFIL depth of field
DPHFOU depth of focus
DPLMRS depolymerise
DPLMRZ depolymerize
DPLRHF Doppler shift
DPLTCS depoliticise
DPLTCZ depoliticize
DPNNEO do penance for
DPPLTO depopulation
DPRMNA departmental
DPSTOA depositional
DPTOGS diphthongise
DPTOGZ diphthongize
DRCACS direct access
DRCATO direct action
DRCLBU direct labour

DRCLUE dark-coloured
DRCNTO deracination
DRCOJC direct object
DRCOSI directorship
DRCSEC direct speech
DRETAE Derwent Water
DREWNO dormer window
DRGLTO deregulation
DRGTRL derogatorily
DRGTVL derogatively
DRIGAG Darling Range
DRKACL Derek Malcolm
DRKACT Derek Walcott
DRSESN Doris Lessing
DRSVNS derisiveness
DRVTOA derivational
DRVTVL derivatively
DRYAHN dirty washing
DRYANR dirty laundry
DRYLTE dirty clothes
DRYNJA Darby and Joan
DRYZNC Darryl Zanuck
DSACCS dispatch case
DSADRN discandering
DSAIFE dissatisfied
DSAMNS disharmonise
DSAMNZ disharmonize
DSANUL disdainfully
DSAPRS dispauperise
DSAPRZ dispauperize
DSARNL despairingly
DSBDEC disobedience
DSCHRD disaccharide
DSDATG disadvantage
DSDRTV desiderative
DSEADN disregarding
DSEADU disregardful
DSEAEO desperate for
DSEBAC dissemblance
DSEBRN dismembering
DSEEMN dishevelment
disseverment
DSEIAO disseminator
DSEIVN disbelieving
DSEPRT distemperate
DSEREE disheartened
DSESTO dispensation
DSESWT dispense with
DSETNL dissentingly
DSETPO dessertspoon
DSETTO dissertation
DSEUAL disreputable
disreputably
DSFETO disaffection
DSFIIT disaffiliate
DSGEAE desegregated
DSGEAL disagreeable
disagreeably
DSGEDU designer drug
DSGEMN disagreement
DSGEWT disagree with
DSGRGT disaggregate
DSHIGL Das Rheingold

DSIAEL dissipatedly
DSICNS distinctness
DSIEUL dispiteously
DSIIAL dissimilarly
DSIIAT dissimilar to
DSIIEL dispiritedly
DSILNR disciplinary
DSILSI discipleship
DSILTO distillation
DSISVL dismissively
DSIUAO dissimulator
DSLAEL displeasedly
DSLCMN displacement
DSLHRS desulphurise
DSLHRT desulphurate
DSLHRZ desulphurize
DSLNTO desalination
DSLOAC disallowance
DSLTNS desolateness
DSMARS disembarrass
DSMELS disembellish
DSMIUT disambiguate
DSNAGE disentangled
DSNEMN disinterment
DSNERT disintegrate
DSNETN disinfectant
DSNETO disinfection
DSNETV disincentive
DSNEUU disingenuous
DSNHNE disenchanted
DSNIIE desensitizer
DSNRCT disintricate
DSOAEL dislocatedly
DSOCRE disconcerted
DSODNL despondently
despondingly
discordantly
DSOEAL discoverable
DSOEYA Discovery Bay
DSOFTN discomfiting
DSOFTR discomfiture
DSOGMN dislodgement
DSOIAL despotically
DSOILS dissocialise
DSOILZ dissocialize
DSOITO despoliation
dissociation
DSONAL discountable
DSONCE disconnected
DSONEL disjointedly
DSONRT discount rate
DSOORN dishonouring
DSOPSR discomposure
DSOREU discourteous
DSORGN discouraging
DSORPE discographer
DSOSLT disconsolate
DSOSSE dispossessed
DSOTNE discontented
discontinued
DSPERN disappearing
DSPONE disappointed
DSPRVN disapproving

DSPRVO disapprove of
DSPYLU dasyphyllous
DSRAIE disorganised
disorganized
DSRBLT desirability
DSRBTO distribution
DSRBTV distributive
DSRCEL distractedly
DSRCIL destructible
DSRDTN discrediting
DSRENS discreetness
DSRETT disorientate
DSRIMN distrainment
DSRMNT discriminate
DSRNHS disfranchise
DSROCI Desert Orchid
DSRTNS discreteness
DSRTOA discretional
DSRTVL discretively
DSRVLG disprivilege
DSSALS disestablish
DSSEAE disaster area
DSSOIT disassociate
DSSRUL disastrously
DSUAIU disputatious
DSUBTV disturbative
DSUHRS disauthorise
DSUHRZ disauthorize
DSULFE disqualified
DSUMTO desquamation
DSUMTR desquamatory
DSUMTV desquamative
DSUSMN disbursement
DSUSTO disquisition
DSUSVL discursively
dissuasively
DSUTNL disgustingly
DSUTUL disgustfully
DSUTVL disruptively
DSYMTI dissymmetric
DTATNL detractingly
DTATVL detractively
DTEITO do the dirty on
DTEOOR do the honours
DTHORG Dutch courage
DTHRUH Dutch Draught
DTHUTO Dutch auction
DTMSEC detumescence
DTRIAL determinable
determinably
DTRIEB determined by
DTRIEL determinedly
DTRIET determined to
DTRNMN dethronement
DTROAE deteriorated
DTUCTO detruncation
DUHUTN doughnutting
DUKSLR drunk as a lord
DUKSNW drunk as a newt
DULBIE double boiler
DULCAG double-charge
DULDAE double-dealer
DULDCE double-decker

DULDGE double dagger
DULFUE double fluked
DULGAE double-glazed
DULSAE Douglas Bader
DULSDM Douglas Adams
DULTNU double-tongue
DULVSO double vision
DUSHMR Deutsche Mark
Deutsche mark
DUSUGE drug-smuggler
DUTUNS doubtfulness
DUVBSU Deus vobiscum
DVAINS deviationism
deviationist
DVDAPS David Campese
DVDARC David Garrick
DVDDNW divided in two
DVDEKA David Beckham
DVDELM David Bellamy
DVDIAD David Ricardo
DVDIBR David Hilbert
DVDNLN dividing-line
DVDNWL dividing wall
DVDOKE David Hockney
DVDRML David Trimble
DVLACR devil-may-care
DVLFMS devil of a mess
DVLILN Devil's Island
DVLPET developments
DVLSNS devilishness
DVNPTE diving petrel
DVNTCL divinity calf
DVNZTO divinization
DVRCTO divarication
DVREOR divorce court
DVRIET divertimenti
divertimento
DVRINR diversionary
DVRIUA diverticular
DVRIUU diverticulum
DVRIYN diversifying
DVSVNS divisiveness
DVTOAL devotionally
DWTEAC down the hatch
DWTERI down the drain
DXEGRO Dexter Gordon
DXRUNS dextrousness
EACLTO emasculation
EACPTO emancipation
EAEBTO exacerbation
EAECNL evanescently
EAGLSI evangelistic
EAGRTO exaggeration
EAITAU Erasistratus
EALNBL enabling bill
EAMBAC elasmobranch
EAMGEO Ewan McGregor
EAOTEE Eratosthenes
EAOTOE epanorthoses
EAPRTN exasperating
EAPRTO exasperation
EBAOMN emblazonment
EBEAIA emblematical
EBLIHN embellishing
EBODRN embroidering
EBRASN embarrassing
EBRUMN embarquement
EBTEMN embitterment
EBTLMN embattlement
EBUGOS embourgeoise
EBYLGS embryologist
EBZLMN embezzlement
ECADVR each and every
ECAGAL exchangeable
exchangeably
ECAGRT exchange rate
ECATNL enchantingly
ECCOEI encyclopedia
encyclopedic
ECEILG ecclesiology
ECEISE Ecclesiastes
ECEISI ecclesiastic
ECGTTO excogitation
ECIELN eccrine gland
ECIIAL enclitically
ECLPUE eucalyptuses
ECMASN encompassing
ECMNEO encomenderos
ECNRCT eccentricity
ECOCMN encroachment
ECODOA enchondromas
ECPAII encephalitis
ECPCAS escape clause
ECPLGS escapologist
ECRINS excursionise
excursionist
ECRINZ excursionize
ECRLMN encirclement
ECSHLI eschscholzia
ECTBLT excitability
ECUINR exclusionary
ECUITN excruciating
ECUITO excruciation
ECUTRA Encounter Bay
ECUTTO encrustation
EDAORN endeavouring
EDCRII endocarditis
EDEDAD Eddie Edwards
EDEOHA Eddie Cochran
EDFHLN end of the line
EDMTII endometritis
EDNEMN endangerment
EDPNMK end up in smoke
EDSEEA endoskeletal
EDSEEO endoskeleton
EECAGN ever-changing
EECSBK exercise bike
EEEIAL exegetically
EEETHU eleventh-hour
EEHNCR elephant cord
EEHNEL even-handedly
EEHNSA elephant seal
EEIGRS evening dress
evening-dress
EELSRA evenly spread
EEMSNR eleemosynary
EENRDS Eleonora Duse
EENRIB Eleanor Rigby
EENRRS Eleanor Cross
EENTRN eternity ring
EEPIYN exemplifying
EERTVL execratively
EETBLT electability
EETIAL electrically
EETIBU electric blue
EETIYN electrifying
EETMEE even-tempered
EETNSL exert oneself
EETOCP electroscope
EETOEE electrometer
EETOER electrometry
EETOHC electroshock
EETOHL electrophile
EETOIO event horizon
EETOLT electroplate
EETOPI electro-optic
EETOTB electron tube
EETOYI electrolysis
electrolytic
EEUOSI executorship
EEWDSU Eyes Wide Shut
EEYAJC every man Jack
EEYEDY every few days
EEYOFE every so often
EFCUTO effectuation
EFELMN enfeeblement
EFMNTL effeminately
EFNTOV enfant trouvé
EFOECN efflorescent
EFRECN effervescent
EFRLSL effortlessly
EFSVNS effusiveness
EGATTO engraftation
EGBNDC eggs Benedict
EGIHOA Englishwoman
EGNABE Elgin marbles
EGNDIE engine driver
engine-driver
EGNOEI Eugene Onegin
EGNOEL Eugene O'Neill
EGRVRS Edgard Varèse
EGTETL eighteenthly
EHATNN enheartening
EHBTOE exhibitioner
EHBTVL exhibitively
EHLRTN exhilarating
EHLRTO exhilaration
EHLRTV exhilarative
EHMRLT ephemerality
EHNDRA echinodermal
EHNIAI ethanoic acid
EHOCEC ethnoscience
EHOETI ethnocentric
EHOOIA ethnological
EHORPE ethnographer
EHORPI ethnographic
EHRAIN exhortations
EHSUDN echo-sounding
EHUTAV exhaust valve

EHUTVL	exhaustively
EIAEHR	Elizabeth Fry
EICRTO	evisceration
EIECIA	epideictical
EIEIAL	epidemically
EIEILG	epidemiology
EIETAL	evidentially
EIHHRO	Edith Wharton
EIHIWL	Edith Sitwell
EIHLMA	epithalamial
EIHLOA	epitheliomas
EIHNMN	epiphenomena
EIHRSO	Édith Cresson
EIIYIE	epididymides
EIMNEL	evil-mindedly
EIOIAL	episodically
EIOILS	editorialise
EIOILZ	editorialize
EIRMAI	epigrammatic
EISAET	Elias Canetti
EISELN	evil-smelling
EITMEE	evil-tempered
EITMLG	epistemology
EIUENS	Epicureanism
EIUUNS	exiguousness
EIYAIO	Emily Davison
EJYNSL	enjoy oneself
EJYRAL	enjoy greatly
ELCIAL	eclectically
ELGTNN	enlightening
ELNCMD	Ealing comedy
ELPIAL	elliptically
EMMROT	Edmé Mariotte
EMNHLE	Edmond Halley
EMNRBR	Edmund Rubbra
EMNWLE	Edmund Waller
EMNWLO	Edmund Wilson
EMTOPO	Emma Thompson
ENIPOL	E Annie Proulx
ENTACE	Ernst Haeckel
EOADAE	Edouard Manet
EOAELN	eco-labelling
EOBTNL	exorbitantly
EOEIAL	esoterically
	exoterically
EOHHLI	exophthalmia
	exophthalmic
EOHHLO	exophthalmos
EOHHLU	exophthalmus
EOHRAL	exothermally
EOIDNE	exotic dancer
EOIDSR	erotic desire
EOILGS	exobiologist
EOINLS	emotionalism
EOMUNS	enormousness
EOOERC	econometrics
EOOIAL	ecologically
	economically
EOPEIA	exospherical
EOSIAL	egoistically
EOUETR	emolumentary
EOUINR	elocutionary
	evolutionary
EOUINS	elocutionist
	evolutionism
	evolutionist
EPAEET	emplacements
EPAIAL	emphatically
EPATTO	explantation
EPCAIN	expectations
EPDETA	expediential
EPESMN	empressement
EPESOC	express coach
EPESRI	express train
EPESVL	expressively
EPIINS	explicitness
EPNETP	expanded type
EPNINR	expansionary
EPNINS	expansionism
	expansionist
EPOEVE	exploded view
EPOIUL	euphoniously
EPORAO	expropriator
EPOTTO	exploitation
EPOTTV	exploitative
EPRETA	experiential
EPRMNA	experimental
EPRMNE	experimenter
EPRRJC	export reject
EPRSSE	expert system
EPSTOA	expositional
EPSTRS	expose to risk
EPSTVE	expose to view
EPSTVL	expositively
EPSUAO	expostulator
EPTITO	expatriation
ERCCRS	Enrico Caruso
ERCREC	Eurocurrency
ERHCEC	earth science
ERHHKN	earth-shaking
ERPAPA	European plan
ERPITN	ear-splitting
ERRESG	error message
ERYLSN	early closing
ERYNLS	Early English
ERYNLT	early and late
ESAIAL	ecstatically
ESARHR	East Ayrshire
ESEDOA	eisteddfodau
ESEDOI	eisteddfodic
ESEILN	Easter Island
ESESNA	Easter Sunday
ESFISA	East Friesian
ESFLTO	exsufflation
ESKLRD	East Kilbride
ESLBOE	easily broken
ESLSLE	easily solved
ESNNBU	Eisen und Blut
ESNUNT	exsanguinate
ESOTEY	easy on the eye
ESRIEA	ex-serviceman
ESTDGS	easy to digest
ETAAAC	extravagance
ETAAAZ	extravaganza
ETAAIA	extramarital
ETACHL	entrance hall
	entrance-hall
ETAESO	extraversion
ETAESR	extrasensory
	extra-sensory
ETAEUL	extraneously
ETAGMN	estrangement
ETAIAL	extraditable
ETAOAO	extrapolator
ETATRA	extractor fan
ETECMN	entrenchment
ETEHGL	esteem highly
ETERNU	entrepreneur
ETETNL	entreatingly
ETMLGS	entomologise
	entomologist
ETMLGZ	entomologize
ETMOIE	extemporized
ETMPOI	entomophobia
ETNLMN	entanglement
ETNSEM	eat one's terms
ETNSOD	eat one's words
ETNUSE	extinguished
	extinguisher
ETOESO	extroversion
ETRANN	entertaining
ETRANR	entertainers
ETRCPO	exteroceptor
ETRIAE	exterminated
ETRIAO	exterminator
ETRINS	extortionist
ETRINT	extortionate
ETRISE	entertissued
ETRLEB	enthralled by
ETRNMN	enthronement
ETRRSN	enterprising
ETRYOC	enter by force
ETUBEI	eat humble pie
	eat humble-pie
ETUISI	enthusiastic
EUAINS	educationist
EUDSAC	equidistance
EUEIAL	ecumenically
EUEOON	eau de Cologne
	eau-de-cologne
EULBAO	equilibrator
EULOTN	equal footing
EULZTO	equalization
EUNMUL	equanimously
EUSREN	equestrienne
EUTRAL	equatorially
EUVCLT	equivocality
EUVCTN	equivocating
EUVCTO	equivocation
EUVLNL	equivalently
EUVLNT	equivalent to
EVSRPE	eavesdropper
EVSRSE	Elvis Presley
EWNORS	Edwin Forrest
EWNUYN	Edwin Lutyens
EWRALY	Edward Alleyn
EWRDBN	Edward De Bono
EWRFRE	Edward Forbes
EWRGBO	Edward Gibbon

EWRJNE Edward Jenner
EWRTLE Edward Teller
EWRTOA Edward Thomas
EWRVRO Edward Vernon
EWRWLO Edward Wilson
EYAHDA Ely Cathedral
EYHOYI erythromycin
EYOOIA etymological
EYTLGS Egyptologist
EZMLGS enzymologist
FAADIO feal and divot
FABDRS flat-bed press
FABYNL flamboyantly
FACIRD François Rude
FACSAD Francis Maude
FACSAL Francis Baily
FACSAO Francis Bacon
FACSRC Francis Crick
FACSRK Francis Drake
FADLNL fraudulently
FAEHOE flame-thrower
FAELTO flagellation
FAENZN fraternizing
FAGBLT frangibility
FAHOWR flash forward
flashforward
FAHRNS featheriness
FAIIUL flagitiously
FAKEMD Frank Kermode
FAKHTL Frank Whittle
FAKIAR Frank Sinatra
FAKNES frankincense
FAKNTI Frankenstein
FAKOSE Frank Loesser
FALSNS fearlessness
flawlessness
FAMBLT flammability
FAOFYN Fear of Flying
FATFEO Feast of Herod
FATGAH fractography
FATOAL fractionally
FATOAO fractionator
FATRNL flatteringly
FAZLME Franz Klammer
FBILTO fibrillation
FBIOYI fibrinolysin
FBLUNS fabulousness
FCATSU facial tissue
FCIIUL factitiously
fictitiously
FCINLS factionalism
fictionalise
FCINLZ fictionalize
FCLSNS fecklessness
FCLTTO facilitation
FCLZTO focalization
FCOYWE factory-owner
FCTEUI face the music
FDLAON fiddle around
FDLFDL fiddle-faddle
FDLSIK fiddlesticks
FDNNRI fide non armis
FDRLOR federal court
FDSCAE fidus Achates
FEBDBU feel bad about
FECGIN French Guiana
FECLTE French letter
FECPLS French polish
French-polish
FECWNO French window
FEDASA field marshal
FEDASI Freudian slip
FEDEAE Freddie Laker
FEDETR Freddie Starr
FEDFIE field officer
FEDFTD field of study
FEDLSE field glasses
field-glasses
FEDOOR field colours
FEDSNS fiendishness
FEEIAL frenetically
FEEISA Frederikstad
FEGTIE freightliner
FEGTRI freight-train
FEHSAN fresh as paint
FEICIE feel inclined
FEIJCO fuel injector
FEKSNS freakishness
FELMNE feeble-minded
FEOCAG free of charge
FEOEFC feed one's face
FEOEFE feel one's feet
FEOELG feel one's legs
FEOEOT feel one's oats
FESADN free-standing
FESRYO feel sorry for
FETDIA fleet admiral
FETEIC feel the pinch
FETIKN freethinking
free-thinking
FETNNS fleetingness
FETODA Fleetwood Mac
FEUNNS frequentness
FEZNCL freezing cold
FFYECN fifty per cent
FGRSAE figure skater
FGRTVL figuratively
FGTNCC fighting cock
FGTNFS fighting fish
FGTVNS fugitiveness
FGYUDN figgy pudding
FHGRCT Fehmgerichte
FIACML fait accompli
FIHEEB frightened by
FIHELN Faith Healing
faith healing
FIHUNS faithfulness
FIKHOG flick through
FIKRNL flickeringly
FININE friend in need
FINLFR friendly fire
FINLNS friendliness
FINLTL friendly talk
FINLWT friendly with
FIOIIO frigorificos
FIRBLA friar's balsam
FITERE faint-hearted
flint-hearted
FITNTC fail to notice
FITOLS frictionless
FLAELN foliage plant
FLAIUL fallaciously
FLBCUO fall back upon
FLBSEE filibusterer
FLCTTO felicitation
FLCTUL felicitously
FLEERE false-hearted
fille des rues
FLEINS false witness
FLEIPA false display
FLEITR false picture
FLEOOR false colours
FLGNUL fuliginously
FLHALN fall headlong
FLIGOE folding money
FLIGPR falling apart
FLLNSA Falklands War
FLOEEG full of energy
FLOTEE follow the sea
FLOWRE fellow worker
fellow-worker
FLTPEE fall to pieces
FLTRAE full-throated
FLUTDL fill untidily
FLYLDE fully fledged
fully-fledged
FMLAIE familiarized
FMLANM familiar name
FMLAWT familiar with
FMLCEI family credit
FMLCNO female condom
FMLCRL family circle
FMLDCO family doctor
FMNNNS feminineness
FMUPRO famous person
FNAETL fundamentals
FNAKHL finback whale
FNATCE fantasticoes
FNATCT fantasticate
FNBCAC find by chance
FNEBFE finger buffet
FNELCI fingerlickin'
FNEPIT fingerprints
FNEPPE finger puppet
FNESAE funnel-shaped
FNHFAE fan the flames
FNIUNS fancifulness
FNLZTO finalization
FNNEOS finance house
FNNILI financial aid
FNNILS financialist
FNOEFE find one's feet
FNOELG find one's legs
FNOTBU find out about
FNPESN find pleasant
FNSEWT finished with
FNSRTO fenestration
FNTOAL functionally
FNTOLS functionless

FNTOWR function word
FNYELN funny feeling
FNYNSL fancy oneself
FNYRDC Fanny Cradock
FOADOT foot-and-mouth
FOAERI fromage frais
FOBLBO football boot
FOCLTO flocculation
FODSEC frondescence
FODYOA from day to day
FOEPOL flower people
FOIHIT foolish-witty
FOIHRA Frobisher Bay
FOISML frolicsomely
FOIUTR floriculture
FOOAGN Frodo Baggins
FORRDE flour dredger
FOSNOU from sun to sun
FOTATM from that time
FOTEER from the heart
FOTESA frontiersman
FOTNDC floating dock
FOTSIC frontispiece
FRADEE Fernand Léger
FRADFE fore-and-after
FRADHD formaldehyde
FRADWR fire and sword
FRAENS forsakenness
FRAHRN forgathering
FRAMNS fore-admonish
FRBDMN forebodement
FRBDNL forebodingly
FRCONO for account of
FRDFAC Fort de France
Fort-de-France
FREAER force majeure
FREESK for pete's sake
FREHPC force the pace
FRENFA force and fear
FRENSA force one's way
FRENSL force oneself
FREOEV force to leave
FRERNL forbearingly
FRESAD Faroe Islands
FRESLE forset-seller
FRETNL forgettingly
FRETTO fermentation
FRETTV fermentative
FREUNS forcefulness
FRHAKN for the asking
FRHBTE for the better
FRHGOO for the good of
FRHIHL forthrightly
FRHMMN for the moment
FRHRCR for the record
FRHSBC furthest back
FRHSKO for the sake of
FRHTMO for the time of
FRIDNL forbiddingly
FRIGOS forcing-house
FRIHEL far-sightedly
FRILNS forcibleness
FRINGN foreign agent
FRINOD foreign goods
FRINRD foreign trade
FRIUEA furniture van
FRKOAL foreknowable
FRLNTM for a long time
FRLSNS formlessness
FRMNLF fireman's lift
FRNIAL forensically
FRNNTN for an instant
FRNOMN for enjoyment
FRNSAN for one's pains
FRODIE foreordained
FRSALN forestalling
FRSASI forestaysail
FRSENL foreseeingly
FRTEDN first reading
FRTEUA first refusal
FRTFIE first officer
FRTHWN first showing
FRTOCR first concern
FRUAEU furfuraceous
FRUTUL fortuitously
FSADHP fish and chips
FSEPRN foster parent
FSESLE fosset-seller
FSIAEB fascinated by
FSIIUL fastidiously
FSINLT fashion plate
FSINOE fashion model
FSINOS fashion house
FSONLN festoon blind
FTEFGR father-figure
FTESNA fathers-in-law
FTGERS fatigue-dress
FTSFDL fit as a fiddle
FUDTOA foundational
FUDZTO fluidization
FUFUTM four-four time
FULNUG foul language
FUPNYN fourpenny one
FUQATT Four Quartets
FURCRO fluorocarbon
FURSEC fluorescence
FURSOI fluoroscopic
FUSELN foul-smelling
FUTERN fruit-bearing
FUTETL fourteenthly
FUTETT fourth estate
FUTFRU fructiferous
FUTIDN fault-finding
FUTIHA fountainhead
fountain-head
FUTUNS fruitfulness
FUTVRU fructivorous
FVNAWN Favonian wind
FVRHRP fever therapy
FVRSNS feverishness
FVUEWT favoured with
FXDAIA fixed capital
FYNBIG flying bridge
FYNCLM flying column
FYNDCO flying doctor
FYNLZR flying lizard
FYNNSA fry in one's fat
FYNORG fly into a rage
FYNSUE flying saucer
GAAGEN Graham Greene
GAAQII Guadalquivir
GABRSL Glauber's salt
GACMTU glaucomatous
GADASI guardianship
GADCMR Grande Comore
GADGIS guard against
GADLUL glandulously
GADNSL guard oneself
GADUGO Grand Guignol
GADUHS grand duchess
GAELTE graveclothes
GAEUDA Grateful Dead
GAEUNS gracefulness
gratefulness
GAHCOE graphic novel
GAHLGS graphologist
GAIAEU graminaceous
GAICSL Glamis Castle
GAITRA gladiatorial
GAIUNS graciousness
GAIYNL gratifyingly
GAMGRE Graeme Garden
GAMTCS grammaticise
GAMTCZ grammaticize
GANGTV Gram-negative
GANLOO grain alcohol
GAOOAZ Giacomo Manzú
GAPNNS graspingness
GAPSTV Gram-positive
GARUNS glabrousness
GASELN glass ceiling
GASLWN glass-blowing
GASOEA Gladstone bag
GATEPI Giant Despair
GAUTUL gratuitously
GAYKIH Gladys Knight
GBILAR Gabriel Fauré
GBIMRE Goblin Market
GBLDGO gobbledegook
gobbledygook
gobblydegook
GBLIII go ballisitic
GBTEOR go by the board
GBTEOS go by the worse
GCETRO G K Chesterton
GDRYVN Godfrey Evans
GDWATR go down a storm
GEAIUL gregariously
GECAPL Greg Chappell
GEIHRW greyish-brown
GEMNIO Gherman Titov
GENADE Greenland Sea
GENIGR green fingers
GENODS Green Goddess
GENOLG Green College
GENRCR greengrocery
GEOMNE Gregor Mendel
GERLEO guerrilleros
GERSDK Greg Rusedski

GESMNE grease monkey
GESURE grey squirrel
GETATR Great Eastern
GETAVR Great Malvern
GETELE great-bellied
GETETR Great Western
GETMKE Great Smokies
GETRTI Great Britain
GETSPR greatest part
GETUBR great numbers
GETYAI Great Pyramid
GFFYIT go fifty-fifty
GFLTFS gefüllte fish
GFOTEA gift of the gab
GFROHN go for nothing
GGNIAL gigantically
GGNINS giganticness
GHNIHN go hand in hand
GIBATN grit blasting
GIDNTR Guildenstern
GIEBSA Guinea-Bissau
GIEFLI griseofulvin
GIEUNS guilefulness
GIGHOG going-through
GIGIHU going-without
GIGOWR going forward
GIIGIH guiding light
GILTNN guillotining
GIMMNU gain momentum
GIMRNL glimmeringly
GISETB Geissler tube
GISOOG Gainsborough
GISRNT gain strength
GITDTI go into detail
GITHDN go into hiding
GITRNL glisteringly
glitteringly
GITTEE go into the red
GIVUNS grievousness
GLAIAL galvanically
GLAOEE galvanometer
GLCLUE gold-coloured
GLEDRI Gilles de Rais
GLEFEC golden fleece
GLEHIE golden-haired
GLEPOE golden plover
GLETHT Gilbert White
GLETML Golden Temple
GLETNA Galveston Bay
GLEWTL golden wattle
GLFSBW goldfish bowl
GLIAEU gallinaceous
GLKARA go like a dream
GLSADR gold standard
GMLNGM gambling game
GMPEEV game preserve
GMPTLU gamopetalous
GMSASI gamesmanship
GNAMRA Gunnar Myrdal
GNAOIA genealogical
GNCLTL geniculately
GNERGR Ginger Rogers
GNFETO genuflection
GNRLTF general staff
GNRTIE generatrices
GNRTOA generational
GNRUNS generousness
GNWNLN Gondwanaland
GOALOR go on all fours
GOANTS geomagnetism
GOBEDN good breeding
GOEHAR Globe Theatre
GOEIAL geodetically
GOEIDM geodesic dome
GOEILN geodesic line
GOEIPE goose-pimples
GOEONA go one's own way
GOEQEI grotesquerie
GOERCA geometrician
GOERTE globetrotter
GOETEO go over the top
GOFEHL Geoffrey Hill
GOFEHW Geoffrey Howe
GOFTCR go off at score
GOGAIU good gracious
GOGBAL George Beadle
GOGCAB George Crabbe
GOGCCT George C Scott
GOGCRE George Carver
GOGCRO George Curzon
GOGGAA George Graham
GOGGLU George Gallup
GOGHNE George Handel
GOGLGT György Ligeti
GOGOWL George Orwell
GOGPRE George Porter
GOGPTO George Patton
GOGSIE Georges Bizet
GOGSOE George Stokes
GOGSUB George Stubbs
GOGUHE Georg Büchner
GOHMSR geochemistry
GOHMUE good-humoured
GOHSCS geophysicist
GOIEIA globigerinae
GOIOPR Goodison Park
GOIUNS gloriousness
GOKNPE glockenspiel
GOLSNS ghoulishness
GONBEL ground beetle
GONLSL groundlessly
GOOIAL geologically
gnomonically
GOOIIA geopolitical
GOPATI group captain
GOPFEE Group of Seven
GOPFOD group of words
GOPHRP group therapy
GORPIA geographical
GOSADN good standing
GOSRAL glossarially
GOTEHU go on the shout
GOTELN go on the blink
GOTETG go on the stage
GOTFIH go out of sight
GOTGTE grow together
GOTMEE good-tempered
GOTMRE growth market
GOTUTR Ghostbusters
GRADZN gormandizing
GRAIAL Germanically
GRARCA geriatrician
GRECNR garden centre
GREOEE Garden of Eden
GRESBR garden suburb
GREUNS gorgeousness
GRITVN Geraint Evans
GRKSAO Gary Kasparov
GRLRTE Gerald Ratner
GRLSAF Gerald Scarfe
GRMGEI gyromagnetic
GRNORC gerontocracy
GROSTE Gordon setter
GRRDBE Gerard Debreu
GRRKIE Gerard Kuiper
GSABIE gastarbeiter□
GSADNL Gus Macdonald
GSAMHE Gustav Mahler
GSEDWT go steady with
GSEMAL gas-permeable
GSFCTO gasification
GSICLM gossip column
GSIMNE gossip-monger
GSRCEI gastrocnemii
GSRCUC gastric juice
GSRNMS gastronomist
GTCAHN gatecrashing
GTEBET gather breath
GTEGON gather ground
GTETEE go to extremes
GTGENE get a guernsey
GTHFNE get the finger
GTHHNO get the hang of
GTHMTE get the mitten
GTHNEL get the needle
GTHOGT get through to
GTHSAE get the shakes
GTHWNO get the wind of
GTHWNU get the wind up
GTIGHR getting there
GTIHUC get-rich-quick
GTLAEU get cleaned up
GTLBRG Gottlob Frege
GTLGAL gateleg table
GTLNWT get along with
GTLSEE get flustered
GTNOEO get one over on
GTNOHP get into shape
GTNORG get into a rage
GTNRSE get undressed
GTNSAD get one's cards
GTNSOK get one's books
GTOEHA go to one's head
GTOEHR get somewhere
GTOELE get some sleep
GTPUEU get spruced up
GTRSEI get dressed in
GTSFET gates of death
GTTAEU get steamed up

Words marked □ can also be spelled with an initial capital letter

GTTCIT get stuck into
GTTEAL go to the walls
GTTEEI go to the devil
GTTEOL go to the polls
go to the world
GTTFWT get it off with
GTTREO get started on
GTUBEU get jumbled up
GTUSDO get outside of
GTWGLO get a wiggle on
GUDRAE go under water
GUGNNS grudgingness
GUHHTA Gough Whitlam
GUIFAE go up in flames
GUITEI go up in the air
GUSIFN glue-sniffing
GUSMNS gruesomeness
GUTNUL gluttonously
GVAEAT give a medal to
GVAERU give an earful
GVAEUT give a leg up to
GVAOST give a boost to
give a loose to
GVCEIT give credit to
GVEFCT give effect to
GVEIEC give evidence
GVGIAC give guidance
GVIAHR give it a whirl
GVICAG give in charge
GVIRTR give in return
GVIWLI give it wellie
GVNRST giving rise to
GVODRT give orders to
GVOELF give one's life
GVOEWR give one's word
GVPITT give points to
GVRMNA governmental
GVROSI governorship
GVTEEV give the heave
GVTEIL give the title
GVTEIT give the lie to
GVTELO give the elbow
GVTEOK give the works
GVTEOT give the nod to
GVTOHR give to others
GVWIHT give weight to
GYADOL Guys and Dolls
GYTGAH glyptography
HAEFRI heaven forbid
HAEHLA heave the lead
HAELBD heavenly body
HAELCT heavenly city
HAELNS heavenliness
HAENIH heave in sight
HAESBV heavens above
HAHNSL heathenishly
HAIYUL heavily built
HAMSRS headmistress
HAQATR headquarters
HARGSE head register
HASRAL heads or tails
HASRNE headshrinker
HATAMN heartwarming
heart-warming
HATCNR health centre
HATEDN heart-rending
HATGVN health-giving
HATIES heart disease
HATNHN heart and hand
HATNSU heart and soul
HATOER heart-to-heart
HATRAE heart-breaker
HATRSR health resort
HAUHRI hiatus hernia
HAYERE heavy-hearted
HAYRNE heavy drinker
HBACRU habeas corpus
HBIIAL hybridizable
HBIVGU hybrid vigour
HBLBBL hubble-bubble
HBOAAL hebdomadally
HBRIAL Hibernically
HBTAET habituated to
HBTANS habitualness
HBTBLT habitability
HBTOMN habit-forming
HCEUON hoc genus omne
HCNYOC hackney coach
HCORPI hectographic
HDALCA hydraulic ram
HDERME hedgetrimmer
HDESIL Huddersfield
HDINWL Hadrian's Wall
HDOAHS hydropathist
HDOEBM hydrogen bomb
HDOEBN hydrogen bond
HDOEHA hide one's head
HDOEUA Hydromedusae
HDOHOI hydrochloric
HDOHRP hydrotherapy
HDOIEI hydrokinetic
HDOLOI hydrofluoric
HDOOIA hydrological
HDORPE hydrographer
HDORPI hydrographic
HDORPS hydrotropism
HDOTTC hydrostatics
HDOUNN hydroquinone
HDOYAI hydrodynamic
HEACIA hierarchical
HEAOYI haematolysis
HELSNS heedlessness
HEOHLA haemophiliac
HEOLPI hieroglyphic
HEOOIA hierological
HFZLSA Hafez al-Assad
HGCLUE high-coloured
HGEIAL hygienically
HGEIRN higher in rank
HGEMGE hugger-mugger
HGETLC highest place
HGETON highest point
HGFDLT high fidelity
HGFLTN highfaluting
HGLGTN highlighting
HGLHGL higgle-haggle
HGLSRN highly-strung
HGLVLE highly valued
HGOOIA hagiological
HGORPI hagiographic
HGPESR high-pressure
HGPIRT high-priority
HGSIIE high-spirited
HGSUDN high-sounding
HGYEDN high-yielding
HIDESN hairdressing
HIHOLN height of land
HILSNS hairlessness
HIRCBL Heinrich Böll
HIRCLN Heinrich Lenz
HIRSOE hair restorer
HISLTE hair-splitter
HISRAT hair's-breadth
HLBCFO hold back from
HLDYAE holidaymaker
HLDYUM holiday tummy
HLEFOE helmet flower
HLESOE Halley's comet
HLETNR Heldentenöre
Helden-tenors
HLFRCU Hell-fire Club
HLIGAD holding hands
HLLSNS helplessness
HLMRTO half marathon
half-marathon
HLNHRA Helen Sharman
HLOAAU Heliogabalus
HLOETI heliocentric
HLOHLE holy of holies
HLOHRP heliotherapy
HLORPI heliographic
HLORPS heliotropism
HLORVR heliogravure
HLPCWT hold pace with
HLPIOE hold prisoner
HLSAOE half-seas-over
hold sway over
HLSASI helmsmanship
HLSIAL holistically
HLSTRA Holy Saturday
HLTELO hold the floor
HLTGTE hold together
HLTMEE half-timbered
HLTRNO hold to ransom
HLUIOE hallucinogen
HLWYON halfway point
HLWYOS halfway house
HLYODS Hollywoodise
HLYODZ Hollywoodize
HMASJL Hammarskjöld
HMCUTE home counties
HMEIGU hammering-out
HMESAI homoeostasis
HMFCTO humification
HMFOHM home from home
HMGTCI Homage to Clio
HMLGTO homologation
HMLSNS homelessness
HMMRHS homomorphism

HMMRHU homomorphous
HMNMUL homonymously
HMNOIT human society
HMNPEA hymenopteran
HMNTRA humanitarian
HMNZTO humanization
HMODNE Hammond Innes
HMRUNS humorousness
HMSCNS homesickness
HMTDMT Humpty-Dumpty
humpty-dumpty
HMTELE hump the bluey
HNADLV hand and glove
HNAONI hang around in
HNCAPN handclapping
HNEAOA hendecagonal
HNEKLE hunter-killer
HNEOWR henceforward
HNESRK hunger strike
hunger-strike
HNFRMS hindforemost
HNIAIS Henri Matisse
HNIEFG hang in effigy
HNIGOG hunting-lodge
HNIGOS hanging loose
HNKRHE handkerchief
HNOEAE hand-operated
HNOEFS hand over fist
HNOEHA hand over head
hang one's head
HNOEHN hand over hand
HNOKIL Hancock Field
HNQATR hindquarters
HNSBOE honest broker
HNSBTU hunt saboteur
HNSMNS handsomeness
HNSRAT hand's breadth
HNTESI henotheistic
HNTGTE hang together
HNUBIH honour bright
HNUSFA honours of war
HNVNUO Hans von Bülow
HNYABR Henry Raeburn
HNYACN Henry Mancini
HNYAGA Henry Vaughan
HNYECE Henry Mencken
HNYERV Henry Segrave
HNYHRA Henry Thoreau
HNYIGN Henry Higgins
HNYOGE honey-tongued
HNYREE honeycreeper
HNYTNE Henry Stanley
HNYUCL Henry Purcell
HOMNLN hoodman-blind
HPCIIA hypocritical
HPCLRT hypochlorite
HPCODI hypochondria
HPCRSI hypocoristic
HPESAC happenstance
HPGYEI hypoglycemia
HPLSNS hopelessness
HPOHRP hypnotherapy
HPOIAL hypnotically
hypnotizable
HPOOAU hippopotamus
HPORTS Hippocratise
HPORTZ Hippocratize
HPRCDT hyperacidity
HPRESO hypertension
HPRESV hypertensive
HPRHRA hyperthermal
HPRHRI hyperthermia
HPROEN Hyperboreans
HPRRPI hypertrophic
HPSAIA hypostatical
HPSLHT hyposulphite
HPTAAI hypothalamic
HPTAAU hypothalamus
HPTEIA hypothetical
HPTLGS hepatologist
HPYEES happy release
HPYOUK happy-go-lucky
HPYSAR happy as Larry
HRACRE Hernán Cortés
HRADHR here and there
HRAESU her name is mud
HRANES Hermann Hesse
HRANOD Hermann Bondi
HRANOE Hermann Vogel
HRCREC hard currency
HRDCMA hors de combat
HRDEVE hors d'oeuvres
HRDGIP Herod Agrippa
HRDIKN hard drinking
HRDNIA Herod Antipas
HRDODE hired soldier
HRDSIO hors de saison
HRDTMN hereditament
HRDTRL hereditarily
HREASI horsemanship
HREDUL horrendously
HREETC hermeneutics
HREETS hermeneutist
HREIAL hermetically
HREODE horse soldier
HRERDN horsetrading
horse-trading
HRETOS harvest mouse
HREUND harlequinade
HRFAUE hard-featured
HRFEIG hard feelings
HRFVUE hard-favoured
HRIAEA Hermitage Bay
HRIIAL horrifically
HRILNS horribleness
HRIOAC horrisonance
HRIOFR Harrison Ford
HRISIC herd instinct
HRIUTR horticulture
HRIYNL horrifyingly
HRLIAL heraldically
HRLPNE Harold Pinter
HRLSNS harmlessness
HRLTLA Harold Tilman
HRLWLO Harold Wilson
HRMAUE hard measures
HROIAL harmonically
HROIMA harmonic mean
HROIUL harmoniously
HROPET horn of plenty
HROSRC horror-struck
HRPRHS hire purchase
hire-purchase
HRSADN hard-standing
HRSCOE hard-sectored
HRSOLE hard shoulder
HRTBLT heritability
HRTCMB hard to come by
HRTOAE Horatio Gates
HRTPES hard to please
hard-to-please
HRYEOB Harry Secombe
HRYHOG hurry through
HRYNIL Harry Enfield
HRYTUA Harry S Truman
HRZNAL horizontally
HSAAIT hasta la vista
HSAESU his name is mud
HSAIAL Hispanically
HSAILS hispaniolise
HSAILZ hispaniolize
HSCMUE host computer
HSEETM hysterectomy
HSEIAL hysterically
HSIUAA Hosni Mubarak
HSOEEI histogenesis
histogenetic
HSOIAL historically
HSOOIA histological
HSTTNL hesitatingly
HTBDAC hit a bad patch
HTEADO hither and yon
HTHBTL hit the bottle
HTHCLT hot chocolate
HTHNKC hitch and kick
HTHNPS hitching post
HTHTAE hatchet-faced
HTOPLE hot gospeller
HTRCCI heterocyclic
HTRGMU heterogamous
HTRGNU heterogonous
HTRLGU heterologous
HTRMRH heteromorphy
HTRMRU heteromerous
HTRNMU heteronomous
HTRPAI heteroplasia
HTRPAT heteroplasty
HTRPYL heterophylly
HTRSXA heterosexual
HTRSXS heterosexism
heterosexist
HTRTCI heterotactic
HTRTOH heterotrophy
HTRZGT heterozygote
HTRZGU heterozygous
HTTFWT hit it off with
HUDTNU hound's-tongue
HUEAMN housewarming
house-warming

HUEEPN housekeeping
HUEFAD house of cards
HUEFOD House of Lords
HUEHUE housey-housey
HUEITN house-sitting
HUEOTR haute couture
HUERAE housebreaker
house-breaker
HUERIE house-trained
HUEUGO house-surgeon
HUEUSN haute cuisine
HUEUTN house-hunting
HUSANS haussmannise
HUSANZ haussmannize
HVAAAI have as a basis
HVAAFI have an affair
HVAAGA have as an goal
HVAAOB have as a hobby
HVAAWT have a way with
HVAEFC have an effect
HVAEGO have an edge on
HVAHRI have a share in
HVAIEA have a nice day
HVAIHT have a right to
HVALTE have a flutter
HVAOKE have a look-see
HVARNE have arranged
HVARSO have a crush on
HVBUHI have bought it
HVCAGO have charge of
HVDNWT have done with
HVEOGO have enough of
HVICMN have it coming
HVISEN have its being
HVNAHN having a thing
HVNAOO having a lot on
HVNLTL having little
HVNNLF have none left
HVOEGA have one's goal
HVOEHM have one's home
HVOTEI have on the hip
HVRCUS have recourse
HVSAEO have space for
HVTDWT have to do with
HVTEAO have the law on
HVTEER have the heart
HVTEOO have the job of
HVTEOS have the worse
HVTESO have the use of
HVTOAE have two faces
HWRCRE Howard Carter
HWRHGE Howard Hughes
HWROTN Hawk Roosting
IAABRI Isaiah Berlin
IAAIYA in a family way
IAARAT in a fair way to
IACBLT irascibility
IACIEO Isaac Dineson
IACLEI Isaac Albéniz
IACRAC in accordance
IACRTL inaccurately
IACRWT in accord with
IACSIL inaccessible
inaccessibly
IADBLT inaudibility
IADTOT in addition to
IAEFFL in a kerfuffle
IAEIHU in an evil hour
IAERAE image-breaker
IAEUTL inadequately
IAGRTO inauguration
IAHRTM in a short time
IAIHSO in a tight spot
IALUNM in all but name
IAMSIL inadmissible
inadmissibly
IAOAVN Italo Calvino
IAODIH in a good light
IAODWA in a cold sweat
IAPIAL inapplicable
inapplicably
IAPLAL inappellable
IAPSTL inappositely
IASIIU inauspicious
IATAFC in actual fact
IATALF in actual life
IATCLC inarticulacy
IATCLT inarticulate
IATEET in at the death
IATREE Ivan Turgenev
IAUDLU iracundulous
IAVREC inadvertence
inadvertency
IAWNLN in a twinkling
IBNOEI in banco regis
ICDNAL incidentally
ICESNL increasingly
ICGIAC incognizance
ICGIAL incognizable
ICHRNL incoherently
ICIIAE incriminated
ICLUAL incalculable
incalculably
ICMAAL incomparable
incomparably
ICMAIL incompatible
incompatibly
ICMAIO in comparison
ICMEEC incompetence
incompetency
ICMISO in commission
ICMLTL incompletely
ICMOIU incommodious
ICMUAL incommutably
incomputable
ICNECN incandescent
ICNEEC in conference
ICNEIN inconvenient
ICNEUN inconsequent
ICNIEC in confidence
incontinence
incontinency
ICNIRS incendiarism
ICNITN inconsistent
ICNLSO in conclusion
ICNLSV inconclusive
ICNOAL inconsolable
inconsolably
ICNRST in contrast to
ICNRTO incineration
ICNTNL inconstantly
ICNUAL inconsumably
ICOSRE incrossbreed
ICPBLT incapability
ICPCTT incapacitate
ICRBLT incurability
ICREAE incarcerated
ICRIIL incorrigible
incorrigibly
ICRNTO incoronation
ICROAE incorporated
ICROET incorporeity
ICSVNS incisiveness
ICUIUL incautiously
ICUTTO incrustation
ICVLTE incivilities
IDAAEL India Pale Ale
IDAAOI Indianapolis
IDARNE Indian runner
IDASME Indian summer
IDBENS indebtedness
IDCIAL indeclinably
IDCRNT indoctrinate
IDCRUL indecorously
IDCSVL indecisively
IDCTTL induce to talk
IDCTVL indicatively
IDERPA Indo-European
IDEWTR in deep waters
IDFACO in defiance of
IDFAIL indefeasible
indefeasibly
IDFEEC indifference
IDFNIL indefensible
indefensibly
IDFNTL indefinitely
IDGNUL indigenously
IDGSIL indigestible
indigestibly
IDHSEC indehiscence
IDLCTL indelicately
IDPNEC independence☐
independency
IDRCNS indirectness
IDRGNH Indira Gandhi
IDSICL indistinctly
IDSILN indiscipline
IDSOUL indissoluble
indissolubly
IDSRAL industrially
IDSREL indiscreetly
IDSRTL indiscretely
IDSRTO indiscretion
IDSUAL indisputable
indisputably
IDVDAL individually
IDXIKN index-linking
IEAIAL ineradicable
ineradicably

Words marked ☐ can also be spelled with an initial capital letter

IEATCT inelasticity
IEATTD inexactitude
IEFBLT ineffability
IEFCAL ineffaceable
ineffaceably
IEFCEC inefficiency
IELZTO idealization
IEOUNL ineloquently
IEPDEC inexpedience
inexpediency
IEPESV inexpressive
IEPGAL inexpugnably
IEPIAL inexplicable
inexplicably
IEPOMN in employment
IEPREC inexperience
IEPRNS inexpertness
IETFAL identifiable
IETFWT identify with
IETIAL inextricable
inextricably
IETOAL ideationally
IETTCR identity card
IFAINR inflationary
IFAINS inflationism
inflationist
IFAMTO inflammation
IFAMTR inflammatory
IFBLTO infibulation
IFCEWT infected with
IFCIUL infectiously
IFETOA inflectional
IFEUNL infrequently
IFIGMN infringement
IFLCTU infelicitous
IFLRTO infiltration
IFNFTL in fine fettle
IFNIIA infanticidal
IFNIUA infundibular
IFNSHO infant school
IFNTNS infiniteness
IFNTVL infinitively
IFTIMN infotainment
IGAITN ingratiating
IGAITO ingratiation
IGOHAT in good health
IGOIUL ingloriously
IGVRMN in government
IHBTTO inhabitation
IHROIU inharmonious
IHSIAL inhospitable
inhospitably
IHSUTN in his buttons
IHTUSI in hot pursuit
IHUDOO I should cocoa
IHUDOR I should worry!
IIAONN Irina Rodnina
IIECNL iridescently
IIHRUH Irish Draught
IISNRS idiosyncrasy
IIUTUL iniquitously
IJDCAL injudicially
IJNTVL injunctively
IKNRLE inking roller
ILAUEL ill-naturedly
ILBRLS illiberalise
ILBRLT illiberality
ILBRLZ illiberalize
ILDIEL ill-advisedly
ILEEMN ill-beseeming
ILGBLT illegibility
ILGCLT illogicality
ILGTMC illegitimacy
ILGTMT illegitimate
ILKMNE in like manner
ILMNTN illuminating
ILMNTO illumination
ILMNTV illuminative
ILMZTO Islamization
ILOCAE ill-concealed
ILOCIE ill-conceived
ILRAMN ill-treatment
ILSRTO illustration
ILSRTR illustratory
ILSRTV illustrative
ILSVNS illusiveness
ILTRTL illiterately
ILWPRT in low spirits
IMAUAL immeasurable
immeasurably
IMCLTL immaculately
IMDRTL immoderately
IMDRTO immoderation
in moderation
IMMRAL immemorially
IMNEKN Immanuel Kant
IMNGOI immunoglobin
IMNLGS immunologist
IMNSSE immune system
IMNZTO immunization
IMTBLT immutability
IMTRAL immaterially
IMTRNS immatureness
IMVBLT immovability
IMYEDE it may be added
INCECA Ian McGeechan
INNOEC Ion Antonescu
INTIIU innutritious
INTOCI ignition coil
IOAEAE isolated area
IOAINS isolationism
isolationist
IOARUL idolatrously
IOCADN iron-cladding
IODNTL inordinately
IOEINL inobediently
IOEPCE in one's pocket
IOESNE in one's senses
IOETAK in one's tracks
IOHOAL isochronally
IOHRAL isothermally
IOHROD in other words
IOIMTI isodiametric
IOIOPI isodimorphic
IOLNKO I wouldn't know
IOOLSI iconoclastic
IOPSTO in opposition
IORCAD Ivor Richards
IOSKRK Igor Sikorsky
IPATTO implantation
IPDMNA impedimental
IPEAIN imprecations
IPEEEC in preference
IPENTO impregnation
IPESVL impressively
IPIAIN implications
IPIINS implicitness
IPIOMN imprisonment
IPLEUE impulse buyer
IPLTNS impoliteness
IPNEAL imponderable
IPNTAL impenetrable
impenetrably
IPNTNL impenitently
IPOHAT in poor health
IPOIEC improvidence
IPRAEC impermanence
impermanency
IPRETO imperfection
IPRETV imperceptive
IPREUT in perpetuity
IPRIAC impertinance
IPRIEC impertinence
IPRIIN impercipient
IPRILT impartiality
IPRIUA in particular
IPRIUL imperviously
IPROAL impersonally
IPROAO impersonator
IPRSAL imperishable
imperishably
IPRTVL imperatively
IPSHMT imposthumate
IPTEHO it pitieth you
IPTGNU impetiginous
IPTTVL imputatively
IPVRSE impoverished
IQIEBU inquire about
IQIEFE inquire after
IRBTAL irrebuttable
IRDEAL irredeemable
irredeemably
IRFAAL irrefragable
irrefragably
IRFRAL irreformable
irreformably
IRGLRT irregularity
IRLTOT in relation to
IRLTVL irrelatively
IRLVNL irrelevantly
IRMDAL irremediable
irremediably
IRMSIL irremissible
IRPAAL irrepealably
IRPOAL irreprovably
IRSETV irrespective
IRSLAL irresolvably
IRSLTL irresolutely
IRSLTO irresolution

IRSSIL irresistible
irresistibly
IRTBLT irritability
IRTOAL irrationally
IRTOPC in retrospect
IRVRIL irreversible
irreversibly
IRVRNL irreverently
ISALDY it's early days
ISALTO installation
ISCESO in succession
ISETNL inspectingly
ISETRA inspectorial
ISETRT inspectorate
ISFEAL insufferable
insufferably
ISFIIN insufficient
ISILTO instillation
ISLBIU insalubrious
ISLBLS insolubilise
ISLBLT insolubility
ISLBLZ insolubilize
ISMNTO insemination
ISMOEC insomnolence
ISNPRO insane person
ISOTRE in short order
ISPESR it's a pleasure
ISRCIL instructible
ISRCIN instructions
ISRCRS instructress
ISRETO insurrection
ISRMNA instrumental
ISSESO in suspension
ISUINL insouciantly
ISYUEA it's my funeral
ITARNU intrapreneur
ITASGN intransigent
ITASTV intransitive
ITATRN intrauterine
ITEAAC in the balance
ITEAEA in the same way
ITEAHO in the fashion
ITEAIO in the habit of
ITEETO in the teeth of
ITEHCO in the thick of
ITEHLO in the whole of
ITEHPO in the shape of
ITEIHO in the light of
in the sight of
ITEINS intrepidness
ITEISO in the midst of
ITEITR in the picture
ITELDY in the old days
ITENEI in the interim
ITEODO in the mood for
ITEOEO in the power of
ITEOGU in the long run
ITEONE in the boonies
ITEONN in the morning
ITEPNI in the open air
ITEREO in the order of
ITEUNN in the running
ITEVNO in the event of
ITEXRM in the extreme
ITEYON in the by-going
ITGAPR integral part
ITIRGR in this regard
ITISCT intrinsicate
ITIUNL intriguingly
ITLETA intellectual
ITLIEC intelligence
ITLIGO I'm telling you
ITLIIL intelligible
intelligibly
ITLRNL intolerantly
ITMDTN intimidating
ITMDTO intimidation
ITMDTR intimidatory
ITMEAC intemperance
ITMETV intempestive
ITMRTL intemerately
ITMSEC intumescence
ITNIYN intensifying
ITOESO introversion
ITOISO intromission
ITOUIL introducible
ITOUTO introduction
ITOUTR introductory
ITREAE interrelated
ITREEC interference
ITREIN intervenient
ITREIR intermediary
ITREIT intermediate
ITRELT interpellate
ITRENM interregnums
ITRESO intercession
ITRESR intercessory
ITRETA intertextual
ITRETN intercepting
intersecting
ITRETO interception
interjection
intersection
intervention
ITRETV interceptive
ITRHNE interchanged
ITRIAL interminable
interminably
ITRIKN interlinking
ITRISO intermission
ITRITN intermittent
ITRITO interdiction
ITRITR interdictory
intermixture
ITROAO interrogator
ITROIT interfoliate
ITROKN interlocking
ITROMN intercommune
ITRONC interconnect
ITROUO interlocutor
ITROVR interconvert
ITRRAH interwreathe
ITRRTV interpretive
ITRSEI interested in
ITRSEL interestedly
ITRTLA interstellar
ITRUCO internuncios
ITRURN intercurrent
ITRUTN interrupting
ITRUTO interruption
ITRUTV interruptive
ITSUCP intussuscept
ITXCTN intoxicating
ITXCTO intoxication
IVGLTO invigilation
IVGNTO invagination
IVGRTN invigorating
IVGRTO invigoration
IVILMN inveiglement
IVLDTN invalidating
IVLDTO invalidation
IVLEAL invulnerable
invulnerably
IVNBRI Irving Berlin
IVRERT invertebrate
IVRESO inverted snob
IVSBEN invisible ink
IVSBLT invisibility
IVSIAO investigator
IVTRTL inveterately
IWAADO in weal and woe
IWSOHN it was nothing
JACAFR Joan Crawford
JADBFE Jean Dubuffet
JAHMUA Joachim Murat
JANLME Joanna Lumley
JANMRA Jeanne Moreau
JAPNEE Jean Poncelet
JASBLU Jean Sibelius
JATNUL Jean Tinguely
JBLTAN Jubilate Agno
JCBLDE Jacob's ladder
JCBPTI Jacob Epstein
JCIOFC jack-in-office
JCITEO jack-in-the-box
JCNCLU Jack Nicklaus
JCSEPR Jack Sheppard
JCSNIL Jacksonville
JCUSAI Jacques David
JCUSOO Jacques Monod
JDPROT jodhpur boots
JHAASF John Atansoff
JHBRYA John Berryman
JHBTEA John Betjeman
JHCANE John Charnley
JHCLRN John Coltrane
JHCRSI John Christie
JHEISO John Ericsson
JHFECE John Fletcher
JHFEND John F Kennedy
JHFLTF John Falstaff
JHGLIN John Galliano
JHHMHY John Humphrys
JHHRCE John Herschel
JHJRDC John Jarndyce
JHLLUN John Lilburne
JHMCRH John McCarthy
JHMRIE John Mortimer
JHNBOD Johnny B Goode

Code	Word
JHNCUF	Johann Cruyff
JHNEBR	Johannesburg
JHNFCT	Johann Fichte
JHNGEH	Johann Goethe
JHNIKA	Jahangir Khan
JHNRHO	John Northrop
JHNUIA	Johnny Unitas
JHOLYE	John of Leyden
JHPECT	John Prescott
JHPRHN	John Pershing
JHSCLN	John Suckling
JHSSIN	John Sessions
JHSTEB	John Sotherby
JHTAOT	John Travolta
JHVNRG	John Vanbrugh
JHWCIF	John Wycliffe
JHWIGF	John Whitgift
JHWITE	John Whittier
JHWLIM	John Williams
JITCON	joint account
JITETR	joint venture
JITGTE	join together
JLAAEO	Julia Cameron
JLAHXE	Julian Huxley
JLAOET	Julia Roberts
JLELIE	jolies laides
JLENRW	Julie Andrews
JLSAAI	Jules Mazarin
JLSAGE	Jules Maigret
JLUCEA	Julius Caesar
JMKNAT	Jomo Kenyatta
JMOEBI	jump one's bail
JMSACA	James Mancham
JMSADI	James Baldwin
JMSAEO	James Cameron
JMSAIO	James Madison
JMSALA	James Earl Ray
JMSAMT	James Nasmyth
JMSAWL	James Maxwell
JMSEDL	James Weddell
JMSHRE	James Thurber
JMSKNE	James Skinner
JMSLVL	James Clavell
JMSOWL	James Boswell
JMSTWR	James Stewart
JMTEEO	jump the besom
JMTEUU	jump the queue
JMUAHI	Jammu-Kashmir
JMYABC	Jimmy Tarbuck
JMYONR	Jimmy Connors
JMYRAE	Jimmy Greaves
JNIBRE	Jan Tinbergen
JNLJNL	jingle-jangle
JNMTHL	Joni Mitchell
JNSAIB	Jonas Savimbi
JNTAKO	Janet Jackson
JRDIMN	Jared Diamond
JRMIAC	Jeremy Isaacs
JRMPXA	Jeremy Paxman
JRMTOP	Jeremy Thorpe
JRSIAL	juristically
JRSIPR	Jurassic Park
JRSITO	jurisdiction
JRSITV	jurisdictive
JRSOSL	jurisconsult
JRSRDN	jurisprudent
JRYAWL	Jerry Falwell
JSCREA	José Carreras
JSEAKO	Jesse Jackson
JSECNA	Jasper Conran
JSFAII	Jusuf Habibie
JSIAAG	Jessica Lange
JSIIAL	jesuitically
JSIIAO	justificator
JSIMRY	Justin Martyr
JSLKTA	just like that
JSPCNA	Joseph Conrad
JSPDME	Joseph Damien
JSPHLE	Joseph Heller
JSPHOE	Joseph Hooker
JSPLSE	Joseph Lister
JSPNEC	Joseph Niepce
JSPPXO	Joseph Paxton
JSPSAI	Joseph Stalin
JSPTRE	Joseph Turner
JSPWIH	Joseph Wright
JSSOLG	Jesus College
JSSRMG	José Saramago
JUNLSI	journalistic
JUNYAE	journey-bated
JVNLNS	juvenileness
JVNSEC	juvenescence
JYEOVL	Jayne Torvill
JYORSE	Jay Forrester
JZWRIR	Jazz Warriors
KAEKUA	Kwame Nkrumah
KBEOLG	Keble College
KCIWCI	kickie-wickie
KCTEAI	kick the habit
KCUSAR	kick upstairs
KDIWNI	kiddiewinkie
KEAAFO	keep away from
KEAEEU	keep an eye out
KEAOKU	keep a lookout
KEBECE	knee-breeches
KECOKN	knee-crooking
KEDRAE	Kielder Water
KEDSAC	keep distance
KEFIWT	keep fair with
KEFOHR	keep from harm
KEGOTM	keep good time
KEOECO	keep one's cool
KEOEHA	keep one's head
KEOEMN	keep one's mind
KEOEWR	keep one's word
KEORCR	keep on record
KEPCWT	keep pace with
KETEEC	keep the peace
KETEIL	keep the field
KETEOS	keep the house
KETEUE	keep the rules
KETMNA	kleptomaniac
KEUTDT	keep up to date
KIHART	Keith Jarrett
KIHAUT	Krishnamurti
KIHERN	knight-errant
KIOFLO	Keiron Fallon
KISRNE	klipspringer
KITASN	Kristiansand
KLBICE	kill by inches
KLBPIO	kill by poison
KLCUTS	kill-courtesy
KLEIOU	Kylie Minogue
KLENCT	Kilkenny cats
KLIOCP	kaleidoscope
KLWTHU	kilowatt hour
KMALHR	Kimball O'Hara
KMDDAO	Komodo dragon
KNALRN	Konrad Lorenz
KNEGRE	kindergarten
KNEHAE	Kenneth Baker
KNEHLE	Kenneth Olsen
KNEHLR	Kenneth Clark
KNETEI	kinaesthesia
	kinaesthesis
	kinaesthetic
KNOBAT	king of beasts
KNOMTL	king of metals
KNSEAI	Kingsley Amis
KNSIHA	King's highway
KNSNLS	King's English
KNSOLG	King's College
KNSONE	King's Counsel
KNYVRT	Kenny Everett
KOKNCP	knocking copy
KOKNDW	knocking-down
KOKNSO	knocking shop
	knocking-shop
KOLDAL	knowledgable
	knowledgably
KOTECR	know the score
KOTEOE	know the ropes
KOWAII	know what it is
KRCWSE	kirschwasser
KRELIO	Kyrie eleison
KRHTVU	kurchatovium
KRLSAD	Kuril Islands
KRMRHN	kerb-merchant
KROIEI	karyokinesis
KRSHLE	Karl Schiller
KRTGNU	keratogenous
KRTKNW	Kiri Te Kanawa
KRVNEU	Kurt Vonnegut
KRWLHI	Kurt Waldheim
KTAOEE	katharometer
KTEJME	katzenjammer
KTHNEC	kitchen-wench
KTHNHI	kitchen chair
KTKNBL	Kota Kinabalu
KTLOFS	kettle of fish
KTRNWT	Katerina Witt
KTYOFE	Kitty Godfree
KUKENE	knuckle under
KVNOTE	Kevin Costner
KYINTR	key signature
LAAAFO	lead away from
LAEHRO	leave the room
LAENCL	leave one cold
LAENUN	leave in ruins

LAEODA leave for dead
LAEUCL leave quickly
LAEUEL leave quietly
LAEWIE leader-writer
LAFOGN leap-frogging
LAGRBN Luang Prabang
LAHUNS loathfulness
LAIGAG loading gauge
LAIGCO leading actor
LAIGIH leading light
LAIGOS leaping-house
LAIPAE lead in prayer
LANYER learn by heart
LASNLG leads and lags
LBDNUL libidinously
LBERVS l'Abbé Prévost
LBRLAT Liberal Party
LBRLSI liberalistic
LBRNHN labyrinthine
LBUOLV labour of love
LBUSVN labour-saving
LCAECS lack an excuse
LCEIMT Lucretia Mott
LCETWL Lucie Attwell
LCEYPI lickety-split
LCIADC lacrimal duct
LCLZTO localization
LCMBLT locomobility
LCMTVT locomotivity
LCNARE Lucinda Green
LCNELT license plate
LCNIUL licentiously
LCOCAG lack of change
LCOEEG lack of energy
LCOELP lick one's lips
LCRMSL lachrymosely
LCSRNC Lucas Cranach
LCTEIS lick the birse
LCTGTE lock together
LCTNTI Lichtenstein
LCYUIN Lucky Luciano
LDIEHR Ludwig Erhard
LDIGOS lodging house
LDLKNS ladylikeness
LDOCSL Ludlow Castle
LDSLPE lady's slipper
lady's-slipper
LEFHLN lie of the land
LENATO lie in wait for
LETABR Lee Strasberg
LETNNR lieutenantry
LFADET life-and-death
LFHNEL left-handedly
LFITEI left in the air
LFLKNS lifelikeness
LFLSNS lifelessness
LFOCRS life of Christ
LFSINE life sciences
LFSNEC life sentence
LFTELO lift the elbow
LGBIUL lugubriously
LGCICI logic circuit
LGDEAU logodaedalus
LGLDIE legal adviser
LGLOIA legal holiday
LGLSTO legalisation
LGLZTO legalization
LGOEIG leg-coverings
LGTERE light-hearted
LGTIGO lightning-rod
LGTKNE light-skinned
LGTMTL legitimately
LIEISO Leif Eriksson
LIIAVN Luigi Galvani
LISRAR laisser-faire
LISZAR laissez-faire
LKALNS likeableness
LKAUAI like a lunatic
LKAYHN like anything
LKBLHS Lake Balkhash
LKGLDS like gold dust
LKHYOA like hey-go-mad
LKMCIA Lake Michigan
LKMGIR Lake Maggiore
LKODOT like old boots
LKSPRO Lake Superior
LKTBRA Lake Tiberias
LKTTCC Lake Titicaca
LKVCOI Lake Victoria
LKVRMC like very much
LKWNIE Lake Winnipeg
LLIOLD lollipop lady
LLIUIN Lilliputians
LLORGD Lollobrigida
LLQELS Lalique glass
LMETDN Lamberto Dini
LMNAIN Lamentations
LMNSEC luminescence
LMNUFU luminous flux
LMOACN limbo-dancing
LMOOIA limnological
LNADHR long-and-short
LNBOKN lino blocking
LNCAWC Lynn Chadwick
LNDANU long-drawn-out
LNELTL lanceolately
LNENAE lantern-jawed
LNEWNO lancet window
LNIGIL landing-field
LNIGRF landing craft
landing-craft
LNIGTG landing-stage
LNIGTI landing-strip
LNISLT lend itself to
LNIUAL lenticularly
LNIUIA longitudinal
LNOATC line of attack
LNOATO line of action
LNOHLA Land o' the Leal
LNONHR Lincolnshire
LNONRE Lincoln green
LNRASI lunar caustic
LNSADN long-standing
LNSALN Linus Pauling
LNSMNS lonesomeness
LNTGTE link together
LNTODY length of days
LNTOTM length of time
LNUDCA langue de chat
LNUFAC lingua franca
LNUGLS languageless
LNURUL languorously
LOADIO Leonard Nimoy
LOADOE Leonard Cohen
LOAKLN Leo Baekeland
LODRDE Lloyd Bridges
LOEITN loose-fitting
LOEJSI Lionel Jospin
LOEONE loose-jointed
LOERCI Lionel Richie
LOEYOE loosely woven
LOIEHM Leonine rhyme
LOIGFE looking after
looking-after
LOIGLS looking-glass
LOODLO Leopold Bloom
LOOTOE lookout tower
LPIENS lopsidedness
LPOEHL leptocephali
LPOOAI leptosomatic
LQAIUL loquaciously
LQEATO liquefaction
LQIAST liquid assets
LRCHAR Lyric Theatre
LREERE large-hearted
LRIGBU larking about
LSAJSE loss adjuster
LSAVNE less advanced
LSBETE lust-breathed
LSFROD lost for words
LSFRWL last farewell
LSGEED lasagne verde
LSIIUL lasciviously
LSIUNS lusciousness
LSLSNS listlessness
LSOECO lose one's cool
LSOEHA lose one's head
LSOEHI lose one's hair
LSOELF lose one's life
LSOESA lose one's seat
LSRIAI lysergic acid
LSRRNE laser printer
LSTELC lose the place
LSYPIE Les Sylphides
LTEBSE litter basket
LTEEMN Lotte Lehmann
LTELLN let well alone
LTITEA late in the day
LTLDRI Little Dorrit
LTLFNE little finger
LTLHTE little Hitler
LTLPOL little people
LTNPRO latent period
LTNSLG let oneself go
LTOOIA lithological
LTOPEI lithospheric
LTORPE lithographer
lithotripter
LTORPI lithographic

LTORPO lithotriptor
LTORTS lithotritise
LTORTZ lithotritize
LTPNET lite pendente
LTRIAL liturgically
LTTBAK lots to blanks
LTTDNU latitudinous
LTTENW let it be known
LUCIGA launching-pad
LUCWNO launch window
LUEBCL Lauren Bacall
LUGAON lounge around
LUGLZR lounge-lizard
LUHOCR laugh to scorn
LUHOOG Loughborough
LUHUEL laugh quietly
LURWNO louvre window
LUSATU Louis Pasteur
LUSGSI Louis Agassiz
LUSLRO Louis Blériot
LVADER live and learn
LVALWT liveable with
LVENAS levée en masse
LVIARA live in a dream
LVICOE live in clover
LVLEGN level pegging
LVLUFC level surface
LVNLGN living legend
LVNTIG living things
LVRASG liver sausage
LVRSAL livery stable
LVRULA Liverpudlian
LVTGTE live together
LWAEMR low-watermark
LWFHLN law of the land
LWNPRT low in spirits
LWOMTO laws of motion
LWRAKN lower-ranking
LWREIN lower regions
LWRLSE lower classes
LWRNSL lower oneself
LWRQEC low frequency
LWSARL Lewis Carroll
LWSNME lowest number
LXCGAH lexicography
LYFNEO lay a finger on
LYNHLN lay on the line
LYNNHC lay in on thick
LYRSHL Layard's whale
LYTNHC lay it on thick
LZIBRE Lizzie Borden
LZMNEL Liza Minnelli
MAADRN meat and drink
MABSNS mean business
MAIGUL meaningfully
MARTIE meat retailer
MASFNR means of entry
MASIIE mean-spirited
MAUEET measurements
MAUIGU measuring jug
MAYOTE mealy-mouthed
MBLZTO mobilization
MCAIAL mechanically
MCALAI Michael Palin
MCALAN Michael Caine
MCALOL Michael Foale
MCALRD Michael Grade
MCALUR Michael Buerk
MCEAGL Michelangelo
MCEFKN Michel Fokine
MCEMNL Mickey Mantle
MCEROE Mickey Rooney
MCETKN mickey-taking
MCEZEA Mackenzie Bay
MCIAIN machinations
MCIGBU mucking about
MCLGNU mucilaginous
MCLSIL Macclesfield
MCOAAL microwavable
MCOAIA microhabitat
MCOCPU Microscopium
MCOEHL macrocephaly
MCOICI microcircuit
MCOILG microbiology
MCOITC macrobiotics
MCOLMT microclimate
MCORNE microprinted
MCORVT microgravity
MCOUGO microsurgeon
MCOUGR microsurgery
MCPAMT mycoplasmata
MCSRAE muckspreader
MCTENF Mack The Knife
MDCNBL medicine ball
MDFCTO modification
MDIHMS Midnight Mass
MDLCUS middle course
MDLGON middle ground
MDLMRA Mid Glamorgan
MDLSHO middle school
MDLWIH middleweight
MDMBVR Madame Bovary
MDMIEL mademoiselle□
MDNNSY mud in one's eye
MDOLVN mode of living
MDRTNS moderateness
MDSHTE mad as a hatter
MDSIED modus vivendi
MDTTVL meditatively
MDUMRA Midsummer Day
MDUSER medium sherry
MDYETE muddy-mettled
MEBCAC meet by chance
MEIGLC meeting-place
MEIGON meeting-point
MEIGOS meeting-house
MESCAL meet socially
MGCATR magic lantern
MGCOET Magic Moments
MGCOML magic formula
MGCONO Magic Johnson
MGEIAL magnetically
magnetizable
MGEIDS magnetic disk
MGEIDU magnetic drum
MGEIFU magnetic flux
MGEIMN magnetic mine
MGEITP magnetic tape
MGEOEE magnetometer
MGEOER magnetometry
MGESHO magnet school
MGIIAL magnifically
MGIIEC magnificence
MGIOOS Magnitogorsk
MGIOUN magniloquent
MGLMNA megalomaniac
MGLSUU megalosaurus□
MGTNMI might and main
MGUBNM magnum bonums
MIOHNU maid of honour
MIOSNA Mail on Sunday
MIRDOE maître d'hôtel
MITIAL maintainable
MITRLS moistureless
MJRABR Major Barbara
MJREEA major general
major-general
MJRRMS major premise
MJRTRL majority rule
MJRTVE majority view
MJSIAL majestically
MKAAEO make a case for
MKAAIO make a habit of
MKAALO make a balls of
MKAAOI make a day of it
MKAAWT make away with
MKAEAA make a getaway
MKAEFR make an effort
MKAERN make an errand
MKAHNO make a thing of
MKAHRO Mike Atherton
MKAILN make a killing
MKAITK make a mistake
MKAIWT make a hit with
MKALYO make a play for
MKAODO make a good job
MKAONO make a point of
MKARFC make a wry face
MKARIH make airtight
MKATOG make as though
MKAVNE make advances
MKBIHE make brighter
MKBNRP make bankrupt
MKCERU make cheerful
MKCMLT make complete
MKCNET make converts
MKCOCO make choice of
MKDFNT make definite
MKEDME make ends meet
MKEIIL make eligible
MKFEFO make free from
MKFEWT make free with
MKFMLA make familiar
MKFUTU make fruitful
MKGOTM make good time
MKIHTO make it hot for
MKISAP make it snappy
MKIVLE make involved
MKLTLO make little of

MKLVWT make love with
MKNPBI making public
MKODIL Mike Oldfield
MKODOE make old bones
MKOEHM make one's home
MKOEMR make one's mark
MKOEPL make one's pile
MKOHRH Miklós Horthy
MKPASO make plans for
MKPENN make pregnant
MKPORS make progress
MKPRLE make parallel
MKPSIL make possible
MKQETO make question
MKRAYO make ready for
MKSAEO make space for
MKSIAL make suitable
MKSRCE make stricter
MKSRNE make stronger
MKTERD make the grade
MKUATR make up a story
MKULEA make up leeway
MLADOE milk and honey
MLCLRT molecularity
MLDAAI melodramatic
MLDCIN maledictions
MLEBLT malleability
MLEEIL millefeuille
MLEERS Maltese cross
MLEIAL millesimally
MLESTO malversation
MLFADR Moll Flanders
MLIAAN mulligatawny
MLIAEA multilateral
MLIAEC multivalence
MLIAEE multifaceted
MLIAIU multifarious
MLIAKN multitasking
MLIATT multipartite
MLIIGA multilingual
MLILAL multipliable
MLILCN multiplicand
MLILCT multiplicity
MLILSO multiple shop
MLIOMT multiformity
MLIOUN multiloquent
MLIOUU multiloquous
MLIRVD multigravida
MLIUPS multipurpose
MLNELI Melanie Klein
MLNHLA melancholiac
MLNUDR Milan Kundera
MLOKYE Milton Keynes
MLOMOR Malcolm Lowry
MLOMTO malformation
MLOREU Melbourne Cup
MLORSE malnourished
MLOTNE malcontented
MLPRNS malapertness
MLRAMN maltreatment
MLSXEC mill-sixpence
MLTRSI militaristic
MLURTO malnutrition
MLVLNL malevolently
MLYODE mollycoddled
MMAYLN mammary gland
MMILRA mammillarias
MMRBLT memorability
MMRJGE memory-jogger
MMRZTO memorization
MNAIDC mandarin duck
MNAINC mandarin neck
MNAIUL mendaciously
MNAUTG Montague Tigg
MNAWRE manual worker
MNBGLN mind-boggling
MNBUTW man about town
man-about-town
MNCLUA monocultural
MNCLUE many-coloured
MNCMUE minicomputer
MNCPLS municipalise
MNCPLT municipality
MNCPLZ municipalize
MNEAON monkey around
MNEASN Monte Cassino
MNEEVU mendeleevium
MNEIIT monte di pietà
MNELNS mannerliness
MNEOTE mangetout pea
MNEPZL monkey puzzle
MNETIK monkey tricks
monkey-tricks
MNEVAL manoeuvrable
MNEWRE mangel-wurzel
MNFCNL munificently
MNFCUE manufactured
manufacturer
MNFETR man of letters
MNFLMN monofilament
MNFLNS manifoldness
MNFLWR man-of-all-work
MNFORG man of courage
MNFSAL manifestable
MNGAHS monographist
MNGARI ménage à trois
MNGTHA manage to hear
MNHWOG mind how you go
MNIIIT monti di pietà
MNLMNL mingle-mangle
MNLNUS monolinguist
MNLSNS mindlessness
MNLUHE manslaughter
MNMNAA monomaniacal
MNMNAL monumentally
MNMRHU monomorphous
MNMZTO minimization
MNNECU Manon Lescaut
MNNHMO man in the moon
MNOEWY mend one's ways
MNPDAL monopodially
MNPLSI monopolistic
MNPLTO manipulation
MNPLTR manipulatory
MNPLTV manipulative
MNPLZN monopolizing
MNRFEC minor offence
MNRLAE mineral water
MNRLGS mineralogise
mineralogist
MNRLGZ mineralogize
MNSEIT monts-de-piété
MNSIAL monastically
MNSLAI monosyllabic
MNSLAL monosyllable
MNSRTO ministration
MNSRTV ministrative
MNTESI monotheistic
MNTNUL monotonously
MNTRAL monitorially
MNTRUI monetary unit
MNTUTO menstruation
MNYATN money-wasting
MNYEDN moneylending
money-lending
MNYPNE moneyspinner
money-spinner
MNYRBE money-grubber
MOLGTN moonlighting
MQIAOA maquiladoras
MRAEMA Margaret Mead
MRAIUL mordaciously
MRATLS mercantilism
mercantilist
MRAWLE Murray Walker
MRCLUL miraculously
MRCMEA Morecombe Bay
MRDOAL meridionally
MREABR Marie Rambert
MREATU Morte d'Arthur
MREEBN Mercedes-Benz®
MREEET Marie Celeste
MREEID Mircea Eliade
MREFRE market forces
MREGRE market garden
MRELAE market leader
MRELUL marvellously
MREPOS Marcel Proust
MRESUR market square
MREWTA marked with a T
MRHGAA Martha Graham
MRHLGS morphologist
MRHNAL merchantable
MRHNBN merchant bank
MRHNIE merchandiser
MRHNLK merchantlike
MRHNNV merchant navy
MRHUNS mirthfulness
MRIACS marginal cost
MRIANT marginal note
MRIDTT married state
MRIEAG mortise gauge
MRIGAG marking gauge
MRIGAL marriageable
MRIGFE morning after
MRIGRS morning dress
MRILTE Martin Luther
MRINYN Mercian Hymns
MRIUNS mercifulness

MRLTPA morality play
MRLUPR moral support
MRLZTO moralization
MRMAES Mary McAleese
MRNMRN Marino Marini
MRNWRE Marina Warner
MROBAD Marlon Brando
MROFTE marrowfat pea
MROIRP marconigraph
MRPCFR Mary Pickford
MRPILP Mark Phillips
MRRBNO Mary Robinson
MRSASI marksmanship
MRTAHL more than half
MRTCAI meritocratic
MRTIIU meretricious
MRUBDE Murrumbidgee
MRUGRE Marcus Garvey
MRUILS mercurialise
MRUILZ mercurialize
MRUPTP Marius Petipa
MRVLAL more valuable
MRYEDA Marty Feldman
MRYILN mercy killing
MRYOON merry-go-round
MRYSGI merry as a grig
MSACLT miscalculate
MSAEIA Mesoamerican
MSAENS mistakenness
MSCASI musicianship
MSCHAR music theatre
MSCHRP music therapy
MSCLGS musicologist
MSCLRU musical group
MSDETR misadventure
MSDIEL misadvisedly
MSEAAM master-at-arms
MSEAIU misbehaviour
MSEBML Mister Bumble
MSEDNL misleadingly
MSEENU misdemeanour
MSEGER Messeigneurs
MSEGRN messenger RNA
MSEIUL mysteriously
MSELNS masterliness
miscellanist
MSEPTT mashed potato
MSERSN misrepresent
MSESRK masterstroke
MSEWPL Mister Wopsle
MSHVSA Miss Havisham
MSIETO misdirection
MSIGBU messing about
MSIGOI misdiagnosis
MSINRE missionaries
MSINRS missionarise
MSINRZ missionarize
MSIYNL mystifyingly
MSLCMN misplacement
MSMREE mass murderer
MSMRHU mesomorphous
MSNEPE misinterpret
MSNHOI misanthropic
MSNHOO misanthropos
MSOCIE misconceived
MSOSRC misconstruct
MSOSRE misconstrued
MSPOUE mass-produced
MSPRHN misapprehend
MSRAMN mistreatment
MSRCNL most recently
MSRNLT mistranslate
MSRNUC mispronounce
MSRSFR Mistress Ford
MSRSPG Mistress Page
MSTEON miss the point
MSUBTO masturbation
MSUCUT mispunctuate
MSUGMN misjudgement
MSULKL most unlikely
MSURDA masquerade as
MSUTTO misquotation
MSVIVI moshvei ovdim
MTCLUL meticulously
MTCODI mitochondria
MTEAIA mathematical
MTELNS motherliness
MTEMNE motley-minded
MTENTR mother nature
MTEOFC matter-of-fact
MTEOFR matter of form
MTESNA mothers-in-law
MTETNU mother tongue
MTHWAI Matthew Paris
MTIYAE Matti Nykanen
MTLIAL metallically
MTLIBN metallic bond
MTLNUG metalanguage
MTLUGS metallurgist
MTMRHS metamorphism
metamorphose
MTNUNS mutinousness
MTOATN method acting
MTOHAE mutton-headed
MTOIAL meteorically
methodically
MTOMLC mute of malice
MTOOIA metropolitan
mythological
MTOOIE metropolises
MTOSOE meteor shower
MTPOIA metaphorical
MTPYIA metaphysical
MTRANS materialness
MTRDTS mithridatise
MTRDTZ mithridatize
MTREIL motor vehicle
MTRERN motor neurone
MTRIYL motor-bicycle
MTRYLS motorcyclist
MTRZTO motorization
MTTOAL mutationally
MTVTOA motivational
MUHOOT mouth-to-mouth
MUIEAE Maurice Ravel
MUNUNS mournfulness
MUTANE Mount Rainier
MUTIBK mountain bike
MUTIGA mountain goat
MUTIHG mountain-high
MUTILO mountain lion
MUTISD mountainside
MUTLMU Mount Olympus
MUTOAM Mount Roraima
MUTTNE Mount Stanley
MUTVRS Mount Everest
MVALNS moveableness
MVEHAR movie theatre
MVNARA moving abroad
MVNSII moving spirit
MVSEDL move steadily
MVSOTL move smoothly
MVTADR move to and fro
MXDAMN mixed farming
MXDBLT mixed-ability
MXDCNM mixed economy
MXDELN mixed feeling
MXDOBE mixed doubles
MXEMXE mixter-maxter
MZLLAE muzzle-loader
MZOORN mezzo-soprano
MZRNHO mazarine hood
NAAAAL Niagara Falls
NAAAOC near as a touch
NAADMI near as dammit
NATADT near that date
NBLUNS nebulousness
NCABLS noctambulism
noctambulist
NCERAT nuclear waste
NCEROE nuclear power
NCIRPS nyctitropism
NCIUEC noctilucence
NCLKDA Nicole Kidman
NCLPSN Nicola Pisano
NCOACG Nicholas Cage
NCOARW Nicholas Rowe
NCOAYE nectocalyces
NCOHGU necrophagous
NCOHLA necrophiliac
NCOOIE necropolises
NDFCTO nidification
NDLNDL niddle-noddle
NEAIAL noematically
NELSNS needlessness
NGETNL neglectingly
NGETUL neglectfully
NGLASL Nigel Mansell
NGLEND Nigel Kennedy
NGTAIN negotiations
NGTFOE Night of Power
NGTLBE nightclubber
NGTLTE nightclothes
NGTRNS nugatoriness
NGTVNS negativeness
NGTVPL negative pole
NGTVSG negative sign
NGTVSI negativistic
NIHORN neighbouring

NISNBT no ifs and buts
NKLIOO Nikolai Gogol
NLNEHV no longer have
NLNVLN nolens volens
NLONLO Nelson Nelson
NLOPQE Nelson Piquet
NMDOPN name-dropping
NMDZTO nomadization
NMELSL numberlessly
NMETER number theory
NMLFOE nimble-footed
NMLSNS namelessness
NMLWTE nimble-witted
NMNLAU nominal value
NMNLTR nomenclature
NMNPMN niminy-piminy
NMNTVL nominatively
NMNUNS numinousness
NMOTAU nimbostratus
NMRBLT numerability
NMRLGS numerologist
NMRUNS numerousness
NMTEWA no matter what
NMYABE namby-pambies
NNAINN non-malignant
NNBETV non-objective
NNCEUE non-scheduled
NNDMTI Nunc Dimittis
nunc dimittis
NNEHIA non-technical
NNEIEC non-residence
NNEIIU non-religious
NNEITN non-resistant
NNELSI non-realistic
NNFETV non-effective
NNGNRA nonagenarian
NNHLNL nonchalantly
NNITOA non-fictional
NNLGMN non-alignment
NNLMAL non-flammable
NNLOOI non-alcoholic
NNOBTN non-combatant
NNODCO non-conductor
NNOMTA non-committal
NNOSNU non-poisonous
NNPRTA non-spiritual
NNSETA non-essential
NNTEIE none the wiser
NNTETL nineteenthly
NNUTDA non-custodial
NNXRMS nonextremist
NNXSEC non-existence
NNYIFR Nancy Mitford
NOAWNA neo-Darwinian
NOAWNS neo-Darwinism
neo-Darwinist
NOEIAL neoterically
NOELSI neorealistic
NOLSIA neoclassical
NOLTNS Neoplatonism
Neoplatonist
NOOIAL neologically
NPEOEE nephelometer
NPEOER nephelometry
NPEYLO Naples-yellow
NPOOIA nephological
NRAFSE Norman Foster
NRAFWE Norman Fowler
NRALMN Norman Lamont
NRAMIE Norman Mailer
NRAMNE Norman Manley
NRASHO normal school
NRASRC Norway spruce
NRATBI Norman Tebbit
NRAWSO Norman Wisdom
NRDEAI noradrenalin
NREAKN nerve-racking
NREINE Norwegian Sea
NREYHM nursery rhyme
NREYUS nursery nurse
NRHATR north-eastern
NRHETR north-western
NRHMRA Northumbrian
NRHMRC North America
NRHRMS northernmost
NRISSI narcissistic
NROECP narrow escape
NROIAL narcotically
NROMNE narrow-minded
NROTEA narrow the gap
NROZNE Norton Zinder
NSEMAA Nasseem Hamad
NSLCYA nasolacrymal
NSLZTO nasalization
NSOETA no sooner than
NSRNET no stranger to
NTADOT nuts and bolts
NTAECU not have a clue
NTAETA not later than
NTAKNI not hacking it
NTALDO not called for
NTEGAE nutmeg grater
NTELNE Netherlander
NTELNI Netherlandic
NTESBU not mess about
NTFCTO notification
NTFETN not affecting
NTFMNT not of a mind to
NTIEDM not give a damn
NTIGFO nothing if not
NTIGON nothing doing
NTIGOT nothing loath
NTIINS nutritionist
NTIIUL nutritiously
NTITNN not listening
NTLHRP natal therapy
NTLMAL not flammable
NTNILN not unwilling
NTNLDN not including
NTOABN national bank
NTOACD national code
NTOACL national call
NTOACU National Club
NTOADB national debt
NTOAGI national grid
NTOAIE nationalized
NTOAPR national park
NTOETO not to mention
NTOJSP not for Joseph
NTOPEE not completed
NTOSXD nitrous oxide
NTPRTV not operative
NTRLHL natural child
NTRLIH natural light
NTRLSI naturalistic
NTRPBI notary public
NTRPTI naturopathic
NTSICO not a stitch on
NTUKBU not muck about
NTUNHI not turn a hair
NTUOTO not cut out for
NTWRHL noteworthily
NUETNL nauseatingly
NUEUIH nouveau riche
NUEUNS nauseousness
NUIAML nautical mile
NUIHNL nourishingly
NUOIAL neurotically
NUOOIA neurological
NUOTRN neuropterans
NURLZN neutralizing
NVGBLT navigability
NVGTOA navigational
NVLFIE naval officer
NVMRAU Novum Organum
NVRALN never-failing
NVRHLS nevertheless
NWAEOI New Caledonia
NWAGEL newfangledly
NWAGLR New Mangalore
NWAHOE new-fashioned
NWAPHR New Hampshire
NWCETS New Scientist
NWCVRG news coverage
NWETMN New Testament
NWMNOR No Woman, No Cry
NWMTRA New Amsterdam
NWNLNE New Englander
NWONLN Newfoundland
NWPPRA newspaperman
NWPPRE newspapermen
NWRNWC New Brunswick
NWTTSA New Statesman
NXNNHN Nixon in China
NZFCTO Nazification
OADNNO on and on and on
OAEEKE on an even keel
OAGSUS orange squash
OALIEO on all sides of
OANFEG on a knife edge
OAOIAL oratorically
OASSAC of assistance
OAYCON on any account
OBTNBD orbiting body
OCADGI once and again
OCDNAL occidentally
OCETAI orchestra pit
OCETAO orchestrator
OCIAHL once in a while

OCLOCP oscilloscope
OCLORP oscillograph
OCPEWT occupied with
OCPTOA occupational
OCSOAL occasionally
OCSOEB occasioned by
ODAHLC Old Catholics
ODAHOE old fashioned
old-fashioned
ODASER old man's beard
ODCOLI old school tie
old-school tie
ODETMN Old Testament
ODIETL old wives' tale
ODNRNS ordinariness
OEADBV over and above
OEAIAL operatically
OEALSE opera-glasses
OEAOIU opéra comique
OEAUDN overabundant
OEBREE overburdened
OEBSSO one's best shot
OECAGN overcharging
OECIIA overcritical
OECMWT overcome with
OECODN overcrowding
OECPFE one's cup of tea
OEDAAI overdramatic
OEDLCT overdelicate
OEEPAI overemphasis
OEEPSR overexposure
OEETMT overestimate
OEETNE overextended
OEFINL over-friendly
OEFLNS overfullness
over-fullness
OEFMLA overfamiliar
over-familiar
OEFORS overflourish
OEFOWT overflow with
OEHNKO overhand knot
OEIENS one-sidedness
OEIGIH opening night
OELANN open learning
OELRSI overlordship
OEMLIL overmultiply
OEMRIG open marriage
OENGAH oceanography
OENGTA overnight bag
overnight-bag
OENLGS oceanologist
OEOEHA over one's head
OEOHSO one for his nob
OEOSRC one-horse race
OEOSTW one-horse town
OEOVNN Ode to Evening
OEPASI one-upmanship
OEPRUD overpersuade
OEPWRN overpowering
OEQETO open question
OERATO overreaction
OERCMN one-track mind
OESEDN overspending
OESEPN overstepping
OESNWC open sandwich
OESRIE overstrained
OESVRU of easy virtue
OETATC open to attack
OETDBT open to debate
OETRAO open to reason
OETUTN overtrusting
OEWEMN overwhelming
OFCAMR official mark
OFCBAE office-bearer
OFCHLE office-holder
OFCRNC olfactronics
OFCUIG offscourings
OFCWRE office worker
OFHBTL off the bottle
OFHHNE off the hinges
OFHRCR off the record
off-the-record
OFNSAD off one's hands
OFNSHM off one's chump
OFNSNO off one's onion
OFNSUR off one's guard
OFRNSL offer oneself
OFROSL offer for sale
OGNRNE organ-grinder
OGNSTO organisation
OGNZTO organization
OGORPT of good repute
OHGRPT of high repute
OHILAS Othniel Marsh
OHOHBA ochlophobiac
OHROLL otherworldly
other-worldly
OIACIA oligarchical
OIEDBI Oliver de Bois
OIEDCU obiter dictum
OILOLG Oriel College
OINERN orienteering
OIORPI oligotrophic
OIPRAC of importance
OJTEET objet de vertu
OLGNNS obligingness
OLGTRL obligatorily
OLHMCT Oklahoma City
OLHWEL oil the wheels
OLTRTO obliteration
OLTRTV obliterative
OLVSEC obliviscence
OMCADE Of Mice and Men
OMXDRE of mixed breed
ONMNAL ornamentally
ONPEEC omnipresence
ONPTNL omnipotently
ONSINL omnisciently
ONTICI Ornithischia
ONTOIU Ornithomimus
OOAOOI onomatopoeia
onomatopoeic
OOEPRO on one's person
OOEUPR on one's uppers
OOTLGS odontologist
OPESVL oppressively
OPOETM oophorectomy
OPSBLT opposability
OPSNSD opposing side
OPSTNS oppositeness
OPSTOA oppositional
ORFETO on reflection
OSAKSA on Shanks's nag
OSALRC obstacle race
OSERCA obstetrician
OSFCTO ossification
OSFEAC on sufferance
OSLSEC obsolescence
OSLTNS obsoleteness
OSQIUL obsequiously
OSRCIN obstructions
OSRPRT obstreperate
OSRPRU obstreperous
OSSEWT obsessed with
OSSINS obsessionist
OSTUPS of set purpose
OSUATS obscurantism
obscurantist
OTADSL outlandishly
OTAEUL outrageously
OTAOUR outmanoeuvre
OTBEKN oath-breaking
OTCLIR optical fibre
OTEAIO on the basis of
OTEALB on the wallaby
OTEAPG on the rampage
OTEAPT on the warpath
OTEEGO on the verge of
OTEELN on the decline
OTEELO on the heels of
OTEHLE on the shelves
OTEIEO on the lines of
OTELNE on the blanket
OTEMRV on the improve
OTENCE on the knocker
OTENHN on the one hand
OTENTN on the instant
OTEOIO on the horizon
OTEOKU on the lookout
OTEONO on the point of
OTEPNU on the up and up
OTEREO of the order of
OTERNO on the brink of
OTESEC of the essence
OTETET on the streets
OTEUFC on the surface
OTEUSD on the outside
OTEUVV on the qui vive
OTFAGO out of range of
OTFAHO out of fashion
OTFECO out of reach of
OTFEPN out of keeping
OTFEVC out of service
OTFHBU out of the blue
OTFHNI out of thin air
OTFHRA out of the road
OTFHWO out of the wood
OTFLNC out of all nick
OTFOHR out of nowhere

OTFOTO out of control
OTFPRT out of spirits
OTFRWN out of drawing
OTGNRA octogenarian
OTHWNO out the window
OTIEIH outside right
OTMYRO Otto Meyerhof
OTMZTO optimization
OTNAIU ostentatious
OTNNME octane number
OTNRTN octane rating
OTOAAI osteomalacia
OTOADC orthopaedics
OTOADS orthopaedist
OTOEEI orthogenesis
orthogenetic
osteogenesis
osteogenetic
OTOHMI orthorhombic
OTOLSI osteoplastic
OTOOAL orthogonally
OTOOIA osteological
OTOOOI osteoporosis
OTOOTC orthodontics
OTOOTS orthodontist
OTORPE orthographer
OTORPI orthographic
OTOTRU orthopterous
OTREIN outer regions
OTRMNE out from under
OTRUFC outer surface
OTSAGE obtuse-angled
OTSLAI octosyllabic
OTSLAL octosyllable
OTTECE outstretched
OUAMSL ocular muscle
OWLMSE Oswald Mosley
OYPCAE Olympic Games
OYTLGN oryctolagine
PAALNS placableness
PAATAC Peasant Dance
PAAWSE play at waster
PAEDMU praseodymium
PAEETN place setting
PAEEWE place between
PAEFIT place of birth
PAELSL prayerlessly
PAESUU Plateosaurus
PAETAA Placentia Bay
PAEUDN pease pudding
PAEUNS peacefulness
PAFRHE platform heel
PAFROE play for money
PAHLSO peach blossom
PAHLWT play hell with
PAIGIL playing-field
PAIUDS platinum disc
PALABU Pearl Harbour
PAMCLG pharmacology
PAMCUI pharmaceutic
PAMSMT plasmosomata
PANALN plain sailing
PANELN plain-dealing
PANRCE prawn cracker
PAOATO plan of action
PAOIAL platonically
PAOKTI peacock's tail
PAOOCV plano-concave
PAOYIA phagocytical
PAOYOI phagocytosis
PASBLT plausibility
PASWRH praiseworthy
PATCLS practicalism
practicalist
PATCLT practicality
PATEEI play the devil
PATEIL play the field
PATEOA play the woman
PATRAN plaster saint
PATROR plasterboard
PATSAL phantasmally
PATTOE practitioner
PAUBTE peanut butter
PAURDE plague-ridden
PAWTFR play with fire
PAYGLG pharyngology
PBIFGR public figure
PBISCO public sector
PBISHO public school
PBOIAS Pablo Picasso
PCAILE peccadilloes
PCFCTO pacification
PCFCTR pacificatory
PCIGRE pecking order
PCORPI pictographic
PCRAIU picornavirus
PCSIFA Pecksniffian
PCTPEE pick to pieces
PCUEOS picture-house
PCUTEA pick up the tab
PDIGAI pudding basin
PDLNPO paddling-pool
PDNIAL pedantically
PDNUAE pedunculated
PDSADS pedestal desk
PDYSDW Paddy Ashdown
PEAAIN preparations
PEAENS preparedness
PEAIAL prelatically
PEAIAO prevaricator
PEAIUL precariously
PEALNL prevailingly
PEARCT prefabricate
PEBTRA presbyterian
PECAPI pre-eclampsia
PECITO prescription
PECITV prescriptive
PECUYN preoccupying
PEDCEI pseudocyesis
PEDMND pseudomonads
PEDNMU pseudonymous
PEDPDU pseudopodium
PEEDNL pretendingly
PEEEMN predetermine
PEEETA preferential
PEEFIH piece of eight
PEEFOD piece of goods
PEEIAE premeditated
PEEINT predesignate
PEESLT prehensility
PEESOA precessional
PEESRA premenstrual
PEETAL presentially
PEETMN presentiment
PEETNT predestinate
PEETRA preceptorial
prefectorial
PEETSN prevent using
PEETTO presentation
PEETTV preventative
PEETVL preventively
PEEUST prerequisite
PEEVTO preservation
PEEVTV preservative
PEHLGS psephologist
PEICTR plebiscitary
PEIETA presidential
PEIETO predilection
PEIIAC precipitance
precipitancy
PEIINS precisianist
precisionist
PEIOEC plenipotence
PEIOHT pteridophyte
PEITVL predictively
PEIUNS preciousness
PELSNS peerlessness
PELSVL preclusively
PELUET poet laureate
PEMLFE preamplifier
PEMNNL pre-eminently
PEMNRA Piet Mondrian
PEMRHS pleomorphism
PENNSL preen oneself
PENSIA pleonastical
PEOAIE prerogatived
PEOCIE preconceived
PEODRN preponderant
PEODRT preponderate
PEODTO precondition
PEOEAL phenomenally
PEOIAC predominance
PEOIUL precociously
PEONTO precognition
PEONTV precognitive
PEOOIA phenological
PEOOPI paedomorphic
PEOTRU preposterous
PEOYIA phenotypical
PEPESR peer pressure
PEPSLN Pier Pasolini
PERBUE Pierre Boulez
PERCRI Pierre Cardin
PERDPN Pierre Du Pont
PERLCO Pierre Laclos
PESALR press gallery
PESALS pre-establish
PESEES press release
PESFIE press officer

PESHRE press charges
PESLWA Piers Plowman
PESNNS pleasantness
PESNRE pleasantries
PESRCO pressure-cook
PESRTI pleasure trip
PESRZN pressurizing
PESUTN press cutting
PETCRE Puerto Cortes
PETGAO prestigiator
PETPET pretty-pretty
PETSIO prestissimos
PETVCN Pretty Vacant
PEUGMN prejudgement
PEUPUU presumptuous
PEUSSE plenum system
PEYAAI phenylalanin
PGAIUL pugnaciously
PGETTO pigmentation
PGMGTL pigs might fly
PIADRN philandering
PIAEAT private parts
PIAEEN private means
PIAEIE Private Lives
PIAEOE private hotel
PIAEPI Philadelphia
PIAEPU philadelphus
PIAEUO private tutor
PIATRP philanthrope
philanthropy
PIAYSU primary issue
PICABR Prince Albert
PICPLO principal boy
PICPLT principality
PICRPR Prince Rupert
PIEAAO primeval atom
PIEAAP Phi Beta Kappa
PIEFLC pride of place
PIEFOE price of money
PIEIHE prizefighter
prize-fighter
PIEINN prize-winning
PIENSL pride oneself
PIEOTO price control
PIGSNS priggishness
PIHROI philharmonic
PIILRI Philip Larkin
PIIRVD primigravida
PIISDE Philip Sidney
PIITES pain in the ass
PIITNS Philistinise
philistinism
PIITNZ Philistinize
PILSNS painlessness
PIODAL primordially
PIOEIA primogenital
PIOEIO primogenitor
PIOOHS philosophise
PIOOHZ philosophize
PIOOIA philological
PIOUAU Philo Judaeus
PIRSPT primrose path
PISLLN Plimsoll line
PISLMR Plimsoll mark
PITDOK printed works
PITFRE point of order
PITHLL paint the lily
PITOON point-to-point
PITTLC Paint It Black
PITTSU point at issue
PITYON point by point
PIUMBL primum mobile
PIYONI Privy Council
PJRTVL pejoratively
PLAATN pull a fast one
PLABXE pillar-box red
PLALNE pull a flanker
PLARFC pull a wry face
PLATUE polyanthuses
PLAWRE Pelham Warner
PLBTMS phlebotomise
PLBTMZ phlebotomize
PLEBTN palaeobotany
PLEGAH palaeography
PLEHLN polyethylene
PLEIAL pulverizable
PLELTI palaeolithic❑
PLGAIA phlegmatical
PLGESN palm-greasing
PLGMUL polygamously
PLIGOT polling-booth
PLIGRL pelvic girdle
PLMRHS polymorphism
PLMRHU polymorphous
PLNEEE palingeneses
PLNRMS palindromist
PLNUII polyneuritis
PLPSTO pole position
PLRSTO polarisation
PLRZTO polarization
PLSLAI polysyllabic
PLSLAL polysyllable
PLTBLT palatability
PLTEIE pull the wires
PLTENF palette knife
PLTESI polytheistic
PLTFIE pilot officer
PLTGTE pull together
PLTPEE pull to pieces
PLUEHN polyurethane
PLUINS pellucidness
PLUSAE pull up stakes
PLYNAS pollyannaish
PMENCE pumpernickel
PNAECA Pentateuchal
PNAEGD Ponta Delgada
PNAERN pentahedrons
PNAOAL pentagonally
PNCLTL paniculately
PNEHIO pantechnicon
PNELNS Panhellenism
Panhellenist
PNEMNS pan-Germanism
PNETLT pendente lite
PNHNJD Punch and Judy
PNHNLO Punchinellos
PNHOAI panchromatic
PNHRAO panpharmacon
PNIIAE pontificater
PNIIAL pontifically
PNINDF pensioned off
PNLETN panel heating
PNLYEC penalty bench
PNLZTO penalization
PNOECA pine overcoat
PNOIIA pantomimical
PNSLAI Pennsylvania
PNTNIR penitentiary
PNYICE penny-pincher
POAADS propagandise
propagandist
POAADZ propagandize
POADUI propaedeutic
POAHDA procathedral
POAINR probationary
POATNU protactinium
POCITO proscription
POCITV proscriptive
PODERE proud-hearted
POEBAL proverbially
POEDGI proceed again
POEHZN promethazine
POEIAL phonemically
phonetically
POEIRS progenitress
POEMTO proper motion
POEOEA prolegomenal
POEOEO prolegomenon
POESOA processional
professional
POESRA professorial
POETNL protectingly
protestingly
POETRA prosectorial
POETRN progesterone
POETRT protectorate
POETTO protestation
POETVL protectively
POEUAL prosecutable
POEYIE proselytizer
POEYOE Ptolemy Soter
POFORC proof-correct
POGMNA Plough Monday
POHLCI prophylactic
POHLMO prothalamion
POICAL provincially
POIELN promised land
POIERN profiteering
POIETA providential
POIIAL prolifically
POIINI proficient in
POIINL proficiently
POIINS prolificness
POIITO propitiation
POIITR propitiatory
POIITV propitiative
POIIUL prodigiously
propitiously
POILSL profitlessly

POIMKN profit-making
POIMRI profit margin
POIMTO phonic method
POISRL promissorily
POLETN people-eating
POLGTL profligately
POLMTO proclamation
POLMTR proclamatory
POLSRN people's front
POLTIE proglottides
POOAPI phonocamptic
POOCEL Paolo Uccello
POOGTO prolongation
POOHMS photochemist
POOIAL pronominally
prosodically
POOLSA protoplasmal
POOLSI protoplasmic
POONEL pronouncedly
POONNS profoundness
POOOIA phonological
POOOYN photocopying
POORPE photographer
POORPI photographic
POORPS phototropism
POOTOA proportional
POOYIA prototypical
POPCUE prospectuses
POPOEC phosphoresce
POPRUL prosperously
PORCEL protractedly
PORERS proprietress
PORMAL programmable
PORSVL protrusively
POTGTE pool together
POTLGS proctologist
POTRAL proctorially
POTTTO prostitution
POUEAC protuberance
POUGTN promulgating
POUGTO promulgation
POUNTO propugnation
POUTVL productively
POUTVT productivity
PPADAO pipe and tabor
PPCTPT Popocatepetl
PPLRRN popular front
PPNSLG pop one's clogs
PPRLGS papyrologist
PPRRFT paper profits
PPSIAL papistically
PRAEAD Port Adelaide
PRAEEU pergameneous
PRAETA permanent way
PRAGNT permanganate
PRAPIC Port-au-Prince
PRAUTR permaculture
PRCIIA paroccipital
PRCILS parochialise
parochialism
PRCILT parochiality
PRCILZ parochialize
PRCNEI paracentesis
PRCRII pericarditis
PRCRNS parachronism
PRDETR peradventure
PRDGAI paradigmatic
PRDSIA paradisaical
PRDSLS Paradise Lost
PREABN parietal bone
PREALB parietal lobe
PREANS porcelainise
PREANZ porcelainize
PREBLT permeability
PRECAG part-exchange
PREEAC perseverance
PRELNS porcellanise
PRELNZ porcellanize
PREOHU porte-bonheur
PRERTO perpetration
PRESNS perverseness
PRETEI paraesthesia
PRETIC perfect pitch
PRETIT perfect fifth
PRETOA perceptional
PRETUL portentously
PRETVL perceptively
perfectively
PRETVT perceptivity
PREUTO perpetuation
PRFCTO purification
PRFCTR purificatory
PRGIAO peregrinator
PRHETS parchmentise
PRHETZ parchmentize
PRHROR Port Harcourt
PRIAIU pertinacious
PRIASI partisanship
PRIATR port in a storm
PRIGEE parking meter
PRIGIH parking-light
PRIIAO participator
PRIIAT participants
PRIIDA Porfirio Díaz
PRIINF partition off
PRIINN partitioning
PRIIUL perfidiously
perniciously
PRIOIU parsimonious
PRISNS parkinsonism
PRISVL permissively
PRITNL persistently
persistingly
PRITVT permittivity
PRIUAL particularly
PRLEBR parallel bars
PRLEWS parallelwise
PRLNCU Portland Club
PRLNUG paralanguage
PRLPMN paralipomena
PRLUNS perilousness
PRLXNL perplexingly
PRMLTR paramilitary
PRMNEU portmanteaus
portmanteaux
PRMRHT pyromorphite
PRMTIA parametrical
perimetrical
PRMTRL peremptorily
PRMUAO perambulator
PRNEAL parenterally
PRNHSS parenthesise
PRNHSZ parenthesize
PRNILT perenniality
PRNLGS phrenologise
phrenologist
PRNLGZ phrenologize
PRNMSI paronomastic
PRNPRU perinephrium
PROABS personal best
PROAIE personalized
PROBFR period before
PROEUL purpose-built
purposefully
PROFIA person Friday
PROIAL periodically
PROITO perfoliation
PROMAI perform magic
PROOTC periodontics
PROOTS periodontist
PRORPE pornographer
PRORPI pornographic
PROSEC part of speech
PROTTO pernoctation
PRPCCT perspicacity
PRPPYE parapophyses
PRPRSI periphrastic
PRPRTO perspiration
PRSCUC parish church
PRSEDN parascending
PRSIAL puristically
PRSINR parishioners
PRSMNE phrasemonger
PRSNHT parasyntheta
PRSTLG parasitology
PRTCNC pyrotechnics
PRTDLN parotid gland
PRUAEU percutaneous
PRUBTO perturbation
PRUSOA percussional
PRUSVL percussively
persuasively
PRVCOI Port Victoria
PRYNBS Porgy and Bess
PSAERV passage grave
PSAETM postage stamp
PSALNS passableness
PSASSE postal system
PSAWRE postal worker
PSEATU passe-partout
PSEORE pas de bourrée
PSERLA Pasteurellae
Pasteurellas
PSESVL possessively
PSFRBN pisiform bone
PSGAUT postgraduate
PSHMUL posthumously
PSIETA pestilential
PSINRI passion fruit

PSINTL passionately
PSISRM past its prime
PSIUTR pisciculture
PSMRDA postmeridian
PSMRDE post meridiem
PSOAHA pastoral head
PSOEBS past one's best
PSOELC push one's luck
PSOEWR pass one's word
PSPADA postprandial
PSPNMN postponement
PSPSTO postposition
PSPSTV postpositive
PSRCTE pastry cutter
PSSNEC pass sentence
PSTOHR pass to others
PSTVNS positiveness
PSYOTN pussyfooting
PTALNS pitiableness
PTDMEO put a damper on
PTEATO putrefaction
PTEATV putrefactive
PTEIAL pathetically
PTEIDO put behind you
PTEPTE pitter-patter
PTESHE potter's wheel
PTETSO patient as Job
PTFNEO put a finger on
PTHAIO put the acid on
PTHBOI put the boot in
PTHBTO put the bite on
PTHMKO put the make on
PTHNPT pitch and putt
PTHOWR pitch forward
PTHWNU put the wind up
PTIATO petrifaction
PTIKHT Patrick White
PTIKOR Patrick Moore
PTINES Pythian verse
PTIOGN pettifogging
PTIOGR pettifoggery
PTIRHT patriarchate
PTLSNS pitilessness
PTNHBC pat on the back
PTNHBO put in the boot
PTNHFI put on the foil
PTNHLN put on the line
PTNHMI put in the mail
PTNHPS put in the post
PTNHRC put on the rack
PTNHRT put on the Ritz
PTNHSO put on the spot
PTNILT potentiality
PTNIPA put on display
PTNNSD put on one side
PTNOEO put one over on
PTNOFC Patent Office
PTNOOD put into words
PTNRTN put in writing
PTNSAI put one's oar in
PTOEEI pathogenesis
PTOEIT put money into
PTOETO Pat Robertson
PTOHHR put to the horn
PTONOT put down roots
PTONSD put to one side
PTOODS put to good use
PTOOIA pathological
PTPHHI put up the hair
PTPOSL put up for sale
PTRARE Peter Gabriel
PTRBLR Peter Abelard
PTRCRY Peter Ackroyd
PTREAA Peter Medawar
PTRELR Peter Sellers
PTRERN Peter Behrens
PTRHFE Peter Shaffer
PTRHLO Peter Shilton
PTROBR Peter Lombard
PTROOG Peterborough
PTRSIO Peter Ustinov
PTRUHN Peter Cushing
PTSCII put a sock in it
PTSIES Pott's disease
PTTBIH potato blight
PTTELE Pitt the elder
PTTFNE potato finger
PTTMSE potato masher
PTYFIE petty officer
PUDFLS pound of flesh
PUEENE Paule Régnier
PUETAL prudentially
PUIGNF pruning-knife
PUIOUN pauciloquent
PULNEI Paul Langevin
PUOIAI Paulo DiCanio
PUSABU Prussian blue
PUSOIL Paul Scofield
PUTUNE Paul Tournier
PUVRAN Paul Verlaine
PWEMNE powder monkey
PWRALR power failure
PWRHRN power-sharing
PWRTAB powers that be
PWRTTO power station
PWRUNS powerfulness
PYETWR Payne Stewart
PYHARS psychiatrist
PYHATV psychoactive
PYHBBL psychobabble
PYHLGS psychologise
psychologist
PYHLGZ psychologize
PYHPTI psychopathic
PYHSCA psychosocial
PYHSXA psychosexual
PYHTOI psychotropic
PYIGAH physiography
PYIGOI physiognomic
PYILGS physiologist
PYLTCI phyllotactic
PYNDAC pay in advance
PYOATI phycoxanthin
PYOEEI phylogenesis
phylogenetic
phytogenesis
PYOTRC Plymouth Rock
PYRBTT pay tribute to
PYSOER pay-as-you-earn
PYTETO pay attention
QARGSM Quadragesima
QARMNU quadrumanous
QARNMA quadrinomial
QARNUA quadrangular
QARPEI quadriplegia
quadriplegic
QARPOI quadraphonic
quadrophonic
QARVLN quadrivalent
QATFAL quantifiable
QATOET quattrocento
QATRIE quarter-miler
QATRIH quarterlight
QATRLO quarter-blood
QATRON quarter bound
QATTTV quantitative
QATTVL quantitively
QATZTO quantization
QAUVRA quaquaversal
QECLSL quenchlessly
QEEUPN queue-jumping
QENETI Queen Beatrix
QENFHB Queen of Sheba
QENLNE Queenslander
QENSEC Queen's Speech
QETOAL questionable
questionably
QETOLS questionless
QETOMR question mark
QETOTM question time
QIKIVR quicksilvery
QIKYUL quickly built
QILROC Quiller-Couch
QIOIAL quixotically
QIQENA quinquennial
QIQENU quinquennium
QITSEC quintessence
QIZCLT quizzicality
RAALNS readableness
RAIGRN roaring drunk
RAPAAC reappearance
re-appearance
RASRNL reassuringly
RASSMN reassessment
RATVNS reactiveness
RATVTO reactivation
RAYOMR ready for more
RBECEU rubber cheque
RBECMN rubber cement
RBERLE Robbe-Grillet
RBHUDR rub shoulders
RBIIAL rabbinically
RBISCE rabbit-sucker
RBLATN R M Ballantyne
RBLGIS rebel against
RBLIUL rebelliously
RBLRUE rabble-rouser
RBNCES ribonuclease
RBNOSN Robin Cousins

RBNSAD rub one's hands
RBRALC Roberta Flack
RBRATA Robert Altman
RBRBNE Robert Bunsen
RBRBON Robert Browne
RBRDNR Robert De Niro
RBRGAE Robert Graves
RBRGBO Robert Gibson
RBRGEN Robert Greene
RBRLWL Robert Lowell
RBRMGB Robert Mugabe
RBRMGW Robert Mugawe
RBRNPE Robert Napier
RBRRNI Robert Runcie
RBRWRE Robert Warren
RBSIUL robustiously
RCADCT Richard Scott
RCADDM Richard Adams
RCADED Richard Meade
RCADIO Richard Nixon
RCADRO Richard Pryor
RCAGAL rechargeable
RCCIBN rock-climbing
RCEBCE Rickenbacker
RCECRO Rachel Carson
RCEEGN rocket engine
RCEERN racketeering
RCETIE racket-tailed
RCETOA recreational
RCGIAC recognisance
recognizance
RCGIAL recognisably
recognizable
recognizably
RCIBNU Richie Benaud
RCICII rachischisis
RCIESI receivership
RCIGHI rocking-chair
RCIIAO recriminator
RCIIGE receiving-set
RCLETO recollection
RCLETV recollective
RCLIRN recalcitrant
RCLIRT recalcitrate
RCLSEC recalescence
RCLSNS recklessness
RCMEDN recommending
RCMOTR recomforture
RCMZTO racemization
RCNERN raconteuring
RCNIAL reconcilable
reconcilably
RCNOTE reconnoitrer
RCNTTT reconstitute
RCPINS receptionist
RCPOAL reciprocally
RCPOAO reciprocator
RCPRTN recuperating
RCPRTO recuperation
RCPRTV recuperative
RCPTLS recapitalise
RCPTLT recapitulate
RCPTLZ recapitalize
RCREMI recorded mail
RCRKEE record-keeper
RCROFL record on film
RCRPAE record-player
RCTRCL Richter scale
RCUECN recrudescent
RDAEGN radial engine
RDCBLT reducibility
RDCINS reductionism
reductionist
RDCIRN reduce in rank
RDCLUL ridiculously
RDCRTO redecoration
RDECSE Red Leicester
RDEPDL rudder pedals
RDEPRE Rodney Porter
RDFRFL ride for a fall
RDIHRW reddish-brown
RDLCRA Rudolf Carnap
RDLDEE Rudolf Diesel
RDMNAE rodomontader
RDNERT redintegrate
RDNEWN red underwing
RDNSLO rid oneself of
RDOHNC radiophonics
RDOHNS radiophonist
RDOHRP radiotherapy
RDOILG radiobiology
RDOLMN radioelement
RDOOIA radiological
RDOOPS radio compass
RDOPSL red corpuscle
RDORPE radiographer
RDORPI radiographic
RDOSTP radioisotope
RDOULD radionuclide
RDSRBT redistribute
RDTHUD ride to hounds
RDULMN redoublement
RDUVCO radius vector
REAUTO re-evaluation
REMTLG rheumatology
REOIAL rhetorically
REUFCO rhesus factor
REUMNE rhesus monkey
RFAINR reflationary
RFATRL refractorily
RFATVT refractivity
RFECMR reflex camera
RFEHET refreshments
RFEHNL refreshingly
RFEHNN refreshening
RFEHUL refreshfully
RFETNL reflectingly
RFETVL reflectively
RFETVT reflectivity
RFIEAO refrigerator
RFLTCE raffle-ticket
RFREPI referred pain
RFRIHN refurbishing
RFSINN refashioning
RFSTVT refuse to vote
RGAFIC Ragnar Frisch
RGESHO ragged school
RGESVL regressively
RGESVT regressivity
RGLROT regular costs
RGLRRN regular drink
RGNRTN regenerating
RGNRTO regeneration
RGNRTR regeneratory
RGNRTV regenerative
RGRCOG Roger McGough
RGRERS Roger Penrose
RGRHFE Roger Chaffee
RGRHGL regard highly
RGRLSL regardlessly
RGRLSO regardless of
RGRUNS rigorousness
RGSRTO registration
RGTADA right-hand man
RGTFNR right of entry
RGTHHL right the helm
RGTNLF right-and-left
RGTUNS rightfulness
RHBLTT rehabilitate
RIBRAL reimbursable
RIBWRU rainbow trout
RIDEMS reindeer moss
RIEAEL reiteratedly
RIEHAT raise the ante
RIEHNT raise a hand to
RIEHRO raise the roof
RIEHWN raise the wind
RIENSA raise one's hat
RIEOEO raise money on
RIOAPU rhizocarpous
RIOEOE rhinoceroses
rhinocerotes
RIOEOI rhinocerotic
RIOLSI rhinoplastic
RIOOIA rhinological
RIVGRT reinvigorate
RJNAOE rejoneadores
RJVNTN rejuvenating
RJVNTO rejuvenation
RLESAE roller-skater
RLETNO rallentandos
RLHINE Ralph Fiennes
RLIGIC rolling hitch
RLIGTN rolling stone
RLITEA roll in the hay
RLNLSL relentlessly
RLTEOS rule the roast
rule the roost
RLTOAL relationally
RLTOSI relationship
RLTVNS relativeness
RLTVSI relativistic
RLTVSZ relative size
RLTVTS relativitist
RLYNCL rallying call
RMDLSL remedilessly
RMFCTO ramification
RMMEAL rememberably
RMMRNE remembrancer

remembrances
RMNCNR remand centre
RMNIAL romantically
RMNRLS remineralise
RMNRLZ remineralize
RMNRTO remuneration
RMNRTR remuneratory
RMNRTV remunerative
RMNSEC reminiscence
RMNTAC remonstrance
RMNTAO remonstrator
RMNTNL ruminatingly
RMNTOE ruminate over
RMNTVL ruminatively
RMNZTO Romanization
RMPTEU Ramapithecus
RMREUL remorsefully
RMTIDT rumpti-iddity
RMTSAE remotest area
RMUMNE rumour-monger
RMVBLT removability
RNENSL range oneself
RNFHML run of the mill
run-of-the-mill
RNHRSO run the risk of
RNIBRE Ronnie Barker
RNIGFE running after
RNIGHM running a home
RNIGIL running title
RNIGOR running-board
RNIGOT running costs
RNIGRC running-track
RNIGUO running out on
RNLFSE Ronald Fisher
RNLRAA Ronald Reagan
RNLSAL Ronald Searle
RNMGIT René Magritte
RNNITO renunciation
RNNITR renunciatory
RNNITV renunciative
RNNUUE ranunculuses
RNOACS random access
RNONET run counter to
RNOSML random sample
RNREWO Ron Greenwood
RNRWHR Renfrewshire
RNTCUS run its course
RNUCMN renouncement
ROAOEA rhopaloceral
ROATEO Room at the Top
ROBHDA rhombohedral
ROBHDO rhombohedron
ROEAER Rio de Janeiro
ROEALT Rio de la Plata
ROEBYO Rhodes Boyson
ROIGOS rooming-house
ROLSNS rootlessness
ROOEDO rhododendron
RPAISL repeat itself
RPAWNL Rip Van Winkle
RPEESO reprehension
RPEESR reprehensory
RPEETN representing
RPESVL repressively
RPLEFC ripple effect
RPLMRE ripple-marked
RPOCAL reproachable
RPOESN reprocessing
RPORPE reprographer
RPORPI reprographic
RPOUIL reproducible
RPOUTO reproduction
RPOUTV reproductive
RPRBOK Rupert Brooke
RPRUSO repercussion
RPRUSV repercussive
RPSESO repossession
RPTITO repatriation
RPTTVL repetitively
reputatively
RQIEET requirements
RQIETN requite atone
RRLZTO ruralization
RSAAYI risk analysis
RSADHN rise and shine
RSARTU restaurateur
RSCLUE rose-coloured
rust-coloured
RSDGER ruse de guerre
RSDNIR residentiary
RSEOCT Rosie Boycott
RSETUL respectfully
RSETVL respectively
RSGENS resignedness
RSHSAA Rosh Hashanah
RSINAA Russian salad
RSINRS Russian cross
RSIOEE respirometer
RSLENS resolvedness
RSLNAO Rosalyn Yalow
RSLNEC resplendence
resplendency
RSLSNS restlessness
RSLTNS resoluteness
RSLTOE resolutioner
RSMCUA Rose Macaulay
RSMRWS Rosemary West
RSMTVL resumptively
RSNGON rising ground
RSOSLS responseless
RSOSRA responsorial
RSOSVL responsively
RSPNTO resupination
RSRAIN reservations
RSRCEL restrictedly
RSRCIN restrictions
RSRELS reserved list
RSRENS reservedness
RSRERC reserve price
RSRETO resurrection
RSRIEL restrainedly
RSRIET risorgimento
RSRPVC Rostropovich
RSSIAE resuscitated
RSSIAL resuscitable
RSSIAO resuscitator
RSSLSL resistlessly
RSTADR rush to and fro
RSUCLS resourceless
RSUDNL resoundingly
RTATLT retractility
RTATTO retractation
RTATVL retractively
RTCLTL reticulately
RTCLTO reticulation
RTECMN retrenchment
RTFCTO ratification
RTHTHE ratchet-wheel
RTHYOT Rita Hayworth
RTIIGE retaining fee
RTIOTE retail outlet
RTLHAE rattle-headed
RTLSNS ruthlessness
RTNINS retentionist
RTOAIE rationalized
RTOESO retrocession
retroversion
RTOESV retrocessive
RTOLXO retroflexion
RTROPS return of post
RTRTCE return ticket
RUDBUL roundaboutly
RUDHBN round the bend
RUDPRO roundsperson
RUHAKI rough hawkbit
RUHASG rough passage
RUHIMN rough diamond
RUHUTC rough justice
RVCBLT revocability
RVNEUL revengefully
RVNUNS ravenousness
RVREAO reverberator
RVRERC river-terrace
RVRHEI River Phoenix
RVRINR reversionary
RVROPI river dolphin
RVSEWT ravished with
RVTLZN revitalizing
RVVLSI revivalistic
RYEOET rhyme to death
RYHIAL rhythmically
RYIETM rhytidectomy
RYIGLN rhyming slang
RYLARN royal warrant
RYLOLO Royal Doulton
RYODLN Raymond Blanc
RZLDZL razzle-dazzle
SAAAFO stay away from
SAAAUE scarabaeuses
SACEGN search engine
SACLEE scarcely ever
SADAKO stand back for
SADGIS stand against
SADHPC stand the pace
SADLUL scandalously
SADNDW standing-down
SADNJK standing joke
SADNVA Scandinavian
SADNWO stand in awe of

SADNWV standing wave
SADPIH stand-up fight
stand upright
SADPOI stand-up comic
SADRIE standardized
standardizer
SADRLM standard lamp
SADRTM standard time
SADRUL slanderously
SADSRD stand astride
SAEAEL shamefacedly
SAEESO state pension
SAEEWN Siamese twins
SAEFHC state of shock
SAEFIG state of siege
SAEHCS share the cost
SAEHRE snake-charmer
SAEHSE stage whisper
SAEHTL space shuttle
SAEHVE share the view
SAEIEL stare fixedly
SAEILN Staten Island
SAEODN shareholding
SAEOET scare to death
SAEPRO statesperson
SAERPE sharecropper
SAERWN scale drawing
SAETTO space station
SAEUNS shamefulness
SAFAIE Sea of Galilee
SAFAMR Sea of Marmara
SAFEBR Stauffenburg
SAFKOS Sea of Okhotsk
SAFOLG staff college
SAFSEE snap-fastener
SAGEET snaggleteeth
SAGEOT snaggletooth
SAGRNL staggeringly
swaggeringly
SAGRTC swagger-stick
SAGTRU slaughterous
SAHIBN scaphoid bone
SAHNGA smash-and-grab
SAHUKE swashbuckler
SAIGOE staying power
SAIHTP Spanish Steps
SAIHUM Spanish tummy
SAILVK Stanislavsky
SAINAO station wagon
SAINOS station house
SAITCA statistician
SAIUNS spaciousness
SAKGIS stack against
SAKNTY slack in stays
SALODN smallholding
SALOTN small fortune
SALTEE scarlet fever
SALTOA scarlet woman
SALYNF Stanley knife®
SAMNWT swarming with
SAMRNL stammeringly
SANDAD Shaun Edwards
SANDLS stained glass

SAOBXN shadow-boxing
SAOEWO seasoned wood
SAOOIA scatological
SAOTCE season ticket
SAPHOE sharpshooter
SAPOGE sharp-tongued
SAPOKN sharp-looking
SAPSNS scampishness
snappishness
SARNAI Sharron Davis
SARNPR starring part
SARUNS scabrousness
SARWRS sparrow-grass
SASAGE star-spangled
SASPHR star sapphire
SATNGT starting gate
SATNWY slantingways
SATOKN start working
SATRNL scatteringly
smatteringly
SATROO starter motor
SATRRI scatterbrain
SATRRO shatterproof
SAUHAE Seamus Heaney
SAUMLO Seamus Mallon
SAUOZU Statue of Zeus
SAUSMO status symbol
SAUSUL statuesquely
SAWRNS stalwartness
SBAILR submaxillary
SBCIAL subscribable
SBCITO subscription
SBDTRA subeditorial
SBERNA subterranean
SBETVL subjectively
SBETVS subjectivise
subjectivism
subjectivist
SBETVZ subjectivize
SBEUNL subsequently
SBEUNT subsequent to
SBEVEC subservience
subserviency
SBIIAL subliminally
SBIIIL subdivisible
SBIIRL subsidiarily
SBIIRT subsidiarity
SBISVL submissively
SBLCAL subglacially
SBNEDT subinfeudate
SBNRDC subintroduce
SBNTHL St Benet's Hall
SBOMLT subnormality
SBOSIU subconscious
SBOTNN subcontinent
SBRCFO subtract from
SBRZTO suberization
SBSINO Sebastian Coe
SBTNIA substantival
SBTNIT substantiate
SBTTTO substitution
SBTTTV substitutive
SBTUTR substructure

SBUAEU subcutaneous
SBUTRL subsultorily
SCADIE sick and tired
SCAGAE social graces
SCAIAL saccadically
Socratically
SCAINS sectarianise
sectarianism
SCAINZ sectarianize
SCALNS sociableness
SCASAU social status
SCAWRE social worker
SCEAEU succedaneous
SCEDAL succeed rally
SCEPLC secret police
SCESNL successantly
SCESOA successional
SCESSE secret system
SCESTR success story
SCESUL successfully
SCESVL successively
SCEWEC socket-wrench
SCHAAH sick headache
SCICNS succinctness
SCIEIU sacrilegious
SCIIAI succinic acid
SCINLS sectionalise
sectionalism
SCINLZ sectionalize
SCLSAE sickle-shaped
SCNBLO second ballot
SCNCMN Second Coming
SCNCUI second cousin
SCNFDL second fiddle
SCNGOT second growth
SCNNTR second nature
SCNSRK second strike
SCNSRN second string
SCNTNN second to none
second-to-none
SCOILG sociobiology
SCOOIA sociological
SCPATS sycophantise
SCPATZ sycophantize
SCROAL sacerdotally
SCRTRS security risk
SCSINS secessionist
SDEABE sedge warbler
SDEBCE Sidney Bechet
SDESEL Sadler's Wells
SDEWAT sudden wealth
SDEWTE sodden-witted
SDFNED se defendendo
SDLBCE saddlebacked
SDLSIC saddle stitch
SDLUNS sedulousness
SDRATM sidereal time
SDRAYA sidereal year
SDTAKN sidetracking
SDWIKR side whiskers
SEAEBR Stefan Edberg
SEAHTE see each other
SECDFC speech defect

SECIYN speechifying
SECLSL speechlessly
SECMKN speech-making
SEEAKE Steve Backley
SEECUE Steve McQueen
SEEGAH stereography
SEEIOE stereoisomer
SEELGS speleologist
SEEMTI stereometric
SEENRI Steven Norris
SEEOST Steve Fossett
SEEPOI stereophonic
SEESOI stereoscopic
SEETPN stereotyping
SEGHME sledgehammer
SEHBCO see the back of
SEHNEE Stephen Benét
SEHNRN Stephen Crane
SEHRLN shepherdling
SEHRSI shepherd's pie
SEHSOI stethoscopic
SEIEPG specimen page
SEIFOR sheriff court
SEIIAL specifically
SEILFE special offer
SEILIH special right
SEILSI specialistic
SEIUNS speciousness
SEIWNE Stevie Wonder
SEKASL speak harshly
SEKATR steak tartare
SEKLIL speak plainly
SEKOUE speak volumes
SEKUEL speak quietly
SELEIH she'll be right
SELHCE spellchecker
SELHNS stealthiness
SELHSO steal the show
SELIDN spellbinding
SELNOC Stellenbosch
SELNPN Shetland pony
SELNSL steel oneself
SELNWO Shetland wool
SELOPN shell company
SEMHSL steam whistle
SEMNHL St Edmund Hall
SEMRDL Skelmersdale
SEMTCT spermatocyte
SEMTZA spermatozoal
spermatozoan
SEMTZI spermatozoic
spermatozoid
SEMTZO spermatozoon
SEMUBN steam turbine
SENTTO sternutation
SENTTR sternutatory
SENTTV sternutative
SEOAON see you around
SEORPE stenographer
SEORPI stenographic
SEOTEA step on the gas
SEPAKN sleepwalking
SEPEHS steeplechase
SEPHLO Sleepy Hollow
SEPIHL sleep lightly
SEPNDW stepping-down
SEPNPL sleeping pill
sleeping-pill
SEPSNS sheepishness
SEPSRE sheep's sorrel
SERARE spear-carrier
SERATC smear tactics
SERLAO steer clear of
SERNGA steering gear
SERNVD Sierra Nevada
SERYYO so early by now
SESOWR steps forward
SETAKN sweet-talking
SETCNE sweet-scented
SETHOG see it through
SETILA sweet william
SETLSU sweet alyssum
SETNSU sweet-and-sour
SETOCP spectroscope
spectroscopy
SETOEE spectrometer
SETOER spectrometry
SETOHN sweet nothing
SETORP spectrograph
SETOTE sweet-toothed
SETPGU steatopygous
SETRHE steatorrhoea
SETRUL stertorously
SETTRA spectatorial
SETUKL sweet fuck all
SETUKT sweat buckets
SFADON safe and sound
SFAHUE safe as houses
SFEDFA suffer defeat
SFFAHR soft feathers
SFGADN safeguarding
SFIINL sufficiently
SFLSFL softly-softly
SFOKUC Suffolk Punch
Suffolk punch
SFPDLE soft-pedalled
SFTFCO safety factor
SGATSO signal to stop
SGETTO segmentation
SGETVL suggestively
SGIIAC significance
significancy
SGLNUG sign language
SGRHPL sugar the pill
SGTEDN sight-reading
SGUDRU Sigmund Freud
SHAAEL Schiaparelli
SHAITC sphragistics
SHGOEE sphygmometer
SHGORP sphygmograph
SHHRZD Schéhérézade
SHMOWR scheme of work
SHNTRA sphincterial
SHOLAE school-leaver
SHOMSE schoolmaster
SHPNAE Schopenhauer
SHRCLT sphericality
SHSAIA schismatical
SHZCRI schizocarpic
SHZMCT schizomycete
SHZTYI schizothymia
schizothymic
SIACLM spinal column
SIADOE skin and bones
SIALNS suitableness
SIAORN slip a mooring
SIBETO stilboestrol
SIBIDN shipbuilding
SIDEUO swindle out of
SIEHLE spine-chiller
SIEMNE spider monkey
SIETHE stiletto heel
SIEUNS spitefulness
SIGHLA swing the lead
SIGLIE spiegeleisen
SIGRNL sniggeringly
SIHLWR slightly warm
SIHMTI stichomythia
SIIENS spiritedness
SIIGCL sliding scale
SIILSL spiritlessly
SIIOSL spirit of salt
SIIOWN spirit of wine
SIIULS spiritualise
spiritualism
spiritualist
SIIULT spirituality
SIIULZ spiritualize
SIIUST spirituosity
SIKBLT stickability
SIKELK stickler-like
SIKHPC stick the pace
SIKNRC stinking rich
SIKNSA spick and span
spick-and-span
SIKNSE snick and snee
SIKOTV stick-to-it-ive
SIKWCE sticky wicket
SILBBU spill a bibful
SILCTO spiflication
SILERN still-peering
SILNAO still and anon
SILNMS Stirling Moss
SILSAL shilly-shally
SIMGAH seismography
SIMLGS seismologist
SIMNBT swimming-bath
SIMNPN swimming-pond
SIMNPO swimming-pool
SINDPE skinny-dipper
SIOEBO suit one's book
SIOEMN slip one's mind
SIOEWY slip one's ways
SIOTEE slip of the pen
SIPNRP skipping-rope
SIPRNS slipperiness
SIPTNS snippetiness
SISEHO spinsterhood
SISICI ship's biscuit

SISRKC scissors kick
SITASE shirtwaister
SITEAL slip the cable
SITERE Saint George's
SITGAH scintigraphy
SITSNS skittishness
SITXPR Saint-Exupéry
SIUAIN stipulations
SIZETC swizzle-stick
SLAAYI self-analysis
SLAFCE self-affected
SLAHSV self-adhesive
SLAIAL syllabically
SLAINS saltationism
saltationist
Salvationist
SLALNS saleableness
SLAMRN self-admiring
SLAODL Salvador Dali
SLAOIU saltatorious
SLAPOA self-approval
SLASRE self-absorbed
SLAUEI Silva Eusebio
SLBIUL salubriously
SLCLUE self-coloured
SLCSIA solecistical
SLCTOE solicit votes
SLCTRN self-catering
SLCTTO solicitation
SLCTUL solicitously
SLDCIE self-deceiver
SLDPNE salad spinner
SLDSRC self-destruct
SLDSRS self-distrust
SLEDAE self-endeared
SLEDLA silver dollar
SLEFCN self-effacing
SLEIEC self-evidence
SLELNN silver lining
SLEPAE silver-plated
SLEPOE self-employed
SLESRE silver screen
SLETBS solvent abuse
SLETON salient point
SLGOIU self-glorious
SLHNMD sulphonamide
SLHNTY Solzhenitsyn
SLHRTO sulphuration
SLIBNO saltimbancos
SLIGLT selling plate
SLIGRC selling price
SLIIAL salvifically
SLILSI salpiglossis
SLITRS self-interest
SLIUTR silviculture
SLIVLE self-involved
SLLKCT Salt Lake City
SLLQIE soliloquizer
SLLSNS selflessness
SLMNSA solomon's seal❑
SLNGAH selenography
SLNIAL solenoidally
SLNINS splendidness
SLNLGS selenologist
SLNSRN Silent Spring
SLOESA sell overseas
SLOLDE salmon ladder
SLORTR sale or return
SLPESN self-pleasing
SLPRRI self-portrait
SLRATR solar battery
SLRDRI sclerodermia
sclerodermic
SLRLAC self-reliance
SLRNHM sclerenchyma
SLRPOC self-reproach
SLSASI salesmanship
SLSATN self-starting
SLSMNS selfsameness
SLTEFL splatter film
SLTEUM sell the dummy
SLTHVT split the vote
SLTNRC split on a rock
SLTRNS salutariness
solitariness
SLTTAL solstitially
SLTTOA salutational
SLTTRL salutatorily
SLYUNL Sally Gunnell
SMABLN somnambulant
SMABLS somnambulism
somnambulist
SMABLT somnambulate
SMANAL semi-annually
SMCRUA semicircular
SMDRNS semi-darkness
SMDSAC some distance
SMDTCE semi-detached
SMEBTE Samuel Butler
SMECNR Samuel Cunard
SMEKNA Sam Peckinpah
SMEPEP Samuel Phelps
SMEPLE Samuel Palmer
SMESHO summer school
SMETAE Simmenthaler
SMEWLE Samuel Weller
SMFNLS semifinalist
SMIOUS somniloquise
SMIOUZ somniloquize
SMLAET simultaneity
SMLAEU simultaneous
SMLMNE simple-minded
SMNAAL simoniacally
SMNFRU seminiferous
SMNIAL semantically
SMNOIA Simon Bolivar
Simón Bolívar
SMNUNT Simon Kuznets
SMODLC same old place
SMODON same old round
SMOELE someone else's
SMOIAL symbolically
SMPEIU semi-precious
SMRALE somersaulter
SMTMTS symptomatise
SMTMTZ symptomatize
SMTOIA semi-tropical
SNAABR Santa Barbara
SNADAC song and dance
SNADIE Sunday driver
SNAODN senza sordino
SNASHO Sunday school
SNCARE sonic barrier
SNCIAL synectically
SNCLUE sand-coloured
SNEATA San Sebastian
SNEFAT sense of taste
SNEFIH sense of right
sense of sight
SNEIAL syndetically
SNETAL sententially
SNHOIE synchronizer
SNILNS sensibleness
SNIOEE sensitometer
SNLCMA single combat
SNLDCE single-decker
SNLETT single entity
SNLFGR single-figure
SNLHNE single-handed
SNLMNE single-minded
SNLPRN single parent
SNNMUL synonymously
SNNPAE sun-and-planet
SNOOIG Santo Domingo
SNOPAS song of praise
SNPIAL synoptically
SNRHOE synarthroses
SNRNIC San Francisco
SNRTSI syncretistic
SNRUNS sonorousness
SNSEWS sinisterwise
SNSIAL sinusoidally
SNSRRA sinistrorsal
SNSRUL sinistrously
SNTFEL sanctifiedly
SNTOAL sanctionable
SNTPIO send to prison
SNTRAL senatorially
SNTRNS sanitariness
SNTUIR son et lumière
SNTZTO sanitization
SNUNLN sanguinolent
SNUNNS sanguineness
SNUNRL sanguinarily
SNUNTR sinful nature
SNUUNS sensuousness
SNXELN sun-expelling
SNYCTN sand-yachting
SNYOLN Sonny Rollins
SOAIAL sporadically
SOBADN snowboarding
SOBLTE snowball tree
SOBSNS show business
snobbishness
SOEAEN shove ha'penny
SOEAOR stonemasonry
SOEIEA stovepipe hat
SOELNS slovenliness
SOENRN Stoke-on-Trent

Words marked ❑ can also be spelled with an initial capital letter

SOEPAD slope upwards
SOEPOL spokespeople
SOEPRO spokesperson
SOFGTN stop fighting
SOFURE snow flurries
SOGAON stooge around
SOGFNE sponge finger
SOHRNL smotheringly
SOHUNS slothfulness
SOITER shot in the arm
SOITRS show interest
SOKATC shock tactics
SOKHRP shock therapy
SOKNMS stocking mask
SOKNRD stock-in-trade
SOKUIH stockpunisht
SOLEHG shoulder-high
SOLSNS spotlessness
SOMANN storm warning
SOMPTE stormy petrel
SONUNS scornfulness
SOOEFC show one's face
SOOEHA show one's head
SOOEHN show one's hand
SOPGTM stoppage time
SOPHPO scoop the pool
SOPNLS shopping list
SOPNML shopping mall
SOPOFS scorpion fish
SOPRCP snooperscope
SOTCSE sportscaster
SOTEMS short-termism
SOTERE stout-hearted
SOTESO short version
SOTGON sports ground
SOTHCO shoot the crow
SOTHNE short-changer
SOTHOD shout the odds
SOTICI short circuit
short-circuit
SOTIHE shortsighted
short-sighted
SOTJCE sports jacket
SOTKVC Shostakovich
SOTNIO shooting iron
SOTNSA shooting star
shooting-star
sport one's oak
SOTOMN short commons
SOTPRO sportsperson
SOTSFL Scottish Fold
SOTSOE smooth-spoken
SOTTEA smooth the way
SOTTFE short-staffed
SOTVNS sportiveness
SOYELN story-telling
SOYERE stony-hearted
SOZBTO snooze button
SPARIA supraorbital
SPAUDN supramundane
SPEEAC supreme sauce
SPEEEN Supreme Being
supreme being
SPEEOR Supreme Court
supreme court
SPENAL septennially
SPETAL sapientially
SPIHAE Sopwith Camel
SPITCT sophisticate
SPLCTN supplicating
SPLCTO supplication
SPLCTR supplicatory
SPLMNA supplemental
SPOTRU support group
SPOTVL supportively
SPOTVT supportive to
SPRAGE supercargoes
SPRAUA supernatural
SPRAUU supernaculum
SPRBLT separability
SPREEC supersedence
SPREIN supervenient
SPRESO supersession
SPRETO supervention
SPRHRE supercharger
SPRIHA superhighway
SPRIIR superciliary
SPRIIU supercilious
SPRMOE superimposed
SPRNUT superannuate
SPRODC superconduct
SPRSEL suppressedly
SPRSIL suppressible
SPRTFO separate from
SPRTIE separatrices
SPRTNS separateness
SPRTRO superstardom
SPRTTO superstition
SPRUAL superhumanly
SPRUDN supermundane
SPRUIA superluminal
SPRVLT superovulate
SPTRBR St Petersburg
SPUGSM Septuagesima
SQETAL sequentially
SQETAO sequestrator
SRAAIL sarsaparilla
SRAALT spread a plate
SRAAON spread around
SRAEAE surface water
SRAEGE spread-eagled
SRAEOI surface-to-air
SRAEOS surface noise
SRAGSI spread gossip
SRAKLE serial killer
SRANME serial number
SRASNL surpassingly
SRASRA Sirhan Sirhan
SRBCLT scrobiculate
SRBLNL scribblingly
SRBSIA strabismical
SRBSOI stroboscopic
SRCDMU Sir Scudamour
SRCNNS strychninism
SRDLBC straddleback
SRDLGE stridelegged
SRDLNL stridulantly
SRDLTO stridulation
SRDLTR stridulatory
SRDVRU Stradivarius
SREAIN sorbefacient
SREHCE street hockey
SREHTR serve the turn
SRELAC surveillance
SRELSI surrealistic
SRENKO surgeon's knot
SRENTO Sergeant Troy
SREOWR surge forward
SREPRE Street-Porter
SRETAE street-trader
SRETFR serpentiform
SRETNL serpentinely
SRETNS serpentinise
SRETNZ serpentinize
SRETTR serve its turn
SREWIE screen writer
screenwriter
SREWLE streetwalker
street-walker
SRFOEL surefootedly
SRGLNL stragglingly
strugglingly
SRGLWT struggle with
SRGTUL sprightfully
SRHAGA Sarah Vaughan
SRHIDN Sarah Siddons
SRIAMS surgical mask
SRIAON strain a point
SRIEOA servicewoman
SRIEOE servicewomen
SRIGRI Sergio Garcia
SRIHAA straight away
straightaway
SRIHDW straight down
SRIHEE straightened
SRIHEG straightedge
SRIHEU straighten up
SRIHFA skreigh of day
SRIHNS straightness
SRIHWY straightways
SRIJCE straitjacket
SRKAAC strike a match
SRKAIH strike a light!
SRKIRC strike it rich
SRKOLC stroke of luck
SRLBUG Struldbruggs
SRLGRE shrill-gorged
SRMLNL scramblingly
SRNCUS string course
SRNLHL stranglehold
SRNLQO strong liquor
SRNMNE strong-minded
SRNRYH sprung rhythm
SRNTEE strengthener
SRNTMN spring to mind
SRNWLE strong-willed
SROAOI sarcomatosis
SROIAL sardonically
SROLSI sarcoplasmic

Code	Entry
SRONAL	surmountable
SRONEB	surrounded by
SRONIG	surroundings
SRPATO	strip cartoon
SRPEGA	strippergram
SRPIAL	seraphically
SRPLST	scrupulosity
SRPLUL	scrupulously
SRPOOC	streptococci
SRPOYI	streptomycin
SRPROR	scraperboard
SRPRUL	streperously
SRPSTV	seropositive
SRPTNL	strepitantly
SRPUAL	scripturally
SRPWIE	scriptwriter
SRRSNL	surprisingly
SRTGAH	stratigraphy
SRTHAK	stretch marks
SRTHDU	stretched out
SRTHNL	scratchingly
SRTHNS	scratchiness
	stretchiness
SRTHUL	scratchbuild
SRTNUL	scrutinously
SRTNZN	scrutinizing
SRTSHR	stratosphere
SRUOHN	sarrusophone
SRVLEU	shrivelled up
SRVNTM	shriving-time
SSACEA	Saskatchewan
SSEAIE	systematized
SSELNS	sisterliness
SSESNA	sisters-in-law
SSESVL	suspensively
SSIIUL	suspiciously
SSIIUO	suspicious of
SSMIBN	sesamoid bone
SSNNHN	Susan Anthony
SSOATI	so soon as this
STAINS	situationism
STFLTE	set of clothes
STHLAG	Satchel Paige
STIGPR	setting apart
STLACR	settle a score
STLUWT	settle up with
STNSAA	set one's cap at
STNSET	set one's teeth
STSATO	satisfaction
STSATR	satisfactory
STSYNL	satisfyingly
SUAYLA	squeaky clean
	squeaky-clean
SUBRNL	slubberingly
	slumberingly
SUBRNS	stubbornness
SUBRUL	slumberously
SUDNSI	studdingsail
SUDRNL	shudderingly
SUDSBL	sound as a bell
SUEAIN	stupefacient
SUEATO	stupefaction
SUEATV	stupefactive
SUEDUL	stupendously
SUFDHR	stuffed shirt
SUFNSL	stuff oneself
SUGSNS	sluggishness
SUHAII	South Pacific
SUHATR	south-eastern
SUHERI	South Georgia
SUHETR	south-western
SUHHED	South Shields
SUHMRC	South America
SUHRAP	Southern Alps
SUHRMS	southernmost
SUHRWO	southernwood
SUIUNS	spuriousness
	studiousness
SULSNS	soullessness
SUPUAL	sculpturally
SURLUL	scurrilously
SURNME	square number
SURRGE	square-rigged
	square-rigger
SURTNE	slurry tanker
SUSIRN	soul-stirring
SUSTNI	squash tennis
SUTRNL	saunteringly
	sputteringly
	stutteringly
SUTSNS	sluttishness
SVNYIH	seventy-eight
SVOEFC	save one's face
SVOENC	save one's neck
SVOESI	save one's skin
SVRNEA	severance pay
SVYABG	savoy cabbage
SVYHAR	Savoy Theatre
SWHSEO	sow the seed of
SWOTRO	sawtooth roof
SXAAUE	sexual abuser
SXADSR	sexual desire
SXAOGN	sexual organs
SXFHBS	six of the best
SXGNRA	sexagenarian
SXHRPS	sex therapist
SXIHTM	six-eight time
SXOEIO	sextodecimos
SYEFRS	style of dress
SYHSOA	scyphistomae
	scyphistomas
TAAOAI	thanatomania
TAASEI	thalassaemia
TACERO	thatched roof
TAEAEC	travel agency
TAEARS	travel across
TAEBLT	traceability
TAECNI	tradescantia
TAELMN	trace element
TAEOER	trapezohedra
TAEORA	trade journal
TAEOTO	traded option
TAEPOL	tradespeople
TAEPRO	tradesperson
TAETRL	travesty role
TAETWR	travel to work
TAEUAE	trabeculated
TAEULA	Tracey Ullman
TAEWDL	travel widely
TAHOTM	tracheostomy
TAIGTM	trading stamp
TAIINS	traditionist
TAIOIA	tragicomical
TAKGVN	thanksgiving
TAKNDW	tracking-down
TAKUNS	thankfulness
TALHOG	trawl through
TALNET	to all intents
TANPTE	train-spotter
TAOEHI	tear one's hair
TAPLNN	trampolining
TAPLNS	trampolinist
TAPOFL	teaspoonfuls
TAQILS	tranquillise
TAQILT	tranquillity
TAQILZ	tranquillize
TAQINS	tranquilness
TASAAL	translatable
TASAEC	transparency
TASAII	transpacific
TASCAI	transoceanic
TASCIN	transactions
TASDTO	transudation
TASEAL	transferable
TASEDN	transcendent
TASEEC	transference
TASELS	transfer list
TASESL	transversely
TASETS	transvestism
TASETT	transvestite
TASIAL	transpirable
TASIMN	transhipment
TASIPN	transhipping
TASIRT	transmigrate
TASISO	transmission
TASISV	transmissive
TASLNE	transplanter
TASOAL	transposable
TASOMN	transforming
TASORF	transmogrify
TASOTN	transmontane
	transporting
TASRSO	transgressor
TASSAB	that's as may be
TASTOA	transitional
TASTRL	transitorily
TASTVL	transitively
TASUAC	transhumance
TASUAL	transmutable
	transmutably
TASUEC	translucence
	translucency
TATBLT	tractability
TATNFR	toasting-fork
TATPEE	tear to pieces
TATRUL	traitorously
TATSRD	tear to shreds
TBEIEC	table licence
TBEPCE	to be expected

Code	Word
TBLREL	tubular bells
TBRFRU	tuberiferous
TBRUAE	tuberculated
TBRUOI	tuberculosis
TBRURO	tuberous root
TBSEII	to be specific
TBTLTA	Tibet Plateau
TCEWNO	ticket window
TCLSNS	tactlessness
	ticklishness
TCNBBL	technobabble
TCNCAI	technocratic
TCNCLT	technicality
TCNPOI	technophobia
	technophobic
TCOIAL	tectonically
TCYRPE	tachygrapher
TCYRPI	tachygraphic
TDRHVO	Todor Zhivkov
TEACHR	The March Hare
TEADHR	then and there
TEADTF	the hard stuff
TEAEAE	The Caretaker
TEAECT	The Naked City
TEAEER	teenage years
TEAETC	therapeutics
TEAHTE	The Mad Hatter
TEAIAL	thematically
TEAKRE	The Valkyries
TEAPNE	The Carpenter
TEASNE	The Passenger
TEATLN	The Waste Land
TEATNM	the last enemy
TEATTA	the last straw
TECMRA	trench mortar
TECNMS	The Economist
TECPGA	The Scapegoat
TECPOG	trench-plough
TECRCO	The Scarecrow
TEDESR	the Adversary
TEDETN	trendsetting
TEDNAT	thés dansants
TEEDUL	tremendously
TEEESA	the Seven Seas
TEEESR	the necessary
TEEGIS	thereagainst
TEEKIH	The Red Knight
TEELCO	the real McCoy
TEELHN	the real thing
TEENFE	thereinafter
TEENTE	there and then
TEEODE	The Second Sex
TEESNE	the bee's knees
TEEYHN	the very thing
TEFHIH	Twelfth Night
TEFRSI	the aforesaid
TEGRGT	the aggregate
TEHNRN	teething ring
TEIABO	the final blow
TEIDIE	The Pied Piper
TEIDOE	The Windhover
TEIEFA	the time of day
TEIHMR	The Nightmare
TEIKAE	The Pink Paper
TEIKDN	the wicked one
TEITCE	Themistocles
TEITRN	the bitter end
TEIYFO	The City of God
TEKNAO	tree kangaroo
TELBIE	the Old Bailey
TELCAC	treble chance
TELHMS	The Alchemist
TEMCUL	thermocouple
TEMGAH	thermography
TEMRLA	The Umbrellas
TEMSAI	thermostatic
TEMSHR	thermosphere
TEMSLS	Thermos® flask
TENHOI	theanthropic
TEOBIE	Trevor Bailey
TEODNS	The Golden Ass
TEOEHN	the done thing
TEOEWE	The Go-Between
TEOFIN	The Boy Friend
TEOFTE	The Godfather
TEOHWR	Trevor Howard
TEOLIM	the world is my
TEOLOE	the world over
TEOLSN	the world's end
TEONMR	the morn's morn
TEONOE	The Young Ones
TEONOK	the boondocks
TEOQEO	the Conqueror
TEOSHL	the Household
TEOSTA	The Mousetrap
TEOTOL	The Lost World
TEPCAO	The Spectator
TEPRMN	The Apartment
TEPRSU	Theophrastus
TERAMN	the treatment
TERNDK	The Grand Duke
TERNSO	the wrong shop
TERTCA	theoretician
TERZRN	the prize-ring
TESLNK	Thessaloníki
TESRHN	treasure hunt
TESRNT	treasury note
TESWES	teensy-weensy
TETEOA	Theatre Royal
TETESD	the other side
TETIAL	theatrically
TETORM	Treaty of Rome
TETRGE	the story goes
TETSHR	treat as a hero
TETTET	twenty-twenty
TEUARC	the human race
TEUYOM	The Lucy Poems
TEVOLC	twelve o'clock
TEYPSU	The Symposium
TGLSIC	toggle switch
TGTENS	togetherness
TGTEWT	together with
TGTITN	tight-fitting
TIAEAL	trilaterally
TIATTO	tripartition
TIBULN	thin blue line
TIDEDN	third reading
TIEPOL	tribespeople
TIETNR	tricentenary
TIETSU	toilet tissue
TIGISD	things inside
TIGMYI	thingummyjig
TIGMYO	thingummybob
TIGRAP	trigger-happy
TIHHNA	triphthongal
TIHLGS	trichologist
TIHNLA	trichinellae
	trichinellas
TIHNPL	Trichinopoly
TIHOAI	trichromatic
TIHRAD	thitherwards
TIHTMS	trichotomise
TIHTMU	trichotomous
TIHTMZ	trichotomize
TIIHZN	twilight zone
TIILTE	trivialities
TIIYOS	Trinity House
TIKALO	think badly of
TIKFIH	trick of light
TIKHOG	think through
TIKIHE	thick-sighted
TIKKNE	thick-skinned
TIKNBC	thinking back
TIKRRA	trick or treat
TIKYLS	trick cyclist
TILAAC	trial balance
TILALO	trial balloon
TILCRD	triglyceride
TILCTO	triplication
TILSRT	to illustrate
TILTNU	triple-tongue
TILTRE	triple-turned
TIMHLS	triumphalism
	triumphalist
TIMHNL	triumphantly
TINUAL	triangularly
TIOILS	trinomialism
	trinomialist
TIOOER	trigonometry
TIOTEY	tail of the eye
TISLHT	thiosulphate
TITETL	thirteenthly
TITNTR	twist and turn
TITRNL	twitteringly
TITTOO	thirty-twomos
TIUAIN	tribulations
TIUCTO	trifurcation
TIUERU	Tribune group
TIVSNS	thievishness
TKAAFO	take away from
TKAAOE	take as a model
TKAEKA	take a dekko at
TKAELN	take a telling
TKAETN	take a beating
TKAHNT	take a shine to
TKARDI	take a pride in
TKCAGO	take charge of
TKDWAE	take down a peg
TKFIHA	take fright at

TKFRRD take for a ride
TKIFOM take it from me
TKIKNL take it kindly
TKKNLT take kindly to
TKMAUE take measures
TKNCRO taking care of
TKNTCO take notice of
TKOCSO take occasion
TKOEES take one's ease
TKOEFO take over from
TKOEHO take one's hook
TKOESA take one's seat
TKOETM take one's time
TKOETR take one's turn
TKOTLA take out a loan
TKPESR take pleasure
TKPRWT take part with
TKTEEN take the reins
TKTEHE take the wheel
TKTEHI take the chair
TKTEIL take the field
TKTEIT take the Fifth
TKTELO take the floor
TKTPEE take to pieces
TKUAAE take unawares
TLCMUE telecommuter
TLDOSA till doomsday
TLETEI telaesthesia
TLEVLE tilley-valley
TLGAHS telegraphese
telegraphist
TLIGED Talking Heads
TLIGON talking point
talking-point
TLNNES talk nonsense
TLOCNL tallow-candle
TLOOIA teleological
TLPOEO telephone box
TLPOPE Teleprompter
TLRBLT tolerability
TLRIAL telergically
TLSOPN teleshopping
TLTERT tell the truth
TLUPWE talcum powder
TLVSAL televisually
TLVVAF Tel Aviv-Jaffa
TLYAAA Telly Savalas
TMADGI time and again
TMADHL time and a half
TMBWSE time-bewasted
TMEAII temperalitie
TMEPSR time exposure
TMHNUE time-honoured
TMLOHR Temple of Hera
TMLPRE timely-parted
TMLSNS timelessness
TMLUUL tumultuously
TMMGZN Time Magazine
TMOABN temporal bone
TMOALB temporal lobe
TMOAYS temporary use
TMRUNS timorousness
TMYADE Tommy Handley
TNALNA ten-gallon hat
TNAONT tantamount to
TNATRE Tennant Creek
TNDANS tone-deafness
TNEAON tinker around
TNEHFE tender-hefted
TNENBE Tintern Abbey
TNETAL tangentially
TNEVSO tunnel vision
TNILNS tangibleness
TNINBL tintinnabula
TNLNUG tone language
TNMRIO Toni Morrison
TNNFRE tenant farmer
TNSELM tungsten lamp
TOABCE Thomas Becket
TOABON Thomas Browne
TOADKE Thomas Dekker
TOAEIO Thomas Edison
TOAENS two-facedness
TOAHBE Thomas Hobbes
TOAHGE Thomas Hughes
TOAHXE Thomas Huxley
TOAIDC thoracic duct
TOALDE Two Fat Ladies
TOAMRE Thomas Murner
TOASVR Thomas Savery
TOAWLE Thomas Waller
Thomas Wolsey
TOAWRO Thomas Warton
TOBEAE troublemaker
TOBEHO troubleshoot
TOGTUL thoughtfully
TOHDHE toothed wheel
TOHDHL toothed whale
TOHNEI trochanteric
TOHNNI tooth and nail
TOLDTS troglodytism
TOLYAE troll-my-dames
TOODLT two-toed sloth
TOOGBE thoroughbred❑
TOOGFR thoroughfare
TOOGNS thoroughness
TOONCI two pound coin
TOOPEI tropospheric
TOTUNE Trout Quintet
TPATEI tapsalteerie
TPEETO to prefection
TPFCTO typification
TPFHTE top of the tree
TPIEUV topside-turvy
TPITEI tapsieteerie
TPRCRE tape recorder
TPRETO to perfection
TPSEIE type specimen
TPYUVL topsy-turvily
TRAEAC tartare sauce
TRAEFA turn a deaf ear
TRAEOS terrace house
TRAIAI tartaric acid
TRAOLF thread of life
TRAPRL Tyrian purple
TRBAUA terebratulae
terebratulas
TRCTNA turn cat in pan
TRDWCL turn down cold
TRECRE Turkey carpet
TREICE Three Witches
TRELRA turbellarian
TRETAL torrentially
TRETNL tormentingly
TRETNR tercentenary
TREURE three-quarter
TRFLSL thriftlessly
TRIEST tergiversate
TRIGON turning-point
TRIGSD turning aside
turning-aside
TRIIAL terrifically
TRITCS turn into cash
TRIYNL terrifyingly
TRLSNS tirelessness
TRMNSA Turkmenistan
TRMSLT taramasalata
TRNEWT thronged with
TRNIAL tyrannically
TROEBC turn one's back
TROECA turn one's coat
TROEET turn of events
TROEHA turn one's head
TROHRE turbocharged
turbocharger
TROOFC term of office
TROPRS turn of phrase
TRSIGU thrashing-out
TRSMNS tiresomeness
TRTECE turn the screw
TRTECL turn the scale
TRUHTE through-other
TRUTUP turn up trumps
TRUUNS tortuousness
TRWIHO throw light on
TRWNAA throwing-away
TRWWBL throw a wobbly
TRYILA Terry Gilliam
TSAETR testamentary
TSEGNL tassel-gentle
TSELTO tessellation
TSEUNS tastefulness
TSMDGE to some degree
TSMETN to some extent
TSMSRS taskmistress
TSOTRN testosterone
TSTBBB test-tube baby
TSTEAE test the water
TTAEFC to that effect
TTAERN tetrahedrons
TTAERT tetrahedrite
TTAOAL tetragonally
TTAYLN tetracycline
TTEUPS to the purpose
TTFESV Tet Offensive
TTLCIS total eclipse
TTLTRA totalitarian
TTLTTL tittle-tattle
TUACPT Truman Capote

TUBHOG thumb through
TUDFAC Tour de France
TUDRLS thunderflash
TUDRLU thundercloud
TUDRTN thunder-stone
TUDRTR thunderstorm
TUDRUL thunderously
TUHIHL touch lightly
TUHNNS touchingness
TUHUNS truthfulness
TUITLS tourist class
TUITOT tourist route
TUOEAO tour operator
TUOIAL Teutonically
TUOOIA tautological
TUTUNS trustfulness
TWITWO tu-whit tu-whoo
TWRALT Tower Hamlets
TWRFAE Tower of Babel
TXCLGS toxicologist
TYODLN thyroid gland
TYORPI thyrotrophin
UAAYAL unanalysable
UACPAL unacceptable
unacceptably
UACSOE unaccustomed
UADUNN up and running
UAFCEB unaffected by
UAFCEL unaffectedly
UAFLAE unaffiliated
UAGESV unaggressive
UAHEAL unachievable
UALVAE unalleviated
UAOOEI unapologetic
UAORPE uranographer
UAORPI uranographic
UAPAAL unappeasable
UAPTZN unappetizing
UAQANE unacquainted
UASCAE unassociated
UASEAL unanswerable
unanswerably
UASIAL unassailable
UASIIU unauspicious
UASMNL unassumingly
UATATV unattractive
UATIAL unattainable
UATOIE unauthorized
UAVRIE unadvertised
UBAENS unbiasedness
UBAEUL umbrageously
UBCMNL unbecomingly
UBFINE unbefriended
UBIKNL unblinkingly
UBLCTO umbilication
UBLEAL unbelievable
unbelievably
UBNEEA urban renewal
UBNZTO urbanization
UBOENS unbrokenness
UBUHNL unblushingly
UCAGAL unchangeable
unchangeably
UCAIAL uncharitable
UCALNE unchallenged
UCASFE unclassified
UCATNS unchasteness
UCIIAL uncritically
UCLBAE uncelebrated
UCLIAE uncultivated
UCLIAL uncultivable
UCLUAE uncalculated
UCMECA uncommercial
UCMONS uncommonness
UCNERT unconsecrate
UCNESN unconversant
UCNICN unconvincing
UCNIEE unconsidered
UCNIEL unconfinedly
UCNOMT unconformity
UCNRLE uncontrolled
UCNTAN unconstraint
UCNUAL unconsumable
UCUUNS unctuousness
UDCIAL undeceivable
UDFAAL undefeatable
UDLTNL undulatingly
UDMCAI undemocratic
UDMNSE undiminished
UDPNAL undependable
UDPOAI undiplomatic
UDRAMN undergarment
underpayment
UDRCIV underachieve
UDRCRN underscoring
UDREDN underfeeding
UDREEO under-develop
UDREFR underperform
UDREPE underpeopled
UDRHHE under the heel
UDRINN underpinning
UDRKNE underskinker
UDRLNE underblanket
UDRLTE underclothed
underclothes
UDRLYN underplaying
UDRNSA under one's hat
UDROTO under control
UDRRDC under-produce
UDRRSE underdressed
UDRRTN underwriting
UDRRTS under protest
UDRRUH underwrought
UDRRWN underdrawing
UDRTFE understaffed
UDRUDN underfunding
UDRURN undercurrent
UDSENN undiscerning
UDSGAE undesignated
UDSGEL undesignedly
UDSOEE undiscovered
UDSRBE undesirables
UDSREL undeservedly
UDSUEL undisputedly
UDTCAL undetectable
UDTREB undeterred by
UDTRIE undetermined
UDUTNL undoubtingly
UDVSEL undivestedly
UEAEUL use carefully
UEFINL user-friendly
UEHOCP urethroscope
urethroscopy
UENSRI use one's brain
UEOOIA uneconomical
UEPCEL unexpectedly
UEPESV unexpressive
UEPOAL unemployable
UEPOMN unemployment
UEPRAE unexpurgated
UEPRNL use sparingly
UERNNS unerringness
UFATRN unflattering
UFEUNE unfrequented
UFIHUL unfaithfully
UFINLL unfriendlily
UFMNNT unfemininity
UFRIAL unforgivable
UFTOAL unfathomable
unfathomably
UFVUAL unfavourable
unfavourably
UGAEUL ungratefully
UGAIUL ungraciously
UGILNS ungainliness
UGNLNS ungentleness
UGONEL ungroundedly
UGVRAL ungovernable
ungovernably
UHNSML unhandsomely
UHROIU unharmonious
UHSTTN unhesitating
UIAEAL unilaterally
UIAIAL unimaginable
unimaginably
UIAINS Unitarianism
UIEITL uniseriately
UIESAE United States
UIESLS universalise
universalism❑
Universalist
UIESLT universality
UIESLZ universalize
UIESTE universities
UIETFE unidentified
UIEULT unisexuality
UIFUNE uninfluenced
UIIDIL unified field
UIOEIA urinogenital
UIPESV unimpressive
UIPRAC unimportance
UIPRAL unimpartable
UIPRIL unimpartible
UITRSE uninterested
UIUTUL ubiquitously
ULDCLN ugly duckling
ULENIE uillean pipes
ULFCTO uglification
ULKLHO unlikelihood

Words marked ❑ can also be spelled with an initial capital letter

ULKLNS unlikeliness
ULVLNS unloveliness
ULWUNS unlawfulness
UMAUAL unmeasurably
UMITIE unmaintained
UMNGAL unmanageable
UMRIUL unmercifully
UMSAAL unmistakable
unmistakably
UMTOIA unmethodical
UNTCAL unnoticeable
unnoticeably
UNTRLS unnaturalise
UNTRLZ unnaturalize
UOESEV up one's sleeve
UOESRE up one's street
UOFCAL unofficially
UOIUNS uxoriousness
UOMHNU upon my honour
UONMNE unornamented
UOOELG upon one's legs
UOSRCE unobstructed
UOSREL unobservedly
UOTEHL upon the whole
UOTELR upon the alert
UOTENI upon the anvil
UOTIAL unobtainable
UPBIIE unpublicized
UPEAEL unpreparedly
UPESNL unpleasantly
unpleasingly
UPEUIE unprejudiced
UPICPE unprincipled
UPNTAL unpunctually
UPOETN unprotesting
UPOIAL unprofitable
UPOIEL unprovidedly
UPOIIN unproficient
UPOIIU unpropitious
UPOLIE unproclaimed
UPOOEL unprovokedly
UPOONE unpronounced
UPOUTV unproductive
UPPLRT unpopularity
UPRLEE unparalleled
UPRLSE upper classes
UPROAL unpardonable
UPSESN unpossessing
UQECAL unquenchable
UQETOE unquestioned
URAIUL uproariously
URAOAL unreasonable
unreasonably
URCGIE unrecognized
URCLAL unrecallable
URGNRC unregeneracy
URGNRT unregenerate
URGTUL unrightfully
URMMEE unremembered
URMRAL unremarkable
URMREU unremorseful
URMTEL unremittedly
URPAAL unrepeatable
URPIAL unrepairable
URPOCE unreproached
URQIEL unrequitedly
URSLAL unresolvable
URSOSV unresponsive
URSRCE unrestricted
URSREL unreservedly
URSRIE unrestrained
USACAL unsearchable
unsearchably
USAOAL unseasonable
unseasonably
USAUAL unstatutably
USBISV unsubmissive
USCESU unsuccessful
USEDNS unsteadiness
USELNS unseemliness
USEVNL unswervingly
USINII unscientific
USITNL unstintingly
USMNRE unseminaried
USNTFE unsanctified
USNTOE unsanctioned
USNULS unsensualise
USNULZ unsensualize
USPLNS unsuppleness
USPRIE unsupervised
USRCUE unstructured
USRPLU unscrupulous
USRRSN unsurprising
USSEAI unsystematic
USSETN unsuspecting
USSIIU unsuspicious
USTSYN unsatisfying
UTAMLE untrammelled
UTAOTN ultramontane
UTAUDN ultramundane
UTIKNL unthinkingly
UTMLNS untimeliness
UTNBLT untenability
UTOBEL untroubledly
UTOEEE up to one's eyes
UTOENC up to one's neck
UTOEUL ultroneously
UTRRDS Uttar Pradesh
UTTITM up to this time
UTUHUL untruthfully
UTWRNS untowardness
UVNIAE unventilated
UVNUSE unvanquished
UVREAE unvariegated
UVRFAL unverifiable
UVRUUL unvirtuously
UWEDNS unwieldiness
UWITNA unwritten law
UWNENS unwontedness
UWRHNS unworthiness
UWVRNL unwaveringly
UYEDNL unyieldingly
VBAHNS vibraphonist
VBAINL vibratiuncle
VBAUAI vibracularia
VCFRTO vociferation
VCFRUL vociferously
VCLZTO vocalization
VCODJU Victor de Jouy
VCOINS Victorianism
VCOIPA Victoria Peak
VCOIUL victoriously
VCOIWO Victoria Wood
VCREEA vicar-general
VCTOAL vocationally
VCUPCE vacuum-packed
VGRUNS vigorousness
VGTBEA vegetable fat
vegetable wax
VGTBEI vegetable oil
VGTTVL vegetatively
VIEULT voice quality
VIGOIU vainglorious
VLAEMS Villahermosa
VLAIAL volcanically
VLALNS valuableness
VLANUL villainously
VLCRPO Velociraptor
VLEALT vulnerable to
VLEGAD velvet-guards
VLERAL value greatly
VLESOE velvet-scoter
VLFCTO vilification
VLMNUL voluminously
VLNAYS voluntaryism
VLOIEL Valpolicella
VLPUUL voluptuously
VLRZTO valorization
velarization
VLTAKN valet parking
VLTLNS volatileness
VLTOAL volitionally
VMTRTO vomiturition
VNAEON vantage point
VNCLUA vinicultural
VNETRC Vincent Price
VNEUNS vengefulness
VNFCUL veneficously
VNITVL vindictively
VNMMUH venom'd-mouth'd
VNMUNS venomousness
VNPNTR venepuncture
venipuncture
VNRIAR vin ordinaire
VNUECU Venture Scout
VNUSAL vanquishable
VNUSMN vanquishment
VOAAAB viola da gamba
VOOCLO violoncellos
VPRUNS vaporousness
VPRZTO vaporization
VRALNS variableness
VRALSA variable star
VRAUAL vernacularly
VRBITI Vera Brittain
VRCLUE varicoloured
VRDCLT veridicality
VRDSEC viridescence
VREMNE vervet monkey

VRERTO vertebration
VRFCTO verification
VRFCTR verificatory
VRIANS verticalness
VRIIAO versificator
VRIILN Virginia Leng
VRIILT verticillate
VRIIRE Virginia reel
VRIIWD Virginia Wade
VRIMRI Vernis Martin
VRIUAE vermiculated
VRIUTR vermiculture
VRLSEC virilescence
VRUUNS virtuousness
VSAVRI vestal virgin
VSONSI viscountship
VSTRBO visitors' book
VSTTRA visitatorial
VTCLUA viticultural
VTEUNS vitreousness
VTIFVU vote in favour
VTLTGT vitilitigate
VTLZTO vitalization
VTNRGT voting rights
VTPRTO vituperation
VTPRTV vituperative
VTSRIH vote straight
VUEILA vaudevillian
VVFCTO vivification
VVPRUL viviparously
WABLNE weal-balanced
WAEFTM whale of a time
WAHRHR weather chart
WAHRLN weather along
WAHRLS weather glass
WAHRON weather-bound
WAHROR weatherboard
WAHRRO weatherproof
WAHRTI weather strip
WAHUNS wrathfulness
WAMNEL weak-mindedly
WAMTEI what matter if
WASENM what's-her-name
WASHOD what's the odds?
WASINM what's-his-name
WASOKN what's cooking?
WASONO what's going on
WASTNM what's-its-name
WATEEI what the devil
WCEKEE wicket-keeper
WCIFHL Wycliffe Hall
WDIGAC wedding march
WDIGOE wedding-dower
WDIGRS wedding dress
WDRCIE wide receiver
WECENS wretchedness
WECSEE whencesoever
WEHRRO whether or not
WELNAL wheel and axle
WELNDA wheel and deal
WFSAPN wife-swapping
WIADTA waif and stray
WIEAPO white campion
WIEDIA white admiral
WIEETE white feather
WIENCL white-knuckle
WIERTC write protect
write-protect
WIESRM writer's cramp
WIEUCL write quickly
WIEUDN white pudding
WIEUSA White Russian
WIEWYO write away for
WIGEUO wriggle out of
WIHGIS weigh against
WIHNAO weighing a ton
WIHRAD whitherwards
WIHSHC which is which?
WIIGAL writing-table
WIKGLR Whisky Galore
WIKRNO whiskerandos
WIPRNL whimperingly
whisperingly
WIPRUL whisperously
WISCLT whimsicality
WISOPO whip scorpion
WISOTN wainscotting
WKTEIH wake the night
WLAAFO walk away from
WLAAWT walk away with
WLADIB Willard Libby
WLAETT welfare state
WLAJSE well-adjusted
WLARNE well-arranged
WLAVNE well-advanced
WLBLNE well balanced
well-balanced
WLDRCE well-directed
WLDSGE well-designed
WLDSOE well-disposed
WLDSRE well-deserved
WLECNO Walter Cannon
WLEMUN Wilhelm Kühne
WLEPYO Walter Payton
WLEUAE well-educated
WLEWIH welterweight
WLGONE well-grounded
WLHAEI welsh rarebit❑
WLHAIT wild hyacinth
WLHRES Walther Nerst
WLHRSE Welsh dresser
WLICRO Willie Carson
WLIELR well I declare!
WLIFRE well-informed
WLIGNI walking on air
WLIGOI Wellingtonia
WLIGRM walking-frame
WLIGTC walking stick
walking-stick
WLIMAE William Carey
William James
William Paley
WLIMAU William Hague
WLIMBR Williamsburg
WLIMLG William Bligh
WLIMLK William Blake
WLIMLR William Clark
WLIMON William Johns
WLIMOT William Booth
WLIMRG William Bragg
WLIMRU William Prout
WLIMSO William Astor
WLIMUK William Burke
WLIMYE William Wyler
WLITLI walkie-talkie
WLLDSA Will Ladislaw
WLLFPR wildlife park
WLMNEE well-mannered
WLOFAA Waldorf salad
WLOHWS will-o'-the-wisp
WLOIAO wallop in a tow
WLPOIE well-provided
WLRAOE well-reasoned
WLSAOE well-seasoned
WLSPLE well-supplied
WLTEHL walk the chalk
WLTELN walk the plank
WLTETL Wilt the Stilt
WLUEEL walk unevenly
WLUWIH Wilbur Wright
WLVREI well-versed in
WLYUSL Willy Russell
WMLYRN Wembley Arena
WMNOOA woman-to-woman
WMNRGT women's rights
WMNSNS womanishness
WMNZWT womanize with
WNADDW win hands down
WNECER winter cherry
WNEEGN Wankel engine
WNEGON winter-ground
WNEGRE winter garden
WNEIGE wandering Jew
WNEKNE wunderkinder
WNESOT winter sports
WNESRC wonder-struck
WNEWRE wonder-worker
WNGASU wineglassful
WNHMEI Wyndham Lewis
WNIGHE winding-sheet
WNNCNE win in a canter
WNNSPR win one's spurs
WNOCAG wind of change
WNRUNS wondrousness
WNTNAE Winston-Salem
WNTNMT Winston Smith
WNVRMC want very much
WNYALN Wendy Darling
WOEERE wholehearted
whole-hearted
WOGIEU wrong side out
WOGUNS wrongfulness
WOHDEO wood hedgehog
WOLHIE woolly-haired
WOTEER whortleberry
WOYUHI Woody Guthrie
WRALNE work a flanker
WRALNS workableness
WRDETN world-beating

WRDHKN world-shaking
WRDIEE World Wide Web
WREBAT Warren Beatty
WREHRO Werner Herzog
WREPIS worker priest
WRHEDN worth reading
WRHPUL worshipfully
WRHUEA warehouseman
WRIDBU worried about
WRIGAT working parts
working party
WRIGIH warning light
WRIGLS working class
working-class
WRIGOA working woman
WRIGOE working model
WRIGOR working hours
WRIGRE working order
WRIGUC working lunch
WRIKHR Warwickshire
WRLSNS wordlessness
WROGRN warmongering
war-mongering
WROHNU word of honour
WROWSO word of wisdom
WRSONI works council
WRTGTE work together
WSBOWC West Bromwich
WSEFPC waste of space
WSENAO Western Samoa
WSENSE Western Isles
WSERDC waste product
WSEUNS wastefulness
WSIGOD Washington DC
WSIGOI Washingtonia
WSIGOS Westinghouse
WSIGSE wasting asset
WSMDAD West Midlands
WSSILN West Stirling
WSVRII West Virginia
WTAINS with a witness
WTALPE with all speed
WTBDRC with bad grace
WTDAFO withdraw from
WTESTN witness stand
WTGNTI Wittgenstein
WTHLSL watch closely
WTHNOE watching-over
WTHNWR watch and ward
WTHSRO witches' broom
WTHUNS watchfulness
WTIBUD within bounds
WTIGGN wetting agent
WTILMT within limits
WTIRAO within reason
WTITEA within the law
WTNIAD Withnail and I
WTNRSL with no result
WTOEAM with open arms
WTOEOC with one voice
WTOTAL without fault
WTOTEA without delay
WTOTEN without means
WTOTIH without sight
WTOTII without limit
WTOTOB without doubt
WTOTQA without equal
WTOTRC without price
WTOTRO without error
WTPESR with pleasure
WTRALF water bailiff
WTRARE Water-carrier
WTRGRT with regard to
WTRHNE water-channel
WTRICI water biscuit
WTRIFI water milfoil
WTRIIE water-diviner
WTRLSE water blister
WTRNHL watering-hole
WTROTA water boatman
WTROTR water torture
WTROUL water-soluble
WTRRNE water-drinker
WTRUFL water buffalo
WTSADN withstanding
WTTEIO with the aid of
WUDOMN would you mind?
WVFNTO wave function
WYADEN ways and means
WYEHRE Wayne Shorter
WYERTK Wayne Gretzky
XNHCRI xanthochroic
XNHPEI xanthopterin
YCTTTO yacht station
YEDNNS yieldingness
YKOIHM Yukio Mishima
YLOHME yellowhammer
YLOJRE yellow jersey
YLORBO yellow ribbon
YLORCE yellow rocket
YLOSRA yellow streak
YMIPRA Yom Kippur War
YMUSUR Yamoussoukro
YONCWE Yvonne Cawley
YRADOO Yuri Andropov
YRSIEO Yorkshire fog
YSEAAA Yasser Arafat
YTHKAI Yitzhak Rabin
YUBSSO your best shot
YUEECM you're welcome
YUEEKO you never know
YUGUBN Younghusband
YUHUNS youthfulness
YULDSI your ladyship
ZGPPYE zygapophyses
ZLPEES Zola Pieterse
ZNABOK Zinzan Brooke
ZNOCTU Zeno of Citium
ZNONMN zinc ointment
ZNRROE Zandra Rhodes
ZOEGAH zoogeography
ZOOIAL zoologically
zootomically
ZUSPLA Zsuzsa Polgar

13 letters – odd

AAACBUN Alan Ayckbourn
AAAEPAE at a later place
AAAVNAE at an advantage
AADOTHE a hard row to hoe
AAFLFID a capful of wind
AAFOIAL away from it all
AAHMTZD anathematized
AAHOHBA arachnophobia
AAHOITC anachronistic
AAHOOIT arachnologist
AAHOOSY anachronously
AAHRCLY anaphorically
AAHTCLY apathetically
AAINIHS Arabian Nights
AAJYENR Alan Jay Lerner
AANISAE at a snail's pace
AANNAAN again and again
AANORIR Alain-Fournier
AANTHLW against the law
AAOERNE Anatole France
AAOIAIN anatomization
AAOOSES analogousness
AAOTGIE à la Portugaise
AAOYAPV Anatoly Karpov
AARBCLY anaerobically
AARFHDG a hair of the dog
AARMAIE anagrammatise
anagrammatize
AASHTZD anaesthetized
AASISUY Alan Sainsbury
AATADSE avant-gardiste
AATINHT a Parthian shot
AATNSIL at a standstill
AAUUEAE at a future date
AAUUEIE at a future time
ABEHDRR Albrecht Dürer
ABGOSES ambiguousness
ABOEIRE Ambrose Bierce
ABRCLUE arboriculture
ABRHGET Akbar the Great
ABRHRIG Albert Herring
ABSAOIL ambassadorial
ABTAIES arbitrariness
ABTOSES ambitiousness
ACAOERC archaeometric
ACAOOIT archaeologist
ACAOTRX archaeopteryx
ACBSORC archbishopric

ACDNPOE accident-prone
ACEIAIN accreditation
ACEROPE Arc de Triomphe
ACIADIE archimandrite
ACIEAOS archipelagoes
ACIETNC architectonic
ACIETRL architectural
ACIICNL archidiaconal
ACINRDE auction bridge
ACLUAIN acculturation
ACMAIET accompaniment
ACMOAIG accommodating
ACMOAIN accommodation
ACPAIIY acceptability
ACPEGRY accept eagerly
ACRANBE ascertainable
ACRANET ascertainment
ACSFLEY accuse falsely
ACSIIIY accessibility
ACURMNS accoutrements
ACUTEPR account-keeper
ACUTNFR accounting for
ADCOSES audaciousness
ADEGOYO Andrei Gromyko
ADEHPUN Audrey Hepburn
ADEIHLN André Michelin
ADEJCSN Andrew Jackson
ADEJHSN Andrew Johnson
ADEMREL Andrew Marvell
ADESADR Andreas Baader
ADESGVA Andrés Segovia
ADETPLV Andrei Tupolev
ADLVUIG add flavouring
ADNMCIE adding machine
ADOIULY audiovisually
ADRCLIS Anders Celsius
ADRPAEH Andhra Pradesh
ADTQEEA audita querela
ADTRCNL auditory canal
ADTRNRE auditory nerve
AEADRAG Alexander Haig
AEADRLK Alexander Blok
AEADROE Alexander Pope
AEAEESN average person
AEAEUTR average punter
AEDEAGS Aberdeen Angus
AEDESIE Aberdeenshire
AEDPRUE a new departure
AEEKSGN Alexei Kosygin
AEIACUT American crust
AEIAEGE American eagle
AEIASMA American Samoa
AEIERAT Amelia Earhart
AEISGNS Alec Issigonis
AETEFIH a kettle of fish
AETGNRL agents-general
AFEAVRZ Alfred Alvarez
AFEDEFS Alfred Dreyfus
AFEDNIG Alfred Denning
AFEHRHY Alfred Hershey
AFEWLAE Alfred Wallace
AFLAEIH affiliate with
AFRAIEY affirmatively
AFRAIIY affordability
AFRSAIN afforestation
AGAAIGY aggravatingly
AGAILNS Aegean Islands
AGBACLY algebraically
AGIIAIN anglicization
AGLADUE Argyll and Bute
AGLGCLY algologically
AGMNAIE argumentative
AGMNAIN argumentation
AGNIEOS argentiferous
AGOAHLC Anglo-Catholic
AGOEAIN agglomeration
AGOOOIL Anglo-Colonial
AGSUPGN Augustus Pugin
AGUIAIE agglutinative
AGUIAIN agglutination
AHEAIIY achievability
AHITCLY atheistically
AHMTCLY athematically
AHOAIIY achromaticity
AHRTMAO a short time ago
AHTNHAM a shot in the arm
AIARONR Anita Brookner
AIAUOAA Akira Kurosawa
AIAVRIN animadversion
AIBTCLY adiabatically
AIDFOIG A Kind of Loving
AIGRPAH A Bigger Splash
AIHEIIN arithmetician
AIIIAIN acidification
AIIMROA Alicia Markova
AIMTCLY axiomatically
AIOEISE adipose tissue
AIOTEIE a bit on the side
AITICOE Alistair Cooke
AIWUDEM as it would seem
AJSAIIY adjustability
AKONIIY ask for noisily
AKOTOBE ask for trouble
ALALWDY All Hallows' Day
ALGDESN alleged reason
ALGEHAS at loggerheads
ALGRCLY allegorically
ALIEEOD all-time record
ALKLANT as likely as not
ALNISEG Allen Ginsberg
ALNNPEE all in one piece
ALNODIE all in good time
ALOCNAE all you can take
ALOTEAL a fly on the wall
ALRESIE as large as life
AMADHBY Arms and the Boy
AMADHMN Arms and the Man
AMDOFIT armed conflict
AMLFRUE a small fortune
AMNSEIG administering
AMNSRTR administrator
AMRDCIN arms reduction
AMRLYRH Admiralty Arch
AMSHRCL atmospherical
AMSIIIY admissibility
AMSUOYU almost upon you
AMUOPOF armour of proof
ANAHAOA Anna Akhmatova
ANETAOT at no extra cost
ANIDCME Ann Widdecombe
ANIKATE Alnwick Castle
ANLBNET Arnold Bennett
ANLTYBE Arnold Toynbee
ANOETSS amniocentesis
ANOIFUD amniotic fluid
ANSNUKI Aung San Suu Kyi
AOAOSES anomalousness
AOARSUE Avogadro's rule
AOAYSNW Apocalypse Now
AODHISE avoid the issue
AODIDNE a good riddance
AOECMAD at one's command
AOEERAH above reproach
AOELIUE at one's leisure
AOENSED above one's head
AOESRIE at one's service
AOEWTED at one's wits' end
AOFIHAN Adolf Eichmann
AOGNDNE a song and dance
AOHGAIE apothegmatise
apothegmatize
AOITCLY agonistically
apodictically
apomictically
atomistically
AOLTETE Apollo Theatre
AOPOSES amorphousness
AOTECED Apostles' Creed
AOTFCET abortifacient
AOTLCLY apostolically
AOTOAPN about to happen
AOYFESS a copy of verses
APAATCE alpha particle
APAETUI Alpha Centauri
APANOEA alpha and omega
APAOTNN appear often in
APCSFOE Aspects of Love
APEFHEE apple of the eye
APEOLYR Appleton layer
APEUPIG apple dumpling
APIAIIY applicability
APIIAIN amplification
APITFAE at point of sale
APLAIEY appellatively
APLUEPE appel au peuple
APOIAEO approximate to
APOIAEY approximately
APOIAIG approximating
APOIAIN approximation
APORAEO appropriate to
APORAEY appropriately
APORAIN appropriation
APOSMCA Alphonse Mucha
APRANET appertainment
APREACS appurtenances
APRINET apportionment
APRTWRS aspire towards
AQIETSE acquired taste
AQIIIEY acquisitively

AQIOEEF acquit oneself
AQISETY acquiescently
AQISIGY acquiescingly
ARADRCS airs and graces
ARBTCLY acrobatically
ARCLUIT agriculturist
ARCNILT African violet
ARCOSES atrociousness
ARCRBEN Afro-Caribbean
AREBEES agreeableness
AREOIFR agree to differ
ARETROM air letter form
ARGTNLS at right angles
ARHMBSM Abraham's bosom
ARMNOSY acrimoniously
ARNLOTX adrenal cortex
AROPESR air-compressor
AROTIES airworthiness
ARRFWMN aircraftwoman
ASCAEIH associate with
ASDOSES assiduousness
ASEAIIY answerability
ASHTCLY aesthetically
ASIHRIS Austin hermits
ASLTLNT absolutely not
ASLTPTH absolute pitch
ASLTPWR absolute power
ASLTRLR absolute ruler
ASMLTDN assimilated in
ASNEFID absence of mind
ASNOEEF absent oneself
ASOTOIE at short notice
ASRABID Austrian blind
ASRAIIY absorbability
ASRCIEY abstractively
ASRCVRE abstract verse
ASRIEES assertiveness
ASROEEF assert oneself
ASROOIT Assyriologist
ASSIAIN assassination
ASTTIPR asset-stripper
ASUTFRS assault of arms
ASUTORE assault course
ASUTTRS assault at arms
ATADRFS Arts and Crafts
ATAIAIN actualization
ATBORPY autobiography
ATCAUAT anticoagulant
ATCIATC anticlimactic
ATCOKIE anticlockwise
ATCPAOS autocephalous
ATCTLSS autocatalysis
ATCTOOS autochthonous
ATEAEIE at the same time
ATEEETF at the behest of
ATEHRED at the sharp end
ATEIPIT at the midpoint
ATEMNHC anthelminthic
ATEOIIM autoeroticism
ATEOLAE at the coalface
ATEOPEE asthenosphere
ATEOTMF at the bottom of
ATEOTOS at the controls
ATETCLY authentically
ATETCTD authenticated
ATETCTR authenticator
ATFCAIE artificialise
artificialize
ATFCAIY artificiality
ATGAHOK autograph book
ATGNCLY antigenically
ATHSAIE antihistamine
ATIAIIY attainability
ATIUIEY attributively
ATLGRTM antilogarithm
ATMTCLY asthmatically
automatically
ATNBCLI actinobacilli
ATNEAFF act on behalf of
ATNGRLY Antony Gormley
ATNIEES attentiveness
ATNMAIM antinomianism
ATNNSIS Antoninus Pius
ATNNVRK Antonín Dvorák
ATNOAOA Antonio Canova
ATNOIAN Anton Mosimann
ATNOPDA Antony of Padua
ATNPRTC antinephritic
ATNRCNR Anton Bruckner
ATNSIGY astonishingly
ATOHSCL astrophysical
ATOIAIE authoritative
ATOIAIN authoritarian
authorization
ATOYOAA astrocytomata
ATOYOEL Anthony Dowell
Anthony Powell
ATOYOKR Anthony Fokker
ATOYUYE Anthony Quayle
ATPRONL anti-personnel
ATRAIEY alternatively
ATRFSIN after a fashion
ATRHTIE after that time
ATRPMTY anthropometry
ATRPPAY anthropophagy
ATRPSPY anthroposophy
ATSCAIY antisociality
ATSEITR act as mediator
ATSHDAE autoschediaze
ATSHDAM autoschediasm
ATSHIMN act as chairman
ATSOBTC antiscorbutic
ATSPIIE antisepticise
antisepticize
ATTDNZR attitudinizer
ATTHNIE a stitch in time
ATUBLOR Arthur Balfour
ATUCLRE Arthur C Clarke
ATUCMTN Arthur Compton
ATURCHM Arthur Rackham
ATURMAD Arthur Rimbaud
ATURNOE Arthur Ransome
ATVSRIE active service
AUBAIEY adumbratively
AUDLATE Arundel Castle
AUDNCOS arundinaceous
AUEETAK amusement park
AUOSUOR aqueous humour
AUTMETS ayuntamientos
AUUCUIT acupuncturist
AVNELVL Advanced level
AVNELWY advance slowly
AVNEOIE advance notice
AVNUOSY adventurously
AVRIEET advertisement
AVSAANT advise against
AVSRGOP advisory group
AXLAYEB auxiliary verb
AXNRVNE Aix-en-Provence
AYDLCOS amygdalaceous
AYOYGES anybody's guess
BAAOSED be at a loose end
BACELNS Blanc de Blancs
BACEUOS Blanche Du Bois
BADNHUE boarding-house
BADSMNS blandishments
BAEESES blamelessness
BAEEWRD Brave New World
BAFRSAE Beaufort scale
BAHOARS brachiosaurus ❑
BAIGNID bearing in mind
BAIIAIN beatification
BAITSAE beat into shape
BAKNWIE black and white
black-and-white
BAKTBAK blankety-blank
BAKTTTH blanket stitch
BAKYDEN black-eyed bean
BALCONS by all accounts
BANESES brainlessness
BANHLRN brainchildren
BANTRIG brainstorming
BAPEOSY blasphemously
BASATIG brass farthing
BATCNET beauty contest
BATEEOD beat the record
BATEONS beat the bounds
BATFUDN beast of burden
BATOSES beauteousness
BATPROR beauty parlour
BAWTESO bear witness to
BBEHMIG Bible-thumping
BBESDIH be blessed with
BBEUCIG Bible-punching
BBLCABR bubble-chamber
BBNCLGE bubonic plague
BBTEFAT Babette's Feast
BBUDPIH be bound up with
BBYHRTN Bobby Charlton
BCAESUE béchamel sauce
BCCLUAE back-calculate
BCEIPAE bacteriophage
BCFRAIN back-formation
BCLUAIM biculturalism
BCMAAEF become aware of
BCMBURD become blurred
BCMETNT become extinct
BCMFINS become friends
BCMGETR become greater

BCMILIH become ill with
BCMIVLD become invalid
BCMOVOS become obvious
BCMPPLR become popular
BCMPUPR become plumper
BCMSALR become smaller
BCMSOTR become shorter
BCMTDOS become tedious
BCMTINR become thinner
BCMUSUK become unstuck
BCMVSBE become visible
BCRANFR be curtains for
BCSIVLE bicuspid valve
BCSRTHR backscratcher
back-scratcher
BCYHTHR Becky Thatcher
BDCATYU bad scran to you
BDEACUT budget account
BDEINEO bid defiance to
BDIEANR bedside manner
BDMSIDX body mass index
BDOSINE bad conscience
BDOSPOT body of support
BDXEINE bad experience
BECLAIG breech-loading
BECOTUT breach of trust
BEDIEPG bleed like a pig
BEDNHAT bleeding heart
BEHRSAM blepharospasm
BEKBEES breakableness
BEKHBLS break the balls
BEKNFIH breaking faith
BEKNSOD break one's word
BEKRERM break free from
BESEKLB Beefsteak Club
BESTEAE breast the tape
BETEAIY breathe easily
BETEREY breathe freely
BEZTRUH breeze through
BFINSIH be friends with
BFRTEAT before the mast
BFRTEEM before the beam
BFRTEID before the wind
BGAGHOY Big Bang theory
BGEDDES bigheadedness
big-headedness
BGNBGAE bag and baggage
BGNUDNY begin suddenly
BGOCMAY be good company
BGSFIIL bogus official
BHAIYNO be heavily into
BHRPESD be hard pressed
BHVORLY behaviourally
BHVTWRS behave towards
BIADWTH bait and switch
BIDASUF blind man's buff
BIDNBOK building block
BIGAEBY Bridgwater Bay
BIGBIDR bridge-builder
BIGNOAD bring in to land
BIGNOLY bring into play
BIGOAEO bring solace to
BIGOBAS bridge of boats
BIGOCOE bring to a close
BIGOEHR bring together
BIGOORO bring honour to
BIGPOAE bring up to date
bring up-to-date
BIIHUEM British Museum
BIKMNHP brinksmanship
BINARHN Brian Hanrahan
BINORCS Brian Horrocks
BINURNY Brian Mulroney
BISAMNS by instalments
BITELST be in the closet
BITIGIH bristling with
BLADOKT ball and socket
BLADRCS belt-and-braces
BLAIAIN Balkanization
BLAURET beleaguerment
BLEDNIG ballet-dancing
BLEIBAD bulletin board
BLELTRS belles-lettres
BLIEETY belligerently
BLIHLDY Billie Holiday
BLLGTIG ball lightning
BLNEFID balance of mind
BLORGIG ballot-rigging
BLOSOED bellows to mend
BLSAECN Belisha beacon
BLUGRMN Bildungsroman
BLWTEGH below strength
BLWTNAD below standard
BLYONLY Billy Connolly
BMATCLY bombastically
BMOCRAN bamboo curtain
BMOZEET bamboozlement
BMTOSES bumptiousness
BNAISIH Benjamin Smith
BNASRNE bancassurance
BNEILRS banderilleros
BNEJMIG bungee jumping
BNTRUIE bone turquoise
BNZRHTO Benazir Bhutto
BOADADE boot and saddle
BODESES bloodlessness
BODIDDY broadmindedly
BODRSUE blood pressure
BODRTES Blood Brothers
BODUDIG bloodcurdling
BOEHATD brokenhearted
broken-hearted
BOEHOOY biotechnology
BOERDBE biodegradable
BOETEDE be over the edge
BOGETUS blow great guns
BOHLEPR brothel-keeper
BOHMCLY biochemically
BOHRIES brotherliness
BOHRILW brothers-in-law
BOHRYOE brotherly love
BOKBRUH Brookeborough
BONEUDR Brownie Guider
BONREIS bioenergetics
BOSTRUH browse through
BOTEIOF blow the lid off
BPIMFIE baptism of fire
BPIMLAE baptismal name
BRAAATE Barbara Castle
BRACABR burial chamber
BRACAIE bureaucratise
bureaucratize
BRADOEL Bernard Lovell
BRALGOE barnacle goose
BRAOSES barbarousness
BRCSIOA Baruch Spinoza
BRECETD barrel-chested
BREOPOF burden of proof
BRETEMN Barnett Newman
BRETRIR Border terrier
BREVUTD barrel-vaulted
BRHFAOY burgh of barony
BRHMRST Berthe Morisot
BRIGAIE Birminghamise
Birminghamize
BRIGETE burying beetle
BRINLSN Birgit Nilsson
BRIWOTR Bertie Wooster
BRLNATR Burt Lancaster
BRLROSY burglariously
BROPSAE bird of passage
BRORCTR Burton Richter
BROTRCT Bertolt Brecht
BRSALBY Barnstaple Bay
BRTNOOG burst into song
BRUAHRS Bermuda shorts
BRYCUGN Barry McGuigan
BRYSEDY born yesterday
BSCNTNT Basic Instinct
BSDOEEF beside oneself
BSDTEAK beside the mark
BSIGMYL Bashir Gemayel
BSLHGET Basil the Great
BSMOEMN be someone's man
BSNSWMN businesswoman
BSORFNO basso profondo
basso profundo
BSOTFED Bosworth Field
BSTLGAH bush telegraph
BSYEKLY Busby Berkeley
BTAAIMY be that as it may
BTADICS bits and pieces
BTEADGS butter-and-eggs
BTEFNES butterfingers
BTEFYIH butterfly fish
BTEFYIS butterfly kiss
BTEGNYF by the agency of
BTENHLS betweenwhiles
BTHRBOM butcher's broom
BTLCUSR battle-cruiser
BTLFTGE battle fatigue
BTLOCEY Battle of Crécy
BTLOISS Battle of Issus
BTLOPVA Battle of Pavia
BTLOSDN Battle of Sedan
BTLOVRA Battle of Varna
BTLOYRS Battle of Ypres
BTLSARD battle-scarred
BTOETUB bite one's thumb

BTOLSPT bottomless pit
BTOOELP button one's lip
BTPRILS beta particles
BTTEULT bite the bullet
BUAIAIN brutalization
BUANILA bougainvillea
BUBRYIL Blueberry Hill
BUDESES boundlessness
BUDOAPN bound to happen
BUELFED Bruce Oldfield
BULAASE bouillabaisse
BUMUTIS Blue Mountains
BUTFLES bountifulness
BUTOHDN boustrophedon
BUTOSES bounteousness
BWLEIGY bewilderingly
BWLOEET bowel movement
BWROMUH by word of mouth
BXHCMAS box the compass
BYNCMAE beyond compare
BYNDSUE beyond dispute
BYNMAUE beyond measure
BYNOEKN beyond one's ken
BYNTEAE beyond the pale
CAAEGTY Clara Peggotty
CAATRAT character part
CAATRES characterless
CACOEAM chance one's arm
CACTSEK chance to speak
CADAEHR Chandrasekhar
CADCARL Claude Chabrol
CADDBSY Claude Debussy
CADDRIR Claude Dornier
CADLRAN Claude Lorrain
CADOBAO Claudio Abbado
CADSANN Claude Shannon
CADSIEY clandestinely
CAEANOS chase rainbows
CAEENIE chameleon-like
CAEUAIE Château Lafite
CAEUOGN Château Bougon
CAEURAD Chateaubriand
CAGAIIY changeability
CAGDESN changed person
CAGNPAE changing place
CAGNPEE changing-piece
CAGOEEF change oneself
CAGOHAT change of heart
CAGOSAE change of state
CAGOVNE change of venue
CAGRNIG change-ringing
CAIEBLS clavicembalos
CAIIAIN clarification
CAIIAOY clarificatory
CALEAKR Charlie Parker
CALNIGY challengingly
CALSAKY Charles Mackay
CALSAWN Charles Darwin
CALSHFT Charles the Fat
CALSIGS Charles Mingus
CALSNOS Charles Onions
CALSODN Charles Gordon
CALSOND Charles Gounod
CALSORD Charles Conrad
CALTEON Charlottetown
CAMEZAN Chaim Weizmann
CAMRCLT charm bracelet
CANECIN chain reaction
CAOILNS Chagos Islands
CAOOSES clamorousness
CAOTUDR clap of thunder
CAPOEHR clasp together
CAPTHBT champ at the bit
CASFSIG coarse fishing
CATMNHP craftsmanship
CBAITCL cabbalistical
CBLIEET cobelligerent
CCESAIL cocker spaniel
CCLALWS Cecil Day-Lewis
CCLDMLE Cecil B De Mille
CCOTEAK cock of the walk
CCOTEOT cock of the loft
CCTIAIN cicatrization
CCTIDES cocktail dress
CCTISIK cocktail stick
CCUSLIG co-counselling
CDIMELW cadmium yellow
CDOCNUT code of conduct
CEAEKBY Chesapeake Bay
CEASAAE Caesar's Palace
CEEEETE crème de menthe
CEENLIE crème anglaise
CEETTLE Clement Attlee
CEHEULC Czech Republic
CEISUEE credit squeeze
CELWIOZ Czeslaw Milosz
CEMFATR cream of tartar
CEMOORD cream-coloured
CENNWMN cleaning woman
CEOEETR chemoreceptor
CEPNNSY cheap and nasty
CERESES cheerlessness
CERHDCS clear the decks
CERHNIG clear-thinking
CERPCIG cherry-picking
CETRIIZ Chester Nimitz
CETRRHR Chester Arthur
CEUAINL coeducational
CEUOSES credulousness
CEURDLG chequered flag
CEVBEES cleavableness
CGRTEUT cigarette butt
CIAOOIT climatologist
CIATCLY climactically
CIATRCL climacterical
CIBNFAE climbing-frame
CIBNPAT climbing plant
CIDESOE children's home
CIDIEES childlikeness
CIEEEVS Chinese leaves
CIEEUZE Chinese puzzle
CIEICAR Clive Sinclair
CIFANHP chieftainship
CIFIITR chief minister
CIFROES Clifford Odets
CIHALVR clishmaclaver
CIIACUT criminal court
CIIAPIT critical point
CIIAWRD criminal world
CIIOOIT criminologist
CIKTCIK clickety-click
CINHUGU Chien-Shiung Wu
CINKIHK Chiang Kai Shek
Chiang Kai-Shek
CIOILNS Caicos Islands
CIORPIT chirographist
CITATOD Clint Eastwood
CITRATE Caister Castle
CITRHLS Chiltern Hills
CLACAIY cold as charity
CLAOAIE collaborative
CLAOAIG collaborating
CLAOAIN collaboration
CLBODDY cold-bloodedly
CLBSOKY colobus monkey
CLEEFRS College of Arms
CLETDES collectedness
CLFCOIS calefactories
CLFRRMS call for trumps
CLHATDY cold-heartedly
CLIIAIN calcification
CLIITCL Calvinistical
CLIRPIT calligraphist
CLITEIS callisthenics
CLMIRVR Columbia River
CLNAPEL Colin Campbell
CLNEBOK cylinder block
CLNEPES cylinder press
CLNRCLY cylindrically
CLOTEID Call of the Wild
CLOUAIM colloquialism
CLRDRVR Colorado River
CLSILOY celestial body
CLTACUT call to account
CLUAIGY calculatingly
CLUARDO cellular radio
CLUEEIM culture medium
CLUFLES colourfulness
CLUIAIN colourization
CLUTEAY colour therapy
CMAAIEY comparatively
CMAAIIY comparability
CMADEIG commandeering
CMADOUE command module
CMAFTGE combat fatigue
CMAIEES combativeness
CMAIIIY compatibility
CMAINBE companionable
CMAINBY companionably
CMAINES companionless
CMAINHP companionship
CMAOGIH come along with
CMAOOIT campanologist
CMASIDW compass window
CMASOAE compassionate
CMECAIE commercialise
commercialize
CMECAIM commercialism
CMECAIY commerciality

CMEDOSY compendiously
CMEOAIE commemorative
CMEOAIN commemoration
CMESRBE commensurable
CMESRBY commensurably
CMESTFR compensate for
CMIEAIG commiserating
CMIEAIN commiseration
CMIEOCS combine forces
CMIGRUD camping-ground
CMIIGOM combining form
CMIOEEF commit oneself
CMIPRUY commit perjury
CMISIIE commit suicide
CMISOIG commissioning
CMITBIG come into being
CMITFRE come into force
CMITSGT come into sight
CMLIATY complaisantly
CMLIIGY complainingly
CMLMNAY complementary
complimentary
CMLMNIG complementing
CMLXDES complexedness
CMLXUBR complex number
CMOBROK common burdock
CMOCUTC common caustic
CMOETAT component part
CMOIEES compositeness
CMOIGOM composing room
CMOTIHT come out with it
CMRHNIE comprehensive
CMRHNIN comprehension
CMROSUA camera obscura
CMRSEAR compressed air
CMSGAHS Compsognathus
CMTALMX come to a climax
CMTNTIG come to nothing
CMTOEEF come to oneself
CMTTEOL come to the boil
CMUAANT come up against
CMUAIEY commutatively
CMUAINL computational
CMUECIE computer crime
CMUESEK computerspeak
CMUIAIE communicative
CMUIAIN communication
communitarian
CMUIMEK Communism Peak
CMUIYOE community home
CMUIYOK community work
CMYOATR campylobacter
CNACIBR canvas-climber
CNAEAIN concatenation
CNAECNE convalescence
CNAGIIY consanguinity
CNAIAIG contaminating
CNAIAIN contamination
CNAIRSN cannabis resin
CNANRHP container ship
CNATESS contact lenses
CNAUAIE connaturalise
connaturalize
CNAUAIN confabulation
CNBYEOE Can't Buy Me Love
CNCETOS conscientious
CNCOSES consciousness
CNDARVR Canadian River
CNECNIG condescending
CNECNIN condescension
CNEEAIN confederation
CNEEEET concede defeat
CNEILES congenialness
CNEINFR convenient for
CNENDES concernedness
CNENDIH concerned with
CNEPAIE contemplative
CNEPAIN contemplation
CNESDIK condensed milk
CNESOAY concessionary
CNESZOI conversazioni
CNETAAT Conceptual Art
CNETAEN concentrate on
CNETAIE conceptualise
conceptualize
contextualise
contextualize
CNETAIG concentrating
CNETAIM conceptualism
CNETAIN concentration
CNETDES conceitedness
contentedness
CNETDIH connected with
CNETIIY concentricity
CNETNRD connecting rod
CNETOAH convert to cash
CNETOBY Conception Bay
CNETOEY confectionery
CNETOSY contentiously
CNETRLY conjecturally
CNEUIEY consecutively
CNEUNIL consequential
CNEVTIE conservatoire
CNIAITC cannibalistic
CNIEAEY considerately
CNIEAIN consideration
CNIEIGY consideringly
CNIETBD confined to bed
CNIEUUL consider usual
CNIGSFX cunning as a fox
CNIINLN conditional on
CNIINLY conditionally
CNIUAIN configuration
CNIUTMN continuity man
CNLCLTD canaliculated
CNLGAIN conflagration
CNMTGAH cinematograph
CNOIAIE consolidative
CNOIAIN consolidation
CNOIATY concomitantly
CNONIGY confoundingly
CNOTOIT contortionist
CNPCOSY conspicuously
CNRBNIT contrabandist
CNRBSON contrabassoon
CNRBTBE contributable
CNRBTOS contributions
CNRCPIE contraceptive
CNRCPIN contraception
CNRDCIG contradicting
CNRDCIN contradiction
CNRDCOY contradictory
CNRFGLY centrifugally
CNRFRAD centre-forward
CNRILNS Canary Islands
CNRLEIN Central Region
CNRLOUN control column
CNRNAIN confrontation
CNRPNIT contrapuntist
CNRPOTS contrappostos
CNRSINL congressional
CNRSWMN congresswoman
CNRTRIY confraternity
CNRVNIN contravention
CNRVRIL controversial
CNSOWTR Coniston Water
CNTANDY constrainedly
CNTIGNY constringency
CNTLAIN constellation
CNTNEPY Constance Spry
CNTRAIN consternation
CNTUTBE constructable
constructible
CNUCIEY conjunctively
CNUEGOS consumer goods
CNUICNE concupiscence
CNUPIEY consumptively
CNUPIIY consumptivity
CNUSAOS conquistadors
CNUSOTD cinque-spotted
CNYLCLY concyclically
COADHNE chop and change
COAFNAY Choral Fantasy
COCOWRS choice of words
COEAEIH co-operate with
COEAIEY co-operatively
COEGAHC choreographic
COEGAHR choreographer
COHIWRS clothe in words
COKHEBW crook the elbow
CONMEIL crown imperial
CONNGOY crowning glory
CONNPIT crowning point
CONRNES crown princess
COOEHES cool one's heels
COPNBAD chopping-board
COSATRD cross-gartered
COSDHQE crossed cheque
COSHFOR cross the floor
COSNSID cross one's mind
COSREIG cross-breeding
COSRSIG cross-dressing
COSUSIN cross-question
COSUTRL cross-cultural
COUAHRE cook up a charge
CPAIIDX cephalic index
CPCOSES capaciousness
CPEPRTS copper pyrites
CPETUPT copper trumpet

CPRGTBE copyrightable
CPRNRHP copartnership
CPSVNET Cape St Vincent
CPTLETR capital letter
CPTLSES capital assets
CPUENIM capture on film
CRANASR curtain-raiser
CRATEBY Carmarthen Bay
CRBADIY cardboard city
CRBAPLY cerebral palsy
CRBOPNL cerebrospinal
CRBRSEN Carl Bernstein
CREAIEY correlatively
CREAITN cornet-à-piston
CRELDRH corbelled arch
CREPNET correspondent
CREPNIG corresponding
CRESEPR carpet-sweeper
CRIACOS cardinal cross
CRIAIOS cartilaginous
CRIAPIT cardinal point
CRIASER cervical smear
CRIAUAA Carmina Burana
CRICRET cardiac arrest
CRIGAHR cardiographer
CRIGCOK carriage clock
CRIIAIN certification
CRIIDIK certified milk
CRIOOSY carnivorously
CRLNDFY Carol Ann Duffy
CRLOLGT circle of light
CRLORER Cyril Tourneur
CRMNOSY ceremoniously
CRMTCLY chromatically
CRMTPOE chromatophore
CRNCELY chronicle play
CRNGAHR chronographer
CRNHAIE corinthianise
corinthianize
CRNLGCL chronological
CRNRCUT coroner's court
CRODOIE carbon dioxide
CROIAIN carbonisation
carbonization
CROIEES corrosiveness
CROIEOS carboniferous❑
CROOAIE corroborative
CROOAIN corroboration
CRSEALT corps de ballet
CRSIGOY Christ in Glory
CRSINAE christian name❑
CRSINIR Christian Dior
CRSINUE Christian Duve
CRSMNTR Christminster
CRSMSAD Christmas card
CRSMSAE Christmas cake
CRSMSOE Christmas rose
CRSMSOG Christmas song
CRSMSRE Christmas tree
CRSNHMM chrysanthemum
CRSORMN Chris Boardman
CRTDREY carotid artery
CRTOARS Corythosaurus

CRUABET circumambient
CRUCRSI Corpus Christi
CRUFRNE circumference
CRUSACS circumstances
CRUSETY circumspectly
CRUSRBD circumscribed
CRUVLAE circumvallate
CRUVNIN circumvention
CRYHTRH carry the torch
CRYOXES carry to excess
CRYUTSS carry out tests
CRZNQIO Corazon Aquino
CSAAIIY cast a nativity
CSAALVR cast a pall over
CSAEEVR cast an eye over
CSDSESR cash dispenser
CSEFCIE cost-effective
CSIBNRM cessio bonorum
CSITCLY casuistically
CSLISAN castle in Spain
CSOIAIN customization
CSOINHP custodianship
CSRISEN Cesar Milstein
CTAEHEE cottage cheese
CTCITCL catechistical
CTEIEAR Catherine Parr
CTGRCLY categorically
CTHETRA catchment area
CTHFGAD catch off guard
CTHHDIT catch the drift
CTHMSAD cut the mustard
CTHNHAT catch in the act
CTHNHHP catch on the hip
CTHNWRS catch unawares
CTHPITR cut the painter
CTHTSRW catch at a straw
CTHTTAS catch at straws
CTLTCLY catalytically
CTNNTIS cat-o'-nine-tails
CTNOICS cut into pieces
CTNSHOT cut one's throat
CTNSOSS cut one's losses
CTOHQIK cut to the quick
CTOITMS Catholic Times
CTONOIE cut down to size
CTOPCIG cotton-picking
CTRONRD catercornered
CUCIWLS Church in Wales
CUDEETR could be better
CUEIAIN cauterization
CUEOAPN cause to happen
CUSCNRL cruise control
CUSMSIE cruise missile❑
CUSOSUY course of study
CUSREGT cruiserweight
CUTATAS court martials
CUTBRUH county borough
CUTEOTR court reporter
CUTESES countlessness
CUTFEOD court of record
CUTFLIS court of claims
CUTFPEL Court of Appeal
CUTFRHS Court of Arches

CUTMRIL courts martial
CUTOSES courteousness
CUTRATR counter-caster
CUTRCIE counteractive
CUTRCIN counteraction
CUTREGT counter-weight
CUTRETR counterfeiter
CUTRETY counterfeitly
CUTRHRE countercharge
CUTRTAK counter-attack
CUTSLGT courtesy light
CUTSTTE courtesy title
CUTYESN country person
CUTYOSN country cousin
CUUTDPN C Auguste Dupin
CVLARAE civil marriage
CVLNIER civil engineer
CXOBCLY coxcombically
CYAILNS Cayman Islands
CYBOOIT cryobiologist
CYEOBUH Clyde Tombaugh
CYLEUDR cry blue murder
CYNEEPR cayenne pepper
CYOTEON cry for the moon
CYTGAHC cryptographic
CYTGAHR cryptographer
CYTLAAE Crystal Palace
CYTLAIG crystal-gazing
CYTNLSS cryptanalysis
DAAELVR draw a veil over
DAAHLCN diacatholicon
DAAIAIN dramatization
DAAIIOY dramatic irony
DAAUGCL dramaturgical
DACTONE dead-cat bounce
DAERCLY diametrically
DAETCLY dialectically
DAFLOAR Dwarf Allosaur
DAGTWMN draughtswoman
DAHAMTC diaphragmatic
DAHESES deathlessness
DAHETNE death sentence
DAHNEIE Death in Venice
DAITCLY dualistically
DALTEBX dead-letter box
DALVLIH draw level with
DAMNPDL dead man's pedal
DAMNSOS dead men's shoes
DANSIIN diagnostician
DAODUNO do a good turn to
DAOEEFP draw oneself up
DAOEHES drag one's heels
DATEIET draw the line at
DBUHDES debauchedness
DCAAIEY declaratively
DCAAOIY declamatorily
declaratorily
DCAENAE declare unsafe
DCAEPNY declare openly
DCAOILY dictatorially
DCDAANT decide against
DCDNTOO decide not to do
DCDOSES deciduousness

DCEIAIN decrepitation
DCIFLES deceitfulness
DCIIAIE decriminalise
decriminalize
DCLSGAD ductless gland
DCMLYTM decimal system
DCMNAIE documentarise
documentarize
DCMNAIN documentation
DCMNAIY documentarily
DCMOIIN decomposition
DCMRSIE decompressive
DCMRSIN decompression
DCNAIAE decontaminate
DCNAIAT decontaminant
DCNETAE deconcentrate
DCNRLZD decentralized
DCOFUTS Doctor Faustus
DCOOOSY dichotomously
DCOPODE Doctor Proudie
DCOZIAO Doctor Zhivago
DCPIEES deceptiveness
DCSNRGT Dickson Wright
DCSOTBE decision table
DDADEES Dido and Aeneas
DDCBEES deducibleness
DDYOGES daddy longlegs
daddy-long-legs
DEBRYOE Drew Barrymore
DEIFUTS dies infaustus
DEISDYU deep inside you
DEITEOL dyed in the wool
dyed-in-the-wool
DEITOGT deep in thought
DELDRAS Die Fledermaus
DELNHUE dwelling-house
DELNPAE dwelling-place
DEOAAOA Diego Maradona
DEOEWID dree one's weird
DESDOIL dressed to kill
DESNTBE dressing-table
DESRCUE deep structure
DEVUGRE Dieu vous garde
DFASUDY defeat soundly
DFBILTR defibrillator
DFCIEES defectiveness
DFEETAE differentiate
DFEETRM different from
DFNEESY defencelessly
DFNIIIY defensibility
DFNOEEF defend oneself
DFNTLNT definitely not
DFRECNE defervescence
DFRECNY defervescency
DFRNILY deferentially
DFRSAIN deforestation
DFUIEES diffusiveness
DFUIIIY diffusibility
DGBEKAT dog's breakfast
DGEROYE daguerreotype
DGSIIIY digestibility
DIGORDE doing porridge
DIGWYIH doing away with
DIKFEIG drink offering
DIKNGAS drinking-glass
DINSPIT deipnosophist
DISNDAS dribs and drabs
DIYRDCS dairy products
DKELNTN Duke Ellington
DKFEEIK Duke Frederick
DKVNETO Duke Vincentio
DLAIAIN dollarization
DLCAIIY delectability
DLGTDES delightedness
DLHNRUS dolphinariums
DLODUCE deltoid muscle
DLOSEKY Daltons Weekly
DLQECNE deliquescence
DLROSES deliriousness
DLTROSY deleteriously
DLYALIG dilly-dallying
DLYDCIN delayed action
DLYHMSN Daley Thompson
DMAOEEF demean oneself
DMCLAIN domiciliation
DMGAIIY damageability
DMIIAIN damnification
DMNFEIG demand feeding
DMNSIGY diminishingly
DMNTAIE demonstrative
DMNTAIG demonstrating
DMNTAIN demonstration
DMOTEOK Dome of the Rock
DMSIAIN domestication
DMSITBY domestic tabby
DMSUSEL Damascus steel
DMTOOIE demythologise
demythologize
DMTRAIE dematerialise
dematerialize
DMUGCLY demiurgically
DNAFRUA dental formula
DNBTEOK done by the book
DNEAAMI Daniel arap Moi
DNEDRNA Daniel Deronda
DNEOSES dangerousness
DNESRIE dinner service
DNICMTN Dennis Compton
DNIDNOT Dandie Dinmont
DNISINR Dennis Skinner
DNIUAIN denticulation
DNLDULS Donald Douglas
DNLMCEN Donald Maclean
DNMNINT don't mention it
DNRLGCL dendrological
DNTOAIE denationalise
denationalize
DNTRATE Dunster Castle
DOATNAT door attendant
DOIIAIN deoxidization
DOITCLY dioristically
DONWRIK Dionne Warwick
DOOIAIN deodorization
DOTLGCL deontological
DPEAIGY deprecatingly
DPEAOIY deprecatorily
DPLRFET Doppler effect
DPNAIIY dependability
DPOAIBG diplomatic bag
DPOAIIY deplorability
DPROAIE depersonalise
depersonalize
DPTOGLY diphthongally
DRAOOIT dermatologist
DRCCRET direct current
DRCGIIN derecognition
DRCINES directionless
DRCTWRS direct towards
DREBSEL Darcey Bussell
DRFRYTS Dornford Yates
DRICLEE Darwin College
DRIGEDE darning-needle
DRIOYON dormitory town
DRLGOIE dereligionise
dereligionize
DRQIIIN derequisition
DRSRCIN derestriction
DRSUPRY Doris Humphrey
DRYELNS dirty dealings
DSAAEES disparateness
DSAAEET disparagement
DSAAIAE discapacitate
DSAAIGY disparagingly
DSACRDR dispatch rider
DSAEIDN disease-ridden
DSAIFIG dissatisfying
DSAIIAE dishabilitate
DSAMNOS disharmonious
DSASOAE dispassionate
DSATFLY distastefully
DSAUAIE disnaturalise
disnaturalize
DSBDETY disobediently
DSBIIGY disobligingly
DSDATGD disadvantaged
DSEAEES desperateness
DSEBIGY dissemblingly
DSEBRET dismemberment
DSEIAIN dissemination
DSELWHP disfellowship
DSEOROA dysmenorrhoea
DSEPCFL disrespectful
DSEREIG disheartening
DSETCLY dyspeptically
DSEUAIN disreputation
DSFETDY disaffectedly
DSFIMNE disaffirmance
DSGEAIN desegregation
DSGELBL designer label
DSHREUE discharge tube
DSICIEY distinctively
DSIGIHD distinguished
DSIGODR dusting powder
DSIHFMN Dustin Hoffman
DSIIAIY dissimilarity
DSIIIGY dispiritingly
DSIIIUE dissimilitude
DSILNBE disciplinable
DSIUAIG dissimulating

DSIUAIN disfiguration
dissimulation
DSIUEET disfigurement
DSLAIGY displeasingly
DSLOIES desultoriness
DSLUIAE disilluminate
DSLUIND disillusioned
DSNAEET disengagement
DSNAGIG disentangling
DSNEETD disinterested
DSNEIIG disinheriting
DSNERTD disintegrated
DSOCRIG disconcerting
DSOCRIN disconcertion
DSODORS Desmond Morris
DSOEYEL discovery well
DSOFRIY disconformity
DSOIIEY dispositively
DSONCIN disconnection
DSONHUE discount house
DSOOAIN discoloration
DSOORBE dishonourable
DSOORBY dishonourably
DSOSSIN dispossession
DSOTNIG discontinuing
DSOTNIY discontinuity
DSOTNOS discontinuous
DSOUEES dissoluteness
DSPERNE disappearance
DSPONIG disappointing
DSQIIRA disequilibria
DSRCCUT district court
DSRCFLY disgracefully
DSRCIEY destructively
distractively
DSRCIGY distractingly
DSRCNRE district nurse
DSRDTBE discreditable
DSRDTBY discreditably
DSRETTD disorientated
DSRIAEY disordinately
DSRIIGY dispraisingly
DSRIUAE disarticulate
DSRMNTR discriminator
DSRPIEY descriptively
DSRPIIM descriptivism
DSRPRIN disproportion
DSRSFLY distressfully
distrustfully
DSRSIGY distressingly
DSRTOAY discretionary
DSSIIAE disassimilate
DSSOITD disassociated
DSUAIEY disputatively
DSUCIEY disjunctively
DSUCINL dysfunctional
DSUEIGY disquietingly
DTEHPIG do the shopping
DTHOOIL Dutch Colonial
DTIETLO detrimental to
DTIETLY detrimentally
DTRIAEY determinately
DTRIAIE determinative
DTRIAIN determination
DTRIITC deterministic
DTROAIG deteriorating
DTROAIN deterioration
DTSAIIY detestability
DUDPNET drug-dependent
DUEMCIA deus ex machina
DUHEILW daughter-in-law
DUKSPPR drunk as a piper
DULCCNT double coconut
DULCOSR double-crosser
DULDAIG double dealing
double-dealing
DULDNAE doubly dentate
DULFGRS double figures
DULGAIG double-glazing
DULJITD double-jointed
DULMAIG double meaning
double-meaning
DULOQIS double or quits
DULWDIG double wedding
DUSUGIG drug-smuggling
DUTESES dauntlessness
DUUSPOT drum up support
DVDEULY divide equally
DVDHPAD David Sheppard
DVDIBEY David Dimbleby
DVDITTO divide into two
DVDLNET David Blunkett
DVLPETL developmental
DVLTOAY devolutionary
DVLTOIT devolutionist
DVROEEF divert oneself
DVSAIGY devastatingly
DVTOEEF devote oneself
DWIGTET Downing Street
DWSYDOE Down's syndrome
DWTTEIE down to the wire
DXEOSES dexterousness
DYAEETE day care centre
EAAILSS epanadiploses
EAGLCLY evangelically
EAGRTDY exaggeratedly
EAHCATR edaphic factor
EAIAIIY examinability
EAOAEES elaborateness
EATCISE elastic tissue
EATIEES exact likeness
EATORMA enantiodromia
EATYNIE exactly on time
EBLIHET embellishment
EBRASET embarrassment
EBYLGCL embryological
ECAGVES exchange views
ECAOOIT eschatologist
ECCOADA encyclopaedia
ECCOEIT encyclopedist
ECMASET encompassment
ECMATCL encomiastical
ECMUIAE excommunicate
ECNRCLY eccentrically
ECOCIGY encroachingly
ECODOAA enchondromata
ECOEODR enclosed order
ECPINBE exceptionable
ECPINBY exceptionably
ECPINLY exceptionally
ECPUAIN encapsulation
ECRIEES excursiveness
ECSBGAE excess baggage
ECSHLZA eschscholtzia
ECSIEES excessiveness
ECSLGAE excess luggage
ECSOEEF excuse oneself
ECTBEES excitableness
ECUAEET encouragement
ECUAIGY encouragingly
ECUIEES exclusiveness
EDCIOOY endocrinology
EDEHEGE Eddie The Eagle
EDFHERH end of the earth
EDMTISS endometriosis
EEECLEE Exeter College
EEEECOE Ebenezer Cooke
EEGNYXT emergency exit
EEGTCLY energetically
EEHNISS elephantiasis
EEHNSRW elephant shrew
EELMTHD evenly matched
EELSIGY everlastingly
EEPAIES exemplariness
EEPIIBE exemplifiable
EERGNSS epeirogenesis
EESPOIG even supposing
EETIFED electric field
EETIFNE electric fence
EETIMTR electric motor
EETIOGN electric organ
EETISOM electric storm
EETOAET electrovalent
EETOANT electromagnet
EETOCPC electroscopic
EETOERC electrometric
EETOHLC electrophilic
EETOHRS electrophorus
EETOOIE electromotive
EETOPIS electro-optics
EETOPOE electron probe
EETOTTC electrostatic
EETOUIN electrocution
EETRLOL electoral roll
EEUAIIG eke out a living
EEYAHOD Evelyn Ashford
EEYEHUS every few hours
EEYGENE Evelyn Glennie
EEYHCWY every which way
EFCCOSY efficaciously
EFCIEES effectiveness
EFCOEEF efface oneself
EFOECNE efflorescence
EFRECNE effervescence
EGNINSO Eugène Ionesco
EGNMCLY ergonomically
EGNOSVY Eugene of Savoy
EGRLAPE Edgar Allan Poe
EGTOEEL eightsome reel

EHBTOIM exhibitionism
EHBTOIT exhibitionist
EHCLAUS ethical values
EHLGCLY ethologically
EHOETIM ethnocentrism
EHOETIT ethnocentrist
EHOIGIT ethnolinguist
EHPSAIE enhypostatise
enhypostatize
EIAEHYN Elizabeth Ryan
EIATCLY epinastically
EIECGIE éminence grise
EIETOAN eminent domain
EIHEAQE Erich Remarque
EIHLOAA epitheliomata
EIHNMNN epiphenomenon
EIHOEKR Erich Honecker
EILNLTR Eric Linklater
EIMRCME Eric Morecombe
EIMTCLY enigmatically
EIPRRDE Eric Partridge
EIRMAIE epigrammatise
epigrammatize
EITNILY existentially
EITOODR eviction order
ELGTNET enlightenment
ELNILAS Emlyn Williams
ELSEEOT Ellesmere Port
EMNBUDN Edmund Blunden
EMNEAEA Éamon de Valera
EMNHLAY Edmund Hillary
EMNHSEL Edmund Husserl
EMNOARS Edmontosaurus
EMNRSAD Edmond Rostand
EMNSESR Edmund Spenser
EMWOHUE Emma Woodhouse
ENTOBIH Ernst Gombrich
ENTOFAN Ernst Hoffmann
ENTUISH Ernst Lubitsch
EOADATT Edouard Lartet
EOAIEES evocativeness
EOETIIY egocentricity
EOILGCL exobiological
EOITCLY egotistically
EOOERCL econometrical
EOOIAIN economization
EOOIOOY ecotoxicology
EORNGAD exocrine gland
EPAAOIY explanatorily
EPCOAIN expectoration
EPDTOAY expeditionary
EPDTOSY expeditiously
EPESOBS express doubts
EPESOIM expressionism❑
EPESOIT Expressionist
EPIDCRS esprit de corps
EPNAIIY expendability
EPNEMTL expanded metal
EPNIEES expansiveness
expensiveness
EPNIIIY expansibility
EPNINAD expansion card
EPNINOT expansion bolt

EPNNILY exponentially
EPOIEES explosiveness
EPOIGTR exploding star
EPORAIN expropriation
EPRAIIY exportability
EPRBIDR empire-builder
EPRECDN experienced in
EPREGOS exported goods
EPRUAIE empyreumatise
empyreumatize
EPSRMTR exposure meter
EPSUAIE expostulative
EPSUAIN expostulation
EPSUAOY expostulatory
EPTIEIH empathize with
EPYEAOS emphysematous
EQIIEES exquisiteness
ERAIIGS earn a living as
ERGOSES egregiousness
ERHOEET earth-movement
ERHOHRY earth-motherly
ERIJHSN Earvin Johnson
ERNOSES erroneousness
ESAWNIG easy as winking
ESIDALB East India Club
ESLDCDD easily decided
ESLDMGD easily damaged
ESLNTCD easily noticed
ESLSEIG easy listening
ESMNEEL Epsom and Ewell
ESNILAT essential part
ESNRHAT east-north-east
ESSUHAT east-south-east
ETAAAIN extravasation
ETAAATY extravagantly
ETAELLR extracellular
ETAOAIE extrapolative
ETAOAIN extrapolation
ETAOAOY extrapolatory
ETARIAY extraordinary
ETBIHBE establishable
ETBIHET establishment❑
ETEEUGR extreme hunger
ETERNUE entrepreneuse
ETISCLY extrinsically
ETMLGCL entomological
ETMOAIY extemporarily
ETMOIIG extemporizing
ETNAIGY extenuatingly
ETNAIIY extendability
ETNIEES extensiveness
ETNIIIY extendibility
ETNINLY extensionally
ETOLDRW eat boiled crow
ETRANET entertainment
ETRBGTI Ettore Bugatti
ETRHLSS enter the lists
ETRIAIG exterminating
ETRIAIN extermination
ETRNSED enter one's head
ETROAGE exterior angle
ETRPOET enter a protest
ETRSTAS Ettore Sotsass

EUAAIIY educatability
EUAIGIA Educating Rita
EUAINLY educationally
EUDSATY equidistantly
EUEIAIM ecumenicalism
EUEOLTE eau-de-toilette
EUNCILY equinoctially
EUPNEAE equiponderate
EURBCNR Eduard Buchner
EUSOPIT emulsion paint
EUSRAIM equestrianism
EUTBEES equitableness
EVRNETL environmental
EVSOTLO Elvis Costello
EVSRPIG eavesdropping
EWNADER Edwin Landseer
EWNAOSY Erwin Panofsky
EWNHRAF Erwin Chargaff
EWRBRAD Edward Barnard
EWRKNEY Edward Kennedy
EWRWYPR Edward Whymper
EYIMILS elysium fields
EYINILS elysian fields
FABRATD flabbergasted
FACSAIR Francis Xavier
FACSATN Francis Galton
FACSOEH Francis Joseph
FAELTEN flageolet bean
FAHLOIG flash flooding
FAHNHPN flash in the pan
FAHREGT featherweight
FAJTDMN Franjo Tudjman
FAKEEID Frank Wedekind
FAKEOED Frankie Howerd
FAKILAS Frank Williams
FAKURAH Frank Auerbach
FAMNAIN fragmentation
FAMNAIY fragmentarily
FANCLUS fear no colours
FATCMLS fractocumulus
FATOAIE fractionalise
fractionalize
FATOAIN fractionation
FATOAIT fractionalist
FATOSES fractiousness
FATSRTS fractostratus
FAUEEGH feature-length
FAUERTR feature-writer
FAZCUET Franz Schubert
FBUMXMS Fabius Maximus
FCINLZD fictionalized
FCINRTR fiction writer
FCLAIEY facultatively
FCOIAIN factorization
FCTOSES facetiousness
FDEFDCA fide et fiducia
FDLRGEN fiddler's green
FDOHTEH fed to the teeth
FECCIKT French cricket
FECMAIN free companion
FECTOTR French Trotter
FEDFATE field of battle
FEDFIIN field of vision

Words marked ❑ can also be spelled with an initial capital letter

Code	Entry
FEDODUH	field wood rush
FEDOPTL	field hospital
FEEIKAE	Frederick Jane
	Frederick Page
FEEISAN	Frederikshavn
FEHNBOD	flesh and blood
FEHSDIY	fresh as a daisy
FEIGOTE	feeding bottle
FEIGRUH	feeding trough
FEIJCIN	fuel-injection
FEKFAUE	freak of nature
FEMSRBE	feel miserable
FETEOSF	feel the loss of
FEUNAIE	frequentative
FEZNPIT	freezing point
FGATUEM	Fogg Art Museum
FGRHGIG	figure-hugging
FGROEGT	figure of eight
FGRSAIG	figure skating
FIADQAE	fair and square
	fair-and-square
FIGBNFT	fringe benefit
FIGDELR	fringe-dweller
FIGFEZR	fridge-freezer
FIGHOMD	fling throw mud
FIGTETE	fringe theatre
FIHEIGY	frighteningly
FIHESES	faithlessness
FIHFAHR	flight-feather
FIHFLES	frightfulness
FIHOFNY	flight of fancy
FILDIAD	frilled lizard
FIRARNE	Friar Laurence
FITMNIN	fail to mention
FITRDWY	frittered away
FITTOSY	flirtatiously
FLASRNE	full assurance
FLCTTOS	felicitations
FLETNIN	file extension
FLETRUH	filter through
FLEVDNE	false evidence
FLEWAIG	false swearing
FLEWRIR	Fallen Warrior
FLFAORD	full-flavoured
FLFOGAE	fall from grace
FLIGOIS	falling to bits
FLIIAIN	falsification
FLITPAE	fall into place
FLNCBNT	filing cabinet
FLNOSES	feloniousness
FLOCOEY	follow closely
FLOCTZN	fellow citizen
FLOFEIG	fellow feeling
	fellow-feeling
FLOOEEF	full of oneself
FLOTRUH	follow through
	follow-through
FLPOETR	film projector
FLSMOEN	fill someone in
FLTTERM	full to the brim
FMLHSOY	family history
FMNNRYE	feminine rhyme
FNAARUD	find a way round
FNAETLY	fundamentally
FNAHDOK	finnan haddock
FNANBEU	Fontainebleau
FNATCLY	fantastically
FNEAABY	Fontenay Abbey
FNEASAE	Finnegans Wake
FNEJYBE	find enjoyable
FNFUTIH	find fault with
FNIGATR	fencing-master
FNLEIIN	final decision
FNNILEP	financial help
FNNILER	financial year
FNNILUN	financial ruin
FNOELVL	find one's level
FNSIGOT	finishing post
FNTOAIM	functionalism
FNTOAIT	functionalist
FNTOHOB	fine-tooth comb
FNYEUIR	funny peculiar
	funny-peculiar
FNYUIES	funny business
FOALLCS	from all places
FOANFUA	flora and fauna
FOAOTIH	fool about with
FODIHIG	floodlighting
FOHRIES	foolhardiness
FOIGRUD	fooling around
FOITCLY	floristically
FOLNRKR	foot-land-raker
FOPIOIG	food poisoning
FOPOESR	food processor
FOROEIG	floor-covering
FORSIGY	flourishingly
FOSAAIE	fool's paradise
FOTAELR	foot-traveller
FOTEODO	from the word go
FOTGNSS	frontogenesis
FOTNOAR	floating on air
FOTNSOK	floutingstock
FRADFRG	fore-and-aft rig
FRAIAIN	formalization
FRAOIIN	form an opinion
FRAVRIT	formal verdict
FRCOSES	ferociousness
FRECSAE	for mercy's sake
FREFLES	forgetfulness
FREHISE	force the issue
FREOEEF	forget oneself
FRFEIGY	forefeelingly
FRHACUT	for the account
FRHPEET	for the present
FRHSESN	for this reason
FRHTATR	for that matter
FRHTESN	for that reason
FRIADOH	Ferdinand Foch
FRIADON	Ferdinand Cohn
FRIAIIY	formidability
FRIIAIN	fertilisation
	fertilization
	fortification
FRIIDIE	fortified wine
FRIIYRG	fertility drug
FRINFIE	foreign office
FRISRNE	fire insurance
FRKOIGY	foreknowingly
FRKOLDE	foreknowledge
FRLFTUK	fork-lift truck
FRLYUAE	for all you care
FRLYUNW	for all you know
FRMDXOD	Ford Madox Ford
FRMNIND	forementioned
FROADES	form of address
FROANTC	ferromagnetic
FRODNAL	for good and all
FROOCEE	ferroconcrete
FRRFRNE	for preference
FRROTCS	furor poeticus
FRRSSAT	fire-resistant
FRSAOIG	foreshadowing
FRSOTIE	for a short time
FRTACVR	first-day cover
FRTFEDR	first offender
FRTIITR	first minister
FRTOLWR	First World War
FRUEELR	fortune-teller
FRUEOKE	fortune cookie
FRUEUTR	fortune-hunter
FRVRNAE	for ever and aye
FRWRPRY	firework party
FSIAOSY	fissiparously
FSIIAIN	fossilization
FSIIEOS	fossiliferous
FSINITM	fashion victim
FSORATR	fusion reactor
FTCAPTE	fête champêtre
FTHCMAS	fetch a compass
FTHCRUT	fetch a circuit
FTHNCRY	fetch and carry
FTIEGOE	fit like a glove
FTRHSAD	future husband
FTSAATS	Fêtes Galantes
FUANFOA	fauna and flora
FUDRIIE	feux d'artifice
FUETROS	frumentarious
FUTAIGY	frustratingly
FUTATLE	fruit pastille
FUTESES	faultlessness
	fruitlessness
FUTOKAL	fruit cocktail
FUTYPOY	Faust Symphony
FVPSTOS	five positions
FVUIEPT	favourite spot
FVUSOOE	favours to come
FXHPIET	fix the price at
FYNCLUS	flying colours
FYNMCIE	flying machine
FYNOFCR	flying officer
FZYEOAE	fizzy lemonade
GAACAMN	Graham Chapman
GAAINLY	gradationally
GAAPLOK	Graham Pollock
GACTRUH	glance through
GADAAGL	guardian angel
GADAGTR	granddaughter
GADAHRY	grandfatherly
GADAINL	Grand National

GADCCTE grande cocotte
GADDXNE Grande Dixence
GADFOOR guard of honour
GADLQET grandiloquent
GADLQOS grandiloquous
GADOHRY grandmotherly
GAEAAIY Guatemala City
GAEESES gracelessness
GAERSIG grade crossing
GAEYCNH grape hyacinth
GAHLGCL graphological
GAHNCLY gnathonically
GAIAINL gravitational
GAIIAIN gratification
GAIIOOS graminivorous
GAILEID glacial period
GAIUAIN graticulation
GAMSUES Graeme Souness
GAMTCLY grammatically
GANGASS granny glasses
GANVRAE Gianni Versace
GAOIAIN glamorization
GAPIGOK grappling-hook
GAPIGRN grappling-iron
GAPTSRW grasp at a straw
GAPTTAS grasp at straws
GATOTIE giant tortoise
GAYALAD Gladys Aylward
GBRAOIL gubernatorial
GDLTERM Gödel's theorem
GDOMNEL Gideon Mantell
GDWIVLE go down in value
GDWTEUE go down the tube
GEDJCSN Glenda Jackson
GEILWNE Greville Wynne
GENIHNY green with envy
GENOSGS greenhouse gas
GEOYICS Gregory Pincus
GETAMUH Great Yarmouth
GETATAE Great Salt Lake
GETBATR ghetto-blaster
GETERAE Great Bear Lake
GETIBBE Great Zimbabwe
GETITNE great distance
GETITRA Great Victoria
GETNAHD great unwashed
GETRODN Greater London
GETRUBR greater number
GIADERT grin and bear it
GICNRLF gain control of
GIECUTR Geiger counter
GIEESES guilelessness
GIEMSIE guided missile
GIFTIKN grief-stricken
GIGOAOG going for a song
GIGOICS going to pieces
GIOESUS gain one's spurs
GISUIIS Gaius Lucilius
GITDTIS go into details
GITESES guiltlessness
GLAEHPC Gilgamesh Epic
GLAHETE goliath beetle
GLAIAIN galvanization
GLCIPAE galactic plane
GLEJBLE golden jubilee
GLESCIN golden section
GLNUAOA Galina Ulanova
GLOSUOR gallows humour
GMALBLN gamma globulin
GMATCLY gymnastically
GMTIHET Gemütlichkeit
GNDTOHC gonadotrophic
GNDTOHN gonadotrophin
GNEANIG genre painting
GNEBNIG gender-bending
GNEOOIT gynaecologist
GNINILT gentian violet
GNISOMS gentilshommes
GNLMNIE gentlemanlike
GNRLEGR general ledger
GNRLSIO generalissimo
GNRLULC general public
GNRTOGP generation gap
GNTPCLY genotypically
GNTTEAL gone to the wall
GNTUIAY genito-urinary
GOATCLY geotactically
GOATRON good afternoon
GOAVLAE global village
GOAWRIG global warming
GOCNIIN good condition
GODNBUO Giordano Bruno
GODSHRE glow discharge
GOEBGIH go over big with
GOEQEES grotesqueness
GOERCLY geometrically
GOERTIG globetrotting
globe-trotting
GOETEDE go over the edge
GOETIIM geocentricism
GOFHRIS go off the rails
GOGAKEE Georgia O'Keefe
GOGBDEL George Biddell
GOGBNHM George Bentham
GOGCAMN George Chapman
GOGCDUY George Cadbury
GOGCNIG George Canning
GOGEEAN Georg Telemann
GOGESHM George Eastham
GOGESMN George Eastman
GOGFRMN George Foreman
GOGGSIG George Gissing
GOGHRET George Herbert
GOGIOOM Georg Simon Ohm
GOGMCAL George Michael
GOGMCEH George Macbeth
GOGMLOY George Mallory
GOGORAI Giorgio Armani
GOGSATN Georges Danton
GOGSERT Georges Seurat
GOGSIIZ George Stibitz
GOGSRQE Georges Braque
GOGSUIR Georges Cuvier
GOGTOSN George Thomson
GOGWCHM George Wickham
GOGYHKV Giorgiy Zhukov
GOHMCLY geochemically
GOHOOOY geochronology
GOIIAIN glorification
GOISENM Gloria Steinem
GOLKTPY grow like Topsy
GONBEKR groundbreaker
ground-breaker
GONTRDY good-naturedly
GOOPOOY geomorphology
GOPOEHR group together
GOPRCIE group practice
GOPYAIS group dynamics
GORPCLY geotropically
GOSMRTN good Samaritan
GOTEAZE go on the razzle
GOTFHWY go out of the way
GOTHROE growth hormone
GOTTOAY geostationary
GPYUHOM gypsy mushroom
GRADEGR Gerhard Berger
GRAMALS German measles
GRANGER Germaine Greer
GRATOTR German Trotter
GRIMRUZ García Márquez
GRLDREL Gerald Durrell
GRLEEMN Gerald Edelman
GRLKUMN Gerald Kaufman
GRMGEIM gyromagnetism
GRNOOIT gerontologist
GRNORTC gerontocratic
GROBNET Gordon Bennett
GROCLEE Girton College
GRTEWRS Gareth Edwards
GRUOSES garrulousness
GRYAFRY Gerry Rafferty
GRYULGN Gerry Mulligan
GSAEIFL Gustave Eiffel
GSIUAIN gesticulation
GSMOEWY go someone's way
GSNGIES gas and gaiters
GSRCEIS gastrocnemius
GTAYEGH go to any length
GTCUTMD get accustomed
GTEEGHF go the length of
GTEHLHG go the whole hog
GTEITNE go the distance
GTETAED gather to a head
GTFMCOD Get Off My Cloud
GTGRVTD get aggravated
GTHHAEO get the heave-ho
GTHJTES get the jitters
GTHKAKF get the knack of
GTHMSAE get the message
GTHPCUE get the picture
GTHWLIS get the willies
GTIGETR getting better
GTIGSDO getting used to
GTNELIH get on well with
GTNHWYF get in the way of
GTNNHAT get in on the act
GTNNSET get on one's feet
GTNNSIK get on one's wick
GTNOHAT get into the act

GTNSADN	get one's hand in
GTNSAKP	get one's back up
GTNSWWY	get one's own way
GTNYFLF	get an eyeful of
GTOGDON	get bogged down
GTOJSIE	gate of justice
GTOLDPN	get dolled up in
GTONSET	get to one's feet
GTPNSOE	get up one's nose
GTRGLRY	go to regularly
GTRUHIH	go through with
GTTEOTM	go to the bottom
GTTOEHR	get it together
GTUPRFR	get support for
GUEPPAO	Giuseppe Peano
GUEPVRI	Giuseppe Verdi
GUIOSES	glutinousness
GUMNIIG	gourmandizing
GVAAADO	give an award to
GVAAEIT	give a facelift
GVAEAPE	give an example
GVAETNE	give a sentence
GVAIIGO	give a hiding to
GVAMSIN	give admission
GVANEVR	give a once-over
GVAOAIN	give a donation
GVAOIIN	give an opinion
GVAOKTO	give a rocket to
GVAOORO	give a honour to
GVAOSIG	give a roasting
GVAPEHO	give a speech to
GVAREEN	give a free rein
GVAUSER	give a bum steer
GVCEIFR	give credit for
GVCUAEO	give courage to
GVDTISF	give details of
GVLSOSN	give lessons in
GVNATNS	Gavin Hastings
GVNOPIN	given no option
GVRIGOY	governing body
GVTEAKO	give the sack to
GVTEOEN	give the come-on
GVTEOEO	give the vote to
GVTEOTO	give the boot to
GVTEUHO	give the push to
GVTEUKT	give the bucket
GVTOGTO	give thought to
GVTTEOS	give to the dogs
GWTTELW	go with the flow
HAECAGR	heat exchanger
HAEHGRE	heave the gorge
HAEKSIG	heaven-kissing
HAELBIG	heavenly being
HAEOERH	heaven on earth
HAHOISN	Heath-Robinson
HAIIAIN	hyalinization
HAOEHES	head over heels
HARSRIT	head restraint
HASILOL	heads will roll
HATESES	heartlessness
HATFERS	heart of hearts
HATIKES	heart-sickness
HATRAIG	heartbreaking
	heart-breaking
HATTRIG	heart-stirring
HATVSTR	health visitor
HAUDSLY	head-up display
HAYATCE	heavy particle
HAYNUTY	heavy industry
HAYYRGN	heavy hydrogen
HBIIAIN	hybridization
HBITCLY	hubristically
HBOSHIE	Hobson's choice
HBRDBRH	Hubert de Burgh
HBTBEES	habitableness
HCADAGR	heck and manger
HCIIHIY	Ho Chi Minh City
HCOBRIZ	Hector Berlioz
HDALCLY	hydraulically
HDEMAIG	hidden meaning
HDENSES	hedge one's bets
HDOEAIN	hydrogenation
HDOEHLC	hydrocephalic
HDOEHLS	hydrocephalus
HDOERCL	hydrometrical
HDOIEIS	hydrokinetics
HDOLCRC	hydroelectric
HDOTTCL	hydrostatical
HDOYAIS	hydrodynamics
HEAOOIT	haematologist
HEIJEIS	heebie-jeebies
HEOILSS	haemodialysis
HEOLPIS	hieroglyphics
HEORODL	haemorrhoidal
HESEGWY	heels o'er gowdy
HFUGUEM	Hofburg Museum
HGADIHY	high and mighty
	high-and-mighty
HGCNTBE	High Constable
HGEPOIE	high explosive
HGFEUNY	high frequency
HGGISEL	Hugh Gaitskell
HGKNSIL	Hugh Kingsmill
HGLNDES	Highland dress
HGLNFIG	Highland fling
HGOCPCL	hygroscopical
HGOERCL	hygrometrical
HGORPIT	hagiographist
HGPISES	high priestess
HGSOAHD	high-stomached
HGWTRAK	high-water mark
HIEEASE	Haile Selassie
HIEEGSU	Haile Mengistu
HIHTPPR	height to paper
HIRCBRH	Heinrich Barth
HIRCHIE	Heinrich Heine
HIRCHRZ	Heinrich Hertz
HISLTIG	hair-splitting
HIZOLGR	Heinz Holliger
HLAADEO	hold a candle to
HLADERY	hale and hearty
HLADONR	hole-and-corner
HLAHSAE	hold as hostage
HLCMUIN	Holy Communion
HLCRASS	Halicarnassus
HLDYETE	holiday centre
HLEITCL	Hellenistical
HLESETR	helter-skelter
HLHATDY	half-heartedly
HLICSOY	held in custody
	hold in custody
HLIEELC	Hilaire Belloc
HLINCNS	Holy Innocents
HLITEAL	hole in the wall
HLITISS	helminthiasis
HLMTIOY	Holy Matrimony
	holy matrimony
HLNKNEY	Helena Kennedy
HLOCEKD	hollow-cheeked
HLOEEFO	help oneself to
HLOEPAE	hold one's peace
HLORPCL	heliotropical
HLSMOEO	hold someone to
HLSVRIN	half sovereign
HLTACUT	hold to account
HLTEATE	half the battle
HLUIAIG	hallucinating
HLUIAIN	hallucination
HLUIAOY	hallucinatory
HLUSHIT	Helmut Schmidt
HLUTSAE	hold up to shame
HMBCWAE	humpback whale
HMCLUOE	hemicellulose
HMEOOIS	home economics
HMEOOIT	home economist
HMETEMC	homoeothermic
HMITEML	homoiothermal
HMLGCLY	homologically
HMLOEEF	humble oneself
HMLTCLY	homiletically
HMMRHSS	homomorphosis
HMNNEET	human interest
HMNPEOS	hymenopterous
HMSHRCL	hemispherical
HMSXAIY	homosexuality
HNAOTIH	hang about with
HNBAHED	hang by a thread
HNBTEAL	hang by the wall
HNBTEEK	hang by the neck
HNEMRHR	hunger-marcher
HNESRKR	hunger-striker
HNIABSE	Henri Barbusse
HNIENUT	Henri Regnault
HNIGALY	hanging valley
HNIGREY	hanging freely
HNILGLY	hunt illegally
HNITEID	hang in the wind
HNKRHES	handkerchiefs
HNLRUHY	handle roughly
HNRDEGT	hundredweight
HNRDUIR	Honoré Daumier
HNRFCLY	honorifically
HNTEETR	hunt the letter
HNUAIIY	honourability
HNUOEHT	hang up one's hat
HNYEMLN	honeydew melon
HNYESMR	Henry Bessemer
HNYIGIK	Henry Sidgwick
HNYILIG	Henry Fielding

HNYOISN Henry Robinson
HOOHLAD Hook of Holland
HPAADES haphazardness
HPAYLBC heptasyllabic
HPCCODL hypocycloidal
HPCODIC hypochondriac
HPCODIM hypochondrium
HPEIGON happening soon
HPGYAMA hypoglycaemia
HPGYAMC hypoglycaemic
HPPOPIE hypophosphite
HPRCIIY hyperactivity
HPRERCL hypermetrical
HPRERPA hypermetropia
HPRHSCL hyperphysical
HPRRPID hypertrophied
HPRRTCL hypercritical
HPYADNS happy landings
HPYAIIS happy families
HRADODR here and yonder
HRADOPD her jaw dropped
HRAHOIE hermaphrodite
HRDHGET Herod the Great
HRDYNGT Hard Day's Night
HREAARS Herrerasaurus
HREAKRL horse mackerel
HRECSIG Harvey Cushing
HREETCL hermeneutical
HREETES horsefeathers
HREHATE Harlech Castle
HREHERB horseshoe crab
HREHERH horseshoe arch
HREHPIG horsewhipping
HREHSNT horse chestnut
HRELSOE horseflesh ore
HRENHUD Horse and Hound
HREODES horse soldiers
HREOHBA herpetophobia
HREOOIT herpetologist
HRETEEK harden the neck
HRETOVR Herbert Hoover
HRETPDR harvest spider
HREUHOM horse mushroom
HRFRSIE Herefordshire
Hertfordshire
HRHATDY hard-heartedly
HRICULT heroic couplet
HRIHNOK Herbie Hancock
HRIIAIN horripilation
HRITAMN Harriet Harman
HRITUMN Harriet Tubman
HRIUTRL horticultural
HRLBBOK Harold Babcock
HRLLROD Harold Larwood
HRLRBIS Harold Robbins
HRLSIMN Harold Shipman
HRLTEIE hardly the time
HROHAIG hard of hearing
HROIAIN harmonization
HROIEIH harmonize with
HROSALY Harlow Shapley
HRSIAIN haruspication
HRTBLEE hard to believe

HRTOESN Horatio Nelson
HRUBRSP her number is up
HRUEORT Hercule Poirot
HRWGAAN here we go again
HRZNABR horizontal bar
HRZNAIY horizontality
HSADOPD his jaw dropped
HSIGBNA Hastings Banda
HSUBRSP his number is up
HTAECUT hot-water crust
HTEADOD hither and yond
HTEDDES hot-headedness
HTHBGIE hit the big time
HTHCIIG hit the ceiling
HTHJCPT hit the jackpot
HTIBLON hot-air balloon
HTIJCUS Hattie Jacques
HTNHHES hot on the heels
HTNSTIE hit one's stride
HTOKOTM hit rock bottom
HTOPLIG hot gospelling
HTRGNIY heterogeneity
HTRGNOS heterogeneous
HTRGNSS heterogenesis
HTRGNTC heterogenetic
HTRMRHC heteromorphic
HTRPATC heteroplastic
HTRPEOS heteropterous
HTRTOHC heterotrophic
HUEFRYR house of prayer
HUEFTTS House of States
HUEITES housemistress
HUEODAE household name
HUEODOD household word
HUERAIG housebreaking
house-breaking
HUIGCEE housing scheme
HUIGSAE housing estate
HUITCLY heuristically
HVAAEIH have a game with
HVAAIFL have a basinful
HVAHNFR have a thing for
HVAIEFT have a time of it
HVAIMUH have a big mouth
HVAISOE have as its home
HVAODID have a good mind
HVAODIE have a good time
HVAODIH have a word with
HVAORRF have a horror of
HVAULOE have a dual role
HVCMADF have command of
HVCNRLF have control of
HVCSOYF have custody of
HVDSGSN have designs on
HVEITNE have existence
HVEOGFR have enough for
HVHDNUH have had enough
HVHDTDY have had its day
HVHLAID have half a mind
HVIFUNE have influence
HVIOEWY have it one's way
HVIOFIH have it off with
HVIOTIH have it out with

HVNFIHN have no faith in
HVNKTES having kittens
HVNRPOT having rapport
HVNTIGN have nothing on
HVNTMFR have no time for
HVSMOEN have someone on
HVTEDEN have the edge on
HVTEIDF have the wind of
HVTEOKF have the look of
HVTOEEF have to oneself
HWIGOKY howling monkey
HWRHDKN Howard Hodgkin
HYESAIM Heysel Stadium
HZROSES hazardousness
IACUTIH in account with
IAEEGNY in an emergency
IAHRWIE in a short while
IAIAIEY imaginatively
IAIEHNS imagine things
IAIIAIN italicization
IALARES in all fairness
IALEPCS in all respects
IALFSIK in a cleft stick
IALOSEL if all goes well
IAOAUCN Isadora Duncan
IAPEIBE inappreciable
IAPEIBY inappreciably
IAPORAE inappropriate
IARWSUY in a brown study
IATNIEY inattentively
IAVRETY inadvertently
IAYNSOK in anyone's book
ICEIIIY incredibility
ICEUOSY incredulously
ICIEPAE inclined plane
ICIIAIG incriminating
ICIIAIN incrimination
ICIIAOY incriminatory
ICLAIIY inculpability
ICMAYIH in company with
ICMEETY incompetently
ICMEIIN in competition
ICMSOIY incomes policy
ICMSPOT income support
ICMUIAO incommunicado
ICMUTBE incombustible
ICMUTBY incombustibly
ICNATIH in contact with
ICNCETY inconsciently
ICNECNE incandescence
ICNEINE inconvenience
ICNETBE incontestable
ICNETBY incontestably
inconvertibly
ICNETIH in concert with
ICNEUNE in consequence
inconsequence
ICNEVBE inconceivable
ICNEVBY inconceivably
ICNIEAE inconsiderate
ICNIETY incontinently
ICNITNY inconsistency
ICNOATY inconsonantly

ICNPCOS inconspicuous
ICNROSY incongruously
ICNUAIM in contumaciam
ICNUCIN in conjunction
ICOEAIN in co-operation
ICPCTTD incapacitated
ICREAIN incarceration
ICRETES incorrectness
ICROAIN incorporation
ICROELY incorporeally
ICROSES incuriousness
ICRUAIN in circulation
ICRUTBE incorruptible
ICRUTBY incorruptibly
ICSATES incessantness
ICUTNNE in countenance
IDCINOL induction coil
IDCRNTR indoctrinator
IDCTSEK induce to speak
IDFEETY indifferently
IDFTGBE indefatigable
IDFTGBY indefatigably
IDPNETY independently
IDRCRUE indirect route
IDRSRIS in dire straits
IDSENBE indiscernible
IDSENBY indiscernibly
IDSESBE indispensable
IDSESBY indispensably
IDSOIIN indisposition
IDSRAIE industrialise
industrialize
IDSRAIM industrialism
IDSRAIT industrialist
IDSRBBE indescribable
IDSRBBY indescribably
IDSROSY industriously
IDSUDBY indissuadably
IDTRIAE indeterminate
IDTRIAY indeterminacy
IDVDAIE individualise
individualize
IDVDAIM individualism
IDVDAIN individuation
IDVDAIT individualist
IDVDAIY individuality
IEAOAEY inelaborately
IECAGFR in exchange for
IEEYATF in every part of
IEEYEAL in every detail
IEFBEES ineffableness
IEFCCOS inefficacious
IEFCETY inefficiently
IEFCIEY ineffectively
IEFCULY ineffectually
IEHUTBE inexhaustible
IEHUTBY inexhaustibly
IEIAIIY inevitability
IEIIIIY ineligibility
IEOAIIY inexorability
IEPDETY inexpediently
IEPESBE inexpressible
IEPESBY inexpressibly
IEPNIEY inexpensively
IEPRECD inexperienced
IETCLES identicalness
IEUAIIY ineducability
IFAIIIY infeasibility
IFCIEES infectiveness
IFEIIIY inflexibility
IFLFAHR in full feather
IFLIIIY infallibility
IFNIUAE infundibulate
IFNTSML infinitesimal
IFOECNE inflorescence
IFRAANT inform against
IFRAIGY infuriatingly
IFRAINL informational
IFREAOT informed about
IFRNILY inferentially
IFUNILY influentially
IFUTOSY infructuously
IGABRMN Ingmar Bergman
IGEILGS in gremio legis
IGETEAD in great demand
IGETEAL in great detail
IGIBRMN Ingrid Bergman
IGNOSES ingeniousness
ingenuousness
IGOSIIS in good spirits
IHGDDEN in high dudgeon
IHGFAHR in high feather
IHGSIIS in high spirits
IHHOOIT ichthyologist
IHNUBUD in honour bound
IHROYIH in harmony with
IIAIEES imitativeness
IIALPIH it is all up with
IIIAIIY inimitability
IIMTCLY idiomatically
IISNIEY in its entirety
IISNRTC idiosyncratic
IJDCOSY injudiciously
IJRDESN injured person
IJROSES injuriousness
IKEIGIH in keeping with
IKEPITR ink-jet printer
ILAORDY ill-favouredly
ILHNHMO I'll thank him to
ILHNHRO I'll thank her to
ILHNYUO I'll thank you to
ILMNTOS illuminations
ILNHPIG island-hopping
ILNRVNE Inland Revenue
ILOSDRD ill-considered
ILQIAIN in liquidation
ILSFCLY Isles of Scilly
ILSROSY illustriously
IMDAEES immediateness
IMMRAOD immemorial old
IMNLGCL immunological
IMNTEAY immunotherapy
IMRECBE immarcescible
IMTBEES immutableness
IMTRAIE immaterialise
immaterialize
IMTRAIY immateriality
INAILNS Ionian Islands
INCOSES innocuousness
INIXNKS Iannis Xenakis
INMNOSY ignominiously
INRERDS Inner Hebrides
INROKNS inner workings
INTMAAL in no time at all
INVTOIT innovationist
IOEAIIY inoperability
IOEEEET in one's element
IOEONIE in one's own time
IOERCLY isometrically
IOFCOSY inofficiously
IOFNIEY inoffensively
IOGNCLY inorganically
IOHOOSY isochronously
IOIOPIM isodimorphism
IOIOPOS isodimorphous
IOPRUEY inopportunely
IOTEERT in on the secret
IOTTCLY isostatically
IOTUIEY inobtrusively
IPAAIIY implacability
IPATCBE impracticable
IPATCBY impracticably
IPATCLY impractically
IPCAIIY impeccability
IPCNOIY impecuniosity
IPCNOSY impecuniously
IPEAAIN in preparation
IPEIEES impreciseness
IPESOIM Impressionism
IPESOIT impressionist
IPIAIEY implicatively
IPITFAT in point of fact
IPLAIIY impalpability
IPLEUIG impulse buying
IPLIEES impulsiveness
IPOAIIY improbability
IPOIAIN improvisation
IPOIETY improvidently
IPOORPS in photographs
IPRAETY impermanently
IPRAITC imperialistic
IPREGOS imported goods
IPRETBE imperceptible
IPRETBY imperceptibly
IPREVBE imperceivable
IPRIETY impertinently
IPRILES impartialness
IPRISBE impermissible
IPRISBY impermissibly
IPRNHSS in parenthesis
IPRNRHP in partnership
IPROAIE impersonalise
impersonalize
IPROAIN impersonation
IPROAIY impersonality
IPROSES imperiousness
IPRPCIE in perspective
IPRUAEY importunately
IPRUBBE imperturbable

IPRUBBY imperturbably
IPSAIIY impassability
IPSIEES impassiveness
IPSIIIY impossibility
IPTEHHM it pitieth them
IPTOSES impetuousness
IQERTET in queer street
IQIIIEY inquisitively
IQIIINL inquisitional
IQIIOIL inquisitorial
IRCAMBE irreclaimable
IRCAMBY irreclaimably
IRCVRBE irrecoverable
IRCVRBY irrecoverably
IREIEYT Israel in Egypt
IRFAGBY irrefrangibly
IRLGOIT irreligionist
IRLGOSY irreligiously
IRLVNIS irrelevancies
IRPAEBE irreplaceable
IRPAEBY irreplaceably
IRPESBE irrepressible
IRPESBY irrepressibly
IRSNUNS iure sanguinis
IRSOSBE irresponsible
IRSOSBY irresponsibly
IRTBEES irritableness
IRTIVBE irretrievable
IRTIVBY irretrievably
IRTOAIE irrationalise
irrationalize
IRTOAIY irrationality
IRVRNIL irreverential
ISALTOS installations
ISATNIY instantaneity
ISATNOS instantaneous
ISBRIAE insubordinate
ISBTNIL insubstantial
ISCIOOS insectivorous
ISDOSES insidiousness
ISFIINY insufficiency
ISGIIAT insignificant
ISIAIGY instigatingly
ISIAINL inspirational
ISICIEY instinctively
ISICULY instinctually
ISIEFHS in spite of this
ISIEFHT in spite of that
ISIHRES in smithereens
ISIIIGY inspiritingly
ISIUIEY institutively
ISIUINL institutional
ISMMAUE in some measure
ISMNWRS in so many words
ISNAEES insensateness
ISNAIGY insinuatingly
ISNIIEY insensitively
ISNIIIY insensibility
insensitivity
ISOTUPY in short supply
ISPOTBE insupportable
ISPOTBY insupportably
ISRCIEY instructively
ISRCINL instructional
ISRPIEY inscriptively
ISRPINL inscriptional
ISSETBY insusceptibly
ISTAIIY insatiability
ITAELLR intracellular
ITASGNE intransigence
ITAUCLR intramuscular
ITEAEOT in the same boat
ITEANRF in the manner of
ITEATRF in the matter of
ITEAUEF in the nature of
ITEBTAT in the abstract
ITEEINF in the region of
ITEENIE in the meantime
ITEHREF in the charge of
ITEHRRN in the short run
ITEIDEE in the wind's eye
ITEIDEF in the middle of
ITEIEIE in the pipeline
ITEIIIY in the vicinity
ITEITNE into existence
ITEMLET in the smallest
ITENEVL in the interval
ITEODUS in the doldrums
ITEOHUE in the doghouse
ITEOREF in the course of
ITERWWY in their own way
ITGMNAY integumentary
ITIAEES intricateness
ITIIEES intuitiveness
ITISCLY intrinsically
ITLETAS intellectuals
ITLIETY intelligently
ITMEAEY intemperately
ITMSOEY in times gone by
ITNIEAE intensive care
ITNIEES intensiveness
ITNIIIY intangibility
ITNINLY intentionally
ITOPCIE introspective
ITOPCIN introspection
ITRAAIN intercalation
ITRAATC intergalactic
ITRAEET interlacement
ITRAIAE interlaminate
ITRAILY interradially
ITRAINL international
ITRARAE intermarriage
ITRAUAE interjaculate
ITRCPLR interscapular
ITREAIN interrelation
ITREEIH interfere with
ITREIGY interferingly
ITRELLR intercellular
ITRESNL interpersonal
ITRETLY interdentally
ITRHNIG interchanging
ITRIGIG intermingling
ITRIIAE interdigitate
ITRITNE intermittence
ITROAGE interior angle
ITROAIE interrogative
ITROAIN interpolation
interrogation
ITROAOY interrogatory
ITROIIN interposition
ITROUIN interlocution
ITROUOY interlocutory
ITRPRIN interspersion
ITRREIG interbreeding
ITRRTBE interpretable
ITRRXML interproximal
ITRSIGY interestingly
ITRSUAE interosculate
ITRTAIY interstratify
ITRURNE intercurrence
ITRUTDY interruptedly
ITUIEES intrusiveness
IVDOSES invidiousness
IVLNAIY involuntarily
IVNIEES inventiveness
IVNIIIY invincibility
IVNOILY inventorially
IVOAIIY inviolability
IVRAIIY invariability
IVSIAIE investigative
IVSIAIG investigating
IVSIAIN investigation
IVSIAOY investigatory
IWRLOIG inward-looking
IYUOTID if you don't mind
IZAPRMN Itzhak Perlman
JAFOSAT Jean Froissart
JALCOAD Jean-Luc Godard
JAPUGTY Jean Paul Getty
JAPUMRT Jean Paul Marat
JBCMOTR Job's comforter
JCBNCLY Jacobinically
JCBPEGR Jacob Sprenger
JCISEAT Jackie Stewart
JCNCOSN Jack Nicholson
JCTAADN Jack Teagarden
JCTEIPR Jack the Ripper
JCUSEKR Jacques Necker
JCUSHRC Jacques Chirac
JDCOSES judiciousness
JDITCLY Judaistically
JDSSAIT Judas Iscariot
JDUGABY Jedburgh Abbey
JFESNIY Jefferson City
JFRYRHR Jeffrey Archer
JGESIPE jogger's nipple
JGEYOEY jiggery-pokery
JGNSEOY jog one's memory
JHCNTBE John Constable
JHDLIGR John Dillinger
JHDNWRH John Dankworth
JHDSASS John Dos Passos
JHFASED John Flamsteed
JHLEOKR John Lee Hooker
JHMSFED John Masefield
JHNHECR Johnny H Mercer
JHNSRUS Johann Strauss
JHSENEK John Steinbeck
JIHUEOK Jailhouse Rock

JKLADYE Jekyll and Hyde
JLEUCIL Julie Burchill
JLIIAIN jollification
JLSAOGE Jules Laforgue
JLSASNT Jules Massenet
JLSIHLT Jules Michelet
JLSONAE Jules Poincaré
JLUAERD Julius Axelrod
JLUNEEE Julius Nyerere
JMIGHGN jumping the gun
JMIGOJY jumping for joy
JMRWCOL Jim Crow school
JMSAALN James Van Allen
JMSAGTE James Naughtie
JMSARTY James Hanratty
JMSHDIK James Chadwick
JMSHITE James Christie
JMSHSLR James Whistler
JMSIHNR James Michener
JMSIRES James Mirrlees
JMSNXOK James Knox Polk
JMSOIRY James Moriarty
JMSUHNN James Buchanan
JMYWTHR Jemmy Twitcher
JNLWRAE jungle warfare
JNTASIT Jonathan Swift
JNWIFED June Whitfield
JRMBNHM Jeremy Bentham
JRMGSOT Jeremy Guscott
JRMKEOE Jerome K Jerome
JRMUTIS Jura Mountains
JROIAIN jargonisation
jargonization
JRSRDNE jurisprudence
JRYALNS Jerry Rawlings
JRYELWS Jerry Lee Lewis
JRYENED Jerry Seinfeld
JSECROT Jasper Carrott
JSHHIEZ Jascha Heifetz
JSIIAIE justificative
JSIIAIN justification
JSIIAOY justificatory
JSPADES Joseph Andrews
JSPADSN Joseph Addison
JSPBOSY Joseph Brodsky
JSPKNEY Joseph Kennedy
JSPRTLT Joseph Rotblat
JSPRZIO Josip Broz Tito
JSPSRAE Joseph Surface
JSSCEDN just succeed in
JSSSOIS Just So Stories
JSSVNEN Just Seventeen
JSTIKFT just think of it
JVNLCUT juvenile court
JWLONAN Jewel Mountain
JWNSIGR jow one's ginger
JWRAIGY jawbreakingly
JWRPIGY jawdroppingly
JXAOEIH juxtapose with
JXAOIIN juxtaposition
KACAUIN Khatchaturian
KCOEHES kick one's heels
KCTEUKT kick the bucket
KCUAHNY kick up a shindy
KDEMCIE kidney machine
KDEMNTR Kidderminster
KEAEODF keep a record of
KEAMSAD keen as mustard
KECSSON keep costs down
KEDWCSS keep down costs
KEFIHIH keep faith with
KEGOHUS keep good hours
KEICSOY keep in custody
KEIGNID keeping in mind
KEIRSRE keep in reserve
KEITEAK keep in the dark
KEOEEDP keep one's end up
KEOEHUE keep open house
KESPLIG keep supplying
KETOEEF keep to oneself
KEWTHVR keep watch over
KIHSRAT knights-errant
KIOEBOS knit one's brows
KLICAKE Killiecrankie
KLIOCPC kaleidoscopic
KNAOCUT kangaroo court
KNAOGAS kangaroo grass
KNCEJNA Kangchenjunga
KNEHANA Kenneth Kaunda
KNEHLRE Kenneth Clarke
KNHATDY kind-heartedly
KNMTGAH kinematograph
KNOTROS king of terrors
KNSOOIT kinesiologist
KNSVDNE King's evidence
KNTCNRY kinetic energy
KNUKDRY Kentucky Derby
KNYAGIH Kenny Dalglish
KOISDOT know inside out
KOKAKFW knock back a few
KOKDOSX knocked for six
KOKIEAS knock sideways
KOKNFET knock-on effect
KOKNKES knocking knees
KOKOEHR knock together
KOKPTOF knock spots off
KOKUDOS knockout drops
KOLDEAE knowledge base
KOLDEBE knowledgeable
KOLDEBY knowledgeably
KOOEPAE know one's place
KOOESUF know one's stuff
KOWASHT know what's what
KPLMITR kapellmeister
KRCDRGT Kirkcudbright
KREIEDR Kornelia Ender
KRITLOH Kirkintilloch
KRVNRSH Karl von Frisch
KSADAEP kiss and make up
KSOHSLS kist o' whistles
KTGENWY Kate Greenaway
KTHNCLS kitchen scales
KTHNEIS Kitchen Devils®
KTYONRD kitty-cornered
KUKEONO knuckle down to
KUKEUTR knuckleduster
KURSUSN Knud Rasmussen
KZOSIUO Kazuo Ishiguro
LABTEOE lead by the nose
LAENSOE leave one's home
LAEOGAS Leaves of Grass
LAETNIG leave standing
LAETTHT leave it at that
LAHOEES loathsomeness
LAHRAKT leatherjacket
leather-jacket
LAIGEID leaving behind
LAIGOSA Leamington Spa
LAITEAK leap in the dark
LANNCRE learning curve
LATUTBE least suitable
LBAINHP librarianship
LBLEEEE La Belle Hélène
LBROSES laboriousness
LBRTOIM liberationism
LBRTOIT liberationist
LBRYOIE liberty bodice
LCAASCL lackadaisical
LCCVNIH Lucy Cavendish
LCEOSES lecherousness
LCEOSOK lecherous look
LCITSAE lick into shape
LCLALNE local parlance
LCMEETS locum tenentes
LCNIVTM licentia vatum
LCOCNEN lack of concern
LCOEOIN lack of emotion
LCOFEIG lack of feeling
LCOSCES lack of success
LCUTETE Lyceum Theatre
LDBAKEL Lady Bracknell
LDCOSES ludicrousness
LDIWIIG lady-in-waiting
LDOSAOT Lady of Shalott
LEFAMLH Liebfraumilch
LEHESEN Liechtenstein
LENNSAS lie on one's oars
LEONWRE lied ohne worte
LEOOAIN laevorotation
LFASRNE life assurance
LFISRNE life insurance
LFRNEIG life-rendering
LFSINIT life scientist
LFTEIOF lift the lid off
LFVNRCE left ventricle
LGCHPIG logic-chopping
LGFHTDS lag of the tides
LGLAAIY legal capacity
LGOOMRT Legion of Merit
LGSAIEY legislatively
LGSAOIL legislatorial
LGTFAUE light of nature
LGTIGRD light-fingered
LGTOORD light-coloured
LGTOSMN lighthouseman
LGTPRTD light-spirited
LIHAISS leishmaniases
leishmaniasis
leishmanioses

LISZASR	laissez-passer
LIUEETE	leisure centre
LKCNTNE	Lake Constance
LKCOKOK	like clockwork
LKCTNDG	like cat and dog
LKGIDAH	like grim death
LKLGTIG	like lightning
LKMRCIO	Lake Maracaibo
LKNCRGA	Lake Nicaragua
LKNUHTL	Lake Neuchâtel
LLILNTY	Lillie Langtry
LLOTEIE	lily of the nile
LMHTCLY	lymphatically
LMLIRNH	lamellibranch
LMNQEZR	lemon squeezer
LMSNHOE	Le Misanthrope
LMTESES	limitlessness
LNDWELB	Lansdowne Club
LNEOPRL	lance-corporal
LNFROTN	long-forgotten
LNIDNGN	Lonnie Donegan
LNODSET	line of descent
LNSFEIG	long-suffering
LNTCRNE	lunatic fringe
LNTCSLM	lunatic asylum
LNUFACE	lingue franche
LNUSIGY	languishingly
LNUSIIN	linguistician
LOACOEY	look at closely
LOBIFYT	look briefly at
LODGEST	look daggers at
LOEHMTN	Lionel Hampton
LOFRADO	look forward to
LOHRELR	Leonhard Euler
LOITEAE	look in the face
LOQIKYT	look quickly at
LOUADON	look up and down
LPDPEIT	lepidopterist
LPDPEOS	lepidopterous
LPULNUE	lapsus linguae
LQICYTL	liquid crystal
LRANCOS	Lorraine cross
LREULIG	large building
LREUNIY	large quantity
LRPEIET	Lord President
LRPIYEL	Lord Privy Seal
LRSEPRL	Lords Temporal
LSEPGOT	Lester Piggott
LSIEALS	Les Miserables
	Les Misérables
LSIPRAT	less important
LSISAMN	Leslie Scarman
LSITOGT	lost in thought
LSMNIND	last-mentioned
LSOCAGS	list of charges
LSOCNRL	loss of control
LSOENRE	lose one's nerve
LSOEPAE	lose one's place
LSOESIT	lose one's shirt
LSRRNIG	laser printing
LTAGCLY	lethargically
LTASANS	Lytham St Anne's
LTEBRAK	Luther Burbank
LTECRIR	letter-carrier
LTEOPAE	letter of peace
LTEPRET	letter-perfect
LTFTEOK	let off the hook
LTGOSES	litigiousness
LTLBGON	Little Bighorn
LTLRCAD	Little Richard
LTNMRCN	Latin-American
LTOENUE	let someone use
LTRRAET	literary agent
LTSOIIN	lotus position
LUCVHCE	launch vehicle
LUETAIS	Laurent Fabius
LUHNSOK	laughing-stock
LUSANIE	Louis MacNeice
LUSAURE	Louis Daguerre
LUSHLPE	Louis Philippe
	Louis-Philippe
LUSUTRE	Louis-Quatorze
LVADEDE	Live and Let Die
LVIPRNR	live-in partner
LVLKAOD	live like a lord
LVRCMAY	livery company
LWECBAG	Lawrence Bragg
LWECOTS	Lawrence Oates
LWFVRGS	law of averages
LWSLNOD	Lewis Alan Hoad
LXCGAHC	lexicographic
LXCGAHR	lexicographer
LXGAHCL	lexigraphical
LXROSES	luxuriousness
LYNAEDR	lay in lavender
LYNHTBE	lay on the table
LYONHLW	lay down the law
LYYHHES	lay by the heels
MAIGINE	moaning minnie
MAOSFRN	meadow saffron
MASFCES	means of access
MASLRIE	mean solar time
MASMTIG	mean something
MATOAPN	meant to happen
MAUEWRS	measure swords
MCAIAIN	mechanization
MCALALY	Michael Manley
MCALASY	Michael Ramsay
MCALFET	Michael of Kent
MCALOAD	Michael Howard
MCALODN	Michael Jordan
MCALOEL	Michael Powell
MCEAIII	Michela Figini
MCEESAK	mackerel shark
MCIEUNR	machine-gunner
MCIVLIN	Machiavellian
MCOAEBE	microwaveable
MCOAEVN	microwave oven
MCOASTE	microcassette
MCOCNMC	macroeconomic
	microeconomic
MCOEHLC	macrocephalic
MCOOEUE	macromolecule
MCOOPTR	microcomputer
MCORAIM	micro-organism
MCOUGCL	microsurgical
MCOURET	micronutrient
MCRNCLY	macaronically
MDAILNS	Midway Islands
MDAOILY	mediatorially
MDCLETE	medical centre
MDCNWMN	medicine woman
MDLAEIA	Middle America
MDLEGAD	Middle England
MDLSRUH	Middlesbrough
MDLTRUH	muddle through
MDMDSAL	Madame de Staël
MDODSAE	mad cow disease
MDRIAIN	modernization
MDRTAAL	moderate a call
MDRTRHP	moderatorship
MDSPRNI	modus operandi
MDTMAUE	made to measure
	made-to-measure
MDTRAEN	Mediterranean
MDUJFRY	Madhur Jaffrey
MDYPAEH	Madhya Pradesh
MEIGEPE	meeting people
MEOEMKR	meet one's maker
METEOTF	meet the cost of
MGAIOSY	magnanimously
MGCLOES	magical powers
MGCUHOM	magic mushroom
MGEIAIN	magnetization
MGEIFED	magnetic field
MGEINRH	magnetic north
MGEISOM	magnetic storm
MGEOOIE	magnetomotive
MGEOPEE	magnetosphere
MGIIAIN	magnification
MGIIETY	magnificently
MGIOUNE	magniloquence
MGRFNEN	Magersfontein
MGSEILY	magisterially
MGSOAGA	megasporangia
MGTAEEN	might-have-been
MHMASOB	Muhammad's Tomb
MHMEAIE	Mohammedanise
	Mohammedanize
MICAATR	main character
MIECNUY	maiden century
MIETNUD	maiden-tongued
MIEWDWD	maiden-widowed
MIOALOK	maid of all work
	maid-of-all-work
MISPRTD	mains-operated
MITRIGR	Meistersinger
MJRICEL	Major Mitchell
MJRNEVL	major interval
MKAAJBF	make a bad job of
MKAAKNN	Mikka Hakkinen
MKAALBE	make available
MKAATRF	make a martyr of
MKAATUK	make a fast buck
MKACUTF	make account of
MKAEDFR	make amends for
MKAEIIN	make a decision
MKALLNA	Mikhail Glinka
MKAOAIN	make a donation

MKAODEL make a good meal
MKAOGOE make a long nose
MKAOKYF make a monkey of
MKAREDF make a friend of
MKARGNT make arroganat
MKARMUH make a wry mouth
MKAUFRT make a run for it
MKCNETD make conceited
MKCPTLF make capital of
MKCRANF make certain of
MKDFEET make different
MKDFIUT make difficult
MKDMNSN make demands on
MKDPESD make depressed
MKFRTAE make first base
MKFUWTR make foul water
MKHSIEO make hostile to
MKHZLOD Mike Hazelwood
MKIFRIE make infertile
MKISLET make insolvent
MKISRNE make it strange
MKMNINF make mention of
MKMRSLD make more solid
MKMSRBE make miserable
MKNBNSF make no bones of
MKNCSAY make necessary
MKNTIGF make nothing of
MKOEPAE make one's peace
MKOESNE make obeisance
MKOETRS make overtures
MKPAEIH make peace with
MKPOIIN make provision
MKPWRES make powerless
MKRDNAT make redundant
MKSAKFY make sparks fly
MKTAKFR make tracks for
MKTEETF make the best of
MKTEFOT make the effort
MKTEONS make the rounds
MKTEOTF make the most of
MKTIGHM make things hum
MKTOUHF make too much of
MLCOOAE milk chocolate
MLCOSES maliciousness
MLDAAIE melodramatise
melodramatize
MLDIITR maladminister
MLDOSES melodiousness
MLDOTES maladroitness
MLDPAIN maladaptation
MLDUTET maladjustment
MLEBEES malleableness
MLIAINL multinational
MLIELLR multicellular
MLIIAIN mollification
MLIIGIT multilinguist
MLIKLIG multiskilling
MLILBTO multiply by two
MLILCBE multiplicable
MLILETY mellifluently
MLILOSY mellifluously
MLILSOE multiple store
MLILWRS multiply words
MLIOORD multicoloured
multi-coloured
MLIOUNE multiloquence
MLIRVDE multigravidae
MLIRVDS multigravidas
MLIUIOS multitudinous
MLIUTRL multicultural
MLMNPUE male menopause
MLOKNYE Mull of Kintyre
MLSTNIH Myles Standish
MLTRCOS Military Cross
MLTRMDL Military Medal
MLYODIG mollycoddling
MMEOSAF member of staff
MMESIFE membership fee
MMIIAIN mummification
MMNOSES momentousness
MMNOTUH moment of truth
MMRMIIE membrum virile
MNAAEET man-management
MNAILES mental illness
MNAPCUE mental picture
MNCEBGN Menachem Begin
MNCRMTC monochromatic
MNCTLDN monocotyledon
MNEBOST Mandelbrot set
MNECLOS minced collops
MNEDFLA Manuel de Falla
MNEVNRS montes veneris
MNFAACA Man of La Mancha
MNFCUIG manufacturing
MNFEDAK Mansfield Park
MNFHCOH man of the cloth
MNFHMTH man of the match
MNFHWRD man of the world
MNFIHNS man of his hands
MNFSAIN manifestation
MNFUIES man of business
MNFYEGT mini-flyweight
MNGAHCL monographical
MNGAIIY manageability
MNGAMTC monogrammatic
MNGWTOT manage without
MNIIAIE mundificative
MNMMEGT minimum weight
MNNCESS mononucleosis
MNNOOCC meningococcic
MNNOOCL meningococcal
MNOTSIE Monmouthshire
MNPLMNY Monopoly money
MNPLTBE manipulatable
MNRLGCL mineralogical
MNRNEVL minor interval
MNSEILY ministerially
MNSRTOS ministrations
MNTOSES monstrousness
MNTRIAD monitor lizard
MNTULLW menstrual flow
MNUAIIY mensurability
MNYEEVD money received
MNYHNEL Manny Shinwell
MNYRBIG money-grabbing
money-grubbing
MPADROS mops and brooms
MRAALSR Maria Walliser
MRAECUT Margaret Court
MRAETDR Margaret Tudor
MRASAIG mortal-staring
MRCEOKR miracle-worker
MREAIIY marketability
MREDCAP Marcel Duchamp
MREEEII Marie de Médici
MREEOOY market economy
MRELTWR martello tower
MREMREU Marcel Marceau
MREMSEY murder mystery
MREOSES murderousness
MREWLOT murder will out
MRHAIOD marsh marigold
MRHESES mirthlessness
MRHGNSS morphogenesis
MRHGNTC morphogenetic
MRHLGCL morphological
MRHNIIG merchandising
MRHPOEE morphophoneme
MRHRYFL Merthyr Tydfil
MRIAIGS Martina Hingis
MRIBRAN Martin Bormann
MRIBUDE Martin Brundle
MRIDNIG morris dancing
MRIESES mercilessness
MRIIAIN mortification
MRLHOOY moral theology
MRLNORE Marilyn Monroe
MRLSMSN Myrtle Simpson
MRLUETN Mary Lou Retton
MRMGAEE Mary Magdalene
MROCLEE Merton College
MROFNEN Margot Fonteyn
MRONRTI Mario Andretti
MROSLCS marrons glacés
MROYRSR Marjory Fraser
MRPEIEY more precisely
MRTROSY meritoriously
MRUSEAE Marquis de Sade
MSAAEET mismanagement
MSAHSTS Massachusetts
MSAOENS Missa Solemnis
MSAOTIH mess about with
MSCLGCL musicological
MSCLHIS musical chairs
MSCLOEY musical comedy
MSDPRUE mass departure
MSEBIDR master builder
MSEBTEY masked battery
MSEEAIN miscegenation
MSEFLES masterfulness
MSEJGES Mister Jaggers
MSELNIY miscellaneity
MSELNOS miscellaneous
MSEMNIG masterminding
MSESHIT Messerschmidt
Messerschmitt
MSEWMIK Mister Wemmick
MSHEMKR mischief-maker
MSHEOSY mischievously

MSHPNES misshapenness
MSIGHSA Missing the Sea
MSIIAIN mystification
MSINBIK mashie niblick
MSIPRAT most important
MSMLYET misemployment
MSMREIG mass-marketing
MSNEHLN mesencephalon
MSNESAD misunderstand
MSNESOD misunderstood
MSNHOIT misanthropist
MSOCPIN misconception
MSOENET misgovernment
MSOJCUE misconjecture
MSOPEED miscomprehend
MSOPTAE mess of pottage
MSPRCAE misappreciate
MSROCOD mushroom cloud
MSRPRIN misproportion
MSRSFLY mistrustfully
MSRSIGY mistrustingly
MTCODIL mitochondrial
MTCODIN mitochondrion
MTEAIIE mathematicise
mathematicize
MTEAIIN mathematician
MTECUTY mother country
mother-country
MTEOPAL mother-of-pearl
MTESITN Mother Shipton
MTETEEA Mother Theresa
MTGAOIE metagrabolise
metagrabolize
MTGOOIE metagrobolise
metagrobolize
MTHESES matchlessness
MTHWAKR Matthew Parker
MTHWROD Matthew Arnold
MTIIELY matrilineally
MTIOILY matrimonially
MTIUAIN matriculation
MTLEETR metal detector
MTLIAIN metallization
MTLUGCL metallurgical
MTMRHSS Metamorphoses
metamorphosis□
MTNEAKT matinée jacket
MTNMCLY metonymically
MTOOOIT meteorologist
MTOPCUE motion picture
MTPYIIT metaphysicist
MTRACUE material cause
MTRAIIS materfamilias
MTRAITC materialistic
MUEOORD mouse-coloured
MUHAEIG mouthwatering
mouth-watering
MUIEEAT Maurice Béjart
MUIEIKS Maurice Wilkes
MUISSHR Maurits Escher
MUTAEON Mount Cameroon
MUTBNEY mountebankery
MUTBNIM mountebankism
MUTCILY Mount McKinley
MUTIRNE mountain range
MUTISIH mountains-high
MUTTEES Mount St Helens
MUTUHOE Mount Rushmore
MVBCWRS move backwards
MVDWWRS move downwards
MVNFRAD moving forward
MVNWLWY moving walkway
MVUADON move up and down
MVUNTCD move unnoticed
MXDARAE mixed marriage
MXDEAHR mixed metaphor
MXDLSIG mixed blessing
MXELAIS Maxwell Davies
MZLLAIG muzzle-loading
MZOORNS mezzo-sopranos
NAOIAIE Neapolitan ice
NASGTDY near-sightedly
NBLARAE Nobel laureate
NCEPAIG nickel-plating
NCERAIY nuclear family
NCEREPN nuclear weapon
NCERITR nuclear winter
NCERNRY nuclear energy
NCERUIN nuclear fusion
NCLUSEO Nicolaus Steno
NCOASOT Nicholas Scott
NCONTIG neck or nothing
NCSIAIN necessitarian
NCSIOSY necessitously
NCTNCCD nicotinic acid
NDAOAEI Nadia Comaneci
NDIGOKY nodding donkey
NELSTSY needless to say
NFROSES nefariousness
NGADIES niggardliness
NGETHKS no great shakes
NGIIIIY negligibility
NGIMHOZ Naguib Mahfouz
NGTACMN night-watchman
NGTAIHY nightmarishly
NGTAIIY negotiability
NGTFSET Night of Ascent
NGTLBIG nightclubbing
NGTRPIG night-tripping
NHLSARD no holds barred
no-holds-barred
NIAMTOG Neil Armstrong
NIEESES noiselessness
NIHOROD neighbourhood
NLERSQI nolle prosequi
NLIIAIN nullification
NLNEIUE no longer in use
NLOMNEA Nelson Mandela
NLOSOUN Nelson's Column
NMESAKT numbers racket
NMNOPRS Naming of Parts
NMNTVLY nominatively
NMRCEPD numeric keypad
NMRLGCL numerological
NNBEVNE non-observance
NNEADNE non-regardance
NNECITY nondescriptly
NNEITNE non-resistance
NNEITRD non-registered
NNEOIBE non-negotiable
NNESCLY nonsensically
NNESSET non-persistent
NNESVRE nonsense verse
NNEUNBE non-returnable
NNGRSIE non-aggressive
NNGRSIN non-aggression
NNLSIID non-classified
NNNUGNE non-indulgence
NNODCIG non-conducting
NNOFRIT nonconformist
non-conformist
NNOFRIY nonconformity
non-conformity
NNOLNTN nannoplankton
NNONZBE non-cognizable
NNOPINE non-compliance
NNPCAIT non-specialist
NNPERNE non-appearance
NNRDCIE non-productive
NNTEDNE non-attendance
NNUCINL non-functional
NNUFLET non-fulfilment
NNUGETL non-judgmental
NNYERGN Nancy Kerrigan
NOLANIG no oil painting
NOLSIIM neoclassicism□
NOOITCL neological
NPEOERC nephelometric
NRABOKS Norman Brookes
NRAIAIN normalization
NRALCYR Norman Lockyer
NRAMCAG Norman MacCaig
NRDEAIE noradrenaline
NREESES nervelessness
NRERCIG nerve-wracking
NRETINR Norbert Wiener
NREYCOL nursery school
NREYLPS nursery slopes
NRHAOIA North Carolina
NRHATAD north-eastward
NRHATRY north-easterly
NRHETAD north-westward
NRHETRY north-westerly
NRHNSUH North and South
NRHRCON Northern Crown
NRHRIES northerliness
NRHYSIE North Ayrshire
NROCSIG narrowcasting
NROIAIN narcotization
NROKAKT Norfolk jacket
NROKSAD Norfolk Island
NROSYTM nervous system
NSAGCLY nostalgically
NSEHSAN Nasser Hussain
NTAEATN not take part in
NTELNIH Netherlandish
NTEOEIE not before time
NTIGAET nothing patent
NTIIAIN nitrification

Words marked □ can also be spelled with an initial capital letter

NTNNSIE	not on one's life
NTNWRBE	not answerable
NTOAFOT	National Front
NTOAGAD	National Guard
NTOAITC	nationalistic
NTOAOET	not for a moment
NTOATUT	National Trust
NTODNUH	not good enough
NTOECCE	nitrogen cycle
NTOGTIG	not forgetting
NTOOEHR	not go together
NTOPOIE	not compromise
NTOTAAN	not worth a damn
NTRIIIL	not artificial
NTRLASS	natural causes
NTRLUBR	natural number
NTROSES	notoriousness
NTRRSRE	nature reserve
NTRUHOD	no through road
NTSNLOE	not a single one
NTVCUTY	native country
NTVSEKR	native speaker
NUANTOK	neural network
NUIATBE	nautical table
NUOIGIT	neurolinguist
NUOIRMS	neurofibromas
NURLESN	neutral person
NVCLROE	navicular bone
NVLIGIK	Nevil Sidgwick
NVRHWSR	never the wiser
NWEEOUN	nowhere to turn
NWEINNS	new beginnings
NWOTWLS	New South Wales
NWUTAIN	New Australian
NWXRSIN	new expression
NXTNTIG	next to nothing
OAHETIG	on a shoestring
OAPOAIN	on approbation
OAYCAIN	on any occasion
OBRSTEL	Osbert Sitwell
OCADOAL	once and for all
OCDNAIE	occidentalise
	occidentalize
OCETAIN	orchestration
OCETAIT	orchestralist
OCNEUNE	of consequence
OCPOEEF	occupy oneself
OCPTLOE	occipital bone
	occipital lobe
OCREESN	Oscar Peterson
OCSOAIM	occasionalism
OCSOAIT	occasionalist
OCUEFOT	occluded front
OCUOAIE	once upon a time
ODACDPT	ordnance depot
ODACDTM	ordnance datum
ODGPNIN	old-age pension
ODNLUBR	ordinal number
ODNRGAE	Ordinary grade
ODONTOK	old-boy network
ODRFATE	order of battle
ODRFHDY	order of the day
ODRFVNS	order of events
ODROEUN	order to return
ODSHHLS	old as the hills
OEABTOS	overambitious
OEAIEES	operativeness
OEASRIE	over-assertive
OEAUDNE	overabundance
OEBAIGY	overbearingly
OECNIET	overconfident
	over-confident
OEDAAIE	overdramatize
OEDCRTD	overdecorated
OEEAOAE	overelaborate
	over-elaborate
OEEOINL	overemotional
	over-emotional
OEEPAIE	overemphasize
OEETMTD	overestimated
OEEYIEF	on every side of
OEFOIGY	overflowingly
OEIDLET	overindulgent
OEIGABT	opening gambit
OEMRAIE	oleomargarine
OENGAHC	oceanographic
OENGTTY	overnight stay
OENLGCL	oceanological
OENMLIN	one in a million
OENTEAE	one and the same
OEOHRAF	one's other half
OEOTEOD	one for the road
OEPEIIN	over-precision
OEPPLTD	overpopulated
OEQAIID	overqualified
OESAEET	overstatement
OESAOIG	overshadowing
OESBCIE	oversubscribe
OESNIIE	oversensitive
	over-sensitive
OESRTHD	overstretched
OESUAIH	over-squeamish
OETEIKT	over the wicket
OETEORO	open the door to
OFADDES	offhandedness
OFCASAP	official stamp
OFCOSES	officiousness
OFCRFRS	officer of arms
OFNIEES	offensiveness
OFNSOKR	off one's rocker
OFNSTOE	off one's stroke
OFNSUTR	off one's nutter
OFNSWBT	off one's own bat
OFRYPTY	offer sympathy
OHHLOOY	ophthalmology
OHORTCL	ochlocratical
OHRARUD	other way round
OHREMNS	on her beam-ends
OIOOITC	oligopolistic
OISATES	on its last legs
OJCIEES	objectiveness
OJCIEET	objective test
OJCIITC	objectivistic
OJCINBE	objectionable
OJCINBY	objectionably
OJCOVRU	object of virtu
OJTDVRU	objets de vertu
OJTTOVS	objets trouvés
OKEILNS	Orkney Islands
OLTEOEY	Only the Lonely
OLVOSES	obliviousness
ONMNAIN	ornamentation
ONRCUID	owner-occupied
ONRCUIR	owner-occupier
ONTICIN	ornithischian
ONTOETS	Ornitholestes
ONTOOIT	ornithologist
ONXOSES	obnoxiousness
OOATCLY	onomastically
OOECAIN	on one occasion
OOEONOK	on one's own hook
OOEREDY	ozone-friendly
OOIEOSY	odoriferously
OOIIAOS	ovoviviparous
OOTLGCL	odontological
OPETWMN	Oh, Pretty Woman
OPOROSY	opprobriously
OPRUEES	opportuneness
OPRUITC	opportunistic
OSAKSAE	on Shanks's mare
OSAKSOY	on Shanks's pony
OSECTHR	oystercatcher
OSERCLY	obstetrically
OSRAINL	observational
OSRCIEY	obstructively
OSRUCCE	oestrous cycle
OSSIEES	obsessiveness
OSSIINF	on suspicion of
OSSINLY	obsessionally
OTCHLMS	optic thalamus
OTCNEAY	octocentenary
OTEAEET	on the pavement
OTEAEFT	on the face of it
OTEAEID	of the same kind
	of the same mind
OTEAKGS	of the Dark Ages
OTEAUEF	of the nature of
OTEEBUS	or thereabouts
OTEEOTF	on the report of
OTEIHSF	on the wishes of
OTEIKIT	on the sick list
OTENRAE	on the increase
OTEOGIE	on the long side
OTEOTAY	on the contrary
OTEOTEM	on the port beam
OTETEGH	on the strength
OTETOEF	on the stroke of
OTFAMWY	out of harm's way
OTFEUNE	out of sequence
OTFHWOS	out of the woods
OTFNSED	out of one's head
OTFNSID	out of one's mind
OTFNSOD	out of one's road
OTFNSRE	out of one's tree
OTFRCIE	out of practice
OTFUSIN	out of question
OTGNCLY	ontogenically
OTIELGT	out like a light
OTJSESN	Otto Jespersen

OTKEPRR	Otto Klemperer
OTLGCLY	ontologically
OTNEHOS	on tenterhooks
OTNIIIY	ostensibility
OTNNSET	out on one's feet
OTORPIT	orthographist
OTOYLTS	osteomyelitis
OTPEIGR	Otto Preminger
OTPKNES	outspokenness
OTRERDS	Outer Hebrides
OTTNIGY	outstandingly
OTUIEES	obtrusiveness
OUSUDID	of unsound mind
OVLERGT	Orville Wright
OWNOKDE	On Wenlock Edge
PAAOTIH	play about with
PAAWSES	play at wasters
PAEBEES	peaceableness
PAEFAEY	place of safety
PAEFLES	prayerfulness
PAEFRGN	place of origin
PAEIIED	peace dividend
PAEOEHR	place together
PAEOOIT	planetologist
PAFRAEY	play for safety
PAHRTGT	play hard to get
PAHVCIH	play havoc with
PAIACLY	pharisaically
PAIGATS	praying mantis
PAIGRUD	playing around
PAISSIO	pianississimo
PAITCLY	pianistically
PAIUBAK	platinum black
PAIUBOD	platinum-blond
PAIUIIE	platitudinise
	platitudinize
PAIUIOS	platitudinous
PALCNRC	phallocentric
PALFIDM	pearl of wisdom
PAMCPEA	pharmacopoeia
PAMCUIS	pharmaceutics
PAMDSAA	plasmodesmata
PAMTCLY	pragmatically
PANIEES	plaintiveness
PANOKAL	prawn cocktail
PANPAIG	plain speaking
	plain-speaking
PAOEHNH	play one's hunch
PAOISLD	Platonic solid
PASBEES	plausibleness
PATCLES	practicalness
PATCLOE	practical joke
PATCULT	plastic bullet
PATEATF	play the part of
PATEATN	play the wanton
PATEOEF	play the role of
PATEOSS	play the horses
PAUOWRS	play upon words
PBIAFIS	public affairs
PBICMAY	public company
PBIHLDY	public holiday
PBIIQIY	public inquiry
PBILKON	publicly known
PBISEKR	public speaker
PBISRAT	public servant
PBIUIIY	public utility
PCADHOE	pick and choose
PCCRNIM	pococurantism
PCCRSIH	pack cards with
PCEBRUH	pocket borough
PCOACOS	pectoral cross
PCUEAAE	picture-palace
PCUEQEY	picturesquely
PDCLAIE	pedicellariae
PDGGCLY	pedagogically
PDIEGIH	pidgin English
PDLSEMR	paddle steamer
	paddle-steamer
PDSRAIE	pedestrianise
	pedestrianize
PEAAIEY	preparatively
PEAAOIY	preparatorily
PEAAOYO	preparatory to
PEAHEIE	Pre-Raphaelite
PEAIAIG	prevaricating
PEAIAIN	prevarication
PEAOIES	predatoriness
PEAOILY	prefatorially
PEATOAY	precautionary
PEAYOES	plenary powers
PECCIIE	phencyclidine
PECUAIN	preoccupation
PEDMRHC	pseudomorphic
PEECAGS	prefer charges
PEEEMND	predetermined
PEEFDIE	piece of advice
PEEFRUD	piece of ground
PEEIAIE	premeditative
PEEIAIN	premedication
	premeditation
PEENTRL	preternatural
PEEOEHR	piece together
PEETOSY	pretentiously
PEETTEF	present itself
PEEUSTS	prerequisites
PEGOEEF	pledge oneself
PEHLGCL	psephological
PEHRCLY	plethorically
PEIAIEY	predicatively
PEIIAEY	precipitately
PEIIAIN	precipitation
PEIIAIS	preliminaries
PEIIAIY	preliminarily
PEIIATY	precipitantly
PEIIOSY	precipitously
PEIJSIE	poetic justice
PEILCNE	poetic licence
PEITIIN	paediatrician
PEITRCL	prehistorical
PEIUAIN	prefiguration
PEIUMTL	precious metal
PEIUSOE	precious stone
PEMTCLY	pneumatically
PEMTCYE	pneumatic tyre
PEMUAOY	preambulatory
PEOAIEY	prerogatively
PEOCPIN	preconception
PEODRNE	preponderance
PEOEAIE	phenomenalise
	phenomenalize
PEOEAIM	phenomenalism
PEOEAIT	phenomenalist
PEOEOOY	phenomenology
PEOHAIE	phenothiazine
PEOIATY	predominantly
PEOIIEY	prepositively
PEOIINL	prepositional
PEOIOIY	premonitorily
PEOLCRC	piezoelectric
PEOOPIM	paedomorphism
PEOSSIG	prepossessing
PERAEIO	Pietro Aretino
PERBNAD	Pierre Bonnard
PERIAIN	preordination
PERTUEU	Pierre Trudeau
PERVRIR	Pierre Vernier
PESFAVS	press of canvas
PESHFEH	press the flesh
PESOEEF	please oneself
PESOEHR	press together
PESRGOP	pressure group
PESRGUE	pressure gauge
PESRPIT	pressure point
PETFLES	plentifulness
PETOSES	plenteousness
PEUIILY	prejudicially
PEUPIEY	presumptively
PEYAAIE	phenylalanine
PGBEKAT	pig's breakfast
PGEDDES	pig-headedness
PGOCETD	pigeon-chested
PGOHATD	pigeon-hearted
PGYSCOT	Peggy Ashcroft
PIADRIH	philander with
PIAEABD	private pay bed
PIAEATR	private matter
PIAECOL	private school
PIAEETR	private sector
PIAENOE	private income
PIAIAIN	privatization
PIATCLY	peirastically
PIATRPC	philanthropic
PIAYCOL	primary school
PIAYTES	primary stress
PICCNOT	prince consort
PICMUIE	Prince Maurice
PICNSEM	Prince Nasseem
PICOPAE	Prince of Peace
PICOWLS	Prince of Wales
PICPLAT	principal part
PICSRYL	Princess Royal
PIEEIIN	prime meridian
PIEESES	pricelessness
PIEIHIG	prizefighting
	prize-fighting
PIEIITR	prime minister
PIIIEES	primitiveness
PIIMROE	Philip Marlowe
PIIPSLA	Philippe Sella

PIIRVDE primigravidae
PIIRVDS primigravidas
PIITEEK pain in the neck
PIITERE pain in the arse
PIITEUT pain in the butt
PIMTCLY prismatically
PIOCLUS pair of colours
PIODAIY primordiality
PIOEIAY primogenitary
PIOEIIE primogenitive
PIOEIUE primogeniture
PIOEOWR prisoner of war
PIOOFCR prison officer
PIOOHCL philosophical
PIOOHZR philosophizer
PIOOSES poisonousness
PISAIGY painstakingly
PITDATR printed matter
PITESES pointlessness
PITFOOR point of honour
PITNERR printing error
PITNPES point-and-press
printing press
PKMLOKT poke mullock at
PLAIGTR pulsating star
PLALGOS palpable-gross
PLAOGAE pull a long face
PLARMUH pull a wry mouth
PLCOFCR police officer
PLCRMTC polychromatic
PLCROAE polycarbonate
PLCSAIN police station
PLEBOOY palaeobiology
PLEEOOY palaeoecology
PLEGAHR palaeographer
PLEIAIN pulverization
PLENOOY palaeontology
PLGSIAE phlogisticate
PLIDDNE palais de danse
PLIOTIK pile in on thick
pile it on thick
PLOYLTS poliomyelitis
PLPOYEE polypropylene
PLTCMET polite comment
PLTELGN pull the plug on
PMLADES Pamela Andrews
PMRKSIE Pembrokeshire
PNAEAEP pancake make-up
PNAPEED pineapple weed
PNAPEOL Pineapple Poll
PNCTIKN panic-stricken
PNEOSES ponderousness
PNFIAIM pan-Africanism
PNGRCLY panegyrically
PNHITCL pantheistical
PNHNLOS Punchinelloes
PNIESES pennilessness
PNIGHAS pinking shears
pinking-shears
PNIIAIG pontificating
PNISIAE Pontius Pilate
PNLYONR penalty corner
PNNUAWR Peninsular War
PNOEAEA pinhole camera
PNONRDE pontoon bridge
PNPRAIM panspermatism
PNPRAIT panspermatist
PNRMAIT pangrammatist
PNROSES penuriousness
PNTAIEY penetratively
PNTAIGY penetratingly
PNTAIIY penetrability
PNTLOSY punctiliously
PNTNILY penitentially
PNUOSES pendulousness
PNYATIG penny farthing
penny-farthing
PNYICIG penny-pinching
PNYRAFL penny dreadful
POAIIIS probabilities
POAOCCD propanoic acid
POEAEEK promenade deck
POEBAIE proverbialise
proverbialize
POEOEAY prolegomenary
POEOEOS prolegomenous
POETAET property agent
POETCLY proleptically
POETNIE Protestantise
Protestantize
POETNIM Protestantism
POETODY protest loudly
POETOIT projectionist
protectionist
POEURCS prosecutrices
POEURXS prosecutrixes
POEVRAX procès-verbaux
POEYIIG proselytizing
POGTRUH plough through
POHTCES propheticness
POHTCLY prophetically
POHTFOM prophet of doom
POIAIIY profitability
POICAIE provincialise
provincialize
POICAIM provincialism
POICAIT provincialist
POICAIY provinciality
POICOSY promiscuously
POIEAIN proliferation
POIEOSY proliferously
POIERAH promise-breach
POIIAIN poor imitation
POIIIEY prohibitively
POIINLY provisionally
POINCCD propionic acid
POISAIG profit-sharing
POLMTCL problematical
POLSRED People's Friend
PONSIAE prognosticate
POOAIEY provocatively
POOEETR photoreceptor
POOEOEE Paolo Veronese
POOHMCL photochemical
POOLCRC photoelectric
POONEBE pronounceable
POONEET pronouncement
POOORPY prosopography
POORPES photographers
POOTOAE proportionate
POPCIEY prospectively
POPOYAE phosphorylate
POREOIL proprietorial
POROETR proprioceptor
PORSIAE procrastinate
PORSIEY progressively
PORSIIM progressivism
PORSIIT progressivist
POTGADN prostaglandin
POUCAIN pronunciation
POUEATY protuberantly
PPEADAT pepper-and-salt
PPEMNTA peppermint tea
PPETETE puppet theatre
PPIGRAE popping crease
popping-crease
PPLIEOS papilliferous
PPLOAOS papillomatous
PPNHSOT Pepin the Short
PPRATLS paper nautilus
PPRHHUE paper the house
PRADACL part and parcel
PRADIPE pure and simple
PRAEKIT Pär Lagerkvist
PRAETAE permanent wave
PRAIEES pervasiveness
PRBASAS part brass rags
PRBLCLY parabolically
PRBLCRH parabolic arch
PRCILES parochialness
PRCODIM perichondrium
PRDXCLY paradoxically
PREDCLR perpendicular
PREEIGY perseveringly
PREIAEH Port Elizabeth
PRETNET perfect insect
PRETOAE perfectionate
PRETOIM perfectionism
PRETOIT perfectionist
PRETORH perfect fourth
PRETUBR perfect number
PRGIAIG peregrinating
PRGIAIN peregrination
PRHPTTS perihepatitis
PRIDTAD Per Lindstrand
PRIIAEN participate in
PRIIAIG participating
PRIIAIN participation
PRIIAOY participatory
PRIIATY participantly
PRIIILY participially
PRIMNAY parliamentary
PRINAPT Persian carpet
PRIOORD particoloured
parti-coloured
PRISNLW Parkinson's law
PRIUAIE particularise
particularize
PRIUAIM particularism

PRIUAIY particularity
PRLATCL parallactical
PRLEORM parallelogram
PRLEPRR purple emperor
PRLERLR parallel ruler
PRLIOEA paraleipomena
PRMDCLY pyramidically
PRMDHPD pyramid-shaped
PRMUAIN perambulation
PRMUAOY perambulatory
PRNCMAY parent company
PRNEHLN parencephalon
PRNHTCL parenthetical
PRNLGCL phrenological
PRNPRTS perinephritis
PRNTCLY phrenetically
PROAAAM personal alarm
PROEESY purposelessly
PROFSIN parrot-fashion
PROIEES purposiveness
PROITBE periodic table
PROMRCS perform tricks
PROOMAS person of means
PROOTTS periodontitis
PRPCCOS perspicacious
PRPCIEY perspectively
PRPCIIM perspectivism
PRPCOSY perspicuously
PRPEATY pork-pie pastry
PRPENLA paraphernalia
PRPRSUE piri-piri sauce
PRSAIIY perishability
PRSCUCL parish council
PRSOATL perissodactyl
PRSTCLY parasitically
PRTNCLY puritanically
PRUAIIY permutability
PRUCOIY perfunctorily
PRUDNTO persuade not to
PRUSOIT percussionist
PRXELNE par excellence
PRYOIIS party politics
PRYRIGR Percy Grainger
PSAEFRS passage of arms
PSAETNE pass a sentence
PSASRIE postal service
PSCEDEE Passchendaele
PSEETNE poste restante
PSEETRE passementerie
PSFOSGT pass from sight
PSIEOSY pestiferously
PSIIERE pesticide-free
PSIIIIS possibilities
PSINUDY Passion Sunday
PSIUTRL piscicultural
PSJDEET pass judgement
PSLAIIY pusillanimity
PSLAIOS pusillanimous
PSMDRIM Post-Modernism
Post-modernism
PSMNKOK postman's knock
PSOEAIE post-operative
PSOEPIE past one's prime
PSPRPOO passport photo
PSTEACL pass the parcel
PSTEOTE push the bottle
PSTEUTN push the button
PSTTEAL push to the wall
PSUDIIS push up daisies
PTACBAE pe-tsai cabbage
PTCETPN put a cheat upon
PTEIDAS put behind bars
PTFOWOG put a foot wrong
PTHBAEN put the blame on
put the brake on
PTHBAKN put the black on
PTHLDNT put the lid on it
PTHMVSN put the moves on
PTHNSWY put things away
PTHSISN put the skids on
PTIAYOY pituitary body
PTIGPIH putting up with
PTIIAIN petrification
PTIIELY patrilineally
PTIKASN Patrick Manson
PTIKWYE Patrick Swayze
PTIOILY patrimonially
PTITCLY patriotically
PTMHSSN put emphasis on
PTNBYNE put in abeyance
PTNEPRY put in jeopardy
PTNEWTR put under water
PTNGLOS pit and gallows
PTNHSAE put in the shade
PTNHSRW put on the screw
PTNHWOG put in the wrong
PTNIMTR potentiometer
PTNLAHR patent leather
PTNNSAE put on one's face
PTNOCIN put into action
PTNOFET put into effect
PTNOIIN put in position
PTNSADO put one's hand to
PTNSAEN put one's face on
PTNSETP put one's feet up
PTNSIDO put one's mind to
PTOEIIY pathogenicity
PTOHMCL petrochemical
PTOHSOD put to the sword
PTOHTRH put to the torch
PTOHWRE put to the worse
PTOIIGY patronisingly
patronizingly
PTOSAIN petrol station
PTPATRN put a plaster on
PTPEIMN put a premium on
PTPNONS put upon points
PTRAIIS paterfamilias
PTRAITC paternalistic
PTRSUEN put pressure on
PTSRCUE Pott's fracture
PTTOEHR put it together
PTUOJIT put out of joint
PTUOPAE put out of place
PTUOSGT put out of sight
PTUTGAS put out to grass
PTUTNRE put out to nurse
PUAIAIN pluralization
PUASCEY plural society
PUDTRIG pound sterling
PUEIAIN pauperization
PUGSOGE Paul Gascoigne
PUHNEIH Paul Hindemith
PUIGHAS pruning-shears
PUMCRNY Paul McCartney
PUTREIR Paul Tortelier
PUWTRVR pour water over
PVMNLGT pavement light
PVRLATE Peveril Castle
PVTEAFR pave the way for
PWRESES powerlessness
PWRFEIG power of seeing
PWROIIS power politics
PWRRSIG power dressing
PWRTEIG power steering
PWRTUGE power struggle
PYEOEAD pay beforehand
PYHAAYE psychoanalyse
PYHAAYT psychoanalyst
PYHCOES psychic powers
PYHDNMC psychodynamic
PYHGNSS psychogenesis
PYHGNTC psychogenetic
PYHLGCL psychological
PYHMTIS psychometrics
PYHSMTC psychosomatic
PYHSREY psychosurgery
PYHTEAY psychotherapy
PYIAJRS physical jerks
PYIGAHC physiographic
PYIGAHR physiographer
PYIGOIT physiognomist
PYILGCL physiological
PYITEAY physiotherapy
PYLQIOE phylloquinone
PYOHMCL phytochemical
PYOLIIG payroll giving
PYOLNTN phytoplankton
QACBTOK quatch-buttock
QAIAIEY qualitatively
QAIIAIN qualification
QAIIAOY qualificatory
QAIYFIE quality of life
QARGSML quadragesimal
QARLINH quadrillionth
QARLOEY quarrelsomely
QARLTRL quadrilateral
QARNILY quadrennially
QARPEIE quadruple time
QARPIAE quadruplicate
QARPOIS quadraphonics
quadrophonics
QARPRIE quadripartite
QARTCOS quadrate cross
QATCYTL quartz crystal
QATIEOS quartziferous
QATMHOY quantum theory
QATRATR quartermaster
QATROLR quarter dollar

QATRORY	quarter-hourly
QENCLEE	Queens' College
QENCUSL	Queen's Counsel
QENEEVS	Queenie Leavis
QENEGIH	Queen's English
QENFHMY	Queen of the May
QENLNNT	Queensland nut
QERHPTH	queer the pitch
QETNASS	Quentin Massys
QETOIGY	questioningly
QETONIE	questionnaire
QEUOSES	querulousness
QICNEAY	quincentenary
QICNILY	quincuncially
QIEOSBY	quite possibly
QIKEPRD	quick-tempered
QIKHNIG	quick-thinking
QIKITDY	quick-wittedly
QIKNWRD	quick-answered
QIQAEIA	Quinquagesima
QIQEAET	quinquevalent
QITLINH	quintillionth
QITNDON	quietened down
QITPIAE	quintuplicate
QITSNIS	Quintus Ennius
RADMNIT	rhabdomantist
RADMNSN	Roald Amundsen
RAESIET	Reader's Digest
RAFRAIN	reaffirmation
RAIGATR	reading matter
RAITCLY	realistically
RALKAOK	read like a book
RAOEEFN	read oneself in
RARNEET	rearrangement
RASDCLY	rhapsodically
RAYEKNR	ready reckoner
RAYTAYO	ready, steady, go
RBFHGEN	rub of the green
RBIADOK	rabbit and pork
RBLRUIG	rabble-rousing
RBNHGEN	rub on the green
RBNILAS	Robin Williams
RBNODBY	Robin Hood's Bay
RBRADIH	Robert Aldrich
RBRBIGS	Robert Bridges
RBRBRLY	Robert Barclay
RBRCTSY	Robert Catesby
RBRGDAD	Robert Goddard
RBRHRIK	Robert Herrick
RBRKNEY	Robert Kennedy
RBRMLON	Robert Muldoon
RBRMTHM	Robert Mitchum
RBRMXEL	Robert Maxwell
RBROAGO	Roberto Baggio
RBRRDOD	Robert Redford
RBRSUHY	Robert Southey
RBRWLOE	Robert Walpole
RBRWNTN	Robert Winston
RCADALE	Richard Hadlee
RCADANR	Richard Wagner
RCADANY	Richard Hannay
	Richard Tawney
RCADATN	Richard Martin
RCADECN	Richard Deacon
RCADEKY	Richard Leakey
RCADIIN	rack and pinion
RCADODN	Richard Cobden
RCADOES	Richard Rogers
RCADOKR	Richard Hooker
RCADRGT	Richard Bright
RCADTEE	Richard Steele
RCADULR	Richard Butler
RCADUTN	Richard Burton
RCAGLRY	rectangularly
RCIAIIY	receivability
RCIEAMY	receive warmly
RCIIAIE	recriminative
RCIIAIN	recrimination
	rectification
RCIIAOY	recriminatory
RCIIERY	rectilinearly
RCIIGIE	receiving-line
RCIUIOS	rectitudinous
RCLETDY	recollectedly
RCLETOS	recollections
RCLIRNE	recalcitrance
RCMEDBE	recommendable
RCMEDBY	recommendably
RCMIAIN	recombination
RCNIEES	reconditeness
RCNIEET	reconcilement
RCNOTIG	reconnoitring
RCNTTET	reconstituent
RCNTUTR	reconstructor
RCPIEES	receptiveness
RCPINOM	reception room
RCPOAIE	reciprocative
RCPOAIN	reciprocation
RCPOAIY	reciprocality
RCRLTOS	race relations
RCSIEES	recessiveness
RCUECNE	recrudescence
RCUIEES	reclusiveness
RCYACAO	Rocky Marciano
RCYTLIE	recrystallise
	recrystallize
RDAAEIG	rude awakening
RDAPYYE	radial-ply tyre
RDATEIG	ride at the ring
RDATNRY	radiant energy
RDCIEES	reductiveness
RDCNAET	reducing agent
RDCTAHS	reduce to ashes
RDIHELW	reddish-yellow
RDINYEN	red kidney bean
RDIOOGA	Rodrido Borgia
	Rodrigo Borgia
RDLNRYV	Rudolf Nureyev
RDLPIRS	Rudolf Peierls
RDLSENR	Rudolf Steiner
RDMNAIY	rudimentarily
RDNERTD	redintegrated
RDNOFCR	rodent officer
RDNTEAR	riding the fair
RDOAELD	radiolabelled
RDOCIIY	radioactivity
RDOOAIN	radiolocation
RDPDRIE	red spider mite
RDPIAIE	reduplicative
RDPIAIN	reduplication
REAIAIN	re-examination
REALABY	Rievaulx Abbey
REMTCLY	rheumatically
RFATMTR	refractometer
RFEIEES	reflexiveness
RFEIIIY	reflexibility
RFEOOIT	reflexologist
RFIEAIE	refrigerative
RFIEAIN	refrigeration
RFIEAOY	refrigeratory
RFRAIIY	reformability
RFRIHET	refurbishment
RFRJDIM	Reform Judaism
RFRNEOK	reference book
RFRNILY	referentially
RFSLOOE	refusal to vote
RGEFLES	regretfulness
RGEGLEY	rogues' gallery
RGIJCSN	Reggie Jackson
RGMNAIN	regimentation
RGRIAIN	regurgitation
RGSRRHP	registrarship
RGTEEED	Right Reverend
RGTFCES	right of access
RGTOSES	righteousness
RGYOTAL	rugby football
RHBLTTR	rehabilitator
RIBREET	reimbursement
RIBWHSR	rainbow-chaser
RICRAIN	reincarnation
RIEEERW	raised eyebrow
RIEHDVL	raise the devil
RIFREET	reinforcement
RINFERR	Reign of Terror
	reign of terror
RISAEET	reinstatement
RITEAKT	raid the market
RIVGRTD	reinvigorated
RIWYRDE	railway bridge
RJVNSET	rejuvenescent
RLECATR	rollercoaster
RLEITOE	rolled into one
RLESAIG	roller-skating
RLGOSES	religiousness
RLGOSOY	religious body
RLIGTNS	Rolling Stones
RLMNSEY	Rila Monastery
RLNBRHS	Roland Barthes
RLNPSIN	ruling passion
RLOTEOD	rule of the road
RLYNPIT	rallying-point
RMAERUD	rummage around
RMNAHLC	Roman Catholic
RMNEAOE	Roman de la Rose
RMNIIIG	romanticizing
RMNOASI	Roman Polanski
RMNSECS	reminiscences
RMNSETY	reminiscently
RMNTAIE	remonstrative

RMNTAIN remonstration
RMNTATY remonstrantly
RMPTEIE ramapithecine
RMREESY remorselessly
RMSIIIY remissibility
RMTCNRL remote control
RMTSNIG remote sensing
RNDRAMR René de Réaumur
RNDSATS René Descartes
RNEFIIN range of vision
RNICRET Ronnie Corbett
RNIGATE running battle
RNIGIHS running lights
RNIGRUD run rings round
RNNHBOD run in the blood
RNOIAIN randomization
RNOOSES rancorousness
RNTGTHP run a tight ship
RNUOSEM run out of steam
ROADRNH root and branch
root-and-branch
ROAOEOS rhopalocerous
ROBHDOS rhombohedrons
ROOHOIE rhodochrosite
ROVGTBE root vegetable
RPBIAIE republicanise
republicanize
RPBIAIM republicanism
RPCOSES rapaciousness
RPEESBE reprehensible
RPEESBY reprehensibly
RPEETBE representable
RPEIHET replenishment
RPIIEOS reptiliferous
RPLIEES repulsiveness
RPOCFLY reproachfully
RPRCEET rapprochement
RPRMROH Rupert Murdoch
RPRUSOS repercussions
RPSTOIG repositioning
RPTTOSY repetitiously
RQIIEES requisiteness
RRCAHET Rorschach test
RRUDROD Rory Underwood
RSGOEEF resign oneself
RSIIAIN Russification
RSILAHR russia leather❑
RSLAIIY resolvability
RSLNETY resplendently
RSLXMUG Rosa Luxemburg
RSNFLES resentfulness
RSOAIEY restoratively
RSOEOIE restore to life
RSRCIEY restrictively
RSRCUIG restructuring
RSRIETS risorgimentos
RSROROK reservoir rock
RSROROS Reservoir Dogs
RSSIAIE resuscitative
RSSIAIN resuscitation
RSSIIIY resistibility
RSTTEAT rise to the bait
RSVOETY rush violently

RTAIAIN ritualization
RTALVLE rateable value
RTEBRUH rotten borough
RTEFRIM rutherfordium
RTIIGAL retaining wall
RTIUIEY retributively
RTLBAND rattle-brained
RTLNSAD Rathlin Island
RTLTEAE rattle the cage
RTNIEES retentiveness
RTNSOIT retinoscopist
RTOAITC rationalistic
RTOCIEY retroactively
RTOCIIY retroactivity
RTOIAIE ratiocinative
RTOIAIN ratiocination
RTOLCIN retroflection
RTOPCIE retrospective
RTOPCIN retrospection
RTOPSAE rite of passage
RTORSIE retrogressive
RTORSIN retrogression
RTRDEPE retired people
RTRDESN retired person
RUDHCOK round the clock
round-the-clock
RUDHTIT round the twist
RUEDLSE Rouget de Lisle
RUETWEL roulette wheel
RUHNRAY rough and ready
rough-and-ready
RVAOEEF reveal oneself
RVLERUD revolve around
RVLIGOR revolving door
RVLTOAY revolutionary
RVLTOIE revolutionise
revolutionize
RVLTOIM revolutionism
RVLTOIT revelationist
revolutionist
RVNEUTR revenue cutter
RVREAIE reverberative
RVREAIG reverberating
RVREAIN reverberation
RVREAOY reverberatory
RVRIIIY reversibility
RVRINLY reversionally
RVRNILY reverentially
RVRRDNS River Eridanus
RWNTISN Rowan Atkinson
RYATESY Roy Hattlersey
RYLIKAE Royal Birkdale
RYLTNAD royal standard
RYODAVR Raymond Carver
RYRESAE Roy Greenslade
RYSYDOE Reye's syndrome
SAADIKE slap and tickle
SACLYOE Stan Collymore
SACTSIO staccatissimo
SACWRAT search warrant
SADARIH stand fair with
SADFADN stand off and on
SADLOGR scandalmonger

SADNIFR standing in for
SADNODR standing order
SADNSAD stand one's hand
SADNSOE standing stone
SADNTSE standing to sue
SADOEHR stand together
SADOESN stand to reason
SADRERR standard error
SADRGAE Standard grade
SADRGUE standard gauge
SADUALT Spandau Ballet
SAEAAIY spare capacity
SAEESES shamelessness
shapelessness
SAEFEAR state of repair
SAEFELH state of health
SAEFHAT state of the art
state-of-the-art
SAEMNHP statesmanship
SAEMNIE statesmanlike
SAENETY stare intently
SAENOLD State Enrolled
SAENSED shake one's head
SAEPAEN Shakespearean
SAEPAIN Shakespearian
SAETDAH scared to death
SAFEGAT staff sergeant
SAFRMOE Stanford Moore
SAFRSIE Staffordshire
SAGMLCP shaggy milk cap
SAGNMTH slanging match
slanging-match
SAGPRSL shaggy parasol
SAHLCCI staphylococci
SAHOICS smash to pieces
SAHUKIG swashbuckling
SAIIAIN scarification
stabilization
SAIIEOS staminiferous
SAITCLY statistically
SAITEAE slap in the face
SAITEAK stab in the back
SAKMNES shark's manners
SAKNSIS smack one's lips
SALAIAS small capitals
SALRMUT smaller amount
SALTETR scarlet letter
SALTOAA Scarlett O'Hara
SALTUNR scarlet runner
SALWDPN swallowed up in
SALYILR Stanley Miller
SAMDCLY spasmodically
SANESES stainlessness
SANSDOE star-nosed mole
SAOCBNT shadow cabinet
SAOODAH shadow of death
SAOTEAK slap on the back
SAOTIES seaworthiness
SAPHOIG sharpshooting
SAPRCIE sharp practice
SAPTEOD sharp's the word
SASICIG stay stitching
SATEORE stay the course

Code	Entry
SATNAAN	starting again
SATNPIE	starting price
SATNPIT	starting point
	starting-point
SATTEKN	soak to the skin
SAUEARD	statute-barred
SAYUIES	shady business
SBAHNGN	submachine-gun
SBEATIG	sabre-rattling
SBETATR	subject matter
SBETOAY	subventionary
SBETTOS	subreptitious
SBEVETO	subservient to
SBEVETY	subserviently
SBIIAIN	subtilization
SBIIINL	subdivisional
SBIUEAT	sublieutenant
SBLVCLR	subclavicular
SBOTATR	subcontractor
SBRIAEO	subordinate to
SBRIAEY	subordinately
SBRIAIE	subordinative
SBRIAIN	subordination
SBRPCLY	subtropically
SBRSJDE	sober as a judge
SBTNIEY	substantively
SBTNIIE	substantivise
	substantivize
SBTNILY	substantially
SBTTTBE	substitutable
SBTTTFR	substitute for
SBTUTRL	substructural
SBUCIEY	subjunctively
SCAAART	sick as a parrot
SCACATR	Social Chapter
SCACIBR	social climber
SCACMAT	social compact
SCACNAT	social contact
SCACNEN	social concern
SCAETLY	sacramentally
SCAIAIN	socialisation
	socialization
SCAIEIH	socialize with
SCAIIOY	Socratic irony
SCAOTAT	social outcast
SCEAYID	secretary bird
SCEIEES	secretiveness
SCEMEIG	secret meeting
SCEMSAE	secret message
SCESCEY	secret society
SCESESY	successlessly
SCESRIE	secret service
SCEWIIG	secret writing
SCHRMTR	saccharimeter
SCHRMTY	saccharimetry
SCIIILY	sacrificially
SCNAIES	secondariness
SCNAYEL	secondary cell
SCNRAIG	second reading
SCOACIY	sacrosanctity
SCOATEP	Sack of Antwerp
SCROAIE	sacerdotalise
	sacerdotalize
SCROAIM	sacerdotalism
SCROAIT	sacerdotalist
SCRTAAM	security alarm
SCRTGAD	security guard
SCTEOKY	suck the monkey
SCTOGTD	sick-thoughted
SCVLEET	Sackville-West
SDAHSEN	Saddam Hussein
SDCIEES	seductiveness
SDEPIIR	Sidney Poitier
SDEPLAK	Sydney Pollack
SDIPCBR	side-impact bar
SDMNAIN	sedimentation
SDMSCIM	sado-masochism
SDMTCLY	sodomitically
SDRAMNH	sidereal month
SDSLTIG	side-splitting
SDTOSES	seditiousness
SDUNTAE	sodium nitrate
SEATSAD	Stewart Island
SECEBBZ	Sketches By Boz
SECRCOS	stercoraceous
SECRRCY	Spencer Tracey
SECTEAY	speech therapy
SEDATES	steadfastness
SEDECAT	speed merchant
SEDIEIH	spend time with
SEDNMNY	spending money
SEEEGAE	Steve Redgrave
SEELGCL	speleological
SEEOOHE	Steve Donoghue
SEETPCL	stereotypical
SEFOCNO	see if you can do
SEGTFAD	sleight of hand
	sleight-of-hand
SEHNEDY	Stephen Hendry
SEHNOTR	Stephen Foster
SEHNRAS	Stephen Frears
SEHRSLB	shepherd's club
SEHTCNO	see what I can do
SEIFLRS	sheriff clerks
SEIIAIN	specification
	sterilisation
	sterilization
SEILCOL	special school
SEILRED	special friend
SEILRNH	Special Branch
SEIRIWY	scenic railway
SEKIHYF	speak highly of
SEKNCOK	speaking clock
SEKNSID	speak one's mind
SELGBOS	Stella Gibbons
SELMRHN	steal a march on
SELOORD	steel-coloured
SEMTPOE	spermatophore
SEMTPYE	spermatophyte
SENOEOT	stern-foremost
SENSIEY	sue one's livery
SEOTFIE	step out of line
SEPEHSR	steeplechaser
SEPESES	sleeplessness
SEPHBAD	sweep the board
SEPIELG	sleep like a log
SEPNCAH	sleeping coach
SEPNGPY	Sleeping Gypsy
SEPNSOE	stepping-stone
SEPNUIG	sleep-inducing
SEPOEHR	sleep together
SEPRNIG	step-parenting
SEPTNIG	Sherpa Tenzing
SEPUDOS	sleep outdoors
SERAPIN	smear campaign
SERHPAE	swear the peace
SERNWEL	steering-wheel
SETCLRY	spectacularly
SETDAOR	sweated labour
SETEADF	seek the hand of
SETFWMN	Scent of a Woman
SETHSNT	sweet chestnut
SETIEPG	sweat like a pig
SETMLIG	sweet-smelling
SETOERC	spectrometric
SETOHNS	sweet nothings
SETONIG	sweet-sounding
SETORPY	spectrography
SETTRHP	spectatorship
SEUAIEY	speculatively
SFIINFR	sufficient for
SFITEED	soft in the head
SFOAIGY	suffocatingly
SFRGTIM	suffragettism
SFTCRAN	safety curtain
SFTDPST	safety-deposit
SGAUEUE	signature tune
SGCOSES	sagaciousness
SGETLRH	segmental arch
SGETOIE	suggestionise
	suggestionize
SGETTEF	suggest itself
SGIIAIE	significative
SGIIAIN	signification
SGIIATY	significantly
SGRIBTS	sugar diabetes
SGTELDE	sign the pledge
SGTESES	sightlessness
SHDNRUE	schadenfreude
SHEEGEN	Scheele's green
SHGORPY	sphygmography
SHLRIES	scholarliness
SHLSIIM	scholasticism
SHMTCLY	schematically
SHNLRAK	Schindler's Ark
SHNUVLE	Sihanoukville
SHOGRIH	schoolgirlish
SHOMRIH	school-marmish
SHOTAHR	schoolteacher
SHRCLES	sphericalness
SHRIIIY	spheroidicity
SHZCROS	schizocarpous
SHZMCTC	schizomycetic
SHZPRNA	schizophrenia
SHZPRNC	schizophrenic
SIBOQIT	Stig Blomquist
SIEESES	spinelessness
SIEHLIG	spine-chilling
SIEILGN	Spike Milligan

SIERMOE slide trombone
SIESEPE Smiley's People
SIGAKHE slingback shoe
SIGHOMD sling throw mud
SIGNSOK sling one's hook
SIHLDUK slightly drunk
SIHRHNA Soichiro Honda
SIISFAT spirits of salt
SIISFIE spirits of wine
SIIULES spiritualness
SIIULZR spiritualizer
SIKNHMD stick-in-the-mud
SIKNPIT sticking-point
SIKOEHR stick together
SIKUAIE stick out a mile
SILDESN skilled person
SILDOKR skilled worker
SILDSAE Still's disease
SILHBAS spill the beans
SILNRNE Stirling Range
SILVLAO shield volcano
SILYASY Shirley Bassey
SILYEPE Shirley Temple
SIMGAHR seismographer
SIMLGCL seismological
SIMNBTS swimming-baths
SIMTCLY stigmatically
SINDPIG skinny-dipping
SINEUEM Science Museum
SINNJNY spinning-jenny
SINNWEL spinning-wheel
SITEOSM stir the possum
SITEOTE spin the bottle
SITESES shiftlessness
SITLAIG scintillating
SITLAIN scintillation
SITNBAD skirting-board
SITNIAE spitting image
SIYNETR spiny anteater
SLAAEET self-abasement
SLAAEKM salaam aleikum
SLAAYIG self-analysing
SLADESD self-addressed
SLADEUN sale and return
SLAIAIN syllabication
SLAINRY Salvation Army
SLAPITD self-appointed
SLAPOIG self-approving
SLARSDE Salman Rushdie
SLASRIE self-assertive
SLASRIG self-asserting
SLASRIN self-assertion
SLASRNE self-assurance
SLAWKMN Selman Waksman
SLCLCCD salicylic acid
SLCLETD self-collected
SLCNAND self-contained
SLCNCOS self-conscious
SLCNESD self-confessed
SLCNETD self-conceited
SLCNIET self-confident
SLCOSES salaciousness
SLDCPIN self-deception
SLDFAIG self-defeating
SLDFNIE self-defensive
SLDNCIE salade niçoise
SLDNIGY self-denyingly
SLDRCIN self-direction
SLDRSIG salad dressing
SLEAIIG self-examining
SLEIGRN soldering-iron
SLEJBLE silver jubilee
SLENTAE silver nitrate
SLESAKT seller's market
sellers' market
SLESRIE silver service
SLETCLY sylleptically
SLETNUD silver-tongued
SLFNNIG self-financing
SLGVRIG self-governing
SLHDAIE sulphadiazine
SLHNCCD sulphonic acid
SLHRCCD sulphuric acid
SLHROSY sulphureously
SLHROTM sulphur-bottom
SLIDCIN self-induction
SLIDLET self-indulgent
SLIFITD self-inflicted
SLIGCOY salpingectomy
SLIGILM Sylvie Guillem
SLIPRAT self-important
SLMIAIN solemnization
SLMTCIS salami tactics
SLNEGOP splinter group
SLNEPOF splinter-proof
SLNFTES Solon of Athens
SLNGAHC selenographic
SLNGAHR selenographer
SLNIEOS splendiferous
SLNLGCL selenological
SLNTCLY splenetically
SLOSRIG self-observing
SLPOELD self-propelled
SLPSESD self-possessed
SLRGTOS self-righteous
SLRPOEN scleroprotein
SLRSRIT self-restraint
SLSAGTR self-slaughter
SLSCIIE self-sacrifice
SLSFIIG self-sufficing
SLSTSID self-satisfied
SLTEIGY splutteringly
SLTEMVE splatter movie
SLTNSOE split one's vote
SLVRGAD salivary gland
SLYCLEE Selwyn College
SMAIAIN summarization
SMATMTC semi-automatic
SMAULUE summa cum laude
SMCNCOS semiconscious
SMCNUTR semiconductor
SMEBCET Samuel Beckett
SMEGLWN Samuel Goldwyn
SMEJHSN Samuel Johnson
SMELNLY Samuel Langley
SMEPDIG summer pudding
SMERCLY symmetrically
SMESEIG summer-seeming
SMESUKY Samuel Slumkey
SMIENLY sempiternally
SMITCLY symbiotically
SMLKIHT Some Like It Hot
SMOHRIE some other time
SMOIAIN symbolization
SMOILGC symbolic logic
SMOPISN Siméon Poisson
SMPLTNK Semipalatinsk
SMPREBE semi-permeable
SMTIGIE something like
SMTIGOO something to do
SMTIGSP something is up
SMTMTCF symptomatic of
SMTOSES sumptuousness
SMWEELE somewhere else
SMYAIJR Sammy Davis Jnr
SNAACUT send an account
SNADOES Sons and Lovers
SNAEERM send a telegram
SNAINLY sensationally
SNAIVIE send an invoice
SNATCLY syntactically
SNBRSRM Sune Bergström
SNCLTIM sansculottism
SNCLTIT sansculottist
SNEESES senselessness
SNETOSY sententiously
SNFHMNE son of the manse
SNGETNS send greetings
SNHNRSS synchondroses
SNHOIIY synchronicity
SNHOOSY synchronously
SNHTCLY synthetically
SNIETLY sentimentally
SNIIAIN sensitization
SNIIEES sensitiveness
SNIIIIS sensitivities
SNLAAKR Sunil Gavaskar
SNLFGRS single figures
SNLHATD single-hearted
SNLILWS Sinclair Lewis
SNOBTHS sons of bitches
SNOCTZN senior citizen
SNOSLMN Song of Solomon
SNOSRIE senior service
SNROONR Sandra O'Connor
SNSRREY sinistrorsely
SNTFIGY sanctifyingly
SNTMNOS sanctimonious
SNTTEOS send to the dogs
SNTTOIT sanitationist
SOADERH stop-and-search
SOAEDNY show a tendency
SOAEEIE storage device
SOAEETR storage heater
SOANTIG stop at nothing
SOASSAT shop assistant
shop-assistant
SOBIDES snow blindness
SOCIMTY stoichiometry

SODMNHP swordsmanship
SOEEETR smoke detector
SOEESOE smokeless zone
SOEHCOS stone the crows
stone the crows!
SOEHQER shove the queer
SOEHTIH score a hit with
SOEOLTR sooner or later
SOEPROS spokespersons
SOGPDIG sponge pudding
SOHNAIS Siobhan Davies
SOITEAK shot in the dark
SOKBOBR shock absorber
shock-absorber
SOKXHNE stock exchange
SOLEBAE shoulder blade
SOLESRP shoulder strap
SOLNEDD swollen-headed
SONRNES Sloane Rangers
SOOECRS show one's cards
SOOEHES show one's heels
SOOEPCS show one's paces
SOOETEH show one's teeth
SOPNPAE stopping-place
SORGRFR show regard for
SOTBRGT show to be right
SOTEORO show the door to
SOTEPRD short-tempered
SOTHWRS shoot the works
SOTMNHP sportsmanship
SOTMNIE sportsmanlike
SOTNDOM shortened form
SOTNMTH shouting match
shouting-match
SOTNOSY spontaneously
SOTNRNE shooting range
SOTNSET short and sweet
SOTNSIK shooting stick
SOTRNIG smooth-running
SOTTLIG smooth-talking
SOTTNUD smooth-tongued
SPEBROG September Song
SPEEATR supreme matter
SPEEOIT Supreme Soviet
SPETINL septentrional
SPIGISN Sophie Grigson
SPISHIE Sophie's Choice
SPITCLY sophistically
SPITCTD sophisticated
SPLMNAY supplementary
SPLNAIN supplantation
SPLTAHR supply teacher
SPOIGHT supposing that
SPOIINL suppositional
SPRAEDR supercalender
SPRAIEY superlatively
SPRAUAE supersaturate
SPRBEES separableness
SPRBNAT superabundant
SPRDIIN superaddition
SPREAIN superfetation
SPRESBY supersensibly
SPRHSCL superphysical
SPRIILY superficially
SPRLIIY superfluidity
SPRLOSY superfluously
SPRNUTD superannuated
SPROMLY supernormally
SPROPTR supercomputer
SPRRIAE superordinate
SPRTTOS superstitions
superstitious
SPRUAIE superhumanise
superhumanize
SPRUEAY supernumerary
SPRYMTY supersymmetry
SPTRCOS St Peter's cross
SQETAIN sequestration
SQETAIY sequentiality
SRAAUOR spread a rumour
SRAECIE surface-active
SRAIAIN serialization
SRAQIKY spread quickly
SRARMUS spread rumours
SRATCLY sarcastically
SRATEOD spread the word
SRATRUH spread through
SRCEWEL sprocket wheel
SRCLUIT sericulturist
SRCUAIM structuralism
SRCUAIT structuralist
SREMCEN Sorley MacLean
SRENMJR sergeant-major
SRENSIE serve one's time
SRENSUN serve one's turn
SREPITS sur les pointes
SREPOES screen process
SRETETE street theatre
SRETTOS surreptitious
SREWLIG street-walking
SRGTIES sprightliness
SRHREET surchargement
SRIAIIY survivability
SRIEHRE service charge
SRIHAGE straight angle
SRIHEIG straightening
SRIHEOT straighten out
SRIHFCD straight-faced
SRIHFGT straight fight
SRIHFRH straightforth
SRIHPGT straight-pight
SRIOEEF strain oneself
SRKTEEM strike the beam
SRKTRUH strike through
SRLGCLY serologically
SRMADAE scrimp and save
SRMTOSY scrumptiously
SRNBLNE spring balance
SRNCIKN spring chicken
SRNETES stringentness
SRNEUNX spring equinox
SRNFEIG strong feeling
SRNIIOS serendipitous
SRNOSES strenuousness
SRNQATT string quartet
SRNTEIG strengthening
SRNUAIN strangulation
SROAEHP surrogateship
SROFLES sorrowfulness
SROHGSS sarcophaguses
SRONSUD surround sound
SROOEEF sure of oneself
SRORAIN Serbo-Croatian
SROSIDD serious-minded
SRPAIIG scrape a living
SRPIHIG strip lighting
SRPOOCC streptococcic
SRPOOCL streptococcal
SRPOOCS streptococcus
SRPTRUH scrape through
SRTCMLS stratocumulus
SRTGAHC stratigraphic
SRTGAHR stratigrapher
SRTGCLY strategically
SRTHPIT stretch a point
SRTSHRC stratospheric
SRVTEDY Shrove Tuesday
SRYANIG spray-painting
SSECLAE supercollate
SSEDRET suspender belt
suspender-belt
SSIHNDY St Swithin's Day
SSIINES suspicionless
STEDAOE Satyendra Bose
STHPIET set the price at
STIGAGT sitting target
STIGEAT sitting tenant
STLIEIH satellite dish
STLIEON satellite town
STNHFNE sit on the fence
STNNSAS set in one's ways
STNSADO set one's hand to
STNSAKP set one's back up
STNSELN set one's seal on
STNSELO set one's seal to
STNSIDN set one's mind on
STNSIDO set one's mind to
STPCSIF Seth Pecksniff
STSIDIH satisfied with
STTAINE set at variance
STXRSIN set expression
STYHHES set by the heels
SUAIHES squeamishness
SUBECOS stumble across
SUDESES soundlessness
SUDHAAM sound the alarm
SUDNIER sound engineer
SUEAIIY squeezability
SUHAOIA South Carolina
SUHATAD south-eastward
SUHATRY south-easterly
SUHETRY south-westerly
SUHHNSA South China Sea
SUHRCON Southern Crown
SUHRCOS Southern Cross
SUHROEN Southern Ocean
SUHYSIE South Ayrshire
SUMRIPN Sturmer Pippin
SUNEIGY squanderingly

SUPUEQE sculpturesque
SURBAKT square bracket
SURBSIG square-bashing
SURDNIG square-dancing
SUSACIG soul-searching
SVAYUAN save as you earn
SVEOOIT sovietologist
SVNENHY seventeenthly
SVNERWR Seven Years' War
SVNHEVN seventh heaven
SVOEBCN save one's bacon
SWHSESF sow the seeds of
SWNMCIE sewing-machine
SXAASUT sexual assault
SXENPEE sixpenny piece
SXGSMLY sexagesimally
SXHOOOE sex chromosome
SXLIAIN sexploitation
SXTRCIN sex attraction
SXYHLIG sixty shilling
SYAOARS Styracosaurus
SYELOEO say well done to
SYNIETY say indirectly
TAASOUN Trajan's Column
TAATIOF tear a strip off
TAATXET to a vast extent
TACNEOE that can be done
TAEERIT trapeze artist
trapeze-artist
TAEICUT trade discount
TAELNBG travelling bag
TAELRJY traveller's joy
TAENOIM trade unionism
TAENOIT trade unionist
TAETITD travel-tainted
TAETRUH travel through
TAETWRS travel towards
TAFCADN traffic warden
TAIGSAE trading estate
TAIINLY traditionally
TAITEOE toad in the hole
toad-in-the-hole
TAKESES thanklessness
TALNPAT trailing plant
TALNSOT trail one's coat
TALTAHE that'll teach me
TALTAHS that'll teach us
TAMTCLY traumatically
TAMTRIS thaumaturgics
TAMTRIT thaumaturgist
TANEEID trainee period
TANPTIG Trainspotting
train-spotting
TAOELVL to a lower level
TAOFSRP tear off a strip
TAQILSR tranquilliser
TAQILZR tranquillizer
TASAETY transparently
TASAINL translational
transnational
TASCIIE transactinide
TASEDNE transcendence
TASEDNY transcendency
TASERBE transferrable
TASESLY transversally
TASESNL transpersonal
TASHSUF that's the stuff!
TASIAIN transpiration
TASIEAE transliterate
TASIOHM that's big of him
TASIRTR transmigrator
TASISBE transmissible
TASITBE transmittable
TASLNIG transplanting
TASOAIN translocation
TASOIIN transposition
TASOMBE transformable
TASOTAE transport café
TASOTBE transportable
TASOTDY transportedly
TASOTNE transportance
TASRPIE transcriptive
TASRPIN transcription
TASRSIE transgressive
TASRSIN transgression
TASSOIE transistorise
transistorize
TASTATC transatlantic
TASTOAY transitionary
TASTONE transit lounge
TASUAIN transmutation
TASUETY translucently
TASUIEY transfusively
TASUIIY translucidity
TATBEES tractableness
TATITES toastmistress
TAUEXET to a huge extent
TBEONAN Table Mountain
TBEOTAL table football
TBEPOFL tablespoonful
TBEUIAT tableau vivant
TBRUAIN tuberculation
TCEOLAE ticket of leave
TCLTDAH tickle to death
TCNCLES technicalness
TCNLGCL technological
TCNUEIH to conjure with
TCOLUEX tic douloureux
TCTNCRE to cut and carve
TDOEEFP tidy oneself up
TEAAAAE The Pajama Game
TEABROK The Jabberwock
TEABSES The Dam Busters
TEACTWR The Watchtower
TEAELNH The Naked Lunch
TEAETOD the latest word
TEAIFUE The Magic Flute
TEAIOIN The Mabinogion
TEANHNE the main chance
TEARQEN The Fairy Queen
TEASREX très au sérieux
TEATRIH the matter with
TEATSVR the party's over
TEATUPR The Last Supper
TEATYON The Last Tycoon
TEAZIGR The Jazz Singer
TEBLSIH Theobald Smith
TEBVNMD the above-named
TECEOSY treacherously
TECFRAD thenceforward
TECWRAE trench warfare
TEDMAUE tread a measure
TEDPNGS tread upon eggs
TEDROEI Theodor Boveri
TEDSAIE The Odessa File
TEEENNW the here and now
TEEITPY the devil to pay
TEELAKY the real Mackay
TEENDOS the penny drops
TEENEOE thereinbefore
TEEOMLA The Jew of Malta
TEERUTR The Deer Hunter
TEHLSOT the whole shoot
TEHLWRD the whole world
TEHMSON the thumbs-down
TEHNEAE the chances are
TEHSWLS the ghost walks
TEHTDVL The White Devil
TEIEFAH The Wife of Bath
TEIGNAS The Virginians
TEIHSUF The Right Stuff
TEIHWTH The Night Watch
TEIONAN Trevi Fountain
TEISFIE the kiss of life
TEISOBY The Winslow Boy
TEITDZN The Dirty Dozen
TEIWOMN The Tin Woodman
TELETAL The Albert Hall
TELGCLY theologically
TELGUEA theologoumena
TELOEHR the altogether
TELSRET the old serpent
TELUSPN the clouds open
TELVNOF the cloven hoof
TEMDNMC thermodynamic
TEMLPIT the small print
TEMNCER thermonuclear
TEMPATC thermoplastic
TEMSTIG thermosetting
TENEWRD The Underworld
TEODLES The Gondoliers
TEODNOL The Golden Bowl
TEOGSDY The Longest Day
TEOISOK Thelonius Monk
TEOKELR The Bookseller
TEOKFHL The Book of Thel
TEOKUTE The Mock Turtle
TEOMNEL the common weal
TEOMNOD the common good
TEONNCT the morn's nicht
TEOSAET the noes have it
TEOSNLE the boys in blue
TEOTIHS the footlights
TEOTMIE the bottom line
TEOTNAS The Bostonians
TEPECUT the upper crust
TEPOIIN the opposition
TERETOD the priesthood
TERMEPR the grim reaper

TEROFGE The Art of Fugue
TERPRYF the property of
TERSNDY the present day
TERTCLY theoretically
TESLNAS Thessalonians
TESRBNH Treasury bench
TESRRHP treasurership
TESRSOE treasure-store
TESRTOE treasure-trove
TETEWRD the other world
TETIAIE theatricalise
theatricalize
TETIAIY theatricality
TETIEHT treat like shit
TETIEIT treat like dirt
TETODVR Treaty of Dover
TETOGET Treaty of Ghent
TETROAT The Story of Art
TEUCAKR The Nutcracker
TEUGEOK The Jungle Book
TEULCEL the public weal
TEUOSES tremulousness
TEWWRAE The Awkward Age
TGOPROE to good purpose
TGTYAKD tightly packed
TIAEAIM trilateralism
TIAEAIT trilateralist
TIATRON this afternoon
TIGRIGR trigger finger
TIHITCL tritheistical
TIHLGCL trichological
TIHOAIM trichromatism
TIHPEOS trichopterous
TIIGAIM trilingualism
TIIYUDY Trinity Sunday
TIKEHRE trickle-charge
TIKETRF think better of
TIKIHYF think highly of
TIKITDY thick-wittedly
TIKITEF think little of
TIKLAHD thick-pleached
TIKOOEF think no more of
TIKSPAK thick as a plank
TILETNE Triple Entente
TILFHPX trial of the pyx
TILNERR trial and error
trial-and-error
TILYEOD trial by record
TIMHLRH triumphal arch
TINUAEY triangulately
TINUAIN triangulation
TINUAIY triangularity
TIOESIS trim one's sails
TIOTHDA trisoctahedra
TITMCLY triatomically
TIUTOSY triquetrously
TKAADRT take a gander at
TKAAKET take a back seat
TKACUTF take account of
TKAHFIT take a shufti at
TKAHSAE take as hostage
TKAIIGO take a liking to
TKAOEON take as one's own

TKAQITT take a squint at
TKARAHR take a breather
TKCMUIN take communion
TKECPIN take exception
TKIISUF take it in snuff
TKIITRS take it in turns
TKISEIH take issue with
TKISOLF take its toll of
TKISOLN take its toll on
TKISORE take its course
TKLBRIS take liberties
TKLIGON take lying down
TKMWTYU take me with you
TKNCPIE taking captive
TKNOBAD taking on board
TKOELAE take one's leave
TKOELMS take one's lumps
TKOEPAE take one's place
TKOFNET take offence at
take offense at
TKRGLRY take regularly
TKTEATF take the part of
TKTEIEF take the side of
TKTEIKY take the mickey
TKTEIOF take the lid off
TKTELDE take the pledge
TKTELNE take the plunge
TKTOEBD take to one's bed
TKTTEOD take to the road
TKUBAET take umbrage at
TKUTEOD take up the word
TLAIEES talkativeness
TLATEIG tilt at the ring
TLCMUIG telecommuting
TLCTAIG telecottaging
TLLKAOK talk like a book
TLMAOHR tell me another
TLMREIG telemarketing
TLNSOTR talent spotter
TLOEBAS tell one's beads
TLPOEOK telephone book
TLPOOES telephoto lens
TLRBEES tolerableness
TLRTOIT tolerationist
TLTOEEF talk to oneself
TLVNEIT televangelist
TMATRIE time after time
TMBTEIG time-bettering
TMCNUIG time-consuming
TMEAEES temperateness
TMEAETL temperamental
TMEEIET tamper-evident
TMETETN tempest-beaten
TMETOSD tempest-tossed
TMETOSY tempestuously
TMNFTES Timon of Athens
TMOAIES temporariness
TMOIAIN temporization
TMOIHES tomboyishness
TMOIIGY temporisingly
temporizingly
TMOTFID time out of mind
TMRROSY temerariously

TMSGAUE time signature
TMYIFGR Tommy Hilfiger
TMYOHRY Tommy Docherty
TNAIAIN tantalization
TNAIEES tentativeness
TNAIIGY tantalisingly
tantalizingly
TNCOSES tenaciousness
TNECPEE ten pence piece
TNEHATD tender-hearted
TNENPEE tenpenny piece
TNETAIY tangentiality
TNETOSY tendentiously
TNIBWIG tenpin bowling
ten-pin bowling
TNIGOGY Tenzing Norgay
TNILCOY tonsillectomy
TNOEPPS tune one's pipes
TNSNVTS tenosynovitis
TNUICEK tongue in cheek
tongue-in-cheek
TNULSIG tongue-lashing
TNUTITR tongue-twister
TNUWGIG tongue-wagging
TOAADSN Thomas Addison
TOAAEKT Thomas à Becket
TOAAEPS Thomas à Kempis
TOAAUDL Thomas Arundel
TOAAUNS Thomas Aquinas
TOABDOS Thomas Beddoes
TOABEHM Thomas Beecham
TOACAMR Thomas Cranmer
TOACMIN Thomas Campion
TOACRYE Thomas Carlyle
TOAESIE Thomas Erskine
TOAJCSN Thomas Jackson
TOAMLHS Thomas Malthus
TOAPAHM Thomas Peachum
TOAPNHN Thomas Pynchon
TOASPIH Thomas Sopwith
TOATLOD Thomas Telford
TOBEAIG troublemaking
TOBEOEY troublesomely
TOECPEE two pence piece
TOEKTDY two weeks today
TOENPEE twopenny piece
TOGTESY thoughtlessly
TOHYRAL Thor Heyerdahl
TOIASOM tropical storm
TOILSNO Trofim Lysenko
TOLDTCL troglodytical
TOOGGIG thoroughgoing
TOUHOER too much to bear
TPEDETE top dead-centre
TPFHWRD top of the world
TPGAHCL topographical
typographical
TPIEUVY topside-turvey
TPLGCLY topologically
TPRCRIG tape-recording
TRAEHUE terraced house
TRAEIGY threateningly
TRAHOTR Tarka the Otter

Code	Entry
TRALNEE	turn a blind eye
TREAEET	three-day event
TREBZAD	turkey buzzard
TREENBT	threepenny bit
TREIEHP	three-line whip
TREIPPR	turmeric paper
TREONRD	three-cornered
TREORIE	three-four time
TRETILY	terrestrially
TRETNIL	tercentennial
TREVLUE	turkey vulture
TRHNASA	Tyrrhenian Sea
TRIAIEY	terminatively
TRIAIIY	terminability
TRIESTR	tergiversator
TRIHNOA	Turkish Angora
TRIHOFE	Turkish coffee
TRIOILY	territorially
TRISDOT	turn inside out
	turn inside-out
TRMAOOY	thremmatology
TRNEORN	Terence Conran
TRNFAHR	tar and feather
TRNIAIN	tyrannization
TRNOARS	tyrannosaurus□
TROIAIN	terrorization
TROSSEL	tortoiseshell□
TROTEER	turn of the year
TROTEET	turn on the heat
TRSCOEN	terpsichorean
TRSNCLY	thrasonically
TRSOAIA	Teresa of Avila
TRSOEEF	thrust oneself
TRTACUT	turn to account
TRTEALS	turn the tables
TRTECLS	turn the scales
TRTEETN	turn the heat on
TRTEONR	turn the corner
TRTGNSS	teratogenesis
TRUHHDY	through the day
TRUTTSO	Torquato Tasso
TRWOBSN	throw doubts on
TRWOEHR	throw together
TRWTNRM	throw a tantrum
TSAINOF	Tasmanian wolf
TSEESES	tastelessness
TSMPROE	to some purpose
TSTEAES	test the waters
TSUCLUE	tissue culture
TSYHLAT	to say the least
TTAERLY	tetrahedrally
TTEAKOE	to the backbone
TTEOTAY	to the contrary
TTERFTF	to the profit of
TTLAIGY	titillatingly
TTLTTLR	tittle-tattler
TTNUWIE	titanium white
TUBNSOE	thumb one's nose
TUCTDOM	truncated form
TUDRATR	thunder-darter
	thunder-master
TUDRERR	thunder-bearer
TUDRTIE	thunderstrike
TUDRTOE	thunder-stroke
TUDRTUK	thunderstruck
TUDSOIG	true-disposing
TUGTRUH	trudge through
TUOOOSY	tautologously
TUPTRWN	trumpeter swan
TUTOTIY	trustworthily
TWRFODN	Tower of London
TXCLGCL	toxicological
TXEUTBE	tax-deductible
TXNMCLY	taxonomically
TXPAMSS	toxoplasmosis
TYAIEOF	thylacine wolf
TYNSADT	try one's hand at
TYNSUKT	try one's luck at
TYTNPAE	trysting-place
UABEITD	unabbreviated
UABGOSY	unambiguously
UACMAID	unaccompanied
UACUTBE	unaccountable
UACUTBY	unaccountably
UAEAIIY	unamenability
UAEIAIE	un-Americanise
	un-Americanize
UAMUTIS	Ural Mountains
UAPEEDD	unapprehended
UAPEITD	unappreciated
UAPOIGY	unapprovingly
UATCPTD	unanticipated
UAUTRTD	unadulterated
UAVNUOS	unadventurous
UAVSDES	unadvisedness
UBAEOTY	unblameworthy
UBELGOP	umbrella group
UBELSAD	umbrella-stand
UBLCLOD	umbilical cord
UBLEIGY	unbelievingly
UBLIEOS	umbelliferous
UBNIGES	unbendingness
UBNITIT	urban district
UBSEIGY	unbeseemingly
UBUDDES	unboundedness
UCENIES	uncleanliness
UCMLCTD	uncomplicated
UCMLIAT	uncomplaisant
UCMLIIG	uncomplaining
UCMOTBE	uncomfortable
UCMOTBY	uncomfortably
UCNANBE	uncontainable
UCNCOSY	unconsciously
UCNELBE	unconcealable
UCNENDY	unconcernedly
UCNERTD	unconsecrated
UCNEVBY	unconceivably
UCNIIND	unconditioned
UCNIINL	unconditional
UCNOMBE	unconformable
UCNOMBY	unconformably
UCNTAND	unconstrained
UCNURBE	unconquerable
UCODNTD	uncoordinated
	unco-ordinated
UCOEAIE	unco-operative
UCRMNOS	unceremonious
UCRSINY	unchristianly
UCRUCSD	uncircumcised
UCRUSET	uncircumspect
UDLNFVR	undulant fever
UDMSIAE	undomesticate
UDRADDY	underhandedly
UDRAMNS	undergarments
UDRANIG	underpainting
UDRARAE	undercarriage
UDRCIVR	underachiever
UDRHKIE	under the knife
UDRHLIG	underwhelming
UDRHTBE	under the table
UDRIKOD	Under Milk Wood
UDRINNS	underpinnings
UDRLSMN	underclassman
UDRLTIG	underclothing
UDRNSAD	under one's hand
UDRNSET	under one's belt
UDRNSOE	under one's nose
UDRRDAE	undergraduate
UDRRPRD	underprepared
UDRRSUE	under pressure
UDRSIAE	underestimate
UDRTNIG	understanding
UDRXOUE	underexposure
UDSEBIG	undissembling
UDSENBE	undiscernible
UDSENBY	undiscernibly
UDSENDY	undiscernedly
UDSICIE	undistinctive
UDSILND	undisciplined
UDSORGD	undiscouraged
UDSRALS	undesireables
UDSRBBE	undescribable
UDSRIGY	undeservingly
UDSUSDY	undisguisedly
UDUTDES	undauntedness
UEAGRTD	unexaggerated
UEBLIHD	unembellished
UEBRASD	unembarrassed
UECPINL	unexceptional
UEFREBE	unenforceable
UEHOCPC	urethroscopic
UEITRAE	user interface
UELGTND	unenlightened
UENUTBY	use unsuitably
UEOINLY	unemotionally
UEPANBE	unexplainable
UEPANBY	unexplainably
UERHIES	unearthliness
UESDOMT	use as a doormat
UETBIHD	unestablished
UEUVCLY	unequivocally
UFEIGES	unfeelingness
UFICIGY	unflinchingly
UFLEIGY	unfalteringly
UFMLAIY	unfamiliarity
UFRETBE	unforgettable
UFRHOIG	unforthcoming
UFRSEBE	unforeseeable
UFRUAEY	unfortunately

Words marked □ can also be spelled with an initial capital letter

UFSINBE unfashionable
UFSINBY unfashionably
UGADDES unguardedness
UGAMTCL ungrammatical
UGNLMNY ungentlemanly
UHATFLY unhealthfully
UHATIES unhealthiness
UHATYIT unhealthy diet
UHRIDES unhurriedness
UIAEAIM unicameralism
unilateralism
UIAEAIT unicameralist
unilateralist
UIAEAIY unilaterality
UIAIAIE unimaginative
UIEKNDM United Kingdom
UIENTOS United Nations
UIESLES universalness
UIESLUE universal cure
UIFAMBE uninflammable
UIFRAIE uninformative
UIGNSOF using one's loaf
UIHBTBE uninhabitable
UILMNTD unilluminated
UIOACUT unit of account
UIPAHBE unimpeachable
UIPSIND unimpassioned
UISRCIE uninstructive
UITLIET unintelligent
UITNINL unintentional
UITRSIG uninteresting
UITRUTD uninterrupted
UJSIIBE unjustifiable
UJSIIBY unjustifiably
ULANDES unlearnedness
ULWUGOS unlawful goods
UMAIGES unmeaningness
UMDCNBE unmedicinable
UMNFLES unmindfulness
UMNINBE unmentionable
UMTGTDY unmitigatedly
UNCSAIY unnecessarily
UNIHORY unneighbourly
UNTRLES unnaturalness
UOFNIGY unoffendingly
UOIIAIY unoriginality
UOTUIEY unobtrusively
UPEEETD unprecedented
UPEETBE unpreventable
UPEETOS unpretentious
UPEITBE unpredictable
UPEITBY unpredictably
UPESRBY unpleasurably
UPIAONS unpaid amounts
UPNTAIY unpunctuality
UPORSIE unprogressive
UPROEIE Upper Yosemite
UPRUBBE unperturbable
UPRUDBE unpersuadable
UPTONBE unputdownable
UQETOIG unquestioning
URAOIGY unreasoningly
URCIIBE unrectifiable
URCVRBE unrecoverable
URGNRTD unregenerated
URGTOSY unrighteously
uprighteously
URLAIIY unreliability
URLNIGY unrelentingly
URLTDES unrelatedness
URMTETY unremittently
URMTIGY unremittingly
URPIADD unreprimanded
URSETBE unrespectable
URSSIGY unresistingly
USAIGES unsparingness
USBTNIL unsubstantial
USCAIIY unsociability
USETCLR unspectacular
USGTIES unsightliness
USIAIIY unsuitability
USIFLES unskilfulness
USIIULY unspiritually
USLADES Ursula Andress
USLAEBE unsalvageable
USLCIEY unselectively
USLIHES unselfishness
USMAHTC unsympathetic
USMERCL unsymmetrical
USNIETL unsentimental
USOTNOS unspontaneous
USPOTDY unsupportedly
USRASBE unsurpassable
USRASDY unsurpassedly
USRIEBE unserviceable
USSANBE unsustainable
USSETBE unsusceptible
USSETDY unsuspectedly
USTLDES unsettledness
USTSIBE unsatisfiable
USUHATR unsought-after
USVUIES unsavouriness
UTAIINL untraditional
UTAITOS ultra-virtuous
UTITDES untaintedness
UTLHEDF until the end of
UTNBEES untenableness
UTNICAR Upton Sinclair
UTRFIES unthriftiness
UTTEIEF up to the time of
UTTEIUE up to the minute
up-to-the-minute
UTTELOS up to the elbows
UTTEOET up to the moment
up-to-the-moment
UTTIPIT up to this point
UTUTOTY untrustworthy
UWLIGES unwillingness
UWMNIES unwomanliness
UWOEOEY unwholesomely
UWRAIIY unworkability
UWRATBE unwarrantable
UWRATBY unwarrantably
UWRATDY unwarrantedly
UWRDIES unworldliness
UWRMNIE unworkmanlike
UWTIGES unwittingness
UYSSGAT Ulysses S Grant
VAIIPTN Vladimir Putin
VBAINES vibrationless
VCIIAIN victimization
VCLAIGY vacillatingly
VCOICOS Victoria Cross
VCOIFLS Victoria Falls
VCOLDRM victor ludorum
VCOSICE vicious circle
VCPEIET vice-president
VCRFHIT Vicar of Christ
VCUCENR vacuum cleaner
VDOASTE videocassette
VDOEODR video recorder
VDONEAD video-on-demand
VIECEET void excrement
VIEESES voicelessness
VLAIAIN vulcanization
vulgarization
VLAOOIT vulcanologist
VLDCOIN valedictorian
VLEAIIY vulnerability
VLEDETX value-added tax
VLEOMNY value for money
VLTLZBE volatilizable
VNCLUIT viniculturist
VNEOBRI Vince Lombardi
VNETBIN Vincent O'Brien
VNETEAL Vincent de Paul
VNFCOSY veneficiously
VNIAOIY vindicatorily
VNRBEEE Venerable Bede
VNRBEES venerableness
VNRLQIE ventriloquise
ventriloquize
VNRLQIM ventriloquism
VNRLQIT ventriloquist
VNSILAS Venus Williams
VNTABID Venetian blind
VNUEOEY venturesomely
VODGMOS viol-de-gamboys
VOOCLIT violoncellist
VPRBGOS viper's bugloss
VPUDNIY vapour density
VRAEUNX vernal equinox
VRAIAIN verbalization
vernalisation
vernalization
VRAIEES versatileness
VRALCSS variable costs
VRAUAIE vernacularise
vernacularize
VRCOSES voraciousness
VRCSASA Vera Caslavska
VREYRIT variety artist
VRFAIIY verifiability
VRIIAIN versification
VRIIBAH Virginia Beach
VRIILNS Virgin Islands
VRIIOSY vertiginously
VRIIWOF Virginia Woolf
VRIOORD versicoloured

VRMNAUS verumontanums
VRSMLRY verisimilarly
VRSOTIE very short time
VSAIAIN visualization
VSOAIES visionariness
VTCLUIT viticulturist
VTIIAIN vitrification
VUTFEVN vault of heaven
VVCOSES vivaciousness
VVSCINL vivisectional
VXDUSIN vexed question
VXTOSES vexatiousness
WAALHMT what ails him at?
WADYUNW what do you know?
WAEVRIN weaker version
WAHRETN weather-beaten
WAHRIDW weather window
WAHRPIT weather a point
WAIGAEP wearing make-up
WAIOEES wearisomeness
WATELGE what the plague
WDACLEE Wadham College
WDBODIW wide-broad view
WDOTEAK wide of the mark
WDSRTHD wide-stretched
WEIGILW weeping willow
WEIWEOT week in week out
WELRELR wheeler-dealer
WEYUATO when you want to
WIEAPIE white sapphire
WIEATAE White Hart lane
WIELPAT white elephant
WIENSAE write one's name
WIHLFIG weightlifting
WIHROVR whithersoever
WIIHELW whitish-yellow
WIITSAE whip into shape
WITELWR whistle-blower
WITEWYT whittle away at
WLADOLY wild and woolly
WLAKADY walk awkwardly
WLAPITD well-appointed
WLBOGTP well-brought-up
WLCNUTD well-conducted
WLDVLPD well-developed
WLEBGHT Walter Bagehot
WLEGOIS Walter Gropius
WLEHMTN Wolverhampton
WLEMNAE Walter Mondale
WLEMRUD Wilhelm Freund
WLEMTHU Walter Matthau
WLEPESD well-expressed
WLERLIH Walter Raleigh
WLESCET Walter Sickert
WLFRIID well-fortified
WLGNPUI Wolfgang Pauli
WLHMOET Waltham Forest
WLICLIS Wilkie Collins
WLIMABT William Talbot
WLIMAFN William Baffin
WLIMANS William Barnes
WLIMATN William Walton
WLIMAVY William Harvey

WLIMBIE Willie McBride
WLIMEPE William Temple
WLIMEVN William Kelvin
WLIMFYE William of Tyre
WLIMMSN William Empson
WLIMOIG William Boeing
WLIMOPR William Cowper
WLIMORS William Morris
WLIMORT William Dorrit
WLIMOVR William Hoover
WLIMOWN William Godwin
WLIMUBR William Dunbar
WLIRNHW Willie Renshaw
WLMNOIZ Wolf Mankowitz
WLNTERF will not hear of
WLOGNZD well-organized
WLOHWSS will-o'-the-wisps
WLOPCET Wilson Pickett
WLOPTEN willow pattern□
WLPEEVD well preserved
well-preserved
WLPOETD well-protected
WLQAIID well-qualified
WLRDHDS Wilfred Rhodes
WLRGLTD well-regulated
WLRSETD well-respected
WLSAEAS walls have ears
WLSTEIP wills-o'-the-wisp
WLTAELD well-travelled
WLTOGTF well-thought-of
WLTREOT well-turned-out
WLUADON walk up and down
WLWTAIP walk with a limp
WMNHLRN women-children
WNCMADR wing commander
WNEAOIE winter aconite
WNEIAIN winterization
WNEWRIG wonder-working
WNIGOAE wanting to have
WNITEOH Winnie-the-Pooh
WNOHNIG window hanging
WNSFHNE winds of change
WNSRATE Windsor Castle
WNTNRHM Winston Graham
WOEAODE whole caboodle
WOEGAIG wood engraving
WOEOEES wholesomeness
WOGARUD wrong way round
WOGEDDY wrong-headedly
WOGTEIG woolgathering
wool-gathering
WOLMLCP woolly milk cap
WOPNCUH whooping cough
WORWISN Woodrow Wilson
WRBIDES word-blindness
WRDAGAE world language
WRDYELH worldly wealth
WRDYIDD worldly-minded
WREHRIG Warren Harding
WRHATDY warm-heartedly
WRHESES worthlessness
WRHFRUE worth a fortune
WRHNSAT worth one's salt

WRIGESN working person
WRIGINL warning signal
WRIKATE Warwick Castle
WROEWYN worm one's way in
WROHKIE war to the knife
WRPOESR word processor
WRTERCE work the oracle
WSEAEBN wastepaper bin
WSENHRH Western Church
WSGAOGN West Glamorgan
WSHNBSN washhand basin
WSIGODR washing powder
WSIHEDD waspish-headed
WSNRHET west-north-west
WSOEHNS wash one's hands
WSSDSOY West Side Story
WSSUHET west-south-west
WSYRSIE West Yorkshire
WTAAGAE with a bad grace
WTAFCIN with affection
WTAIEAY with a siserary
WTFLFRE with full force
WTGETOS with great loss
WTGOGAE with good grace
WTHHCOK watch the clock
WTHNBIF watching brief
WTHNSAK watch one's back
WTHNSED with hands held
WTHNSGT with hindsight
WTHNSTP watch one's step
WTIAAEF within an ace of
WTIMAUE within measure
WTIRAHF within reach of
WTITGIY with integrity
WTKDLVS with kid gloves
WTLADAB wattle and daub
WTNTIGN with nothing on
WTOECOD with one accord
WTOEHNS with one's hands
WTOTBEK without a break
WTOTDUT without a doubt
WTOTESN without reason
WTOTHRE without charge
WTOTIIN without vision
WTOTPEH without speech
WTOTRLS without frills
WTOTSUD without a sound
WTOTUBR without number
WTRHSNT water chestnut
WTRLNAN water plantain
WTRSETO with respect to
WTRTNIG water-standing
WTSADBE withstandable
WTTEANR with the manner
WTTEEPF with the help of
WTTEEUT with the result
WTWOEKN with whole skin
WUDOEVN would to heaven
WVMCAIS wave mechanics
WYAIGRE wayfaring-tree
WYFEAIG way of behaving
WYFHCOS Way of the Cross
WYFHNIG way of thinking

13 W_Y_F

WYFPAIG way of speaking
XAATOOY X-ray astronomy
XRPTAMA xerophthalmia
YAIYAOT year in year out
YESLUET Yves St Laurent
YHDMNHN Yehudi Menuhin
YHIAAOO Yohji Yamamoto
YKTRNUG Yekaterinburg
YLOBLID yellow-bellied
YPIIAIN yuppification
YTHKHMR Yitzhak Shamir
YUGFEDR young offender
YUSLAAN yourself again
ZBARSIG zebra crossing
ZCAYALR Zachary Taylor
ZGMTCOE zygomatic bone
ZLIAOSN Zuleika Dobson
ZOEGAHC zoogeographic
ZRAHGEK Zorba the Greek

14 letters – odd

AAAEFNT at a rate of knots
AAATESI as a partnership
AADRHWT Alan Dershowitz
AADUODS A Handful of Dust
AAEMTDU Anaheim Stadium
AAENHHL an ace in the hole
AAEPORS A Rake's Progress
AAERSNS amateurishness
AAGNMEO a large number of
AAHCRSI Agatha Christie
AAHOIAL anachronically
AAHOOIA arachnological
AAIIUNS avariciousness
AALNSLO avail oneself of
AAMEETO a warm reception
AANSIAL anamnestically
AANTHHA against the head
AANTHWO against the wool
AAOUSGA analogue signal
AARSRDE Alan Rusbridger
AATIBRE Alastair Burnet
AATNATO awaiting action
AATOEFR a waste of effort
ABDXRUL ambidextrously
ABRCLUA arboricultural
ABRENTI Albert Einstein
ABRMMRA Albert Memorial
ABROOAI Alberto Moravia
ABRRYOD Albert Reynolds
ABSAOSI ambassadorship
ABSOCMN asbestos cement
ACAOOIA archaeological
ACETITR ancient history
ACIAIET acclimatized to
ACIETNC architectonics
ACIPSOA archiepiscopal
ACMAIET accompaniments
ACMLSAL accomplishable
ACMLSMN accomplishment
ACMLTVL accumulatively
ACNIGOT ascending aorta
ACPALNS acceptableness
ACSOENS accustomedness
ACUTBLT accountability
ADBASAD Aldabra Islands
ADEBNRA Andrew Bonar Law
ADECREI Andrew Carnegie
ADEDLAT Andrea del Sarto
ADEMNEN Andrea Mantegna
ADEPLAI Andrea Palladio
ADESKAO Andrei Sakharov
ADGESRW at daggers drawn
ADGLWRH Andy Goldworthy
ADHTAEO and what have you
ADLTAJZ and all that jazz
ADRAAEL Andorra-la-Vella
ADRAGTO Anders Ångström
ADTOATM additional time
ADYHHAR Aldwych Theatre
AEADEUA Alexandre Dumas
AEADOAI Alexandr Oparin
AEADROD Alexander Korda
AEADROR Alexander Monro
AEEAOAR Amedeo Avogadro
AEHFAKI Aretha Franklin
AEIABAT American Beauty
AEIAIDA American Indian
AEKFUDY a week of Sundays
AEOATVT area of activity
AEOCNLC area of conflict
AEOITRS area of interest
AEPIHAR Adelphi Theatre
AETIPRO a certain person
AFCINTL affectionately
AFCSRNL affect strongly
AFETNYO Alfred Tennyson
AFIDREE auf Wiedersehen
AFIOHNU affair of honour
AFISFTT affairs of state
AFLTRTL at full throttle
AFTSFDL as fit as a fiddle
AGADEIU au grand sérieux
AGADZMN aggrandizement
AGESVNS aggressiveness
AGMNIAS argumenti causa
AGSEICR Auguste Piccard
AGSEUIR Auguste Lumière
AGSIINS Augustinianism
AGSOADN Augusto Sandino
AGSSHEE August Schlegel
AGSWIMN August Weismann
AHCNOGU à chacun son goût
AHEEETG achievement age
AHEEUCS achieve success
AHLETNO Achilles' tendon
AHNRPAI achondroplasia
AHOAIAL achromatically
AHOSIEA A Shropshire Lad
AHRSIAL aphoristically
AIACAKR Animal Crackers
AIAVRIN animadversions
AIDENAO Ariadne on Naxos
AIEHNTD a wise thing to do
AIHEIAL arithmetically
AIHUEAT acid-house party
AILKKIE at it like knives
AIOALIH a bit of all right
AIOHMDN azidothymidine
AIOSMER axis of symmetry
AKIFRNL ask differently
AKNOMTO ask information
AKOGVNS ask forgiveness
AKOLDMN acknowledgment
AKOOEON ask to come round
ALANNSA a flea in one's ear
ALCITEU a place in the sun
ALERIBK all-terrain bike
ALITVNO Adlai Stevenson
ALKNNBN all skin and bone
ALNDYWR all in a day's work
ALONCMR all-round camera
ALPTIAL allopathically
ALSONAN Atlas Mountains
ALVRHSO all over the shop
ALWOUCE allow to succeed
AMIAHAR Almeida Theatre
AMLMTTO arms limitation
AMLNMEO a small number of
AMMNAIM armamentariums
AMNSRTO administration
AMNSRTV administrative
AMNTODM ammunition dump
AMSILNS admissibleness
ANBASRE Anne Bradstreet
ANEEBVT Annie Leibovitz
ANHWRSA Anna Howard Shaw
ANLRCIS annular eclipse
ANSIAII annus mirabilis
AOAHRPS aromatherapist
AOCOTEU a touch of the sun
AODFABG a load of garbage
AODFUBS a load of rubbish
AODONNA avoid going near
AOECIAL apodeictically
AOEDSOA at one's disposal
AOEELWO at one fell swoop
AOEETOE above-mentioned
aforementioned
AOENBYN above and beyond
AOEUPCO above suspicion
AOFOBEE Adolf von Baeyer
AOFUEAD Adolf Butenandt
AOHHGAI apophthegmatic

AOIMSUI atomic mass unit
AOLCIAL apoplectically
AOMFNSW A Room of One's Own
AOMIHVE A Room with a View
AONIELC A Town Like Alice
AOOEIAL apologetically
AOSIGIA acoustic guitar
AOSLHIE Alois Alzheimer
AOTCREU a sop to Cerberus
AOTNHDO a foot in the door
APAATCE alpha particles
APAEIAL alphabetically
alphamerically
APASDEL appear suddenly
APAUEIA alphanumerical
APEADER apples and pears
APEESVL apprehensively
APEFICR apple of discord
APEFNSY apple of one's eye
APEHROT apple charlotte
APEITVL appreciatively
APETCHO apprenticehood
APETCSI apprenticeship
APIDHSC applied physics
APIOOIA amphibological
APNIETM appendicectomy
APYNSLT apply oneself to
AQANEWT acquainted with
AQIEKLI acquire skill in
ARADSAC a great distance
ARANMEO a great number of
ARAYTRE already started
ARBOIAL aerobiotically
ARCLUAL agriculturally
ARHMICL Abraham Lincoln
ARIEASA air-vice-marshal
ARNENAR arrange in pairs
ARNUIAL aeronautically
ARODTOE air-conditioned
air-conditioner
ARPEIWE a prophetic week
ARRBRAI aurora borealis
ARRFSOA aircraftswoman
ARSTEOR across-the-board
ARVSDEL arrive suddenly
ASCAEWT associated with
ASEBCCD answer back code
ASEIUNS abstemiousness
ASIIIUL adscititiously
ASIIUNS auspiciousness
ASNMNEL absent-mindedly
ASRCENS abstractedness
ASRLAAP Australian Alps
ASTTIPN asset-stripping
ASUTIKE Afsluitdijk Sea
ASVRTNL asseveratingly
ATATVNS attractiveness
ATBORPE autobiographer
ATCAAET attach a label to
ATCAIAL autocratically
ATCEFAT article of faith
ATCLTNS articulateness
ATCNUSN anticonvulsant
ATCPTRL anticipatorily
ATCPTVL anticipatively
ATCSRNL attack strongly
ATDLVAL antediluvially
ATDPESN antidepressant
ATEEINN at the beginning
ATEEUSO at the request of
ATEHLFC at the chalkface
ATEIDNO at the bidding of
ATEIHTM at the right time
ATEOMNO at the command of
ATERWLE as the crow flies
ATETCTO authentication
ATEXESO at the expense of
ATFUPRI a stiff upper lip
ATGAHLU autograph album
ATGAIAL astigmatically
ATGNSIT antagonistic to
ATGNZTO antagonization
ATIALNS attainableness
ATIEATA Antoine Watteau
ATIONAN Altai Mountains
ATMTCIO automatic pilot
ATMTIAL altimetrically
ATNHNMO act in the name of
ATNOAIR Antonio Salieri
ATNOIAD Antonio Vivaldi
ATNOWBR Anton von Webern
ATOGTMC a strong stomach
ATOHSCS astrophysicist
ATOOIAL astrologically
astronomically
ATOPITN action painting
ATOSAIN action stations
ATOYEKN Anthony Perkins
ATOYFAU Anthony of Padua
ATOYOKN Anthony Hopkins
ATOYUGS Anthony Burgess
ATPOIAL antiphonically
ATPRPRN antiperspirant
anti-perspirant
ATPTEIA antipathetical
ATRPLGS anthropologist
ATRPMTI anthropometric
ATRSRGL after a struggle
ATRTCCA Antarctic Ocean
ATSGETO auto-suggestion
ATSPIAL antiseptically
ATTDNZN attitudinizing
ATTEIAL antithetically
ATUGIFT Arthur Griffith
ATUHNGE Arthur Honegger
ATUKETE Arthur Koestler
ATUKRBR Arthur Kornberg
ATUSIAL altruistically
ATUSLIA Arthur Sullivan
ATVIMNT active immunity
AVNAEUL advantageously
AVNEATR advance factory
AVNEOAD advance towards
AVNIGER advancing years
AVNIIUL adventitiously
AWOHUDA as who should say
AYCRNUL asynchronously
AYMTIAL asymmetrically
AYMTIBR asymmetric bars
AYPOIAL asymptotically
BACMAIO bear comparison
BADRAPO bladder campion
BAHODNL Blashford-Snell
BAIIVSO beatific vision
BAKACSU Black Narcissus
BAKAKTE black-marketeer
BAKATIG blank cartridge
BAKNHFC black in the face
BAKYDUA black-eyed Susan
black-eyed susan
BANIEAC Béarnaise sauce
BAOEBAN beat one's brains
BAOEBES beat one's breast
BAOFHBL bear off the bell
BAOSRCO boa constrictor
BAPOTTO blaxploitation
BASANPP boatswain's pipe
BATEERA beat the retreat
BATELSE Bran the Blessed
BATFCTO beautification
BBEEIVN Bible-believing
BBIZIMN Bob Fitzsimmons
BBNKEFC Babinski effect
BBOGTOE be brought to bed
BCEADPD bucket and spade
BCEILGS bacteriologist
BCLYCAC Buckley's chance
BCMAPRN become apparent
BCMARON become airborne
BCMCUBE become chubbier
BCMDFNT become definite
BCMECTN become exciting
BCMEPUE become espoused
BCMOSLT become obsolete
BCMPENN become pregnant
BCMSANN become stagnant
BCMSNIL become sensible
BCSADIE back-seat driver
BCSRTHN backscratching
BDADRTN bad handwriting
BDIHMTN Bedrich Smetana
BDLFNTO bodily function
BDYRAIE badly organized
BECDLVR breech delivery
BECOTEA breach of the law
BEDNGON breeding-ground
BEDRECO breeder reactor
BEHIPLC Blenheim Palace
BEHRPAT blepharoplasty
BEKATWT break faith with
BEKEGON break new ground
BEKHBCO break the back of
BEKHRCR break the record
BEKNSER break one's heart
BEKOQAE break no squares
BEKOSFO break loose from
BEKTFWT break it off with
BETIGPC breathing space
breathing-space

BETLSNS	breathlessness
BFROETM	before one's time
BFRTELO	before the flood
BGAEADE	baggage-handler
BGAEARE	baggage-carrier
BGAEELI	baggage reclaim
BGERENS	big-heartedness
BGILBOS	big girl's blouse
BHMAFRS	Bohemian Forest
BHNOEBC	behind one's back
BHNSHDL	behind schedule
BHNTEHE	behind the wheel
BHNTEIE	behind the times
BIANAEA	Britannia metal
BIEROTB	bridegroom-to-be
BIFNONE	Brief Encounter
BIGAITT	bring variety to
BIGBIDN	bridge-building
BIGCLIT	bring acclaim to
BIGELWT	being dealt with
BIGICSE	being discussed
BIGIDUO	being mindful of
BIGNOEN	bring into being
BIGNOOU	bring into focus
BIGNSLT	bring oneself to
BIGNSOT	bringings forth
BIGOCON	bring to account
BIGOHBI	bring to the boil
BIGOHFR	bring to the fore
BIGOUTC	bring to justice
BIGPHRA	bring up the rear
BIHADAL	bright and early
BIHSIES	Bright's disease
BIIHHLR	British cholera
BIITBRO	Brigitte Bardot
BITEAIO	be in the habit of
BITNAEA	Brittania metal
BITRUNS	boisterousness
BLAOGLA	balsam of Gilead
BLHAENS	bald-headedness
	bull-headedness
BLIGMTO	Billings method
BLIJAKN	Billie Jean King
BLILOLG	Balliol College
BLMAEVS	bulimia nervosa
BLMOATR	Belém Monastery
BLNEFOE	balance of power
BLNEFRD	balance of trade
BLOACSL	Balmoral Castle
BLODMPM	Bolson de Mapimi
BLOECAG	bill of exchange
BLPRFGR	ballpark figure
BLSFRLN	bells of Ireland
BLSYWNO	bull's eye window
BMUGCSL	Bamburgh Castle
BNAIBTE	Benjamin Butler
BNAIOIL	Beniamino Gigli
BNDCANL	Benedict Arnold
BNDTORC	Benedetto Croce
BNEHALN	banner headline
BNFTOIT	benefit society
BNIGNAD	bending inwards
BNLOLUH	bundle of laughs
BNLONRE	bundle of nerves
BNNRPBI	banana republic
BNOIZPN	benzodiazepine
BNOTFHP	bend out of shape
BODARFC	blood-sacrifice
BODHRTL	bloodthirstily
BODNHBA	broad in the beam
BODNNGA	Brobdingnagian
BODOSMN	blood-consuming
BOENLER	Boolean algebra
BOERDTO	biodegradation
BOGTOWR	brought forward
BOHRAFE	Brother Cadfael
BOKIHFO	block light from
BOKNTCL	block and tackle
BOKRBNO	Brooks Robinson
BONIERN	bioengineering
BOPSTWT	be opposite with
BORPIAL	biographically
BOTEHSL	blow the whistle
BRAAAKO	Barbara Jackson
BRADAAU	Bernard Malamud
BRADANN	Bernard Manning
BRADATN	Bernard Haitink
BRADCAG	bureau de change
BRADIAL	Bernard Hinault
BRATETK	burn at the stake
BRESMNS	burdensomeness
BRHSKNE	Burrhus Skinner
BRIACNR	Barbican Centre
BRIRUSN	barrier nursing
BRIUIAI	barbituric acid
BRMTIAL	barometrically
BROEEFU	burn oneself out
BROEFGO	burn one's faggot
BROOEDA	Bartolomeu Diaz
BROPRDS	Bird of Paradise
	bird of paradise
BRSATRA	Boris Pasternak
BRSFMRC	Birds of America
BRTEACE	bury the hatchet
BRTNOER	burst into tears
BRTOCNE	burnt to a cinder
BRYODAE	Barry Goldwater
BSADZTO	bastardization
BSASOIA	busman's holiday
BSBFRDT	best-before date
BSDTEON	beside the point
BSLOIER	Basil D'Oliveira
BSNSPOL	businesspeople
BSOHROE	Bustopher Jones
BSORFNO	basso profundos
BTEAEOE	by the same token
BTEESRO	be the measure of
BTEETRO	be the better for
BTEFNEE	butter-fingered
BTETOWO	Betsey Trotwood
BTEYFET	battery of tests
BTIGOTM	bathing costume
	bathing-costume
BTLAELC	battle-axe block
BTLOANE	Battle of Arnhem
BTLOATU	Battle of Actium
BTLOCNA	Battle of Cannae
BTLOKSV	Battle of Kosovo
BTLOMCL	Battle of Mycale
BTLOMDA	Battle of Midway
BTLONSB	Battle of Naseby
BTLOPNI	Battle of Pinkie
BTLOSIO	Battle of Shiloh
BTLOVRU	Battle of Verdun
BTLOWGA	Battle of Wagram
BTMNUCA	bituminous coal
BTOMSRO	button mushroom
BTYOTRY	Betty Boothroyd
BUANILE	bougainvillaea
BUBNICI	Bourbon biscuit
BUSLSRU	brussels sprout□
BVRAFRS	Bavarian Forest
BWLRZTO	bowdlerization
BXEDREK	Bix Beiderbecke
BXREELO	Boxer Rebellion
BYNQETO	beyond question
BYNRPOC	beyond reproach
BYWLBBY	boys will be boys
CAATRCO	character actor
CAATRSI	characteristic
CABRONI	chamber council
CABRYAC	cranberry sauce
CABTEEL	clap by the heels
CACLOSI	chancellorship
CACOELC	chance one's luck
CACROFC	Chancery Office
CAECDRO	Clarence Darrow
CAEHDAO	chase the dragon
CAEPRTN	cease operating
CAGALNS	changeableness
CAGLSNS	changelessness
CAGNCUS	changing course
CAGNPAE	changing places
CAGOEMN	change one's mind
CAGOETN	change one's tune
CAGOEWY	change one's ways
CAHALVR	clash-ma-clavers
CAHMSAD	Chatham Islands
CAIALNS	charitableness
CAITOFR	Chariots of Fire
CALEHPI	Charlie Chaplin
CALOHSO	Charlton Heston
CALSABG	Charles Babbage
CALSACE	cradle-snatcher
CALSAGE	Charles Haughey
CALSANL	Charles Parnell
CALSASE	Charles Causley
CALSASN	Charles Parsons
CALSEND	Charles Kennedy
CALSHBL	Charles the Bald
CALSIFN	Charles Tiffany
CALSIKN	Charles Dickens
CALSLNI	Charles Blondin
CALSOCT	Charles Boycott
CALSOGO	Charles Dodgson
CALSORO	Charles Bourbon
CALSRNO	Charles Bronson
CALSUFC	Charles Surface
CALSUIN	Charles Luciano

CALTEOG Charlotte Yonge
CALTEUS charlotte russe
CAMFESV charm offensive
CANFOMN chain of command
CANLOPN channel hopping
CANLSAD Channel Islands
CANLUFN channel surfing
CAOOAAI cyanocobalamin
CASFCTO classification
CASFCTR classificatory
CASNEET chanson de geste
CASOSIU class-conscious
CASRPOI claustrophobia
claustrophobic
CAUAOGU chacun à son goût
CBAEOTL cabbage-root fly
CBAEREA cabbage-tree hat
CBLTGTE cobble together
CCAODEO cock-a-doodle-doo
CCEESCN cycle per second
CCHNENS cack-handedness
CCLAKNO Cecil Parkinson
CDOPATC code of practice
CDRIHOI Cider with Rosie
CDVRUNS cadaverousness
CEAXERS chevaux-de-frise
CECNSAE crescent-shaped
CEEEARM crème de la crème
CEESZTE crêpes suzettes
CEGMNKE clergyman's knee
CEIACLA clerical collar
CEIATIE chemical toilet
CEICIES coeliac disease
CEIIIYA credibility gap
CEITASE credit transfer
CEKUPRO checkout person
CENNSLU clean oneself up
CENPNSC clean up one's act
CENSNWI clean as a new pin
CERHGON clear the ground
CERHWYO clear the way for
CEROHEH cheer to the echo
CETFRWR chest of drawers
chest-of-drawers
CETVSII creative spirit
CIAOOIA climatological
CIARUNS chivalrousness
CICDNAL coincidentally
CICEICE chincherinchee
CIDEITN child-resistant
CIDESOR children's court
CIEEABG Chinese cabbage
CIEEATR Chinese lantern
CIEEEYA Chinese New Year
CIFHRCE chief character
CIFOSAL chief constable
CIFXCTV chief executive
CIIAMMN critical moment
CIKNERE chicken-hearted
CIKNIEE chicken-livered
CILCNAN chilli con carne
CINFATG coign of vantage
CIOIETM clitoridectomy
CIOOSAT Chilon of Sparta
CLASBLT collapsability
collapsibility
CLDNACU Caledonian Club
CLDRMTE cold dark matter
CLEFATR Colles' fracture
CLETDOK collected works
CLETNSL collect oneself
CLETRIE collector's item
CLETTEA called to the bar
CLETVFR collective farm
CLETVNU collective noun
CLICOIG Calvin Coolidge
CLIMABD calcium carbide
CLIQETO call in question
CLITATO call into action
CLMNAKN Coleman Hawkins
CLNLADF Colonel Gaddafi
CLNLKMR Colin Blakemore
CLRDBEL Colorado beetle
CLRFCAU calorific value
CLSOLEE cold shouldered
CLUACNR cultural centre
CLUAERS calculated risk
CLUEUTR culture vulture
CMADCNM command economy
CMADVEO command a view of
CMAILWT compatible with
CMAYESO company pension
CMDWHRO come down hard on
CMEEGIS compete against
CMESRTL commensurately
CMFLCRL come full circle
CMFOBHN come from behind
CMIEEFR combined effort
CMISOAR commissionaire
CMITEFC come into effect
CMITETG committee stage
CMITMMR commit to memory
CMLPRAI Camelopardalis
CMNITVE coming into view
CMOETAT component parts
CMOIUNS commodiousness
CMOLBUE common labourer
CMOOGRE common or garden
common-or-garden
CMOSNIA commonsensical
CMOTAFA common toadflax
CMOTECN come on the scene
CMOTNSL comport oneself
CMOTTTO comfort station
CMRDEHR Cambridgeshire
CMRHNIL comprehensible
comprehensibly
CMTMTRT come to maturity
CMTNUNT Compton-Burnett
CMTOEHN come to one's hand
CMTTERN come to the front
CMUCIUL compunctiously
CMUEDTN computer dating
CMUFSEE come unfastened
CMUIAIN communications
CMUTBLT combustibility
CNAGIEU consanguineous
CNAKRUL cantankerously
CNDADLA Canadian dollar
CNECNUO condescend upon
CNEECHL conference hall
CNELNSL conceal oneself
CNENNSL concern oneself
CNEPUUL contemptuously
CNESNWT conversant with
CNESOAR concessionaire
CNESTOA conversational
CNESZOE conversaziones
CNETBLT convertibility
CNETGOS concerto grosso
CNETIAL concentrically
CNETOAL conventionally
CNEVBLT conceivability
CNEVTOA conservational
CNEVTVL conservatively
CNIEHGL consider highly
CNIENRA consider normal
CNIETAL confidentially
CNIINLT conditionality
CNITNWT consistent with
CNIUTGR continuity girl
CNIUUNS continuousness
CNLMRTO conglomeration
CNLSVNS conclusiveness
CNMPRDS Cinema Paradiso
CNMTGAH cinematography
CNNCLOR canonical hours
CNNFHMS canon of the mass
CNOBHLE cannot be helped
CNOIUNS censoriousness
CNOMBLT conformability
CNPRTRA conspiratorial
CNPYOTA Can't Pay, Won't Pay
CNRCBIG contract bridge
CNRFGLS centrifugalise
CNRFGLZ centrifugalize
CNRFGTO contrafagottos
CNRGTOA congregational
CNRIDCN contraindicant
CNRIDCT contraindicate
CNRLETN central heating
CNRLNSL control oneself
CNRLOKN central locking
CNRLZTO centralization
CNRPSTO contraposition
CNRTJNL concrete jungle
CNRTLTO congratulation
CNRTLTR congratulatory
CNRTLTV congratulative
CNRTPER concrete poetry
CNRVRIL controvertible
controvertibly
CNSRSIN con espressione
CNTTTOA constitutional
CNTUTOA constructional
CNTUTVL constructively
CNTUTVS Constructivism
CNUAIUL contumaciously
CNUCIII conjunctivitis

CNUEIUL contumeliously
CNUSAOE conquistadores
CNUSEEA consuls general
CNUTDNR consuetudinary
CNUTNRO consulting room
CNUTNSL conduct oneself
COAERLD chorale prelude
COASMHN Choral Symphony
COEHDOT close the door to
COEHRCR close the record
COENONE close encounter
COEOHBN close to the bone
COEYEAE closely related
COHAENS cool-headedness
COIGEAK closing remarks
COKNDGE cloak-and-dagger
CONNACO crown and anchor
COOIEER crocodile tears
COSATRE cross batteries
COSEEEC cross-reference
COSETLZ cross-fertilize
COSETOA cross-sectional
COSNSER cross one's heart
COSOLNT cross-pollinate
COTNFCO clotting factor
CPADACR cups and saucers
CPCIMNE capuchin monkey
CPDNUNS cupidinousness
CPEBTOE copper-bottomed
CPECLUE copper-coloured
CPESLHT copper sulphate
CPIIUNS capriciousness
CPTLZTO capitalization
CQETSNS coquettishness
CRAENUT curtate annuity
CRAEUNS curvaceousness
CRANNUT certain annuity
CRBACRE cerebral cortex
CRCRIUU core curriculum
CREAITN cornet-à-pistons
CREISEO Cornelius Nepos
CREPNEC correspondence
CREPNET correspondents
CREPNWT correspond with
CRETCON current account
CRFRLIL cure for all ills
CRIANME cardinal number
CRIANWA Cardinal Newman
CRIAVRU cardinal virtue
CRICASG cardiac massage
CRIOEEI carcinogenesis
CRIOTRI corticosteroid
CRIRRSO Cartier-Bresson
CRIVSUA cardiovascular
CRKLEAA care killed a cat
CRLAAHS Cyril Ramaphosa
CRLNNIN Carolina Nairne
CRLYMRS Curtley Ambrose
CRMLZTO caramelization
CRMTCCL chromatic scale
CRMTGAH chromatography
CRMTSHR chromatosphere
CRNBRAI Corona Borealis
CRNMTIA chronometrical
CRNRATR coronary artery
CRNRBPS coronary bypass
CROAALS corpora callosa
CROADTC carrot and stick
CROAETT corporate state
CROAINA corporation tax
CROIEFC Coriolis effect
CROMNXD carbon monoxide
CROYIAI carboxylic acid
CRSINEE Christian de Wet
CRSINTA Christian Stead
CRSOHLC Christoph Gluck
CRSOHRE Christopher Lee
CRSOHRL Christopher Sly
CRSOHRR Christopher Fry
CRSOIGO Chris Bonington
CRSSOLG Christ's College
CRUABLT circumambulate
CRUAEIO corrugated iron
CRUCLOU corpus callosum
CRUGRTO circumgyration
CRULCTO circumlocution
CRULCTR circumlocutory
CRUNVGT circumnavigate
CRUSATA circumstantial
CRUSETO circumspection
CRUTBLT corruptibility
CRUTRAE circuit-breaker
CRUTUNS circuitousness
CRYNSON carry one's point
CRYTRHO carry a torch for
CSACUTN cost-accountant
cost-accounting
CSAOOCP cast a horoscope
CSAPLUO cast a spell upon
CSAPRIN cast aspersions
CSETPAE cassette player
cassette-player
CSETSNL cassette single
CSIFBOI cystic fibrosis
CSLITEI castle in the air
CSLSNPI castles in Spain
CSMDMDC Cosimo de' Medici
CSMNWNO casement window
CSOOLLN castor oil plant
CSTTEID cast to the winds
CTCEIAL catechetically
CTEIEHE Catherine wheel
CTGRSTO categorisation
CTGRZTO categorization
CTHEHNE catch red-handed
CTHLEAL catch illegally
CTHNSET catch one's death
CTLVRCU City Livery Club
CTNSETO cut one's teeth on
CTOEATB cathode-ray tube
CTOIHRL Catholic Herald
CTXEDTR cut expenditure
CTZNARS citizen's arrest
CUAEUNS courageousness
CUCAATA clutch at a straw
CUCASML Church Assembly
CUCASRW clutch at straws
CUCILAL Churchill Falls
CUCLFTT Council of State
CUDAAOS could eat a horse
CUECLBE causes célèbres
CUEHLSO cause the loss of
CUEONEG cause to undergo
CUILWRA cauliflower ear
CUSOATO course of action
CUTFESO Court of Session
CUTFPEL court of appeals
CUTFUTC court of justice
CUTHCSO count the cost of
CUTRAAC counterbalance
CUTRADN countermanding
CUTRESR countermeasure
CUTRETN counterfeiting
CUTRIOT counter-riposte
CUTRUTR counter-culture
CUTYUPI country bumpkin
CVRHBCL cover the buckle
CVRNLTE covering letter
CYNSYSU cry one's eyes out
CYUTBDN cry out to be done
CYUTBUE cry out to be used
DAAAERN dead as a herring
DAAIATS dramatic artist
DAAIGOT dramatic growth
DAETLGS dialectologist
DAHHAMT death's-head moth
DAHNHNL Death on the Nile
DAHNUNS diaphanousness
DAHOIAL diachronically
DAHRCIE death-practised
DAJHLTE Dear John letter
DAMNHNL dead man's handle
DAODEDN diamond wedding
DAODUIE diamond jubilee
DAOOEFE dead on one's feet
DARMAIA diagrammatical
DASACOL Dead Sea Scrolls
DASTGIS dead set against
DATEETO draw the teeth of
DATEOGO draw the long bow
DATEUTI draw the curtain
DATTEOL dead to the world
DAYURTL do as you are told
DCAMGIS declaim against
DCEASLT decree absolute
DCIENFL Decline and Fall
DCIIGER declining years
DCLNZTO decolonization
DCMISOE decommissioner
DCMLZTO decimalization
DCMNRAE document reader
DCMONAL decompoundable
DCNAIAE decontaminated
DCNAIAO decontaminator
DCNERTO deconsecration
DCNTUTO deconstruction
DCRSINS dechristianise
DCRSINZ dechristianize
DCRTDTL Decorated style

DCRTVNS decorativeness
DCSOMKN decision-making
DCSVMMN decisive moment
DDEHCLM dodge the column
DDYFHML daddy of them all
DEEMNRI Dieu et mon droit
DENNSHE die in one's shoes
DENNSOT die in one's boots
DEOCVNN deed of covenant
DEOEAQE Diego Velázquez
DESFOIT dregs of society
DFBILTO defibrillation
DFEETAL differentially
DFEETAO differentiator
DFNSRTO defenestration
DFNTVNS definitiveness
DGNHMNE dog in the manger
DGNNSEL dig in one's heels
DGNRTNS degenerateness
DGNSELI dig one's heels in
DGSIERC digestive tract
DIEAKAD drive backwards
DIEOEPI drive to despair
DIEOHWL drive to the wall
DIEPHWL drive up the wall
DIIGIEC driving licence
DIKIEFS drink like a fish
DIKNUTM drinking-up time
DLBRTNS deliberateness
DLBRTUO deliberate upon
DLBRTVL deliberatively
DLCALNS delectableness
DLEANET dolce far niente
DLGTUNS delightfulness
DLVRPRO delivery-person
DLVRSEC deliver a speech
DMBLZTO demobilization
DMCAIAL democratically
DMNTVNS diminutiveness
DMRLZTO demoralization
DMSMQAE demisemiquaver
DNEDYEI Daniel Day-Lewis
DNEGJUE Daniel Gajdusek
DNELGIR Dante Alighieri
DNELSEL Danielle Steele
DNERNBE danseurs nobles
DNGTERN don't get me wrong
DNIBRKM Dennis Bergkamp
DNLCMBL Donald Campbell
DNLJHNO Donald Johanson
DNMNTOA denominational
DNMNTVL denominatively
DNTBAAT Donato Bramante
DNTOAIE denationalized
DNZFCTO denazification
DOEBSNS do one's business
DOEHMWR do one's homework
DOEONHN do one's own thing
DOITECA drop in the ocean
DOOEBNL drop one's bundle
DPEITNL depreciatingly
DPFHNEL dip of the needle
DPIEFIH deprive of sight

DPLRZTO depolarization
DPNSTHO Daphnis et Chloé
DPOAIAL diplomatically
DPOALNS deplorableness
DPRMNAL departmentally
DPRTILF depart this life
DPSTCON deposit account
DRCDILN direct drilling
DRCOSHI director's chair
DRGSRTO deregistration
DRGTRNS derogatoriness
DRIRESR dernier ressort
DRNEPRO deranged person
DRTEBOK Dorothea Brooke
DRTYOGI Dorothy Hodgkin
DRTYSYR Dorothy L Sayers
DSANUNS disdainfulness
DSCNWEG disacknowledge
DSCOMDT disaccommodate
DSEADUL disregardfully
DSEFCTO Disneyfication
DSESTRL dispensatorily
DSESTVL dispensatively
DSFIITO disaffiliation
DSFIMTO disaffirmation
DSGEGNE design engineer
DSIGIHN distinguishing
DSIIENS dispiritedness
DSILNRA disciplinarian
DSLNSTO desalinisation
DSLNZTO desalinization
DSLUINS disillusionise
DSLUINZ disillusionize
DSMAKTO disembarkation
DSMIUTO disambiguation
DSMOEIH do someone right
DSMOEMN disembowelment
DSMOERN do someone wrong
DSMOERU do someone proud
DSMOUMN disemboguement
DSMTIGO do something for
DSNACRT disincarcerate
DSNEIAC disinheritance
DSNERTN disintegrating
DSNERTO disintegration
DSNEUUL disingenuously
DSNHNMN disenchantment
DSNLNTO disinclination
DSNOMTO disinformation
DSNOPRT disincorporate
DSNRNHS disenfranchise
DSOBBLT discombobulate
DSOBBRT discomboberate
DSOIBLT dissociability
DSOITFO dissociate from
DSONCEL disconnectedly
DSONEAC discountenance
DSONENS disjointedness
DSOORTO discolouration
DSOREUL discourteously
DSORGMN discouragement
DSORGNL discouragingly
DSOSLTL disconsolately

DSOSLTO disconsolation
DSOTNAC discontinuance
DSOTNEL discontentedly
DSOTNMN discontentment
DSPONMN disappointment
DSPRBTO disapprobation
DSPRBTR disapprobatory
DSPRBTV disapprobative
DSPRPIT disappropriate
DSPRVNL disapprovingly
DSQIIRT disequilibrate
DSRAGMN disarrangement
DSRBTVL distributively
DSRELNS disorderliness
DSRETTO disorientation
DSRIUAE disarticulated
DSRMNTL discriminately
DSRMNTN discriminating
DSRMNTO discrimination
DSRMNTR discriminatory
DSRMNTV discriminative
DSRNLMN disgruntlement
DSRSSGA distress signal
DSRTOAL discretionally
DSSESFA Disasters of War
DSSOITO disassociation
DSTRBTO disattribution
DSUAIUL disputatiously
DSUSTOA disquisitional
DSUSVNS discursiveness
DSYMTIA dissymmetrical
DTCIETR detective story
DTEAEHN do the same thing
DTPOESN data processing
DTPOETO data protection
DTSALNS detestableness
DTXFCTO detoxification
DUEIMXD deuterium oxide
DUHELNS daughterliness
DUHESNA daughters-in-law
DULBESE double-breasted
DULCNET double concerto
DULCOSN double-crossing
DULDCUC double-declutch
DULEPSR double exposure
DULETNR double entendre
DULNGTV double negative
DULSADN Douglas Jardine
DULSADR double standard
DULSUEA double saucepan
DUTNCSL Doubting-Castle
DUTNTOA doubting Thomas
DVDEGRO David Ben-Gurion
DVDEKWT David Berkowitz
DVDNSRE dividing screen
DVDOLHR David Coulthard
DVDSLNC David O Selznick
DVLAVCT devil's advocate
DVNCMEI Divina Commedia
DVNFCTO divinification
DVRISMN divertissement
DVRIUII diverticulitis
DVTLZTO devitalization

DWIGOLG Downing College
DWITEOT down in the mouth
DWITEUP down in the dumps
DWOOELC down on one's luck
DXRRTTR dextrorotatory
DYFTNMN Day of Atonement
DZYILSI Dizzy Gillespie
EAEBSEC exacerbescence
EAGLCLS evangelicalism
EAGLZTO evangelization
EAIAINS egalitarianism
EAIELSL examine closely
EAIENHE examine-in-chief
EAITGLI Évariste Galois
EAOAEML evaporated milk
EBEAIAL emblematically
EBLIHNL embellishingly
EBWNSAI elbow one's way in
EBYTASE embryo transfer
ECAOOIA eschatological
ECEILGS ecclesiologist
ECEISIA ecclesiastical
ECEISIU Ecclesiasticus
ECMUIAO excommunicator
ECPVLCT escape velocity
ECSMFEC excuse my French
ECUIEIH exclusive right
ECUINRE exclusion order
ECUITNL excruciatingly
ECUTRRU encounter group
EDCIELN endocrine gland
EDMAEHC Eudemian Ethics
EDRTTSA elder statesman
EDSOIAL endosmotically
EEEEBEE Ebenezer Brewer
EEEEIAL epexegetically
EEETRNS elementariness
EEHNAAE Elephanta caves
EEHNENS even-handedness
EEIGEVC evening service
EELBOHR Everly Brothers
EENLZTO eternalization
EETAOPE Electra complex
EETIGIA electric guitar
EETIWNO electric window
EETOAEC electrovalency
EETOERN electioneering
EETOHMS electrochemist
EETOHRP electrotherapy
EETOIAL electronically
EETOILG electrobiology
EETOIMI electronic mail
EETOLTN electroplating
EETOPIA electro-optical
EETOSOI electro-osmosis
EETOTTC electrostatics
EEYEODA every second day
EEYTHDO enemy at the door
EFCETAS efficient cause
EFMNTNS effeminateness
EFNTRIL enfant terrible
EFRECNL effervescingly
EFRLSNS effortlessness

EGGMNBO engagement book
EGNGOSN Eugene Goossens
EGNRQEC eigen-frequency
EGTSILN eighty shilling
EGTYASA Eighty Years' War
EHBTOAE exhibition area
EHCRIGA echocardiogram
EHLNGYO ethylene glycol
EHLOEBR Ethel Rosenberg
EHLRTNL exhilaratingly
EHOOIAL ethnologically
EHORPIA ethnographical
EHROIAL enharmonically
EIAEHAI Elizabeth David
EIAEHEN Elizabeth Kenny
EIAEHIL Elisabethville
EIAEHRN Elizabeth Frink
EIAOLTL Eliza Doolittle
EIEILGS epidemiologist
EIINZPT Emiliano Zapato
EILDROS edible dormouse
EITMLGS epistemologist
EITNILS existentialism
existentialist
EIVNERN Emil von Behring
EIYIKNO Emily Dickinson
EJYOHFL enjoy to the full
ELFTGRL Ella Fitzgerald
ELGSIAL eulogistically
EMNELSE Emmanuel Lasker
EMNIOSD Edmund Ironside
EOCSMHN Eroica Symphony
EOHRIAL exothermically
EPAHZWT emphathize with
EPDETAL expedientially
EPESNSL express oneself
EPESOLS expressionless
EPESOMR expression mark
EPESOUE express volumes
EPESVNS expressiveness
EPNECON expense account
EPNINON expansion joint
EPNINOR expansion board
EPRBIDN empire-building
EPRETAL experientially
EPRMNAL experimentally
EPRREGI emperor penguin
EPSTDNE expose to danger
EPUSIAL euphuistically
ERMNCSL Egremont Castle
EROELVN earn one's living
EROSNWC Earl of Sandwich
ERYAMTO early day motion
ESAHATB eustachian tube❑
ESEACDN ens per accidens
ESESTRA Easter Saturday
ESLDCIE easily deceived
ESLPEAE easily prepared
ESRIEOA ex-servicewoman
ETAEIUA extravehicular
ETAEUNS extraneousness
ETAOPRA extracorporeal
ETATBLT extractability

ETEENTO extreme unction
ETEEYAG extremely large
ETEEYML extremely small
ETEEYUN extremely funny
ETMOAEU extemporaneous
ETNAYHN eating anything
ETNEFML extended family
ETNSEDF eat one's head off
ETNUSAL extinguishable
ETOHCTO eutrophication
ETRANNL entertainingly
ETRFCTO esterification
ETRHDAO Enter the Dragon
ETRINTL extortionately
ETRLEAL enter illegally
ETRRSNL enterprisingly
ETRRSZN enterprise zone
ETTSEEA Estates General
EUAGLRT equiangularity
EUAINLS educationalist
EUPNEAC equiponderance
EUSFCTO emulsification
EVNRSMR en ventre sa mère
EWRAPEO Edward Appleton
EWRCSUO Edward Casaubon
EWRTELE Edward the Elder
EYOOIAL etymologically
FAAAACK flat as a pancake
FAATEOT foam at the mouth
FABRATN flabbergasting
FACIEAA Françoise Sagan
FACIVLO François Villon
FACSIAI Francis Picabia
FACSOLN Francis Poulenc
FAEEADN flame-retardant
FAEEITN flame-resistant
FAENSTO fraternisation
FAENZTO fraternization
FAENZWT fraternize with
FAFOENS flat-footedness
FAHLNNS flash blindness
FAHRRIE feather-brained
FAIIUNS flagitiousness
FAKAKNO Frank Tarkenton
FAKEETR Frankie Dettori
FAKHRHL Frank Churchill
FAKIPEC Franklin Pierce
FAOOEBC flat on one's back
FATRNSL flatter oneself
FAUERTN feature-writing
FAZLXNE Franz Alexander
FCIIUNS factitiousness
FCLYFIH faculty of sight
FDRLZTO federalization
FECDESN French dressing
FECKIKR French knickers
FEDEECR Freddie Mercury
FEDMIHE freedom fighter
freedomfighter
FEDMUAC field ambulance
FEDRILR field artillery
FEEICOI Frédéric Chopin
FEEIKBR Fredericksburg

FEEIKOD Frederick Soddy
FEEIKOW Frederick Loewe
FEETRRS free enterprise
free-enterprise
FEHNENS free-handedness
FELMNEL feeble-mindedly
FERMREO feel remorse for
FESOENS free-spokenness
FETERUH feel the draught
FFHOUNS fifth columnist
FGROSEC figure of speech
FGRTVNS figurativeness
FGTIDIL fight windmills
FGTNCAC fighting chance
FIDIHRP Friedrich Krupp
FIDRPTI Flinders Petrie
FIDRRNE Flinders Ranges
FIGBNFT fringe benefits
FIHEGNE flight engineer
FIINSAD Frisian Islands
FIMNENS fair-mindedness
FINLRMR friendly remark
FINLSNS friendlessness
FITEREL faint-heartedly
FITMDLN fair to middling
FITONNE Fridtjof Nansen
FITRMME fail to remember
FIYOMTE fairy godmother
FLAIUNS fallaciousness
FLAOPAN file a complaint
FLEETMN false testimony
FLERGAC false pregnancy
FLETTMN false statement
FLIAOMO fill in a form for
FLIGHOG falling-through
FLIIBLT falsifiability
FLILVWT fall in love with
FLOINUE Fallopian tubes
FLONTOA fellow national
FLOOEFE fall on one's feet
FLOOENS follow one's nose
FLOTERW follow the crowd
FLOTEUE follow the rules
FLPGNAE Felipe González
FLPIOIP Filippino Lippi
FLSEMHA full steam ahead
FLTBRTN full to bursting
FLYAHOE fully-fashioned
FLYEEOE fully-developed
FLYEOEE fully recovered
FLYTECE fully stretched
FMLPANN family planning
FNAAAIR Fontana Magiore
FNAAAON find a way around
FNADSTO Finlandisation
FNADZTO Finlandization
FNAETLS fundamentalism❑
fundamentalist
FNAETLT fundamentality
FNATATV find attractive
FNEHTBE fence the tables
FNEPITN finger-pointing
FNIARBE find it a problem

FNLTTMN final statement
FNMCUHI Finn mac Cumhail
FNNEOPN finance company
FNNILIE Financial Times
FNNILTT financial state
FNRLALU funeral parlour
FNRLRTO funeral oration
FNYRSBL fancy dress ball
FOAEDOS flog a dead horse
FOAONWT fool around with
FOBDOOS from bad to worse
FOBNTBN from bank to bank
FOESOLE frozen shoulder
FOPUDOC foot-pound force
FORXRIE floor exercises
FOSDTSD from side to side
FOTESOA frontierswoman
FOTITMO from this time on
FOTMTTM from time to time
FOTNBAO floating beacon
FOTNILN floating island
FRADDST Fernando de Soto
FRADOKN forward-looking
FRAITRO form a picture of
FRECENS far-fetchedness
FRENSAI force one's way in
FRETBLT fermentability
FREVNSK for heaven's sake
FRHDRTO for the duration
FRHHGJM for the high jump
FRHHLOI for the hell of it
FRHIHNS forthrightness
FRHLFOM for the life of me
FRHLSTM for the last time
FRHLVOI for the love of it
FRHMSPR for the most part
FRHRULO further outlook
FRHSBHN farthest behind
FRIALNS formidableness
FRIDNNS forbiddingness
FRIDNRI forbidden fruit
FRIHENS farsightedness
far-sightedness
FRILFEL forcible feeble
FRINRDC foreign product
FRITEAN forbid the banns
FRIYNSL fortify oneself
FRLTEOL for all the world
FRMDXRW Ford Madox Brown
FRMNGMN farm management
FRNSWHN for one's own hand
FROANTS ferromagnetism
FRODESR for good measure
FRODNTO foreordination
FROEROE for love or money
FRRCIED furor scribendi
FRSAIIT forisfamiliate
FRSOTNN foreshortening
FRTEODN first recording
FRTETOE first-mentioned
FRTPALN fore-topgallant
FRUEELN fortune-telling
FRUEUTN fortune-hunting

FRUSATR Fergus Slattery
FRUTUNS fortuitousness
FRVRNAA for ever and a day
FRVRNEE for ever and ever
FSADUIU fast and furious
FSEMNBN fisherman's bend
FSEMNKO fisherman's knot
FSIIUNS fastidiousness
FSINOGN fashionmonging
FSOTFAE fish out of water
FTESNSN Fathers and Sons
FTETGTE fitted together
FUDNFTE founding father
FUFNSIE fluff one's lines
FULTEWR four-letter word
FUTFCTO fructification
FUTISBE Fountains Abbey
FUWELRV four-wheel drive
FVPNEIC five pence piece
FVUALNS favourableness
FVUIERN favourite drink
FXDAELT fixed satellite
FYNBTRS flying buttress
FYNDTHA Flying Dutchman
FYNHFCO fly in the face of
FYNSURE flying squirrel
GADFEEC goal difference
GADLQEC grandiloquence
GADLREE glandular fever
GADTENR Grand St Bernard
GAEBRSO Gräfenberg spot
GAHCOML graphic formula
GAHCTBE graphics tablet
GAMRHCE grammar checker
GAOGIHO go along with you
GAOIIMS Glagolitic Mass
GAOOUCN Giacomo Puccini
GAPHNTL grasp the nettle
GASOENU grass someone up
GATCUEA Giant's Causeway
GATNUYO Glastonbury Tor
GAVLEIK Granville Hicks
GDAEHMR God save the mark
GDONONR God's own country
GDWTERI go down the drain
GDWTEUE go down the tubes
GEAIUNS gregariousness
GEGDHAR Gielgud Theatre
GEHUDEB Greyhound Derby
GEIFOBL Gaelic football
GELTRTR grey literature
GENADHL Greenland whale
GENRSCD Green Cross Code
GEOYFOR Gregory of Tours
GEOYFYS Gregory of Nyssa
GETHTHP great white hope
GETLVLK Great Slave Lake
GETSAON greatest amount
GETSEFR greatest effort
GETSETN greatest extent
GFRHDCO go for the doctor
GIACNAC gain ascendancy
GIFTJYE Griffith-Joyner

Words marked ❑ can also be spelled with an initial capital letter

GIGLNWT going along with
GIGOHWL going to the wall
GIGWYRS going-away dress
GIGYHBO going by the book
GITOHML grist to the mill
GLEPESN golden pheasant
GLEPVLO Golden Pavilion
GLETHLO Gilbert Sheldon
GLETSAD Gilbert Islands
GLINERN Gillian Wearing
GLKHTAE go like hot cakes
GLLOAIE Galileo Galilei
GLTNZTO gelatinization
GMLEPCL Gamaliel Pickle
GNAFHGE Gandalf the Grey
GNAOIAL genealogically
GNAYAAE Gennady Yanayev
GNEOOIA gynaecological
GNESEII gender-specific
GNFRBRO gone for a Burton
GNRFCTO gentrification
GNRLONI general council
GNRLSIO generalissimos
GNRLUPS general-purpose
GNRLZTO generalization
GNRTVNS generativeness
GNTCAET genetic parents
GNTLAAL genethliacally
GOACSOE grow accustomed
GOADNBU go on and on about
GOANPSN Giovanni Pisano
GOAOEWR good as one's word
GOCNCEC good conscience
GOERIHK globe artichoke
GOETIAL geocentrically
GOFEFSE Geoffrey Fisher
GOFETYO Geoffrey Taylor
GOFLOSI good fellowship
GOFROHN good-for-nothing
GOGBREE George Berkeley
GOGGRHI George Gershwin
GOGHRIO George Harrison
GOGJFRY George Jeffreys
GOGKIHL George Knightly
GOGLNBR George Lansbury
GOGMGVR George McGovern
GOGMRDT George Meredith
GOGMRHL George Marshall
GOGOAAI Giorgio Vasarib
GOGSIEO Georges Simenon
GOGTEEE Georgette Heyer
GOHMUEL good-humouredly
GONBEKN ground-breaking
GONLSNS groundlessness
GONSIAL geognostically
GOOIATM geological time
GOOIIAL geopolitically
GORPIAL geographically
GOSOONS goods for own use
GOTEAPG go on the rampage
GOTFNSA go out of one's way
GOTIDSR growth industry
GOTNHTW go out on the town
GOVBAIN Good Vibrations
GOYFHSO glory of the snow
GOYODNS goody-goodiness
GRASEHR German Shepherd
GRIHERE garnishee order
GRIKHAR Garrick Theatre
GRLGRIE Gerald Gardiner
GRNOOIA gerontological
GROLNDL Gordon Lonsdale
GRORCAD Gordon Richards
GRTOOKE Gareth of Orkney
GRYIORN Garry Winogrand
GSAEORE Gustave Courbet
GSPRTWY go separate ways
GSUEOAD gesture towards
GTALEGH go to all lengths
GTAYEGH go to any lengths
GTEMRHN gutter-merchant
GTETGTE gather together
GTFEUNL go to frequently
GTFOEBK get off one's bike
GTHBEZU get the breeze up
GTHBTEO get the better of
GTIGHOG getting-through
GTNOCWT get in touch with
GTNRNWT get in wrong with
GTNSADO get one's hands on
GTNSEET get one's deserts
GTNSEOE get one's leg over
GTNSLOU get one's blood up
GTNSNAA get one's end away
GTNSWBC get one's own back
GTOEHTY get some shut-eye
GTOENAI get someone at it
GTOENDW get someone down
GTOISBS get to first base
GTORPWT get to grips with
GTPRVLO get approval for
GTTEONR go to the country
GTTNHNC get it in the neck
GUEPGUT Giuseppe Giusti
GUGAHUH grudge a thought
GUITEOL go up in the world
GVAAKNT give a talking-to
GVAAMRN give a hammering
GVAANMT give a bad name to
GVAESNO give a reason for
GVAIHNT give a big hand to
GVAITLO give a dirty look
GVAONOE give a going-over
GVAUGMN give a judgement
GVAUMRO give a summary of
GVAUSDT give a subsidy to
GVCEECT give credence to
GVCRECT give currency to
GVFERIT give free rein to
GVIECAG give in exchange
GVIORNI Gavrilo Princip
GVPESRT give pleasure to
GVPRISO give permission
GVRAOSO give reasons for
GVSFRGT give suffrage to
GVSRNTT give strength to
GVTEENT give the reins to
GVTEEVH give the heave-ho
GVTELOT give the elbow to
GVTEODW give the low-down
GVTEOHA give the go-ahead
GVUOELF give up one's life
GVUOEPS give up one's post
GVUTEHS give up the ghost
GWLTGTE go well together
GWTTEOS go with the worse
HAEAAPC Hoare-Laval Pact
HAEECAG heated exchange
HAELBDE heavenly bodies
HAIIEAE Heaviside layer
HASNTRW heads and thraws
HATERHN heart-searching
HATYOKN healthy-looking
HAYRAHN heavy breathing
HBASIAL Hebraistically
HBICMUE hybrid computer
HBLCNTN Hubble constant
HBLDHYS hobbledehoyish
HBRHMHE Hubert Humphrey
HBTNRPT habit and repute
HCSMOEF hack someone off
HDALCRK hydraulic brake
HDALCRS hydraulic press
HDETESR hidden treasure
HDLTGTE huddle together
HDOEHLU hydrocephalous
HDOHBCT hydrophobicity
HDOOIAL hydrologically
hydroponically
HDOYAIA hydrodynamical
HDTDIES hydatid disease
HEACIAL hierarchically
HEOLPIA hieroglyphical
HGCMISO High Commission
HGEGEMN Hague Agreement
HGHNENS high-handedness
HGLETEE highly esteemed
HGLNCTL Highland cattle
HGLRGRE highly regarded
highly-regarded
HGLSAOE highly seasoned
highly-seasoned
HGMCIRI Hugh MacDiarmid
HGMNENS high-mindedness
HGOCPCT hygroscopicity
HGORPIA hagiographical
HGPICPE high-principled
HGSREBN high-street bank
HGYLVUE highy-flavoured
HIRCOBR Heinrich Olbers
HIRCRHE Heinrich Rohrer
HLDRANS Halldór Laxness
HLETATO holier-than-thou
HLFRETE hell for leather
HLIAEAC hold in abeyance
HLICNEP hold in contempt
HLIGATR holding pattern
HLIGOPN holding company
HLITEER hole in the heart

HLNBIFO hold no brief for
HLOEGON hold one's ground
HLOEHRE hold one's horses
HLOETNU hold one's tongue
HLOEWIH hold one's whisht
HLORPIA heliographical
HLOTGIS hold out against
HLPNYOT halfpennyworth
HLSELON hold spellbound
HLSRPUE holy Scriptures
HLTEOTO hold the fort for
HLUIOEI hallucinogenic
HLUOEHA hold up one's head
HMBCBIG humpback bridge
HMDFCTO humidification
HMEADOG hammer and tongs
HMEAFIE homme d'affaires
HMETUBR Humbert Humbert
HMGNZTO homogenization
HMHEBGR Humphrey Bogart
HMHYLNE Humphry Clinker
HMLEPTA Hemel Hempstead
HMNEORE human resources
HMRLYAG Hamersley Range
HMSMCNE Hamish MacInnes
HMULSNS humourlessness
HNAOFRB Hans Adolf Krebs
HNAONWT hang around with
HNEGTEE hunter-gatherer
HNEOTAE Henley-on-Thames
HNIGNHR hanging in there
HNIHNWT hand in hand with
HNIRFSA handicraftsman
HNITAAI Henrietta Maria
HNIURCE Henri Dutrochet
HNKRHEE handkerchieves
HNRDBLA Honoré de Balzac
HNRKOET Hendrik Lorentz
HNSFPLC hands-off policy
HNUALNS honourableness
HNUYEIO Hanbury-Tenison
HNYAEDS Henry Cavendish
HNYISNE Henry Kissinger
HNYONEN Henry John Heinz
HOYNFIL hooly and fairly
HPCIIAL hypocritically
HPCODIS hypochondriast
HPCRSIA hypocoristical
HPDRIAL hypodermically
HPEIGFE happening often
HPETGTE happen together
HPEYOPT hippety-hoppety
HPKPNJM hop, skip and jump
HPRAIAL hyperbatically
HPRESTS hypersensitise
HPRESTV hypersensitive
HPRESTZ hypersensitize
HPRETEI hyperaesthesia
HPRETLT hyperventilate
HPRLCEI hyperglycaemia
HPRNLTO hyperinflation
HPROIAL hyperbolically
HPRRTCS hypercriticise
hypercriticism
HPRRTCZ hypercriticize
HPSAIAL hypostatically
HPTEIAL hypothetically
HPTPNJM hop, step and jump
HPTYODS hypothyroidism
HRADDST Hernando de Soto
HRADENE Hero and Leander
HRAHOII hermaphroditic
HRAMLIL Herman Melville
HRANORN Hermann Goering
HRDTBLT hereditability
HRDTRNS hereditariness
HREAIUE horse latitudes
HREDUNS horrendousness
HRETACS Herbert Marcuse
HRETPNE Herbert Spencer
HRETSUT Herbert Asquith
HRHAENS hard-headedness
HRIGACU Hurlingham Club
HRINFAO Heraion of Samos
HRIUTRS horticulturist
HRLHRFO Harold Harefoot
HRLIDVC heraldic device
HRLSOLG Herald's College
HRLTELC hardly the place
HROIMTO harmonic motion
HROIUNS harmoniousness
HROSRCE horror-stricken
HRSNSIE herbs and spices
HRSSXAL harass sexually
HRTSMSE hard taskmaster
HRUEBEL Hercules beetle
HRYEFIG Harry Selfridge
HRYNOHL harrying of hell
HSADNWF husband and wife
HSAESOG his cake is dough
HSEETMS hysterectomise
HSEETMZ hysterectomize
HSEHERO Hesketh Pearson
HSIADCO hospital doctor
HSIALNS hospitableness
HSOEIAL histogenically
HSOIGAH historiography
HSOOIAL histologically
HSOYIAL histolytically
HSROIAL histrionically
HTAEBTL hot-water bottle
HTFTERS hot off the press
HTNBTEE hot and bothered
HTRCRMU heterochromous
HTRPYLU heterophyllous
HUEADKE housemaid's knee
HUEFLFM house of ill fame
HUEFOMN House of Commons
HUEFOSI house of worship
HUEHSCA house-physician
HUEODOD household goods
HVAEFCO have an effect on
HVAERNO have a bearing on
HVAHPON have a whip-round
HVAIEOS have a tile loose
HVAIIGO have a liking for
HVAIPCO have an impact on
HVAISLC have as its place
HVAOEHM have as one's home
HVAOIGY have a roving eye
HVARAMN have a great mind
HVARIWV have a brainwave
HVBEAON have been around
HVCMTSA have come to stay
HVCNIEC have confidence
HVEEYHN have everything
HVFRYIK have forty winks
HVHDGTU have had a gutful
HVHDNSA have had one's day
HVIAAWT have it away with
HVIBTWY have it both ways
HVIOEHN have in one's hand
HVISOTI have its roots in
HVMSIIG have misgivings
HVNAOTD having a lot to do
HVNNQAM having no qualms
HVNPOLM having problems
HVNWRSO have no words for
HVOATVT hive of activity
HVOEEEO have one's eyes on
HVOEFLO have one's fill of
HVOEHMI have one's home in
HVOEOMN have one too many
HVRCUST have recourse to
HVSLRGT have sole rights
HVTEAGO have the laugh of
HVTEOSO have the hots for
HWHLNLE how the land lies
HWHWNLE how the wind lies
IACOEBR Isaac Rosenberg
IAEIAEO Isabelita Perón
IAELAJN Isabelle Adjani
IAEOVRE image converter
IAIELOL in an ideal world
IAINBLT inalienability
IAITEHL in a little while
IAIUERW in a minute or two
IALIHJC I'm all right, Jack
IANSEAA Ioannis Metaxas
IAOETRW in a moment or two
IAOHRLC in another place
IAPISCN in a split second
IAPOCAL inapproachably
IAPSTNS inappositeness
IASIIUL inauspiciously
IATCLTL inarticulately
IATCPTO in anticipation
IATFCAL inartificially
IATRBLT inalterability
IATSIAL inartistically
IATTOFU in a state of flux
IAVSBLT inadvisability
IBDODTO in bad condition
IBERSOS inbred response
IBIAERO imbricated roof
ICEILNS incredibleness
ICESISZ increase in size
ICESMTE Increase Mather
ICMESRT incommensurate

ICMLTNS incompleteness
ICMOIUL incommodiously
ICMUIAL incommunicable
incommunicably
ICNEINE inconvenienced
ICNEINL inconveniently
ICNEUNL inconsequently
ICNIEAL inconsiderable
inconsiderably
ICNIRBM incendiary bomb
ICNITNL inconsistently
ICNIUUL incontiguously
ICNLSVL inconclusively
ICNRLAL incontrollably
ICPCTTN incapacitating
ICPCTTO incapacitation
ICROELT incorporeality
ICUIUNS incautiousness
IDACVLA Indian Civil War
IDAEEHN Indian elephant
IDAURSN Indian Uprising
IDBTBLT indubitability
IDCINOO induction motor
IDCPEAL indecipherable
IDCRNTO indoctrination
IDCRUNS indecorousness
IDCSVNS indecisiveness
IDCTORL indication rule
IDFIUTE in difficulties
IDFNTNS indefiniteness
IDMNTAL indemonstrable
indemonstrably
IDMTBLT indomitability
IDOFRWR indoor firework
IDRCOJC indirect object
IDRCSEC indirect speech
IDSEPIL indiscerptible
IDSGEMN in disagreement
IDSICNS indistinctness
IDSRCIL indestructible
indestructibly
IDSRMNT indiscriminate
IDTRIAL indeterminable
indeterminably
IDVSBLT indivisibility
IECPBLT inescapability
IECTBLT inexcitability
IEEGETC iceberg lettuce
IEEYEPC in every respect
IEFCULT ineffectuality
IEIALNS inevitableness
IELSIAL idealistically
IEPESBE inexpressibles
IETAELN inertia selling
IETFCTO identification
IETTCII identity crisis
IEYUPRO I beg your pardon?
IFAMBLT inflammability
IFATUTR infrastructure
IFCIUNS infectiousness
IFEILNS inflexibleness
IFRINAT in foreign parts
IFTAEWT infatuated with
IGAITNL ingratiatingly
IGETUBR in great numbers
IGOIUNS ingloriousness
IHHOOIA ichthyological
IHROIUL inharmoniously
IHRTNEA inheritance tax
IIGNHCK icing on the cake
IIHOFON Irish wolfhound
IIIALNS inimitableness
IIPTIAL idiopathically
IKEPITN ink-jet printing
ILCPRNI in loco parentis
ILGLRFI illegal traffic
ILGTMTL illegitimately
ILHNTET I'll thank them to
ILOAGEE Isle of Anglesey
ILOTNAN ill-gotten gains
ILREUBR in large numbers
ILSRTOA illustrational
ILSRTVL illustratively
ILVNMMR in living memory
IMBLZTO immobilization
IMCLTNS immaculateness
IMDRTNS immoderateness
IMIMRHN Ismail Merchant
IMNRSOS immune response
IMNSPRS immunosuppress
IMTOIAL immethodically
INMNTBN innominate bone
INMRBLT innumerability
INVTVNS innovativeness
IODNTNS inordinateness
IOEALNS inoperableness
IOEBRDY in one's born days
IOEELWO in one fell swoop
IOEMNSY in one's mind's eye
IOEONIH in one's own right
IOIMTIA isodiametrical
IOPSTOT in opposition to
IOSRVNK Igor Stravinsky
IOTEIVS I don't believe so
IOWRHPE idol-worshipper
IPAALNS implacableness
IPANNLS in plain English
IPASBLT implausibility
IPATCLT impracticality
IPEEECT in preference to
IPEETTO implementation
IPENBLT impregnability
IPESOAL impressionable
IPESRAL impress greatly
IPESVNS impressiveness
IPNYUBR in penny numbers
IPOOTOT in proportion to
IPRAPLC Imperial Palace
IPREBLT impermeability
IPRETVL imperfectively
IPRIUNS imperviousness
IPRTVNS imperativeness
IPSALNS impassableness
IPVRSMN impoverishment
IRCNIAL irreconcilable
irreconcilably
IRFTBLT irrefutability
IRMVBLT irremovability
IRPOCAL irreproachable
irreproachably
IRPRBLT irreparability
IRSETVL irrespectively
IRSETVO irrespective of
IRSLTNS irresoluteness
IRSOSVL irresponsively
IRSRIAL irrestrainable
IRSSIAL irresuscitably
IRTOAFA irrational fear
IRUDUBR in round numbers
IRVCBLT irrevocability
ISAMNPA instalment plan
ISBRANS in sober sadness
ISDRELN insider dealing
ISETROS Inspector Morse
ISFIINL insufficiently
ISGIIAC insignificance
ISLBIUL insalubriously
ISLTNTP insulating tape
ISMAHWT in sympathy with
ISMOEDB in someone's debt
ISNTRNS insanitariness
ISORUEA it's your funeral
ISPRBLT inseparability
insuperability
ISPRSIL insuppressible
insuppressibly
ISRMNAL instrumentally
ISRONAL insurmountable
insurmountably
ISRTBLT inscrutability
ISSETVL insusceptively
ISTALNS insatiableness
ITASGNL intransigently
ITASTVL intransitively
ITASUAL intransmutable
ITATBLT intractability
ITEAEAA in the same way as
ITEAEAO in the same canoe
ITEAIYA in the family way
ITEAKTO in the market for
ITEBECO in the absence of
ITEEINN in the beginning
ITEENHL in the meanwhile
ITENWBU in the know about
ITEOERN in the forefront
ITEOFIH in the top flight
ITEONOK in the boondocks
ITEOTOO in the control of
ITERCSO in the process of
ITLETAL intellectually
ITLIETI intelligentsia
ITLRBLT intolerability
ITMETVL intempestively
ITOUTRL introductorily
ITRAOGN internal organs
ITREEDN interdependent
ITREERT interpenetrate
ITREITL intermediately
ITREITO intermediation

ITRELTO interpellation
ITREOEE interferometer
ITRESOA intercessional
ITRESRA intercessorial
ITRETOA interjectional
intersectional
ITRIETO interlineation
ITRIGAL interlingually
ITRITNL intermittently
ITRLNTR interplanetary
ITRMUAR interambulacra
ITRODSG interior design
ITRONCE interconnected
ITRPTAL interspatially
ITRRTTO interpretation
ITRRTTV interpretative
ITRRTVL interpretively
ITRUCUT interpunctuate
ITRUTVL interruptively
ITTEAGI into the bargain
IVIHGIS inveigh against
IVNLNMI Irving Langmuir
IVOALNS inviolableness
IVRECMA inverted commas
IWIHEEV In Which We Serve
IWRIGRE in working order
IYSTKGW Ieyasu Tokugawa
JAHNIAR Jean Henri Fabre
JAISLNE J David Salinger
JALCEAN Jean-Luc Dehaene
JANTOLP Joanna Trollope
JAPUSRR Jean-Paul Sartre
JASTELN Joan Sutherland
JBFRHBY jobs for the boys
JCBRNWK Jacob Bronowski
JCCNIGA Jack Cunningham
JCICALO Jackie Charlton
JCSNOLC Jackson Pollock
JCUSERD Jacques Derrida
JDTEBCR Jude the Obscure
JHBYDNO John Boyd Dunlop
JHCRSSO John Chrysostom
JHCUHDM John Couch Adams
JHDNSOU John Duns Scotus
JHGLWRH John Galsworthy
JHLGEAR John Logie Baird
JHMLUHI John McLaughlin
JHNEBAM Johannes Brahms
JHNEFGE Johannes Fugger
JHNEKPE Johannes Kepler
JHNEMLE Johannes Müller
JHNLEEC Johnny Lee Bench
JHOTERS John of the Cross
JHRTEFR John Rutherford
JHSURML John Stuart Mill
JHTEATS John the Baptist
JHVNEMN John Von Neumann
JIEXRCO juice extractor
JITEOOR join the colours
JLACLNA Julian calendar
JLPNPPE jalapeño pepper
JLRVLTO July Revolution
JLUDDKN Julius Dedekind
JLUVNAH Julius von Sachs
JMETGTE jammed together
JMSAKNO James Parkinson
JMSALGA James Callaghan
JMSDIWB James Edwin Webb
JMSGRIL James A Garfield
JNEDIOR Jan Hendrik Oort
JNOSIAL jingoistically
JPNSWRO Japanese War God
JRSITOA jurisdictional
JRSLMRS Jerusalem cross
JRYRTWK Jerzy Grotowski
JSCPBAC José Capablanca
JSHAICE Joschka Fischer
JSIIBLT justifiability
JSPGEBL Joseph Goebbels
JSPGIAD Joseph Grimaldi
JSPIEAE Josephine Baker
JSPMCRH Joseph McCarthy
JSPNSMN just punishment
JSPPLTE Joseph Pulitzer
JSPRWTE Joseph Rowntree
JSRMSOT José Ramos-Horta
JSTEEES just the reverse
JSURYOD Joshua Reynolds
JUNYHOG journey through
JWLESOG jeweller's rouge
JWSCLNA Jewish calendar
JYEASIL Jayne Mansfield
JZFISDK Józef Pilsudski
KAPLSTP Krapp's Last Tape
KCITEAT kick in the pants
KCITEET kick in the teeth
KEAAMOG keep a calm sough
KEAIHRI keep a tight rein
KEAODOS keep a good house
KEERYOR keep early hours
KEOECIU keep one's chin up
KEOEHIO keep one's hair on
KEOEHNI keep one's hand in
KEOEMNO keep one's mind on
KEOEWOO keep one's wool on
KEOTFIH keep out of sight
KETAELN keep travelling
KEUDRRP keep under wraps
KIHBCEO knight bachelor
knight-bachelor
KIHSEPA Knights Templar
KIKROKR knickerbockers
KITNNEL knitting needle
KIYRSHO kailyard school
KLIGNSL killing oneself
KLOGOLG Kellogg College
KLOTERS kill on the cross
KNAAEAE Konrad Adenauer
KNEHRHM Kenneth Grahame
KNEHRNG Kenneth Branagh
KNIIGTN Ken Livingstone
KOAOERW know a move or two
KOKNHHA knock on the head
KOOEOIN know one's onions
KPSSACM Kaposi's sarcoma
KRAHMLO Karma Chameleon
KRLGRIL Karl Lagerfield
KRSHITR Kurt Schwitters
KRTNZTO keratinization
KTHNAIE kitchen cabinet
KTYHTOT Kathy Whitworth
KYOEUGR keyhole surgery
KYTNEFC keystone effect
KZNAHDA Kazan Cathedral
LAAEIHL lead apes in hell
LAEFBEC leave of absence
LAEOFET leave no effects
LAEQETO loaded question
LAIGCRS leading actress
LALYAAR Leaellynasaura
LASNFIE liaison officer
LATTELA lead to the altar
LBAYDTO library edition
LBAYIDN library binding
LBDNUNS libidinousness
LBRAINS libertarianism
LBRLZTO liberalization
LBUECAG labour exchange
LCIAHIT Lacrima Christi
LCLUHRT local authority
LCNIUNS licentiousness
LCOBNVL lector benevole
LCOEWUD lick one's wounds
LCOITRS lack of interest
LCOVTLT lack of vitality
LCRMLLN lachrymal gland
LCSALYE Lucas van Leyden
LCSLSIU locus classicus
LCUAUEU Lucius Apuleius
LDADHSA Leda and the Swan
LDDYOIA Lady Day Holiday
LDOTEIH lady of the night
LDVCEND Ludovic Kennedy
LEADSAD Leeward Islands
LEUKRVN Lee Buck Trevino
LFATRET life after death
LFEPCAC life expectancy
LFITEUC left in the lurch
LGADAAR Le Grand Macabre
LGBIUNS lugubriousness
LGLSIAL legalistically
LGTEREL light-heartedly
LGTLWIH light-flyweight
LGTMSTO legitimisation
LGTMTNS legitimateness
LGTMZTO legitimization
LGTNUTM lighting-up time
LGTOLTO light pollution
LIETRHR Leicestershire
LIUEUSI leisure pursuit
LKIOLMI like it or lump it
LKMNENS like-mindedness
LKOECOE Lake Okeechobee
LKTNAYK Lake Tanganyika
LKWNEMR Lake Windermere
LMAPNTR lumbar puncture
LMEGLIE Lemuel Gulliver
LMTDDTO limited edition
LMTDOPN limited company

LMTNFCO limiting factor
LNCEOLG Linacre College
LNEITRS landed interest
LNHRBEL longhorn beetle
LNIGIRR lending library
LNITEOT long in the tooth
LNIUIAL longitudinally
LNJHSLE Long John Silver
LNMNGMN land management
LNOBONO Lyndon B Johnson
LNOBREE Lennox Berkeley
LNOBSNS line of business
LNOEPCE line one's pocket
LNOMRTO London Marathon
LNONOLG Lincoln College
LNOOEFE land on one's feet
LNPRIMN Long Parliament
LNUSIAL linguistically
LNWNENS long-windedness
LOADOLE Leonard Woolley
LOALVRO look all over for
LODOEGA Lloyd Honeyghan
LOETILN Lionel Trilling
LOFRRUL look for trouble
LOHRHTE Leonhard Hutter
LOIBEHE Leonid Brezhnev
LOIEASN Léonide Massine
LOIGOWR looking forward
LOIKACU Leonid Kravchuk
LQAIUNS loquaciousness
LQIPRFI liquid paraffin
LRCACLO Lord Chancellor
LRCLALD Lyrical Ballads
LRETALF larger than life
LRLETNN Lord Lieutenant
LROTELE Lord of the Flies
LRSNLDE lords and ladies
lords-and-ladies
LRSPRTA Lords Spiritual
LSETRAO listen to reason
LSIIUNS lasciviousness
LSLUSUA Les Fleurs du Mal
LSNOEHI losing one's hair
LSOCNET list of contents
LSOEBTL lose one's bottle
LSOETME lose one's temper
LSOETNU lose one's tongue
LSRIHSO laser-light show
LSTANTM less than no time
LTAMTHU Lothar Matthaus
LTEOCEI letter of credit
LTEOTEA letter of the law
LTEVNRS Luther Vandross
LTHSDDW let the side down
LTLADAG Little and Large
LTLBLTL little by little
LTLGENE little green men
LTOENHV let someone have
LTOENKO let someone know
LTOSRCE Lytton Strachey
LTRLZTO lateralization
LTRRRVE Literary Review
LTTDNRA latitudinarian
LUCLTOB Launcelot Gobbo
LUCLTUA Launcelot du Lac
LUEADAD Laurel and Hardy
LUECBNO Laurence Binyon
LUECESE Laurence Eusden
LUECSEN Laurence Sterne
LUSHVOE Louis Chevrolet
LUSLHSE Louis Althusser
LUSOBLA Louis Roubiliac
LUSRSRN Louis Armstrong
LVADELV live and let live
LVADRAH live and breathe
LVNKNNS loving-kindness
LVNQATR living quarters
LVOTEHA live on the cheap
LVOTEOK Love on the Rocks
LVSNSNG Love Songs in Age
LWFHJNL law of the jungle
LWSOTEO lowest of the low
LXCGAHS lexicographist
LYFLECN lay a false scent
LYNSADO lay one's hands on
LYONEPN lay down weapons
MAIGUNS meaningfulness
MAMRADF Muammar Gaddafi
MASFEES means of release
MASFUPR means of support
MBTSZSK Mobutu Seze Seko
MCALAAA Michael Faraday
MCALAKO Michael Jackson
MCALATR Michaelmas term
MCALECE Michael Meacher
MCALETI Michael Ventris
MCALETN Michael Bentine
MCALIPT Michael Tippett
MCALODN Michael Holding
MCALODR Michael Hordern
MCALOGA Michael Douglas
MCALOLN Michael Collins
MCALONO Michael Johnson
MCALORY Michael Holroyd
MCECERU Michel Chevreul
MCEFUAL Michel Foucault
MCESILN Mickey Spillane
MCEZEAG' Mackenzie Range
MCEZEIE Mackenzie River
MCHRIAL mock-heroically
MCIEOEE machine-powered
MCOCNMC macroeconomics
microeconomics
MCOEHLU macrocephalous
MCOILGS microbiologist
MCOOIAL micrologically
MCOPRNI microsporangia
MCORAIM micro-organisms
MCORCSO microprocessor
MCRNCES macaroni cheese
MCSHPUE mocks the pauses
MCTRLSU mock turtle soup
MCUACLI Macaulay Culkin
MCUMMRN mucous membrane
MDCLCEC medical science
MDCLFIE Medical Officer
medical officer
MDCMNAL medicamentally
MDIHCWO Midnight Cowboy
MDLDSAC middle distance
MDLHAEL muddleheadedly
MDLNSLO model oneself on
MDLSMNS meddlesomeness
MDRPITR Modern Painters
MGEATRA Miguel Asturias
MGEIDRI Miguel Indurain
MGEINEL magnetic needle
MGEISRP magnetic stripe
MGIOUNL magniloquently
MGITLIE Maggie Tulliver
MHMASAI Muhammad Sharif
MHMEADE Mohammed Aideed
MHNAGNH Mohandas Gandhi
MHYNSTA Mahayana Sutras
MIIGEIN main ingredient
MITRIGR Meistersingers
MKAALUO make a balls-up of
MKACSIL make accessible
MKAEDEA make a dead set at
MKAEINN make a beginning
MKAIHOI make a night of it
MKAISAO make a pig's ear of
MKALAUI Mikhail Bakunin
MKALWNE make allowances
MKAODOO make a good job of
MKAOGBU make a song about
MKAOROT make a poor mouth
MKAOTOI make a bolt for it
MKAQANE make acquainted
MKATTMN make a statement
MKBETLS make breathless
MKCNESN make conversant
MKDSODN make despondent
MKFIHEE make frightened
MKIDSIC make indistinct
MKJKSBU make jokes about
MKLSSCR make less secure
MKMRSAL make more stable
MKMRSCR make more secure
MKMRWTR make more watery
MKOEECP make one's escape
MKOEHMI make one's home in
MKOERUD make one's rounds
MKRNSON make rings round
MKRPRTO make reparation
MKSFEAT make so free as to
MKSMOEA make someone pay
MKTEITM make the big time
MKTEUNN make the running
MKUDRTO make understood
MKUOEMN make up one's mind
MKVLEAL make vulnerable
MKWTHOG make wet through
MKWTRIH make watertight
MKYUHNO make you think of
MLCAVNS male chauvinism
male chauvinist
MLEAINS millenarianism
MLIAILS multiracialism

Words marked ☐ can also be spelled with an initial capital letter

MLIAIUL multifariously
MLIGAHN milking machine
MLILCOC multiple-choice
MLILCTO multiplication
MLOFIDA Milton Friedman
MLOMAGN Malcolm Sargent
MLOMIKN Malcolm Rifkind
MLOTNEL malcontentedly
MLPRPIT malappropriate
MLTRPLC Military Police
military police
MLTRZTO militarization
MLUCINN malfunctioning
MMSOFLE Mr Mistoffelees
MNAATTD mental attitude
MNADSRE mental disorder
MNAHNIA mental handicap
MNAHSIA mental hospital
MNAICLA mandarin collar
MNCPLOR municipal court
MNEBSNS monkey business
MNEOLVN manner of living
MNFHMMN man of the moment
MNFSISL manifest itself
MNGALNS manageableness
MNLNULS monolingualism
MNNHSRE man in the street
MNNOSBC man on horseback
MNNRYUT men in grey suits
MNNSPRA Man and Superman
MNOEFNE mend one's fences
MNPTOGS monophthongise
MNPTOGZ monophthongize
MNRLZTO mineralization
MNSCHRD monosaccharide
MNTULYL menstrual cycle
MPITPEE Mephistopheles
MRAAIAL morganatically
MRACPAL more acceptable
MRADEOT Maria Edgeworth
MRADHAR Mermaid Theatre
MRAEAWO Margaret Atwood
MRAEFLE Margaret Fuller
MRAESNE Margaret Sanger
MRAGLMN Murray Gell-Mann
MRCLUNS miraculousness
MRELUNS marvellousness
MRERSAC market research
MRGRREL Marc Girardelli
MRHGLHR Martha Gellhorn
MRHNODR marching orders
marching-orders
MRIGBRA marriage bureau
MRIGEVC morning service
MRIGRYR morning prayers
MRIKART Martin Klaproth
MRISOSS Martin Scorsese
MRISRST Martin Sarasate
MRIVNUE Martin Van Buren
MRLETIT moral certainty
MRLTNAD moral standards
MROABSE Marco Van Basten
MROIPOP Marjorie Proops
MROSMER mirror symmetry
MROTEES mark of the Beast
MRTAEOG more than enough
MRTIIUL meretriciously
MRUARLU Marcus Aurelius
MRUATNU Marcus Antonius
MRUGIES Marburg disease
MRWTARS mark with a cross
MSACLTO miscalculation
MSAEBLE mistaken belief
MSAENSA mistake one's man
MSAONWT mess around with
MSEAUTO mass evacuation
MSEIUNS mysteriousness
MSEOSLE Mesdemoiselles
MSERSNE misrepresented
MSFVUAL most favourable
MSIGWNL Mrs Tiggy-Winkle
MSITEHN mose in the chine
MSJABOI Miss Jean Brodie
MSJNMRL Miss Jane Marple
MSNEPEE misinterpreted
MSNIOLN Mason-Dixon Line
MSNOMTO misinformation
MSNTCAL most noticeable
MSPLCTO misapplication
MSPOUTO mass production
mass-production
MSPRCAE misappreciated
MSPRPIT misappropriate
MSRNLTO mistranslation
MSRVRNE Musgrave Ranges
MSUOLNO Museum of London
MSUSIAL most unsuitable
MTAIDCO mutual inductor
MTAONAN Matra Mountains
MTCLUNS meticulousness
MTEAIAL mathematically
MTEFMLA matresfamilias
MTENBIE motte and bailey
MTEOCUS matter of course
MTEOFCL matter-of-factly
MTESPRO mother superior
MTHWRML Matthew Bramble
MTLOPST metal composite
MTMSCOE metempsychoses
MTMSCOI metempsychosis
MTOIANS methodicalness
MTOLSNS motionlessness
MTOOHNU matron of honour
MTOOIAL mythologically
MTOOOIA meteorological
methodological
MTOSCNS motion sickness
MTPOIAL metaphorically
MTPYHLG metapsychology
MTPYIAL metaphysically
MTRIYEV maternity leave
MTVTOAL motivationally
MUIETIL Maurice Utrillo
MUTIBAE mountain beaver
MUTIBKN mountain biking
MUTIERN mountaineering
MVRNSAE mover and shaker
MVSELHL move stealthily
MVUSEDL move unsteadily
MXEVRRO Max Beaverbrook
MYTLAEO may it please you
NATANME near that number
NATENCL near the knuckle
NBCANZA nebuchadnezzar[□]
NBESOLG noblesse oblige
NCABLTO noctambulation
NCBRSAD Nicobar Islands
NCERECO nuclear reactor
NCERHSC nuclear physics
NCERISO nuclear fission
NCEROEE nuclear-powered
NCERZTO nuclearization
NCLSOSI Nicolas Poussin
NCOARDE Nicholas Ridley
NCOTEOD neck of the woods
NDAOLNE Nadia Boulanger
NDNGRIE Nadine Gordimer
NEZCENS Nietzscheanism
NGETUNS neglectfulness
NGOPRTA Negro spiritual
NGTAEBE Nightmare Abbey
NGTLNNS night-blindness
NGTVEUT negative equity
NGTVNME negative number
NHNKPLE Nihanj Kapil Dev
NHRFEIG no hard feelings
NIEOLTO noise pollution
NKLIAIO Nikolai Vavilov
NLCNEDR nolo contendere
NLNESOE no longer spoken
NMECUCE number-cruncher
NMLFNEE nimble-fingered
NMSAIAL numismatically
NNDYWNE nine days' wonder
NNELGRN nonbelligerent
NNESCLT nonsensicality
NNETITV non-restrictive
NNEUNAV non-return valve
NNMNMRI nine men's morris
NNNEECO Ninon de Lenclos
NNNEFRN non-interfering
NNNLMAL non-inflammable
NNNOVMN non-involvement
NNOEOEI non-comedogenic
NNOMNCN non-communicant
NNOMTAL non-committally
NNRDMRE non-trademarked
NNRDTOA nontraditional
NNRPITR non-proprietary
NNUCINN non-functioning
NNUGMNA non-judgemental
NOIICIO Naomi Mitchison
NOOOILS neocolonialism
neocolonialist
NPLOIWR Napoleonic Wars
NRHATAD north-eastwards
NRHETAD north-westwards
NRHMELN Northumberland
NRHOKHR North Yorkshire

NRHOTES north-north-east
NRHOTWS north-north-west
NRIGFIE nursing officer
NROERRS narcoterrorism
NROMNEL narrow-mindedly
NROSESO nervous tension
NROYTEI narcosynthesis
NTAAEEI not bat an eyelid
NTATOEV not want to leave
NTBIDIO not a blind bit of
NTEAEIB not be taken in by
NTEAIGN not be having any
NTEEEOY not see eye to eye
NTEPNIL not responsible
NTHFLQI not the full quid
NTIGHRO nothing short of
NTIGOAT nothing to say to
NTIGPCA nothing special
NTIIUNS nutritiousness
NTITFNE not lift a finger
NTNEETN not interesting
NTNPRTO not in operation
NTNTEWR not another word
NTOAATE national anthem
NTOHRBU not bother about
NTOLCRN nitroglycerine
NTOOEHN not do something
NTOTEOL not for the world
NTOTSUK not worth shucks
NTPOCAC not up to scratch
NTRLATG natural wastage
NTRLBLT natural ability
NTRLCEC natural science
NTRLITR natural history
NTRLZTO naturalization
NTRRCRE not prerecorded
NTUCINN not functioning
NTVAEIA Native American
NTVLNUG native language
NTWRHNS noteworthiness
NUEURCE nouveaux riches
NUOIRMT neurofibromata
NUOLSOA neuroblastomas
NUOOIAL neurologically
NURLZTO neutralization
NVREELN Never-Never Land
never-never land
NWAGENS newfangledness
NWCNEEC news conference
NWHMOLG Newnham College
NWNIUTO no-win situation
NWOTEOL News of the World
NWPPROA newspaperwoman
NWPPROE newspaperwomen
OAKONAN Ozark Mountains
OCOECAI onchocerciasis
OCSOANS occasionalness
ODACSRE Ordnance Survey
ODADSNS old-maidishness
ODAOTEE old man of the sea
ODEPEHM old people's home
ODETRNM Old Deuteronomy
ODNRPRO ordinary person
ODNRSAA ordinary seaman
ODPSOPE Oedipus complex
ODRFHBT Order of the Bath
OEAIGAL operating table
OEAIGOT operating costs
OEBTEHL one's better half
OECMEST overcompensate
OECNIEC overconfidence
over-confidence
OECPTLS overcapitalise
OECPTLZ overcapitalize
OEETMTO overestimation
OEFHSDY one of these days
OEFSIIU overfastidious
over-fastidious
OEFTOSN one of a thousand
OEGNUNS oleaginousness
OEGREIE one's gorge rises
OEHNENS open-handedness
OEIDLEC overindulgence
OEIHNTE one with another
OEMDABD over my dead body
OEMNENS open-mindedness
OEMTCLU over-meticulous
OENTOSN one in a thousand
OEOFCAL open officially
OEOTMSI over-optimistic
OEPOETV overprotective
over-protective
OEPRIUA overparticular
over-particular
OEPWRNL overpoweringly
OEREBNI one-armed bandit
OERFNMN over-refinement
OESMLFE oversimplified
OESRPLU overscrupulous
OETGPSR one-stage pastry
OETQETO open to question
OETXNSL overtax oneself
OEUPHAO one jump ahead of
OEWEMNL overwhelmingly
OFEPITN offset printing
OFHBCFO off the back foot
OFHSOLE off the shoulder
OFNSRLE off one's trolley
OFRMVMN Oxford Movement
OGETRIL of great article
OGNZDRM organized crime
OGNZTOA organizational
OHHLOCP ophthalmoscope
OHRPRHS on hire purchase
OIECOWL Oliver Cromwell
OIINTVL opinionatively
OIIRHAR Olivier Theatre
OIOSNSI oligopsonistic
OITIERL obiit sine prole
OJCLNUG object language
OKEFLSE Oak-leaf Cluster
OKROOCK Oskar Kokoschka
OLGTRNS obligatoriness
OLNOUIS Orlando Furioso
OMRGLTO osmoregulation
ONBSDTO omnibus edition
ONFXDBD of no fixed abode
ONRCUAC owner-occupancy
ONTEOEA Ornette Coleman
ONTOOIA ornithological
ONUGTEU omnium-gatherum
OOAYGLG otolaryngology
OOEBAED on one's beam ends
on one's beam-ends
OOEDAHE on one's deathbed
OOEDOSE on one's doorstep
OOEHABI on one's head be it
OOELSLG on one's last legs
OONKILN Oroonoko Island
OPESVNS oppressiveness
OPOETMS oophorectomise
OPOETMZ oophorectomize
OPSTNME opposite number
OPSTPOP opposite prompt
OSEILFE on special offer
OSEMSRO oyster mushroom
OSGIIAC of significance
OSMOETI on someone's tail
OSQIUNS obsequiousness
OSRAINA observation car
OSRCINS obstructionism
obstructionist
OSRELSL observe closely
OSRPRUL obstreperously
OTADOKN outward-looking
OTADSNS outlandishness
OTAEUNS outrageousness
OTEASDO on the far side of
OTECAHA on the scrap heap
OTEHPLO on the shop floor
OTEHRSD on the short side
OTEIDSD on the windy side
OTEIHOE on the high ropes
OTEIHSD on the tight side
OTEIHTC on the right tack
OTERALN on the breadline
OTERNTC on the wrong tack
OTETEHN on the other hand
OTEUJCO on the subject of
OTFHRCE out of character
OTFHSOL out of this world
OTFHWNO out of the window
OTFNSET out of one's depth
OTFODTO out of condition
OTLLETA Otto Lilienthal
OTMLZTO optimalization
OTMSIAL optimistically
OTNAIUL ostentatiously
OTOHOAI orthochromatic
OTONPRO outgoing person
OTOOCUC Orthodox Church
OTORHII osteoarthritis
OTORHOI osteoarthrosis
OTORPIA orthographical
OTOTEON out for the count
OWLSEGE Oswald Spengler
OWRMVMN onward movement
OYECLNE oxygen cylinder
PAAONWT play around with

PAATEDN Peasant Wedding
PADAOPE Phaedra complex
PAEETNC plate tectonics
PAEFOSI place of worship
PAEFTEH Peace of Utrecht
PAIOOIG Plácido Domingo
PAMCLGS pharmacologist
PAMCUIA pharmaceutical
PAMPEEI plasmapheresis
PAOFGIS play off against
PASWRHL praiseworthily
PATCBLT practicability
PATCETS plant scientist
PATCLOE practical joker
practical jokes
PATCLTE practicalities
PATCUGO plastic surgeon
PATCUGR plastic surgery
PATRFAI plaster of Paris
PATSAOI phantasmagoria
phantasmagoric
PAUSMHN Prague Symphony
PBIHDOK published works
PBIIAET Public Image Ltd
PBINIAC public nuisance
PBISEDN public spending
PBISEKN public speaking
PBISIIE public-spirited
PCAEOIA package holiday
PCCRNES pococuranteism
PCEAISL pocket an insult
PCLDERN pickled herring
PCOTEUC pick of the bunch
PDEEVLP padded envelope
PDOLOOA Pedro Almodovar
PEAENSL prepare oneself
PEAIUNS precariousness
PEALNWN prevailing wind
PEARCTO prefabrication
PEBTRAL presbyterially
PECITVL prescriptively
PECITVS prescriptivism
PEDMRHS pseudomorphism
PEDNMUL pseudonymously
PEDOGIT plead not guilty
PEEBEGE Pieter Breughel
PEEBUGE Pieter Brueghel
PEECOMN presence of mind
PEEEMNT predeterminate
PEEETAL preferentially
PEEIAEL premeditatedly
PEETNSL present oneself
prevent oneself
PEETNTO predestination
PEETOSL present for sale
PEETSFL present as a film
PEETSPA present as a play
PEIPSTO predisposition
PEITBLT predictability
PELIIEV Pier Luigi Nervi
PEMCNOI pneumoconiosis
PENSIAL pleonastically
PEOABTN phenobarbitone
PEOCREL preconcertedly
PEODRNL preponderantly
PEOIRSN phenolic resins
PEOIUNS precociousness
PEOOEMN prey on one's mind
PEOTRUL preposterously
PEPRLEE puerperal fever
PERAGMN prearrangement
PERBDGI Pietro Badaglio
PERDFRA Pierre de Fermat
PERLRUS Pierre Larousse
PERPODO Pierre Proudhon
PERPPYE pleurapophyses
PESDSUC pleased as Punch
PESHBTO press the button
PESRCOE pressure cooker
PESRGON pleasure ground
PESRLVN pleasure-loving
PESRSEE pleasure-seeker
PETFCTO prettification
PETPETE pretty-pretties
PEUPSTO presupposition
PEUPUUL presumptuously
PGLSIAL pugilistically
PGOBESE pigeon-breasted
PIAALRN prima ballerina
PIAEATS private baptism
PIAEODE private soldier
PIAEOPN private company
PIATRPS philanthropist
PIAYATR primary battery
PIAYOOR primary colours
PICCAMN Prince Charming
PICPLAT principal parts
PIENSLO pride oneself on
PIIAGSU Philip Augustus
PIIOHRI poikilothermic
PIIPPTI Philippe Pétain
PIISEIA Philip Sheridan
PILYATR paisley pattern
PIOOIAL philologically
PITDICI printed circuit
PITFOTC point of contact
PITRITR Pointer Sisters
PKOENSI poke one's nose in
PLAATNO pull a fast one on
PLENHOI palaeanthropic
PLGAIAL phlegmatically
PLMRSTO polymerisation
PLMRZTO polymerization
PLNCETD polynucleotide
PLOAYAV pulmonary valve
PLOEWIH pull one's weight
PLOTEGN pile on the agony
PLSCHRD polysaccharide
PLTCLIW political views
PLTCZTO politicization
PLTEOGO pull the long bow
PLTETIG pull the strings
PLUTEGN pile up the agony
PMLPRIA Pamulaparti Rao
PNADEDE pins and needles
PNEOTLS Pentecostalism
Pentecostalist
PNERCCK Pontefract cake
PNHGNAE Pancho Gonzales
PNLEVTD penal servitude
PNLPLVL Penelope Lively
PNMRCNS pan-Americanism
PNNSATO pin one's faith on
PNNSOEO pin one's hopes on
PNOABTN pentobarbitone
PNOENDW pin someone down
PNOIIAL pantomimically
PNORGAI pantopragmatic
PNRMCIH panoramic sight
PNTNOEN pin it on someone
POAADZN propagandizing
POCITVL proscriptively
POCNUAC proscenium arch
POEAIAL phonematically
POEAINS proletarianise
POEAINZ proletarianize
POEESAI proceleusmatic
POEFATO proper fraction
POELRHF propeller shaft
POESOAL professionally
POESRAL professorially
POETVNS protectiveness
POGTEAD plough the sands
POIALNS profitableness
POIEEPN promise-keeping
POIERAE promise-breaker
POIERME promise-crammed
POIETAL providentially
POIIINR prohibitionary
POIIINS prohibitionist
POIITRL propitiatorily
POIIUNS propitiousness
POISRNT promissory note
PONSIAO prognosticator
PONXHAR Phoenix Theatre
PONXSAD Phoenix Islands
POOEIDS photoperiodism
POOESTS photosensitise
POOESTZ photosensitize
POOHMSR photochemistry
POOLSAI protoplasmatic
POONRVN photoengraving
POOOULC pro bono publico
POOTOAL proportionably
proportionally
POOUIEC photoluminesce
POOYTEI photosynthesis
photosynthetic
POPOECN phosphorescent
POPOIAI phosphoric acid
POREOSI proprietorship
PORMEUI programme music
PORPIAL procryptically
PORSIAO procrastinator
PORSTOI pro aris et focis
POUAOSI procuratorship
POUCAET pronunciamento
POUEEUT produce results
POUEOGL produce roughly

POUEUCL produce quickly
POUTOLN production line
POUTVNS productiveness
PPAEGIE Papua New Guinea
PPHQETO pop the question
PPLOAEU papilionaceous
PPLRZTO popularization
PRDGAIA paradigmatical
PREICRL parhelic circle
PRETAEC perfect cadence
PRETBLT perceptibility
perfectibility
PRETLRN percentile rank
PRETUNS portentousness
PRETVNS perceptiveness
PRETXML perfect example
PREULHC perpetual check
PRGOGTW Port Georgetown
PRHCITR Pyrrhic victory
PRHETAE parchment paper
PRIAIUL pertinaciously
PRIIUNS perfidiousness
perniciousness
PRIKTNS pernicketiness
PRIOIUL parsimoniously
PRISBLT permissibility
PRISVNS permissiveness
PRIUANS particularness
PRJCSNA Port Jackson Bay
PRLEMTO parallel motion
PRLESAO parallel slalom
PRLNUSI paralinguistic
PRLWTRG purple with rage
PRMDELN pyramid selling
PRMTRNS peremptoriness
PROACLM personal column
PROALNS personableness
PROASEE personal stereo
PROEUNS purposefulness
PROMFEC pardon my French
PROMNAT performing arts
PROMNER performance art
PROTPRO person-to-person
PROUINR perlocutionary
PRPYHLG parapsychology
PRSOOIA phraseological
PRSRGSE parish register
PRSTLGS parasitologist
PRTCIAL paratactically
PRUAEUL percutaneously
PRUENSL perjure oneself
PRUSBLT persuasibility
PRUSVNS persuasiveness
PRYOIIA party political
PSADRSN Past and Present
PSERLOE Pasteurelloses
PSERSTO pasteurisation
PSERZTO pasteurization
PSESVNS possessiveness
PSIEMKN passive smoking
PSIETAL pestilentially
PSIGAHO passing fashion
PSIGHBC passing the buck
PSINTNS passionateness
PSIUTRS pisciculturist
PSOEEFF pass oneself off
PSPAIGO past praying for
PSPOUTO post-production
PSPSTVL postpositively
PSSMOEF piss someone off
PSTEOTU push the boat out
PSTTEII push to the limit
PSTVNME positive number
PSTVRSL positive result
PTAKORN put back to front
PTAOENS Pythagoreanism
PTCLOHL put a call on hold
PTDFIGA pâté de foie gras
PTEFMLA patresfamilias
PTGOFCO put a good face on
PTHBAEO put the brakes on
PTHFASU put the flags out
PTHKBSO put the kibosh on
PTHSRWO put the screws on
PTHTNAO put the tin hat on
PTHTNIO put the tin lid on
PTHWAMO put the whammy on
PTIAYLN pituitary gland
PTIGHSO putting the shot
PTIGOET putting to death
PTNBDIH put in a bad light
PTNHMRE put on the market
PTNMDCN patent medicine
PTNNSUR put on one's guard
PTNNTHL put in a nutshell
PTNPDSA put on a pedestal
PTNSHRO put one's shirt on
PTOEHNA put something at
PTOEMEL petroleum jelly
PTOENWS put someone wise
PTOHMSR petrochemistry
PTOOIAL pathologically
petrologically
PTQETOT put a question to
PTRACLA Peter Pan collar
PTRADLO Peter Mandelson
PTRCDMR Peter Scudamore
PTRERBC Peter Henry Buck
PTRIYEV paternity leave
PTROSUS Paterson's curse
PTRREAA Peter Greenaway
PTRUCIF Peter Sutcliffe
PTTEONE Pitt the younger
PTTOREI petit bourgeois
PTULERE pit bull terrier
PTUOATO put out of action
PTYOSAL petty constable
PUENSLO plume oneself on
PUIEETR Pauline Letters
PUKPORG pluck up courage
PVLHRNO Pavel Cherenkov
PVMNATS pavement artist
PWRFHKY power of the keys
PWRORCL powers of recall
PWRRAFS power breakfast
PYHAAYE psychoanalyser
PYHAAYI psychoanalysis
psychoanalytic
PYHDNMC psychodynamics
PYHNUOE psychoneuroses
PYHPIEO pay the price for
PYIANTR physical nature
PYIGOIA physiognomical
PYLTCIA phyllotactical
PYOAHLG phytopathology
PYOENBC pay someone back
PYPNLYO pay a penalty for
PYTETOT pay attention to
QAIIAIN qualifications
QAIYOTO quality control
QARGNRA quadragenarian
QARNUAL quadrangularly
QATFCTO quantification
QATOETS quattrocentism
quattrocentist
QATTTVL quantitatively
QAUVRAL quaquaversally
QEIOIUL querimoniously
QENEIEC Queen's evidence
QENLZBT Queen Elizabeth
QETOOFC question of fact
QICNENA quincentennial
QIEOEHN quite something
QIKIVRN quicksilvering
QIKNHDA quick on the draw
QIQENAL quinquennially
QITSETA quintessential
RAHDCSO reach a decision
RAIGAHN reading-machine
RAOALNS reasonableness
RAOLMMR read only memory
RASDIBU Rhapsody in Blue
RATEITC read the riot act
RAVEMRO rear-view mirror
RAWRHNS roadworthiness
RAYOAIH ready for a fight
RBHWOGA rub the wrong way
RBIWLIM Robbie Williams
RBLIINS Rabelaisianism
RBLIUNS rebelliousness
RBNOCUO Robinson Crusoe
RBRBKWL Robert Bakewell
RBRBONN Robert Browning
RBRDLUA Robert Delaunay
RBRHLMN Robert Helpmann
RBRKLEE Robert Koldewey
RBRMLIA Robert Millikan
RBRMLIE Robert Mulliken
RBRMNMR Robert McNamara
RBRPTAR Robert Pitcairn
RBRSHMN Robert Schumann
RBRTERC Robert the Bruce
RBSEHMR robes-de-chambre
RCADAKN Richard Dawkins
RCADALY Richard Hakluyt
RCADEIL Richard Neville
RCADENA Richard Feynman
RCADLMN Richard Ellmann
RCADNRM Richard Ingrams

RCADOGR Richard Hoggart
Richard Rodgers
RCADRNO Richard Branson
RCADTAS Richard Strauss
RCADUBG Richard Burbage
RCAGLRT rectangularity
RCEOTNE roche moutonnée
RCIALNS receivableness
RCIEAEL receive eagerly
RCIEWSO received wisdom
RCIIERT rectilinearity
RCIIGOS receiving-house
RCLETVL recollectively
RCMECMN recommencement
RCMEDTO recommendation
RCMEDTR recommendatory
RCMIATN recombinant DNA
RCNASAC reconnaissance
RCNIINN reconditioning
RCNIITO reconciliation
RCNIITR reconciliatory
RCNTTTO reconstitution
RCNTUTO reconstruction
RCNTUTV reconstructive
RCOEBAN rack one's brains
RCPINLS reception class
RCPINRE reception order
RCPRTFO recuperate from
RCPTLTO recapitulation
RCPTLTR recapitulatory
RCPTLTV recapitulative
RCRBEKN record-breaking
RCVRBLT recoverability
RCYONAN Rocky Mountains
RDADILN Rudyard Kipling
RDASMER radial symmetry
RDAVLCT radial velocity
RDCLSTO radicalisation
RDCLUNS ridiculousness
RDCLZTO radicalization
RDLBLMN Rudolf Bultmann
RDLVNAA Rudolf von Laban
RDNTETN riding the stang
RDOEECP radio telescope
RDOEERP radiotelegraph
RDOESTS radiosensitise
RDOESTV radiosensitive
RDOESTZ radiosensitize
RDOHMSR radiochemistry
RDORQEC radio frequency
RDOSRNM radio astronomy
RDRCRNO Roderick Random
RDSMOEF ride someone off
RDSRBTO redistribution
REAPOCU Roehampton Club
REMTCEE rheumatic fever
REMTLGS rheumatologist
RFAGBLT refrangibility
RFATRNS refractoriness
RFCOYAL refectory table
RFEHNSL refresh oneself
RFETALO reflect badly on
RFETVNS reflectiveness
RFRAINS reformationist
RFRNEON reference-point
RGESVNS regressiveness
RGLRAMN regular payment
RGLRIIO regular visitor
RGNRTVL regeneratively
RGOAOFC regional office
RGRANSE Roger Bannister
RGRLSNS regardlessness
RGSEEMI registered mail
RGSEEPS registered post
RGSEOFC register office
RGTADOA right-hand woman
RGTBUFC right about face!
RGTETIL right ventricle
RGTFTEA right off the bat
RGTNCNR right and centre
RGTOSNA Rogation Sunday
RGTSESO right ascension
RGTSTIE right as a trivet
RHBLTTO rehabilitation
RHBLTTV rehabilitative
RIEHMRE raise the market
RIENSLS raise one's glass
RIENSOC raise one's voice
RIENYBO raise an eyebrow
RISAHDA Reims Cathedral
RISALTO reinstallation
RITOUTO reintroduction
RIVGRTN reinvigorating
RIVGRTO reinvigoration
RJNRPAA Rajendra Prasad
RJVNSEC rejuvenescence
RKIIKTV Rikki-Tikki-Tavi
RLEENSL relieve oneself
RLEPITN relief printing
RLGOSOS religious house
RLGOSRU religious group
RLNLSNS relentlessness
RLNUSMN relinquishment
RLPIGEE relapsing fever
RMAEHOG rummage through
RMAEUNS rampageousness
RMICMOE remain composed
RMKKRAO Rimsky-Korsakov
RMNICMD romantic comedy
RMONJLE Romeo and Juliet
RMPRIMN Rump Parliament
RMRALNS remarkableness
RMREUNS remorsefulness
RMTJBNR remote job entry
RMUCIUL rambunctiously
RNFOEFE run off one's feet
RNHICUS run their course
RNIGAON run rings around
RNIGEAR running repairs
RNLHINE Ranulph Fiennes
RNNHFML run in the family
RNNSYOE run one's eye over
RNOOELF run for one's life
RNOVRAL random variable
RNTEHNE ring the changes
ROESADE Rhode Island Red
ROGNZTO reorganization
RPEESVL reprehensively
RPEETTO representation
RPEETTV representative
RPNAHDA Ripon Cathedral
RPOUTVL reproductively
RPOUTVT reproductivity
RPRESEC reported speech
RPTTVNS repetitiveness
RQIIINR requisitionary
RQIIINS requisitionist
RSAAINS Rastafarianism
RSCNRRS ruse contre ruse
RSETBLS respectabilise
RSETBLT respectability
RSETBLZ respectabilize
RSETUNS respectfulness
RSICPTL rustic capitals
RSINZTO Russianization
RSLIGOE resolving power
RSNFCTO resinification
RSOAINS restorationism
RSOEFNE rush one's fences
RSOOEOR rest on one's oars
RSOSBEO responsible for
RSOSBLT responsibility
RSOSVNS responsiveness
RSRCEAE restricted area
RSRCENS restrictedness
RSTOEFE rise to one's feet
RTOANME rational number
RTOECAG rate of exchange
RTOICES rate of increase
RTOPORS rate of progress
RTOPRTV retro-operative
RTORDTO retrogradation
RTRMNHM retirement home
RTSFASG rites of passage
RUDBUEL roundaboutedly
RUDBUNS roundaboutness
RUDHCRE round the corner
RUDHWCE round the wicket
RUHNTML rough-and-tumble
RUHRAHN rough breathing
RVASDEL reveal suddenly
RVLIGTG revolving stage
RVNENSL revenge oneself
RVNEUNS revengefulness
RVREAIN reverberations
RVRIGIH reversing light
RVSDESO Revised Version
RVTLZTO revitalization
RVVFCTO revivification
RYHADLE rhythm and blues
RYLEIEC royal residence
RYLIGOT Ray Illingworth
RYLOCSE Royal Worcester
RYODNME Reynolds number
RZRAKHL razorback whale
SADESRS St Andrew's cross
SADLZTO scandalization
SADNHGT stand in the gate
SADOFSE stand confessed

SADPGIS	stand up against	SBTNILS	substantialise	SEMTGNU	spermatogonium
SADPNEM	stand upon terms		substantialism	SEMTPYI	spermatophytic
SADRBAE	standard-bearer		substantialist	SEOTEUC	step on the juice
SADUEYO	stand surety for	SBTNILT	substantiality	SEPHSLN	sheep-whistling
SADUROE	stand guard over	SBTNILZ	substantialize	SEPNTBE	sleeping tablet
SAEADWT	shake hands with	SBTNITN	substantiating	SERNCLM	steering column
SAEAENS	shamefacedness	SBTNITO	substantiation		steering-column
SAEEFRE	stage performer	SBTTTVL	substitutively	SETCLRT	spectacularity
SAEEMTG	State Hermitage	SBUAEUL	subcutaneously	SETIHNN	sheet lightning
SAEFFAR	state of affairs	SCACNRC	social contract	SETORPI	spectrographic
SAEFNRS	state of undress	SCADIEO	sick and tired of	SETRUNS	stertorousness
SAEILNL	shake violently	SCADMCA	social democrat	SETTRPR	spectator sport
SAENHFC	stare in the face	SCADVSO	social division	SFCNCEC	soft-conscienc'd
SAENHNC	skate on thin ice	SCAEGNE	social engineer	SFEAEZR	suffer a seizure
SAENOPC	stare into space	SCAETLS	sacramentalism	SFIETOA	suffice it to say
SAENSIE	shake one's sides		sacramentalist	SGAAAII	Sagrada Familia
SAEOGRN	scaremongering	SCALPRO	sociable person	SGEAINS	segregationist
SAERVLE	space traveller	SCASADN	social standing	SGETBLT	suggestibility
SAFRBIG	Stamford Bridge	SCASCRT	social security	SGETVNS	suggestiveness
SAFRCIP	Stafford Cripps	SCELNUG	secret language	SGOGSRS	St George's cross
SAGTROS	slaughterhouse	SCESOAL	successionally	SGOTERS	sign of the cross
SAGTRUL	slaughterously	SCESOLS	successionless	SGTASTR	sagittal suture
SAHLCCA	staphylococcal	SCESUNS	successfulness	SGUDOBR	Sigmund Romberg
SAHLCCU	staphylococcus	SCESVNS	successiveness	SHAZNGE	Schwarzenegger
SALNETN	small intestine	SCEYFEU	Society of Jesus	SHEEMCE	Schleiermacher
SALYADI	Stanley Baldwin	SCEYSAD	Society Islands	SHGSOLG	St Hugh's College
SALYPNE	Stanley Spencer	SCIEIUL	sacrilegiously	SHLSIAL	scholastically
SALYURC	Stanley Kubrick	SCLRZTO	secularization	SHMTZTO	schematization
SANESTE	stainless steel	SCNTOGT	second thoughts	SHNLRLS	Schindler's List
SANNGON	spawning-ground	SCNWRDA	Second World War	SHOMSRS	schoolmistress
SANSOLG	St Anne's College	SCOACNS	sacrosanctness	SHOTAHN	schoolteaching
SAOALNS	seasonableness	SCOSOLG	St Cross College	SHSAIAL	schismatically
SAOAPOA	seal of approval	SCPATSL	sycophantishly	SHZMCTU	schizomycetous
SAOIDNE	Slavonic Dances	SCRTCMR	security camera	SIDEHNE	spindle-shanked
SAOTERS	slap on the wrist	SDEICES	sudden increase	SIEFHCK	slice of the cake
SAPNGON	stamping-ground	SDUCLRD	sodium chloride	SIERJCO	slide projector
SAPNTRL	snapping turtle	SECLSNS	speechlessness	SIGNHTI	sting in the tail
	snapping-turtle	SEDIEAE	spend like water	SIGNNTL	stinging nettle
SAPOLCO	stamp collector	SEDNLSO	Sheldon Glashow	SIIGOIH	Sailing Tonight
SAPRCIE	sharp practices	SEEFREN	Siege of Orléans	SIILSNS	spiritlessness
SATNSAL	starting stalls	SEEIOEI	stereoisomeric	SIIULSI	spiritualistic
SATRIGA	scatter diagram	SEEMTIA	stereometrical	SIIUUNS	spirituousness
SATRLNS	slatternliness	SEEWIBR	Steven Weinberg	SIKFNEE	sticky-fingered
SATRRIE	scatterbrained	SEHNAGO	Stephen Langton	SIKNSAI	stick one's oar in
	scatter-brained	SEHNAKN	Stephen Hawking	SIKTOHN	stick at nothing
SATYRSE	smartly dressed	SEHNEAU	Stephen Dedalus	SILNCSL	Stirling Castle
SAUSUNS	statuesqueness	SEHNORL	Stephen Dorrell	SILSALE	shilly-shallier
SBAAINS	Sabbatarianism	SEHNPNE	Stephen Spender	SIMNTUK	swimming trunks
SBCITOT	subscription TV	SEHRSUS	shepherd's purse	SIMTZTO	stigmatization
SBCOSLN	sebaceous gland	SEIFEUE	sheriff deputes	SINEITO	science fiction
SBEEIAL	subgenerically	SEIFFIE	sheriff officer		science-fiction
SBEGBLT	submergibility	SEIIAIN	specifications	SINIIAL	scientifically
SBESBLT	submersibility	SEILETO	special mention	SIOESUP	stir one's stumps
SBETEDN	subject heading	SEILIEC	special licence	SISRYNF	Swiss army knife
SBETVNS	subjectiveness	SEILSAE	specialist area	SITONES	Saint-John Perse
SBETVSI	subjectivistic	SEILZTO	specialization	SITRDSA	Saint Bride's Bay
SBISVNS	submissiveness	SEKHRLT	speak sharply to	SJHSOLG	St John's College
SBLEEFR	Sybille Bedford	SEKNLAL	speak unclearly	SLACSTO	self-accusation
SBLHRDK	Sybil Thorndike	SEKNOGE	speak in tongues	SLAFIHE	self-affrighted
SBLIEOK	Sibylline Books	SEKYHCR	speak by the card	SLAMRTO	self-admiration
SBOSIUL	subconsciously	SELCHLE	Sherlock Holmes	SLANGTN	self-abnegating
SBSINAO	Sebastian Cabot	SELFHLM	smell of the lamp	SLANGTO	self-abnegation
SBTNIAL	substantivally	SELMRIG	steal a marriage	SLASRTO	self-absorption

SLATVTN self-activating
SLAVRIE self-advertiser
SLBIUNS salubriousness
SLCFCTO silicification
SLCMAIO self-comparison
SLCNEUN self-consequent
SLCNIEC self-confidence
SLCNRLE self-controlled
SLCSIAL solecistically
SLCTUNS solicitousness
SLDFCTO solidification
SLDSILN self-discipline
SLEATTO self-exaltation
SLEFCMN self-effacement
SLEPANN self-explaining
SLEPESO self-expression
SLEPOMN self-employment
SLFATRN self-flattering
SLFLILN self-fulfilling
SLFLIMN self-fulfilment
SLFRETN self-forgetting
SLGVRMN self-government
SLHNLMD sulphanilamide
SLHRIXD sulphur dioxide
SLHRUAI sulphurous acid
SLIDLEC self-indulgence
SLIMLTO self-immolation
SLIPRAC self-importance
SLITRSE self-interested
SLJSIYN self-justifying
SLMNELK salamander-like
SLMNSAD Solomon Islands
SLNMJRT silent majority
SLOTEAT salt of the earth
SLPNSMN self-punishment
SLPOELN self-propelling
SLPOLIE self-proclaimed
SLPSESO self-possession
SLRGLTN self-regulating
SLRSETN self-respecting
SLRSRIE self-restrained
SLSFIIN self-sufficient
SLSPOTN self-supporting
SLSSANN self-sustaining
SLSSEAC self-sustenance
SLSSITN sales assistant
SLSXCTV sales executive
SLTDNRA solitudinarian
SLTEUMT sell the dummy to
SLTNSIE split one's sides
SLTNSOE split one's votes
SMABLTO somnambulation
SMAHZWT sympathize with
SMAYFEC summary offence
SMCNUTN semiconducting
SMCRUAL semicircularly
SMEPCWC Samuel Pickwick
SMESLTC summer solstice
SMHWRTE somehow or other
SMLAEUL simultaneously
SMLFATO simple fraction
SMLFATR simple fracture
SMLFCTO simplification
SMLITRS simple interest
SMLQIFO semi-liquid food
SMLSIAL simplistically
SMLSNEC simple sentence
SMNAKKB Simon Bar Kokhba
SMNHZAO Simon the Zealot
SMOERTE someone or other
SMOFCAL semi-officially
SMPOIAL semaphorically
SMTIGIE something like a
SMTMTLG symptomatology
SNAINLS sensationalism
sensationalist
SNAOELN singapore sling
SNATTMN send a statement
SNBSWSE send best wishes
SNEFUPS sense of purpose
SNFRKUA Sandford Koufax
SNGOWSE send good wishes
SNHOIAL synchronically
SNIETLS sentimentalise
sentimentalism
sentimentalist
SNIETLT sentimentality
SNIETLZ sentimentalize
SNIGDCB Santiago de Cuba
SNIIELN sensitive plant
SNLBESE single-breasted
SNLDMNI senile dementia
SNLHNEL single-handedly
SNLHOTN single hoop tent
SNLMNEL single-mindedly
SNOCTZN senior citizens
SNOHAAH Song of Hiawatha
SNOLCUE senior lecturer
SNSRRAL sinistrorsally
SNTCVNR send to Coventry
SNTFCTO sanctification
SNUNRNS sanguinariness
SNWCCUS sandwich course
SOAEATR storage battery
SOAHUNN stomach-turning
SOCEOER stoicheiometry
SOCIMTI stoichiometric
SOEACSL Stokesay Castle
SOEAFEN shove-halfpenny
SOEFETN Stone of Destiny
SOENWGA score an own goal
SOEODOE stone-cold sober
SOEONSF score points off
SOKARCN stock-car racing
SOKNBRE stock and barrel
SOKNFLE stocking filler
SOKOOTE Stockton-on-Tees
SOKRAMN shock treatment
SOLEEAC shouldered arch
SOLEHIH shoulder-height
SOMNTAU storm in a teacup
SOPNCNR shopping centre
SOPTKLK swoopstake-like
swoop-stake-like
SORNPWE scouring powder
SOTADOT stouth and routh
SOTEOTO stop the mouth of
SOTEREL stout-heartedly
SOTGOFO shortage of food
SOTHBEZ shoot the breeze
SOTIHEL short-sightedly
SOTNCAC sporting chance
SOTSEKN smooth-speaking
SPITCTO sophistication
SPLCTNL supplicatingly
SPNFCTO saponification
SPOIIIU supposititious
SPOTNSL support oneself
SPRAGSI supercargoship
SPRAUAL supernaturally
SPRBNAC superabundance
SPRCITO superscription
SPRFRUL soporiferously
SPRHSHT superphosphate
SPRIILS superficialise
SPRIILT superficiality
SPRIILZ superficialize
SPRIIUL superciliously
SPRLVTO superelevation
SPRLWIH super-flyweight
SPRMNNL supereminently
SPRNEDN superintendent
SPRNUTO superannuation
SPRODCO superconductor
SPROIAL supersonically
SPROTNN supercontinent
SPRRGTO supererogation
SPRRGTR supererogatory
SPRTUTR superstructure
SPUGNRA septuagenarian
SRAEESO surface tension
SRAEMSL striated muscle
SRAOTAD spread outwards
SRBLGTN strobe lighting
SREDRAU surrender value
SREKRLO Sergei Korolyov
SREMSCA street-musician
SRENEEA surgeon general
SREPITN screen printing
SRESHAO streets ahead of
SRETNNL serpentiningly
SRHENAD Sarah Bernhardt
SRIASII surgical spirit
SRICUTS strain courtesy
SRIEBLT serviceability
SRIETTO service station
SRIHAAI straight as a die
SRKAAAC strike a balance
SRKAAGI strike a bargain
SRKOGNU stroke of genius
SRMEAII serum hepatitis
SRNCENN spring-cleaning
SRNEETN Strange Meeting
SRNLNUG strong language
SRNMTRS spring mattress
SRNSELN strong-smelling
SRNTOMN strength of mind
SRNTOWL strength of will
SRNWLIM Serena Williams

SRORSRU Sartor Resartus
SROSRNE serious drinker
SRPLUNS scrupulousness
SRPTGTE scrape together
SRRSATC surprise attack
SRRSNNS surprisingness
SRTFCTO stratification
SRTGAHS stratigraphist
SRTNSNL scrutinisingly
SRTNSTF strut one's stuff
SRTNZNL scrutinizingly
SRTNZTO scrutinization
SRWERMR strawberry mark
SRWERTE strawberry tree
SRWNHWN straw in the wind
SRWRPLE screw propeller
SSANBLT sustainability
SSEAIAL systematically
SSEBIDN system building
SSEOWAT system of wealth
SSETBLT susceptibility
SSIEAON Sistine Madonna
SSIIUNS suspiciousness
SSUPDLA sesquipedalian
SSUPDLT sesquipedality
STHSEEO set the scene for
STLIETT satellite state
STLTECR settle the score
STNHSLC sit on the splice
STNHTRN sit on the throne
STNMSRO satan's mushroom
STNNSAD sit on one's hands
STNPDSA set on a pedestal
STNSERO set one's heart on
STNUGMN sit in judgement
STROOIA soteriological
STSATRL satisfactorily
SUBIGLC stumbling-block
SUCNIMN soul-confirming
SUCOICM source of income
SUDOLAE squadron leader
SUDSRYN soul-destroying
SUEDUNS stupendousness
SUETECE student teacher
SUHETAD south-westwards
SUHLMRA South Glamorgan
SUHOKHR South Yorkshire
SUHOTES south-south-east
SUHOTWS south-south-west
SUHUTAI South Australia
SUINNLN Sauvignon Blanc
SUMBELN Sturmabteilung
SUOEEET shut one's eyes to
SUREMNE squirrel monkey
SURLUNS scurrilousness
SUTEOTO shut the mouth of
SUTFCTO stultification
SUYFHMN study of the mind
SUYNESL study intensely
SVOEBET save one's breath
SVRINTT sovereign state
SXAAPTT sexual appetite
SXFAAEU saxifragaceous

SYIFRNL say differently
SYNSRYR say one's prayers
SYOAEOR say you are sorry
SZNEEGE Suzanne Lenglen
TAAGETN to a large extent
TADOSIE trapdoor spider
TAELNFL travelling folk
TAELRCU Travellers Club
TAEOERN trapezohedrons
TAESCNS travel sickness
TAIINLS traditionalism
traditionalist
TAIINLT traditionality
TAIOIAL tragicomically
TALBTEA That'll Be The Day
TALTAHE that'll teach her
TALTAHI that'll teach him
TALTAHO that'll teach you
TAMTZTO traumatization
TANFHUH train of thought
TANNGON training ground
TANSMAH tea and sympathy
TAOHRLC to another place
TAQILZN tranquillizing
TARADGE to a great degree
TARAETN to a great extent
TASEDNA transcendental
TASEDNL transcendently
TASESWV transverse wave
TASETTS transvestitism
TASHTCE that's the ticket
TASIEAO transliterator
TASIRTO transmigration
TASIRTR transmigratory
TASISOA transmissional
TASISVL transmissively
TASISVT transmissivity
TASIUUL transpicuously
TASLNAL transplantable
TASOMTO transformation
TASOMTV transformative
TASOTNL transportingly
TASOTTO transportation
TASTOAL transitionally
TASTRNS transitoriness
TATOEGN traction engine
TATRUNS traitorousness
TBASOLT Tobias Smollett
TBEPOFL tablespoonfuls
TCIAVTN tactical voting
TCNCLIC technical hitch
TCYRPIA tachygraphical
TDYOSVL Teddy Roosevelt
TEADLYR The Card Players
TEAEBBE The Water-Babies
TEAEOHL The Gates of Hell
TEAKNFL the rank and file
TEASYAA the cat's pyjamas
TEATMEO The Last Emperor
TEATSAE the Earthshaker
TEAYILR The Ladykillers
TECAIAL theocratically
TEDRCWN Theodor Schwann

TEDROME Theodor Mommsen
TEEDUNS tremendousness
TEEEAWA the general weal
TEEFSGN The Selfish Gene
TEEHRAD The Netherlands
TEEIADL the devil and all
TEERFRC the Year of Grace
TEERTGN The Secret Agent
TEETERF the gentle craft
TEEVTLV the velvet glove
TEEYRPS The New York Post
TEGOBOZ The Age of Bronze
TEGORAO The Age of Reason
TEHRDGE the third degree
TEHRETT the third estate
TEHTRBI The White Rabbit
TEICUTE the Six Counties
TEIEAHN The Time Machine
TEIEFEU The Life of Jesus
TEIEFIE the life of Riley
TEIENSU the life and soul
TEIGFIG The King of Kings
TEIHSFA The Rights of Man
TEITEOA the little woman
TEITRTL The Winter's Tale
TELAPTT the clean potato
TELPATA The Elephant Man
TEMASDR The Ambassadors
TEMDNMC thermodynamics
TEMEETI thermoelectric
TEMLECO thermal reactor
TEMLMGN thermal imaging
TEMLRNE thermal printer
TENEEDN The Independent
TEOAILN The Coral Island
TEODADR The Woodlanders
TEODLDY the good old days
TEODNEG the wooden wedge
TEODNOG The Golden Bough
TEODPAE the Lord's Prayer
TEODTKN the Lord's tokens
TEOEOLV The Power of Love
TEOEYEU The Rokeby Venus
TEOGODY The Long Goodbye
TEOLTCM the world to come
TEOMATR the worm may turn
TEOMDNL Trevor McDonald
TEOMTET The Commitments
TEONRWF The Country Wife
TEONXDO the boy next door
TEOPLRT the gospel truth
TEOPTTO the competition
TEORESN The Four Seasons
TEORNGM the roaring game
TEOSTSG The Forsyte Saga
TEOUETR The Lotus-Eaters
TERABYN the Great Beyond
TERAGTB The Great Gatsby
TERDGLO The Prodigal Son
TERDLUG Tierra del Fuego
TERKNAE The Kraken Wakes
TERLTRA the proletariat
TERSNTM the present time

TESPIAL theosophically
TESRILN Treasure Island
TETOAIN Treaty of Amiens
TEUDEDY the Hundred Days
TEUESEC the queen's peace
TEUHRTE the authorities
TEUILVR The Music Lovers
TFRINAT to foreign parts
TIDIESO third dimension
TIDNTSE tried and tested
TIGNFON toing and froing
TIHMNAI trichomoniasis
TIHTMUL trichotomously
TIIAINS Trinitarianism
TIILUSI Trivial Pursuit®
TIILZTO trivialization
TIIYOLG Trinity College
TIKEESR think necessary
TIKEHOG trickle through
TIKOHNO think nothing of
TILNRFE twin-lens reflex
TINLSAE triangle-shaped
TISQECE thirst-quencher
TITASAD Tristram Shandy
TITNAUH Tristan da Cunha
TITYASA Thirty Years' War
TIUPDAV tricuspid valve
TKAAMRN take a hammering
TKAANHC take a raincheck
TKACNET take a scunner to
TKAIEUO take a mike out of
take a rise out of
TKAITRO take a picture of
TKAIVEO take a dim view of
TKBSRRS take by surprise
TKFRRNE take for granted
TKGOCRO take good care of
TKNNTCO take no notice of
TKNPIOE taking prisoner
TKODRFO take orders from
TKOEBET take one's breath
TKOECAC take one's chance
TKOECOC take one's choice
TKOTNSA take out one's bat
TKPEEEC take precedence
TKPESRI take pleasure in
TKPROAL take personally
TKRVNEO take revenge for
TKTEDEF take the edge off
TKTEICI take the biscuit
TKTEIET take the liberty
TKTELCO take the place of
TKTEUSO take the guise of
TKTIGES take things easy
TKTOETE take to one's toes
TKTTEOT take to the boats
TKUAURE take up a quarrel
TKUPSTO take up position
TLILKII tell it like it is
TLISWTL tell its own tale
TLMRLUL talk more loudly
TLOOIAL teleologically
TLOTEEI talk of the devil
TLPOEOT telephone booth
TLPOIAL telephonically
TLPTIAL telepathically
TLSAIAL telesmatically
TLSOIAL telescopically
TMEAEOE temperate zones
TMIMMRA time immemorial
TMLNBRE tumbling-barrel
TMLOAHN Temple of Athena
TMLOAOL Temple of Apollo
TMLOAOR Temple of Amon-Ra
TMLUUNS tumultuousness
TMOMUOU Tomb of Mausolus
TNAECSL Tintagel Castle
TNINBLT tintinnabulate
TNRDEEL Tunbridge Wells
TNUTENS tongue-tiedness
TOACOWL Thomas Cromwell
TOAKNAL Thomas Keneally
TOAMCUA Thomas Macaulay
TOANWOE Thomas Newcomen
TOASAWL Thomas Shadwell
TOBEHOE troubleshooter
TOGTUNS thoughtfulness
TOHEREV trochlear nerve
TOIAFRS tropical forest
TOIESOA two-dimensional
TOIOCNE Tropic of Cancer
TONOWLE Thornton Wilder
TOOHSEL two for his heels
TOOOIAL tropologically
TPCLULT typical quality
TPIGNSL topping oneself
TPTTREL to put it briefly
TPYUVNS topsy-turviness
TQIAURS tequila sunrise
TRAADHU thread and thrum
TRACUTN turf accountant
TRAEFAT turn a deaf ear to
TREADRC three-card trick
TRELNUG target language
TREODLT three-toed sloth
TREONTR three-point turn
TRETNTE turpentine tree
TRFLSNS thriftlessness
TRIALNS terminableness
TRIESTO tergiversation
TRIHEIH Turkish delight
TRINAAC torsion-balance
TRIOILS territorialise
TRIOILT territoriality
TRIOILZ territorialize
TRIOOIA terminological
TRLETBT thrilled to bits
TROEBCO turn one's back on
TROEHNT turn one's hand to
TROOEHE turn on one's heel
TROSRCE terror-stricken
TRTEAAC turn the balance
TRTEIBU turn the air blue
TRTETMC turn the stomach
TRUHHNS through the nose
TRUOETE turn up one's toes
TRUSDDW turn upside down
turn upside-down
TRWHBOA throw the book at
TRWHSIC throw the switch
TRWNNSO throw in one's lot
TRWNSLA throw oneself at
TRWNSLO throw oneself on
TRWOHDG throw to the dogs
TRWPNSA throw up one's cap
TRWTGTE thrown together
thrown-together
TRYOELN terry towelling
TRYRTHT Terry Pratchett
TSAADRO Tessa Sanderson
TSAETRL testamentarily
TSAINEI Tasmanian devil
TSAINIE Tasmanian tiger
TSEOHFL taste to the full
TSIOILS testimonialise
TSIOILZ testimonialize
TSYOHNO to say nothing of
TTAONAN Tatra Mountains
TTARMAO Tetragrammaton
TTEDMLO tatterdemalion
TTENOTM to the end of time
TUACOSN Toucan crossing
TUHSETE tough as leather
TUOOIAL tautologically
TUPTOGE trumpet-tongued
TWCUCLO town councillor
TYOCUIN try conclusions
TYOOOMC try to do too much
UAALBLT unavailability
UACMLSE unaccomplished
UACSOET unaccustomed to
UACUTDO unaccounted-for
UAFCENS unaffectedness
UAKOLDE unacknowledged
UAMDGIS unarmed against
UAODBLT unavoidability
UAORPIA uranographical
UAPEESV unapprehensive
UAPEITV unappreciative
UAPOCAL unapproachable
unapproachably
UAPORAE unappropriated
UASMNNS unassumingness
UBCMNNS unbecomingness
UBNURIL urban guerrilla
UCASFAL unclassifiable
UCEOSAI Uncle Tom's Cabin
UCIIANS uncriticalness
UCMRMSN uncompromising
UCNAIAE uncontaminated
UCNCOAL unconscionable
unconscionably
UCNEILT uncongeniality
UCNETAE unconcentrated
UCNETOA unconventional
UCNRLAL uncontrollable
uncontrollably
UCNRLEL uncontrolledly
UCROOAE uncorroborated

UCRSINS unchristianise
UCRSINZ unchristianize
UCRUCSO uncircumcision
UDMNTAL undemonstrable
UDMSIAE undomesticated
UDNALNS undeniableness
UDRAUTO undervaluation
UDREATO under penalty of
UDREEOE underdeveloped
UDRERTR under-secretary
UDRETOE undermentioned
UDRHHME under the hammer
UDRHNMO under the name of
UDRNSHM under one's thumb
UDROEWR undercover work
UDRORSE undernourished
UDROUAE underpopulated
UDRSIAE underestimated
UDRTNAL understandable
UDRTTMN understatement
UDRTUTR understructure
UEALNUG use bad language
UECTBLT unexcitability
UEEPRRL use temporarily
UEETUNS uneventfulness
UEPCENS unexpectedness
UETRRSN unenterprising
UETUISI unenthusiastic
UFAPBLT unflappability
UFIHUNS unfaithfulness
UFINLNS unfriendliness
UFMLAWT unfamiliar with
UFUTUNS unfruitfulness
UGAEUNS ungratefulness
UGAIUNS ungraciousness
UGNRUNS ungenerousness
UHREDAO Uther Pendragon
UHSTTNL unhesitatingly
UIESLON universal joint
UIESTRA universitarian
UIETFAL unidentifiable
UIGNSAD using one's hands
UIIAINS utilitarianise
utilitarianism
UIIAINZ utilitarianize
UIIETOA unidirectional
UINAAOU union catalogue
UIOMTRA uniformitarian
UITLETA unintellectual
UITLIEC unintelligence
UITLIIL unintelligible
UIVTDUS uninvited guest
ULDLKNS unladylikeness
UMITIAL unmaintainable
UMNELNS unmannerliness
UMNINBE unmentionables
UMRIDTT unmarried state
UMRIUNS unmercifulness
UMTOIAL unmethodically
UOTEELO upon the heels of
UOTNAIU unostentatious
UPEAENS unpreparedness
UPEEDNL unpretendingly
UPEEIAE unpremeditated
UPESNNS unpleasantness
UPOESOA unprofessional
UQEDASA usque ad nauseam
UQETOAL unquestionable
unquestionably
URAALNS unreadableness
URAIUNS uproariousness
URCGIAL unrecognizable
URCNIAL unreconcilable
URMNRTV unremunerative
URMREUL unremorsefully
URSRENS unreservedness
URSRIAL unrestrainable
URSRIEL unrestrainedly
USCALNS unsociableness
USCESUL unsuccessfully
USDDWCK upside-down cake
USIALNS unsuitableness
USIIULS unspiritualise
USIIULZ unspiritualize
USNHOIE unsynchronized
USOKBLT unshockability
USPRSIL unsuppressible
USRONAL unsurmountable
USRPLUL unscrupulously
USRPUAL unscripturally
USSEAIE unsystematized
USSETNL unsuspectingly
USSIIUL unsuspiciously
USTSATR unsatisfactory
UTAKUNS unthankfulness
UTAOIAL ultrasonically
UTAOTNS ultramontanist
UTARPDT ultracrepidate
UTASEAL untransferable
UTATUTR ultrastructure
UTIKNNS unthinkingness
UTMGNTR ultimogeniture
UTOETIK up to one's tricks
UTOGTUL unthoughtfully
UTTERSN up to the present
UTUHUNS untruthfulness
UWLOEUS unwelcome guest
UWRALNS unworkableness
UWRMBLT upward mobility
VCFRUNS vociferousness
VCOEMNE Victor Emmanuel
VCOIILN Victoria Island
VCOISOG Victoria sponge
VCOIUNS victoriousness
VCRPSOI vicar-apostolic
VDOEODN video recording
VDUQILN Vidkun Quisling
VEICNIE Vreni Schneider
VGTTVNS vegetativeness
VIGOIUL vaingloriously
VKOKRHO Viktor Korchnoi
VLAFATO vulgar fraction
VLAOOIA vulcanological
VLEALNS vulnerableness
VLEUGMN value judgement
VLMNUNS voluminousness
VLMTIAL volumetrically
VLPUUNS voluptuousness
VLTDNRA valetudinarian
VLTEHMR valet de chambre
VLTLZTO volatilization
VNETAGG Vincent Van Gogh
VNIGAHN vending machine
VNITVNS vindictiveness
VNSIGON vanishing point
VNSIGRA vanishing cream
VNUEAIA venture capital
VRIAAGE vertical angles
VRIACRL vertical circle
VRSMLTD verisimilitude
VRULELT virtual reality
VRUUCRL virtuous circle
VSANJNK Vaslav Nijinsky
VSBEMOT visible imports
VSBEXOT visible exports
VSDFRNI vasa deferentia
VSEITRS vested interest
VSTEUAL visit regularly
VSUABNL vascular bundle
VSUATSU vascular tissue
VTCNUEM Vatican Museums
VTEUHMU vitreous humour
VTLSIAL vitalistically
VTLTGTO vitilitigation
VTOIDSC Vittorio De Sica
VTPRTVL vituperatively
VVPRUNS viviparousness
VVSCINS vivisectionist
VWLRDTO vowel gradation
WAAEGAC what a vengeance
WAAOHRA wear another hat
WAATENE weak at the knees
WADOCLI what-d'you-call-it
WADYUAT what do you say to?
WAEOEHL whalebone whale
WAHRRPE weather prophet
WAHRTTO weather station
WAMIIKE What Maisie Knew
WAMNENS weak-mindedness
WAOEEFU wear oneself out
WASAIGO what's eating you?
WASHDMG what's the damage?
WASIIGO what's biting you?
WASPIHO what's up with you?
WATEIKN what the dickens
WAYUEEV what you deserve
WDEPREC wide experience
WEKAOWT wreak havoc with
WELFOTN wheel of Fortune
wheel of fortune
WELRELN wheeler-dealing
WEOTTEA woe worth the day
WGOTERE wigs on the green
WIATNAC wait attendance
WIELOCL white blood cell
WIEOPSL white corpuscle
WIHLSNS weightlessness
WIHOHBA weigh to the beam
WIHTANN weight-training

WINYOSO Whitney Houston
WIPRNDM whispering dome
WIPRNPE whippersnapper
WISNSRY waifs and strays
WITEHTI whittie-whattie
WLAETVN Wallace Stevens
WLAFCEL walk affectedly
WLAIHRP walk a tightrope
WLASHUN Weltanschauung
WLECOKT Walter Cronkite
WLEDLMR Walter De La Mare
Walter de la Mare
WLELPMN Walter Lippmann
WLEMOTE Wilhelm Röntgen
WLGOEHS wild-goose chase
WLIGOBO wellington boot
WLIGONE walking wounded
WLIMAEO William Bateson
WLIMAET William Barentz
WLIMAKN William Rankine
WLIMALC William Wallace
WLIMALT William Hazlitt
WLIMAPE William Dampier
WLIMBNE William H Bonney
WLIMHRA William Sherman
WLIMHTE William Shatner
WLIMIBR William Gilbert
WLIMIMN William Siemens
WLIMOAT William Hogarth
WLIMOBT William Cobbett
WLIMODN William Golding
WLIMPOE William Spooner
WLIMRII William Craigie
WLIMRNA William Brennan
WLIMUKE William Buckley
WLIMYDL William Tyndale
WLIWIEA Willie Whitelaw
WLOECAK walk one's chalks
WLRSACE well-researched
WLSAHDA Wells Cathedral
WLSNOLG Wolfson College
WLSOERF Wollstonecraft
WLSRCUE well-structured
WLTETET walk the streets
WLTOGTU well-thought-out
WLUSEDL walk unsteadily
WLVNIAE well-ventilated
WMLYTDU Wembley Stadium
WMNFETR woman of letters
WMNFHTW woman of the town
WMNFORG woman of courage
WMNMVMN women's movement
WNEFLOL Wonderful World
WNESLTC winter solstice
WNESRCE wonder-stricken
WNFEHLB Winifred Holtby
WNHECAG win the exchange
WNIGOER wanting to learn
WNISRMN wind instrument
WNODESN window dressing
window-dressing
WNOMRAI Wynton Marsalis
WNOSOPN window-shopping
WOEAGHO whole bang shoot
WOEEREL wholeheartedly
whole-heartedly
WOEOECA wooden overcoat
WOGNHHA wrong in the head
WONGTHD wood nightshade
WOPEUHO whoopee cushion
WOPGLBR Whoopi Goldberg
WRAPRNR work as partners
WRATFIE warrant officer
WRDERNS world-weariness
WRDYIEA Worldly Wiseman
WREPREC work experience
WRETRAC Worcester sauce
WRETRHR Worcestershire
WRFTRTO war of attrition
WRHNSHL worth one's while
WRHPUNS worshipfulness
WRHUEAT warehouse party
WRIGAIA working capital
WRIGLSE working classes
WRIGRWN working drawing
WRORLGO Wars of Religion
WROTEOE Wars of the Roses
WRPOESN word-processing
WRRBMSE wardrobe master
WRSOMTE works committee
WRTARZL worn to a frazzle
WSENZTO westernization
WSFLHNE wishful thinker
WTAADEC with an audience
WTAEGAC with a vengeance
WTAILRC with an ill grace
WTAODRC with a good grace
WTAOEMN with an open mind
WTDFIUT with difficulty
WTHAEUL watch carefully
WTHIEHW watch like a hawk
WTIAICO within an inch of
WTNSHSL wet one's whistle
WTOEOSN with one consent
WTOTANN without warning
WTOTEEV without reserve
WTOTELN without feeling
WTOTEPT without respite
WTOTESR without measure
WTOTIPT without dispute
WTOTLMS without blemish
WTOTRUN without arguing
WTREELN water-repellent
WTREITN water-resistant
WTRLTOT with relation to
WTRNHKE water on the knee
WTROORS watercolourist
WTTERVS with the proviso
WTTEUPS with the purpose
WTTMTKL with time to kill
WUDOHAO would not hear of
WYADSIH Wayland's Smithy
XNHMLNU xanthomelanous
YKNERTR Yukon Territory
YLOIHHT yellowish-white
YLOIHRW yellowish brown
yellowish-brown
YSEAAAA Yasser Ar Arafat
YUEELNM you're telling me
YUGDLHO young adulthood
YUGOHAT your good health
YUHATET your heart melts
YUHOTLE youth hosteller
YUSICRL yours sincerely
YUSOOMN yours to command
YWRMSVN Yoweri Museveni
ZRATINS Zoroastrianism
ZRCUOBN zero-coupon bond
ZRZROTO zero-zero option

15 letters – odd

AAATRAIE as an alternative
AAATRFAT as a matter of fact
AADUTCAK a hard nut to crack
AAEELORS A Farewell to Arms
AAERIRIE at an earlier time
AANTHCOK against the clock
AANTHGAN against the grain
AAOSOWRS at a loss for words
AASGTIDA A Passage to India
AASHTCLY anaesthetically
AATBTFOK a nasty bit of work
AATSOOOA Anastasio Somoza
ABEBADLY Aubrey Beardsley
ABOEUNIE Ambrose Burnside
ABRCLUIT arboriculturist
ABRIAUEM Albertina Museum
ABRMCESN Albert Michelson
ABROUIOI Alberto Fujimori
ACECTERL Aachen Cathedral
ACETOUET ancient monument
ACIADARD Archibald Garrod
ACIAIAIN acclimatization
ACIETRLY architecturally
ACMOAIGY accommodatingly
ACNTEHOE ascend the throne
ACOEURES at close quarters
ACRINLAS accordion pleats
ACSOWRHP ancestor-worship
ACUTBEES accountableness
ADESEAIS Andreas Vesalius
ADEVSISY Andrei Vyshinsky
ADISIHFY and pigs might fly
ADLAIRHM Abdullah Ibrahim

ADOEAEUA Andromeda nebula
AEADRADR Alexander Calder
AEADRESI Alexander Nevski
AEADRESY Alexander Nevsky
AEADRRIE Alexander Irvine
AEADRUCK Alexander Dubcek
AEDFCEUE ahead of schedule
AEDFHTMS ahead of the times
AEDFNSIE ahead of one's time
AEDULSOE Alec Douglas-Home
AEFICEIN age of discretion
AEIATOTR American Trotter
AEIOEPCI Amerigo Vespucci
AESECOLY Aleister Crowley
AESNRVLA Alessandro Volta
AESOTEAY aversion therapy
AETAILNS Aleutian Islands
AFEHTHOK Alfred Hitchcock
AFESIGIZ Alfred Stieglitz
AFEWIEED Alfred Whitehead
AFLXEINE awful experience
AFUNSCEY affluent society
AGMNAIEY argumentatively
AGSEAITE Auguste Mariette
AGSIFENL Augustin Fresnel
AGSOIOHT Augusto Pinochet
AHITACRL A Christmas Carol
AHLONUMR al-hallown summer
AHLOORIE A Child of our Time
AHNPOAHS Athena Promachos
AHNRPATC achondroplastic
AHOENUEM Ashmolean Museum
AHRSLRSS atherosclerosis
AHUADNOE a thousand and one
AIAECEET animal excrement
AIAECRON animated cartoon
AIAMGEIM animal magnetism
AIEFCIIY a hive of activity
AIEFNUTY a hive of industry
AIENKCIG alive and kicking
AIETRCNL alimentary canal
AIGRNHPE a finger in the pie
AIHUOWTR a fish out of water
AIOBWTHD a widow bewitched
AITIDRIG Alistair Darling
AITIMCEN Alistair Maclean
AIWUDPER as it would appear
AKEPEOIE ask people to give
AKOENTPY ask someone to pay
AKOLDEET acknowledgement
ALHSMTYU all the same to you
ALHWYCOS all the way across
ALKNNBNS all skin and bones
ALNOPSIG all-encompassing
ALNUTRAN Allan Quatermain
ALOEFLES all-powerfulness
ALOLCLEE All Souls College
ALPNHWIT a slap on the wrist
ALSIAAMA aplastic anaemia
ALVRHPAE all over the place
AMADAYLB Army and Navy Club
AMDOHTEH armed to the teeth
AMRLRFPE Admiral Graf Spee
AMSHRCLY atmospherically
AMUEVHCE armoured vehicle
ANBAEIDE Anne Bracegirdle
ANEEYUGN Annie Get Your Gun
ANSORBLS annus horribilis
AOAITCLY anomalistically
AOAYTCLY apocalyptically
AODSHHLS as old as the hills
AOEFHDVL abode of the devil
AOEHWAHR above the weather
AOEINROA anorexia nervosa
AOELMAUE above all measure
AOENNSOT a hole in one's coat
AOGHLNSF along the lines of
AOHHGAIE apophthegmatize
AOHRUOTA another cup of tea
AOISRCUE atomic structure
AOSICULR acoustic coupler
AOTNSESN about one's person
AOTOSNAS a month of Sundays
APITETOK appointment book
APOCAIIY approachability
APOIAEES approximateness
APOIAEOT approximate cost
APORAEES appropriateness
AQIIIEES acquisitiveness
ARAEMNSN Adrian Edmondson
ARAOLVTI Adriano Olivetti
ARCLUAIT agriculturalist
ARCNLPAT African elephant
ARDLTRIR Airedale terrier
ARDNMCLY aerodynamically
ARHEMRHL air-chief-marshal
ARNEKNEK Aaron Temkin Beck
ARODTOIG air-conditioning
AROIOELT a crook in one's lot
ARPNHOEN a drop in the ocean
ARRASRLS aurora australis
ARRFCRIR aircraft carrier
ARSTERCS across the tracks
ARWOSNRG arrow-poison frog
ASRLARLS Australian Rules
ASUDSRAH as sound as a roach
ASUTEULY assault sexually
ATCEIAIM anticlericalism
ATEAEIES at the same time as
ATEAEOET at the same moment
ATEATIUE at the last minute
ATEISBUH at the first blush
ATENTNEF at the instance of
ATERASAE at the trial stage
ATERPFHT at the drop of a hat
ATFALAET Act of Parliament
ATFGRSIN act of aggression
ATHGDYOT act the giddy goat
ATIKSPAK as thick as a plank
ATMAEUNX autumnal equinox
ATNUISEN Anton Rubinstein
ATOAIAIN astro-navigation
ATOAJUNL Acts of Adjournal
ATOCMITE action committee
ATOIAIEY authoritatively
ATOPTNIL action potential
ATOYRLOE Anthony Trollope
ATPNLIAE antepenultimate
ATRAIEOE Alternative Vote
ATRDORPY autoradiography
ATREUTOS after deductions
ATRIAECP a storm in a teacup
ATROCABR anterior chamber
ATRPCNRC anthropocentric
ATRPLGCL anthropological
ATRPMRHC anthropomorphic
ATRPPAIE anthropophagite
ATRPSPIT anthroposophist
ATRTSAII Arturo Toscanini
ATRUISEN Artur Rubinstein
ATSECMKR act as peacemaker
ATSHIWMN act as chairwoman
ATTETELB Arts Theatre Club
ATUEDNTN Arthur Eddington
ATUPNENS Arthur Pendennis
ATVTHLDY activity holiday
AUEETRAE amusement arcade
AULADRSA Aquila and Prisca
AVNEIYAS advanced in years
AVNEOIIN advance position
AVNUOSES adventurousness
BAAATEEL bear away the bell
BAARBEDH by a hair's breadth
BADAEADR brandy Alexander
BADNUGAE Brandenburg Gate
BAEAIAIN bear examination
BAEOTDNS bearer of tidings
BAEOTIES blameworthiness
BAHAIYPN bear heavily upon
BAKAEFVR blackwater fever
BAKHNCRS black rhinoceros
BAKIHSAE black nightshade
BAKTOEHR bracket together
BAMRSATE Beaumaris Castle
BASMOEOT beat someone to it
BASOENOF brass someone off
BBDCUAIR Baby Doc Duvalier
BBLADQEK bubble and squeak
bubble-and-squeak
BCEILGCL bacteriological
BCIGASIE Buckinghamshire
BCMAALBE become available
BCMAEBRF become a member of
BCMAINTD become alienated
BCMDFEET become different
BCMEAITD become emaciated
BCMETAGD become estranged
BCMHSIEO become hostile to
BCMIDGAT become indignant
BCMISLET become insolvent
BCMMRSLD become more solid
BCMOCNET by common consent
BCMOEAIE become operative
BCOOEHES back on one's heels
BCTSUROE back to square one
BCTTEUUE Back to the Future
BCWRLOIG backward-looking
BDNBEKAT bed and breakfast
BDYETLTD badly ventilated

BEADKTLS beer and skittles
BECIGODR bleaching powder
BECOPOIE breach of promise
BEKLNEIH break a lance with
BEKNOICS break into pieces
BENNSONT bee in one's bonnet
BESEKUGS beefsteak fungus
BETENSAT breathe one's last
BFRYUNWT before you know it
BFTADTRS by fits and starts
BHNTECNS behind the scenes
BHOOBCOK by hook or by crook
BHVFOIHY behave foolishly
BIDNSCEY building society
BIGAKOIE bring back to life
BIGNBYAE bring and buy sale
BIGNTLGT bringing to light
BIGOAUIY bring to maturity
BIGONOIE bring down to size
BIGOSDRD being considered
BIHAAUTN bright as a button
BIHADREY bright and breezy
BIIHOGAR British longhair
BIIHOUBA British Columbia
BITNHCEP built on the cheap
BLAIILNS Balearic Islands
BLFOTELE bolt from the blue
BLNEFAUE balance of nature
BLNTERGN Bel and the Dragon
BLWHSRAE below the surface
BLWNSRAH below one's breath
BMTLISRP bimetallic strip
BNAIBITN Benjamin Britten
BNEWRHUE bonded warehouse
BNFTFLRY benefit of clergy
BNIGUWRS bending outwards
BNMATERM binomial theorem
BNTMSOII Benito Mussolini
BODEVDOK broad-leaved dock
BODIDDES broad-mindedness
BODNNGAS Brobdingnagians
BODUDIGY bloodcurdlingly
BOHLREES brothel-creepers
BOIITEID Blowin' in the Wind
BOKNSIIN block one's vision
BOOECACS blow one's chances
BOOEONON blow one's own horn
BOOIACOK biological clock
BORSBRIS blow raspberries
BOSNSDLS boots and saddles
BOTEAEIE be on the safe side
BOUIECNE bioluminescence
BOVIAIIY bioavailability
BPTUTGAS be put out to grass
BRAAATAD Barbara Cartland
BRAAEWRH Barbara Hepworth
BRHAHNUS birthday honours
BRHFEAIY burgh of regality
BRHLMWAR Bartholomew Fair
BRHRREAN Bernhard Riemann
BRHSGLEY Borghese Gallery
BRITEHOT burr in the throat
BRITEUPE born in the purple
BRLANRDE Beryl Bainbridge
BRNAOTUS Berengar of Tours
BROIFRES Barrow-in-Furness
BROUOTET Burton-upon-Trent
BRRNRSEL Bertrand Russell
BRRSRIAD Barbra Streisand
BRSFFAHR birds of a feather
BRTEATOF bore the pants off
BRTNOLMS burst into flames
BRTOFAZE burnt to a frazzle
BRUARAGE Bermuda Triangle
BRWTPSIN burn with passion
BSALNSAL by small and small
BSCRNILS basic principles
BSDECOHR beside each other
BSEEPOES Bessemer process
BSPROMNE best performance
BTEFYTOE butterfly stroke
BTEHRHIS by the short hairs
BTENOADE between you and me
BTESMOEP butter someone up
BTETOGAD by the strong hand
BTEYPRTD battery-operated
BTHRCSIG batch processing
BTILNERR by trial and error
BTLNSWAE bottlenose whale
BTLOBIAN Battle of Britain
BTLOCLNO Battle of Colenso
BTLOCMRI Battle of Cambrai
BTLOCRNA Battle of Corunna
BTLODEDN Battle of Dresden
BTLOFODN Battle of Flodden
BTLOIOIA Battle of Iwo Jima
BTLOJTAD Battle of Jutland
BTLOLPNO Battle of Lepanto
BTLOLUTA Battle of Leuctra
BTLOMRNO Battle of Marengo
BTLOPASY Battle of Plassey
BTLOSLMS Battle of Salamis
BTLOSLRO Battle of Salerno
BTLOTASS Battle of Thapsus
BTLOTEEA Battle of the Neva
BTLOTEIE Battle of the Nile
BTLSFORK Battles of Tobruk
BTOTERDE bite on the bridle
BTOTEULT bite on the bullet
BUFOEBOY blue-footed booby
BWAADNVR bowl a maiden over
BYHFEDMF buy the freedom of
BYNEDRNE beyond endurance
CAATRKTH character sketch
CAATRSIS characteristics
CADUDRIR Claudius Dornier
CAEPRTOS cease operations
CAGDATCE charged particle
CAGDFARS chargé d'affaires
CAGOADES change of address
CAISHROE Clarissa Harlowe
CAKNTEOR chalking the door
CALSAEFX Charles James Fox
CALSAGTN Charles Laughton
CALSALRY Charles Earl Grey
CALSAOSY Charles Yanofsky
CALSEALE Charles de Gaulle
CALSIGLY Charles Kingsley
CALSODER Charles Goodyear
CALSRVLE Charles Greville
CALTEMLE Charlotte Amalie
CALTEODY Charlotte Corday
CALTERNE Charlotte Brontë
CALTEVLE Charlottesville
CATRNVRE chapter and verse
CBCETMTE cubic centimetre
CBEEEIIN cable television
CBLDOEHR cobbled together
CBNTIITR cabinet minister
CCLAESAP Cecil James Sharp
CDOBHVOR code of behaviour
CEESRNAO Clemens Brentano
CEIAEEET chemical element
CEIAWRAE chemical warfare
CEKFHCUT clerk of the court
CEKFHWRS clerk of the works
CEMNFRAD Clermont-Ferrand
CENSWITE clean as a whistle
CERNSHOT clear one's throat
CESARSLB Chelsea Arts Club
CETHGLOS cheat the gallows
CETRETET Chester-le-Street
CFETBEOK coffee-table book
CIDAEYET child-safety seat
CIDESONR Children's Corner
CIEEAEDR Chinese calendar
CIEEHQES Chinese chequers
CIEEHSES Chinese whispers
CIEOADEL Clive Howard Bell
CIIABPIM clinical baptism
CIIAIAIN criminalisation
criminalization
CLATNINO call attention to
CLBODDES cold-bloodedness
CLCMOIIN cold composition
CLCMOTAM Cold Comfort Farm
CLEEETRR college lecturer
CLETRPEE collector's piece
CLHATDES cold-heartedness
CLIINORE collision course
CLRDSRNS Colorado Springs
CLSILPEE celestial sphere
CMAGAANT campaign against
CMASOAEY compassionately
CMAYFOVS Company of Wolves
CMDOMNES comedy of manners
CMDWHAYN come down heavy on
CMECABEK commercial break
CMEDOSES compendiousness
CMEIIEES competitiveness
CMELNSUE Cumberland sauce
CMHMTROT come home to roost
CMIAINOK combination lock
CMIEAEIH commiserate with
CMIEELIH combine well with
CMITCNAT come into contact
CMITEEBR committee member
CMITOEON come into one's own
CMLEISRO Camille Pissarro

CMLMNAIY complementarily
CMLTANIY complete annuity
CMLTSUIS complete studies
CMLXETNE complex sentence
CMNTNTIG coming to nothing
CMOITEOL common in the soil
CMOKOLDE common knowledge
CMOLWPUE common-law spouse
CMOOPSUE common of pasture
CMOTEAKT come on the market
CMOWATDY Commonwealth Day
CMRHNIEY comprehensively
CMRHNIIE comprehensivise
comprehensivize
CMRIOSIE come rain or shine
CMRRAYOY camera-ready copy
CMRSIIIY compressibility
CMSMOEWY come someone's way
CMTAEIIN come to a decision
CMTEAPAN come the raw prawn
CMTGISIH come to grips with
CMTONTOS comity of nations
CMTTEIDF come to the mind of
CMTTRSIH come to terms with
CMUEIAIN computerization
CMUESINE computer science
CMUIAEIH communicate with
CMUIAIEY communicatively
CMUIYCOL community school
CMUIYETE community centre
CMUIYHRE community charge
CMUIYIDD community-minded
CMUTBEES combustibleness
CMUTSRTH come up to scratch
CNBDIGIH can't be doing with
CNCECMNY conscience money
CNCECPOF conscience-proof
CNCETOSY conscientiously
CNEBRTLS Canterbury Tales
CNECNIGY condescendingly
CNEINEOD convenience food
CNEPAIEY contemplatively
CNEPIIIY contemptibility
CNEPOCUT contempt of court
CNEPRNIY contemporaneity
CNEPRNOS contemporaneous
CNESBEES conversableness
CNETDCIN concerted action
CNETNAUT consenting adult
CNETOAIE conventionalise
conventionalize
CNETOAIM conventionalism
CNETOAIT conventionalist
CNETOAIY conventionality
CNETOSES contentiousness
CNEUIEES consecutiveness
CNEUNILY consequentially
CNEVTOIT conservationist
CNIEAEES considerateness
CNIECTIK confidence trick
CNIEIGHT considering that
CNIETAIY confidentiality
CNIUAINL configurational
CNLITEID Candle in the Wind
CNMTGAHC cinematographic
CNMTGAHR cinematographer
CNPCOSES conspicuousness
CNRBNOWR contraband of war
CNRDCOIY contradictorily
CNRLAIIY controllability
CNROGAIY centre of gravity
CNROIETA centre of inertia
CNRTLTOS congratulations
CNRVRILY controversially
CNTNLMET Constant Lambert
CNTTETAT constituent part
CNUESCEY consumer society
CNUPIEES consumptiveness
CNUSATAE consubstantiate
COAAUUBR cool as a cucumber
CODUKOAD Cloudcuckooland
cloud-cuckoo-land
COEACFRL cholecalciferol
COEADDES close-handedness
COEITDES close-fistedness
COENSYSO close one's eyes to
COEOHCET close to the chest
COEYOEHR closely together
COHSNUTY clothes industry
COOAECAR chocolate éclair
COOIEUDE Crocodile Dundee
COSFTERE Cross of St George
COSHRBCN cross the Rubicon
COSODUZE crossword puzzle
COSONRRN cross-country run
COSWRSIH cross swords with
CPANAHAH Captain MacHeath
CPANBOUE Captain Absolute
CPCTFRET capacity for heat
CPEDAIBE Cepheid variable
CPLAYCIN capillary action
CPTLANTX capital gains tax
CRAKOLDE carnal knowledge
CRATESIE Carmarthenshire
CREFCTAD curse of Scotland
CREISASN Cornelius Jansen
CREPNIGO corresponding to
CREPNIGY correspondingly
CRETNFUD correcting fluid
CRIFRSAK Cardiff Arms Park
CRIGADAR carriage and pair
CRIIDHQE certified cheque
CRIPLOAY cardiopulmonary
CRIUUVTE curriculum vitae
CRLALNTN Cyril Darlington
CRLEILNS Coral Sea Islands
CRLSINES Carolus Linnaeus
CRMNOSES ceremoniousness
CRMOIOEE coram domino rege
CRNASRLS Corona Australis
CRNLGCLY chronologically
CROAEADR corporate raider
CROMCLES Carson McCullers
CRSAEPIN Christadelphian
CRSIMJSY Christ in Majesty
CRSINEUE Christian de Duve
CRSMSATS Christmas cactus
CRSMSSAD Christmas Island
CRSNHTBE cards on the table
CRSOHREN Christopher Dean
CRSOHRRN Christopher Wren
CRUJCNIS circumjacencies
CRUNVGTR circumnavigator
CRUSATAE circumstantiate
CRUSRPIN circumscription
CRUTRIIG circuit training
CRUTURUE circuitous route
CRYAORIH curry favour with
CRYFTEEL carry off the bell
CRYOVCIN carry conviction
CRYUOEBT carry out one's bat
CSAADAIN Cosmas and Damian
CSABRHLN Caspar Bartholin
CSAFIDIH Caspar Friedrich
CSAHDWVR cast a shadow over
CSCNIIND cask-conditioned
CSEISREY cosmetic surgery
CSIGHERH costing the earth
CSIOECIS cash in one's chips
CSLSNHAR castles in the air
CSOEEEVR cast one's eye over
CSOILAET custodial parent
CTAENUTY cottage industry
CTEADIHD catted and fished
CTEIEOAD Catherine Howard
CTHGIPEF catch a glimpse of
CTHNSRAH catch one's breath
CTIAICCE citric acid cycle
CTNCMAAN cut and come again
CTZNTETE Citizen's Theatre
CUAIEUNN causa sine qua non
CUCLFTTS Council of States
CUCLFUOE Council of Europe
CUCOEGAD Church of England
CUDTAEES couldn't care less
CUEEETET cause resentment
CUEITRES cause bitterness
CUEOAEAT cause to take part
CUEOOEAE cause to lose face
CUHADOLD caught and bowled
CUINRTLS Cautionary Tales
CUSOSUIS course of studies
CUTRRUET counter-argument
CUTYFRGN country of origin
CVNNOGAE covenant of grace
CVNNOWRS covenant of works
CVRNSRCS cover one's tracks
CWOADNIN cowboy and Indian
CYLPOARS Cryolophosaurus
CYNSEROT cry one's heart out
CYPEIIAE cryoprecipitate
CYTLIAIN crystallisation
crystallization
CYTLORPY crystallography
CYTNIGIH cry stinking fish
DAAAORAL dead as a doornail
dead as a door-nail
DAACEJBN do a hatchet job on
DAATNINO draw attention to

DACRIGWY dual carriageway
DAGRIHRT Django Reinhardt
DAGTMNHP draughtsmanship
DAIOEHRS draw in one's horns
DAMNFNES dead men's fingers
DATOEHAT dear to one's heart
DAWTQIKY deal with quickly
DBRADSOE Dr Barnardo's home
DCAENOET declare innocent
DCAOILES dictatorialness
DCESQIKY decrease quickly
DCIIGOOE declining to vote
DCLIIAIN decalcification
DCMISOIG decommissioning
DCMLRCIN decimal fraction
DCMLURNY decimal currency
DCNAIAIE decontaminative
DCNAIAIN decontamination
DCPEAIIY decipherability
DCROIAIN decarbonization
DCRTDIDW decorated window
DCRUIAIN decarburization
DDIGHISE dodging the issue
DEETELNS deepest feelings
DEOACSIN deed of accession
DFEETAIG differentiating
DFEETAIN differentiation
DFIUTOID difficult to find
DFNEESES defencelessness
DFNTCMET definite comment
DFREANIY deferred annuity
DFREPYET deferred payment
DGAMRKOD Dag Hammarskjöld
DGEOFEDM degree of freedom
DGTZNBAD digitizing board
DIDSRAIE deindustrialise
deindustrialize
DLADPOAY dollar diplomacy
DLRUTEES delirium tremens
DLVRHGOS deliver the goods
DLVROFCR delivery officer
DLVRVRIT deliver a verdict
DLYNTCIS delaying tactics
DMCAIAIN democratization
DMGEIAIN demagnetization
DMNIPYET demand in payment
DMNOTETE Dominion Theatre
DMNTAIEY demonstratively
DMRAINIE demarcation line
DMSIIAIN demystification
DMSIMTES domestic matters
DMSISINE domestic science
DNAWRHUE Donmar Warehouse
DNEBRNOM Daniel Barenboim
DNEBROLI Daniel Bernoulli
DNETEDNE dance attendance
DNGVAUGR don't give a bugger
DNLPESNE Donald Pleasance
DNMKMLUH don't make me laugh
DOEDMEET do one's damnedest
DOELVLET do one's level best
DONOENOT drown someone out
DOOEATHS drop one's aitches
DOOUSCLS Diodorus Siculus
DOPIOAIO Deo Optimo Maximo
DPFHHRZN dip of the horizon
DPHSCOOY depth psychology
DPIEFIIN deprive of vision
DPIMVMNO doppio movimento
DPLGSIAE dephlogisticate
DPNDMUIR Daphne Du Maurier
DPNETLUE dependent clause
DPNSNCLE Daphnis and Chloe
DPOAICRS diplomatic corps
DPRMNAIE departmentalise
departmentalize
DPRMNAIM departmentalism
DPRMNSOE department store
DRACTERL Durham Cathedral
DRCMREIG direct marketing
DRIGUHOM darning mushroom
DRTYATSN Dorothy Pattison
DSAIFCIN dissatisfaction
DSASOAEY dispassionately
DSDATGOS disadvantageous
DSEPCFLY disrespectfully
DSESLRSN dispersal prison
DSFETDES disaffectedness
DSFOETET disafforestment
DSGEAIIY disagreeability
DSICIEES distinctiveness
DSIGIHBE distinguishable
DSIGIHET distinguishment
DSILHMET Dashiell Hammett
DSLCDESN displaced person
DSLUINET disillusionment
DSNAGEET disentanglement
DSNEETDY disinterestedly
DSNIIAIN desensitization
DSODFONS discord of sounds
DSOIBEES dissociableness
DSONEACD discountenanced
DSOTNAIN discontinuation
DSOTNOSY discontinuously
DSRAIAIN disorganization
DSRCIEES destructiveness
DSRCIIIY destructibility
DSRPIEES descriptiveness
DSRTOAIY discretionarily
DSRYNAGL destroying angel
DSUSOGOP discussion group
DTHLDSAE Dutch elm disease
DTIAIAIN detribalization
DTNINETE detention centre
DULIDMIY Double Indemnity
DULPEMNA double pneumonia
DUOADCIN drug of addiction
DUSHSUEM Deutsches Museum
DVDRBIIS David Frabricius
DVDRNNEG David Cronenberg
DVLPETLY developmentally
DVLPETRA development area
DVNHRCEM Devonshire cream
DVNMSEGR divine messenger
DVRIIAIN diversification
DVTATNIN devote attention
DWHATDES downheartedness
DYIHRBEY daylight robbery
EBRADCOX embarras de choix
embarras du choix
ECAAINAK exclamation mark
ECADVROE each and every one
ECAGADAT Exchange and Mart
ECAGAIIY exchangeability
ECAGCNRL exchange control
ECAGLTES exchange letters
ECAGSUET exchange student
ECAGTAHR exchange teacher
ECAGVESN exchange views on
ECEETTOS excrementitious
ECEIHAOI Escherichia coli
ECEILGCL ecclesiological
ECEISIIM ecclesiasticism
ECLTRLUE escalator clause
ECMATCLY encomiastically
ECMUIAIN excommunication
ECNRCESN eccentric person
ECUAEOAK encourage to talk
ECUIEIHS exclusive rights
EDCIOOIT endocrinologist
EDXSFNDS Eudoxus of Cnidus
EECSBCCE exercise bicycle
EEECTERL Exeter Cathedral
EEEESROE Ebenezer Scrooge
EEIGRMOE evening primrose
EEIGTNAD Evening Standard
EELSIGES everlastingness
EELSIGIE everlasting life
EENLRAGE eternal triangle
EEPIIAIN exemplification
EETIASOM electrical storm
EETIBAKT electric blanket
EETIBTEY electric battery
EETICRET electric current
EETIIAIN electrification
EETIPWRD electric-powered
EETOANTC electromagnetic
EETOCUTC electroacoustic
EETOEAIE electronegative
EETOEHIS electrotechnics
EETOERCL electrometrical
EETOHMCL electrochemical
EETOHRSS electrophoresis
EETOHRTC electrophoretic
EETOIFAH electronic flash
EETOIMSC electronic music
EETOYAIS electrodynamics
EEYEODEK every second week
EEYNIIUL every individual
EEYOADHN every now and then
EEYOHRSN every mother's son
EFACIEET enfranchisement
EFCCOSES efficaciousness
EGIMOSIE eggs in moonshine
EGNDLCOX Eugène Delacroix
EGNSONAE egg-and-spoon race
EGOSNAED engrossing a deed
EHAMHMES Ephraim Chambers
EHBTOITC exhibitionistic

EHICENIG ethnic cleansing
EHNDRAOS echinodermatous
EHOIGITC ethnolinguistic
EHOUIOOY ethnomusicology
EIAEHALR Elizabeth Taylor
EIAEHENT Elizabeth Bennet
EIAEHIHP Elizabeth Bishop
EIBRHATE Edinburgh Castle
EICPLAIM episcopalianism
EIEILGCL epidemiological
EITMLGCL epistemological
ELSEESAD Ellesmere Island
EMNECLEE Emmanuel College
ENSHMNWY Ernest Hemingway
ENTATRAR Ernst Walter Mayr
EOADAAIR Edouard Daladier
Édouard Daladier
EOOIOOIT ecotoxicologist
EOOIRFGE economic refugee
EPDTOSES expeditiousness
EPEITCLY euphemistically
EPESEIEY express delivery
EPESOITC expressionistic
EPESYPTY express sympathy
EPRCQTQE emperick qutique
EPREPOUT exported product
EPRETAIM experientialism
EPRETAIT experientialist
EPRMNAIE experimentalise
experimentalize
EPRMNAIM experimentalism
EPRMNAIN experimentation
EPRMNAIT experimentalist
EPRROCRO Emperor Concerto
ERHHTEIG earth-shattering
ERPACUCL European Council
ERPAIAIN Europeanization
ESERBLIN Easter Rebellion
ESETPESN Elsie Stephenson
ESIEHLES Erskine Childers
ESNILATR essential factor
ESTGTNIH easy to get on with
ETAAIASX extramarital sex
ETALUTAE extra-illustrate
ETARIAIY extraordinarily
ETBIHDOK established work
ETERNUIL entrepreneurial
ETMLGCLY entomologically
ETMOAIES extemporariness
ETMOIAIN extemporization
ETNEODAE entente cordiale
ETNIIAIN extensification
ETNSEROT eat one's heart out
ETRAIAIN externalization
ETRASRAE external surface
ETROIAIN exteriorization
EUROALZI Eduardo Paolozzi
EWRGOISN Edward G Robinson
EWRRCETR Edward Rochester
EWRTEATR Edward the Martyr
FACIBUHR François Boucher
FACIFNLN François Fénelon
FACIMUIC François Mauriac
FACSAGAE Francis Palgrave
FACSEUOT Francis Beaufort
Francis Beaumont
FACSFSII Francis of Assisi
FACSOEOA Francisco de Goya
FACSORNO Francisco Franco
FAHRNSET feather one's nest
FAIGHWRT fearing the worst
FAIIPLPI Fra Filippo Lippi
FAISOEHS Flavius Josephus
FAKUTMAN Frankfurt am Main
FAKWOWRH Frank W Woolworth
FAMNAIES fragmentariness
FATFRMES feast of trumpets
FCSNFGRS facts and figures
FCSNSIDN focus one's mind on
FDRCFLII Federico Fellini
FDSTUTTA fides et justitia
FEAGIVDT feel aggrieved at
FEASCAIN free association
FEBTEAOT feel bitter about
FECPLNSA French Polynesia
FEDMRMAN freedom from pain
FEEIKAGR Frederick Sanger
FEEIKALR Frederick Taylor
FEEIKEIS Frederick Delius
FEEIKLNA Frederick Blanda
FEEIKRVS Frederick Treves
FEEIKSTN Frederick Ashton
FEEIRPAL Frederic Raphael
FEIOEBNS feel in one's bones
FEOEMSLS flex one's muscles
FERVLINT feel revulsion at
FFYECPEE fifty pence piece
FGRADLUS Figure and Clouds
FGTNSONR fight ones corner
FGTOHRPS fight to the ropes
FIBRIIBT flibbertigibbet
FIDIHNES Friedrich Engels
FIGOHWNS fling to the winds
FIHATNAT flight attendant
FIHITEYT Flight into Egypt
FIKOLCIN Frick Collection
FINLSCEY friendly society
FLDWIVLE fall down in value
FLEERNER folie de grandeur
FLEMRSIN false impression
FLIGOICS falling to pieces
FLLNILNS Falkland Islands
FLMTLAKT Full Metal Jacket
FLOEOEEF fall over oneself
FLOOEKES fall on one's knees
FLOTAELR fellow-traveller
FLTOEKES fall to one's knees
FMLAIAIN familiarization
FMLAIEIH familiarize with
FMLALWNE family allowance
FNAETLNT fundamental unit
FNATCOAE Fantastic Voyage
FNAYOTAL fantasy football
FNDSICIN fine distinction
FNEWBPDR funnel-web spider
FNITRSIG find interesting
FNLOTFAL final port of call
FNNILYTM financial system
FNOEACUT find one's account
FNRLIETR funeral director
FNSIGTOE finishing stroke
FNTENWRO find the answer to
FNTOAGOP functional group
FNYRSPRY fancy-dress party
FOFRTOAT from first to last
FOHNTMUH from hand to mouth
FOOCAIPN Fyodor Chaliapin
FOTEHUDR from the shoulder
FOTFHHUE front of the house
FOTNCPTL floating capital
FOTPOOTM from top to bottom
FRADHNIG forward-thinking
FRADLNIG forward planning
FRADOEET forward movement
FRELGTIG forked lightning
FRENOPAE force into a place
FREOELNS forget one's lines
FRHBNFTF for the benefit of
FRHLFOHM for the life of him
FRHLFOHR for the life of her
FRHTMBIG for the time being
FRIADACS Ferdinand Marcos
FRIDNLNT Forbidden Planet
FRIERSET Fertile Crescent
FRINXHNE foreign exchange
FRIOEBLY fire in one's belly
FRLTMSAE for old time's sake
FRODESAE for goodness sake
FRTIUEAT first-lieutenant
FRTPERNE first appearance
FRTRNILS first principles
FRWAOEEF forswear oneself
FSAPOCIG fast approaching
FSINBEES fashionableness
FSINUIES fashion business
FSITRUIE fossil turquoise
FTECRSMS Father Christmas
FTMWIBED Fatima Whitbread
FUDTOSOE foundation stone
FUHNMAOS Flushing Meadows
FUTDMNIN fourth dimension
FXDEOIES fixed set of ideas
FXDXRSIN fixed expression
FYFTEADE fly off the handle
FYNPAAGR flying phalanger
GAANISAE go at a snail's pace
GADLQETY grandiloquently
GAHCEINR graphic designer
GAIAINLY gravitationally
GAIYLTOM gravity platform
GAOHNCLY gramophonically
GAOOEPRI Giacomo Leopardi
GAOOGSII Giacomo Agostini
GASOPRID grasshopper mind
GATMUIYO grant immunity to
GAUAESGR granulated sugar
GBSAKSOY go by shanks's pony
GDLSTEAK God bless the mark
GECEASCE Glencoe Massacre

GEFIRBBY Greyfriars Bobby
GEHUDAIG greyhound-racing
GESTEHES grease the wheels
GETITRAE Great Bitter Lake
GETRUNIY greater quantity
GFRHJGLR go for the jugular
GFRSOTIE go for a short time
GIGNSWWY going one's own way
GIGONSED going to one's head
GIKOLDEF gain knowledge of
GIMSEYVR gain mastery over
GINHGLNS Guiana Highlands
GITCMITE go into committee
GLEDLCOS Golden Delicious
golden delicious
GLEHNCFS golden handcuffs
GLEHNSAE golden handshake
GLEPRCUE golden parachute
GLERTIVR golden retriever
GLINHPED Gillian Shepherd
GLLEGLLI Galilieo Galilei
GLSIHETE goldsmith beetle
GNEBEPAT ginger beer plant
GNELUIES genteel business
GNLMNAMR gentleman farmer
GNLMNIES gentlemanliness
GNMRNMAL Gene Myron Amdahl
GNNRMRHC gynandromorphic
GNRLEGAO General Belgrano
GNRLLCIN general election
GNRLRCIE general practice
GNRLSEBY General Assembly
GNWTTEID Gone With the Wind
Gone with the Wind
GOAIKTIE go on a picket line
GOANBLII Giovanni Bellini
GOANCMBE Giovanni Cimabué
GOANCSII Giovanni Cassini
GOCSESIE Gloucestershire
GOECEEAD Grover Cleveland
GOEETRHN go one better than
GOFEBYOT Geoffrey Boycott
GOFECACR Geoffrey Chaucer
GOFHDEED go off the deep end
GOFHSBET go off the subject
GOFRNTIG good for anything
GOFTAFOK go off at half cock
GOFTTNET go off at a tangent
GOGDMUIR George Du Maurier
GOGGEVLE George Grenville
GOGGOSIH George Grossmith
GOGRBRSN George Robertson
GOGSEATE Georges Lemaître
GOGSNAAA George Santayana
GOGSOPDU Georges Pompidou
GOGTEEYN George Trevelyan
GOGVNEEY George von Hevesy
GOGVNOVR George Vancouver
GOGVNUAS György von Lukacs
GOGYAEKV Giorgiy Malenkov
GOHOOOIT geochronologist
GOOPOOIT geomorphologist
GOSNPRVL goods on approval
GOTFUIES go out of business
GOTIELGT go out like a light
GOUACUTR globular cluster
GRACTOIS German Catholics
GRADCRDR Gerhard Schröder
GRIMGZNS girlie magazines
GRLMCRAO Girolamo Cardano
GRRDPRIU Gérard Depardieu
GRUDNRUD go round and round
GRUOELIS gird up one's loins
GSADETIG Giscard d'Estaing
GSAELUET Gustave Flaubert
GSICLMIT gossip columnist
GSRETRTS gastroenteritis
gastro-enteritis
GTAIIRIH get familiar with
GTAKOOML get back to normal
GTEDMEUG Götterdämmerung
GTFIDEPR Gottfried Semper
GTFOECET get off one's chest
GTFTERUD get off the ground
GTHDOOOE get the drop on one
GTHFNEOT get the finger out
GTHNSOIG get things moving
GTHRNRUD get the runaround
GTHWOGDA get the wrong idea
GTHWRTFT get the worst of it
GTIOCDRM get divorced from
GTLEDILR Gottlieb Daimler
GTLSEMDP get all steamed up
GTNNHWRD get on in the world
GTNNSEVS get on one's nerves
GTNSADRP get one's dander up
GTNSERNS get one's bearings
GTNSHROT get one's shirt out
GTNSKTSN get one's skates on
GTNSOKYP get one's monkey up
GTOEACUT go to one's account
GTOENSOT get someone's goat
GTOIDADF get to windward of
GTPOICIF get up to mischief
GTRCADUN go to rack and ruin
GUIADETI Giulio Andreotti
GVAADIEO give a hard time to
GVAAEITO give a facelift to
GVAASRNE give an assurance
GVAOAINO give a donation to
give an ovation to
GVARLIGO give a grilling to
GVATOIYO give authority to
GVITSMOE give it to someone
GVNWNRYO give new energy to
GVOEBCIG give one's backing
GVOECNET give one's consent
GVOEEFIS give oneself airs
GVOEEFWY give oneself away
GVOEOIIN give one's opinion
GVOESPOT give one's support
GVROGNRL governor-general
GVSGETOS give suggestions
GVSMOEEL give someone hell
GVSMOEIE give someone five
GVTEAEWY give the game away
GVTEEDEO give the needle to
GVTEHMSP give the thumbs-up
GVTEHWWY give the show away
GVTENEVR give the once-over
GVTEOLFR give the world for
GVTERSOF give the brush-off
GVUTEHOE give up the throne
GWRZRMNR Gewürztraminer
GWTECOHR go with each other
GWTOTAIG go without saying
GWTTETEM go with the stream
GYEAPSAT Guy de Maupassant
HAEOHAES heaven of heavens
HAHRTLAY heath fritillary
HAIGITNE hearing distance
HAODEBAE hyaloid membrane
HBLDHYOD hobbledehoyhood
HBLSOSAT Hubble's constant
HCLBRYIN Huckleberry Finn
HCNYARAE hackney carriage
hackney-carriage
HCNYDHAE hackneyed phrase
HDKNDSAE Hodgkin's disease
HDOAHCLY hydropathically
HDOMUTIS Hudson Mountains
HDOYAIIT hydrodynamicist
HDOYNCCD hydrocyanic acid
HEOYUBSH Hieronymus Bosch
HGEEUAIN higher education
HGGAEBID high-gravel-blind
HGLDVLPD highly-developed
HGTEORPR Hugh Trevor-Roper
HGTMEAUE high temperature
HLAAARTR Haleakala Crater
HLCUTUEM Holocaust Museum
HLECUFED Holden Caulfield
HLEITCLY Hellenistically
HLGLNBGT Heligoland Bight
HLIGHRIS holding the reins
HLIGOEHR holding together
HLIRVRNE hold in reverence
HLNBAASY Helena Blavatsky
HLOEAARL hold over a barrel
HLORPCLY heliotropically
HLRMNMIE Holy Roman Empire
HLRSOSBE hold responsible
HMBCEWAE humpbacked whale
HMEADIKE Hammer and Sickle
hammer and sickle
HMNTRAIM humanitarianism
HMOAHCLY homeopathically
HMROCLEE Homerton College
HMSHNESN Hamish Henderson
HNEADRTL Hansel and Gretel
HNEAYLBC hendecasyllabic
HNEAYLBE hendecasyllable
HNETCEGE Hanseatic League
HNITSMOE hand it to someone
HNNHTIDE hen on a hot girdle
HNRDERWR Hundred Years' War
HNRIHNAH Hans Reichenbach
HNRKEWED Hendrik Verwoerd
HNYETEEL Henry Kettlewell

HPAANTOE hope against hope
HPCODICL hypochondriacal
HPCODISS hypochondriasis
HPOIAIIY hypnotizability
HPORTCAH Hippocratic oath
HPRHRIIM hyperthyroidism
HPRRTCLY hypercritically
HPYSSNBY happy as a sandboy
HRAHLEIH Herman Hollerith
HRAHOIIM hermaphroditism
HRATOOLW hard act to follow
HREETCLY hermeneutically
HREFRSOE Harvey Firestone
HRENHTOK horse and hattock
HRESNQEN Harpers and Queen
HRETETVL harvest festival
HRETORSN Herbert Morrison
HRFRCLEE Hertford College
HRHATDES hard-heartedness
HRIAEUEM Hermitage Museum
HRLMCILN Harold Macmillan
HRLNCOSN Harold Nicholson
HROIGFEL harrowing of hell
HROOETIG harp on one string
HRORFEUE harbour of refuge
HROROPIE harbour porpoise
HRSFDLMA horns of a dilemma
HRSFHATR horns of the altar
HRWRTEAE Hereward the Wake
HSIAIAIN hospitalization
HSLADUTE hustle and bustle
HSOIANVL historical novel
HSOIGAHC historiographic
HSOIGAHR historiographer
HTEADODR hither and yonder
HTEOTEET hit below the belt
HTHHALNS hit the headlines
HTHHGSOS hit the high spots
HTNHHESF hot on the heels of
HTRCRMTC heterochromatic
HTRGNOSY heterogeneously
HTRSXAIY heterosexuality
HUEFSEBY House of Assembly
HUOEWEST haud one's wheesht
HUSFAKES hours of darkness
HVAAAIYF have a capacity of
HVAAEPNE have as a response
HVAAWTOE have a way with one
HVACELOE have a screw loose
HVAICSIN have a discussion
HVAISORE have as its source
HVAISRGN have as its origin
HVAODIDO have a good mind to
HVAOEOIK have a bone to pick
HVAOGNFR have a longing for
HVAOLCIN have a collection
HVARVNFR have a craving for
HVATEORE have as the source
HVBTEHOT have by the throat
HVDUTAOT have doubts about
HVHLAIDO have half a mind to
HVIOEHNS have in one's hands
HVISRGNN have its origin in
HVNNBAIG having no bearing
HVNTUKIH have no truck with
HVOCSOFR have occasion for
HVOEAARL have over a barrel
HVOEEDWY have one's end away
HVOEKIEN have one's knife in
HVOEMRLS have one's marbles
HVOEROSN have one's roots in
HVQAMAOT have qualms about
HVSESRIE have seen service
HVTEUAIY have the audacity
HVWAITKS have what it takes
HWHWNBOS how the wind blows
HWIAILNS Hawaiian Islands
HXCLRPEE hexachlorophene
IACSIIIY inaccessibility
IAEAINHP in a relationship
IAEFCWRD in a perfect world
IAEKOIIN in a weak position
IAELHPET Isabelle Huppert
IAIAIEES imaginativeness
IAIAYUBR imaginary number
IAIFRNWY in a different way
IALIEIOD in all likelihood
IALIETOS in all directions
IALOSINE in all conscience
IAMSIIIY inadmissibility
IAPEESBE inapprehensible
IAPEIODR in apple-pie order
IAPIAIIY inapplicability
IAPORAEY inappropriately
IAREETIH in agreement with
IATAGTIE in a straight line
IATEERBE Ivan the Terrible
IATNIEES inattentiveness
IATRBEES inalterableness
IBAKNWIE in black and white
IBTENHLS in between whiles
ICDNAMSC incidental music
ICESQIKY increase quickly
ICEUOSES incredulousness
ICLAOAIN in collaboration
ICLUAIIY incalculability
ICMAAIIY incomparability
ICMAIIIY incompatibility
ICMESRBE incommensurable
ICMRHNIN incomprehension
ICNEUNEF in consequence of
ICNEUNIL inconsequential
ICNIEAEY inconsiderately
ICNIEAIN inconsideration
ICNOAIIY inconsolability
ICNPCOSY inconspicuously
ICNRNAIN in confrontation
ICNROSES incongruousness
ICRIIIIY incorrigibility
IDBTBEES indubitableness
IDCNASUT indecent assault
IDENTATR it does not matter
IDFAIIIY indefeasibility
IDFNIIIY indefensibility
IDGSIIIY indigestibility
IDISNDAS in dribs and drabs
IDMIIAIN indemnification
IDMTBEES indomitableness
IDPNECDY Independence Day
IDSOUIIY indissolubility
IDSROSES industriousness
IDTRIAEY indeterminately
IDVDAITC individualistic
IEFCCOSY inefficaciously
IEFCIEES ineffectiveness
IEFCULES ineffectualness
IEGAHCLY ideographically
IEPCAINF in expectation of
IEPIAIIY inexplicability
IEPNIEES inexpensiveness
IEPRECDN inexperienced in
IETFIGAK identifying mark
IETTEEET identity element
IEUTBEES inequitableness
IFNTSMLY infinitesimally
IFRARGOS infernal regions
IFRINLMS in foreign climes
IFTADTRS in fits and starts
IGOCNIIN in good condition
IHTHSEIF I Shot the Sheriff
IIOIACAI Isidor Isaac Rabi
IIUIPRAT it is unimportant
IJDCOSES injudiciousness
ILMTBEES illimitableness
ILRPRIND ill-proportioned
ILRULYUO I'll trouble you to
ILSROSES illustriousness
IMNLGCLY immunologically
IMRAIAIN immortalization
IMRINETR immersion heater
INMLNAIN ion implantation
INMRBEES innumerableness
IOERGTID in one's right mind
IOESAEIE in one's spare time
IOFNIEES inoffensiveness
IOHREPCS in other respects
IOLNTIKF I wouldn't think of
IOPRUEES inopportuneness
IOWRHPIG idol-worshipping
IPCNOSES impecuniousness
IPESOITC impressionistic
IPNTAIIY impenetrability
IPREPOUT imported product
IPRETELH in perfect health
IPRSAIIY imperishability
IQIIIEES inquisitiveness
IQIIOILY inquisitorially
IRCGIINF in recognition of
IRFAAIIY irrefragability
IRLGOSES irreligiousness
IRMMRNEF in remembrance of
IRMSIIIY irremissibility
IRPEESBE irreprehensible
IRSSIIIY irresistibility
IRVRIIIY irreversibility
ISATNOSY instantaneously
ISBRIAEY insubordinately
ISBRIAIN insubordination
ISBTNILY insubstantially

ISESAEET issue a statement
ISFECUTY it's a free country
ISGIIATY insignificantly
ISIAINLY inspirationally
ISMOEPWR in someone's power
ISMOETEH in someone's teeth
ISRCIEES instructiveness
ISRCINOK instruction book
ISRETOAY insurrectionary
ISRETOIT insurrectionist
ISRMNAIN instrumentation
ISRMNAIT instrumentalist
ISRMNAIY instrumentality
ISRMNPNL instrument panel
ISVNHEVN in seventh heaven
ITEAEFOE In the Name of Love
ITEAERAH in the same breath
ITEAKRUD in the background
ITEATEOT in the last resort
ITEERUUE in the near future
ITEETNPT in the melting-pot
ITEIIIYF in the vicinity of
ITEIKFIE in the nick of time
ITEISFUH in the first flush
ITEISPAE in the first place
ITELOEHR in the altogether
ITENEETF in the interest of
ITERSNEF in the presence of
ITESEDNY in the ascendancy
ITIDYNAE in this day and age
ITLETAIE intellectualise
intellectualize
ITLETAIM intellectualism
ITLETAIY intellectuality
ITLIIIIY intelligibility
ITLRBEES intolerableness
ITNIIAIN intensification
ITRAIAIN internalization
ITRAINLY internationally
ITRCOATC interscholastic
ITREEDNE interdependence
ITRETAIY intertextuality
ITRETOIM interventionism
ITRETOIT interventionist
ITRHNEBE interchangeable
ITRHNEBY interchangeably
ITRHNEET interchangement
ITROAIEY interrogatively
ITRONCIG interconnecting
ITRONCIN interconnection
ITRRTRHP interpretership
ITSUCPIN intussusception
IVLEAIIY invulnerability
IVSMNTUT investment trust
IYLOTEIG Idylls of the King
JAAMTAIG Joan Armatrading
JACADKLY Jean Claude Killy
JACAPLIN Jean Champollion
JANTEAKN Jeannette Rankin
JCBUCHRT Jacob Burckhardt
JCOALRDS jack-of-all-trades❑
JCULNDPE Jacqueline du Pré
JCUSOSEU Jacques Cousteau
JDSACBES Judas Maccabaeus
JEESREES jeepers creepers
JEILEAAH Joe Willie Namath
JHBNELWS John Bennet Lawes
JHHNYEMN John Henry Newman
JHHREJNS John Harvey-Jones
JHNEEKAT Johannes Eckhart
JHNPCEBL Johann Pachelbel
JHNVNEDR Johann von Herder
JHPIISUA John Philip Sousa
JHQICAAS John Quincy Adams
JHSHEIGR John Schlesinger
JHWLEBOH John Wilkes Booth
JIIMTIOY join in matrimony
JITEEVCS join the services
JLAONRIH Julian of Norwich
JLURSNEG Julius Rosenberg
JLUSRIHR Julius Streicher
JLYOLOTN Jelly Roll Morton
JMIJCFAH Jumpin' Jack Flash
JNHARNTN Jonah Barrington
JNOFYEGT junior-flyweight
JNTAEWRS Jonathan Edwards
JPNSBBAL Japanese Bobtail
JPTRYPOY Jupiter Symphony
JREKISAN Jurgen Klinsmann
JREUSOGS Jorge Luis Borges
JRMBNPRE Jérôme Bonaparte
JRSASIET Jaroslav Seifert
JRSRDNIL jurisprudential
JSABUDRY Josiah Bounderby
JSIIBEES justifiableness
JSMNGTGT just manage to get
JSPGILTN Joseph Guillotin
JSPPISLY Joseph Priestley
JSPWIWRH Joseph Whitworth
JSTEPOIE just the opposite
JSULDREG Joshua Lederberg
JSUVNIBG Justus von Liebig
JVNLHROE juvenile hormone
JWHRANHU Jawaharlal Nehru
JWLNHCON jewel in the crown
JXAOIINL juxtapositional
KCUOEHES kick up one's heels
KEAOKUFR keep a lookout for
KEAOPOIE keep a low profile
KECMAYIH keep company with
KEIGOODR keep in good order
KELCNETD keenly contested
KENTIGAK keep nothing back
KEOESITN keep one's shirt on
KEOETUBN keep one's thumb on
KIHAEHUE Keith Waterhouse
KIHOTEHP knight of the whip
KIHOTEOD knight of the road
KIHOTEOT knight of the post
KLIGEOTY Killing Me Softly
KNAOCOUE kangaroo closure
KNEHILAS Kenneth Williams
KNHATDES kind-heartedness
KNOTEATE king of the castle
KNOTEOET king of the forest
KOAHNOTO know a thing or two
KOKHSCSF knock the socks of
KOKLOAEP knock all of a heap
KOOEONID know one's own mind
KRGTEASY Karl Guthe Jansky
KSSMOEAS kiss someone's ass
KTLEFRIR Kathleen Ferrier
KUKEADIH knuckle sandwich
LAAERDNE lead a merry dance
LAEADIHS loaves and fishes
LAEIHNDY leave high and dry
LAENBYNE leave in abeyance
LAENHLRH leave in the lurch
LAEPEHES leave speechless
LAHRNILW leather on willow
LAIGAEAT leading male part
LAIGAEOE leading male role
LAIGOIIN leading position
LAIGUSIN leading question
LANNSPOT learning support
LATASAIN loan-translation
LBRLEORT Liberal Democrat
LCAASCLY lackadaisically
LCGAXOLS La Cage aux Folles
LCIOICNI Luchino Visconti
LCLOENET local government
LCMTRTXA locomotor ataxia
LCNSMNTR Loch Ness monster
LCOEEAIN lactovegetarian
LDECMLIT lodge a complaint
LDEIWIIG ladies-in-waiting
LDIBLZAN Ludwig Boltzmann
LDIFURAH Ludwig Feuerbach
LDIVNOHL Ludwig von Köchel
LDVCAISO Ludovico Ariosto
LEAVYSAD Lee Harvey Oswald
LENNSHOT lie in one's throat
LFTRAEIG life-threatening
LGEOEIKT leg before wicket
LGRTMCLY logarithmically
LGTEDDES light-headedness
LGTIDDES light-mindedness
LGTIGTIE lightning strike
LGTMTDAA legitimate drama
LIIIADLO Luigi Pirandello
LIUECIIY leisure activity
LKAOSINR like a dog's dinner
LKGNBSES like gangbusters
LKTELPES like the clappers
LLOTEALY lily of the valley
lily-of-the-valley
LMHTCYTM lymphatic system
LMUGRHEE limburger cheese
LNENETVL Lantern Festival
LNETBIHD long-established
LNHOVUHR luncheon voucher
LNIONETE longicorn beetle
LNODHITE Linford Christie
LNOEPCES line one's pockets
LNONEOIL Lincoln Memorial
LNOOEBRH land of one's birth
LNOPLAIM London Palladium
LNREESAL Leni Riefenstahl
LOADDVNI Leonardo da Vinci

Words marked ❑ can also be spelled with an initial capital letter

LOADOHUE	Leonard Hobhouse
LOBCIAGR	Look Back in Anger
LOEBRYOE	Lionel Barrymore
LOHATDES	lion-heartedness
LOODORNE	Leopold von Ranke
LOTETEWY	look the other way
LOWOTLIG	look who's talking
LPAGOCOG	lapsang souchong
LRCABRAN	Lord Chamberlain
LRHGAMRL	Lord High Admiral
LRNOHBRI	Lorenzo Ghiberti
LRPTRISY	Lord Peter Wimsey
LRSAAYIA	Larissa Latynina
LSECLNIE	lesser celandine
LSECRFLY	listen carefully
LSEIGEIE	listening device
LSICATRS	Leslie Charteris
LSOEBLNE	lose one's balance
LSOEFOIG	lose one's footing
LSOEHATO	lose one's heart to
LSOEMRLS	lose one's marbles
LSTEXHNE	lose the exchange
LTAIJCIN	lethal injection
LTLEGADR	little Englander
LTLGECLS	little grey cells
LTLNLTET	Little Nell Trent
LTNSARON	let one's hair down
LTRLHNIG	lateral thinking
LTTLHNOT	let it all hang out
LUECOIIR	Laurence Olivier
LUHIEDAN	laugh like a drain
LUHNLEON	laugh and lie down
LUHNLYON	laugh and lay down
LUSBUGOS	Louise Bourgeois
LUSMYLOT	Louisa May Alcott
LVIALRUD	Love is All Around
LVLEDDES	level-headedness
LVSFHPES	Lives of the Poets
LWECDREL	Lawrence Durrell
LWFASCIN	law of mass action
LWPRTDES	low-spiritedness
LWRNAKHN	lower in rank than
LXCGAHCL	lexicographical
LYNOOHNS	laying-on of hands
LYNSIGRN	lay one's finger on
LYONNSRS	lay down one's arms
LYRASOEY	lay great store by
LZRSAEHF	Lazarus Zamenhof
MAADOAOS	meat and potatoes
MAIGESES	meaninglessness
MASFPRAH	means of approach
MAUETEGH	measure strength
MAUIGYTM	measuring system
MCAITCLY	mechanistically
MCALATKV	Michail Saltykov
MCALEGAE	Michael Redgrave
MCALNATE	Michael Ondaatje
MCALOTLO	Michael Portillo
MCIEAGAE	machine language
MCOAUHES	much of a muchness
MCOCPCLY	macroscopically
	microscopically
MCOLCRNC	microelectronic
MCOOMCLY	macrocosmically
MDIHEPES	Midnight Express
MDLONWEE	middle of nowhere
MDLOTEOD	middle-of-the-road
MDMBTEFY	Madame Butterfly
MDNAEPAO	Madonna del Prato
MDNANCID	Madonna and Child
MDRTIAAL	moderate in a call
MDTTTEUE	meditate the muse
MGAECLEE	Magdalen College
MGAIOSES	magnanimousness
MGEICMAS	magnetic compass
MGEIEUTR	magnetic equator
MGIYNGAS	magnifying glass
MGUMGUSN	Magnus Magnusson
MIDRHBEA	Meindert Hobbema
MKACSTOS	make accusations
MKAEAPEF	make an example of
MKAECPIN	make an exception
MKAELNFR	make a beeline for
MKAETLOE	make a mental note
MKAIFRNE	make a difference
MKAITIGF	make a big thing of
MKAIVNOY	make an inventory
MKAJSMNS	make adjustments
MKALABEK	make a clean break
MKALASEP	make a clean sweep
MKALGTOS	make allegations
MKALUGKV	Mikhail Bulgakov
MKAODINR	make a good dinner
MKAODITF	make a good fist of
MKAONCIN	make a connection
MKARAFRT	make a break for it
MKCMOCUE	make common cause
MKCMOTBE	make comfortable
MKCNATIH	make contact with
MKCNCOSF	make conscious of
MKCNESOS	make concessions
MKCNIINL	make conditional
MKEEYFOT	make every effort
MKFINSIH	make friends with
MKFIWAHR	make fair weather
MKGETLYF	make great play of
MKIRASNO	make inroads into
MKLFHLFR	make life hell for
MKLSETEE	make less extreme
MKMNEETF	make mincemeat of
MKNTEETF	making the best of
MKOEGTWY	make one's getaway
MKOETRSO	make overtures to
MKRFRNEO	make reference to
MKSGETOS	make suggestions
MKSMOEDY	make someone's day
MKSOTOKF	make short work of
MKTIGWRE	make things worse
MKUCNCOS	make unconscious
MLADILOE	Millard Fillmore
MLGATRWH	malignant growth
MLIAEAIM	multilateralism
MLIAEAIT	multilateralist
MLIIGAIM	multilingualism
MLILOSES	mellifluousness
MLINDIDW	mullioned window
MLIUIOSY	multitudinously
MLOMAPEL	Malcolm Campbell
MLOMRDUY	Malcolm Bradbury
MLRCIINR	malpractitioner
MLSPEAIT	male supremacist
MLTRHNUS	military honours
MLTRTOTP	military two-step
MLTTAANT	militate against
MLTVOKAL	Molotov cocktail
MMRASRIE	memorial service
MNAAIIIS	mental abilities
MNABEKON	mental breakdown
MNACEITY	mental chemistry
MNAUIAIN	miniaturization
MNCAREET	Munich Agreement
MNCERSIE	manic-depressive
MNEALRLY	Monte Carlo Rally
MNEITCLY	manneristically
MNEVAIIY	manoeuvrability
MNGMRCIT	Montgomery Clift
MNHNOTOT	month in month out
MNIUDPRS	Monsieur de Paris
MNMRLOIE	montmorillonite
MNOEMNES	mind one's manners
MNOEPADS	mind one's p's and q's
MNRDYPOY	Manfred Symphony
MNSEOSAE	Minister of State
MNSITIHL	Mont-Saint-Michel
MNSLNORD	many-splendoured
MNYAAEET	money management
MNYONTIG	Money for Nothing
MNYOODOE	money for old rope
MNYRETTD	money-orientated
MPITPEIN	Mephistophelian
MRAEBCET	Margaret Beckett
MRAEDABE	Margaret Drabble
MRAEFRTR	Margaret Forster
MRAEOAJU	Margaret of Anjou
MREARCLR	Mordecai Richler
MREEITIH	Marlene Dietrich
MRENONTE	Marie Antoinette
MREUNNHM	Merce Cunningham
MRHLILNS	Marshall Islands
MRHNFRAD	marching forward
MRHNSRIE	merchant service
MRHNTLSI	Marghanita Laski
MRHSIEAD	Martha's Vineyard
MRIEWELR	Mortimer Wheeler
MRIFOIHR	Martin Frobisher
MRIGAAOE	Marriage à la Mode
MRIGIKES	morning sickness
MRIGPRIN	marriage portion
MRIGPRNR	marriage partner
MRIGSRIE	marriage service
MRIHIEGR	Martin Heidegger
MRINEOLR	Martin Niemöller
MRIURLAE	merciful release
MRLHLSPY	moral philosophy
MRLRNILS	moral principles
MRNRCMAS	Mariner's Compass
MRTROSES	meritoriousness
MRWTELWS	Meriwether Lewis
MSADNCES	mustard and cress

MSAEFHIT message of Christ
MSAHAAUK Mustapha Atatürk
MSCLIETR musical director
MSCONSAS music to one's ears
MSDSRCIN mass destruction
MSEFZIIG Mister Fezziwigg
MSELNOSY miscellaneously
MSHEOSES mischievousness
MSIFUNIL most influential
MSOSRCIN misconstruction
MSPRHNIE misapprehensive
MSPRHNIN misapprehension
MSQEOCEE musique concrète
MSRPRIND misproportioned
MSRSQIKY Mistress Quickly
MSSAMNDS Moses Maimonides
MSSGIIAT most significant
MSUOMNID Museum of Mankind
MTAPEAIE methamphetamine
MTHWLNES Matthew Flinders
MTMORNMN Mr Tambourine Man
MTOOIAIE metropolitanise
metropolitanize
MTRAIAIN materialization
MTRAMDES motorway madness
MTTSUADS mutatis mutandis
MUENONLY Maureen Connolly
MUNMUTIS Mourne Mountains
MUSLNSUE mousseline sauce
MVNSARAE moving staircase
MVUTEADR move up the ladder
NAANNPNE near as ninepence
NAHOTABT Neath Port Talbot
NAIGOLPE nearing collapse
NATOEHAT near to one's heart
NCEREBAE nuclear membrane
NCERECIN nuclear reaction
NCEREIIE nuclear medicine
NCOATCLY necromantically
NCOAWSMN Nicholas Wiseman
NCOOAAII Niccolò Paganini
NDIGGERH nodding ogee arch
NEIGEYUH needing very much
NFILCLEE Nuffield College
NIHORIES neighbourliness
NIOEEHTC noisomemephitic
NKLIUGNN Nikolai Bulganin
NKLUPVNR Nikolaus Pevsner
NKLYUHRN Nikolay Bukharin
NMECUCIG number-crunching
NNATSNHP non-partisanship
NNESCLES nonsensicalness
NNNEFRNE non-interference
NNNEVNIN non-intervention
NNOENETL non-governmental
NNOPSETS non compos mentis
NNRFSINL non-professional
NNRFTAIG non-profit-making
NNRNFRBE non-transferable
NNTEEAOS Ninette De Valois
Ninette de Valois
NNTEOSFR none the worse for
NRHNEABY Northanger Abbey

NROSIODR nervous disorder
NSRNCIKN no spring chicken
NTAALREE Nathanael Greene
NTAATNIN not pay attention
NTAEIDYO not take kindly to
NTAENUHF not have enough of
NTAIGNUH not having enough
NTEEEVDY not be deceived by
NTHWRFRT not the word for it
NTIGASIE Nottinghamshire
NTIGESHN nothing less than
NTIGOIBT nothing for it but
NTIHTNIG notwithstanding
NTNNSELE not on one's nellie
NTOAEGOT not to have a ghost
NTOAGLEY National Gallery
NTOAIAIN nationalization
NTOALTEY National Lottery
NTOASRIE national service
NTOATETE National Theatre
NTOIGNOT not coming into it
NTPNOESN not open to reason
NTRLAGAE natural language
NTRLEPNE natural response
NTRLHOOY natural theology
NTRLMUIY natural immunity
NTUHHWSR not much the wiser
NTUHOOKT not much to look at
NUELCIIE nouvelle cuisine
NUOIGITC neurolinguistic
NVLERTES Neville Brothers
NVREOEEN never before seen
NWGTAELR New Age traveller
NWORTLIG now you're talking
NWYICVRD newly discovered
NXTECOHR next to each other
NZNYOGRD Nizhniy Novgorod
OAEAIAIN oral examination
OBRLNATR Osbert Lancaster
OCIALEON once in a blue moon
OCNIINHT on condition that
OCSOATBE occasional table
ODESNSOE Old Red Sandstone
ODGPNINR old-age pensioner
ODNRCTZN ordinary citizen
ODREEAIN older generation
OEADOEIH over and done with
OEAETAIY one-parent family
OEAIGYTM operating system
OEAOAOHR one way or another
OECABRAN Owen Chamberlain
OEDVLPET overdevelopment
OEFHICOD one of the in-crowd
OEFMLAIY overfamiliarity
over-familiarity
OEFOIGIH overflowing with
OEHAADAS over head and ears
OENEACOY Ode on Melancholy
OENGAHCL oceanographical
OENTVHAH one's native heath
OEUDEHUS one hundred hours
OEVRHEGT one over the eight
OFCRFHDY officer of the day

OFINLTRS on friendly terms
OFRPNSIE offer up one's life
OHGEQAIY of higher quality
OHHLOCPC ophthalmoscopic
OHHLOOIT ophthalmologist
OIEGLSIH Oliver Goldsmith
OIEHAIIE Oliver Heaviside
OIINTDES opinionatedness
OIIRESAN Olivier Messiaen
OJCIIAIN objectification
OLOENSAM oil someone's palm
OMNOCSOS on many occasions
OMTCRSUE osmotic pressure
ONCNEUNE of no consequence
ONDRCINL omnidirectional
ONTOHNHS ornithorhynchus
OOEHGHRE on one's high horse
OOEONCOD of one's own accord
OOEPNALS on one's pantables
OOIEOSES odoriferousness
OPRUIYOT opportunity cost
OPSTETEE opposite extreme
ORUULRED Our Mutual Friend
OSEKNTRS on speaking terms
OSRAINLY observationally
OSRAINOT observation post
OSRCIEES obstructiveness
OTCLLUIN optical illusion
OTEAEFOT On the Waterfront
OTEAGRIT on the danger list
OTEAKUNR on the back burner
OTEEENVR on the never-never
OTEIDEGS of the Middle Ages
OTEIHTAK on the right track
OTEISWTR of the first water
OTETEGHF on the strength of
OTFHCUTY out of the country
OTFHLCOH out of whole cloth
OTFHRNIG out of the running
OTFIFCLY out of difficulty
OTFNSEGE out of one's league
OTFNSESS out of one's senses
OTFOMSIN out of commission
OTFRPRIN out of proportion
OTGNTCLY ontogenetically
OTPFHWRD on top of the world
PACSOSAT Planck's constant
PAEBTEOK played by the book
PAEFUIES place of business
PAEIEYIE place side by side
PAENREFR place an order for
PAEOAAIH Prayer of Azariah
PAFOSEIH play footsie with
PAFRTIDE play first fiddle
PAIACLES pharisaicalness
PAIGHFED playing the field
PATCBEES practicableness
PATRAGAD praetorian guard
PBIATNIN public attention
PBIRLTOS public relations
PCEAAFOT pocket an affront
PCEOEPIE pocket one's pride
PCGTESED pick gather speed

PCOAIMJR pectoralis major
PCOAIMNR pectoralis minor
PCRSUNVL picaresque novel
PCUEOTAD picture postcard
PCUEQEES picturesqueness
PCUTEICS pick up the pieces
PDGGIHES pedagoguishness
PEBTRAIE Presbyterianise
Presbyterianize
PEBTRAIM Presbyterianism
PEEDOTSE pretend not to see
PEEEMNBE predeterminable
PEEFNSID piece of one's mind
PEENTRLY preternaturally
PEETECIG prevent reaching
PEETNEIG prevent entering
PEETOSES pretentiousness
PEEVTOIT preservationist
PEIIAEES precipitateness
PEIIOSES precipitousness
PEIOETAY plenipotentiary
PEITRCLY prehistorically
PEMNCLGE pneumonic plague
PEOEOOIT phenomenologist
PEOIINLY prepositionally
PEOPTAEN phenolphthalein
PERCRELE Pierre Corneille
PERDRNAD Pierre de Ronsard
PERTEAUT Pierre Trésaguet
PESDOEHR pressed together
PESOFRNE press conference
PESRSEIG pleasure-seeking
PETDGTTR prestidigitator
PETDMQIK pretty damn quick
PEYKTNRA phenylketonuria
PEYKTNRC phenylketonuric
PGADHSLS pigs and whistles
PIAEODES private soldiers
PIATRPCL philanthropical
PIHOETOH plight one's troth
PIIEECAS privileged class
PIKPNSAS prick up one's ears
PIOOHCLY philosophically
PISAIGES painstakingness
PITFOEUN point of no return
PITHTWRD paint the town red
PITNMCIE printing-machine
PIYONILR Privy Councillor
PLAEALRA Palma de Mallorca
PLCNRSIG pelican crossing
PLENOOIT palaeontologist
PLHIUIOS pulchritudinous
PLIOEHRS pull in one's horns
PLOEPNHS pull one's punches
PLSMOELG pull someone's leg
PLTCLSLM political asylum
PLUOESCS pull up one's socks
PLUSTRTD polyunsaturated
PMRKCLEE Pembroke College
PNAKNSAS pin back one's ears
PNRAIJIE pancreatic juice
PNRMCAEA panoramic camera
PNTAIEES penetrativeness
PNTLOSES punctiliousness
PNUMUTIS Pindus Mountains
POCIEGOS proscribed goods
POEHUBUD Prometheus Bound
POESNPAT processing plant
POESOAIE professionalise
professionalize
POESOAIM professionalism
POETOMNY protection money
POEYIAIN proselytization
POFFDNIY proof of identity
POFFUCAE proof of purchase
POGMNLNH ploughman's lunch
POIAETUI Proxima Centauri
POIEOENY promise solemnly
POIIEGOS prohibited goods
POIIIEES prohibitiveness
POLMTCLY problematically
POLSOGES People's Congress
POLSSEBY People's Assembly
POMNFUTN poor man of mutton
PONSIAIN prognostication
POOCSOKY proboscis monkey
POOETATO propose a toast to
POOTOAEY proportionately
POOUTPIR photomultiplier
POPCIEIE prospective wife
POPOECNE phosphorescence
POREAYAE proprietary name
PORSIAIG procrastinating
PORSIAIN procrastination
PORSIEES progressiveness
PPDCUAIR Papa Doc Duvalier
PPEMNCEM peppermint cream
PPEOATIG Puppet on a String
PPRAKRTR Paperback Writer
PRAETANT permanent magnet
PRAGNCCD permanganic acid
PRAMNDVD Père Armand David
PRCMAYIH part company with
PREDCLRY perpendicularly
PRETNEVL perfect interval
PRETOITC perfectionistic
PREULOIN perpetual motion
PRGIEACN peregrine falcon
PRGIEIKE Peregrine Pickle
PRHNGNSS parthenogenesis
PRHNGNTC parthenogenetic
PRHNKNOS Perth and Kinross
PRILPYIS particle physics
PRILRCIN partial fraction
PRIMNAIM parliamentarism
PRIMNAIN parliamentarian
PRIMNAIY parliamentarily
PRISOTSE permission to see
PRLNUSIS paralinguistics
PRLOOABN perfluorocarbon
PRMDFHOS Pyramid of Cheops
PRMDFHSN Pyramid of the Sun
PRNAMSLS peroneal muscles
PRNHTCLY parenthetically
PROAEFCS personal effects
PROAIAIN personalization
PROAIYUT personality cult
PROAOGAA persona non grata
PROAPNIN personal pension
PROAPOON personal pronoun
PROEESES purposelessness
PROIIAIN personification
PROOCUAE person of courage
PROTEORE par for the course
PRPCCOSY perspicaciously
PRPCOSES perspicuousness
PRSLUHOM parasol mushroom
PRSUOOHS Parasaurolophus
PRUCOIES perfunctoriness
PSASRAGE Pascal's triangle
PSEGRIEN passenger pigeon
PSHFHCOS Pasch of the Cross
PSIEEITR passive resister
PSIEMUIY passive immunity
PSIITCLY pessimistically
PSITEONR puss in the corner
PSJDEETN pass judgement on
PSLAIOSY pusillanimously
PSOALTES Pastoral Letters
PSOEFRUE push one's fortune
PSPROMNE past performance
PSRUDHHT pass round the hat
PSSNHOIE post-synchronise
post-synchronize
PSTVVTIG positive vetting
PTAKHCOK put back the clock
PTAKOEHR put back together
PTARILNS Pitcairn Islands
PTBAEAEN put a brave face on
PTEATRPS Pithecanthropus
PTEIFLAY pathetic fallacy
PTETRSLA Patient Griselda
PTFSOEVR put a fast one over
PTHCOKAK put the clock back
PTHEEOTF put the eyes out of
PTHMCESN put the mockers on
PTIFEUDR put six feet under
PTIGHSOE putting the stone
PTIGOEHR putting together
PTNBAEAE put on a brave face
PTNHPCUE put in the picture
PTNHPYOL put on the payroll
PTNILNRY potential energy
PTNNREFR put in an order for
PTNOHSAE put into the shade
PTNORCIE put into practice
PTNSAEON put one's name down
PTNSAKNO put one's back into
PTNSIGRN put one's finger on
PTNSOTNT put one's foot in it
PTNSOTON put one's foot down
PTNTEWRS put in other words
PTOEIENO put some life into
PTRALUES Peter Paul Rubens
PTRNTEOF Peter and the Wolf
PTTCAANT put a tick against
PTVRNSNE put over one's knee
PUCLWTRN pour cold water on
PUPERBOA Paul Pierre Broca

PUTRMAUE poulters' measure
PVRYTIKN poverty stricken
poverty-stricken
PWRFTONY power of attorney
PWRULBIT powerfully built
PYFODCRS pay off old scores
PYHLGCLY psychologically
PYHPTOOY psychopathology
PYHTEAIT psychotherapist
PYIGAHCL physiographical
PYILGCLY physiologically
PYITEAIT physiotherapist
PYORGLRY pay for regularly
QAIIDESN qualified person
QAIYNRUD qualifying round
QARLOEES quarrelsomeness
QARPIAIN quadruplication
QENFUDNS queen of puddings
QIEHRVRE quite the reverse
QIKITDES quick-wittedness
QIKOCIIG quick-conceiving
QIKYRPRD quickly prepared
QITPIAIN quintuplication
RAETTAET real-estate agent
RAFNLCNE road fund licence
RAFRSAIN reafforestation
RAHOKOTM reach rock bottom
RBATNWUD rub salt in a wound
RBNCECCD ribonucleic acid
RBNOCLEE Robinson College
RBNODELW Robin Goodfellow
RBROLMNE Roberto Clemente
RBRSUHEL Robert Southwell
RCADAITN Richard Hamilton
RCADIBEY Richard Dimbleby
RCADOEAE Richard Lovelace
RCADRYUS Richard Dreyfuss
RCADUWOY Richard Dunwoody
RCAPEUIE racial prejudice
RCESINIT rocket scientist
RCEWIEED Rachel Whiteread
RCIEEGIH Received English
RCMEDTOS recommendations
RCMETIUE Recumbent Figure
RCMLRMTN Richmal Crompton
RCNIAIIY reconcilability
RCNIEAIN reconsideration
RCPINETE reception centre
RCVRBEES recoverableness
RDMNAIES rudimentariness
RDOIRPOE radio microphone
RDVNAAZC Radovan Karadzic
REMTLGCL rheumatological
RETBIHET re-establishment
RFATVIDX refractive index
RGLRUTMR regular customer
RGOAIAIN regionalisation
regionalization
RGRATEAE regard as the same
RGTADESN right-hand person
RGTFTEEL right off the reel
RGTIDDES right-mindedness
RGTOORBE Right Honourable
RGTTEARS Roget's Thesaurus
RIBWOORD rainbow-coloured
RICTADOS rain cats and dogs
RIENSADO raise one's hand to
RIENSIHS raise one's sights
RIEOHBNH raise to the bench
RIHATEAY reichian therapy□
RLHBRRMY Ralph Abercromby
RLHCUAHR Ralph Schumacher
RLHIHRSN Ralph Richardson
RLRGTTNS Rollright Stones
RLTVDNIY relative density
RLXOPEEY relax completely
RMAMCOAD Ramsay MacDonald
RMNIFCIN romantic fiction
RMNIIAIN romanticization
RMNTAEIH remonstrate with
RMREESES remorselessness
RMVGITRM remove guilt from
RNICERUD run circles round
RNNSYSVR run one's eyes over
RNRAIAIN renormalisation
renormalization
RNTIELMR ring-tailed lemur
RNTMEAUE run a temperature
RNWBENRY renewable energy
ROTMEAUE room temperature
ROTSIGCT room to swing a cat
RPEETTVS representatives
RPIAIAIN reprivatization
RPOCFLES reproachfulness
RPTTOSES repetitiousness
RSDNILOE residential home
RSDNILRA residential area
RSGAINRM resignation from
RSINIIWR Russian Civil War
RSINOLTE Russian roulette
RSRETOAY resurrectionary
RSRETOIE resurrectionise
resurrectionize
RSRETOIT resurrectionist
RSREURNY reserve currency
RSUCFLES resourcefulness
RTAITCLY ritualistically
RTEFRHYS Rutherford Hayes
RTOAIAIN rationalization
RTOPCIEY retrospectively
RTORSIEY retrogressively
RTROTEEI Return of the Jedi
RUDBURUE roundabout route
RVLIGRDT revolving credit
RVLTOAIS revolutionaries
RVREAEVR reverse takeover
RVROBBLN Rivers of Babylon
RYADDSAE Raynaud's disease
RYLOMSIN Royal Commission
royal commission
RYODHNLR Raymond Chandler
RYODILAS Raymond Williams
RYODONAE Raymond Poincaré
RZTTERUD raze to the ground
SADNEEOY stand on ceremony
SADNOAIN standing ovation
SADNSONR stand one's corner
SADNSRUD stand one's ground
SADONSUS stand to one's guns
SADPNONS stand upon points
SADREGIH Standard English
SADRIAIN standardization
SAEEHOOY space technology
SAEEITRD State Registered
SAEERAGE scalene triangle
SAEESESN stateless person
SAENHGAS snake in the grass
SAENSORE shape one's course
SAETTEKN soaked to the skin
SAHNCOHS swathing-clothes
SAIGELNS sharing feelings
SAIGHUHS sharing thoughts
SAIHIIWR Spanish Civil War
SAKNAORF stack in favour of
SALIDDES small-mindedness
SALYATES Stanley Matthews
SALYOASI Stanley Kowalski
SAPFPRVL stamp of approval
SARNPRNR sparring partner
SASNSRPS Stars and Stripes
SATAREIS Svante Arrhenius
SATOOKAD start to work hard
SAUOLBRY Statue of Liberty
SBITNEAE subsistence wage
SBRAIAIN suburbanization
SBSINALS Sebastian Faulks
SBTNIEES substantiveness
SBTTTOAY substitutionary
SCAAAEES social awareness
SCACENIG social cleansing
SCADMCAY social democracy
SCAETRVR Sacramento River
SCAISRNE social insurance
SCAITCLY socialistically
SCASCEAY social secretary
SCEDNAIY succeed in easily
SCNAYASS secondary causes
SCNAYCOL secondary school
SCNAYOOR secondary colour
SCNCIDOD second childhood
SCNICMAD second-in-command
SCNSBNFT sickness benefit
SCPATCLY sycophantically
SCRTBAKT security blanket
SCRTCUCL Security Council
SDNASHRA Sydenham's chorea
SDUCROAE sodium carbonate
SDUHDOIE sodium hydroxide
SEAWSYSI Stefan Wyszynski
SECRECVL Spencer Perceval
SECTEAIT speech therapist
SEDFRUEN spend a fortune on
SEDNSRAH spend one's breath
SEECEITY stereochemistry
SEECTERL Speyer Cathedral
SEEFAEIG Siege of Mafeking
SEEIOEIM stereoisomerism
SEESILEG Steven Spielberg
SEHNAGUD Stephen Jay Gould

Words marked □ can also be spelled with an initial capital letter

SEHNODEM Stephen Sondheim
SEIFRAIN seek information
SEIIGAIY specific gravity
SEILEIEY special delivery
SEILLAIG special pleading
SEILZDRA specialized area
SEKFTEUF speak off the cuff
SEKNEAFF speak on behalf of
SEKNIETY speak indirectly
SEKOHHAT speak to the heart
SEKUAANT speak out against
SELMCRNY Stella McCartney
SELNILNS Shetland Islands
SELNMSAE spelling mistake
SELNORSS smelling of roses
SEMTGNSS spermatogenesis
SEMTGNTC spermatogenetic
SEOENRGT see someone right
SEPNPRNR sleeping partner
SERNCERF steering clear of
SETANAAS sweet Fanny Adams
SETEHSOD sheathe the sword
SETFNSRW sweat of one's brow
SEUAIEES speculativeness
SEUTEADR step up the ladder
SFCMOIIS soft commodities
SFFRIHNS soft furnishings
SFHATDES soft-heartedness
SFLSRGTD softly-sprighted
SGRALOAD Sugar Ray Leonard
SHDLDATS scheduled castes
SHOOTOGT school of thought
SHSOOISS schistosomiasis
SIEMTMES shiver my timbers
SIIARCNS Scipio Africanus
SIIOAMNA spirit of ammonia
SIKNNSRW stick in one's craw
SIKNPATR sticking-plaster
SIKNPRSL stinking parasol
SIKNSANW spick and span new
SIKNSOEN stick one's nose in
SIKOHRLS stick to the rules
SIKONSUS stick to one's guns
SILMLVIE still small voice
SILSALIG shilly-shallying
SILYALIE Shirley MacLaine
SILYILAS Shirley Williams
SIMNCSUE swimming costume
SINATEID sail near the wind
SIOTEEET ship of the desert
SIOTEOGE slip of the tongue
SIPOIEIE stilpnosiderite
SITNSRUD shift one's ground
SITOOEEF shift for oneself
SIWTTEIE swim with the tide
SKTSNNVS St Kitts and Nevis
SLAIIAIN syllabification
SLAOALNE Salvador Allende
SLAPOAIN self-approbation
SLBTEADE sell by the candle
SLCCMITE select committee
SLCNEUNE self-consequence
SLCNRDES self-centredness
SLDPEAIG self-deprecating
SLDPEAIN self-deprecation
SLDSILND self-disciplined
SLDSRCIN self-destruction
SLDTRIIG self-determining
SLEAIAIN self-examination
SLEPAAOY self-explanatory
SLLGSAIG self-legislating
SLOIINTD self-opinionated
SLOITCLY syllogistically
SLOSRAIN self-observation
SLRPOCFL self-reproachful
SLSBTNIL self-substantial
SLSCIIIG self-sacrificing
SLSEITNE sales resistance
SLSFIINY self-sufficiency
SLSIUAIN self-stimulation
SLSRIEAE self-service café
SLSSANET self-sustainment
SLSVRINY self-sovereignty
SLTNIIIE split infinitive
SLUUNCTR Seleucus Nicator
SLYADMRL Süleyman Demirel
SMAHTCLY sympathetically
SMAKOSED Sam Jackson Snead
SMEHHEAN Samuel Hahnemann
SMELGTIG summer lightning
SMNEOTOT Simon de Montfort
SMNSBTNE sum and substance
SMOEBBLS Summoned by Bells
SMREMUHM Somerset Maugham
SMTMTCLY symptomatically
SMWEEOIE somewhere to live
SNADACAT song-and-dance act
SNAOHROG sing another song
SNAOHRUE sing another tune
SNBTLGAH send by telegraph
SNCNOECS send condolences
SNEBUEAD Sunset Boulevard
SNEFDNIY sense of identity
SNETOSES sententiousness
SNHOIAIN synchronization
SNIENUTY sunrise industry
SNOERGRS send one's regards
SNPIGSES Synoptic Gospels
SNRNICBY San Francisco Bay
SNRUDHHT send round the hat
SNTMNOSY sanctimoniously
SNTTEIBT send to the gibbet
SNUAIAIN singularization
SNWCILNS Sandwich Islands
SOAEAAIY storage capacity
SOAONCIN show a connection
SOCNEPFR show contempt for
SODFAOLS sword of Damocles
SOENHWTR Smoke on the Water
SOETAUUL slower than usual
SOEUDRIH snowed under with
SOGODSOD slough of despond
SOKADTNS stocks and stones
SOLBTUEY slowly but surely
SOLECAPR shoulder-clapper
SOLESOTN shoulder-shotten
SOOEGTOT slog one's guts out
SOOEIOIS show one's ivories
SOOTEPAE slow on the uptake
SOTAVNAE show to advantage
SOTHRSOK short sharp shock
SOTLEUDR shout blue murder
SOTMOAIY stop temporarily
SOTNGLEY shooting gallery
SOTNOSES spontaneousness
SOTRMHHP shoot from the hip
SOTSBRES Scottish Borders
SOTSTRIR Scottish terrier
SOYFNSIE story of one's life
SOYIHMRL story with a moral
SPLMNAIN supplementation
SPLMNAIS supplementaries
SPOIINLY suppositionally
SPRAUAIE supernaturalise
supernaturalize
SPRAUAIM supernaturalism
SPRAUAIT supernaturalist
SPRBNATY superabundantly
SPREEOYE superheterodyne
SPRIILES superficialness
SPRLOSES superfluousness
SPRMOIIN superimposition
SPRNEDNE superintendence
SPRNEDNY superintendency
SPRODCIE superconductive
SPRTTOSY superstitiously
SPRTUTRL superstructural
SRADWWRS spread downwards
SRAOEWNS spread one's wings
SRATEOPL spread the gospel
SREDAHLV Sergei Diaghilev
SREPOOIV Sergei Prokofiev
SRETTOSY surreptitiously
SRIEBEES serviceableness
SRIENUTY service industry
SRIHFRAD straightforward
SRKAAPTH strike a bad patch
SRKATTDS strike attitudes
SRKOBDUK stroke of bad luck
SRNESAIL springer spaniel
SRNIGILT shrinking violet
SRNIIOSY serendipitously
SRNLRYTM sprinkler system
SROAEOHR surrogate mother
SRONIGRA surrounding area
SROSRNIG serious drinking
SRPEFRAH strapped for cash
SRSOWAHR stress of weather
SRTHHTUH stretch the truth
SRTHNSES stretch one's legs
SRVNRPLY scrivener's palsy
SSANNPDL sustaining pedal
SSEAIAIN systematization
SSESACUT suspense account
SSESNLSS systems analysis
SSETBEES susceptibleness
SSUCNEAY sesquicentenary
STAINOEY situation comedy
STAINTIS situation ethics

STLODCRS settle old scores
STNSIHSN set one's sights on
STOCLFED Sutton Coldfield
STRASOEY set great store by
STRTOPIT saturation point
SUBRAAUE stubborn as a mule
SUDESFID soundness of mind
SUHAKETE South Bank Centre
SUOTEOET spur of the moment
spur-of-the-moment
SURKLMTE square kilometre
SURLGMIE square leg umpire
SURTEANY Squire Trelawney
SVBLETRS Seve Ballesteros
SVLNIEDY St Valentine's Day
SVNYHLIG seventy shilling
SWNSIDAS sow one's wild oats
SXAISICS sexual instincts
SXALASUT sexually assault
SXARLTOS sexual relations
SYEFPAIG style of speaking
SYHMGCOD say the magic word
TAASTEAY thalassotherapy
TAEDCMNS travel documents
TAEISUCE trapezius muscle
TAEOMLTS Thales of Miletus
TAESRERE to a lesser degree
TAESRXET to a lesser extent
TAETADRM travel to and from
TAKNSAIN tracking station
TALTAHHM that'll teach them
TANNCLEE training-college
TAOEHIOT tear one's hair out
TASAETES transparentness
TASEAIIY transferability
TASIEAIN transliteration
TASIUAIN transfiguration❑
TASIUEET transfigurement
TASLNAIN transplantation
TASLUIAE transilluminate
TASNFINS to absent friends
TASOEIET that's more like it
TASOIINL transpositional
TASRPINL transcriptional
TASRSINL transgressional
TASUAIIY transmutability
TASUAINL transmutational
TBGIGNIH to be going on with
TCNLGCLY technologically
TDOENTPR Tadpole and Taper
TEAASSES the fatal sisters
TEACODAH The Dance of Death
TEADNFDN The Garden of Eden
TEAEFUOA The Rape of Europa
TEAELSOY the same old story
TEAETCLY therapeutically
TEAICMUE the Paris Commune
TEAKFEOD the back of beyond
TEAREUEE The Faerie Queene
TEASHSES the cat's whiskers
TEASOHUE the Mansion House
TEATFEUA The Raft of Medusa
TEAXRTES The Marx Brothers
TEAYAIHS The Lady Vanishes
TEBIGOLR trembling poplar
TECEOSES treacherousness
TECMNOEH The Iceman Cometh
TEDRILOH Theodor Billroth
TEDRREHE Theodore Roethke
TEDRVDEG Theodor Svedberg
TEEAEUUH The Female Eunuch
TEEGROEA The Beggar's Opera
TEEISATO the devil's tattoo
TEEKRESL the weaker vessel
TEENTLIG there's no telling
TEEODOIG The Second Coming
TEERFSES The Pearl Fishers
TEERSSES the Weird Sisters
TEERTADN The Secret Garden
TEETOMRT The Death of Marat
TEETRATF the better part of
TEEYRTMS The New York Times
TEFIAQEN The African Queen
TEGOAXEY The Age of Anxiety
TEHESSES The Three Sisters
TEHEWSMN the Three Wise Men
TEHEWTHS The Three Witches
TEHLSEAG the whole shebang
TEHSNEPE the chosen people
TEICGDES the bitch goddess
TEIEFPIG The Rite of Spring
TEIGFOEY The King of Comedy
TEIIEOEY The Divine Comedy
TEIOTEAD the lie of the land
TEITERNE The Little Prince
TEITFHGB the gift of the gab
TEITOVNS The Birth of Venus
TEIYLTIF The Bicycle Thief
TEKSHLMT the sky's the limit
TELGLAIN The Flagellation
TELVSROF the gloves are off
TEMADOIE Thelma and Louise
TEMOIVLE thermionic valve
TENIILMN The Invisible Man
TENOTEOD the end of the road
TENUCAIN The Annunciation
TEOADHWY the how and the why
TEOADYIN The Cowardly Lion
TEOAIWIE The Woman in White
TEOAOAES The Potato Eaters
TEODHPED the Good Shepherd
TEOEOBBL The Tower of Babel
TEOESHTE the powers that be
TEOKOLDE tree of knowledge
TEOLSINE the noble science
TEOMNEPE the common people
TEONMRIG the morn's morning
TEONNATR the morning after
TEONOMSC The Sound of Music
TEOSFRER the worse for wear
TEOSICER the coast is clear
TERECLNS the Greek calends
TERFLOGR The Artful Dodger
TERGTIHS the bright lights
TESASFLA The Essays of Elia
TESEFVLN The Isle of Avalon
TESNBEES treasonableness
TETEOPRS Treaties of Paris
TEUENTRL the supernatural
TEVOSANS The Eve of St Agnes
TFRINLMS to foreign climes
TGAPTOIN Tigran Petrosian
TGTITDES tight-fistedness
TGTNNSET tighten one's belt
TGTOEAKR tight-rope walker
TIEIANRE trigeminal nerve
TIEXRSIN trite expression
TIIRTLEE trinitrotoluene
TIKFOEHR think of together
TIKHWRDF think the world of
TIKNNSET think on one's feet
TILFTEGH trial of strength
TILNSHMS twirl one's thumbs
TIOTERUD thin on the ground
TISQECIG thirst-quenching
TKAABFRE take away by force
TKAAENAN take a name in vain
TKAAVNAE take at advantage
TKANPHTF take a snapshot of
TKAUCEST take a butcher's at
TKAVNAEF take advantage of
TKECPINO take exception to
TKFECLAE take French leave
TKIFOTEE take it from there
TKIOLAET take it or leave it
take-it-or-leave-it
TKIOTEHN take it on the chin
TKITACUT take into account
TKITCSOY take into custody
TKNACUTF take no account of
TKNAOEON taking as one's own
TKNAVNAE taking advantage
TKOELAEF take one's leave of
TKPEATOS take precautions
TKPRIAAE take part in a race
TKSMBAIG take some beating
TKSMOEPN take someone up on
TKTEEGTF take the weight of
TKTEHLOF take the chill off
TKTEHNOF take the shine off
TKTERNWY take the wrong way
TKTERORE take their course
TKTERPOF take the wraps off
TKTOEHAT take to one's heart
TKTOEHES take to one's heels
TKUOOEEF take upon oneself
TKURSDNE take up residence
TKVNENEN take vengeance on
TLAANTIE talk against time
TLGAHCLY telegraphically
TLKNDMOE till kingdom come
TLOEONAE tell one's own tale
TLPOEUBR telephone number
TLPOORPY telephotography
TLSOISGT telescopic sight
TMEAETLY temperamentally
TMETOSES tempestuousness
TMLOATMS Temple of Artemis
TMLOHTOR Temple of Hathoor

Words marked ❑ can also be spelled with an initial capital letter

TMLOSLMN Temple of Solomon
TMZNDSAE time-zone disease
TMZNFTGE time-zone fatigue
TNOMNMNS Ten Commandments
TOADQICY Thomas De Quincey
TOAGAGID Thomas Gradgrind
TOAJFESN Thomas Jefferson
TOAMDLTN Thomas Middleton
TOBEHOIG troubleshooting
TOBEOEES troublesomeness
TOEKOLDE to one's knowledge
TOGTESES thoughtlessness
TOGTIHYF thought highly of
TOINSHRO Thojib N J Suharto
TONNHFEH thorn in the flesh
TONNNSIE thorn in one's side
TOODOERE too good to be true
TOSNGZLE Thomson's gazelle
TOUDEHUS two hundred hours
TOUHOYUG Too Much Too Young
TPFHIEEG tip of the iceberg
TPGAHCLY topographically
typographically
TRALNEEO turn a blind eye to
TRAOTEPS Tarzan of the Apes
TRATEPMN Tarzan the Ape Man
TRBCTFOT turn back to front
TREEIAOT Three Men in a Boat
TREENPEE threepenny piece
TREIETRE three times three
TRIOEGAE turn in one's grave
TRIOILRY Territorial Army
TRIOOEEF turn in on oneself
TRNEATGN Terence Rattigan
TROESOAH turn one's stomach
TRSTTEAL thrust to the wall
TRTAVNAE turn to advantage
TRUHHNGT through the night
TRWFBLNE throw off balance
TRWNHCRS throw in the cards
TRWNHTWL throw in the towel
TRWNNSAD throw in one's hand
TRWNOEIF throw into relief
TRWOHLOS throw to the lions
TRWOHWNS throw to the winds
TRWPHCRS throw up the cards
TSDREFED Tess Durbeyfield
TSIGHCBR tossing the caber
TSMOETEH to someone's teeth
TTEANRON to the manner born
TTEIHAOT to the right about
TTEIHHUE To the Lighthouse
TTEULXET to the full extent
TTLOYUDN total body burden
TTLTRAIM totalitarianism
TTSNRNCS Titus Andronicus
TUBALKTH thumbnail sketch
TUHSLBOS tough as old boots
TUOSLURC Toulouse-Lautrec
TUPDPHRE trumped-up charge
TUTOTIES trustworthiness
TUUMUTIS Taurus Mountains
TWRFTEGH tower of strength

TXCLGCLY toxicologically
TYAOOISS trypanosomiasis
UABGOSES unambiguousness
UACMOAIG unaccommodating
UACPAIIY unacceptability
UACRANBE unascertainable
UAODBEES unavoidableness
UASIAIIY unassailability
UASRIEES unassertiveness
UATETCTD unauthenticated
UATRBEES unalterableness
UCAGAIIY unchangeability
UCALNEBE unchallengeable
UCANDEOY Unchained Melody
UCMASOAE uncompassionate
UCMLMNAY uncomplimentary
UCMRHNIG uncomprehending
UCMUIAIE uncommunicative
UCNCOSEF unconscious self
UCNCOSES unconsciousness
UCNIINLY unconditionally
UCRMNOSY unceremoniously
UCVLZDES uncivilizedness
UDMNTAIE undemonstrative
UDRADDES underhandedness
UDRBIAIN under obligation
UDRFLEAE under a false name
UDRHAGSF under the aegis of
UDRHBTNF under the baton of
UDRHCUTR under the counter
under-the-counter
UDRHVLAO Under the Volcano
UDRHWAHR under the weather
UDRICSIN under discussion
UDRMLYET underemployment
UDRNSRAH under one's breath
UDROEAET undercover agent
UDROKNKY under lock and key
UDROPLIN under compulsion
UDRORCIN under correction
UDRRVLGD underprivileged
UDRSIAIN underestimation
UDRTNIGY understandingly
UDSIGIHD undistinguished
UDSRBEES undesirableness
UECPINBE unexceptionable
UECPINBY unexceptionably
UEUVCLES unequivocalness
UFIBHVOR unfair behaviour
UFRIIGES unforgivingness
UFTOAIIY unfathomability
UGVRAIIY ungovernability
UIESLEEY universal remedy
UITNINLY unintentionally
UITRSIGY uninterestingly
UITRUTDY uninterruptedly
UKONUNIY unknown quantity
UNCSAIES unnecessariness
UOJCINBE unobjectionable
UOJCINBY unobjectionably
UOTUIEES unobtrusiveness
UPEEETDY unprecedentedly
UPEETOSY unpretentiously

UPEOSSIG unprepossessing
UPOETNIE unprotestantise
unprotestantize
UPRAEETR upper-case letter
UPRIMNAY unparliamentary
UPRTOPEE upper atmosphere
UQETOIGY unquestioningly
URCNIIBE unreconciliable
URGTOSES unrighteousness
URLNIGES unrelentingness
URMTIGES unremittingness
USBTNITD unsubstantiated
USILDOKR unskilled worker
USLCNCOS unselfconscious
USPITCTD unsophisticated
USSETDES unsuspectedness
UTAETIUE ultracentrifuge
UTAIRSOE ultramicroscope
UTAIRSOY ultramicroscopy
UTUSAEET untrue statement
UWOEOEES unwholesomeness
VAIINBKV Vladimir Nabokov
VCCARESN vice-chairperson
VCSIUIOS vicissitudinous
VDOOFRNE videoconference
VIERDCIN voice production
VLATOTUH Valiant-for-Truth
VLNAYUCE voluntary muscle
VLOGAOGN Vale of Glamorgan
VNEZBLII Vincenzo Bellini
VNSAEGAE Vanessa Redgrave
VOEAHMRO Violeta Chamorro
VRADAROA verbal diarrhoea
VRERLOUN vertebral column
VRIICEPR Virginia creeper
VRIIOSES vertiginousness
VSBEPCRM visible spectrum
VSCNTITR vasoconstrictor
VSIUANRE vestibular nerve
VSUADSAE vascular disease
VTLTTSIS vital statistics
VTMNCMLX vitamin B complex
VUHNILAS Vaughan Williams
VXOUIODI vox populi vox Dei
WAEEITKS whatever it takes
WAEETEOT whatever the cost
WAHRHSOM weather the storm
WAHROEAT weather forecast
WAHRORIG weatherboarding
WASVRLAS wear several hats
WATEREHS wear the breeches
WATERUES wear the trousers
WCFRSUES Wackford Squeers
WEDHSETE wield the sceptre
WEEALSAE Where Eagles Dare
WEESHIZL Wiener schnitzel
WELNMLUE wheel animalcule
WEOGOSIH Weedon Grossmith
WIEASUDN white man's burden
WIEHNCRS white rhinoceros
WIEHPLAT Whitechapel cart
WIESPLHE whited sepulchre
WIETAWIE whiter than white

WIIGOGDT Waiting For Godot
WILGGETE whirligig beetle
WITENFUE whistle and flute
WITEOAID whistle for a wind
WLCABRAN Wilt Chamberlain
WLEDKOIG Willem De Kooning
WLEENHVN Willem Einthoven
WLEMTIIZ Wilhelm Steinitz
WLETBIHD well-established
WLHRAHNU Walther Rathenau
WLIADUUA Wallis and Futuna
WLIMAEAT William Davenant
WLIMAGAD William Langland
WLIMALNR William Faulkner
WLIMARSN William Harrison
WLIMCILY William McKinley
WLIMEEIH William Meredith
WLIMEKOD William Beckford
WLIMESHL William Herschel
WLIMESOG William Rees-Mogg
WLIMETNK William Bentinck
WLIMEUOT William Beaumont
WLIMFCHM William of Ockham
WLIMFRNE William of Orange
WLIMHCLY William Shockley
WLIMHTLW William Whitelaw
WLIMOGAE William Cosgrave
WLIMOGEE William Congreve
WLIMOLDE William Coolidge
WLIMREKN William Friedkin
WLIMRNIE William Ironside
WLISIABR Wilkins Micawber
WLISOMKR Willie Shoemaker
WLOIAEHR wallop in a tether
WLRDHSGR Wilfred Thesiger
WLUHLTRD well-upholstered
WLUMUTCE walrus moustache
WMNFHCOH woman of the cloth
WMNFHWRD woman of the world
WMNISIUE Women's Institute
WNFOTESY win effortlessly
WNIGEYUH wanting very much
WNOGREIG window gardening
WNSREWPR windscreen-wiper
WNWRILNS Windward Islands
WNYSOTED win by a short head
WOGEDDES wrong-headedness
WOYIHSAE woody nightshade
WRALHMSN Worrall Thompson
WRDHTEIG world-shattering
WRDIHUED world without end
WRDULTDS work double tides
WRFHPCFC War of the Pacific
WRHATDES warm-heartedness
WRHHWITE worth the whistle
WRHROBAN Wernher von Braun
WRIGAOIY working majority
WRIGOEHR working together
WRLKARJN work like a Trojan
WROEGTOT work one's guts out
WROEPSAE work one's passage
WROTHTTL work out the total
WSENSRAH waste one's breath
WSFLHNIG wishful thinking
WSHPIESO wish happiness to
WSIGPIUD washing-up liquid
WSIYENIF Wassily Leontief
WSLKNISY Wasily Kandinsky
WSOEHNSF wash one's hands of
WSOOSLMN Wisdom of Solomon
WSOSPRAE Weston-super-Mare
WSYUEEEE Wish You Were Here
WTACELOE with a screw loose
WTAIFRNE with a difference
WTBTDRAH with bated breath
WTHBBSED wet the baby's head
WTHNSOND with hands joined
WTIAMRAH within arm's reach
WTMNYOUN with money to burn
WTNTIGNT with nothing in it
WTNTIGOO with nothing to do
WTOTAALL without parallel
WTOTBEKN without a break in
WTOTEEOY without ceremony
WTOTHCIG without checking
WTOTHNIG without thinking
WTOTLNIG without planning
WTOTPRNR without a partner
WTOTSRTH without a scratch
WTOTUSIN without question
WTRFRNEO with reference to
WTRNHBAN water on the brain
WTRTHMUH water at the mouth
WTSLCNRL with self-control
WTTMTSAE with time to spare
WTUSNDWS with ups and downs
WYFXRSIG way of expressing
YLOBIKOD yellow brick road
YLOSBAIE Yellow Submarine
YONGOAOG Yvonne Goolagong
YRSIEIPR Yorkshire Ripper
YUEOMTEE you've got me there
YUSATFLY yours faithfully
ZGOMUTIS Zagros Mountains